TEACHER'S WRAPAROUND EDITION

WORLD HISTORY

THE HUMAN EXPERIENCE

NATIONAL GEOGRAPHIC SOCIETY

Mounir A. Farah
Andrea Berens Karls

GLENCOE
McGraw-Hill
New York, New York   Columbus, Ohio   Mission Hills, California   Peoria, Illinois

About the Authors

The **National Geographic Society**, founded in 1888 for the increase and diffusion of geographic knowledge, is the world's largest nonprofit scientific and educational organization. Since its earliest days, the Society has used sophisticated communication technologies and rich historical and archival resources to convey knowledge to a worldwide membership. The Educational Media Division supports the Society's mission by developing innovative educational programs—ranging from traditional print materials to multimedia programs including CD-ROMs, videodiscs, and software.

Mounir A. Farah, Ph.D. is a research historian and Associate Director of the Middle East Studies Program at the University of Arkansas, Fayetteville. Dr. Farah taught history and social science at New York University and Western Connecticut State University and has lectured at many teachers' conferences and workshops in the United States and abroad. He was a consultant to the Ministry of Education in Jordan and served as Coordinator of Social Studies in the Monroe, Connecticut public schools. Named Outstanding History Scholar-Teacher in New England and a recipient of the Connecticut Social Studies Annual Award, Dr. Farah is a past president of the Connecticut Council for the Social Studies and of the Middle East Outreach Council and a board member of the Arkansas Council for Social Studies. He is a contributing writer to several books and has authored numerous articles and reviews. Dr. Farah also is coauthor of Glencoe's *Global Insights.*

Andrea Berens Karls is an educator and coauthor of Glencoe's *Global Insights.* Educated at Wellesley College and Harvard University, she has taught at both the elementary and secondary levels. Ms. Karls was formerly Program Associate at Global Perspectives in Education, Inc., where she edited and wrote curriculum materials and worked with teachers. She is a member of the National Council for the Social Studies and the American Historical Association.

About the Cover

The temple of Amon-Ra—ancient Egypt's most important god—was the major building in Thebes, a city of Egypt. Between the 1300s B.C. and the 1100s B.C., Egyptian builders constructed the temple at the site of the present-day city of Luxor.

The part of the temple shown is an outer court, decorated with colossal images of the great Egyptian pharaoh Ramses II. A pair of granite obelisks covered with hieroglyphics also graced the outer court. One obelisk (shown in the cover photo) still stands. The other was removed to the Place de la Concorde in Paris, France, in 1831.

Glencoe/McGraw-Hill

A Division of The ***McGraw-Hill*** *Companies*

Design and Production: DECODE, Inc.

Cover photograph: Temple of Amon-Ra, Luxor, Egypt; Mark D. Phillips/Photo Researchers, Inc.

Send all inquiries to:

Glencoe/McGraw-Hill, 936 Eastwind Drive, Westerville, Ohio 43081

ISBN 0-02-823219-4 (Student Edition) ISBN 0-02-823387-5 (Teacher's Wraparound Edition)

Printed in the United States of America.

1 2 3 4 5 6 7 8 9 10 VH/LP 01 00 99 98 97 96

Academic Consultants

Stephen Chicoine
Author/Lecturer, World Affairs
Vice President
Bechtel Energy Resources Corporation
Houston, Texas

Paula Fredricksen, Ph.D.
Aurelio Professor of Scripture
Boston University
Boston, Massachusetts

Madhulika S. Khandelwal, Ph.D.
Research Historian
Asian/American Center
Queens College
City University of New York
New York City, New York

George Demetrius Knysh, Ph.D.
Associate Professor of Political Studies
University of Manitoba
Winnipeg, Manitoba
Canada

Frances Malino, Ph.D.
Professor of History
Wellesley College
Wellesley, Massachusetts

Ali A. Mazuri, Ph.D.
Professor of History
State University of New York
Binghamton, New York

Jesus Mendez, Ph.D.
Associate Professor of History
Barry University
Miami Shores, Florida

Brendan Nagle, Ph.D.
Associate Professor
University of Southern California
Los Angeles, California

Al Naklowycz, Ph.D.
President, Ukrainian-American Academic Association of California
Carmichael, California

Donald Niewyk, Ph.D.
Professor of History
Southern Methodist University
Dallas, Texas

Boniface Obichere, Ph.D.
Professor of History
University of California
Los Angeles, California

Sayyid M. Syeed, Ph.D.
Secretary General
The Islamic Society of North America
Plainfield, Indiana

Frank De Varona
Region 1 Superintendent
Dade County Public Schools
Hileah, Florida

Teacher Reviewers

Christine Allen
North Salem High School
Salem, Oregon

Mattie Collins
Pine Bluff High School
Pine Bluff, Arkansas

Louis Gallo
West High School
Knoxville, Tennessee

Mark Heinig
Reitz Memorial High School
Evansville, Indiana

Paul Horton
Williamsville East High School
East Amherst, New York

Jim Lloyd
Department Chair, History-Social Science
Bullard High School
Fresno, California

Patti Long
Forrest City High School
Forrest City, Arkansas

Willis M. Overton III
Warren Central High School
Indianapolis, Indiana

Table of Contents

Student Edition Table of Contents T5

Professional Notes

Answering the Issue of Relevancy T12
Seeing the Big Picture T14
The Story of History T16
Cultural Perspectives T17
Visualizing History T18
Geography in History T20
Integrating Literature and Writing into History T21
Addressing Multiple Learning Styles T22
Implementing Block Scheduling T24
Utilizing Performance Assessment T25
Using Technology in the Classroom T26
Surfing the History Net T27
Correlation to NCSS Ten Thematic Strands T28
Six Alternative Course Outlines T30
Scope and Sequence Chart T32

Classroom Resources

Applications and Hands-On Activities
History Simulations T40
Historical Significance Chapter Activities T41
Skill Reinforcement Activities T42
People in World History T43

Review and Reinforcement Activities
Vocabulary Activities T44
Vocabulary PuzzleMaker Software T44
Guided Reading Activities T45
Time Line Activities T46
Chapter Themes: Graphic Organizers T47
Reteaching Activities T48

Spanish Language Resources T49

Geography Activities
Mapping History Activities T50
Geography and History Activities T51
Outline Map Resource Book T52
Student Desk Map T52

Interdisciplinary Connections
World Literature Selections T53
World Art and Music T54
World Music: Cultural Traditions T54
World History and Art Transparencies T55
Focus on World Art Prints T55

Enrichment and Extension Activities
Enrichment Activities T56
Critical Thinking Activities T57
Source Readings T58

Assessment and Evaluation
Performance Assessment Strategies and Activities T59
Section Quizzes T60
Chapter and Unit Tests: Forms A and B T61
Testmaker Software T61

Multimedia and Technology
Student Self-Test and Review Software T62
MindJogger Videoquiz T63
Teaching Transparencies T64
Section Focus Transparencies T65
Chapter Digests Audiocassettes T66

NATIONAL GEOGRAPHIC SOCIETY Resources T67

ABCNEWS INTERACTIVE™ Resources T71

STUDENT EDITION

Table of Contents

Reference Atlas A1
Geography Handbook 1
Themes in World History 12

Unit 1 The Rise of Civilizations 14

Chapter 1
Human Beginnings 18
1 Discovery of Early Humans in Africa 20
2 The Appearance of *Homo Sapiens* 26
3 Emergence of Civilization 32

Chapter 2
Early Civilizations 44
1 The Nile Valley 46
2 The Fertile Crescent 58
3 Early South Asia 66
4 Early China 69

Chapter 3
Kingdoms and Empires in the Middle East 78
1 Trading Peoples 80
2 Early Israelites 83
3 Empire Builders 88

Unit 2 Flowering of Civilizations 100

Chapter 4
The Rise of Ancient Greece 104
1 Beginnings 106
2 The Polis 112
3 Rivals 115
4 War, Glory, and Decline 120

Chapter 5
The Height of Greek Civilization 128
1 Quest for Beauty and Meaning 130
2 The Greek Mind 135
3 Alexander's Empire 140

Chapter 6
Ancient Rome and Early Christianity 152
1 The Roman Republic 154
2 Expansion and Crisis 159
3 The Roman Empire 164
4 The Rise of Christianity 171
5 Roman Decline 175

Chapter 7
Flowering of African Civilizations 182
1 Early Africa 184
2 Kingdoms in West Africa 189
3 African Trading Cities and States 194

Chapter 8
India's Great Civilization 200
1 Origins of Hindu India 202
2 Rise of Buddhism 208
3 Indian Empires 211

Chapter 9
China's Flourishing Civilization 218
1 Three Great Dynasties 220
2 Three Ways of Life 225
3 Society and Culture 228

Unit 3 **Regional Civilizations** 240

Chapter 10
Byzantines and Slavs **244**
1 The New Rome 246
2 Byzantine Civilization 251
3 The Eastern Slavs 258

Chapter 11
Islamic Civilization **268**
1 A New Faith 270
2 Spread of Islam 277
3 Daily Life and Culture 282

Chapter 12
The Rise of Medieval Europe **292**
1 Frankish Rulers 294
2 Medieval Life 298
3 The Medieval Church 303
4 Rise of European Monarchy 308

Chapter 13
Medieval Europe at Its Height **316**
1 The Crusades 318
2 Economic and Cultural Revival 322
3 Strengthening of Monarchy 329
4 The Troubled Church 334

Chapter 14
East and South Asia **340**
1 Central Asia 342
2 China 346
3 Southeast Asia 351
4 Korea and Japan 358

Chapter 15
The Americas **372**
1 The Early Americas 374
2 Early Mesoamerican Cultures 379
3 The Aztec and Inca Empires 388

Unit 4 **Emergence of the Modern World** 398

Chapter 16
Renaissance and Reformation **402**
1 The Italian Renaissance 404
2 The Northern Renaissance 412
3 The Protestant Reformation 415
4 The Spread of Protestantism 418
5 The Catholic Reformation 422

Chapter 17
Expanding Horizons **432**
1 Early Explorations 434
2 Overseas Empires 440
3 Changing Ways of Life 446

Chapter 18
Empires of Asia **454**
1 Muslim Empires 456
2 Chinese Dynasties 462
3 The Japanese Empire 468
4 Southeast Asia 474

Chapter 19
Royal Power and Conflict **480**
1 Spain 482
2 England 485
3 France 490
4 The German States 494
5 Russia 498

STUDENT EDITION

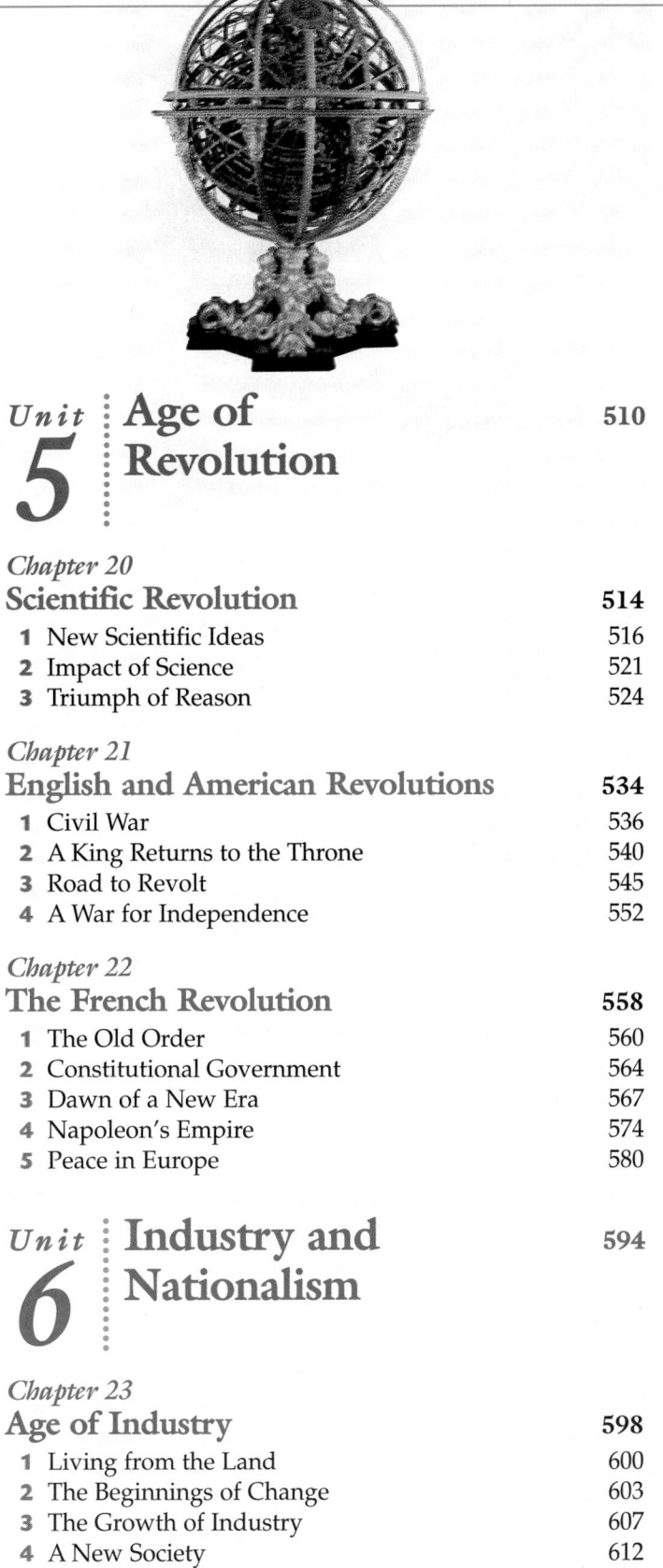

Unit 5 Age of Revolution 510

Chapter 20
Scientific Revolution 514
1 New Scientific Ideas 516
2 Impact of Science 521
3 Triumph of Reason 524

Chapter 21
English and American Revolutions 534
1 Civil War 536
2 A King Returns to the Throne 540
3 Road to Revolt 545
4 A War for Independence 552

Chapter 22
The French Revolution 558
1 The Old Order 560
2 Constitutional Government 564
3 Dawn of a New Era 567
4 Napoleon's Empire 574
5 Peace in Europe 580

Unit 6 Industry and Nationalism 594

Chapter 23
Age of Industry 598
1 Living from the Land 600
2 The Beginnings of Change 603
3 The Growth of Industry 607
4 A New Society 612

Chapter 24
Cultural Revolution 620
1 New Ideas 622
2 The New Science 626
3 Popular Culture 629
4 Revolution in the Arts 635

Chapter 25
Democracy and Reform 646
1 Reform in Great Britain 648
2 The Dominions 652
3 Political Struggles in France 655
4 Expansion of the United States 660
5 Latin American Independence 666

Chapter 26
Reaction and Nationalism 674
1 The Unification of Italy 676
2 The Unification of Germany 681
3 Bismarck's Realm 686
4 Empire of the Czars 690
5 Austria-Hungary's Decline 695

Chapter 27
The Age of Imperialism 702
1 Pressures for Expansion 704
2 The Partition of Africa 707
3 The Division of Asia 713
4 Imperialism in the Americas 721

STUDENT EDITION

Unit 7 World in Conflict 732

Chapter 28
World War I 736
1 The Seeds of War 738
2 The Spark 741
3 The War 744
4 The Russian Revolution 756
5 Peace at Last 760

Chapter 29
Between Two Fires 768
1 The Postwar World 770
2 The Western Democracies 776
3 Fascist Dictatorships 781
4 The Soviet Union 788

Chapter 30
Nationalism in Asia, Africa, and Latin America 794
1 New Forces in the Middle East and Africa 796
2 India's Struggle for Independence 801
3 China's Drive for Modernization 804
4 Militarism in Japan 807
5 Nationalism in Latin America 811

Chapter 31
World War II 824
1 The Path to War 826
2 War in Europe 831
3 A Global Conflict 838
4 Turning Points 842
5 Allied Victories 846

Unit 8 The Contemporary World 858

Chapter 32
The Cold War 862
1 The East–West Split 864
2 The Communist Bloc 872
3 Western Europe 878
4 The United States and Canada 882

Chapter 33
Asia and the Pacific 894
1 Japan's Economic Rise 896
2 China in Revolution 901
3 A Divided Korea 906
4 Southeast Asia 909
5 South Asia 916
6 The Pacific 920

Chapter 34
Africa 926
1 African Independence 928
2 Africa Today 935
3 Africa's Challenges 941

Chapter 35
The Middle East 948
1 Nationalism in the Middle East 950
2 War and Peace in the Middle East 954
3 Challenges Facing the Middle East 962

Chapter 36
Latin America 972
1 Latin American Challenges 974
2 Mexico and the Caribbean 979
3 Central America 985
4 South America 990

Chapter 37
The World in Transition 996
1 The End of the Cold War 998
2 The Crumbling Wall 1004
3 Toward a European Union 1010
4 National and Ethnic Conflicts 1014
5 Global Interdependence 1018

Appendix 1030
English Glossary 1030
Index 1040
Spanish Glossary 1073
Acknowledgments 1086

STUDENT EDITION

NATIONAL GEOGRAPHIC SOCIETY

Special Report

The Iceman	38
The Egyptians	54
The Maya	384
The *Lusitania*	752

Picturing History

Hominid Hunter	23
Ramses the Great	50
Merchants of the Mediterranean	81
Trojan Horse	109
Greek Soldier	133
Roman Forum	169
West African Empire	192
The Buddha's First Sermon	209
Silk Road	223
Rurik the Rus	261
Tower Mosque	274
Life in the Castle	300
Cathedral of Chartres	331
Kublai Khan and Marco Polo	349
Serious Sport	382
"The Last Supper"	410
"Little Girl"	437
Taj Mahal	460
Peter's Great City	500
Tower Physics	522
Tarred and Feathered	549
Guillotine	572
Steel	610
French Impressionists	637
Pioneers	661
Mad Ludwig's Castle	688
Panama Canal	723
In the Trenches	750
Flying High	774
Sending in the Marines	815
Japanese Americans	840
Cold War	867
Boat People	913
Africa and Independence	930
Mortal Enemies	959
Rich Heritage	983
Seeing Red	1002

The Spread of Ideas

Farming and Civilization	16
Systems of Law	102
Mathematics	242
Music	400
Revolution	512
Industrialization	596
International Peacekeeping	734
Communications	860

Bridge to the Past: Literature

Gilgamesh	72
Antigone by Sophocles	146
Four Poems by Li Bo	366
The Prince by Machiavelli	426
Les Misérables by Victor Hugo	584
The Beggar by Anton Chekhov	640
Gifts of Passage by Santha Rama Rau	818
Modern Poems: "The Window" by Jaime Torres Bodet; "The World, My Friends, My Enemies, You, and the Earth" by Nazim Hikmet; and "Once Upon a Time" by Gabriel Okara	966

Images of the Times

Early Human Technology 28
Mesopotamia 62
Ancient Persepolis 90
The Glory of Greece 116
The Hellenistic Age 142
Pompeii, A.D. 79 166
Africa's Religious Heritage 190
Hindu Beliefs 204
Han China 230
Byzantine Art 252
Islamic Art and Architecture 278
Monastic Life 304
Medieval Life 324
Angkor Wat 352
Native Americans 376
Art of the Italian Renaissance 406
The Dutch Republic 442
Chinese Life 464
Tudor England 486
Salon Society 526
Colonial America 546
Revolutionary Life 570
The Industrial Age 614
Leisure Time 630
The Civil War 662
Uniting Italy 678
The British Empire 716
Industry Generates War Materials 746
Life in Nazi Germany 784
Mexican Murals 812
The Blitz 834
Rebuilding Europe 868
Vietnam War, 1964–1975 910
Toward a New Africa 936
Living in the Middle East 956
Mexico Today 980
A New Era 1006

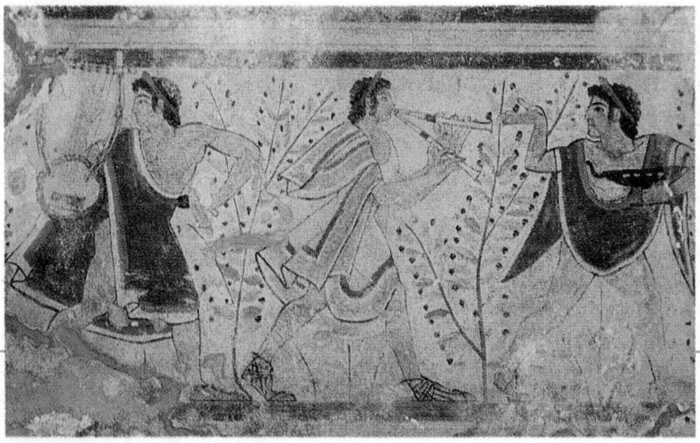

Connections To...

Geography

First Migration to America 35
Stemming the Flood 47
Sailing the Aegean 113
The Trail of the Black Death 327
Development of Industrial Cities 605
A Divided Land 683
Coastal Trading Centers 712
The Dust Bowl 777
Imperialist Boundaries 799
The Moving Sahara 943
Booming Buenos Aires 976

Economics

An Economic Region 144
East African Trading Cities 195
The Commercial Revolution 448
Feeding the Empire 466
Rebuilding Japan's Steel Industry 899
Global Economy 1020

Science and Technology

Counting the Days 85
The First Seismograph 226
At the Doctor's 286
Movable Metal Type and Printing 416
Bubbling Waters 519
Triumph Over an Ancient Enemy 627
The Development of Photography 658
Flaming Coffins 748
Water From the Euphrates 964

The Arts

Etruscan Culture 155
The Ajanta Caves 213
Hagia Sophia 249
The Bayeux Tapestry 309
The Art of Feudal Japan 361
Mayan Monuments 381
Johann Sebastian Bach 496
Rebuilding London 541
Music of Revolutions 578
Let Us Never Forget 850
Abstract Painting 884

Around the World

Early Oceangoing Navigation 24
Stonehenge Religious Site 53
Spread of Celtic Culture 92
Zapotec Temple Complex at Monte Albán 119
Palace of Persepolis 132
Sassanids Establish an Empire 178
Rebuilding of the Kremlin 188
"Song of Deborah" 206
Aesop's Fables 229
Simplified Alphabet Becomes Popular 250
Heraclius Recaptures the True Cross 271
Founding of Cairo 311
Kano Becomes a Walled City 326
Temple of Kailasa 362
Chocolate Is Introduced to Europe 389
Timur Lenk Rebuilds Central Mosque 409
Galileo Improves the Telescope 444
First Public Opera House Opens 472
The War of Jenkins' Ear 497
Franklin Experiments with Electricity 520
Religious Revolution in the Colonies 542
Revolution in Saint Domingue 566
World's Highest Railroad Is Built 611
Futabatei Publishes *The Drifting Clouds* 638
Greeks Fight for Independence 669
Slavery Is on Its Way Out 694
The Hague Peace Conference 725
Race to the South Pole 739
Jordan Gains Independence 780
Major Oil Discovery 816
Chemist Invents Nylon 833
Edmund Hillary Climbs Mount Everest 881
Free Speech Movement 902
Kwanzaa Celebrates African American Culture 939
SALT II Pact Signed 965
Live Aid Concert 993
Castro Allows Flood of Refugees 999

SKILLS

Social Studies Skills

Understanding Map Projections 37
Finding Exact Location on a Map 139
Interpreting Demographic Data 289
Analyzing Historical Maps 337
Comparing Thematic Maps 451
Interpreting Graphs 579
Reading a Cartogram 671
Interpreting Military Movements on Maps 765
Analyzing Trends 989
Interpreting Statistics 1023

Critical Thinking Skills

Classifying Information 65
Making Comparisons 125
Relevant and Irrelevant Information 179
Determining Cause and Effect 215
Identifying Central Issues 233
Distinguishing Between Fact and Opinion 265
Making Inferences 313
Making Generalizations 357
Hypothesizing 391
Identifying Evidence 421
Analyzing Primary and Secondary Sources 473
Interpreting Point of View 531
Detecting Bias 617
Analyzing Political Cartoons 720
Identifying an Argument 810
Synthesizing Information 837
Understanding World Time Zones 891

Study and Writing Skills

Taking Notes 87
Answering Test Questions 197
Recognizing a Stereotype 503
Outlining 551
Paraphrasing Information 634
Selecting and Using Research Sources 699
Preparing Note Cards for a Research Report 787
Conducting Interviews 923
Writing a Research Report 940
Preparing a Bibliography 961

"Why do we have to study this?"

Answering the Issue of Relevancy

Links to Today

Revolution … expansion … imperialism … How do you get your students to see that these concepts changed the world before *and during* their lifetimes? It's true that, unless your students see relevant reasons to study about the history of the world, they will not learn the lessons that history reveals. Your challenge every day is to generate high enthusiasm for learning by making strong connections between today's reality and the most telling stories and messages of the past.

Glencoe's *World History: The Human Experience* is your primary tool for successful student motivation, second only to your masterful talents of instruction. It continually reminds students why the content *must* matter to them. Every unit opens with **Then & Now,** recognizing how history is directly embedded in our everyday lives. Each chapter and section opens with **The Storyteller,** personalizing the historical period by disclosing the thoughts and ideas of people from that time in their own words. Pivotal questions pointing to the era's **Historical Significance** open each chapter, and the Chapter Review imparts more relevancy in **Linking Past and Present.**

Then & Now

Historical Significance

The Storyteller

Living the History

You want your students to *experience* history, to comprehend another's situation from a different perspective, and to develop more active empathy with people from another time. You raise the level of authentic instruction by increasing the students' interactions with the content and with each other. Your students begin and end the study of each chapter in Glencoe's *World History: The Human Experience* by writing in **Your History Journal,** where they explore real-world problems of another era, learning that no problem is totally objective and every point of view comes with a bias. **Footnotes to History** pique interest by revealing fascinating yet little-known facts about people, places, and events. And the classroom resource **History Simulations** take your students that much closer to actually being a part of history.

For Further Professional Reading

Adams, D., and M. Hamm. 1994. *New Designs for Teaching and Learning: Promoting Active Learning in Tomorrow's Schools.* San Francisco: Jossey-Bass Publishers.

Bower, B., J. Lobdell, and L. Swenson. 1994. *History Alive! Engaging All Learners in the Diverse Classroom.* New York: Addison-Wesley Publishing Company.

Newmann, F. M., and G. G. Wehlage. 1993. "Five Standards of Authentic Instruction." *Educational Leadership* 50(7): 8–12.

Other Program Resources

Rely on these additional resources to help students understand the relevancy of world history.

Teacher's Wraparound Edition

- Then & Now
- Linking Past and Present
- Global Gourmet
- You Don't Say…

Classroom Resources

- Historical Significance Chapter Activities
- Turning Points in World History Videodisc
- National Geographic Society CD-ROMs
- World Music: Cultural Traditions

Linking Past and Present

Seeing the Big Picture

> **Who? What? Where? When?**
>
> **Rasputin** was a hard man to kill. The conspirators who murdered him first tried poisoned wine and cakes. When these methods did not work, Prince Felix Yusupov, organizer of the plot, shot Rasputin. The bullets did not kill him either. He was finally drowned by plotters in the Neva River.

Learning for Understanding

Your students want to know what is most important among the millions of facts, key figures, significant events, and revealing interpretations in world history. You want them to know what it *all* means—recognizing the common themes from era to era and relating this information to today's hottest world headlines. Especially in this Information Age where data is at our fingertips, today's gauge of successful learning is not the quantity of information your students know but how well they understand. As coach and facilitator, your collaboration helps students become proficient in how to access information and derive meaning from it.

Find Out

World History: The Human Experience provides depth of understanding by consistently reinforcing historical trends, themes, and concepts. Beginning the unit with **A Global Chronology**, students see the relationships among important political, scientific, and social and cultural events. The text consistently puts events in perspective with time lines at the beginning of each chapter and section, too. Each unit ends with the **Unit Digest**, a synthesis of the important concepts discussed in each chapter.

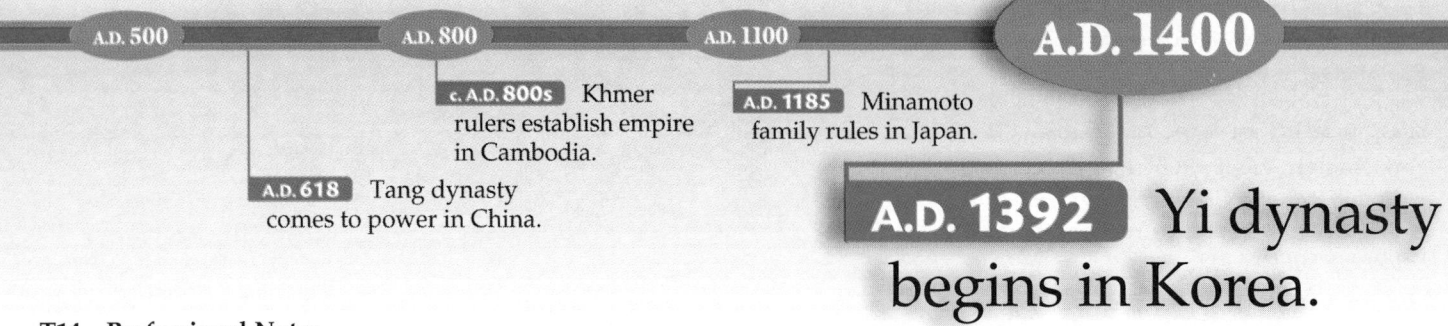

A.D. 500 — A.D. 800 — A.D. 1100 — A.D. 1400

A.D. 618 Tang dynasty comes to power in China.

c. A.D. 800s Khmer rulers establish empire in Cambodia.

A.D. 1185 Minamoto family rules in Japan.

A.D. 1392 Yi dynasty begins in Korea.

The Spread of Ideas

Comprehending Concepts

You are convinced that knowing the "big picture" empowers students to learn more and to find new ways to learn. Investing them with the power of historians—to determine the essential questions, investigate for answers in a variety of sources, draw conclusions, and present their interpretations with vigor—builds critical thinkers, able researchers, and participating citizens. Through such work, students grasp the "big ideas" and understand how important they are in the study of history. Glencoe's *World History: The Human Experience* opens each unit with **The Spread of Ideas**, which identifies an important concept in world history and explains how people from different parts of the world learned and reacted to these ideas during the epoch. Questions at the end of the feature help students in **Linking the Ideas**. The program communicates concepts by identifying **Chapter Themes** at the beginning of the chapter and reinforcing them in **Understanding Themes** in the Chapter Review. Students start each section of study with a **Find Out** question that channels their search for meaning.

Other Resources

Rely on these additional resources to help students see the "big picture."

Teacher's Wraparound Edition
- Section Theme Activity in Guided Practice
- Who?What?Where?When?

Classroom Resources
- Time Line Activities
- Chapter Themes: Graphic Organizers

For Further Professional Reading

Chuska, K. R. 1995. *Improving Classroom Questions: A Teacher's Guide to Increasing Student Motivation, Participation, and Higher-Level Thinking*. Bloomington, Ind.: Phi Delta Kappa Educational Foundation.

Thompson, L. J. 1995. *Habits of the Mind: Critical Thinking in the Classroom*. Lanham, Md.: University Press of America.

Williams, J. A. 1994. *Classroom in Conflict: Teaching Controversial Subjects in a Diverse Society*. Albany, N.Y.: State University of New York Press.

The Story of History

Telling the Story

Students' world views are only as broad as their life experiences. Once your students hear the powerful stories of the world's peoples, you know their views will broaden further. What's magical about the history of the world is that each story is brought to a personal level at which your students can ponder their ancestors' options. Through this personal identification, students imagine what it was like for people in that particular time and place—and learn from it. They are touched by the magic of the past through authentic voices, showcased in **The Storyteller** in Glencoe's *World History: The Human Experience*, which dramatically open each new chapter study. Primary source quotations, integrated generously throughout the narrative, sustain the story's momentum. With so many stories to read and incredible people to learn about, students extend their world views and move toward acceptance of the many sides of the global story.

Other Program Resources

Rely on these additional resources to help students understand the world's many cultural perspectives.

Teacher's Wraparound Edition

- Cultural Diffusion
- Cultural Perspectives

Classroom Resources

- People in World History
- World Music: Cultural Traditions

The Storyteller

The caravan halted for the night. Chaghatai, the leader, before retiring posted a sign and fastened bells around the animals' necks. Maffeo, a young foreigner, wondered at these precautions. Chaghatai explained that strange things may happen in the Desert of Lop. "When a man is riding by night through this desert and something happens to make him … lose touch with his companions … he hears spirits talking…. Often these voices make him stray from the path…. For this reason bands of travellers make a point of keeping very close together…. And round the necks of all their beasts they fasten little bells, so that by listening to the sound they may prevent them from straying from the path."

—adapted from *The Travels of Marco Polo*, Marco Polo, translated by Ronald Latham, 1958

Cultural Perspectives

Learning more about how world cultures of today and yesterday are interrelated is an important aspect of understanding the world's history. *World History: The Human Experience* helps you make those intercultural connections. As our global community shrinks in size because of high-speed communication and transportation, it becomes increasingly important for students to see people different from themselves as interesting neighbors who have different ideas, customs, and languages, but who share many of the same values. In analyzing the progress and struggles of these groups over the course of human history—and witnessing the humanity throughout—students develop more positive attitudes toward others.

Cultural Diffusion

The Circle Is Unbroken The diffusion of African-influenced music continues. In the 1960s, British groups such as the Beatles, the Rolling Stones, and Led Zeppelin recorded blues and rhythm and blues classics written by Muddy Waters, Howlin' Wolf, and Willie Dixon, among others. The British versions of such songs as "Little Red Rooster" and "Seventh Son" became popular among American fans who had never heard the originals.

At the same time, blues and soul have traveled back across the Atlantic Ocean to influence Ali Farka Toure of Mali and other popular African musicians. Similarly, Caribbean musicians have incorporated elements of rap into merengue, from the Dominican Republic, and reggae, from Jamaica.

Cultural Perspectives

Navajo Code Talkers In 1943 the U.S. Marines recruited the Navajo to develop a military code that the Japanese could not break. Based on their oral language, the Navajo code talkers created the only unbreakable code in military history.

For Further Professional Reading

Brown, C. S. 1988. *Like It Was. A Complete Guide to Writing Oral History*. New York: Teachers and Writers Collaborative.

Davidman, L., and P. T. Davidman. 1994. *Teaching With a Multicultural Perspective: A Practical Guide.* New York: Longman.

Gay, G. 1994. *At the Essence of Learning: Multicultural Education*. West Lafayette, Ind.: Kappa Delta Pi.

Sherritt, C. 1990. *What Not To Do in the Name of Multiculturalism*. Contemporary Education 61(4): 215–16.

Visualizing History

Seeing is Believing

Your students were raised on cable TV and remote controls. It's plain and simple from students' perspectives—if they can't see it, they *don't* believe it. But bringing the people, places, and events of world history to your students is what Glencoe's *World History: The Human Experience* does best. Interesting text and features are accompanied by colorful illustrations, maps, charts, and photos. With the help of giants such as the National Geographic Society and ABCNews InterActive™, students witness the rich pageantry of the world's past through **STV Videodiscs**, **PictureShow CD-ROMs**, and **Turning Points in World History**. The ***Picturing History*** and ***NGS Special Report*** features in the student text are brought to you from the National Geographic Society, unveiling exciting visuals and high-interest descriptions.

NATIONAL GEOGRAPHIC SOCIETY

Other Program Resources

Rely on these additional resources to help students visualize the spectacles of history.

Teacher's Wraparound Edition

- Visualizing History
- Images of the Times
- Making Connections Activities
- History & Art
- Curriculum Connection
- Connections: The Arts

Classroom Resources

- National Geographic Society Videodiscs
- NGS PictureShow CD-ROMs
- NGS Poster Sets and PicturePack Transparencies
- ABCNews InterActive™ Videodiscs
- Focus on World Art Prints
- Chapter Transparencies
- World History and Art Transparencies

ABCNEWS INTERACTIVE™

Images of the Times

Art as Experience

Nothing conveys the meaning of "god-king" more emphatically than examining the gold and precious stones on the stunning mask of Egyptian pharaoh Tutankhamen, one of the breathtaking posters in the **Focus on World Art Prints** collection. Prints displaying eighth-century Mayan civilization, medieval Europe, and nineteenth-century Africa, for example, bring students the color and artistry of times long ago. **Images of the Times**, a collection of art, sculpture, and other artifacts, also reveal the majesty of each period. Fine art appears continually throughout the text as illustrations and **History & Art**. Captions pose higher-order thinking questions that help students analyze what the art discloses about the people and the time in which they lived.

History & Art

Visualizing History

For Further Professional Reading

Epstein, T. L. 1994. "Sometimes a Shining Moment: High School Students' Representations of History Through the Arts." *Social Education* 58(3): 136–41.

Schubert, W., and G. Willis. 1991. *Understanding Curricula and Teaching Through the Arts*. Albany, N. Y.: State University of New York Press.

Geography in History

From the study of the emerging river valley civilizations in ancient times to the devastation of late twentieth-century natural disasters, the story of human history cannot be told without the influence of geographic features. Whether we talk about physical features—mountains blocking movement—or cultural features—dozens of ethnic groups and languages within a small region—geography has a significant impact on where and how people live.

Glencoe's *World History: The Human Experience* understands that there is no time to teach geography separately from world history. By integrating important geographic information and the five geographic themes within the narrative and providing in-depth focus on geography in **Connections: Geography** features, this program helps students see the undeniable tie between geography and history. The extensive map program and accompanying **Map Study** questions help students improve their map-reading skills while recognizing the importance of location, place, region, movement, and human/environment interaction. The **Geography in History** questions in the Chapter Review reinforce themes and key concepts. The best in the field—the National Geographic Society—offers special multimedia resources that extend the student text—CD-ROMs, videodiscs, transparencies, posters, related references to *National Geographic*, and more!

NATIONAL GEOGRAPHIC SOCIETY

Other Program Resources

Rely on these additional resources to help students understand the importance of geography in history.

Teacher's Wraparound Edition
- Geography Connection
- Map Study

Classroom Resources
- Geography and History Activities
- Student Desk Map
- Mapping History Activities
- Mapping History Overlay Transparencies

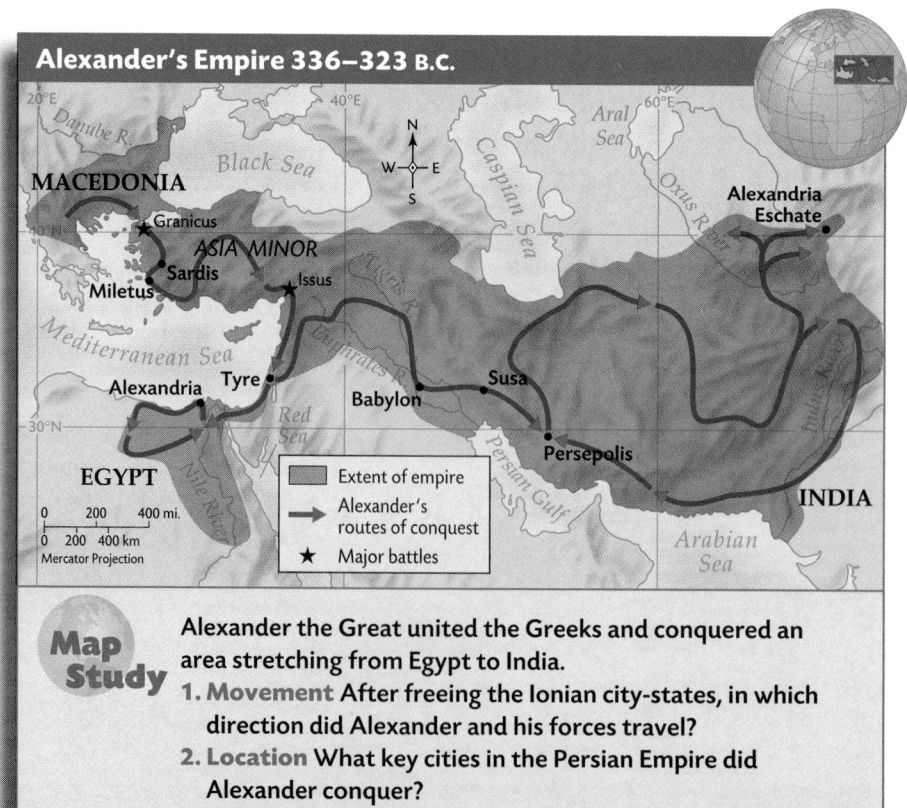

Alexander's Empire 336–323 B.C.

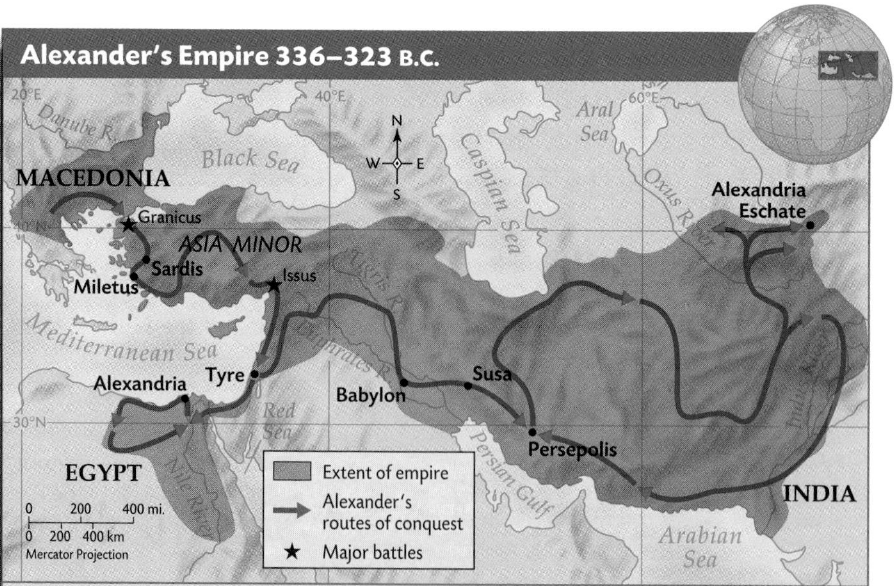

Map Study

Alexander the Great united the Greeks and conquered an area stretching from Egypt to India.

1. **Movement** After freeing the Ionian city-states, in which direction did Alexander and his forces travel?
2. **Location** What key cities in the Persian Empire did Alexander conquer?

Integrating Literature and Writing into History

Concepts are better understood when information is presented in context rather than in unrelated bits and pieces. This means that integrating the important literature of particular eras within the study of history not only assists students in understanding the context of the people's lives but also reinforces verbal skills when completing writing assignments, such as the **Portfolio Project** at the beginning of each unit and **Your History Journal** at the start of each chapter.

Glencoe's *World History: The Human Experience* provides an extensive excerpt from world literature for each unit in **Literature: Bridge to the Past**. This selection represents the time, the people, and the issues of the period, exposing students to literature of interdisciplinary consequence. Discussions and activities related to the selection assist the student in understanding its **Historical Connection** and **Contemporary Connection**. Information about the author and further examples of literature from the period extend student knowledge and understanding.

Bridge to the Past
Literature

Other Program Resources

Rely on these additional resources to help students understand the importance of literature and writing in history.

Teacher's Wraparound Edition
- History and the Humanities
- About the Author
- Additional Literary Works of the Period

Classroom Resources
- World Literature Selections
- Source Readings

Your History Journal

Portfolio Project

For Further Professional Reading

Danks, C. 1995. "Using Holocaust Short Stories and Poetry in the Social Studies Classroom." *Social Education* 59(6): 358–61.

Irvin, J. L., J. P. Lunstrum, C. Lynch-Brown, and M. F. Shepard. 1995. *Enhancing Social Studies Through Literary Strategies*. Washington, D.C.: National Council for the Social Studies.

Addressing Multiple Learning Styles

With the advent of the 1980s and throughout the past 15 years, new discoveries about the inner workings and development of the brain and the nature of intelligence have replaced traditional beliefs that intelligence is entirely predetermined at birth. One of the most noted theories, advanced by Howard Gardner, is the theory of multiple intelligences, which contends that there are at least seven forms of intelligence that help us understand the world around us.

MULTIPLE LEARNING STYLES

Glencoe's *World History: The Human Experience* provides you with a chapter activity for seven types of intelligences in each **Chapter Planning Guide**.

1 Verbal/Linguistic Learners

Students who exhibit this intelligence can argue, persuade, entertain, or instruct others effectively with words. They read regularly, can write clearly, and easily understand the written word. They retain facts readily, and love to play with the sounds of language.

Teachers can help develop this intelligence by using overhead projectors to convey information, providing audiocassettes for Chapter Digests, as well as assigning reading and writing. Writing a journal, like the **Your History Journal** in *World History: The Human Experience*, will exercise linguistic intelligence.

2 Logical/Mathematical Learners

Students who exhibit this intelligence demonstrate the ability to reason, sequence, identify cause and effect, and create hypotheses. They see numerical patterns and can spot conceptual irregularities. They generally have a very rational outlook toward life, and love to develop "what if" scenarios.

Teachers can help develop this intelligence by discussing the pros and cons of important decisions made in world history and eliciting rationales for each side. To exercise this intelligence, students, for example, could sequence events in the **Time Line Activities** booklet.

3 Visual/Spatial Learners

Students who exhibit this intelligence think in terms of pictures and images. They are acutely aware of visual details and need to draw or sketch their ideas graphically. They easily see three-dimensional space and can transform content into images.

Teachers can help develop this intelligence by planning videodisc and CD-ROM presentations or by assigning readings in the NATIONAL GEOGRAPHIC ***Magazine***, which depicts historical events with beautiful illustrations.

4 Auditory/Musical Learners

Students who exhibit this intelligence can produce rhythms and melodies. They sing in tune, keep time to music, and listen perceptively to different kinds of music. They can discern subtle differences in sounds and have "good ears."

Teachers can help develop this intelligence by incorporating more technology into lessons. Having students listen to the **Chapter Digests Audiocassettes** will exercise this intelligence. CD-ROMs also provide students with instant auditory directions and feedback.

5 Kinesthetic Learners

Students who exhibit this intelligence coordinate their body movements well, must move their bodies frequently, and can maneuver objects with skill. They have good tactile sensitivity, needing to touch things in order to learn about them, and can sense with their physical body.

Teachers can help develop this intelligence by asking students to perform basic tasks, such as constructing models, charts, or graphs that apply new knowledge. Students also practice new skills by using the **Student Self-Test and Review Software**.

6 Interpersonal Learners

Students who exhibit this intelligence understand and work well with other people. They demonstrate abilities to perceive others' moods, intentions, and desires. They can comfortably step into another's perspective of the world. Many class leaders have this intelligence.

Teachers can help develop this intelligence by integrating **History Simulations** and **Cooperative Learning Activities** into their plans. In such settings, students can seek help from another student or learn with a partner.

7 Intrapersonal Learners

Students who exhibit this intelligence can easily assess their own feelings, are very introspective, and enjoy meditation and soul-searching. They use their self-understanding to guide their lives and can be very goal-directed. They can be fiercely independent and highly self-disciplined. These students are likely to have opinions that set them apart from others and prefer to work alone. They take themselves very seriously yet have a realistic understanding of their strengths and weaknesses.

Teachers can help develop this intelligence by encouraging the use of a personal journal, asking for students' opinions on important issues, and encouraging the reading of autobiographies and biographies of important historical figures, such as those featured in **People in World History**. Analyzing the traits of figures who have been successful will help students analyze their own personal strengths.

What multiple intelligences mean to history teachers is that you must assign activities to students that accommodate their strongest intelligences but frequently exercise their weakest intelligences. Although students may experience some difficulty by engaging in work from a different domain, they can strengthen the weaker intelligence over time. And by stretching their comfort zones, you help them strengthen their overall thinking and problem-solving abilities.

The resources available in *World History: The Human Experience* guarantee that your classroom will be a multisensory environment, providing multiple paths for student learning.

Other Program Resources

Rely on these additional resources to help you provide for individual student needs.

Teacher's Wraparound Edition

- Multiple Learning Styles Chapter Activities
- Cooperative Learning Activities
- Key to Ability Levels
- Meeting Special Needs Activities

For Further Professional Reading

Armstrong, T. 1993. *Seven Kinds of Smart: Identifying and Developing Your Many Intelligences.* New York: Plume/Penguin Books Inc.

Csikszentmihalyi, M., K. Rathunde, and S. Whalen. 1993. *Talented Teenagers: The Roots of Success and Failure.* New York: Cambridge University Press.

Gardner, H. G. 1993. *Multiple Intelligences: The Theory in Practice.* New York: Basic Books, Inc.

Johnson, D. W., R. Johnson, E. J. Holubec, and P. Roy. 1984. *Circles of Learning: Cooperation in the Classroom.* Alexandria, Va.: Association for Supervision and Curriculum Development.

Kagan, S. 1990. *Cooperative Learning: Resources for Teachers.* San Juan Capistrano, Calif.: Resources for Teachers.

Implementing Block Scheduling

Advantages for Schools

For the schools themselves, the greatest advantage of block scheduling is a better use of resources. The schedule change does not require additional teachers or classrooms. It eliminates half of the time needed for class changes, which results in fewer discipline problems. Schools also report an increase in the overall quality of teacher instruction and student's time on task.

Advantages for Teachers

With block scheduling, teachers instruct fewer students each term, so students and teachers get to know each other better, and relationships improve. Teachers have time to provide additional one-on-one help and other resources for meeting the individual needs of students. Because block scheduling cuts in half the time needed for introducing and closing classes, teachers have more time to teach the key concepts of their discipline and become more focused themselves. Some schools report improved teacher morale, increased teacher effectiveness, and decreased burn-out.

Block scheduling results in more frequent use of varied teaching approaches and more student-centered environments. Teachers venture away from discussion and lecture and use more productive models of teaching. Flexibility allows more opportunities for cooperative teaching strategies such as team teaching and interdisciplinary studies. Block scheduling also encourages activity-centered instruction; in Glencoe's *World History: The Human Experience* Teacher's Wraparound Edition, such activities and research projects are specially coded for block schedules.

Advantages for Students

Student success rate is greater in a block scheduling format because students interact more with their teachers and the content, learning more and retaining it longer. Students develop better problem-solving skills because they have more time to think.

In a block students study fewer subjects each term, making them better able to manage their workload. Students experience fewer outside distractions and are better able to concentrate. They voice that there is more time to learn and more time to ask questions.

Students maximize use of the curriculum with a block schedule. They schedule required courses during the first term, and, if they do not pass the course, they can repeat it during the second term. Better students move ahead more quickly; block scheduling increases the number of students who take upper-level classes and earn advanced studies diplomas.

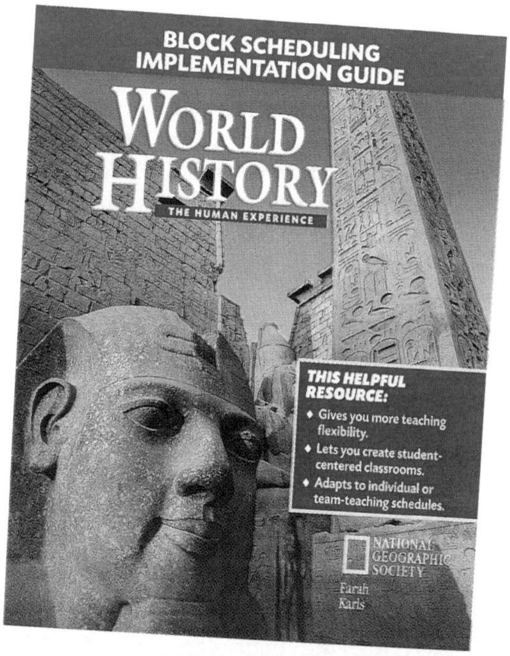

BLOCK SCHEDULING IMPLEMENTATION GUIDE
WORLD HISTORY
THE HUMAN EXPERIENCE
THIS HELPFUL RESOURCE:
• Gives you more teaching flexibility.
• Lets you create student-centered classrooms.
• Adapts to individual or team-teaching schedules.
NATIONAL GEOGRAPHIC SOCIETY
Farah
Karls

Utilizing Performance Assessment

Traditionally, in the social studies classroom, assessment has been at the end of study to measure how well students have learned the objectives of the unit of study. But today, in order to prepare students for future success in the adult world, more authentic forms of assessment, consisting of ongoing demonstrations of worthwhile, meaningful tasks, are in order.

Traditional Measures

Glencoe's *World History: The Human Experience* provides you with both types of assessment. Traditional forms—**Chapter and Unit Tests**, **Section Quizzes**, and **Testmaker Software**—are available to evaluate knowledge of factual content and some forms of thinking skills.

Performance Measures

The alternative measures most often utilized by classroom teachers are projects, teacher observation, performance-based essays, and portfolios.

Tasks may be divided into three broad types: teacher-directed tasks, student-directed tasks, and collections over time. In **teacher-directed tasks**, students may be guided step-by-step through various phases of a task. For example, the teacher leads the class in brainstorming, but when students realize that they do not have enough information in order to be successful, the teacher serves as coach or facilitator.

Student-directed tasks are typically used at the end of a unit of study in the place of or in concert with traditional tests. The teacher explains clearly what is expected of the students in process and product and makes known the essential criteria.

Collections over time require longer periods to develop but are helpful in allowing the student to discover a broader application for what is learned than can be accomplished within a one-time task. The **Portfolio Project** assigned at the beginning of each unit in *World History: The Human Experience* is an example.

Journals are often used as performance assessment because they contain samples of students' work collected over a period of time—often an entire grading period or even a semester. **Your History Journal**, assigned at the beginning of every chapter, provides students an opportunity not only to find information but also to make sense of it and put that information in context. The most common form of assessing authentic performance is by rubric, or by percent or points. You determine the components of the product, process, or task, and weight the completion of each according to its merits. A three-point rubric would show Score Point One as unacceptable performance and Score Point Three as completely successful. Each chapter's **Performance Assessment Activity**, suggested in *World History: The Human Experience*, is accompanied with possible rubric features to help you plan your assessment strategies.

Other Resources

Rely on these additional resources to help students prepare portfolio items for assessment.

Teacher's Wraparound Edition

- Performance Assessment Activities
- Extra Credit Project

Classroom Resources

- Performance Assessment Strategies and Activities
- Student Self-Test and Review Software

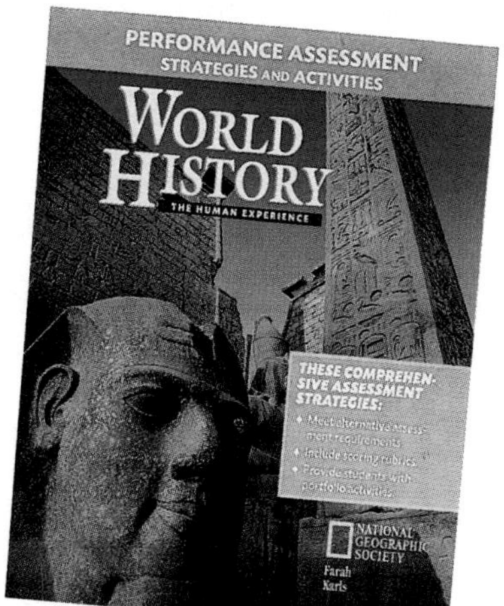

Glencoe's software HOTLINE is 1-800-437-3715

Using Technology in the Classroom

Advances in technology continually debut, dramatically affecting all aspects of the social studies. Social studies instruction can include such advances, and Glencoe has developed many programs for successful integration of technology into your classroom.

Software

Student Self-Test and Review Software This highly motivational program allows students to check their comprehension by answering questions using the computer. If a student chooses a wrong answer, the computer explains why the choice is incorrect. The student may then try again. This process continues until the student chooses the correct answer. Chapter Summaries and a Glossary are also integrated in this software.

Testmaker Glencoe's Testmaker allows you to customize tests to fit your students' special needs. The software allows you to edit, reorder, and add questions as you desire and is available in Macintosh and DOS formats.

Vocabulary PuzzleMaker Because vocabulary development and comprehension is such an important part of social studies instruction, Glencoe has developed a special vocabulary program. The Vocabulary PuzzleMaker helps you create high-interest crossword puzzles and word searches.

NATIONAL GEOGRAPHIC SOCIETY

The National Geographic Society has prize-winning resources. Fascinating audio and video clips exhibit history, languages, music, and cultural traditions of nations and civilizations.

Picture Atlas of the World

PictureShow CD-ROMs

- **Egypt and the Fertile Crescent**
- **India and China**
- **Greece and Rome**
- **The Middle Ages**
- **The Renaissance**
- **Age of Exploration**

Videodiscs

If your school has a basic system consisting of a videodisc player and a television receiver, the videodiscs provide an effective and interesting tool for classroom presentations.

MindJogger Videoquiz The MindJogger Videoquiz uses a game show format for review of key concepts. A bar code scanner allows you immediate access to specific chapters on the videodisc. The bar codes are placed on the Chapter Opener and Chapter Review pages of the Teacher's Wraparound Edition. The MindJogger Videoquiz is also available in a VHS format.

NATIONAL GEOGRAPHIC SOCIETY

- **STV: World Geography**
- **STV: North America**
- **STV: Maya**

ABCNEWS INTERACTIVE™ The following videodiscs help students in their understanding of world history.

- **Turning Points in World History**
- **In the Holy Land**
- **Lessons of War**
- **Communism and the Cold War**

Computer Training for Teachers

You must have a general knowledge of computer operation, but you do not need to have a knowledge of internal hardware elements or programming languages. Call Glencoe's software hotline as your best resource when using any type of software.

For Further Professional Reading

Brady, H. R. 1994. "Overview of Computer Integration Into Social Studies Instruction." *Social Education* (58): 312.

Jonassen, D. H. 1996. *Computers in the Classroom: Mindtools for Critical Thinking*. Englewood Cliffs, N.J.: Prentice Hall

Surfing the History Net

You can join three history list servers:

- Send this message **Subscribe NCSS-L Your Name** to listproc2@bgu.edu to share information and ideas about K–12 social studies education, sponsored by the Instructional Technology Committee of the National Council for the Social Studies.
- Send **sub H-High-S Your Name Your School** to LISTSERV@msu.edu for inclusion in an ongoing discussion of curriculum, instructional strategies, and educational resources involved in teaching history.
- Send **Sub Histnews Your Name** tolistserv@ukanvm.cc.ukans.edu for a newsletter for historians.

The Internet

Think of the Internet as similar to using the telephone. If you know the name of the computer you want to contact, you look up its number, have your computer dial it, and talk to it. Sending messages from person to person is one of the Net's most popular uses. You can reach a specific person by using E-mail, be on a list server that sends information to its subscribers, or you can subscribe to bulletin boards where messages are posted for all to read. The Internet, however, is used for much more than just receiving and sending messages.

World Wide Web

Getting information through the Internet became much easier with the development of the World Wide Web in 1992. The Web is an exciting region of the Internet that contains pictures, sound, and video as well as text. You can scan the Web using "browsers"—programs such as Netscape and Mosaic. You can go directly to one of the million sources of information if you know an address called the Uniform Reference Locator (URL).

On-line Resources

Each Chapter Planning Guide in *World History: The Human Experience* offers you easy-to-use Internet Connections. In addition to this unique feature, you may also wish to use the following Internet sites.

On-line resources for world history teachers are limitless. Sites are listed below with their URLs. When you type the address, you will reach the organization's "home-page," which tells you what is available at its site. Some are clearinghouses for other sources.

- **Armadillo from Rice University**
  http://chico.rice.edu/armadillo/about.html
- **CNN**
  http://www.cnn.com
- **ERIC Clearinghouses**
  http://www.cua.edu/www/eric_ae/home.html
  http://ericir.syr.edu/ERIC/eric.hmtl
- **Joint Education Initiative at Maryland**
  http://jei.umd.edu/
- **Library of Congress**
  http://lcweb.loc.gov/homepage/lchp.html
- **Western European Studies (since 1945) Homepage**
  http://www.pitt.edu/~wwwes/
- **Yahoo**
  http://www.yahoo.com/

The following sites are particularly relevant to world history:

- **CIA's 1995 World Factbook, indexed by country**
  http://www.odci.gov/cia/publications/95fact/index.html
- **Dewey Web, which is geared for students of global education**
  http://ics.soe.umich.edu/
- **EuroDocs for primary historical documents**
  http://library.byu.edu/~rdh/eurodocs/
- **Historical Atlas**
  http://www.ma.org/maps/map.html
- **KidLink encourages dialogue among students ages 10–15 worldwide.**
  http://www.kidlink.org/home-std.html
- **Medieval Studies**
  http://sunsite.berkeley.edu/OMACL/
- **Program in International Educational Resources**
  http://www.yale.edu/pieris
- **Resources on Asia**
  http://coombs.anu.edu.au/WWWVL/AsianStudies.html
- **Resources on Japan**
  http://www.indiana.edu/~japan/odata.html
- **Resources on Latin America**
  http://www.cmcc.muse.digital.ca/cmc/cmceng/mminteng.html
- **Resources on Africa**
  http://www.sas.upenn.edu/African_Studies/Home_Page/Country.html
- **Resources on Saudi Arabia**
  http://imedl.saudi.net/
- **Ultimate History**
  http://history.cc.ukans.edu/history/index.html

Newspapers from other countries summarize daily news:

German News in English
http://www.uni-karlsruhe.de/misc/de-news/

ANSA News Agency summaries (Italy) in English
http://www.ansa.it/inglese2.html

The Times (London)
http://www.the-times.co.uk/

Glencoe's unique Internet Connections are a continuing source of exploration. The sites listed here and elsewhere in the Teacher's Wraparound Edition are not under the control of Glencoe/McGraw-Hill and, therefore, Glencoe makes no representation concerning the content of the sites. We encourage teachers to preview these sites before students access them. Internet sites are sometimes under construction and may be incomplete and not always available. Sites may move or be removed.

Correlation to NCSS Ten Thematic Strands

In *Curriculum Standards for Social Studies: Expectations of Excellence*, the National Council for the Social Studies (NCSS) identified ten themes that serve as organizing strands for the social studies curriculum at every school level. These themes are interrelated and draw from all of the social science disciplines. Below is a correlation chart showing where the social studies themes are incorporated in *World History: The Human Experience*.

Social Studies Theme	**Incorporated Within *World History: The Human Experience***			
I. Culture				
Human beings create, learn, and adapt culture. Human cultures are dynamic systems of beliefs, values, and traditions that exhibit both commonalities and differences. Understanding culture helps us understand ourselves and others.	Ch. 1; S. 2, 3 Ch. 2 Ch. 3 Ch. 4; S. 1, 4 Ch. 5 Ch. 6; S. 1, 3, 4 Ch. 7; S. 1, 2 Ch. 8 Ch. 9; S. 2, 3	Ch. 10; S. 1, 2, 3 Ch. 11; S. 1, 3 Ch. 12; S. 1, 3 Ch. 13; S. 1, 2, 4 Ch. 14 Ch. 15; S. 2, 3 Ch. 16 Ch. 17; S. 7 Ch. 18	Ch. 19; S. 1, 2, 3, 5 Ch. 20 Ch. 21; S. 1, 2, 4 Ch. 22; S. 2, 3, 4 Ch. 23; S. 1, 4 Ch. 24; S. 1, 3, 4 Ch. 25; S. 1, 3 Ch. 26; S. 3 Ch. 27; S. 1, 2	Ch. 29; S. 1, 4 Ch. 28; S. 4 Ch. 30; S. 2, 4 Ch. 32; S. 4 Ch. 33; S. 2, 5 Ch. 35; S. 2, 3 Ch. 36; S. 1 Ch. 37; S. 1, 4
II. Time, Continuity, and Change				
Human beings seek to understand their historic roots and to locate themselves in time. Such understanding involves knowing what things were like in the past and how things change and develop—allowing us to develop historic perspective and answer important questions about our current condition.	Ch. 1 Ch. 2 Ch. 3 Ch. 4; S. 1 Ch. 6; S. 1, 4 Ch. 7; S. 1 Ch. 8; S. 1 Ch. 9; S. 1	Ch. 10; S. 1 Ch. 11; S. 1 Ch. 12; S. 1 Ch. 14 Ch. 15 Ch. 16; S. 1 Ch. 17; S. 1, 3 Ch. 20	Ch. 21; S. 1, 3, 4 Ch. 22; S. 1, 3 Ch. 23 Ch. 24 Ch. 27; S. 1 Ch. 28; S. 1, 2, 4, 5 Ch. 29; S. 1 Ch. 30	Ch. 31; S. 1, 5 Ch. 32; S. 1 Ch. 33; S. 1 Ch. 34; S. 1 Ch. 35; S. 3 Ch. 36; S. 1 Ch. 37
III. People, Places, and Environment				
Technological advancements have insured that students are aware of the world beyond their personal locations. As students study content related to this theme, they create their spatial views and geographic perspectives of the world; social, cultural, economic, and civic demands mean that students will need such knowledge, skills, and understandings to make informed and critical decisions about the relationship between human beings and their environment.	Ch. 1 Ch. 2 Ch. 3; S. 1, 2 Ch. 4; S. 1, 2, 3 Ch. 5; S. 3 Ch. 6; S. 1 Ch. 7; S. 1, 3	Ch. 8; S. 1 Ch. 10; S. 1, 3 Ch. 11; S. 1 Ch. 12; S. 2 Ch. 13; S. 2 Ch. 14; S. 1, 4 Ch. 15; S. 1, 2	Ch. 17; S. 1, 2 Ch. 21; S. 3 Ch. 23; S. 1, 2, 5 Ch. 24; S. 3 Ch. 26; S. 3, 5 Ch. 27; S. 1, 3 Ch. 32; S. 2	Ch. 33; S. 2 Ch. 34; S. 3 Ch. 35; S. 3 Ch. 36; S. 1 Ch. 37; S. 5
IV. Individual Development and Identity				
Personal identity is shaped by one's culture, by groups, and by institutional influences. Examination of various forms of human behavior enhances understanding of the relationships between social norms and emerging personal identities, the social processes which influence identity formation, and the ethical principles underlying individual action.	Ch. 1; S. 3 Ch. 2 Ch. 3 Ch. 4; S. 2 Ch. 5; S. 1, 2 Ch. 6; S. 3, 4 Ch. 7; S. 1 Ch. 8; S. 1, 2	Ch. 9; S. 2, 3 Ch. 10 Ch. 11; S. 1, 3 Ch. 12; S. 2, 3 Ch. 15 Ch. 16; S. 1, 4, 5 Ch. 17; S. 3 Ch. 20; S. 2, 3	Ch. 21; S. 1, 3, 4 Ch. 22; S. 2, 3 Ch. 23; S. 1, 3, 4 Ch. 24; S. 1, 3 Ch. 28; S. 1, 3, 4 Ch. 29; S. 1 Ch. 30 Ch. 31; S. 1, 3, 4	Ch. 32; S. 1 Ch. 34; S. 3 Ch. 35; S. 3 Ch. 36; S. 1 Ch. 37

Ch. = Chapter   S. = Section

V. Individuals, Groups, and Institutions

Institutions exert enormous influence over us. Institutions are organizational embodiments to further the core social values of those who comprise them. It is important for students to know how institutions are formed, what controls and influences them, how they control and influence individuals and culture, and how institutions can be maintained or changed.

Ch. 1; S. 3	Ch. 11; S. 1, 2	Ch. 21	Ch. 32
Ch. 2	Ch. 12; S. 1, 3, 4	Ch. 22	Ch. 33
Ch. 3	Ch. 13; S. 2, 3, 4	Ch. 23; S. 4	Ch. 34
Ch. 4; S. 2	Ch. 14	Ch. 25	Ch. 35
Ch. 6; S. 1, 3, 4	Ch. 15	Ch. 26	Ch. 36
Ch. 7; S. 1, 2	Ch. 16; S. 4, 5	Ch. 28; S. 4	Ch. 37
Ch. 8; S. 1, 3	Ch. 17; S. 2	Ch. 29; S. 2, 3, 4	
Ch. 9; S. 1	Ch. 18	Ch. 30	
Ch. 10; S. 2, 3	Ch. 19	Ch. 31; S. 5	

VI. Power, Authority, and Governance

Understanding of the historical development of structures of power, authority, and governance and their evolving functions in contemporary society is essential for the emergence of civic competence.

Ch. 1; S. 3	Ch. 9; S. 1	Ch. 18	Ch. 29; S. 2, 3, 4
Ch. 2	Ch. 10	Ch. 19	Ch. 30
Ch. 3	Ch. 11; S. 2	Ch. 21	Ch. 32
Ch. 4	Ch. 12; S. 1, 4	Ch. 22	Ch. 33
Ch. 5; S. 3	Ch. 14	Ch. 25	Ch. 34
Ch. 6; S. 1, 2, 3, 5	Ch. 15	Ch. 26	Ch. 35
Ch. 7	Ch. 16; S. 1, 4, 5	Ch. 27; S. 2, 3, 4	
Ch. 8; S. 3	Ch. 17; S. 2	Ch. 28; S. 4	

VII. Production, Distribution, and Consumption

Decisions about exchange, trade, and economic policy and well-being are global in scope, and the role of government in policy making varies over time and from place to place. The systematic study of an interdependent world economy and the role of technology in economic decision making is essential.

Ch. 1; S. 3	Ch. 12; S. 2	Ch. 22; S. 1, 2, 4	Ch. 32
Ch. 2; S. 1, 2, 3	Ch. 13; S. 2	Ch. 23; S. 1, 2, 4	Ch. 33; S. 1, 3
Ch. 3; S. 1, 3	Ch. 14; S. 2, 4	Ch. 24; S. 1	Ch. 34; S. 2, 3
Ch. 4; S. 2, 3, 4	Ch. 15; S. 2, 3	Ch. 25; S. 4, 5	Ch. 35; S. 1, 2, 3
Ch. 6; S. 3, 5	Ch. 16; S. 1, 2	Ch. 26; S. 3	Ch. 36; S. 1, 2, 4
Ch. 7; S. 2	Ch. 17; S. 1, 3	Ch. 27; S. 1, 2	Ch. 37; S. 1, 2, 3, 5
Ch. 9; S. 1, 3	Ch. 18; S. 2, 3, 4	Ch. 28; S. 1, 4, 5	
Ch. 10; S. 2	Ch. 19; S. 1, 2, 3	Ch. 29	
Ch. 11; S. 3	Ch. 21; S. 1, 2, 3	Ch. 30; S. 4, 5	

VIII. Science, Technology, and Society

Technology is as old as the first crude tool invented by prehistoric humans, and modern life as we know it would be impossible without technology and the science which supports it. Today's technology forms the basis for some of our most difficult social choices.

Ch. 1; S. 2, 3	Ch. 10; S. 2	Ch. 20; S. 1, 2	Ch. 30; S. 4
Ch. 2; S. 1, 2	Ch. 11; S. 3	Ch. 22; S. 3	Ch. 31; S. 2, 4, 5
Ch. 3; S. 2, 3	Ch. 13; S. 3	Ch. 23; S. 1, 2, 3	Ch. 32; S. 3, 4
Ch. 4; S. 3	Ch. 14; S. 2	Ch. 24; S. 2, 3	Ch. 33; S. 1, 2
Ch. 5; S. 2, 3	Ch. 15; S. 2	Ch. 26; S. 3	Ch. 37; S. 5
Ch. 6; S. 3	Ch. 16; S. 1	Ch. 27; S. 4	
Ch. 8; S. 2, 3	Ch. 17; S. 1	Ch. 28; S. 3	
Ch. 9; S. 1, 3	Ch. 19; S. 5	Ch. 29; S. 1	

IX. Global Connections

The realities of global interdependence require understanding of the increasingly important and diverse global connections among world societies before there can be analysis leading to the development of possible solutions to persisting and emerging global issues.

Ch. 1	Ch. 7; S. 2, 3	Ch. 13; S. 1	Ch. 24; S. 4
Ch. 2	Ch. 8; S. 2	Ch. 14; S. 3	Ch. 3; S. 1, 3
Ch. 9; S. 3	Ch. 16; S. 2, 4	Ch. 25; S. 2	Ch. 27; S. 1
Ch. 4; S. 2	Ch. 10; S. 3	Ch. 17; S. 2	Ch. 33; S. 6
Ch. 5; S. 3	Ch. 11; S. 2, 3	Ch. 18; S. 2, 3, 4	Ch. 35; S. 3
Ch. 6; S. 3, 4	Ch. 12; S. 2, 3	Ch. 22; S. 4	Ch. 37; S. 5

X. Civic Ideals and Practices

All people have a stake in examining civic ideals and practices across time, in diverse societies, as well as in determining how to close the gap between present practices and the ideals upon which our democratic republic is based. An understanding of civic ideals and practices of citizenship is critical to full participation in society.

Ch. 2; S. 1, 2	Ch. 10; S. 1, 3	Ch. 20; S. 2, 3	Ch. 30
Ch. 3	Ch. 11; S. 1, 2	Ch. 21	Ch. 31; S. 1, 2, 5
Ch. 4; S. 1, 2, 3	Ch. 12; S. 1, 2, 4	Ch. 22; S. 1, 2, 4	Ch. 32; S. 2, 3, 4
Ch. 5; S. 2, 3	Ch. 13; S. 2, 3	Ch. 25; S. 1, 2, 3, 5	Ch. 33; S. 1, 2, 5, 6
Ch. 6; S. 1, 2, 3, 5	Ch. 14	Ch. 26	Ch. 34; S. 1, 2
Ch. 7; S. 2	Ch. 15; S. 2, 3	Ch. 28; S. 2, 3, 4	Ch. 35
Ch. 9; S. 1, 2	Ch. 19	Ch. 29	Ch. 36

Six Alternative Course Outlines

World History: The Human Experience may be taught in a variety of courses. Listed below are six examples.

OUTLINE 1

World History Survey

Unit 1 **The Rise of Civilizations** Chapters 1, 2, 3
Unit 2 **Flowering of Civilizations** Chapters 4, 5, 6, 7, 8, 9
Unit 3 **Regional Civilizations** Chapters 10, 11, 12, 13, 14, 15
Unit 4 **Emergence of the Modern World** Chapters 16, 17, 18, 19
Unit 5 **Age of Revolution** Chapters 20, 21, 22
Unit 6 **Industry and Nationalism** Chapters 23, 24, 25, 26, 27
Unit 7 **World in Conflict** Chapters 28, 29, 30, 31
Unit 8 **The Contemporary World** Chapters 32, 33, 34, 35, 36, 37

OUTLINE 2

Western Civilization

Unit 2 **Flowering of Civilizations** Chapters 4, 5, 6
Unit 3 **Regional Civilizations** Chapters 12, 13
Unit 4 **Emergence of the Modern World** Chapters 16, 17, 19
Unit 5 **Age of Revolution** Chapters 20, 21, 22
Unit 6 **Industry and Nationalism** Chapters 23, 24, 25, 26
Unit 7 **World in Conflict** Chapters 28, 29, 31
Unit 8 **The Contemporary World** Chapters 32, 37

OUTLINE 3

Non-Western Civilization

Unit 1 **The Rise of Civilizations** Chapters 1, 2, 3
Unit 2 **Flowering of Civilizations** Chapters 7, 8, 9
Unit 3 **Regional Civilizations** Chapters 10, 11, 14, 15
Unit 4 **Emergence of the Modern World** Chapter 18
Unit 6 **Industry and Nationalism** Chapter 27
Unit 7 **World in Conflict** Chapter 30
Unit 8 **The Contemporary World** Chapters 33 34, 35

OUTLINE 4

World Cultures/Global Studies

Unit 1 The Rise of Civilizations Chapters 2, 3
Unit 2 Flowering of Civilizations Chapters 5, 6, 7, 8, 9
Unit 3 Regional Civilizations Chapters 10, 11, 14, 15
Unit 4 Emergence of the Modern World Chapter 18
Unit 5 Age of Revolution Chapter 20
Unit 6 Industry and Nationalism Chapters 24, 27
Unit 7 World in Conflict Chapter 30
Unit 8 The Contemporary World Chapters 33, 34, 35, 36, 37

OUTLINE 5

Ancient History

Unit 1 The Rise of Civilizations Chapters 1, 2, 3
Unit 2 Flowering of Civilizations Chapters 4, 5, 6, 7, 8, 9
Unit 3 Regional Civilizations Chapters 10, 11, 12, 13, 14, 15
Unit 4 Emergence of the Modern World Chapters 16, 18

OUTLINE 6

Modern History

Unit 4 Emergence of the Modern World Chapters 16, 17, 19
Unit 5 Age of Revolution Chapters 20, 21, 22
Unit 6 Industry and Nationalism Chapters 23, 24, 25, 26, 27
Unit 7 World in Conflict Chapters 28, 29, 30, 31
Unit 8 The Contemporary World Chapters 32, 33, 34, 35, 36, 37

Scope and Sequence

Historical Themes

Students need to understand and be able to recognize the themes that appear throughout history. Students also need to develop the ability to apply these themes as they examine the effect of the past on the present and the future.

The central theme highlighted in each section appears in red. Related themes are listed in black.

Content Knowledge

Students need to have a knowledge of the disciplines that play an integral role in the social studies: history, literature, art and culture, science and technology, government and civics, geography, economics, and religion. Students also need to develop a keen understanding of how these subjects interact with one another.

Skills

Students need to learn and practice skills, in groups and independently, to participate effectively in society.

	Chapter 1	2	3	4
Historical Themes				
Movement	Sections 1, 2	Sections 1, 2, 4	Sections 1, 3	Sections 1, 2
Innovation	Sections 2, 3	Sections 1, 2, 4	Sections 1, 2	Section 1
Conflict/ Cooperation		Sections 1, 2	Sections 2, 3	Sections 3, 4
Revolution/ Reaction		Section 1		Section 2
Change	Sections 2, 3	Section 1	Section 2	
Diversity/ Uniformity		Section 1	Sections 1, 2, 3	Section 1
Cultural Diffusion		Sections 1, 2, 3, 4	Sections 1, 3	Section 2
Relation to Environment	Sections 1, 2, 3	Sections 1, 2, 3, 4	Sections 1, 2	Sections 1, 2, 3
Regionalism/ Nationalism/ Internationalism		Sections 1, 2, 3, 4	Section 3	Sections 1, 3
Content Knowledge				
Literature, Art, and Culture	Sections 2, 3	Sections 1, 2, 3, 4	Sections 1, 2, 3	Sections 1, 4
Science and Technology	Sections 2, 3	Sections 1, 2	Sections 2, 3	Section 3
Geography and Environment	Sections 1, 2, 3	Sections 1, 2, 3, 4	Sections 1, 2, 3	Sections 1, 2, 3
Economics	Section 3	Sections 1, 2, 3	Sections 1, 3	Sections 2, 3, 4
Government/ Civics	Section 3	Sections 1, 2, 3, 4	Sections 1, 2, 3	Sections 1, 2, 3
Religion	Section 2	Sections 1, 2, 3, 4	Sections 2, 3	Section 1
Skills				
Critical Thinking Skills		Section 2		Section 4
Social Studies Skills	Section 3			
Study and Writing Skills			Section 2	

5	6	7	8	9	10	11
Section 3	Sections 2, 3, 5	Section **1**	Sections **1**, 2, 3	Section 1	Section 3	Sections 1, **2**
Sections **1, 2**	Section **4**	Section **3**	Section **2**	Section **2**	Section **2**	Section **1**
Section 3	Sections **2**, 5	Section 1		Section 1	Sections **1**, 2	Sections 1, 2
	Section 5					
	Sections **1, 5**				Section 3	
Section 3	Sections 1, 3	Section 3	Section 2	Section **1**	Section 3	Section 2
Section **3**	Sections **3**, 4	Sections **2**, 3	Sections 2, **3**	Section **3**	Section **3**	Sections 2, **3**
Section 3	Section 1	Sections 1, 3	Section 1		Sections 1, 3	Section 1
Section 3	Section 2		Section 3		Section 3	
Sections 1, 2, 3	Sections 1, 3	Section 1	Sections 1, 2, 3	Section 3	Sections 1, 2	Section 3
Sections 2, 3	Section 3		Sections 2, 3	Sections 1, 3	Section 2	Section 3
Section 3	Sections 1, 2	Sections 1, 2, 3	Section 1		Sections 1, 3	Section 1
	Sections 3, 5	Section 2		Sections 1, 3	Section 2	Section 3
Sections 2, 3	Sections 1, 2, 3, 5	Section 2	Section 3	Sections 1, 2	Sections 1, 3	Sections 1, 2
Section 1	Sections 1, 4	Sections 1, 2	Sections 1, 2, 3	Section 2	Sections 1, 2, 3	Section 1
	Section 5		Section 3	Section 3	Section 3	Section 3
Section 2						
		Section 3				

Scope and Sequence

	12	13	14	15	16	17
Movement	Section 1		Sections 1, 2	Section 1	Sections 1, 2, 4, 5	Section 2
Innovation		Section 2	Section 4	Section 2	Section 1	Section 1
Conflict/ Cooperation	Sections 2, 3, 4	Sections 1, 3, 4	Sections 1, 3, 4		Sections 3, 4	Section 2
Revolution/ Reaction		Section 4			Section 5	Section 3
Change		Section 2		Section 3	Sections 1, 5	Section 3
Diversity/ Uniformity	Sections 1, 3	Section 3	Sections 2, 3			Section 2
Cultural Diffusion	Section 4	Section 1	Section 3		Sections 2, 4	Sections 1, 2
Relation to Environment	Section 2	Section 2	Sections 1, 4	Sections 1, 2		Sections 1, 2
Regionalism/ Nationalism/ Internationalism	Section 4	Sections 2, 3, 4	Section 1	Section 3		
Literature, Art, and Culture		Section 2	Sections 1, 2, 4	Section 2	Sections 1, 2, 3	
Science and Technology		Section 3	Section 2	Section 2	Section 1	Section 1
Geography and Environment	Section 2	Section 2	Sections 1, 4	Sections 1, 2		Sections 1, 2
Economics	Section 2	Section 2	Sections 2, 4	Sections 2, 3	Sections 1, 2	Sections 1, 3
Government/ Civics	Sections 1, 2, 4	Sections 2, 3	Sections 1, 2, 3, 4	Sections 2, 3	Section 1	Section 2
Religion	Sections 1, 3	Sections 1, 4	Sections 3, 4	Sections 2, 3	Sections 1, 2, 3, 4, 5	Section 3
Critical Thinking Skills	Section 4		Section 3	Section 3	Section 4	
Social Studies Skills		Section 4				Section 3
Study and Writing Skills						

	18	19	20	21	22	23	24
	Section 1	Section 3	Section 3	Section 2	Sections 4, 5	Sections 2, 3	Section 3
		Section 5	Sections 1, 2			Sections 2, 3	Sections 2, 3, 4
	Section 1	Sections 1, 2, 3, 4, 5	Section 2	Sections 1, 3	Sections 2, 3, 4, 5	Section 4	
	Sections 1, 3	Sections 4, 5	Section 3	Sections 2, 4	Sections 1, 3, 5	Sections 2, 3	
	Sections 1, 4	Section 2	Section 1	Section 2	Sections 2, 3, 4	Sections 2, 3	Section 1
		Sections 1, 3					
	Sections 2, 3, 4				Section 4		Section 4
				Section 3		Sections 1, 2, 5	Section 3
		Sections 1, 2, 3		Section 3	Sections 4, 5		
	Section 2	Sections 2, 3	Section 3	Section 4	Sections 2, 3	Sections 1, 4	Sections 1, 3, 4
		Section 5	Sections 1, 2		Section 3	Sections 1, 2. 3, 4	Sections 2, 3
		Sections 4, 5		Section 3	Sections 4, 5	Sections 1, 2, 5	Section 3
	Sections 2, 3, 4	Sections 1, 2, 3, 5		Sections 1, 2, 3	Sections 1, 2, 3, 4	Sections 1, 2, 4	Section 1
	Sections 1, 2, 3	Sections 1, 2, 3, 4, 5	Sections 2, 3	Sections 1, 2, 3, 4	Sections 1, 2, 3, 4		Section 1
	Sections 1, 3	Sections 1, 2, 3, 5	Sections 1, 2, 3	Sections 1, 2	Sections 2, 3, 4		
	Section 3		Section 3			Section 4	
					Section 4		
		Section 5		Section 3			Section 3

Scope and Sequence

	25	26	27	28	29	30
Movement	Section 2		Sections 1, 2			Section 4
Innovation	Section 4	Section 3	Section 4	Section 3	Sections 1, 3	Section 4
Conflict/ Cooperation	Sections 2, 3, 4	Sections 1, 2, 4	Sections 3, 4	Sections 1, 2, 3, 4, 5		Sections 1, 2, 3, 4
Revolution/ Reaction	Section 3	Sections 4, 5	Section 3	Section 4		Section 3
Change	Sections 1, 4	Sections 3, 4	Section 2	Sections 4, 5	Section 2	Sections 2, 5
Diversity/ Uniformity		Section 5		Section 5	Sections 3, 4	
Cultural Diffusion	Section 2		Section 1			
Relation to Environment		Sections 3, 5	Sections 1, 3			
Regionalism/ Nationalism/ Internationalism	Section 5	Sections 1, 2	Sections 3, 4	Sections 1, 5	Section 1	Sections 1, 2, 5
Literature, Art, and Culture			Sections 2, 3		Sections 1, 4	Section 4
Science and Technology		Section 3	Section 4	Section 3	Section 1	Section 4
Geography and Environment	Sections 2, 4	Sections 3, 5	Sections 1, 3	Sections 3, 5		
Economics	Sections 4, 5	Section 3	Sections 1, 2	Sections 1, 4, 5	Sections 1, 2, 3, 4	Sections 4, 5
Government/ Civics	Sections 1, 2, 3, 5	Sections 1, 2, 3, 4, 5	Sections 1, 2, 3, 4,	Sections 2, 3, 4	Sections 1, 2, 3, 4	Sections 1, 2, 3, 4, 5
Religion	Sections 1, 3, 5	Section 3	Section 1	Section 4		Section 2
Critical Thinking Skills			Section 3			Section 4
Social Studies Skills	Section 5			Section 5	Section 3	
Study and Writing Skills		Section 5				

	31	32	33	34	35	36	37
	Sections 1, 3				Section 2		Section 2
	Section 5	Section 3					Section 5
	Sections 2, 3, 4	Sections 1, 2, 4	Sections 3, 4, 5	Sections 1, 2	Sections 1, 2, 3	Sections 1, 2, 3, 4	Sections 1, 3, 4
			Section 2		Section 2	Sections 2, 3	Section 4
		Sections 1, 2, 4	Section 1	Sections 1, 2, 3		Sections 2, 4	Sections 1, 2
	Section 3	Sections 2, 4	Section 5	Section 3			Sections 3, 5
			Section 6		Section 3		Section 5
		Section 2	Section 1	Section 3	Sections 1, 2	Section 1	Section 5
	Section 1	Sections 2, 3, 4	Sections 3, 4, 6	Sections 1, 2, 3	Section 1	Sections 1, 2, 3, 4	Sections 1, 2, 3, 4, 5
		Section 4	Section 2		Section 3		Sections 1, 4
	Sections 2, 4, 5	Sections 3, 4	Sections 1, 2				Section 5
		Sections 1, 2	Section 1	Section 3	Sections 1, 2	Section 1	Section 5
		Sections 1, 2, 3, 4	Sections 1, 3	Sections 2, 3	Sections 1, 2, 3	Sections 1, 2, 4	Sections 1, 2, 3, 5
	Sections 1, 2, 5	Sections 2, 3, 4	Sections 1, 2, 5, 6	Sections 1, 2	Sections 1, 2, 3	Sections 1, 2, 3, 4	Sections 1, 2, 3, 4
			Section 5		Sections 2, 3	Section 1	Section 4
	Section 2	Section 4					
						Section 3	Section 5
			Section 6	Section 2	Section 2		

Glencoe Gives You a

World of Resources

Easy-to-use **Reproducible Lesson Plans** help you integrate the Classroom Resources into your daily lessons.

HISTORY SIMULATION 22

Where Do They Stand?

One of the reasons for France's difficulties during the late 1700s was the people's inability to reconcile the many different political opinions that existed. In this activity, students will examine a range of political opinions.

History Simulations:

- Make history relevant.
- Examine a variety of realistic problems.
- Provide opportunities for cooperative learning.

Ob
star
s re
ench
Prep
al C
and
renc
Stu
levi
nd?
evo
path
isior
chart based
Opinion" ch
chart, studen
should indic
where the le
have chosen
view falls in
ical spectrum
whether that
can best be d
as (1) a radic
moderate, (3
servative, (4
or (5) a react
preparing fo
interviews, e
sive paragra
position. Me
pare intervie
ject.

Activity Gu

1. Introduc
steps inv
Political

Name .... Date .... Class ....

HISTORY SIMULATION 22

HANDOUT MATERIAL

"Where Do They Stand?"—A Television Special

Select one of these individuals to be the subject of your interview:

- ☐ Louis XVI
- ☐ Maximilien Robespierre
- ☐ The Girondist leader
- ☐ One of the women who led the march for bread
- ☐ Napoleon Bonaparte
- ☐ George-Jacques Danton

Group Activity A Draw your own version of the political opinion chart and any other visual materials you think would help your television special; fill in information on the chart as determined by your group.	**Group Activity C** Create questions to ask the person you will interview.	**Group Activity E** Select the news team who will conduct the interview.
Group Activity B Write a description of the political position of the person your group selected to interview.	**Individual Activity D** Select the person who acts as the political leader.	**Individual Activity F** Select a timekeeper.

Group Assessment

When the activity is complete, your group will answer these questions:

1. Did the members of your group agree on the selection of the leader?
2. Did each member contribute ideas and participate in the activity?
3. Did group members work well together?
4. Was the information presented by the other groups clear to you? Why or why not?
5. Did you find this a helpful way to study this material? Why or why not?
6. What would you do to improve this assignment?

Name .... Date .... Class ....

Historical Significance ACTIVITY 22

Three Ways Napoleon Changed the World

Although assessments of Napoleon differ widely, no one denies that he was one of the most colorful and famous people in all of history. He was also among the most influential. Napoleon helped spread the ideas of the French Revolution throughout Europe. The passages below discuss three additional ways Napoleon changed the world. Read them and then answer the questions. Use a separate sheet of paper if necessary.

1. The Napoleonic Code

"One of Napoleon's reforms . . . was destined to have an impact far beyond the borders of France. That was the creation of the French civil code, the [Napoleonic Code]. In many ways the code embodied the ideals of the French Revolution. For example, under the code there were no privileges of birth, and all men were equal under the law. At the same time, the code was sufficiently close to the older French laws and customs to be acceptable to the French public and the legal profession. On the whole, the code was moderate, well organized, and written with commendable brevity and outstanding lucidity. As a result, the code has not only endured in France (the French civil code today is strikingly similar to the original [Napoleonic Code]) but has been adopted, with local modifications, in many other countries."

2. The Invasion of Spain

"Napoleon also had a large, though indirect, effect on the history of Latin America. His invasion of Spain so weakened the Spanish government that for a period of several years it lost effective control of its colonies in Latin America. It was during this period of *de facto* autonomy that the Latin American independence movements commenced."

3. The Louisiana Purchase

"Of all Napoleon's actions . . . the one that has perhaps had the most enduring and significant consequences was one that was almost irrelevant to his main plans. In 1803, Napoleon sold a vast tract of land to the United States. He realized that the French possessions in North America might be difficult to protect from British conquest, and besides he was short of cash. The Louisiana Purchase, perhaps the largest peaceful transfer of land in all of history, transformed the United States into a nation of near-continental size. It is difficult to say what the United States would have been like without the Louisiana Purchase; certainly it would have been a vastly different country than it is today. Indeed, it is doubtful whether the United States would have become a great power without the Louisiana Purchase.

Napoleon, of course, was not solely responsible for the Louisiana Purchase. The American government clearly played a role as well. But the French offer was such a bargain that it seems likely that any American government would have accepted it, while the decision of the French government to sell the Louisiana territory came about through the arbitrary judgment of a single individual, Napoleon Bonaparte."

— from *The 100: A Ranking of the Most Influential Persons in History* by Michael H. Hart. © 1978, Hart Publishing Company

1. Which change has affected the most people? Explain your answer.
2. Which change was the most significant one for your ancestors? Explain your answer.
3. Which has had the most significant effect on your life? Explain your answer.
4. Which change do you think is the most significant? Why?

Historical Significance Chapter Activities:

- Emphasize the relevance of the past.
- Answer the question "Why do we need to learn this?"
- Provide a basis for classroom discussion.

Skill Reinforcement Activities:

- Extend all skills taught in the student edition.
- Reinforce social studies, critical thinking, and study and writing skills.

Name .... Date .... Class ....

SKILL REINFORCEMENT Activity 22

Interpreting Graphs

Graphs can show a great deal of information in a single, easy-to-read format. The graph below illustrates an important aspect of the situation in France just prior to the revolution. To interpret the graph, follow these steps: First, read the title. Then, read the captions and text. Finally, determine the relationships among all sections of the graph. When you have done so, use the graph to answer the questions that follow. Use a separate sheet of paper for your answers.

Population and Land Ownership by Estate 1789

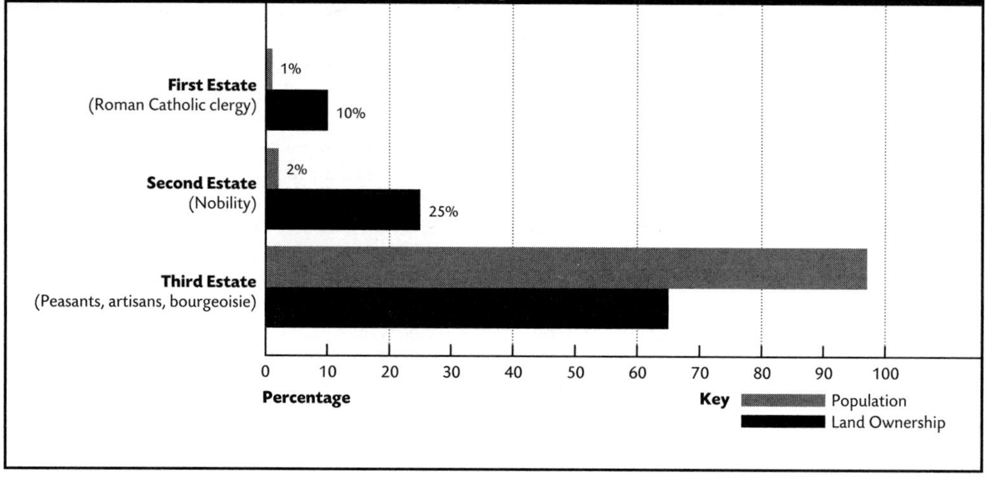

1. What does the horizontal axis of the graph represent?
2. a. What percentage of the French population comprised the First Estate?
   b. What percentage of land did they own?
3. a. What percentage of the French population comprised the Second Estate?
   b. What percentage of land did they own?
4. a. Calculate the percentage of the French population that comprised the Third Estate. Write the value on the graph.
   b. Calculate the percentage of land owned by the Third Estate. Write the value on the graph.
5. Why was land a good measure of wealth at this time?
6. Which estate had the greatest land ownership in proportion to its population?
7. a. How was the relationship between population and land ownership fundamentally different in the Third Estate?
   b. How might this fact have helped lead to the Revolution?

Name .... Date .... Class ....

PEOPLE IN WORLD HISTORY PROFILE 41

Marie Antoinette (1755–1793)

Courage! I have shown it for years; think you I shall lose it at the moment when my sufferings are to end?
—on the way to the guillotine, 1793

From childhood, Marie had been told that she would someday be a queen. At the age of 15, she was married to the French *dauphin,* or crown prince. In only four years, he became King Louis XVI, and Marie Antoinette—at the age when people today graduate from high school—became the queen of France.

Like many royal marriages of the day, the one between Marie and Louis was based not on love, but on politics. The marriage was arranged to strengthen France's ties to Marie's native Austria. Unhappy in her marriage, Marie sought comfort in elaborate balls at Versailles, horse races, expensive parties, and lavish theater productions. In her extravagance, Marie became an important symbol of royal excess and indifference. As such, her influence on the French Revolution was incalculable.

Marie's reputation was under attack for much of her reign, although not always justifiably. The quotation most commonly associated with Marie is "Let them eat cake." This was supposedly her unthinking reply to a courtier's remark that the peasants were rioting outside her palace because they had no bread. She never said these words, but the fact that people were willing to believe otherwise says much about the way she was perceived by the public. Many French citizens viewed Marie as simply frivolous. Others thought she was dangerous, an untrustworthy foreigner who would plot against France. Indeed, Marie tried constantly to influence French foreign policy to benefit her native Austria. When France went to war with Austria in 1792, Marie, who hoped for the defeat of the French revolutionaries, passed information to the enemy. Her treason gave the Republicans their reason to try and convict the queen. She was guillotined on October 16, 1793.

The last years of Marie's life were full of heartache. She spent four years as a virtual prisoner of the revolutionaries. In her final months, her husband was executed and her surviving son was taken from her. Surprisingly, the superficial queen demonstrated remarkable character during these tragedies. Accounts of the time portray her as courageous, steadfast, and above all else, dignified as she approached the guillotine. Her noble death, in such contrast to her frivolous life, is one reason why Marie Antoinette has intrigued people for generations.

Reviewing the Profile

Answer the following questions on a separate sheet of paper.

1. How did Marie Antoinette come to be queen of France?
2. Why was she so unpopular with the French people?

Critical Thinking

3. **Evaluating Information** Make a list of adjectives you think apply to Marie Antoinette.
4. **Drawing Conclusions** Does it surprise you that Marie Antoinette, famous for her frivolity, demonstrated such character toward the end of her life? Explain your answer.

People in World History:

- Personalize world history.
- Emphasize the role that people played in major historical events.
- Include people of all backgrounds in the human story.

Review and Reinforcement Activities

Name .... Date .... Class ....

Vocabulary Activity 22

Select and write the term that best completes each sentence.

1. Before the revolution, French society was divided into three ____________________ (estates/émigrés).

2. Although the Catholic Church in France used ____________________ (tithe/coup d'état) money for charitable activities, some of the money supported the grand lifestyles of the higher clergy.

3. The Constitution of 1791 created a ____________________ (unicameral legislature/ bicameral legislature), or one-house assembly, to represent the people.

4. In 1815, the Congress of Vienna established ____________________ (buffer states/tithes), or neutral territories, to isolate France.

5. As France grew more unstable, many nobles, called ____________________ (émigrés/plebiscites), fled France to live in neighboring countries.

6. The ____________________ (bourgeoisie/coup d'état), or French middle class, supported the revolution.

7. After the French armies suffered a string of losses, the leaders of the revolution were forced to adopt ____________________ (nationalism/conscription), or the draft.

8. The delegates of the Congress of Vienna were mostly ____________________ (liberals/reactionaries), who opposed change in Europe.

9. The popular general Napoleon Bonaparte seized control of France in a ____________________ (bourgeoisie/coup d'état).

10. To help secure his rule, Napoleon held a ____________________ (plebiscite/coup d'état), or popular vote, to ap

11. The Congress of Vien ____________________ (nationalism/liberalis that celebrated indivi

12. Although Napoleon

Vocabulary Activities:

- Reinforces chapter vocabulary terms.
- Help students practice and master new words.

Also available in Spanish

Vocabulary PuzzleMaker Software:

- Reinforces vocabulary terms.
- Lets you create your own word puzzles.
- Includes DOS and Macintosh software.

Name ____________ Date ____________ Class ____________

Guided Reading Activity 22-1

The Old Order

As you read Section 1, answer the following questions.

1. What were the estates? ____________

2. Who were the members of the First Estate? ____________

3. Who were the members of the Second Estate? ____________

4. Who were the members of the Third Estate? ____________

5. Which estate had the most members but the least money, rights, and privileges? ____________

6. Why was each group of the French population growing increasingly unhappy during the 1780s?
   a. peasants: ____________
   b. artisans: ____________
   c. bourgeoisie: ____________
   d. nobility: ____________

7. a. What financial crisis did King Louis XVI face? ____________
   b. Why did he call the Estates-General? ____________

8. How did the National Assembly form out of the Estates-General? ____________

9. What led to the fall of the Bastille? ____________

10. What was the "Great Fear"? ____________

Guided Reading Activities help students:

- Master new material as they read each section.
- Read with a purpose.
- Prepare for quizzes and tests.

Also available in Spanish

Time Line Activities help students:

- Put historical events in chronological perspective.
- Reinforce major events.
- Provide a visual/spatial learning strategy.

Name .... Date .... Class ....

Time Line Activity 22

The French Revolution

In France, the years from 1789 to 1815 were turbulent. You can trace the changes that took place during this time in French history on a time line. Read the time line below. Then answer the questions that follow, adding information to the time line as directed.

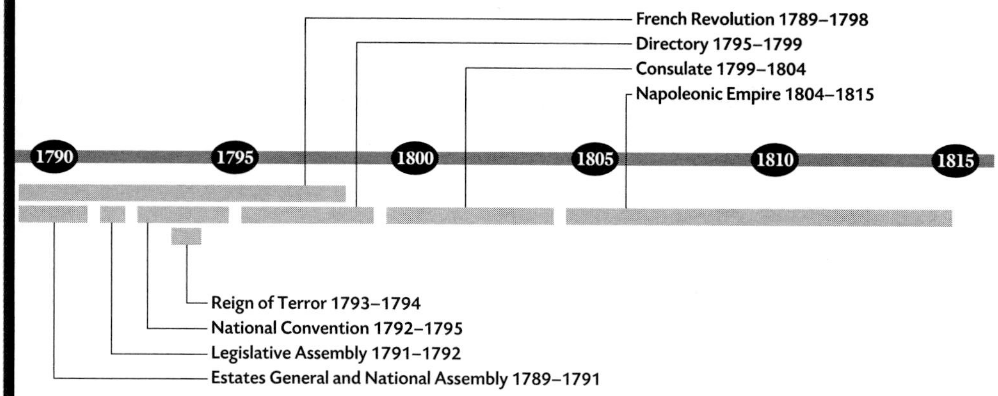

1. a. What event marked the beginning of the French Revolution? Add this point to the time line.

____

b. How long did the French Revolution last? ______________________________

2. a. What event marked the beginning of Napoleon's rule? Add this point to the time line.

____

b. What event marked the end of Napoleon's rule? Add this point to the time line.

____

3. Napoleon ruled from 1799 to 1815. The Consulate accounts for the years 1799 to 1804. The remaining years are called the Napoleonic Empire. What 1804 event caused the change? Write your answer below, then mark this point on your time line.

____

____

4. A French historian once said that the French Revolution "turned out badly." How does your time line illustrate this concept?

____

____

Name .... Date .... Class ....

CHAPTER THEMES
GRAPHIC ORGANIZER 22

The French Revolution

The French Revolution is one of the great turning points in history. The years from 1789 to 1815 in France were chaotic. Change came swiftly and in unexpected ways. The chart below will help you understand and remember some of the major events of this time and the changes they caused. To complete the chart, identify at least one change that resulted from each event.

Event	Change(s) Resulting from Event
Meeting of the Estates-General	
The Great Fear	
The Declaration of Rights	
The March on Versailles	
The Reign of Terror	
Napoleon's coup d'état	
The Battle of Trafalgar	
The Invasion of Russia	
The Congress of Vienna	
The Concert of Europe	

Chapter Themes: Graphic Organizers help students:

- Learn in a visual way.
- Reinforce key chapter themes.
- Stimulate critical thinking.

Reteaching Activities:
- Reinforce key chapter content.
- Help students prepare for quizzes and tests.
- Build students' study skills.

Name .... Date .... Class ....

Reteaching Activity ...22

The French Revolution

The increasingly bitter division of French society in the late 1700s was a fundamental cause of the French Revolution. Understanding these divisions, then, is essential to your understanding of this turning point in history. To help you understand the divisions of French society, complete the activity below.

1. What were the estates? ____________________

2. Complete the diagram by copying each phrase into the appropriate space below.

- comprised about 1 percent of the population
- comprised about 2 percent of the population
- comprised about 97 percent of the population
- held high posts in government and the military
- made up of higher and lower Roman Catholic clergy
- made up of nobility
- made up of peasants, artisans, and the bourgeoisie
- main income was feudal dues
- most were very poor
- often enjoyed grand lifestyles paid for by tithe money
- owned 10 percent of French land
- owned 25 percent of French land
- owned 65 percent of French land

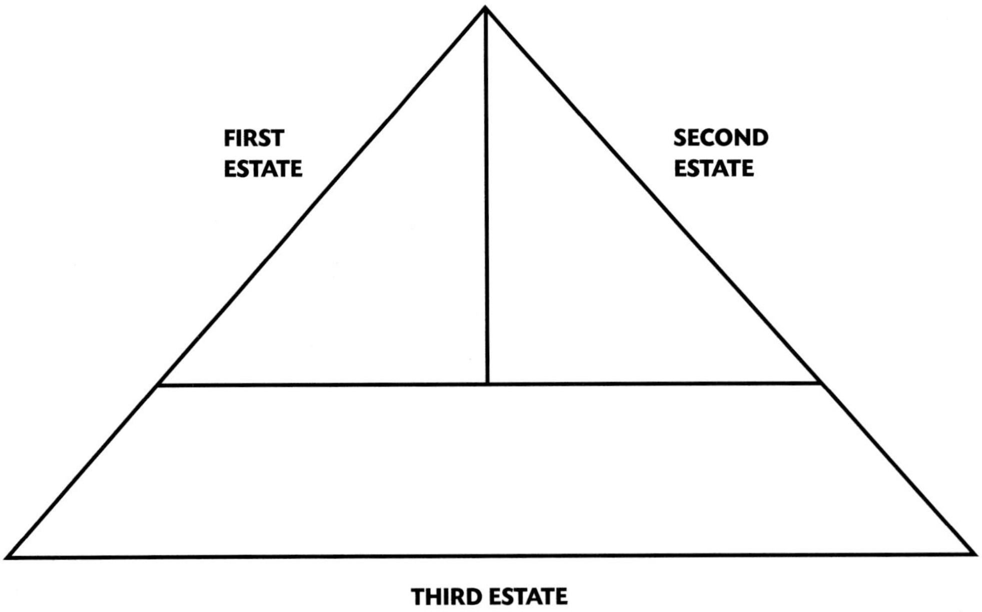

Spanish Language Resources

Spanish Resources help Spanish-speaking students process dual-language instruction. Resources include:

- *Spanish Chapter Summaries*
- *Spanish Guided Reading Activities*
- *Spanish Section Quizzes*
- *Spanish Vocabulary Activities*
- *Spanish Chapter Digests Audiocassettes Activities and Tests*

SPANISH GUIDED READING ACTIVITIES
SPANISH VOCABULARY ACTIVITIES
SPANISH CHAPTER SUMMARIES
SPANISH SECTION QUIZZES
WORLD
SPANISH CHAPTER DIGESTS AUDIOCASSETTES ACTIVITIES AND TESTS
WORLD HISTORY
THE HUMAN EXPERIENCE
SPANISH RESOURCES
WORLD HISTORY
THE HUMAN EXPERIENCE
THIS COMPREHENSIVE PACKAGE OF RESOURCES INCLUDES:
Spanish Chapter Summaries
Spanish Guided Reading Activities
Spanish Section Quizzes
Spanish Vocabulary Activities
ISBN 0-02-823246-1
GLENCOE
McGraw-Hill
SPANISH RESOURCES
WORLD HISTORY
SPANISH CHAPTER DIGESTS AUDIOCASSETTES
WORLD HISTORY
THE HUMAN EXPERIENCE
THIS COMPREHENSIVE PACKAGE INCLUDES:
Chapter summaries on audiocassettes.
Activities for each chapter summary.
Tests for each ch summary.
GLENCOE
Chapters 9-10
Spanish

Mapping History Activities help students:

- Get hands-on practice using maps.
- Integrate world history with map skills.
- Make the history-geography connection.

Name .... Date .... Class ....

MAPPING HISTORY Activity 22

The French Revolution

Napoleon so dominated Europe that the years 1800 to 1815 are often called "the Napoleonic Era." At the height of his power, Napoleon controlled virtually the entire continent. The map below illustrates the remarkable extent of his influence. Use it to complete the activities that follow. Write your answers on a separate sheet of paper.

Europe at Height of Napoleon's Power 1812

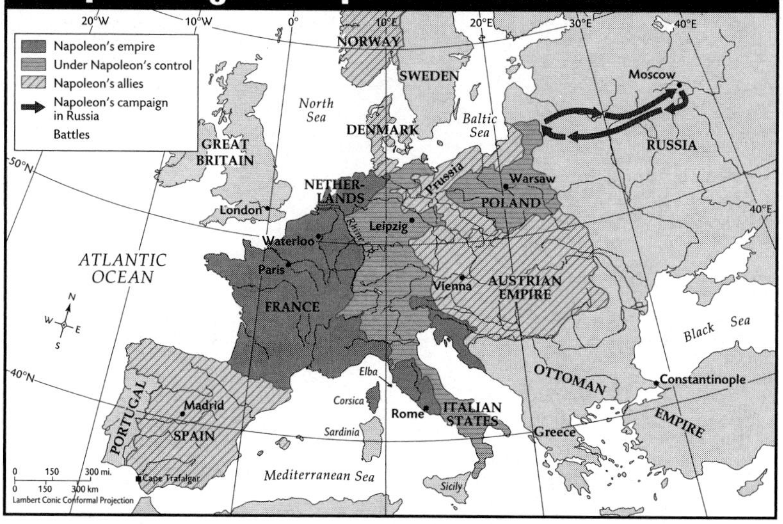

1. **a.** In what year was Napoleon at the height of his power?
   b. What nations did he control?
   c. What nations did he make his allies?
2. What parts of Europe did he fail to conquer?
3. Napoleon's major battles are listed in the chart at right.
   a. Create a map symbol for a battle, and add the symbol to the map key.
   b. Using the symbol you created, mark the location of each battle on the map. Write the date of each battle next to its symbol.
   c. One historian said that between 1800 and 1815 "warfare ravaged Europe." Study the map. Do you agree? Explain your answer.

Battle	Date	Approximate Location
Marengo	1800	300 miles northwest of Rome
Trafalgar	1805	off the coast of Cape Trafalgar
Austerlitz	1805	250 miles southwest of Warsaw
Auerstedt	1806	just southwest of Leipzig
Jena	1806	just southeast of Auerstedt
Friedland	1807	extreme northern Poland, about 100 miles from the Baltic Sea
Peninsular War	1808–1814	throughout Spain
Wagram	1809	just north of Vienna
Aspern	1809	just northeast of Vienna
Borodino	1812	about 100 miles west of Moscow
Lützen	1813	about 100 miles west of Leipzig
Leipzig	1813	at Leipzig
Ligny	1815	about 100 miles southeast of Waterloo
Waterloo	1815	at Waterloo

Name .... Date .... Class ....

GEOGRAPHY and HISTORY Activity 22

Movement: *A Doomed March to Russia*

Napoleon gathered troops from all quarters of his European empire in his quest to conquer the Russian Empire. By June 1812 his "Grand Army," numbering 600,000 men, confidently began to march east across the vast, level Russian plain. Yet six months later, these same troops were making a desperate escape from Russia—having lost more than 500,000 men. What caused this panicked retreat and massive loss of life?

Napoleon had underestimated the Russian troops and his most bitter rival, the fierce Russian winter. To resist Napoleon, the Russians used a new strategy. Instead of meeting the French in open battle, the Russian army retreated slowly, drawing the French army deeper and deeper into Russia.

In September, Napoleon's forces finally reached Moscow, which the Russians had evacuated. The day after the French entered Moscow, a huge fire, probably started by Russian patriots, destroyed the city. With the Russian winter looming, Napoleon faced a difficult decision. He could either chase the Russian army farther to the east or turn back to the west.

Napoleon waited too long to make his decision to retreat. Bitter cold and driving snow plagued the Grand Army as it crossed the vast Russian plain once again. Temperatures plunged and Russians began attacking French forces without mercy.

The Grand Army's Retreat

The strongest threw into the river those who were weaker, and . . . trampled underfoot all the sick whom they found in their way. . . . Others, hoping to save themselves by swimming, were frozen in the middle of the river, or perished by placing themselves on pieces of ice, which sunk to the bottom. Thousands and thousands . . . were lost.

—French officer's account

Napoleon's Russian Campaign

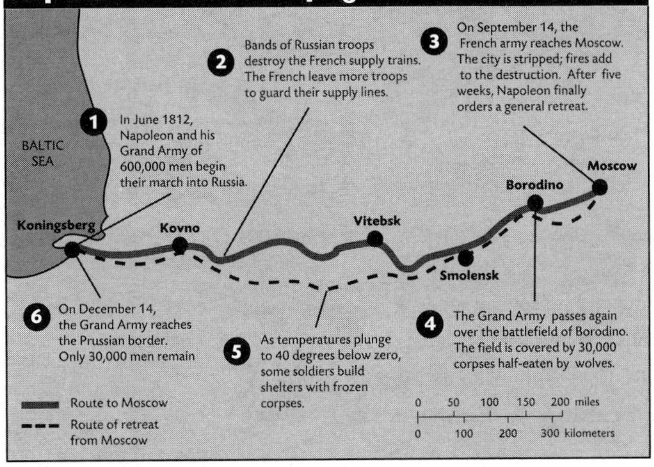

BALTIC SEA
Koningsberg
Kovno
Vitebsk
Smolensk
Borodino
Moscow
1 In June 1812, Napoleon and his Grand Army of 600,000 men begin their march into Russia.
2 Bands of Russian troops destroy the French supply trains. The French leave more troops to guard their supply lines.
3 On September 14, the French army reaches Moscow. The city is stripped; fires add to the destruction. After five weeks, Napoleon finally orders a general retreat.
4 The Grand Army passes again over the battlefield of Borodino. The field is covered by 30,000 corpses half-eaten by wolves.
5 As temperatures plunge to 40 degrees below zero, some soldiers build shelters with frozen corpses.
6 On December 14, the Grand Army reaches the Prussian border. Only 30,000 men remain
Route to Moscow
Route of retreat from Moscow
0 50 100 150 200 miles
0 100 200 300 kilometers

With the help of the severe winter of their homeland, Russian forces wiped out 80 percent of the Grand Army by the time it returned to Germany in December 1812.

f barriers to

ately how
rder to
r this dis-

hing that
conse-
n leaders

6. How might geographical barriers to movement hinder a nation's development? How might they help it?

Activity

7. Research the settlement of the area in which you live. What factors encouraged settlement? What factors prohibited settlement? What affects the movement of people in and out of your area today?

Geography and History Activities:

- Show the important role of geography in history.
- Improve students' geography skills.
- Relate the five geography themes to world history.

Geography Activities

Glencoe Social Studies Outline Map Resource Book provides a variety of updated, reproducible regional outline maps.

The laminated **World Desk Map** allows individual, hands-on practice of place location.

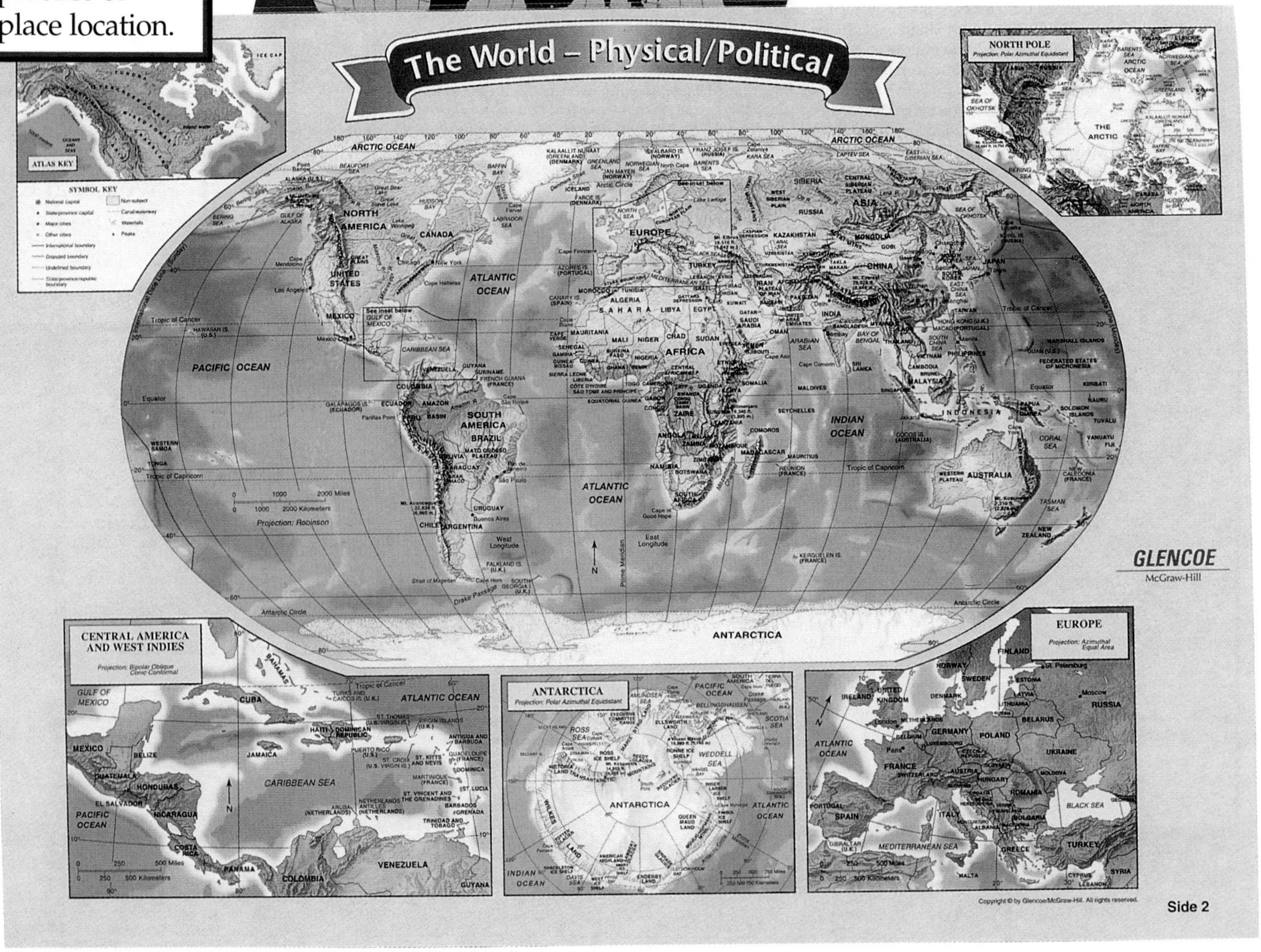

Interdisciplinary Connections

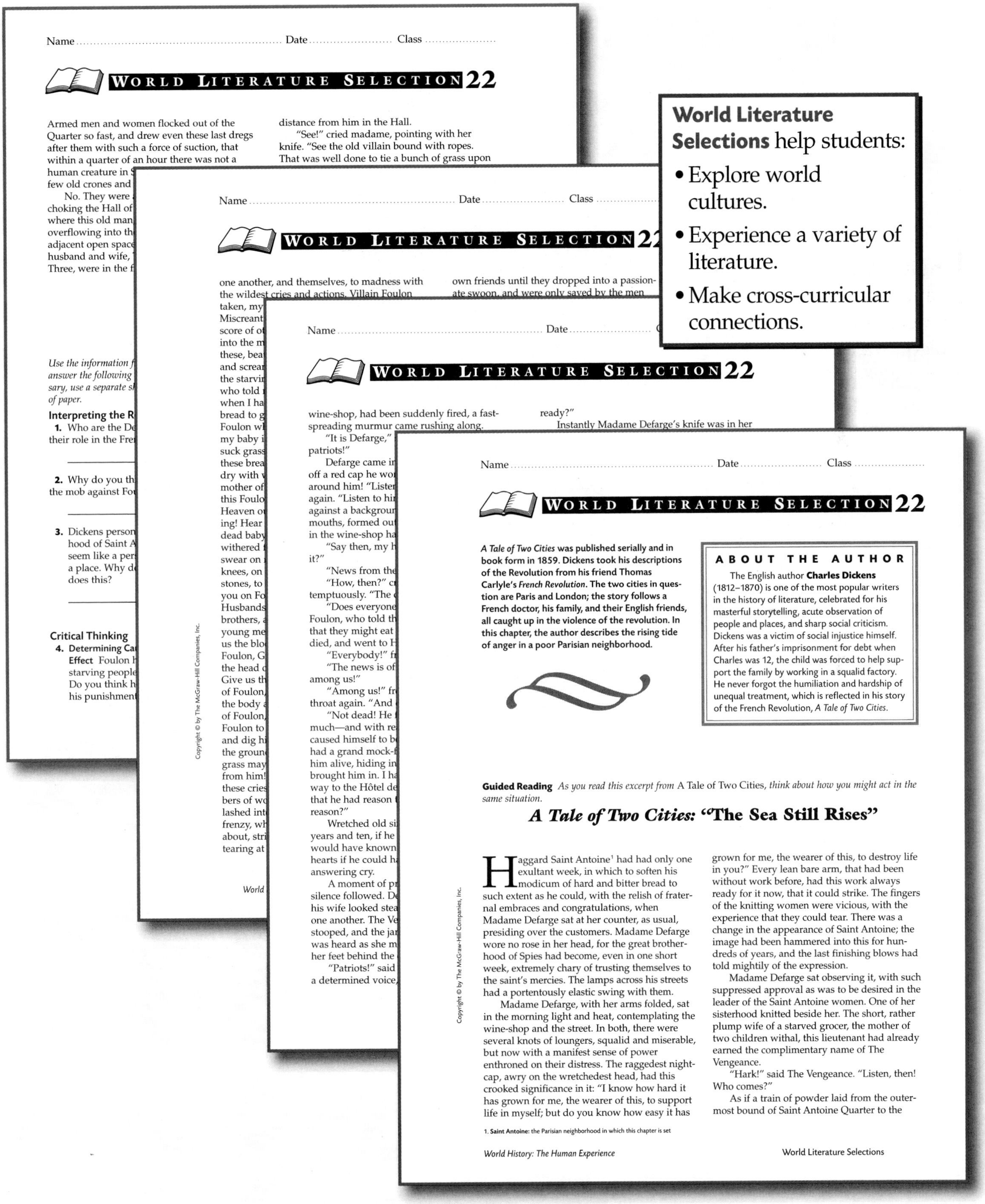

Name .... Date .... Class ....

WORLD LITERATURE SELECTION 22

A Tale of Two Cities **was published serially and in book form in 1859. Dickens took his descriptions of the Revolution from his friend Thomas Carlyle's *French Revolution*. The two cities in question are Paris and London; the story follows a French doctor, his family, and their English friends, all caught up in the violence of the revolution. In this chapter, the author describes the rising tide of anger in a poor Parisian neighborhood.**

ABOUT THE AUTHOR

The English author **Charles Dickens** (1812–1870) is one of the most popular writers in the history of literature, celebrated for his masterful storytelling, acute observation of people and places, and sharp social criticism. Dickens was a victim of social injustice himself. After his father's imprisonment for debt when Charles was 12, the child was forced to help support the family by working in a squalid factory. He never forgot the humiliation and hardship of unequal treatment, which is reflected in his story of the French Revolution, *A Tale of Two Cities.*

Guided Reading *As you read this excerpt from* A Tale of Two Cities, *think about how you might act in the same situation.*

A Tale of Two Cities: "The Sea Still Rises"

Haggard Saint Antoine[1] had had only one exultant week, in which to soften his modicum of hard and bitter bread to such extent as he could, with the relish of fraternal embraces and congratulations, when Madame Defarge sat at her counter, as usual, presiding over the customers. Madame Defarge wore no rose in her head, for the great brotherhood of Spies had become, even in one short week, extremely chary of trusting themselves to the saint's mercies. The lamps across his streets had a portentously elastic swing with them.

Madame Defarge, with her arms folded, sat in the morning light and heat, contemplating the wine-shop and the street. In both, there were several knots of loungers, squalid and miserable, but now with a manifest sense of power enthroned on their distress. The raggedest nightcap, awry on the wretchedest head, had this crooked significance in it: "I know how hard it has grown for me, the wearer of this, to support life in myself; but do you know how easy it has grown for me, the wearer of this, to destroy life in you?" Every lean bare arm, that had been without work before, had this work always ready for it now, that it could strike. The fingers of the knitting women were vicious, with the experience that they could tear. There was a change in the appearance of Saint Antoine; the image had been hammered into this for hundreds of years, and the last finishing blows had told mightily of the expression.

Madame Defarge sat observing it, with such suppressed approval as was to be desired in the leader of the Saint Antoine women. One of her sisterhood knitted beside her. The short, rather plump wife of a starved grocer, the mother of two children withal, this lieutenant had already earned the complimentary name of The Vengeance.

"Hark!" said The Vengeance. "Listen, then! Who comes?"

As if a train of powder laid from the outermost bound of Saint Antoine Quarter to the

1. **Saint Antoine:** the Parisian neighborhood in which this chapter is set

World Literature Selections help students:

- Explore world cultures.
- Experience a variety of literature.
- Make cross-curricular connections.

World Art and Music activities and profiles:

- Tell the story of history through the arts.
- Introduce important personalities in the arts.
- Make cross-curricular connections.

Name .... Date .... Class ....

WORLD ART and MUSIC Activity 22

Jacques-Louis David

In the painting below, Jacques-Louis David depicts one of the turning points in the history of Europe and of the world. Interestingly, the painting itself carries a historic importance all its own. Explore the painting's many details. Pay particular attention to its formal style and the faces of the individuals in the scene. Then read the accompanying article and respond to the questions at the bottom of the next page.

The Consecration of Emperor Napoleon I and the Cor

The painting you are looking at w... Napoleon's favorites. When he first s... exclaimed "How great! What relief! H... This is not a painting; one can walk a... this picture; life is everywhere!"

World Music: Cultural Traditions brings students into contact with music representing many cultures and regions of the world.

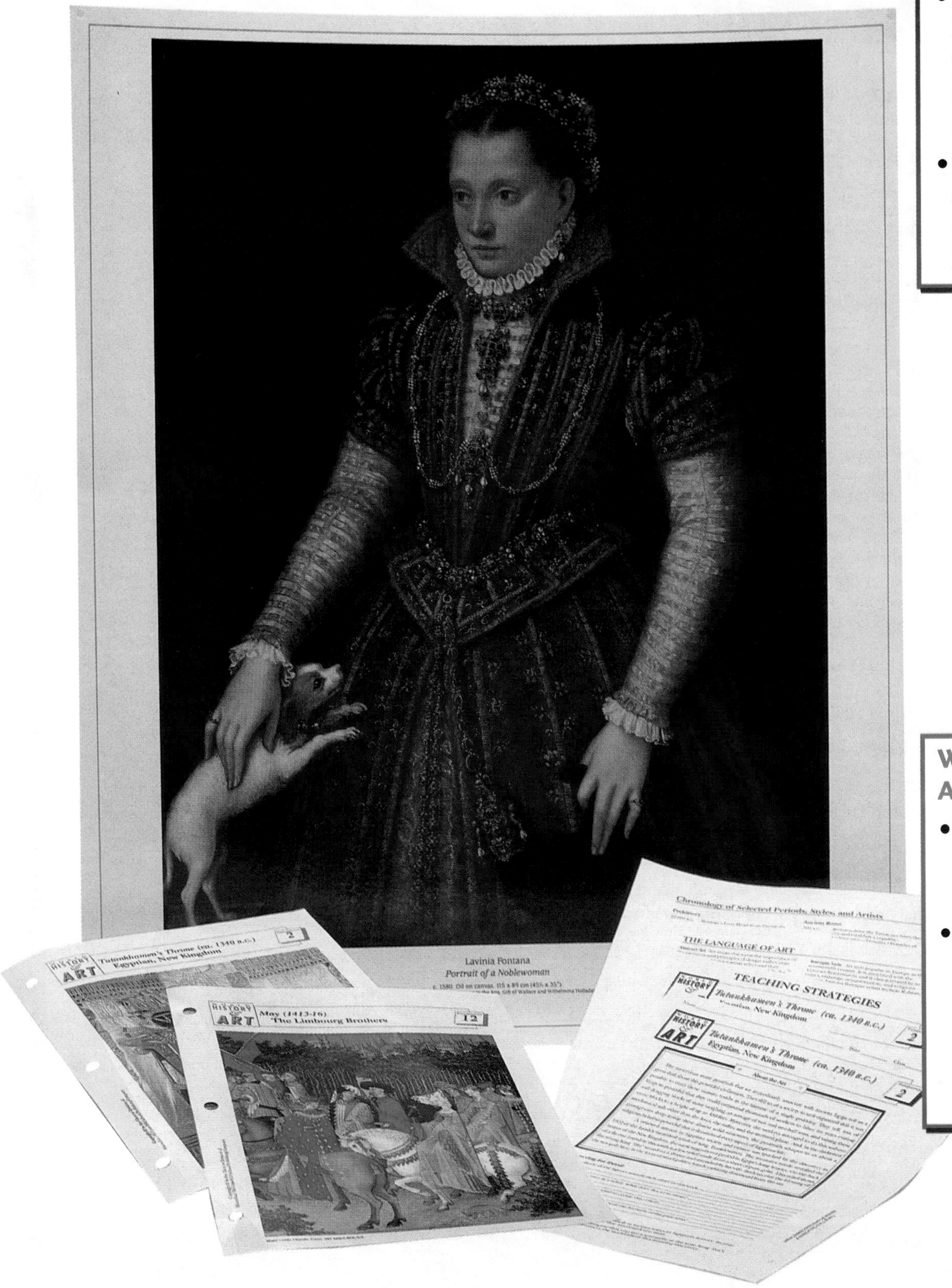

Focus on World Art Prints:

- Provides you with 25 display-quality prints, teaching strategies, and study activities.
- Offers your students a cultural perspective of history.

World History and Art Transparencies:

- Introduce your students to the world of fine art.
- Captivate students with the wonder, majesty, and intrigue of breathless works of art.

Name .... Date .... Class ....

Enrichment Activity 22

The *Levée en Masse*

Four months after the French Revolutionaries proclaimed the first day of the "Year I of Liberty," they faced fierce attacks from European monarchies that feared the spread of the revolution. Desperate, the leaders of the revolution made a decision that would change the face of warfare forever. Read the excerpt below and answer the questions that follow.

Enrichment Activities:

- Help you expand chapter themes.
- Stimulate critical thinking.
- Engage students in meaningful interpretations of history.

most all of the monarchies of Europe ed their armies against France to stamp e sacrilegious revolutionaries, and when vas left of the old royal army, aided by vol- s, proved unable to stem the attacks, the al Convention decided on conscription: *ée en masse.*

. the convention issued the call for a *levée se* in August [1793]. By New Year's Day, he French armies numbered about 777,000 nd the wars of mass armies that ensued d Europe for the next two decades.

Conscription was not an entirely new idea . . . but it had never really amounted to more than compulsory selection of an unfortunate minority, nor had it lasted long or been extended to an entire country. But the French Revolution, with its principles of liberty and equality, first stimulated and then exploited a fervent nationalism which made conscription acceptable. It also made French troops behave differently.

The "nation in arms" produced poorly trained soldiers . . . who had no time to master the intricate drill of close-order formations, but their enthusiasm and numbers made up for it: attacking in clouds of skirmishers and disorderly columns, they often simply overwhelmed their better-trained adversaries. . . . Battles rarely ended in draws any more—Carnot of the Committee of Public Safety instructed the French armies in 1794 "to act in mass formations and take the offensive. . . . Give battle on a large scale and pursue the enemy until he is utterly destroyed."

The basic principle underlying all this was that whereas the prerevolutionary regular soldiers had been scarce and expensive, the lives of conscripts were plentiful and cheap. The disdain for casualties grew even greater once Napoleon had seized control of France in 1799. "You cannot stop me," he boasted to Count Metternich, the Austrian diplomat. "I spend thirty thousand men a month." It was not an idle boast: the losses of France in 1793–1814 amounted to 1.7 million dead—almost all soldiers—out of a population of 29 million.

—from *War* by Gwynne Dyer. ©1985, Media Resources

1. Why did French revolutionary leaders institute the *levée en masse*? ____________

2. How did the *levée en masse* change the French armies? ____________

____

3. What "basic principle" does the author refer to? ____________

____

4. France's enemies were reluctant to introduce conscription. Why do you think this was so?

____

5. What do you think about Napoleon's statement? How do you think this reflects on him?

____

____

Name .... Date .... Class ....

CRITICAL THINKING Activity 22

Analyzing Information

To the French people today, the Revolution of 1789 remains a lively topic of discussion and debate. No one disputes that it was a watershed in French—and human—history. In fact, historians generally that 1789 marks the beginning of the modern era. Yet the true meaning and legacy of the French Revolution continues to be debated. To sort through the many opinions about the French Revolution, or any historical event, you need to analyze information. Analyzing information means studying it carefully in order to learn as much as possible about what is being presented.

Below are three recent statements about the French Revolution. Answer the questions after each statement to help you analyze it. Then answer the final two questions, which will guide you in analyzing the quotations as a group. Use a separate sheet of paper for your answers.

> *The revolution is a complex whole, like life itself, with the inspiring and the unacceptable, with hope and fear, violence and fraternity.*
>
> —François Mitterrand, president of France, speaking at the Bicentennial Celebration of the French Revolution

1. Mitterrand said the Revolution included "the inspiring," "the unacceptable," "hope," "fear," "violence," and "fraternity." From your knowledge of the Revolution, identify at least one historical fact that fits each category.
2. What might have motivated Mitterrand to emphasize both the positive and negative aspects of the Revolution?

> *The French have come to realize that the revolution was a magnificent event that turned out badly."*
>
> —François Furet, historian at Paris's Ecole des Hautes Etudes

3. What do you think was "magnificent" about the French Revolution?
4. Why do you think Furet says it "turned out badly"?

> *One of my ancestors stormed the Bastille, and I feel both thrilled and proud to be French whenever I walk past the place where it once stood.*
>
> —Jacques Delmas, a lawyer from Reims

5. What is the source of Jacques Delmas's pride?
6. Do you think he would agree with Furet's statement? Why or why not?

7. Which of the three statements is the most positive statement about the Revolution? The most negative? Explain your choices.
8. Which one do you think best summarizes the Revolution? Why?

Critical Thinking Activities help students:

- Practice vital critical thinking skills.
- Enrich essential chapter themes.

Name .... Date .... Class ....

SOURCE READING 22

10. No one should be disturbed on account of his opinions, even religious, provided their manifestation does not trouble the public order as established by law.

11. The free communication of thoughts and opinions is one of the most precious of the rights of man; ever... write, and print fr... responsibility for t...

tax is indispensable; it should be equally apportioned among all the citizens according to their means.

14. All citizens have the right to ascertain, by themselves or through their representatives, the necessary amount of public taxation, to...

Use information from th...

1. What does the Dec...

2. According to the D... from that in the Am...

3. If the Declaration h...

Source Readings:

- Reinforce and extend chapter content.
- Make connections across the curriculum.
- Let students experience the story of history.

Name .... Date .... Class ....

SOURCE READING 22

Declaration of the Rights of Man and of the Citizen

Although the French Revolution later turned to violence and terror, the first bold public statement of the revolutionary National Assembly echoes the high ideals of John Locke, the Enlightenment, and the American Declaration of Independence. The Declaration of the Rights of Man and of the Citizen was issued in August 1789.

Guided Reading *In this selection, read to learn what problems and rights the Declaration addresses.*

The representatives of the French people, constituted in National Assembly, considering that ignorance, forgetfulness, or contempt of the rights of man are the sole causes of public misfortunes and the corruption of governments, have resolved to set forth in a solemn declaration the natural, inalienable, and sacred rights of man so that this declaration, being constantly before all members of the social body, may unceasingly recall to them their rights and their duties; so that the acts of the legislative power and those of the executive power may always be compared with the true aim of political organization and thus may be more respected; and so that the demands of the citizens, founded henceforth upon simple and incontestable principles, may always be aimed at maintaining the constitution and the happiness of all.

In consequence, the National Assembly recognizes and declares, in the presence and under the auspices of the Supreme Being, the following rights of man and citizen.

1. Men are born and remain free and equal in rights. Social distinctions can be based only upon the common good.

2. The aim of every political association is the preservation of the natural and imprescriptible rights of man. These rights are liberty, property, security, and resistance to oppression.

3. The source of all sovereignty is essentially in the nation [that is, the people]; no body, no individual can exercise authority that does not emanate from it expressly.

4. Liberty consists in the power to do anything that does not injure others; accordingly, the exercise of the natural rights of each man has no limits except those that assure to the other members of society the enjoyment of these same rights. These limits can be determined only by law.

5. The law can forbid only such actions as are injurious to society. Nothing can be forbidden that is not forbidden by the law, and no one can be constrained to do that which it does not decree.

6. Law is the expression of the general will. All citizens have the right to take part personally, or by their representatives, in its enactment. It must be the same for all, whether it protects or punishes. All citizens being equal in its eyes, are equally eligible to all public dignities, places, and employments, according to their capacities, and without other distinction than that of their merits and their talents.

7. No man can be accused, arrested, or detained, except in the cases determined by the law and according to the forms which it has prescribed. Those who call for, expedite, execute, or cause to be executed arbitrary orders should be punished; but every citizen summoned or seized by virtue of the law ought to obey instantly; he makes himself culpable by resistance.

8. The law ought to establish only punishments that are strictly and obviously necessary, and no one should be punished except by virtue of a law established and promulgated prior to the offence and legally applied.

9. Every man being presumed innocent until he has been declared guilty, if it is judged indispensable to arrest him, all severity that may not be necessary to secure his person ought to be severely suppressed by law.

Name .... Date .... Class ....

PERFORMANCE ASSESSMENT Activity 22

The French Revolution

Background
The Declaration of the Rights of Man and of the Citizen shocked the world. Its adoption by the National Assembly on August 26, 1789, trumpeted the success of the radical ideas of the revolutionary leaders. The inspiring document was to have dramatic effects beyond the borders of France. "This single page of print," the British statesman Lord Acton later said, "is stronger than all the armies of Napoleon." Today, the Declaration of Rights forms the preamble to the French Constitution and continues to serve as a model of liberal thought and government.

Task
You are a member of the National Assembly in the summer of 1789. You and other Assembly members are to compile a list of all the rights due to individuals and citizens.

Audience
Your audience is the people of France, present and future, and people around the world who will look to this document for inspiration as they struggle to end oppression in their own nations.

Purpose
The purpose is to determine the specific rights that will be included in the final Declaration of Rights adopted by the National Assembly.

Procedures

1. Working with a group, begin two lists. Title one list "Rights of Man"and the other list "Rights of the Citizen." (In the original document, the word *man* was used to refer to people in general, not to men only.)
2. Ask yourself, How do the rights of the individual (as a person) differ from the rights of a citizen (as a member of a nation)? Decide on the types of rights to be included in each list and write this at the beginning of each list.
3. Remember the historical situation: You are working in the National Assembly as feudalism is ending in France. Keeping this in mind, brainstorm a list of rights that you think all individuals should have. Then brainstorm a list of rights that you think all citizens should have.
4. Review and revise your lists. Working together, decide whether to eliminate some rights and add others.
5. Combine your two lists into a single list titled "Rights of Man and of the Citizen." List the rights in order of importance.
6. Revise each right on the list so its meaning is clear.
7. Prepare a final copy of your list and post it. Compare your list to the text of the actual Declaration of the Rights of Man and of the Citizen.

Performance Assessment Strategies and Activities:

- Meet alternative assessment requirements.
- Include scoring rubrics.
- Provide students with activities to include in their portfolios.

Section Quizzes:
- Monitor day-to-day student progress.
- Offer section-by-section evaluation.
- Limit your preparation time.

Also available in Spanish

Name ______ Date ______ Class ______

Section Quiz 22-1

Score ____

The Old Order

Matching

Match each item in Column A with an item in Column B by writing the correct letters in the blanks. (3 points each)

Column A

____ **1.** the middle class

____ **2.** a Paris prison that symbolized the injustices of the French monarchy

____ **3.** a lavish palace where French royalty lived

____ **4.** the orders or classes of French society

____ **5.** a tax paid by church members

Column B

a. estates

b. bourgeoisie

c. tithe

d. Versailles

e. the Bastille

Multiple Choice

In the blank at the left, write the letter of the choice that best completes the statement or answers the question. (4 points each)

____ **6.** All of the following people belonged to the Third Estate EXCEPT

a. peasants.
b. artisans.
c. members of the bourgeoisie.
d. members of the nobility.

____ **7.** The King of France during the French Revolution was

a. Louis XIV.
b. Louis XV.
c. Louis XVI.
d. Louis XVII.

____ **8.** What was the Estates-General?

a. a lavish palace in the French countryside
b. an assembly of delegates
c. a prison that was attacked by a French mob
d. the court of the King of France

____ **9.** Who took the Tennis Court Oath?

a. representatives of the First Estate
b. representatives of the Second Estate
c. representatives of the Third Estate
d. the King of France

____ **10.** The violence that rocked the French countryside in 1789 was called the

a. Terror.
b. French Revolution.
c. Great Fear.
d. fall of the Bastille.

Chapter and Unit Tests: Forms A and B:

- Evaluate student understanding of chapter ideas.
- Offer students a variety of question formats.
- Give you alternate tests to choose from.

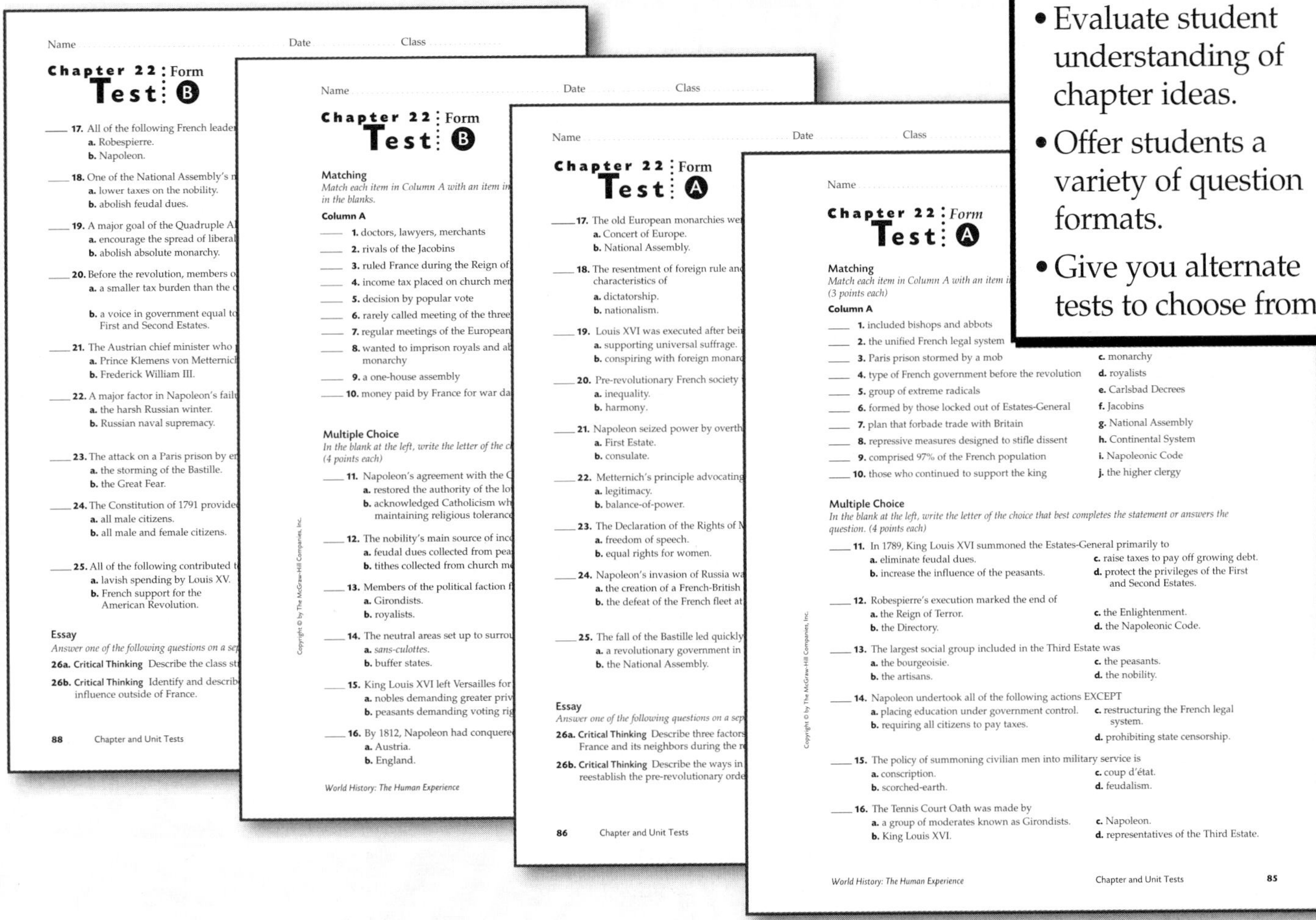
Name Date Class

Chapter 22 Form Test A

Matching
Match each item in Column A with an item in Column B. Write the correct letters in the blanks. (3 points each)

Column A

____ 1. included bishops and abbots
____ 2. the unified French legal system
____ 3. Paris prison stormed by a mob
____ 4. type of French government before the revolution
____ 5. group of extreme radicals
____ 6. formed by those locked out of Estates-General
____ 7. plan that forbade trade with Britain
____ 8. repressive measures designed to stifle dissent
____ 9. comprised 97% of the French population
____ 10. those who continued to support the king

c. monarchy
d. royalists
e. Carlsbad Decrees
f. Jacobins
g. National Assembly
h. Continental System
i. Napoleonic Code
j. the higher clergy

Multiple Choice
In the blank at the left, write the letter of the choice that best completes the statement or answers the question. (4 points each)

____ 11. In 1789, King Louis XVI summoned the Estates-General primarily to
a. eliminate feudal dues. c. raise taxes to pay off growing debt.
b. increase the influence of the peasants. d. protect the privileges of the First and Second Estates.

____ 12. Robespierre's execution marked the end of
a. the Reign of Terror. c. the Enlightenment.
b. the Directory. d. the Napoleonic Code.

____ 13. The largest social group included in the Third Estate was
a. the bourgeoisie. c. the peasants.
b. the artisans. d. the nobility.

____ 14. Napoleon undertook all of the following actions EXCEPT
a. placing education under government control. c. restructuring the French legal system.
b. requiring all citizens to pay taxes. d. prohibiting state censorship.

____ 15. The policy of summoning civilian men into military service is
a. conscription. c. coup d'état.
b. scorched-earth. d. feudalism.

____ 16. The Tennis Court Oath was made by
a. a group of moderates known as Girondists. c. Napoleon.
b. King Louis XVI. d. representatives of the Third Estate.

World History: The Human Experience Chapter and Unit Tests 85

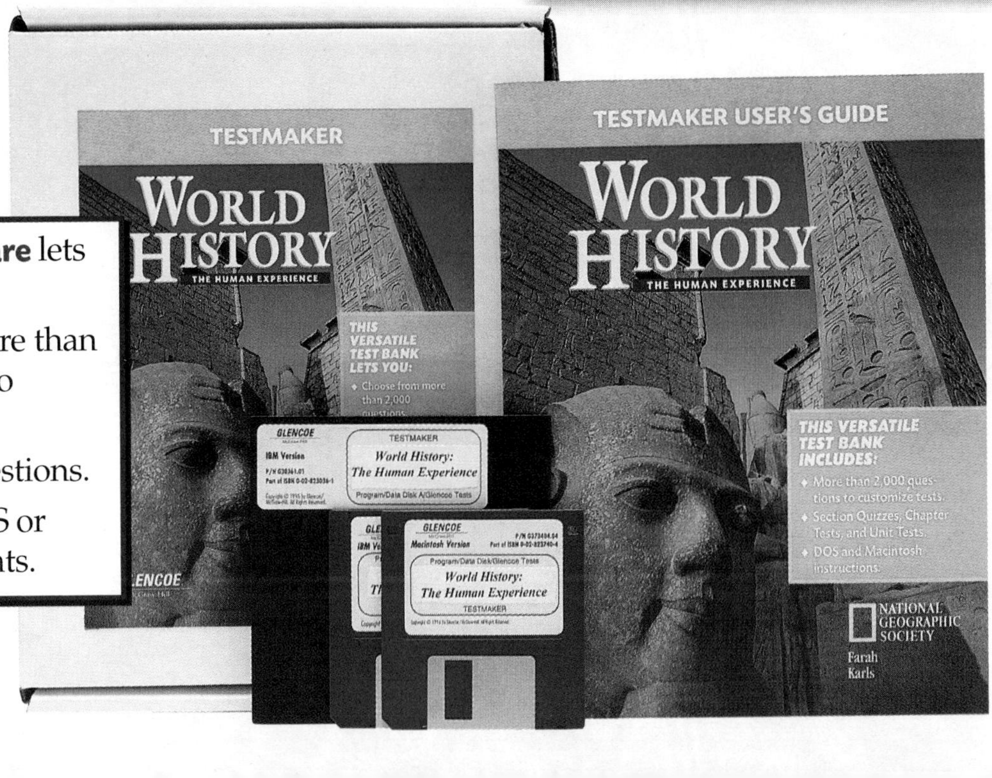

TESTMAKER
WORLD HISTORY
THE HUMAN EXPERIENCE
TESTMAKER USER'S GUIDE
THIS VERSATILE TEST BANK INCLUDES:
More than 2,000 questions to customize tests.
Section Quizzes, Chapter Tests, and Unit Tests.
DOS and Macintosh instructions
NATIONAL GEOGRAPHIC SOCIETY
Farah
Karls
GLENCOE
World History: The Human Experience
TESTMAKER

Testmaker Software lets you:

- Choose from more than 2,000 questions to customize tests.
- Edit existing questions.
- Select either DOS or Macintosh formats.

Student Self-Test and Review Software helps students:

- Review and reinforce chapter concepts, people, and events.
- Take responsibility for their learning.
- Pinpoint and correct their own mistakes.

Available in DOS and Macintosh

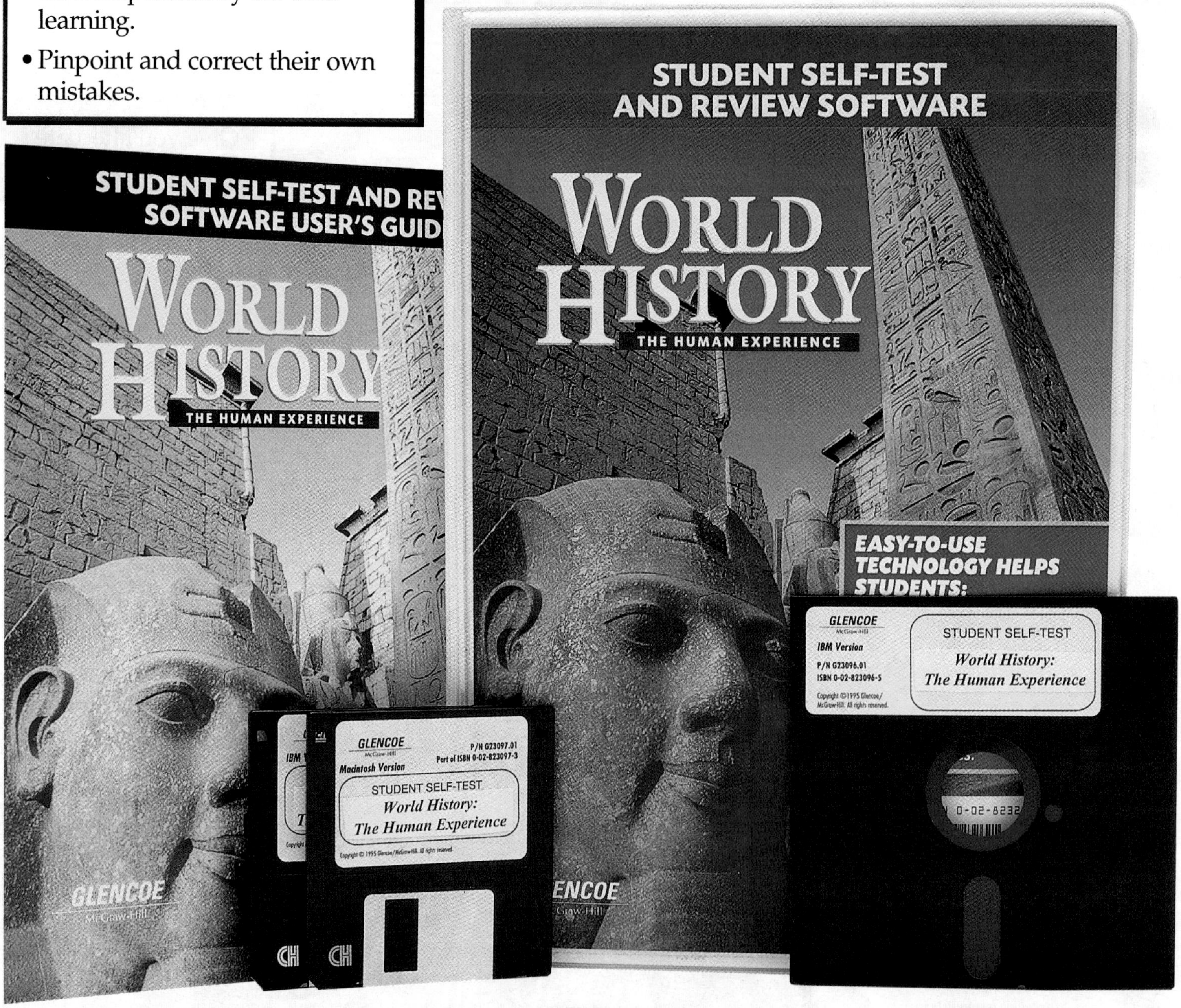

MindJogger Videoquiz offers preview, review, and reinforcement of chapter content in a game-show format.

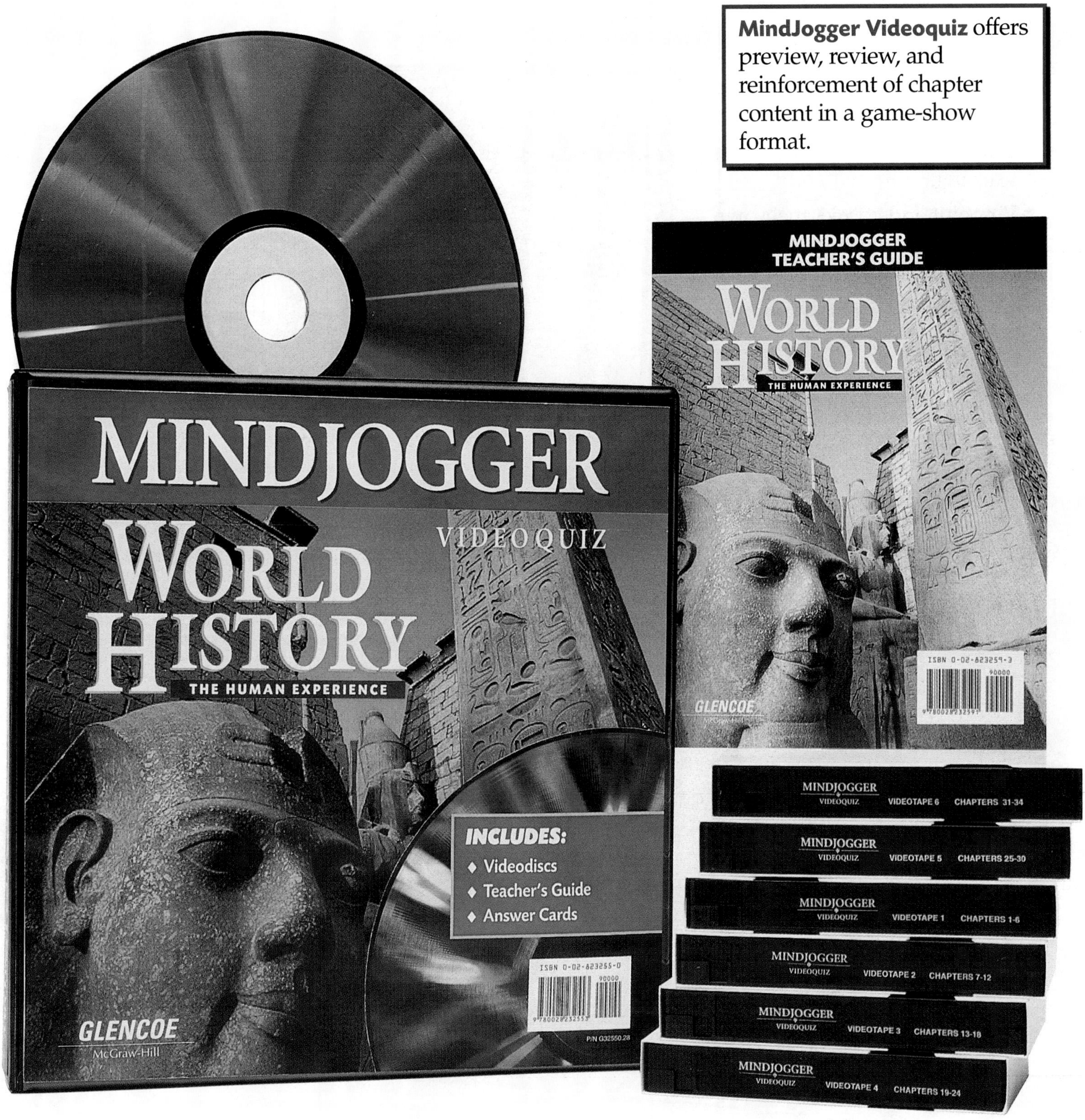

MINDJOGGER
WORLD HISTORY
VIDEOQUIZ
THE HUMAN EXPERIENCE
INCLUDES:
♦ Videodiscs
♦ Teacher's Guide
♦ Answer Cards
GLENCOE
McGraw-Hill
MINDJOGGER TEACHER'S GUIDE
WORLD HISTORY
THE HUMAN EXPERIENCE
MINDJOGGER VIDEOQUIZ VIDEOTAPE 6 CHAPTERS 31-34
MINDJOGGER VIDEOQUIZ VIDEOTAPE 5 CHAPTERS 25-30
MINDJOGGER VIDEOQUIZ VIDEOTAPE 1 CHAPTERS 1-6
MINDJOGGER VIDEOQUIZ VIDEOTAPE 2 CHAPTERS 7-12
MINDJOGGER VIDEOQUIZ VIDEOTAPE 3 CHAPTERS 13-18
MINDJOGGER VIDEOQUIZ VIDEOTAPE 4 CHAPTERS 19-24

Multimedia and Technology

The following multiple-use **Teaching Transparencies** with teaching strategies and activities are included in this binder:

- Unit Digest Transparencies
- Mapping History Overlay Transparencies
- Chapter Transparencies

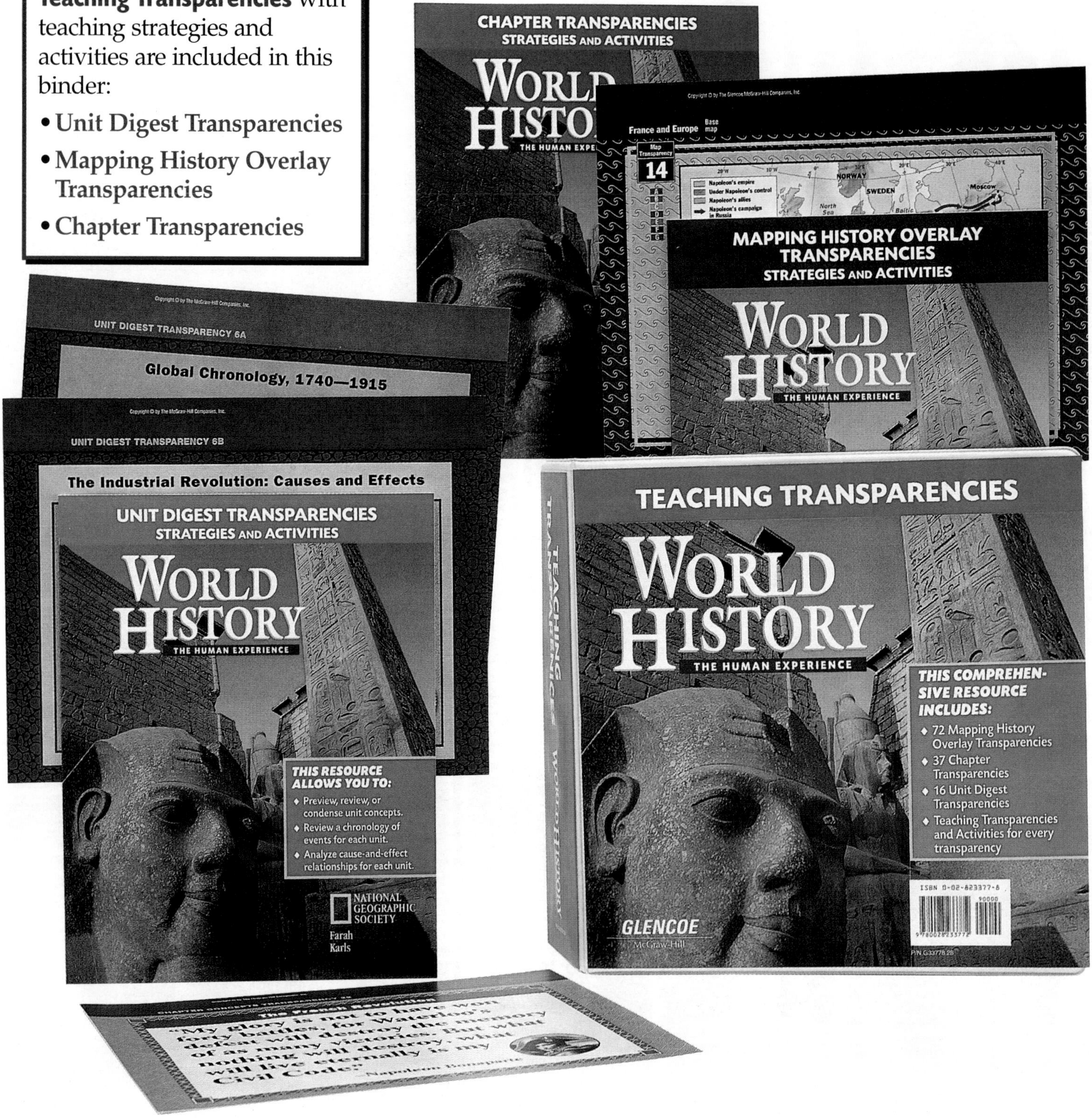

Section Focus Transparencies include 147 high-interest and colorful transparencies and blackline masters.

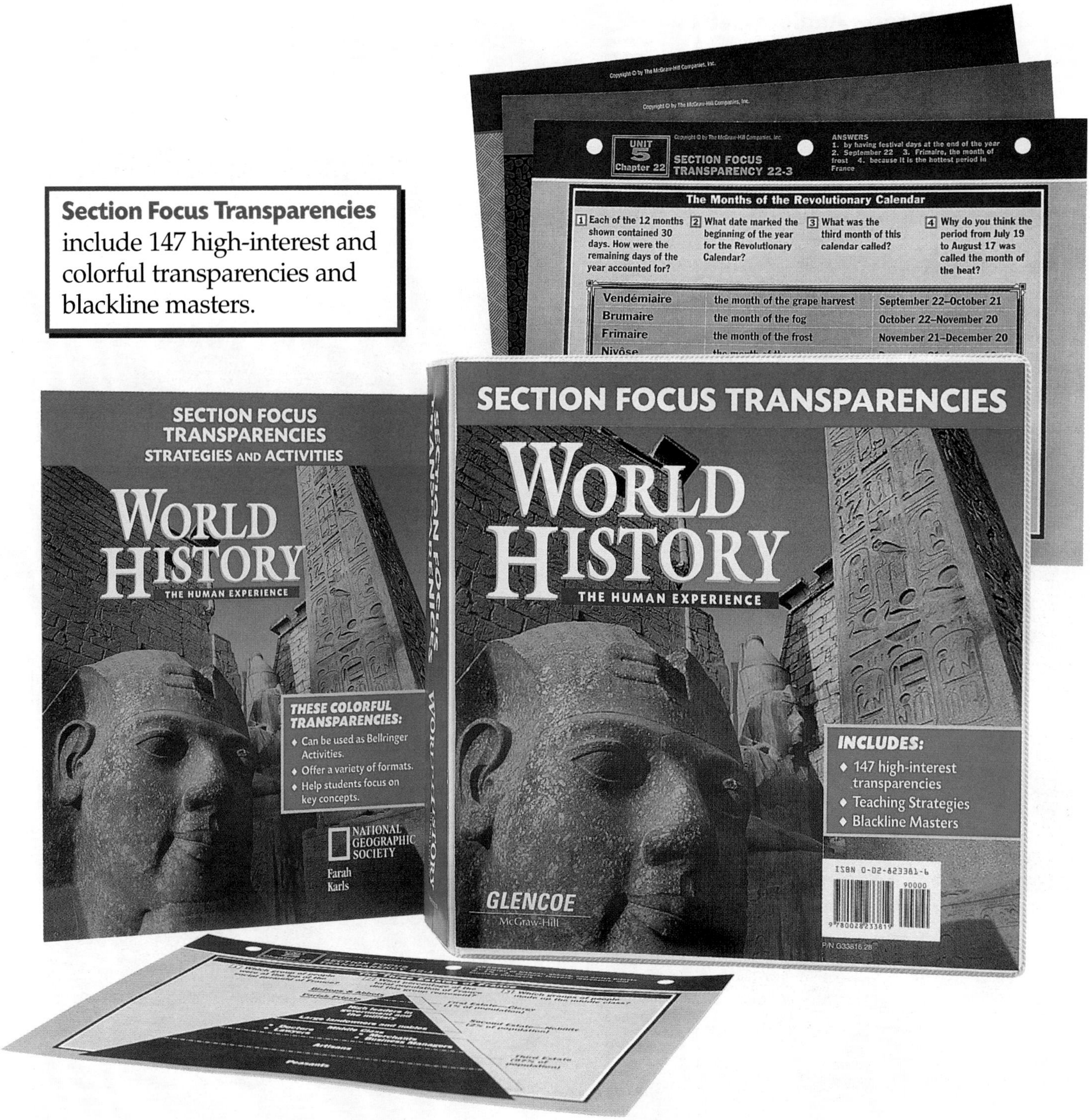
UNIT 5
Chapter 22
SECTION FOCUS TRANSPARENCY 22-3
ANSWERS
1. by having festival days at the end of the year
2. September 22 3. Frimaire, the month of frost 4. because it is the hottest period in France
The Months of the Revolutionary Calendar
1 Each of the 12 months shown contained 30 days. How were the remaining days of the year accounted for?
2 What date marked the beginning of the year for the Revolutionary Calendar?
3 What was the third month of this calendar called?
4 Why do you think the period from July 19 to August 17 was called the month of the heat?
Vendémiaire the month of the grape harvest September 22–October 21
Brumaire the month of the fog October 22–November 20
Frimaire the month of the frost November 21–December 20
SECTION FOCUS TRANSPARENCIES
STRATEGIES AND ACTIVITIES
WORLD HISTORY
THE HUMAN EXPERIENCE
THESE COLORFUL TRANSPARENCIES:
Can be used as Bellringer Activities.
Offer a variety of formats.
Help students focus on key concepts.
NATIONAL GEOGRAPHIC SOCIETY
Farah
Karls
SECTION FOCUS TRANSPARENCIES
WORLD HISTORY
THE HUMAN EXPERIENCE
INCLUDES:
147 high-interest transparencies
Teaching Strategies
Blackline Masters
ISBN 0-02-823381-6
GLENCOE
McGraw-Hill

Multimedia and Technology

Chapter Digests Audiocassettes Activities and Tests:

- Includes activities to accompany the audiocassettes.
- Provides tests to assess comprehension of the audiocassettes.

Also available in Spanish

NATIONAL GEOGRAPHIC SOCIETY

The prestigious National Geographic Society has teamed with Glencoe to provide your students with a variety of interactive videodiscs, CD-ROMs, transparencies, and posters to extend and enrich the study of world history.

STV: Maya includes the National Geographic television special ***Lost Kingdoms of the Maya*** and more than 130 archival images.

Multimedia and Technology

NATIONAL GEOGRAPHIC SOCIETY

STV: World Geography videodiscs opens the world to your students and allows them to see the environments in which the events they are studying took place. This series includes the following:

- *Volume 1: Asia and Australia*
- *Volume 2: Africa and Europe*
- *Volume 3: South America and Antarctica*

Also available is **STV: North America**.

NGS PictureShow™ CD-ROMs let students explore ancient civilizations, their powerful rulers, and their achievements in art, technology, and government.

- *Ancient Civilizations: Egypt and the Fertile Crescent*
- *Ancient Civilizations: India and China*
- *Ancient Civilizations: Greece and Rome*
- *Ancient Civilizations: The Americas*
- *The Middle Ages*
- *The Renaissance*
- *Great Explorers, Parts 1 and 2*

Picture Atlas of the World CD-ROM is also available.

NATIONAL GEOGRAPHIC SOCIETY

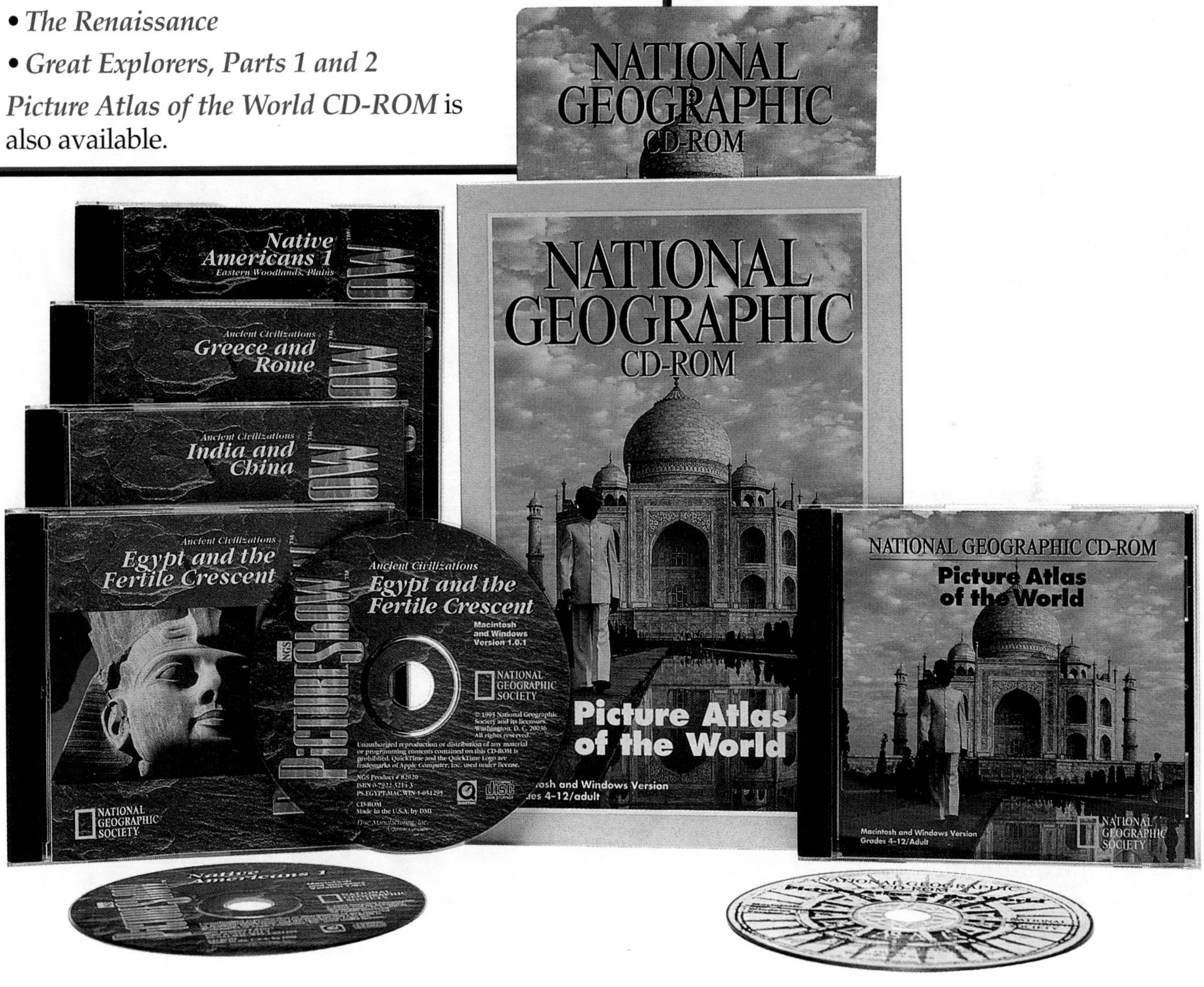

NATIONAL GEOGRAPHIC SOCIETY

NGS PicturePack Transparency Sets and **Poster Sets** visually display the beauty and grandeur of the following:

PicturePack Transparencies

- *Ancient Egypt*
- *The Fertile Crescent*
- *Ancient China*
- *Ancient India*
- *Ancient Greece*
- *Ancient Rome*
- *The Middle Ages*
- *The Renaissance*
- *Age of Exploration*

Physical Geography of the World Transparencies are also available.

Poster Sets

- *Ancient Egypt*
- *The Fertile Crescent*
- *Ancient Greece*
- *Ancient Rome*
- *The Middle Ages*
- *The Renaissance*
- *Age of Exploration*

Multimedia and Technology

ABCNEWS INTERACTIVE™

ABCNews InterActive ™ videodiscs are excellent tools to aid students in visualizing and understanding history. The following titles are available:

- *In the Holy Land*
- *Lessons of War*
- *Communism and the Cold War*

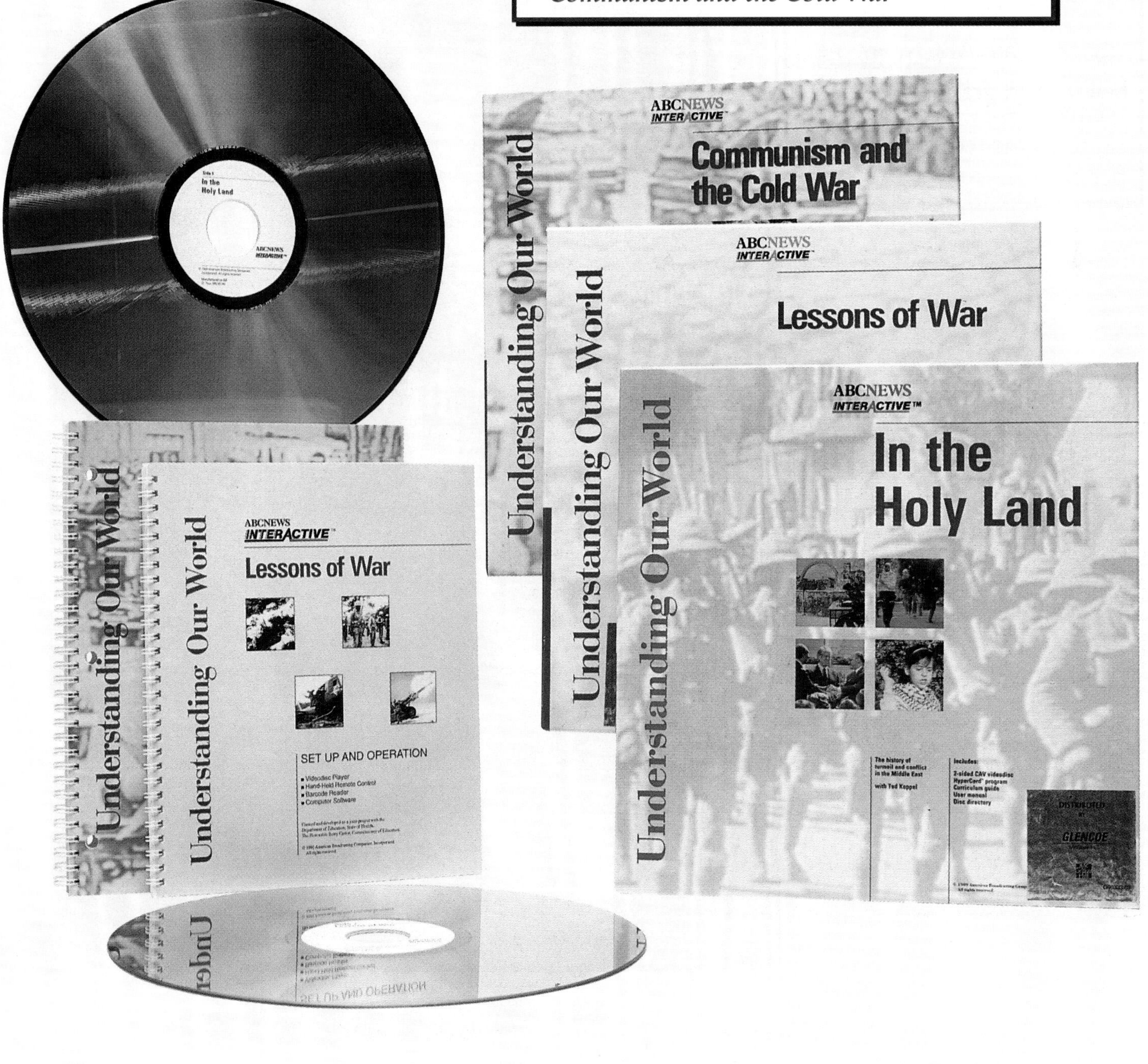

ABCNEWS INTERACTIVE™

Turning Points in World History from ABCNews InterActive™ highlights the historical events that changed the world and its people.

Reference Atlas

The World: Physical/Political	A2
The World: Political	A4
The United States: Physical/Political	A6
Mexico, the Caribbean, and Central America	A8
North America	A10
South America	A11
Europe	A12
Russia and the Republics	A14
Eurasia	A16
Middle East	A18
Africa	A20
South Asia	A21
The Pacific Rim	A22
Oceania	A24
Polar Regions	A26

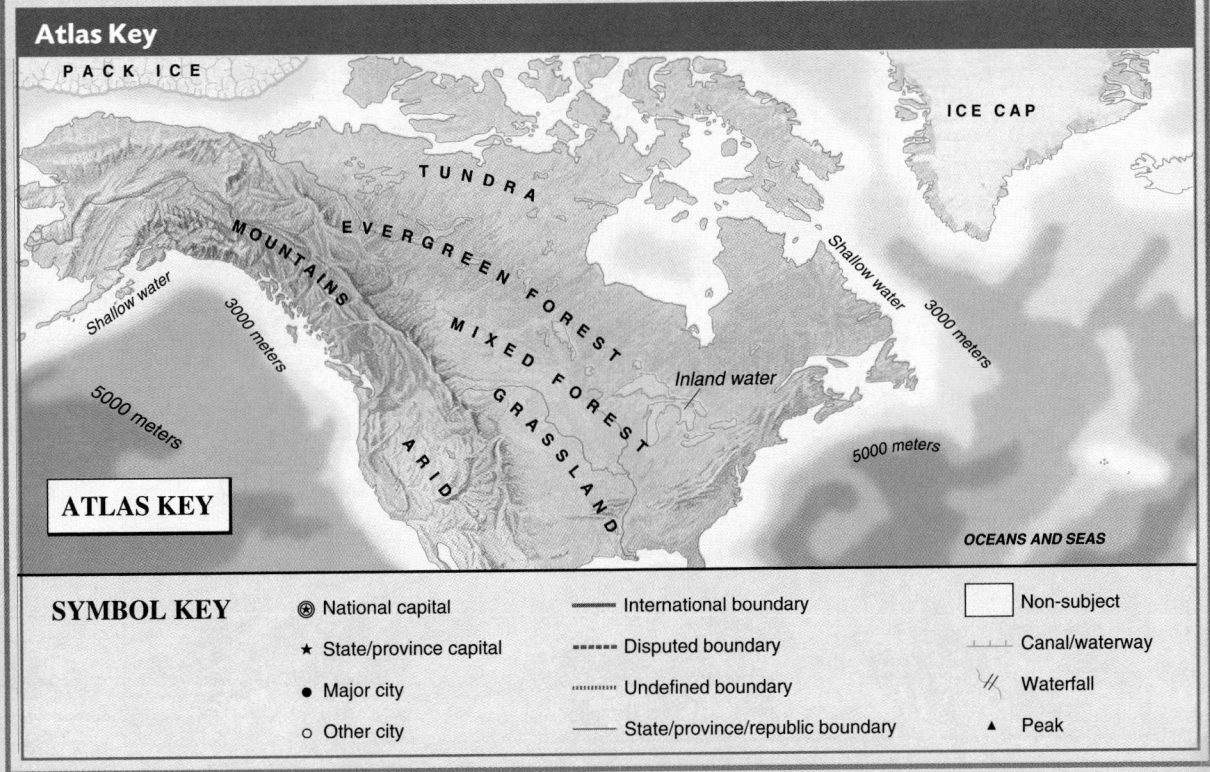

Atlas Key

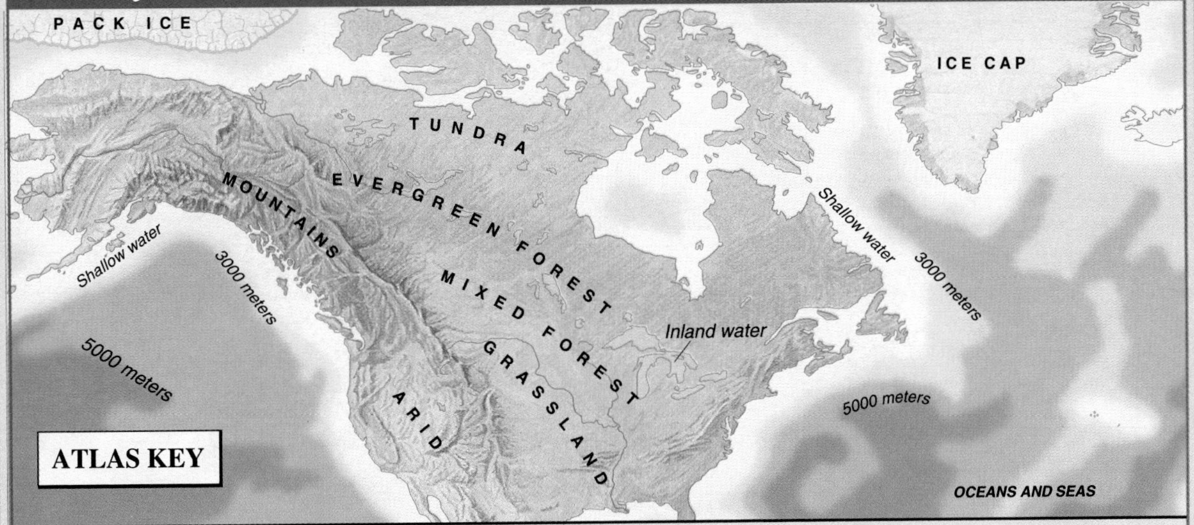

SYMBOL KEY

- National capital
- ★ State/province capital
- ● Major city
- ○ Other city
- International boundary
- Disputed boundary
- Undefined boundary
- State/province/republic boundary
- Non-subject
- Canal/waterway
- Waterfall
- ▲ Peak

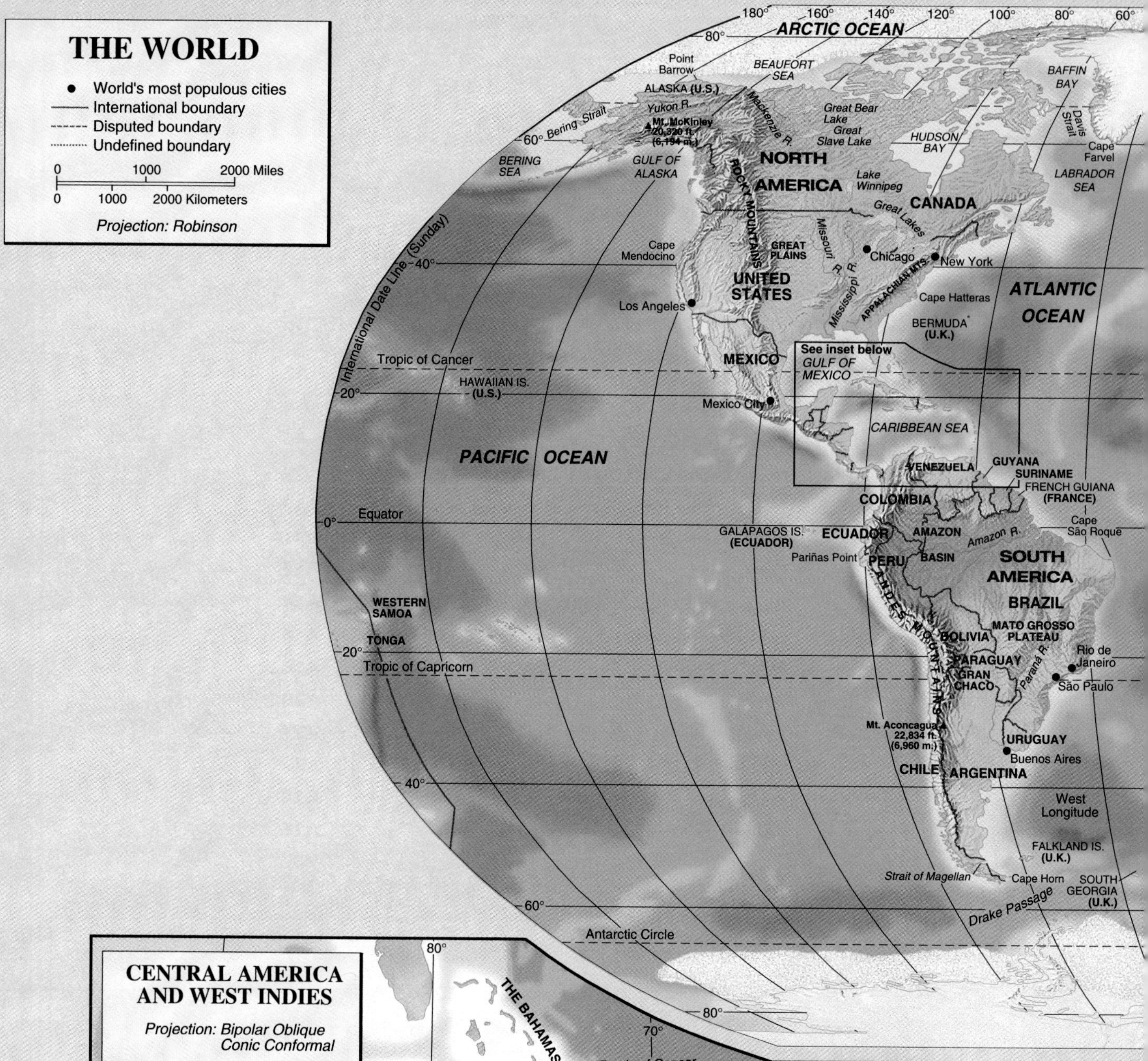
THE WORLD
World's most populous cities
International boundary
Disputed boundary
Undefined boundary
0
1000
2000 Miles
0
1000
2000 Kilometers
Projection: Robinson
ARCTIC OCEAN
Point Barrow
BEAUFORT SEA
ALASKA (U.S.)
Yukon R.
Bering Strait
Mt. McKinley 20,320 ft. (6,194 m.)
Mackenzie R.
Great Bear Lake
Great Slave Lake
BERING SEA
GULF OF ALASKA
NORTH AMERICA
ROCKY MOUNTAINS
HUDSON BAY
BAFFIN BAY
Davis Strait
Cape Farvel
LABRADOR SEA
Lake Winnipeg
Great Lakes
CANADA
Missouri R.
Cape Mendocino
GREAT PLAINS
Chicago
New York
International Date Line (Sunday)
UNITED STATES
Mississippi R.
APPALACHIAN MTS.
Los Angeles
Cape Hatteras
ATLANTIC OCEAN
BERMUDA (U.K.)
MEXICO
See inset below
GULF OF MEXICO
Tropic of Cancer
HAWAIIAN IS. (U.S.)
Mexico City
CARIBBEAN SEA
PACIFIC OCEAN
VENEZUELA
GUYANA
SURINAME
FRENCH GUIANA (FRANCE)
COLOMBIA
Equator
Cape São Roque
GALÁPAGOS IS. (ECUADOR)
ECUADOR
AMAZON BASIN
Amazon R.
Pariñas Point
PERU
SOUTH AMERICA
ANDES MOUNTAINS
BRAZIL
WESTERN SAMOA
TONGA
MATO GROSSO PLATEAU
BOLIVIA
Rio de Janeiro
PARAGUAY
Tropic of Capricorn
GRAN CHACO
Paraná R.
São Paulo
Mt. Aconcagua 22,834 ft. (6,960 m.)
URUGUAY
Buenos Aires
CHILE
ARGENTINA
West Longitude
FALKLAND IS. (U.K.)
Strait of Magellan
Cape Horn
SOUTH GEORGIA (U.K.)
Drake Passage
Antarctic Circle

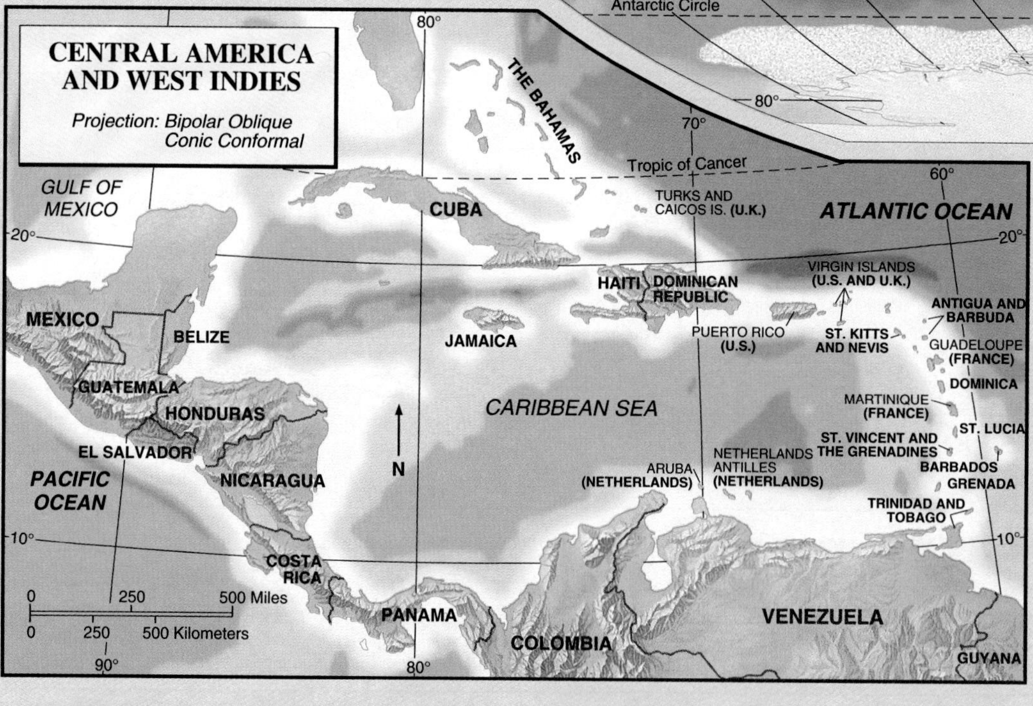
CENTRAL AMERICA AND WEST INDIES
Projection: Bipolar Oblique Conic Conformal
THE BAHAMAS
Tropic of Cancer
GULF OF MEXICO
CUBA
TURKS AND CAICOS IS. (U.K.)
ATLANTIC OCEAN
HAITI
DOMINICAN REPUBLIC
VIRGIN ISLANDS (U.S. AND U.K.)
ANTIGUA AND BARBUDA
MEXICO
BELIZE
JAMAICA
PUERTO RICO (U.S.)
ST. KITTS AND NEVIS
GUADELOUPE (FRANCE)
DOMINICA
GUATEMALA
HONDURAS
CARIBBEAN SEA
MARTINIQUE (FRANCE)
ST. LUCIA
EL SALVADOR
N
ST. VINCENT AND THE GRENADINES
BARBADOS
GRENADA
PACIFIC OCEAN
NICARAGUA
ARUBA (NETHERLANDS)
NETHERLANDS ANTILLES (NETHERLANDS)
TRINIDAD AND TOBAGO
COSTA RICA
0
250
500 Miles
0
250
500 Kilometers
PANAMA
VENEZUELA
COLOMBIA
GUYANA

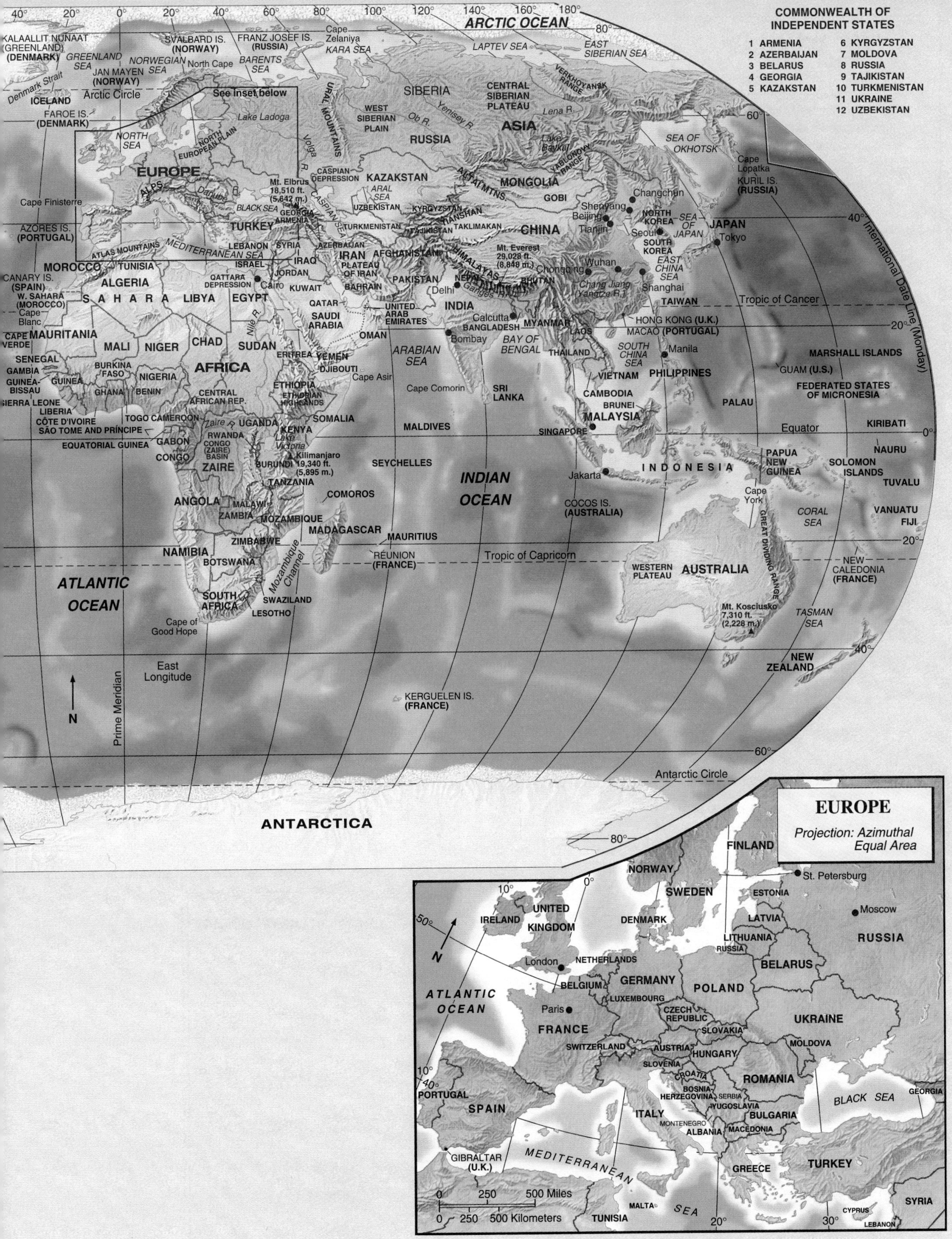

COMMONWEALTH OF INDEPENDENT STATES
1 ARMENIA
2 AZERBAIJAN
3 BELARUS
4 GEORGIA
5 KAZAKSTAN
6 KYRGYZSTAN
7 MOLDOVA
8 RUSSIA
9 TAJIKISTAN
10 TURKMENISTAN
11 UKRAINE
12 UZBEKISTAN
ARCTIC OCEAN
KALAALLIT NUNAAT (GREENLAND) (DENMARK)
SVALBARD IS. (NORWAY)
FRANZ JOSEF IS. (RUSSIA)
Cape Zelaniya
KARA SEA
LAPTEV SEA
EAST SIBERIAN SEA
GREENLAND SEA
NORWEGIAN SEA
BARENTS SEA
North Cape
JAN MAYEN (NORWAY)
Denmark Strait
ICELAND
Arctic Circle
See Inset below
FAROE IS. (DENMARK)
Lake Ladoga
SIBERIA
CENTRAL SIBERIAN PLATEAU
VERKHOYANSK RANGE
WEST SIBERIAN PLAIN
URAL MOUNTAINS
Ob R.
Yenisey R.
Lena R.
ASIA
RUSSIA
NORTH SEA
NORTH EUROPEAN PLAIN
Volga R.
Lake Baykal
YABLONOVY RANGE
SEA OF OKHOTSK
Cape Lopatka
KURIL IS. (RUSSIA)
EUROPE
ALPS
Danube R.
Mt. Elbrus 18,510 ft. (5,642 m.)
CASPIAN DEPRESSION
KAZAKSTAN
ARAL SEA
ALTAI MTNS.
MONGOLIA
GOBI
Changchun
Shenyang
Beijing
Tianjin
NORTH KOREA
SOUTH KOREA
Seoul
SEA OF JAPAN
JAPAN
Tokyo
Cape Finisterre
BLACK SEA
GEORGIA
ARMENIA
CASPIAN SEA
UZBEKISTAN
KYRGYZSTAN
TIANSHAN
TURKMENISTAN
TAJIKISTAN
TAKLIMAKAN
CHINA
AZORES IS. (PORTUGAL)
TURKEY
AZERBAIJAN
ATLAS MOUNTAINS
MEDITERRANEAN SEA
LEBANON
SYRIA
IRAN
AFGHANISTAN
HIMALAYAS
Mt. Everest 29,028 ft. (8,848 m.)
Chongqing
Wuhan
EAST CHINA SEA
International Date Line (Monday)
MOROCCO
TUNISIA
ISRAEL
IRAQ
PLATEAU OF IRAN
CANARY IS. (SPAIN)
ALGERIA
QATTARA DEPRESSION
JORDAN
Cairo
KUWAIT
BAHRAIN
PAKISTAN
NEPAL
BHUTAN
Chang Jiang (Yangtze R.)
Shanghai
Delhi
Ganges R.
W. SAHARA (MOROCCO)
SAHARA
LIBYA
EGYPT
QATAR
INDIA
TAIWAN
Tropic of Cancer
Cape Blanc
Nile R.
SAUDI ARABIA
UNITED ARAB EMIRATES
Calcutta
BANGLADESH
MYANMAR
HONG KONG (U.K.)
MACAO (PORTUGAL)
CAPE VERDE
MAURITANIA
MALI
NIGER
CHAD
SUDAN
OMAN
Bombay
BAY OF BENGAL
LAOS
ARABIAN SEA
THAILAND
SOUTH CHINA SEA
Manila
MARSHALL ISLANDS
SENEGAL
GAMBIA
GUINEA-BISSAU
GUINEA
SIERRA LEONE
LIBERIA
BURKINA FASO
GHANA
BENIN
NIGERIA
AFRICA
ERITREA
YEMEN
DJIBOUTI
Cape Asir
VIETNAM
PHILIPPINES
GUAM (U.S.)
FEDERATED STATES OF MICRONESIA
ETHIOPIA
ETHIOPIAN HIGHLANDS
CENTRAL AFRICAN REP.
Cape Comorin
SRI LANKA
CAMBODIA
BRUNEI
PALAU
CÔTE D'IVOIRE
TOGO
CAMEROON
Zaire R.
UGANDA
SOMALIA
MALAYSIA
MALDIVES
SÃO TOME AND PRÍNCIPE
GABON
RWANDA
KENYA
SINGAPORE
Equator
KIRIBATI
EQUATORIAL GUINEA
CONGO
CONGO (ZAIRE) BASIN
Lake Victoria
Kilimanjaro 19,340 ft. (5,895 m.)
NAURU
ZAIRE
BURUNDI
SEYCHELLES
Jakarta
INDONESIA
PAPUA NEW GUINEA
SOLOMON ISLANDS
TANZANIA
INDIAN OCEAN
TUVALU
COMOROS
Cape York
ANGOLA
MALAWI
ZAMBIA
MOZAMBIQUE
COCOS IS. (AUSTRALIA)
VANUATU
CORAL SEA
FIJI
GREAT DIVIDING RANGE
MADAGASCAR
MAURITIUS
ZIMBABWE
NAMIBIA
Mozambique Channel
RÉUNION (FRANCE)
Tropic of Capricorn
NEW CALEDONIA (FRANCE)
BOTSWANA
WESTERN PLATEAU
AUSTRALIA
ATLANTIC OCEAN
SOUTH AFRICA
SWAZILAND
LESOTHO
Mt. Kosciusko 7,310 ft. (2,228 m.)
TASMAN SEA
Cape of Good Hope
NEW ZEALAND
East Longitude
N
Prime Meridian
KERGUELEN IS. (FRANCE)
Antarctic Circle
ANTARCTICA
EUROPE
Projection: Azimuthal Equal Area
FINLAND
NORWAY
St. Petersburg
SWEDEN
ESTONIA
Moscow
UNITED KINGDOM
IRELAND
DENMARK
LATVIA
LITHUANIA
RUSSIA
London
NETHERLANDS
BELARUS
GERMANY
POLAND
BELGIUM
LUXEMBOURG
ATLANTIC OCEAN
Paris
CZECH REPUBLIC
UKRAINE
FRANCE
SLOVAKIA
SWITZERLAND
AUSTRIA
HUNGARY
MOLDOVA
SLOVENIA
CROATIA
ROMANIA
BOSNIA-HERZEGOVINA
SERBIA
YUGOSLAVIA
PORTUGAL
SPAIN
BLACK SEA
GEORGIA
ITALY
MONTENEGRO
BULGARIA
ALBANIA
MACEDONIA
GIBRALTAR (U.K.)
MEDITERRANEAN SEA
GREECE
TURKEY
0 250 500 Miles
0 250 500 Kilometers
MALTA
TUNISIA
CYPRUS
SYRIA
LEBANON

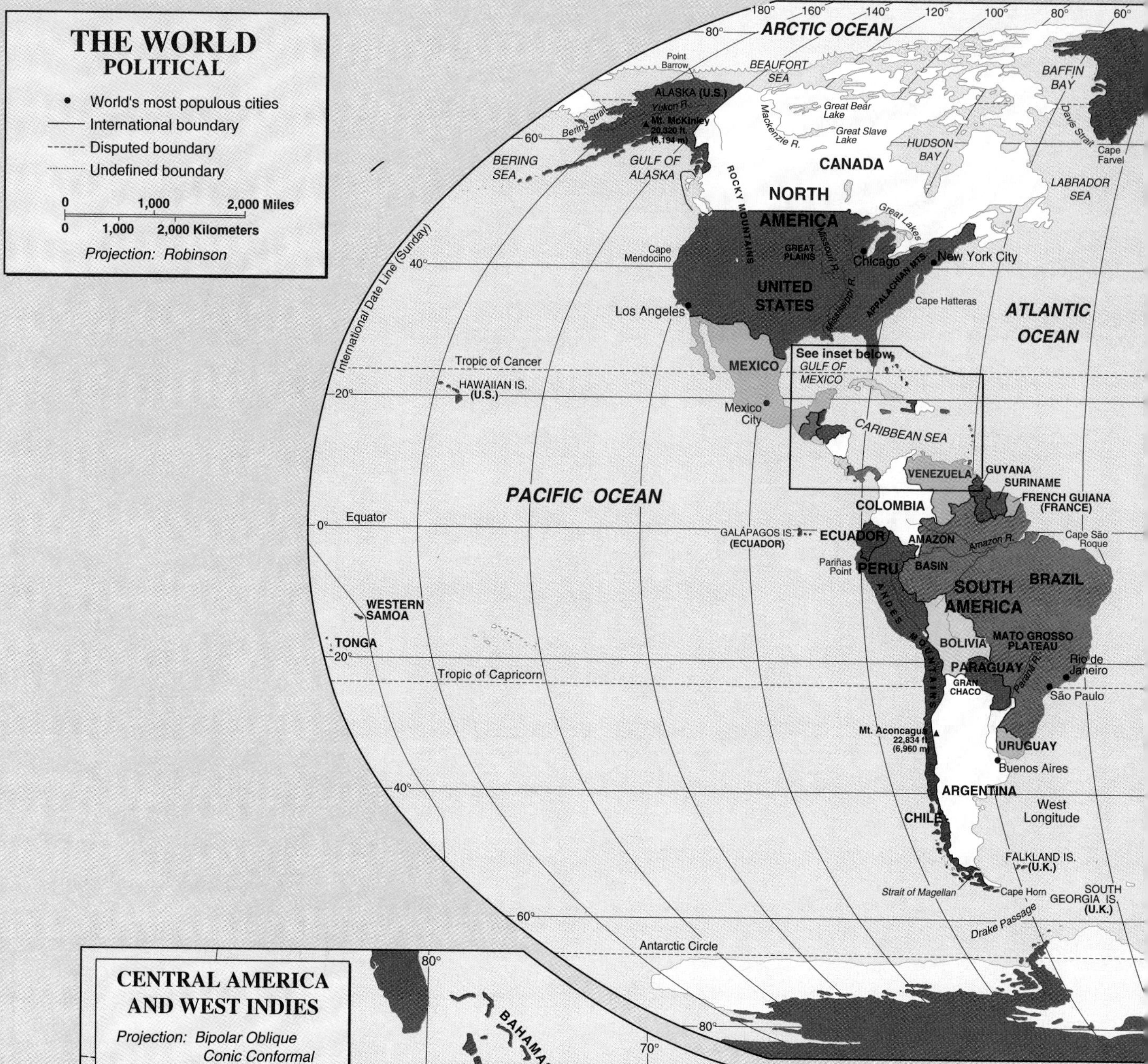
THE WORLD
POLITICAL
World's most populous cities
International boundary
Disputed boundary
Undefined boundary
0 1,000 2,000 Miles
0 1,000 2,000 Kilometers
Projection: Robinson
ARCTIC OCEAN
Point Barrow
BEAUFORT SEA
ALASKA (U.S.)
Yukon R.
Mt. McKinley 20,320 ft. (6,194 m)
Bering Strait
BERING SEA
GULF OF ALASKA
Great Bear Lake
Great Slave Lake
Mackenzie R.
HUDSON BAY
BAFFIN BAY
Davis Strait
Cape Farvel
CANADA
LABRADOR SEA
ROCKY MOUNTAINS
NORTH AMERICA
Great Lakes
Cape Mendocino
GREAT PLAINS
Missouri R.
Chicago
APPALACHIAN MTS.
New York City
UNITED STATES
Mississippi R.
Los Angeles
Cape Hatteras
ATLANTIC OCEAN
International Date Line (Sunday)
Tropic of Cancer
MEXICO
See inset below
GULF OF MEXICO
HAWAIIAN IS. (U.S.)
Mexico City
CARIBBEAN SEA
VENEZUELA
GUYANA
SURINAME
FRENCH GUIANA (FRANCE)
PACIFIC OCEAN
COLOMBIA
Equator
GALÁPAGOS IS. (ECUADOR)
ECUADOR
AMAZON BASIN
Amazon R.
Cape São Roque
Pariñas Point
PERU
ANDES MOUNTAINS
SOUTH AMERICA
BRAZIL
WESTERN SAMOA
TONGA
BOLIVIA
MATO GROSSO PLATEAU
PARAGUAY
GRAN CHACO
Paraná R.
Rio de Janeiro
São Paulo
Tropic of Capricorn
Mt. Aconcagua 22,834 ft. (6,960 m)
URUGUAY
Buenos Aires
ARGENTINA
CHILE
West Longitude
FALKLAND IS. (U.K.)
Strait of Magellan
Cape Horn
SOUTH GEORGIA IS. (U.K.)
Drake Passage
Antarctic Circle
80° 60° 40° 20° 0° 20° 40° 60° 80°
180° 160° 140° 120° 100° 80° 60°

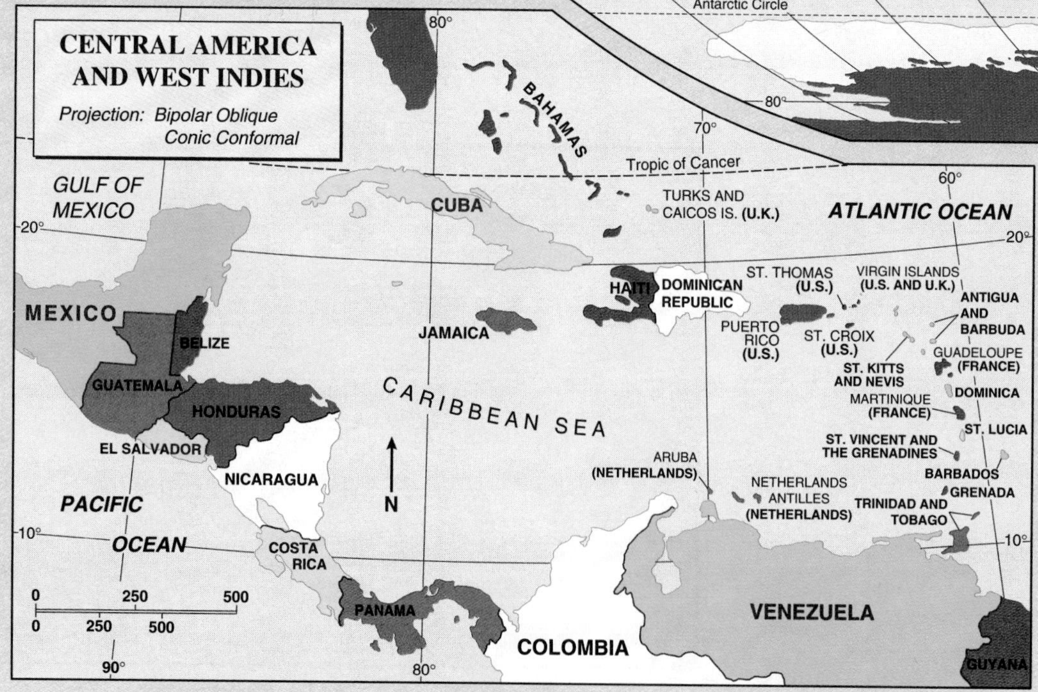
CENTRAL AMERICA AND WEST INDIES
Projection: Bipolar Oblique Conic Conformal
BAHAMAS
Tropic of Cancer
GULF OF MEXICO
CUBA
TURKS AND CAICOS IS. (U.K.)
ATLANTIC OCEAN
HAITI
DOMINICAN REPUBLIC
ST. THOMAS (U.S.)
VIRGIN ISLANDS (U.S. AND U.K.)
ANTIGUA AND BARBUDA
MEXICO
BELIZE
JAMAICA
PUERTO RICO (U.S.)
ST. CROIX (U.S.)
ST. KITTS AND NEVIS
GUADELOUPE (FRANCE)
GUATEMALA
DOMINICA
HONDURAS
CARIBBEAN SEA
MARTINIQUE (FRANCE)
ST. LUCIA
EL SALVADOR
ST. VINCENT AND THE GRENADINES
ARUBA (NETHERLANDS)
BARBADOS
NICARAGUA
GRENADA
PACIFIC OCEAN
N
NETHERLANDS ANTILLES (NETHERLANDS)
TRINIDAD AND TOBAGO
COSTA RICA
0 250 500
0 250 500
PANAMA
VENEZUELA
COLOMBIA
GUYANA
20° 10° 90° 80° 70° 60°

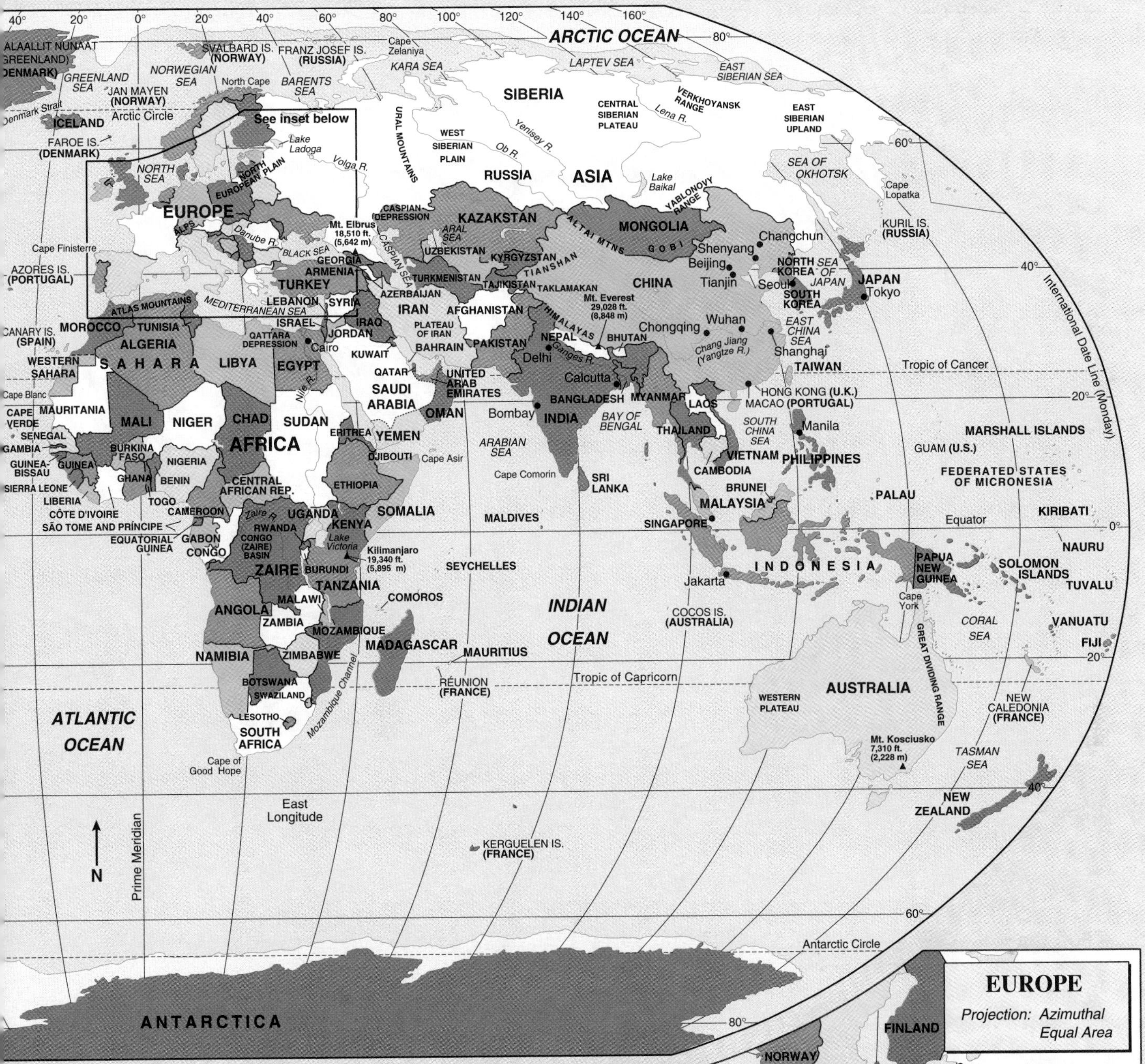
ARCTIC OCEAN
SVALBARD IS. (NORWAY)
FRANZ JOSEF IS. (RUSSIA)
GREENLAND SEA
NORWEGIAN SEA
BARENTS SEA
KARA SEA
LAPTEV SEA
EAST SIBERIAN SEA
JAN MAYEN (NORWAY)
North Cape
Cape Zelaniya
ICELAND
Arctic Circle
See inset below
FAROE IS. (DENMARK)
NORTH SEA
EUROPE
ALPS
NORTH EUROPEAN PLAIN
Lake Ladoga
Volga R.
URAL MOUNTAINS
SIBERIA
WEST SIBERIAN PLAIN
Ob R.
Yenisey R.
CENTRAL SIBERIAN PLATEAU
Lena R.
VERKHOYANSK RANGE
EAST SIBERIAN UPLAND
SEA OF OKHOTSK
Cape Lopatka
KURIL IS. (RUSSIA)
RUSSIA
ASIA
Lake Baikal
YABLONOVYY RANGE
CASPIAN DEPRESSION
KAZAKSTAN
ARAL SEA
MONGOLIA
GOBI
Mt. Elbrus 18,510 ft. (5,642 m)
Danube R.
BLACK SEA
CASPIAN SEA
UZBEKISTAN
KYRGYZSTAN
TIAN SHAN
TURKMENISTAN
TAJIKISTAN
TAKLAMAKAN
ALTAI MTNS.
Shenyang
Changchun
Beijing
Tianjin
NORTH KOREA
SEA OF JAPAN
JAPAN
Tokyo
Seoul
SOUTH KOREA
CHINA
Cape Finisterre
AZORES IS. (PORTUGAL)
GEORGIA
ARMENIA
TURKEY
AZERBAIJAN
LEBANON
SYRIA
MEDITERRANEAN SEA
ATLAS MOUNTAINS
IRAN
AFGHANISTAN
Mt. Everest 29,028 ft. (8,848 m)
HIMALAYAS
Chongqing
Wuhan
EAST CHINA SEA
Shanghai
Chang Jiang (Yangtze R.)
TAIWAN
CANARY IS. (SPAIN)
MOROCCO
TUNISIA
ISRAEL
IRAQ
JORDAN
QATTARA DEPRESSION
Cairo
KUWAIT
PLATEAU OF IRAN
BAHRAIN
PAKISTAN
NEPAL
BHUTAN
Delhi
Ganges R.
ALGERIA
WESTERN SAHARA
SAHARA
LIBYA
EGYPT
QATAR
SAUDI ARABIA
UNITED ARAB EMIRATES
Calcutta
BANGLADESH
MYANMAR
LAOS
HONG KONG (U.K.)
MACAO (PORTUGAL)
Tropic of Cancer
International Date Line (Monday)
Cape Blanc
CAPE VERDE
MAURITANIA
SENEGAL
GAMBIA
MALI
NIGER
CHAD
SUDAN
Nile R.
ERITREA
YEMEN
OMAN
Bombay
INDIA
BAY OF BENGAL
THAILAND
SOUTH CHINA SEA
Manila
PHILIPPINES
MARSHALL ISLANDS
GUAM (U.S.)
GUINEA-BISSAU
GUINEA
BURKINA FASO
AFRICA
NIGERIA
DJIBOUTI
Cape Asir
ARABIAN SEA
VIETNAM
CAMBODIA
FEDERATED STATES OF MICRONESIA
SIERRA LEONE
LIBERIA
GHANA
BENIN
TOGO
CENTRAL AFRICAN REP.
ETHIOPIA
Cape Comorin
SRI LANKA
BRUNEI
MALAYSIA
PALAU
CÔTE D'IVOIRE
SÃO TOME AND PRÍNCIPE
CAMEROON
Zaire R.
UGANDA
KENYA
SOMALIA
MALDIVES
SINGAPORE
Equator
KIRIBATI
EQUATORIAL GUINEA
GABON
CONGO
CONGO (ZAIRE) BASIN
RWANDA
Lake Victoria
Kilimanjaro 19,340 ft. (5,895 m)
SEYCHELLES
INDONESIA
PAPUA NEW GUINEA
NAURU
SOLOMON ISLANDS
TUVALU
ZAIRE
BURUNDI
TANZANIA
Jakarta
COMOROS
MALAWI
ANGOLA
ZAMBIA
INDIAN OCEAN
COCOS IS. (AUSTRALIA)
Cape York
CORAL SEA
VANUATU
FIJI
MOZAMBIQUE
MADAGASCAR
NAMIBIA
ZIMBABWE
MAURITIUS
GREAT DIVIDING RANGE
BOTSWANA
RÉUNION (FRANCE)
Tropic of Capricorn
SWAZILAND
Mozambique Channel
WESTERN PLATEAU
AUSTRALIA
NEW CALEDONIA (FRANCE)
ATLANTIC OCEAN
LESOTHO
SOUTH AFRICA
Cape of Good Hope
Mt. Kosciusko 7,310 ft. (2,228 m)
TASMAN SEA
NEW ZEALAND
East Longitude
N
Prime Meridian
KERGUELEN IS. (FRANCE)
Antarctic Circle
ANTARCTICA

EUROPE
Projection: Azimuthal Equal Area
FINLAND
NORWAY
SWEDEN
St. Petersburg
ESTONIA
IRELAND
DENMARK
LATVIA
Moscow
UNITED KINGDOM
LITHUANIA
RUSSIA
N
London
BELARUS
NETHERLANDS
ATLANTIC OCEAN
BELGIUM
GERMANY
POLAND
Paris
LUXEMBOURG
CZECH REPUBLIC
UKRAINE
FRANCE
LIECHTENSTEIN
SLOVAKIA
SWITZERLAND
AUSTRIA
MOLDOVA
HUNGARY
SLOVENIA
CROATIA
ROMANIA
MONACO
BOSNIA-HERZEGOVINA
SERBIA
PORTUGAL
ANDORRA
SAN MARINO
YUGOSLAVIA
BLACK SEA
GEORGIA
SPAIN
ITALY
BULGARIA
VATICAN CITY
MONTENEGRO
MACEDONIA
ALBANIA
GIBRALTAR (U.K.)
MEDITERRANEAN SEA
GREECE
TURKEY
MOROCCO
TUNISIA
MALTA
ALGERIA
SYRIA
CYPRUS
LEBANON

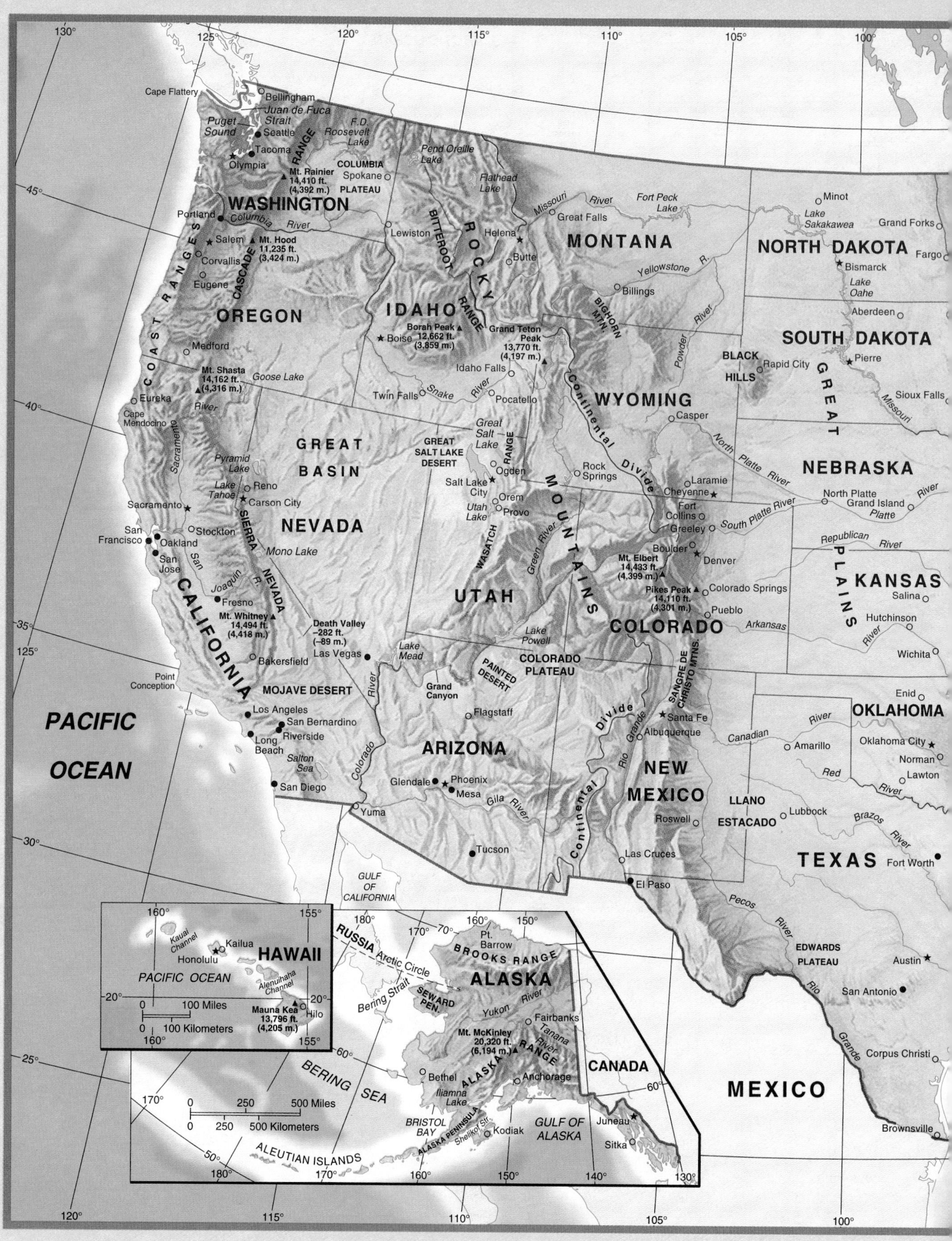

PACIFIC OCEAN
WASHINGTON
OREGON
CALIFORNIA
NEVADA
IDAHO
MONTANA
WYOMING
UTAH
COLORADO
ARIZONA
NEW MEXICO
NORTH DAKOTA
SOUTH DAKOTA
NEBRASKA
KANSAS
OKLAHOMA
TEXAS
MEXICO
CANADA
ALASKA
HAWAII
Cape Flattery
Bellingham
Juan de Fuca Strait
Puget Sound
Seattle
Tacoma
Olympia
F.D. Roosevelt Lake
Mt. Rainier 14,410 ft. (4,392 m.)
COLUMBIA PLATEAU
Spokane
Pend Oreille Lake
Flathead Lake
Portland
Columbia River
Salem
Mt. Hood 11,235 ft. (3,424 m.)
Corvallis
Eugene
CASCADE RANGE
COAST RANGES
Medford
Mt. Shasta 14,162 ft. (4,316 m.)
Goose Lake
Eureka
Cape Mendocino
Sacramento River
Pyramid Lake
Lake Tahoe
Reno
Carson City
Sacramento
Stockton
San Francisco
Oakland
San Jose
San Joaquin R.
SIERRA NEVADA
Mono Lake
Fresno
Mt. Whitney 14,494 ft. (4,418 m.)
Death Valley −282 ft. (−89 m.)
Las Vegas
Bakersfield
Point Conception
MOJAVE DESERT
Los Angeles
San Bernardino
Riverside
Long Beach
Salton Sea
San Diego
Yuma
GREAT BASIN
Lewiston
BITTERROOT RANGE
ROCKY MOUNTAINS
Missouri River
Great Falls
Helena
Butte
Fort Peck Lake
Yellowstone R.
Billings
BIGHORN MTN.
Powder River
Borah Peak 12,662 ft. (3,859 m.)
Boise
Grand Teton Peak 13,770 ft. (4,197 m.)
Idaho Falls
Snake River
Twin Falls
Pocatello
Continental Divide
Casper
Great Salt Lake
GREAT SALT LAKE DESERT
Ogden
Salt Lake City
Orem
Provo
Utah Lake
WASATCH RANGE
Green River
Rock Springs
Laramie
Cheyenne
Fort Collins
Greeley
North Platte River
South Platte River
Boulder
Denver
Mt. Elbert 14,433 ft. (4,399 m.)
Pikes Peak 14,110 ft. (4,301 m.)
Colorado Springs
Pueblo
Arkansas River
Lake Powell
Lake Mead
COLORADO PLATEAU
PAINTED DESERT
Grand Canyon
Flagstaff
Colorado River
SANGRE DE CHRISTO MTNS.
Santa Fe
Albuquerque
Rio Grande
Glendale
Phoenix
Mesa
Gila River
Tucson
Las Cruces
El Paso
Roswell
GULF OF CALIFORNIA
Minot
Lake Sakakawea
Grand Forks
Fargo
Bismarck
Lake Oahe
Aberdeen
BLACK HILLS
Rapid City
Pierre
Sioux Falls
GREAT PLAINS
North Platte
Grand Island
Platte River
Republican River
Salina
Hutchinson
Wichita
Enid
Oklahoma City
Norman
Lawton
Canadian River
Amarillo
Red River
LLANO ESTACADO
Lubbock
Brazos River
Fort Worth
Pecos River
EDWARDS PLATEAU
Austin
San Antonio
Corpus Christi
Brownsville
Kauai Channel
Kailua
Honolulu
PACIFIC OCEAN
Alenuihaha Channel
Mauna Kea 13,796 ft. (4,205 m.)
Hilo
0 100 Miles
0 100 Kilometers
RUSSIA
Arctic Circle
Pt. Barrow
BROOKS RANGE
Bering Strait
SEWARD PEN.
Yukon River
Fairbanks
Tanana River
Mt. McKinley 20,320 ft. (6,194 m.)
ALASKA RANGE
Bethel
Anchorage
Iliamna Lake
BERING SEA
BRISTOL BAY
ALASKA PENINSULA
Shelikof Str.
Kodiak
GULF OF ALASKA
Juneau
Sitka
ALEUTIAN ISLANDS
0 250 500 Miles
0 250 500 Kilometers

UNITED STATES
National capital
State capital
Major city
International boundary
State boundary
0
150
300 Miles
0
150
300 Kilometers
Projection: Albers Equal Area
CANADA
ATLANTIC OCEAN
GULF OF MEXICO
CUBA
THE BAHAMAS
Straits of Florida
MAINE
N.H.
VT.
MASS.
R.I.
CONN.
NEW YORK
N.J.
PENNSYLVANIA
MD.
DEL.
D.C.
WEST VIRGINIA
VIRGINIA
NORTH CAROLINA
SOUTH CAROLINA
GEORGIA
FLORIDA
ALABAMA
MISSISSIPPI
LOUISIANA
ARKANSAS
TENNESSEE
KENTUCKY
OHIO
INDIANA
ILLINOIS
MICHIGAN
WISCONSIN
MINNESOTA
IOWA
MISSOURI
CENTRAL LOWLAND
OZARK PLATEAU
APPALACHIAN MOUNTAINS
CUMBERLAND PLATEAU
COASTAL PLAIN
ADIRONDACK MTNS.
Mt. Washington 6,288 ft. (1,905 m.)
Mt. Mitchell 6,684 ft. (2,037 m.)
Lake of the Woods
Red Lake
Lake Superior
Lake Michigan
Lake Huron
Lake Erie
Lake Ontario
Lake Champlain
Moosehead Lake
St. Lawrence River
Hudson R.
Susquehanna River
Mississippi River
Ohio River
Wabash R.
Cumberland River
Tennessee R.
Chattahoochee R.
Alabama R.
Roanoke River
Harry S. Truman Res.
R.S. Kerr Res.
Lake Eufaula
Lake Texoma
Toledo Bend Res.
Sam Rayburn Reservoir
Lake Pontchartrain
Lake Okeechobee
DELAWARE BAY
CHESAPEAKE BAY
Cape Cod
Cape Hatteras
Cape Canaveral
Cape Sable
Niagara Falls
Duluth
Minneapolis
St. Paul
Rochester
Green Bay
Appleton
Madison
Milwaukee
Racine
Rockford
Dubuque
Cedar Rapids
Davenport
Des Moines
Sioux City
Omaha
Council Bluffs
Lincoln
Chicago
Aurora
Joliet
Gary
Hammond
South Bend
Peoria
Springfield
Decatur
Grand Rapids
Lansing
Flint
Detroit
Ann Arbor
Toledo
Fort Wayne
Muncie
Indianapolis
Evansville
Owensboro
Louisville
Frankfort
Lexington
Cincinnati
Dayton
Columbus
Cleveland
Akron
Canton
Youngstown
Parkersburg
Charleston
Huntington
Wheeling
Pittsburgh
Erie
Buffalo
Rochester
Syracuse
Utica
Albany
Binghamton
Harrisburg
Allentown
Philadelphia
Newark
Yonkers
New York
Trenton
Camden
Wilmington
Dover
Baltimore
Annapolis
Washington
Arlington
Richmond
Newport News
Norfolk
Roanoke
Burlington
Montpelier
Concord
Manchester
Augusta
Lewiston
Portland
Bangor
Boston
Worcester
Springfield
Hartford
New Haven
Providence
Greensboro
Winston-Salem
Durham
Raleigh
Charlotte
Knoxville
Nashville
Chattanooga
Memphis
Spartanburg
Greenville
Columbia
Charleston
Augusta
Atlanta
Macon
Savannah
Columbus
Albany
Huntsville
Birmingham
Tuscaloosa
Montgomery
Mobile
Pensacola
Tallahassee
Jacksonville
Orlando
Tampa
St. Petersburg
Palm Beach
Miami Beach
Miami
Key West
Biloxi
Meridian
Jackson
Hattiesburg
Greenville
Baton Rouge
Lafayette
Lake Charles
New Orleans
Shreveport
Houston
Dallas
Tulsa
Fort Smith
Little Rock
North Little Rock
Hot Springs
Pine Bluff
Topeka
Lawrence
Kansas City
Independence
Jefferson City
St. Louis
East St. Louis
Springfield
95°
90°
85°
80°
75°
70°
65°
50°
45°
40°
35°
30°
25°
N

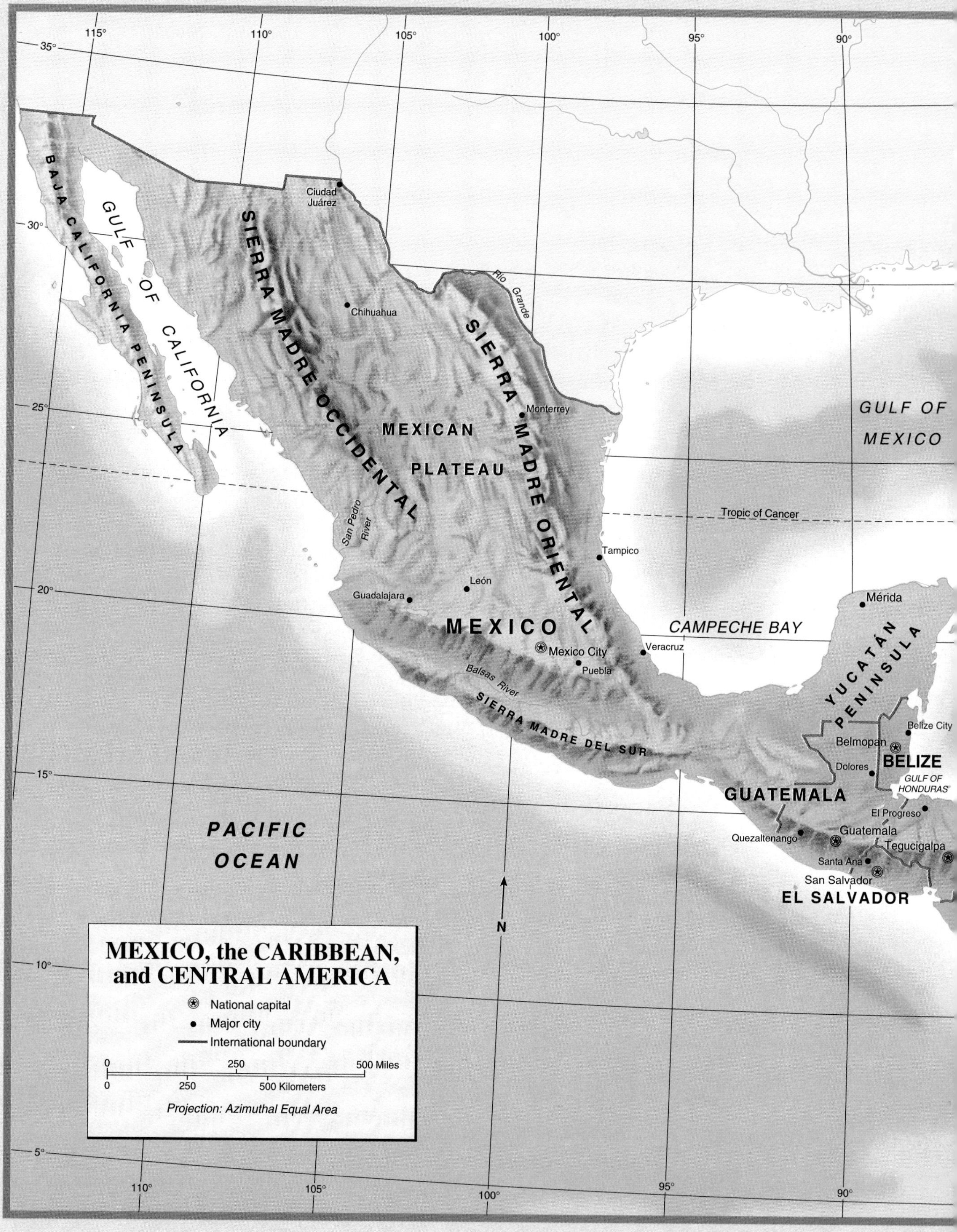

MEXICO, the CARIBBEAN, and CENTRAL AMERICA
National capital
Major city
International boundary
0 250 500 Miles
0 250 500 Kilometers
Projection: Azimuthal Equal Area
115° 110° 105° 100° 95° 90°
35° 30° 25° 20° 15° 10° 5°
BAJA CALIFORNIA PENINSULA
GULF OF CALIFORNIA
SIERRA MADRE OCCIDENTAL
SIERRA MADRE ORIENTAL
SIERRA MADRE DEL SUR
MEXICAN PLATEAU
MEXICO
Ciudad Juárez
Chihuahua
Rio Grande
Monterrey
Tampico
San Pedro River
Guadalajara
León
Mexico City
Puebla
Veracruz
Balsas River
CAMPECHE BAY
GULF OF MEXICO
Tropic of Cancer
Mérida
YUCATÁN PENINSULA
Belize City
Belmopan
BELIZE
Dolores
GULF OF HONDURAS
GUATEMALA
El Progreso
Guatemala
Quezaltenango
Tegucigalpa
Santa Ana
San Salvador
EL SALVADOR
PACIFIC OCEAN
N

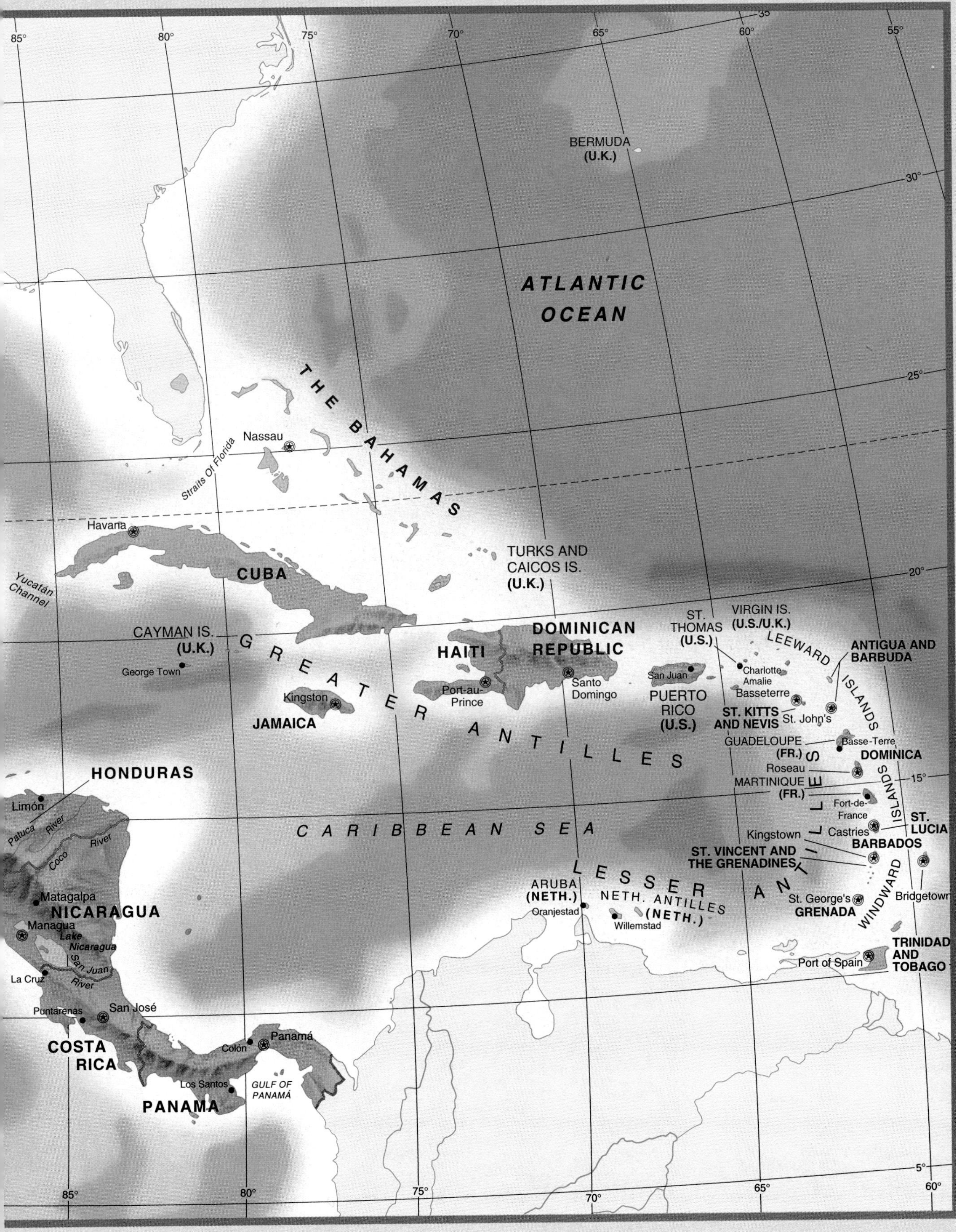
ATLANTIC OCEAN
BERMUDA (U.K.)
THE BAHAMAS
Nassau
Straits Of Florida
Havana
CUBA
Yucatán Channel
TURKS AND CAICOS IS. (U.K.)
CAYMAN IS. (U.K.)
George Town
GREATER ANTILLES
HAITI
Port-au-Prince
DOMINICAN REPUBLIC
Santo Domingo
Kingston
JAMAICA
ST. THOMAS (U.S.)
VIRGIN IS. (U.S./U.K.)
Charlotte Amalie
San Juan
PUERTO RICO (U.S.)
LEEWARD ISLANDS
ANTIGUA AND BARBUDA
Basseterre
ST. KITTS AND NEVIS
St. John's
GUADELOUPE (FR.)
Basse-Terre
DOMINICA
Roseau
MARTINIQUE (FR.)
Fort-de-France
WINDWARD ISLANDS
ST. LUCIA
Castries
Kingstown
BARBADOS
ST. VINCENT AND THE GRENADINES
Bridgetown
St. George's
GRENADA
TRINIDAD AND TOBAGO
Port of Spain
LESSER ANTILLES
ARUBA (NETH.)
Oranjestad
NETH. ANTILLES (NETH.)
Willemstad
CARIBBEAN SEA
HONDURAS
Limón
Patuca River
Coco River
Matagalpa
NICARAGUA
Managua
Lake Nicaragua
San Juan River
La Cruz
Puntarenas
San José
COSTA RICA
Colón
Panamá
Los Santos
GULF OF PANAMÁ
PANAMA
85°
80°
75°
70°
65°
60°
55°
35°
30°
25°
20°
15°
5°

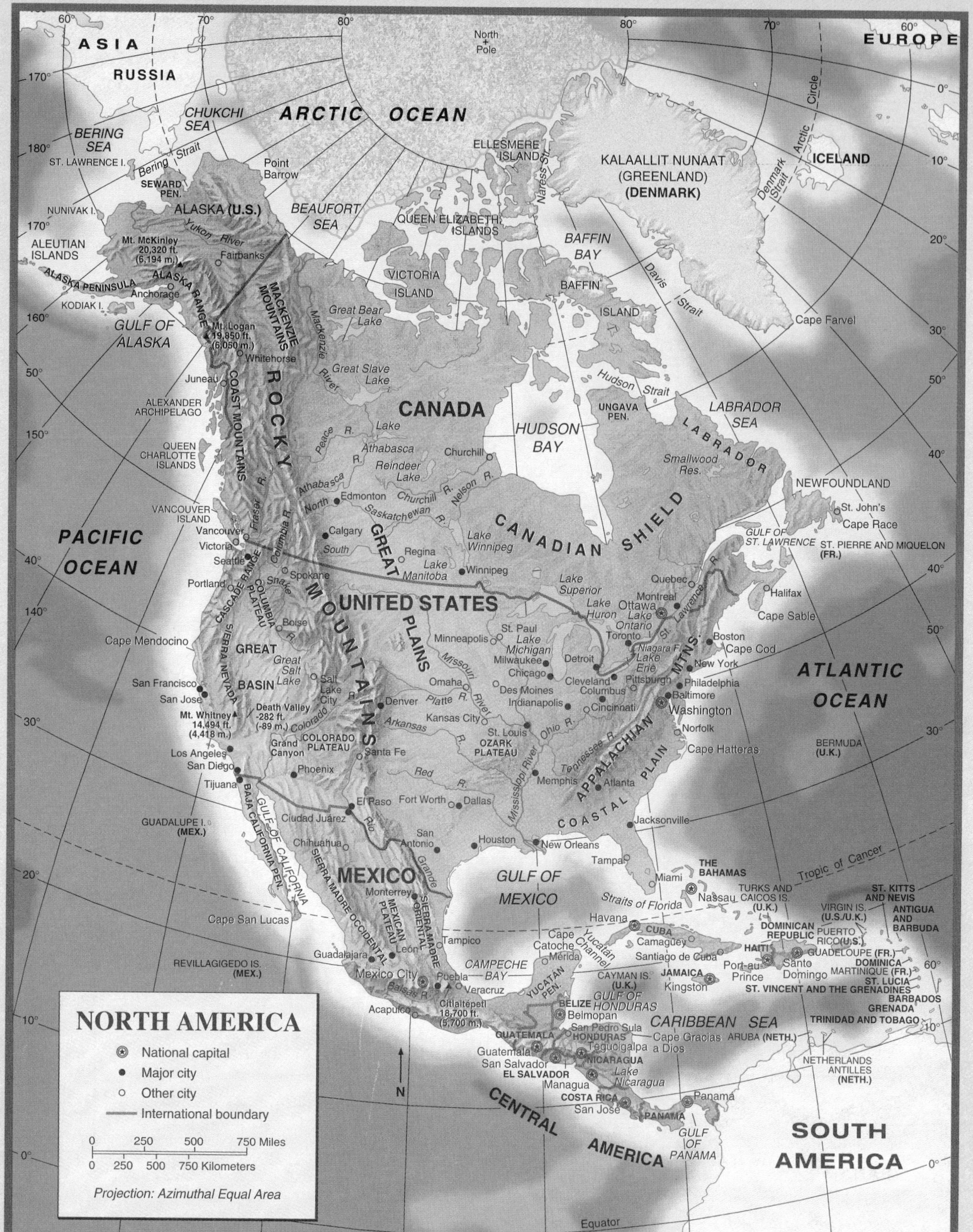
NORTH AMERICA
National capital
Major city
Other city
International boundary
0 250 500 750 Miles
0 250 500 750 Kilometers
Projection: Azimuthal Equal Area
ASIA
RUSSIA
EUROPE
ARCTIC OCEAN
North Pole
CHUKCHI SEA
BERING SEA
Bering Strait
ST. LAWRENCE I.
SEWARD PEN.
NUNIVAK I.
ALASKA (U.S.)
Point Barrow
BEAUFORT SEA
ALEUTIAN ISLANDS
Mt. McKinley 20,320 ft. (6,194 m.)
Yukon River
Fairbanks
ALASKA PENINSULA
ALASKA RANGE
Anchorage
KODIAK I.
GULF OF ALASKA
Mt. Logan 19,850 ft. (6,050 m.)
Whitehorse
MACKENZIE MOUNTAINS
Mackenzie River
Great Bear Lake
Great Slave Lake
ELLESMERE ISLAND
Nares Str.
QUEEN ELIZABETH ISLANDS
VICTORIA ISLAND
BAFFIN BAY
BAFFIN ISLAND
Davis Strait
KALAALLIT NUNAAT (GREENLAND) (DENMARK)
Denmark Strait
Arctic Circle
ICELAND
Cape Farvel
Juneau
ALEXANDER ARCHIPELAGO
COAST MOUNTAINS
ROCKY MOUNTAINS
QUEEN CHARLOTTE ISLANDS
CANADA
Peace R.
Lake Athabasca
Athabasca R.
Reindeer Lake
Churchill
HUDSON BAY
Hudson Strait
UNGAVA PEN.
LABRADOR SEA
LABRADOR
Smallwood Res.
NEWFOUNDLAND
St. John's
Cape Race
GULF OF ST. LAWRENCE
ST. PIERRE AND MIQUELON (FR.)
Halifax
Cape Sable
CANADIAN SHIELD
VANCOUVER ISLAND
Vancouver
Victoria
Seattle
Portland
Fraser R.
Columbia R.
Edmonton
North Saskatchewan
Churchill R.
Nelson R.
Calgary
South
Regina
Lake Winnipeg
Lake Manitoba
Winnipeg
GREAT PLAINS
PACIFIC OCEAN
Spokane
Snake
CASCADE RANGE
COLUMBIA PLATEAU
Boise
UNITED STATES
Lake Superior
Quebec
Montreal
Ottawa
St. Lawrence
Lake Huron
Lake Ontario
Toronto
Cape Mendocino
SIERRA NEVADA
GREAT BASIN
Great Salt Lake
Salt Lake City
St. Paul
Minneapolis
Lake Michigan
Milwaukee
Chicago
Detroit
Niagara F.
Lake Erie
Boston
Cape Cod
New York
San Francisco
San Jose
Omaha
Missouri River
Des Moines
Cleveland
Columbus
Pittsburgh
Philadelphia
Baltimore
Washington
Denver
Platte R.
Kansas City
Indianapolis
Cincinnati
ATLANTIC OCEAN
Mt. Whitney 14,494 ft. (4,418 m.)
Death Valley -282 ft. (-89 m.)
Colorado
Arkansas
St. Louis
Ohio R.
Norfolk
OZARK PLATEAU
COLORADO PLATEAU
Grand Canyon
Santa Fe
Los Angeles
San Diego
Tijuana
Phoenix
Red R.
Mississippi River
Memphis
Tennessee R.
APPALACHIAN MTNS.
Atlanta
COASTAL PLAIN
Cape Hatteras
BERMUDA (U.K.)
BAJA CALIFORNIA PEN.
GULF OF CALIFORNIA
GUADALUPE I. (MEX.)
El Paso
Ciudad Juárez
Fort Worth
Dallas
Rio Grande
Jacksonville
San Antonio
Houston
New Orleans
Tampa
Chihuahua
SIERRA MADRE OCCIDENTAL
MEXICO
Monterrey
MEXICAN PLATEAU
SIERRA MADRE ORIENTAL
GULF OF MEXICO
Miami
THE BAHAMAS
Nassau
Straits of Florida
Tropic of Cancer
TURKS AND CAICOS IS. (U.K.)
ST. KITTS AND NEVIS
ANTIGUA AND BARBUDA
VIRGIN IS. (U.S./U.K.)
Cape San Lucas
Havana
CUBA
Camaguey
DOMINICAN REPUBLIC
PUERTO RICO (U.S.)
Tampico
Cape Catoche
Mérida
Yucatan Channel
Santiago de Cuba
HAITI
GUADELOUPE (FR.)
Guadalajara
León
REVILLAGIGEDO IS. (MEX.)
Mexico City
Puebla
CAMPECHE BAY
Veracruz
YUCATAN PEN.
CAYMAN IS. (U.K.)
JAMAICA
Kingston
Port-au-Prince
Santo Domingo
DOMINICA
MARTINIQUE (FR.)
ST. LUCIA
ST. VINCENT AND THE GRENADINES
BARBADOS
GRENADA
Balsas R.
Acapulco
Citlaltépetl 18,700 ft. (5,700 m.)
BELIZE
Belmopan
GULF OF HONDURAS
CARIBBEAN SEA
TRINIDAD AND TOBAGO
GUATEMALA
San Pedro Sula
HONDURAS
Tegucigalpa
Cape Gracias a Dios
ARUBA (NETH.)
Guatemala
San Salvador
EL SALVADOR
NICARAGUA
Lake Nicaragua
NETHERLANDS ANTILLES (NETH.)
Managua
COSTA RICA
San José
Panama
PANAMA
CENTRAL AMERICA
GULF OF PANAMA
SOUTH AMERICA
Equator
N

SOUTH AMERICA
National capital
Major city
Other city
International boundary
0 250 500 Miles
0 250 500 Kilometers
Projection: Azimuthal Equal Area
NORTH AMERICA
CENTRAL AMERICA
CARIBBEAN SEA
GULF OF DARIÉN
GULF OF PANAMÁ
Pt. Gallinas
GUAJIRA PEN.
GRENADA
MARGARITA I.
PARIA PEN.
TRINIDAD AND TOBAGO
Delta of the Orinoco
Barranquilla
Cartagena
Maracaibo
Lake Maracaibo
Maracay
Valencia
Caracas
Barquisimeto
Cumaná
VENEZUELA
MÉRIDA RANGE
Cúcuta
San Cristóbal
Bucaramanga
Orinoco River
Ciudad Guayana
Ciudad Bolívar
Guri Res.
Angel Falls
LLANOS
GUIANA HIGHLANDS
Georgetown
Paramaribo
Cayenne
GUYANA
SURINAME
FRENCH GUIANA (FR.)
Van Blommestein Res.
PACARAIMA MOUNTAINS
TUMUCUMAQUE MOUNTAINS
Essequibo R.
Medellín
Manizales
Bogotá
Cali
Tolima Peak 17,109 ft. (5,215 m.)
Meta R.
Orinoco R.
Branco R.
CORDILLERA OCCIDENTAL
CORDILLERA ORIENTAL
Magdalena R.
COLOMBIA
Cape San Francisco
Equator
Quito
Ambato
Chimborazo 20,561 ft. (6,267 m.)
Portoviejo
ECUADOR
Guayaquil
Cuenca
GULF OF GUAYAQUIL
Pariñas Point
Caquetá R.
Putumayo R.
Negro River
AMAZON BASIN
Manaus
Amazon River
Delta of the Amazon
Cape Maquarinho
Belém
São Luís
Fortaleza
Cape São Roque
Teresina
Natal
PLATEAU OF BORBOREMA
Recife
Maceió
Aracaju
Salvador
TODOS OS SANTOS BAY
Esperança Reservoir
Sobradinho Reservoir
Parnaíba R.
Tocantins River
Araguaia River
Xingu River
Tapajós River
Madeira River
Purus R.
Iquitos
Marañón River
Ucayali River
SELVAS
BRAZIL
Rio Branco
PERU
Chiclayo
Trujillo
Chimbote
Huascarán Peak 22,204 ft. (6,768 m.)
CORDILLERA ORIENTAL
Callao
Lima
ANDES
Cuzco
Lake Titicaca
Point Carreta
Arequipa
Ancohuma Peak 21,489 ft. (6,550 m.)
La Paz
BOLIVIA
BOLIVIAN PLATEAU
Cochabamba
Santa Cruz
Lake Poopó
Oruro
Sucre
Potosí
Arica
Guaporé R.
Mamoré R.
MATO GROSSO PLATEAU
BRAZILIAN HIGHLANDS
Brasília
Goiânia
São Francisco R.
Simão Res.
Tres Marias Reservoir
Belo Horizonte
Bandeira Peak 9,481 ft. (2,890 m.)
Juiz de Fora
Petrópolis
Niterói
Rio de Janeiro
Nova Iguaçu
Volta Redonda
Campinas
Osasco
São Paulo
Santos
Santo André
Furnas Reservoir
Ilha Solteira Res.
Jupiá Res.
Campo Grande
Curitiba
Tropic of Capricorn
PACIFIC OCEAN
ATLANTIC OCEAN
ATACAMA DESERT
Antofagasta
Salta
GRAN CHACO
Pilcomayo R.
Paraguay River
PARAGUAY
Concepción
Asunción
Itaipu Res.
Iguaçu Falls
Paraná River
Mt. Ojos del Salado 22,516 ft. (6,863 m.)
San Miguel de Tucumán
Resistencia
Corrientes
Santiago del Estero
Salado R.
Mar Chiquita Lake
Uruguay R.
Pôrto Alegre
Rivera
Lake dos Patos
Lake Mirim
SAN FÉLIX I. (CHILE)
SAN AMBROSIO I. (CHILE)
Mt. Aconcagua 22,834 ft. (6,960 m.)
CÓRDOBA RANGE
Córdoba
Santa Fe
Paysandú
Negro Res.
URUGUAY
Rosario
Mendoza
Viña del Mar
Valparaíso
Santiago
JUAN FERNÁNDEZ IS. (CHILE)
Buenos Aires
Montevideo
Punta del Este
La Plata
RÍO DE LA PLATA
Cape San Antonio
ARGENTINA
PAMPAS
CHILE
Talcahuâno
Concepción
Temuco
Salado River
Colorado River
Mar del Plata
Bahía Blanca
BLANCA BAY
Negro River
Rasa Point
GULF OF SAN MATÍAS
VALDÉS DEPRESSION
VALDÉS PEN.
Chubut R.
CHILOÉ ISLAND
CHONOS ARCHIPELAGO
Comodoro Rivadavia
GULF OF SAN JORGE
Cape Tres Puntas
PATAGONIA
Lake Buenos Aires
PENAS GULF
Lake San Martín
Lake Argentino
GRANDE BAY
QUEEN ADELAIDE ARCH.
Strait of Magellan
Punta Arenas
TIERRA DEL FUEGO
FALKLAND ISLANDS (U.K.)
Stanley
ESTADOS ISLAND
Cape Horn
SOUTH GEORGIA (U.K.)
MOUNTAINS

EUROPE
National capital
Major city
Other city
International boundary
Republic boundary
Canal
0 100 200 300 Miles
0 100 200 300 Kilometers
Projection: Azimuthal Equal Area
ICELAND
Reykjavík
Arctic Circle
Prime Meridian
NORWEGIAN SEA
FAROE IS. (DEN.)
SHETLAND IS. (U.K.)
ORKNEY ISLANDS
Cape Wrath
OUTER HEBRIDES IS.
SCANDINAVIAN HIGHLANDS
Trondheim
NORWAY
Goldhöpiggen 8,097 ft. (2,468 m.)
Bergen
Oslo
SWEDEN
Lake Vänern
Uppsala
Stockholm
GULF OF BOTHNIA
ÅLAND I.
HIIUMAA I.
SAAREMAA I.
GOTLAND I.
Lake Vättern
Göteborg
Skagerrak
Kattegat
ÖLAND I.
BALTIC SEA
NORTH SEA
N
NORTHERN IRELAND (U.K.)
SCOTLAND
Glasgow
Edinburgh
PENNINE RANGE
Belfast
IRISH SEA
ISLE OF MAN
UNITED KINGDOM
Dublin
IRELAND
Cork
Cape Clear
Manchester
Liverpool
Leeds
Sheffield
St. George's Channel
ENGLAND
WALES
Birmingham
Cardiff
Bristol
London
JUTLAND
Copenhagen
DENMARK
Odense
Malmö
BORNHOLM I.
Kiel
Kiel Canal
Rostock
Gdańsk
RUSSIA
Szczecin
NETHERLANDS
Amsterdam
The Hague
Rotterdam
Hamburg
Bremen
Mittelland Canal
Elbe R.
Hannover
Berlin
NORTH
POLAND
Vistula
Poznań
Warsaw
Łódź
English Channel
Strait of Dover
GUERNSEY I. (U.K.)
JERSEY I. (U.K.)
ATLANTIC OCEAN
Antwerp
BELGIUM
Brussels
Liège
Essen
Dortmund
Magdeburg
Cologne
Bonn
GERMANY
Leipzig
Dresden
Wrocław
Le Havre
Seine River
BRETON PEN.
Paris
Marne R.
LUXEMBOURG
Luxembourg
Frankfurt
Chemnitz
Prague
Katowice
Marne-Rhine Canal
Rhine R.
CZECH REPUBLIC
Ostrava
Nantes
Loire River
Strasbourg
Stuttgart
Danube River
Brno
FRANCE
Munich
Bodensee
LIECHTENSTEIN
Vienna
Linz
Salzburg
Bratislava
SLOVAKIA
Zürich
Bern
Vaduz
Innsbruck
AUSTRIA
Miskolc
Cape Finisterre
BAY OF BISCAY
Lausanne
Geneva
L. Geneva
SWITZERLAND
ALPS
Budapest
Bordeaux
Lyon
Mt. Blanc 15,771 ft. (4,807 m.)
Mt. Rosa 15,203 ft. (4,634 m.)
Graz
HUNGARY
L. Balaton
CANTABRIAN MTNS.
Bilbao
Garonne R.
CENTRAL MASSIF
Rhône R.
Ljubljana
SLOVENIA
Zagreb
Pécs
Tisza
Porto
Ebro River
PYRENEES
Toulouse
Canal du Midi
Milan
PO VALLEY
Turin
Venice
Po R.
CROATIA
Sava R.
Novi Sad
Valladolid
Duero River
Genoa
Montpellier
Bologna
Belgrade
PORTUGAL
IBERIAN
Aneto Peak 11,168 ft. (3,404 m.)
ANDORRA
Andorra la Vella
Marseille
GULF OF LION
Nice
Monaco
MONACO
SAN MARINO
San Marino
DINARIC ALPS
BOSNIA-HERZEGOVINA
Sarajevo
Tagus River
Zaragoza
Madrid
Florence
APENNINES
ADRIATIC SEA
Split
Lisbon
Setúbal
Barcelona
CORSICA (FR.)
VATICAN CITY
MONTENEGRO
Guadiana River
PENINSULA
Rome
ITALY
Cape St. Vincent
SIERRA MORENA
SPAIN
Valencia
MACEDONIA
Seville
Palma
SARDINIA (IT.)
Naples
Bari
Tiranë
ALBANIA
BALEARIC IS. (SP.)
TYRRHENIAN SEA
Málaga
Granada
Murcia
G. OF TARANTO
Strait of Gibraltar
GIBRALTAR (U.K.)
Cagliari
MEDITERRANEAN
Strait of Sicily
Palermo
IONIAN SEA
KEFALLINIA I.
SICILY
Catania
PANTELLERIA (IT.)
MALTA
Valletta
AFRICA
SEA
40°
60°
30°
20°
10°
70°
0°
50°

North Cape
BARENTS SEA
Murmansk
KOLA PENINSULA
WHITE SEA
TIMAN RIDGE
Pechora R.
URAL MOUNTAINS
Arkhangel'sk
White Sea-Baltic Waterway
N. Dvina River
Vychegda River
Kama R.
Mt. Konzhakovskiy
5,147 ft.
(1,569 m.)
FINLAND
Lake Onega
Sukhona River
Perm
ASIA
Tampere
Lake Saimaa
Lake Ladoga
Volga-Baltic Waterway
Turku
Helsinki
Espoo
GULF OF FINLAND
St. Petersburg
Rybinsk Reservoir
Kama River
Ufa
Ural River
Tallinn
ESTONIA
Chudskoye Lake
Yaroslavl
Kazan
Nizhniy Novgorod
Kuybyshev Reservoir
GULF OF RIGA
LATVIA
Riga
W. Dvina
Volga River
Volga-Baltic Waterway
Moscow
Samara
Orenburg
BALTIC PLAIN
EUROPEAN PLAIN
River
Oka River
Tula
LITHUANIA
Kaunas
Vilnius
Smolensk
CENTRAL RUSSIAN UPLAND
RUSSIA
VOLGA UPLAND
Volga River
Saratov
Volgograd Reservoir
Minsk
BELARUS
Don River
Voronezh
Kursk
R.
KAZAKSTAN
ARAL SEA
Pripet River
Desna
Volgograd
Volga River
DEPRESSION
Kiev
Kremenchug Reservoir
Kharkov
Lugansk
Tsimlyansk Reservoir
Astrakhan
UKRAINE
Lvov
DNEIPER UPLAND
Dniester R.
Dnepropetrovsk
Donetsk
Don River
Krivoy Rog
Zaporozhye
Rostov
CASPIAN
Delta of the Volga
CARPATHIAN MTNS.
Prut River
MOLDOVA
Chisinau
DNIEPER LOWLAND
Dnieper River
Kakhovka Res.
SEA OF AZOV
CASPIAN SEA
Debrecen
Cluj-Napoca
Odessa
Krasnodar
Grozny
ROMANIA
Timişoara
Braşov
CRIMEA
CAUCASUS MTNS.
Mt. Elbrus
18,510 ft.
(5,642 m.)
Bucharest
WALLACHIA PLAIN
Danube River
Constanţa
BLACK SEA
SERBIA
Ruse
Varna
Niš
BULGARIA
Sofia
Burgas
Plovdiv
Skopje
Musala Peak
9,536 ft.
(2,926 m.)
BALKAN PENINSULA
TURKEY
Bosporus
Salonika
Dardanelles
SEA OF MARMARA
Larissa
AEGEAN SEA
GREECE
ASIA
Patras
Athens
Piraeus
PELOPONESE PEN.
RHODES
CRETE (GR.)
Iraklion
30°
40°
50°
60°
70°
80°

ARCTIC OCEAN
FRANZ JOSEF ISLANDS
EUROPE
BARENTS SEA
Cape Zelaniya
NOVAYA ZEMLYA
KARA SEA
Kara Strait
BALTIC SEA
GULF OF FINLAND
Murmansk
KOLA PENINSULA
WHITE SEA
(RUSSIA)
Lake Ladoga
Baltic-White Sea Canal
St. Petersburg
Lake Onega
Arkhangel'sk
TIMAN RIDGE
YAMAL PEN.
GYDAN PENINSULA
VALDAI HILLS
Volga-Baltic Waterway
Minsk
BELARUS
Yenisey River
Lvov
DNIEPER UPLAND
Rybinsk Res.
Vologda
Sukhona R.
Vychegda R.
N. Dvina R.
Pechora River
Yaroslavl
NORTHERN HILLS
Moscow
Ivanovo
Volga
URAL MOUNTAINS
WEST SIBERIAN PLAIN
Urengoy
Ob River
Kiev
DNIEPER LOWLAND
UKRAINE
Tula
Ryazan'
Nizhniy Novgorod
MOLDOVA
Chisinau
Kamsk Res.
Mt. Konzhakovskiy 5,147 ft. (1,569 m.)
Kazan
Kharkov
Don River
Voronezh
Kuybyshev Res.
Izhevsk
Perm
Kama
Odessa
Nikolayev
Krivoy Rog
Dnepropetrovsk
Zaporozh'ye
Ul'yanovsk
Penza
Vakh R.
Donetsk
Lugansk
VOLGA UPLAND
Saratov
Tol'yatti
Samara
Yekaterinburg
Irtysh River
SEA OF AZOV
Mariupol
Rostov
Ufa
Chelyabinsk
Tobol R.
BLACK SEA
Volgograd Reservoir
Volgograd
Krasnodar
Tsimlyansk Res.
Ural R.
Orenburg
Ishim
Omsk
L. Chany
Tomsk
Novosibirsk
Kemerovo
CAUCASUS MTS.
Mt. Elbrus 18,510 ft. (5,642 m.)
CASPIAN DEPRESSION
Astrakhan
KYRGYZ STEPPE
TURGAY PLATEAU
Novosibirsk Res.
Novokuznetsk
Barnaul
GEORGIA
Tbilisi
KAZAKSTAN
KAZAKH UPLAND
Karaganda
Semipalatinsk
Mt. Belukha 14,783 ft. (4,506 m.)
ARMENIA
Yerevan
AZERBAIJAN
CASPIAN SEA
ARAL SEA
L. Zaysan
Baku
USTYURT PLATEAU
Syr Darya
Kzyl-Orda
BETPAK-DALA DESERT
Lake Balkhash
PLAINS OF TURAN
KARA BOGAZ GOL GULF
TURKMENISTAN
UZBEKISTAN
Ili R.
L. Alakol
ASIA
KARAKUM DESERT
Amu Darya
Ashkhabad
Bishkek
Almaty
Tashkent
KYRGYZSTAN
L. Issyk-Kul
Samarkand
ALAY MOUNTAINS
Dushanbe
TAJIKISTAN
Communism Pk. 24,590 ft. (7,495 m.)
Arctic Circle
60°
70°
80°
50°
40°
30°
20°
10°
0°

RUSSIA AND
THE EURASIAN REPUBLICS
National capital
Major city
Other city
International boundary
0 250 500 Miles
0 250 500 Kilometers
Projection: Two-Point Equidistant
North Pole
ARCTIC OCEAN
CHUKCHI SEA
Bering Strait
WRANGEL ISLAND
Long Strait
CHUKOTSK PEN.
BERING SEA
EAST SIBERIAN SEA
NEW SIBERIAN ISLANDS
Sannikov Strait
Laptev Strait
Cape Arkticheski
SEVERNAYA ZEMLYA
Vil'kitskiy Strait
TAYMYR PEN.
BYRRANGA MTNS.
L. Taymyr
LAPTEV SEA
Cherskiy
KOLYMA PLAIN
Kolyma
KOLYMA RANGE
Anadyr R.
KORYAK MTNS.
Evensk
KARAGIN ISLAND
KOMANDORSKIY ISLANDS
SHELIKHOV GULF
SREDINNY RA.
KAMCHATKA PENINSULA
Mt. Klyuchevsk 15,584 ft. (4,750 m.)
Petropavlovsk-Kamchatskiy
Cape Lopatka
Magadan
SEA OF OKHOTSK
Indigirka River
CHERSKIY RANGE
Verkhoyansk
VERKHOYANSK RANGE
SIBERIA
Lena River
Olenëk R.
Kotuy R.
Noril'sk
Vilyuy R.
Markha R.
Yakutsk
CENTRAL SIBERIAN PLATEAU
Tura
Lower Tunguska River
Vilyuysk Reservoir
Vilyuy R.
LENA PLATEAU
Aldan River
ALDAN MTNS.
DZHUGDZHUR RA.
STANOVOY RANGE
Uda R.
Cape Yelizavety
SAKHALIN ISLAND
Tatar Strait
Terpeniya Point
KURIL ISLANDS
La Pérouse Strait
Amur River
Komsomol'sk
Khabarovsk
SIKHOTE-ALIN RA.
L. Khanka
Vladivostok
SEA OF JAPAN
ASIA
Vitim
Angara R.
Yenisey River
Bratsk
Bratsk Reservoir
Krasnoyarsk
Krasnoyarsk Reservoir
STANOVOY UPLAND
Lake Baikal
YABLONOVY RANGE
Chita
Shilka R.
Ulan-Ude
Irkutsk
SAYAN MOUNTAINS
ALTAI MTNS.
80° 70° 60° 170° 180° 170° 160° 150° 40° 140° 30° 130° 120° 110° 100° 90°

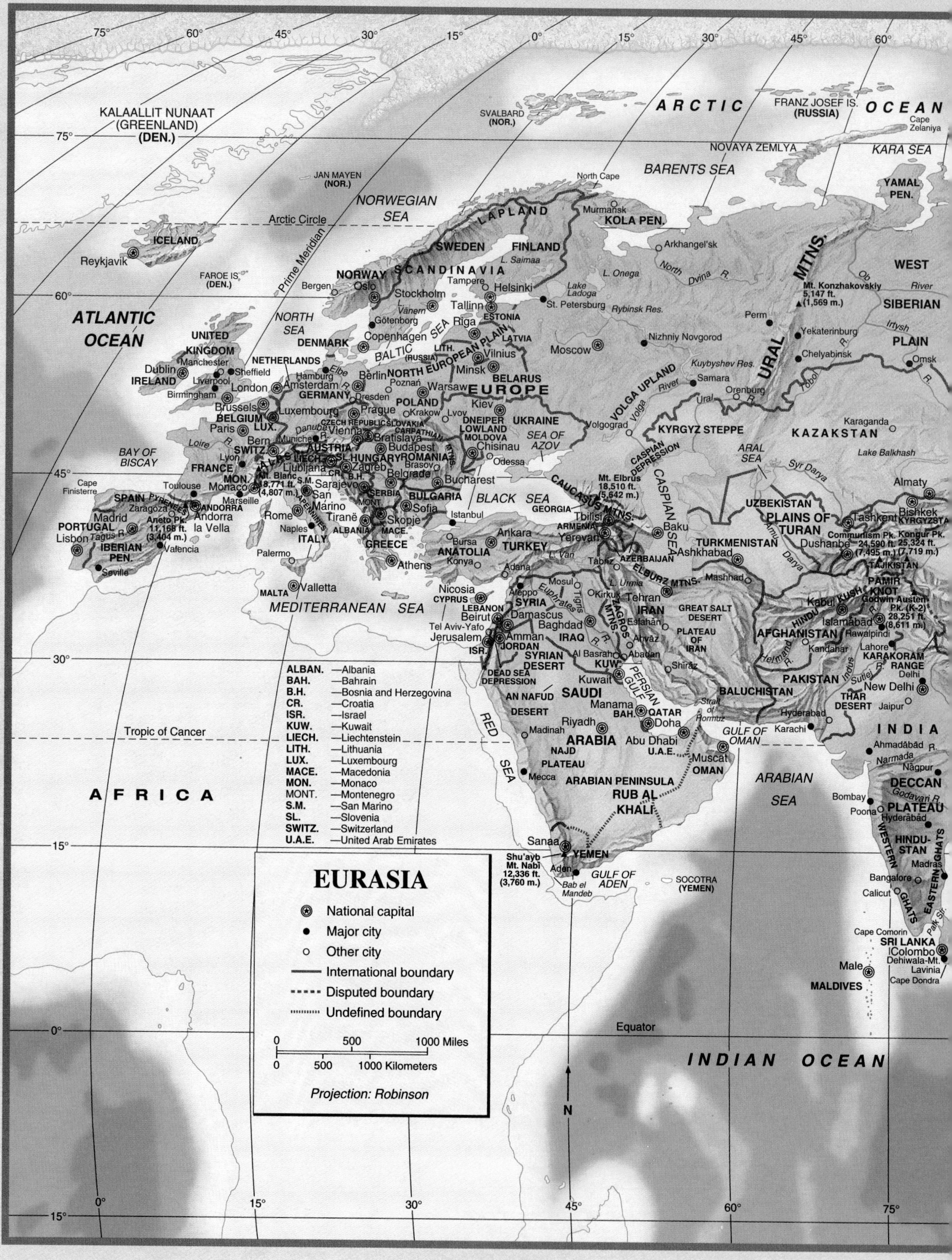
EURASIA
National capital
Major city
Other city
International boundary
Disputed boundary
Undefined boundary
0 500 1000 Miles
0 500 1000 Kilometers
Projection: Robinson
ALBAN. —Albania
BAH. —Bahrain
B.H. —Bosnia and Herzegovina
CR. —Croatia
ISR. —Israel
KUW. —Kuwait
LIECH. —Liechtenstein
LITH. —Lithuania
LUX. —Luxembourg
MACE. —Macedonia
MON. —Monaco
MONT. —Montenegro
S.M. —San Marino
SL. —Slovenia
SWITZ. —Switzerland
U.A.E. —United Arab Emirates
ARCTIC OCEAN
KALAALLIT NUNAAT (GREENLAND) (DEN.)
SVALBARD (NOR.)
FRANZ JOSEF IS. (RUSSIA)
Cape Zelaniya
NOVAYA ZEMLYA
KARA SEA
BARENTS SEA
North Cape
JAN MAYEN (NOR.)
NORWEGIAN SEA
YAMAL PEN.
Arctic Circle
LAPLAND
Murmansk
KOLA PEN.
ICELAND
Reykjavik
SWEDEN
FINLAND
Arkhangel'sk
Prime Meridian
FAROE IS. (DEN.)
NORWAY
SCANDINAVIA
L. Saimaa
L. Onega
North Dvina R.
URAL MTNS.
Ob
WEST
Bergen
Oslo
Tampere
Helsinki
Lake Ladoga
Mt. Konzhakovskiy 5,147 ft. (1,569 m.)
River
ATLANTIC OCEAN
Stockholm
Vänern
Tallinn
St. Petersburg
Rybinsk Res.
SIBERIAN
NORTH SEA
Göteborg
Riga
ESTONIA
Perm
Irtysh
UNITED KINGDOM
DENMARK
Copenhagen
BALTIC SEA
LATVIA
Nizhniy Novgorod
Yekaterinburg
PLAIN
LITH.
(RUSSIA)
NORTH EUROPEAN PLAIN
Vilnius
Moscow
Chelyabinsk
Omsk
Manchester
NETHERLANDS
Dublin
Sheffield
Hamburg
Elbe
Minsk
Kuybyshev Res.
IRELAND
Liverpool
Amsterdam
Berlin
Poznań
BELARUS
Samara
Tobol
London
Birmingham
GERMANY
Warsaw
EUROPE
VOLGA UPLAND
Volga River
Orenburg
Ural R.
Dresden
POLAND
Kiev
Brussels
Prague
Krakow
Lvov
BELGIUM
Luxembourg
LUX.
CZECH REPUBLIC
SLOVAKIA
DNIEPER LOWLAND
UKRAINE
Volgograd
KYRGYZ STEPPE
Karaganda
Paris
Danube R.
Vienna
CARPATHIAN MTNS.
MOLDOVA
SEA OF AZOV
KAZAKSTAN
Loire R.
Bern
Munich
Bratislava
Budapest
CASPIAN DEPRESSION
ARAL SEA
BAY OF BISCAY
SWITZ.
AUSTRIA
Chisinau
Lake Balkhash
Lyon
ALPS
LIECH.
SL.
HUNGARY
ROMANIA
Odessa
Syr Darya
FRANCE
Ljubljana
Zagreb
Brasov
CASPIAN SEA
Cape Finisterre
MON.
Mt. Blanc 15,771 ft. (4,807 m.)
S.M.
CR.
B.H.
Belgrade
Bucharest
Mt. Elbrus 18,510 ft. (5,642 m.)
Almaty
Toulouse
Monaco
Sarajevo
San Marino
SERBIA
BULGARIA
BLACK SEA
CAUCASUS MTS.
UZBEKISTAN
Bishkek
SPAIN
PYRENEES
Marseille
MONT.
Sofia
GEORGIA
PLAINS OF TURAN
Tashkent
KYRGYZSTAN
Zaragoza
ANDORRA
Andorra la Vella
APENNINES
Rome
Tiranë
Skopje
Istanbul
Tbilisi
Madrid
Aneto Pk. 11,168 ft. (3,404 m.)
ALBANIA
MACE.
ARMENIA
Yerevan
Baku
Amu Darya
Communism Pk. 24,590 ft. (7,495 m.)
Kongur Pk. 25,324 ft. (7,719 m.)
PORTUGAL
Tagus R.
Naples
ITALY
Ankara
TURKMENISTAN
Dushanbe
Lisbon
IBERIAN PEN.
Valencia
GREECE
Bursa
ANATOLIA
TURKEY
L. Van
Ashkhabad
AZERBAIJAN
TAJIKISTAN
Seville
Palermo
Athens
Konya
Tabriz
ELBURZ MTNS.
Mashhad
PAMIR KNOT
Adana
Mosul
L. Urmia
MALTA
Valletta
Nicosia
Aleppo
Kirkuk
Tehran
HINDU KUSH
Kabul
Godwin Austen Pk. (K-2) 28,251 ft. (8,611 m.)
MEDITERRANEAN SEA
CYPRUS
SYRIA
Euphrates R.
Tigris R.
ZAGROS MTNS.
IRAN
GREAT SALT DESERT
Islamabad
LEBANON
Beirut
Damascus
Baghdad
Esfahan
PLATEAU OF IRAN
Tel Aviv-Yafo
IRAQ
Ahvaz
AFGHANISTAN
Rawalpindi
Jerusalem
Amman
Abadan
Kandahar
Lahore
ISR.
JORDAN
SYRIAN DESERT
Al Basrah
Shiraz
Helmand R.
KARAKORAM RANGE
KUW.
Indus
Delhi
DEAD SEA DEPRESSION
Kuwait
PERSIAN GULF
BALUCHISTAN
PAKISTAN
Sutlej
New Delhi
AN NAFUD DESERT
SAUDI ARABIA
Manama
BAH.
QATAR
Doha
Strait of Hormuz
THAR DESERT
Jaipur
Tropic of Cancer
RED SEA
Riyadh
Hyderabad
Karachi
INDIA
Madinah
NAJD PLATEAU
Abu Dhabi
U.A.E.
GULF OF OMAN
Ahmadabad
Muscat
OMAN
Narmada R.
Nagpur
AFRICA
Mecca
ARABIAN PENINSULA
ARABIAN SEA
DECCAN PLATEAU
RUB AL KHALI
Bombay
Godavari R.
Poona
Hyderabad
Sanaa
YEMEN
WESTERN GHATS
HINDUSTAN
Shu'ayb Mt. Nabi 12,336 ft. (3,760 m.)
Aden
GULF OF ADEN
SOCOTRA (YEMEN)
Madras
Bab el Mandeb
Bangalore
Calicut
EASTERN GHATS
Palk St.
Cape Comorin
SRI LANKA
Colombo
Dehiwala-Mt. Lavinia
Male
MALDIVES
Cape Dondra
Equator
INDIAN OCEAN
N

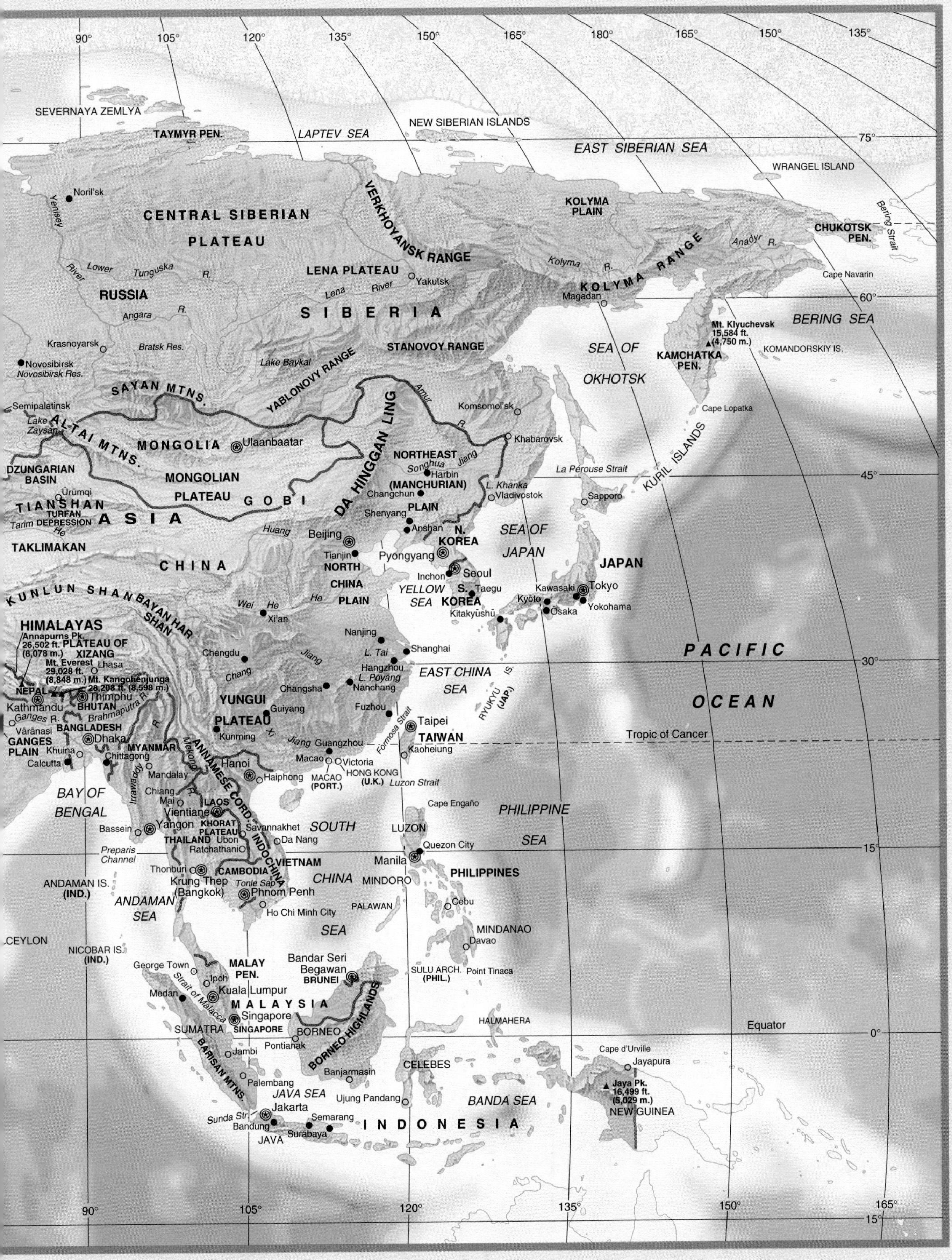
SEVERNAYA ZEMLYA
TAYMYR PEN.
LAPTEV SEA
NEW SIBERIAN ISLANDS
EAST SIBERIAN SEA
WRANGEL ISLAND
Noril'sk
Yenisey
CENTRAL SIBERIAN
PLATEAU
VERKHOYANSK RANGE
KOLYMA
PLAIN
CHUKOTSK
PEN.
Bering Strait
Anadyr R.
Kolyma R.
KOLYMA RANGE
Cape Navarin
Lower Tunguska R.
River
LENA PLATEAU
Yakutsk
Lena River
RUSSIA
Angara R.
S I B E R I A
Magadan
BERING SEA
Mt. Klyuchevsk
15,584 ft.
(4,750 m.)
KOMANDORSKIY IS.
KAMCHATKA
PEN.
SEA OF
OKHOTSK
Krasnoyarsk
Bratsk Res.
Lake Baykal
STANOVOY RANGE
Novosibirsk
Novosibirsk Res.
SAYAN MTNS.
YABLONOVY RANGE
Amur R.
Komsomol'sk
Cape Lopatka
KURIL ISLANDS
Semipalatinsk
Lake Zaysan
ALTAI MTNS.
MONGOLIA
Ulaanbaatar
DA HINGGAN LING
Khabarovsk
DZUNGARIAN
BASIN
MONGOLIAN
PLATEAU
NORTHEAST
Songhua Jiang
Harbin
(MANCHURIAN)
La Pérouse Strait
L. Khanka
Vladivostok
Sapporo
Ürümqi
TIANSHAN
TURFAN
Tarim DEPRESSION
He
GOBI
A S I A
Changchun
PLAIN
Shenyang
Anshan
N.
KOREA
SEA OF
JAPAN
TAKLIMAKAN
Huang
Beijing
Tianjin
NORTH
CHINA
PLAIN
Pyongyang
Seoul
Inchon
JAPAN
C H I N A
YELLOW
SEA
S.
KOREA
Taegu
Kitakyūshū
Kawasaki
Tokyo
Kyōto
Ōsaka
Yokohama
KUNLUN SHAN
BAYAN HAR
SHAN
Wei He
Xi'an
He
HIMALAYAS
Annapurna Pk.
26,502 ft.
(8,078 m.)
PLATEAU OF
XIZANG
Mt. Everest
29,028 ft.
(8,848 m.)
Lhasa
Mt. Kangchenjunga
28,208 ft. (8,598 m.)
Nanjing
Shanghai
L. Tai
Chengdu
Jiang
Hangzhou
L. Poyang
Nanchang
EAST CHINA
SEA
RYUKYU IS.
(JAP.)
PACIFIC
OCEAN
NEPAL
Kathmandu
Thimphu
BHUTAN
Brahmaputra R.
Ganges R.
Vārānasi
Chang
YUNGUI
PLATEAU
Guiyang
Changsha
Fuzhou
Formosa Strait
Taipei
TAIWAN
Kaohsiung
Tropic of Cancer
BANGLADESH
Dhaka
GANGES
PLAIN
Khulna
Calcutta
Chittagong
MYANMAR
Mekong
Kunming
Xi
Jiang
Guangzhou
Macao
Victoria
MACAO
(PORT.)
HONG KONG
(U.K.)
Luzon Strait
ANNAMESE CORD.
Hanoi
Haiphong
Irrawaddy R.
Mandalay
Chiang Mai
BAY OF
BENGAL
Vientiane
LAOS
Cape Engaño
PHILIPPINE
SEA
Bassein
Yangon
KHORAT
PLATEAU
Savannakhet
SOUTH
LUZON
THAILAND
Ubon
Ratchathani
Da Nang
INDOCHINA
Quezon City
Preparis
Channel
Thonburi
CAMBODIA
VIETNAM
Manila
PHILIPPINES
ANDAMAN IS.
(IND.)
Krung Thep
(Bangkok)
Tonle Sap
CHINA
MINDORO
ANDAMAN
SEA
Phnom Penh
Ho Chi Minh City
PALAWAN
Cebu
SEA
MINDANAO
Davao
CEYLON
NICOBAR IS.
(IND.)
George Town
MALAY
PEN.
Ipoh
Bandar Seri
Begawan
BRUNEI
SULU ARCH.
(PHIL.)
Point Tinaca
Medan
Strait of Malacca
Kuala Lumpur
M A L A Y S I A
BORNEO HIGHLANDS
HALMAHERA
Equator
Singapore
SINGAPORE
SUMATRA
BORNEO
Pontianak
Jambi
BARISAN MTNS.
Banjarmasin
CELEBES
Cape d'Urville
Jayapura
Jaya Pk.
16,499 ft.
(5,029 m.)
Palembang
JAVA SEA
Ujung Pandang
BANDA SEA
NEW GUINEA
Sunda Str.
Jakarta
Semarang
Bandung
Surabaya
JAVA
I N D O N E S I A
90°
105°
120°
135°
150°
165°
180°
75°
60°
45°
30°
15°
0°

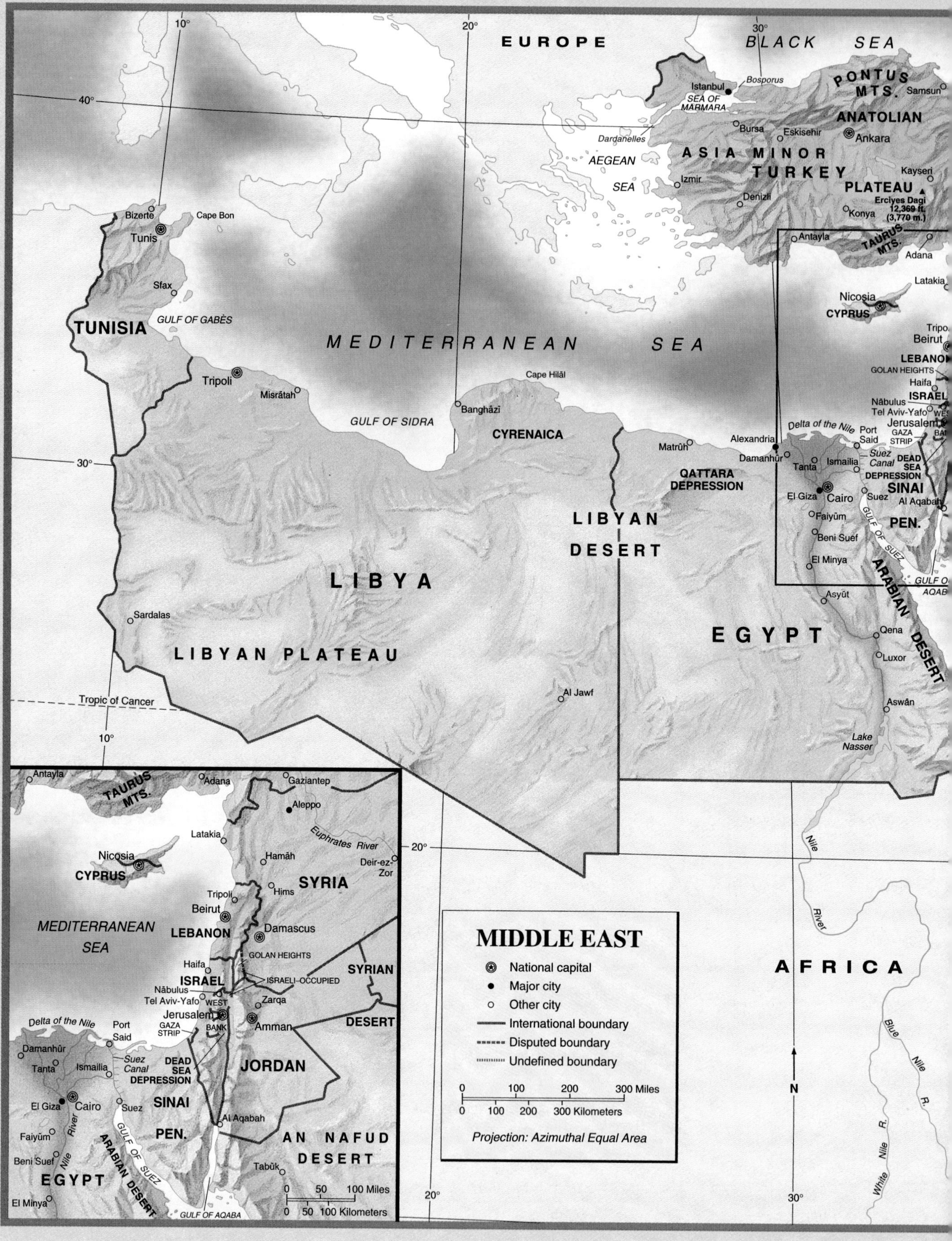

MIDDLE EAST
National capital
Major city
Other city
International boundary
Disputed boundary
Undefined boundary
0 100 200 300 Miles
0 100 200 300 Kilometers
Projection: Azimuthal Equal Area
EUROPE
BLACK SEA
PONTUS MTS.
Samsun
Istanbul
Bosporus
SEA OF MARMARA
Bursa
Eskisehir
Ankara
ANATOLIAN
Dardanelles
AEGEAN SEA
ASIA MINOR
TURKEY
PLATEAU
Kayseri
Izmir
Denizli
Erciyes Dagi 12,369 ft. (3,770 m.)
Konya
Antayla
TAURUS MTS.
Adana
Latakia
Nicosia
CYPRUS
Tripoli
Beirut
LEBANON
GOLAN HEIGHTS
Haifa
ISRAEL
Nâbulus
Tel Aviv-Yafo
Jerusalem
Bizerte
Cape Bon
Tunis
Sfax
TUNISIA
GULF OF GABÈS
MEDITERRANEAN SEA
Tripoli
Misrātah
Cape Hilāl
Banghāzī
GULF OF SIDRA
CYRENAICA
Delta of the Nile
Port Said
GAZA STRIP
Alexandria
Matrūh
Damanhûr
Tanta
Ismailia
Suez Canal
DEAD SEA DEPRESSION
QATTARA DEPRESSION
El Giza
Cairo
Suez
SINAI PEN.
Al Aqabah
Faiyūm
Beni Suef
El Minya
GULF OF SUEZ
ARABIAN DESERT
GULF OF AQABA
LIBYAN DESERT
LIBYA
Sardalas
LIBYAN PLATEAU
EGYPT
Asyūt
Qena
Luxor
Aswân
Lake Nasser
Al Jawf
Tropic of Cancer
Nile River
AFRICA
Blue Nile R.
White Nile R.
N
10°
20°
30°
40°
Gaziantep
Aleppo
Euphrates River
Hamāh
Deir-ez-Zor
Hims
SYRIA
Damascus
SYRIAN DESERT
ISRAELI-OCCUPIED
WEST BANK
Zarqa
Amman
JORDAN
AN NAFUD DESERT
Tabūk
0 50 100 Miles
0 50 100 Kilometers

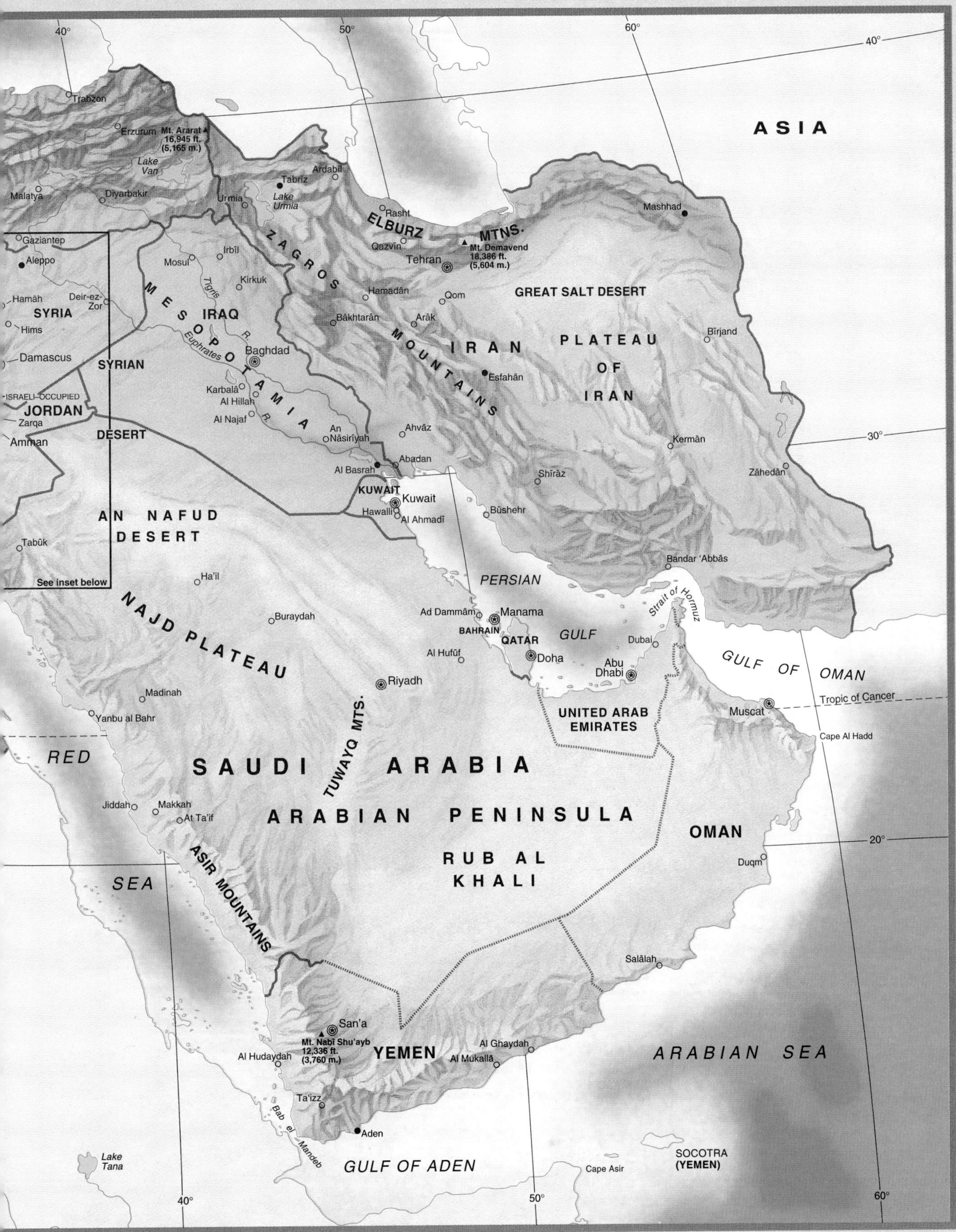
ASIA
Trabzon
Erzurum
Mt. Ararat 16,945 ft. (5,165 m.)
Lake Van
Malatya
Diyarbakir
Tabriz
Ardabil
Lake Urmia
Urmia
Rasht
ELBURZ MTNS.
Mt. Demavend 18,386 ft. (5,604 m.)
Qazvin
Tehran
Mashhad
Gaziantep
Aleppo
Mosul
Irbil
Kirkuk
Tigris
ZAGROS MOUNTAINS
Hamadān
Qom
GREAT SALT DESERT
Hamāh
SYRIA
Deir-ez-Zor
Hims
MESOPOTAMIA
IRAQ
Bākhtarān
Arāk
Euphrates R.
Baghdad
Damascus
SYRIAN
DESERT
IRAN
PLATEAU OF IRAN
Bīrjand
Esfahān
ISRAELI-OCCUPIED
JORDAN
Zarqa
Amman
Karbalā
Al Hillah
Al Najaf
An Nāsirīyah
Ahvāz
Kermān
Abadan
Al Basrah
Shīrāz
Zāhedān
KUWAIT
Kuwait
Hawalli
Al Ahmadī
Būshehr
AN NAFUD DESERT
Tabūk
See inset below
Bandar 'Abbās
Ha'il
PERSIAN GULF
Strait of Hormuz
NAJD PLATEAU
Buraydah
Ad Dammām
Manama
BAHRAIN
QATAR
Doha
Al Hufūf
Dubai
Abu Dhabi
GULF OF OMAN
Riyadh
Madinah
Yanbu al Bahr
TUWAYQ MTS.
UNITED ARAB EMIRATES
Muscat
Tropic of Cancer
Cape Al Hadd
RED SEA
SAUDI ARABIA
ARABIAN PENINSULA
Jiddah
Makkah
At Ta'if
ASIR MOUNTAINS
OMAN
RUB AL KHALI
Duqm
Salālah
San'a
Mt. Nabī Shu'ayb 12,336 ft. (3,760 m.)
YEMEN
Al Hudaydah
Al Ghaydah
Al Mukallā
ARABIAN SEA
Ta'izz
Bab el Mandeb
Aden
Lake Tana
GULF OF ADEN
Cape Asir
SOCOTRA (YEMEN)
40°
50°
60°
30°
20°

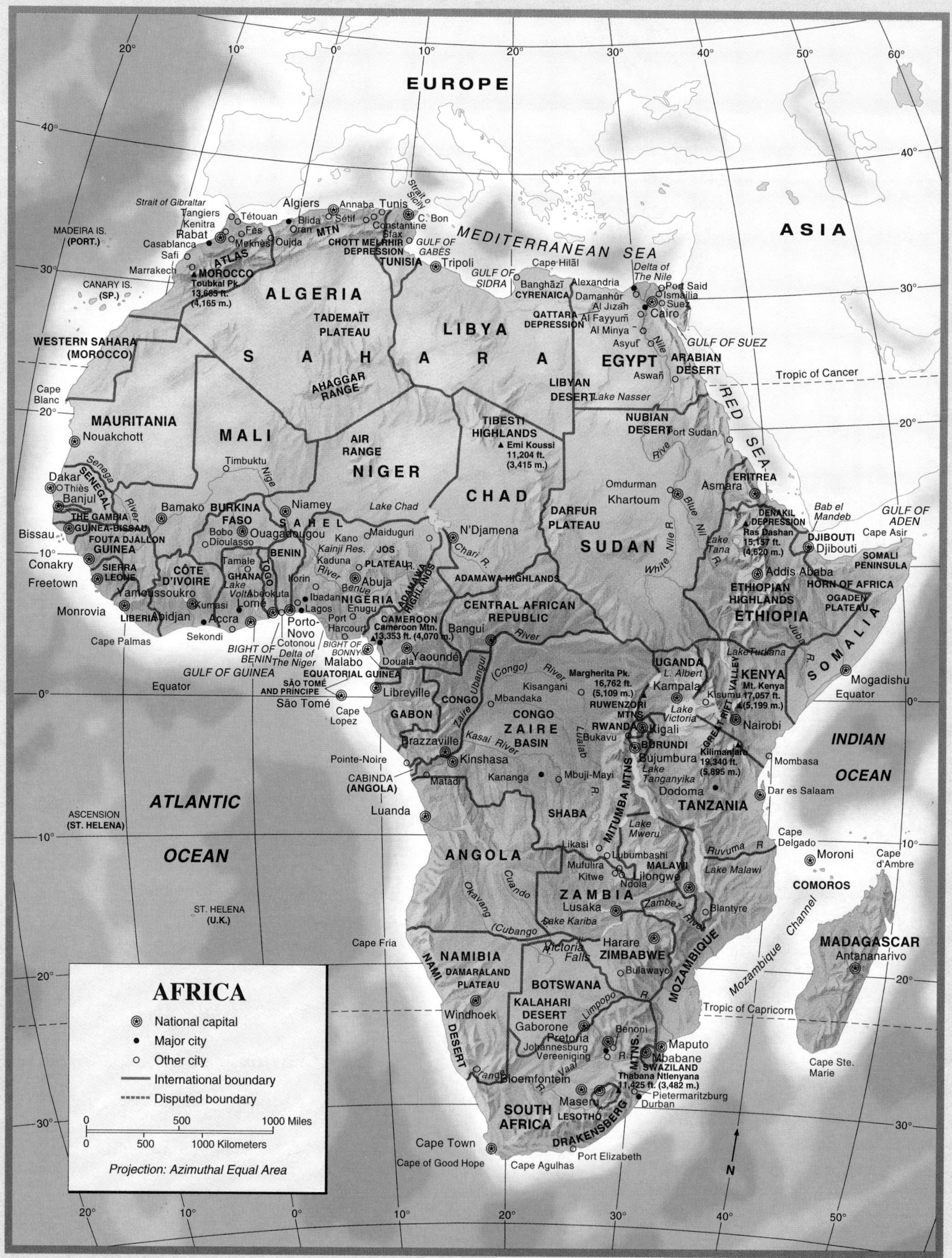

AFRICA
National capital
Major city
Other city
International boundary
Disputed boundary
0 500 1000 Miles
0 500 1000 Kilometers
Projection: Azimuthal Equal Area
EUROPE
ASIA
MEDITERRANEAN SEA
RED SEA
ATLANTIC OCEAN
INDIAN OCEAN
GULF OF GUINEA
GULF OF ADEN
GULF OF SUEZ
GULF OF SIDRA
GULF OF GABÈS
BIGHT OF BENIN
BIGHT OF BONNY
Mozambique Channel
Strait of Gibraltar
Strait of Sicily
Bab el Mandeb
Tropic of Cancer
Tropic of Capricorn
Equator
MADEIRA IS. (PORT.)
CANARY IS. (SP.)
WESTERN SAHARA (MOROCCO)
ASCENSION (ST. HELENA)
ST. HELENA (U.K.)
MOROCCO
ALGERIA
TUNISIA
LIBYA
EGYPT
MAURITANIA
MALI
NIGER
CHAD
SUDAN
ERITREA
DJIBOUTI
ETHIOPIA
SOMALIA
SENEGAL
THE GAMBIA
GUINEA-BISSAU
GUINEA
SIERRA LEONE
LIBERIA
CÔTE D'IVOIRE
BURKINA FASO
GHANA
TOGO
BENIN
NIGERIA
CAMEROON
CENTRAL AFRICAN REPUBLIC
EQUATORIAL GUINEA
SÃO TOMÉ AND PRINCIPE
GABON
CONGO
ZAIRE
UGANDA
KENYA
RWANDA
BURUNDI
TANZANIA
CABINDA (ANGOLA)
ANGOLA
ZAMBIA
MALAWI
MOZAMBIQUE
ZIMBABWE
NAMIBIA
BOTSWANA
SOUTH AFRICA
LESOTHO
SWAZILAND
MADAGASCAR
COMOROS
S A H A R A
SAHEL
ATLAS MTN
Toubkal Pk. 13,665 ft. (4,165 m.)
TADEMAÏT PLATEAU
AHAGGAR RANGE
AIR RANGE
TIBESTI HIGHLANDS
Emi Koussi 11,204 ft. (3,415 m.)
CHOTT MELRHIR DEPRESSION
QATTARA DEPRESSION
CYRENAICA
LIBYAN DESERT
ARABIAN DESERT
NUBIAN DESERT
DARFUR PLATEAU
DENAKIL DEPRESSION
Ras Dashan 15,157 ft. (4,620 m.)
ETHIOPIAN HIGHLANDS
SOMALI PENINSULA
HORN OF AFRICA
OGADEN PLATEAU
FOUTA DJALLON
JOS PLATEAU
ADAMAWA HIGHLANDS
Cameroon Mtn. 13,353 ft. (4,070 m.)
Margherita Pk. 16,762 ft. (5,109 m.)
RUWENZORI MTNS.
Mt. Kenya 17,057 ft. (5,199 m.)
Kilimanjaro 19,340 ft. (5,895 m.)
GREAT RIFT VALLEY
CONGO ZAIRE BASIN
SHABA
MITUMBA MTNS.
DAMARALAND PLATEAU
NAMIB DESERT
KALAHARI DESERT
DRAKENSBERG MTNS.
Thabana Ntlenyana 11,425 ft. (3,482 m.)
Delta of The Nile
Delta of The Niger
Nile
Blue Nile
White Nile
Niger River
Senegal River
Benue River
Chari R.
Ubangi
Congo River
Zaire
Kasai River
Lualaba
Cuando
Okavango (Cubango)
Zambezi River
Limpopo R.
Orange R.
Vaal R.
Juba R.
Ruvuma R.
Lake Nasser
Lake Chad
Kainji Res.
Lake Volta
Lake Tana
Lake Turkana
L. Albert
Lake Victoria
Lake Tanganyika
Lake Mweru
Lake Malawi
Lake Kariba
Victoria Falls
Cape Blanc
Cape Palmas
Cape Lopez
Cape Fria
Cape of Good Hope
Cape Agulhas
Cape Hilāl
C. Bon
Cape Asir
Cape Delgado
Cape d'Ambre
Cape Ste. Marie
Tangiers
Kenitra
Rabat
Casablanca
Safi
Marrakech
Tétouan
Fès
Meknès
Oujda
Algiers
Blida
Oran
Annaba
Sétif
Constantine
Tunis
Sfax
Tripoli
Banghāzī
Alexandria
Damanhûr
Al Jīzah
Cairo
Port Said
Ismailia
Suez
Al Fayyum
Al Minya
Asyut
Aswan
Port Sudan
Omdurman
Khartoum
Asmara
Djibouti
Addis Ababa
Mogadishu
Nouakchott
Dakar
Thiès
Banjul
Bissau
Conakry
Freetown
Monrovia
Timbuktu
Bamako
Bobo Dioulasso
Ouagadougou
Niamey
Yamoussoukro
Abidjan
Kumasi
Tamale
Accra
Sekondi
Lomé
Porto-Novo
Cotonou
Abeokuta
Ibadan
Ilorin
Lagos
Kano
Kaduna
Maiduguri
Abuja
Enugu
Port Harcourt
N'Djamena
Malabo
Douala
Yaoundé
Bangui
Libreville
São Tomé
Kisangani
Mbandaka
Brazzaville
Kinshasa
Pointe-Noire
Matadi
Kananga
Mbuji-Mayi
Bukavu
Kigali
Bujumbura
Kampala
Kisumu
Nairobi
Mombasa
Dodoma
Dar es Salaam
Luanda
Likasi
Lubumbashi
Mufulira
Kitwe
Ndola
Lilongwe
Lusaka
Blantyre
Harare
Bulawayo
Moroni
Antananarivo
Windhoek
Gaborone
Pretoria
Johannesburg
Vereeniging
Benoni
Maputo
Mbabane
Bloemfontein
Maseru
Pietermaritzburg
Durban
Cape Town
Port Elizabeth
N

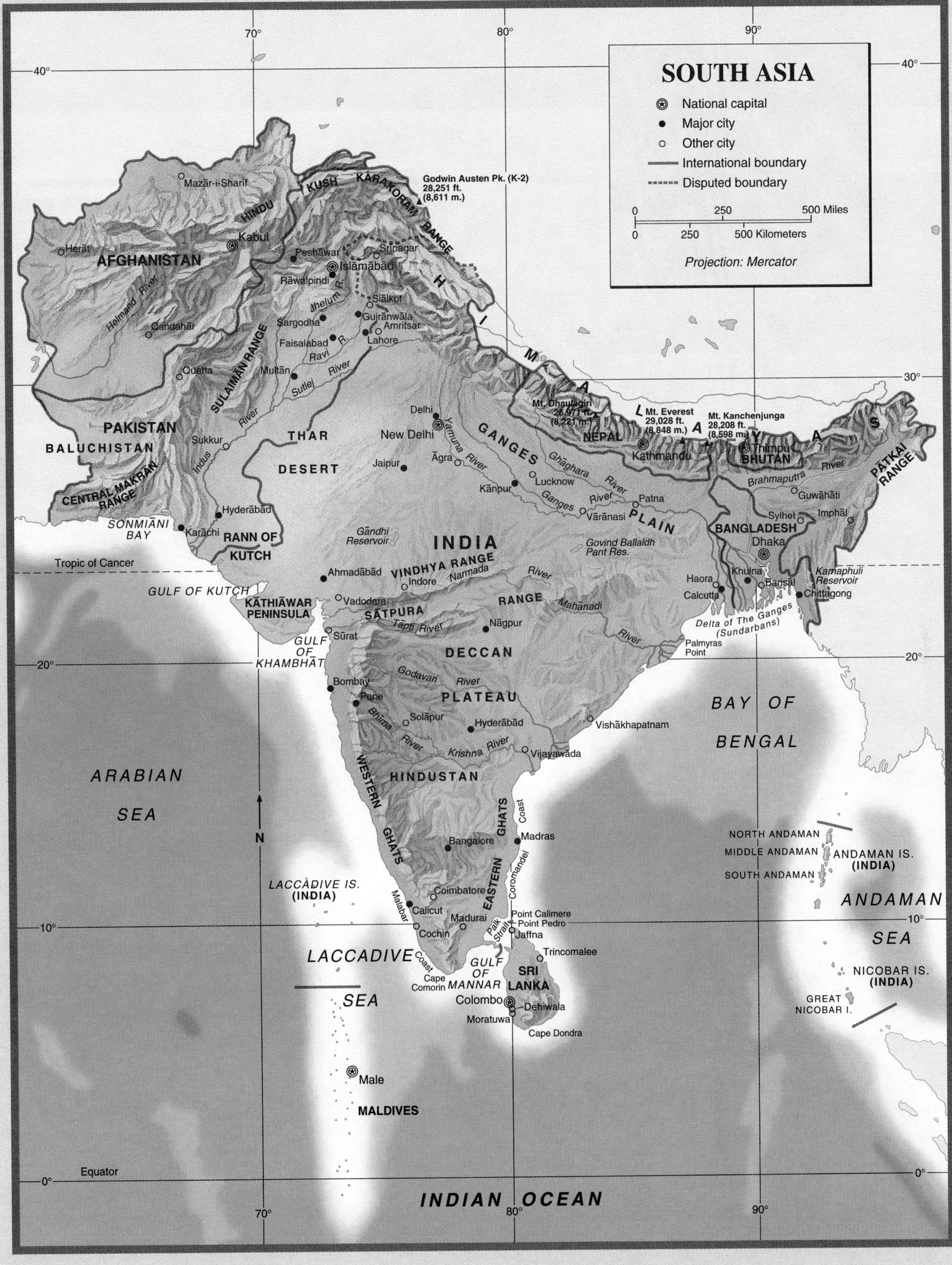
SOUTH ASIA
National capital
Major city
Other city
International boundary
Disputed boundary
0 250 500 Miles
0 250 500 Kilometers
Projection: Mercator
70°
80°
90°
40°
30°
20°
10°
0°
Godwin Austen Pk. (K-2)
28,251 ft.
(8,611 m.)
Mazār-i-Sharif
KUSH
KARAKORAM
RANGE
HINDU
Herāt
Kabul
AFGHANISTAN
Peshāwar
Srinagar
Islāmābād
Rāwalpindi
H
I
M
A
L
A
Y
A
S
Helmand River
Jhelum R.
Siālkot
Gujrānwāla
Amritsar
Qandahār
Sargodha
Faisalabad
Lahore
Ravi R.
Quetta
SULAIMAN RANGE
Multān
Sutlej River
Mt. Dhaulagiri
26,971 ft.
(8,221 m.)
Mt. Everest
29,028 ft.
(8,848 m.)
Mt. Kanchenjunga
28,208 ft.
(8,598 m.)
PAKISTAN
BALUCHISTAN
Sukkur
Indus River
THAR
DESERT
Delhi
New Delhi
Yamuna River
Jaipur
Āgra
GANGES
Ghāghara River
NEPAL
Kathmandu
Thimpu
BHUTAN
PĀTKAI RANGE
Brahmaputra River
CENTRAL MAKRAN RANGE
Hyderābād
Kānpur
Lucknow
Ganges River
Vārānasi
Patna
PLAIN
Guwāhāti
Imphāl
Sylhet
SONMIĀNI BAY
Karāchi
RANN OF KUTCH
Gāndhi Reservoir
INDIA
Govind Ballaldh Pant Res.
BANGLADESH
Dhaka
Tropic of Cancer
Ahmadābād
VINDHYA RANGE
Narmada River
Indore
Khulna
Haora
Calcutta
Barisāl
Karnaphuli Reservoir
Chittagong
GULF OF KUTCH
KATHIĀWAR PENINSULA
Vadodara
SĀTPURA RANGE
Mahānadi River
Tāpti River
Nāgpur
Delta of The Ganges (Sundarbans)
Sūrat
GULF OF KHAMBHĀT
DECCAN
Palmyras Point
Godavari River
Bombay
Pune
PLATEAU
BAY OF BENGAL
Solāpur
Bhīma River
Hyderābād
Vishākhapatnam
Krishna River
Vijayawāda
ARABIAN SEA
WESTERN GHATS
HINDUSTAN
EASTERN GHATS
Coast
Coromandel
Madras
N
Bangalore
NORTH ANDAMAN
MIDDLE ANDAMAN
SOUTH ANDAMAN
ANDAMAN IS. (INDIA)
LACCADIVE IS. (INDIA)
Coimbatore
Malabar Coast
Calicut
Madurai
Cochin
Point Calimere
Point Pedro
Palk Strait
Jaffna
ANDAMAN SEA
Trincomalee
LACCADIVE SEA
GULF OF MANNAR
SRI LANKA
Cape Comorin
Colombo
Dehiwala
Moratuwa
Cape Dondra
NICOBAR IS. (INDIA)
GREAT NICOBAR I.
Male
MALDIVES
Equator
INDIAN OCEAN

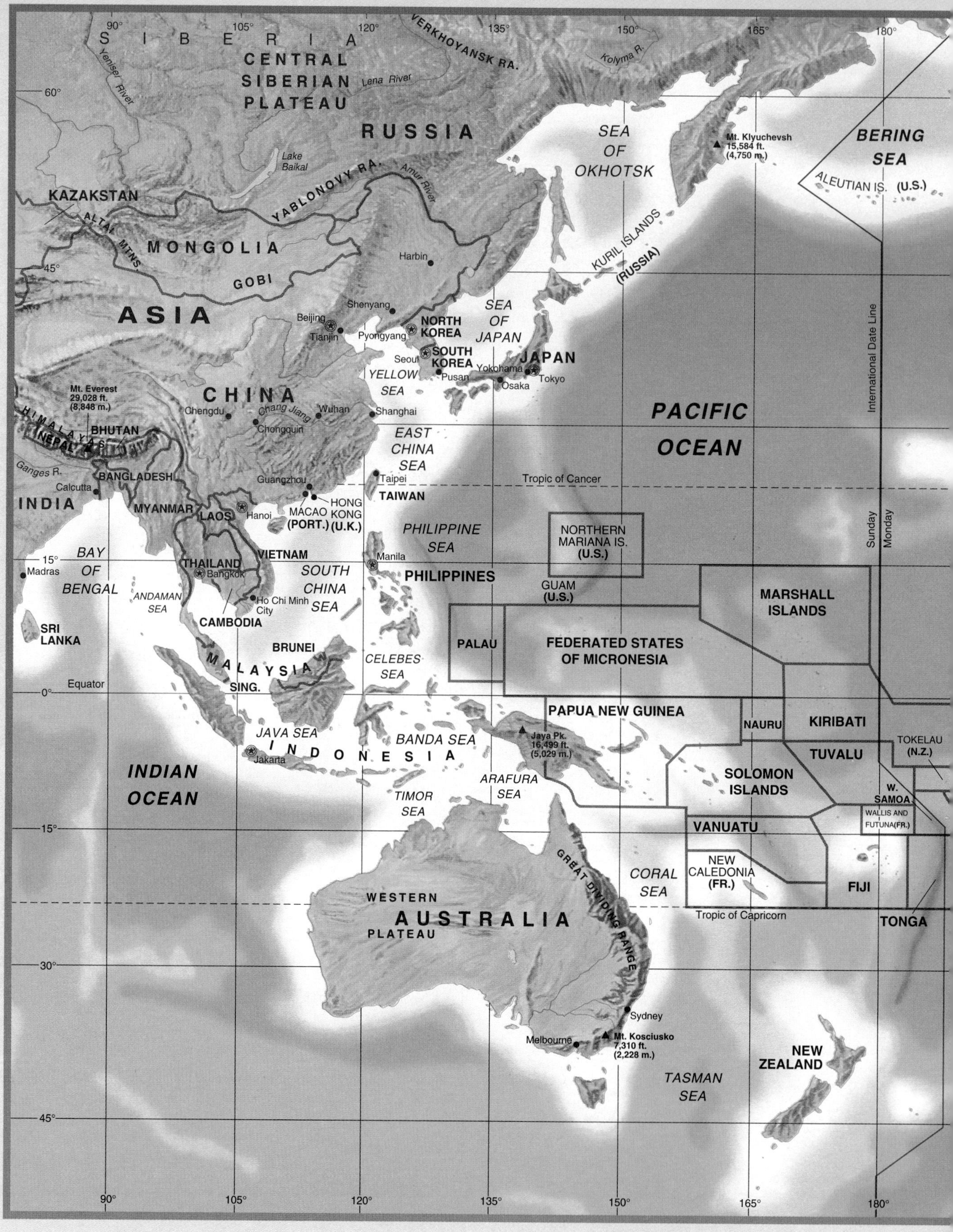

SIBERIA
CENTRAL SIBERIAN PLATEAU
Yenisei River
Lena River
VERKHOYANSK RA.
Kolyma R.
RUSSIA
SEA OF OKHOTSK
Mt. Klyuchevsh 15,584 ft. (4,750 m.)
BERING SEA
ALEUTIAN IS. (U.S.)
Lake Baikal
YABLONOVY RA.
Amur River
KAZAKSTAN
ALTAI MTNS.
MONGOLIA
GOBI
Harbin
KURIL ISLANDS (RUSSIA)
ASIA
Shenyang
Beijing
Tianjin
Pyongyang
NORTH KOREA
SEA OF JAPAN
Seoul
SOUTH KOREA
JAPAN
Yokohama
Tokyo
Pusan
Osaka
YELLOW SEA
International Date Line
CHINA
Mt. Everest 29,028 ft. (8,848 m.)
Chengdu
Chang Jiang
Wuhan
Shanghai
Chongquin
HIMALAYAS
NEPAL
BHUTAN
EAST CHINA SEA
PACIFIC OCEAN
Ganges R.
BANGLADESH
Calcutta
Guangzhou
Taipei
TAIWAN
Tropic of Cancer
INDIA
MYANMAR
LAOS
Hanoi
MACAO (PORT.)
HONG KONG (U.K.)
PHILIPPINE SEA
NORTHERN MARIANA IS. (U.S.)
Sunday
Monday
BAY OF BENGAL
Madras
THAILAND
Bangkok
VIETNAM
SOUTH CHINA SEA
Manila
PHILIPPINES
GUAM (U.S.)
MARSHALL ISLANDS
ANDAMAN SEA
Ho Chi Minh City
CAMBODIA
SRI LANKA
PALAU
FEDERATED STATES OF MICRONESIA
BRUNEI
CELEBES SEA
MALAYSIA
Equator
SING.
PAPUA NEW GUINEA
NAURU
KIRIBATI
JAVA SEA
BANDA SEA
Jaya Pk. 16,499 ft. (5,029 m.)
TOKELAU (N.Z.)
INDONESIA
Jakarta
TUVALU
INDIAN OCEAN
ARAFURA SEA
SOLOMON ISLANDS
W. SAMOA
TIMOR SEA
WALLIS AND FUTUNA(FR.)
VANUATU
GREAT DIVIDING RANGE
CORAL SEA
NEW CALEDONIA (FR.)
FIJI
WESTERN PLATEAU
AUSTRALIA
Tropic of Capricorn
TONGA
Sydney
Melbourne
Mt. Kosciusko 7,310 ft. (2,228 m.)
NEW ZEALAND
TASMAN SEA
60°
45°
15°
0°
15°
30°
45°
90°
105°
120°
135°
150°
165°
180°

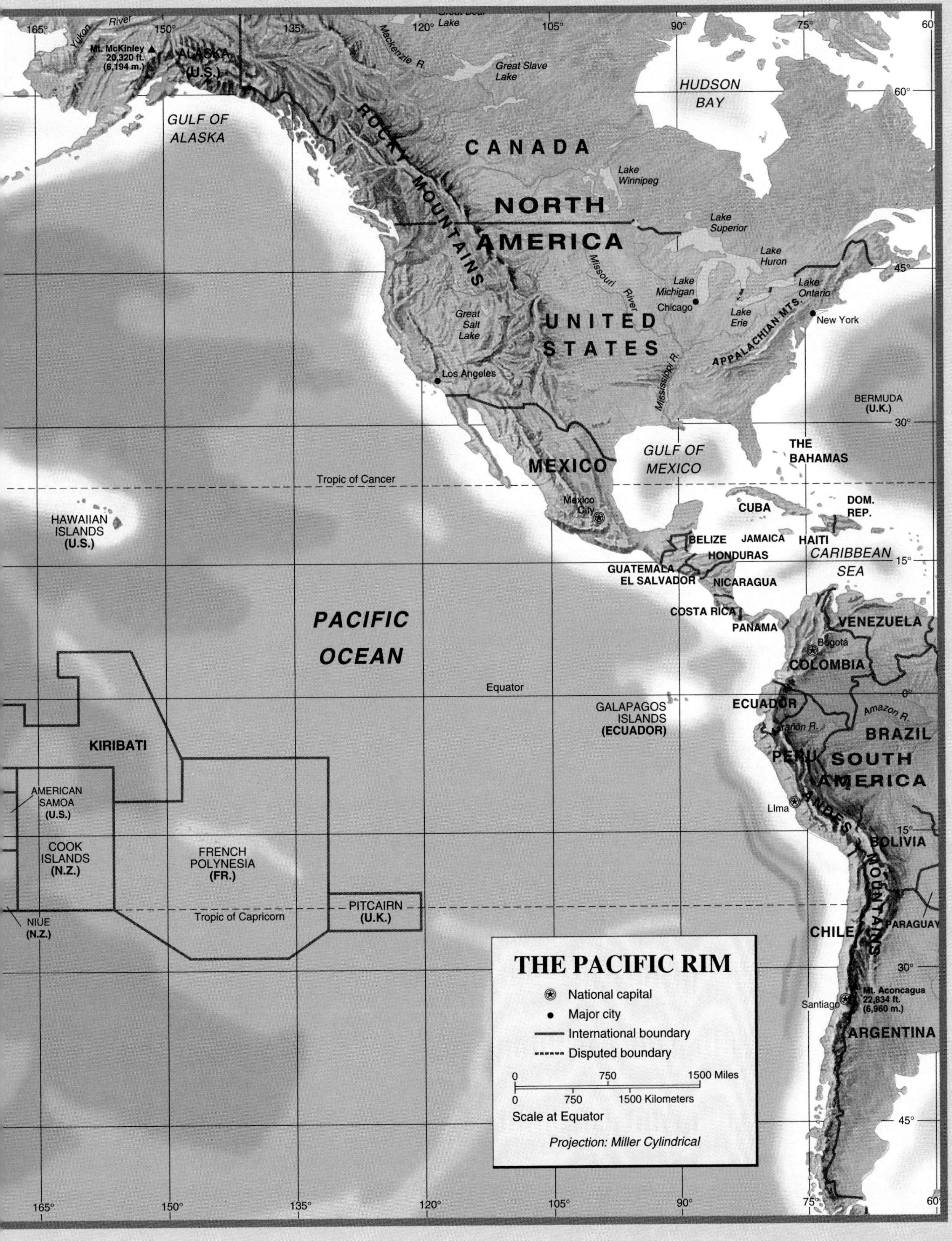
THE PACIFIC RIM
National capital
Major city
International boundary
Disputed boundary
0 750 1500 Miles
0 750 1500 Kilometers
Scale at Equator
Projection: Miller Cylindrical
PACIFIC OCEAN
NORTH AMERICA
CANADA
UNITED STATES
MEXICO
SOUTH AMERICA
ALASKA (U.S.)
Mt. McKinley 20,320 ft. (6,194 m.)
Yukon River
Mackenzie R.
Great Slave Lake
HUDSON BAY
GULF OF ALASKA
ROCKY MOUNTAINS
Lake Winnipeg
Lake Superior
Lake Huron
Lake Michigan
Lake Ontario
Lake Erie
Chicago
New York
Missouri River
Mississippi R.
Great Salt Lake
APPALACHIAN MTS.
Los Angeles
BERMUDA (U.K.)
THE BAHAMAS
GULF OF MEXICO
Tropic of Cancer
Mexico City
CUBA
DOM. REP.
HAITI
JAMAICA
BELIZE
HONDURAS
GUATEMALA
EL SALVADOR
NICARAGUA
COSTA RICA
PANAMA
CARIBBEAN SEA
HAWAIIAN ISLANDS (U.S.)
VENEZUELA
Bogotá
COLOMBIA
Equator
GALAPAGOS ISLANDS (ECUADOR)
ECUADOR
Amazon R.
Marañón R.
BRAZIL
PERU
Lima
ANDES MOUNTAINS
BOLIVIA
PARAGUAY
CHILE
Santiago
Mt. Aconcagua 22,834 ft. (6,960 m.)
ARGENTINA
KIRIBATI
AMERICAN SAMOA (U.S.)
COOK ISLANDS (N.Z.)
NIUE (N.Z.)
FRENCH POLYNESIA (FR.)
PITCAIRN (U.K.)
Tropic of Capricorn
165° 150° 135° 120° 105° 90° 75° 60°
60° 45° 30° 15° 0° 15° 30° 45°

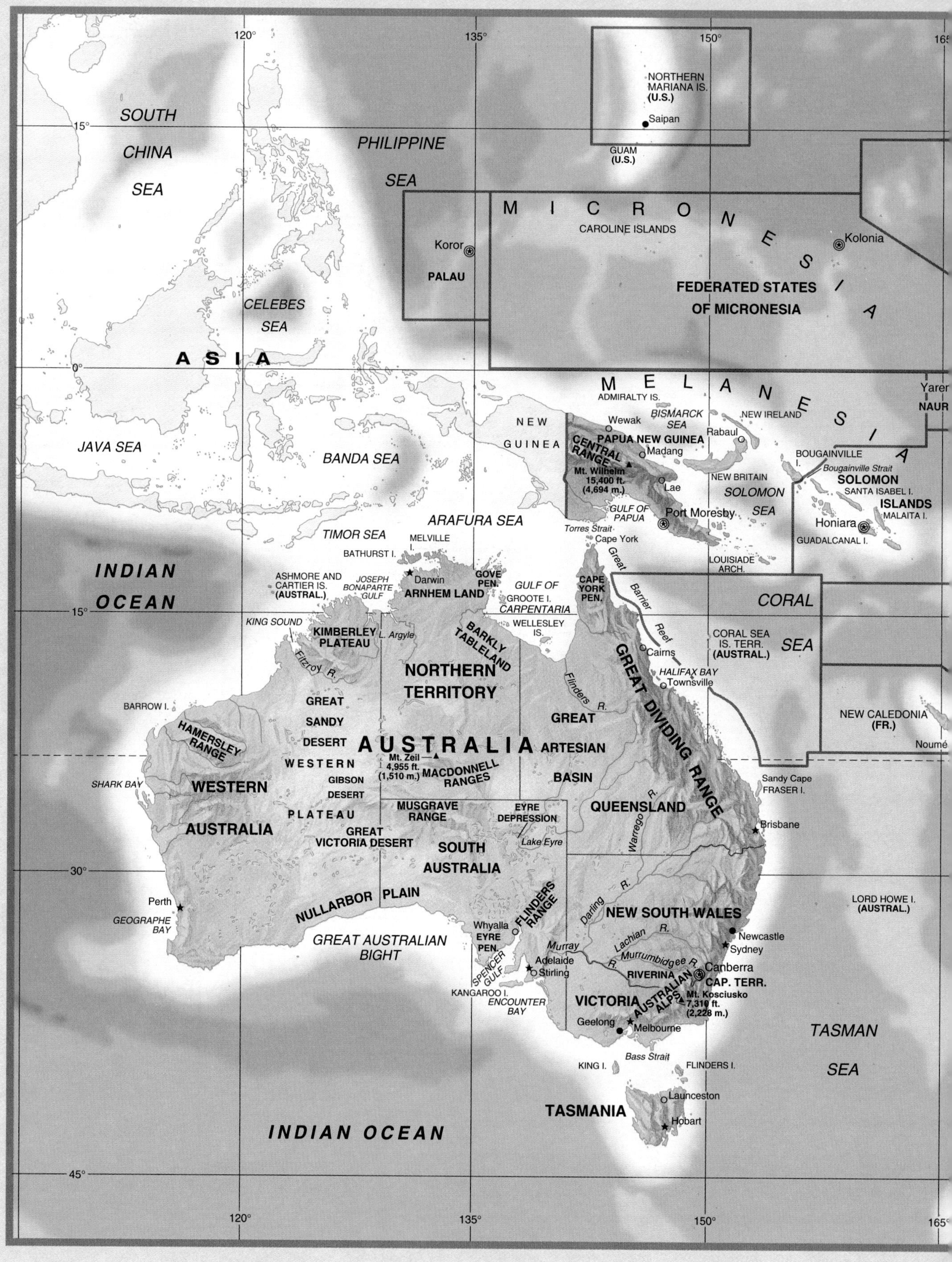

SOUTH CHINA SEA
PHILIPPINE SEA
NORTHERN MARIANA IS. (U.S.)
Saipan
GUAM (U.S.)
M I C R O N E S I A
CAROLINE ISLANDS
Koror
PALAU
Kolonia
FEDERATED STATES OF MICRONESIA
CELEBES SEA
A S I A
M E L A N E S I A
ADMIRALTY IS.
BISMARCK SEA
NEW IRELAND
Yaren
NAURU
Wewak
Rabaul
NEW GUINEA
PAPUA NEW GUINEA
Madang
CENTRAL RANGE
Mt. Wilhelm 15,400 ft. (4,694 m.)
Lae
BOUGAINVILLE I.
Bougainville Strait
NEW BRITAIN
SOLOMON ISLANDS
SANTA ISABEL I.
SOLOMON SEA
MALAITA I.
Honiara
GUADALCANAL I.
JAVA SEA
BANDA SEA
ARAFURA SEA
GULF OF PAPUA
Port Moresby
Torres Strait
Cape York
TIMOR SEA
MELVILLE I.
BATHURST I.
LOUISIADE ARCH.
INDIAN OCEAN
ASHMORE AND CARTIER IS. (AUSTRAL.)
JOSEPH BONAPARTE GULF
Darwin
ARNHEM LAND
GOVE PEN.
GULF OF CARPENTARIA
GROOTE I.
CAPE YORK PEN.
Great Barrier Reef
CORAL SEA
KING SOUND
KIMBERLEY PLATEAU
L. Argyle
BARKLY TABLELAND
WELLESLEY IS.
Cairns
CORAL SEA IS. TERR. (AUSTRAL.)
Fitzroy R.
NORTHERN TERRITORY
Flinders R.
GREAT DIVIDING RANGE
HALIFAX BAY
Townsville
BARROW I.
GREAT SANDY DESERT
GREAT ARTESIAN BASIN
NEW CALEDONIA (FR.)
Nouméa
HAMERSLEY RANGE
AUSTRALIA
Mt. Zeil 4,955 ft. (1,510 m.)
MACDONNELL RANGES
WESTERN PLATEAU
GIBSON DESERT
SHARK BAY
WESTERN AUSTRALIA
Sandy Cape
FRASER I.
MUSGRAVE RANGE
EYRE DEPRESSION
QUEENSLAND
Warrego R.
Brisbane
GREAT VICTORIA DESERT
SOUTH AUSTRALIA
Lake Eyre
Perth
GEOGRAPHE BAY
NULLARBOR PLAIN
FLINDERS RANGE
Darling R.
NEW SOUTH WALES
LORD HOWE I. (AUSTRAL.)
Whyalla
EYRE PEN.
GREAT AUSTRALIAN BIGHT
Murray R.
Lachian R.
Murrumbidgee R.
Newcastle
Sydney
Canberra
Adelaide
Stirling
SPENCER GULF
RIVERINA
CAP. TERR.
KANGAROO I.
ENCOUNTER BAY
VICTORIA
AUSTRALIAN ALPS
Mt. Kosciusko 7,310 ft. (2,228 m.)
Geelong
Melbourne
TASMAN SEA
Bass Strait
KING I.
FLINDERS I.
Launceston
TASMANIA
Hobart
INDIAN OCEAN
120°
135°
150°
165°
15°
0°
30°
45°

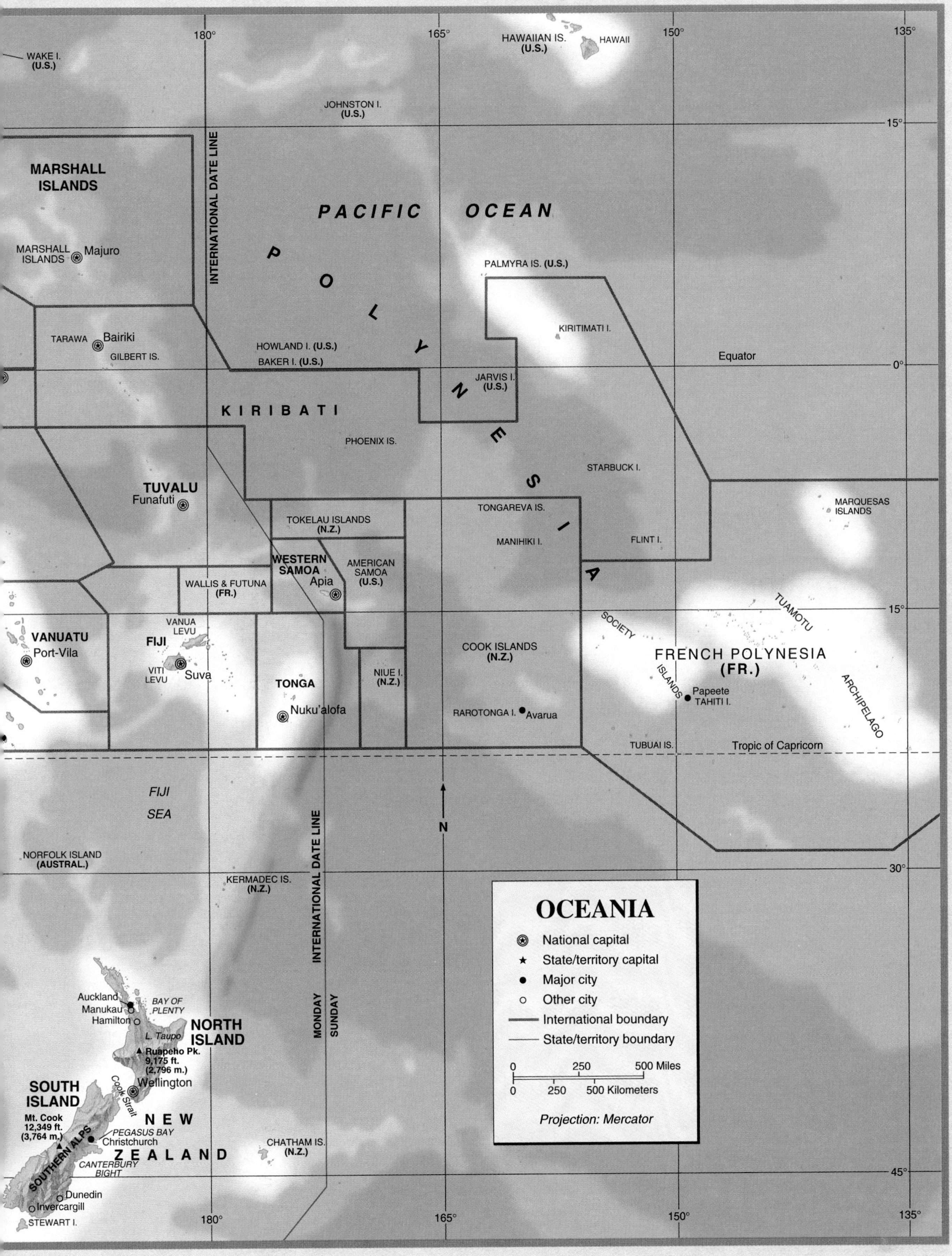
OCEANIA
National capital
State/territory capital
Major city
Other city
International boundary
State/territory boundary
0 250 500 Miles
0 250 500 Kilometers
Projection: Mercator
PACIFIC OCEAN
POLYNESIA
WAKE I. (U.S.)
HAWAIIAN IS. (U.S.)
HAWAII
JOHNSTON I. (U.S.)
MARSHALL ISLANDS
MARSHALL ISLANDS
Majuro
INTERNATIONAL DATE LINE
PALMYRA IS. (U.S.)
KIRITIMATI I.
TARAWA
Bairiki
GILBERT IS.
HOWLAND I. (U.S.)
BAKER I. (U.S.)
Equator
JARVIS I. (U.S.)
KIRIBATI
PHOENIX IS.
STARBUCK I.
TUVALU
Funafuti
TOKELAU ISLANDS (N.Z.)
TONGAREVA IS.
MARQUESAS ISLANDS
MANIHIKI I.
FLINT I.
WESTERN SAMOA
Apia
AMERICAN SAMOA (U.S.)
WALLIS & FUTUNA (FR.)
VANUATU
Port-Vila
VANUA LEVU
FIJI
VITI LEVU
Suva
TONGA
Nuku'alofa
NIUE I. (N.Z.)
COOK ISLANDS (N.Z.)
RAROTONGA I.
Avarua
SOCIETY ISLANDS
TUAMOTU ARCHIPELAGO
FRENCH POLYNESIA (FR.)
Papeete
TAHITI I.
TUBUAI IS.
Tropic of Capricorn
FIJI SEA
N
NORFOLK ISLAND (AUSTRAL.)
KERMADEC IS. (N.Z.)
MONDAY
SUNDAY
Auckland
Manukau
Hamilton
BAY OF PLENTY
L. Taupo
NORTH ISLAND
Ruapeho Pk. 9,175 ft. (2,796 m.)
Wellington
Cook Strait
SOUTH ISLAND
Mt. Cook 12,349 ft. (3,764 m.)
SOUTHERN ALPS
PEGASUS BAY
Christchurch
NEW ZEALAND
CANTERBURY BIGHT
CHATHAM IS. (N.Z.)
Dunedin
Invercargill
STEWART I.
180°
165°
150°
135°
15°
0°
15°
30°
45°

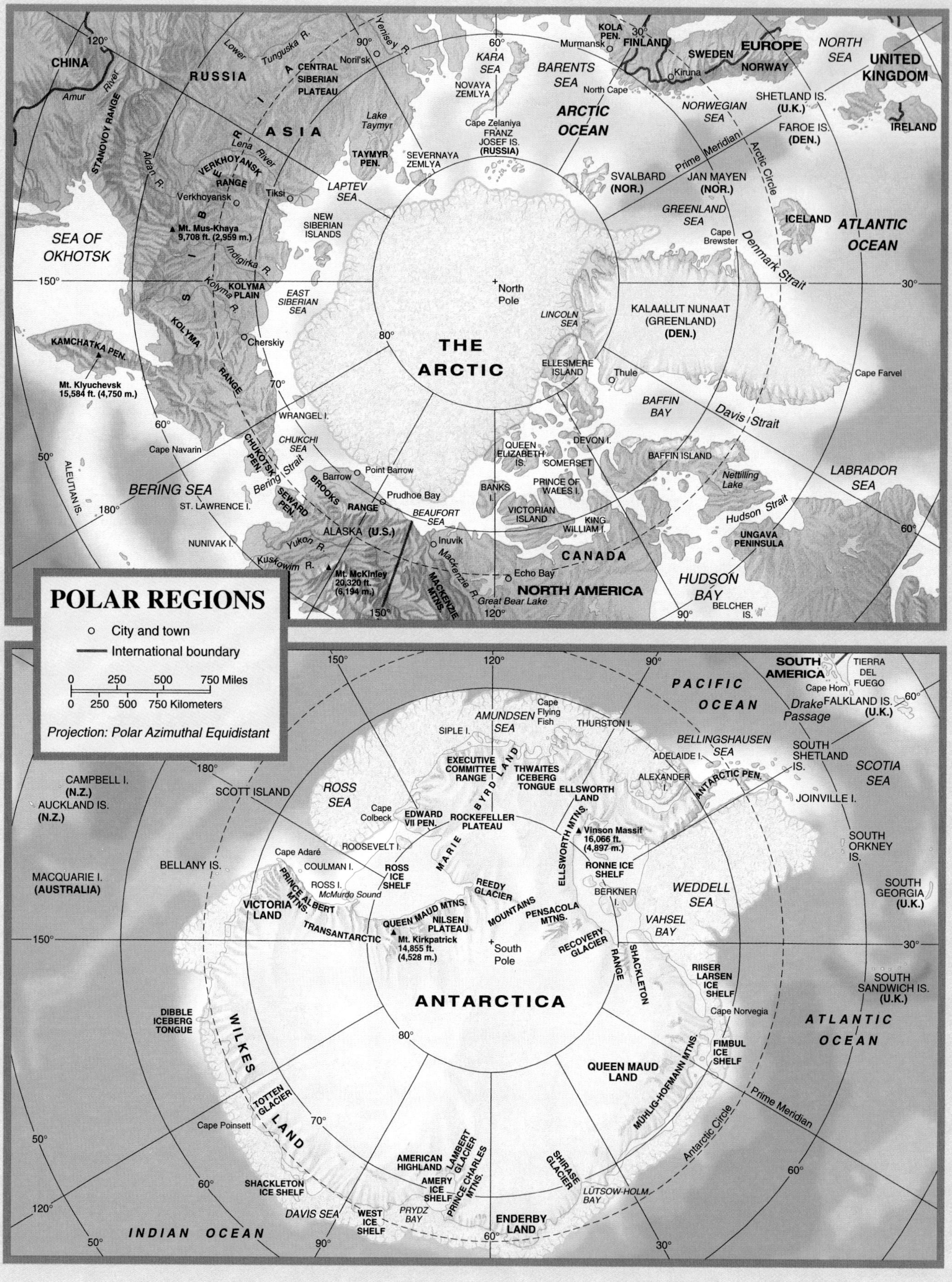
POLAR REGIONS
City and town
International boundary
0 250 500 750 Miles
0 250 500 750 Kilometers
Projection: Polar Azimuthal Equidistant
THE ARCTIC
North Pole
ARCTIC OCEAN
CHINA
RUSSIA
ASIA
SIBERIA
CENTRAL SIBERIAN PLATEAU
Lower Tunguska R.
Yenisey R.
Noril'sk
Amur River
STANOVOY RANGE
Aldan R.
Lena River
VERKHOYANSK RANGE
Verkhoyansk
Tiksi
Mt. Mus-Khaya 9,708 ft. (2,959 m.)
SEA OF OKHOTSK
Indigirka R.
Kolyma R.
KOLYMA PLAIN
KOLYMA RANGE
Cherskiy
KAMCHATKA PEN.
Mt. Klyuchevsk 15,584 ft. (4,750 m.)
Lake Taymyr
TAYMYR PEN.
SEVERNAYA ZEMLYA
LAPTEV SEA
NEW SIBERIAN ISLANDS
EAST SIBERIAN SEA
KARA SEA
NOVAYA ZEMLYA
Cape Zelaniya
FRANZ JOSEF IS. (RUSSIA)
Murmansk
KOLA PEN.
FINLAND
SWEDEN
Kiruna
NORWAY
EUROPE
NORTH SEA
UNITED KINGDOM
IRELAND
SHETLAND IS. (U.K.)
FAROE IS. (DEN.)
BARENTS SEA
North Cape
NORWEGIAN SEA
Prime Meridian
Arctic Circle
SVALBARD (NOR.)
JAN MAYEN (NOR.)
GREENLAND SEA
Cape Brewster
ICELAND
ATLANTIC OCEAN
Denmark Strait
KALAALLIT NUNAAT (GREENLAND) (DEN.)
LINCOLN SEA
ELLESMERE ISLAND
Thule
Cape Farvel
BAFFIN BAY
Davis Strait
DEVON I.
QUEEN ELIZABETH IS.
SOMERSET I.
BAFFIN ISLAND
Nettilling Lake
LABRADOR SEA
PRINCE OF WALES I.
BANKS I.
VICTORIAN ISLAND
KING WILLIAM I.
Hudson Strait
UNGAVA PENINSULA
CANADA
HUDSON BAY
BELCHER IS.
NORTH AMERICA
Echo Bay
Great Bear Lake
Mackenzie R.
MACKENZIE MTNS.
Inuvik
BEAUFORT SEA
Prudhoe Bay
Point Barrow
Barrow
BROOKS RANGE
ALASKA (U.S.)
Yukon R.
Kuskowim R.
Mt. McKinley 20,320 ft. (6,194 m.)
SEWARD PEN.
Bering Strait
CHUKOTSK PEN.
CHUKCHI SEA
WRANGEL I.
Cape Navarin
BERING SEA
ST. LAWRENCE I.
NUNIVAK I.
ALEUTIAN IS.
120° 90° 60° 30° 150° 180° 80° 70° 60° 50°
ANTARCTICA
South Pole
SOUTH AMERICA
TIERRA DEL FUEGO
Cape Horn
Drake Passage
FALKLAND IS. (U.K.)
PACIFIC OCEAN
AMUNDSEN SEA
Cape Flying Fish
THURSTON I.
SIPLE I.
BELLINGSHAUSEN SEA
ADELAIDE I.
ALEXANDER I.
ANTARCTIC PEN.
SOUTH SHETLAND IS.
SCOTIA SEA
JOINVILLE I.
SOUTH ORKNEY IS.
SOUTH GEORGIA (U.K.)
SOUTH SANDWICH IS. (U.K.)
EXECUTIVE COMMITTEE RANGE
BYRD LAND
MARIE BYRD LAND
THWAITES ICEBERG TONGUE
ELLSWORTH LAND
ELLSWORTH MTNS.
Vinson Massif 16,066 ft. (4,897 m.)
RONNE ICE SHELF
BERKNER I.
WEDDELL SEA
VAHSEL BAY
ROSS SEA
Cape Colbeck
EDWARD VII PEN.
ROCKEFELLER PLATEAU
ROOSEVELT I.
ROSS ICE SHELF
REEDY GLACIER
Cape Adaré
COULMAN I.
ROSS I.
McMurdo Sound
PRINCE ALBERT MTNS.
VICTORIA LAND
TRANSANTARCTIC MOUNTAINS
QUEEN MAUD MTNS.
NILSEN PLATEAU
Mt. Kirkpatrick 14,855 ft. (4,528 m.)
PENSACOLA MTNS.
RECOVERY GLACIER
SHACKLETON RANGE
RIISER LARSEN ICE SHELF
Cape Norvegia
ATLANTIC OCEAN
FIMBUL ICE SHELF
QUEEN MAUD LAND
MÜHLIG-HOFMANN MTNS.
Prime Meridian
Antarctic Circle
SHIRASE GLACIER
LÜTSOW-HOLM BAY
ENDERBY LAND
PRINCE CHARLES MTNS.
LAMBERT GLACIER
AMERICAN HIGHLAND
AMERY ICE SHELF
PRYDZ BAY
WEST ICE SHELF
DAVIS SEA
SHACKLETON ICE SHELF
INDIAN OCEAN
Cape Poinsett
TOTTEN GLACIER
WILKES LAND
DIBBLE ICEBERG TONGUE
SCOTT ISLAND
BELLANY IS.
CAMPBELL I. (N.Z.)
AUCKLAND IS. (N.Z.)
MACQUARIE I. (AUSTRALIA)
150° 120° 90° 60° 30° 180° 80° 70° 60° 50°

Historical Atlas AND World Data Bank

Early Civilizations 3500 B.C.–1700s B.C.	A27
Ancient Empires A.D. 1–A.D. 500	A28
A New Global Age A.D.800–A.D. 1500	A28
Age of Imperialism 1870–1914	A29
Global Civilization Today	A29
World Trade Power (cartogram)	A30
World Population (cartogram)	A32

Early Civilizations 3500 B.C –1700s B.C.

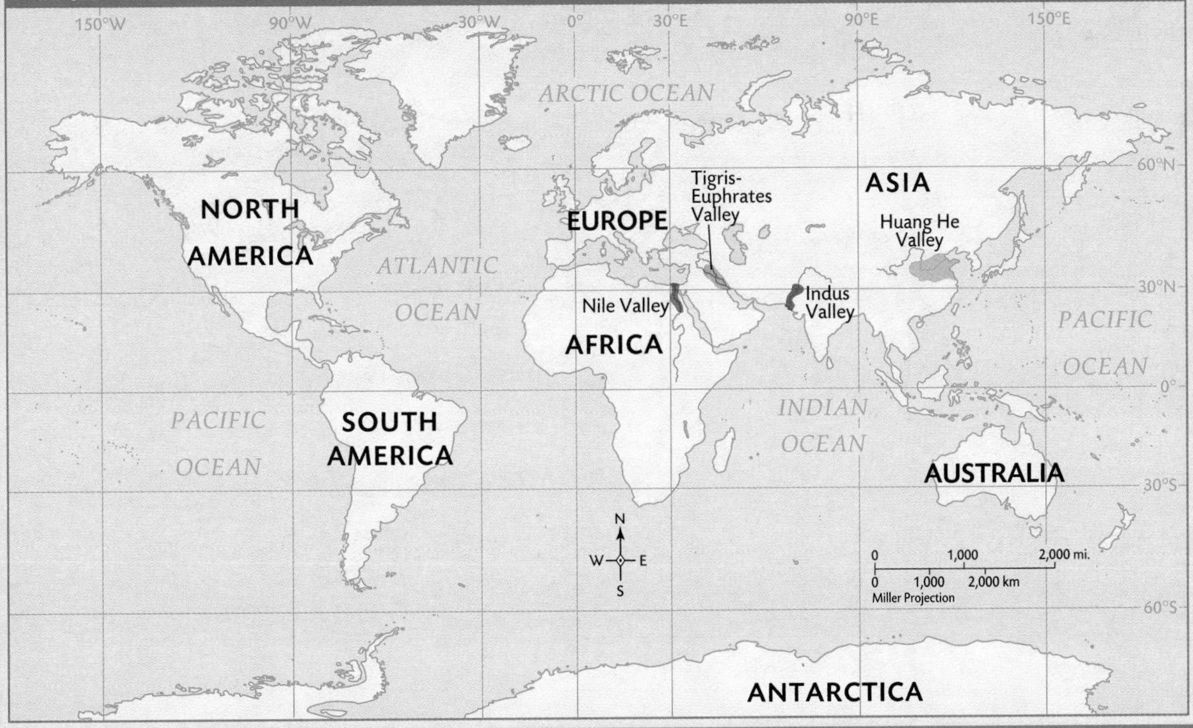

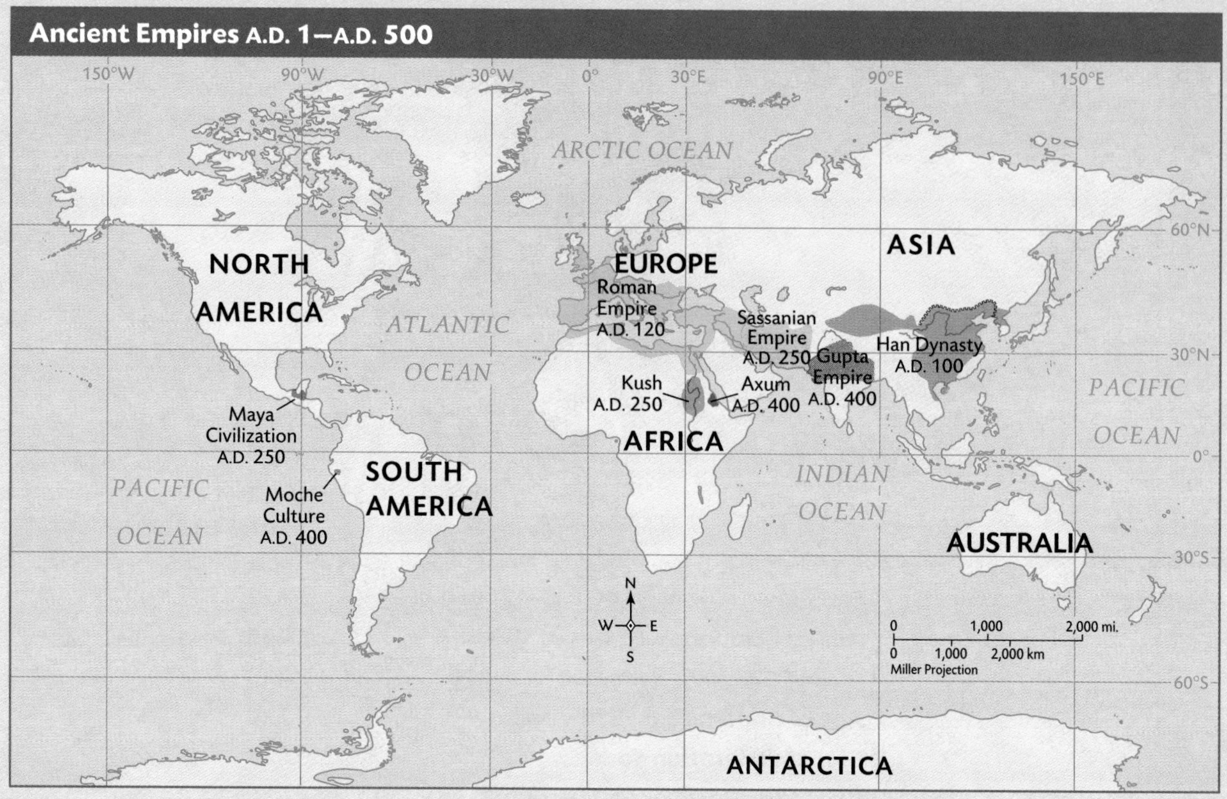
Ancient Empires A.D. 1—A.D. 500
150°W
90°W
30°W
0°
30°E
90°E
150°E
60°N
30°N
0°
30°S
60°S
ARCTIC OCEAN
NORTH AMERICA
EUROPE
ASIA
Roman Empire A.D. 120
Sassanian Empire A.D. 250
Gupta Empire A.D. 400
Han Dynasty A.D. 100
ATLANTIC OCEAN
PACIFIC OCEAN
Kush A.D. 250
Axum A.D. 400
Maya Civilization A.D. 250
AFRICA
SOUTH AMERICA
Moche Culture A.D. 400
INDIAN OCEAN
AUSTRALIA
N
W
E
S
0 1,000 2,000 mi.
0 1,000 2,000 km
Miller Projection
ANTARCTICA

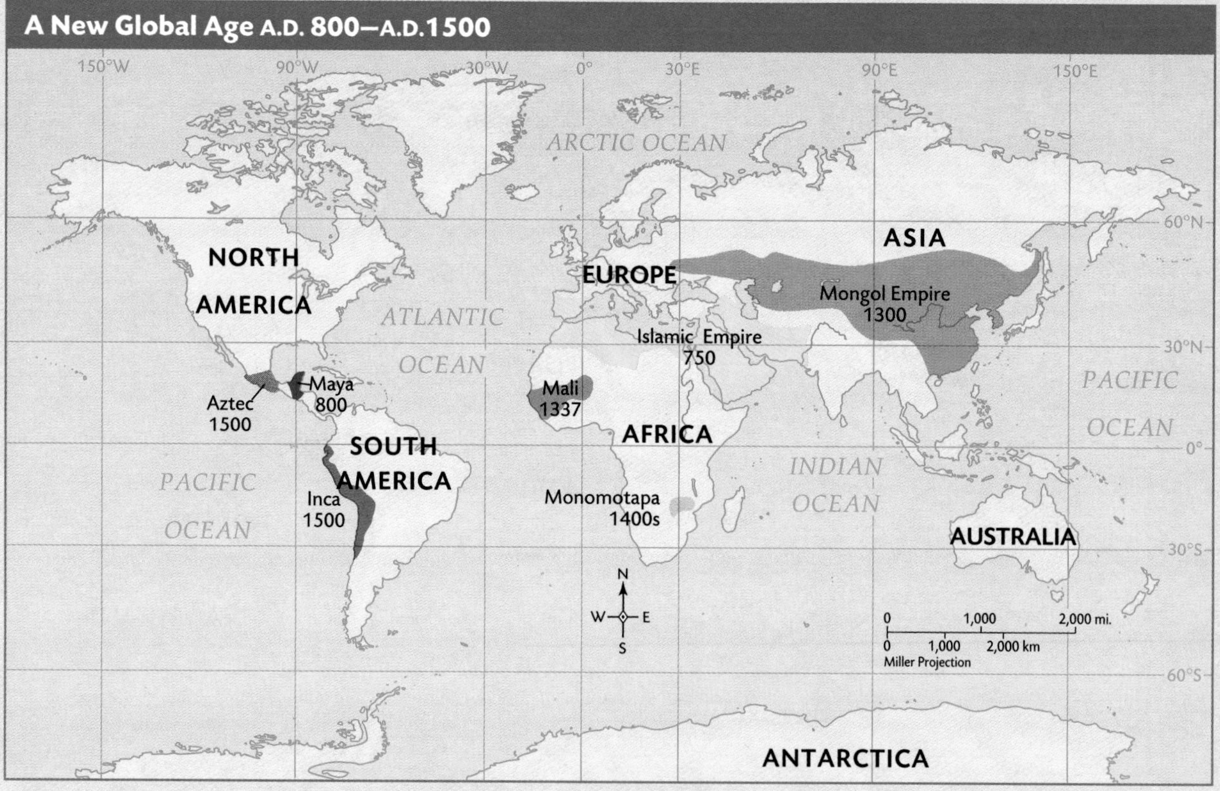
A New Global Age A.D. 800—A.D. 1500
150°W
90°W
30°W
0°
30°E
90°E
150°E
60°N
30°N
0°
30°S
60°S
ARCTIC OCEAN
ASIA
NORTH AMERICA
EUROPE
Mongol Empire 1300
Islamic Empire 750
ATLANTIC OCEAN
PACIFIC OCEAN
Aztec 1500
Maya 800
Mali 1337
AFRICA
SOUTH AMERICA
Inca 1500
Monomotapa 1400s
INDIAN OCEAN
AUSTRALIA
N
W
E
S
0 1,000 2,000 mi.
0 1,000 2,000 km
Miller Projection
ANTARCTICA

Age of Imperialism 1870–1914

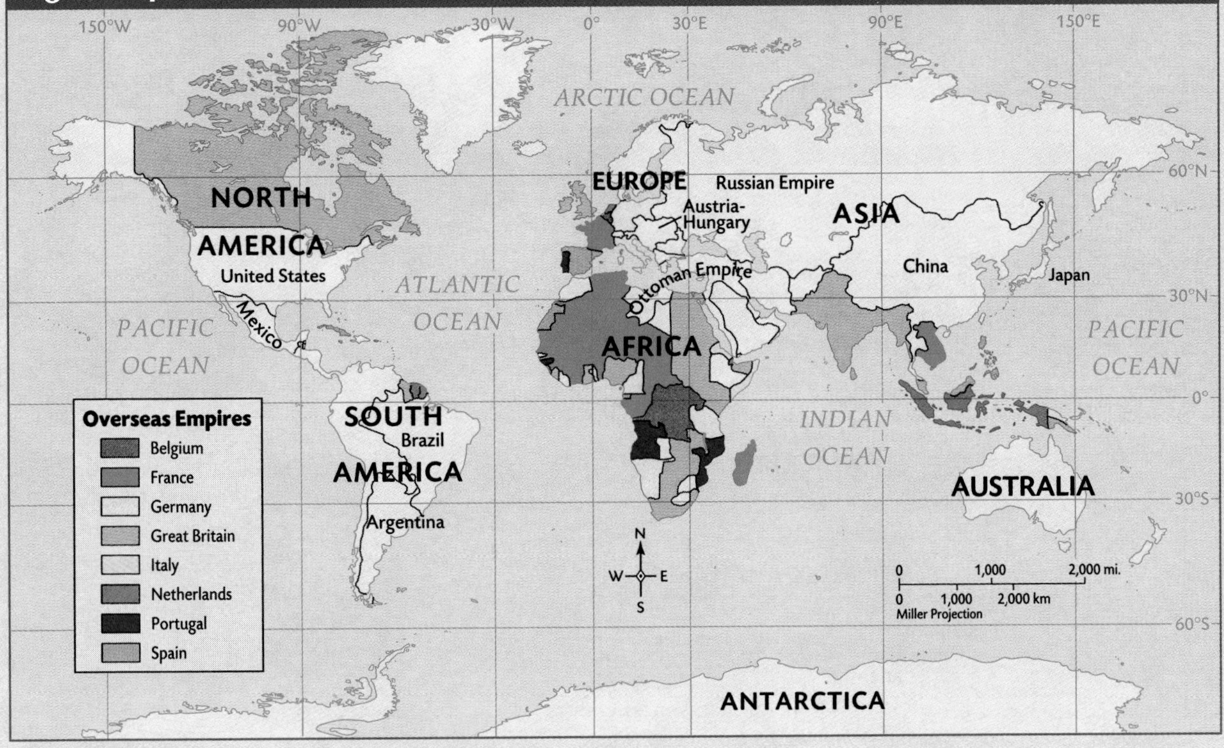
150°W
90°W
30°W
0°
30°E
90°E
150°E
60°N
30°N
0°
30°S
60°S
ARCTIC OCEAN
NORTH AMERICA
United States
Mexico
PACIFIC OCEAN
ATLANTIC OCEAN
SOUTH AMERICA
Brazil
Argentina
EUROPE
Russian Empire
Austria-Hungary
Ottoman Empire
ASIA
China
Japan
AFRICA
INDIAN OCEAN
PACIFIC OCEAN
AUSTRALIA
ANTARCTICA
Overseas Empires
Belgium
France
Germany
Great Britain
Italy
Netherlands
Portugal
Spain
N
W
E
S
0
1,000
2,000 mi.
0
1,000
2,000 km
Miller Projection

Global Civilization Today

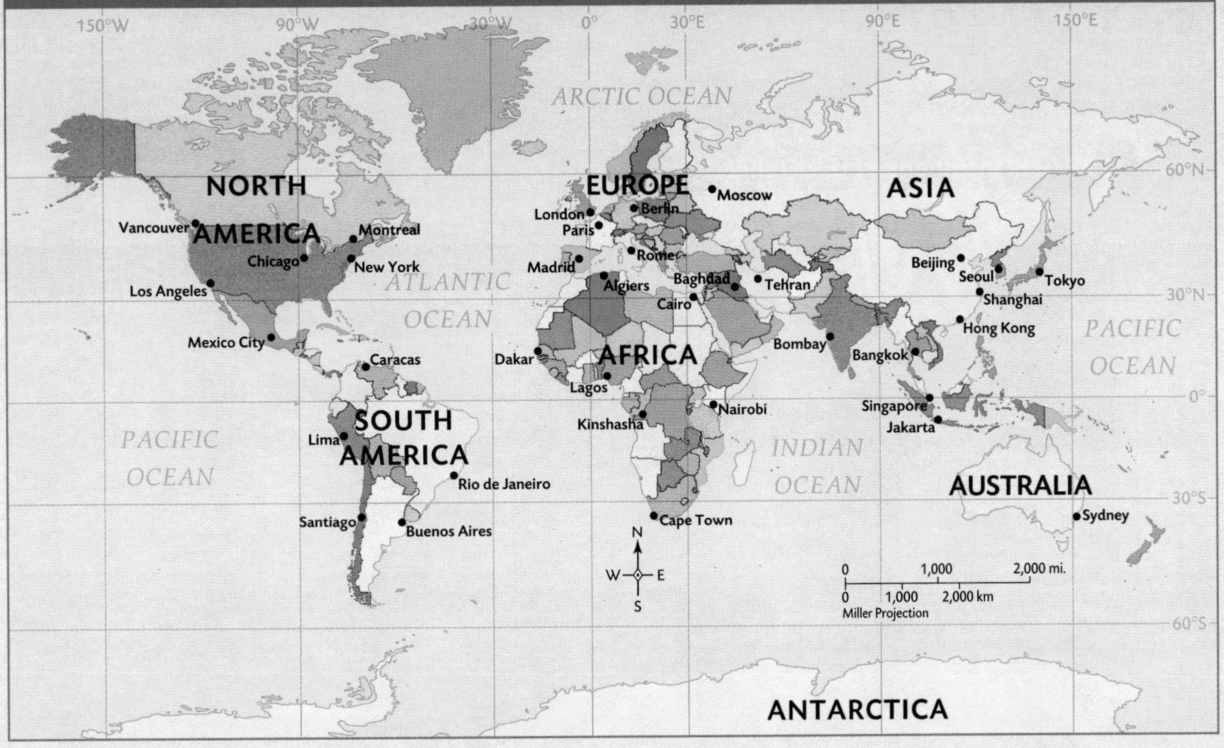
150°W
90°W
30°W
0°
30°E
90°E
150°E
60°N
30°N
0°
30°S
60°S
ARCTIC OCEAN
NORTH AMERICA
Vancouver
Montreal
Chicago
New York
Los Angeles
Mexico City
ATLANTIC OCEAN
PACIFIC OCEAN
Caracas
SOUTH AMERICA
Lima
Rio de Janeiro
Santiago
Buenos Aires
EUROPE
London
Paris
Berlin
Moscow
Madrid
Rome
Algiers
Baghdad
Tehran
Cairo
AFRICA
Dakar
Lagos
Kinshasha
Nairobi
Cape Town
ASIA
Beijing
Seoul
Tokyo
Shanghai
Hong Kong
Bombay
Bangkok
Singapore
Jakarta
INDIAN OCEAN
PACIFIC OCEAN
AUSTRALIA
Sydney
ANTARCTICA
N
W
E
S
0
1,000
2,000 mi.
0
1,000
2,000 km
Miller Projection

World Trade Power

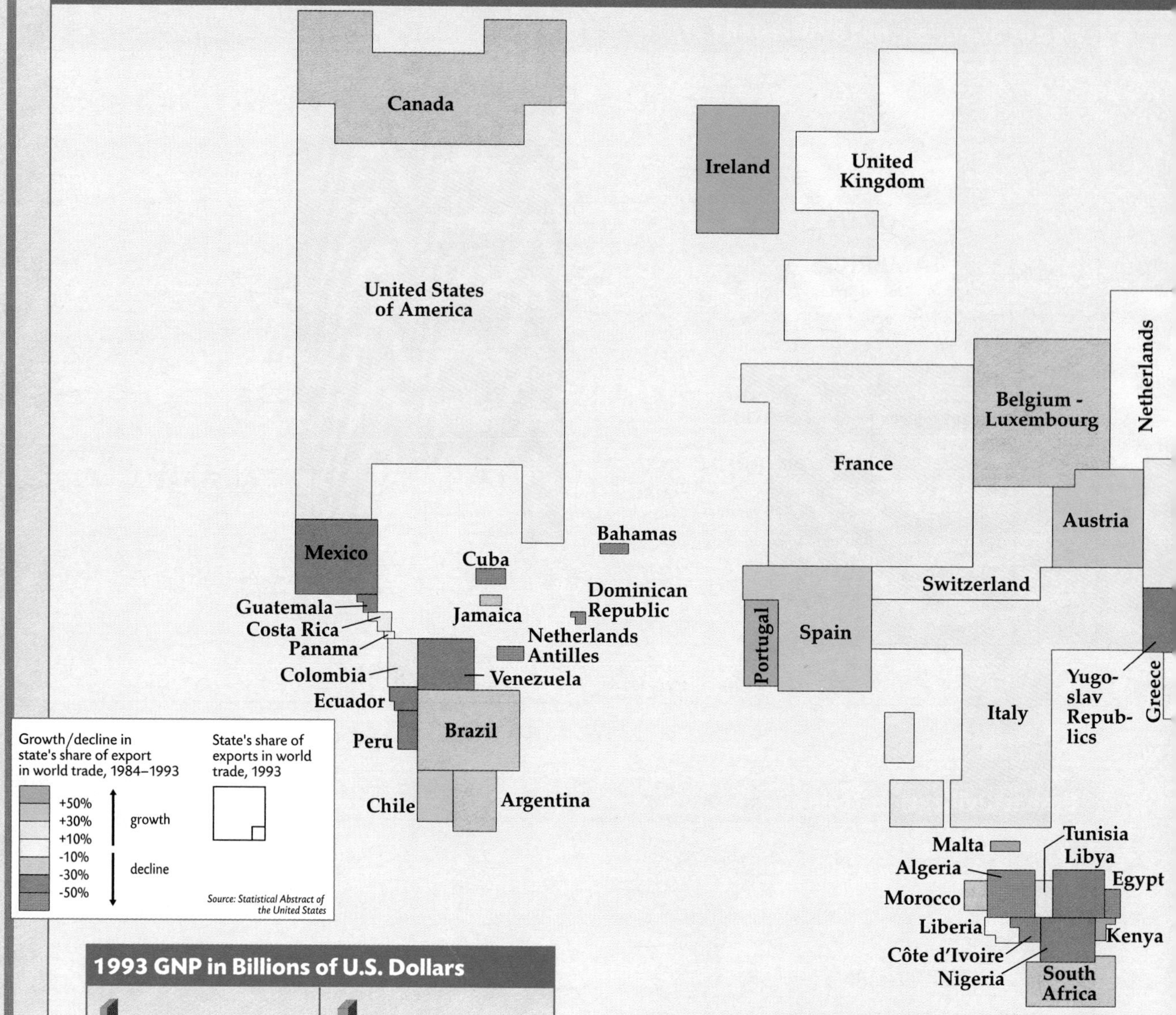

1993 GNP in Billions of U.S. Dollars

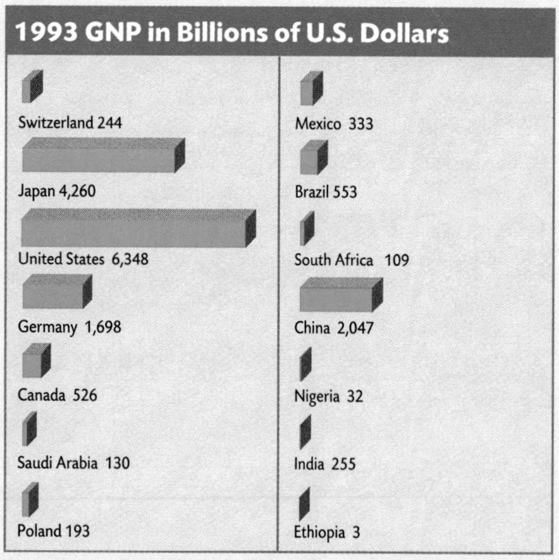

1993 Per Person GNP in U.S. Dollars

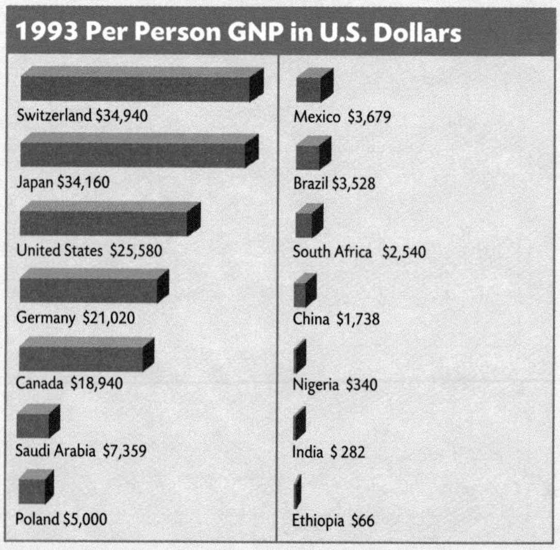

World Trade Power

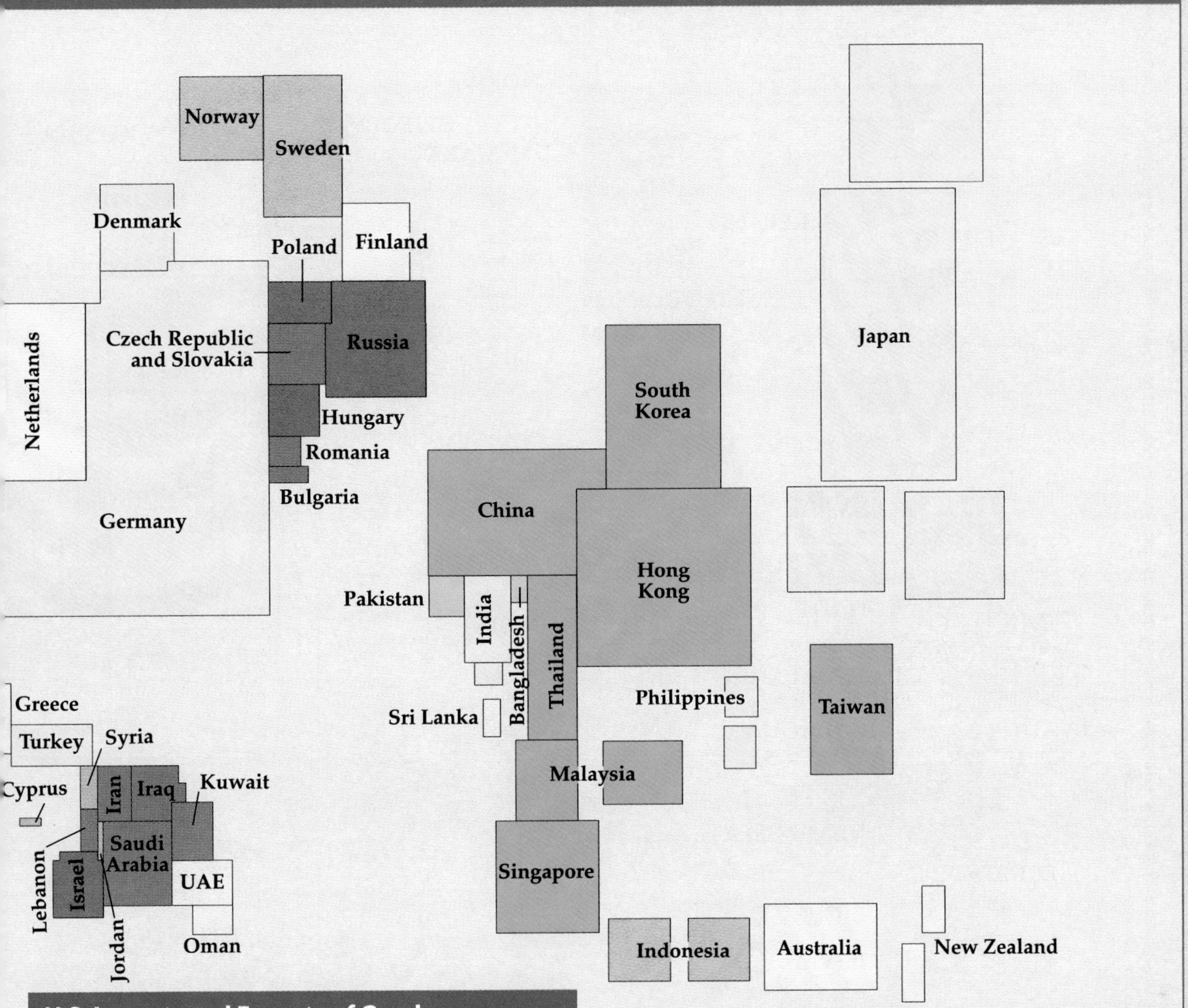

U.S. Imports and Exports of Goods

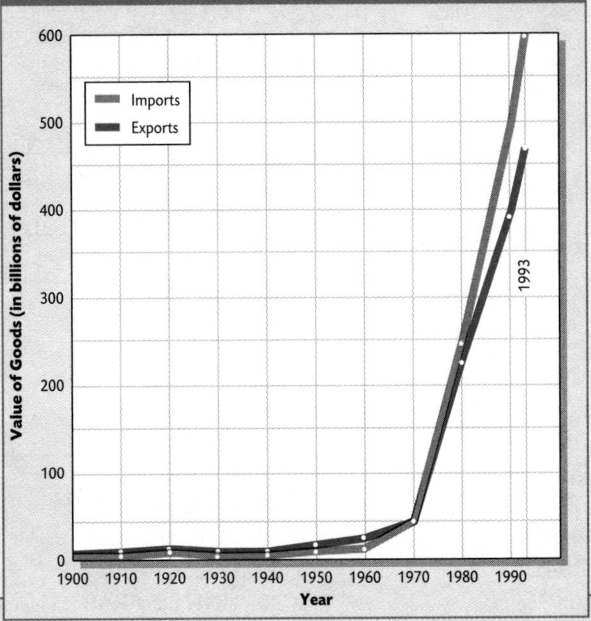

U.S Trade Balance

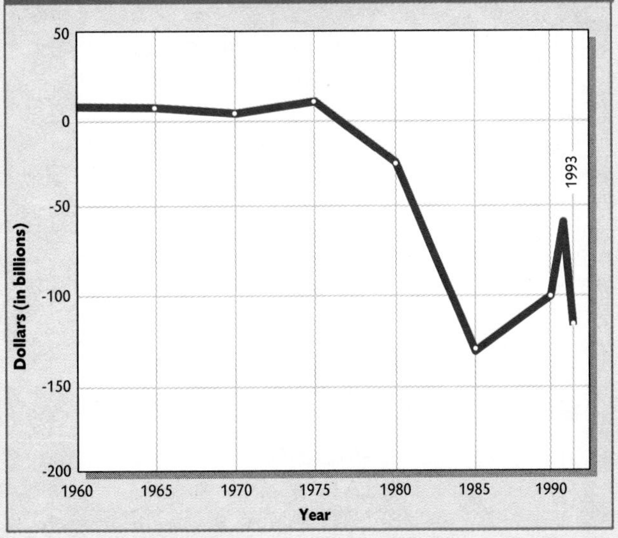

World Population

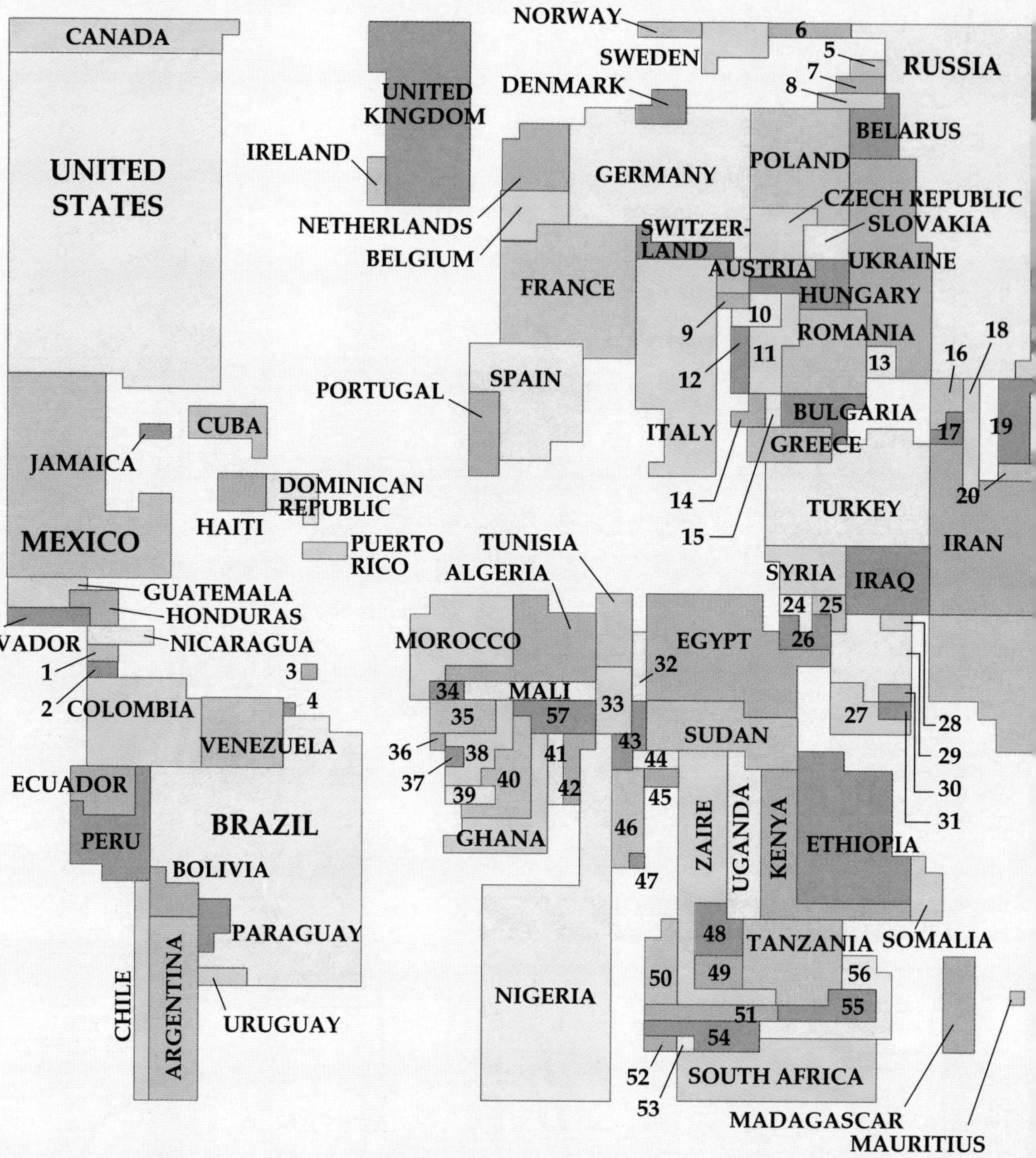

EACH AREA'S SIZE IS PROPORTIONATE TO ITS POPULATION.

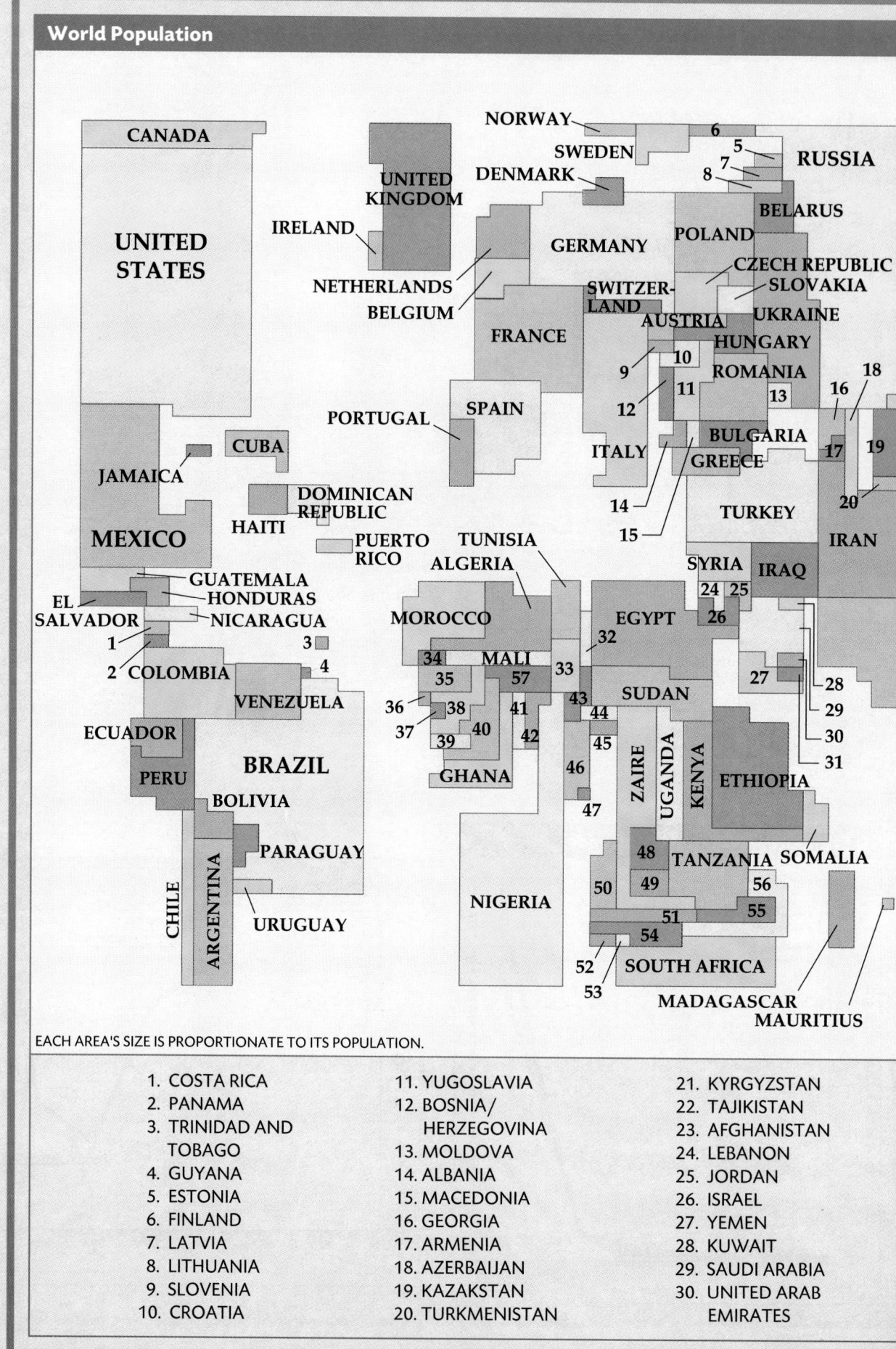

1. COSTA RICA
2. PANAMA
3. TRINIDAD AND TOBAGO
4. GUYANA
5. ESTONIA
6. FINLAND
7. LATVIA
8. LITHUANIA
9. SLOVENIA
10. CROATIA
11. YUGOSLAVIA
12. BOSNIA/ HERZEGOVINA
13. MOLDOVA
14. ALBANIA
15. MACEDONIA
16. GEORGIA
17. ARMENIA
18. AZERBAIJAN
19. KAZAKSTAN
20. TURKMENISTAN
21. KYRGYZSTAN
22. TAJIKISTAN
23. AFGHANISTAN
24. LEBANON
25. JORDAN
26. ISRAEL
27. YEMEN
28. KUWAIT
29. SAUDI ARABIA
30. UNITED ARAB EMIRATES

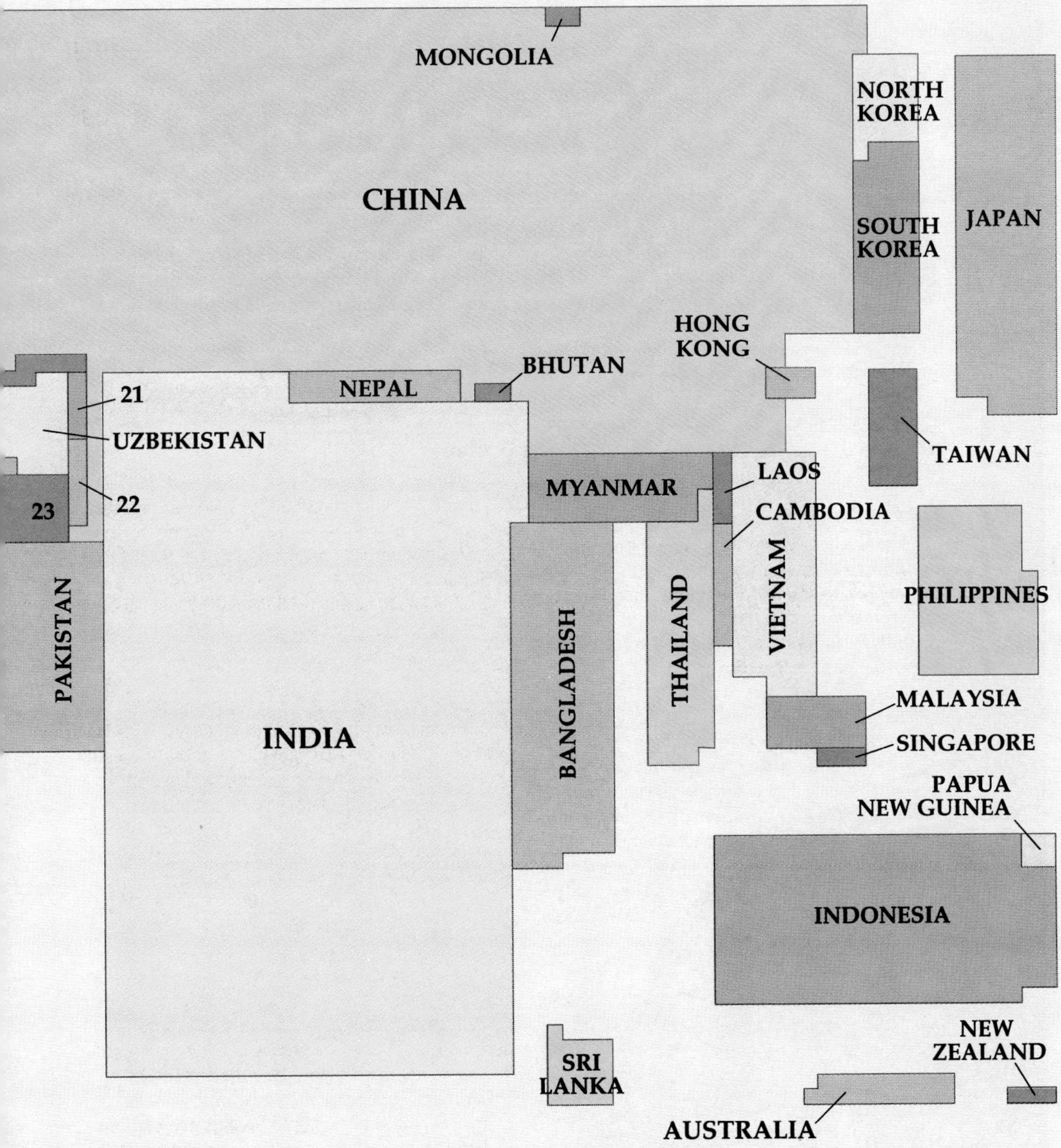

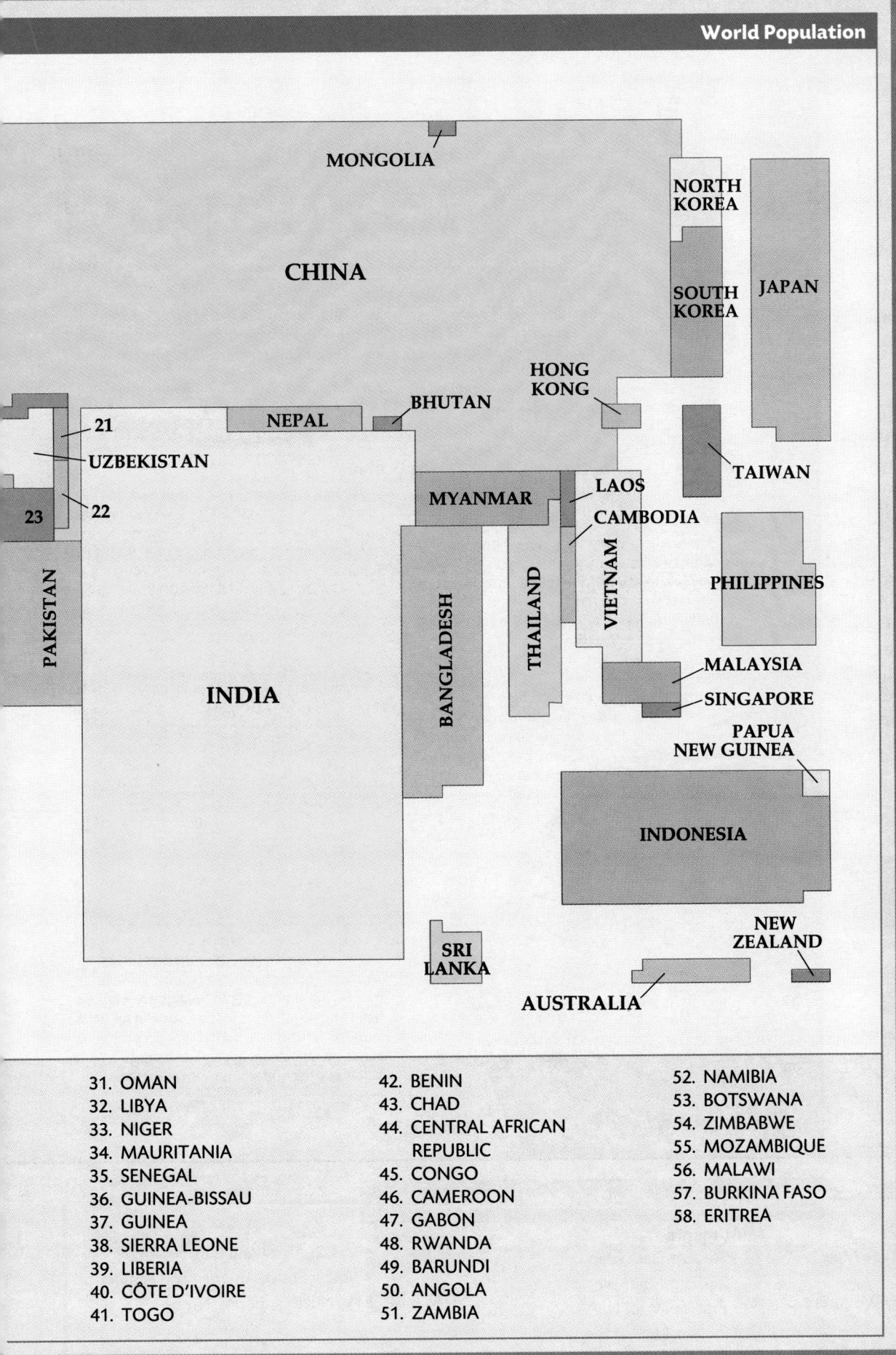

31. OMAN
32. LIBYA
33. NIGER
34. MAURITANIA
35. SENEGAL
36. GUINEA-BISSAU
37. GUINEA
38. SIERRA LEONE
39. LIBERIA
40. CÔTE D'IVOIRE
41. TOGO
42. BENIN
43. CHAD
44. CENTRAL AFRICAN REPUBLIC
45. CONGO
46. CAMEROON
47. GABON
48. RWANDA
49. BARUNDI
50. ANGOLA
51. ZAMBIA
52. NAMIBIA
53. BOTSWANA
54. ZIMBABWE
55. MOZAMBIQUE
56. MALAWI
57. BURKINA FASO
58. ERITREA

Introducing the Geography Handbook

Handbook Objectives

1. **Understand** the purpose and uses of globes and map projections.
2. **Identify** most commonly used geographic terms.
3. **Analyze** geographic factors that have shaped the course of historic events.

Vocabulary Pre-check

Survey the students' knowledge of geographic terms. Create three columns on the chalkboard with the following headings: *landforms*, *map elements*, and *bodies of water*.

List one term that fits each column, such as "canyon," "meridian," and "bay." Ask students to volunteer as many other terms for each column as they can.

Have students turn to page 4 and read the geographic dictionary. Then have them close their books and continue suggesting terms for each column on the chalkboard.

TEACH

NATIONAL GEOGRAPHIC SOCIETY

CD-ROM

PICTURE ATLAS OF THE WORLD

You and your students can see the challenges and solutions involved in making maps by viewing the Mapping Our World animation "Round Earth on Flat Paper."

What Is Geography?

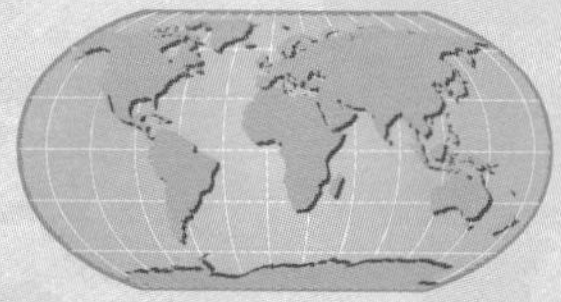

The story of humanity begins with **geography**—the study of the earth in all of its variety. Geography concerns the earth's land, water, and plant and animal life. It also tells you about the people who live on the earth, the places they have created, and how these places differ. The earth is a planet of diverse groups of people. A study of geography can help you see why the people of the earth are so diverse.

The Five Themes of Geography

The study of geography can be organized around five themes: **location**, **place**, **human/environment interaction**, **movement**, and **region**. Geographers use these five themes to study and classify all parts of the earth and its variety of human activity.

Geography and World History

World geography is especially important to the study of world history. Historians use geography to explain connections between the past and the present. They study how places looked in the past, how places and patterns of human activity have changed over time, and how geographic forces have influenced these changes.

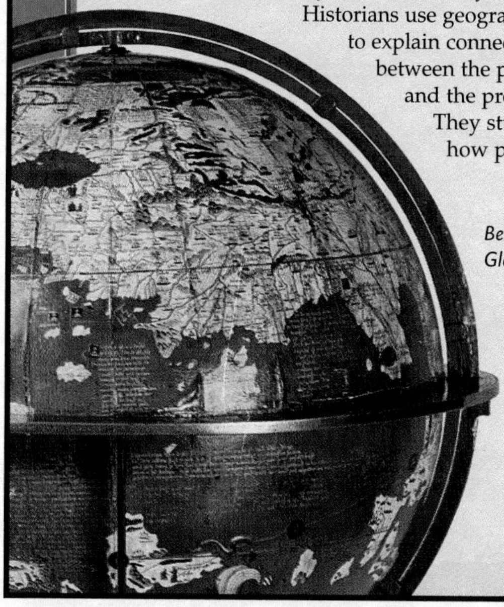

Behaim's Globe

GLOBES AND MAPS

Globes

Photographs from space show the earth in its true form—a great ball spinning around the sun. The only accurate way to draw the earth is as a globe, or a round form. A globe gives a true picture of the earth's size and the shape of the earth's landmasses and bodies of water. Globes also show the true distances and true directions between places.

Maps

A map is a flat drawing of the earth's surface. People use maps to locate places, plot routes, and judge distances. Maps can also display useful information about the world's peoples.

What advantages does a map have over a globe? Unlike a globe, a map allows you to see all areas of the world at the same time. Maps also show much more detail and can be folded and more easily carried.

Maps, however, have their drawbacks. As you can imagine, drawing a round object on a flat surface is very difficult. Cartographers, or mapmakers, have drawn many **projections**, or kinds of maps. Each map projection is a different way of showing the round earth on a flat map. This is because it is impossible to draw a round planet on a flat surface without distorting or misrepresenting some parts of the earth. As a result, each kind of map projection has some distortion. Typical distortions involve distance, direction, shape, and/or area.

GEOGRAPHY HANDBOOK RESOURCES

Reproducible Masters
- Glencoe Social Studies Outline Map Resource Book
- Building Skills in Geography Workbook

Transparencies
- NGS PictureПack Transparencies: Physical Geography of the World

Multimedia
- Student Desk Map
- Zip!Zap!Map! World
- Zip!Zap!Map! USA
- Picture Atlas of the World
- STV: World Geography:
  - Vol. 1: Asia and Australia
  - Vol. 2: Africa and Europe
  - Vol. 3: South America and Antarctica
- STV: North America

Geography Handbook

The Hemispheres

To determine location, distance, and direction on a map or globe, geographers have developed a network of imaginary lines that crisscross the earth. One of these lines, the **Equator**, circles the earth midway between the **North Pole** and the **South Pole**. It divides the earth into "half spheres," or **hemispheres**. The Northern Hemisphere includes all of the land and water between the Equator and the North Pole. The Southern Hemisphere includes all of the land and water between the Equator and the South Pole.

Another imaginary line running from north to south divides the earth into half spheres in the other direction. This line is called the **Prime Meridian**. Every place east of the Prime Meridian is in the Eastern Hemisphere. Every place west of the Prime Meridian is in the Western Hemisphere.

Latitude and Longitude

The Equator and the Prime Meridian are the starting points for two sets of lines used to find any location. The two sets measure distances north or south of the Equator, and east and west of the Prime Meridian.

One set of lines called **parallels** circle the earth and show **latitude**, which is distance measured in degrees (°) north and south of the Equator at 0° latitude. The letter *N* or *S* following the degree symbol tells you if the location is north or south of the Equator. The North and South Poles are at 90° North (*N*) and South (*S*) latitude.

Two important parallels in between the poles are the **Tropic of Cancer** at 23 1/2°N latitude and the **Tropic of Capricorn** at 23 1/2°S latitude. You can also find the **Arctic Circle** at 66 1/2°N latitude and the **Antarctic Circle** at 66 1/2°S latitude.

The second set of lines called **meridians** run north to south from the North Pole to the South Pole. These lines signify **longitude**, which is distance measured in degrees east (*E*) or west (*W*) of the Prime Meridian at 0° longitude. On the opposite side of the earth is the International Date Line, or the 180° meridian.

Hemispheres

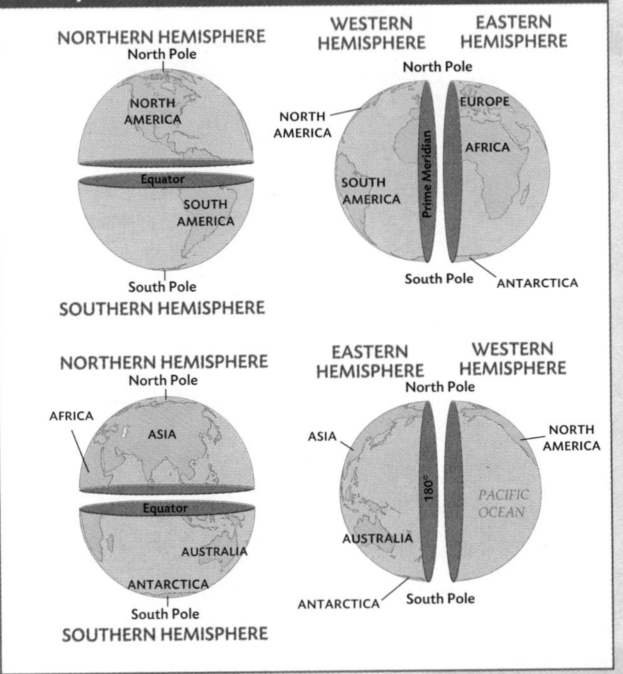

The Grid System

Lines of latitude and longitude cross one another in the form of a **grid system**. You can use the grid system to find where places are exactly located on a map or globe. Each place on Earth has an address on the grid. This grid address is the place's **coordinates**—its degrees of latitude and longitude. For example, the coordinates of the city of San Francisco are 38°N latitude and 122°W longitude. This means that San Francisco lies about 38 degrees (°) north of the Equator and 122 degrees (°) west of the Prime Meridian. Where those two lines cross is called the **absolute location** of the city.

Map Symbols

Maps can direct you down the street, across the country, or around the world. There are as many different kinds of maps as there are uses for them. Being

NATIONAL GEOGRAPHIC SOCIETY

CD-ROM

PICTURE ATLAS OF THE WORLD

Have students view the Mapping Our World animation "Where in the World," which introduces the concepts of latitude and longitude.

Skills Practice

Reading a Diagram Have students look at the illustrations on this page. **What hemisphere contains most of the landmass of the earth?** *(the Northern Hemisphere)* **What continents are entirely in the Western Hemisphere?** *(North America and South America)* **What line divides the earth into the Northern and Southern Hemispheres?** *(Equator)* **What line divides the earth into the Eastern and Western Hemispheres?** *(Prime Meridian)*

Cultural Perspectives

Universal Language The grid system provides a kind of universal language. Citizens of all countries, no matter how different their cultures, speak the same language of latitude and longitude.

COOPERATIVE LEARNING ACTIVITY

Game Have students prepare a game called "My Grid Address." Students should write out grid address question cards, with each card containing one multiple-choice question regarding the grid address of a well-known location—a city, lake, mountain, and so on. A sample question format is "My grid address is 36° north latitude and 140° east longitude. What city am I? a. Madrid b. Tokyo c. New York d. Cairo." After students have completed at least 30-40 cards, organize them into teams and play "My Grid Address." Allow five points for each correct answer. **L1**

Geography Handbook

Types of Maps Explain that general-purpose maps may include both physical and political information. Students should always carefully read the map title and key to determine the purpose of the map. Because of changes that occur in history, political maps should always identify the time period that they represent. If a political map does not identify a date, we usually assume that it is a current map.

Map Study

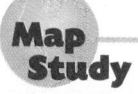

Have students look at the LANDSAT map and the San Francisco Bay Area map. Both maps are of the same general area.

Map Skills Practice

Reading a Map What is the value of the LANDSAT map? *(Changes to the earth's environment can be tracked by comparing LANDSAT maps over a period of time.)*

Have students each write a paragraph detailing the information about San Francisco that can be learned from the San Francisco Bay Area map. Have students read a detail from their paragraphs that they believe no other student recorded.

Who?What?Where?When?

Antarctica covers about 3.2 million square miles (8.3 million sq. km) of landmass. Including the islands and shelf ice, it is about 5.4 million square miles (14 million sq. km). No nation owns this territory. The Antarctica Treaty, signed by 16 nations, allows only the exploration of the continent.

able to read a map begins with learning about its parts.

The **map key** explains the symbols used on the map. On a map of the world, for example, dots mark cities and towns. On a road map, various kinds of lines stand for paved roads, dirt roads, and interstate highways. A pine tree symbol may represent a state park, while an airplane is often the symbol for an airport.

An important first step in reading any map is to find the direction marker. A map has a symbol that tells you where the **cardinal directions**—north, south, east, and west—are positioned. Sometimes all of these directions are shown with a **compass rose**.

A measuring line, often called a **scale bar**, helps you find distance on the map. The map's **scale** tells you what distance on the earth is represented by the measurement on the scale bar. For example, 1 inch on a map may represent 100 miles on the earth. Knowing the scale allows you to visualize how large an area is, as well as to measure distances. Map scales are usually given in both miles and kilometers, a metric measurement of distance.

TYPES OF MAPS

Maps of many different kinds are used in this text to help you see the connection between world geography and the history of humanity.

General-Purpose Maps

Maps that show a wide range of general information about an area are called **general-purpose maps**. Two of the most common general purpose maps are physical maps and political maps. **Physical maps** show natural features, such as rivers and mountains. **Political maps** show places that people have created, such as cities or the boundaries of countries and states.

Special-Purpose Maps

Special-purpose maps show information on specific topics, such as climate, land use, or vegetation. Human activities, such as exploration routes, territorial expansion, or battle sites, also appear on special purpose maps. Colors and map key symbols are especially important on this type of map.

LANDSAT Maps

LANDSAT maps are made from photographs taken by camera-carrying LANDSAT satellites in space. The cameras record millions of energy waves invisible to the human eye. Computers then change this information into pictures of the earth's surface. With LANDSAT images, scientists can study whole mountain ranges, oceans, and geographic regions. Changes to the earth's environment can also be tracked using the satellite information.

LANDSAT map of San Francisco Bay area

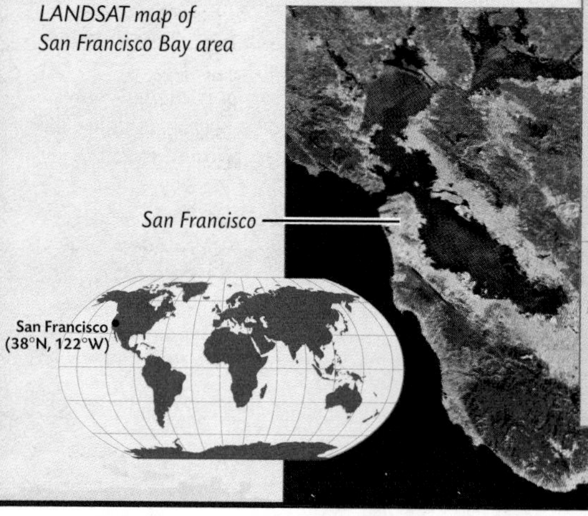

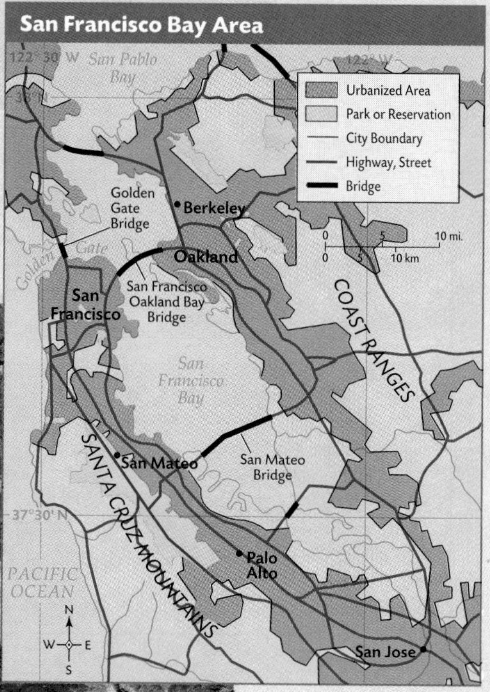

MORE ABOUT...

Cartography British sea captain James Cook was the greatest explorer and cartographer of the eighteenth century. In three voyages, undertaken between 1769 and 1779, Cook surveyed and charted huge areas of the Pacific Ocean. He also verified the existence of the continent of Antarctica and provided a wealth of information about the south Atlantic, south Indian, and Arctic Oceans. Using the latest scientific developments, Cook created incredibly accurate charts of his journeys. These charts revolutionized cartographic knowledge and practices.

CONTINENTS

Geographers divide most of the earth's land surface into seven large landmasses called **continents**. The continents are North America, South America, Europe, Africa, Asia, Australia, and Antarctica. Asia is the largest continent in size, and Australia is the smallest.

LANDFORMS

Landforms cover about 30 percent of the surface of the earth. **Landforms**, or the natural features of the earth's surface, include **mountains**, **hills**, **plateaus**, and **plains**. Geographers describe each landform by its **elevation**, or height above sea level, and by its **relief**, or changes in height.

Mountains

Mountains are the highest of the world's landforms. They rise from about 2,000 feet (610 m) to more than 20,000 feet (6,100 m) above sea level. One of the peaks in the Himalaya mountain ranges of central Asia is Mount Everest, the world's highest mountain. It towers 29,028 feet (8,848 m) above sea level. Other mountains, such as the Appalachians in eastern North America, are not as high. Mountains generally have high relief.

Hills, Plateaus, and Plains

Hills are lower than mountains and generally rise from about 500 to 2,000 feet (152 to 610 m) above sea level. They generally have moderate relief.

Plateaus are raised areas of flat or almost flat land. Most plateaus have low relief and vary in elevation from about 300 to 3,000 feet (91 to 914 m) above sea level. The world's largest plateau area is the Tibetan Plateau in central Asia. It covers about 715,000 square miles (1,852,000 sq. km) and has an average altitude of 16,000 feet (4,877 m) above sea level.

Plains are large areas of flat or gently rolling land that generally rise less than 1,000 feet (305 m) above sea level and have low relief. The world's largest plain is the North European Plain, which stretches for more than 1,000 miles (1,609 km) from the western coast of France to the Ural Mountains in Russia.

BODIES OF WATER

About 70 percent of the earth's surface is covered with water. Geographers identify bodies of water by their shapes and sizes. The major types include oceans, seas, bays, gulfs, lakes, and rivers.

Oceans and Seas

The largest bodies of water in the world are the four saltwater **oceans**—the Pacific, the Atlantic, the Indian, and the Arctic. The Pacific Ocean is the largest ocean, covering about 64 million square miles (165,760,000 sq. km)—more than all the land areas of the earth combined.

Seas are smaller bodies of salt water that are usually in part surrounded by land. The world's largest sea is East Asia's South China Sea, with an area of 1,148,500 square miles (2,975,000 sq. km).

Bays and Gulfs

Still smaller bodies of salt water are gulfs and bays. **Bays** are extensions of a sea usually smaller than a gulf. The largest bay in the world measured by shoreline is Hudson Bay, Canada, with a shoreline of 7,623 miles (12,265 km) and an area of 476,000 square miles (1,233,000 sq. km). Measured by area, the Bay of Bengal, in the Indian Ocean and bordering South Asia and part of Southeast Asia, is larger at 839,000 square miles (2,173,000 sq. km).

Lakes and Rivers

Other water features of the earth include lakes and rivers. A **lake** is a body of water completely surrounded by land. The world's largest freshwater lake is Lake Superior, one of the five Great Lakes between the United States and Canada. It has an area of 31,820 square miles (82,414 sq. km). The world's largest inland body of water, however, is the Caspian Sea, often considered a saltwater lake. Lying between Europe and Asia and east of the Caucasus Mountains, the Caspian Sea has a total area of 143,550 square miles (371,795 sq. km).

A **river** is a waterway flowing through land and emptying into another body of water. The world's longest river is the Nile River in Africa, which flows into the Mediterranean Sea from the highlands of Ethiopia. The Nile's length is about 4,160 miles (6,690 km).

TEACHER NOTES

Geography Handbook

CURRICULUM CONNECTION

SCIENCE
It tastes really salty, but ocean water averages only about 3.5 percent salt. Of this, nearly 3 percent is sodium chloride (regular salt). The rest contains almost every chemical element on earth.

Landforms Mountains have fascinated people throughout history. They have provided refuge and asylum for those in danger; they have served as a buffer between warring states; they have challenged people for the sheer thrill of climbing them. **How many mountain ranges or peaks can you name?** Allow students a few minutes to list on the chalkboard several of the world's best known mountains. **What historic event can you associate with any of the mountains on our list?** *(Accept all legitimate answers such as Hannibal crossing the Alps, American settlers crossing the Rocky Mountains, the Inca building a refuge at Machu Picchu.)*

Cultural Perspectives

Terminology To promote communication, geographers the world over use the same terminology. The terms they use come from many different languages. For example, *tsunami* is a Japanese word meaning "overflowing wave," and *fjord* is a Norwegian word meaning "long, narrow bay."

Geography Handbook

you don't say...

The word *longitude* comes from the Latin word for "length," and *latitude* comes from the Latin word "breadth."

Who?What?Where?When?

There is a point on Earth with **"no" latitude and "no" longitude**. The absolute location where the Prime Meridian and the Equator intersect, off the African coast in the Atlantic Ocean, is 0° N-S, 0° E-W.

CURRICULUM CONNECTION

COMPUTER LITERACY

Computers have revolutionized cartography. They reduce distortions and calculate changes at incredible speeds. They gather, process, and store data about contour reliefs, ethnicities, economics, waterways, and much more. They even produce animated "flow maps," such as those that show storm movement.

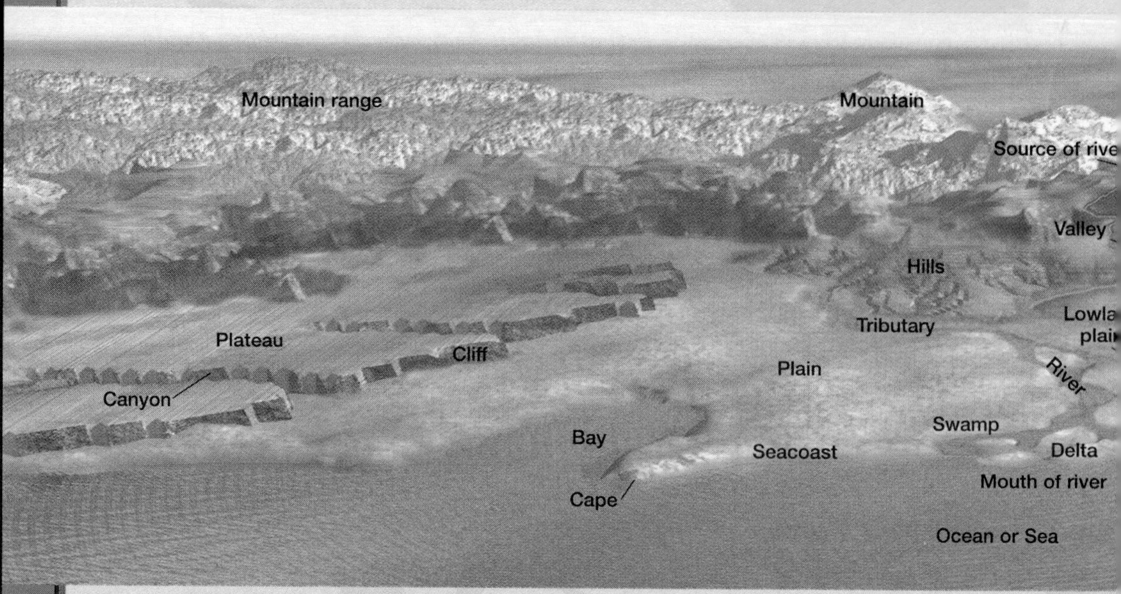

GEOGRAPHIC DICTIONARY

As you read about the world's geography and history, you will discover most of the terms listed and explained below. Many of the terms are pictured in the diagram above. Others you learned earlier in this Geography Handbook.

absolute location–exact location of a place on the earth described by global coordinates
basin–area of land drained by a given river and its branches; area of land surrounded by lands of higher elevations
bay–part of a large body of water that extends into a shoreline
canyon–deep and narrow valley with steep walls
cape–point of land surrounded by a body of water
channel–deep, narrow body of water that connects two larger bodies of water; deep part of a river or other waterway
cliff–steep, high wall of rock, earth, or ice
continent–one of the seven large landmasses on the earth
cultural feature–characteristic that humans have created in a place, such as language, religion, and history
delta–land built up from soil carried downstream by a river and deposited at its mouth
divide–stretch of high land that separates river basins
downstream–direction in which a river or stream flows from its source to its mouth
elevation–height of land above sea level
Equator–imaginary line that runs around the earth halfway between the North and South Poles; used as the starting point to measure degrees of north and south latitude
glacier–large, thick body of slowly moving ice, found in mountains and polar regions
globe–sphere-shaped model of the earth
gulf–part of a large body of water that extends into a shoreline, larger than a bay
harbor–a sheltered place along a shoreline where ships can anchor safely
highland–elevated land area with sloping sides such as a hill, mountain, or plateau hill, smaller than a mountain
island–land area, smaller than a continent, completely surrounded by water
isthmus–narrow stretch of land connecting two larger land areas
lake–a sizable inland body of water
latitude–distance north or south of the Equator, measured in degrees
longitude–distance east or west of the Prime Meridian, measured in degrees
lowland–land, usually level, at a low elevation
map–drawing of all or part of the earth shown on a flat surface
meridian–one of many lines on the global grid

MORE ABOUT...

Geographers work for the federal government in the Defense Mapping Agency, United States Geologic Survey, Central Intelligence Agency, Army Corps of Engineers, National Science Foundation, Smithsonian Institution, and Office of the Geographer in the Department of State.

State environmental and transportation agencies hire geographers as analysts, planners, and cartographers. In the private sector, geographers work as professors, researchers, and cartographers for high-tech computer mapmakers. Businesses as varied as fast-food chains and ski resorts consult geographers about optimal locations for new restaurants and effects of pollution on the slopes.

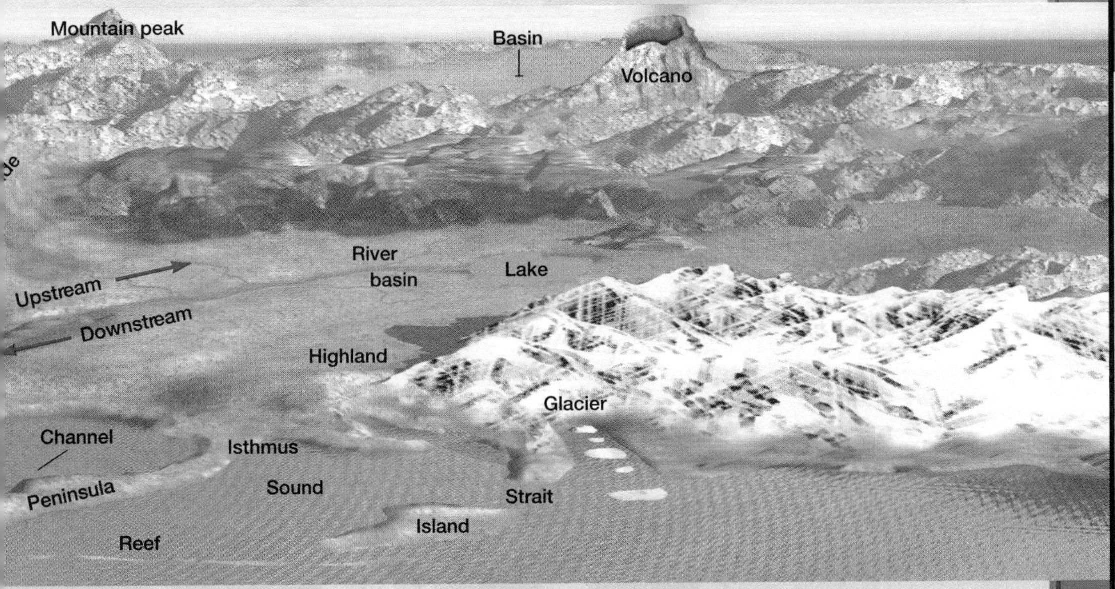

running from the North Pole to the South Pole, used to measure degrees of longitude

mesa–area of raised land with steep sides; smaller than a plateau

mountain–land with steep sides that rises sharply from surrounding land; larger and more rugged than a hill

mountain peak–pointed top of a mountain

mountain range–a series of connected mountains

mouth–(of a river) place where a stream or river flows into a larger body of water

ocean–one of the four major bodies of salt water that surrounds a continent

ocean current–stream of either cold or warm water that moves in a definite direction through an ocean

parallel–one of many lines on the global grid that circle the earth north or south of the Equator; used to measure degrees of latitude

peninsula–body of land almost surrounded by water

physical feature–characteristic of a place occurring naturally, such as a landform, body of water, climate pattern, or resource

plain–area of level land, usually at a low elevation

plateau–area of flat or rolling land at a high elevation

Prime Meridian–line of the global grid running from the North Pole to the South Pole at Greenwich, England; used as the starting point for measuring degrees of east and west longitude

relative location–position of a place on the earth in relation to other places

relief–changes in elevation, either few or many, that occur over a given area of land

river–large stream of water that runs through the land

sea–large body of water completely or partly surrounded by land

seacoast–land lying next to a sea or ocean

sea level–average level of an ocean's surface

sound–body of water between a shoreline and one or more islands off the coast

source–(of a river) place where a river or stream begins, often in high lands

strait–narrow stretch of water joining two larger bodies of water

tributary–small river or stream that flows into a large river or stream; a branch of the river

upstream–direction opposite the flow of a river; toward the source of a river or stream

valley–area of low land between hills or mountains

volcano–mountain created as liquid rock or ash are thrown up from inside the earth

TEACHER NOTES

Geography Handbook

Who?What?Where?When?

Flemish mathematician, geographer, and cartographer **Gerardus Mercator** created his well-known projection in 1568. This projection exaggerates areas as they increase in distance from the Equator, and has been favored by sailors for more than 400 years.

CURRICULUM CONNECTION

CIVICS

Geographic knowledge and perspectives help people be responsible citizens, especially when making decisions that affect their community, region, country, and world.

Who?What?Where?When?

One of the most violent **volcanic eruptions** in history occurred in 1883 on the island of Krakatau in Indonesia. The volcano collapsed from a height of 2,640 feet (692 meters) to 1,000 feet (300 meters) below sea level. Its collapse triggered a tidal wave that killed 36,000 people in nearby Java and Sumatra.

Linking Past and Present

Climate The early Greeks established a classification of climate based only on what they knew of differences between where they lived and lands to the north and south of Greece. They called their own climate *temperate* because it posed few problems of shelter and clothing. They believed that the area south of the Mediterranean became increasingly hotter, so they called these lands *torrid*. Stories told by travelers from the north and the cold winter winds that came from that direction led the Greeks to call that area *frigid*.

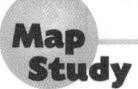

Map Study

Map Skills Practice

Reading a Map What are four classifications that may be used to describe climate today? *(tropical, mid-latitude, high latitude, and dry)* What projection is this map? *(Robinson)*

Who?What?Where?When?

Climatologists agree that the **United States** has the most varied climate on Earth. With its tornadoes, hurricanes, thunderstorms, and blizzards, the climate of the United States also is one of the most violent and unpredictable.

CLIMATE

Climate is the usual pattern of weather events that occurs in an area over a long period of time. Climate is determined by distance from the Equator, by location near large bodies of water, and sometimes by positions near mountain ranges

The world's climates can be organized into four major regions: **tropical, mid-latitude, high latitude**, and **dry**. Some of these regions are determined by their latitude; others are based on the vegetation that grows in them.

Tropical Climates

Tropical climates get their name from the tropics, the areas along the Equator. Temperatures in the tropics change little from season to season. The warm tropical climate region can be separated into two types: tropical rain forest and tropical savanna.

The tropical rain forest climate region is wet in most months, with up to 100 inches (254 cm) of rain a year. In these areas, rain and heat produce lush vegetation and **rain forests**, dense forests that are home to millions of kinds of plant and animal life. The Amazon River basin in South America is the world's largest rain forest area.

The tropical **savanna** climate has two seasons—one wet and one dry. Savannas, or grasslands with few trees, occur in this region. Among the leading tropical savanna climate areas are southern India and eastern Africa.

Mid-Latitude Climates

Mid-latitude, or moderate, climates are found in the middle latitudes of the Northern and Southern Hemispheres. Most of the world's people live in this climate region. The mid-latitude region has a greater variety of climates than other regions. This variety results from the mix of air masses—warm air coming from the tropics and cool air coming from the polar regions. In most places, temperatures change with the seasons.

High Latitude Climates

High latitude, or polar, climate regions lie in the high latitudes of each hemisphere. Climates are cold everywhere in the high latitude regions, some more severe than others.

High latitude climate regions also include highland or mountainous regions even in lower

World Climates

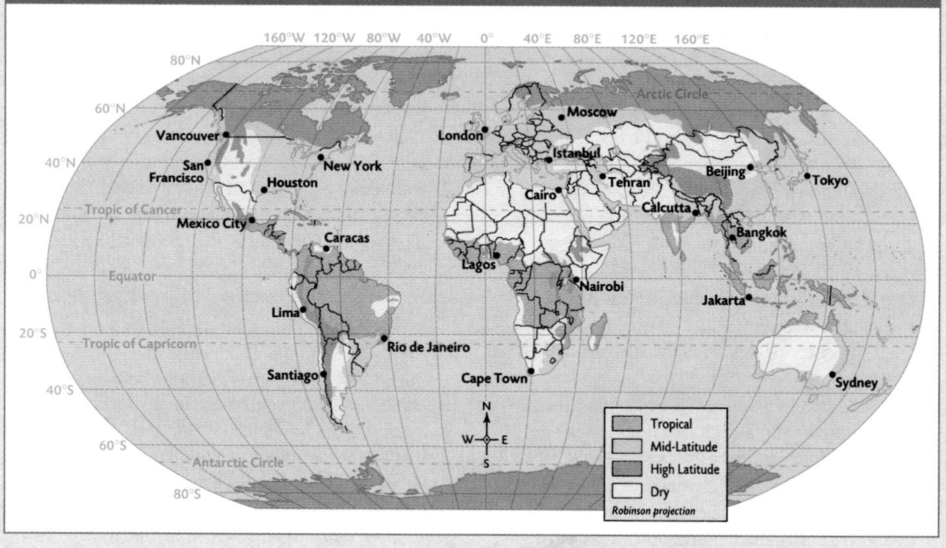

COOPERATIVE LEARNING ACTIVITY

Survival Strategy Organize students into four or more groups. Assign each group a climate type. Encourage group members to imagine that they will be stranded for one year in a remote area that has their assigned climate type. Have groups plan a survival strategy to live in that climate. Each group should identify at least the following: (1) the type of shelter they need and will be able to make or obtain; (2) the type of clothing they need and will be able to make; and (3) the way they will obtain food and water. Have each group present their survival plan to the class, and have the class challenge each plan with situations or conditions likely to arise in the climate region. **L2**

World Land Use and Resources

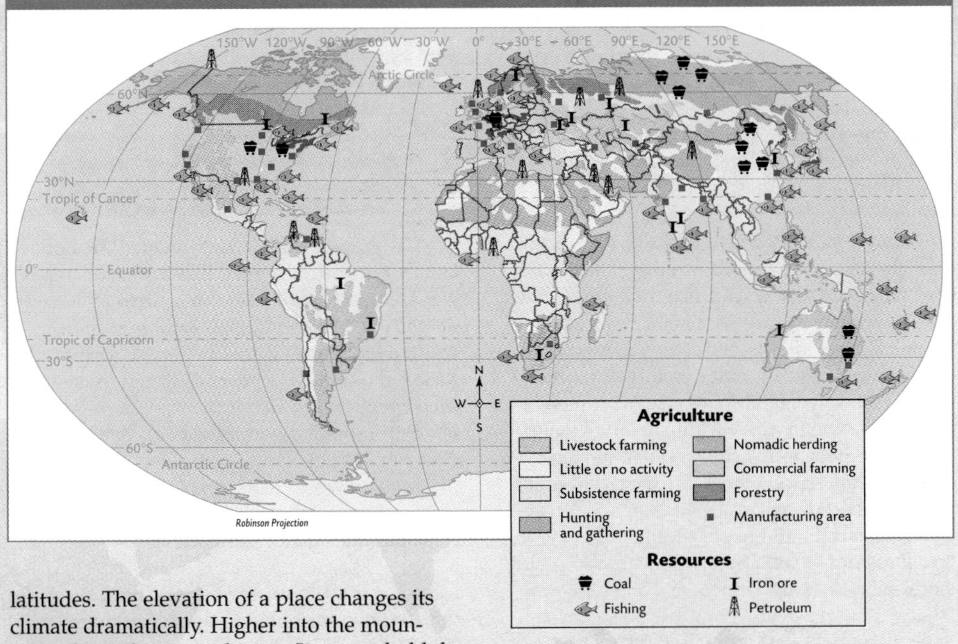

latitudes. The elevation of a place changes its climate dramatically. Higher into the mountains, the air becomes thinner. It cannot hold the heat from the sun, so the temperature drops. Even in the tropics, snow covers the peaks of high mountains.

Dry Climates

Dry climate refers to dry or partially dry areas that receive little or no rainfall. Temperatures can be extremely hot during the day and cold at night. Dry climates can also have severely cold winters.

Nearly an eighth of the world's land surface is dry, with a rainfall of less than 10 inches (25 cm) per year. The Sahara in North Africa is the largest desert in the world. The area covered by the Sahara—3,579,000 square miles (9,270,000 sq. km)—is about the size of the United States.

NATURAL RESOURCES

Natural resources refer to anything from the natural environment that people use to meet their needs. Natural resources include fertile soil, clean water, minerals, trees, and energy sources. Human skills and labor are also valuable natural resources.

Renewable Resources

Some natural resources can be replaced as they are used up. These renewable resources can be replaced naturally or grown fairly quickly. Forests, grasslands, plant and animal life, and rich soil all can be renewable resources if people manage them carefully. A lumber company concerned about future growth can replant as many trees as it cuts. Fishing and whaling fleets can limit the number of fish and whales they catch in certain parts of the ocean.

Nonrenewable Resources

Metals and other minerals found in the earth's crust are nonrenewable resources. They cannot be replaced because they were formed over millions of years by geologic forces within the earth.

One important group of nonrenewable resources is fossil fuels—coals, oil, and natural gas. Industries and people depend on these fuels for energy and as raw materials for plastics and other goods. We also use up large amounts of other metals and minerals, such as iron, aluminum, and phosphates. Some of these can be reused, but they cannot be replaced.

Geography Handbook

Natural Resources Forests are considered renewable natural resources, but they are renewable only if people manage them carefully. Depletion of forests causes changes to both ground and climate. **What are the possible consequences of deforestation?** *(Deforestation causes erosion. It might also cause a change in the world's heating balance or in its water cycle. It could cause many plants and animals to become extinct.)*

Map Study

Help students understand the uneven distribution of resources by studying the map on this page. Point out that the symbols show only the major concentrations of four resources. **Why have coal and petroleum been important natural resources in the last 200 years?** *(The Industrial Revolution depended on these energy sources for its development.)*

Explain that natural resources are only one factor in an area's standard of living. Japan, for example, must import most of its energy resources, yet it has one of world's highest standards of living. Technology, or the ability to use resources effectively, has been the key to development.

TEACHER NOTES

Geography Handbook

Environmental Challenges Efforts to preserve a healthy environment date back hundreds of years. In A.D. 1253 the English Parliament placed bans on burning coal. The increasing use of fossil fuels, expanding populations, and the use of chemicals, however, present new challenges. Discuss the challenges presented on this page. Ask students to talk about how they view the future. Will people be able to preserve a healthy environment?

Who?What?Where?When?

Europe has few areas that have not been affected by human interaction. In recent years Europeans have taken steps to control pollution, despite the high costs. In some areas progress is slow. The estimated cost of cleaning up air pollution in eastern Europe ranges from $200 to $500 billion.

Geography's Impact on World History

Use the examples given for each unit as a launch pad for a general overview of world history.

Unit 1 Explain that most early civilizations developed near water. The Egyptians used the Nile, and many civilizations developed around the Mediterranean and near rivers in China. What are the essential needs that rivers and seas provided to early peoples? *(water for daily use, irrigation, transportation, fishing)*

Unit 2 Waves of Aryans from Europe swept into the Indus River valley around 1500 B.C. From there they spread into northern India. Why were river valleys good routes for early peoples to move from one location to another? *(Before roads, rivers and the lowlands near rivers were the easiest routes to travel.)*

Unit 3 Large oceans helped to separate people into regional civilizations. The Atlantic, the Indian, and the Pacific Oceans kept civilizations in the Americas, Asia, and Africa from much contact with each other. What people were most isolated from the rest of the world until the A.D. 1500s? *(the people in the Americas; some contact took place between Asia and Africa, Europe and Asia, and Europe and Africa in this period.)*

Unit 4 The modern world emerged largely as a result of

ENVIRONMENTAL CHALLENGES

When people use natural resources to make a living, they affect the environment. The unmanaged use of resources is a threat to the environment. Many human activities can cause pollution—putting impure or poisonous substances into the land, water, and air.

Land and Water

Only about 11 percent of the earth's surface has land good enough for farming. Chemicals that farmers use may improve their crops, but some also may damage the land. Pesticides, or chemicals that kill insects, can pollute rivers and groundwater, or water that fills tiny cracks in the rock layers below the earth's surface.

Other human activities also pollute soil and water. Oil spills from tanker ships threaten ocean coastal areas. Illegal dumping of dangerous waste products causes problems. Untreated sewage reaching rivers pollutes lakes and groundwater as well. Salt water can also pollute both soil and groundwater.

Air

Industries and vehicles that burn fossil fuels are the main sources of air pollution. Throughout the world, fumes from cars and other vehicles pollute the air. The chemicals in air pollution can seriously damage people's health.

These chemicals combined with precipitation may fall as acid rain, or rain carrying large amounts of sulfuric acid. Acid rain eats away the surfaces of buildings, kills fish, and can destroy entire forests.

Energy

All of the world nations need safe, dependable sources of energy. Fossil fuels are most often used to generate electricity, heat buildings, run machinery, and power vehicles. Fossil fuels, however, are nonrenewable resources. In addition, they contribute to air pollution. So today many countries are trying to discover new ways of using renewable energy sources. Two of these ways are hydroelectric power, the energy generated by falling water, and solar energy, or energy produced by the heat of the sun.

GEOGRAPHY'S IMPACT ON WORLD HISTORY

Geographic factors have shaped the outcome of historical events. Landforms, waterways, climate, and natural resources all have helped or hindered human activities. In many cases, people have learned either to adapt to their environment or to transform it to meet their needs.

Throughout the units of your text, you will discover how geography has shaped the course of events in world history. Here are some examples of the role that geographic factors have played in the story of humanity.

Unit 1 The Rise of Civilizations

Rivers contributed to the rise of many of the world's early civilizations. By 3000 B.C. the Sumerians of the Middle East had set up 12 prosperous city-states in the Tigris-Euphrates River valley. The Fertile Crescent, as the area is often called because of its relatively rich topsoil and its curved shape, was able to support city-state populations ranging from 20,000 to 250,000 people.

Unit 2 Flowering of Civilizations

Landforms and waterways also affected the political relationships of the world's ancient peoples. For example, the rugged landscape of Greece divided the ancient Greeks into separate city-states instead of uniting them into a single nation. Furthermore, closeness to the sea caused the Greek city-states to expand their trade, culture, and sense of civic pride to other parts of the Mediterranean world.

Unit 3 Regional Civilizations

From about A.D. 400 to A.D. 1500, regional civilizations developed at the crossroads of trade between different areas of the world. The city of Makkah (Mecca), in the Middle East's Arabian Peninsula, was a crossroads for caravans from North Africa, Palestine, and the

Persian Gulf. The religion of Islam established a firm base in Makkah, from which it spread to other areas of the Middle East, North Africa, South Asia, and Southeast Asia.

Unit 4 Emergence of the Modern World

The desire to control or to obtain scarce natural resources has encouraged trade and stimulated contact among the world's peoples. At the dawn of the modern era, Asians and Europeans came into contact with one another partly because Europeans wanted Asia's spices and silks. When the Asiatic people known as the Mongols could no longer guarantee safe passage for traders on overland routes, Europeans were forced to consider new water routes to Asia. This opened a new global age that brought the peoples of Europe, Asia, Africa, and the Americas into closer contact with each other.

Unit 5 Age of Revolution

Climate often affects the way a country behaves toward its neighbors. For example, many of Russia's harbors stay frozen during much of the year. In the past, Russia has often gone to war with other countries to capture land for warm water ports. Climate was also one reason why the Russians were able to stop the invasions of French ruler Napoleon Bonaparte in 1812 and the German dictator Adolf Hitler in 1941. The Russians were used to the bitter cold and snow of their country's winter, whereas the invaders were not.

Unit 6 Industry and Nationalism

Exploiting natural resources, such as coal and iron, was an important factor in the growth of the Industrial Revolution. Modern industry started in Great Britain, which had large amounts of coal and iron ore for making steel. Throughout Europe and North America, the rise of factories that turned raw materials into finished goods prompted people eager for employment to move from rural areas to urban centers.

Also, the availability of land and the discovery of minerals in the Americas, Australia, and South Africa caused hundreds of thousands of Europeans to move to these areas in hope of improving their lives. These mass migrations were possible because of improvements in industrial technology and transportation that enabled people to overcome geographic barriers.

Unit 7 World in Conflict

Environmental disasters during the first part of the 1900s affected national economies in various parts of the world. For example, during the 1930s, winds blew away so much of the soil in the Great Plains of central North America that the area became known as the Dust Bowl. Ruined by the drought, many farmers packed up their belongings and headed west. It took many years of normal rainfall and improved farming techniques to transform the Great Plains from a Dust Bowl into productive land once again.

Unit 8 The Contemporary World

As the year 2000 approaches, the world's peoples have become more aware of the growing scarcity of nonrenewable resources. Oil takes millions of years to form, and the earth's supply is limited. Industrialized countries like the United States consume far more oil than they produce and must import large amounts. Many experts believe that the world's fossil fuels will be used up if steps are not taken to limit their consumption and to find alternative sources.

Geography and History Journal

You are about to journey to the past to learn about the people and events that have shaped the world you live in today. Throughout your course of study, keep a record of the events discussed above and any other events in world history that have been affected by geography. When you come to the last unit, you may also want to explore how geography impacts current events or issues: For example, how has geography influenced peacekeeping missions in Bosnia and other parts of the world, or what would happen to Canada geographically if the province of Quebec were to separate and form an independent nation? On a world map locate the places where these historical events have occurred, and identify the units of study in your text in which they are discussed.

cultural exchange among people who had once been separated from each other. **In what ways are cultural contacts increasing today?** *(increased trade, travel, and telecommunications)*

Unit 5 Ideals of the American Revolution and the French Revolution affected people in other lands. Within a few years revolution spread through Latin America. **Why did ideals of these revolutions spread so quickly?** *(People had overcome the barriers that had separated civilizations—oceans and communications.)*

Unit 6 Available land and abundant natural resources helped to attract millions of people to the United States. **How did the seemingly inexhaustible resources of the North American continent affect people's attitude toward these resources?** *(Resources were exploited without much concern for their replacement or for the environment.)*

Unit 7 World War I grew out of national rivalries and the effects of imperialism. Imperialism was, in part, a quest for resources. **What is a better way than conquest for a nation to obtain resources?** *(Trade has been an effective means for Japan and many other nations.)*

Unit 8 As the world's population grows and more nations develop industrially, the demand for resources will increase. **How can the world ensure adequate resources and avoid conflict over them?** *(Science can research the use of alternative fuels; recycling can extend the use of resources; nations should consider the long-term costs and negative effects of war and explore the benefits of cooperation.)*

Using Your Geography and History Journal

An interesting and purposeful ***Geography and History Journal*** may be formatted using two columns in a notebook. For each chapter the student could list one or more events that were affected by specific geography listed in the first column. In the second column, the student could write a sentence explaining how geography helped shape history.

To help illustrate the link between history and geography, geographers have identified five themes that can be used to examine the role that geography plays.

Modern mapmaking uses photography as a tool. A LANDSAT satellite provided data for this image of Miami, Florida.

1 **Location** serves as a starting point by asking, "Where is it?" To be more specific, there are two types of location. **Absolute location** refers to the exact location on the earth's surface as measured by latitude (lines north and south of the Equator) and longitude (lines east and west of the Prime Meridian). Every location on the earth can be found in this way.

Relative location is less precise. It helps you orient yourself to a location that is relative to something else. Relative location has been important historically as people decided where to build their cities and establish their civilizations.

This village in Tunisia, North Africa, is at the northern edge of the Sahara. Stone and mud brick buildings give the village and its surroundings a sense of place.

2 The idea of **Place** includes more than just where something is located. It includes those features and characteristics that give an area its own identity or personality. These can be *physical* characteristics—such as landforms, weather, plants, and animals—or *human* characteristics—language, religion, architecture, music, politics, and way of life.

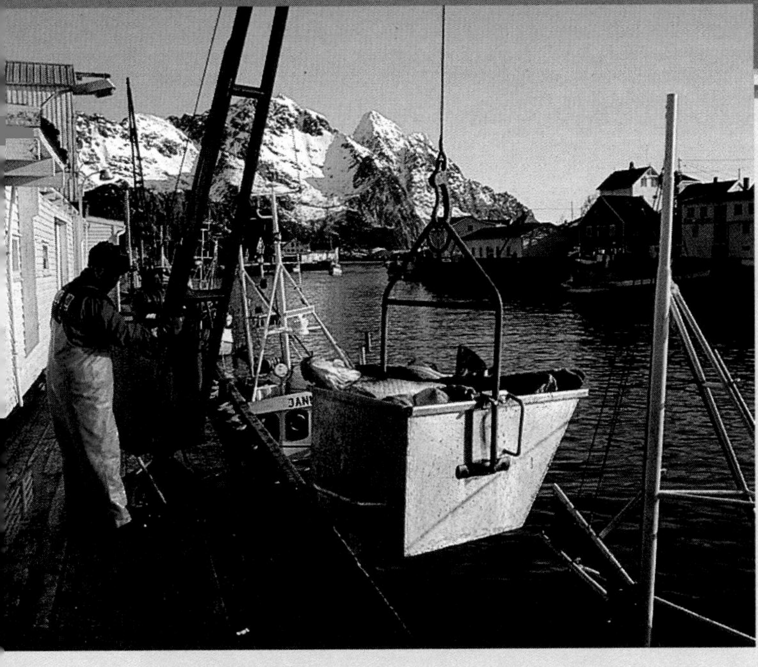

3 **Human/Environment Interaction** focuses on how people respond to and alter their environment. To live comfortably or even to survive in many parts of the world, people must make changes in the environment or adapt to conditions they cannot change, or both.

How people choose to change their environment depends on their attitude toward the natural setting and on the technology they have available to change it.

Fishing is a major industry in Denmark, a small European nation nearly surrounded by water.

4 The **Movement** of people and things between places means that events in other places can have an impact on you personally. Transportation routes, communication systems, and trade connections link people and places throughout the world. Products, ideas, and information are sent around the globe, either slowly by ship or almost instantaneously by electronics.

The movement of people is particularly important because it can spread ideas and cultural characteristics from one place to another. Sometimes those ideas or characteristics are accepted in the new location, and the culture is changed by that linkage.

On the southern coast of China is Hong Kong, one of Asia's busiest ports.

Street signs and buildings in a historical area of Montreal reveal the French character of the Canadian province of Quebec.

5 A **Region** is an area that is unified by some feature or a mixture of features. It is used to generalize about parts of the earth's surface in either physical or human terms. A neighborhood is an example of a small region, while a cultural region that shares a common language would be a larger region. Other regions could be economic, where a particular economic activity is dominant, or political, where the same type of political system is followed.

Geography's Impact on History

While studying the history of the world, you will be learning about the people and events that have shaped the past and provide the framework for the future. As you read *World History: The Human Experience*, pay special attention to the ways in which geography has influenced history and fashioned the world in which you live.

Themes IN WORLD HISTORY

Relation to Environment
The ancient Egyptians develop a civilization in northeastern Africa's Nile River Valley.

Bust of infant sun god

Uniformity
Early Chinese dynasties establish and maintain a strong central government in East Asia.

Terra cotta warriors–Qin dynasty

Change
Early modern Europe enjoys a cultural awakening based on ancient Greek and Roman ideas as well as on Christianity and Judaism.

Renaissance musicians

The Gas Factory

Cultural Diffusion
The Industrial Revolution begins in Great Britain and gradually spreads to other parts of the world.

Innovation
New technology transforms many aspects of life in the modern world.

Shuttle lift-off

World history is a record of the adventures of humankind—both the famous and the ordinary—throughout thousands of years. By studying world history—by gazing across time—you can understand the past and recognize its contribution to the present and the future. World history tells of significant people and events. It also encompasses broad historical themes that happen again and again, providing meaning for events in the past and showing how they affect contemporary life.

World History: The Human Experience introduces 9 key historical themes. Each chapter highlights and develops several of these themes that demonstrate the interconnectedness of ideas and events. These events help organize your study of world history and make connections across time.

Cooperation/Conflict focuses on how people relate to each other throughout history—sometimes in cooperation, working together to accomplish a common goal, at other times in conflict, struggling against one another.

Revolution/Reaction deals with revolution, or the sudden overthrow of long-established ideas and organizations, contrasted with reaction, or the efforts to oppose new ideas and preserve traditional ways.

Change includes political, social, religious, cultural, and economic transformations that influence human activities throughout the centuries.

Diversity/Uniformity focuses on the diversity or variety of world peoples and customs, contrasted with the desire for uniformity or commonality in some societies.

Regionalism/Nationalism deals with a sense of loyalty and belonging, expressed in ties to a region, to a nation, or to the world as a whole—to the global community.

Innovation includes cultural, scientific, and technical breakthroughs that increase knowledge and impact the way people live and think.

Cultural Diffusion focuses on the spread of cultural expressions through a variety of means across nations, regions, and the world.

Movement involves the movement of people throughout history, including patterns of migration, exploration, and colonization as well as imperialism—people in one place on the globe exercising control over people in another place.

Relation to Environment emphasizes human-environment interchange—how people are affected by their environment and, in turn, how they affect that same environment.

Horn player, Benin

Introducing Unit 1

0:00 OUT OF TIME?

If time does not permit teaching each chapter in Unit 1, you may use the Unit Digest beginning on page 96, in conjunction with the Unit Digest Transparencies and Chapter Digest Audiocassettes with activities and tests.

Introducing the Unit

Unit 1 traces the development of humankind from prehistoric groups to early river valley civilizations in Egypt, the Fertile Crescent, the Indus Valley, and China. It then focuses on the kingdoms and empires of the ancient Middle East.

Unit Objectives

After reading Unit 1, students will be able to:

1. describe how prehistoric peoples lived, the development of agriculture and other technological achievements, and the growth of civilizations.
2. explain the achievements of early river valley civilizations in Egypt, the Fertile Crescent, and South Asia.
3. discuss the lasting contributions of ancient Middle Eastern peoples, including the development of monotheism.

History *and the* Humanities

- Focus on World Art Print 7, Egyptian. *Mask of Tutankhamen*
- World History and Art Transparency 1, *Woman's Head;* 3, *Terra-cotta Warriors;* 4, *Standard of Ur: Peace*

Unit 1 **Prehistory–500 B.C.**

Rise of Civilizations

Chapter 1 Human Beginnings

Chapter 2 Early Civilizations

Chapter 3 Kingdoms and Empires in the Middle East

Then & Now *Scholars have divided history into periods according to environmental changes on Earth and cultural developments of mankind. The Paleolithic period or Old Stone Age began about 2 million years ago and lasted until about 12,000 B.C. The earliest evidence of human cultural development was discovered by four teenagers, quite by accident. Jacques Marshal and three young friends entered a cave near Lascaux, France, in 1940 and found the most spectacular cave paintings from Ice Age Europe, created some 17,000 years ago. Cave paintings have been discovered in many parts of the world, but the Lascaux paintings provide the most dramatic and best preserved "snapshots" of early human life yet to be discovered.*

A Global Chronology

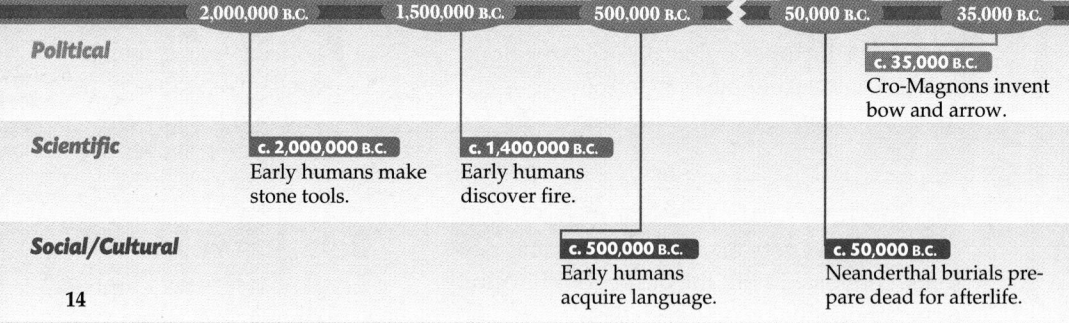

	2,000,000 B.C.	1,500,000 B.C.	500,000 B.C.	50,000 B.C.	35,000 B.C.
Political					c. 35,000 B.C. Cro-Magnons invent bow and arrow.
Scientific	c. 2,000,000 B.C. Early humans make stone tools.	c. 1,400,000 B.C. Early humans discover fire.			
Social/Cultural			c. 500,000 B.C. Early humans acquire language.	c. 50,000 B.C. Neanderthal burials prepare dead for afterlife.	

Then & Now **Art and Society** Unlike early river valley civilizations, which left pyramids and other large monuments, Paleolithic peoples left few traces. The paintings at Lascaux and other sites were not discovered until the twentieth century because they were hidden deep inside caves. The paintings show bison, reindeer, and other animals that Paleolithic peoples hunted. Because Stone Age peoples depended on these animals for food, the cave paintings were probably meant to bring success to the hunters. (See student page 29 for a discussion of cave paintings.) What things do you create that can be considered "art"? *(Answers may include drawings and doodles, homemade gifts such as Christmas or birthday cards, handmade clothing, jewelry, and so on.)* What do these artistic creations show about

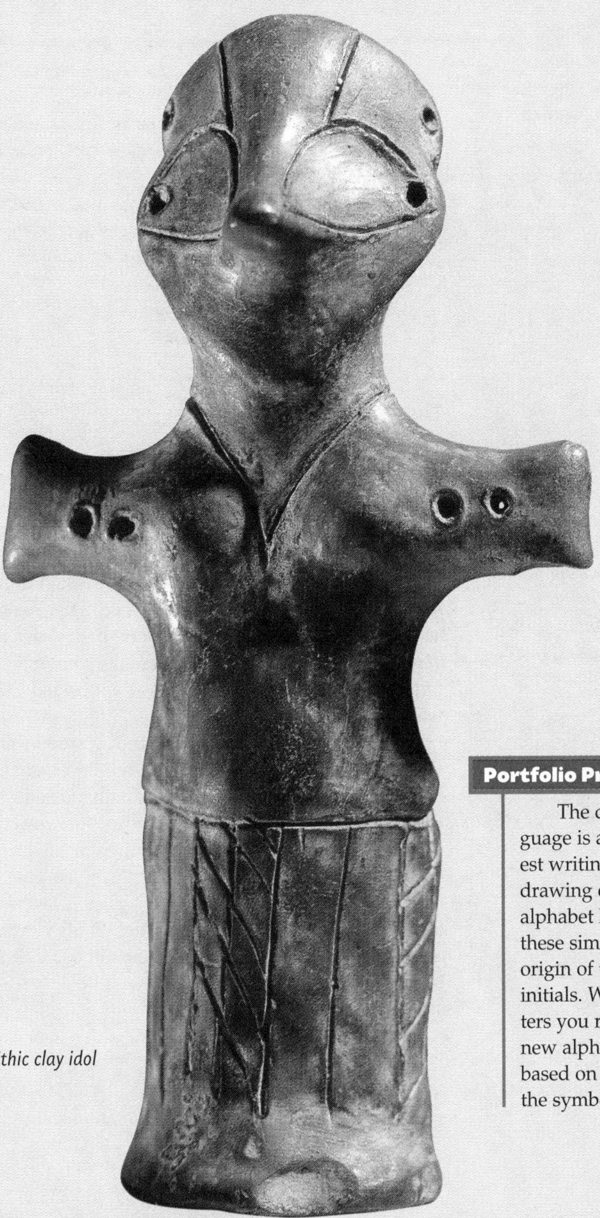

Neolithic clay idol

Portfolio Project

The development of written language is a fascinating study. The earliest writing was a simplified form of drawing objects. The letters of our alphabet have a history going back to these simple drawings. Research the origin of the letters that are your own initials. Write a brief history of the letters you researched. Then create several new alphabet letters using symbols based on modern inventions. Explain the symbols you chose.

4000 B.C. — 3000 B.C. — 2000 B.C. — 1000 B.C.

- **c. 3500 B.C.** Sumerians build first cities.
- **c. 3400 B.C.** Corn and beans cultivated in the Americas.
- **c. 3000 B.C.** Narmer unites Upper Egypt and Lower Egypt.
- **c. 2000 B.C.** Chinese write on oracle bones.
- **c. 1800 B.C.** Stonehenge monument is built.
- **c. 1200 B.C.** Sumerians record *Gilgamesh* epic.
- **c. 1150 B.C.** Olmec civilization begins in Mexico.

your lives? *(Current fashion trends and feelings about others, among other things.)* Do you create anything that has symbolic meaning, as the cave paintings did? *(Answers will vary, but students will probably say no.)* In the United States today, who creates art and symbols? *(Professional artists and performers, the media, the entertainment industry, sports, and companies produce most art and symbols today.)* Why do you think this is so? *(Answers may include that "art" has a broader meaning now than historically, and that the many common symbols of our culture originate in a variety of mediums.)*

Introducing Unit 1

ABC NEWS INTERACTIVE™

VIDEODISC
Turning Points in World History

Side One, Chapter 3

Title: *The Rise of Cities*
Subject: The inventions of the Sumerians in Mesopotamia enabled people to live together in communities for the first time.
Ask: What practice did the Sumerians create when they attempted to keep records of trading transactions? *(They created writing with symbols, which led to the creation of the alphabet.)*

History & Art Neolithic peoples sculpted figures from soft clay and then baked them rock-hard in ovens. These clay statuettes are the most common artifacts of early civilizations. Point out to students that most ancient art had symbolic or religious meaning.

Portfolio Project

Students may find information about the evolution of English letters by looking at the first entry for each letter in a good dictionary or an encyclopedia. The letters invented by students should be based on widely recognized symbols. This activity may be an appropriate method of authentic assessment.

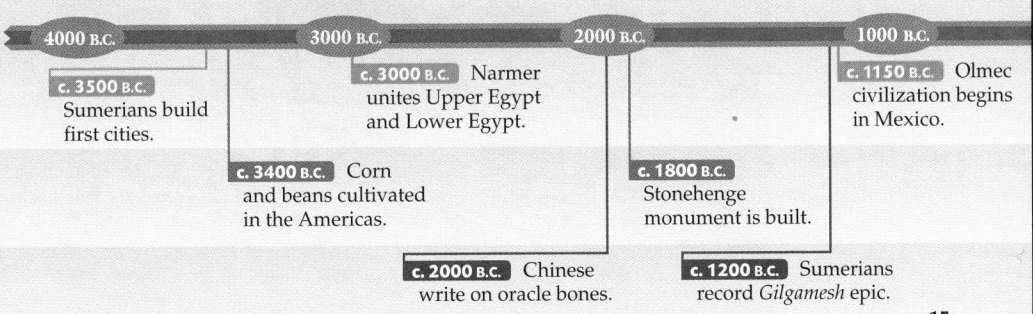

The Spread of Ideas

TEACH

Introduction

This feature focuses on a revolutionary breakthrough in human history—the invention of agriculture. Before they learned to farm, our ancestors spent nearly all their time hunting and gathering food. Because farming is much more efficient than hunting, it created food surpluses that allowed people to live in larger, permanent communities and dedicate themselves to activities besides mere survival.

Who?What?Where?When?

Women and Agriculture Many archaeologists believe that women invented the practice of agriculture. In hunter-gatherer societies, women collected fruit, nuts, and seeds. As they did so, women probably noticed that plants sprouted where seeds fell. Women probably invented the hoes they used to tend early farms. Only after the invention of the plow did men take over the job of raising crops.

Background Notes

Linking Past and Present

Farmers As farming methods have improved, fewer people are needed to produce the food we eat. In the nineteenth century, most Americans lived and worked on farms. Today, less than 10 percent of Americans are farmers. In developing countries, farming is still the primary occupation of most people. In China, India, Nigeria, and Zaire, for example, more than half the people are farmers.

The Spread of Ideas

Farming and Civilization

Between 8,000 and 10,000 years ago, a quiet revolution took place. In scattered pockets of the Middle East, Asia, Africa, and the Americas, people learned to cultivate food-producing plants for the first time. As knowledge of farming gradually spread, it dramatically changed human culture. Farming encouraged the growth of permanent communities, which in turn became the seedbeds for the world's first civilizations.

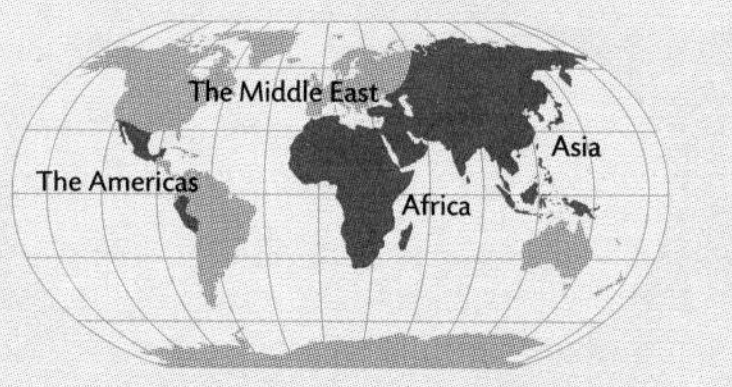

The Middle East

Breadbasket of the Ancient World

Greek grain storage jar

Today only sparse vegetation covers the foothills of Iraq's Zagros Mountains. Erosion and overgrazing by sheep and goats have taken their toll. Around 8000 B.C., however, wild wheat known as emmer covered the hills. Experts believe it was here that the world's first farmers may have watched seeds fall to earth and sprout. This observation led these ancient wanderers to plant seeds.

Over time, knowledge of farming spread in a broad arc of fertile land that curved from the Persian Gulf to the Mediterranean Sea. Farmers gradually added other foods to their diets—barley, chickpeas, lentils, figs, apricots, pistachios, walnuts, and more. A hunger for these foods kept people in one place. Hunting and gathering lifestyles changed as people began to develop new ideas and skills. Slowly—very slowly—farming settlements grew into cities. Known by names such as Ur, Babylon, and Jericho, these cities were the centers of Earth's oldest civilizations.

Foothills of the Zagros Mountains

16

COOPERATIVE LEARNING ACTIVITY

Research Organize the class into groups of four or five students. Have each group select an agricultural product, such as corn, wheat, rice, soybeans, apples, bananas, or potatoes. Using encyclopedias and other reference works, as well as outline maps of the world, each group should identify the regions of the world that produce the product they selected. After students have completed the unit, lead a discussion about the importance of agriculture in the development of civilization. Have students discuss which farm products are most important today in their region, and then rank the products they investigated. **L1**

The Americas

Mexico and Peru: Farming and Diversity

For much of world history, distance separated the Americas from the rest of the world. But the independent invention of farming in the areas of present-day Mexico and Peru created cities as sophisticated as those in other regions. The crops that spurred their growth, however, differed from crops elsewhere. Few of the wild grains found on other continents grew in the Americas. The first farmers in the Americas used the seeds of other plants, especially squash and beans. They also developed two high-yield foods unknown to the rest of the world—potatoes and maize (corn). When distant civilizations made contact, ideas about agriculture accompanied the wide distribution of foods that early peoples had developed and cultivated.

Corn Dance *by Frank Reed Whiteside*

Asia and Africa

Expansion of Earth's Gardens

The farming revolution did not happen just once. It occurred several times in widely separated regions. More than 6,000 years ago, farmers along the upper Huang He in present-day northern China started planting millet. About 5,000 years ago, farmers near the mouth of the Chang Jiang in southern China learned to grow rice. At roughly the same time, farmers along the Nile River in the northern part of Africa harvested their first crops of wheat and barley.

Wood relief of farming activities, Yoruba peoples

Like the gardens of the Middle East, the gardens of China and northern Africa grew more diverse. By 3000 B.C., farmers cultivated soybeans, bananas, and sugarcane. Supported by the harvests, people had more time to think and dream. Soon they created things that were used by the civilizations of the Middle East—calendars, systems of writing, forms of art and government.

LINKING THE IDEAS

1. How do experts think farming probably began?
2. Why is farming considered one of the most important inventions of human history?

Critical Thinking

3. **Cause and Effect** What is the connection between farming and the rise of ancient civilizations?

The Spread of Ideas

Geography

Place Ask students to look at the small map on this page. Ask them to locate the early American civilizations that developed farming. *(Modern-day Mexico and Peru)* Have them identify other continents and regions where early societies learned to farm. *(Middle East, China, Africa)* What crops were grown in each region? *(Americas: squash, beans, corn, potatoes; Middle East: wild wheat, barley, chickpeas, lentils; China: rice; Africa: wheat, barley, soybeans, bananas, sugarcane)* Then have students use larger, specialized world maps, such as relief and rainfall maps, to describe conditions in these areas that may have contributed to the development of agriculture.

Cultural Diffusion

The Columbian Exchange After 1492, Europe and the Americas exchanged plants, animals, and microbes. The potato, a tuber of the Americas, became a staple food in Ireland and other parts of Europe. The potato, like corn, yields far more food per acre than does wheat. The growth of Europe's population after 1500 is partly due to the introduction of nutritious, hardy crops of the Americas—such as the potato, corn, and manioc (also called cassava or tapioca).

ANSWERS TO LINKING THE IDEAS

1. In the Middle East, people watched seeds sprout, then tried planting seeds themselves.
2. Farming produced food surpluses that allowed larger, permanent communities to develop, which became the world's first civilizations.
3. Early civilizations grew in areas that had pioneered farming and were well suited to agriculture because increasing numbers of people were freed to devote their time and energy to other pursuits.

Teach, Reinforce, and Extend CHAPTER Content

Human Beginnings

CHAPTER RESOURCES

	Reproducible Resources	Multimedia Resources
Chapter Opener	Chapter Themes: Graphic Organizer 1 Historical Significance Chapter Activity 1	MindJogger Videoquiz
Chapter Enrichment	Vocabulary Activity 1* Time Line Activity 1 Mapping History Activity 1 History Simulation 1 Geography and History Activity 1 Source Reading 1 Enrichment Activity 1 Critical Thinking Activity 1 Skill Reinforcement Activity 1 Building Skills in Geography Workbook, Unit 1, Lesson 12 Performance Assessment Activity 1	World History and Art Transparency 1, *Woman's Head* Chapter Transparency 1 Vocabulary PuzzleMaker Software Turning Points in World History: *The Rise of Cities*
Chapter Review/Reteaching	Reteaching Activity 1 Skill Reinforcement Activity 1 Spanish Chapter Summary 1	Chapter 1 Digest Audiocassette, Activity, Test* Vocabulary PuzzleMaker Software Student Self-Test and Review Software MindJogger Videoquiz
Chapter Evaluation/Testing	Performance Assessment Activity 1 Chapter 1 Test, Forms A and B	Testmaker

* *Also available in Spanish*

0:00 **OUT OF TIME?** Assign the Chapter 1 summary in the Unit 1 Digest on pages 96–99, and the Chapter 1 Audiocassettes.

Block Schedule

Block scheduling differs from traditional class scheduling in the amount of time allotted to each period. The extended time frame provided by block scheduling affords you the opportunity to implement a greater number of research-oriented and activity-intense projects to motivate and involve your students. Activities that are particularly suited to use within the block scheduling framework are identified throughout this chapter by the following designation.

KEY TO ABILITY LEVELS

Teaching strategies have been coded for varying learning styles and abilities.

- **L1** **BASIC** activities for all students
- **L2** **AVERAGE** activities for average to above-average students
- **L3** **CHALLENGING** activities for above-average students
- **LEP** **LIMITED ENGLISH PROFICIENCY** activities

Chapter 1 Planning Guide

A complete, 1-page lesson plan is provided for each section in the *Reproducible Lesson Plans* booklet.

SECTION RESOURCES

Daily Objectives	Reproducible Resources	Multimedia Resources
Section 1 Discovery of Early Humans in Africa Explain how recent archaeological finds have contributed to our understanding of human origins.	Reproducible Lesson Plan 1-1 Guided Reading Activity 1-1* Time Line Activity 1 Section Quiz 1-1*	Section Focus Transparency 1-1 Chapter Transparency 1 Vocabulary PuzzleMaker Software Student Self-Test and Review Software Testmaker
Section 2 The Appearance of *Homo Sapiens* Describe some of the achievements of the earliest humans.	Reproducible Lesson Plan 1-2 Vocabulary Activity 1* Guided Reading Activity 1-2* History Simulation 1 Section Quiz 1-2*	Section Focus Transparency 1-2 World History and Art Transparency 1, *Woman's Head* Student Self-Test and Review Software Testmaker
Section 3 Emergence of Civilization Specify the kinds of economic, political, and social changes that resulted from the rise of cities.	Reproducible Lesson Plan 1-3 Guided Reading Activity 1-3* Reteaching Activity 1 Enrichment Activity 1 Section Quiz 1-3* Performance Assessment Activity 1 Spanish Chapter Summary 1	Section Focus Transparency 1-3 Vocabulary PuzzleMaker Software Student Self-Test and Review Software Testmaker Turning Points in World History: *The Rise of Cities*

** Also available in Spanish*

Chapter Activities

Performance Assessment Activity

Planning a Documentary Have students take the roles of producers who must plan a documentary on early people. Have pairs of students prepare proposals for three thirty-minute segments, including where and when filming will take place, who will narrate, what types of people will be interviewed, what information will be presented and the manner in which it will be presented (interview, graph, photo, and so on). Students may present proposals either in written or oral form, and should keep in mind that their audience will be potential financial backers for the project.

Possible Rubric Features
Content information, concept attainment, decision-making skills, quality and clarity of product

• *For an additional activity, refer to Activity 1 in the* Performance Assessment Strategies and Activities *booklet.*

Activity

From the Classroom of...

Nancy Sue Romerdahl, EdD.
Everett High School
Everett, WA

An Archaeological "Dig"

Materials: Pen and paper, and a woman's purse, with most contents (except personal items) remaining.

Procedure: Ask students to brainstorm how people and particularly history book authors come to "know" what they know.

Explain that this simulation is designed to show how historians and archaeologists use artifacts to make observations and then inferences from those observations. The "dig" is a woman's purse. Have the class list and describe items in the purse. Next, see how many inferences students can make about the purse and its owner. For example, if the purse contains contact lens solution, they might infer that the owner wears contacts; however, she might also be holding the solution for a relative. The class would discuss which is the stronger possibility. Then, if there is also an optometrist appointment card with her name on it this, added to the lens solution "find," becomes stronger evidence that she wears contacts.

After all the items are cataloged, and all reasonable inferences listed, have students write a probable description of the woman.

Following this activity, help students understand how archaeologists generate knowledge about people who left no written record.

MULTIPLE LEARNING STYLES

Verbal/Linguistic
Have students read outside sources about the origin and development of writing. Ask one or more students to report orally on the information obtained.

Auditory/Musical
Have students identify and bring to class one or more musical selections that they think would provide suitable background music for a visit to a cave in which prehistoric paintings have been found.

Kinesthetic
Have students mime the movements of a Neanderthal hunter or gatherer or both. Ask students to explain how they decided what movements would be appropriate.

Interpersonal
Have students form a panel to discuss this question: *As a small group of cave dwellers who have just begun to grow a few crops for food, how shall we divide up the work necessary to keep us alive?*

Additional Resources

TEACHER'S CORNER

NATIONAL GEOGRAPHIC SOCIETY

INDEX TO NATIONAL GEOGRAPHIC MAGAZINE

The following articles may be used for research relating to this chapter:

- "The Dawn of Humans," by Meave Leakey, September 1995.
- "The Brindisi Bronzes: Classical Castoffs Reclaimed from the Sea," by O. Louis Mazzatenta, April 1995.
- "Chile's Chinchorro Mummies," by Bernardo Arriaza, March 1995.
- "A Mummy Unearthed from the Pastures of Heaven," by Natalya Polosmak, October 1994.
- "The Ice Man: Lone Voyager from the Copper Age," by David Roberts, June 1993.
- "The Search for Modern Humans," by John J. Putnam, October 1988.
- "Lascaux Cave: Art Treasures from the Ice Age," by Jean-Philippe Rigaud, October 1988.
- "Oasis of Art in the Sahara," by Henri Lhote, August 1987.
- "The Search for Our Ancestors," by Kenneth F. Weaver, November 1985.
- "Homo Erectus Unearthed," by Richard Leakey and Alan Walker, November 1985.

Bibliography

Literature About the Period

Auel, Jean M. ***The Clan of the Cave Bear.*** New York: Bantam, 1984 (paperback). A Cro-Magnon girl is adopted by a Neanderthal tribe.

Readings for the Student

Johanson, Donald, and James Shreeve. ***Lucy's Child: The Discovery of a Human Ancestor*.** New York: William Morrow and Company, Inc., 1989. An account of Johanson's return to Africa in 1986.

Readings for the Teacher

Gowlett, John. ***Ascent to Civilization: The Archaeology of Early Man.*** New York: Knopf, 1984. The rise and development of human culture as revealed by archaeological finds.

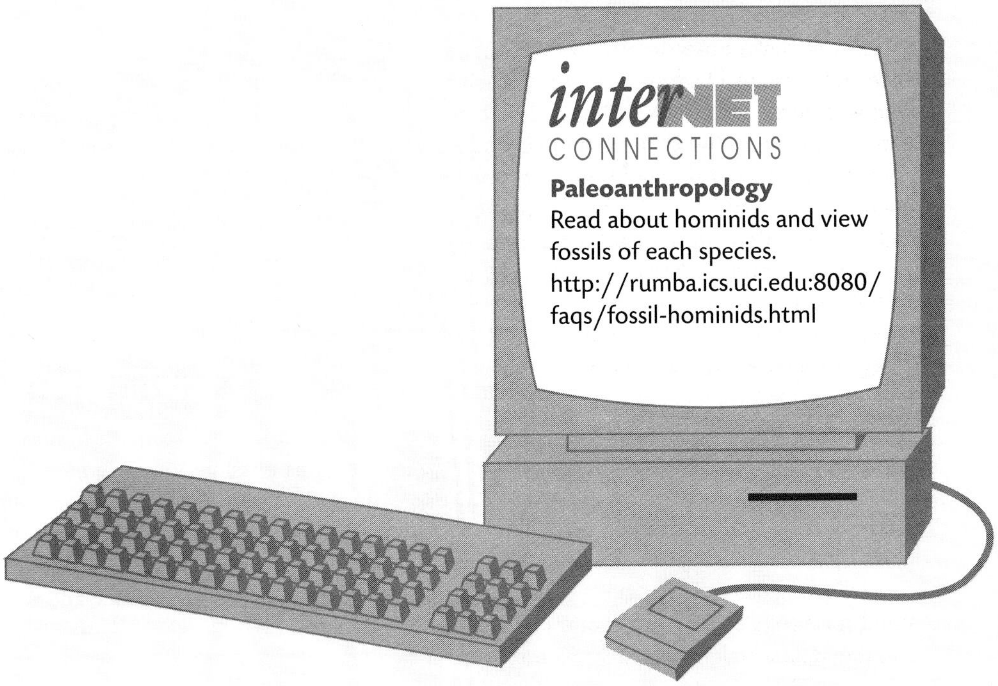
interNET
CONNECTIONS
Paleoanthropology
Read about hominids and view fossils of each species.
http://rumba.ics.uci.edu:8080/faqs/fossil-hominids.html

Introducing Chapter 1

CHAPTER THEMES

Chapter Themes are listed by section on this chapter opening page of the Student Edition. A corresponding theme-based activity is available under "TEACH," and a theme-based question is asked in the Section and Chapter Reviews.

The Storyteller

Historical Setting Finding the remains of the earliest hominids can be a daunting task. The famous anthropological team of Louis and Mary Leakey spent 30 years in Olduvai Gorge, Tanzania, before they finally found a hominid in 1959. (More than 60 hominids have since been found in the same general area.) The Leakeys felt certain they were searching in the right place, because they had been finding stone tools there—a sure sign of the presence of hominids. Their many discoveries in East Africa were the result of scientific knowledge, close observation, and perseverance.

Historical Significance

Answers: *Early people learned to make fire, clothing, and tools as they struggled to survive. They learned how to preserve food for future use. In time they learned to domesticate plants and animals.*

Early civilizations developed with the rise of cities. The cities grew because advances in agriculture—including irrigation—allowed specialization of labor, which in turn led to advanced technology.

Chapter 1

Prehistory–1000 B.C.

Human Beginnings

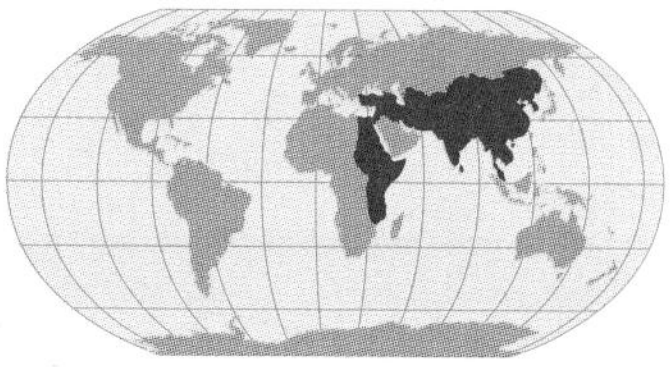

Chapter Themes

- **Movement** Migrations of prehistoric peoples result in their spread throughout the world. *Section 1*
- **Innovation** Early humans produce tools and domesticate animals and crops. *Section 2*
- **Change** The earliest civilizations begin with the evolution of farming settlements into the first cities. *Section 3*

The Storyteller

On the coast of southern Africa, in caves and rock shelters, lived some of the world's first communities of prehistoric people. The region enjoyed a mild climate and abundant food from both the land and the sea. Women gathered supplies, while men made longer journeys inland, hunting for big animals such as antelope, buffalo, and wildebeest. Both men and women searched the coast at each low tide for small sea animals.

The cave dwellers preserved food for times of scarcity by drying leftover meat in smoke from fires. They did not know that more than 70,000 years later scientists and other people exploring the same area would uncover the remains of their long-vanished way of life.

Historical Significance

How did early peoples develop skills that became the basic elements of human ways of life? What developments led to the rise of the world's first civilizations?

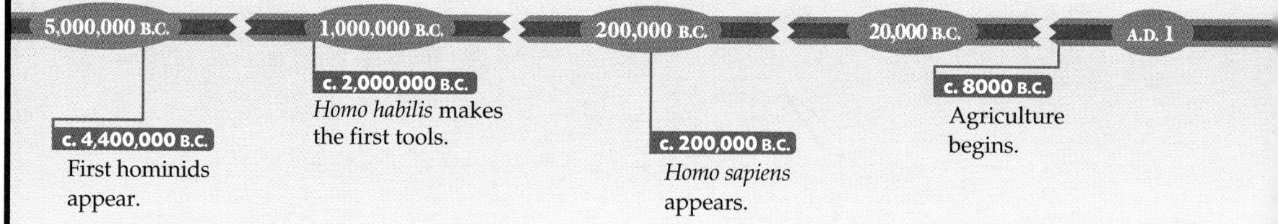

5,000,000 B.C.
1,000,000 B.C.
200,000 B.C.
20,000 B.C.
A.D. 1
c. 4,400,000 B.C.
First hominids appear.
c. 2,000,000 B.C.
Homo habilis makes the first tools.
c. 200,000 B.C.
Homo sapiens appears.
c. 8000 B.C.
Agriculture begins.

18

GEOGRAPHY CONNECTION

Location Have students brainstorm a list of conditions that would have made it as easy as possible for early people to survive. *(Answers may include: warm climate all year long, plentiful water supply, abundant vegetation and wildlife.)* Next, have students use the Atlas of their text to locate areas of the world where these conditions exist. *(Answers may include: parts of South America, Africa, and South Asia.)* Finally, have students locate Ethiopia, northern Tanzania, and Kenya, where the remains of early people were actually found.

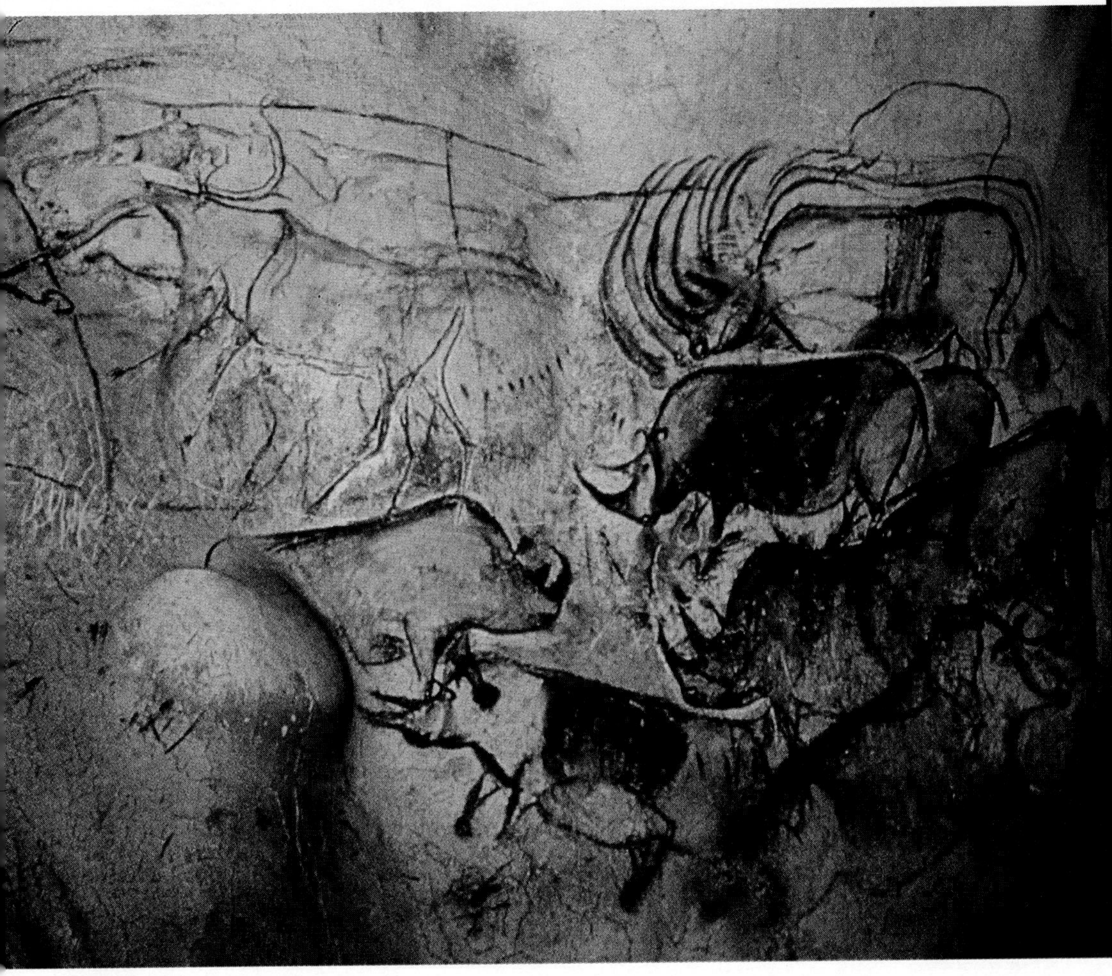

History & Art Cro-Magnon cave paintings from Vallon-Pont-d'Arc near Avignon, France

Your History Journal

Imagine that you and a friend are stranded on a large uninhabited island. You have no tools except a pocket knife. There are many species of small animals, a stream of fresh water, a sandy beach, and a dense forest. You must survive until rescued, perhaps a month later. Write a journal account of your first seven days.

EXTRA CREDIT PROJECT

Essay Ask students why it is important to have an understanding of past events and their significance. Write on the chalkboard the following quotation from Cicero, a Roman statesman and orator: "To be ignorant of what happened before you were born is to be ever a child." Have students write an essay in which they explain the meaning of Cicero's words. In the paper, have them explore the meaning and importance of history, discussing its relevance in today's world.

Introducing Chapter 1

History & Art Paleolithic artists used three basic colors: black, red, and yellow. The pigments came from natural sources such as charcoal, clay, and minerals such as iron. How does this cave painting compare in color, composition, and technique to other art you have seen? *(fewer colors and simpler rendering of figures than in other paintings, but lively, with sense of movement and impression of three-dimensional form)*

Performance Assessment

Refer to the activity on page 18C of the Planning Guide.

For an additional activity, refer to Activity 1 in the *Performance Assessment Strategies and Activities* booklet.

Using Your History Journal

Journal entries may be in diary form. Remind students that the survival methods they use will parallel those of the earliest humans.

GLENCOE TECHNOLOGY

VIDEODISC
Use MindJogger to preview chapter content.

MindJogger Videoquiz
Chapter 1
Disc 1 Side A

Also available in VHS.

Chapter 1 Section 1

SECTION THEME

▶ **Movement** Migrations of prehistoric peoples result in their spread throughout the world.

Find Out

Answer: *They have shown more clearly than before when, where, and how the earliest humans lived and developed.*

FOCUS

Section Objective

Explain how recent archaeological finds have contributed to our understanding of human origins.

BELLRINGER
Motivational Activity

Before taking roll at the beginning of the class period, project Section Focus Transparency 1-1 and have students answer the activity questions. Discuss students' responses.

This activity is also available as a blackline master.

Vocabulary Pre-check

Use the Vocabulary PuzzleMaker to create a puzzle that reinforces the vocabulary terms in this section. **L1**

5,000,000 B.C. — 3,000,000 B.C. — 1,000,000 B.C.

c. 4,400,000 B.C. Earliest known human ancestor lives in East Africa.

c. 2,000,000 B.C. *Homo habilis* develops first stone tools.

c. 1,700,000 B.C. *Homo erectus* reaches Asia.

Section 1

Discovery of Early Humans in Africa

Setting the Scene

▶ **Terms to Define**
prehistory, hominid, anthropologist, paleontologist, archaeologist, artifact, radiocarbon dating, nomad, culture, technology

▶ **People to Meet**
Gen Suwa, Tim D. White, Donald C. Johanson, Louis Leakey, Mary Leakey

▶ **Places to Locate**
Aramis, Hadar, Olduvai Gorge

Find Out How have recent archaeological finds contributed to our understanding of human origins?

The Storyteller

On the slab lies the shriveled corpse of a man.... Alongside him lies a long wooden stave with a fibrous end. Laid out on the slab ... are the other finds—the axe with its elbow-shafting and metal blade, a stone bead with a strange tassel of twisted hide thongs, the small dagger ... a wooden stick with holes in it, a scrap of leather, and a nut-sized stone.... Archaeologist Konrad Spindler's assessment: 'Roughly four thousand years old ... [or] even earlier.'

—adapted from *The Man in the Ice*, Konrad Spindler, 1994

Excavation of an ancient site in Lake Kinneret, Galilee

History tells the story of humankind. Because historians mostly use written records to gather information about the past, history is said to begin with the invention of writing about 5,500 years ago. But the story of humankind really begins in the time *before* people developed writing—the period called **prehistory**.

Using the best available evidence, scientists have traced the existence of the first humanlike creatures back to about 4.4 million years ago in Africa. Human beings and the humanlike creatures that preceded them together belong to a group of beings named **hominids** (HAH•muh•nuhds). The scientific study of hominids—their physical features, development, and behavior—is called anthropology. Physical **anthropologists** (AN•thruh•PAH•luh•jihsts) compare hominid bones and other fossil remains, looking for changes in such features as brain size and posture. Anthropologists work closely with other scientists. **Paleontologists** (PAY•lee•AHN•TAH•luh•jihsts), for example, study fossil remains to determine the characteristics of various prehistoric periods. **Archaeologists** (AHR•kee•AH•luh•jihsts) investigate prehistoric life by unearthing and interpreting the objects left behind by prehistoric people. These **artifacts** include any objects that were shaped by human hands—tools, pots, and beads—as well as other remains of human life, such as bits of charcoal.

Dating Early Artifacts

As they unearth the remains of prehuman and human settlements, archaeologists and physical anthropologists face the additional problem of dating what they find. It is easy to determine the relative sequence in which events happened: More

SECTION RESOURCES

Reproducible Masters
- Reproducible Lesson Plan 1-1
- Guided Reading Activity 1-1
- Time Line Activity 1
- Section Quiz 1-1

Transparencies
- Section Focus Transparency 1-1
- Chapter Transparency 1

Multimedia
- Vocabulary PuzzleMaker Software
- Student Self-Test and Review Software
- Testmaker

recent remains are usually found above older ones. The problem lies in assigning a definite age to fossil bones, tools, and other remains.

Among the techniques for determining the age of organic remains is radiocarbon dating. Organic matter includes once-living things like wood artifacts, campfire ashes, bone, and cotton cloth. A very small percentage of the carbon atoms absorbed by every living thing is radioactive. When any living thing dies, it stops absorbing carbon. Then, because radioactive carbon decays at a known rate, archaeologists can measure how much the radioactive carbon in organic remains has decayed and figure out when the animal or plant died.

Radiocarbon dating, however, can be used only for organic matter that is less than 50,000 years old. Researchers have devised other techniques for studying earlier periods. By measuring the rate of decay for chemical elements other than carbon, researchers can date older fossils as far back as 2.6 billion years. These extremely sophisticated methods are not infallible, of course, but they do enable scientists to peer far into the past.

Prehistoric Finds in Africa

On December 17, 1992, a paleontologist from Japan named **Gen Suwa** walked across the rugged desert landscape of Ethiopia in East Africa. At a site called **Aramis**, an object in the ground caught Suwa's eye. It turned out to be one of the oldest hominid teeth ever found—a link to the origins of our human ancestors!

The Oldest Human Ancestor

Over the next two years, Suwa, his colleague **Tim D. White** of the University of California, and a 20-person team uncovered additional remains. They came up with teeth, arm bones, and parts of a skull and jaw that belonged to 17 individuals. Analyzing the fossils, the scientists determined that they were about 4.4 million years old and came from the oldest direct human ancestor known. The small creatures would have weighed about 65 pounds (30 kg) and stood 4 feet (1.2 m) tall. Scientists have yet to determine whether they walked upright.

Discovery of Lucy

About 45 miles (73 km) north, at **Hadar**, two scientists—**Donald C. Johanson** and Tom Gray—in 1974 had uncovered the 3.2 million-year-old skeleton of a hominid nicknamed "Lucy." Lucy received her name from a popular Beatles song of the period, "Lucy in the Sky with Diamonds." Hers was the most nearly complete skeleton of any erect-walking prehuman found up to that time.

Since then, Johanson and his team of researchers have made further discoveries. In 1994 they assembled, from other fossils found at the Hadar site, the first reasonably complete skull of a Lucy-like hominid. The scientists claimed that the skull provided evidence that males and females in this early hominid group were of significantly different sizes. The evidence also indicated that Lucy-like hominids spent some time climbing in trees and could also walk upright.

The earliest known direct evidence of upright walking comes from Kenya, where archaeologists in 1995 discovered a fossilized hominid shin bone about 4 million years old. The shape and size of the bone indicate upright walking.

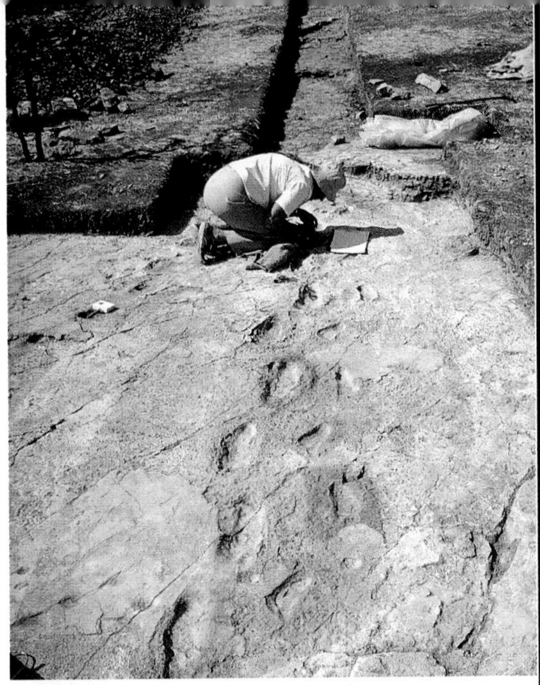

Visualizing History **Mary Leakey, a noted paleoanthropologist, follows a trail of hominid footprints fossilized in volcanic ash.** *What are hominids?*

Human Origins

Scientists disagree about many aspects of the story of human beginnings. As scientists unearth more clues, newer evidence may require them to reinterpret older evidence.

COOPERATIVE LEARNING ACTIVITY

Bulletin Board Organize the class into three groups to prepare a bulletin board display showing the development of hominids from *Australopithecus* to *Homo habilis* to *Homo erectus*. Each group's contributions should include an illustration from a reliable source such as the *World Book Encyclopedia*, *Scientific American*, or *National Geographic*. Displays should also include an indication of the dates of the hominid category and a brief paragraph describing each type. Have students describe individual contributions and cite their sources before posting the bulletin board display. **L1**

TEACH

Guided Practice

THEME **Movement**

Have students look at the map on page 22. Ask them to brainstorm a list of reasons why early *Homo sapiens* migrated from place to place. *(Answers may include: to find better sources of food; changes in climate; knowing how to make fire and clothing made life in colder climates possible.)* **L1**

Visualizing History Burial in volcanic ash is just one of a number of ways in which fossils are formed. Other conditions that led to the formation of fossils include quick burial in moist sediment, freezing (in cold areas), and engulfment in asphalt pits.

Answer to Caption: *All human beings as well as the humanlike creatures that preceded them are part of this group.*

Geography: Human/Environment Interaction Have students locate the middle latitudes on a world map or globe. *(30°N to 30°S)* Then ask a volunteer to point out Ethiopia on a classroom map. Discuss how the discoveries of Suwa, White, Johanson, and the Leakeys are consistent with the theory about where humans lived during the Ice Ages. *(Only the middle latitudes remained warm enough to support human and animal life.)* **L2**

Chapter Transparency 1

you don't say...

Australopithecus The Latin word *australis* means "southern." It is familiar to many people only in the name *Australia* ("southern land"), so students may jump to the erroneous conclusion that *Australopithecus* lived in Australia. Point out that the diminutive "southern ape" was, like all the earliest hominids, native to Africa–specifically, as the name shows, to southern Africa.

Who?What?Where?When?

Willard F. Libby, an American chemist, devised the radiocarbon dating method in 1946 while at the University of Chicago. The technique is also known as C-14 dating. In 1960 Dr. Libby won the Nobel Prize in chemistry for developing radiocarbon dating.

Map Study

Answers

1. *Asia and Australia*
2. *The two continents are so close at the Bering Strait that it is reasonable to assume they were once joined by a land bridge.*

Map Skills Practice

Reading a Map How many skeletal sites are there between the latitudes of 0° and 60°N? *(12)*

The First Hominids

According to one of the generally accepted theories, the first prehuman hominids, of whom the discoveries in Ethiopia are an example, date back about 4.4 million years. Known as *Australopithecus* (aw•STRAY•loh•PIH•thuh•kuhs), or "southern ape," they stood about 3.5 to 5.0 feet (1.1 to 1.6 m) tall and walked on two legs. They had large faces that jutted out. The brain was small, the nose flat, and the teeth large. The back teeth were suitable for grinding food.

Australopithecus lived in the humid forests of eastern and southern Africa, where they fed on fruits, leaves, and nuts. They probably also ate fish caught in streams and meat from animals killed by lions or other predators. *Australopithecus* were most likely **nomads**—moving constantly in search of food. They probably had few, if any, possessions and may have shared food with one another. Fossil evidence shows that family groups lived in temporary camps. Perhaps they lived together for protection from large animals. No evidence exists showing that *Australopithecus* made or used tools. They may have used grass stems and twigs as tools and sticks or bones to dig roots, however.

Hominid Groups

Scientists use the Latin word *Homo,* which means "human," to name these hominids and all later human beings as well. Anthropologists today are still not certain whether a direct relationship connected *Australopithecus* and human beings or exactly when hominids became truly human. Scientists divided *Homo*—the genus of humans—into three species that differ somewhat in body structures. These three human or humanlike species arose at different times in prehistory. The earliest of the three was *Homo habilis,* or "person with ability," who lived until about 1.5 million years ago. After *Homo habilis* lived the second type

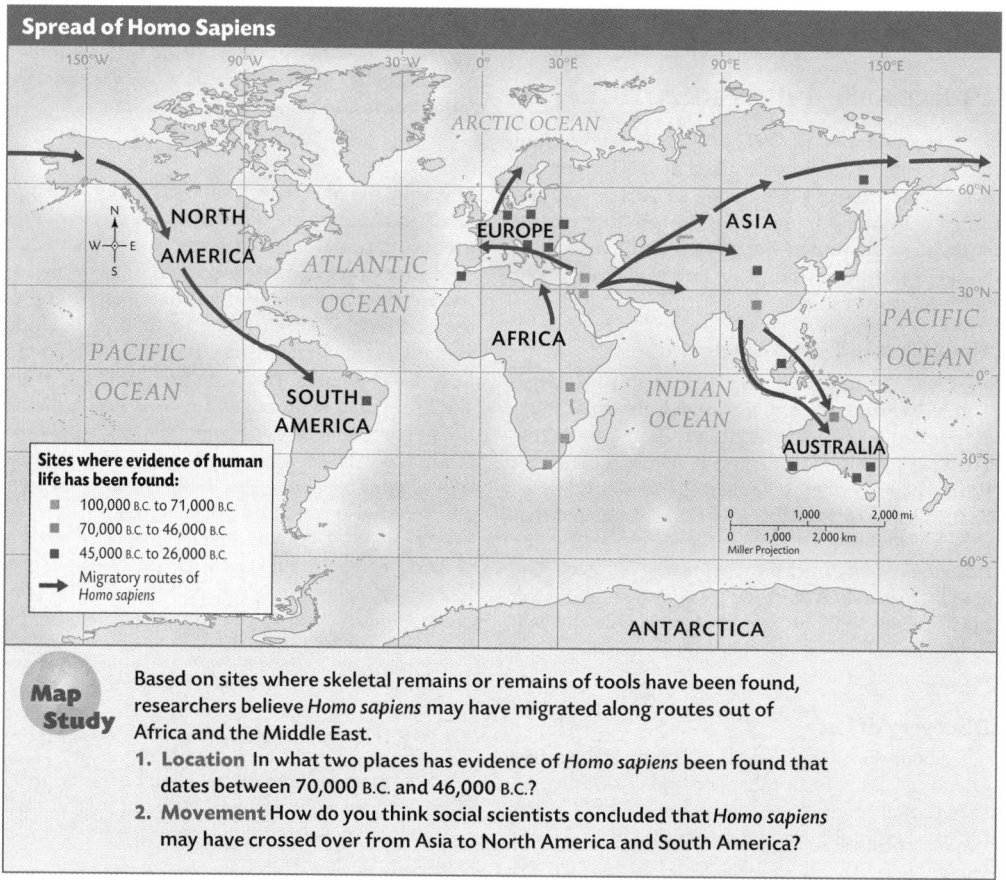

Spread of Homo Sapiens

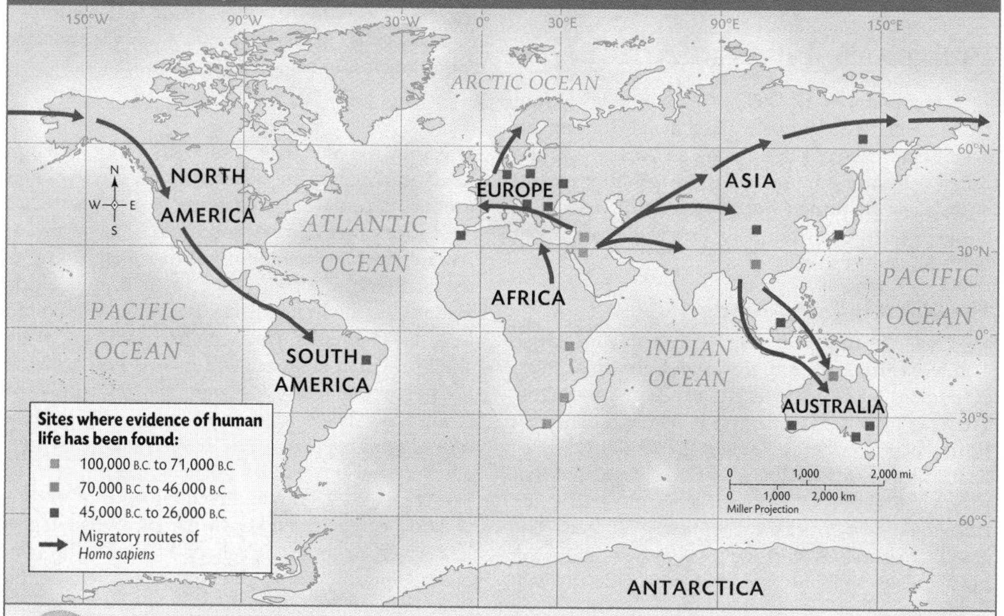

Map Study Based on sites where skeletal remains or remains of tools have been found, researchers believe *Homo sapiens* may have migrated along routes out of Africa and the Middle East.

1. **Location** In what two places has evidence of *Homo sapiens* been found that dates between 70,000 B.C. and 46,000 B.C.?
2. **Movement** How do you think social scientists concluded that *Homo sapiens* may have crossed over from Asia to North America and South America?

MEETING SPECIAL NEEDS ACTIVITY

Learning Style: Logical/Mathematical 4.4 million years–the approximate age of *Australopithecus*–may be hard for students to comprehend. Have them think of a grandmother-mother-daughter relationship. Three generations = 100 years. Add the word *great* to each previous generation–great-grandmother, great-great-grandmother, and so on. Have students calculate how many times *great* would have to be added to the word *grandmother* to name the ancestor that lived 1,000 years ago. *(27; the word* great *is not added for the first three generations)* Then have them figure how many times *great* would be used for a woman who lived 4.4 million years ago. *(132,000 less 3)* **L3**

© Bob Campbell

Hominid Hunter

Meave Leakey, daughter-in-law of famed fossil hunters Mary and Louis Leakey, sifts through e soil near Lake Turkana in north- n Kenya, a site in the East African ft System famous for its treasury of e fossils of early humans. In recent ars a wide range of scholars have ntinued to push back the date for e origin of the earliest humans. olecular biologists, through the udy of human, chimpanzee, and gorilla genes and ood proteins, speculate that hominids, or early

Kenneth Garrett

humans, originated somewhere between five and seven million years ago. One of a number of scientists influenced by this research, Meave Leakey and her team began exploring for new evidence. They now theorize that a jawbone found near Lake Turkana in 1994 may be 4.1 million years old. Before that discovery there was little evidence of hominids older than 3.6 million years. Some researchers believe that a 5.6 million-year-old jaw fragment (left) discovered in 1967 may be the oldest hominid fossil yet found.

TEACH

Tell students that in 1970 Meave Leakey found the first fossil hominid femur (thigh bone) to be recovered in Kenya. Her husband, Richard E. Leakey, a paleoanthropologist, has written that before her discovery, he sometimes walked right past fossil leg bone fragments, as skulls, jaws, and teeth were easier to recognize. Skulls, jaws, and teeth can provide much interesting information, such as clues to diet and brain size. But they cannot tell the whole story. Ask students what information might be gained from a femur. *(A femur could provide information on the posture and movement of the hominid.)*

CURRICULUM CONNECTION

SCIENCE

Scientists have made great strides in dating fossil bones. Between 1908 and 1912, fragments of a supposed hominid were found in a gravel pit near Piltdown Common, England. Not until 1959, using fluorine tests and other analyses, was it proved conclusively that "Piltdown man" was a hoax.

Chapter 1
Section 1

Independent Practice

Guided Reading Activity 1-1 **L1**

Time Line Activity 1

Environment Have students draw pictures of and report on some of the giant mammals that became extinct as the Ice Age ended. These could include the mammoth, giant beaver, and giant sloth. **L1 LEP**

Archaeology Have students choose one of these archaeological sites to research: Altamira, Spain; Tassili n'Ajjer, Algeria; Stonehenge, England. Have them report their research in the form of a magazine article explaining site location and the importance of the discovery. **L2**

Linking Past and Present

Global warming is a topic of concern today. Some scientists predict gradual increases in world temperatures. Unlike the natural forming and melting of glaciers in prehistory, global warming stems from human activities, such as burning fossil fuels. The result is heat trapped in the atmosphere.

AROUND THE WORLD

Early Oceangoing Navigation

Australia, c. 50,000–30,000 B.C.

Early people used boats to travel from Southeast Asia to Australia, crossing about 50 miles of open seas. A land bridge, formed during the Ice Ages, enabled them to make part of the journey by land. The early adventurers reached a landmass called Sahul, which consisted of Australia, New Guinea, and Tasmania. There they encountered animals such as kangaroos that were previously unknown to humans.

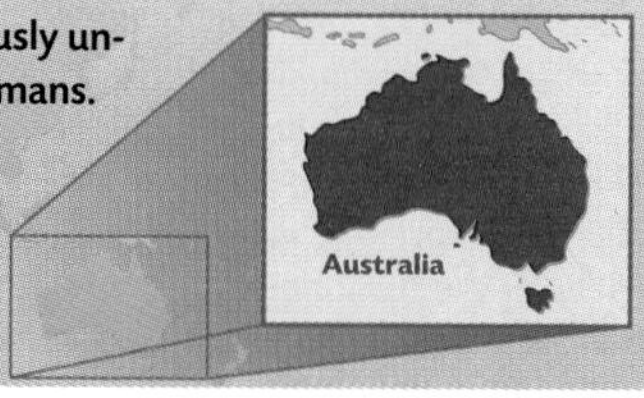

of early human—*Homo erectus*, or "person who walks upright"—who was, in turn, followed between 100,000 and 200,000 years ago by *Homo sapiens*, or "person who thinks." All people living today belong to the species *Homo sapiens*.

The Ice Ages

Climatic changes played an important part in the development of early humankind. Between 2 million and 10,000 years ago, Earth experienced four long periods of cold climate, known as the Ice Ages. During each such period, average temperatures in many parts of the world fell to below freezing, and massive glaciers spread out from the Poles, scarring the landforms over which they crept. The northern glaciers covered large portions of Europe, Asia, and North America, and the ice fields of Antarctica stretched over wide regions in the Southern Hemisphere. Only the middle latitudes remained warm enough to support human and animal life. Between glacial periods, Earth's climate warmed overall, and abundant rains brought lush plant growth—until the next glacial period began.

As the sheets of ice formed, the level of the oceans dropped more than 300 feet (90 m). As a result, some areas that are now separated by water were connected then by bridges of land. One such land bridge joined Japan and mainland Korea, another connected Great Britain and Ireland to western Europe, a third led from the Malay Peninsula through the Indonesian islands almost all the way to Australia, and a fourth connected Asia and North America at the Bering Strait.

Early human beings responded to the environmental changes of the Ice Ages in several ways. Some migrated to warmer places. Others found strategies for keeping warm, such as clothing and fire. Those who could not adapt died from starvation or exposure.

Human Culture

Clothing and fire had become part of the **culture**, or way of life, of prehistoric people. Culture also includes the knowledge a people have, the language they speak, the ways in which they eat and dress, their religious beliefs, and their achievements in art and music.

Toolmaking

One of the earliest aspects of culture that people formed was the use of tools. At first they dug roots and tubers out of the ground with wooden digging sticks. Later, they made crude tools of stone, which enabled them to skin small animals and cut off pieces of meat. Improving their **technology**—the skills and useful knowledge available to them for collecting material and making the objects necessary for survival—early people began to create specialized tools, such as food choppers, skin scrapers, and spear points.

The Stone Age

The use of stone tools by early people led historians to apply the name Stone Age to the period before writing became established. Scholars divided the Stone Age into three shorter periods, depending on differences in toolmaking techniques. The earliest period, the Paleolithic (PAY•lee •uh•LIH•thihk) or Old Stone Age, began about 2 million years ago with the first toolmaking by *Homo habilis* and lasted until about 12,000 B.C. The Mesolithic (MEH•zuh•LIH•thihk) period or Middle Stone Age is usually dated from 12,000 B.C. to about 8000 B.C. The Neolithic (NEE•uh•LIH•thihk) period or New Stone Age lasted from about 8000 B.C. to 5000 B.C.

Paleolithic Hunter-Gatherers

Archaeologists as yet do not know a great deal about the culture of the early humans called *Homo habilis* and *Homo erectus*. Their knowledge, however, widens as new discoveries are made.

MAKING CONNECTIONS ACTIVITY

Environment For many years people thought the remains of a vast river system lay hidden under the Sahara. When scientists studied the radar scan of the Sahara by the space shuttle *Columbia* in 1981, they saw a network of waterways, floodplains, and broad river valleys throughout southern Egypt and northern Sudan. Prompted by these images, in 1982 an Egyptian-American team excavated along the banks of an ancient river. They found tools and other artifacts believed to have been used by *Homo erectus* who lived and hunted in the fertile Sahara 200,000 years ago. Have students research to find other areas in which the climate has changed markedly in the past 200,000 years. **L2**

Homo Habilis

Homo habilis lived during the first quarter of the Paleolithic period. It seems probable, however, that these prehistoric people are the oldest hominids known to manufacture tools. They lived in Africa from about 2.5 million to 1.5 million years ago, alongside *Australopithecus*. Their larger brains indicate that they were more physically and mentally advanced. Much of the evidence for *Homo habilis* has come from research by **Louis and Mary Leakey**, and later their son Richard, at **Olduvai** (OHL•duh•VY) **Gorge** and other sites in the eastern part of Africa.

Homo Erectus

Scientists have gathered much more information about *Homo erectus* than about *Homo habilis*. *Homo erectus* first appeared in Africa and lived from 1.6 million years ago to about 250,000 years ago. Their living areas covered a variety of environments from woodlands and grasslands in Africa to forests and plains in Europe and Asia.

Homo erectus at first were mostly food gatherers. Scientists think the females gathered fruits, nuts, and seeds, and the males scavenged for meat—either searching for an animal that had died of natural causes or yelling and waving their arms to frighten carnivores away from a kill. By about 500,000 years ago, however, the males had become hunters, using spears and clubs to kill such small prey as deer, pigs, and rabbits. The females, whose movements were restricted by the constant demands of child care, continued to forage close to home for vegetable food.

Meanwhile, these early humans also had learned how to make fire. This discovery allowed them to keep warm, cook food, and scare away threatening animals. It also enabled them to live in caves. Before, they had protected themselves from the weather by digging shallow pits and covering these with branches. Now, they could drive animals out of caves and use the caves themselves.

Homo erectus by this time not only had fire but also made clothing. Initially they simply wrapped themselves in animal skins, having first scraped hair and tissue off the inner side of the skins. Later, they laced the skins together with strips of leather.

Migrations

Scientists disagree on when prehistoric peoples left Africa and moved to other parts of the world. Some experts believe that *Homo habilis* may have been the earliest to migrate to Europe and Asia; however, clear evidence to support this view is lacking. Scientists do know, however, that *Homo erectus* migrated from their native Africa to Europe and Asia. Skeletal remains found in Java have led anthropologists to conclude that *Homo erectus* reached the Indonesian islands about 1.6 to 1.8 million years ago. *Homo erectus* was clearly well established in China by 460,000 years ago, and the earliest skeletal traces in Europe may also date back around 400,000 years.

Language

Homo erectus may have been talking to each other about 500,000 years ago instead of just making sounds to indicate emotions and directions. Language was one of humanity's greatest achievements. It enabled individuals to work with one another—to organize a hunting group, for example, or to give specific instructions about where to find a spring of fresh water. It allowed individuals to exchange ideas, such as how the world began or what caused animals to migrate across the plains. Individuals could sit around a hearth fire, eat together, and talk about the day's events. They could talk about the best way to fell a tree or build a shelter. Perhaps most significantly, spoken language made it possible for the older generation to pass its culture on to the younger generation, enabling new generations to build upon the knowledge of the past.

SECTION 1 REVIEW

Recall

1. **Define** prehistory, hominid, anthropologist, paleontologist, archaeologist, artifacts, radiocarbon dating, nomad, culture, technology.
2. **Identify** Gen Suwa, Tim D. White, Donald C. Johanson, Louis Leakey, Mary Leakey.
3. **Locate** each of these prehistoric sites and explain their importance: Aramis, Hadar, Olduvai Gorge.

Critical Thinking

4. **Making Comparisons** Compare and contrast the culture of *Homo habilis* and *Homo erectus*. Consider housing, technology, and mobility.

Understanding Themes

5. **Movement** How did changes in climate affect the migration of early peoples from one part of the world to another?

Chapter 1 Section 1

ASSESS

Check for Understanding

Assign Section 1 Review as homework or as an in-class activity.

Use Student Self-Test and Review Software to review Section 1.

Evaluate

Section Quiz 1-1

Use the Testmaker to create a customized quiz for Section 1.

Reteach

Discuss with students the meaning of the word *innovation*. Have them name innovations discussed in this section, and examine how each innovation changed the lives of prehistoric people.

Enrich

Have each student list what he or she thinks are the five most basic tools needed for human survival. Discuss and compare the lists.

CLOSE

Have students describe in their own words the migrations pictured on the map on page 22. Remind them to pay close attention to the symbols on the map that represent prehistoric time.

SECTION 1 REVIEW ANSWERS

1. All vocabulary words are defined in the Glossary.
2. Suwa, 21; Tim D. White, 21; Johanson, 21; Louis Leakey, 25; Mary Leakey, 25
3. Aramis, site in Ethiopia where remains of oldest human ancestors were found; Hadar, site in Ethiopia where oldest most nearly complete skeleton of a hominid was found; Olduvai Gorge, site in eastern Africa where Leakeys conducted research on *Homo habilis*
4. *Homo habilis*: earliest toolmakers, may have migrated to Europe and Asia; *Homo erectus*: cave dwellers, made fire and clothing, migrated to Europe and Asia
5. **MOVEMENT** In Ice Ages, people migrated to warmer climates; answers should also mention land bridges during periods of glaciation.

Chapter 1
Section 2

SECTION THEME

▶ **Innovation** Early humans produce tools and domesticate animals and crops.

Find Out

Answer: *They developed improved tools, invented the wheel and the loom, and discovered how to work metal. They domesticated both plants and animals. They began to live and work together in larger groups, cared for their sick and aged, and developed religious beliefs and practices.*

FOCUS

Section Objective

Describe some of the achievements of the earliest humans.

BELLRINGER Motivational Activity

Before taking roll at the beginning of the class period, project Section Focus Transparency 1-2 and have students answer the activity questions. Discuss students' responses.

This activity is also available as a blackline master.

Vocabulary Pre-check

Use Vocabulary Activity 1 to introduce vocabulary terms.
L1 LEP

100,000 B.C. — 75,000 B.C. — 50,000 B.C. — 25,000 B.C.

c. 100,000 B.C. Neanderthals spread from Africa into Europe and Asia.

c. 50,000 B.C. Modern humans originate in Africa.

c. 15,000 B.C. World population reaches about 2 million.

Section 2

The Appearance of *Homo Sapiens*

Setting the Scene

▶ **Terms to Define**
domesticate, deity

▶ **People to Meet**
Neanderthals, Cro-Magnons

▶ **Places to Locate**
Neander Valley, Lascaux, Vallon-Pont-d'Arc, Jericho, Çatal Hüyük

Find Out What were the achievements of the earliest humans?

The Storyteller

The first sign of animal domestication we have discovered, at some of the earliest human settlements, is not of something that pulled a plow, or was eaten; it is the dog. This creature, which willingly chooses a human as the leader of its life-long pack, was humankind's first friend, it seems, as well as its best. Certain species began to thrive under human care; and humans rearranged their lives to care for the animals that now came to depend on them.

—adapted from *Women's Work: The First 20,000 Years,* Elizabeth Wayland Barber, 1994

Neolithic scraper

Homo erectus discovered, used, and improved upon numerous aspects of culture that are basic to present-day life. These accomplishments occurred extremely slowly, however, taking place over many thousands of years. When *Homo sapiens,* the modern human species, appeared, cultural changes began occurring with much greater frequency and took on greater sophistication. In 1995 archaeologists uncovered in Zaire, Central Africa, a number of 80,000-year-old barbed points and blades. This find indicates that humans made the first sophisticated tools in Africa and at a much earlier date than had been believed.

The Neanderthals

Evidence of early *Homo sapiens* dates back about 200,000 years. The first *Homo sapiens* probably were the **Neanderthals** (nee•AN•duhr•THAWLZ). Anthropologists named them after the **Neander Valley** in Germany where their remains were first discovered in the A.D. 1850s. Fossil evidence indicates that Neanderthal people originated in Africa and began spreading into Europe and Asia about 100,000 years ago.

Neanderthals stood about 5.5 feet (1.7 meters) tall. Their brains were slightly larger than those of modern human beings, and their bodies were stocky, with thick bones and very muscular necks and shoulders. Some scientists today believe that these distinctive physical characteristics enabled Neanderthals to adapt to colder climates.

Technological Skills

Like their predecessors, Neanderthals were nomadic hunter-gatherers who used fire for warmth and for cooking their food, but their tool-

SECTION RESOURCES

Reproducible Masters
- Reproducible Lesson Plan 1-2
- Vocabulary Activity 1
- Guided Reading Activity 1-2
- History Simulation 1
- Section Quiz 1-2

Transparencies
- Section Focus Transparency 1-2
- World History and Art Transparency 1, *Woman's Head*

Multimedia
- Student Self-Test and Review Software
- Testmaker

making ability was more sophisticated than that of *Homo erectus*. Neanderthals skillfully crafted stone knives, spear points, and bone tools. Hide-cleaning and food-preparing tools were made of flakes struck from flint or whatever other kind of stone was available. The flakes were delicately shaped by chipping away small pieces from one or more edges of the stone.

Ways of Life

Most Neanderthals lived in small groups of 35 to 50 people. Because they were nomads, Neanderthals did not live in permanent homes. In good weather or warm climates, they lived in open-air camps along the shores of lakes or rivers. In several places, archaeologists have found the remains of Neanderthal shelters built of branches and animal skins. In colder climates, Neanderthals lived together in caves or under the overhangs of cliffs. Heavy clothing made from animal skins must have been worn to fight off the cold.

Culture and Beliefs

The Neanderthals were advanced culturally. They cared for their sick and aged, and may have been the first to practice medicine. A number of Neanderthal fossils shows signs of serious injuries that had completely healed before death. Neanderthals also apparently had a belief in life after death. They covered the bodies of their dead with flowers and buried them in shallow graves with food, tools, and weapons.

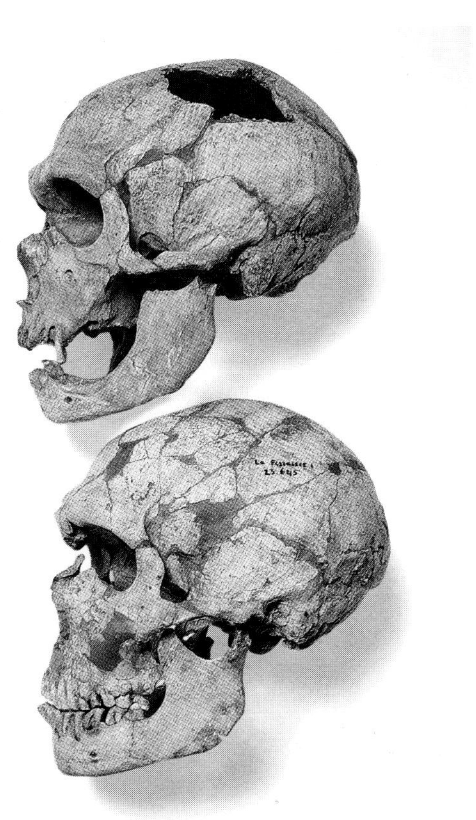

Visualizing History ***Homo neanderthalensis*** **fossil skulls found in caves in France resemble the original fossil skull from the Neander Valley in Germany. Neanderthals were short, sturdy hunter-gatherers.** *How did Neanderthals adapt to cold weather?*

Homo Sapiens Sapiens

Most scientists believe that modern humans, or *Homo sapiens sapiens*, originated in Africa about 50,000 years ago. Within 20,000 years, this new group had migrated to almost every continent in the world, including Australia and North America and South America. Many scientists believe that as *Homo sapiens sapiens* moved slowly from Africa into Europe and Asia, they intermarried with Neanderthals and gradually absorbed them. With the extinction of the Neanderthals, *Homo sapiens sapiens* became the only hominids left on Earth.

Footnotes to History **The First Razors** Archaeologists have unearthed evidence that prehistoric men were shaving as early as 18,000 B.C. Some Cro-Magnon cave paintings portray beardless men, and early Cro-Magnon grave sites contain sharpened shells that were the first razors. Later, people hammered razors out of bronze, and eventually, out of iron.

The Cro-Magnons

The earliest *Homo sapiens sapiens* in Europe are called **Cro-Magnons**, after the rock shelter in France where their remains were first found in the A.D. 1860s. Since then, a wealth of Cro-Magnon remains have been found in other parts of Europe and in eastern and central Asia. Similar forms of modern humans have been discovered in Russia, China, Southeast Asia, and all over Africa.

The Cro-Magnons were taller but less robust than the Neanderthals. They brought with them improved technology and a more sophisticated

Chapter 1 Section 2

TEACH

Guided Practice

THEME Innovation

Write the word *innovation* on the chalkboard. Review its meaning with students. Elicit that an innovation can be more than just a device or contrivance. Have students give examples of various kinds of innovations that they are aware of from their own lifetime. Especially try to elicit examples of customs or methods of doing something. **L1**

Visualizing History The evolution of the brain, teeth, and jaw of hominids has determined the shape of the skull. From *Australopithecus* on, the teeth of hominids have become progressively smaller, the jaw less heavy, and the brain case larger (except for the Neanderthal brain, which was larger than that of modern humans).

Answer to Caption: *They lived together in caves and used animal skins for heavy clothing.*

Religion Have students discuss why the evidence of food, tools, and weapons at burial sites suggests to scientists a prehistoric belief in the afterlife. *(Answers might include the point that, since the articles would no longer be useful in the person's life, they must have been meant for an afterlife.)* **L2**

COOPERATIVE LEARNING ACTIVITY

Role Play Have students work with partners. Have them role-play an interview with an archaeologist at one of the following sites: Neander Valley, Lascaux, Vallon-Pont-d'Arc, Jericho, Çatal Hüyük. To prepare for the interview, students should read the *archaeology* entry in a good encyclopedia. They should also find additional information on the particular site they have chosen. Have them write specific questions they would like to ask the archaeologist they are interviewing. Students can take turns being interviewer and interviewee. When all interviews have taken place, ask the class to summarize what they have learned from them. **L1**

Chapter 1
Section 2

Critical Thinking Have students discuss how people's attitudes toward their environment might have changed as they began to raise crops and domesticate animals. *(One conclusion that students might draw is that hunter-gatherers live in nature, but farmers set out to control nature.)* **L3**

World History and Art Transparency 1, *Woman's Head*

Linking Past and Present

Beards Men's beards have gone in and out of fashion throughout history. The ancient Egyptians considered a clean-shaven face a symbol of high status. The ancient Persians, however, wore their beards long and curled.

culture. Although they still made their living by hunting and gathering, their methods of food gathering were more efficient, and their hunting techniques were more effective than those of earlier groups.

Cro-Magnon Technology

The many advances the Cro-Magnons made in their toolmaking technology transformed human life. Their blades were thinner and had sharper cutting edges than those of the Neanderthals. The Cro-Magnons used bone, antler, and ivory to make new kinds of tools—hammers, hoes, and pincers. Soon they were fishing with bone fishhooks and using bone needles to sew fitted leather clothes.

With the invention of the stone ax, Cro-Magnons could chop down trees and shape them into canoes. Soon they were traveling down rivers and along seacoasts. They even crossed 50 miles (80 kilometers) of open sea to reach Australia.

Cro-Magnon hunters also invented long-distance weapons—the spear-thrower and the bow and arrow. Now they could hunt several animals at once and larger animals, too, such as woolly mammoths and bison. The food supply increased and with it the number of people on Earth. Anthropologists estimate that by 15,000 B.C., the world population of human beings stood at a little more than 2 million.

Social Life

The Cro-Magnons' increased food supply had political and social consequences as well. Because it was not possible for a lone band of Cro-Magnons to carry out a big-game hunt, it became necessary for four or five unrelated bands to cooperate, often for weeks at a time. The cooperating bands probably needed formal rules in order to get along, giving rise in turn to leaders who devised and enforced the rules. The evidence for Cro-Magnon leaders consists of high-status burials. Archaeologists have discovered certain Cro-Magnons buried with ivory daggers, amber beads, and other signs of high rank.

Cro-Magnons at first lived in a variety of temporary structures. Some lived inside cave

Images of the Times

Early Human Technology

Although they are difficult to date precisely, ancient artifacts provide important clues to early human life.

Discovered in France, this bison licking its flank was carved from bone during the Middle Stone Age–12,000–8000 B.C.

A Neolithic scraper, c. 70,000–50,000 B.C., flaked by repeated blows, helped ancient people dig up roots, shape wood, and cut meat.

28

Images of the Times **Early Human Technology**

Just as plastics are the wonder materials of the modern age, the Cro-Magnon era also had its wonder materials. Among these were bone, antler, and ivory. They were much more versatile than wood. They could be cut, carved, and shaped into implements from needles to shovels. They were strong and durable. They could be sharpened. Ivory could even be steamed and bent. Other Stone-Age wonder materials included flint, a type of quartz, and obsidian, a kind of glass formed when lava cools quickly. Both could be used to produce very sharp edges and were fashioned into knives, even razors.

entrances, while others built huts in forested areas. As better hunting methods developed, Cro-Magnons built more permanent homes. Long houses holding many families were made of stone blocks. There is archaeological evidence that communities of 30 to 100 people lived together.

Cave Paintings

To their technological advances, the Cro-Magnons added accomplished artistry. They created cave paintings like those found at **Lascaux** (la •SKOH) and **Vallon-Pont-d'Arc** (vah•YOHN pohn DAHRK), both in France, as well as those at numerous other cave sites in Spain and Africa. Researchers so far can only speculate on the purpose behind the mysterious wall images. Perhaps the hunting scenes were educational, designed to teach young hunters how to recognize prey. On the other hand, the Cro-Magnon painters may have been reaching out to the spiritual world, creating images meant to have mystical powers that would help the hunters.

Archaeologists have discovered some Cro-Magnon figures sculpted from clay or carved from reindeer antlers. They have also found figures of ivory and bone decorated with animal drawings and abstract designs. Some of these artifacts may well have been used in magic rituals and probably reflect Cro-Magnon beliefs about spirits thought to live in animals, plants, the earth, and the sky.

The Neolithic Revolution

During the Neolithic period and immediately after, humanity made one of its greatest cultural advances. New environments had developed with the end of the last Ice Age, and forests and grasslands appeared in many areas. Over some 5,000 years, people gradually shifted from gathering and hunting food to producing food. Because new agricultural methods led to tremendous changes in peoples' lifestyles, this period is usually called the Neolithic Revolution.

Sumerian cuneiform laid the foundation of writing about 3000 B.C.

REFLECTING ON THE TIMES

1. What clue to early human life does the bison licking its flank provide?
2. How did people store information about the past before writing began?

ANSWERS TO REFLECTING ON THE TIMES

1. Early peoples had tools capable of fine carving.
2. by painting and drawing on cave walls and by memorizing stories and passing them on

Chapter 1 Section 2

Independent Practice

Guided Reading Activity 1-2 **L1**

History Simulation 1

Art Have students research and report on the cave paintings of French, Spanish, or African sites such as Vallon-Pont-d'Arc in France or the Altamira Cave in Spain. They might include illustrations in the report. **L2**

Daily Life Have students use the information in the text as a guide to building a model of a Neolithic village such as the one discovered at Çatal Hüyük. **L2 LEP**

CURRICULUM CONNECTION

THE ARTS

Paleolithic cave painters used a variety of techniques, including painting with fingers, sticks, and pads of fur or moss. They daubed, dotted, and sketched, using charcoal or pigments from the earth. Sometimes they spray-painted through hollow bone. Painters of different eras often worked on the same cave walls. At Lascaux, 13 eras are evident.

Chapter 1 Section 2

The Arts Have students create comic strips illustrating their conception of Neolithic people's lives. Have them share their comic strips with the class. Then discuss these questions: What is the basis for the information presented in your comic strip? Is it based on your reading in this section? Is it completely imaginary? Does it reflect the popular media as represented by television *(The Flintstones)* or the movies *(History of the World–Part 1)*? **L3**

Chart Study

Answer

They can compare their ideas about prehistoric cultures with the records of more recent cultures–and with cultures from around the world today–to infer which social behaviors typically go along with specific technological innovations.

Practice

Reading a Chart How long ago did people learn to make tools out of bone? *(42,000–10,000 years ago)* What other technological innovation did bone tools make possible? *(sewing clothing, using a needle)*

ASSESS

Check for Understanding

Assign Section 2 Review as homework or as an in-class activity.

Use Student Self-Test and Review Software to review Section 2.

In a sense, the Mesolithic period was a forerunner of the Neolithic Revolution. Most of the cultural changes of the Mesolithic period came in methods of obtaining food. People domesticated, or tamed for human purposes, the dog and used it to help them hunt small game. They also domesticated the goat to use for meat and milk. Early farmers invented the sickle for cutting wild grains so that they could eat the seeds. Pottery, made from sun-hardened clay, was far more effective for carrying and storing food and water than the pouches of animal skin people had used previously.

The Dawn of Agriculture

The Neolithic Revolution not only took place slowly, but also began at different times in different parts of the world. Archaeologists have found evidence of agriculture in the Middle East dating as far back as 8000 B.C. In contrast, China did not have agriculture until about 5000 B.C.

The crops that Neolithic people domesticated varied from place to place, depending on the varieties of wild plants and on the crops best adapted to the region's climate—wheat and barley in the Middle East, rice in Southeast Asia, and corn in the Americas. Farmers in Africa cultivated bananas and yams, and farmers in South America grew potatoes. Neolithic people also domesticated animals. They used cattle, pigs, and sheep for meat and sometimes milk. Chickens provided eggs as well as meat.

Farming in many ways made life easier. It brought a steady food supply and enabled people to stay longer in one place. However, farmers had to work harder and longer than earlier hunters and gatherers.

Early Humans

	Homo Habilis	Homo Erectus	Homo Sapiens	
Years B.C.	2.5–1.5 million	1.5 million–200,000	200,000–35,000	40,000–8,000
			Neanderthal	Cro-Magnon
TECHNOLOGICAL INNOVATIONS	• Crude stone tools	• Hand axes and other flaked stone tools • Caves used and pits dug • Clothing of animal skins • Fire controlled for warmth, protection, and cooking	• Spear points and hide scrapers • Shelters built or caves improved • Skins laced for clothing	• Knives, chisel, spear-thrower, bow and arrow • Bone tools: needle, fish hook, harpoon • Fish nets, canoes • Sewed leather clothing • Sun-hardened pottery
SOCIAL BEHAVIORS	• Limited speech • Food gathering and scavenging	• Language • Nomadic bands • Hunting-gathering	• Planned burials of dead • Care for disabled members of the community	• Cooperative big-game hunts • Status burials for leaders • Possible magic rituals with cave painting and carved, sculpted artifacts

Chart Study **The category "Technological Innovations" describes items found in archaeological digs and dated to a specific period. Interpretation of likely prehistoric social behaviors, however, depends mostly on inferences made by archaeologists and anthropologists.**
What evidence do researchers have to support the theory that the social behaviors listed above really existed?

MEETING SPECIAL NEEDS ACTIVITY

Language Delayed Play a "What's My Meaning?" word game. Organize students into two teams and have each team survey the section and list five terms to be defined. The first team gives a term for the second team to define or explain. The moderator (who can be the teacher) assigns points–from one to five for the answer given. The team with the most points is the winner. For the benefit of students with limited English proficiency, have a volunteer write the terms on the board as they are defined. Have students write the terms and their meanings in a notebook for future reference. **L1 LEP**

The First Villages

Now that they could produce food, many more people survived. Anthropologists estimate that by 4000 B.C. the world population had risen to 90 million. Once they had agriculture, people could also settle in communities instead of wandering as nomads. Soon, agricultural villages of about 200 or so inhabitants began to develop where soil was fertile and water abundant. Archaeologists date one of the earliest such villages—**Jericho**, in the modern Israeli-occupied West Bank—back to 8000 B.C. Another village, **Çatal Hüyük** (CHAH•tuhl hoo•YOOK), in present-day Turkey, dates from 7000 to 6300 B.C.

Çatal Hüyük is the largest Neolithic village that archaeologists have so far discovered. Its people built rectangular, flat-roofed houses of mud bricks placed in wooden frames. Houses of several related families made up a compound with shared walls. People had to walk across roofs. The villagers also painted the interior walls of their windowless houses with vivid scenes of hunting and other activities.

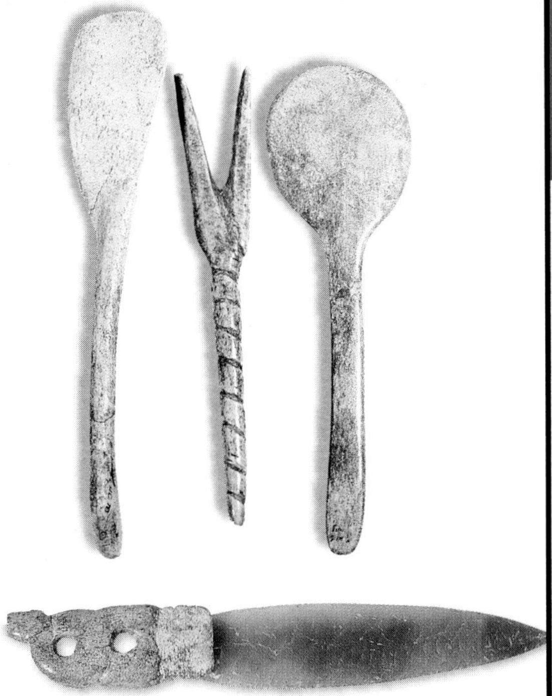

Visualizing History **This Neolithic flint knife and these cooking utensils are from Çatal Hüyük.** *What evidence tends to show that these people enjoyed art?*

Technological Advances

Neolithic farmers eventually made their agricultural work easier and more productive by inventing the plow and by training oxen to pull it. They also learned how to fertilize their fields with ashes, fish, and manure.

The relatively steady food supply quickened the pace of technological advance. Neolithic villagers invented the loom and began weaving textiles of linen and wool. They invented the wheel and used it for transportation. They found a way to bake clay bricks for construction. They learned how to hammer the metals copper, lead, and gold to make jewelry and weapons. In 1991, for example, the frozen body of a late Neolithic Age man was discovered in the Italian Alps. The 5,000-year-old "Iceman" wore well-made fur and leather clothing and shoes stuffed with grass. He carried a wooden backpack, a copper ax, a bow, and arrows.

The agricultural way of life led to many other changes. People created calendars to measure the seasons and determine when to plant crops. Because their food supply depended on land ownership, people now cared about such matters as boundary lines and rules of inheritance. Warfare probably came into being as villages competed for land and water.

Neolithic people also believed in many **deities**, or gods and goddesses. The spirits that supposedly surrounded them throughout nature were transformed into humanlike gods and goddesses with the power to help or hurt people. The people of Çatal Hüyük, for example, set up shrines at which they offered gifts in honor of their deities.

SECTION 2 REVIEW

Recall

1. **Define** domesticate, deity.
2. **Identify** Neanderthals, Cro-Magnons, Neolithic Revolution.
3. **List** the innovations made during the Neolithic period.

Critical Thinking

4. **Evaluating Information** Does the use of agriculture by Neolithic peoples deserve to be called a revolution? Give reasons.

Understanding Themes

5. **Innovation** Discuss how technological developments affected the food supplies of early peoples in various parts of the world.

Chapter 1 Section 2

Visualizing History Also found in Çatal Hüyük was the earliest known landscape painting. Created by a Neolithic artist, it consists of a series of squares representing the mud-brick houses of the city. An erupting volcano appears in the background. **Answer to Caption:** *the artistic shape and decoration of the knife and cooking utensils*

Evaluate

Section Quiz 1-2

Use the Testmaker to create a customized quiz for Section 2.

Reteach

Review students' understanding of the word *innovation*. Then have them name and discuss the significance of some of the innovations covered in this section. *(clothing, tools, agriculture, houses)*

Enrich

Have students obtain from the guidance office or library a course catalog of a university. Have them report to the class on some of the courses offered by the anthropology department.

CLOSE

Have students describe the progression in food-procurement methods discussed in this section. *(gathering, scavenging for meat, hunting, agriculture)* Then have them list innovations that helped in this progression. *(for example, knives, fishhooks, domestication of animals)*

SECTION 2 REVIEW ANSWERS

1. All vocabulary words are defined in the Glossary.
2. Neanderthals, 26; Cro-Magnons, 27; Neolithic Revolution, 29
3. agriculture, villages, plow, fertilizer, loom, wheel, bricks, metalworking, calendars
4. Yes: agriculture led to huge and important changes in people's lives, such as living in villages.
5. **INNOVATION** Improved technology made farming easier, brought higher crop yields, and helped ensure a steady food supply.

Chapter 1 Section 3

SECTION THEME

▶ **Change** The earliest civilizations begin with the evolution of farming settlements into the first cities.

Find Out

Answer: *Among the changes were the introduction or growth of specialized labor and long-distance trade, the development of government and armies, and the division of society into classes.*

FOCUS

Section Objective

Specify the kinds of economic, political, and social changes that resulted from the rise of cities.

BELLRINGER Motivational Activity

Before taking roll at the beginning of the class period, project Section Focus Transparency 1-3 and have students answer the activity questions. Discuss students' responses.

This activity is also available as a blackline master.

Vocabulary Pre-check

Use the Vocabulary PuzzleMaker to create a puzzle that reinforces the vocabulary terms in this section. L1

10,000 B.C.		5000 B.C.	1000 B.C.
c. 10,000 B.C. Last Ice Age ends.	**c. 8000 B.C.** Agriculture begins in various places.	**c. 3500 B.C.** Cities develop along the Tigris and Euphrates Rivers.	**c. 1500 B.C.** First urban communities in East Asia appear.

Section 3

Emergence of Civilization

Setting the Scene

▶ **Terms to Define**
civilization, economy, artisan, cultural diffusion, myth

▶ **People to Meet**
the Sumerians

▶ **Places to Locate**
Nile, Tigris-Euphrates, Indus, and Huang River valleys

Find Out What economic, political, and social changes resulted from the rise of cities?

The Storyteller

Archaeological evidence leaves little doubt that women played key roles in every aspect of life in Old Europe. "In the temple workshops … females made and decorated quantities of various pots appropriate to different rites. Next to the altar of the temple stood a vertical loom on which were probably woven the sacred garments.… The most sophisticated creations of Old Europe—the most exquisite vases, sculptures, etc. now extant—were women's work."

—from *The Early Civilizations of Europe*, (Monograph for Indo-European Studies, UCLA, 1980), Marija Gimbutas

Mohenjo-Daro mother goddess

Over thousands of years, some of the early farming villages evolved slowly into complex societies, known as **civilizations**. The people of a civilization lived in a highly organized society with an advanced knowledge of farming, trade, government, art, and science. The word *civilization* comes from the Latin word *civitas*, meaning "city," and most historians equate the rise of civilizations with the rise of cities. Because most city dwellers learned the art of writing, the development of cities also marks the beginning of history.

River Valley Civilizations

As with agriculture, cities formed at different times in different parts of the world. Many of the earliest civilizations, however, had one thing in common: They rose from farming settlements in river valleys like that of the **Nile** River in northeastern Africa. The earliest cities that archaeologists have uncovered so far lie in the valley of the **Tigris and Euphrates** (yoo•FRAYT•eez) Rivers in the Middle East and date back to about 3500 B.C. Cities arose in the **Indus** River valley in South Asia some 1,000 years later. The first urban communities in East Asia appeared about 1500 B.C. in the **Huang He** (HWONG HUH) valley. By about 1000 B.C. cities were flourishing in Europe and in the Americas, and by 750 B.C. in sub-Saharan Africa.

Early river valley civilizations also shared several other basic features. People's labor was specialized, with different men and women doing different jobs. The civilization depended on advanced technology, such as metalworking skills. Each civilization always had some form of government to coordinate large-scale cooperative efforts such as building irrigation systems. The people in each

---

SECTION RESOURCES

Reproducible Masters
- Reproducible Lesson Plan 1-3
- Guided Reading Activity 1-3
- Reteaching Activity 1
- Enrichment Activity 1
- Section Quiz 1-3
- Performance Assessment Activity 1
- Spanish Chapter Summary 1

Transparencies
- Section Focus Transparency 1-3

Multimedia
- Vocabulary PuzzleMaker Software
- Student Self-Test and Review Software
- Testmaker
- Turning Points in World History

Visualizing History **Behind high baked-brick walls the people of the ancient city of Mohenjo-Daro, near the Indus River in Pakistan, used four-wheeled carts to carry grain to a large granary.** *What was the value of surplus food to the development of a civilization?*

civilization also shared a complex system of values and beliefs.

Not all societies formed civilizations, however. Some people continued to live in small agricultural villages, while others lived by hunting and gathering. Some nomadic people built a specialized culture that relied on moving herds of domesticated animals in search of good pasture.

The Economy of a Civilization

The ways in which people use their environment to meet their material needs is known as an economy. The economy of early civilizations depended on their farmers' growing surplus food. With extra food, fewer men and women had to farm and more could earn their living in other ways.

First Irrigation Systems

A major reason that farmers could produce surpluses of grain crops was that early civilizations built massive irrigation systems. Neolithic farmers had relied at first on rainfall to water their crops. Later, farmers transported water to grow the crops by digging ditches from a nearby river to their fields. Then they began building small canals and simple reservoirs.

Farmers also built earthen dikes and dams to control flooding in their valley by the river itself. They could now count on a reasonably steady flow of water and prevent destructive flooding.

Specialization of Labor

As men and women continued to specialize in ways of earning a living, artisans—workers skilled in a craft—became increasingly productive and creative. The longer they worked at one task, such as producing storage vessels, the more they learned about how to handle available materials, such as different types of clay. Gradually they turned out larger quantities of goods and improved the quality of their products.

Jewelry, eating utensils, weapons, and other goods were made by hammering copper, lead, and gold. Later, metalworkers in the early civilizations

COOPERATIVE LEARNING ACTIVITY

Newspaper Article Organize the class into small groups. Have each group brainstorm ideas about how life in an early city differed from life in a small Neolithic village. Contrasts include size, complexity of life, occupations, standard of living, government, and social structure. Have each group write an article for a newspaper about the differences. Students may supplement the text content with library research. Have each group member contribute ideas, information, and help in organizing the article. Assign one or two members to research or write, others to create a headline, and still others to create an illustration to accompany the article. Have one group member orally present the article to the entire class. **L2**

TEACH

Guided Practice

THEME Change

Have students list some of the changes that evolved in early civilizations. Discuss the results of these changes. *(Irrigation made food surpluses possible; metalworking provided tools and weapons; ships promoted long-distance trading.)* **L1**

Visualizing History Mohenjo-Daro was a great urban center that flourished from about 2500 B.C. to about 1500 B.C. A city with a perimeter of 3 miles (5 km), its streets were laid out in rectangular patterns. Houses, many of them two stories high, lined the streets. Drainage systems led into these brick-lined streets. The city had hilltop fortresses for protection and baths, probably for sacred rites.

Answer to Caption: *The economy depended on it; with surplus food fewer people had to farm and more could perform other types of work.*

Critical Thinking Have students explain why a system of writing that uses letters to represent sounds is superior to one that uses symbols or pictures to represent ideas or words. *(The former system is easier to encode and decode and is more efficient in communicating abstract ideas.)* **L3**

Independent Practice

Guided Reading Activity 1-3 **L1**

History Have students research one topic about the Bronze Age and write a short report about it. Topics may include specific tools, hunting practices, ritual art objects, jewelry, food preparation, and so on. **L1**

Global Gourmet

Sumeria As methods of raising foods grew more sophisticated, so did methods of preparing it. The first ovens with burners on top were developed by the Sumerians. When Sir Leonard Woolley excavated the Sumerian city of Ur, he found one ancient stove so perfectly preserved that he was able to light it and prepare food on it.

ABCNEWS INTERACTIVE™

VIDEODISC
Turning Points in World History

Side One
Chapter 3

Title: *The Rise of Cities*
Subject: The inventions of the Sumerians in Mesopotamia enabled people to live together in communities for the first time.
Ask: What led to the need for new forms of government in Mesopotamia? *(population growth)*

learned to make alloys, or mixtures of metals. The most important alloy was bronze, a reddish-brown metal made by mixing melted copper and tin. Historians refer to the period that followed the Stone Age as the Bronze Age, when bronze replaced flint and stone as the chief material for weapons and tools.

Bronze, harder than either copper or tin alone, took a sharper cutting edge. Artisans also found it much easier to cast bronze, or shape the liquid metal by pouring it into a mold to harden. Because the copper- and tin-containing ores needed to make bronze were scarce, however, the metal was expensive and therefore used only by kings, priests, and soldiers.

Long-Distance Trade

The search for new sources of copper and tin is an example of the long-distance trade that accompanied the rise of early civilizations. At first farmers and artisans traded within their own communities. They eventually began traveling to nearby areas to exchange goods. After a while merchants, a specialized class of traders, began to handle trade, and expeditions soon were covering longer routes.

Some long-distance trade moved overland by means of animal caravans. Some goods were transported by water. People floated down rivers on rafts. They made boats, propelling them in shallow water with poles and, in deeper water, with paddles and oars. After a time, people learned how to harness the force of the wind, and rivers and seacoasts became filled with sailing ships.

Along with goods, ideas were actively shared. This exchange of goods and ideas when cultures come in contact is known as **cultural diffusion**. Although early civilizations developed many similar ideas independently, other ideas arose in a few areas and then spread throughout the world by cultural diffusion. When ancient peoples learned about the technology and ideas of different civilizations, the new knowledge stimulated them to improve their own skills and way of life.

Living Together in Cities

Civilizations grew both more prosperous and more complex. Early cities had from 5,000 to 30,000 residents. A population of this size could not function in the same way that a Neolithic village of 200 inhabitants had.

Planning and Leadership

Ancient cities faced several problems unknown in the Neolithic period. Because city residents depended on farmers for their food, they had to make certain that farmers regularly brought their surplus food to city markets. At the same time, farmers could not build dams, dig irrigation ditches, and maintain reservoirs on their own. As civilizations prospered, they drew the envy of nomadic groups, who would repeatedly raid and pillage farms and attack caravans. In short, the first cities needed a way of supervising and protecting agriculture and trade.

The early city dwellers found two solutions to these problems. First, ancient cities organized a group of government officials whose job it was to oversee the collection, storage, and distribution of farming surpluses. These officials also organized and directed the labor force needed for large-scale construction projects, such as irrigation systems and public buildings. Second, ancient cities hired professional soldiers to guard their territory and trade routes.

Army, government officials, and priests belonged to a ruling class often led by a king, although women also held positions of authority. The ruling class justified its power by means of religion. According to ancient beliefs, the land produced food only if the gods and goddesses looked on the people with favor. One of the king's main functions, therefore, was to assist priests in carrying out religious ceremonies to ensure an abundant harvest. The first kings were probably elected, but in time they inherited their positions.

Levels of Social Standing

Archaeological evidence for the position of the ruling class can be found both in the treasures with which they were buried and in the physical layout of the ancient cities. At the city's center was an area that held the most imposing religious and government buildings. Nearby stood the residences of the ruling class. Next to these came the houses of the merchants. Farther out, the shops and dwellings of specific groups of artisans—such as weavers or smiths—were established in special streets or quarters. Farmers, as well as sailors and fishers, lived on the city's outskirts. Archaeological evidence suggests too that slaves, who were probably captured in battle, lived in many parts of the city.

Invention of Writing

Many archaeologists think that writing originated with the records that priests kept of the wheat, cloth, livestock, and other items they received as religious offerings. At first the priests used marks and pictures, called pictograms, to represent products. After a time they used the marks and pictures to represent abstract ideas and, later

MEETING SPECIAL NEEDS ACTIVITY

Study Strategy Students may benefit from being shown how to find key ideas in the text. Go through the levels of headings with them, beginning with the section title, "Emergence of Civilization." Next point out the major headings ("River Valley Civilizations," "The Economy of a Civilization," and so on) and the subheadings ("First Irrigation Systems," "Specialization of Labor," and so on). Be sure they understand how this organizational structure helps them as readers to focus on main ideas and subordinate ideas. Have them write in their own words a one-sentence summary of content under several of the subheadings. **L2**

still, to represent sounds. Priestly records listed the individual men and women who were heads of households, landowners, and merchants. Soon the priests were also recording such information as the king's battle victories, along with legal codes, medical texts, and observations of the stars.

Systems of Values

Among the materials recorded by the priesthoods in early civilizations were myths, traditional stories explaining how the world was formed, how people came into being, and what they owed their creator. The priests of **the Sumerians** in the Tigris-Euphrates River valley wrote their myth of creation, for example, on seven clay tablets.

According to the Sumerian story, before creation there were two gods, Apsu the First Father and Tiamat the First Mother. They married and had many children. "But each generation of gods grew taller than its parents ... [and] the younger gods could do things their parents had never tried to do." Eventually Apsu's great-grandson Ea made a magic spell and killed Apsu. Ea's son Marduk killed Tiamat. Then:

> "Marduk turned again to the body of Tiamat.
> He slit her body like a shellfish into two parts.
> Half he raised on high and set it up as sky....
> He marked the places for the stars....
> He planned the days and nights, the months and years.
> From the lower half of Tiamat's body, Marduk made the earth.
> Her bones became its rocks.
> Her blood its rivers and oceans....
> 'We need creatures to serve us,' he said.
> 'I will create man and woman who must learn to plow land to plant, and make the earth bring forth food and drink for us.
> I will make them of clay.'..."
>
> —"Enuma Elish," Sumerian account of creation from *The Seven Tablets of Creation*, date unknown

After relating how the people drained marshes

Connections: Geography

First Migration to America

One of the land bridges that formed during the Ice Ages joined Siberia, the easternmost part of Asia, with Alaska, the westernmost part of the Americas. Modern historians have named this land bridge Beringia, after the shallow Bering Strait that covers it today.

Approximately 30,000 years ago, groups of Cro-Magnons began crossing Beringia from Asia to the Americas. According to most anthropologists, these groups were nomadic hunting bands who came in search of migrating herds of animals. We do not know whether the migrants crossed all at once or in successive waves.

From the north the migrants gradually moved south into new territory. Anthropologists estimate that their journey all the way to the southernmost tip of South America took about 600 generations. This equals a rate of migration of about 18 miles (29 kilometers) per generation, over 18,000 years.

About 10,000 years ago, while the migrants were moving south through the Americas, the last Ice Age ended and the glaciers retreated toward the Poles. As the ice sheets melted, large quantities of water poured into the oceans and the sea level rose, covering Beringia and similar land bridges. As a result, the Inuit, or Eskimos, who migrated to North America from Asia about 2,000 years ago, arrived by boat rather than on foot.

Little Diomedes Island, Bering Strait

MAKING THE CONNECTION

1. Why were the Inuit unable to migrate from Asia to North America by land?
2. Predict the effects on human life today of major changes in global climate, either warmer or colder.

Chapter 1 Section 3

ASSESS

Check for Understanding

Assign Section 3 Review as homework or as an in-class activity.

Use Student Self-Test and Review Software to review Section 3.

Connections: Geography

First Migration to America

Although water now separates Siberia and Alaska, the Bering Strait is narrow enough (only about 55 miles wide) that small boats can easily cross it during the warmer months of the year.

Answers to Making the Connection

1. *By the time the Inuit migrated, the Beringia land bridge had been covered with water.*
2. *Warmer: Polar ice would melt and oceans would rise, submerging low-lying coastal land. Colder: New glaciers might form, and people would migrate toward tropical regions.*

MAKING CONNECTIONS ACTIVITY

Literature Have students engage in a roundtable discussion about creation myths from various civilizations, such as the story of Marduk in this section. Have students prepare by finding out as much as they can about these various creation myths. Each student should become a resource person for one myth. The myths can be discussed one at a time or thematically in class. Focus the discussion on the myths' similarities and differences. Have students speculate about the nature and beliefs of the different civilizations. Have excerpts from some of the myths read aloud in class. Creation myths from greatly differing civilizations will enhance this activity. For example: Greek theogony, Scandinavia's Ymir (or Imir), Ghana's Nyame, and China's cosmic egg. **L2**

Visualizing History The stone sculptures discovered at Tel Amar give us some idea of what the ancient Sumerians looked like. They were tall, and the men wore both their hair and their beards long. **Answer to Caption:** *Marduk*

Evaluate

Section Quiz 1-3

Use the Testmaker to create a customized quiz for Section 3.

Reteach

Have students review the roles of the following people in early cities: farmers, merchants, artisans, soldiers, rulers, priests.

Reteaching Activity 1

Enrich

Have students research cuneiform writing. Direct them to find out how different pictograms evolved into abstract symbols and how people of modern times learned to decode and read cuneiform inscriptions.

Enrichment Activity 1

CLOSE

Have students write four topic sentences that express main ideas about the first civilizations. *(Examples: The first civilizations began along river valleys. Farmers in early civilizations produced surpluses of food. Early civilizations traded with one another. City living created specialization of labor.)* Have students read and discuss their sentences in class.

Visualizing History **Statue of the god Abu and his consort from the temple at Tel Asmar.** *What god was worshiped by the ancient Sumerians as creator of the earth?*

for farmland, built walled cities, learned to make bricks, and built a great temple at the center of their biggest city, the myth continues:

> "Daily they sang praises to Marduk,
> supreme among the gods
> He who created the vast spaces and fashioned
> earth and men;
> He who both creates and destroys; who is god
> of storms and of light;
> He who directs justice; a refuge for those in
> trouble;
> From whom no evil doer can escape;
> His wisdom is broad. His heart is wide. His
> sympathy is warm."

Creation myths have been found in every civilization. Because these myths vary from place to place, historians often examine them for evidence of a people's customs and values. For example, the seven Sumerian clay tablets could easily imply information about Sumer's values and beliefs. The clay tablets reveal that Marduk, though not the first god, had become—at the time the tablets were recorded—the leading one by supplanting the goddess Tiamat. The Sumerians seemed to believe too that evil should—and would—be punished. Apparently they also thought it was effective to praise and worship Marduk. Of course, the inferences an archaeologist can reasonably make from a myth are often limited and leave many unanswered questions.

SECTION 3 REVIEW

Recall

1. **Define** civilization, economy, artisan, cultural diffusion, myth.
2. **Identify** the Sumerians.
3. **Name** the four river valleys in which the world's earliest civilizations developed. Where are these river valleys located?

Critical Thinking

4. **Synthesizing Information** Imagine that you rule a city in an early civilization. What instructions would you give to your government officials to improve the living conditions of your people?

Understanding Themes

5. **Change** How did technological changes of the first civilizations improve toolmaking skills and the transportation of trade goods?

SECTION 3 REVIEW ANSWERS

1. All vocabulary words are defined in the Glossary.
2. a people who lived in the Tigris-Euphrates River valley and wrote their myth of creation on clay tablets
3. Nile: northeastern Africa; Tigris and Euphrates: southwest Asia; Indus: south Asia; Huang He: east Asia
4. Students should consider basic needs of city's people. Answers may include issuing orders to build walls around the city; beginning project to develop adequate sewage system and so on.
5. **CHANGE** toolmaking: ability to make alloys such as bronze; transportation: advances in boatbuilding, such as sails

Social Studies SKILLS

Understanding Map Projections

Greenland appears to be a larger landmass than Australia on some maps, yet Australia actually has a larger land area than Greenland. Have you ever wondered why?

Learning the Skill

When mapmakers attempt to transfer the three-dimensional surface of Earth to a flat surface, some inaccuracies occur. To accomplish this mapmakers use *projections*—an image produced when light from within the globe projects the globe's surface on a flat paper. These projections may stretch or shrink Earth's features, depending on the map's intended use.

Projections create two major kinds of maps. A *conformal map* shows land areas in their true shapes, while distorting their actual size. An *equal-area map* shows land areas in correct proportion to one another, but distorts shapes.

The map on this page is a *Cylindrical Projection (Mercator)*. Imagine wrapping a paper cylinder around the globe. A light from within projects the globe's surface on the paper. The resulting conformal projection makes Alaska appear larger than Mexico. Distortion is greatest near the Poles.

A *Conic Projection* is formed by placing a cone of paper over a lighted globe. This produces a cross between a conformal and an equal-area map. This projection is best to show areas in middle latitudes.

To understand map projections use the following steps:

- Compare the map to a globe.
- Determine the type of projection used.
- Identify the purpose of the projection.

Practicing the Skill

Turn to the map of the world in the Atlas. Compare the sizes and shapes of the features on this map to those on a globe. Based on this comparison, answer the following questions:

1. What is the map's projection?
2. How does the map distort Earth's features?
3. In what way does the map accurately present Earth's features?
4. Why did the mapmaker use this projection?

Applying the Skill

Compare the size of Antarctica as it appears on a map with Antarctica on a globe.

For More Practice

Turn to the Skill Practice in the Chapter Review on page 43 for more practice in understanding map projections.

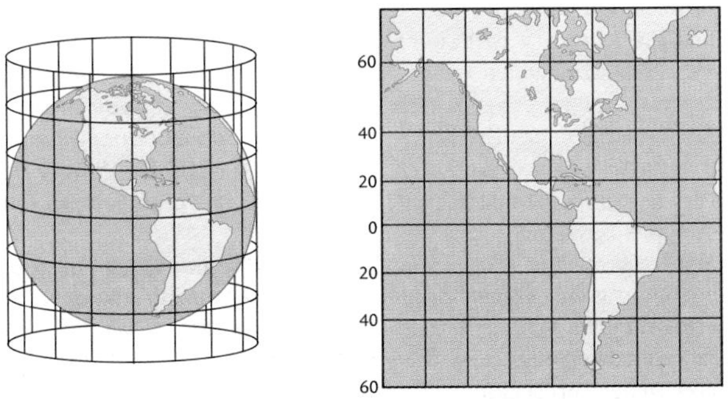

***Cylindrical Projection** (Mercator): This projection is accurate along the line where the cylinder touches the globe, with great distortions near the Poles.*

Social Studies SKILLS

TEACH

Understanding Map Projections To help students see how maps distort our view of the world, have them plot the shortest, most direct route from New York City to Rome on a Mercator map. Then have them use a piece of string to do the same thing on a globe. Compare the two results. *(On the Mercator map, it looks like the route would be over the middle of the Atlantic Ocean, when in fact the shortest route is up the Canadian coast towards Greenland and down.)* Be sure to have a globe available while teaching this skill.

Additional Practice

Skill Reinforcement Activity 1

Building Skills in Geography Workbook, Unit 1, Lesson 12

ANSWERS TO PRACTICING THE SKILL

1. a Robinson projection (created recently by American cartographer Arthur Robinson)
2. The Robinson projection distorts Earth's features less than other projections have. For example, Australia looks as if it has a larger land area than Greenland, which indeed it does.
3. The sizes and shapes of continents and the distances between places are fairly accurate, and visually disturbing distortions have been minimized.
4. The Robinson projection is a good compromise.

Special Report Summary

In 1991 two German hikers discovered the body of a prehistoric man who had been frozen in a glacier in the Alps.

↓

Scientists determined that the "Iceman" was at least 5,000 years old.

↓

The Iceman lived during the Copper Age, which in Europe lasted from 4000 to 2200 B.C.

↓

From the Iceman's possessions we have learned that he was a member of a community which knew how to sew, make finely hewn tools of metal and flint, and use natural substances to combat illness.

TEACH

Points to Discuss

After students have read the selection, discuss the following: **What two methods did scientists use to determine the Iceman's age? Which of the two is more exact?** *(estimating by style of ax, radiocarbon dating; the latter is more exact)* **What factors led the Iceman and others of his time to**

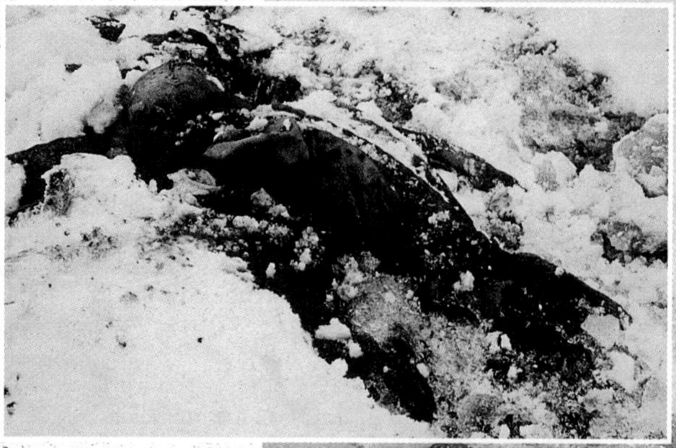

Sygma

The Iceman

On September 19, 1991, Helmut and Erika Simon, a German couple hiking near the border between Austria and Italy, wandered slightly off the trail. Suddenly Erika Simon caught sight of a small head and pair of shoulders emerging from the ice. The Simons thought they had stumbled across a discarded doll. In fact, they had found the solitary prehistoric traveler now known around the world as the Iceman.

At first the Iceman was thought to be 4,000 years old—which would have made the discovery remarkable enough. Scientists later discovered that the Iceman was at least 5,000 years old! In comparison, Tutankhamen, Egypt's boy-king, was born some 2,000 years later.

The Iceman is the oldest body ever retrieved from an Alpine glacier; the next-oldest was only 400 years old. At 10,530 feet (3,210 m),

Overcome by fatigue and cold, a mountaineer (above) lies down to die high in the Alps. Some 5,000 years later, the discovery of his well-preserved body, along with clothes and a copper ax, offers startling clues about how humans greeted the metal age in Europe.

The Iceman (top) emerges from under a melting glacier.

TEACHER NOTES

Greg Harlin/Wood Ronsaville Harlin, Inc.

Sygma

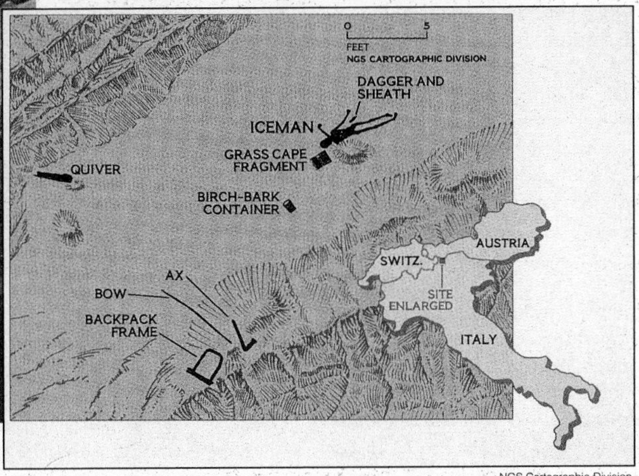

NGS Cartographic Division

ıe site where the Iceman lay is the ghest elevation in Europe in which rehistoric human remains have een found. Not even traces of a ımpfire have ever been discovered that height.

The body of the Iceman was preırved through sheer luck. Shortly ter he died, the rocky hollow here he lay filled with snow. For ıousands of years a glacier covered ıis pocket of snow, only a few ırds over the Iceman's head. More ommonly, a body caught in a glaer would be crushed and torn by ıe movement of the ice. Instead, the eman was naturally mummified.

In the four days following the discovery, many well-meaning hikers and officials tried to free the Iceman from the glacier. They took turns hacking and prodding around the body with ice axes and ski poles. Unfortunately, they damaged the Iceman and the artifacts found with him—in ways that 5,000 years of glaciation had not. One of the "rescuers" seized a stick to dig with, breaking it in the process; the stick turned out to be part of the hazel-wood-and-larch frame of the Iceman's backpack, a type of ancient artifact never seen before. Workers also snapped off the top

The local coroner (above) and an assistant remove the corpse from his icy grave.

The Iceman was found at an elevation of 10,530 feet (3,210 m) on the Austrian-Italian border. His tools and backpack frame were located near his body.

climb high into the Alps? *(climatic warming made higher and higher altitudes good locations for hunting game or pasturing sheep; large veins of copper found there)* How did the discovery of copper change life for the prehistoric people who lived in the Alps? *(led to the development of trade routes, and of new, specialized occupations such as smelters and axmakers)* What evidence is there that the Iceman had a spiritual life? *(He had tattoo-like marks in places that no one could see, which suggests they were to confer supernatural power; he carried two pieces of fungi on a leather thong, an artifact which also might have been believed to confer power or protection, as it has no other more utilitarian purpose.)*

Linking Past and Present

Archaeological Evidence Since the discovery of the Iceman, archaeologists have looked for other signs of prehistoric people in the high Alpine valleys where he died. They have found remains of campsites and flint tools from hunters who lived thousands of years before the Iceman. Many of these remains, as well as the Iceman's body, were found along a path which local shepherds still use.

FUN FACTS

- Although lung disease is often thought of as a symptom of modern life with its cigarette smoke and pollution, doctors found that the Iceman's lungs were as black as a smoker's. They attribute his condition to living in a shelter with an open fire.
- The development of metalworking increased contact between peoples, as the early metalsmiths were traveling specialists. The Iceman had large amounts of copper in his hair, and may have been such a traveling coppersmith.
- Copper is the first metal prehistoric people put to utilitarian use. The oldest known human-made metal is a copper pendant that dates from around 9500 B.C.
- Animals as well as humans have been preserved in ice. In Siberia, some 50 specimens of the long-extinct woolly mammoth have been found preserved in ice with their skin and flesh still intact.

CURRICULUM CONNECTION

MEDICINE

Doctors and scientists have used special instruments and techniques to study the Iceman's physical remains. Their studies have shown that he may have been in a weakened condition when he died, as he suffered from worms. X-rays of the Iceman's shinbones revealed that he endured several periods of illness or extreme hunger during the course of his life that arrested his growth.

you don't say...

Copper Age The Copper Age is also sometimes called the Chalcolithic Age, which means "Copper-Stone" Age. This name is fitting because in the early stages of this period, copper was used mainly for small precious objects, while many tools continued to be made of stone. Some of the Iceman's tools, for example his dagger, were made of flint, not metal.

end of the Iceman's six-foot-long bow. What remained of the Iceman's clothing was torn off, as were parts of his body, and an officer using a jackhammer left a gaping hole in the Iceman's hip. To be sure, none of the salvagers suspected how old the Iceman was.

Not until five days after the discovery did an archaeologist examine the Iceman's body. Basing his estimate on the style of the ax found with the body, the archaeologist guessed that the Iceman was 4,000 years old.

Once officials knew the Iceman's approximate age, a rigorous effort to stabilize his condition began. The mummy was placed in a freezer, where the temperature was kept at a constant 21°F (-6°C) and the humidity at 98 percent—conditions much the same as those of the ice in which he had lain. The Iceman was not removed from the freezer for more than 20 minutes at a time, and then only for the most important scientific research. Part of that research was carbon-dating the Iceman to verify how old he was. Further chemical analysis revealed that the blade of his ax was not bronze, but nearly pure copper. He was, in fact, unique: a mummy from the Copper Age, which lasted in central Europe roughly from 4000 to 2200 B.C. Two different laboratories concluded that he was 5,000 to 5,500 years old.

THE ICEMAN'S DOMAIN was the Alps, stretching from southeast France to the Swiss-German border, and from Austria to northern Italy. Five thousand years ago these mountains were a vast wilderness. In the Copper Age, hardy voyagers trekked these ranges, and the goods they traded traveled even farther. We know from his tools and clothes that the Iceman was one of these rugged mountaineers.

The first half of the Copper Age was an era of climatic warming, when humans penetrated higher than ever into the Alps. The tree line climbed during the warming, game followed the forests, and hunters followed the game. Meadows above the tree line offered the best pastures for sheep, goats, and cattle and contained great green veins of a newly valued metal—which today we call copper. Copper changed the Alpine world forever, leading to the development of major trade routes between isolated valleys. Earlier, wealth was made through cattle or wheat. Copper was not only a form of portable wealth but also a stimulus for the development of specialized occupations. Men became smelters, axmakers, possibly even salesmen. The world's earliest known manmade copper objects—beads, pins, and awls—were made about 8000 B.C. in Turkey and Iran. There is evidence of copper mining in the Balkans by 5000 B.C. From there the technology spread west, reaching the Alps a thousand years later.

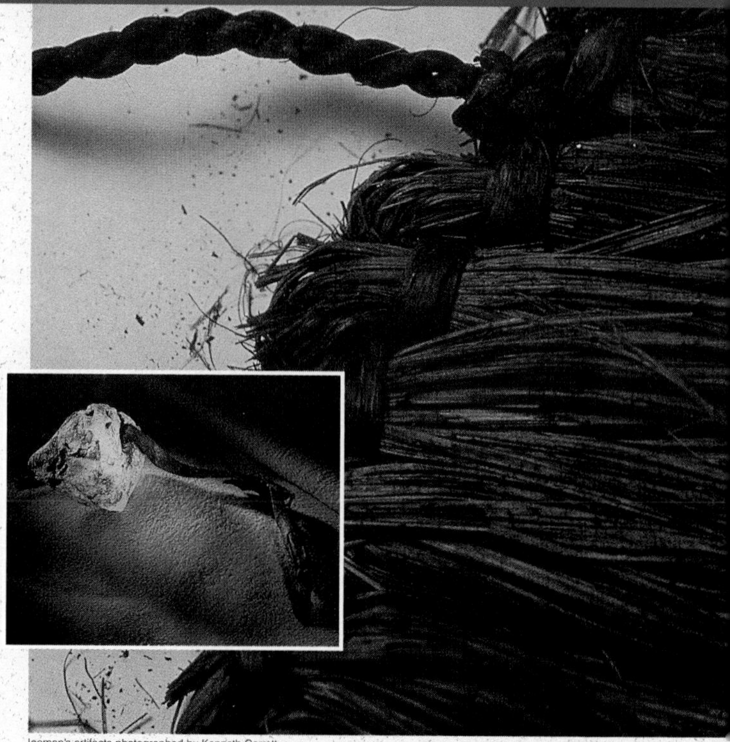

Iceman's artifacts photographed by Kenneth Garrett

A fragment of the Iceman's plaited-grass cape (above) was found next to his head.

This stone disk threaded with a leather thong (inset, top right) may have been worn to protect against evil.

The Iceman's copper ax is the oldest ever found in Europe with its bindings and handle intact (inset, bottom right).

A fungus on a string may have been a first-aid kit (inset, above left).

TEACHER NOTES

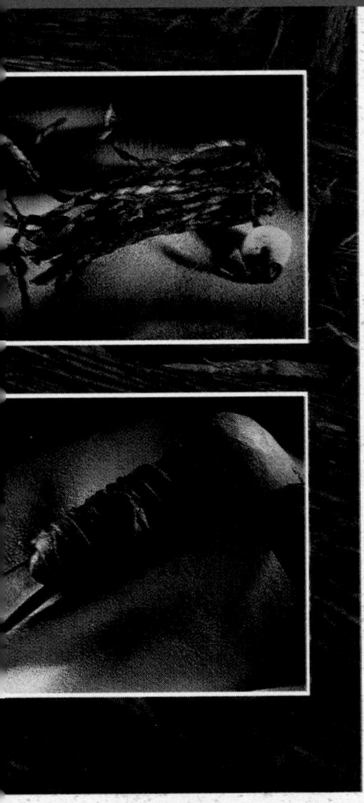

The work of many researchers over the past 30 years tells us much about life during the Copper Age. Excavations have yielded bones that indicate that by around 5000 B.C. Alpine people had domesticated five animals: dogs, which were originally more important for food than companionship, cattle, sheep, goats, and pigs. Horses and chickens were still unknown in the Alps. Villagers grew wheat and barley and made linen clothes from flax. They had only recently discovered how to milk a cow and how to make cheese and butter. Their sheep may have been used for meat but not yet for wool. Many staple foods of today were still unknown, including potatoes, onions, and oats.

EVENTUALLY, THE ICEMAN'S possessions may tell us more than his body will. Of those possessions, his copper ax may tell us most. Its yew-wood handle ends in a gnarled joint, where a notch holds the blade. Dark birch gum held the blade firmly in position beneath a tightly wrapped thong of rawhide. It is a ribbed ax, rather than the more primitive flat ax that archaeologists would have expected to find.

Researchers who reconstructed what remained of the Iceman's clothing observed that his garment had been skillfully stitched together with sinew. Cruder repairs had been made, probably by the Iceman himself on his travels. This led researchers to believe that the Iceman had been part of a community, although he was used to fending for himself. Also, tiny pieces of a wheat that grew only at low altitudes, and bits of charcoal from a variety of trees found throughout the Alps were discovered with the Iceman, indicating that he may have come the South Tirol.

Included among the Iceman's possessions were a stick with a tip of antler used to sharpen flint blades; a deerskin quiver that contained 14 arrows; and an unfinished bow. His small flint dagger was similar to those found at other Copper Age sites, but no one had ever seen the kind of delicately woven sheath that held the dagger.

Central Europe's oldest known plow is more than a thousand years younger than the Iceman. Yet Copper Age artists cut images of plows on rocks. Rows of furrows have been found preserved at a major Copper Age religious complex excavated in northwest Italy, though experts believe plowing was ritualistic rather than agricultural.

The Iceman also had tattoo-like marks that might imply something about his spiritual life. Located on normally hidden places—his lower back, behind his knee, and on his ankle—the marks were not for show. Perhaps they were meant to confer supernatural power or protection. So might the pair of fungi he carried, each pierced by a leather thong. Archaeologists have never seen anything like this artifact from that period. The fungi contain chemical substances now known to be antibiotic. If the Iceman used them to counteract illness, perhaps they also seemed magical to him.

We may never know what drew the Iceman to the mountain pass where he died. Perhaps he was a shepherd, a trader, or an outcast. But, in the late 20th century, it is our good fortune to have the opportunity to learn from this ambassador of the Copper Age.

Kenneth Garrett

The Iceman's head was reconstructed by John Gurche, an anthropologically trained artist. He first sculpted a replica of the skull by using computer images, X rays, and CT scans of the Iceman. Gurche then added clay to duplicate the Iceman's mummified face, complete with smashed nose and lip. Next, he added muscles and fatty tissue, nasal cartilage, and glass eyes. Finally he made a new model of the head with soft urethane, tinted to suggest windburned skin. He completed the replica of the Iceman's head by adding human hair.

Who?What?Where?When?

Copper From the time of the Iceman until the A.D. 1800s, methods for processing copper didn't change much. But in the late 1800s, the spread of telephone lines and electric power lines greatly increased the demand for copper, and deposits of high-grade ore were soon depleted. Around 1900, a new method for processing low-grade ore was invented by a young American engineer. Today, about 9 million short tons (8.3 million metric tons) of copper are mined each year.

Cultural Perspectives

Human Development The era in which the Iceman lived, the Copper Age, represented the first stage of human development beyond the Stone Age. In addition to the discovery of metalworking techniques, people made numerous other advances. In some communities of the time, people wore clothes of woven fabric, extracted oil from plants, ate out of stone and wooden bowls, and lived in houses.

MORE ABOUT...

Metal How did early people learn how to make metal? Scientists speculate that the discovery was probably made in a pottery kiln, because ordinary cooking fires do not get hot enough. Copper oxides in powdered form were sometimes used as a glaze on pots. After firing such a pot, a potter may have discovered a small piece of copper in his kiln. If this happened more than once, he might eventually figure out that it was made when the heat interacted with the copper oxide.

Chapter 1 Review

GLENCOE TECHNOLOGY

VIDEODISC

Use MindJogger to review students' knowledge of the chapter.

MindJogger Videoquiz

Chapter 1
Disc 1 Side A

Also available in VHS.

Answers

Using Key Terms

1. h	**6.** b
2. i	**7.** l
3. e	**8.** j
4. d	**9.** a
5. m	**10.** c

Using Your History Journal

Students should understand that early humans had survival skills that people in industrialized societies seldom need; for example, how to make tools from stone and bone; how to start a fire without matches; how to hunt and fish without today's manufactured equipment.

Reviewing Facts

1. connecting Japan and mainland Korea, Great Britain and Ireland to western Europe, the Malay Peninsula almost to Australia, Asia and North America at the Bering Strait
2. Europe and eastern and central Asia
3. Language enabled people to work together, exchange ideas, and pass on culture from generation to generation.
4. Cro-Magnons could hunt larger animals and also more animals at

CHAPTER 1 REVIEW

Historical Significance

Prehistoric people created the basics of human culture—for example, tools, language, and religious belief. In time, increased food supplies and a diverse labor force led to the rise of cities and civilizations. In ancient times, cities enabled large numbers of people to live together, to cooperate with each other, and to carry out many cultural activities. Today the populations of many cities are more than 100 times that of these first cities. Modern cities serve as complex economic, cultural, and political centers in a world that has become, in many ways, one global civilization.

Using Key Terms

Write the key term that completes each sentence.

a. technology
b. artisan
c. myth
d. civilization
e. nomad
f. economy
g. anthropologist
h. prehistory
i. radiocarbon dating
j. archaeologist
k. artifact
l. cultural diffusion
m. culture

1. The period of time before people developed writing is called ______.
2. Among the techniques used by scientists for determining the age of organic remains is ______________.
3. A _______ is a person who uses up the food supply in one place and then moves on to another place.
4. Over thousands of years, some of the early agricultural villages evolved into highly complex societies, known as __________ .
5. _______ includes the knowledge people have, the language they speak, the ways in which they eat and dress, their religious beliefs, and their achievements in art and music.
6. An _______ is a worker who is skilled in a particular craft.
7. The exchange of goods and ideas when different peoples come in contact is known as ___________.
8. A scientist known as an _________ unearths and interprets remains left behind by prehistoric people.
9. _______ includes the skills and useful knowledge available to people for collecting materials and making objects necessary for survival.
10. A ______ is a traditional story explaining the origins of the world and civilization.

Using Your History Journal

Evaluate your journal account of being stranded on a deserted island. What skills and knowledge, known to early humans but not to you, may have helped you survive?

Reviewing Facts

1. **Name** the four land bridges used by prehistoric people during the Ice Ages.
2. **Locate** the two places in which Cro-Magnons seem to have originated before spreading into other parts of the world.
3. **Explain** why the acquisition of language is one of humanity's greatest achievements.
4. **Describe** how the invention of the spear-thrower and the bow and arrow changed the Cro-Magnons' food supply.
5. **List** two major problems faced by inhabitants of ancient cities that Neolithic village dwellers did not face.
6. **State** what many archaeologists consider to be the relationship between religion and the origin of writing.

Critical Thinking

1. **Apply** How did climatic changes affect the development of humankind?
2. **Analyze** What were the major cultural features of each period in the Stone Age?
3. **Synthesize** How do you think the invention of the stone ax might have changed the culture of

a time.

5. coordinating large-scale irrigation projects, guarding territory and trade routes
6. Priests kept written records of religious offerings.

Critical Thinking

1. Colder climates led early humans to develop strategies for keeping warm; Ice Age land bridges led to migration into previously uninhabited areas.
2. Paleolithic: hunting and food gathering, use of fire, making clothing, acquisition of language and religion, invention of tools; Mesolithic: domestication of dog and goat, invention of pottery and sickle; Neolithic: agriculture, settled villages, inventions (plow, loom, wheel, calendar), rules of inheritance, belief in many deities
3. because the stone ax would have enabled

a people who lived along the banks of a navigable river?

4. **Evaluate** What do you think was the most valuable skill that prehistoric people learned during the Paleolithic period? What was the most valuable skill learned during the Neolithic period?

Geography in History

1. **Location** Refer to the map below. What is the relative location of Mesopotamia?
2. **Human/Environment Interaction** Where in this area would ancient peoples have likely begun farming?
3. **Human/Environment Interaction** Why did early farmers build dikes and dams in the river valleys where they raised their crops?

Mesopotamian Civilizations

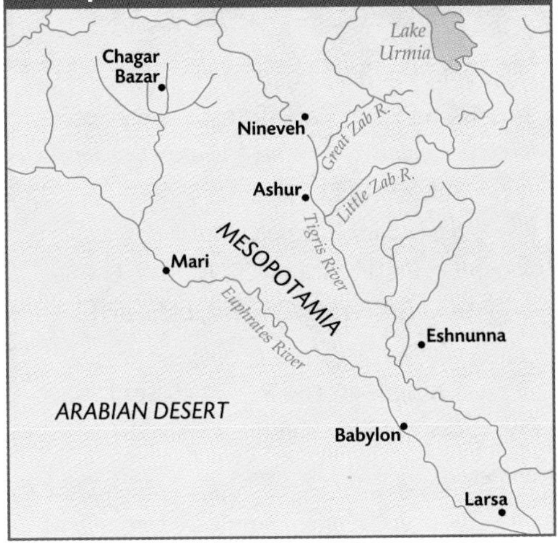

Understanding Themes

1. **Movement** Describe the migrations of human beings from their place of origin to other parts of the world.
2. **Innovation** How did improvements in toolmaking affect the way in which prehistoric people lived?
3. **Change** How did city life differ from village life in early civilizations?

Linking Past and Present

1. Many aspects of human culture are passed down from generation to generation. What cultural achievements of *Homo erectus*—from more than 200,000 years ago—do people still use today?
2. Government officials 5,000 years ago directed the large labor forces needed for large-scale construction projects such as irrigation systems and city walls. They oversaw the collection, storage, and distribution of agricultural surpluses. How do government officials' activities in early civilizations compare with those of government officials in your community?

Skill Practice

Using a small tennis ball, place a dot on each side to represent the North and South Poles. Cut paper strips so that they could completely cover this "globe." (See the example below.)

1. Why are the strips wider at the middle than at the ends?
2. If the strips are laid side-by-side on a flat surface, what pattern do they form?
3. What does this show about the problem of creating an accurate map on a flat surface?
4. The earth is a sphere, but it is somewhat pear-shaped—not a perfect sphere. What additional problem does this create for the cartographer who wants to make a very accurate map of the world?

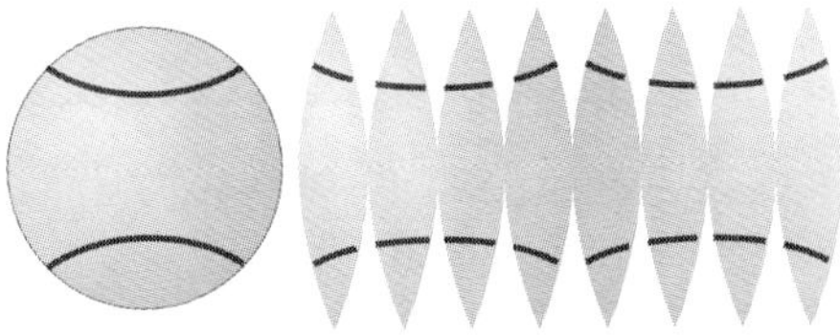

Chapter 1 Review

them to make canoes, it might have led to trading with other peoples and cultural diffusion

4. Paleolithic: language; Neolithic: agriculture

Geography in History

1. between the Tigris and Euphrates Rivers
2. in the fertile river valleys
3. to control flooding and make the water supply steady

Understanding Themes

1. **MOVEMENT** Human beings originated in eastern Africa; spread by land to Europe and Asia and by land bridge to Americas; crossed to Australia by sea.
2. **INNOVATION** Improvements in toolmaking led to greater efficiency in hunting, fishing, making clothing, building homes, vehicles and boats, and, in time, in farming.
3. **CHANGE** number of people in one community averaged 5,000 to 30,000 instead of 200; large-scale irrigation projects needed; labor more specialized; long-distance trade and large ruling class developed; writing invented

Linking Past and Present

1. hunting, making fire, wearing clothing, and talking
2. Students may discuss the modern equivalents of supervision or protection of agriculture, public construction, and trade.

Skill Practice

1. The distance around the ball decreases as the strips get closer to the "poles."
2. a series of football shapes, joined at the middle
3. An accurate map may be difficult to read.
4. Even a projection such as the one described here would not reflect this slight deviation from a perfect sphere.

Chapter Bonus Test Question

Ask students: In seeking the remains of early hominids, how does a paleontologist know where to look? *(It is important for the paleontologist to search in the right rock stratum [for geologic age], the right region [for habitable prehistoric climate], and the right area for fossilization [very rare, and determined by a variety of factors, including soil and environmental conditions].)*

Teach, Reinforce, and Extend CHAPTER Content

Early Civilizations

CHAPTER RESOURCES

	Reproducible Resources	Multimedia Resources
Chapter Opener	Chapter Themes: Graphic Organizer 2 Historical Significance Chapter Activity 2	MindJogger Videoquiz
Chapter Enrichment	Vocabulary Activity 2* Time Line Activity 2 Mapping History Activity 2 History Simulation 2 Geography and History Activity 2 Source Reading 2 People in World History Profiles 1, 2 World Art and Music Activity 2 Enrichment Activity 2 Critical Thinking Activity 2 Skill Reinforcement Activity 2 Performance Assessment Activity 2	Focus on World Art Print 7, Egyptian. *Mask of Tutankhamen* World History and Art Transparencies 2, 3 Mapping History Overlay Transparencies 1, 2, 3 Chapter Transparency 2 NGS PicturePack Transparency Sets: *Ancient Egypt, Fertile Crescent, Ancient China, Ancient India* Vocabulary PuzzleMaker Software NGS PictureShow CD-ROMS: *Egypt and the Fertile Crescent*, *India and China* Turning Points in World History: *The Code of Hammurabi*
Chapter Review/Reteaching	Reteaching Activity 2 Skill Reinforcement Activity 2 Spanish Chapter Summary 2	Chapter 2 Digest Audiocassette, Activity, Test* Vocabulary PuzzleMaker Software Student Self-Test and Review Software MindJogger Videoquiz
Chapter Evaluation/Testing	Performance Assessment Activity 2 Chapter 2 Test, Forms A and B	Testmaker

* *Also available in Spanish*

0:00 **OUT OF TIME?** Assign the Chapter 2 summary in the Unit 1 Digest on pages 96–99, and the Chapter 2 Audiocassettes.

Block Schedule

Block scheduling differs from traditional class scheduling in the amount of time allotted to each period. The extended time frame provided by block scheduling affords you the opportunity to implement a greater number of research-oriented and activity-intense projects to motivate and involve your students. Activities that are particularly suited to use within the block scheduling framework are identified throughout this chapter by the following designation.

KEY TO ABILITY LEVELS

Teaching strategies have been coded for varying learning styles and abilities.

- L1 **BASIC** activities for all students
- L2 **AVERAGE** activities for average to above-average students
- L3 **CHALLENGING** activities for above-average students
- LEP **LIMITED ENGLISH PROFICIENCY** activities

A complete, 1-page lesson plan is provided for each section in the *Reproducible Lesson Plans* booklet.

SECTION RESOURCES

Daily Objectives	Reproducible Resources	Multimedia Resources
Section 1 **The Nile Valley** Understand why Egypt was called the "gift of the Nile."	Reproducible Lesson Plan 2-1 Guided Reading Activity 2-1* Section Quiz 2-1*	Focus on World Art Print 7, Egyptian. *Mask of Tutankhamen* Section Focus Transparency 2-1 World History and Art Transparency 2, *Tutankhamen's Throne* Mapping History Overlay Transparency 2, *Ancient Egypt* Vocabulary PuzzleMaker Software Student Self-Test and Review Software Testmaker Egypt and the Fertile Crescent
Section 2 **The Fertile Crescent** Summarize how Sumer's achievements enriched the early culture of the Middle East.	Reproducible Lesson Plan 2-2 Guided Reading Activity 2-2* Section Quiz 2-2*	Section Focus Transparency 2-2 Mapping History Overlay Transparency 1, *River Valley Civilizations* Student Self-Test and Review Software Testmaker Egypt and the Fertile Crescent Turning Points in World History: *The Code of Hammurabi*
Section 3 **Early South Asia** Relate how people of the Indus River valley civilization built cities.	Reproducible Lesson Plan 2-3 Vocabulary Activity 2* Guided Reading Activity 2-3* Reteaching Activity 2 Enrichment Activity 2 Section Quiz 2-3*	Section Focus Transparency 2-3 Mapping History Overlay Transparency 3, *Ancient India and Ancient China* Student Self-Test and Review Software Testmaker India and China
Section 4 **Early China** Examine the major contributions of early Chinese civilization.	Reproducible Lesson Plan 2-4 Guided Reading Activity 2-4* Reteaching Activity 2 Enrichment Activity 2 Section Quiz 2-4* Performance Assessment Activity 2 Spanish Chapter Summary 2	Section Focus Transparency 2-4 Mapping History Overlay Transparency 3, *Ancient India and Ancient China* World History and Art Transparency 3, *Terra-cotta Warriors* Ancient China Student Self-Test and Review Software Testmaker India and China

* *Also available in Spanish*

Chapter Activities

Performance Assessment Activity

Time Travel Have students assume the roles of time-traveling archaeologists who would like to go back in time to learn more about one of the civilizations in this chapter. Have students choose one of the civilizations and justify their decision with both facts and arguments. Tell them to indicate why they rejected the other civilizations as a choice. The final product should be a grant proposal for funding for the trip. It should include a rationale for the expenses incurred.

Possible Rubric Features
Accuracy and extent of content information, persuasiveness, organization and clarity, appropriateness of product for purpose, elaboration and detail.

• *For an additional activity, refer to Activity 2 in the* Performance Assessment Strategies and Activities *booklet.*

ACTIVITY

From the Classroom of...

John Tabb
Central Hardin High School, Cecilia, KY

Save the Temples

Before assigning reading from Chapter 2, present students with the following situation in modern-day Egypt: A new dam is nearly completed and water is beginning to rise behind it. In about two years it will flood temples built by Ramses II; archaeologists and others want to preserve the temples for posterity. Because Egypt needs the dam for hydroelectricity and irrigation, there is no chance the dam will be stopped before the area is flooded.

Students are instructed to write a short essay on how to save the temples. Have them consider such questions as what machinery to use or how to house the workers. Tell students that this was a real problem Egypt faced in the 1960s, but you would like to see how they would solve it today.

Have students read one another's work within small groups. One group member should briefly summarize for the class the idea selected by each group as its best plan to save the temples. Play the following video,"Touring Egypt," Chicago: Questar Video, 1988, which shows how the Temples of Abu Simbel were moved to higher ground (1964–1966).

MULTIPLE LEARNING STYLES

Verbal/Linguistic
Have students write and deliver a short oral presentation comparing and contrasting the earliest known deities. The speech should define and discuss monotheism and polytheism.

Logical/Mathematical
In a short oral or written report, have students speculate on the practical reasons why early civilizations showed a great interest in astronomy. Ask them to assess how important astronomy is to people today.

Visual/Spatial
Have students find examples of the art of early China. Then have them draw or paint a picture in the early Chinese style. Ask them to describe how this style differs from that of modern Western art.

Intrapersonal
Have students imagine themselves as a pharaoh in the Valley of the Kings. They are having a pyramid built that is bigger than all the other pyramids in Egypt. Have them explain, orally or in writing, why they have undertaken this massive project.

Additional Resources

TEACHER'S CORNER

NATIONAL GEOGRAPHIC SOCIETY

INDEX TO NATIONAL GEOGRAPHIC MAGAZINE

The following articles may be used for research relating to this chapter:

- "Age of Pyramids: Egypt's Old Kingdom," by David Roberts, January 1995.
- "Iraq: Crucible of Civilization," by Merle Severy, May 1991.
- "Ramses the Great," by Rick Gore, April 1991.
- "Kingdom of Kush," by Timothy Kendall, November 1990.
- "Finding a Pharaoh's Funeral Bark," by Farouk El-Baz, April 1988.
- "Riddle of the Pyramid Boats," by Peter Miller, April 1988.

NATIONAL GEOGRAPHIC SOCIETY PRODUCTS AVAILABLE FROM GLENCOE

To order the following products for use with this chapter, contact your local Glencoe sales representative or call Glencoe at 1-800-368-7344:

NGS PICTURESHOW CD-ROMS
- Egypt and the Fertile Crescent
- India and China

NGS PICTUREPACK TRANSPARENCY SETS
- Ancient Egypt
- Fertile Crescent
- Ancient China
- Ancient India

ANCIENT CIVILIZATIONS POSTER SETS
- Ancient Egypt
- The Fertile Crescent

ADDITIONAL NATIONAL GEOGRAPHIC SOCIETY PRODUCTS

To order the following products for use with this chapter, call National Geographic Society at 1-800-368-2728:

- *Ancient Civilizations*, "Africa," "Mesopotamia and Egypt." (Filmstrip)
- *Egypt: Quest for Eternity* (Video)

BIBLIOGRAPHY

Literature About the Period

Drury, Allen. ***A God Against the Gods.*** New York: Doubleday, 1976. Historical novel about the pharaoh Akhenaton and his attempt to establish a single god.

Readings for the Student

Perl, Lila. ***Mummies, Tombs, and Treasure: Secrets of Ancient Egypt.*** New York: Clarion Books, 1990. An account of ancient Egyptian beliefs about death and the afterlife.

Romer, John. ***Ancient Lives: Daily Life in Egypt of the Pharaohs.*** New York: Henry Holt, 1984. Social life and customs in the Valley of the Kings.

Readings for the Teacher

Hawkes, Jaquetta, ed. ***Atlas of Ancient Archaeology.*** New York: McGraw-Hill, 1974. Traces the patterns of ancient cultures and civilizations around the world.

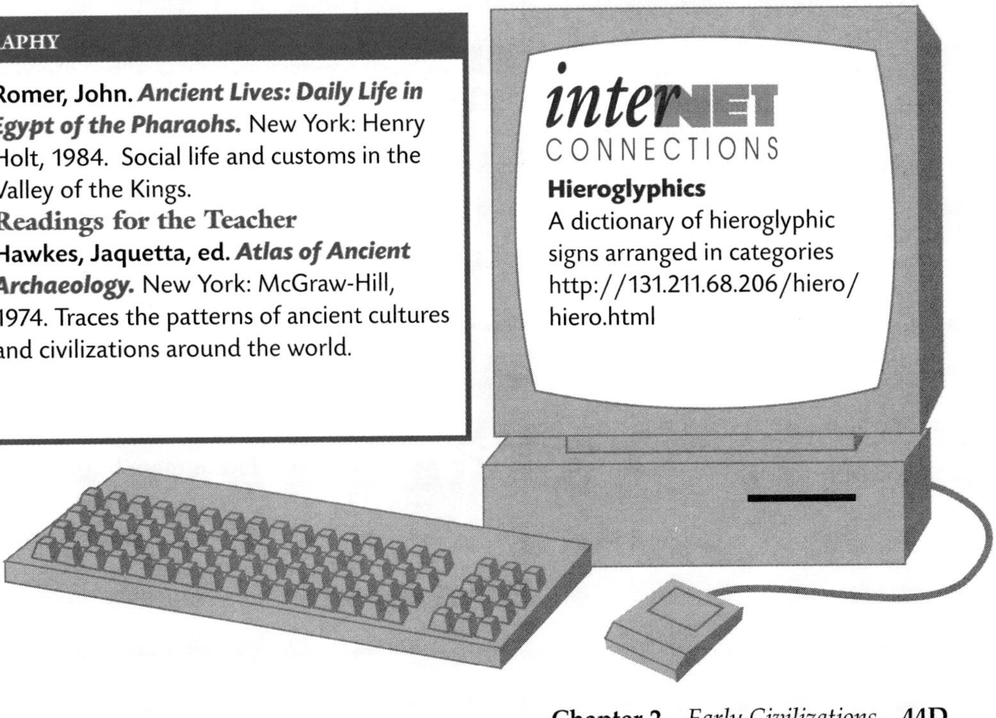
interNET
CONNECTIONS
Hieroglyphics
A dictionary of hieroglyphic signs arranged in categories
http://131.211.68.206/hiero/hiero.html

Introducing Chapter 2

CHAPTER THEMES

Chapter Themes are listed by section on this chapter opening page of the Student Edition. A corresponding theme-based activity is available under "TEACH," and a theme-based question is asked in the Section and Chapter Reviews.

The Storyteller

Historical Setting Although Khufu was responsible for the largest monument ever built, surprisingly little is known about him, except for the length of his reign. He ruled for 23 years, around 2500 B.C. Much can be said about the extraordinary dimensions of his pyramid, however. It was originally 481 feet (147 meters) high. At its base, which covers about 13 acres (5.3 hectares), it is almost perfectly square, 755 feet (230 meters) to a side. The more than 2 million blocks of limestone in the pyramid average more than 2.5 short tons (2.3 metric tons) each. Most of them came from nearby quarries.

Historical Significance

Answers: *Each civilization had unique features—Egypt, pyramids; Sumer, irrigation; Indus River valley, urban planning; China, metal casting. Although these four civilizations all developed in river valleys, worshiped many gods, and wrote with pictograms, they also differed in various ways, depending on climate, topography, and traditions. All contributed to the growth of cities, government, literacy, and technology—keys to the rise of a global civilization.*

Chapter 2

4000–1000 B.C.

Early Civilizations

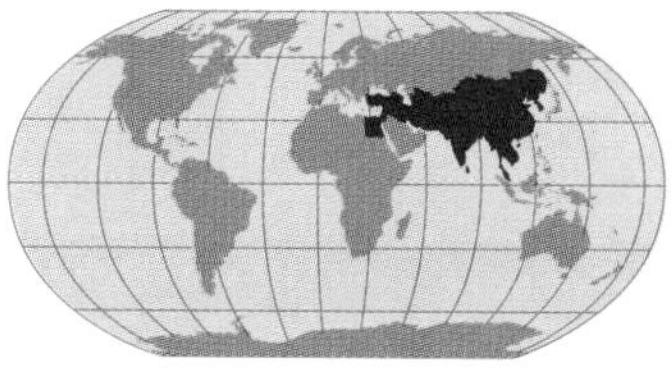

Chapter Themes

- **Relation to Environment** The Egyptians learn to control the floodwaters of the Nile River upon which their agriculture relies. *Section 1*
- **Cooperation** The peoples of the Fertile Crescent work together to build irrigation systems and cities. *Section 2*
- **Cultural Diffusion** Cities in early India develop close trading and cultural ties with the Fertile Crescent area. *Section 3*
- **Innovation** Early Chinese civilization excels in metal-casting skills. *Section 4*

The Storyteller

Under the blazing sun, a gigantic stone structure began to take shape on the desert sands of Egypt in northeastern Africa. A hundred thousand men toiled together, building a burial pyramid for Khufu, a king of Egypt about 2500 B.C. Gangs of laborers dragged huge blocks of limestone up winding ramps of dirt and brick to pile layer upon layer of stone. Farmers during the rest of the year, these laborers were compelled to work for the 3 or 4 months during which the annual flooding of the Nile River made farming impossible. It would take 20 years of their forced labor and more than 2 million blocks of stone before the Egyptians completed the massive pyramid. Today, the Great Pyramid built almost 5,000 years ago still stands at Giza, near the city of Cairo.

Historical Significance

In what ways were each of the early civilizations unique? How were they different? How did the river valley civilizations lay the foundations for the global civilization that we know today?

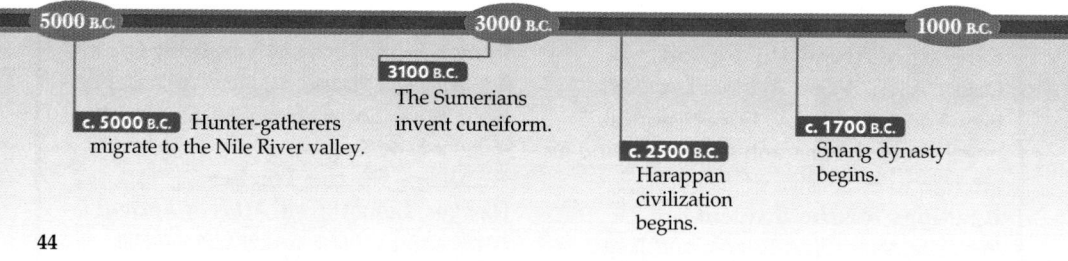

5000 B.C. — 3000 B.C. — 1000 B.C.

- **c. 5000 B.C.** Hunter-gatherers migrate to the Nile River valley.
- **3100 B.C.** The Sumerians invent cuneiform.
- **c. 2500 B.C.** Harappan civilization begins.
- **c. 1700 B.C.** Shang dynasty begins.

GEOGRAPHY CONNECTION

GEOGRAPHIC THEMES

Location The civilizations discussed in this chapter arose along river valleys. Have students locate these historic rivers on the appropriate map in the Atlas of their text: Nile, Tigris, Euphrates, Indus, and Huang He. Why were river valleys vital to the development of civilizations? *(Water is essential to human life and agriculture. The flooding of rivers produced rich soil, which enabled farmers to grow more than they needed for their own consumption, thus permitting the rise of cities.)*

History & Art Fowling scene from a tomb at Thebes along the Nile River, Egypt

Your History Journal

Sumerian scribes studied at special schools called eddubas. *There they learned cuneiform writing. After reading Section 2, write a short creative account of a scribe's day at an* edduba.

EXTRA CREDIT PROJECT

Essay The invention of writing is part of the development of the four early civilizations in this chapter. Have students write an essay in which they compare and contrast Egyptian hieroglyphics, Sumerian cuneiform, Harappan pictograms, and Chinese written script. In their paper, students should explain why writing was important to the growth of these civilizations.

Introducing Chapter 2

History & Art Scenes depicting the sport of fowling are common in Egyptian tomb paintings. Here, a noble prepares to hurl a throwing stick at a flock of geese. Notice one woman clasping the man's waist and another holding his leg. What do you think these poses were intended to illustrate? *(personal attachment to the man; more than just a fowling scene, this is also a family scene)*

Performance Assessment

Refer to the activity on page 44C of the Planning Guide.

For an additional activity, refer to Activity 2 in the *Performance Assessment Strategies and Activities* booklet.

Using Your History Journal

Advise students that an *edduba* was a very strict school. Sumerian youths attended from sunrise to sunset, and teachers used discipline.

GLENCOE TECHNOLOGY

VIDEODISC

Use MindJogger to preview chapter content.

MindJogger Videoquiz

Chapter 2
Disc 1 Side A

Also available in VHS.

Chapter 2 Section 1

SECTION THEME

▶ **Relation to Environment** The Egyptians learn to control the floodwaters of the Nile River upon which their agriculture relies.

Find Out

Answer: *The Nile enabled the early Egyptians to farm and thus to settle and develop a civilization.*

FOCUS

Section Objective

Understand why Egypt was called the "gift of the Nile."

BELLRINGER
Motivational Activity

Before taking roll at the beginning of the class period, project Section Focus Transparency 2-1 and have students answer the activity questions. Discuss students' responses.
This activity is also available as a blackline master.

Vocabulary Pre-check

Use the Vocabulary PuzzleMaker to create a puzzle that reinforces the vocabulary terms in this section. **L1**

3000 B.C. — c. 3000 B.C. King Narmer unifies Egypt.
2000 B.C. — c. 1700s B.C. The Hyksos invade Egypt.
c. 1480 B.C. Queen Hatshepsut comes to power.
1000 B.C. — c. 945 B.C. Egypt enters long period of foreign rule.

Section 1

The Nile Valley

Setting the Scene

▶ **Terms to Define**
monarchy, dynasty, theocracy, bureaucracy, pharaoh, empire, polytheism, hieroglyphics

▶ **People to Meet**
Narmer, Hatshepsut, Thutmose III, Akhenaton, Ramses II

▶ **Places to Locate**
Nile River valley, Memphis, Thebes

Find Out Why was Egypt called the "gift of the Nile"?

The Storyteller

Live for today; the afterlife will come soon enough! The following message about the brief pleasures of this life demonstrates that Egyptian poets sometimes sang what their wealthy patrons liked to hear:

"The pharaohs, those ancient gods, rest now in their pyramids. The people who built houses; their walls have crumbled, as if they had never been! Listen! Put perfume upon your head, wear fine linen. Make holiday! … No one who has died has ever returned."

—freely adapted from "Song of the Harper," *Journal of Near Eastern Studies* 4, 1945, translated by Miriam Lichtheim

King Narmer

One of the world's first civilizations developed along the banks of the Nile River in northeastern Africa. The **Nile River valley**'s early inhabitants called their land *Kemet*, meaning "black land," after the dark soil. Later, the ancient Greeks would name the Nile area *Egypt*. Of the four early river valley civilizations, people today probably know the most about the ancient Egyptian civilization. People still marvel at its remains in modern Egypt—especially the enormous Sphinx, the wondrous pyramids, and the mummies buried in lavish tombs.

A River Valley and Its People

Running like a ribbon through great expanses of desert, the Nile River for thousands of years has shaped the lives of the Egyptians. The land of Egypt receives little rainfall, but its people have relied instead on the Nile's predictable yearly floods to bring them water.

At 4,160 miles (6,690 km) in length, the Nile River is the world's longest river. Several sources in the highlands of East Africa feed the Nile. The river then takes a northward route to the Mediterranean Sea. On its course through Egypt the Nile crosses six cataracts, or waterfalls. Because of the cataracts the Nile is not completely navigable until it reaches its last 650 miles (1,040 km). Before emptying into the Mediterranean, the Nile splits into many branches, forming a marshy, fan-shaped delta.

The Gifts of the River

The green Nile Valley contrasts sharply with the vast desert areas that stretch for hundreds of miles on either side. Rich black soil covers the river's banks and the Nile Delta. From late spring through summer, heavy tropical rains in central Africa and melting mountain snow in East Africa add to the Nile's volume. As a result the river overflows its banks and floods the land nearby. The

SECTION RESOURCES

Reproducible Masters
- Reproducible Lesson Plan 2-1
- Guided Reading Activity 2-1
- Section Quiz 2-1

Transparencies
- Section Focus Transparency 2-1
- Ancient Egypt
- World History and Art Transparency 2
- Mapping History Overlay Transparency 2

Multimedia
- Ancient Egypt
- Focus on World Art Print 7
- Vocabulary PuzzleMaker Software
- Student Self-Test and Review Software
- Testmaker
- Egypt and the Fertile Crescent

floodwaters recede in late fall, leaving behind thick deposits of silt.

As early as 5000 B.C., nomadic hunter-gatherers of northeastern Africa began to settle by the Nile. They took up a farming life regulated by the river's seasonal rise and fall, growing cereal crops such as wheat and barley. The Nile also provided these Neolithic farmers with ducks and geese in its marshlands and fish in its waters. The early Egyptians harvested papyrus growing wild along the banks of the Nile, using the long, thin reeds to make rope, matting, sandals, baskets, and later on, sheets of paperlike writing material.

Uniting Egypt

Protected from foreign invasion by deserts and cataracts, the early farming villages by the Nile prospered. In time a few strong leaders united villages into small kingdoms, or **monarchies**, each under the unrestricted rule of its king. The weaker kingdoms eventually gave way to the stronger. By 4000 B.C. ancient Egypt consisted of two large kingdoms: Lower Egypt in the north, in the Nile Delta, and Upper Egypt in the south, in the Nile Valley.

Around 3000 B.C., **Narmer**, also known as Menes (MEE•neez), a king of Upper Egypt, gathered the forces of the south and led them north to invade and conquer Lower Egypt. Narmer set up the first government that ruled all of the country. He governed both Lower Egypt and Upper Egypt from a capital city he had built at **Memphis**, near the border of the two kingdoms.

Narmer's reign marked the beginning of the first Egyptian **dynasty**, or line of rulers from one family. From 3000 B.C. until 332 B.C., a series of 30 dynasties ruled Egypt. Historians have organized the dynasties into three great periods: the Old Kingdom, the Middle Kingdom, and the New Kingdom.

The Old Kingdom

The Old Kingdom lasted from about 2700 B.C. to 2200 B.C. During the first centuries of the unified kingdom, Upper Egypt and Lower Egypt kept their separate identities as kingdoms. In time, however, Egypt built a strong national government under its kings. It also developed the basic features of its civilization.

CONNECTIONS

Geography

Stemming the Flood

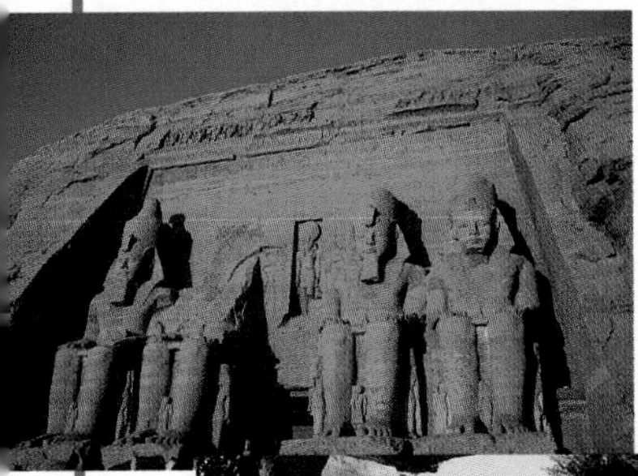

Ancient Egyptians had to take control of their river environment. Over the years farmers built ditches and canals to carry the floodwaters to basins. There the silt settled and served as fertilizer for planting crops. Machines, such as the shadoof, lifted water to cultivated land. Farmers eventually built dams and reservoirs, making year-round irrigation possible.

Built in the 1960s, the Aswan High Dam in southeastern Egypt trapped the waters of the Nile in a huge reservoir for later irrigation. When the rising waters of the Nile behind the dam threatened to destroy statues of Ramses II, engineers had to move the statues to higher ground. Today, the dam generates electrical power and protects against flooding. Because the dam prevents the Nile from flowing over the valley land, however, the floodwaters no longer deposit fertile silt annually. Farmers must add expensive chemical fertilizers to their fields. The absence of silt has also increased land erosion along the Nile.

MAKING THE CONNECTION

1. How did the Egyptians gradually manage to control the waters of the Nile?
2. Why might people today object to the building of a dam?

Chapter 2
Section 1

TEACH

Guided Practice

THEME Relation to Environment

On the map on page 48, have students trace the boundaries of the Old, Middle, and New Kingdoms. **What is the position of the Nile in relation to the three kingdoms of Egypt?** *(flows through the center of each of them)* **L1**

Geography: Location Have students study the map of ancient Egypt on page 48. Then ask them to use the Atlas in this text to find modern nations that fall within the boundaries of ancient Egypt during the New Kingdom. *(Egypt, Lebanon, Israel, Sudan, Cyprus, and part of Turkey)* **L1**

CONNECTIONS

Geography

Stemming the Flood

Rivers typically overflow their usual channels about once every two years. At their worst, floods can destroy whole communities.

Answers to Making the Connection

1. *At first they built ditches and canals to control the annual floodwaters. Later they built dams and reservoirs.*
2. *Answers may include: Dams are costly. They upset the ecology of a river. They may displace people who live in the lake or reservoir created. Sometimes they break, resulting in loss of life and property damage.*

COOPERATIVE LEARNING ACTIVITY

A Play Have the class write and perform a play about one of the people listed in the section. Organize the class into small groups. Have each group be responsible for a specific task in the project, such as researching the person chosen and the way of life during his or her time, writing the script, acting, making costumes, finding props, writing and designing programs, and designing sets (if needed). At each stage of the project, all students should be given an opportunity to react to the group task. Then have the students present the play to other classes. **L1**

Map Study

Answer

by supporting irrigation projects

Map Skills Practice

Reading a Map Why does the map suggest that ancient Egyptians made advances in transportation? *(parts of the New Kingdom are located across a large body of water, indicating ability to navigate and sail)*

NATIONAL GEOGRAPHIC SOCIETY

Use these materials to enrich student understanding of ancient Egyptian culture.

- **NGS PICTURESHOW CD-ROM**
  Egypt and the Fertile Crescent
- **NGS PICTUREPACK TRANSPARENCY SET**
  Ancient Egypt
- **ANCIENT CIVILIZATIONS POSTER SET**
  Ancient Egypt

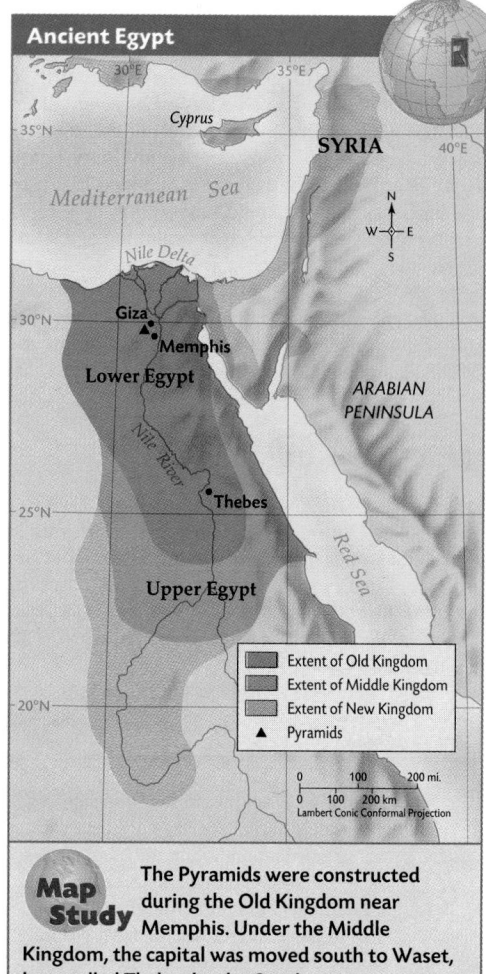

Ancient Egypt

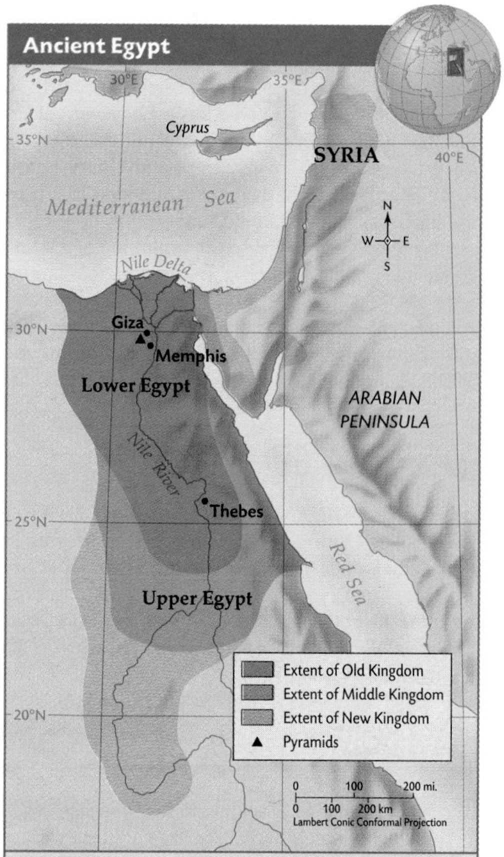

Map Study The Pyramids were constructed during the Old Kingdom near Memphis. Under the Middle Kingdom, the capital was moved south to Waset, later called Thebes by the Greeks. **Human/Environment Interaction** How did Theban kings add thousands of acres to the land under cultivation?

The Egyptian Monarchy

The Egyptian people regarded their king as a god who ruled over all Egyptians. Such a government, in which the same person is both the religious leader and the political leader, is called a theocracy. As a god, the king performed many ritual acts believed to benefit the entire kingdom, such as cutting the first ripe grain to ensure a good harvest. As political leader, the king wielded absolute power, issuing commands regarded as the law of the land.

Unable to carry out all official duties himself, the king delegated many responsibilities to a bureaucracy, a group of government officials headed by the king's vizier, or prime minister. Through the vizier and other bureaucrats the king controlled trade and collected taxes. He also indirectly supervised the building of dams, canals, and storehouses for grain—all crucial to survival for an agriculture-based civilization.

The Pyramids: A Lasting Legacy

To honor their god-kings and to provide them with an eternal place of rest, the Egyptians of the Old Kingdom built lasting monuments—the Pyramids. The Step Pyramid was built for King Djoser in the mid-2600s B.C. Overlooking Memphis, it was the first large, all-stone building in the world. Later the Egyptians constructed the three Pyramids at Giza, which stand today as testimony to Egyptian engineering skills. The Great Pyramid, the largest of the three, stands 481 feet (144 m) high. Long, narrow passageways lead to the king's burial chamber deep within the pyramid.

The Egyptians believed that a king's soul continued to guide the kingdom after death. Before entombing a dead king in his pyramid, they first preserved the king's body from decay by a procedure called embalming. Next they wrapped the dried, shrunken body—called a mummy—with long strips of linen and placed it in an elaborate coffin. Only then could the coffin lie in the burial chamber of the pyramid along with the king's clothing, weapons, furniture, and jewelry—personal possessions the king could enjoy in the afterlife.

The Middle Kingdom

Around 2200 B.C., the kings in Memphis began to lose their power as ambitious nobles fought each other for control of Egypt. The stable, ordered world of the Old Kingdom entered a period of upheaval and violence. Then, around 2050 B.C., a new dynasty reunited Egypt and moved the capital south to **Thebes**, a city in Upper Egypt. This new kingdom, known as the Middle Kingdom, would last until after 1800 B.C.

In time Theban kings became as powerful as the rulers of the Old Kingdom and brought unruly local governments under their control. They supported irrigation projects that added thousands of acres to the land already under cultivation. The Theban dynasty seized new territory for Egypt, setting up fortresses along the Nile to capture Nubia (part of modern Sudan) and launching military campaigns against Syria. Theban kings also

MEETING SPECIAL NEEDS ACTIVITY

Language Delayed Ask several students who read English well to go through this section to find words related to the natural environment, such as *river*, *riverbank*, *source*, *highland*, and so on. Working with partners who are language delayed, these students can help find pictures of the listed natural features in resource materials. Next, ask language-delayed students to prepare and present a simple natural-features map of their native country. Have students find similarities and differences between the geographic features of the student's country and those of Egypt. **L1 LEP**

ordered construction of a canal between the Nile and the Red Sea, and as a result, Egyptian ships traded along the coasts of the Arabian Peninsula and East Africa.

In the 1700s B.C., local leaders began to challenge the kings' power again, shattering the peace and prosperity of the Middle Kingdom. At the same time, Egypt also faced its first serious threat—invasion by the Hyksos (HIHK•SAHS), a people from western Asia. The Hyksos swept across the desert into Egypt with new tools for war—bronze weapons and horse-drawn chariots. So armed, they easily conquered the Egyptians, who fought on foot with copper and stone weapons. The Hyksos established a new dynasty that ruled for about 110 years.

Visualizing History **This tomb painting from the Valley of the Kings, Deir El Bahri, Egypt, shows Queen Hatshepsut wearing the traditional false beard of the pharaohs.** *What does the term "pharaoh" mean?*

The New Kingdom

The Egyptians despised their Hyksos masters. To overthrow Hyksos rule, the Egyptians learned to use Hyksos weapons and adopted the fighting style of their conquerors. About 1600 B.C. Ahmose (ah•MOH•suh), an Egyptian prince, raised an army and drove the Hyksos out.

Pharaohs Rule an Empire

Ahmose founded a new Egyptian dynasty—the first of the New Kingdom. He and his successors assumed the title **pharaoh**, an Egyptian word meaning "great house of the king." Ahmose devoted his energies to rebuilding Egypt, restoring abandoned temples, and reopening avenues of trade. The pharaohs who followed him, however, used large armies to realize their dreams of conquest. They pressed farther to the east and into the rest of Africa than had the kings of the Middle Kingdom.

Around 1480 B.C. Queen **Hatshepsut** (hat•SHEHP•soot) came to power in Egypt. She first ruled with her husband and then ruled on behalf of her stepson **Thutmose** (thoot•MOH•suh) **III**, who was too young to govern. Finally she had herself crowned pharaoh. Hatshepsut assumed all the royal trappings of power, including the false beard traditionally worn by Egyptian kings. Hatshepsut carried out an extensive building program, which included a great funeral temple and a tomb built into the hills of what is now called the Valley of the Kings.

Thutmose III did reclaim the throne at Hatshepsut's death and soon after marched with a large army out of Egypt toward the northeast. He conquered Syria and pushed the Egyptian frontier to the northern part of the Euphrates River. In a short time, Thutmose III had conquered an **empire** for Egypt, bringing many territories under one ruler.

The Egyptian Empire grew rich from commerce and tribute from the conquered territories. The capital of Thebes, with its palaces, temples, and carved stone obelisks, reflected the wealth won by conquest. No longer isolated from other cultures, Egyptians benefited from cultural diffusion within their empire.

Akhenaton Founds a Religion

A new ruler, Amenhotep (AH•muhn•HOH•TEHP) IV, assumed power about 1370 B.C. Supported by his wife, Nefertiti, Amenhotep broke with the Egyptian tradition of worshiping many

Chapter 2 Section 1

Visualizing History Deir el Bahri, called Djeser-djeseur or "holy of holies," at the time of Queen Hatshepsut, contains, in addition to tomb paintings, more than 190 statues and relief carvings glorifying the queen's reign.
Answer to Caption: *great house of the king*

Focus on World Art Print 7, Egyptian. *Mask of Tutankhamen*

World History and Art Transparency 2, *Tutankhamen's Throne*

Mapping History Overlay Transparency 2, *Ancient Egypt*

Government Write this quotation from the Persian poet Sadi on the chalkboard: "[A King] requires a prudent and able man." Discuss the meaning of the quotation and how it applies to the pharaohs. Lead the class to consider how choosing wise people to help govern can ensure good government. Draw a parallel between the bureaucracy of Egypt and that of the United States today. **L2**

MAKING CONNECTIONS ACTIVITY

Technology In 1987 scientists from Egypt and the United States used advanced technology to view the remains of an ancient Egyptian boat that had been sealed inside a chamber for 4,600 years. To see inside without excavating and damaging the chamber, the scientists employed a special drill with technology invented for moon exploration. After drilling through the outer rock, they inserted a miniature video camera. Have students research other techniques used to handle and explore ancient Egyptian remains and report to the class on their findings. **L2**

TEACH

Not every well-preserved body from prehistoric times is a true mummy. Strictly speaking, a mummy is a dead body preserved by embalming. The technique of embalming seems to have been developed in Egypt about 2600 B.C. Bodies preserved from earlier times were the result of natural drying in the hot Egyptian sand. Mummification was costly, and at first only the wealthy could afford it. Still, mummified corpses of bulls, cats, and ibis have been found. Ask students why they think the Egyptians preserved these animals. *(The bull, cat, and ibis were sacred, associated with certain Egyptian gods.)*

CURRICULUM CONNECTION

ARCHAEOLOGY
One of the impressive temple sites of Ramses II is Abu Simbel, located near the Nile River about 762 miles south of Cairo. In the 1960s the High Dam at Aswan would have flooded the site, but 51 countries contributed funds to move the temples block by block to higher ground farther inland.

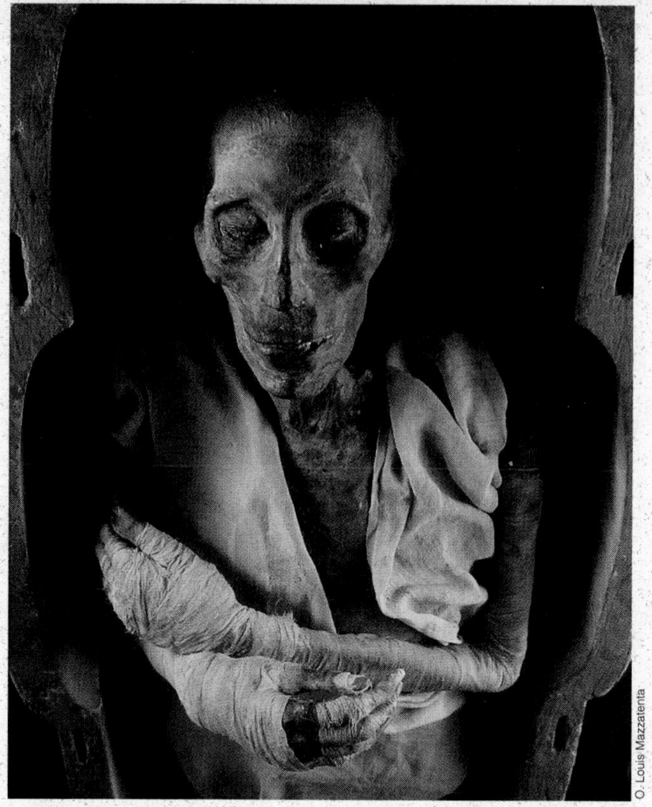

O. Louis Mazzatenta

Ramses the Great

O. Louis Mazzatenta

The mummy of Ramses the Great (above) lies in a display case on the second floor of the Egyptian Museum in Cairo. For many centuries before Ramses was brought to Cairo, the great pharaoh lay in his tomb near Luxor in a richly decorated coffin (left), embellished with symbols of Osiris, god of the afterlife. Ramses was nearly 90 when he died in 1237 B.C. His mummy has remained intact for the last 3,000 years.

Egyptians believed strongly in the afterlife and took great care to preserve the bodies of their pharaohs. Embalmers spent 70 days preparing the corpse of Ramses the Great. First they removed the internal organs and placed them in sacred jars. The heart was sealed in the body because Egyptians believed that it was the source of intellect as well as feeling and was needed in the afterlife. The brain, on the other hand, was thought to be useless and embalmers drew it out through the nose and threw it away. The body was then dried with salt, washed, coated with preserving resins, and wrapped in hundreds of yards of linen. Recent medical tests show that Ramses suffered from arthritis, dental abscesses, gum disease, and poor circulation. ⊕

deities. He declared that Egyptians should worship only Aton, the sun-disk god, as the one supreme deity. Claiming to be Aton's equal, Amenhotep changed his royal name to **Akhenaton** (AHK •NAH•tuhn), which means "spirit of Aton." To stress the break with the past, Akhenaton moved the capital from Thebes to a new city in central Egypt dedicated to Aton.

These controversial changes had an unsettling effect on Egypt. Many of the common people rejected the worship of Aton, a god without human form, and continued to believe in many deities. The priests of the old religion resented their loss of power. At the same time, the army was unhappy about Egypt's loss of territories under Akhenaton's weak rule.

After Akhenaton's death, the priests restored the old religion. They also made Akhenaton's successor, Tutankhamen, move the capital to Memphis. Shortly thereafter, the head of the Egyptian army overthrew the dynasty and created a new one.

Recovery and Decline

During the 1200s B.C. the pharaohs regained some of the territory and prestige that Egypt had lost during the previous century. One of these pharaohs, **Ramses II**, or Ramses the Great, reigned for 67 years. He erected large statues of himself and built many temples and tombs. In A.D. 1995, archaeologists uncovered a vast underground tomb with at least 67 chambers that they believed to be the burial place of 50 of the 52 sons of Ramses II. The find, located near Ramses' own tomb, was hailed as one of the most historically significant discoveries in Egypt in the twentieth century.

In the 1100s B.C., another pharaoh also named Ramses led Egypt into a long and costly war for the control of Syria. Ramses III barely escaped assassination, and after his war, Egypt entered a long period of decline. It eventually split into two kingdoms. Beginning in 945 B.C., Egypt came under control by foreigners—among them the Libyans from the west and the Kushites from the south.

Life in Ancient Egypt

At the height of its glory, ancient Egypt was home to some 5 million persons, most of whom lived in the Nile Valley and the Nile Delta. Even though Egyptian society was divided into classes, ambitious people in the lower classes could improve their social status somewhat.

Levels of Egyptian Society

Royalty, nobles, and priests formed the top of the social order. They controlled religious and political affairs. Members of the wealthy upper class lived in the cities or on estates along the Nile River. There they built large, elaborately decorated homes surrounded by magnificent gardens, pools, and orchards.

Below the upper class in social rank was the middle class. Its members—artisans, scribes, merchants, and tax collectors—carried out the business activities of Egypt. Middle-class homes—mostly in the cities—were comfortable but not elegant.

The majority of Egyptians belonged to the poor lower class. Many were farmers. For the land they farmed, they paid rent to the king—usually a large percentage of their crop. Farmers also worked on building projects for the king, and some members of the lower class served the priests and the nobles. They lived in small villages of simple huts on or near the large estates along the Nile.

Egyptian Families

In the cities and in the upper class the husband, wife, and children made up the family group.

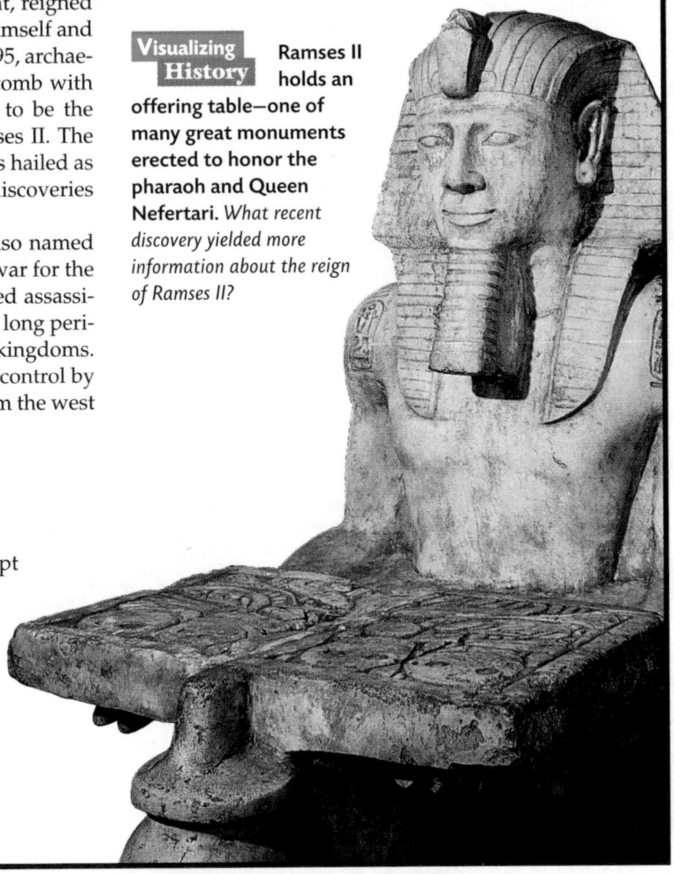

Visualizing History **Ramses II holds an offering table—one of many great monuments erected to honor the pharaoh and Queen Nefertari.** *What recent discovery yielded more information about the reign of Ramses II?*

Chapter 2 Section 1

Cultural Diffusion Have students locate Egypt on the map of the Middle East in the Atlas of this text. Discuss how Egypt's location at the crossroads between Africa and Asia provided opportunities for cultural diffusion. **L2**

Critical Thinking Remind students about the consensus that a writing system, a well-organized government, art and literature, and specialization of labor are the earmarks of civilization. Have students explain how ancient Egypt met these criteria. **L3**

Who?What?Where?When?

Nile Surroundings On the east bank of the Nile stood the commercial city of Thebes. On the west bank lay irrigated fields of black alluvium and green crops. At the edge of the fields rose a row of temples, each surrounded by a cluster of buildings. Several of these buildings were the homes of priests and scribes, but most were great storerooms holding the riches of the empire.

Visualizing History A modern historian calls the inscriptions on the monuments of Ramses II some of "the greatest propaganda pieces of all time." They impressed poets, too. "Ozymandias," the sonnet by Shelley, takes its title from the Greek name for Ramses.

Answer to Caption: *1995 discovery of tomb where 50 of 52 sons of Ramses II are believed to be buried.*

CRITICAL THINKING ACTIVITY

Making Generalizations In Chapter 1, students studied these themes as they relate to early human beings: movement, innovation, and change. The same three themes apply to many civilizations. Have students write a paragraph on each theme as it relates to ancient Egypt. Ask volunteers to read their paragraphs in class. Then discuss the question: **How do these three themes also apply to the history of the United States?** **L2**

Chapter 2
Section 1

Independent Practice

Guided Reading Activity 2-1 **L1**

Economics Have students write a want ad for a vizier, a tax collector, an artisan, a scribe, or a construction laborer. Have them describe the qualifications needed for the job. Display the ads on a bulletin board. **L2**

Religion Have students write an editorial explaining their position on this question: Did religion play a greater role in Egyptian society than it does in our society today? Tell students to respond according to their perception of the role of religion in today's society. **L3**

ASSESS

Check for Understanding

Assign Section 1 Review as homework or as an in-class activity.

Use Student Self-Test and Review Software to review Section 1.

Visualizing History Throughout Egyptian history, the falcon god Horus was personally identified with the ruler. Each pharaoh in turn used the name Horus as the first of his titles.

Answer to Caption: *Osiris was god of the Nile; he and his wife Isis together were rulers of the realm of the dead.*

Outside the cities, especially among farmers and laborers, a family also included grandparents and other relatives, who took an active part in the life of the household. An Egyptian child was taught great respect for his or her parents, with a son particularly expected to maintain his father's tomb.

The status of Egyptian women changed somewhat as the centuries passed. Literature of the Old Kingdom portrayed women as the property of their husbands and as valued producers of children. Wise men reminded children to cherish their mothers for bearing them, nourishing them, and loving and caring for them. By the time of the empire, documents indicate that women's legal rights had improved. Women could buy, own, and sell property in their own names, testify in court, and start divorce and other legal proceedings. The lives of Hatshepsut and some of the queens of the later pharaohs, like Nefertiti, suggest that privileged women of the royalty could attain prominence.

Worshiping Many Deities

Religion guided every aspect of Egyptian life. Egyptian religion was based on **polytheism**, or the worship of many deities, except during the controversial rule of Akhenaton. Gods and goddesses were often represented as part human and part animal—Horus, the sky god, had the head of a hawk. The Egyptians in each region worshiped local deities, but rulers and priests promoted the worship of specific gods and goddesses over all of Egypt. These deities included Ra, the sun god, whom the Theban pharaohs joined with their favorite god Amon to make one god, Amon-Ra.

The popular god Osiris, initially the powerful god of the Nile, became the god responsible for the life, death, and rebirth of all living things. The Egyptians worshiped Osiris and his wife, the goddess Isis, as rulers of the realm of the dead. They believed that Osiris determined a person's fate after death.

Because their religion stressed an afterlife, Egyptians devoted much time and wealth to preparing for survival in the next world. At first they believed that only kings and wealthy people could enjoy an afterlife. By the time of the New Kingdom, however, poor people could also hope for eternal life with Osiris's help.

Visualizing History **This statue of the falcon god Horus served both as a protector and symbol of the pharaoh, who ruled as the incarnation of Horus, son of the divine king.** *Who were Osiris and Isis?*

Writing With Pictures

In their earliest writing system, called **hieroglyphics**, the Egyptians carved picture symbols onto pieces of slate. These picture symbols, or hieroglyphs, stood for objects, ideas, and sounds. For everyday business, however, the Egyptians used a cursive, or flowing, script known as hieratic, which simplified and connected the picture symbols.

Few people in ancient Egypt could read or write. Some Egyptians, though, did prepare at special schools for a career as a scribe in government or commerce. Scribes learned to write hieratic script on paper made from the papyrus reed.

MORE ABOUT...

Deciphering the Rosetta Stone Jean-François Champollion, who deciphered the Rosetta stone, had a thorough knowledge of Coptic, the modern Egyptian language. He knew Greek as well, so he was able to read the entire text of the stone. The stone's inscription is a decree by Ptolemy V Epiphanes, king of Egypt from 203 to 181 B.C. The two forms of Egyptian writing on the stone are hieroglyphics and Demotic, the language of Egypt at the time the stone was inscribed. The black basalt stone—3 feet 9 inches (114 centimeters) high, 2 feet 4 1/2 inches (72 centimeters) thick—is on view at the British Museum in London.

After the decline of ancient Egypt, hieroglyphs fell from use, and their meaning remained a mystery to the world's scholars for nearly 2,000 years. Then in A.D. 1799 French soldiers in Egypt found a slab of stone dating to the 200s B.C. near the town of Rosetta. The stone was carved with Greek letters and two forms of Egyptian writing. In A.D. 1822 a young French archaeologist named Jean-François Champollion (shahn•pawl•YOHN) figured out how the Greek text on the Rosetta stone matched the Egyptian texts. Using the Greek version, he was able to decipher the Egyptian hieroglyphics.

Some of the oldest writings from the Old Kingdom were carved on the inner walls of the Pyramids. Scribes also copied many prayers and hymns to deities. The Book of the Dead collected texts telling how to reach a happy afterlife, recording more than 200 prayers and magic formulas.

The ancient Egyptians also wrote secular, or nonreligious, works such as collections of proverbs. One vizier gave this advice: "Do not repeat slander; you should not hear it, for it is the result of hot temper. Repeat a matter seen, not what is heard." The Egyptians also enjoyed adventure stories, fairy tales, and love stories:

> "Now I'll lie down inside
> and act as if I'm sick.
> My neighbors will come in to visit,
> and with them my girl.
> She'll put the doctors out,
> for she's the one to know my hurt."
>
> –a love poem by a young Egyptian, date unknown

Achievements in Science

Pyramids, temples, and other monuments bear witness to the architectural and artistic achievement of Egyptian artisans. These works, however, would not have been possible without advances in disciplines such as mathematics. The Egyptians developed a number system that enabled them to calculate area and volume, and they used principles of geometry to survey flooded land.

The Egyptians worked out an accurate 365-day calendar by basing their year not only on the movements of the moon but also on Sirius, the bright Dog Star. Sirius rises annually in the sky just before the Nile's flood begins.

Egyptians also developed medical expertise, having first learned about human anatomy in their practice of embalming. Egyptian doctors wrote directions on papyrus scrolls for using splints, bandages, and compresses when treating fractures, wounds, and diseases. Other ancient civilizations would acquire much of their medical knowledge from the Egyptians.

AROUND THE WORLD — Stonehenge Religious Site

Salisbury Plain, England, c. 1700 B.C.
Ancient people created a religious monument in southwestern England by dragging huge stones from miles away and arranging them in giant circles. The work probably took hundreds of years to complete. The layout of stones suggests that they were used in ceremonies linked to the rising of the sun on the longest day of the year.

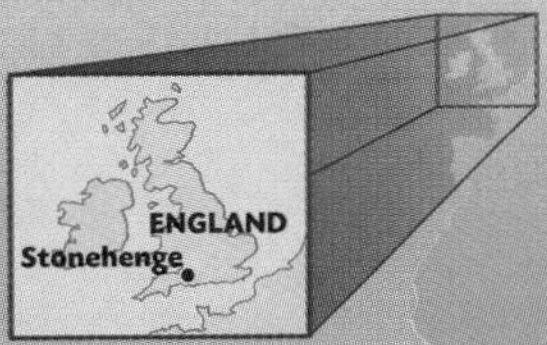

SECTION 1 REVIEW

Recall
1. **Define** monarchy, dynasty, theocracy, bureaucracy, pharaoh, empire, polytheism, hieroglyphics.
2. **Identify** Narmer, the Hyksos, Ahmose, Hatshepsut, Thutmose III, Akhenaton, Ramses II.
3. **Explain** how a bureaucracy became part of government in ancient Egypt.

Critical Thinking
4. **Making Comparisons** Compare the reigns of Ahmose, Hatshepsut, and Thutmose III. Which reign do you think contributed most to Egypt? Support your opinion.

Understanding Themes
5. **Relation to Environment** How did geography and climate affect where people lived in ancient Egypt? How did the ancient Egyptians make use of the environment to meet their economic and cultural needs?

Evaluate

Section Quiz 2-1

Use the Testmaker to create a customized quiz for Section 1.

Reteach

Organize the class into groups and assign each one a topic, such as Old Kingdom, Middle Kingdom, New Kingdom, family and society, religion, writing, technology. Have each group devise review questions on their topic to ask the rest of the class.

Enrich

Have students research Nefertiti and write a one-page biographical sketch.

CLOSE

Have students list factors that account for the growth and longevity (3,000 years) of civilization along the Nile River. *(fertile soil, favorable climate, easy transportation by boat, development of irrigation, presence of outlying desert and five cataracts as natural defense barriers, growth of strong national government, rise of cities, evolution of writing)* Discuss which of these factors can be found in any river valley and which are unique to Egypt's location or unrelated to geography.

SECTION 1 REVIEW ANSWERS

1. All vocabulary words are defined in the Glossary.
2. Narmer, 47; the Hyksos, 49; Ahmose, 49; Hatshepsut, 49; Thutmose III, 49; Akhenaton, 51; Ramses II, 51
3. because the king was not able to carry out all official duties, he delegated many responsibilities
4. Students might mention Ahmose driving the Hyksos out of Egypt, the significance of a woman as pharaoh, or Thutmose's development of an empire.
5. **RELATION TO ENVIRONMENT** The favorable climate and geographic features of the Nile River valley—warm, with rich soil due to annual flooding—led people to settle there. The ancient Egyptians grew crops in the soil and learned to control the Nile's floodwaters so they could farm year-round. They also used the lower Nile for travel and trade. They used stone from the nearby desert for the Pyramids and other buildings.

Special Report Summary

Discoveries at the Valley of the Kings in 1922 revealed the magnificence of ancient royalty in Egypt.

↓

Discoveries made in 1988 and the early 1990s revealed details of lives of Egyptian commoners.

↓

A bakery and skeletons reveal the diet and hard labor of the commoners.

↓

Art, culture, and faith may have developed up from the average man and woman, rather than down from royalty.

TEACH

Points to Discuss

After students have read the feature, ask the following: **What archaeological remains indicate differences in life for royalty and for commoners?** *(Royal tombs and relics indicate great wealth; skeletons of workers reveal years of hard labor.)* **Why would people be willing to spend a life of toil and perhaps injury to build monumental tombs for their**

NATIONAL GEOGRAPHIC Special Report

The Egyptians

The Valley of the Kings has seen more than its share of visitors. For thousands of years, travelers, warriors, and more recently, archaeologists have descended on this area on the outskirts of what is now Luxor to marvel at the magnificence of ancient Egypt. It was thought that most of what there was to discover had been found after British explorer Howard Carter opened up the tomb of Tutankhamen in 1922.

Then in 1988, plans were made to build a parking lot over the site of Tomb 5, which had been discovered—and looted—years earlier. Wanting to make sure that the parking facility would not seal off anything important, Egyptologist Kent Weeks of the American University of Cairo decided to make one last exploration of the tomb. To his surprise, beyond a few debris-choked rooms, he opened a door that led t the mostly unexcavated tomb of perhaps 50 of the sons of Ramses II the powerful pharaoh who ruled Egypt from 1279 to 1212 B.C.

Though the tomb was emptied of valuables long ago, archaeologists consider Weeks's discovery a major find. Scientists and researchers hope

TEACHER NOTES

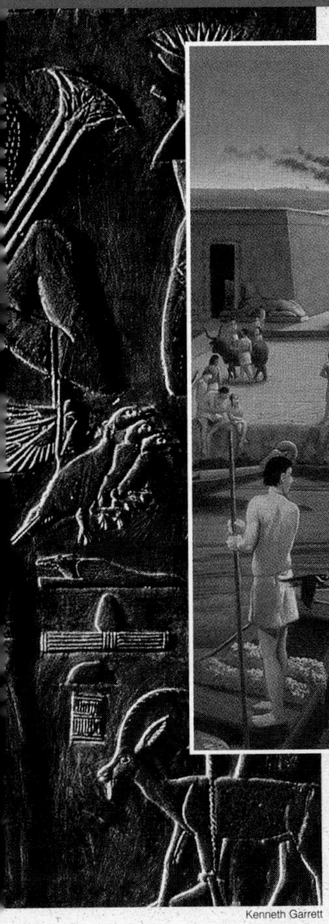

Kenneth Garrett

Illustration by C.F. Payne

that artifacts found in the tomb will provide clues about Egyptian civilization during Egypt's last golden age.

For students of Judeo-Christian history, any information on Ramses' oldest son, Amen-hir-khopshef, would be a most important discovery. Ramses was in power when, in retribution for the enslavement of the Israelites, according to the Book of Exodus, the Lord "...smote all the firstborn in the land of Egypt, from the firstborn of Pharaoh that sat on his throne unto the firstborn of the captive that was in the dungeon."

The tomb and pyramids of ancient Egypt hold many answers: These stone monuments have certainly established the immortality of the pharaohs. But what about the commoners, who vastly outnumbered the royalty? What of the men and women who gave their strength, sweat, and lives to create Egypt's lasting monuments? The widespread fame of the Sphinx and the three Great Pyramids at Giza make it easy to forget that basic questions about Egyptian history have remained unanswered. Only recently have Egyptologists begun to fill in those gaps.

SEVERAL YEARS AGO, archaeologists began to excavate two sites—located about half a mile from the Sphinx—searching for signs of the

Offerings of food are carved in relief on an official's tomb (left).

Another pyramid nears completion about 2500 B.C. (above). Limestone facing blocks were quarried across the Nile and ferried to the work site. Teams then dragged the blocks to ramps made of rubble that were built around the pyramid during construction. Some experts believe that it took only 10,000 men—far below earlier estimates of up to 100,000—and 25 years to lay 5 million tons of rock. Half lion, half pharaoh, the Sphinx (in the foreground) is carved from an outcropping left unexcavated in a U-shaped quarry.

pharaohs? *(Some scholars believe that the divine aspect of Egyptian society was expressed through the pharaoh, and building a tomb for the leader may have been an act of religious faith for the workers.)* **Why was the discovery of the bakery and the cemetery significant?** *(These finds were rich sources of information about the life of common Egyptians.)*

Cultural Perspectives

Burial Chambers Ancient Egyptians buried their kings in a secret chamber inside or beneath a pyramid. The pyramids protected and preserved the bodies, which the Egyptians believed was necessary for the soul to live forever. They filled the chamber with gold and other treasures as well as practical, everyday items. Egyptians believed that the king would need these things in the afterlife.

Focus on World Art Print 7, Egyptian. *Mask of Tutankhamen*

World History and Art Transparency 2, *Tutankhamen's Throne*

Mapping History Overlay Transparency 2, *Ancient Egypt*

FUN FACTS

- The Pyramids are one of the Seven Wonders of the Ancient World.
- A broken section of the head of the Great Sphinx indicates that it may have been used as a target for gun practice at various times throughout history.
- The ancient Egyptians were among the first to use clocks and calendars, to produce books, and to devise formulas for finding the area and volume of geometric figures.
- One of the greatest treasures ever found in ancient Egypt was the tomb of the boy-king Tutankhamen. When the tomb was opened in 1922, nearly 5,000 items from the fourteenth century B.C. came to light.

Linking Past and Present

Tourism is an important economic activity in Egypt today. The warm, dry climate and magnificent relics from ancient times attract visitors from all over the world.

NATIONAL GEOGRAPHIC SOCIETY

Use these materials to enrich student understanding of ancient Egyptian culture.

- **NGS PICTURESHOW CD-ROM**
  Egypt and the Fertile Crescent
- **NGS PICTUREPACK TRANSPARENCY SET**
  Ancient Egypt
- **ANCIENT CIVILIZATIONS POSTER SET**
  Ancient Egypt

NATIONAL GEOGRAPHIC Special Report

ordinary people who built the pyramids. Within months they uncovered the remains of many mud-brick buildings, including the oldest bakery yet discovered in Egypt.

This was a significant find. While the pyramids built Egypt by drawing its provinces together in a unified effort, it can be said that bread built the pyramids. For thousands of workers, a loaf of emmer–wheat bread—washed down with beer—was most likely the dietary staple.

At about the time the bakery was discovered, searchers also unearthed a cemetery of 600 graves of workers. Their skeletons revealed years of hard labor: Vertebrae were compressed and damaged from years of carrying heavy loads. Some skeletons were missing fingers and even limbs. A few of the tombs were adorned with mini-pyramids several feet high, made of mud brick. Nothing like these tiny pyramids had been found before. In the past, scholars believed that the pyramid form was invented as the shape for a royal tomb. However, Zahi Hawass, director general of the Giza Pyramids, thinks that the pyramid form actually may have arisen among the common people. He believes that the mini-pyramids evolved from sacred rectangular mounds found in tombs even older than the pharaohs' pyramids.

Life for most ancient Egyptians was hard. Society was built around a preoccupation with the pharaohs' immortality. But perhaps there were spiritual rewards for the common people in this devotion to their pharaohs. Some scholars think that ancient Egyptians believed not so much that the pharaoh was divine,

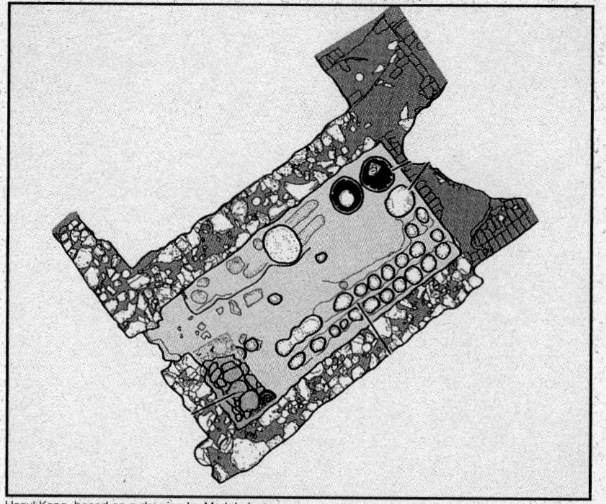

Hosul Kang, based on a drawing by Mark Lehner

Kenneth Garrett

A drawing of an ancient bakery (top) was used to build this replica of an ancient Egyptian bakery near Saqqara, Egypt (bottom).

but that through the pharaoh the divine nature of their society was expressed. Building a pyramid might have been an act of faith much as building a cathedral was in the Middle Ages.

Such recent discoveries about the life of the common people may lead to a new way of seeing ancient Egypt: not only as a brilliant civilization of the elite trickling down to the masses but also as a culture built from the bottom up—a culture that stood on the daily toil of the workers and the beliefs of ordinary men and women.

Much of the emerging picture of daily life in ancient Egypt is one of arduous toil. The villages were crowded and dirty. Huts were made of thatch and mud brick. Men wore loincloths; women dressed in long sheaths with wide shoulder straps; and children went naked. On wooden sledges workers hauled the giant granite blocks that built the pyramids. Egypt created a vast agricultural empire, yet all the irrigation was done by hand. Farmers filled two heavy jars from the canals, then hung them from a yoke over their shoulders. Oxen dragging wooden plows tilled the fertile soil along the Nile, followed by lines of sowers who sang in cadence as they cast grains of emmer wheat from baskets.

There is much still to be learned and understood about daily life in ancient Egypt. The discovery of the bakery has provided insight into what sustained the masses; the bones in the commoners' graveyard tell us that life was not easy; the mini-pyramids illustrate that art, culture, and faith may have developed up from the average man and woman, rather than down from the royalty. For years Egyptologists have focused on the grandiose—and thereby disregarded most of Egyptian society. Eventually, however, our view of ancient Egyptian culture is broadening to encompass those responsible for creating it.

MORE ABOUT...

Recreation Although the ancient Egyptians were hard workers as farmers and pyramid builders, they also found time for leisure activities. Sailing on the Nile was a popular family pastime. Egyptians also enjoyed swimming and fishing on the Nile. Many Egyptians also liked to watch wrestling matches. The more adventurous hunted crocodiles, lions, hippopotamuses, and wild cattle with spears or bows and arrows. At home, Egyptians liked to play *senet*, a board game much like backgammon.

Kenneth Garrett

Kenneth Garrett

Kenneth Garrett

A potter was hired to make replicas of the old baking pots. A local worker (top left) heats the tops in a wood fire in preparation for baking.

A kind of wheat known as emmer was supplied by a Californian who collects and grows ancient grains. The wet flour made from the emmer was left outside to collect free-floating native yeast spores and bacteria. (Store–bought yeast was not known to ancient Egyptians.) On baking day, the dough was placed into the pot bottoms and allowed to rise (bottom left). A hole for each pot was dug in the hot coals. The heated pot tops were then placed on the heated bottom halves and were placed in the coals to bake.

Success! For perhaps the first time in more than 4,000 years, a loaf of emmer bread popped out of an Old Kingdom-style pot. Edward Wood (above), who has been baking ancient breads for 50 years, holds up a perfect loaf.

CURRICULUM CONNECTION

MATHEMATICS
The Pyramid of Khufu contains more than 2 million stone blocks that average 2 1/2 short tons (2.3 metric tons) each. The pyramid was originally 481 feet (147 meters) high. Its base covers about 13 acres (5 hectares).

Global Gourmet

Egypt Just as emmer-wheat bread was the staple in the pyramid builders diet, most villagers and poor city dwellers today eat a simple diet based on bread and *fool* (broad beans). For a typical evening meal, each person dips bread into a large communal bowl of vegetable stew.

Portfolio Project

Tell students that the study of ancient Egypt is called "Egyptology." Have students choose one of the following categories—architecture, woodworking, metalworking, or written records, and list five facts that they have learned about life in ancient Egypt.

TEACHER NOTES

Chapter 2 *Early Civilizations* 57

SECTION THEME

- **Cooperation** The peoples of the Fertile Crescent work together to build irrigation systems and cities.

Find Out

Answer: *Sumer enriched early Middle Eastern cultures with its legacy of cities and city life, a writing system, and such important inventions as the wagon wheel, bronze, and the twelve-month calendar.*

FOCUS

Section Objective

Summarize how Sumer's achievements enriched the early culture of the Middle East.

BELLRINGER
Motivational Activity

Before taking roll at the beginning of the class period, project Section Focus Transparency 2-2 and have students answer the activity questions. Discuss students' responses.

This activity is also available as a blackline master.

Vocabulary Pre-check

Use Vocabulary Activity 2 to introduce vocabulary terms.
L1 LEP

3000 B.C. — **2000 B.C.** — **1000 B.C.**

- **c. 3000 B.C.** Sumerians set up city-states.
- **c. 2300 B.C.** Akkadian king Sargon I begins conquests.
- **c. 1700 B.C.** Hammurabi develops code of laws.

Section 2

The Fertile Crescent

Setting the Scene

- **Terms to Define**
  city-state, cuneiform
- **People to Meet**
  the Sumerians, Sargon I, the Akkadians, Hammurabi
- **Places to Locate**
  Fertile Crescent, Mesopotamia, Tigris and Euphrates Rivers

Find Out How did Sumer's achievements enrich the early culture of the Middle East?

The Storyteller

Sumerians honored the sun god Shamash as a defender of the weak, giver of life, and even as a judge of business deals, as in this hymn:

"The whole of mankind bows to you,
Shamash the universe longs for your light....
As for him who declines a present, but
nevertheless takes the part of the weak,
It is pleasing to Shamash, and he will prolong
his life....
The merchant who practices
trickery as he holds the
balances...
He is disappointed in the matter
of profit and loses his capital.
The honest merchant who holds
the balances and gives good
weight—
Everything is presented to him in
good measure."

—from *Babylonian Wisdom Literature*, W. B. Lambert, in *Readings in Ancient History* (2nd ed.), N. Bailkey

Sumerian board game

Around 5000 B.C.—at about the same time as Egyptian nomads moved into the Nile River valley—groups of herders started to journey north from the Arabian Peninsula. Rainfall in the area had declined over the years, and the lakes and grasslands had begun to dry up. Other peoples—from the highlands near present-day Turkey—moved south at this time. Driven by poor weather, they also fled war and overpopulation.

Both groups of migrants headed into the crescent-shaped strip of fertile land that stretched from the Mediterranean Sea to the Persian Gulf, curving around northern Syria. Called the **Fertile Crescent**, this region included parts of the modern nations of Israel, Jordan, Lebanon, Turkey, Syria, and Iraq.

Many of the peoples migrating from the north and south chose to settle in **Mesopotamia** (MEH•suh•puh•TAY•mee•uh), the eastern part of the Fertile Crescent. Located on a low plain lying between the **Tigris and Euphrates Rivers**, the name *Mesopotamia* means "land between the rivers" in the Greek language. The two rivers begin in the hills of present-day eastern Turkey and later run parallel to each other through present-day Iraq on their way to the Persian Gulf. In this region, the newcomers built villages and farmed the land.

The Twin Rivers

Beginning with Neolithic farmers, people used the Tigris and Euphrates Rivers to water their crops. Unlike the Nile River, however, the twin rivers did not provide a regular supply of water. In the summer no rain fell, and the Mesopotamian plain was dry. As a result, water shortages often coincided with the fall planting season. By the spring harvest season, however, the rivers swelled with rain and melting snow. Clogged with deposits of silt, the Tigris and Euphrates Rivers often overflowed onto the plain. Strong floods sometimes

SECTION RESOURCES

Reproducible Masters
- Reproducible Lesson Plan 2-2
- Vocabulary Activity 2
- Guided Reading Activity 2-2
- Section Quiz 2-2

Transparencies
- Section Focus Transparency 2-2
- Mapping History Overlay Transparency 1
- Fertile Crescent

Multimedia
- The Fertile Crescent
- Student Self-Test and Review Software
- Testmaker
- Egypt and the Fertile Crescent
- Turning Points in World History

swept away whole villages and fields. The time of year of such flooding, however, was never predictable, and the water level of the rivers often varied from year to year.

The early Mesopotamian villages cooperated in order to meet the rivers' challenges. Together they first built dams and escape channels to control the seasonal floodwaters and later constructed canals and ditches to bring river water to irrigate their fields. As a result of their determined efforts, Mesopotamian farmers were producing food, especially grain crops, in abundance by 4000 B.C.

The Sumerian Civilization

Around 3500 B.C. a people from either central Asia or Asia Minor—**the Sumerians**—arrived in Mesopotamia. They settled in the lower part of the Tigris-Euphrates river valley, known as Sumer. Sumer became the birthplace of what historians have considered the world's first cities.

The Sumerian City-States

By 3000 B.C. the Sumerians had formed 12 city-states in the Tigris-Euphrates valley, including Ur, Uruk, and Eridu. A typical Sumerian city-state consisted of the city itself and the land surrounding it. The population of each city-state ranged from 20,000 to 250,000.

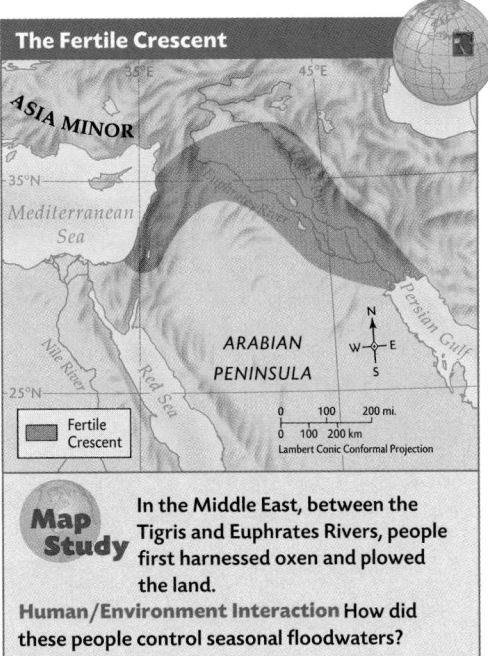

The Fertile Crescent

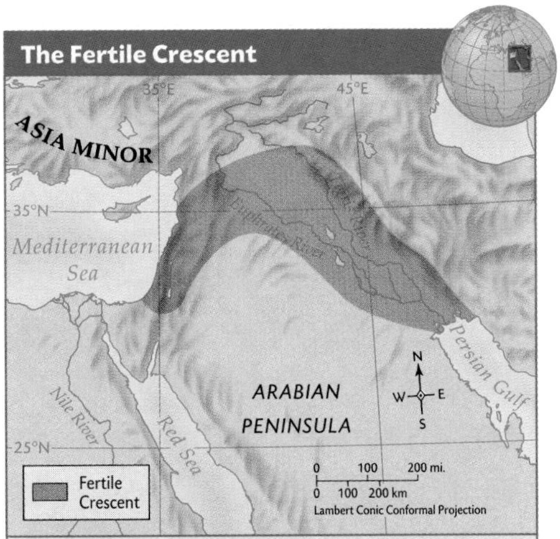

Map Study **In the Middle East, between the Tigris and Euphrates Rivers, people first harnessed oxen and plowed the land.**
Human/Environment Interaction How did these people control seasonal floodwaters?

The people of Sumer shared a common culture, language, and religion. Sumerian city-states also shared some physical features. A ziggurat (ZIH •guh•RAT), or temple, made of sun-dried brick and decorated with colored tile, was built in each city-state. Sumerians built a ziggurat as a series of terraces, with each terrace smaller than the one below. A staircase climbed to a shrine atop the ziggurat. Only priests and priestesses were allowed to enter the shrine, which was dedicated to the city-state's chief deity. In form a ziggurat resembled a pyramid—both being massive stepped or peaked structures—but the feeling and emphasis of the two differed. A pyramid hid an inner tomb reachable only through passageways. A ziggurat raised a shrine to the sky, reached by mounting outer stairs.

Sumerian Government

Each Sumerian city-state usually governed itself independently of the others. In the city-state of Uruk, for example, a council of nobles and an assembly of citizens ran political affairs at first. But later, as city-states faced threats of foreign invaders and began to compete for land and water rights, the citizens of each city-state typically chose a military leader from among themselves. By 2700 B.C. the

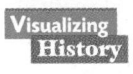

Visualizing History **A bull-headed lyre from Sumer, c. 2500 B.C.** *What was a ziggurat, and how was it built?*

COOPERATIVE LEARNING ACTIVITY

Team Presentation Organize the class into teams of five or six students. Have each team research one aspect of life in ancient Sumer, Akhad, or Babylon. Have teams prepare a class presentation, the subject and format of which they determine cooperatively. Students could include lifestyles, occupations, religious practices, or achievements. Formats could include skits, plays, and lectures. Assign specific tasks or have teams decide what role each team member will play in gathering and presenting the material. Provide time after each presentation for discussion and questions. Have a volunteer record on the board the main points brought out in the presentation. **L1**

TEACH

Guided Practice

THEME Cooperation

Ask why public works projects, such as dams and irrigation canals, require organization and cooperation. *(No one person can do them alone; they are too large, and many such projects require a number of different specialized skills.)* **L1**

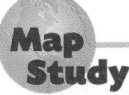

Map Study

Answer

They built dams and escape channels.

Map Skills Practice

Reading a Map Using the Atlas in this text, name a state or states in the United States that are approximately the same distance from the Equator as is the Fertile Crescent. *(Possible answers include: Georgia, Alabama, Mississippi, Texas, Arizona, New Mexico, southern California)*

Visualizing History The lyre, a stringed musical instrument with a sound box, was common to many early civilizations, including those of Mesopotamia, Egypt, and Israel. The word *lyre* comes from a Greek word for the instrument.

Answer to Caption: *a pyramid-shaped temple with steep sides, made of sun-dried brick and decorated with colored tile*

Map Study

Answers

1. *Euphrates River*
2. *two rivers that supplied water, fertile land for farming*

Map Skills Practice

Reading a Map Have students locate the modern countries in the Fertile Crescent region in the Atlas in their text.

Mapping History Overlay Transparency 1, *River Valley Civilizations*

Religion Three of the world's great religions—Judaism, Christianity, and Islam—originated in the Middle East. Several of the countries, peoples, regions, natural features, or cities mentioned in this section are also mentioned in the Bible or the Quran. Have students identify and describe three of these places. *(Ur, Uruk [Erech], Babylon)* **L3**

Independent Practice

Guided Reading Activity 2-2 **L1**

Time Line Have students create a time line of Mesopotamian history from 5000 B.C. (arrival of Akkadians) to 1600 B.C. (end of Hammurabi's empire). Encourage students to make the time line visually appealing by adding illustrations. **L1 LEP**

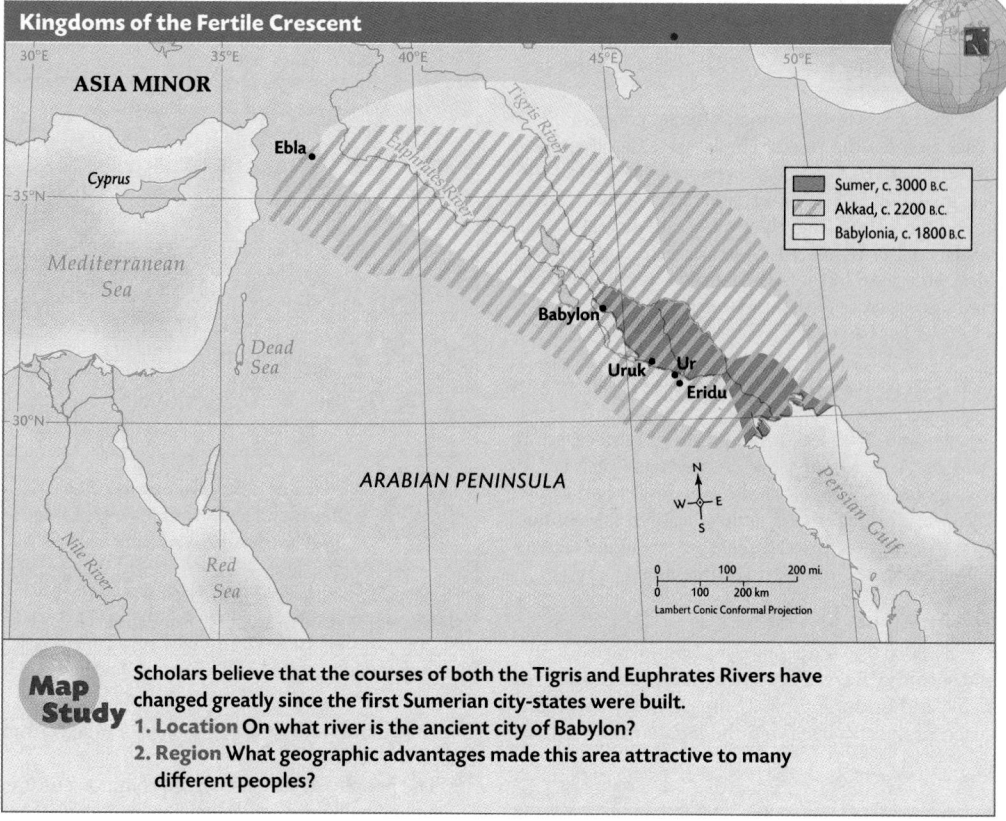

Kingdoms of the Fertile Crescent

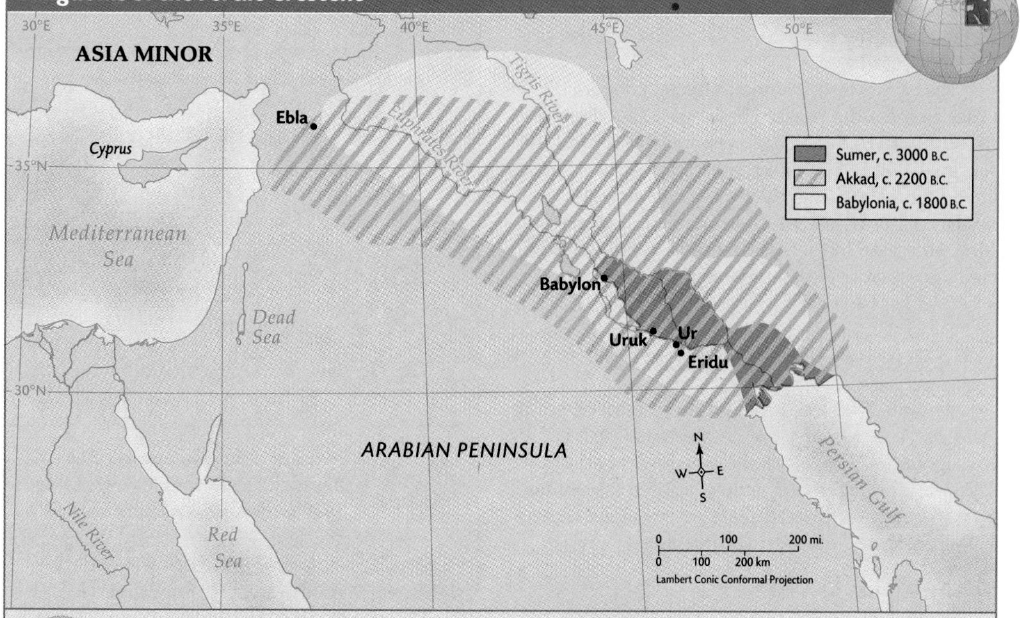

Map Study Scholars believe that the courses of both the Tigris and Euphrates Rivers have changed greatly since the first Sumerian city-states were built.

1. **Location** On what river is the ancient city of Babylon?
2. **Region** What geographic advantages made this area attractive to many different peoples?

leaders of several city-states ruled as kings. Soon after, the kingships became hereditary.

A Sumerian king served not only as military leader but as the high priest, who represented the city-state's deity. Thus the governments of the city-states were not only monarchies but theocracies. Because the Sumerians believed that much of the land belonged to a city-state's god or goddess, a king and his priests closely supervised farming. A king also enforced the law and set penalties for lawbreakers. Most punishments consisted of fines and did not involve bodily injury or loss of life.

The Roles of Men and Women

Sumerian law extensively regulated family life and outlined the roles of men and women. As the heads of households, men exercised great authority over their wives and children. According to Sumerian law codes, a man could sell his wife or children into slavery if he needed the money to pay a debt. He could also divorce his wife for the slightest cause. For a Sumerian woman, in contrast, the law codes made divorce much more difficult. Women did enjoy some legal rights, however. Like Egyptian women, they could buy and sell property. They could also operate their own businesses and own and sell their own slaves.

Writing on Clay Tablets

Commerce and trade dominated the Sumerian city-states. The Sumerians developed a system of writing so they could keep accounts and prepare documents. Archaeologists believe that the writing system the Sumerians invented is the oldest in the world, dating to about 3100 B.C. The **cuneiform** (kyoo•NEE•uh•FAWRM) system began with pictograms—as did Egyptian hieroglyphics—and consisted of hundreds of wedge-shaped markings made by pressing the end of a sharpened reed on wet clay tablets. Then the Sumerians dried or baked the tablets until they were hard. Eventually cuneiform evolved into a script that became—about 2,000 years later—a model for alphabetic systems of writing.

MEETING SPECIAL NEEDS ACTIVITY

Study Strategy Have students who need help synthesizing and summarizing information research ancient Mesopotamian cities and write an in-depth report about one of them. Encourage students to illustrate the reports. These cities are possible research topics: Eridu, the first of the five cities that existed before the Flood; Uruk, the biblical city called Erech in Genesis; Ur, one of the important religious centers of ancient Sumer; Kish, the first seat of kingship after the Flood; Mari, a city on the trade route between Mesopotamia and Syria; Babylon, capital of the Amorite dynasty after the fall of the Ur empire. **L2**

Visualizing History **Medical remedies are inscribed on this Sumerian clay tablet—a cuneiform writing tablet that was baked until hard.** *How is cuneiform different from alphabetic writing?*

Sumerians wishing to learn cuneiform and become scribes studied for many years at special schools called *eddubas*. As educated professionals, scribes rose to high positions in Sumerian society. They produced business records, lists of historical dates, and literary works.

One of these literary works, the epic poem *Gilgamesh*, was written down before 1800 B.C. Scholars believe that the *Gilgamesh* epic may be the oldest story in the world. The scribes probably based the stories of Gilgamesh, a godlike man who performs heroic deeds, on an actual king of the city-state of Uruk.

Sumer's Many Deities

The Sumerians, like the Egyptians, practiced a polytheistic religion. Each Sumerian deity presided over a specific natural force—rain, moon, air—or over a human activity—plowing or brick making, for example. An, the highest Sumerian deity, was responsible for the seasons. Another important god—Enlil, god of winds and agriculture—created the hoe. Although Sumerians honored all the deities, each city-state claimed as its own one god or goddess, to whom its citizens prayed and offered sacrifices.

The Sumerians pictured their gods and goddesses as unpredictable, selfish beings who had little regard for human beings. The Sumerians believed that if deities became angry, they would cause misfortunes such as floods or famine. To appease their temperamental gods and goddesses, Sumerian priests and priestesses performed religious ceremonies and rituals.

Unlike the Egyptians, the Sumerians felt that humans had little control over their daily lives and could not look forward to a happy life after death. Only a grim underworld, without light or air, awaited them—an afterlife where the dead were only pale shadows.

Sumerian Inventions

Historians credit the Sumerians with numerous technological innovations. The Sumerians developed the wagon wheel, for example, to better transport people and goods, the arch to build sturdier buildings, the potter's wheel to shape containers, and the sundial to keep time. They developed a number system based on 60 and devised a 12-month calendar based on the cycles of the moon. The Sumerian civilization also was the first to make bronze out of copper and tin and to develop a metal plow. They produced an abundance of finely crafted metal work, some of which has been discovered in the Royal Cemetery at Ur. These and other Sumerian achievements have prompted one scholar to observe that "history begins at Sumer."

First Mesopotamian Empires

After a long period of conquest and reconquest, the Sumerian city-states eventually fell to foreign invaders in the 2000s B.C. The invaders of Sumer, like the Egyptians of the New Kingdom, were inspired by dreams of empire.

Footnotes to History **The Umbrella**

1400 B.C.—Umbrellas actually originated under the sunny skies of Mesopotamia. Sumerians used palm fronds or feather umbrellas to shield their heads from the harsh rays and scorching heat of the Middle Eastern sun.

Visualizing History Clay tablets with cuneiform writing on them have given us more information about Mesopotamia than any other artifact. They explain many aspects of Mesopotamian life.
Answer to Caption: *Cuneiform began as pictograms, or pictures representing ideas. In alphabetic writing, symbols (not pictures) represent sounds.*

Technology Have students find out more about a Sumerian invention, such as the wagon wheel or the arch, and write a television commercial script about it. The script should explain the benefits of the invention to the Sumerian people. Have students write descriptions of the visuals that would accompany the script. **L3**

NATIONAL GEOGRAPHIC SOCIETY

Use these materials to enrich student understanding of Mesopotamian civilizations.

- **NGS PICTURESHOW CD-ROM** Egypt and the Fertile Crescent
- **NGS PICTUREPACK TRANSPARENCY SET** Fertile Crescent
- **ANCIENT CIVILIZATIONS POSTER SET** Fertile Crescent

MAKING CONNECTIONS ACTIVITY

Global Issues The Louvre in Paris owns and displays a stone pillar inscribed with Hammurabi's legal decisions. The British Museum in London has an extensive collection of Mesopotamian art. The University Museum at the University of Pennsylvania has a collection of early Sumerian literary works. Have students debate whether a museum should return artifacts such as these to their places of origin. **L1**

Chapter 2
Section 2

Linking Past and Present

Barley Most Sumerians were farmers. Indeed, the world's oldest agricultural manual was written in Sumer. It tells farmers how to grow barley, Mesopotamia's staple food. Barley is still an important crop throughout the world. It is the fourth most widely grown grain, after wheat, corn, and rice.

Critical Thinking Have students research Hammurabi's code of laws. Ask volunteers to present their findings in class. Students should understand that the code was an attempt to deal fairly with people in a political state made up of former independent states with different traditions. The code set up a social order based on individual rights. **L3**

Who?What?Where?When?

Cuneiform Whereas Egyptian hieroglyphics were used by a homogenous group of people, cuneiform was used by heterogenous groups who spoke different languages. Cuneiform served as the writing system for diverse cultures for some 3,000 years. Sumerians, Akkadians, Babylonians, Assyrians, Hittites, and Old Persians are among the peoples whose language was written in cuneiform. In its time, cuneiform was as widely used as the Latin alphabet is today.

Sargon Leads the Akkadians

The first empire builder in Mesopotamia—**Sargon I**—may have been born a herder or a farmer's son. According to legend his mother abandoned him as a baby, setting him out on the Euphrates River in a reed basket. Downstream a farmer irrigating his fields pulled Sargon ashore and raised him as his own.

Sargon's people, **the Akkadians**, were Semites, one of the nomadic groups that had migrated from the Arabian Peninsula to the Fertile Crescent around 5000 B.C. The Akkadians established a kingdom called Akkad (AH•KAHD) in northern Mesopotamia. When Sargon assumed power in Akkad around 2300 B.C., he immediately launched a military campaign of expansion. Sargon's conquests united all of the city-states of Mesopotamia in one empire, which predated the empire of the Egyptian New Kingdom by more than 800 years.

Under Sargon's rule the people of Mesopotamia began to use the Akkadian language instead of Sumerian. But the Akkadians adopted various Sumerian religious and farming practices. After Sargon's death and the successful rule of his grandson, however, the Akkadian Empire disintegrated.

The Kingdom of Ebla

No one really knows how far Sargon's empire extended. Historians do know, however, that Ebla, a kingdom located in what is now northern Syria, fought unsuccessfully against Sargon for control of the Euphrates River trade. When Sargon's grandson captured Ebla, he burned the royal archives. Yet fire did not destroy the thousands of clay tablets stored there. These tablets and other finds from Ebla have convinced historians that highly developed Semitic civilizations prospered in that area of Syria earlier than previously believed.

The overland trade that passed between Egypt and Mesopotamia made Ebla a wealthy and powerful city-state. Ebla controlled a number of neighboring towns, from which it exacted tribute.

The kings of Ebla were elected for seven-year terms. In addition to their political role, they looked

Images of the Times

Mesopotamia

For many centuries, beginning about 4000 B.C., enterprising civilizations rose and fell in the fertile valley of the Tigris and Euphrates Rivers.

The Royal Standard of Ur is an oblong decorated box with panels that represent scenes of war and peace. The war panel celebrates a military victory by the Sumerian city of Ur.

62

Images of the Times

Mesopotamia

Our knowledge of life in Mesopotamia depends heavily on cuneiform studies. Translations were begun nearly 150 years ago and are still continuing. Tens of thousands of clay tablets have been found inscribed with the wedge-shaped script. They include business, legal, and administrative documents, as well as hymns, myths, epic tales, proverbs, fables, and essays. A thousand years before the Hebrews wrote their Bible or the Greeks their *Iliad* and *Odyssey*, writers in Mesopotamia had produced a rich and mature literature.

after the welfare of the poor. If the kings failed, they could be removed by a council. After 2000 B.C., Ebla declined and eventually was destroyed by the Amorites, a Semitic people from western Syria.

Hammurabi's Babylonian Empire

Around the same time that they destroyed Ebla, the Amorites also expanded beyond Syria. After the Akkadian Empire disintegrated, the Sumerian civilization had briefly recovered under the leadership of the kings of Ur, but soon it was again in decline. The Amorites poured into Mesopotamia and overran many Sumerian centers, including Babylon. The dynasty that they founded at Babylon later produced a ruler who would dominate Mesopotamia: **Hammurabi**.

Hammurabi used his might to put down other Mesopotamian rulers. He eventually brought the entire region under his control, reorganizing the tax system and ordering local officials to build and repair irrigation canals. Hammurabi organized a strong government and worked to increase the economic prosperity of his people. Under Hammurabi's rule, Babylon became a major trade center. Merchants from as far away as India and China paid gold and silver for the grain and cloth the Babylonians produced.

Hammurabi's Law Code

Historians consider Hammurabi's greatest achievement his effort "to make justice appear in the land." Hammurabi collected laws of the various Mesopotamian city-states and created a law code covering the entire region. When completed, Hammurabi's code consisted of 282 sections dealing with most aspects of daily life. It clearly stated which actions were considered violations and assigned a specific punishment for each. Hammurabi's code penalized wrongdoers more severely than did the old Sumerian laws. Instead of fining violators, it exacted what the Bible later expressed as "an eye for an eye, and a tooth for a tooth." According to the harsh approach of Hammurabi's code:

This goddess, one of many similar preserved relics, along with discovered temple sites, reveals the significance of religion in early Mesopotamian civilizations.

The Kassite stela fragment shows animals that were important to a vigorous agricultural people, the Kassites, who emerged as a dominant force after 2000 B.C.

REFLECTING ON THE TIMES

1. What evidence reveals the importance of religion in Mesopotamian cities?
2. What role might gods and goddesses have in times of war?

ANSWERS TO REFLECTING ON THE TIMES

1. Many religious relics have been found.
2. They could help ensure victory for their side, or, if angered, bring about defeat.

ABCNEWS INTERACTIVE™

VIDEODISC
Turning Points in World History

Side One
Chapter 4

Title: *The Code of Hammurabi*
Subject: Hammurabi's written code of laws established justice and became the basis for rules and laws throughout the world.
Ask: How were punishments for crimes decided? *(Punishments were to fit the crimes, like the biblical saying, "an eye for an eye.")*

ASSESS

Check for Understanding

Assign Section 2 Review as homework or as an in-class activity.

Use Student Self-Test and Review Software to review Section 2.

Evaluate

Section Quiz 2-2

Use the Testmaker to create a customized quiz for Section 2.

Reteach

Have students write two sentences about each of the three Mesopotamian civilizations. Each sentence should present an important fact about the civilization being described. Ask students to read their sentences in class. Discuss.

Visualizing History The god Shamash, the supreme judge, was one of a pantheon of deities, humanlike in form but superhuman and immortal, who guided the activities of the universe. Although Shamash appears on this stone slab, the god of judgment—like all the gods in the pantheon—was invisible to mere mortals.

Answer to Caption: *They dealt with many aspects of daily living and had to be known by all citizens.*

Enrich

Have students draw to scale an Egyptian pyramid, a Sumerian ziggurat, and a large building in their area. Have them compare the dimensions and report on what they find.

CLOSE

Have students write a paragraph about each of the three civilizations in this section—Sumerian, Akkadian, and Babylonian—that begins with this sentence: We influenced the course of human history. Have students summarize in these paragraphs the contributions of each civilization. Ask volunteers to read their paragraphs aloud in class.

Visualizing History **King Hammurabi stands in front of the sun god Shamash at the top of the stone slab upon which is inscribed Hammurabi's code of laws. Shamash—the supreme judge—delivers the laws to the king.** *Why were Hammurabi's laws carved in stone for public display?*

> "If a builder has built a house for a man and has not made his work sound, so that the house he has made falls down and causes the death of the owner of the house, that builder shall be put to death. If it causes the death of the son of the owner of the house, they shall kill the son of that builder."

Other sections of Hammurabi's code covered the property of married women, adoption and inheritance, interest rates on loans, and damage to fields by cattle. Some laws were attempts to protect the less powerful—for example, protecting wives against beatings or neglect by their husbands. The development of written law in Mesopotamia was a major advance toward justice and order. Before this achievement, people who had been offended or cheated often acted on their own and used violence against their opponents. Now, crimes against people or property became the concern of the whole community. Government assumed the responsibility of protecting its citizens in return for their loyalty and service.

Babylonian Society

Historians have been able to infer from Hammurabi's code a threefold division of Babylonian social classes—the kings, priests, and nobles at the top; the artisans, small merchants, scribes, and farmers next; and slaves as the lowest group. His laws varied according to the class of the person offended against, with more severe penalties for assaulting a landowner than for hurting a slave. Most slaves had been captured in war or had failed to pay their debts.

The Babylonians borrowed heavily from Sumerian culture. They used the cuneiform script for their Semitic language and wrote on clay tablets. Babylonian literature was similar to that of Sumer.

Decline and Fall

After Hammurabi's death, the Babylonian Empire declined, and Mesopotamia was again divided into a number of small states. Hammurabi's dynasty finally ended and his empire fell apart when the Hittites, a people from Asia Minor, raided Babylon about 1600 B.C. Babylon, however, would again play a role in Mesopotamian civilization in the 600s B.C. as the capital of a new empire under the Chaldeans.

SECTION 2 REVIEW

Recall

1. **Define** city-state, cuneiform.
2. **Identify** the Sumerians, Gilgamesh, Sargon I, the Akkadians, Hammurabi.
3. **Explain** the purpose of the religious ceremonies and rituals performed by Sumerian priests and priestesses.

Critical Thinking

4. **Making Comparisons** Contrast Hammurabi's code with earlier Sumerian law. Which do you think served justice better? Explain your answer.

Understanding Themes

5. **Cooperation** Identify an economic or cultural achievement of one of the civilizations of the Fertile Crescent region that must have required skillful planning and organization of many people.

SECTION 2 REVIEW ANSWERS

1. All vocabulary words are defined in the Glossary.
2. Sumerians, 59; Gilgamesh, 61; Sargon I, 62; Akkadians, 62; Hammurabi, 63
3. They were performed to please the gods and goddesses, who, if angered, would bring disaster.
4. Hammurabi's code was more severe. Sumerian law fined wrongdoers; Hammurabi's code exacted "an eye for an eye and a tooth for a tooth." Students should give reasons for their choice.
5. **COOPERATION** Answers may include: irrigating the land, governing city-states, building ziggurats, administering schools for scribes, conducting military operations

Critical Thinking SKILLS

Classifying Information

Imagine shopping in a store where shoes, rugs, dishes, and books are all mixed together in piles. To find the item you need, you would have to comb through each pile. How frustrating!

Dealing with large quantities of information about a subject likewise can be frustrating. It is easier to understand information if you put it into groups, or classify it.

Learning the Skill

In classifying anything, we put together items with shared characteristics. Department stores group items according to their uses. For example, shoes and boots are in the footwear department, while pots and pans are in the kitchen department.

We can classify written information in the same way.

1. As you read about a topic, look for items that have similar characteristics. List these items in separate columns or on separate notecards.
2. Label these categories with an appropriate heading.
3. Add facts to the categories as you continue reading.
4. Review the groups. If necessary, subdivide the categories into smaller groups or combine categories that overlap.

Once you have classified the material, look for patterns and relationships in the facts. Make comparisons, draw conclusions, and develop questions or hypotheses for further study.

Practicing the Skill

Use the information in the passage below to answer the following questions:

1. The passage describes two groups of children in ancient Egypt. What are these groups?
2. Classify the educational opportunities available to each group.
3. Classify the occupations available to each group.
4. From your classifications, what conclusions can you draw about Egyptian society?

> "The royal children ... were privately tutored ... frequently joined by the sons of great noble families.... The most sought-after profession in Egypt was that of scribe.... The most important subjects were reading and writing ... history, literature, geography, [and] ethics. Arithmetic was almost certainly part of the curriculum.... Boys who were to specialize in medicine, law or religious liturgy would perhaps have devoted some of their time to elementary studies in these fields.
>
> Formal education for [a son from] the lower classes ... was not selected for him because he wished to become an artist or goldsmith or a farmer ... he entered a trade because it was his father's work. The sons of artists and craftsmen were apprenticed and went to train at one of the temples or state workshops ... the sons of peasants would have joined their fathers in the field at an early age."
>
> —A. Rosalie David, *The Egyptian Kingdoms*, 1975

Applying the Skill

Find two newspaper or magazine articles about a topic that interests you. Classify the information on notecards or in a chart.

For More Practice

Turn to the Skill Practice in the Chapter Review on page 77 for more practice in classifying information.

Critical Thinking SKILLS

TEACH

Classifying Information Elicit from students how they organize various aspects of their personal life. You might mention such things as closets and bureau drawers; stamp, coin, or sports card collections; school papers, notes and assignments. Focus discussion on how they have grouped similar items together. The skills feature teaches a four-step process for classifying data. Emphasize how sorting items based on shared characteristics is a common method of classification and is simply part of being well organized.

Additional Practice

Skill Reinforcement Activity 2

ANSWERS TO PRACTICING THE SKILL

1. nobles' children, children of the lower classes
2. nobles: private tutoring in subjects such as reading , writing, history, ethics, literature, geography, arithmetic; lower classes: apprenticeships, field work, determined by their fathers' work
3. nobles: scribes, priests, doctors, lawyers; lower classes: artisans, farmers, craftspeople
4. It was rigidly divided by class.

Chapter 2 Section 3

SECTION THEME

- **Cultural Diffusion** Cities in early India develop close trading and cultural ties with the Fertile Crescent area.

Find Out

Answer: *People of the Indus River valley civilization built centrally planned cities with multistory houses, grid-patterned streets, and sewer systems.*

FOCUS

Section Objective

Relate how people of the Indus River valley civilization built cities.

BELLRINGER Motivational Activity

Before taking roll at the beginning of the class period, project Section Focus Transparency 2-3 and have students answer the activity questions. Discuss students' responses.

This activity is also available as a blackline master.

Vocabulary Pre-check

Use Vocabulary Activity 2 to introduce vocabualry terms.
L1 LEP

- **2500 B.C.**
- **c. 2500 B.C.** Settlements develop in the Indus River valley.
- **2000 B.C.**
- **c. 2300 B.C.** Harappan people trade with Mesopotamia.
- **1500 B.C.**
- **c. 1500 B.C.** Indus Valley civilization declines.

Section 3

Early South Asia

Setting the Scene

- **Terms to Define**
  subcontinent, monsoon
- **People to Meet**
  the Harappans
- **Places to Locate**
  Indus River valley, Harappa, Mohenjo-Daro

Find Out How did people of the Indus River valley civilization build cities?

The Storyteller

For a long time, it had been known that the mounds of Mohenjo-Daro and Harappa contained archaeological remains. But neighborhood construction workers actually used the ancient mounds as sources for bricks, until practically none remained above ground. As Sir Alexander Cunningham, the first Director General of the Archaeological Survey records, "Perhaps the best idea of the extent of the ruined brick mounds of Harappa may be formed from the fact that they have more than sufficed to furnish brick ballast for about 100 miles of Lahore and Multan Railway."

—adapted from *Indus Valley Civilization*, Ashim Kumar Ron N.N. Gidwani (Cunningham, 1875), 1982 and *Harappan Civilization*, Gregory Possehl, 1982

Harappan jar lid

A third civilization, larger than both Egypt and Sumer in land area, arose in the **Indus River valley** far to the east, in South Asia. It reached its height at about the time of the Akkadian and Babylonian Empires between about 2500 B.C. and 1500 B.C.

The Subcontinent

Three modern nations—India, Pakistan, and Bangladesh—trace their roots to the Indus Valley civilization. These countries lie on the subcontinent of South Asia, a large, triangular-shaped landmass that juts into the Indian Ocean.

Bounded by Mountains

Natural barriers separate the South Asian subcontinent from the rest of Asia. Water surrounds the landmass on the east and west. To the north rise two lofty mountain ranges—the Himalayas and the Hindu Kush. Throughout history, invaders entering the subcontinent by land have had to cross the few high mountain passes of the Hindu Kush.

Plains sweep across the landscape to the south of the mountains. Across the plains flow three rivers, fed by rain and melting mountain snows. The Indus River drains into the Arabian Sea, and the Ganges (GAN•JEEZ) and Brahmaputra (BRAH•muh•POO•truh) Rivers join and empty into the Bay of Bengal, forming a wide delta. The Ganges-Brahmaputra Delta and the Indus-Ganges plain are formed from soils left by the rivers. Like the Nile Valley and Delta and the Tigris-Euphrates plains, fertile river areas of South Asia have supported vast numbers of people over the ages.

Seasonal Winds

The northern mountains ensure generally warm weather in South Asia. Like a wall, they block blasts of cold air from central Asia. Two seasonal winds called monsoons affect the climate,

SECTION RESOURCES

Reproducible Masters
- Reproducible Lesson Plan 2-3
- Vocabulary Activity 2
- Guided Reading Activity 2-3
- Section Quiz 2-3

Transparencies
- Section Focus Transparency 2-3
- Mapping History Overlay Transparency 3
- Ancient India

Multimedia
- Student Self-Test and Review Software
- Testmaker
- India and China

Early Asian Civilizations

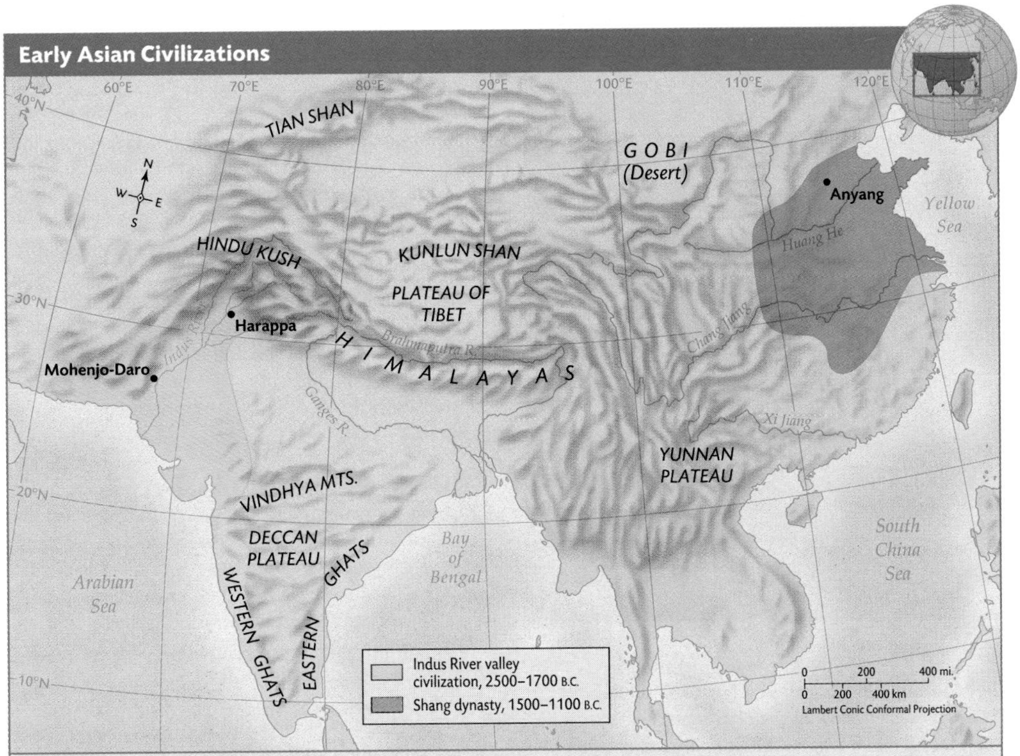

Map Study The urban Harappan civilization emerged in the Indus Valley about 2500 B.C. The Shang dynasty ruled China from 1700 B.C. to 1000 B.C.
Human/Environment Interaction What may have caused the collapse of the Harappan civilization?

however, and shape the pattern of life on the subcontinent.

The northeast, or winter, monsoon blows from November to March; the southwest, or summer, monsoon from June to September. The northeast wind brings dry air from the mountains, and the average winter temperatures of the Indus-Ganges plain remain mild—about 70°F (21°C). By June, temperatures have soared, sometimes exceeding 100°F (38°C), and South Asians welcome the rain-bearing southwest wind blowing off the ocean.

Because of the heavy downpours of the southwest monsoon, the rivers swell rapidly, then widen across the flat plains and rush to the sea. The flooding enriches the soil, but in some years unusually heavy rains drown people and animals and destroy whole villages. In other years the monsoon arrives late or rainfall is light; then crops are poor and people go hungry. The people of the plains are dependent on the monsoons.

The Indus Valley Civilization

Less than a century ago, archaeologists working in the Indus River valley first identified an ancient civilization in South Asia. They dated this early civilization to about 2500 B.C.

Centrally Planned Cities

Archaeologists named the Indus Valley settlements "the Harappan civilization" after one of its major cities, **Harappa** (huh•RA•puh), located in present-day Pakistan. **Mohenjo-Daro** (moh •HEHN•joh DAHR•oh), another important Harappan city, lay nearer the Arabian Sea.

The ruins of Harappa and Mohenjo-Daro are outstanding examples of urban planning. A citadel, or fortress, built on a brick platform overlooked each city—possibly serving as a government and religious center. Below the citadel Harappan engineers skillfully laid out each city in a grid pattern of

COOPERATIVE LEARNING ACTIVITY

Visual Presentations Organize the class into groups of five or six students. Have each group choose a topic from this list of suggestions: religion, architecture, city planning, farming, textiles, arts and crafts, commerce, and geography. Have groups research their topic as it pertains to Harappan civilization. They should then prepare visuals illustrating what they have learned about their topic. The items may be labeled, but the emphasis should be on a visual presentation. Each group should decide what task the members of the group will perform. Provide space for the groups to display their completed work. Discussion of the displays should include a time for questions and answers. **L2**

TEACH

Guided Practice

THEME Cultural Diffusion

Using information in the text, have students trace on a relief map a possible route taken by the traders who traveled to Mesopotamia and brought ideas such as writing back to Harappa and Mohenjo-Daro. *(Routes should cross through a pass in the Hindu Kush.)* **L1 LEP**

Map Study

Answer

floods caused by climate changes, or violence—perhaps at the hands of invaders

Map Skills Practice

Reading a Map What features of physical geography, common to Egypt and Mesopotamia, were also vital to the Harappan and early Chinese civilizations? *(rivers)*

Independent Practice

Guided Reading Activity 2-3 **L1**

NATIONAL GEOGRAPHIC SOCIETY

Use these materials to enrich student understanding of Indus River valley civilizations.

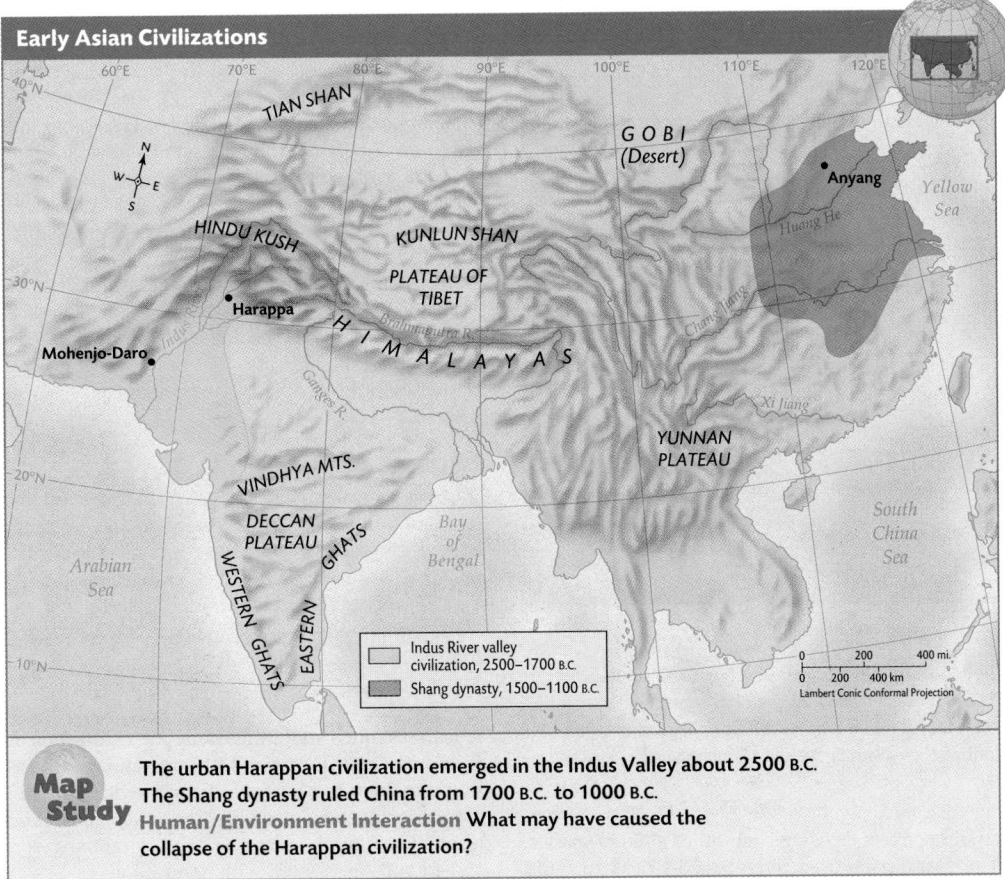

- **NGS PICTURESHOW CD-ROM**
  India and China
- **NGS PICTUREPACK TRANSPARENCY SET**
  Ancient India

Visualizing History Among the many art objects from the Indus River valley civilization are statuettes made of soapstone and limestone, square soapstone seals decorated with a variety of animals, ceramic storage jars, and toys with wheels. **Answer to Caption:** *lack of written records from the Harappans*

ASSESS

Check for Understanding

Assign Section 3 Review as homework or as an in-class activity.

Use Student Self-Test and Review Software to review Section 3.

Evaluate

Section Quiz 2-3

Use the Testmaker to create a customized quiz for Section 3.

Reteach

Have a discussion on the achievements of Harappan civilization.

Enrich

Have students find out more about monsoons, including their causes, and write a one-page report on the subject.

CLOSE

Have students write a paragraph describing the features of Harappan civilization that made it attractive to invaders, such as its thriving agricultural enterprise. Have students read their paragraphs in class.

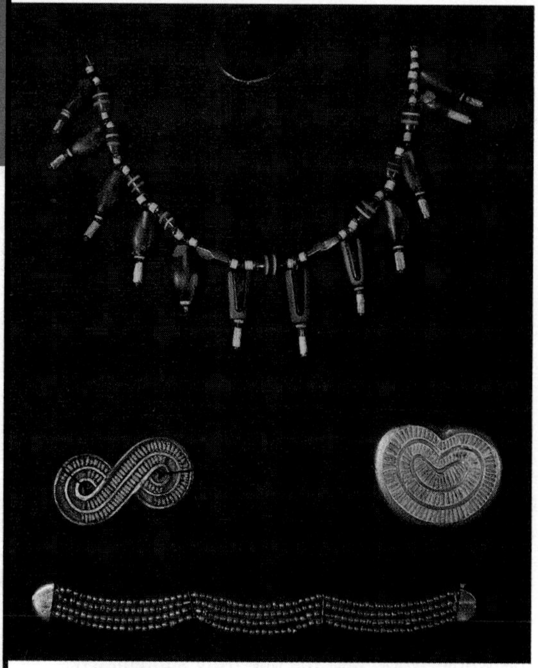

Visualizing History **Some fine jewelry crafted by Harappan artisans has survived. These pieces are now in the National Museum at New Delhi, India.** *Why is less known about Harappan civilization than about Egypt and Mesopotamia?*

straight streets crossing each other at right angles. **The Harappans** used oven-baked bricks to build houses with flat wooden roofs, and some houses rose to several stories and enclosed courtyards. Almost every house had at least one bathroom, with drains and chutes connected to a brick sewer system beneath the streets.

Harappan Life

Most of the Harappan people worked the land. In the fields of the Indus Valley floodplain they grew wheat, barley, rice, and cotton. Farmers planted at the beginning or end of the flood season and relied on the drenched land to provide the necessary water for their crops.

Supported by a food surplus, Harappan city dwellers engaged in industry and commerce. Some artisans worked bronze and copper into tools, while others made silver vessels and gold, shell, and ivory jewelry. The Harappans also mass-produced clay pots, and they spun and wove cotton cloth. Merchants who handled these goods used soapstone seals to identify bundles of merchandise. The discovery by archaeologists of Harappan seals in Mesopotamia indicates that Indus Valley people traded with the people of Mesopotamia as early as 2300 B.C.

Language and Religion

The Harappans inscribed pictograms on the seals they placed on packages of goods. Scientists have yet to decipher these inscriptions—almost the only known examples of the written language of the Harappan civilization. Some believe that the Harappans made their pictograms after adopting the idea of writing from the people of Mesopotamia.

The lack of written records has made it difficult to learn as much about the Harappan civilization as is known about Egypt and Mesopotamia. Artifacts found in the ruins, however, have provided archaeologists with some clues. For example, animal and humanlike figures suggest that the Harappans worshiped gods associated with natural forces.

Collapse of a Civilization

By 1500 B.C. the Harappan civilization had disappeared. Historians have many theories for what caused this collapse. Evidence of floods, for example, suggests possible climate changes. In the Mohenjo-Daro ruins are signs that some of its people may have met a violent end, possibly at the hands of invaders.

SECTION 3 REVIEW

Recall
1. **Define** subcontinent, monsoon.
2. **Identify** the Harappans.
3. **Name** three modern nations of South Asia that trace their roots to the Indus Valley civilization. In what present-day nation were the cities of Harappa and Mohenjo-Daro located?

Critical Thinking
4. **Analyzing Information** What do archaeological clues suggest about the decline and collapse of the Indus Valley civilization?

Understanding Themes
5. **Cultural Diffusion** How might the Indus Valley civilization at Mohenjo-Daro and the civilization at Harappa have been influenced by the Mesopotamian city-states and empires?

SECTION 3 REVIEW ANSWERS

1. All vocabulary words are defined in the Glossary.
2. Harappans, 67
3. India, Pakistan, Bangladesh; Pakistan
4. Historians theorize destructive natural disasters. At Mohenjo-Daro there are signs of a violent end.
5. **CULTURAL DIFFUSION** Trade existed between the Indus Valley and Mesopotamia; some believe the Harappans learned about writing from the people of Mesopotamia.

2500 B.C. — 2000 B.C. — 1500 B.C. — 1000 B.C.

- **c. 2500 B.C.** Lung-shan culture begins in China.
- **c. 2000 B.C.** Yu founds the legendary Xia dynasty.
- **c. 1700 B.C.** Tang establishes the Shang, the first historical dynasty.
- **c. 1000s B.C.** The Zhou dynasty comes to power.

Section 4

Early China

Setting the Scene

▶Terms to Define
mandate

▶People to Meet
Yu the Great

▶Places to Locate
Huang He valley, Anyang

Find Out What were the major contributions of early Chinese civilization?

The Storyteller

What would the oracle say this time? Tang tried not to lean too far forward to watch as the fortune-teller began to apply red-hot coals to the turtle shell. A man of his station should not appear too anxious: his confidence in divine support should be seen by all. On the shell was inscribed a question known only to him: "Shall I attack before harvest?" So much depended on the answer. There was nothing to do now but wait for the fire to work on the brittle shell covered with scratchings, containing the destiny of China.

—adapted from *Ancient Records of Assyria and Babylon*, Volume 1, edited by Daniel David Luckenbill, 1968

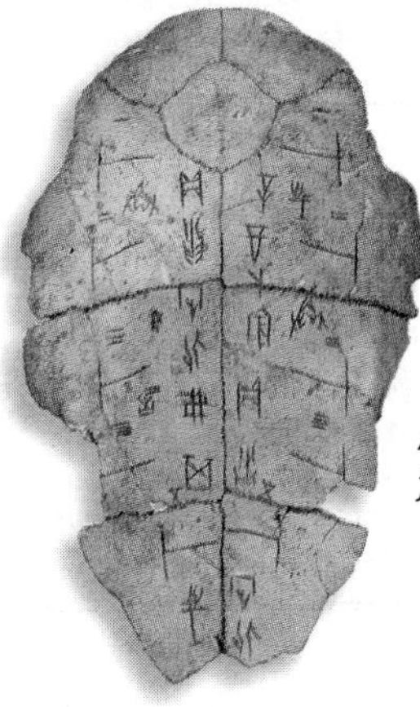

A tortoise shell oracle bone from the Shang Dynasty

Even as the Harappans were meeting their mysterious fate, China's first dynasty had begun to assert its power over another river valley. This fourth river valley civilization has endured to the present day.

For many centuries the Chinese lived in relative isolation from the rest of the world. They called their homeland *Zhong Guo* (JOONG GWAH), or "the Middle Kingdom." To them it was the center of the whole world and the one truly supreme civilization. The lack of outside contacts allowed the Chinese to develop one culture across many regions and a strong sense of national identity as well. As a result, China has the oldest continuous civilization in the world.

China's Geography

China's varied geography has affected its historical development. Mountains make up about one-third of China's area. The Himalayas close off China to the southwest, and on the western border rise the Kunlun Shan and Tian Shan ranges. To the east of the Tian Shan lie the vast desert wastes of the Gobi. These rugged physical features hindered cultural diffusion both into and out of China for many centuries.

On the east, China's coastline touches the Pacific Ocean. Although some Chinese became devoted seafarers, they mostly focused on developing the agriculture of eastern China's fertile river valleys and plains. Unlike the land to the west with its forbidding terrain, the east welcomed life. For centuries large numbers of Chinese have farmed in the region's North China Plain.

Three major rivers drain eastern China: the Huang He (HWONG HUH); the Chang Jiang (CHAHNG JYAHNG), known also as the Yangtze (YANG•SEE); and the Xi Jiang (SHEE JYAHNG), also called the West River. The Huang He flows more than 2,900 miles (4,640 km) from the northern

SECTION THEME

▶ **Innovation** Early Chinese civilization excels in metal-casting skills.

Find Out

Answer: *a writing system, metal-casting skills, silk weaving, and pottery making*

FOCUS

Section Objective

Examine the major contributions of early Chinese civilization.

BELLRINGER
Motivational Activity

Before taking roll at the beginning of the class period, project Section Focus Transparency 2-4 and have students answer the activity questions. Discuss students' responses.

This activity is also available as a blackline master.

Vocabulary Pre-check

Use Vocabulary Activity 2 to introduce vocabulary terms. **L1 LEP**

* This book uses the pinyin system for writing most Chinese names. Since 1979, pinyin spellings have been used in many reference works and books in China.

SECTION RESOURCES

Reproducible Masters
- Reproducible Lesson Plan 2-4
- Guided Reading Activity 2-4
- Reteaching Activity 2
- Enrichment Activity 2
- Section Quiz 2-4
- Performance Assessment Activity 2
- Spanish Chapter Summary 2

Transparencies
- Section Focus Transparency 2-4
- Mapping History Overlay Transparency 3
- World History and Art Transparency 3
- Ancient China

Multimedia
- Student Self-Test and Review Software
- Testmaker
- India and China

TEACH

Guided Practice

THEME Innovation

Have students explain in class the distinctive features of early Chinese writing and metal casting. *(writing: characters represented objects, ideas, or sounds; large number of written characters limited the number of people who could read and write; metal casting: Chinese produced some of finest objects ever made from bronze.)* **L1**

Independent Practice

Guided Reading Activity 2-4 **L1**

Visualizing History Oracle-bone inscriptions were usually made on the shoulder blades of animals, mainly oxen, or else on turtle shells. The questions that were asked the priest concerned sacrifices, weather, war, hunting, travel, or luck. The form of the question had to yield a yes or no answer.

Answer to Caption: *to have a record of the king's question and the answer*

NATIONAL GEOGRAPHIC SOCIETY

Use these materials to enrich student understanding of early China.

NGS PICTURESHOW CD-ROM
India and China

NGS PICTUREPACK TRANSPARENCY SET
Ancient China

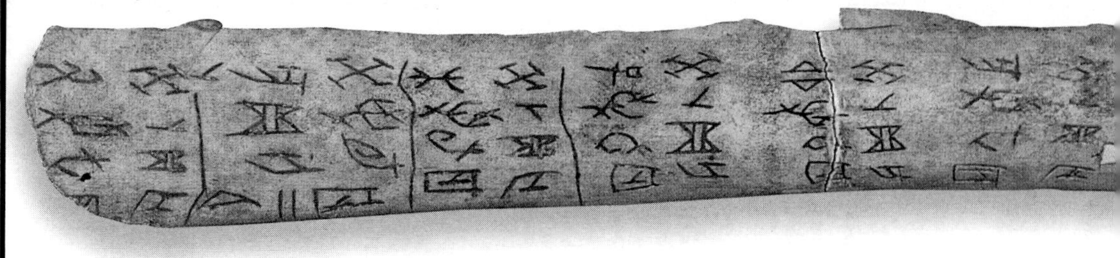

Visualizing History **Oracle bones used to obtain advice about military campaigns were often inscribed with the question and answer and preserved as part of the king's records.** *Why were such oracle bones stored by the rulers?*

highlands eastward to the Yellow Sea. On its way it cuts through thick layers of loess (LEHS), a rich yellow soil. The river carries away large amounts of loess, which it deposits farther downstream. The abundance of yellow soil in the Huang's waters gives it its name—Yellow River. The Chinese sometimes call the Huang He "the Great Sorrow" because of the tragedy brought by its floods. However, the silt deposits brought by the flooding river have made the North China Plain a rich agricultural area.

A favorable climate also contributes to successful farming on the North China Plain. Melting snow from the mountains and the monsoon rains between July and October feed the Huang He. Farmers of the region have long depended on the seasonal rhythm of temperature and rainfall.

The Shang Dynasty

Very little is known about the origins of Chinese civilization. In the A.D. 1920s, archaeologists in the Huang He valley uncovered traces of Neolithic life in China. The magnificent painted pots of the Yang-shao (YAHNG•SHOW) culture found by the archaeologists date back to 3000–1500 B.C. Archaeologists have discovered that the Lung-shan culture, from about 2500–2000 B.C., used a potter's wheel to make delicate pots and goblets. These and other Neolithic finds dated to earlier than 5000 B.C. make it clear that the **Huang He valley**, like the river valleys of Egypt, the Fertile Crescent, and South Asia, invited settlement from very early times.

Chinese Myths

Over the centuries the Chinese developed many myths to explain their remote past. One myth tells how the universe was created from the body of a giant named Pan Gu (PAHN GOO), who hatched from an egg. Other legends celebrate the deeds of hero-kings. These larger-than-life rulers included Yao (YOW), a person in the form of a mountain, and Shun, the master of elephants. Another, **Yu the Great**, was a miraculous engineer. According to a myth about Yu:

> "When widespread waters swelled to Heaven and serpents and dragons did harm, Yao sent Yu to control the waters and to drive out the serpents and dragons. The waters were controlled and flowed to the east. The serpents and dragons plunged to their places."

The myth about Yu—written much later than the first oral tellings—may reflect stories about the attempts of one or many early rulers to channel the floodwaters of the Huang He.

According to tradition, Yu the Great founded China's first dynasty, named Xia (SYAH), around 2000 B.C. Archaeologists, however, have yet to find evidence of the legendary Xia. The first dynasty to be dated from written records in China is the Shang (SHAHNG). The Shang ruled China from about 1700 B.C. to 1000 B.C.

Early Religion

Though the Shang kings were political leaders, they also performed religious duties. As high priests, they could communicate with nature deities on behalf of the people. They prayed, made offerings, and performed sacrifices to gain a good harvest, a change in the weather, or victory in battle. Kings also had special powers for calling upon their ancestors. To do so, they had a priest scratch a question on an animal bone or sometimes on a

COOPERATIVE LEARNING ACTIVITY

Bulletin Board Have students prepare a bulletin board depicting the early history of China. Have the class discuss what should be included in the display. Possibilities are maps showing areas of China ruled by early dynasties, maps showing what crops were grown, drawings of artifacts, and illustrations of the layout of an excavated city or cities. After the topics have been determined, assign small groups to research and prepare each one. Group members should assume responsibility for a specific task in connection with their part of the display. When the parts are completed, have the class design the bulletin board display and assemble it. **L2**

tortoise shell. The priest then applied intense heat to the bone. The bone would crack, and the priest would interpret the splintered pattern of cracks as the answer to the king's question. The bones helped the kings to predict the future. The scratchings on the oracle bones, as they are called, are the first known examples of writing in China.

Important Achievements

The priests writing on the oracle bones used a script with many characters. These characters represented objects, ideas, or sounds and were written in vertical columns. To use the script with ease, a writer had to memorize each character. Because only a small percentage of the population could master all the characters, few people in ancient China could read and write.

Not only did the Chinese of the Shang period develop a written script, but they also perfected their metal-casting skills and produced some of the finest bronze objects ever made. These included bronze daggers, figurines, and ritual urns. They built massive ceremonial cauldrons that stood on legs. Bronze fittings adorned hunting chariots, and warriors carried bronze daggers. Artisans also carved beautiful ivory and jade statues. They wove silk into elegantly colored cloth for the upper class and fashioned pottery from kaolin, a fine white clay.

The Chinese built their first cities under the Shang. Archaeologists today have identified seven capital cities, including the city of **Anyang** (AHN•YAHNG). Their excavations reveal the general layout of Anyang. A palace and temple stood at the center of the city, as in the cities of other early civilizations, and public buildings and homes of government officials circled the royal sanctuary. Beyond the city's center stood various workshops and other homes.

Expansion and Decline

Shang kings at first ruled over a small area in northern China. Later, their armies, equipped with bronze weapons and chariots, conquered more distant territories and finally took over most of the Huang He valley.

The Shang dynasty lacked strong leaders, however, and in time grew weak. Around 1000 B.C., Wu, a ruler of a former Shang territory in the northwest, marshaled his forces and marched on the capital. Wu killed the Shang king and established a new dynasty. Wu's dynasty, known as the Zhou (JOH), ruled China for 800 years.

Many Centuries of Dynasties

From the beginning of its recorded history until the early 1900s, dynasties ruled China. When writing about China's past, Western historians have followed the Chinese practice of dividing Chinese history into periods based on the reigns of these ruling families.

The Chinese believed that their rulers governed according to a principle known as the Mandate of Heaven. If rulers were just and effective, they received a **mandate**, or authority to rule, from heaven. If rulers did not govern properly—as indicated by poor crops or losses in battle—they lost the mandate to someone else who then started a new dynasty. The principle first appeared during the Zhou dynasty. Indeed the Zhou, as did later rebels, probably found the Mandate of Heaven a convenient way to explain their overthrow of an unpopular dynasty.

SECTION 4 REVIEW

Recall

1. **Define** mandate.
2. **Identify** Yu the Great, Xia dynasty, Shang dynasty, Mandate of Heaven.
3. **Use** the map on page 67 to list the major physical features of China. Explain how these physical features affected the development of Chinese civilization.

Critical Thinking

4. **Making Comparisons** Compare the Mandate of Heaven with the way Egyptian kings justified their rule.

Understanding Themes

5. **Innovation** Explain the basic features of the Chinese writing system as it developed in early times. How widespread was the use of this method of writing in China under the early dynasties?

Chapter 2
Section 4

ASSESS

Check for Understanding

Assign Section 4 Review as homework or as an in-class activity.

Use Student Self-Test and Review Software to review Section 4.

Evaluate

Section Quiz 2-4

Use the Testmaker to create a customized quiz for Section 4.

Reteach

Have students survey the chapter and make a list of questions to test their knowledge. Have students quiz partners.

Enrich

Have students find out more about the Huang He and report their findings orally in class.

Enrichment Activity 2

CLOSE

Write on the chalkboard this statement from page 69: *China has the oldest continuous civilization in the world*. Have students explain what this statement means. Ask students to consider how isolation has affected China. *(Possible answer: It has built a strong national identity.)*

SECTION 4 REVIEW ANSWERS

1. All vocabulary words are defined in the Glossary.
2. Yu the Great, 70; Xia dynasty, 70; Shang dynasty, 70; Mandate of Heaven, 71
3. Himalayas, Plateau of Tibet, Kunlun Shan, Tian Shan, Gobi, Huang He, Chang Jiang, and Xi Jiang; isolated the Chinese and encouraged development of a common culture and strong national identity; deposits of loess created fertile land capable of supporting a large population
4. Chinese rulers claimed their right to rule was given by the gods; Egyptian pharaohs claimed to be gods or descended from gods. Chinese rulers used the Mandate of Heaven to justify overthrowing an unjust ruler. Egyptian pharaohs expected to be worshiped as gods.
5. **INNOVATION** consisted of many characters representing objects, ideas, or sounds; written in vertical columns. Very few people in ancient China could read or write.

Bridge to the Past
Literature

Block Schedule

Team Teaching This excerpt from *Gilgamesh* may be presented in a team-teaching context, in conjunction with English or Language Arts.

Gilgamesh

Historical Connection

The story of Gilgamesh shows the variety of deities worshiped by the Sumerians and the humanlike emotions of these deities.

Background Information

Setting Storytellers set the Gilgamesh tales in the distant past. By the time the stories were written, they probably were different from the original versions.

Characters Gilgamesh: Sumerian hero based on a king of the city-state of Uruk who lived in about 2700 B.C. He was considered part human and part god. Utnapishtim: an elderly man chosen by the gods to survive the great flood sent to the city of Shurrupak.

Plot Utnapishtim tells Gilgamesh how the gods directed him to build a boat on which he and selected animals survived a great flood. After finishing the tale of horrible destruction, Utnapishtim considers how he might help Gilgamesh search for eternal life.

Literary Element The story of Gilgamesh is an epic, a long poem telling about a legendary figure. The *Iliad*, the *Odyssey*, and the *Song of Roland* are among the most famous epics in European

Bridge to the Past
Literature

from

Gilgamesh

retold by Herbert Mason

Like people today, ancient Sumerians loved adventure tales featuring extraordinary heroes battling the forces of evil. Many Sumerian myths featured a king, Gilgamesh, who lived around 2700 B.C. The earliest known written accounts of Gilgamesh's adventures date from about 1850 B.C., making them the oldest surviving examples of epic poetry. An epic is a long poem recalling the exploits of a legendary hero. Gilgamesh, after the death of his friend Enkidu, searched for the secret of eternal life, which he hoped to share with his departed friend. In the following excerpt, Gilgamesh, hoping to learn how to escape death, listens to a mysterious elderly man, Utnapishtim, recount how he survived a great flood.

There was a city called Shurrupak
On the bank of the Euphrates.
It was very old, and so many were the gods
Within it. They converged in their complex
hearts
On the idea of creating a great flood.
There was Anu, their aging and weak-minded
father,
The military Enlil, his adviser,
Ishtar, the sensation-craving one,
And all the rest. Ea, who was present
At their council, came to my house
And, frightened by the violent winds that filled
the air,
Echoed all that they were planning and had said.
Man of Shurrupak, he said, tear down your
house
And build a ship. Abandon your possessions
And the works that you find beautiful and crave,
And save your life instead. Into the ship
Bring the seed of all living creatures.

I was overawed, perplexed,
And finally downcast. I agreed to do
As Ea said, but I protested: What shall I say
To the city, the people, the leaders?

About the Author

It is not known who first told the story of Gilgamesh. In ancient civilizations, stories were passed orally from generation to generation. With the development of writing in Mesopotamia, people began to record stories. The earliest tablets inscribed with the tales of Gilgamesh date from 1850 B.C., but the most complete set of stories was found in a library that belonged to an Assyrian monarch, Ashurbanipal, who ruled Nineveh from about 669 to 630 B.C.

Tell them, Ea said, you have learned that Enlil
The war god despises you and will not
Give you access to the city anymore.
Tell them for this Ea will bring the rains.

This is the way gods think, he laughed. His tone
Of savage irony frightened Gilgamesh
Yet gave him pleasure, being his friend.
They only know how to compete or echo.
But who am I to talk? He sighed as if
Disgusted with himself; I did as he
Commanded me to do. I spoke to them,
And some came out to help me build the ship
Of seven stories, each with nine chambers.
The boat was cube in shape, and sound; it held
The food and wine and precious minerals
And seed of living animals we put
In it. My family then moved inside,
And all who wanted to be with us there:
The game of the field, the goats of the steppe,
The craftsmen of the city came, a navigator
Came. And then Ea ordered me to close
The door. The time of the great rains had come.
O there was ample warning, yes, my friend,
But it was terrifying still. Buildings
Blown by the winds for miles like desert brush.
People clung to branches of trees until
Roots gave way. New possessions, now debris,
Floated on the water with their special
Sterile vacancy. The riverbanks failed
To hold the water back. Even the gods
Cowered like dogs at what they had done.
Ishtar cried out like a woman at the height
Of labor: O how could I have wanted
To do this to my people! They were *hers*,
Notice. Even her sorrow was possessive.
Her spawn that she had killed too soon.
Old gods are terrible to look at when
They weep, all bloated like spoiled fish.
One wonders if they ever understand

Other Works about Gilgamesh

Gardner, John, and John Maier, trans. ***Gilgamesh.*** New York: Knopf, 1984.
Konacs, Maureen Gallery, trans. ***The Epic of Gilgamesh.*** Stanford: Stanford University Press, 1989.
Silverberg, Robert. ***Gilgamesh the King.*** New York: Arbor House, 1984.
Picard, Barbara Leonie. ***Three Ancient Kings: Gilgamesh, Hrolf Kraki, Conary.*** New York: Warne, 1972.
Westwood, Jennifer. ***Gilgamesh and Other Babylonian Tales.*** New York: Coward-McCann, 1970.

Bridge to the Past
Literature

literature. Some modern movies, such as *Star Wars*, could be considered epics as well.

FOCUS

Ask students to consider the type of deities worshipped by the Sumerians. Tell students that the story of the flood suggests that gods and goddesses had human emotions. Point out that the story gives little explanation for why the floods came, other than "Enlil/The war god despised you."

TEACH

Comparison

Students may be familiar with the story of the great flood in the Bible: Noah built an ark and filled it with animals. Encourage students to compare the Sumerian and Hebrew accounts. *(Students may note, for example, that the line "O the dove, the swallow, and the raven/Found their land" seems to parallel the Bible's mention of the raven and dove.)*

Interpretation

Ask students how they interpret "Abandon your possessions/And the works that you find beautiful and crave,/And save your life instead." *(Some students may see this passage as evidence that the gods were angered by the materialism of Sumerian society. Others may argue that it shows that the gods cared little for human achievements.)*

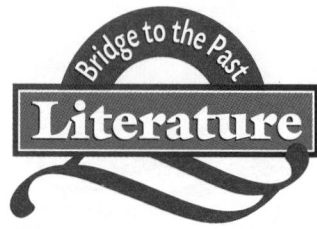

Bridge to the Past

Literature

Clarification

Refer students to "Bodies lay like alewives … , dead/And in the clay." Explain to students that alewives live in the Atlantic Ocean off the coast of North America and in the Great Lakes. Although alewives are not actually found in Mesopotamia, they are similar to small fish that are found there.

Evaluation

Ask students to evaluate Utnapishtim's questions about the flood: "Why? Why did they/Have to die? I couldn't understand. I asked/ Unanswerable questions a child asks/When a parent dies—for nothing." Point out that the gods chose to save someone who would ask questions rather than someone who was unconcerned.

World Literature Selection 1

Visualizing History The most complete version of the Gilgamesh tales, found in the library of the Assyrian king Ashurbanipal, consists of 12 tablets, totaling some 3,000 lines. Each tablet describes one adventure of the hero.

Answer to Caption: *He says that they shall be like gods.*

ASSESS

Assign **Responding to Literature** questions.

That they have caused their grief. When the
    seventh day
Came, the flood subsided from its slaughter
Like hair drawn slowly back
From a tormented face.
I looked at the earth and all was silence.
Bodies lay like alewives [a type of fish], dead
And in the clay. I fell down
On the ship's deck and wept. Why? Why did they
Have to die? I couldn't understand. I asked
Unanswerable questions a child asks
When a parent dies—for nothing. Only slowly
Did I make myself believe—or hope—they
Might all be swept up in their fragments
Together
And made whole again
By some compassionate hand.
But my hand was too small
To do the gathering.
I have only known this feeling since
When I look out across the sea of death,
This pull inside against a littleness—myself—
Waiting for an upward gesture.

O the dove, the swallow and the raven
Found their land. The people left the ship.
But I for a long time could only stay inside.
I could not face the deaths I knew were there.
Then I received Enlil, for Ea had *chosen* me;
The war god touched my forehead; he blessed
My family and said:
Before this you were just a man, but now
You and your wife shall be like gods. You
Shall live in the distance at the rivers' mouth,
At the source. I allowed myself to be
Taken far away from all that I had seen.
Sometimes even in love we yearn to leave mankind.
Only the loneliness of the Only One
Who never acts like gods
Is bearable.

Visualizing History **Gilgamesh subdues a lion. By the 700s B.C. Gilgamesh had become a mythological hero. The real Gilgamesh ruled over ancient Uruk.** *What blessing did the war god give Gilgamesh and his family?*

Additional Literary Works of the Period

The Torah. The first five books of the Bible cover the history of the Jews until about 1200 B.C. The written texts of the Torah were collected and organized in the 400s B.C.

I am downcast because of what I've seen,
Not what I still have hope to yearn for.
Lost youths restored to life,
Lost children to their crying mothers,
Lost wives, lost friends, lost hopes, lost homes,
I want to bring these back to them.
But now there is you.
We must find something for you.
How will you find eternal life
To bring back to your friend?
He pondered busily, as if
It were just a matter of getting down to work
Or making plans for an excursion.
Then he relaxed, as if there were no use
In this reflection. I would grieve
At all that may befall you still,
If I did not know you must return
And bury your own loss and build
Your world anew with your own hands.
I envy you your freedom.

As he listened, Gilgamesh felt tiredness again
Come over him, the words now so discouraging,
The promise so remote, so unlike what he sought.
He looked into the old man's face, and it seemed changed,
As if this one had fought within himself a battle
He would never know, that still went on.

RESPONDING TO LITERATURE

1. How did Utnapishtim of Shurrupak survive the great flood?
2. How were the reactions of the gods and of Utnapishtim similar?
3. What questions would you ask Utnapishtim if you could meet him?
4. **Applying Information** What aspects of this tale about the great flood in Mesopotamia might apply to other cultures in other places and at other times?

Bridge to the Past
Literature

CLOSE

Discuss what the tale about Gilgamesh and the flood might mean for people today. For example, ask students to consider how people today react to disasters such as floods, earthquakes, or explosions. Also ask students how people today try to escape death. *(exercise, diet)*

Contemporary Connection

For hundreds of years before it was written down, the *Gilgamesh* epic was passed from generation to generation. Ask students what makes a good story and a good storyteller. **What modern equivalents are there to heroic epics such as *Gilgamesh*?** *(Students may name books or movies that deal with a big, important topic; a long time span; or characters that behave heroically.)*

Portfolio Project

Have students research the archaeological investigations that have attempted to determine whether the great flood mentioned in *Gilgamesh* and the Bible actually occurred. Then have students write an essay on their position. Instruct students to support their position with evidence from their research. This activity may be an appropriate method of authentic assessment.

ANSWERS TO RESPONDING TO LITERATURE

1. At the command of the god Ea, Utnapishtim tore down his house and built a ship.
2. Both the gods and Utnapishtim were horrified by the death and destruction the flood caused and wondered why it had happened.
3. Students might want to ask Utnapishtim why he thought he was selected to survive the flood, whether he tried to discourage the gods from causing the flood, and what he thought of Gilgamesh.
4. A terrible disaster happening for no apparent reason and the struggle for survival of one individual are themes that could apply to other cultures in other eras.

Chapter 2 Review

GLENCOE TECHNOLOGY

VIDEODISC

Use MindJogger to review students' knowledge of the chapter.

MindJogger Videoquiz

Chapter 2
Disc 1 Side A

Also available in VHS.

Historical Significance

The world's first civilizations developed along the banks of river valleys—the Nile, Tigris-Euphrates, Indus, and Huang. They faced similar challenges in explaining the mysteries of nature, using their resources, and providing for defense. They all sought answers through cooperation, government, technology, and religion. They built cities, created dynasties, developed writing systems, and devised laws. Their political ideas, social institutions, and cultural achievements were inherited by later peoples and became the foundation of the civilization we know today.

Using Key Terms

Write the key term that completes each sentence.

a. bureaucracy	g. mandate
b. city-state	h. monarchy
c. cuneiform	i. monsoon
d. dynasty	j. pharaoh
e. empire	k. polytheism
f. hieroglyphics	l. theocracy

1. Each ancient ____ was directed by a hereditary ruler known as a king or queen.
2. In ancient China, the first historical ______, or line of rulers from one family, was called the Shang.
3. The ancient Egyptians carved onto pieces of slate a variety of picture symbols, or _____, that stood for objects, ideas, and sounds.
4. The Sumerian form of writing, _________, consisted of hundreds of wedge-shaped markings made by pressing the end of a sharpened reed on wet clay tablets.
5. The southwest ________ brings plenty of seasonal rain to India and other countries of the South Asian subcontinent.
6. The title _______, meaning "great house of the king," was used by Egyptian monarchs.
7. Historians consider ancient Egyptian government a _______ because the Egyptian ruler was both god and king.
8. A typical Sumerian ____ included the city itself and surrounding land.
9. Egyptian religion was based on ____, or the worship of many gods and goddesses, except during the brief, controversial reign of Akhenaton.
10. Sargon I united all of the Mesopotamian city-states in a single ____, which consisted of many different territories under one ruler.

Using Your History Journal

Choose one event from this chapter. Describe the event in picture-writing (cuneiform). Exchange your description with other students and try to guess what each person's event is.

Reviewing Facts

1. **Explain** how the early Mesopotamians controlled the Tigris and Euphrates Rivers.
2. **Describe** how the southwest monsoon affects life on the South Asian subcontinent.
3. **Identify** the archaeological discovery that indicates that there was contact between the Mesopotamian and Harappan cultures.
4. **List** the achievements of the ancient Chinese that exemplify their artistic innovation.
5. **Describe** how the Himalayas affected two early river valley civilizations.
6. **Identify** the first ruler who conquered Lower Egypt and set up the first government in that country.
7. **Name** the capital of Upper Egypt that was established in 2050 B.C.
8. **Explain** why Amenhotep changed his royal name to Akhenaton.
9. **Describe** the main powers and responsibilities of a typical king of a Sumerian city-state around 2700 B.C.
10. **List** four examples of the kinds of laws that Hammurabi's code addressed in attempting to provide people with a systematic and easily understood set of laws.

Answers

Using Key Terms

1. h	6. j
2. d	7. l
3. f	8. b
4. c	9. k
5. i	10. e

Using Your History Journal

Mention to students that their picture-writing will be personal and may therefore be harder for others to translate than the more standardized cuneiform would have been for the Sumerians.

Reviewing Facts

1. built dams and escape channels to prevent floods; constructed canals and ditches for irrigation
2. Rivers swell, widen across plains, and rush to the sea, causing floods; crops get nourished from the rain but can also be destroyed if monsoons are too heavy; sometimes people and animals drown.
3. Harappan soapstone seals
4. bronze works such as figurines and urns, which are considered some of the finest ever made; ivory and jade statues; pottery; silk cloth
5. protected Harappan and ancient Chinese civilizations
6. Narmer
7. Thebes
8. Amenhotep declared that Egyptians should worship only one god, Aton. To show he was equal to Aton, he changed his name to Akhenaton, which means "spirit of Aton."
9. A Sumerian king served as both military leader and high priest. The king and his priests supervised farming, enforced the law, and set penalties for offenders.
10. Answers may include: laws governing the building of houses, the property of married women, protection of women against beating by their husbands, adoption and inheritance, interest rates on loans, and damage to fields by cattle.

CHAPTER 2 REVIEW

Critical Thinking

1. **Apply** What clues do artifacts found in the ruins at Harappa and Mohenjo-Daro provide about the Harappan religion?
2. **Compare** How did the powers of the Egyptian kings differ from those of the Shang kings? How were their powers the same?
3. **Synthesize** What reaction would you have had to Akhenaton's reforms if you had been a priest of Amon-Ra?
4. **Evaluate** What do you think might have happened if the Sumerians had never invented cuneiform?

Geography in History

1. **Location** Refer to the map below. What is the relative location of the Sinai Peninsula? Find this peninsula on the Middle East map in the Atlas. What is its absolute location?
2. **Place** Why was most agricultural production in ancient Egypt and in that nation today found along the Nile River?
3. **Movement** Why would travel in ancient Egypt have been easier for a person who was going from south to north than for a person going from east to west? What might make travel from east to west less difficult today?

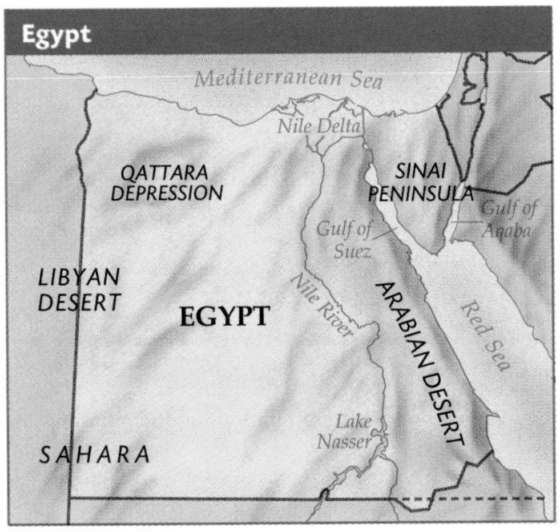

Skill Practice

Read about life in Harappan civilization in the Indus River valley on pages 67 and 68 in Section 3. Use this information to complete the following chart.

Harappan Life

Occupations	Artifacts	Theories of Decline

Understanding Themes

1. **Relation to Environment** What flood-control methods of the ancient Egyptians and other river valley peoples are still in use today?
2. **Cooperation** In what areas of city life today is cooperation as important as it was when the Sumerians built the earliest cities?
3. **Cultural Diffusion** What advances in the twentieth century have made cultural diffusion easier and faster than in ancient times?
4. **Innovation** Why would you consider each of the following developments in ancient China an innovation: a writing script with many characters, bronze vessels and tools, pottery, and silk cloth?

Linking Past and Present

1. Hatshepsut was only one of the women who held prominent positions in ancient Egypt. What women have held high government positions in modern times?
2. Physical features isolated the Chinese from the rest of the world for centuries. What moves have the Chinese made recently to make greater contact with other cultures? To what extent have they maintained their traditional isolation?

Chapter 2 Review

Skill Practice

occupations: farmer, trader, metalworker, pottery maker, weaver, jeweler, merchant, engineer, builder; artifacts: soapstone seals, jewelry, animal and humanlike figurines; theories of decline: climate changes, destruction caused by invading peoples

Understanding Themes

1. **RELATION TO ENVIRONMENT** dams, canals, reservoirs
2. **COOPERATION** Answers may include building and maintaining public buildings and areas, fighting societal problems such as crime, poverty and drugs.
3. **CULTURAL DIFFUSION** Answers may include telecommunications devices, computers, jet travel.
4. **INNOVATION** a writing script with many characters: some represented sounds, unlike cuneiform; bronze vessels and tools: metal-casting skills were superior to those of other civilizations; pottery: artisans used a fine white clay called kaolin; silk cloth: earliest use of silk

Linking Past and Present

1. Margaret Thatcher, Indira Gandhi, Golda Meir, Corazon Aquino, Benazir Bhutto
2. China now allows foreign firms to do business there, and Chinese citizens may study abroad. Curbs on freedom of movement remain for both citizens and foreigners within China.

Critical Thinking

1. Harappan deities were associated with natural forces.
2. Egyptian kings were regarded as gods, while Shang kings were not. Both were political and religious leaders, and both performed ritual acts in order to benefit their people.
3. Priests resented the loss of their power.
4. Answers should discuss effect of communication and writing ability on Sumerian society.

Geography in History

1. northeastern Egypt; 28°–31° N, 32°–35° E
2. The Nile River valley is fertile, while the rest of Egypt is desert.
3. south to north: could travel by boat or by land in Nile River valley; east to west: would have to cross vast desert; easier today because of modern roads and air travel

Chapter Bonus Test Question

Ask students: What factors can lead to the decline or fall of a civilization or dynasty? *(weak rulers, foreign invasion, natural disasters, climate changes)*

Kingdoms and Empires in the Middle East

CHAPTER RESOURCES

	Reproducible Resources	Multimedia Resources
Chapter Opener	Chapter Themes: Graphic Organizer 3 Historical Significance Chapter Activity 3	MindJogger Videoquiz
Chapter Enrichment	Vocabulary Activity 3* Time Line Activity 3 Mapping History Activity 3 History Simulation 3 Geography and History Activity 3 Source Reading 3 People in World History Profiles 3, 4 World Art and Music Activity 3 Enrichment Activity 3 Critical Thinking Activity 3 Skill Reinforcement Activity 3 Writer's Guidebook, Lesson 10 Performance Assessment Activity 3	Ancient Civilizations Poster Set: *The Fertile Crescent* Chapter Transparency 3 NGS PicturePack Transparency Set: *Fertile Crescent* Vocabulary PuzzleMaker Software NGS PictureShow CD-ROM: *Egypt and the Fertile Crescent*
Chapter Review/Reteaching	Reteaching Activity 3 Skill Reinforcement Activity 3 Spanish Chapter Summary 3	Chapter 3 Digest Audiocassette, Activity, Test* Vocabulary PuzzleMaker Software Student Self-Test and Review Software MindJogger Videoquiz
Chapter Evaluation/Testing	Performance Assessment Activity 3 Chapter 3 Test, Forms A and B	Testmaker

* *Also available in Spanish*

0:00 **OUT OF TIME?** Assign the Chapter 3 summary in the Unit 1 Digest on pages 96-99, and the Chapter 3 Audiocassettes.

Block Schedule

Block scheduling differs from traditional class scheduling in the amount of time allotted to each period. The extended time frame provided by block scheduling affords you the opportunity to implement a greater number of research-oriented and activity-intense projects to motivate and involve your students. Activities that are particularly suited to use within the block scheduling framework are identified throughout this chapter by the following designation.

KEY TO ABILITY LEVELS

Teaching strategies have been coded for varying learning styles and abilities.

- **L1** **BASIC** activities for all students
- **L2** **AVERAGE** activities for average to above-average students
- **L3** **CHALLENGING** activities for above-average students
- **LEP** **LIMITED ENGLISH PROFICIENCY** activities

A complete, 1-page lesson plan is provided for each section in the *Reproducible Lesson Plans* booklet.

SECTION RESOURCES

Daily Objectives	Reproducible Resources	Multimedia Resources
Section 1 Trading Peoples Explain how trading peoples influenced the development of the Middle East.	Reproducible Lesson Plan 3-1 Vocabulary Activity 3* Guided Reading Activity 3-1* Time Line Activity 3 Source Reading 3 Section Quiz 3-1*	Section Focus Transparency 3-1 NGS PicturePack Transparency Set: *Fertile Crescent* Student Self-Test and Review Software Testmaker NGS PictureShow CD-ROM: *Egypt and the Fertile Crescent*
Section 2 Early Israelites Describe the role that slavery, exile, and return play in the history of the Israelites.	Reproducible Lesson Plan 3-2 Guided Reading Activity 3-2* Geography and History Activity 3 History Simulation 3 Mapping History Activity 3 Section Quiz 3-2*	Section Focus Transparency 3-2 NGS PicturePack Transparency Set: *Fertile Crescent* Vocabulary PuzzleMaker Software Student Self-Test and Review Software Testmaker NGS PictureShow CD-ROM: *Egypt and the Fertile Crescent*
Section 3 Empire Builders Explain how a series of powerful empires extended their rule throughout the Middle East.	Reproducible Lesson Plan 3-3 Guided Reading Activity 3-3* Reteaching Activity 3 Enrichment Activity 3 Section Quiz 3-3* Performance Assessment Activity 3 Spanish Chapter Summary 3	Ancient Civilizations Poster Set: *Fertile Crescent* Section Focus Transparency 3-3 NGS PicturePack Transparency Set: *Fertile Crescent* Student Self-Test and Review Software Testmaker NGS PictureShow CD-ROM: *Egypt and the Fertile Crescent*

* *Also available in Spanish*

Chapter Activities

Performance Assessment Activity

Creating a Children's Book Have students take the roles of authors for a then-and-now children's book illustrating the concepts of trade, migration, cultural diffusion, and empires. Each set of facing pages should have an ancient example on the left accompanied by a modern-day example on the right. Illustrations and short explanatory paragraphs appropriate to an audience of young children should be included. Books may be sent to an elementary school.

Possible Rubric Features
Concept attainment, accuracy and extent of content information used, appropriateness to audience, visual appeal of product, clarity of text, relevance of modern-day examples.
• *For an additional activity, refer to Activity 3 in the* Performance Assessment Strategies and Activities *booklet.*

Activity

From the Classroom of...

Terry Pollack
Shaker Heights High School
Shaker Heights, OH

Time Capsule
Make a "time capsule" by bringing in a wide-mouth bottle or a can and filling it with the following items, then covering all with sand:

1. a chart comparing several letters of the Hebrew, Greek, and German alphabets;
2. a map of early Israel and a map of modern Israel;
3. a copy of the Ten Commandments

Have students uncover the items one at a time and perform the following tasks:

1. Research the remaining letters in the alphabet and trace how many of them began their journey through the western world in ancient Israel.
2. Locate the cities of Jerusalem, Tyre, Sidon, and Petra on the maps of both modern and ancient Israel. Figure approximately how long these cities have been continuously occupied.
3. Discuss which commandments have been codified into contemporary law.

When students have completed the activities, discuss the many benefits the ancient Hebrews bestowed on the world.

MULTIPLE LEARNING STYLES

Verbal/Linguistic
Have students find copies of the Greek alphabet and the Hebrew alphabet. (Most dictionaries include these.) Ask students to make a chart displaying both alphabets, including both the symbol for each letter and the name of each letter. Discuss the similarities and differences between letters in these two alphabets and our own Roman alphabet.

Kinesthetic
Have students make a diorama portraying an event described in the chapter.

Interpersonal
Have students debate opposing sides of the following statement: The destruction of the Temple benefited the Jews.

Intrapersonal
Have students imagine that they are members of a people conquered by one of the kings described in the chapter. Ask them to write a short essay describing their experiences and emotions.

Additional Resources

TEACHER'S CORNER

NATIONAL GEOGRAPHIC SOCIETY

INDEX TO NATIONAL GEOGRAPHIC MAGAZINE

The following articles may be used for research relating to this chapter:

- "Iraq: Crucible of Civilization," by Merle Severy, May 1991.
- "The Phoenicians: Sea Lords of Antiquity," by Samuel W. Mattews, August 1974.

NATIONAL GEOGRAPHIC SOCIETY PRODUCTS AVAILABLE FROM GLENCOE

To order the following products for use with this chapter, contact your local Glencoe sales representative or call Glencoe at 1-800-368-7344:

NGS PICTURESHOW CD-ROM
- Egypt and the Fertile Crescent

NGS PICTUREPACK TRANSPARENCY SET
- Fertile Crescent

ANCIENT CIVILIZATIONS POSTER SET
- The Fertile Crescent

ADDITIONAL NATIONAL GEOGRAPHIC SOCIETY PRODUCTS

To order the following for use with this chapter, call National Geographic Society at 1-800-368-2728

- *Nations of the World Series,* "Israel." (Video)

BIBLIOGRAPHY

Literature About the Period

Tanakh—The Holy Scriptures. Philadelphia, New York, Jerusalem: The Jewish Publication Society, 1988. The standard Jewish Bible for the English-speaking world.

Readings for the Student

Saggs, H. W. ***Everyday Life in Babylonia and Assyria.*** New York: Dorset Press, 1987. Describes the life and customs of ancient Babylonians and Assyrians.

Readings for the Teacher

Pritchard, James B., ed. ***Ancient Near Eastern Texts Relating to the Old Testament.*** Princeton, NJ: Princeton University Press, 1969. Interesting parallels between Israelite culture and others.

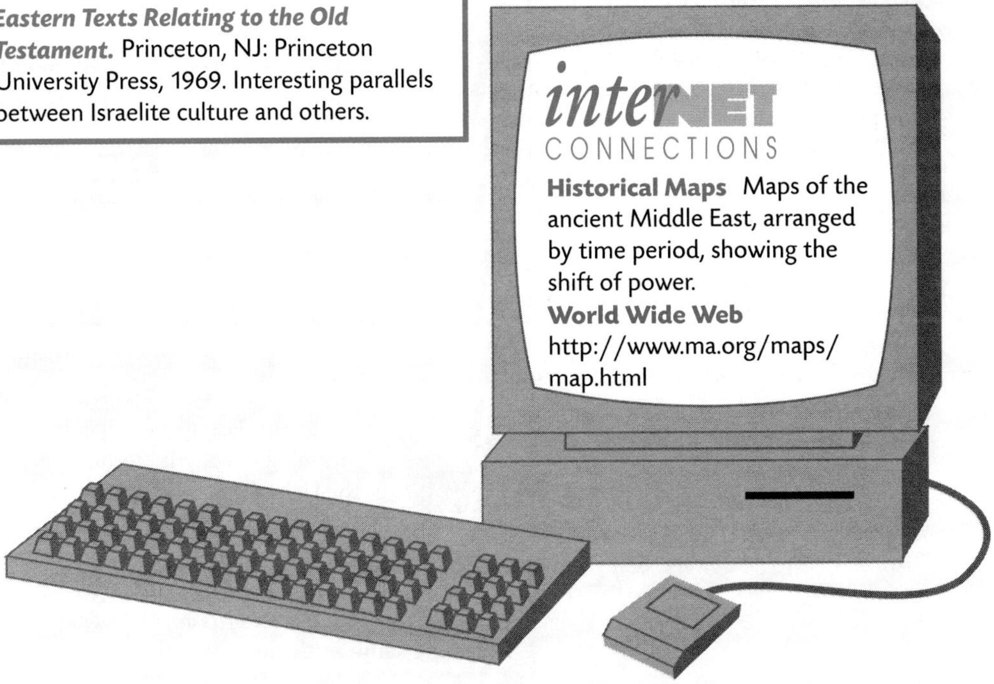
interNET
CONNECTIONS
Historical Maps Maps of the ancient Middle East, arranged by time period, showing the shift of power.
World Wide Web
http://www.ma.org/maps/map.html

Introducing Chapter 3

CHAPTER THEMES

Chapter Themes are listed by section on this chapter opening page of the Student Edition. A corresponding theme-based activity is available under "TEACH," and a theme-based question is asked in the Section and Chapter Reviews.

The Storyteller

Historical Setting Archaeologists began to map the Assyrian city of Nineveh in 1820. During 1845–1851 British archaeologist Henry Layard studied the ruins of Nineveh. Layard brought back to England thousands of cuneiform tablets from the library of the palace of Ashurbanipal. The tablets provide examples of literature, religious thought, and administrative decrees. They also shed light on ancient Middle Eastern concepts of mathematics, botany, and chemistry. Scholars continue to learn about the ancient world by studying these tablets.

Historical Significance

Answers: *Traders spread languages, alphabets, commercial practices, customs, and ideas; religious thinkers introduced the concept of monotheism and ideas of human worth and accountability; empire builders developed methods of warfare, introduced legal systems, and organized complex societies.*
The alphabet, the concept of monotheism, and ethical laws that developed in the ancient Middle East have had lasting effects on civilization.

Chapter 3

2000–400 B.C.

Kingdoms and Empires in the Middle East

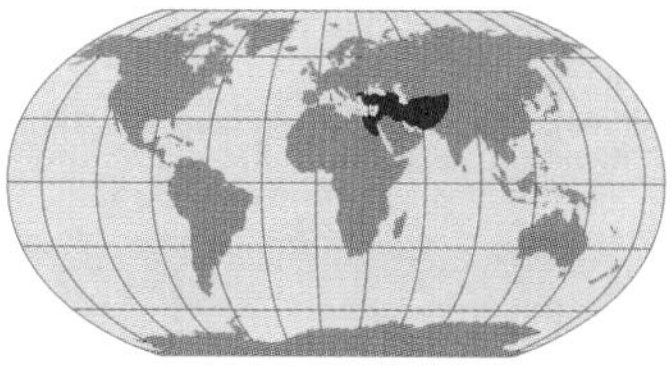

Chapter Themes

- **Cultural Diffusion** Aramaean and Phoenician merchants spread ideas throughout the Middle East. *Section 1*
- **Innovation** The Israelites contribute to the world the concept of monotheism. *Section 2*
- **Conflict** A series of empires—Hittite, then Assyrian, then Chaldean, then Persian—each conquers the previous one. *Section 3*

The Storyteller

Ashurbanipal, the last great Assyrian king, reigned in the mid-600s B.C. The dim rooms were almost still in Ashurbanipal's great palace at Nineveh, the splendid capital of his empire. Men with shoulder-length hair and squared-off beards glided in their tunics and sandals through the vast hallways. But the stone reliefs that decorated the palace walls told a less peaceful story. In intricately carved scenes, the impassive hunter in his chariot lets fly with a volley of arrows into a staggering lion, and the valiant general on the battlefield proudly waves his sword above the defeated enemy legions. Ashurbanipal followed a long line of ruthless Assyrian conquerors who boasted of their military exploits and cruelty.

Historical Significance

How did traders, religious thinkers, and empire builders shape the development of the ancient Middle East? How have their achievements influenced cultural and religious life today?

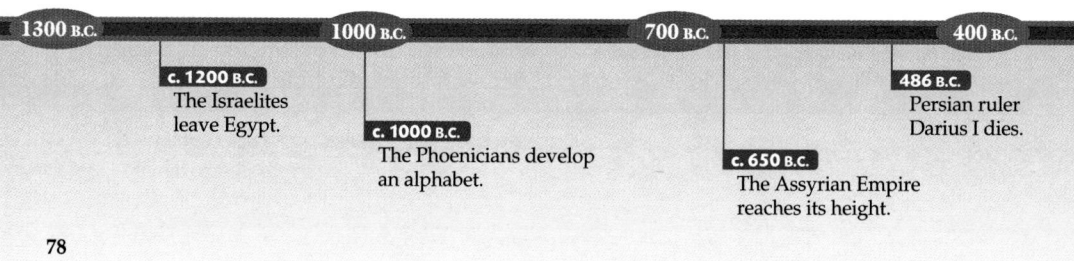

1300 B.C. — 1000 B.C. — 700 B.C. — 400 B.C.

- c. 1200 B.C. The Israelites leave Egypt.
- c. 1000 B.C. The Phoenicians develop an alphabet.
- c. 650 B.C. The Assyrian Empire reaches its height.
- 486 B.C. Persian ruler Darius I dies.

78

GEOGRAPHY CONNECTION

Location Using the Atlas in their texts, students should find the Middle East, including Iraq, Syria, Jordan, Israel, Turkey, Iran, Saudi Arabia, and Egypt, as well as the United States. How do the different countries compare in size with the states of the United States? *(Iraq: larger than California; Syria: slightly larger than North Dakota; Jordan: slightly larger than Indiana; Israel: about the size of New Jersey; Turkey: twice the size of California; Iran: slightly larger than Alaska; Saudi Arabia: one-third the size of the United States; Egypt: about the size of Texas, Oklahoma, and Arkansas combined)* Were boundaries in ancient times the same as those today? *(No.)*

History & Art Ashurbanipal hunting on horseback. Relief from the NW Palace at Nineveh, c. 640 B.C.

Your History Journal

The kingdoms of the Middle East provide rich accounts of the struggle for peace and justice. Read the quotations on pages 86 and 93 and write similar verses about several events in this chapter.

Introducing Chapter 3

History & Art Tell students that the main purpose of the designs on Assyrian reliefs was to glorify the king. Why do you think the Assyrian kings preferred scenes of military conquest or of hunting? *(to frighten their enemies)*

Performance Assessment

Refer to the activity on page 78C of the Planning Guide.

For an additional activity, refer to Activity 3 in the *Performance Assessment Strategies and Activities* booklet.

Using Your History Journal

Suggest to students that their verses focus on the achievements of individual biblical figures or of individual kings.

GLENCOE TECHNOLOGY

VIDEODISC
Use MindJogger to preview chapter content.

MindJogger Videoquiz
Chapter 3
Disc 1 Side A

Also available in VHS.

EXTRA CREDIT PROJECT

Research Report Have students research and report to the class on one or more of the gods worshiped by Assyrians, such as Ashur (chief god), Nabu (god of learning), Ninurta (god of war), and Ishtar (goddess of love). Suggested resources: H.W. Saggs, *Everyday Life in Babylonia and Assyria*.

Chapter 3
Section 1

SECTION THEME

- **Cultural Diffusion** Aramaean and Phoenician merchants spread ideas throughout the Middle East.

Find Out

Answer: *Trading peoples spread their languages, customs, and ideas.*

FOCUS

Section Objective

Explain how trading peoples influenced the development of the Middle East.

BELLRINGER
Motivational Activity

Before taking roll at the beginning of the class period, project Section Focus Transparency 3-1 and have students answer the activity questions. Discuss students' responses.
This activity is also available as a blackline master.

Vocabulary Pre-check

Use Vocabulary Activity 3 to introduce vocabulary terms.
L1 LEP

1200 B.C. — 1000 B.C. — 800 B.C. — 600 B.C.

- **c. 1200 B.C.** Aramaeans settle in central Syria.
- **c. 1100 B.C.** Phoenicians reach Spain and western Africa.
- **c. 600s B.C.** Lydians develop a wealthy kingdom in Asia Minor.

Section 1

Trading Peoples

Setting the Scene

- **Terms to Define**
  confederation, alphabet, colony, barter
- **People to Meet**
  the Aramaeans, the Phoenicians, the Lydians
- **Places to Locate**
  Syria, Damascus, Tyre

Find Out How did trading peoples influence the development of the Middle East?

The Storyteller

King Hiram was pleased. Tyre, his capital city, was a bustling seaport: sophisticated, cosmopolitan, and rich. Not only did the kings of Egypt and Babylon send ambassadors to Hiram's court, they also brought business to his land. Gold, copper, ivory, and linen from Egypt; precious stones from Babylon; silver from Asia Minor; and pottery from Crete enriched Tyre. In return, Tyre exchanged cedar, cut from the nearby mountains, and a vivid purple dye, harvested from murex shells found in the seas near the rocky coast. Hiram's people were Phoenicians, the people of the purple, the color—beautiful, costly, and rare—which throughout the ancient world marked an individual as one of immense wealth and high rank.

—adapted from *The Bible as History*, Werner Keller, translated by William Neil, 1969

Phoenician ship

The magnificent civilizations of Mesopotamia and Egypt greatly influenced neighboring peoples in the Fertile Crescent—among them **the Aramaeans** (AR•uh•MEE•uhnz) and **the Phoenicians** (fih •NEE•shuhnz). In turn, these trading peoples helped to spread their own cultures throughout the region and into much of the ancient world. Traveling on sailing ships and by caravan, traders from the Fertile Crescent brought languages, customs, and ideas along with their trade goods.

The Aramaeans

One of the most active peoples in early Middle Eastern trade, the Aramaeans settled in central **Syria** around 1200 B.C. Although Aramaean kings established a capital at **Damascus**, provincial leaders frequently challenged their authority. Despite political weaknesses, the Aramaeans gained control of the rich overland trade between Egypt and Mesopotamia.

Because Aramaean caravans crossed and recrossed the Fertile Crescent on business, people throughout the region learned Aramaic, the language of the Aramaeans. Until the A.D. 800s, the majority of the people living in the Fertile Crescent spoke Aramaic, a language closely related to Hebrew and Arabic. In addition, some parts of the Bible were written in Aramaic.

The Phoenicians

Between ancient Egypt and Syria lay the land of Canaan, today made up of Lebanon, Israel, and Jordan. The Phoenicians, one of the Semitic groups that migrated from the Arabian Peninsula about 3000 B.C., settled in the northern part of Canaan. Their neighbors in Canaan, the Philistines, came from the eastern Mediterranean. The Greeks would

SECTION RESOURCES

Reproducible Masters
- Reproducible Lesson Plan 3-1
- Vocabulary Activity 3
- Guided Reading Activity 3-1
- Time Line Activity 3
- Source Reading 3
- Section Quiz 3-1

Transparencies
- Section Focus Transparency 3-1
- Fertile Crescent

Multimedia
- Student Self-Test and Review Software
- Testmaker
- Egypt and the Fertile Crescent

NATIONAL GEOGRAPHIC PICTURING HISTORY

Lloyd K. Townsend

Merchants of the Mediterranean

In this illustration sturdy cargo boats dock in their North African home port of Carthage, and war galleys in the harbor lie in wait for any rivals caught in Phoenician waters. A captain argains over the price of a bale of purple cloth for he next voyage as his crew unloads grain from ardinia and cedar logs from North Africa. Above eck sit clay jars of olive oil and wine; below, silver, in, gold, and ivory are stored. Departing vessels ake on terra-cotta figurines, decorated ostrich eggshells, metal utensils, and perfume vials.

From their cities nestled along the coast of the eastern Mediterranean Sea, Phoenicians launched a trading empire. They soon became middlemen for their neighbors in Mesopotamia, Arabia, and Egypt. By 800 B.C., Phoenician trade had spread into the western Mediterranean. From Carthage and other Mediterranean cities, the Phoenicians manned supply depots, guarded sea lanes, and expanded their trading empire. ⊕

PICTURING HISTORY

TEACH

Guided Practice

THEME Cultural Diffusion

Ask students for a definition of the word *diffusion. (spreading or scattering widely)* Then ask if they know of other kinds of diffusion. *(scattering of light, spreading of different weather properties by air)* **L1**

Independent Practice

Guided Reading Activity 3-1 **L1**

Picturing History

Ask students what is distinctive about the construction of the ships in the picture. *(The ships are much higher at the front and back; there is one large sail.)* As early as 1000 B.C. stemposts and sternposts were carved and painted as a way of identifying ships. Mediterranean peoples often placed a figurehead on the bow of their vessels. On Phoenician ships, the figurehead frequently was a carving of their principal god. The Carthaginians often featured a carving of their god Amon. The Phoenicians marked their trading route with lighthouses, which were illuminated by wood fires or torches.

NATIONAL GEOGRAPHIC SOCIETY

Use these materials to enrich student understanding of Phoenician culture.

NGS PICTURESHOW CD-ROM
Egypt and the Fertile Crescent

Chapter 3 Section 1

ASSESS

Check for Understanding

Assign Section 1 Review as homework or as an in-class activity.

Use Student Self-Test and Review Software to review Section 1.

Evaluate

Section Quiz 3-1

Use the Testmaker to create a customized quiz for Section 1.

Reteach

Have students summarize the business practices of the trading peoples discussed in this section and state how these practices made trade more efficient.

Enrich

Ask students to write a short scenario describing how using a system of record keeping could affect the relationship between trading partners.

CLOSE

Organize the class into two "nations": one with a bartering system and one with a monetary system. Ask each group to decide on a product to trade with the other group, the product's value, and a record-keeping system. Then ask them to role-play a trading situation, first using the bartering system and then the monetary system. Discuss the results.

later call Canaan *Palestine*, the Greek name for the Philistines.

In contrast to the Aramaeans, who trekked overland to reach their markets, the Phoenicians sailed the seas. On a narrow strip of land between the mountains of western Syria and the Mediterranean Sea, Phoenicia lacked enough arable land for farming, and many Phoenicians turned to the sea to earn a living. They harvested timber from the cedar forests on nearby slopes to build strong, fast ships.

By 1200 B.C. the Phoenicians had built a string of cities and towns along their coast. Many of these scattered ports grew to become city-states, the largest of which were **Tyre**, Byblos, Sidon, and Berytus (modern Beirut). The city-state of Tyre often provided the leadership for what remained a **confederation**, or loose union, of independent Phoenician city-states. According to the Bible:

> "Who was like Tyre.... In the midst of the sea? When your wares were unloaded from the seas, You satisfied many peoples; With your great wealth and merchandise You enriched the kings of the earth."
>
> —Ezekiel 27:32-33

The Phoenicians sailed from their coastal city-states throughout the Mediterranean. Expert navigators, they learned to plot their voyages with great accuracy by means of the sun and the stars. By 1100 B.C. Phoenicians reached the southern coast of Spain and the western coast of Africa. Some historians believe they even ventured as far as the British Isles in northwestern Europe.

Astute traders and businesspeople, the Phoenicians soon took charge of Mediterranean shipping and trade. At ports of call, they exchanged cedar logs, textiles dyed a beautiful purple, glass objects, and elegant jewelry for precious metals. They also brought new business practices, such as bills of sale and contracts.

An advantage that Phoenician merchants held over their competitors when keeping track of complex business deals was an improved **alphabet**—a series of written symbols that represent sounds. Phoenicians developed their efficient alphabet about 1000 B.C. from earlier, more complicated systems from southern Canaan and northwest Syria. The concise Phoenician alphabet used just 22 characters, each character representing a consonant sound. Readers mentally supplied vowels in the proper places.

The Phoenician system later became the foundation of several alphabets, including Greek, which in turn became the basis of all Western alphabets. Because the Phoenician alphabet did not require years of study to master, merchants no longer needed the services of specially trained scribes to keep records.

To protect and resupply their ships, Phoenician sailors and traders set up along the coasts of the Mediterranean a network of temporary trading posts and **colonies**, or settlements of Phoenician emigrants. For example, about 814 B.C., people from Tyre founded a colony named Carthage on the coast of present-day Tunisia. Carthage eventually became the most powerful city in the western Mediterranean.

The Lydians

The Lydians (LIH•dee•uhnz) lived in Asia Minor—the peninsula jutting westward between the Mediterranean, Aegean, and Black Seas. Lydian merchants and artisans were well situated to prosper in the growing regional trade. By the late 600s B.C., the Lydians had developed a wealthy and independent kingdom famous for its rich gold deposits.

Most traders from neighboring cultures still relied on a system of **barter** for their transactions, exchanging their wares for other goods. The Lydians, however, began to set prices and developed a money system using coins as a medium of exchange. Soon Greek and Persian rulers began to stamp their own coins, and the concept of money spread beyond Lydia.

SECTION 1 REVIEW

Recall

1. **Define** confederation, alphabet, colony, barter.
2. **Identify** the Aramaeans, the Phoenicians, the Lydians.
3. **Describe** the bodies of water bordering the regions of Canaan and Asia Minor.

Critical Thinking

4. **Evaluating Information** What factors enabled the Phoenician city-states to remain independent of each other and to prosper?

Understanding Themes

5. **Cultural Diffusion** Why was the Phoenician alphabet a significant development?

SECTION 1 REVIEW ANSWERS

1. All vocabulary words are defined in the Glossary.
2. Aramaeans, 80; Phoenicians, 80; Lydians, 82
3. Canaan: Mediterranean; Asia Minor: Mediterranean, Black Sea, and Aegean Sea
4. The city-states were each able to prosper economically on their own and were not oriented toward developing a united home country.
5. **CULTURAL DIFFUSION** It was more efficient for record keeping and correspondence and easier to learn than the previous system.

2000 B.C. | 1500 B.C. | 1000 B.C. | 500 B.C.

c. 1900 B.C. Abraham settles in Canaan.

c. 1200 B.C. The Israelites first celebrate Passover.

c. 1000 B.C. David sets up capital at Jerusalem.

c. 530s B.C. Jews rebuild the Temple in Jerusalem.

Section 2

Early Israelites

Setting the Scene

- **Terms to Define** monotheism, covenant, exodus, prophet, Diaspora
- **People to Meet** the Israelites, Abraham, Moses, Deborah, David, Solomon
- **Places to Locate** Canaan, Jerusalem

Find Out What part do slavery, exile, and return play in the history of the Israelites?

The Storyteller

This battle would be decisive, Jael was certain. Before the sun set, the Israelites would be recognized as Yahweh's chosen people. Unlike the nomads who had passed through Canaan for generations, the 12 tribes of Israel now sought permanent settlement. However, to remain and prosper, the Israelites had to join together and defeat the threatening Canaanites. Several tribes of Israel, held together only by their common covenant with Yahweh, were sending armed men to battle. Jael, resolving to take action herself, if necessary, was sure that Yahweh would muster the heavens themselves to confound the enemies of the covenant, give victory to the Israelites, and bring peace to the land.

—adapted from the *Holy Bible*, Judges

Mount Sinai

People in the ancient world usually worshiped many deities. The Phoenicians, for example, worshiped a chief god known as El, Baal, or Melqart; an earth-mother goddess called Astarte; and a young god of rebirth named Adonis.

The Israelites—another people living in **Canaan**—were an exception among the polytheistic cultures of the ancient world. They brought a new idea to the world, **monotheism**, or the belief in one all-powerful God. The Israelites believed that God, whom they called Yahweh, determined right and wrong and expected people to deal justly with each other and to accept moral responsibility for their actions. The teachings of the Israelites exist today as the religion of Judaism, which in turn has influenced two other monotheistic religions—Christianity and Islam.

The Land of Canaan

The Bible remains one of the main sources of ancient history in the Fertile Crescent. As a record of the early Israelites, the Bible traces their origins to Abraham, a herder and trader who lived in the Mesopotamian city of Ur. Around 1900 B.C. **Abraham** and his household left Ur and settled in Canaan at the command of Yahweh, or God. The Israelites believed that God made a **covenant**, or agreement, with Abraham at this time. "I will make of you a great nation" was God's promise to bless Abraham and his descendants if they would remain faithful to God.

According to the Bible, once in the land of Canaan, the descendants of Abraham shared the land with other related peoples, such as the Phoenicians and Philistines. Canaan contained rocky hills and desert, fertile plains and grassy slopes, with the best farming in the valley of the Jordan River. Many people lived as nomads herding sheep and goats.

Chapter 3
Section 2

SECTION THEME

- **Innovation** The Israelites contribute to the world the concept of monotheism.

Find Out

Answer: *Their troubled past led Jews to believe that history had a God-directed purpose.*

FOCUS

Section Objective

Describe the role that slavery, exile, and return play in the history of the Israelites.

BELLRINGER
Motivational Activity

Before taking roll at the beginning of the class period, project Section Focus Transparency 3-2 and have students answer the activity questions. Discuss students' responses.

This activity is also available as a blackline master.

Vocabulary Pre-check

Use the Vocabulary PuzzleMaker to create a puzzle that reinforces the vocabulary terms in this section. **L1**

SECTION RESOURCES

Reproducible Masters
- Reproducible Lesson Plan 3-2
- Guided Reading Activity 3-2
- Geography and History Activity 3
- History Simulation 3
- Mapping History Activity 3
- Section Quiz 3-2

Transparencies
- Section Focus Transparency 3-2
- Fertile Crescent

Multimedia
- Vocabulary PuzzleMaker Software
- Student Self-Test and Review Software
- Testmaker
- Egypt and the Fertile Crescent

Chapter 3 Section 2

TEACH

Guided Practice

THEME Innovation

Have students focus on the two Greek roots of the term for the early Israelites' major innovation: *monotheism.* After explaining that *monos* means "alone" or "single" and *theos* means "god," ask students for other words that incorporate either of the two roots. *(Answers may include* monocle, monogamy, monologue, monorail, *and* theocracy *and* theologian.*)* **L1**

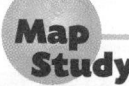

Map Study

Answer

Canaan lay northeast of Egypt and west of Babylon.

Map Skills Practice

Reading a Map How did the size of David's kingdom compare to that of Judah and Israel? *(David's kingdom was more than twice the size of Judah and Israel.)*

NATIONAL GEOGRAPHIC SOCIETY

Use these materials to enrich student understanding of Mesopotamian cultures.

NGS PICTURESHOW CD-ROM
Egypt and the Fertile Crescent

The Exodus From Egypt

Abraham's grandson Jacob, also known as Israel, raised 12 sons in Canaan, and each son led a separate family group, or tribe. These groups became the 12 tribes of Israel. After a severe drought brought a terrible famine to Canaan, the Israelites migrated to Egypt, perhaps during the time that the Hyksos ruled. The Israelites lived peacefully there for several generations, until the pharaohs decided to enslave them.

In the 1200s B.C., the Israelite leader **Moses** led his people out of Egypt in an exodus, or departure, into the Sinai Desert. Every year during the festival of Passover, Jews today retell the story of the Exodus from Egypt.

According to the Bible, during the long trek across the desert of the Sinai Peninsula, God renewed the covenant made with Abraham. Moses and the Israelites pledged to reject all gods other than the one true God and to obey God's laws, the most important of which would be called the Ten Commandments.

> "I the Lord am your God who brought you out of the land of Egypt, the house of bondage: You shall have no other gods beside Me.
> You shall not make for yourself a sculptured image....
> You shall not swear falsely by the name of the Lord your God....
> Remember the sabbath day and keep it holy....
> Honor your father and your mother, that you may long endure on the land that the Lord your God is giving you.
> You shall not murder.
> You shall not commit adultery.
> You shall not steal.
> You shall not bear false witness against your neighbor.
> You shall not covet ... anything that is your neighbor's."
>
> —Exodus 20:2–14

In return for their loyalty, God promised the Israelites a safe return to the land of Canaan.

Settling the Land

Moses died before reaching Canaan, but his successor, Joshua, led the Israelites across the Jordan River into Canaan. For about 200 years, the Israelites fought the Philistines and the Canaanites who now occupied the land.

The Fighting Judges

Lack of unity among the 12 tribes of Israel prolonged the campaign to acquire Canaan. Leaders known as "judges" ruled each tribe. Serving as both judicial and military leaders, some of the judges attempted to rally the Israelites. The Bible relates how **Deborah**, a judge widely admired for her wisdom, planned an attack on a Canaanite army camped near Mount Tabor. Through God's help, the Israelites won the battle.

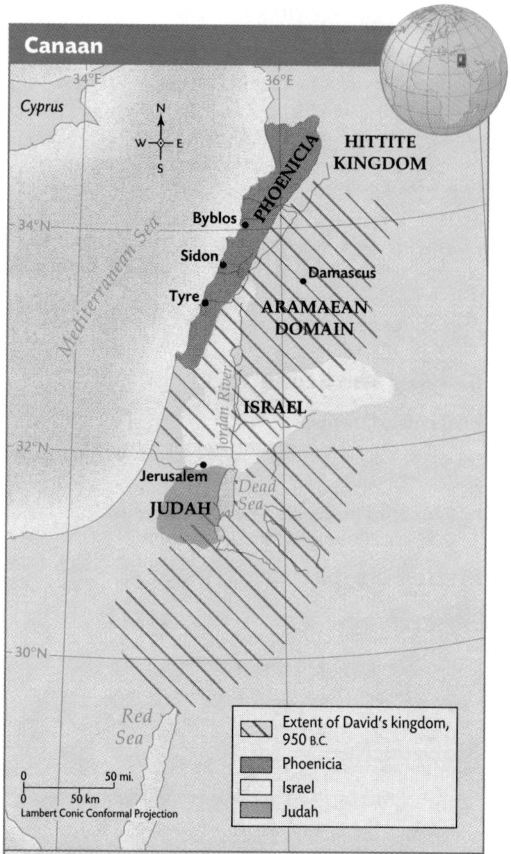

Map Study The Canaanites settled in Canaan about 3000 B.C. Before the Israelites conquered them in about 1200 B.C., some Canaanites settled along the coast and became known as Phoenicians.

Location Where was Canaan in relation to Egypt and to Babylon?

COOPERATIVE LEARNING ACTIVITY

Reading and Summarizing Organize the class into small groups. Give each group a copy of *Exodus*: Chapters 1–13. Have all groups read Chapters 3–4 and summarize the points made in the dialogue between God and Moses. Divide the remaining chapters among the groups. Ask each group to read its section and work together to summarize the arguments Moses used to convince Pharaoh to let the Hebrews leave Egypt. Regroup students so that each chapter has been read by someone in each new group. Tell students to learn from other group members about the chapters they did not read. Ask students to write a paragraph comparing the arguments in later chapters with the original dialogue between God and Moses. **L2**

The Davidic Monarchy

Around 1020 B.C. continual warfare led most of the Israelite tribes to unite under one king, Saul. Although he was popular at first, Saul's power waned when he proved unable to defeat the Philistines. **David**, who had once fought the Philistine Goliath on Saul's behalf, took the throne in 1012 B.C. and ruled for the next 40 years. King David set up a capital at **Jerusalem**, organized a central government, and enlarged his kingdom's borders. During his reign, the Israelites enjoyed economic prosperity.

David's son **Solomon** succeeded his father in 973 B.C. Solomon founded new cities and lavished money on the construction of a magnificent temple to God in Jerusalem. The Israelites resented Solomon's high taxes and harsh labor requirements. After Solomon's death in 922 B.C., the 10 northern tribes broke away from the 2 tribes in the south. The northern tribes continued to call their kingdom Israel. The 2 southern tribes called their kingdom Judah, and kept Jerusalem as their capital. The word *Jew* comes from the name *Judah*.

Exile and Return

Although split politically, the people of Israel and Judah continued to share one religion. The 2 kingdoms, however, were too weak to resist invasions by powerful neighbors. In 722 B.C. the Assyrians of Mesopotamia swept in and conquered Israel, scattering the people of the 10 northern tribes throughout the Assyrian Empire. Then, in 586 B.C., another Mesopotamian people, the Chaldeans (kal•DEE•uhnz), gained control of Judah and destroyed the Temple in Jerusalem. They enslaved some of the city's residents and carried them off to exile in the Chaldean capital city of Babylon.

Exile in Babylon

During this difficult period, **prophets**—preachers who interpreted God's will—arose among the Israelites, who were called Jews after the Babylonian exile. Some prophets, such as Jeremiah, condemned abuses in society and blamed the exile on the Jews' forgetting their duties to God and to one another. The prophets also helped the people of

CONNECTIONS **Science and Technology**

Counting the Days

How many days are there in a week? Different ancient peoples had more than one answer to this question. The Assyrians used a five-day week, while the Egyptians favored groupings of seven.

The modern week may trace its origins to the Jewish custom of observing a Sabbath day every seven days. Alternatively, our week may have originated in the Babylonian belief in the sacredness of the number seven—a belief probably linked either to the four seven-day phases of the moon or to the seven planets then visible in the heavens.

A modern sundial

Ancient peoples often developed lunar calendars, based on the length of time it takes the moon to circle Earth, about 29 days. Of course, the lunar year of about 354 days did not correspond to the solar, or agricultural, year of 365 days. To solve this problem, Babylonian rulers added an extra month to certain years by royal decree.

Astronomers continued to try to adjust calendars to match the annual cycle of seasons. In 46 B.C. the Roman ruler Julius Caesar decreed that months should be longer than a lunar month. He also introduced January 1 as the first day of a new year. But not until A.D. 1582 were errors in the Julian calendar corrected by Pope Gregory XIII, who formalized a self-correcting system of leap years. The Gregorian calendar used today by most people in the Western world closely matches the solar year.

MAKING THE CONNECTION

1. How did the Babylonians resolve differences between the lunar year and the solar year?
2. How does our modern calendar differ from the ancient Babylonian calendar?

Chapter 3 Section 2

Independent Practice

Guided Reading Activity 3-2 **L1**

Daily Life Ask students to find out some differences between the Hebrew alphabet and the English alphabet. *(The Hebrew alphabet is read from right to left and has essentially no vowels.)* **L2**

CONNECTIONS **Science and Technology**

Counting the Days

Our names for the days of the week also can be traced back to ancient times. The Babylonians named each of the seven days after a god who ruled one of the seven planets then visible. The Romans and the Anglo-Saxons simply substituted the names of their gods. The Babylonian god that ruled Jupiter, for example, was Marduk, who gave his name to the fifth day. The ancient Romans gave the name Jove to this day (in French, it is *jeudi*). The Anglo-Saxons in turn called it after their god Thor—*Thursday*.

Answers to Making the Connection

1. *by adding an extra month to certain years*
2. *Our months are one or two days longer than the lunar month, and we add a day each leap year.*

ASSESS

Check for Understanding

Assign Section 2 Review as homework or as an in-class activity.

Use Student Self-Test and Review Software to review Section 2.

MEETING SPECIAL NEEDS ACTIVITY

Language Delayed Organize students with limited English proficiency into two groups. Have one group prepare a poster on King David and the other a poster on King Solomon. Explain that each poster should summarize information about the king. Have students work together to choose the information and then decide on a format for presenting it on the poster. Encourage the students to include copies of art depicting "their" king. Pair students from the two groups and have them describe their posters. **L1 LEP**

Chapter 3 Section 2

Visualizing History To this day, after a scribe finishes copying the Torah onto parchment sheets, the sheets are sewn together with special thread made from animal muscles. The connected sheets are then attached to rollers. Ask students why scribes are not allowed to write from memory. *(to avoid mistakes)*

Answer to Caption: *Micah envisioned a peaceful world.*

Evaluate

Section Quiz 3-2

Use the Testmaker to create a customized quiz for Section 2.

Reteach

Have students select three major figures from early Hebrew history and write several paragraphs describing their contributions.

Enrich

Have students research the Jewish festival of Passover and write a report on its origin and significance. Encourage them to interview a person of the Jewish faith to get a personal perspective.

CLOSE

Organize the class into small groups. Ask the groups to describe how Jews changed their rituals when they no longer had the Jerusalem Temple. Have them compare these methods of worship with those of other religions.

Judah retain their culture during the exile.

While in Babylon, the Jews no longer had a temple in which to worship God. Instead, small groups of Jews began to meet on the Sabbath, the holy day of rest, for prayer and discussion. The rise of local synagogues developed from these gatherings.

Rebuilding Jerusalem

Many Jews continued to hope for a return to Jerusalem. Finally, in 539 B.C., the Persians conquered the Chaldeans. The Persian king, Cyrus II, allowed the Jewish exiles to return to Judah and to rebuild the Temple in Jerusalem. In the 400s B.C., Jewish holy writings were collected and organized into the Torah, made up of the first five books of the Bible: Genesis, Exodus, Leviticus, Numbers, and Deuteronomy.

Although a new Jewish community arose in Jerusalem, many Jews chose to remain in Babylon, and some migrated to other areas in the Middle East. Ever since this time, communities of Jews have existed outside their homeland in what has become known as the **Diaspora**, a Greek word meaning "scattered."

Visualizing History **Scribes recopied the Torah carefully, comparing each letter and word to the original copy.** *What was the prophet Micah's vision for the world?*

A Lasting Legacy

Their troubled history—with cycles of slavery, exile, and return—made the Jews keenly aware of their past. Seeing events as having a God-directed purpose, the Jews recorded their history and examined it for meaning. The Jewish Scriptures begin with the Torah and include the writings of the prophets. As the Jews scattered beyond Canaan, they took the Torah with them, and its teachings spread around the world.

From the Torah has come the concept that every human being, made in the image of God, has infinite worth. Further, humans work in partnership with God, striving to achieve a perfect world, and this link makes people accountable for what happens in the world. The Jewish prophet Micah expressed his vision for the world as follows:

> "And they shall beat their swords
> into plowshares,
> And their spears into pruning hooks.
> Nation shall not take up
> Sword against nation;
> They shall never again know war;
> But every man shall sit
> Under his grapevine or fig tree
> With no one to disturb him."
>
> —Micah 4:3–4

SECTION 2 REVIEW

Recall

1. **Define** monotheism, covenant, exodus, prophet, Diaspora.
2. **Identify** the Israelites, Abraham, Moses, Deborah, David, Solomon.
3. **Locate** Jerusalem on the map on page 84. What was the significance of Jerusalem to Jews in exile in Babylon?

Critical Thinking

4. **Analyzing Information** Create a chronology of the migrations of the Israelites.

Understanding Themes

5. **Innovation** What religious beliefs set the Israelites apart from other ancient peoples? How have these beliefs helped the Jews to survive in spite of exile and persecution?

SECTION 2 REVIEW ANSWERS

1. All vocabulary words are defined in the Glossary.
2. the Israelites, 83; Abraham, 83; Moses, 84; Deborah, 84; David, 85; Solomon, 85
3. The Jews longed to return to Jerusalem, the site of Solomon's Temple.
4. Chronology should begin with Abraham departing Mesopotamia about 1900 B.C. and end with the return to Judah under Cyrus.
5. **INNOVATION** beliefs in one all-powerful God and moral responsibility; belief that their existence as a people had a God-directed purpose.

Study and Writing
SKILLS

Taking Notes

Your history teacher has assigned 20 pages of text to read for homework tonight. You will be tested on the material tomorrow. How will you remember all those facts?

Learning the Skill

Taking notes will help you remember what you have read. Effective note taking, however, is more than just writing facts in short phrases. When taking notes, you must group facts in a logical order. This order can be chronological—what happened first, next, last. It can be based on relationships between events—for example, causes and effects or problems and solutions. By arranging notes logically, you will have better recall and understanding of the information.

Before taking notes, read the material to identify the main ideas. Look for patterns and connections between ideas. Then decide on a note-taking method. Whenever possible, use a graphic organizer to take notes. For example, use a time line to take notes on the sequence of events. A cause-and-effect chart with arrows identifies connections between events. A semantic web shows different aspects of a general topic or theme. A category chart arranges data about groups of people and places into specific categories. Once you have selected an appropriate method, paraphrase your notes in brief headings and short phrases.

Practicing the Skill

Reread Section 2 on pages 83-86 about the early Israelites. Use that information and the semantic web below to answer the following questions.

1. What subtopics belong in the two upper boxes of this web?
2. What religions belong in the lower boxes?
3. What subtopics can you add to the upper left box?
4. What subtopics can you add to the upper right box?

Applying the Skill

Use a semantic web to take notes on Section 1, Trading Peoples.

For More Practice

Turn to the Skill Practice in the Chapter Review on page 95 for more practice in taking notes.

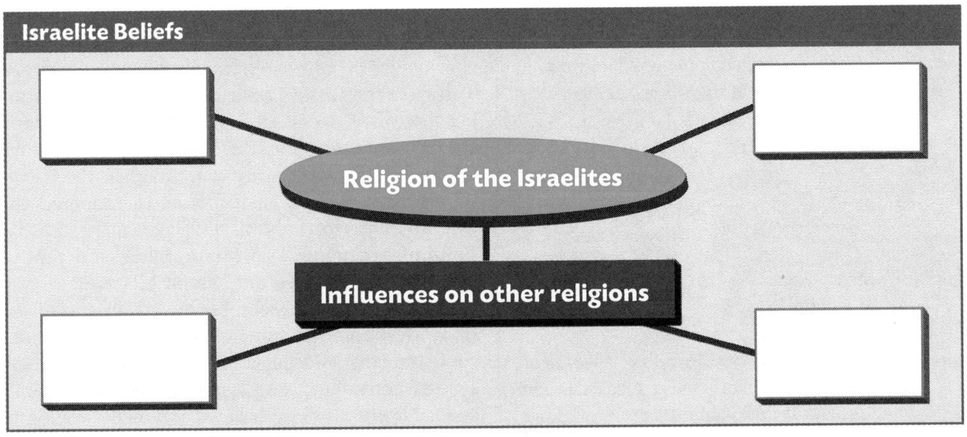

Study and Writing
SKILLS

TEACH

Taking Notes Ask a student to read *Learning the Skill* aloud. Then, to illustrate the three note-taking methods other than the semantic-web, ask students some simple questions about their daily lives and show them how to organize the data they provide by modeling simple graphic organizers on the chalkboard. For a time line, ask them to identify the years they were born, began grade school and high school. Organize this material in a simple time line under the heading *Significant Dates in a Student's Life.* For a cause-and-effect chart, ask them to suggest three cause-and-effect events in their lives this past week. *(Examples: short of cash—did odd jobs; slipped on ice—bruised knee; yelled at sibling—was rebuked by parent.)* For a category chart, ask them to identify some categories that help distinguish among different members of the class and write them on the board. *(Examples: age, gender, hair color, eye color, handedness, height.)* After you have reviewed these three note-taking strategies, have students read the skill to themselves and complete the practice questions.

Additional Practice

Skill Reinforcement Activity 3

Writer's Guidebook, Lesson 10

ANSWERS TO PRACTICING THE SKILL

1. monotheism, human responsibility to treat others justly
2. Christianity, Islam
3. Answers may include: "God's covenant with the Israelites"; "history has a God-directed purpose"
4. Answers may include: "humans are made in God's image, so each individual is of infinite worth"; "people are God's partners in perfecting the world"

2000 B.C. — 1500 B.C. — 1000 B.C. — 500 B.C.

c. 1600 B.C. Hittite Empire reaches its height.

c. 605 B.C. Nebuchadnezzar begins reign in Babylon.

525 B.C. Persian armies conquer Egypt.

SECTION THEME

▶ **Conflict** A series of empires—Hittite, then Assyrian, then Chaldean, then Persian—each conquers the previous one.

Find Out

Answer: *They used their military power to conquer other peoples.*

FOCUS

Section Objective

Explain how a series of powerful empires extended their rule throughout the Middle East.

BELLRINGER Motivational Activity

Before taking roll at the beginning of the class period, project Section Focus Transparency 3-3 and have students answer the activity questions. Discuss students' responses.

This activity is also available as a blackline master.

Vocabulary Pre-check

Use Vocabulary Activity 3 to introduce vocabulary terms.
L1 LEP

Section 3

Empire Builders

Setting the Scene

▶ **Terms to Define**
satrap

▶ **People to Meet**
the Hittites, the Assyrians, the Chaldeans, Nebuchadnezzar, the Persians, Cyrus II, Darius I, Zoroaster

▶ **Places to Locate** Anatolia, Babylon, Nineveh, Persepolis

Find Out How did a series of powerful empires extend their rule throughout the Middle East?

The Storyteller

The scribe carefully recorded King Ashurbanipal II's proclamation. The royal archives would preserve an accurate account of the actions taken against the cities that had dared to revolt. The king dictated: "With the fury of my weapons I stormed the city. I flayed all the chief men who had revolted, and I covered a pillar with their skins. Some I impaled on the pillar on stakes.... I fashioned a heroic image of my royal self, my power and my glory I inscribed thereon...." Ashurbanipal called the gods to destroy all who opposed him, overthrowing their kingdoms and blotting out their names from the land.

—from *Ancient Records of Assyria and Babylonia*, Volume 1, edited by Daniel David Luckenbill, 1968

Hittite hunting scene

The Phoenicians, Aramaeans, Lydians, and Israelites gave the world their alphabets, languages, commercial practices, and religious beliefs. These peoples, however, lacked the military power of their neighbors, and the conquering armies of a series of warlike empires came to rule the Fertile Crescent.

The Hittites

Around 2000 B.C., **the Hittites**—perhaps coming from areas beyond the Black Sea—conquered the local people of Asia Minor. The Hittites set up several city-states on a central plateau called **Anatolia**, and by about 1650 B.C., they had built a well-organized kingdom. Archaeologists have deciphered the writing on some of the clay tablets found in the ruins of Hattusas, the Hittite capital. Other information about the Hittites comes from records of peoples they confronted as they expanded their empire. An Egyptian source, for example, described the Hittites' custom of wearing their hair in a long, thick pigtail that hung down in the back.

Hittite kings assembled a fearsome army—the first in the Middle East to wield iron weapons extensively. The army used light, spoked-wheel chariots that could carry two soldiers and a driver. This gave the Hittites a decided advantage in battle, because they were able to field twice as many troops as their foes in two-person chariots. Overwhelming any army that stood in their way, the Hittites pushed eastward and conquered the city of **Babylon** about 1595 B.C. The Hittite Empire—spanning Asia Minor, Syria, and part of Mesopotamia—lasted until about 1200 B.C.

The Hittites largely borrowed their culture from Mesopotamia and Egypt. However, they did contribute to Middle Eastern civilization a legal system considered less harsh than Hammurabi's code. Hittite law emphasized payments for damages rather than harsh punishments.

SECTION RESOURCES

Reproducible Masters
- Reproducible Lesson Plan 3-3
- Guided Reading Activity 3-3
- Reteaching Activity 3
- Enrichment Activity 3
- Section Quiz 3-3
- Performance Assessment Activity 3
- Spanish Chapter Summary 3

Transparencies
- Section Focus Transparency 3-3
- Fertile Crescent

Multimedia
- The Fertile Crescent
- Student Self-Test and Review Software
- Testmaker
- Egypt and the Fertile Crescent

88 Chapter 3 *Kingdoms and Empires in the Middle East*

The Assyrians

The Assyrians, a people living in northern Mesopotamia, had faced constant invasions from adjoining Asia Minor—including those by the Hittites. About 900 B.C. the Assyrians finally became strong enough to repel attacks from the west. They also began to launch their own military campaigns to subdue their Mesopotamian neighbors.

A Powerful Army

The Assyrian army earned a reputation as the most lethal fighting force in the Middle East. The Assyrians organized their warriors into units of foot soldiers, charioteers, and fast-moving cavalry fighting on horseback. They were described as fighters "whose arrows were sharp and all their bows bent, the horses' hooves were like flint, and their [chariot] wheels like a whirlwind." The Assyrians fought with iron weapons and used battering rams against the walls of the cities they attacked.

The Assyrians treated conquered peoples cruelly. They burned cities and tortured and killed thousands of captives. The Assyrians routinely deported entire populations from their homelands. Resettling the land with people from other parts of the empire, the Assyrians forced these settlers to pay heavy taxes.

The Assyrian Empire

By about 650 B.C., the Assyrian kings governed an empire stretching from the Persian Gulf to Egypt and into Asia Minor. They divided their empire into provinces, each headed by a governor directly responsible to the king. Officials sent from the central government collected taxes to support the army and to fund building projects in **Nineveh**, the Assyrian capital. To improve communication, the Assyrians built a network of roads linking the provinces. Government messengers and Aramaean merchants traveled these roads, protected by soldiers from bandits.

In spite of these links, the Assyrian Empire eventually began to fracture as conquered peoples continually rebelled. In 612 B.C. **the Chaldeans**, who lived in the ancient city of Babylon, formed an alliance with the Medes from the east. The alliance captured Nineveh and brought down the Assyrian Empire.

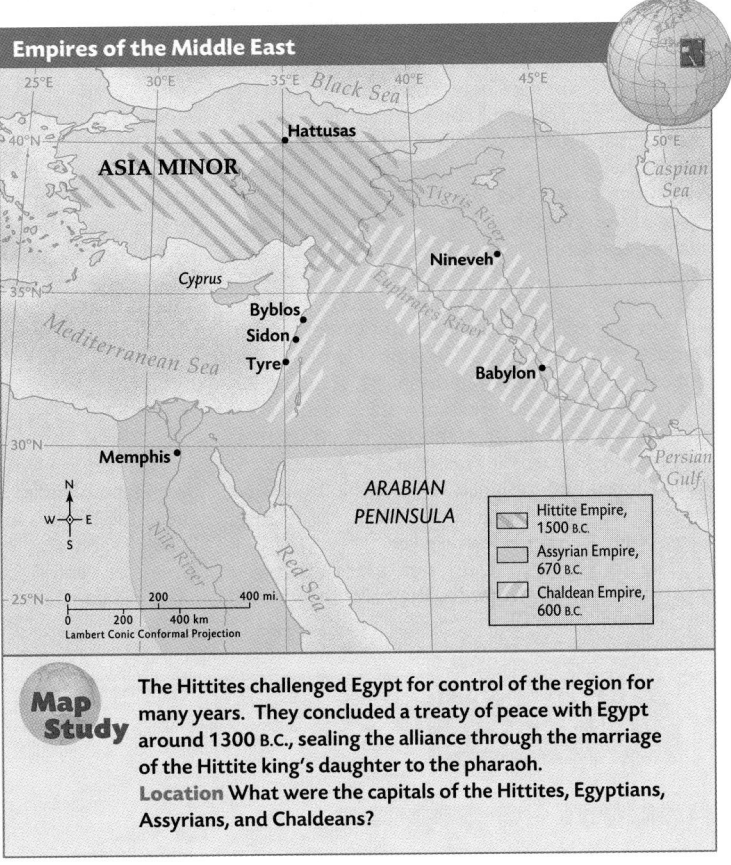

Empires of the Middle East

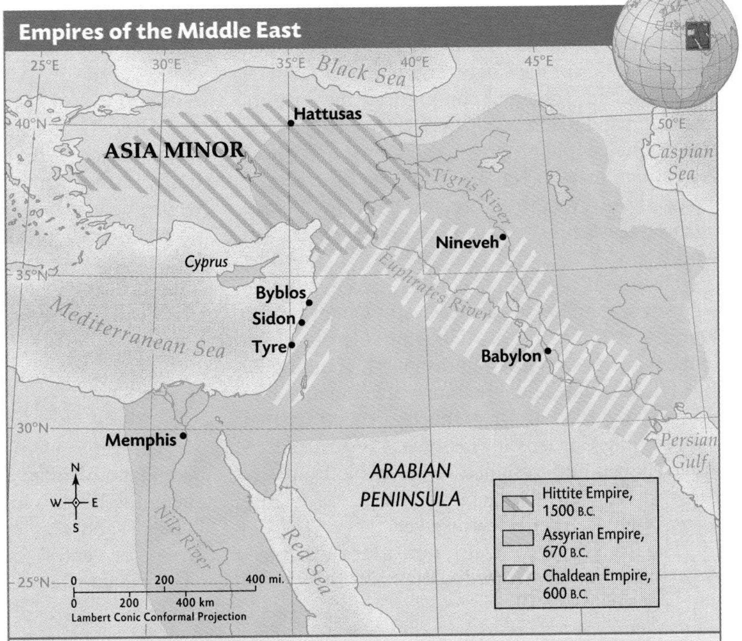

Map Study **The Hittites challenged Egypt for control of the region for many years. They concluded a treaty of peace with Egypt around 1300 B.C., sealing the alliance through the marriage of the Hittite king's daughter to the pharaoh.**
Location What were the capitals of the Hittites, Egyptians, Assyrians, and Chaldeans?

The Chaldeans

Soon after the Assyrians fell, the Chaldean Empire succeeded in dominating the entire Fertile Crescent. Most of the Chaldeans—sometimes called the New Babylonians—were descended from people of Hammurabi's Babylonian Empire of the 1700s B.C.

The Chaldeans reached the height of their power during the reign of one of their greatest

Chapter 3 Section 3

TEACH

Guided Practice

THEME Conflict
Have students compare the ways in which conquered peoples were treated by the Assyrians and the Persians. Discuss: Which methods are more likely to lead to conflict? **L1**

Critical Thinking Have students discuss if governments today might profit from certain principles of governmental organization of ancient Middle Eastern empires. **L3**

Geography: Movement Have students make travel plans for an ancient Greek who wants to visit one of the empires discussed in this section. Have them plot the route on an outline map, and then write a detailed description of it, including method of travel and a description of each site to be visited. **L2**

Map Study

Answer
Hittites: Hattusas; Egyptians: Memphis; Assyrians: Nineveh; Chaldeans: Babylon

Map Skills Practice

Reading a Map Which empire included the former Egyptian capital? *(Assyrian)*

COOPERATIVE LEARNING ACTIVITY

Interview Organize the class into groups of four to six to plan interviews. Have students first work cooperatively to research and create a character who lived in Nebuchadnezzar's Babylon. Then have them plan an interview that elicits details about the character's life in the city of the Hanging Gardens. In planning and carrying out the interview, each student should assume one of these roles: interviewer, costume designer, editor, photographer, keyboardist, and interviewee. Tell students that the final product is to be a printed version of the interview with accompanying photographs. Display these on the bulletin board. **L2**

Chapter 3 Section 3

Independent Practice

Guided Reading Activity 3-3 **L1**

Geography: Environment In the Hanging Gardens, Nebuchadnezzar put plants that would remind his wife of her home in the mountains of Media (northwestern Iran). Have students make a catalog of plants that Nebuchadnezzar might have placed in the Hanging Gardens had his wife come from the students' own region. **L1 LEP**

NATIONAL GEOGRAPHIC SOCIETY

Use these materials to enrich student understanding of Middle Eastern civilizations.

- **NGS PICTURESHOW CD-ROM** Egypt and the Fertile Crescent
- **NGS PICTUREPACK TRANSPARENCY SET** Fertile Crescent
- **ANCIENT CIVILIZATIONS POSTER SET** The Fertile Crescent

rulers, King **Nebuchadnezzar** (NEH•byuh•kuhd•NEH•zuhr), from 605 B.C. to 562 B.C. He extended the boundaries of the Chaldean Empire as far west as Syria and Canaan, conquering the city of Jerusalem and the Phoenician city-state of Tyre and forcing the people of the kingdom of Judah into a Babylonian exile in 586 B.C. Nebuchadnezzar also amassed great wealth and rebuilt Babylon into one of the largest, most beautiful cities of the ancient world.

Historians of the time counted two features of Babylon among the so-called Seven Wonders of the World—its wall and its Hanging Gardens. An immense wall snaked around the city, standing 50 feet (15 m) high and bristling with watchtowers every 100 yards (90 m). Nebuchadnezzar created the Hanging Gardens for his wife. Constructed on several levels and designed to be visible from any point in Babylon, the elaborate park was fed by water pumped from a nearby river.

The Chaldeans were also noted for their interest in astrology. They recorded their observations of the stars and made maps that showed the position of the planets and the phases of the moon. Their studies laid the foundations for the science of astronomy.

After Nebuchadnezzar's death, a series of weak kings held the throne. Poor harvests and slow trade further sapped the strength of an empire whose people had been severely taxed and plundered. Then, in 539 B.C., **the Persians** under **Cyrus II** came from the mountains to the northeast, seized Babylon, and then conquered the rest of the Chaldean Empire.

The Persians

The Persians originated from a larger group of people now called Indo-Europeans. As warriors and cattle herders in search of new grasslands, the Persians and the Medes, another Indo-European group, left central Asia about 2000 B.C. They settled on a plateau between the Persian Gulf and the

Images of the Times

Ancient Persepolis

The most luxurious palace of Darius was built at Persepolis. Completed by Xerxes, the palace was a monument to the king's power.

Alexander the Great destroyed most of the palace in 331 B.C., but the stone monumental gateways and terraces survived.

Bronze image of a Persian chariot

90

Images of the Times **Ancient Persepolis**

The location of Persepolis, in a remote and mountainous region, limited its use as a royal residence mainly to springtime. Among the cuneiform inscriptions archaeologists found cut in stone at Persepolis is one on the south retaining wall. The inscription gives Darius's prayer for his people: "God protect this country from foe, famine, and falsehood."

Caspian Sea, in the area of present-day Iran.

Cyrus's Conquests

During the 540s B.C., Cyrus had developed a strong army, conquered the Medes, and advanced into neighboring lands. He added northern Mesopotamia, Syria, Canaan, and the Phoenician cities to his empire. Cyrus also took over the kingdom of Lydia and the Greek city-states in Asia Minor. In 525 B.C. Cyrus's son Cambyses (kam•BY•seez) conquered Egypt, bringing all of the Middle East under Persian control.

The Persian Empire, then second to none, stretched from the Nile River to the Indus River, a distance of 3,000 miles (4,800 km). Within this immense empire, the Persians ruled more than 50 million people.

Darius's Empire

The best organizer among the Persian kings was **Darius I**, who reigned from 522 B.C. to 486 B.C. To administer his empire, Darius effectively divided the realm into provinces and assigned satraps, or provincial governors, to rule. Military officials and tax inspectors, chosen by the king from among the conquered people themselves, assisted the satraps in carrying out the king's decrees in the provinces. In addition, inspectors called "Eyes and Ears of the King" made unannounced tours of the provinces and reported directly to the king on the activities of officials. In this way, the king's court was able to keep watch on local government.

In contrast to the Assyrians, the Persians were tolerant rulers who allowed conquered peoples to retain their own languages, religions, and laws. The Persians won the loyalty of conquered peoples by respecting local customs. They believed that this loyalty could be won more easily with fairness than by fear or force. When faced with rebellion, however, the Persians did not hesitate to take extreme military measures.

Commerce and Roads

Darius brought artisans from many of his

Persian god and goddess protecting a palm tree

More than 1,000 years after Alexander destroyed Persepolis, the first curious travelers rediscovered the impressive remains of the city. The Apadana hall at the northern end of the palace contains stairways with beautiful reliefs of Persian nobles, guards, and tribute bearers.

REFLECTING ON THE TIMES

1. About what year did travelers rediscover Persepolis?
2. What ruins reveal the wealth of Persian kings?

The Arts Have students set up a gallery show of Persian art and architecture, using photocopies or sketches of actual artwork. Ask them to label and give background information on each item in the show. **L2**

Multicultural Have students read the following sections of the Hebrew Bible to see how the Israelites and the Hittites intermingled: Genesis 23, Genesis 26:34–35, II Samuel 11. Ask students to describe each interaction of the two peoples. **L2**

Who?What?Where?When?

Nineveh According to the Hebrew Bible, God sent the prophet Jonah to warn the people of Nineveh that they would be destroyed for their wickedness. The Ninevites repented, however, and God spared the city.

ANSWERS TO REFLECTING ON THE TIMES

1. Travelers rediscovered Persepolis after A.D. 670.
2. The ruins of Darius's palace at Persepolis reveal the wealth of Persian kings.

Chapter 3 Section 3

Map Study

Answer

by respecting local customs

Map Skills Practice

Reading a Map What was the distance between Susa and Sardis along the Royal Road? *(about 1,400 miles or 2,253 kilometers)*

Linking Past and Present

Zoroastrians The Parsees of the Bombay area in India are modern Zoroastrians. Their ancestors traveled to India from Iran in the A.D. 700s to avoid Muslim persecution. The Parsees represent an important economic group in India. From about 1850 on, they proved successful in such industries as shipbuilding and the railways.

ASSESS

Check for Understanding

Assign Section 3 Review as homework or as an in-class activity.

Use Student Self-Test and Review Software to review Section 3.

Evaluate

Section Quiz 3-3

Use the Testmaker to create a customized quiz for Section 3.

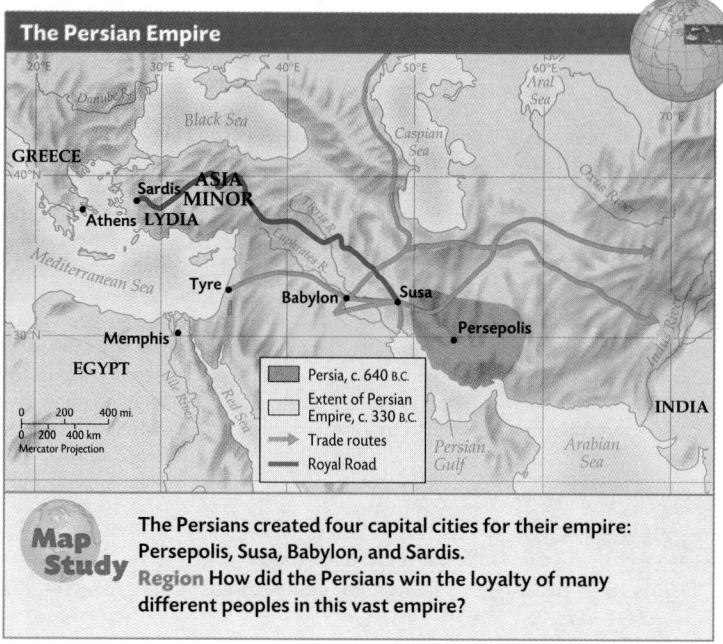

The Persian Empire

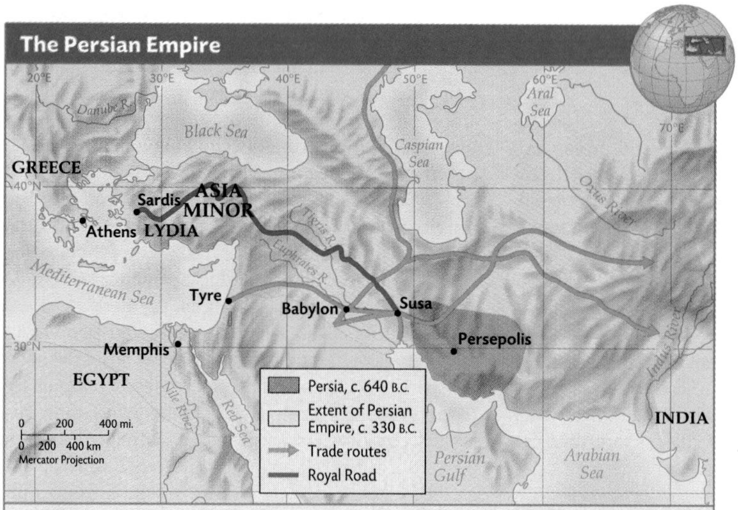

Map Study The Persians created four capital cities for their empire: Persepolis, Susa, Babylon, and Sardis.
Region How did the Persians win the loyalty of many different peoples in this vast empire?

conquered lands to build **Persepolis**, the most magnificent city in the empire. The Persians themselves did not engage in trade, which they considered an indecent occupation. However, they did encourage trade among the peoples of their empire. To advance trade throughout the empire and aid the movement of soldiers, Darius had Persian engineers improve and expand the network of roads first laid down by the Assyrians. Royal messengers also journeyed on the roads allowing "neither snow, nor rain, nor heat, nor the darkness of night to hinder them in the prompt completion of their . . . tasks."

The Royal Road, the most important thoroughfare in the Persian Empire, stretched more than 1,500 miles (2,400 km) from Persia to Asia Minor. Every 14 miles (22.4 km), stations along the Royal Road provided travelers with food, water, and fresh horses. Royal messengers could travel the length of the road in just seven days, a journey that had taken three months before the road was built.

A Persian Disaster

During his reign, Darius waged war against the Greeks over the control of city-states in Asia Minor. After Darius died, his son Xerxes (ZUHRK •SEEZ) led the forces of Persia in a disastrous campaign to conquer Greece in 480 B.C., crippling the Persian Empire in the process.

Persian Religion and Culture

The Persians followed a strict moral code that stressed bravery and honesty. They taught their sons to "ride horses, to draw a bow, and to speak the truth." Before the 500s B.C., the Persian people worshiped many deities associated with the sky, sun, and fire. Then, about 570 B.C., a prophet named **Zoroaster** (ZOHR•uh•WAS•tuhr) began to call for reform of the Persian religion. Zoroaster preached that the world was divided by a struggle between good and evil. The god Ahura Mazda led the forces of good, and another god, Ahriman, commanded the forces of evil. At the end of time, Ahura Mazda would triumph over Ahriman.

Zoroaster also taught that humans were caught up in this struggle and had to choose between good and evil. All humans who fought on the side of Ahura Mazda against evil would be rewarded with eternal life. Those who chose Ahriman would be condemned after death to eternal darkness and

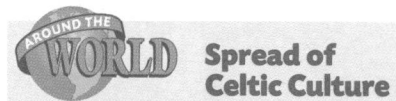

AROUND THE WORLD — Spread of Celtic Culture

Central Europe, c. 600 B.C.

The Hallstatt Celts spread their influence from Austria to the British Isles. They were among the first people in northern Europe to make iron. Their warlike chieftains relied on horses and slept on animal skins in crude houses. Their weapons and artifacts, however, were decorated with elaborate patterns. Celtic art featured highly stylized plants and animals.

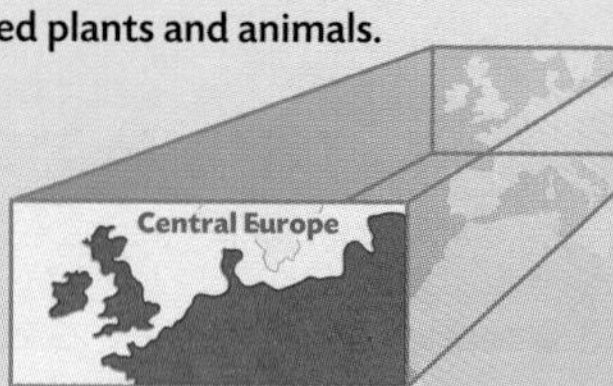

MEETING SPECIAL NEEDS ACTIVITY

Learning Style: Visual/Spatial Have students trace the Chaldean Empire from the map (p. 89), including the labeled cities and the bodies of water abutting it. Ask them to name the rivers on which Babylon is located *(Euphrates)* and on which Nineveh is located *(Tigris)*, and the body of water into which the rivers empty *(Persian Gulf)*. Now have them use a ruler and the distance scale to figure out the distance Babylon-Nineveh. *(The distance is 3/4 of an inch, or, based on the distance scale, 300 miles.)* Ask them to compare the distances Babylon-Nineveh and New York-Los Angeles. *(New York and Los Angeles are 10 times farther apart.)*

Visualizing History This relief of King Darius and Xerxes is one of many at the palace of King Darius. The rigidity of posture and arrogance of the figures conveys the grandeur and ceremony of the royal court. *How did the Royal Road affect travel time?*

misery. These teachings were contained in a book called the Avesta.

Persian rulers believed that they ruled by the power of Ahura Mazda and were responsible to him alone. Darius I had the following statement carved on a cliff:

> “On this account Ahura Mazda brought me health.... Because I was not wicked, nor was I a liar, nor was I a tyrant, neither I nor any of my line. We had ruled according to righteousness.”

Zoroaster's teachings were eventually linked to the glorification of the Persian monarchy. Because the monarchy was viewed as a sacred institution, Persian kings commanded great respect and were surrounded by pomp and pageantry. This style of kingship later shaped the development of monarchies in the Western world.

Zoroaster's beliefs also may have shaped beliefs in the Mediterranean world. Some scholars believe that Zoroaster's teachings about paradise, hell, and the Last Judgment—or the separation of good and evil at the end of time—may have influenced Judaism, Christianity, and Islam. Other aspects of Persian culture lived on as well, and mixed with Greek culture when Alexander the Great absorbed the Persians into his own empire in the 300s B.C.

SECTION 3 REVIEW

Recall

1. **Define** satrap.
2. **Identify** the Hittites, the Assyrians, the Chaldeans, Nebuchadnezzar, the Persians, Cyrus II, Darius I, Zoroaster.
3. **Locate** the Hittite, Assyrian, Chaldean, and Persian Empires on the maps on pages 89 and 92. Rank them in order of approximate size.

Critical Thinking

4. **Evaluating Information** Why might other religions have adopted features of the Zoroastrian religion?

Understanding Themes

5. **Conflict** How did the military exploits of the Hittites and the Assyrians both change the way peoples of the time fought military battles and the way in which they dealt with conquered peoples?

SECTION 3 REVIEW ANSWERS

1. All vocabulary words are defined in the Glossary.
2. Hittites, 88; Assyrians, 89; Chaldeans, 89; Nebuchadnezzar, 90; Persians, 90; Cyrus II, 90; Darius I, 91; Zoroaster, 92
3. from smallest to largest: Hittite, Chaldean, Assyrian, Persian
4. Allow for personal opinion. Many people have found meaning in the idea of conflict between the forces of good and evil and a final day of judgment.
5. **CONFLICT** The Hittites introduced iron weapons; the Assyrians introduced cavalry. Both taxed conquered peoples heavily, a practice that endured.

Chapter 3 Section 3

Visualizing History The Persians operated a postal system along the Royal Road much like the American Pony Express. Postal stations were set up along the road a day's ride apart. At each station, a fresh rider and horse would wait to take the mail from the incoming rider.
Answer to Caption: *A three-month journey took only seven days on the Royal Road.*

Reteach

Prepare a chart on the chalkboard requesting the following information about each of the empires described in this section: beginning and ending dates, territorial extent of empire, names of rulers, significant achievements. Organize the class into four groups. Assign each group responsibility for filling in the chart of one of the four empires described in the section.

Reteaching Activity 3

Enrich

Have students find and summarize further information about ancient Susa (which the biblical book of Esther calls Shushan), where a stele containing the Code of Hammurabi was discovered.

Enrichment Activity 3

CLOSE

Ask students to reflect on the transitory nature of the empires built by the Hittites, Assyrians, Chaldeans, and Persians. **What remains of the original empire in each case?** *(Little remains of these empires; students might discuss ways in which each empire has indirectly affected later cultures.)*

Chapter 3 Review

GLENCOE TECHNOLOGY

VIDEODISC

Use MindJogger to review students' knowledge of the chapter.

MindJogger Videoquiz

Chapter 3
Disc 1 Side A

Also available in VHS.

Answers

Using Key Terms

1. b	6. i
2. g	7. a
3. j	8. c
4. h	9. e
5. f	10. d

Using Your History Journal

Remind students that an epic is a long poem that recounts the adventures of a hero who contributed to the formation of a nation. Suggest that they incorporate such conventions of epic poetry as describing warfare and referring to the nation's gods.

CHAPTER 3 REVIEW

Historical Significance

Trading peoples and empire builders both enriched the culture of the ancient Middle East and strongly influenced later civilizations. One of the most significant innovations, for example, was the concise and easy-to-learn Phoenician alphabet, which spread communication, enhanced trade, and eventually evolved into the alphabet used to spell the words on this page.

Spiritual life also evolved dramatically, through the adherence of the Israelites to a belief in one God, who required people to live justly. The concepts of monotheism and ethical laws have endured in the modern religions of Judaism, Christianity, and Islam.

Using Key Terms

Write the key term that completes each sentence.

a. alphabet	f. satraps
b. monotheism	g. exodus
c. colony	h. prophets
d. covenant	i. Diaspora
e. barter	j. confederation

1. The belief in one all-powerful god is known as ________ .
2. In the 1200s B.C., the Israelite leader Moses rallied his people and led them out of Egypt in a ______ into the Sinai Desert.
3. The Phoenicians were organized into a ________ of independent city-states along the coast of northern Canaan.
4. Israelite ________ condemned abuses in society and urged people not to forget their duties to God and to one another.
5. Persian kings appointed a number of ________ to govern the provinces of the Persian Empire.
6. Jewish communities existing outside of their homeland have become known as the ________, after a Greek word meaning "scattered."
7. The Phoenicians developed an improved, efficient________—a series of written symbols that represent sounds.
8. About 814 B.C. Phoenician emigrants founded the ______ of Carthage on the coast of present-day Tunisia in North Africa.
9. In early Asia Minor, most traders relied on a system of ______ for their transactions—exchanging their wares for other goods.
10. According to the Bible, God made a ______ with Abraham, stating that Abraham's descendants would be blessed as a great nation if they remained faithful to God.

Using Your History Journal

Choose one of the verses that you have written for your journal dealing with an event mentioned in the chapter. After research expand the verse into an epic poem about the event.

Reviewing Facts

1. **Explain** how Aramaic came to be spoken throughout the Fertile Crescent.
2. **Identify** the practices that the Phoenicians introduced to Mediterranean business and trade. What advantage did the Phoenicians have over their competitors?
3. **Describe** how the Israelites interpreted and applied the new idea of monotheism.
4. **List** the peoples with whom the Israelites came into conflict after the Exodus from Egypt and the return to Canaan.
5. **Identify** the contribution that the Hittites made to Middle Eastern civilization.

Critical Thinking

1. **Apply** What natural resource supported the Lydians' development of a money system to replace the barter system?
2. **Analyze** How were the deities and beliefs of the Phoenicians, the Israelites, and the Persians different from one another?
3. **Analyze** What actions taken by Darius I made his rule so effective?

Reviewing Facts

1. Aramaeans controlled overland trade between Egypt and Mesopotamia and traveled throughout the entire region.
2. bills of sale and contracts; alphabet allowed them to correspond with others and keep better track of business dealings
3. One God determined right and wrong, expected people to deal fairly with one another and be morally responsible.
4. Philistines, Canaanites, Assyrians, Chaldeans, Persians
5. introduced legal system that emphasized payment for damages rather than harsh punishments

Critical Thinking

1. rich gold deposits
2. Phoenician: polytheistic, with three main deities; Hebrew: monotheistic, with God expecting moral behavior; Persian: polytheistic, with gods associated with sky, sun, fire
3. divided Persian Empire into provinces; appointed military officials and tax inspectors from among conquered peoples; ordered surprise inspections of provinces; improved roads to encourage trade
4. Students should support their answers.

Geography in History

1. the Chaldeans' defeat of Judah in 586 B.C.
2. through a network of canals

4. **Evaluate** Which development of this period do you believe was most important for the future of world history? Why?

Geography in History

1. **Movement** What event led to the establishment of a large Jewish community in Babylon after 586 B.C.?
2. **Human/Environment Interaction** How did the people of Babylon provide water to various locations inside the city walls?
3. **Human/Environment Interaction** How did the people of Babylon fortify the city against attack from outsiders?

Babylon c. 500s B.C.

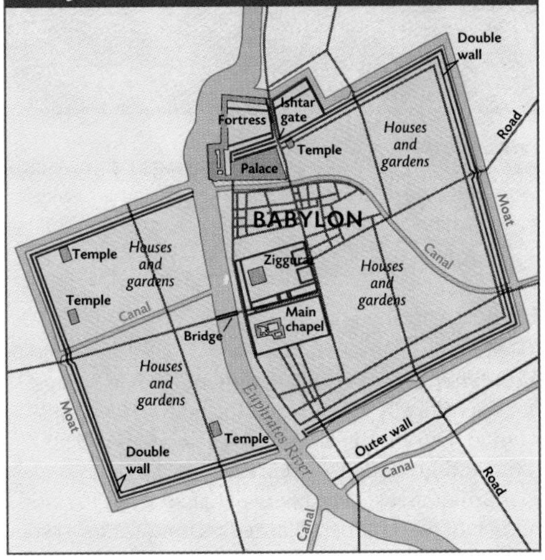

Understanding Themes

1. **Cultural Diffusion** Based on your knowledge of the ancient trading peoples of the Middle East, what kinds of ideas might people be likely to adopt from other cultures?
2. **Innovation** From a modern perspective, do you see any advantages or disadvantages to the development of a religious belief system based on monotheism?
3. **Conflict** Make a list of what aims might have motivated conquerors such as the Hittites, Assyrians, Chaldeans, and Persians to incorporate their neighbors into empires.

Linking Past and Present

1. Does the legal system of our country parallel Hittite law or Hammurabi's code? Provide a brief explanation of your view.
2. The Israelites, ancestors of the Jews, shared Canaan with several other peoples, such as the Phoenicians and the Philistines. What peoples live today in what was formerly the land of Canaan? Give a brief summary of their history in recent decades.
3. Solomon built a magnificent temple at Jerusalem. The last Jewish temple on the Temple Mount was destroyed in A.D. 70. What building stands on that site now?

Skill Practice

The various peoples in this chapter all lived in the Middle East. The beginning dates of their civilizations, the achievements of their cultures, and their contributions to history all differ. Use the category chart below to arrange data about each group.

Peoples	Beginning Dates	Cultural Achievements and Contributions
Aramaeans		
Phoenicians		
Lydians		
Israelites		
Hittites		
Assyrians		
Chaldeans		
Persians		

3. a powerful double wall, reinforced by a moat

Understanding Themes

1. **CULTURAL DIFFUSION** ideas that simplify or improve daily life
2. **INNOVATION** advantage: a single God who demands moral behavior of people is a better role model than a pantheon of gods who do not always act morally. disadvantage: with one God responsible for both good and evil, people may have difficulty understanding why "bad things happen to good people."
3. **CONFLICT** desire for power, for enslaved persons, for more natural resources, for control of trade routes.

Linking Past and Present

1. Fines levied for misdemeanors resemble Hittite code; capital punishment parallels Hammurabi's code.
2. Canaan is now split into Lebanon, Israel, Syria, Jordan; inhabitants of these areas: Lebanese, Syrians, Palestinians, Israelis, Jordanians. Since the state of Israel was created in 1948, ongoing conflicts between the Israelis and the Palestinian Arabs. Arabs in Syria, Jordan, and Lebanon sided with the Palestinians against Israel. Israel and the Palestinian Arabs began to work to resolve their conflicts peacefully in the 1990s. Other Arab states began to make peaceful overtures toward Israel.
3. the Dome of the Rock and al-Aqsa Mosque

Skill Practice

Aramaeans: 1200 B.C., controlled overland trade between Egypt and Mesopotamia; Phoenicians: 3000 B.C., built coastal cities, sailed on Mediterranean; Lydians, 600s B.C., wealth based on gold, first to use coins; Israelites, 1900 B.C., monotheism, Ten Commandments; Hittites, 2000 B.C., strong army, iron weapons; Assyrians, 900 B.C., built empire, network of roads linking provinces; Chaldeans, 1700s B.C., made Babylon a large and beautiful city, studied astrology; Persians, 2000 B.C., built large empire, tolerance of local cultures, Zoroastrianism

Chapter Bonus Test Question

Ask students: According to a well-known maxim, "the pen is mightier than the sword." What information in this chapter supports that view? *(The militarily weak ancient Hebrew culture, through its written scriptures, has had the most lasting effect on later civilizations.)*

Unit 1 Digest

The Unit Digest offers a chapter-by-chapter summary that can be used for any of the following teaching purposes:

- ***Preview*** one chapter or an entire unit,
- ***Review*** some or all of the chapters,
- ***Condense*** when specific chapters or units have not been taught, or
- ***Reteach*** chapters that students have studied in the unit.

PREVIEW

Use the Unit 1 Digest Transparencies to preview the highlights of the unit.

Visualizing History The term *archaeology* comes from the Greek word *arche*, meaning "the beginning." Among the earliest archaeological digs were the excavations in the 1700s of the ancient Roman cities of Pompeii and Herculaneum in southern Italy. When Napoleon invaded Egypt in 1798–1799, he took with him scholars who sparked European interest in ancient Egyptian civilization.

Answer to Caption: *agriculture*

Unit 1 Digest

The bones of early human beings as well as other fossil remains, archaeological artifacts, and written records hold many clues for researchers studying the past. Although historians consider history to have begun about 5,500 years ago, when early civilizations created writing systems, the human story extends much further into the past—into more than 2 million years of prehistory.

In prehistoric times, early human beings set many cultural patterns that continued into historic times. They adapted to their changing environment. They migrated in search of more hospitable living conditions. They cooperated with one another to obtain food and came into conflict over land and water. They invented new ways of doing things and adopted from one another new methods and ideas.

Some early peoples quit their wandering life and settled down as farmers. They began to live together in villages and later built cities. Many historians set the beginning of history at the formation of cities, for it was there that writing and other activities of early civilization evolved. The ancient cities founded in the river valleys of the Nile, the Tigris-Euphrates, the Indus, and the Huang spawned several great civilizations. Some of these civilizations shared their ideas and way of life with other peoples through trade, conquest, and empire. Some disappeared; some were overcome but rose again; some have continued in one form or another to the present day.

Visualizing History **Archaeologist working at a grave site in Jerusalem.** *What allowed people to give up their nomadic life and settle in cities?*

Chapter 1 Human Beginnings

Using research techniques such as radiocarbon dating to date plant and animal matter, anthropologists and archaeologists have been able to establish a time frame for prehistoric human life. Scientists do not agree about all aspects of how or when the first human beings became truly human, but fossil evidence suggests that the first prehuman hominids lived about 4.4 million years ago. Over the next few million years, the hominids gradually adapted to changes in their environment, such as a colder climate, in various ways. Some hominids evolved larger brains.

Early Humans

Two large-brained hominids, *Homo habilis* and *Homo erectus*, as well as all modern human beings, are scientifically classified in the genus *Homo*—human. During the Ice Ages—periods of cold climate and glaciation—some early people migrated to warmer areas, and others perished from the cold or lack of food. Others learned techniques for staying warm. Clothing and fire became part of the culture of prehistoric people, as did the use of stone tools. The early human beings of the Stone Age invented many new technological and social skills, including spoken language. Changes were relatively slow, however, until the modern human species, *Homo sapiens*, appeared around 200,000 years ago. Two groups of *Homo sapiens*, the Neanderthals and Cro-Magnons, made significant advances in housing and in tool and weapon making, but the greatest achievement came late in the Stone Age, during the Neolithic period, with the shift from hunting and food gathering to agriculture. This change in

CLASSROOM RESOURCES FOR UNIT 1 DIGEST

Preview
- Unit 1 Digest Transparencies

Review
- Time Line Activities 1, 2, 3
- Student Self-Test and Review Software, Chapters 1, 2, 3
- MindJogger Videoquiz, Chapters 1, 2, 3

Condense
- Chapter Digests Audiocassettes, Chapters 1, 2, 3

Reteach
- Reteaching Activities 1, 2, 3
- Chapter Digests Audiocassettes, Chapters 1, 2, 3
- Turning Points in World History

the way of life was so radical that it is often referred to as the Neolithic Revolution.

Civilizations

The development of agriculture was an essential stepping-stone to civilization. Initially farming allowed people to give up their nomadic life and settle in communities. Eventually, with a relatively steady food supply, many men and women could devote their time to economic activities other than farming. As time passed, some of the early agricultural villages grew into the first cities, which were home to highly organized societies, or civilizations. All early civilizations shared some basic features. They had specialized labor; cooperative methods for producing surplus food, such as irrigation; and metalworking technology. Under an organized government they formed social classes and maintained an army. They undertook long-distance trade. With a system of values and religious beliefs, they were sophisticated enough to have written records.

SURVEYING CHAPTER 1

1. **Analyzing Information** How did climate affect where early hominids lived?
2. **Making Connections** How did the Neolithic Revolution become a stepping-stone to the rise of the first civilizations?

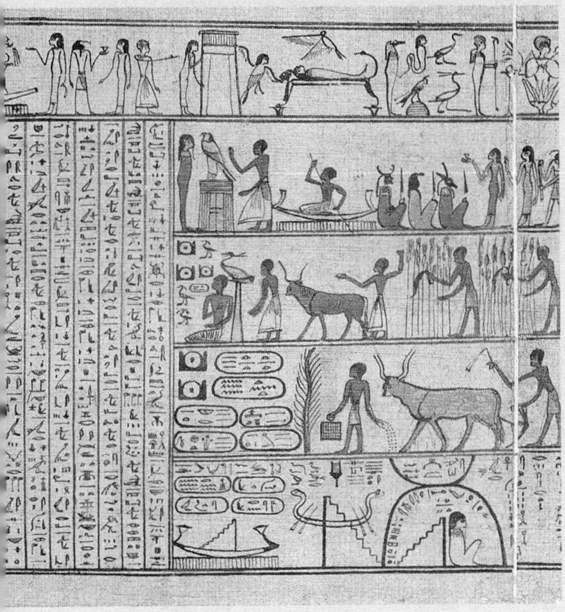

Visualizing History **A funeral papyrus from the *Book of the Dead*, Egypt.** *Along what river are most ancient Egyptian monuments found?*

Chapter 2
Early Civilizations

Cities and civilizations arose at different times in different parts of the world. Many of the earliest civilizations had one thing in common, however: they grew out of agricultural settlements in river valleys. Civilization appeared around 3500 B.C. in the Tigris-Euphrates River valley in the Fertile Crescent, but it also arose soon thereafter in the Nile River valley of Egypt, and again later in the Indus River valley of the South Asian subcontinent and in the Huang He valley in China.

Ancient Egypt and Mesopotamia

In northeastern Africa, nomads left the desert to settle along the fertile banks of the Nile and founded villages. These villages then banded together in small kingdoms, which were later united under a king, who was a religious and political leader and head of a government bureaucracy.

The ancient Egyptians built a magnificent civilization. With innovative irrigation and flood control techniques, they used the seasonally fluctuating Nile waters to their advantage. They undertook ambitious building projects, such as the Pyramids, which required new engineering skills. The writing system early Egyptians invented and the script that formed from it were put to use both for everyday purposes and for decorating their massive monuments. The prosperity achieved by Egyptian civilization encouraged later pharaohs to expand the frontiers of their country and to build an empire. The cultural diffusion made possible by the empire further enriched Egyptian civilization.

In Mesopotamia, the land between the Tigris and Euphrates Rivers, the pattern of development was much the same. Peoples fleeing war and overpopulation, as well as poor climate, settled in villages on the fertile river plain. Although the early peoples of Mesopotamia, unlike the Egyptians, could not depend on a regular supply of water, they managed to meet the challenges of the twin rivers by cooperating with one another and devising methods of irrigation and flood control. The Sumerians, a group who migrated to the region from central Asia, built the world's first cities and a civilization that reached its height sometime before that of the Egyptians. The complex organization of

Unit 1 Digest

REVIEW

GLENCOE TECHNOLOGY

VIDEODISC
Use MindJogger to review any chapter in Unit 1.

MindJogger Videoquiz

Chapter 1
Disc 1 Side A

Chapter 2
Disc 1 Side A

Chapter 3
Disc 1 Side A

Also available in VHS.

Use Student Self-Test and Review Software to review any chapters that students have studied in Unit 1.

Visualizing History Egyptian scribes copied prayers and images, later collected in the *Book of the Dead*, onto pieces of papyrus, like the one shown here. These sheets were buried with well-to-do Egyptians to help them in the afterlife. **Answer to Caption:** *the Nile*

ANSWERS TO SURVEYING THE CHAPTER

CHAPTER 1 ANSWERS

1. The first hominids appeared in the warm forests of Africa, then spread throughout the world. During the Ice Ages, many migrated to warmer climates in the middle latitudes; others crossed land bridges to North America from Asia.
2. The development of agriculture allowed people to give up their nomadic life and to settle in communities, some of which grew into cities that spawned civilizations. Crucial to the rise of the first civilizations was the ability to maintain a food surplus, which freed many men and women for other activities.

Unit 1 Digest

Visualizing History Shang metalworkers added lead to the usual ingredients used in bronze—copper and tin—to create an alloy unique to ancient China. Lead made the molten metal flow more easily, allowing Shang artisans to cast intricate bronzes.
Answer to Caption: *the Huang He*

Cultural Diffusion Have students brainstorm examples of ways that cultural diffusion took place during the period covered in Unit 1. Discuss the examples and decide which three were the most important. (*Answers may include: Migrating peoples spread their culture; trading peoples exchanged ideas as well as goods; empire builders brought large territories under the control of one ruler.*) **L2**

CONDENSE

Use Chapter Digest Audiocassettes to introduce chapters that students have not studied in Unit 1. Spanish Chapter Digest Audiocassettes are also available.

Discuss Have students read the **Unit Digest** and discuss the **Surveying Chapter** questions. **L1**

RETEACH

Time Line Have students summarize Unit 1 by creating a time line that shows at least 10 key events and developments from 10,000 B.C. to 1000 B.C.

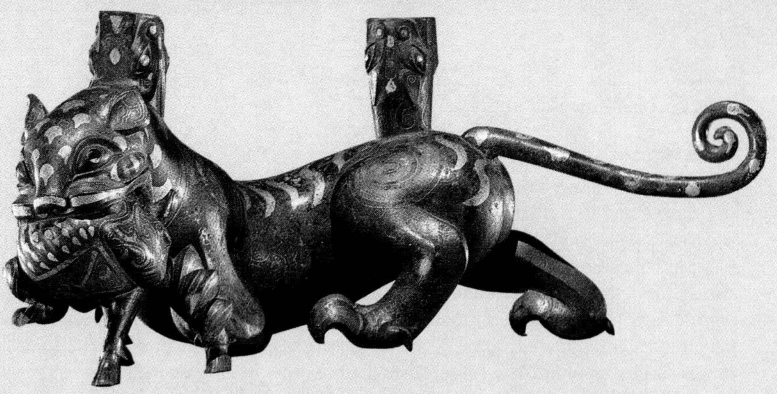

Visualizing History **Shang ritual vessel in the form of a tiger protecting a man.** *In what river valley did the Shang dynasty flourish?*

their civilization was evident in the governments of the Sumerian city-states and their laws and religion. The innovative Sumerians created cuneiform, perhaps the world's oldest writing system, and they also invented the wheel. The prosperous Sumerian city-states eventually fell to empire builders, first the Akkadians and later the Babylonians.

South and East Asian Civilizations

At about the same time as the rise of empires in Mesopotamia, a third river valley civilization to the east, the Harappans, reached its peak. Adapting to the unique seasonal winds and flood patterns of their environment, the people of the South Asian subcontinent prospered in the Indus River valley. They produced a surplus of food and various goods, which they traded with the people of Mesopotamia, among others. The pictograms on the seals used to identify merchandise from the Indus Valley suggest that the Harappan people also exchanged ideas with their trading partners. Although the remains of Harappan cities such as Mohenjo-Daro indicate that the people of the Indus Valley were expert urban planners, why the cities were destroyed and what caused their civilization to collapse remains a mystery.

The fourth river valley civilization, which began in ancient China, has continued to the present day. Isolated from other cultures for many centuries by formidable landforms, the Chinese formed one culture and a strong sense of national identity. From Neolithic times, people settled and flourished in the Huang He valley. Written records and other finds indicate that under the Shang dynasty, which controlled the river valley from about 1700 B.C. to 1000 B.C., the Chinese built their first cities, created a complex writing system, and perfected their skill in casting bronze. The replacement of the Shang dynasty by the Zhou dynasty was just one of many transitions between the dynasties that successively ruled China.

SURVEYING CHAPTER 2

1. **Relating to the Environment** How did the ancient Egyptians and Sumerians meet the challenges of their river environments?
2. **Defending a Point of View** Do you think cultural diffusion benefits or hinders the growth of a civilization? Explain your reasoning, supporting your point of view by citing examples from ancient Egypt and Mesopotamia.

Chapter 3
Kingdoms and Empires in the Middle East

The Fertile Crescent, where civilization began, continued to be home for diverse peoples after the earliest river valley civilizations fell. Many people in the region were active in trade and thus promoted cultural diffusion and also made lasting cultural and economic contributions to later civilizations.

Traders and Herders

Prominent among the trading peoples of the Middle East were the Phoenicians. They not only navigated the Mediterranean Sea and beyond with ease, controlling shipping and trade and founding colonies, but created an alphabet that was a major breakthrough in writing and the model for later alphabets. Among the other trading peoples in the region, the Aramaeans introduced the Aramaic language into the everyday life of many other peoples, and the Lydians left a lasting mark on the economies of other civilizations by using coins as a medium of exchange.

The Israelites, a nomadic people in this region, made lasting cultural contributions. Foremost among these was monotheism—the belief in one

ANSWERS TO SURVEYING THE CHAPTER

CHAPTER 2 ANSWERS

1. To control the Nile's annual flooding, Egyptians built canals to carry floodwaters to basins. Later they built dams and reservoirs to irrigate their farmlands. In Mesopotamia, which experienced droughts during summer months, the Sumerians cooperated to build dams and canals to irrigate their fields.
2. Benefits: Egyptian and Mesopotamian civilizations were enriched by cultural diffusion, and the interchange of ideas about technology and government advanced the development of civilization. Hindrances: Cultural diffusion was often accompanied by war or conflict.

Visualizing History **Ruins of ancient Babylon, capital of the Chaldeans.** *How long did the Chaldean Empire last before being overthrown by the Persians?*

all-powerful God—an idea that formed the basis of Judaism, Christianity, and Islam. During their long history, the Israelites several times came into conflict with neighboring peoples. Although they were enslaved and exiled, they kept close ties to their homeland.

Empire Builders

Many peoples in the Fertile Crescent suffered as warlike empires successively dominated the region and neighboring regions as well.

In spite of their emphasis on war, these empires also advanced trade, created new methods of government, and carried out building projects. The Hittites were the first of these aggressors, coming to Asia Minor from Europe or central Asia. With many advantages in military tactics, the Hittites established an empire spanning Asia Minor, Syria, and part of Mesopotamia.

The Assyrians, a Mesopotamian people, were the next conquerors in the Middle East. They too had great expertise on the battlefield, and cruelly treated the peoples they conquered. They controlled an empire stretching from the Persian Gulf to Egypt and into Asia Minor.

The well-organized and extensive Assyrian Empire fell to the Chaldeans (descendants of the Babylonians). The Chaldeans built their capital, Babylon, into one of the largest, most stunning cities of the ancient world. In less than 100 years, however, the Chaldean Empire was in turn overthrown by the Persians.

The Persians, who originated in central Asia and settled in the area of present-day Iran, built an empire that was second to none, stretching from the Nile River to the Indus River. The Persians surpassed their predecessors in administering a vast area and in tolerating the languages, religions, and customs of subject peoples. Communication and cooperation characterized the Persian approach to ruling an empire. The teachings of the Persian prophet Zoroaster may have later influenced certain beliefs of the religions of Judaism, Christianity, and Islam.

SURVEYING CHAPTER 3

1. **Analyzing Information** How did the Hittites, Assyrians, Chaldeans, and Persians acquire their empires?
2. **Making Comparisons** Compare and contrast the empires that came to dominate the Fertile Crescent and neighboring regions, from the Akkadians to the Persians.

Unit 1 Digest

Reteaching Activities 1, 2, 3

Chapter Digests Audiocassettes, Chapters 1, 2, 3

Visualizing History Whereas the Assyrians had used stone slabs cut from rock for their buildings, the Chaldeans used baked brick, which allowed them to create more complicated shapes and ornate surfaces.
Answer to Caption: *fewer than 100 years (from 612 B.C. to 539 B.C.)*

ABCNEWS INTERACTIVE™

VIDEODISC
Turning Points in World History

Side One
Chapter 3

Title: *The Rise of Cities*
Subject: The inventions of the Sumerians in Mesopotamia enabled people to live together in communities for the first time.
Ask: What did the Sumerians use to help them draw maps? *(They studied the stars.)*

ANSWERS TO SURVEYING THE CHAPTER

CHAPTER 3 ANSWERS

1. The Hittites first conquered Asia Minor, built a well-organized kingdom and a powerful army, then pushed east to take Syria and Mesopotamia. The Assyrians had long fought against invaders in northern Mesopotamia and by 900 B.C. had an army able to subdue an empire stretching from the Persian Gulf to Asia Minor. The Chaldeans allied with the Medes to bring down the Assyrian Empire. Under Cyrus, the Persians developed a powerful army and spread from Iran into neighboring regions.
2. Students should include the Akkadians, Babylonians, Hittites, Assyrians, Chaldeans, and Persians. Although the Chaldeans were descended from the Babylonians, foreign empire builders moved into the Fertile Crescent . Students may compare the military efficacy of the Hittites with the Assyrians and contrast how the Assyrians and Persians treated their subjects.

Introducing Unit 2

0:00 OUT OF TIME?

If time does not permit teaching each chapter in Unit 2, you may use the Unit Digest beginning on page 236, in conjunction with the Unit Digest Transparencies and Chapter Digest Audiocassettes with accompanying activities and tests.

Introducing the Unit

Unit 2 traces the growth of Hellenic civilization in Greece, the rise of Rome and of Christianity and their legacy to the West, and the development of civilizations in Africa, India, and China.

Unit Objectives

After reading Unit 2, students will be able to:

1. describe the development of the civilization of Greece.
2. give examples of the achievements of the ancient Greeks and tell how these were spread by Alexander.
3. explain the rise and decline of Rome and the spread of Roman culture, including Christianity, throughout Europe.
4. trace the rise of wealthy and powerful kingdoms in Africa.
5. summarize the development of Indian civilization and the importance of Hinduism and Buddhism.
6. discuss the achievements of Chinese civilization and the meaning of Confucianism and Daoism.

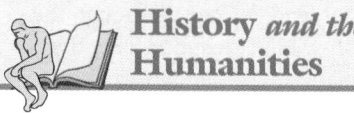

History *and the* Humanities

- Focus on World Art Prints 6, 8, 9, 12
- World History and Art Transparencies 5-11

Unit 2 **2000 B.C.–A.D. 500**

Flowering of Civilizations

Chapter 4 The Rise of Ancient Greece
Chapter 5 The Height of Greek Civilization
Chapter 6 Ancient Rome and Early Christianity
Chapter 7 Flowering of African Civilizations
Chapter 8 India's Great Civilization
Chapter 9 China's Flourishing Civilization

Then & Now *As people developed agricultural technology, nomadic life gave way to living in communities. Emerging cities became centers of trade and commerce, characterized by highly organized social structures and governments. Commerce brought wealth that allowed more people time for leisure and study. Ancient civilizations contributed much that remains in the modern world. China developed a civil service system based on merit. The city of Alexandria in Egypt had a great library. The Greeks refined geometry to calculate the size of the earth. Architecture, theater, and education all have their roots in ancient civilizations.*

A Global Chronology

2000 B.C. — 1500 B.C. — 1000 B.C.

Political
- c. 1500 B.C. Aryans cross the Hindu Kush into South Asia.

Scientific
- c. 1700 B.C. Babylonian Empire adopts Sumerian calendar.

Social/Cultural
- c. 1200 B.C. Vedic Age begins in India.

100

Then & Now **Classical Legacy** The influence of ancient civilizations, particularly the classical civilizations of Greece and Rome, is visible in many aspects of modern American society. Examples include the use of Latin mottoes such as *E pluribus unum* inscribed on our currency, the neoclassical architecture of many public buildings, especially in Washington, D.C., and in state capitals, and even our form of government, which adopted the concepts of the senate and veto from the Roman Republic.

Have students brainstorm a list of things today that reflect the influence of ancient civilizations, prompting them from the examples above as necessary. Ask students why they think classical civilizations, especially Rome, have influenced the United States. Why was neoclassical

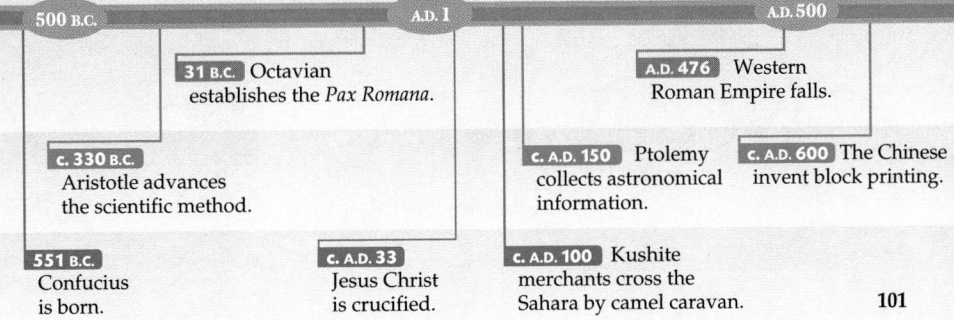

The gold mask of King Agamemnon found in the royal grave circle at Mycenae, National Archaeological Museum, Athens, Greece

Portfolio Project

The Greeks refined the study of philosophy—the seeking of wisdom. They were interested in the big questions such as: What is truth? What is an ideal society? Choose a topic or an issue that you have thought deeply about and write a two-page essay about what you believe. Remember to organize your thoughts into an outline before writing the first draft.

500 B.C. — A.D. 1 — A.D. 500

- **551 B.C.** Confucius is born.
- **c. 330 B.C.** Aristotle advances the scientific method.
- **31 B.C.** Octavian establishes the *Pax Romana*.
- **c. A.D. 33** Jesus Christ is crucified.
- **c. A.D. 100** Kushite merchants cross the Sahara by camel caravan.
- **c. A.D. 150** Ptolemy collects astronomical information.
- **A.D. 476** Western Roman Empire falls.
- **c. A.D. 600** The Chinese invent block printing.

101

architecture a popular style for public buildings? *(reflects power and solemnity, recalls the golden age of the Roman Republic)* Why was Latin often used for inscriptions and mottoes? *(Latin was the language of the learned for many centuries.)* Why do certain features of the federal and state governments stem from Roman institutions? *(Classical republican ideas influenced the Founders of the United States.)*

Introducing Unit 2

ABC NEWS INTERACTIVE™

VIDEODISC
Turning Points in World History

Side One, Chapter 5

Title: *Democracy in Greece*
Subject: Athenian democracy laid the foundation for the concept of democratic government in which the majority rules, but the minority still has rights.
Ask: What are the basic ideals behind democracy? *(individual equality and freedom)*

Visualizing History According to Greek myth, Agamemnon was the brother of Menelaus, whose wife, Helen, was abducted by Paris. Agamemnon led the Mycenaean army that lay siege to Troy for 10 years. After the war, Agamemnon was murdered by his wife, Clytemnestra. The murder and its consequences are related by Aeschylus in the three-play cycle known as the *Oresteia*. What might be a prominent theme in this cycle of plays? *(revenge)*

Portfolio Project

Have students tell you what topic or issue they have chosen before they begin writing. Ask students to explain in the essay what their point of view is based on—moral or religious principles, values they learned from their families, or their own observations of the world. This activity may be an appropriate method of authentic assessment.

The Spread of Ideas

TEACH

Introduction

This feature focuses on the influence of Roman law and government on the development of legal and political systems in the West. Although the Greeks pioneered the idea of democratic government, it was Roman law, spread across Europe by Roman armies, that shaped the legal systems of most of the West.

Who?What?Where?When?

Early Roman law was severe, especially toward families. Fathers had nearly absolute control over their wives and children. A father even had the right to execute his child. All property belonged to the father, who could divorce his wife at will. By the classical period, these laws had all been moderated.

Background Notes

Linking Past and Present

Roman history was a common reference point for educated American colonists. At the Constitutional Convention of 1787, delegates cited the fall of the Roman Republic as proof that a government allowing too much direct participation could not survive. Alexander Hamilton reminded delegates that when the Roman tribunes "levelled the boundary between the *patricians and plebeians*," disaster followed. The Constitution's limits on direct democracy reflect the fears of the founders that, as in Rome, too much democracy would destroy the new nation.

The Spread of Ideas

Systems of Law

Law is a code of conduct and rights accepted or formally recognized by a society. Law provides social control, order, and justice. It enables people to know their rights and responsibilities. Law also forms the cornerstone of constitutional government. A constitutional government based upon law helps ensure justice, or the fair treatment of all citizens. "Where law ends, tyranny begins," said William Pitt, an English leader, in A.D. 1770.

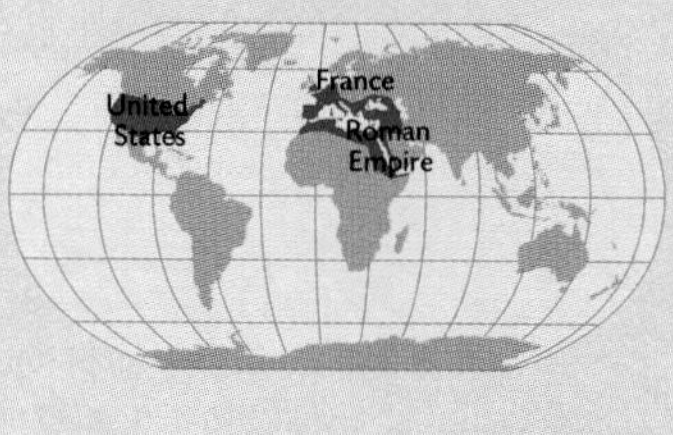

Roman Empire

Laying the Foundation

Sometime around 451-450 B.C., a group of judges posted 12 tablets in Rome's main forum, or marketplace. According to legend, the common people of Rome had demanded that the laws be written down for all to see. People would then know their rights. The tablets listed the unwritten laws that guided judges. They also included penalties imposed on people who broke the law.

Although a group of invaders smashed the so-called Twelve Tables in 390 B.C., the basic code of law remained in effect for almost 1,000 years. When Roman armies marched out to conquer a huge empire, they carried their belief in law with them. By A.D. 120 Roman law governed the entire Mediterranean world and much of western Europe.

In theory, Roman law applied to all people, regardless of wealth or power. Not everyone honored Roman legal ideals. Nonetheless, the Romans developed an important democratic principle. They believed people should be ruled by law rather than by the whims of leaders. In A.D. 533-534 the Byzantine emperor Justinian consolidated all Roman law into a single written code. The Justinian Code became the foundation of the present civil law system. Civil law and common law, which originated in England, are two of the major legal systems in the world today.

Cicero

COOPERATIVE LEARNING ACTIVITY

Writing a Constitution Ask students to imagine what school would be like if it had no rules. Ask students why rules are important for a nation or an organization. Then have students brainstorm a list of the most important rules that govern their behavior at school. Based on the list, have groups of students write a "Constitution" that embodies the school's "fundamental principles" and the goals these laws seek to accomplish. **L1**

Independence Hall, Philadelphia

The United States
A Model for Constitutional Government

The Founders of the United States knew about and admired the Romans. They understood what the Roman orator Cicero meant when he spoke of the need to limit the power of government. When it came time to draw up a plan of government, they wrote a constitution that balanced the powers of government among three branches.

To ensure that rulers did not place themselves above the law, the Framers included a provision that made the Constitution "the supreme law of the land." The Framers used the example of Rome to defend the Constitution. "The Roman republic attained … the utmost height of human greatness," declared Alexander Hamilton. He then explained how government under the Constitution would do the same.

A second system of legal justice, common law, evolved in England. Trial by jury, the right to petition the government, and many other rules governing trials originated in this system. Common law is not a written code but rather is based on written judicial decisions. Common law was established in the American colonies and continued to develop when the colonies became states of the United States.

France
Unifying the Law

In A.D. 1799 a French general named Napoleon Bonaparte set out to build an empire even larger than Rome's. By A.D. 1802 he had conquered much of Europe. Napoleon then tried to extend his reach into the Americas.

In seeking to rule this empire, Napoleon followed the Roman example. He took part in a commission to draw up a uniform code of laws. This code, known as the Napoleonic Code, was completed in A.D. 1807.

Although Napoleon ruled as emperor, the code named in his honor reaffirmed the principle that the same laws should be used to govern all people. In drafting these laws, Napoleon drew upon many of the legal precedents first introduced by the Romans. Under Napoleon, this code became applied in lands as far-flung as present-day Belgium, Quebec, Spain, and some Latin American nations.

Assemblée Nationale, Paris

LINKING THE IDEAS

1. What important democratic principle did the Romans develop?

Critical Thinking

2. How did the United States hope to ensure that rulers would not place themselves above the law?

The Spread of Ideas

Geography

Movement Have students look at the small map on this page and identify the areas that are highlighted. *(Roman Empire, France, U.S.)* How did Roman law spread through Europe? *(Roman armies carried the law with them to conquered regions.)* How did the influence of Roman law and government cross the Atlantic to the United States? *(the Founders knew about and admired the Roman Republic)*

Cultural Diffusion

Roman Influence The influence of Roman law is evident today in American law schools and courthouses. The familiar vocabulary of the legal world, including *court*, *judge*, *jury*, *crime*, *verdict*, and *punish*, are all from Latin, the language of Rome. Lawyers often use terms taken directly from Latin, such as *stare decisis*, which means to follow precedent.

Despite the influence of Roman law, the U.S. legal system is based largely on the English common law tradition. The previous decisions of judges, together known as "case law," rather than legislative enactments or administrative codes, guide the decisions of the courts.

ANSWERS TO LINKING THE IDEAS

1. that people should be ruled by law rather than by the whims of rulers
2. They made the Constitution the supreme law of the land.

Unit 2 *Flowering of Civilizations* 103

The Rise of Ancient Greece

CHAPTER RESOURCES

	Reproducible Resources	Multimedia Resources
Chapter Opener	Chapter Themes: Graphic Organizer 4 Historical Significance Chapter Activity 4	MindJogger Videoquiz
Chapter Enrichment	Vocabulary Activity 4* Time Line Activity 4 Mapping History Activity 4 History Simulation 4 Geography and History Activity 4 Source Reading 4 People in World History Profiles 5, 6 World Art and Music Activity 4 Enrichment Activity 4 Critical Thinking Activity 4 Skill Reinforcement Activity 4 Performance Assessment Activity 4	Focus on World Art Print 6, Early Cycladic II. *Cycladic Harpist* NGS Ancient Civilizations Poster Set: *Ancient Greece* World History and Art Transparency 5, *Amphora from Vulci* Mapping History Overlay Transparency 4, *Ancient Greece* Chapter Transparency 4 NGS PicturePack Transparency Set: *Ancient Greece* Vocabulary PuzzleMaker Software NGS PictureShow CD-ROM: *Greece and Rome* Turning Points in World History: *Democracy in Greece*
Chapter Review/Reteaching	Reteaching Activity 4 Skill Reinforcement Activity 4 Spanish Chapter Summary 4	Chapter 4 Digest Audiocassette, Activity, Test* Vocabulary PuzzleMaker Software Student Self-Test and Review Software MindJogger Videoquiz
Chapter Evaluation/Testing	Performance Assessment Activity 4 Chapter 4 Test, Forms A and B	Testmaker

* *Also available in Spanish*

0:00 OUT OF TIME? Assign the Chapter 4 summary in the Unit 2 Digest on pages 236–239, and the Chapter 4 Audiocassettes.

Block Schedule

Block scheduling differs from traditional class scheduling in the amount of time allotted to each period. The extended time frame provided by block scheduling affords you the opportunity to implement a greater number of research-oriented and activity-intense projects to motivate and involve your students. Activities that are particularly suited to use within the block scheduling framework are identified throughout this chapter by the following designation.

KEY TO ABILITY LEVELS

Teaching strategies have been coded for varying learning styles and abilities.

- L1 **BASIC** activities for all students
- L2 **AVERAGE** activities for average to above-average students
- L3 **CHALLENGING** activities for above-average students
- LEP **LIMITED ENGLISH PROFICIENCY** activities

A complete, 1-page lesson plan is provided for each section in the *Reproducible Lesson Plans* booklet.

SECTION RESOURCES

Daily Objectives	Reproducible Resources	Multimedia Resources
Section 1 **Beginnings** Describe where and how the early civilizations of Greece developed.	Reproducible Lesson Plan 4-1 Vocabulary Activity 4* Guided Reading Activity 4-1* Time Line Activity 4 Section Quiz 4-1*	Focus on World Art Transparency 6, Early Cycladic II. *Cycladic Harpist* Section Focus Transparency 4-1 Mapping History Overlay Transparency 4, *Ancient Greece* Student Self-Test and Review Software Testmaker
Section 2 **The Polis** Explain how economic prosperity brought significant political and social changes to the Greek city-states.	Reproducible Lesson Plan 4-2 Guided Reading Activity 4-2* Mapping History Activity 4 Geography and History Activity 4 Section Quiz 4-2*	Section Focus Transparency 4-2 Chapter Transparency 4 Vocabulary PuzzleMaker Software Student Self-Test and Review Software Testmaker
Section 3 **Rivals** Differentiate between the values represented by Sparta and those represented by Athens.	Reproducible Lesson Plan 4-3 Vocabulary Activity 4* Guided Reading Activity 4-3* Source Reading 4 Section Quiz 4-3*	NGS Ancient Civilizations Poster Set: *Ancient Greece* Section Focus Transparency 4-3 World History and Art Transparency 5, *Amphora from Vulci* Student Self-Test and Review Software Testmaker NGS PictureShow CD-ROM: *Greece and Rome* Turning Points in World History: *Democracy in Greece*
Section 4 **War, Glory, and Decline** Discuss how the Persian and Peloponnesian Wars affected democracy in Greek city-states.	Reproducible Lesson Plan 4-4 Vocabulary Activity 4* Guided Reading Activity 4-4* Reteaching Activity 4 Enrichment Activity 4 Section Quiz 4-4* Performance Assessment Activity 4 Spanish Chapter Summary 4	Section Focus Transparency 4-4 Mapping History Overlay Transparency 4, *Ancient Greece* Student Self-Test and Review Software Testmaker

* *Also available in Spanish*

Chapter Activities

Performance Assessment Activity

Composing a Political Speech Have students take the roles of candidates running for a political office. They are interested in transforming American democracy so that it resembles the original Athenian state. Have them prepare and present a speech using information from the chapter—as well as problems from current events—to make connections between past theories and modern life. While students are presenting their speeches, their classmates should take the roles of voters who will fill out an "exit poll" regarding the nature of the speeches.

Possible Rubric Features

Persuasiveness, content information, clarity, relevance of current events, appropriateness to audience

- For an additional activity, refer to Activity 4 in the *Performance Assessment Strategies and Activities* booklet.

Activity

From the Classroom of...

Ray Barron
Heritage High School
Littleton, CO

Comparing Pericles' *Funeral Oration* and Lincoln's *Gettysburg Address*

The purpose of this activity is to enable students to see the similarities among all civil wars and realize that there are connections between the American Civil War and that of the ancient Greeks.

Have students read both Pericles' *Funeral Oration* and Abraham Lincoln's *Gettysburg Address*. As they read each, have them list the qualities of individuals, government, and war that are mentioned. Next have them list those qualities of individuals, government, and war which seem to be mentioned in both orations. A Venn diagram is a helpful graphic organizer for this part of the activity. After they have done this, organize students into small groups and have each group reach a consensus as to which qualities are present in both orations and why this is so.

Have students write a paragraph explaining why these two speeches were made to the people of Greece and the United States, respectively, and summarize what we can learn about civil war from the speeches.

MULTIPLE LEARNING STYLES

Verbal/Linguistic

Have students write their own "Odyssey" in three or more pages, using prose or poetry. They should imagine a soldier traveling home from the Trojan War, and describe a few of his adventures.

Logical/Mathematical

Have students compute the distances, in miles and kilometers, between each of the Greek mainland cities shown on the map on page 107 and the following: Knossos, Phaestus, Troy.

Visual/Spatial

Have students prepare a class book about Minoan and Mycenaean culture, with each student contributing a page on some aspect of either culture: art, artifacts, clothing, food, transportation, and so on. Have each student sketch the chosen object.

Interpersonal

Have students research the prosecution against Aspasia. Then have them stage a hearing at which charges are brought against her, and she is successfully defended by Pericles.

Additional Resources

TEACHER'S CORNER

NATIONAL GEOGRAPHIC SOCIETY

INDEX TO NATIONAL GEOGRAPHIC MAGAZINE

The following articles may be used for research relating to this chapter:

- "Oldest Known Shipwreck Reveals Splendors of the Bronze Age," by George F. Bass, December 1987.
- "The Quest for Ulysses," by Tim Severin, August 1986.
- "Drama of Death in a Minoan Temple," by Yannis Sakellarakis and Efi Sapouna-Sakellaraki, February 1981.

NATIONAL GEOGRAPHIC SOCIETY PRODUCTS AVAILABLE FROM GLENCOE

To order the following products for use with this chapter, contact your local Glencoe sales representative or call Glencoe at 1-800-368-7344:

NGS PICTURESHOW CD-ROM
- Greece and Rome

NGS PICTUREPACK TRANSPARENCY SET
- Ancient Greece

ANCIENT CIVILIZATIONS POSTER SET
- Ancient Greece

ADDITIONAL NATIONAL GEOGRAPHIC SOCIETY PRODUCTS

To order the following products for use with this chapter, call National Geographic Society at 1-800-368-2728:

- *Ancient Civilizations*, "Greece." (Filmstrip)

Bibliography

Literature About the Period

Renault, Mary. ***The King Must Die.*** New York: Random House, 1988. Retells the legend of Theseus's struggle with the Minotaur.

Readings for the Student

Hamilton, Edith. ***The Greek Way.*** New York: Norton, 1983. The Greek spirit and mind as seen by great writers.

Readings for the Teacher

Grant, Michael. ***The Rise of the Greeks.*** New York: Scribner's, 1988. An examination of Greek civilization from the collapse of Mycenae to the Peloponnesian War.

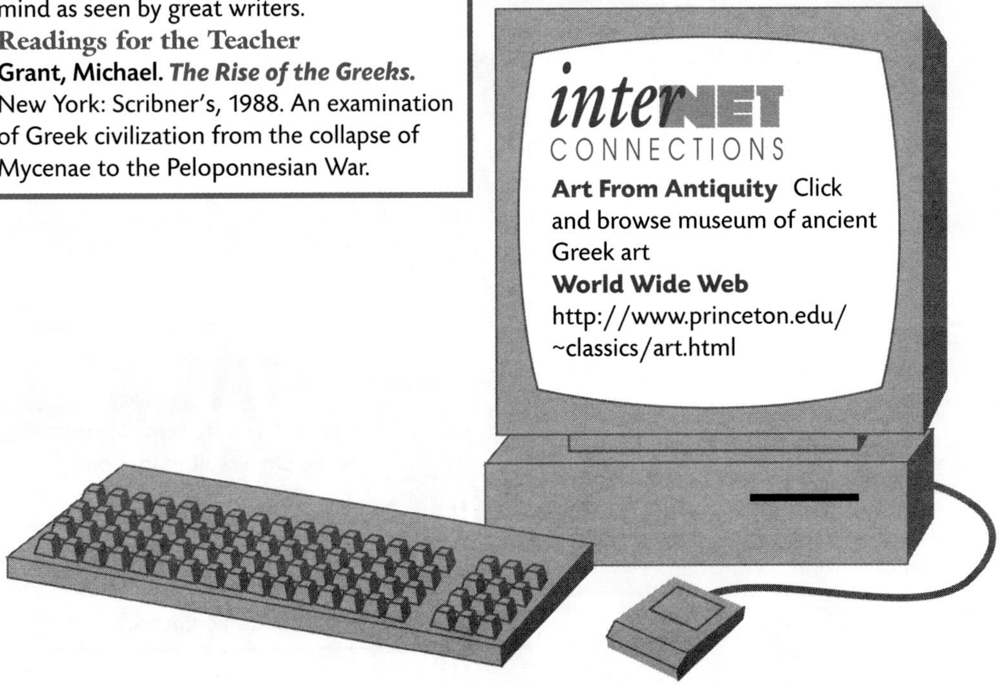
interNET
CONNECTIONS
Art From Antiquity Click and browse museum of ancient Greek art
World Wide Web
http://www.princeton.edu/~classics/art.html

Introducing Chapter 4

CHAPTER THEMES

Chapter Themes are listed by section on this chapter opening page of the Student Edition. A corresponding theme-based activity is available under "TEACH," and a theme-based question is asked in the Section and Chapter Reviews.

The Storyteller

Historical Setting The first European civilization, the Minoan, arose on the island of Crete, achieving a splendor comparable to the contemporary civilizations of Egypt and Mesopotamia. According to some ancient Greek legends, Zeus himself was born on Crete, died on the island, and was buried there.

Minoan Crete strongly influenced the early Greeks of the mainland and the classical culture that was to arise there.

Bulls were important in Minoan religion. Altars and shrine roofs were often surmounted by hornlike shapes, probably representing sacred bulls.

Historical Significance

Answers: *Governments of ancient Greece included kingdoms, aristocracies, tyrannies, oligarchies, and democracies. Most societies were based on trade and commerce, although Sparta emphasized militarism.*

The most important Greek political idea to influence later Western civilization was citizen participation in government.

Chapter 4

2000–350 B.C.

The Rise of Ancient Greece

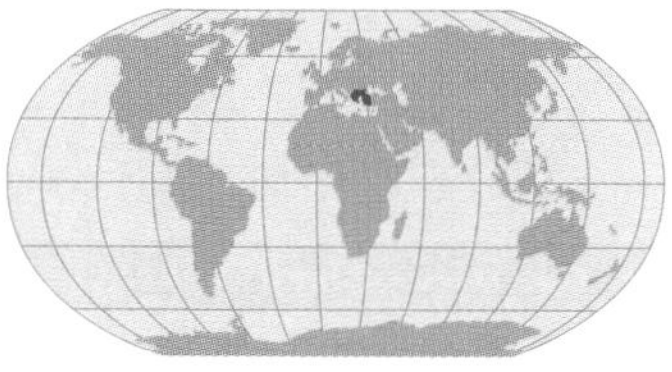

Chapter Themes

- **Relation to Environment** Closeness to the sea helps make the early Greeks seafarers. *Section 1*
- **Movement** The Greeks found colonies throughout the area of the Mediterranean and Black Seas. *Section 2*
- **Regionalism** Two leading Greek city-states—Athens and Sparta—differ greatly from each other in their values, cultures, and achievements. *Section 3*
- **Conflict** Greek city-states together fight the Persians; then the city-states, led by rivals Athens and Sparta, fight each other. *Section 4*

The Storyteller

An eager crowd gathered in the sun-drenched sports arena just outside King Minos's palace at Knossos on the Aegean island of Crete. According to legend, Minos ruled over the Minoan civilization in the 2000s B.C. *The Minoans' favorite event—bull leaping—was about to begin. The crowd gasped as a raging bull, representing the earthquakes that shook Crete, charged a young male gymnast who stood motionless. Just before the collision, the gymnast grabbed the bull's horns and somersaulted onto the bull's back. Then his body arched into the air, and he completed a back flip, landing in the arms of his female partner waiting nearby. The crowd cheered at the end of this spectacle, part sport and part religious ritual. By leaping over the bull, the gymnast had shown that no matter how much the earth trembled, the Minoans would stay on Crete.*

Historical Significance

What kinds of governments and societies developed in ancient Greece? How have Greek political ideas shaped the development of Western civilization?

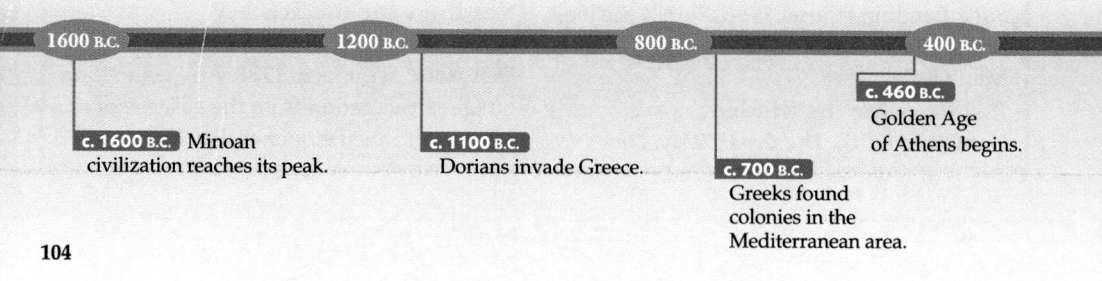

1600 B.C. — 1200 B.C. — 800 B.C. — 400 B.C.

- **c. 1600 B.C.** Minoan civilization reaches its peak.
- **c. 1100 B.C.** Dorians invade Greece.
- **c. 700 B.C.** Greeks found colonies in the Mediterranean area.
- **c. 460 B.C.** Golden Age of Athens begins.

104

GEOGRAPHY CONNECTION

Place Have students locate the eastern Mediterranean region in the Atlas of their texts. On a wall map, point out the location of the Balkan Peninsula, the Aegean Sea, Asia Minor, and Crete while students follow along on their maps. How did geography affect the life of the ancient Greeks? *(Mountains protected the people from foreign attack, but limited communication within the region. Numerous harbors and the proximity of the sea led many people to take up fishing, trading, and piracy. Because of the mild climate, many activities were carried on outdoors.)*

History & Art Minoan wall painting of a fleet of ships entering port. National Archaeological Museum, Athens, Greece

Your History Journal

Athens laid the foundation for the Western concept of democratic government. After reading about Athenian democracy, write an essay entitled "What Democracy Means to Me."

EXTRA CREDIT PROJECT

Report The Greek alphabet and the Greek language played an important role in the development of our own alphabet and language. Have students research and report to the class on some aspect of one of these topics. For example, one student might wish to report on Greek words in government *(aristocracy, democracy, politics)*, another on Greek words in science *(atom, botany, zoology)*, a third on Greek words in the arts *(architecture, music, poetry)*. Standard reference works, such as encyclopedias, should provide adequate information.

Introducing Chapter 4

History & Art

This painting was created by the Minoans, the people of the ancient Aegean island of Crete. Much of what we know about this civilization comes from its art works; although the Minoans had a form of writing, it has not been deciphered. What can you guess about Minoan culture from looking at the painting? *(The Minoans were skilled at constructing buildings and ships; the sea was important to them; they had a division of labor and were skilled artists.)*

Performance Assessment

Refer to the activity on page 104C of the Planning Guide.

For an additional activity, refer to Activity 4 in the *Performance Assessment Strategies and Activities* booklet.

Using Your History Journal

Students may want to refer to this essay as they read about later societies, especially those that were not democratic.

GLENCOE TECHNOLOGY

VIDEODISC

Use MindJogger to preview chapter content.

MindJogger Videoquiz

Chapter 4
Disc 1 Side A

Also available in VHS.

Chapter 4 Section 1

SECTION THEME

▶ **Relation to Environment** Closeness to the sea helps make the early Greeks seafarers.

Find Out

Answer: *They developed on the Greek mainland and on nearby islands; among factors influencing their development were a favorable climate, trade networks, and the movement and interaction of different peoples.*

FOCUS

Section Objective

Describe where and how the early civilizations of Greece developed.

BELLRINGER Motivational Activity

Before taking roll at the beginning of the class period, project Section Focus Transparency 4-1 and have students answer the activity questions. Discuss students' responses.

This activity is also available as a blackline master.

Vocabulary Pre-check

Use Vocabulary Activity 4 to introduce vocabulary terms. **L1 LEP**

2000 B.C. — 1500 B.C. — 1000 B.C. — 500 B.C.

c. 2000 B.C. Mycenaean civilization begins.

c. 1450 B.C. Mycenaeans control the Aegean area.

c. 750 B.C. Homer composes epics.

Section 1

Beginnings

Setting the Scene

▶ **Terms to Define**
labyrinth, bard

▶ **People to Meet**
Sir Arthur Evans, the Minoans, the Mycenaeans, Homer, Heinrich Schliemann

▶ **Places to Locate**
Crete, Mycenae

Find Out Where and how did the early civilizations of Greece develop?

The Storyteller

The hero Sarpedon was a son of Zeus, but destined to die in the Trojan War. He held before him the perfect circle of his shield, a lovely thing of beaten bronze, which the bronze-smith had hammered out for him. On its inward side were stitched ox-hides in close folds with golden staples all around the circle.... And now Sarpedon spoke to Glaukos, son of Hippolochos: "Glaukos, why are we honored before others with the best seats, choice cuts of meat, brimming wine cups, and the best plots of land? Because we stand in the front line of blazing battle. Friend, if we could escape, and live forever ageless and immortal, I would not go on fighting, or encourage you to fight. But now, since the spirits of death stand close by us, let us go win glory for ourselves, or yield it to others."

—adapted from *The Iliad of Homer*, translated by Richmond Lattimore, 1951

Entrance to the ancient silver mines at Siphnos, Greece

The ancient Greeks became the people who set their stamp on the Mediterranean region and who also contributed greatly to the way we live today. Every time you go to the theater or watch the Olympic Games on television, you enjoy an activity that has its roots in ancient Greece. Modern public buildings often reflect Greek architectural styles. Above all, the ancient Greeks developed the Western concept of democracy.

The Aegean Area

Ancient Greece included the southern part of Europe's Balkan Peninsula and a group of small, rocky islands, most of which dot the Aegean (ih •JEE•uhn) Sea near Asia Minor. Low-lying, rugged mountains make up about three-fourths of the Greek mainland. Between the mountain ranges and along the coast lie fertile plains suitable for farming. Short, swift rivers flow from the interior to the sea, and the long, indented coastline provides many fine harbors. The climate is mild, with rainy winters. Afternoon breezes carrying cooler air from the sea offset the hot, dry summers.

The mountains both protected and isolated Greeks on the mainland. Besides making attacks by foreigners difficult, the mountains limited travel and communication between communities. The Greek people, therefore, never united under one government, although they spoke one language and practiced the same religion.

Because of the numerous harbors and since no place in Greece is more than 50 miles (80 km) from the coast, many Greeks turned to the sea to earn their living. They became fishers, traders, and even pirates.

In addition, the mild climate allowed the ancient Greeks to spend much of their time outdoors. People assembled for meetings in the public square, teachers met their students in public gardens, and actors performed plays in open-air theaters.

SECTION RESOURCES

Reproducible Masters
- Reproducible Lesson Plan 4-1
- Vocabulary Activity 4
- Guided Reading Activity 4-1
- Time Line Activity 4
- Section Quiz 4-1

Transparencies
- Section Focus Transparency 4-1
- Mapping History Overlay Transparency 4

Multimedia
- Focus on World Art Print 6
- Student Self-Test and Review Software
- Testmaker

Visualizing History **Chalices such as these are evidence that Mycenaean kings were rich and powerful.**
What evidence suggests that these kings were meticulous about collecting taxes?

Aegean Civilizations

Greek myths referred to an early civilization on the island of **Crete**, southeast of the Greek mainland, but for a long time historians disputed this claim. Then, about A.D. 1900, British archaeologist **Sir Arthur Evans** unearthed remains of the Minoan civilization, which flourished from about 2500 B.C. to 1450 B.C.

The Minoans

At Knossos (NAH•suhs) on Crete, Evans uncovered the palace of legendary King Minos. Throughout the palace, passageways twist and turn in all directions to form a labyrinth, or maze. Brightly colored murals that decorate palace walls show that **the Minoans**—both men and women—curled their hair, bedecked themselves with gold jewelry, and set off their narrow waists with wide metal belts. The murals also show that they were fond of dancing and sporting events, such as boxing matches.

Minoan women apparently enjoyed a higher status than women in other early civilizations. For example, Minoan religion had more goddesses than gods. The chief deity of Crete was the Great Goddess, or Earth Mother, whom the Minoans believed caused the birth and growth of all living things.

The Minoans earned their living from sea trade. Crete's oak and cedar forests provided wood for ships. In addition, the island's location enabled Minoan traders to reach Egypt and Mesopotamia. By 2000 B.C., Minoan fleets dominated the eastern Mediterranean, carrying goods and keeping the seas free from pirates. The ships also guarded Crete against outside attack, which explains why the Minoans did not build walls around their cities.

Minoan civilization reached its peak around 1600 B.C. About 250 years later it collapsed. Some historians think its cities were destroyed by huge tidal waves resulting from an undersea earthquake. Others think that a people from the Greek mainland, **the Mycenaeans** (MY•suh•NEE•uhnz), succeeded in invading Crete.

The Mycenaeans

The Mycenaeans originated among the Indo-European peoples of central Asia. About 2000 B.C., as a result of the rapid growth of their population, the Mycenaeans began moving out from their homeland. Upon entering the Balkan Peninsula, they gradually intermarried with the local people——known as Hellenes (HEH•leenz)—and set up a group of kingdoms.

Each Mycenaean kingdom centered around a hilltop on which was built a royal fortress. Stone walls circled the fortress, providing a shelter for the people in time of danger. Nobles lived on their estates outside the walls. They would turn out in armor when the king needed them to supply horse-drawn chariots. The slaves and tenants who farmed the land lived in villages on these estates.

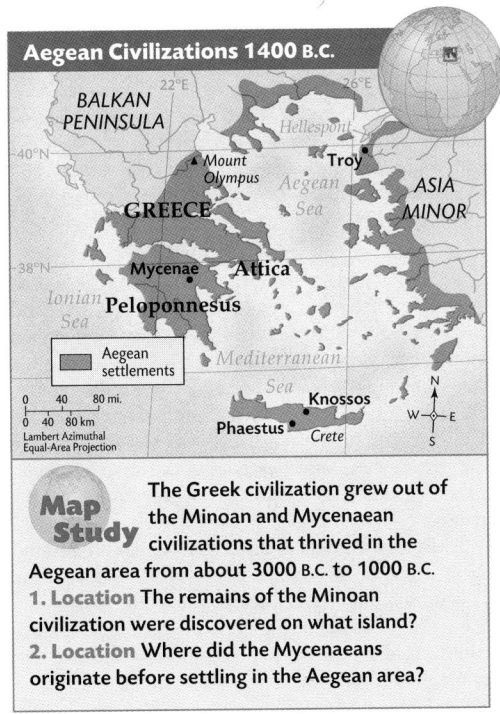

Aegean Civilizations 1400 B.C.

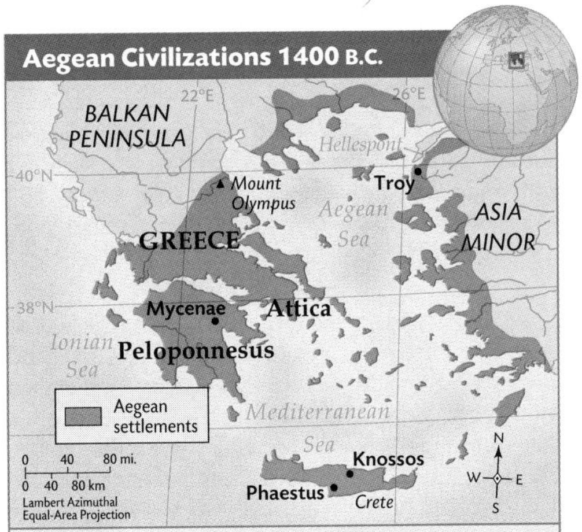

Map Study **The Greek civilization grew out of the Minoan and Mycenaean civilizations that thrived in the Aegean area from about 3000 B.C. to 1000 B.C.**
1. Location The remains of the Minoan civilization were discovered on what island?
2. Location Where did the Mycenaeans originate before settling in the Aegean area?

Chapter 4 Section 1

TEACH

Guided Practice

THEME Relation to Environment

Have students respond to these questions: What geographical features offered protection to Minoan cities? *(bodies of water)* to Mycenaean cities? *(mountains)* How did the Minoans and Mycenaeans further protect their cities? *(Minoans had ships to guard against attack; Mycenaeans built walls around their cities.)* **L1**

Visualizing History Other Mycenaean treasures include gold masks and jewelry.
Answer to Caption: *Government officials kept records of the wealth of everyone in the kingdom.*

Multicultural Have students explain how Hellenic civilization depended on contributions from at least three cultures: Minoan, Mycenaean, and Phoenician. Ask what cultures have contributed to American society. *(English, Spanish, German, Italian, and others)*

Map Study

Answers
1. *Crete*
2. *central Asia*

Map Skills Practice

Reading a Map What bodies of water border mainland Greece on the west, east, and south? *(Ionian Sea, Aegean Sea, Mediterranean Sea)*

COOPERATIVE LEARNING ACTIVITY

Class Presentation Organize the class into small groups and have each group find additional information about a Greek hero—either from the *Iliad* or the *Odyssey* or from myths. Each group should decide how best to present its information to the class and should assign tasks for the final presentation. Encourage students to be as inventive as possible. Some suggestions include: acting out a myth about a hero; recording information about the hero on audiotape; recording an oral/graphic presentation on videotape; delivering an oral/graphic presentation live; drawing and displaying posters that include a brief description of what is depicted. **L1**

Chapter 4 Section 1

Focus on World Art Print 6

Mapping History Overlay Transparency 4

Visualizing History After finding the rich tombs at Mycenae, Schliemann announced that they were the remains of the legendary king Agamemnon and his companions, from the time of the Trojan War. We now know that they are much older, dating from the 1500s B.C.

Answer to Caption: *fighting among the Mycenaeans themselves and invasions by the Dorians*

Independent Practice

Guided Reading Activity 4-1 **L1**

Time Line Activity 4 **L1**

Critical Thinking Have students write two paragraphs explaining why they would rather be a Mycenaean or a Minoan in the period before 1400 B.C. Have them consider such things as lifestyle, economics, and location. Ask several students to read their paragraphs aloud. **L2**

Who?What?Where?When?

The labyrinth, or maze, in the palace at Knossos was supposedly constructed by King Minos to house a dangerous monster, the Minotaur. A legendary hero named Theseus killed the Minotaur and married Ariadne, Minos's daughter.

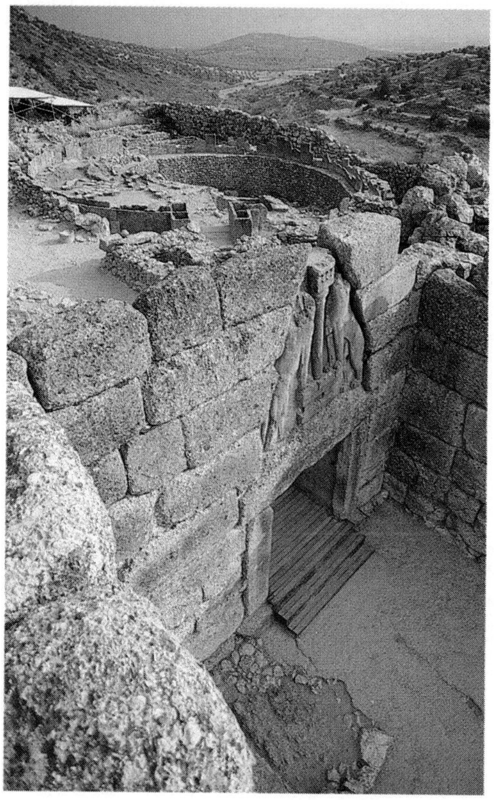

Visualizing History **Heinrich Schliemann discovered six tombs at the royal grave circle near the lion gate at Mycenae. They contained 16 skeletons and a large hoard of gold.** *What events ended Mycenaean civilization?*

The palaces in the city of **Mycenae** served as centers of both government administration and production. Inside, artisans tanned leather, sewed clothes, fashioned jars for storing wine and olive oil, and made bronze swords and ox-hide shields. To help in collecting taxes, government officials kept records of the wealth of every person in the kingdom. They collected taxes in the form of wheat, livestock, and honey, which were stored in the palace.

Minoan traders visited the Greek mainland soon after the Mycenaeans set up their kingdom. Gradually, the Mycenaeans adopted many elements of Minoan culture—metalworking and shipbuilding techniques and navigation by the sun and stars. The Mycenaeans worshiped the Minoan Earth Mother as well.

By the mid-1400s B.C., the Mycenaeans had conquered the Minoans and controlled the Aegean area. By 1100 B.C., however, fighting among the Mycenaeans had destroyed the great hilltop fortresses. Soon after, a new wave of invaders, the Greek-speaking Dorians, entered Greece from the north. Armed with iron weapons, the Dorians easily overran the mainland.

Historians call the next 300 years of Greek history a "dark age." During this period, overseas trade stopped, poverty increased, and people lost skills such as writing and craft making. Thousands of refugees fled the mainland and settled in Ionia—the west coast of Asia Minor and its adjoining islands.

By 750 B.C. the Ionians had reintroduced culture, crafts, and skills to their homeland, including the alphabet used by Phoenician traders. The "dark age" of the Dorians ended, and a new Greek civilization with Mycenaean elements emerged. The new civilization—called Hellenic, after the original people of Greece—flourished from about the 700s B.C. until 336 B.C.

Poets and Heroes

During the "dark age," bards, or singing storytellers, had kept alive Mycenaean traditions. With their new ability to write, the Greeks began to record the epic poems that the bards had passed from generation to generation.

The *Iliad* and the *Odyssey*

According to tradition, a blind poet named **Homer** who lived during the 700s B.C. composed the two most famous Greek epics—the *Iliad* and the *Odyssey*. Homer set the *Iliad* and the *Odyssey* during and after the legendary Trojan War. The Mycenaeans had supposedly fought the people of Troy in the mid-1200s B.C. In A.D. 1870 **Heinrich Schliemann**, a German archaeologist, proved that Troy actually existed and was a major trading city in Asia Minor.

The *Iliad* begins when a Trojan prince named Paris falls in love with Helen, the wife of a Mycenaean king, and takes her with him to Troy. To avenge Helen's kidnapping, the Mycenaeans lay siege to Troy for 10 years, but they cannot capture the city. Finally, they trick the Trojans by building a huge, hollow wooden horse. The best Mycenaean soldiers hide inside the horse, while the rest board their ships and pretend to sail away. The joyful Trojans, thinking themselves victorious, bring the gift horse into the city. That night, the Greeks creep out of the horse, slaughter the Trojan men, enslave

MEETING SPECIAL NEEDS ACTIVITIES

Language Delayed Have students who find it hard to define and use larger words look for difficult words in the text and copy them into a notebook. Assign partners to work with them to define each word. Then use each word in another context to promote understanding. **L1**

Learning Style: Verbal/Linguistic For students who need a challenge, have them find and read sections of the *Iliad* or the *Odyssey* and present interpretations of what they have read to the class. Have students place the section they will interpret in context for their listeners. **L2**

Erich Lessing, Magnum

Trojan Horse

On this Greek vase from the 600s B.C. the Trojan horse of myth and epic stands tall. According to the Greek poet Homer—who described the Trojan War in his epic poem he *Iliad*—for ten long years the Mycenaeans of Greece attled their enemies who lived within the walls of the Turkish city of Troy. The two sides were so well natched that only a clever strategy of war could produce victory. So the Greeks came up with one: They uilt a great wooden horse, so large that a cargo of soliers could hide in its belly. Then they set the horse on wheels and gave it to Troy as a "gift." Having tricked their way into Troy, the Greek soldiers leapt out of the horse and conquered their foe.

While time has blurred the line between historic fact and Homeric epic (written centuries after the struggle), an important war did take place in which a loose federation of Greek kings set out to conquer the city-state of Troy. Homer's epic reveals that piracy and plunder were part of that era's commerce. Archaeologists have uncovered the ruins of a mighty Turkish fortress that once commanded the narrows of the Hellespont. Modern opinions, however, differ as to whether or not this was the site of Homer's Troy. ⊕

TEACH

Remind students that the *Iliad* and the *Odyssey* are epic poems, not reliable historic accounts of the Trojan War. According to scholars, Homer's totals—1,186 Greek ships carrying at least 60,000 soldiers who fought for 10 years—are gross exaggerations. Ask students why they think the poet, or poets, used those inflated figures. *(They wanted to make the heroes seem grand; the figures had probably been increased in oral retellings little by little over the years.)*

CURRICULUM CONNECTION

LITERATURE

The story of the Trojan horse is only touched upon in Homer; in its fullest version, it is found in the *Aeneid*, the Latin epic poem by Virgil. The hero, Aeneas, supposedly founded Rome after having fought in the Trojan War.

Chapter 4 The Rise of Ancient Greece 109

Chapter 4 Section 1

you don't say...

"Achilles' heel" is used to indicate a person's weak point. It is just one of several phrases still used in English derived from Greek legends about the Trojan War. When the Greek hero Achilles was a baby, his mother dipped him into a sacred river to make him invulnerable, but she did not wet the heel she held onto; it was in this heel that Achilles was mortally wounded at Troy.

Linking Past and Present

Tubs and Toilets The Minoans were one of the first civilizations to use bathtubs. They also had toilets. Both tubs and toilets bore a noticeable similarity to modern bathroom appointments.

Visualizing History No one knows what Homer looked like, or even if there was such a person. But because the ancient epics were so much admired, artists and sculptors have imagined the appearance of their author.

Answer to Caption: *The wife of a Mycenaean king, seized and taken to Troy; her kidnapping brought on the Trojan War.*

ASSESS

Check for Understanding

Assign Section 1 Review as homework or as an in-class activity.

Use Student Self-Test and Review Software to review Section 1.

---

the women and children, and burn the city to the ground.

The *Odyssey* describes the homeward wanderings of the Mycenaean king Odysseus after the fall of Troy. Because it took him 10 years to return to Greece, people refer to any long, adventure-filled journey as an *odyssey*.

Teaching Greek Values

Eventually, schools in ancient Greece used the *Iliad* and the *Odyssey* to present to students many of the values of Hellenic civilization. For example, in an exciting description of men marching to war, the *Iliad* taught students to be proud of their Greek heritage and their heroic ancestors:

> "As a ravening fire blazes over a vast forest and the mountains, and its light is seen afar, so while they marched the sheen from their forest of bronze [spears] went up dazzling into high heaven.
>
> As flocks of wildfowl on the wing, geese or cranes or long-necked swans fly this way and that way over the Asian meadows, proud of the power of their wings, and they settle on and on honking as they go until they fill the meadow with sound: so flocks of men poured out of their camp onwards over the Scamandrian plain, and the ground thundered terribly under the tramp of horses and of men."
>
> —Homer, from the *Iliad*, mid-700s B.C.

The *Iliad* and the *Odyssey* also represented other values of Hellenic civilization, such as a love for nature, the importance of husband-wife relationships and tender feelings, and loyalty between friends. Hellenic schools also used the two epics to teach students to always strive for excellence and to meet with dignity whatever fate had in store.

A Family of Deities

In Greek religion, the activities of gods and goddesses explained why people behaved the way they did and why their lives took one direction rather than another. The Greeks also believed that their powerful deities caused the events of the physical world to occur—such as the coming of spring or violent storms with thunder and lightning.

Most ancient peoples feared their deities. They believed that people were put on the earth only to obey and serve the gods and goddesses. The Greeks were the first people to feel differently. They placed importance on the worth of the individual. Because they believed in their own value, the Greeks had a great deal of self-respect. This allowed them to approach their gods with dignity.

Much more than other civilizations did, the Greeks humanized their deities. Unlike the half-animal gods and goddesses of Egypt, Greek deities had totally human forms. They behaved like humans, too—marrying, having children, lying, and murdering. Frequently jealous of one another, the Greek deities quarreled and sometimes played tricks on one another. They also possessed superhuman powers. Since the Greeks saw their deities as sources of power, both physical and mental, they tried to be like them by doing everything to the best of their ability.

Gods and Goddesses

The gods and goddesses of ancient Greece combined features of both Minoan and Mycenaean deities. For example, different Greek goddesses took over different aspects of the Earth Mother. Athena became the goddess of wisdom and art, Demeter became the goddess of agriculture, and Aphrodite became the goddess of love and beauty. Each community chose a particular god or goddess as its patron and protector, but all Greeks worshiped as their chief deity the Mycenaean god Zeus.

Visualizing History **The Greek poet Homer (below) wrote of the ancient Mycenaean king Agamemnon. Nineteenth-century discoveries raised Homer's work from the rank of myth to that of history.** *Who was Helen of Troy?*

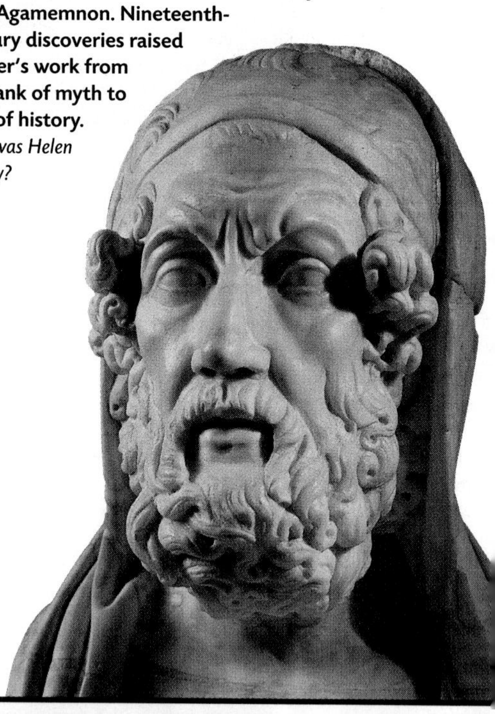

MAKING CONNECTIONS ACTIVITY

Religion Most peoples of the ancient world were polytheistic, worshiping many gods. Have students make three lists: one of the major gods of ancient Egypt, a second of the important Sumerian deities, and a third of the Greek gods. Have them point out similarities and differences. Both the Greeks and the Egyptians, for example, had a god of the sun, but Greek attitudes toward their gods differed from those of the Egyptians. **L2**

Visualizing History Dionysus shown riding a leopard. Greek tragedy was developed from the odes sung by choruses in honor of the god Dionysus. *What is an amphitheater?*

Greeks believed that the 12 most important Greek deities lived on high Mount Olympus, an actual mountain in Greece. Each of the deities controlled a specific part of the natural world. For example, Zeus, the chief god, was thought to rule the sky, weather, and thunderstorms. His brother Pluto was thought to rule the underworld, where the dead spent eternity.

Zeus's son Apollo, the god of light, drove the sun across the sky every day in his chariot. Because the Greeks also considered Apollo to be the god of prophecy, they would bring gifts to the oracle at Delphi—a holy place to honor Apollo—and ask to have hidden knowledge revealed. Like the Shang in ancient China, the Greeks believed that oracles could predict the future. At the Delphic oracle, they would ask questions, and the priests and priestesses would interpret Apollo's replies.

Festivals

As Hellenic civilization developed, certain religious festivals became an important part of Greek life. Every four years the Greeks held a series of athletic contests "for the greater glory of Zeus." Because these contests were held at the city of Olympia, they were called the Olympic Games. The Greeks also originated the play—a celebration in honor of Dionysus, the god of wine and fertility. At these events, the audience sat on a hillside around an open space, where a chorus chanted a story about Dionysus and danced to the sound of a flute. As the years passed, cities began building permanent amphitheaters, carving a hillside into a semicircle, adding rows of stone seats, and paving the stage area. Actors began to recite poems explaining the songs and dances of the chorus. The words they recited eventually evolved into dialogue.

SECTION 1 REVIEW

Recall

1. **Define** labyrinth, bard.
2. **Identify** Sir Arthur Evans, the Minoans, the Mycenaeans, Homer, Heinrich Schliemann.
3. **Describe** the routes the Mycenaeans would have taken to reach Troy and Knossos from their home city of Mycenae.

Critical Thinking

4. **Applying Information** Using Zeus, Athena, and Apollo, illustrate how the Greeks viewed their gods and goddesses.

Understanding Themes

5. **Relation to Environment** How did the geography and climate of Greece and the Aegean islands affect the development of the Minoan and Mycenaean civilizations?

Chapter 4 Section 1

Visualizing History According to legend, Dionysus was associated with leopards and panthers after his mythical conquest of India.
Answer to Caption: *a semicircular theater, with seats often built into the side of a hill* (amphi *is the Greek word for "around."*)

Evaluate

Section Quiz 4-1

Use the Testmaker to create a customized quiz for Section 1.

Reteach

Have students review the environmental factors that influenced early Aegean civilizations.

Enrich

Have students find information about other Aegean settlements near Troy and present it to the class.

CLOSE

Have students speculate about the position of women in a society that worshiped an Earth Mother *(the Minoan, the Mycenaean)* and whose chief god was male *(such as the Greeks' Zeus).*

SECTION 1 REVIEW ANSWERS

1. All vocabulary words are defined in the Glossary.
2. Sir Arthur Evans, 107; Minoans, 107; Mycenaeans, 107; Homer, 108; Heinrich Schliemann, 108
3. Troy: they would have sailed northeast across the Aegean Sea. Knossos: they would have traveled southeast across the Mediterranean.
4. Zeus: ruled the sky, weather, and thunderstorms; Athena: goddess of wisdom and art; Apollo: god of the sun and prophecy. Greeks believed that their deities caused the events of the physical world, and the activities of the gods explained the behavior of people.
5. **RELATION TO ENVIRONMENT** Minoan civilization was strategically located for trade with Egypt, Mesopotamia, and the Greek mainland; the sea protected the island from invaders. The mainland offered Mycenaeans high places to build their cities. Warm climate meant activities outdoors.

Chapter 4 Section 2

SECTION THEME

▶ **Movement** The Greeks found colonies throughout the area of the Mediterranean and Black Seas.

Find Out

Answer: *Farmers, artisans, and merchants, as they became more important to Greek society, demanded more of a say in the government of the polis. This led to struggles with the aristocrats and the rise of tyrants.*

FOCUS

Section Objective

Explain how economic prosperity brought significant political and social changes to the Greek city-states.

BELLRINGER Motivational Activity

Before taking roll at the beginning of the class period, project Section Focus Transparency 4-2 and have students answer the activity questions. Discuss students' responses.

This activity is also available as a blackline master.

Vocabulary Pre-check

Use the Vocabulary PuzzleMaker to create a puzzle that reinforces the vocabulary terms in this section. **L1**

---

700 B.C. — **c. 700s B.C.** Greek kings lose power to aristocrats.

600 B.C. — **c. 600s B.C.** Greeks learn coinage from the Lydians.

500 B.C. — **c. 500 B.C.** The rule of tyrants in Greek city-states ends.

Section 2

The Polis

Setting the Scene

▶ **Terms to Define**
polis, citizen, aristocrat, phalanx, tyrant, oligarchy, democracy

▶ **Places to Locate**
Athens, Sparta

Find Out How did economic prosperity bring significant political and social changes to the Greek city-states?

The Storyteller

An Athenian ruler had to be careful of plots hatched by jealous nobles. The tyrant Hippias, the once-mild ruler of Athens, learned this lesson. He was with his bodyguard, arranging a citywide parade, when two assassins approached. Pretending to take part in the procession, they had daggers ready, hidden behind their shields. Suddenly, seeing one of their accomplices casually talking with Hippias, they halted, thinking that he had betrayed the plot to the tyrant. Turning, they rushed within the gates, met Hippias's brother, and killed him. Afterward, Athenians found Hippias harsher, ever fearful of revolt.

—adapted from *The Peloponnesian War*, Thucydides, Crawley translation revised by T.E. Wick, 1892

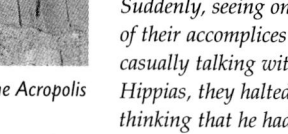

The Parthenon on the Acropolis

The English language offers evidence of how ancient Greeks have influenced modern life. Words such as *police* and *politics*, for example, derive from the Greek word *polis*. The **polis**, or city-state, was the basic political unit of Hellenic civilization. Each polis developed its own pattern of life independently but shared certain features with other city-states.

The Typical Polis

A typical polis included a city and the surrounding villages, fields, and orchards. At the center of the city on the top of an acropolis (uh•KRAH•puh •luhs), or fortified hill, stood the temple of the local deity. At the foot of the acropolis the agora, or public square, served as the political center of the polis. **Citizens**—those who took part in government—gathered in the agora to carry out public affairs, choose their officials, and pass their laws. Artisans and merchants also conducted business in the agora.

The citizens of a polis had both rights and responsibilities. They could vote, hold public office, own property, and speak for themselves in court. In return, the polis expected them to serve in government and to defend the polis in time of war.

Citizens, however, made up only a minority of the residents of a polis. In Athens, slaves and those who were foreign-born were excluded from citizenship, and before 500 B.C. so were men who did not own land. Greek women had no political or legal rights.

Greek Colonies and Trade

The return of prosperity after the "dark age" led to an increase in Greece's population. By 700 B.C. Greek farmers no longer grew enough grain to feed everyone. As a result, each polis sent out groups of people to establish colonies in coastal areas around the Mediterranean and Black Seas.

SECTION RESOURCES

Reproducible Masters
- Reproducible Lesson Plan 4-2
- Guided Reading Activity 4-2
- Mapping History Activity 4
- Geography and History Activity 4
- Section Quiz 4-2

Transparencies
- Section Focus Transparency 4-2
- Chapter Transparency 4

Multimedia
- Vocabulary PuzzleMaker Software
- Student Self-Test and Review Software
- Testmaker

112 Chapter 4 *The Rise of Ancient Greece*

Colonies

Each colony kept close ties with its metropolis, or "parent city." A colony supplied its metropolis with grain—wheat and barley. Farmers on the Greek mainland produced wine, olive oil, and other cash crops for export. Because vineyards and olive groves needed fewer workers than did grain fields, many farmers moved to the cities, where they learned crafts. With more goods to sell, Greek merchants began trading throughout the Mediterranean region.

Economic Growth

During the 600s B.C. the Greeks replaced their barter system with a money economy, and their overseas trade expanded further. Merchants issued their own coins, but eventually individual city-states took over this responsibility.

The cities of Ionia in Asia Minor assumed leadership in a growing textile industry. Sheep in the interior of Asia Minor furnished the raw material. Purple dye obtained from mollusks, a type of shellfish, gave the woven materials color.

Pottery developed as a local industry wherever sufficient clay was found. Pottery made in Ionia was the earliest Greek pottery to be exported. Ionian pottery styles were based on Mycenaean and Middle Eastern influences. The artists who made and decorated the vases painted figures of birds and humans interspersed with line or geometric decorations.

Political and Social Change

Economic growth changed Greek political life. Greek communities at first were ruled by kings. By the 700s B.C., however, the kings had lost power to landholding aristocrats, or nobles, who as members of the upper class provided cavalry for the king's military ventures.

By 650 B.C. disputes arose between the aristocrats and the common people. Farmers often needed credit until harvest time. To obtain loans from the wealthy aristocrats, they had to pledge their fields as security. When they could not repay the loans, many farmers lost their land to the aristocrats and became either sharecroppers or day laborers in the cities. Some even had to sell themselves into slavery. In protest, farmers demanded political reforms.

CONNECTIONS Geography

Sailing the Aegean

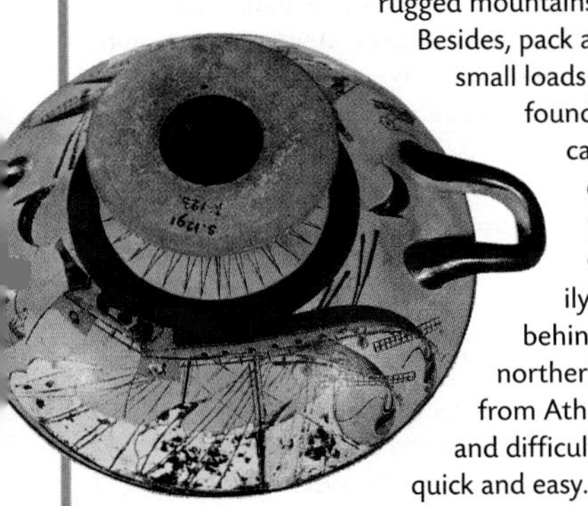

Pottery jar showing a merchant ship

Because of their many natural harbors, the Greeks transported most goods by sea. Sea travel made good sense, given the rugged mountains of the Greek mainland. Besides, pack animals could carry only small loads short distances. Merchants found sea transport of bulky cargo—grain, timber, and even jugs of olive oil—to be practical and inexpensive. Greek sailors could sail easily only when the wind was behind them. The prevailing northerly winds made the voyage from Athens to the Black Sea slow and difficult, but the return trip was quick and easy. Likewise, Greek ships could coast to Egypt, but they had to struggle to get home. Most ships managed only one round-trip per year.

The typical Greek freighter was broad—about 25 feet (7.5 m) wide compared to a length of 80 feet (24 m). Rigged with a large square sail, this sturdy ship averaged only about 5 knots with the wind. Merchant ships usually sailed in fleets escorted by warships—galleys propelled by oarsmen.

Compare the ancient ships with today's diesel-driven giants. A container ship makes the round-trip between the United States and Europe in 21 days. It holds cargo in 1,000 containers—four of which are the size of one Greek freighter. Some things have not changed, however. The Greek merchant fleet of today ranks among the largest in the world.

MAKING THE CONNECTION

1. Why were the prevailing winds a problem for Greek sailors?
2. Besides larger, faster ships, how has cargo transport changed since ancient times?

Chapter 4 Section 2

TEACH

Guided Practice

THEME **Movement**

Ask: What types of movement resulted from colonization? *(Greeks left their polis to establish colonies. Farmers on the mainland moved to cities. Greek traders sailed throughout the region.)* **L1**

Independent Practice

Guided Reading Activity 4-2 **L1**

CONNECTIONS Geography

Sailing the Aegean

Because Greek ships were small, they could carry very few provisions. As much as possible, ships hugged the coasts so that they could land frequently to take on food and water.

Answers to Making the Connection

1. *because Greek ships could sail easily only with the wind behind them; since the winds usually blew from north to south, sailing south was easy but sailing north was hard*
2. *Cargo today is transported by ships, trains, planes, and trucks.*

ASSESS

Check for Understanding

Assign Section 2 Review as homework or as an in-class activity.

Use Student Self-Test and Review Software to review Section 2.

COOPERATIVE LEARNING ACTIVITY

Skit Have students write and produce a skit that shows typical activity in an agora, with parts for women, enslaved people, children, aristocrats, artisans, and merchants. Assign groups to handle various activities: scriptwriting; designing and producing a simple set, costumes, program, and promotional materials; acting; and directing.

The skit should clearly convey through dialogue and action the operation of democracy in the polis. After the skit, have students conduct a poll to see whether this aim was accomplished. **L1**

Chapter 4 Section 2

Map Study

Answer

wine and olive oil

Map Skills Practice

Reading a Map How far from Greece were the most distant Greek colonies? *(around 1,200 miles [about 1,900 kilometers])*

Evaluate

Section Quiz 4-2

Use the Testmaker to create a customized quiz for Section 2.

Reteach

Have students summarize the chief political and social changes in Greece between 700 and 500 B.C.

Enrich

Have students write letters as if they were early Greek merchants promoting trade.

CLOSE

Ask students to compare the advantages and disadvantages of living in a Greek city-state with those of modern city life.

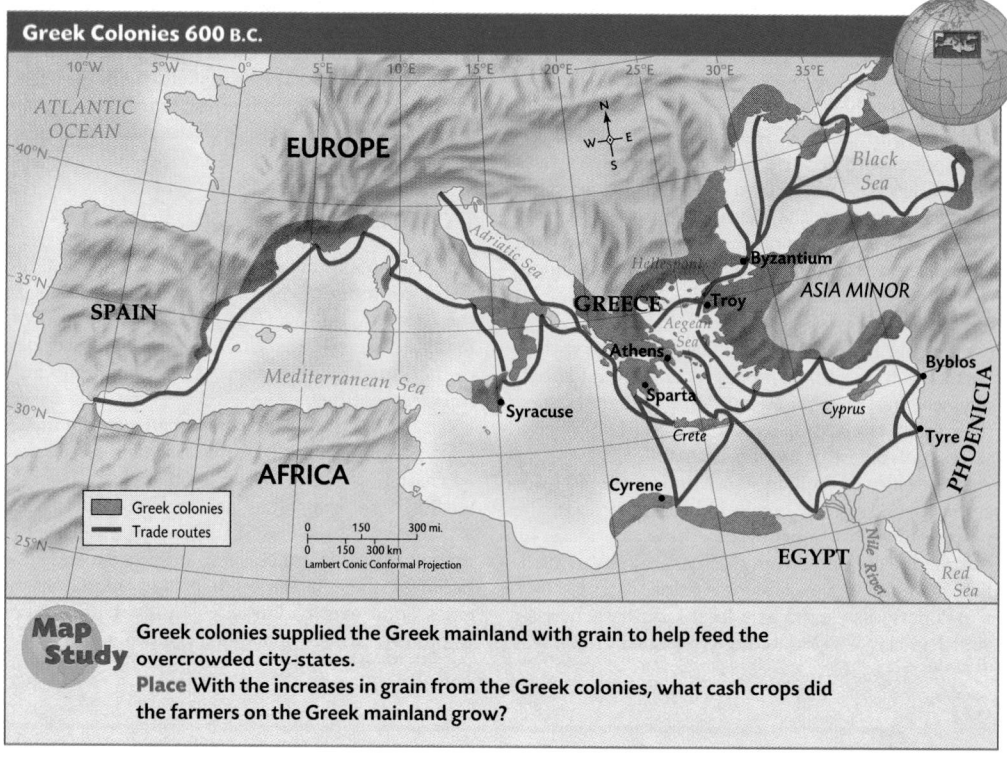

Greek Colonies 600 B.C.

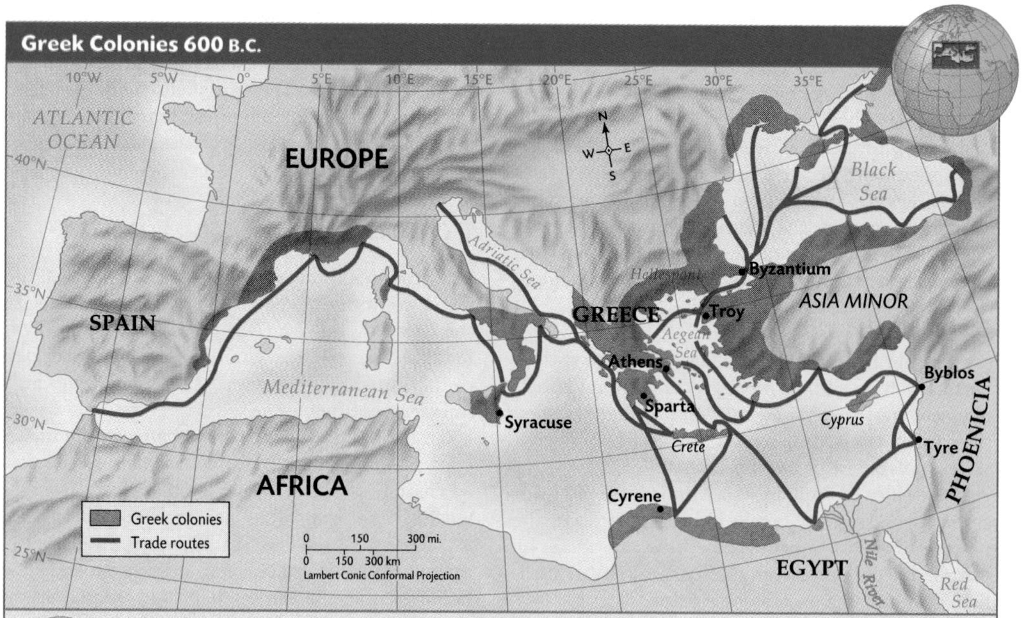

Map Study Greek colonies supplied the Greek mainland with grain to help feed the overcrowded city-states.

Place With the increases in grain from the Greek colonies, what cash crops did the farmers on the Greek mainland grow?

The farmers, who were foot soldiers, were becoming more valuable to Greek armies than the aristocrats, who were cavalry. As Greek armies came to rely on the **phalanx**—rows of foot soldiers closely arrayed with their shields forming a solid wall—aristocrats began to lose influence. Middle-class, non-landowning merchants and artisans, thus far excluded from citizenship, wanted a voice in the government and joined the farmers in their demands. Merchants and artisans also wanted the polis to advance their interests by encouraging industry and by protecting profitable overseas trade routes.

As a result of the unrest, tyrannies arose. A tyranny was created when one man, called a **tyrant**, seized power and ruled the polis single-handedly. Although most tyrants ruled fairly, the harshness of a few gave *tyranny* its present meaning—rule by a cruel and unjust person.

Tyrants ruled various Greek city-states until about 500 B.C. From then until 336 B.C., most city-states became either oligarchies or democracies. In an **oligarchy**, a few wealthy people hold power over the larger group of citizens. In a **democracy**, or government by the people, power lies in the hands of all the citizens. Two democracies of ancient Greece—**Athens** and **Sparta**—became the most famous of the city-states.

SECTION 2 REVIEW

Recall

1. **Define** polis, citizen, aristocrat, phalanx, tyrant, oligarchy, democracy.
2. **Identify** Athens, Sparta.
3. **Describe** the social and political functions of an acropolis and an agora in a Greek polis.

Critical Thinking

4. **Synthesizing Information** What arguments might a citizen of a polis present for or against changing citizenship?

Understanding Themes

5. **Movement** What kind of relationship existed between a Greek colony and its metropolis on the Greek mainland?

SECTION 2 REVIEW ANSWERS

1. All vocabulary words are defined in the Glossary.
2. Athens, 114; Sparta, 114
3. An acropolis was a fortified hill in the center of a polis with a temple to the local deity; an agora was a public square used as a political and business center.
4. Students might argue that citizenship should be extended to foot soldiers, merchants, and artisans because of their contributions to the polis; or they might argue that the polis should follow tradition and continue to restrict citizenship.
5. **MOVEMENT** A Greek colony kept close religious, cultural, and economic ties with its metropolis, usually supplying it with grain and buying products from its merchants.

114 Chapter 4 *The Rise of Ancient Greece*

650 B.C. — 600 B.C. — 550 B.C. — 500 B.C.

c. 650 B.C. Slaves revolt in Sparta.

621 B.C. Draco enacts code of laws in Athens.

594 B.C. Tyrant Solon becomes leader of Athens.

507 B.C. Athens becomes a democracy.

Section 3

Rivals

Setting the Scene

- **Terms to Define**
  rhetoric
- **People to Meet**
  Draco, Solon, Peisistratus, Cleisthenes
- **Places to Locate**
  Peloponnesus, Attica

Find Out What different Greek values did Athens and Sparta each represent?

The Storyteller

Pausanias darted among the bushes to avoid the moonlight. Finally, stumbling, he plunged behind a large rock, his lungs heaving. Having managed to steal just one loaf of fresh bread, he knew that he must ration it out for at least two days. The ephors had declared that those caught with stolen food would be beaten severely. But, if he could just survive for two more days, he would finish the initiation and join the other young men in the barracks. He shivered quietly, trying to imagine where he might spend the next two cold nights.

—adapted from *The Ancient World*, edited by Esmond Wright, 1979

Spartan female athlete

The two leading city-states in ancient Greece—Sparta and Athens—stood in sharp contrast to each other. Though citizens of both Sparta and Athens participated in polis government, the two city-states differed greatly from each other in their values, cultures, and accomplishments.

Sparta

The descendants of the Dorian invaders of the dark age founded Sparta. It was located in the **Peloponnesus** (peh•luh•puh•NEE•suhs), a peninsula of southern Greece. Like other city-states, Sparta based its economy on agriculture.

Instead of founding overseas colonies, the Spartans invaded neighboring city-states and enslaved the local people. The polis of Sparta owned many slaves, known as helots (HEH•luhts), who farmed the estates of individual Spartans. In addition, a group of free individuals called *perioeci* (peh•REE•ee•sy)—artisans and merchants from the conquered territories—worked for the Spartans. Helots and *perioeci* together outnumbered Spartans by about 200,000 to 10,000.

Around 650 B.C., the helots revolted against their Spartan masters. It took 30 years, but the Spartans managed to suppress the revolt. They then decided that the only way they could maintain power was to establish a military society.

A Military Society

All life in Sparta revolved around the army. Spartan men strove to become first-rate soldiers, and Spartan women aspired to become mothers of soldiers. Spartans despised the other Greeks who lived behind city walls, believing that a city defended by Spartan soldiers did not need walls.

In Sparta, government officials examined newborn infants to see if they were healthy. If not, an official left the sickly infant on a hillside to die. At

Chapter 4 Section 3

SECTION THEME

- **Regionalism** Two leading Greek city-states—Athens and Sparta—differ greatly from each other in their values, cultures, and achievements.

Find Out

Answer: *Spartan life revolved around the army and physical prowess, while the Athenians stressed public service and, at least for men, education.*

FOCUS

Section Objective

Differentiate between the values represented by Sparta and those represented by Athens.

BELLRINGER Motivational Activity

Before taking roll at the beginning of the class period, project Section Focus Transparency 4-3 and have students answer the activity questions. Discuss students' responses.

This activity is also available as a blackline master.

Vocabulary Pre-check

Use Vocabulary Activity 4 to introduce vocabulary terms. **L1 LEP**

SECTION RESOURCES

Reproducible Masters
- Reproducible Lesson Plan 4-3
- Vocabulary Activity 4
- Guided Reading Activity 4–3
- Source Reading 4
- Section Quiz 4-3

Transparencies
- Section Focus Transparency 4-3
- World History and Art Transparency 5
- Ancient Greece

Multimedia
- Ancient Greece
- Student Self-Test and Review Software
- Testmaker
- Greece and Rome
- Turning Points in World History

TEACH

Guided Practice

THEME Regionalism

Ask students to brainstorm definitions of the term *regionalism.* Then read this definition: "consciousness of and loyalty to a distinct region that has its own special characteristics." Ask students how this concept applies to their own lives and locality today. **L1**

Conflict Ask students to write a few sentences telling how they think 10,000 Spartans could keep many times that number of helots subjugated. Discuss the students' opinions. **L2**

World History and Art Transparency 5

NATIONAL GEOGRAPHIC SOCIETY

Use these materials to enrich student understanding of ancient Greek culture.

- **NGS PICTURESHOW CD-ROM**
  Greece and Rome
- **NGS PICTUREPACK TRANSPARENCY SET**
  Ancient Greece
- **ANCIENT CIVILIZATIONS POSTER SET**
  Ancient Greece

the age of 7, Spartan boys were taken away from their homes and placed in military barracks. Their training included learning to read, write, and use weapons.

At age 20, Spartan men became soldiers and were sent to frontier areas. At age 30, they were expected to marry. But Spartan men did not maintain households of their own. Instead, they continued to live in military barracks until age 60, when they could retire from the army.

The Role of Women

The Spartans brought up women to be, like the Spartan men, as healthy and strong as possible. Female infants received as much food as their brothers, which was not the case elsewhere in Greece. Young Spartan girls trained in gymnastics, wrestling, and boxing. The women in Sparta married at age 19 rather than at 14—the average marrying age in most of Greece—which increased the likelihood that their children would be healthy.

Sparta gave its women more personal rights and freedoms than the women of other Greek city-states received. Spartan women could go shopping in the marketplace, attend dinners at which non-family members were present, own property in their own names, and express opinions on public issues. They could not, however, take part in the government of the polis.

Sparta's Government

Two kings, who ruled jointly, officially governed Sparta. Except for leading the army and conducting religious services, however, Spartan kings had little power. The Assembly, made up of all male citizens over the age of 20, passed laws and made decisions concerning war and peace. Each year the Assembly elected five overseers, known as ephors (EH•fuhrs), to administer public affairs. The ephors could also veto legislation. A Council of Elders, consisting of 28 men over the age of 60, proposed laws to the Assembly and served as a supreme court. It also assisted the ephors in supervising citizens and in training the young.

Images of the Times

The Glory of Greece

Archaeological treasures and architectural remains remind the world of the achievements of Greek civilization.

The Parthenon crowns the Acropolis at Athens.

Greek sculptors in the classical period depicted living and moving people in natural poses.

Images of the Times **The Glory of Greece**

We tend to think of Greek buildings and sculptures as white or cream-colored—the color of old marble. In ancient times, however, they were much more colorful. The Greeks painted both buildings and statues in reds, blues, and other bright colors.

The Acropolis in Athens has suffered extensive damage in its long history. Over the centuries, various buildings were used as a mosque, an official residence, and a Turkish harem. At one time, when the Parthenon was being used as a powder magazine, it was hit by a bombardment that caused a huge explosion. Today air pollution poses a serious threat to the architectural remains.

Results of Militarism

The Spartans succeeded in maintaining their power over the helots and *perioeci* for nearly 250 years. They paid a price, however. Suspicious of any new ideas that might change their society, the Spartans lagged far behind other city-states in developing trade and manufacturing. As a result, they were much poorer than the other Greeks. The Spartans also lagged in intellectual accomplishments. The Athenians created a vast body of literature and made important discoveries in science. The Spartans did not. The Spartans were, however, exceptional athletes who almost always won the Olympic Games, and Spartan soldiers played key roles in defending Greece against invaders.

Athens

Northeast of the Peloponnesus—on a peninsula of central Greece named **Attica**—people descended from the Mycenaeans established the city-state of Athens. They named their polis after the goddess Athena. Like the early rulers of the other city-states, Athenian kings and aristocrats in the 600s B.C. faced demands by small farmers, merchants, and artisans for economic and political reforms.

Around this time, the governing methods of Athens and Sparta diverged. Athens gradually expanded its definition of citizenship to encompass more people. Initially, only a man whose father and maternal grandfather had been citizens could be a citizen; however, non-landowning citizens could not participate in Athens's Assembly. Athenians called the many free (non-enslaved) foreigners who lived in Athens *metics*. These people could not own land or participate in government. By 507 B.C., however, the constitution of Athens stated that all free men were citizens regardless of what class they belonged to, and that they could participate in the Assembly regardless of whether they owned land. This political change reduced much of the friction between social classes and enabled Athens to forge ahead.

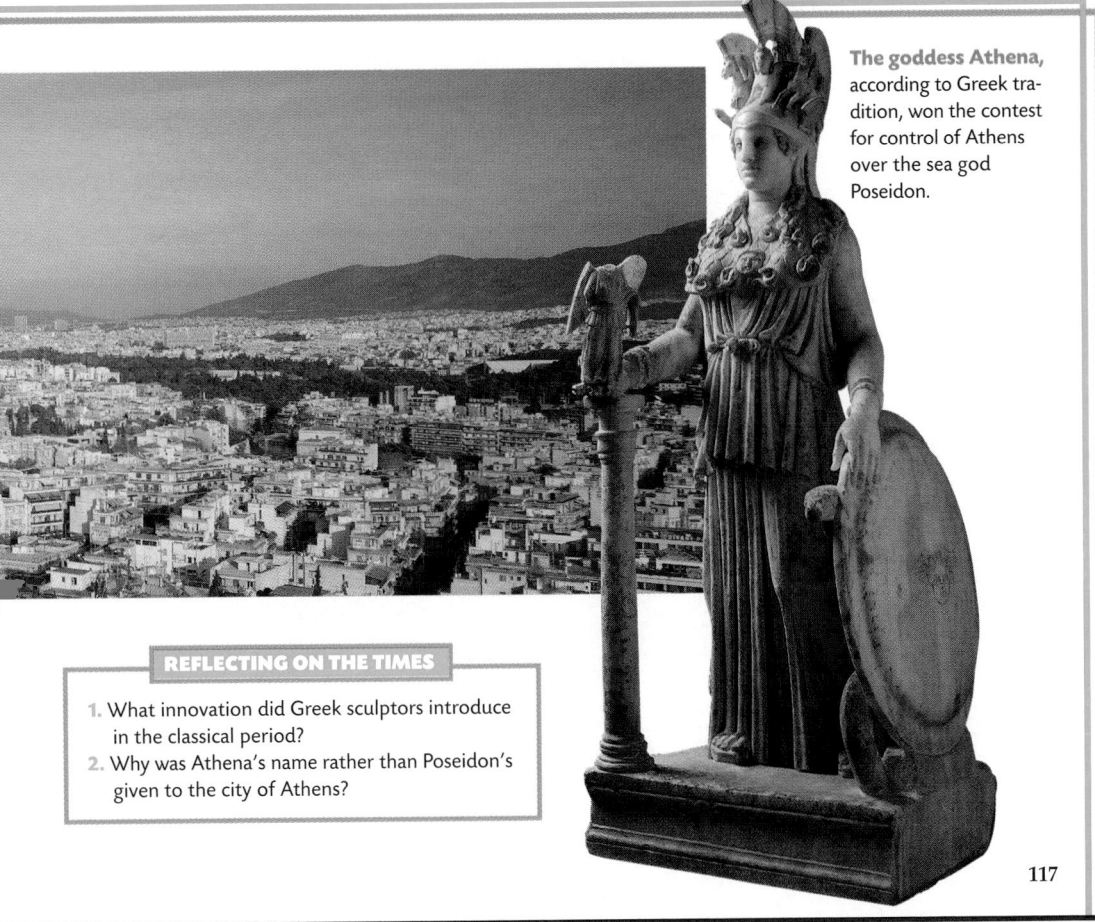

The goddess Athena, according to Greek tradition, won the contest for control of Athens over the sea god Poseidon.

REFLECTING ON THE TIMES

1. What innovation did Greek sculptors introduce in the classical period?
2. Why was Athena's name rather than Poseidon's given to the city of Athens?

117

ANSWERS TO REFLECTING ON THE TIMES

1. They depicted living and moving people in natural poses.
2. According to tradition, she defeated Poseidon in a contest for control of the city.

Chapter 4
Section 3

Independent Practice

Guided Reading Activity 4-3 **L1**

Source Reading 4

History Have students imagine that they are Athenian citizens organizing a protest march against the hated laws of the tyrant Draco. Have them create picket signs that express their points of view. Display the signs in the classroom. **L1 LEP**

City-States Have students research information about Greek city-states other than Athens and Sparta and report their findings to the class. Among the many that reward research are Argos, Corinth, Sicyon, Olympia, Delphi, Thebes, Miletus, and Ephesus. **L3**

Global Gourmet

Greece Olives were a staple of the Greek diet because olive trees grow well in dry, rocky soil. Olive oil was so important to the Greek economy that when the Spartans attacked Athens, their first move was to destroy the olive groves surrounding the city in order to weaken the Athenian economy.

Linking Past and Present

Language The Spartans of ancient times were taught to behave modestly and to say only what was necessary. They were known for their brusqueness of speech. Today we use the word *laconic* to describe someone who speaks little. The word comes from Laconia, the plain on which Sparta was located.

Visualizing History All important lawsuits tried anywhere in territories under Athenian control—including faraway colonies—could be appealed to the people's courts in Athens.
Answer to Caption: *Athenians hoped that the large size would prevent jurors from being influenced by threats, bribes, or prejudice.*

ABC NEWS INTERACTIVE™

VIDEODISC
Turning Points in World History

Side One
Chapter 5

Title: *Democracy in Greece*
Subject: Athenian democracy laid the foundation in which the majority rules, but the minority still has rights.
Ask: What is the meaning of democracy? (Democracy *literally means "rule by the people."*)

Draco's Law Code

Four successive tyrants brought most of the changes in Athenian government. **Draco**, the first of these tyrants, issued an improved code of laws in 621 B.C. The penalties given to offenders were extremely harsh. Even minor offenses, like stealing a cabbage, were punishable by death.

Over time, the word *draconian* has come to describe something that is very cruel and severe. On the other hand, because Draco's laws were written down, everyone knew exactly what the laws were. Aristocrats could no longer dictate what was legal and what was not.

Solon's Reforms

The next series of reforms took place under the tyrant **Solon**, who became the leader of Athens in 594 B.C. To improve economic conditions, Solon canceled all land debts and freed debtors from slavery. He also placed limits on the amount of land any one individual could own. By urging farmers to grow cash crops rather than grain, Solon promoted trade. He also promoted industry by ordering fathers to teach their sons a trade and by extending citizenship to artisans and merchants who were not born Athenians.

Next, Solon turned his attention to the political conflict between aristocrats and commoners. He did this by setting up a two-house legislature. Aristocrats belonged to the Council of 400, while landowning commoners made up the Assembly. The Council drafted measures that then went to the Assembly for approval.

Radical Reformers

In 546 B.C. the tyrant **Peisistratus** (pih•SIHS•truh•tuhs) took over the government of Athens. Peisistratus pushed reforms in an even more radical direction than had Solon. He divided large estates among landless farmers and extended citizenship to men who did not own land. Peisistratus provided the poor with loans and put many of them to work building temples and other public works projects.

Cleisthenes (KLYS•thuh•NEEZ), the fourth tyrant to help reform Athens, came to power in 508 B.C. The following year he introduced a series of laws that established democracy for Athens. Through his reforms, Cleisthenes sought to end local rivalries, break the power of the aristocracy, and extend citizenship guarantees to more people living in Athens. He also set out to reorganize the structure of Athenian government.

Athenian Democracy

The Assembly remained the major political institution in Cleisthenes' democracy. All citizens could belong to the Assembly, in which they were considered equal before the law and guaranteed freedom of speech. The Assembly passed laws and also served as a supreme court. In addition, each year the Assembly chose 10 generals to run the army and navy. A Council of 500 administered everyday government business such as taxes, treaties, and public works.

Each year in a lottery, Athenians chose members of the Council. They favored a lottery over the ballot, believing that, except for running a military campaign, all citizens were competent to hold public office. In addition, they considered elections unfair because rich men, men who boasted a well-known family name, or men who spoke effectively in public would have an advantage. Besides, all citizens were supposed to take part in government.

Athenian democracy included a jury system to decide court cases. Juries contained from 201 to

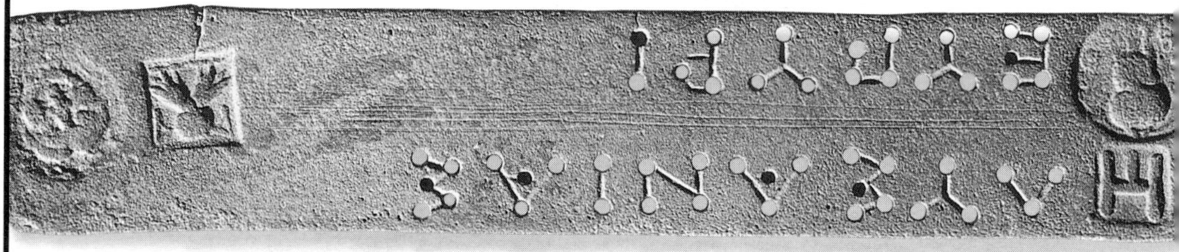

Visualizing History **A juror's token is shown above. Athenian courts demonstrated faith in the ordinary man's ability. Groups of hundreds of citizens sat on panels called *dicasteries* and decided cases by majority vote.** *Why were juries so large?*

COOPERATIVE LEARNING ACTIVITY

Role Play Organize the class into groups of seven or eight. Have four or five in each group play the roles of typical residents of Athens and the remaining group members play newspaper reporters who ask them questions about their lives and times. Have the groups prepare by doing library research to find out all they can about an Athenian merchant, one of the tyrants, an upper-class woman, a priestess of Athena, or an enslaved person. Have the group work together to frame questions reporters might ask and answers that might be given. Each group should present its questions and answers to the whole class. Encourage students to strive for realism in their assumed roles. Have the audience take notes and write a summary. **L1**

1,001 members, with a majority vote needed to reach a verdict. The Athenians reasoned that the large size of their juries would keep jurors from being influenced by threats, bribes, or prejudice.

Athenian democracy also included a system called ostracism. Each year, citizens could write the name of an undesirable politician on a piece of baked clay called an ostracon. If a person's name appeared on 6,000 ostraca, the polis exiled him for 10 years.

Cleisthenes' reforms lasted for almost 200 years, until the Macedonians living to the north conquered the Greeks. Even though the Athenians excluded several groups from citizenship, ancient Athens nevertheless laid the foundation for the Western concept of democratic government.

Athenian Education

The training an Athenian received depended on social and economic status. About a week after being born, a male child received a name and was enrolled as a citizen. Because Athens expected every citizen to hold public office at some time in his life, it required Athenian citizens to educate their sons. With few exceptions, Athenian girls—who would not participate in governing the democracy of Athens—did not receive a formal education. Instead, a girl learned household duties, such as weaving and baking, from her mother.

Private tutors educated the boys from wealthy upper-class families, while other students paid a small fee to attend a private school. Much of their education was picked up in the agora, through daily conversations and discussions in the Assembly.

Athenian boys entered school at age 7 and graduated at age 18. Their main textbooks were the *Iliad* and the *Odyssey*, and students learned each epic by heart. They studied arithmetic, geometry, drawing, and music in the morning and gymnastics in the afternoon. When boys reached their teens, they added rhetoric, or the art of public speaking, to their studies. Because lawyers did not represent participants in a court case, an Athenian needed to be accomplished in rhetoric to argue his own position.

When young Athenian men reached 18, they left for two years of military service. Before entering the army, however, they went with their fathers to the temple of Zeus, where they swore the following oath:

> "I will not bring dishonor upon my weapons nor desert the comrade by my side. I will strive to hand on my fatherland greater and better than I found it. I will not consent to anyone's disobeying or destroying the constitution but will prevent him, whether I am with others or alone. I will honor the temples and the religion my forefathers established."
>
> —oath of enrollment in Epheboi corps, early 400s B.C.

AROUND THE WORLD

Zapotec Temple Complex at Monte Albán

Mexico, c. 500 B.C.

Monte Albán in the valley of Oaxaca in southern Mexico became an important center of Zapotec culture. The Zapotecs flattened the mountaintop to create a large plaza, around which they designed a temple complex. They carved the slopes of the mountain into terraces for agriculture and housing. An estimated 5,000 people, or about 50 percent of the valley's population, lived at Monte Albán.

SECTION 3 REVIEW

Recall

1. **Define** rhetoric.
2. **Identify** Draco, Solon, Peisistratus, Cleisthenes.
3. **Locate** Athens and Sparta on the map on page 121. In which peninsula was each located?

Critical Thinking

4. **Evaluating Information** Do you think the reasons the Athenians gave for choosing government officials by lottery were good reasons? What other method would you propose if you were an Athenian reformer?

Understanding Themes

5. **Regionalism** Contrast Athens and Sparta in their idea of citizenship, type of education, and position of women.

Chapter 4 Section 3

ASSESS

Check for Understanding

Assign Section 3 Review as homework or as an in-class activity.

Use Student Self-Test and Review Software to review Section 3.

Evaluate

Section Quiz 4-3

Use the Testmaker to create a customized quiz for Section 3.

Reteach

Have students write a paragraph that explains in what areas Sparta failed to develop and why. *(trade, manufacturing, intellectual achievement; because they were suspicious of new ideas and devoted energies to becoming a military society)*

Enrich

Have students write a two-page essay that compares the Athenian practice of ostracism with the modern process of impeachment in the United States.

CLOSE

Write these headings on the chalkboard: *Sparta, Athens*. Have volunteers write facts about political, social, and economic life under the correct heading.

SECTION 3 REVIEW ANSWERS

1. All vocabulary words are defined in the Glossary.
2. Draco, 118; Solon, 118; Peisistratus, 118; Cleisthenes, 118
3. Athens in Attica, Sparta in the Peloponnesus
4. Yes: being rich or being a good speaker may win votes but may not reflect how good a job a person can do; or, no: different people have different abilities. Other methods might include choosing officials from men who apply for the jobs or having the Assembly nominate and elect candidates.
5. **REGIONALISM** In Athens, citizenship was open to more men than in Sparta, and Athenian men received a broader education, but Athenian women had fewer rights than Spartan women.

Chapter 4
Section 4

SECTION THEME

▶ **Conflict** Greek city-states together fight the Persians; then the city-states, led by rivals Athens and Sparta, fight each other.

Find Out

Answer: *The Persian Wars led to the development of an Athenian empire, undermining democracy in other city-states. The Peloponnesian War destroyed the Greeks' ability to govern themselves.*

FOCUS

Section Objective

Discuss how the Persian and Peloponnesian Wars affected democracy in Greek city-states.

BELLRINGER Motivational Activity

Before taking roll at the beginning of the class period, project Section Focus Transparency 4-4 and have students answer the activity questions. Discuss students' responses.

This activity is also available as a blackline master.

Vocabulary Pre-check

Use Vocabulary Activity 4 to introduce vocabulary terms.
L1 LEP

550 B.C.	500 B.C.	450 B.C.	400 B.C.
546 B.C. Persian armies conquer Ionia.	**499 B.C.** Athenians and Persians fight the Battle of Marathon.	**447 B.C.** Pericles begins rebuilding of Athens.	**431 B.C.** Peloponnesian War begins.

Section 4

War, Glory, and Decline

Setting the Scene

▶ **Terms to Define**
symposium, mercenary

▶ **People to Meet**
Darius I, Xerxes, Themistocles, Leonidas, Pericles, Aspasia

▶ **Places to Locate**
Marathon, Thermopylae, Salamis, Delos

Find Out How did the Persian Wars and the Peloponnesian War affect democracy in the Greek city-states?

The Storyteller

The Greek historian Herodotus reported that during the Persian Wars, some Greek deserters approached the Persian king Xerxes. Questioned about what the Greeks were about to do, they told him the truth: The Olympic Games were being held. They were going to watch the athletic competitions and chariot races. When asked what the prize was for such contests, they responded that the Olympic prize was an olive wreath. Upon hearing this, a Persian noble cried out in fear: "What kind of men are these? How can we be expected to fight against men who compete with each other for no material reward, but only for honor!"

—adapted from *The Histories*, Herodotus, translated by Aubrey de Selincourt

Themistocles

As the 400s B.C. opened, the Persian Empire—then the strongest military power in the ancient world—stood poised to extend its influence into Europe. Surprisingly, the Greek city-states not only cooperated with each other in resisting the Persian attack, but they also succeeded in throwing Persia's armed forces back into Asia.

After their victory against Persia, the Greeks—especially the Athenians—enjoyed a "golden age" of remarkable cultural achievements. Then, the Greek city-states began to fight among themselves. This bitter and devastating war lasted for more than 27 years.

The Persian Wars

In 546 B.C. the Persian armies, led by Cyrus II, conquered the Greek city-states of Ionia, in Asia Minor. Despite the mildness of Persian rule, the Ionians disliked the conquerors. The Ionians considered the non-Greek-speaking Persians to be barbarians. In addition, an all-powerful king ruled the Persian Empire, whereas the Greek population of Ionia believed that citizens should choose their own government.

Finally, in 499 B.C., the Ionians revolted against the Persians. Even though Athens and another mainland polis sent some warships to help the Ionians, **Darius I** of Persia soon defeated the Ionians. Darius then decided to punish the mainland Greeks for helping the rebels.

Marathon

Darius first tried to send an army around the northern coast of the Aegean Sea. However, a storm destroyed his supply ships, forcing him to turn back. Two years later, in 490 B.C., Darius tried again.

SECTION RESOURCES

Reproducible Masters
- Reproducible Lesson Plan 4-4
- Guided Reading Activity 4-4
- Reteaching Activity 4
- Enrichment Activity 4
- Section Quiz 4-4
- Performance Assessment Activity 4
- Spanish Chapter Summary 4

Transparencies
- Section Focus Transparency 4-4
- Mapping History Overlay Transparency 4

Multimedia
- Student Self-Test and Review Software
- Testmaker

This time he sent his fleet directly across the Aegean to the coastal plain of **Marathon**, about 25 miles (40 km) north of Athens. For several days the Persians awaited the Athenians. However, the Athenians, outnumbered 20,000 to 10,000, did nothing. Finally, the Persians decided to attack Athens directly. They loaded their ships with the cavalry—the strongest part of their army—and then began loading the infantry.

Not waiting for the Persians to take the offensive, the Athenians struck. The Athenian general ordered his well-disciplined foot soldiers to charge down the hills above Marathon at the Persian infantry, which stood in shallow water waiting to board the ships. This tactic astounded the Persians, who believed that infantrymen would fight only with the support of horsemen and archers. Marathon was a terrible defeat for the Persians, who reportedly lost 6,400 men compared to only 192 Greek casualties.

Persian Wars

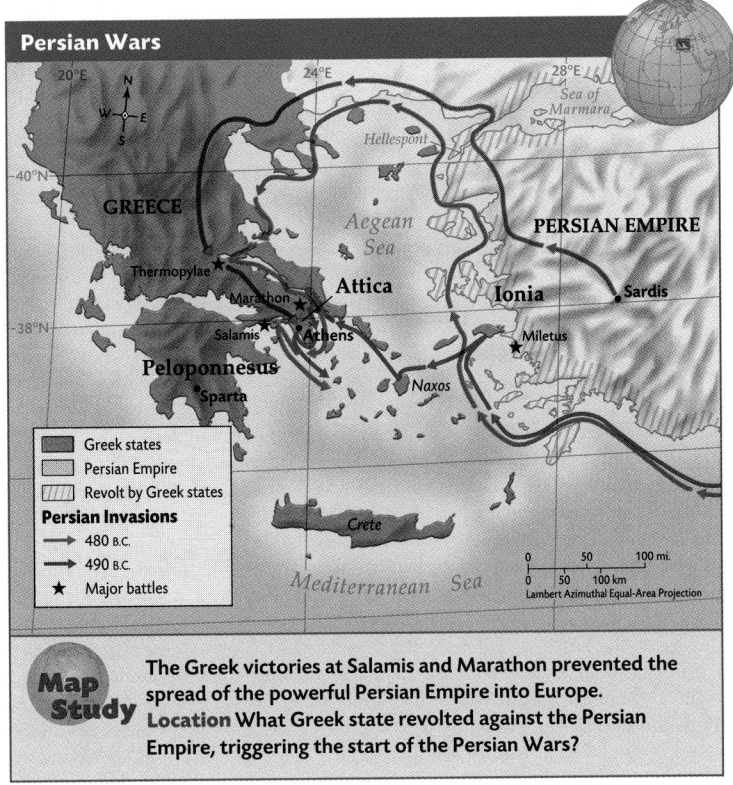

Map Study The Greek victories at Salamis and Marathon prevented the spread of the powerful Persian Empire into Europe. **Location** What Greek state revolted against the Persian Empire, triggering the start of the Persian Wars?

Salamis

After Marathon, the Persians withdrew to Asia Minor, but they returned 10 years later. In 480 B.C. Darius's son and successor, **Xerxes**, invaded Greece from the north, this time with 200,000 soldiers. Because so huge an army could not live off the land, offshore supply ships accompanied them.

Once again the Greeks, this time under the leadership of Sparta, faced the Persians. A few years before, the oracle at Delphi had said that Greece would be safe behind a "wooden wall." The Athenian general **Themistocles** (thuh•MIHS•tuh •KLEEZ) tried to convince his Greek allies that a "wooden wall" meant a fleet of ships and that the way to defeat the Persians was to challenge them at sea.

To do this, the Greek army had to set up a delaying action on land. They chose **Thermopylae** (thuhr•MAH•puh•lee) as the place—a mountain pass north of Athens. There, 7,000 Greeks led by King **Leonidas** of Sparta stood firm against the Persians for three days. Then a Greek traitor showed the enemy a trail over which they could attack the Greeks from the rear. Realizing that he would soon be surrounded, Leonidas sent off most of his troops. But he and 300 fellow Spartans remained obedient to the law of their polis—never

Footnotes to History

Marathon
According to legend, a messenger named Pheidippides (fy•DIH•puh•DEEZ) carried the news of the victory at Marathon back to Athens. Because Pheidippides had previously run 280 miles (448 km) in four days, he barely managed to reach the city and deliver his message before he fell to the ground, dead from exhaustion. Ever since, people have used the word *marathon* to describe a long-distance race.

TEACH

Guided Practice

THEME Conflict

Have students name some of the reasons that other city-states came to resent Athens and eventually went to war with Athens. *(Answers should include: Pericles' use of Delian League money to build the Parthenon, his insistence that criminal cases be tried only in Athens, and his forcing other city-states to adopt the Athenian coinage system.)* **L1**

Map Study

Answers
Ionia

Map Skills Practice

Reading a Map How did Persian strategy in 480 B.C. differ from that in 490 B.C.? *(In 480 B.C., the Persians attacked from the north, rather than from the east. They also divided their forces in 480 B.C., with some on land and some at sea.*

Pericles Point out that many great men and women have both positive and negative aspects to their lives and characters. Have students list positive and negative aspects of Pericles' life and accomplishments. *(positive: led Athens through its Golden Age, built the Parthenon and other buildings, spoke out for democracy; negative: used Delian League money to build Parthenon, tried to force other city-states to accept Athenian leadership, helped push Sparta to start Peloponnesian War.)* **L2**

COOPERATIVE LEARNING ACTIVITY

Oral-Visual Presentations Organize the class into two groups for further study of the Persian Wars and the Peloponnesian War. Each group should prepare an oral and visual presentation for the other group. Organize each group into subgroups to research facets of the topic, such as the impact of geography on the battles and the leaders involved. Subgroups should also prepare visuals to add interest to the group presentation, including drawings of soldiers, weapons, battle formations, fortifications, and ships. Each group should prepare a large time line of the events. Have groups cooperatively decide how to present their completed report to the other group. Encourage them to use discussion rather than a written report. **L2**

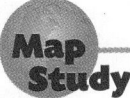

Mapping History Overlay Transparency 4

Independent Practice

Guided Reading Activity 4-4 **L1**

Daily Life Have students draw floor plans for a typical Athenian home. Point out that most rooms looked inward to a courtyard, rather than outward to the noisy and smelly streets. **L1 LEP**

Editorial Have students imagine that they witnessed the battle of Salamis. Have them write a newspaper editorial glorifying the Greek victory. They may do outside reading. Editorials should be historically accurate but may reflect personal observations and feelings. **L3**

you don't say...

"Barbarians" is a word that goes back to the Greeks who applied the term to all non-Greeks. It was not a pejorative term, but simply a way of approximating a foreign language, which to the Greeks sounded like "bar-bar-bar."

Visualizing History Pericles gave his great funeral oration in 430 B.C., in honor of Athenian soldiers killed in the Peloponnesian War.
Answer to Caption: *Democracy meant that power was in the hands of the many, not the few.*

surrender on the battlefield, but fight until victory or death.

> "They [the Spartans] defended themselves to the last, such as still had swords using them, and the others resisting with their hand and teeth; till the barbarians [Persians] ... overwhelmed and buried the remnant left beneath showers of missile weapons."
>
> —Herodotus, from *History*, 400s B.C.

The heroic stand of Leonidas and the Spartans gave Themistocles enough time to carry out his plan. He drew the Persian fleet into the strait of Salamis, a narrow body of water between Athens and the island of **Salamis**. Themistocles reasoned that the heavy Persian ships would crowd together in the strait and make easy targets for the lighter but faster and more maneuverable Greek ships. The plan worked, and the outnumbered ships of the Greek navy destroyed almost the entire Persian fleet.

After the battle at Salamis, the Greeks gained the upper hand. By 479 B.C., the Persians had once again retreated to Asia Minor, this time for good. With the end of the Persian Wars, the Greek city-states resumed their traditional quarrels.

The Golden Age of Athens

Greek culture reached its peak after the Persian Wars. Most historians refer to the period from 461 B.C. to 429 B.C. as the Golden Age of Athens because most Greek achievements in the arts and sciences took place in Athens during this time.

Pericles in Charge

The Athenian general **Pericles**, beginning in the 450s B.C., led Athens through its Golden Age. The Persians had burned Athens during the Persian Wars, but beginning in 447 B.C., Pericles was determined to rebuild the city. When the rebuilt temples and palaces crowned its acropolis, Athens became the most beautiful city in Greece. The most famous structure built under Pericles, the Parthenon (the temple of Athena), still stands.

Pericles wanted the polis of Athens to stand for all that was best in Greek civilization. A persuasive speaker, he expressed his ideas in a famous funeral oration quoted by the Greek historian Thucydides (thoo•SIH•duh•DEEZ):

> "We are called a democracy [because power] is in the hands of the many and not the few.... When it is a question of putting one person before another in positions of public responsibility, what counts is not membership of a particular class, but the actual ability which the man possesses.... We are prevented from doing wrong by respect ... for the laws.... We are lovers of the beautiful, yet simple in our tastes, and we cultivate the mind without loss of manliness.... To avow poverty with us is no disgrace; the true disgrace is in doing nothing to avoid it.... Athens is the school of Hellas [Greece]."

Visualizing History **Pericles held virtual control over Athenian affairs for the last 15 years of his life, being elected each year as one of the 10 city generals.** *How did Pericles identify his faith in democracy?*

Athenian Daily Life

Athenians lavished money on public buildings, but they kept their individual homes simple. The typical Athenian house contained two main rooms and several smaller ones built around a central courtyard. In one main room, the dining room, the men entertained guests and ate while reclining on couches. An Athenian woman joined her husband for dinner only if company was not invited. In the other main room, the wool room, the women spun and wove cloth. In the courtyard stood an altar, a wash basin, and sometimes a well. The courtyard also contained the family's chickens and goats.

Athenian men usually worked in the morning as farmers, artisans, and merchants. Then they spent the afternoon attending the Assembly or exercising in the gymnasium. Slaves—who were mostly foreigners and prisoners of war and who made up one-third of the population—did most of

MEETING SPECIAL NEEDS ACTIVITY

Learning Style: Logical/Mathematical Many students have trouble understanding dates. This is especially true in the pre-Christian era (B.C.), when numbers grow smaller as the time advances—just the opposite of what happens in more recent history when dates are A.D.

Have students reproduce the time line on page 120 and then add the following events in the appropriate places: battle of Salamis, Golden Age of Athens, Pericles' funeral oration, end of the Peloponnesian War. **L2** the heavy work in craft production and mining. Many slaves also worked as teachers and household servants. Most Athenian women spent their time at home, cooking and making wool cloth, but poor women worked in the open-air markets as food sellers and cloth weavers.

Upper-class Athenian men—as well as citizens from other city-states—enjoyed the symposium as a form of recreation. Wives were excluded from a **symposium**, which was a drinking session following a banquet. The men at a symposium were entertained by female dancers and singers as well as by acrobats and magicians. The guests also spent much of the evening entertaining each other, telling riddles and discussing literature, philosophy, and public issues.

Athenian Women

In spite of restrictions, many Athenian women were able to participate in public life—especially in city festivals—and learned to read and write. Public opinion allowed greater freedom to women of the *metic* class than to those of other groups. The most famous of *metic* women was **Aspasia**, who was known for her intelligence and personal charm. To her house came many of the women of Athens, and she apparently gave advice on home life while attempting to gain more education and greater freedom for Athenian women. Her views aroused great opposition among some Athenians of both sexes, and she was prosecuted on a charge of "impiety," or disloyalty to the gods. Aspasia was finally acquitted after an impassioned plea to the jury by Pericles himself.

The Peloponnesian War

Even after the Persian Wars ended, the Persian threat remained. Athens persuaded most of the city-states—but not Sparta—to ally against the enemy. This alliance became known as the Delian League because the treasury was kept on the sacred island of **Delos**. Athens provided the principal naval and land forces, while the other city-states furnished money and ships. Over the next several decades, the Delian League succeeded in freeing Ionia from Persian rule and sweeping the Aegean free of pirates. Overseas trade expanded, and Greece grew richer.

The Athenian Empire

Athens gradually began to dominate the other city-states. Pericles, for example, used part of the Delian League's treasury to build the Parthenon. He insisted that criminal cases be tried only in Athens and that other city-states adopt the Athenian coinage system. He also sent Athenian troops to support revolts by commoners against aristocrats in other city-states. In short, the policies of Pericles more or less transformed the Delian League from what had been an anti-Persian defense league into an Athenian empire.

As Athen's trade and political influence grew, several city-states reacted by forming an alliance opposed to Athens. Sparta, a long-standing Athenian rival, became the leader of the anti-Athens alliance. Since Sparta was located in the Peloponnesus, historians have called the war against Athens and its allies the Peloponnesian War.

The Conflict

The Peloponnesian War lasted from 431 B.C. to 404 B.C., excluding one brief period of peace. At first it seemed as if Athens could hold out indefinitely, since Sparta had no navy. Sparta's fear and jealousy of Athens, however, were so strong that the Spartans made a deal with the Persians to return Ionia to Persian control. In exchange, Sparta received gold to build its own fleet. Then, in 430 B.C., a disastrous plague—probably typhus—weakened Athens. More

Visualizing History **A Spartan soldier poises for battle. The Spartans developed a chain of orders to be shouted above the din of battle.** *How did Sparta attain a navy?*

Chapter 4 Section 4

Visualizing History Physical prowess alone was not responsible for Spartan military victories. Spartans also developed an early flame-throwing weapon.
Answer to Caption: *Persia gave Sparta enough gold to build its own fleet in exchange for being allowed to retake control of Ionia.*

Linking Past and Present

The Peloponnesian War demanded great sacrifice from Athens. It has been estimated that almost a third of its population was mobilized. By contrast, World War I mobilized 10 percent of the population of the countries involved.

ASSESS

Check for Understanding

Assign Section 4 Review as homework or as an in-class activity.

Use Student Self-Test and Review Software to review Section 4.

Evaluate

Section Quiz 4-4

Use the Testmaker to create a customized quiz for Section 4.

MAKING CONNECTIONS ACTIVITY

Sports The first modern marathon—named after the battle that led to the famous run of Pheidippides—was held at the Olympic Games in Athens in 1896. The length of the marathon varied until it was officially set, in 1908, at 26 miles, 385 yards (45.37 kilometers). Have students research and report on famous marathons of today, such as those of Boston and New York City. Their reports should include the history of the event, the time and place in which it is staged, the average number of runners, the names of important recent winners, and the time it took these people to run the race. **L2**

Chapter 4 Section 4

Map Study

Answers

1. *They feared and were jealous of Athens.*
2. *Ionia*

Map Skills Practice

Reading a Map What strategic advantage can you see in the geographic location of Sparta's allies? The allies of Athens? *(Sparta's allies not only surrounded Attica but also included a territory in the north (Macedonia), in the midst of regions linked to Athens. The allies of Athens dominated the Aegean Sea.)*

Reteach

Have students write two brief paragraphs describing Athenian political life, the first as it was before the Peloponnesian War, the second as it was after the war.

Reteaching Activity 4

Enrich

Have students research the clothing and weapons used by the typical Greek soldier.

Enrichment Activity 4

CLOSE

Ask students which event discussed in this chapter was the most important for Greek civilization.

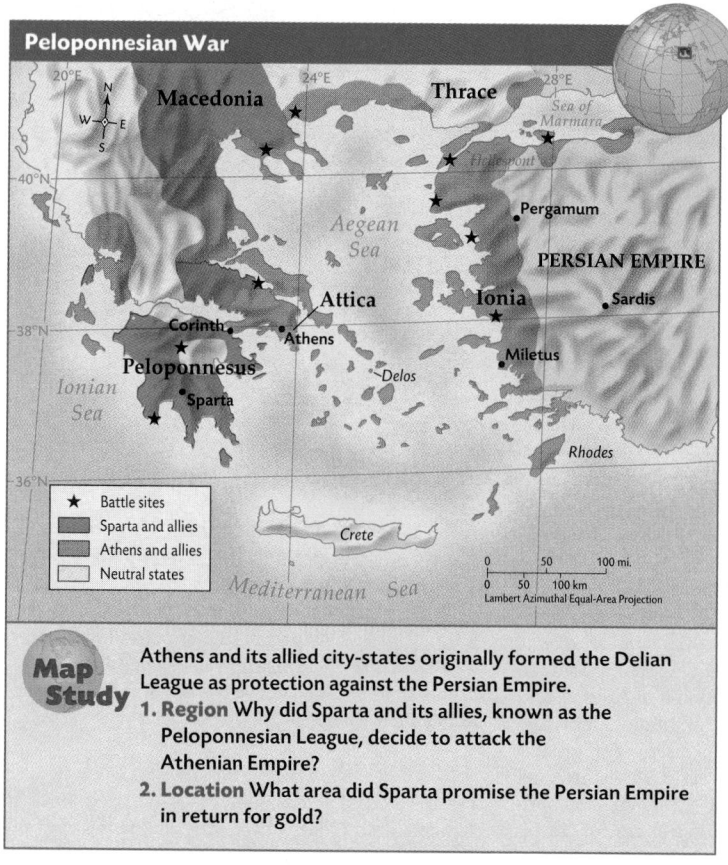

Peloponnesian War

Map Study Athens and its allied city-states originally formed the Delian League as protection against the Persian Empire.

1. **Region** Why did Sparta and its allies, known as the Peloponnesian League, decide to attack the Athenian Empire?
2. **Location** What area did Sparta promise the Persian Empire in return for gold?

fleet. After the Spartans laid siege to Athens itself, the Athenians finally surrendered in 404 B.C.

Effects of the War

The Peloponnesian War brought disaster to the Greek city-states, both victors and vanquished. Many city-states declined in population. Fighting had destroyed many fields and orchards. Unemployment became so widespread that thousands of young men emigrated and became **mercenaries**, or hired soldiers, in the Persian army.

Worst of all, the Greeks lost their ability to govern themselves. The length and cost of the war made people forget about the common good of their polis and think only about making money. Feelings between aristocrats and commoners grew increasingly bitter. Many Greeks, losing faith in democracy, even came to look down on free political discussion and began to believe that

than a third of its population died, including Pericles.

After Pericles died in 429 B.C., some Athenians wanted to make peace with Sparta and its allies, while other Athenians wanted to keep on fighting. No decision was made, and the war continued deadlocked for many more years. Eventually, several allies of Athens switched sides and joined the Spartan-led alliance. Then, with their Persian-financed navy, the Spartans destroyed the Athenian

might makes right.

For a time, Sparta tried to rule the other city-states. Then, in 371 B.C., a new alliance of city-states led by Thebes overthrew the harsh, incompetent Spartan rulers. The Thebans, however, also made poor rulers and were also overthrown. As a result of almost continual fighting, the city-states became weaker than ever. When a new invader, the Macedonians, threatened Greece in the 350s B.C., the city-states were unable to resist.

SECTION 4 REVIEW

Recall

1. **Define** symposium, mercenary.
2. **Identify** Ionia, Darius I, Marathon, Xerxes, Themistocles, Thermopylae, Leonidas, Salamis, Pericles, Aspasia.
3. **Describe** the daily activities of an Athenian husband. What were those of an Athenian wife?

Critical Thinking

4. **Evaluating Information** Judge whether Pericles' rule was beneficial for Athens. Give reasons to support your answer.

Understanding Themes

5. **Conflict** Why didn't loyalty to the polis prevent Greeks from uniting against Persia?

SECTION 4 REVIEW ANSWERS

1. All vocabulary words are defined in the Glossary.
2. Ionia, 120; Darius, 120; Marathon, 121; Xerxes, 121; Themistocles, 121; Thermopylae, 121; Leonidas, 121; Salamis, 122; Pericles, 122; Aspasia, 123
3. Husband: work, go to agora, attend Assembly, exercise in gymnasium, enjoy symposium (upper class); wife: cook, spin and weave, sell in agora (lower class), remain at home (upper class)
4. Yes: he rebuilt Athens and extended Athenian power and influence; no: by transforming the Delian League into an Athenian Empire, he helped bring on the disastrous Peloponnesian War.
5. **CONFLICT** The Greeks felt so threatened by the Persians that they overcame rivalries in order to oppose the enemy.

Critical Thinking SKILLS

Making Comparisons

In shopping for athletic shoes, you have narrowed your selection to two pairs. Which pair should you buy? To decide this question, you must make a comparison.

Learning the Skill

Making comparisons means finding similarities and differences. In the above example, you might first notice the similarities between the shoes. Both pairs are the same price and the same color. Then, you would look for differences. One pair extends above the ankle, the other pair does not. One pair is designed for jogging, the other for aerobics. Once you have compared the shoes, you can draw a conclusion about which pair will best suit your needs.

Apply the same method in comparing any two objects, groups, or concepts. First, determine the purpose of your comparison. What question do you want to answer? Then determine the bases for comparison. In the shoe example, we compared on the bases of price, color, style, and athletic function. Then identify similarities and differences in each of these categories. Finally, use the comparison to draw conclusions or to answer your question.

Practicing the Skill

The excerpts on this page discuss the military strength of Sparta and Athens. Read the excerpts and answer the questions below.

1. Identify three bases for comparing the military strength of Athens and Sparta.
2. Do both city-states have armies and navies?
3. What are two differences in the military strength of Athens and Sparta?
4. Based on this comparison, which city-state has greater military strength? Why?

> "We [Spartans] have many reasons to expect success,—first, superiority in numbers and in military experience, and second, our general and unvarying obedience in the execution of orders. The naval strength which they [Athens] possess shall be raised by us from ... the monies at Olympia and Delphi. A loan from these enables us to seduce their foreign sailors by the offer of higher pay.... A single defeat at sea is in all likelihood their ruin."
>
> —Thucydides, account of a Corinthian envoy to the Congress at Sparta, 432 B.C.

> "Personally engaged in the cultivation of their land, without funds either private or public, the Peloponnesians [Spartans] are also without experience in long wars across the sea.... Our naval skill is of more use to us for service on land, than their military skill for service at sea. Even if they were to ... try to seduce our foreign sailors by the temptation of higher pay ... none of our foreign sailors would consent to become an outlaw from his own country, and to take service with them."
>
> —Pericles, account to Athenian Ecclesia, 432 B.C.

Applying the Skill

Choose a topic or activity that interests you, such as baseball, rock music, politics, etc. Research and compare two individuals, groups, or organizations involved in this activity. Write a short essay or make a chart outlining at least five similarities and five differences.

For More Practice

Turn to the Skill Practice in the Chapter Review on page 127 for more practice in making comparisons.

ANSWERS TO PRACTICING THE SKILL

1. number of soldiers; experience; naval strength
2. yes
3. The Spartans claim to have a bigger army of more experienced soldiers; the Athenians claim to have a navy that is loyal and more skilled.
4. Students might make the case either for Sparta, with a better and larger army or for Athens, with a superior navy.

Critical Thinking SKILLS

TEACH

Making Comparisons Many television ads are based on comparisons. Have two volunteers with different preferences in morning cereal bring in the box or copy of the nutrition information, net weight, and price each displays. Other volunteers can transfer the nutritional data to the chalkboard. Then write on the chalkboard the price per ounce of the two cereals. Ask students to draw conclusions from the comparison.

Additional Practice

Skill Reinforcement Activity 4

CHAPTER 4 REVIEW

Historical Significance

Ancient Greece provided the world with its first example of democratic government. Because the limited number of citizens in a Greek polis permitted direct participation by all citizens, Athens can be described as a *direct* democracy. In the United States today, where we elect senators and representatives who are responsible to us, the form of government is called a *representative* democracy. In contrast to citizenship in ancient Greece, United States citizenship has broadened to include women and people of all races, as well as naturalized foreign-born citizens.

Using Key Terms

Write the key term that completes each sentence.

a. aristocrats	g. rhetoric
b. citizen	h. tyrant
c. democracy	i. symposiums
d. oligarchy	j. labyrinth
e. mercenary	k. phalanx
f. polis	l. bards

1. The _____, the basic political unit of ancient Greece, included a city and the surrounding villages, fields, and orchards.
2. A woman in ancient Greece was not considered to be a full _______ with the right to take part in political affairs.
3. A leader known as a ______ came to power in many Greek city-states and usually promised to introduce reforms to help farmers, merchants, and artisans.
4. Upon reaching their teens, Athenian boys studied __________, or the art of public speaking, as part of their education.
5. Sir Arthur Evans discovered that intricate passageways in Minos's palace at Knossos on Crete form a ___________, or maze.
6. By the 700s B.C., kings in Greece had lost power to landholding members of the upper class known as __________.
7. Athenian men entertained each other at _____, telling riddles and discussing literature, philosophy, and public issues.
8. In an ______, a few wealthy people hold power over a larger group of citizens.
9. _____, or singing storytellers, kept alive Mycenaean literary traditions during Greece's "dark age."
10. In a ______, or government by the people, political power lies in the hands of all citizens.

Using Your History Journal

Democracy is not easy to achieve or to maintain. Make a list of the issues that challenge democracy in America. Write a paragraph entitled "Maintaining Democracy" or "Achieving Democracy" that responds to this issue.

Reviewing Facts

1. **List** the elements of Minoan culture that were adopted by the Mycenaeans.
2. **State** the values of Hellenic civilization that were found in the *Iliad* and the *Odyssey*.
3. **Explain** how the attitude of the Greeks toward their deities differed from the attitude of the Egyptians.
4. **Explain** how Sparta's response in the 700s B.C. to the problems of increased population and a shortage of arable land differed from the response of most other Greek city-states.
5. **Describe** the major difference between the Greeks and the Persians, according to the Ionians.

Critical Thinking

1. **Apply** How did Sparta's values affect its educational system?
2. **Analyze** How did increased trade affect Greek political life?
3. **Synthesize** What might have been the outcome of the Persian Wars if Themistocles had not convinced the Greeks to build a fleet of ships?

Chapter 4 Review

GLENCOE TECHNOLOGY

VIDEODISC

Use MindJogger to review students' knowledge of the chapter.

MindJogger Videoquiz

Chapter 4
Disc 1 Side A

Also available in VHS.

Answers

Using Key Terms

1. f	6. a
2. b	7. i
3. h	8. d
4. g	9. l
5. j	10. c

Using Your History Journal

Students should consider how actions they take in their own lives serve to maintain or achieve democracy.

Reviewing Facts

1. metalworking techniques, shipbuilding, navigation by sun and stars, worship of the Earth Mother
2. pride in being Greek, love of life, desire for excellence, determination to meet fate with dignity
3. The Greeks humanized their deities and strived to achieve godlike power and excellence.
4. Sparta conquered neighboring city-states and enslaved the inhabitants. Other city-states set up colonies and expanded overseas trade.
5. Greeks believed that citizens should choose their own government, while Persians believed in rule by an all-powerful king.

Critical Thinking

1. Males lived in military barracks after age 7. They learned how to use weapons so that they would be good soldiers. Females trained in gymnastics, wrestling, and boxing so they would be strong and bear healthy children.
2. It led to an increase in the number and wealth of nonlandowning merchants and artisans, who demanded a voice in the government and also wanted the government to encourage industry and promote trade.
3. because the Persians would have controlled the sea, they might have defeated the Greeks
4. They might suggest that women are simply objects, like pillars, or, they might suggest that women are powerful and respected enough to support an important building.

4. **Analyze Art** Shown below, the south porch of the Erechtheum near the Parthenon uses figures of maidens to replace conventional columns. The buildings on the Acropolis are examples of early classical architecture and sculpture. What might these figures suggest about the role of women in Athenian life?

Understanding Themes

1. **Relation to Environment** What aspects of Crete's environment enabled the Minoans to become skilled seafarers?
2. **Movement** What role did trade play in the development of Greek civilization?
3. **Regionalism** What effect did Sparta's emphasis on military values have on its development as a city-state?
4. **Conflict** Why did several Greek city-states, led by Sparta, form an alliance in the mid-400s B.C. to fight against Athens and the Delian League?

Linking Past and Present

1. During times of unrest in ancient Athens, tyrants seized power to introduce political and economic reforms. Do you think a tyrant could establish a dictatorship in the United States at a time of crisis? Explain your answer.
2. Why might students at the United States Naval Academy study the Persian Wars?

Skill Practice

Reread Section 3 and compare the two leading city-states in ancient Greece.

1. What are two similarities in the education of young people in Athens and Sparta?
2. What are two differences in their education?
3. What are two similarities in the political structure of Athens and Sparta?
4. What are two differences in their political structure?
5. What are two differences in the role of women in Athens and Sparta?
6. What are two similarities in women's roles?

Geography in History

1. **Place** Although it is a small island, Crete has what two landforms?
2. **Location** Refer to the map on page 124. What is the relative location of Crete? What is Crete's absolute location?
3. **Location** Where was the palace of the legendary king Minos?
4. **Human/Environment Interaction** How did the early people of Crete earn their living?

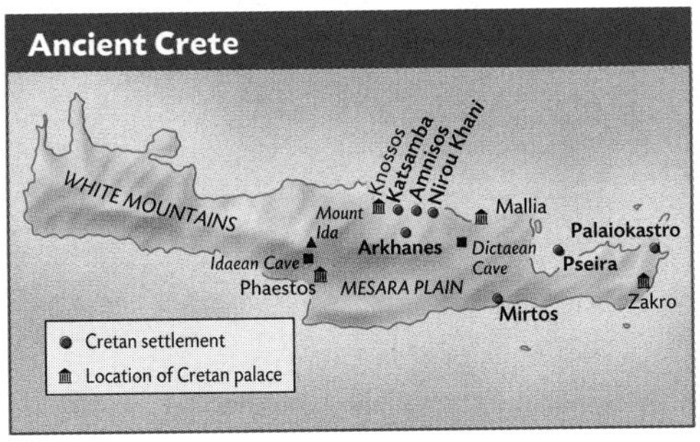

Chapter 4 Review

Linking Past and Present

1. constitutional safeguards against arbitrary power; the operation of a two-party system; and the influence of the mass media for both good and ill
2. to learn about Themistocles' tactics at the battle of Salamis

Skill Practice

1. All boys were educated; education started at age 7.
2. Athens: more subjects were studied; Sparta: girls were trained in athletics
3. Both had an Assembly of all citizens; both had a Council.
4. Sparta had kings and ephors, while Athens did not.
5. Athens: women received no education and stayed at home. Sparta: women married later and had more personal rights.
6. inferior to men in status, had no voice in government

Geography in History

1. mountains, plains
2. southeast of Greece and southwest of Ionia, 35°N latitude, 24°E longitude
3. at Knossos, on Crete's north coast
4. from sea trade

Chapter Bonus Test Question

Ask students: "Beware of Greeks bearing gifts" is a common expression. What event in Greek history or legend does it refer to, and what does it mean? Give an example of a situation in which someone today might use this expression. *(the event is the Trojan War; the "gift" a wooden horse given to the Trojans that secretly contained Spartan soldiers. People should be wary of gifts coming from unlikely givers. People today might use this phrase in reference to the "free" gifts that businesses offer, which are often tied to promises of future purchases.)*

Understanding Themes

1. **RELATION TO ENVIRONMENT** It was an island, and it was located close to other centers of civilization.
2. **MOVEMENT** Minoan traders visited the Greek mainland and brought their culture with them. Trade between the Greek city-states and their colonies flourished. The economic prosperity led those who made the goods traded to demand more rights. Eventually this led to the development of democracy.
3. **REGIONALISM** Because of its concentration on military power, it lagged behind other city-states in trade and manufacturing (and thus was poorer) and created little in the way of intellectual, literary, and scientific accomplishments.
4. **CONFLICT** They resented and feared Athens's growing influence and power.

Chapter 4 *The Rise of Ancient Greece* 127

The Height of Greek Civilization

CHAPTER RESOURCES	Reproducible Resources	Multimedia Resources
Chapter Opener	Chapter Themes: Graphic Organizer 5 Historical Significance Chapter Activity 5	MindJogger Videoquiz
Chapter Enrichment	Vocabulary Activity 5* Time Line Activity 5 Mapping History Activity 5 History Simulation 5 Geography and History Activity 5 Source Reading 5 People in World History Profiles 7, 8 World Art and Music Activity 5 Enrichment Activity 5 Critical Thinking Activity 5 Skill Reinforcement Activity 5 Building Skills in Geography Workbook, Unit 1, Lessons 3, 4, 5 Performance Assessment Activity 5	Focus on World Art Print 8, Greek. *Laocoön* Ancient Civilizations Poster Set: *Ancient Greece* World History and Art Transparency 6, *Nike of Samothrace* Mapping History Overlay Transparencies 4, 5 Chapter Transparency 5 NGS PicturePack Transparency Set: *Ancient Greece* Vocabulary PuzzleMaker Software NGS PictureShow CD-ROM: *Greece and Rome* World Music: Cultural Traditions, Lesson 3
Chapter Review/Reteaching	Reteaching Activity 5 Skill Reinforcement Activity 5 Spanish Chapter Summary 5	Chapter 5 Digest Audiocassette, Activity, Test* Vocabulary PuzzleMaker Software Student Self-Test and Review Software MindJogger Videoquiz
Chapter Evaluation/Testing	Performance Assessment Activity 5 Chapter 5 Test, Forms A and B	Testmaker

* *Also available in Spanish*

0:00 OUT OF TIME? Assign the Chapter 5 summary of the Unit 2 Digest on pages 236–239, and the Chapter 5 Audiocassettes.

Block Schedule

Block scheduling differs from traditional class scheduling in the amount of time allotted to each period. The extended time frame provided by block scheduling affords you the opportunity to implement a greater number of research-oriented and activity-intense projects to motivate and involve your students. Activities that are particularly suited to use within the block scheduling framework are identified throughout this chapter by the following designation.

KEY TO ABILITY LEVELS

Teaching strategies have been coded for varying learning styles and abilities.

- L1 **BASIC** activities for all students
- L2 **AVERAGE** activities for average to above-average students
- L3 **CHALLENGING** activities for above-average students
- LEP **LIMITED ENGLISH PROFICIENCY** activities

A complete, 1-page lesson plan is provided for each section in the *Reproducible Lesson Plans* booklet.

SECTION RESOURCES

Daily Objectives	Reproducible Resources	Multimedia Resources
Section 1 Quest for Beauty and Meaning Describe how the Greeks expressed their love of beauty and meaning.	Reproducible Lesson Plan 5-1 Guided Reading Activity 5-1* Source Reading 5 World Art and Music Activity 5 Section Quiz 5-1*	NGS PicturePack Transparency Set: *Ancient Greece* Section Focus Transparency 5-1 World History and Art Transparency 6, *Nike of Samothrace* NGS PicturePack Transparency Set: *Ancient Greece* Vocabulary PuzzleMaker Software Student Self-Test and Review Software Testmaker NGS PictureShow CD-ROM: *Greece and Rome* World Music: Cultural Traditions, Lesson 3
Section 2 The Greek Mind Identify the achievements of the ancient Greeks in philosophy, history, and science.	Reproducible Lesson Plan 5-2 Vocabulary Activity 5* Guided Reading Activity 5-2* People in World History Profiles 7, 8 History Simulation 5 Section Quiz 5-2*	Section Focus Transparency 5-2 Mapping History Overlay Transparency 4, *Ancient Greece* Chapter Transparency 5 Student Self-Test and Review Software Testmaker
Section 3 Alexander's Empire Outline Alexander's goals and evaluate his success in achieving them.	Reproducible Lesson Plan 5-3 Vocabulary Activity 5* Guided Reading Activity 5-3* Reteaching Activity 5 Enrichment Activity 5 Time Line Activity 5 Mapping History Activity 5 Geography and History Activity 5 Section Quiz 5-3* Performance Assessment Activity 5 Spanish Chapter Summary 5	Focus on World Art Print 8, Greek. *Laocoön* Section Focus Transparency 5-3 Mapping History Overlay Transparency 5, *Empire of Alexander the Great* Student Self-Test and Review Software Testmaker

** Also available in Spanish*

Chapter Activities

Performance Assessment Activity

A Cultural Borrowing Portfolio Have students create a chapter portfolio of modern-day examples of Greek influence. Examples may come from library materials, magazines, television, multimedia, film, or newspapers—each cited and including a short explanation of how the event, process or item can be connected to ancient Greece. Portfolios should include at least ten examples. Students may work together in groups of up to four on the portfolios.

Possible Rubric Features

Accuracy of content information, concept attainment (cultural borrowing), relevancy of modern-day examples, organization of portfolio, clarity of text

• *For an additional activity, refer to Activity 5 in the* Performance Assessment Strategies and Activities *booklet.*

Activity

From the Classroom of...

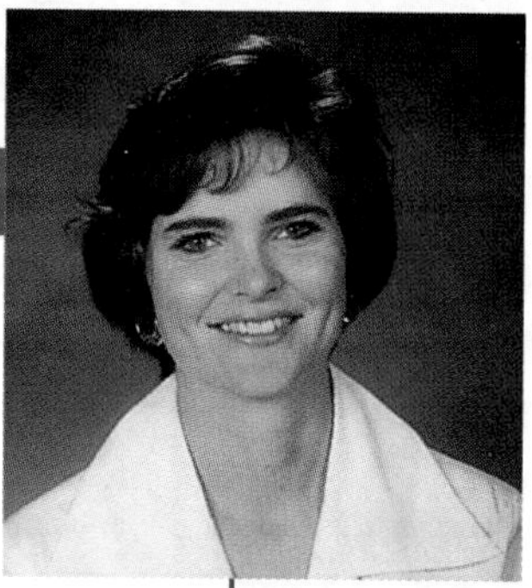

Shannon Heck, Ladue Horton Watkins High School, St. Louis, MO

The Trial of Socrates

Students will simulate "democracy on trial." Socrates, at 70 years old, in 399 B.C., is charged with 1) corrupting the youth of Athens and causing them to doubt the wisdom of Homer; 2) lack of reverence for the Greek gods; and 3) belief in his own gods. In his defense, Socrates claimed to be guided by an inner voice.

The roles in this simulation trial can vary, but may include: "Cleon," an Athenian councilman fearful of Socrates' teachings; "Diodorus," a concerned father who believes that Socrates' teachings are undermining the youth of Athens; "Judge," presides over the trial, keeps order; "Prosecutor," citizen attorney who accuses Socrates of the three crimes; "Defense," advises and counsels Socrates; "Plato" and "Xenophon," students of Socrates; "Agia," a worshiper of Athena.

Students on both teams should work out their strategies in the presentation of their cases. Attorneys for the teams should coach their witnesses for direct examination and prepare for cross-examinations also. Likewise, the jurors and judge should prepare for the case by gaining background knowledge but should reserve judgment prior to the case. After the trial, discuss with students whether they think a case such as Socrates' could ever come to trial in the United States.

MULTIPLE LEARNING STYLES

Verbal/Linguistic

Have students contribute to a "Legacy of Ancient Greece" bulletin board. Ask each student to write on some aspect of architecture, art, history, literature, science, mathematics, or philosophy. They should illustrate their subjects and explain why each is an important contribution to Western civilization.

Logical/Mathematical

Have students construct a time line illustrating the Hellenic and Hellenistic eras. Have them include dates, events, and people. Students may begin with key dates from the chapter opener time line and add to their time line as they progress through the chapter. Have students work on poster-size paper.

Visual/Spatial

Have students draw a base map for the growth of Greek influence (see map on page 141). Then ask them to make two overlays on onionskin paper—one showing Hellenic Greece and its colonies (see map on page 114), the other, the Hellenistic region.

Kinesthetic

Have students find political cartoons in newspapers and magazines. Then have them prepare their own cartoons to illustrate the political philosophy of Plato or Aristotle, or to illustrate political issues from the days of ancient Greece.

Additional Resources

TEACHER'S CORNER

NATIONAL GEOGRAPHIC SOCIETY

INDEX TO NATIONAL GEOGRAPHIC MAGAZINE

The following articles may be used for research relating to this chapter:

- "When the Greeks Went West," by Rick Gore, November 1994.
- "Warriors From a Watery Grave: Glorious Bronzes of Ancient Greece," by Joseph Alsop, June 1983.

NATIONAL GEOGRAPHIC SOCIETY PRODUCTS AVAILABLE FROM GLENCOE

To order the following products for use with this chapter, contact your local Glencoe sales representative or call Glencoe at 1-800-368-7344:

NGS PICTURESHOW CD-ROM
- Greece and Rome

NGS PICTUREPACK TRANSPARENCY SET
- Ancient Greece

ANCIENT CIVILIZATIONS POSTER SET
- Ancient Greece

ADDITIONAL NATIONAL GEOGRAPHIC SOCIETY PRODUCTS

To order the following products for use with this chapter, call National Geographic Society at 1-800-368-2728:

- *Ancient Civilizations*, "Greece." (Filmstrip)

Bibliography

Literature of the Period

Fagles, Robert, trans. ***Sophocles: The Three Theban Plays.*** New York: Penguin, 1984. Included are *Oedipus the King*, *Antigone*, and *Oedipus at Colonus*.

Hamilton, Edith, trans. ***Three Greek Plays.*** New York: Norton, 1958. Included are *The Trojan Women* by Euripides and *Prometheus Bound* and *Agamemnon* by Aeschylus.

Readings for the Student

Harris, Nathaniel. ***Alexander the Great and the Greeks.*** New York: Bookwright Press, 1986. Easy reading, but with well-researched detail about Alexander's contributions.

Renault, Mary. ***The Persian Boy.*** New York: Bantam, 1988. The second of three novels about Alexander the Great.

Readings for the Teacher

Grant, Michael. ***The Classical Greeks.*** New York: Scribner, 1989. Connects culture—art, architecture, philosophy, and drama—with historical events.

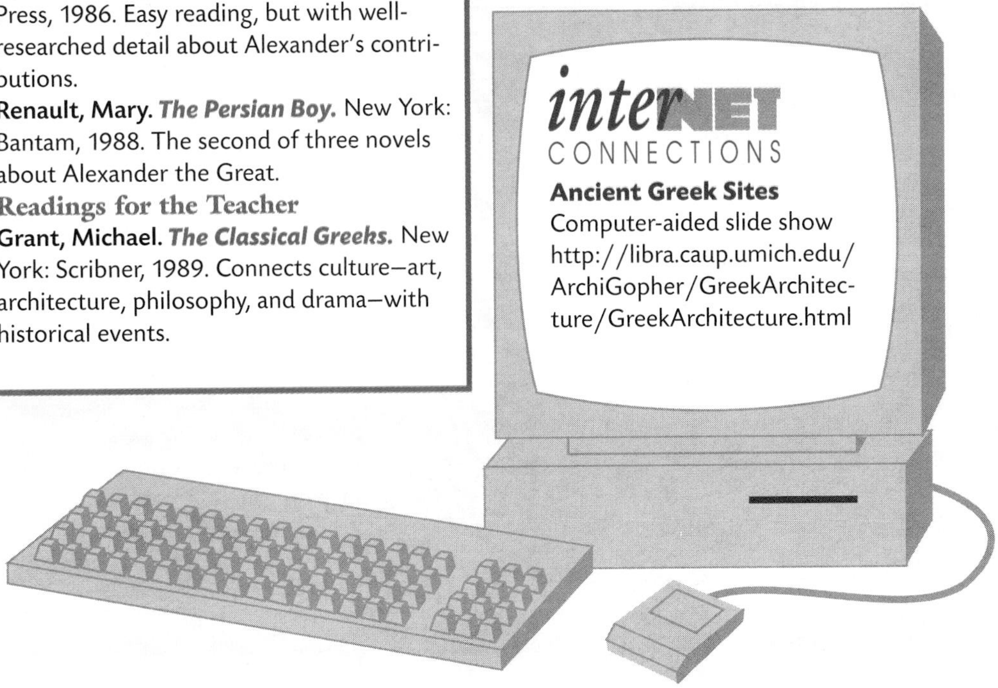

interNET
CONNECTIONS
Ancient Greek Sites
Computer-aided slide show
http://libra.caup.umich.edu/ArchiGopher/GreekArchitecture/GreekArchitecture.html

Introducing Chapter 5

CHAPTER THEMES

Chapter Themes are listed by section on this chapter opening page of the Student Edition. A corresponding theme-based activity is available under "TEACH," and a theme-based question is asked in the Section and Chapter Reviews.

The Storyteller

Historical Setting Much of what we know about the life and teachings of Socrates comes to us from Socrates' most famous student, Plato. But Plato, according to some scholars, may have attributed ideas to Socrates that originated with Plato himself. Ask students why scholars might care whether the ideas should be attributed to Plato or Socrates. *(Scholars want to know how coherent and/or consistent their subject's ideas are, and how they relate to the work of others; uncertain provenance makes this task harder.)*

Historical Significance

Answers: *They valued moderation and balance, loved beauty, stressed the individual, and sought the truth through free inquiry.*

Western architects and sculptors have copied Greek works for centuries; Greek philosophers, historians, and scientists created traditions in these disciplines that are still valid today.

Chapter 5

750–150 B.C.

The Height of Greek Civilization

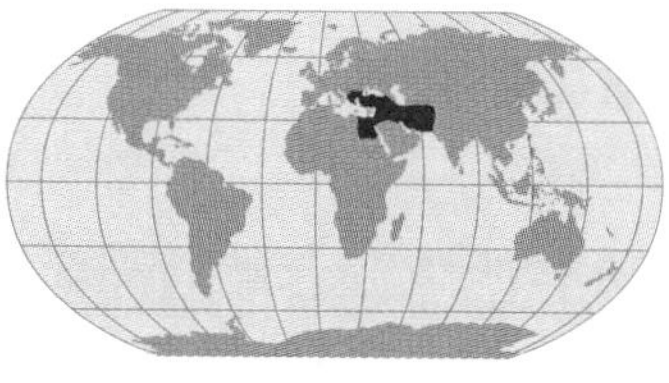

Chapter Themes

- **Innovation** The ancient Greeks develop a culture that becomes one of the foundations of Western civilization. *Section 1*
- **Innovation** Ancient Greek thinkers believe in reason and the importance of the individual. *Section 2*
- **Cultural Diffusion** Alexander's empire brings about a mix of Greek and Middle Eastern cultures. *Section 3*

The Storyteller

An outwardly unimpressive man, Socrates was nonetheless an intellectual giant in the Athens of the late 400s B.C. *One of his devoted followers described Socrates' day: "At early morning he was to be seen betaking himself to one of the promenades or wrestling grounds; at noon he would appear with the gathering crowds in the marketplace; and as day declined, wherever the largest throng might be encountered, there was he to be found, talking for the most part, while anyone who chose might stop and listen." Socrates was a supreme questioner who succeeded in getting people to analyze their own behavior. Today, Socrates' reputation lives on as one of the greatest teachers of all time.*

Historical Significance

What were the principal beliefs and values of the ancient Greeks? How did their achievements in art, philosophy, history, and science shape the growth of Western civilization?

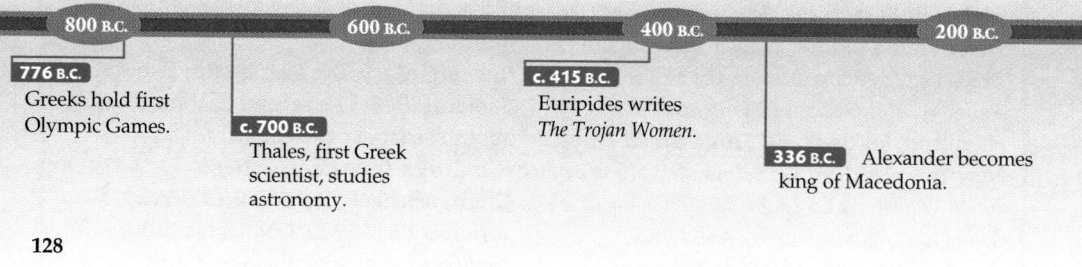

800 B.C. — 600 B.C. — 400 B.C. — 200 B.C.

- **776 B.C.** Greeks hold first Olympic Games.
- **c. 700 B.C.** Thales, first Greek scientist, studies astronomy.
- **c. 415 B.C.** Euripides writes *The Trojan Women.*
- **336 B.C.** Alexander becomes king of Macedonia.

128

GEOGRAPHY CONNECTION

Movement Using a wall map or text maps in Chapter 4, review with students the Mediterranean world of Hellenic civilization. Then, using a wall map or the text map on page 141, contrast it with the empire of Alexander. What are some of the modern countries that belonged, in whole or in part, to Alexander's empire? *(Greece, Serbia, Bulgaria, Turkey, Syria, Lebanon, Israel, Egypt, Libya, Iraq, Iran, Afghanistan, Pakistan)*

History & Art Actors preparing for a performance, a mosaic from the House of the Tragic Poet, Pompeii. National Museum, Naples, Italy

Your History Journal

The word* thespian, *meaning "actor," derives from the Greek dramatist Thespis. Many Greek innovations in staging productions are still used today. Research the history of early Greek drama. Write a comparison with modern theater.

Introducing Chapter 5

History & Art

Tell students that this is a picture of a mosaic—a work formed by fitting together many small pieces of stone and/or glass. Found in the Roman city of Pompeii, it depicts many theater traditions that began with the Greeks, such as the wearing of masks by actors. Why might people have had a work like this in their home? *(They enjoyed attending plays, and so did their guests. Also, such a work displayed the wealth of those who commissioned it.)*

Performance Assessment

Refer to the activity on page 128C of the Planning Guide.

For an additional activity, refer to Activity 5 in the *Performance Assessment Strategies and Activities* booklet.

Using Your History Journal

Topics for comparison include the stage itself, scenery, music, dancing, and the actors (training, costumes, and so on).

GLENCOE TECHNOLOGY

VIDEODISC

Use MindJogger to preview chapter content.

MindJogger Videoquiz

Chapter 5
Disc 1 Side B

Also available in VHS.

EXTRA CREDIT PROJECT

Storytelling Greek writers produced many works other than dramas, although much of their output has been lost. Have students research and report on one of the Greek poets whose writings have survived: Archilochus, Pindar, or Sappho. Another writer who may be of special interest to students is Aesop, known for his fables. Have students prepare a storytelling session for young children, or for the class, using several of Aesop's best-known stories, such as the tale of the goose that laid the golden egg.

Chapter 5
Section 1

SECTION THEME

▶ **Innovation** The ancient Greeks develop a culture that becomes one of the foundations of Western civilization.

Find Out

Answer: *through the arts—buildings, vase paintings, sculptures, and drama—and through sports and games*

FOCUS

Section Objective

Describe how the Greeks expressed their love of beauty and meaning.

BELLRINGER
Motivational Activity

Before taking roll at the beginning of the class period, project Section Focus Transparency 5-1 and have students answer the activity questions. Discuss students' responses.

This activity is also available as a blackline master.

Vocabulary Pre-check

Use the Vocabulary PuzzleMaker to create a puzzle that reinforces the vocabulary terms in this section. **L1**

600 B.C. | 500 B.C. | 400 B.C.

c. 600 B.C. Greeks perform the earliest plays.

459 B.C. Aeschylus writes the *Oresteia.*

432 B.C. Athenians finish building the Parthenon.

Section 1

Quest for Beauty and Meaning

Setting the Scene

▶ **Terms to Define**
classical, sanctuary, perspective, amphora, tragedy, comedy

▶ **People to Meet**
Myron, Phidias, Praxiteles, Aeschylus, Sophocles, Euripides, Aristophanes

▶ **Places to Locate**
Olympia

Find Out How did the Greeks express their love of beauty and meaning?

The Storyteller

An early Greek actor remembers performing in his first tragedy: "I put on the robe of Zeus for the prologue, a lovely thing, purple worked with golden oak leaves.... The next thing I remember is sitting enthroned down center on the god-walk, eagle on left fist, scepter in right hand ... and all the eyes of Athens skinning me to the bone." The actor felt as though he had sleepwalked into the scene. Gripped by fear, he tried to remember his lines: "My father would die of shame.... He was twice the artist I am. At once my lines came back to me. I started my speech...."

—adapted from *The Mask of Apollo,* Mary Renault, 1974

Vase depicting actors preparing for a play

During the mid-400s B.C., Greek civilization reached its cultural peak, particularly in the city-state of Athens. This period of brilliant cultural achievement has been called ancient Greece's Golden Age. Artists of the Golden Age excelled in architecture, sculpture, and painting. They created works characterized by beautiful simplicity and graceful balance, an artistic style now called **classical**.

Classical Greek art, copied soon after in Roman artistic styles, set lasting standards of beauty still admired today. The writers and thinkers of ancient Greece also made enduring achievements in literature and drama, creating works read through the centuries and still considered classics today. Many cultural traditions of Western civilization—the civilization of Europe and those parts of the world influenced by Europeans—began with Greece's Golden Age.

Building for the Gods

The Greeks, wrote the Athenian leader Pericles, were "lovers of the beautiful." Each Greek city-state tried to turn its acropolis into an architectural treasure.

The Parthenon—the temple to Athena built on the summit of the Acropolis in Athens—best exemplified classical Greek architecture. It was begun in 447 B.C. and finished in 432 B.C., under the rule of Pericles. Because the Greeks worshiped either in their homes or at outdoor altars, they did not need large **sanctuaries**, or places of worship. Instead, they built temples as places where their deities would live.

The Parthenon has an ingeniously simple design. It is a rectangle surrounded by 46 fluted columns. At the same time, the Parthenon is extremely beautiful. In the right light, because of

SECTION RESOURCES

Reproducible Masters
- Reproducible Lesson Plan 5-1
- Guided Reading Activity 5-1
- Source Reading 5
- World Art and Music Activity 5
- Section Quiz 5-1

Transparencies
- Section Focus Transparency 5-1
- World History and Art Transparency 6
- Ancient Greece

Multimedia
- Ancient Greece
- Vocabulary PuzzleMaker Software
- Student Self-Test and Review Software
- Testmaker
- Greece and Rome
- World Music: Cultural Traditions, Lesson 3

Visualizing History An ancient Greek krater (vase) illustrates a scene from Odysseus and the Sirens. *What kinds of vases did the Greeks decorate with scenes from mythology?*

iron in its white marble, the Parthenon gleams a soft gold against the blue sky.

The Parthenon's graceful proportions perfectly balance width, length, and height. To the Greeks the Parthenon represented the ideal of "nothing to excess," an ideal sometimes called the Golden Mean, or the midpoint between two extremes.

The architects of the Parthenon also understood optical illusions and perspective, or the artistic showing of distances between objects as they appear to the eye. Thus, they made the temple's columns thicker in the middle and thinner at the top so that the columns appeared straight when viewed from a distance. The steps leading up to the Parthenon, actually lower in the center than at either end, likewise appear straight. The Athenians wanted to create the impression of perfection—and they succeeded.

Greek Arts

The Greek love of beauty was expressed in the fine arts as well as in architecture. In both painting and sculpture, the Greeks—because they emphasized the individual—excelled at portraying the human form.

Painting on Vases

Although the Greeks painted murals, as had the Minoans, no originals have survived. We know of Greek murals only from written descriptions or Roman copies. But today we can still see examples of their work in the paintings on Greek vases.

The Greeks designed their pottery with different shapes that were suited for different functions. For example, Greek potters gave the *krater*—a small two-handled vase—a wide mouth in which it was easy to mix wine with water. On the other hand, they gave the *leythos* a narrow neck so that oil could be poured out slowly and in small quantities.

Most Greek pottery remaining from the classical period is either red on a black background or black on a red background. The varied subjects of the paintings depended on the size and use of the vase. Potters usually decorated an amphora—a large vase for storing oil and other bulk supplies—with scenes from mythology. In contrast, a *kylix*—a wide, shallow two-handled drinking cup—showed scenes of everyday life: children attending school, shoemakers and carpenters plying their trades, a farmer guiding the plow behind a team of oxen, a merchant ship braving the winds. Greek potters skillfully adapted their designs and decorations to the curves and shape of the vase.

Sculpting the Human Body

Greek sculpture, like Greek architecture, reached its height in Athens during the time of Pericles. **Myron**, one of the greatest sculptors of Greece's Golden Age, portrayed in his statues idealized views of what people *should* look like rather than actual persons. When Myron sculpted his *Discus Thrower* poised to hurl the discus, he carved the lines of the body to indicate an athlete's excellent physical condition as well as his mental control over what he was doing.

The great sculptor **Phidias** (FIH•dee•uhs) was in charge of the Parthenon's sculptures. Phidias himself carved the towering statue of Athena that was placed inside the Parthenon. The statue, made of gold and ivory plates attached to a wooden framework, showed the goddess in her warlike aspect, carrying a shield, spear, and helmet.

COOPERATIVE LEARNING ACTIVITY

Cultural Contributions Have students plan and execute a "Greek Heritage Day." Organize the class into groups. Assign or have each group choose a Greek creative achievement to demonstrate to the class. These may include drama (tragedy and comedy can be divided), painting, sculpture, and architecture. The groups may decide what form their demonstrations will take: an actual performance of part of a drama, a model of a vase, a model of a building, and so forth. Consult with the groups to make sure that each member has a specific assignment. **L1**

TEACH

Guided Practice

THEME Innovation

Remind students that the word *innovation* means "something new." Ask them to recall innovations developed by earlier peoples. *(prehistoric: stone tools, agriculture, metalworking, boats; Egyptians: picture writing; Sumerians: cuneiform writing, wagon wheel, potter's wheel; early Chinese: picture writing, silk)* Then ask them what ancient Greek innovation they learned about in the last chapter. *(democracy)* **L1**

Visualizing History On his journey home after the Trojan War, Odysseus passed by the Sirens, half-bird half-woman creatures whose singing lured sailors to their death. He had his sailors stop their ears with wax and tie him to the mast in order to avoid temptation.

Answer to Caption: *amphoras*

The Arts Discuss the enduring legacy of classical Greek architecture. Show the class slides or pictures of classical Greek buildings. Ask if students can think of any well-known buildings in this country or any local buildings that use elements of this style. *(Answers may include the Lincoln Memorial, the Jefferson Memorial, other federal buildings in Washington, D.C.)* **L2**

World History and Art Transparency 6

Independent Practice

Guided Reading Activity 5-1 **L1**

Chapter 5 Section 1

NATIONAL GEOGRAPHIC SOCIETY

Use these materials to enrich student understanding of ancient Greek culture.

- **NGS PICTURESHOW CD-ROM**
  Greece and Rome
- **NGS PICTUREPACK TRANSPARENCY SET**
  Ancient Greece
- **ANCIENT CIVILIZATIONS POSTER SET**
  Ancient Greece

you don't say...

"Orchestra" is a Greek word from the verb "to dance" and was first used to describe the space between the stage and the audience where the chorus performed. In modern times, the term designates both the area in front of the stage and the group of musicians that plays there.

ASSESS

Check for Understanding

Assign Section 1 Review as homework or as an in-class activity.

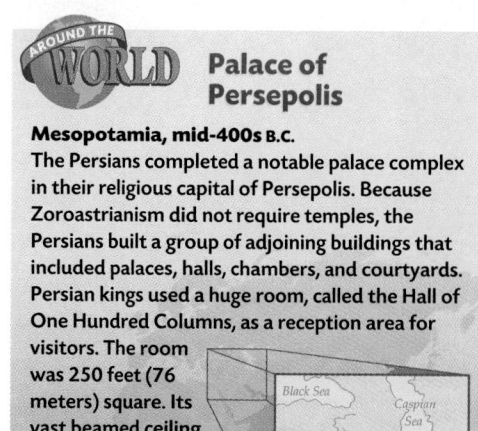

AROUND THE WORLD — Palace of Persepolis

Mesopotamia, mid-400s B.C.
The Persians completed a notable palace complex in their religious capital of Persepolis. Because Zoroastrianism did not require temples, the Persians built a group of adjoining buildings that included palaces, halls, chambers, and courtyards. Persian kings used a huge room, called the Hall of One Hundred Columns, as a reception area for visitors. The room was 250 feet (76 meters) square. Its vast beamed ceiling was supported by columns 60 feet (18 meters) high.

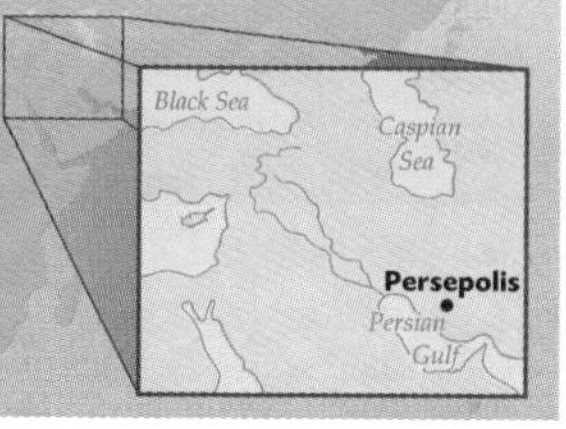

A hundred years after the Golden Age of Athens, the work of another famous Greek sculptor—**Praxiteles** (prak•SIH•tuhl•EEZ)—reflected the changes that had occurred in Greek life. The sculptures of Myron and Phidias had been full of power and striving for perfection, as befitted a people who had defeated the mighty Persian Empire. By the time of Praxiteles, the Greeks had suffered through the Peloponnesian War and had lost their self-confidence. Accordingly, Praxiteles and his colleagues favored life-sized statues rather than massive works. They emphasized grace rather than power. The sculptors of the Golden Age had carved only deities and heroes, but the sculptors of the 300s B.C. carved ordinary people too.

Drama and Theater

The Greeks also explored the human condition through theatrical dramas. They were the first people to write and perform plays, which they presented twice a year at festivals to honor Dionysus, the god of wine and fertility.

Aeschylus

The earliest Greek plays were tragedies. In a tragedy, the lead character struggles against fate only to be doomed—after much suffering—to an unhappy, or tragic, ending. **Aeschylus** (EHS•kuh•luhs), the first of the great writers of tragedies in the 400s B.C., wrote 90 plays. Seven have survived. His *Oresteia* is a trilogy—a set of three plays with a related theme—and is famous for the grandeur of its language.

The *Oresteia* shows how the consequences of one's deeds are carried down from generation to generation. The first play in the trilogy tells about the return of King Agamemnon from the Trojan War and his murder by his wife Clytemnestra in revenge for Agamemnon's sacrifice of their daughter Iphigenia before the Greeks sailed for Troy. The second play describes how Agamemnon's son Orestes in turn avenges his father's death by killing his mother. The third play has Orestes standing trial in Athens for his bloody deed. When the jury splits six to six, the goddess Athena intervenes and casts the deciding vote in favor of mercy. The moral of the trilogy is that the law of the community, not personal revenge, should decide punishment.

Sophocles

The next great tragedian, **Sophocles** (SAH•fuh•KLEEZ), had served as a general in the Athenian army and had lived through most of the Peloponnesian War. Sophocles accepted human suffering as an unavoidable part of life. At the same time, he stressed human courage and compassion.

In one of his most famous plays, *Oedipus Rex*, Sophocles deals with the plight of Oedipus, a king who is doomed by the deities to kill his father and marry his mother. Despite Oedipus's efforts to avoid his fate, the deities' decree comes true. When Oedipus discovers what he has done, he blinds himself in despair and goes into exile.

Euripides

The last of the three great Greek tragedians—**Euripides** (yu•RIH•puh•DEEZ)—rarely dealt with the influence of the gods and goddesses on human lives. Instead, he focused on the qualities human beings possess that bring disaster on themselves.

Euripides also hated war, and many of his 19 surviving plays show the misery war brings. In *The Trojan Women*, the Trojan princess Cassandra explains why the Greeks, despite their victory, are not better off than the Trojans:

> "And when [the Greeks] came to the banks
> of the Scamander those thousands died.
> And why?
> No man has moved their landmarks or
> laid siege to their high-walled towns.
> But those whom war took never saw their
> children.
> No wife with gentle hands shrouded them
> for their grave.
> They lie in a strange land. And in their

MEETING SPECIAL NEEDS ACTIVITY

Language Delayed To benefit students who need help in understanding the vocabulary and concepts in this section, have students create a crossword puzzle on a large laminated surface marked with a permanent grid. Have a student find a word to be included and write it on the grid. Have another student write a clue that defines or explains the word. Have students continue composing the puzzle as long as they can fit words together in crossword form or for a specific time period. Have students copy the puzzle from the large grid to refer to later or to challenge their friends or family. **L1**

NATIONAL GEOGRAPHIC PICTURING HISTORY

Liberto Perugi

Greek Soldier

A Greek warrior, sculpted in bronze, gazes at the world with a determined stare. For more than 1,500 years, the soldier rested under the waters of the Mediterranean Sea. Then in 972 an Italian chemist from Rome, diving off the coast f southern Italy, found this statue and a companion ronze of an older Greek soldier. The statues were robably lost at sea en route to Rome—perhaps thrown verboard to lighten a storm-tossed ship. Rescued by ivers (upper left) and carefully restored, the statues ow stand guard in an Italian museum.

The Greeks began casting statues in bronze in the mid-500s B.C. Within a century ancient Greek civilization entered its Golden Age, the era in which Plato (427–347 B.C.) and Aristotle (384–322 B.C.) laid the foundations of Western philosophy; Sophocles (495–405 B.C.) wrote tragedies; Thucydides (471–c. 400 B.C.) recorded Greek history; and Phidias of Athens (500–431 B.C.) created statues—perhaps even these rare examples. It was an age in which sculptors created new modes of artistic expression and began to depict the human body with precision. ●

TEACH

Remind students that, by the time this statue was cast, ordinary Greek citizens had replaced aristocrats as the most valuable military men. Called *hoplites*, they were so heavily armed that they could fight well only in the tight formation of the phalanx, a group of soldiers close together with their shields overlapping. Ask the class why they think this statue was probably on its way to Rome. *(The Romans greatly admired Greek culture.)*

CURRICULUM CONNECTION

ARCHAEOLOGY
To the archaeologist, an ancient shipwreck like the one that yielded this statue is a sort of time capsule. Objects found under water are often very well preserved because of the lack of airborne bacteria.

Chapter 5 Section 1

Visualizing History This sculpture, like many works of classical Greece, is a Roman copy of a Greek original. **Answer to Caption:** *by crowning them with wreaths of olive leaves and by holding parades in their honor*

Use Student Self-Test and Review Software to review Section 1.

Evaluate

Section Quiz 5-1

Use the Testmaker to create a customized quiz for Section 1.

Reteach

Have students review the artistic accomplishments of Greece's Golden Age.

Enrich

Have students compare the ancient Greek treatment of Olympic athletes with the treatment of professional athletes in the United States.

CLOSE

Write this quotation from the English poet Shelley on the board: "We are all Greeks." Have students discuss what they think the statement means in light of this section.

Visualizing History **A bronze sculpture by Myron, a Greek sculptor, honored the Olympic discus thrower.** *How did the Greeks honor winners of the Olympic Games?*

homes are sorrows, too, the very same.
Lonely women who died, old men who
waited for sons that never came—no
son left to them to make the offering at
their graves.
That was the glorious victory they won. ❞

—Euripides, from his tragedy
The Trojan Women, c. 415 B.C.

A Comedy Tonight

Eventually the Greeks also wrote **comedies**, plays with humorous themes and happy endings. **Aristophanes** (ar•uh•STAH•fuh•NEEZ), the most famous writer of comedies, created imaginative social satire. In his works he made witty comments about leading figures—such as Euripides—and about issues of his day. In his play *The Clouds*, Aristophanes had a character named Strepsiades ask where Athens was on a map. When the polis's location was pointed out to him, Strepsiades replied: "Don't be ridiculous, that can't be Athens, for I can't see even a single law court in session."

The Olympic Games

Believing that healthy bodies made the best use of nature's gifts, the ancient Greeks stressed athletics in their school curriculum. Greek men who could afford the leisure time usually spent all or part of their afternoons practicing sports in their polis's gymnasiums.

The ancient Greeks held the Olympic Games—their best-known sporting event—in **Olympia** every four years. Because the Olympic Games were a religious festival in honor of Zeus, trading and fighting stopped while they were going on. The Greek calendar began with the supposed date of the first Olympic Games: 776 B.C.

Athletes came from all over the Greek-speaking world to compete in the Olympics. Only male athletes, however, were allowed to take part, and women were not permitted even as spectators. Games that honored the goddess Hera were held at a different location than Olympia and gave Greek women an opportunity to participate in races.

In line with the Greek emphasis on the individual, Olympic competition took the form of individual rather than team events. These consisted at first of only a footrace. Later other events—the broad jump, the discus throw, boxing, and wrestling—were added. An activity called the pentathlon (pehn•TATH•luhn) combined running, jumping, throwing the discus, wrestling, and hurling the javelin.

The Greeks crowned Olympic winners with wreaths of olive leaves and held parades in their honor. Some city-states even excused outstanding athletes from paying taxes.

SECTION 1 REVIEW

Recall

1. **Define** classical, sanctuary, perspective, amphora, tragedy, comedy.
2. **Identify** Myron, Phidias, Praxiteles, Aeschylus, Sophocles, Euripides, Aristophanes.
3. **Describe** how worship of Greek deities influenced architecture, art, and athletics.

Critical Thinking

4. **Applying Information** Show how the Greek emphasis on the individual was demonstrated both in the Olympic Games and in the fine arts.

Understanding Themes

5. **Innovation** How was the ancient Greeks' emphasis on reason and individuality revealed in their arts? Cite examples from architecture, sculpture, and drama.

SECTION 1 REVIEW ANSWERS

1. All vocabulary words are defined in the Glossary.
2. Myron, 131; Phidias, 131; Praxiteles, 132; Aeschylus, 132; Sophocles, 132; Euripides, 132; Aristophanes, 134
3. Greek temples were built to venerate the deities. Amphoras often pictured the gods, and many sculptures represented them. Greek plays honored Dionysus, while the Olympic Games honored Zeus.
4. Olympics: individual contests, not team events; fine arts: emphasized the human form
5. INNOVATION Architecture: moderation in balancing proportions, understanding of optical illusions; sculpture: lifelike representation of body; drama: depiction of human emotions, struggles, and weaknesses.

500 B.C. | 450 B.C. | 400 B.C. | 350 B.C.

c. 500s B.C. Pythagoras develops mathematical theories.

435 B.C. Herodotus writes history of the Persian Wars.

399 B.C. Athenians try Socrates for treason.

335 B.C. Aristotle opens the Lyceum in Athens.

Section 2

The Greek Mind

Setting the Scene

▶ **Terms to Define**
philosopher, logic, hygiene

▶ **People to Meet**
Sophists, Socrates, Plato, Aristotle, Herodotus, Thucydides, Thales, Pythagoras, Hippocrates

Find Out What did the ancient Greeks achieve in philosophy, history, and science?

The Storyteller

Socrates was on trial for his life, for crimes against religion and for corrupting the youth of Athens. He spoke in his own defense: "I have done nothing but try to persuade you all, young and old, not to be concerned with body or property first, but to care chiefly about improvement of the soul. I tell you that virtue does not come from money, but that money comes from virtue, as does every other good of man, public and private. This is my teaching, and if this corrupts the youth, then I am a mischievous person. O men of Athens, either acquit me or convict me; but whichever you do, understand that I shall never alter my ways, not even if I have to die many times."

—adapted from *The Apology of Socrates*, Plato

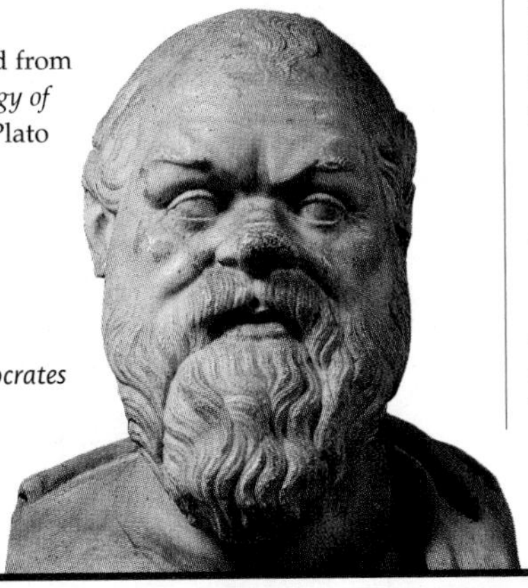

Socrates

The Greeks believed the human mind capable of understanding everything. As a result, the **philosophers**, or thinkers, of ancient Greece produced some of the most remarkable ideas the world has ever known. Through philosophy—which means "the seeking of wisdom"—they laid the foundations for such disciplines as history, political science, biology, and **logic**, or the science of reasoning.

The Sophists

In the 400s B.C. higher education was provided by professional teachers known as **Sophists**. Although Sophists traveled from polis to polis, many gathered in Athens, possibly for the freedom of speech allowed there. Sophists, meaning "knowers," claimed that they could find the answers to all questions.

Many Sophists rejected the belief that the gods and goddesses influenced human behavior. They also did not believe in absolute moral and legal standards. Instead, they asserted that "man is the measure of all things" and that truth is different for each individual.

Not only did Sophists challenge certain traditional Greek beliefs, they also took money for their teaching. Many of them seemed most intent on teaching young men how to win a political argument and get ahead in the world. Many Greeks, including two of Greece's greatest philosophers—**Socrates** (SAH•kruh•TEEZ) and his pupil **Plato**—criticized the Sophists severely.

Socrates

Socrates was born to a poor Athenian family in 470 B.C. Athough a sculptor by trade, he spent most of his time teaching. Unlike the Sophists, Socrates believed in absolute rather than relative truth. His

SECTION THEME

▶ **Innovation** Ancient Greek thinkers believe in reason and the importance of the individual.

Find Out

Answer: *Philosophers laid the foundations of disciplines such as logic and political science; historians investigated and explained events, customs, and beliefs of early Greeks, and established the tradition of accuracy and impartiality in the writing of history; scientists made lasting contributions to the fields of mathematics and medicine.*

FOCUS

Section Objective

Identify the achievements of the ancient Greeks in philosophy, history, and science.

BELLRINGER
Motivational Activity

Before taking roll at the beginning of the class period, project Section Focus Transparency 5-2 and have students answer the activity questions. Discuss students' responses.

This activity is also available as a blackline master.

Vocabulary Pre-check

Use Vocabulary Activity 5 to introduce vocabulary terms. **L1 LEP**

SECTION RESOURCES

Reproducible Masters
- Reproducible Lesson Plan 5-2
- Vocabulary Activity 5
- Guided Reading Activity 5-2
- People in World History Profiles 7, 8
- History Simulation 5
- Section Quiz 5-2

Transparencies
- Section Focus Transparency 5-2
- Mapping History Overlay Transparency 4
- Chapter Transparency 5

Multimedia
- Student Self–Test and Review Software
- Testmaker

TEACH

Guided Practice

THEME Innovation

What two new ideas made the Sophists innovators in Greek thought? *(They rejected the notion that deities influenced human behavior, as well as belief in absolute moral and legal standards.)* **L1**

Philosophy Draw a rectangle on the chalkboard and label it *philosophy*. Have volunteers draw and label within it smaller rectangles to represent other disciplines founded on philosophy. *(history, political science, biology)* Use this graphic organizer to brainstorm with students some fundamental questions in each of these disciplines; questions which a philosopher might address. *(Examples are: Can people uncover the truth about the past? What form of government best serves justice? What qualities define "life"?)* **L2 LEP**

Mapping History Overlay Transparency 4

Chapter Transparency 5

Visualizing History For Plato, there was one criterion by which every public action and institution should be judged: whether or not it made people better than before. **Answer to Caption:** *social disorder*

main interest did not lie in teaching rhetoric or in imparting information. Rather, Socrates was attracted to the process by which people learned how to think for themselves.

To encourage his students to clear away mistaken ideas and discover the truth, Socrates developed a teaching technique known as the Socratic method. He would ask students pointed questions without giving them answers and then oppose the students' answers with clear logical arguments. Through this method, he forced his students to defend their statements and to clarify their thinking. For example, in discussing the topic of justice, Socrates proceeded as follows:

> "Socrates: Does falsehood then exist among mankind?
> Euthydemus: It does assuredly.
> Socrates: Under which head [justice or injustice] shall we place it?
> Euthydemus: Under injustice, certainly.
> Socrates: Well then … if a father, when his son requires medicine, and refuses to take it, should deceive him, and give him the medicine as ordinary food, and, by adopting such deception, should restore him to health, under which head must we place such an act of deceit?
> Euthydemus: It appears to me that we must place it under [justice].… I retract what I said before."
>
> —Xenophon, from *Memorabilia*, early 300s B.C.

Some prominent Athenians viewed Socrates' teachings as a threat to the polis. In 399 B.C. they accused him of "corrupting the young" and of "not worshiping the gods worshiped by the state" and had him brought to trial.

Socrates argued in his own defense that a person who *knew* what was right would always *do* what was right and that the intellectual search for truth was the most important thing in the world. "A man who is good for anything ought not to calculate the chance of living or dying; he ought only to consider whether … he is doing right or wrong."

Despite Socrates' eloquence, a jury of citizens found him guilty and sentenced him to death. Although Socrates had the right to ask for a lesser penalty, such as exile, he refused to do so. He had lived his life under the laws of his polis, and he would not avoid obeying them now.

Socrates carried out the sentence of his fellow citizens himself. He drank poisonous hemlock juice and died quietly among his grieving followers.

Plato

Born an Athenian aristocrat, Plato thought at first of entering politics. However, after Socrates' death, Plato—at age 30—became a teacher and opened his Academy, a school that remained in existence until A.D. 529.

From memory Plato recorded dialogues, or conversations, between Socrates and fellow Athenians, and he also wrote the earliest book on political science, *The Republic*. In this book, he presented a plan for what he considered would be the ideal society and government.

Plato disliked Athenian democracy and preferred the government of Sparta. He gave more importance to the state than to the individual. Like the Spartans, he believed that each person should place service to the community above strictly personal goals. Plato also believed that the result of people having too much freedom is social disorder. He distrusted the lower classes and wanted only the most intelligent and best-educated citizens to participate in government. As he explained in *The Republic*:

> "Until philosophers are kings, or the kings and princes of this world have the spirit and power of philosophy, and political greatness and wisdom meet in one, and those commoner natures who pursue either to the exclusion of the other are compelled to stand aside, cities will never have rest from their evils, no, nor the human race."

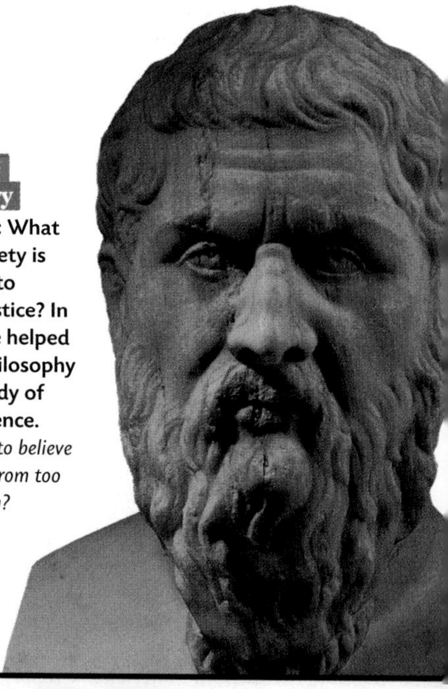

Visualizing History

Plato asked: What type of society is most likely to promote justice? In so doing, he helped to direct philosophy into the study of political science. *What did Plato believe would result from too much freedom?*

COOPERATIVE LEARNING ACTIVITY

Radio Play Assign groups of six or seven students the task of writing and performing a ten-minute radio play about any aspect of Greek civilization presented in this section. For example, a group might choose as its theme Hippocrates and medicine. Encourage students to balance their plays with a mixture of narration and dialogue. Have them follow this plan: (1) choose a theme; (2) write a broad summary of the play; (3) decide on five or six scenes to tell the story; (4) write narration and dialogue for each scene; (5) agree on readers for the material; (6) present the play to the class. Encourage all students to participate in each step of the plan. **L1**

Plato's political views were part of an all-embracing philosophy by which he tried to search for "truth." Plato rejected the senses—seeing, hearing, touch, smell, and taste—as a source of truth, believing that the many things that could be perceived by these senses were only "appearance." Reality, the "real" world, was constructed from ideas, or ideal "forms," which could be understood through logical thought and reasoning.

Aristotle

The third great philosopher of ancient Greece was **Aristotle** (AR•uh•STAH•tuhl), who had studied with Plato at the Academy for 20 years. Aristotle then tutored the young Alexander of Macedonia, who later would be known as Alexander the Great. In 335 B.C. Aristotle opened a school in Athens called the Lyceum. Besides teaching, he wrote or edited more than 200 books on topics ranging from astronomy to poetry and from political science to the weather. Because of Aristotle's wide range of knowledge, the Italian poet Dante later called him "the master of those who know."

Aristotle influenced later philosophers with his work on logic. He developed the syllogism, a means for presenting an argument in such a way that one can determine whether or not the conclusion follows logically from the premises, or basic statements.

Aristotle and Science

Aristotle also influenced scientific work. He was the first person to observe facts, then classify them according to their similarities and their differences, and finally develop generalizations from his data. Some of his specific beliefs—notably, that Earth is the center of our solar system—were incorrect. Aristotle's views and his method of inquiry, however, would continue to dominate European scientific thinking for centuries.

Aristotle and Government

Many of Aristotle's writings were focused on political science. Unlike Plato, he did not theorize about idealized principles of government. Instead, he examined the political structure of various city-states, analyzing their advantages and disadvantages. Only then did he spell out his conclusions in a book called *Politics*. Aristotle believed that democracies, oligarchies, and tyrannies are all workable, depending on circumstances. He preferred, however, to have power rest with the middle class, because they knew both how to command *and* obey.

Writers of History

The Greeks also used their intellectual skills in writing history. Until the 400s B.C. the Greeks had considered literary legends as history. **Herodotus** (hih•RAH•duh•tus), the first Greek historian, decided to separate fact from legend. Historians still consider him "the father of history."

Herodotus

Herodotus chose as his subject the Persian Wars and called his work the *Historia*, or "investigation." Herodotus traveled throughout the Persian Empire and also visited many Greek colonies. Everywhere he went, he asked questions, recorded answers, and checked the reliability of his sources. However, he accepted some statements that were not true, especially exaggerated numbers—such as how many Persians died at Marathon. He also sometimes offered supernatural explanations of events.

Herodotus did not limit himself to describing military and political events. He also wrote about outstanding individuals, social customs, and religious beliefs and practices. Later historians have learned a great deal from the *Historia* about the culture of the period and about the civilizations that Herodotus visited.

Thucydides

The second noted historian of ancient Greece, **Thucydides** (thoo•SIH•duh•DEEZ), wrote about the Peloponnesian War. Thucydides is regarded as the first scientific historian because he completely rejected the idea that the deities played a part in human history. Only human beings make history, Thucydides said. He also was as accurate and impartial as possible. He visited battle sites, carefully examined documents, and accepted only the evidence of actual eyewitnesses to events.

Footnotes to History

The Atom The Greek thinker Democritus came up with the idea of a solid particle of matter so small that it was both invisible and not divisible. He named this particle *atom*, meaning "invisible." Today scientists know that atoms are in fact divisible and include many separate and smaller types of matter. But the basic idea of atomic physics can be traced back to Democritus.

Independent Practice

Guided Reading Activity 5-2 **L1**

People in World History Profiles 7, 8

History Simulation 5

Biography Have students write a one- or two-page biography about any person discussed in this section. Students should research their subject to find information beyond that presented in the text. **L2**

Cultural Perspectives

Greek Influence The Romans borrowed heavily from Greek culture, especially after their conquest of Greece in 146 B.C. The poet Virgil, author of the *Aeneid*—the national epic of Rome—read and was inspired by Homer's works. Roman architects and sculptors imitated Greek styles. The Roman poet Horace put it this way: "Greece, taken captive, captured her savage conqueror."

ASSESS

Check for Understanding

Assign Section 2 Review as homework or as an in-class activity.

Use Student Self-Test and Review Software to review Section 2.

MEETING SPECIAL NEEDS ACTIVITY

Learning Disability Some students have difficulty dealing with abstract philosophical concepts, such as those discussed in this section. Organize the class into small groups and assign each one a statement from the text, such as the one summarizing the Sophists' belief that "truth is different for each individual." Have them restate the idea in other words (such as "Everyone has a special way of looking at things"). Then, using examples, they should agree or disagree. *(Yes, we each have a unique perspective on life. No, certain scientific truths, for example, are the same for everyone.)* **L1**

Chapter 5 Section 2

Visualizing History The medical school founded by Hippocrates published the world's first work on epidemics, as well as a treatise on epilepsy.

Answer to Caption: *proper hygiene, a sound diet, and plenty of rest*

Evaluate

Section Quiz 5-2

Use the Testmaker to create a customized quiz for Section 2.

Reteach

Have students review the major innovations in thought discussed in this section.

Enrich

Have students research the syllogism, the most common form of deductive logic, which Aristotle originated. Have them write and share syllogisms.

CLOSE

Have students discuss who they think was the single most important figure of all those treated in this section. Be sure they support their choice.

Visualizing History **Greek physicians observed the many symptoms of disease and concluded that illnesses are not caused by evil spirits, but have natural causes.** *What three prescriptions for health did Hippocrates suggest?*

Thucydides did not simply recite facts, however. He also offered explanations for why events took place and what motivated political leaders. He believed that future generations could learn from the past.

The First Scientists

The ancient Greeks passed on a great scientific heritage. They believed that the world is ruled by natural laws and that human beings can discover these laws by using reason. Lacking scientific equipment, the Greek scientists made most of their discoveries by observation and thought. They then went on to develop general theories or statements about the workings of nature.

Greek Mathematicians

The Greeks became the first people to distinguish mathematics as a pure science apart from everyday practical uses. They constructed systematic methods of reasoning to prove the truth of mathematical statements. Through the study of mathematics, Greek thinkers believed that they could find absolutely certain and eternal knowledge.

The first prominent Greek scientist was **Thales** (THAY•leez) of Miletus, a Greek city-state in Ionia. Born in the mid-600s B.C., Thales studied astronomy at Babylon and mathematics in Egypt and could foretell a solar eclipse. He also formulated a theory that water was the basic substance of which everything in the world is made.

During the 500s B.C., **Pythagoras** (puh •THA•guh•ruhs) tried to explain everything in mathematical terms. He explored the nature of numbers, especially whole numbers and their ratios. Students of geometry still learn the Pythagorean theorem about the relationship of sides of a right-angled triangle. Pythagoras also taught that the world was round and revolved around a fixed point.

Greek Medicine

Greek scientists also contributed to the field of medicine. Called "the father of medicine," the physician **Hippocrates** (hih•PAH•kruh•TEEZ) believed that diseases had natural, not supernatural, causes and that the body could heal itself. He was the first doctor to view medicine as a science separate from religious beliefs or mythological explanations.

Basing his work in the late 400s B.C. on observation, he traveled all over Greece diagnosing illnesses and treating sick people. He urged fellow doctors to keep records of their cases and to exchange information with one another. He strongly advocated proper **hygiene**, or health care, a sound diet, and plenty of rest.

According to tradition, Hippocrates drafted a code for ethical medical conduct that has guided the practice of medicine for more than 2,000 years. Many doctors today recite the Hippocratic oath when they receive their medical degree.

SECTION 2 REVIEW

Recall

1. **Define** philosopher, logic, hygiene.
2. **Identify** Sophists, Socrates, Plato, Aristotle, Herodotus, Thucydides, Thales, Pythagoras, Hippocrates.
3. **Explain** how Plato, Socrates, and Aristotle were related as philosophers.

Critical Thinking

4. **Making Comparisons** Compare the political views of Plato and Aristotle and their attitudes regarding observations made through the senses.

Understanding Themes

5. **Innovation** How did Socrates and Hippocrates each contribute to the intellectual life of ancient Greece?

SECTION 2 REVIEW ANSWERS

1. All vocabulary words are defined in the Glossary.
2. Sophists, 135; Socrates, 135; Plato, 135; Aristotle, 137; Herodotus, 137; Thucydides, 137; Thales, 138; Pythagoras, 138; Hippocrates, 138
3. Plato studied with Socrates; Aristotle in turn studied with Plato.
4. Plato: government by educated philosopher-kings; Aristotle: government by middle class. Plato: believed senses show only appearance, while reality is in "forms"; Aristotle: observed with his senses and classified what he observed as facts.
5. **INNOVATION** Socrates: developed Socratic method, forcing students to think clearly; Hippocrates: taught that diseases had natural causes and based his work on observation, thereby furthering the use of the scientific method

Social Studies
SKILLS

Finding Exact Location on a Map

Your new friend invites you to her house. In giving directions, she says, "I live at the northwest corner of Vine Street and Oak Avenue." She has pinpointed her exact location. We use a similar system to identify the exact location of any place on Earth.

Learning the Skill

Over many centuries, cartographers developed a grid system of imaginary lines—the lines of latitude and lines of longitude. Lines of latitude run east and west around the earth. Because they always remain the same distance from each other, they are also called parallels. The parallel lines of latitude measure distance north and south of the Equator, located at 0° latitude. Each line of latitude is one degree, or 69 miles (110 km), from the next. There are 90 latitude lines between the Equator and each Pole. For example, New York City lies 41° north of the Equator, or 41° N.

Lines of longitude, or meridians, run north and south from Pole to Pole. Unlike lines of latitude, lines of longitude are not always the same distance from each other. Lines of longitude are farthest apart at the Equator and intersect at each Pole. Longitude measures distance east and west of the Prime Meridian, located at 0° longitude. That line runs through Greenwich, England, in western Europe and through western Africa. Longitude lines increase east and west of the Prime Meridian to 180°. This meridian runs through the Pacific Ocean. New York City, for example, lies 74° west of the Prime Meridian, or 74° W.

With this system, we can pinpoint the "grid address" of any place on Earth. On a map, find the nearest line of latitude to the designated place. Then follow along this line until it crosses the nearest line of longitude. The point where the lines intersect is the grid address. For example, New York City has this grid address: 41° N, 74° W.

Practicing the Skill

Use the map below to answer the following questions:

1. What is the approximate grid address of Babylon?
2. What city is located at approximately 31° N, 30° E?
3. What is the approximate grid address of Nineveh?
4. What is the approximate grid address of Tyre?

Cities of the Middle East

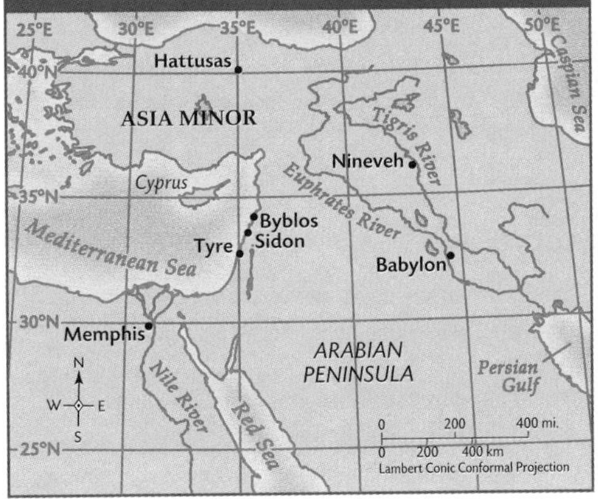

Applying the Skill

Create a travel itinerary for a tour of the ruins of ancient Egypt, Greece, or the Middle East. Choose at least 10 locations you would like to visit. Draw a map of the region, including grid lines. On the map, identify the approximate grid location of each place.

For More Practice

Turn to the Skill Practice in the Chapter Review on page 151 for more practice in finding exact location on a map.

ANSWERS TO PRACTICING THE SKILL

1. 32°N, 44°E
2. Memphis
3. 36°N, 43°E
4. 33°N, 35°E

Social Studies
SKILLS

TEACH

Finding Exact Location on a Map
Have one or more students draw on the chalkboard a simplified map of the area around your school or a nearby residential or business district. (The school, or some other landmark, should be at the center, labeled "0.") With north at the top, the map should include 3-4 streets to the north, south, east, and west of the central point. These should be labeled with the street name and with a grid location: 1, 2, and 3 north, 1, 2, and 3 east, and so on. Then ask students to give grid locations for several street intersections, and vice versa.

Additional Practice

Skill Reinforcement Activity 5

Building Skills in Geography Workbook, Unit 1, Lessons 3, 4, 5

Chapter 5
Section 3

SECTION THEME

▶ **Cultural Diffusion** Alexander's empire brings about a mix of Greek and Middle Eastern cultures.

Find Out

Answer: *He wanted to create an empire that would unite Europe and Asia and combine the best of Greek and Persian cultures; although the unity of his empire died with him, the cities he founded remained centers of Greek culture for many years.*

FOCUS

Section Objective

Outline Alexander's goals and evaluate his success in achieving them.

BELLRINGER
Motivational Activity

Before taking roll at the beginning of the class period, project Section Focus Transparency 5-3 and have students answer the activity questions. Discuss students' responses.

This activity is also available as a blackline master.

Vocabulary Pre-check

Use Vocabulary Activity 5 to introduce vocabulary terms.
L1 LEP

400 B.C. — 300 B.C. — 200 B.C. — 100 B.C.

359 B.C. Philip II becomes king of Macedonia.

331 B.C. Alexander the Great defeats the Persians in the battle of Gaugamela.

250 B.C. Jewish scholars translate the Hebrew Bible into Greek.

c. 100 B.C. Roman Empire begins to conquer the Hellenistic world.

Section 3

Alexander's Empire

Setting the Scene

▶ **Terms to Define**
domain

▶ **People to Meet**
Philip II, Demosthenes, Alexander the Great, Zeno, Menander, Eratosthenes, Euclid, Archimedes

▶ **Places to Locate**
Macedonia, Alexandria

Find Out What were Alexander's goals for his empire, and how successful was he in achieving them?

The Storyteller

Hellenistic poets who lived in bustling cities loved to tell simple fables about love in a countryside setting:

A bee once stung the god of love [Cupid]
as he was stealing honey.
His fingertips began to smart,
and he blew upon his hand,
stamped and danced.
When he showed his wound to his mother,
she laughed. "Aren't you just like the bee,
so small, yet inflicting great pain?"

—adapted from *The Idylls of Theocritus,* (no. 19, "The Honey-Thief"), in *Greek Pastoral Poetry,* Anthony Holden, 1974

Cupid, wall painting, Pompeii, Italy

In the early 400s B.C., the Persians under Darius I, and then under his son Xerxes, had tried to conquer the Greek city-states but failed. Some 150 years later the Macedonians, a people who lived north of Greece in the Balkan Peninsula, made a similar attempt—and succeeded.

Rise of Macedonia

The Macedonians, like the Spartans, were descended from the Dorians, and the Macedonian language incorporated many Greek words. The Greeks, however, looked down on the Macedonians as backward mountaineers.

In 359 B.C. **Philip II** became king of **Macedonia**. During his youth he had been a hostage for three years in the Greek city-state of Thebes. There he had learned to admire both Greek culture and military organization. As king, Philip determined to do three things: create a strong standing army, unify the quarreling Greek city-states under Macedonian rule, and destroy the Persian Empire.

Philip increased his army's fighting power by organizing his infantry into Greek-style phalanxes. Arrayed in close formation 16 rows deep, Philip's lance-bearing foot soldiers fought as a single unit.

For the next 23 years, Philip pursued his ambition. Sometimes he conquered a polis or bribed a polis's leaders to surrender. Sometimes he allied a polis through marriage; Philip had a total of six or seven wives.

The Greek city-states, weakened by the Peloponnesian War, would not cooperate in resisting Philip. The great Athenian orator **Demosthenes** (dih•MAHS•thuh•NEEZ) appealed to his fellow citizens to fight for their liberty. But Demosthenes' words were to no avail. By 338 B.C. Philip had conquered all of Greece except Sparta.

Philip then announced that he would lead the Greeks and Macedonians in a war against Persia. But in 336 B.C., just as he was ready to carry out his

SECTION RESOURCES

Reproducible Masters
- Reproducible Lesson Plan 5-3
- Guided Reading Activity 5-3
- Reteaching Activity 5
- Enrichment Activity 5
- Section Quiz 5-3
- Performance Assessment Activity 5
- Spanish Chapter Summary 5

Transparencies
- Section Focus Transparency 5-3
- Mapping History Overlay Transparency 5

Multimedia
- Focus on World Art Print 8
- Student Self-Test and Review Software
- Testmaker

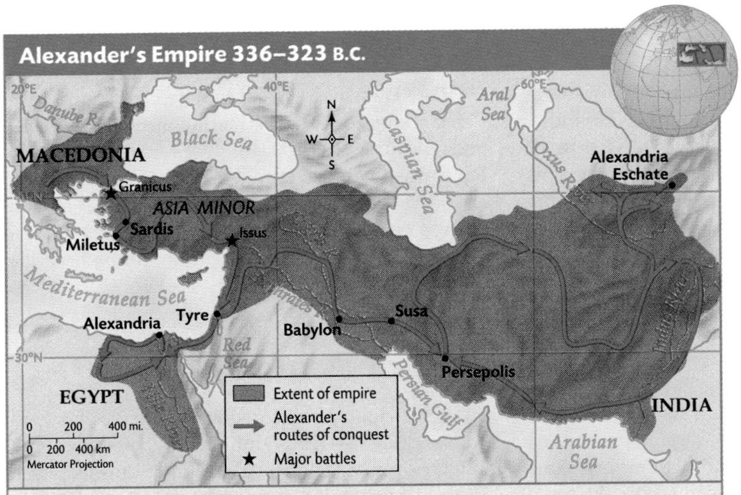

Map Study Alexander the Great united the Greeks and conquered an area stretching from Egypt to India.

1. **Movement** After freeing the Ionian city-states, in which direction did Alexander and his forces travel?
2. **Location** What key cities in the Persian Empire did Alexander conquer?

plans, Philip was murdered—either by a Persian agent or by an assassin hired by his first wife, Olympias. Olympias's son Alexander, later known as **Alexander the Great**, became king.

Alexander the Great

Alexander was only 20 when he became the ruler of Macedonia and Greece. A commander in the Macedonian army since he was 16, Alexander was highly respected by his soldiers for his courage and military skill. He was also extremely well educated, for his father had him tutored by Aristotle for four years.

Early Conquests

In 334 B.C. Alexander led 30,000 soldiers and 5,000 cavalry into Asia to open his campaign of "West against East." The first major encounter with the Persians took place at the Granicus River in western Asia Minor. Alexander's forces won, and he sent 300 suits of Persian armor to Athens as an offering to the goddess Athena. He then marched along the coast of Asia Minor, freeing the Ionian city-states from Persian rule.

The second major battle between the Greeks and Persians took place in 333 B.C. at Issus, Syria. Once again, Alexander's superb tactics resulted in victory, forcing the Persian king Darius III to flee.

Instead of pursuing Darius, Alexander and his troops moved south along the Mediterranean coast. First they captured the seaports of Phoenicia and cut off the Persian fleet from its main supply bases. The fleet soon surrendered. Next, turning west, they invaded Egypt where the people, discontented under Persian rule, welcomed them and declared Alexander a pharaoh. In Egypt, Alexander established a new city and named it **Alexandria** after himself.

Final Campaigns

In 331 B.C. Alexander again turned his attention eastward. He invaded Mesopotamia and smashed Darius's main army in the battle of Gaugamela near the Tigris River. He went on to capture the key cities of the Persian Empire: Babylon, Persepolis, and Susa. When Darius was killed by one of his own

Alexander the Great

Chapter 5 Section 3

TEACH

Guided Practice

THEME Cultural Diffusion

Have students speculate about what elements of Greek culture might be spread into Alexander's empire. *(language, religion, everyday customs, government, technology, military organization and tactics, learning, the arts)* **L1**

Map Study

Answers

1. *south and east*
2. *Babylon, Persepolis, and Susa*

Map Skills Practice

Reading a Map What major bodies of water bordered Alexander's empire? *(the Mediterranean, Black, Caspian, and Arabian Seas and the Persian Gulf)*

Diversity Have students identify the diverse cultures that were part of Alexander's empire. *(Greek, Egyptian, Persian)* Then ask them what steps Alexander took to unify these cultures. *(by example, intermarriage, founding cities)* Have them explain which step they think was most effective. **L2 LEP**

COOPERATIVE LEARNING ACTIVITY

Making a Book Organize the class into groups to prepare pages or sections of a class book illustrating the exploits of Alexander the Great. Assign each group an area of conquest to research, including Thebes, the Granicus River, Issus, Egypt, Gaugamela, and the Indus River valley. Each finished product should include a description of the area, what happened there, and the dates on which the event(s) occurred. It should also include a map, with principal cities and features labeled. Groups may also include drawings showing costumes, weapons, and buildings. **L1**

Chapter 5
Section 3

Critical Thinking Have students identify the major strands of Hellenistic philosophy discussed in this section. *(Cynicism, Epicureanism, Stoicism)* Have them compare these philosophies with those of Plato and Aristotle. *(The Hellenistic philosophers cared more about individual well-being; the earlier philosophers cared about the well-being of the state.)* **L3**

Focus on World Art Print 8

Mapping History Overlay Transparency 5

Who?What?Where?When?

Achilles Alexander the Great's mother told him that Achilles was his ancestor, and the legendary Greek hero became Alexander's model. Alexander, who learned the *Iliad* by heart, carried a copy of it with him wherever he went.

Independent Practice

Guided Reading Activity 5-3 **L1**

Time Line Activity 5

Mapping History Activity 5

Geography and History Activity 5

Advertising Show students examples of advertisements for cities or regions from business or travel magazines. Have them write ad copy for a magazine, to be distributed throughout the Hellenistic world, that extols the virtues of living in Alexandria, Egypt. **L1**

generals, Alexander declared himself ruler of the Persian Empire.

Even this success was not enough for the young conqueror. In 327 B.C. he led his soldiers into India, and after three years they reached the Indus River valley. Alexander hoped to go farther yet, but his Macedonian veterans refused. Alexander therefore reluctantly turned around and went to Babylon, which he had made the capital of his empire. But the hardships of the journey had undermined his health, and he fell ill with a fever, probably malaria. In 323 B.C. Alexander the Great died at the age of 33.

Imperial Goals

When Alexander first set out with his army, his goal was to punish Persia for its invasion of Greece 150 years earlier. But as more and more territory came under his control, Alexander's views changed. His new vision was to create an empire that would unite Europe and Asia and combine the best of Greek and Persian cultures.

Alexander tried to promote this goal by example. He wore Persian dress and imitated the court life of Persian kings. He married a daughter of Darius III and encouraged 10,000 of his soldiers to marry Persian women. He enrolled 30,000 Persians in his army. He also founded about 70 cities that served both as military outposts and as centers for spreading the Greek language and culture throughout his empire.

Divided Domain

Following Alexander's death, three of his generals—Ptolemy (TAH•luh•mee), Seleucus (suh•LOO•kuhs), and Antigonus (an•TIH•guh•nuhs)—eventually divided his vast empire into separate **domains**, or territories. Ptolemy and his descendants ruled Egypt, Libya, and part of Syria. The most famous Ptolemaic ruler was Cleopatra VII, who lost her kingdom to the Romans in 31 B.C.

Images of the Times

The Hellenistic Age

Hellenistic culture blended mythology with real live heroes.

The Greeks retold tales of mythological figures on pottery. This scene shows the god of wine, Dionysus, in a boat.

Bronze statuette of Hellenistic dancer, said to be from Alexandria.

This Pompeiian mosaic honors Alexander the Great, who extended his empire to the Indus River valley.

142

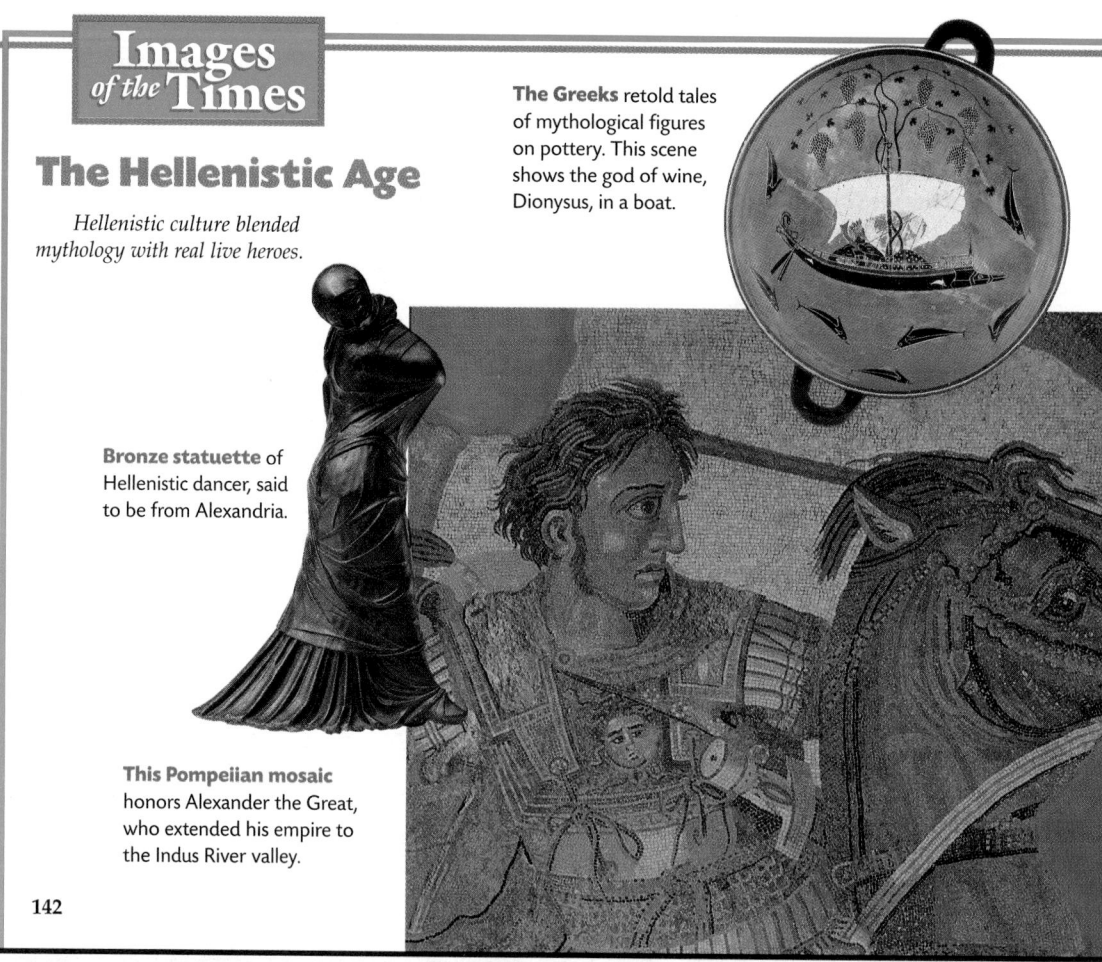

Images of the Times **The Hellenistic Age**

The statue of the Winged Victory shown here is considered the greatest masterpiece of Hellenistic sculpture. It was discovered on the Aegean island of Samothrace in 1863. When found, the statue was in many fragments, which were later pieced together. Today it stands in the Louvre Museum in Paris.

The Winged Victory is just one of many military monuments and statues erected during this age that glorified armed conquest and commemorated victories. Hellenistic art was also characterized by a movement toward more realism in portraits. This reflected the growing tendency to look up to and even worship individuals who boasted great achievements.

Seleucus and his descendants—the Seleucids (suh•LOO•suhds)—at first controlled the rest of Syria, as well as Mesopotamia, Iran, and Afghanistan. After a while, however, they were forced to give up their eastern territory and withdraw to Syria. In 167 B.C. Jewish guerrillas led by Judah Maccabees challenged the Seleucid control of Palestine. The Seleucid Antiochus IV had ordered the Jews to worship the Greek deities, but many Jews refused to abandon their religion. In 165 B.C. Judah Maccabees succeeded in reoccupying Jerusalem and rededicating the Temple, an event commemorated by the Jewish festival of Hanukkah. The kingdom of Judah would remain independent until its defeat by Rome in 63 B.C. The Seleucids likewise ruled in Syria until the Romans came.

The domain of Antigonus and his heirs consisted at first of Macedonia and Greece. But the Greek city-states soon declared their independence and once again began fighting with each other. In the 100s B.C., the growing Roman Empire would conquer Macedonia and Greece.

Hellenistic Culture

The political unity of Alexander's empire disappeared with his death, but the Greek language and culture continued to spread and flourish in the lands he had conquered. There, Hellenic ways of life mixed with elements of Middle Eastern culture to form a new culture, called Hellenistic.

City Life

Hellenistic culture was concentrated in cities. The largest and wealthiest of these was Alexandria in Egypt. Alexandria's straight streets intersected each other at right angles, in contrast to the crooked streets of older cities. Its white stucco stone palaces and temples gleamed brilliantly in the sun.

The city's economic position benefited from a double harbor that could hold 1,200 ships at a time. Another asset to trade was the city's lighthouse, which was visible from 35 miles (56 km) out at sea.

Alexandria also was a major intellectual center. Its museum was the first ever and included a

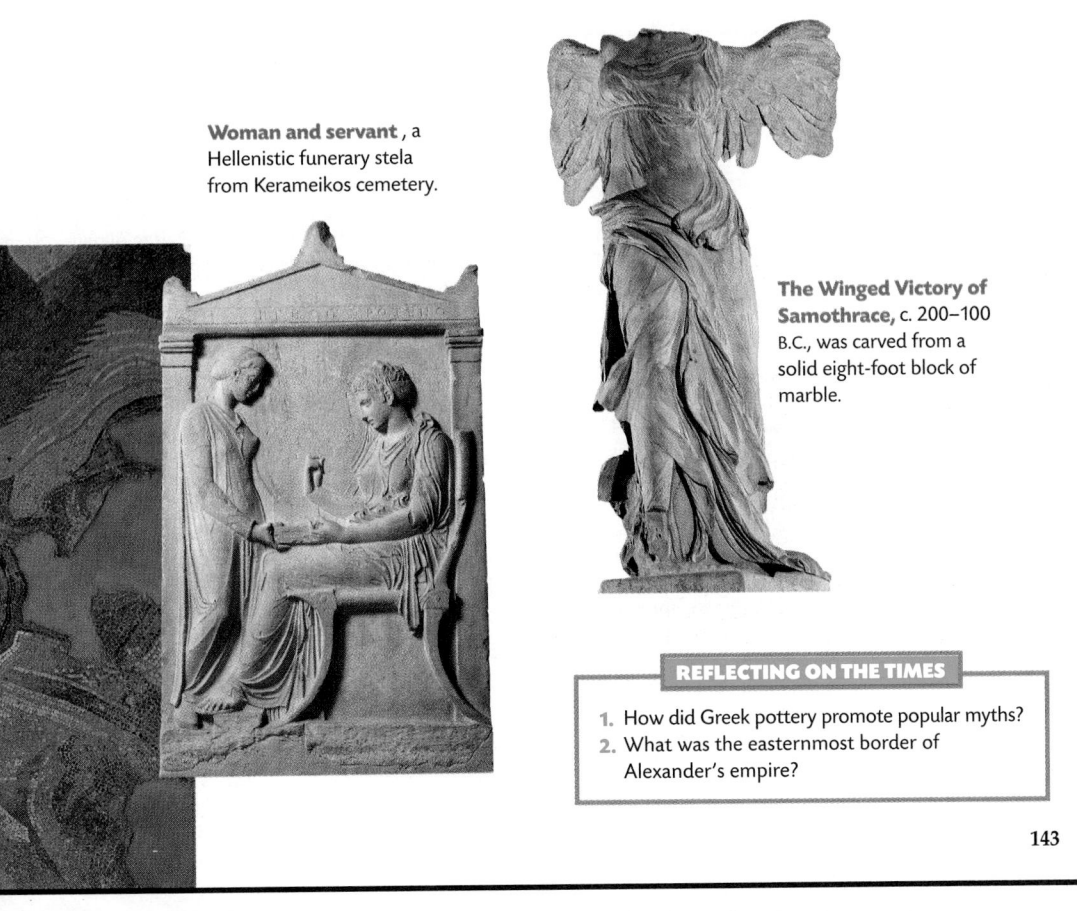

Woman and servant, a Hellenistic funerary stela from Kerameikos cemetery.

The Winged Victory of Samothrace, c. 200–100 B.C., was carved from a solid eight-foot block of marble.

REFLECTING ON THE TIMES

1. How did Greek pottery promote popular myths?
2. What was the easternmost border of Alexander's empire?

ANSWERS TO REFLECTING ON THE TIMES

1. It retold them in pictorial form.
2. the valley of the Indus River

Chapter 5 Section 3

Science Have students work in pairs to find out more about and demonstrate one of Archimedes' inventions or innovations. These can be in addition to the ones mentioned in the section. The demonstrations may include models, prepared drawings, or "chalk talks" in which students illustrate their presentations on the chalkboard. **L2**

Multicultural Have students use what they have learned to prepare a chart that compares the roles of women in the Egyptian, Hellenic, and Hellenistic cultures. Headings could include main role, education, social life, and participation in government. **L3**

you don't say...

"Cynic" comes from the Greek *cynikos* meaning "like a dog." This term probably began as an insult, referring to the philosophers' aggressive manners. But they adopted it with pride, saying that they were the watchdogs of morality. Today the term refers to someone who is doubtful.

Chapter 5
Section 3

ASSESS

Check for Understanding

Assign Section 3 Review as homework or as an in-class activity.

Use Student Self-Test and Review Software to review Section 3.

Evaluate

Section Quiz 5-3

Use the Testmaker to create a customized quiz for Section 3.

CONNECTIONS
Economics

Economics

The basic coin of Alexander's empire was the Athenian drachma. The term comes from the Greek word "handful" because the coin was originally the equivalent of a handful of arrows.

Answers to Making the Connection

1. *thriving sea trade, numerous public works projects, a uniform currency*
2. *Some students will think of geographic boundaries, such as mountains (defining the Rocky Mountain region) or bodies of water (surrounding Hawaii); others may think of political boundaries, such as those dividing the New England states from the Midwest.*

library of nearly a million volumes, an institute for scientific research, a zoo, and a botanical garden. Scientists came from all over the Hellenistic world. Around 250 B.C. Jewish scholars in Alexandria translated the Hebrew Bible into Greek. This translation, known as the Septuagint (sehp•TOO •uh•juhnt), was later used by the apostle Paul and is still used in the Eastern Orthodox Church.

During Hellenic times, the Greeks had been intensely involved with their particular polis. In Hellenistic society, however, the Greeks formed the upper class of Alexandria and other cities in the Middle East and Asia Minor that were ruled by kings. Rather than being loyal to their king or kingdom, professional Greek soldiers and bureaucrats moved from place to place, wherever job opportunities were best.

In Alexandria and other Hellenistic cities, the social status of upper-class Greek women improved over their traditional status in Athens. No longer secluded, women could move about freely. They learned how to read and write and entered such occupations as real estate, banking, and government. Such opportunities were not, however, available to commoners.

Hellenistic Philosophers

Hellenistic philosophers focused on personal behavior, especially the question of how to achieve peace of mind. Three systems of thought attracted most Hellenistic intellectuals: Cynicism, Epicureanism (EH•pih•kyu•REE•uh•NIH•zuhm), and Stoicism.

The best known Cynic was Diogenes (dy•AH •juh•NEEZ). He criticized materialism and asserted that people would be happy if they gave up luxuries and lived simply, in accord with nature. The scholar Epicurus started the philosophy of Epicureanism. He argued that people should avoid both joy and pain by accepting the world as it was, ignoring politics, and living simply and quietly with a few close friends.

Zeno founded Stoicism. The name *Stoicism* comes from the *Stoa Poikile*, or "painted porch," in which Zeno lectured. The Stoics believed that what happened to people was governed by natural laws. Accordingly, people could gain happiness by ignoring their emotions, and instead following their reason. In this way, they were able to accept even the most difficult circumstances of life and do their duty. Stoicism later affected both Roman intellectuals and early Christian thinkers.

CONNECTIONS
Economics

An Economic Region

Geographers, historians, and economists often divide the world into regions based on physical features, political characteristics, or economic factors, such as trade routes and uniform currency. The empire of Alexander the Great came to be one economic region.

International sea trade expanded greatly under Alexander's empire and its successor domains. The Ptolemies, in particular, began using the monsoons to sail directly across the Indian Ocean between Africa and Asia instead of hugging the coast. As a result, luxury items from India and Arabia became common in Mediterranean cities.

Coin bearing the face of Alexander the Great

An increase in public works projects also spread throughout the empire. Alexander and his successors used the vast sums of gold and silver captured in Persia to finance road construction and harbor development.

A uniform currency held Alexander's empire together economically. Before Alexander, the Greek city-states, Egypt, and Persia all had coined their own money. Alexander circulated a coin bearing his profile, which merchants could use everywhere.

After Alexander's death, his empire divided into rival kingdoms. The people in the overall geographic area, however, still enjoyed a common culture. Extensive trade routes also helped to maintain close economic links among the cities built by Alexander.

MAKING THE CONNECTION

1. List three regional economic characteristics of Alexander's empire.
2. What are the boundaries of the region in which you live?

MEETING SPECIAL NEEDS ACTIVITY

Learning Style: Visual/Spatial Many students have problems understanding distances. Have students, in pairs or small groups, "translate" some of the distances of Alexander's time into comparable distances in the United States today. For instance, the extent of Alexander's conquests in Asia, from the Aegean coast to the Indus Valley, is approximately 2,800 miles (4,505 kilometers)—about the same as the east-west distance across the United States. If possible, have students present their findings to the class using a wall map of the United States. **L1**

History & Art Learning philosophy at the School of Plato, a mosaic from Pompeii. National Museum of Archaeology, Naples, Italy *What three systems of thought attracted most Hellenistic intellectuals?*

History & Art The School of Plato, in Athens, was commonly referred to as the Academy. It was located in a grove of trees said to have belonged to a man named Academus, a hero of the Trojan War.
Answer to Caption: *Cynicism, Epicureanism, and Stoicism*

Hellenistic Art and Literature

During the Hellenistic era, artists departed from Hellenic styles. Instead of carving idealized individuals, Hellenistic sculptors showed people in the grip of powerful emotions. They also carved portrait heads, because art had become a business.

Hellenistic playwrights usually wrote comedies rather than tragedies. Like Hellenistic philosophers, they ignored the problems of the outside world as much as possible. **Menander**, the most renowned Hellenistic playwright, specialized in comedies about everyday life. Well-known lines from his works include "Whom the gods love die young" and "We live not as we will, but as we can."

Science, Medicine, and Mathematics

Although limited by their simple instruments, Hellenistic scientists performed many experiments and formed new theories. Aristarchus (AR•uh•STAHR•kuhs) of Samos concluded that the sun is larger than the earth, that the earth revolves around the sun, and that the stars lie at immense distances from both. **Eratosthenes** (EHR•uh•TAHS•thuh•NEEZ) estimated the earth's circumference to within 1 percent of the correct figure. Hellenistic doctors dissected corpses in order to learn more about human anatomy. They discovered the nervous system, studied the brain and the liver, and learned how to use drugs to relieve pain.

The Hellenistic period also saw great developments in mathematics and physics. **Euclid** of Alexandria wrote *The Elements of Geometry*, a book that organized all information about geometry. **Archimedes** (AHR•kuh•MEE•deez) invented the compound pulley, which moves heavy objects easily, and the cylinder-screw, which is still used to lift water for irrigation. He also discovered the principle of buoyancy and demonstrated the principle of the lever.

SECTION 3 REVIEW

Recall
1. **Define** domain.
2. **Identify** Philip II, Demosthenes, Alexander the Great, Zeno, Menander, Eratosthenes, Euclid, Archimedes.
3. **Locate** Macedonia and Alexandria on the map on page 141. What does Alexandria owe to the Macedonians?

Critical Thinking
4. **Making Comparisons** Compare and contrast Alexander the Great's original goal and the goal he finally chose for his empire. Why did his goals change?

Understanding Themes
5. **Cultural Diffusion** Explain how and why Hellenistic arts differed from Hellenic arts.

Reteach

Have volunteers read each heading in this section. After each is read, have other volunteers summarize the main ideas under the heading.

Reteaching Activity 5

Enrich

Have students research the achievements of other Greek scientists of the Hellenistic period, such as Hipparchus, Herophilus, or Erasistratus.

Enrichment Activity 5

CLOSE

Organize the class into three teams to prepare questions and answers for a class quiz game called "It's Greek to Me." Each team takes a section of the chapter and prepares ten questions and answers. Each team also reviews the other two sections to be able to answer questions. Have teams quiz each other.

SECTION 3 REVIEW ANSWERS

1. All vocabulary words are defined in the Glossary.
2. Philip II, 140; Demosthenes, 140; Alexander the Great, 141; Zeno, 144; Menander, 145; Eratosthenes, 145; Euclid, 145; Archimedes, 145
3. Alexandria was founded by Alexander the Great, a Macedonian.
4. His first goal was revenge; later, he wanted to combine different cultures into a new civilization. His goals changed as he subdued more and more territory.
5. **CULTURAL DIFFUSION** Compared to the Hellenic Greeks, Hellenistic sculptors created more emotional, less idealistic works. Hellenistic playwrights wrote comedies rather than tragedies. Causes for these changes may include: the absorption of different peoples into Alexander's empire; a tendency to shun the problems of the outside world and to be less involved in political life.

Bridge to the Past
Literature

Block Schedule

Team Teaching This excerpt from *Antigone* may be presented in a team-teaching context, in conjunction with English or Language Arts.

Antigone

Historical Connection

Sophocles wrote during the Golden Age of Athens, an era in which Greek writers, philosophers, architects, and historians produced works that shaped all subsequent Western civilization. This excerpt from the play *Antigone* shows how thinkers of the time dealt with such basic issues as ethics and justice.

Background Information

Setting During the Golden Age of Athens, writers often set their works in the distant past. *Antigone* takes place in the city of Thebes in a mythological period long before Sophocles lived.

Characters Antigone: daughter of the deceased king of Thebes, niece of Creon, sister of Ismene, Polyneices, and Eteocles; Ismene: sister of Antigone; Creon: brother of the deceased king of Thebes.

Plot The main conflict is between Antigone, who wants to give her brother Polyneices an honorable burial, and Creon, her uncle, who argues that Polyneices was a traitor who does not deserve a burial. Antigone violates Creon's order and buries her brother. Antigone and Creon then debate the morality of her action.

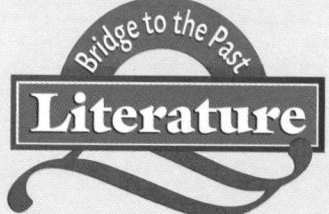

Bridge to the Past
Literature

from Antigone

by Sophocles

The Greek playwright Sophocles, who lived from about 496–406 B.C., wrote about the conflict between conscience and authority in his play Antigone. *After Antigone's two brothers died battling each other for the throne of Thebes, her uncle, Creon, became king. Creon allowed one brother, Eteocles, an honorable burial. He declared, however, that the other brother, Polyneices, was a traitor whose body should be left for the "birds and scavenging dogs." Anyone attempting to bury Polyneices, he warned, would be stoned to death. Antigone's sister, Ismene, obeys Creon. Antigone, however, out of respect for her brother, buries him.*

Creon [*slowly, dangerously*]. And you, Antigone,
You with your head hanging—do you confess this thing?

Antigone. I do. I deny nothing.

Creon [*to* SENTRY]. You may go.
[*Exit* SENTRY] [*To* ANTIGONE] Tell me, tell me briefly:
Had you heard my proclamation touching this matter?

Antigone. It was public. Could I help hearing it?

Creon. And yet you dared defy the law.

Antigone. I dared.
It was not God's proclamation. That final justice
That rules the world below makes no such laws.
Your edict, King, was strong,
But all your strength is weakness itself against
The immortal unrecorded laws of God.
They are not merely now: they were, and shall be,
Operative forever, beyond man utterly.

I knew I must die, even without your decree:
I am only mortal. And if I must die
Now, before it is my time to die,
Surely this is no hardship: can anyone
Living, as I live, with evil all about me,
Think death less than a friend? This death of mine
Is of no importance; but if I had left my brother
Lying in death unburied, I should have suffered.
Now I do not.
You smile at me. Ah Creon.

About the Author

Sophocles was born into a well-to-do family in ancient Greece. Many of his plays focused on one strong-willed individual who challenged authority, tradition, or the gods and goddesses. For example, Antigone defies the authority of the state to defend the honor of her brother. Although Sophocles wrote more than 100 plays, only 7 are known to exist today. Many of the lost plays won awards in the annual writing competition held in ancient Greece. In addition to writing, Sophocles served as a government administrator and a general in the Athenian army.

Think me a fool, if you like; but it may well be
That a fool convicts me of folly. . . .
Creon, what more do you want than my death?

Creon. Nothing.
That gives me everything.

Antigone. Then I beg you: kill me.
This talking is a great weariness: your words
Are distasteful to me, and I am sure that mine
Seem so to you. And yet they should not seem so:
I should have praise and honor for what I have done.
All these men here would praise me
Were their lips not frozen shut with fear of you.
[*Bitterly*] Ah the good fortune of kings,
Licensed to say and do whatever they please!

Creon. You are alone here in that opinion.

Antigone. No, they are with me. But they keep their tongues in leash.

Creon. Maybe. But you are guilty, and they are not.

Antigone. There is no guilt in reverence for the dead.

Creon. But Eteocles—was he not your brother too?

Antigone. My brother too.

Creon. And you insult his memory?

Antigone [*softly*]. The dead man would not say that I insult it.

Creon. He would: for you honor a traitor as much as him.

Antigone. His own brother, traitor or not, and equal in blood.

Creon. He made war on his country. Eteocles defended it.

Antigone. Nevertheless, there are honors due all the dead.

History & Art Actors preparing for a performance (detail), the House of the Tragic Poet, Pompeii. National Museum, Naples, Italy
What is the theme of Antigone?

Other Works by Sophocles

Jebb, Richard Claverhouse, trans. *The Complete Plays of Sophocles.* New York: Bantam, 1982.

Knox, M. W., trans. *Oedipus the King.* New York: Pocket Books, 1972.

Watling, E. F., trans. *Electra and Other Plays.* New York: Penguin Books, 1954.

Williams, C. K., and Gregory W. Dickerson, trans. *Women of Trachus.* New York: Oxford University Press, 1978.

Bridge to the Past
Literature

Literary Element Alliteration occurs when words in a phrase begin with a similar sound. The first line by Creon uses alliteration, as in "head hanging." Later, Antigone uses the phrase "a fool convicts me of folly."

FOCUS

Before students read the excerpt, list on the chalkboard people who students feel have authority over them, such as parents, teachers, and so on. Ask students to describe hypothetical cases in which they might choose to disobey a person having authority. Help them see the difference between ignoring authority and principled disobedience.

TEACH

Interpretation

Ask students if they agree with Antigone's claim that "All these men here would praise me/Were their lips not shut with fear of you." Point out that ordinary people may support a heroic individual against a repressive government. At other times, people see such an individual as a threat to order and stability.

History & Art Pompeii was a provincial Roman city buried in ash and lava when the volcano Vesuvius erupted in August of A.D. 79, killing all its residents but preserving much of the art and architecture.
Answer to Caption: *an individual can stand up to an authority, but at a price*

Chapter 5 *The Height of Greek Civilization* 147

Bridge to the Past

Literature

Clarification

The chorágos is the leader of the chorus, who serves as a narrator to smooth the flow of the story and adds commentary from the author.

Evaluation

Discuss the role of women in Greek society as portrayed in this excerpt. Students might consider how the play would differ if Antigone had been male instead of female. *(She would have taken the throne instead of Creon.)*

History & Art Roman art was strongly influenced by Hellenic styles. Wealthy Romans not only had artists copy Greek originals but also sometimes brought artists from Greece to decorate their homes. **Answer to Caption:** *Students may say that since Ismene feared to act, mere words cannot redeem her.*

Linking Past and Present

Greek Dramas *Antigone* and other tragedies by Sophocles, such as *Oedipus the King*, *Oedipus at Colonus*, and *Electra*, are often staged today by college theater groups and by local repertory companies. Some students may wish to attend a performance in your area.

World Literature Selection 2

ASSESS

Assign **Responding to Literature** questions.

History & Art Wall painting of a Greek woman with flowers. National Museum, Naples, Italy
The Greeks admired beauty and virtue. *Does Ismene regain virtue by confessing a share in the crime?*

Creon. But not the same for the wicked as for the just.

Antigone. Ah Creon, Creon.
Which of us can say what the gods hold wicked?

Creon. An enemy is an enemy, even dead.

Antigone. It is my nature to join in love, not hate.

Creon [*finally losing patience*]. Go join them, then; if you must have your love,
Find it in hell!

Choragos [*leader of a group of 15 citizens*]. But see, Ismene comes:
[*Enter Ismene, guarded.*] Those tears are sisterly, the cloud
That shadows her eyes rains down gentle sorrow.

Creon. You too, Ismene,

Additional Literary Works of the Period

Book of Songs. A collection of 300 poems from China dating to 1000 B.C.
Homer. *Illiad and Odyssey.* Ancient Greek epic poems that have greatly influenced Western literature.
Laozi. *The Classic of the Way and the Virtue.* Writings of the founder of Daoism, who lived in China in the 500s B.C.
Samhitas. Sacred Hindu hymns written in Sanskrit in India and compiled about 1000 B.C.

Snake in my ordered house, sucking my blood
Stealthily—and all the time I never knew
That these two sisters were aiming at my throne!
Ismene,
Do you confess your share in this crime, or deny it?
Answer me.

Ismene. Yes, if she will let me say so. I am guilty.

Antigone [*coldly*]. No, Ismene. You have no right to say so.
You would not help me, and I will not have you help me.

Ismene. But now I know what you meant; and I am here
To join you, to take my share of punishment.

Antigone. The dead man and the gods who rule the dead
Know whose act this was. Words are not friends.

Ismene. Do you refuse me, Antigone? I want to die with you:
I too have a duty that I must discharge to the dead.

Antigone. You shall not lessen my death by sharing it.

Ismene. What do I care for life when you are dead?

Antigone. Ask Creon. You're always hanging on his opinions.

Ismene. You are laughing at me. Why, Antigone?

Antigone. It's a joyless laughter, Ismene.

Ismene. But can I do nothing?

Antigone. Yes. Save yourself. I shall not envy you.
There are those who will praise you; I shall have honor, too.

Ismene. But we are equally guilty!

Antigone. No more, Ismene.
You are alive, but I belong to death.

RESPONDING TO LITERATURE

1. Explain what Antigone means when she says to Creon, "But all your strength is weakness itself against the immortal unrecorded laws of God."
2. Quote a passage that demonstrates Antigone's bravery.
3. Explain whether you would like to live in a society in which individuals followed only their consciences.
4. **Making Inferences** Predict whether Creon actually would have Antigone stoned to death.

Bridge to the Past **Literature**

CLOSE

Ask students to put themselves in the position of Antigone and Creon and have them describe what moral dilemmas each faced. *(As ruler, Creon may feel he cannot back down from sentencing Antigone to death, but as her uncle, he may be reluctant to carry out the punishment. Antigone does not wish to die, but she feels it is dishonorable to leave her brother unburied.)*

Contemporary Connection

One underlying theme of Antigone is loyalty to family. Discuss the idea with students, asking if they feel they have a duty to be loyal to their families. Ask students to consider how far loyalty to family should go.

Portfolio Project

Have students draw on their own experience to write a short essay, agreeing or disagreeing with this statement: *There is no value more important than loyalty to family.*

ANSWERS TO RESPONDING TO LITERATURE

1. Antigone believes that her duty to obey the laws of the gods and goddesses is more important than the laws of the state.
2. Her first line, "I do. I deny nothing," condemns her to die and so shows her courage.
3. Students may recognize that a society in which each person followed his or her conscience would be anarchic; on the other hand, they may sympathize with the right of individuals to determine what is right and wrong.
4. Based on the excerpt, some students may feel that Creon's hard posture implies that he will have Antigone executed; others may feel the fact that he enters into a discussion with her means that he might reconsider Antigone's punishment. At the end of the play, Creon banishes Antigone to a cave, where she commits suicide.

CHAPTER 5 REVIEW

Historical Significance

Greek culture has influenced Western civilization in many ways. The ancient Greeks developed classical models on which later architects, artists, and playwrights have relied. Their thinkers also laid the foundation for the disciplines of history, political science, and logic.

The Founders of the United States took inspiration from ancient Greek ideals, such as belief in the worth and importance of the individual. The Founders' belief in a democratic form of government—as the one best suited to enabling people to enhance their abilities—also has its roots in ancient Greece.

Using Key Terms

Write the key term that completes each sentence.

a. classical	f. domains
b. comedies	g. hygiene
c. logic	h. sanctuaries
d. philosophers	i. amphora
e. tragedies	j. perspective

1. Because the Greeks worshiped either in their homes or at outdoor altars, they did not need large _____, or places of worship.
2. Some Greek playwrights wrote _______, plays that were characterized by humorous themes and happy endings.
3. The architects of the Parthenon in Athens understood ________, the artistic representation of distances between objects as they appear to the eye.
4. Greek potters usually decorated an ________—a large vase for storing bulk supplies such as oil—with scenes from their mythology and legends.
5. Greek artists and architects created works characterized by a ________ style known for its beautiful simplicity and graceful balance.
6. The earliest Greek plays were ______, in which the lead characters experienced great suffering and had unhappy endings.
7. After Alexander's death in 323 B.C., his large multicultural empire was divided into several _________.
8. Greek thinkers, or __________, developed the foundations for disciplines such as history, political science, and logic.
9. The physician Hippocrates advocated proper _____, a sound diet, and plenty of rest.
10. Greek thinkers, such as Aristotle, developed ____, or the science of reasoning.

Using Your History Journal

The Greeks liked to relive historic events through drama. Each actor would wear a large mask to show the age, sex, and mood of each character. Write a short scene for a drama depicting an event from the chapter.

Reviewing Facts

1. **Locate** where the Parthenon was built and explain for what purpose.
2. **Describe** the main philosophical differences between the Sophists and Socrates.
3. **Name** the main steps in the scientific method of inquiry developed by Aristotle.
4. **Explain** why Thucydides is considered the first scientific historian.
5. **List** the major contributions that Hippocrates made to medicine.
6. **Identify** the two major cultural areas that contributed to Hellenistic civilization.
7. **State** the contributions of Archimedes to Hellenistic science.

Critical Thinking

1. **Apply** How did the Peloponnesian War affect Greek drama and philosophy?
2. **Analyze** In what ways did Alexander the Great demonstrate his love of learning?
3. **Evaluate** Whose political ideas does the United States government more closely follow, those of Plato or those of Aristotle?

Chapter 5 Review

GLENCOE TECHNOLOGY

VIDEODISC

Use MindJogger to review students' knowledge of the chapter.

MindJogger Videoquiz

Chapter 5
Disc 1 Side B

Also available in VHS.

Answers

Using Key Terms

1. h	6. e
2. b	7. f
3. j	8. d
4. i	9. g
5. a	10. c

Using Your History Journal

Events that might serve as the bases for short dramas include: the trial or death of Socrates; a speech by Demosthenes; the murder of Philip II of Macedonia; one of Alexander's battles; the death of Alexander.

Reviewing Facts

1. It was built on the Acropolis in Athens as a temple to the goddess Athena.
2. The Sophists believed in relative truth; Socrates believed in absolute truth. The Sophists emphasized the use of rhetoric in political arguments; Socrates aimed to teach people how to think for themselves.
3. observing facts, classifying them according to similarities and differences, and constructing generalizations from data
4. because he rejected the idea that the deities play a part in human history; also, he was as accurate and impartial as possible
5. He taught that diseases have natural rather than supernatural causes; based his work on observation; urged physicians to record their cases and exchange information with one another.
6. the Greek world and the area dominated by Persian culture
7. He invented the compound pulley and the cylinder screw. He also discovered the principle of buoyancy and demonstrated the principle of the lever.

Critical Thinking

1. Both Sophocles and Euripides, who experienced the war, wrote of human suffering and war's miseries.
2. Instead of destroying cultures, he sought to combine the best of Greek and Persian

CHAPTER 5 REVIEW

Geography in History

1. **Place** Refer to the map "Alexander's Empire Divided." Who controlled the area of Macedonia?
2. **Location** What present-day countries make up the part of Alexander's empire ruled by Ptolemy?
3. **Movement** What caused the descendants of Seleucus to lose their holdings in Mesopotamia, Iran, and Afghanistan?

Alexander's Empire Divided

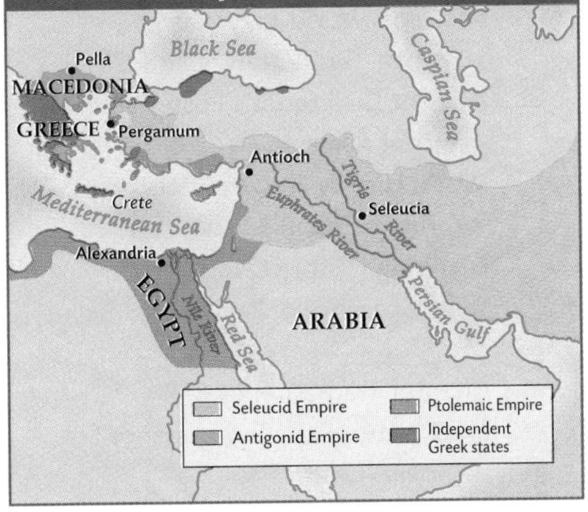

Understanding Themes

1. **Innovation** What might contemporary theater be like if such playwrights as Aristophanes and Menander had not lived?
2. **Innovation** Do you think Herodotus deserves to be called the "father of history"? Explain your answer.
3. **Cultural Diffusion** How did Alexander the Great's founding of cities throughout his empire help spread Greek culture?

Linking Past and Present

1. The Olympic Games were revived in 1896. In what ways do the modern Olympic Games resemble those of ancient Greece? In what ways do they differ?
2. The inclusion of diverse territories in Alexander the Great's empire led to widespread cultural diffusion. What aspects of Greek culture spread during the Hellenistic period?
3. Some American and European theaters have recently staged revivals of Greek plays. What do you think might be the appeal of these ancient plays to modern directors? How might modern audiences react to plays written more than 2,000 years ago?
4. Ideas of Greek civilization have affected much of American culture. Choose one area such as medicine, philosophy, politics, art, or architecture. Reread information about that area in your chapter. Then list as many examples of influences on American culture as you can. Ask friends, parents, or other family members to help complete the list.

Skill Practice

Use the map "Greece and Persia" to answer the following questions.

1. What is the approximate location of Athens?
2. Which body of water lies entirely north of 40° N latitude?
3. What is the approximate location of Sparta?
4. What is the approximate location of Sardis?
5. What is the relative location of Sardis?
6. What Mediterranean island lies along the 35th parallel?

Greece and Persia

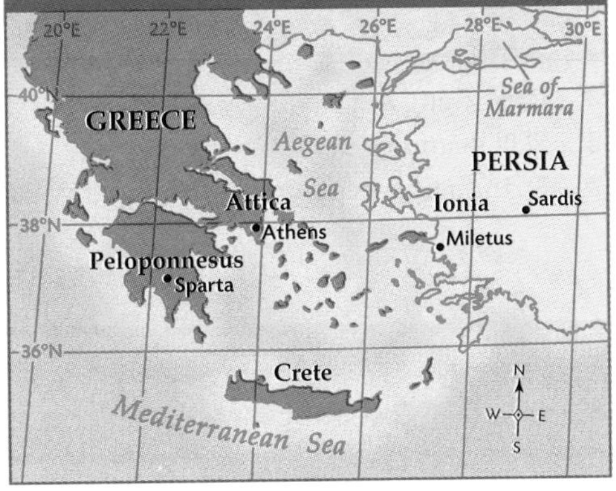

cultures.

3. those of Aristotle

Understanding Themes

1. **Innovation** Perhaps the only type of play would be tragedy.
2. **Innovation** Yes, because he traveled widely, asked questions, and checked his sources; he also wrote about individuals, social customs, and religious practices and beliefs; or no, because he accepted some untrue statements; he also offered supernatural explanations for some events.
3. **Cultural Diffusion** Greek was spoken, and Greek culture flourished in these cities.

Linking Past and Present

1. The modern Olympics are still held every four years; many of the events today are the same as those of ancient times; winners are greatly honored. But today's Olympics feature athletes from all over the world, not just Greeks; women can watch and participate; many additional events have been added, including winter sports; today's winners, celebrated in the mass media, can make millions of dollars by endorsements.
2. the Greek language, Greek art/architecture, drama, science, business practices, and religion
3. Modern directors might enjoy the challenge of adapting ancient plays for a modern stage and audience. If the plays are well staged, modern audiences may find the tragedies moving and the comedies funny.
4. Answers will vary.

Chapter 5 Review

Skill Practice

1. 38°N, 24°E
2. Sea of Marmara
3. 37°N, 22°E
4. 38°N, 29°E
5. east of Ionia, south of the Sea of Marmara, north of Miletus
6. Crete

Geography in History

1. Antigonid Empire
2. Egypt, Libya, and part of Syria
3. They were forced to withdraw from Syria due to an uprising in Palestine led by a group of Jewish guerrillas. The uprising, led by Judah Macabee, was a rebellion against being forced to worship Greek deities.

Chapter Bonus Test Question

Ask students: Which of the many philosophical outlooks discussed in this chapter do you think is most relevant to today's world? Why? *(Answers should include the basic tenets of whichever philosopher or school is chosen.)*

Teach, Reinforce, and Extend CHAPTER Content

Ancient Rome and Early Christianity

CHAPTER RESOURCES

	Reproducible Resources	Multimedia Resources
Chapter Opener	Chapter Themes: Graphic Organizer 6 Historical Significance Chapter Activity 6	MindJogger Videoquiz
Chapter Enrichment	Vocabulary Activity 6* Time Line Activity 6 Mapping History Activity 6 History Simulation 6 Geography and History Activity 6 Source Reading 6 People in World History Profiles 9, 10 World Art and Music Activity 6 Enrichment Activity 6 Critical Thinking Activity 6 Skill Reinforcement Activity 6 Performance Assessment Activity 6	Focus on World Art Print 9, Roman. *Girl With Writing Tablet* Ancient Civilizations Poster Set: *Ancient Rome* World History and Art Transparency 7, *The Pantheon* Mapping History Overlay Transparency 6, *Roman Expansion* Chapter Transparency 6 NGS PicturePack Transparency Set: *Ancient Rome* Vocabulary PuzzleMaker Software NGS PictureShow CD-ROM: *Greece and Rome* Turning Points in World History: *Jerusalem: City of Three Faiths* In the Holy Land
Chapter Review/Reteaching	Reteaching Activity 6 Skill Reinforcement Activity 6 Spanish Chapter Summary 6	Chapter 6 Digest Audiocassette, Activity, Test* Vocabulary PuzzleMaker Software Student Self-Test and Review Software MindJogger Videoquiz
Chapter Evaluation/Testing	Performance Assessment Activity 6 Chapter 6 Test, Forms A and B	Testmaker

* *Also available in Spanish*

0:00 **OUT OF TIME?** Assign the Chapter 6 summary in the Unit 2 Digest on pages 236–239, and the Chapter 6 Audiocassettes.

Block Schedule

Block scheduling differs from traditional class scheduling in the amount of time allotted to each period. The extended time frame provided by block scheduling affords you the opportunity to implement a greater number of research-oriented and activity-intense projects to motivate and involve your students. Activities that are particularly suited to use within the block scheduling framework are identified throughout this chapter by the following designation.

KEY TO ABILITY LEVELS

Teaching strategies have been coded for varying learning styles and abilities.

- L1 **BASIC** activities for all students
- L2 **AVERAGE** activities for average to above-average students
- L3 **CHALLENGING** activities for above-average students
- LEP **LIMITED ENGLISH PROFICIENCY** activities

A complete, 1-page lesson plan is provided for each section in the *Reproducible Lesson Plans* booklet.

SECTION RESOURCES

Daily Objectives	Reproducible Resources	Multimedia Resources
Section 1 The Roman Republic Describe the structure of the Roman Republic and the ways it changed.	Reproducible Lesson Plan 6-1 Guided Reading Activity 6-1* Time Line Activity 6 History Simulation 6 Section Quiz 6-1*	Focus on World Art Print 9, Roman. *Girl With Writing Tablet* Ancient Civilizations Poster Set: *Ancient Rome* Section Focus Transparency 6-1 Chapter Transparency 6 Vocabulary PuzzleMaker Software Student Self-Test and Review Software
Section 2 Expansion and Crisis Outline the economic and social problems that ended the Roman Republic.	Reproducible Lesson Plan 6-2 Vocabulary Activity 6* Guided Reading Activity 6-2* Section Quiz 6-2*	Section Focus Transparency 6-2 Mapping History Overlay Transparency 6, *Roman Expansion* NGS PicturePack Transparency Set: *Ancient Rome* Student Self-Test and Review Software Testmaker
Section 3 The Roman Empire Characterize life under the *Pax Romana*.	Reproducible Lesson Plan 6-3 Vocabulary Activity 6* Guided Reading Activity 6-3* Section Quiz 6-3*	Section Focus Transparency 6-3 World History and Art Transparency 7, *The Pantheon* Student Self-Test and Review Software NGS PictureShow CD-ROM: *Greece and Rome*
Section 4 The Rise of Christianity Summarize the teachings of Jesus of Nazareth and the influence of early Christians on the later Roman Empire.	Reproducible Lesson Plan 6-4 Guided Reading Activity 6-4* Section Quiz 6-4*	Section Focus Transparency 6-4 Vocabulary PuzzleMaker Software Student Self-Test and Review Software Testmaker Turning Points in World History: *Jerusalem: City of Three Faiths* In the Holy Land
Section 5 Roman Decline List the reasons for the decline of the western Roman Empire.	Reproducible Lesson Plan 6-5 Vocabulary Activity 6* Guided Reading Activity 6-5* Reteaching Activity 6 Enrichment Activity 6 Section Quiz 6-5* Performance Assessment Activity 6 Spanish Chapter Summary 6	Section Focus Transparency 6-5 Student Self-Test and Review Software Testmaker

* *Also available in Spanish*

Chapter Activities

Performance Assessment Activity

An Ad Campaign Have students take the roles of ad executives for a museum exhibit about ancient Rome. They should create a series of ten magazine ads (or billboards) showcasing the most important aspects of what can be learned by visiting the exhibit. Ads/billboards may be described or actually drawn and should be placed in priority order for an audience of potential contributors who may decide to fund only a portion of the campaign. Students should write a reflection in which they explain and support their ranking.

Possible Rubric Features
Accuracy of content information, decision-making skills, quality of product, extent of support

• *For an additional activity, refer to Activity 6 in the* Performance Assessment Strategies and Activities *booklet.*

ACTIVITY

From the Classroom of...

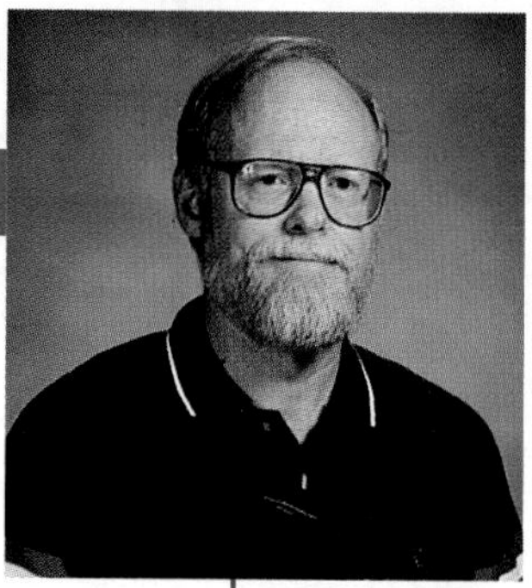

Lawrence J. Emsing
Arapahoe High School
Littleton, CO

The Collapse of the Roman Empire

The purpose of this simulation activity is to get students to analyze and to understand the underlying causes for the eventual collapse of the Roman Empire in the West. Students will appreciate that multiple causation is a more historically satisfying explanation for complex events than single causation theories. This activity is designed to encourage: critical analysis of a major historical event, collaborative decision making within a small group, and advocacy skills.

Organize students into five groups, each representing a segment of the Roman population (wealthy landowners; urban poor in crowded Rome; rural poor in the provinces; the military; Christians, Jews, and other non-Roman religious sects). Groups will research and develop a plan for solving some of the many problems confronting the Empire. Each group will present its grievances and plans for addressing the grievances that will avert the fall as well as enhance their own position. The activity is designed to take 2-3 days depending on whether preparation time is included. After all groups have made their presentations, have students vote on which plan or plans for reform they would approve.

MULTIPLE LEARNING STYLES

Verbal/Linguistic
Have students write a detailed description of the Baths of Caracalla, one of the most elaborate of the Roman public baths.

Logical/Mathematical
Have students prepare a chart of Arabic numerals (1 through 15, then 20, 30, 40, 50, 60, 70, 80, 90, 100, 500, and 1,000), the corresponding Roman numerals, and the Latin names for the numerals. Have students research how Romans performed mathematical calculations using their numerals, and write a few simple examples.

Kinesthetic
Have students prepare a visual presentation of Roman architecture. They should present illustrations, diagrams, and pictures of some of the most important Roman structures from various periods, along with an explanation of each structure.

Intrapersonal
As students read Chapter 6, have them keep brief notes on each person mentioned. Then have them prepare a list of who they believe were the 10 most important Romans and briefly explain why they have chosen each person.

Additional Resources

TEACHER'S CORNER

NATIONAL GEOGRAPHIC SOCIETY

INDEX TO NATIONAL GEOGRAPHIC MAGAZINE

The following articles may be used for research relating to this chapter:

- "The Day the World Ended at Kourion," by David Soren, July 1988.
- "The Eternal Etruscans," by Rick Gore, June 1988.
- "Caesarea Maritima: Herod the Great's City on the Sea," by Robert L. Hohlfelder, February 1987.
- "Arabia's Frankincense Trail," by Thomas J. Abercrombie, October 1985.
- "The Dead Do Tell Tales at Vesuvius," by Rick Gore, May 1984.
- "On the Slope of Vesuvius: A Buried Roman Town Gives Up Its Dead," by Joseph Judge, December 1982.
- "Ancient Aphrodisias Lives Through Its Art," by Kenan T. Erim, October 1981.
- "Down the Ancient Appian Way," by James Cerruti, June 1981.

NATIONAL GEOGRAPHIC SOCIETY PRODUCTS AVAILABLE FROM GLENCOE

To order the following products for use with this chapter, contact your local Glencoe sales representative or call Glencoe at 1-800-368-7344:

NGS PICTURESHOW CD-ROM
- Greece and Rome

NGS PICTUREPACK TRANSPARENCY SET
- Ancient Rome

ANCIENT CIVILIZATIONS POSTER SET
- Ancient Rome

ADDITIONAL NATIONAL GEOGRAPHIC SOCIETY PRODUCTS

To order the following products for use with this chapter, call National Geographic Society at 1-800-368-2728:

- *Ancient Civilizations*, "Rome." (Filmstrip)
- *In the Shadow of Vesuvius* (Video)

BIBLIOGRAPHY

Literature of the Period

Virgil. *Aeneid.* Translated by John Dryden. Edited by Howard Clarke. University Park, PA: Pennsylvania State University, 1989. The national epic of Rome.

Readings for the Student

Wallace, Lewis. *Ben-Hur: A Tale of the Christ.* Uhrichsville, OH: Barbour and Co., 1985. A highly popular book, originally published in 1880, that has been twice made into a movie.

Readings for the Teacher

Hamilton, Edith. *The Roman Way.* New York: Norton, 1984. Originally published in 1932, this famous work by an American classical scholar translates for modern readers the meaning of ancient Roman life as mirrored in its literature.

interNET
CONNECTIONS
SPQR- Senate and the Roman People Explore a virtual reconstruction of Ancient Rome.
http://pathfinder.com/@@oif o6df8twaaqcik/twep/rome

Introducing Chapter 6

CHAPTER THEMES

Chapter Themes are listed by section on this chapter opening page of the Student Edition. A corresponding theme-based activity is available under "TEACH," and a theme-based question is asked in the Section and Chapter Reviews.

The Storyteller

Historical Setting Romans admired and imitated the Greeks—their art, religion, architecture, philosophy, and science. Admiration led to an ambivalent approach to conquest. Rome conquered Greece shortly after 200 B.C., then proclaimed "the freedom of Greece." The Greeks proved to be recalcitrant, and the Romans finally subjugated Greece by destroying Corinth in 146 B.C. Greek influence in Roman culture, however, persisted.

Historical Significance

Answers: *Rome became the center of a vast empire by establishing a common Greco-Roman culture among the diverse peoples.*

Lasting legacies of the Roman Empire are its Latin language, which provided the roots of the Romance languages; its engineering skills; its transmission of Greek culture; and its development of Christianity.

Chapter 6

750 B.C.–A.D. 500

Ancient Rome and Early Christianity

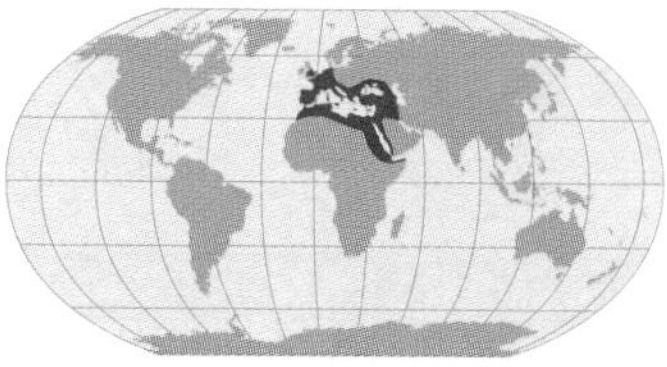

Chapter Themes

- **Change** The Roman political system evolves as Rome allows more of its people to participate in government. *Section 1*
- **Conflict** Roman armies conquer most of the Mediterranean world. *Section 2*
- **Cultural Diffusion** The Romans build an empire and spread Latin culture. *Section 3*
- **Innovation** Christianity becomes the dominant religion in the West. *Section 4*
- **Change** Germanic invasions and cultural weaknesses destroy the Roman Empire. *Section 5*

The Storyteller

War trumpets rang over the cheers of the people of Rome who gathered to view the triumphal grand parade. Then sweating horses jerking at their harnesses rattled the victor's chariot over the paving stones, and the people's cries became louder. On this day in 146 B.C., the Romans were celebrating their conquest of the last of the free Greek city-states.

Ironically, however, over the next several centuries Greek culture would come to form the base of Roman culture and society. Texts written by Greeks would shape Roman knowledge in many areas of study. Even after years of Roman rule, the eastern Mediterranean world would retain Greek as its primary language.

Historical Significance

How did the small city-state of Rome become the center of a vast, diverse empire that spanned the Mediterranean world? What were Rome's last legacies to Europe, Africa, the Middle East, and other parts of the world?

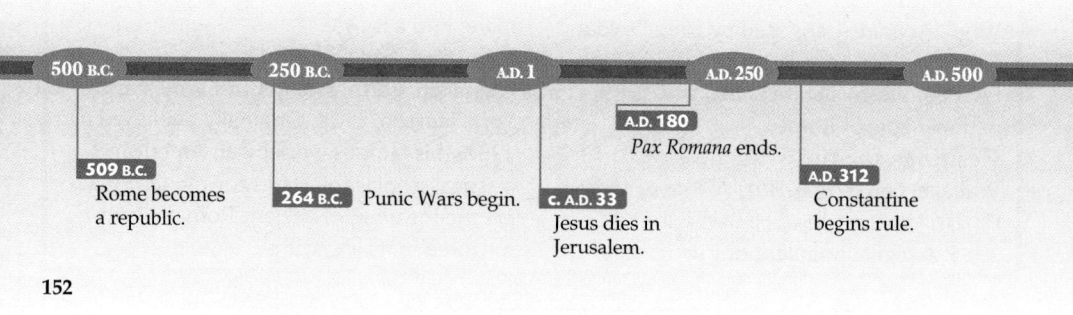

500 B.C. — 250 B.C. — A.D. 1 — A.D. 250 — A.D. 500

- **509 B.C.** Rome becomes a republic.
- **264 B.C.** Punic Wars begin.
- **c. A.D. 33** Jesus dies in Jerusalem.
- **A.D. 180** *Pax Romana* ends.
- **A.D. 312** Constantine begins rule.

GEOGRAPHY CONNECTION

GEOGRAPHIC THEMES

Location Have students use the Atlas in their text to locate Europe, the Mediterranean Sea, Asia Minor, North Africa, and the Middle East—the regions controlled by the Roman Empire by A.D. 130. What problems might arise in governing such a vast area? *(delays in communications, need to provide defense against invaders and rebellions, tax collection)*

History & Art Woman playing the cithera, painted on the east wall of a room in the villa of Publius Fannius Synistor, Pompeii, Italy

Your History Journal

The European cities of Bonn, Vienna, London, and Paris were each founded by the Romans. Research the early history of one of these cities and describe the Roman influence on its early architecture and lifestyle.

Introducing Chapter 6

History & Art Tell students that the Roman use of the cithera was another example of the pervasiveness of Greek culture. The cithera was one of two principal types of ancient Greek lyres, or stringed instruments with a sound box and two curved arms connected by a yoke. How does the painting suggest the cithera was played? *(held upright with the strings plucked by the fingers)* What common instrument derives its name from the cithera? *(guitar; also zither)*

Performance Assessment

Refer to the activity on page 152C of the Planning Guide. For an additional activity, refer to Activity 6 in the *Performance Assessment Strategies and Activities* booklet.

Using Your History Journal

Suggest that students write from the perspective of Roman soldiers involved in the settlement of these outposts.

GLENCOE TECHNOLOGY

VIDEODISC

Use MindJogger to preview chapter content.

MindJogger Videoquiz

Chapter 6
Disc 1 Side B

Also available in VHS.

EXTRA CREDIT PROJECT

Report Several studies focus on the importance of the military in the history of ancient Rome. Have students research and report to the class on the development of the professional army and the role military leaders played in Roman politics. Ask them to evaluate in their reports the importance of the military from the time of the republic through the rule of Constantine. Suggested resources: M. Mulvihill, *Roman Forts*; A. Ferrill, *The Fall of the Roman Empire: The Military Explanation*; and L. Keppie, *The Making of the Roman Army: From Republic to Empire*.

Chapter 6
Section 1

SECTION THEME

▶ **Change** The Roman political system evolves as Rome allows more of its people to participate in government.

Find Out

Answer: *Patrician officials called consuls headed the executive branch. The legislature was composed of the Assembly of Centuries and the Senate, both under patrician control. Over the years the republic became more democratic.*

FOCUS

Section Objective

Describe the structure of the Roman Republic and the ways it changed.

BELLRINGER
Motivational Activity

Before taking roll at the beginning of the class period, project Section Focus Transparency 6-1 and have students answer the activity questions. Discuss students' responses.

This activity is also available as a blackline master.

Vocabulary Pre-check

Use the Vocabulary PuzzleMaker to create a puzzle that reinforces the vocabulary terms in this section. **L1**

800 B.C.		500 B.C.		200 B.C.
c. 753 B.C. Romulus founds Rome.	**c. 620 B.C.** Etruscans gain control of Rome.	**451 B.C.** The patricians of Rome enact the Twelve Tables.	**287 B.C.** The plebeians begin to make laws for Rome.	

Section 1

The Roman Republic

Setting the Scene

▶ **Terms to Define**
patrician, republic, plebeian, consul, dictator, tribune

▶ **People to Meet**
the Etruscans, the Latins, Romulus, the Tarquins

▶ **Places to Locate**
Italy, Sicily, Rome

Find Out How was Rome governed as a republic? How did the Roman Republic change over the years?

The Storyteller

The city of Rome was besieged by Lars Porsena, king of Clusium, and the time had come for decisive action. One young Roman hoped to break the siege by killing Porsena. After laying his plan before the Senate, he set out alone toward enemy lines. However, he was seized as a spy and dragged by guards before the very man he had hoped to kill—Porsena. He spoke boldly: "I am a Roman, my name is Gaius Mucius. I came here to kill you—my enemy. I have as much courage to die as to kill. It is our Roman way to do and to suffer bravely."

—adapted from *Early History of Rome*, Titus Livy, in *The Global Experience, Readings in World History to 1500*, 1987

The Forum

The peoples of **Italy** first came into contact with the Greeks around 900 B.C., when Greek traders sailed up both the east and west coasts of the Italian Peninsula. From about 750 B.C. to 500 B.C., the Greeks set up farming communities in southern Italy and in **Sicily**, an island southwest of the Italian Peninsula. These Greek colonists planted olive trees for the oil yielded and grapevines from which they could produce wine, thus introducing these two major products to Italy. The Greeks also introduced the Greek alphabet to the Italians.

The Italian Peninsula

The Greeks were interested in colonizing Italy for several reasons, one of which was Italy's central location in the Mediterranean. A narrow, boot-shaped peninsula, Italy extends from Europe toward the shores of Africa, dividing the Mediterranean almost in half. Thus, Italy was ideally situated to be the center of trade among three continents: Asia, Europe, and Africa. Italy's rich soil and mild, moist climate also attracted the Greek colonists. Beyond the mountains and foothills that covered three-quarters of the peninsula lay plains with soil enriched by the silt deposits of mountain streams.

However, the silt washing down Italy's short and shallow rivers blocked the mouths of many rivers, creating mosquito-infested swamps. The people of Italy suffered recurrent epidemics of malaria and other diseases carried by mosquitoes.

Because of Italy's mountains, the early inhabitants of the peninsula generally traded among themselves. Italy's only land connection—to the north—was cut off by the Alps. Furthermore, Italy's rocky and marshy coastline lacked good harbors. To increase trade, the Italians eventually turned to the sea, but until that time came, they remained attached to the land.

SECTION RESOURCES

Reproducible Masters
- Reproducible Lesson Plan 6-1
- Guided Reading Activity 6-1
- Time Line Activity 6
- History Simulation 6
- Section Quiz 6-1

Transparencies
- Section Focus Transparency 6-1
- Chapter Transparency 6

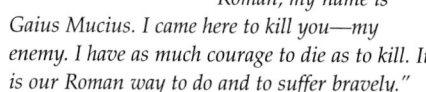

Multimedia
- Focus on World Art Print 9
- Ancient Rome
- Vocabulary PuzzleMaker Software
- Student Self-Test and Review Software
- Testmaker

Early Peoples

Archaeological evidence suggests that people lived in Italy long before the Greeks arrived or Roman civilization began. The remains of human settlements reveal that Neolithic cultures may have begun to form in Italy as early as about 5000 B.C. Early peoples in the Italian Peninsula built villages and farms, moving on whenever they had exhausted the land around their settlements.

Indo-Europeans

Between 2000 B.C. and 1000 B.C., waves of Indo-European immigrants arrived and overwhelmed these Neolithic peoples. By the time Greek colonists came to Italy, many peoples inhabited the peninsula—including Umbrians in the north, Latins in the central plain called Latium (LAY•shee•uhm), and Oscans in the south. Like the Greeks, most of these people spoke Indo-European languages.

The Etruscans

The most mysterious of the early peoples were **the Etruscans** who, from about 900 B.C. to 500 B.C., ruled northern Italy from the plains of Etruria. No one knows definitely where the Etruscans came from. They did not, at any rate, speak an Indo-European language as did many of the inhabitants of the peninsula. Although Etruscans wrote in an alphabet borrowed from the Greeks, modern scholars have been able to decipher only a few Etruscan words.

Although Etruscan writings still baffle our understanding, Etruscan art is expressive, needing no translation. In wall paintings, Etruscan figures dance and play music, enjoying a rich and pleasant life. In Etruscan sculpture, men and women feast and converse, triumphant soldiers revel in their victories, and hauntingly beautiful deities smile and gesture.

Such sculptures ornamented the homes of the Etruscan upper classes. Historians believe that Etruscan society probably consisted of wealthy overlords, aristocratic priests, and a slave labor force made up of conquered peoples. Wealthy overlords enslaved these peoples to provide themselves with comforts, and aristocratic priests sacrificed prisoners of war or forced them to duel to the death to appease angry gods.

After repeated revolts, the Etruscan lower classes and the other Italian peoples under Etruscan rule finally freed themselves from

CONNECTIONS — The Arts

Etruscan Culture

Etruscan tomb art

Although archaeologists have unearthed the remains of some Etruscan cities, these tell little about Etruscan culture. Only the many burial chambers that have been uncovered provide clues about the Etruscans.

The murals and sculptures in these tombs depict the daily life of the Etruscans. Many tomb paintings show sports, religious ceremonies, and people enjoying music and feasts. Some tombs have murals that show funeral banquets. In these, the scene on one wall shows banqueters, and on the other walls dancers or musicians.

The many objects in Etruscan tombs—furniture, clothing, jewelry, pottery, and tools—also reveal much about Etruscan culture. Because many of the objects seem Greek or Middle Eastern, the Etruscans probably traded with these peoples. The luxury items also suggest that Etruscan society had a wealthy upper class.

MAKING THE CONNECTION

1. Why are Etruscan tombs so vital in studying ancient Etruria?
2. What conclusions have historians drawn from objects in Etruscan tombs?

Chapter 6 Section 1

TEACH

Guided Practice

THEME Change Ask students to give two examples of conflict leading to change in ancient Rome. *(overthrow of Etruscan rule, struggle between patricians and plebeians over who ruled the republic)* **L1**

Geography: Region Have the class make a chart comparing the climates and physical characteristics of the Italian Peninsula and the region where you live. The chart should include climate, landforms, and agriculture. Then discuss with students how environmental factors have made their lives similar to or different from the lives of the people of Italy. **L2 LEP**

CONNECTIONS — The Arts

Etruscan Culture

Basic questions about the Etruscans, such as their origin, will remain unanswered as long as scholars cannot translate the Etruscan language. Focus discussion on the problems that archaeologists have in interpreting limited evidence. How might archaeologists' ideas about ancient life be distorted by being limited to artifacts of wealthy Etruscans? *(cannot generalize from wealthy Etruscans to enslaved people)*

Answers to Making the Connection

1. *Murals and sculptures in the tombs provide depictions of daily life.*
2. *The Etruscans probably traded with Greeks and Middle Easterners; luxury items suggest a wealthy upper class.*

COOPERATIVE LEARNING ACTIVITY

Wall Diagram The Romans borrowed extensively from other cultures, adapting Etruscan ritual duels, Etruscan and Greek deities, Greek styles of architecture and sculpture, and Greek medicine and science. Provide students with a wall-sized sheet of paper on which to show a composite of what Romans borrowed. Assign students to small groups. Have each group research one major topic and complete one portion of the wall diagram. Each group should divide tasks among its members: doing research, obtaining pictures or drawing illustrations, writing captions, explaining the group's work to the class. **L1**

Chapter 6 Section 1

NATIONAL GEOGRAPHIC SOCIETY

Use these materials to enrich student understanding of ancient Rome.

ANCIENT CIVILIZATIONS POSTER SET
Ancient Rome

Chapter Transparency 6

History Simulation 6

Focus on World Art Print 9

Who?What?Where?When?

The legend of **Rome's founding** begins when the twin brothers Romulus and Remus were newborns. Their mother was a princess, their father the god Mars. The boys' great-uncle had the baby boys set adrift in a basket on the Tiber River. However, the twins did not die. A female wolf found them and nursed them. When they grew up, they set out to build a new city where they had been rescued from the Tiber.

Map Study

Answer

It would have enabled them to conquer the Etruscans more easily because a divided force can be easier to conquer than a united one.

Map Skills Practice

Reading a Map Why were the Latins ideally positioned to gain control of the entire Italian Peninsula? *(They were in a central location, at the mouth of the Tiber River.)*

domination by these wealthy overlords and priests. Chief among those who overthrew the Etruscans were **the Latins**, whose center was the city of **Rome** in the central plain of Latium.

The Rise of Rome

According to legend, in 753 B.C., a stocky man named **Romulus** was building the wall of a city on a hill overlooking the Tiber River. His twin brother, Remus, came over from the hillside opposite, where he too had been laying the foundations for a city. The Roman historian Livy tells what happened next:

> "Remus, by way of jeering at his brother, jumped over the half-built walls of the new settlement, whereupon Romulus killed him in a fit of rage, adding the threat, 'So perish whoever else shall overleap my battlements.'"
>
> —Livy, *Ab Urbe Condita*, 29 B.C.

Setting more stone on the stains of his brother's blood, Romulus is said to have continued his building. In time, his namesake city—Rome—grew to include his brother's hill and the other nearby hills. Romulus was so effective a military ruler, the myth tells us, that Rome became the greatest city in that part of the peninsula.

In fact, the origins of Rome were probably much less violent. At some time between 800 B.C. and 700 B.C., the Latins huddled in straw-roofed huts in the villages on the seven hills apparently agreed to join and form one community. It was this community that came to be called Rome.

Etruscan Rule

About 620 B.C. the Etruscans gained control of Rome. A wealthy Etruscan family, **the Tarquins**, provided kings to rule over the Romans. The Tarquins taught the Latins to build with brick and to roof their houses with tile. They drained the marshy lowlands around Rome and laid out city streets. At the center of the city they created a square called the Forum, which became the seat of Roman government. The Tarquins also built temples, taught the Romans many of the Etruscans' religious rituals, and elevated Rome to a position among the wealthiest cities in Italy.

Then in 534 B.C. Tarquin the Proud came to the throne. This king's cruelties so angered the Romans that in 509 B.C. they drove the Tarquins out. Skilled Etruscan artisans stayed on in Rome, however, helping the city continue to prosper.

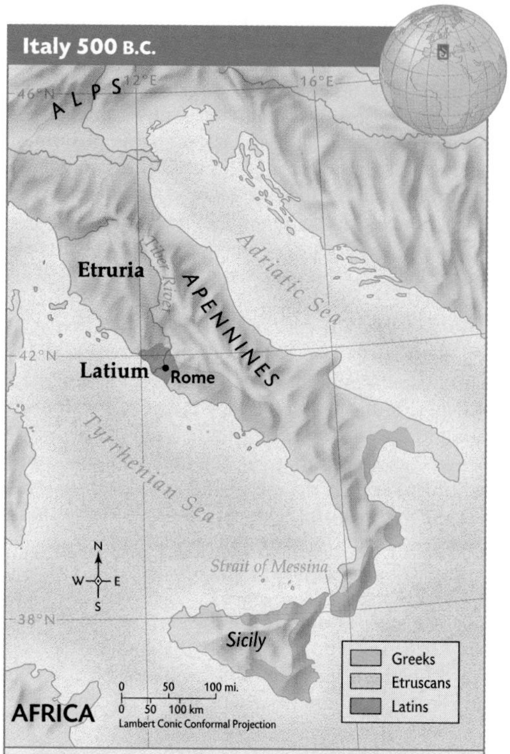

Map Study Notice on the map that Latium divides the Etruscan territory. **Region** What advantage might this location have provided the Latins when they set out to conquer the Etruscans?

Social Groups

Under Etruscan rule, a new wealthy aristocratic class had come into being in Rome—Latin nobles called **patricians**. Once the Etruscan rulers were driven out, the patricians declared Rome a **republic**, a community in which the people elect their leaders.

Most of Rome's inhabitants, however, were **plebeians** (plih•BEE•uhns), who included wealthy, nonaristocratic townspeople and landowners as well as merchants, shopkeepers, small farmers, and laborers. As citizens, both the plebeians and the patricians had rights, such as the right to vote, and responsibilities, such as paying taxes and serving in the military. Plebeians, however, could not hold public office as patricians could.

The Roman Republic

The patricians organized Rome's government into executive and legislative branches. Two

MEETING SPECIAL NEEDS ACTIVITY

Learning Style: Visual/Spatial Encourage students to work in pairs or small groups to develop a pictorial history of events in this chapter. The history could include drawings of events or objects, illustrated maps, diagrams of such things as a Roman bath, charts showing such things as the structure of the Roman government during the republic or the organizational command of the Roman legions, or political cartoons. Make sure each image has a caption explaining the picture. Have students compile all their materials into a book. Upon completion of this chapter, have students share their books with the rest of the class. **L1**

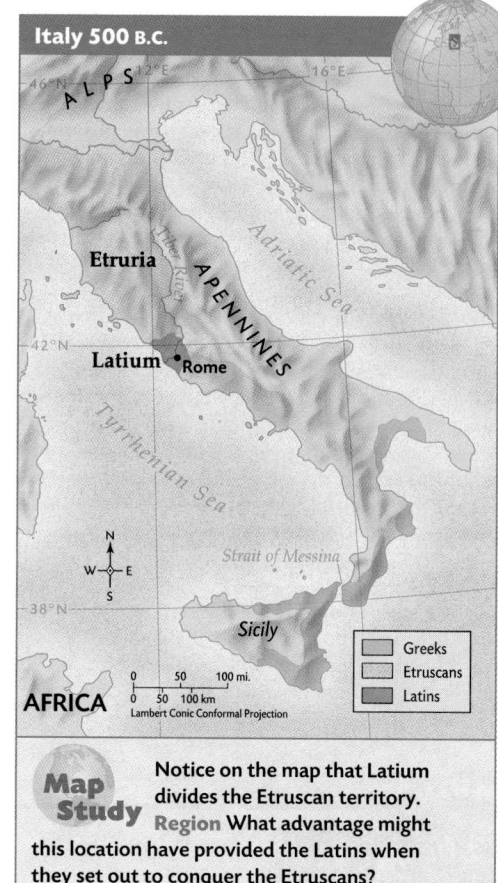

patrician officials elected for one-year terms headed the executive branch, running the city's day-to-day affairs. These officials were called consuls because they had to consult each other before acting. They understood that either consul could veto the other's decisions. The word *veto* is Latin for "I forbid." The consuls oversaw other executive officials, such as praetors, or judges, and censors, or keepers of tax and population records. Only a dictator, a leader whose word was law, could overrule the consuls. But dictators were temporarily appointed to lead the Romans only in time of crisis.

The Roman legislative branch at first consisted of the Assembly of Centuries and the Senate, both under patrician control. Members of the Assembly of Centuries (named for a military formation of 100 soldiers) elected officials of the executive branch. However, the power of the Senate—a group of 300 patrician men who served for life—outweighed the Assembly of Centuries. The senators advised the consuls, debated foreign policy, proposed laws, and approved contracts for constructing roads, temples, and defenses.

Plebeians Against Patricians

The plebeians resented their lack of power in the new republic—especially because they knew that the patricians could not maintain the republic without them. In 494 B.C., to obtain a greater voice in the government, the plebeians went on strike—at first refusing to serve in the army and then leaving the city altogether to set up a republic of their own.

Tribunes

The patricians, frightened at the loss of their military and work forces, soon agreed to meet some of the plebeians' demands. The patricians agreed to recognize the plebeians' chosen representatives, the tribunes. They also granted tribunes the power to veto any government decision and ensured that they would be protected by law. Tribunes could not be arrested, and any person who dared to injure a tribune could be put to death. The patricians also formally recognized the Assembly of Tribes, the plebeians who elected the tribunes.

Old and New Laws

The plebeians did not stop fighting for their rights after winning these concessions. Until that time, no one had ever put Roman laws into writing—and only the patricians knew what the laws said. As a result, plebeians usually found out about a law only upon being charged with breaking that law. To make sure that judges applied the laws fairly, the plebeians insisted that the government write down the laws.

After decades of struggle, the plebeians in 451 B.C. finally got the patricians to engrave the laws on 12 bronze tablets and to set them in the Forum for all to see. The Twelve Tables, as these tablets were called, became the basis for all future Roman law.

Soon after, plebeians also won the right to serve in some public offices, although few of them could bear the cost of an unsalaried public position. Then, in 287 B.C., plebeians won their greatest success, establishing their right to make laws for the republic in the Assembly of Tribes.

Changes for Plebeians

Other changes followed that improved the status of plebeians. Among these, plebeians were allowed to marry patricians, and failure to pay debts was no longer penalized by slavery. In spite of these benefits for the common people, the republic continued to be dominated by a small group of powerful and wealthy citizens. However, through their struggles the plebeians had moved Rome closer to democracy.

Religion

Early Romans worshiped nature spirits. Under Etruscan influence, they came to think of these spirits as gods and goddesses. They also adopted the practice of foretelling the future. Priests known as soothsayers believed that they could gain knowledge of future events by observing the flight of birds or the intestines of animals.

For almost 500 years, Rome thrived as a republic. During this time, the Romans were influenced by Greek culture. They borrowed Greek deities, giving them Roman names. Aphrodite, the Greek

Footnotes to History

A Roman Dinner Party
In ancient Rome, dinner guests of wealthy Romans would recline on couches while slaves served them delicacies. Main course dishes might include boiled stingray garnished with hot raisins; boiled crane with turnips; roast hare in white sauce; leg of boar; wood pigeon baked in a pie; or roast flamingo cooked with dates, onions, honey, and wine.

Chapter 6 Section 1

Independent Practice

Guided Reading Activity 6-1 **L1**

Time Line Activity 6

Government Have students diagram the structure of republican government in Rome, showing the executive and legislative branches as well as the tribunes and Assembly of Tribes. Discuss student diagrams in class, focusing on the special powers of consuls and tribunes. **L2 LEP**

Linking Past and Present

Architecture Many shopping malls today have an atrium, a skylit central court. The concept of the atrium originated in ancient Rome. In a Roman house, the atrium was the central room. Open to the sky at the center, the atrium usually had a pool to collect rainwater.

ASSESS

Check for Understanding

Assign Section 1 Review as homework or as an in-class activity.

Use Student Self-Test and Review Software to review Section 1.

MAKING CONNECTIONS ACTIVITIES

The Calendar Romans helped shape the modern calendar. Have students do research and write a report summarizing Roman contributions to the calendar, including the names of the months and the division of the year into 12 months. Suggest that they also describe the shortcomings leading to calendar reform in the late 1500s. **L1**

Public Speaking The Romans helped define rules of rhetoric, or the art of using words persuasively, for oratory—the art of eloquent speaking. Have students research the life of Cicero, focusing on his contributions to these arts and describing some of his most famous orations. Encourage students to rehearse and deliver parts of his best-known orations. **L2**

Chapter 6 Section 1

Visualizing History According to tradition, the first Roman image of a god dated from the sixth century B.C. during the period of Etruscan domination.

Answer to Caption: *The Romans were outraged by the cruelties of the tyrant Tarquin the Proud.*

Evaluate

Section Quiz 6-1

Use the Testmaker to create a customized quiz for Section 1.

Reteach

Have students work in small groups to prepare time lines of events covered in this section. Then have groups present their time lines to the class, explaining the importance of each event.

Enrich

The Roman goddess Vesta occupied a central role in the religious lives of Roman families. Have students research Vesta and write a brief report on her origins, how she was worshiped, and what values she symbolized.

CLOSE

Ask half the class to imagine that they are tribunes and the other half to imagine that they are senators in the year 250 B.C. Have each group prepare a list of what, from its perspective, are the most important accomplishments of Rome to that time. After each group compares and explains its list, allow one group to challenge items on the other's list. Group members should be prepared to defend the items on their own list.

Visualizing History **An Etruscan farmer and his animals, c. 300 B.C. Etruscan literature, music, painting, metalwork, and jewelry were admired by the Romans.** *Why did the Romans drive the wealthy Etruscan family, the Tarquins, from the city?*

goddess of love, became the Roman goddess Venus. Ares, the Greek god of war, became Mars. They also made their old gods look Greek, giving the Etruscan god Jupiter the characteristics of the Greek Zeus.

Roman life remained distinctly Roman, however. Families privately worshiped their ancestral spirits and their storeroom guardians, as well as Vesta, goddess of the hearth.

Family

The family was the basic unit of Roman society. Roman households were large and close-knit. They included all unmarried children, married sons and their families, all dependent relatives, and household slaves.

In Roman families the father was absolute head of the household. He conducted the religious ceremonies, controlled property, and supervised the education of his sons. He also had the power to sell family members into slavery, or even kill them. However, fathers also felt a deep sense of responsibility for the welfare of all family members.

Roman wives had few legal rights, but they had more freedom than Greek women. They acted as hostesses for parties, did their marketing, and ran their households with little or no interference. Occasionally, however, they did acquire their own property and businesses. Wealthy women, with slaves to do their work, could study Greek literature, arts, and fashions. Lower-class women spent their time at household tasks and in family-run shops.

Roman children grew up with firm discipline and had to give complete loyalty to their family. In early Rome, parents taught their children reading, writing, and moral standards. Boys were trained by their fathers to be good farmers and soldiers. Mothers taught their daughters how to run households.

Rich or poor, most Romans held the same values: thrift, discipline, self-sacrifice, and devotion to the family and the republic. Long after the Roman Republic ended, nostalgic reformers saw these as traditional Roman values.

SECTION 1 REVIEW

Recall
1. **Define** patrician, republic, plebeian, consul, dictator, tribune.
2. **Identify** the Etruscans, the Latins, Romulus, the Tarquins.
3. **Locate** Etruria, Latium, and Rome on the map on page 156. How were the people of these three places connected?

Critical Thinking
4. **Evaluating Information** How might the struggle between patricians and plebeians have weakened Rome? Give examples to support your case.

Understanding Themes
5. **Change** Why did political change occur in the Roman Republic?

SECTION 1 REVIEW ANSWERS

1. All vocabulary terms are defined in the Glossary.
2. the Etruscans, 155; the Latins, 156; Romulus, 156, the Tarquins, 156
3. The Latins of the central plains of Latium founded the Roman city-state, which was ruled by Etruscans from Etruria in the north.
4. Possible answer: The plebeians' strike in 494 B.C. deprived the city of its military and work forces.
5. **CHANGE** The plebeians wanted a greater say in the government. Their key role in the economy and military gave the plebeians the clout to force change.

300 B.C. — 200 B.C. — 100 B.C. — A.D. 1

c. 264 B.C. Rome rules the entire Italian Peninsula.

202 B.C. Roman forces defeat Carthage at the battle of Zama.

133 B.C. The reformer Tiberius Gracchus becomes tribune.

44 B.C. Group of senators assassinate Julius Caesar.

Section 2

Expansion and Crisis

Setting the Scene

- **Terms to Define**
  indemnity, triumvirate
- **People to Meet**
  Hannibal, Scipio, Tiberius Gracchus, Gaius Gracchus, Marius, Sulla, Julius Caesar, Octavian, Marc Antony
- **Places to Locate**
  Carthage

Find Out How did economic and social problems bring down the Roman Republic?

The Storyteller

The government of Rome had become cumbersome and corrupt. Maecenas, the richest man in Rome, was about to propose a radical change. Called before Mark Anthony, Marcus Lepidus, and Octavian, the most powerful men in Rome, he spoke persuasively. "Ever since we were led outside the peninsula, filling the whole earth with our power, nothing good has been our lot. Our city, like a great ship manned with a crew of every race and lacking a pilot, has been rolling and plunging as it has drifted in a heavy sea." Maecenas looked at his hearers. One of them must assume all authority. Rome had to cease being a republic.

—from *Roman History*, Dio Cassius, in *Readings in Ancient History from Gilgamesh to Diocletian*, 1969

Marc Antony

From about 500 B.C. to 300 B.C., Rome faced threats from its many neighbors in Italy. To protect their republic, the Romans either conquered these opponents or forced them to ally with Rome. In this way the Romans subdued one rival after another, until by 264 B.C., Rome ruled the entire peninsula.

Roman Legions

Rome's success in war was due to its strong army. In the early days of the republic, every male citizen had to serve in the military when needed. Early Roman armies also used the tactics of Greek phalanx warfare. Roman generals, however, learned that phalanxes were too large and slow to be effective. They reorganized their troops into legions of 6,000 men and divided these further into small, mobile units of 60 to 120 soldiers. With this new organization, the Romans could shatter the phalanxes of their enemies.

Roman soldiers—called legionaries—were well trained, and deserters were punished by death. With such iron discipline, the legionaries would conquer an empire. In a time when victors routinely slaughtered or enslaved whole cities, Rome treated conquered foes remarkably well. Some conquered peoples were allowed to keep their own governments if they helped fight Rome's wars. Rome gave other peoples partial rights, and to some peoples even granted citizenship.

The Romans set up permanent military settlements—called *coloniae*—throughout Italy to defend strategic heights and river crossings. To link these *coloniae*, the legions forged a chain of roads up and down the Italian Peninsula. As war yielded gradually to peace, some of these roads became major trade routes.

Chapter 6 Section 2

SECTION THEME

- **Conflict** Roman armies conquer most of the Mediterranean world.

Find Out

Answer: *The expense of putting down provincial revolts, unrest among the poor, and conflicts among leaders led to the collapse of the republic.*

FOCUS

Section Objective

Outline the economic and social problems that ended the Roman Republic.

BELLRINGER Motivational Activity

Before taking roll at the beginning of the class period, project Section Focus Transparency 6-2 and have students answer the activity questions. Discuss students' responses.

This activity is also available as a blackline master.

Vocabulary Pre-check

Use Vocabulary Activity 6 to introduce vocabulary terms. **L1 LEP**

SECTION RESOURCES

Reproducible Masters
- Reproducible Lesson Plan 6-2
- Vocabulary Activity 6
- Guided Reading Activity 6-2
- Section Quiz 6-2

Transparencies
- Section Focus Transparency 6-2
- Mapping History Overlay Transparency 6
- Ancient Rome

Multimedia
- Student Self-Test and Review Software
- Testmaker

Chapter 6
Section 2

TEACH

Guided Practice

THEME **Conflict**

Discuss with students various ways of resolving conflicts. *(negotiation, mediation, fighting)* **L1**

Visualizing History The basic unit of the Roman legion was the maniple, which consisted of 120 men in 12 files and 10 ranks. The expression "rank and file," referring to common people, derives from this method of organizing Roman soldiers.

Answer to Caption: *They snared the Carthaginian ships with grappling hooks, boarded them, and used hand-to-hand combat to defeat the enemy.*

Government The Roman Republic was founded to govern a city-state but floundered when Rome governed a vast empire. Have students list political changes occurring from about 300 B.C. that resulted from the growth of Roman territory. *(Answers may include: Rome created a system of proconsuls and publicans to rule non-Italian provinces; generals gained power controlling the provinces and took over government of the republic.)* **L2**

Mapping History Overlay Transparency 6

Who?What?Where?When?

Marcus Portius Cato, a prominent soldier and statesman, was so alarmed by the threat Carthage posed to Rome that he is said to have ended his every speech, regardless of its subject, with the phrase, "Carthage must be destroyed."

Visualizing History **Roman legionaries, shown in a colorful mosaic, were well trained.** *How did Rome defeat the Carthaginian navy?*

Rome Against Carthage

In Chapter 3 you read how **Carthage** became the Mediterranean area's wealthiest city. To expand their commerce, the Carthaginians had then gone on to conquer the Spanish coast and most of Sicily by about 300 B.C. The Romans decided to check the expansion of the Carthaginians—the *Punici*, as the Romans called them.

The First Punic War

In 264 B.C. Carthage threatened to seize the Strait of Messina, a narrow passage between Sicily and Italy. When the Romans sent a force to secure the strategic waterway, a full-scale war erupted.

The Romans' strong army conquered most of Carthage's colonies in Sicily. However, the Carthaginians lashed out at the Romans with their huge and powerful fleet. For a time this naval superiority gave Carthage the advantage.

Undaunted, the Romans built a larger fleet. In a battle off the African coast, they stunned the Carthaginians with a new tactic. They snared the enemy's ships with grappling hooks, boarded them, and defeated the enemy in hand-to-hand combat. This enabled the Romans to fight on sea as well as they did on land. Thus, they were able to force the Carthaginians to retreat.

The war raged on until 241 B.C., but the Carthaginians never regained control of Sicily or the sea. Threatened with invasion of their homeland, they agreed to hand the Romans a huge indemnity, or payment for damages.

The Second Punic War

In 221 B.C. a young soldier named **Hannibal** became general of the Carthaginian army in Spain. In 218 B.C. Hannibal grabbed one of Rome's allied cities in Spain. His next move was even more audacious—to take the war into Italy itself. Leading 40,000 soldiers and about 40 elephants, he marched out of Spain, crossed southern Gaul, and started up the Alps. His soldiers, however, were terrified by the sight of those chilly heights, and their fears were well-founded. Before they reached Italy, cold, snow, hunger, sickness, and attacks by mountain peoples killed half of Hannibal's army and most of the elephants.

Although outnumbered, Hannibal's troops defeated the Roman armies sent against them. By 216 B.C., in a battle at Cannae in southeastern Italy, Hannibal's soldiers had nearly destroyed the Roman army. But the Romans rallied, refusing to admit defeat, and raised dozens of new volunteer legions. Their general, Publius **Scipio** (POO•blee •uhs SIH•pee•OH), attacked Carthage and forced Hannibal's recall to Africa.

In 202 B.C. Scipio's forces defeated Hannibal's army at Zama, near Carthage. At Scipio's demand, the Carthaginians gave up their lands in Spain, handed over most of their warships, and agreed to another indemnity.

The Third Punic War

After 50 years of peace, Carthage regained its prosperity. Although Carthage was still no threat, Rome decided to end Carthaginian independence. In 146 B.C. the Romans burned Carthage, sold its surviving population into slavery, and sowed salt in its soil so that no crops would grow. This victory gave Rome complete control of the western Mediterranean.

The Republic in Crisis

While Roman armies were fighting the Punic Wars in the west, their forces were also engaged in

COOPERATIVE LEARNING ACTIVITY

Debate Organize the class into three groups and stage a debate on the following resolution: The wars with Carthage were worth the short-term and long-term cost. Have two of the groups take opposite sides in the debate. The third group should act as the audience, asking questions and voting for the more persuasive side. Assign one student as moderator and make sure each group member has specific responsibility for research, preparation, and presentation of arguments. Students in the audience should prepare questions in advance, as well as be encouraged to ask spontaneous questions. **L2**

conflicts in the east. Between 230 B.C. and 130 B.C., Rome brought the eastern Mediterranean area under its rule. Although the Romans left Syria and Egypt independent, they forced the rulers into obedient alliances. With these eastern conquests, the Romans emerged as the undisputed masters of the Mediterranean from Spain to Asia Minor. As a result, they had begun to call the Mediterranean *mare nostrum*—"our sea."

Ruling such a vast territory, however, created considerable difficulties. Political leaders could not readily adapt Rome's form of government—which had been created to meet the needs of a small city-state—to govern these numerous peoples. Political problems led to social and economic upheaval as well.

Exploiting the Provinces

Rome organized its non-Italian territories into provinces that had to pay tribute to Rome and recognize its authority. At first the provinces seemed a source of endless wealth. The Senate-appointed governors, called proconsuls, often accepted bribes and robbed the provincial treasuries. The publicans—officials who collected the taxes—also took money from the provinces. Soon, taking money from the provinces became an accepted way for the rich to become richer.

In response to this treatment, the provinces rebelled. It became necessary to permanently station Roman legions in most provinces. Because putting down revolts cost Rome troops and money, the provinces began to strain Rome's resources. While the people in most provinces adjusted to Rome's rule, the Jews in Palestine stubbornly resisted. The Romans sacked Jerusalem in A.D. 70.

Changing the Countryside

By expanding, the Roman government acquired properties in the provinces. These holdings were rented to wealthy Romans, who joined individual units into large estates called latifundia (LA•tuh•FUHN•dee•uh). Latifundia owners used enslaved people to work the land. Because slave labor was less expensive than paid labor, latifundia owners could produce crops that cost less than those grown by small farmers in Italy. By offering low prices for grain, latifundia owners in the provinces captured the grain market and thus brought great wealth to the provinces.

The latifundia owners also forced small farmers out of business. Then, just as they had done in the provinces, proconsuls and publicans began buying up small farms in Rome to create latifundia. Wisely, rather than try to compete in the grain market against provincial latifundia, these owners devoted their estates to sheep ranching and to raising olives and fruits. Thus, latifundia owners captured these markets too, putting even more farmers out of work.

Visualizing History **Rome's legions put down revolts in the provinces, but not without cost. Here, women funeral dancers mourn losses.** *Why were the provinces not an endless source of wealth to Rome?*

Chapter 6 Section 2

NATIONAL GEOGRAPHIC SOCIETY

Use these materials to enrich student understanding of ancient Rome.

NGS PICTUREPACK TRANSPARENCY SET
Ancient Rome

Independent Practice

Guided Reading Activity 6-2 **L1**

Literature Have students work as individuals or in small groups to read and present to the class portions of Shakespeare's *Julius Caesar*. Suggest the following scenes: Caesar's assassination (III, i, 1-95); Marc Antony's address to the plebeians (III, ii); or the farewell of Brutus and Cassius (V, i, 70-125). **L2**

Multicultural Have students research various aspects of Carthage and its history and present short oral reports to the class. Suggest the following topics: the legend of Dido (its legendary queen) and Aeneas; the city's founding as a Phoenician colony; extent of the Carthaginian Empire; type of trade, culture, and religion; styles of art and architecture; famous leaders and rulers. **L3**

Visualizing History When the Roman legions finally suppressed the Jewish Revolt in A.D. 70, they had killed many thousands of Jews. Many legionaries also died in the five-year struggle.
Answer to Caption: *The cost of suppressing rebellions in the provinces began to strain Rome's resources.*

MEETING SPECIAL NEEDS ACTIVITY

Study Strategy Have students work in small groups to develop a chart on the chalkboard summarizing the three Punic Wars. Have them begin the chart by answering **Where Does the Name "Punic" Come From?** (Help them find the answer on page 160.) For each war, instruct them to include the dates, the areas where the war was fought, the major battle, and the final outcome. For the Second Punic War, have them also include the names of the opposing generals. Leave the chart on the board for the entire class to refer to. **L1**

Cultural Perspectives

Caesar The German title *kaiser* and the Russian title *czar* both derive from Caesar's family name.

Linking Past and Present

Calendar More than 2,000 years after Caesar's death, our calendar continues to commemorate him. Already during his lifetime, Romans had changed the name of the month of Caesar's birth, Quintilis, to July in his honor.

Visualizing History

Even though Caesar's family traced its lineage back to the goddess Venus, the family was not snobbish, rich, or influential.

Answer to Caption: *By crossing the Rubicon, Caesar committed treason by disregarding the orders of Pompey and the Senate.*

ASSESS

Check for Understanding

Assign Section 2 Review as homework or as an in-class activity.

Use Student Self-Test and Review Software to review Section 2.

Crowding the Cities

Landless farmers streamed into Rome, where bread was cheap and public shows were free. In the cities the poor discovered that many jobs were already being done by enslaved people. Angry and without hope, the free poor eked out a living and voted for any leader who promised cheaper food and more amusements. Although often jobless, these people clung proudly to their status as free citizens.

While the urban poor increased in numbers, so too did a new class between the plebeians and the patricians. Made up of people who had obtained wealth in working their latifundia or in business, this new social class took the old title of *equites* (EH•kwuh•TEEZ). The title *equites*, or knights, had once applied to those wealthy enough to ride horses in battle but not noble enough to be patricians. The new *equites* saw more value in wealth than in nobility or character, influencing most Romans to adopt similar values.

Reformers and Generals

Many Romans viewed with dismay the changes brought on by Roman expansion. They feared that the growth of latifundia and the spread of corruption threatened the republic's institutions. They also thought that someone had to help the urban poor before these plebeians toppled the state.

The Gracchi

As grandson of General Scipio, a patrician career lay open to **Tiberius Gracchus**. Instead, he threw in his lot with the plebeians, winning the office of tribune in 133 B.C. As tribune, Tiberius at once proposed a law to limit the size of the latifundia and to redistribute land to the poor. Despite stiff opposition from the patrician Senate, Tiberius passed the law through the plebeian Assembly of Tribes. Opponents organized a riot in which Tiberius and 300 of his followers were killed. His murder, the first political violence in Rome in 400 years, would begin a trend.

Elected tribune a decade later, Tiberius's brother **Gaius** pushed through more reforms. A fiery orator, he persuaded the plebeian Assembly to give more land to farmers. To help the urban poor, he set up a government program to sell grain at low prices. Because the Senate refused to convict corrupt provincial governors, Gaius started a new court with members drawn from the *equites*.

Gaius too met with a violent end. In 121 B.C. he was killed in a riot planned by his enemies. By 111 B.C., the Senate had put a stop to the land reforms.

Marius and Sulla

In 107 B.C. General Gaius **Marius** was elected consul. A reformer, he gave poor people jobs by enlisting them in the army. He paid them money for their service and promised them land when they were discharged. For the first time, Rome had a professional army in which soldiers owed allegiance to their commander, not to the republic.

In 88 B.C. this new army was used against Gaius Marius. General Lucius Cornelius **Sulla** sought to end his dispute with Marius over who should command the army in the east. Sulla persuaded his legions to capture Rome and drive Marius into exile. After seven years of civil war, Sulla appointed himself dictator. He tried to strengthen the Senate and take power away from the Assembly of Tribes. But by then the army had become the most powerful element in Roman politics, and violence overtook law.

Visualizing History **Political strife in the period following the murders of the Gracchi gave the young Julius Caesar the opportunity to rise to power.** *Why did Caesar's crossing the Rubicon River lead to civil war?*

MAKING CONNECTIONS ACTIVITIES

Human Rights Different cultures enslaved human beings for a variety of reasons. Have students use reference books to compare and contrast the practice of slavery in ancient Rome with that in ancient Egypt, ancient Greece, or ancient Israel. **L2**

Education Ancient Rome had no public schools, but most boys and some girls received some formal instruction. Have students use reference books to compare and contrast educational methods in ancient Rome with those in ancient Egypt, ancient Israel, ancient Greece, or ancient Persia. **L1**

The First Triumvirate

In 70 B.C. General Gnaeus Pompey (NEE•uhs PAHM•pee) and the politician Marcus Licinius Crassus were elected consuls. They gained the support of **Julius Caesar**, a rising young aristocrat. Then, in 60 B.C., the three formed a **triumvirate**, a group of three persons with equal power, to control the government. The triumvirate proved to be unstable, however.

Politically ambitious, Caesar took a military command in Gaul, which was inhabited by Indo-Europeans known as Celts (KEHLTS). Caesar conquered the Celts, forcing them to accept Roman rule. He then pushed northward, greatly increasing Rome's landholdings in northwestern Europe and elevating his own status as well.

Meanwhile Crassus, attempting to prove that he too was a great military leader, was killed in battle in 53 B.C. Fearing that Caesar might use his own legions to seize power, Pompey and the Senate then ordered Caesar to leave his legions north of the Rubicon River, the legal border of Roman Italy, and return to Rome. According to legend, however, upon arriving at the Rubicon, Caesar saw a vision that encouraged him to cross, and exclaimed to his troops, "Let us accept this as a sign from the gods, and follow where they beckon, in vengeance on our double-dealing enemies. The die is cast."

By crossing the Rubicon, Caesar officially committed treason and started civil war. Within two months he had captured all of Italy and driven Pompey and his allies out of the country. The fighting eventually spread to the entire Mediterranean region, with Caesar finally overwhelming Pompey's armies.

Julius Caesar

In 45 B.C. Caesar took over the government as dictator for life, to rule very much like a monarch. Under his leadership, the government gave jobs to the unemployed, public land to the poor, and citizenship to many people in the provinces. Caesar also added representatives from the provinces to the Senate. Finally, Caesar adopted a new calendar based on the Egyptian year of $365\frac{1}{4}$ days. This calendar was called Julian in honor of Caesar. It was used in western Europe until early modern times.

Many Romans believed that Caesar was a wise ruler who had brought order and peace back to Rome. Others, however, considered him to be a tyrant who meant to end the republic and make himself king. To prevent this, on March 15, 44 B.C., a group of senators led by Marcus Brutus and Gaius Cassius assassinated Caesar as he entered the Senate.

End of the Republic

After the death of Julius Caesar, his 18-year-old grandnephew **Octavian** joined forces with **Marc Antony** and Marcus Lepidus, two of Caesar's top government officers. Together this second triumvirate defeated Caesar's assassins in 42 B.C. Then, while keeping up the appearance of republican government, these three generals divided the Roman world among themselves. Octavian took command in Italy and the west, Antony ruled in Greece and the east, and Lepidus took charge of North Africa.

The second triumvirate did not last long, however. Octavian forced Lepidus to retire from political life. When Antony married Cleopatra, the queen of Egypt, Octavian persuaded the Romans that Antony intended to rule them with his foreign queen by his side, and so Octavian declared war on Antony in Rome's name. In 31 B.C. Octavian scattered the forces of his enemies in a critical naval battle at Actium in Greece. A year later, to evade capture by Octavian, Antony and Cleopatra committed suicide in Egypt. With Antony dead, Octavian became the undisputed ruler of Rome.

SECTION 2 REVIEW

Recall

1. **Define** indemnity, triumvirate.
2. **Identify** Hannibal, Scipio, Tiberius Gracchus, Gaius Gracchus, Marius, Sulla, Julius Caesar, Octavian, Marc Antony.
3. **Locate** Carthage and Gaul on the map on page 165. What was the importance of each place in the military history of the Roman Republic?

Critical Thinking

4. **Making Comparisons** Compare the events that started the First and Third Punic Wars. Why might one war be called justified and the other unjustified?

Understanding Themes

5. **Conflict** Explain how Roman conquests overseas affected Rome's development.

Chapter 6 Section 2

you don't say...

"Cross the Rubicon," meaning "take a decisive, irrevocable step," derives from Caesar's irrevocable decision to embark on civil war by crossing the Rubicon River.

Evaluate

Section Quiz 6-2

Use the Testmaker to create a customized quiz for Section 2.

Reteach

Have students briefly summarize the importance of the Punic Wars, Hannibal, latifundia, *equites*, the Gracchi, Marius, Sulla, the triumvirate, Julius Caesar, and Octavian.

Enrich

Have students prepare a report on the Roman legions, focusing either on the army's structure and the legionaries' training and duties or on the legions' military siege machines. Encourage students to illustrate their reports.

CLOSE

Work with students to prepare a chronology of events and issues that led to the fall of the republic. Have students choose two or three events or issues that they think were the most significant.

SECTION 2 REVIEW ANSWERS

1. All vocabulary words are defined in the Glossary.
2. Hannibal, 160; Scipio, 160; Tiberius Gracchus, 162; Gaius Gracchus, 162; Marius, 162; Sulla, 162; Julius Caesar, 163; Octavian, 163; Marc Antony, 163
3. Victory over Carthage gave Rome complete control of the western Mediterranean. The conquering of Gaul by Julius Caesar enabled him to greatly expand Rome's land holdings in northwestern Europe.
4. First: justified, Rome needed to control Straits of Messina; Third: unjustified, Carthage no longer a threat to Rome
5. **CONFLICT** Provincial wealth was used to establish latifundia, displacing peasant farmers. New social class, the *equites*, arose.

A.D. 1 | A.D. 50 | A.D. 100 | A.D. 150 | A.D. 200

A.D. 14 Augustus Caesar dies.
A.D. 79 Volcanic eruption destroys Pompeii.
A.D. 96 Rule of the Good Emperors begins.
A.D. 180 *Pax Romana* ends.

Section 3

The Roman Empire

SECTION THEME

▶ **Cultural Diffusion** The Romans build an empire and spread Latin culture.

Find Out

Answer: *Life was orderly and peaceful in the Roman Empire during the* Pax Romana.

FOCUS

Section Objective

Characterize life under the *Pax Romana.*

BELLRINGER
Motivational Activity

Before taking roll at the beginning of the class period, project Section Focus Transparency 6-3 and have students answer the activity questions. Discuss students' responses.

This activity is also available as a blackline master.

Vocabulary Pre-check

Use Vocabulary Activity 6 to introduce vocabulary terms.
L1 LEP

Setting the Scene

▶ **Terms to Define**
aqueduct

▶ **People to Meet**
Augustus, Tiberius, Claudius, Nero, Marcus Aurelius, Galen, Ptolemy, Virgil, Livy

▶ **Places to Locate**
Appian Way

Find Out What was life like in the Roman Empire during the *Pax Romana*?

The Storyteller

The visitor, Aelius Aristides, an educated and well-travelled man, had never seen anything to rival Rome. And it was not just the city—it was everything that Rome represented: military might, sensible government, and an elegant lifestyle. Who could help but admire an empire that commanded vast territories and diverse peoples, a military that conquered both armed forces and selfish ambition, a government where officials ruled not through arbitrary power but by law. Romans "measured out the world, bridged rivers, cut roads through mountains, filled the wastes with posting stations, introduced orderly and refined modes of life." They were, he declared, natural rulers.

—adapted from *Oration on the Pax Romana,* Aelius Aristides, reprinted in *Sources of the Western Tradition,* Marvin Perry, 1991

Augustus Caesar

Under the Roman Republic, laws had proven too weak to control social changes, while generals had taken power away from elected officials. Thus, Octavian believed that Rome needed one strong leader. The Senate agreed and appointed Octavian consul, tribune, and commander in chief for life in 27 B.C. Octavian gave himself the title *Augustus,* or "Majestic One."

The First Emperors

Augustus claimed to support the republic, but he actually laid the foundation for a new state called the Roman Empire. In practice, he became Rome's first emperor, or absolute ruler.

Augustus Caesar

In the 40 years of his reign—from 27 B.C. to A.D. 14—Augustus rebuilt the city of Rome and became a great patron of the arts. He also introduced many reforms to the empire. Proconsuls could no longer exploit the provinces. Publican tax collectors were replaced with permanent government employees. Grain was imported from North Africa so that all in Rome would be fed. New roads were built and old ones repaired. Magnificent public buildings were constructed throughout the empire. Augustus boasted that he had "found Rome a city of brick and left it a city of marble."

In 31 B.C. there began the *Pax Romana,* or Roman Peace, which lasted about 200 years. The only major disturbances during those years occurred when new emperors came to power. For, although Augustus chose his own successor carefully, he failed to devise any law for the selection of later emperors.

The Julian Emperors

Historians call the four emperors who ruled from A.D. 14 to A.D. 68 the Julians because each was

SECTION RESOURCES

Reproducible Masters
- Reproducible Lesson Plan 6-3
- Vocabulary Activity 6
- Guided Reading Activity 6-3
- Section Quiz 6-3

Transparencies
- Section Focus Transparency 6-3
- World History and Art Transparency 7

Multimedia
- Student Self-Test and Review Software
- Testmaker
- Greece and Rome

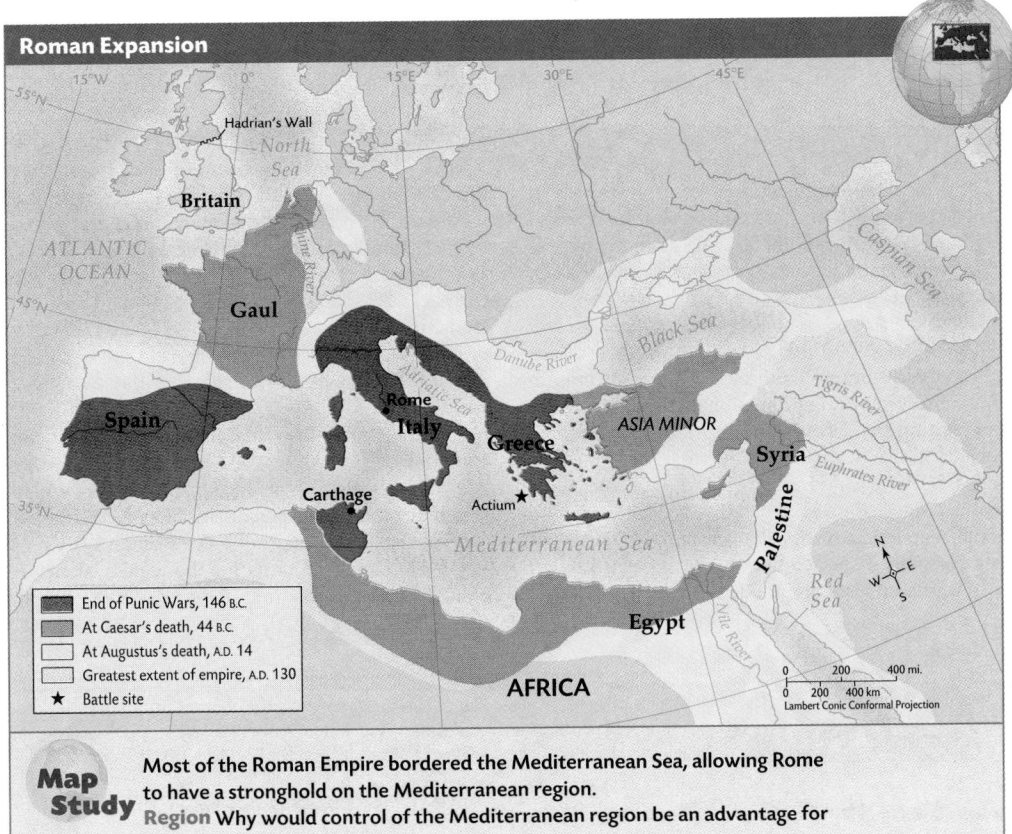

Roman Expansion

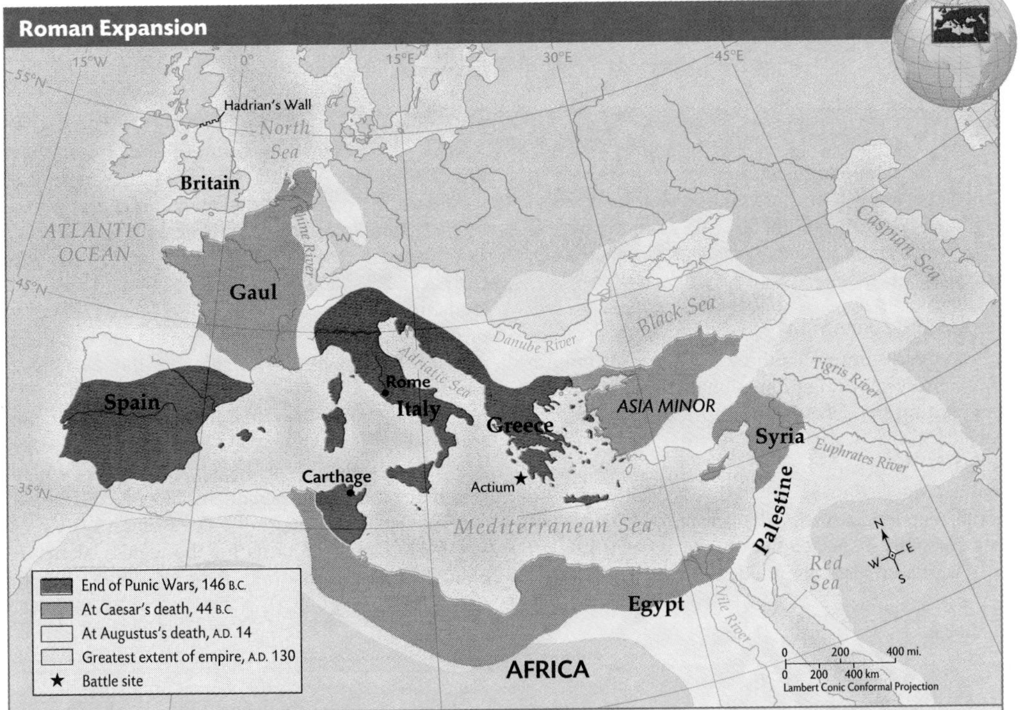

Map Study Most of the Roman Empire bordered the Mediterranean Sea, allowing Rome to have a stronghold on the Mediterranean region.
Region Why would control of the Mediterranean region be an advantage for Rome's economy?

related in some way to Julius Caesar. Each showed promise when he became emperor, but later revealed great faults.

Augustus's adopted son **Tiberius**, who succeeded Augustus Caesar as emperor, spoiled his able leadership by accusing many innocent people of treason against him. Caligula, Tiberius's grandnephew and successor in A.D. 37, became mentally disturbed and was killed by a palace guard in A.D. 41. Caligula's uncle, **Claudius**, was a renowned scholar, but as he grew older he had difficulty focusing on affairs of state.

Nero, Claudius's stepson, who became emperor in A.D. 54, was cruel and probably insane. Nero was willing to bankrupt Rome to pay for his twin pleasures—horse racing and music. Suspecting others of plotting against him, he killed his wife and his mother and executed many senators. In A.D. 68 the Senate sentenced Nero to death for treason. Before he committed suicide, reportedly he cried, "What a loss I shall be to the arts!"

The Good Emperors

For 28 years following Nero's death, Rome was governed by a number of emperors who were backed by the army. Then, in A.D. 96 the Senate chose its own candidate for emperor: Nerva. Historians consider Nerva the first of the so-called Good Emperors; the others were Trajan, Hadrian, Antoninus Pius, and **Marcus Aurelius** (aw•REE •lee•uhs). The Good Emperors were known for their skills as effective administrators and their support of large building projects.

The Emperor Trajan, who succeeded Nerva, increased the empire to its greatest size. Hadrian then strengthened Rome's fortifications along the frontiers. Antoninus Pius succeeded him, maintaining the empire's prosperity. The philosopher-ruler Marcus Aurelius brought the empire to the height of its economic prosperity. All of these Good Emperors lived by the principle of Stoic philosophy best expressed by Marcus Aurelius in *Meditations*: "Every moment think steadily as a Roman and a

TEACH

Guided Practice

THEME Cultural Diffusion

Have students cite specific examples of cultural diffusion mentioned in this section. *(diffusion of Roman religion and law throughout the empire; Roman adaptation of Etruscan architecture, Egyptian astronomy, and Greek literature)* Discuss how Roman roads encouraged the diffusion of Roman culture throughout the empire, and ask what technologies in our world are important factors in cultural diffusion. *(satellite transmission of television signals; computer technology; ease and speed of world travel)* **L1**

Map Study

Answer

It ensured access to a wide variety of resources and products, without the expense of foreign tariffs or the danger of naval attack.

Map Skills Practice

Reading a Map What is the distance of the farthest point of the empire from the city of Rome? *(about 2,500 miles, or 4,000 kilometers)*

COOPERATIVE LEARNING ACTIVITY

Roman Life Assign students to groups that will research specific areas of life and culture during the *Pax Romana*. Divide each broad topic into smaller areas to be covered by individual students within each group. Members of each group should organize their reports into a coordinated presentation. Have each group choose a spokesperson to explain how each report contributes to the central topic. Suggest the following topics and subtopics: Roman daily life *(food, housing, amusements, household deities, women's lives, education)*; law *(ideas of citizenship, judges, effect on modern law)*; language and literature *(Romance languages, specific authors)*; science or technology *(Roman roads, the arch)*. **L2**

Cultural Perspectives

Pax Romana Expressions modeled on the term *Pax Romana* have come to mean a state of peace imposed by a strong nation on weaker ones. In the decade 1610-20, Spain's domination of Europe led to a "Pax Hispanica." From about 1815 to 1850, Great Britain was able to impose a "Pax Britannica" over Europe because of its industrial dominance.

Chapter 6
Section 3

List Work with students to prepare a list of contributions Augustus Caesar made to the empire. Discuss how these contributions helped to establish the *Pax Romana*. **L2**

Government Discuss the ways in which Roman government in the days of the empire had changed from the government of the Roman Republic. *(Answers may include: emperor appointed governors rather than let Senate choose proconsuls; emperor ruled with absolute power for life, rather than elected consuls who served one-year terms.)* Explore with students the pros and cons of these changes in the structure of Roman government. **L3**

NATIONAL GEOGRAPHIC SOCIETY

Use these materials to enrich student understanding of everyday life in ancient Rome.

NGS PICTURESHOW CD-ROM
Greece and Rome

World History and Art Transparency 7

Independent Practice

Guided Reading Activity 6-3 **L1**

Geography: Place Have students trace a map of Italy. Ask them to research in an encyclopedia or other library reference books the Appian Way and other Roman roads and draw these on their maps. Have students include the names of the towns or cities connected by the Appian Way. **L2** **LEP**

human being how to do what you have in hand with perfect and simple dignity."

Roman Rule

By the time Augustus had come to power in 27 B.C., between 70 and 100 million people were living in the Roman Empire. To rule so many people effectively, Augustus had to make many changes in government.

Imperial Government

Augustus improved the working of the empire by carefully choosing professional governors rather than letting the Senate appoint inexperienced proconsuls every year. In some provinces, such as Judea, he left local kings in charge under his command. Augustus ordered new roads built so that he could keep in touch with all parts of the empire, and he personally inspected the provinces frequently.

Augustus also dignified his own position by serving as *pontifex maximus*, or chief priest of Rome. Thus he and each later emperor became the head of a national, unifying religion.

The Law

As the Romans won more provinces, they found that they needed a new kind of law that would apply to noncitizens. They therefore created the *jus gentium*, or law that dealt with noncitizens, as opposed to the *jus civile*, or citizen law. By the early A.D. 200s, however, emperors had granted citizenship to the peoples of so many nearby provinces that all free males in the empire had been made full citizens of Rome, and the two laws became one.

In their laws Romans generally stressed the authority of the state over the individual. They also accorded people definite legal rights, one of which was that an accused person should be considered innocent until proven guilty. The Roman system of law has formed the basis for the legal systems of many Western nations and of the Christian Church.

Images of the Times

Pompeii, A.D. 79

On August 23-25, A.D. 79, the volcano Vesuvius erupted in southern Italy. The city of Pompeii was buried in a single day.

A detail from the Villa of the Mysteries shows that life for many in Pompeii offered many comforts and pleasures.

Images of the Times **Pompeii, A.D. 79**

After the eruption of Vesuvius, Pompeii was buried under 19 to 23 feet (6 to 7 meters) of ash and debris. Herculaneum was covered by mud-lava to a depth of about 65 feet (20 meters).
An architect in the 1500s who was building a channel for drinking water discovered the ruins at Pompeii. Excavations of Herculaneum and Pompeii were begun in the 1700s and have continued, with interruptions, until the present. The earliest diggers were primarily treasure seekers, but in the mid-1800s archaeologists began to document their findings with care. Archaeologists have unearthed statue-covered public buildings, homes, shops, and luxurious villas.

An Imperial Army

Augustus and later emperors maintained the professional army. As conditions became more peaceful, however, Augustus reduced the number of legions and supplemented this fighting force with troops recruited from the provincial peoples. Even with forces combined, the emperor could count on having only about 300,000 troops, which was not enough to defend a border with a length of about 4,000 miles (6,440 km). Therefore, by A.D. 160, invasions by peoples outside the empire had become a continuing problem.

Roman Civilization

From about 31 B.C. to A.D. 180, the Roman world enjoyed a period of prosperity known as the *Pax Romana*, or Roman Peace. The stability of the *Pax Romana* boosted trade, raised standards of living, and generated many achievements in the arts. The Latin author Tertullian described this time:

> “Everywhere roads are built, every district is known, every country is open to commerce … the [fields] are planted; the marshes drained. There are now as many cities as there were once solitary cottages.… Wherever there is a trace of life, there are houses and human habitations, well-ordered governments, and civilized life.”
>
> —Tertullian, *Concerning the Soul*, c. A.D. 180

The Empire's Economy

Tertullian's description of economic growth under the empire was not exaggerated. In the first century A.D., artisans in Italy made pottery, woven cloth, blown glass, and jewelry for sale throughout the empire. The provinces in turn sent to Italy luxury items, such as silk cloth and spices, gathered in trade with China, India, and Southeast Asian countries. Dockworkers at Rome's harbor, Ostia, unloaded raw materials such as tin from Britain,

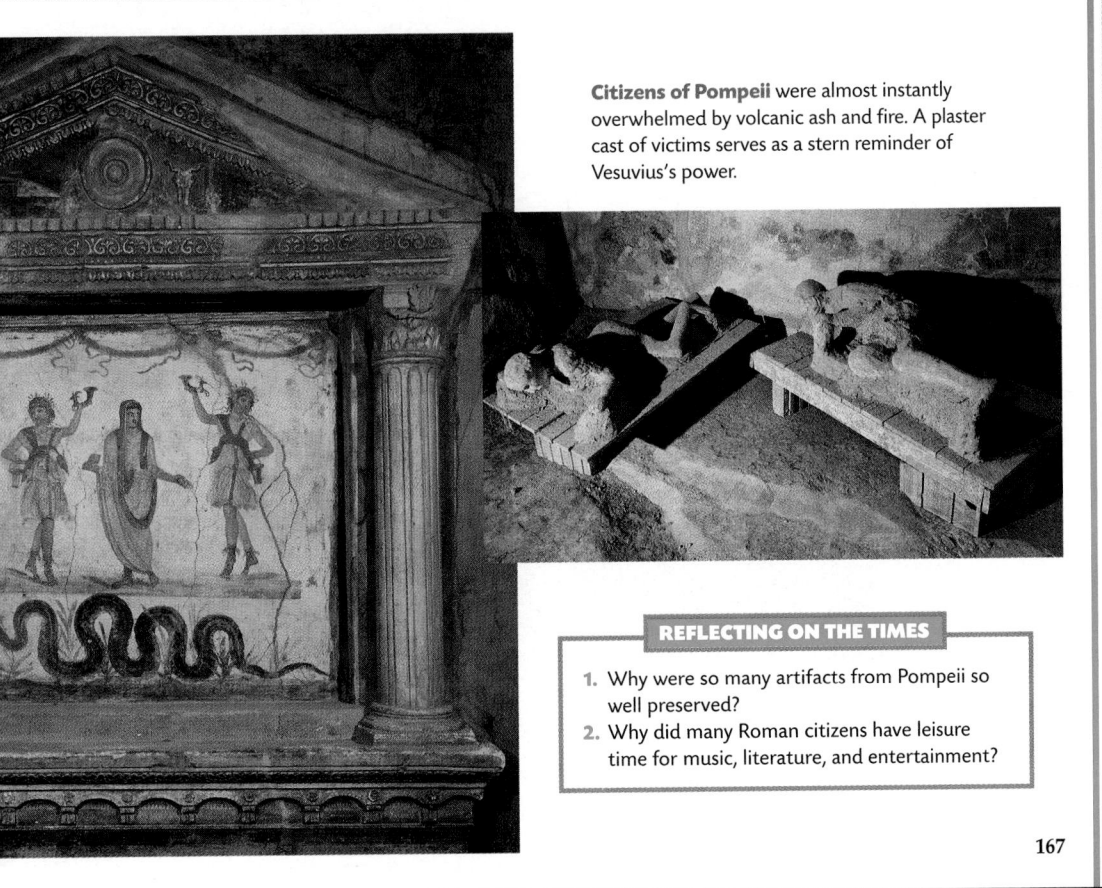

Citizens of Pompeii were almost instantly overwhelmed by volcanic ash and fire. A plaster cast of victims serves as a stern reminder of Vesuvius's power.

REFLECTING ON THE TIMES

1. Why were so many artifacts from Pompeii so well preserved?
2. Why did many Roman citizens have leisure time for music, literature, and entertainment?

167

Chapter 6 Section 3

Daily Life Have students choose the role of a person in the Roman Empire and then write a first-person narrative of a typical day. A student might choose to be a Roman legionary, a shopkeeper, a senator, a public official in the provinces, or an enslaved person. Students should research the daily life of the person they have chosen and include in their narrative details of his or her occupational functions, family life, and social life. **L2**

Military History Although Romans made significant accomplishments during the *Pax Romana*, the period had its dark side as well. Have students research and report orally on gladiator matches, the behavior of Roman legions toward defeated enemies or revolting provinces, or the practice of decimation used to discipline cowardly or mutinous troops. **L3**

Who?What?Where?When?

Augustus had such handsome features that artists in the employ of Napoleon based their sculptures of the French ruler on busts of the Roman emperor crafted centuries earlier.

Linking Past and Present

Calendar The calendar used by much of the world today reflects the intervention of Augustus. During his lifetime, the Romans renamed the sixth month, Sextilis, in his honor. Some scholars believe that Augustus borrowed a day from February, reducing it to 28 days, so that the month named in his honor would have at least as many days as the month named for Julius Caesar.

ANSWERS TO REFLECTING ON THE TIMES

1. The remains at Pompeii were preserved intact when the volcanic ash covering them hardened.
2. Many Romans became prosperous during the *Pax Romana*, and the government offered free entertainment to all.

Who?What?Where?When?

The Appian Way, dubbed "queen of long-distance roads," was named for the outstanding Roman statesman Appius Claudius, who undertook its construction in 312 B.C. Appius also completed Rome's first aqueduct, Aqua Appia, to bring water from the Sabine Hills. Appius Claudius, one of the first significant personalities in Roman history, was also the first individual to have building projects named in his honor.

Visualizing History Although nothing but the site of the Circus Maximus remains today, it was one of the largest sports arenas ever constructed. In the fourth century A.D., under the emperor Constantine, it was enlarged to a seating capacity of about 250,000.
Answer to Caption: *concrete*

ASSESS

Check for Understanding

Assign Section 3 Review as homework or as an in-class activity.

Use Student Self-Test and Review Software to review Section 3.

iron from Gaul, and lead from Spain. Soon skillful Greek traders within the empire were doing business in distant areas, such as eastern Africa, Southeast Asia, and China.

Life During the *Pax Romana*

These economic changes brought changes in lifestyles. The family gradually became less significant than it had been during the republic. Romans had fewer children and were likely to divorce and remarry several times. Fathers lost some of the absolute power they had during the republic, and wives gained some legal rights. Society became less stable. Patricians might go bankrupt, *equites* might take a place in the Senate, and a poor man might even make a fortune in manufacturing.

Within each class, a consistent pattern of life formed. The wealthy often held public office, owned large farms outside the cities, ran factories, or directed trading firms. They lived comfortably in luxurious homes with marble walls, mosaic floors, running water, and baths.

The prosperity of the *Pax Romana* sometimes reached people of average means—shopkeepers and artisans. Although fewer people became very rich, more became moderately well off. The majority in Rome, however, were still poor. There were no private baths for them; instead they bathed at crowded public areas built under Augustus and later emperors. Most Romans lived in flimsy wooden apartment buildings of six or seven stories that readily collapsed or caught fire.

Public Amusements

Despite these trying conditions, the poor did not rebel against the government, because it offered them both free bread and free entertainment. By A.D. 160, Romans were celebrating 130 holidays a year. On some days, teams of charioteers competed in races in the Circus Maximus, an arena seating more than 150,000. On other holidays, crowds could watch gladiators fight each other to the death or battle wild animals in stadiums like the Colosseum.

Architecture, Engineering, and Science

The Romans erected many impressive buildings during the *Pax Romana* besides the Circus Maximus and the Colosseum. Between A.D. 118 and A.D. 128, Hadrian rebuilt the Pantheon, a temple for all the deities, with a soaring dome and a huge skylight. To build the Pantheon, the Romans mixed concrete—a new building material—with various kinds of stone.

The Romans also excelled in road building. The first major Roman road was the **Appian Way**. Constructed in the 300s B.C., it connected Rome and southeastern Italy. During the *Pax Romana*, a network of roads was built to link Rome with the provinces. Reaching a total length of 50,000 miles (80,000 km), the road network contributed to the empire's unity.

As they constructed public buildings and a vast network of roads, the Romans engineered aqueducts, or artificial channels for carrying water.

Visualizing History **Entertainment at the giant arena Circus Maximus, depicted in this bas-relief, was free to Roman citizens.** *What new building material did the Romans use to construct the Pantheon?*

MEETING SPECIAL NEEDS ACTIVITY

Learning Style: Visual/Spatial Encourage students who are visual learners to find pictures of sites in today's Rome that date back to ancient times. Ask them to make copies of the pictures or to draw renditions of them, arrange them in a book with captions to identify them, and provide information about when and why they were built. Have them share their completed books with the rest of the class. Suggested sites include the Colosseum, the Arch of Constantine, the Arch of Titus, the Pantheon, the Baths of Caracalla. **L1 LEP**

© Sonia Halliday Photographs

Roman Forum

The ruins of the Roman Forum are a major tourist attraction of modern Rome. In ancient times, the Forum was the center of both politics and commerce. The Forum contained a number of separate buildings: In the foreground the Temple of Castor and Pollux, built in the 400s B.C., honored Roman gods. Behind is the Arch of Titus, the ruler whose military victory is enshrined in the arch built about A.D 70. Beyond the Arch stand the walls of the Colosseum. The largest amphitheater built in ancient Rome, the Colosseum took a decade to construct and could seat 50,000. Here the Romans watched gladiators battle lions and later vanquish Christians.

The rise of the Roman state began with the city of Rome itself hundreds of years before the birth of Christ. Slowly the Romans consolidated control over Italy and built a great army. By 200 B.C. Rome had become a vast empire. Power brought wealth and great monuments such as these in the Forum. ⊕

TEACH

Tell students that Castor and Pollux were twin brothers of the same mother (Leda) but different fathers. Castor was the son of a mortal (Tyndareus, Leda's husband), while Pollux was the son of Jupiter (the Roman name for Zeus), the king of the gods. According to legend, the twins brought the news to Rome of the Roman victory at the 484 B.C. battle of Lake Regillus.

Explain to students that the Arch of Titus commemorates the Roman victory in the Jewish war, in which one million Jews were said to have died. **What do these buildings tell us about Roman society?** *(Possible answers: The Romans valued military conquests.)* **What buildings in our nation's capital do you think will still be standing 2,000 years from now, and what can they tell people about our country?** *(Answers may include the Capitol, the Washington Monument, the Lincoln and Jefferson Memorials; these buildings show that the United States values democratic government and honors those leaders who have built and supported it.)*

CURRICULUM CONNECTION

ASTRONOMY

According to Greek myth, when Castor, who was mortal, died, Pollux refused immortality, which would have separated him from his brother. To unite them forever, Zeus transformed Castor and Pollux into the constellation Gemini, which means "twins" in Latin.

Chapter 6 Section 3

Evaluate

Section Quiz 6-3

Use the Testmaker to create a customized quiz for Section 3.

Reteach

Have students work in small groups to make a list of the Roman emperors and the accomplishments of each.

Enrich

Have students imagine that they are contemporaries of one of the early Roman emperors and write a feature article about the life of that emperor. Students should research in the library the daily life of the emperor, as well as his contributions. Have students compile the completed reports into a "Book of Caesars" to be shared with the class.

CLOSE

Write these headings on the board: *Trade, Science and Technology, Literature, Government, Law, Religion, Entertainment, Military, Architecture*. Work with the class to describe the characteristics of each of these aspects of life during the *Pax Romana*.

These lofty arches built out of stone enabled water to flow into Rome from as far away as 57 miles (about 92 km). One Roman-built aqueduct in Segovia, Spain, was so well constructed that it is still used today—nearly 1,900 years after it was completed.

The Romans excelled at adapting the discoveries of others and using them in new and more practical ways. They made use of the Etruscan arch and dome to build aqueducts and the Pantheon, and borrowed the Greek design for columns to support porches built around city squares.

Roman scientists also relied upon information that had been gathered from other cultures. The medical ideas of the ancient world compiled by the Greek physician **Galen** formed the basis of Roman medical science. Likewise, the observations of the Egyptian astronomer **Ptolemy** formed the foundation of Roman astronomy. Galen's works influenced medical science for many centuries, and Ptolemy's work made it possible for later astronomers to predict with accuracy the motion of the planets.

Roman Education

The Romans studied their borrowed knowledge avidly. Wealthy boys and girls received private lessons at home. Young men from wealthy families went on to academies—where former Greek slaves often taught—to learn geometry, astronomy, philosophy, and oratory. The daughters of the wealthy did not attend academies. Many upper-class women continued to study at home, however, and often became as well educated as Roman men. People in the lower classes usually had at least the basic knowledge of reading, writing, and arithmetic they needed to conduct business.

Language and Literature

Latin, Rome's official language, had a vocabulary far smaller than that of Greek or modern English; thus, many words expressed several meanings. Nevertheless, Latin remained the *lingua franca*, or common language, of Europe as late as the A.D. 1500s. Latin also forms the basis of the so-called Romance languages, such as Italian, French, Spanish, Portuguese, and Romanian, and supplies the roots for more than half of English words.

Although Romans learned from Greek literature, during the reign of Augustus Latin literature achieved an elegance and power of its own. Cicero, a Roman senator, published beautifully written speeches. Ovid wrote the *Metamorphoses*, a collection of verses based on Greek mythology. Horace, a poet, wrote about the shortness of life and the rewards of companionship. Horace's friend **Virgil** wrote the *Aeneid*, an epic poem comparable to those of Homer. In one passage of this poem, Virgil expresses both the humility and pride of Romans:

> "Others, no doubt, will better mould the bronze
> To the semblance of soft breathing, draw, from marble,
> The living countenance; and others plead
> With greater eloquence, or learn to measure,
> Better than we, the pathways of the heaven,
> The risings of the stars: remember, Roman,
> To rule the people under law, to establish
> The way of peace, to battle down the haughty,
> To spare the meek. Our fine arts, these, forever."
>
> —Virgil, the *Aeneid*, c. 20 B.C.

Livy, a later writer, wrote a monumental history of Rome that glorified the early Romans. The historian Tacitus, on the other hand, condemned the tyranny of the Julian emperors with subtle but scathing irony. In *Germania*, Tacitus contrasted the robust life of the Germans with what he felt was the weak and pleasure-loving life of the Romans.

SECTION 3 REVIEW

Recall

1. **Define** aqueduct.
2. **Identify** Augustus, *Pax Romana*, Tiberius, Claudius, Nero, Marcus Aurelius, Galen, Ptolemy, Virgil, Livy.
3. **Use** the map on page 165 to identify Roman expansion. When did the empire reach its greatest extent?

Critical Thinking

4. **Synthesizing Information** The expression "bread and circuses" has been used to describe hasty measures taken by a government to prevent discontent among the poor. Explain whether you believe this expression applies to any aspects of life in the modern United States. If so, to what aspects does it apply?

Understanding Themes

5. **Cultural Diffusion** List some of the advantages and disadvantages to a province of adopting Roman culture.

SECTION 3 REVIEW ANSWERS

1. All vocabulary words are defined in the Glossary.
2. Augustus, 164; Tiberius, 165; Claudius, 165; Nero, 165; Marcus Aurelius, 165; *Pax Romana*, 167; Galen, 170; Ptolemy, 170; Virgil, 170; Livy, 170
3. in A.D. 130
4. Answers may include public welfare or televised professional sports displays as "bread and circuses."
5. CULTURAL DIFFUSION advantages: education and comforts to wealthy provincials; disadvantages: loss of local laws, customs, and language

A.D. 1 — A.D. 150 — A.D. 300 — A.D. 450

- **c. A.D. 30** Jesus preaches in Palestine.
- **A.D. 70** Jews in Palestine unsuccessfully revolt against Roman rule.
- **A.D. 312** Constantine becomes Roman emperor.
- **A.D. 392** Christianity becomes Rome's official religion.

Section 4

The Rise of Christianity

Setting the Scene

- **Terms to Define**
  sect, messiah, disciple, martyr, bishop, patriarch, pope
- **People to Meet**
  Jesus, Paul, Peter, Constantine, Theodosius, Augustine

Find Out What did Jesus of Nazareth teach, and how did the early Christians influence the later Roman Empire?

The Storyteller

How could Justin, a man well versed in philosophy and intellectual pursuits, explain to the emperor why he had embraced Christianity? He had opened a school to teach others about this religion, although most educated people dismissed it as a dangerous superstition. He had to convince the emperor that, just as the ancient philosophers had sought truth, Christians sought it too. Since both scholars and Christians shared this quest, following Christian teachings could only help in the search for understanding. He set his pen to paper and began to write a defense of the Christian faith.

—from *Apology*, Justin, reprinted in *Readings in Ancient History from Gilgamesh to Diocletian*, Nels M. Bailkey, 1969

Mosaic of Jesus as shepherd

The early Romans worshiped nature spirits. Under Etruscan influence they came to think of these spirits as deities. Later, the Romans adopted much of Greek religion, identifying Greek deities with their own. Beginning with Augustus, the government also expected people to honor the emperor as Rome's chief priest. Nevertheless, the empire's people were still allowed to worship freely, and a variety of religions flourished.

Meanwhile, a new monotheistic religion called Christianity began to be practiced by some of the Jews in the eastern Mediterranean. At first, both the Romans and the earliest Christians thought of the new religion as a **sect**, or group, within Judaism. As Christians won over non-Jewish followers, however, the faith diverged from its Jewish roots and became a separate religion.

Judaism and the Empire

In A.D. 6 the Emperor Augustus turned the kingdom of Judah into the Roman province of Judea. The Romans in Judea still allowed the Jews to practice their religion, but they treated them cruelly. Many Jews therefore strengthened their hope that a **messiah**, or savior, would help them regain their freedom. The coming of a messiah had long been foretold by Jewish prophets.

Believing that God would intervene on their behalf, some Jews took matters into their own hands. In A.D. 66 they rebelled against the Romans and overpowered the small Roman army in Jerusalem. But only four years later, in A.D. 70, the Romans retook Jerusalem, destroying the Temple and killing thousands of Jews.

Then, after another unsuccessful rebellion in A.D. 132, the Romans banned the Jews from living

SECTION THEME

- **Innovation** Christianity becomes the dominant religion in the West.

Find Out

Answer: *Jesus taught that people should turn away from their mistakes and that God would forgive all who truly repented. More people turned to Christianity for comfort, and eventually it became the official religion of the Roman Empire.*

FOCUS

Section Objective

Summarize the teachings of Jesus of Nazareth and the influence of early Christians on the later Roman Empire.

BELLRINGER Motivational Activity

Before taking roll at the beginning of the class period, project Section Focus Transparency 6-4 and have students answer the activity questions. Discuss students' responses.

This activity is also available as a blackline master.

Vocabulary Pre-check

Use the Vocabulary PuzzleMaker to create a puzzle that reinforces the vocabulary terms in this section. **L1**

SECTION RESOURCES

Reproducible Masters
- Reproducible Lesson Plan 6-4
- Guided Reading Activity 6-4
- Section Quiz 6-4

Transparencies
- Section Focus Transparency 6-4

Multimedia
- Vocabulary PuzzleMaker Software
- Student Self-Test and Review Software
- Testmaker
- Turning Points in World History
- In the Holy Land

TEACH

Guided Practice

THEME **Innovation**

Review with students the meaning of innovation and the way in which Christianity grew out of Judaism. Ask students to explain how Christianity could be considered an innovation. *(Although like Judaism it was monotheistic and stressed ethical behavior, it was an innovation in teaching that Jesus was the Messiah and that the kingdom of God was close at hand.)* **L1 LEP**

Visualizing History The word *apostle* comes from the Greek for "one who is sent out." Jesus sent his original followers out into the world to preach the gospel, which literally means "good news."

Answer to Caption: *They formed churches for worship, fellowship, and instruction.*

ABCNEWS INTERACTIVE™

VIDEODISC
Turning Points in World History

Side One
Chapter 6

Title: *Jerusalem: City of Three Faiths*
Subject: Christian, Muslim, and Jewish scholars discuss the importance of Jerusalem to their three faiths.
Ask: Why is the land of Israel significant to Christianity? *(The events of Jesus' life took place there.)*

Visualizing History An engraving of the apostles Peter and Paul decorates the sepulchre of the child Asellus. *Why did the apostles form churches?*

in Jerusalem. The Jews were forced to live in other parts of the Mediterranean and the Middle East. In their scattered communities, the Jews continued to study the Torah, the entire body of Jewish religious law and learning. They set up special academies called yeshivas to promote its study. Furthermore, between A.D. 200 and A.D. 500, rabbis—scholars trained in the yeshivas—assembled their various interpretations of the Torah into a book known as the Talmud. To this day the Talmud remains an important book of Jewish law.

Jesus of Nazareth

A few decades before the Jewish revolts, a Jew named **Jesus** grew up in the town of Nazareth. With deep spiritual fervor, Jesus traveled through Galilee and Judea from about A.D. 30 to A.D. 33, preaching a new message to his fellow Jews and winning disciples, or followers.

Proclaiming that God's rule was close at hand, Jesus urged people to turn away from their sins and practice deeds of kindness. He said that God was loving and forgiving toward all who repented, no matter what evil they had done or how lowly they were. In his teaching, Jesus often used parables, or symbolic stories. With the parable below, Jesus urged his followers to give up everything so that they would be ready for God's coming:

> "The kingdom of heaven is like treasure lying buried in a field. The man who found it, buried it again; and for sheer joy went and sold everything he had, and bought that field."
>
> —Matthew 13:44-46

Jesus' disciples believed that he was the messiah; other Jews, believing that the messiah had yet to come, disputed this claim. The growing controversy over Jesus troubled Roman officials in Palestine. They believed that anyone who aroused such strong public feelings could endanger Roman rule in the region. In about A.D. 33, the Roman governor Pontius Pilate arrested Jesus as a political rebel and ordered that he be crucified—hung from a cross until dead. This was a typical Roman way of punishing criminals.

The Spread of Christianity

After Jesus' death, his disciples proclaimed that he had risen from the dead and had appeared to them. They pointed to this as evidence that Jesus was the messiah. His followers began preaching that Jesus was the Son of God and the way of salvation. Small groups in the Hellenistic cities of the eastern Mediterranean world accepted this message. Jews and non-Jews who accepted Jesus and his teachings became known as Christians—*Christos* was Greek for "messiah." They formed churches—communities for worship, fellowship, and instruction.

A convert named **Paul** aided Christianity's spread, especially among non-Jews. He traveled widely and wrote on behalf of the new religion. Paul's letters to various churches were later combined with the Gospels, or stories about Jesus, and the writings of other early Christian leaders. Together, these works form the New Testament of the Bible.

Meanwhile, other apostles, or Christian missionaries, spread Christianity throughout the Roman world. It is believed that **Peter**, the leader of the group, came to Rome and helped found a church in that city. Other churches were set up in Greece, Asia Minor, Egypt, and later in Gaul and Spain.

COOPERATIVE LEARNING ACTIVITY

Religions Organize students into several groups. Have each group research one of the various religions practiced in the Roman Empire. Make sure each group member is responsible for either research, compiling information, providing illustrations, preparing answers for possible questions, or presentation to the class. Religions to be researched include the official religion of Rome, Judaism, and the Persian and Egyptian mystery religions, such as Mithraism and the cult of Isis. Have each group choose one of its members to deliver its report to the class. The entire group should act as a panel, answering questions from the class about the religion it studied. **L2**

Persecution and Competition

Christians taught that their religion was the only true faith. They refused to honor the emperor as a god and rejected military service. As a result, many Romans disliked the Christians and accused them of treason.

The Romans feared that Christian rejection of their deities would bring divine punishment. Therefore, although they did not hunt out the Christians, if local officials thought Christians were causing trouble, they might have the Christians killed. The Romans frequently threw these Christian martyrs—people who chose to die rather than give up their beliefs—into the stadiums to be killed by wild beasts in front of cheering crowds.

Such persecution, which lasted until the early A.D. 300s, kept many people from becoming Christians. To win converts, Christians had to overcome this obstacle. Christianity also had to compete for followers with polytheistic religions and mystery religions—so named for their mythical heroes and secret rituals—and with Judaism.

During the A.D. 200s and 300s, different varieties of Christianity flourished in the Mediterranean world along with these other religions. Like Judaism, Christianity was mainly a religion of the cities, while traditional Roman religions retained their hold in the countryside. Even though the number of Christians was relatively small during this period, their strength in the cities of the Roman Empire gave Christianity an influence that was far beyond its size.

Romans Adopt Christianity

According to legend, in A.D. 312, as the Roman general **Constantine** led his army into battle, a flaming cross appeared in the sky and beneath it in fiery letters appeared the Latin words *In hoc signo vinces*: "With this as your standard you will have victory." Apparently because of this vision, Constantine ordered his soldiers to paint the Christian symbol of the cross on their shields. When his army won the battle, Constantine credited the victory to the Christian God.

Named emperor of Rome in A.D. 312, Constantine thus became a protector of Christianity. Through his influence all religious groups throughout the empire, including Christians, gained complete freedom to worship as they pleased. Constantine attended meetings of Christian leaders and ordered churches to be built in Rome and Jerusalem.

Because of effective missionary work and growing government support, Christianity further increased in size and influence throughout the entire Roman world. It became as important in the western part of the empire as it was in the eastern part. In A.D. 392 the Emperor **Theodosius** (THEE•uh•DOH•shuhs) made Christianity the official religion of the Roman Empire. At the same time, he banned the old Hellenistic and Roman religions.

The Early Church

From early times Christians recognized that their organization, the Church, would prosper only if it was united. They also felt that Christian teachings had to be stated clearly to avoid differences of opinion that might divide the Church. Consequently, Christians turned to important religious thinkers who attempted to explain many Christian beliefs. Between A.D. 100 and A.D. 500, various scholars known as Church Fathers wrote books explaining Christian teachings. They greatly influenced later Christian thinkers.

Teachings of Augustine

Christians in the western part of the empire especially valued the work of **Augustine**, a scholar born in North Africa in A.D. 354. Augustine is considered to have written one of the world's first great autobiographies. In this work called *Confessions*, Augustine describes how he was converted to Christianity:

> "I heard from a neighboring house a voice, as of a boy or girl, I know not, chanting, and oft repeating, 'Take up and read; Take up and read.'… So … I arose, interpreting it to be no other than a command from God, to open the book [the Bible], and read the first chapter I should find."
>
> —Augustine, *Confessions*, c. A.D. 398

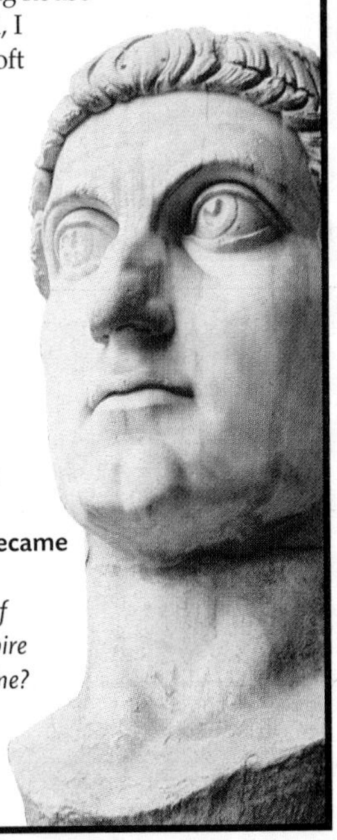

Visualizing History **Constantine became a defender of Christianity.** *How did the status of Christians living in the Roman Empire change under the rule of Constantine?*

Chapter 6 Section 4

ABC NEWS INTERACTIVE™

VIDEODISC
In the Holy Land

Side One, Chapter 9
Frame: 9487
Title: *Ted Koppel: Three Religions*
Subject: Introduction to Islam, Christianity, and Judaism
Ask: Which of the three religious groups controls most of Israel today? *(Jewish religion)*

Geography: Movement Have students trace a map of the Roman Empire. Then have them read in the New Testament portions of the Acts of the Apostles that record the apostles' travels. Have students record on their map some of the place names mentioned in the Acts. Have students display and explain their maps to the class. **L3**

Visualizing History Constantine believed he was God's chosen servant and responsible to God for good government of the Church. **Answer to Caption:** *Christians gained complete freedom to worship as they pleased.*

MEETING SPECIAL NEEDS ACTIVITY

Learning Style: Visual/Spatial Many movies have been made about the life of Jesus or the impact of Christianity on the people of imperial Rome. Have students who are visual learners or have limited English proficiency view a videotape of *The Robe, Ben Hur, The Silver Chalice*, or *The Greatest Story Ever Told* and then write a report. Instruct them to include descriptions of details about life under the *Pax Romana* (for example, in *Ben Hur*, the chariot races; in *The Silver Chalice*, the Greek artisan and enslaved person; in *The Robe*, the Roman legionaries). Ask students to deliver their reports to the rest of the class. **L1**

ASSESS

Check for Understanding

Assign Section 4 Review as homework or as an in-class activity.

Use Student Self-Test and Review Software to review Section 4.

Chapter 6 Section 4

Visualizing History The catacombs, found in and near Rome, were the underground burial chambers of the early Christians. **Answer to Caption:** *a history of humanity told from the Christian viewpoint*

Evaluate

Section Quiz 6-4

Use the Testmaker to create a customized quiz for Section 4.

Reteach

Work with students to create a time line on the chalkboard of significant events in Judaism and Christianity covered in this section.

Enrich

Have students interview a local Christian minister or priest or a Jewish rabbi about the Jewish roots of Christianity. Encourage students to tape-record the interview and to prepare a list of questions in advance. (Sample questions: What beliefs do Judaism and Christianity share? What are the significant differences? Why do you think Christianity arose out of Judaism at that particular moment in history?) Have students report orally on their interviews.

CLOSE

Have groups of five or six students summarize one of the following: the teachings of Jesus, the spread of Christianity throughout the Roman world, or the evolution of the early Church. Have each group present its summary to the class.

Visualizing History **The walls of Roman catacombs host many depictions of Christian art such as the Eucharist Banquet version of the Last Supper.** *What kind of literature was the* City of God*?*

So powerful was Augustine's influence that he became a leading church official in North Africa. In this post he wrote books, letters, and sermons that shaped Christian thought during his own time and afterward. For instance, he wrote *City of God*—the first history of humanity from the Christian viewpoint.

Church Structure

By Augustine's time, Christian leaders had organized the Church as a hierarchy—into levels of authority, each level more powerful than the level below it. Local gatherings of Christians, called parishes, were led by priests. Priests conducted worship services and supervised parish activities. Several parishes together formed a diocese, each overseen by a bishop. Bishops interpreted Christian beliefs and administered regional church affairs. The most powerful bishops governed Christians in the empire's larger cities. The bishops of the five leading cities—Rome, Constantinople, Alexandria, Antioch, and Jerusalem—were called patriarchs.

The bishops of the Christian Church met in councils to discuss questions and disputes about Christian beliefs. The decisions they reached at these councils came to be accepted as doctrine, or official teachings. The points of view the council did not accept were considered heresy, or false doctrine.

During the A.D. 400s, the bishop of Rome began to claim authority over the other patriarchs. Addressed by the Greek or Latin word *papa*, his name today is rendered *pope* in the English language. Latin-speaking Christians in the West regarded the pope as head of all of the churches. Greek-speaking Christians in the East, however, would not accept the authority of the pope over their churches. The bishops of Alexandria and Antioch claimed to exercise a paternal rule equal to that of the pope. Eventually these churches and those of the Latin West separated from each other. In time, the Latin churches as a group became known as the Roman Catholic Church. The Greek churches as a group became known as the Eastern Orthodox Church.

SECTION 4 REVIEW

Recall

1. **Define** sect, messiah, disciple, martyr, bishop, patriarch, pope.
2. **Identify** the Talmud, Jesus, Paul, Peter, Constantine, Theodosius, Augustine.
3. **Use** a chart to describe the hierarchy of the Christian Church by the time of Augustine. What were the functions of bishops? Of priests?

Critical Thinking

4. **Evaluating Information** Why might the Romans in Judea especially have responded harshly toward anyone arousing strong feelings among the Jewish people?

Understanding Themes

5. **Innovation** List some of the ways in which Christianity diverged from Judaism to become a distinct religion rather than a sect.

SECTION 4 REVIEW ANSWERS

1. All vocabulary words are defined in the Glossary.
2. Talmud, 172; Jesus, 172; Paul, 172; Peter, 172; Constantine, 173; Theodosius, 173; Augustine, 173
3. Chart should include priest, bishop, patriarch, pope, in that order. Bishop oversaw diocese, interpreted beliefs, administered regional church affairs; priest oversaw parish, conducted worship services
4. Romans feared a Jewish rebellion.
5. INNOVATION Unlike Jews, Christians believed Jesus was the Messiah. When Christianity spread to non-Jews, it stopped being a Jewish sect.

A.D. 200 — A.D. 300 — A.D. 400 — A.D. 500

- A.D. 284 Diocletian becomes Roman emperor.
- A.D. 330 Constantine moves capital to Byzantium, renamed Constantinople.
- A.D. 395 Theodosius divides Roman Empire.
- A.D. 476 German soldier Odoacer seizes Rome.

Section 5

Roman Decline

Setting the Scene

- **Terms to Define**
  inflation
- **People to Meet**
  Diocletian, Constantine, Theodosius I, Alaric, Attila
- **Places to Locate**
  Constantinople

Find Out What caused the decline of the western Roman Empire?

The Storyteller

The old world had ended. There was no longer any doubt of that. Gregory, whose family had for countless generations served Rome as Senators and consuls, looked out the window at the city which had once ruled the world. Now it was in the hands of warlike tribes who had no appreciation for Roman virtue, achievements, or culture.

"Cities are destroyed," he mused, "fortifications razed, fields devastated. Some men are led away captive, others are mutilated, others slain before our eyes." The pride of Rome was reduced to memories of a vanished glory.

—from *Homiliarum in Ezechielem*, Pope Gregory I, reprinted in *Sources of the Western Tradition*, Marvin Perry, Joseph Peden, and Theodore Von Laue, 1991

Marcus Aurelius

During the A.D. 200s, while Christianity was spreading through the Roman Empire, Germanic tribes began to overrun the western half of the empire. Many inhabitants in this area reported widespread devastation and chaos. The Germanic tribes had always been a threat to the empire. Why were they so much more successful now than they were during the times of Marcus Aurelius?

The Empire's Problems

The Romans had a brief rest from political violence during the reign of the five Good Emperors. When Marcus Aurelius died in A.D. 180, however, a new period of violence and corruption brought the *Pax Romana* to an end.

Political Instability

The time of confusion began with the installation of Emperor Commodus, Marcus Aurelius's son. Like Nero, he spent so much state money on his own pleasures that he bankrupted the treasury. In A.D. 192 Commodus's own troops plotted to kill him.

From A.D. 192 to A.D. 284, army legions installed 28 emperors, only to kill most of them off in rapid succession. During this time of political disorder, Rome's armies were busier fighting each other than they were defending the empire's borders. Germanic tribes such as the Goths, the Alemanni, the Franks, and the Saxons repeatedly and successfully attacked the empire.

Economic Decline

Political instability led to economic decline. Warfare disrupted production and trade. For artisans and merchants, profits declined sharply, forcing many out of business. Warfare also destroyed farmland, causing food shortages that sent food prices soaring.

Chapter 6 Section 5

SECTION THEME

- **Change** Germanic invasions and cultural weaknesses destroy the Roman Empire.

Find Out

Answer: *Political instability, economic problems, unsuccessful reforms, and barbarian invasions destroyed the Roman Empire.*

FOCUS

Section Objective

List the reasons for the decline of the western Roman Empire.

BELLRINGER Motivational Activity

Before taking roll at the beginning of the class period, project Section Focus Transparency 6-5 and have students answer the activity questions. Discuss students' responses.

This activity is also available as a blackline master.

Vocabulary Pre-check

Use Vocabulary Activity 6 to introduce vocabulary terms. **L1 LEP**

SECTION RESOURCES

Reproducible Masters
- Reproducible Lesson Plan 6-5
- Vocabulary Activity 6
- Guided Reading Activity 6-5
- Reteaching Activity 6
- Enrichment Activity 6
- Section Quiz 6-5
- Performance Assessment Activity 6
- Spanish Chapter Summary 6

Transparencies
- Section Focus Transparency 6-5

Multimedia
- Student Self-Test and Review Software
- Testmaker

TEACH

Guided Practice

THEME **Change**

Work with students to make a list of some of the changes that took place in the empire from the days of the *Pax Romana* to the decline of the western empire. Then discuss with them which changes were positive and which contributed to the decline of the empire. *(positive: spread of Christianity, Constantinople established as eastern capital; negative: economic decline, Germanic invasions)* **L1**

Economics Have students name the economic reforms instituted by Diocletian and Constantine. For each, ask what specific problem(s) the reform was meant to solve. *(freezing wages and prices—inflation; ordering farmers not to leave their land or allowing land owners to chain them—farmers were leaving farms and food shortages were occurring; requiring people to stay at their jobs and making jobs hereditary—people leaving heavily taxed professions)* Have students suggest other methods the emperors might have used to solve these problems. **L2**

Critical Thinking Ask students how the lack of orderly succession affected the Roman Empire. *(political instability, process controlled by armies)* Ask how power is passed on in our country and what might happen if we did not have a method of selection. **L3**

Visualizing History Relief sculpture is carved or cast so it projects from the surface of which it is a part. **Answer to Caption:** *to cover the expense of defending the vast empire*

To cope with falling incomes and rising prices, the government minted more coins. It hoped the increase would make it easier to pay its soldiers. However, because the government had already drained its stores of gold and silver, the new coins contained less of the precious metals—cutting their value. To continue getting the same return for their goods, merchants raised prices. Thus, the government's policy sparked severe inflation—a rise in prices corresponding to a decrease in the value of money.

The spiraling decline in wealth affected almost all parts of the empire. To sustain a fighting force, the Roman government had to continually raise soldiers' wages. Taxing landowners heavily seemed the only way to meet this expense, but as increased taxes made farming less profitable, more and more farmers abandoned their lands. As a result, the output of crops shrank even more, worsening the food shortage.

Unsuccessful Reforms

During the late A.D. 200s and early A.D. 300s, two emperors—**Diocletian** (DY•uh•KLEE•shuhn) and later, **Constantine**—struggled to halt the empire's decline. Their reforms preserved the government in the eastern part of the empire for more than 1,000 years. In the west, they succeeded only in briefly delaying the Germanic tribes' invasion of Rome.

Diocletian

General Diocletian came to power in A.D. 284 by slaying the murderer of the preceding emperor. To hold back invasions, he raised the number of legions in the army and spent his time traveling throughout the empire to oversee defenses. Recognizing, however, that the empire was too large for one person to govern, Diocletian divided the empire into two administrative units. Diocletian set himself up as coemperor of the eastern provinces and set up General Maximian as coemperor of the western provinces.

Diocletian also tried to stop the empire's economic decline. To slow inflation, he issued an order called the Edict of Prices. In this edict, Diocletian froze wages and set maximum prices for goods. Yet, even though the penalty for breaking the law was death, his effort failed completely. Citizens merely sold their goods through illegal trade. To stop farmers from leaving their lands and heavily taxed people from changing their

Visualizing History **As this relief sculpture shows, tax collectors in Roman times were very visible.** *Why did the Roman government have to increase taxes?*

COOPERATIVE LEARNING ACTIVITY

Role Play Organize the class into small groups and assign each group to role-play one of the following: Franks, Vandals, Visigoths, or Huns. Have each group research and prepare a presentation to the class on the group they are role-playing. The presentation should include information on the following: social structure and culture, homeland, methods of battle, and reasons for invading the empire. Make sure each group member is assigned a specific area of research and presentation. Have groups present their role plays to the class. Encourage them to use props such as maps and pictures in their presentations, and if they wish, to dress the part. Have the audience prepare questions in advance. **L1**

professions to avoid taxation, Diocletian required farmers who rented land never to leave their property and all workers to remain at the same job throughout their lives.

Constantine

When Diocletian retired in A.D. 305, civil wars broke out again. They continued until Constantine came to power in A.D. 312.

Constantine worked to stabilize the empire once more. He made it legal for landowners to chain their workers to keep them on the farm. He declared most jobs hereditary; sons had to follow their fathers' occupations. In A.D. 330 he moved the capital of the eastern empire to the Greek town of Byzantium—an ideal site for trade and well protected by natural barriers—and renamed it **Constantinople**.

Theodosius

After Constantine's death in A.D. 337, civil war flared anew until **Theodosius I** succeeded Constantine. During Theodosius's rule, the empire still suffered internal problems, and again the western half suffered more. To lessen the problems, Theodosius willed upon his death that the eastern and western parts should be declared separate empires. In A.D. 395 this division came to pass. To distinguish the two, historians refer to the eastern empire as the Byzantine Empire—after Byzantium, the town that became the capital—and the western empire as the Roman Empire.

Germanic Invasions A.D. 200–500

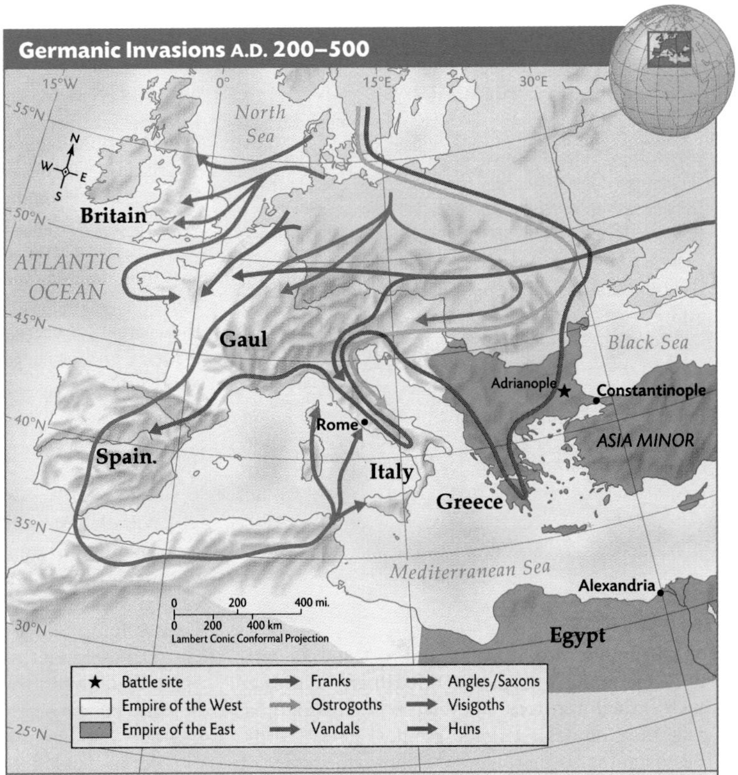

Map Study Between A.D. 410 and A.D. 476 Visigoths, Huns, and Vandals invaded Italy.
Movement What was the area of origin and the destination of the Angles and Saxons during this period?

Barbarian Invasions

Germanic tribes entered the Roman Empire for many reasons. Beginning in the late A.D. 300s, large numbers of Germanic peoples migrated into the empire because they sought a warmer climate and better grazing land. Others crossed the empire's borders wanting a share of Rome's wealth. Most, however, came because they were fleeing the Huns, fierce nomadic invaders from central Asia.

Warrior Groups

Germanic warriors lived mostly by raising cattle and farming small plots. Despite their interest in the empire's goods, they themselves had little surplus to trade and were poor compared to the Romans. Each warrior group consisted of warriors, their families, and a chief. This chief governed the group and also led the warriors into battle. As the bands of warriors were numerous, so too were the chiefs. Often the only unifying factor among these Germanic groups was their language, which to the Romans sounded like unintelligible babbling. The Romans labeled the Germanic peoples barbarians, a reference to the sounds they made.

Map Study

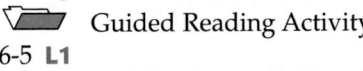

Answer
northern European mainland (present-day Denmark); Britain

Map Skills Practice

Reading a Map Which invading groups must have been skilled seafarers as well as warriors? *(Vandals, Angles/Saxons)*

Independent Practice

Guided Reading Activity 6-5 **L1**

News Reports Have students imagine that they are anchorpersons for the Rome Evening News in August A.D. 410. The Visigoths, led by Alaric, are camped outside the walls ready to attack. Have students write news reports, including background information on Alaric and his Goths, and present their newscast to the class. **L2**

Economics Have students write an in-depth report on economic factors that led to the decline of the empire. Have students explain how the interaction of factors, such as increased taxes and inflation, caused further decline. Encourage students to discuss whether there are any similar economic problems today. **L3**

MEETING SPECIAL NEEDS ACTIVITY

Mixed Learners To make certain that students with learning difficulties understand the unsuccessful reforms that failed to halt the decline of the Roman Empire, have them imagine that they are farmers living in one of Rome's western provinces during the rule of Diocletian. Have them write letters to relatives in Rome describing the difficulties they are having and their worries. Then ask the students to read their letters to the rest of the class. **L2**

Linking Past and Present

The Vandals so thoroughly looted and destroyed Rome that today we call someone who willfully destroys valuable objects a *vandal* and deliberate destruction of property *vandalism*.

Chapter 6 Section 5

ASSESS

Check for Understanding

Assign Section 5 Review as homework or as an in-class activity.

Use Student Self-Test and Review Software to review Section 5.

Evaluate

Section Quiz 6-5

Use the Testmaker to create a customized quiz for Section 5.

Reteach

Work with students to create on the chalkboard a time line of significant events from A.D. 180-476.

Reteaching Activity 6

Enrich

Have students research to find out more about the culture of the Visigoths, Huns, and Vandals.

Enrichment Activity 6

CLOSE

Have students summarize the factors that led to the fall of Rome and discuss their relative importance. For example, did invasions have a greater impact than economic problems?

AROUND THE WORLD: Sassanids Establish an Empire

Persia, A.D. 200s

Ardashir I, king of Persis, defeated the Parthian army in a decisive victory, then entered the capital of Ctesiphon in triumph. There he was crowned King of Kings and established the Sassanid Empire, which lasted until A.D. 651. Ardashir founded or rebuilt many cities and made Zoroastrianism the state religion. A rock carving at Naqshi-Rustam shows Ardashir taking the symbol of royalty from the supreme Zoroastrian god.

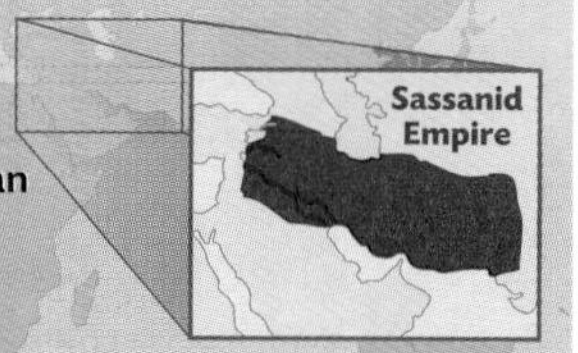

The Visigoths

During the late A.D. 300s and A.D. 400s, a variety of Germanic groups extended their hold over much Roman territory. They were the Ostrogoths, Visigoths, Vandals, Franks, Angles, and Saxons. The Visigoths, at first, were the most important of these groups. In A.D. 378 they rebelled against Roman rule and defeated a large Roman army at Adrianople in the Balkan Peninsula, killing the eastern Roman emperor. His successor managed to buy peace by giving the Visigoths land in the Balkans. Then in A.D. 410 the Visigothic chief, **Alaric**, led his people into Italy, capturing and sacking Rome. After Alaric's death the Visigoths retreated into Gaul.

The Huns

The next threat to the empire was invasion by the Huns. This nomadic group streamed westward from the grasslands of central Asia. Led by their chief, **Attila**, the Huns raided the eastern empire; then they moved north into Gaul. In A.D. 451 the Romans and the Visigoths combined to fight and stop the Huns in central Gaul. Foiled in the provinces, Attila turned upon Italy. There his horde plundered the larger cities and terrified the people. Eventually plague and famine took their toll on the Huns. After Attila died in A.D. 453, they retreated to eastern Europe.

The end of the empire of the Huns brought new troubles to the Romans. Wandering Germans, Persians, Slavs, and Avars battered continually at the Roman Empire's eastern frontier. Diplomacy, bribery, and warfare kept them at bay for only a short time.

End of the Western Empire

With the Huns gone and Italy devastated, nothing remained to prevent Germanic tribes from taking over. The Vandals raided and thoroughly sacked Rome in A.D. 455. Franks and Goths divided Gaul among themselves. Finally, in A.D. 476, a German soldier named Odoacer (OH•duh•WAY•suhr) seized control of Rome by killing the emperor and keeping the emperor's son from power. Odoacer then named himself king of Italy.

Because Odoacer called himself king and never named a substitute emperor, people today refer to A.D. 476 as the year in which the Roman Empire "fell." However, this event no more signifies the collapse of the empire than any other event. Its end was caused by a complex interaction of events between A.D. 200 and A.D. 500.

More accurately, the Roman Empire ended in the late A.D. 400s. Yet it did not mean the end of Roman culture, for the new Germanic rulers accepted the Latin language, Roman laws, and the Christian Church. In the Byzantine Empire, however, aspects of Roman culture were gradually supplanted by Hellenistic culture. By the A.D. 700s, Greek had even replaced Latin as the language of the Byzantine Empire.

SECTION 5 REVIEW

Recall

1. **Define** inflation.
2. **Identify** Diocletian, Constantine, Theodosius I, Alaric, Attila, Odoacer.
3. **Locate** Adrianople on the map on page 177. What significant event occurred there during the time of the "fall" of the Roman Empire?

Critical Thinking

4. **Synthesizing Information** Which do you think had a greater impact on the fall of the Roman Empire, internal difficulties or outside invaders? Why?

Understanding Themes

5. **Change** How did warfare both create and destroy the Roman Empire?

SECTION 5 REVIEW ANSWERS

1. All vocabulary words are defined in the Glossary.
2. Diocletian, 176; Constantine, 176; Theodosius I, 177; Alaric, 178; Attila, 178; Odoacer, 178
3. The Visigoths defeated a large Roman army at Adrianople in A.D. 378.
4. Answers will vary. Internal difficulties opened empire to outside invaders. Economic decline made maintaining armies difficult.
5. CHANGE Romans brought territories into the empire through warfare. The cost of maintaining armies and putting down rebellions weakened the empire. Outside invaders destroyed the empire through warfare.

178 Chapter 6 *Ancient Rome and Early Christianity*

Critical Thinking SKILLS

Relevant and Irrelevant Information

Suppose you go to a department store sale and see a CD player that you like. You ask the salesperson, "How much does it cost?"

"It's a great price—lower than it has been all year!"

"But how much is it?" you repeat.

"It comes with a two-year warranty."

"You've told me that it's discounted and has a warranty, but how much is it?" you insist.

"It's on sale for $129.95 plus tax."

Finally, you have the information you need.

Learning the Skill

For any subject or area of interest, information that is available may be either relevant or irrelevant. Relevant information is connected, or related, to the subject. Any facts that define, explain, or illustrate the subject are relevant. Irrelevant information is just the opposite—facts unrelated to the subject. Irrelevant information is not necessarily wrong; it is just not useful to the subject. In the example above, you wanted to know the price of the CD player. All other information was irrelevant.

History contains masses of factual information. To avoid being overwhelmed by the quantity, you must learn to distinguish between relevant and irrelevant material. This is very important when studying for an exam or writing a report. First, clearly define your topic, question, or main idea. Write this topic in your own words. When studying written material, examine each sentence and look for facts that define, explain, or illustrate your topic. Take notes on these items. When listening to a lecture or other oral presentation, look for the same kinds of material and take notes on relevant statements. As soon as possible, rewrite your notes in full sentences.

Practicing the Skill

Decide whether each statement below is relevant or irrelevant to the following topic: the decline of the Roman Empire. Explain each answer.

1. During the A.D. 200s, Germanic peoples began to overrun the western half of the empire.
2. From A.D. 192 to A.D. 284, army legions installed 26 emperors, only to kill most of them off in rapid succession.
3. The Romans built aqueducts throughout Europe.
4. The Roman baths served as popular meeting places for social and business purposes.
5. Political instability led to economic decline.
6. Long after the collapse of the empire, Latin remained the written language of the Roman Catholic Church.
7. Corruption and disunity within the Roman Empire made it easier for external forces to overrun it.
8. Roman citizens had the duty to be ready for army service at any time.
9. As the empire grew, the rule limiting citizenship to members of the original peoples of Rome was changed.
10. The emperors of Rome became so weak that they were puppets of the army—a military that allowed men of German birth to become commanders.

Applying the Skill

Choose one of the following aspects of the Roman Empire: economy, daily life, public amusement, science and engineering, arts and literature. Using books and/or encyclopedias, find at least five pieces of relevant information on your chosen topic. List your sources for each piece of information.

For More Practice

Turn to the Skill Practice in the Chapter Review on page 181 for more practice in distinguishing between relevant and irrelevant information.

Critical Thinking SKILLS

TEACH

Relevant and Irrelevant Information Organize the class into three groups, and assign one of these topics to each group: the advantages or disadvantages of having a school sports team, the purpose of the student government, the need or lack of need for a school prom. Ask each group to write a paragraph of at least six sentences about the topic it has been assigned. Instruct them to include at least two irrelevant statements. When all the groups have completed the task, ask a representative of each group to read its paragraph, stopping briefly between sentences to allow the rest of the class to write down whether the information in each sentence was relevant or irrelevant. After each paragraph is read, go over the responses of the other class members. Then have students read the skill and complete the practice questions.

Additional Practice

Skill Reinforcement Activity 6

ANSWERS TO PRACTICING THE SKILL

1. relevant
2. relevant
3. irrelevant
4. irrelevant
5. relevant
6. irrelevant
7. relevant
8. irrelevant
9. irrelevant
10. relevant

Chapter 6 Review

GLENCOE TECHNOLOGY

VIDEODISC
Use MindJogger to review students' knowledge of the chapter.

MindJogger Videoquiz
Chapter 6
Disc 1 Side B

Also available in VHS.

Answers

Using Key Terms

1. g
2. i
3. f
4. a
5. d
6. j
7. b
8. c
9. e
10. h

Using Your History Journal

Remind students who was emperor in A.D. 130 (Hadrian). Suggest they use reference books to amplify their knowledge of Rome's domestic and foreign policies at that time.

Reviewing Facts

1. Rome and Carthage competed for control of trade and political power in the Mediterranean.
2. Rome ceased to be a republic and became an empire.
3. The *jus gentium* applied to noncitizens and was derived from the *jus civile*, code of law for Roman citizens.
4. used Roman engineering and architecture; staged Roman amusements
5. ordered new roads built, made inspection trips, named self head of religion practiced throughout empire

CHAPTER 6 REVIEW

Historical Significance

The Romans established a common culture among the diverse peoples of the Mediterranean world. Their legal system, forms of government, engineering feats, and arts formed the foundation of many provincial cities. Frequent civil wars triggered a chain of events that ultimately led to the Roman Empire's economic and political ruin.

The lasting legacies of the Roman Empire, however, are its Latin language, which provided the root of the Romance languages; its engineering skills; its transmission of Greek culture; and Christianity.

Using Key Terms

Write the key term that completes each sentence.

a. indemnity
b. bishop
c. plebeians
d. sect
e. inflation
f. aqueducts
g. republic
h. patricians
i. triumvirate
j. messiah
k. pope
l. consul
m. dictator

1. After years of rule by kings, the Romans declared their city-state a _____, a form of government in which people elect their leaders.
2. In 60 B.C. Pompey, Crassus, and Julius Caesar formed a _________, a group of three persons with equal power, to control the government.
3. Throughout the Roman Empire, Roman engineers built ________, or artificial channels for carrying water from one area to another.
4. After their defeat, the people of Carthage agreed to pay the Romans a huge _______, or payment for damages.
5. Early Christianity was thought of as a _______, or group, within Judaism.
6. Many Jews hoped for a ______, or savior, to deliver them from Roman rule.
7. A church official known as a _____ oversaw a diocese, interpreted Christian beliefs, and administered church affairs.
8. The majority of people in the Roman Republic were ______ —nonaristocratic landowners, merchants, shopkeepers, small farmers, and laborers.
9. During the period of economic decline, the Roman government's debasing of coinage sparked severe ______ —a rise in prices that reflected a decrease in the value of money.
10. Latin nobles called ______ drove out the Etruscans and changed Rome's form of government.

Using Your History Journal

Imagine that you are either a young Roman legionary stationed in a remote outpost of the empire in A.D. 130 or you are a friend of the legionary, awaiting his return to Rome. Write a letter describing what you have been doing in the past week.

Reviewing Facts

1. **Explain** what was the main source of conflict between Rome and Carthage.
2. **Describe** how Rome's political system changed when Augustus Caesar came to power.
3. **Explain** the difference between the *jus gentium* and the *jus civile.*
4. **Discuss** how Roman governors made provincial cities throughout the empire more like Rome.
5. **Tell** how Augustus strengthened the bonds between the city of Rome and provincial cities.

Critical Thinking

1. **Apply** How did the reforms introduced during Marius's rule hasten the end of the Roman Republic?
2. **Analyze** What evidence suggests that Roman society was more stable during the republic than during the time of the empire?
3. **Evaluate** In what ways did the Romans' treatment of the peoples they conquered differ from the ways in which other victors usually treated the peoples they conquered? How might Roman attitudes have strengthened the empire?

Critical Thinking

1. Marius instituted a professional army. Soldiers owed first allegiance to commanders who used the army to seize power. Perpetual instability resulted.
2. During the republic the family unit was stable, and people held similar values.
3. Romans treated conquered people better, gave citizenship to some, and built cities; winning provincial loyalty.
4. Unlike most migrant peoples from Asia Minor, the Etruscans did not speak an Indo-European language.

Geography in History

1. east
2. credited military victories to Christian God; gave Christians freedom of worship; resolved differences among Christian leaders; ordered churches constructed at Christian shrines
3. Rome

4. **Analyze** The vase shown here incorporates the Etruscan alphabet. Why have scholars been unable to decipher Etruscan words?

Geography in History

1. **Location** Refer to the map below. Which area (east or west) was more heavily influenced by Christianity by A.D. 200?
2. **Movement** How did Constantine encourage the spread of the Christian religion in the Roman Empire?
3. **Place** According to the map below, which city in western Europe had the largest concentration of Christians by A.D. 200?

The Spread of Christianity

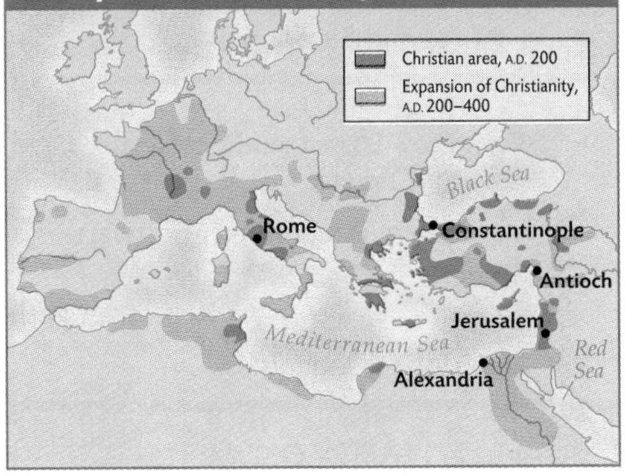

Understanding Themes

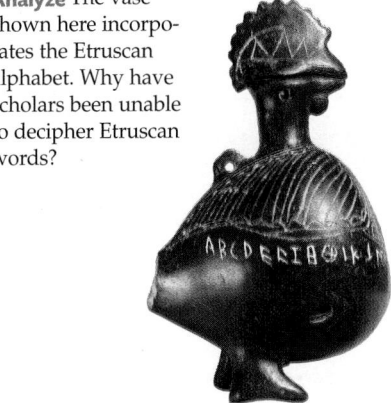

1. **Change** How did the Roman government change from the time of the Etruscans to Augustus Caesar?
2. **Conflict** Describe a conflict between nations that has occurred in the recent past and explain the ways in which it is similar to conflicts between the Romans and other peoples of the Mediterranean region.
3. **Cultural Diffusion** How might Roman roads have helped to foster cultural diffusion?
4. **Innovation** What was the basis of the religious controversy between Jesus' followers and some of the Jews in Palestine? How might this division have furthered Christianity's evolution as a separate religion?
5. **Change** Which half of the Roman Empire would have benefited most by becoming politically separate from the other? Why?

Linking Past and Present

United States government officials recently have proposed legislation to allow the President to veto parts of budget laws passed by Congress. Do you think the President should be granted this power? Why or why not? Use examples from Roman history to support your answer.

Skill Practice

Read the following paragraph of numbered sentences. For each sentence, determine whether or not it is relevant to this topic: the importance of the Italian Peninsula in ancient times. Explain each answer.

1. The Greeks were interested in colonizing Italy for several reasons, the most important of which was Italy's central location in the Mediterranean. 2. A narrow boot-shaped peninsula, Italy extends from Europe toward Africa, dividing the Mediterranean almost in half. 3. Thus Italy was ideally suited to be the center of trade among three continents.
4. Italy's rich soil and moist climate also attracted Greek colonists. 5. The silt washing down Italy's rivers, however, created mosquito-infested swamps at the mouths of rivers. 6. By the time Greek colonists arrived, many peoples inhabited Italy, including Umbrians, Latins, and Oscans.

Chapter 6 Review

Linking Past and Present

Students should show their understanding that giving the executive branch a line veto would take power over the budget process away from the legislative branch. Students should refer to the veto power as used in the Roman Republic.

Skill Practice

1. relevant (cause)
2. relevant (cause)
3. relevant (consequence)
4. relevant (cause)
5. irrelevant
6. irrelevant

Chapter Bonus Test Question

Ask students: According to French philosopher Blaise Pascal, who lived in the 1600s, "Cleopatra's nose, had it been shorter, the whole face of the world would have been changed." How is Pascal's statement connected with the events of this chapter? Do you agree with his point of view? *(Antony's marriage to Cleopatra triggered events that led to the end of the republic and the rise of the empire; answers will vary as to the effect of beauty on love and of love on politics.)*

Understanding Themes

1. **CHANGE** It changed from a republic with elected leaders to an empire headed by an absolute ruler.
2. **CONFLICT** Answers will vary.
3. **CULTURAL DIFFUSION** Ease of travel between Rome and the provinces facilitated trade and other contacts.
4. **INNOVATION** Many Jews rejected the idea that Jesus was the Messiah. The controversy forced Christian Jews to reach out to non-Jews.
5. **CHANGE** Political separation would have benefited the eastern half most because its Greek-speaking Christians did not accept the pope's authority.

Flowering of African Civilizations

CHAPTER RESOURCES

	Reproducible Resources	Multimedia Resources
Chapter Opener	Chapter Themes: Graphic Organizer 7 Historical Significance Chapter Activity 7	MindJogger Videoquiz
Chapter Enrichment	Vocabulary Activity 7* Time Line Activity 7 Mapping History Activity 7 History Simulation 7 Geography and History Activity 7 Source Reading 7 People in World History Profiles 11, 12 World Art and Music Activity 7 Enrichment Activity 7 Critical Thinking Activity 7 Skill Reinforcement Activity 7 Writer's Guidebook, Lesson 7 Performance Assessment Activity 7	Focus on World Art Print 12, Fang, Gabon. *Ngi Society Mask* World History and Art Transparency 8, *Gold Pendant Mask* Mapping History Overlay Transparency 7, *African Regions* Chapter Transparency 7 NGS PicturePack Transparencies: Physical Geography of the World, *Africa South of the Sahara* Vocabulary PuzzleMaker Software STV: World Geography, Vol. 2, Africa and Europe: *Africa*
Chapter Review/Reteaching	Reteaching Activity 7 Skill Reinforcement Activity 7 Spanish Chapter Summary 7	Chapter 7 Digest Audiocassette, Activity, Test* Vocabulary PuzzleMaker Software Student Self-Test and Review Software MindJogger Videoquiz
Chapter Evaluation/Testing	Performance Assessment Activity 7 Chapter 7 Test, Forms A and B	Testmaker

* *Also available in Spanish*

0:00 **OUT OF TIME?** Assign the Chapter 7 summary in the Unit 2 Digest on pages 236–239, and the Chapter 7 Audiocassettes.

Block Schedule

Block scheduling differs from traditional class scheduling in the amount of time allotted to each period. The extended time frame provided by block scheduling affords you the opportunity to implement a greater number of research-oriented and activity-intense projects to motivate and involve your students. Activities that are particularly suited to use within the block scheduling framework are identified throughout this chapter by the following designation.

KEY TO ABILITY LEVELS

Teaching strategies have been coded for varying learning styles and abilities.

- L1 **BASIC** activities for all students
- L2 **AVERAGE** activities for average to above-average students
- L3 **CHALLENGING** activities for above-average students
- LEP **LIMITED ENGLISH PROFICIENCY** activities

A complete, 1-page lesson plan is provided for each section in the *Reproducible Lesson Plans* booklet.

SECTION RESOURCES

Daily Objectives	Reproducible Resources	Multimedia Resources
Section 1 Early Africa Investigate what kinds of societies emerged in early Africa.	Reproducible Lesson Plan 7-1 Guided Reading Activity 7-1* Time Line Activity 7 Source Reading 7 Section Quiz 7-1*	Focus on World Art Print 12, Fang, Gabon. *Ngi Society Mask* Section Focus Transparency 7-1 Mapping History Overlay Transparency 7, *African Regions* Vocabulary PuzzleMaker Software Student Self-Test and Review Software Testmaker STV: World Geography, Vol. 2: Africa and Europe: *Africa*
Section 2 Kingdoms in West Africa Describe how trade was carried out in West Africa.	Reproducible Lesson Plan 7-2 Vocabulary Activity 7* Guided Reading Activity 7-2* Mapping History Activity 7 Geography and History Activity 7 Section Quiz 7-2*	Section Focus Transparency 7-2 Chapter Transparency 7 Student Self-Test and Review Software Testmaker
Section 3 African Trading Cities and States Discuss how areas in East, Central, and South Africa developed as a result of inland and overseas trade.	Reproducible Lesson Plan 7-3 Vocabulary Activity 7* Guided Reading Activity 7-3* Reteaching Activity 7 Enrichment Activity 7 Section Quiz 7-3* Performance Assessment Activity 7 Spanish Chapter Summary 7	Section Focus Transparency 7-3 Mapping History Overlay Transparency 7, *African Regions* Student Self-Test and Review Software Testmaker

* *Also available in Spanish*

Chapter Activities

Performance Assessment Activity

Creating a News Report Have students assume the roles of news reporters. They should create a fictitious news event set in a modern-day area once inhabited by early African civilizations. The task is then to create a short news segment of two to three minutes in which they inform the public of the significance and history of the area and how it relates to the event. The report may be submitted on audiotape or videotape, or as a written or oral presentation.

Possible Rubric Features

Accuracy of content information, clarity of presentation, appropriateness of inferences and connections

• *For an additional activity, refer to Activity 7 in the* Performance Assessment Strategies and Activities *booklet.*

ACTIVITY

From the Classroom of...

Umbisa Kendeli-Gusa
Mifflin International School
Columbus, OH

Contemporary Lifestyle of African Teenagers

Have students make a direct link with a school in Africa and communicate one-on-one with an African teenager. This can be facilitated through E-mail, or by calling an African embassy in Washington, D.C., which will provide the link between the schools in Africa and the United States. It is recommended that students communicate with the English-speaking countries south of the Sahara.

Using their knowledge from Chapter 7, have students ask their African counterparts to focus on the way life is now as compared to the way it was in the past. Students should investigate in detail the interaction between the church, parents, the government, and any other agencies that affect the lives of youth from early childhood through adolescence. Students may also wish to inquire about age sets.

Have students write to the local newspaper and share this experience and their new knowledge with the community at large.

MULTIPLE LEARNING STYLES

Verbal/Linguistic
Have students think up words associated with daily life in early African cultures, such as *grasslands, cattle, gods, spirits, family,* and *traditions*, and record their responses on the chalkboard. Each student should write a poem using words from the list.

Visual/Spatial
Students may choose one African culture that they studied and create drawings that focus on a specific art form or aspect of that culture. Bind the artwork together to create a book.

Kinesthetic
Challenge students to create a dance through which they can teach others about some aspect of African culture. Dancing groups may have a narrator who helps interpret the symbolic meaning of their dance steps.

Intrapersonal
Have students write several paragraphs describing how their life would be different if our society were organized on matrilineal lines and stating whether they would prefer this type of social organization.

Additional Resources

TEACHER'S CORNER

NATIONAL GEOGRAPHIC SOCIETY

INDEX TO NATIONAL GEOGRAPHIC MAGAZINE

The following articles may be used for research relating to this chapter:

- "The Cruelest Commerce: African Slave Trade," by Colin Palmer, September 1992.

NATIONAL GEOGRAPHIC SOCIETY PRODUCTS AVAILABLE FROM GLENCOE

To order the following products for use with this chapter, contact your local Glencoe sales representative or call Glencoe at 1-800-368-7344:

VIDEODISC
- STV: World Geography, Vol. 2: Africa and Europe

NGS PICTUREPACK TRANSPARENCIES
- Physical Geography of the World

ADDITIONAL NATIONAL GEOGRAPHIC SOCIETY PRODUCTS

To order the following products for use with this chapter, call National Geographic Society at 1-800-368-2728:

- *Ancient Cities, A Geographic Perspective,* "Cities of Africa." (Filmstrip)
- *Ancient Civilizations,* "Africa." (Filmstrip)

Bibliography

Literature About the Period

Davidson, Basil. ***African Civilization Revisited.*** Trenton: Africa World Press, 1991. Presents the story of Africa through a collection of historic chronicles and records.

Readings for the Student

McKissack, Patricia and Fredrick. ***The Royal Kingdoms of Ghana, Mali, and Songhay.*** New York: Henry Holt, 1994. Examines the civilizations of the Western Sudan.

Shinnie, Margaret. ***Ancient African Kingdoms.*** New York, St. Martin's Press, 1966. Combines archaeological and historical insights into the history of African states.

Readings for the Teacher

Davidson, Basil. ***African Kingdoms.*** New York, Time-Life Books, 1971. Reevaluation of the achievements of African civilizations from ancient Egypt through A.D. 1500.

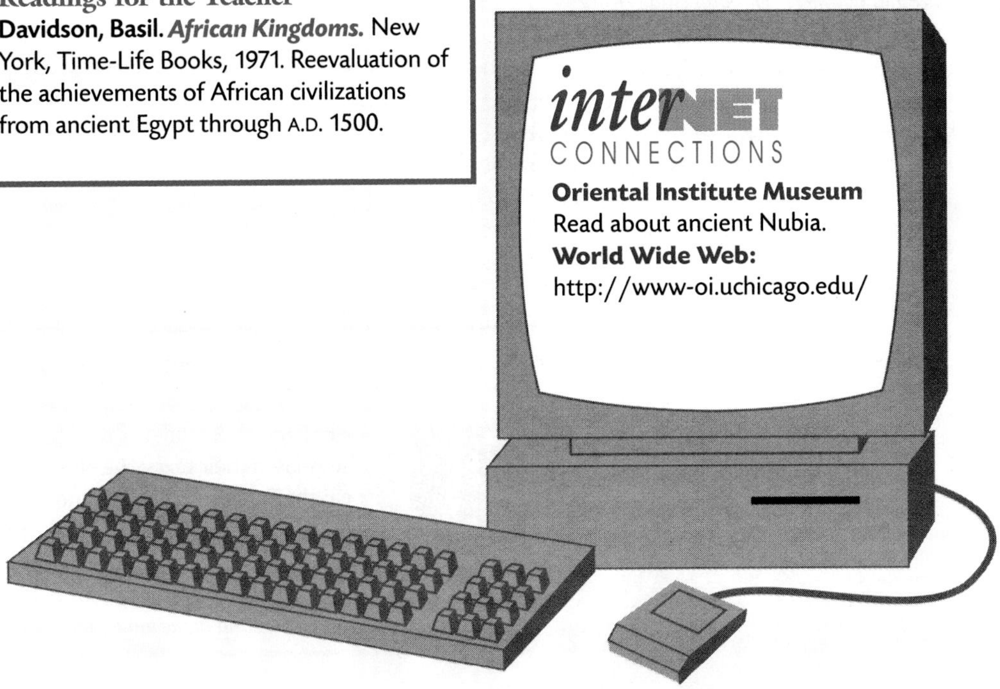
interNET
CONNECTIONS
Oriental Institute Museum
Read about ancient Nubia.
World Wide Web:
http://www-oi.uchicago.edu/

Introducing Chapter 7

CHAPTER THEMES

Chapter Themes are listed by section on this chapter opening page of the Student Edition. A corresponding theme-based activity is available under "TEACH," and a theme-based question is asked in the Section and Chapter Reviews.

The Storyteller

Historical Setting That the legend of Ogun is still told at festivals in West Africa illustrates how important the knowledge of iron technology was to African peoples. Both the Egyptians and the Kushites knew how to make iron, but they did little with the knowledge for many years. Only when the Kushites were attacked by the Assyrians, who were using superior iron weapons, did the Kushites begin making iron tools and weapons.

Historical Significance

Answers: *They traded their plentiful supplies of salt, gold, copper, iron ore, and ivory to obtain resources and goods they did not have. Through trade traffic, Islamic culture spread through much of Africa.*

Chapter 7

1500 B.C.–A.D. 1500

Flowering of African Civilizations

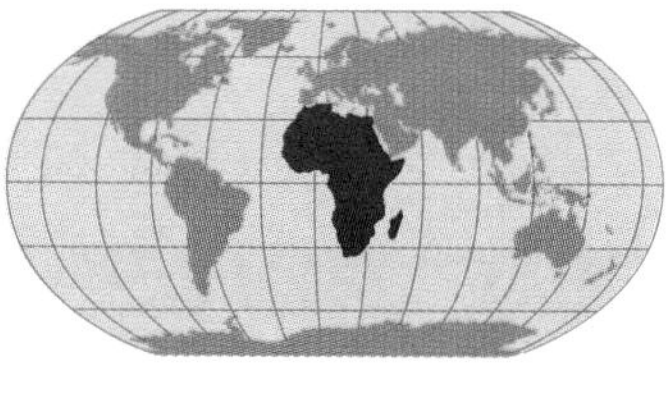

Chapter Themes

- **Movement** Migrations of Bantu-speaking people influence Africa's cultural development. *Section 1*
- **Cultural Diffusion** Africa's trade contacts with Europe and Asia affect African cultures. *Section 2*
- **Innovation** East African city-states develop a new culture based on African and Arab cultures. *Section 3*

The Storyteller

The Yoruba—West Africans living by the Niger River—gather each winter to hear storytellers recount a legend that tells of how their ancestors struggled to clear their land with tools made of wood and soft metal. Even orishas, *or gods, could not cut through vines or trees with these tools until the god Ogun appeared, carrying his bush knife.*

"He slashed through the heavy vines, felled the trees and cleared the forest from the land.... So [the people] made [Ogun] their ruler.... He built forges for them and showed them how to make spears, knives, hoes, and swords."

Legends such as this describe experiences that early people valued most. Early Africans built civilizations that have left rich traditions for today's peoples.

Historical Significance

How did early Africans use the natural resources of their environment to develop trade networks? What impact did their cultures have on other lands?

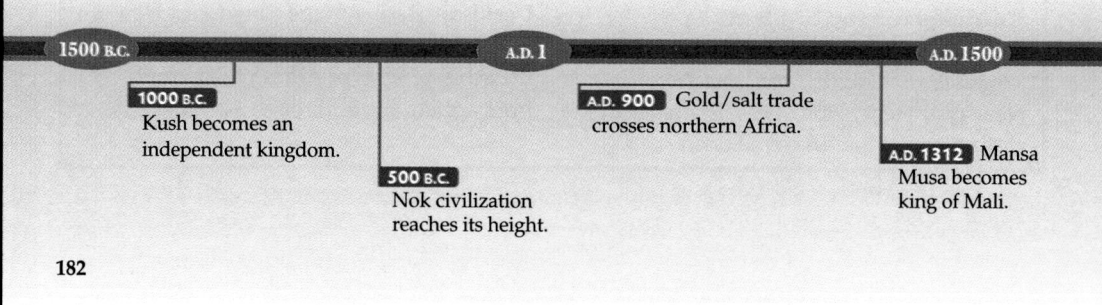

1500 B.C. — A.D. 1 — A.D. 1500

- **1000 B.C.** Kush becomes an independent kingdom.
- **500 B.C.** Nok civilization reaches its height.
- **A.D. 900** Gold/salt trade crosses northern Africa.
- **A.D. 1312** Mansa Musa becomes king of Mali.

182

GEOGRAPHY CONNECTION

Location Ask students to locate the following physical features on a wall map or in the Atlas in their texts: the Nile, Niger, Senegal, Zambezi, and Limpopo Rivers; the Red Sea; the Sahara; the Sahel; and the Great Rift Valley. Why didn't Africa's rivers provide easy routes into and out of the interior? *(Many contain rapids and great waterfalls.)* Lead students to notice how few natural harbors are found on the African continent. Discuss the significance of this lack of harbors. *(The lack of protected harbors and navigable rivers would tend to isolate cultures and make land transport the major access route into the interior of the continent.)*

History & Art Prehistoric cave art from Tassili N'Ajjer Plateau, Algeria

Your History Journal

Draw an outline map of Africa. Place the kingdoms of Kush, Axum, Nok, Ghana, Mali, Songhai, and Karanga on the map along with the dates when each kingdom existed.

EXTRA CREDIT PROJECT

Investigate Ask students to select one culture on the African continent to research and investigate further. Specifically, have them find out in what ways the culture's heritage has survived to the present. Have them present their findings to the class, using photographs or other visual aids to accompany their reports.

Introducing Chapter 7

History & Art An early African people left a record of Stone Age life in the frescoes they carved and painted on rock walls at Tassili N'Ajjer Plateau in Algeria. These paintings were preserved by the dry air and the isolation of the plateau. What do these paintings reveal about conditions in the Sahara at the dawn of African culture? *(During this period, the Saharan region was a fertile land with abundant wildlife.)*

Performance Assessment

Refer to the activity on page 182C of the Planning Guide.

For an additional activity, refer to Activity 7 in the *Performance Assessment Strategies and Activities* booklet.

Using Your History Journal

Have students name each civilization and share what they already know about it. Maps should include a title and legend. Students may use their maps to trace the major African trade routes.

GLENCOE TECHNOLOGY

VIDEODISC

Use MindJogger to preview chapter content.

MindJogger Videoquiz

Chapter 7
Disc 1 Side B

Also available in VHS.

2000 B.C. — 1000 B.C. — A.D. 1 — A.D. 1000

c. 750 B.C. Kushite kings rule over Egypt.

c. 250 B.C. Merchants from Egypt, Rome, Persia, and India trade with Axum.

A.D. 330 Christianity becomes Axum's official religion.

Chapter 7 Section 1

SECTION THEME

▸ **Movement** Migrations of Bantu-speaking people influence Africa's cultural development.

Find Out

Answer: *trading societies and close-knit agricultural communities with a wide variety of religious customs and traditions*

FOCUS

Section Objective

Investigate what kinds of societies emerged in early Africa.

BELLRINGER Motivational Activity

Before taking roll at the beginning of the class period, project Section Focus Transparency 7-1 and have students answer the activity questions. Discuss students' responses.

This activity is also available as a blackline master.

Vocabulary Pre-check

Use the Vocabulary PuzzleMaker to create a puzzle that reinforces vocabulary terms in this section. **L1**

Section 1

Early Africa

▸ **Terms to Define**
oral tradition, plateau, savanna, matrilineal, age set

▸ **People to Meet**
Piankhi, Ezana, the Nok

▸ **Places to Locate**
Nubia, Kush, Axum

Find Out What kinds of societies emerged in early Africa?

The Storyteller

African oral tradition contained stories full of wisdom, to be enjoyed by all. For example, where did death come from? A myth from Madagascar gave this answer. One day God asked the first couple what kind of death they wanted, one like that of the moon, or that of the banana? The couple was puzzled. God explained: The banana creates young plants to take its place, but the moon itself comes back to life every month. After consideration, the couple prayed for children, because without children they would be lonely, would have to do all the work, and would have no one to provide for. Since that time, human life is short on this earth.

—freely adapted from *The Humanistic Tradition,* Gloria K. Fiero, 1992

Mount Kilimanjaro

Africa's earliest civilizations left few written records of their existence. It was through **oral traditions**—legends and history passed by word of mouth from one generation to another—that early African peoples communicated knowledge about their culture. Thus, archaeologists and historians have had to rely on legends and artifacts to learn about the culture of African civilizations between 1100 B.C. and A.D. 1500.

Archaeologists have discovered that early African cultures developed technologies and trade based on regional natural resources. Civilizations rose and declined, and were influenced by the movement of people and by the way in which natural resources were developed.

Geography and Environment

Africa's geography and climate are a study in contrasts. Africa, the world's second-largest continent, is three times larger than the United States. Within its huge expanse lie desolate deserts, lofty mountains, rolling grasslands, and fertile river valleys.

Regions of Africa

The African continent can be divided into two large regions—North Africa, the region along the Mediterranean Sea; and sub-Saharan Africa, the vast area south of the Sahara. North Africa, bordering the Mediterranean Sea, has mild temperatures and frequent rainfall. In contrast, the area south of this thin green belt is a vast expanse of sand: the Sahara, the world's largest desert. Extending across the continent, the Sahara is a region of shifting dunes and jagged rock piles.

African Landscapes

The sub-Saharan region, which embraces all of the continent that lies south of the Sahara, features

SECTION RESOURCES

Reproducible Masters
- Reproducible Lesson Plan 7-1
- Guided Reading Activity 7-1
- Time Line Activity 7
- Source Reading 7
- Section Quiz 7-1

Transparencies
- Section Focus Transparency 7-1
- Mapping History Overlay Transparency 7, *African Regions*

Multimedia
- Focus on World Art Print 12
- Vocabulary PuzzleMaker Software
- Student Self-Test and Review Software
- Testmaker
- STV: World Geography

History & Art Wall painting from the Metropolitan Museum of Art, New York City, New York. **Four late Bronze Age Nubian princes offer rings and gold to an Egyptian ruler.** *What happened to the Nubian River civilization after 2000 B.C.?*

a great central plateau—a relatively high, flat area known as the Sahel. This region receives moderate rainfall to sustain the savannas, or treeless grasslands, that cover the plateau. The sub-Saharan savannas constitute about 40 percent of Africa's land area.

On the eastern edge of the Sahel, the land splits into a deep crack known as the Great Rift Valley. It extends 40 miles (65 km) in width and 2,000 feet (610 m) in depth. The Great Rift Valley runs 3,000 miles (4,827 km) from the Red Sea in the north all the way to South Africa. Rising above the plateau east of the valley are two mountain peaks—Mount Kenya and Mount Kilimanjaro. Kilimanjaro is Africa's highest mountain, with an elevation of 19,340 feet (5,895 m).

In West Africa, the Sahel rises above a narrow coastal plain that has a relatively unbroken coastline. The major rivers that do flow through the coastal plain—the Niger and the Zaire (Congo)—are navigable only for short distances. The few natural harbors and limited river travel isolated early African civilizations and made foreign invasions difficult in some areas.

Near the Equator is a lush tropical rain forest so thick that sunlight cannot penetrate to the forest floor. Although the climate of the rain forest is hot and humid, 1,500 miles (2,413 km) farther south the land again turns into a desert. Still farther south, the desert gives way to a cool, fertile highland in the present-day country of South Africa.

The African continent has provided rich resources for its people. Early cultures developed where rainfall was plentiful, or near lakes or along rivers like the Nile.

Nubia and Kush

By 3000 B.C., a people called the Nubians established a kingdom called **Nubia** in the southern part of the Nile River valley in present-day Sudan. The Nubian people mastered the bow and arrow and became warriors. With their military skills, they conquered smaller neighboring territories in the Nile Valley.

The Nubians maintained close contacts with Egypt to the north. Archaeologists have uncovered the tombs of Nubian kings, which contained precious stones, gold, jewelry, and pottery. These are as ornate as those found in Egypt from the same period. Some scholars believe that political ideas, such as monarchy, and various objects, like boats and eating utensils, were really the creations of the Nubians and later were passed on to the Egyptians.

By 2000 B.C., the Nubian river civilization had developed into the kingdom of **Kush**. After defeat in warfare, Kush was under Egyptian rule for 500 years. Egyptian pharaohs stationed soldiers in Kush to collect duties on goods moving through the region.

The people of Kush used their location along the Upper Nile River to develop a strong trade

COOPERATIVE LEARNING ACTIVITY

Archaeology Organize the class into groups of three to four students. Have each group select one culture covered in this section–Kush, Axum, Nok, or Bantu–for further study. Each group should work together to write a journal of an imaginary archaeological expedition that has uncovered artifacts from the selected culture. Each member of the group should participate in collecting and recording the information, drawing pictures of the artifacts, and drawing the location of the finds on maps of the site. **L2**

Chapter 7
Section 1

TEACH

Guided Practice

THEME **Movement**

Ask students what the main reason for the Bantu migration was. *(population increase, leading to a shortage of arable land)* Discuss with students how this reason for moving compares with other reasons. Point out that an inability to provide for themselves and their families, whether due to natural disaster, climate changes, or lack of local resources, is a common reason people migrate.

Focus on World Art Print 12

Mapping History Overlay Transparency 7

History & Art Egyptian civilization obtained luxury items such as gold, ivory, and ebony as tribute from Nubia to the south.

Answer to Caption: *After 2000 B.C. the Nubian River civilization developed into the kingdom of Kush.*

NATIONAL GEOGRAPHIC SOCIETY

VIDEODISC

STV: World Geography, Vol 2: Africa and Europe

Side One, Frames 00001-49739

Title: *Africa*

Subject: Geographic contrasts and how people and animals have affected the natural environment of Africa

Ask: What continues to happen geologically in the Great Rift Valley? *(volcanic activity)*

Independent Practice

Guided Reading Activity 7-1 **L1**

Time Line Activity 7

Source Reading 7

Geography: Movement Have students imagine that they are West African farmers who moved during the Bantu migrations to the grassland plateau around Lake Chad. Have them write a story about their experiences. Ask them what might have affected them the most—meeting new cultures or adapting to a new environment. **L3**

Global Gourmet

Tropical Africa None of the food crops that today form the staple food supply of the forest regions of Africa was originally native to the continent. Bananas and yams were brought to Africa from Indonesia. Peanuts, maize, and cassava were introduced by Europeans from the Americas. Fou-fou, served in many African countries, is made from cassava root, yams, and rice or cornmeal. It has the consistency of pudding and is served as a main dish.

Visualizing History The kingdom of Axum was located in the northern part of modern Ethiopia. Emperor Haile Selassie was a member of Ethiopia's Amhara dynasty. Generations of this proud people are bound together by their Christian faith and traditional ways of life.

Answer to Caption: *When King Ezana of Axum converted to Christianity during the A.D. 300s, it became a state religion.*

economy. The Kushite cities of Napata and Meroë stood where trade caravans crossed the Nile, bringing gold, elephant tusks, and timber from the African interior. This strategic location brought wealth to the merchants and kings of Kush.

Around 1000 B.C. Kush broke away from Egypt and became politically independent. In time Kush grew strong enough that a Kushite king named **Piankhi** (pee•AHNK•hee) in 724 B.C. led a powerful army from Kush into Egypt and defeated the Egyptians. After this victory, Kushite kings ruled over both Egypt and Kush from their capital at Napata. The city boasted white sandstone temples, monuments, and pyramids fashioned in styles similar to those of the Egyptians.

In 671 B.C. the Assyrians invaded Egypt, easily defeating the Kushites, whose bronze weapons were no match against Assyrian iron swords. The Kushites were forced to leave Egypt and return to their home territory at the bend of the Upper Nile. In spite of their defeat, the Kushites learned from their enemies the technology of making iron. They built a new capital at Meroë that became a major center for iron production. Kush merchants traded iron, leopard skins, and ebony for goods from the Mediterranean and the Red Sea regions. They also conducted business throughout the Indian Ocean area. Meroë's merchants used their wealth to construct fine houses built around a central courtyard and public baths modeled after ones they had seen in Rome.

For about 150 years, the Kushite kingdom thrived. Then a new power—**Axum**, a kingdom located near the Red Sea—invaded Kush and ended Kushite domination of northeastern Africa.

Axum

Because of its location along the Red Sea, Axum also emerged as a trading power. During the 200s B.C., merchants from Egypt, Greece, Rome, Persia, and India sent ships laden with cotton cloth, brass, copper, and olive oil to Axum's main seaport at Adulis. Traders exchanged their goods for cargoes of ivory that the people of Axum hauled from Africa's interior.

Through trade Axum absorbed many elements of Roman culture, including a new religion:

Visualizing History **Church of St. Mary of Zion. According to tradition, this church contains the original tablets of Moses, brought by King Menelik I to Axum. Emperor Haile Selassie I of Ethiopia built a new church of the same name near the old one in 1965.** *How did Christianity come to Axum about A.D. 330?*

MEETING SPECIAL NEEDS ACTIVITY

Study Strategy Have students review the section and make note of natural resources or trade goods and locations where they can be found. Have students make a chart listing the name of the natural resource, its location(s), and the people who made use of the resource. They may use graphic symbols to represent the resources. **L1**

Christianity. A remarkable event led to the conversion of Axum's King **Ezana** to Christianity. Shipwrecked off the coast of Ethiopia, two Christians from Syria were picked up and brought to King Ezana's court, where they lived for several years. The young men convinced Ezana that he should become a Christian. About A.D. 330 the king made Christianity the official religion in Axum. During this time, Christianity also became dominant in other areas of northeastern Africa—Kush and Egypt.

Axum began its decline when Muslim merchants and soldiers from Arabia raided Axum's trading ships and ports in the A.D. 600s. As a result, Axum lost much of its coastal territory and trade. Confined to the remote interior of East Africa, the rulers of Axum set up a Christian kingdom that became known as Ethiopia.

Kingdoms of Kush and Axum

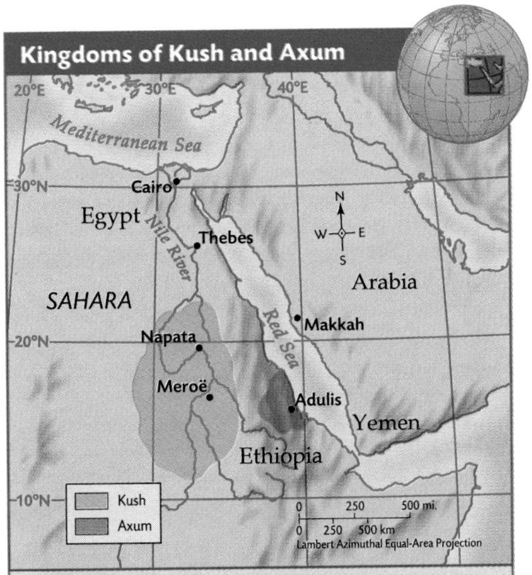

Map Study The kingdoms of Kush and Axum developed along the Nile River and the Red Sea.
Location Because of its location, Axum was influenced by merchants and traders from what areas of the world?

Sub-Saharan Africa

Between 700 B.C. and 200 B.C., during Axum's rise to power, a West African culture called **the Nok** had already established itself in the fertile Niger and Benue River valleys. In the 1940s archaeologists working in present-day central Nigeria found terra-cotta, or baked clay, figurines that provided evidence of the Nok culture. Working in the Nok sites and other areas of West Africa, archaeologists also unearthed iron hoes and ax-heads. This latter discovery provided evidence that metal production had enabled sub-Saharan cultures to farm their land more effectively.

As West African farmers used their iron tools to produce more food, the population increased. In time, arable land became scarce, causing widespread food shortages. Small groups of Africans began to migrate from West Africa to less populated areas. Other groups followed. Over about a thousand years a great migration took place.

Bantu Migrations

Historians call this mass movement the Bantu migrations because descendants of the people who migrated into central, eastern, and southern parts of the continent share elements of a language known as Bantu.

The Bantu migrations did not follow a single pattern. Some villagers followed the Niger or other rivers, settling in one spot to farm for a few years and moving on as the soil became less fertile. Other groups penetrated the rain forests and grew crops along the riverbanks. Still others moved to the highland savannas of East Africa and raised cattle. Groups that settled on the eastern coastal plain grew new crops, such as bananas and yams that had been brought to East Africa by traders from Southeast Asia.

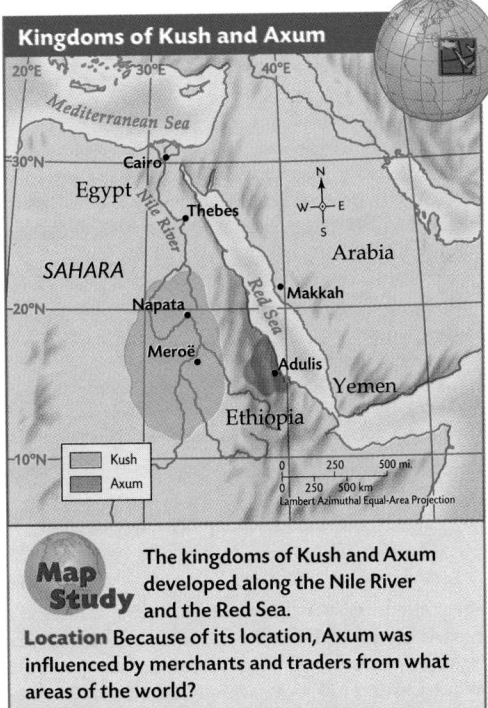

As people pushed into new areas, they met other African groups that joined the migrants and adopted their ways of life. In time, Bantu-speaking peoples became the dominant group of sub-Saharan Africa.

Village Life

Africans who spoke Bantu languages became divided into thousands of ethnic groups, each with its own religious beliefs, marriage and family customs, and traditions. Ethnic groups living around A.D. 1000 formed close-knit communities where most families were organized into large households that included descendants of one set of grandparents.

Many villages were **matrilineal** societies in which villagers traced their descent through mothers rather than through fathers. However, when a girl married, she became a member of her husband's family. To compensate the bride's family for the loss of a member, the husband's family gave the bride's family gifts of iron tools, goats, or cloth.

Even before marriage, specific jobs were assigned to groups of males and females of a similar

Chapter 7 Section 1

Map Study

Answer

Egypt, Greece, Rome, Persia, India, Arabia, and the African interior

Map Skills Practice

Reading a Map Where was Meroë located in relation to Thebes? With respect to Axum? *(south of Thebes; west of Axum)*

Linking Past and Present

Mancala Anthropologists consider *mancala* the world's oldest game. It was played in ancient Egypt at least 3,000 years ago. The name means "to transfer" in Arabic, which is exactly how the game is played: Players move game pieces from one bin to another. Versions of the game are played in nearly every African country.

you don't say...

Swahili is a Bantu language originally spoken on the east coast of Africa. The word comes from an Arabic word meaning "coast." It is the only Bantu language with a written literature. The name "Uhura," a character from the original Star Trek series, comes from the Swahili word *uhuru*, meaning "freedom."

MAKING CONNECTIONS ACTIVITY

Geology When the first reliable world maps were made, several scientists noted the remarkable fit between the west coast of Africa and the east coast of South America. The suggestion was made that the two continents might once have been joined but had broken apart and moved to their present locations. Guide students to discover this for themselves by taking an outline map of the world, cutting out the continents, and fitting them together like a jigsaw puzzle. Then, by researching African and South American landforms, fossils, and natural resources, have students present evidence other than shapes of the continents that might confirm the idea that the continents were once joined. **L2**

Chapter 7 *Flowering of African Civilizations* 187

Chapter 7 Section 1

ASSESS

Check for Understanding

Assign Section 1 Review as homework or as an in-class activity.

Use Student Self-Test and Review Software to review Section 1.

Evaluate

Section Quiz 7-1

Use the Testmaker to create a customized quiz for Section 1.

Reteach

Distribute outline maps of Africa. Have students indicate the name, dates, and approximate location of the following: the kingdoms of Kush and Axum, Nok culture, and the Bantu-speaking peoples. Students may use the text or historical atlases.

Enrich

Have students read traditional African folktales. Have them work in groups of three or four to prepare an oral reading or dramatization of a tale they have read.

CLOSE

Have students create posters illustrating what they have learned about early African civilizations and ways of life. Display on a bulletin board.

AROUND THE WORLD — Rebuilding of the Kremlin

Moscow, A.D. 1340

Many medieval Russian cities were built around a kremlin, or fortress, surrounded by a wall and a moat. The Moscow Kremlin originally was built of wood in A.D. 1156. In the A.D. 1300s it was rebuilt in brick. It is triangular in shape and has four gateways. Its back gate conceals a secret passage to the Moscow River. Italian architects designed some of the Kremlin's impressive towers and cathedrals in the late A.D. 1400s.

age, called age sets. Boys younger than 10 or 12 herded cattle; girls of the same age helped their mothers plant as well as tend and harvest crops. At about 12 years old, boys and girls took part in ceremonies initiating them into adulthood. A boy remained with his age set throughout his life. After marriage, a girl joined an age set in her husband's village.

Religious Beliefs

To most Africans, marriage customs and all other social laws and traditions were made by a single supreme god who created and ruled an orderly universe. The god rewarded those who followed social rules with abundant harvests and the birth of healthy children, and punished those who violated tradition with accidents, crop failures, or illness.

Beneath the supreme god were many lesser deities who influenced the daily affairs of men and women. These deities were present in natural phenomena such as storms, mountains, and trees. Many Africans also believed that spirits of dead ancestors lived among the people of the village and guided their destiny.

The religious beliefs and family loyalties of most Africans maintained stability and support within villages. Most communities expected their members to obey the social rules they believed to have come from the supreme god.

Although African communities relied heavily on religious and family traditions to maintain a stable social structure, outside influences through trade and learning still affected them. North Africans absorbed influences from the Arab world, whereas sub-Saharan people adapted to Persian, Indian, and later, European influences. From these outsiders, African communities adopted many new customs, ideas, and languages.

The Arts

Various arts developed in early sub-Saharan Africa. Sculpture was an important art form. African sculpture included figures, masks, decorated boxes, and objects for ceremonial and everyday use. Most of these items were made of wood, bronze, ivory, or baked clay. The wearing of masks at ceremonial dances symbolized the link between the living and the dead. Those wearing the masks and performing the dances called upon ancestral spirits to guide the community.

Music rich in rhythm was interwoven with the fabric of everyday African life. It included choral singing, music performed at royal courts, and songs and dances for ceremonies. In villages, where many activities were performed by groups, music often provided the motivation and rhythm for various tasks, such as digging ditches or pounding grain. African musicians used a variety of drums as well as harps, flutes, pipes, horns, and xylophones.

Early sub-Saharan Africa excelled in oral literature passed down from one generation to another. The stories included histories, fables, and proverbs. Oral literature not only recorded the past but also taught traditions and values.

SECTION 1 REVIEW

Recall

1. **Define** oral tradition, plateau, savanna, matrilineal, age set.
2. **Identify** Sahel, Nubia, Kush, Piankhi, Axum, Ezana, the Nok, Bantu.
3. **Locate** the Nile River valley on the map on page 187. Why did the Nubians settle in the Upper Nile Valley?

Critical Thinking

4. **Applying Information** Explain how Mediterranean trade influenced the economy of the kingdom of Axum.

Understanding Themes

5. **Movement** How does the Bantu migration in early sub-Saharan Africa contrast with the Aryan migration in early South Asia?

SECTION 1 REVIEW ANSWERS

1. All vocabulary words are defined in the Glossary.
2. Sahel, 185; Nubia, 185; Kush, 185; Piankhi, 186; Axum, 186; Ezana, 187; the Nok, 187; Bantu, 187
3. The Nile provided water for crops, as well as a means of transportation.
4. Mediterranean trade brought many resources and manufactured goods to Axum and stimulated the local production of ivory.
5. **MOVEMENT** Both migrations took place over long periods. The Bantu migration was peaceful, whereas the Aryan one was the result of conquest. Both the Aryan and Bantu languages and customs blended with those of native peoples.

A.D. 300 — A.D. 700 — A.D. 1100 — A.D. 1500

A.D. 300 Ghana begins to build a trading empire.

c. A.D. 1275 Mali conquers surrounding territory.

A.D. 1493 Askia Muhammad begins rule in Songhai.

Section 2

Kingdoms in West Africa

Setting the Scene

- **Terms to Define**
  monotheism, ghana, mosque
- **People to Meet**
  Sundiata Keita, Mansa Musa, Askia Muhammad
- **Places to Locate**
  Ghana, Mali, Timbuktu, Songhai

Find Out How was trade carried out in West Africa?

The Storyteller

The poets of Mali preserved the history of their people. Hear one speak: "I teach kings the history of their ancestors so that the lives of the ancients might serve them as an example, for the world is old, but the future springs from the past. My word is pure and free of all untruth.... Listen to my word, you who want to know, by my mouth, you will learn the history of Mali. By my mouth you will get to know the story of the ancestor of great Mali, the story of him who ... surpassed even Alexander the Great.... Whoever knows the history of a country can read its future."

—from *Sundiata: An Epic of Old Mali* in *The Humanistic Tradition*, Gloria K. Fiero, 1992

Horn player, Benin

Sub-Saharan Africa provided rich natural resources for the early kingdoms of West Africa. Africans living in this area between A.D. 300 and A.D. 1500 mined gold and other mineral resources found in the region. An active trade developed between them and peoples outside the region who practiced a religion called Islam. Islam preached **monotheism**, or the belief in one God, and spread throughout the Middle East, North Africa, and Spain during the A.D. 600s and A.D. 700s. Through their trade contacts with Muslims, the followers of Islam, African cultures gradually adopted Islamic cultural elements such as language and religion.

Kingdom of Ghana

The kingdom of **Ghana** became one of the richest trading civilizations in sub-Saharan Africa due to its location midway between Saharan salt mines and tropical gold mines. Between A.D. 300 and A.D. 1200 the kings of Ghana controlled a trading empire that stretched more than 100,000 square miles (260,000 sq. km). They prospered from the taxes they imposed on goods that entered or left their kingdom. Because the **ghana**, or king, ruled such a vast region, the land became known by the name of its ruler—Ghana.

There was two-way traffic by caravan between cities in North Africa and Ghana. Muslim traders from North Africa sent caravans loaded with cloth, metalware, swords, and salt across the western Sahara to northern settlements in Ghana. Large caravans from Ghana traveled north to Morocco, bringing kola nuts and farming produce. Ghanaian gold was traded for Saharan salt brought by Muslim traders.

Salt was an important trade item for the people of Ghana. They needed salt to preserve and flavor their foods. Using plentiful supplies of gold as a

SECTION THEME

- **Cultural Diffusion** Africa's trade contacts with Europe and Asia affect African cultures.

Find Out

Answer: *There was two-way traffic overland by caravan between North Africa and the West African trading kingdoms. Gold was used as a medium of exchange.*

FOCUS

Section Objective

Describe how trade was carried out in West Africa.

BELLRINGER Motivational Activity

Before taking roll at the beginning of the class period, project Section Focus Transparency 7-2 and have students answer the activity questions. Discuss students' responses.

This activity is also available as a blackline master.

Vocabulary Pre-check

Use Vocabulary Activity 7 to introduce vocabulary terms. **L1 LEP**

SECTION RESOURCES

Reproducible Masters
- Reproducible Lesson Plan 7-2
- Vocabulary Activity 7
- Guided Reading Activity 7-2
- Mapping History Activity 7
- Geography and History Activity 7
- Section Quiz 7-2

Transparencies
- Section Focus Transparency 7-2
- Chapter Transparency 7

Multimedia
- Student Self-Test and Review Software
- Testmaker

Chapter 7
Section 2

TEACH

Guided Practice

THEME Cultural Diffusion

Develop a working definition of the term *cultural diffusion* by asking students to think of ways they have changed as a result of contact with other persons or groups. *(the transfer of religion, customs, traditions, arts, and language from one people to another)* How did trade contacts with Arabs affect the development of African cultures? *(The Arabs brought with them the religion of Islam, written language, and other elements of Islamic culture that were adopted by West Africans.)* **L1 LEP**

Economics List the products the West Africans exchanged for Arab goods. *(gold, kola nuts, and farm produce)* Ask what Arab goods they chiefly traded for. *(cloth, metalware, swords, salt)* Challenge students to name items people use today that come from Africa. *(gold, diamonds for jewelry, agricultural products such as cocoa and coffee, petroleum, and carvings)* Discuss ways early and modern African trading patterns are similar. *(Africans still trade precious metals and agricultural products for items they need.)* **L3**

Chapter Transparency 7

Who?What?Where?When?

The Silent Trade The trade exchange described by Masudi is also known as "the silent trade." It has been described by other writers, including Herodotus, as the method often used by peoples who have no common language.

medium of exchange, Ghanaian merchants traded the precious metal for salt and other goods from Morocco and Spain.

Masudi, a Muslim traveler, writing about A.D. 950, described how trade was conducted:

> "The merchants ... place their wares and cloth on the ground and then depart, and so the people of [Ghana] come bearing gold which they leave beside the merchandise and then depart. The owners of the merchandise then return, and if they are satisfied with what they have found, they take it. If not, they go away again, and the people of [Ghana] return and add to the price until the bargain is concluded."

Ghana reached the height of its economic and political power as a trading kingdom in the A.D. 800s and A.D. 900s. The salt and gold trade moving through Ghana brought Islamic ideas and customs to the kingdom. Muslim influence increased as Muslims held court positions, and many Ghanaians converted to Islam.

At the end of the A.D. 1000s, an attack on the Ghanaian trade centers by the Almoravids, a Muslim group from North Africa, led to the eventual decline of Ghana as a prosperous kingdom. Groups of Ghanaians broke away to form Islamic communities that developed into many small independent states.

Footnotes to History

Golden Monarchs Ghana's rulers became very wealthy from the taxes they imposed on the gold and salt trade. They wore elaborate gold headdresses and adorned themselves with jewelry. One ruler's dogs even wore collars and bells made of silver and gold.

Images of the Times

Africa's Religious Heritage

Religion played a central role in the development of African cultures. Islam became the dominant religion in the north.

The Great Mosque at Timbuktu
Founded around A.D. 1100, the city of Timbuktu became a major center of trade and site of an important Islamic school.

Altar of the Hand, Benin
Beginning in the A.D. 1200s the kingdom of Benin emerged as a wealthy trading state. The *oba*, or king, became the political, economic, and spiritual leader of the people.

190

Images of the Times **Africa's Religious Heritage**

Africa's indigenous religious beliefs were not universal but ethnic in scope. Thus, each ethnic group had its own name for the supreme being, its own account of the creation and the origin of death, and its own magic, initiation rites, and rituals. Nearly all Africans, however, believed in a supreme being that was the origin of all things and presided over a realm of lesser beings and a host of animate and inanimate forces. These religious beliefs and practices permeated every phase of life on the African continent.

Kingdom of Mali

Mali, one of the small states to break away from Ghana, became a powerful kingdom that eventually ruled much of West Africa. The word *Mali* means "where the king resides" and is an appropriate name for a kingdom that gained much of its power and influence from its kings. **Sundiata Keita**, one of Mali's early kings, defeated his leading rival in A.D. 1235 and began to conquer surrounding territories. By the late A.D. 1200s, Mali's territory included the old kingdom of Ghana.

Sundiata worked to bring prosperity to his new empire. He sought to improve agricultural production, and he restored the trans-Saharan trade routes that had been interrupted by the Almoravid attacks. Sundiata ordered soldiers to clear large expanses of savanna and burn the grass that had been cleared to provide fertilizer for crops of peanuts, rice, sorghum, yams, beans, onions, and grains. With the benefit of adequate rainfall, agriculture flourished in Mali. With larger tracts of land under cultivation, farmers produced surplus crops that Mali's kings then collected as taxes.

Mali's greatest king was **Mansa Musa**, who ruled from A.D. 1312 to A.D. 1332. By opening trade routes and protecting trade caravans with a powerful standing army, Musa maintained the economic prosperity begun by Sundiata. He also introduced Islamic culture to Mali.

A Muslim himself, Musa enhanced the prestige and power of Mali through a famous pilgrimage to Makkah in A.D. 1324. Arab writers report that Musa traveled in grand style. He took with him 12,000 slaves, each dressed in silk or brocade and carrying bars of gold. Musa gave away so much gold on his journey that the world price of gold fell. At Makkah, Musa persuaded a Spanish architect to return with him to Mali. There the skilled architect built great mosques—Muslim houses of worship—and other fine buildings, including a palace for Musa in the capital of **Timbuktu** (TIHM•BUHK•TOO). Timbuktu became an important center of Muslim art and learning mainly through the efforts of Mansa Musa, who

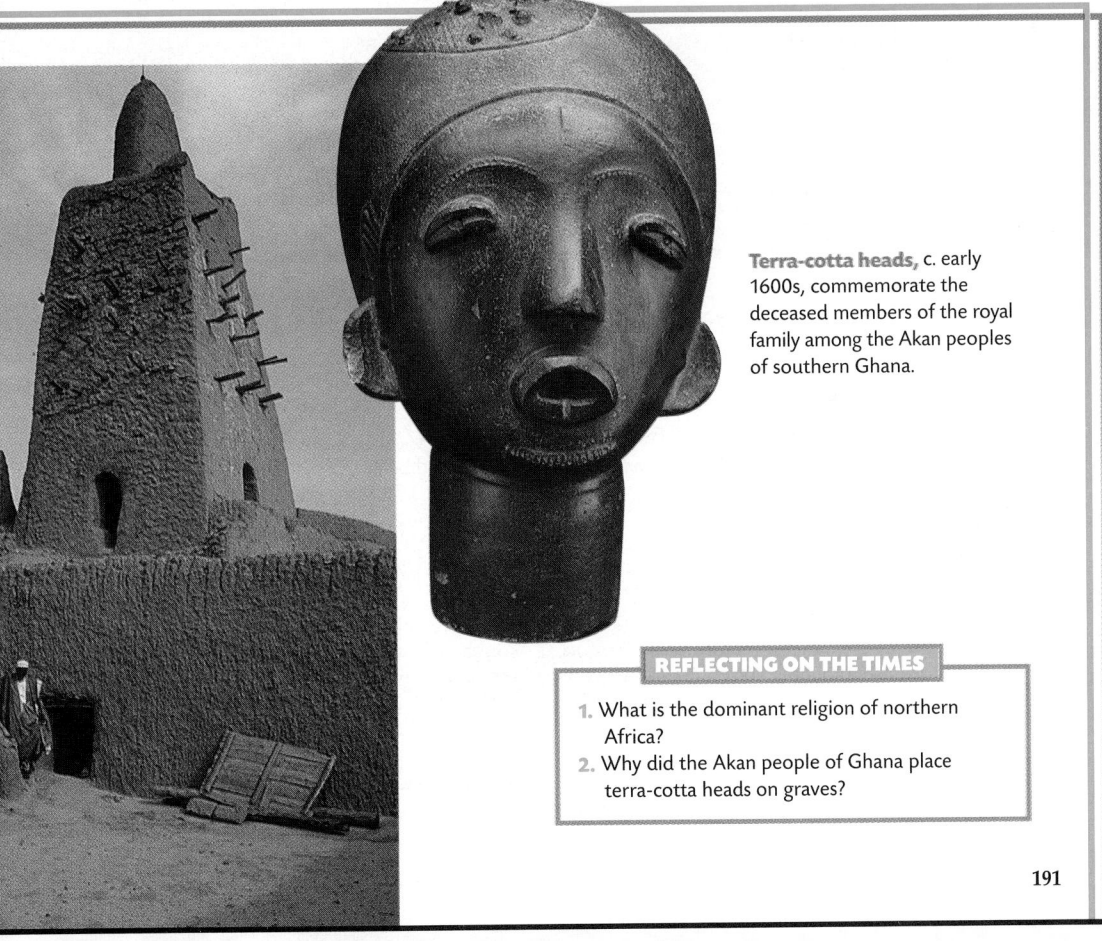

Terra-cotta heads, c. early 1600s, commemorate the deceased members of the royal family among the Akan peoples of southern Ghana.

REFLECTING ON THE TIMES

1. What is the dominant religion of northern Africa?
2. Why did the Akan people of Ghana place terra-cotta heads on graves?

191

Chapter 7 Section 2

Independent Practice

Guided Reading Activity 7-2 **L1**

Mapping History Activity 7

Geography and History Activity 7

Linking Past and Present

Timbuktu At the time of the kingdom of Mali, Timbuktu became a major center for trade, learning, and scholarship. Merchants, religious leaders, and scholars mingled in this Muslim city. After it was attacked by Moroccan invaders in 1593, Timbuktu was never again a leading city. Today Timbuktu is a small provincial town; however, hints of its former glory are visible in its mosques and monuments.

ASSESS

Check for Understanding

Assign Section 2 Review as homework or as an in-class activity.

Use Student Self-Test and Review Software to review Section 2.

Evaluate

Section Quiz 7-2

Use the Testmaker to create a customized quiz for Section 2.

ANSWERS TO REFLECTING ON THE TIMES

1. Islam
2. to memorialize members of the royal family

TEACH

Tell students that the main religion of the Republic of Mali is still Islam. Today 90 percent of the people are of that faith. Another mosque has been built recently in Niomo, Mali, as a monument to Islam. What might have attracted a traveler like Battuta to Timbuktu? *(It was on an important caravan route and was a center of Islamic culture.)*

Who?What?Where?When?

Timbuktu was an important site for the gold-salt trade in the A.D. 1300s. Today it is the administrative center of Mali. Small salt caravans are still evident, but no gold trade exists. The city has air service, but it is more accessible by camel or boat.

CURRICULUM CONNECTION

GEOGRAPHY

Mali is within three climatic zones: the Sudanic of the south with temperatures of 75° to 86°F; the Sahel with temperatures of 73° to 97°F; and the Saharan area with temperatures ranging from 117°F in the daytime to 39°F at night.

NATIONAL GEOGRAPHIC PICTURING HISTORY

West African Empire

This turreted mosque in Djenné, Mali, harks back to the A.D. 1300s, when the town thrived as a center of trade and Islamic learning. A masterpiece of African-Muslim architecture, the great mosque boasts massive mud ramparts broken by patterns of protruding beams. Its tall spires are crowned not with the traditional Islamic crescent but with ostrich eggs, symbol of fertility and fortune. Every year, after the rainy season, the town turns out 4,000 people to replaster the walls of the mosque with their bare hands. The job is done in a day.

Almost two centuries before Columbus set off for the Americas, an Arab traveler and author named Ibn Battuta began his travels in A.D. 1325 to the far corners of the Islamic world—from North Africa to China and back. He returned home three decades later as one of history's great travelers and travel writers. His journeys totaled 75,000 miles (121,000 km)—three times the distance logged by his European predecessor, Marco Polo. Ibn Battuta's final journey brought him here to the West African empire of Mali where he praised the piety of the Muslims. Battuta sought out the ruler, Mansa Sulayman, at his capital but was not impressed with the king's generosity. Mansa Sulayman, he wrote, "is a miserly king." Battuta also traveled to Timbuktu—about a hundred years before the city really started to prosper. At its height, in the A.D. 1500s, the city could boast three universities and perhaps 50,000 residents.

encouraged Muslim scholars to teach at his court.

After Mansa Musa died in A.D. 1332, the empire came under attack by Berbers, a people living in the Sahara region to the north. They raided Mali and captured Timbuktu. From the south, warriors from the rain forest also attacked Mali. Inside the kingdom, people living in the **Songhai** region of the Niger River valley had long resented losing control over their region and rebelled against the empire. By the middle of the A.D. 1500s, Mali had split into several independent states.

Kingdom of Songhai

The rebellious Songhai, who were skilled traders, farmers, and fishers, were led by strong leaders. During the late A.D. 1400s their ruler, Sunni Ali, fought many territorial wars and managed to conquer the cities of Timbuktu and Djenné, expanding his empire to include most of the West African savanna. Sunni Ali was a Muslim ruler, but when he died, rule fell to his son, a non-Muslim. The Muslim population of Songhai overthrew Ali's son and brought a Muslim ruler to the throne.

Under the new ruler, **Askia Muhammad**, the Songhai Empire reached the height of its glory. Ruling from A.D. 1493 to A.D. 1528, Askia Muhammad divided Songhai into five huge provinces, each with a governor, a tax collector, a court of judges, and a trade inspector—very much like the government structure of China in the A.D. 1400s. The king maintained the peace and security of his realm with a cavalry and a navy. Timbuktu became a center of learning.

Devoted to Islam, Muhammad introduced laws based on the teachings of the holy book of Islam, the Quran (kuh•RAHN). Lesser crimes were sometimes overlooked, but those who committed major crimes such as robbery or idolatry received harsh punishments. Askia Muhammad appointed Muslim judges, assuring that Islamic laws would be upheld.

In A.D. 1528 Askia Muhammad was overthrown by his son. A series of struggles for the throne followed, leading to a weakened central government. Around A.D. 1589 the rulers of Morocco sent an army across the Sahara to attack Songhai gold-trading centers. Moroccan soldiers, armed with guns and cannons, easily defeated the Songhai forces fighting with only swords, spears, and bows and arrows. By A.D. 1600 the Songhai Empire had come to an end.

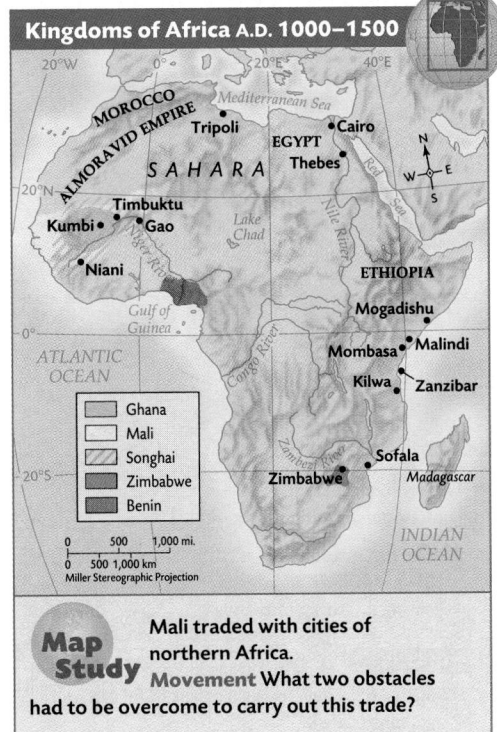

Kingdoms of Africa A.D. 1000–1500

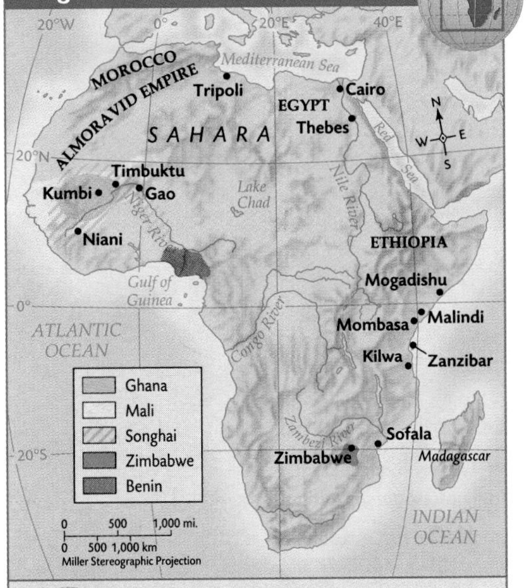

Map Study Mali traded with cities of northern Africa.
Movement What two obstacles had to be overcome to carry out this trade?

SECTION 2 REVIEW

Recall

1. **Define** monotheism, ghana, mosque.
2. **Identify** the Almoravids, Sundiata Keita, Mansa Musa, Askia Muhammad.
3. **Locate** Timbuktu on the map on this page. How did Timbuktu become an important center of Islamic art and learning during the A.D. 1300s?

Critical Thinking

4. **Analyzing Information** Why was trade vital to the economies of the West African kingdoms?

Understanding Themes

5. **Cultural Diffusion** What goods were traded, and how did trade between West Africa and the Islamic world influence the development of West African cultures between A.D. 900 and A.D. 1500?

Chapter 7 Section 2

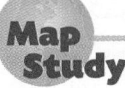

Map Study

Answer

the Sahara and attacks by the Almoravids

Map Skills Practice

Reading a Map Have students determine how far it is across the Sahara from Timbuktu north to Morocco. *(about 1,000 miles [1,700 km])* Discuss how long such a journey might have taken when traveling on foot or by camel.

Reteach

Hold a class discussion in which students compare the bartering practices of the Ghanaian and Arab traders with their own experiences buying and selling.

Enrich

Have students use library resources to find interesting details and insights about early African leaders such as Sundiata Keita, Mansa Musa, Sunni Ali, or Askia Muhammad. Students may prepare oral or written reports on their findings.

CLOSE

Hold a class discussion about why the kingdoms of West Africa declined. *(Almoravid invaders, leadership struggles, interruption of vital trade routes, death of strong leaders)*

SECTION 2 REVIEW ANSWERS

1. All vocabulary words are defined in the Glossary.
2. Almoravids, 190; Sundiata Keita, 191; Mansa Musa, 191; Askia Muhammad, 193
3. Mansa Musa encouraged Islamic scholars to teach in his capital and hired a skilled architect to build great mosques.
4. They needed salt to preserve their food and could procure it only through trade.
5. **CULTURAL DIFFUSION** Trade goods were gold, salt, metalware, swords, farm products, and cloth. North African Arab merchants brought the teachings of the Quran and other Islamic customs and learning to West Africa. Islamic scholars came to live there. Arab traders helped convert many West Africans to Islam.

Chapter 7
Section 3

SECTION THEME

▶ **Innovation** East Africa's city-states develop a new culture based on African and Arab cultures.

Find Out

Answer: *East African trading centers developed to enable Arab and Persian merchants to control trade between the interior of Africa and India and China. The areas in central and southern Africa that produced the gold and copper these traders wanted became wealthy kingdoms.*

FOCUS

Section Objective

Discuss how areas in East, Central, and South Africa developed as a result of inland and overseas trade.

BELLRINGER
Motivational Activity

Before taking roll at the beginning of the class period, project Section Focus Transparency 7-3 and have students answer the activity questions. Discuss students' responses.

This activity is also available as a blackline master.

Vocabulary Pre-check

Use Vocabulary Activity 7 to introduce vocabulary terms.
L1 LEP

A.D. 500 — A.D. 1000 — A.D. 1500

A.D. 900 Arab and Persian merchants trade in East Africa.

c. A.D. 1200 Kilwa thrives as East African coastal city-state.

c. A.D. 1300 People of Karanga build stone-walled fortresses.

Section 3

African Trading Cities and States

Setting the Scene

▶ **Terms to Define**
monopoly, multicultural

▶ **Places to Locate**
Kilwa, Malindi, Mombasa, Sofala, Zanzibar, Karanga, Great Zimbabwe

Find Out How did areas in East, Central, and South Africa develop as a result of inland and overseas trade?

The Storyteller

The first trained engineer ever to see the ruins of the Great Zimbabwe reported: "For fifty miles I saw the ruins.... The ruins are principally terraces, which rise up continually from the base to the apex of all the hills.... The terraces are all made very flat and of dry masonry.... The way the ancients seem to have levelled off the contours of the various hills around which the water courses are laid is very astonishing, as they seem to have been levelled with as much exactitude as we can accomplish with our best mathematical instruments.

—from *The Mystery of the Great Zimbabwe,* Wilfrid Mallows, 1984

Ruins of the Great Zimbabwe

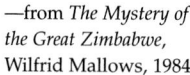

During the same time that West African kings ruled their empires, important trading communities developed along the coast of East Africa and in the interior of Central and South Africa. Inland African kingdoms mined copper and iron ore and traded these minerals and ivory with city-states that had developed along the East African coast. There Muslim traders brought cotton, silk, and Chinese porcelain from India and Southeast Asia to exchange for the products from Africa's interior. As in West Africa, trade contracts with the Muslim world enabled East African coastal areas to adopt the religion of Islam and Islamic cultural practices.

East Africa

As early as 500 B.C., coastal areas of East Africa were trading with the Arabian Peninsula and South Asia. East Africans used monsoon winds to sail across the 2,500-mile (4,023-km) stretch of Indian Ocean that separates Africa from India. By the A.D. 900s Arab and Persian merchants had settled on the East African coast and controlled the trade there. Traders from the interior of Africa brought ivory, gold, iron, and rhinoceros horn to the east coast to trade for Indian cotton and silk and Chinese porcelain.

Coastal City-States

By A.D. 1200 small East African trading settlements had become thriving city-states taxing the goods that passed through their ports. The port of **Kilwa** had a virtual **monopoly**, or sole control or ownership, of the gold trade with the interior. **Malindi** and **Mombasa**, both ports farther north on the coast, were also important centers, as was **Sofala**, a port in what is present-day Mozambique. The iron mined in the surroundings of these three

SECTION RESOURCES

Reproducible Masters
- Reproducible Lesson Plan 7-3
- Guided Reading Activity 7-3
- Reteaching Activity 7
- Enrichment Activity 7
- Section Quiz 7-3
- Performance Assessment Activity 7
- Spanish Chapter Summary 7

Transparencies
- Section Focus Transparency 7-3
- Mapping History Overlay Transparency 7

Multimedia
- Student Self-Test and Review Software
- Testmaker

city-states was widely used in the Arabian Peninsula and South Asia.

The island of **Zanzibar** was also an important center of trade. Sailors from the islands of Southeast Asia as well as India and China came to Zanzibar in search of ivory and gold, which was brought to Zanzibar ports from the coastal city-states of East Africa.

Blending of Cultures

By the A.D. 1300s, the city-states of East Africa had reached the height of their prosperity. They had become truly multicultural centers—populated by a variety of cultural groups. Within each city-state, Islamic and African cultures blended. For the most part, Arab and Persian merchants ruled the trading states. They converted many Africans to Islam.

Arab merchants married local women who had converted to Islam. Families having members with African and Islamic cultural backgrounds began speaking Swahili, a Bantu language that included Arabic and Persian words. The people of the East African coastal city-states also developed an Arabic form of writing that enabled them to write about their history.

East African rulers were either Arab governors or African chieftains. They used coral from Indian Ocean reefs to build mosques, palaces, and forts.

The Bantu Kingdoms

The Indian Ocean trade was not limited to the coastal trading states. It reached far inland, contributing to the rise of wealthy Bantu kingdoms in Central and South Africa. The inland kingdoms mined rich deposits of copper and gold. During the A.D. 900s, traders from the East African coast made their way to the inland mining communities in Central Africa and began an active trade among the people living there. The traders brought silk and porcelain from China, glass beads from India, carpets from Arab lands in the Middle East, and fine pottery from Persia.

Great Zimbabwe

The people of **Karanga**, a Bantu kingdom located on a high plateau between the Zambezi and Limpopo Rivers, built nearly 300 stone-walled fortresses throughout their territory between A.D. 1000 and A.D. 1500. The largest was called the **Great Zimbabwe**—meaning "stone house"—and served as the political and religious center of the kingdom. The oval stone wall of the Zimbabwe enclosure was 30 feet (9.15 m) high and was made from 900,000 stones fitted together without mortar. Within the wall was a maze of interior walls and hidden

CONNECTIONS

Economics

East African Trading Cities

In the A.D. 700s Arab merchants arrived on the coast of East Africa to establish a flourishing trade in gold, ivory, and tortoise shells. The descendants of the Arab immigrants and the local inhabitants became known as the Swahili (an Arabic word for "coastland"). By the late A.D. 1100s thriving city-ports began to develop along the East African coast. More than 40 such cities established trade with peoples across the Indian Ocean. Kilwa, set in an enclosed bay in southern Tanzania, developed into a mercantile and military power dominating the region's trade. The Swahili people became the intermediaries between the gold and ivory producers of the East African interior and traders from ports in India, Ceylon, and even China. Cotton, porcelain, and pottery were the principal imports. In A.D. 1414 an East African giraffe, a gift from the Swahili city of Malindi, was delivered to the reigning emperor of the Ming dynasty. Not many years after this, however, China changed its policy. A new law forbade all ocean sailing, and trade ended. Europeans would soon reach Africa's east coast. Their dominion marked a rapid decline in Swahili's eastern trade.

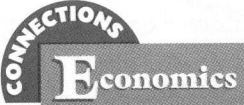

Port of Lamu, Kenya

MAKING THE CONNECTION

1. Who are the ancestors of the people known as the Swahili?
2. What two significant events marked the rapid decline of East Africa's trade with Asia?

Chapter 7 Section 3

TEACH

Guided Practice

THEME **Innovation**

Ask students to identify some aspects of the East African or Bantu cultures that represented an innovation. **L1**

Independent Practice

Guided Reading Activity 7-3 **L1**

ASSESS

Check for Understanding

Assign Section 3 Review as homework or as an in-class activity.

Use Student Self-Test and Review Software to review Section 3.

Evaluate

Section Quiz 7-3

Use the Testmaker to create a customized quiz for Section 3.

CONNECTIONS

Economics

East African Trading Cities

The organization of seagoing trade was largely in the hands of the visiting Arabs, Chinese, Persians, and Indians because the Africans had no ships of their own. Merchant trading cities such as Kilwa and Sofala, however, controlled trade between interior and coastal Africa.

Answers to Making the Connection

1. *Bantu-speaking people and Arabs*
2. *China's passage of a law forbidding all ocean sailing and the appearance of European traders on the scene*

COOPERATIVE LEARNING ACTIVITY

Simulation Game Have students role-play the interactions between the various groups that made up the East African trading community: coastal traders; traders from inland kingdoms; and merchants and traders from Muslim lands, India, and China. Organize the class into groups of three or four for this activity.

Create game cards to represent trade articles such as ivory, gold, copper, iron tools, carvings, cotton, silk, glass beads, and porcelain. Allow time for small groups to meet to discuss and plan strategies for their trading activities. Discuss the impact of this trade on the economies of the various African empires and city-states. **L1**

Chapter 7
Section 3

Visualizing History The Great Zimbabwe is located in what was once the British colony of Rhodesia. When Rhodesia became independent, it took Zimbabwe as its new name.
Answer to Caption: *political and religious center; fortress*

Reteach

Have students make a resource map that presents the information in the section.

Reteaching Activity 7

Enrich

Have students research to learn more about the archaeological excavation of the Great Zimbabwe or similar stone building sites at Khami, Natetali, and Mapungubwe. Encourage artistic students to create visual representations.

Enrichment Activity 7

CLOSE

Have students create a chart that compares the achievements of the early African cultures with another civilization that they have studied. Headings should include *Religion, Agriculture, Architecture, Literature, Trade Networks,* and *Science and Technology.*

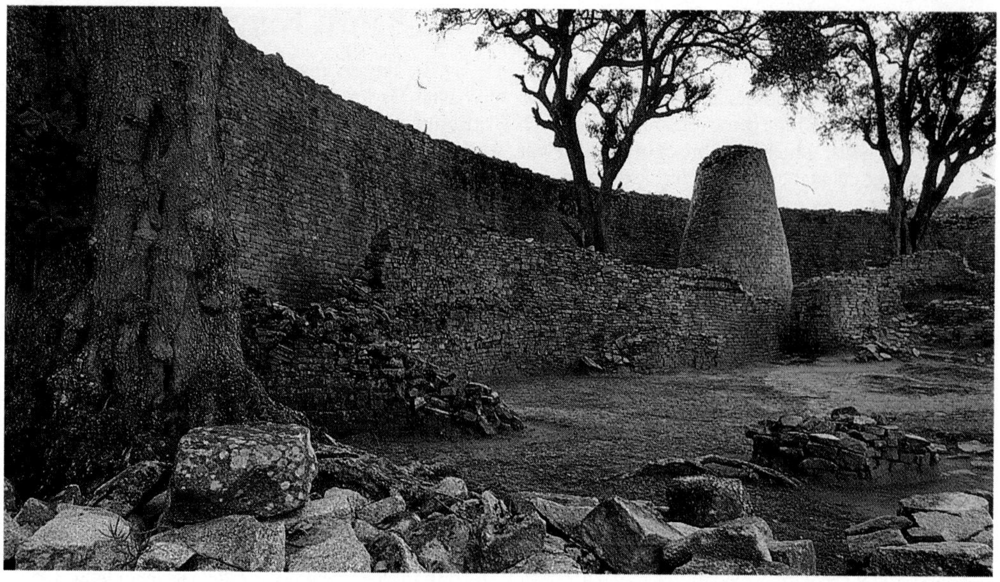

Visualizing History **This view shows the circular stone ruins of the Great Zimbabwe with an exterior wall more than 800 feet in circumference.**
What functions did this "stone house" serve?

passages that protected the circular house of the Zimbabwe chief. Near the house, archaeologists have uncovered a platform with several upright stones that may have been the place where the chief held court.

Territorial Divisions

For nearly five centuries, Karanga and the other Bantu states grew wealthy from their control of the chief routes between the gold mines and the sea. However, during the A.D. 1400s, Bantu states in South Africa struggled in civil wars that brought disorder to the kingdoms and disrupted trade. The Karanga territories were split between two rival forces. The northern territory was called Monomotapa. The southern territory was taken over by the Changamire dynasty.

The Changamire Empire became stronger than the Monomotapa Empire. Changamire rulers took over Great Zimbabwe and built the fortress's largest structures. At the same time, European explorers arrived along the East African coast. Eager to control the sources of gold, ivory, and copper, the Europeans attacked the Monomotapa Empire, threatening the survival of the African civilizations in the continent's interior.

SECTION 3 REVIEW

Recall
1. **Define** monopoly, multicultural.
2. **Identify** Kilwa, Malindi, Mombasa, Sofala, Zanzibar, Karanga, Great Zimbabwe.
3. **Explain** why the Bantu kingdoms of Central and South Africa prospered.

Critical Thinking
4. **Synthesizing Information** Imagine that you are an Arab merchant visiting an East African coastal city-state in the A.D. 1300s. What aspects of the people's culture would be familiar to you? What parts might seem different?

Understanding Themes
5. **Innovation** What new aspect of cultural life developed in the city-states of East Africa as a result of African and Middle Eastern contacts?

SECTION 3 REVIEW ANSWERS

1. All vocabulary words are defined in the Glossary.
2. Kilwa, 194; Malindi and Mombasa, 194; Sofala, 194; Zanzibar, 195; Karanga, 195; Great Zimbabwe, 195
3. The inland Bantu kingdoms mined rich deposits of copper and gold and began an active trade with traders from the East African coast.
4. Sample answer: The Arabs and Africans in the coastal city-states who practice Islam and speak Swahili would make you feel at home. Some of the exotic goods from the interior of Africa might seem strange.
5. **INNOVATION** the Swahili language, a Bantu language with a written form

Study and Writing
SKILLS

Answering Test Questions

How do you react when your teacher announces a test? For many students, taking a test is a dreaded ordeal. Learning test-taking strategies, however, can make this unavoidable experience easier and more successful.

Learning the Skill

Preparation: Good test preparation requires time. Don't try to cram all the facts into your mind at the last minute. Before beginning to study, identify what material the test will cover.

Review: To review the material, list main topics and concepts from your class notes and other material. From your textbook, list headings, map and graph titles, preview items, and review questions. These textbook items usually contain the main concepts of the chapter. Under each main topic or concept, add important details such as terms, people, places, events, movements, and dates. Finally, review previous tests and quizzes to find out what kinds of questions to expect.

Practice: Now turn your list of topics into questions and test yourself. Write your answers and evaluate them. Find areas that require further study. If you need help, ask a parent, teacher, or friend to resolve confusing issues or to quiz you again. Repeat the process of self-testing and checking your answers until you can answer most questions quickly and easily.

Taking the Test: When taking a test, preview all of its parts. Estimate how much time you will need to complete each section. Allow more time for essay questions than for short answer questions. Answer easy questions first. Then complete those that need more work. Read all test directions carefully and follow them correctly. Allow time at the end to review your answers and make additions or corrections.

A. Multiple-Choice Questions: Read all choices before marking one. If you are not sure of an answer, make your best guess.

B. Analogy Questions: First identify the relationship between the first set of items. Then look for a term that will show the same relationship in the second pair of items. Here's an example: Mansa Musa is to Mali as Askia Muhammad is to ____________. Mansa Musa was Mali's greatest king. This is the relationship between the first pair. To complete this analogy, you must know that Askia Muhammad was the greatest king of another African kingdom—Songhai.

C. Essay Questions: Make sure you understand the question. In the margin or on a notepad, briefly jot down the main points to include in your answer. Decide how to arrange these ideas and then write a complete answer.

Practicing the Skill

Imagine that you are taking a test on Chapter 7. Answer the following questions about preparing for and taking the test.

1. What topics, terms, and concepts would you list as study topics for Section 1, "Early Africa"?
2. Write a self-test question for each subheading in Section 2, "Kingdoms in West Africa."
3. How would you study the information in the map entitled "Kingdoms of Kush and Axum"?
4. Suppose you expect a test question comparing the Bantu and Ghana kingdoms. How would you study for this question?

Applying the Skill

Write five self-test questions on the material in Chapter 7. Without consulting the textbook, write answers to all questions. Then refer to the textbook to decide which topics need further study and rewrite your answers to those questions.

For More Practice

Turn to the Skill Practice in the Chapter Review on page 199 for more practice in answering test questions.

Study and Writing
SKILLS

TEACH

Answering Test Questions Discuss different ways to study for tests. Point out that some people study well alone and others do best with a partner. Ask students to share how they prefer to study for tests. Suggest that it is sometimes helpful to try to teach the material you are studying to a partner as preparation for answering test questions. Encourage students to use study methods that work best for them but to be sure to allow plenty of study time and rest before a test.

Additional Practice

Skill Reinforcement Activity 7

Writer's Guidebook, Lesson 7

ANSWERS TO PRACTICING THE SKILL

1. Answers will vary. Possible answers: Topics: regions, kingdoms, sub-Saharan cultures, village life, art; terms: oral tradition, plateau, savanna, matrilineal, age set; concepts: religious views
2. Why were gold and salt important to Ghana? What did Sundiata Keita and Mansa Musa achieve as kings of Mali? What did Askia Muhammad do for the Songhai Empire?
3. Learn the important cities and their locations on the map and their relationships to the waterways, each other, and nearby territories.
4. Make a list of all important facts about each kingdom and arrange them in categories so that they can be easily compared.

Chapter 7 Review

GLENCOE TECHNOLOGY

VIDEODISC

Use MindJogger to review students' knowledge of the chapter.

MindJogger Videoquiz

Chapter 7
Disc 1 Side B

Also available in VHS.

Answers

Using Key Terms

1. c	6. b
2. f	7. i
3. h	8. a
4. d	9. e
5. g	10. j

Using Your History Journal

Encourage students to notice how many modern African states have taken the names of early kingdoms.

Reviewing Facts

1. North Africa and sub-Saharan Africa
2. It made farming and hunting easier, which encouraged population growth. This growth eventually led to mass migrations.
3. Located in central Nigeria, the Nok produced terra-cotta figurines and iron tools.
4. Ghana's trade with North African cities made it wealthy. The kingdom taxed all goods that entered or left its territory.
5. introduced Islamic culture to Mali; reopened trade routes and protected caravans with a huge standing army
6. Timbuktu
7. divided his kingdom into five separate provinces, each with its own governor, tax collector, court, and trade inspector
8. copper, iron ore, gold, ivory, rhinoceros horn, cotton, silk, and fine porcelain
9. When Arab merchants intermarried with women from local Bantu-speaking groups on the east coast of Africa, Swahili resulted. It is a Bantu language that includes Arabic and Persian words.
10. trading communities along the coast and inland kingdoms in Central and South Africa
11. the stone fortress that served as the political and religious center of the Karanga kingdom

Critical Thinking

1. Climate and geography determine which crops can or cannot be grown, whether a community has resources useful to trade, and whether travel and exchanges with other civilizations are easy.

CHAPTER 7 REVIEW

Historical Significance

Throughout the early history of Africa, civilizations developed religious beliefs, agriculture, and trade networks in harmony with their environment. Some African peoples mined gold, iron, and other minerals from the land and then turned the raw ores into trade items. Others grew surplus crops to sell at local markets. Trade networks brought Africa, Europe, the Middle East, South Asia, and East Asia into contact with each other and encouraged the exchange of ideas and practices. This set the stage for the later development of global trading links.

Using Key Terms

Write the key term that completes each sentence.

a. multicultural	f. oral traditions
b. matrilineal	g. monopoly
c. plateau	h. age sets
d. savanna	i. monotheism
e. ghana	j. mosque

1. The sub-Saharan region of Africa includes a large central ______—a relatively high, flat area called the Sahel.
2. Early African peoples communicated knowledge about their culture through _______ —legends and history passed by word of mouth from one generation to another.
3. Before marriage, specific jobs in African communities were assigned to groups of males and females of a similar age, called ______.
4. Much of Africa's landscape is covered by ____, or treeless grasslands.
5. The city-state of Kilwa had a near ______, or sole control, of the gold trade along the East African coast.
6. Many African villages were ________ societies in which villagers traced their descent through mothers rather than through fathers.
7. Along with Judaism and Christianity, the religion of Islam upholds __________, the belief in one all-powerful God.
8. A society is said to be ___________ when it has people of many different cultural backgrounds.
9. In the earliest of the three great West African kingdoms, the ruler's title ______ was also the name of the kingdom.
10. The fine buildings constructed in the Malian capital of Timbuktu included a palace and ______, or Muslim houses of worship.

Using Your History Journal

On your map of Africa draw in the modern states where each ancient kingdom that you identified was located. Use the map of Africa in the Atlas of your text.

Reviewing the Facts

1. **List** the two major geographical regions of Africa.
2. **Discuss** how iron technology was important to the development of early West African cultures.
3. **Identify** the Nok people, their location, and their major cultural achievements.
4. **Explain** how Ghana became a wealthy nation.
5. **Discuss** the major accomplishments of Mansa Musa in Mali.
6. **Name** the city that became a major center of trade and Islamic art and learning in Mali.
7. **Explain** how ruler Askia Muhammad kept order and control over his huge empire of Songhai.
8. **List** the products traded in the coastal city-states of East Africa.
9. **State** how the East African language of Swahili originated.
10. **Name** the three areas of Africa that prospered from the Indian Ocean trade between Africa and Asia.
11. **Identify** Great Zimbabwe and discuss its importance to the Bantu kingdom of Karanga.

Critical Thinking

1. **Apply** How do climate and geography affect the development of a civilization?

2. **Evaluate** The Bantu language changed as people moved into central, eastern, and southern regions of Africa. Why do you think this happened?
3. **Making Comparisons** Compare the causes for the decline of each of the three West African kingdoms.
4. **Synthesize** Discuss how a typical Bantu-speaking village in sub-Saharan Africa was organized around A.D. 1000.
5. **Analyze** What two cultural values does this artifact of a Benin horn player reveal?

Horn player, Benin

Understanding Themes

1. **Movement** How did population movements affect the development of early Africa?
2. **Cultural Diffusion** How did trade affect cultural diffusion in West Africa? From what areas did the West African kingdoms receive new ideas and practices?
3. **Innovation** What two examples can you give that illustrate how the peoples of coastal East Africa and of the interior of Central Africa and South Africa made creative use of their resources?

Linking Past and Present

1. Gold helped make Ghana a powerful empire. Name another natural resource that has made African countries wealthy today.
2. Ancient peoples adapted to their environments in order to survive. Explain ways we adapt today.
3. How do strong central governments affect a nation's economic and social structures? What factors often lead to a weakening of central governments?

Skill Practice

Suppose that you are taking a five-part test on Chapter 7 divided in the following way.

- Part A: eight completion questions
- Part B: multiple choice
- Part C: true-false
- Part D: analogy
- Part E: essay

Parts A–D have five items each; and Part E has three essay questions. Describe how you would schedule your time (40 minutes).

Geography in History

1. How does the continent of Africa compare with the United States in land area?
2. Why has communication and travel always been difficult between the northwest African interior and northeast Africa?
3. Why has Egypt had nearly continual contact with peoples of Asia and Europe?

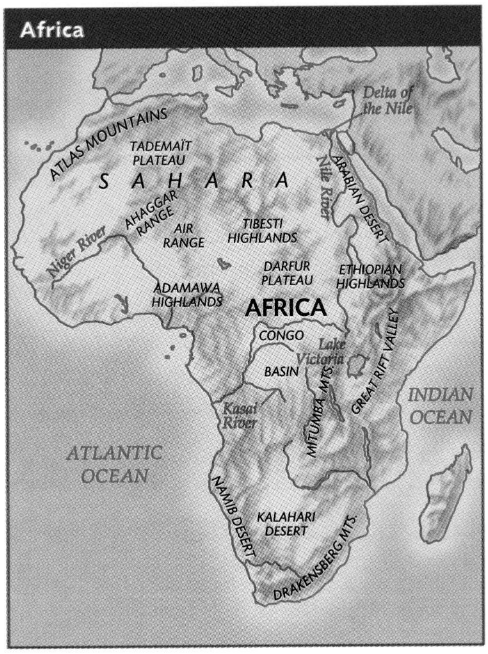

2. They encountered new environments and objects, which needed new words, and they adopted words from the languages of the peoples they met.
3. Ghana: Islamic peoples from North Africa attacked Ghanaian trade centers, which led to the empire's decline; Mali: attacked from north and south and faced internal rebellion; Songhai: the central government weakened and Morocco attacked with superior weapons
4. A typical Bantu village was organized into households that included descendants of one set of grandparents. Males and females joined groups of young people about their age, called age sets. When a girl married, she joined her husband's family and age set.
5. love of music, artistic skill

Understanding Themes

1. **MOVEMENT** They brought Bantu peoples, language, and culture to most of sub-Saharan Africa.
2. **CULTURAL DIFFUSION** Trade brought the culture of the Islamic world to West Africa.
3. **INNOVATION** The peoples of the eastern coast used coral to produce handsome mosques and palaces. The inhabitants of Karanga used stone to build Great Zimbabwe.

Chapter 7 Review

Linking Past and Present

1. diamond and gem mining
2. Answers may include: We use air conditioning in hot climates, burn oil and gas to provide heat in cold climates; build dams to irrigate farmland in dry regions.
3. Strong central governments may improve a nation's economy but may impose rigid control of its social structures; conflicts between ethnic groups or other factions can lead to a weakening of central governments.

Skill Practice

Answers should allow more time for essay questions than for short answer questions and should include time for reviewing answers.

Geography in History

1. Africa has approximately three times the land area of the U.S.
2. They were separated by the Sahara and travel had to be overland by caravan.
3. Egypt had ports on the Mediterranean and Red Seas.

Chapter Bonus Test Question

Ask students: How might the history of Africa have been different if the rivers that flow through the West African coastal plain were easily navigable? *(The kingdoms might have had more contact with other cultures; they might have been attacked by foreign invaders more often.)*

Chapter 7 *Flowering of African Civilizations* 199

Teach, Reinforce, and Extend CHAPTER Content

India's Great Civilization

CHAPTER RESOURCES

	Reproducible Resources	Multimedia Resources
Chapter Opener	Chapter Themes: Graphic Organizer 8 Historical Significance Chapter Activity 8	MindJogger Videoquiz
Chapter Enrichment	Vocabulary Activity 8* Time Line Activity 8 Mapping History Activity 8 History Simulation 8 Geography and History Activity 8 Source Reading 8 People in World History Profiles 13, 14 World Art and Music Activity 8 Enrichment Activity 8 Critical Thinking Activity 8 Skill Reinforcement Activity 8 Performance Assessment Activity 8	World History and Art Transparency 9, *Siva Nataraja* Chapter Transparency 8 NGS PicturePack Transparency Set: *Ancient India* Vocabulary PuzzleMaker Software NGS PictureShow CD-ROM: *India and China* World Music: Cultural Traditions, Lesson 7
Chapter Review/Reteaching	Reteaching Activity 8 Skill Reinforcement Activity 8 Spanish Chapter Summary 8	Chapter 8 Digest Audiocassette, Activity, Test* Vocabulary PuzzleMaker Software Student Self-Test and Review Software MindJogger Videoquiz
Chapter Evaluation/Testing	Performance Assessment Activity 8 Chapter 8 Test, Forms A and B	Testmaker

** Also available in Spanish*

0:00 **OUT OF TIME?** Assign the Chapter 8 summary in the Unit 2 Digest on pages 236-239, and the Chapter 8 Audiocassettes.

Block Schedule

Block scheduling differs from traditional class scheduling in the amount of time allotted to each period. The extended time frame provided by block scheduling affords you the opportunity to implement a greater number of research-oriented and activity-intense projects to motivate and involve your students. Activities that are particularly suited to use within the block scheduling framework are identified throughout this chapter by the following designation.

KEY TO ABILITY LEVELS

Teaching strategies have been coded for varying learning styles and abilities.

- L1 **BASIC** activities for all students
- L2 **AVERAGE** activities for average to above-average students
- L3 **CHALLENGING** activities for above-average students
- LEP **LIMITED ENGLISH PROFICIENCY** activities

A complete, 1-page lesson plan is provided for each section in the *Reproducible Lesson Plans* booklet.

SECTION RESOURCES

Daily Objectives	Reproducible Resources	Multimedia Resources
Section 1 Origins of Hindu India Describe how the cultures of the Aryans and the peoples they conquered developed into the culture of Hindu India.	Reproducible Lesson Plan 8-1 Guided Reading Activity 8-1* Time Line Activity 8 Source Reading 8 Geography and History Activity 8 Section Quiz 8-1*	Section Focus Transparency 8-1 World History and Art Transparency 9, *Siva Nataraja* Chapter Transparency 8 NGS PicturePack Transparency Set: *Ancient India* Vocabulary PuzzleMaker Software Student Self-Test and Review Software Testmaker
Section 2 Rise of Buddhism Analyze why Buddhism appealed to many people in India, Southeast Asia, and East Asia.	Reproducible Lesson Plan 8-2 Vocabulary Activity 8* Guided Reading Activity 8-2* History Simulation 8 Section Quiz 8-2*	Section Focus Transparency 8-2 Student Self-Test and Review Software Testmaker
Section 3 Indian Empires List the cultural achievements of the Mauryan and Gupta Empires.	Reproducible Lesson Plan 8-3 Vocabulary Activity 8* Guided Reading Activity 8-3* Mapping History Activity 8 Reteaching Activity 8 Enrichment Activity 8 Section Quiz 8-3* Performance Assessment Activity 8 Spanish Chapter Summary 8	Section Focus Transparency 8-3 Student Self-Test and Review Software Testmaker NGS PictureShow CD-ROM: *India and China* World Music: Cultural Traditions, Lesson 7

* *Also available in Spanish*

Chapter Activities

Performance Assessment Activity

A Guide for India Have students take the roles of advisers hired to help educate employees of a company that is transferring many Americans to a newly opened branch in India. The company is very hopeful that the two cultures will be able to respect each other in order to create a well-functioning corporate operation. The students should work in groups to develop guides to be used in a course for the American employees. Included should be the information and concepts the students feel are most vital to developing true understanding. Students should work under the assumption that Hinduism is by far the dominant religion in India today.

Possible Rubric Features

Accuracy of content information, concept attainment, clarity, decision-making skills, collaborative skills

- *For an additional activity, refer to Activity 8 in the* Performance Assessment Strategies and Activities *booklet.*

Activity

From the Classroom of...

Mary Beth Craddock
Grandview Senior High School
Grandview, MO

Indian Wedding

Point out that in India many marriages are arranged through a family decision, just as they were centuries ago. Have students create an ad for a bride to be placed by a family in a newspaper in Bombay (or other major Indian city). Discuss what qualities the family might advertise. *(education, caste,* jati*)* Also discuss the importance of the dowry (bride's price) the bride brings to the marriage. Then ask students what qualities might be stressed in an ad for a groom.

Have students use library resources to make a plan for a wedding. Have them detail who would come; what kinds of music, dance, and food would be involved; what the bride and groom would wear; what kinds of gifts would be given; and what rituals would be followed. If there are Indian families in the community, they might be asked for advice.

Conclude by having students generate a class list of qualities that make for good relationships and families. Discuss how arranged marriages might help or hinder building good family relationships. Have students consider to what degree parents in the United States indirectly have a role in arranging marriages.

MULTIPLE LEARNING STYLES

Verbal/Linguistic
Have one or more students lead a discussion on the early caste system in India. Suggest that they compare and contrast the ranking of social classes in a modern democracy.

Visual/Spatial
Have students illustrate, draw, paint, sketch, sculpt, or construct an image of the Buddha. This can be either representational (similar to existing Buddha images) or purely imaginative.

Kinesthetic
Have students make flash cards for their classmates to use in identifying and studying the terms, people, and places introduced in this chapter.

Intrapersonal
Point out that many people might find unappealing the idea of having one's marriage partner or future career largely determined by their family and the social position to which one is born. Have students consider all sides of these issues and write a paragraph in defense of one of these practices.

Additional Resources

TEACHER'S CORNER

NATIONAL GEOGRAPHIC SOCIETY

INDEX TO NATIONAL GEOGRAPHIC MAGAZINE

The following articles may be used for research relating to this chapter:

- "Banaras: India's City of Light," by Santha Rama Rau, February 1986.

NATIONAL GEOGRAPHIC SOCIETY PRODUCTS AVAILABLE FROM GLENCOE

To order the following products for use with this chapter, contact your local Glencoe sales representative or call Glencoe at 1-800-368-7344:

CD-ROMS
- Picture Atlas of the World
- NGS PictureShow CD-ROM: India and China

NGS PICTUREPACK TRANSPARENCY SETS
- Ancient India
- Physical Geography of the World

BIBLIOGRAPHY

Literature About the Period

van Buitenen, J. A. B., trans. and ed. ***The Mahabharata: I. The Book of the Beginning.*** Chicago: University of Chicago Press, 1973. Indian and Hindu culture and history are represented in this epic Sanskrit poem that is a collection of legends, romance, theology, and ethics.

Readings for the Student

DeRoin, Nancy, ed. ***Jataka Tales: Fables from the Buddha.*** Boston: Houghton Mifflin, 1975. A retelling of 30 tales told by the Buddha.

Readings for the Teacher

Miller, Barbara Stolar, trans. ***The Bhagavad Gita: Krishna's Council in Time of War.*** New York: Columbia University Press, 1986. An Indian culture and Sanskrit literature scholar's translation of the philosophical dialogue between Krishna and Arjuna.

Introducing Chapter 8

CHAPTER THEMES

Chapter Themes are listed by section on this chapter opening page of the Student Edition. A corresponding theme-based activity is available under "TEACH," and a theme-based question is asked in the Section and Chapter Reviews.

The Storyteller

Historical Setting The *Mahabharata,* a national epic of India and the world's longest poem, depicts heroes and their adventures and was the basis for the Hindus' religious, moral, and political duties. Some of these beliefs are still prevalent today. Ask students what other epic poems in world literature they know. *(Answers may include:* Iliad, Odyssey, Aeneid, Beowulf, Song of Roland.)

Historical Significance

Answers: *India's early civilization saw the introduction of Sanskrit; the evolution of hymns, epics, and holy books (Vedas); and the development of the caste system. Hinduism and Buddhism emerged in early India.*

Chapter 8

1500 B.C.–A.D. 500

India's Great Civilization

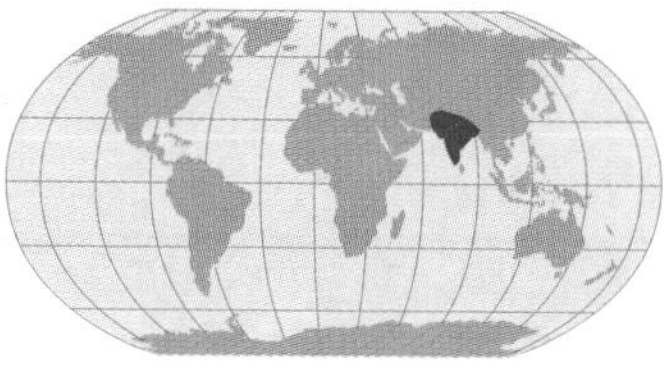

Chapter Themes

- **Movement** Aryans invade the Indian subcontinent and bring new ideas and practices. *Section 1*
- **Innovation** Hinduism and Buddhism emerge and become the dominant religions in much of Asia. *Section 2*
- **Cultural Diffusion** Mauryan and Gupta rulers bring unity to northern India and encourage cultural achievements. *Section 3*

The Storyteller

The Mahabharata, *an epic poem of ancient India, relates an amazing event. A battle raged, but the prince Arjuna did not want to fight. After all, among his foes were relatives. Arjuna took his case to the god Krishna: "O Krishna, when I see my own people ... eager for battle, my limbs shudder, my mouth is dry, my body shivers, and my hair stands on end.... I can see no good in killing my own kinsmen."*

Krishna answered, "As a [warrior], your duty is to fight a righteous battle.... Arise, O Arjuna, and be determined to fight. Get ready for battle without thought of pleasure and pain, gain and loss, victory and defeat."

As a warrior, Arjuna understood Krishna's words. A warrior must fight. It was his duty.

Historical Significance

What were the achievements of India's early civilization? What religions emerged from early India that have shaped the cultures of Asia and, in many ways, the rest of the world?

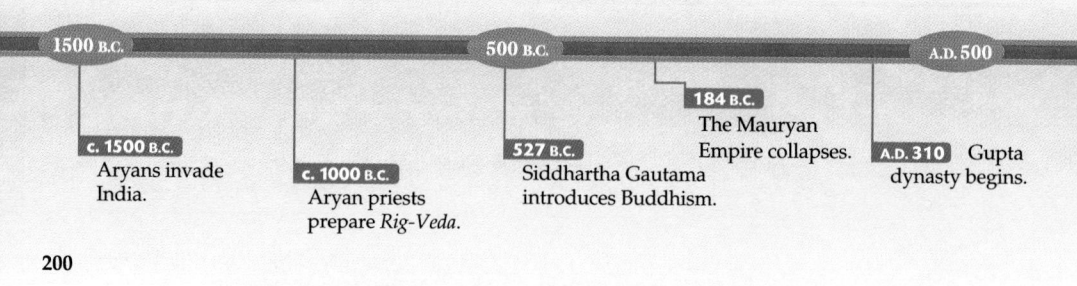

1500 B.C. — 500 B.C. — A.D. 500

- **c. 1500 B.C.** Aryans invade India.
- **c. 1000 B.C.** Aryan priests prepare *Rig-Veda.*
- **527 B.C.** Siddhartha Gautama introduces Buddhism.
- **184 B.C.** The Mauryan Empire collapses.
- **A.D. 310** Gupta dynasty begins.

GEOGRAPHY CONNECTION

Location This chapter focuses on events that occurred in the Indian peninsula and parts of Central and Southeast Asia. Have students locate the Indus and Ganges Rivers, the Khyber Pass, the Deccan Plateau, and the Himalayas in the Atlas in their text and/or on a large wall map. Ask them to point out the following major cities and to specify their relative location within India: Delhi *(north central),* Calcutta *(east),* Bombay *(west central),* Hyderabad *(south central),* Madras *(southeast),* Bangalore *(south central).*

Visualizing History Hindus communicated their beliefs through poems, tales, songs, and art. This painting of Vishnu on a bird honors one of the three main gods of Hinduism.

Your History Journal

Using a recent edition of an almanac, make a chart of the world's major religions, including the number of people who today are adherents of each religion.

EXTRA CREDIT PROJECT

Quotation Booklet In this chapter students learn about the beginnings of two of the world's major religions: Hinduism and Buddhism. Have students compile a group of 20 quotations from the sacred texts of the world's four major religions: five quotations from the Holy Bible (Christianity), five quotations from the Quran (Islam), five quotations from the Vedas and/or *Upanishads* (Hinduism), and five quotations from the Sutras (Buddhism). If several students work on this project, have them combine their efforts to create a small booklet of the quotations they find.

Introducing Chapter 8

Visualizing History Vishnu was usually depicted as blue in color, wearing a crown, and having four hands. He was often shown riding an eagle, as in this picture. Some worshipers regarded him as the supreme deity.

Performance Assessment

Refer to the activity on page 200C of the Planning Guide.

For an additional activity, refer to Activity 8 in the *Performance Assessment Strategies and Activities* booklet.

Using Your History Journal

Students' charts should include the four religions with the greatest number of adherents worldwide. They are:
Christianity (1,900,174,000),
Islam (1,033,453,000),
Hinduism (764,000,000), and
Buddhism (338,621,000).

GLENCOE TECHNOLOGY

VIDEODISC
Use MindJogger to preview chapter content.

MindJogger Videoquiz
Chapter 8
Disc 1 Side B

Also available in VHS.

Chapter 8 Section 1

SECTION THEME

▶ **Movement** Aryans invade the Indian subcontinent and bring new ideas and practices.

Find Out

Answer: *The Aryan conquerors and the early Indus River valley people merged into a single culture, developing Hinduism, which is both a religion and a way of life.*

FOCUS

Section Objective

Describe how the cultures of the Aryans and the peoples they conquered developed into the culture of Hindu India.

BELLRINGER Motivational Activity

Before taking roll at the beginning of the class period, project Section Focus Transparency 8-1 and have students answer the activity questions. Discuss students' responses.

This activity is also available as a blackline master.

Vocabulary Pre-check

Use the Vocabulary PuzzleMaker to create a puzzle that reinforces the vocabulary terms in this section. **L1**

1500 B.C. | 1000 B.C. | 500 B.C.

c. 1200 B.C. Vedic Age begins.

c. 1000 B.C. *Rig-Veda* records Aryan legends.

c. 700 B.C. Religious thinkers compile the *Upanishads*.

Section 1

Origins of Hindu India

Setting the Scene

▶ **Terms to Define**
rajah, epic, *varna*, *jati*, dharma, reincarnation, karma, ahimsa

▶ **People to Meet**
the Aryans

▶ **Places to Locate**
Hindu Kush, Ganges Plain

Find Out How did the cultures of the Aryans and the peoples they conquered develop into the culture of Hindu India?

The Storyteller

The bleeding warrior lay helpless with a broken arm. Only proper words and medicines could save him now. The priest, sprinkling him with water and herbs chanted: "He who drinks you, medicine, lives. Save the man. You are mender of wounds inflicted by club, arrow, or flame. Mend this man. O most beautiful one, go to the fracture." Next would come the grass and termite mud mixture to drink, then water in a cow's horn, and pepper-corns to eat. The warrior breathed quietly, thankful that he had found a healer who knew the ritual.

—adapted from *Religious Healing in the Veda*, Kenneth Zysk, 1985

Hindu Kush

Into the Indus River valley raced horse-drawn chariots carrying tall, light-skinned warriors—**the Aryans** from areas north of the Black and Caspian Seas. The invasion began around 1500 B.C. For several generations, waves of Aryans swept through passes in the mountains known as the **Hindu Kush** into the Indus River valley and from there into northern India.

Aryans

After conquering the people of the Indus River valley, the Aryans moved southeast into the **Ganges Plain**. There they subdued the local inhabitants and developed a new civilization that eventually spread over much of South Asia. Aspects of this civilization—especially its religious contributions—endure today.

Ways of Life

The Aryans were loosely organized into tribes of nomadic herders. Each tribe was led by a rajah, or chief. Ancient Aryan legends and hymns describe people who delighted in waging war, gambling on chariot races, and singing and dancing at festivals. Cattle were the basis of their diet and economy, even serving as money. Wealth was measured in cattle, and so the Aryans raided each other's herds. They were often at war.

The fertile Indus Valley was ideal for farming, and the Aryans soon settled down into an agricultural way of life. Dozens of Aryan words describe cattle, indicating their continued prominence in Aryan life. Cattle provided meat, fresh milk, and ghee, or liquid butter. The Aryans also hunted game and butchered sheep and goats from their herds. Later, their herds would be considered so sacred that a ban was placed on eating meat. The

SECTION RESOURCES

Reproducible Masters
- Reproducible Lesson Plan 8-1
- Guided Reading Activity 8-1
- Time Line Activity 8
- Source Reading 8
- Geography and History Activity 8
- Section Quiz 8-1

Transparencies
- Section Focus Transparency 8-1
- World History and Art Transparency 9
- Chapter Transparency 8
- Ancient India

Multimedia
- Vocabulary PuzzleMaker Software
- Student Self-Test and Review Software
- Testmaker

Aryans also ate cucumbers, bananas, and barley cakes.

Men dominated the Aryan world. Although a woman had some say in choosing a husband, the man she married expected no challenge to his authority. Even so, women took part in religious ceremonies and social affairs, and they were allowed to remarry if they were widowed—freedoms they would lose in the centuries to come. Both girls and boys from families of high rank attended school, where they learned Aryan traditions.

Language and Traditions

As a nomadic people, the Aryans had no written language. Sanskrit, their spoken language, evolved slowly and became one of the major languages of India. As part of the great Indo-European language family, Sanskrit has many of the same root words as English, Spanish, French, and German. It also includes many words from the languages of the peoples living in India before the Aryan invasions.

The Aryan warrior-herders sang rousing hymns and recited **epics**, long poems celebrating their heroes. For centuries these hymns and poems were passed by word of mouth from generation to generation. Families of warriors and priests were responsible for preserving this oral heritage. Over and over they repeated the legends, striving for complete accuracy.

Eventually, the Aryans developed a written form of Sanskrit. Priests collected the hymns, poems, legends, and religious rituals into holy books known as Vedas (VAY•duhz), or "Books of Knowledge," which formed the basis of Aryan religious practices.

Indeed, the Vedas are extremely valuable sources of knowledge, for without them historians would know little about the Aryans. Unlike the Indus River valley people, the Aryans left no artifacts or structures. Whatever we know of their life and culture we know from the Vedas. Indeed, Indian history from 1200 B.C. to 500 B.C. is known as the Vedic Age. The oldest of the four Vedas, the *Rig-Veda*, dates from around 1000 B.C. It records legends that tell us about Aryan life. The *Rig-Veda* is one of the world's oldest religious texts still in use.

Social Structure

The Vedas reveal the complex social system of ancient India. The invading Aryans brought a system of four main social classes, or ***varnas***. At first the warriors, called Kshatriyas (KSHA•tree•uhz), were the most honored *varna*. They were followed by the priests, or Brahmans; merchants, artisans, and farmers, called Vaisyas (VYSH•yuhz); and

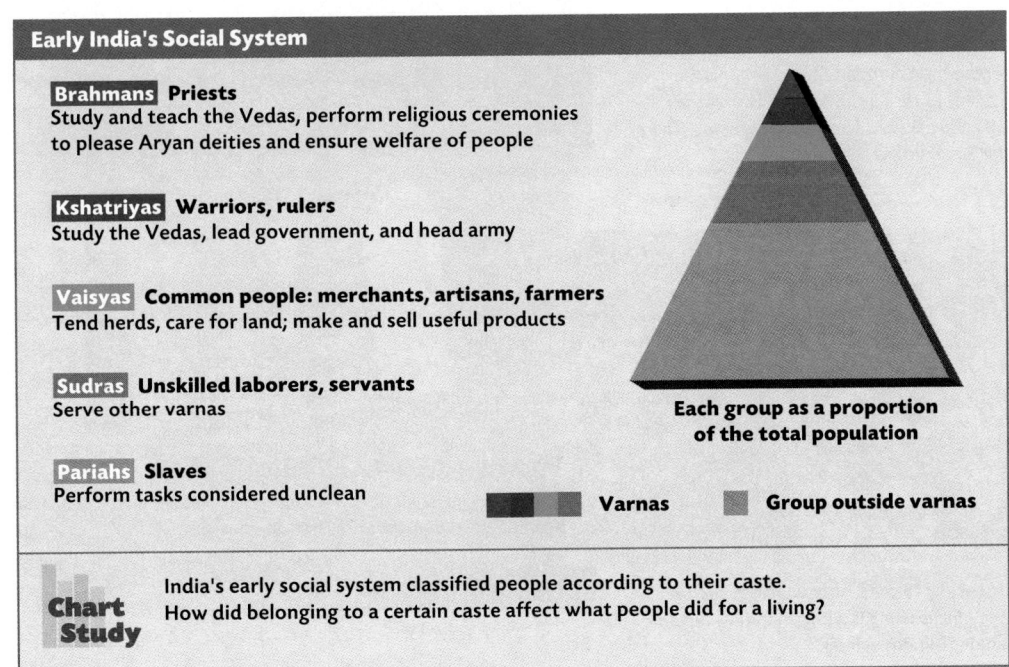

Early India's Social System

Brahmans Priests
Study and teach the Vedas, perform religious ceremonies to please Aryan deities and ensure welfare of people

Kshatriyas Warriors, rulers
Study the Vedas, lead government, and head army

Vaisyas Common people: merchants, artisans, farmers
Tend herds, care for land; make and sell useful products

Sudras Unskilled laborers, servants
Serve other varnas

Pariahs Slaves
Perform tasks considered unclean

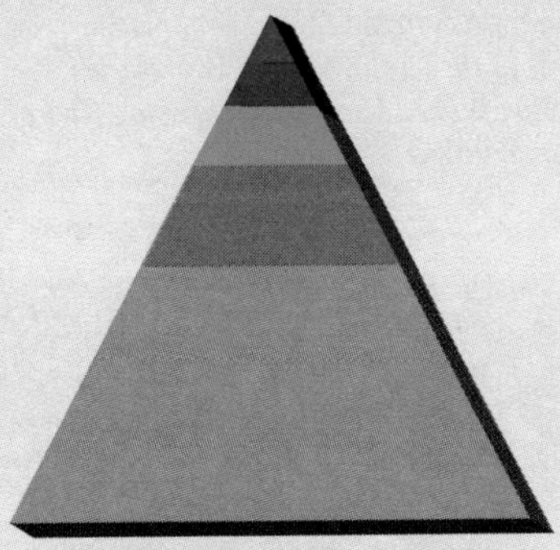

Each group as a proportion of the total population

Varnas **Group outside varnas**

Chart Study India's early social system classified people according to their caste. How did belonging to a certain caste affect what people did for a living?

Chapter 8 Section 1

TEACH

Guided Practice

THEME Movement

Have students locate India on a map (in the text Atlas or other resource) and trace the route of conquering Aryans from central Asia to the northwestern part of the South Asian subcontinent (today's Pakistan and northern India). Also have them locate the area to which the Indus River valley people fled to escape Aryan capture (southern part of Indian peninsula). **L1 LEP**

World History and Art Transparency 9

Chapter Transparency 8

NATIONAL GEOGRAPHIC SOCIETY

Use these materials to enrich student understanding of ancient India.

NGS PICTUREPACK TRANSPARENCY SET
Ancient India

Chart Study

Answer

A person's occupation was determined by varna.

Practice

Reading a Chart Why is a pyramid an appropriate geometric form to use for this chart? *(In going from the base to the peak, the number of people in each group decreases.)*

COOPERATIVE LEARNING ACTIVITY

Role Play Organize the class into the four *varnas* and the "untouchables" shown in the chart on this page. To assure fairness, be sure that students are put into groups at random, counting off 1-2-3-4-5 or pulling numbers out of a box. Have students discuss and write how the group members should act and what their duties and rights would be in their particular social group, according to ancient Indian beliefs. Also have each group discuss how its members should react to the following hypothetical situation: In ancient India, a cow from a small herd dies in a crowded street in front of a Hindu temple or shrine. Have one person from each group explain the group's responses to the entire class. **L1**

Adaptation Change occurs as people migrate, bringing ideas and customs with them and adapting to new surroundings. Over time, some traditions are adopted and some rejected. Remind students that the Aryans, formerly nomadic herders and hunters, became farmers. Ask what effects this had on Indian life, religion, and culture. Write answers on the chalkboard. *(Answers may include: Aryans settled in fertile valleys, began to farm, conquered Indus River valley people; brought caste system of* varnas; *beliefs changed as political and social organizations evolved.)* **L2**

Critical Thinking India is known for its rigid caste system. Sociologists in recent times have counted as many as 3,000 *jati*, some with marriage exclusions so strict that caste members cannot marry outside of 15 families. By contrast, the "American Dream" in the United States is based on the idea that everyone should have the opportunity to achieve a higher socioeconomic status. Have students discuss how different the United States is from India in terms of social mobility. **L3**

Independent Practice

Guided Reading Activity 8-1 **L1**

Time Line Activity 8

Source Reading 8

Geography and History Activity 8

unskilled laborers and servants, known as Sudras (SHOO•druhz).

Only priests and warrior families were allowed to hear and recite the Vedas. Over the years, rituals grew more secret and complex, and priests replaced warriors as the most honored members of society. The priests alone knew how to make sacrifices properly and to repeat the appropriate hymns. The social system changed to reflect the importance of priests.

Each *varna* had its own duties and took pride in doing them well. The Brahmans performed the elaborate rituals and studied the Vedas; only they could teach the Vedas. As warriors, Kshatriyas took charge of the army and the government. They led the councils of elders who ran small villages. Kshatriyas could study the Vedas but were not allowed to teach them. Vaisyas had the important tasks of tending the cattle, lending money, trading goods, and caring for the land. The Sudras' job was to serve the other varnas. They worked in the fields and acted as servants.

By 500 B.C. the division among the four *varnas* had become more rigid. Varnas were divided into smaller groups knows as *jati*. *Jati* were formed according to occupations: shoemakers, potters, farmers, and so on. Priests were higher than cultivators, and cultivators were higher than carpenters, for example. *Jati* had their own rules for diet, marriage, and social customs. Groups lived in separate neighborhoods and did not mix socially with others.

Centuries later, Europeans named the Indian system of *varnas* and *jati* the caste system. The word *caste* has no one definition, but how it worked is clear. Within the system people were always ranked. They were born into a group, and that group could not be changed. People married within their own group. Moreover, that group determined a great deal about people's everyday lives. Members of the group lived in the same neighborhoods and did not mix socially with those outside.

Outside the system of *varnas* and *jati* were a group later called the pariahs. They did work that

Images of the Times

Hindu Beliefs

The three main gods of Hinduism are Brahma, Vishnu, and Siva. Brahma is creator of the world, Vishnu is preserver, and Siva is destroyer. These three are part of the same universal spirit.

Meeting to read holy writings such as the *Mahabharata* is a long-standing custom among Hindus in India.

204

Images of the Times

Hindu Beliefs

The Hindu religion is polytheistic, which means that followers worship many gods. Early Hindus worshiped gods that represented powers in nature—the sun and the rain, for example. In time, some Hindus began to believe that gods appear in various forms, and that these separate forms are part of one universal spirit called Brahman. These Hindus believed that Brahman consists of many divinities. The creation of religious art was itself regarded as an act of worship. Many Hindu shrines are literally covered with stone sculptures of nymphs, dwarfs, serpents, and demons. Sometimes these figures represent one of the principal gods, often Vishnu or Siva.

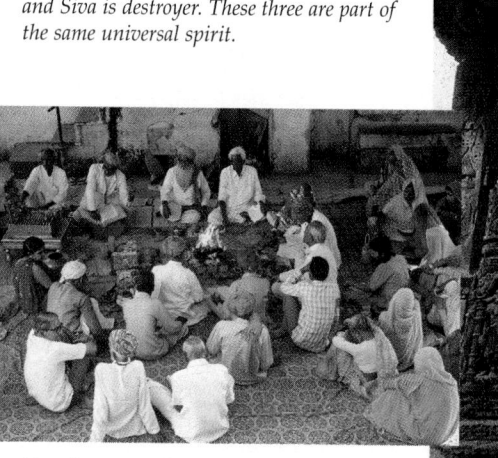

was considered unclean, such as skinning animals and tanning their hides for leather. Sometimes called "outcastes" or "untouchables," the pariahs lived outside the villages and were shunned by most other people.

Concept of Duty

The Vedas outlined the dharma, or duties, of the males who belonged to each *varna*. Members of each *varna* were urged to do their duty. The epic poem called the *Mahabharata* (muh•HAH•BAH •ruh•tuh) makes the concept clear. One eloquent section, called the *Bhagavad Gita* (BAH•guh•VAHD GEE•tuh), or "Song of the Lord," includes the story you read at the beginning of this chapter. Arjuna's decision—to fight no matter what the personal cost—illustrates the importance of dharma in Indian life. As a warrior, Arjuna had to do his duty, even if it meant fighting against family.

The concept of dharma included doing what was proper for one's age. For instance, a male student would follow an occupation that was appropriate for his class. He then took a wife, and assumed responsibility for a family. In old age, he retired. As he neared death, he withdrew from his friends and family to pray. A woman was educated in household tasks. She married and served her husband and family until he died or retired, at which time she was expected to retire from active life and be taken care of by her sons and daughters-in-law. This concept of duty affected every member of society.

India's Two Epics

Two epics addressed the concepts of good and evil and became the spiritual forebears of India's main religions. The tale of Arjuna is a small part of the *Mahabharata*, which is 100,000 verses in length—as long as the first five books of the Bible. The epic—like the Bible—is a collection of writings by several authors. Some characters are historical, while others represent human ideals and various deities. Woven into the story of two families' struggle for power are discussions of religion and philosophy.

Much of India's fine art is related to its religions. Hindus built elaborate temples, such as this Mehsana Sun Temple (interior shown).

This sculpture of Ganesha, god of good fortune and auspicious beginnings, was done in the A.D. 1700s.

REFLECTING ON THE TIMES

1. How did Hinduism contribute to the development of fine art in India?
2. What epic describes the concept of duty that affects every member of Hindu society?

205

Chapter 8 Section 1

Daily Life Have students select one *varna*, or social group, to which they would want to belong (assuming they had a choice). Then have them tell or write a short explanation of why they chose the particular group. Students should mention the daily roles, rights, and duties of members of the category they have chosen. **L1 LEP**

Critical Thinking Have students write a short paper that supports or opposes Krishna's advice to Arjuna, "Get ready for battle without thought of pleasure and pain, gain and loss, victory and defeat." **L3**

Who?What?Where?When?

Concepts of Time Western and Hindu beliefs differ profoundly. Consider the concept of time. Westerners see time as a steady, fixed progression. To Westerners, when a moment is gone, it is gone forever. Hindus see time as a revolving, endless circle. To Hindus, everything that happens today has happened before and will happen again.

ANSWERS TO REFLECTING ON THE TIMES

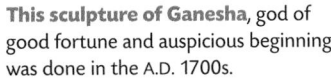

1. The many divinities of Hinduism inspired much Indian art.
2. the *Mahabharata*

Chapter 8 Section 1

Cultural Perspectives

Yoga A system of mental and physical exercises, yoga—which means "discipline" in Sanskrit—was developed to achieve isolation of the soul from the mind and body, and union with the universal spirit. Today, many people outside India practice various forms of yoga for exercise and relaxation.

Linking Past and Present

Hinduism Considered by many to be the world's oldest religion, Hinduism is not identified with the teachings of a single individual, as is the case with Christianity, Buddhism, and Islam. The Hindu religion has evolved over many centuries, and today it has about 750 million followers in India alone.

ASSESS

Check for Understanding

Assign Section 1 Review as homework or as an in-class activity.

Use Student Self-Test and Review Software to review Section 1.

Evaluate

Section Quiz 8-1

Use the Testmaker to create a customized quiz for Section 1.

AROUND THE WORLD "Song of Deborah"

Israel, c. 1100s B.C.
Deborah was a Biblical prophet in the 1100s B.C. Acting upon Deborah's advice, the Israelites fought the Canaanite army on the plain of Esdraelon. A rainstorm turned the plain to mud, trapping the enemy's chariots. The Canaanite leader, Sisera, escaped on foot but was later murdered. The "Song of Deborah" records the victory in the Old Testament Book of Judges. One of the oldest sections of the Bible, it provides a valuable record of Israelite civilization around 1100 B.C.

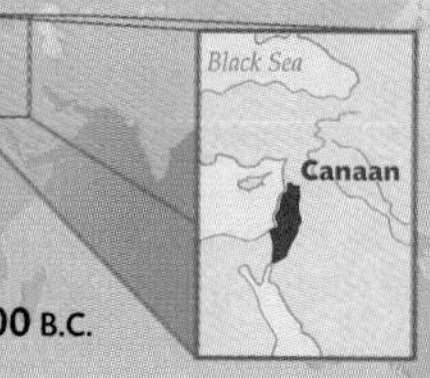

One passage tells of how the need for a king arose when dharma no longer guided people in everyday life:

> "Bhishma said: ... Neither kingship nor king was there in the beginning, neither scepter nor the bearer of the scepter. All people protected one another by means of righteous conduct (dharma). Thus, while protecting one another by means of righteous conduct, O Bharata, men eventually fell into a state of spiritual lassitude [weariness]. Then delusion overcame them ... their sense of righteous conduct was lost. When understanding was lost, all men ... became victims of greed."

Later, the God Vishnu chooses "... that one person among mortals who alone is worthy of high eminence." A man named Virajas is brought forth, and he becomes the first king.

A second epic, the well-loved *Ramayana*, grew to 24,000 verses before it was written down. It presents the moving tale of Rama and Sita (SEE•tuh). Rama was the ideal king; Sita, his faithful wife. Vividly describing the struggle between good and evil, the *Ramayana* tells how the demon Ravana captures Sita. When Rama finds that she is missing, he cries:

> "Sita! Gentle Sita! If you have wanted to prove my love, if you are hiding from us, let the agony of my fear suffice. Come to me, my love, come to me!"
>
> He stood there, both his arms held wide, as though half hoping she might run forward to his embrace. The country lay very still around him. Only the old tree shivered in every leafy spray and seemed to wring its hands for pity.
>
> Slowly that gleam of hope quite faded, and his arms fell to his sides."

Rama at first doubts Sita; but later she is saved, and they reunite. Like other Indian epics, the *Ramayana* ends with good winning over evil.

Indian Beliefs

The Aryan conquerors believed in many deities and thought their gods and goddesses had power over the forces of nature. They worshiped Agni, the god of fire; Indra, the god of thunder and war; and Usha, the goddess of dawn. Aryan priests created elaborate rituals and offered sacrifices to appease the gods and win their favor.

Over the centuries, as political and social organizations evolved, the Aryan religion slowly changed into Hinduism and became the national religion of India.

Universal Spirit

Hinduism was not founded on the teachings of one person, nor did it have one holy book. Instead it was based on different beliefs and practices, many of which had their roots in the Vedas and the Indian epics.

Other ideas that became part of Hinduism came from religious thinkers who had grown discontented with complex Vedic rituals. Between 800 B.C. and 400 B.C., their search for wisdom and truth was reflected in the religious writings known as the *Upanishads* (oo•PAH•nih•SHAHDZ).

The *Upanishads* tell of a universal spirit present within all life, "a light that shines beyond all things on earth." All living things, according to these writings, have souls. Thus, Hindus came to regard animals as sacred and forbade killing them. All souls, say the *Upanishads*, are part of the one eternal spirit, sometimes called Brahman Nerguna. Their bodies tie them to the material world, but only for a short time. To know true freedom, a soul must be separated from the material world and united with Brahman Nerguna: "As a lump of salt thrown in water dissolves, and cannot be taken out again as salt, though wherever we taste the water it is salt."

MEETING SPECIAL NEEDS ACTIVITY

Learning Style: Visual/Spatial Students who need additional guidance in following the chronology of the development of Hinduism, the emergence of Buddhism, and the growth of the Mauryan and Gupta Empires might prepare a list of major events and dates from this chapter. (The list can also be written on the chalkboard.) Then have students place the events on a time line. Visual learners might benefit from drawing small pictures or symbols to illustrate events or people listed. Have students compare their time lines with the one on page 200 of Chapter 8. Students, working in pairs or small groups, may add important historical events from previous chapters. **L1**

The authors of the *Upanishads* taught that forms of self-denial such as fasting helped people achieve union with the universal spirit. They encouraged the practice of yoga, a discipline that combines physical and mental exercises designed to help one achieve a state of tranquility.

Cycle of Rebirth

Another idea that came from the *Upanishads* was that of reincarnation, or the rebirth of the soul. Hindus believe the soul passes through many lifetimes before it finally achieves union with the universal spirit. The *Upanishads* offer this picture of rebirth:

> "As a caterpillar, having reached the end of a blade of grass, takes hold of another blade, then draws its body from the first, so the Self, having reached the end of his body, takes hold of another body, then draws itself from the first."

The cycle of rebirth is determined by a principle called karma. According to this principle, how a person lives his or her life determines what form the person will take in the next life. To move toward the universal spirit, one must live a good life and fulfill one's dharma. For example, a conscientious diplomat, a Kshatriya, might be reborn as a Brahman. The souls of those who fail to fulfill their dharma, however, might be reborn in a lower *varna*, or perhaps even as snakes or insects.

The concept of karma creates the desire to live a good life, for "By good deeds a man becomes what is good, by evil deeds what is bad." Out of that desire arose the practice of nonviolence toward all living things—still important to Hindus today. Called ahimsa (uh•HIHM•SAH), this practice requires the believer to protect humans, animals, and even insects and plants.

The cycle of reincarnation continues until a person reaches spiritual perfection. The ultimate aim of life is *moksha*, or release from the pain and suffering of rebirth after rebirth. In *moksha* a person finds freedom from reincarnation in a state of complete oneness with Brahman Nerguna. Hindus teach that a life committed to prayer, religious rituals, strict self-denial, and rejection of all worldly possessions will help a person to achieve the final goal of *moksha*.

History & Art **Siva, ringed by a circle of flames, dances on the back of the dwarf Apasmara.** *Why do Hindus regard animals as sacred?*

SECTION 1 REVIEW

Recall

1. **Define** rajah, epic, *varna*, *jati*, dharma, reincarnation, karma, ahimsa.
2. **Identify** the Aryans, Sanskrit, Vedas, *Mahabharata*, *Bhagavad Gita*, *Ramayana*, Hinduism, *Upanishads*.
3. **Explain** how geography affected the life of the Aryan groups that invaded India.

Critical Thinking

4. **Applying Information** Illustrate the Hindu concept of dharma by telling the story of the warrior-prince Arjuna.

Understanding Themes

5. **Movement** How did the Aryan invasion beginning about 1500 B.C. affect the development of Indian culture?

Chapter 8 Section 1

History & Art Have students notice that in two of his four hands Siva holds symbols of his divine nature—the drum of creation and the flame of destruction. Apasmara, the dwarf beneath his foot, represents the illusions that Siva dispels. Why do you think Siva is ringed by flames? *(He is the god of destruction.)*

Answer to Caption: *Since all living things have souls, animals are sacred and cannot be killed.*

Reteach

Ask students to explain why Hinduism was not just a religion but a way of life for Indians. *(Answers may include: Religion was the basis for daily life, social groups, duties; religious texts explained life and culture; duty [dharma] was placed above all else; beliefs in self-denial and reincarnation influenced people's daily behavior.)*

Enrich

Have students write a short essay supporting or rejecting the Hindu idea of ahimsa, the practice of nonviolence toward all living things.

CLOSE

Have students summarize the major Hindu beliefs and terms used in Section 1.

SECTION 1 REVIEW ANSWERS

1. All vocabulary words are defined in the Glossary.
2. Aryans, 202; Sanskrit, 203; Vedas, 203; *Mahabharata*, 205; *Bhagavad Gita*, 205; *Ramayana*, 206; Hinduism, 206; *Upanishads*, 206
3. fertile soil ideal for agriculture so they changed from nomadic herding to settled agriculturalists
4. Sample answer: Dharma means doing whatever is required of one's *varna*; Arjuna was a Kshatriya, or warrior. He made a decision to fight even if it meant fighting against his family.
5. **MOVEMENT** brought new language, customs, and traditions to Indian society

SECTION THEME

▶ **Innovation** Hinduism and Buddhism emerge and become the dominant religions in much of Asia.

Find Out

Answer: *Many Hindus had become dissatisfied with external rituals and wanted a more spiritual faith. Disciples and traveling monks spread the Buddha's message throughout India and beyond.*

FOCUS

Section Objective

Analyze why Buddhism appealed to many people in India, Southeast Asia, and East Asia.

BELLRINGER Motivational Activity

Before taking roll at the beginning of the class period, project Section Focus Transparency 8-2 and have students answer the activity questions. Discuss students' responses.

This activity is also available as a blackline master.

Vocabulary Pre-check

Use Vocabulary Activity 8 to introduce vocabulary terms.
L1 LEP

600 B.C. — 550 B.C. — 500 B.C.

- **c. 566 B.C.** Siddhartha Gautama is born.
- **c. 540 B.C.** Gautama begins spiritual search.
- **c. 500 B.C.** Gautama (the Buddha) dies.

Section 2

Rise of Buddhism

Setting the Scene

▶ **Terms to Define**
nirvana, stupa

▶ **People to Meet**
Siddhartha Gautama

Find Out Why did Buddhism appeal to many people in India, Southeast Asia, and East Asia?

The Storyteller

Siddhartha stood still, as if a snake lay in his path. Suddenly the icy thought stole over him: he must begin his life completely afresh. "I am no longer what I was, ... I am no longer a hermit, no longer a priest, no longer a Brahmin. How can I return home? What would I do at home with my father? Study? Offer sacrifices? Practice meditation? All this is over for me now." He realized how alone he was. Now he was Siddhartha, the awakened. He must begin his life afresh. He began to walk quickly, no longer homewards, no longer looking back.

—from *Siddhartha,* Herman Hesse, translated by Hilda Rosner, 1957

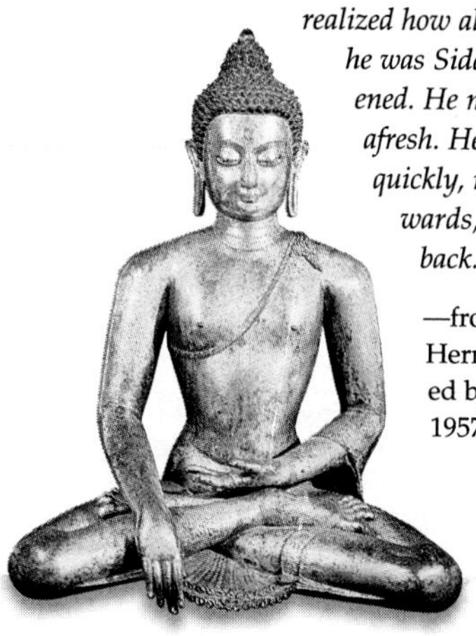

Gautama, the Buddha

During the 500s B.C., changes occurred in Indian religious life. Many devout Hindus became dissatisfied with external rituals and wanted a more spiritual faith. They left the towns and villages and looked for solitude in the hills and forests. Through meditation, many of these religious seekers developed new insights and became religious teachers. Their ideas and practices often led to the rise of new religions. The most influential of the new religions was Buddhism.

The Buddha

Siddhartha Gautama (sih•DAHR•tuh GOW•tuh•muh), the founder of Buddhism, began his life as a Kshatriya prince. Born around 566 B.C., Gautama was raised in luxury. As a young man he continued to live a sheltered life, shielded from sickness and poverty. Tradition states that one day Gautama's charioteer drove him around his estates, and for the first time Gautama saw sickness, old age, and death. Shocked at these scenes of misery, Gautama decided to find out why people suffered and how suffering could be ended. At the age of 29, he left his wife and newborn son and wandered throughout India.

For seven years Gautama lived as a hermit, seeking the truth through fasting and self-denial. This did not lead him to the truth, however. One day, while meditating under a tree, Gautama gained a flash of insight that he felt gave him an answer to the problem of suffering. He began to share with others the meaning of his "enlightenment." Dressed in a yellow robe, he preached his message to people and began to gather followers. His closest friends began calling him the Buddha, or "Enlightened One."

SECTION RESOURCES

Reproducible Masters
- Reproducible Lesson Plan 8-2
- Vocabulary Activity 8
- Guided Reading Activity 8-2
- History Simulation 8
- Section Quiz 8-2

Transparencies
- Section Focus Transparency 8-2

Multimedia
- Student Self-Test and Review Software
- Testmaker

Rajesh Bedi

The Buddha's First Sermon

From this stupa, or domed shrine, in Isipatana, a village in northern India, the Buddha is said to have delivered his first sermon. Once a small village, Isipatana is now Sarnath, a suburb of the city of Varanasi. Here, Buddhists believe, in the 500s B.C. the Buddha delivered his first sermon to five followers. A large monastery, which once housed 1,500 monks, was founded on this sacred spot. Today the shrine stands empty.

The Buddha began India's second religion, after the far older Hindu religion had become entrenched. He lived in a unique moment of history. The 500s B.C. gave birth not only to Buddhism in India but also to Confucianism in China and to new rationalist philosophies in Greece. Buddhism became one of the world's major religions and the Buddha one of the most notable spiritual leaders in the history of the world. ⊕

TEACH

Guided Practice

THEME Innovation
Have students list the religious ideas taught by the Buddha that were different from Hindu beliefs. *(no sacrifices to gods; rejection of the* varna *system)* **L1 LEP**

History Simulation 8

← Picturing History

The site of the Buddha's first sermon can be identified, and so can the circumstances of his death—although both events are based on tradition. The story goes that the 80-year-old Buddha accepted a piece of pork from a dedicated follower. Even though the Enlightened One knew the meat was spoiled, he ate it out of politeness. He sickened and died in a park, telling his followers in his last breath, "Work out your own salvation with diligence." What other famous person's last words do you know? *(Possible answers: Julius Caesar's "Et tu, Brute," Nathan Hale's "I only regret that I have but one life to lose for my country.")*

CURRICULUM CONNECTION

LITERATURE
Hermann Hesse's novel *Siddhartha*, published in 1922, is a poetic expression of Indian philosophy. Hesse, a German, narrates how his young hero, the Brahman Siddhartha, after encountering the Buddha, sets off in search of self-fulfillment. His goal is to conquer suffering and fear, to attain serene contentment, and to see the unity in seeming contrasts—in short, to reach nirvana.

Chapter 8 Section 2

Independent Practice

Guided Reading Activity 8-2 **L1**

ASSESS

Check for Understanding

Assign Section 2 Review as homework or as an in-class activity.

Use Student Self-Test and Review Software to review Section 2.

Evaluate

Section Quiz 8-2

Use the Testmaker to create a customized quiz for Section 2.

Reteach

Ask students to summarize in their own words the Four Noble Truths and the Eightfold Path that the Buddha taught.

Enrich

Have students write a brief statement in which they explain why they agree or disagree with the Buddha's teaching that desire causes suffering. Discuss answers in class.

CLOSE

Discuss possible reasons Buddhism did not flourish in India as Hinduism had. *(Answers may include: resistance from leaders such as Brahmans and Kshatriyas, strength of caste system, strictness regarding poverty and nonviolence.)*

Four Noble Truths

The Buddha developed a new religious philosophy. He outlined his main ideas in the Four Noble Truths. First, as he had discovered, all people suffer and know sorrow. Next, said the Buddha, people suffer because their desires bind them to the cycle of rebirth. He told his followers:

> "The thirst for existence leads from rebirth to rebirth; lust and pleasure follow. Power alone can satisfy lust. The thirst for power, the thirst for pleasure, the thirst for existence; there, O monks, is the origin of suffering."

The third truth, said the Buddha, was that people could end their suffering by eliminating their desires. And according to the fourth truth, one could eliminate desire by following the Eightfold Path.

The Eightfold Path

The Buddha urged his disciples to do eight things: know the truth, resist evil, say nothing to hurt others, respect life, work for the good of others, free their minds of evil, control their thoughts, and practice meditation. By avoiding extremes and following the Eightfold Path, a person could attain **nirvana**, a state of freedom from the cycle of rebirth. Nirvana is not a place, like heaven, but a state of extinction. In fact, the root meaning of the word *nirvana* is a "blowing out," as of a candle. In nirvana, a person would be in a state of oneness with the universe.

The Buddha rejected the *varna* system. He taught that a person's place in life depended on the person, not on the person's birth. He taught that anyone, regardless of caste, could attain enlightenment. He did not believe in the Hindu deities. He believed in reincarnation but taught that one could escape the cycle of suffering and reach nirvana by following the Eightfold Path.

Spread of Buddhism

The Buddha spent 45 years teaching the Four Noble Truths and the Eightfold Path. He gathered thousands of disciples around him. After their master's death, traveling monks carried the new religion beyond India to other parts of Asia, especially to China, Japan, Korea, and the Middle East.

Architecture and the Arts

The rise of Buddhism led to a flowering of architecture and the arts. Buddhist architects built **stupas**, or large stone mounds, over the bones of Buddhist holy people. Stupas were known for their elaborately carved stone railings and gateways. Paintings and statues of the Buddha, carved of polished stone or wood covered with gilt, adorned stupas and cave temples. Exquisite smaller statues were made from fine porcelain. Books about the Buddha's life and teachings were often beautifully illustrated.

Divisions

As Buddhism spread, disagreements developed among the Buddha's followers. Two distinct branches of Buddhism soon arose. One branch, known as Theravada, was established in South Asia and Southeast Asia. It remained fairly close in practice to the original teachings of the Buddha, regarding him as simply a teacher.

The other branch of Buddhism was known as Mahayana. It became dominant in China, Korea, and Japan. Mahayana encouraged the worship of the Buddha as a divine being and savior.

Today, only a few Indians are Buddhists. Most are Hindus. Muslims, Jains, Christians, and others make up the rest of the population. Recently, however, Buddhism has gained new followers in India, especially among the pariahs. Outside India, Buddhism has followers in the West as well as in the East.

SECTION 2 REVIEW

Recall

1. **Define** nirvana, stupa.
2. **Identify** Siddhartha Gautama, Four Noble Truths.
3. **Locate** on a map in the Atlas the Asian countries to which monks and merchants carried the teachings of the Buddha: China, Japan, Korea, Burma, Malaysia, Indonesia. How did the monks and merchants help to assure the survival of Buddhism as a worldwide religion?

Critical Thinking

4. **Synthesizing Information** Compare the religions of Hinduism and Buddhism, explaining which Hindu beliefs and practices the Buddha accepted and which he rejected in his teaching.

Understanding Themes

5. **Innovation** Decide how your own life and goals would be different if you tried to live by the Four Noble Truths and the Eightfold Path.

SECTION 2 REVIEW ANSWERS

1. All vocabulary words are defined in the Glossary.
2. Siddhartha Gautama, 208; Four Noble Truths, 210
3. They carried it to other Asian lands, where it still has a large following.
4. Hinduism: many gods, make sacrifices, *varnas*; Buddhism: no gods, sacrifices, or *varnas*, Eightfold Path. Both believe in rebirth, *moksha* for Hindus and nirvana for Buddhists; both believe in nonviolence.
5. **INNOVATION** Answers might include: less materialistic, less ambitious for worldly success, more compassionate.

400 B.C. — A.D. 1 — A.D. 400

321 B.C. Chandragupta Maurya founds Mauryan dynasty.

254 B.C. Asoka sends Buddhist missionaries throughout Asia.

A.D. 380 Chandragupta II unites northern India.

Section 3

Indian Empires

Setting the Scene

- **Terms to Define**
  "Arabic numerals"
- **People to Meet**
  Chandragupta Maurya, Asoka, Chandragupta I, Chandragupta II
- **Places to Locate**
  Magadha

Find Out What were the cultural achievements of the Mauryan and Gupta Empires?

The Storyteller

It troubled King Asoka that criminals continued their wrongdoing within his empire. Therefore he was proud of his latest merciful decree, carved on stone monuments: "Thus speaks the Beloved of the Gods.... This is my instruction from now on: Men who are imprisoned or sentenced to death are to be given three days respite. Thus their relations [relatives] may plead for their lives, or, if there is no one to plead for them, they may make their donations or undertake a fast for a better rebirth in the next life. For it is my wish that they should gain the next world."

—from *Asoka and the Decline of the Mauryas,* Romila Thapar, 1961

Lion-headed capital atop a Rock Edict pillar of Asoka

Despite the high mountain barriers in the north, India has never been completely cut off from other lands. The Aryans marched through the mountain passes to invade the Indus River valley; later, others followed. In the 500s B.C., Persian ruler Darius I conquered lands in the Indus River valley. Alexander the Great invaded the same area in 327 B.C., and Indian merchants carried on a busy trade with the Roman Empire. In all that time, however, no Indian king or foreign conqueror had ever succeeded in uniting the separate kingdoms into one Indian nation.

At the time of Darius's invasion, one Indian kingdom, **Magadha**, was expanding in the north. King Bimbisara, who ruled Magadha from 542 B.C. to 495 B.C., added to its territory by conquest and marriage. Although Magadha declined after Bimbisara's death, it was to become the center of India's first empire.

The Mauryan Empire

At the time of Alexander's invasion, Magadha was only one of many small warring states in northern India. Then, in 321 B.C., a military officer named **Chandragupta Maurya** (CHUHN•druh•GUP•tuh MAH•oor•yuh) overthrew the Magadhan king and proclaimed himself ruler.

Chandragupta Maurya was a skilled administrator whose achievements included the development of an efficient postal system. He kept control of his empire by maintaining a strong army and by using an extensive spy network. He founded a Mauryan kingdom that included most of northern and central India and lasted until 184 B.C.

Asoka's Enlightened Rule

Indian civilization blossomed during the reign of Chandragupta's grandson, **Asoka** (uh•SHOH•kuh). Asoka's rule began in 274 B.C. with fierce wars of conquest. His merciless armies swept

Chapter 8 Section 3

SECTION THEME

Cultural Diffusion Mauryan and Gupta rulers bring unity to northern India and encourage cultural achievements.

Find Out

Answer: *Mauryas developed an efficient postal system, free hospitals, and fine roads; Guptas encouraged art, literature, math, and science.*

FOCUS

Section Objective

List the cultural achievements of the Mauryan and Gupta Empires.

BELLRINGER Motivational Activity

Before taking roll at the beginning of the class period, project Section Focus Transparency 8-3 and have students answer the activity questions. Discuss students' responses.

This activity is also available as a blackline master.

Vocabulary Pre-check

Use Vocabulary Activity 8 to introduce vocabulary terms. **L1 LEP**

SECTION RESOURCES

Reproducible Masters
- Reproducible Lesson Plan 8-3
- Vocabulary Activity 8
- Guided Reading Activity 8-3
- Mapping History Activity 8
- Reteaching Activity 8
- Enrichment Activity 8
- Section Quiz 8-3
- Performance Assessment Activity 8
- Spanish Chapter Summary 8

Transparencies
- Section Focus Transparency 8-3

Multimedia
- Student Self-Test and Review Software
- Testmaker
- India and China
- World Music: Cultural Traditions, Lesson 7

Chapter 8 Section 3

TEACH

Guided Practice

THEME **Cultural Diffusion**

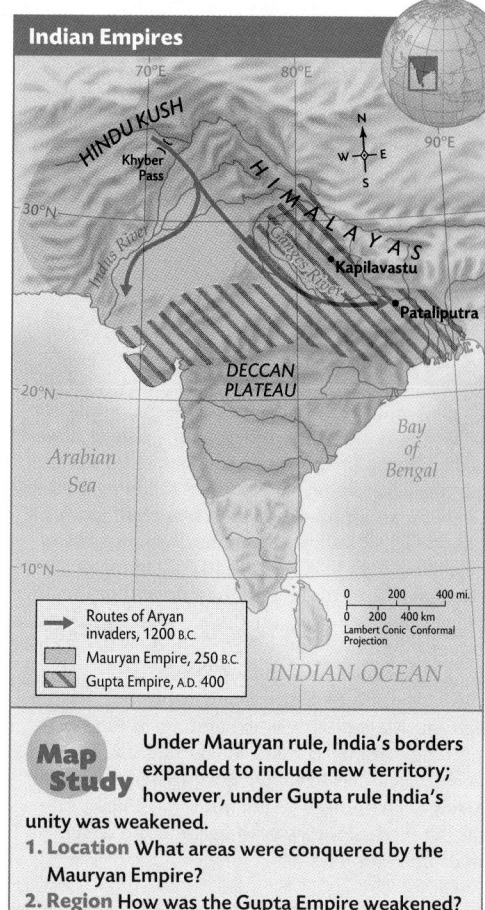

Discuss how the cultures of the early Indian empires influenced the cultures of visitors from the West. **L2**

Map Study

Answers

1. *north and central India*
2. *invasions along northwestern border*

Map Skills Practice

Reading a Map What areas of India that the Mauryas had controlled did the Guptas fail to conquer? *(Indus Valley and the Deccan Plateau)*

Economics Discuss how rulers in both empires financed their governments and provided for Indian citizens. Remind students of the harsh policies of some rulers and the compassion of others. **L3**

World Music: Cultural Traditions, Lesson 7

CURRICULUM CONNECTION

EDUCATION

Learning in the Gupta Empire was furthered by several fine universities in northern India. One of them, the university at Nalanda, with eight colleges and three libraries, attracted students from all over Asia.

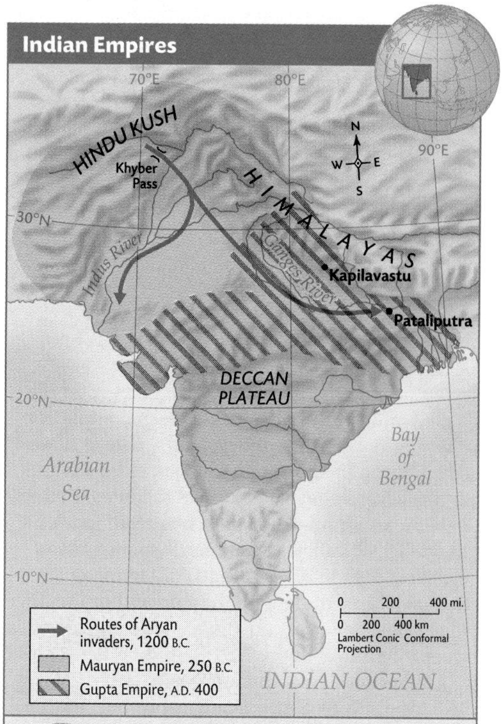

Map Study Under Mauryan rule, India's borders expanded to include new territory; however, under Gupta rule India's unity was weakened.

1. **Location** What areas were conquered by the Mauryan Empire?
2. **Region** How was the Gupta Empire weakened?

across the plains and into the forests and cities, hunting down and killing their enemies. He built an empire that covered two-thirds of the Indian subcontinent.

After one particularly brutal battle, Asoka rode out to view the battlefield. The experience changed his life. As he looked on the bloodied bodies of the dead and maimed, the Indian ruler was horrified. Determined never again to rule by force and terror, Asoka renounced war. Henceforth, he announced, he would follow the teachings of the Buddha and become a man of peace. Asoka kept his word. During his reign, missionaries spread Buddhism throughout India and other parts of Asia.

Asoka issued laws stressing concern for other human beings. To make sure these laws became widely known, Asoka wrote them in the local languages rather than in Sanskrit. The laws, known today as the Rock Edicts, were carved on rocks and on tall stone pillars throughout the vast empire.

Asoka's public projects reflected the same care for people. He provided free hospitals and veterinary clinics. He built fine roads, with rest houses and shade trees for the travelers' comfort.

Although he promoted Buddhism, Asoka permitted his non-Buddhist subjects to continue to practice Hinduism if they wished. The Hindu caste system continued.

Collapse of Mauryan Empire

The Mauryan Empire declined after Asoka's death in 232 B.C. because his successors were not as enlightened as he was. They levied heavy taxes on the goods sold by merchants and seized large portions of the crops grown by peasants. Such harsh policies caused the people to turn against the Mauryas. When the last Mauryan ruler was murdered in 184 B.C., northern India again split into many small warring kingdoms.

The Gupta Empire

After the Mauryan Empire, 500 years passed before much of India was again united. About A.D. 310, **Chandragupta I** began to build an empire. He was not related to Chandragupta Maurya, but like that earlier ruler he made Magadha the base of his kingdom.

Chandragupta I introduced the Gupta dynasty, which ruled northern India for more than 200 years. The arts and sciences flourished, and the Gupta period would later be called India's Golden Age.

The Guptas governed a much smaller empire than the Mauryas. They never gained control of the Indus Valley or of the Deccan, the broad plateau that forms most of India's southern peninsula. The Guptas did manage to build a strong state, however, and worked to maintain unquestioned authority. They trained soldiers and used spies and political assassins. In short, they did whatever they felt had to be done to maintain power.

Gupta Religion

The Gupta rulers encouraged learning based on the ideas found in the *Upanishads*. They made Hinduism the religion of their empire. Hindu temples were built—elaborate structures with brightly painted sculptures depicting tales in the *Mahabharata* and the *Ramayana*. Although each temple had its presiding god or goddess, the Hindus viewed the many deities as different ways of worshiping Brahman Nerguna, the eternal spirit.

COOPERATIVE LEARNING ACTIVITY

Debate Have students form two groups, one to support Asoka and his followers, who opposed war, and the other to defend the Gupta rulers and warriors, who wanted to conquer more land. Be sure the groups are balanced in research and communications skills. Have each group break into smaller teams to discuss such issues as politics, law, religion, and economics. Then have students rejoin the larger groups to discuss findings. Key ideas should be written down and presented to the class in oral arguments by one or two spokespersons. Following the debate, discuss the major points made by both sides. Take a poll to see if the debate changed students' minds about the rulers and the peace-versus-war issue. **L1**

CONNECTIONS

The Arts

The Ajanta Caves

On the inner side of a 70-foot (22-m) granite cliff in central India are a number of spectacular caves carved into the rock. Known today as the Ajanta caves, these wonders were built by Buddhist monks between A.D. 300 and A.D. 600.

Royal Procession, cave 17

The monks carved out the caves to serve as monasteries and temples. They first fashioned the ceilings of the chambers. Then they worked their way downward, cutting out the walls and floors. Finally, sculptors and painters decorated cave entrances and interiors with murals, statues, and carved pillars.

Most of the Ajanta cave paintings illustrate tales and stories from the Buddha's previous lives. Some paintings show everyday life in early India. Others show Gupta kings and queens and their royal courts. Still others are images of ships, elaborate buildings, and animals such as elephants, bulls, and tigers. Art historians believe that the styles and subjects of the Ajanta cave paintings spread to other parts of India and eventually influenced Buddhist art throughout Asia.

MAKING THE CONNECTION

1. Who built the Ajanta caves? How and why did they build them?
2. What subjects do the sculptures and paintings show?

Gupta Life

The Gupta Empire reached its height under **Chandragupta II**, who ruled from A.D. 375 to A.D. 415. Faxian (FAH•SYEN), a Buddhist monk from China, traveled to India and recorded in his diary:

> "In the Gupta Empire, people are numerous and happy; only those who cultivate the royal land have to pay [in] grain.... If they want to go, they go; if they want to stay, they stay. The king governs without decapitation [cutting off heads] or corporal [bodily] punishment.... The leaders of Vaisya families have houses in the cities for dispensing charity and medicine."

Faxian may have exaggerated the benefits of Gupta rule, but he provided a useful glimpse into Indian life. By easing tax burdens, Chandragupta II gave people more freedom. Of all the Gupta monarchs, he was the most chivalrous and heroic. Though he expanded the empire, he is remembered for more than conquest. Gupta rulers believed they had reached a high level of civilization. They began to write down rules for everything, from grammar to drama to politics. The Sanskrit of the Gupta court became the major language in the north.

In one respect, though, daily life did not improve during the Gupta period. The status of Indian women had declined since Aryan times. Aryan women at first often had a say about whom they would marry. By Gupta times, parents were choosing mates for their children, and child marriages were common. Women and mothers were

Footnotes to History

Highway Rest Stops
Asoka's highway rest stops were marked by stone pillars engraved with Buddhist teachings. On one of these pillars, Asoka explained:

I have ordered banyan trees to be planted along the roads to give shade to men and animals. I have ordered mango groves to be planted. I have ordered wells to be dug every [half-mile], and I have ordered rest houses built.

—The Edicts of Asoka

CONNECTIONS

The Arts

The Ajanta Caves

Point out that the Ajanta caves were carved and decorated during the Gupta period, when Hinduism was the religion of the empire. **Why might such elaborate art and architecture be created at a time when Buddhism was declining in influence in India?** *(Possible answer: The Ajanta caves were built by Buddhist monks, who remained dedicated to the faith despite the loss of Buddhist followers in India during the Gupta period.)*

Answers to Making the Connection

1. *Buddhist monks; carved from top to bottom, then decorated, to serve as monasteries and temples*
2. *the Buddha's lives, everyday life, Gupta royalty, ships, buildings, and animals*

NATIONAL GEOGRAPHIC SOCIETY

Use these materials to enrich student understanding of ancient India.

NGS PICTURESHOW CD-ROM
India and China

Independent Practice

Guided Reading Activity 8-3 **L1**

Politics Have students make lists of the "positive" *(public projects, art, learning)* and the "negative" *(wars, repression)* historical developments that occurred during the Mauryan and Gupta Empires. **L2**

MEETING SPECIAL NEEDS ACTIVITY

Learning Disability For students who need extra help and additional reinforcement with the material in this section, read aloud to them (or have other students read aloud) relevant entries about the Indian empires from a children's encyclopedia. *The World Book Encyclopedia* is a good choice. Ask students to explain in their own words the main points of some or all of the following entries: Mauryan Empire, Chandragupta Maurya, Asoka, Gupta dynasty, Sanskrit literature. **L1**

Chapter 8
Section 3

Visualizing History The *Ramayana*, or "Story of Rama," tells the tale of an exile and his patient, faithful wife. Rama, a crown prince, is the embodiment of the Hindu concept of dharma. Sita, his wife, is a flawless princess from a nearby kingdom. Both undergo many trials and emerge with honor.

Answer to Caption: *to present moral lessons*

ASSESS

Check for Understanding

Assign Section 3 Review as homework or as an in-class activity.

Use Student Self-Test and Review Software to review Section 3.

Evaluate

Section Quiz 8-3

Use the Testmaker to create a customized quiz for Section 3.

Reteach

Ask students to name the important people from this section and several contributions from each of the major empires.

Reteaching Activity 8

Enrich

Have students discuss some of the reasons that "golden ages" end, using the Mauryan and Gupta Empires as examples.

Enrichment Activity 8

CLOSE

Ask students to speculate on why Hindu religion, social structure, and customs remain deeply embedded in Indian life, even though the Gupta rulers were India's last Hindu rulers.

Visualizing History **Gupta rulers decorated Hindu temples with elaborate scenes from the *Ramayana*, such as this painting of Rama and Lakshamana accompanied by Visvamitra.** *What was the purpose of the* Panchatantra?

highly respected, but they had little power or independence.

Art and Learning

Learning flourished under the Guptas. The court welcomed poets, playwrights, philosophers, and scientists. Much of the writing was concentrated on religion, but folk tales were also popular. A collection of tales called the *Panchatantra* presented moral lessons through animals who acted like humans. Many of these stories eventually spread to the Middle East and the West, where they were retold by other authors. Drama was also important during Gupta times. Kalidasa, the most famous playwright, wrote *Shakuntala*, a play about romantic love between a king and a forest maiden.

Gupta mathematicians contributed significantly to mathematics as it is today, making major advances in developing the principles of algebra. They also explained the concept of infinity and invented the concept of zero. The symbols they devised for the numbers 1 to 9 were adopted by traders from the Middle East and so came to be called **"Arabic numerals"** in the West.

Gupta astronomers used these mathematical discoveries to advance their understanding of the universe. They realized that the earth is round, and they had some knowledge of gravity. In medicine, Gupta doctors set bones, performed operations, and invented hundreds of medical instruments.

Many countries benefited from Gupta achievements, as both ideas and products traveled the land and sea trade routes that connected India to the rest of the world. Indian exporters traded such items as gems, spices, cotton, teak, and ebony for horses from Arabia and central Asia, silk from China, and gold from Rome.

The Golden Age Ends

After Chandragupta II's death in A.D. 415, the Gupta Empire began to fail. As the government weakened, the Guptas faced invasions along India's northwestern border. By A.D. 600, the Gupta Empire had dissolved into a collection of small states.

However, much of the culture that was uniquely Indian survived. Many aspects of India's life today grew out of the social structures and religions, the arts and sciences, that were born during the 2,000 years that followed the Aryan invasions.

SECTION 3 REVIEW

Recall

1. **Define** "Arabic numerals."
2. **Identify** Chandragupta Maurya, Asoka, Chandragupta I, Chandragupta II, *Panchatantra*, *Shakuntala*.
3. **Locate** the map on page 212, and find the Mauryan Empire and the Gupta Empire. Compare and contrast their sizes and features.

Critical Thinking

4. **Analyzing Information** How did the rulers of India's empires have an effect on the religious life of the Indian people?

Understanding Themes

5. **Cultural Diffusion** What aspects of early Indian empires have had a lasting impact on India and the rest of the world?

SECTION 3 REVIEW ANSWERS

1. All vocabulary words are defined in the Glossary.
2. Chandragupta Maurya, 211; Asoka, 211; Chandragupta I, 212; Chandragupta II, 213; *Panchatantra*, 214; *Shakuntala*, 214
3. Mauryan Empire covered more territory than Gupta; unlike Mauryas, Guptas never controlled Indus River valley.
4. Asoka encouraged Buddhism; Guptas supported Hinduism.
5. CULTURAL DIFFUSION religious, social, intellectual aspects

Critical Thinking
SKILLS

Determining Cause and Effect

As you read a mystery novel, you may try to figure out which events or actions caused the main character to act in specific ways. Understanding history is a similar process. We try to find reasons behind people's actions. Looking for cause-effect relationships unlocks the mystery of history.

Learning the Skill

To identify cause-effect relationships in history, first select an event. Then examine the situation before this event. How was it different? Look for related problems and actions. These are likely causes of the event. Suppose you select the following event: Asoka's renunciation of war. What events preceded Asoka's decision? In earlier years, Asoka had led many brutal wars of conquest. Eventually, he was horrified by the bloody results of war. This combination of underlying and specific events caused him to renounce war altogether.

Now examine what happened after Asoka renounced war. He became a Buddhist, promoted Buddhist ideas of compassion, and passed laws based on this philosophy. He also built hospitals and roads and worked to improve conditions for his people. These were direct and indirect effects of Asoka's change of direction.

Certain words and phrases often indicate cause-effect relationships; these include *because, due to, therefore, as a result of, led to, and brought about*. It can be hard to determine causes and effects of historical events. Facts may be missing. Moreover, we can't test our ideas as we can in science experiments. Instead, we must rely on logic and common sense.

Lion-headed capital atop a Rock Edict pillar of Asoka

Practicing the Skill

Read the paragraph below. Then answer the questions that follow.

> "Cattle were the basis of the Aryan diet and economy, even serving as money. Wealth was measured in cattle, and so the Aryans raided each other's herds. They were often at war.... Dozens of Aryan words describe cattle, indicating their continued prominence in Aryan life. Later, their herds would be considered so sacred that a ban was placed on eating meat."

1. What were causes of conflict among Aryans?
2. How did the importance of cattle affect the culture and language of Aryans?

Applying the Skill

Reread Section 2, "Rise of Buddhism." Then describe causes of Buddhism's rise in India and its effects on India and other parts of the world.

For More Practice

Turn to the Skill Practice in the Chapter Review on page 217 for more practice in determining cause and effect.

Critical Thinking
SKILLS

TEACH

Determining Cause and Effect

To show students a few clear-cut cases of cause and effect, use examples from biology. Have students explain how or why the following diseases occur in human beings: malaria *(bite of infected mosquito)*, rickets *(lack of vitamin D)*, beri-beri *(lack of thiamine)*, typhoid *(contaminated food or water)*, rabies *(bite of infected animal)*, scurvy *(lack of vitamin C)*. Ask how the causes of these diseases were discovered. *(observation, experimentation, logic)* Emphasize, as the text does, that cause-and-effect relationships in history may be less certain than those in science and medicine. Have students read the skill and complete the practice questions.

Additonal Practice

Skill Reinforcement Activity 8

ANSWERS TO PRACTICING THE SKILL

1. Aryans were nomadic herders who delighted in waging war. Since their wealth was measured in cattle, they often raided one another's herds.
2. Cattle became the basis of the Aryans' diet and economy. Their language had dozens of words to describe cattle. Cattle were so important that they would in time be considered sacred and could not be eaten.

Chapter 8 Review

GLENCOE TECHNOLOGY

VIDEODISC

Use MindJogger to review students' knowledge of the chapter.

MindJogger Videoquiz

Chapter 8
Disc 1 Side B

Also available in VHS.

Answers

Using Key Terms

1. f	**6.** h
2. g	**7.** e
3. j	**8.** i
4. b	**9.** d
5. c	**10.** a

Using Your History Journal

The 1996 *World Almanac* shows that 23,000 Buddhists live in Africa, 337 million in Asia, 279,000 in Europe, 559,000 in Latin America, 578,000 in North America, 26,000 in Oceania, and 401,000 in Eurasia; of the world's Hindus, 1.6 million live in Africa, 759 million in Asia, 725,000 in Europe, 912,000 in Latin America, 1.3 million in North America, 379,000 in Oceania, and 2,000 in Eurasia.

CHAPTER 8 REVIEW

Historical Significance

The civilization that developed in India between 1500 B.C. and A.D. 500 produced two of the world's great religions: Hinduism and Buddhism. Hinduism became not only India's major faith but also its way of life. Buddhism rejected many Hindu social practices and affirmed a disciplined life to achieve peace and deliverance from suffering. The belief in nonviolence has influenced modern leaders in their struggle for peace and human rights. Over the centuries, the two religions have inspired magnificent achievements in architecture and the arts.

Using Key Terms

Write the key term that completes each sentence.

a. ahimsa	f. nirvana
b. dharma	g. rajah
c. epics	h. reincarnation
d. *jati*	i. stupas
e. karma	j. *varna*

1. In following the Buddha's teachings, Buddhists strive to attain freedom from the cycle of rebirth, a state called _____.
2. The Aryans were loosely organized into a number of tribes, each of which was led by a _____, or chief.
3. The invading Aryans brought to the Indian subcontinent a system of four main social classes, or _______.
4. To ensure rebirth in a higher state, people in each Hindu group must properly perform their duty, or ______.
5. Early literary works, such as the *Mahabharata* and the *Ramayana*, are _____ that reflect basic Hindu beliefs and values.
6. Hindus believe in ______, a process of rebirth in which the soul resides in many bodies before it finally unites with Brahman Nerguna, or the universal spirit.
7. A person's ______ determines whether he or she will be closer to the universal spirit in the next life.
8. For purposes of prayer, Buddhist architects built large elaborate ____ over the remains of holy people.
9. Each *varna* was made up of social groups called _____ that were defined and ranked by occupation.
10. The practice of ______, or nonviolence, requires the believer to protect all living things—humans, animals, and even insects and plants—from harm.

Using Your History Journal

Refer to a world almanac to determine how many Buddhists and how many Hindus live in each region of the world today. Build a graph or create a world map that illustrates this information.

Reviewing Facts

1. **Identify** Chandragupta Maurya and his role in developing early Indian civilization.
2. **Explain** in your own words the Four Noble Truths of Buddhism.
3. **Define** *ahimsa* and describe how it is practiced in Indian society.
4. **Identify** the *Bhagavad Gita* and its major theme.
5. **Locate** where the Aryan invaders came from, and how they entered what later became Pakistan and northern India.
6. **List** some of the achievements of Indian mathematicians during the Gupta Empire.
7. **Identify** Siddhartha Gautama and his social background.

Critical Thinking

1. **Apply** How could a person use the principle of nonviolence, or ahimsa, as a force for social change?
2. **Analyze** How did ideas in the Hindu religion help to maintain the separation of classes in Indian society?
3. **Synthesize** What might have happened if Asoka had not been horrified while viewing the carnage after a fierce battle?

Reviewing Facts

1. Military officer who in 321 B.C. overthrew Magadhan king and founded Mauryan Empire, which lasted until 184 B.C.
2. Answers should include: All people suffer; people suffer because desire binds them to cycle of rebirth; eliminating desires will end suffering; and desire is eliminated by following Eightfold Path.
3. Concept of karma creates desire to live a good life, and from that arose practice of nonviolence toward all living things, or ahimsa.
4. portion of the *Mahabharata*; importance of dharma
5. Eastern Europe, north of Black and Caspian Seas; through passes in the Hindu Kush
6. Achievements include: made advances in principles of algebra; explained concept of infinity and invented concept of zero; devised symbols for numbers 1 to 9.
7. Kshatriya prince who, following his enlightenment, became known as the Buddha.

Critical Thinking

1. to force better treatment of humans
2. The Hindu concept of dharma said that people had to perform the specific duties of their social class.
3. Fierce wars might have continued to

216 Chapter 8 *India's Great Civilization*

4. **Analyze** Here, two Brahman cattle stand in a street of Bombay, India. Why do Hindus abstain from eating meat?

Understanding Themes

1. **Movement** How was India affected by the Aryan invasions?
2. **Innovation** What might make Buddhism attractive to people from different cultures?
3. **Cultural Diffusion** Why did Gupta achievements in science and the arts spread quickly to other parts of the world, both Eastern and Western?

Linking Past and Present

1. The *varna* system created a huge underclass that Europeans called "the untouchables." How do you think this system created problems for modern India?
2. Religion has always had a major part in Indian society. How have religious differences hindered Indian unity in modern times?
3. Early in the 1900s, India applied the Hindu principle of nonviolence to help win its independence from Great Britain. Do you think people can still use nonviolence effectively to win freedom and human rights?

Geography in History

1. **Location** What mountain range forms India's northern border?
2. **Movement** What routes did the Aryan invaders take to the interior of India?
3. **Region** What effect did the invasion of the Aryans have on the developing culture of India?
4. **Human/Environment Interaction** What physical features made it difficult for one empire to unify all of northern and southern India?

Modern India

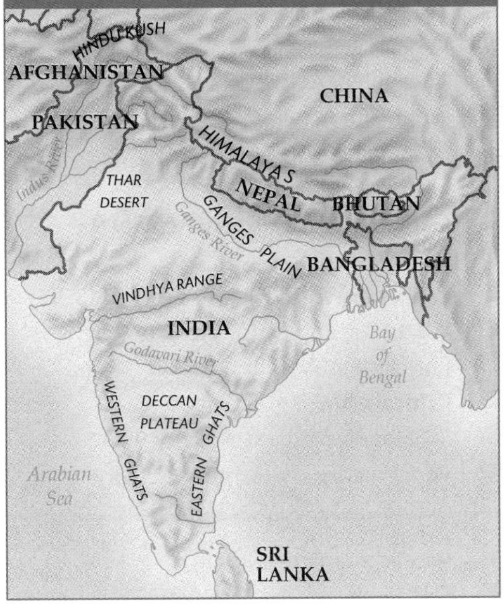

Skill Practice

Reread the discussion of "The Gupta Empire" in Section 3. Then answer the following questions.

1. What caused the Gupta rulers to use spies and assassins?
2. The Guptas adopted Hinduism as India's religion. What effects did this have on art and architecture?
3. What were the effects of Gupta culture on science and mathematics?
4. What caused the breakup of the Gupta Empire?

Chapter 8 Review

characterize the Indian empire; it would have encompassed more territory but had less cultural advancement.

4. Animals are considered sacred, and killing them is forbidden.

Understanding Themes

1. **MOVEMENT** cultural, social, linguistic influences
2. **INNOVATION** emphasis on nonviolence, social equality
3. **CULTURAL DIFFUSION** Trade extended achievements to other parts of the world.

Linking Past and Present

1. Answers may include: the *varna* system created vast social inequalities; it burdened the government with a large, needy underclass.
2. Clashes between Hindus and Muslims have led to wars and tensions on the Indian subcontinent throughout the twentieth century.
3. Students should weigh consequences of violent action against those of nonviolence in today's world. They might mention successful uses of nonviolence in the American civil rights movement.

Geography in History

1. Himalaya
2. through the passes in the Hindu Kush onto the Ganges Plain and from there into northern India
3. The Aryans brought religious ideas and a rigid caste system to India as well as Sanskrit.
4. the Vindhya Range, the Godavari River, and the Thar Desert

Skill Practice

1. They wanted to maintain unquestioned authority.
2. Many beautiful temples were built, adorned with pictures and statues of Hindu gods and goddesses.
3. Gupta mathematicians made advances in algebra, invented the concept of zero, and explained the concept of infinity. They also devised the symbols for the numbers 1 to 9 we use today. Gupta astronomers knew the earth was round, Gupta doctors invented many surgical instruments.
4. The government began to fail and also faced invaders on the empire's northwest border.

Chapter Bonus Test Question

Ask students: The philosophy of nonviolence has been espoused by many Hindus. How do you reconcile this fact with the fact that Hindu India has been involved in many wars and armed struggles? *(Answers might suggest that not all Hindus believed in nonviolence, or that some believed there could be instances of justifiable exceptions.)*

Teach, Reinforce, and Extend CHAPTER Content

China's Flourishing Civilization

CHAPTER RESOURCES

	Reproducible Resources	Multimedia Resources
Chapter Opener	Chapter Themes: Graphic Organizer 9 Historical Significance Chapter Activity 9	MindJogger Videoquiz
Chapter Enrichment	Vocabulary Activity 9* Time Line Activity 9 Mapping History Activity 9 History Simulation 9 Geography and History Activity 9 Source Reading 9 People in World History Profiles 15, 16 World Art and Music Activity 9 Enrichment Activity 9 Critical Thinking Activity 9 Skill Reinforcement Activity 9 Performance Assessment Activity 9	World History and Art Transparency 10, *Buddha*; 11, *Ming Phoenix Crown* Chapter Transparency 9 NGS PicturePack Transparency Set: *Ancient China* Vocabulary PuzzleMaker Software NGS PictureShow CD-ROM: *India and China* World Music: Cultural Traditions, Lesson 8
Chapter Review/Reteaching	Reteaching Activity 9 Skill Reinforcement Activity 9 Spanish Chapter Summary 9	Chapter 9 Digest Audiocassette, Activity, Test* Vocabulary PuzzleMaker Software Student Self-Test and Review Software MindJogger Videoquiz
Chapter Evaluation/Testing	Performance Assessment Activity 9 Chapter 9 Test, Forms A and B	Testmaker

* *Also available in Spanish*

0:00 **OUT OF TIME?** Assign the Chapter 9 summary in the Unit 2 Digest on pages 236–239, and the Chapter 9 Audiocassettes.

Block Schedule

Block scheduling differs from traditional class scheduling in the amount of time allotted to each period. The extended time frame provided by block scheduling affords you the opportunity to implement a greater number of research-oriented and activity-intense projects to motivate and involve your students. Activities that are particularly suited to use within the block scheduling framework are identified throughout this chapter by the following designation.

KEY TO ABILITY LEVELS

Teaching strategies have been coded for varying learning styles and abilities.

- **L1** **BASIC** activities for all students
- **L2** **AVERAGE** activities for average to above-average students
- **L3** **CHALLENGING** activities for above-average students
- **LEP** **LIMITED ENGLISH PROFICIENCY** activities

Chapter 9 Planning Guide

A complete, 1-page lesson plan is provided for each section in the *Reproducible Lesson Plans* booklet.

SECTION RESOURCES

Daily Objectives	Reproducible Resources	Multimedia Resources
Section 1 Three Great Dynasties Summarize the major advances the Chinese made under the Zhou, the Qin, and the Han dynasties.	Reproducible Lesson Plan 9-1 Vocabulary Activity 9* Guided Reading Activity 9-1* Time Line Activity 9 Mapping History Activity 9 Section Quiz 9-1*	Section Focus Transparency 9-1 Chapter Transparency 9 World History and Art Transparency 11, *Ming Phoenix Crown* Student Self-Test and Review Software Testmaker
Section 2 Three Ways of Life Describe the philosophic ideals that helped to shape China's government.	Reproducible Lesson Plan 9-2 Vocabulary Activity 9* Guided Reading Activity 9-2* History Simulation 9 Geography and History Activity 9 Section Quiz 9-2*	Section Focus Transparency 9-2 World History and Art Transparency 10, *Buddha* Student Self-Test and Review Software Testmaker
Section 3 Society and Culture Explain how early Chinese society was organized and summarize the scientific and technological break-throughs.	Reproducible Lesson Plan 9-3 Vocabulary Activity 9* Guided Reading Activity 9-3* Source Reading 9 People in World History Profiles 15, 16 World History Art and Music Activity 9 Reteaching Activity 9 Enrichment Activity 9 Section Quiz 9-3* Performance Assessment Activity 9 Spanish Chapter Summary 9	Section Focus Transparency 9-3 NGS PicturePack Transparency Set: *Ancient China* Student Self-Test and Review Software Testmaker World Music: Cultural Traditions, Lesson 8 NGS PictureShow CD-ROM: *India and China*

* *Also available in Spanish*

Chapter Activities

Performance Assessment Activity

A Last Will and Testament Have students take the roles of lawyers who help the philosophers and people of early China prepare wills in which they leave their artifacts, beliefs, and so on, to those nations, groups, or individuals in most need of them today. Students should use news media to find modern-day recipients in order to make connections with the past. Students should produce a document similar to an actual will and then present an oral "reading of the will" to classmates.

Possible Rubric Features
Concept attainment, content information, inferences and connections, decision-making skills, clarity, and appropriateness to purpose and audience

• *For an additional activity, refer to Activity 9 in the* Performance Assessment Strategies and Activities *booklet.*

ACTIVITY

From the Classroom of...

Robert W. Gardner
New Canaan High School
New Canaan, CT

Ancient China

The purpose of this activity is to have students understand that Chinese civilization evolved as a result of varied political, social, economic, and geographic forces. It makes a good wrap-up activity for the chapter.

Organize students into groups of three or four and have them brainstorm four or five topics such as: the Great Wall, Confucianism, Daoism, the Silk Road, and the role of the family in Chinese culture. Students should take notes. Then give each student a copy of three short readings (either from periodicals or teacher-prepared), each one of which focuses on one of the three great dynasties. Have the class devote the remainder of the period to reading and studying them. The next day, have students write in-class essays of several paragraphs using assigned reading from the text, notes taken during brainstorming, and the teacher-provided readings. Pose essay questions that encourage students to integrate these sources. Samples: "To what degree did economic need and opportunity–along with the forces of geography–shape the political behavior of the great dynasties?" "What were the most outstanding aspects of Chinese culture and why did they develop at the time when they did?"

MULTIPLE LEARNING STYLES

Verbal/Linguistic
Have students research myths and legends of the ancient Chinese and then write a series of stories recounting the myths in their own words.

Kinesthetic
Have students find an ancient Chinese nature painting that they admire. Then ask them to try painting a similar scene that is consistent with the Daoist emphasis on harmony with nature.

Interpersonal
Have students work in small groups to create a newsmagazine about this chapter. The magazine could carry news stories of significant events; profiles of important people; feature articles on family life, art, religion, and literature; and articles on significant achievements in science and technology. Have students illustrate the magazine with their own drawings or pictures cut from magazines.

Intrapersonal
Have students imagine that they are members of an ancient Chinese family. Ask them to keep a journal in which they recount interactions that reflect their position in their family.

Additional Resources

TEACHER'S CORNER

NATIONAL GEOGRAPHIC SOCIETY

INDEX TO NATIONAL GEOGRAPHIC MAGAZINE

The following articles may be used for research relating to this chapter:

- "A Chinese Emperor's Army for Eternity," by O. Louis Mazzatenta, August 1992.

NATIONAL GEOGRAPHIC SOCIETY PRODUCTS AVAILABLE FROM GLENCOE

To order the following products for use with this chapter, contact your local Glencoe sales representative or call Glencoe at 1-800-368-7344:

NGS PICTURESHOW CD-ROM
- India and China

NGS PICTUREPACK TRANSPARENCY SET
- Ancient China

ADDITIONAL NATIONAL GEOGRAPHIC SOCIETY PRODUCTS

To order the following products for use with this chapter, call National Geographic Society at 1-800-368-2728:

- *Ancient Civilizations*, "China." (Filmstrip)

BIBLIOGRAPHY

Literature of the Period

Shih-Ching: The Classical Anthology Defined by Confucius. Translated by Ezra Pound. Cambridge: Harvard University Press, 1954. The *Book of Songs*, with songs and poetry from the 1100s to the 200s B.C.

Readings for the Student

Temple, Robert. ***The Genius of China: 3,000 Years of Science, Discovery, and Invention.*** New York: Simon and Schuster, 1989. Includes such inventions as the wheelbarrow, the stirrup, and the umbrella.

Readings for the Teacher

Fairbank, John King. ***China: A New History.*** Cambridge: Harvard University Press, 1992. A survey of Chinese history from antiquity to the Tiananmen Square protests by the Harvard sinologist.

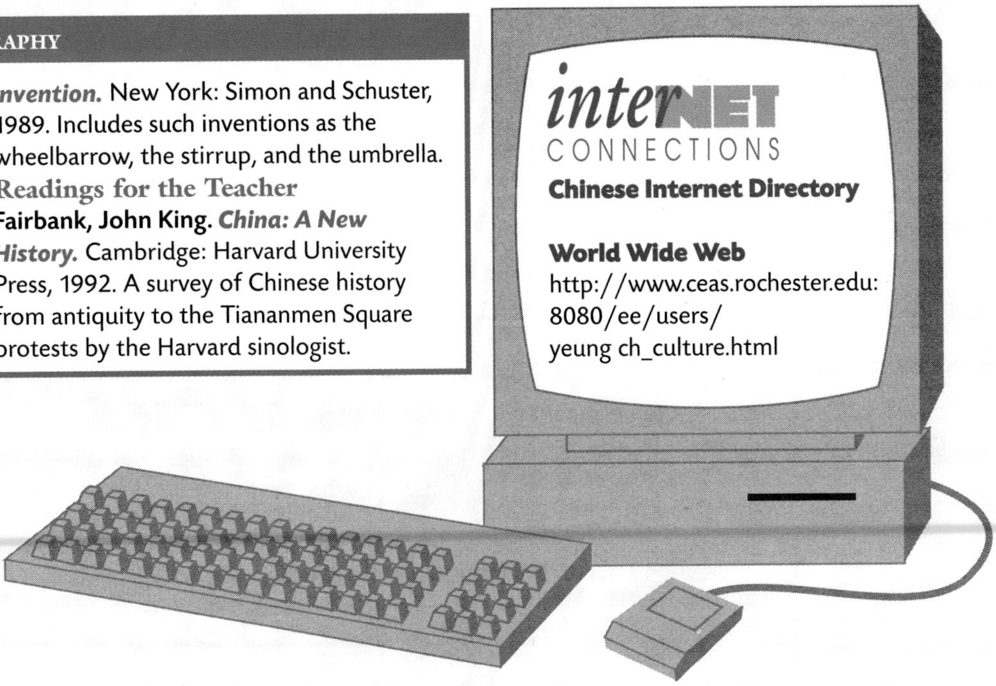
interNET
CONNECTIONS
Chinese Internet Directory
World Wide Web
http://www.ceas.rochester.edu:
8080/ee/users/
yeung ch_culture.html

Introducing Chapter 9

CHAPTER THEMES

Chapter Themes are listed by section on this chapter opening page of the Student Edition. A corresponding theme-based activity is available under "TEACH," and a theme-based question is asked in the Section and Chapter Reviews.

The Storyteller

Historical Setting Most ancient Chinese would have agreed "straightness" meant being loyal to family first. The family was the most important social unit in China, not only supplying basic human needs but also serving as the focus of religious practice through ancestor worship. Confucius was once asked why he did not take part in government. In response, he quoted from an ancient classic, the *Shu Ching* (Classic of History), "Simply by being a good son and friendly to his brothers a man can exert an influence upon government!" He thus made clear his belief that the public good is served by the practice of family ethics.

Historical Significance

Answers: *For centuries, Chinese society centered around the family and esteemed just government and ethical behavior, in keeping with the teachings of Confucius. Chinese arts have reflected the Daoist ideal of harmony with nature.*

Confucius's teachings served as a basis for Chinese society and government until the 1900s. The Daoist concept of yin and yang helped China accept new ideas, such as those of Buddhism, brought by traders and other foreigners.

Chapter 9

1100 B.C.–A.D. 200

China's Flourishing Civilization

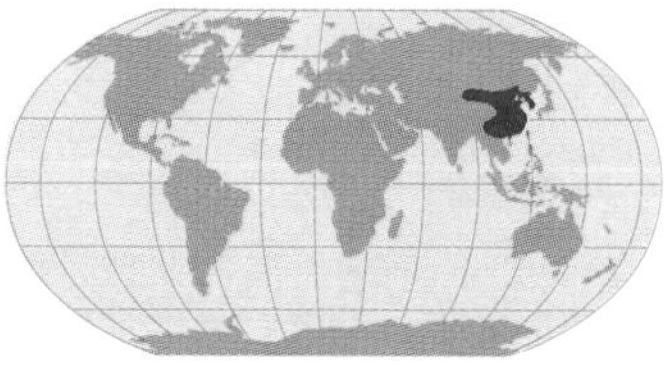

Chapter Themes

- **Uniformity** The Qin and Han dynasties establish and maintain a strong central government. *Section 1*
- **Innovation** The Chinese formulate ethical philosophies and make scientific and technological advances. *Section 2*
- **Cultural Diffusion** Traders carry ideas and products along the Silk Road. *Section 3*

The Storyteller

Whom do you agree with in the following conversation, dating from the 500s B.C.*? What is right, or "straightness," in this case?*

The Governor of She said to Confucius: "In our village there is a man nicknamed Straight Body. When his father stole a sheep, he gave evidence against him." Confucius answered, "In our village those who are straight are quite different. Fathers cover up for their sons, and sons cover up for their fathers...."

This conversation involves a conflict between law and family. Confucius's view—that family should always take precedence—reflects an attitude toward families that was dominant in Chinese culture for a long time.

Historical Significance

How did the ideas of Confucius and other Chinese thinkers affect behavior in Chinese society for centuries? How have their ideas influenced China's development and its relationship with other parts of the world?

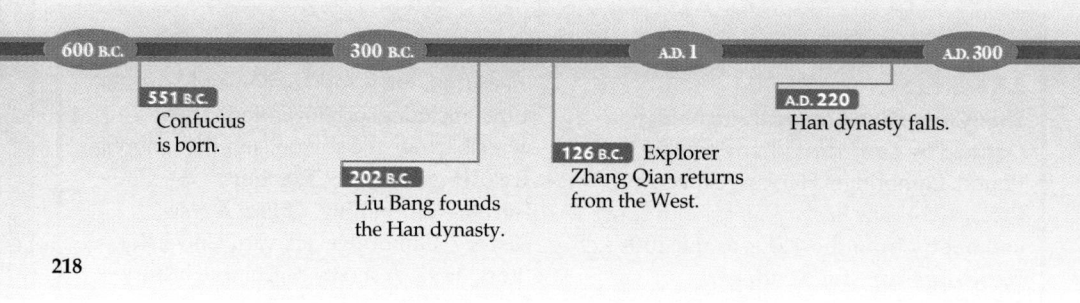

600 B.C. — 300 B.C. — A.D. 1 — A.D. 300

- **551 B.C.** Confucius is born.
- **202 B.C.** Liu Bang founds the Han dynasty.
- **126 B.C.** Explorer Zhang Qian returns from the West.
- **A.D. 220** Han dynasty falls.

218

GEOGRAPHY CONNECTION

GEOGRAPHIC THEMES

Place Have students locate China on a world map. How does China rank among the nations of the world in terms of size? *(third largest, after Russia and Canada)* What bodies of water encircle its coastline from north to south? (Yellow Sea, East China Sea, Taiwan Strait, South China Sea) With what countries does it share its land frontier to the south? *(Hong Kong, Vietnam, Laos, Myanmar)* To the southwest? *(India, Bhutan, Nepal, Kyrgyzstan, Tajikistan, Afghanistan)* To the north? *(Kazakstan, Russia, Mongolia)* To the northeast? *(North Korea)*

Visualizing History The Great Wall of China at Huang Ya Guan, a view of a section of the 1400-mile-long wall

Your History Journal

Chinese inventions and discoveries include many "firsts" such as printed books, the compass, and gunpowder. Choose one Chinese invention or discovery reported in this chapter and write a short research report on its early history.

EXTRA CREDIT PROJECT

Research Over the course of history, China's Great Wall has been transformed from a defense against invaders to a lure for tourists. Have students research the history of the Great Wall from ancient times to the present. Suggested resources: J. Fryer, *The Great Wall of China*; A. Waldron, *The Great Wall of China: From History to Myth*; C. Capa, ed., *Behind the Great Wall of China*.

Introducing Chapter 9

Visualizing History Although the Chinese had built protective walls since the 600s B.C., Qin ruler Shihuangdi was, according to tradition, the first Chinese ruler to build a Great Wall to deter invasion. Most of the Qin wall, however, was north of the Great Wall tourists visit today, which was built mostly during the Ming dynasty (A.D. 1368–1644).

Performance Assessment

Refer to the activity on page 219C of the Planning Guide.

For an additional activity, refer to Activity 9 in the *Performance Assessment Strategies and Activities* booklet.

Using Your History Journal

Instruct students to include the approximate date of the invention, the need that led to it, and the approximate date the invention made its way beyond China.

GLENCOE TECHNOLOGY

VIDEODISC
Use MindJogger to preview chapter content.

MindJogger Videoquiz
Chapter 9
Disc 2 Side A

Also available in VHS.

Chapter 9 Section 1

SECTION THEME

▶ **Uniformity** The Qin and Han dynasties establish and maintain a strong central government.

Find Out

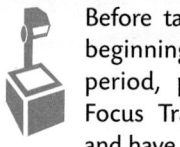

Answer: *The Zhou made a variety of technological advances; the Qin strengthened central government; the* Pax Sinica *under the Han had many lasting effects, including the civil service.*

FOCUS

Section Objective

Summarize the major advances the Chinese made under the Zhou, the Qin, and the Han dynasties.

BELLRINGER Motivational Activity

Before taking roll at the beginning of the class period, project Section Focus Transparency 9-1 and have students answer the activity questions. Discuss students' responses.

This activity is also available as a blackline master.

Vocabulary Pre-check

Use Vocabulary Activity 9 to introduce vocabulary terms.
L1 LEP

1000 B.C. | 500 B.C. | A.D. 1 | A.D. 500

771 B.C. Zhou political power begins to decline.

221 B.C. Qin Shihuangdi founds the Qin dynasty.

141 B.C. Wudi becomes the sixth Han emperor.

Section 1

Three Great Dynasties

Setting the Scene

▶ **Terms to Define**
cavalry, civil service, mandarin

▶ **People to Meet**
Qin Shihuangdi, Liu Bang, Wudi, Zhang Qian

▶ **Places to Locate**
Great Wall of China, Silk Road

Find Out What major advances did China make under the Zhou, Qin, and Han dynasties?

The Storyteller

Seeing the Marquis Chao of Han asleep on the cold floor, the keeper of the royal hat covered him with a robe. Upon awakening, the marquis demanded to know who had covered him. Learning the keeper of the hat was responsible, the marquis punished the keeper of the robe for failing to perform his duty. Then he punished the keeper of the hat for undertaking tasks not his to perform. The trespass of one official upon the duties of another was considered a great danger.

—adapted from *Basic Writing of Mo Tzu, Hsün Tzu, and Han Fei Tzu,* reprinted in *The Global Experience: Readings in World History to 1500*, 1987

Late Zhou jade dragon

Around 1100 B.C., the Chinese people were fashioning ideas that would result in a unique civilization. From then until the A.D. 200s, the Chinese lived under three dynasties, or ruling families—the Zhou (JOH), the Qin (CHIN), and the Han (HAHN). The first of these, the Zhou, ruled the nation for more than 800 years, longer than any other Chinese dynasty.

The Enduring Zhou

The Zhou conquered the last Shang dynasty king around 1028 B.C., claiming the Mandate of Heaven, or heaven's approval. They called their king the Son of Heaven, saying that the Shang had lost the mandate by ruling poorly.

Eventually, the Zhou held a vast realm. To control their holdings, Zhou kings set up an agricultural system in which nobles owned the land and peasants worked it. They appointed their relatives to govern, giving each one a city-state.

Each local lord had total authority on his own lands and built his own army. At first all the lords pledged allegiance to the Son of Heaven. In time, though, some grew strong enough to challenge the king's authority.

In 771 B.C. the Zhou suffered a severe defeat in a conflict with their enemies. After that, political power fell increasingly to local nobles. In the next centuries, the nobles fought small wars until by the 200s B.C., several city-states were locked in a struggle that ended the Zhou era.

Even though Zhou rulers lost their power, the Zhou are remembered for many technological advances. During the Zhou period the Chinese built roads and expanded foreign trade. They obtained horses from western nomads, forming a

---

SECTION RESOURCES

Reproducible Masters
- Reproducible Lesson Plan 9-1
- Vocabulary Activity 9
- Guided Reading Activity 9-1
- Time Line Activity 9
- Mapping History Activity 9
- Section Quiz 9-1

Transparencies
- Section Focus Transparency 9-1
- Chapter Transparency 9
- World History and Art Transparency 11

Multimedia
- Student Self-Test and Review Software
- Testmaker

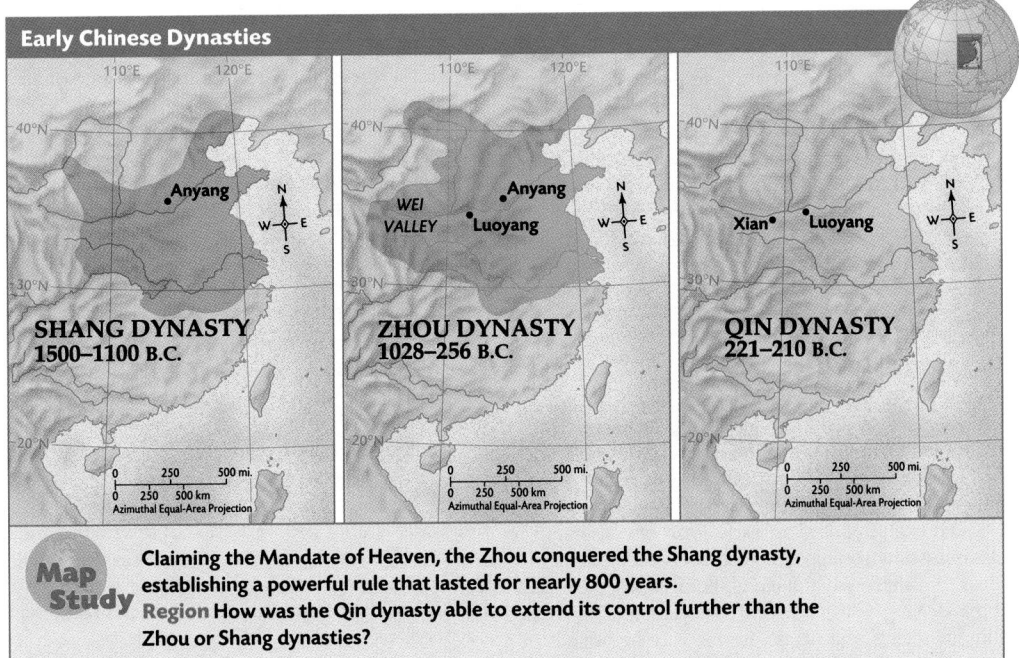

Early Chinese Dynasties

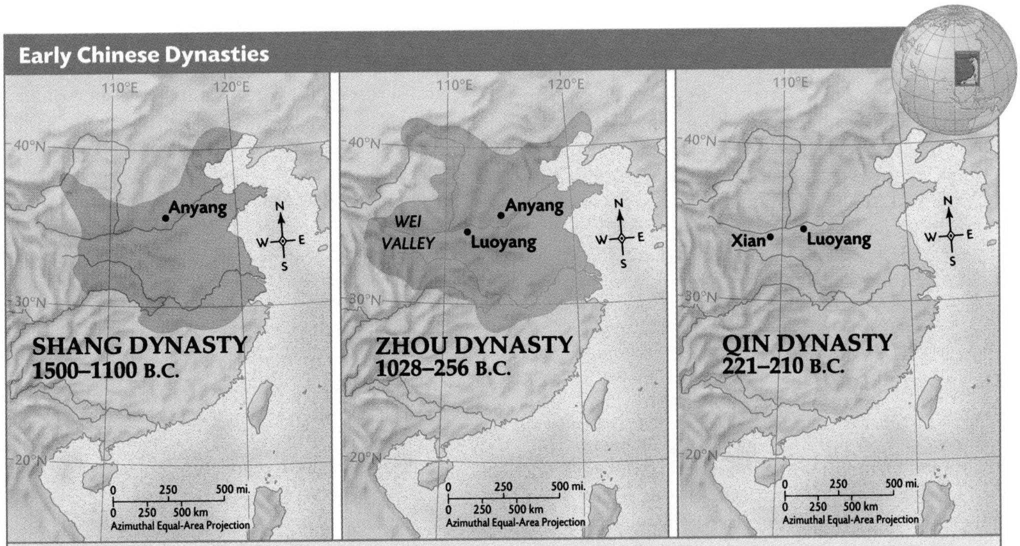

Map Study Claiming the Mandate of Heaven, the Zhou conquered the Shang dynasty, establishing a powerful rule that lasted for nearly 800 years.
Region How was the Qin dynasty able to extend its control further than the Zhou or Shang dynasties?

cavalry, or group of mounted warriors, along with horse-drawn chariots. The Zhou also added a deadly weapon: the crossbow. They further elaborated the system of picture writing begun by the Shang, a system that is the ancestor of modern Chinese writing. Under the Zhou, iron plows were invented, irrigation systems were developed, and flood-control systems were initiated. These and other advances led to population growth, and Zhou China became the world's most densely populated country.

The Mighty Qin

Meanwhile, several small states were struggling for control in China. Among them was a state on the western border ruled by the Qin. By 221 B.C., the Qin had wiped out the Zhou and conquered the rest of northern China, uniting much of the nation under a strong central authority for the first time. Westerners would later call the nation *China* after the Qin, whose first ruler added the title Shihuangdi (SHUR•HWONG•DEE), or First Emperor, to his name.

A tireless ruler, **Qin Shihuangdi** set out to create a government directly under his control. He reorganized the empire into military districts, appointing officials to govern them. This system prevented local lords from becoming strong enough to challenge the power of the central government—the problem that had led to the downfall of the Zhou.

The First Emperor made other changes to further centralize his control. He devised a system of weights and measures to replace the various systems used in different regions. He standardized coins, instituted a uniform writing system, and set up a law code throughout China.

Qin had grandiose plans for his empire, and he used forced labor to accomplish them. Gangs of Chinese peasants dug canals and built roads.

Footnotes to History

Court Magic

A court magician made a potion for Wudi, claiming that it would give immortality. Before the emperor got the potion, a scholar drank it. The scholar was immediately sentenced to death but told Wudi that, if the potion was genuine, Wudi would not be able to kill him. If the potion was a fake, he had done no harm. Wudi had to agree. Needless to say, the scholar had exposed a fraud.

TEACH

Guided Practice

THEME Uniformity

Have students assemble a list of the main features of the Qin empire. *(central government that controlled all districts, standardized system of weights and measures, uniform writing system, uniform law code, built roads and canals, began building Great Wall)* Help students to see how these features contributed to uniformity in China. **L1**

Map Study

Answer

by centralizing control of the empire

Map Skills Practice

Reading a Map About how far apart were the Zhou capitals? *(about 1/4" apart on the map, or about 125 miles [201 km] apart)* The Qin capitals? *(about 1/2" apart on the map, or about 250 miles [402 km])*

Critical Thinking Have students name the many technological advances of the Zhou dynasty. *(roads, horses, crossbow, improved writing system, iron plows, irrigation systems, flood control)* Have students suggest ways these advances could have led to population growth. **L2**

Chapter Transparency 9

World History and Art Transparency 11

COOPERATIVE LEARNING ACTIVITY

An Interview Assign two groups of students the task of preparing a *Meet the Press* interview with either Qin Shihuangdi or the Han emperor Wudi. Remind students that each group member must contribute to the research effort. One student should play the person to be interviewed, and the other group members should act as reporters. All group members should prepare a list of questions, such as "What did you learn from your predecessors?" "What reforms are you planning and how will they affect the people?" Each group should work together to prepare answers for their questions. Have each group present their interview to the class. **L2**

Chapter 9 Section 1

Independent Practice

Guided Reading Activity 9-1 **L1**

Time Line Activity 9

Mapping History Activity 9

Geography: Place Have students examine a physical map of China and then write a brief explanation of why the ancient Chinese thought of their country as the "Middle Country" or the center of the civilized world. *(China is isolated by geographic barriers)* **L2**

> ***Cultural Perspectives***
>
> **Highways** The imperial highways built under the Qin totaled more than 4,000 miles, as many as in the Roman Empire.

ASSESS

Check for Understanding

Assign Section 1 Review as homework or as an in-class activity.

Use Student Self-Test and Review Software to review Section 1.

Evaluate

Section Quiz 9-1

Use the Testmaker to create a customized quiz for Section 1.

Reteach

Work with students to make lists summarizing the main activities and contributions of the three dynasties studied in this section. Have students explain how each activity served to help or harm the country.

The Great Wall

To Qin, one building project seemed especially urgent—shoring up China's defenses to the north. Earlier rulers had built walls to prevent attacks by nomadic invaders. Qin ordered those walls connected. Over several years some 300,000 peasants toiled—and thousands died—before the work was done. Eventually the wall stretched more than 1,400 miles (2,254 km). Rebuilt by later rulers, the **Great Wall of China** stands today as a monument to Qin's ambition and to the peasants who carried out their emperor's will.

Qin's Strict Rule

Qin Shihuangdi imposed a new order on China. He ended the power of the local lords by taking land from many of them and imposing a tax on landowners. He appointed educated men instead of nobles as officials to run his government.

Qin even imposed an early form of censorship, clamping down on scholars who discussed books and ideas. In 213 B.C. he ordered all books burned except those dealing with "practical" subjects like agriculture, medicine, and magic. In this way he hoped to break people's ties to the past. He agreed with his adviser, who said, "anyone referring to the past to criticize the present … should be put to death." About 460 scholars resisted and were executed.

Qin's subjects saw him as a cruel tyrant who had lost the Mandate of Heaven. Nobles were angry because he had destroyed the aristocracy; scholars detested him for the burning of books; and peasants hated his forced-labor gangs. In 210 B.C. Qin died, and soon the dynasty itself came to an end. Even so, the rule of the Qin brought lasting changes. The most influential changes were new ways of organizing the nation, establishing foundations for the Chinese state that would last 2,000 years.

The Glorious Han

In 207 B.C. **Liu Bang** (LYOH BONG) overthrew the Qin government. A military official from a peasant background, Liu defeated his most powerful rival in 202 B.C. and declared himself the emperor of a new dynasty, the Han.

The Han governed China until A.D. 220, more than 400 years. The Han emperors used the same forms of centralized power that the Qin had set up, but without the harshness of Qin rule. Han China rivaled the Roman Empire in its power and achievement.

Advances Under Wudi

The Han dynasty reached its peak during the reign of **Wudi** (WOO•DEE), who ruled from 141 B.C. to 87 B.C. Wudi, one of the most talented and dynamic rulers in Chinese history, personally supervised all aspects of his government.

An ambitious ruler, Wudi extended his empire. He sent huge armies against the nomadic invaders and other non-Chinese peoples. He conquered lands to the north, including Korea and Manchuria, south into Southeast Asia, and west as far as northern India.

In 139 B.C. Wudi sent out an expedition led by **Zhang Qian** (JAHNG CHYEN), a general and explorer. Thirteen years later, Zhang staggered back. His troops had been nearly wiped out by barbarian attacks, and the general had endured more than 10 years of captivity.

Although he had made no conquests, Zhang brought back amazing tales he had heard on his travels. He told of a great empire to the west, with huge cities full of people "who cut their hair short, wear embroidered garments, and ride in very small chariots." Zhang, who was describing Rome, gave Han rulers their first hint of another civilization as advanced as their own.

Wudi's new interest in the West, fed by news of Zhang Qian's explorations, led to the expansion of trade routes later known as the **Silk Road**. Winding past deserts and through mountain passes, the Silk Road linked East and West. It allowed traders to exchange China's fine silk for Middle Eastern and European products, such as gold, glassware, and wool and linen fabrics.

Pax Sinica

Under the Han, China enjoyed a 400-year period of prosperity and stability, later referred to as the *Pax Sinica* (PAHKS SIH•nuh•kuh), the Chinese Peace. The *Pax Sinica* coincided with the *Pax Romana* in the West.

During the *Pax Sinica*, Wudi adopted an economic policy designed to prevent food shortages and high prices. Government agents stored surplus food during years of plenty and sold it when harvests were poor. Under this system, China was able to feed its growing population.

Before Wudi, emperors had chosen as their officials members of their families or of the aristocracy, a practice that led easily to corruption in government. Wudi wanted talented people to govern, and so he initiated changes. First, he asked people to recommend candidates for public posts. These candidates took long, difficult written examinations. After an official "graded" the tests, the emperor evaluated the results and appointed those with the highest scores.

MEETING SPECIAL NEEDS ACTIVITY

Learning Style: Visual/Spatial Have students trace a map of the area from East Asia to western Europe as far as Rome. Have them draw in and label on the map the physical features of the area, the primary cities of the dynasties covered in this section, and the Silk Road between China and Rome. **L1**

NATIONAL GEOGRAPHIC PICTURING HISTORY

Thomas J. Abercrombie

Silk Road

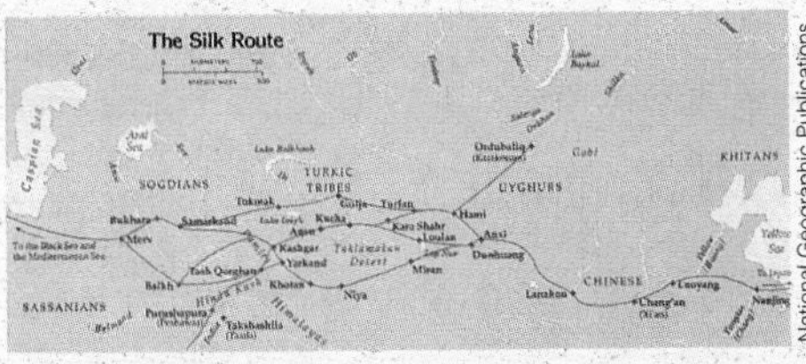

National Geographic Publications Art Division

A caravan of men and mules walk a trail that once formed part of the old Silk Road, a network of paths cutting across Asia from the Pacific coast of China to the Mediterranean Sea. The route, first traveled many years before the Christian era, was the passageway not only for Chinese silk but for a great range of products including jade and fruit, ideas and paintings. Today it is still possible to see how poles and rocks created the actual highway over which goods moved throughout many centuries—before ships, trains, buses, and airplanes replaced mules and packs.

You can trace the length of the trip on the accompanying map. A trader setting forth from the Chinese city of Nanjing would soon leave Chinese territory and enter a world of Muslim ethnic groups and treacherous terrain. The trail loops south and north of the scorching Takla Makan Desert and rises high through mountain passes across the Pamir Mountains. The whole trip was far too long for a single caravan to undertake. Instead, Chinese or Persian merchants dealt with central Asian middlemen from lands such as Afghanistan and Turkestan. ⊕

PICTURING HISTORY

TEACH

Tell students that for more than 2,000 years, the Silk Road and its extensions westward into Roman territory made up the world's longest road. The travel distance along the length of the road and its western extensions totaled 8,000 miles (12,800 km). Ask students in which direction the silk traveled. *(westward)* Point out to students that among the ideas China received via the road were Christianity and Buddhism.

CURRICULUM CONNECTION

ENGINEERING

Part of the Silk Road is currently in use as a paved highway linking Pakistan and Sinkiang Uihgur Autonomous Region, China. The ancient trade route was the inspiration for a United Nations' plan for a trans-Asian highway.

Map Study

Answer

China is isolated by mountains to the north and west, the Gobi to the northwest, and the sea to the east.

Map Skills Practice

Reading a Map From what regions does the Great Wall separate China? *(Manchuria, Mongolia, and the Gobi)*

Enrich

Students may wonder why the spelling of the names *Qin* and *Zhou*, as well as other Chinese personal and place names, appear in different spellings in different books. Have students research the Wade-Giles and pinyin systems for writing Chinese in languages using the Latin alphabet.

CLOSE

Organize the class into two teams. Appoint one person as scorekeeper. Have the teams take turns challenging each other by giving specific names or occurrences and having the other team identify the ruler or dynasty under which the person lived or the event occurred.

The Han Dynasty 202 B.C.–A.D. 220

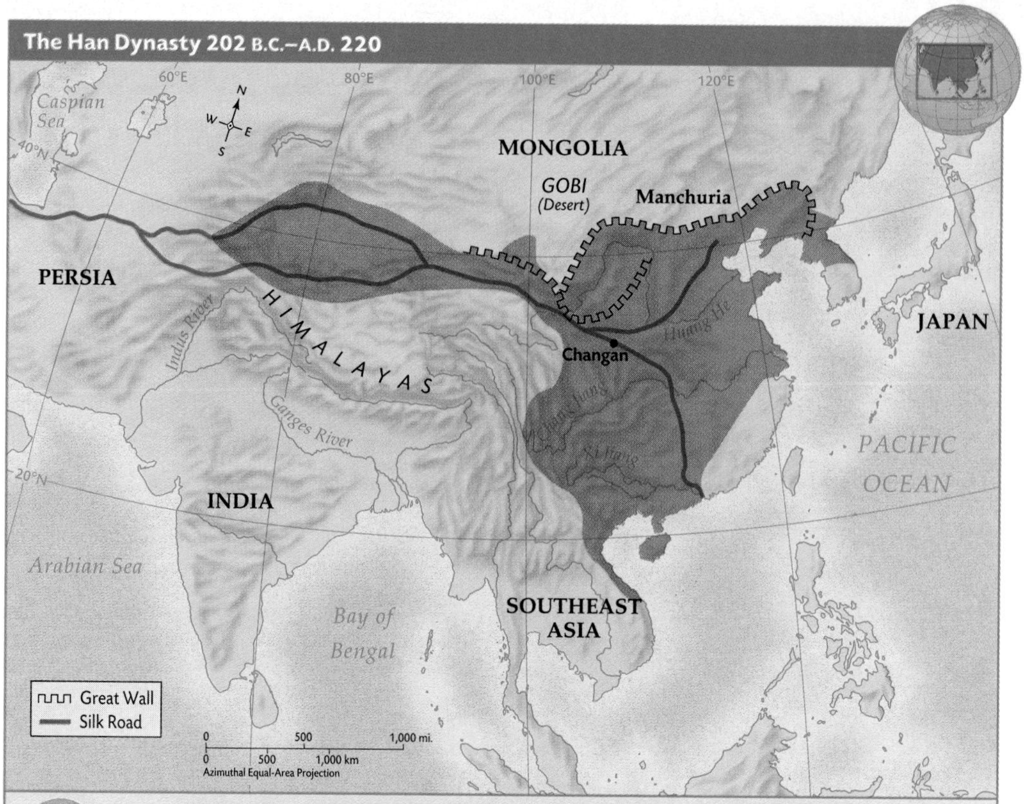

Map Study The Han dynasty stretched from northern India into Manchuria and south into Southeast Asia.
Region What natural features isolated China from the rest of the world?

Wudi's examinations evolved into the **civil service**, a system that allowed anyone with ability to attain public office. At least, that was the theory. In practice, the system favored the wealthy, for education was expensive, and usually only the wealthy could afford to obtain enough education to pass the exams.

The civil service system made scholars the most respected members of Chinese society. A new class of well-educated civil servants, called **mandarins**, controlled the government, and they would continue to do so until the early 1900s.

After Wudi's reign, Han power declined until the dynasty eventually fell in A.D. 220. However, Han achievements in government, technology, science, and the arts were lasting.

SECTION 1 REVIEW

Recall

1. **Define** cavalry, civil service, mandarin.
2. **Identify** Qin Shihuangdi, Liu Bang, Wudi, Zhang Qian.
3. **List** two of the major achievements the Chinese people made under each dynasty—the Zhou, the Qin, and the Han.

Critical Thinking

4. **Analyzing Information** Did Wudi's civil service system offer equal opportunity to all Chinese? Explain.

Understanding Themes

5. **Uniformity** How did Qin Shihuangdi unify China?

SECTION 1 REVIEW ANSWERS

1. All vocabulary words are defined in the Glossary.
2. Qin Shihuangdi, 221; Liu Bang, 222; Wudi, 222; Zhang Qian, 222
3. Zhou: cavalry and cross-bows, iron plows and flood control; Qin: strong central government, plan for Great Wall; Han: exploration and Silk Road, civil service system
4. No: it abolished the system whereby rulers chose family members as officials, but it discriminated against those who could not afford education in the classics.
5. UNIFORMITY standardized coins; uniform tax system, writing system, weights and measures

500 B.C. | A.D. 1 | A.D. 500

c. 522 B.C. Confucius begins to teach.

c. 500 B.C. Daoism emerges as a major Chinese philosophy.

c. A.D. 400 Buddhism becomes a popular religion in China.

Chapter 9
Section 2

Section 2

Three Ways of Life

Setting the Scene

▶ **Terms to Define**
ethics, filial piety, yin and yang

▶ **People to Meet**
Confucius (Kongzi), Laozi

Find Out What philosophic ideals shaped China's government, and how did they shape it?

The Storyteller

One of the duties of Prince Wei-hui's cook was to slaughter cattle for the royal table. When he performed this task, all his movements were harmonious, like a dance. The prince was amazed and asked his servant how he was able to do such heavy work so effortlessly. The cook explained, "What your servant loves is the Tao, which I have applied to the skill of carving. I work with my mind, and not with my eyes." In this way, the toughest cuts yielded easily before his skill. He had learned how to nurture his spirit while maintaining his livelihood.

—adapted from *A Source Book in Chinese Philosophy*, reprinted in *Lives and Times: A World History Reader*, James P. Holoka and Jiu-Hwa L. Upshur, 1994

Confucius

In the latter half of the Zhou era, two major philosophies appeared in China—Confucianism and Daoism. Neither dealt with the supernatural or with eternal life; both were focused instead on life in this world.

Confucianism

Confucianism grew out of the teachings of **Kongzi** (KOONG•DZUH), a government official from Shandong Province. Known in the West as **Confucius**, he was born about 551 B.C. to a poor family. For over 12 years, Confucius traveled throughout northern China, seeking a position as an adviser to a ruler. He hoped that in such a position he could help end China's political and social disorder. Never able to get the post he wanted, Confucius finally found a way to spread his ideas by becoming a teacher.

Family and Government

Promoting order was Confucius's principal concern. He believed that everyone had a proper role in society. If each person would accept that role and perform the related duties, social and political disorder would end. Confucius did not write books, but his followers collected his sayings and later published them in a collection called the *Analects*.

Individuals, Confucius taught, should live according to principles of ethics—good conduct and moral judgment. Ethics began with respect for family, especially elders, and reverence for the past and its traditions. Ethics should govern each person's behavior in these five primary relationships: ruler and subject, parent and child, husband and wife, old and young, friend and friend. Each person, Confucius believed, owed respect and obedience to those above him or her. Those above were expected to set a good example for those below.

Confucius cared especially about filial piety, or children's respect for their parents. For Confucius,

SECTION THEME

▶ **Innovation** The Chinese formulate ethical philosophies and make scientific and technological advances.

Find Out

Answer: *Confucian ideals helped shape China's government by emphasizing order and ethics.*

FOCUS

Section Objective

Describe the philosophic ideals that helped to shape China's government.

BELLRINGER
Motivational Activity

Before taking roll at the beginning of the class period, project Section Focus Transparency 9-2 and have students answer the activity questions. Discuss students' responses.

This activity is also available as a blackline master.

Vocabulary Pre-check

Use Vocabulary Activity 9 to introduce vocabulary terms.
L1 LEP

SECTION RESOURCES

Reproducible Masters
- Reproducible Lesson Plan 9-2
- Vocabulary Activity 9
- Guided Reading Activity 9-2
- History Simulation 9
- Geography and History Activity 9
- Section Quiz 9-2

Transparencies
- Section Focus Transparency 9-2
- World History and Art Transparency 10

Multimedia
- Student Self-Test and Review Software
- Testmaker

TEACH

Guided Practice

THEME **Innovation**

Have students explain the new ideas put forth by Confucius and Laozi. *(Confucius: filial piety, ethical conduct toward others, importance of accepting one's role in society, reverence for the past; Laozi: renouncing worldly ambitions, harmony with nature, yin/yang)* **L1**

Independent Practice

Guided Reading Activity 9-2 **L1**

ASSESS

Check for Understanding

Assign Section 2 Review as homework or as an in-class activity.

Use Student Self-Test and Review Software to review Section 2.

CONNECTIONS
Science and Technology

The First Seismograph

The seismograph in the picture is not the actual one invented by Zhang Heng. Experts have been able to make a model of it based upon available descriptions.

Answers to Making the Connection

1. *When a tremor occurred, a mechanism caused one of the balls to fall into a toad's mouth. This action showed that somewhere an earthquake was taking place. The side of the seismograph where the toad was sitting indicated the quake's direction. The loudness of the ball indicated the tremor's strength.*
2. *to understand divine messages; to provide help for those affected by disaster*

the family represented society in miniature. He said:

> "The superior man spreads his culture to the entire nation by remaining at home.... The teaching of filial piety is a preparation for serving the ruler of the state; the teaching of respect for one's elder brothers is a preparation for serving all the elders of the community; and the teaching of kindness in parents is a training for ruling over people.... When individual families have learned kindness, then the whole nation has learned kindness."

Governments too had a duty: to set an example of right conduct. The ethical ruler had integrity, was righteous, inspired loyalty, understood proper behavior, and appreciated culture.

When a student asked Confucius for one single word that could serve as a principle for conduct, he responded: "Perhaps the word *reciprocity* will do. Do not do unto others what you would not want others to do unto you." This rule is similar to a familiar teaching of Judaism and Christianity, sometimes called the Golden Rule: "Do unto others as you would have others do unto you."

Confucianism After Confucius

The Zhou government did not accept Confucius's teachings during his lifetime. Within a century after his death in 479 B.C., however, Confucian ethics were widely followed in China. Later scholars added their ideas, and Confucianism eventually became a religion.

During the Han dynasty, Confucius's teachings provided the basis for Wudi's civil service system. Though Han scholars reinterpreted Confucianism, they retained its devotion to ethical behavior and just government. Indeed, Confucius's teachings would serve as a basis for Chinese society and government until the 1900s.

Daoism

During the time of Confucius, a man called **Laozi** (LOW•DZUH), or "Old Master," taught ideas that in some ways seem the opposite of Confucianism. He rejected formal social structures and the idea that people must fill specific roles in society. Unlike Confucius, Laozi shunned public

CONNECTIONS
Science and Technology

The First Seismograph

Zhang Heng's seismograph

In 1994 a powerful earthquake struck Los Angeles, California. A year later, the city of Kobe in Japan was rocked by a major quake that brought death and destruction throughout the city's metropolitan area.

Today we know that shifting in the earth's crust causes earthquakes. This movement sends seismic waves across the earth's surface, much as dropping a pebble in a pond sends ripples across water.

People in Han China believed that angry spirits caused earthquakes to express their displeasure with society. Scholars studied quakes closely in hope of finding a divine message.

In A.D. 132 Zhang Heng invented the world's first seismograph, an instrument for detecting and measuring earthquakes. Zhang's device resembled a domed, cylindrical urn. Each of eight dragons around the top held a ball in its jaws. At the base of the urn sat eight toads with upturned heads and open mouths, each directly under a dragon.

When a tremor occurred, a mechanism caused one of the balls to fall into a toad's mouth. This action showed that somewhere an earthquake was taking place. The side of the seismograph where that toad was sitting indicated the quake's direction. As the ball popped into the toad's mouth, the loudness indicated the tremor's strength.

MAKING THE CONNECTION

1. How did Zhang Heng's seismograph work?
2. Why might Han emperors want to know about earthquakes?

COOPERATIVE LEARNING ACTIVITY

Panel Discussion Organize the class into three groups. Assign one of the following thinkers to each group: Confucius, Laozi, the Buddha. Have each group research the teachings of its thinker. (Alert students that they may find variant spellings: *Kongzi*, *Kungfuzi*, or *Kung-fu-tzu* for *Confucius*; *Tao* instead of *Dao*; and *Lao-tzu* or other variants for *Laozi*.) Ask each group to prepare for a panel discussion in which each thinker will explain how his ideas can benefit individuals and society. Each group should appoint one student to role-play the thinker. Other students should be prepared to ask questions of the panel members. You or a student should act as panel moderator. **L2**

life, leaving anything we know of him heavily mixed with legend.

Daoist Ideas

Laozi's ideas were recorded in the *Dao De Jing*, one of the Chinese classics. Daoists believed that people should renounce worldly ambitions and turn to nature and the Dao—the eternal force that permeates everything in nature. They followed examples from nature, as these lines suggest:

> "The highest good is like water.
> Water gives life to the ten thousand things
> and does not strive.
> It flows in places men reject and so is like
> the Dao.
> In dwelling, be close to the land.
> In meditation, go deep in the heart.
> In dealing with others, be gentle and kind.
> In speech, be true.
> In ruling, be just."

By emphasizing harmony with nature, Daoists deeply influenced Chinese arts, particularly painting and poetry.

Daoist simplicity seems to oppose Confucian formalism, but a person could be both a Confucianist and a Daoist. Confucianism provided the pattern for government and one's place in the social order, and Daoism emphasized harmony within the individual attuned to nature. Because the emphasis of each was different, a person could easily be both.

Yin and Yang

A Chinese theory related to Daoist ideas was the concept of yin and yang, the two opposing forces believed to be present in all nature. Yin was cool, dark, female, and submissive, while yang was warm, light, male, and aggressive. Everything had both elements. For harmony the two elements had to be in balance. Human life and natural events, including the changing seasons, resulted from the interplay between yin and yang.

History & Art Laozi on his buffalo. Guimet Museum, Paris, France. *How did the teaching of Laozi as recorded in the Dao De Jing influence Chinese arts and poetry?*

The concept of yin and yang helped the Chinese reconcile seeming opposites—like Dao simplicity and Confucian formalism. It also helped them accept Buddhist ideas brought to China by monks and traders from India.

Buddhism

Buddhism reached China just as the Han Empire was collapsing, and its emphasis on personal salvation in nirvana appealed to many people seeking an escape from suffering. Confucianists could follow its Eightfold Path, and Daoists admired its use of meditation. By the A.D. 400s, Buddhism was widely embraced in China.

SECTION 2 REVIEW

Recall

1. **Define** ethics, filial piety, yin and yang.
2. **Identify** Confucius, Laozi.
3. **Explain** why Confucius wanted to become an adviser to a ruler. What was his goal in life, and was he successful?

Critical Thinking

4. **Making Comparisons** How would you compare the philosophers Confucius and Laozi in their ideas and also in their ways of life?

Understanding Themes

5. **Innovation** How did the concept of yin and yang help the Chinese people reconcile ideas in the thought of Daoism that seemed opposed to Confucianism?

Chapter 9 Section 2

History & Art Laozi was a scholar at the royal court of the Zhou dynasty. When he realized that the Zhou dynasty was in decline, he made a legendary voyage to the state of Qin. The guardian of the pass to the Qin state begged Laozi to write a book for him. The result was the *Dao De Jing*.

Answer to Caption: *Laozi's teachings influenced Chinese arts by emphasizing harmony with nature.*

Evaluate

Section Quiz 9-2

Use the Testmaker to create a customized quiz for Section 2.

Reteach

Have students meet in small groups to discuss the three belief systems of ancient China. Have the groups identify the primary teachings of each system.

Enrich

Have students write a report on Buddhism today, describing each of the major traditions, its beliefs, and where it is practiced.

CLOSE

Have students explain briefly how a Han Chinese family might have practiced Confucianism, Daoism, and Buddhism simultaneously.

SECTION 2 REVIEW ANSWERS

1. All vocabulary words are defined in the Glossary.
2. Confucius, 225; Laozi, 226
3. Confucius wanted to help end China's political and social disorder—his goal in life. He never got the post he wanted, but he was able to spread his ideas by becoming a teacher. These ideas became the basis of Han government and continued to shape China for many centuries.
4. Confucius was a public man with strong ideas about a structured, orderly society; Laozi was a private man who looked to nature for the Dao, or way.
5. **INNOVATION** The concept of yin and yang taught that opposing forces were present in all of nature.

Chapter 9 Section 3

SECTION THEME

▶ **Cultural Diffusion** Traders carry ideas and products along the Silk Road.

Find Out

Answer: *Early Chinese society was organized according to Confucian values. In addition to breakthroughs in astronomy, medicine, farming, and transport, the ancient Chinese invented silk and paper.*

FOCUS

Section Objective

Explain how early Chinese society was organized and summarize the scientific and technological breakthroughs.

BELLRINGER Motivational Activity

Before taking roll at the beginning of the class period, project Section Focus Transparency 9-3 and have students answer the activity questions. Discuss students' responses.

This activity is also available as a blackline master.

Vocabulary Pre-check

Use Vocabulary Activity 9 to introduce vocabulary terms. **L1 LEP**

1000 B.C. | 500 B.C. | A.D. 1

1000 B.C. Chinese begin poems in the *Book of Songs*.

240 B.C. Chinese astronomers record appearance of Halley's comet.

c. 100 B.C. Chinese invent paper.

Section 3

Society and Culture

Setting the Scene

▶ **Terms to Define**
hierarchy, extended family, nuclear family, acupuncture

▶ **People to Meet**
Sima Qian

Find Out How was early Chinese society organized, and what scientific and technological breakthroughs took place in early China?

The Storyteller

Wu Phu was a physician, trained by Hua Tho, an outstanding medical theorist. Hua Tho impressed upon his pupils the importance of physical exercise as a means of obtaining good health. He compared an exercised body to running water, which never became stale. "When the body feels ill," he counseled, "one should do one of these exercises. After perspiring, one will sense the body grow light and the stomach will manifest hunger." There was merit in those recommendations. Wu Phu had carefully followed his master's regimen, and although he was past ninety years of age, his hearing, vision, and even his teeth were all still excellent.

—adapted from "Hygiene and Preventive Medicine in Ancient China," reprinted in *Reflections on World Civilization*, edited by Ronald H. Fritze, James S. Olson, and Randy W. Roberts, 1994

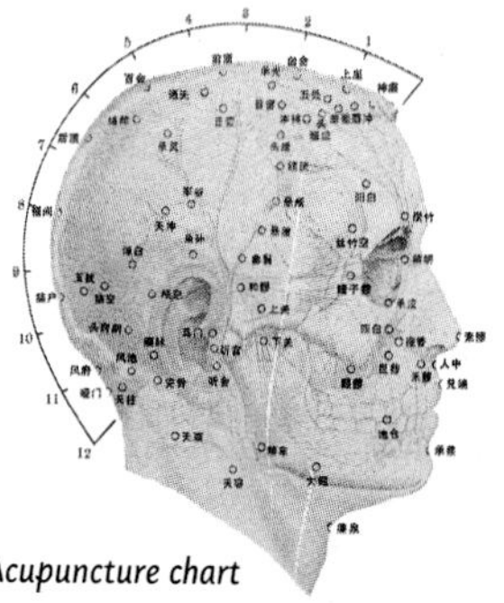

Acupuncture chart

Confucian values governed all aspects of personal and social life in Han China. "With harmony at home, there will be order in the nation," Confucius had said. "With order in the nation, there will be peace in the world." And indeed, the family was supreme in Chinese society. It was the focus of life, bound together strongly by mutual love, loyalty, and dependence.

Family Life

The members of a Chinese family of the Han era lived and worked together. In an ideal family every member knew his or her role and the duties that went with it.

Relationships

Family members did not relate to each other as equals; instead, the family was a strict **hierarchy**, organized into different levels of importance. The oldest male in the home, usually the father, was dominant. Next in rank was the oldest son, followed by all the younger sons and all the females. The mother came before the daughters, and finally—at the bottom—the youngest daughter or childless daughter-in-law. Each family member expected obedience from those who were further down in the hierarchy, and each obeyed and respected those who were above.

Family Rules

Strict rules governed the relationships between husbands and wives, parents and grandparents, uncles and aunts, brothers and sisters, and other relatives. Each family member knew his or her place and understood its duties, and each was careful not to bring dishonor on the family by failing in those duties. Moreover, the duty to family members did not stop at death; all were expected to pay respect to departed ancestors.

SECTION RESOURCES

Reproducible Masters
- Reproducible Lesson Plan 9-3
- Vocabulary Activity 9
- Guided Reading Activity 9-3
- Source Reading 9
- People in World History Profiles 15, 16
- World History Art and Music Activity 9
- Reteaching Activity 9
- Enrichment Activity 9
- Section Quiz 9-3
- Performance Assessment Activity 9
- Spanish Chapter Summary 9

Transparencies
- Section Focus Transparency 9-3
- Ancient China

Multimedia
- Student Self-Test and Review Software
- Testmaker
- World Music: Cultural Traditions, Lesson 8
- India and China

228 Chapter 9 *China's Flourishing Civilization*

Typical homes in Han China did not have the extended families, or families of many generations living together, that would later be typical. Rather, they had what we call today nuclear families, each consisting of parents and their children. The father assigned his children's careers, determined their education, arranged their marriages, meted out rewards or punishments, and controlled the family finances. The family also provided support for members who themselves could not contribute—the aged, the young, the sick, and even the lazy.

No doubt the system offered many opportunities for exploiting those further down in the hierarchy. Nevertheless, few fathers were tyrants. Like other family members, they practiced ethical principles of kindness and compassion, either from genuine love or from fear of the disapproval of others and the scorn of their ancestors.

AROUND THE WORLD **Aesop's Fables**

Greece, c. 500 B.C.
A collection of stories told by an enslaved Greek named Aesop features animals who talk and act like people. Each of Aesop's fables ends with a proverb that teaches a moral. For example, the proverb "The Tortoise and the Hare" teaches that slow and steady wins the race. Aesop's fables were not written down until nearly three centuries after his death.

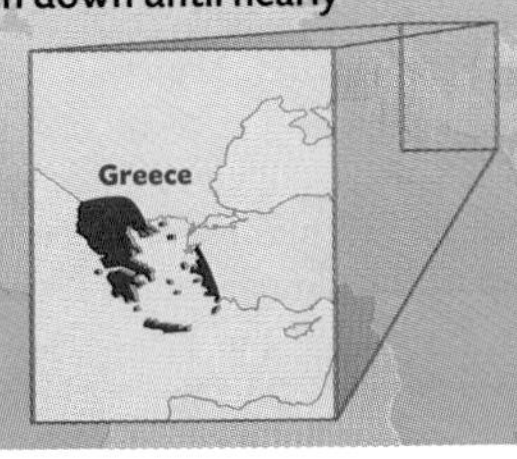

Status of Women

Under the Confucian social system, women were subordinate to men. Confucius himself had little regard for women, saying, "Women and uneducated people are the most difficult to deal with."

Girls began life subservient to their fathers and brothers. Later their husbands and in-laws were their superiors, and eventually even a mother came under the authority of her own sons. Parents valued baby girls far less than baby boys. A poor family had to work hard to raise and support a child, and if that child was a daughter, she left home to become part of her husband's family as soon as she married.

Some women were able to gain respect in Chinese homes. With marriage and motherhood, they became revered. Other opportunities for women, such as education, were limited. In spite of Confucianism's predominance, women fared far better under the Han than they would in later centuries. They could inherit property, even own it after they married, and they could remarry after a husband's death.

Society and Economy

Chinese society consisted of three main classes: landowners, peasants, and merchants. Landowning families were wealthy. They lived in tile-roofed mansions with courtyards and gardens. They surrounded their homes with walls to protect them from bandits. They filled their rooms with fine furniture and adorned them with silk wall hangings and carpets. Wealthy families feasted on a rich variety of foods.

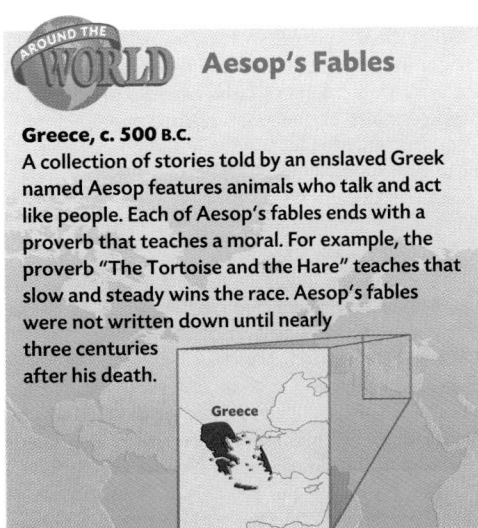

The landholders' wealth was generally limited, however, and families rarely kept their holdings for more than a few generations. When a family's land was divided, it went to all the sons, not just the oldest, with the result that in time individual landowners had less and less property.

Probably 90 percent of the Chinese people were peasants. The wealth that supported the lifestyles of the rich was gained from the hard labor of the peasants who cultivated the land. Unlike Western farmers, who usually lived on the land they farmed, most Chinese peasants lived in rural villages and worked fields outside their mud walls. Their homes were simple, and they ate a plain diet that featured millet, rice, beans, turnips, and fish.

The peasants raised livestock and toiled long hours in the grain fields. They faced constant threats from floods and from famines. As rent for the land, peasants turned over part of their produce to the landowner. The government required them to pay taxes and to work one month each year on public works projects such as road building. In times of conflict, peasants were drafted into the army as soldiers.

At the bottom of the social hierarchy were merchants—a group that included shopkeepers, traders, service workers, and even bankers. The merchants lived in towns and provided goods and services for the wealthy. In spite of the great wealth that many merchants accumulated, Chinese society generally held them in contempt. Confucianism taught that the pursuit of profit was an unworthy pastime for the "superior" individual. Merchants were not allowed to take the civil service examinations and enter government service.

TEACH

Guided Practice

THEME **Cultural Diffusion**

Have students list inventions and discoveries made by the ancient Chinese. Then have them list things in their homes that originated in China. *(Possible items: kite, firecrackers, abacus, paper, silk, compass, paper money, chinaware or porcelain.)* Have students compare their lists in class. Discuss how and why certain inventions might have spread to other cultures. **L1 LEP**

Social Class Work with students to organize a chart showing the social classes in ancient China. List the classes in order of hierarchy. Next to each class, list its characteristics. **L2**

World Music: Cultural Traditions, Lesson 8

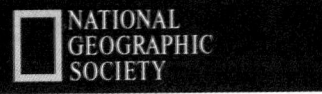

NATIONAL GEOGRAPHIC SOCIETY

Use these materials to enrich student understanding of Chinese culture.

NGS PICTURESHOW CD-ROM
India and China

COOPERATIVE LEARNING ACTIVITY

Making Posters Organize the class into small groups to create posters that illustrate the costumes and decorations worn by ancient Chinese of various social classes. Make sure each student is assigned a specific task, such as reading, drawing, designing, framing, and so on. Students should research costumes worn by groups such as mandarins, women of the royal family, peasants, merchants, and so on. Students should include a brief explanation under each illustration. Students may also illustrate groups' hair styles or personal grooming habits (such as makeup). Display the completed posters. **L1**

Independent Practice

Guided Reading Activity 9-3 **L1**

Source Reading 9

People in World History Profiles 15, 16

World Art and Music Activity 9

The Arts Have students research and write a report on some of the poetry and songs from the *Book of Songs* or *Shih Ching*. Have students share the poems or songs with the class. **L2**

Global Gourmet

China The Chinese have been drinking tea since about 50 B.C. Tea was originally used as a medicine—to help keep awake and alert, or to counteract the effects of too much food or drink. But eventually the Chinese came to appreciate tea for its own merits, and an elaborate culture grew up around the drinking of tea.

NATIONAL GEOGRAPHIC SOCIETY

Use these materials to enrich student understanding of ancient Chinese culture.

NGS PICTUREPACK TRANSPARENCY SET
Ancient China

For all the people in Han society except merchants, the civil service system provided opportunities for advancement, though the expense of education blocked most of the poor from competing. Still, poor but talented individuals sometimes rose to positions of power and influence.

Literature

Although the Qin burned thousands of books, many survived in royal libraries and secret private collections. Particularly prized was a collection of books called the Five Classics, some of which were written before Confucius. All candidates for the civil service were required to master them. No better example is recorded of the Chinese reverence for history.

The oldest of the Five Classics, the *Book of Songs*, preserves 305 of the earliest Chinese poems, written between 1000 B.C. and 600 B.C. The poems deal with political themes, ritual, and romance. Many seem modern, with their everyday topics and simple, concrete imagery—this one, for example:

> "Near the East Gate
> Young women go
> Like so many clouds all day.
> Like drifting clouds
> A thought of them
> Soon blows away.
>
> There. White robe
> and a blue scarf—
> she makes my day.
>
> Near the Great Tower and Wall
> Go slender girls
> Like reeds by river's edge:
> Like bending reeds
> A thought of them
> Soon passes by."

The *Book of Documents* records political speeches

Images of the Times

Han China

The Han dynasty was a golden age of Chinese history. Important political, economic, and cultural changes took place.

Wudi's examinations developed into a civil service system, leading to a wealthy class of mandarins who controlled the government.

230

Images of the Times **Han China**

The terra-cotta horseman in the photograph is only one example of Han tomb sculpture. Han tombs were very elaborate, in many cases constructed of brick or stone and divided into several chambers. The tombs of Han emperors were enclosed in giant mounds of earth that are still visible today. In addition to statues, the tombs often contained bronze mirrors. The ancient Chinese believed that mirrors were sources of light and as such could brighten the darkness of the tomb through all eternity. A great deal of pottery has also been unearthed from Han tombs, including both household items and pots made especially for burial, called *ming ch'i*, or "spirit utensils."

and documents from early in the Zhou dynasty, including the earliest statement of the Mandate of Heaven. The *Book of Changes* presents a complex system for foretelling the future and choosing a course of action. In *Spring and Autumn Annals* Confucius reported major events that occurred in the state of Lu between 722 B.C. and 481 B.C.

The Five Classics were thought to carry solutions to most problems. Officials studied them closely to find support for their positions, such as the conduct of political leaders. Accounts of solar eclipses, meteor showers, and droughts were used to show what terrifying events and disasters could befall poor political leaders.

Another great collection of books, the Thirteen Classics, included the *Analects*—Confucius's sayings compiled by his students after his death. Many appeared as answers to questions. For example, Confucius was asked about the gentleman, or the "superior man." Among other replies he gave this one: "What the gentleman seeks, he seeks within himself; what the small man seeks, he seeks in others."

The Han Chinese encouraged literary pursuits and made literature available to everyone. An especially valuable work produced during the Han dynasty period was the *Historical Record*. Written by **Sima Qian** during the reign of Wudi, it is the first true history of ancient China.

Science and Technology

Besides literature and philosophy, China made major contributions in science and technology. By the 300s B.C., Chinese astronomers had calculated the length of the solar year as $365\frac{1}{4}$ days. They gazed through bronze tubes equipped with a device that divided the sky into measured segments, allowing them to make accurate measurements. They kept valuable records of solar and lunar eclipses and comet sightings. In 240 B.C. Chinese astronomers recorded the appearance of the object that would later be called Halley's comet—many centuries before Halley's birth.

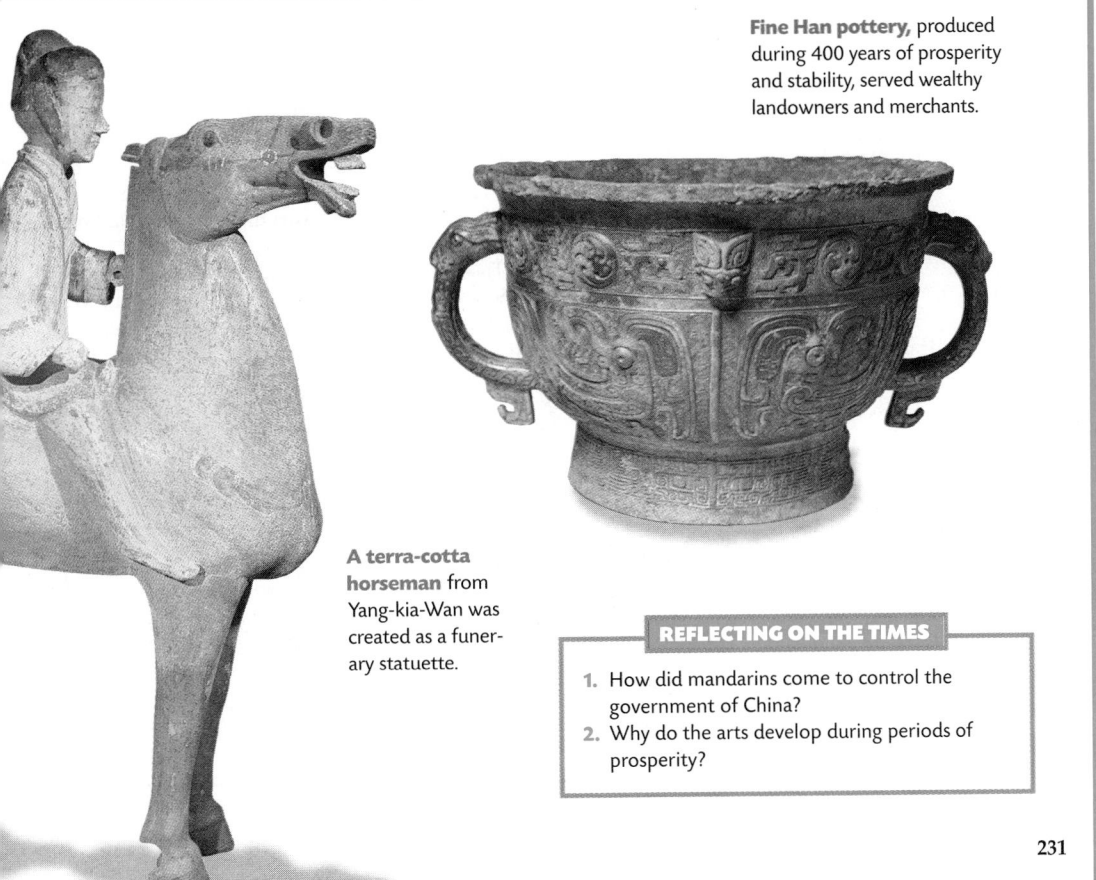

Fine Han pottery, produced during 400 years of prosperity and stability, served wealthy landowners and merchants.

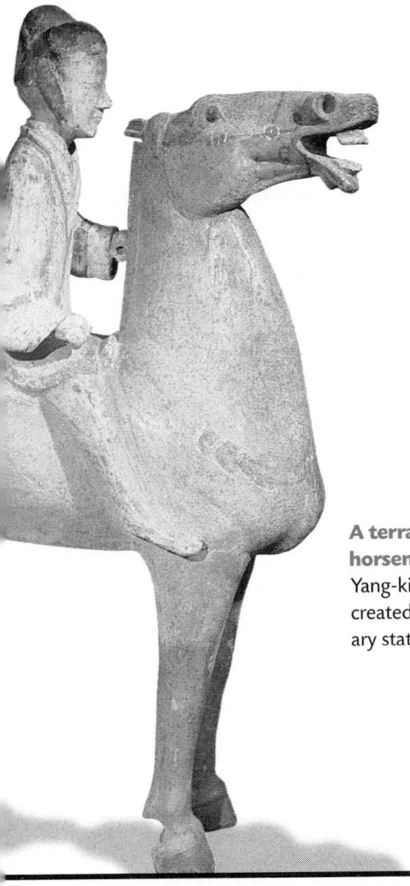

A terra-cotta horseman from Yang-kia-Wan was created as a funerary statuette.

REFLECTING ON THE TIMES

1. How did mandarins come to control the government of China?
2. Why do the arts develop during periods of prosperity?

231

Chapter 9 Section 3

Linking Past and Present

Acupuncturists today treat pain and a variety of disorders: headache, sinusitis, chronic respiratory infections, digestive problems, and drug addictions. Modern Chinese surgeons also use acupuncture instead of anesthetics. The patient remains conscious during surgery but reportedly does not feel pain. Some doctors in Europe and the United States have begun to use acupuncture.

ASSESS

Check for Understanding

Assign Section 3 Review as homework or as an in-class activity.

Use Student Self-Test and Review Software to review Section 3.

Evaluate

Section Quiz 9-3

Use the Testmaker to create a customized quiz for Section 3.

Reteach

Have students work in pairs to make a chart summarizing the main topics of this section. Headings should include *Family Structure, Social Structure, Literature,* and *Science and Technology*. Have students list the important points and illustrate the chart.

Reteaching Activity 9

ANSWERS TO REFLECTING ON THE TIMES

1. Mandarins came to control the government of China as a result of Wudi's civil service examinations.
2. The arts develop during periods of prosperity because people have the money to patronize artists.

Chapter 9
Section 3

Visualizing History According to legend, in about 2700 B.C. Chinese emperor Huangdi ordered his wife to find out what was killing his mulberry trees. Finding white worms eating and spinning shiny cocoons on the leaves, she accidentally dropped a cocoon into hot water. When she removed a thin thread unwinding from the cocoon, she discovered silk.
Answer to Caption: *the Silk Road*

Enrich

Have students research the status of merchants in one or more other ancient civilizations. Ask students to prepare a report that summarizes their findings and highlights areas of comparison/contrast with the status of merchants in ancient China.

Enrichment Activity 9

CLOSE

Ask students to imagine that they live in China in A.D. 200. Have them decide which family role (father, mother, eldest son, youngest son, daughter, daughter-in-law) they would like best and which they would like least. Ask them to explain why.

Visualizing History **Women prepare newly woven silk. Han weavers created beautiful damasks of many colors.** *What was the name of one of history's greatest trade routes out of China?*

Medicine

Chinese physicians recognized nutrition as vital and realized that some diseases resulted from vitamin deficiencies. Although they did not identify vitamins as such, they discovered and prescribed foods that would correct some problems. They also understood that many herbs had medicinal value.

Chinese doctors treated ailments and relieved pain with **acupuncture**, a technique in which the skin is pierced with thin needles at vital points. They believed acupuncture restored the balance between yin and yang in a person's body.

Farming and Transport

Under the Han, many improvements occurred in agriculture and transportation. Complex irrigation systems drained swamps and diverted rivers to quench parched fields. Advances in fertilizing crops helped farmers produce enough to feed China's growing population. Veterinary medicine helped save many farm animals. New canals and improved roadways reduced the cost of distributing food and permitted ideas to spread more rapidly.

Inventions

Many inventions in ancient China were especially vital to Chinese life and the economy. Made by the Chinese since prehistoric times, silk was in great demand as a trade item; its worth was attested to by the name of one of history's greatest trade routes—the Silk Road. Caravans carried the precious cargo as far as Rome.

Paper was probably invented by 100 B.C., although it was officially credited to an inventor of about 200 years later. Artisans pounded tree bark, hemp, or rags into a pulp. By treating it with gelatin, they discovered that they could then make paper. Used first for wrapping and clothing, paper was soon recognized as an ideal writing material.

The invention of paper benefited the bureaucratic Han government. Its centralized structure resulted in an explosion in the number of documents. Most were written on strips of wood, which were fragile and cumbersome to work with. The use of paper had many obvious advantages.

Other inventions improved mining and construction. Miners, using iron drill bits driven by workers on seesawlike levers, drilled boreholes to obtain salt from the earth. Another invention was the wheelbarrow, which was first used on building sites around 100 B.C.

These are only a few examples from a list of Chinese "firsts," which also includes the first printed books, the earliest technologies for casting bronze and iron, the suspension bridge, the compass, and gunpowder. Such achievements caused China to remain far ahead of Europe in science and technology until the A.D. 1300s.

SECTION 3 REVIEW

Recall

1. **Define** hierarchy, extended family, nuclear family, acupuncture.
2. **Identify** the Five Classics, *Spring and Autumn Annals*, the *Analects*, Sima Qian.
3. **Explain** how families and government during the Han era reflected the Confucian idea of order.

Critical Thinking

4. **Making Comparisons** Compare a typical Han Chinese family with families you consider typical of America today.

Understanding Themes

5. **Cultural Diffusion** What ideas and products from ancient China have become popular in the West in recent years? What factors account for their popularity among Western thinkers and consumers?

SECTION 3 REVIEW ANSWERS

1. All vocabulary words are defined in the Glossary.
2. Five Classics, 230; *Spring and Autumn Annals*, 231; the *Analects*, 231; Sima Qian, 231
3. Both were highly structured hierarchies.
4. Answers will vary. Students may refer to the strict Han family hierarchy with the father at the top, obedience and respect due to those above, and limited opportunities for women.
5. **CULTURAL DIFFUSION** Answers may include: acupuncture, herbal medicine, ancient philosophies; popularity linked to perception that Western products and ideas have failed to prevent social decline.

Critical Thinking

SKILLS

Identifying Central Issues

The saying "He can't see the forest for the trees" refers to someone so focused on separate details that he cannot see the entire situation. Sometimes we face this problem when studying history. It is easy to focus on details such as names, dates, and places, thus losing sight of the bigger picture. To avoid this, it is important to identify the central issues. Central issues are the main ideas of historical material.

Learning the Skill

First, skim the material to identify its general subject. Look for headings and subheadings; often they highlight central issues. A central issue may also appear in the topic sentence of a paragraph. The other sentences in the paragraph usually explain and support the central issue.

When looking for central issues, ask yourself these questions: What is the general topic of this material? What ideas have the greatest emphasis? What main idea holds the details together? If I had to summarize this material in one sentence, what would it be? If you can answer one or more of these questions, you can identify central issues.

Practicing the Skill

Read the passage about the *Book of Changes* and answer the questions that follow.

> "The *Book of Changes—I Ching* in Chinese—is unquestionably one of the most important books in the world's literature.... Nearly all that is greatest and most significant in the three thousand years of Chinese cultural history has either taken its inspiration from this book, or has exerted an influence on the interpretation of its text.... Indeed, not only the philosophy of China but its science and statecraft as well have never ceased to draw from the spring of wisdom in the *I Ching*.... Even the commonplaces of everyday life in China are saturated with its influence. In going through the streets of a Chinese city, one will find, here and there at a street corner, a fortune teller sitting behind a neatly covered table, brush and tablet at hand, ready to draw from the ancient book of wisdom pertinent counsel and information on life's minor perplexities...."

1. What is the general subject of the passage?
2. Which idea has the greatest emphasis?
3. What are some details that support this idea?
4. Which sentence states the central issue of the passage?

Applying the Skill

Find a newspaper or magazine article that interests you. Identify the central issues in this article and summarize them in your own words.

For More Practice

Turn to the Skill Practice in the Chapter Review on page 235 for more practice in identifying central issues.

Critical Thinking

SKILLS

TEACH

Identifying Central Issues Before asking students to read the skill, distribute copies of a newspaper editorial. Ask students which sentence best indicates the subject of the editorial. Ask them what such a sentence is called. *(topic sentence)* Have them restate the point of the topic sentence in their own words. Now ask them to identify sentences in the editorial that support the main point. After you are satisfied with the students' ability to locate the central issue, have students read the skill and complete the practice questions.

Additional Practice

Skill Reinforcement Activity 9

ANSWERS TO PRACTICING THE SKILL

1. the *Book of Changes*, or *I Ching*
2. The book's influence has permeated all levels of Chinese life.
3. Fortune tellers on city streets base their message on the *I Ching*. Science and statecraft have drawn on the wisdom of the *I Ching*.
4. Students may name either the first sentence or the second sentence as the topic sentence. As long as students can argue convincingly to support their choice, either is an acceptable answer.

Chapter 9 Review

GLENCOE TECHNOLOGY

VIDEODISC
Use MindJogger to review students' knowledge of the chapter.

MindJogger Videoquiz
Chapter 9
Disc 2 Side A

Also available in VHS.

Answers

Using Key Terms

1. b	**6.** g
2. c	**7.** d
3. a	**8.** e
4. f	**9.** i
5. j	**10.** h

Using Your History Journal

For a multicultural perspective, suggest to students that they also look at the Old Testament book of Proverbs, or at Benjamin Franklin's *Poor Richard's Almanack* for ideas for wise sayings.

Reviewing Facts

1. Confucius was a thinker from Zhou times who stressed order, ethics, and filial piety.
2. Daoism rejects social hierarchies and emphasizes harmony with nature.
3. ruler-subject, parent-child, husband-wife, old-young, friend-friend
4. *Book of Songs*: oldest of Five Classics; *Spring and Autumn Annals*: Confucius's account of major events in state of Lu from 722 B.C. to 481 B.C.; *Historical Record*: first true history of ancient China, written by Sima Qian in Han era
5. to protect China's border from invaders
6. landowners, peasants, merchants
7. Zhou: local lords were powerful; Qin: strong central government; Han: civil servants called mandarins controlled government
8. a ruler had to be ethical and set an example of right conduct for those beneath him
9. The Qin would have disliked the Confucian reverence for the past and emphasis on the need for rulers to exhibit ethical behavior; since Han rulers like Wudi treated their subjects well, they would have approved of Confucius's teachings.
10. silk, paper

Critical Thinking

1. Students should support their answers.
2. positive: social order, loyalty, sense of duty; negative: low status of women, lack of

CHAPTER 9 REVIEW

Historical Significance

Confucian ideas have had a major impact on China's development. On the negative side, some historians point to the Confucian denial of women's rights and its stress on total obedience to authority. On the positive side, others state that the Confucian emphasis on stability helped early China build a strong government and that Confucius's ideas about relationships resulted in a more compassionate society. Confucius also left a revolutionary legacy. He considered it a society's duty to overthrow an unjust ruler and to ensure a fair distribution of wealth.

Using Key Terms

Write the key term that completes each sentence.

a. acupuncture	f. mandarin
b. civil service	g. yin and yang
c. extended family	h. filial piety
d. hierarchy	i. cavalry
e. ethics	j. nuclear family

1. The Chinese emperor Wudi created a school that helped students prepare for examinations for positions in the _______, a system that allowed anyone with abilities to attain public office.
2. An ___________ consists of parents, children, grandparents, and other relatives living together in one household.
3. Chinese doctors treated ailments and relieved pain with _______, a technique in which the skin is pierced with thin needles at vital points.
4. The administration of China's government came under the control of the _______, a class of well-educated officials.
5. The typical household in Han China was made up of a ___________, which included only parents and children.
6. A Chinese theory related to Daoism was the concept of ___________, the two opposing forces believed to be present in all of nature.
7. The Chinese family was a strict _____ in which members were ranked in order of importance under the father.
8. Confucius taught that individuals should live according to principles of _____.
9. During the Zhou period, the Chinese organized their military, forming a _____ of mounted warriors and horse-drawn chariots.
10. The Chinese cared especially about _________, or children's respect for their parents.

Using Your History Journal

Many of Confucius's sayings compiled by his students after his death are similar to proverbs, or wise sayings. Write a set of your own proverbs about everyday decisions and situations.

Reviewing Facts

1. **Identify** Confucius (Kongzi) and his principal ideas.
2. **State** the differences between Confucianism and Daoism.
3. **List** the five important relationships in Chinese society that were identified by Confucius.
4. **Describe** the *Book of Songs*, the *Spring and Autumn Annals*, and the *Historical Record*.
5. **Explain** why Qin Shihuangdi ordered the construction of the Great Wall of China.
6. **Identify** three main groups that made up Chinese society during the Han era.
7. **List** the characteristics of China's government and politics under the Zhou, Qin, and Han dynasties.
8. **Analyze** how Confucius applied the idea of filial piety to governments as well as families.
9. **Explain** why Qin rulers strongly opposed the teachings of Confucius, though Han rulers like Wudi promoted Confucianism.
10. **List** three inventions that were especially important to Chinese life.

Critical Thinking

1. **Evaluate** Do you think merchants deserved the

low status they held in Chinese society?
2. **Evaluate** Was a strong family structure a positive or a negative influence on Chinese society?
3. **Apply** How does your society make use of the Han concept of appointing officials by ability?
4. **Synthesize** How would you respond if your government adopted the social policies of the Qin dynasty?
5. **Contrast** How did the Zhou and Qin systems of government differ?
6. **Synthesize** Think about how merchants were viewed in Han society and why. How might the United States be different if we felt that way about merchants?

Geography in History

1. **Movement** Refer to the map below. Buddhism came to China from which area of the world?
2. **Location** What cities became major Buddhist sites in China?
3. **Movement** From what area did Daoism spread into China?
4. **Region** What Daoist concepts made it possible for much of China to accept the teachings of Confucius, Laozi, and the Buddha into a unified belief system?

Buddhism and Daoism in China

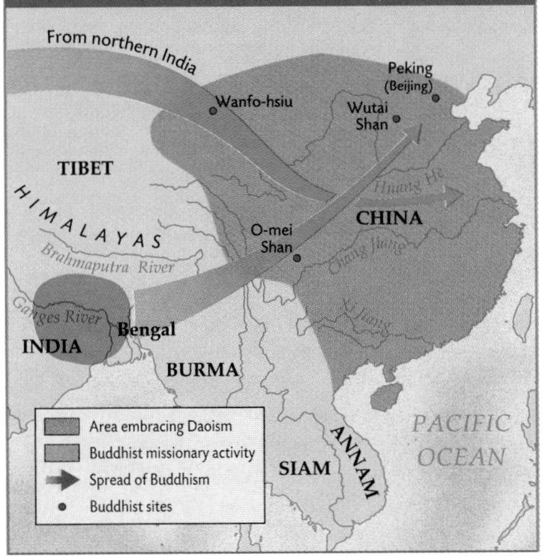

Understanding Themes

1. **Uniformity** What methods did Qin Shihuangdi use to unify China?
2. **Innovation** How did the ethical philosophy of Confucius influence Chinese society?
3. **Cultural Diffusion** How did Buddhism reach China?

Linking Past and Present

1. The Qin tried to control people's ideas by limiting the books they could read. Provide an example of a modern government that limits the information its people receive.
2. The Han government forced peasants to work one month of each year on public projects. Was forced labor justified?
3. All candidates for China's civil service were required to master the Five Classics. Can you think of literature from our own culture that everyone should know? Why would it be difficult for Americans to agree on five classics?

Skill Practice

Read the passage below and answer the questions that follow.

> "Females should be strictly grave and sober, and yet adapted to the occasion. Whether in waiting on her parents, receiving or reverencing her husband, rising up or sitting down, when pregnant, in times of mourning, or when fleeing in war, she should be perfectly decorous. Rearing the silkworm and working cloth are the most important employments of the female; preparing food for the household and setting in order sacrifices follow next, each of which must be attended to. After that, study and learning can fill up the time."
>
> *Book of Changes (I Ching)*

1. What is the general topic of this passage?
2. What details are offered on this topic?
3. Which sentence, if any, states the central issue of this passage?
4. State the central issue in your own words.

individual choice, submissiveness to authority
3. federal and state civil service systems, jobs and promotions based on merit
4. Answers will vary.
5. Zhou: feudal system, weak central government; Qin: strong central authority, social uniformity
6. The country might be less productive if merchants were held in contempt.

Geography in History

1. India
2. Wanfo-hsiu, Peking, Wutai Shan, O-mei Shan
3. from southeastern India
4. the yin-yang concept

Understanding Themes

1. **UNIFORMITY** centralizing government; standardizing weights, measures, coins, writing

Chapter 9 Review

2. **INNOVATION** Confucian emphasis on order made Chinese society submissive to authority.
3. **CULTURAL DIFFUSION** Buddhist monks and traders from India crossed mountains to bring their message to China

Linking Past and Present

1. Iran, Iraq, Syria, Libya, Singapore, China, Cuba
2. Students might argue that forced labor is a kind of tax, or mention workfare (requiring welfare recipients to work in exchange for their checks) as it is being practiced in the United States today.
3. Answers might include works by Hawthorne, Thoreau, Emerson, Melville, or Twain; there are so many from which to choose.

Skill Practice

1. woman's role in society
2. Details are listed in the second through fourth sentences.
3. the first sentence
4. Accept well-phrased summaries.

Chapter Bonus Test Question

Ask Students: In ancient China, either birth or individual talent and achievement might be the basis for an individual's standing in society. How did Confucianism support these seemingly contradictory positions? *(One's standing was largely determined by the family to which one was born: the father chose careers and arranged marriages; a wealthy family gave a person the educational opportunities needed to prepare for the civil service exam. Among those who could afford the necessary education, the civil service system gave one the chance to achieve public office on the basis of one's own talents/performance.)*

Unit 2 Digest

The Unit Digest offers a chapter-by-chapter summary that can be used for any of the following teaching purposes:

- **Preview** one chapter or an entire unit,
- **Review** some or all of the chapters,
- **Condense** when specific chapters or units have not been taught, or
- **Reteach** chapters that students have studied in the unit.

PREVIEW

Use the Unit 2 Digest Transparencies to preview the highlights of the unit.

Visualizing History The rulers of Mycenae were wealthy enough to import gold from Nubia (present-day Sudan) and ivory from India.
Answer to Caption: *Minoans and Ionians*

Unit 2 Digest

From about 2000 B.C. to about A.D. 500, major civilizations arose throughout the world. Although each civilization had unique traits, they all had common features, such as a stable political system, one or more major religions, and an interest in the arts and sciences. These civilizations produced many achievements that still influence the world today.

Visualizing History **Chalices from the court of a wealthy Mycenaean king.** *Besides the Mycenaeans, what other peoples influenced the development of Greek civilization?*

Chapter 4 The Rise of Ancient Greece

Although Greece's mountains protected against invaders, they also limited travel and communication among the Greeks and prevented them from uniting under one government. Numerous harbors and closeness to the sea encouraged the Greeks to become traders, and eventually they founded colonies around the Mediterranean Sea.

Early Civilizations

Greek civilization had its origins in the Minoan civilization of Crete and the Mycenaean civilization brought in by Indo-Europeans. The Greeks immortalized their legends and early history in two epic poems, the *Iliad* and the *Odyssey*. These epics taught such values as courage, dignity, and love of beauty. The Greeks worshiped gods and goddesses—who were both humanlike and superpowerful—and imitated their deities by themselves striving for excellence.

The City-States

The polis—the Greek city-state—served as the center of Greek life. Each polis, especially Athens, encouraged participation by its citizens in government. Women, however, had no political rights, and slaves and foreign-born men were excluded from citizenship.

After years of rule by kings, aristocrats, and tyrants, most city-states became either oligarchies or democracies. The two major Greek democracies were Sparta and Athens. Sparta was a warlike society that used its army to control its noncitizens. Athens built a much freer society that introduced the Western concept of democracy.

During the 500s B.C., the Greeks defeated the Persians in a series of wars. A golden age of cultural achievement in Athens followed the Persian conflicts. Later, resentment against Athenian control led to the Peloponnesian War between Athens and an alliance of city-states led by Sparta. The war brought defeat for Athens and decline for the Greek city-state system.

SURVEYING CHAPTER 4

1. **Making Comparisons** How did the peoples of Sparta and Athens differ in their general attitudes toward life?
2. **Making Connections** How did Greece's geography affect the development of its political institutions?

Chapter 5 The Height of Greek Civilization

During the 400s B.C., Athens became the center of Greek civilization. Its classical style of art, architecture, and literature have endured in Western civilization. The Athenians expressed their love of beauty and harmony in such buildings as the Parthenon. They decorated their pottery with paintings and created masterpieces of sculpture. The Greeks were the first to write and perform plays—comedies and tragedies. They held the Olympic Games as a religious festival in honor of Zeus, the chief Greek god.

CLASSROOM RESOURCES FOR UNIT 2 DIGEST

Preview
- Unit 2 Digest Transparencies

Review
- Time Line Activities 4, 5, 6, 7, 8, 9
- Student Self-Test and Review Software, Chapters 4, 5, 6, 7, 8, 9
- MindJogger Videoquiz, Chapters 4, 5, 6, 7, 8, 9

Condense
- Chapter Digests Audiocassettes, Chapters 4, 5, 6, 7, 8, 9

Reteach
- Reteaching Activities 4, 5, 6, 7, 8, 9
- Chapter Digests Audiocassettes, Chapters 4, 5, 6, 7, 8, 9

Thinkers and Writers

Greek thinkers believed in the power of reason to explain all things. Socrates constructed a way of teaching known as the Socratic method. His student Plato studied human behavior and wrote the first book on political science. Aristotle wrote on logic, rhetoric, poetry, and political science, among other topics. The Greeks also gave us the first true historians, Herodotus and Thucydides, and the father of medicine, Hippocrates.

Alexander the Great

By 330 B.C., Alexander of Macedonia had defeated the Persian Empire and conquered an area from Egypt to India. His goal was to combine the best of Greek and Persian cultures into one civilization. After Alexander's death, the empire was divided among three of his generals.

Although political unity vanished, Greek culture spread and mixed with Middle Eastern culture to form the Hellenistic civilization. This new civilization formed around newly built cities, such as Alexandria, Egypt. During the Hellenistic era, the Greeks excelled in the sciences.

SURVEYING CHAPTER 5

1. **Identifying Trends** In what ways did the ancient Greeks lay the foundation of the arts and sciences of the West?
2. **Analyzing Viewpoints** Do you think Alexander of Macedonia deserves to be called "the Great"? Explain your answer.

Chapter 6
Ancient Rome and Early Christianity

In 509 B.C. the Romans established a republic that lasted almost 500 years. The republic was ruled by upper-class patricians, although after a while representatives of the plebeians—the common people—also played a part in government.

The Roman Empire

Rome conquered the Italian Peninsula by 264 B.C. It then fought the Punic Wars against Carthage, finally defeating the North African city-state in 149 B.C. Rome's military conquests brought the Roman Republic wealth but also substituted slave labor on large estates for small, independent citizen-farmers. The latter crowded into Rome, where they voted for any leader who promised cheaper food and more public amusements. Rome's failure to reform brought Julius Caesar to power in 45 B.C. In 27 B.C. his grandnephew Octavian, or Augustus, became the first Roman emperor.

From 27 B.C. to A.D. 180, the Roman Empire enjoyed a time of peace and prosperity known as the *Pax Romana*. During this period the Romans developed their system of laws and built roads, aqueducts, and public buildings. Great literary figures include the poets Horace and Virgil and the historians Livy and Tacitus.

Christianity

Christianity, based on the life and teachings of Jesus, began as a sect of Judaism but quickly spread through the Roman world as a new religion. After great persecution, Christianity became the official religion of the empire in A.D. 392. During the A.D. 400s, the bishop of Rome began to claim authority over the Christian Church and eventually became known as pope. His claims, however, were rejected by the non-Latin speaking churches in the eastern part of the empire.

Visualizing History

Octavian, known as Augustus, preferred to be called "first citizen." *What was the period that began with his reign called?*

Unit 2 Digest

REVIEW

GLENCOE TECHNOLOGY

VIDEODISC

Use MindJogger to review any chapter in Unit 2.

MindJogger Videoquiz

Chapter 5
Disc 1 Side B

Chapter 6
Disc 1 Side B

Chapter 7
Disc 1 Side B

Chapter 8
Disc 1 Side B

Chapter 9
Disc 2 Side A

Also available in VHS.

Visualizing History This sculpture of Augustus was modeled on a Greek statue of a young athlete. **Answer to Caption:** *the Roman Empire*

ANSWERS TO SURVEYING THE CHAPTER

CHAPTER 4 ANSWERS

1. Sparta, a military society, emphasized physical prowess and service in the army. Athenians stressed education and public service.
2. The mountains and islands of Greece hindered contact among communities, encouraging the growth of city-states rather than a unified government.

CHAPTER 5 ANSWERS

1. Greek ideals of beauty and harmony profoundly influenced Western art, and their belief in reason became a basic principle of science.
2. Answers may vary. Students may see Alexander's effort to combine Greek and Persian culture as valid but find his imperial goals exaggerated.

Unit 2 Digest

Use the Student Self-Test and Review Software to review any chapters that students have studied in Unit 2.

Religion Ask students to identify the religions that arose during the time period of Unit 2 that are still practiced today. Have students tell where each religion originated and where it first spread. *(Christianity: began among Jewish disciples of Jesus in Judea, spread through Roman Empire. Hinduism: evolved in India from early Aryan beliefs. Buddhism: the Buddha lived in India; Buddhism spread to China and Southeast Asia.)* **L1**

CONDENSE

Use Chapter Digest Audiocassettes to introduce chapters that students have not studied in Unit 2. Spanish Chapter Digest Audiocassettes are also available.

Discuss Have students read the **Unit Digest** and discuss the **Surveying Chapter** questions. **L1**

Visualizing History Ancient statues of the Buddha are found throughout the areas where Buddhism spread, including Sri Lanka, Cambodia, Vietnam, and Indonesia.

Answer to Caption: *the Buddha's rules for reaching nirvana*

Roman Decline

During the A.D. 200s, political chaos, economic crisis, and Germanic invasions led to the decline of the Roman Empire. Reform efforts by Diocletian and Constantine preserved the eastern part of the empire but only delayed the downfall of the western part of the empire until the late A.D. 400s.

SURVEYING CHAPTER 6

1. **Relating Ideas** How did Christianity begin and later develop?
2. **Predicting Developments** What do you think might have happened if Diocletian and Constantine had lived about 100 years earlier than they did?

Chapter 7
Flowering of African Civilizations

Africa's diverse geography has influenced the development of civilizations. In a land of scarce rainfall, cultures arose near lakes or rivers, such as the Nile. Trading cultures, like Kush and Axum in eastern Africa, imported new ideas and religions along with goods. Movement of people, such as the Bantu migrations, spread culture to other parts of Africa. Family traditions and customs were built around religious beliefs in many African villages.

West Africa

Ghana was one of the wealthiest nations, trading gold for salt brought by Muslim traders. Mali, a nation that broke away from Ghana, also became a powerful kingdom. Its king, Mansa Musa, created a rich trading empire through his contacts with Muslims. Islamic culture spread throughout Africa. Songhai, the last of the great West African kingdoms, expanded its territory and developed a strong legal system based on Islam.

East, Central, and South Africa

Trade contacts also brought power and wealth to city-states along the coast of East Africa. There Arab traders brought cotton, silk, and Chinese porcelain from India and Southeast Asia to exchange for ivory and metals from Africa's interior.

Meanwhile, powerful Bantu kingdoms thrived in Central Africa and South Africa. These inland areas mined rich deposits of copper and gold.

Traders from the East African coast made their way to the Bantu kingdoms and began an active trade there.

SURVEYING CHAPTER 7

1. **Relating Ideas** How did the spread of new religions affect various cultures in Africa?
2. **Analyzing Trends** Why was trade so important to early African kingdoms and city-states?

Chapter 8
India's Great Civilization

About 1500 B.C. Aryan invaders conquered northern India, bringing with them the Sanskrit language and a social structure that divided people into *varnas*, four social classes. The *Rig-Veda*, dating from the Aryan period, is one of the oldest religious texts still in use. Between 900 B.C. and 500 B.C., two epic poems, the *Mahabharata* and the *Ramayana*, were recorded. These epics and later religious writings, the *Upanishads*, taught the principles of Hinduism, India's major religion. Hinduism includes belief in many deities and the concepts of an eternal spirit, reincarnation, and the obligation to perform the duties of one's caste.

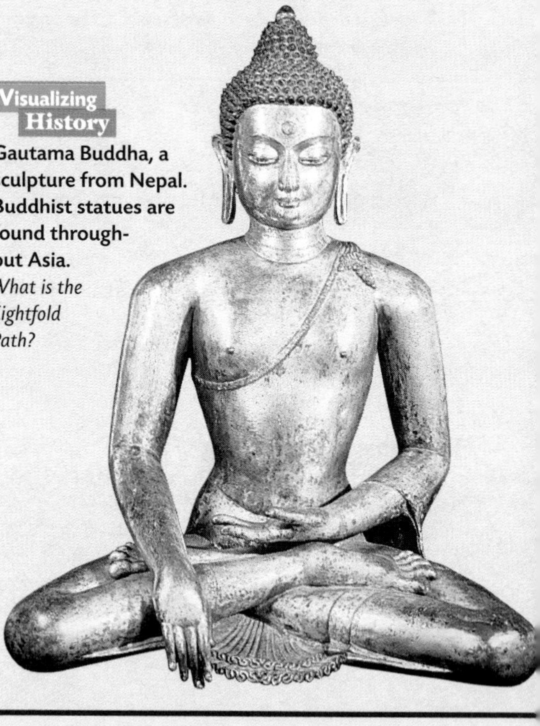

Visualizing History
Gautama Buddha, a sculpture from Nepal. Buddhist statues are found throughout Asia.
What is the Eightfold Path?

ANSWERS TO SURVEYING THE CHAPTER

CHAPTER 6 ANSWERS

1. Christianity began as a sect of Judaism, spread through the Roman Empire, and eventually became the state religion.
2. Some students may feel that if these emperors had lived earlier their reforms might have saved the empire; others may say that Rome's decline was inevitable for economic reasons.

CHAPTER 7 ANSWERS

1. Axum adopted Christianity in what later became Ethiopia; Mali, Songhai, and the east African city-states became part of the Islamic world.
2. African civilizations, including Kush, Axum, Ghana, Mali, Songhai, Zimbabwe, and the east African city-states, grew by trading salt, gold, iron, ivory, and other goods.

Rise of Buddhism

During the 500s B.C., Siddhartha Gautama founded Buddhism, which spread to India, East Asia, and Southeast Asia. Known as the Buddha, or Enlightened One, Gautama taught that people can escape the cycle of rebirth by eliminating desire and by following rules of behavior, the Eightfold Path. Buddhist artists created paintings and statues of the Buddha throughout Asia. Since Buddha's death, Buddhism has become one of the world's great religions.

Indian Empires

The Mauryas, who ruled from 322 B.C. to 184 B.C., founded an empire in northern India, and the Mauryan ruler Asoka helped spread Buddhism throughout India. About 500 years later, the Guptas reunited India, and their empire lasted from A.D. 320 to A.D. 600. Under the Guptas, scholars made numerous advances—including the invention of "Arabic numerals" and the concept of zero.

SURVEYING CHAPTER 8

1. **Making Comparisons** In what ways do ancient Greece and ancient India compare in their cultural achievements?
2. **Relating Ideas** What mathematical advances did early India pass on to other parts of the world?

Chapter 9 China's Flourishing Civilization

The Zhou, who replaced the Shang about 1000 B.C., ruled China until 256 B.C.—their dynasty lasting longer than any other Chinese dynasty. Under the Zhou, China made many technological advances and began to experience steady population growth.

Qin and Han Dynasties

The Qin and Han dynasties united China under powerful central governments that enacted strict laws, expanded China's borders, and increased Chinese contacts with the outside world. The Qin ruler Shihuangdi standardized weights and measures, built the Great Wall, and tried to control people's thinking by burning many books. Under the Han emperor Wudi, the government adopted a civil service system in which officials were appointed on the basis of examinations.

Visualizing History **A treasure of 6,000 terra-cotta soldiers from the Qin dynasty was uncovered in Shensi Province.** *What other large structure was built during this time?*

Chinese Beliefs

Two major philosophies appeared in early China: Confucianism and Daoism. Confucianism was developed by Confucius, or Kongzi. He stressed basic ethical relationships, especially those between ruler and ruled and between parent and child. Confucianism also emphasized the ideal of a courteous, knowledgeable individual. Daoism, another philosophy, emphasized living in harmony with nature. Toward the end of the Han dynasty, Buddhism entered China.

Society and Culture

The Chinese family of the Han era played an important role in Chinese society and was dominated by the oldest male. The family functioned as an economic unit to which all members gave their earnings and which supported the old, the young, and the sick. Chinese society was divided into three main groups—landowners, peasants, and merchants.

Producing numerous literary works, the Chinese also made great contributions in science and technology. These include the first printed book and the invention of paper, gunpowder, and acupuncture.

SURVEYING CHAPTER 9

1. **Making Comparisons** In what ways did the people of China differ from the people of India in their general attitudes toward life?
2. **Analyzing Viewpoints** How do you think Qin Shihuangdi's book burning would have been regarded by the ancient Greeks?

Unit 2 Digest

Visualizing History In 1975, in a vast pit in Shensi Province, a literal army of clay figures was discovered. The 6,000 life-size figures of soldiers, horses, and chariots were individually sculpted during the Qin dynasty, about 210 B.C. The Shensi find ranks as one of the most remarkable archaeological discoveries in history.

Answer to Caption: *the Great Wall*

RETEACH

Comparing Historical Maps Using outline maps of Europe, Africa, and Asia, students should draw in, label, and indicate the years for the following kingdoms and empires discussed in Unit 2: Alexander's empire; the Roman Empire at its height; the kingdoms of Kush, Axum, Ghana, Songhai, Zimbabwe; the Mauryan and Gupta Empires; and the Han dynasty. (Refer to maps on pages 141, 165, 187, 193, 212, 224.)

Reteaching Activities 4, 5, 6, 7, 8, 9

Chapter Digests Audiocassettes, Chapters 4, 5, 6, 7, 8, 9

ANSWERS TO SURVEYING THE CHAPTER

CHAPTER 8 ANSWERS

1. Both produced important epic poems that embodied their society's values; they also created sophisticated art and architecture and made contributions to science and mathematics.
2. Gupta mathematicians developed algebra and invented the concept of zero, as well as devising the numbers 1 to 9.

CHAPTER 9 ANSWERS

1. In India, both Hindus and Buddhists focused on spiritual matters. In China, Confucianism and Daoism were ethical philosophies that emphasized proper conduct.
2. Because Greeks valued learning and tolerated differing opinions, they probably would have condemned the book burning of Qin Shihuangdi.

Introducing Unit 3

0:00 OUT OF TIME?

If time does not permit teaching each chapter in Unit 3, you may use the Unit Digest beginning on page 394, in conjunction with the Unit Digest Transparencies and Chapter Digest Audiocassettes with activities and tests.

Introducing the Unit

Unit 3 traces the economic, political, religious, and cultural development of Europe, the Middle East, Asia, and the Americas from A.D. 500 to 1500.

Unit Objectives

After reading Unit 3, students will be able to:

1. trace the rise and fall of the Byzantine Empire and the development of Slavic culture in Kiev and Moscow.
2. understand Islam and describe the spread of Islamic civilization.
3. define feudalism and discuss the influence of the Church in early medieval Europe.
4. explain the effects of the Crusades and the development of Europe in the later Middle Ages.
5. summarize the achievements of the Tang and Song dynasties and the influence of China on other Asian cultures.
6. describe the well-organized civilizations that arose in Mexico, Central America, and South America.

Portfolio Project

You may wish to have students work in groups to create their maps. Have them skim the chapters of this unit to find products, inventions, and ideas from different regions.

Unit 3 A.D. 400–1500

Regional Civilizations

Chapter 10 Byzantines and Slavs

Chapter 11 Islamic Civilization

Chapter 12 The Rise of Medieval Europe

Chapter 13 Medieval Europe at Its Height

Chapter 14 East and South Asia

Chapter 15 The Americas

Then & Now

As this period opened, advanced civilizations began to develop in many regions of the world. Although some cultures were cut off from other regions, trade and migrations spread ideas across continents and among several different peoples. Emerging centers of trade and commerce brought more highly organized social structures and governments. These regional civilizations contributed many ideas that influenced the development of the modern world. Christianity, Islam, Confucianism, and Buddhism spread over wide areas. Scientific discoveries crossed cultures. Some contact between cultures caused conflict that lasted for decades or centuries.

A Global Chronology

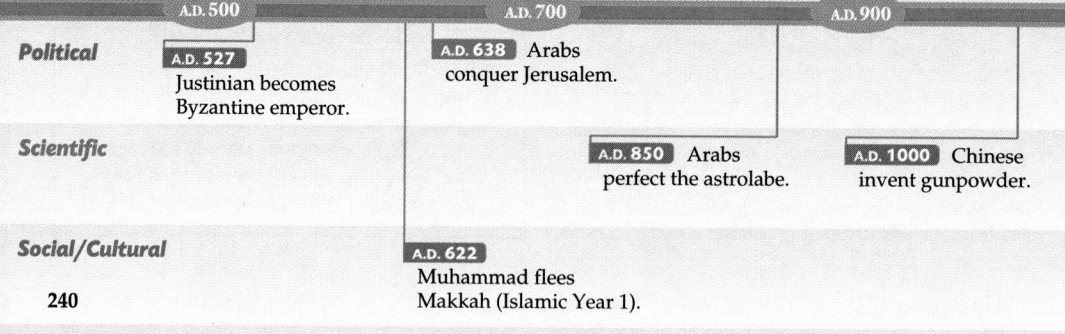

A.D. 500 — A.D. 700 — A.D. 900

Political
- A.D. 527 Justinian becomes Byzantine emperor.
- A.D. 638 Arabs conquer Jerusalem.

Scientific
- A.D. 850 Arabs perfect the astrolabe.
- A.D. 1000 Chinese invent gunpowder.

Social/Cultural
- A.D. 622 Muhammad flees Makkah (Islamic Year 1).

Then & Now

Religion One theme of this unit is contact and conflict between followers of different religions. Point out to students that in some epochs, people of different religions have interacted and lived side by side without conflict. At other times, during the spread of Islam and the Crusades, for example, religious differences led to violence and war.

Have students brainstorm a list of places in the world today where people of different religions live together in peace and other areas where there is religious conflict. In what areas does a

Mayan clay figurine of a man and a woman wrapped in a blanket, c. A.D. 700–1000. Campeche, Mexico

Portfolio Project

Americans share the benefits of foods, inventions, discoveries, and ideas from all over the world. Often we do not think about the cultures that contributed these things. Create a map on which you show some products or ideas that originated in each of the following areas: the Middle East, Asia, Africa, South America, or Europe.

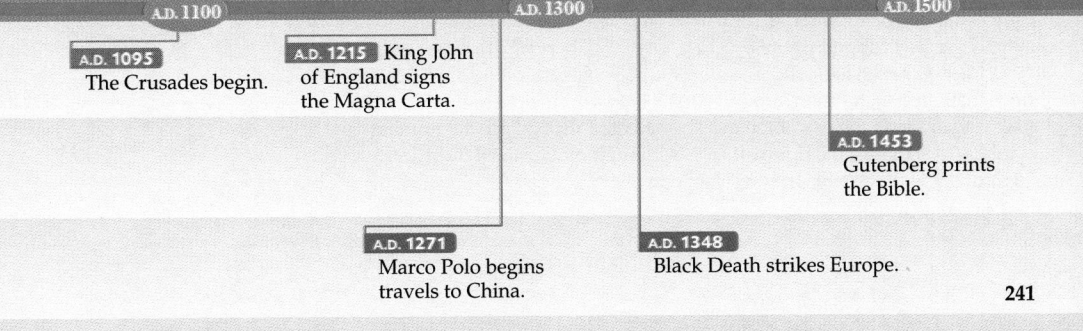

A.D. 1100 — A.D. 1300 — A.D. 1500

- **A.D. 1095** The Crusades begin.
- **A.D. 1215** King John of England signs the Magna Carta.
- **A.D. 1271** Marco Polo begins travels to China.
- **A.D. 1348** Black Death strikes Europe.
- **A.D. 1453** Gutenberg prints the Bible.

history of religious conflict spur violence today? *(former Yugoslavia, Northern Ireland, Indian subcontinent, Middle East [Israel])* What factors besides religion may contribute to conflict among religious groups? *(differences in wealth in Northern Ireland and Middle East; issues of political power in all four regions)* In what countries do people of different religious backgrounds live together peacefully? *(United States, Argentina, most of Europe)* What explains the peaceful coexistence of different groups in those areas? *(Answers may include: traditions of pluralism, lessons learned from past intolerance.)*

Introducing Unit 3

ABC NEWS INTERACTIVE™

VIDEODISC
Turning Points in World History

Side One
Chapter 7

Title: *The Crusades*
Subject: The Crusades affected Europe's economic and political development.
Ask: Why did the Crusades encourage western Europeans to increase trade? *(Increased knowledge of Middle Eastern civilizations led to an increase in demand for imported goods.)*

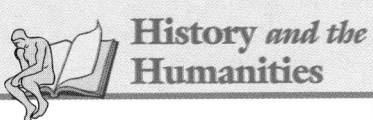

History & Art The Maya produced remarkably detailed sculptures and relief carvings using only stone tools.

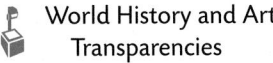

History and the Humanities

Focus on World Art Prints
- 13 *Mantik et-Tayr*
- 14 *Bayeux Tapestry*
- 15 *Saint George and the Dragon*
- 17 *Saint Jerome in His Study*
- 11 *Presentation of Captives to a Maya Ruler*

World History and Art Transparencies
- 12 *Theodora and Attendants*
- 13 *Ukrainian Easter Eggs*
- 14 *Court of the Lions, the Alhambra*
- 15 *Cover of the Lindau Gospels*
- 16 *May*
- 17 *Angkor Wat*
- 18 *Mola Stitchery*
- 19 *Quilled Buckskin Robe*

The Spread of Ideas

TEACH

Introduction

This feature focuses on the contributions of Hindu and Arab mathematicians to Western civilization. To impress upon students the importance of the Hindu-Arab system, discuss the efficiencies of using only nine digits, place value, and zero as a placeholder. Have students invent and write numerals for the first 20 numbers without using place value or zero as a placeholder.

Background Notes

Linking Past and Present

Italian merchants were the first Europeans to adopt the Hindu-Arabic numerals. In Venice and other cities, schools of mathematics drew students from across Europe. A German father told his son "to rise early, go to church regularly, and pay attention to his arithmetic teacher." The schools focused on practical mathematics for use in business. Students had to learn the multiplication tables up to 99 x 99; they also learned to calculate interest, compute land areas, and handle fractions.

Geography

Movement Two great centers of learning developed in the Islamic world: one in Baghdad, in modern-day Iraq; the other in Córdoba, in Spain. The caliphs of Baghdad gathered mathematical and scientific works from Greece and India and had them translated into Arabic. These translations, as well as original works by Muslim scholars, then traveled across the Islamic world, often reaching Europeans through Spain.

The Spread of Ideas

Mathematics

The invention of mathematics changed the course of civilization. Astronomers used mathematics to account for the movements of the sun and moon so they could mark the seasons. Geometry enabled people to calculate the volume of a cylindrical granary. Mathematics supported travel, from the earliest sea travel to the development of the space program. It all began with the Sumerians.

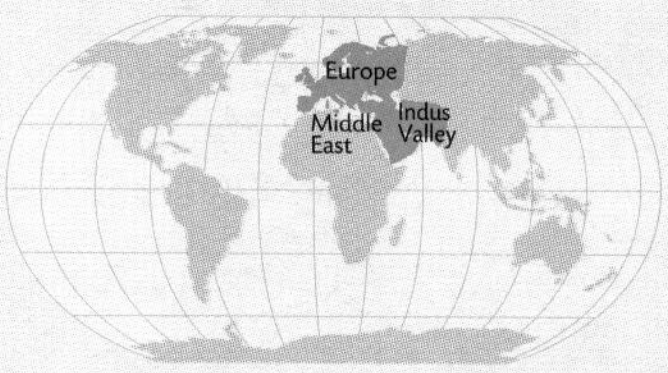

Sumerian cuneiform tablet

Indus Valley

The Use of Numerals

The Sumerians devised one of the earliest numbering systems based on cuneiform. They used two wedge-like symbols for counting. One symbol stood for 1, the other for 10. But these symbols—and others to follow—basically came from the Sumerian alphabet. The wedges served double-duty for symbolizing words and figures.

Other early peoples who invented numbering systems also used letters from their alphabets. Then, around A.D. 500, Hindu people in the Indus River valley abandoned the use of letters. They created instead special number symbols to stand for the figures 1 to 9. Although modernized over time, these 9 Hindu symbols are the ones we use today.

COOPERATIVE LEARNING ACTIVITY

Create a New Numeric System Have students discuss why Europe was so slow to adopt Hindu-Arabic numerals. Point out that the United States has still not converted to the metric system despite its simplicity and widespread use. Then organize students into two groups. Have one group create new symbols for the numbers 1–5, the other for 6–9 and zero. Combine the symbols and have volunteers attempt to carry out different mathematical functions with the new system. After students complete this activity, have them project how difficult it might be to switch numbering systems. **L1**

The Spread of Ideas

Persian astronomer

Astrolabe

The Middle East

The Rise of Algebra

Trade introduced people in the Middle East to the Hindu number system. About A.D. 825 an Arab mathematician, al-Khowarizmi of Baghdad, wrote a book recommending the new system to everyone. In a second book, al-Khowarizmi showed how the system could be used. He called the book *al-jabr w'al-muqabalah*, which roughly means "the art of bringing together unknowns to match a known quantity." The word *algebra* comes from the key word in the title—*al-jabr*, or "bringing together."

The wonder of the system caught Arab imaginations. Arabs especially liked the concept of zero—developed by the Hindus after they created the symbols for 1-9. In explaining this concept, one Arab mathematician wrote: "When [in subtraction] nothing is left over, then write the little circle so that the place does not remain empty." With the use of zero, mathematicians could build numbers of astronomical size using just 10 symbols.

Book of Hours *with Arabic numerals*

Europe

The Triumph of Arabic Numerals

Arab conquerors arrived in Spain in the A.D. 700s. Their presence opened the door for use of the new number system. At first, many Europeans rejected it. They clung instead to Roman numerals. The Italian city-state of Florence even passed a law banning the use of the Hindu-Arab system.

Later, however, "Arabic numerals," as they were called, proved a more powerful conqueror than Arab soldiers. European merchants embraced the new numbers first. They found it easier to do their tallies using the symbols for 1-10. European mathematicians soon learned the new arithmetic too. By the A.D. 1400s, the numbers could even be found in popular art.

As you will read in this unit, Europeans began to adopt other practices from the Middle East as well. The pace of change quickened as wars and trade brought more people in contact with each other.

LINKING THE IDEAS

1. How did the Hindu system of numbers differ from earlier systems?
2. What was the importance of the invention of zero?

Critical Thinking

3. **Cause and Effect** What was the role of conquest and trade in spreading the use of the Hindu-Arab number system?

ANSWERS TO LINKING THE IDEAS

1. It used special number symbols instead of letters.
2. With zero, mathematicians could create large numbers using only 10 symbols.
3. With the Muslim conquest of Spain in the A.D. 700s, Hindu-Arabic numbers began to penetrate Europe. Merchants who traded with the Arab world hastened the process.

Who?What?Where?When?

Al-Khowarizmi His short work on algebra, al-Khowarizmi said, was meant to be a practical guide for "the measuring of lands, the digging of canals, geometrical computation, and other objects of various sorts." The work became so widely known that for centuries Europeans assumed that al-Khowarizmi had invented Hindu-Arabic numerals. The word *algorithm* is derived from al-Khowarizmi's name.

Cultural Diffusion

The Spread of Arabic Numerals
Europeans resisted the use of Hindu-Arabic numerals well into the A.D. 1400s. An Italian bookkeeping manual insisted that Roman numerals "cannot be falsified as easily as those of the new art of computation, of which one can, with ease, make one out of another, such as turning the zero into a 6 or a 9."

During the age of exploration, Europeans came into contact with societies that used the more advanced numerals. For practical reasons they had to adopt the new system. The Portuguese author of a mathematics text published in 1519 explained: "I am printing this arithmetic because it is a thing so necessary in Portugal for transactions with the merchants of India, Persia, Arabia, Ethiopia, and other places." After A.D. 1450, the printing press helped spread the use of Hindu-Arabic numerals across Europe.

Unit 3 *Regional Civilizations* **243**

Teach, Reinforce, and Extend CHAPTER Content

Byzantines and Slavs

CHAPTER RESOURCES

	Reproducible Resources	Multimedia Resources
Chapter Opener	Chapter Themes: Graphic Organizer 10 Historical Significance Chapter Activity 10	MindJogger Videoquiz
Chapter Enrichment	Vocabulary Activity 10* Time Line Activity 10 Mapping History Activity 10 History Simulation 10 Geography and History Activity 10 Source Reading 10 People in World History Profiles 17, 18 World Literature Selection 3 World Art and Music Activity 10 Enrichment Activity 10 Critical Thinking Activity 10 Skill Reinforcement Activity 10 Performance Assessment Activity 10	World History and Art Transparencies 12, *Theodora and Attendants*; 13, *Ukrainian Easter Eggs* Chapter Transparency 10 Vocabulary PuzzleMaker Software Picture Atlas of the World World Music: Cultural Traditions, Lesson 4
Chapter Review/Reteaching	Reteaching Activity 10 Skill Reinforcement Activity 10 Spanish Chapter Summary 10	Chapter 10 Digest Audiocassette, Activity, Test* Vocabulary PuzzleMaker Software Student Self-Test and Review Software MindJogger Videoquiz
Chapter Evaluation/Testing	Performance Assessment Activity 10 Chapter 10 Test, Forms A and B	Testmaker

* *Also available in Spanish*

0:00 **OUT OF TIME?** Assign the Chapter 10 summary in the Unit 3 Digest on pages 394–397, and the Chapter 10 Audiocassettes.

Block Schedule

Block scheduling differs from traditional class scheduling in the amount of time allotted to each period. The extended time frame provided by block scheduling affords you the opportunity to implement a greater number of research-oriented and activity-intense projects to motivate and involve your students. Activities that are particularly suited to use within the block scheduling framework are identified throughout this chapter by the following designation.

KEY TO ABILITY LEVELS

Teaching strategies have been coded for varying learning styles and abilities.

- L1 **BASIC** activities for all students
- L2 **AVERAGE** activities for average to above-average students
- L3 **CHALLENGING** activities for above-average students
- LEP **LIMITED ENGLISH PROFICIENCY** activities

A complete, 1-page lesson plan is provided for each section in the *Reproducible Lesson Plans* booklet.

SECTION RESOURCES

Daily Objectives	Reproducible Resources	Multimedia Resources
Section 1 The New Rome Explain what made the Byzantine Empire rich and powerful.	Reproducible Lesson Plan 10-1 Guided Reading Activity 10-1* Geography and History Activity 10 Time Line Activity 10 History Simulation 10 Section Quiz 10-1*	Section Focus Transparency 10-1 Chapter Transparency 10 World History and Art Transparency 12, *Theodora and Attendants* Vocabulary PuzzleMaker Software Student Self-Test and Review Software Testmaker
Section 2 Byzantine Civilization Investigate the role of Christianity in Byzantine, Armenian, and Georgian societies.	Reproducible Lesson Plan 10-2 Guided Reading Activity 10-2* Section Quiz 10-2*	Section Focus Transparency 10-2 World History and Art Transparency 12 Vocabulary PuzzleMaker Software Student Self-Test and Review Software Testmaker Picture Atlas of the World
Section 3 The Eastern Slavs Describe how the Eastern Slavs developed separate cultures from those of western Europe.	Reproducible Lesson Plan 10-3 Vocabulary Activity 10* Guided Reading Activity 10-3* Reteaching Activity 10 Enrichment Activity 10 Section Quiz 10-3* Performance Assessment Activity 10 Spanish Chapter Summary 10	Section Focus Transparency 10-3 World History and Art Transparency 13, *Ukrainian Easter Eggs* Student Self-Test and Review Software Testmaker World Music: Cultural Traditions, Lesson 4

** Also available in Spanish*

Chapter Activities

Performance Assessment Activity

An Itinerary for a Trip Have students assume the roles of travelers to the area of the world where the Byzantine and Slavic civilizations once existed. (Refer students to the maps on pages 247, 254, and 259 to identify these historical boundaries.) Then, using current maps and researching the geography of the area today, students should plan an itinerary that would take them to areas, cities, and landmarks of historic significance during a 5- to 10-day trip. Included should be a list of the types of artifacts or information that a traveler might hope to find at each stop. Students should be called on to explain their choices of destinations.

Possible Rubric Features
Accuracy and extent of content information, research skills, decision-making skills, organization

• *For an additional activity, refer to Activity 10 in the* Performance Assessment Strategies and Activities *booklet.*

Activity

From the Classroom of...

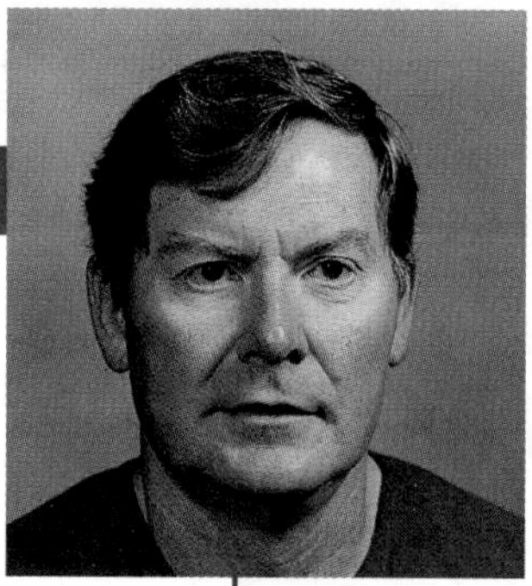

Bud Robertson
C.M. Russell High School
Great Falls, MT

Cyrillic Alphabet
One of the easiest ways to introduce students to the Byzantine and Slavic cultures is to teach them the Cyrillic (Russian) alphabet. For a week or so before presenting the activity, spend a few minutes a day memorizing and practicing the alphabet.

Begin by showing students how to make the letters. Using all capital letters is easiest, and spelling the names of a few students helps pique interest. Here, for example, is John (Ivan) written in Cyrillic:

ИВАН

The name "Robertson" looks like this:

РОБЭРТСОН

Hand out copies of the alphabet. Allow students time to practice. By the end of one period, everyone should be able to write his or her name.

MULTIPLE LEARNING STYLES

Verbal/Linguistic
Have students think up words that describe Byzantine culture and record their responses on a flip chart. Each student should use these word lists to write a description of his or her impression of everyday life in the Byzantine Empire.

Visual/Spatial
Students may use colored stones or pieces of paper to create a mosaic portrait. They may choose a subject illustrated in the text or from another source and represent it in the Byzantine style.

Auditory/Musical
Have students find examples of music from the areas of study in this chapter. These might be Turkish folk tunes, Russian ballets, or religious music. Have the class listen and compare the different styles.

Interpersonal
Suggest that students imagine that they are visitors to Russia from the Byzantine Empire. Have them prepare the script for a speech to the Russians about the benefits of Byzantine civilization and present the speech to their classmates.

Additional Resources

TEACHER'S CORNER

NATIONAL GEOGRAPHIC SOCIETY

INDEX TO NATIONAL GEOGRAPHIC MAGAZINE

The following articles may be used for research relating to this chapter:

- "Viking Trail East," by Robert Paul Jordan, March 1985.
- "Rome of the East: The Byzantine Empire," by Merle Severy, December 1983.

NATIONAL GEOGRAPHIC SOCIETY PRODUCTS AVAILABLE FROM GLENCOE

To order the following products for use with this chapter, contact your local Glencoe sales representative or call Glencoe at 1-800-368-7344:

VIDEODISC
- STV: World Geography, Vol. 2: Africa and Europe

CD-ROMS
- Picture Atlas of the World
- NGS PictureShow CD-ROM: The Middle Ages

TRANSPARENCIES
- Physical Geography of the World
- NGS PicturePack Transparency Set: The Middle Ages

NGS POSTER SET
- The Middle Ages

BIBLIOGRAPHY

Literature About the Period

Procopius. The Secret History. Translated by G.A. Williamson. London: Penguin Books, 1966. Political commentaries by a contemporary historian.

Readings for the Student

Sherrard, Philip. *Byzantium.* New York: Time-Life Books, 1966. Traces the history of the Byzantine Empire from the establishment of New Rome to the fall of Constantinople.

Readings for the Teacher

Norwich, John Julius. *Byzantium: The Early Centuries.* New York: Knopf, 1989. Popular history of Byzantine Empire through the reign of Empress Irene.

interNET
CONNECTIONS
Byzantine Studies Sites A comprehensive list of sites related to the Byzantine Empire.
World Wide Web:
http://www.bway.net/
%7Ehalsall/other.html

Introducing Chapter 10

CHAPTER THEMES

Chapter Themes are listed by section on this chapter opening page of the Student Edition. A corresponding theme-based activity is available under "TEACH," and a theme-based question is asked in the Section and Chapter Reviews.

The Storyteller

Historical Setting First built in A.D. 360, about 30 years after Byzantium had become the capital of the Roman Empire, Hagia Sophia was twice destroyed by fire. The second time it was rebuilt, in A.D. 532–537, under Justinian, it was made fireproof. Earthquakes caused the dome to collapse in A.D. 558, but this, too, was rebuilt.

For a millennium, the Hagia Sophia was the spiritual center of the empire, first as a church and then as a mosque for the Ottoman Turks. It remains an architectural masterpiece, presenting a magnificent interplay of stone and marble, light and color.

Historical Significance

Answers: *The old Roman laws were organized and classified under Justinian, and they eventually served as the foundation for the legal systems of Europe. By preserving the writings of ancient Greeks and Romans, the Byzantines made the learning of the past available to the Western world.*

The Byzantine Empire's greatest achievement may lie in the civilizing influence it exercised over all the peoples it encompassed. The Eastern Slavic peoples of the Balkans and Russia received written language, Christianity, and the basis of their art and culture from Byzantium.

Chapter 10

A.D. 400–1500

Byzantines and Slavs

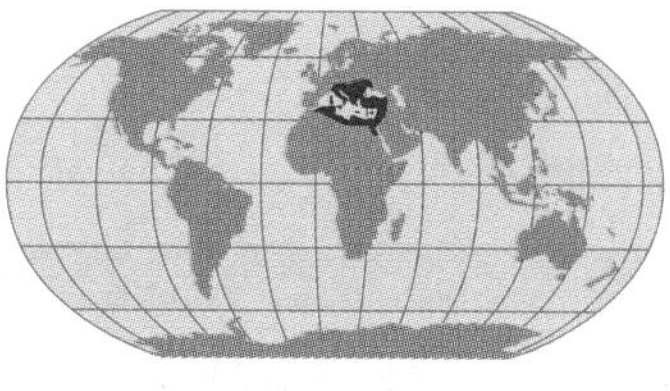

Chapter Themes

- **Conflict** Byzantines fight off invaders and struggle over use of icons. *Section 1*
- **Innovation** Byzantines develop Eastern Orthodox theology and distinctive art forms. *Section 2*
- **Cultural Diffusion** Trade routes and invasions spread beliefs and ideas. *Section 3*

The Storyteller

The awestruck visitor arriving in A.D. 600 in the city of Constantinople in southeastern Europe scarcely knew where to turn. Splendid public buildings as well as simple private homes lined the streets; the scent of rare spices perfumed the air; people dressed in fine silk thronged the church of Hagia Sophia. "One might imagine that one has chanced upon a meadow in full bloom," the Greek historian Procopius wrote about the newly built church. "For one would surely marvel at the purple hue of some [columns], the green of others, at those on which the crimson blooms, at those that flash with white, at those, too, which nature, like a painter, has varied with the most contrasting colors." The church's grandeur reflected that of Constantinople, "city of the world's desire," capital of a prosperous empire that controlled east-west trade and laid the basis for the Greek and Slavic cultures of modern Europe.

Historical Significance

What cultural achievements did the Byzantines pass on to western Europe? How did their civilization affect the development of the peoples of eastern Europe?

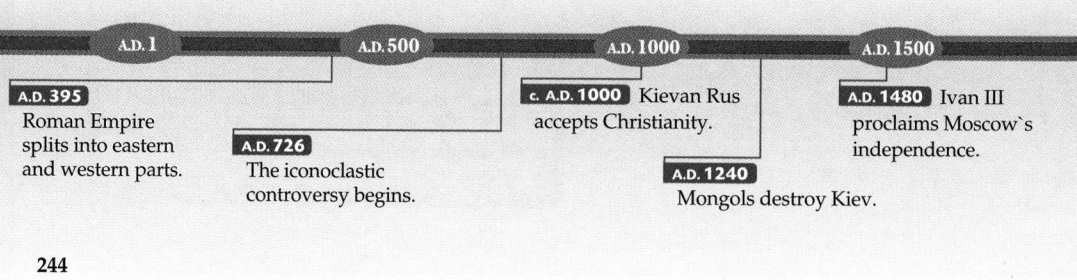

A.D. 1 — A.D. 500 — A.D. 1000 — A.D. 1500

A.D. 395 Roman Empire splits into eastern and western parts.

A.D. 726 The iconoclastic controversy begins.

c. A.D. 1000 Kievan Rus accepts Christianity.

A.D. 1240 Mongols destroy Kiev.

A.D. 1480 Ivan III proclaims Moscow's independence.

GEOGRAPHY CONNECTION

GEOGRAPHIC THEMES

Location Explain to students that they will be studying the Mediterranean area, focusing on the Balkan Peninsula, Asia Minor, ancient Russia, and the waterways from the Mediterranean Sea to the Black Sea. Have students locate the Balkan Peninsula, Asia Minor, and the Caucasus Mountains in the Atlas of their text and identify the seas bordering on those areas. Find the present-day site of Constantinople. *(Istanbul)* What made this site ideal for trade? *(It was situated on a natural harbor where Asia and Europe meet. By sailing north, contact could be made with ports on the Black Sea, and trade developed with Russia, India, and China. Turning south, ships could enter the Mediterranean Sea.)*

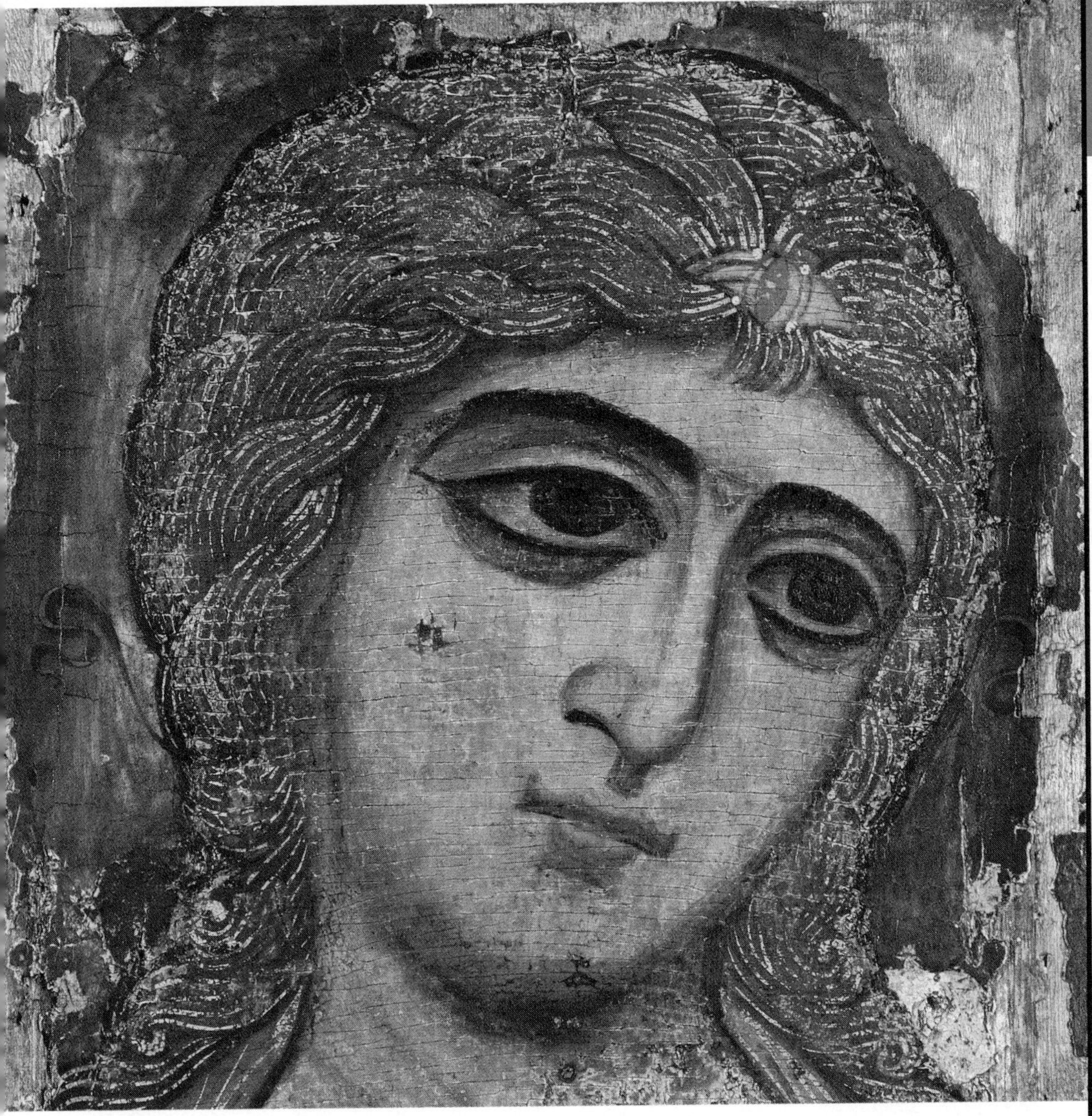

History & Art The archangel Gabriel, an icon on wood, from the Russian State Museum, St. Petersburg, Russia

Your History Journal

Find out about a specific law in Justinian's Code in an encyclopedia or a book on the history of legal systems. Write the law as an illuminated manuscript, an art form described in this chapter.

Introducing Chapter 10

History & Art The word *icon* is Greek for "image." In Byzantine art the image on an icon is of a holy person. The artist attempted to portray the person's sanctity. Icons can be found in church frescoes, mosaics, and paintings on wood panels, such as this one of the archangel Gabriel. What other religions that you have studied used images of deities or holy people? *(Answers may include ancient Sumerian, Egyptian, Greek, and Roman religions.)*

Performance Assessment

Refer to the activity on page 244C of the Planning Guide.

For an additional activity, refer to Activity 10 in the *Performance Assessment Strategies and Activities* booklet.

Using Your History Journal

Entries should incorporate appropriate penalties for violations of the chosen law. Illuminations may be full page or use decorative capital letters and margin adornments.

EXTRA CREDIT PROJECT

Preparing a Biography Suggest that students do further library research about a notable person introduced in this chapter, such as Justinian, Constantine, Theodora, Sultan Mehmet, Queen Tamara, Tiridates III, or Alexander Nevsky. Ask students to prepare a written report detailing what they have learned about the life, politics, and contributions of this person to Byzantine or Slavic history.

GLENCOE TECHNOLOGY

VIDEODISC
Use MindJogger to preview chapter content.

MindJogger Videoquiz
Chapter 10
Disc 2 Side A

Also available in VHS.

SECTION THEME

▶ **Conflict** Byzantines fight off invaders and struggle over use of icons.

Find Out

Answer: *The Byzantine Empire flourished as a result of strong imperial leadership, the strategic location of its capital, successful military conquests, and its strong ties to the Church.*

FOCUS

Section Objective

Explain what made the Byzantine Empire rich and powerful.

BELLRINGER
Motivational Activity

Before taking roll at the beginning of the class period, project Section Focus Transparency 10-1 and have students answer the activity questions. Discuss students' responses.

This activity is also available as a blackline master.

Vocabulary Pre-check

Use the Vocabulary PuzzleMaker to create a puzzle that reinforces the vocabulary terms in this section. **L1 LEP**

A.D. 300 — A.D. 600 — A.D. 900 — A.D. 1200

A.D. 330 Constantine builds city of Constantinople.

A.D. 527 Justinian becomes eastern Roman emperor.

A.D. 787 Church council at Nicaea approves use of icons.

A.D. 1054 Eastern and Western Churches split.

Section 1

The New Rome

Setting the Scene

▶ **Terms to Define**
clergy, laity, icon, iconoclast, schism

▶ **People to Meet**
Constantine, Justinian, Theodora, Leo III

▶ **Places to Locate**
Byzantine Empire, Constantinople

Find Out What made the Byzantine Empire rich and powerful?

The Storyteller

Byzantium [Constantinople] was in flames. A mob was screaming insults at Emperor Justinian and Empress Theodora. The emperor swiftly ordered the imperial treasury loaded onto ships to prepare for escape. Half crazed and without hope, Justinian held a final council of a few loyal friends; Theodora was present. After the military generals expressed their fears, Theodora suddenly rose and broke the silence. "I do not choose to flee," she said. "Never shall I see the day when I am not saluted as the empress.... You have the money, the ships are ready, the sea is open. As for me, I shall stay." Hearing her, the others took heart. That day, Theodora saved Justinian's throne.

—adapted from *Theodora, Empress of Byzantium*, Charles Diehl, 1972

Theodora, detail of mosaic

As you read in Chapter 6, after the Roman Empire was divided in A.D. 395, the eastern half became known as the **Byzantine Empire**. At its height in the A.D. 500s, the Byzantine Empire included most of the Balkan Peninsula, Asia Minor, Syria, and Egypt. Its major population group, the Greeks, lived mainly in the central part of the empire. Also included in the empire were Egyptians, Syrians, Arabs, Armenians, Jews, Persians, Slavs, and Turks. These varied peoples and cultures gave Byzantine civilization an international character.

Byzantine Foundations

The location of **Constantinople**, the Byzantine capital, reinforced this multicultural character. The city was located near the centers of early Christianity as well as on major trade routes.

A Strategic City

In A.D. 330 the Roman emperor **Constantine** built Constantinople at a strategic place where Europe and Asia meet. Located on a peninsula, Constantinople overlooked the Bosporus, the narrow strait between the Sea of Marmara and the Black Sea. A second strait, the Dardanelles, connects the Sea of Marmara and the Aegean Sea, which leads to the Mediterranean. These straits gave the occupiers of the peninsula control over movement between the Mediterranean and the Black Seas and, as a result, over the routes leading east to Asia and north to northern Europe. The site of Constantinople itself offered natural protection from attack at a time when Germanic invaders were assaulting Rome to the west. Water protected the city on three sides, and triple walls fortified the side open to attack by land. Eventually a huge chain was strung across the narrow mouth of the deep harbor on Constantinople's north side for still greater protection.

SECTION RESOURCES

Reproducible Masters
- Reproducible Lesson Plan 10-1
- Guided Reading Activity 10-1
- Geography and History Activity 10
- Time Line Activity 10
- History Simulation 10
- Section Quiz 10-1

Transparencies
- Section Focus Transparency 10-1
- Chapter Transparency 10
- World History and Art Transparency 12

Multimedia
- Vocabulary PuzzleMaker Software
- Student Self-Test and Review Software
- Testmaker

The straits also made the peninsula a natural crossroads for trade. By Constantine's time the Byzantine capital had become the wealthiest part of the Roman Empire, handling rich cargoes from Asia, Europe, and Africa.

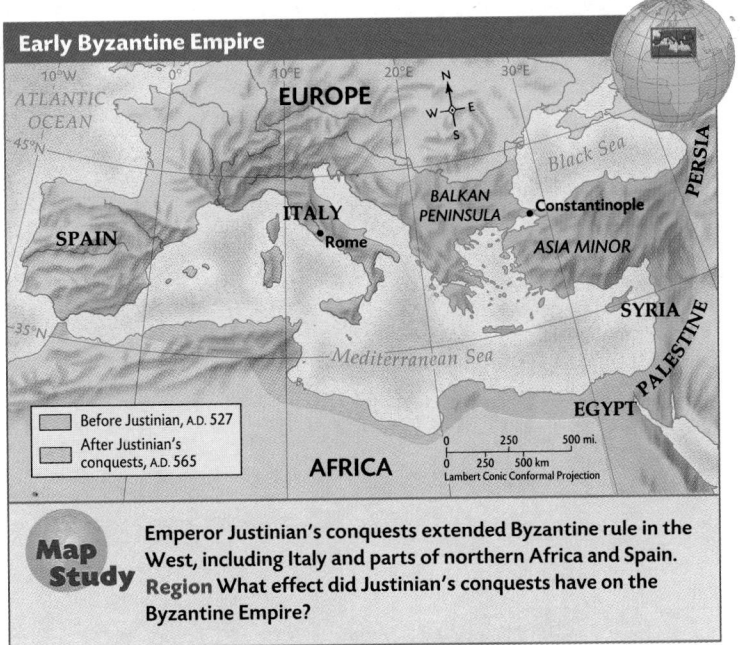

Early Byzantine Empire

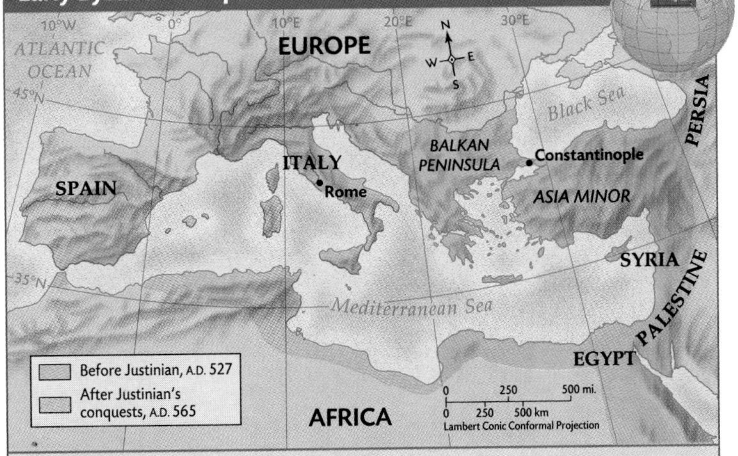

Map Study Emperor Justinian's conquests extended Byzantine rule in the West, including Italy and parts of northern Africa and Spain. **Region** What effect did Justinian's conquests have on the Byzantine Empire?

Cultural Blend

After Rome's fall, the Byzantine Empire was regarded as heir to Roman power and traditions. Constantinople was known as the New Rome because its emperors were Romans who spoke Latin and many of its wealthy families came from Rome. Despite these ties, the Byzantine Empire was more than a continuation of the old Roman Empire.

Lands once part of the Greek world formed the heart of the Byzantine Empire. The Byzantine people not only spoke Greek but also stressed their Greek heritage. Eventually Byzantine emperors and officials also used Greek rather than Latin. Religious scholars expressed their ideas in Greek and developed a distinct form of Christianity known as Eastern Orthodoxy. In addition to the Byzantine Empire's classical Greek heritage and Christian religion came cultural influences from eastern civilizations such as Persia. This mixture of cultures created a distinct Byzantine civilization. Between A.D. 500 and A.D. 1200, this civilization was one of the most advanced in the world and had a higher standard of living than western Europe.

Justinian's Rule

At its height the Byzantine Empire was ruled by **Justinian**, the son of prosperous peasants from Macedonia in the western part of the empire. Justinian was called the Emperor Who Never Sleeps. While a young man in the court of his uncle, Emperor Justin I, he worked late into the night at his studies of law, music, religion, and architecture. His enthusiasm for knowledge and hard work continued after he became emperor in A.D. 527, at age 44.

Theodora's Support

Justinian's wife, **Theodora**, was beautiful, intelligent, and ambitious. Justinian had married her in spite of court objections to her occupation as an actress—a profession held in low esteem in the empire. A capable empress, Theodora participated actively in government, rewarding friends with positions and using dismissals to punish enemies.

Theodora was especially concerned with improving the social standing of women. She persuaded Justinian to issue a decree giving a wife the right to own land equal in value to the wealth she brought with her at marriage. This land gave a widow the income she needed to support her children without the assistance of the government.

In A.D. 532 Theodora's political talents helped save Justinian's throne. When a revolt of taxpayers in Constantinople threatened the government, Justinian's advisers urged him to leave the city. As flames roared through Constantinople and the rebels battered at the palace gates, Justinian prepared to flee. Theodora, however, persuaded him to remain in control.

Inspired by his wife's determination, Justinian reasserted his power. His army crushed the rebels, killing 30,000 people. From that time until his death in A.D. 565, Justinian ruled without challenge.

Chapter 10 Section 1

TEACH

Guided Practice

THEME Conflict

Have students name the various issues that led to conflict between the Eastern and Western Churches. Discuss which of these were primarily religious and which primarily political. *(religious: iconoclastic controversy, source of religious authority, points of doctrine; political: control over new churches in Balkans)* **L1**

Map Study

Answer

Justinian's conquests were very expensive. The empire had little money left to protect its eastern borders.

Map Skills Practice

Reading a Map By how much did the Byzantine Empire grow after Justinian became emperor? *(Justinian's conquests nearly doubled the size of his empire.)*

Mock Trial Have students research a section of the Justinian law code that interests them and work in small groups to prepare a mock court session in which someone is tried for breaking the chosen law. **L2**

COOPERATIVE LEARNING ACTIVITY

Geography Organize a travel agency in which teams of students provide information to people traveling to Constantinople during Justinian's rule. One team can plan important stops on a tour of the city; another can provide information on climate and food; while a third can prepare travel posters. The team that plans the stops should prepare a map showing the route the tour will take. Each team should research the various points of interest (such as the Hagia Sophia and the Hippodrome). On completion of the project, display the map, posters, travel brochures, and itineraries. **L1**

Who?What?Where?When?

Justinian's wife, **Theodora**, had remarkable intellectual gifts and an indomitable will. She actively helped Justinian shape his policies. Theodora also built hospitals for the poor and homes for destitute women.

Chapter 10
Section 1

History & Art This mosaic portrait panel is a contemporary representation of Emperor Justinian. He is standing with officials of his court and the church during Communion service.

Answer to Caption: *As a young man, Justinian worked late into the night at his studies. His reputation for hard work and attention to every detail continued after he became emperor.*

Critical Thinking Have students make a chart comparing the elements of the Old Rome with Byzantium. They can title the columns *Rome* and *New Rome* (Constantinople), and under each heading list cultural elements that show contrasts such as language, daily life, religion, and architecture. **L3**

Art Have students draw an icon. They should choose a subject from an illustration in the text or another source and copy it in the Byzantine manner. Students should try to use the same colors as those used by Byzantine artists. Ask students to observe the motionless aspect of the faces. **L2 LEP**

Chapter Transparency 10

World History and Art Transparency 12

Independent Practice

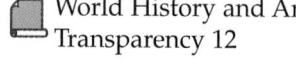

Guided Reading Activity 10-1 **L1**

History Simulation 10

Time Line Activity 10

Geography and History Activity 10

History & Art The Emperor Justinian, a mosaic from the A.D. 500s from Ravenna, Italy. *Why was Justinian called the Emperor Who Never Sleeps?*

Military Campaigns

During Justinian's reign, the Byzantines faced a serious military threat from the East. The Sassanian Empire of Persia, under Chosroes (kaz•ROH•eez) I, grew in strength and threatened to conquer the eastern provinces of the Byzantine Empire. The Byzantines rallied their forces and threw back the Persians. Justinian gained a brief period of security for the eastern borders by agreeing to pay tribute in return for peace.

Justinian dreamed of restoring the Roman Empire. In A.D. 533 he began the reconquest of Italy, North Africa, and Spain—Roman lands that had fallen to Germanic invaders. Under the general Belisarius, the Byzantine armies were strengthened and reorganized. Between A.D. 533 and A.D. 555, they fought a series of wars against the Vandals in North Africa, the Ostrogoths in Italy, and the Visigoths in southern Spain. The Byzantines conquered these Germanic groups and extended Byzantine rule in the west.

The successful reconquest, however, proved costly for the empire. The wars exhausted most of the Byzantine resources. Funds were low for defending the eastern borders, which faced attack by an expanding Persian Empire. Justinian's conquests did not last. Within a generation of his death, the empire lost many of its outlying territories.

Code of Laws

Justinian's legal reforms did last, affecting Western law even today. Shortly after becoming emperor, Justinian appointed a commission to codify, or classify, the empire's Roman laws. For centuries, these laws had accumulated without organization or classification.

The commission was made up of 10 scholars headed by a legal expert named Tribonian. For more than 6 years, the commission collected and organized vast numbers of laws. It threw out the ones that were outdated, simplified many, and put the remainder into categories. The commission's work was recorded in a collection of books known as the *Corpus of Civil Law*, or the Justinian Code. This massive work preserved Rome's legal heritage and later became the basis for most European legal systems.

The Arts

Under Justinian, Byzantine art and architecture

MEETING SPECIAL NEEDS ACTIVITIES

Reading Comprehension Have students work in pairs to create comprehension questions for each part of the section. Students can then use these to quiz each other over section content. **L1**

Learning Style: Verbal/Linguistic Have students read the poem "Ozymandias" by Percy Bysshe Shelley. Direct them to use this as a springboard for writing a one-page paper on what kinds of accomplishments by a political leader endure the longest. Have them apply this question to Justinian's accomplishments. **L3**

thrived and achieved their distinct character. The emperor ordered the construction of new roads, fortresses, aqueducts, monasteries, and other buildings. His most famous project was the church of Hagia Sophia, "Holy Wisdom," in Constantinople. The largest and most beautiful church in the empire, Hagia Sophia still stands today as one of the world's great architectural landmarks.

Byzantine Religion

Strong ties linked Byzantine emperors and the Church. The emperors were regarded as God's representatives on earth. Starting in the A.D. 400s, Byzantine emperors and empresses were crowned by the patriarch of Constantinople and took an oath to defend the Christian faith.

Church and State

Byzantine emperors frequently played a major role in church affairs. They appointed church officials, defined the style of worship, and used the wealth of the Church for government purposes.

Justinian strengthened this control over the Church by intervening in disputes over church beliefs. He also tried to unify the empire under one Christian faith, a practice that sometimes led to persecution of Jews and non-Greek Christians.

Religious Controversy

Both Byzantine **clergy**—church officials such as priests and bishops—and **laity**—church members who were not clergy—were intensely interested in religious matters. In their homes, markets, and shops, Byzantines often engaged in heated religious discussions. Visitors to Constantinople saw shoppers in the marketplaces having lively discussions about such topics as the exact relationship of Jesus the Son to God the Father. Such arguments often became political issues and led to fights and riots.

In the A.D. 700s, a dispute broke out over the use of **icons** (EYE•KAHNZ), or religious images, in worship. Although Christians had disagreed about this practice since the A.D. 400s, the use of icons in churches became a political issue by the A.D. 700s.

Those who objected to the use of icons in Christian worship argued that the Bible, in the Ten Commandments, prohibited such images. Defenders stressed that icons were symbols of

CONNECTIONS The Arts

Hagia Sophia

Hagia Sophia

Justinian ordered his architects to create the most spectacular building of all time. The construction of Constantinople's church of Hagia Sophia, or Holy Wisdom, began in A.D. 532. Workers completed the church in five years.

For Justinian, building this church was important for religious and political reasons. First, as the church of the imperial court, Hagia Sophia symbolized the importance of Orthodox Christianity in the Byzantine Empire. Second, by commissioning important buildings and art, Justinian asserted his authority as well as the Church's role in Byzantine society.

The design of Hagia Sophia was radically new. Its dome, supported by four arches, was larger and more prominent than any the world had ever known. Pierced by windows and covered with glimmering mosaics, the dome appeared to hover, weightless, above the vast church. Light streamed into the church from all directions and reflected off decorated surfaces.

To an extent, Justinian succeeded in his goal of creating the greatest religious monument of his time. It was centuries before a building of equal size and splendor was built in the Mediterranean world.

MAKING THE CONNECTION

1. What sort of effect did the interior of Hagia Sophia have on its viewers?
2. How did the splendor of the church of Hagia Sophia serve Justinian's goals?

Chapter 10 Section 1

ASSESS

Check for Understanding

Assign Section 1 Review as homework or as an in-class activity.

Use Student Self-Test and Review Software to review Section 1.

CONNECTIONS The Arts

Hagia Sophia

Justinian chose a plan common in eastern areas of the empire: a cross-shaped domed church. This became the prevailing form of church architecture in the Byzantine Empire. The central dome blended harmoniously with every part of the building. The walls were covered with mosaics.

Answers to Making the Connection

1. *an effect of mystery, light, and splendor*
2. *The church symbolized the importance of Orthodox Christianity to the empire; by commissioning public works, Justinian asserted imperial authority.*

MAKING CONNECTIONS ACTIVITIES

Religion Since the schism of A.D. 1054, the Eastern Orthodox and Roman Catholic Churches have continued to develop their own doctrine and traditions. Have students research the principal differences in doctrine and religious practices between the two churches today and report their findings to the class. **L2**

The Arts Numerous conventions governed the painting of Byzantine icons to ensure that an icon would have a particular effect on its viewers. Have students research the conventions and report to the class on their findings. Have them illustrate their report with examples of Byzantine art. **L3**

Chapter 10 *Byzantines and Slavs* 249

Chapter 10 Section 1

Evaluate

Section Quiz 10-1

Use the Testmaker to create a customized quiz for Section 1.

Reteach

Have students create cards with questions and answers such as the following and encourage them to play a Jeopardy-style game with the question cards.

1. walled harbors and fortified gates *(What protected Byzantium from outside attack?)*
2. the iconoclast controversy *(What conflict involved the use of images in the Church?)*

Enrich

Have students research the epidemic of plague that struck Constantinople in A.D. 542. Encourage them to prepare a brief essay or oral report on the devastation caused by the epidemic and its impact on political affairs in the empire.

CLOSE

Discuss the importance of Christianity in the Byzantine Empire. Explain that the emperor was never questioned and that the emperor and the patriarch of the Church were very close. Organize a class discussion about how religious disagreements, such as the schism with Rome and the iconoclastic controversy, affected politics.

Around the World: Simplified Alphabet Becomes Popular

Japan, A.D. 860

The Japanese alphabet, hiragana, became popular around A.D. 860. It consisted of characters developed by simplifying the Chinese alphabet. Hiragana was popularized by women of the Heian court, who used the system in writing poetry, diaries, and novels. It was called "letters of women" because men continued to use kanji, or the Chinese system.

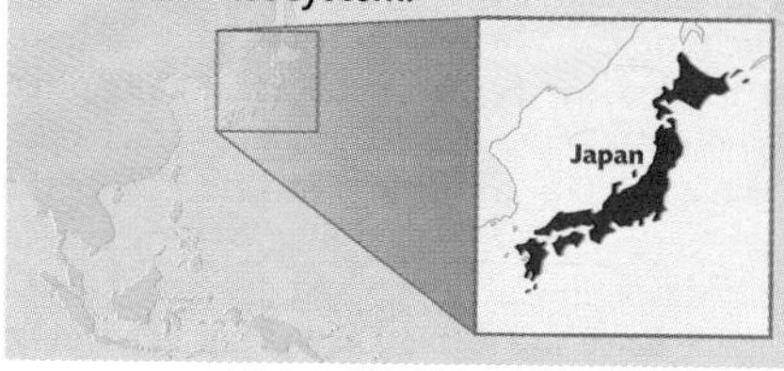

God's presence in human affairs. The leading champion of icons was the Byzantine theologian John of Damascus. Although a resident of the Islamic Empire, he wrote many religious articles defending the use of icons.

Believing that icons encouraged superstition and the worship of idols, in A.D. 726 Emperor **Leo III** ordered all icons removed from the churches. The emperor's supporters—mostly military leaders, government officials, and many of the people in Asia Minor—became known as iconoclasts, or image breakers.

Church leaders and other Byzantines resisted the order, and were supported by the Church in Rome, which was as important a center of Christianity as Constantinople. The Roman pope's involvement in the controversy strained relations between the Eastern and Western Churches.

Feeling his authority was being challenged, Leo asserted his power and suppressed demonstrations in favor of icons. Although several later emperors followed Leo's lead, they were not supported by the people. In A.D. 787 a church council at Nicaea approved the use of icons. Soon after, the Empress Irene—the first woman to hold the Byzantine throne in her own right—allowed the use of icons as long as they were not given the worship due to God. The Eastern Church further settled the issue in A.D. 843, allowing the use of pictures, but not statues, in worship.

Conflict With Rome

Since the A.D. 300s, the Eastern and Western Churches had disagreed on a number of religious and political issues. As centuries passed, the disagreements intensified.

The iconoclastic controversy was but one of many reasons that divided the two churches. The most serious issue concerned the source of religious authority. The pope in Rome and the patriarch of Constantinople did not agree on their roles in the Christian Church. The pope stated that he was supreme leader of the Church; the patriarch of Constantinople opposed this claim. The two church leaders also disagreed over points of doctrine. They challenged each other for control of new churches in the Balkan Peninsula.

Relations between Eastern and Western Churches worsened in the A.D. 700s when the Germanic Lombards invaded central Italy. When the Byzantine emperor refused to give the pope in Rome military protection, the pope turned to the Franks, a Germanic Catholic people in western Europe. After the Franks defeated the Lombards, the pope gave the Frankish leader, Charlemagne, the title of emperor—a title which only the Byzantine ruler could legally grant. This action made the Byzantines even more bitter toward the pope and the Western Church.

By A.D. 1054 doctrinal, political, and geographical differences finally led to a schism (SIH•zuhm), or separation, of the Church into the Roman Catholic Church in the West and the Eastern Orthodox Church in the East. The split further weakened the Byzantine Empire, which had faced attacks from numerous peoples since its founding.

SECTION 1 REVIEW

Recall

1. **Define** clergy, laity, icon, iconoclast, schism.
2. **Identify** Constantine, Justinian, Theodora, Leo III.
3. **Locate** Constantinople on the map on page 247. Why was Constantinople's location significant?

Critical Thinking

4. **Analyzing Information** How were Byzantine emperors and the Christian Church linked?

Understanding Themes

5. **Conflict** How did religious disputes, such as the iconoclastic controversy, affect Byzantine political affairs?

SECTION 1 REVIEW ANSWERS

1. All vocabulary words are defined in the Glossary.
2. Constantine, 246; Justinian, 247; Theodora, 247; Leo III, 250
3. Constantinople's location offered protection from attack and access to trade routes from three continents.
4. Byzantine emperors played a major role in church affairs by appointing church officials, setting the style of worship, and intervening in church disputes.
5. CONFLICT Religious disputes such as the iconoclastic controversy helped produce the schism between the Eastern and Western Churches. This split weakened the Byzantine Empire.

250 Chapter 10 *Byzantines and Slavs*

A.D. 500 — A.D. 1000 — A.D. 1500

A.D. 550 Byzantines send expedition to China.

A.D. 863 Cyril develops alphabet for the Slavs.

A.D. 1184 Queen Tamara begins her reign in Georgia.

A.D. 1453 Constantinople falls to Ottoman Turks.

Section 2

Byzantine Civilization

Setting the Scene

- **Terms to Define**
  theology, regent, mosaic, illuminated manuscript, monastery, missionary
- **People to Meet**
  Cyril, Methodius, the Seljuk Turks, the Ottoman Turks, Tiridates III, Tamara
- **Places to Locate**
  Venice, Armenia, Georgia

Find Out What role did Christianity play in Byzantine, Armenian, and Georgian societies?

The Storyteller

A bishop from Italy wrote home describing the Byzantine court: "In the audience-hall sat the Emperor on a throne before which stood an artificial tree, all gilded, on whose branches mechanical birds perched, singing. To either side of the throne stood a mighty lion, which, as the visitor approached, lashed the ground with its tail and from whose open jaws … there came a terrifying roar." The visitor threw himself to the ground three times, and looking up beheld the Emperor raised by an invisible mechanism to the roof of the hall, where he sat glittering among his jewels.

—adapted from *Istanbul*, Martin Heurlimann, 1958

Emperor Constantine IX

From A.D. 500 to A.D. 800, when western Europe was in decline, the Byzantine Empire was a brilliant center of civilization. Its scholars preserved Greek philosophy and literature, Roman political and legal ideas, and Christian **theology**, or religious teachings. The Byzantines also created new art forms and spread the religion of the Eastern Orthodox Church into eastern Europe.

Byzantine Life

Byzantine society was divided into a hierarchy of social groups. Yet, there were few barriers to prevent a person from moving from one group to another. This flexibility brought variety and change to Byzantine life.

Family Life

The family was the center of social life for most Byzantines. Both the Church and the government supported marriage as a sacred institution. Divorce was difficult to obtain, and the Church generally forbade more than one remarriage.

Byzantine women were expected to live partly in seclusion, and so rooms in homes and churches were set aside for their sole use. Nevertheless, women had gained some rights through Theodora's efforts. Like the empress herself, some women became well educated and influential in the government. Several governed as **regents**, or temporary rulers, and a few ruled in their own right as empresses.

The Economy

Most Byzantines made a living through farming, herding, or working as laborers. Farmers paid heavy taxes that supported the government.

Chapter 10 Section 2

SECTION THEME

- **Innovation** Byzantines develop Eastern Orthodox theology and distinctive art forms.

Find Out

Answer: *Christianity provided the peoples of the Byzantine Empire, Armenia, and Georgia with a sense of national identity and unity and served as the basis for innovations in the arts and architecture.*

FOCUS

Section Objective

Investigate the role of Christianity in Byzantine, Armenian, and Georgian societies.

BELLRINGER Motivational Activity

Before taking roll at the beginning of the class period, project Section Focus Transparency 10-2 and have students answer the activity questions. Discuss students' responses.

This activity is also available as a blackline master.

Vocabulary Pre-check

Use the Vocabulary PuzzleMaker to create a puzzle that reinforces the vocabulary terms in this section. **L1 LEP**

SECTION RESOURCES

Reproducible Masters
- Reproducible Lesson Plan 10-2
- Guided Reading Activity 10-2
- Section Quiz 10-2

Transparencies
- Section Focus Transparency 10-2
- World History and Art Transparency 12

Multimedia
- Vocabulary PuzzleMaker Software
- Student Self-Test and Review Software
- Testmaker
- Picture Atlas of the World

TEACH

Guided Practice

THEME Innovation

Refer students to the description of Hagia Sophia on page 249 and discuss Byzantine architectural innovation: the large central church dome. Explain that although domes were not a new architectural feature, Byzantine domes were used in a new geometrical setting—flanked by smaller domes—and were higher and wider than any previous domes. If possible, bring to class pictures of ancient Roman domed buildings for students to compare. **L1 LEP**

Daily Life Ask students to consider such aspects of Byzantine civilization as art, religion, the economy, education, politics, and family life. Have small groups of students each choose two areas of interest and examine how these areas affected Byzantine culture. Then ask groups to share their findings with their classmates. **L3**

World History and Art Transparency 12, *Theodora and Attendants*

Although the base of the Byzantine economy was agricultural, commerce thrived in cities such as Constantinople, which was the site of a natural crossroads for trade. Byzantine ships loaded with cargo sailed between the Mediterranean and Black Seas by way of the Bosporus and Dardanelles. At the eastern shore of the Black Sea, goods could be shipped overland through Asia. Rivers such as the Dnieper, which flows from the Black Sea north to the Baltic, provided access to northern Europe.

Merchants traded Byzantine agricultural goods and furs and enslaved people from northern Europe for luxury goods from the East. To Constantinople's busy harbor, called the Golden Horn, ships brought cloves and sandalwood from the East Indies; pepper, copper, and gems from India and Ceylon (present-day Sri Lanka); and silk from China.

The major Byzantine industry was weaving silk. It developed after A.D. 550, when Justinian sent two monks to China, the center of the silk industry. On a visit to a silk factory the monks stole some silkworm eggs, hid them in hollow bamboo canes, and smuggled their precious cargo out of China. Brought to Constantinople, the silkworms fed on mulberry leaves and spun the silk that made the empire wealthy.

Byzantine Art and Learning

Among the products of Byzantine culture were beautiful icons, jewel-encrusted crosses, and carved ivory boxes for sacred items. These art forms were adopted by eastern Europe and also influenced western Europe and the Middle East.

Art

Religious subjects were the sources of most Byzantine art. Icons, the most popular art form, portrayed saints and other religious figures. Icons were displayed on the walls of churches, homes, and shrines. Magnificent churches were

Images of the Times

Byzantine Art

Byzantine art reflected the strong influence of Christianity.

The crucifix was a familiar Byzantine icon both in churches and in homes.

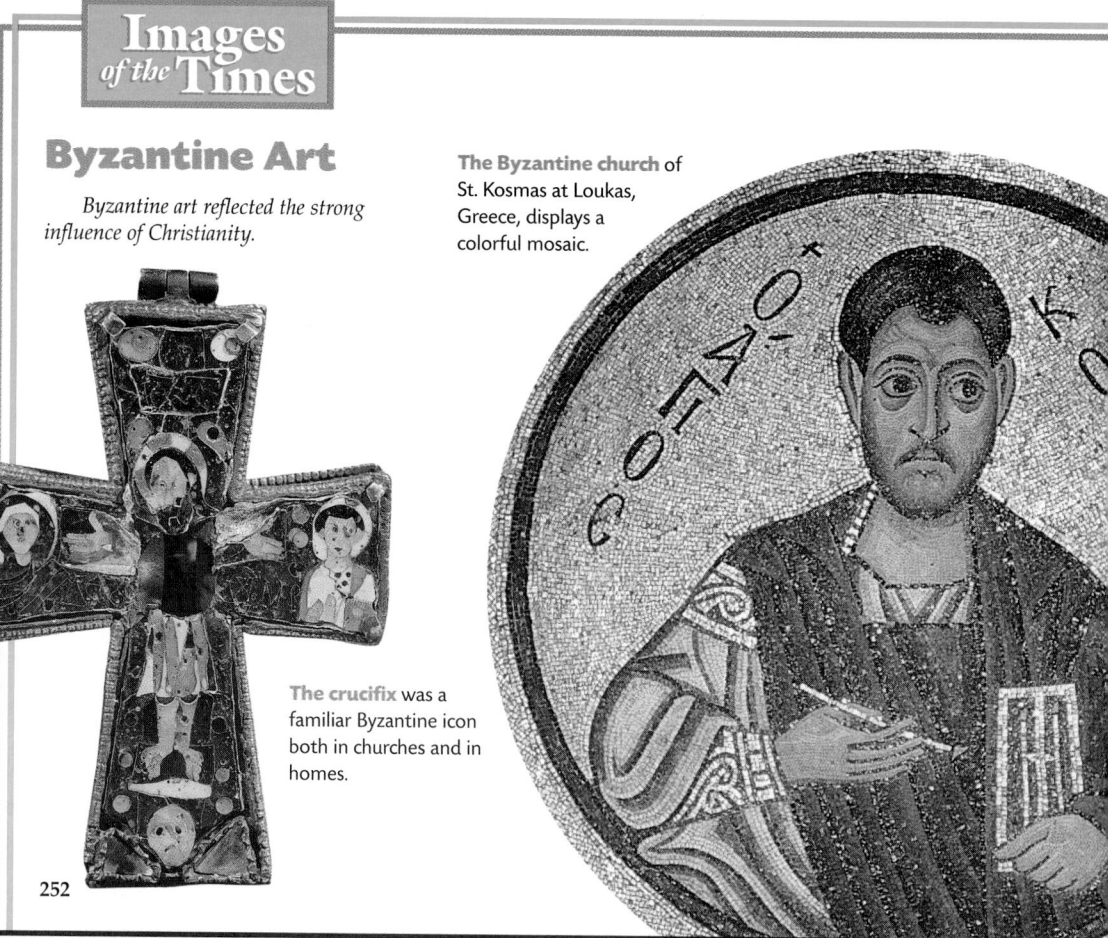

The Byzantine church of St. Kosmas at Loukas, Greece, displays a colorful mosaic.

Images of the Times **Byzantine Art**

The creative artists of the Byzantine Empire painted frescoes and icons, carved ivories, illuminated manuscripts, created reliquaries with precious jewels and metalwork, embroidered tapestries, and used tiny bits of stone and glass to produce superb mosaics. The mood of much of this art was reverent, with religious themes. But secular forms existed alongside the religious: sculptures, woven silk, textiles, dishes, enamelwork, and glass.

embellished with gold and silver, polished and carved marble, ivory, and jewels, as well as icons and other religious images.

The Byzantines also excelled in the art of **mosaic**, or pictures made of many tiny pieces of colored glass or flat stone set in plaster. The most masterly mosaics captured the finest gradations of skin tones and textures of clothing—a skill even painters found difficult to master. Byzantine emperor Constantine VII, historian, painter, and author, described one mosaic:

> "As you move, the figures seem to move, too. You could swear that their eyes are turning and shining and that their garments are rustling … the Byzantine mosaicist has succeeded in creating the illusion that his jig-saw puzzle has come to life."

Religious scholars of the Byzantine Empire created another art form, the **illuminated manuscript**. These were books decorated with elaborate designs, beautiful lettering, and miniature paintings. The brilliantly colored paintings portrayed religious themes as well as scenes of Byzantine daily life. Adopted in western Europe, the art of illuminating manuscripts provided a vivid record of daily life between A.D. 300 and A.D. 1200.

Education

Schools and learning also played an important role in Byzantine culture. The government-supported University of Constantinople, established in A.D. 850, trained scholars and lawyers for government jobs; the Eastern Orthodox Church provided religious schools to train priests and theological scholars. Beyond the religious subjects that reflected the primary role of the Church, areas of study included medicine, law, philosophy, arithmetic, geometry, astronomy, grammar, and music. Wealthy people sometimes hired tutors to instruct their children, particularly their daughters, who were usually not admitted to schools and universities.

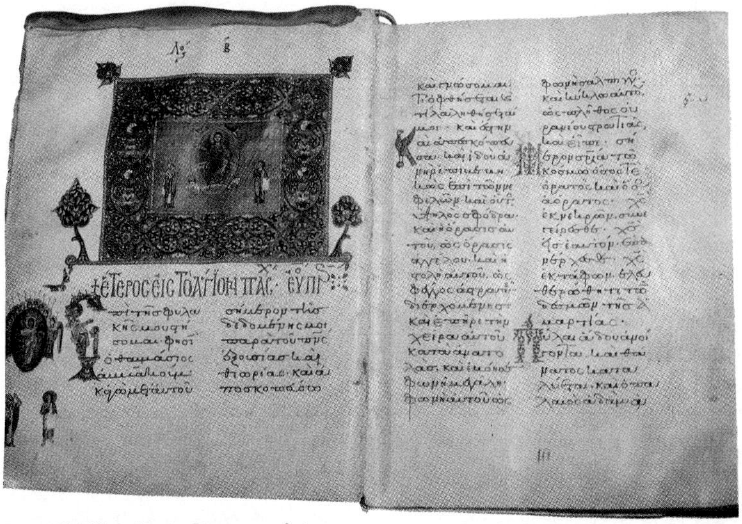

Beautiful illuminated manuscripts, such as this from St. Catherine's Monastery at Sinai, were the work of religious scholars. Monasteries were financed by the emperor and by wealthy citizens.

REFLECTING ON THE TIMES

1. How do these images reveal the prosperity of the Byzantine Empire?
2. Who paid to have much of the religious art at churches and monasteries created?

253

Chapter 10 Section 2

Independent Practice

Guided Reading Activity 10-2 **L1**

The Arts Have students select a letter of the alphabet (one of their own initials, for example) to be illuminated. They will need to check resources for examples of illuminated manuscripts. Encourage students to be creative and decorate the letter with as much color and detail as possible. **L2 LEP**

Who?What?Where?When?

Education The Byzantine Empire provided free schools open to all children regardless of nationality or class as early as the eleventh century. Children of upper-class families, however, were often educated by private tutors.

Global Gourmet

Byzantine Empire Byzantine eating habits were similar to our own. Three meals a day (breakfast, midday, and supper) were common. Most people ate simply: bread and cheese, and vegetables cooked in olive oil. The wealthy enjoyed banquets of meats roasted or cooked in herbs and spices. A variety of meat, game, poultry, and fish was eaten. Soups and stews were often on the menu. Fruits such as apples, melon, figs, and dates were staple items of the diet.

ANSWERS TO REFLECTING ON THE TIMES

1. Jewel-encrusted crosses and gold and glass mosaics reflected the great wealth of resources from the empire's trade.
2. The emperor and wealthy citizens financed this religious art.

Map Study

Answer

unending attacks by many peoples, both in the east and in the west; losing control of trade

Map Skills Practice

Reading a Map Between what latitudes on the map does Constantinople lie? *(between 40°N–45°N latitudes)*

Religion and the Arts Students may work in small groups to list specific examples of how Byzantine art and architecture were strongly influenced by religion. Have all students then write individual short essays explaining the relationship. **L3**

NATIONAL GEOGRAPHIC SOCIETY

CD-ROM
PICTURE ATLAS OF THE WORLD

You and your students can see the present-day skyline of Istanbul and the beautiful Hagia Sophia by clicking the "Photos" button of Istanbul, Turkey.

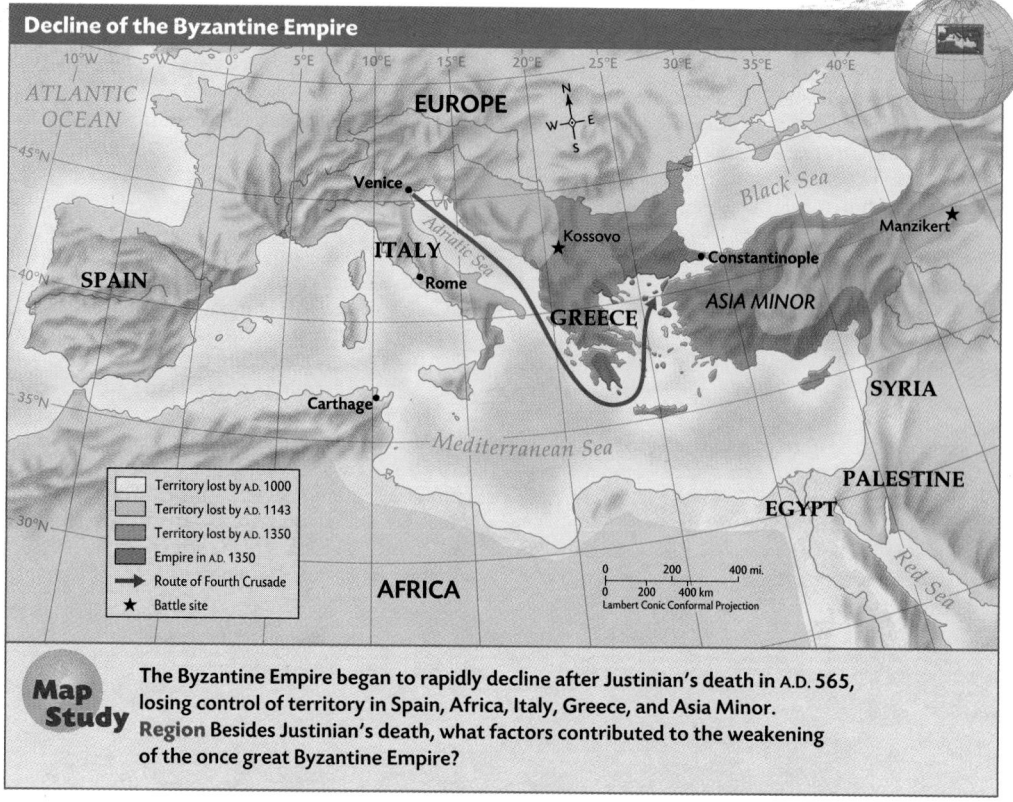

Decline of the Byzantine Empire

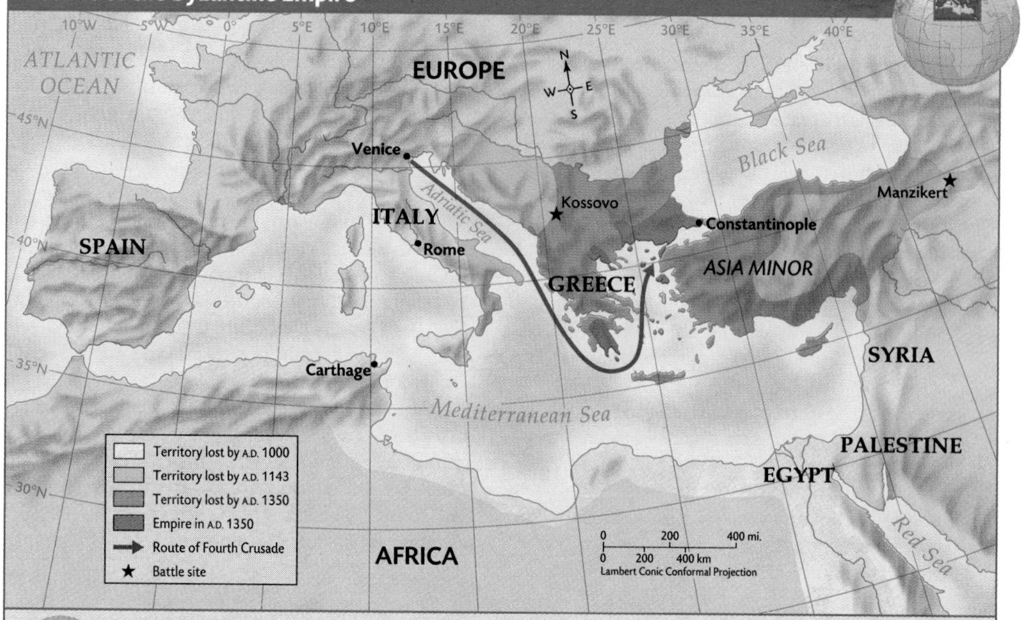

Map Study **The Byzantine Empire began to rapidly decline after Justinian's death in A.D. 565, losing control of territory in Spain, Africa, Italy, Greece, and Asia Minor.**
Region Besides Justinian's death, what factors contributed to the weakening of the once great Byzantine Empire?

Byzantine literature focused on salvation of the soul and obedience to God's will. Writers composed hymns and poems in praise of Christ and his mother, Mary. Instead of popular fiction, Byzantine authors wrote books about the lives of the saints, which provided readers with moral lessons as well as accounts of the saints' miracles and adventures.

The foremost occupation of Byzantine scholars, however, was copying the writings of the ancient Greeks and Romans. By preserving ancient works on science, medicine, and mathematics, the Byzantines helped spread classical knowledge to the Western world.

Footnotes *to* History

Greek Fire

In fighting their enemies, the Byzantines used a terrifying weapon known as Greek fire, one of the earliest uses of chemicals in warfare. This chemical mixture exploded when it came into contact with fire or water. The formula remains a mystery; it probably included highly flammable oil, pitch, quicklime, sulfur, and resin.

Spread of Christianity

Near the end of the A.D. 300s, devout Christians throughout the Byzantine Empire formed religious communities called **monasteries**. In the monasteries, men called monks sought to develop a spiritual way of life apart from the temptations of the world. At the same time, they could help other people by doing good deeds and by setting an example of Christian living. Christian women who did the same were called nuns and lived in quarters of their own known as convents.

Monasteries and convents soon played an important role in Byzantine life. They helped the poor and ran hospitals and schools for needy children. They also spread Byzantine arts and learning. Monasteries also sent **missionaries**—people who carry a religious message—to neighboring peoples to convert them to the Christian faith.

COOPERATIVE LEARNING ACTIVITY

Role Play Organize the class into two large groups—one representing citizens of the Byzantine Empire and the other representing visitors from northern Europe. Have each group prepare a presentation. The Byzantines should prepare a speech welcoming their visitors. The speech should stress the virtues and achievements of Byzantine culture. Then the visitors from northern Europe should respond by acknowledging their hosts' achievements and commenting on what they have seen during their visit. The visitors should compare features of their homeland with those of the Byzantine Empire. Conclude the presentations with a discussion of various social, religious, political, and economic concerns and conflicts facing both groups. **L1**

Among the most successful missionaries were the brothers **Cyril** and **Methodius**. They reasoned that Christianity would be more acceptable to the Slavic peoples who lived north of the empire if it were presented in their own language. About A.D. 863 Cyril devised an alphabet for the Slavic languages. Known today as the Cyrillic (suh•RIH•lihk) alphabet in honor of its inventor, this script is still used by Russians, Ukrainians, Bulgarians, and Serbs. When Cyril and Methodius presented the Slavs with Cyrillic translations of the Bible and church ceremonies, they won many converts.

Decline and Fall

From its founding, the Byzantine Empire suffered frequent attacks by invading armies. Among them were Germanic Lombards, Slavs, Avars, Bulgars, Persians, and Arabs.

Unending Attacks

After Justinian died in A.D. 565, the Germanic Lombards took over most of Italy, the Avars attacked the northern frontier, Slavic peoples moved into the Balkans, and the Persians resumed their attacks in the east. By A.D. 626 the Slavs were at the walls of Constantinople. Although a brilliant counterattack stopped their advance, a new enemy—the Arabs from the Middle East—entered the scene. Followers of the new religion of Islam, the Arabs sought to spread their faith and acquire wealth. By the A.D. 630s, they occupied Syria and Palestine and had expanded into Persia and across North Africa. The Byzantines stopped the Arabs at Constantinople, but could not regain the lost territories in the Middle East and North Africa.

By A.D. 700 the Byzantine Empire was reduced to the territories that were primarily Greek. The loss of the non-Greek lands actually helped strengthen the empire because it now had one religion, one language, and one culture.

Christian Conquest

In A.D. 1071 northern European people called Normans seized the Byzantine lands in southern Italy. **Venice**, an Italian trading city on the Adriatic Sea, agreed to help the Byzantines' effort to regain the lands in return for trading privileges in Constantinople. The attempt failed, however, and the Byzantines soon lost control of trade, badly weakening an economy already strained by war.

In the same year, **the Seljuk** (SEHL•JOOK) **Turks**, who had come from central Asia and converted to Islam, defeated the Byzantines at the town of Manzikert. As the invaders advanced, the Byzantine emperor asked the pope's help in defending Christianity. Expeditions sent by the pope against the Islamic forces were more interested in taking over Palestine.

Visualizing History **St. Jacob holding script in the Cyrillic alphabet, a modified form of the Greek alphabet.** *What peoples use the Cyrillic alphabet today?*

In A.D. 1204 Christian soldiers from western Europe agreed to help the Venetians attack Constantinople. For three days the attackers burned and looted the city, stealing and destroying priceless manuscripts and works of art. Their actions were so brutal that Pope Innocent III publicly condemned them:

> "These defenders of Christ, who should have turned their swords only against the infidels [followers of Islam], have bathed in Christian blood. They have respected neither religion, nor age, nor sex.... It was

Visualizing History The Russian language and other Slavic languages are closely related. The Cyrillic alphabet, which is based largely on the Greek alphabet and originally had 43 letters, eventually became the basis for the culture of the entire Slavic world.
Answer to Caption: *A modified form of the Cyrillic alphabet, containing 33 letters, is used by the Russians, Ukrainians, Bulgarians, and Serbs today.*

Politics Encourage students to consider the factors that led to the fall of the Byzantine Empire. Have them create a time line tracing the decline of the empire after the reign of Justinian. Students may need to do library research to fill in some of the details. Time lines should include the reigning emperor, economic factors, internal and external conflicts, and a list of territories lost at each stage. **L2**

MEETING SPECIAL NEEDS ACTIVITY

Language Delayed Encourage students who have difficulty defining terms to search through the text for new words and jot them down on index cards. Assign partners to work together to define the terms on the back of the cards. Have students use the words in another context to ensure understanding. The entire class can use the set of cards for review at the end of the chapter and before the unit test. **L1 LEP**

Chapter 10 *Byzantines and Slavs* 255

Chapter 10 Section 2

CURRICULUM CONNECTION

LITERATURE
Georgia enjoyed a golden age during the reign of Queen Tamara. Her court welcomed artists and poets, including Shota Rustaveli, whose epic poem, *The Knight in the Tiger Skin*, was dedicated to the queen. Set in Arabia, the poem tells a tale of courtly love, emphasizing courage, loyalty, and patriotism. It has been translated into French, Russian, Japanese, and other languages.

Visualizing History Mahmet set about rebuilding the newly renamed capital, Istanbul. He constructed new buildings and converted some of the city's finest churches into mosques.
Answer to Caption: *The city held out for six weeks under siege until their last emperor was slain.*

ASSESS

Check for Understanding

Assign Section 2 Review as homework or as an in-class activity.

Use Student Self-Test and Review Software to review Section 2.

not enough for them to squander the treasures of the Empire and to rob private individuals, whether great or small.... They have dared to lay their hands on the wealth of the churches. They have been seen tearing from the altars the silver adornments, breaking them in fragments, over which they quarrelled, violating the sanctuaries, carrying away the icons, crosses, and relics. ”

The western Christians established "a Latin empire" in Constantinople. The Byzantine people resisted this rule successfully and reestablished their own culture in A.D. 1261.

Fall of Constantinople

The years of fighting had severely weakened the Byzantine Empire. Soon Serbs and Bulgars took over Balkan territory. New invaders from central Asia, **the Ottoman Turks**, attacked the eastern provinces. By the late A.D. 1300s, the Byzantine Empire consisted of only Constantinople and part of Greece.

About 100,000 people still lived in the capital; food was scarce, and wealth was gone. In A.D. 1453 the Ottomans laid siege to Constantinople. For six weeks their huge cannon blasted away at the city's walls. The Byzantines fought fiercely until their last emperor was killed.

For a thousand years, the Byzantine Empire had protected the Christian lands to its north. With the fall of Constantinople, central Europe lay open to attack by Islamic forces. Despite the empire's fall, the Byzantine heritage lived on in the civilization developed by the Eastern Slavs.

Visualizing History **Portrait of Sultan Mahmet II, who conquered Constantinople and renamed it Istanbul.** *How long did the Byzantine city hold out against the sultan's siege?*

Neighboring Kingdoms

During the time of the Byzantine Empire, two neighboring kingdoms—**Armenia** and **Georgia**—went through periods of prosperity and decline. Both Armenia and Georgia lay south of the rugged, snow-capped Caucasus Mountains between the Black and Caspian Seas. Although the mountains made travel by land difficult, plains and valleys between the mountains allowed traders and invaders to pass between Europe and Asia. Over the centuries, the peoples of Armenia and Georgia faced a repeated pattern of conquest by larger neighboring powers that rivaled each other for control of the region.

Armenia

Historians believe that the first Armenians settled the area that is present-day Armenia in about the 700s B.C. Within 200 years, these settlers had intermarried with the local people, built walled towns, and prospered from the growing of wheat and other cereal crops. By about 400 B.C., the Persians who lived to the south absorbed Armenia into their empire and forced the Armenians to pay tribute to the Persian ruler.

When Alexander the Great conquered Persia in the 330s B.C., his armies also gained control of Armenia. The country, however, was allowed a degree of independence. King Tigran II, who came to power in 95 B.C., built an independent Armenian kingdom that reached from the Caspian Sea to the Mediterranean Sea. The Romans defeated Tigran in 55

MAKING CONNECTIONS ACTIVITY

Daily Life Have students bring in works of folk art, literature, and music and examples of foods from the Balkan Peninsula and Slavic areas. Some might prepare recipes from Turkey, Armenia, and Russia. Other students can locate collections of folktales and perform a dramatic reading. Still others might play recordings of typical folk music of the region. Possibly someone from the community can share a traditional costume or perform a folk dance. **L1**

B.C., and Armenia became part of the Roman Empire.

In the early A.D. 300s, Armenia came under the influence of Christianity, which was spreading throughout the Roman Empire. One of the Christian missionaries working in Armenia was Gregory, an Armenian nobleman. Eventually known as Gregory the Illuminator, he converted the Armenian king **Tiridates** (TEER•uh•DAH•teez) **III** to Christianity. Most Armenians soon accepted the new faith, and Armenia became the first officially Christian country in the world.

Christianity gave Armenians a sense of national identity. Mesorb (MEH•zohrb), an Armenian monk and scholar, developed the Armenian alphabet in the early A.D. 400s. In A.D. 451, Armenians under Vartan Mamikonian (VAHR•tahn mah•mih•KOH•nee•uhn) defended their religion against the Persians in the battle of Avarair (ah•vah•RAHR). To gain peace, the Persians finally offered the Armenians religious and political freedom.

In the A.D. 600s another religion—Islam—arose among Arab peoples in the Middle East, which lay south of Armenia. Islam's followers, called Muslims, invaded Armenia, but failed to completely conquer the country. By the late A.D. 800s, an independent Armenian kingdom was thriving in the northern region. In the A.D. 1000s, peace was again interrupted when the Seljuk Turks, who had earlier conquered parts of the Byzantine Empire, won control of Armenia. The Seljuks were followed in the A.D. 1400s by other conquerors—the Ottoman Turks. Within 100 years, Armenia had become a battlefield between the Ottomans and their rivals, the Persians. Centuries later, in the A.D. 1800s, Armenia became a part of the Russian Empire to the north.

Georgia

People have lived in the area of present-day Georgia for thousands of years. By the 600s B.C., most of the present-day Black Sea coast of Georgia was part of a kingdom known as Colchis (KAHL•kuhs). Known for its riches, Colchis attracted the seafaring Greeks, who described the kingdom in their epic of the Golden Fleece. Another kingdom, Iberia, arose in the central part of present-day Georgia. In 65 B.C. Iberia and Colchis both came under the rule of the Romans.

The Roman conquerors built new roads and introduced their laws and customs to the region of Georgia. The Silk Road, which passed through the Caucasus Mountains, allowed the Georgians to prosper from trade between Europe and Asia. Caravans of silk cloth, spices, and other goods reached ports on Georgia's Black Sea coast and continued on to the Middle East and Europe.

Georgians accepted Christianity in the A.D. 300s. According to Georgian tradition, a Christian woman named Nino converted the people of Iberia to the new religion, which eventually spread to other parts of Georgia. Meanwhile, Georgia became a battleground between two opposing neighbors: the Persians and the Byzantines.

During the A.D. 1000s and A.D. 1100s, a series of Georgian rulers gradually freed Georgia of foreign influences and strengthened its government. These efforts eventually produced Georgia's golden age during the reign of Queen **Tamara** (tah•MAH•rah), who ruled from A.D. 1184 to A.D. 1212. During this time, the Georgians made great advances in culture, science, and the arts.

Beginning in the early A.D. 1200s, however, Georgia again suffered attacks from other nations. Mongol armies from central Asia raided Georgian lands from the A.D. 1220s to the early A.D. 1400s. These attacks sent Georgia into a period of decline. From the A.D. 1500s to the A.D. 1700s the Ottomans and the Persians fought over Georgian territory. In the late A.D. 1700s, the ruler of a small kingdom in eastern Georgia accepted partial control by the Russians to the north in return for military help. By the early A.D. 1800s, all of Georgia became part of the Russian Empire.

SECTION 2 REVIEW

Recall

1. **Define** theology, regent, mosaic, illuminated manuscript, monastery, missionary.
2. **Identify** Cyril, Methodius, the Seljuk Turks, Manzikert, the Ottoman Turks, Tiridates III, Tamara.
3. **Explain** why the Bosporus and the Dardanelles are strategic waterways.

Critical Thinking

4. **Analyzing Information** Examine how the doctrinal and cultural split between the Roman Catholic Church and the Eastern Orthodox Church contributed to the Byzantine Empire's decline.

Understanding Themes

5. **Innovation** How did Christianity affect culture in the Byzantine Empire, Armenia, and Georgia? What was the role of art and religion in these lands?

Chapter 10 Section 2

Evaluate

Section Quiz 10-2

Use the Testmaker to create a customized quiz for Section 2.

Reteach

Ask students to make a list of key elements of Byzantine culture during Emperor Justinian's time. *(religion, art, architecture, and trade)*

Enrich

Have students research the life of the Empress Theodora. Direct them to focus especially on what she did to improve the lives of women in the empire.

CLOSE

Help the class summarize the section by asking them to list three important contributions of Byzantine civilization. Ask whether they agree with historian Will Durant that the Byzantine Empire protected western Europe from Islam, transmitted the literature of ancient Greece, and passed Christianity along to the Slavs.

SECTION 2 REVIEW ANSWERS

1. All vocabulary words are defined in the Glossary.
2. Cyril, 255; Methodius, 255; Seljuk Turks, 255; Manzikert, 255; Ottoman Turks, 256; Tiridates III, 257; Tamara, 257
3. They link the Mediterranean and Black Seas, and they provide access to trade between Europe and Asia.
4. Constant conflict and friction disrupted and distracted religious and political leadership, eventually leading to an attack on Constantinople by western Christians.
5. **INNOVATION** Religious devotion stimulated and inspired cultural creativity. Religion and art played a central role in these societies and helped give them a sense of identity and unity.

SECTION THEME

▶ **Cultural Diffusion** Trade routes and invasions spread beliefs and ideas.

Find Out

Answer: *Eastern Slavs developed cultures separate from those of western Europe because of the influence of Byzantine religion and culture, the influence of Asian cultures, and the fact that many Slavic peoples never adopted Latin or Greek but instead used their native tongues.*

FOCUS

Section Objective

Describe how the Eastern Slavs developed separate cultures from those of western Europe.

BELLRINGER
Motivational Activity

Before taking roll at the beginning of the class period, project Section Focus Transparency 10-3 and have students answer the activity questions. Discuss students' responses.

This activity is also available as a blackline master.

Vocabulary Pre-check

Use Vocabulary Activity 10 to introduce vocabulary terms. **L1 LEP**

A.D. 900 — A.D. 1100 — A.D. 1300 — A.D. 1500

A.D. 980 Vladimir becomes Grand Prince of Kiev.

A.D. 1240 Alexander Nevsky defeats the Swedes.

A.D. 1380 Moscow defeats Mongols at the Battle of Kulikovo.

A.D. 1472 Ivan III of Moscow takes title of czar.

Section 3

The Eastern Slavs

Setting the Scene

▶ **Terms to Define**
steppe, principality, boyar, czar

▶ **People to Meet**
the Slavs, Rurik, Olga, Vladimir, Yaroslav, the Mongols, Alexander Nevsky, Ivan III

▶ **Places to Locate**
Dnieper River, Kiev, Novgorod, Moscow

Find Out How did the Eastern Slavs develop separate cultures from those of western Europe?

The Storyteller

As a pagan prince, Vladimir behaved kindly; once he became a Christian, his generosity became unlimited. Beggars assembled in his courtyard every day for food, drink, clothing, and money. For the sick and weak, supply wagons were loaded up and driven around the city of Kiev. Once, when his friends showed disgust at having to eat with plain wooden spoons, Vladimir laughed and had silver ones cast for them. He was also the first Kiev prince to mint gold and silver coins. The first of these, made by inexperienced Russian crafts workers, were slightly lumpy and uneven, but bore Vladimir's picture and the inscription, "Here is Vladimir on his throne. And this is his gold."

—from *Vladimir the Russian Viking,* Vladimir Volkoff, 1985

Eastern Orthodox church

After the fall of Constantinople in A.D. 1453, the leadership of the Eastern Orthodox world passed from the Byzantines to **the Slavs**. The Slavs were among the largest groups living in eastern Europe. Because of their location, the Slavs had been in close contact with the Byzantines since the A.D. 900s.

This relationship made a lasting mark on the development of Slavic history. The Slavs, especially those living in the areas that are today the Balkan Peninsula, Ukraine, and Russia, borrowed much from the Byzantines. On the foundation of Byzantine religion, law, and culture, the Slavs built a new civilization. They also borrowed heavily from western European and Asian cultures. As a result of these different influences, Russia—the farthest north and east of the Slavic lands—never became a completely European or completely Asian country.

The Setting

One of the Byzantine trade routes ran north across the Black Sea and up the **Dnieper River**, then overland to the Baltic Sea. From trading posts along the river grew the roots of early Slavic civilization.

The Steppe

North of the Black Sea are vast plains, thick forests, and mighty rivers. Much of the land is an immense plain called the steppe. Ukrainian author Nikolay Gogol vividly captures its spirit in his *Cossack Tales*:

> "The farther the steppe went the grander it became … one green uninhabited waste. No plow ever furrowed its immense wavy plains of wild plants; the wild horses, which herded there, alone trampled them down. The whole extent of the steppe was nothing but a green-gold ocean, whose surface seemed besprinkled with millions of different colored flowers."

SECTION RESOURCES

Reproducible Masters
- Reproducible Lesson Plan 10-3
- Vocabulary Activity 10
- Guided Reading Activity 10-3
- Reteaching Activity 10
- Enrichment Activity 10
- Section Quiz 10-3
- Performance Assessment Activity 10
- Spanish Chapter Summary 10

Transparencies
- Section Focus Transparency 10-3
- World History and Art Transparency 13

Multimedia
- Student Self-Test and Review Software
- Testmaker
- World Music: Cultural Traditions, Lesson 4

Although the steppe has rich black soil, the harsh climate makes farming difficult and crop failures common. Too far inland to be reached by moist ocean breezes, the steppe often has scanty rainfall. In addition, most of the land lies in the same latitudes as Canada and has the same short growing season. During the long, hard winter, blasts of Arctic air roar across the land and bury it deep in snow.

Forests and Rivers

North of the steppe stretch seemingly endless forests of evergreens, birch, oak, and other hardwoods. North–south flowing rivers such as the Dnieper, Dniester, and Volga cross the steppe and penetrate the forests, providing the easiest means of transportation. Yet travel is difficult for much of the year. In winter, deep drifts of snow cover the ground, and in the spring thaw the land turns to knee-deep mud.

The People

Historians know little about the origin of the first Slavic peoples. Some believe the Slavs came from present-day eastern Poland. Others think they may have been farmers in the Black Sea region. It is known that by about A.D. 500 the Slavs had formed into three distinct groups and had settled in different parts of eastern Europe.

Slavic Groups

One group, known as the West Slavs, lived in the marshlands, plains, and mountains of east-central Europe. They successfully fought the Germans to the west and the Scandinavians to the north for control of territory. Today the descendants of the West Slavs are the peoples of Poland, the Czech Republic, and Slovakia. Their religious ties came to be with the Roman Catholic Church, and their cultural ties were with western Europe.

Another group, known as the South Slavs, settled in the Balkan Peninsula, and had frequent contacts with the Byzantines. Today, their descendants are the Serbs, Croats, and Slovenes, whose languages and cultures were shaped by both the Roman Catholic West and the Orthodox East. One group of South Slavs—the Bosnians—were influenced by the religion of Islam from the Middle East.

The third and largest Slavic group, the Eastern Slavs, includes those now known as Ukrainians, Russians, and Belarussians. They lived north of the Black Sea between the Dnieper and Dniester Rivers and traded with the Byzantine Empire and northern Europe. From A.D. 500 to A.D. 800, some Eastern Slavs moved eastward toward the Volga River.

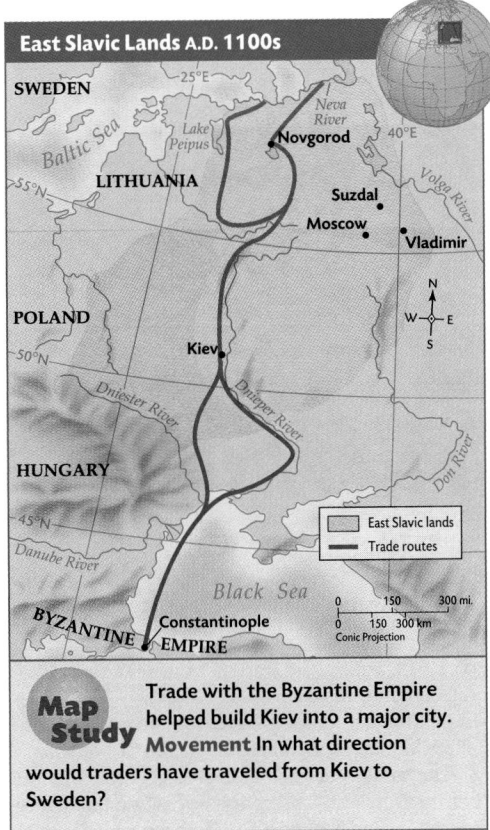

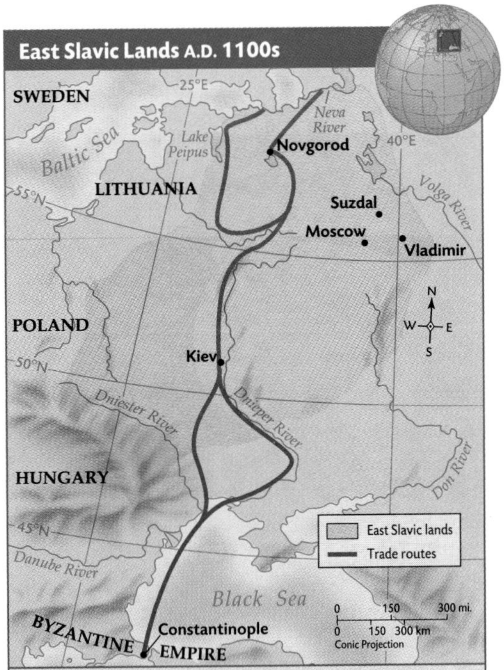

Map Study Trade with the Byzantine Empire helped build Kiev into a major city. **Movement** In what direction would traders have traveled from Kiev to Sweden?

Early Ways of Life

The early Eastern Slavs lived in villages made up of related families. They were farmers who hunted wild game and birds to supplement the wheat, rye, and oats they grew. In the forests they cleared land by cutting and burning trees and scattering the ash to enrich the soil. On the steppes they ignited a "sea of flame" to burn off the grass for planting.

Most farm homes were sturdy log houses called *izbas*. With knife, chisel, and ax the peasants skillfully shaped the logs, notching them so that they would fit together without nails. Many *izbas* had wooden gables and window frames decorated with painted carvings of flowers and animals. Skilled artisans also used wood to make furniture, cooking utensils, musical instruments, boats, and images of favorite deities.

The Eastern Slavs used the many rivers in their region for transportation and trade. They set up trading towns along the riverbanks. By the A.D. 800s, a trade route ran from the Baltic Sea in the north to the Black Sea in the south.

TEACH

Guided Practice

THEME Cultural Diffusion

Discuss with the class the influences of the Byzantines on early Slavic peoples: trade items such as silk, jewels, and food; the Cyrillic alphabet; and Christianity. Ask students to consider how the early Slavic people might have felt about these influences on their traditional culture and practices. **L1**

World History and Art Transparency 13

Map Study

Answer

Traders would have traveled northwest from Kiev to Sweden.

Map Skills Practice

Reading a Map How would Kiev's location have been favorable to Byzantine trade? *(Kiev was centrally located along the Dnieper River between Sweden and Constantinople.)*

Who?What?Where?When?

Slash-and-Burn A farming technique known as slash-and-burn was used by the Eastern Slavs to clear forests. After the trees were hauled away, remaining stumps and brush were set on fire. The ashes provided rich fertilizer that produced good harvests. After a few years the land was exhausted, however, and the Slavs were compelled to move to new locations at frequent intervals.

COOPERATIVE LEARNING ACTIVITY

Cultural Influences Organize the class into three groups—one representing the West Slavs, the second representing the South Slavs, and the third representing the Eastern Slavs. Group members should work together to research and prepare a family chronicle that reveals the cultural and religious influences on their group and then present the results of their work to the rest of the class. All members should participate in gathering and recording the information by using the text and library resources, preparing the chronicle, finding appropriate illustrations, and making the oral report. Conclude with a discussion of similarities and differences and any conflicts that divide the three groups. **L2**

Geography: Movement Have students trace an outline map of eastern Europe. Ask them to use the Atlas in their textbook as a guide for drawing and labeling the Dnieper, Dniester, Volga, Danube, and Neva Rivers; Moscow, Kiev, Novgorod, and Constantinople; and the Baltic and Black Seas. Have them also label land features such as the Ural Mountains. Trace the trade routes from Constantinople to Novgorod and discuss the vast openness of the land that invited movement and attack from the east and west. **L2 LEP**

World Music: Cultural Traditions, Lesson 4

Visualizing History An *izba* was a traditional type of log house found in rural Russia. A typical *izba* had an unheated entrance room and a single room for living and sleeping, heated by a clay or brick stove.
Answer to Caption: *The Eastern Slavs shaped logs with knives, chisels, and axes, notching the logs so they fit together without nails.*

Independent Practice

Guided Reading Activity 10-3 **L1**

Biography Have students write a short report about the life and achievements of one of the following: Prince Oleg, Prince Vladimir, Prince Yaroslav, or Ivan the Great. Have volunteers present oral summaries of their reports. **L1 LEP**

Visualizing History This *izba* in Russian Siberia's Lake Baikal region evidences the decorative style of Eastern Slav houses. *How did these people build without nails?*

Kievan Rus

The early Eastern Slavs were not warlike. During the late A.D. 800s, they relied on Vikings, a group of warriors and traders from Scandinavia, to protect their trade routes. The Vikings not only provided military aid, they also helped to lay the foundations of Slavic government.

The arrival of the Vikings is recorded in the *Primary Chronicle*, a collection of Eastern Slavic history, tales, and legends written around A.D. 1100. According to the *Chronicle*, in about A.D. 860 the Slavic people from the northern forest village of Novgorod asked Vikings from Scandinavia for aid: "Our land is great and rich, but there is no order in it. Come to rule and reign over us." The Viking leader **Rurik** accepted the invitation. The Slavs called the Vikings and the area they controlled *Rus*; the word *Russia* is probably derived from this name.

Rise of Kiev

In about A.D. 880, Rurik's successor, Prince Oleg, conquered the fortress-village of **Kiev** to the south. Built high on a bluff where the forest meets the steppe, Kiev prospered because it lay on the Dnieper River trade route. Some still call it the mother of Eastern Slavic cities.

Control of Kiev enabled Oleg to dominate the water trade route. Towns along the route were brought together under his leadership. Kiev soon became the major city of a region of Slavic territories known as Kievan Rus. The rulers of Kiev, known as Grand Princes, conducted raids against Constantinople. They were attracted by the wealth and civilization of the Byzantine capital. In A.D. 911 a treaty ended these raids and established trade between the Byzantines and the Eastern Slavs. During the summer months, Slavic merchants carried furs, honey, and other forest products by boat to Constantinople. There they traded their goods for cloth, wine, weapons, and jewelry.

Kievan Government

By A.D. 900, Kievan Rus had organized into a collection of city-states and **principalities**, or territories ruled by princes. Each region enjoyed local self-government; however, they all paid special respect to the Grand Prince of Kiev. The Grand Prince collected tribute from the local princes to support his court and army. The major duties of these princes were to administer justice and to defend the frontiers. The princes were assisted by councils of wealthy merchants and landed nobles, who were known as **boyars**. Assemblies represented all free adult male citizens. They handled daily affairs and had the power to accept or remove princes.

These three institutions—the princely office, the council, and the assembly—varied in power from region to region. In the northeastern territories, the prince wielded a great deal of political power. In the southeastern areas, the boyars had the greatest political influence. In Novgorod and a few northern trading towns and cities, the assemblies overshadowed both princes and boyars. In these areas, the assemblies came close to establishing a tradition of representative government in the Eastern Slavic lands. However, later princes limited the powers of the assemblies.

MEETING SPECIAL NEEDS ACTIVITY

Physical Disability Students with hearing impairments may need extra visual help to learn the material in this section. Select an advanced student to prepare a simple outline of the section using key words and ideas from the class. Have the resulting outline typed and provide it to students with special needs. (You may want to distribute the outline to the class as a whole, since this is an effective study method for everyone.) **L1**

260 Chapter 10 *Byzantines and Slavs*

NATIONAL GEOGRAPHIC PICTURING HISTORY

Jim Brandenburg

Rurik the Rus

This 19th-century statue of Russia's ancient ruler Rurik the Rus stands in the center of the city of Novgorod. The bronze Rurik, a mighty Prince, holds symbols of military might and political power: a shield and sword. His fur cape sweeps proudly over his shoulders. Founder of a nation, the Viking warrior proclaims a glorious past.

Rurik and his Viking warriors came from Scandinavia to what is now northern Russia in the A.D. 800s, perhaps invited there by native Slavic tribes constantly warring with each other. Russia during the A.D. 800s had no political stability, which made farming and commerce difficult. The Vikings changed that. Trading with the strong, plundering the weak, they moved south from Novgorod to Kiev, where they founded a political state, and from there they moved on to Odessa on the shores of the Black Sea. It took them two centuries. By then the Vikings had lost their Scandinavian ways and had become assimilated into the local cultures. ⊕

PICTURING HISTORY

TEACH

Explain to students that the Vikings were capable sailors and had already been carrying out raids and expeditions to establish settlements beyond their own territory—present-day Scandinavia. They settled as far away as North America. After Rurik went to Novgorod, he took complete control. Twenty years later his successor Oleg set himself up as prince of Kiev but retained control of Novgorod. **Why would Novgorod have been a desirable place for the Vikings to become established?** *(It gave them control of and access to the trade route with Constantinople.)*

Linking Past and Present

St. Sophia Cathedral Kiev is the capital of the Republic of Ukraine. The St. Sofia Cathedral in Kiev, one of the city's oldest structures, dates back to Kievan Rus.

CURRICULUM CONNECTION

ARCHAEOLOGY
Recent discoveries suggest that there was already a flourishing grain trade in Kiev when the Scandinavians took over. The native Slavs grew wheat, rye, barley, and oats.

Chapter 10 *Byzantines and Slavs* 261

Chapter 10 Section 3

Daily Life Direct students to imagine that they are going to be exchange students from Kiev to a city in another country. Have them write letters to their host families describing their own city, home, family, and daily life. **L2**

you don't say...

Pravda commonly means "truth," but during Yaroslav's reign it also meant "justice." The Kievan legal system that Yaroslav organized during his reign was known as the *Russkaya Pravda*. Yaroslav's *Pravda* was based on Byzantine models and was notable for being mild by medieval standards, not using corporal or capital punishment. The word *pravda* is familiar to the West through its association with the Moscow newspaper of the same name.

Visualizing History Monasteries played a key role in the revival of Russian civilization, much as they did in medieval Europe. Early Russian monasteries were often built near cities, and many monks took part in local political, economic, or military activities outside the monastery. **Answer to Caption:** *Legend states that Prince Vladimir sent observers abroad to examine various religions and, upon their recommendation, converted to Eastern Orthodoxy.*

Arrival of Christianity

Before the late A.D. 900s, the Eastern Slavs honored nature spirits and ancestors, and worshiped many deities. The most popular gods were Perun, god of thunder and lightning, and the Great Mother, goddess of the land and harvest. Images of the deities were built on the highest ground outside the villages.

Vladimir's Conversion

Because of contact with the Byzantine Empire, many Eastern Slavs were influenced by Eastern Orthodoxy. **Olga**, a princess of Kiev, became the first member of the Kievan nobility to accept the faith. Her grandson, Prince **Vladimir** of Kiev, decided to abandon the old beliefs and to adopt a new religion that he thought would help the Eastern Slavs become a more powerful civilization. An old Slavic legend states that Vladimir sent observers abroad to examine Judaism, Roman Catholicism, Eastern Orthodoxy, and Islam. Only the beautiful ceremony in the splendid Byzantine church of Hagia Sophia impressed the observers. In A.D. 989, after his own conversion to Eastern Orthodoxy, Vladimir ordered a mass baptism in the Dnieper River for his people.

Visualizing History **This ancient monastery stands as a symbol of the influence of Byzantine Christianity.** *How was Eastern Orthodoxy introduced in Kievan Rus?*

Effects of Conversion

The conversion to Eastern Orthodoxy brought Byzantine culture to Kievan Rus. Byzantine priests and bishops introduced the Eastern Slavs to colorful rituals and taught them the art of painting icons. The Eastern Slavs also learned to write their language in the Cyrillic alphabet. Schools were established in the towns for the sons of boyars, priests, and merchants. Byzantine architects arrived in Kiev to build stone churches with onion-shaped domes. Monasteries also were founded in the towns and countryside, and attracted many of the new converts.

Acceptance of Eastern Orthodoxy, however, tended to isolate the Eastern Slavs from the outside world. Following the split between the Eastern and Western Churches, Kievan Rus was separated from western Europe. Its people lost contact with developments that took place in that area after A.D. 1200. At the same time, the Byzantine practice of translating the Bible and Orthodox church services into local languages had an important impact. Because Kievan scholars had translations of some classical and Christian writings in their own language, they did not learn Greek or Latin. As a result, they did not deepen their knowledge of the heritage of western European civilization. Instead, they turned for inspiration to the traditions of their own local culture.

Kiev's Golden Age

Vladimir, who ruled from A.D. 980 to A.D. 1015, was one of the most important grand princes of Kiev. Known for his skills as a warrior, he successfully defended Kievan Rus's eastern frontiers against nomadic invaders. He also expanded its western borders by capturing lands in Poland and near the Baltic Sea.

Yaroslav's Reign

After a time of dynastic conflict, Vladimir's son **Yaroslav** became Grand Prince in A.D. 1019. Under Yaroslav's rule, Kievan culture reached its height. Yaroslav encouraged the spread of learning by establishing the first library in Kiev. Yaroslav also organized the Kievan legal system, drawing from Justinian's Code. Written primarily for the princes and merchants, the code treated crimes against property as well as against persons.

A skilled diplomat, Yaroslav arranged for his daughters and sisters to marry kings in Norway, Hungary, France, and Poland. To the Europeans, who were just arising from the isolation and

MAKING CONNECTIONS ACTIVITIES

The Arts Have students find examples of the following: Russian folktales or legends, Russian music, or Russian art. Have them prepare a brief presentation to the class on the subject of their research, including examples or audiovisual aids. Those who select folktales may want to read selections to the class. **L1 LEP**

Geography Encourage students to discover more about how the lack of natural barriers affected the Russian national character and how Russian leaders coped with invasions. Have students write essays focusing on the influence of geography on Russian history. Students might look at the Kremlin or the establishment of buffer zones. **L2**

disorder of the early Middle Ages, Kiev was a glittering capital whose culture outshone that of any in western Europe.

Kiev's Decline

After Yaroslav's death, Kiev declined in power and wealth for several reasons. First, Yaroslav began the practice of dividing up his lands among all his sons instead of willing them to one heir. Since no law established a clear line of succession, the heirs battled one another over control of Kiev. Second, the Latin Christian state created in Constantinople disrupted trade with the Byzantines and weakened Kiev's economy. Finally, in A.D. 1240 Mongol invaders from central Asia captured Kiev and completely destroyed it.

Mongol Rule

The Mongols, or Tatars, as the Slavs called them, defeated the armies of the Russian princes and conquered most of the country except for Novgorod. They sacked towns and villages and killed thousands. Mongols sought to tax the peoples they conquered, rather than impose their culture. The Slavs were allowed to practice their Christian faith, but the Mongols required allegiance to the Mongol ruler and service in the Mongol army.

For two centuries, Mongol rule isolated most of the Eastern Slavs from European civilization. Although the occupation helped unify the Eastern Slavs, it also further distanced them from ideas and trends of the Western world.

Rise of Muscovy

As city life in the south declined after the fall of Kiev, many Eastern Slavs—led by monks, farmers, and artisans—moved into the remote northern forests in order to escape Mongol rule. By the late A.D. 1200s, the principalities of Vladimir–Suzdal and **Novgorod** were the strongest Eastern Slavic territories.

Alexander Nevsky

The Mongols had never advanced as far north as Novgorod because the spring thaw turned the land into a swamp they could not cross. Instead, the city faced attacks in the Baltic Sea area from Swedes and Germans who wanted to convert the Eastern Slavs to Roman Catholicism. In a ferocious battle on the Neva River in A.D. 1240, Alexander, prince of Novgorod, defeated the invading Swedes. This victory earned him the nickname **Alexander Nevsky**, Alexander "of the Neva," and his victory established Novgorod as a strong, independent principality.

Visualizing History **Alexander Nevsky, ruler of Novgorod, fought the German Teutonic Knights in A.D. 1242.** *Why did the Germans and Swedes attack the Eastern Slavs?*

Moscow's Beginnings

Daniel, the youngest son of Alexander Nevsky, became ruler of **Moscow**, a small but prosperous town located near vital land and water routes. Using war and diplomatic marriages, the princes of Moscow, or Muscovy, gradually expanded their state's territory. Muscovy's importance grew in A.D. 1325 when the metropolitan, or leader of the Orthodox Church in the Eastern Slavic lands, was transferred there. By about A.D. 1350, Moscow had become the most powerful city. Cooperation with Mongol policies had kept it free from outside interference. Daniel's son, Prince Ivan I, became known as Money Bag because the Mongols even trusted him to collect taxes for them.

Muscovite forces defeated the Mongols at the Battle of Kulikovo in A.D. 1380. The tide had turned in favor of Muscovy. Over the next hundred years, the Eastern Slavs steadily drove out the Mongols. In A.D. 1480 during the rule of **Ivan III**, Moscow finally refused to pay taxes to the Mongols. The

Visualizing History Nevsky defended his frontiers against Christian invaders but was forced to pay tribute to the Mongol Batu Khan, the grandson of Genghis Khan.
Answer to Caption: *The Germans and Swedes wanted to convert the Eastern Slavs to Roman Catholicism.*

Global Gourmet

Russia The diet of the Russian peasant was very starchy. Staples included cabbage dishes; cooked grains such as barley, buckwheat, and millet; dark bread; and smoked and pickled herring.

ASSESS

Check for Understanding

Assign Section 3 Review as homework or as an in-class activity.

Use Student Self-Test and Review Software to review Section 3.

Evaluate

Section Quiz 10-3

Use the Testmaker to create a customized quiz for Section 3.

Linking Past and Present

Moscow From a small trading post on the Moskva River, Moscow grew to be the center of the Commonwealth of Independent States. Today the golden-domed Kremlin has walls of stone and brick instead of the wooden ones of the thirteenth century.

CRITICAL THINKING ACTIVITY

Synthesizing Information Have students think about the unique culture that developed among the Eastern Slavs and in Russia in particular. Have them create a chart that includes the following headings: *Geography, Religion, Economic Activities, Arts and Architecture,* and *Politics.* In each column, have students note the historic factors that influenced the development of Slavic culture. Ask students to identify which elements resulted from contacts with Asia and which came from the West. **L3**

Chapter 10 Section 3

Visualizing History Throughout the disruptive invasions, the Church kept the people of Russia united. More than a dozen churches and cathedrals stood within the protective walls of the Kremlin.
Answer to Caption: *The Kremlin was a fortress located within the city of Moscow.*

Reteach

Ask students to explain the significance of waterways and mobility in early Russia.

Reteaching Activity 10

Enrich

Encourage students to research the history of the Kremlin and the role it has played as a symbol of Russian unity. Students may write essays or brief reports. Artistic students can create posters or models.

Enrichment Activity 10

CLOSE

In this section, Byzantine influence spread to Russia, and Ivan III declared a "Third Rome" as the final and eternal Rome of all the land. Ask the class to discuss Ivan's declaration. Ask how students view the Commonwealth of Independent States, its lands, and its governments today.

Visualizing History **Gold-domed spires of the Church of the Annunciation reach toward the sky behind the Kremlin's walls.** *What was the original purpose of the Kremlin?*

long submission to the Asian rulers was over. Today, Ivan is known as Ivan the Great because he was able to bring all the Russian principalities under his rule. His major gain was Novgorod, which controlled territory all the way east to the Ural Mountains, the traditional division between Europe and Asia.

The Third Rome

Other factors helped to strengthen the power of Moscow's rulers. After Constantinople fell to the Ottoman Turks in A.D. 1453, Muscovy stood alone as the center of the Eastern Orthodox Church. In A.D. 1472 when Ivan III married Sophia, niece of the last Byzantine emperor, he took the title czar, or "caesar," the title used by the Roman and Byzantine emperors. Ivan also made the two-headed Byzantine eagle the symbol of his rule.

In A.D. 1493 Ivan added the title Sovereign of All Russia. The lands he ruled, now known as Russia, were a hundred times as large as the original Muscovite state. The people spoke one language, and the princes served one czar. The Russian Orthodox Church, which identified its interests with those of the Muscovite ruler, proclaimed that Moscow was the Third Rome. The Church regarded Ivan as both the successor of the Byzantine emperor and protector of the Eastern Orthodox Church, a claim all succeeding Russian czars would also make.

Moscow's Culture

Eastern Orthodoxy shaped the development of Moscow's culture. Its leaders stressed the importance of obedience to the czar and the government. The Church taught the people that submission to authority was a Christian duty. Joseph Sanin, an influential church leader during Ivan III's reign, wrote that "although the [ruler] was like other men in his physical characteristics, in his power he was similar to God in heaven."

Although western European influences reached Russia, they were transformed by local Russian styles and tastes. Instead of using Greek, Latin, or other classical languages, the Church used the Russian language in its worship and writings. Russia's religious leaders and political rulers also encouraged the development of a unique national style of icon painting and building construction. Ivan III had western European and Russian architects rebuild the Moscow Kremlin, or fortress. In spite of Western influences on its construction, the Kremlin became known for the typically Russian splendor of its beautiful onion-domed churches and ornately decorated palaces. Today the Kremlin in Moscow is still a center of government, religion, and culture for Russia.

SECTION 3 REVIEW

Recall
1. **Define** steppe, principality, boyar, czar.
2. **Identify** the Slavs, Rurik, Olga, Vladimir, Yaroslav, the Mongols, Alexander Nevsky, Ivan III.
3. **Locate** Kiev on the map on page 259. Why did Kiev prosper?

Critical Thinking
4. **Making Comparisons** Compare Kievan Rus with Muscovy. How was each dependent on geography? What role did the Orthodox Church play in each?

Understanding Themes
5. **Cultural Diffusion** What traditions that had originated with Rome became part of Russian culture? How did Russian culture differ from the civilization of western Europe? Why?

SECTION 3 REVIEW ANSWERS

1. All vocabulary words are defined in the Glossary.
2. the Slavs, 258; Rurik, 260; Olga, 262; Vladimir, 262; Yaroslav, 262; the Mongols, 263; Alexander Nevsky, 263; Ivan III, 263
3. Kiev: fortress-city on the Dnieper; Kiev prospered because it was on the trade route between the Slavs and the Byzantines.
4. Both Kievan Rus and Muscovy were located on rivers. Kiev saw the arrival of Christianity; Moscow became an important Christian center.
5. **CULTURAL DIFFUSION** Sample answers: Christian faith and title of Caesar; geography, differences in language, and the schism between Eastern and Western churches tended to isolate Russian culture, compounded by Russia's use of its native language rather than Greek or Latin.

Critical Thinking
SKILLS

Distinguishing Between Fact and Opinion

Imagine that you are watching two candidates for President debate the merits of the college loan program. One candidate says, "In my view, the college loan program must be reformed. Sixty percent of students do not repay their loans on time."

The other candidate replies, "College costs are skyrocketing, but only 30% of students default on their loans for more than one year. I believe we should spend more money on this worthy program."

How can you tell who or what to believe? First, you must learn to distinguish between fact and opinion.

Learning the Skill

A fact is a statement that can be proved to be true or false. In the example above, the statement "Sixty percent of students do not repay their loans on time" is a fact. By reviewing statistics on the number of student loan recipients who repay their loans, we can determine whether it is true or false. To identify facts, look for words and phrases indicating specific people, places, events, dates, times.

An opinion, on the other hand, expresses a personal belief, viewpoint, or emotion. Because opinions are subjective, we cannot prove or disprove them. In the opening example, most statements by the candidates are opinions.

Opinions often include qualifying words and phrases such as *I think, I believe, probably, seems to me, may, might, could, ought, in my judgment*, or *in my view*. Also, look for expressions of approval or disapproval such as *good, bad, poor*, and *satisfactory*. Be aware of superlatives such as *greatest, worst, finest*, and *best*. Notice words with negative meanings and implications such as *squander, contemptible*, and *disgrace*. Also, identify generalizations such as *none, every, always*, and *never*.

Practicing the Skill

For each pair of statements below, determine which is fact and which is opinion. Give a reason for each choice.

1. (a) The Byzantine Empire came to a pitiful end at the hands of the savage Turks.
   (b) The Byzantine Empire ended when Constantine XI died while defending Constantinople from invading Turks in A.D. 1453.
2. (a) The alliance with the Byzantine Empire made Kiev a major trading link between Europe and Asia and between Scandinavia and the Middle East.
   (b) In the A.D. 900s Kiev was the most isolated, uncivilized place and possessed little in the way of culture.
3. (a) The Byzantine culture was more advanced than any other of its day.
   (b) Vladimir's conversion to Eastern Orthodoxy brought Byzantine culture to Kievan Rus.

Applying the Skill

In a newspaper, find a news article and an editorial on the same topic or issue. Identify five facts and five opinions from these sources.

For More Practice

Turn to the Skill Practice in the Chapter Review on page 267 for more practice in distinguishing between fact and opinion.

Critical Thinking
SKILLS

TEACH

Distinguishing Between Fact and Opinion Point out to students that they are confronted with facts and opinions every day in newspapers and magazines. Ask where they would look for opinions in newspapers. *(editorial pages, book and movie reviews)* Where would solid facts be? *(news stories, sports scores, weather reports from day before)* Have students consider headlines and suggest that they bring in samples of fact and opinion headlines for a bulletin-board display.

Additional Practice

Skill Reinforcement Activity 10

ANSWERS TO PRACTICING THE SKILL

1. (a) opinion: uses negative words *pitiful* and *savage* to imply disapproval
   (b) fact: can be verified by reading a historical text
2. (a) fact: can be verified by studying reports of archaeologists in Sweden who have unearthed Arabic and Byzantine coins, evidence that extensive trade occurred
   (b) opinion: uses negative words *uncivilized* and *little* with superlative *most*
3. (a) opinion: does not give any specific facts to prove statement or allow checking
   (b) fact: can be verified by reading historical documents and studying arts of that era

Chapter 10 Review

GLENCOE TECHNOLOGY

VIDEODISC
Use MindJogger to review students' knowledge of the chapter.

MindJogger Videoquiz
Chapter 10
Disc 2 Side A

Also available in VHS.

Answers

Using Key Terms

1. d	6. g
2. b	7. a
3. l	8. f
4. c	9. k
5. i	10. e

Using Your History Journal

Student stories should incorporate information on how the law was administered in Justinian's time. They might use stories to show daily life at the time.

Reviewing Facts

1. preserved the legal heritage of Rome; served as the basis for later European legal systems
2. Some believed icons violated the biblical injunction against idols.
3. Byzantine court appointed church officials, built churches, intervened in doctrinal disputes.
4. The focus was on religion.
5. Nino converted the people of Iberia to Christianity.
6. West Slavs became Poles, Czechs, and Slovaks; South Slavs became Serbs, Croats, and Slovenes; Eastern Slavs became Russians, Ukrainians, and Belarussians.
7. Mongol rule, cultural and language barriers, and Eastern Orthodox Church isolated Russia.
8. brought Byzantine art and culture to Eastern Slavs, but local languages kept them isolated
9. Vikings protected Eastern Slavs' trade routes between Novgorod and Byzantine Empire, provided military aid, provided foundations of Slavic government.

Critical Thinking

1. Constantinople adopted some of its Roman heritage, but also had other influences.
2. served to unite people in a common heritage and provided the basis for further innovations
3. They reveal a civilization advanced in trade, metallurgy, mining, and religious thought.
4. use of icons, disagreements over the roles of the Roman pope and the Eastern patriarch. Compromise might have prevented the split; doubtful because of doctrinal differences.
5. had language and customs in common;

CHAPTER 10 REVIEW

Historical Significance

As a crossroads of trade, the Byzantine Empire was a center for cultural diffusion. Its scholars transmitted Roman law and classical and Christian learning to western Europe. The Byzantine Church spread Christianity by sending missionaries to convert the Slavs and other neighboring peoples.

In addition, the Byzantines were cultural innovators who made a lasting impact. Their icons and mosaics became part of the Christian artistic heritage of Europe, and their architecture inspired building styles in eastern Europe and the Middle East.

Using Key Terms

Write the key term that completes each sentence.

a. boyar	g. missionary
b. clergy	h. regent
c. mosaic	i. schism
d. iconoclasts	j. laity
e. monasteries	k. czar
f. illuminated manuscripts	l. steppe

1. Wanting to prevent superstition and idol worship, ______, or image breakers, supported the removal of all images from churches.
2. Church officials, such as bishops and priests, are referred to as members of the _______.
3. North of the Black Sea are thick forests, mighty rivers, and a vast plain known as the ______.
4. The Byzantines excelled in the art of _____, or pictures made of many tiny pieces of colored glass or flat stone set in plaster.
5. In A.D. 1054 doctrinal, political, and geographic differences led to a ______ between the Roman Catholic Church in the West and the Eastern Orthodox Church in the East.
6. The _______ Cyril and Methodius brought Eastern Orthodox Christianity and the Byzantine culture to the Slavs of eastern Europe.
7. In Kievan Rus, wealthy nobles and landowners who assisted the princes were called _____.
8. Religious scholars of the Byzantine Empire often preserved ancient writings in the form of _____________.
9. In A.D. 1472 the Muscovite ruler Ivan III took the title _____, the title used by the Roman and Byzantine emperors.
10. _____ were communities of devout Christians set apart from the world.

Using Your History Journal

Write a short story describing a fictional case that may have come before an official of Justinian's court. Base the story on the law you described in Your History Journal at the beginning of this chapter.

Reviewing Facts

1. **Explain** the significance of the Justinian Code to later generations.
2. **Describe** how the use of religious art became the center of a controversy in the Eastern Orthodox Church.
3. **Analyze** how the Byzantine Empire promoted Christianity.
4. **Explain** the focus of Byzantine art as revealed in mosaics and icons.
5. **Explain** the contribution that Nino made to the development of the kingdom of Georgia.
6. **Identify** the three groups of Slavs and the part of modern Europe in which each is found.
7. **Explain** how the Russians became isolated from the rest of Europe.
8. **Describe** how Christianity affected the East Slavs.
9. **Explain** the role of the Vikings in Slavic and Byzantine history.

Critical Thinking

1. **Analyze** How was the title of New Rome both suitable and unsuitable for the city of Constantinople?
2. **Evaluate** Why was the preservation of Greek

and Roman learning a significant contribution of Byzantine civilization?

3. **Analyze** What do these Byzantine coins reveal about the level of development of Byzantine civilization?

4. **Analyze** What were the causes of the schism in the Christian Church? Could the split have been prevented? Explain.
5. **Compare/Contrast** How were the Byzantine Empire and the Roman Empire alike? How were they different?
6. **Synthesize** What were Constantine's reasons for his location of Constantinople? What other factors are of concern in the location of a city?
7. **Analyze** How did trade affect the Byzantine Empire?
8. **Synthesize** Imagine you are a Russian boyar under Ivan III. Would you resist calling him Czar? Explain.

Understanding Themes

1. **Conflict** How does conflict—such as the iconoclastic controversy in the Byzantine Empire—weaken a government?
2. **Innovation** Using Byzantine civilization as an example, explain how one civilization's ideas can be adapted to other societies.
3. **Cultural Diffusion** How can two societies be enriched by sharing cultural aspects? Give examples from the cases of Kievan Rus and Muscovy.

Linking Past and Present

1. Investigate the role the Bosporus played in World War I and World War II.
2. Explain the historical reasons why Russia has a continuing interest in the affairs of eastern European nations.
3. Investigate the historical roots of religious controversies in modern societies, such as Bosnia and Northern Ireland.

Skill Practice

Read the following statements. Determine which are facts and which are opinions. Give a reason for each choice.

1. The *Primary Chronicle* states that in A.D. 911 Grand Prince Oleg agreed on a peace treaty with the Byzantine emperors Leo and Alexander.
2. The Volga River is longer than the Danube River.
3. The Russian Orthodox Church is the most spiritually uplifting faith in the world.
4. Nomads wandered aimlessly throughout the steppes and lived in flimsy shelters.

Geography in History

1. **Location** Refer to the map below. By what year had the area around the Volga River been added to Moscow's holdings?
2. **Place** What enabled the princes of Muscovy to expand the city of Moscow?
3. **Region** By A.D. 1493 Moscow's ruler claimed to be "Sovereign of All Russia." About how far did Moscow's territory stretch from north to south in A.D. 1462?

The Rise of Moscow

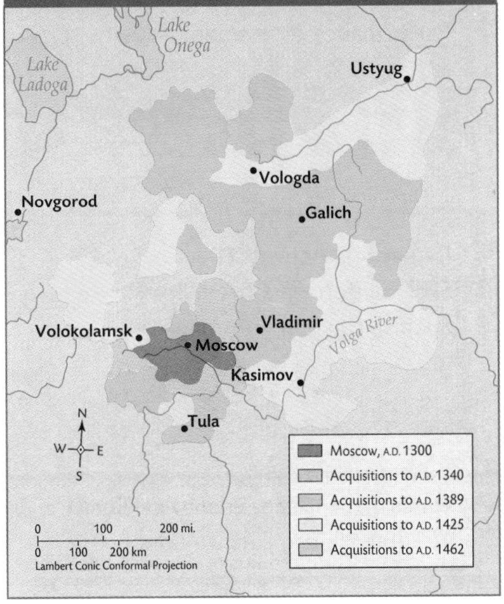

Chapter 10 Review

3. **CULTURAL DIFFUSION** Kiev encountered Byzantine culture when it converted to Eastern Orthodoxy. Muscovy's culture was also shaped by the Eastern Orthodox Church.

Linking Past and Present

1. During World War I, the Russians made a secret agreement with their Western allies to annex Constantinople along with the Bosporus and Dardanelles Straits. In World War II, the Russians again pressed for joint control of the Turkish straits.
2. Both the Russians and the peoples of eastern Europe share a common past as Slavic peoples.
3. the long-standing religious conflicts between Christian and Muslim groups in Bosnia; Catholic and Protestant groups in Ireland

Skill Practice

1. fact—names specific people, dates, event
2. fact—can be proved by comparing measurements
3. opinion—contains a superlative; cannot be proved
4. opinion—contains words with negative, judgmental connotations

Geography in History

1. by A.D. 1425
2. As medieval Moscow grew outward, Muscovy princes also expanded the fortified Kremlin. When Muscovy finally defeated the Mongols in A.D. 1380, Muscovy expanded its territory.
3. about 600 miles

differences emerged as Constantinople grew as the focus of Byzantine power; Rome remained important Western religious center.

6. Constantinople's control over the Bosporus and Dardanelles Straits made the city a natural crossroads for trade. Water protected the city on three sides; trade and defense, access to food and natural resources.
7. made it wealthy and prosperous, provided funds to finance cultural growth
8. Yes; it implied a loss of power by the boyars.

Understanding Themes

1. **CONFLICT** can distract leaders' attentions from other important matters and can cause divisions in society
2. **INNOVATION** The Byzantine Church used architectural ideas from Eastern sources; Byzantine culture was modified when its civilization mingled with other sources.

Chapter Bonus Test Question

Ask students: Use your knowledge of the early history of either Georgia or Armenia to explain, at least in part, the turmoil that followed the breakup of the Soviet Union in the 1990s.

Islamic Civilization

CHAPTER RESOURCES

	Reproducible Resources	Multimedia Resources
Chapter Opener	Chapter Themes: Graphic Organizer 11 Historical Significance Chapter Activity 11	MindJogger Videoquiz
Chapter Enrichment	Vocabulary Activity 11* Time Line Activity 11 Mapping History Activity 11 History Simulation 11 Geography and History Activity 11 Source Reading 11 People in World History Profiles 19, 20 World Art and Music Activity 11 Enrichment Activity 11 Critical Thinking Activity 11 Skill Reinforcement Activity 11 Performance Assessment Activity 11	Focus on World Art Print 13, Habib Allah. *Mantik et-Tayr* World History and Art Transparency 14, *Court of the Lions, The Alhambra* Chapter Transparency 11 Vocabulary PuzzleMaker Software World Music: Cultural Traditions, Lesson 5 Turning Points in World History: *Jerusalem: City of Three Faiths* In the Holy Land: *Ted Koppel: The Holy Land* In the Holy Land: *Ted Koppel: Three Religions*
Chapter Review/Reteaching	Reteaching Activity 11 Skill Reinforcement Activity 11 Spanish Chapter Summary 11	Chapter 11 Digest Audiocassette, Activity, Test* Vocabulary PuzzleMaker Software Student Self-Test and Review Software MindJogger Videoquiz
Chapter Evaluation/Testing	Performance Assessment Activity 11 Chapter 11 Test, Forms A and B	Testmaker

* *Also available in Spanish*

0:00 **OUT OF TIME?** Assign the Chapter 11 summary in the Unit 3 Digest on pages 394–397, and the Chapter 11 Audiocassettes.

Block Schedule

Block scheduling differs from traditional class scheduling in the amount of time allotted to each period. The extended time frame provided by block scheduling affords you the opportunity to implement a greater number of research-oriented and activity-intense projects to motivate and involve your students. Activities that are particularly suited to use within the block scheduling framework are identified throughout this chapter by the following designation.

KEY TO ABILITY LEVELS

Teaching strategies have been coded for varying learning styles and abilities.

- L1 **BASIC** activities for all students
- L2 **AVERAGE** activities for average to above-average students
- L3 **CHALLENGING** activities for above-average students
- LEP **LIMITED ENGLISH PROFICIENCY** activities

A complete, 1-page lesson plan is provided for each section in the *Reproducible Lesson Plans* booklet.

SECTION RESOURCES

Daily Objectives	Reproducible Resources	Multimedia Resources
Section 1 A New Faith Identify the basic beliefs and practices of Islam.	Reproducible Lesson Plan 11-1 Guided Reading Activity 11-1* History Simulation 11 Time Line Activity 11 Section Quiz 11-1*	Section Focus Transparency 11-1 Chapter Transparency 11 Vocabulary PuzzleMaker Software Student Self-Test and Review Software Testmaker Turning Points in World History: *Jerusalem: City of Three Faiths* In the Holy Land: *Ted Koppel: The Holy Land* In the Holy Land: *Ted Koppel: Three Religions*
Section 2 Spread of Islam Explain how the Islamic state expanded and then declined.	Reproducible Lesson Plan 11-2 Vocabulary Activity 11* Guided Reading Activity 11-2* Mapping History Activity 11 Section Quiz 11-2*	Section Focus Transparency 11-2 World History and Art Transparency 14, *Court of the Lions, the Alhambra* Student Self-Test and Review Software Testmaker
Section 3 Daily Life and Culture Name the achievements of Islamic civilization and explain how they were spread to other parts of the world.	Reproducible Lesson Plan 11-3 Guided Reading Activity 11-3* Geography and History Activity 11 Reteaching Activity 11 Enrichment Activity 11 Section Quiz 11-3* Performance Assessment Activity 11 Spanish Chapter Summary 11	Focus on World Art Print 13, Habib Allah. *Mantik et-Tayr* Section Focus Transparency 11-3 Student Self-Test and Review Software Vocabulary PuzzleMaker Software Testmaker World Music: Cultural Traditions, Lesson 5

** Also available in Spanish*

Chapter Activities

Performance Assessment Activity

A Cultural Contract Have small groups of students produce a contract for tolerance and understanding between their culture and the Islamic culture. Students should first research how Islamic life has changed since the time of early Islamic civilizations. Groups should synthesize their information in order to produce a contract of conduct for both cultures to follow in respecting each other.

Possible Rubric Features Concept attainment, research skills, clarity and organization, content information

• *For an additional activity, refer to Activity 11 in the* Performance Assessment Strategies and Activities *booklet.*

ACTIVITY

From the Classroom of...

Eric Hahn
Ladue Horton Watkins High School
St. Louis, MO

Lessons Through Islamic Literature

The purpose of this activity is to learn about history and social science concepts utilizing children's stories from *The Arabian Nights*. You will need a copy of *The Arabian Nights*, which is readily available in most libraries and many bookstores. If you can obtain multiple copies, students can read in groups.

Allow students to select a story from *The Arabian Nights*. There are many stories to choose from, but a few favorites include "Ali Baba and the Forty Thieves" and "Sinbad the Sailor and the Mudpies". After students read the story, ask them the following questions:

What does this story teach? Explain that these stories usually had a moral to them, just like *Aesop's Fables, Grimm's Fairy Tales*, or even Dr. Seuss stories.

What technologies are identified? (For example, Sinbad's ships are often described in detail, depending on the translation; the thieves in "Ali Baba" hide inside large containers of oil—ask students about the uses of oil.)

Finally, ask students for any comparisons they can make with recently studied units. This allows for some review and synthesis.

A great follow-up homework assignment is to have students write a short story utilizing the vocabulary learned in Chapter 11.

MULTIPLE LEARNING STYLES

Auditory/Musical
Ask students to modify any song they know by writing new lyrics that describe some aspect of Islamic history or culture presented in this chapter. Ask one student to accompany the singing by playing the tune on an instrument.

Kinesthetic
Have students draw poster-size pictures of calligraphy, arabesques, or a combination of the two for a bulletin-board display. They may find examples of Islamic art in reference materials to serve as a guide.

Interpersonal
Have students work together to make a wall map of the Islamic state at its peak. The map should include enough surrounding territory to show the context of the Islamic state. Students should label places discussed in Chapter 11, including Tours in France, Seville and Córdoba in Spain, the North African states, and India, and then show the path of Islamic expansion. Display the map for students to refer to as they study this chapter.

Intrapersonal
Ask students to research ceremonies involved in the hajj. Have them use their research to write a day-by-day journal account of their own imaginary participation in the hajj. Choose several journal accounts to be read aloud in class.

Additional Resources

TEACHER'S CORNER

NATIONAL GEOGRAPHIC SOCIETY

INDEX TO NATIONAL GEOGRAPHIC MAGAZINE

The following articles may be used for research relating to this chapter:

- "Ibn Battuta: Prince of Travelers," by Thomas J. Abercrombie, December 1991.
- "When the Moors Ruled Spain," by Thomas J. Abercrombie, July 1988.
- "Morocco's Ancient City of Fez," by Harvey Arden, March 1986.

NATIONAL GEOGRAPHIC SOCIETY PRODUCTS AVAILABLE FROM GLENCOE

To order the following products for use with this chapter, contact your local Glencoe sales representative or call Glencoe at 1-800-368-7344:

NGS PICTUREPACK TRANSPARENCY SET
- Physical Geography of the World

CD-ROM
- Picture Atlas of the World

Bibliography

Literature of the Period

Arabian Nights: The Thousand and One Nights. New York: Norton, 1990. The classic tales including those of Sinbad and Aladdin.

Readings for the Student

Gordon, Matthew S. *Islam.* New York: Facts on File, 1991. The history, religious practices, and political influence of Islamic sects.

Readings for the Teacher

Esposito, John L. *Islam: The Straight Path.* Expanded ed. New York: Oxford University Press, 1991. Clear, up-to-date survey of Islam.

Hourani, Albert. *A History of the Arab Peoples.* Cambridge: Harvard University Press, 1991. A comprehensive study.

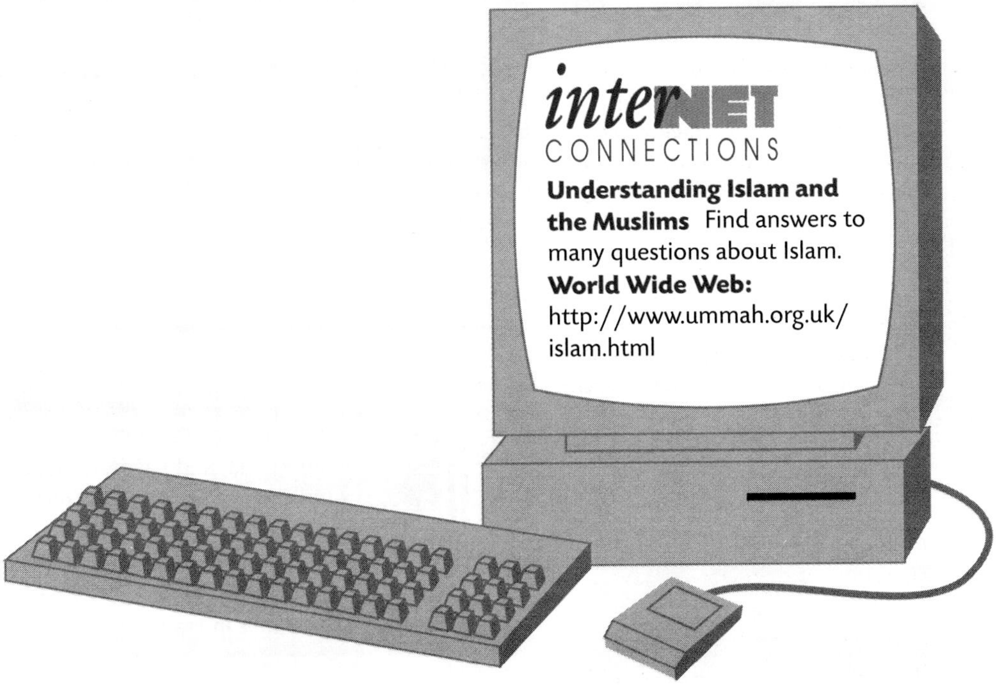
interNET
CONNECTIONS
Understanding Islam and the Muslims Find answers to many questions about Islam.
World Wide Web:
http://www.ummah.org.uk/islam.html

Introducing Chapter 11

CHAPTER THEMES

Chapter Themes are listed by section on this chapter opening page of the Student Edition. A corresponding theme-based activity is available under "TEACH," and a theme-based question is asked in the Section and Chapter Reviews.

The Storyteller

Historical Setting The woman quoted is describing her participation in the hajj, the pilgrimage to Makkah, the holy city in Saudi Arabia. The white-robed pilgrims the woman describes are wearing two white seamless sheets wrapped around the body. This special garb is prescribed for pilgrims when they are about 6 miles (10 kilometers) from the holy city, at which point they are said to enter the state of holiness and purity known as *ihram.* The white clothes symbolize not only the pilgrims' purity but also the equality of all members of the Muslim community, regardless of their station in life.

Historical Significance

Answers: *Islamic principles include belief in one all-powerful, just, and merciful God, the belief that God's message was revealed to Muhammad and recorded in the Quran, and basic moral values similar to those of Christianity and Judaism.*

Islamic civilization has made significant contributions in fields ranging from mathematics and the physical and biological sciences to literature and the arts.

Chapter 11

A.D. 600–1300

Islamic Civilization

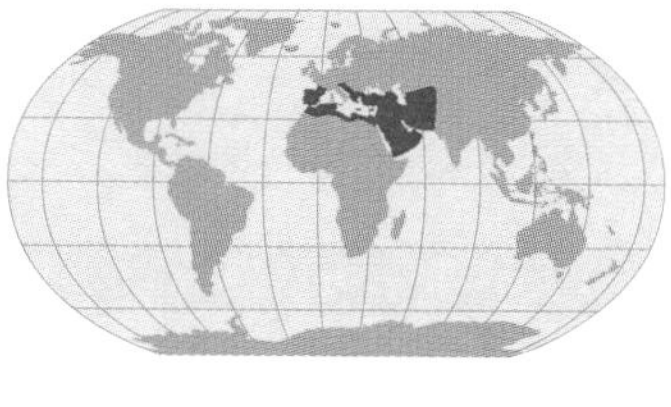

Chapter Themes

- **Innovation** The faith and principles of Islam become the basis of a new civilization. *Section 1*
- **Movement** Armies and merchants spread Islam through the Middle East and North Africa, and into Spain and Asia. *Section 2*
- **Cultural Diffusion** Contributions from many cultures and peoples enrich the Islamic state. *Section 3*

The Storyteller

"I was in Makkah at last," writes a devout Muslim woman about her pilgrimage to Makkah, the holiest city of the religion of Islam. She continues, "Before me was the Kaaba, a great black cube partly submerged in a torrent of white-robed pilgrims circling round and round. Around us, like a great dam containing the torrent, stood the massive walls and the seven slim minarets of the Sacred Mosque. High above, the muezzin began the evening call to prayer: 'Allahu Akbar! ... God is Most Great!'...

"Around the Kaaba ... repeating the customary prayers, swirled men and women of every race and nation, from every corner of the earth...."

All believers of Islam hope to share in this event at least once in their lives. Since the A.D. 600s, it has been one of the unifying celebrations for all Muslims.

Historical Significance

What are the basic beliefs and principles of Islam? What contributions has Islamic civilization made to world knowledge and culture?

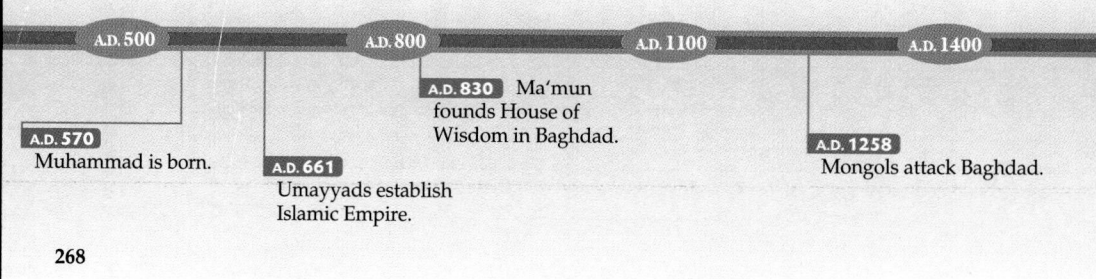

A.D. 500 — A.D. 800 — A.D. 1100 — A.D. 1400

- **A.D. 570** Muhammad is born.
- **A.D. 661** Umayyads establish Islamic Empire.
- **A.D. 830** Ma'mun founds House of Wisdom in Baghdad.
- **A.D. 1258** Mongols attack Baghdad.

268

GEOGRAPHY CONNECTION

Location Have students locate a number of Arab nations on a map, including Iran, Saudi Arabia, and Egypt. Explain that, contrary to what many people believe, these countries are not home to the majority of the world's Muslims. The majority of the world's 1 billion Muslims are not Arab but rather Asian and African. Have students locate Indonesia, Bangladesh, Pakistan, India, central Asia, and Nigeria. Where are the world's largest Muslim communities found? *(in these regions)* Point out that there are also large Muslim communities in France and England, in Bosnia, and in the United States.

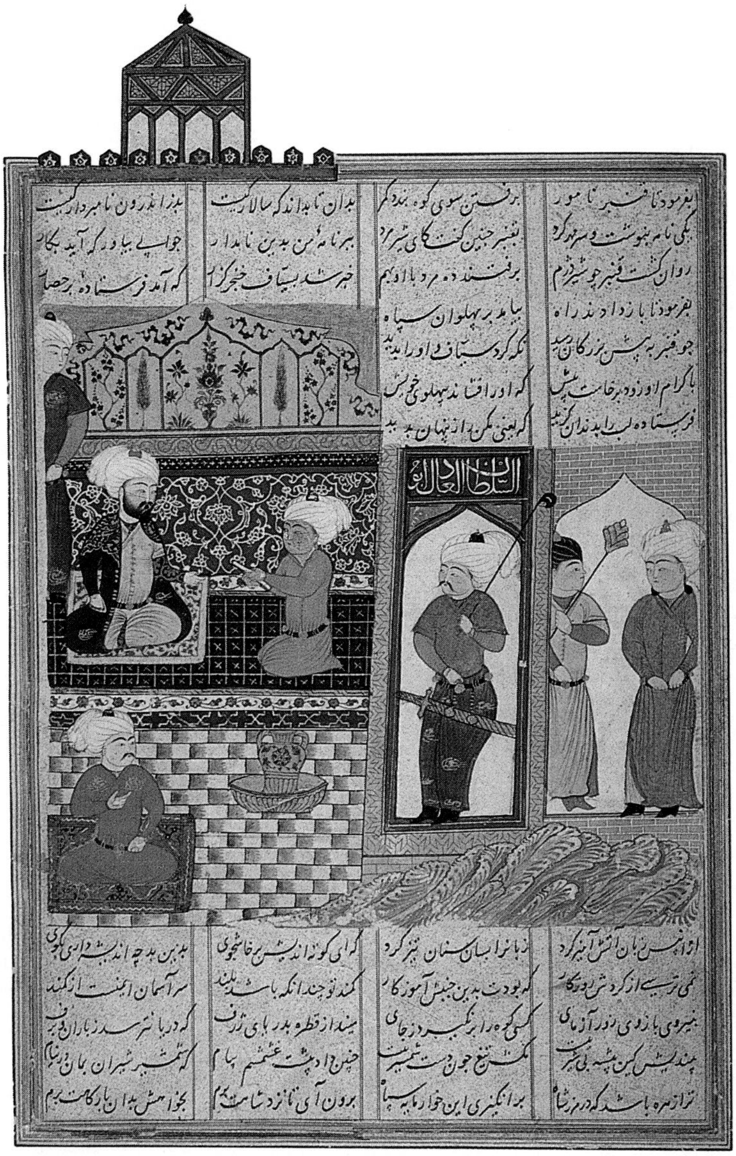

History & Art *Apocryphal Life of Ali*, from the *Kharar-nama*, late A.D. 1400s

Your History Journal

Choose a topic from the text headings on astronomy and geography, chemistry and medicine, or art and architecture in the Muslim world. Research the subject in a library and write a short report.

EXTRA CREDIT PROJECT

Compare and Contrast Students can learn about some of the similarities and differences between the Judeo-Christian tradition and the Islamic tradition by comparing and contrasting the Bible and the Quran. There are many translations of the latter, but A. J. Arberry's *The Koran* is the most poetic. Ask students to consider whether the Quran is tied to the history of a single nation in the way the Bible is. Suggest that they compare the accounts of Joseph, Moses, Noah, or Jonah in the Quran with those in the Bible's Old Testament.

Introducing Chapter 11

History & Art Tell students that Islam, like Judaism and Christianity, includes a number of different branches. One of the two major Muslim groups—the Shiites—has a particular connection to Ali, who was the son-in-law of Muhammad, the prophet of Islam. The name "Shiite" derives from the Arabic words *shi'at Ali*, which means "party of Ali." Shiites revere Ali as the only true successor to Muhammad.

Performance Assessment

Refer to the activity on page 268C of the Planning Guide.

For an additional activity, refer to Activity 11 in the *Performance Assessment Strategies and Activities* booklet.

Using Your History Journal

Advise students to avoid overgeneralization in their reports by focusing on the work of an individual, such as Ibn Sina, or on a particular advance, such as algebra.

GLENCOE TECHNOLOGY

VIDEODISC

Use MindJogger to preview chapter content.

MindJogger Videoquiz

Chapter 11
Disc 2 Side A

Also available in VHS.

SECTION THEME

▶ **Innovation** The faith and principles of Islam become the basis of a new civilization.

Find Out

Answer: *belief in one all-powerful, just, and merciful God; belief that God's message was revealed to Muhammad and recorded in the Quran; the governing of all aspects of public and private life by the law contained in the Quran and in Muhammad's sayings (Hadith); praying five times a day facing Makkah; giving alms; fasting during Ramadan; and making a pilgrimage to Makkah*

FOCUS

Section Objective

Identify the basic beliefs and practices of Islam.

BELLRINGER Motivational Activity

Before taking roll at the beginning of the class period, project Section Focus Transparency 11-1 and have students answer the activity questions.

This activity is also available as a blackline master.

Vocabulary Pre-check

Use the Vocabulary PuzzleMaker to create a puzzle that reinforces the vocabulary terms in this section. **L1**

A.D. 600 — A.D. 625 — A.D. 650

A.D. 610 Muhammad has his first revelation.

A.D. 622 Muhammad and followers depart on the *Hijrah*.

A.D. 630 The people of Makkah accept Islam.

A.D. 632 Muhammad dies at Madinah.

Section 1

A New Faith

Setting the Scene

▶ **Terms to Define**
sheikh, revelation, *shari'ah*, mosque, imam, hajj

▶ **People to Meet**
Muhammad

▶ **Places to Locate**
Arabian Peninsula, Makkah

Find Out What are the basic beliefs and practices of Islam?

The Storyteller

Ubadah sat on the only chair in the crowded room and began to recite. The men sitting on the floor did not seem to pay much attention at first, but soon conversation died away. As imam, Ubadah described the rewards awaiting the pious after death. The Paradise he described was vastly different from the baked, dusty town where they sat. He spoke of a green garden with fruit trees of every kind and fountains of water, milk, wine, and honey. In Paradise everyone would rest on silken couches, have beautiful wives, and all his sins would be pardoned. "Which, therefore, of your Lord's benefits will you ungratefully deny?" Ubadah concluded.

—freely adapted from *The Short Koran*, George M. Lamsa, editor, reprinted in *Sources of World History*, Mark A. Kishlansky, 1995

A reading from the Quran

South of Asia Minor lies the **Arabian Peninsula**, home of the Arabs. This location placed the Arabs at the margins of the great Middle Eastern civilizations. Like the ancient Israelites, Phoenicians, and Chaldeans, the Arabs were descended from Semitic tribes. Archaeologists have traced Arab civilizations in the Arabian Peninsula to at least 3000 B.C.

Arab Life

The relative geographic remoteness of the Arabian Peninsula kept the empires in the northern part of the region from invading Arab lands. Their isolation allowed the Arabs to create their own civilization.

The Setting

The Arabian Peninsula is a wedge of land of about 1 million square miles (2.6 million sq. km) between the Red Sea and the Persian Gulf. It is made up of two distinct regions. The southwestern area, across from the northeast coast of Africa, has well-watered valleys nestled between mountains. The rest of the peninsula, however, consists of arid plains and deserts.

Yet the peninsula is not entirely forbidding. Grass grows quickly during the showers of the rainy season, and oases, the fertile areas around springs and water holes, provide a permanent source of water for farmers, herders, and travelers. For centuries, nomadic herders and caravans have crisscrossed the desert, traveling from oasis to oasis.

Lives of the Bedouin

In ancient times many of the Arabs were bedouin (BEH•duh•wuhn), nomads who herded sheep, camels, and goats and lived in tents made of felt from camel or goat hair. They ate mainly fresh or dried dates, and they drank milk from their herds; on special occasions they also ate mutton.

SECTION RESOURCES

Reproducible Masters
- Reproducible Lesson Plan 11-1
- Guided Reading Activity 11-1
- History Simulation 11
- Time Line Activity 11
- Section Quiz 11-1

Transparencies
- Section Focus Transparency 11-1
- Chapter Transparency 11

Multimedia
- Vocabulary PuzzleMaker Software
- Student Self-Test and Review Software
- Testmaker
- Jerusalem: City of Three Faiths
- Ted Koppel: The Holy Land
- Ted Koppel: Three Religions

The bedouin lived in tribes, each made up of related families. Arabs valued family ties because they ensured protection and survival in the harsh desert environment. Leading each tribe was a sheikh (SHAYK), or chief, appointed by the heads of the families. A council of elders advised the sheikh, who ruled as long as he had the tribe's consent. Warfare was part of bedouin life. The Arab tribes went on raids to gain camels and horses and battled one another over pastures and water holes, the most precious resources in the desert. To protect their honor and their possessions, the bedouin believed in retaliation—"an eye for an eye, and a tooth for a tooth."

For entertainment the bedouin enjoyed many activities. Camel and horse races and other games sharpened the men's abilities as warriors, and then everyone enjoyed an evening of storytelling around the campfires. Poets composed and recited poems about battles, deserts, camels and horses, and love. In these lines an Arab sheikh states his view of war:

> "From the cup of peace
> drink your fill;
> but from the cup of war
> a sip will suffice."

Growth of Towns

By the A.D. 500s, many tribes had settled around oases or in fertile valleys to pursue either farming or trade. Groups of merchants soon founded prosperous market towns. The most important of these towns was **Makkah**, a crossroads of commerce about 50 miles (80 km) inland from the Red Sea.

People from all over the Arabian Peninsula traveled to Makkah to trade animal products for weapons, dates, grain, spices, jewels, ivory, silk, and perfumes. Enormous caravans from the fertile southeast passed through Makkah en route to Syria, Iraq, and as far away as China. Arabs also visited Makkah to worship at the peninsula's holiest shrine, the Kaaba, which contained statues of the many Arab deities. The business the pilgrims brought to Makkah made its merchants wealthy.

Signs of Change

As business ties replaced tribal ties in the trading towns, the old tribal rules were no longer adequate. At the same time, the Byzantine and Persian Empires were threatening to take over Arab lands. The Arabs had a common language, but they lacked a sense of unity and had no central government to solve these new problems.

Religious ideas were also changing. Contacts with the Byzantines, the Persians, and the Ethiopians introduced the teachings of the monotheistic religions of Judaism and Christianity. Moreover, a number of Christian and Jewish Arabs lived in the peninsula. Dissatisfied with their old beliefs, many idol-worshiping Arabs searched for a new religion. Holy men known as hanifs (hah•NEEFS) denounced the worship of idols and believed in one god. They rejected Judaism and Christianity, however, preferring to find a uniquely Arab form of monotheism.

This ferment in Arab religious life contributed to the emergence of the religion known as Islam, which means "submission to the will of Allah (God)." This faith would bring the Arabs into contact with other civilizations and change Arab history.

AROUND THE WORLD

Heraclius Recaptures the True Cross

Jerusalem, A.D. 630

In A.D. 622 the Emperor Heraclius set out from Constantinople to recapture what was believed to be the "True Cross" on which Christ died. The cross had been taken by the Persians when they conquered Jerusalem. Heraclius advanced on the Persian capital of Ctesiphon, demanding the return of the cross. In A.D. 630, a triumphant Heraclius restored the True Cross to the Church of the Holy Sepulchre in Jerusalem.

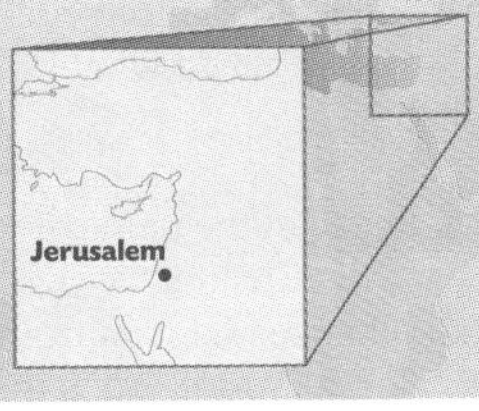

Muhammad and His Message

The prophet of Islam, **Muhammad**, was born in the bustling city of Makkah around A.D. 570. Muslim traditions state that Muhammad was orphaned at an early age and raised by an uncle.

Life of Muhammad

During his teens, Muhammad worked as a caravan leader on a trade route. His reputation as an exceptionally honest and able person prompted his employer, a wealthy widow of 40 named Khadija (kuh•DEE•juh), to put him in charge of her business affairs. When Muhammad was about 25 years old, Khadija proposed marriage to him.

Muhammad's marriage to Khadija relieved

COOPERATIVE LEARNING ACTIVITY

Oral Report Organize the class into three groups. Have each group research one of the three main holy places in Jerusalem—the Western Wall, the Church of the Holy Sepulchre, or the Dome of the Rock. Each group should present an oral report that traces the site's history and explains its importance to Jews, Christians, or Muslims. Suggest that students include drawings or photographs and a diagram of the city showing the site's location. After the presentations, ask why it is significant that these sites are all in the same city. Students should not only understand that the Middle East was the birthplace of three major world religions, but also consider the sensitive political question of who should control Jerusalem today. **L2**

TEACH

Guided Practice

THEME **Innovation**

Discuss how innovations can occur in any field—in religion as well as in science and technology. Ask students to name some of Muhammad's innovative ideas. *(belief in one God, the equality of all who believe in God, the responsibility of the wealthy to help the poor; placing loyalty to the Islamic community above tribal loyalty)* **L1**

ABC NEWS INTERACTIVE™

VIDEODISC
In the Holy Land

Side One, Chapter 3
Title: *Ted Koppel: The Holy Land*
Subject: Introduction to the geography and history of the Holy Land
Ask: Where is the Holy Land located? *(in modern-day Israel)*

Side One, Chapter 9
Frame: 9487
Title: *Ted Koppel: Three Religions*
Subject: Introduction to Islam, Christianity, and Judaism
Ask: What is the hajj? *(annual pilgrimage to Makkah)*

Chapter 11
Section 1

Geography: Movement Have students draw or trace a map of the Arabian Peninsula. Have them locate and label Madinah, Makkah, the Red Sea, the Arabian Sea, and the Persian Gulf. Then ask students to look at the trade routes on the map on page 284. Why was the Arabian Peninsula a good starting point for the spread of Islam? *(near overland trade routes and Red Sea and Persian Gulf water routes)* **L2**

Government Discuss the meaning of *compact* as it relates to the Madinah Compact. Then have a volunteer find the Mayflower Compact in an encyclopedia and read aloud from it. Have students discuss the similarities and differences between the compacts. *(Similarities: Both established a form of government; both had religious connections. Differences: The Mayflower Compact was agreed to and signed by the people involved; the Madinah Compact was decreed by Muhammad.)* **L3**

History Simulation 11

Chapter Transparency 11

Visualizing History The Ottomans controlled almost the whole of the Arab world from 1520 until the nineteenth century. Ottoman architects skillfully used colored tiles to transform smaller buildings, such as Istanbul's mosque of Rustem Pasa, into strikingly colorful edifices.
Answer to Caption: *The second revelation commanded Muhammad to "rise and warn" the people about divine judgment.*

him of financial worries and gave him time to reflect on the meaning of life. Muhammad was troubled by the greed of Makkah's wealthy citizens, the worship of idols, and the mistreatment of the poor. Seeking guidance, Muhammad spent time alone praying and fasting in a cave outside the city.

Revelation

Islamic tradition holds that, in A.D. 610, Muhammad experienced a revelation, or vision. He heard a voice calling him to be the apostle of the one true deity—Allah, the Arabic word for God. Three times the voice proclaimed, "Recite!" When Muhammad asked what he should recite, the voice replied:

> "Recite in the name of your Lord,
> the Creator,
> Who created man from clots of blood.
> Recite! Your Lord is the most bountiful
> One
> Who by the pen has taught mankind
> things they did not know."

A second revelation commanded Muhammad to "rise and warn" the people about divine judgment. Although Muhammad had doubts about the revelations, he finally accepted his mission and returned to Makkah to preach.

In A.D. 613 Muhammad began sharing his revelations with his family and friends. He preached to the people of Makkah that there was only one God and that people everywhere must worship and obey him. He also declared that all who believed in God were equal. Therefore the rich should share their wealth with the poor. Muhammad also preached that God measured the worth of people by their devotion and good deeds. He told the people of Makkah to live their lives in preparation for the day of judgment, when God would punish evildoers and reward the just.

Muhammad made slow progress in winning converts. Khadija and members of Muhammad's family became the first Muslims, or followers of Islam. Many of the other converts came from Makkah's poor, who were attracted by Muhammad's call for social justice.

Opposition to Islam

Most Makkans rejected Muhammad's message. Wealthy merchants and religious leaders were upset by the prophet's attacks on the images at the Kaaba. They feared that monotheistic worship would end the pilgrimages to Makkah. Wealthy Makkans believed that this development would ruin the city's economy and lead to the loss of their prestige and wealth. Driven by these fears, the merchants persecuted Muhammad and the Muslims.

Muhammad persisted in his preaching until threats against his life forced him to seek help outside the city. He found it in Yathrib, a small town north of Makkah. In A.D. 622 Muhammad sent about 60 Muslim families from Makkah to Yathrib; soon after, he followed them in secret. His departure to Yathrib is known in Muslim history as the *Hijrah* (HIH•jruh), or emigration. The year in which the *Hijrah*

Visualizing History **Nineteenth-century Turkish decorative tile with inscription "Allah is Great." The Ottoman Turks built an Islamic state that lasted until 1918.** *What was the command Muhammad received in the second revelation?*

MEETING SPECIAL NEEDS ACTIVITY

Learning Style: Visual/Spatial Have students work individually to prepare posters that highlight aspects of daily life and culture in the Islamic Empire. Encourage them to embellish their drawings with decorative borders using a floral design similar to the one on the tile pictured on this page. Have students write brief captions to identify the subject of each scene. Display the completed posters in the classroom. **L1**

took place, A.D. 622, marks the beginning of the Islamic era and is recognized as the first year of the Muslim calendar.

The Islamic Community

Many of the people of Yathrib accepted Muhammad as the messenger of God and the ruler of their city. As the center of Islam, Yathrib became known as Madinat al-Nabi, "the city of the prophet," or Madinah (muh•DEE•nuh).

Origin of the Islamic State

Muhammad proved that he was a skilled political as well as religious leader. In the Madinah Compact of A.D. 624, Muhammad laid the foundation of an Islamic state. He decreed that all Muslims were to place loyalty to the Islamic community above loyalty to their tribe. Disputes were to be settled by Muhammad, who was declared the community's judge and commander in chief. All areas of life were placed under the divine law given to Muhammad and recorded in the Quran (kuh•RAHN), the holy scriptures of Islam. Muhammad also extended protection to Jews and Christians who accepted the political authority of the Islamic community.

Acceptance of Islam

Eventually the Makkans invaded Yathrib, forcing the Muslims to retaliate in self-defense. In the resulting battles, the Muslims defeated the Makkans, and the Muslims won the support of many Arab groups outside Madinah.

When Muhammad and his followers entered Makkah in A.D. 630, they faced little resistance. The Makkans accepted Islam and acknowledged Muhammad as God's prophet. The Muslims destroyed the idols in the Kaaba and turned the shrine into a place of worship for Muslim pilgrims. Makkah became the spiritual capital of Islam, and Madinah remained its political capital.

The Muslims also extended their control into other parts of Arabia. By A.D. 631 the Islamic state included the entire Arabian Peninsula and was supported by a strong army recruited from all of the Arab tribes.

After a brief illness, Muhammad died at Madinah in A.D. 632. He left behind two major achievements: the growth of a monotheistic religion that stood on an equal level with Judaism and Christianity, and a well-organized political-religious community that increased the Arabs' power and influence.

Visualizing History **Because the Quran was written in Arabic, Muslims of many cultures adopted Arabic as a universal language.** *What does the name "Quran" mean?*

Beliefs and Practices of Islam

Muhammad established beliefs and practices for his followers based on his revelations. In spite of social and political changes, these Islamic beliefs and practices have remained remarkably stable through the centuries.

The Quran

According to Muslim tradition, the angel Gabriel revealed divine messages to Muhammad over a 22-year period. Faithful Muslims wrote down or memorized these messages, but they were not compiled into one written collection until after Muhammad died. Then his successor, Abu Bakr, ordered Muslims to retrieve these messages from wherever they could be found, from the "ribs of palm-leaves and tablets of white stone and from the breasts of men." It took 20 years before the messages were compiled into the Quran, whose name means "recital." For all Muslims, the Quran is the final authority in matters of faith and life style.

Written in Arabic, the Quran is believed to contain God's message as revealed to Muhammad. This message is expressed in stories, legends, teachings, and exhortations. Some of the stories—such as

Chapter 11 Section 1

ABC NEWS INTERACTIVE™

VIDEODISC
Turning Points in World History

Side One
Chapter 6

Title: *Jerusalem: City of Three Faiths*
Subject: Discussion of the importance of the Holy City to three faiths
Ask: Why is Jerusalem important to Muslims? *(because Muhammad ascended from Jerusalem to heaven)*

Visualizing History Arabic is the religious language of all Muslims. Although classical Arabic—the form of the language found in the Quran—is uniform throughout the Arab world, colloquial Arabic includes several different dialects, some of which may not be intelligible to speakers of another Arabic dialect.
Answer to Caption: *The name "Quran" means "recital."*

Independent Practice
Guided Reading Activity 11-1 **L1**

MAKING CONNECTIONS ACTIVITIES

The Arts Muslims reproduced their sacred text, the Quran, in beautiful handwritten script. Other cultures have done likewise. Have students work together to create a bulletin-board display showing examples of how Christian, Jewish, and Islamic sacred scriptures have been written by scribes over the ages. **L2**

Religion Have students research the Muslim celebration that occurs on the last day of Ramadan. Have them write short reports in which they compare customs for that holiday with those for Christmas or Hanukkah. **L2**

PICTURING HISTORY

TEACH

Tell students that a minaret is always associated with a mosque. The mosque associated with the minaret in the picture, Samarra's Great Friday Mosque, is now in ruins, although the minaret itself still stands. Samarra was the Abbasid capital from 836, when the caliph al-Mutasim was forced to leave Baghdad, until 892. Ask students to describe the minaret in the picture. *(The tower is composed of thick, squat spiral ramps.)*

CURRICULUM CONNECTION

ARCHITECTURE
Minarets are not always constructed in the same form as the great minaret of Samarra. Some have very thin, delicate spires. The crowning feature also varies from minaret to minaret, ranging from a round dome to an open pavilion to a metal-covered cone.

Linking Past and Present

The **Islamic calendar** was instituted in A.D. 622 and is still used today by Muslims. The calendar is a lunar one, with 12 months and 354 days. The Muslim Era, which counts years from the year of the *Hijrah*, is the official era in Saudi Arabia, Yemen, and the Persian Gulf principalities. Even in Muslim countries where the Christian Era is in official use, people use the Muslim Era in private.

NATIONAL GEOGRAPHIC PICTURING HISTORY

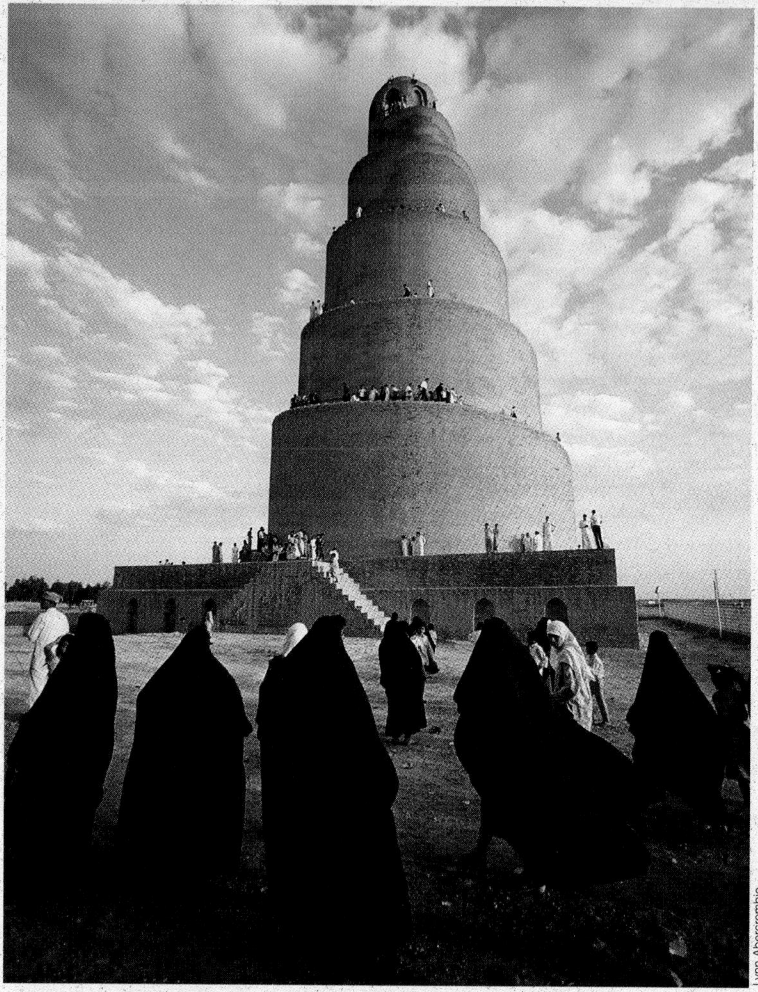

Lynn Abercrombie

Tower Mosque

In Samarra, Iraq, modern Muslim worshipers make their way up the spiral of a mosque built in the A.D. 800s. Some of the women, clothed from head to foot in black, are in purdah, or fully veiled from the public eye.

After Muhammad's death in A.D. 632, Islam spread through the Middle East, into Africa and Europe, and to the borders of India and China. This mosque was built during Islam's golden age, after the Abbasid caliphs assumed power over the Muslim Empire in A.D. 750 The new rulers shifted the capital of the stil expanding Muslim Empire to the brand-new city o Baghdad and ended the legal distinctions between Aral Muslims and non-Arab Muslims, a division that ha long deprived the non-Arabs of many legal rights. Th peoples of the empire were now given greater freedom and the Abbasids ruled over a period of great cultura flowering, peace, and order.

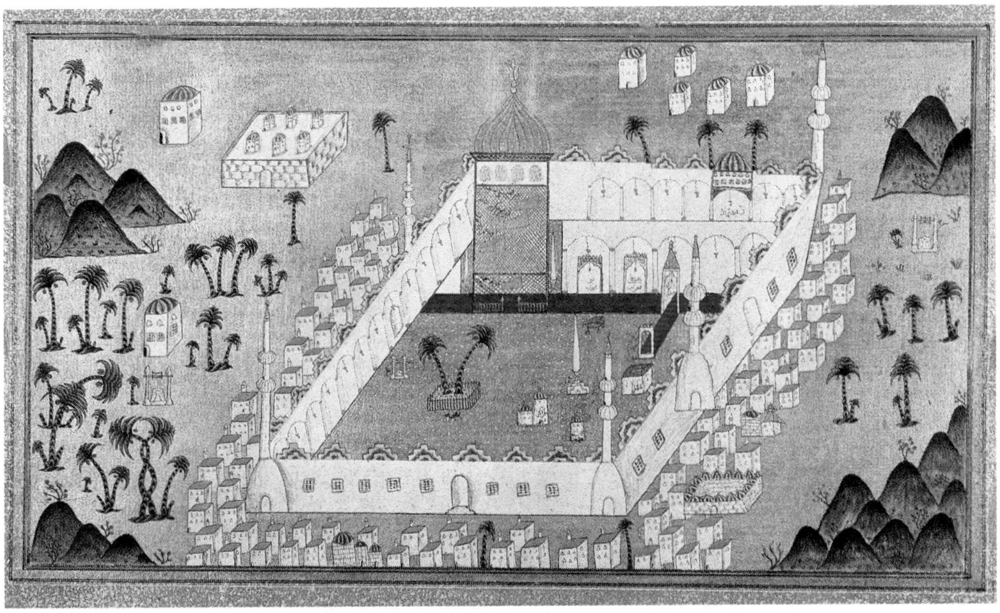

Visualizing History **A tile from the A.D. 1600s depicts the plan for the mosque and the Kaaba at Makkah.** *What is the fifth pillar of Islam?*

Noah's ark and Jonah in the belly of the whale—are variations of those found in the Bible.

Values

The Quran presents the basic moral values of Islam, which are similar to those of Judaism and Christianity. Muslims are commanded to honor their parents, show kindness to their neighbors, protect orphans and widows, and give generously to the poor. Murder, stealing, lying, and adultery are condemned.

The Quran also lays down specific rules to guide Muslims in their daily activities. It forbids gambling, eating pork, or drinking alcoholic beverages. It also contains rules governing marriage, divorce, family life, property inheritance, and business practices.

Law

Law cannot be separated from religion in Islamic society. Although Islam has no ranked order of clergy, generations of legal scholars and theologians have organized Islamic moral rules into a code of law known as the *shari'ah* (shuh•REE•uh). Based on the Quran and the Hadith (huh •DEETH), or sayings of Muhammad, the *shari'ah* covers all aspects of Muslim private and public life.

Five Pillars of Islam

The Quran presents the Five Pillars of Islam, or the five essential duties that all Muslims are to fulfill. They are the confession of faith, prayer, almsgiving, fasting, and the pilgrimage to Makkah.

Faith

The first pillar is the confession of faith that affirms the oneness of an all-powerful, just, and merciful God. All Muslims are required to submit to God's will as given in the Quran.

The confession stresses Muhammad's role as a prophet; he is not considered divine. Muslims view him as the last and most important of several prophets who have brought God's word to different peoples. To Muslims, Allah is the same god as the God of the Jews and the Christians; and Abraham, Moses, and Jesus are considered prophets.

Prayer

Muslims express their devotion in prayers offered five times each day—sunrise, noon, afternoon, sunset, and evening. Worshipers pray while facing Makkah, always using the same set of words and motions—kneeling, bowing, and

CRITICAL THINKING ACTIVITY

Making Comparisons Have students practice their skill at comparing and contrasting by devising a list of points on which various religions might be compared. The lists could include such things as the nature of God, worship, and religious leaders. Then have students use their lists to compare Islam, Christianity, and Judaism. **L2**

Chapter 11 Section 1

Time Line Activity 11

Daily Life Have students write a letter to a bedouin cousin from the viewpoint of a former bedouin who now lives in pre-Islamic Makkah. The letter should describe how the cousin's life has changed since the move to the city. **L1**

Visualizing History The tile shown here is an example of Persian art. The landscape setting is typical of Persian painting of the time. With the high horizon line, the artist essentially tilts the ground up, as though we are looking down upon it.

Answer to Caption: *the annual pilgrimage, or hajj, to Makkah*

Who?What?Where?When?

The **confession of faith** in the first pillar is called the *shahada*. The English translation of the *shahada* is "There is no God but God and Muhammad is the Prophet [messenger] of God."

ASSESS

Check for Understanding

Assign Section 1 Review as homework or as an in-class activity.

Use Student Self-Test and Review Software to review Section 1.

Chapter 11
Section 1

Visualizing History The Sulmaniyeh Mosque, also known as the Mosque of Suleyman, was inspired by Istanbul's Hagia Sophia.
Answer to Caption: *A mosque may serve as a place of worship, a school, a court of law, and a shelter.*

Evaluate

Section Quiz 11-1

Use the Testmaker to create a customized quiz for Section 1.

Reteach

Have students outline the central ideas in each of the five main divisions of this section. Discuss the outlines in class, correcting any misconceptions students have about the content.

Enrich

Have students find out about the Feast of Sacrifice, or *Id al-Adha*, which concludes the hajj. Have them write a brief report summarizing what the sacrifice commemorates and symbolizes.

CLOSE

Explain to students that, in the next section, they will learn about the spread of Islam. Then ask students to name Muhammad's achievements as described in this section. Write the achievements on the chalkboard.

Visualizing History **Islamic mosque lamp from the Sulmaniyeh Mosque in Istanbul, Turkey** *What are the various uses that a mosque may serve in an Islamic community?*

touching one's forehead to the ground as a sign of submission to God.

Muslims can offer their daily prayers outside or inside, at work or at home. At noon on Fridays, many Muslims pray together in a mosque, a building that may serve as a place of worship, a school, a court of law, and a shelter.

An imam (ih•MAHM), or prayer leader, guides believers in prayer, and a sermon sometimes follows. Any male Muslim with the proper religious education can serve as an imam.

Alms

The third pillar of Islam is the giving of alms, or charity. It reflects the Islamic view that the wealthy should assist the poor and weak. Almsgiving is practiced privately through contributions to the needy and publicly through a state tax that supports schools and aids the poor.

Fasting

The fourth pillar of Islam, fasting, occurs in the month of Ramadan (RAH•muh•DAHN), the ninth month in the Muslim calendar. During Ramadan, Muhammad received the first revelation. From sunrise to sunset Muslims neither eat nor drink, although they work as usual. Children, pregnant women, travelers, and the sick are exempt from fasting. At sunset the call for prayer—and in large cities the sound of a cannon—announces the end of the fast. Muslims then sit down to eat their "evening breakfast." In the cool evening hours, people stream out into the streets to greet their friends. At the end of Ramadan, there is a three-day celebration for the end of the fast.

Pilgrimage

The fifth pillar of Islam is the annual pilgrimage, or hajj, to Makkah. Every able-bodied Muslim who can afford the trip is expected to make the pilgrimage at least once in his or her lifetime. Those who perform the hajj are especially honored in the community.

The hajj takes place two months and ten days after the Ramadan fast and involves three days of ceremony, prayer, and sacrifice. Today, hundreds of thousands of Muslims come together to worship at the Kaaba and other shrines of Islam in Makkah and Madinah. The hajj is more than a religious pilgrimage. A visible expression of Muslim unity, the hajj allows a continuing exchange of ideas among the peoples of Africa, Europe, Asia, and the Americas who follow Islam.

SECTION 1 REVIEW

Recall

1. **Define** sheikh, revelation, *shari'ah*, mosque, imam, hajj.
2. **Identify** Arabian Peninsula, Makkah, Muhammad, Muslims, *Hijrah*, Madinah Compact, Quran.
3. **Explain** What made life possible in the harsh environment of the Arabian Peninsula?

Critical Thinking

4. **Analyzing Information** In what ways was Islam a new religion? In what ways was it an extension or a continuation of other religions that were also founded in this region—Judaism and Christianity?

Understanding Themes

5. **Innovation** Describe the Five Pillars of Islam and the Madinah Compact, and tell how they changed life in the Arabian Peninsula.

SECTION 1 REVIEW ANSWERS

1. All vocabulary words are defined in the Glossary.
2. Arabian Peninsula, 270; Makkah, 271; Muhammad, 271; Muslims, 272; *Hijrah*, 272; Madinah Compact, 273; Quran, 273
3. oases, tribal ties, cooperation
4. new: rejects Jewish doctrine that Moses is the greatest prophet and Christian doctrine that Jesus is divine; extension: monotheistic, stresses moral conduct, Quran includes many of the same people and stories as the Bible
5. INNOVATION Five Pillars: faith, prayer, almsgiving, fasting, pilgrimage; Madinah Compact: basis for the Islamic state. Attention to the duties outlined by the Five Pillars replaced worship of many deities and a greedy lifestyle among the wealthy; loyalty to the Islamic community replaced tribal loyalty.

A.D. 600 — A.D. 800 — A.D. 1000 — A.D. 1200

A.D. 632 Abu Bakr becomes the first caliph.

A.D. 732 Muslims and Christians fight the Battle of Tours.

A.D. 750 The Abbasid dynasty comes to power.

c. A.D. 1050 The Abbasids enter period of decline.

Section 2

Spread of Islam

Setting the Scene

- **Terms to Define**
  caliph, jihad
- **People to Meet**
  Abu Bakr, Ali, Mu'awiyah, the Shiites, Husayn, the Sunnis, Harun al-Rashid
- **Places to Locate**
  Damascus, Baghdad

Find Out How did the Islamic state expand, and how did it decline?

The Storyteller

From the far reaches of the Mediterranean to the Indus River valley, the faithful approached the holy city. All had the same objective—to worship together at the holiest shrine of Islam, the Kaaba in Makkah. One such traveler was Mansa Musa, king of Mali in western Africa. Musa had prepared carefully for the long journey he and his attendants would take. He was determined to go, not only for his own religious fulfillment, but also for recruiting teachers and leaders, so that his land could learn more of the Prophet's teachings.

—adapted from *The Chronicle of the Seeker*, Mahmud Kati, reprinted in *The Human Record*, Alfred J. Andrea and James H. Overfield, 1990

Pilgrimage to Makkah

When Muhammad died in A.D. 632, he had left no clear instructions about who was to succeed him as the leader of Islam. Muslims knew that no one could take Muhammad's place as the messenger of God. They realized, however, that the Islamic community needed a strong leader who could preserve its unity and guide its daily affairs. A group of prominent Muslims met and chose a new type of leader, whom they called *khalifah* (kuh•LEE•fuh) or caliph (KAY•luhf), meaning "successor."

"The Rightly Guided Caliphs"

The first four caliphs were elected for life. All were close friends or relatives of Muhammad. The first caliph was Muhammad's father-in-law and close friend, **Abu Bakr** (uh•BOO BA•kuhr). The last, his son-in-law Ali, was married to Muhammad's daughter Fatimah (FAH•tuh•muh). The first four caliphs followed Muhammad's example, kept in close touch with the people, and asked the advice of other Muslim leaders. For these reasons, Muslims have called them "the Rightly Guided Caliphs."

Early Conquests

The Rightly Guided Caliphs sought to protect and spread Islam. Their military forces carried Islam beyond the Arabian Peninsula. In addition to religious motives, the Arabs were eager to acquire the agricultural wealth of the Byzantine and Persian Empires to meet the needs of their growing population.

Arab armies swept forth against the weakened Byzantine and Persian Empires. By A.D. 650, these armies had acquired Palestine, Syria, Iraq, Persia, and Egypt. The conquests reduced the Asian part of the Byzantine Empire to Asia Minor and the Constantinople area and brought the Persian Empire completely under Muslim control.

Chapter 11
Section 2

SECTION THEME

▶ **Movement** Armies and merchants spread Islam through the Middle East and North Africa, and into Spain and Asia.

Find Out

Answer: *It expanded through the conquests of the early caliphs and declined when many of the lands won by these caliphs broke free and set up their own states.*

FOCUS

Section Objective

Explain how the Islamic state expanded and then declined.

BELLRINGER Motivational Activity

Before taking roll at the beginning of the class period, project Section Focus Transparency 11-2 and have students answer the activity questions. Discuss students' responses.

This activity is also available as a blackline master.

Vocabulary Pre-check

Use Vocabulary Activity 11 to introduce vocabulary terms. **L1 LEP**

SECTION RESOURCES

Reproducible Masters
- Reproducible Lesson Plan 11-2
- Vocabulary Activity 11
- Guided Reading Activity 11-2
- Mapping History Activity 11
- Section Quiz 11-2

Transparencies
- Section Focus Transparency 11-2
- World History and Art Transparency 14

Multimedia
- Student Self-Test and Review Software
- Testmaker

Chapter 11
Section 2

TEACH

Guided Practice

THEME **Movement**

Ask students to what regions Islam spread under "the Rightly Guided Caliphs." *(Palestine, Syria, Iraq, Persia, Egypt, bringing the Persian Empire under Muslim control and reducing the Byzantine Empire)* Under the Umayyads? *(eastward to the borders of India and China, westward across North Africa and into Spain)* Ask why the Arabs were able to conquer such a vast, diverse area. *(religious duty to spread Islam to other peoples; promise of paradise for those who died in jihad; weakened condition of defeated empires)* **L1**

Critical Thinking Have students list reasons for the rise of the Abbasids. Have them single out the reason they consider most important and defend it in a written paragraph or in a class discussion. *(Choices might include Shiite opposition to the Umayyads, or non-Arab Muslims' dissatisfaction with Umayyad policies.)* **L2**

World History and Art Transparency 14, *Court of the Lions, The Alhambra*

The Arab armies were successful for several reasons. Their faith united them in seeking a common goal—to carry Islam to other peoples. According to the Quran, Muslims had a duty to follow their faith and to struggle for its expansion. The Islamic state, therefore, viewed the conquests as a jihad (jih•HAHD), or struggle to introduce Islam to other lands. The Quran forbade the use of force in winning converts to Islam. Islamic teaching, however, promised that warriors who died in a jihad would immediately enter paradise. Furthermore, the Byzantine and Persian Empires had been weakened militarily and economically by the wars they had been fighting with each other for many years.

Division Within Islam

While Muslim armies were achieving military success, rival groups fought for the caliphate, or the office of the caliph. The struggle began when **Ali** was elected the fourth caliph in A.D. 656.

One of Ali's most powerful rivals was **Mu'awiyah** (moo•UH•wee•uh), governor of Syria and nephew of the third caliph, Uthman, who had been murdered. Mu'awiyah wanted revenge for that murder and accused Ali's supporters of encouraging it. When Ali tried to depose the Syrian governor, Mu'awiyah refused to step down.

In the battle that followed, Mu'awiyah's defeat seemed certain. Then the Syrian soldiers tied copies of pages from the Quran to the tips of their lances and charged, shouting, "Let Allah decide!" Unwilling to strike an enemy bearing the word of God, Ali was forced to negotiate with Mu'awiyah.

While Ali was trying to reassert his control as caliph, Mu'awiyah took over Egypt and raided Iraq. In A.D. 661 Ali was fatally stabbed by a disillusioned follower, and his older son renounced his claim to the caliphate. Mu'awiyah became the first caliph of the powerful Umayyad (oo•MY•uhd) dynasty.

Followers of Ali, known as **the Shiites** (SHEE•EYETS), never accepted Mu'awiyah's rule. When he died in A.D. 680, they claimed the caliphate for Ali's son, **Husayn** (hoo•SAYN), then in Madinah. Husayn's followers in Iraq invited him

Images of the Times

Islamic Art and Architecture

Inspired by their faith, artists and architects of Islam created unequaled geometric designs, floral patterns, and calligraphy.

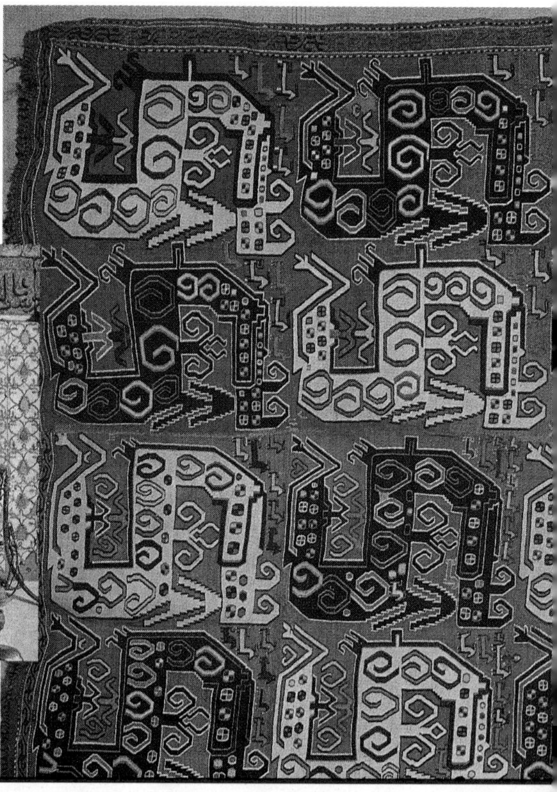

Carpets and other textiles were turned into fine art pieces by the skilled hands of Islamic weavers.

Shoes of the Faithful by Charles Robertson is a reminder of the centrality of religious belief in Muslim daily life.

278

Images of the Times **Islamic Art and Architecture**

Although the Quran neither prohibits nor allows the representation of living things, by the middle of the eighth century such a prohibition became a standard element of Islamic thought. In spite of this prohibition, Islamic artists produced elaborate arabesques and developed a stylistic form of calligraphy.

The Alhambra (in Arabic, "the red," probably from the color of the outer wall's bricks) was built in Granada, Spain, mainly between 1238 and 1358. The Alhambra has six courts, of which the Court of the Myrtles is the most famous. It leads into the huge Hall of Ambassadors.

to lead them as caliph. When he arrived in Iraq with his family and a small group of followers, Umayyad troops massacred all but the women and a young son in a battle at Karbala. The leader sent Husayn's head to Mu'awiyah's son, who had assumed the caliphate.

The murders of Ali and Husayn led to a permanent schism in the Islamic world. The majority of Muslims, known as **the Sunnis** (SU•neez), or "followers of the way," follow the teachings of Muhammad, the tradition followed by the Rightly Guided Caliphs. In Sunni Islam, the caliph may be any devout Muslim who is accepted by the people.

The Shiites, the smaller group of Muslims, followed a series of leaders who aimed to destroy the existing caliphate and establish a new one in its place. Living mostly in Iraq and Iran, the Shiites believe the caliphate should be held only by descendants of Muhammad through his daughter Fatimah and her husband Ali. The Shiites stress the imam's power as a spiritual leader.

The Islamic State

The Umayyad dynasty, which was founded by Mu'awiyah, ruled from A.D. 661 to A.D. 750. The Umayyads moved the capital from Madinah to **Damascus**, Syria, which was more centrally located in the expanding state.

Umayyad Conquests

In the next century, Umayyad warriors carried Islam east, to the borders of India and China. In the west, they swept across North Africa and into Spain, the southernmost area of Christian western Europe.

By A.D. 716 the Muslims ruled almost all of Spain. They advanced halfway into France before the Frankish leader Charles Martel stopped them at the Battle of Tours in A.D. 732. This battle halted the spread of Islam into western Europe.

Life in the Umayyad State

The Umayyads built a powerful Islamic state that stressed the political, rather than the religious,

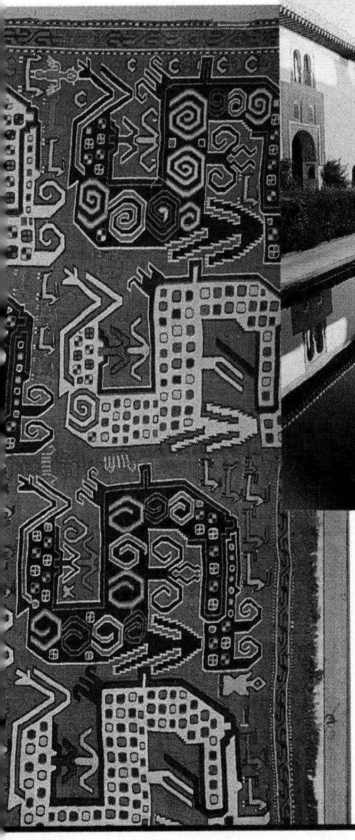

Court of the Myrtles, Alhambra, Granada, Spain remains as a striking example of intricate Islamic architectural design.

REFLECTING ON THE TIMES

1. What details characterize the interior walls of the Court of the Myrtles?
2. Why do you think the decorative arts flourished in the Islamic world during this period?

Chapter 11 Section 2

Economics Have students discuss how they think the spread of Islam enriched the Islamic state. They may discuss such topics as new tax monies, trading opportunities, natural resources, and skills of conquered peoples. Explain that the Arabs also absorbed the traditions of the conquered peoples and synthesized them into a unique culture. **L3**

Independent Practice

Guided Reading Activity 11-2 **L1**

Mapping History Activity 11 **L1**

Time Line Ask students to chart the chronology of the Islamic state. Have them find the year of as many significant events as possible and arrange the events in chronological order on their charts. Provide these dates to get students started:

- ***ca. 570*** birth of Muhammad
- ***632*** death of Muhammad; succession of Abu Bakr as first caliph
- ***1258*** Mongols capture Baghdad, ending Abbasid caliphate **L1**

Linking Past and Present

Mujahedeen Students may recognize the word *mujahedeen*, the Islamic guerrilla fighters who fought in Afghanistan, Iran, and Bosnia. The word is related to *jihad*. The mujahedeen think of themselves as warriors in a holy war against unbelievers.

ANSWERS TO REFLECTING ON THE TIMES

1. geometric designs, calligraphy, floral patterns
2. The Islamic state was prosperous; as it expanded into new territories, it synthesized local traditions into Islamic forms.

Map Study

Answer
The Muslim defeat at the Battle of Tours prevented the spread of Islam into France.

Map Skills Practice

Reading a Map Which caliphs added most of the territory in Europe and North Africa? *(Umayyads)* Which added most of the territory in Asia and North Africa? *(the Rightly Guided Caliphs)*

Geography: Place Have students make a visual representation of their interpretation of Baghdad as described in this section. Have them use information from the diagram on page 281 and the text to illustrate a poster, develop a clay model, render a sketch, or complete another type of visual. **L2**

Poetry Have students compose a poem celebrating Mu'awiyah's achievements in a lofty style, suitable for delivery after one of his victories. **L3**

ASSESS

Check for Understanding

Assign Section 2 Review as homework or as an in-class activity.

Use Student Self-Test and Review Software to review Section 2.

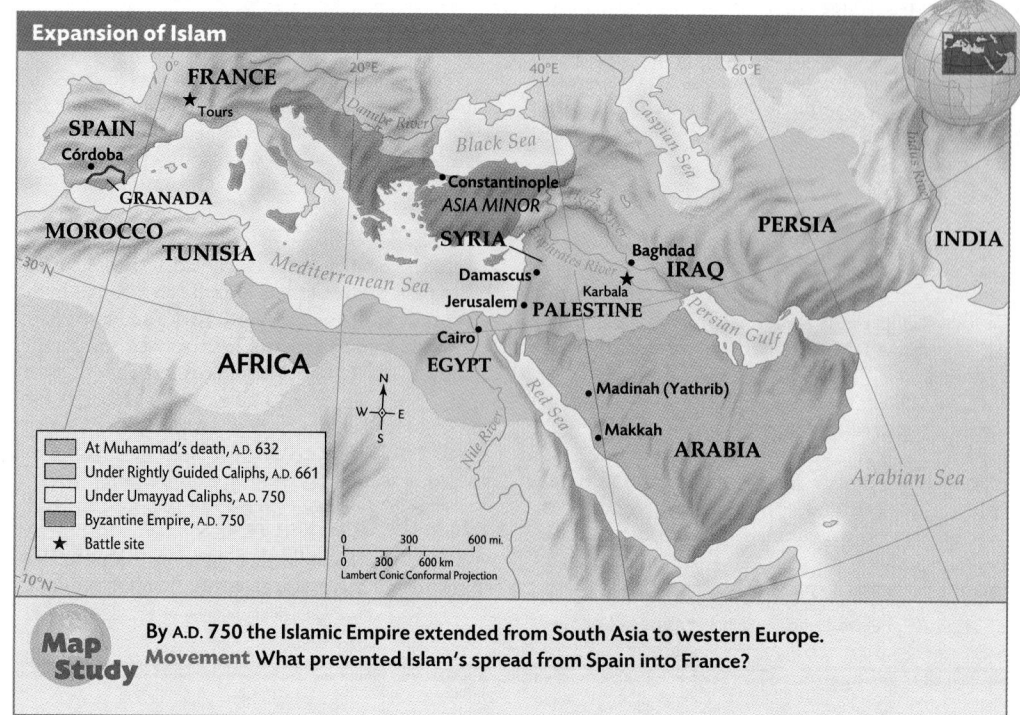

Expansion of Islam

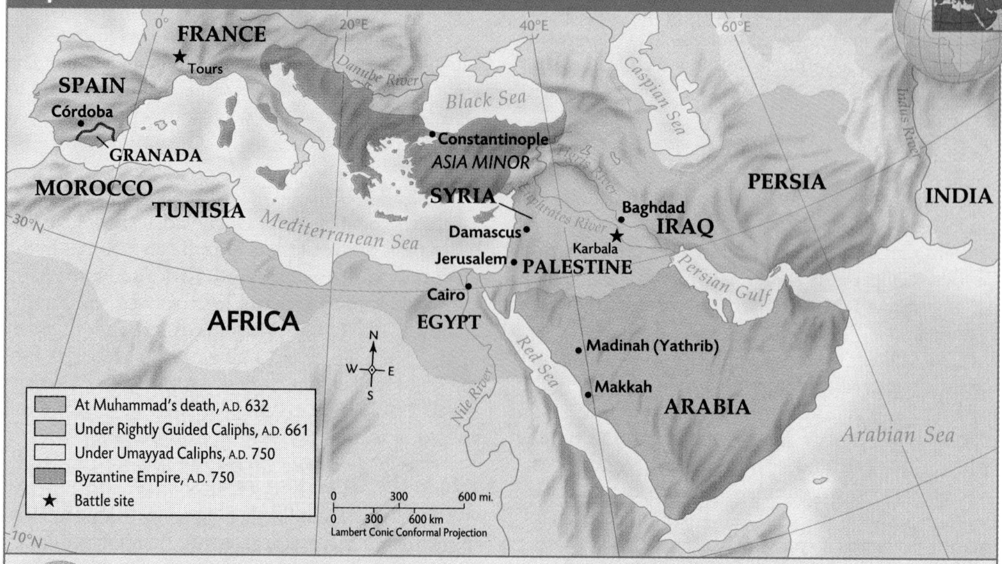

Map Study By A.D. 750 the Islamic Empire extended from South Asia to western Europe.
Movement What prevented Islam's spread from Spain into France?

aspect of their office. As time went by, they ruled more like kings and less like the earlier caliphs.

The Umayyads did, however, help to unite the lands they ruled. They made Arabic the official language, minted the first Arabic currency, built roads, and established postal routes. Their administration depended on a civil service made up of well-trained bureaucrats who had served as officials in the Byzantine and Persian Empires.

Umayyad rule also improved conditions for many, particularly Jews and non-Greek Christians, who had often suffered under Byzantine rule. They had to pay a special tax, but they were tolerated because they believed in one God. The great Arab commander Khalid ibn al-Walid, who had led the conquest of Syria and Persia, described Muslim policy:

> "In the name of Allah, the compassionate, the merciful, this is what Khalid ibn al-Walid would grant to the inhabitants of Damascus.... He promises to give them security for their lives, property and churches. Their city wall shall not be demolished, neither shall any Muslim be quartered in their houses. Thereunto we give to them the pact of Allah and the protection of His Prophet, the Caliphs and the believers. So long as they pay the tax, nothing but good shall befall them."

Opposition to Umayyad Rule

Despite this enlightened outlook, Umayyad rule caused dissatisfaction among non-Arab Muslims. They paid higher taxes, received lower wages in the army and government, and were discriminated against socially. Discontent was particularly strong in Iraq and Persia, the center of the Shiite opposition to Umayyad rule.

The Abbasids

In the year A.D. 747, the anti-Umayyad Arabs and the non-Arab Muslims in Iraq and Persia joined forces, built an army, and, in three years of fighting, overwhelmed the Umayyads. The new caliph, Abu'l-'Abbas, was a descendant of one of Muhammad's uncles. He established the Abbasid (uh•BA•suhd) dynasty and had a new city, **Baghdad**, built on the banks of the Tigris River. By the A.D. 900s, about 1.5 million people lived in Baghdad.

Baghdad lay at the crossroads of the land and

COOPERATIVE LEARNING ACTIVITY

The Arts To understand the role and influence of Islamic crafts and decorative arts, have students form two groups. Have one group research and prepare a presentation on the different styles of art and architecture in the Islamic world. Ask students to offer illustrations of each kind of art and to explain the significance of the different styles. Have students choose two members of the group to present the material and lead a classroom discussion after their presentation. The second group of students should investigate the ways Islamic art influenced European art. They should organize their presentation in the same fashion as the first group. **L3**

280 Chapter 11 *Islamic Civilization*

water trade routes that stretched from the Mediterranean Sea to East Asia. The city was shaped like a circle and surrounded by walls. Highways led from Baghdad's center to different parts of the empire and divided the city into districts. At Baghdad's heart stood the great mosque and the caliph's magnificent palace, where he ruled in splendor like the Persian rulers. Surrounding areas contained the luxurious homes of court members and army officials. Outer districts of the city were made up of the homes of the common people.

Abbasid Diversity

The Abbasid Empire reached its height under Caliph **Harun al-Rashid** (ha•ROON ahl•rah •SHEED), who ruled from A.D. 786 to A.D. 809. During this time, the Abbasids developed a sophisticated urban civilization based on the diversity of the empire's peoples. Harun and his successors worked to ensure equality among all Muslims, Arab and non-Arab. They set up a new ruling group that included Muslims of many nationalities. Persians became the dominant group in the government bureaucracy, while the Turks became the leading group in the army. Arabs, however, continued to control religious life and administration of law.

Breakup of the Islamic State

The Abbasids ruled the Islamic state from A.D. 750 to A.D. 1258; during this time, however, many of the lands that had been won by the Umayyads broke free from Baghdad. In central Asia, during the A.D. 800s, Persian Muslims set up the Samanid dynasty in the city of Bukhara (boo•KAHR•uh). Under Samanid rule, Bukhara and other central Asian cities, such as Samarkand and Tashkent, became major commercial, religious, and educational centers. Their wealth was based on caravans that traveled through the region, bringing silk, spices, and animal products from East Asia to European areas as far north as the Baltic Sea.

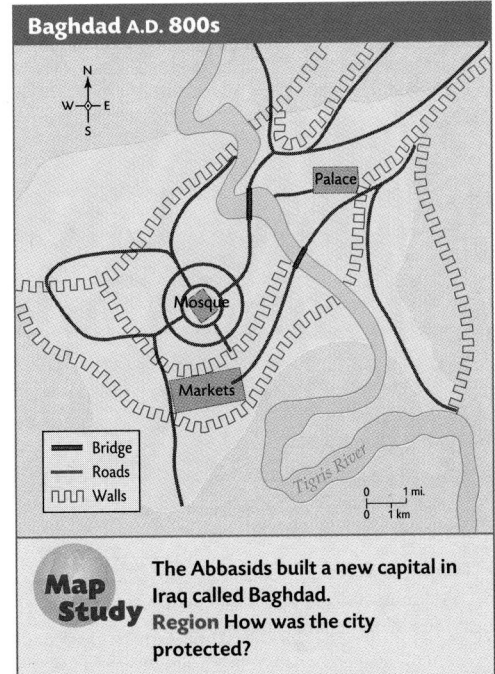

Baghdad A.D. 800s

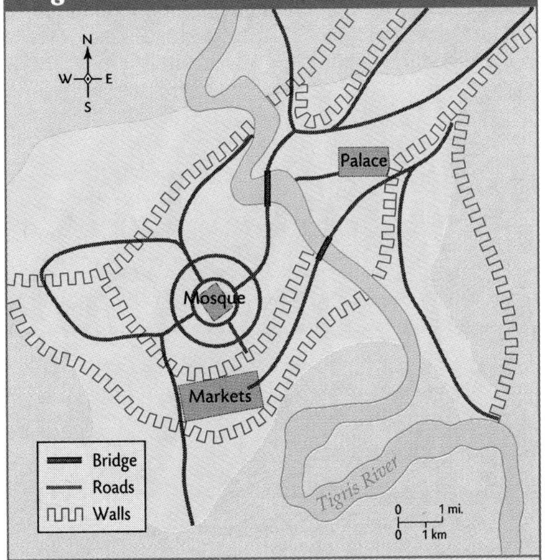

Map Study The Abbasids built a new capital in Iraq called Baghdad.
Region How was the city protected?

Independent states also emerged in other parts of the crumbling Abbasid Empire. One of the last Umayyad princes fled to Spain and continued Umayyad rule there. The Egyptian dynasty, the Fatimids, gained control over areas in North Africa and the Middle East, rivaling Baghdad for power. Much of Persia also came under the control of rival rulers. By the A.D. 1000s, the Abbasids ruled little more than the area around Baghdad.

During the next 200 years, Baghdad and its Abbasid rulers came under the control of the Seljuk Turks and later, the Mongols. In their ferocious assault on the city in A.D. 1258, the Mongols burned buildings and slaughtered 50,000 inhabitants, among them the last Abbasid caliph.

SECTION 2 REVIEW

Recall

1. **Define** caliph, jihad.
2. **Identify** Abu Bakr, Ali, Mu'awiyah, the Shiites, Husayn, the Sunnis, the Umayyads, the Abbasids, Harun al-Rashid.
3. **Locate** the cities of Damascus and Baghdad on the map on page 280. Why did the caliphs move the capital of the Islamic state to each of these cities?

Critical Thinking

4. **Evaluating Information** What were the strengths and weaknesses of Umayyad rule?

Understanding Themes

5. **Movement** How did expansion affect the ethnic diversity of the Islamic Empire? How did expansion affect the empire's stability?

SECTION 2 REVIEW ANSWERS

1. All vocabulary words are defined in the Glossary.
2. Abu Bakr, 277; Ali, 277; Mu'awiyah, 278; the Shiites, 278; Husayn, 278; the Sunnis, 279; the Umayyads, 279; the Abbasids, 280; Harun al-Rashid, 281
3. Damascus: more centrally located than Madinah in expanding state; Baghdad: built in Iraq by conquering group that included Iraqi and Persian Muslims
4. strengths: efficient government, tolerance for non-Muslims; weaknesses: emphasis on politics over religion, discrimination against non-Arab Muslims
5. **MOVEMENT** Expansion increased diversity but led to instability.

Chapter 11 Section 2

Map Study

Answer

Walls surrounded the city.

Map Skills Practice

Reading a Map How far from the mosque was the palace? *(about 4 miles [6 km])* How far from the mosque were the markets? *(less than 2 miles [3 km])*

Evaluate

Section Quiz 11-2

Use the Testmaker to create a customized quiz for Section 2.

Reteach

Ask students to imagine they have moved to a foreign country. Have them speculate about the changes they would have to make in their lives to adapt to a new culture. What facets of the students' culture would people in the new environment be likely to absorb? Have them relate these concepts to the expansion of the Islamic state.

Enrich

Have students find out more about the four Rightly Guided Caliphs and write a two-page report about them.

CLOSE

Write these names from the section on the chalkboard: Abu Bakr, Ali, Umayyads, Abbasids. Have students identify the names and explain the importance of each in the history of Islam and the expansion of the Islamic state.

Chapter 11 Section 3

SECTION THEME

- **Cultural Diffusion** Contributions from many cultures and peoples enrich the Islamic state.

Find Out

Answer: *Islamic civilization made advances in the arts and in many of the sciences. These advances spread to other parts of the world through the extensive trade and travel of the peoples of the Abbasid state.*

FOCUS

Section Objective

Name the achievements of Islamic civilization and explain how they were spread to other parts of the world.

BELLRINGER Motivational Activity

Before taking roll at the beginning of the class period, project Section Focus Transparency 11-3 and have students answer the activity questions. Discuss students' responses.

This activity is also available as a blackline master.

Vocabulary Pre-check

Use the Vocabulary PuzzleMaker to create a puzzle that reinforces the vocabulary terms in this section. **L1**

A.D. 600 — A.D. 800 — A.D. 1000 — A.D. 1200

- **c. A.D. 635** The Quran is compiled.
- **c. A.D. 830** Baghdad reaches its height as a major center of learning.
- **c. A.D. 910** Arab chronicler al Tabari writes a history of the world.
- **A.D. 1135** The Jewish philosopher Maimonides is born.

Section 3

Daily Life and Culture

Setting the Scene

- **Terms to Define**
  madrasa, bazaar, calligraphy, arabesque, chronicle
- **People to Meet**
  Ma'mun, al-Razi, Ibn Sina, Omar Khayyám, Moses Maimonides, Ibn Khaldun

Find Out What were the achievements of Islamic civilization, and how did they spread to other parts of the world?

The Storyteller

One hundred and twenty camels were required to transport Ismail's books as he prepared to move from Baghdad to Cairo. It was not that he would be unable to obtain books in Cairo. That city, like Baghdad, was lavishly supplied with both public and private libraries whose collections numbered in the tens of thousands. Like many scholars in the Muslim world, Ismail had amassed a collection of works on topics from poetry, history, and law to medicine, mathematics, and astronomy. Now it would take a major effort to move them.

—adapted from *The Mind of the Middle Ages*, Frederick B. Artz, 1990

An astrolabe

In the Abbasid state, the arts and learning flourished despite political disunity. The time of conquest had ended, and the people had enough leisure to enjoy cultural activities. Because Arabic was the language of the Quran, it became the common language. Its widespread use enabled scientists, rulers, and writers from different lands to communicate with one another. This blend of people and ideas gave the Islamic state a new multicultural character and created a golden age.

Muslim Society

Islam set the guidelines for the way people lived. It laid down rules for family life and business as well as for religious practices.

Family Life

Early Islam stressed the equality of all believers before God; however, as in the case of contemporary Christian and Jewish communities, in Islamic communities men and women had distinct roles and rights. The Quran told Muslims that "men are responsible for women." A woman's social position was therefore defined by her relationship as wife, mother, daughter, or sister to the male members of her family.

Islam did, however, improve the position of women. It forbade the tribal custom of killing female infants and also limited polygamy (puh•LIH•guh•mee), or the practice that allowed a man to have more than one wife. A Muslim could have as many as four wives, but all were to be treated as equals and with kindness. Also, a woman had complete control over her own property. If she were divorced, she could keep the property she had brought with her when she married. A woman could also inherit property from her father and remarry.

SECTION RESOURCES

Reproducible Masters
- Reproducible Lesson Plan 11-3
- Guided Reading Activity 11-3
- Geography and History Activity 11
- Reteaching Activity 11
- Enrichment Activity 11
- Section Quiz 11-3
- Performance Assessment Activity 11
- Spanish Chapter Summary 11

Transparencies
- Section Focus Transparency 11-3

Multimedia
- Focus on World Art Print 13
- Student Self-Test and Review Software
- Vocabulary PuzzleMaker Software
- Testmaker
- World Music: Cultural Traditions, Lesson 5

282 Chapter 11 *Islamic Civilization*

Many Muslim women learned to read and write, and several women in the caliph's court were renowned for their poetry. Some of them were not always happy with their lives, though, as indicated by this poem written by Maisuna, the bedouin wife of Mu'awiyah. Her comments made Mu'awiyah so furious that he sent her back to the desert:

> "The coarse cloth worn in the serenity
> of the desert
> Is more precious to me than the luxurious
> robes of a queen;
> I love the bedouin's tent, caressed by the
> murmuring breeze, and standing amid
> boundless horizons,
> More than the gilded halls of marble in
> all their royal splendor.
> I feel more at ease with my simple crust,
> Than with the delicacies of the court;
> I prefer to rise early with the caravan,
> Rather than be in the golden glare of
> the sumptuous escort.
> The barking of a watchdog keeping away
> strangers
> Pleases me more than the sounds of the
> tambourine played by the court singers;
> I prefer a desert cavalier, generous and
> poor,
> To a fat lout in purple living behind closed
> doors."
>
> —Najib Ullah, *Islamic Literature*

Women usually stayed at home and did household tasks, and they did not participate in public life except to go shopping and sometimes to go to the mosque on Friday. In the mosque, women were assigned a special room for prayer.

At home, a married woman was entitled to her own rooms. Household servants, some of them enslaved, helped with the housekeeping. Girls usually married young; they prepared for marriage by learning from their mothers or servants how to manage a household.

Outside the home, Muslim men worked at a variety of businesses or in the fields. For leisure they visited public baths and meeting places where they relaxed and talked. Men also played chess, practiced gymnastics, or watched horse racing.

Education

When Muslim boys reached age seven, they entered mosque schools, which cost little and were open to all boys. Wealthier families paid tuition, but many poor children were admitted without charge. Being able to speak Arabic fluently and to write with grace and ease were skills that Muslims valued. For all but the sons of the wealthy, however, schooling ended with learning to read and write. Some young men continued their studies at ***madrasas***, or theological schools. Those who were to become leaders in Muslim society studied the classical literature of Islam, memorized poetry, and learned to compose original verses.

City and Country

Most Arabs lived in rural or desert places. The leadership of the Islamic state, however, came from the cities.

Many cities, such as Damascus, in Syria, developed as trading centers even before the rise of Islam. Others, such as Kufa, in Iraq, developed from military towns set up during the early conquests. Muslim cities were divided into distinct business and residential districts. A maze of narrow streets, often covered to protect pedestrians from the scorching sun, separated the closely packed buildings.

Urban Centers

City homes were designed to provide maximum privacy and to keep the occupants cool in the blazing heat. Houses were centered around courtyards; in wealthy homes, these courtyards had fountains and gardens. Thick walls of dried mud or brick and few windows kept the interior dim and cool.

The interiors of most Muslim homes were plain with few pieces of furniture. They were decorated with beautiful carpets and small art objects. Most people sat on carpets or leaned on cushions or pillows. At mealtime, household members sat in a circle and ate from large trays of breads, meats, and fruits.

Footnotes to History

Magic Carpets

The magic carpet gliding through the air is a familiar form of transportation in *The Arabian Nights*. The real magic of Islamic carpets, however, is their glowing colors and intricate designs. During the Islamic Empire, carpets adorned both caliphs' palaces and shepherds' tents. Today, carpets from the Islamic world still give their magic to modern walls and floors.

Chapter 11
Section 3

TEACH

Guided Practice

THEME Cultural Diffusion

Write this sentence on the chalkboard: *Merchants traded freely throughout the Islamic world.* Have students give examples from the section to illustrate this statement. Then have them write two sentences explaining how such trade influenced Islamic civilization. Ask several students to read their sentences aloud. Students should conclude that contact with many different cultures modified and expanded the original Islamic civilization. **L1**

Social Life Have students write paragraphs defending or rebutting the following statement: "Outside the home, Islamic society was a man's world." Use students' paragraphs as a springboard for a class discussion of gender roles in Muslim society. **L2**

Daily Life Have students contrast their education with early Islamic education. **How do public schools today differ from the Islamic schools of a thousand years ago?** *(Islamic schools available only to boys, free only to boys from poor families, mission was to teach literacy only, advanced schooling mainly religious)* **What conclusions about Islamic society can you draw from its educational system?** *(Possible conclusion: No distinction was made between religious life and secular life.)* **L3**

World Music: Cultural Traditions, Lesson 5

Focus on World Art Print 13, Habib Allah. *Mantik et-Tayr*

COOPERATIVE LEARNING ACTIVITY

Role Play Have students write and perform plays about life in Islamic society. Organize the class into small groups and have each group select a theme for its play. Themes could include family life, education, religion, business activities, or bazaars. Have students in each group pool their information and collectively decide what to use in the play. Some group members should be responsible for writing the play, including the dialogue. Other members should perform the play. Each group should choose a student to act as director, as well as an announcer to introduce the play by setting it in time and place. **L2**

Map Study

Answer

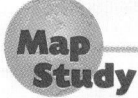

Trade routes from Baghdad to Asia include overland routes through Persia; to Europe, overland routes through Syria, Egypt, and the Byzantine Empire; across the Mediterranean Sea.

Map Skills Practice

Reading a Map About how far did a caravan travel overland to go from Makkah to Constantinople? *(about 1,600 miles [2,574 km])*

Independent Practice

Guided Reading Activity 11-3 **L1**

Geography and History Activity 11

Puzzle Have students make a crossword puzzle by using Islamic words from this section. The puzzle may include proper nouns, common nouns, adjectives, and verbs. Students should construct a grid for their puzzle and write short clues for the words. Have students solve each other's puzzles. **L2**

you don't say...

Originally, **"bazaar"** referred to the public market districts of Persian towns. The word spread from Persia to Arabia and other parts of the Islamic state, including Turkey, North Africa, and India. In current English usage it may mean a store offering many types of goods for sale, a sale of contributed articles to benefit a cause, or a Middle Eastern marketplace.

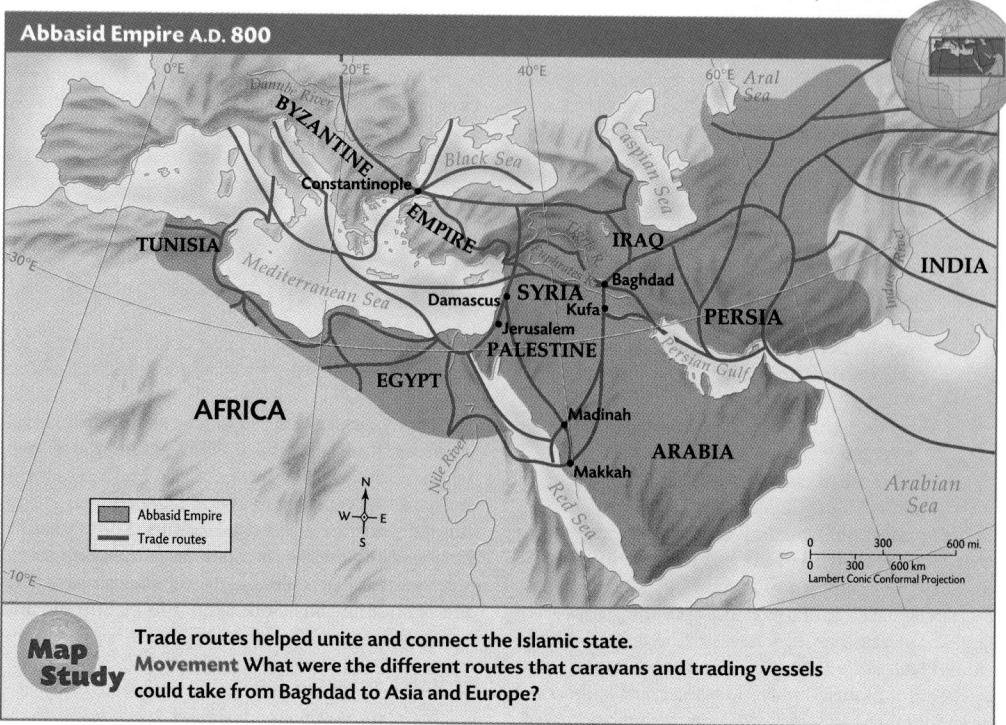

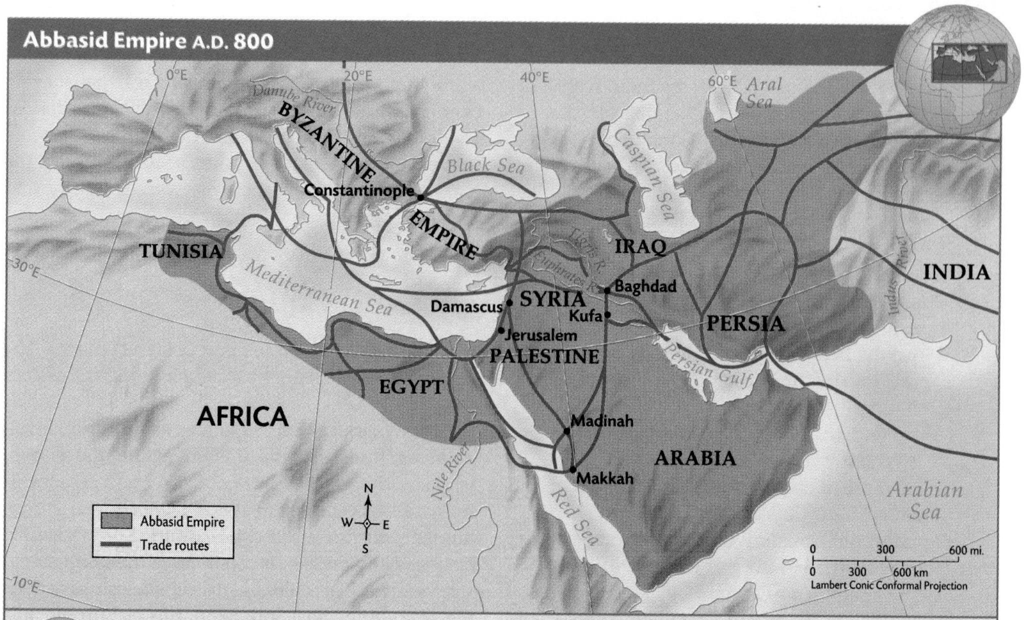

Map Study Trade routes helped unite and connect the Islamic state.
Movement What were the different routes that caravans and trading vessels could take from Baghdad to Asia and Europe?

The main religious, government, and business buildings were at the center of the city. Dominating the skyline were graceful mosques and their slender minarets, or towers from which people were called to prayer. Mosques usually included a prayer hall where worshipers gathered on Fridays. At one end of this hall a mihrab, or niche, marked the direction of Makkah. Often mosques included schools and shelters for travelers.

Trade and the Bazaar

Muslim merchants dominated trade throughout the Middle East and North Africa until the A.D. 1400s. Caravans traveled overland from Baghdad to China. Muslim traders crossed the Indian Ocean gathering cargoes of rubies from India, silk from China, and spices from Southeast Asia. Gold, ivory, and enslaved people were brought from Africa, Asia, and Europe. From the Islamic world came spices, textiles, glass, and carpets.

The destination of these goods were the city bazaars, or marketplaces. In major cities, such as Baghdad, Damascus, and Cairo, the bazaars consisted of mazes of shops and stalls, often enclosed to shut out the glare of the sun. Buyers at the major bazaars included Europeans who purchased Asian goods, shipped them across the Mediterranean Sea to Italy and then on to other parts of Europe. Islamic men also met at the bazaars for conversation as well as business. Nearby were large warehouses and lodging houses that served traveling merchants.

Rural Areas

Because of the dry climate and the scarcity of water, growing food was difficult in most of the Islamic state. Farmers, however, made efficient use of the few arable areas. They produced good yields by irrigating their fields, rotating crops, and fertilizing the land. Most productive land was held by large landowners who received grants from the government. They had large estates and employed farmers from nearby villages to work the land. Muslim farms produced wheat, rice, beans, cucumbers, celery, and mint. Orchards provided almonds, blackberries, melons, apricots, figs, and olives. Farmers also cultivated flowers for perfume.

After Arab irrigation methods were introduced into Spain, Muslims there could cultivate valuable new crops, including cherries, apples, pears, and bananas. Seville, Córdoba, and other Spanish Islamic cities grew rich from the produce they sold in international trade.

MEETING SPECIAL NEEDS ACTIVITY

Learning Style: Verbal/Linguistic Ask students to imagine that they are followers of Muhammad in Madinah during his lifetime. Have them write letters to Muhammad praising him for the improved status of women under Islam. Letters should mention specific improvements, such as abolishing the killing of female infants. Proofread each student's letter individually, pointing out mistakes in grammar, fuzzy passages, and unclear statements. Give specific suggestions as to how to improve these weaknesses. **L2**

Islamic Achievements

The use of Arabic not only promoted trade but also encouraged communication among the different peoples in the Islamic state. From these peoples the Islamic state built a rich storehouse of knowledge and scientific discovery.

Between the A.D. 800s and A.D. 1300s, Islamic scientists made important contributions in several scientific areas, such as mathematics, astronomy, chemistry, and medicine. They based their work on two main intellectual traditions. The first, and most important, was that of Greece. The second was that of India, which came to the Arabs by way of Persia.

The House of Wisdom

The Islamic world experienced a scientific awakening under the Abbasids. During the A.D. 800s, Baghdad became a leading intellectual center.

According to Muslim tradition, the Abbasid caliph **Ma'mun** (mah•MOON) founded the House of Wisdom at Baghdad in A.D. 830. This research center specialized in the translation into Arabic of Greek, Persian, and Indian scientific texts. Ma'mun staffed the institute with Christian, Jewish, and Muslim scholars who shared ideas from different intellectual traditions. They performed scientific experiments, made mathematical calculations, and built upon the ideas of the ancients. The House of Wisdom, therefore, sparked many of the mathematical and scientific achievements in the Islamic world.

Muslim science involved more than just theory; it was put to practical use. For example, mathematics was used to solve daily problems in business and agriculture. Astronomy was used to determine the hours of prayer and the time period of celebrations.

Mathematics

As you read in Chapter 7, Gupta mathematicians in India devised the numerals we know as Arabic numerals and the concept of zero. Muslim mathematicians adopted these numerals and used them in a place-value system. In this system, today used worldwide, a number's value is determined by the position of its digits. The place-value system made possible great achievements in mathematics.

Muslim mathematicians invented algebra and expressed equations to define curves and lines. Their work in geometry led to the development of trigonometry, which was used to calculate the distance to a star and the speed of a falling object. Mathematicians also were interested in practical applications, such as devising pumps and fountains and applying their skills to building and surveying.

Astronomy and Geography

At Ma'mun's observatory in Baghdad, astronomers checked the findings of the ancient Greeks, made observations of the skies, and produced physical and mathematical models of the universe. They accurately described solar eclipses and proved that the moon affects the oceans.

Muslim astronomers improved on a Greek device called the astrolabe, with which they determined the positions of stars, the movements of planets, and the time. The astrolabe made navigation easier and safer. It was also useful in religious practices, enabling Muslims to ascertain the direction of Makkah, the beginning of Ramadan, and the hours of prayer.

Using the astrolabe, Muslim geographers measured the size and circumference of the earth with accuracy unmatched until the 1900s. From such studies, geographers concluded that the earth was round, although most continued to accept the Greek theory that heavenly bodies revolve around the earth.

By the A.D. 1100s, Muslim geographers had determined the basic outlines of Asia, Europe, and North Africa and had produced the first accurate maps of the Eastern Hemisphere. They also traveled widely to gain firsthand knowledge of the earth's surface, its climates, and its peoples.

Chemistry and Medicine

Muslims developed alchemy, the branch of chemistry that attempted to change lead into gold. Although alchemists never succeeded in their goal, they did develop the equipment and methods that are still used in modern chemistry.

The renowned chemist and physician **al-Razi** (ahl•RAH•zee), who lived from A.D. 865 to A.D. 925, classified chemical substances as animal, mineral, or vegetable, a classification system that remains in use today. Al-Razi also made invaluable contributions to medicine. Among his nearly 200 works are a medical encyclopedia that describes the origin of disease and a handbook identifying the differences between smallpox and measles.

In the A.D. 900s, the doctor **Ibn Sina** (IH•buhn SEE•nuh) produced the *Canon of Medicine*, a monumental volume that attempted to summarize all the medical knowledge of that time. It described the circulation of the blood and the functions of the kidneys and the heart. It also offered diagnosis and treatment for many diseases.

Muslim physicians founded the science of optics, or the study of light and its effect on sight. Ibn al-Haytham, the founder of optics, discovered that the eye sees because it receives light from the object seen. Earlier physicians had believed the

Social Life Ask students to research the status of women in the Islamic state and in another culture such as that of Native Americans. Have students write a paper that compares the status and the relative freedom and independence of women in both cultures. Display the papers or have several students read their papers aloud in class. **L2**

CURRICULUM CONNECTION

MATHEMATICS

About A.D. 825 al-Khowarizmi (ahl KWAHR•eez•mee), a teacher of mathematics in Baghdad, wrote a book titled *Kitab al-jabr wa al-muqabalah*. His work was a presentation of what was known about algebra at the time. The Arab mathematician improved and expanded algebra, the mathematics that uses symbols to solve complex mathematical problems. Al-Khowarizmi—and readers of his book—invented so many things that scholars consider algebra an Arab creation. Even the name *algebra* comes from part of the title of al-Khowarizmi's book—*al-jabr.*

MAKING CONNECTIONS ACTIVITY

Mathematics To help students appreciate the Muslim innovation of the place-value system, have them try adding the following Roman numerals without writing down their Arabic equivalents: CXLVIII + LXXXII + CCXXXVII. *(467)* You may need to review Roman numerals with students. (M=1,000, C=100, L=50, X=10, V=5) Then have them add these Arabic numbers : 342 + 79 + 175. *(596)* Have students make similar comparisons with multiplication and division. Discuss the results. **L3**

Cultural Perspectives

Paper Trail The Abbasids' capture of a group of Chinese papermakers at the Battle of Talas in 751 helped foster the blossoming of Islamic literature during the reign of this dynasty.

CONNECTIONS **Science and Technology**

At the Doctor's

The accounts of Mansur's stomach distress and Muslim pioneering work in hygiene illustrate the contributions of physicians from the Muslim empire to the advancement of medical science. Not all the physicians in the empire were Muslim, however. Some, including Maimonides, whose religious work is described on pages 287–288, were Jewish, while others were Christian. An early physician was the ninth-century Persian Rhazes, whose most famous book clearly described and distinguished between smallpox and measles. Ibn Sina, introduced on page 285, was also a Persian. His *Canon of Medicine* was used as late as 1650 in medical schools at Montpellier, France, and elsewhere.

Answers to Making the Connection

1. *Muslim doctors based their medical practices on scientific methods; western European doctors continued to rely on superstition to explain and treat illnesses until Islamic knowledge spread westward.*
2. *Answers will vary but may include organ transplants, vaccines against such diseases as polio, as well as treatments and diagnostic techniques based on technological breakthroughs, such as laser surgery, sonograms, and CAT scans.*

opposite: that the eye sees because it produces rays that give light to the object seen. Muslim medicine, in fact, was centuries ahead of the medicine practiced in the West.

Art and Architecture

Like mathematics and science, Islamic art and architecture benefited from the cultural diversity of the Islamic Empire. Muslim theologians, fearful of idol worship, did not allow artists to make images or pictures of living creatures. Instead, artists used the beautiful script of written Arabic in an art form known as **calligraphy** (kuh•LIH•gruh•fee), or the art of elegant handwriting, to decorate public walls with passages from the Quran. Often calligraphy was accompanied by geometric designs entwined with plant stems, leaves, flowers, and stars. These **arabesques** (AR•uh•BEHSKS) decorated books, carpets, swords, and entire walls.

Islamic architects and artists did their best work in architecture, particularly in building and decorating mosques. Gardens and water, both precious in the arid Islamic lands, became artistic objects. Sun-drenched courtyards in mosques, palaces, and wealthy homes had trees to provide cool shade and flowers to delight the eye and nose; splashing fountains and running water refreshed both eye and ear.

Literature

Until the A.D. 600s, Arabic literature consisted mostly of poetry passed orally from one generation to the next. After the rise of Islam, religion had much influence in the creation of Arabic literature. The Quran, the first and greatest work in Arabic prose, was familiar to every Muslim, and its style influenced Islamic writing.

During the A.D. 700s, nonreligious prose appeared that both taught and entertained. The most famous of these writings was *Kalila and Dimna*, a collection of animal fables that presented moral lessons.

During the Abbasid period, Islamic literature blossomed as a result of contact with Greek thought, Hindu legends, and Persian court epics.

CONNECTIONS **Science and Technology**

At the Doctor's

Today we take it for granted that the doctor can make us better when we get sick. In A.D. 765, however, the caliph Mansur was not so fortunate. His personal physicians—the best in Baghdad—could find no remedy for his chronic indigestion.

Medicinal herb from an Islamic manuscript

The caliph had heard that physicians in a Persian medical school based their practices on rational Greek methods of treatment. Traditional Arab medicine was based mainly on magic or superstition.

When the caliph asked the medical school for help, the chief physician, a Christian named Jurjis ibn Bakhtishu, cured Mansur. This encouraged other Muslim doctors to practice medicine based on the methods of the Greeks and Persians.

Muslim doctors were the first to discover the functions of internal organs and to diagnose illnesses such as meningitis. They also advanced surgery, carrying out head and stomach operations with the aid of anesthetics such as opium.

Believing that medicine required long training, Muslim doctors studied in hospitals and medical schools. Doctors based their treatments upon careful observation of their patients rather than superstition. They also diagnosed diseases such as measles and smallpox, prescribed treatments, and performed surgery. Such practices were unknown in the West until the A.D. 1100s and A.D. 1200s, when Islamic knowledge reached western Europe.

MAKING THE CONNECTION

1. Why was Islamic medicine far ahead of Western medicine during the Middle Ages?
2. What new methods of treatment have doctors developed in the past 50 years?

CRITICAL THINKING ACTIVITY

Making Comparisons and Drawing Conclusions The Muslims made important contributions in many fields of human knowledge and endeavor: mathematics, astronomy, geography, chemistry, medicine, philosophy. Have students decide in which area they think Muslim contributions were the most significant. Have them write one-page papers defending their choice. Their arguments should include comparisons with Islamic achievements in other fields. **L2**

The upper classes valued elegant speech and the ability to handle words cleverly. Reading and appreciating literature became the sign of a good upbringing; every wealthy person took pride in having a well-stocked library. Córdoba, the Umayyad capital in Spain, had 70 libraries and more than half a million books. In contrast, the largest library in the Christian monasteries, at that time the center of European learning, held only a few hundred volumes.

In the A.D. 1000s, Persian became a second literary language in the Muslim world. Persian authors wrote epics about warrior-heroes, religious poetry, and verses about love. One of the best known works of this period is the *Rubaiyat* of **Omar Khayyám** (OH•MAHR KY•YAHM), a Persian mathematician and poet. You may also have heard some of the stories found in *A Thousand and One Nights*, also known as *The Arabian Nights*—stories such as "Sinbad the Sailor," "Aladdin and His Lamp," and "Ali Baba and the Forty Thieves." Originating in Arabia, India, Persia, Egypt, and other lands, the tales reflect the multinational character of the Islamic state.

Philosophy and History

Muslim philosophers tried to reconcile the teachings of the Quran with Greek philosophy. They believed that religious truths could be analyzed and defended using logic. Many of their works were translated into Latin and later brought a new understanding of philosophy to western Europe. Ibn Sina, known for his work in medicine, also wrote numerous books on logic and theology. Ibn-Rushd, a judge in Córdoba, was the most noted Islamic philosopher, and Christian scholars in western Europe later used his commentaries on Aristotle.

Moses Maimonides (my•MAH•nuh•DEEZ), a Spanish Jew born in A.D. 1135, fled to Morocco and then Egypt to escape persecution. Maimonides became a leader in the Jewish community and a doctor to the Egyptian ruler. Like several Muslim scholars, Maimonides attempted to reconcile his faith with the teachings of Aristotle.

One of Maimonides' major contributions was the *Mishne Torah*, a 14-volume work on Jewish law

History & Art Turkish miniature depicting angels, from the *Ajac, ib Mahlukat* by Sururi, A.D. 1500s. British Museum, London, England
Why did Muslim theologians forbid images of living creatures in works of art?

Chapter 11 Section 3

Who? What? Where? When?

Kufic script is the earliest Islamic style of calligraphy used to transcribe the Quran. The script's name comes from the Iraqi city of Kufa, where it may have originated. Kufa was a center of Arab culture and learning from the eighth to the tenth centuries. From about the twelfth century, Kufic script was no longer generally used except as a decorative border around later scripts.

ASSESS

Check for Understanding

Assign Section 3 Review as homework or as an in-class activity.

Use Student Self-Test and Review Software to review Section 3.

History & Art According to Islamic myth, God created angels from light before creating Adam from clay. With the exception of Iblis (Satan), all the angels obeyed God's order to bow down to Adam. Upon dying, a person is questioned by two angels. The archangel Israfil will blow a trumpet to awaken the dead for the day of resurrection.
Answer to Caption: *They wanted to avoid idol worship.*

MORE ABOUT...

Omar Khayyám and the *Rubaiyat* The name *Khayyám* refers to Omar's father's trade, tentmaking. Omar's fame as a scholar spread widely. One of eight experts chosen to revise the calendar, he also prepared astronomical tables and a book on algebra. The *Rubaiyat*, his collection of quatrains or *rubais* (four-line stanzas), was never popular in his own country. The English translation, discovered only after the death of the translator, Edward Fitzgerald (1809–1883), is a masterpiece of English poetry. The most famous quatrain is:

A Book of Verses underneath the Bough,
A Jug of Wine, a Loaf of Bread—and Thou
Beside me singing in the Wilderness—
Oh, Wilderness were Paradise enow!

Chapter 11 *Islamic Civilization* 287

Chapter 11 Section 3

Visualizing History In 642 the Arabs conquered Isfahan, which is about 210 miles (340 kilometers) south of Tehran. The founder of the Seljuk dynasty made Isfahan its capital. Although Isfahan declined after the fall of the Seljuks in about 1200, the city's fortunes began to rise in 1598, when Shah Abbas I the Great transformed it into one of the most magnificent cities of the seventeenth century. Today the city is a major textile center.
Answer to Caption: *The early historical events of Islam are traced in chronicles.*

Evaluate

Section Quiz 11-3

Use the Testmaker to create a customized quiz for Section 3.

Reteach

Ask students to write five sentences that describe specific Islamic achievements in areas such as mathematics, astronomy, and medicine. Have students read their sentences in class and correct any misstatements.

Reteaching Activity 11

Enrich

Ask students to find out more about Ibn Sina, often referred to as Avicenna, and write a one-page summary of their findings.

Enrichment Activity 11

CLOSE

Have students make a chart that compares the major features of Islamic civilization with those of another civilization they have studied, such as Egyptian, Greek, Roman, or Byzantine.

Visualizing History **A modern Islamic mosque in Isfahan, Iran, one of the most magnificent cities in the early Muslim world.** *What kind of writings traced the early historical events of Islam?*

and tradition, written in Hebrew. His other major religious work, *The Guide of the Perplexed,* was written in Arabic and later translated into Hebrew and Latin. After his death in A.D. 1204, Maimonides was recognized as one of the world's great philosophers.

Like Judaism and Christianity, Islam traces its origins to historical events. Therefore, Islamic scholars were interested in writing history. At first they wrote **chronicles**, or accounts in which events are arranged in the order in which they occurred. The most famous of the Islamic chroniclers were al Tabari (al tah•BAH•ree), who in the early A.D. 900s wrote a multivolume history of the world, and Ibn al-Athir (IH•buhn ahl•ah•THEER), who wrote an extensive history during the early A.D. 1200s.

Later, historians began to organize their accounts around events in the lives of rulers and others. The first Muslim historian to examine history scientifically was a North African diplomat named **Ibn Khaldun** (IH•buhn KAL•DOON). He looked for laws and cause-and-effect relationships to explain historical events. Ibn Khaldun believed that history was a process in which human affairs were shaped by geography, climate, and economics, as well as by moral and spiritual forces. His work later influenced European historical writing.

SECTION 3 REVIEW

Recall

1. **Define** *madrasa*, bazaar, calligraphy, arabesque, chronicle.
2. **Identify** Ma'mun, House of Wisdom, al-Razi, Ibn Sina, Omar Khayyám, Moses Maimonides, Ibn Khaldun.
3. **Locate** on the map on page 284 the major trade routes used by Muslim merchants. What features gave the Islamic state its multicultural character?

Critical Thinking

4. **Evaluating Information** Were Islamic theologians justified in their fear that people might worship paintings or sculptures of people or animals? Explain your answer.

Understanding Themes

5. **Cultural Diffusion** What examples of cultural diffusion in the Islamic state can you find in these areas: (a) art, (b) mathematics, (c) commerce, and (d) literature?

SECTION 3 REVIEW ANSWERS

1. All vocabulary words are defined in the Glossary.
2. Ma'mun, 285; House of Wisdom, 285; al-Razi, 285; Ibn Sina, 285; Omar Khayyám, 287; Moses Maimonides, 287; Ibn Khaldun, 288
3. to India in east, to Spain in west; trade and conquest fostered multiculturalism
4. Answers may refer to pre-Islamic idol worship or to Christian reverence for icons.
5. CULTURAL DIFFUSION Answers may include (a) calligraphy; (b) algebra; (c) bazaars; (d) fables, legends.

Social Studies

SKILLS

Interpreting Demographic Data

Demographic data are statistics about a population, or group of people. Demographic data can tell us a great deal about where and how people live.

Learning the Skill

Demographers measure populations in different ways. Sometimes they simply count the number of people living in a country or region. By comparing these numbers, we can determine which countries have more people than others.

Suppose, however, that country A and country B each has five million people, but country A has five times more land area than country B. Country B would be more crowded, or more densely populated, than country A. Population density measures the number of people living within a certain area. Demographers also measure the population distribution, or the pattern of settlement within a country. For example, in Egypt most people live in the fertile Nile River valley and few people live in the desert.

Demographic data also describe population growth. Zero population growth occurs when births equal deaths. If births exceed deaths, the population is growing; if deaths exceed births, the population is shrinking. Population growth is expressed as a percentage rate. Demographers use growth rates to predict the future size of a population. A population pyramid is a graph showing the age distribution of a population. If the pyramid is wider at the bottom than at the top, the population is growing. If a pyramid is smaller at the bottom, the population is shrinking.

Practicing the Skill

The graphs on this page show demographic data for seven countries in the modern Islamic world. Use the graphs to answer these questions.

1. What kind of demographic data appears in each graph?
2. Which three countries have the largest total populations?
3. Which three countries are growing fastest?
4. How is population size related to growth rates in the graphs of these countries?

Applying the Skill

At the library, find demographic data about your city or county and illustrate it in a table, graph, or map. You could show population increase or decrease, population distribution, population growth rates, or age distribution. Write a short paragraph interpreting your data.

For More Practice

Turn to the Skill Practice in the Chapter Review on page 291 for more practice in interpreting demographic data.

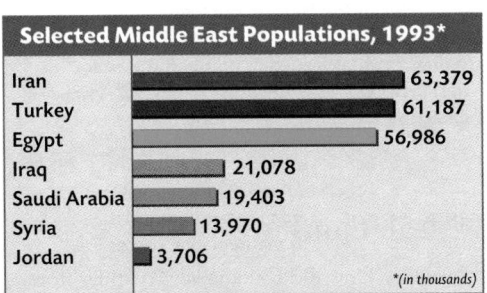

Selected Middle East Populations, 1993*

Country	Population
Iran	63,379
Turkey	61,187
Egypt	56,986
Iraq	21,078
Saudi Arabia	19,403
Syria	13,970
Jordan	3,706

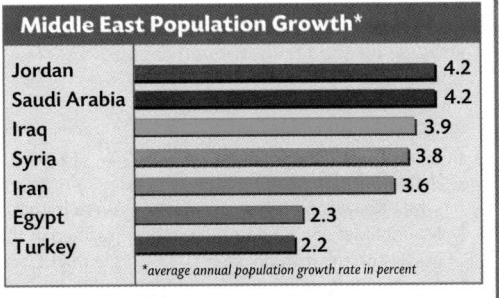

*(in thousands)

Middle East Population Growth*

Country	Growth
Jordan	4.2
Saudi Arabia	4.2
Iraq	3.9
Syria	3.8
Iran	3.6
Egypt	2.3
Turkey	2.2

*average annual population growth rate in percent

Critical Thinking

SKILLS

TEACH

Interpreting Demographic Data

Before the class reads the skill, ask students if they know the meaning of the word *demography*. *(the science of the statistics of populations)* Ask them what other words they can think of that share one of the two roots of the word *demography*. *(for example,* democracy, geography, biography*)* Then ask them what conclusions they might reach from the following information:

1. The number of students entering twelfth grade in the imaginary country of Utopia has been on the decline since 1990.
2. The number of students entering kindergarten in Utopia has been on the rise since 1995. *(They will probably conclude that after a decline in the birthrate for a number of years, Utopia is witnessing a rise in the birthrate.)* Now have students read the skill and complete the practice questions.

Additional Practice

Skill Reinforcement Activity 11

Building Skills in Geography Workbook, Unit 2, Lesson 4

ANSWERS TO PRACTICING THE SKILL

1. The graph on the left presents a simple count of the number of people in each country. The graph on the right compares the rate of population growth in the same countries.
2. Iran, Turkey, Egypt
3. Jordan, Saudi Arabia, Iraq
4. The four countries with the smallest populations are experiencing the highest rates of growth. The three countries with the largest populations are experiencing a lesser percentage rate of growth.

Chapter 11 Review

GLENCOE TECHNOLOGY

VIDEODISC

Use MindJogger to review students' knowledge of the chapter.

MindJogger Videoquiz

Chapter 11
Disc 2 Side A

Also available in VHS.

CHAPTER 11 REVIEW

Historical Significance

From Muhammad's revelations in the A.D. 600s grew the religion of Islam, which now includes more than a billion worshipers and ranks as one of the world's leading faiths. Today, Muslims predominate in the Middle East, North Africa, and parts of sub-Saharan Africa and Southeast Asia. Other areas of the world have significant numbers of Muslims.

During the Islamic Empire, Muslims preserved much ancient knowledge and made advances in the arts and sciences. Their achievements have enriched the cultures of the world.

Using Key Terms

Write the key term that completes each sentence.

a. arabesques
b. caliph
c. chronicle
d. hajj
e. imam
f. jihad
g. *madrasa*
h. bazaars
i. revelations
j. calligraphy
k. *shari'ah*
l. sheikh
m. mosque

1. Islamic scholars and theologians organized Islamic moral rules into the ________, or code of law.
2. Each Arab tribe was led by a ______, or chief, appointed by the heads of tribal families.
3. Islamic tradition holds that, in A.D. 610, Muhammad experienced the first of his ________.
4. At noon on Fridays, many Muslims pray together in a __________ .
5. Islamic artists used the beautiful script of Arabic in ____________ , or the art of elegant handwriting.
6. The fifth pillar of Islam is the annual pilgrimage, or __________, to Makkah.
7. After Muhammad's death in A.D. 632, a group of prominent Muslims chose a _______ to head the Muslim community.
8. Muslims believed they had a religious duty to struggle for their faith through conquests known as ______.
9. Products obtained from trade in the Islamic world were often sold in city _________, or marketplaces that consisted of mazes of shops and stalls.
10. Islamic geometric designs entwined with plant stems, leaves, flowers, and stars that decorate walls, books, and various objects are known as ________.

Using Your History Journal

Calligraphy, an elegant form of handwriting, is still used as an art form. Look at samples of calligraphy in an encyclopedia. Then, in calligraphy, reproduce the beginning page of your short report on Muslim life.

Reviewing Facts

1. **Identify** the changes that took place in the Arabian Peninsula during the A.D. 600s.
2. **Explain** how the Madinah Compact formed the basis for the Islamic state.
3. **Outline** the events that led to the schism between Muslims.
4. **Explain** why some Muslims revolted against the Umayyads.
5. **Describe** the status of women in the Islamic Empire.
6. **List** some achievements of the Islamic Empire in science and the arts.
7. **Describe** the career of Moses Maimonides. In what ways did he reflect the multicultural character of the Islamic Empire?
8. **Name** the author and work in which a person would find tales such as "Sinbad the Sailor" and "Ali Baba and the Forty Thieves."
9. **Describe** the change in writing history that was introduced by Ibn Khaldun.

Critical Thinking

1. **Contrast** How did bedouin society differ from the society that formed under Islam?

Answers

Using Key Terms

1. k	6. d
2. l	7. b
3. i	8. f
4. m	9. h
5. j	10. a

Using Your History Journal

Encourage students to use one kind of calligraphy for the text and another as a border around the text, just as Kufic script was often used as a decorative element around other scripts that superseded it.

Reviewing Facts

1. growth of towns and trade; new religious ideas
2. called for loyalty to Islamic state rather than to tribe
3. murders of Ali and Husayn
4. Umayyad discrimination against non-Arab Muslims
5. women's social position defined by their relationship to men; women did exert control over their property; expected to stay at home, do household tasks; girls married young
6. Answers may include advances in astronomy, geography, medicine, chemistry, math, literature, decorative arts, architecture.
7. outstanding Jewish legal scholar and philosopher, physician to Egyptian ruler; born in Spain but later lived in Morocco and Egypt; a Jewish leader yet involved in the Muslim community
8. *The Arabian Nights*; originated in many lands by many authors
9. first to examine scientifically the effects of geography, climate, and economics on history

Critical Thinking

1. bedouins: polytheistic, tribal loyalty paramount; Muslims: monotheistic, loyalty to God and Islamic state
2. Possible answer: A successor appointed by Muhammad would not have encountered opposition, at least initially.
3. Possible answer: to prevent revelations from being lost or corrupted; to unify Islamic scripture.

2. **Apply** Would there have been a struggle for the caliphate if Muhammad had named a successor before his death?
3. **Analyze** Why do you think Abu Bakr wanted to compile Muhammad's revelations into one written collection?
4. **Synthesize** If the hajj was not among the Five Pillars of Islam, how might its omission have affected the Islamic state?
5. **Evaluate** How did Muslim scholars contribute to the world's knowledge?
6. **Contrast** How did the Islamic Empire under the Abbasids differ from the early Islamic community under Muhammad?

Geography in History

1. **Movement** Refer to the map below. Identify how far the Abbasid Empire had spread by A.D. 800 by naming the areas that it encompassed.
2. **Place** What was the capital city of the Abbasid Empire, and where was it located?
3. **Location** How did the city of Baghdad fortify itself against invasion?

Abbasid Empire A.D. 800

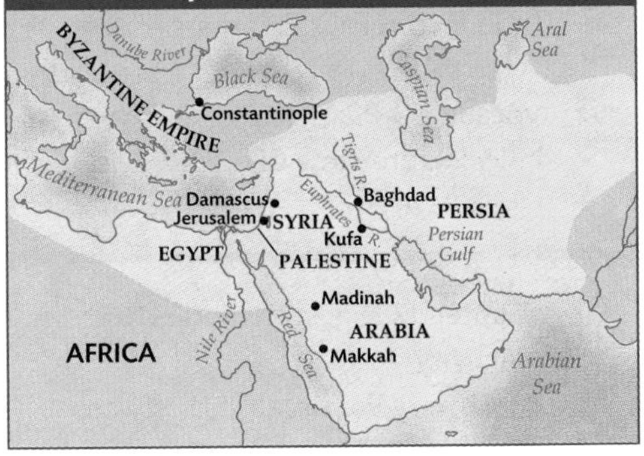

Understanding Themes

1. **Innovation** Why was Islam an innovation in the way the people of the Arabian Peninsula worshiped?
2. **Movement** How was the Umayyads' decision to move the nation's capital from Madinah to Damascus a result of Islamic expansion?
3. **Diversity** How did the failure of the Umayyad government to embrace non-Arab Muslims destroy Umayyad rule?

Linking Past and Present

1. What evidence can you find in today's world of the split between Sunnis and Shiites?
2. How have students today benefited from the work done at the House of Wisdom?
3. What words in the English language have their origins in the Arabic language?

Skill Practice

Study the population pyramid below and then answer these questions.

1. What is the general shape of the graph?
2. What percentage of the female population is between 0 and 19 years old?
3. Are there equal numbers of males and females in this population? How can you tell?
4. What conclusion can you draw about the growth rate in this population? On what data do you base this conclusion?

Age Distribution in Jordan

Age	% of Pop'n	Male	Female	% of Pop'n	Age
70+	0.8%			0.8%	70+
60-69	1.2%			1.1%	60-69
50-59	2.4%			2.2%	50-59
40-49	3.8%			3.4%	40-49
30-39	4.5%			4.2%	30-39
20-29	8.1%			7.3%	20-29
10-19	13.9%			12.4%	10-19
0-9	17.6%			16.3%	0-9
		640 320 0	320 640		

Total Population: 3,413,000
Total Male Population: 1,785,000
Total Female Population: 1,628,000
Life Expectancy (Male): 70 years
Life Expectancy (Female): 73 years

Source: Broderbund Software, Inc.

Chapter 11 Review

Understanding Themes

1. **INNOVATION** Arabs had been polytheistic.
2. **MOVEMENT** As the Islamic state expanded, its central location changed.
3. **DIVERSITY** Dissatisfaction among non-Arab Muslims was particularly strong in Iraq and Persia, the center of Shiite opposition to Umayyad rule.

Linking Past and Present

1. Students may point to Iran's Shiite fundamentalists.
2. Answers may mention algebra and lab equipment.
3. Answers may include *bazaar* and *algebra*.

Skill Practice

1. bottom-heavy pyramid
2. 28.7 percent
3. No, the male bars of the pyramid are longer—signifying more males in the population.
4. The population growth rate is high; the population pyramid is much wider at the bottom than at the top.

Chapter Bonus Test Question

Ask students: What role may Muhammad's personal life have played in making the Muslim attitude toward merchants different from that of the ancient Chinese? *(Answers will vary but may include: Since Muhammad was a successful merchant himself, Muslims respected merchants, while the ancient Chinese held them in contempt.)*

4. would have deprived state of the unifying effect of hajj and of the economic and cultural benefits travelers making the hajj provided
5. Translations into Arabic of Greek and Indian works transmitted previous knowledge; Muslim achievements in arts and sciences; House of Wisdom brought scholars together.
6. Early Islamic state made up mostly of Arabs; under Abbasids, population was larger and very diverse, and people had more leisure for cultural pursuits.

Geography in History

1. Egypt, Arabia, Palestine, Syria, Persia
2. Baghdad, Iraq
3. surrounded city with walls

Teach, Reinforce, and Extend CHAPTER Content

The Rise of Medieval Europe

CHAPTER RESOURCES

	Reproducible Resources	Multimedia Resources
Chapter Opener	Chapter Themes: Graphic Organizer 12 Historical Significance Chapter Activity 12	MindJogger Videoquiz
Chapter Enrichment	Vocabulary Activity 12* Time Line Activity 12 Mapping History Activity 12 History Simulation 12 Geography and History Activity 12 Source Reading 12 People in World History Profiles 21, 22 World Art and Music Activity 12 Enrichment Activity 12 Critical Thinking Activity 12 Performance Assessment Activity 12	Focus on World Art Print 14, French. *William Exhorts His Troops,* from the Bayeux Tapestry NGS Poster Set: *The Middle Ages* World History and Art Transparency 15, *Cover of the Lindau Gospels* Mapping History Overlay Transparency 9 Chapter Transparency 12 NGS PicturePack Transparency Set: *The Middle Ages* Vocabulary PuzzleMaker Software NGS PictureShow CD-ROM: *The Middle Ages*
Chapter Review/Reteaching	Reteaching Activity 12 Skill Reinforcement Activity 12 Spanish Chapter Summary 12	Chapter 12 Digest Audiocassette, Activity, Test* Vocabulary PuzzleMaker Software Student Self-Test and Review Software MindJogger Videoquiz
Chapter Evaluation/Testing	Performance Assessment Activity 12 Chapter 12 Test, Forms A and B	Testmaker

* *Also available in Spanish*

0:00 **OUT OF TIME?** Assign the Chapter 12 summary in the Unit 3 Digest on pages 394–397, and the Chapter 12 Audiocassettes.

Block Schedule

Block scheduling differs from traditional class scheduling in the amount of time allotted to each period. The extended time frame provided by block scheduling affords you the opportunity to implement a greater number of research-oriented and activity-intense projects to motivate and involve your students. Activities that are particularly suited to use within the block scheduling framework are identified throughout this chapter by the following designation.

KEY TO ABILITY LEVELS

Teaching strategies have been coded for varying learning styles and abilities.

- L1 **BASIC** activities for all students
- L2 **AVERAGE** activities for average to above-average students
- L3 **CHALLENGING** activities for above-average students
- LEP **LIMITED ENGLISH PROFICIENCY** activities

A complete, 1-page lesson plan is provided for each section in the *Reproducible Lesson Plans* booklet.

SECTION RESOURCES

Daily Objectives	Reproducible Resources	Multimedia Resources
Section 1 Frankish Rulers Explain what made Frankish rulers, such as Charlemagne, exceptional rulers for their time.	Reproducible Lesson Plan 12-1 Vocabulary Activity 12* Guided Reading Activity 12-1* Time Line Activity 12 Section Quiz 12-1*	Section Focus Transparency 12-1 Chapter Transparency 12 Student Self-Test and Review Software Testmaker
Section 2 Medieval Life Describe how loyalties were maintained in a divided and often violent Europe.	Reproducible Lesson Plan 12-2 Guided Reading Activity 12-2* Source Reading 12 History Simulation 12 Section Quiz 12-2*	NGS Poster Set: *The Middle Ages* Section Focus Transparency 12-2 Vocabulary PuzzleMaker Software Student Self-Test and Review Software Testmaker NGS PictureShow CD-ROM: *The Middle Ages*
Section 3 The Medieval Church Summarize the role of the Catholic Church in shaping the development of medieval Europe.	Reproducible Lesson Plan 12-3 Guided Reading Activity 12-3* People in World History Profiles 21, 22 World Art and Music Activity 12 Section Quiz 12-3*	Section Focus Transparency 12-3 World History and Art Transparency 15, *Cover of the Lindau Gospels* NGS PicturePack Transparency Set: *The Middle Ages* Vocabulary PuzzleMaker Software Student Self-Test and Review Software Testmaker NGS PictureShow CD-ROM: *The Middle Ages*
Section 4 Rise of European Monarchy Name the achievements of medieval European monarchs.	Reproducible Lesson Plan 12-4 Vocabulary Activity 12* Guided Reading Activity 12-4* Time Line Activity 12 Mapping History Activity 12 Geography and History Activity 12 Reteaching Activity 12 Enrichment Activity 12 Section Quiz 12-4* Performance Assessment Activity 12 Spanish Chapter Summary 12	Focus on World Art Print 14, French. *William Exhorts His Troops,* from the Bayeux Tapestry Section Focus Transparency 12-4 Mapping History Overlay Transparency 9, *Europe in A.D. 1160* Student Self-Test and Review Software Testmaker

** Also available in Spanish*

Chapter Activities

Performance Assessment Activity

Writing a Historical Fiction Narrative Have students take the role of authors to develop a historical fiction story set in medieval Europe. Students should combine accounts of actual leaders and situations with those of fictitious characters. You may wish to have on hand a dictionary of old English terms from which students can draw words to make their narratives more authentic. Have students share their narratives with the class.

Possible Rubric Features
Accuracy and extent of content information, concept attainment, elaboration and detail, clarity and organization

• *For an additional activity, refer to Activity 12 in the* Performance Assessment Strategies and Activities *booklet.*

ACTIVITY
From the Classroom of...

Amy Chevalier
Sun Prairie High School
Sun Prairie, WI

Be a Medieval
Have students identify with an individual from medieval Europe by assuming a role and communicating a message to another party.

Have students choose the character whose identity they will assume, the type of communication they wish to use, their audience, and the subject matter of the message they will convey. They may choose from the following list, or use ideas of their own.

Characters: a ruler (Clovis, Pepin, Charlemagne), a noble (a mayor of the palace, a knight, a lord or a lady), a member of the clergy (Pope Gregory, an abbot, monk, cardinal, or friar), a Viking, a serf
Communication: letter, poem, speech, decree, sermon, editorial, song
Audience: a family member (for example, a cousin in Constantinople), a church congregation, peasants on the manor, the king, the pope
Subject of Message: Viking raids, feudal battles, living conditions on the manor, change in taxation, new laws for the manor, heresy in the Church, life in the castle

Students may also choose to authenticate their document when they present it. For example, they may choose to write it in an old-style script.

MULTIPLE LEARNING STYLES

Verbal/Linguistic
As students study the people of the Middle Ages, read portraits from Chaucer's Prologue to *The Canterbury Tales* aloud to them. Discuss the details provided by Chaucer on the following characters in relation to information provided in the text: the Knight, the Wife of Bath, the Squire, the Monk, the Friar, the Parson, and the Prioress.

Visual/Spatial
Have the class work together to create a mural in the fashion of the Bayeux Tapestry. Have them include portraits of people from the chapter, including details of their dress and objects that symbolize their station in life. For instance, students might depict a knight in full armor with a shield showing his coat of arms.

Kinesthetic
Have students research a key medieval ceremony, such as homage or the admission of a squire to knighthood. Then have them stage a reenactment, with a narrator explaining the steps in the ceremony.

Interpersonal
Have students work in groups to create advertisements for some of the many technological improvements that date from the Middle Ages. Have one or two students in each group research, one student draw or create other visuals, and another student write the text for the ad. Students should work together to divide and coordinate the various tasks. Some possible subjects for the ads are trousers, barrels, skis, the horse collar, horseshoes, and the water mill. Display the ads in the classroom as you cover Chapter 12.

Additional Resources

TEACHER'S CORNER

NATIONAL GEOGRAPHIC SOCIETY

INDEX TO NATIONAL GEOGRAPHIC MAGAZINE

The following articles may be used for research relating to this chapter:

- "The Hanseatic League: Europe's First Common Market," by Edward Von Der Porten, October 1994.

NATIONAL GEOGRAPHIC SOCIETY PRODUCTS AVAILABLE FROM GLENCOE

To order the following products for use with this chapter, contact your local Glencoe sales representative or call Glencoe at 1-800-368-7344:

NGS PICTURESHOW CD-ROM
- The Middle Ages

NGS PICTUREPACK TRANSPARENCY SET
- The Middle Ages

NGS POSTER SET
- The Middle Ages

Bibliography

Literature of the Period

Sayers, Dorothy, trans. *The Song of Roland.* New York: Penguin, 1957. Chronicles the events and legends of Charlemagne's life and that of his young nephew Roland.

Readings for the Student

Guerber, H. A., ed. *Middle Ages.* New York: Avenel Books, 1985. From the Myths and Legends Series, covers Beowulf, Charlemagne, Arthur and his knights, and other tales of the Middle Ages.

Readings for the Teacher

Ehrenreich, Barbara, and Deirdre English. *Witches, Midwives, and Nurses: A History of Women Healers.* New York: Feminist Press, 1972. Covers the roles of women in medicine during the Middle Ages.

Power, Eileen. *Medieval People.* New York: Barnes and Noble, 1963. Includes detailed portraits of medieval people from different social classes, including peasants, merchants, and clergy.

interNET CONNECTIONS
The Magna Carta View an excerpt, the whole manuscript, or the English translation.
World Wide Web:
http://www.bl.uk/access/treasures/magna-carta.html

Introducing Chapter 12

CHAPTER THEMES

Chapter Themes are listed by section on this chapter opening page of the Student Edition. A corresponding theme-based activity is available under "TEACH," and a theme-based question is asked in the Section and Chapter Reviews.

The Storyteller

Historical Setting Training for knighthood began early for boys of noble birth. When a boy reached the age of 7, he was usually sent away to the home of a nobleman or knight. There he served the lord of the manor and received formal training to become a squire and then a knight—learning to ride and manage a horse, to wield a heavy sword, to hurl a lance, to shoot a bow, and to clean and care for his armor.

Historical Significance

Answers: *A new European civilization took shape with the interaction of the deep and widespread influence of Roman Catholicism, the learning of classical times, and the political innovations of Frankish rulers.*

The civilization developed through a number of institutions, including feudalism, manorialism, and monasticism. Modern European countries such as France and England had their beginnings in the Middle Ages.

Chapter 12

A.D. 500–1300

The Rise of Medieval Europe

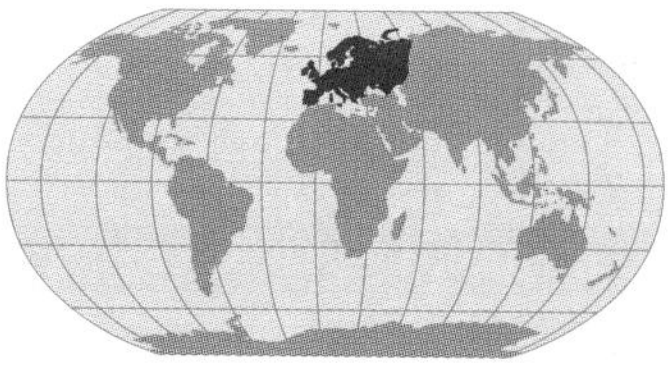

Chapter Themes

- **Movement** Invasions by Vikings, Magyars, and Muslims influence medieval Europe. *Section 1*
- **Cooperation** Nobles, church officials, and peasants develop ties of loyalty and service to one another. *Section 2*
- **Uniformity** The Catholic Church affects every aspect of medieval life. *Section 3*
- **Conflict** European kings, feudal lords, and popes struggle for political dominance. *Section 4*

The Storyteller

It was tournament day. As trumpets flourished, the marshal shouted, "In the name of God and St. Michael, do your battle!" Knights on horseback thundered toward each other and met with a deafening clash. Lords and ladies cheered as their favorite unhorsed his opponents. The victor was awarded a prize from the lady whose colors he wore.

Such tournaments provided more than just entertainment. They also trained soldiers for combat. After the fall of Rome, wars were frequent. A professional warrior class—the knights—led the new, vigorous, competitive society that would reshape western Europe.

Historical Significance

How did Christianity, the classical heritage, and Germanic practices combine to form a new European civilization? How did this civilization develop and lay the foundation for modern European life?

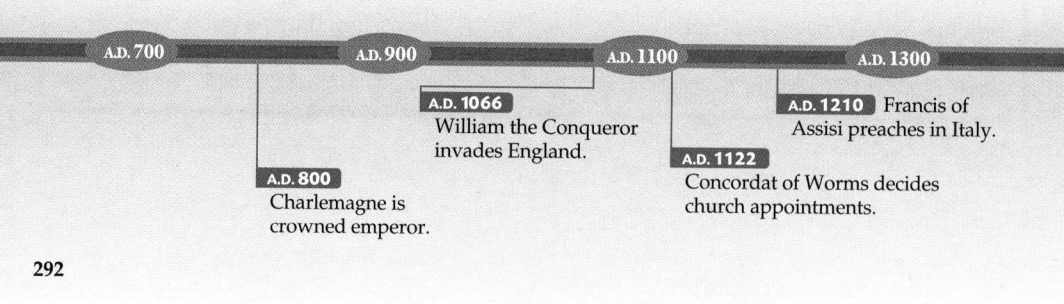

A.D. 700 — A.D. 900 — A.D. 1100 — A.D. 1300

- **A.D. 800** Charlemagne is crowned emperor.
- **A.D. 1066** William the Conqueror invades England.
- **A.D. 1122** Concordat of Worms decides church appointments.
- **A.D. 1210** Francis of Assisi preaches in Italy.

GEOGRAPHY CONNECTION

GEOGRAPHIC THEMES

Movement Have students consult the map on page 297. Make sure that they understand the use of different colors to indicate movement by Vikings, Magyars, and Muslims. What region was the original home of the Vikings? *(Scandinavia)* On which continent did the Magyars originate? *(Asia)* In which direction did the Muslims travel to reach Europe? *(north)* What physical obstacles did the invaders have to overcome? *(mountains, seas)*

History & Art *The Effect of Good Government on a City* by Ambrogio Lorenzetti. Palazzo Pubblico, Siena, Italy

Your History Journal

Medieval life was governed by many mutual obligations. Build a diagram that shows the relationships among lords and ladies, knights, and vassals.

EXTRA CREDIT PROJECT

Music Among the best-loved figures of the Middle Ages were the poet-musicians known variously as minstrels, troubadours, minnesingers, skalds, or bards. Have students research the lives of these men, paying special attention to their role in society and the tales they sang or told. Students should write summaries of their research, then present them to the class. If possible, have them obtain and play recordings of music typical of the period. Then have students write their own lyrics to music composed in the medieval style. The songs may be presented live in class or audiotaped.

Introducing Chapter 12

History & Art Siena was one of a number of Italian city-states that became centers of art and trade during the Middle Ages. Siena is especially famous for its medieval painters, of whom Lorenzetti was one.

Performance Assessment

Refer to the activity on page 292C of the Planning Guide.

For an additional activity, refer to Activity 12 in the *Performance Assessment Strategies and Activities* booklet.

Using Your History Journal

Given the complexity of medieval relationships, this diagram might be easiest to construct if the student concentrated on one (imagined) noble family and its manor.

GLENCOE TECHNOLOGY

VIDEODISC
Use MindJogger to preview chapter content.

MindJogger Videoquiz
Chapter 12
Disc 2 Side A

Also available in VHS.

Chapter 12
Section 1

SECTION THEME

▶ **Movement** Invasions by Vikings, Magyars, and Muslims influence medieval Europe.

Find Out

Answer: *They tried to maintain a large territory as a stable, united domain.*

FOCUS

Section Objective

Explain what made Frankish rulers, such as Charlemagne, exceptional rulers for their time.

BELLRINGER
Motivational Activity

Before taking roll at the beginning of the class period, project Section Focus Transparency 12-1 and have students answer the activity questions. Discuss students' responses.

This activity is also available as a blackline master.

Vocabulary Pre-check

Use Vocabulary Activity 12 to introduce vocabulary terms. **L1 LEP**

A.D. 400 | A.D. 600 | A.D. 800 | A.D. 1000

A.D. 496 Frankish King Clovis accepts Catholicism.

A.D. 768 Charlemagne becomes Frankish king.

A.D. 843 Treaty of Verdun divides Carolingian lands.

c. A.D. 850 Vikings begin explorations.

Section 1

Frankish Rulers

Setting the Scene

▶ **Terms to Define**
mayor of the palace, count

▶ **People to Meet**
Clovis, Charles Martel, Pepin the Short, Charlemagne, the Vikings

▶ **Places to Locate**
Frankish Empire, Scandinavia

Find Out What made Frankish rulers, such as Charlemagne, exceptional rulers for their time?

The Storyteller

The men of medieval times, including Charlemagne, loved hunting. It was a cruel sport, but at least it provided meat for the royal tables. When Charlemagne sat down to dinner, the main course was usually a roast of game from the morning hunt. During the meal, one of the poets of the royal court might rise to read aloud a poem—to the dismay of the king's soldiers, who sometimes clapped their hands over their ears and glared at the poet until Charlemagne scolded them. With dinner, the king enjoyed "the wine of learning."

—freely adapted from *Charlemagne*, Richard Winston, 1968

Charlemagne

By A.D. 500, Germanic invasions had all but destroyed the urban world of the Roman Empire. Trade declined. Cities, bridges, and roads fell into disrepair and disuse. Law and order vanished, and education almost disappeared. Money was no longer used. For most people, life did not extend beyond the tiny villages where they were born, lived, and died.

Western Europe was so backward because of this decline that the early part of this period was once called "the Dark Ages." Scholars later combined the Latin terms *medium* (middle) and *aevum* (age) to form the term *medieval*, recognizing that this period was an era of transition between ancient and modern times. Out of this violent medieval period, or Middle Ages, a dynamic civilization arose. It combined elements of classical and Germanic cultures with Christian beliefs.

Merovingian Rulers

During the A.D. 400s the Franks, who settled in what is now France and western Germany, emerged as the strongest Germanic group. Their early rulers, known as Merovingian (MEHR•uh•VIHN•jee•uhn) kings for the ruler Merowig, held power until the early A.D. 700s.

Clovis

In A.D. 481 a brutal and wily warrior named **Clovis** became king of the Franks. Fifteen years later, Clovis became the first Germanic ruler to accept Catholicism. Clovis's military victories and his religious conversion gave his throne stability.

A century later the Frankish kingdom began to decline. Frankish kings had followed the custom of dividing the kingdom among their heirs. Heirs became rivals and fought each other for land. By A.D. 700 political power had passed from kings to government officials known as **mayors of the palace**

SECTION RESOURCES

Reproducible Masters
- Reproducible Lesson Plan 12-1
- Vocabulary Activity 12
- Guided Reading Activity 12-1
- Time Line Activity 12
- Section Quiz 12-1

Transparencies
- Section Focus Transparency 12-1
- Chapter Transparency 12

Multimedia
- Student Self-Test and Review Software
- Testmaker

Charles Martel

In A.D. 714 **Charles Martel**, or "Charles the Hammer," became mayor of the palace. When Muslim forces threatened Europe in A.D. 732, Charles led the successful defense of Tours, in France. This victory won him great prestige. As you read in Chapter 11, the victory ensured that Christianity would remain the dominant religion of Europe.

Pepin the Short

In A.D. 752, with the backing of nobles and church officials, **Pepin the Short**, the son of Charles Martel, became king of the Franks. The pope anointed, or put holy oil on, Pepin, making him a divinely chosen ruler in the eyes of the people.

In return for the Church's blessing, Pepin was expected to help the pope against his enemies. In A.D. 754 Pepin forced the Lombards, a Germanic people, to withdraw from Rome. He then gave the pope a large strip of Lombard land in central Italy. In appreciation, the pope cut his political ties to the Byzantine Empire and looked to the Franks as his protector. As a result, the fortunes of western Europe and Catholicism were bound more closely together.

Visualizing History Shown here, a decorated Merovingian buckle. Gregory, bishop of Tours, wrote the best source of the history of the Merovingian kings. *Why did the political power of these kings fade?*

Charlemagne's Empire

In A.D. 771 Pepin's son, **Charlemagne**, became the Frankish king. Charlemagne, or Charles the Great, was one of Europe's great monarchs. In Latin his name is written *Carolus Magnus*, which gave the name Carolingian to his dynasty. The king cut an imposing figure. His biographer, a monk named Einhard, described him this way:

> "Charles was large and strong, and of lofty stature, though not disproportionally tall ... nose a little long, hair fair, and face laughing and merry.... He used to wear the national, that is to say, the Frankish, dress—next his skin a linen shirt and linen breeches, and above these a tunic fringed with silk; white hose fastened by bands covered his lower limbs and shoes his feet, and he protected his shoulders and chest in winter by a close-fitting coat of otter or marten skins. Over all he flung a blue cloak, and he always had a sword girt about him."

Charlemagne nearly doubled the borders of his kingdom to include Germany, France, northern Spain, and most of Italy. His enlarged domain became known as the **Frankish Empire**. For the first time since the fall of Rome, most western Europeans were ruled by one government.

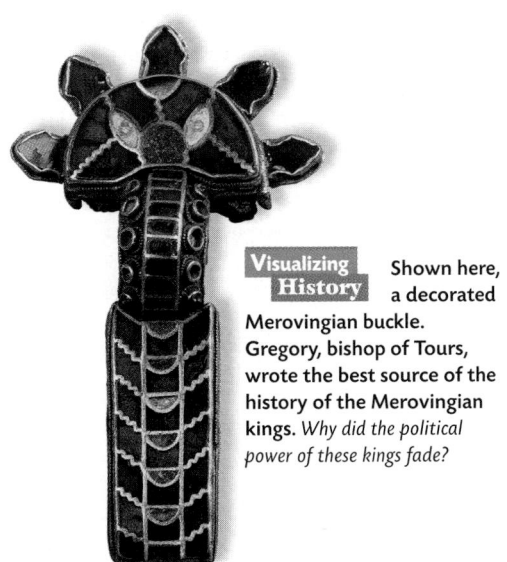

Because few western Europeans could read and write, Charlemagne encouraged the formation of schools in churches and monasteries. He gathered scholars from all over Europe to teach in his palace school. These scholars helped preserve classical learning by making accurate Latin copies of ancient religious manuscripts and Roman classics. When knowledge spread from Charlemagne's court to other areas of Europe, western Europeans became united by a common set of ideas.

A Christian Realm

One of the ideas that united western Europeans was the creation of a Christian Roman Empire. Church leaders believed that Charlemagne could turn this idea into reality. In A.D. 800 Charlemagne came to Rome to militarily defend Pope Leo III against the Roman nobles. To show his gratitude, Leo crowned Charlemagne the new Roman emperor. As protector of the Church and ruler of much of western Europe, Charlemagne wanted the title, but he had misgivings about receiving it from the pope. By crowning a monarch, the pope seemed to be saying that church officials were superior to rulers.

In spite of his concern, Charlemagne accepted his duties as emperor and worked to strengthen the empire. Because the central bureaucracy was small, he relied on local officials called **counts** to assist him. Each count was carefully instructed in the duties of office. The counts solved local problems, stopped feuds, protected the weak, and raised

Chapter 12
Section 1

TEACH

Guided Practice

THEME **Movement**

Ask students to list other movements of peoples they have already studied. *(Answers will vary but might include those of the Dorians into Greece, the Aryans into the Indus Valley, and the Germanic tribes into the Roman Empire.)* Then have them discuss some important population movements of the present day. *(Possibilities include: famine victims or war refugees in Africa, war refugees in the former Yugoslav republics, immigration to the United States.)* **L1 LEP**

Visualizing History The history written by Gregory of Tours, who lived in the A.D. 500s, included ancient chronicles, legends, and his own eyewitness observations. **Answer to Caption:** *because the Frankish kingdom was divided among rivals, and because of outside invasions*

Government Have students make a list on the chalkboard of Charlemagne's major personality traits, as described in the text. Then have them compare these with traits desirable in present-day politicians. What similarities and differences do they see? **L2**

Chapter Transparency 12

COOPERATIVE LEARNING ACTIVITY

Role Play Have the class create a historical account of a medieval village under Viking attack. Some students should take on the roles of Vikings, keeping a record of their voyage, their intentions, and their strategies for attack. Other students may assume the roles of clergy members, keeping the village's official records. Still others may represent the villagers, recording the raid with drawings of the encounter. Encourage students to research and to include vivid details in their projects. Conclude the activity with a class presentation. **L1 LEP**

Chapter 12 Section 1

Map Study

Answer

France, Belgium, the Netherlands, most of Germany and Austria, northern Italy

Map Skills Practice

Reading a Map How far from north to south did the Frankish Empire stretch at its greatest extent? *(about 1,000 miles [1,600 kilometers])*

Independent Practice

Guided Reading Activity 12-1 **L1**

Time Line Activity 12

Literature Have students read the *Song of Roland* and write a report on the characters of Charlemagne and Roland as presented in the poem. Ask students to comment on the mythical and legendary quality given to historical figures in the poem. **L3**

Who?What?Where?When?

Charlemagne was such an important ruler that legends about him soon spread. According to one legend, he did not die but was only sleeping, and would awake in the hour of his country's need.

Frankish Empire

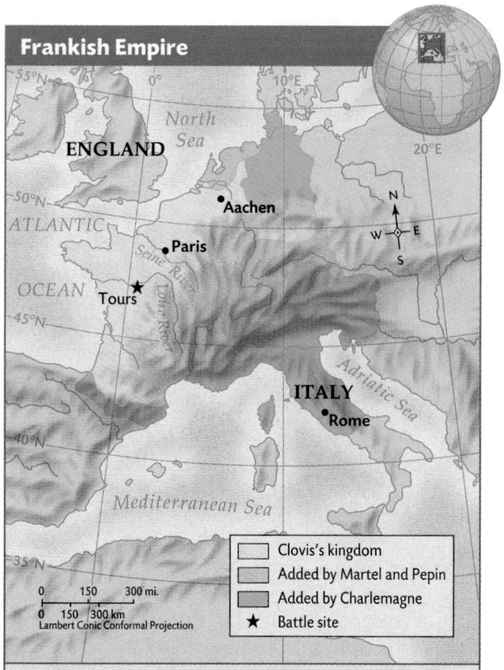

Map Study During the A.D. 400s, the Franks emerged as the strongest of all Germanic peoples.

Location What modern countries did the Franks control?

armies for the emperor. Each year royal messengers, the *missi dominici*, went on inspections in which they informed Charlemagne about the performance of the counts and other local administrators. The emperor also traveled throughout the empire observing the work of his officials firsthand.

Collapse of Charlemagne's Empire

More than anything else, Charlemagne's forceful personality held his empire together. His death in A.D. 814 left a void that his only surviving son, Louis the Pious, could not fill. After Louis's death, Charlemagne's three grandsons fought one another for control of the empire.

In A.D. 843 the three brothers agreed in the Treaty of Verdun to divide the Carolingian lands. Charles the Bald took the western part, which covered most of present-day France. Louis the German acquired the eastern portion, which today is Germany. Lothair, who became the Holy Roman emperor, took a strip of land in the middle of the empire stretching from the North Sea southward to Italy.

Invasions Increase Disunity

While internal feuding weakened the Carolingian kingdoms, outside invasions nearly destroyed them. Muslims from North Africa seized parts of southern Italy and gained control of the western Mediterranean. The Slavs marched out of the east to invade central Europe. From Asia a new group of fierce nomads called Magyars galloped west, leaving a trail of destruction. The most threatening attacks, however, came from **the Vikings**, raiders from **Scandinavia** to the north.

Viking Invasions

In medieval Scandinavian, to go *a-viking* means to fight as a warrior. Viking warriors traveled in long, deckless ships with one sail that were designed to slide swiftly through the water propelled by long oars. These boats were sturdy enough to cross the Atlantic Ocean, shallow enough to navigate Europe's rivers, and light enough to be carried past fortified bridges. The Vikings became known for surprise attacks and speedy retreats. What they could not steal they burned. No place in Europe was safe from attack.

Boasting names like Eric Bloodax and Harald Bluetooth, the Vikings sought riches and adventure. In the A.D. 800s they left their overpopulated homeland, which later became the kingdoms of Norway, Denmark, and Sweden. Viking warriors fought ferociously and showed their victims no mercy.

Viking Trade

The Vikings, however, were more than just raiders. They were also explorers and settlers. Skilled in sailing and trading, they moved along the Atlantic and Mediterranean coasts of Europe. The Norwegians settled the North Atlantic islands of Greenland and Iceland, and even reached North America. The Danes temporarily held England and established the Viking state of Normandy in northwestern France. The Swedes settled in present-day Ukraine and Russia.

Viking Culture

In Scandinavia and their new homelands, the Vikings worshiped many deities. They were proud of their gods and told stories of the gods' great deeds. These stories became written poems called *Eddas*. The Vikings also made up sagas, or long tales. At first, storytellers recited them at special feasts. After A.D. 1100 the Vikings wrote down their sagas. By this time they had converted to Christianity. With their acceptance of the new religion, the Vikings began to write their languages with Roman letters.

ASSESS

Check for Understanding

Assign Section 1 Review as homework or as an in-class activity.

Use Student Self-Test and Review Software to review Section 1.

MEETING SPECIAL NEEDS ACTIVITY

Study Strategy Ask students with strong organizational skills to work in small groups with students who are having difficulty understanding this material. Ask the groups to create descriptive flowcharts that show the movement of power from Clovis to the heirs of Charlemagne. Have students add boxed features that give biographical details, relationships to other rulers, major accomplishments, and important events for each ruler. Then ask the groups to compare their information in a class discussion. **L1 LEP**

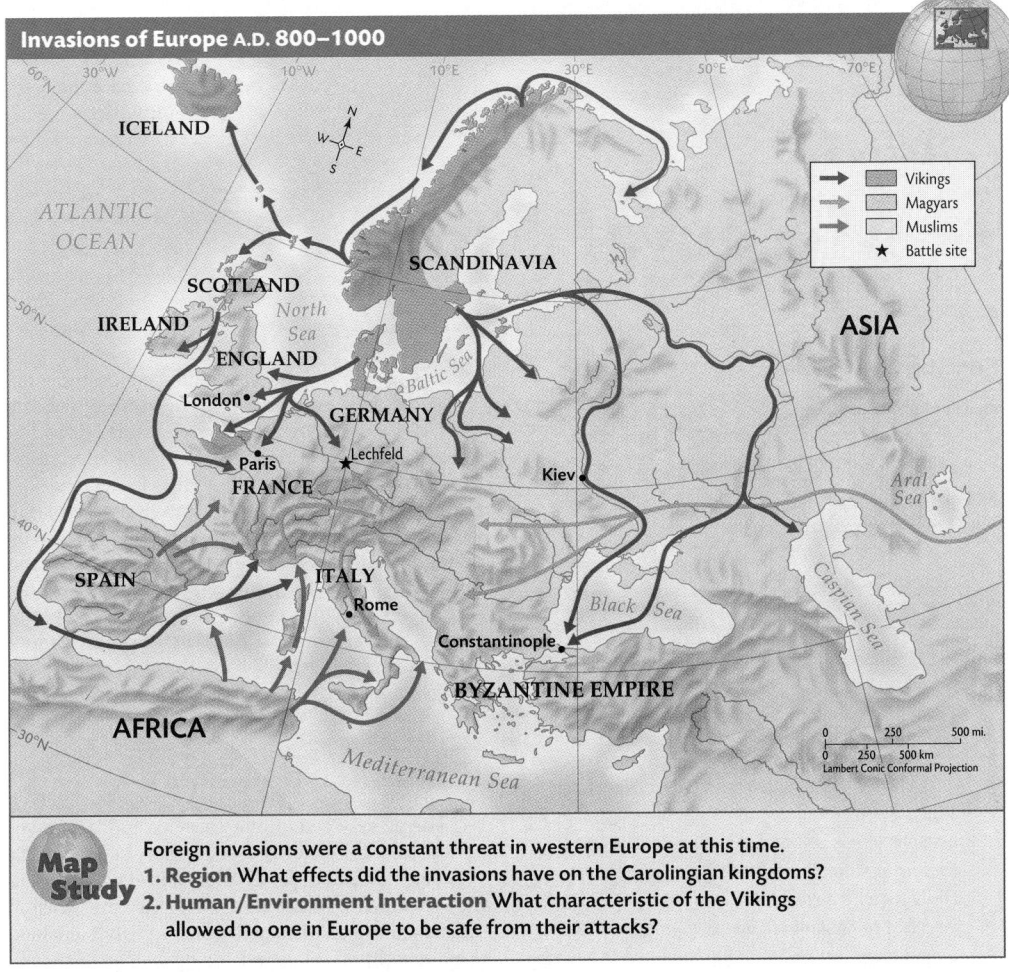

Invasions of Europe A.D. 800–1000

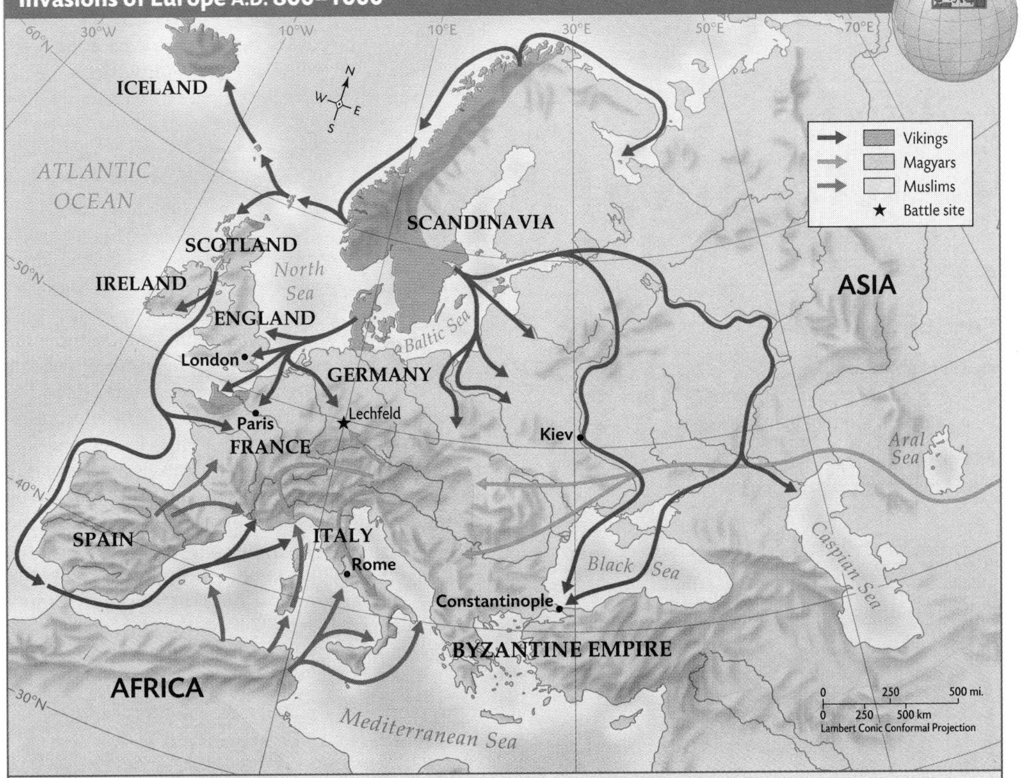

Map Study Foreign invasions were a constant threat in western Europe at this time.
1. **Region** What effects did the invasions have on the Carolingian kingdoms?
2. **Human/Environment Interaction** What characteristic of the Vikings allowed no one in Europe to be safe from their attacks?

A New Europe

The people of western Europe suffered at the hands of Vikings and other invaders. These raids isolated communities and severely weakened the central authority of monarchs. Trade declined, and many areas faced economic collapse. As a result of royal weakness, nobles and local officials took over the local defense. Beginning in the A.D. 900s, a new political and social system brought more stability to western Europe.

SECTION 1 REVIEW

Recall
1. **Define** mayor of the palace, count.
2. **Identify** Clovis, Charles Martel, Pepin the Short, Charlemagne, Treaty of Verdun, the Vikings.
3. **Explain** what problem resulted when Charlemagne was crowned by the pope.

Critical Thinking
4. **Making Comparisons** Contrast Charlemagne with his weak successors. Why do you think Charlemagne was successful in enlarging and maintaining his empire?

Understanding Themes
5. **Movement** Why did the Vikings, the Magyars, and the Slavs leave their homelands and invade western Europe?

Map Study

Answers
1. *They nearly destroyed them.*
2. *They attacked by surprise and retreated swiftly.*

Map Skills Practice

Reading a Map Name five European seas across or to which the Vikings traveled. *(Baltic, North, Mediterranean, Black, and Caspian)*

Evaluate

Section Quiz 12-1

Use the Testmaker to create a customized quiz for Section 1.

Reteach

Ask students to explain how each of the following influenced the early Middle Ages: Germanic invasions, the donation of papal states by Pepin to the pope, Charlemagne's dedication to education, the Viking raids.

Enrich

Have students render a sketch of a Viking ship as it looked when setting out on a raid.

CLOSE

Discuss the term "Middle Ages." What were the Middle Ages in the middle of? *(a dark age and the Renaissance)* Did people living at the time think of the era as the "middle"? *(no)*

SECTION 1 REVIEW ANSWERS

1. All vocabulary words are defined in the Glossary.
2. Clovis, 294; Charles Martel, 295; Pepin the Short, 295; Charlemagne, 295; Treaty of Verdun, 296; the Vikings, 296
3. The crowning could be interpreted to mean that the Church had more power than secular rulers.
4. Charlemagne had a more forceful personality than his successors. His empire owed its success to the emperor's personality, to his wise use of local officials and royal messengers, and to his firsthand contact with all areas of his realm.
5. **MOVEMENT** They were looking for riches, adventure, and land.

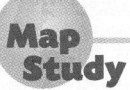

Chapter 12
Section 2

SECTION THEME

▶ **Cooperation** Nobles, church officials, and peasants develop ties of loyalty and service to one another.

Find Out

Answer: *They were maintained through feudal relationships and the manorial system.*

FOCUS

Section Objective

Describe how loyalties were maintained in a divided and often violent Europe.

BELLRINGER
Motivational Activity

Before taking roll at the beginning of the class period, project Section Focus Transparency 12-2 and have students answer the activity questions. Discuss students' responses.

This activity is also available as a blackline master.

Vocabulary Pre-check

Use the Vocabulary PuzzleMaker to create a puzzle that reinforces the vocabulary terms in this section. **L1**

A.D. 700 — A.D. 900 — A.D. 1100

c. A.D. 750 Charles Martel grants warriors landed estates with peasants.

c. A.D. 900 Feudalism takes hold in northern France.

c. A.D. 1000 Peasants begin to use three-field system in farming.

Section 2

Medieval Life

Setting the Scene

▶ **Terms to Define**
feudalism, fief, vassal, homage, tournament, chivalry, manorialism, serf

▶ **People to Meet**
knights, lords, ladies, peasants

Find Out How were loyalties maintained in a divided and often violent Europe?

The Storyteller

Medieval law laid down rules for marriage. When a young woman arrived at marriageable age, one of her brothers or male relatives had to find her a suitable husband. If he did not, she could register a complaint, and her relative could be called to the king's court and given a year and a day to find her one. The husband had to be suited to her social status and property. If the relative did not do this, the king would step in and assign the woman a part of the family inheritance. Then she could marry whomever she wished.

—from *Women's Lives in Medieval Europe, A Sourcebook*, edited by Emile Amt, 1993

Medieval tournament

With the weakening of central government, a new political system known as **feudalism** developed in western Europe. Feudalism was a highly decentralized form of government that stressed alliances of mutual protection between monarchs and nobles of varying degrees of power. The system was based on giving land to nobles in exchange for loyalty and military aid. With the land came peasants to farm it and many powers usually reserved for governments. Feudalism took hold in northern France around A.D. 900 and spread through the rest of western Europe by the A.D. mid-1000s.

Feudal Relationships

The tie between military service and land ownership that characterized feudalism began in the A.D. 700s. At that time, Charles Martel was fighting the Muslims. Unlike the Europeans, the Muslim soldiers used saddles with stirrups that enabled them to fight on horseback, using a sword or lance. Charles wanted to adopt the stirrup and develop a cavalry. However, the cost of keeping such a force required a new type of military system. To support the cavalry, Martel began granting warriors **fiefs**, or estates with peasants. From these fiefs, warriors got the income to buy horses and battle equipment.

Frankish kings later enlarged this system by giving fiefs to counts and local officials. In time, such nobles assumed many of the powers usually held by government: raising armies, dispensing justice, and in some cases even minting coins. In return, the nobles swore an oath of loyalty and pledged military support to the king.

By the A.D. 900s, such arrangements among nobles and monarchs emerged as feudalism. Lords who had been granted fiefs were allowed to pass their lands on to their heirs. In return, these nobles were to provide **knights**, or mounted warriors, for the royal army.

SECTION RESOURCES

Reproducible Masters
- Reproducible Lesson Plan 12-2
- Guided Reading Activity 12-2
- Source Reading 12
- History Simulation 12
- Section Quiz 12-2

Transparencies
- Section Focus Transparency 12-2

Multimedia
- The Middle Ages
- Vocabulary PuzzleMaker Software
- Student Self-Test and Review Software
- Testmaker
- The Middle Ages

In theory, feudal relationships were like a pyramid. The king was at the top. In the middle were various ranks of lords. Each lord was a **vassal**—a noble who served a lord of the next higher rank. At the bottom were the knights. In practice, however, a noble might be both a lord and a vassal, since a noble could pledge his allegiance to more than one lord. In fact, one German warrior, Siboto of Falkenstein, was vassal to 20 different lords. Of course, conflicts of loyalty arose if one of a vassal's lords went to war with another.

Feudal Obligations

Ties between a lord and a vassal were made official in a solemn ceremony known as **homage**. In return for a fief, the vassal pledged to perform certain duties. The most important obligation was military service. The vassal agreed to provide his lord with a certain number of knights for battle during a period of 40 to 60 days each year. In addition, the vassal agreed to serve in the lord's court, to provide food and lodging when the lord came visiting, and to contribute funds when the lord's son became a knight or when his oldest daughter married. Vassals also pledged to pay ransom in the event of the lord's capture in battle.

Castles for Defense

Because of the lack of a strong central government, warfare occurred frequently in feudal society. As a result, every noble built a castle, or fortified manor house, for defense against enemies. The first castles were wooden buildings with high fences of logs or mounds of hard-packed earth around them. By the A.D. 1100s castles were built of stone, with thick walls and turrets, or small towers. Each castle was built on a hill or mound surrounded by a deep moat. Castles had a square tower called a keep. The keep, located in the strongest part of the castle, contained many rooms, a hall, and a dungeon. Surrounding the keep was a large open area called a bailey. Within the bailey were various buildings, including barracks, storerooms, workshops, and a chapel.

Visualizing History **An illustration from the *Trés Riches Heures du Duc de Berry* shows peasants at work outside a castle.** *Why did feudal lords need castles?*

Life of the Nobility

Lords, ladies, and knights made up the nobility of the Middle Ages. Although the nobles lived much easier lives than the peasants who worked for them, their lives can hardly be called luxurious or glamorous. Castles were built for security, not comfort, and were largely cold, dingy, and damp places.

Within his fief, a **lord**, or nobleman, had almost total authority. He collected rents from peasants and administered justice in disputes between his vassals. Any outside attempt to seize the land or control the inhabitants of his fief was met with violent resistance.

In contrast, a **lady**, or noblewoman, had few, if any, rights. A noblewoman could be wed as early as her twelfth birthday to a man her father selected. Her primary duties lay in bringing up children and taking care of the household. Noblewomen took pride in their needlework, turning out cloth and fine embroidery. They also learned to make effective medicines from plants and herbs. Some women shared the supervision of the estate with the lord and took over their husband's duties while the men were away at war.

Entertainment

Nobles looked forward to **tournaments**—mock battles between knights—as a show of military

TEACH

Guided Practice

THEME **Cooperation**

Review with students the political situation in Europe after the invasions that ended Frankish rule. *(no central authority; danger from marauding bands of thieves and murderers)* **Why would cooperation be important at such a time?** *(Individuals could not defend themselves on their own; they needed the strength of others to withstand attack.)* **L1 LEP**

Visualizing History One of the most famous works of the Middle Ages, the *Trés Riches Heures du Duc de Berry* (Very Rich Hours of the Duke of Berry) is a book of hours, or devotional prayer book, illustrated by the Limbourg Brothers. It includes a beautiful painting for each of the twelve months of the year.
Answer to Caption: *They needed them because warfare was frequent, and, being fortified, castles provided defense against enemies.*

NATIONAL GEOGRAPHIC SOCIETY

Use these materials to enrich student understanding of the Middle Ages.

- **NGS PICTURESHOW CD-ROM**
  The Middle Ages
- **NGS POSTER SET**
  The Middle Ages

COOPERATIVE LEARNING ACTIVITY

Building Castles Have the class work in small groups to create plans for a medieval castle like those described in the text. Refer to David Macaulay's book *Castle* and the videocassette that accompanies it. Tasks may be divided in several ways: researching medieval architecture, organizing data, writing plans, and illustrating the finished design by blueprint and sketch on poster board. Special attention should be paid to the outer wall, the turrets, surrounding fields, the drawbridge, the keep and well, the chapel, and the great hall. **L1 LEP**

TEACH

Tell students that the center of castle activity was the great hall, which changed greatly during the castle-building period. Though initially drafty, smoky, and dark, it gradually became more comfortable with tapestries on the walls and balconies for musicians. Ask students which part of the castle they think was the most important. *(Answers will vary. Without walls and a moat, a castle could be stormed. But without a well, livestock, and gardens, the inhabitants would starve during a siege.)*

CURRICULUM CONNECTION

LITERATURE
One of Europe's best-preserved castles is the Castle of Chillon, built in Switzerland on an island in Lake Geneva. A famous poem by Lord Byron, published in 1816, tells the story of "The Prisoner of Chillon," who was imprisoned in the castle for so long that he lost his desire for freedom.

Cultural Perspectives

Castles Medieval castles had their origins in the early Byzantine Empire. Byzantine general Belisarius constructed square forts with tall corner towers during his North African campaigns. Muslim conquerors of North Africa copied the idea and built similar structures in Spain. Castles spread from there to France during the tenth century, where they were first used as private fortresses.

1–Moat; 2–Drawbridge; 3–Guardroom; 4–Latrine; 5–Armory; 6–Soldiers' quarters; 7–Kitchen garden; 8–Storerooms and servants' quarters; 9–Kitchen; 10–Great hall; 11–Chapel; 12–Lord and lady's quarters; 13–Inner ward

Harry Bl

Life in the Castle

The medieval castle was both fortress and home. The first castles, raised in the A.D. 900s, were square towers encircled by wooden ramparts. By the A.D. 1100s, castles had become mighty stone fortresses. From the towers and walls archers took aim and soldiers dumped boiling liquids on attackers. The castle was surrounded by a moat—a body of water encircling the castle—that could be crossed when a drawbridge was let down.

Inside it was crowded, smelly, dirty, and damp The animals ate and slept with the people, and th smell of animal and human waste was everywher The occupants of the castle had to contend with col earthen or stone floors, drafty halls, smoky room and windows without glass that let in cold and hea along with light. Not even the lord and lady had thei own private room. Grand but never comfortable, th castle's main purpose was military security.

300 Chapter 12 *The Rise of Medieval Europe*

skills. They also loved to hunt, and both men and women learned the art of falconry and archery. A dinner featuring several dishes of game and fish might follow. In a castle's great hall, nobles and their guests ate while being entertained by minstrels, or singers.

Becoming a Knight

A nobleman's son began training for knighthood at age 7. Beginning as a page, or assistant, in the house of a lord, he learned manners and the use of weapons. At 15, the page became a squire who assisted a knight and practiced using weapons. Once he proved himself in battle, the squire was knighted in an elaborate ceremony.

The behavior of knights was governed by a code of chivalry. This code called for knights to be brave in battle, fight fairly, keep promises, defend the Church, and treat women of noble birth in a courteous manner. Chivalry eventually became the basis for the development of good manners in Western society.

Visualizing History **A suit of armor made of steel, brass, and leather belonging to an English knight, Master Jacobe.** *What knightly code became the basis of good manners in Western society?*

The Manorial System

The wealth of a feudal lord came from the labor of the **peasants** who lived on and worked the lord's land. Since the last years of the Roman Empire, many peasants had worked for large landowners, in part because they could not afford their own land and in part for protection. By the Middle Ages, economic life across Europe centered around a system of agricultural production called manorialism. It provided lords and peasants with food, shelter, and protection.

Manors, or estates, varied in size from several hundred to several hundred thousand acres. Each manor included the lord's manor house, pastures for livestock, fields for crops, forest areas, and a village where the peasants lived. While feudalism describes the political relationships between nobles, manorialism concerns economic ties between nobles and peasants.

Work on a Manor

In return for the lord's protection, the peasants provided various services for the lord. Chief among the obligations were to farm the lord's land and to make various payments of goods. For example, each time a peasant ground grain at the lord's mill, he was obligated to leave a portion for the lord. If he baked in the lord's oven, he left a loaf behind for the lord. In addition, peasants were obligated to set aside a number of days each year to provide various types of labor, such as road or bridge repair.

Warfare and invasions made trade almost impossible, so the manor had to produce nearly everything its residents needed. Most of the peasants farmed or herded sheep. A few worked as skilled artisans, for each manor needed a blacksmith to make tools, a carpenter for building, a

Footnotes to History **Identifying a Knight** To identify themselves, knights had individual designs painted on their shields and tunics. His particular design became known as the knight's coat of arms. In noble families, coats of arms were passed down from one generation to the next. The flags of some modern countries are based on the system of designs that were developed by the knights.

Chapter 12 Section 2

Visualizing History Early medieval armor, called chain mail, consisted of small metal rings linked closely together. With the development of more deadly weaponry—crossbows, maces, and axes—heavier protection was needed. By the 1300s, most knights wore plate armor, made of large metal sheets.
Answer to Caption: *chivalry*

Critical Thinking Review with students the principal values of medieval nobles as set forth in the code of chivalry. Have students identify practices regarded as good manners today and the social values these practices reflect. Then compare and contrast the two lists. **L3**

Who?What?Where?When?

Fairs served as centers of trade in medieval Europe, attracting merchants from all over the continent. During the year, there were four major fair seasons: one in the winter, one at Easter, one in midsummer, and one in October.

Independent Practice

- Guided Reading Activity 12-2 **L1**
- Source Reading 12
- History Simulation 12

Women in History Have students research the roles of medieval women from different classes and write reports on what they find. Have them include in their reports a comparison of the roles, goals, and beliefs of medieval women with those of women today. **L3**

MEETING SPECIAL NEEDS ACTIVITY

Learning Style: Verbal/Linguistic Some students may have difficulty differentiating between feudalism, a political system, and manorialism, an economic system. Have students write on the chalkboard the headings *Political* and *Economic*. Then introduce various activities and ask students to place them in the appropriate column. Activities might include voting, shopping, baby-sitting, eating a restaurant meal, depositing a check, and writing a letter to the editor of the local paper. **L1**

Chapter 12 Section 2

ASSESS

Check for Understanding

Assign Section 2 Review as homework or as an in-class activity.

Use Student Self-Test and Review Software to review Section 2.

Evaluate

Section Quiz 12-2

Use the Testmaker to create a customized quiz for Section 2.

Reteach

Have students review the workings of feudalism as a political system.

Enrich

Have students read one of the King Arthur legends and present an oral report on it to the class.

CLOSE

Have students summarize the main advantages and disadvantages of the manorial system.

shoemaker, a miller to grind grain, a vintner to make wine, and a brewer to make beer. Peasant women made candles, sheared sheep, spun wool, and sewed clothing.

Peasants rarely left the manor. Most were serfs, people who were bound to the manor and could not leave it without permission. But the serfs were not slaves—they could not be "sold" apart from the land they lived on.

Increased Production

The manorial system normally produced only enough food to support the peasants and the lord's household. However, a number of improvements gradually boosted productivity and eased the threat of famine.

The first improvement was the development of a new, heavier type of plow. The new plow made deeper cuts in the ground and had a device called a mould-board that pushed the soil sideways. The heavier plow meant less time in the fields for peasant farmers. As a result, farmers developed a better method of planting.

Instead of dividing plots of land into two fields, one of which lay fallow, or unsown, each year, farmers in the A.D. 1000s began to use a three-field system. One field might be planted with winter wheat, a second with spring wheat and vegetables, and a third left fallow. The next year, different crops were planted in the fallow field. One of the two remaining fields was planted, and the other one was left fallow until the next year. This system produced more crops than the old system and helped to preserve the soil.

Peasant Life

Poverty and hardship characterized peasant life, and few serfs lived beyond the age of 40. Famine and disease were constant dangers. In times of war, the peasants were the first and hardest hit. Invading knights trampled crops and burned villages, causing famine and loss of life. To support the war, their lord might require additional payments of crops or labor. A monk of Canterbury described an English serf's account of his day:

> "I work very hard. I go out at dawn, driving the oxen to the field, and I yoke them to the plough; however hard the winter I dare not stay home for fear of my master; but, having yoked the oxen and made the ploughshare and coulter fast to the plough, every day I have to plough a whole acre or more."
>
> —Aelfric, *Colloquy*, A.D. 1005

Serfs like this man lived in tiny, one-room houses with dirt floors, no chimney, and one or two crude pieces of furniture—perhaps a table and stools. People slept huddled together for warmth. Coarse bread, a few vegetables from their gardens, and grain for porridge made up their usual diet. Meat was a rarity.

In spite of hardships, peasants were able to relax on Sundays and holy days. They enjoyed dancing, singing, and such sports as wrestling and archery. In addition, there were other amusements, such as religious plays, pageants, and shows by minstrels.

Despite the obvious differences between serfs and nobles, the two groups did share a common interest in the land. Medieval Europeans believed that every person was equal in the "eyes of God." In practice, however, society was viewed as a hierarchy with ranked leaders from top to bottom. Each person—no matter what his or her place might be in the hierarchy—had certain duties that were attached to his or her position in life. In general, people did not question their standing or obligations. Although the manorial system seemed to lack freedom and opportunity for most of the people involved in it, it did create a very stable and secure way of life during a time that was generally violent and uncertain.

SECTION 2 REVIEW

Recall

1. **Define** feudalism, fief, vassal, homage, tournament, chivalry, manorialism, serf.
2. **Identify** knight, lord, lady, peasant.
3. **Explain** the stages that were necessary for a medieval nobleman to become a knight.

Critical Thinking

4. **Making Comparisons** Compare and contrast the feudal class structure in medieval Europe with the *varna* system in early India discussed in Chapter 8.

Understanding Themes

5. **Cooperation** Diagram the ways nobles, knights, and peasants cooperated during the medieval period.

SECTION 2 REVIEW ANSWERS

1. All vocabulary words are defined in the Glossary.
2. knight, 298; lord, 299; lady, 299; peasant, 301
3. service as a page, squire, proving himself in battle, and the ceremony conferring knighthood
4. Both systems clearly defined a person's place in society and attached certain duties to that position. The *varna* system, however, was based more on occupation, feudalism on political relationships.
5. COOPERATION Diagrams should emphasize interdependency while illustrating the various rights, responsibilities, levels, and relationships that characterized medieval life.

A.D. 500 — A.D. 900 — A.D. 1300

A.D. 520 Benedict introduces rule for monasteries.

c. A.D. 650 Irish missionaries win converts in western Europe.

A.D. 1073 The monk Hildebrand becomes Pope Gregory VII.

A.D. 1232 The Inquisition begins.

Section 3

The Medieval Church

Setting the Scene

- **Terms to Define**
  sacrament, abbot, abbess, cardinal, lay investiture, heresy, excommunication, friar
- **People to Meet**
  Benedict, Gregory I, Gregory VII, Innocent III, Francis of Assisi, Dominic
- **Places to Locate**
  Monte Cassino, Cluny

Find Out How did the Catholic Church shape the development of medieval Europe?

The Storyteller

Alcuin, a Benedictine monk, arose to begin his day. The day's work in a monastery depended on sunlight hours, for candles were expensive and no one in medieval times had access to cheap artificial light. Because it was winter, Alcuin had to get up at 2:30 A.M., and go to bed at 6:30 P.M. after sunset. Sometimes he was already tired by noon! His workday included reading, choir practice, bookbinding, sewing, gardening, and worship services—which were the only times during the day that he was permitted to break his vow of silence and speak.

—from *Monastic Life in Medieval England*, J.C. Dickinson, 1962

Ancient monastery in Glendalough, Ireland

During the Middle Ages, the Catholic Church was the dominant spiritual influence in western Europe. For most people, the Church was the center of their lives. A small number of Europeans, however, were Jews, Muslims, or non-Catholic Christians.

The Medieval Church

Although the Church's primary mission was spiritual, the decline of Rome in the A.D. 400s led the Church to assume many political and social tasks. During this time, the bishop of Rome, now called the pope, became the strongest political leader in western Europe. The pope claimed spiritual authority over all Christians, basing this claim on the belief that Peter the Apostle, Rome's first bishop, had been chosen by Jesus to lead the Church.

Religious Role

The Catholic Church taught that all people were sinners and dependent on God's grace, or favor. The only way to receive grace was by taking part in the **sacraments**, or church rituals: baptism, penance, eucharist, confirmation, matrimony, anointing of the sick, and holy orders. One of the most important sacraments was the eucharist, or holy communion, which commemorated Christ's death. People shared in the eucharist at a mass, or worship service. At each mass, the priest blessed wheat wafers and a cup of wine that stood on an altar. According to Catholic teaching, the priests and the worshipers received Jesus' invisible presence in the forms of the bread and the wine.

During the Middle Ages, people generally had a limited understanding of church rituals. Masses were said in Latin, a language few people understood. Also, many priests were poorly educated

Chapter 12 Section 3

SECTION THEME

- **Uniformity** The Catholic Church affects every aspect of medieval life.

Find Out

Answer: *It provided religious support, spiritual guidance, and such social services as education, medical care, and charity.*

FOCUS

Section Objective

Summarize the role of the Catholic Church in shaping the development of medieval Europe.

BELLRINGER Motivational Activity

Before taking roll at the beginning of the class period, project Section Focus Transparency 12-3 and have students answer the activity questions. Discuss students' responses.

This activity is also available as a blackline master.

Vocabulary Pre-check

Use the Vocabulary PuzzleMaker to create a puzzle that reinforces the vocabulary terms in this section. **L1**

SECTION RESOURCES

Reproducible Masters
- Reproducible Lesson Plan 12-3
- Guided Reading Activity 12-3
- People in World History Profiles 21, 22
- World Art and Music Activity 12
- Section Quiz 12-3

Transparencies
- Section Focus Transparency 12-3
- World History and Art Transparency 15
- The Middle Ages

Multimedia
- Vocabulary PuzzleMaker Software
- Student Self-Test and Review Software
- Testmaker
- The Middle Ages

TEACH

Guided Practice

THEME **Uniformity**

The goal of the medieval Church was to unify western Europe in accordance with the teachings and beliefs of Christianity. Does the Catholic Church play the same role today in the Western world? *(No, because it is not the only Christian church, and there are other non-Christian religions as well.)* What factors tend to create uniformity in the United States today? *(Answers will vary but might include: the English language, our government under the Constitution, and the mass media.)* **L2**

World History and Art Transparency 15, *Cover of the Lindau Gospels*

Global Gourmet

Southern Europe The knot-shaped pretzels that we enjoy today were the creation of medieval monks, given as rewards to children for memorizing their prayers. (The Latin word *pretiola* means "small reward.") The shape represented the folded arms of children at prayer.

NATIONAL GEOGRAPHIC SOCIETY

Use these materials to enrich student understanding of the culture of the Middle Ages.

NGS PICTURESHOW CD-ROM
The Middle Ages

NGS PICTUREPACK TRANSPARENCY SET
The Middle Ages

and did not preach effectively. Moreover, few worshipers could read or write. What the average person learned about the Christian faith came from the statues, paintings, and later the stained glass windows that adorned most medieval churches.

Church Organization

The church hierarchy, which was described in Chapter 6, remained largely the same during the Middle Ages. The contact most people had with the Church was through parish priests, who conducted services and oversaw the spiritual life of the community. Occasionally bishops visited a parish to supervise the priests.

The pope, bishops, and priests formed what is called the secular clergy because they lived *in saeculo*, a Latin phrase that means "in the world." Other clergy, known as regular clergy, lived by a *regula*, or rule. Regular clergy included monks and nuns who lived apart from society. These Christians played an important role in strengthening the medieval Church.

Benedict's Rule

In A.D. 520 a Roman official named **Benedict** founded a monastery at **Monte Cassino** in Italy. His monastery became a model for monks in other communities. Benedict drew up a list of rules that provided for manual work, meditation, and prayer. According to the Benedictine rule, monks could not own goods, must never marry, and were bound to obey monastic laws. Their life was one of poverty, chastity, and obedience to the directives of an abbot, or monastery head.

Monastic Life

Monks dressed in simple, long robes made of coarse material and tied at the waist by a cord. They ate one or two plain meals each day. Most monasteries had a rule of silence; monks could not converse with one another except for a short time each day. In some monasteries total silence was the rule. During meals, one monk might read passages from

Images of the Times

Monastic Life

Although monasteries were closed religious communities, their members often worked in the outside world.

An illustrated page from a book copied by monks shows the careful, artistic writing that became the manuscript before printing was developed.

St. Benedict and his monks, like all those who lived at the monasteries, ate together in a refectory.

Mont St. Michel presents a view of the beautiful old monastery's lower ramparts.

304

Images of the Times **Monastic Life**

According to St. Benedict's *Rule for Monasteries*, all monks took a vow of obedience to their abbot. This was intended to help them develop humility. Abbots, in turn, were responsible for the care of the souls of all the men in their monastery. It was their job to set a good example, to teach, coax, and admonish the monks so as to best ensure their spiritual development.

St. Benedict did much to foster the important social role monasteries were to play during the Middle Ages. "Let all guests who arrive be received like Christ ...," he wrote. "In the reception of the poor and of pilgrims the greatest care and solicitude should be shown."

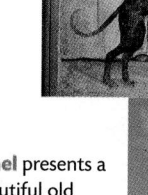

the Bible while the others meditated.

Women took part in monastic life by living in a convent under the direction of an abbess. Known as nuns, they wore simple clothes and wrapped a white cloth called a wimple around their face and neck. They alternated prayer with spinning, weaving, and embroidering items such as tapestries and banners. They also taught needlework and the medicinal use of herbs to the daughters of nobles.

Influence of Monastics

Although monks and nuns lived apart from society, they were not completely isolated. Indeed, they played a crucial role in medieval intellectual and social life. Since few people could read or write, the regular clergy preserved ancient religious works and the classical writings. Scribes laboriously copied books by hand, working in a small drafty room with only a candle or small window for light. Illuminated manuscripts decorated with rich colors and intricate pictures indicate that, although the task was tedious, it was lovingly done.

Monasteries and convents provided schools for young people, hospitals for the sick, food for the needy, and guest houses for weary travelers. They taught peasants carpentry and weaving and made improvements in agriculture that they passed on to others. Some monks and nuns became missionaries who spread Christian teachings to non-Christians.

Missionary Efforts

Pope **Gregory I** was so impressed with the Benedictine Rule that he adopted it to spread Christianity in Europe. In A.D. 597 he sent monks to England, where they converted the Anglo-Saxons to Catholicism. From England, missionaries carried Christianity to northern Germany. During the A.D. 600s, monasteries in Ireland sent missionaries throughout the North Atlantic and western Europe. Although the Irish were isolated from the pope in Rome, their missionaries won many converts. By the A.D. mid-1000s, most western Europeans had become Catholics.

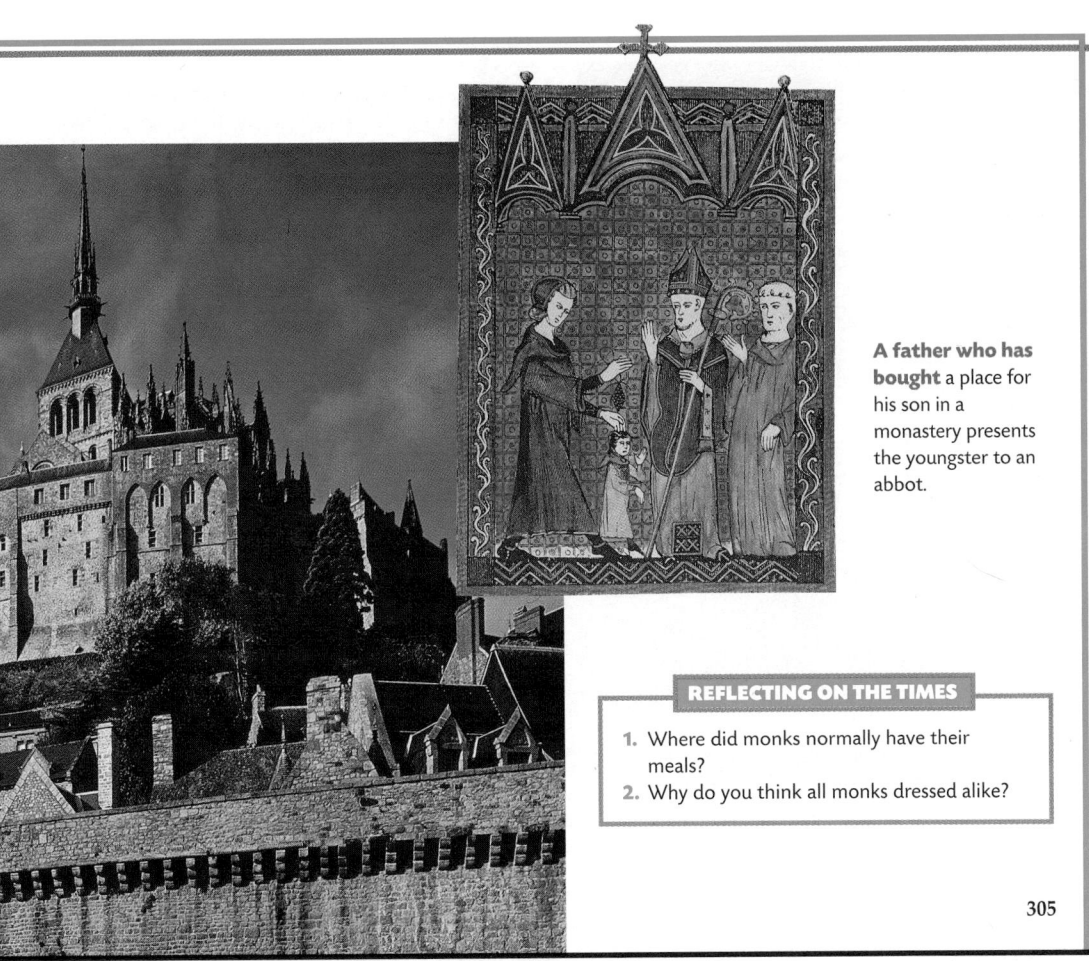

A father who has bought a place for his son in a monastery presents the youngster to an abbot.

REFLECTING ON THE TIMES

1. Where did monks normally have their meals?
2. Why do you think all monks dressed alike?

305

ANSWERS TO REFLECTING ON THE TIMES

1. in a refectory
2. All were equal in the eyes of God.

Chapter 12 Section 3

Independent Practice

Guided Reading Activity 12-3 **L1**

Religion Have students speculate on what the various attractions of the monastic life might have been to young medieval men and women. *(Answers may include: opportunity to better serve and worship God; desire to study or to develop the particular skills used in monasteries and convents; for women, a chance to escape a life of childbearing and child rearing.)* Discuss which of these were spiritual in nature and which were worldly. **L3**

The Arts Have students create posters in the style of medieval stained glass to tell a story about people or events they have studied in this section. Possible subjects include Francis of Assisi, missionary efforts in Europe, a church ritual, or the Albigensian crusade. **L2 LEP**

Who?What?Where?When?

Iona The great center of Irish monasticism was the island of Iona, off the western coast of Scotland. From its monastery, founded in the A.D. 500s by St. Columba, missionaries traveled over northern Scotland, converting the Scots to Christianity.

Chapter 12 Section 3

Biography Have students select one of the popes discussed in this section—Gregory I, Gregory VII, or Innocent III. Have them research his life, write a brief summary of his major accomplishments, and share their findings with the class. **L3**

People in World History Profiles 21, 22

World Art and Music Activity 12

Linking Past and Present

Electing a Pope The pope today is still elected by a gathering of cardinals, called a "conclave." They meet no later than the twentieth day after the death of a pope and vote by secret ballot until they can achieve a two-thirds majority on a given candidate.

Visualizing History Relics were an important object of devotion in medieval times. Remains of the bodies or clothes of the saints, or splinters from Jesus' cross or his crown of thorns were housed in special receptacles called reliquaries. Reliquaries were often decorated with jewels and precious metals.
Answer to Caption: *He criticized the practice of lay investiture.*

Power of the Church

During the Middle Ages, the Catholic Church helped to govern western Europe. Bishops and abbots played an important part in the feudal system. Because many of them were nobles, they received land from kings in return for military service. Since they were religious leaders, however, these vassals could not fight. They fulfilled their military duty by giving some of their land to knights who would fight for them.

These feudal ties boosted the Church's wealth and political power. The Church also received donations of land and money from rich nobles who wanted to perform acts of piety. As a result, local lords began to control many church offices and lands, contrary to church tradition. They often appointed relatives as bishops or abbots, instead of awarding those offices to the most qualified people. Furthermore, as religious leaders and monasteries grew wealthier, many church officials became increasingly careless about carrying out their religious duties.

Visualizing History **A young boy, having obtained the office of bishop, carries sacred church relics.** *How did Pope Gregory try to stop the selection of church officials by secular rulers?*

Church Reform

By the A.D. 900s, many devout Christians were calling for reform. The reform movement began in the monasteries and spread throughout much of western Europe. Most famous was the monastery at **Cluny** in eastern France, whose monks won respect for leading lives of pious simplicity. The abbots of Cluny sent representatives to other monasteries to help them undertake similar reforms.

Other church leaders tried to free the Church from the control of feudal lords. They wanted the Church, not the state, to be the final authority in Western society. In A.D. 1059 a church council declared that political leaders could no longer choose the pope. Instead, the pope would be elected by a gathering of cardinals—high church officials in Rome ranking directly below the pope. In addition, the reformers insisted that the pope, not secular rulers such as lords and kings, should be the one to appoint bishops and other officials to church offices.

In A.D. 1073 the cardinals elected a reform-minded monk named Hildebrand as Pope **Gregory VII**. Gregory believed that the pope should have complete jurisdiction over all church officials. He especially criticized the practice of lay investiture, in which secular rulers gave the symbols of office, such as a ring and a staff, to the bishops they had appointed.

Fighting Heresy

Innocent III, one of the most powerful popes, also tried to reform the Catholic Church. In A.D. 1215 he convened a council that condemned drunkenness, feasting, and dancing among the clergy. The council also laid down strict rules for stopping the spread of heresy, or the denial of basic church teachings. Heresy had increased as corruption and scandal had rocked the Church. In the Middle Ages, heresy was regarded as seriously as the crime of treason is viewed today.

At first, the Catholic Church tried to convert heretics, or those who challenged its teachings. When that failed, however, heretics were threatened with excommunication, or expulsion from the Church. An excommunicated person was not allowed to take part in the sacraments and was also outlawed from any contact with Christian society. Since receiving the sacraments was considered to be essential for salvation, banishment was an especially severe penalty.

Early in the A.D. 1200s, for example, the Church became concerned about a group of heretics in France known as Albigensians (AL•buh•JEHN•shuhnz). The Albigensians believed that the

COOPERATIVE LEARNING ACTIVITY

Role Play Organize the class into three groups. One group will represent missionaries who have been ordered by Pope Gregory I to convert the people of England, and should describe their thoughts and goals as they prepare to leave continental Europe. The second group will represent monks and nuns who teach the young and help the sick and needy, and should explain how their work benefits others. The third group will represent the regular clergy who copy books by hand in order to preserve ancient learning, and should portray the life of a scribe. The members of each group should explain why their work is important, what their goals are, and how their work reflects their Christian beliefs. **L2**

material world was evil and rejected church sacraments. To end this heresy, Pope Innocent III sent French knights to crush the group.

The Inquisition

In order to seek out and punish people suspected of heresy, the Church set up a court in A.D. 1232 known as the Inquisition. Those brought before the court were urged to confess their heresy and to ask forgiveness. Often, however, Inquisition officials accused people without sufficient proof; sometimes they even used torture to obtain confessions. The Church welcomed back those who repented, but those who did not repent were punished. Punishment ranged from imprisonment to loss of property and even execution. According to church officials, these punishments were needed to save the souls of the heretics.

Friars Inspire Reform

Other reformers of the Church during the early A.D. 1200s were friars, or wandering preachers. At a time when church leaders were criticized for their love of wealth and power, the friars lived simply, owned no possessions, and depended on gifts of food and shelter to survive.

The friars followed monastic rules but did not isolate themselves from the rest of the Christian community. Instead, they lived in towns and preached Christianity to the people. The best-known friars were the Franciscans and the Dominicans. Because they were well known and liked, the friars kept many people loyal to the Catholic Church.

Francis of Assisi, the son of a wealthy Italian cloth merchant, founded the Franciscan friars about A.D. 1210. Francis and his followers sought to follow the simple life of Jesus and his disciples. They became known for their cheerful trust in God and their respect for nature as a divine gift.

A Spanish priest named **Dominic** organized the Dominican friars in A.D. 1215. Like the Franciscans, the Dominicans lived a life of poverty, simplicity, and service. In addition, they were well-educated, persuasive preachers who could reply to the arguments of heretics.

Church councils, the Inquisition, and the efforts of the friars were all signs of the Church's power during the Middle Ages. By the A.D. 1000s, however, that power was increasingly being challenged by secular rulers.

History & Art *St. Dominic and Albigensians, c. 1450–1504. Museo Del Prado, Madrid, Spain*

Here, St. Dominic tests books in the campaign against heresy. *How did the life of a friar differ from that of other clergy?*

SECTION 3 REVIEW

Recall

1. **Define** sacrament, abbot, abbess, cardinal, lay investiture, heresy, excommunication, friar.
2. **Identify** Benedict, Gregory I, Gregory VII, Innocent III, Francis of Assisi, Dominic.
3. **Explain** how the Catholic Church provided the link between the ancient world and the medieval world.

Critical Thinking

4. **Synthesizing Information** Imagine that you are a religious, but superstitious, peasant living during the Middle Ages. Invent an explanation for the famine that has struck your village.

Understanding Themes

5. **Uniformity** How effective were the actions of the Catholic Church in trying to make all western Europeans believe and practice one faith?

SECTION 3 REVIEW ANSWERS

1. All vocabulary words are defined in the Glossary.
2. Benedict, 304; Gregory I, 305; Gregory VII, 306; Innocent III, 306; Francis of Assisi, 307; Dominic, 307
3. It preserved much of the learning of the classical world.
4. Possible answer: It is a punishment from God because you and/or your neighbors have disobeyed the teachings of the Church.
5. UNIFORMITY On the whole, they were effective; for 1,500 years the Church retained its power and influence over western Europe.

Chapter 12 Section 3

History & Art The Dominican order grew very quickly. By the time St. Dominic died in A.D. 1221, there were more than 500 friars, based at 60 friaries located throughout western Europe.

Answer to Caption: *They did not isolate themselves from the rest of the Christian community; they preached to the people.*

ASSESS

Check for Understanding

Assign Section 3 Review as homework or as an in-class activity.

Use Student Self-Test and Review Software to review Section 3.

Evaluate

Section Quiz 12-3

Use the Testmaker to create a customized quiz for Section 3.

Reteach

Ask students to summarize the contributions that monasteries and convents made to society during the Middle Ages.

Enrich

Have students research the life of St. Francis of Assisi or St. Dominic and present their findings to the class.

CLOSE

Have the class summarize the various elements of church reform mentioned in this section. Discuss which reform would seem to be the most effective and which the least effective.

SECTION THEME

▶ **Conflict** European kings, feudal lords, and popes struggle for political dominance.

Find Out

Answer: *They strengthened their power by establishing royal departments of finance and royal law courts, extending privileges to towns, and adding land to their domains.*

FOCUS

Section Objective

Name the achievements of medieval European monarchs.

BELLRINGER Motivational Activity

Before taking roll at the beginning of the class period, project Section Focus Transparency 12-4 and have students answer the activity questions. Discuss students' responses.

This activity is also available as a blackline master.

Vocabulary Pre-check

Use Vocabulary Activity 12 to introduce vocabulary terms. **L1 LEP**

A.D. 700 — A.D. 900 — A.D. 1100 — A.D. 1300

A.D. 871 Alfred the Great begins rule in England.

A.D. 955 German King Otto defeats the Magyars at Lechfeld.

A.D. 1180 Philip Augustus becomes king of France.

A.D. 1215 English King John and his barons sign the Magna Carta.

Section 4

Rise of European Monarchy

Setting the Scene

▶ **Terms to Define**
common law, grand jury, petit jury, middle class

▶ **People to Meet**
Alfred the Great, William the Conqueror, Henry II, Thomas à Becket, Philip Augustus, Otto the Great, Henry IV

▶ **Places to Locate**
England, France, Germany

Find Out What were the achievements of medieval European monarchs?

The Storyteller

The English throne was at stake as the Battle of Hastings approached. William decided to provoke Harold to fight in single combat and called on him to spare the blood of his followers. Under Norman law, personal combat decided difficult cases, looking for the judgment of God to settle the matter. Harold refused because he knew the cause was not personal, but national. It would take a full-scale invasion to decide who would wear the English crown.

—adapted from *William the Conqueror*, Edward A. Freeman, 1927

William the Conqueror

After the decline of the Roman Empire, central authority in western Europe disappeared. Except for Charlemagne's reign in the late A.D. 700s, kings were rulers in name only, their lands and power gradually lost to nobles. However, beginning in the A.D. 1100s, many European monarchs began to build strong states.

England

After the Romans abandoned Britain in the A.D. 400s, the island was invaded by Germanic Angles, Saxons, and Jutes. These groups took over much of Britain from the native Celts (KEHLTZ) and set up several kingdoms. In the late A.D. 800s, the Danish Vikings from Scandinavia posed another threat. King Alfred of Wessex, known as **Alfred the Great**, united the Anglo-Saxon kingdoms and defeated the Danes in A.D. 886. His united kingdom eventually became known as "Angleland," or **England**.

The Anglo-Saxons

Alfred ruled Anglo-Saxon England from A.D. 871 to A.D. 899. Like Charlemagne, he was interested in the revival of learning. The English king founded schools and hired scholars to translate many books from Latin to Anglo-Saxon. He also had the scholars write a history of England, known as the *Anglo-Saxon Chronicle*.

The kings who followed Alfred were weak rulers. When the last Anglo-Saxon king, Edward the Confessor, died in A.D. 1066, three rivals claimed the throne.

The Norman Conquest

One of the claimants to the throne was William, the Duke of Normandy. A cousin of the late English

SECTION RESOURCES

Reproducible Masters
- Reproducible Lesson Plan 12-4
- Vocabulary Activity 12
- Guided Reading Activity 12-4
- Time Line Activity 12
- Mapping History Activity 12
- Geography and History Activity 12
- Reteaching Activity 12
- Enrichment Activity 12
- Section Quiz 12-4
- Performance Assessment Activity 12
- Spanish Chapter Summary 12

Transparencies
- Section Focus Transparency 12-4
- Mapping History Overlay Transparency 9

Multimedia
- Focus on World Art Print 14
- Student Self-Test and Review Software
- Testmaker

king and vassal of the king of France, William had a strong feudal organization in the area of northwestern France. Gathering a force of several hundred boats and some 6,000 soldiers, he invaded England in A.D. 1066. At the Battle of Hastings, William defeated Harold Godwinson, another rival for the throne. The victory won William the English crown and the name **William the Conqueror**.

To keep the loyalty of his Norman vassals, William gave them the lands of Anglo-Saxon church leaders and nobles. He also set up a Great Council of royal officials, bishops, and nobles to advise him and used local officials called sheriffs to collect taxes.

To find out how much money he could collect, William sent officials throughout the land to conduct the first census in western Europe since Roman times. Every person, every farm, every town and manor, every cow and pig, every horse and sheep became an entry in the *Domesday Book*.

Royal Power

William's son, Henry I, ruled from A.D. 1100 to A.D. 1135 and further strengthened the English monarchy. He set up the Exchequer, or department of royal finances, and a system of royal courts.

The court system developed under Henry's grandson, **Henry II**. In place of the old feudal rules, which differed from lord to lord, Henry II established a common law throughout the kingdom. In each community, judges began to meet with a grand jury, a group of men who submitted the names of people suspected of crimes. Soon a system of trial by jury was developed to establish the guilt or innocence of the accused. The kind of jury used in these cases was called a petit jury.

The Magna Carta

Thomas à Becket, the Archbishop of Canterbury, however, opposed Henry's reform that brought priests under the jurisdiction of the royal courts. Becket's resistance surprised the king, who had counted on Becket as a friend. Their quarrel lasted many years until four of Henry's knights heard the king declare in a fit of rage that he wished Becket dead. The knights murdered the archbishop in his own cathedral during the Christmas season.

CONNECTIONS *The Arts*

The Bayeux Tapestry

The Bayeux Tapestry, made between A.D. 1073 and A.D. 1083, is a remarkable work of medieval art. In fact, the Bayeux Tapestry is not a tapestry at all. By definition, a tapestry is a textile woven of different-colored threads to produce a design or picture. The Bayeux Tapestry is really a work of embroidery, a band of linen upon which pictures and patterns are stitched in colored wool. Twenty inches high and 230 feet long, it probably once decorated the walls of an entire room.

Bayeux Tapestry (detail)

The 72 scenes on the tapestry illustrate William the Conqueror's invasion of England in A.D. 1066. The story is shown in a series of individual scenes, much as a story is told in a comic book today. The tapestry even includes words to indicate what is happening in each scene. The images are lively and simple. No complicated settings are shown; only the people or objects necessary to the story appear. The figures themselves are outlined in a cartoonlike fashion, giving a sense of movement and vitality.

The Bayeux Tapestry was probably the work of Matilda (the wife of William the Conqueror) and the ladies of her court. Such textiles seem to have been common in the Middle Ages, and were often used to decorate castles and the homes of wealthy clerics. The Bayeux Tapestry is a part of this decorative tradition.

MAKING THE CONNECTION

1. What story is told by the Bayeux Tapestry?
2. How did the artists of the Bayeux Tapestry convey a sense of movement in the scenes depicted?

COOPERATIVE LEARNING ACTIVITY

Pictorial Record Have students choose a historical event presented in this chapter and plan the presentation of a pictorial record. Organize the class into three groups. One group should determine the style and nature of the record and how it will be produced, choose particular scenes to present, and make recommendations during its execution. A second group should be responsible for the actual production. The third group should create a narrative to accompany the record. Have students select one person from each group to work together on a class presentation when the record is finished. **L2 LEP**

Chapter 12 Section 4

TEACH

Guided Practice

THEME **Conflict**

Discuss the word *conflict* as it applies to England in this section. What specific conflicts are mentioned in the text? *(military conflicts between the Anglo-Saxons and the Danes and between the English and the Normans; political conflicts between the monarchy and the Church and between the monarchy and the nobility)* **L1 LEP**

Who?What?Where?When?

The ***Domesday Book*** apparently got this popular name because people said that there was no appeal from its records. In other words, its determination was final, like that of God on the Day of Judgment (doomsday).

CONNECTIONS *The Arts*

The Bayeux Tapestry

The Bayeux Tapestry is named after the Norman town where, for many years, it was displayed annually in the cathedral. It is now preserved in the Bayeux Museum.

In fact, the Bayeux Tapestry is not a tapestry at all, but rather an embroidered piece of linen.

Answers to Making the Connection

1. *that of the Norman Conquest*
2. *The figures are outlined like cartoons.*

Map Study

Answers

1. *Holy Roman Empire*
2. *Kingdom of Poland, Kingdom of Hungary*

Map Skills Practice

Reading a Map What three kingdoms were located in what is now Spain? *(Aragon, Castile, and Navarre)*

Government Have students make a chart on the chalkboard listing the actions taken by the English and the French monarchs to increase their power. What was the name of the national assembly in each country? *(England: Parliament; France: the Estates-General)* **L2**

Focus on World Art Print 14, French. *William Exhorts His Troops*, from the Bayeux Tapestry

Mapping History Overlay Transparency 9

CURRICULUM CONNECTION

GOVERNMENT
Unlike the United States, the United Kingdom has no single written constitution. Instead, it is governed according to a series of laws and charters. The oldest of them is the Magna Carta.

Kingdoms of Europe A.D. 1160

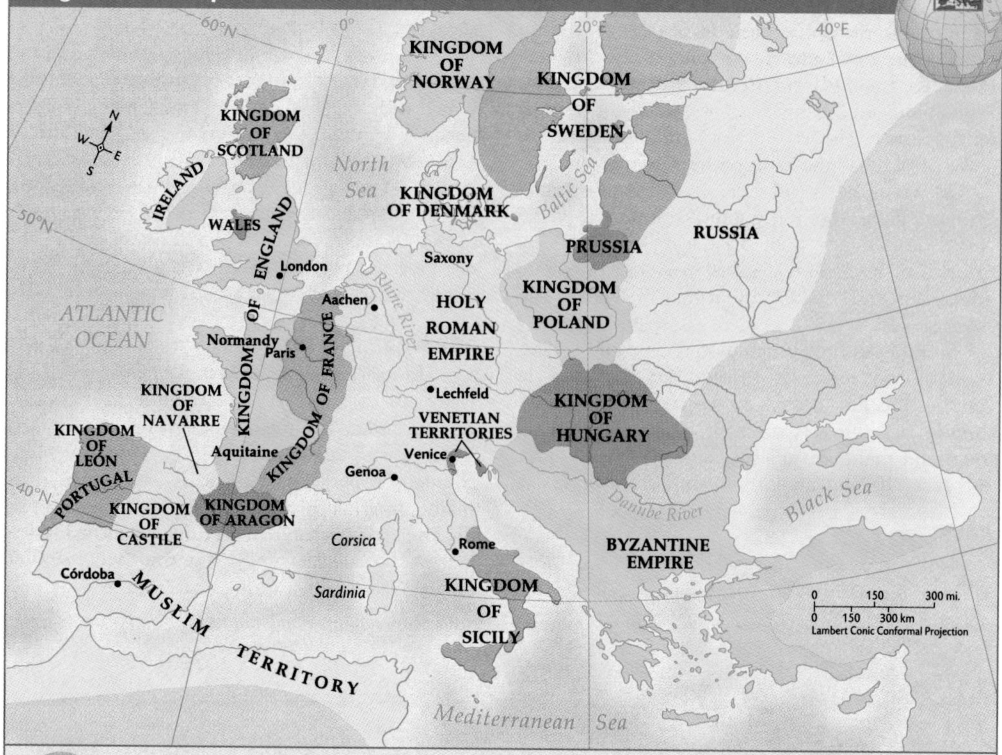

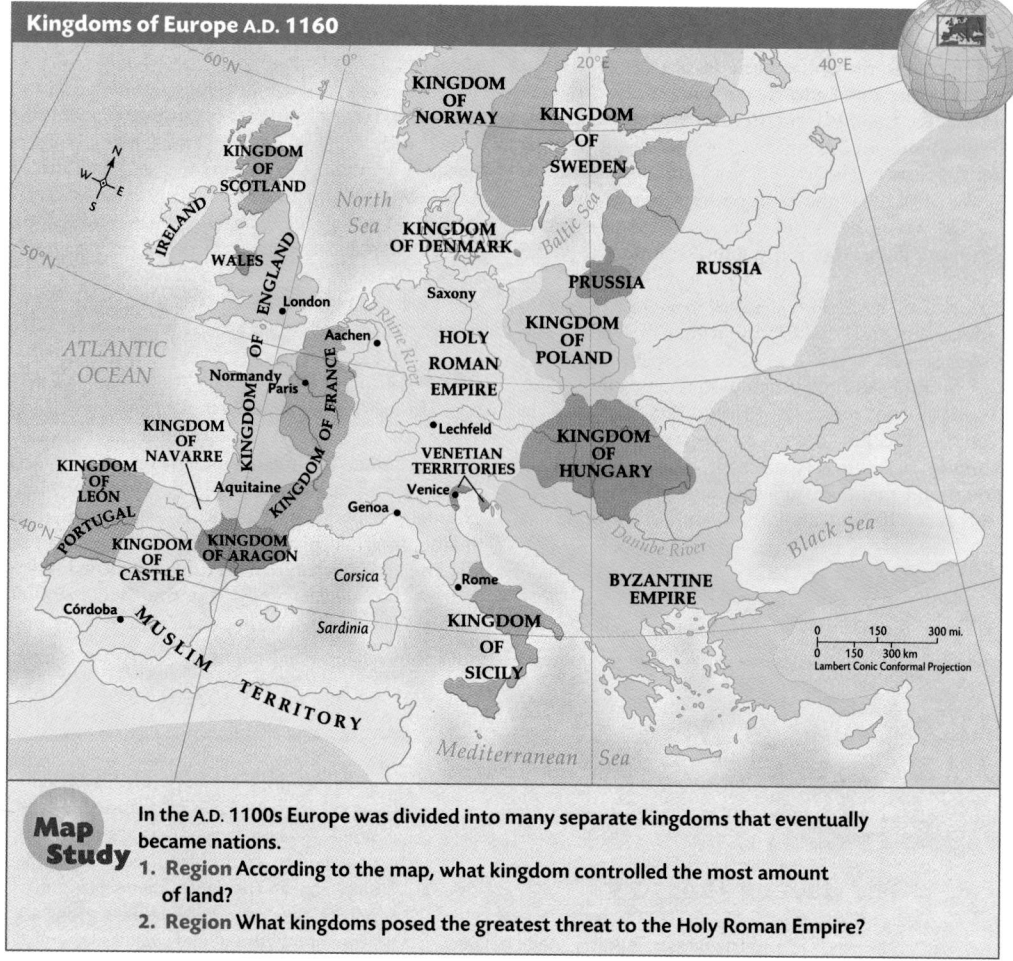

Map Study In the A.D. 1100s Europe was divided into many separate kingdoms that eventually became nations.

1. **Region** According to the map, what kingdom controlled the most amount of land?
2. **Region** What kingdoms posed the greatest threat to the Holy Roman Empire?

Within months, Becket was honored like a saint, and pilgrims reported miracles at his tomb.

Henry's sons, Richard I and John, were ineffective rulers. John lost some English land to France and became unpopular when he increased taxes and punished his enemies without trial. Alarmed at the loss of their feudal rights, a group of nobles met at Runnymede in A.D. 1215. They forced John to sign the Magna Carta, or Great Charter, one of the most important documents in the history of representative government.

The Magna Carta placed clear limits on royal power. Now even a king was bound by law. The charter prevented the king from collecting taxes without the consent of the Great Council. It also assured freemen the right of trial by jury. Article 39 stated:

> "No freeman shall be taken, or imprisoned, or disseized [dispossessed], or outlawed, or exiled, or in any way harmed—nor will we go upon or send upon him—save by the lawful judgment of his peers [equals] or by the law of the land."

The nobles intended the Magna Carta to protect their feudal rights. Over time, however, it guaranteed the rights of all English people.

Rise of Parliament

During the reign of John's son, Henry III, an increase in population encouraged the growth of towns. A new social class—the middle class—was emerging. The middle class did not fit in the medieval social order of nobles, clergy, and

MEETING SPECIAL NEEDS ACTIVITY

Study Strategy Have students make a list of each of the major figures discussed in this section. In a second column, they should write the name of the person or group with which the first figure was in conflict. Then students should make a check mark next to the victor. For instance, Alfred the Great (checked) would be paired with Danes; William of Normandy (checked) with Harold Godwinson; and so on. **L1**

peasants. Its income came from business and trade, not from the land. This group played an increasingly important role in government.

Recognizing the towns' growing power, Henry III added knights and burgesses, or important townspeople, to the Great Council that advised the king. By that time the Great Council was called Parliament, the name by which it is still known.

In A.D. 1295 Henry's son, Edward I, called into session the Model Parliament, which included representatives from the clergy, nobility, and burgesses. As England's government became more representative, Edward encouraged members of Parliament to advise him on business matters, submit petitions to him, and meet frequently.

By A.D. 1400 Parliament had divided into two chambers. Nobles and clergy met as the House of Lords, while knights and burgesses met as the House of Commons.

France

Like England, **France** developed a strong monarchy in the Middle Ages. The type of government that emerged in France, however, differed considerably from the increasingly representative government in England.

Beginnings of Central Government

After Charlemagne's death, the Frankish lands disintegrated into separate territories governed by feudal lords. These lords defended their own lands and were virtually independent rulers.

In A.D. 987 a noble named Hugh Capet seized the French throne from the weak Carolingian king. Capet controlled only the city of Paris and a strip of land between the Seine and Loire Rivers in northern France. The Capetian (kuh•PEE•shuhn) dynasty he established, however, lasted for more than three centuries. By the A.D. 1100s Capetian kings had established the principle of the eldest son inheriting the throne. The Capetians strengthened the power of the monarchy and brought French feudal lords under royal control.

As in England, the number of towns in France increased during the A.D. 1100s. Louis VI, who became king in A.D. 1108, used the townspeople to strengthen the royal government at the expense of the nobles. Louis awarded both the townspeople and the clergy positions on his court of advisers and also granted self-government to towns, freeing them from obligations to feudal lords. These measures led local officials to be loyal to the monarch rather than to feudal lords.

Strengthening the Monarchy

Philip II, known as **Philip Augustus**, ruled France from A.D. 1180 to A.D. 1223. Barely 15 when he succeeded to the throne, Philip was determined to strengthen the monarchy. During his 43-year reign Philip doubled the area of his domain, acquiring some territory through marriage and recapturing French land from England. By appointing local officials who were loyal to the king and forming a semipermanent royal army, Philip further weakened the power of feudal lords.

A Saintly Ruler

Philip's grandson became King Louis IX in A.D. 1226. Louis made royal courts dominant over feudal courts and decreed that only the king had the right to mint coins. Bans on private warfare and the bearing of arms further promoted the French monarch.

A very religious man, Louis was regarded as the ideal for his chivalry and high moral character. His advice to his son reveals these characteristics:

> "[Have] a tender pitiful heart for the poor ... [and] hold yourself steadfast and loyal toward your subjects and your vassals, without turning either to the right or to the left, but always straight, whatever may happen. And if a poor man have a quarrel with a rich man, sustain the poor rather than the rich, until the truth is made clear, and when you know the truth, do justice to them."

AROUND THE WORLD

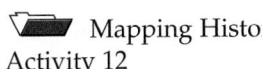

Founding of Cairo

Egypt, A.D. 968

The Fatimids, who claimed to be descendants of Muhammad's daughter Fatima, conquered Egypt around A.D. 968. They founded the city of El Qahira, which means "The Victorious." The name later was shortened to Cairo. The Fatimids made Cairo their capital, and it soon became one of the most important cities in the Arab world. By the late Middle Ages, Cairo had a population of nearly 500,000.

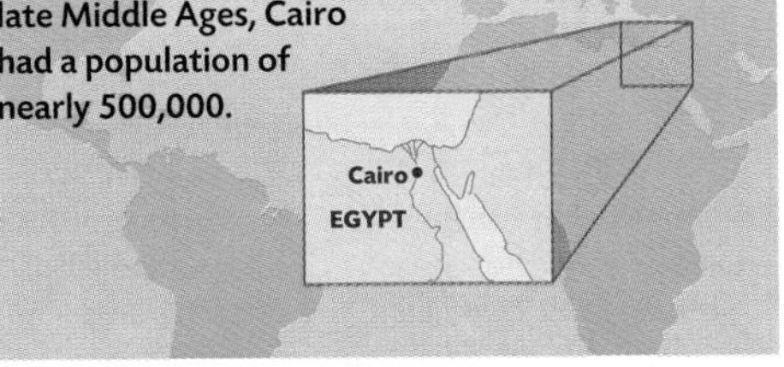

Chapter 12 Section 4

Independent Practice

Guided Reading Activity 12-4 **L1**

News Report Assign students to prepare a TV report on Henry IV's plea before the gates of Gregory VII's castle. Designate a news anchor, reporters, Henry, Gregory, and passersby for on-the-spot interviews. Have students present the report to the class. **L2**

Time Line Activity 12

Mapping History Activity 12

Geography and History Activity 12

Cultural Perspectives

Language For years after the Norman Conquest, two languages were spoken in England—Norman French by the upper classes and Anglo-Saxon English by the lower classes. This double heritage is preserved in the English language today. The words for animals in the field (in the Middle Ages, tended by the lower classes) are Anglo-Saxon: *ox, pig,* and *sheep*. The words for cooked meat (served to the upper classes) are French: *beef, pork,* and *mutton*.

MAKING CONNECTIONS ACTIVITIES

Religion The tomb of Thomas à Becket became a popular destination for pilgrims soon after Becket's murder. (It was the goal of the pilgrims in Chaucer's *The Canterbury Tales*.) Have students research other medieval pilgrimage sites that are still popular today, notably Rome, Italy, and Santiago de Compostela, Spain. Students should report on the nature of the pilgrimages in the Middle Ages, comparing them with journeys made today. **L2**

Government Hold a mock debate between representatives of the English monarchy and the Church of Rome. Organize the class into three groups. Have one group prepare arguments defending the position of the monarchy and another group defend the position of the Church. These two groups should make use of outside sources as well as information in the text. The third group should hear the arguments by both sides, determine the most persuasive position, and write a statement defending its decision. **L3**

Chapter 12 *The Rise of Medieval Europe* 311

Chapter 12
Section 4

ASSESS

Check for Understanding

Assign Section 4 Review as homework or as an in-class activity.

Use Student Self-Test and Review Software to review Section 4.

Evaluate

Section Quiz 12-4

Use the Testmaker to create a customized quiz for Section 4.

Reteach

Have students review the major theme of this section, conflict, as it applies to England, France, and the Holy Roman Empire.

Reteaching Activity 12

Enrich

Have students read and discuss T. S. Eliot's *Murder in the Cathedral,* a play about the martyrdom of Thomas à Becket.

Enrichment Activity 12

CLOSE

Have students review the time lines for the four sections of Chapter 12 and discuss which one of the highlighted events on each time line was most important.

Signs of a Strong Monarchy

Louis IX's grandson, Philip IV, was so handsome he was nicknamed Philip the Fair. The blond, blue-eyed Philip increased France's territory and trade by defeating both England and Flanders in war. To pay for the wars, he raised taxes and taxed new groups, such as the clergy. Although Pope Boniface VIII opposed taxing the clergy, he could not force Philip to back down.

Before he died in A.D. 1314, Philip summoned the Estates-General, an assembly of nobles, clergy, and townspeople. He wanted to use the assembly to raise taxes on a national level rather than locally. The assembly, however, never became as powerful as Parliament in England. French kings kept a firm hand on government affairs.

The Holy Roman Empire

While monarchs in England and France were building strong central governments, rulers in **Germany** remained weak and often powerless. Among the major reasons were their disputes with the pope and with powerful German nobles.

"Emperor of the Romans"

During the A.D. 1000s and A.D. 1100s, German kings posed the biggest threat to the pope's authority. King Otto I, or **Otto the Great**, of Germany tried to restore Charlemagne's empire. After defeating the Magyars at the Battle of Lechfeld in A.D. 955, King Otto set his sights on Italy. In A.D. 962 Pope John XII sought Otto's help against Roman nobles who opposed the pope. In return for the German king's help, the pope in Rome crowned Otto Emperor of the Romans.

Problems of the Holy Roman Empire

Otto and his successors claimed the right to intervene in the election of popes, and Otto himself appointed and deposed several popes. The pope, as you have read, claimed the right to anoint and depose kings. These two conflicting claims led to centuries of dispute between the Holy Roman emperors and the Roman Catholic popes.

Powerful German lords also prevented the Holy Roman emperors from building a strong, unified state. Their challenges to imperial power caused several civil wars. Numerous wars with the Slavic states—Poland and Bohemia—and with Hungary also weakened the Holy Roman emperor's power.

Emperor and Pope Collide

During the rule of **Henry IV**, a major quarrel broke out with Pope Gregory VII. In A.D. 1073 the pope condemned lay investiture, hoping to free the Church from secular control. Since the bishops supported Henry in his struggle with feudal lords, the emperor refused to halt the practice.

The pope promptly proclaimed Henry deposed and urged the German nobles to elect another ruler. Henry gave in. In A.D. 1077 he made his way southward in bitter January weather across the snowy mountains to Canossa, Italy. There he sought forgiveness from the pope. He showed his repentance by standing before the gate of the castle begging for mercy for three days.

Gregory pardoned Henry, but the struggle between the Holy Roman emperor and the pope resumed later. Finally, in A.D. 1122, church officials and representatives of the Holy Roman emperor reached a compromise at the German city of Worms. This agreement, known as the Concordat of Worms, allowed the emperor to name bishops and grant them land. It also gave the pope the right to reject unworthy candidates.

Popes and monarchs would continue to struggle over power and territory in the coming years. The increasing strength of Europe's monarchies not only threatened the authority of the Church, but it also paved the way toward other changes on the European scene.

SECTION 4 REVIEW

Recall
1. **Define** common law, grand jury, petit jury, middle class.
2. **Identify** Alfred the Great, William the Conqueror, Henry II, Thomas à Becket, Magna Carta, Philip Augustus, Otto the Great, Henry IV.
3. **Explain** what factors account for the differences in the way French and English monarchs built strong states.

Critical Thinking
4. **Evaluating Information** Judge the importance of the English Parliament in the development of representative government.

Understanding Themes
5. **Conflict** Why did conflicts develop between popes and monarchs? Could their disputes have been resolved peacefully?

SECTION 4 REVIEW ANSWERS

1. All vocabulary words are defined in the Glossary.
2. Alfred the Great, 308; William the Conqueror, 309; Henry II, 309; Thomas à Becket, 309; Magna Carta, 310; Philip Augustus, 311; Otto the Great, 312; Henry IV, 312
3. England developed representative government whereas the French weakened the power of feudal lords.
4. It became more representative when townspeople were added to the original membership of nobles and clergy, and more important as it assumed additional functions.
5. CONFLICT Conflicts developed over whether ecclesiastical or secular leaders had supreme authority, especially in the appointment of religious officials. Answers will vary as to whether conflicts could have been resolved peacefully.

Critical Thinking SKILLS

Making Inferences

Just as you leave home to catch your school bus, you hear a news flash. Firefighters are battling a blaze near the bus garage. Your bus arrives 45 minutes late. Though no one told you directly, you know that the fire disrupted the bus schedule.

Learning the Skill

In the situation above, you made an *inference*. That is, from the limited facts at hand, you formed a conclusion. You knew that the fire was near the garage. From past experience, you knew that fire trucks often create traffic jams. By combining immediate facts and general knowledge, you inferred that the fire trucks delayed your bus.

To make accurate inferences, follow these steps:

- Read or listen carefully for stated facts and ideas.
- Then review what you already know about the same topic or situation.
- Use logic and common sense to form a conclusion about the topic.
- If possible, find specific information that proves or disproves your inference. In the example above, you could determine whether your inference was correct by asking the bus driver why she was late. Or you could read news reports describing the fire and its consequences.

Practicing the Skill

Read the passage about Pepin the Short and then answer the questions that follow.

> "Charles's son, Pepin the Short, succeeded his father and became mayor of the palace in A.D. 741. Pepin ... wished to be named king of the Franks. Since he had no blood claim to the throne, Pepin used his influence with the Frankish bishops and the pope to bring about a change in dynasties. In a show of support, the pope journeyed to France and anointed King Pepin I with holy oil.
>
> In return for the Church's blessing, Pepin was to defend the pope against his enemies. In A.D. 754 the new king forced the Lombards, a Germanic people, to withdraw from Rome. Pepin seized a large tract of Lombard territory around Rome and gave it to the pope."

1. What facts are stated about Pepin the Short's acquisition of the title King of the Franks?
2. Using these facts, what inference can you make about the pope's power in Europe at this time?
3. What facts are stated about Pepin's actions on behalf of the pope?
4. Using these facts, what inference can you make about the Lombards' relations with the pope and with the Franks?

Applying the Skill

Review the sections on "Monastic Life" and the "Influence of Monastics" on pages 304-305. Many men and women adopted the monastic lifestyle during the Middle Ages. What inferences can you make about their motivations? Also, do you think motivations were the same for men and women? How might you prove or disprove these inferences?

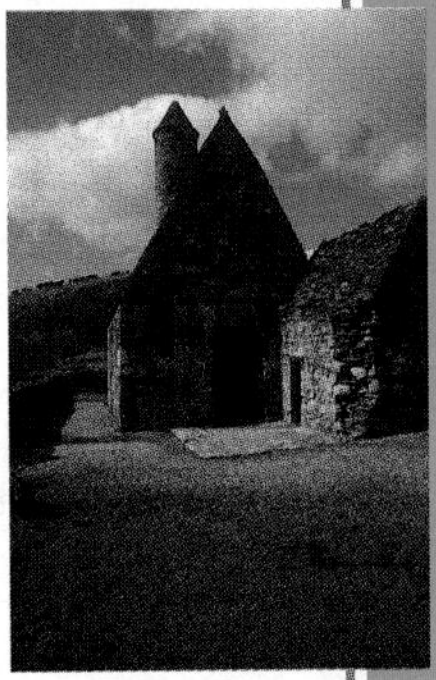

Ancient monastery

For More Practice

Turn to the Skill Practice in the Chapter Review on page 315 for more practice in making inferences.

Critical Thinking SKILLS

TEACH

Making Inferences Bring to class a short news story from the local newspaper or, if appropriate, from the school newspaper. Duplicate and circulate it, or read it aloud to the class. Have students summarize the facts as stated, review what they already know about the situation, and then form one or more conclusions about the topic. If time permits, have the class follow up later if additional information appears to support or refute the conclusion(s).

Additional Practice

Skill Reinforcement Activity 12

ANSWERS TO PRACTICING THE SKILL

1. He had no blood claim to the throne, but he persuaded Frankish bishops and the pope to make a change in dynasties. The pope anointed Pepin with holy oil.
2. The pope must have been powerful.
3. He forced the Lombards out of Rome and gave the pope territory.
4. The Lombards were enemies of the pope; they had more power than the pope. Relations with the Franks were hostile; the Franks exerted power over the Lombards.

Chapter 12 Review

GLENCOE TECHNOLOGY

VIDEODISC

Use MindJogger to review students' knowledge of the chapter.

MindJogger Videoquiz

Chapter 12
Disc 2 Side A

Also available in VHS.

Answers

Using Key Terms

1. k	6. m
2. b	7. f
3. l	8. j
4. a	9. c
5. h	10. i

Using Your History Journal

Encourage students to be as specific as possible about the work monks or nuns did, what they ate, and the religious duties they performed.

Reviewing Facts

1. Muslims, Slavs, Magyars, Vikings
2. In the A.D. 700s, Charles Martel wanted cavalry; he helped warriors pay for their equipment by granting them land.
3. Many bishops and abbots were nobles and thus served as vassals; they could not fight, but they gave land to knights to fight for them.
4. Pope Gregory I sent missionaries to England; from there missionary journeys were made to northern Germany. Irish missionaries traveled throughout North Atlantic and western Europe.
5. church hierarchy, the Church's feudal ties, fighting heresy
6. Monks could not converse with one another except in some cases during a brief period each day.
7. preserved learning; provided schools, hospitals, and guest houses; taught skills to peasants; improved agriculture; did missionary work
8. the *Anglo-Saxon Chronicle*
9. individuals, farmland, towns, manors, livestock

Critical Thinking

1. They grew out of that part of the chivalric code that required knights to treat ladies of noble birth in a courteous manner.
2. In medieval times, most of these problems were dealt with by the Church. Today, although religious organizations and charities play an important role, the responsibility is largely borne by government.
3. It should outline feudalism and manorialism.

CHAPTER 12 REVIEW

Historical Significance

Many of today's European nations, such as Great Britain and France, as well as many of the Western world's legal procedures and forms of government, trace their origins to the political struggles of medieval times.

The medieval Catholic Church wove Christianity into the fabric of Western culture and laid the basis for modern scholarship by preserving and transmitting the learning of the ancient world. Debates today concerning the relationship of Church and state have their echoes in the contest of medieval popes and monarchs for political supremacy.

Using Key Terms

Write the key term that completes each sentence.

a. counts	h. manorialism
b. cardinals	i. abbess
c. chivalry	j. common law
d. fief	k. excommunication
e. feudalism	l. sacraments
f. friars	m. serfs
g. heresy	n. vassal

1. The medieval Catholic Church threatened heretics with ______, or expulsion from the Church.
2. Popes were elected by a gathering of _____, or high church officials in Rome.
3. _______ are formal church rituals, such as baptism, eucharist, confirmation, marriage, anointing of the sick, and holy orders.
4. Charlemagne relied on local officals called ____ to help him rule his large empire.
5. During the Middle Ages, economic life in Europe centered around a system of agricultural production called _________.
6. Peasants in medieval Europe often were _____, people who were bound to the manor.
7. _____, such as the Franciscans and the Dominicans, followed monastic rules but did not isolate themselves from the rest of the Christian community.
8. In place of old feudal rules, Henry II of England established a ______ that applied throughout his kingdom.
9. The code of ________ called for knights to be brave in battle, fight fairly, keep promises, defend the Church, and treat noblewomen courteously.
10. Medieval women took part in monastic life by living in a convent under the supervision of an ______.

Using Your History Journal

The Church had a significant role in medieval life. Imagine living as a monk or a nun. Write a short diary entry called "Today at the Monastery" or "Today at the Convent," describing the life of a monk or a nun.

Reviewing Facts

1. **List** the invading groups that attacked the Carolingian Empire.
2. **Describe** how and when the tie between military service and landownership began.
3. **Explain** the role that church leaders played in the feudal system.
4. **Outline** briefly how missionaries carried Christianity across Europe.
5. **List** the factors that helped maintain religious uniformity during medieval times.
6. **Explain** the monks' rule of silence that was kept in many monasteries.
7. **List** several services that monasteries and convents provided for the community in medieval times.
8. **Name** the history of England that Alfred had scholars write.
9. **List** the various kinds of entries that were recorded in the *Domesday Book.*

Critical Thinking

1. **Apply** Until the 1970s, "good manners" required a man to help a woman with her coat, and push in her chair. How do these customs

relate to chivalry?

2. **Evaluate** Every society has to develop ways to deal with ignorance, ill health, hunger, and homelessness. How did feudal society handle these problems compared to the way modern society handles them?
3. **Synthesize** Use a diagram to describe what goods and services were exchanged among nobles, knights, and peasants.

Geography in History

1. **Place** Refer to the map below. Where did Leif Eriksson's journey lead him?
2. **Movement** What reasons did Vikings have for leaving Scandinavia and venturing out into the Atlantic?
3. **Human/Environment Interaction** Why did the Vikings sail across the far northern part of the Atlantic rather than through the warmer waters to the south?
4. **Location** After leaving Scandinavia, which landmasses did the Vikings explore?

Viking Exploration A.D. 1000

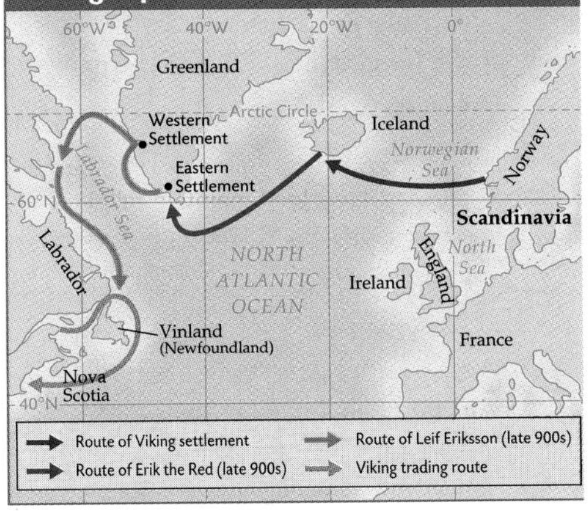

Understanding Themes

1. **Movement** How can the movement of people both have created and crippled Frankish society?
2. **Cooperation** How were lords and peasants mutually dependent?
3. **Uniformity** How is uniformity implied in the term *regular clergy*?
4. **Conflict** How did the conflict between King John and the nobles eventually have positive results for all English people?

Linking Past and Present

1. Great Britain, defended by its island location, has not been invaded since A.D. 1066. What structure has recently been built that will reduce Great Britain's physical isolation from the rest of Europe?
2. People often cherish a romantic view of medieval life: for example, medieval Europeans lived in elegant castles, wore beautiful clothes, and enjoyed festivals. Do you think such a view is justified by historical evidence?
3. Improvements changed farming in Europe around A.D. 1000. What improvements today will increase farm productivity? What far-reaching effects will they have?

Skill Practice

Read the passage about knights. Use stated facts and your knowledge to answer the questions that follow.

> "A knight cannot distinguish himself in [war] if he has not trained for it in tourneys. He must have seen his blood flow, heard his teeth crack under fist blows, felt his opponent's weight bear down upon him as he lay on the ground and, after being twenty times unhorsed, have risen twenty times to fight."

1. From this passage, what can you infer about the physical appearance of many European knights?
2. What fact(s) or observations helped you make this inference?
3. What can you infer about the average length of a knight's career?

Chapter 12 Review

4. **CONFLICT** It resulted in the Magna Carta, which limited the power of the monarch.

Linking Past and Present

1. the Chunnel, the tunnel between England and France under the English Channel
2. No, historical evidence shows that medieval life was harsh and difficult.
3. Hybridization and gene splicing will increase productivity by developing hardier strains of plants. Better pesticides will prevent crop loss due to insects and other pests. Both may reduce hunger and famine.

Skill Practice

1. They probably looked scarred and battered, with broken noses and missing teeth.
2. The passage mentions blood flowing and teeth cracking.
3. It probably was not very long.

Chapter Bonus Test Question

Ask students: Medieval society operated under a system of mutual obligations. What kinds of mutual obligations exist in our own society today? *(Answers will vary. An example might be government: citizens pay taxes and in return are provided with such services as defense and transportation networks.)*

Geography in History

1. to Labrador (Canada) and possibly Vinland (Newfoundland)
2. They were looking for riches, adventure, and land.
3. Their homeland bordered the northern Atlantic.
4. Iceland, Greenland, North America

Understanding Themes

1. **MOVEMENT** Expansion increased power and wealth but made governing more difficult.
2. **COOPERATION** Without lords, peasants would not have had land or protection; without peasants, lords would not have had laborers.
3. **UNIFORMITY** All the members of a given order abided by its rule *(regula)*.

Medieval Europe at Its Height

CHAPTER RESOURCES

	Reproducible Resources	Multimedia Resources
Chapter Opener	Chapter Themes: Graphic Organizer 13 Historical Significance Chapter Activity 13	MindJogger Videoquiz
Chapter Enrichment	Vocabulary Activity 13* Time Line Activity 13 Mapping History Activity 13 History Simulation 13 Geography and History Activity 13 Source Reading 13 People in World History Profiles 23, 24 World Literature Selection 13 World Art and Music Activity 13 Enrichment Activity 13 Critical Thinking Activity 13 Skill Reinforcement Activity 13 Building Skills in Geography Workbook, Unit 1, Lesson 13 Performance Assessment Activity 13	Focus on World Art Prints 15, 17 NGS Poster Set: *The Middle Ages* World History and Art Transparency 16, *May* Mapping History Overlay Transparencies 8, 9 Chapter Transparency 13 NGS PicturePack Transparency Set: *The Middle Ages* Vocabulary PuzzleMaker Software NGS PictureShow CD-ROM: *The Middle Ages* Turning Points in World History: *The Crusades*
Chapter Review/Reteaching	Reteaching Activity 13 Skill Reinforcement Activity 13 Spanish Chapter Summary 13	Chapter 13 Digest Audiocassette, Activity, Test* Vocabulary PuzzleMaker Software Student Self-Test and Review Software MindJogger Videoquiz
Chapter Evaluation/Testing	Performance Assessment Activity 13 Chapter 13 Test, Forms A and B	Testmaker

* *Also available in Spanish*

0:00 OUT OF TIME? Assign the Chapter 13 summary in the Unit 3 Digest on pages 394–397, and the Chapter 13 Audiocassettes.

Block Schedule

Block scheduling differs from traditional class scheduling in the amount of time allotted to each period. The extended time frame provided by block scheduling affords you the opportunity to implement a greater number of research-oriented and activity-intense projects to motivate and involve your students. Activities that are particularly suited to use within the block scheduling framework are identified throughout this chapter by the following designation.

KEY TO ABILITY LEVELS

Teaching strategies have been coded for varying learning styles and abilities.

- L1 **BASIC** activities for all students
- L2 **AVERAGE** activities for average to above-average students
- L3 **CHALLENGING** activities for above-average students
- LEP **LIMITED ENGLISH PROFICIENCY** activities

A complete, 1-page lesson plan is provided for each section in the *Reproducible Lesson Plans* booklet.

SECTION RESOURCES

Daily Objectives	Reproducible Resources	Multimedia Resources
Section 1 The Crusades Summarize how the Crusades began and what their results were.	Reproducible Lesson Plan 13-1 Vocabulary Activity 13* Guided Reading Activity 13-1* Mapping History Activity 13 Time Line Activity 13 Section Quiz 13-1*	NGS Poster Set: *The Middle Ages* Section Focus Transparency 13-1 Chapter Transparency 13 Mapping History Overlay Transparency 8, *Early Christian Communities* Student Self-Test and Review Software Turning Points in World History: *The Crusades*
Section 2 Economic and Cultural Revival Explain how the growth of towns affected the society of medieval Europe.	Reproducible Lesson Plan 13-2 Guided Reading Activity 13-2* Geography and History Activity 13 Section Quiz 13-2*	Focus on World Art Prints 15, 17 Section Focus Transparency 13-2 World History and Art Transparency 16, *May* Mapping History Overlay Transparency 9, *Europe in A.D. 1160* NGS PicturePack Transparency Set: *The Middle Ages* Vocabulary PuzzleMaker Software Student Self-Test and Review Software NGS PictureShow CD-ROM: *The Middle Ages*
Section 3 Strengthening of Monarchy Describe how European monarchs increased their powers during the Middle Ages.	Reproducible Lesson Plan 13-3 Vocabulary Activity 13* Guided Reading Activity 13-3* Section Quiz 13-3*	Section Focus Transparency 13-3 Student Self-Test and Review Software
Section 4 The Troubled Church List the reasons the Church was under pressure to reform.	Reproducible Lesson Plan 13-4 Vocabulary Activity 13* Guided Reading Activity 13-4* History Simulation 13 Reteaching Activity 13 Enrichment Activity 13 Section Quiz 13-4* Performance Assessment Activity 13 Spanish Chapter Summary 13	Section Focus Transparency 13-4 Student Self-Test and Review Software Testmaker

* *Also available in Spanish*

Chapter Activities

Performance Assessment Activity

Starting a Modern-Day Crusade Have students expand their concept of *crusade* by researching modern-day crusades such as the women's movement, the March of Dimes crusade against polio, and so forth. After students have developed various perspectives on crusades, have them choose an issue for which they would "crusade." Students should take the roles of social activists and develop a plan for their crusade, including major events, strategies, people they would involve, and so on. Students should also complete a reflection in which they compare their crusade to that of medieval times.

Possible Rubric Features
Accuracy of content information, research skills, organization of plan, decision-making skills

• *For an additional activity, refer to Activity 13 in the* Performance Assessment Strategies and Activities *booklet.*

Activity

From the Classroom of...

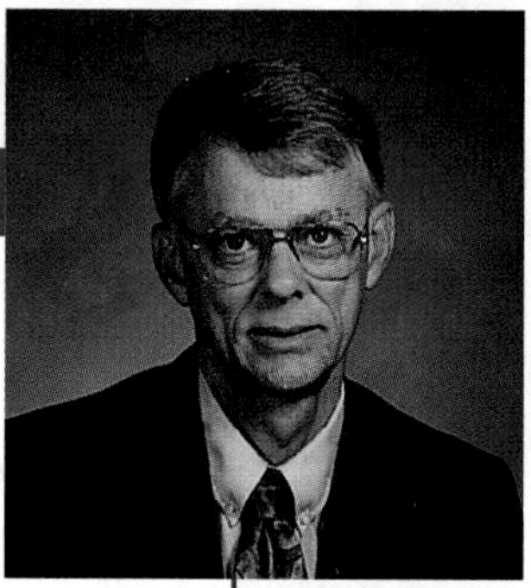

Hank Poehling
Central High School
La Crosse, Wisconsin

Compare and Contrast

The purpose of this project is to acquaint students with the historical impact of the Black Death on medieval European society. In comparing the Black Death to AIDS, students will understand the relevance of history as they also examine a contemporary problem. In addition, they receive beneficial AIDS education.

Have students produce a project comparing and contrasting the Black Death (bubonic plague) with AIDS, working either individually or in groups of up to four. The type of project can be left up to each individual or group—a display, a video newscast, a reenactment, a news-style magazine. Tell students that the following areas must be addressed in the project:

- causes of both diseases
- symptoms of both diseases
- how both are spread
- any known or possible cures for both
- the effects of each disease on the individual
- the effects of each disease on society

Allow about two weeks for the projects. On the due date, have all groups and individuals make a formal presentation of their projects to the class.

MULTIPLE LEARNING STYLES

Verbal/Linguistic
Have students prepare a talk show program about dissent within the Church during the High Middle Ages. The guests to be interviewed might include a corrupt clergyman, Pope Clement V, John Wycliffe, and Jan Hus. Students should research the lives of these figures. Then some students may act the parts of each of these figures, based on the research, and others may serve as panel members and the host of the show. Both host and panel members should research sufficiently to enable them to prepare a set of questions in advance of the show.

Visual/Spatial
Have the class work together to create a mural in the fashion of the tapestries that were popular as wall hangings during the Middle Ages. First have them research the art of tapestry and the tapestries of the Middle Ages. Then they can design a tapestry or set of tapestries, depicting some motif or event from this chapter. Students may choose such themes as the Crusades, a medieval fair, a battle of the Hundred Years' War, or some other theme. Display the completed tapestry designs in class.

Auditory/Musical
Have students present a short musical based on portraits from the General Prologue to Chaucer's *The Canterbury Tales.* Students may choose to write their lyrics either to music typical of the Middle Ages or to contemporary music.

Intrapersonal
Have students write essays in which they state whether they would have supported or opposed Wycliffe or Hus during the late Middle Ages. Ask them to explain the reasons for their stand.

Additional Resources

TEACHER'S CORNER

NATIONAL GEOGRAPHIC SOCIETY

INDEX TO NATIONAL GEOGRAPHIC MAGAZINE

The following articles may be used for research relating to this chapter:

- "The Power of Money," by Peter T. White, January 1993.
- "Retracing the First Crusade," by Tim Severin, September 1989.
- "A Castle Under the Louvre," by Peter Miller, July 1989.
- "The Gothic Revolution," by James L. Stanfield and Victor R. Boswell, Jr., July 1989.

NATIONAL GEOGRAPHIC SOCIETY PRODUCTS AVAILABLE FROM GLENCOE

To order the following products for use with this chapter, contact your local Glencoe sales representative or call Glencoe at 1-800-368-7344:

NGS PICTURESHOW CD-ROM
- The Middle Ages

NGS PICTUREPACK TRANSPARENCY SET
- The Middle Ages

NGS POSTER SET
- The Middle Ages

ADDITIONAL NATIONAL GEOGRAPHIC SOCIETY PRODUCTS

To order the following products for use with this chapter, call National Geographic Society at 1-800-368-2728:

- *The Middle Ages*, "A Historical Overview," "Feudal Life," "The Rise of Towns." (Filmstrip)
- *Money: Summing It Up* (Video)

BIBLIOGRAPHY

Literature of the Period

Chauncer, Geoffrey. *The Canterbury Tales.* In *The Complete Poetry and Prose of Geoffrey Chaucer*, 2nd ed. New York: Holt, Rinehart and Winston, 1989. This masterpiece of English literature gives insight into the character of the Middle Ages.

Readings for the Student

Gies, Frances and Joseph. *Life in a Medieval Village.* New York: HarperCollins, 1991. Describes everyday life and real people in a medieval village.

Readings for the Teacher

Armstrong, Karen. *Holy War: The Crusades and Their Impact on Today's World.* New York: Doubleday, 1991. Analyzes the effect of the Crusades on current relations among Christians, Jews, and Muslims.

Tuchman, Barbara. *A Distant Mirror: The Calamitous Fourteenth Century.* New York: Alfred A. Knopf, 1979. An illustrated analysis of life and problems in the turbulent 1300s.

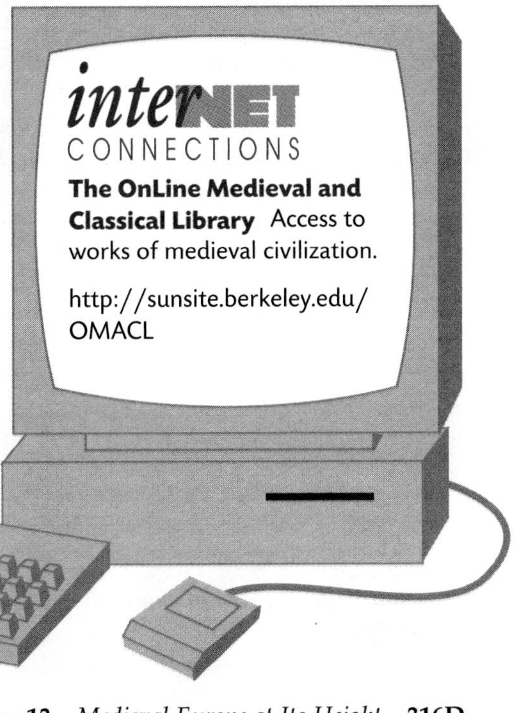

interNET
CONNECTIONS
The OnLine Medieval and Classical Library Access to works of medieval civilization.
http://sunsite.berkeley.edu/OMACL

Introducing Chapter 13

CHAPTER THEMES

Chapter Themes are listed by section on this chapter opening page of the Student Edition. A corresponding theme-based activity is available under "TEACH," and a theme-based question is asked in the Section and Chapter Reviews.

The Storyteller

Historical Setting In medieval Latin, the word *universitas* meant "corporation," and the earliest universities were corporations of students and masters. These corporations received charters from popes and emperors but were entitled to govern themselves as long as they stayed away from heretical or atheistic teachings. Along with this freedom came financial independence, which meant that teachers had not only to charge fees but also to please those they taught in order to attract enough students to guarantee themselves a living. As the letter from the student to his father shows, students also had financial worries. Some colleges offered room and board to the poorest students.

Historical Significance

Answers: *Modern nations, national languages, many of Europe's great cities, international trade networks, the predecessors of modern labor unions, the middle class, and the university all had their beginnings during the height of the Middle Ages.*

The Crusades, the breakdown of the feudal system and the growth of towns, the Hundred Years' War, and dissension within the Church changed European society during the High Middle Ages.

Chapter 13

A.D. 1050–1500

Medieval Europe at Its Height

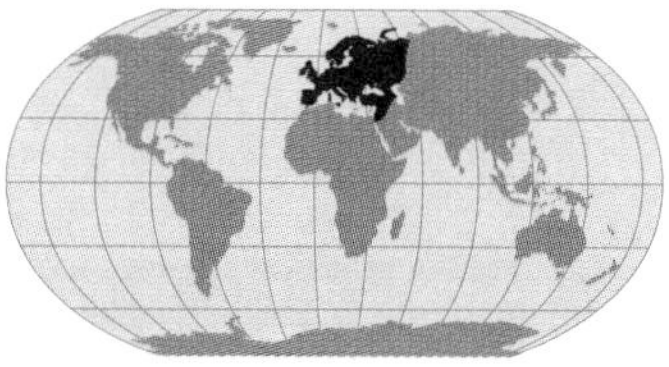

Chapter Themes

- **Cultural Diffusion** The Crusades increase European contact with other areas. *Section 1*
- **Innovation** Advances in commerce, learning, and the arts change Europe. *Section 2*
- **Conflict** England and France battle while their monarchs gain power. *Section 3*
- **Conflict** The Church faces a split from within and opposition from without. *Section 4*

The Storyteller

"Well-beloved father," wrote a medieval student, "I have not a penny, nor can I get any save through you, for all things at the University are so dear: nor can I study in my [law books], for they are all tattered. Moreover, I owe ten crowns in dues to the [university administrator], and can find no man to lend them to me.

"Well-beloved father, to ease my debts ... at the baker's, with the doctor ... and to pay ... the laundress and the barber, I send you word of greetings and of money."

This letter from a medieval student sounds very much like something a modern student might write. At that time, however, the university was something new. It was part of the cultural awakening that took place in the High Middle Ages.

Historical Significance

What features of modern Western civilization had their beginnings during the height of the Middle Ages in western Europe? What new developments changed European society during the High Middle Ages?

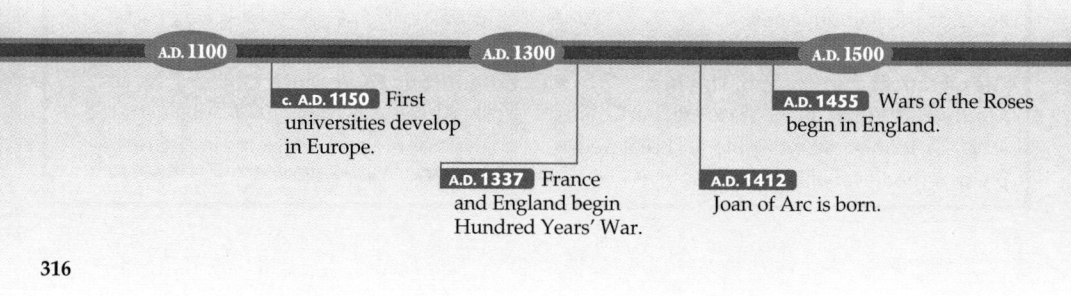

A.D. 1100 — A.D. 1300 — A.D. 1500

- c. A.D. 1150 First universities develop in Europe.
- A.D. 1337 France and England begin Hundred Years' War.
- A.D. 1412 Joan of Arc is born.
- A.D. 1455 Wars of the Roses begin in England.

316

GEOGRAPHY CONNECTION

GEOGRAPHIC THEMES

Movement Have students use a map to locate the city of Jerusalem (in the present country of Israel), as well as England, France, Germany, and Italy. Have students discuss some of the difficulties that physical geography presented to medieval armies traveling from Europe to Jerusalem. *(crossing the Alps, crossing the mountains of the Macedonian peninsula, traveling through the Syrian and Palestinian deserts, the dangers of open sea voyages on the Mediterranean)*

History & Art *The Church Militant and Triumphant,* a fresco from the A.D. 1300s by Andrea de Bonaiuto. The Spanish Chapel in Santa Maria Novella, Florence, Italy

Your History Journal

Medieval literature contains epics that were put into writing for the first time. Read an excerpt from Beowulf, *the* Song of Roland, *or* The Canterbury Tales *and take notes about life in Europe at the time.*

Introducing Chapter 13

History & Art The church of Santa Maria Novella was founded by the Dominicans, who were named after a Spanish priest. But in Latin the words *Domini Canes* mean the "dogs of God." Why did de Bonaiuto include dogs in his fresco? *(The Dominicans served God in hunting out heresy like hounds served hunters by tracking prey.)*

Performance Assessment

Refer to the activity on page 316C of the Planning Guide.

For an additional activity, refer to Activity 13 in the *Performance Assessment Strategies and Activities* booklet.

Using Your History Journal

Suggest that students look for details of medieval life in the descriptions of the feasts in *Beowulf*; in the General Prologue to *The Canterbury Tales*; or in the description of the battle at Roncesvalles in the *Song of Roland*.

GLENCOE TECHNOLOGY

VIDEODISC

Use MindJogger to preview chapter content.

MindJogger Videoquiz

Chapter 13
Disc 2 Side B

Also available in VHS.

EXTRA CREDIT PROJECT

Research Report The Crusades are of interest from a military as well as a religious perspective. Ask students to prepare a report that compares and contrasts the organization, tactics, and effectiveness of the Crusader and Muslim armies. Suggested resources: R. C. Finucane, *Soldiers of the Faith: Crusaders and Moslems at War*; J. Godfrey, *1204: The Unholy Crusade*; H. E. Mayer, *The Crusades*; and J. Riley-Smith, *The Crusades: A Short History.*

Chapter 13 Section 1

SECTION THEME

▶ **Cultural Diffusion** The Crusades increased European contact with other areas.

Find Out

Answer: *The Crusades were organized to free the Holy Land from the Muslims. They did not establish lasting Christian control over the area but stimulated economic and intellectual growth in Europe.*

FOCUS

Section Objective

Summarize how the Crusades began and what their results were.

BELLRINGER
Motivational Activity

Before taking roll at the beginning of the class period, project Section Focus Transparency 13-1 and have students answer the activity questions. Discuss students' responses.

This activity is also available as a blackline master.

Vocabulary Pre-check

Use Vocabulary Activity 13 to introduce vocabulary terms.
L1 LEP

A.D. 1050 — A.D. 1150 — A.D. 1250

- **A.D. 1095** Pope Urban II calls for First Crusade.
- **A.D. 1147** Second Crusade begins.
- **A.D. 1204** Crusaders sack Constantinople.
- **A.D. 1212** Children's Crusade begins.

Section 1

The Crusades

Setting the Scene

▶ **Terms to Define**
the Crusades

▶ **People to Meet**
the Seljuk Turks, Pope Urban II, Saladin, Richard I

▶ **Places to Locate**
Jerusalem, Constantinople

Find Out How did the Crusades begin, and what were their results?

The Storyteller

Geoffrey de Renneville was footsore, thirsty, and covered with dust. He had joined the Crusade as an adventure. The Crusaders had traveled for weeks and were beset by flies, bandits, disease, poor food, and limited drink. The cavalcade stopped and the weary men dropped into an uneasy slumber. Suddenly, they were startled awake by the cry "Help for the Holy Sepulchre!" One by one the knights took up the cry. Shouting with the others, Geoffrey was reminded of the Crusade's purpose.

—adapted from *The Dream and the Tomb*, Robert Payne, 1984

Leaving for the Crusades

Life in the Early Middle Ages was characterized by decentralized and destabilized government, warfare and invasions, cultural isolation, famine, and wretched living conditions. Trade was sparse, and agricultural production—the mainstay of the European economy—was inefficient.

By A.D. 1100, however, conditions in Europe had begun to improve. Some European monarchs succeeded in building strong central governments. Better farming methods led to larger crop yields and a growth in population. Towns and trade began to reappear. The Church held a powerful sway over the emotions and energies of the people. Changes in religion, society, politics, and economics made the High Middle Ages—the period between A.D. 1050 and A.D. 1270—a springboard for a new and brilliant civilization in western Europe.

The transformation of medieval society began with a holy war over the city of **Jerusalem**. European Christians undertook a series of military expeditions—nine in all—to recover the Holy Land from the Muslims. These expeditions were called **the Crusades**, from the Latin word *crux*, meaning "cross." Those who fought were called Crusaders because they vowed to "take up the cross."

Call for a Crusade

Jerusalem was a holy city for people of three faiths. Jews treasured it as Zion, God's own city, and as the site of the ancient temple built by Solomon. To Christians, the city was holy because it was the place where Jesus was crucified and resurrected. Muslims regarded Jerusalem as their third holiest city, after Makkah and Madinah. According to Muslim tradition, Muhammad ascended to heaven from Jerusalem.

Jerusalem and the entire region of Palestine fell to Arab invaders in the A.D. 600s. Mostly Muslims, the Arabs tolerated other religions. Christians and

SECTION RESOURCES

Reproducible Masters
- Reproducible Lesson Plan 13-1
- Vocabulary Activity 13
- Guided Reading Activity 13-1
- Mapping History Activity 13
- Time Line Activity 13
- Section Quiz 13-1

Transparencies
- Section Focus Transparency 13-1
- Chapter Transparency 13
- Mapping History Overlay Transparency 8

Multimedia
- The Middle Ages
- Student Self-Test and Review Software
- Testmaker
- The Crusades

Jews were allowed to live in Jerusalem as long as they paid their taxes and followed certain regulations. European traders and religious pilgrims traveled to Palestine without interference.

In the late A.D. 1000s, however, **the Seljuk Turks**—a Muslim people from central Asia—took control of Jerusalem and closed the city to Jewish and Christian pilgrims. The Seljuks also threatened the Byzantine Empire, especially **Constantinople**. As a result of this threat, the Byzantine emperor wrote to the pope in A.D. 1095 requesting military assistance from the West. Reports of persecution against Christians in Palestine gave added urgency to the emperor's request.

First Crusade

On a cold November day in A.D. 1095, **Pope Urban II** mounted a platform outside the church at Clermont, France. His voice shaking with emotion, he addressed the assembled throng, asking for a volunteer army to take Jerusalem and Palestine from the Seljuks:

> "I exhort you ... to strive to expel that wicked race from our Christian lands.... Christ commands it. Remission of sins will be granted for those going thither.... Let those who are accustomed to wage private war wastefully even against believers go forth against the infidels.... Let those who have lived by plundering be soldiers of Christ; let those who formerly contended against brothers and relations rightly fight barbarians; let those who were recently hired for a few pieces of silver win their eternal reward."

"Deus vult!" (God wills it!) shouted the crowd in response to the pope's plea. Knights and peasants alike vowed to join the expedition to the Holy Land. For knights, the Crusade was a welcome chance to employ their fighting skills. For peasants, the Crusade meant freedom from feudal bonds while on the Crusade. All were promised immediate salvation in heaven if they were killed freeing the Holy Land from non-Christians. Adventure and the possibility of wealth were other reasons to join the Crusade. In preparation for the holy war, red crosses of cloth were stitched on clothing as a symbol of service to God.

This First Crusade heightened already existing hatred of non-Christians and marked the onset of a long period of Christian persecution of the Jews. During the First Crusade, which began in A.D. 1096, three armies of Crusader knights and volunteers

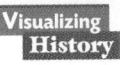

Visualizing History **Pope Urban II arrives at the Council of Clermont.** *What did the pope ask the people to do?*

traveled separately from western Europe to the eastern Mediterranean. On the way, many of them killed Jews and sometimes massacred entire Jewish communities.

Led by French nobles, the three armies finally met in Constantinople in A.D. 1097. From there the Crusaders made their way to Jerusalem, enduring the hardships of desert travel as well as quarrels among their leaders. In June A.D. 1099, the Crusaders finally reached the city. After a siege of almost two months Jerusalem fell. Crusaders swarmed into the city and killed most of its Muslim and Jewish inhabitants.

The success of the First Crusade reinforced the authority of the Church and strengthened the self-confidence of western Europeans. The religious zeal of the Crusaders soon cooled, however, and many knights returned home. Those who stayed set up feudal states in Syria and Palestine. Contact between the Crusaders and the relatively more sophisticated civilizations of the Byzantines and the Muslims would continue for the next 100 years and become a major factor in ending the cultural isolation of western Europe.

Chapter 13 Section 1

TEACH

Guided Practice

THEME Cultural Diffusion

Have students provide examples of cultural diffusion that resulted from the Crusades. *(exposure of Europe to classic texts preserved by the Muslims and Byzantines, to Muslim expertise in cartography and shipbuilding technology, and to many luxury goods from the East)* **L1**

Chapter Transparency 13

Mapping History Overlay Transparency 8, *Early Christian Communities*

Visualizing History When he was born to noble parents about 1035 in the Champagne region of France, the baby who would become pope some 53 years later was named Odo.
Answer to Caption: *to wage war against the infidels*

ABCNEWS INTERACTIVE™

VIDEODISC
Turning Points in World History

Side One
Chapter 7

Title: *The Crusades*
Subject: Western Europeans warred against the Muslim Turks to secure Jerusalem.
Ask: How did the Crusades encourage Europeans to increase trade? *(increased knowledge of Asia's civilizations increased the demand for imported goods)*

COOPERATIVE LEARNING ACTIVITY

Drawing Maps Have students work in small groups to research and prepare maps of the various routes used by the Crusaders to reach the Middle East. (For example, early Crusaders from France and Germany sailed from Italy to Greece or crossed Europe to Constantinople, then marched across present-day Turkey. Later Crusaders sailed from the Mediterranean coast to ports in Palestine.) Assign each student a task, such as tracing the area from western Europe to the Middle East, drawing in topographic features, drawing the routes used by the Crusaders, or illustrating maps with pictures pertaining to the Crusaders or dangers they encountered. Display and discuss the completed maps in class. **L2**

Map Study

Answer

about 1,875 miles (3,017 km)

Map Skills Practice

Reading a Map About how far did Crusaders on the First Crusade travel before reaching Jerusalem? *(about 2,000 miles [3,218 km])*

Independent Practice

Guided Reading Activity 13-1 **L1**

Mapping History Activity 13

Time Line Activity 13

Daily Life Ask students to report on how the European lifestyle of a knight differed from his lifestyle in the Middle East. Have students report on differences in housing, food, and clothing. **L2**

Literature Have students read Sir Walter Scott's *Ivanhoe*, whose main character is a Crusader. Ask them to report to the class on the Christian-Jewish interactions depicted in the novel. **L3**

NATIONAL GEOGRAPHIC SOCIETY

Use these materials to enrich student understanding of the Middle Ages.

NGS POSTER SET
The Middle Ages

ASSESS

Check for Understanding

Assign Section 1 Review as homework or as an in-class activity.

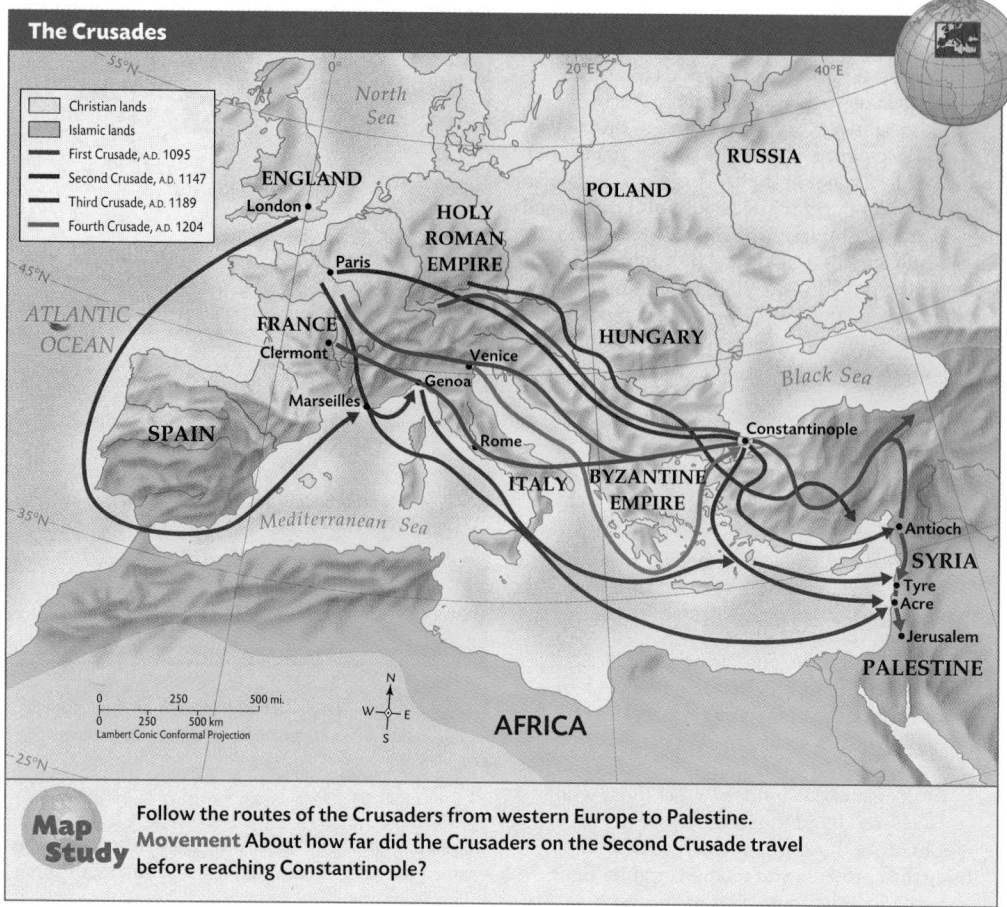

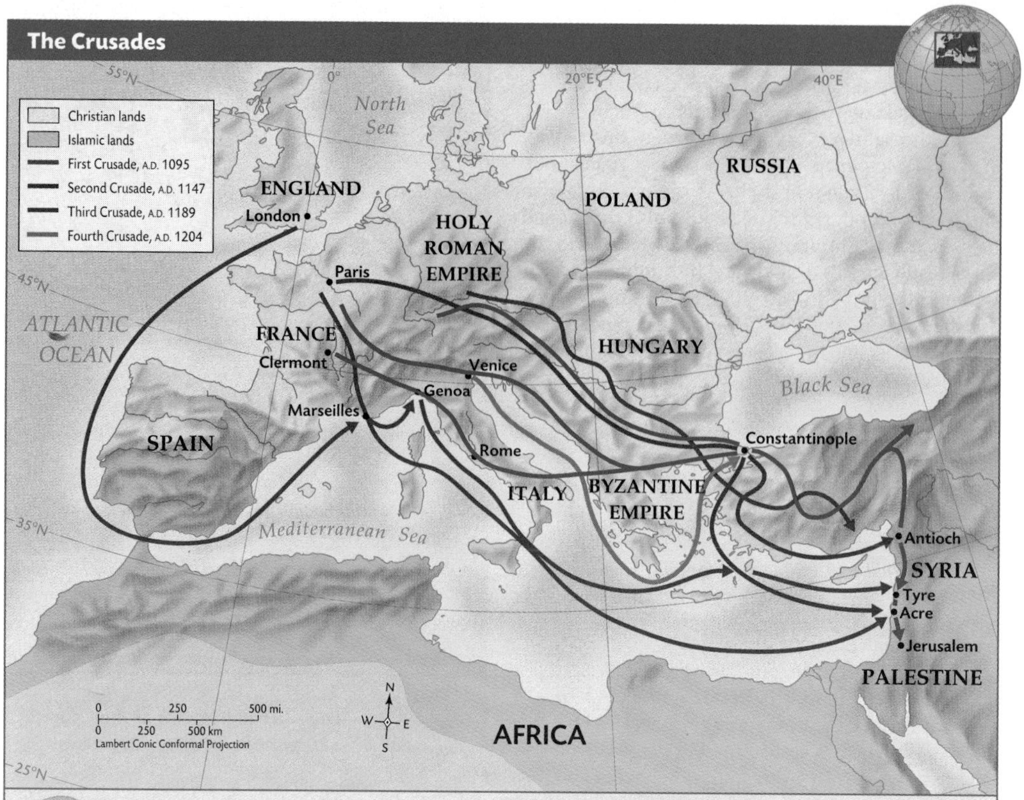

Map Study Follow the routes of the Crusaders from western Europe to Palestine.
Movement About how far did the Crusaders on the Second Crusade travel before reaching Constantinople?

Second Crusade

Less than 50 years after the First Crusade, the Seljuks conquered part of the Crusader states in Palestine. Pope Eugenius IV called for a Second Crusade to regain the territory. Eloquent sermons by the monk Bernard of Clairvaux (KLAR•VOH) persuaded King Louis VII of France and Holy Roman Emperor Conrad III to lead armies to Palestine. The Second Crusade, which lasted from A.D. 1147 to A.D. 1149, was unsuccessful. Louis VII and Conrad III quarreled constantly and were ineffective militarily. They were easily defeated by the Seljuks.

Third Crusade

A diplomatic and forceful leader named **Saladin** (SA•luh•DEEN) united the Muslim forces and then captured Jerusalem in A.D. 1187. The people of western Europe were stunned and horrified. Holy Roman Emperor Frederick Barbarossa of Germany, King Philip Augustus of France, and King **Richard I** of England assembled warriors for the Third Crusade. This "Crusade of Kings" lasted from A.D. 1189 to A.D. 1192 and was no more successful than the Second Crusade. Frederick Barbarossa died on the way to Palestine, and his army returned home. Philip Augustus returned to France before the army reached Jerusalem. Richard continued the struggle alone.

Although his army defeated the Muslims in several battles, Richard could not win a decisive victory over Saladin's well-trained and dedicated forces. After three years of fighting, Richard signed a truce with the Muslims and tried to persuade Saladin to return Jerusalem to the Christians. "Jerusalem," he wrote to the Muslim leader, "we are resolved not to renounce as long as we have a single man left." Saladin's reply to Richard showed his equal determination to keep the city:

MEETING SPECIAL NEEDS ACTIVITY

Learning Style: Visual/Spatial To reinforce the ideas presented in this section, have students who are visual learners draw a series of illustrations depicting important events and people. Illustrations could include Pope Urban II delivering his call for the First Crusade, a series of drawings depicting the journeys of Crusaders to the Holy Land, or a portrait of King Richard I of England. Ask the artists to work with other students to create text that explains their drawings. Display the completed drawings and accompanying text in the classroom. **L1 LEP**

"To us Jerusalem is as precious, aye and more precious, than it is to you, in that it was the place whence our Prophet made his journey by night to heaven and is destined to be the gathering place of our nation at the last day. Do not dream that we shall give it up to you.... It belonged to us originally, and it is you who are the real aggressors. When you seized it, it was only because of the suddenness of your coming and the weakness of those [Muslims] who then held it. So long as the war shall last God will not suffer you to raise one stone upon another."

Although Saladin refused to turn over Jerusalem, he allowed Christian pilgrims access.

Other Crusades

Other Crusades followed in the A.D. 1200s, but none succeeded in winning permanent Christian control of Palestine. In fact, the Muslims slowly conquered all the remaining Christian territories. In A.D. 1291 they captured Acre, the last Christian stronghold in Palestine. By this time, western Europeans had lost sight of the religious goal of the Crusades. They were now more concerned about political and economic gain. As a result, European rulers lost interest in regaining Palestine and shifted their attention to other matters.

Effects of the Crusades

The Crusades failed to free the Holy Land from the Muslims. Nonetheless, the Crusades had a major impact on the development of western Europe. In Europe, the Crusades helped break down feudalism and increase the authority of kings. Kings levied taxes and raised large armies of fighting forces. Some nobles died in battle without leaving heirs, and their lands passed to kings. To raise money for weapons and supplies, many lesser nobles sold their estates or allowed their serfs to buy their freedom to become freeholders on the land or artisans in the towns.

European contact during the Crusades with the more advanced Byzantine and Muslim civilizations helped to bring classical texts back to the West. This knowledge fueled a renewed interest in literature and art that later swept across Europe.

In addition, European cities—especially Venice and Genoa in Italy—became more prosperous and powerful due to increased trading in the Mediterranean. Contact with the East spurred a new demand for luxury goods: spices, sugar, melons, tapestries, silk, and other items previously hard to come by.

Finally, the Crusades improved European technology. From the Muslims, the Crusaders learned how to build better ships and make more accurate maps. They began to use the magnetic compass to tell direction. The Crusaders also learned new military skills, especially in siege techniques. Weaponry significantly improved as well.

History & Art *Return from the Crusade* by Karl Friedrich Lessing. Rheinland Museum, Bonn, Germany *How did the Crusades help to break down feudalism?*

SECTION 1 REVIEW

Recall

1. **Define** the Crusades.
2. **Identify** the Seljuk Turks, Pope Urban II, Saladin, Richard I.
3. **Explain** why both Christians and Muslims of the A.D. 1000s and A.D. 1100s felt that Jerusalem should belong to them.

Critical Thinking

4. **Analyzing Information** In what ways were the Crusades a success? In what ways were they a failure?

Understanding Themes

5. **Cultural Diffusion** Describe how cultural diffusion in the Middle Ages occurred throughout Europe and the Mediterranean world as a result of the Crusades.

Chapter 13 Section 1

History & Art By bringing the knights of Christian Europe together in a joint undertaking sponsored by the Church, the Crusades did much to transform the Christian ideal of knightly behavior into reality. **Answer to Caption:** *They weakened feudal lords, whose lands passed to kings when the lords died heirless in battle. The lords sometimes raised money for weapons and supplies by selling their estates or allowing their serfs to buy their freedom.*

Use Student Self-Test and Review Software to review Section 1.

Evaluate

Section Quiz 13-1

Use the Testmaker to create a customized quiz for Section 1.

Reteach

Have students work in small groups to list the important features of each Crusade discussed in this section. Have the groups compare and discuss their lists.

Enrich

Have students read an account of Saladin and Richard I during the Third Crusade. Ask them to give a brief oral report comparing the character of the two men, their motives for fighting, and the regard in which they held each other.

CLOSE

Have students evaluate the positive and negative effects of the Crusades on Western civilization. *(gains: increased trade and knowledge; losses: heavy casualties, bitterness and distrust between Muslims and Christians)*

SECTION 1 REVIEW ANSWERS

1. All vocabulary words are defined in the Glossary.
2. Seljuk Turks, 319; Pope Urban II, 319; Saladin, 320; Richard I, 320
3. For Christians, the city was the site of Jesus' crucifixion and resurrection; for Muslims, of Muhammad's ascent to heaven.
4. They brought new ideas and goods to western Europe, broke down feudalism and strengthened monarchies, but they were very costly in terms of human life and failed to achieve their goal.
5. **CULTURAL DIFFUSION** Contact with eastern cultures improved European learning, technology, and trade.

Chapter 13
Section 2

SECTION THEME

▸ **Innovation** Advances in commerce, learning, and the arts change Europe.

Find Out

Answer: *The middle class arose, feudalism declined, and the need for educated town officials stimulated an interest in learning.*

FOCUS

Section Objective

Explain how the growth of towns affected the society of medieval Europe.

BELLRINGER Motivational Activity

Before taking roll at the beginning of the class period, project Section Focus Transparency 13-2 and have students answer the activity questions. Discuss students' responses.

This activity is also available as a blackline master.

Vocabulary Pre-check

Use the Vocabulary PuzzleMaker to create a puzzle that reinforces the vocabulary terms in this section. **L1**

A.D. 1000 — A.D. 1200 — A.D. 1400

- **c. A.D. 1000** Europe's economy begins to revive.
- **c. A.D. 1150** French architects begin to build in the Gothic style.
- **c. A.D. 1348** The Black Death spreads throughout Europe.
- **c. A.D. 1386** Geoffrey Chaucer begins writing *The Canterbury Tales.*

Section 2

Economic and Cultural Revival

Setting the Scene

▸ **Terms to Define**
money economy, guild, master, apprentice, journeyman, charter, scholasticism, troubadour, vernacular

▸ **People to Meet**
Thomas Aquinas, Dante Alighieri, Geoffrey Chaucer

▸ **Places to Locate**
Venice, Flanders, Champagne, Bologna

Find Out How did the growth of towns affect the society of medieval Europe?

The Storyteller

To help rebuild the cathedral, people for miles around brought their goods. So that the church might rise swiftly, larger and more beautiful than any they had seen, peasants, skilled workers, and even nobles pulled heavy carts filled with wood and stone. Religious fervor motivated the people, and the reward was a renewed spirit in the community. Perfect harmony reigned. During the night, the workers formed a camp with their wagons, and by the light of candles, they sang canticles and psalms. Everyone was doing penance and forgiving their enemies.

—adapted from *Chronique*, Robert de Torigni, in *Chartres*, Emil Mâle, translated by Sarah Wilson, 1983

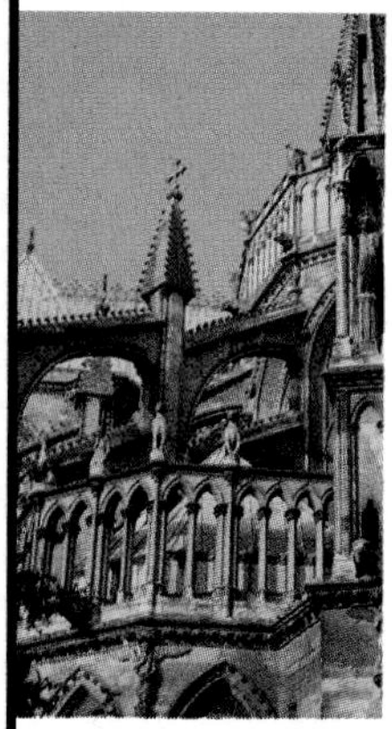

Cathedral at Reims, France

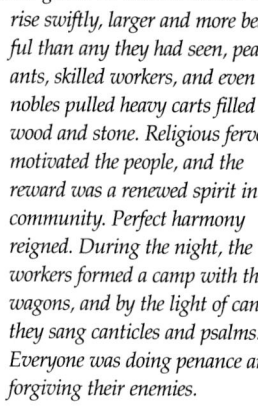

The Crusades accelerated the transformation of western Europe from a society that was crude, backward, and violent—showing little cultural and technological advancement—to a civilization that exhibited some early features of modern Western civilization. Towns grew, trade expanded, and learning and the arts thrived.

Economic Expansion

The economy of western Europe had begun to show vigor around A.D. 1000. Agricultural production increased. Expanding opportunities in trade encouraged the growth of towns, and the lively atmosphere of the towns in turn stimulated creative thought and innovations in art.

Agricultural Advances

Plows during the Early Middle Ages were light and did not cut much below the surface of the soil. The invention of a new, heavier plow made it possible to cut through the rich, damp soils of northwestern Europe. This plow enabled farmers to produce more and to cultivate new lands, increasing food production. Nobles and freeholders—peasants not bound to the land—migrated to new areas, clearing forests, draining swamps, and building villages. In one of the largest migrations of the time, the Germans moved to areas of eastern Europe, doubling the territory they controlled.

About the same time, the collar harness replaced the ox yoke. Horses were choked by the ox yoke, but the new harness shifted weight off the neck and onto the shoulders, allowing farmers to replace oxen with horses. Horses pulled the plow faster than oxen, allowing farmers to plant and plow more crops.

SECTION RESOURCES

Reproducible Masters
- Reproducible Lesson Plan 13-2
- Guided Reading Activity 13-2
- Geography and History Activity 13
- Section Quiz 13-2

Transparencies
- Section Focus Transparency 13-2
- World History and Art Transparency 16
- Mapping History Overlay Transparency 9
- The Middle Ages

Multimedia
- Focus on World Art Prints 15, 17
- Vocabulary PuzzleMaker Software
- Student Self-Test and Review Software
- Testmaker
- The Middle Ages

As you read in Chapter 12, the three-field system of planting also made the land more productive. As the land began to feed more people, the population naturally increased.

Expansion of Trade

The revival of towns caused a rapid expansion of trade. Soon the sea-lanes and roads were filled with traders carrying goods to market. Important sea and river routes connected western Europe with the Mediterranean, eastern Europe, and Scandinavia. The repaired and rebuilt Roman road system carried international traders to and from Europe.

Italian towns such as **Venice**, Pisa, and Genoa controlled the Mediterranean trade after A.D. 1200, bringing silks and spices from Asia to Europe. The town of **Flanders**, a region that includes present-day northern France and southern Belgium, became the center of trade on Europe's northern coast. The textiles produced by these towns were traded at Middle Eastern markets for porcelain, velvet and silk, and silver. Towns along the Baltic coast controlled trade between eastern Europe and the North Atlantic.

The merchandise for sale in a town was varied and seemingly endless. This was especially true during trade fairs. Each year hundreds of traders met at large trade fairs in places convenient to land and water routes. Feudal lords charged the merchants fees, charged taxes on goods, and offered protection to the merchants. The most famous fair was at **Champagne** in eastern France, located in almost the exact center of western Europe. For four to six weeks each year, Champagne was a distribution point for goods from around the world.

Banking

Early merchants used the barter system, trading goods without using money. Before long, however, merchants found this system impractical. Moreover, some of the merchants who supplied luxury goods such as silk would only accept money in payment. European merchants therefore needed a common medium of exchange.

The rise of a money economy, or an economy based on money, had far-reaching consequences. Initially, it led to the growth of banking. Since traders came from many countries, they carried different currencies with different values. Moneychangers—often Jews or Italians—determined the value of the various currencies and exchanged one currency for another. They also developed procedures for transferring funds from one place to another, received deposits, and arranged loans, thus becoming the first bankers in Europe. Indeed, the word *bank* comes from the *banca*, or bench, that the moneychangers set up at fairs.

As the money economy grew, it put the feudal classes in an economic squeeze. Kings, clergy, and nobles became dependent on money from banks to pay their expenses. To pay off their loans, they had to raise taxes, sell their lands, or demand money in place of traditional feudal services. As serfs became able to buy their freedom, the feudal system declined.

Visualizing History **Italian bankers, from *Treatise on the Seven Vices: Avarice*. The Church viewed lending with the intent to charge interest as evil.** *What is the origin of the term "bank"?*

Growth of Towns

The number of towns in western Europe grew tremendously in the A.D. 1000s and A.D. 1100s. Many grew up beside well-traveled roads or near waterways. Although warfare had declined,

Chapter 13 Section 2

TEACH

Guided Practice

THEME Innovation

Have students give some examples of innovations that developed during the High Middle Ages. *(heavier plows and collar harnesses, trade fairs, money economy, universities)* **L1 LEP**

Economics Have students explain the consequences of the rise of a money economy. Ask how it affected banking. *(led to the growth of banking)* How did a money economy affect the feudal system? *(It weakened feudalism by forcing lords to become dependent on money for expenses and by enabling serfs to buy their freedom.)* **L2**

Visualizing History Medieval scholars associated the demon Mammon, whose name means "riches" in Aramaic, with the sin of avarice, or insatiable greed for riches.

Answer to Caption: *It derives from the* banca*, or bench, that money changers set up at medieval fairs.*

you don't say...

Burg The term *burg* originally meant a fortified town or castle. As part of town names, it appeared in the German *-burg*, the French *-bourg*, and the English *-borough* and *-bury*. Today in Europe one can find Hamburg, Strasbourg, Edinburgh, and Canterbury; in the United States there is Pittsburgh, Harrisburg, Jonesboro, and Salisbury.

COOPERATIVE LEARNING ACTIVITY

Role Play Have students write and present a brief play showing daily life in a medieval town. Assign small groups to research the daily work, clothing, food, and homes of townspeople. Assign each student a specific task such as selecting an event and characters, outlining and writing parts of the script, and obtaining or making props.

Students may choose to portray such characters as apprentices, journeymen, masters of various guilds, university students, clergy, moneychangers, or troubadours. When students have completed their research, writing, costumes, and set, have them present the play. If possible, videotape the play for viewing by students in other classes. **L2**

Chapter 13
Section 2

Critical Thinking Have students discuss the benefits of the guild system. How did guilds help not only guild members but also society at large? *(ensured high quality)* What were some disadvantages? *(Students may answer that guilds could fix prices at an unfair level or that discouraging competition also discouraged growth of business.)* **L3**

NATIONAL GEOGRAPHIC SOCIETY

Use these materials to enrich student understanding of the Middle Ages.

NGS PICTURESHOW CD-ROM
The Middle Ages

NGS PICTUREPACK TRANSPARENCY SET
The Middle Ages

World History and Art Transparency 16, *May*

Mapping History Overlay Transparency 9, *Europe in A.D. 1160*

Focus on World Art Print 15, Master Guillebert de Mets and Others. *Saint George and the Dragon*

Focus on World Art Print 17, Jan van Eyck. *Saint Jerome in His Study*

settlements still faced bandits. To protect themselves, townspeople built walls around their towns. At first these enclosures were simple wooden fences. As the population grew, stone walls were built, with guard towers at the gates.

Inside the walls narrow, winding streets bustled with people, carts drawn by horses and oxen, and farm animals on the way to market. A din of noise and overpowering smells attacked the senses. Church bells chimed the hours; carts piled high with goods creaked and rumbled through streets that were little more than alleys. Shops lined the streets at ground level, and the shop owners often lived in quarters above. Most buildings were of wood and had thatch roofs, making fire a constant hazard.

Medieval towns had almost no sanitation, and a constant stench assailed the people from the garbage and sewage tossed into the streets. These conditions caused the rapid spread of diseases such as diphtheria, typhoid, influenza, and malaria. In crowded towns such diseases often turned into epidemics and took many lives. The worst of these epidemics—the bubonic plague—ravaged Europe between A.D. 1348 and 1350, killing one-third of the population and earning the name the Black Death.

Guilds

During the A.D. 1100s, merchants and artisans organized themselves into business associations called guilds. The primary function of the merchant guild was to maintain a monopoly of the local market for its members. To accomplish this end, merchant guilds severely restricted trading by foreigners in their city and enforced uniform pricing. The following regulations from Southampton, England, indicate the power of the merchant guilds:

> “And no one shall buy honey, fat, salt herrings, or any kind of oil, or millstones, or fresh hides, or any kind of fresh skins, unless he is a guildsman; nor keep a tavern for wine, nor sell cloth at retail, except in market or fair days …”

Images of the Times

Medieval Life

The recovery of commerce and the beginnings of industries stimulated the growth of European towns.

Market scene in a medieval town is the subject of this fresco from Castello de Issogne, Val d' Aosta, Italy.

324

Images of the Times

Medieval Life

Craft and merchant guilds often controlled different aspects of a given industry. In a wool-processing town, for example, the merchant guild would control the purchase of raw wool along with the production and sale of the processed fiber. The craft guilds, by contrast, would control such aspects of the industry as wool carding, dyeing, and weaving.

The word *romance* originally referred not to romantic love but to narratives written in the vernacular rather than in Latin. Although love stories often played a part in these tales of chivalric adventure, they were not essential to this literary genre.

Craft guilds, by contrast, regulated the work of artisans: carpenters, shoemakers, blacksmiths, masons, tailors, and weavers. Women working as laundresses, seamstresses and embroiderers, and maidservants had their own trade associations.

Craft guilds established strict rules concerning prices, wages, and employment. A member of the shoemakers' guild could not charge more (or less) for a pair of shoes than other shoemakers, nor could he advertise or in any way induce people to buy his wares. Although the guilds prohibited competition, they set standards of quality to protect the public from shoddy goods.

Craft guilds were controlled by **masters**, or artisans who owned their own shops and tools and employed less-skilled artisans as helpers. To become a master at a particular craft, an artisan served an apprenticeship, the length of which varied according to the difficulty of the craft. **Apprentices** worked for a master without pay. An apprentice then became a **journeyman** and received pay. However, a journeyman could only work under a master. To become a master, a journeyman submitted a special sample of his work—a masterpiece—to the guild for approval. If the sample was approved, the journeyman became a master and could set up his own shop.

Aside from business activities, guilds provided benefits for their members such as medical help and unemployment relief. Guilds also organized social and religious life by sponsoring banquets, holy day processions, and outdoor plays.

Rise of the Middle Class

The medieval town, or burg, created the name for a new class of people. In Germany they were called *burghers*; in France, the *bourgeoisie* (BURZH•WAH•ZEE); and in England, *burgesses*. The name originally referred to anyone living in a town. Gradually it came to mean the people who made money through the developing money economy. They were a middle class made up of merchants, bankers, and artisans who no longer had to rely on the land to make a living.

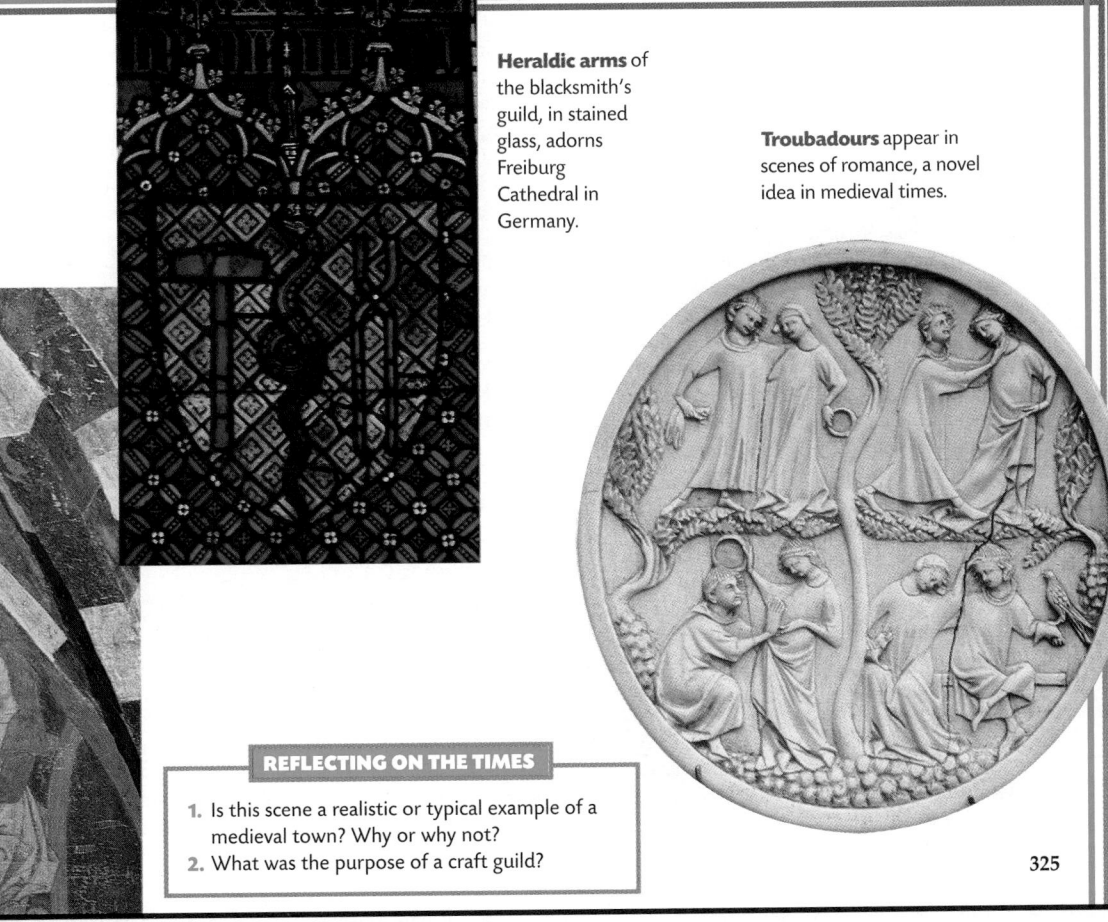

Heraldic arms of the blacksmith's guild, in stained glass, adorns Freiburg Cathedral in Germany.

Troubadours appear in scenes of romance, a novel idea in medieval times.

REFLECTING ON THE TIMES

1. Is this scene a realistic or typical example of a medieval town? Why or why not?
2. What was the purpose of a craft guild?

325

Chapter 13 Section 2

Global Gourmet

France The first important French cookbook was written during the Middle Ages. Taillevent, the chef of King Charles VI, wrote *Le Viander* around 1375. Although Taillevent is the name of one of the finest restaurants in modern Paris, the recipes in Taillevent's cookbook aim not at bringing out the flavor of food but rather at disguising it, since the lack of refrigeration often led to spoilage.

you don't say...

Journeyman Because a journeyman had proved his competence by serving an apprenticeship but still had to work under a master, today the word has come to mean an experienced and capable—but routine—worker or performer.

Who? What? Where? When?

Hospitals became more widespread during the Middle Ages. During the Crusades military hospitals were established along the Crusaders' routes and in the Holy Land. Although most medieval hospitals were established by Benedictine monks, cities and towns also began to set up health-care institutions.

ANSWERS TO REFLECTING ON THE TIMES

1. Students may argue that the scene is not realistic because it doesn't show the crowding and poor sanitation of typical medieval towns.
2. Craft guilds regulated the work of artisans, establishing rules governing prices, wages, and employment; setting standards of quality; and providing other social benefits for their members.

Chapter 13 Section 2

Independent Practice

Guided Reading Activity 13-2 **L1**

Daily Life Have students write two paragraphs describing what it might have been like to live in a medieval town. Have them mention both advantages *(jobs, safety, intellectual opportunity)* and disadvantages *(crowded conditions, lack of sanitation, disease).* **L2**

Literature Have students read the General Prologue to Chaucer's *The Canterbury Tales* and write a character sketch of three different pilgrims. Select several students to read their character sketches aloud. **L3**

Geography and History Activity 13

Cultural Perspectives

Early Universities Although modern universities had their origins in medieval Europe, Arabs had founded universities nearly 200 years earlier. The Fatimids founded Cairo's al-Azhar University in A.D. 970. It remains the world's chief center of Islamic and Arabic learning.

AROUND THE WORLD

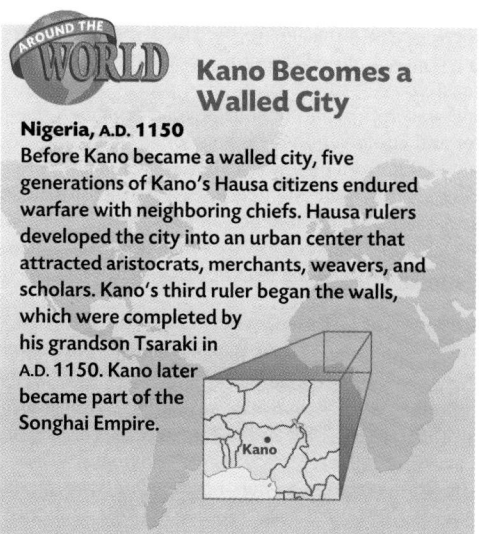

Kano Becomes a Walled City

Nigeria, A.D. 1150

Before Kano became a walled city, five generations of Kano's Hausa citizens endured warfare with neighboring chiefs. Hausa rulers developed the city into an urban center that attracted aristocrats, merchants, weavers, and scholars. Kano's third ruler began the walls, which were completed by his grandson Tsaraki in A.D. 1150. Kano later became part of the Songhai Empire.

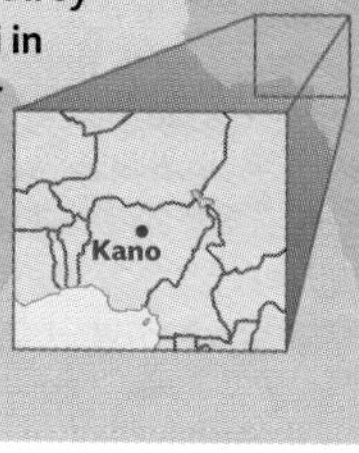

The middle class helped turn towns into organized municipalities. Businessmen created councils to administer town affairs and gained political power for themselves. As the money economy spread, kings began to depend on the middle class for loans and for income from the taxes they paid. The leading merchants and bankers became advisers to lords and kings.

Town Government

Conflict gradually developed between the feudal classes and the burghers. City dwellers did not fit into the feudal system; they resented owing taxes and services to lords. They wanted to run their own affairs and have their own courts and laws. At the same time, feudal lords feared the growing wealth and power of the middle class. To try to keep the burghers in line, the lords began to strictly enforce feudal laws.

The money economy gave the towns the income and power they needed to win the struggle against the lords. In the A.D. 1000s Italian towns formed groups called communes. Using the political power they gained from the growing money economy, the communes ended the power of feudal lords and made the Italian towns into independent city-states. In other areas of Europe, kings and nobles granted townspeople charters, documents that gave them the right to control their own affairs. At the same time, many towns remained a part of a kingdom or feudal territory.

Education

During the Early Middle Ages, most people were illiterate. Education was controlled by the clergy. In monastery and cathedral schools, students prepared for monastery life or for work as church officials. In addition to religious subjects, students learned grammar, rhetoric, logic, arithmetic, geometry, astronomy, and music.

As towns grew, the need for educated officials stimulated a new interest in learning. The growth of courts and other legal institutions created a need for lawyers. As a result, around A.D. 1150, students and teachers began meeting away from monastery and cathedral schools. They formed organizations that became known as universities.

Universities

At first the university was not so much a place as it was a group of scholars organized like a guild for the purpose of learning. Classes were held in rented rooms or churches or in the open air. Books were scarce. In most classes a teacher read the text and discussed it, while students took notes on slates or committed as much information as possible to memory. Classes did, however, meet on a regular schedule. University rules established the obligations of students and teachers toward each other. To qualify as a teacher, students had to pass an examination leading to a degree, or certificate of completion.

By the end of the A.D. 1200s, universities had spread throughout Europe. Most southern European universities were modeled after the law school at **Bologna** (buh•LOH•nyuh), Italy, and specialized in law and medicine. Universities in northern Europe, on the other hand, specialized in liberal arts and theology. These were generally modeled after the University of Paris.

New Learning

At medieval universities, scholars studied Latin classics and Roman law in depth. They also acquired knowledge from the works of the Greek philosopher Aristotle and from Islamic scholarship in the sciences. This interest in the physical world eventually led to the rise of Western science.

Many church leaders opposed the study of Aristotle's works, fearing that his ideas threatened Christian teachings. In contrast, some scholars thought the new knowledge could be used to support Christian ideas. They applied Aristotle's philosophy to theological questions and developed a system of thought called scholasticism. This new type of learning emphasized reason as well as faith in the

MEETING SPECIAL NEEDS ACTIVITY

Learning Style: Auditory/Musical Medieval guilds did much more than regulate people's work lives. Ask students who are particularly sensitive to or have a special interest in music to listen to Richard Wagner's opera *Die Meistersinger von Nürnberg.* Ask them to prepare a presentation for the class including a description of the Meistersingers who arose among the burghers of late thirteenth-century Germany. Students also may describe selections from the opera, a summary of its libretto, and some biographical information about its main character, the German poet and composer Hans Sachs, who was the most famous of the Meistersingers. **L3**

326 Chapter 13 *Medieval Europe at Its Height*

interpretation of Christian doctrine. Scholastics sought to reconcile classical philosophy with the Church's teachings. They believed all knowledge could be integrated into a coherent whole.

One early scholastic teacher, Peter Abelard, taught theology in Paris during the early A.D. 1100s. In his book *Sic et Non* (Yes and No), he collected statements from the Bible and the writings of early Christian leaders that showed both sides of controversial questions. Abelard then had his students reconcile the differences through logic.

In the A.D. 1200s the most important scholastic thinker was **Thomas Aquinas** (uh•KWY•nuhs), a brilliant theologian and philosopher who taught philosophy in Paris and Naples. In his work *Summa Theologica* (a summary of religious thought), Aquinas claimed that reason was a gift from God that could provide answers to basic philosophical questions. The Catholic Church later accepted and promoted Aquinas's way of teaching and thinking.

Medieval Literature and Art

The spread of universities and the revival of intellectual endeavor stimulated advances in literature and the arts. Songs and epics of the Early Middle Ages were put in writing for the first time.

Epics and Romances

One of the earliest surviving literary works of the feudal world was the Anglo-Saxon epic *Beowulf.* A tale of grim battle and gloomy scenery, *Beowulf* reveals the harshness of life in northern Europe. Handed down by oral tradition for two centuries, it was finally written down in Old English (Anglo-Saxon) by an unknown poet in about A.D. 700. In colorful verses and exciting narrative, the epic describes how the Anglo-Saxon warrior Beowulf defeats a horrible monster named Grendel.

French epics called *chansons de geste,* or songs of high deeds, celebrated the courage of feudal warriors. The *Song of Roland,* written around A.D. 1100, gives an account of the chivalrous defense of Christianity by Charlemagne's knights.

Romances about knights and ladies were also popular. In southern France in the A.D. 1100s and A.D. 1200s, traveling poet-musicians called troubadours composed lyric poems and songs about love and the feats of knights. They helped define the ideal knight celebrated in the code of chivalry.

CONNECTIONS Geography

The Trail of the Black Death

Outbreaks of the Black Death—today known as the bubonic plague—erupted throughout Europe in the A.D. 1340s. It continued at 10-year intervals throughout the Middle Ages. The worst epidemic, which claimed nearly 25 million lives between A.D. 1348 and A.D. 1350, began in China and spread swiftly across Asia.

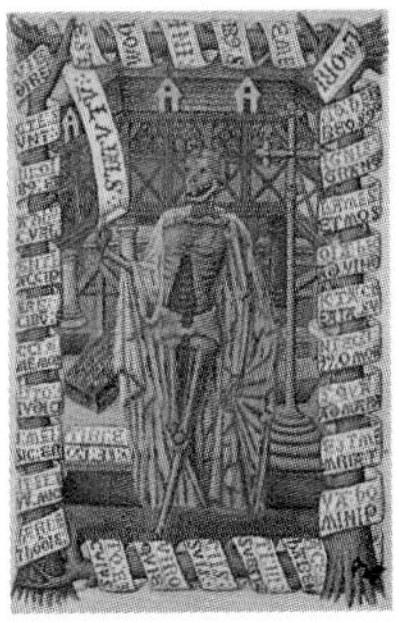
The Black Death

When ships from Asia reached the Mediterranean, the disease spread to Sicily, North Africa, and western Europe. People in crowded towns with poor sanitation—and rats—were at greater risk than those in the countryside. About one-third of Europe's population died in this single epidemic. It was not until A.D. 1906 that flea-infested rats were identified as the carrier of the Black Death.

The plague brought many changes to Europe. Wars stopped, and trade slowed. People were forbidden to gather in groups, religious services were suspended, and infected homes were sealed off. Businesses shut their doors, and many city people fled to the country. It would take two centuries for Europe to regain its pre-1348 level of population.

MAKING THE CONNECTION

1. How was the plague brought to western Europe?
2. How is the spread of disease still related to human movement?

Chapter 13 Section 2

CONNECTIONS Geography

The Trail of the Black Death

In addition to the physical effects, the psychological effects of the Black Death were also significant. Many people, searching for answers to the scourge, turned to mysticism and superstitious practices. They often found little spiritual guidance among the clergy, who fell ill and died at the same alarming rate as the general population. As the number of educated priests declined, religious orders began to recruit less qualified individuals, which lowered the overall intellectual level of the Church.

Answers to Making the Connection

1. *on flea-infested rats aboard ships from Asia*
2. *When people exposed to an infection in one part of the world travel to another part, they can infect people with whom they come into contact.*

ASSESS

Check for Understanding

Assign Section 2 Review as homework or as an in-class activity.

Use Student Self-Test and Review Software to review Section 2.

MAKING CONNECTIONS ACTIVITIES

Health Have students research and write a short report on other plague epidemics, such as the biblical plague of Ashdod, reported in I Samuel; epidemics in ancient Greece and Rome; the plague in London in the mid-1600s; and the plague in China in the mid-1800s. **L2**

The Arts Have students peruse art books to find several styles of manuscript illumination, such as Byzantine, Indian, Islamic, and one or more of the styles of medieval Europe, including Gothic, Romanesque, and Irish. Encourage students to make photocopies of works that reveal the distinctive characteristics of each style. Have them put together illustrated reports and then display them in the classroom. **L2 LEP**

Chapter 13
Section 2

Visualizing History Despite the fact that Reims's cathedral of Notre-Dame was built over the course of more than a century, it is remarkably unified in style. Carefully restored after sustaining heavy damage in World War I, the cathedral is considered among France's most beautiful Gothic churches.

Answer to Caption: *Gothic style featured flying buttresses instead of Romanesque heavy walls and low arches. It also featured higher ceilings and stained glass windows.*

Evaluate

Section Quiz 13-2

Use the Testmaker to create a customized quiz for Section 2.

Reteach

Have students work in small groups to prepare charts describing the significant people discussed in the chapter, as well as important innovations in agriculture, economics, trade, education, literature, and art.

Enrich

Have students read David Macaulay's *Cathedral: The Story of Its Construction* and prepare an oral report on how and why cathedrals were built, paying special attention to the role of craft guilds.

CLOSE

Have students write summaries of how the focus of medieval life gradually shifted from the feudal manor to the towns.

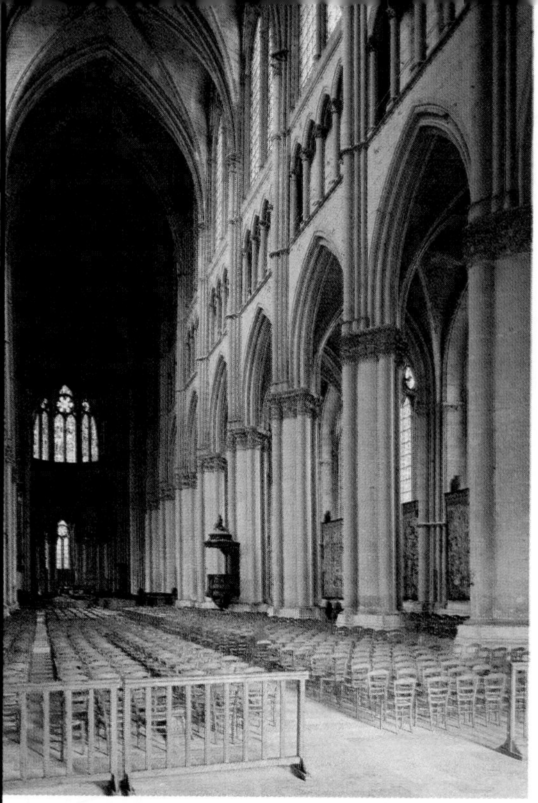

Visualizing History **Interior of a Gothic cathedral at Reims, France.** *How did the Gothic style differ from the Romanesque?*

Vernacular Literature

Most medieval literature was written in the vernacular, or language of everyday speech, of the writer. Instead of using Latin as a common language, people spoke the language of their own country—English, German, French, Italian, or Spanish. These vernacular languages helped give each kingdom of Europe a separate identity. Use of vernacular languages in writing made literature accessible to more people.

Some outstanding works of literature were written in the vernacular in the A.D. 1300s. **Dante Alighieri** (DAHN•tay A•luh•GYEHR•ee) wrote *The Divine Comedy*, an epic poem in Italian. Written over a period of several years, the poem discusses medieval ideas of life after death by describing an imaginary journey from hell to heaven.

In England a government official named **Geoffrey Chaucer** started writing *The Canterbury Tales* in A.D. 1386, and continued the series of tales probably right up to his death in A.D. 1400. The narrative poems describe a group of pilgrims, representing people of various classes and occupations, who tell stories to amuse one another on their way to a shrine at Canterbury, England.

Medieval Art

Early medieval churches were built in a style called Romanesque, which combined features of Roman and Byzantine structures. Romanesque churches had thick walls, columns set close together, heavy curved arches, and small windows. About A.D. 1150, French architects began to build in a new style called Gothic. They replaced the Romanesque heavy walls and low arches with flying buttresses. These stone beams, extending out from the walls, took the weight of the building off the walls. This allowed the walls to be thinner, with space for stained-glass windows. The ceiling inside was supported by pointed arches made of narrow stone ribs reaching out from tall pillars. These supports allowed architects to build higher ceilings and more open interiors.

Medieval painters, by contrast, turned their attention to a much smaller art form, the illuminated manuscript. Adorned with brilliantly colored illustrations and often highlighted with gold leaf, these works were miniature masterpieces whose beauty has endured to the present day.

SECTION 2 REVIEW

Recall

1. **Define** money economy, guild, master, apprentice, journeyman, charter, scholasticism, troubadour, vernacular.
2. **Identify** Peter Abelard, Thomas Aquinas, Beowulf, Dante Alighieri, Geoffrey Chaucer.
3. **Explain** why membership in a guild was advantageous for a medieval artisan. Why was it disadvantageous?

Critical Thinking

4. **Synthesizing Information** Create an imaginary medieval town. Briefly explain its physical characteristics. Then describe what a typical day for an artisan working there would be like.

Understanding Themes

5. **Innovation** Choose one of the following and trace its effect on medieval society: three-field system, money economy, guilds.

SECTION 2 REVIEW ANSWERS

1. All vocabulary words are defined in the Glossary.
2. Abelard, 327; Aquinas, 327; *Beowulf*, 327; Dante, 328; Chaucer, 328
3. protected members against outside competition offering lower prices; provided social benefits, but prevented competition and innovation
4. Answers should refer to protective walls, crowding, poor sanitation, markets, and guilds.
5. **INNOVATION** Answers should reflect chosen topic's significance.

328 Chapter 13 *Medieval Europe at Its Height*

A.D. 1300 — A.D. 1400 — A.D. 1500

A.D. 1347 France and England fight the Battle of Crécy.

A.D. 1469 Ferdinand of Aragon and Isabella of Castile marry.

c. A.D. 1485 Henry VII founds England's Tudor dynasty.

Section 3

Strengthening of Monarchy

Setting the Scene

- **Terms to Define**
  cortes
- **People to Meet**
  Joan of Arc, Louis XI, Richard III, Henry VII, Ferdinand of Aragon, Isabella of Castile
- **Places to Locate**
  Crécy, Agincourt, Burgundy, Castile, Aragon

Find Out How did European monarchs strengthen their powers during the Middle Ages?

The Storyteller

A popular legend in English history is the story of the first Prince of Wales. Edward, King of England, desired to make the proud chieftains of Wales acknowledge his power. He campaigned against them, soon controlling their lands. The Welsh chiefs refused to accept Edward as their prince. They agreed, however, to serve a prince whom Edward would choose—provided he was noble and spoke neither English nor French. Edward accepted these terms and showed them their prince, his newborn son, who was indeed of noble birth and could speak neither language. The chiefs accepted the baby as their lawful lord, the Prince of Wales.

—adapted from *The Three Edwards*, Thomas Costain, 1964

The Tower of London

During the Middle Ages, power rested in the hands of nobles who owned feudal estates. But as trade flourished and towns grew, feudalism weakened. Beginning in the A.D. 1100s, power in western Europe began to shift from nobles to kings or queens. Gradually the influence of the clergy and nobles diminished as educated common people and laymen became advisers to monarchs. At the outset, however, a period of violent warfare swept through western Europe.

The Hundred Years' War

During the A.D. 1300s, feudal disputes often led to wars among Europe's monarchs. The Hundred Years' War between England and France grew out of such a dispute. The war—actually a series of wars—lasted from A.D. 1337 to A.D. 1453, before the French claimed victory.

Causes

After William of Normandy conquered England in A.D. 1066, conflicting feudal claims caused great bitterness between the English and French kings. Because William had been duke of Normandy—an area in northwestern France—before becoming king of England, his successors in England saw themselves as rulers of Normandy and England. English control over French lands increased in A.D. 1152, when Henry II married Eleanor of Aquitaine, heir to lands in southwestern France. As a result of the marriage, Henry II controlled more land in France than did the French king.

The French monarch Philip II regained most of the northern lands held by England by defeating Eleanor's son, King John, in the early A.D. 1200s. The French kings, however, wanted all of the lands claimed by the English.

Chapter 13 Section 3

SECTION THEME

▶ **Conflict** England and France battle while their monarchies gain power.

Find Out

Answer: *They centralized their power through warfare, diplomacy, and religious control.*

FOCUS

Section Objective

Describe how European monarchs increased their powers during the Middle Ages.

BELLRINGER
Motivational Activity

Before taking roll at the beginning of the class period, project Section Focus Transparency 13-3 and have students answer the activity questions. Discuss students' responses.

This activity is also available as a blackline master.

Vocabulary Pre-check

Use Vocabulary Activity 13 to introduce vocabulary terms. **L1 LEP**

SECTION RESOURCES

Reproducible Masters
- Reproducible Lesson Plan 13-3
- Vocabulary Activity 13
- Guided Reading Activity 13-3
- Section Quiz 13-3

Transparencies
- Section Focus Transparency 13-3

Multimedia
- Student Self-Test and Review Software
- Testmaker

TEACH

Guided Practice

THEME Conflict

Ask students to refer to pages 329–330, then give examples of conflicting claims and name the outright conflict that arose from those claims. *(dispute between France and England over lands in Normandy and southern France, and over the French throne, which led to the Hundred Years' War)* **L1**

Critical Thinking Have students recap the developments they learned about in Section 2 that led to the decline of feudalism. Then have them explain how the Hundred Years' War further hastened its decline. *(revival of trade and growth of towns; new ways of fighting led to need for standing armies rather than feudal soldiers)* **L3**

History & Art *La Pucelle* is French for "the Maid." How is Joan dressed? *(in men's clothes)* Among the charges of blasphemy brought against Joan in her trial was her wearing of men's clothes.
Answer to Caption: *Her courage rallied the French around the king and drove the English out of France.*

History & Art *"La Pucelle!" Jeanne d' Arc Leads Her Army* by Franck Craig, 1907. Musée d' Orsay, Paris, France *What did the "Maid of Orléans" accomplish for the French?*

Matters between the English and the French worsened in A.D. 1328, when the French king died without leaving a direct heir. King Edward III of England, a grandson of the French king, declared himself king of France and announced that he would not recognize French sovereignty over his feudal lands in France. The successor to the French throne, Philip of Valois—himself only a nephew of the dead king—quietly began to prepare for war with England.

Major Battles

Despite being poorer and less populated than France, England won the early battles of the Hundred Years' War. English unity contributed to this success. English kings received popular support from the nation and financial support from Parliament. Superior military tactics also gave England an edge.

When French knights arrived at the small village of **Crécy** (kray•SEE) in A.D. 1346, they outnumbered the English two to one. They were surprised to see foot soldiers fighting alongside the English knights. These soldiers carried a new weapon, the Welsh longbow. As tall as a man, longbows could shoot steel-tipped arrows capable of piercing heavy armor at 300 yards (274 m). French swords and crossbows were useless at such a distance. French historian Jean Froissart described the battle:

> "Then the English archers stept forth one pace and let fly their arrows so wholly [together] and so thick, that it seemed snow. When the [soldiers] felt the arrows piercing through heads, arms and breasts, many of them cast down their cross-bows and did cut their strings and [retreated]...."

At Crécy the English forces also used the first portable firearm in European warfare: a long iron tube mounted on a pole. This cumbersome firearm led to the development of the cannon, which became a major weapon in later fighting.

By the late A.D. 1300s, France was in disarray. War and plague were ravaging the country. Although a peasant revolt was quickly put down, it added to the disorder. At the battle of **Agincourt** (A•juhn•KORT) in A.D. 1415, the English army once more triumphed, though again outnumbered, this time by a margin of three to one. Just as French fortunes had sunk to their lowest, a young woman helped bring about a dramatic reversal.

Joan of Arc

Born just three years before the French defeat at Agincourt, **Joan of Arc** grew up in the small French village of Domremy. Like most peasants, she did not learn to read or write. Joan left home at the age of 17,

COOPERATIVE LEARNING ACTIVITY

Readers' Theater Have groups of students prepare and present readings from the play *Saint Joan* by George Bernard Shaw, choosing suitable passages for presentation, assigning and reading the roles, preparing and presenting a synopsis of the play, and explaining the scenes.

Advanced students may prefer to present readings from Shakespeare's *Henry V*, Act IV, Scenes iii–viii, which dramatize the Battle of Agincourt from the English point of view. Much of the dialogue in this scene is in French; students taking French classes might especially enjoy the challenge. Make sure they use an edition with adequate footnotes, such as the Arden Shakespeare, and that they do not overlook the humor in Scene iv. **L3**

Adam Woolfitt

Cathedral of Chartres

The cathedral stands out against a lowering sky. The old town of Chartres, France, crowds the foreground, where artisans, merchants, bakers, and stonemasons once lived, clustered near the great church. At the center of the photograph, the rose window provides a perfect example of medieval stained glass. The two towers, one ornate, the other plain, were finished in different periods. They pierce the sky—giving form to the faith and spirit of Europe's Middle Ages.

The cathedral reflects the technology of the High Middle Ages. Built before A.D. 1300, Chartres Cathedral, located about 50 miles southwest of Paris, is one of many works of Gothic architecture expressing both the fervor of the medieval era and the revival of the European economy, beginning around A.D. 1000. The growth of towns such as Chartres was a result of such changes. The combination of new building techniques, financial resources, and professional skills enabled the construction of the great cathedrals of Europe.

TEACH

Tell students that the rose window (also called a wheel window) was a richly decorated circular window. Toward the mid-1100s the rose window began to be used widely in Gothic churches. Ask students to explain why stained glass art is not static. *(As sunlight changes in intensity, direction, and color during the day, the effect of the stained glass changes.)* Ask students which windows of Chartres Cathedral are the first to come fully to life. *(the east windows, because the sun rises in the east)*

CURRICULUM CONNECTION

RELIGION

Numerous street names in today's Chartres, such as *Rue aux Juifs*, recall the presence of an important medieval Jewish community there. The city's Saint-Hilaire Hospital probably originated as a synagogue.

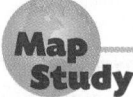

Map Study

Answer

Conflicting feudal claims to French lands and to the French throne fueled the Hundred Years' War.

Map Skills Practice

Reading a Map Why was control of Calais particularly important? *(It is the French port closest to England.)*

Independent Practice

Guided Reading Activity 13-3 **L1**

The Arts When Ferdinand and Isabella captured the Moorish province of Granada, they gained some remarkable examples of Moorish art and architecture, such as the Alhambra. Have students research and report on the art and architecture of Moorish Spain. Have them give an oral summary, bringing pictures to share with the class. **L2**

Biography The French estates of Eleanor of Aquitaine were a source of dispute during the Hundred Years' War. An extraordinary woman in her own right, Eleanor was more than the wife and mother of French and English kings. Have students research the life of Eleanor of Aquitaine and write a brief summary of their findings. **L2**

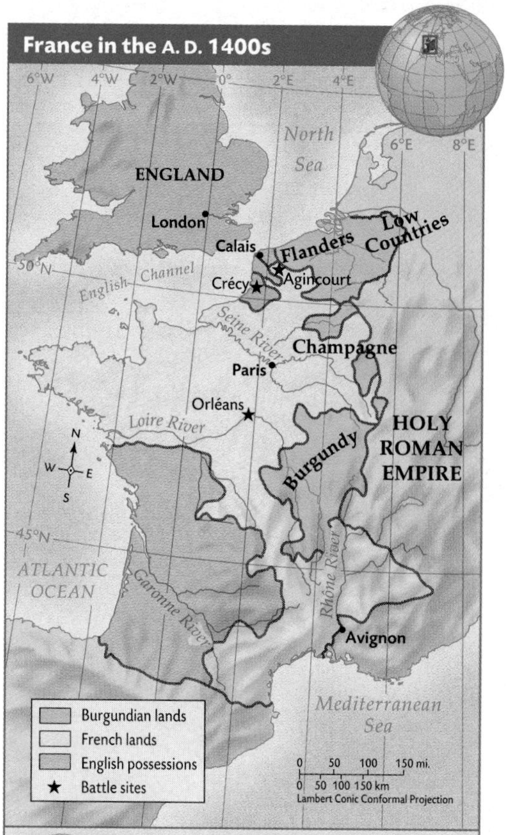

Map Study The Hundred Years' War was actually a series of conflicts between England and France that lasted from A.D. 1337 to A.D. 1453.

Region What were some of the reasons for the ongoing conflict between these countries?

insisting that she had received messages from God telling her to help drive the English from France.

In A.D. 1429 Joan arrived at Chinon (shee•NAW) to persuade Charles, heir to the French throne, to give her command of his troops. After several tests of her unique powers, Charles gave her armor, a banner, and command of troops.

Joan then set off to Orléans (AWR•lay•AHN), a town in northern France that had been besieged by English troops for several months. Inspired by her piety and sincerity, French soldiers broke the siege of Orléans in only 10 days, and the English fled. Under the leadership of the Maid of Orléans, as Joan of Arc came to be known, French soldiers fought their way to Reims, where Charles was officially crowned King Charles VII.

In A.D. 1430 Joan was captured by rivals of the French king and sold to the English. After nearly a year in prison and a long trial in which she steadfastly insisted on the truth of her visions, Joan of Arc was condemned to be burned at the stake as a witch and a heretic. On a mild May day in A.D. 1431, onlookers wept as Joan calmly went to her fate. Twenty-four years after her death, a new trial proclaimed her innocence.

Joan's courage rallied the French around the king and drove the English out of France. When the war ended in A.D. 1453, the port of Calais was the only French territory still in English hands.

Effects of the War

During the Hundred Years' War, France suffered more severely than England, since all of the fighting occurred on French soil. Yet victory gave the French a new sense of unity that enabled them to rebuild their country.

Although England had been spared destruction, English nobles who had owned lands in France were bitter about the defeat. For the rest of the A.D. 1400s, England was torn by civil war. In the long run, however, the loss of French lands contributed to national unity for England and encouraged the English to concentrate on problems at home.

The Hundred Years' War also hastened the decline of feudalism. The use of the longbow and firearms made feudal methods of fighting based on castles and mounted knights obsolete. Monarchs replaced feudal soldiers with national armies made up of hired soldiers. Maintaining these armies, however, was expensive. Monarchs turned to townspeople and the lower nobility for new sources of revenue. These groups willingly paid taxes and made loans in return for security and good government.

France

By the end of the Hundred Years' War, the French monarchy had gained much power and prestige. Warfare emergencies allowed kings to collect national taxes and maintain standing, or permanent, armies. Therefore, after Charles VII defeated the English, he was able to renew the royal tradition of ruling the country assertively.

Louis XI, son of Charles VII, set out to unite France by taking back lands once part of the royal territory but now held by French nobles. Louis especially wanted **Burgundy,** one of the most prosperous regions of Europe. However, its ruler, Charles the Bold, wanted Burgundy to be an independent state.

Linking Past and Present

Religion Not until 1990 did Spain officially overturn the 1492 order calling for the expulsion or conversion of the Jews. The 1990 accord places not only Judaism but also Protestantism on par with Roman Catholicism in Spain.

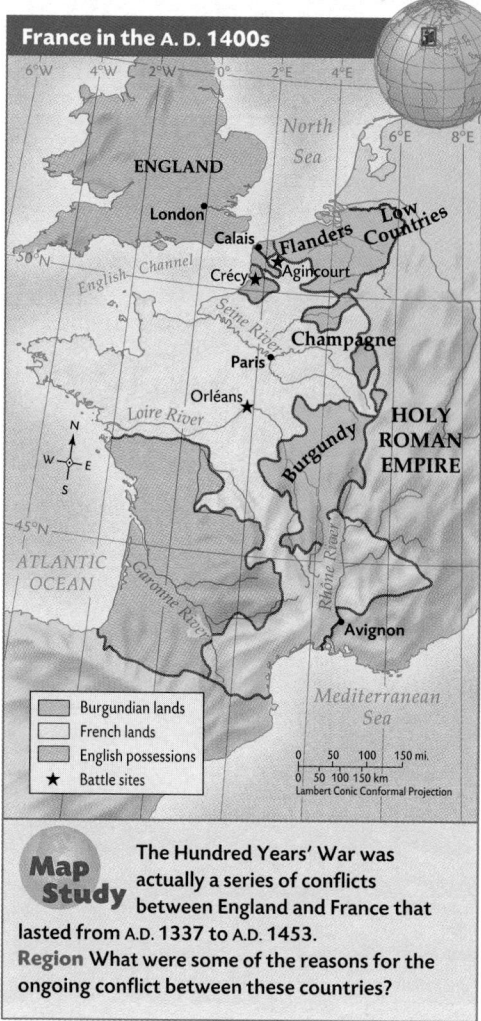

MEETING SPECIAL NEEDS ACTIVITY

Learning Style: Visual/Spatial Organize the class into small groups of three to five students. Each group should include one student who draws well. Have each group choose a topic related to medieval life and draw several designs for stained glass treatment. Each group should then select a single design to prepare for presentation using poster board and colored tissue paper. After the design has been sketched in pencil on the poster board, students should work together to cut out the design and glue the tissue paper to the back of the poster. Have each group present its finished project to the class. **L1 LEP**

Louis was a shrewd diplomat. Rather than fight Charles openly, he encouraged quarrels between Burgundy and the neighboring Swiss. After Charles was killed in a battle with the Swiss in A.D. 1477, Burgundy was divided into two parts: the northern half, Flanders, went to Charles's daughter Mary; the remainder became part of France.

Through a series of reforms, Louis strengthened the bureaucracy of government, kept the nobles under royal control, and promoted trade and agriculture. By the end of his reign, France was strong and unified, and its monarch ruled with increased power.

England

After the Hundred Years' War, England became mired in a struggle for the English throne. The 30-year conflict, known as the Wars of the Roses (because of the symbols of the rival royal families), began in A.D. 1455. The royal house of Lancaster bore the red rose; its rival, the house of York, a white rose.

During the Wars of the Roses, Edward, duke of York, overthrew the weak Lancaster dynasty and became King Edward IV. As king, Edward worked to strengthen royal government and to promote trade. Edward's death in A.D. 1483 brought uncertainty to England. The heirs to the throne were the late king's two sons. Edward's brother, Richard, however, proclaimed himself **Richard III** and locked his young nephews in the Tower of London. Not long after, the boys were found murdered. Many suspected Richard—who himself fell to the forces of Henry Tudor, a Lancaster noble, on Bosworth Field in A.D. 1485.

Henry became King **Henry VII**, the first Tudor king. Henry steadily eliminated rival claimants to the throne, avoided expensive foreign wars, and gradually reasserted royal power over the lords and nobles. As a result, the English monarchy emerged from the Wars of the Roses strengthened and with few challengers. The Tudor dynasty ruled England for more than 100 years until 1603.

Spain

During the late A.D. 1400s, Spain emerged from a period of turmoil and warfare to become an important European power. Even before Pope Urban called for the Crusades, the Christian kingdoms of northern Spain were engaged in the *Reconquista* (RAY•kohn•KEES•tuh), or reconquest, of the lands the Muslims had taken in the A.D. 700s. By A.D. 1250 the Iberian Peninsula consisted of three Christian kingdoms: Portugal in the west, **Castile** in the center, and **Aragon** on the Mediterranean coast. Only Granada in the south remained in the hands of the Moors, or Spanish Muslims.

In A.D. 1469 **Ferdinand of Aragon** and **Isabella of Castile** were married. The two kingdoms maintained separate governments, however, and the power of their monarchs was limited by local interests and large minority religious groups. The Christian settlers who had been moved into the reconquered territories and the large Jewish and Muslim communities in Castile and Aragon had their own laws and elected their own officials. Special royal charters allowed many towns to keep their own courts and local customs. Finally, assemblies known as *cortes* (KOR•tays), in which nobles were powerful, had the right to review the monarchs' policies.

The two monarchs strengthened the powers of the Crown in Castile. Royal officials governed the towns, and special courts enforced royal laws. In A.D. 1492 their armies forced the surrender of the last Moorish stronghold at Granada. Shortly afterward, Ferdinand and Isabella ended the traditional policy of toleration for minority groups. They believed that all Spaniards had to be Catholic if Spain was to become one nation. Spanish Jews and Muslims were given the choice to convert to Catholicism or leave Spain. Later the two monarchs set up the Spanish Inquisition, a court that enforced Catholic teachings. The fear caused by the Inquisition further strengthened the power and authority of the Spanish monarchs over their people. However, it limited Spanish contacts with other parts of Europe.

SECTION 3 REVIEW

Recall

1. **Define** *cortes*.
2. **Identify** Joan of Arc, Louis XI, Richard III, Henry VII, Ferdinand of Aragon, Isabella of Castile.
3. **Explain** the causes and results of the Hundred Years' War.

Critical Thinking

4. **Applying Information** Relate how one European monarchy changed during the Middle Ages.

Understanding Themes

5. **Conflict** Explain the reasons for the struggles between the various European monarchies.

Chapter 13 Section 3

ASSESS

Check for Understanding

Assign Section 3 Review as homework or as an in-class activity.

Use Student Self-Test and Review Software to review Section 3.

Evaluate

Section Quiz 13-3

Use the Testmaker to create a customized quiz for Section 3.

Reteach

Have students prepare a time line of significant events covered in this section, including a brief explanation next to each event listed.

Enrich

The son of the English king Edward III was known as the Black Prince because he wore black armor. Have students research the Black Prince and his role in the Hundred Years' War. Ask them to summarize his career in a brief written report.

CLOSE

Summarize the ways the monarchy was strengthened during the period covered in this section and the causes for this change. Have students debate the advantages and disadvantages of a strong monarchy.

SECTION 3 REVIEW ANSWERS

1. All vocabulary words are defined in the Glossary.
2. Joan of Arc, 330; Louis XI, 332; Richard III, 333; Henry VII, 333; Ferdinand, 333; Isabella, 333
3. Causes included feudal disputes over land and sovereignty; results included unity in England and France and decline of feudalism.
4. Answers should describe that country's social, political, and economic life.
5. **CONFLICT** Answers should include analysis of feudalism and of shifting political interests in Europe during the Middle Ages.

Chapter 13 Section 4

SECTION THEME

▶ **Conflict** The Church faces a split from within and opposition from without.

Find Out

Answer: *Abuses such as simony and the princely lifestyles of clergy led to the call for reform.*

FOCUS

Section Objective

List the reasons the Church was under pressure to reform.

BELLRINGER Motivational Activity

Before taking roll at the beginning of the class period, project Section Focus Transparency 13-4 and have students answer the activity questions. Discuss students' responses.

This activity is also available as a blackline master.

Vocabulary Pre-check

Use Vocabulary Activity 13 to introduce vocabulary terms. **L1 LEP**

A.D. 1300 — A.D. 1400 — A.D. 1500

- **A.D. 1305** Pope's court moves to Avignon, France.
- **A.D. 1378** Great Schism in the Church occurs.
- **A.D. 1415** Church authorities burn Jan Hus as a heretic.
- **A.D. 1436** Compromise reached between the Church and Hussites.

Section 4

The Troubled Church

Setting the Scene

▶ **Terms to Define**
pilgrimage, simony

▶ **People to Meet**
Pope Clement V, John Wycliffe, the Lollards, Jan Hus

▶ **Places to Locate**
Avignon, Bohemia

Find Out Why was the Church under pressure to reform?

The Storyteller

The situation was intolerable, Nicholas of Clèmanges thought angrily. The Church was increasingly corrupt. Greed, pride, and love of luxury prevailed in place of humility and charity. Comparing the current priests and bishops with the holy leaders of antiquity, he reflected, was like comparing mud to gold. What would come of such ills? "So great a flood of evils must assuredly be crushed and utterly destroyed by God's most righteous judgment. It does not seem possible in any other way to chasten it." Nicholas prayed that the Church might be spared from complete destruction—that a little seed might remain in the world.

—adapted from *On the Ruin and the Repair of the Church*, Nicholas Clèmanges, reprinted in *Readings in Western Civilization*, 1986

The Church besieged by evil forces

During the upheavals of the Late Middle Ages—caused by warfare, the plague, and religious controversy—many people turned to the Church for comfort and reassurance. Religious ceremonies multiplied, and thousands of people went on religious pilgrimages, or journeys to holy places. In spite of this increase in religious devotion, the temporal authority of the Church was weakening due to the influence of strong monarchs and national governments. A growing middle class of educated townspeople and a general questioning of the Church's teachings also contributed to this decline.

Babylonian Captivity

During the early A.D. 1300s, the papacy came under the influence of the French monarchy. In A.D. 1305 a French archbishop was elected **Pope Clement V.** Clement decided to move his court from Rome to **Avignon** (A•veen•YOHN), a small city in southern France, to escape the civil wars that were disrupting Italy. While in France, the pope appointed only French cardinals. Pope Clement V and his successors—all French—remained in Avignon until A.D. 1377.

This long period of the exile of the popes at Avignon came to be known as the Babylonian Captivity, after the period of the exile of the Jews in Babylon in the 500s B.C. For centuries, Rome had been the center of the western Church. With the pope in France, people feared that the papacy would be dominated by French monarchs. Others disliked the concern the Avignon popes showed for increasing church taxes and making church administration more efficient. They believed the popes had become corrupted by worldly power and were neglecting their spiritual duties. The Italian poet Petrarch complained:

> "Here reign the successors of the poor fishermen of Galilee; they have strangely

SECTION RESOURCES

Reproducible Masters
- Reproducible Lesson Plan 13-4
- Vocabulary Activity 13
- Guided Reading Activity 13-4
- History Simulation 13
- Reteaching Activity 13
- Enrichment Activity 13
- Section Quiz 13-4
- Performance Assessment Activity 13
- Spanish Chapter Summary 13

Transparencies
- Section Focus Transparency 13-4

Multimedia
- Student Self-Test and Review Software
- Testmaker

forgotten their origin. I am astounded … to see these men loaded with gold and clad in purple, boasting of the spoils of princes and nations. ”

The Great Schism

Finally, in A.D. 1377, Pope Gregory XI left Avignon and returned to Rome. After his death, Roman mobs forced the College of Cardinals to elect an Italian as pope. The cardinals later declared the election invalid, insisting they had voted under pressure. The cardinals then elected a second pope, who settled in Avignon. When the Italian pope refused to resign, the Church faced the dilemma of being led by two popes.

This controversy became known as the Great Schism because it caused serious divisions in the Church. The Great Schism lasted from A.D. 1378 until A.D. 1417 and seriously undermined the pope's authority. People wondered how they could regard the pope as the divinely chosen leader of Christianity when there was more than one person claiming to be the single, unquestioned head of the Church.

Calls for a Council

Many kings, princes, and church scholars called for a reform of church government. The most popular remedy was a general church council. However, this solution posed many problems. First, such councils were traditionally called by popes. No pope was willing to call a council that would limit his authority. However, the legality of a council would be questionable if it did not receive papal approval. Second, different rulers in Europe supported particular popes for political reasons. Such political divisions made it almost impossible to reach agreement on even the site of a council, let alone to reach agreement on the deeper and more important issues involved.

By A.D. 1400 many western Europeans were committed to the idea of a church council. In A.D. 1409 a council met at Pisa, Italy, to unite the Church behind one pope. It resulted in the election of a third pope, since neither the pope at Rome nor the pope at Avignon would resign. Finally, in A.D. 1414, another council met at Constance, Germany. It forced the resignation of all three popes and then elected Pope Martin V, ending the Great Schism. The long period of disunity, however, had seriously weakened the political influence of the Church. Moreover, many Europeans had come to feel a greater sense of loyalty to their monarchs than to the pope.

Calls for Reform

Church authority was also weakened by people's dislike of abuses within the Church. The clergy used many unpopular means to raise money. Fees were charged for almost every type of service the Church performed. Common people especially disliked simony—the selling of church positions—because the cost of buying these positions was passed on to them. The princely lifestyles of the clergy further eroded regard for the Church. Many Europeans called for reform. Two of the clearest voices belonged to an English scholar and a Bohemian preacher.

John Wycliffe

John Wycliffe (WIH•KLIHF), a scholar at England's Oxford University, criticized the Church's wealth, corruption among the clergy, and the pope's claim to absolute authority. He wanted secular rulers to remove church officials who were immoral or corrupt.

Wycliffe claimed that the Bible was the sole authority for religious truth. He began to translate the Bible from Latin into English so people could read it themselves. Since church doctrine held that only the clergy could interpret God's word in the Bible, this act was regarded as revolutionary. Some of Wycliffe's followers, known as **the Lollards**, angrily criticized the Church. They destroyed images of saints, ridiculed the Mass, and ate communion bread with onions to show that it was no different from ordinary bread.

Widespread antipapal feelings made it difficult for the English government to suppress Lollards. Wycliffe was persuaded to moderate his views and received only a mild punishment. He died peacefully in A.D. 1384, but his ideas spread.

Among those who supported the Lollards was Bohemian-born Queen Anne, the wife of King

Footnotes to History

Silver Spoons
During the Middle Ages, pewter spoons became common utensils for eating. In the A.D. 1400s silver "apostle spoons," bearing the image of a child's patron saint, were favored gifts for newborns in Italy. Only the wealthy could afford such a luxury. From these apostle spoons came the saying that a privileged child is "born with a silver spoon in his or her mouth."

Chapter 13 Section 4

TEACH

Guided Practice

THEME Conflict
After students have read this section, ask them to name specific examples of conflict within the medieval Church that led to changes. *(Students should mention the teachings of John Wycliffe and the Lollards, and Jan Hus and the Hussites. Changes include the translation of the Bible into vernacular languages and some religious liberties for Hussites.)* **L1**

Philosophy Tell students that Wycliffe's belief that people could and should think for themselves was not original. Ask students to name other historical or contemporary figures who have advocated the same belief. *(Answers may include Socrates and Thoreau.)* **L3**

History Simulation 13

Independent Practice

Guided Reading Activity 13-4 **L1**

Political Cartoon Have students draw a political cartoon about an event or issue in this section, such as the Babylonian Captivity, the Great Schism, or the behavior of corrupted clergy. Display the cartoons in class. **L3**

ASSESS

Check for Understanding

Assign Section 4 Review as homework or as an in-class activity.

Use Student Self-Test and Review Software to review Section 4.

COOPERATIVE LEARNING ACTIVITY

Role Play Have students work in small groups to write and present a play about an incident related in this section. Each student in the group should be responsible for a specific task, such as researching, writing dialogue, preparing props, or acting in the play itself. Students could present a play about the refusal of Urban VI to resign as pope, thus causing the Great Schism; Jan Hus defending his views to church leaders; John Wycliffe discussing his views with a group of his students; or some other incident related to this section. Encourage students to research the material thoroughly. Have students present their play for the class and, if possible, videotape their presentation. **L2**

Chapter 13 Section 4

History & Art John of Gaunt (1340–1399) was the fourth son of the English king Edward III. His political aspirations were opposed by a group of powerful clergymen. In opposition to them, John formed an alliance with Wycliffe. *Gaunt* refers to Ghent, where John was born.
Answer to Caption: *It encouraged people to search the Bible for religious truths on their own, rather than rely on the clergy.*

Evaluate

Section Quiz 13-4

Use the Testmaker to create a customized quiz for Section 4.

Reteach

Have students identify two major events that destroyed people's confidence in the Church and two main dissenters who called for reform.

Reteaching Activity 13

Enrich

Ask students to find out why Wycliffe's followers were called Lollards and to summarize their findings in a brief paragraph. *(from the Middle Dutch* lollaert, *"mumbler," a name given to earlier European groups considered heretical)*

Enrichment Activity 13

CLOSE

Lead a discussion about the problems within the medieval Church. Ask students to identify the most serious problems.

History & Art *John Wycliffe Reading His Translation of the Bible to John of Gaunt* by Ford Madox Brown. *Why was Wycliffe's translation of the Bible revolutionary?*

Richard II. Anne sent copies of Wycliffe's writings to her homeland in the Holy Roman Empire, where they influenced another great religious reformer.

Jan Hus

During the late A.D. 1300s and A.D. 1400s, the Slavs of **Bohemia**, known as Czechs, became more aware of their own national identity. They wanted to end German control of their country and backed sweeping reforms in the Catholic Church in Bohemia, which had many German clergy. Their religious and political grievances combined to produce an explosive situation.

The Czechs produced religious pamphlets and copies of the Bible in Czech and criticized the corruption of leading church officials, many of whom were German. The leader of the Czech religious reform movement was **Jan Hus**, a popular preacher and professor at the University of Prague. When Hus and his works were condemned by the Church and political leaders, a violent wave of riots swept across Bohemia.

Faced with a possible full-scale rebellion against the Church, in A.D. 1415 the council at Constance demanded that Hus appear before them to defend his views. The Holy Roman emperor promised Hus safe conduct to Constance, Germany, but this guarantee was ignored. Hus was burned at the stake as a heretic, but his heroic death caused many Czechs to rally around their new martyr.

From A.D. 1420 to A.D. 1436, Hus's supporters, called Hussites, resisted the Church and the Holy Roman emperor, and the Church launched five crusades against the Hussites. All five failed. Using firearms and the tactic of forming movable walls with farm wagons, the Hussites defeated the crusading knights.

In A.D. 1436 representatives of the pope and the Holy Roman emperor reached a compromise with the Hussite leaders. They gave the Hussites certain religious liberties in return for their allegiance to the Church. The ideas of Jan Hus, however, continued to spread throughout Europe to influence later and more radical reformers. While this agreement gave the appearance that the Church had successfully met the challenges to its authority, the basic spiritual questions raised by Hus and others did not go away.

SECTION 4 REVIEW

Recall

1. **Define** pilgrimage, simony.
2. **Identify** Pope Clement V, Babylonian Captivity, Great Schism, John Wycliffe, the Lollards, Jan Hus, the Hussites.
3. **Explain** the effects of the Babylonian Captivity and the Great Schism on the Church.

Critical Thinking

4. **Synthesizing Information** Imagine you are a follower of Jan Hus just after his execution. How would you feel about carrying on his work?

Understanding Themes

5. **Conflict** Explain the rise of dissent among many devout Europeans. Why were they against the Church and its leadership?

SECTION 4 REVIEW ANSWERS

1. All vocabulary words are defined in the Glossary.
2. Clement V, 334; Babylonian Captivity, 334; Great Schism, 335; Wycliffe, 335; Lollards, 335; Hus, 336; Hussites, 336
3. seriously undermined pope's authority; aroused resentment against papal power; led to call for reform within Church
4. would have continued resistance to Church and Holy Roman Emperor in order to attain goal of ridding Bohemia of German influence
5. **CONFLICT** People were angered by corruption within Church and abuse of power by church leaders.

Social Studies
SKILLS

Analyzing Historical Maps

When you walk through your town, you may see changes in progress. Perhaps a new restaurant has opened, or an old factory has been torn down. Change also takes place on a larger scale across nations and continents. Historical maps illustrate political, social, and cultural changes over time.

Learning the Skill

To analyze a historical map, first read the title to identify its theme. Then identify the chronology of events on the map. Many historical maps show changes in political boundaries over time. For example, the map below of the Frankish Empire uses colors to show land acquisitions under three different rulers. On the other map, however, colors represent areas controlled by different rulers at the same time. Read the map key, labels, and captions to determine what time periods and changes appear on the map.

To compare historical maps of the same region in different time periods, first identify the geographic location and time period of each map. Then look for similarities and differences. Which features have remained the same and which have changed? What groups control the area in each map? Has the country grown larger or smaller over time? Have other features changed?

After analyzing the information on historical maps, try to draw conclusions about the causes and effects of these changes.

Practicing the Skill

The two maps on this page show the same region in different time periods. Study both maps and answer these questions.

1. What is the time period of each map?
2. How did the Frankish Empire change from A.D. 500 to A.D. 800?
3. Did France grow larger or smaller between A.D. 800 and A.D. 1400?
4. What other changes appear on these maps?

Applying the Skill

Compare a map of Europe today with a map of Europe in 1985 or earlier. Identify at least five changes that have occurred since the early 1980s.

For More Practice

Turn to the Skill Practice in the Chapter Review on page 339 for more practice in analyzing historical maps.

Frankish Empire A.D. 481–814

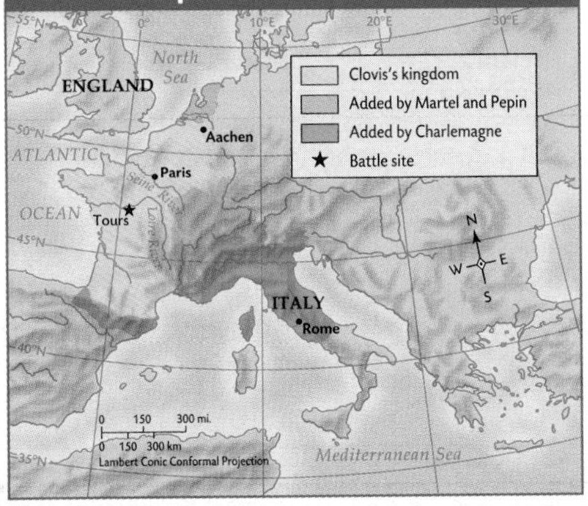

France in the A.D.1400s

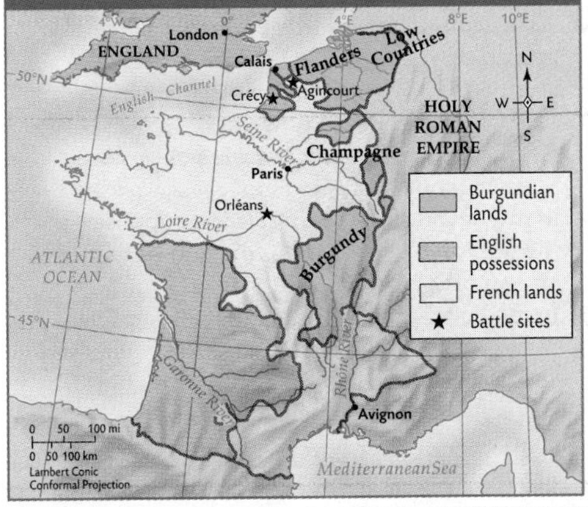

ANSWERS TO PRACTICING THE SKILL

1. The map on the left shows the Frankish Empire from A.D. 481 to A.D. 814; the map on the right shows France in the 1400s.
2. It spread eastward and south to include parts of present-day Spain, Italy, Switzerland, and the Benelux countries.
3. smaller
4. Answers may include that France was divided up among various rulers, that its boundaries changed over time, and so on.

Social Studies
SKILLS

TEACH

Analyzing Historical Maps Before students read the skill, ask them whether they think of maps as static or changing and to justify their answers. Then ask them to name some other kinds of maps with which they are familiar. *(Students might mention weather maps, topographic maps, astronomical maps.)* Ask them to indicate what kinds of changes those maps can illustrate. *(Weather maps clearly show changing weather patterns; changes in topographic maps of the same region over time might show the formation of a new island from vulcanism; changes in astronomical maps of the same region over time might show the appearance of a comet.)* When students are sufficiently familiar with the idea that maps of different kinds can serve as records of change, have them read the skill and complete the practice questions.

Additional Practice

Skill Reinforcement Activity 13

Building Skills in Geography Workbook, Unit 1, Lesson 13

Chapter 13 Review

GLENCOE TECHNOLOGY

VIDEODISC

Use the Chapter 13 Mind-Jogger Videoquiz to preview chapter content.

MindJogger Videoquiz

Chapter 13
Disc 2 Side B

Also available in VHS.

Answers

Using Key Terms

1. e	**6.** a
2. d	**7.** b
3. j	**8.** h
4. f	**9.** l
5. i	**10.** g

Using Your History Journal

Students should consider how military or religious motives shaped the characters of the Europeans whose values these works describe.

Reviewing Facts

1. First: 1096–1099, captured Jerusalem; Second: 1147–1149, attempt to regain territory in Palestine failed; Third: 1189–1192, failed to regain complete control of Jerusalem; others: 1200s, Muslims conquered remaining Christian territories in Palestine.
2. heavier plow, collar harness, three-field system
3. worked without pay to learn craft and become a journeyman, who received pay but worked under a master; he could become a master himself if the guild approved his masterpiece
4. English king claimed throne of France when French king died in 1328 without a direct heir; England won early battles but France eventually prevailed.
5. Wycliffe began translating Bible into English; Hus was burned at stake as heretic.
6. dirty, crowded, smelly, noisy, constant threat of fire and disease
7. middle class, merchants; helped turn towns into cities, weakened feudal system, strengthened monarchies
8. wiped out about a third of Europe's population; disrupted warfare, business
9. served as advisers to monarchs; received freedom from feudal obligations in exchange for financial support of monarchs
10. decline in religious/political authority as result of Babylonian Captivity and Great Schism
11. strengthened bureaucracy, kept nobles under royal control, promoted trade/farming
12. English monarchy emerged strengthened.
13. reconquest of Muslim lands in Spain; nearly all of Spain shared same religion
14. development of a money economy, banking;

CHAPTER 13 REVIEW

Historical Significance

Many features of modern Western civilization arose during the Middle Ages. The medieval history of Europe's great cities can still be seen in great cathedrals. Modern labor unions and institutions of higher learning are related to medieval guilds and universities. Today's national languages in Europe first appeared during the Middle Ages. Finally, the middle class, which plays an important role in the world today, also had its beginnings during this period.

Using Key Terms

Write the key term that completes each sentence.

a. apprentice	g. vernacular
b. cortes	h. simony
c. charter	i. money economy
d. scholasticism	j. pilgrimages
e. Crusade	k. master
f. guilds	l. troubadours

1. A military expedition of Christian Europeans to free the Holy Land from the Muslims was known as a ____________.
2. Church scholars developed a system of thought known as __________ that sought to reconcile faith and reason.
3. During the Late Middle Ages, many devout people demonstrated their faith by going on ____________.
4. During the A.D. 1100s merchants and artisans organized themselves into business associations called ________.
5. The rise of a ___________ led to the growth of banking and put the feudal classes in an economic squeeze.
6. To become an expert in a particular craft, an artisan served for a certain period of time as an _________ without pay.
7. In Spain, assemblies known as ______ at first had the right to review the policies of Spanish monarchs.
8. Many devout European Catholics opposed the practice of______—the buying and selling of church offices.
9. In medieval France, traveling poet-musicians called __________ composed lyric poems and songs about love and the feats of knights.
10. During the Middle Ages, the rise of ______ languages gave each kingdom of Europe a separate identity.

Using Your History Journal

From your notes on* Beowulf, *the* Song of Roland, *or* The Canterbury Tales, *write a short description of the manners, customs, and values of the Europeans described in the work.

Reviewing Facts

1. **List** the various medieval Crusades and their results.
2. **Describe** several agricultural improvements in the Middle Ages.
3. **Outline** the steps taken by an apprentice to become a master.
4. **List** the key events in the Hundred Years' War.
5. **Identify** two church reformers and a major event in the life of each.
6. **Describe** what a typical medieval town was like.
7. **Identify** the bourgeoisie and state their role in late medieval Europe.
8. **Discuss** the impact of the Black Death on western Europe.
9. **Explain** why townspeople and the lower nobility supported the rise of strong monarchies in western Europe.
10. **List** the problems that the Catholic Church faced at the end of the Middle Ages.
11. **State** how Louis XI strengthened the French monarchy.
12. **Discuss** the major result of the Wars of the Roses.
13. **Identify** the *Reconquista.* How did it contribute to the unity of Spain?
14. **List** new business methods that developed in western Europe during the A.D. 1300s and A.D. 1400s. How did they change western European life?

CHAPTER 13 REVIEW

Critical Thinking

1. **Apply** How did the medieval middle class change European society?
2. **Analyze** What various forces led to Europe's economic growth during the Middle Ages?
3. **Evaluate** How would Europe be different today if there had been no Crusades?
4. **Apply** How did European monarchies change during the Middle Ages? What were the effects of this change on culture, religion, and politics in Europe?

Geography in History

1. **Place** Refer to the map "Trade Routes A.D. 1400s." Name the major trading cities in western Europe during the 1400s.
2. **Human/Environment Interaction** Why did most European traders avoid overland routes whenever possible?
3. **Location** With which two areas to the east did the cities of Europe most want to trade?
4. **Movement** How did the desire for luxuries from the East lead to changes in transportation in the West?

Trade Routes A.D. 1400s

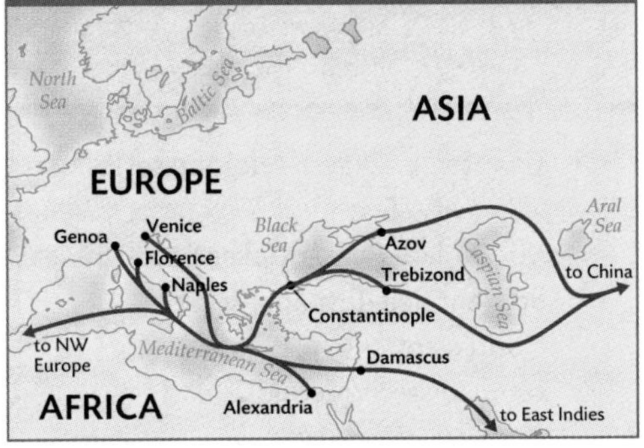

Understanding Themes

1. **Cultural Diffusion** How did a mix of cultures affect medieval Europe?
2. **Innovation** Choose one medieval innovation and describe its influence on medieval society. Do the same for a modern innovation and modern society.
3. **Conflict** How did continual conflict between England and France strengthen the monarchies of those countries?
4. **Conflict** Why was there religious dissent in the Catholic Church of the Late Middle Ages?

Linking Past and Present

1. The Crusades were a series of "holy wars" conducted by Christians against Muslims. Can you find examples of holy wars in modern times?
2. Compare the rise of towns in medieval Europe with the rise of towns in America.
3. How do medieval European universities compare to today's higher educational institutions?

Skill Practice

Study the map "Spread of the Black Death" and answer the questions below.

1. What is the topic and time period of this map?
2. What does color represent?
3. When and where did the Black Death begin?
4. In which direction did the Black Death spread? How does the map show this?
5. What factor do you think caused this pattern of the epidemic?

Spread of the Black Death

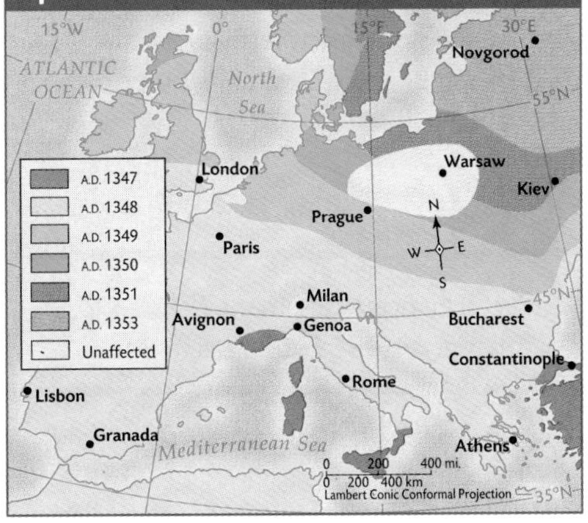

Chapter 13 Review

Understanding Themes

1. **CULTURAL DIFFUSION** brought new ideas and influences to political, technological, and social spheres
2. **INNOVATION** Computer technology today has strengthened interdependence among nations.
3. **CONFLICT** Victory in the Hundred Years' War gave power to French monarchy. Civil war in England culminated in rise of strong Tudor monarchy.
4. **CONFLICT** Doctrinal differences as well as internal abuses of power led to dissent.

Linking Past and Present

1. Some Palestinians and other Arabs reject peace negotiations with Israel because of what they deem holy war.
2. similar process in America, with political, social, and economic growth leading to new opportunities as towns prospered
3. Medieval universities had to be careful not to offend the Church. Admission based on ability to pay. Only males admitted.

Skill Practice

1. spread of the Black Death in 1300s
2. where plague spread to at different times
3. China in 1347
4. north and west; colors correspond to dates, showing northern and westward movement
5. As ships sailed from Asia to Mediterranean, the plague spread from China to ports in southern Europe and beyond.

led to growth of towns, undermined feudalism

Critical Thinking

1. helped turn towns into organized municipalities; businessmen gained power; stimulated new interest in learning, founded universities
2. money economy, rise of middle class, improved agricultural methods
3. lack of cultural diffusion and hostility between Christians and Muslims
4. Monarchies became stronger, leading to greater control over religion and politics, and to stronger national cultures.

Geography in History

1. Venice, Florence, Naples, Genoa
2. sea travel was safer and faster
3. East Indies and China
4. New sea and river routes were developed; the Roman road system was repaired and rebuilt.

Chapter Bonus Test Question

Ask students: How do you think the Church felt about the growth of medieval towns? *(positive–applauded the building of cathedrals; negative–disapproved of practices believed to stem from avarice)*

Chapter 13 *Medieval Europe at Its Height* 339

Teach, Reinforce, and Extend CHAPTER Content

East and South Asia

CHAPTER RESOURCES

	Reproducible Resources	Multimedia Resources
Chapter Opener	Chapter Themes: Graphic Organizer 14 Historical Significance Chapter Activity 14	MindJogger Videoquiz
Chapter Enrichment	Vocabulary Activity 14* Time Line Activity 14 Mapping History Activity 14 History Simulation 14 Geography and History Activity 14 Source Reading 14 People in World History Profiles 25, 26 World Literature Selection 14 World Art and Music Activity 14 Enrichment Activity 14 Critical Thinking Activity 14 Skill Reinforcement Activity 14 Performance Assessment Activity 14	World History and Art Transparency 17, *Angkor Wat* Chapter Transparency 14 PicturePack Transparency Set: Physical Geography of the World Vocabulary PuzzleMaker Software Picture Atlas of the World World Music: Cultural Traditions, Lessons 8, 9 STV: World Geography, Vol. 1, *Asia*
Chapter Review/Reteaching	Reteaching Activity 14 Skill Reinforcement Activity 14 Spanish Chapter Summary 14	Chapter 14 Digest Audiocassette, Activity, Test* Vocabulary PuzzleMaker Software Student Self-Test and Review Software MindJogger Videoquiz
Chapter Evaluation/Testing	Performance Assessment Activity 14 Chapter 14 Test, Forms A and B	Testmaker

** Also available in Spanish*

0:00 **OUT OF TIME?** Assign the Chapter 14 summary in the Unit 3 Digest on pages 394-397, and the Chapter 14 Audiocassettes.

Block Schedule

Block scheduling differs from traditional class scheduling in the amount of time allotted to each period. The extended time frame provided by block scheduling affords you the opportunity to implement a greater number of research-oriented and activity-intense projects to motivate and involve your students. Activities that are particularly suited to use within the block scheduling framework are identified throughout this chapter by the following designation.

KEY TO ABILITY LEVELS

Teaching strategies have been coded for varying learning styles and abilities.

- **L1** **BASIC** activities for all students
- **L2** **AVERAGE** activities for average to above-average students
- **L3** **CHALLENGING** activities for above-average students
- **LEP** **LIMITED ENGLISH PROFICIENCY** activities

Chapter 14 Planning Guide

A complete, 1-page lesson plan is provided for each section in the *Reproducible Lesson Plans* booklet.

SECTION RESOURCES

Daily Objectives	Reproducible Resources	Multimedia Resources
Section 1 Central Asia Describe how the Mongols acquired the world's largest land empire.	Reproducible Lesson Plan 14-1 Vocabulary Activity 14* Guided Reading Activity 14-1* Time Line Activity 14 Section Quiz 14-1*	Section Focus Transparency 14-1 Chapter Transparency 14 Student Self-Test and Review Software Testmaker STV: World Geography, Vol. 1, *Asia*
Section 2 China Summarize the achievements of the Tang, Song, and Yuan dynasties.	Reproducible Lesson Plan 14-2 Vocabulary Activity 14* Guided Reading Activity 14-2* History Simulation 14 Section Quiz 14-2*	Section Focus Transparency 14-2 Student Self-Test and Review Software Testmaker World Music: Cultural Traditions, Lesson 8 Picture Atlas of the World
Section 3 Southeast Asia Explain how Southeast Asians were influenced by the cultures of China and India.	Reproducible Lesson Plan 14-3 Vocabulary Activity 14* Guided Reading Activity 14-3* Geography and History Activity 14 Section Quiz 14-3*	Section Focus Transparency 14-3 World History and Art Transparency 17, *Angkor Wat* Student Self-Test and Review Software Testmaker World Music: Cultural Traditions, Lesson 9 Picture Atlas of the World
Section 4 Korea and Japan Explain how the Koreans and Japanese accepted Chinese culture.	Reproducible Lesson Plan 14-4 Guided Reading Activity 14-4* Reteaching Activity 14 Enrichment Activity 14 Section Quiz 14-4* Performance Assessment Activity 14 Spanish Chapter Summary 14	Section Focus Transparency 14-4 Vocabulary PuzzleMaker Software Student Self-Test and Review Software Testmaker

* *Also available in Spanish*

Chapter Activities

Performance Assessment Activity

Modern-Day Dynasties and Empires Have students expand their understanding of the concepts of dynasty, empire, and kingdom by researching and finding modern-day examples, such as publishing dynasties and entertainment empires. Have students work in pairs or trios to conduct their research and complete a collage, mural, or other complex visual to show the many examples. Students should also include information about dynasties, empires, and kingdoms from the chapter as well as historic examples previously studied.

Possible Rubric Features
Concept attainment, accuracy of content information, research skills, relevance and appropriateness of examples, creative and visual appeal of product

• *For an additional activity, refer to Activity 14 in the* Performance Assessment Strategies and Activities *booklet.*

Activity

From the Classroom of...

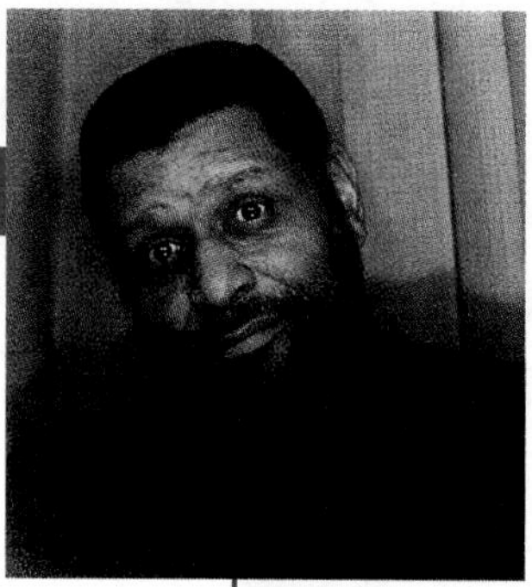

Ken Austin
Friends Academy
Locust Valley, NY

Steppe People Mural and Time Line
Organize students into three groups—illustrators, historians, and scribes. The illustrators will create a 3' x 20' mural, beginning by drawing a map on the mural of East and South Asia. Meanwhile, the historians will gather facts concerning the steppe peoples' way of life, interests, and activities. They should also trace chronologically the rise and movement of these peoples. The historians will share their information with the illustrators, who will add drawings and pictures to the mural, and the scribes, who will prepare a time line and brief fact sheets to accompany the illustrations. Place the time line along the bottom of the mural and the fact sheets near appropriate illustrations.

Multiple Learning Styles

Verbal/Linguistic
Ask students to look for a collection of Chinese or Japanese myths or children's stories in the school or public library. Have them prepare a selection from the works to present to the class.

Logical/Mathematical
Direct students to create a three-part time line of the major events that occurred in China, Korea, and Japan during the period covered in this chapter. Have them label each event as political, cultural, or other.

Visual/Spatial
Have students plan a special Asian Arts day when each person brings to class and displays or reports on the origin of an item from China, Japan, Korea, or Southeast Asia. Suggest items such as a musical recording, pottery, clothing, a special book, or even an ethnic food. This project provides an opportunity for Asian students to share their heritage.

Kinesthetic
Remind students that Chinese writing was originally pictographic—it used pictures to convey the meaning of the words. Ask students to research Chinese writing and make a poster showing examples of Chinese characters. Have them include the character, its Chinese pronunciation, and its meaning.

Additional Resources

TEACHER'S CORNER

NATIONAL GEOGRAPHIC SOCIETY

INDEX TO NATIONAL GEOGRAPHIC MAGAZINE

The following articles may be used for research relating to this chapter:

- "The Golden Hoard of Bactria," by Viktor Ivanovich Sarianidi, March 1990.
- "The Queen of Textiles," by Nina Hyde, January 1984.
- "Indonesia Rescues Ancient Borobudur," by W. Brown Morton III, January 1983.
- "The Lost Fleet of Kublai Khan," by Torao Mozai, November 1982.
- "The Temples of Angkor: Ancient Glory in Stone," by Peter T. White, May 1982.

NATIONAL GEOGRAPHIC SOCIETY PRODUCTS AVAILABLE FROM GLENCOE

To order the following products for use with this chapter, contact your local Glencoe sales representative or call Glencoe at 1-800-368-7344:

VIDEODISC
- STV: World Geography, Vol. 1, *Asia*

CD-ROM
- Picture Atlas of the World

NGS PICTUREPACK TRANSPARENCY SET
- Physical Geography of the World

BIBLIOGRAPHY

Literature of the Period

Murasaki, Shikibu. *The Tale of Genji.* New York: Knopf, 1992. Novel considered to be one of Japan's greatest works of fiction.

Readings for the Student

Van den Heuvel, Cor. *The Haiku Anthology.* Garden City, N.Y.: Anchor Press, 1974. A diverse collection of haiku poetry.

Bynner, Witter, trans. *The Way of Life According to Lao Tzu.* New York: Putnam, 1986. Sayings that were the basis for Daoism.

Readings for the Teacher

Bloodworth, Dennis. *The Chinese Looking Glass.* New York: Farrar, Straus and Giroux, 1980. A historical look at the Chinese people and their customs.

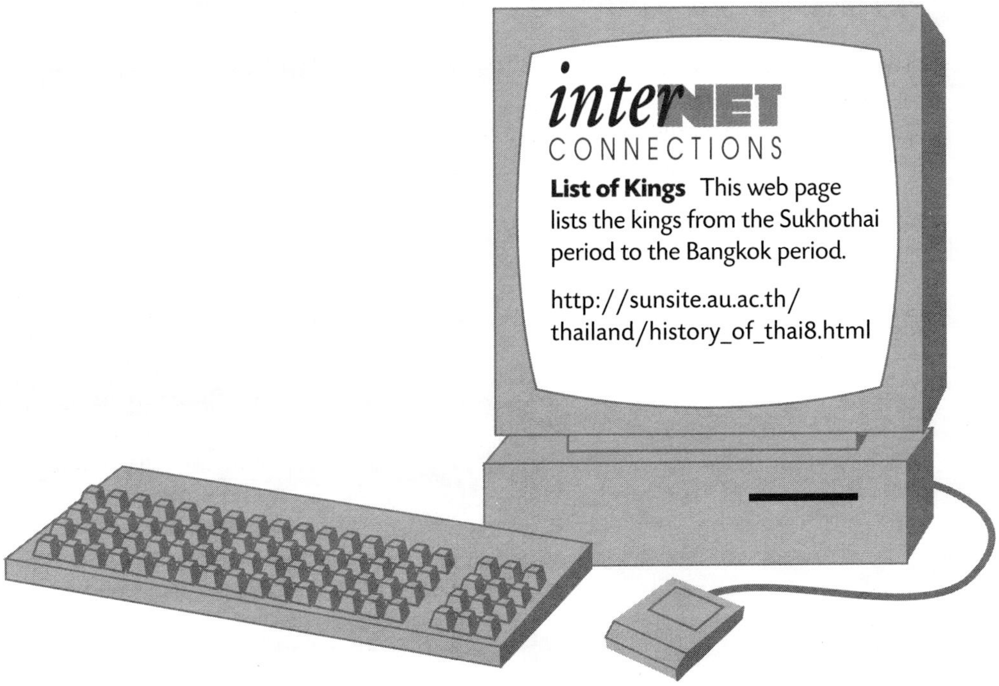
interNET
CONNECTIONS
List of Kings This web page lists the kings from the Sukhothai period to the Bangkok period.
http://sunsite.au.ac.th/thailand/history_of_thai8.html

Introducing Chapter 14

CHAPTER THEMES

Chapter Themes are listed by section on this chapter opening page of the Student Edition. A corresponding theme-based activity is available under "TEACH," and a theme-based question is asked in the Section and Chapter Reviews.

The Storyteller

Historical Setting For more than 2,000 years, the Chinese used competitive exams as a way of selecting government workers. The civil service exam such as the one described here was the last in a series of tests a Chinese student had to pass in order to be offered a government post. First the student took a local exam. If he passed it, he took a provincial exam. The final step was an empirewide exam, given every three years. Applicants were tested on their knowledge of Chinese poetry and the writings of Confucius. Of the hundreds of thousands of men who took these exams, only a few hundred passed.

Historical Significance

Answer: *Indian culture strongly affected Southeast Asia, while Chinese civilization had a strong impact on Southeast Asia, Korea, and Japan. Many aspects of Asian culture reached other parts of the world during the time of the Mongol Empire.*

Chapter 14

500 B.C.–A.D. 1400

East and South Asia

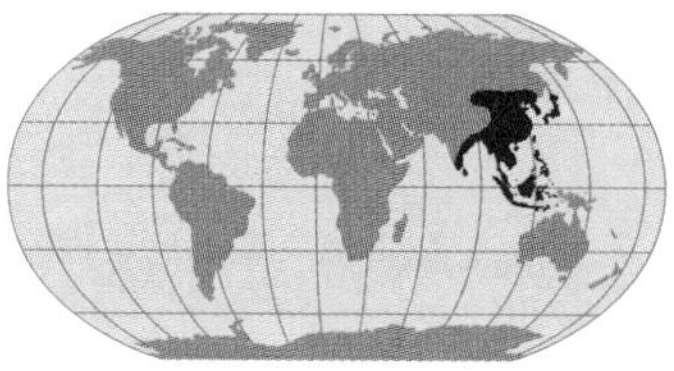

Chapter Themes

- **Movement** The Mongols of central Asia conquer China and parts of Europe. *Section 1*
- **Uniformity** A centralized government, a state religion, and a common language maintain China's cultural continuity. *Section 2*
- **Cultural Diffusion** The civilizations of Southeast Asia reflect the influences of India and China. *Section 3*
- **Innovation** Japan and Korea produce innovations from a blend of Chinese and local traditions. *Section 4*

The Storyteller

In China, in the year A.D. 1200, a lone student sat behind a desk in a room furnished only with a lamp, some paper, a writing brush, and an inkstone. He labored over a grueling government exam designed to test his knowledge of Confucian texts. He worried because examiners could fail a person for even a single misquotation. If he passed, he would be one of the Song emperor's officials. If he failed, he would have to hawk cheap goods in the streets.

Civil service examinations helped ancient China to maintain a consistent government no matter which dynasty was in power. Later, the neighboring countries of Korea and Japan adopted these civil service examinations as well as other aspects of Chinese culture.

Historical Significance

How did the civilizations of East and South Asia influence each other and the rest of the world?

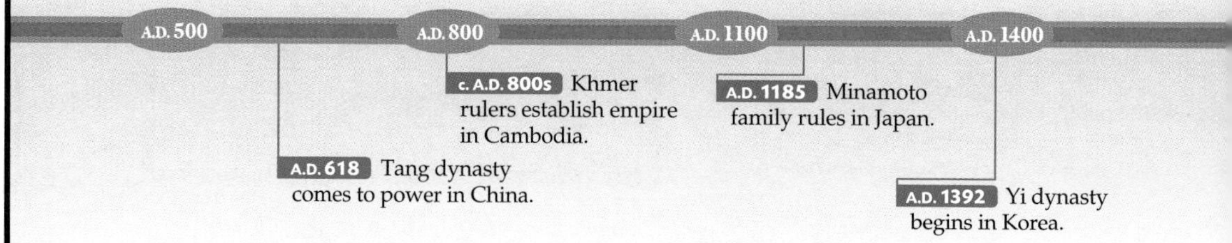
A.D. 500
A.D. 800
A.D. 1100
A.D. 1400
c. A.D. 800s Khmer rulers establish empire in Cambodia.
A.D. 1185 Minamoto family rules in Japan.
A.D. 618 Tang dynasty comes to power in China.
A.D. 1392 Yi dynasty begins in Korea.

340

GEOGRAPHY CONNECTION

Location Have students look at a wall map to locate the geographic boundaries of China, Southeast Asia, Korea, and Japan. *(China: the Gobi, the Tibetan plateau; Southeast Asia: water boundaries including the Bay of Bengal and the Pacific Ocean; Korea: Yellow Sea, Sea of Japan; Japan: Pacific Ocean, Sea of Japan)* Ask which boundaries might serve as barriers and which might encourage interaction. *(Difficult landforms tend to impede movement, while water encourages it.)*

Visualizing History A partial view of the summer palace constructed under Emperor Ch'ien Lung. Bibliothèque Nationale, Paris, France

Your History Journal

Copy or obtain a blank map of East Asia. As you read the chapter, place 10 to 20 key events on your map in the countries or areas where they occurred. Include the dates of these events.

Introducing Chapter 14

Visualizing History Members of the Chinese imperial family lived in elaborate palace complexes. Secluded and sheltered from the outside world, most of them knew little about the lives of their subjects.

Performance Assessment

Refer to the activity on page 340C of the Planning Guide.

For an additional activity, refer to Activity 14 in the *Performance Assessment Strategies and Activities* booklet.

Using Your History Journal

Students may want to use different colors to represent different types of events, such as red for military engagements, blue for political matters (the founding of cities and/or dynasties), and so on.

GLENCOE TECHNOLOGY

VIDEODISC

Use MindJogger to preview chapter content.

MindJogger Videoquiz

Chapter 14
Disc 2 Side B

Also available in VHS.

EXTRA CREDIT PROJECT

Martial Arts Asian civilizations developed several different systems of martial arts. Have students research one or more of these: tai chi chuan (Chinese), tae kwon do (Korean), or karate (Japanese). They should find out where, how, and when the discipline originated and what role it plays in society today. If possible, have students demonstrate or show pictures of some of the basic principles and movements of the system they choose. **L2**

Chapter 14 Section 1

SECTION THEME

- **Movement** The Mongols of central Asia conquer China and parts of Europe.

Find Out

Answer: *At the time, their armies formed the most skilled fighting force in the world. They employed terror and Chinese techniques of siege warfare.*

FOCUS

Section Objective

Describe how the Mongols acquired the world's largest land empire.

BELLRINGER Motivational Activity

Before taking roll at the beginning of the class period, project Section Focus Transparency 14-1 and have students answer the activity questions. Discuss students' responses.

This activity is also available as a blackline master.

Vocabulary Pre-check

Use Vocabulary Activity 14 to introduce vocabulary terms. **L1 LEP**

A.D. 1200 — A.D. 1300 — A.D. 1400

- **c. A.D. 1206** Genghis Khan becomes ruler of all Mongol tribes.
- **c. A.D. 1270** The Mongols establish rule in China.
- **A.D. 1398** Timur Lenk (Tamerlane) sacks Samarkand in central Asia.

Section 1

Central Asia

Setting the Scene

- **Terms to Define**
  clan, yurt, *yasa*, khan
- **People to Meet**
  the Seljuk Turks, the Mongols, Genghis Khan, Timur Lenk (Tamerlane)
- **Places to Locate**
  Mongolia

Find Out How did the Mongols acquire the world's largest land empire?

The Storyteller

The caravan halted for the night. Chaghatai, the leader, before retiring posted a sign and fastened bells around the animals' necks. Maffeo, a young foreigner, wondered at these precautions. Chaghatai explained that strange things may happen in the Desert of Lop. "When a man is riding by night through this desert and something happens to make him … lose touch with his companions ... he hears spirits talking.... Often these voices make him stray from the path.... For this reason bands of travellers make a point of keeping very close together.... And round the necks of all their beasts they fasten little bells, so that by listening to the sound they may prevent them from straying from the path."

—adapted from *The Travels of Marco Polo*, Marco Polo, translated by Ronald Latham, 1958

Porcelain figure on camel

From the A.D. 1000s to the A.D. 1400s, invaders from the steppe of central Asia conquered territories in eastern Asia, the Middle East, and eastern Europe. Originally nomads, the invaders settled in many of the conquered areas. They adapted to the local cultures, advanced trade, and encouraged the exchange of goods and ideas.

The Steppe Peoples

At the beginning of the A.D. 1000s, large numbers of nomadic groups roamed the steppe of central Asia. Loosely organized into clans, or groups based on family ties, they depended for their livelihood on the grazing of animals. To protect their pastures and provide for a growing population, they organized under powerful chiefs. The chiefs formed cavalry units of warriors armed with bows and arrows. The nomadic peoples became a military threat to neighboring territories that were more culturally developed. They carried out a series of invasions that transformed the cultures of eastern Asia, the Middle East, and eastern Europe.

The Seljuk Turks

The first people of the steppes to engage in conquest were the Turks. Around A.D. 800, weak Abbasid rulers centered in Baghdad hired Turkish warriors to fight in their armies. As a result, the Turks became powerful and soon controlled the Abbasid government. Later, about A.D. 1000, a group of Muslim Turks called **the Seljuk Turks** moved from central Asia into the Middle East. There they formed settlements and restored the Sunni caliphate. The Seljuks also gained control of the main trade routes between eastern Asia, the Middle East, and Europe. They benefited from this trade and used their wealth to build an empire.

SECTION RESOURCES

Reproducible Masters
- Reproducible Lesson Plan 14-1
- Vocabulary Activity 14
- Guided Reading Activity 14-1
- Time Line Activity 14
- Section Quiz 14-1

Transparencies
- Section Focus Transparency 14-1
- Chapter Transparency 14

Multimedia
- Student Self-Test and Review Software
- Testmaker
- STV: World Geography, Vol. 1, *Asia*

Mongol Empire at Its Height

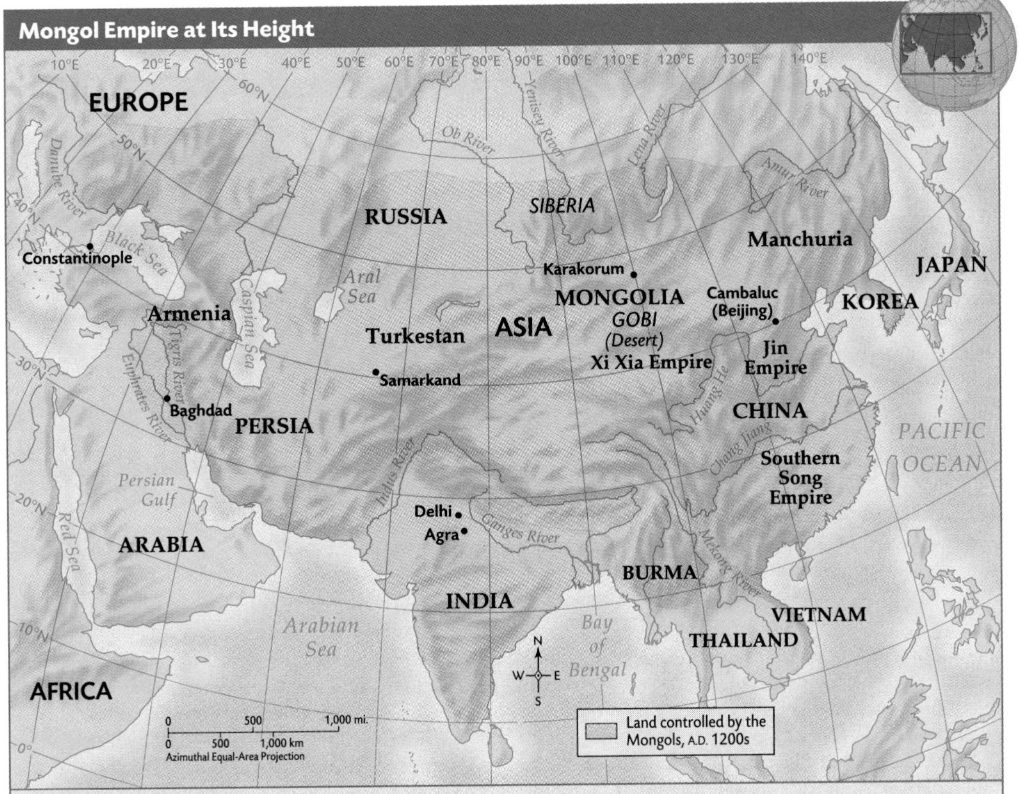

Map Study Genghis Khan's empire extended nearly 5,000 miles from Europe to the Pacific.
Region How did Mongol rule foster trade with the Middle East and Europe?

Seljuk warriors also invaded the plains and highlands of Asia Minor. There they defeated the Byzantines at the Battle of Manzikert in A.D. 1071. The Byzantine emperor Alexius I Comnenus feared the loss of Byzantine territory to the Seljuks and appealed to the pope and the monarchs of western Europe for aid. About 20 years later, the Seljuk conquest of Palestine led to Pope Urban II's calling of the First Crusade.

Though the Seljuks were skilled warriors, they were unable to develop a well-organized government to rule their territories. Seljuk rulers lacked strong traditions of government administration and had difficulties holding the empire together. Local officials ignored the central government and acted like independent rulers. They began to fight each other for control of land. Weakened by internal upheavals, the Seljuks became prey to new nomadic invaders from central Asia.

The Mongols

During the late A.D. 1100s, **the Mongols** became the dominant nomadic group in central Asia. Their homeland was **Mongolia**, a region of forests and steppe northwest of China. In this wild and isolated area, they wandered from pasture to pasture with their herds of sheep, horses, and yaks, or long-haired oxen. Because of their nomadic life, the Mongols lived in movable tents called yurts. Their principal foods were meat and mare's milk. In a few fertile areas, Mongol farmers established small communities. There women raised grains while men herded animals.

Genghis Khan

Like other nomads, the Mongols at first were divided into clans. They were expert fighters on horseback, using bow and arrow. About A.D. 1206

Chapter 14 Section 1

TEACH

Guided Practice

THEME **Movement**

Explain that the steppes are a region of dry, treeless plains covered with grass. They are very hot in summer and bitter cold in winter. Why would this kind of topography encourage the movement of peoples? *(The harsh environment could not long support a large population; people would have to move to find new sources of food for themselves and their animals.)* **L1**

Chapter Transparency 14

Map Study

Answer

by bringing peace

Map Skills Practice

Reading a Map What Mongol settlement is today the capital of China? *(Cambaluc [Beijing])*

NATIONAL GEOGRAPHIC SOCIETY

VIDEODISC
STV: World Geography, Volume 1

Side One, Frames 13631-17712
Title: *Asia*
Subject: Interior and North Asia
Ask: What is the winter climate of the taiga like? *(Winters are long, very cold, and days are short.)*

COOPERATIVE LEARNING ACTIVITY

TV Interview Organize the class into five teams and assign each a Mongol leader: Genghis Khan, Ogadai, Batu, Helagu, Timur Lenk. One member of each team should play the role of announcer, one should act as interviewer, and one should be the guest. Team members should research the man to be interviewed and write questions and answers for the interview. Allow time for team members to share what they have learned and to plan the interview. Then have each team present its interview to the class. **L2**

Military History Ask students to list the military tactics the Mongols developed *(disciplined cavalry units, officers chosen for ability)* and those they learned from the Chinese *(siege warfare, gunpowder, storming ladders, battering rams).* **L1**

Time Line Have students construct a time line showing the major Mongol conquests, beginning with the Turkish steppe peoples and continuing through the conquest of China. **L2**

Visualizing History Some modern yurts have stoves and wooden floors and are even equipped with electricity. **Answer to Caption:** *because the Mongols were nomads and yurts are easily moved*

Independent Practice

Guided Reading Activity 14-1 **L1**

Time Line Activity 14

Daily Life The horse was basic to the culture of the Mongols. Have one or more students research (a) the kind of horses the Mongols rode, and (b) what made the Mongols such good riders. **L2**

Linking Past and Present

Mogul Rule In the 1500s, a descendant of both Genghis Khan and Timur Lenk led a Mongol conquest of India. His people, who ruled India for 200 years, were called Moguls, from the Persian word for Mongol. A Mogul ruler named Shah Jahan built the Taj Mahal, one of the most beautiful buildings in the world.

Visualizing History **Some people in Mongolia still live in yurts, circular domed tents of skins or felt stretched over a lattice frame.** *Why did ancient Mongols choose this kind of housing?*

a Mongol leader named Temujin (teh•MOO•juhn) organized the scattered clans under one government. He brought together Mongol laws in a new code known as the *yasa*. Under Temujin's guidance, an assembly of tribal chiefs met for the first time to plan military campaigns and to appoint future leaders.

Temujin's greatest achievement was in military affairs. He organized the Mongol armies into disciplined cavalry units. These units were then placed under the command of officers chosen for their abilities and not for their family ties. These changes made the Mongols the most skilled fighting force in the world at that time. As a result of his efforts, Temujin was recognized as khan, or absolute ruler. Now called **Genghis Khan** (JEHN•guhs KAHN), he set out to create a large empire.

Mongol Conquests

The Mongol armies under Genghis Khan first conquered the other steppe peoples, most of whom were Turks. These victories brought tribute money to the Mongol state as well as new recruits for the Mongol armies. By A.D. 1211 the Mongols were strong enough to attack major civilizations. In that year, 100,000 Mongol horsemen invaded China. While fighting against the Chinese, the Mongols learned Chinese techniques of siege warfare. Using gunpowder, storming ladders, and battering rams, they won significant victories against their opponents. In spite of Genghis Khan's death in A.D. 1227, the Mongols continued their advance. By A.D. 1270 all of China's territory was in their hands, and a Mongol dynasty ruled the entire country.

Under Ogadai (OH•guh•DY) Khan, the other Mongol forces moved westward. During the A.D. 1230s and A.D. 1240s, a Mongol army led by the commander Batu (bah•TOO) conquered Russian territories and then crossed the Carpathian Mountains into eastern and central Europe. Upon hearing of Ogadai's death, Batu's army returned to Russia. There they awaited the selection of a new khan. Meanwhile, Ogadai's widow ruled the Mongols.

During the same period, another group of Mongols invaded the Middle East. Using terror to subdue the region, the Mongols destroyed cities and killed large numbers of people. In A.D. 1258 the commander Helagu (heh•lah•GOO) captured Baghdad, the old Abbasid capital, and enslaved its inhabitants. The destruction of Baghdad represented a major setback to Islamic civilization. However, the Mongol advance was finally halted by the Mamluks, a Muslim military group that ruled Egypt.

The Mongol Empire

The Mongols created the largest land empire in history. Their territories extended from China to the frontiers of western Europe. Many of the great trade routes between Europe and Asia passed through Mongol lands. During the A.D. 1200s

MEETING SPECIAL NEEDS ACTIVITY

Language Delayed To help make studying easier for students with limited English proficiency, ask other students to record this chapter on tape for home study. Have several students divide the chapter, with each student recording a few paragraphs. Ask students who use the tapes to summarize orally the main ideas of each section. These same students could prepare questions about the chapter and quiz their classmates. **L1 LEP**

Mongol rule brought peace to the region. This advanced the growth of trade and encouraged closer cultural contacts between East and West.

The Mongols respected the highly advanced culture of conquered groups and learned from them. In China, Mongol rulers gradually adopted Chinese ideas and practices. In Persia and central Asia, Mongol settlers converted to Islam and intermarried with the local Turkish population. Turkish became the principal language of the region. The Mongols of Russia, however, kept their traditional customs and lived apart from the Slavs. They settled in the empty steppe region north of the Caspian Sea. From there, they controlled the Slavic principalities located in the northern forests.

The unity of the Mongol Empire did not last long. All Mongols gave allegiance to the khan in Mongolia. However, local rulers became increasingly independent. By the end of the A.D. 1200s, Mongol territories in Russia, central Asia, Persia, and China had developed into separate and independent domains.

Visualizing History **Timur Lenk, or Tamerlane, devoted much of his life to conquest, from India to Russia to the Mediterranean.** *What city was the center of his empire?*

Timur Lenk

About 100 years later, another powerful nomadic force emerged from central Asia. In the A.D. 1390s a Turkish-Mongol chief named **Timur Lenk** (in English, Tamerlane) rose to power in the region. As a youth, Timur was known for his athletic abilities, especially in horse riding. He began his rise as leader of a small nomadic tribe and extended his rule through numerous wars with neighboring tribes.

A devout Muslim, Timur hoped to spread Islam to new areas. His religious zeal also made him oppose Muslims who differed with his understanding of Islam. Claiming descent from Genghis Khan, Timur united the Turkish-Mongols by conquest and eventually extended their rule over much of the Middle East.

Although Timur was ruthless, the people under his rule created important centers of civilization in central Asia. The most influential city in the region was Samarkand. A wealthy trading and craft center, it became known for its beautifully decorated mosques and tombs.

In A.D. 1402 Timur and his armies swept into Asia Minor, defeating another Turkish group—the Ottomans—at Ankara. However, Timur's effort to gain territory in Asia Minor never succeeded. In A.D. 1405 Timur died and was buried at Samarkand. The huge empire that he had created soon collapsed. The Ottomans were then able to regain their lost lands and began the building of their state.

SECTION 1 REVIEW

Recall

1. **Define** clan, yurt, *yasa*, khan.
2. **Identify** the Seljuk Turks, the Mongols, Genghis Khan, Batu, Helagu, Timur Lenk.
3. **Explain** why the empire of the Seljuk Turks declined quickly.

Critical Thinking

4. **Synthesizing Information** What factors led the steppe peoples to expand their territories and to create empires?

Understanding Themes

5. **Movement** How did the Mongol conquests contribute to the spread of culture and ideas throughout Asia and parts of Europe?

SECTION 1 REVIEW ANSWERS

1. All vocabulary words are defined in the Glossary.
2. Seljuk Turks, 342; Mongols, 343; Genghis Khan, 344; Batu, 344; Helagu, 344; Timur Lenk, 345
3. The Seljuk Turks failed to develop an efficient means of governing, especially at the local level, which was essential to holding their empire together.
4. The steppe could not support an expanding population.
5. MOVEMENT By creating a large, peaceful empire, the Mongols encouraged the spread of culture.

Cultural Perspectives

Burial Secrets No one knows where Genghis Khan is buried. According to Mongol tradition, a ruler's grave was hidden and kept secret. The ground was trampled over, trees were planted on it, and those who actually buried the ruler were executed.

History & Art The name Timur Lenk means "Timur the Lame." This Mongol leader was wounded by an arrow when he was a young man.
Answer to Caption: *Samarkand*

ASSESS

Check for Understanding

Assign Section 1 Review as homework or as an in-class activity.

Use Student Self-Test and Review Software to review Section 1.

Evaluate

Section Quiz 14-1

Use the Testmaker to create a customized quiz for Section 1.

Reteach

Have students summarize the main conquests of the Mongols.

Enrich

Have students research and report on present-day Mongolia, especially its people's way of life.

CLOSE

Ask students to summarize the positive and negative consequences of Mongol rule.

Chapter 14 Section 2

SECTION THEME

- **Uniformity** A centralized government, a state religion, and a common language maintain China's cultural continuity.

Find Out

Answer: *Tang: expanded borders, gave farmers land, enforced peace, built roads and waterways, fostered arts; Song: funded public works, fostered arts and sciences, encouraged technological advances; Yuan: expanded territory, promoted peace and stability*

FOCUS

Section Objective

Summarize the achievements of the Tang, Song, and Yuan dynasties.

BELLRINGER Motivational Activity

Before taking roll at the beginning of the class period, project Section Focus Transparency 14-2 and have students answer the activity questions. Discuss students' responses.

This activity is also available as a blackline master.

Vocabulary Pre-check

Use Vocabulary Activity 14 to introduce vocabulary terms. **L1 LEP**

A.D. 600 — A.D. 1000 — A.D. 1400

- c. A.D. 649 Empress Wu begins to control the Chinese Empire.
- A.D. 907 Tang dynasty ends.
- A.D. 1271 Marco Polo arrives in China.
- A.D. 1368 Yuan dynasty collapses.

Section 2

China

Setting the Scene

- **Terms to Define**
  meritocracy, mandarin
- **People to Meet**
  Tai Cong, Empress Wu, Xuanzang, Duo Fu, Li Bo, Zhao Kuangyin, Kublai Khan, Marco Polo
- **Places to Locate**
  Changan, Hangzhou

Find Out What were the significant achievements of the Tang, Song, and Yuan dynasties?

The Storyteller

Thoughtfully, Gui Xi considered the civil service examination. He was to select a single line of poetry and, using his finest calligraphy, write it on a silk scroll. Then he must create a painting linked to the chosen text, filling the scroll. To pass this vital test a man needed to be able to read, drawing conclusions and inferences. He also needed to demonstrate proficiency in the brush arts, a discipline requiring many years to master. Gui Xi recollected the steps essential to writing and painting. One must first find the spirit, rhythm, and thought, then one could seek to control the scenery, brush, and ink. For good work to result, mental and physical aspects must balance.

—adapted from *Record of Brush Methods: Essay on Landscape Painting*, Ching Hao, reprinted in *Varieties of Visual Experience*, 1991

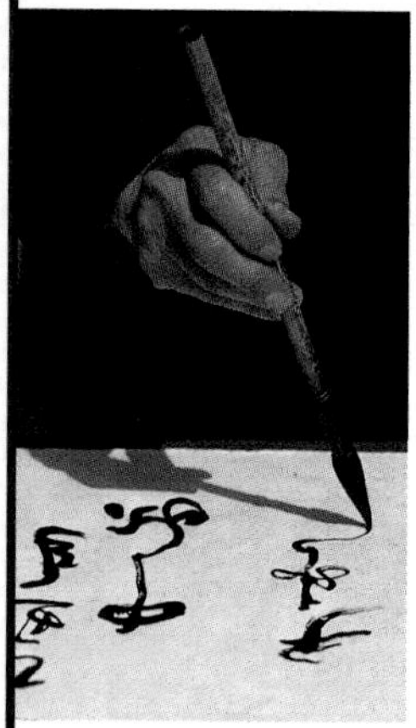

Chinese calligraphy

For more than 350 years after the collapse of the Han dynasty in A.D. 220, Chinese kingdoms and invaders from the north rivaled each other for control of China. Then in A.D. 589, a northern official named Yang Jian (YAHNG JYEN) united China by conquering both the north and the south. Yang Jian took the title Emperor Wen and founded the Sui (SWAY) dynasty. Emperor Wen renewed many of the goals and traditions that had been accepted during the reign of the Han dynasty. He organized public works projects such as the rebuilding of the former Han capital city at **Changan** (CHONG•ON), the repair of the Great Wall, and the construction of a Grand Canal to link northern and southern China. However, to accomplish these projects Emperor Wen used crews of forced laborers, which made him quite unpopular with the peasants.

The Tang Dynasty

In A.D. 618 peasant uprisings against the Sui dynasty enabled a rebellious lord named Li Yuan (LEE YOO•AHN) to take control of the country and proclaim himself emperor. He established the Tang (TONG) dynasty, which lasted from A.D. 618 to A.D. 907. Under the Tang, the Chinese Empire expanded its borders to include new territories.

Government and Society

The military genius behind the early Tang expansion was a son of Li Yuan who took the name **Tai Cong** (TIE TSOONG). Not only was Tai Cong a warrior, but he was also a shrewd administrator. By restoring a strong central government in China, he maintained control of his enormous empire while continuing to expand it.

To obtain a position in the Tang government, candidates had to pass civil service examinations. Under Tang rule, these tests measured the degree to which candidates had mastered Confucian

SECTION RESOURCES

Reproducible Masters
- Reproducible Lesson Plan 14-2
- Vocabulary Activity 14
- Guided Reading Activity 14-2
- History Simulation 14
- Section Quiz 14-2

Transparencies
- Section Focus Transparency 14-2

Multimedia
- Student Self-Test and Review Software
- Testmaker
- World Music: Cultural Traditions, Lesson 8
- Picture Atlas of the World

principles. According to Confucianism, an individual was expected to obey the emperor just as a son was expected to obey his father.

Because almost any male could take these examinations, the Chinese government claimed that it was a meritocracy—a system in which people are chosen and promoted for their talents and performance. But in practice it did not meet that ideal. Few boys from poor families could afford to pay tutors to help them prepare for the exams. Most could not spare the time away from their labor to study on their own.

Nevertheless, some peasants benefited from the Tang dynasty's rule. The Tang government gave land to farmers and enforced the peace that enabled them to till their land. In the Chang Jiang (Yangtze River) region, farmers were able to experiment with new strains of rice and better methods for growing it—both of which led to greater crop yields. With more food available, the Chinese population increased as well.

Foreign Influences

Tang rulers also devoted resources to the construction of roads and waterways. These routes made travel within China and to neighboring countries much easier. New and improved routes helped government officials to perform their duties. They also enabled Chinese merchants to increase trade with people from Japan, India, and the Middle East.

Chinese luxury goods, such as silk and pottery, passed through central Asia along the Silk Road. Beginning in central China, traders' camel caravans traveled north to the Great Wall and then headed west, crossing into central Asia just north of the Tibetan plateau. Some traveled as far west as Syria. These caravans brought Chinese goods and ideas to other cultures and returned with foreign products and new ideas as well. The Buddhist, Christian, and Islamic religions came to China by way of the Silk Road. During the Tang dynasty, Buddhism especially became very popular in China.

As trade increased the wealth of the empire, the Tang capital at Changan grew into the largest city in the world. Dazzling tales attracted merchants and scholars from countries throughout Asia to this city of 2 million people. Visitors to Changan spoke of wide, tree-shaded avenues and two vast market squares where merchants sold goods from Asia and the Middle East. They said that acrobats, jugglers, and dancers performed in the streets and that wealthy Chinese—including women—played the Persian games of chess and polo.

The Arts

In A.D. 649 Gaozong (GOW•DZOONG) succeeded Tai Cong as emperor of China. But Gaozong's wife, **Empress Wu**, actually controlled the empire. She was a brilliant political leader. Under Wu's control China continued to thrive.

History & Art *Four Travelers on Horseback*, porcelain figures from the Tang dynasty
Chinese potters discovered how to make porcelain in the A.D. 800s by firing pieces at very high temperatures. *What constructions helped merchants trade fine Chinese wares with other countries?*

Chapter 14 Section 2

TEACH

Guided Practice

THEME Uniformity
List on the chalkboard some of the factors that made for a uniform Chinese culture: a strong centralized government, good transportation between the different parts of the country, written literature available. Ask students who restored strong central government in China *(Tai Cong)*, who improved transportation *(Emperor Wen, Tang rulers)*, and what invention made it easier to make literature available to people in China *(block printing)*. **L1**

Economy Ask students what three groups of people benefited under Tang rule and why. *(peasants: received land and, in Jiang region, benefited from farm improvements; government officials: improved travel routes; merchants: improved travel routes)* **L2**

Cultural Diffusion Ask students how religions—Buddhism, Christianity, Islam—might come to China "by way of the Silk Road."*(Answers will vary but might include via missionaries, by books, and by traders who practiced these religions.)* **L3**

World Music: Cultural Traditions, Lesson 8

History Simulation 14

History & Art Tang porcelain and other crafts were widely admired. In many Asian languages, the word for "Chinese" became a synonym for "superior."
Answer to Caption: *roads and waterways*

COOPERATIVE LEARNING ACTIVITY

Technology Organize the class into four groups. Ask each group to choose one of the technological advances of the Tang and Song dynasties: porcelain, block printing, the compass, or gunpowder. Have each group research its topic to learn more about when and how the invention came about, how it was used, and how knowledge of it spread. If possible, each group should find illustrations of its subject. Then have the groups present their findings to the class. **L2**

Chapter 14
Section 2

NATIONAL GEOGRAPHIC SOCIETY

CD-ROM
PICTURE ATLAS OF THE WORLD

You and your students can see the Grand Canal, the Great Wall, and the Silk Road by clicking China's "Photos" button.

Independent Practice

Guided Reading Activity 14-2 **L1**

Literature Encourage students to find a poem by Duo Fu or Li Bo or another poet of the Tang or Song dynasty. Ask them to copy their selection so that it can be displayed on a bulletin board. **L1 LEP**

Biography Assign a brief written biography of Tai Cong, the Empress Wu, Kublai Khan, or Marco Polo. Students should use and cite several research sources. **L3**

Global Gourmet

China Chopsticks, the eating implements used by Asians, originated in China as early as the Shang dynasty. Most Asian food is served in bite-sized pieces making it easier to handle with the slender sticks. The Chinese word for chopsticks, *kuai-zi*, is a pun on the word *kuai*, which means both "quick" and "piece."

In A.D. 712 Empress Wu's grandson, **Xuanzang** (SEE•WAHN•DZONG), became emperor of China. Because Xuanzang welcomed artists to his splendid court, the arts flourished during his reign. Tang artisans made a fine translucent pottery that became a prized commodity known in the West as "china."

Two of China's greatest poets, **Duo Fu** (DWA FOO) and **Li Bo** (LEE BWAW), produced their works in Xuanzang's court. Scholars compiled encyclopedias, dictionaries, and official histories of China. Writers popularized stories about ghosts, crime, and love. And while European monks were still slowly and laboriously copying texts by hand, Chinese Buddhist monks invented the more efficient technique of block printing. They carved the text of a page into a block of wood. Then they reproduced the page by inking the wood and pressing a piece of paper onto it.

Tang Decline

For a time the cultural splendor of Xuanzang's court masked its military weakness. However, the Tang ruler's vulnerability to attack was revealed in A.D. 751, when Turkish armies in central Asia successfully revolted against China. They cut off China's trade routes to the Middle East, and they put an end to the thriving exchange of goods and ideas along the Silk Road. Border wars with the Tibetans and rebellions in famine-stricken provinces plagued the Tang from A.D. 766 on. In A.D. 907 this turmoil finally caused the fall of the Tang dynasty.

The Song Dynasty

From A.D. 907 to 960, China was ruled by military dynasties. Then a military general named **Zhao Kuangyin** (JOW KWONG•YIN) seized the throne and established the Song (SOONG) dynasty.

Footnotes to History

Pasta

Almost everyone associates noodles, or pasta, with Italy. Pasta, however, actually originated in China. About 3,000 years ago, the Chinese were making noodles out of bean and rice flour. The Italians had their first taste of pasta in the late A.D. 1200s, when Marco Polo's father and uncle brought Chinese noodle recipes to Italy.

Song emperors kept peace with a group of Mongols in the north, the Khitan, by paying them generously in silver. But in A.D. 1127 the Jurchen, a nomadic people, captured the Song capital of Kaifeng (KIE•FUHNG). The Song rulers set up their royal court in the southern city of **Hangzhou** (HONG•JOH).

Cultural Contributions

Song scholars, resentful of foreign influences, produced an official state philosophy called neo-Confucianism. This philosophy combined Confucian values with elements of Buddhism and Daoism.

Song rulers also more firmly entrenched the civil service system that the Tang had resurrected. They made determining one's knowledge of Confucian curriculum the main focus of these tests. The scholars who had passed the tests eventually formed a wealthy elite group, called **mandarins** by Westerners.

Rich and Poor

During the Song dynasty, China experienced unprecedented economic growth, partly because Song rulers used tax revenues to fund several public-works projects that benefited the economy. For example, they used these revenues to fund the digging of irrigation ditches and canals, which in turn helped farmers increase their crop yields.

The introduction of new crops from Southeast Asia, such as tea and a faster-growing rice plant, further boosted China's farming economy. The new crops also led to an increase in China's trade with India and Southeast Asia. With farming, trade, and commerce all thriving, urban centers prospered.

The urban wealthy lived in spacious homes and enjoyed going to teahouses, restaurants, and luxurious bathhouses. The capital of the dynasty, Hangzhou, grew to nearly 1 million residents.

Of course, the country still had many urban poor. The urban poor lived in flimsy houses. To survive they hawked cheap goods in the streets, worked as manual laborers, begged, or stole.

Song Arts and Sciences

Song achievements in the arts and sciences were many. The cuisine which people recognize today as distinctively Chinese originated during the Song dynasty. Experts regard Song porcelain as the best ever made. Landscape painting reached its peak during Song rule. Song inventors perfected the compass, a tool that enabled Chinese sailors to navigate on journeys far offshore. They also produced gunpowder that was first used in fireworks. Bamboo-tube rocket launchers charged with gunpowder made the Song army a powerful fighting force.

MEETING SPECIAL NEEDS ACTIVITY

Attention Deficiency Chinese food is very popular in the United States. Students who have trouble focusing their attention should enjoy learning more about some of their favorite dishes. They might use cookbooks or other library resources. (These students might be helped in their research by other students with longer attention spans.) If possible, a Chinese meal could be prepared for the class and presented along with informative commentary. **L2 LEP**

348 Chapter 14 *East and South Asia*

NATIONAL GEOGRAPHIC

PICTURING HISTORY

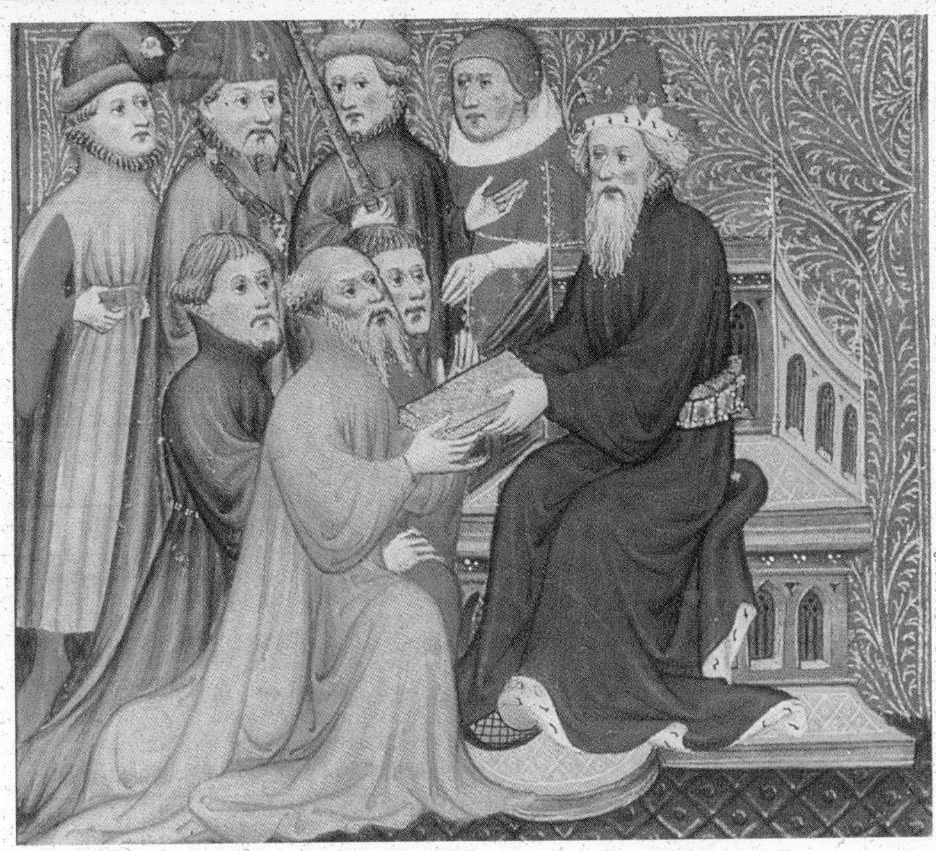

The Bodleian Library, Oxford, Ms. Bodl. 264, fol.219r

Kublai Khan and Marco Polo

This medieval English manuscript shows the Chinese emperor Kublai Khan presenting golden tablets to Marco Polo and his family to ensure their safe passage back to the West. In A.D. 1297 Marco Polo wrote an account of his 17 years in China, and his book eventually became popular with the small literate class in Europe. The painter who embellished this manuscript had never met Marco Polo nor had he ever seen a picture of an Asian. Maybe that's why the emperor looks European rather than Asian.

The Mongol rulers of China put the country in closer touch with the Middle East and Europe. The Mongolian khans were outsiders who distrusted, and were distrusted by, their Chinese subjects. The khans turned to outsiders to help them rule, especially after Kublai Khan moved the Chinese capital to Beijing. The Polos (Marco Polo's father and uncle accompanied him to China) were but three of hundreds of European and Muslim merchants and artisans who moved in and out of China. But Marco Polo became famous, both in his time and in ours, because he wrote a book about his adventures. The Polos brought Chinese noodles back to Europe, and other European and Muslim travelers brought Chinese inventions such as gunpowder and the compass back to the West. This transfer of technology had a major impact on the history of Europe. ⊕

PICTURING HISTORY

TEACH

Tell students that, after Marco Polo's return, he was captured and imprisoned by the Genoese, archrivals of the Venetians. There he dictated his book, known in English as the *Travels of Marco Polo*, to a fellow prisoner. It was instantly popular and soon known all over Europe (even though this was before the days of printing). **Why do you think Europeans of Polo's time were eager to read his book?** *(Answers will vary but should include the fact that East Asia was practically unknown to Europe at the time.)*

CURRICULUM CONNECTION

LITERATURE

One of the most famous poems of the English Romantic period is "Kubla Khan," by Samuel Taylor Coleridge. Published in 1816, it portrays Kublai Khan's court as a place of fantastic beauty.

Chapter 14 Section 2

Map Study

Answer

the mountain ranges of eastern Tibet

Map Skills Practice

Reading a Map At their greatest extent, how far did the domains of the Tang dynasty stretch from east to west? *(about 3,000 miles [4,825 kilometers])*

ASSESS

Check for Understanding

Assign Section 2 Review as homework or as an in-class activity.

Use Student Self-Test and Review Software to review Section 2.

Evaluate

Section Quiz 14-2

Use the Testmaker to create a customized quiz for Section 2.

Reteach

Have students recall one important contribution each from the Tang, Song, and Yuan dynasties.

Enrich

Have students create a bulletin-board display of Chinese porcelain and china from various dynasties.

CLOSE

Guide students in outlining this section. Put key headings on the chalkboard: *I. Tang dynasty, II. Song dynasty, III. Yuan dynasty.* Students can suggest entries under the headings. *(Example: I. Tang; A. Government and Society; B. Foreign Influences; C. The Arts)*

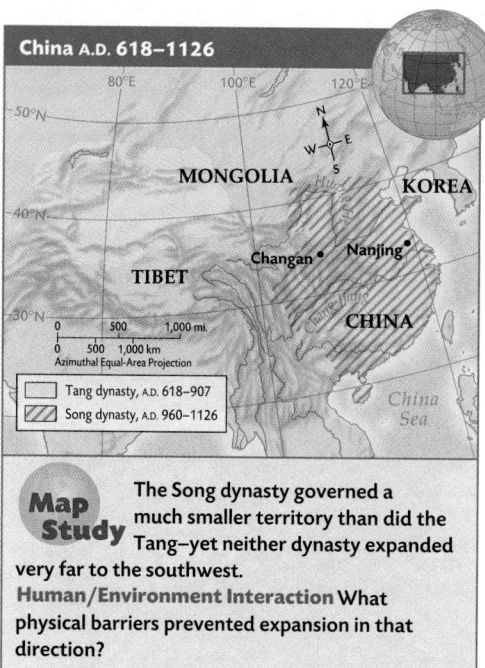

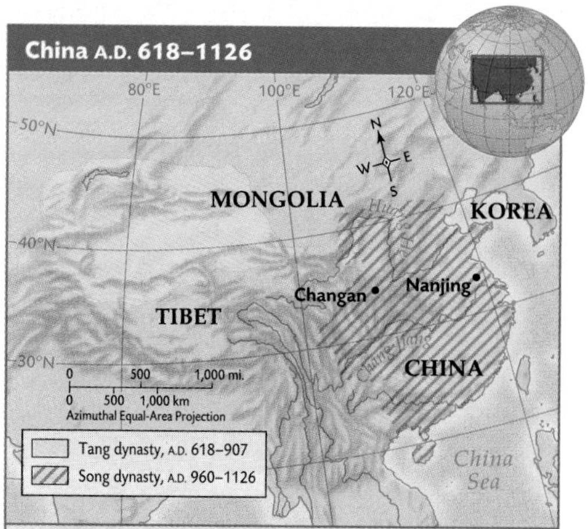

Map Study The Song dynasty governed a much smaller territory than did the Tang—yet neither dynasty expanded very far to the southwest.
Human/Environment Interaction What physical barriers prevented expansion in that direction?

China's enemies, however, were eventually able to obtain the secrets of Song military technology. Thus, using the Song Empire's own technology against it, the Mongols were able to completely capture northern China in A.D. 1234 and bring about the fall of the Song dynasty in southern China in A.D. 1279.

The Yuan Dynasty

During the A.D. 1200s, the Mongols invaded China and overthrew the Jurchen and Song rulers. They established the Yuan (YOO•AHN), or Mongol, dynasty. They became the first conquerors to rule most of the country.

Kublai Khan

The first great Mongol emperor of China was **Kublai Khan** (KOO•BLUH KAHN). A grandson of Genghis Khan, Kublai ruled from A.D. 1260 to A.D. 1294. Kublai Khan extended Mongol rule beyond China's borders. He conquered Korea in the north and part of Southeast Asia. He made two attempts to invade Japan, using Chinese and Korean ships. Both efforts failed because the Mongols were not skilled in naval warfare.

Although Kublai complied with some Chinese traditions to better control the Chinese, he tried to maintain Mongol culture. Government documents were written first in Mongolian, then translated into Chinese. Moreover, the highest positions in the emperor's court were given to Mongols or foreigners.

The most famous of these foreigners appointed to government posts was a Venetian named **Marco Polo**. Polo arrived in China in A.D. 1271 and stayed 17 years, traveling through Mongol territory on the Khan's missions. After Polo returned to Italy, his tales of the splendor of Chinese civilization astounded Europeans.

Mongol Peace and Decline

Marco Polo was able to travel throughout China because the Mongols enforced a relatively stable order. Merchants could safely travel the roads built by the Mongols. Mongol rule thus fostered trade and connections with Europe.

Through contact with the Middle East, Russia, and Europe, the Chinese obtained enslaved people as well as products such as glass, hides, clothes, silver, cotton, and carpets. In return, Europeans got exotic products such as silk, porcelain, and tea.

After Kublai Khan died in A.D. 1294, a series of weak successors took over the throne. The Chinese, still resentful of foreign rule, began to stage rebellions against these rulers. Finally, in A.D. 1368, a young Buddhist monk named Zhu Yuanzhang (JOO YOO•AHN•JAHNG) led an army against the capital and overthrew the Yuan dynasty.

SECTION 2 REVIEW

Recall

1. **Define** meritocracy, mandarin.
2. **Identify** Tai Cong, Empress Wu, Xuanzang, Duo Fu, Li Bo, Zhao Kuangyin, Kublai Khan, Marco Polo.
3. **Locate** the city of Changan in central China on the map above. How was Changan restored years after the Han dynasty collapsed?

Critical Thinking

4. **Evaluating Information** Do you think the Tang and Song systems of government were true meritocracies? Explain.

Understanding Themes

5. **Uniformity** What methods did the rulers of the Tang, Song, and Yuan dynasties use to unite China?

SECTION 2 REVIEW ANSWERS

1. All vocabulary words are defined in the Glossary.
2. Tai Cong, 346; Empress Wu, 347; Xuanzang, 348; Duo Fu, 348; Li Bo, 348; Zhao Kuangyin, 348; Kublai Khan, 350; Marco Polo, 350
3. Emperor Wen had the city rebuilt as a public works project.
4. Bureaucrats were selected through civil service exams open to all, but, because of the time and money involved in studying for them, the system favored the wealthy.
5. UNIFORMITY strong central governments, good roads, civil service system

A.D. 800 — A.D. 1100 — A.D. 1400

A.D. 802 The Khmer people establish capital at Angkor.

A.D. 938 The Vietnamese defeat the Chinese in the Battle of Bach Dang River.

c. A.D. 1200s The Mongols destroy Burman city of Pagan.

A.D. 1350 The Thai establish kingdom of Ayutthaya.

Chapter 14 Section 3

Section 3

Southeast Asia

Setting the Scene

- **Terms to Define**
  archipelago, animism
- **People to Meet**
  the Khmer, Suryavarman II, the Trung sisters, Ngo Quyen, Ramkhamhaeng
- **Places to Locate**
  Angkor Wat, Pagan, Sukhothai, Ayutthaya, Melaka

Find Out How were Southeast Asians influenced by the cultures of China and India?

The Storyteller

The situation was a general's nightmare, T'u Sui thought despairingly. His lord, the Chinese emperor, was determined to subjugate the land of Yueh [Vietnam]. T'u Sui had gladly accepted the command of five hundred thousand men of ability to complete the task. However, when he attacked the Yueh fled into the mountains and forests where it was impossible to fight them or even to find them. Gradually, the troops grew weary of their duties. The Yueh would then attack, inflicting great losses upon the powerful Chinese army.

—from *Huai Nan Tzu*, reprinted in *Ancient Vietnam*, Keith W. Taylor

Mountains of Vietnam

Although China was the most culturally diverse and influential society in Asia from about A.D. 220 until A.D. 1400, other Asian civilizations were creating distinct and influential cultures of their own at the same time. Southeast Asian cultures were among these new societies.

Crossroads of Asia

South of China and east of India is the region known as Southeast Asia. Southeast Asia includes the present-day countries of Myanmar (Burma), Thailand, Vietnam, Laos, Cambodia, Malaysia, Singapore, Brunei, Indonesia, and the Philippines. Located in the tropics, many of these countries have fertile soils, warm climates, and abundant rainfall. Geographically, Southeast Asia is divided into mainland and maritime Southeast Asia. The latter includes more than 10,000 islands of the Philippine and Indonesian **archipelagos**, or chains of islands.

During the A.D. 100s, an exchange of goods and ideas began between India and Southeast Asia. This exchange led Southeast Asia to adopt many elements of Indian culture. For instance, at that time, traveling Indian traders and scholars introduced to Southeast Asia the Sanskrit language and the religions of Hinduism and Buddhism. Indian epics such as the *Ramayana* were interwoven with Southeast Asian stories and legends. Indian architecture, law codes, and political ideas also deeply influenced the cultures of the region. As contact with India increased, Indian culture gradually spread throughout Southeast Asia.

Southeast Asians nevertheless retained many of their own traditions. They continued to perform the art of shadow puppetry, to make intricately patterned cloth called batik, and to play their own unique instruments and music. They also believed in **animism**, the idea that spirits inhabit living and nonliving things.

SECTION THEME

- **Cultural Diffusion** The civilizations of Southeast Asia reflect the influences of China and India.

Find Out

Answer: *Through traveling traders, artisans and scholars, and as a result of military conquest, Southeast Asia adopted languages, literature, religious beliefs, building techniques, artistic forms, and political ideas from China and India.*

FOCUS

Section Objective

Explain how Southeast Asians were influenced by the cultures of China and India.

BELLRINGER Motivational Activity

Before taking roll at the beginning of the class period, project Section Focus Transparency 14-3 and have students answer the activity questions. Discuss students' responses.

This activity is also available as a blackline master.

Vocabulary Pre-check

Use Vocabulary Activity 14 to introduce vocabulary terms. **L1 LEP**

SECTION RESOURCES

Reproducible Masters
- Reproducible Lesson Plan 14-3
- Vocabulary Activity 14
- Guided Reading Activity 14-3
- Geography and History Activity 14
- Section Quiz 14-3

Transparencies
- Section Focus Transparency 14-3
- World History and Art Transparency 17, *Angkor Wat*

Multimedia
- Student Self-Test and Review Software
- Testmaker
- World Music: Cultural Traditions, Lesson 9
- Picture Atlas of the World

TEACH

Guided Practice

THEME Cultural Diffusion

Using a wall map if possible, point out the major origins of cultural influence *(India, China)*, the region affected *(the countries of Southeast Asia)*, and the water routes by which cultural elements traveled *(Bay of Bengal, South China Sea, Mekong River)*. **L1 LEP**

Religion Review with students the major precepts of the religious and ethical teachings "imported" into Southeast Asia from India and China. *(Hinduism: Brahman as eternal spirit, reincarnation based on karma; Buddhism: Four Noble Truths and Eightfold Path; Confucianism: right conduct, especially filial piety; Daoism: harmony with nature)* **L2**

World History and Art Transparency 17, *Angkor Wat*

World Music: Cultural Traditions, Lesson 9

Who?What?Where?When?

Tran Hung Dao One of the greatest of all Vietnamese heroes is Tran Hung Dao, a military leader who defeated the Mongol forces of Kublai Khan. His biggest victory was a naval engagement in 1288. Kublai Khan's fleet was ripped apart by iron-tipped spears that Hung Dao had planted upright under water.

The Khmer

In A.D. 802 **the Khmer** (kuh•MEHR) people of the mainland Southeast Asian country of Cambodia established a great Hindu-Buddhist empire with its capital at Angkor. The Khmer Empire reached its height during the A.D. 1100s, when it conquered much of the land that now includes Laos, Thailand, and Vietnam.

The empire's wealth came primarily from its rice production. Elaborate hydraulic engineering projects enabled the Khmer to irrigate and produce three crops of rice a year. With the wealth from this bountiful harvest, Khmer rulers subsidized mammoth construction projects. Adapting Indian building techniques to create their own distinctive architecture, the Khmer built hundreds of temples that glorified Hindu and Buddhist religious figures. They also constructed roads, reservoirs, irrigation canals, harbors, and hospitals. Khmer rulers were known for the splendor of their court. Borrowing from the Indian idea of kingship, Khmer rulers presented themselves as incarnations of the Hindu gods or as future Buddhas, which served to enhance their power. They bedecked themselves in elaborate finery and filled their palaces with ornate thrones and beautiful furnishings. A Chinese traveler named Zhou Dakuan (JOH DAH•KWON) described the splendor of a Khmer king in dress and manner:

> "His crown of gold is high and pointed like those on the heads of the mighty gods. When he does not wear his crown, he wreathes his chignon [hair gathered in a bun] in garlands of sweet-scented jasmine. His neck is hung with ropes of huge pearls (they weigh almost three pounds); his wrists and ankles are loaded with bracelets and on his fingers are rings of gold set with cats' eyes. He goes barefoot—the soles of his feet, like the palms of his hands, are rouged with a red stuff. When he appears in public he carries the Golden Sword."

Images of the Times

Angkor Wat

Angkor Wat (meaning "temple of the capital") was built in the A.D. 1100s by the Khmer ruler Suryavarman II. Suryavarman believed he was the incarnation of the Hindu god Vishnu.

A bas–relief of the Bayon depicts a battle between the Khmer and the Chams.

Seen through a doorway, the pavilion and the central sanctuary reveal a five-headed Naga serpent.

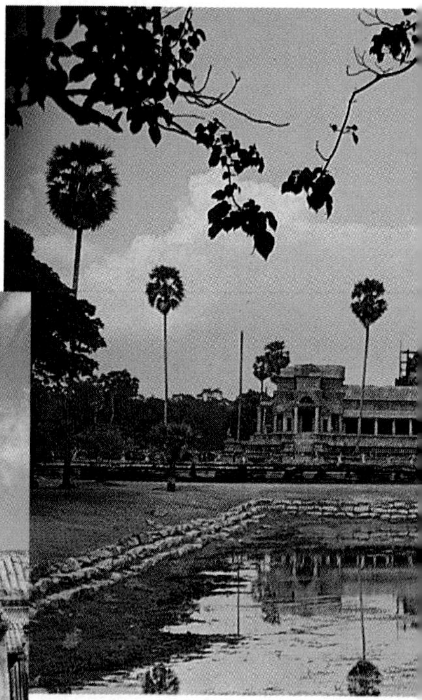

The temple complex at Angkor Wat is encircled by a three-mile moat. The temples and monuments within the complex honored the god-king Suryavarman II and impressed visitors with their size and detailed ornamentation.

352

Images of the Times **Angkor Wat**

The temple complex at Angkor Wat forms the largest single religious building in the world. Its builders were extraordinarily skilled. Modern research indicates that they designed and constructed Angkor Wat so carefully that its walls, built over great distances, deviate from straight lines less than .1 percent.

During the A.D. 1100s, under the rule of King **Suryavarman** (soor•yah•VAHR•mahn) **II**, the Khmer kingdom reached the height of its power. Having expanded Cambodia by conquest to include parts of areas known today as Laos, Vietnam, and Thailand, the king decided to glorify both the Hindu god Vishnu and himself. He ordered the construction of **Angkor Wat**, a temple complex covering nearly a square mile. Carvings depicting the Hindu gods cover the walls of Angkor Wat, and, at the center of the complex, the sanctuary stands 130 feet (40 m) high. Angkor Wat also was used as an astronomical observatory.

The Khmer king poured so much of the empire's wealth into building Angkor Wat, however, that he severely weakened the kingdom. This excess, along with rebellions against Khmer rule and infighting between members of the royal family, further crippled the empire. In A.D. 1431 the Thai, a neighboring Southeast Asian people, captured the capital city of Angkor, bringing an end to Khmer rule there.

Vietnam

East of Cambodia and south of China lies the area of present-day Vietnam. Because of Vietnam's proximity to China and because the Chinese dominated Vietnam for more than 1,000 years, Vietnam's culture in some ways came to resemble that of China.

The Vietnamese absorbed elements of Chinese belief systems such as Confucianism, Daoism, and Buddhism. The Vietnamese also adopted Chinese forms of writing and government. Just as in China, Vietnamese officials were selected through civil service exams based on Confucian principles.

The Vietnamese retained many of their own traditions, however. They adopted Chinese religions and beliefs, but they continued to believe in animism. The Vietnamese built a *dinh*, or spirit house, in each village. This tiny house served as the home for the guardian spirit of a village. The Vietnamese wore their hair long and tattooed their skin. They wrote and spoke their own Vietnamese

A stone bas–relief of elephant and gods helps tell the story of the ancient Khmer civilization.

REFLECTING ON THE TIMES

1. What values of the Khmer are reflected in these images?
2. How did Suryavarman attempt to impress upon visitors that he was an incarnation of Vishnu?

Chapter 14 Section 3

Independent Practice

Guided Reading Activity 14-3 **L1**

Daily Life The cloth known as batik originated in Southeast Asia but is known in many other parts of the world. Have students report on the history of batik and how it is made. Ask a volunteer to bring a piece of batik cloth to class. **L2 LEP**

Religion Encourage students to find out more about animism, the beliefs and practices associated with it, and the areas where it has flourished. Have them compile their findings in a brief written report. **L3**

Architecture After the decline of the Khmer kingdom, the capital city of Angkor fell into ruins and was covered with rain forest growth. Have students research the rediscovery and rebuilding of Angkor, beginning in the late 1800s. **L2**

Geography and History Activity 14

ANSWERS TO REFLECTING ON THE TIMES

1. the importance of religion, pride in the accomplishments of the Khmer, respect for the ruler
2. He built Angkor Wat to glorify both himself and Vishnu.

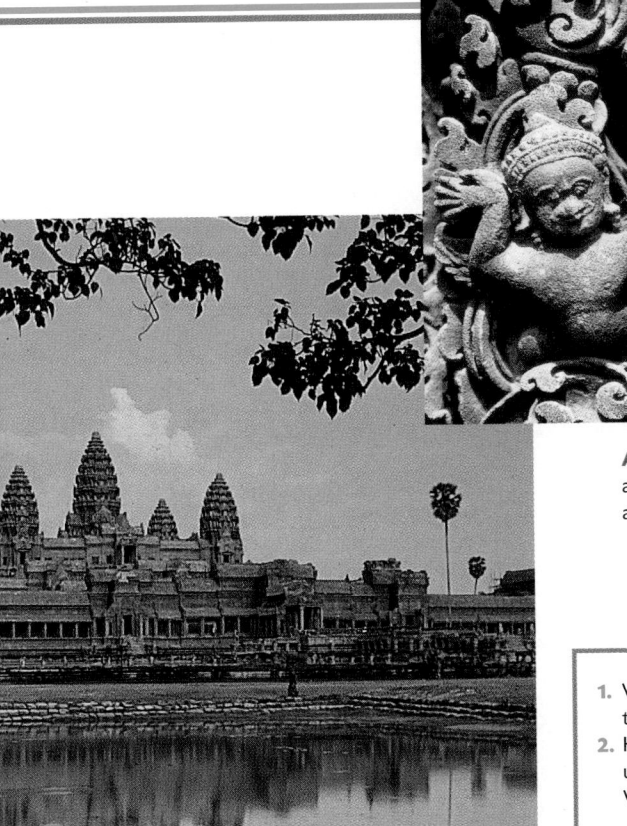

Map Study

Answer

fertile soil, a warm climate, and abundant rain

Map Study Practice

Reading a Map Why do you think Southeast Asia was never united under a single ruler or political system? *(It would be difficult to subdue, much less hold together, a region that includes so many peninsulas and islands scattered over a wide region.)*

Who?What?Where?When?

The city of **Pagan**, in what is now Myanmar, controlled a large area along the Irrawaddy River. Among the visitors to this kingdom was Marco Polo, who was impressed by its magnificent monasteries and temples.

Linking Past and Present

The **shadow puppet theater** of Java, called *wayang kulit*, developed hundreds of years ago. It is still very popular, with several thousand active puppeteers. A single puppeteer works the puppets, chants the story, sings, and recites dialogue. Performances last from 9:00 P.M. until almost dawn.

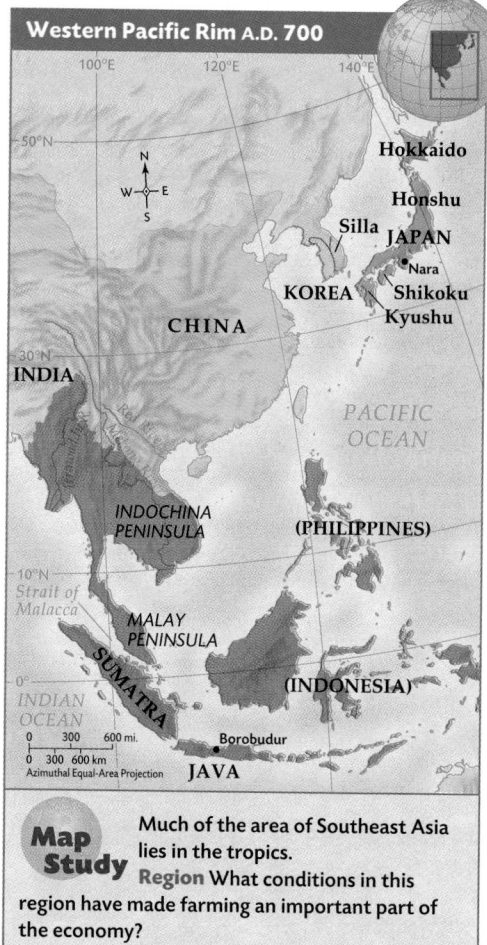

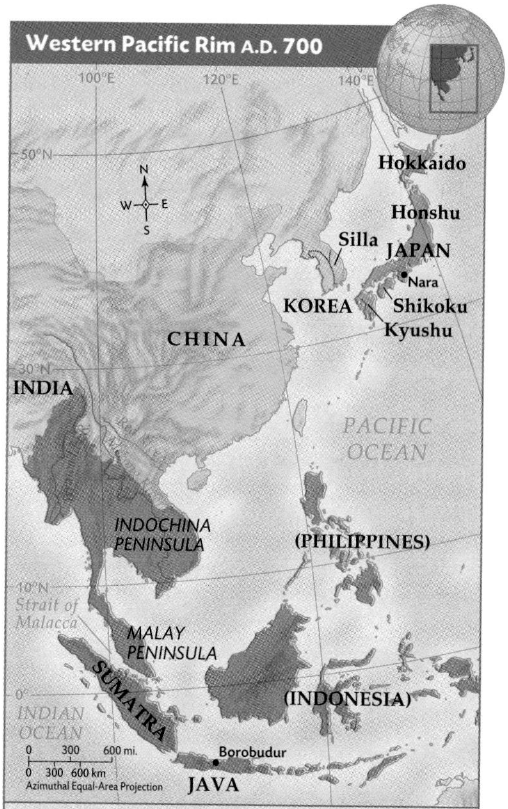

Map Study Much of the area of Southeast Asia lies in the tropics. **Region** What conditions in this region have made farming an important part of the economy?

language, although in writing it they used Chinese characters. Even though the Chinese controlled Vietnam almost continuously from about 200 B.C. to A.D. 939, the Vietnamese fought hard to retain—and then to regain—their independence.

> "The Viets [Vietnamese] were very difficult to defeat. They did not come out to fight, but hid in their familiar mountains and used the jungle like a weapon. As a result, neither side could win.... The Viets would raid suddenly, rob and get away fast, so that just as our army obtained its supplies from the home base, the Viets obtained theirs from our army."
>
> —Chinese general, c. 200 B.C.

In A.D. 39 two Vietnamese sisters called **the Trung**, clad in armor and riding atop elephants, led a successful revolt against the Chinese. For two years Vietnam was independent of China. Then the Chinese returned in greater numbers and defeated the Vietnamese. Rather than surrender to the Chinese, the Trung sisters are said to have drowned themselves in a river.

During the confusion after the overthrow of the Tang dynasty, the Vietnamese took advantage of China's disunity to revolt again. The Chinese sent a fleet of warships to Vietnam to try to subdue the rebels. In A.D. 938, however, under the leadership of **Ngo Quyen** (noo chu•YEHN), the Vietnamese defeated the warships in the Battle of the Bach Dang River. Although Emperor Tai Cong countered this defeat by launching an invasion of Vietnam, the Vietnamese date their independence from the battle, because Tai Cong's invasion failed.

After the Song dynasty gained control of China, the Song emperor threatened the Vietnamese with invasion. To keep peace with China, the Vietnamese agreed to send tribute—gifts—to the Chinese emperor. In return, China agreed not to invade Vietnam. From then on, the Vietnamese ruler called himself emperor at home, but in his messages to the Chinese court he referred to himself merely as a king.

Myanmar

The easternmost area of mainland Southeast Asia today includes the country of Myanmar (Burma). The first peoples to extensively settle most of present-day Myanmar were the Mons and the Tibeto-Burmans. From 200 B.C. to A.D. 100, these two groups gradually occupied different parts of the country. The Mons established villages in southern Burma, while the Tibeto-Burmans lived along the Irrawaddy (IHR•uh•WAH•dee) River in the northern part of the country. Although they developed their own traditions, the Mons and the Tibeto-Burmans accepted Buddhism and other aspects of Indian culture from visiting South Asian sailors and traders.

During the 500s B.C., the Tibeto-Burmans became the dominant group and pushed the Mons southward. In A.D. 849 they set up a capital city called **Pagan** (pah•GAHN), which eventually became a center of Buddhist learning and culture. By the A.D. 1200s, skilled architects had transformed Pagan from a small settlement into a city of elaborate Buddhist temples and monasteries.

During the A.D. 1200s, the Mongol armies of Kublai Khan captured Pagan and ended its glory. To escape Mongol rule, many Burmans moved into

COOPERATIVE LEARNING ACTIVITY

Class Presentation Organize the class into groups of four or five students to prepare a presentation comparing the early governments of Southeast Asian countries with governments in those countries today. After each group selects a country, group members should divide the tasks necessary to research the type of government formed in early years and that of today. Then have groups prepare a fact sheet for both periods and develop a short talk about the differences and similarities between the governments. Allow each group to give a five-minute presentation of their findings and answer any questions classmates have. **L2**

the southern part of Myanmar. There they founded fortified towns along the rivers between their ruined capital and the Andaman Sea. Although Burman culture was preserved, a united kingdom did not arise again in Myanmar until the A.D. 1500s.

Visualizing History Wat Mahathat, an ancient Buddhist temple now restored, is in Sukhothai Historic Park, which was opened to the public in 1980. *What was accomplished in Sukhothai's golden age?*

The Thai

More than four out of every five people who live in the Southeast Asian country of Thailand today belong to the ethnic group called Thai. They are descendants of people who began migrating south from China about A.D. 700. About A.D. 1238 the Thai established their first kingdom at **Sukhothai** (SOO•kah•TY) in the north-central part of the country.

Sukhothai

The Sukhothai kingdom lasted only about 100 years, but it was known for its wise leaders. The kingdom's greatest monarch, King **Ramkhamhaeng** (rahm•KAHM•hong), ruled from A.D. 1275 to A.D. 1317. He made Sukhothai into a center of learning and the arts. During Ramkhamhaeng's reign, the Thai developed an alphabet and writing system based on the Khmer script. Artisans from China taught the making of porcelain, and Buddhist monks from South Asia won most of the Thai people to Buddhism. Beautiful Buddhist temples, with many levels of roofs, rose gracefully above the skyline of Sukhothai. Even during Ramkhamhaeng's lifetime, the Thai saw his reign as a golden age. A stone pillar erected in A.D. 1292 and still standing has the following words engraved on it:

> "This Sukhothai is good. In the water there are fish. In the fields there is rice. The king does not levy a [tax] on his people.... Who wants to trade in elephants, trades. Who wants to trade in horses, trades. Who wants to trade in gold and silver, trades.... "

Ayutthaya

In A.D. 1350 a prince named Ramathibodi (rah•MAH•thee•BOH•dee) overthrew the last Sukhothai ruler and founded a new kingdom known as **Ayutthaya** (ah•YOO•thy•yuh). He set up his capital south of Sukhothai and up the Chao Phraya River (chow PRY•uh) from where Bangkok, the present Thai capital, is today.

The Ayutthaya kingdom lasted for about 400 years, with a succession of 33 kings. At its height, it held control over large areas of Southeast Asia, including parts of Myanmar and the Malay Peninsula. Like Sukhothai, Ayutthaya was an important center of Buddhist learning and culture. Economically prosperous, Ayutthaya carried on trade in teak wood, salt, spices, and hides with China and neighboring Asian kingdoms.

Seafaring Kingdoms

Many kingdoms in early Southeast Asia developed around strategic ports. The Indonesian islands became a crossroads in the expanding international trade that stretched from the Arabian Peninsula to China. Merchants of many lands—Arabs, Chinese, Indians, and Persians—traded such products as porcelain, textiles, and silk for Southeast Asian spices and valuable woods.

The Srivijaya (SHREE•vih•JAY•uh) Empire arose on the islands of Java and Sumatra in present-day Indonesia. Lasting from about A.D. 600 to A.D. 1100, the Srivijaya Empire was one of the region's

Visualizing History The name Sukhothai means "Dawn of Happiness." According to the stone pillar of 1292, all citizens were treated equally and "all its citizenry, all chiefs and nobles, everyone everywhere, all men and women, all groups, believe in Buddhism."

Answer to Caption: *The kingdom became a center of learning and the arts and saw the development of an alphabet and writing system. People learned to make porcelain and built beautiful temples.*

Who?What?Where?When?

Borobudur Another magnificent religious complex in Southeast Asia, Borobudur, is located on the island of Java. Built about A.D. 800, it is not only a temple but also a representation of Buddhist doctrine. As visitors climb its five terraces, they pass from sculptural depictions of the ordinary world to those suggesting the profound truths of Buddhist enlightenment.

NATIONAL GEOGRAPHIC SOCIETY

CD-ROM
PICTURE ATLAS OF THE WORLD

Have students click the "Music" button of Vietnam, Cambodia, Thailand, Myanmar, Malaysia, and Indonesia to hear centuries-old songs played for emperors, rituals, and soldiers.

MEETING SPECIAL NEEDS ACTIVITY

Learning Style: Auditory/Musical Students who have difficulties reading and writing may enjoy staging a musical and/or dance presentation. Have them obtain recordings of gamelan music—the distinctive Indonesian art form that makes extensive use of percussion instruments, including gongs, cymbals, xylophones, and drums. Or, if possible, have them rent a video that combines this music with dance. **L1 LEP**

Visualizing History Temples are everywhere in Bali—in villages, in family courtyards, and on lakeshores or sacred slopes in the countryside.
Answer to Caption: *It remained Hindu when the rest of Indonesia adopted Islam.*

ASSESS

Check for Understanding

Assign Section 3 Review as homework or as an in-class activity.

Use Student Self-Test and Review Software to review Section 3.

Evaluate

Section Quiz 14-3

Use the Testmaker to create a customized quiz for Section 3.

Reteach

Have students identify the countries of Southeast Asia and summarize the major cultural elements they adopted from India *(Hinduism, Buddhism, Sanskrit)* and China *(Confucianism, written language).*

Enrich

Have students do necessary research to create a travel brochure for a Southeast Asian country they would like to visit.

CLOSE

Have students summarize the areas of Southeast Asian culture in which the people retained their own traditions. *(shadow puppetry, batik, music, animism, architectural styles, tattoos, Vietnamese hairstyle, and language)*

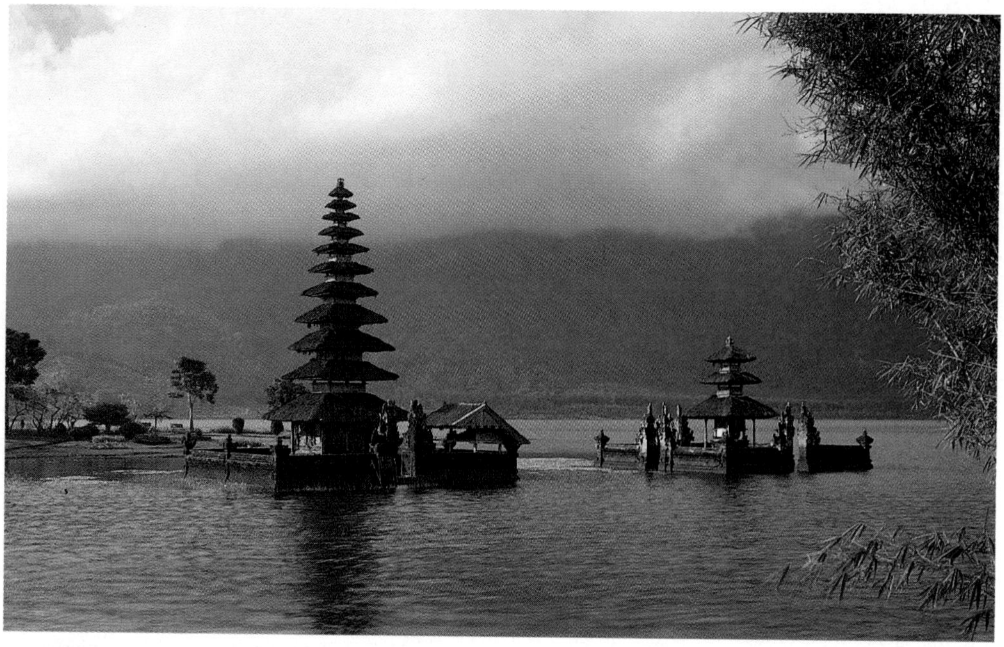

Visualizing History **The Hindu temple of Ulu Danua on Lake Bratan in the Central Mountains of Bali has a typical thatched roof.** *How is Bali's religious heritage different from that of the rest of Indonesia?*

great seafaring powers. It controlled shipping along the Strait of Malacca that separates Sumatra from the Malay Peninsula. By the end of the A.D. 1100s, Srivijaya was reduced to a small kingdom, and the Majapahit (mah•jah•PAH•heet) kingdom began to dominate the Indonesian islands.

From the A.D. 400s to the A.D. 1400s, Buddhism and Hinduism were the dominant religious influences that affected maritime Southeast Asian life. During the early A.D. 1200s Muslim traders from the Arabian Peninsula and India brought Islam to the peoples of the Malay Peninsula and Indonesia.

The first major center of Islam in Southeast Asia was **Melaka**, a port kingdom on the southwestern coast of the Malay Peninsula.

From Melaka, Islam spread throughout the Indonesian islands. The only island to remain outside of Muslim influence was Bali, which has kept its Hindu religion and culture to the present day.

During the A.D. 1500s, a number of Muslim trading kingdoms competed for control of the Indonesian islands. European explorers, beginning with the Portuguese in A.D. 1511, gradually won control by setting local rulers against each other.

SECTION 3 REVIEW

Recall

1. **Define** archipelago, animism.
2. **Identify** the Khmer, Suryavarman II, the Trung sisters, Ngo Quyen, Ramkhamhaeng.
3. **Locate** mainland Southeast Asia on the map on page 354. Why would the mainland, and not the Indonesian and Philippine archipelagos, be more likely to come under the influence of India and China?

Critical Thinking

4. **Synthesizing Information** How might Buddhism or Confucianism complement a belief in animism?

Understanding Themes

5. **Cultural Diffusion** What were some of the ways in which the cultures of China and India influenced the peoples of Southeast Asia?

SECTION 3 REVIEW ANSWERS

1. All vocabulary words are defined in the Glossary.
2. Khmer, 352; Suryavarman II, 353; Trung sisters, 354; Ngo Quyen, 354; Ramkhamhaeng, 355
3. because it lay between India and China and could be reached over land (an easier way to travel)
4. Students should support their answers with facts about the religions in question.
5. **CULTURAL DIFFUSION** China: Confucianism, Daoism, writing, governmental system; India: Hinduism, Buddhism, building techniques, law, political ideas

Critical Thinking

SKILLS

Making Generalizations

Have you heard statements such as "Only tall people play basketball well" or "Dogs make better pets than cats"? Do you consider the validity of such statements? Or do you accept them at face value?

Learning the Skill

These statements, called generalizations, are broad statements about a topic. To be valid, a generalization must be based on accurate information. Let's examine the generalization "Only tall people play basketball well." Is this accurate? We can find many examples of tall basketball players. However, there are also many shorter players who excel at this sport.

In this case, we began with a generalization and looked for facts to support or disprove it. In other cases, you will make a generalization from a group of facts about a topic. To make a valid generalization, first collect information relevant to the topic. This information must be accurate facts, not opinions.

Suppose that you want to make a generalization about the relative danger of air and automobile travel. First, you would collect accident statistics involving airplanes and cars. Then classify the information into categories. Look for relationships between these categories. For example, you might put the airplane and automobile statistics in separate categories. You might also categorize the number of accidents and the number of fatalities. Finally, make a generalization that is consistent with most of the information.

Practicing the Skill

Read the passage about literature in the Tang dynasty and answer the questions that follow.

> "Xuanzang welcomed artists to his splendid court.... Two of China's greatest poets, Duo Fu and Li Bo, produced their works in Xuanzang's court. Scholars compiled encyclopedias, dictionaries, and official histories of China. Writers popularized stories about ghosts, crime, and love. And while European monks were still slowly and laboriously copying texts by hand, Chinese Buddhist monks invented the more efficient technique of block printing."

1. What facts about literature in the Tang dynasty are presented?
2. Organize these facts into categories.
3. How does the invention of block printing relate to the other facts?
4. What generalization can you make about literature during the Tang dynasty?

Chinese pouring vessel

Applying the Skill

Review the information in the chapter about religion in China, Cambodia, Vietnam, Korea, and Japan. Write a generalization about religion in East and Southeast Asia. Then support your generalization with at least five facts.

For More Practice

Turn to the Skill Practice in the Chapter Review on page 371 for more practice in making generalizations.

Critical Thinking

SKILLS

TEACH

Making Generalizations Write the following statement on the chalkboard: "Our school produces great football players [or hockey players or debaters, or whatever]." Ask students what information should be gathered in order to validate this generalization. *(number of team members who have won awards over the years; similar statistics for other schools in the area)* Then have students read the skill and complete the practice questions.

Additional Practice

Skill Reinforcement Activity 14

ANSWERS TO PRACTICING THE SKILL

1. Xuanzang welcomed artists; two great poets wrote in his court; scholars compiled dictionaries and other works; writers popularized stories about ghosts, crime, and love; monks invented block printing.
2. patronage: emperor welcomes artists; types of works produced: encyclopedias, dictionaries, official histories, ghost stories, crime stories, love stories; technology: block printing
3. It made it easier to preserve and transmit writings of the period.
4. Literature flourished during the Tang dynasty.

SECTION THEME

▶ **Innovation** Japan and Korea produce innovations from a blend of Chinese and local traditions.

Find Out

Answer: *The Koreans adopted many elements of Chinese culture because the Chinese controlled the country for a period. The Japanese set up a kind of cultural exchange program through which nobles and scholars learned much from the Chinese.*

FOCUS

Section Objective

Explain how the Koreans and Japanese accepted Chinese culture.

BELLRINGER Motivational Activity

Before taking roll at the beginning of the class period, project Section Focus Transparency 14-4 and have students answer the activity questions. Discuss students' responses.

This activity is also available as a blackline master.

Vocabulary Pre-check

Use the Vocabulary PuzzleMaker to create a puzzle that reinforces the vocabulary terms in this section. **L1**

A.D. 400 · **A.D. 1000** · **A.D. 1600**

c. A.D. 400 Yamato clan founds Japanese imperial dynasty.

A.D. 668 The Silla kingdom conquers all of Korea.

A.D. 1274 Mongols make first attempt to invade Japan.

A.D. 1336 The Ashikaga family rules in Japan.

Section 4

Korea and Japan

Setting the Scene

▶ **Terms to Define**
shamanism, shogun, shogunate, samurai, daimyo

▶ **People to Meet**
Sejong, Yi-Sun-shin, Prince Shotoku, Lady Shikibu Murasaki, Yoritomo Minamoto

▶ **Places to Locate**
Heian Kyo (Kyoto)

Find Out How did the Koreans and the Japanese accept China's culture?

The Storyteller

Zeami Motokiyo was adamant as he lectured his students. "Actors are not thoughtless mimics incapable of intellectualism or philosophy. We seek excellence, as do courtiers and men of letters." Motokiyo had been developing a new form of drama, the Noh play, that had uplifting stories and moral lessons, aspects that appealed to the educated upper classes. "Actors must always bear in mind the correct balance between mental and physical actions. An actor, using his intelligence, will make his presentation seem beautiful." Motokiyo wanted his actors to think as well as to rehearse.

—adapted from *Sources of Japanese Tradition*, Ryusaku Tsunoda, reprinted in *Sources of World History*, Volume 1, edited by Mark A. Kishlansky, 1994

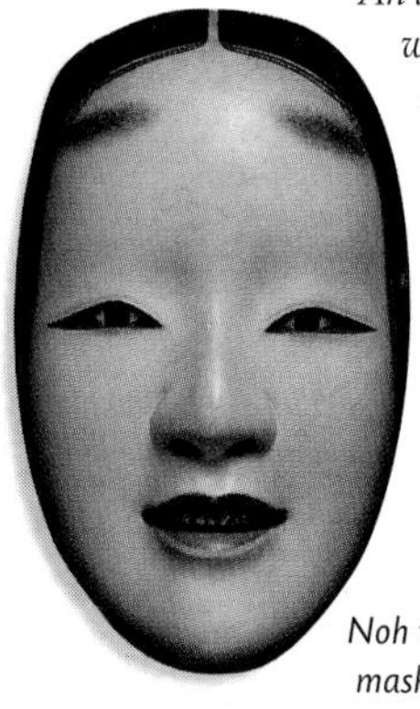

Noh theater mask

Like the nations of Southeast Asia, Korea and Japan adopted elements of Chinese culture. But also like these other nations, they retained their own rich traditions.

Korea

A glance at Korea on the map on page 354 will reveal why a Korean proverb describes the country as "a shrimp between whales." Korea forms a peninsula on the east coast of Asia, extending south toward the western tip of Japan. Thus, it acts as a bridge between its two neighbors, China and Japan.

Early History

By legend, the Koreans claim descent from Tangun, the son of a bear and a god who supposedly founded the first Korean kingdom 5,000 years ago. Historians believe that the first Korean people were immigrants from northern Asia. These settlers lived in villages, grew rice, and made tools and other implements of bronze. They were animists who practiced **shamanism**, a belief that good and evil spirits inhabit both living and nonliving things. Shamans, or priests, interceded between the spirit world and humans.

In 109 B.C. China first invaded Korea, putting Korea under the control of the Han dynasty. From 109 B.C. until the fall of the Han dynasty in A.D. 220, Korea was dominated by China. But after the fall of the Han dynasty, Koreans regained control of their peninsula and, by A.D. 313, eventually formed three kingdoms—Silla, Paekche (pah•EHK•chee), and Koguryo. During the Three Kingdoms period, from 57 B.C. to A.D. 668, the Koreans adopted many elements of Chinese culture. Among these were Confucianism, Buddhism, calligraphy, and ideas about government.

Koreans also used Chinese knowledge of arts and sciences to make their own unique creations. For example, in the A.D. 300s, Koguryo artists

SECTION RESOURCES

Reproducible Masters
- Reproducible Lesson Plan 14-4
- Guided Reading Activity 14-4
- Reteaching Activity 14
- Enrichment Activity 14
- Section Quiz 14-4
- Performance Assessment Activity 14
- Spanish Chapter Summary 14

Transparencies
- Section Focus Transparency 14-4

Multimedia
- Vocabulary PuzzleMaker Software
- Student Self-Test and Review Software
- Testmaker

produced mammoth cave art murals. In Silla, Queen Sondok built an astronomical observatory that still stands today and is the oldest observatory in Asia.

In A.D. 668 the kingdom of Silla conquered all of Korea, ushering in a period of peace, prosperity, and creativity. Korean potters produced superb porcelain decorated with flower designs. Koreans also created a unique mask dance that expressed sentiments of shamanism and Buddhism, which had been adopted as the state religion in A.D. 528. Over a 16-year period, Korean scholars compiled the *Tripitaka Koreana*, the largest collection of Buddhist scriptures in the world today. The *Tripitaka* has 81,258 large wooden printing plates.

The Yi Dynasty

In A.D. 1392 a dynasty called the Yi came to power in Korea. The Yi called their kingdom Choson and built Hanyang—today the city of Seoul—as their capital. They opened schools to teach Chinese classics to civil service candidates and made neo-Confucianism the state doctrine.

The adoption of Korean neo-Confucianism deeply affected people's roles and relationships. According to Korean Confucian doctrine, the eldest son in each family was bound by duty to serve his parents until their death. Korean women—who had been accorded high status under shamanism and Buddhism—were given much lower standing under Korean Confucianism. In fact, women from the higher ranks of society had to stay indoors until nightfall, when a great bell signaled the closing of the city gates. Even then, to go out they had to obtain permission from their husbands.

One of the greatest Yi rulers, King **Sejong**, had two significant accomplishments. He ordered bronze instruments to be used in measuring rain. As a result, Korea now has the oldest record of rainfall in the world. He and his advisers made a greater contribution by creating simplified writing to spread literacy. Together they devised *hangul*, an alphabet that uses 14 consonants and 10 vowels to represent Korean sounds. Although scholars continued to write with Chinese characters after the invention of *hangul*, writers began using *hangul* to transcribe folk tales and popular literature.

Although the Japanese tried to capture Korea in A.D. 1592, the Yi dynasty managed to successfully rebuff the Japanese invaders, mainly because of an invention created by Korea's Admiral **Yi-Sun-shin**. The admiral's ironclad warships, or "turtle ships," devastated the Japanese fleet. The Koreans won the war. However, in the years that followed, they increasingly avoided contact with the outside world and isolated themselves so totally that Korea became known as the Hermit Kingdom.

Japan

Just 110 miles (204 km) east of Korea lies the Japanese archipelago. As the map on page 354 shows, Japan consists of four large islands—Honshu, Shikoku, Kyushu, and Hokkaido—and many smaller ones.

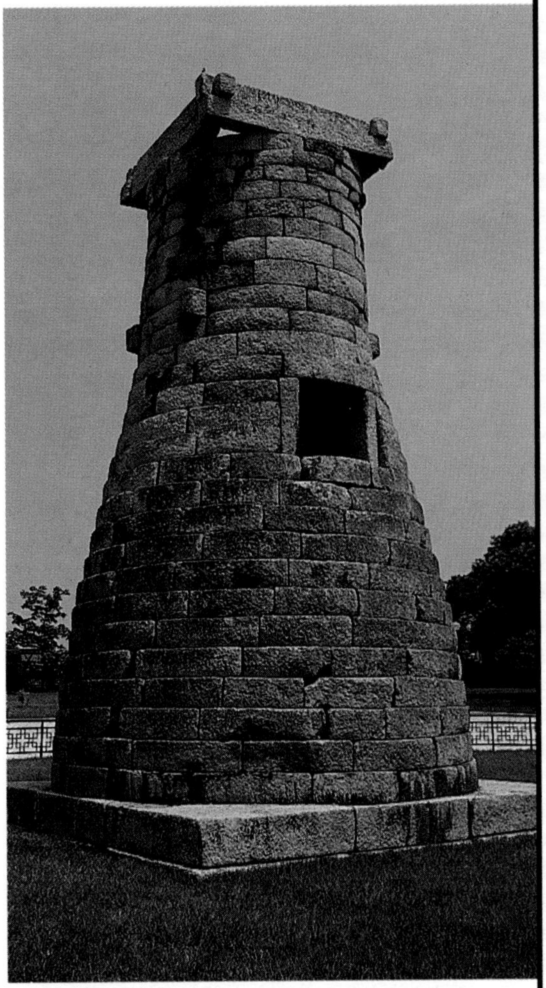

Visualizing History **Shown here is the world's oldest astronomical observatory in Asia. It was built at Silla, Korea, from 365 stones.** *How much territory did the kingdom of Silla hold by A.D. 668?*

Chapter 14 Section 4

TEACH

Guided Practice

THEME Innovation

Explain the difference between a discovery and an innovation. *(To discover is to reveal or find for the first time; to innovate is to introduce something new, or to renew.)* Explain how an innovation can be based on someone else's discovery. **What Korean innovations were based on knowledge gained from the Chinese?** *(cave murals, observatory, new ways to decorate porcelain, mask dance)* **L1**

Technology Review the principles behind the Chinese system of writing. *(Hundreds of characters were needed to represent objects, ideas, and sounds.)* **Why would an innovation like the Korean system of hangul be an improvement?** *(Because it was alphabetic, requiring only 24 symbols. This made it much easier for the average person to learn.)* **L2**

Visualizing History When the kingdom of Silla dominated Korea, absolute monarchy flourished. Although the rulers granted land to aristocrats, the land reverted to the central government when the nobles died.

Answer to Caption: *all of Korea*

COOPERATIVE LEARNING ACTIVITY

Panel Presentation Organize the class into groups of four or five. Each group is to become a panel of experts on a Japanese topic. Subjects may include ikebana (flower arranging); the tea ceremony; Kabuki theater; architecture; the samurai; and various customs relating to food, clothing, manners, or holidays. Choose a leader for each group. Each member of each group should prepare a five-minute presentation on one aspect of the team's subject. **L2**

Visualizing History The graceful shape of Mount Fuji has made this volcanic mountain famous all over the world. The temples and shrines on its slopes—and even in its craters—draw hundreds of thousands of climbers every year.
Answer to Caption: *It inspired Japanese painters and poets with deep reverence for nature.*

Government Ask students to summarize the changes in Japan's form of government from Yamato times to the fourteenth century. *(clan rule: with Taika reforms, stronger central government; Nara: greater centralization; Heian: power struggles and rise of shogunate)* **L3**

Independent Practice

Guided Reading Activity 14-4 **L1**

Cultural Perspectives

The Ainu Because of Japan's geographic isolation, the country today has very few minorities. There is, however, one group that may have descended from the very first inhabitants of Japan. They are called Ainu, and most of them live on the northernmost main island, Hokkaido. Although most of the 15,000 Ainu have intermarried with other Japanese, a few still live in isolated villages, where they follow their traditional way of life.

Visualizing History **Mount Fuji and Ashinto (lake) at Hayoke, Japan.** *How did the physical beauty of the land affect Japanese art?*

Island Geography

Because of its island geography, Japanese culture formed mostly in isolation from mainland Asian cultures, except for that of China. Although the Japanese borrowed from Chinese civilization, their customs and traditions were different from those of most other Asian peoples.

The geography of these islands influenced the formation of Japanese culture in other ways as well. Because much of the land is mountainous—less than 20 percent of it is suitable for farming—the Japanese learned to get most of their food from the sea. They also learned to rely on the sea for protection from invaders—being a natural barrier to invasion from the mainland—and yet to regard it as a route of transport between the islands. The physical beauty of the land inspired deep reverence for nature in works by many Japanese painters and poets. Because these islands are located in an area where earthquakes, typhoons, floods, and volcanic eruptions are frequent, the Japanese long ago created a myth that helped to explain the stormy weather there.

Creation Myth

An ancient Japanese creation myth is the oldest explanation for the origins of Japan, its turbulent weather, and its first emperor. According to the myth, brother and sister gods Izanagi and Izanami dipped a spear into the churning sea. When they pulled it out, the drops of brine that fell upon the water's surface became the islands of Japan. The two gods then created the sun goddess Amaterasu, and because they loved her best of all their children, they sent her to heaven to rule over the world. Next they created Tsuki-yumi, the moon god, and Susanowo, the storm god, to be her companions.

Amaterasu gave life to everything around her. But Susanowo, who had a fierce temper, ruined his sister's rice crop and so frightened her that she hid in a cave. Without her in heaven, the world became dark. The other gods placed a jewel and a mirror on a tree outside the cave to coax Amaterasu back outside. When she came out and told them why she had hidden, the other gods banished Susanowo to the earth.

According to the myth, Susanowo's descendants were the first inhabitants of Japan. Amaterasu sent her grandson, Ninigi, to govern these descendants on the island of Honshu. So that all would acknowledge his divine power, she sent with him her mirror, her jewel, and a great sword. According to legend, Ninigi's grandson, Jimmu, conquered the rest of Susanowo's descendants in 660 B.C., becoming the first emperor of Japan.

By tradition, each successive emperor has received Amaterasu's three gifts: a mirror, a jewel, and a sword. Also by tradition, each emperor—until Hirohito—has claimed to be Amaterasu's descendant. In 1945, after the Japanese defeat in

MEETING SPECIAL NEEDS ACTIVITY

Study Strategy For most Americans, the cultures of East and Southeast Asia are unfamiliar. Students may be helped in studying these peoples if they construct a table summarizing the basic information in the four sections of this chapter. They should put dates along one axis and main categories of information (politics, religion, and so on) along the other. **L2**

World War II, Emperor Hirohito announced that he did not possess divine status.

Early Inhabitants

Among the first people to inhabit the Japanese islands were hunter-gatherers who came there from the mainland more than 10,000 years ago. These people had developed the technology to make pottery but not to make bronze or iron. When Koreans and others from mainland Asia invaded Japan during the 200s B.C. and 100s B.C., they were easily able to defeat the early inhabitants by using iron and bronze weapons.

The invaders introduced the islanders to agricultural methods, such as how to grow rice in flooded paddies. Heavy summer rains in Japan made it the ideal place to grow rice, which soon became Japan's most important crop.

Between A.D. 200 and A.D. 300, another influx of mainlanders came to Japan. According to scholars, these armor-clad warriors who fought on horseback were probably the ancestors of the aristocratic warriors and imperial family of Japan referred to in the creation myth.

In early Japan, though, even before there was an emperor or an imperial family, separate clans ruled their own regions. Clan members practiced a form of animism called Shinto, meaning "the way of the gods." Each clan included a group of families descended from a common ancestor, often said to have been an animal or a god. The clan worshiped this ancestor as its special *kami*, or spirit. Practitioners of Shinto believed that *kami* dwelled within people, animals, and even nonliving objects such as rocks and streams. To honor this *kami*—and the *kami* of their ancestors—they held festivals and rituals. Often these ceremonies were conducted by the chief of the clan, who acted as both military leader and priest.

The Yamato Clan

By about A.D. 400, the military skill and prestige of the Yamato clan, which claimed descent from Amaterasu, enabled it to extend a loose rule over most of Japan. Although other clans continued to rule their own lands, they owed their loyalty to the Yamato chief. In effect, he became the emperor.

Initially, the emperor had a great deal of political power. By the A.D. mid-500s, however, the emperor had become more of a ceremonial figure who carried out religious rituals. The real political power was held by the members of the Soga

CONNECTIONS The Arts

The Art of Feudal Japan

Kiyomatsu, a samurai hero

In A.D. 1185 the rise of military rule in Japan ushered in a new style of art. Japan's shoguns, daimyo, and samurai wanted to see paintings that reflected and glorified their military values. Artists and writers responded by creating art forms highlighting the skill and bravery of soldiers.

Paintings from the Japanese feudal era often show warriors in richly patterned clothing, riding magnificent horses and wielding long swords. The expressions chosen for the rider and his horse often communicate wild, but disciplined, emotions aroused in the moment just before charging into battle. By posing the figures as if on the verge of battle—rather than at rest—artists give their paintings an active quality. The splendor of the soldier coupled with the dramatic intensity of the moment imparted a sense of glamor to doing battle. This artistic approach appealed greatly to a military patron of the arts.

MAKING THE CONNECTION

1. What things identify the subject of this painting as a samurai warrior?
2. Choose one military value reflected in this painting. Explain how the artist has managed to convey this value.

Chapter 14 Section 4

Music Have students find recordings of Korean or Japanese music to share with the class. Samples could include koto (a harplike instrument) or samisen (a three-stringed banjo) music, or a recording of folk songs. **L2 LEP**

Religion Many Japanese practice Shinto along with Buddhism. Have students write a report on Shinto, describing the beliefs and practices of this religion. **L2**

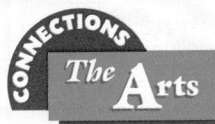

CONNECTIONS The Arts

The Art of Feudal Japan

The samurai's loyalty to his overlord was absolute. Nothing was to come before it—not duties to wife, parents, or children. Although the samurai and the European feudal knight had this tradition of loyalty to one's lord in common, the two were quite different in other ways. The samurai did not go to battle to defend a lady or for religious motives, as his European counterpart often did.

Answers to Making the Connection

1. *rides a horse, wears armor, carries a sword*
2. *Possible answer: fighting spirit; the samurai carries a sword in his hand, ready to fight.*

MAKING CONNECTIONS ACTIVITIES

Religion Have students research the Japanese tea ceremony, focusing especially on the symbolism of the ritual. Encourage students to do a demonstration of a tea ceremony for the rest of the class. **L2**

The Arts Have students research ikebana, the Japanese art of flower arranging. On the basis of the information they find, have students create an arrangement that conforms to the principle of ikebana. Most libraries have books on the subject. **L3**

Politics Have students research the Taika reforms of the Fujiwara family. Ask them to use library resources to describe some of the reforms and draw conclusions about their effects. **L3**

Linking Past and Present

Nara Temples During the Nara period in Japan, hundreds of temples were built at the capital city of Nara. Today, 1,300 years later, many of these temples still stand. Their beauty and historic interest draw some 10 million visitors a year.

Who?What?Where?When?

Early Japanese Writings The earliest known Japanese books are the *Kojiki* (Records of Ancient Matters), completed in A.D. 712, and the *Nihon shoki* (Chronicles of Japan), completed in 720. The two works combine actual events with myths that trace the imperial family to the foundations of the world. Their purpose was to give the court—then under Chinese influence—a history that could compete with that of the Chinese.

family. The emperors kept their position as heads of Japan because people believed that only they could intercede with the gods. But the Soga family controlled the country.

Chinese Influences

In A.D. 552 a Korean king sent a statue of the Buddha and some Buddhist texts to the Japanese court. The king wrote, "This religion is the most excellent of all teachings" and suggested that the emperor make Buddhism the national religion. Buddhism had come to Korea from China, and its introduction to Japan made the Japanese open to Chinese culture. This curiosity about China was especially strong among Japan's nobles and scholars.

Through a kind of cultural exchange program that lasted four centuries, the Japanese learned much from the Chinese. Not only did they learn about the teachings of the Buddha, they also learned a great deal about Chinese art, medicine, astronomy, and philosophy. They incorporated much of this knowledge into Japanese culture. For instance, the Japanese adopted the Chinese characters for writing to create their own writing system.

Prince Shotoku was responsible for much of this cultural exchange. When he became the leading court official in A.D. 593, he instituted programs that encouraged further learning from Chinese civilization. He ordered the construction of Buddhist monasteries and temples and sent officials and students to China to study. When Shotoku heard about the Chinese Confucian ideas of government, he wrote a constitution for Japan in which he set forth general principles that explained how government officials should act.

After Shotoku's death, the Fujiwara family seized power in the name of the emperor and began to urge him to pattern the government more closely on that of China. China had a strong central government at that time.

In A.D. 646 government officials instituted the Taika reforms, or "Great Change." These reforms attempted to do what the Fujiwara family had begun. They proclaimed that all the land was the property of the emperor rather than clan leaders. Clan leaders could oversee the peasants working the land, but they could no longer assign them land or collect taxes from them. Instead, government officials were to allocate plots to peasants and collect part of their harvest in taxes for the emperor.

Although these reforms were somewhat effective at increasing the central government's control over the clans, most clan leaders refused to give up their land. Even after the Taika reforms, Japan remained much divided under the control of regional clan leaders.

The Nara Period

Greater government centralization did not take place until A.D. 710, when Japan built its first permanent capital at Nara. A smaller version of China's Changan, Nara had an imperial palace, broad streets, large public squares, rows of Chinese-style homes, and Buddhist temples.

With the completion of the colossal Todaiji Temple at Nara in A.D. 752, Buddhist fervor in Japan reached its peak. Buddhism, however, did not replace Shinto, for each religion met different needs. Shinto linked the Japanese to nature and their homeland. Buddhism promised spiritual rewards to the good. Therefore, people practiced both.

During the Nara period, the Japanese also produced their first written literature. Scribes wrote histories of ancient Japan that combined the creation myths with actual events. Other writers compiled collections of Japanese poems.

The Heian Period

In A.D. 794 the Japanese established a new capital, **Heian Kyo**, "the City of Peace and Tranquillity," later called **Kyoto**. For more than 1,000 years, this city remained the capital of Japan.

A century after the city was founded, Japan stopped sending cultural missions to China. In the period that followed, a small group of about 3,000 Japanese aristocrats, calling themselves "dwellers among the clouds," created Heian culture.

The focus of Heian court life was the pursuit of

AROUND THE WORLD Temple of Kailasa

India, A.D. 760
Emperor Krishna of the Rashtrakuta dynasty ordered construction of the Kailasa Temple at Ellora. The temple, completed in A.D. 760, was cut from a single outcropping of rock. It was 165 feet (50 m) long and 96 feet (29 m) high. Kailasa was dedicated to the Hindu god Siva. Its elaborate carvings featured Hindu gods and mythological figures in various poses.

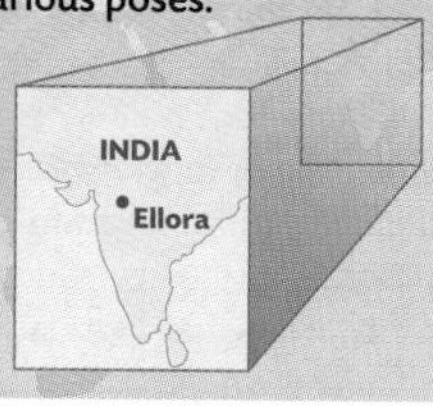

CRITICAL THINKING ACTIVITY

Making Comparisons Although Korea and Japan have many things in common, there are also profound differences between them. Have students compare and contrast the two countries, perhaps using a double-column format with side headings such as: *mythological origins; major historical periods to about 1400; cultural borrowings from China;* and *native cultural contributions.* **L3**

362 Chapter 14 *East and South Asia*

History & Art *The Lady Fujitsubo Watching Prince Genji Departing in the Moonlight* by A. Hiroshige and U. Toyokuni, A.D. 1853. *What author may have written the world's first novel,* The Tale of Genji?

beauty. It pervaded all of life's activities, from wrapping presents to mixing perfumes and colors. People devoted hours each day to writing letters in the form of poems. Calligraphy was as important as the poem itself, for a person's handwriting was taken to be an indication of his or her character. People were even said to fall in love upon seeing each other's handwriting.

During the Heian period, women were the creators of Japan's first great prose literature. **Lady Shikibu Murasaki** wrote *The Tale of Genji*, which some believe to be the world's first novel. The novelist chronicles the life and loves of a fictional prince named Genji. Filled with poems about the beauty of nature, *The Tale of Genji* quickly became very popular.

The Heian aristocrats were so deeply involved in their search for beauty, however, that they neglected tasks of government. Order began breaking down in the provinces. Warlike provincial leaders started running their estates as independent territories, ignoring the emperor's officials and refusing to pay taxes. Thus the Heian aristocrats eventually lost control of the empire completely.

The Way of the Warrior

As Heian power faded, two powerful court families, the Taira and the Minamoto, struggled for control. The families fought a decisive battle in A.D. 1185 in which the Taira were defeated. To **Yoritomo Minamoto**, head of the Minamoto family, the emperor then gave the title shogun, or "general," and delegated to him most of the real political and military power. While the emperor remained with his court in the capital of Kyoto carrying on ritual tasks, Yoritomo and his soldiers ran a shogunate, or military government, from Kamakura near present-day Tokyo.

The shogunate proved to be quite strong. Even though Kublai Khan tried twice to invade Japan—once in A.D. 1274 and again in A.D. 1281—he did not succeed. On the first occasion, Japanese warriors and the threat of a storm forced the Mongols to withdraw. On the second occasion, 150,000 Mongol warriors came by ship, but a typhoon arose and destroyed the fleet. The Japanese thought of the storm as the *kamikaze*, or "divine wind," and took it to be confirmation that their islands were indeed sacred.

In A.D. 1336 the Ashikaga family gained control of the shogunate. But the family failed to get control of regional warriors. Japan soon broke into individual warring states, leaving the shogun and the emperor as mere figureheads.

The powerful landowner-warriors in the countryside were called samurai. The most powerful samurai became daimyo (DY•mee•OH), or lords. Like the medieval knights of feudal Europe who pledged their loyalty to lords, samurai pledged their loyalty and military service to their daimyo. There were many samurai and many daimyo. Poor

Chapter 14 Section 4

History & Art Lady Murasaki's novel depicts Prince Genji and his courtiers as refined members of the nobility. To succeed at court, an aristocrat had to be skilled as a musician, poet, and calligrapher, and be wise in the ways of elegant courtship.
Answer to Caption: *Lady Shikibu Murasaki*

you don't say...

"Tycoon" is an English word that now applies mainly to business leaders. It comes to us from China by way of Japan. The Chinese term for "great prince," *ta kuin*, was adapted by the Japanese as *taikun* and used to describe the shogun.

Linking Past and Present

The ***kamikaze***, or "divine wind" that saved Japan from Mongol defeat in 1281, never lost its importance for the Japanese. During World War II, Allied planes bombed Japan from aircraft carriers. Suicide pilots, their planes loaded with explosives, dived into the aircraft carriers in an effort to stave off defeat. Admired at home and feared by the Allies, they were known as kamikaze pilots.

MORE ABOUT...

Lady Murasaki The author of *The Tale of Genji* was born about 978 and died around 1014. Her real name is unknown; the name by which she is called is that of the heroine of her novel. After the death of her husband, Fujiwara Nobutaka, Lady Murasaki served at court. It was during this time that she wrote *The Tale of Genji.* It has been recognized as a masterpiece ever since. In the thirteenth century, a 54-volume commentary appeared; more recently, a Japanese publisher issued a 1,200-page *Tale of Genji Encyclopedia.*

Chapter 14
Section 4

Visualizing History The Buddha himself did not believe in any god or gods. After his death, however, he was worshiped as a god, surrounded by lesser gods. Buddhism became a complex religion with temples, rituals, priests, monks, and nuns.
Answer to Caption: *by a Korean king who sent a statue of the Buddha and some Buddhist texts to the Japanese court*

ASSESS

Check for Understanding

Assign Section 4 Review as homework or as an in-class activity.

Use Student Self-Test and Review Software to review Section 4.

Evaluate

Section Quiz 14-4

Use the Testmaker to create a customized quiz for Section 4.

Reteach

Ask the class to review the section by volunteering answers to these questions:

1. **What country acted as a bridge between China and Japan?** *(Korea)*
2. **What elements of Chinese culture became part of Korean and Japanese cultures?** *(Confucianism, Buddhism, language, art of making porcelain, use of wood-block printing)*
3. **What kind of military government and class of warriors were unique to Japan?** *(shogunate and samurai)*

Reteaching Activity 14

Visualizing History **Friends mourn the death of the Buddha in this Japanese painting.** *How was Buddhism introduced to Japan?*

rice farmers paid high taxes for the right to farm a daimyo's lands. In return, that daimyo provided the farmers with protection. The system in which large landholders give protection to people in exchange for their services is called feudalism. Japanese feudalism was similar to European feudalism as described in Chapter 12.

The samurai fought on horseback with bows, arrows, and steel swords. They dressed in loose-fitting armor. The samurai followed a strict code of honor called Bushido, meaning "the way of the warrior." Bushido stressed bravery, self-discipline, and loyalty. It demanded that the samurai endure suffering and defend his honor at all costs. If a samurai was dishonored or defeated, he was expected to commit suicide.

Japanese women too could be warriors. This passage from *The Tale of the Heike* describes a female Minamoto samurai:

> "Tomoe had long black hair and a fair complexion, and her face was very lovely; moreover she was a fearless rider whom neither the fiercest horse nor the roughest ground could dismay, and so dexterously did she handle sword and bow that she was a match for a thousand warriors and fit to meet either god or devil. Many times had she … won matchless renown in encounters with the bravest captains, and so in this last fight, when all the others had been slain or had fled, among the last seven there rode Tomoe."
>
> —*The Tale of the Heike*, A.D. 1200s

Growth of a Merchant Class

Despite the political turmoil during its feudal period, Japan developed economically at this time. Workshops on daimyo estates produced arms, armor, and iron tools. Each region began to specialize in goods such as pottery, paper, textiles, and lacquerware. Trade increased between regions.

The increasing trade led to the growth of towns around the castles of the daimyos. Merchants and artisans formed guilds to promote their interests—just as they did in medieval Europe. These guilds, called *za* in Japan, benefited their members in many ways. A *za* might pay a fee to exempt its members from paying tolls for shipping their goods. Over a long period of time, this exemption would save the members quite a bit of money.

Japanese merchants began to trade with Chinese and Korean merchants. Chinese copper coins became the chief means of exchange. The Japanese exported raw materials such as lumber, pearls, and gold, as well as finished goods such as swords and painted fans. The Japanese imported items such as medicines, books, and pictures.

Religion and the Arts

By the A.D. 1200s Buddhism had spread from the nobles to the common people. The opening words of *The Tale of the Heike* describe the Buddhist sentiments that were prevalent in Japan during its feudal period:

> "In the sound of the bell of the Gion Temple echoes the impermanence of all things. The pale hue of the flowers of the teak tree show the truth that they who prosper must fall. The proud do not last long, but vanish like a spring-night's dream. And the mighty ones too will perish in the end, like dust before the wind."

During Japan's feudal age, Buddhist teachings were simplified and gave rise to many religious groups. The new varieties of Buddhism all taught about a personal afterlife in paradise. The way to paradise, they stated, was through simple trust in the Buddha. With salvation so easily available, the influence of priests, monks, and nuns declined. For

TEACHER NOTES

Visualizing History **Zen Buddhist monks sit in a meditation garden at Ryoanji Temple in Kyoto, Japan.** *To a Zen Buddhist, what is the purpose of meditation?*

the first time, the common people began to play an important role in Buddhist life. With widespread support, Japanese Buddhist groups linked religion with patriotism. Some believed that Japanese Buddhism was the only true Buddhism and that Japan was the center of the universe.

While the common people turned to new forms of Buddhism, the samurai followed a form of Buddhism called Zen. The Japanese scholar Eisai had brought Zen to Japan from China late in the A.D. 1100s. Zen taught that the individual had to live in harmony with nature and that this harmony could be achieved through a deep religious understanding called enlightenment. The followers of Zen rejected book learning and logical thought, embracing instead bodily discipline and meditation. They believed that by meditation a student could free his mind and arrive at enlightenment.

Zen was particularly useful for warriors because it taught them to act instinctively, and thinking was a hindrance to action. Samurai could improve skills such as archery by freeing their minds from distractions to better concentrate on the object or target.

Zen also perfected art forms and rituals such as ikebana, or flower arranging, meditation gardens, and the tea ceremony. Ikebana grew out of the religious custom of placing flowers before images of the Buddha. The Zen practice of meditation gave rise to meditation gardens, consisting of carefully placed rocks surrounded by neatly raked sand.

Meditation also sparked the tea ceremony, an elegant, studied ritual for serving tea. One tea master said of the ceremony that it was intended to "cleanse the senses ... so that the mind itself is cleansed from defilements." These and other arts and rituals derived from Buddhism are still popular in Japan today.

SECTION 4 REVIEW

Recall

1. **Define** shamanism, shogun, shogunate, samurai, daimyo.
2. **Identify** Sejong, Yi-Sun-shin, Amaterasu, Jimmu, Shinto, Prince Shotoku, Taika reforms, Lady Shikibu Murasaki, Yoritomo Minamoto, Bushido.
3. **Explain** What is traditionally given to each new emperor of Japan? Why?

Critical Thinking

4. **Evaluating Information** Which would you prefer to follow, the ideals of the Heian court or the samurai code of Bushido? Why? What effects do you think each viewpoint might have had on the people of Japan?

Understanding Themes

5. **Innovation** Identify one Chinese innovation that the Koreans or Japanese borrowed, and describe how they made it their own.

Chapter 14 Section 4

Visualizing History Zen meditation aims at emptying the mind in order to achieve limitless receptivity. **Answer to Caption:** *to free the mind and thus reach enlightenment*

Enrich

Have students research the art of Japanese screens, bringing illustrations to class. Suggest that they also use watercolors to paint a facsimile screen.

Enrichment Activity 14

CLOSE

Discuss the Korean and Japanese acceptance of aspects of Chinese culture that advanced their own cultures. Ask students to give examples. *(Answers may include: Korea: produced superb porcelain with flower designs, compiled world's largest collection of Buddhist scriptures and printed it with wooden plates; Japan: developed stronger central government based on Confucian ideals, used Chinese characters to create their own writing system)*

SECTION 4 REVIEW ANSWERS

1. All vocabulary words are defined in the Glossary.
2. Sejong, 359; Yi-Sun-shin, 359; Amaterasu, 360; Jimmu, 360; Shinto, 361; Prince Shotoku, 362; Taika reforms, 362; Lady Shikibu Murasaki, 363; Yoritomo Minamoto, 363; Bushido, 364
3. mirror, a jewel, and a sword—symbols of divine rule
4. Answers will vary. Students choosing Heian ideals should stress their aesthetic focus, while those who choose Bushido might mention its nobility or enforced self-discipline. Both Heian court and the military required that common people be heavily taxed in order to support them.
5. **INNOVATION** Answers will vary. Sample answer: Japan borrowed Chinese characters to form its own writing system.

Bridge to the Past
Literature

Block Schedule

Team Teaching These poems of Li Bo may be presented in a team-teaching context, in conjunction with English or Language Arts.

Poetry of Li Bo

Historical Connection

Artistic, political, and economic advances often go together. The success of Li Bo was one indication of the prosperity of China during the Tang dynasty.

Background Information

Setting Li Bo often set his poems in natural surroundings. He traveled a great deal and, as a result, he was sensitive to variations in landscape and climate.

Literary Elements Allusion is a reference, often indirect, to something that the writer assumes the reader knows about. For example, in Li Bo's letter to his children, he notes that the silkworms "have now had three sleeps," assuming they would understand how long a time was indicated. When silkworms make their cocoons, they alternate between working and resting.

Simile is the direct comparison of two things. In "Taking Leave of a Friend," Li Bo writes "Sunset like the parting of old acquaintances." He is comparing the setting of the sun with the parting of friends.

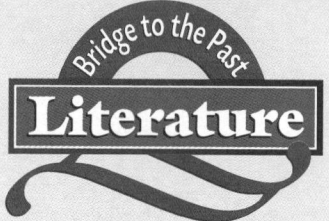

Bridge to the Past
Literature

from Four Poems

by Li Bo

Li Bo was born in A.D. 701 in western China. People began praising his beautiful poems even before he reached adulthood. Throughout his life he traveled extensively in China, amazing people with his ability to compose insightful, touching poems. He usually wrote about the world around him, the people he met, and the emotions he felt. By the time of his death in A.D. 762, he was regarded as one of China's greatest poets, a distinction he still holds today.

In the following poem, Li Bo comments on an experience everyone faces at some time: parting with a close companion.

Taking Leave of a Friend

Blue mountains to the north of the walls,
White river winding about them;
Here we must make separation
And go out through a thousand miles
of dead grass.

Mind like a floating wide cloud,
Sunset like the parting of old acquaintances
Who bow over their clasped hands at a distance.
Our horses neigh to each other
as we are departing.

The following poem is a favorite of many Chinese citizens who have left their homeland and settled in the United States or elsewhere.

On a Quiet Night

I saw the moonlight before my couch,
And wondered if it were not the frost
on the ground.
I raised my head and looked out on the
mountain moon;
I bowed my head and thought of my
far-off home.

About the Author

Li Bo wrote more than 1,000 poems, which are still read today. Many were short poems composed as thank-you notes and gifts to friends. Other poems, usually longer, were more like folk songs. Li Bo wrote them in a traditional ballad style to accompany music. As a follower of Daoism, he believed in intuition and loved nature. According to legend, he died when he jumped out of a boat to grab the reflection of the moon on the water.

Li Bo lived in ancient China's greatest epoch for poetry. Three other revered poets, Wang Wei, Duo Fu, and Bo Juyi, also lived during the Tang dynasty.

Li Bo used extensive symbolism in his writing. In the following poem, he compares life to a traveler on a journey.

Hard Is the Journey

Gold vessels of fine wines,
thousands a gallon,
Jade dishes of rare meats,
costing more thousands,

I lay my chopsticks down,
no more can banquet,
And draw my sword and stare
wildly about me:

Ice bars my way to cross
the Yellow River,
Snows from dark skies to climb
the T'ai-hang Mountains!

At peace I drop a hook
into a brooklet,
At once I'm in a boat
but sailing sunward . . .

(Hard is the Journey,
Hard is the Journey,
So many turnings,
And now where am I?)

So when a breeze breaks waves,
bringing fair weather,
I set a cloud for sails,
cross the blue oceans!

Visualizing History ***Dawn Over Elixir Terrace*** **depicts a tranquil river scene.** *How do the river and mountains present obstacles to the traveler in the poem?*

Bridge to the Past
Literature

FOCUS

Before students read the first poem, describe Li Bo's life and his extensive travels. Ask students to predict what subjects a poet who traveled frequently might emphasize.

Visualizing History Landscape painting became popular in China during the Tang dynasty, the period when Li Bo lived. Artists of this time painted scenes of craggy mountains, rocks, streams, and trees.
Answer to Caption: *The river is iced over, and snow falls in the mountains.*

Other Works of and about Chinese Literature

Bynner, Witter, trans. ***The Jade Mountain.*** New York: Knopf, 1929, 1957.
Grousett, Rene. ***The Rise and Splendor of the Chinese Empire.*** Berkeley: University of California Press, 1953.
Obata, Shigeyoshi. ***The Works of Li Po.*** New York: Paragon, 1965.
Pound, Ezra. ***Personae.*** New York: New Directions, 1926.
Waley, Arthur, trans. ***The Poetry and Career of Li Po.*** New York: Macmillan, 1950.

Chapter 14 *East and South Asia* **367**

Bridge to the Past

Literature

TEACH

Evaluation

In "Taking Leave of a Friend," Li Bo uses hyperbole, or exaggeration. The "thousand miles of dead grass" is an exaggeration used for effect. Ask students if they think hyperbole works to convey the sense of bleakness one might feel if separated from a close friend.

Clarification

In "Hard Is the Journey," Li Bo refers to the Yellow River, now known as the Huang River. It flows through north and central China.

Interpretation

Ask students what the peach tree symbolizes in Li Bo's letter to his children. One view might be that it suggests the poet's role as provider for his family. Another interpretation might be that it symbolizes the changes that affected Li Bo's family during his three-year absence.

World Literature Selection 3

History & Art Artists and poets during the Tang dynasty used natural scenes to express their deepest feelings. "Outwardly, nature has been my teacher," said one Tang landscape painter, "but inwardly I follow the springs of my heart."
Answer to Caption: *spring*

Since Li Bo spent much of his time traveling, he was often separated from his family. He wrote and sent the following poem to his children.

Letter to His Two Small Children Staying in Eastern Lu at Wen Yang Village Under Turtle Mountain

Here in Wu Land mulberry leaves are green,
Silkworms in Wu have now had three sleeps:

My family, left in Eastern Lu,
Oh, to sow now Turtle-shaded fields,
Do the Spring things I can never join,
Sailing Yangtse always on my own—

Let the South Wind blow you back my heart,
Fly and land it in the Tavern court
Where, to the East, there are sprays and leaves
Of one peach-tree, sweeping the blue mist;

History & Art *Landscape of the Four Seasons* by Shen Shih-Ch'ung. *In what season did Li Bo write the above poem?*

Additional Literary Works of the Period

Bede, the Venerable. ***Ecclesiastical History of the English Nation.*** The first important account of English history, written in the early A.D. 700s.

Dante Alighieri. ***The Divine Comedy.*** Epic about Christian views of life after death, written in early A.D. 1300s.

Murasaki, Shikibu. ***The Tale of Genji.*** Japanese tale of romance and political intrigue, written about A.D. 1000.

Nibelungenlied. German epic poems written down in the A.D. 1200s; they formed the basis for several famous operas by Richard Wagner in the 1800s.

Visualizing History **This winter scene is a detail from the Ming dynasty painting *Landscape of the Four Seasons*.** *How many winters have passed since the author was at home?*

This is the tree I myself put in
When I left you, nearly three years past;
A peach-tree now, level with the eaves,
And I sailing cannot yet turn home!

Pretty daughter, P'ing-yang is your name,
Breaking blossom, there beside my tree,
Breaking blossom, you cannot see me
And your tears flow like the running stream;

And little son, Po-ch'in you are called,
Your big sister's shoulder you must reach
When you come there underneath my peach,
Oh, to pat and pet you too, my child!

I dreamt like this till my wits went wild,
By such yearning daily burned within;
So tore some silk, wrote this distant pang
From me to you living at Wen Yang....

RESPONDING TO LITERATURE

1. In "On a Quiet Night," why is the person unhappy?
2. In "Hard Is the Journey," what do the gold vessels and jade dishes symbolize?
3. What types of images did Li Bo use in each of his poems included here?
4. **Supporting an Opinion** Which poem do you like best? Explain why.

Bridge to the Past

Literature

Visualizing History

This painting was done centuries after Li Bo wrote. However, many painters of the Ming dynasty revived older artistic traditions.
Answer to Caption: *three*

ASSESS

Assign **Responding to Literature** questions.

CLOSE

Discuss with students whether Li Bo's poems are relevant today. Point out that people travel more than ever before, which may allow them to more easily identify with the themes in Li Bo's poetry. On the other hand, travel and communication are so much easier today that people may feel less separated from their families when traveling.

Contemporary Connection

Have students think about times they have been away from home or separated from family or friends in some way. Have them use the poem "On a Quiet Night" on page 366 as a model to write a short poem or a paragraph expressing how they felt.

ANSWERS TO RESPONDING TO LITERATURE

1. The person is sad because he or she is far from home.
2. They symbolize the many pleasures, experiences, and fine things to enjoy in life.
3. Li Bo used images from nature: moonlight, frost, blue mountains, white river, mulberry leaves, ice, snow.
4. Students should explain what they like about the poem: for example, that "Hard Is the Journey" has an upbeat ending.

Portfolio Project

Have students select another Chinese poem or a Japanese haiku and write a brief response to it. In their response students should summarize the poem's theme, explain what effects the poet achieves and how he or she achieves them, and discuss the poem's relevance to people today.

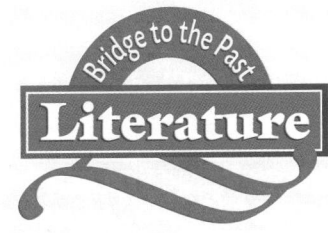

CHAPTER 14 REVIEW

Historical Significance

Contacts among the civilizations of Asia led to an exchange of ideas and practices. The Chinese acquired tea and faster-growing rice plants from the Southeast Asians. The Mongols became an even more powerful fighting force once they learned to use Chinese gunpowder. The Khmer people of Cambodia acquired architectural skills from India and built huge temples. Japan and Korea adopted the Chinese system of civil service examinations.

Today, because of technological advances, cultural diffusion occurs on a global scale. Thus, Westerners learn a great deal from the peoples of Asia, and Asians, likewise, benefit from their encounters with Westerners.

Using Key Terms

Write the key term that completes each sentence.

a. yurts
b. *yasa*
c. daimyo
d. meritocracy
e. samurai
f. shamanism
g. shogun
h. shogunate
i. archipelago
j. mandarins
k. clans

1. Chinese scholars who had passed the civil service examinations eventually formed a wealthy elite group called ________.
2. The Mongol warrior Temujin, later known as Genghis Khan, developed a code of law known as the ______.
3. In A.D. 1185 the Japanese emperor gave the title ________, or "general," to the warrior Yoritomo Minamoto.
4. The early Koreans practiced ________, a belief that priests could intercede between humans and spirits.
5. The Japanese ____________ consists of four large islands and many smaller ones.
6. In feudal Japan, knights known as ______ pledged their loyalty and military service to more powerful landowner-warriors.
7. The early Mongols were organized into _____, or groups based on family ties.
8. Because of its examination system, the Chinese government claimed that it was a ______, or a system in which people are chosen and promoted for their talents and performance.
9. Mongol nomads lived in tent-like structures known as _______.
10. In return for protection, Japanese farmers farmed the lands of powerful landowner-warriors known as ________.

Using Your History Journal

Choose one country from your map of East Asia. Draw that country on a separate sheet of paper. From the section of Chapter 14 that provides information on your chosen country, list 5 to 10 important facts or events beside your map.

Reviewing Facts

1. **Identify** Tai Cong and name his important political achievements.
2. **List** the important scientific and artistic accomplishments made during the Song dynasty.
3. **Explain** the significance of the Battle of the Bach Dang River to the Vietnamese.
4. **Identify** the three most powerful clans in Japan between A.D. 400 and A.D. 1336.
5. **Describe** the code of Bushido and its impact on the Japanese.

Critical Thinking

1. **Apply** How did civil service examinations aid in the development of a strong central government in China?
2. **Analyze** Why did China's economy expand during Song rule?
3. **Synthesize** Do you think the strengths of Mongol society would benefit a nation today? Why or why not?
4. **Evaluate** In what ways did Chinese innovations change the cultures of Korea and Japan?

Chapter 14 Review

GLENCOE TECHNOLOGY

VIDEODISC

Use MindJogger to review students' knowledge of the chapter.

MindJogger Videoquiz

Chapter 14
Disc 2 Side B

Also available in VHS.

Answers

Using Key Terms

1. j	6. e
2. b	7. k
3. g	8. d
4. f	9. a
5. i	10. c

Using Your History Journal

Again, students might want to consider using various colors to represent different types of events.

Reviewing Facts

1. son of the founder of the Tang dynasty; expanded empire and restored strong central government
2. scientific: compass, gunpowder, rocket launchers; artistic: porcelain, landscape painting
3. The Vietnamese won their independence from China.
4. Yamato, Fujiwara, Minamoto
5. the samurai code of honor; stressed bravery, self-discipline, loyalty

Critical Thinking

1. To pass the exams, students had to master Confucianism, which stressed obedience to the emperor; thus, government officials chosen by the exams were loyal and obedient to the emperor.
2. Population increased, making government able to collect more taxes; with increased taxes, government built public works, which in turn helped trade and commerce to expand.
3. Answers will vary, but the Mongols' major asset— military strength—is still regarded as necessary for a strong nation.
4. They altered almost every aspect of society: religion, philosophy, ideas about government, science, and the arts.
5. The islands' beauty inspired writers and artists with a reverence for nature.

Linking Past and Present

1. Heian values, emphasizing taste and beauty, are reflected in simple, elegant design of Japanese buildings, goods, rituals. Bushido,

5. **Analyze** Japanese gardens show a love for nature and order. How did the geography of the islands influence Japanese painting, poetry, and gardening?

Japanese garden

Linking Past and Present

1. How has Japan's possession of Heian and samurai values helped it to become a world leader in industry today?
2. Confucianism spread to many East and South Asian countries. How do Confucian values benefit these countries today?

Skill Practice

Read the passage below and answer the questions that follow.

> "Indian traders and scholars introduced to Southeast Asia the Sanskrit language and the religions of Hinduism and Buddhism. Indian epics such as the *Ramayana* were interwoven with Southeast Asian stories and legends. Indian architecture, law codes, and political ideas also deeply influenced the cultures of the region.... In A.D. 802 the Khmer people of Cambodia established a great Hindu-Buddhist empire.... Borrowing the Indian idea of kingship, Khmer rulers presented themselves as incarnations of the Hindu gods or as future Buddhas...."

1. What facts are presented about India's influence on Southeast Asia in general?
2. What generalization can you make based on these facts?

Understanding Themes

1. **Movement** The Mongols were able to conquer a vast territory, but their empire survived for a relatively short time. Provide a hypothesis that might explain this situation.
2. **Uniformity** What elements of Chinese society remained the same during the Tang, Song, and Yuan dynasties? What effect did this stability have on China's culture?
3. **Cultural Diffusion** What are some of the similarities between Southeast Asian cultures and Chinese culture?
4. **Innovation** Identify one Chinese discovery and explain some of the ways in which it has been used by the Chinese and others. Name things in our culture that derive from this innovation.

Geography in History

1. **Place** Refer to the map below. What river formed a natural border between China and the kingdom of Koguryo?
2. **Region** How did geography contribute to Korea's becoming known as the Hermit Kingdom?

Korea in the Three Kingdoms Period

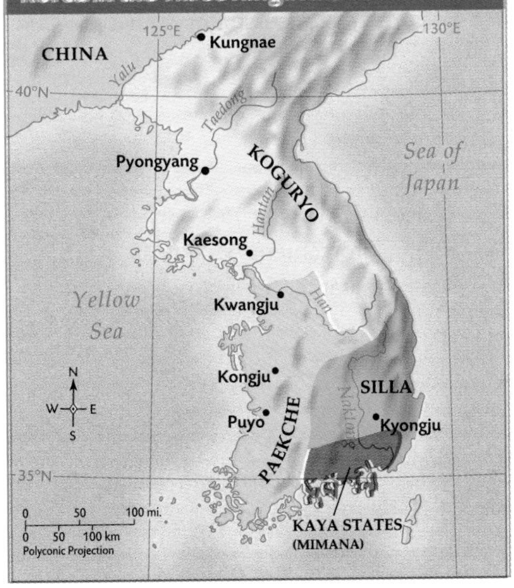

Chapter 14 Review

government, vigorous trade, highly developed art and science, and a common written language; stability meant that China's economy was able to flourish and its cultural life to thrive as a result.

3. **CULTURAL DIFFUSION** Confucian principles and use of civil service exams; systems of writing; arts, such as porcelain
4. **INNOVATION** Many possible answers. One might be the compass, used by Chinese mariners and later adopted throughout the world.

Geography in History

1. the Yalu
2. Because Korea is a peninsula, it had little contact with other peoples.

Chapter Bonus Test Question

Ask students: How does cultural diffusion today differ from what it was in the period covered by this chapter? *(Answers will vary but should make the point that today it is affected by sophisticated systems of communication and transportation and thus happens much more quickly.)*

stressing self-discipline and loyalty, may underlie Japanese work ethic.

2. Confucianism, with focus on deference for authority, inspires respect for teachers and supervisors. Many Asian businesses have educated and efficient workforces.

Skill Practice

1. India contributed Sanskrit, two religions, great epics, architecture, law codes, and political ideas.
2. Indian civilization profoundly influenced the region of Southeast Asia.

Understanding Themes

1. **MOVEMENT** Answers will vary; a possible hypothesis might be that they were skilled fighters but not good administrators, and so could not hold their domains together.
2. **UNIFORMITY** a strong central

Teach, Reinforce, and Extend CHAPTER Content

The Americas

CHAPTER RESOURCES

	Reproducible Resources	Multimedia Resources
Chapter Opener	Chapter Themes: Graphic Organizer 15 Historical Significance Chapter Activity 15	MindJogger Videoquiz
Chapter Enrichment	Vocabulary Activity 15* Time Line Activity 15 Mapping History Activity 15 History Simulation 15 Geography and History Activity 15 Source Reading 15 People in World History Profiles 27, 28 World Art and Music Activity 15 Enrichment Activity 15 Critical Thinking Activity 15 Skill Reinforcement Activity 15 Performance Assessment Activity 15	Focus on World Art Print 11 World History and Art Transparency 18, *Mola Stitchery*; 19, *Quilled Buckskin Robe* Chapter Transparency 15 NGS PicturePack Transparency Sets: *Ancient Central America, Ancient South America* Vocabulary PuzzleMaker Software NGS PictureShow CD-ROM: *The Americas* World Music: Cultural Traditions, Lessons 1, 2 STV: Maya
Chapter Review/Reteaching	Reteaching Activity 15 Skill Reinforcement Activity 15 Spanish Chapter Summary 15	Chapter 15 Digest Audiocassette, Activity, Test* Vocabulary PuzzleMaker Software Student Self-Test and Review Software MindJogger Videoquiz
Chapter Evaluation/Testing	Performance Assessment Activity 15 Chapter 15 Test, Forms A and B	Testmaker

* *Also available in Spanish*

0:00 **OUT OF TIME?** Assign the Chapter 15 summary in the Unit 3 Digest on pages 394–397, and the Chapter 15 Audiocassettes.

Block Schedule

Block scheduling differs from traditional class scheduling in the amount of time allotted to each period. The extended time frame provided by block scheduling affords you the opportunity to implement a greater number of research-oriented and activity-intense projects to motivate and involve your students. Activities that are particularly suited to use within the block scheduling framework are identified throughout this chapter by the following designation.

KEY TO ABILITY LEVELS

Teaching strategies have been coded for varying learning styles and abilities.

- L1 **BASIC** activities for all students
- L2 **AVERAGE** activities for average to above-average students
- L3 **CHALLENGING** activities for above-average students
- LEP **LIMITED ENGLISH PROFICIENCY** activities

Chapter 15 Planning Guide

A complete, 1-page lesson plan is provided for each section in the *Reproducible Lesson Plans* booklet.

SECTION RESOURCES

Daily Objectives	Reproducible Resources	Multimedia Resources
Section 1 The Early Americas Describe how early Native Americans made use of their environment.	Reproducible Lesson Plan 15-1 Vocabulary Activity 15* Guided Reading Activity 15-1* Time Line Activity 15 Section Quiz 15-1*	Section Focus Transparency 15-1 World History and Art Transparency 19, *Quilled Buckskin Robe* Chapter Transparency 15 NGS PicturePack Transparencies: Physical Geography of the World Student Self-Test and Review Software Testmaker World Music: Cultural Traditions, Lesson 1
Section 2 Early Mesoamerican Cultures Explain how trade encouraged the growth of city-states and king-doms in the areas of present-day Mexico and Central America.	Reproducible Lesson Plan 15-2 Vocabulary Activity 15* Guided Reading Activity 15-2* Section Quiz 15-2*	Focus on World Art Print 11, Mayan. *Presentation of Captives to a Maya Ruler* Section Focus Transparency 15-2 Student Self-Test and Review Software Testmaker World Music: Cultural Traditions, Lesson 2 STV: Maya
Section 3 The Aztec and Inca Empires List the factors that led to the rise and decline of the Aztec and Inca Empires.	Reproducible Lesson Plan 15-3 Guided Reading Activity 15-3* Reteaching Activity 15 Enrichment Activity 15 Section Quiz 15-3* Performance Assessment Activity 15 Spanish Chapter Summary 15	Section Focus Transparency 15-3 World History and Art Transparency 18, *Mola Stitchery* Vocabulary PuzzleMaker Software Student Self-Test and Review Software Testmaker World Music: Cultural Traditions, Lesson 2

** Also available in Spanish*

Chapter Activities

Performance Assessment Activity

A Travel Brochure Have students demonstrate their understanding of the concept of adaptation to environment by taking roles of travel agents or advertising executives who have been commissioned to develop a series of travel brochures to entice people to visit areas of North, Central, and South America. Students should work in groups of three to research what the lifestyle is like in each area today and how the people have adapted. They should use both modern-day attractions and historic sites in their brochures, including reasons for visiting each site.

Possible Rubric Features

Concept attainment, extent and accuracy of content information, organization and clarity of product, collaborative skills, research skills, elaboration and detail

• *For an additional activity, refer to Activity 15 in the* Performance Assessment Strategies and Activities *booklet.*

Activity

From the Classroom of...

Sandra Blackman
Dana Center
San Diego, CA

A Woman's Point of View

This activity allows students to experience Cortés's conquest of Mexico from the Mexican perspective and to understand the religious and political influences affecting the decline of the Aztec Empire. Have students read the short novel *The Legend of La Llorona* by Rodolfo Anaya, which tells the story of the Spanish conquest from the point of view of Malintzin, Cortés's interpreter and common-law wife whose actions played a significant role in the conquest.

As students read the novel, discuss some of the issues that arise: using religious belief to gain power; how oppressive rule hastens decline; historical truth vs. historical fiction; conflict of identity when two cultures meet; a woman's voice in history.

Have students write a letter from Malintzin to her friend in her village where she describes the burning of Cortés's ships, her participation in the march across Mexico into Tenochtitlán, the death of Montezuma, and the overthrow and enslavement of the Aztec people. In the letter have them answer the question: How does Malintzin explain the fall of the Aztec Empire?

MULTIPLE LEARNING STYLES

Verbal/Linguistic
Have students research the treatment of the young captive chosen by the Aztec each year to represent the god Tezcatlipoca. Have them keep a journal in which they record monthly entries by an imaginary captive during the year of captivity, culminating in the sacrifice.

Logical/Mathematical
Have students do further research on the complicated calendar used by the early Mesoamericans. Ask them to report to the class on the calendar's combination of a 260-day "year" with the 365-day solar year.

Visual/Spatial
Ask students to research several of the ruins of ancient Native American civilizations. Have them organize an album of photocopied photographs, including short captions describing each picture.

Kinesthetic
Have students design a set of illustrated cards for each of the North American cultures described in the first section. For each culture, include a card depicting geographical location, clothing, buildings and shelters, and crafts and weapons.

Additional Resources

TEACHER'S CORNER

NATIONAL GEOGRAPHIC SOCIETY

INDEX TO NATIONAL GEOGRAPHIC MAGAZINE

The following articles may be used for research relating to this chapter:

- "Maya Masterpiece Revealed at Bonampak," by Mary Miller, February 1995.
- "New Light on the Olmec," by George E. Stuart, November 1993.
- "The Violent Saga of a Maya Kingdom," by Arthur A. Demarest, February 1993.
- "Mural Masterpieces of Ancient Cacaxtla," by George E Stuart, September 1992.
- "Maya Artistry Unearthed," by Ricardo Agurcia Fasquelle, September 1991.
- "New Tomb of Royal Splendor," by Walter Alva, June 1990.
- "Masterworks of Art Reveal a Remarkable Pre-Inca World," by Christopher B. Donnan, June 1990.
- "Copán: A Royal Tomb Discovered," by Ricardo Agurcia Fasquelle, October 1989.
- "Discovering the New World's Richest Unlooted Tomb," by Walter Alva, October 1988.
- "El Mirador: An Early Maya Metropolis Uncovered," by Ray T. Matheny, September 1987.

NATIONAL GEOGRAPHIC SOCIETY PRODUCTS AVAILABLE FROM GLENCOE

To order the following products for use with this chapter, contact your local Glencoe sales representative or call Glencoe at 1-800-368-7344:

VIDEODISC
- STV: Maya

NGS PICTURESHOW CD-ROMS
- Native Americans 1: Eastern Woodlands, Plains
- Native Americans 2: Southwest, Northwest, Arctic
- The Americas

NGS PICTUREPACK TRANSPARENCY SETS
- Native Americans 1: Eastern Woodlands, Plains
- Native Americans 2: Southwest, Northwest, Arctic
- Ancient Central America
- Ancient South America
- Physical Geography of the World

ADDITIONAL NATIONAL GEOGRAPHIC SOCIETY PRODUCTS

To order the following products for use with this chapter, call National Geographic Society at 1-800-368-2728:

- *Digging Up America's Past*, "North America Before Columbus," "Middle America Before Cortés," "South America Before Pizzarro." (Filmstrip)
- *Lost Kingdoms of the Maya* (Video)

BIBLIOGRAPHY

Literature of the Period

Bierhorst, John, ed. ***The Hungry Woman: Myths and Legends of the Aztecs.*** New York: William Morrow, 1984. New versions of more than two dozen traditional tales, with illustrations by Aztec artists.

Readings for the Student

Suzuki, David, and Peter Knudtson. ***Wisdom of the Elders: Honoring Sacred Native Visions of Nature.*** New York: Bantam, 1992. Comparison of Native American beliefs about nature with modern environmental science.

Readings for the Teacher

Coe, Michael, Dean Snow and Elizabeth Benson. ***Atlas of Ancient America.*** New York: Facts on File, 1986. The history of ancient America presented in maps, text, and pictures.

*inter*NET CONNECTIONS

Native American Indian Resources Includes stories, native herbal knowledge, art, astronomy, and more. http://indy4.fdl.cc.mn.us/~isk/mainmenu.html

Introducing Chapter 15

CHAPTER THEMES

Chapter Themes are listed by section on this chapter opening page of the Student Edition. A corresponding theme-based activity is available under "TEACH," and a theme-based question is asked in the Section and Chapter Reviews.

The Storyteller

Historical Setting Inti, the sun god, was the chief deity of the Inca civilization. Farmers adored him for warming the Andean earth and making their crops mature. Inti, who was depicted with a human face on a disk with rays emanating from it, was revered as the divine ancestor of the Inca. The best known Inca temple is the Sun Temple in Cuzco, Peru, where the Inca established their capital in the twelfth century. Other Inca sun temples were built on Titicaca Island in Lake Titicaca and at Latacunga in Ecuador.

Historical Significance

Answers: *Native Americans developed agricultural techniques, religious beliefs, trading networks, and an understanding of astronomy and mathematics.*

The development of the Americas was shaped by the reliance of Native Americans on their environment.

Chapter 15

1500 B.C.–A.D. 1500

The Americas

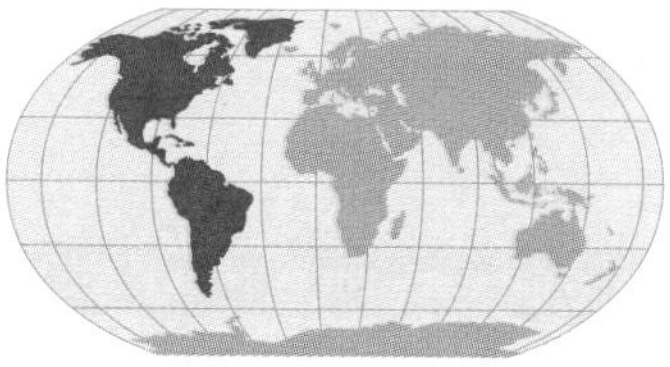

Chapter Themes

- **Relation to Environment** Native Americans in North America adapt to a variety of environments. *Section 1*
- **Innovation** The Mesoamerican civilizations develop an understanding of astronomy and mathematics. *Section 2*
- **Change** The Aztec and the Inca conquer neighboring territories and establish powerful empires in Mexico and South America. *Section 3*

The Storyteller

In the Andes Mountains of South America, an Inca boy begs to hear how the Inca came to be. "The sun was unhappy with the world," the storyteller begins, "for he saw people living like wild beasts among the mountains and cliffs. He decided to send his son and daughter to teach them to adore the sun as their god. He gave special instructions: 'Each day that passes I go around all the world … to satisfy [men's] needs. Follow my example: Do unto all of them as a merciful father would do unto his well-beloved children; for I have sent you on earth for the good of men, that they might cease to live like wild animals.'"

This legend describes what the Inca people believed about the beginnings of their empire. Close to nature and deeply religious, the Inca were only one of a number of Native American groups who built powerful civilizations in the Americas.

Historical Significance

What were the achievements of Native Americans? How did Native American traditions shape the development of the Americas?

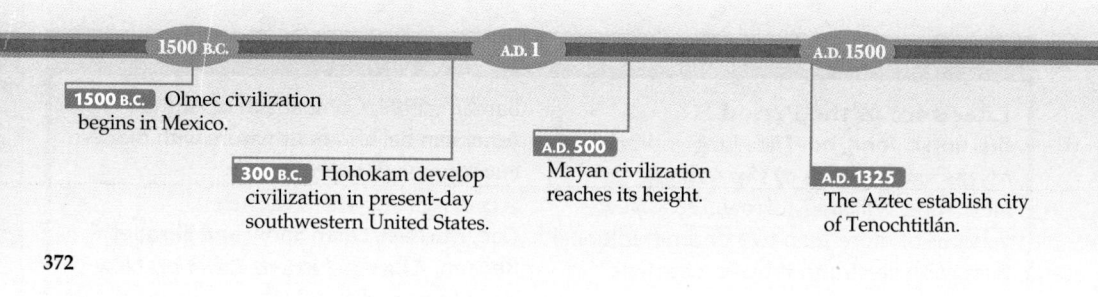

1500 B.C. — A.D. 1 — A.D. 1500

- **1500 B.C.** Olmec civilization begins in Mexico.
- **300 B.C.** Hohokam develop civilization in present-day southwestern United States.
- **A.D. 500** Mayan civilization reaches its height.
- **A.D. 1325** The Aztec establish city of Tenochtitlán.

372

GEOGRAPHY CONNECTION

Location Have students find North America and South America on a map and draw an outline of each continent on tracing paper. Have them look at the map on page 375, find and draw a heavy line around the corresponding area on their traced map, and label it *North American Cultures of the United States*. Next ask the class to draw a heavy line around Mexico, Guatemala, Belize, Honduras, and El Salvador. Tell them that about half of Mexico, all of Guatemala and Belize, and parts of Honduras and El Salvador are included in Mesoamerica, where a variety of civilizations flourished. Have them label this area *Mesoamerican Cultures*. Finally, have them draw a heavy line around Ecuador, Peru, and Bolivia and label this area *Inca Empire*.

History & Art *Afternoon,* a painting by Frank Reed Whiteside. David David Gallery, Philadelphia, Pennsylvania

Your History Journal

Using dates from section time lines and each section narrative, build a time line of important dates in Native American civilizations between 1500 B.C. and A.D. 1500.

EXTRA CREDIT PROJECT

Report and Storytelling In addition to their sun god, Inti, the Inca revered a creator god, Viracocha. Have students research the Inca creation myth and prepare a brief report comparing the Inca account of creation with the creation stories in Genesis and Greek mythology. Students should also be encouraged to present a storytelling session for the rest of the class in which they tell the Inca story of creation. Suggested resource: J. Bierhorst, ed., *Black Rainbow: Legends of the Incas and Myths of Ancient Peru.* **L2**

Introducing Chapter 15

History & Art Frank Reed Whiteside was a Philadelphia artist who visited the Zuni frequently up until 1928. From 1894–1896 he did a series of paintings of the Zuni, recording many aspects of their daily life. What characteristics of the pueblo does the painting suggest? *(The pueblo consisted of multiple structures with more than a single story.)*

Performance Assessment

Refer to the activity on page 372C of the Planning Guide.

For an additional activity, refer to Activity 15 in the *Performance Assessment Strategies and Activities* booklet.

Using Your History Journal

Students might wish to include maps with their time lines.

GLENCOE TECHNOLOGY

VIDEODISC

Use MindJogger to preview chapter content.

MindJogger Videoquiz

Chapter 15
Disc 2 Side B

Also available in VHS.

SECTION THEME

▶ **Relation to Environment** Native Americans in North America adapt to a variety of environments.

Find Out

Answer: *They developed diets, homes, and clothes based on the available natural resources.*

FOCUS

Section Objective

Describe how early Native Americans made use of their environment.

BELLRINGER Motivational Activity

Before taking roll at the beginning of the class period, project Section Focus Transparency 15-1 and have students answer the activity questions. Discuss students' responses.

This activity is also available as a blackline master.

Vocabulary Pre-check

Use Vocabulary Activity 15 to introduce vocabulary terms. **L1 LEP**

5000 B.C. — 2500 B.C. — A.D. 1 — A.D. 2500

c. 5000 B.C. Hunter-gatherers first plant maize in the highlands of Mexico.

c. 3000 B.C. Native Americans make use of stone axes and digging sticks for farming.

c. A.D. 1400 Eastern Woodland peoples form the Iroquois League.

Section 1

The Early Americas

Setting the Scene

▶ **Terms to Define**
maize, weir, potlatch, confederation

▶ **People to Meet**
the Kwakiutl, the Hohokam, the Pueblo, the Apache, the Navajo, the Plains peoples, Mound Builders

▶ **Places to Locate**
Mexico, Great Plains

Find Out How did early Native Americans make use of their environment?

The Storyteller

A Navajo tale describes the origin of the twelve months of the year: First Man and First Woman built a hogan in which to live. Turquoise Boy and White Shell Girl came from the underworld to live with them. "It is not unwise that we plan for the time to come, how we shall live," said First Man. First Woman and First Man whispered together during many nights. They planned that there should be a sun, and day and night. Whenever Coyote, called First Angry, came to make trouble and asked them what they were doing, they told him: "Nothing whatsoever." He said, "So I see," and went away. After he had gone, they planned the twelve months of the year.

—adapted from *The Portable North American Indian Reader*, edited by Frederick W. Turner III, 1974

Navajo rug

When did the earliest humans come to the Americas? Until recently, archaeologists believed that humans arrived in the Western Hemisphere about 12,000 years ago. The theory was that tribes migrated from Asia to North America, following herds of bison and other game across the then-exposed land bridge that today is the Bering Strait.

New evidence, however, challenges this old theory. Archaeologists working in North America and South America have found sites that indicate the presence of humans as early as 40,000 years ago. New theories argue that humans arrived in more than one migratory wave. Some early humans may also have traveled by boat along the Pacific coast from Siberia to Alaska, then to South America.

Once in the Western Hemisphere, the peoples dispersed throughout North America and South America. As they adapted to particular environments, they developed distinct ways of life. Some remained nomadic, while others settled and developed complex civilizations.

The First Americans

The hunter-gatherers who migrated to the Americas used the resources of their particular environment for basic needs of food, clothing, and shelter. If they lived near the ocean, people collected mussels and snails. Some groups fished in rivers and streams, while others hunted. Archaeologists have uncovered evidence of this life in artifacts found in coastal regions throughout the Americas. They have found rounded stones for grinding seeds, bone hooks for fishing, and heaps of snail and mussel shells at campsites.

By about 5000 B.C., a group of hunter-gatherers in a highland area of present-day **Mexico** had discovered that the seeds of maize, or corn, and other native plants could be planted and harvested, providing a reliable source of food. As this discovery

SECTION RESOURCES

Reproducible Masters
- Reproducible Lesson Plan 15-1
- Vocabulary Activity 15
- Guided Reading Activity 15-1
- Time Line Activity 15
- Section Quiz 15-1

Transparencies
- Section Focus Transparency 15-1
- World History and Art Transparency 19
- Chapter Transparency 15
- Physical Geography of the World Transparencies 2, 3, 4, 6, 8, 9

Multimedia
- Student Self-Test and Review Software
- Testmaker
- World Music: Cultural Traditions, Lesson 1

spread from Mexico into the southwestern United States, groups of early people began to settle in permanent villages. About 3000 B.C. farmers made use of stone axes to clear their fields and pointed digging sticks to plant improved varieties of maize, beans, and squash.

As the food supply improved, the population of the Americas grew. By the time Europeans arrived in North America around A.D. 1500, about 30 million to 100 million Native Americans belonging to more than 2,000 different groups were inhabiting the two continents. About 15 to 20 million of these early inhabitants lived in the present-day United States and various parts of Canada.

Map Study Many of the first people to inhabit North America lived near the seacoast or made their homes in river valleys.
Place Why did Native Americans choose to settle in those locations?

North Americans

Much of what we know about the early people of northern North America comes from the work of archaeologists. Archaeological digs have uncovered homes, burial mounds, pottery, baskets, stone tools, and the bones of people and animals in the Arctic and Northwest, California and the Great Basin, the Southwest, the Great Plains, and the Eastern Woodlands. By studying these artifacts, archaeologists discovered that there were distinct regional differences. People who settled in a particular region developed a common culture. Gradually the arts and crafts and religious customs of each region grew to be distinct from those of other regions, a pattern historians call cultural differentiation. In each region, culture reflected the local geography and natural resources.

The Arctic and Northwest

The early people of the Arctic lived in the cold northern regions of present-day Canada and Alaska. The severe climate of this region prohibited farming. Thus, small bands of extended families moved about, hunting and fishing. By 6500 B.C. some Arctic people were living in small villages of pit houses, covered with dome-shaped roofs of whalebone and driftwood. Villagers hunted whales, sea lions, seals, and water birds. They ate the meat and used the skins to make warm, protective clothing.

In contrast to the cold and snow of the Arctic, the thickly forested seacoast of the Pacific Northwest had a milder climate. Rainfall was plentiful, and mild winters and warm ocean currents kept rivers and bays free of ice. Like the people of the Arctic, those who settled along the Pacific Coast—**the Kwakiutl**, for example—hunted whales, fish, and other sea animals as their main source of food. Forests of the Northwest provided additional sources of food—small forest animals and acorns. After about A.D. 500 the people of the Northwest used other resources from the surrounding forests

TEACH

Guided Practice

THEME Relation to Environment Using the map on this page, ask students how the climatic conditions differed for the various North American cultures. *(Arctic and Far North: long winters with subzero temperatures; Northwest: mild winters and a cool, rainy climate much of the year; California Great Basin: warm, mild climate, with rivers making farming possible for most of year; Southwest: dry, desert climate, making farming more difficult; Great Plains: hot summers, very cold winters; Eastern Woodlands: temperate climate)* **L1**

Religion Some Native Americans (Pueblo, Chumash) created community ceremonies to ensure harmony between themselves and the spiritual world. Others (Mound Builders) had burial practices ensuring that the deceased would live on in the afterlife. Ask students to write a two-page description of the practices presented in this section, pointing out why harmonious relations with the spiritual world were so important to these people. **L3**

Map Study

Answer

Rivers and coastal areas provided a supply of fish that people used for food. River valleys and coastlands also provided good land for farming. People living in these areas could use boats for travel and trade.

Map Skills Practice

Reading a Map What two natural boundaries marked the region of the Great Plains people? *(Rocky Mountains, Mississippi River)*

COOPERATIVE LEARNING ACTIVITY

Bulletin Board Organize the class into five groups, corresponding to the five different regions inhabited by native North Americans. Ask each group to select one of the peoples identified in the text as living in "their" region. Have them research and prepare a bulletin-board display on that people, highlighting aspects of daily life and customs. Among the topics students should consider are layout of villages and buildings, the development of crafts, food-gathering techniques, and religious ceremonies. Each group member should have a specific role to play in preparing the display. **L1 LEP**

Chapter 15 Section 1

World History and Art Transparency 19, *Quilled Buckskin Robe*

Chapter Transparency 15

World Music: Cultural Traditions, Lesson 1

NATIONAL GEOGRAPHIC SOCIETY

TRANSPARENCIES

PHYSICAL GEOGRAPHY OF THE WORLD

Display the following to enrich student understanding of Native American environments.

2. Sonoran Desert, U.S.
3. Rocky Mountains, Canada
4. Grand Canyon, U.S.
6. Mississippi River, U.S.
8. Baffin Island, Canada
9. Appalachian Mountains, U.S.

Independent Practice

Guided Reading Activity 15-1 **L1**

Time Line Activity 15

Economics Although Native American cultures did not use a formal monetary system, some used other objects like we use money today. Have students investigate the use of tooth shells by the Native Americans of California and the Northwest Coast and of shell beads by those of eastern North America. *(Seashells, sometimes called* dentalia, *were divided into five sizes according to length, with the longest having the highest value. Wampum, a combination of purple and white beads made from shells, strung into necklaces or belts, served both as money and as a record-keeping device.)* **L1**

and rivers. With stone and copper woodworking tools they split cedar, fir, and redwood trees into planks to make houses and large canoes. They also developed ways to harvest salmon with fiber nets, stone-tipped spears, and elaborate wooden traps called **weirs**.

Society among the Kwakiutl and other Northwest peoples was organized into lineages, each of which claimed to be descended from a mythical ancestor. A lineage group lived together in a single large house and owned the right to use or display special designs, songs, ceremonies, or prized possessions, such as patterned sheets of copper. A lineage maintained exclusive use of its own fishing area and berry-picking grounds. The wealth of each lineage was displayed and given away as gifts at festive gatherings called **potlatches**. At a potlatch a chief might give away canoes, blankets, and other goods. In turn, guests might bring the chief deerskins and food.

To obtain items they themselves could not make, some people of the Northwest developed trading networks with people living farther south. Traders paddled redwood canoes along the coast, stopping at villages along the shore to exchange goods. Trade networks stretched from southern Alaska to northern California.

California–Great Basin

Native Americans living along the California coast enjoyed a warm climate and an abundance of food resources. Many communities lived on diets of abalone and mussels. Near San Francisco Bay, archaeologists have found evidence of this diet in heaps of discarded shells that date from 2000 B.C. In addition to shellfish, the first Californians fished for sea bass, hunted seals, and gathered berries and nuts. Having such abundant resources made food gathering easier for the people living in this region.

Like other Native Americans, they developed elaborate religious ceremonies designed to worship nature spirits believed to inhabit all of the natural world, but especially those spirits related to animals or plants used for food. The Chumash, who

Images of the Times

Native Americans

A variety of peoples have inhabited North America for thousands of years. Some mysteries of the earliest cultures have yet to be revealed.

Georgia's Etowa Mounds sheltered these two-foot high marble images of a man and a woman more than 500 years ago.

376

Images of the Times **Mound Builders**

Native American mounds are found from the Great Lakes to the Gulf of Mexico, and from the Mississippi to the Appalachians. A number of different peoples built mounds over a period spanning hundreds of years. The mounds varied widely in size, shape, and function. Some cover more than 100 acres (40.5 hectares). Others were modest in size. In addition to the serpent-shaped mound shown here, there is one in Wisconsin shaped like an elephant. Other mounds were round; still others long and wall-like.

While many mounds were used as burial places, others served as foundations for temples or as fortresses. The purpose of some mounds, such as the Serpent Mound, is not clear.

lived in the area of present-day southern California, would gather together at harvest festivals to celebrate the goodness of the earth. Villagers participated in dances and games.

Compared with those living along the coast, people living farther inland scratched their living from a harsh desert and mountain environment. Great Basin people moved about in small bands, living in windbreak shelters and eating seeds, grasshoppers, and small animals.

Southwest

People who settled in the high desert regions of present-day Arizona, New Mexico, southern Colorado and Utah, and northern Mexico had fewer resources than those who settled along the Pacific Coast. Nevertheless, the people of the Southwest adapted to their harsh environment by inventing techniques of irrigation to farm the land. For example, around 300 B.C., **the Hohokam** living in the area of present-day Arizona dug an irrigation canal 3 miles (4.8 km) long to draw the waters of the Gila and Salt Rivers onto fields planted with maize, kidney beans, and squash.

Farther north, a group of Southwest people known as **the Pueblo** grew maize in fields terraced like a series of stair steps to check the erosion of topsoil caused by heavy late summer rains. The Pueblo employed a style of building that used adobe, a sun-dried brick easy to produce under desert conditions. The Pueblo often built their villages under ledges on the sides of cliffs to shade residents from the desert sun and to make the villages easier to defend.

Religious leaders governed Pueblo villages. They led religious ceremonies to ensure harmony between humans and the spiritual world. The Pueblo believed that if harmony existed, the spirits would provide small game and rain for crops.

Another Southwest group known as **the Apache** lived in areas that were unsuitable for farming. They hunted wild birds and rabbits and gathered plants. Sometimes they raided Pueblo fields; other times they traded meat and hides with

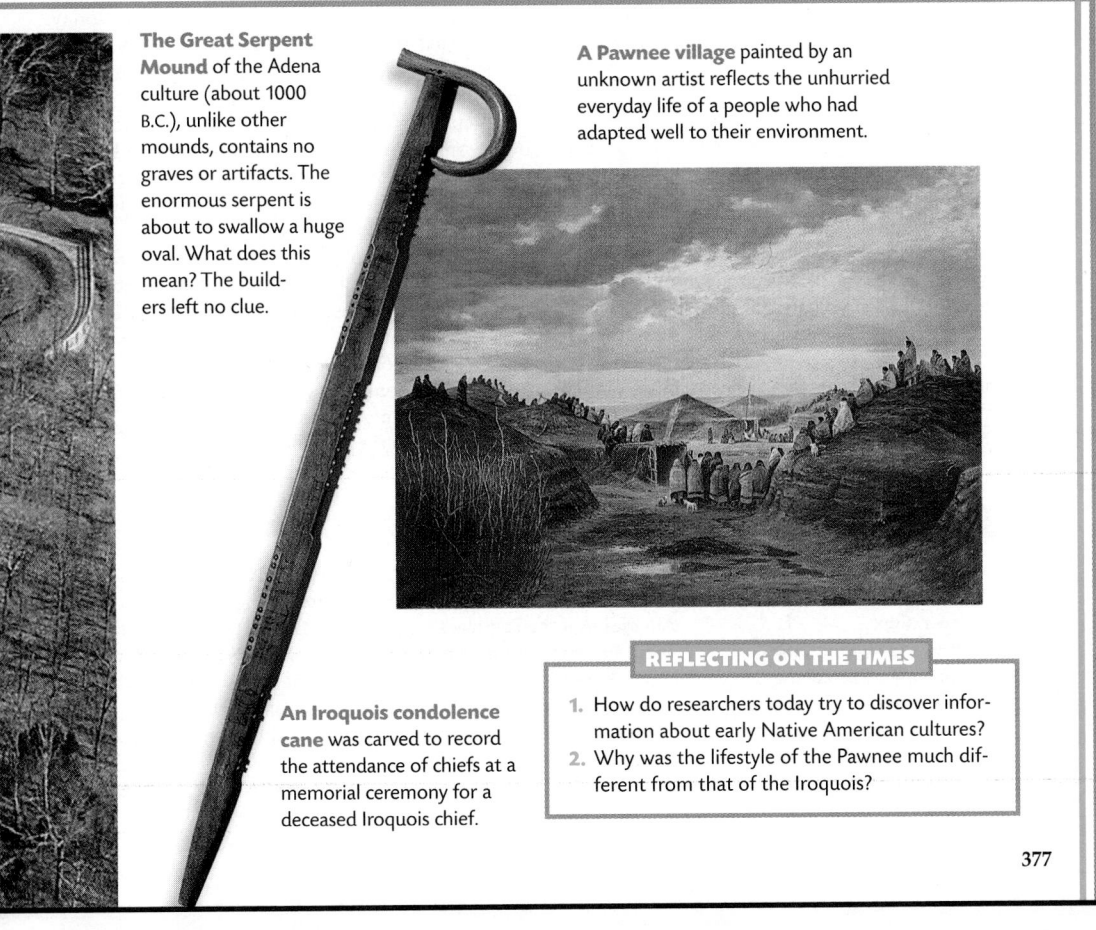

The Great Serpent Mound of the Adena culture (about 1000 B.C.), unlike other mounds, contains no graves or artifacts. The enormous serpent is about to swallow a huge oval. What does this mean? The builders left no clue.

A Pawnee village painted by an unknown artist reflects the unhurried everyday life of a people who had adapted well to their environment.

An Iroquois condolence cane was carved to record the attendance of chiefs at a memorial ceremony for a deceased Iroquois chief.

REFLECTING ON THE TIMES

1. How do researchers today try to discover information about early Native American cultures?
2. Why was the lifestyle of the Pawnee much different from that of the Iroquois?

ANSWERS TO REFLECTING ON THE TIMES

1. by conducting digs and studying the artifacts and bones they uncover
2. The plains environment of the Pawnee was very different from the temperate woodland environment of the Iroquois.

Chapter 15 Section 1

Literature Have students find one or two examples of Native American poetry and stories in the library and share a reading of one with the class. Ask them to explain its purpose in the culture, such as its use in religious ceremonies or celebrations. **L2**

Science Have students research the Bighorn Medicine Wheel in Wyoming and the Anasazi sun dagger in New Mexico and summarize their findings. *(Both show sophisticated understanding of motions of sun and moon.)* **L3**

you don't say...

"Mississippi," the name of the principal river of the United States, comes from an Algonquian word meaning "big river."

Linking Past and Present

Lacrosse, a soccerlike ball game, developed from a war-training exercise called "baggataway" by Native Americans living in today's Canada. The original game was violent, with few rules, and sometimes involved as many as a thousand warriors. Today the game uses 10 players on a men's lacrosse team and 12 on a women's team.

ASSESS

Check for Understanding

Assign Section 1 Review as homework or as an in-class activity.

Use Student Self-Test and Review Software to review Section 1.

Chapter 15
Section 1

Visualizing History Have students design their own totem to either reflect their family history or to show what is important to them. **Answer to Caption:** *in the Iroquois League*

Evaluate

Section Quiz 15-1

Use the Testmaker to create a customized quiz for Section 1.

Reteach

Ask students to outline the section, emphasizing the parallel development of the different Native American cultures.

Enrich

Native Americans made use of plants as health aids, as well as for food and clothing. Have students research the plants Native Americans used for medicinal purposes. Recommend that they use a variety of library resources: encyclopedias, nature magazines, and nonfiction works on medicine or plants.

CLOSE

Conduct a class discussion on how geographic location affects culture. Ask students to give examples from the text and their outside reading. Have them focus on customs, housing styles, clothing, or food preparation that depended on specific resources.

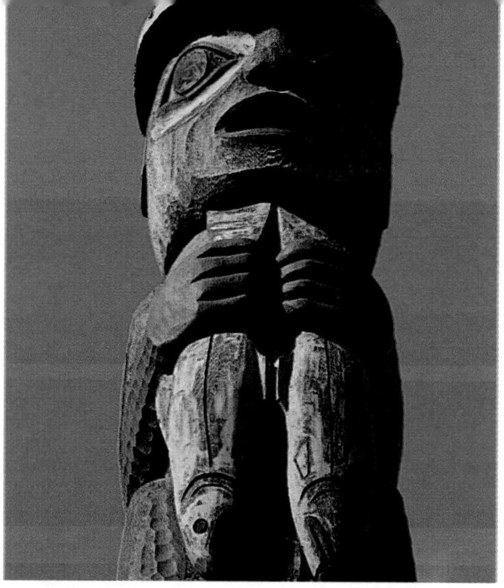

Visualizing History **In the Northwest a totem represented a bond of unity and was the symbol and protector of the group.** *How were Native Americans in the Northeast organized?*

Pueblo villagers for maize and other food supplies. A neighboring people, **the Navajo**, did manage to raise a breed of sheep that could live on the sparse desert vegetation.

Great Plains

In contrast to the sparse Southwestern environment, vast grasslands covered the **Great Plains**, stretching from the Rocky Mountains to the Mississippi River. This environment provided a different challenge for the early people who inhabited the region. Native Americans adapting to life on the plains needed a reliable source of food. Farming in the region was difficult, as the thick plains sod was hard to plow. Moreover, maize needs more water than is naturally available on most parts of the Great Plains.

Although some farming was done along streams, most of **the Plains peoples** depended on one abundant resource—the great herds of bison, or buffalo, that roamed the plains. From earliest times, the Kiowa, Crow, Blackfoot, and other peoples of the plains followed the herds from one grazing ground to another. They used every part of the bison for their food, clothing, shelter, and tools.

Eastern Woodlands

Unlike the Plains peoples who depended on the bison, Native Americans of the woodlands east of the Mississippi River hunted a large variety of animals. Deer, turkeys, geese, and squirrels were common in Eastern forests. Like the Plains peoples, Eastern Woodlands peoples made use of every part of the animals they killed. They ate deer meat, wore deerskin clothing, and made tools out of animal bones and antlers. Since summers were warm, rainfall abundant, and soil fertile throughout most of the Eastern Woodlands, the people of this region lived in farming villages and grew crops such as corn, squash, beans, and tobacco.

In the Ohio and Mississippi Valleys, groups of Native Americans known as **Mound Builders** erected large earthen mounds. Archaeologists today believe that the mounds were used as ceremonial centers or as tombs for leaders. A number of mounds were made in the shape of animals.

Native Americans living in the northeastern part of the present-day United States had a high level of political organization compared with the peoples of the plains and the Southwest. Around A.D. 1500 the Cayuga, Mohawk, Oneida, Onondaga, and Seneca formed the Iroquois League—a confederation, or loose union of groups. A council of representatives from each group discussed and resolved disputes among its members. The Iroquois League predated the formation of United States representative government by more than 200 years. When Europeans invaded Native American land, they met strong resistance from the Iroquois League.

SECTION 1 REVIEW

Recall

1. **Define** maize, weir, potlatch, confederation.
2. **Identify** the Kwakiutl, the Hohokam, the Pueblo, the Apache, the Navajo, the Plains peoples, Mound Builders, Iroquois League.
3. **Describe** how new methods of farming helped Native Americans of the Southwest adapt to living in a dry climate.

Critical Thinking

4. **Analyzing Information** Compare the structure of the Iroquois League with that of the United States government.

Understanding Themes

5. **Relation to Environment** How did Native American peoples within the seven regions of North America depend on their environment and natural resources?

SECTION 1 REVIEW ANSWERS

1. All vocabulary words are defined in the Glossary.
2. Kwakiutl, 375; Hohokam, 377; Pueblo, 377; Plains, 378; Mound Builders, 378; Iroquois League, 378
3. Irrigation canals channeled river water to fields; terraced fields controlled erosion.
4. Each group in the Iroquois League sent representatives to a council; each state in the United States sends elected representatives to Congress.
5. **RELATION TO ENVIRONMENT** Students should give specific examples in their answers.

500 B.C. — A.D. 500 — A.D. 1500

- **c. 400 B.C.** Olmec civilization declines.
- **c. A.D. 300** The Maya begin to expand their territory.
- **c. A.D. 800** Mayan civilization begins to decline.

Section 2

Early Mesoamerican Cultures

Setting the Scene

- **Terms to Define**
  jaguar, slash-and-burn farming, obsidian
- **People to Meet**
  the Olmec, the Maya, the Teotihuacános, the Toltec
- **Places to Locate**
  San Lorenzo, La Venta, Yucatán Peninsula, Teotihuacán, Tula

Find Out How did trade encourage the growth of city-states and kingdoms in the areas of present-day Mexico and Central America?

The Storyteller

How did the world begin? According to Mayan myth, "All was in suspense, all calm, in silence; all motionless, still.... There was nothing standing; only the calm water, the placid sea, alone and tranquil. Nothing existed. There was only silence in the darkness, in the night. Only the Creator[s] were there. By nature they were great thinkers. They decided: when day dawned for the first time, the human being must appear. Thus they spoke. "Let there be light, let there be dawn in the sky and on the earth."

—adapted from *Sources of World History*, edited by Mark A. Kishlansky, 1995

Chichén Itzá temple figure

Between 1500 B.C. and A.D. 1200, a series of sophisticated civilizations emerged in the areas of present-day Mexico, Guatemala, Honduras, El Salvador, and Belize. Amid volcanic mountains, cool valleys, dense rain forests, and dry forested plains, early farmers developed methods that produced plentiful harvests and supported large populations. Maize was their basic crop.

Ruins of ancient cities reveal an astonishing way of life. Ideas from earlier civilizations were adopted and modified by later ones. Although each culture had unique features, they shared common elements. Archaeologists have labeled them together as Mesoamerican civilizations. The prefix *meso-* means "middle" and refers to the fact that these people lived in the middle land area that joins North America and South America. Descendants of the early Mesoamericans continue to live in this region and maintain many of their early traditions.

The Olmec

About 150 years before Tutankhamen ruled Egypt, **the Olmec** emerged as the earliest Mesoamerican civilization. Between 1500 B.C. and 400 B.C., the Olmec flourished in the swampy, lowland river valleys near the Gulf of Mexico. Our knowledge of the Olmec way of life and Olmec beliefs has come primarily from excavations of two principal Olmec sites, **San Lorenzo** and **La Venta**, discovered in the late 1930s. Until then, Olmec culture had been buried by centuries of accumulated layers of earth and rain forest.

Among the objects unearthed at San Lorenzo and La Venta were enormous stone heads carved from basalt, a volcanic rock. Some were more than 9 feet (2.7 m) tall and weighed as much as 40 tons.

Chapter 15 Section 2

SECTION THEME

- **Innovation** The Mesoamerican civilizations develop an understanding of astronomy and mathematics.

Find Out

Answer: *City-states and kingdoms grew up around trading centers.*

FOCUS

Section Objective

Explain how trade encouraged the growth of city-states and kingdoms in the areas of present-day Mexico and Central America.

BELLRINGER Motivational Activity

Before taking roll at the beginning of the class period, project Section Focus Transparency 15-2 and have students answer the activity questions. Discuss students' responses.

This activity is also available as a blackline master.

Vocabulary Pre-check

Use Vocabulary Activity 15 to introduce vocabulary terms. **L1 LEP**

SECTION RESOURCES

Reproducible Masters
- Reproducible Lesson Plan 15-2
- Vocabulary Activity 15
- Guided Reading Activity 15-2
- Section Quiz 15-2

Transparencies
- Section Focus Transparency 15-2

Multimedia
- Focus on World Art Print 11
- Student Self-Test and Review Software
- Testmaker
- World Music: Cultural Traditions, Lesson 2
- STV: Maya

Chapter 15
Section 2

TEACH

Guided Practice

THEME **Innovation**

Ask students to make a written list of the innovations of the Olmec, the Maya, the Teotihuacános, and the Toltec. Ask volunteers to read their lists and have the class point out any omissions. **L1**

Visualizing History The Olmec produced distinctive sculptures that are a combination of jaguars and human infants. Evidently the Olmec believed that in the distant past a union between a woman and a jaguar had produced a race of mythical creatures. What is distinctive about the head of the statue? *(It is cleft at the top; this is a typical feature of Olmec sculptures of mythical creatures.)*
Answer to Caption: *Jade carvings, figurines, and carved stone murals led them to make that inference.*

Economics Mayan farmers produced large surplus crops of maize that they brought to market to trade for other goods made by craftspeople. Ask students to explain what made Mayan trade successful. *(The Maya had trade routes throughout Mexico and Central America; merchants traveled by road, river, and sea.)* **L1**

Focus on World Art Print 11, Mayan. *Presentation of Captives to a Maya Ruler*

World Music: Cultural Traditions, Lesson 2

Visualizing History **This jade ceremonial ax in the form of a feline monster is from the pre-Columbian Olmec culture.** *Why do archaeologists believe that religion played an important role in Olmec life?*

These heads are believed to be portraits of rulers, and may have been part of larger monuments. Without the aid of wheels or beasts of burden, but perhaps using river rafts, the Olmec had moved the heads some 60 miles (97 km) from the mountains to the sites where they were discovered.

Evidence suggests that San Lorenzo and La Venta each had populations of only about 1,000 at their peak. Yet there was clearly organization, planning, and a division of labor. A hilltop at San Lorenzo was sheared off to create a central plaza for market and ceremonial purposes. Stone drains were built to direct water during the rainy season. Early forms of hieroglyphic writings were developed as well as an early calendar.

From jade carvings, figurines, and carved stone murals, archaeologists infer that religion played an important role in the lives of the Olmec. Many carvings show the Olmec god, a being with a human body and the catlike face of a jaguar, the large spotted wild cat that roamed the region. The Olmec believed the jaguar-god controlled their harvests.

Early Olmec farmers practiced what is known as slash-and-burn farming. To clear land, farmers cut down trees, let them dry, and then burned them. They planted maize among the fertile ashes. Since the soil became exhausted after a few years, farmers shifted fields and repeated the cycle on other lands.

Trade with other parts of Mesoamerica was common. Olmec artifacts have been found throughout the region, and Olmec ideas were echoed in later Mesoamerican civilizations.

The Maya

As early as 900 B.C., **the Maya** began to settle the **Yucatán Peninsula** of present-day Mexico. Mayan civilization reached its peak between A.D. 300 and A.D. 900. Mayan ruins can be found throughout the region in diverse terrains: highlands, lowlands, and coastal plains. The Maya adapted to their various environments, developing different farming practices, languages, and governments. The Maya were not unified in one empire. Instead, the patchwork of city-states and kingdoms were linked by culture, political ties, and trade.

Religion

Religion was at the center of Mayan life. The Maya believed in two levels of existence. One level was the daily physical life they lived. The second level was the Otherworld, a spiritual world peopled with gods, the souls of ancestors, and other supernatural creatures. The two levels were closely intertwined. Actions on each level could influence the other. Mayan myths explained the workings of this world and the Otherworld.

Mayan kings were spiritual leaders as well as political leaders. They were responsible for their people's understanding of the Otherworld and for their behaving in ways that would keep the gods pleased. Rulers performed rituals and ceremonies to satisfy the gods. In their great cities, the Maya constructed plazas, temples, and huge pyramids—symbolically sacred mountains—where thousands of people could gather for special religious ceremonies and festivals.

Images on Mayan temples, sacred objects, and pottery provide clues about Mayan beliefs and practices. The maize god, Chac, appears frequently. Images depict other gods in the form of trees, jaguars, birds, monkeys, serpents, reptiles, fish, and shells. Mythical creatures that combine parts of several animals are also shown.

COOPERATIVE LEARNING ACTIVITY

Chart Organize the class into five groups, corresponding to the five subheadings in the section covering the Maya. Distribute a large sheet of poster board to each group. The groups should use the poster board to display information about their subheading that is not found in the text. Each group should select a coordinator responsible for assigning specific tasks to every group member. When each group has filled in its piece of poster board with additional information, mount the display so that it forms a comprehensive chart presenting information on Mayan culture. One member of each group should present its findings to the rest of the class. **L2**

Blood symbols also appear. Human sacrifices and bloodletting rituals were part of Mayan practice. These ceremonies were considered important to appease the gods and to maintain and renew life.

Some festivals also included a ceremonial ball game called *pok-a-tok*. For this game, the Maya invented the use of solid rubber balls about the size of basketballs. Players wearing protective padding batted the balls back and forth across a walled court. These games recalled games played by mythical Mayan heroes.

Sciences

Like the ancient Greeks, the Maya believed that the movements of the sun, moon, and planets were journeys of gods across the sky. Since the gods controlled nature—including harvests—charting the movements of the celestial bodies was essential.

To do this charting, Mayan priests became excellent mathematicians and astronomers. The Maya built on the earlier work of the Olmec. The Maya developed a system of mathematics using the base 20. They used three symbols to represent numbers. A dot stood for the number one; a bar was five; and a shell figure symbolized zero. Rather than expressing place value with the highest place to the left, the Maya expressed their numbers vertically with the largest place at the top. The Maya also developed accurate calendars, a 260-day sacred calendar and another 360-day calendar. The calendars were used to predict eclipses, schedule religious ceremonies, and determine times to plant and harvest.

Economy

The Mayan economy was based on agriculture and trade. In addition to maize, farmers grew beans, squash, pumpkins, chili peppers, and tomatoes. Slash-and-burn farming continued in some areas. Elsewhere the Maya produced larger harvests by intensively farming raised plots surrounded by canals.

Perhaps as often as every five days, farmers brought surplus crops to the open-air markets of the major cities. Maize and other produce was traded for cotton cloth, jade ornaments, pottery, fish, deer meat, and salt.

Mayan merchants participated in long-distance trade throughout Mexico and Central America. Traders transported their cargoes by canoes on rivers and coastal waterways. Overland, goods were carried by humans, for wheeled vehicles and beasts of burden to haul them were unknown.

CONNECTIONS — The Arts

Mayan Monuments

Mayan temple-pyramids were the religious and political centers of Mayan cities. Built of stone, these vast stepped structures were mainly platforms for religious ceremonies. Stone temples at the summit of the pyramids were erected to memorialize dead rulers by associating them with the gods. Religious sacrifices conducted by priests took place outside the temple on top of the pyramid platform.

Archaeologists believe the stepped levels of the pyramids may have represented the harmonious layers of the universe. Mayan astronomers and priests held high administrative positions. Much of a priest's power was in his ability to predict the movements of stars and planets. Thus, a priest would consult with astronomers before major battles or projects were undertaken to see when the heavens would favor such actions.

Further evidence of the Mayan concern with astronomy and proper timing appears in pyramid inscriptions. Carvings found on them often record important dates in the lives of rulers—for example, a ruler's birth date, the date he began his reign, and dates of military victories.

MAKING THE CONNECTION

1. What purpose did the Mayan temple-pyramids serve?
2. How might you compare the Mayan temple-pyramids with public buildings today?

Chapter 15 Section 2

NATIONAL GEOGRAPHIC SOCIETY

VIDEODISC
STV: Maya

Side 1
Frames 00002-34603
Title: *Who Were the Ancient Maya?*
Subject: Exploration and scientific excavation of Copán in an effort to rebuild
Ask: What lands did the Maya once occupy? *(Honduras, Guatemala, El Salvador, Belize, and Mexico)*

Independent Practice

Guided Reading Activity 15-2 **L1**

Daily Life Have students read the article on Teotihuacán in the December 1995 *NATIONAL GEOGRAPHIC*. Ask them to summarize some of the recent discoveries about that city that surprised archaeologists. **L2**

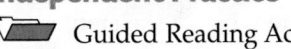

CONNECTIONS — The Arts

Mayan Monuments

Ruined ancient Mayan monuments can still be viewed in such sites as Uxmal, 50 miles south of modern Mérida, Yucatán state, Mexico; Chichén Itzá, in south central Yucatán state; and Tikal, in the northwestern part of the department of Petén, Guatemala.

Answers to Making the Connection

1. *platforms for religious ceremonies*
2. *Public buildings today are political, but not religious, centers of modern cities.*

MEETING SPECIAL NEEDS ACTIVITY

Learning Style: Visual/Spatial Help students distinguish among the cultures described in this section by asking them to draw pictures representing each one. Guide students through the text to make sure they select appropriate images for each culture, such as huge stone heads or jaguar sculptures for the Olmec, ballplayers or pyramids for the Maya, a sharp-edged tool for the Teotihuacános, and a feathered serpent for the Toltec. Students may also use outside sources. **L1 LEP**

TEACH

Tell students that the Mayan ball game was called *pok-a-tok*. The game, which originated not with the Maya but with the Olmec or possibly even earlier, was widespread throughout Mesoamerica, where it was called *ollama*. The ball court, or *tlachtli*, was shaped like a capital I. Oriented in a north-south or east-west direction, the court represented the heavens. Ask students what the ball in the picture resembles. *(the sun or another celestial object)* The serious nature of the sport is especially obvious in art decorating one of the several ball courts of El Tajin in eastern Mexico. Carvings on this court depict scenes in which a skeleton, representing the god of death, observes two men dressed in players' padded clothing.

CURRICULUM CONNECTION

ARCHAEOLOGY

In the early sixteenth century, Spanish explorers in western Honduras near the Guatemalan border discovered the ruins of Copán, an ancient Mayan city. Between 1936 and 1950, archaeologists from the United States and Honduras worked on the ruins. Among the restored sites is a court for playing *pok-a-tok*.

NATIONAL GEOGRAPHIC PICTURING HISTORY

Serious Sport

In this illustration of an ancient Mayan game a rubber ball bounces off the leather pad on the player's chest. The object was to drive the ball through a stone ring, but players could not throw or bat the ball. They had to hit it off a leather pad on their elbow, wrist, torso, or hip. Making a goal was so rare that when a player scored, crowds rewarded the hero with all their clothing and jewelry—unless they could first flee.

Scholars believe that these games were played nc only for sport but also on special holidays as ritu reenactments of Mayan raids. Large cities containe numerous walled courts lined with images of warfar and sacrificial victims. According to Mayan religiou beliefs, ordinary humans could never outwit deatl and so the Mayan ball court became a symbolic mee ing ground—a kind of threshold between earth an the underworld.

Writings

The Maya were one of the first Native American peoples to develop a writing system. They wrote in accordion-folded books made of flattened bark covered with a thin layer of plaster. Four of these books have survived. They also carved inscriptions in clay, and on jade, bone, shells, and large stone monuments. Only within the past 25 years have linguists made major breakthroughs in translating Mayan writing. Linguists discovered that some inscriptions are phonetic syllables, while others represent full words. The Maya recorded the genealogy of their kings and royal families, mythology, history, ritual practices, and trade.

Collapse

By A.D. 900 the Maya in the lowlands showed signs of collapse. They stopped building and moved elsewhere. Why this happened is unclear. There is evidence of increasing conflict and warfare among Mayan royal and nonroyal families. Outsiders were also attacking. Agricultural breakdown, perhaps caused by warfare or by erosion and over-farming, may have produced rising malnutrition, sickness, and death rates.

Visualizing History **The Teotihuacáno rain god Tlaloc is shown in an *incensario* (container for burning incense) from A.D. 400–700.** *Where was the Teotihuacáno civilization located?*

Other Mesoamericans

In a high fertile valley 30 miles (48 km) northeast of present-day Mexico City, **the Teotihuacános** (TAY•oh•TEE•wuh•KAHN•ohs) flourished for about 750 years. By A.D. 100, they dominated the centrally located Mexican Plateau. At its height their main city, **Teotihuacán**, had an estimated 120,000 to 200,000 inhabitants.

Teotihuacán was laid out on a grid. The most important buildings were built along the north-south axis. Excavations of the ruins have revealed 600 pyramids, 2,000 apartment compounds, 500 workshop areas, and a huge marketplace. A valuable source of obsidian was found near Teotihuacán. **Obsidian**, a volcanic glass, was used for sharp-edged tools, arrow points, and other objects. It was easily traded, because Teotihuacán lay on the trade routes east to the Gulf of Mexico.

Teotihuacán declined about A.D. 750. Historians still are uncertain about the reasons for its decline. Drought may have been the cause, or invasion by **the Toltec**, a people from the north.

With a powerful army, the Toltec conquered land as far south as the Yucatán Peninsula. The Toltec capital of **Tula** was the center of a powerful mining and trading empire. Their gods Quetzalcoatl (ket•suhl•KWAH•tuhl), the "plumed serpent" god of the air, and Tezcatlipoca (tehz•KAHT•lee•POH•kuh), the god of war, would be adopted by the Aztec, a later Mesoamerican group. When invaders destroyed Tula in A.D. 1170, the Toltec Empire collapsed.

SECTION 2 REVIEW

Recall

1. **Define** jaguar, slash-and-burn farming, obsidian.
2. **Identify** the Olmec, the Maya, the Teotihuacános, the Toltec, Quetzalcoatl.
3. **Use** the map on page 390 to locate the area settled by the Maya. What large city did the Maya establish? On what landform was it located?

Critical Thinking

4. **Synthesizing Information** What common features linked the Mesoamerican civilizations?

Understanding Themes

5. **Innovation** What were some of the major achievements of the Mesoamerican civilizations?

SECTION 2 REVIEW ANSWERS

1. All vocabulary words are defined in the Glossary.
2. Olmec, 379; Maya, 380; Teotihuacános, 383; Toltec, 383; Quetzalcoatl, 383
3. Chichén Itzá; Yucatán Peninsula
4. maize as basic food; markets for trade; importance of religion; complex cultures
5. INNOVATION writing; folded books; sophisticated calendar; extensive astronomical knowledge

Visualizing History The Aztec borrowed the rain god Tlaloc from the Teotihuacános. At the center of the Aztec capital was a temple where victims were sacrificed to Tlaloc. **Answer to Caption:** *the Mexican Plateau*

ASSESS

Check for Understanding

Assign Section 2 Review as homework or as an in-class activity.

Use Student Self-Test and Review Software to review Section 2.

Evaluate

Section Quiz 15-2

Use the Testmaker to create a customized quiz for Section 2.

Reteach

Write on the board the following sentence from page 379: *Although each culture had unique features, they shared common elements.* Ask students to identify first the unique features of each of the cultures covered in the section and then the elements common to all of them.

Enrich

Have students write a short report comparing Mayan hieroglyphics and pyramids with those of ancient Egypt.

CLOSE

Ask students how a culture is reflected in its art and architecture. Have them describe the types of art and architecture characteristic of the Mesoamerican civilizations.

Special Report Summary

In 1989 archaeologists went to Guatemala to learn why the great Mayan civilization vanished more than 1,000 years ago.

↓

Interpreting artifacts and hieroglyphs, they found that the rulers of the city of Dos Pilas had won control of other cities in the region.

↓

In A.D. 761 the subject kingdoms attacked Dos Pilas. The people of Dos Pilas tore down palaces to build defensive walls, but they were overrun.

↓

Scholars believe that the warfare among rival Mayan kings reduced farming, disrupted trade, and killed young people, contributing to the decline of Mayan civilization.

TEACH

Points to Discuss

After students have read the feature, ask: **Why did a team of archaeologists go to Guatemala in 1989?** *(to learn why the golden age of the Maya ended in the ninth century A.D.)* **What did archaeologists use to learn more about the Maya?** *(potsherds, bones, monuments, spearheads, trash, fortifications, and a hieroglyphic stairway)* **How did the archaeological finds change our view of Maya society?** *(not a series of peaceful kingdoms with ceremonial centers, but wracked by battle and human sacrifice)*

NATIONAL GEOGRAPHIC Special Report

The Maya

Some 2,000 years ago, the lowland Mayan civilization of what is now Central America flourished. A society dating to 1200 B.C., the Maya developed the most complex writing system in the Americas, built majestic temple-pyramids and palaces, and mastered astronomy and mathematics. Then suddenly, in the A.D. 800s, the record of life in the region fell silent: The people stopped erecting monuments, carving hieroglyphic texts, and making pottery. Their cities lay in ruins, their fields and villages were abandoned to the jungle, and the great civilization of the Maya vanished.

What happened to end the golden age of the Maya more than thousand years ago? To answer that question, in 1989 an international team of archaeologists, sponsored in part by the National Geographic Society and Vanderbilt University, went to the Petexbatún rain forest of northern Guatemala. Amid the ruins of the ancient city of Dos Pilas, the team set to work on one of archaeology's greatest mysteries.

TEACHER NOTES

384 Chapter 15 *The Americas*

Enric

Enrico Ferorelli

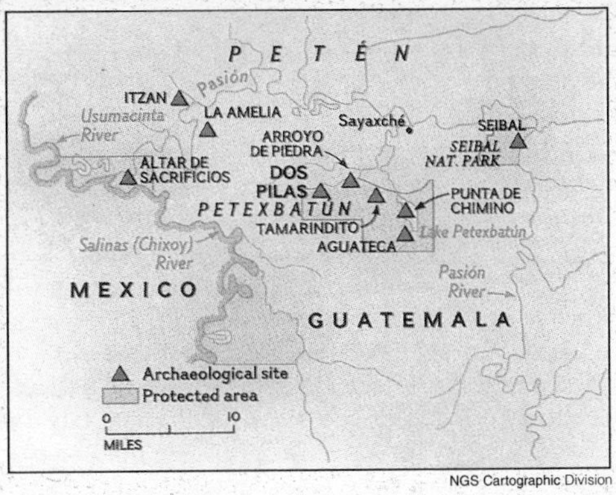

NGS Cartographic Division

After setting up a fully functioning camp complete with a computer lab and drafting workstations, scientists began their task. They studied thousands of potsherds, scores of monuments, bone fragments, spearheads, trash heaps, and miles of fortifications of Dos Pilas—built by renegades from the great Mayan center of Tikal—and nearby cities.

One spectacular find that told the fate of the Maya was a hieroglyphic stairway. Five limestone steps, about 20 feet wide, each with two rows of glyphs carved on the risers, climb to the base of the royal palace near the main plaza at Dos Pilas. Experts at deciphering glyphs were on hand to translate each glyph as it was uncovered. The story on the steps gives an account of the battles of the first ruler of the Petexbatún (referred to as Ruler 1) against his brother at Tikal, some 65 miles northeast of Dos Pilas.

One of the epigraphists summed up the inscription: "It begins by talking about the 60th birthday of

A Mayan warrior-king is portrayed on a stela carved in A.D. 731. Discoveries at Dos Pilas have led to new theories on the collapse of the Mayan civilization along the border of Guatemala and Mexico.

A stairway of five long steps (top) came to light during excavations at the Dos Pilas site.

NATIONAL GEOGRAPHIC **Special Report**

History and the Humanities

Focus on World Art Print 11, Mayan. *Presentation of Captives to a Maya Ruler*

Cultural Perspectives

Mayan Innovations The Maya learned to make a durable cement using burnt lime, which they used for temples and other structures. The pyramids at Tikal rise to 230 feet. Mayan priests also made exact calculations of dates; they estimated the beginning of history to have been August 10, 3113 B.C.

NATIONAL GEOGRAPHIC SOCIETY

VIDEODISC
STV: Maya

Side 2
Frames 15839-38987
Title: *End of Classic Period*
Subject: Evidence of warfare and violence in Mayan society
Ask: What evidence found in 1990 proved that the Maya were violent? *(hieroglyphic text that told of battles)*

FUN FACTS

- At the height of Mayan civilization, the city of Tikal and its environs may have had as many as 60,000 residents.
- The Maya used corbel vaulting in their buildings, a complex technique that supports arches and domes.
- The Maya constructed buildings and carved sculptures without the use of metal tools.
- Mayan farmers experimented with the domestication of many varieties of corn, beans, and other food crops.
- Mayan temples were often built in alignment with astronomical phenomena.

NATIONAL GEOGRAPHIC *Special Report*

NATIONAL GEOGRAPHIC SOCIETY

Use these materials to enrich student understanding of life in the ancient Americas.

NGS PICTURESHOW CD-ROM
The Americas

NGS PICTUREPACK TRANSPARENCY SET
Ancient Central America

Linking Past and Present

Mayan Ruins Until the mid-1800s most Mayan ruins lay hidden and unknown in the jungles of Mexico and Central America. When the sites were discovered, priceless sculptures were often looted and sold. Today, Mayan ruins are protected by the governments of Mexico, Guatemala, and Belize.

NATIONAL GEOGRAPHIC SOCIETY

VIDEODISC
STV: Maya

Side 2
Frames 25914-34042
Title: *Fall of Ancient Maya Cities*
Subject: An attempt to defend Dos Pilas
Ask: How did the Maya of Dos Pilas attempt to defend themselves? *(They built two walls to blockade the city.)*

NATIONAL GEOGRAPHIC *Special Report*

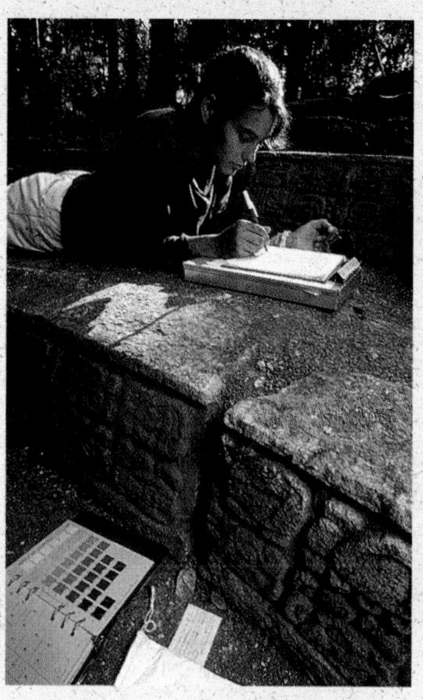

As Vanderbilt graduate student Stacy Symonds excavated a defensive wall, she discovered the hieroglyphic stairway beneath it. Here she records information about the glyphs.

Ruler 1, that he danced a ritual dance. As you read down the steps, the glyphs give a historical sequence to his reign. We think Ruler 1 left Tikal and started a splinter kingdom at Dos Pilas. There's an emblem glyph—which is like a political title—for Tikal, and both brothers claimed it. Ruler 1 was defeated, but then there was another war. This time Dos Pilas won."

Although the glyphs told archaeologists about the origin of a dynasty, what was even more intriguing was a stone wall built on top of the stairs during the kingdom's fall. Less than a hundred years after memorializing their founder, the people of Dos Pilas threw a wall up over his monument in what must have been a desperate attempt to protect themselves. Why did the people of Dos Pilas build defensive walls, which are rarely found at Mayan sites?

The second and third rulers of Dos Pilas changed traditional warfare when they set forth on campaigns of expansion. Digging a 30-foot shaft into the burial temple of Ruler 2, archaeologists discovered hieroglyphs on fine pottery that offered more clues. These glyphs suggest that Ruler 2, who reigned from A.D. 698 to A.D. 726, expanded the influence of Dos Pilas and gained control of other cities through marriage and political alliances.

Ruler 3 went on to wed a royal lady from the city of Cancuén and to dominate the entire region. He traveled to the cities of Tamarindito, Aguateca, Seibal, and others to perform ceremonies and quell unrest. After Ruler 3 died in A.D. 741, Ruler 4 took control, living mostly at Aguateca—by then a twin capital—which rests on a limestone bluff high above Lake Petexbatún.

In A.D. 761 something went wrong. According to hieroglyphs, the kings of the Petexbatún had overextended their domain. There had been hints of trouble for more than a decade: Ruler 4 had spent much of his 20-year reign racing from one end of the realm to the other, performing bloodletting rituals, leading battles, and contracting alliances. He used every technique to sustain the kingdom, but to no avail.

Then the city of Tamarindito threw off the yoke of Dos Pilas. Hieroglyphs at Tamarindito tell us that its warriors attacked the capital and killed Ruler 4.

About that time the citizens of Dos Pilas made a valiant last stand. In desperation they ripped stones from temples and monuments, including the tomb of Ruler 2 and the hieroglyphic stairway. They tore down much of the royal palace to build two walls around the central palaces and temples.

The surviving nobles deserted their citizens and fled to Aguateca, proclaiming themselves the new rulers of the kingdom. They chose Aguateca as its final capital because of its defensive location. The people of Aguateca held out for about 50 years, but disappeared in the early A.D. 800s

IN A SPAN of only a few hundred years the kingdom rose, expanded, and collapsed as a succession of kin[gs] moved from limited conflict to widespread warfare. Scholars have argued that the Mayan civilization simply ou[t]grew its environment, exhausting the soil and creating environmental and economic stress. But another possibility is that intensive warfare forced the Maya, at least in the Petexbatún area, to move close to fortresses such as Aguateca, where they would have soon run out of fertile land. Perhaps farmers were limited to fortified areas near cities that could provide protection, forcing them to forsake traditional agricultural practices that had sustained them for hundreds of years. The wars must have disrupted trade, upset population distribution, destroyed crops, and killed young farmer-warriors, exacting a huge pric[e].

Scholars have added greatly to our view of Mayan society. Once regarded as a network of ceremonial centers ruled by peaceful priest-kings, Mayan civilization is no longer seen that way. Battle and human sacrifice were aspects of lif[e]. Perhaps siege warfare was ultimately too costly for the Maya. For yea[rs] to come, scientists will study the ruins in the Petexbatún rain forest researching changes that may have contributed to the collapse of the lowland Mayan civilization.

386 Chapter 15 *The Americas*

MORE ABOUT...

Mayan Women The archaeologist Tatiana Proskouriakoff (1909–1985) was a leading expert on Mayan civilization. Proskouriakoff pioneered research on the role of women in Mayan society by analyzing female figures in Mayan sculpture. She argued that Mayan women were often the founders of dynasties and suggested that descent among the Maya may have been matrilineal.

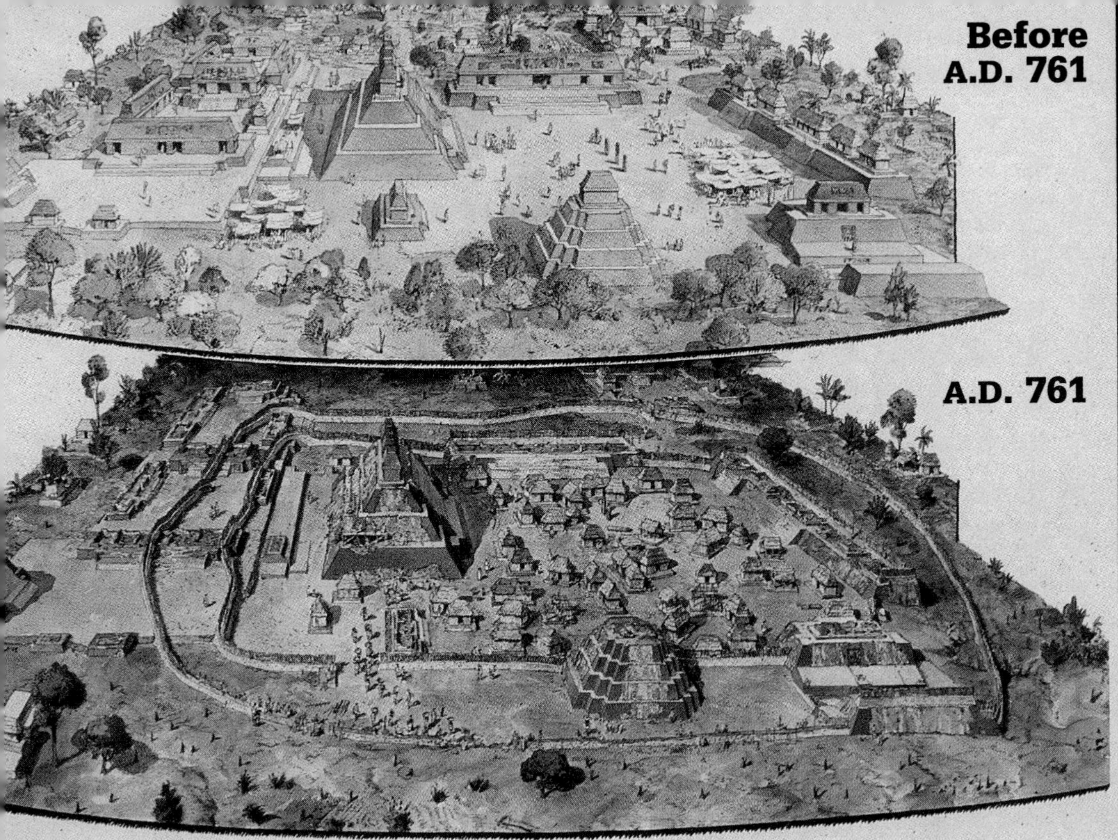

Enrico Ferorelli

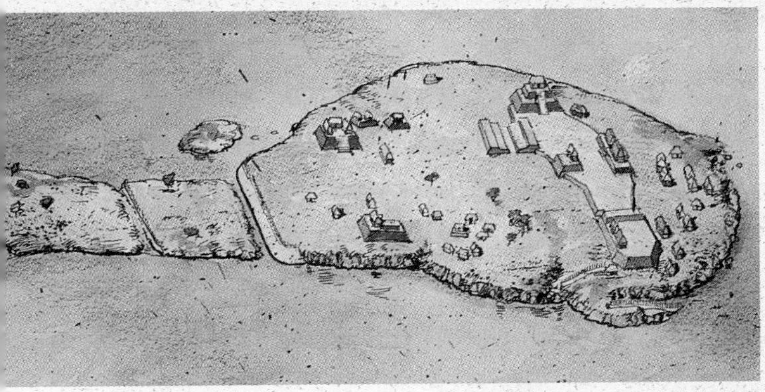

Enrico Ferorelli

In proper Mayan style Dos Pilas's ceremonial precinct (above, top) featured palaces for rulers and temples to the gods. But an apparent golden age came to an abrupt end in A.D. 761 (above, bottom). After the killing of Ruler 4, warfare consumed the region. Residents tore down facades of temples and palaces to raise two walls. A cleared area between the walls likely served as a killing alley. Seeking refuge, farmers moved into the plaza and erected huts. Soon the city was abandoned.

A peninsula became an island (left, top and bottom) as defenders of the Lake Petexbatún port dug three moats across the neck of land. At the tip of the island, a walled wharf protected a canoe landing. Perhaps the enemy proved too strong or conditions too harsh, for the outpost was abandoned.

NATIONAL GEOGRAPHIC *Special Report*

CURRICULUM CONNECTION

LITERATURE

In the A.D. 1500s, Mayan myths were written down in an epic called *Popol Vuh*. The epic describes the universe before the creation of the earth: "There is not yet one person, one animal, bird, fish, crab, tree, rock, hollow, canyon, meadow, forest. Only the sky alone is there; the face of the earth is not clear. Only the sea alone is pooled under all the sky; there is nothing whatever gathered together. It is at rest; not a single thing stirs."

Global Gourmet

Central America Corn and beans remain essential ingredients in the diet of the people of southern Mexico, Guatemala, and Belize. Corn is ground and pounded flat to make tortillas, the pancake-shaped bread popular throughout the region.

Portfolio Project

Remind students of the importance of religion to the Maya. Then ask them to write a brief essay discussing how the people of Dos Pilas probably felt when they tore down temples and palaces to build defensive walls.

TEACHER NOTES

Chapter 15
Section 3

SECTION THEME

▸ **Change** The Aztec and the Inca conquer neighboring territories and establish powerful empires in Mexico and South America.

Find Out

Answer: *Skill in war and governance led to the rise of the empires; the Spanish conquest led to their decline.*

FOCUS

Section Objective

List the factors that led to the rise and decline of the Aztec and Inca Empires.

BELLRINGER
Motivational Activity

Before taking roll at the beginning of the class period, project Section Focus Transparency 15-3 and have students answer the activity questions. Discuss students' responses.

This activity is also available as a blackline master.

Vocabulary Pre-check

Use the Vocabulary PuzzleMaker to create a puzzle that reinforces the vocabulary terms in this section. **L1**

A.D. 1300 — A.D. 1400 — A.D. 1500

A.D. 1325 The Aztec found their capital, Tenochtitlán.

A.D. 1438 The Inca emperor Pachacuti comes to power.

c. A.D. 1500 The Aztec control all of central and southern Mexico.

Section 3

The Aztec and Inca Empires

Setting the Scene

▸ **Terms to Define**
chinampas, hierarchy, quinoa

▸ **People to Meet**
the Aztec, the Inca, the Moche, Pachacuti

▸ **Places to Locate**
Tenochtitlán, Cuzco

Find Out What factors led to the rise and decline of the Aztec and the Inca Empires?

The Storyteller

Cortés captured many Aztec cities. This Aztec song remembers how it was:
"Broken spears lie in the roads;
we have torn our hair in our grief.
The houses are roofless now, and their walls
are red with blood....
We have pounded our hands in despair against
the adobe walls, for our inheritance, our
city, is lost and dead.
The shields of our warriors
were its defense, but they
could not save it.
We have chewed dry twigs
and salt grasses;
We have filled our mouths
with dust and bits of
adobe; we have eaten
lizards, rats and
worms...."

—from *Sources of World History*, edited by Mark A. Kishlansky, 1995

Aztec Stone of the Sun calendar

Both **the Aztec** and **the Inca** were latecomers to power. In scarcely more than 200 years, they transformed themselves from little-known peoples to masters of vast empires. They borrowed from earlier civilizations to create their own distinctive cultures. They developed highly centralized governments and became productive farmers, master builders, artisans, and weavers. Although they held quite different religious beliefs, religion was important to both peoples and motivated their expansion. Both sophisticated civilizations came to sudden ends in the early A.D. 1500s, when they were overwhelmed and destroyed by Spanish invaders from Europe.

The Aztec Empire

The early Aztec were semi-nomadic hunters and warriors who migrated from the north into central Mexico in the A.D. 1200s. They founded what became the capital of their empire in A.D. 1325 on a small, uninhabited island near the western shore of Lake Texcoco. The Aztec named their capital **Tenochtitlán** (tay•NAWCH•teet•LAHN). Today it is the site of Mexico City.

Tenochtitlán

The Aztec turned Tenochtitlán into an agricultural center and marketplace. Since land for farming was scarce on the island, they built *chinampas*, or artificial islands, by piling mud from the bottom of the lake onto rafts secured by stakes. These became floating gardens where farmers grew a variety of crops, including corn and beans. With a plentiful food supply, the population grew and people moved outside the city to the mainland. A network of canals, bridges, and causeways was built to connect the mainland with the capital city.

SECTION RESOURCES

Reproducible Masters
- Reproducible Lesson Plan 15-3
- Guided Reading Activity 15-3
- Reteaching Activity 15
- Enrichment Activity 15
- Section Quiz 15-3
- Performance Assessment Activity 15
- Spanish Chapter Summary 15

Transparencies
- Section Focus Transparency 15-3
- World History and Art Transparency 18

Multimedia
- Vocabulary PuzzleMaker Software
- Student Self-Test and Review Software
- Testmaker
- World Music: Cultural Traditions, Lesson 2

Empire

Strengthened by early alliances with neighboring city-states, the Aztec then conquered more distant rivals. By A.D. 1500 their empire stretched from north-central Mexico to the border of Guatemala, and from the Atlantic Ocean to the Pacific Ocean. Conquered peoples had to pay heavy tribute in the form of food, clothing, raw materials, and prisoners for sacrifice.

As the Aztec Empire expanded, Tenochtitlán prospered. Estimates of the city's population by A.D. 1500 range from 120,000 to 200,000. Goods and tribute came to the city from all parts of the empire.

Government and Society

The Aztec civilization was organized as a hierarchy—divided into levels of authority, each level more powerful than the level below it. At the top was the emperor. His power came from his control of the army and was reinforced by religious beliefs.

The Aztec social order had four classes: nobility, commoners, serfs, and slaves. Land could be owned by noble families and commoners. Commoners included priests, merchants, artisans, and farmers. Serfs were farmworkers tied to noble lands. The lowest class included criminals and debtors, as well as female and children prisoners of war. Male prisoners of war were sacrificed to the Aztec gods.

Religion

Religion was the driving force behind the Aztec emphasis on war and sacrifice. Borrowing religious beliefs from the Maya and the Toltec, the Aztec believed that live human sacrifices were necessary to keep the gods pleased and to ensure abundant harvests.

Much of Aztec art reflected religious and military themes. The walls of temple-pyramids were decorated with scenes of gods or battles. Poets and writers glorified Aztec gods and the legendary history of the Aztec people. The empire, however, proved to be more fragile than the poets dreamed. Tenochtitlán faced rebellions from its outlying territories that weakened the empire. In A.D. 1521 these groups joined Spanish explorers in invading and destroying Aztec villages and cities.

Footnotes to History

Aztec Markets

The market was a very important economic and social institution for the Aztec. The market at Tlateloco was the largest in the Americas. About 60,000 people may have visited the market daily.

AROUND THE WORLD

Chocolate Is Introduced to Europe

Spain, A.D. 1528

According to legend, the Aztec ruler Montezuma had served Hernán Cortés a beverage called *chocolatl*. When Cortés returned to Spain in A.D. 1528, he brought with him the beans of the cacao tree. Spaniards added sugar, vanilla, and cinnamon to sweeten the bitter drink. Chocolate became a favorite with the aristocracy and spread to Italy, France, Austria, and England.

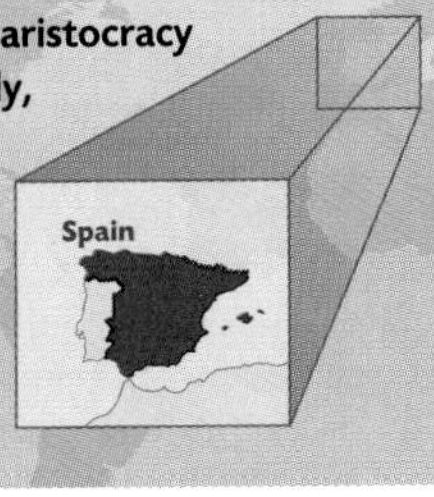

The Inca Empire

In South America, along the Pacific coast and in the mountain ranges of the Andes, other civilizations developed independently of those of Mesoamerica. In the late A.D. 1980s, archaeological finds revealed that complex societies first emerged in South America between 3000 B.C. and 2100 B.C., 2,000 years earlier than previously thought and 1,000 years earlier than in Mesoamerica.

One of the early peoples was **the Moche**, who flourished on the north coast of present-day Peru between A.D. 100 and A.D. 600. In A.D. 1987 the discovery of a noble's pyramid tomb proved that the Moche had a social order based on ranks, skilled artisans who produced ornaments of gold, silver, and copper, and religious beliefs that included a sacrifice ceremony.

Rise of the Inca

The Inca began as one of many small tribes competing for scarce fertile land in the highland valleys of the Andes. Around A.D. 1200 the Inca settled in **Cuzco** (KOOS•koh), which became their capital. They raided other tribes and slowly established a powerful empire.

The decisive period of Inca expansion began in A.D. 1438, when **Pachacuti**, the ninth Inca ruler, came to power. He and his son, Topa Inca Yupanqui, have been compared to Philip and Alexander the Great of Macedonia. By persuasion, threats, and force, they extended Inca boundaries far to the north and south.

TEACH

Guided Practice

THEME Change

Ask students to list the changes instituted by the Aztec and the Inca that enabled them to flourish. *(centralized government, productive farming techniques)* **L1**

Geography: Location Have students locate both the Aztec and Inca Empires, as well as the Mayan civilization studied in the previous section, on a map of Mexico and Central America. Have a class discussion in which students work together to explain why so many civilizations arose in the same area. **L2**

World History and Art Transparency 18, *Mola Stitchery*

World Music: Cultural Traditions, Lesson 2

Independent Practice

Guided Reading Activity 15-3 **L1**

Science, Technology, and Society Encourage students to make a tabletop model or drawing of Aztec *chinampas*. Pair students with limited English proficiency with native-speaking classmates to help with research using an encyclopedia or other resources. After research and completion of the model or drawing, have students summarize the importance of *chinampas* to Aztec society. **L2 LEP**

ASSESS

Check for Understanding

Assign Section 3 Review as homework or as an in-class activity.

Use Self-Test and Review Software to review Section 3.

COOPERATIVE LEARNING ACTIVITY

Model Organize the class into small groups. Propose the task of creating a model of an Aztec city. Groups should approach the task as if they were a city planning committee, including administrators, architects, construction teams, artisans, and researchers. Have groups determine what commercial, residential, governmental, educational, or religious buildings they want to include in addition to water systems, sewers, and roads.

Advise groups to assign a task to each group member. When all the models are completed, have the class evaluate differences in interpretation and materials. Encourage students to consider difficulties the Aztec encountered in building their cities. **L2**

Chapter 15
Section 3

Map Study

Answer

They adjusted to high altitudes.

Map Skills Practice

Reading a Map Where was Machu Picchu located?
(in the Andes Mountains of central Peru, about 50 miles [80 kilometers] northwest of Cuzco)

Evaluate

Section Quiz 15-3

Use the Testmaker to create a customized quiz for Section 3.

Reteach

Have students make a chart on the chalkboard summarizing the religion, economy, and government of the Aztec and Inca.

Reteaching Activity 15

Enrich

Ask students to write short reports comparing Pachacuti and his son, Topa Inca Yupanqui, to Philip and Alexander the Great of Macedonia.

Enrichment Activity 15

CLOSE

Ask students to describe the social classes and hierarchy of government of the Aztec and Inca civilizations.

The Inca Empire eventually included all of present-day Peru, much of Chile, and parts of Ecuador, Bolivia, and Argentina. It stretched more than 2,500 miles (4,020 km) through coastal deserts, dry highlands, fertile river valleys, and rain forests. Most of the Inca lived in the Andes highlands and adjusted to high altitudes. Cuzco was 11,600 feet (3,560 m) above sea level.

Government and Society

Pachacuti created a strong central government to control the vast realm. He permitted local rulers to continue governing conquered territories as long as they were loyal. Rebellious peoples were resettled elsewhere where they could pose less of a threat. Pachacuti instituted a complex system of tribute collections, courts, military posts, trade inspections, and local work regulations to bind outlying territories to the center. To further unite the diverse peoples, the Inca established a common imperial language—Quechua (KEH•chuh•wuh).

The Inca emperor and his officials closely regulated the lives of the common people. As a divine ruler, the emperor owned all land and carefully regulated the growing and distribution of foods, such as potatoes and quinoa (KEEN•WAH), a protein-rich grain. Under the emperor's direction, Inca officials supervised work crews in the building of a network of roads and woven fiber suspension bridges that linked the various parts of the empire.

As a divine ruler, the Inca emperor was believed to have contact with the deities. Like the Aztec, the Inca believed in many deities, including a creator god and a sun god, whom they worshiped in a variety of religious ceremonies. Food and animals were typical sacrificial offerings, but human sacrifices were also made for special events. In A.D. 1995 archaeologists working in the ice fields of the Peruvian Andes discovered the frozen, carefully preserved body of a teenage Inca girl. The food fragments and pottery shards in the girl's coffin seemed to indicate that she was a sacrificial victim offered by Inca priests to appease the gods.

Aztec, Inca, and Maya Empires

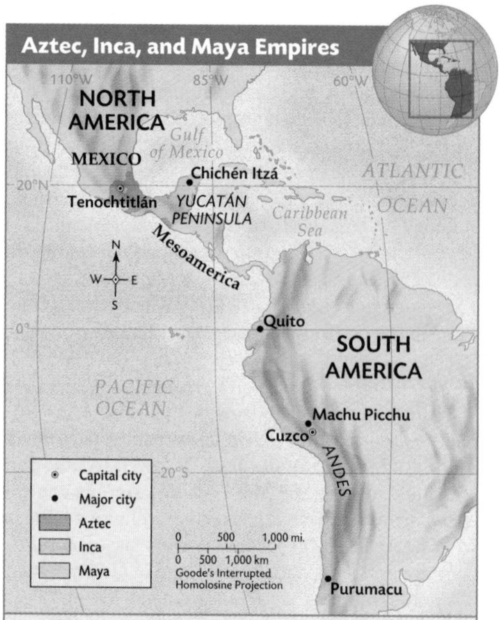

Map Study The Aztec, Inca, and Maya built powerful empires in the Americas.
Human/Environment Interaction
How did the Inca adapt to their environment in order to build their civilization?

Inca Decline

The obedient, well-disciplined Inca would prove to be no match for the Spanish conquerors who arrived in South America in A.D. 1533. In spite of fierce resistance, the Inca Empire declined and eventually disappeared. Aspects of Inca culture, however, have survived among the Inca descendants living today in western areas of South America.

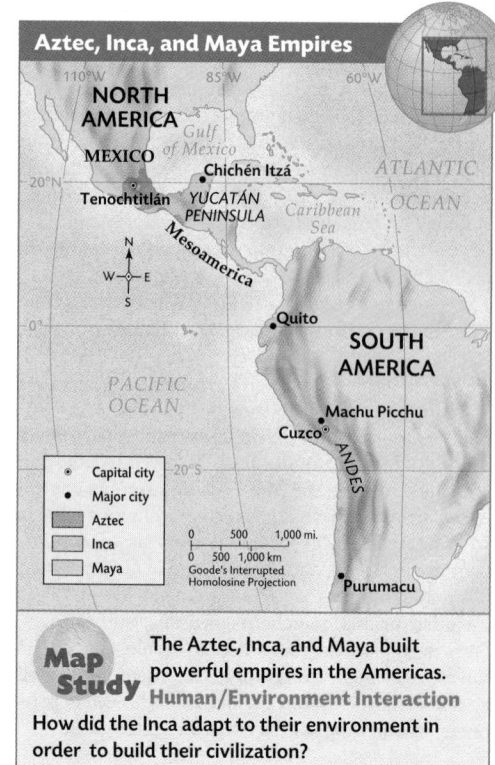

SECTION 3 REVIEW

Recall
1. **Define** *chinampas*, hierarchy, quinoa.
2. **Identify** the Aztec, the Inca, the Moche, Pachacuti.
3. **Use** the maps in the Atlas to describe the physical geography of Mexico and western South America. How did geography affect the early civilizations that arose in each of these two areas?

Critical Thinking
4. **Synthesizing Information** What do modern nations take as tribute after a war? How is this the same as or different from the tribute paid by Aztec people?

Understanding Themes
5. **Change** Contrast the methods used by the Aztec and the Inca to expand and administer their vast empires.

SECTION 3 REVIEW ANSWERS

1. All vocabulary words are defined in the Glossary.
2. Aztec, 388; Inca, 388; Moche, 389; Pachacuti, 389
3. Mexico: diverse terrains, mountain chains, and volcanoes led to innovative farming practices; western South America: coastal deserts, dry highlands, fertile river valleys, and rain forests led to struggle for fertile land and need to adjust to high altitudes.
4. Answers about modern warfare will vary but may include monetary payments or guarantees of future nonaggression. Aztec demanded tribute of food, clothing, raw materials, and sacrificial victims.
5. **CHANGE** Aztec: heavy tribute imposed on conquered peoples; Inca: resettled rebellious peoples

Critical Thinking
SKILLS

Hypothesizing

Imagine that half your history class failed a chapter test. The rest of the students, with one exception, received a grade of D. Can you think of any explanations for this poor showing? Perhaps there was a big basketball game the night before the test, and students spent too little time reviewing. Perhaps the chapter contained a large amount of new information that was difficult to learn. Each possible explanation is called a *hypothesis*.

Learning the Skill

Hypothesizing, or developing possible explanations for events, is an important part of any research process. Each hypothesis forms the basis for further investigation to determine whether it is true or false. In the example above, you could test your hypotheses by interviewing other students to find out why they did so poorly on the test. Once you have more information, you can accept, reject, or revise your hypotheses.

To improve your skill at hypothesizing, first identify the event, trend, or condition you want to explain. Gather information that relates to causes of this event, trend, or condition. Brainstorm all possible hypotheses.

Once you have developed some hypotheses, you have to test each one. There are several ways to do this. First, see if the explanation fits all the known facts. Then, gather more information that can prove or disprove the hypothesis. In the example above, your survey reveals that most of the class attended school events on two evenings just prior to the test, leaving little time for study. This research enables you to revise your explanation.

Practicing the Skill

Read the statement below and answer the questions that follow it.

Despite their great accomplishments, around A.D. 800 the Mayan civilization declined.

1. What event, trend, or condition do you want to explain?
2. What facts do you have that relate to this situation?
3. What are two hypotheses that might explain it?
4. What information could help you prove or disprove each hypothesis?

Applying the Skill

Write a short story using one of the following ideas:

1) You are an archaeologist studying a culture. After finding some unusual artifacts, you hypothesize about the practices and beliefs of the culture.

2) You are a detective investigating a crime. You find some evidence and use it to hypothesize who committed the crime and how.

In either case, include details about the information you need to prove or disprove your hypotheses.

For More Practice

Turn to the Skill Practice in the Chapter Review on page 393 for more practice in hypothesizing.

Artifact–gold chalice

Social Studies
SKILLS

TEACH

Hypothesizing Before students read the skill, explain that historians are social scientists who make and test hypotheses just as physical scientists do, but they use different methods. Have students consider the following situation: You find a new species of plant growing in your backyard one spring. Ask students to draw on their knowledge of ecology and biology to propose possible explanations, or hypotheses, for the appearance of the new plant. *(Answers may include: seeds brought from another area by a bird or animal; unusual weather conditions; building projects in the area affecting drainage and water level.)* Ask students how a biologist might test these hypotheses. *(study past weather reports; investigate records of building permits; find out about habits of local birds and animals)* Point out that this same process of making and testing hypotheses is also used by historians and other social scientists. Then have students read the skill and complete the practice questions.

Additional Practice

Skill Reinforcement Activity 15

ANSWERS TO PRACTICING THE SKILL

1. the decline of Mayan civilization around A.D. 800
2. evidence of increasing warfare and conflict
3. Accept all reasonable hypotheses. The text offers military (civil war and outside attacks) and agricultural (breakdown leading to malnutrition and death) hypotheses.
4. Answers should reflect further research.

Chapter 15 Review

GLENCOE TECHNOLOGY

VIDEODISC

Use MindJogger to review students' knowledge of the chapter.

MindJogger Videoquiz

Chapter 15
Disc 2 Side B

Also available in VHS.

Answers

Using Key Terms

1. d	6. j
2. i	7. g
3. a	8. f
4. h	9. b
5. e	10. c

Using Your History Journal

Suggest that students compare when similar achievements (such as the invention of writing or calendars) were made in different parts of the world.

Reviewing Facts

1. California: abundant resources: fish, shellfish, berries, nuts; Great Basin: limited resources: seeds, grasshoppers, small animals
2. invented irrigation techniques; Pueblo terraced fields to check erosion, built with adobe; Navajo raised sheep adapted to desert
3. ceremonial centers, tombs for leaders
4. San Lorenzo and La Venta
5. plaster-covered, pleated flattened bark
6. Aztec weakened by rebellions from outlying territories; both empires succumbed to the Spanish.

CHAPTER 15 REVIEW

Historical Significance

Throughout the early history of the Americas, Native Americans established a variety of cultures and civilizations. The environment gave these peoples spiritual strength and economic support. Regarding the earth as sacred, they used the land's natural resources to develop agriculture, build ceremonial centers, and advance trade. Several Native American groups in Mesoamerica and South America formed vast empires that linked diverse peoples and spread new ideas and products.

The cultural aspects of these empires are still held by Native Americans living today in Mexico, Central America, and South America. In recent years, Native Americans in North America have reclaimed much of their heritage that had been suppressed with the advance of European civilization in the Americas.

Using Key Terms

Write the key term that completes each sentence.

a. *chinampas*	f. maize
b. weirs	g. obsidian
c. quinoa	h. potlatches
d. confederation	i. hierarchy
e. jaguar	j. slash-and-burn farming

1. Around A.D. 1500 the Cayuga, Mohawk, Oneida, Onondaga, and Seneca formed a __________, or loose union.
2. Aztec society was based on a ______, which consisted of the emperor, nobles, commoners, serfs, and slaves.
3. Because of the scarcity of land to farm, the Aztec devised a way of making __________, or artificial islands.
4. Among Native Americans of the Pacific Northwest, the wealth of each lineage group was given away at _________.
5. Many Olmec jade carvings show the features of a large spotted wild cat called a __________.
6. The early Olmec practiced a form of agriculture known as _____________.
7. Groups in Mexico and Central America used _________, a volcanic glass, to make sharp-edged tools, arrow points, and other objects.
8. By about 5000 B.C., hunter-gatherers in the highland area of present-day Mexico had discovered that the seeds of ______ could be planted.
9. Native Americans in the Pacific Northwest developed ways to harvest salmon with elaborate wooden traps called ______.
10. Native Americans in the Andes mountain ranges grew ________, a protein-rich grain.

Using Your History Journal

Parallel to your time line of important dates in Native American civilizations, add a time line of significant civilizations and achievements in Africa, Asia, and Europe. Use dates from the Unit 3 Digest on pages 394–397.

Reviewing Facts

1. **Explain** how the food resources of Native Americans along the California coast differed from those of Native Americans living in the Great Basin.
2. **Discuss** how the people of southwestern North America adapted to the desert.
3. **Identify** the purposes or possible uses of the large earthen mounds left by the Mound Builders of the Eastern Woodlands.
4. **Name** the two principal sites where excavations have revealed an ancient Olmec culture.
5. **Describe** the four books that have survived from the Mayan civilization.
6. **Identify** the events in the early A.D. 1500s that were responsible for the sudden end to the Inca and the Aztec civilizations.
7. **Explain** the scientific fields in which the Maya excelled.
8. **State** what was unique about the location and geography of the Aztec city of Tenochtitlán.
9. **Discuss** how Inca emperors worked to unify their empire.

7. astronomy, mathematics
8. It was an island city.
9. strong central government; resettled rebels; common imperial language; regulated lives of the common people

Critical Thinking

1. Climate and geography determine which crops can or cannot be grown, what kind of buildings must be built, and whether a community has resources useful to trade.
2. Aztec demanded tribute of conquered peoples; Inca resettled rebellious peoples; Aztec decline hastened by alliance of conquered peoples, whom they had treated brutally, with Spanish; fall of Inca to Spanish eased by obedient national character.
3. hunting, farming
4. to escape the Spaniards

CHAPTER 15 REVIEW

Critical Thinking

1. **Apply** How do climate and geography affect the development of a civilization?
2. **Analyze** How did the rise and decline of the Aztec and Inca Empires differ?
3. **Synthesize** What were some daily activities of the Eastern Woodlands peoples?
4. **Analyze** High in the Andes mountain ranges, the city of Machu Picchu was the last refuge of the Inca. Why did Inca rulers retreat to a city in such a remote location?

Ruins of Machu Picchu

Understanding Themes

1. **Relation to the Environment** How did Native Americans in the Eastern Woodlands differ from the Native Americans of the Great Plains? How were they similar?
2. **Innovation** What were some of the cultural achievements of the Mayan civilization?
3. **Change** How did the arrival of the Spaniards in the Americas affect the development of the Aztec and Inca civilizations?

Linking Past and Present

1. What impact do Native American traditions have on life in the Americas today? In what ways has modern civilization been affected by the early Native Americans?
2. Religion played an important role in early American and other ancient civilizations. What role does religion have in modern societies?
3. Why did ancient civilizations decline? Would the same factors lead to the weakening of civilization today?

Skill Practice

Stelae are vertical shafts of stone, about the height of a human being. They have been found among the ruins of several civilizations around the world. Many stelae found in Mayan ruins were sculpted with portraits and carved with hieroglyphics; archaeologists believe that each stela commemorates a ruler. The Mayan monuments were destroyed, leaving only fragments that archaeologists have put together. Suggest as many hypotheses as you can for this destruction. What evidence would help you prove or disprove your hypotheses?

Geography in History

1. **Movement** Refer to the map below. In the A.D. 1500s and A.D. 1600s Native American civilizations declined as the whole region came under the rule of powerful European nation-states. The triangular trade linked four continents between A.D. 1600 and A.D. 1760. How did trade change the population of the Caribbean Islands?
2. **Human/Environment Interaction** How did farming change when crops such as sugarcane began to be raised for trade?
3. **Movement** What positive and negative changes resulted from the cultural contact of peoples from four different continents?

The Triangular Trade Route

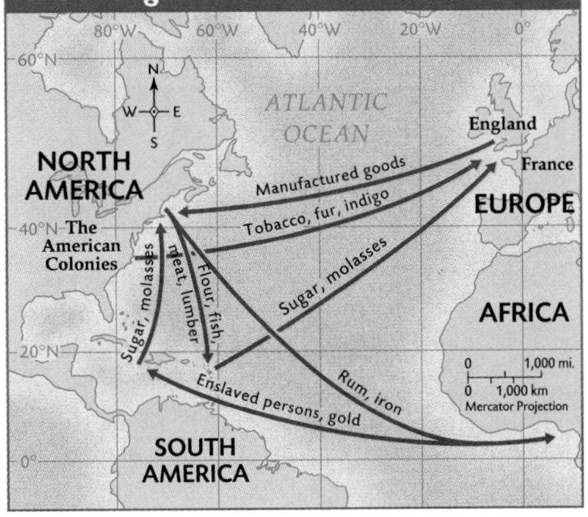

Chapter 15 Review

Understanding Themes

1. **RELATION TO ENVIRONMENT** differences: Great Plains: farming difficult, depended on bison; Eastern Woodlands: lived in farming villages, hunted variety of animals; similarity: made use of every part of animals they killed
2. **INNOVATION** understood concept of zero; developed accurate calendars; wrote books and left written records on monuments
3. **CHANGE** Both civilizations were destroyed.

Linking Past and Present

1. Native American traditions have left their impact on language, recreation (for example, lacrosse, use of hammocks, canoeing), and diet. Respect for the environment, similar to the early Native Americans, has become a concern of modern society.
2. Many modern societies support the separation of church and state, although in others, such as Iran, religion and government are closely connected.
3. Factors that led ancient civilizations to decline, including internal conflicts and invasion, would also weaken civilizations now.

Skill Practice

Accept all reasonable responses. Possible answers include: natural disasters such as earthquakes; enemy invaders; Mayan rebels who wanted to overthrow their own rulers; antiquity hunters; Maya who wanted to prevent others from finding and taking their treasures. Corroborating evidence might include hieroglyphs that support or disprove theories of invasion or rebellion, geological evidence of disaster.

Geography in History

1. Many enslaved Africans were imported; Europeans settled there.
2. Subsistence farming by native peoples gave way to commercial plantations worked by enslaved people.
3. positive: exchange of products, resources, ideas; negative: enslavement of native populations

Chapter Bonus Test Question

Ask students: What similarities do you see between the rise of urban civilization in the Americas and the rise of early urban civilizations in the Near East? *(Answers may include: location in areas that are warm year-round; the building of huge structures such as pyramids; development of astronomy and calendars.)*

Unit 3 Digest

The Unit Digest offers a chapter-by-chapter summary that can be used for any of the following teaching purposes:

- ***Preview*** one chapter or an entire unit,
- ***Review*** some or all of the chapters,
- ***Condense*** when specific chapters or units have not been taught, or
- ***Reteach*** chapters that students have studied in the unit.

PREVIEW

Use the Unit 3 Digest Transparencies to preview the highlights of the unit.

Visualizing History In ancient times, each society had its own standard weights and measures. Through trade and migration, certain weights won wider acceptance. Among the most common in the ancient Middle East were the shekel, drachma, and talent.

Answer to Caption: *Constantinople and Kiev*

Unit 3 Digest

The period from A.D. 500 to A.D. 1500 was one of growth in many areas of the world. Expanded trade routes and missionaries' journeys spread intellectual, cultural, and religious beliefs from one people to another. Such contact between cultures caused conflict that lasted for decades, even centuries; yet at other times, ideas and ideals were peacefully assimilated.

Chapter 10 Byzantines and Slavs

When the Roman Empire was divided in A.D. 395, the eastern half became known as the Byzantine Empire. One of the most advanced civilizations of its time, Byzantine culture blended Greek teachings, Christianity, and influences from Eastern cultures. Emperor Justinian, seeking to restore the Roman Empire, reconquered lands that had been taken by Germanic invaders. He also created great architectural masterpieces in the capital city of Constantinople. But his greatest contribution to posterity was his revision of Roman law known as the Justinian Code.

Following its founding, the Byzantine Empire was repeatedly attacked. In A.D. 1054 after centuries of conflict, the Church, divided over papal rule, split into two separate bodies: the Roman Catholic Church in the west and the Eastern Orthodox Church in the east. The empire, weakened by this schism, was further pressured in the west by Christian Crusaders who had conquered part of Italy, and in the east by attacking Seljuk Turks.

Byzantine culture was spread north by traders and missionaries, who converted the Slavic peoples to Christianity. Schools, churches, and monasteries were constructed in towns and villages throughout the countryside, attracting many Christian converts. Kiev, a fortress-village on the Dnieper River, became the first center of Eastern Slavic civilization. In A.D. 911 Kiev made a trade agreement with the Byzantines, establishing the city as an important trade link between Europe and Asia. But in A.D. 1240, Kiev was destroyed by Mongol invaders in an invasion that isolated the Eastern Slavs from Western influence. The Mongols did, however, allow the Slavs to continue to practice their Christian religion and to govern themselves. Mongols allowed special privileges to the Russian state of Muscovy and its capital, Moscow. Muscovy declared itself the center of the Eastern Orthodox Church after Constantinople fell in A.D. 1453. The Russian czar Ivan III proclaimed Russia the "Third Rome," the protector of Eastern Christianity.

Visualizing History These silver inlaid bronze weights were used by merchants in the Byzantine Empire. *What two cities were major centers of trade between the Byzantines and Slavs?*

SURVEYING CHAPTER 10

1. **Relating Ideas** What cultural influences shaped the development of the Byzantine Empire?
2. **Identifying Trends** How was the Eastern Orthodox Church affected by the decline of the Byzantine Empire?

Chapter 11 Islamic Civilization

While the Byzantine influence was spreading Christianity, another religion was emerging on the Arabian Peninsula. In A.D. 610 Muhammad, a businessman in Makkah, experienced a revelation from Allah (the Arabic name for God), and spread the religion called Islam. Muhammad's religion called for devotion to one God and preparation for the judgment day. Suffering persecution, Muhammad and his followers, known as Muslims, fled Makkah and settled in the town of Madinah. Muhammad

CLASSROOM RESOURCES FOR UNIT 3 DIGEST

Preview
- Unit 3 Digest Transparencies

Review
- Time Line Activities 10, 11, 12, 13, 14, 15
- Student Self-Test and Review Software, Chapters 10, 11, 12, 13, 14, 15
- MindJogger Videoquiz, Chapters 10, 11, 12, 13, 14, 15

Condense
- Chapter Digests Audiocassettes, Chapters 10, 11, 12, 13, 14, 15

Reteach
- Reteaching Activities 10, 11, 12, 13, 14, 15
- Chapter Digests Audiocassettes, Chapters 10, 11, 12, 13, 14, 15
- Turning Points in World History

created an Islamic state in Madinah, putting Islamic law above tribal law.

Muslims eventually won control of Makkah and extended their influence throughout the Arabian Peninsula. The holy book of Islam, the Quran, relates the revelation of God to Muhammad. It outlines moral values and guidelines for daily life and presents the five pillars of Islam: faith, prayer, almsgiving, fasting, and pilgrimage to Makkah.

Islam spread through the efforts of caliphs, the successors of Muhammad. Their military expeditions carried Islam throughout the weakened Byzantine and Persian Empires. While Islam's cultural influence widened abroad, it also suffered from internal strife. Following years of struggle, Islam split into two separate factions, the Sunnis and the Shiites.

The Umayyad dynasty (A.D. 661–750) ruled the Muslim world during a period of tremendous change. Umayyad conquerors carried Islam eastward to India and China, as well as to North Africa and Europe. The Umayyads were later overthrown by the Abbasids, who established the capital city of Baghdad.

During Islam's early centuries, Muslim scholars preserved Greek philosophy and made advances in mathematics, astronomy, geometry, and medicine. Islamic art, architecture, and literature were also deeply influenced by religion. In later centuries western Europe would reflect all these advances.

SURVEYING CHAPTER 11

1. **Explain** What were the two major points of Muhammad's preaching?
2. **Relating Ideas** What were the major cultural contributions of the Islamic Empire?

Chapter 12
The Rise of Medieval Europe

Compared with the Byzantine and Islamic societies of this period, western European culture was relatively backward. This period in western European history has, in fact, been referred to as the Dark Ages. Yet many forces were combining to create a new civilization in Europe.

Charlemagne, king of the Franks (A.D. 768–814) and Holy Roman emperor (A.D. 800–814), united

Visualizing History **Throughout the Islamic world, building complexes known as mosques serve as places of worship, centers of education, courts of law, and shelters.** *What are the Five Pillars of Islam?*

most of Europe for the first time since the fall of Rome. Charlemagne also strengthened the ties between the pope and the monarchy. However, within 50 years of his death, Charlemagne's empire was destroyed by internal strife and external invasion.

The feudal system evolved in Europe as a means of protection against such invaders as Muslims and Vikings. Feudalism joined loyalty between lord and vassals to ownership of land and military service. It provided for mutual protection in an age of conflict. Individual fiefs had their own political and legal rules but had no allegiance to and got no support from a central government. Because the fiefdoms and their knights spent much of their time warring among themselves, trade was limited. The manorial system, onto which feudalism was grafted, formed a self-sustaining unit. Each lord, in his castle on his manor, could in theory dispense with trade.

The Church exerted strong influence, both religious and political, over daily life in the Middle Ages. In A.D. 520 a monk named Benedict established a model monastery at Monte Cassino in Italy. Benedict's monks lived simply, prayed and meditated, and worked in the monastery. Although apart from society, they influenced it by preserving religious writings, establishing schools, and teaching various skills to peasants. Missionaries began spreading Christianity throughout Europe.

Although medieval kings were generally weak rulers, William the Conqueror and his successors began to strengthen the English monarchy. In A.D. 1215 the Magna Carta, the great charter of English

Unit 3 Digest

Visualizing History Mosques usually include a large space for people to assemble, a marker of the direction of Makkah, a pulpit, and a minaret from which the people are called to prayer.
Answer to Caption: *faith, prayer, almsgiving, fasting, and pilgrimage to Makkah*

REVIEW

GLENCOE TECHNOLOGY

VIDEODISC
Use MindJogger to review any chapter in Unit 3.

MindJogger Videoquiz

Chapter 10 Disc 2 Side A

Chapter 11 Disc 2 Side A

Chapter 12 Disc 2 Side A

Chapter 13 Disc 2 Side B

Chapter 14 Disc 2 Side B

Chapter 15 Disc 2 Side B

Also available in VHS.

ANSWERS TO SURVEYING THE CHAPTER

CHAPTER 10 ANSWERS

1. Byzantine culture blended Christianity with the traditions of Greece, Rome, Persia, and other eastern peoples.
2. After the fall of Constantinople in A.D. 1453, leadership of the Eastern Orthodox world passed to the Slavs of Russia.

CHAPTER 11 ANSWERS

1. devotion to one God and preparation for judgment day
2. Muslims preserved Greek philosophy and made important advances in mathematics, geometry, astronomy, and medicine.

Use the Student Self-Test and Review Software to review any chapters that students have studied in Unit 3.

Unit 3 Digest

Visualizing History Under Charlemagne, Frankish troops forcibly converted many Germanic tribes, including the Saxons and Bavarians, to Christianity.

Answer to Caption: *fewer than 50 years*

History Ask students to consider how the decline of a civilization can affect what we know about world history. Ask them to consider efforts by new civilizations to preserve the traditions and knowledge of fallen empires. *(Students should recognize that if a civilization leaves few artifacts, we will know little about it; by preserving useful elements of earlier cultures, newer civilizations preserve our knowledge of the past.)* **L2**

CONDENSE

Use Chapter Digest Audiocassettes to introduce chapters that students have not studied in Unit 3. Spanish Chapter Digest Audiocassettes are also available.

Discuss Have students read the **Unit Digest** and discuss the **Surveying the Chapter** questions. **L1**

Visualizing History **This illuminated manuscript depicts scenes from the life of Charlemagne, including his coronation.** *How long after Charlemagne's death did his empire last?*

political and civil liberties, placed some limits on the king's growing power. A council called Parliament was formed to advise the monarch and pass laws. In France, too, the monarchy was strengthened under Philip II and his grandson, Louis IX. Louis's grandson, Philip IV, established the Estates-General.

While England and France were strengthening their monarchies, the Holy Roman Empire based in Germany continued to struggle with the papacy. A compromise was reached at Worms, but power struggles between popes and emperors continued.

SURVEYING CHAPTER 12

1. **Relating Ideas** What were the major features of feudalism as it developed in early medieval Europe?
2. **Making Comparisons** How did the development of monarchy in England and France differ from the development of monarchy in the Holy Roman Empire?

Chapter 13
Medieval Europe at Its Height

When the Seljuk Turks conquered Jerusalem, Christian pilgrimages were forbidden. The Byzantine emperor's call for help to Pope Urban II resulted in a series of Christian military expeditions to the Holy Land known as Crusades. In A.D. 1099 warriors of the First Crusade recaptured Jerusalem. Other crusades followed, but the goal of making the Holy Land Christian did not succeed in the long run. The Crusades did, however, open Europe to new ways of life and stimulated trade.

Around A.D. 1000 Europe's economy began to revive. Innovations in agriculture increased food production. As trade expanded through annual fairs, banking and a money economy were established. Towns soon grew up along trade routes. Merchants and artisans founded guilds to regulate commerce and protect their interests. Merchants' guilds could buy materials cheaply and keep prices up. Craft guilds set standards for membership, training, quality, and prices.

The money economy created a new wealthy middle class, the bourgeoisie. This class gained political power that led to the decline of the feudal system. The rising middle class also influenced the growth of art, literature, and the universities. Intellectual movements such as scholasticism flourished.

The Hundred Years' War between England and France (A.D. 1337–1453) grew out of a feudal dispute between the English and French monarchies over control of lands in France. England won the major battles, including Crécy, Poitiers, and Agincourt, but in the end was driven out of France. After the long off-and-on war, the French monarchy was firmly established. King Louis XI strengthened the French bureaucracy and created a unified state in France. In Spain, Christians were engaged in reconquering lands taken earlier by the Muslims. Meanwhile, the Holy Roman Empire continued its struggle with the papacy, which was experiencing its own problems.

The Babylonian Captivity, as it was called,

ANSWERS TO SURVEYING THE CHAPTER

CHAPTER 12 ANSWERS

1. A decentralized system of mutual protection, feudalism was based on vassals owing loyalty and military service to lords.
2. In England and France, kings began to create strong central governments, while rulers in the Holy Roman Empire remained weak mainly due to conflicts between popes and emperors.

CHAPTER 13 ANSWERS

1. Improved agriculture and increased trade spurred Europe's economy, as did contact with Byzantine and Muslim societies through the Crusades.
2. a dispute over the control of lands in France

during which French popes lived in France under the king's influence, weakened the Church. Later the Great Schism split the Church for 40 years, supporting a rival pope in Avignon and thus further undermining the authority of the pope in Rome.

SURVEYING CHAPTER 13

1. **Analyzing Trends** How did Europe's economy change during the Middle Ages?
2. **Explain** What was a leading cause of the Hundred Years' War between France and England?

Chapter 14
East and South Asia

Between A.D. 1000 and A.D. 1400, a series of steppe peoples from central Asia conquered vast areas of territory in Europe and Asia. The most important of these peoples were the Mongols, who ruled the world's largest land empire stretching from eastern Europe to China. Internal weaknesses, however, led to the disintegration of the Mongol Empire into smaller units.

In China, the Tang dynasty ruled from A.D. 618 to A.D. 907. It expanded Chinese frontiers and created a stable government. Trade with Japan, India, and the Middle East increased, as well as overland trade to Syria along the Silk Road. The Tang capital, Changan, became the largest city in the world. Later weakened by rebellion and invasion, the Tang dynasty declined.

The Song dynasty then came to power, and with it a golden age of achievement in the arts, literature, science, and technology. Confucianism continued to exert influence on the culture, resulting in social reforms. Great strides were made in economic growth as well as science and technology before China fell to the Mongols about A.D. 1270.

The Mongols established peace in China. Under their rule, trade increased with Europe, Arabia, and Russia. But by A.D. 1300, Mongol society in China had begun to decline.

China's influence extended to Vietnam and Cambodia in Southeast Asia, and to Korea and Japan to the northeast. The Koreans had been influenced by Chinese religion, government, and science. Japan, isolated from mainland Asia because of its island geography, developed traditions different from other Asian countries. Yet it too adopted certain Chinese customs.

Japan developed a feudal system of government that lasted 450 years. Warrior landowners protected their lands by using lesser warriors known as samurai to fight for them. Trade increased and towns were established.

SURVEYING CHAPTER 14

1. **Relating Ideas** What areas of Asia were influenced by the spread of Chinese culture?
2. **Making Comparisons** How was early Japan's society similar to that of medieval Europe?

Chapter 15
The Americas

The earliest inhabitants on the North American continent came from Asia by way of the Beringia land bridge. They eventually settled as far as the southern tip of South America. As in Africa, geography and climate determined ways of life.

A variety of Native American groups flourished in North America. Native Americans in the northeastern part of the continent had a high level of political organization. Around A.D. 1400, several tribes formed the Iroquois League to maintain peace. The Iroquois League's representative structure is believed to have had an influence on the development of American government.

Powerful civilizations ruled in Mexico, Central America, and South America. They built large ceremonial centers that included temple-pyramids, marketplaces, and palaces. Religion played a large part in the Mayan, Aztec, and Inca civilizations. The Maya of Mexico and Central America developed an understanding of science and mathematics. The Inca of South America unified their culture with a strong central government and an official language of culture and trade.

SURVEYING CHAPTER 15

1. **Analyzing Trends** What important political contribution was made by Native Americans in northeastern North America?
2. **Relating Ideas** What were the major achievements of the Native American empires?

Unit 3 Digest

RETEACH

Outline Map Have students use an outline map of the world to locate and give approximate dates for the following: Byzantine Empire, Islamic state, Frankish Empire, Tang dynasty, kingdoms of Kush and Mali, and Aztec and Inca Empires. **L1**

Reteaching Activities 10, 11, 12, 13, 14, 15

Chapter Digests Audiocassettes, Chapters 10, 11, 12, 13, 14, 15

ABCNEWS INTERACTIVE™

VIDEODISC
Turning Points in World History

Side One
Chapter 7

Title: *The Crusades*
Subject: The Crusades affected Europe's economic and political development.
Ask: Why did the Crusades encourage western Europeans to increase trade? *(Increased knowledge of southwest Asia's civilizations led to an increase in demand for imported goods.)*

ANSWERS TO SURVEYING THE CHAPTER

CHAPTER 14 ANSWERS

1. Vietnam, Cambodia, Korea, and Japan
2. Japanese feudalism, in which samurai pledged loyalty and military service to lords, resembled the feudal structure of medieval European society.

CHAPTER 15 ANSWERS

1. The Iroquois League, a federation of five Northeastern peoples, had a council to resolve disputes that may have influenced the American system of government developed later.
2. The Mayan, Aztec, and Incan civilizations developed powerful governments, built large cities, and made advances in science and mathematics.

Introducing Unit 4

0:00 OUT OF TIME?

If time does not permit teaching each chapter in Unit 4, you may use the Unit Digest beginning on page 506, in conjunction with the Unit Digest Transparencies and Chapter Digest Audiocassettes with activities and tests.

Introducing the Unit

Unit 4 focuses on how the Renaissance, the Reformation, and the age of exploration dramatically changed Europe and much of the rest of the world. The unit also explores the way Asian civilizations enriched their own cultures by adapting elements of Western culture.

Unit Objectives

After reading Unit 4, students will be able to:

1. explain how the Renaissance emphasized individualism and how the Protestant Reformation established new forms of Christianity.
2. understand how Europeans explored and colonized the Americas, Asia, and Africa.
3. trace the growing power of monarchs and the rise of strong nation-states in Europe from the 1500s to the 1700s.
4. examine the powerful Ottoman, Persian, Mogul, Chinese, and Japanese Empires and understand the cultural achievements of Asia.

Portfolio Project

Students may work in groups to gather information. Students can learn about early banks on pages 446–447. This activity may be a method of authentic assessment.

Unit 4

1400–1800

Emergence of the Modern World

Chapter 16 Renaissance and Reformation

Chapter 17 Expanding Horizons

Chapter 18 Empires of Asia

Chapter 19 Royal Power and Conflict

Then & Now *The Renaissance and Reformation changed European culture and created powerful political alliances. Europeans set out on uncharted seas to explore the world as powerful European monarchs competed for trade, influence, and territory. While the peoples of the Americas struggled against European invaders, civilizations in Asia reached pinnacles of cultural achievement.*

Every time you use paper money or write a check, you are trusting in a system based on banking that originated during this period. As European trade and commerce increased, merchants turned to bankers for the capital to finance their ventures. Wealthy banking families even made loans to European monarchs. By the 1600s government-chartered banks began to replace family-owned banks. These banks issued banknotes and checks that made trading in heavy coins obsolete.

A Global Chronology

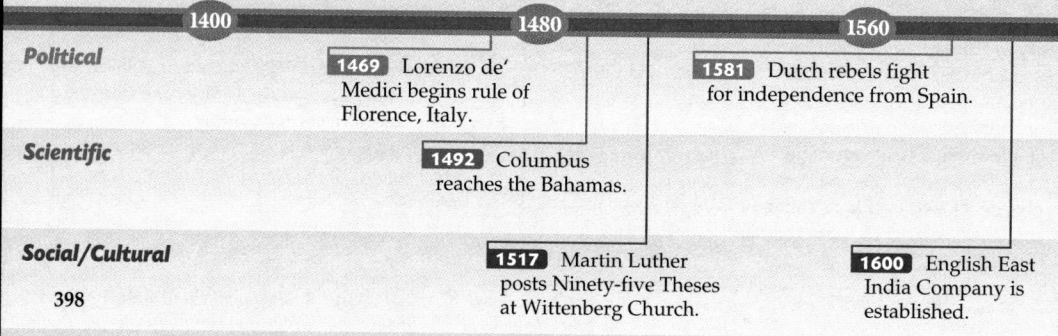

1400 — 1480 — 1560

Political

1469 Lorenzo de' Medici begins rule of Florence, Italy.

1581 Dutch rebels fight for independence from Spain.

Scientific

1492 Columbus reaches the Bahamas.

Social/Cultural

1517 Martin Luther posts Ninety-five Theses at Wittenberg Church.

1600 English East India Company is established.

398

Then & Now

Power In this unit students will learn about the emergence of powerful and wealthy nation-states in Europe and the creation of European colonies in the Americas, Africa, and Asia. Explain that Spain, Portugal, France, Britain, and Holland were the leading commercial and naval powers of the Renaissance and Reformation.

Ask students to make a list of the most powerful nations in the world today, using wealth and

Portfolio Project

Banks originated as places to store money. They then made loans to merchants and others who needed capital. Today banks perform a variety of financial services. Do you know what services your local bank offers? Visit two local banks and pick up several advertising brochures. Compare such things as interest rates, the cost of having a checking account, and the types of loans available. Create a table that shows the different services of early banks and modern banks.

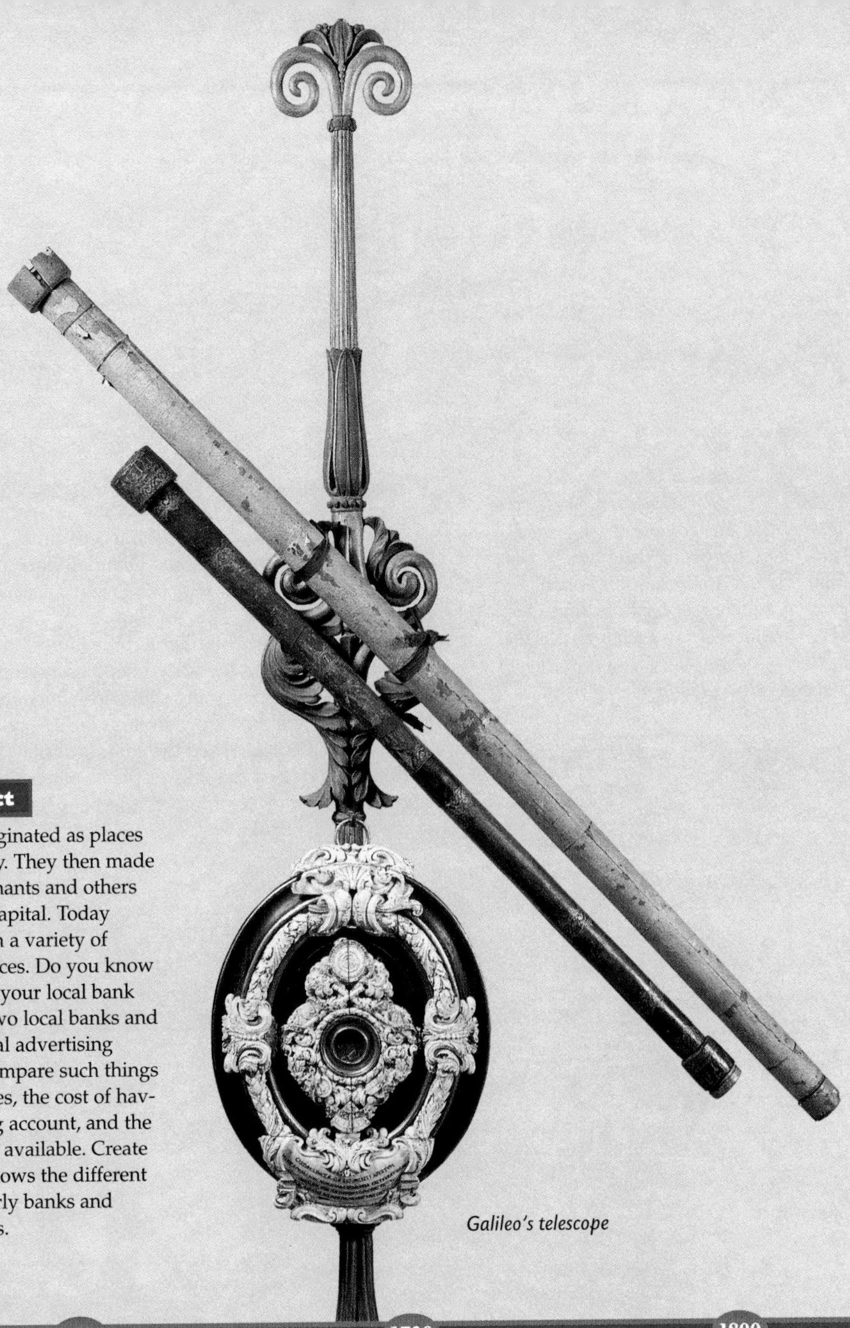

Galileo's telescope

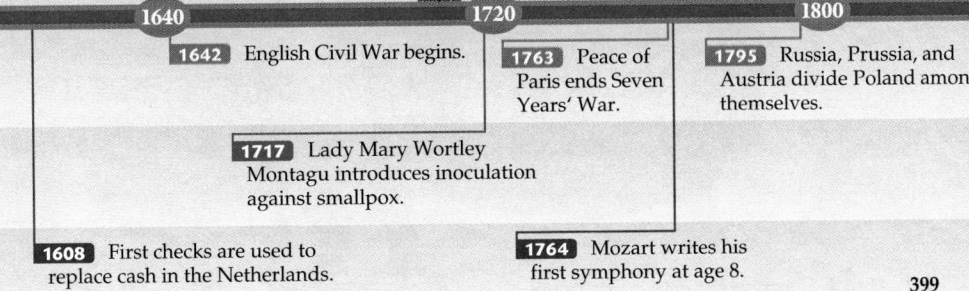

1640 — 1720 — 1800

1608 First checks are used to replace cash in the Netherlands.

1642 English Civil War begins.

1717 Lady Mary Wortley Montagu introduces inoculation against smallpox.

1763 Peace of Paris ends Seven Years' War.

1764 Mozart writes his first symphony at age 8.

1795 Russia, Prussia, and Austria divide Poland among themselves.

military power as their criteria. Are any countries on both lists? Which? *(Britain and France)* Why are some nations wealthy and powerful? *(They possess abundant natural resources, an industrial and technological base, and an educated population.)* What causes nations to lose their position as world leaders? *(loss of economic predominance, limited resources and population, competition of newly industrialized nations)*

Introducing Unit 4

ABCNEWS INTERACTIVE™

VIDEODISC
Turning Points in World History

Side One
Chapter 9

Title: *Age of Exploration*
Subject: Western Europeans seek new routes to Asia.
Ask: In what ways was the age of exploration a turning point? *(Europeans gained territory; indigenous peoples were mistreated, killed, or died from disease; new crops introduced to Europe.)*

History & Art Galileo Galilei was an Italian astronomer, physicist, and mathematician who embodied the Renaissance humanists' ideal of thinking independently. He was tried and convicted of heresy for maintaining that the earth revolved around the sun, rather than vice versa.

History *and the* Humanities

Focus on World Art Prints
- 16 *Portrait of a Noblewoman*
- 20 *The Attributes of Painting*

World History and Art Transparencies
- 20 *Mona Lisa*
- 22 *View of Toledo*
- 24 Taj Mahal
- 25 *Shah Jahan and One of His Sons Riding in Escort*

World Music: Cultural Traditions, Lessons 2, 3, 7

The Spread of Ideas

TEACH

Introduction

This feature focuses on the spread of musical forms from Africa to the Americas as an unintended consequence of the Atlantic slave trade. In North America and the Caribbean, the distinctive African musical forms evolved into spirituals, blues, ragtime, jazz, rock and roll, rap, reggae, calypso, and salsa, among other styles.

Background Notes

Linking Past and Present

Several elements of African music have profoundly influenced modern popular forms, particularly rhythmic polyphony, a more complex and compelling rhythmic style than those of European origin. The minor third, a regular feature of West African music, also became an essential element of blues and rock and roll.

Geography

Movement After reaching North America, African-influenced music was at first found mainly in the Deep South. Early blues masters such as Robert Johnson and Blind Lemon Jefferson came from the Mississippi Basin, and New Orleans and Memphis emerged as centers of the new style. During the Great Depression, millions of African Americans moved north, and the blues traveled with them to St. Louis, Kansas City, Chicago, and New York.

The Spread of Ideas

Music

In the 1400s and 1500s, European ships edged into uncharted waters. These voyages set the stage for one of the greatest cultural exchanges in history, as people from Europe, Africa, and the Americas came face-to-face for the first time. One of the products of this exchange was the birth of "America music," a collection of styles deeply rooted in West Africa.

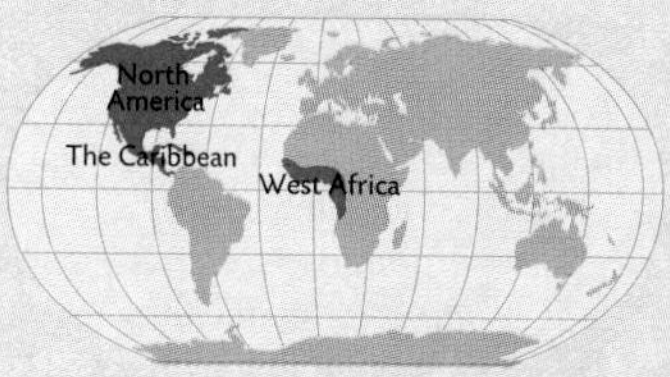

West Africa

Traditional Rhythms

"We are almost a nation of dancers, musicians, and poets," recalled a West African named Olaudah Equiano. "Every great event ... is celebrated ... with songs and music suited to the occasion."

Equiano's words highlighted the importance of music to everyday life among the varied peoples of West Africa. Here musicians won fame for the skill with which they played complicated rhythms on drums, flutes, whistles, and stringed instruments. People added the sounds of their voices to a rhythm known as a call-and-response pattern. A leader would sing out a short piece of music, and people would sing it back to the beat of a drum.

African-style drum

COOPERATIVE LEARNING ACTIVITY

Map Have students use a large outline map of the world to show the diffusion of musical forms from Africa to the Americas, Europe, and back to Africa. Have them label musical centers such as West Africa and New Orleans. Suggest that they use thumbtacks and colored thread to show the paths that music has traveled. Display the finished map in the classroom.

Also encourage students to bring in examples of older forms of music, such as ragtime, blues, jazz, and rhythm and blues, and try to identify similarities and differences in their musical styles. **L1 LEP**

The Spread of Ideas

North America

New Musical Forms

The musical heritage of West Africa traveled to the Americas aboard European slave ships. To endure the pains of slavery, West Africans kept alive musical patterns that reminded them of their ancestral homelands. Because most West Africans came as laborers, work songs took root first. The rhythmic patterns of these songs set the pace for repetitious tasks. West African laborers added field hollers—long calls by a worker in which other workers answered back. Outside the fields, enslaved Africans cried out for freedom in religious folk songs known as spirituals.

Over hundreds of years, these musical forms came together to create new styles. The blues grew out of the field songs and spirituals of slavery. Ragtime echoed the complicated rhythms of West African music. On these foundations grew yet other styles—jazz, rock 'n' roll, and rap.

Chicago 1955 *by Ben Shahn*

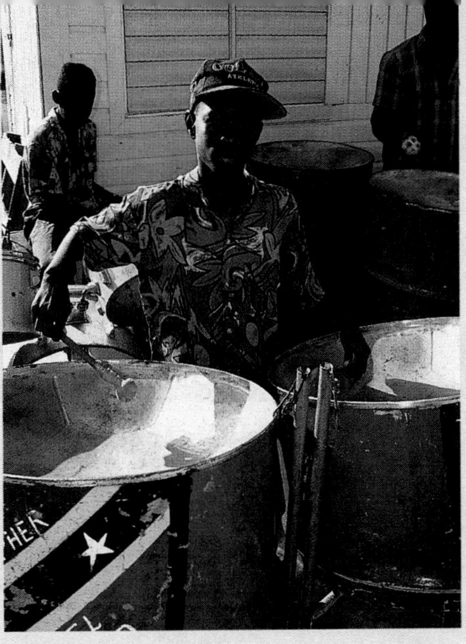

Steel drums of the Caribbean

The Caribbean

Afro-Caribbean Beats

The sounds of West Africa could be heard wherever large enslaved African populations lived in the Americas. On islands in the Caribbean, the beat of bongos, the conga, the tambour, and other West African drums became the soul of Afro-Caribbean music. Added to the drums were European instruments such as the Spanish guitar and a variety of Native American instruments such as the marimba (xylophone), maraca, and wooden rhythm sticks called claves. Out of this blend of influences emerged a range of styles as diverse as the Caribbean islands themselves—reggae, calypso, salsa, and more.

LINKING THE IDEAS

1. What are some of the features of West African music?
2. How did West African music influence musical styles in North America and the Caribbean?

Critical Thinking

3. **Evaluating Information** Which styles of music that you listen to at least once a week are influenced by West African musical patterns?

Who?What?Where?When?

W. C. Handy was a pioneer of jazz and blues. The son of a minister, Handy became a musician over his father's protests. As a young man, he played the cornet in minstrel shows, later forming his own band. In 1912 he published "Memphis Blues," originally composed for a political campaign, and one of the first popular blues songs.

Cultural Diffusion

The Circle Is Unbroken The diffusion of African-influenced music continues. In the 1960s, British groups such as the Beatles, the Rolling Stones, and Led Zeppelin recorded blues and rhythm and blues classics written by Muddy Waters, Howlin' Wolf, and Willie Dixon, among others. The British versions of such songs as "Little Red Rooster" and "Seventh Son" became popular among American fans who had never heard the originals.

At the same time, blues and soul have traveled back across the Atlantic Ocean to influence Ali Farka Toure of Mali and other popular African musicians. Similarly, Caribbean musicians have incorporated elements of rap into merengue, from the Dominican Republic, and reggae, from Jamaica.

ANSWERS TO LINKING THE IDEAS

1. complicated rhythms and call-and-response patterns
2. Musical forms such as work songs, field hollers, and spirituals evolved into modern forms of music such as jazz, rock and roll, rap, salsa, reggae, and calypso.
3. Answers should explain the West African connection.

Teach, Reinforce, and Extend CHAPTER Content

Renaissance and Reformation

CHAPTER RESOURCES	Reproducible Resources	Multimedia Resources
Chapter Opener	Chapter Themes: Graphic Organizer 16 Historical Significance Chapter Activity 16	MindJogger Videoquiz
Chapter Enrichment	Vocabulary Activity 16* Time Line Activity 16 Mapping History Activity 16 History Simulation 16 Geography and History Activity 16 Source Reading 16 People in World History Profiles 29, 30 World Literature Selection 4 World Art and Music Activity 16 Enrichment Activity 16 Critical Thinking Activity 16 Skill Reinforcement Activity 16 Performance Assessment Activity 16	Focus on World Art Print 16, *Portrait of a Noblewoman* NGS Poster Set: *The Renaissance* World History and Art Transparency 20, *Mona Lisa*; 21, *Herzogenburg Monastery* Chapter Transparency 16 NGS PicturePack Transparency Set: *The Renaissance* Vocabulary PuzzleMaker Software NGS PictureShow CD-ROM: *The Renaissance* World Music: Cultural Traditions, Lesson 3 Turning Points in World History
Chapter Review/Reteaching	Reteaching Activity 16 Skill Reinforcement Activity 16 Spanish Chapter Summary 16	Chapter 16 Digest Audiocassette, Activity, Test* Vocabulary PuzzleMaker Software Student Self-Test and Review Software MindJogger Videoquiz
Chapter Evaluation/Testing	Performance Assessment Activity 16 Chapter 16 Test, Forms A and B	Testmaker

** Also available in Spanish*

0:00 **OUT OF TIME?** Assign the Chapter 16 summary in the Unit 4 Digest on pages 506–509, and the Chapter 16 Audiocassettes.

Block Schedule

Block scheduling differs from traditional class scheduling in the amount of time allotted to each period. The extended time frame provided by block scheduling affords you the opportunity to implement a greater number of research-oriented and activity-intense projects to motivate and involve your students. Activities that are particularly suited to use within the block scheduling framework are identified throughout this chapter by the following designation.

KEY TO ABILITY LEVELS

Teaching strategies have been coded for varying learning styles and abilities.

- L1 **BASIC** activities for all students
- L2 **AVERAGE** activities for average to above-average students
- L3 **CHALLENGING** activities for above-average students
- LEP **LIMITED ENGLISH PROFICIENCY** activities

A complete, 1-page lesson plan is provided for each section in the *Reproducible Lesson Plans* booklet.

SECTION RESOURCES

Daily Objectives	Reproducible Resources	Multimedia Resources
Section 1 The Italian Renaissance Identify the factors that inspired the Renaissance.	Reproducible Lesson Plan 16-1 Vocabulary Activity 16* Guided Reading Activity 16-1* People in World History Profile 30 Geography and History Activity 16 Time Line Activity 16 History Simulation 16 Section Quiz 16-1*	NGS Poster Set: *The Renaissance* Section Focus Transparency 16-1 Chapter Transparency 16 World History and Art Transparency 20, *Mona Lisa* NGS PicturePack Transparency Set: *The Renaissance* Student Self-Test and Review Software NGS PictureShow CD-ROM: *The Renaissance*
Section 2 The Northern Renaissance Explain how the Renaissance reached northern Europe.	Reproducible Lesson Plan 16-2 Vocabulary Activity 16* Guided Reading Activity 16-2* Section Quiz 16-2*	Focus on World Art Print 18, Pieter Brueghel. *The Wedding Dance* Section Focus Transparency 16-2 Student Self-Test and Review Software Testmaker
Section 3 The Protestant Reformation Discuss how Luther's religious reforms led to Protestantism, a new branch of Christianity.	Reproducible Lesson Plan 16-3 Vocabulary Activity 16* Guided Reading Activity 16-3* People in World History Profile 29 Section Quiz 16-3*	Section Focus Transparency 16-3 Student Self-Test and Review Software Testmaker Turning Points in World History: *The Reformation*
Section 4 The Spread of Protestantism Identify the different forms of Protestantism that emerged in Europe as the Reformation spread.	Reproducible Lesson Plan 16-4 Vocabulary Activity 16* Guided Reading Activity 16-4* Section Quiz 16-4*	Section Focus Transparency 16-4 Student Self-Test and Review Software Testmaker
Section 5 The Catholic Reformation Describe how the Catholic Church tried to halt the spread of Protestantism.	Reproducible Lesson Plan 16-5 Guided Reading Activity 16-5* Reteaching Activity 16 Enrichment Activity 16 Section Quiz 16-5* Performance Assessment Activity 16 Spanish Chapter Summary 16	Focus on World Art Print 16 Section Focus Transparency 16-5 World History and Art Transparency 21, *Herzogenburg Monastery* Vocabulary PuzzleMaker Software Student Self-Test and Review Software Testmaker

** Also available in Spanish*

Chapter Activities

Performance Assessment Activity

Renaissance and Reformation Have students take the roles of merchants, artisans, and other citizens of Italy and Germany during this era. Pair students and have them write a series of letters to each other in which they give details of the events happening at the time and express their feelings and attitudes regarding the developments and reforms. Each student should write at least five letters that are detailed, persuasive in tone and style, and responsive to the previous letter received.

Possible Rubric Features
Accuracy of content, persuasiveness, concept attainment, appropriateness of inferences and predictions, clarity of organization

- *For an additional activity, refer to Activity 16 in the* Performance Assessment Strategies and Activities *booklet.*

ACTIVITY

From the Classroom of...

Carla Eileen Heckstall
Franklin K. Lane High School
Brooklyn, NY

Renaissance Art and Modern Art

Organize the class into two groups. Have one group review pictures of artwork from the Renaissance. (You may use pictures from the text.) Have the other group review pictures of modern art, preferably from the 1990s. (Use pictures from art magazines or museum or gallery catalogs.)

Ask both groups to select two or three pictures and try to identify values the artists were trying to depict. Have students compare the list of values from the Renaissance art with the list from the modern art.

MULTIPLE LEARNING STYLES

Verbal/Linguistic
Have students research and then debate the following statement: Without the Renaissance, the Reformation could never have taken place.

Logical/Mathematical
Have students create a time line of major events that occurred during the Renaissance and Reformation.

Visual/Spatial
Have students design a bulletin-board display that identifies famous Renaissance paintings, sculptures, and buildings.

Auditory/Musical
Have students collect and present examples of court, church, and popular music that were common in Europe during the Renaissance and Reformation.

Kinesthetic
Have students research and reenact the meeting with Luther at the Diet of Worms in 1521. Remind them to clearly present and defend the points of view of the Catholic Church and of Martin Luther.

Additional Resources

TEACHER'S CORNER

NATIONAL GEOGRAPHIC SOCIETY

INDEX TO NATIONAL GEOGRAPHIC MAGAZINE

The following articles may be used for research relating to this chapter:

- "Out of the Darkness: Michelangelo's Last Judgment," by Meg Nottingham Walsh, May 1994.
- "A Renaissance for Michelangelo," by David Jeffrey, December 1989.
- "Restoration Reveals the Last Supper," by Carlo Bertelli, November 1983.
- "The World of Luther," by Merle Severy, October 1983.
- "Carrara Marble: Touchstone of Eternity," by Cathy Newman, July 1982.

NATIONAL GEOGRAPHIC SOCIETY PRODUCTS AVAILABLE FROM GLENCOE

To order the following products for use with this chapter, contact your local Glencoe sales representative or call Glencoe at 1-800-368-7344:

NGS PICTUREPACK TRANSPARENCY SET
- The Renaissance

NGS POSTER SET
- The Renaissance

NGS PICTURESHOW CD-ROM
- The Renaissance

ADDITIONAL NATIONAL GEOGRAPHIC SOCIETY PRODUCTS

To order the following products for use with this chapter, call National Geographic Society at 1-800-368-2728:

- *Nations of the World Series*, "East Germany." (Video)
- *The Renaissance*, "A Changing World," "The Spirit of an Age," "Art and Architecture." (Filmstrip)

BIBLIOGRAPHY

Literature of the Period

Castiglione, Baldassare. *The Book of the Courtier.* Translated by George Bull. New York: Penguin, 1976. Contemporary handbook of courtly etiquette.

Readings for the Student

Rabb, Theodore K. *Renaissance Lives: Portraits of an Age.* New York: Pantheon, 1993. The Renaissance through the lives of fifteen Renaissance men and women.

Readings for the Teacher

Lucas, Henry. *The Renaissance and the Reformation.* New York: Harper, 1960. Historical survey of the Renaissance, Reformation, and the Catholic Reformation.

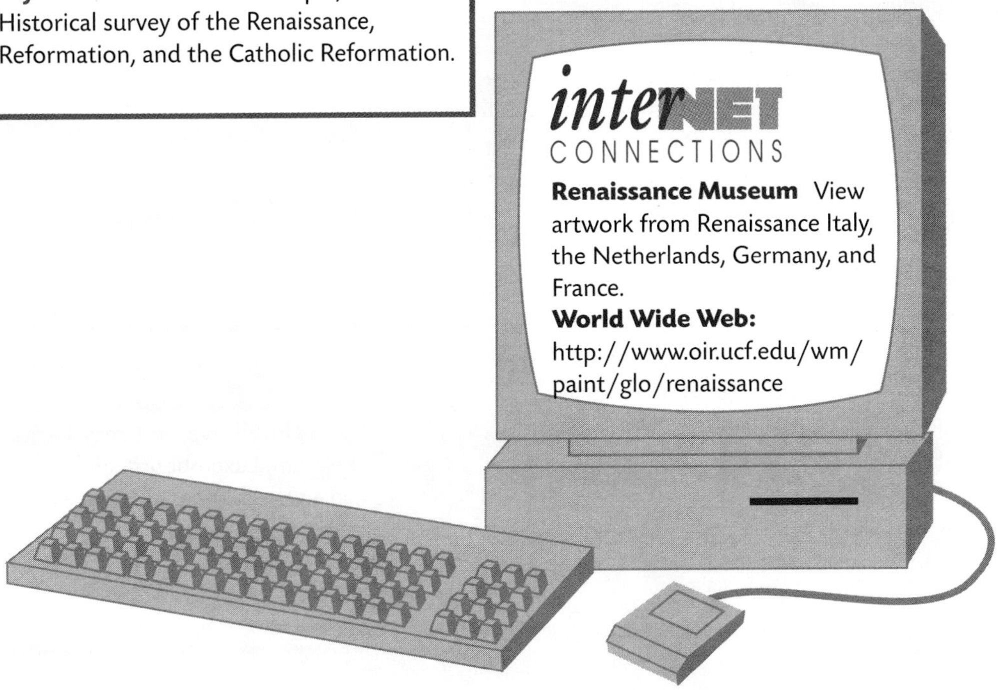
interNET
CONNECTIONS
Renaissance Museum View artwork from Renaissance Italy, the Netherlands, Germany, and France.
World Wide Web:
http://www.oir.ucf.edu/wm/paint/glo/renaissance

Introducing Chapter 16

CHAPTER THEMES

Chapter Themes are listed by section on this chapter opening page of the Student Edition. A corresponding theme-based activity is available under "TEACH," and a theme-based question is asked in the Section and Chapter Reviews.

The Storyteller

Historical Setting The House of Este, which ruled Ferrara from the 1200s through the 1500s, was one of the most influential families in Italian politics. Ercole I, father of Isabella d'Este, used marriage as a means of consolidating his political and military position. He himself had married the daughter of the king of Naples. Not only did he arrange Isabella's marriage to the Marquis of Mantua, Francesco Gonzaga, but his two other daughters married the rulers of Bologna and Milan.

Historical Significance

Answers: *During the Renaissance, interest in the art, literature, and values of classical Greece and Rome caused Europeans to place greater emphasis on life here and now and on the worth of each individual, as well as to view themselves as part of a world larger than their town or village.*

During the Reformation, many northern Europeans left the Catholic Church and joined new Protestant religions. In some countries, the king became head of the new church. In other countries, the church controlled the government. Protestant religions with small numbers of followers were often persecuted. Their members sought religious freedom and separation of church and state.

Chapter 16

1400–1600

Renaissance and Reformation

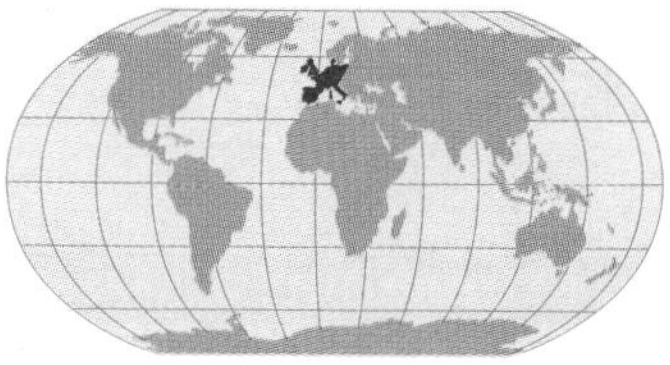

Chapter Themes

- **Innovation** The Renaissance leads to an artistic and intellectual awakening in Europe. *Section 1*
- **Cultural Diffusion** Renaissance ideas and artistic styles spread from Italy to northern Europe. *Section 2*
- **Conflict** Martin Luther's protests against the Catholic Church result in Protestantism. *Section 3*
- **Cultural Diffusion** Protestant religious groups spread reform through northern Europe. *Section 4*
- **Reaction** The Catholic Church enacts its own reform, the Catholic Reformation. *Section 5*

The Storyteller

Isabella d'Este, married in 1490 at the age of 16 to the Marquis of Mantua, played a vital role in ruling the Italian city-state of Mantua. A brilliant and well-educated young woman who loved Latin literature, Isabella gathered a fashionable assemblage of artists and statesmen in her sparkling court. In a room decorated with ornately carved woodwork and paintings that illustrated Greek myths, Isabella entertained her guests to her own lute recitals and poetry readings. Isabella was one of the many Italians of her time who rediscovered and repopularized Greek and Roman classics, educating their contemporaries to the glories of their classical past after a thousand years of neglect. The word Renaissance, *coming from the French word meaning "rebirth," was coined to refer to this rebirth of interest in classical ideas and culture.*

Historical Significance

What happened during the Renaissance that changed Europeans' outlook on the world? How did the Reformation shape the religious and political life of Europe?

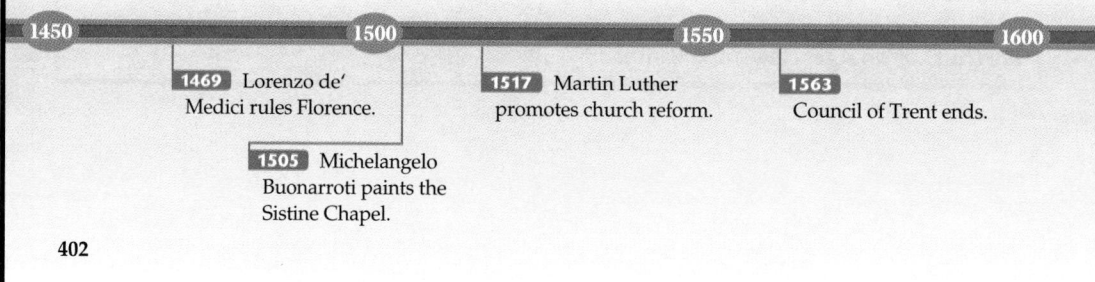

1450 — 1500 — 1550 — 1600

- **1469** Lorenzo de' Medici rules Florence.
- **1505** Michelangelo Buonarroti paints the Sistine Chapel.
- **1517** Martin Luther promotes church reform.
- **1563** Council of Trent ends.

GEOGRAPHY CONNECTION

Location Have students locate Italy, France, the Low Countries (present-day Belgium, Luxembourg, and the Netherlands), Germany, England, and Switzerland on a physical map of Europe in the Atlas of this book. What main geographic barrier separates Italy from these other countries? *(mountains: the Alps)* How could this barrier have affected the spread of new ideas? *(The mountains would have made overland travel difficult.)* **L1**

History & Art Detail of *The Court* by Andrea Mantegna. Palazzo Ducale, Mantua, Italy

Your History Journal

Choose a Renaissance sculptor, architect, or painter mentioned in this chapter. Research and write a short report on the work and influence of this person.

EXTRA CREDIT PROJECT

Research First-person accounts and other information about the Renaissance and Reformation are available in many books. Have students research and report to the class on a person, event, or artwork from this historical period that is not detailed in the chapter. Suggest that students use vivid quotations from the first-person accounts and use descriptive language in their own explanations.

Introducing Chapter 16

History & Art Tell students that Andrea Mantegna served as painter to the Gonzaga court at Mantua from 1460 until his death in 1506. Besides executing large frescoes for the palace, Mantegna painted smaller works for Isabella d'Este's study. How does the artist show Gonzaga's importance in this fresco? *(He is seated in an armchair, surrounded by family and servants, and is being consulted about some kind of business.)*

Performance Assessment

Refer to the activity on page 402C of the Planning Guide.

For an additional activity, refer to Activity 16 in the *Performance Assessment Strategies and Activities* booklet.

Using Your History Journal

Have students use their journals to take notes, organize their ideas, and write a rough draft of the report.

GLENCOE TECHNOLOGY

VIDEODISC

Use MindJogger to preview chapter content.

MindJogger Videoquiz

Chapter 16
Disc 2 Side B

Also available in VHS.

Chapter 16 Section 1

SECTION THEME

▶ **Innovation** The Renaissance leads to an artistic and intellectual awakening in Europe.

Find Out

Answer: *the discovery of Greek and Roman works, rise of humanism, opening of new schools, and the rise of a wealthy middle class in cities*

FOCUS

Section Objective

Identify the factors that inspired the Renaissance.

BELLRINGER Motivational Activity

Before taking roll at the beginning of the class period, project Section Focus Transparency 16-1 and have students answer the activity questions. Discuss students' responses.

This activity is also available as a blackline master.

Vocabulary Pre-check

Use Vocabulary Activity 16 to introduce vocabulary terms. **L1 LEP**

1400 — 1450 — 1500

1436 Filippo Brunelleschi designs dome for Florence Cathedral.

c. 1490 Florence enjoys economic prosperity.

c. 1500 Rome replaces Florence as the leading Renaissance city.

Section 1

The Italian Renaissance

Setting the Scene

▶ **Terms to Define**
humanism, sonnet, doge

▶ **People to Meet**
Niccolò Machiavelli, Lorenzo de' Medici, Michelangelo Buonarroti, Leonardo da Vinci

▶ **Places to Locate**
Florence, Rome, Venice

Find Out What factors inspired the Renaissance?

The Storyteller

Working feverishly for the last few months, Michelangelo finally finished the Sistine Chapel in September 1512. Pope Julius came to see the completed work. One man had covered ten thousand square feet with the greatest wall painting in Italy. He wrote to his father, "I have finished the chapel which I have been painting. The Pope is very satisfied.... Your Michelangelo, sculptor, in Rome." The artist, tired and in poor health, went home to Florence, hoping for rest and relaxation.

—adapted from *Michelangelo The Man*, Donald Lord Finlayson, 1935

Ancestors of Christ, detail from the Sistine Chapel

The Renaissance—the period from about 1350 until 1600 during which western Europeans experienced a profound cultural awakening—was in many ways a continuation of the Middle Ages, but it also signaled the beginning of modern times. The Renaissance caused educated Europeans to develop new attitudes about themselves and the world around them.

The Renaissance began first in the city-states of Italy. Unlike other areas of Europe, Italy had largely avoided the economic crisis of the late Middle Ages. Italian towns remained important centers of Mediterranean trade and boosted their production of textiles and luxury goods.

More than other Europeans, Italians were attached to classical traditions. The ruins of ancient Roman buildings, arches, and amphitheaters constantly reminded them of their heritage. Moreover, through trade Italian towns remained in close contact with the Byzantine Empire, where scholars preserved the learning of ancient Greece.

Humanism

As newly discovered works came to their attention, Italian scholars developed a strong interest in classical writings. This interest in the classics was called **humanism**. Humanists—the scholars who promoted humanism—improved their understanding of Greek and Latin, studied old manuscripts, and tried to copy the classical writing style.

As they studied, humanists came to admire classical culture but also adopted many Greek and Roman beliefs. For example, humanists found the classical idea of seeking fulfillment in daily life more appealing than the medieval belief that people should expect little comfort from life on earth. Humanists also embraced the Greco-Roman belief

SECTION RESOURCES

Reproducible Masters
- Reproducible Lesson Plan 16-1
- Vocabulary Activity 16
- Guided Reading Activity 16-1
- People in World History Profile 30
- Geography and History Activity 16
- Time Line Activity 16
- History Simulation 16
- Section Quiz 16-1

Transparencies
- Section Focus Transparency 16-1
- Chapter Transparency 16
- World History and Art Transparency 20
- The Renaissance

Multimedia
- The Renaissance
- Student Self-Test and Review Software
- Testmaker
- The Renaissance

that each individual has dignity and worth. Humanists also renewed the Greek idea of an ideal person—one who participates in a variety of activities: politics, sports, art, literature, and music.

Education and Literature

To help others gain fulfillment and achieve the Greek ideal, humanists opened schools to teach subjects related to the study of humanity—history, philosophy, Latin, and Greek. These schools soon became so popular that humanists began to replace the clergy as teachers of the sons of wealthy merchants and artisans.

Humanism also inspired new forms of writing—in particular, writing about the daily life and feelings of people. Among the most noted works of humanist Francesco Petrarca, or Petrarch (PEE•TRAHRK), were 366 sonnets, or short poems, that express his love for a woman named Laura who had died during the Black Death. Benvenuto Cellini (chuh•LEE•nee), a goldsmith and sculptor by trade, wrote one of the first modern autobiographies. He encouraged anyone who had done anything of excellence "to describe their life with their own hand," as he had.

Another literary achievement was in political science. In the early 1500s, Florentine diplomat **Niccolò Machiavelli** (mak•ee•uh•VEHL•ee) wrote *The Prince*, a treatise in which he analyzed the politics of Renaissance Italy. Although embraced by power-hungry rulers, the book was attacked by many for the methods Machiavelli advocated. In his analysis he advised rulers to be prepared to use force and deceit to maintain power.

Humanism affected literature in another significant respect. Some humanists broke free of the tradition of writing in Latin, the language of the clergy. By writing in the language of everyday speech, humanists provided literature that was accessible to more people and inspired regional pride in those who read it.

Scholarship

Humanist scholars influenced more than just literature. With their independent thinking, they began to challenge long-accepted traditions, assumptions, and institutions. As they made all sorts of unsettling discoveries, it further validated their desire to challenge and question nearly everything—even long-standing church traditions. For example, in an exciting piece of Renaissance detective work, the scholar Lorenzo Valla determined that a document that supposedly provided the legal basis for the pope's supremacy over kings was actually a forgery.

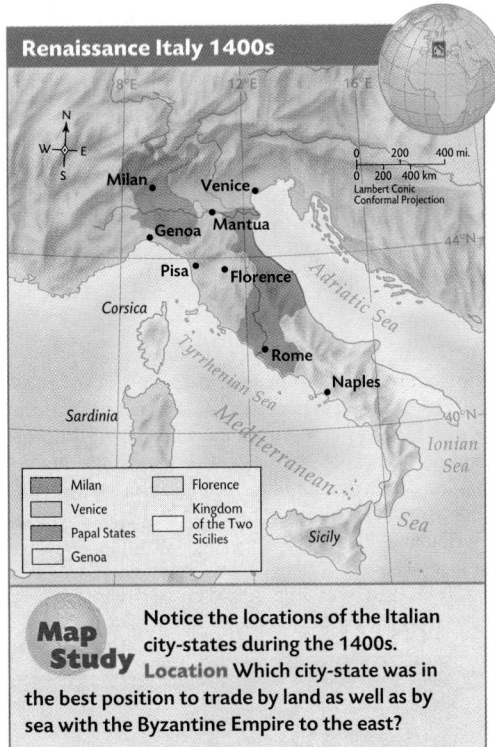

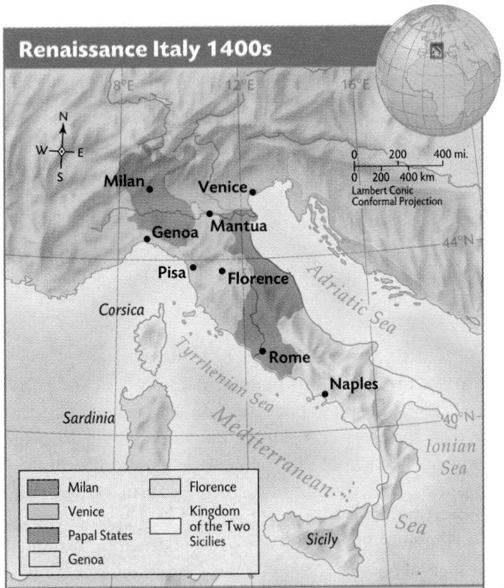

Map Study **Notice the locations of the Italian city-states during the 1400s. Location Which city-state was in the best position to trade by land as well as by sea with the Byzantine Empire to the east?**

Through their teaching and writing, humanists reawakened the educated public to classical values. They also encouraged a ferment of new ideas that eventually spread from Italy throughout Europe and reshaped European civilization.

City Life

Town life was stronger in Italy than in other parts of Europe. As a result, Italians could easily discard feudalism and other medieval institutions that had their origins in the rural north. Italy did not become unified as did France and England. Wealthy and successful, most Italian communes, or communities, resisted the efforts of emperors, kings, and nobles to control them. They became independent city-states, each of which included a walled urban center and the surrounding countryside.

Social Groups

The Italian city-states fashioned a new social order in which wealth and ability mattered more than aristocratic titles and ownership of land. Wealthy merchants and bankers replaced the

Chapter 16 Section 1

TEACH

Guided Practice

THEME Innovation

Ask students to volunteer examples from this section of innovations in literature and art that resulted from the influence of humanism. *(new forms of writing, such as sonnets and autobiography; literature in the common language instead of Latin; more lifelike art; classical as well as religious themes in painting and sculpture)* Write their suggestions on the chalkboard. **L1**

Map Study

Answer

Venice

Map Skills Practice

Reading a Map In which part of Italy were most of its great Renaissance cities located? *(north)*

NATIONAL GEOGRAPHIC SOCIETY

Use these materials to enrich student understanding of the Renaissance.

- **NGS PICTURESHOW CD-ROM**
  The Renaissance
- **NGS PICTUREPACK TRANSPARENCY SET**
  The Renaissance
- **NGS POSTER SET**
  The Renaissance

COOPERATIVE LEARNING ACTIVITY

Oral Reports Have students compare the Renaissance in Milan, Mantua, and Genoa. Organize students into three teams, each studying one city. Have each team split into subgroups to research a topic such as government, economy, patrons of the arts, women, painting, sculpture, or architecture in their city. When research is complete, have subgroups report their findings to the whole team. Then have each team prepare an overall summary of its research. Ask each team to select a member to present orally to the class the team's overall summary of its Renaissance city. **L2**

Chapter 16 Section 1

Geography: Movement Have students review a map of the Byzantine Empire to explain how Italy's trade routes helped maintain the influence of earlier cultures. *(Routes across the Adriatic, Ionian, and Mediterranean Seas led to Greece and Turkey as well as to other countries of the Byzantine Empire.)* **L1**

Government Write the following names on the chalkboard: *Florence, Rome, Venice*. Ask students to compare the governments of these three Renaissance city-states. **What did their governments have in common?** *(The wealthy held power.)* **How did their governments differ?** *(The Medici family ruled Florence; the pope and cardinals ruled Rome; Venice had a republican form of government headed by an elected doge and the Council of Ten.)* **L3**

Chapter Transparency 16

World History and Art Transparency 20, *Mona Lisa*

History Simulation 16

Who?What?Where?When?

Machiavelli's *The Prince* was roundly denounced by the Medici family, even though it had been dedicated to Lorenzo de' Medici. To express his political views to a wider audience, Machiavelli turned to writing plays. His comedy *Mandragola* is considered one of Italy's best Renaissance plays.

landed nobility as the most powerful social and political group—the upper class. Shopkeepers and artisans ranked below the wealthy merchants, forming a moderately prosperous middle class that employed large numbers of poor workers. Most of these workers—who were the majority of town dwellers—came to urban areas from the countryside. At the bottom of the social order were the peasants who worked on the country estates of the upper class.

Government

During the Renaissance, Italy was not under one government, but instead consisted of individual city-states, each ruled by a wealthy family whose fortunes came from commercial trading or banking. Peasants often rebelled against the upper classes. Their demands for equal rights and lower taxes, however, were suppressed.

During the 1400s, social conflicts created upheaval so often that certain city-states felt it necessary to turn over all political authority to a single powerful leader to restore peace. These powerful political leaders were called signori (seen•YOHR •ee). Some signori ruled as dictators, using violence to maintain control. Others successfully ensured popular loyalty by improving city services, supporting the arts, and providing festivals and parades for the lower classes.

While dealing with internal unrest, city-states also fought with each other in territorial disputes. But the prosperous merchants and bankers, unlike the nobility they had supplanted, did not want to fight in these battles. Since military service would interfere with conducting business and trade, the signori chose to replace citizen-soldiers with hired soldiers known as condottieri (KAHN•duh•TYEHR•ee).

Hiring condottieri made wars very costly. To avoid this expense, signori began to seek territorial gain through negotiated agreements. To carry out this policy, they assembled the first modern diplomatic services. Permanent ambassadors were appointed to represent their city-states at foreign

Images of the Times

Art of the Italian Renaissance

The Italian Renaissance produced a host of great Italian artists and sculptors. Among the most notable of these were Michelangelo, Raphael, and Leonardo da Vinci.

Michelangelo created *David*, a gigantic marble sculpture, while at home in Florence between 1501 and 1504. A painter, architect, sculptor, and poet, he has had an unparalleled influence on Western art.

406

Images of the Times **Art of the Italian Renaissance**

Leonardo da Vinci's *Mona Lisa* has fascinated art lovers and the general public for centuries. To this day, art critics and historians still do not know for sure who the woman in the painting is or why she is smiling. Some say that a wealthy Florentine merchant named Giocondo commissioned Leonardo to paint a portrait of his third wife. This painting became the famous *La Gioconda*, also known as *Mona Lisa*. Toward the end of his life, Leonardo sold the painting to Francis I, the king of France, who hung it in the Louvre in Paris where it can still be seen today.

courts. The city-states also worked out an agreement among all the city-states that no one city-state would be allowed enough power to threaten the others. During the 1500s other European states adopted similar agreements with one another and also began to practice diplomacy.

Although the Italian city-states had much in common, each developed its own characteristic life. Three cities in particular played leading roles in the Renaissance: **Florence**, **Rome**, and **Venice**.

Florence

Originally a republic, Florence in the 1400s came under the rule of a prominent banking family known as the Medici (MEH•duh•chee). Medici rulers helped to foster the spirit of humanism among the city-state's scholars and artists. With this spirit alive throughout the city, Florence became the birthplace of the Italian Renaissance.

Cosimo de' Medici was the first Medici to rule Florence. He worked to end peasant uprisings by introducing an income tax that placed a heavier burden on wealthier citizens. He used the tax revenues to make city improvements, such as sewers and paved streets, that benefited everyone. Cosimo also worked to establish peaceful relations between the city and its neighbors.

Cosimo's grandson **Lorenzo de' Medici** ruled Florence from 1469 to 1492, and he continued policies like those of his grandfather. He used his wealth to support artists, philosophers, and writers and to sponsor public festivals. As a result of the city's prosperity and fame, Lorenzo was known as "the Magnificent."

During the 1490s Florence's economic prosperity, based mostly on the banking and textile industries, began to decline with increasing competition from English and Flemish cloth makers. Tired of the Medici rule, discontented citizens rallied in support of a Dominican friar named Girolamo Savonarola (SA•vuh•nuh•ROH•luh). In fiery sermons before hundreds of people, Savonarola attacked the Medici for promoting ideas that he claimed were causing the downfall of Florence:

Leonardo da Vinci painted the *Mona Lisa* during a period of intensive study in Florence in 1503. His talent was also expressed in sculpture, architecture, and engineering.

Raphael painted the *School of Athens* for Pope Julius II. When Raphael died in Rome on his 37th birthday, the whole city mourned. His funeral mass was celebrated at the Vatican.

REFLECTING ON THE TIMES

1. What two Italian cities were centers of artistic development and expression in the early 1500s?
2. Why are there many similarities in style and subject matter among works of the Italian Renaissance?

407

ANSWERS TO REFLECTING ON THE TIMES

1. Florence and Rome
2. The Italian Renaissance artists were all influenced by humanism; because they studied and worked in the same cities, they were in contact with and came to influence one another.

Chapter 16 Section 1

Independent Practice

Guided Reading Activity 16-1 **L1**

The Arts Organize students into small groups. Have each group write brief descriptions of the artworks shown in this section. Also ask students to compare Renaissance art with the medieval art in Chapter 13. **L1 LEP**

Daily Life Have students use outside sources to research one of the following types of Renaissance persons: wealthy banker or merchant, shopkeeper, artisan, manual worker, or peasant. Ask students to write a diary entry for a typical day in their person's life. **L2**

you don't say...

Penknife During the 1400s, penknives were just that—knives for trimming quill pens, whose points quickly became dull. After metal pen points were invented, the term *penknife* came to mean any small blade that could be carried in a pocket.

Linking Past and Present

Tunics, mid-thigh-length garments worn over tights, were fashionable attire for many young Renaissance men. Today, many women favor a similar style of clothing—a long, loose sweater or shirt worn over pants.

Chapter 16
Section 1

History & Art Brunelleschi, a Florentine goldsmith, began his artistic career in 1401 by entering the contest to design the doors of Florence's baptistry. When Ghiberti's design was chosen, Brunelleschi turned to architecture. What characteristics of Renaissance art are shown in his sculpture? *(emotions shown, people and animals look lifelike)*
Answer to Caption: *designing a dome for the Cathedral of Florence*

Critical Thinking Have students research Savonarola's impact on life in Florence. Then have them write a letter to the editor of a Florence newspaper either in support of or in opposition to Savonarola. Encourage students whose letters express opposite points of view to compare them. **L3**

People in World History Profile 30

Geography and History Activity 16

Time Line Activity 16

Global Gourmet

Italy In 1536, François Rabelais, a French writer, discovered a new taste treat in Naples—lettuce. From Naples to his home in France Rabelais sent what he called salad seeds (lettuce seeds) along with instructions on how to plant and cultivate them.

History & Art Brunelleschi's sculpture of the sacrifice of Isaac was a contest entry for the east doors of the Baptistry in Florence. *Brunelleschi lost but is remembered for what architectural feat?*

> "In the mansions of the great prelates and great lords there is no concern save for poetry and the oratorical art. Go … and see; [you] shall find them all with books of the humanities in their hands.… Arise and come to deliver [your] Church from the hands of the devils!"

So many people were won over by Savonarola that the Medici family was forced to turn over the rule of Florence to his supporters. On Savonarola's advice, the city's new leaders imposed strict regulations on public behavior. Parties, gambling, swearing, and horse racing were banned. Savonarola urged his listeners to repent of their "worldly" ways. For a time, he had crowds make bonfires to burn books, paintings, fancy clothes, and musical instruments.

Savonarola soon aroused a great deal of opposition to his preaching. His criticism of church officials angered the pope. Many people in Florence disliked his strict ways. In 1498 Savonarola was hanged for heresy, and the Medici family returned to power. By this time, however, Florence's greatness had passed.

Rome

By 1500 Rome had replaced Florence as the leading Renaissance city. In Rome, the pope and the cardinals living in the Vatican made up the wealthiest and most powerful class.

Eager to increase their prestige, Renaissance popes rebuilt the ancient city. They commissioned architects to construct ornate churches and palaces. They had artists create magnificent paintings and sculptures glorifying religious themes to decorate these buildings. One of their most notable projects was rebuilding St. Peter's Basilica, the largest Christian church in the world. They amassed so many manuscripts and books in the Vatican Library that it attracted scholars from all over Europe.

Renaissance popes lived and behaved more like signori than religious leaders. They often overlooked their religious duties to handle political affairs. They relied on political ambassadors to direct negotiations between their city-state and other city-states in Italy. The popes also collected taxes. The fortunes they spent on architecture and the arts were financed mostly by these taxes.

Although Rome possessed enormous wealth and beauty, by the late 1500s the city of Venice in northeastern Italy rivaled it. Furthermore, as Venetian wealth and power grew, so too did its power to lure artists and scholars away from Rome. By the late 1500s the focus of the Italian Renaissance had shifted from Rome to Venice.

Venice

Perched on a hundred islands at the north end of the Adriatic Sea, Venice was ideally situated to maintain a trade monopoly with Asia. Because it served as the link between western Europe and Asia, this bustling port city also attracted traders from all over the world. These advantages made Venice the wealthiest and most powerful city-state in Italy during the late Renaissance. At the height of its power, the city-state of Venice stretched from the Adriatic Sea in the east to Milan in the west.

Unlike Florence and Rome, Venice had a republican form of government headed by the elected doge (DOHJ), or duke. Although the doge administered the city, the wealthiest merchants held the real power. Indeed, by law the doge could not answer important political correspondence or speak to foreign envoys unless an executive committee of wealthy merchants known as the Council of Ten was present. This council passed laws, elected the doge, and even had to be consulted should the doge's son want to marry.

The city's merchants collected money on all products that passed through their port. Because

MEETING SPECIAL NEEDS ACTIVITY

Learning Style: Visual/Spatial Encourage students who are strong visual learners to draw pictures of some activities representative of the Italian Renaissance. Drawings might include humanist scholars teaching the new learning, Cosimo de' Medici ending a peasant uprising, Savonarola preaching to the people of Florence, a papal banquet, or a meeting of the doge of Venice and the Council of Ten. Have students display their drawings in the classroom. Number each drawing (1, 2, 3, and so on). Then have each class member view the display and identify what activity is illustrated by each drawing. **L1 LEP**

Venice teemed with commercial activity, this income kept them rich enough to afford palazzos, or palaces, overlooking the Grand Canal and luxuries such as beautiful Flemish tapestries to hang on their walls.

Meanwhile, Venice's reputation as the jewel of the Renaissance grew. Shipyards became famous producing huge galleys and graceful gondolas. Venetian printing houses earned a solid reputation for publishing works of high quality, and paintings by Venetian artists came to be in great demand.

Artistic Achievements

What were the unique characteristics of Renaissance art? The humanists' emphasis on cultivating individual talent inspired Italian artists to express their own values, emotions, and attitudes. No longer content with creating symbolic representations of their subjects, artists made their subjects as lifelike and captivating as possible. Although much of the art was still devoted to religious subjects, it had more secular, or worldly, overtones. Interest in ancient Greece and Rome moved artists to include classical mythology as well as biblical themes in their works.

To make their creations lifelike and captivating, artists experimented with new techniques. For example, they learned to create a sense of perspective, which gave their paintings depth. They studied anatomy so they could portray human figures more accurately and naturally. Artists also learned to depict subtleties of gesture and expression to convey human emotions.

The public in Renaissance Italy appreciated works of art and hailed great artists as geniuses. Nobles and townspeople used art to decorate homes as well as churches. They lavishly rewarded artists and gave them a prominent place in society.

Architecture

During the Middle Ages, cathedral architects had pointed soaring arches and spires heavenward for the glory of God. During the Renaissance, however, Italian architects returned to the classical style. On churches, palaces, and villas they substituted domes and columns from classical Greek and Roman architecture for the medieval arches and spires. They sought both comfort and beauty in their buildings, adorning them with tapestries, paintings, statues, finely made furniture, and glass windows. Unlike the anonymous architects of the Middle Ages, Renaissance architects took credit for their fine buildings.

The most famous Italian Renaissance architect was Filippo Brunelleschi (BROO•nuhl•EHS•kee), best known for the dome he designed and completed in 1436 for the Cathedral of Florence. Until Brunelleschi submitted his design, no one had been able to come up with a way to construct a dome large or strong enough to cover the cathedral without the dome collapsing from its own weight. Brunelleschi's design—based on his own study of the domes, columns, and arches of ancient Rome—was considered to be the greatest engineering feat of the time.

Sculpture

Renaissance sculpture reflected a return to classical ideals. The free-standing statues of nude figures sculpted in bronze or marble during the Renaissance resembled ancient Greek and Roman sculptures of nude figures much more than they did medieval sculptures. Human figures in medieval sculptures had usually been portrayed in a stiff, stylized manner.

Some of the best-known Renaissance sculptors—Donatello, Michelangelo, and Ghiberti (gee•BEHR•tee)—came from Florence. There the Medici family opened a school for sculptors. Donatello was the first sculptor since ancient times to cast a statue in bronze. Although the brilliant sculptor **Michelangelo Buonarroti** later moved to Rome to sculpt works for the pope, he learned his craft in Florence. Florentine sculptor Lorenzo Ghiberti took 21 years to create 10 magnificent New Testament scenes on bronze doors for Florence's cathedral baptistry.

AROUND THE WORLD

Timur Lenk Rebuilds Central Mosque

Samarkand, 1404

Timur Lenk (Tamerlane), the Mongol ruler, decided to rebuild the central mosque in Samarkand, making it grander than any in Asia. The Bibi Khanum mosque consisted of 4 vaulted halls. Its 480 marble pillars were carried by teams of elephants from quarries 25 miles (40 km) away. The vault of the central dome was so large that one of its gold inscriptions reportedly could be read a mile away. Shortly after completion the central dome collapsed.

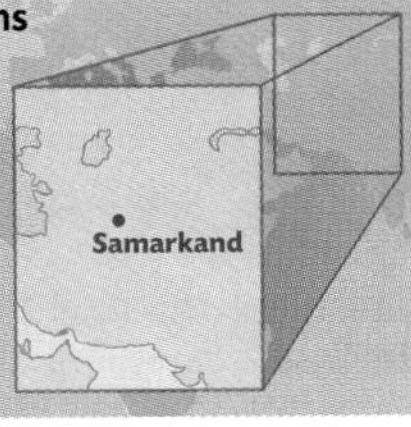

CURRICULUM CONNECTION

THE ARTS

Renaissance artists used perspective to create a three-dimensional effect in their two-dimensional works. Objects in such paintings achieve depth and distance because the artist draws the viewer's eye to an invisible vanishing point.

Cultural Perspectives

Renaissance **palazzi** took their name from the Latin word *palatium*, which meant the area in Rome where the emperors built their homes. The English word *palace*, which also comes from *palatium*, refers to homes of royalty. In Italian, however, *palazzo* simply means a large urban home.

ASSESS

Check for Understanding

Assign Section 1 Review as homework or as an in-class activity.

Use Student Self-Test and Review Software to review Section 1.

MAKING CONNECTIONS ACTIVITY

Sports The Renaissance revived the Greek concept that an ideal person participated in a variety of activities, including sports. Have students research and report to the class on one of the following popular Renaissance games or sports: javelin hurling, tennis, chess, archery, fencing, boxing, falconry, hunting, and gambling. Tell students to explain how these sports or games are alike or different from the same activities today. Ask students to bring props for their reports and, if possible, to give a brief demonstration of the skills needed for their game or sport. **L2**

TEACH

Tell students that to show life and activity, Leonardo chose to illustrate the moment when Jesus says that one of his disciples will betray him. The disciples are caught as they ask, "Is it I?" Encourage students to compare this painting with religious paintings of the Middle Ages and to note the differences in style and subject matter.

More About . . .

The Last Supper A friend of Leonardo's suggested that he leave the face of Jesus incomplete so viewers would not compare Jesus to the disciples.

CURRICULUM CONNECTION

TECHNOLOGY

Because Leonardo believed that an artist's most important work was thinking and planning rather than the actual painting or brush strokes, he didn't use the standard fresco technique of painting on wet plaster, which required quick, certain strokes. Instead, he painted *The Last Supper* on dry plaster with tempera. That is why the painting soon started to deteriorate.

"The Last Supper"

Victor R. Boswell, Jr.

"One of you shall betray me," said Jesus, sitting amid the disciples gathered around in a flurry of worry, gossip, and fear. Between 1495 and 1497 Leonardo da Vinci painted *The Last Supper* on the walls of a monastery in Milan, Italy. Unstable paint and centuries of wear slowly destroyed the mural. In 1977 restoration of the painting began, as shown in the detail (above) depicting the apostles Matthew, Thaddeus, and Simon. The larger view of the masterpiece (left) shows visitors clustered around while restorers continue their work.

Da Vinci was one of the most famous painters of the Italian Renaissance. During the Renaissance the peoples of Europe began to see themselves as Europeans rather than as members of the kingdom of Christendom whose single passport was belief. The Renaissance was a period of upheaval and change in religion, politics, and economy. The arts flourished. Writers began using the language of their own nations instead of Latin. Painters, architects, and sculptors experimented with new techniques. Expressing his belief in the newfound power of paintings, da Vinci boasted that the painter could "even induce men to fall in love with a picture that does not portray any living woman." Indeed, people throughout the ages have fallen in love with *The Last Supper*. ⊕

410 Chapter 16 *Renaissance and Reformation*

Painting

Italian Renaissance painters departed from the flat, symbolic style of medieval painting to begin a more realistic style. This change first appeared in the early 1300s when the Florentine artist-sculptor-architect Giotto (jee•AH•toh) effectively captured human emotions in a series of frescoes portraying the life of Francis of Assisi. In the 1400s Florentine artist Masaccio (muh•ZAH•chee•oh) employed lighting and perspective in his paintings to give depth to the human body and to set off his figures from the background. He thus created an even greater sense of realism than Giotto had.

One of the greatest Renaissance artists was **Leonardo da Vinci** (VIHN•chee). A citizen of Florence, he did much of his work in Milan and Rome. Da Vinci is best known for the *Mona Lisa*, a portrait of a strangely smiling young woman of Florence, and *The Last Supper*, a wall painting of Jesus' last meal with his disciples. In both works, da Vinci skillfully portrayed the subjects' personalities, thoughts, and feelings.

Leonardo da Vinci was also a scientist. He wrote books on astronomy, mathematics, and anatomy. His illustrations of inventions—far ahead of his time—included designs for parachutes, flying machines, mechanical diggers, and artillery.

Another outstanding Renaissance artist—Michelangelo Buonarroti—began his career as a sculptor in Florence. There he did a famous marble statue of David, after the heroic biblical king. Later in Rome he sculpted *La Pietà* (PEE•ay•TAH), which shows the dead Jesus in the arms of his mother, Mary. Most of Michelangelo's sculptures were awesome in size and suggested controlled but intense emotions.

In 1505 Pope Julius II hired Michelangelo to work at the Vatican, painting the ceiling of the Sistine Chapel with scenes from the Bible. All of Michelangelo's painted figures resembled sculptures. They had well-formed muscular bodies that expressed vitality and power. Michelangelo ended his career by designing the dome of the new St. Peter's Basilica.

The Renaissance produced many other artists who overwhelmed the world with their fabulous works. The period's great outpouring of creative genius could not be contained within Italy's boundaries. The ideas of the Renaissance soon filtered northward into France, England, and the Netherlands.

History & Art *La Pietà* by Michelangelo Buonarroti. St. Peter's Basilica, The Vatican, Rome, Italy
Where did Michelangelo learn to do such exceptional work?

SECTION 1 REVIEW

Recall

1. **Define** humanism, sonnet, doge.
2. **Identify** Niccolò Machiavelli, Lorenzo de' Medici, Savonarola, Michelangelo Buonarroti, Leonardo da Vinci.
3. **Locate** Florence, Rome, and Venice on the map on page 405. How did Venice's location affect its economic prosperity?

Critical Thinking

4. **Synthesizing Information** Imagine you were present to hear one of Savonarola's sermons. How would you react?

Understanding Themes

5. **Innovation** Identify one masterpiece in literature or art (painting, sculpture, or architecture) that was accomplished during the Renaissance, and explain how it was an innovative elaboration on some aspect of Greek or Roman culture rather than just an imitation.

Chapter 16 Section 1

History & Art Tell students that Michelangelo executed *La Pietà* in Rome for a French cardinal. The idea for showing the dead Jesus across his mother's lap came from German art, but Michelangelo rendered his work in classic Greek form. From what material is *La Pietà* made? *(marble)*

Answer to Caption: *Florence*

Evaluate

Section Quiz 16-1

Use the Testmaker to create a customized quiz for Section 1.

Reteach

Have students review the characteristics of humanism and give examples of how humanism was expressed by major Renaissance artists and writers.

Enrich

Have students write an essay in which they explain who they think was the most important person of the Italian Renaissance.

CLOSE

Write on the chalkboard: *Important Innovations of the Renaissance.* Ask volunteers to write what they think were the most important innovations in literature, education, art, architecture, and government during this period.

SECTION 1 REVIEW ANSWERS

1. All vocabulary words are defined in the Glossary.
2. Niccolò Machiavelli, 405; Lorenzo de' Medici, 407; Savonarola, 407; Michelangelo Buonarroti, 409; Leonardo da Vinci, 411
3. Venice served as a trade link between western Europe and the Byzantines because it was the nearest city to the Byzantine Empire and connected to it by sea.
4. Answers will vary but should include specific information from the text about Savonarola's sermons.
5. INNOVATION Possible answer: Michelangelo worked in the classical Greek style while rendering religious subjects.

Chapter 16 Section 2

SECTION THEME

▶ **Cultural Diffusion** Renaissance ideas and artistic styles spread from Italy to northern Europe.

Find Out

Answer: *Wars, trade, and the printing press helped bring Renaissance ideas from Italy to northern Europe.*

FOCUS

Section Objective

Explain how the Renaissance reached northern Europe.

BELLRINGER Motivational Activity

Before taking roll at the beginning of the class period, project Section Focus Transparency 16-2 and have students answer the activity questions. Discuss students' responses.

This activity is also available as a blackline master.

Vocabulary Pre-check

Use Vocabulary Activity 16 to introduce vocabulary terms. **L1 LEP**

1400 · 1450 · 1500 · 1550

c. 1440 Johannes Gutenberg uses movable metal type in printing.

1494 Francis I of France invades Italy.

1509 Desiderius Erasmus writes *The Praise of Folly.*

Section 2

The Northern Renaissance

Setting the Scene

▶ **Terms to Define**
châteaux

▶ **People to Meet**
Johannes Gutenberg, François Rabelais, Desiderius Erasmus, Pieter Brueghel, Thomas More, William Shakespeare

▶ **Places to Locate**
the Low Countries

Find Out How did the Renaissance reach northern Europe?

The Storyteller

When Shakespeare's play Hamlet *opened in London, about 2,000 people crowded in to see the performance. Admission was one penny. Down in front of the stage, where it was standing room only, the crowd could be noisy. One writer complained: "Such heaving, and shoving, such pushing and shouldering—especially by the women! Such care for their clothes, that no one step on their dress;.... Such smiling and winking.... Never mind the stage—it is a comedy to watch them!"*

—freely adapted from *Shakespeare: Of an Age For All Time,* The Yale University Festival Lectures, edited by Charles Tyler Prouty, 1954

William Shakespeare

During the late 1400s, Renaissance art and humanist ideas—characterized by a revival of interest in classical antiquity—began to filter northward from Italy to France, England, the Netherlands, and other European countries. War, trade, travel, and a newly invented method of printing helped to promote this cultural diffusion. The people of the Northern Renaissance adapted ideas of the Italian Renaissance to their own individual tastes, values, and needs.

Spreading Ideas

War, as usual, helped disseminate ideas by furthering contact between people of different cultures. When France invaded Italy in 1494, for example, King Francis I and his warrior-nobles became fascinated by Italian Renaissance art and fashions. They brought Leonardo da Vinci and other Italian artists and scholars to their court in France, thus promoting the entry of Renaissance ideas into northern Europe.

Other monarchs soon followed suit. Kings and queens so eagerly supported scholars and artists that the number of humanists in the north grew rapidly. As they grew, so too did the popularity of humanist ideas.

At the same time, Italian traders living in the north set an example for northern European merchants, who began to appreciate wealth, beauty, personal improvement, and other Renaissance values. These northern merchants—having only recently become successful enough to afford lifestyles based upon such values—began to spend their wealth on education, fine houses, and material goods. Some northern Europeans began to travel to Italy to study with Italian masters. Thus began the emergence of a newly educated middle class.

SECTION RESOURCES

Reproducible Masters
- Reproducible Lesson Plan 16-2
- Vocabulary Activity 16
- Guided Reading Activity 16-2
- Section Quiz 16-2

Transparencies
- Section Focus Transparency 16-2

Multimedia
- Focus on World Art Print 18
- Student Self-Test and Review Software
- Testmaker

412 Chapter 16 *Renaissance and Reformation*

This spread of knowledge among the middle class was aided by the invention of the printing press. About 1440 a German metalworker named **Johannes Gutenberg** discovered a revolutionary printing technique using movable metal type. As a result, books were published more quickly and less expensively. Production of humanist texts could now begin to match the newfound desire for such works.

Although Italian Renaissance ideas became quite popular in the north, they were not merely transplanted there. Rather, northern scholars interpreted them according to their own individual ways of thinking. Furthermore, the people of each northern culture adapted these ideas to suit their own needs and traditions.

The French Renaissance

The French Renaissance had a character all its own. French architects blended medieval Gothic towers and windows with the classical columns used by Italian architects to create **châteaux** (sha•TOHZ), or castles, for Francis I and his nobles. These large country estates were erected primarily in the Loire River valley. The château of Chambord is a fine example.

Many French Renaissance writers borrowed extensively from the new literary forms of the Italian Renaissance. Inspired by Petrarch's sonnets, Pierre Ronsard (rohn•SAHR) wrote his own sonnets with common humanist themes such as love, the passing of youth, and the poet's immortality. Michel de Montaigne (mahn•TAYN) may have modeled his informal and direct style on Italian autobiography. He cultivated the literary form called the personal essay, a short prose composition written to express clearly the personal view of a writer on a subject. In his essay "Of the Disadvantages of Greatness," Montaigne analyzed the authority of royalty:

> "The most difficult occupation in the world, in my opinion, is to play the part of a king worthily. I excuse more of their faults than people commonly do, in consideration of the dreadful weight of their burden, which dazes me. It is difficult for a power so immoderate to observe moderation...."

Physician-monk **François Rabelais** (RA•buh•LAY), France's most popular Renaissance author, wrote comic tales, satires, and parodies on a broad spectrum of contemporary life. He rejected the Middle Ages' focus on the afterlife and believed that people should enjoy life to the fullest. Exceptionally knowledgeable and gifted as a writer, he also wrote on such subjects as law, medicine, politics, theology, botany, and navigation.

Visualizing History ***Erasmus* by Quentin Metsys. The "Prince of the Humanists" joined a love for the classics with respect for Christian values.** *What reforms did Christian humanists promote?*

Northern Europe

The Italian Renaissance was enthusiastically accepted by the wealthy towns of Germany and **the Low Countries** (present-day Belgium, Luxembourg, and the Netherlands). Universities and schools promoted humanist learning, and printers produced a large quantity of books. Latin was still the main scholarly language, but writers increased their use of German and Dutch.

Christian Humanism

Unlike in Italy, the Renaissance in northern Europe had a more religious tone. Groups of scholars, known as Christian humanists, wanted reforms in Catholicism that would eliminate abuses and restore the simple piety of the early Church. They believed that humanist learning and Bible study were the best ways to promote these goals.

The most famous Christian humanist, **Desiderius Erasmus** (DEHZ•ih•DEER•ee•uhs ih•RAZ•muhs), inspired his colleagues to study Greek and Hebrew

TEACH

Guided Practice

THEME Cultural Diffusion Ask students how ideas were transported during the time of the Northern Renaissance. *(war, as when France invaded Italy; traveling merchants; new, more affordable printed books)* **L1**

Visualizing History With the help of the printing press, Erasmus became a best-selling author. **Answer to Caption:** *They wanted to eliminate abuses in the Catholic Church and restore piety through humanist learning and Bible study.*

Literature Have students identify the contributions of Ronsard, Montaigne, Erasmus, Thomas More, and Shakespeare. **L2**

Focus on World Art Print 18, Pieter Brueghel. *The Wedding Dance*

Who?What?Where?When?

The Book of Manners by Giovanni della Casa stated, "Anyone whose legs are too thin, or exceptionally fat, ... should not wear vivid or parti-colored hose, in order not to attract attention to his defects."

Independent Practice

Guided Reading Activity 16-2 **L1**

Government Have students research to compare the views of Montaigne and Machiavelli on how a ruler should exercise authority. **L3**

COOPERATIVE LEARNING ACTIVITY

Analyzing Art Assign students to small groups to study the works of one of the following Northern Renaissance artists: Pieter Brueghel the Elder, Jan van Eyck, Albrecht Dürer, Lucas Cranach the Elder, or Hans Holbein the Younger. Tell students to use art history books to analyze their artist's works. Suggest that they record evidence of daily activities, occupations, social classes, entertainment, clothing, hairstyles, and housing shown in these works. Remind groups that each member should be responsible for a task, such as organizing research, recording the group's discussion, making photocopies, or presenting the group's analysis to the class. Tell students to include pictures of artworks in their reports to the class. **L2**

Chapter 16 *Renaissance and Reformation* **413**

Chapter 16
Section 2

History & Art Brueghel, disguised as a peasant, attended village fairs and recorded dances and children's games in his sketchbook.
Answer to Caption: *realistic portraits, landscapes, and scenes of peasant life*

ASSESS

Check for Understanding

Assign Section 2 Review as homework or as an in-class activity.

Use Student Self-Test and Review Software to review Section 2.

Evaluate

Section Quiz 16-2

Use the Testmaker to create a customized quiz for Section 2.

Reteach

Have students create a list on the chalkboard of specific accomplishments and innovations of the Northern Renaissance that show the influence of ideas from Italy.

Enrich

Have students write a report using outside sources on criticisms of Renaissance society by Thomas More, Rabelais, or Montaigne.

CLOSE

Lead students in a brief discussion that summarizes major characteristics of Northern Renaissance literature, painting, and architecture.

History & Art *Peasant's Dance* by Pieter Brueghel the Elder. **The painting emphasizes the enjoyments of common people.** *What three subjects did northern European realistic artists paint?*

so that they could understand older versions of the Bible written in these languages. Erasmus also prompted people to take a more critical view of the Catholic Church. He specifically attacked the extravagance of Renaissance popes. In his noted work, *The Praise of Folly*, he describes these popes, claiming that they were so corrupt they no longer practiced Christianity:

> "Scarce any kind of men live more [devoted to pleasure] or with less trouble.... To work miracles is ... not in fashion now; to instruct the people, troublesome; to interpret the Scripture, [too bookish]; to pray, a sign one has little else to do ... and lastly, to die, uncouth; and to be stretched on a cross, infamous."

Northern European Painters

Artists in northern Europe developed a style of painting that relied more on medieval than classical models. In the early 1400s, a group of Flemish painters, led by the brothers Jan and Hubert van Eyck (EYEK), painted scenes from the Bible and daily life in sharp, realistic detail. They developed the technique of painting in oils. Oils provided artists with richer colors and allowed them to make changes on the painted canvas. Painting in oils soon spread to Italy. Meanwhile, Italian Renaissance art reached northern Europe. Artists such as **Pieter Brueghel** (BROY•guhl) combined Italian technique with the artistic traditions of their homeland. They began painting realistic portraits, landscapes, and scenes of peasant life.

The English Renaissance

Renaissance ideas did not spread to England until 1485, when the Wars of the Roses—bloody conflicts over who was the rightful heir to the throne—ended. Ultimately, the Tudor family defeated the York family, bringing the Tudor king Henry VII to power. Henry invited Italian Renaissance scholars to England, where they taught humanist ideas and encouraged the study of classical texts.

English humanists expressed deep interest in social issues. **Thomas More**, a statesman and a friend of Erasmus, wrote a book that criticized the society of his day by comparing it with an ideal society in which all citizens are equal and prosperous. The book, written in Latin, was called *Utopia*.

The English Renaissance was especially known for drama. The best-known English playwrights were **William Shakespeare** and Christopher Marlowe. They drew ideas for their works from medieval legends, classical mythology, and the histories of England, Denmark, and ancient Rome. Shakespeare dealt with universal human qualities such as jealousy, ambition, love, and despair so effectively that his plays are still relevant to audiences today.

SECTION 2 REVIEW

Recall

1. **Define** châteaux.
2. **Identify** Johannes Gutenberg, Michel de Montaigne, François Rabelais, Desiderius Erasmus, Jan and Hubert van Eyck, Pieter Brueghel,Thomas More, William Shakespeare.
3. **Describe** some elements of Italian Renaissance architecture used by French architects. How did they transform French architecture?

Critical Thinking

4. **Applying Information** Choose one writer or artist from the Northern Renaissance and explain how the works of this writer or artist reflected Renaissance ideas.

Understanding Themes

5. **Cultural Diffusion** How did Italian Renaissance ideas spread to northern Europe?

SECTION 2 REVIEW ANSWERS

1. All vocabulary words are defined in the Glossary.
2. Johannes Gutenberg, 413; Michel de Montaigne, 413; François Rabelais, 413; Desiderius Erasmus, 413; Jan and Hubert van Eyck, 414; Pieter Brueghel, 414; Thomas More, 414; William Shakespeare, 414
3. French architects used classical columns from the Italian Renaissance but blended them with medieval Gothic towers and windows in their châteaux.
4. Answers should incorporate humanistic themes of the Renaissance.
5. CULTURAL DIFFUSION through war, travels, and books

1500 — 1525 — 1550

1517 Martin Luther preaches against indulgences.

1520 The Church condemns Luther's works.

c. 1550 Lutheranism spreads through northern Europe.

Section 3

The Protestant Reformation

Setting the Scene

▶ **Terms to Define**
justification by faith, indulgences, vocation

▶ **People to Meet**
Martin Luther, Pope Leo X

▶ **Places to Locate**
Wittenberg, Worms

Find Out How did Luther's religious reforms lead to Protestantism, a new branch of Christianity?

The Storyteller

In later years, Martin Luther remembered the fateful day he entered the monastery: "Afterwards I regretted my vow, and many of my friends tried to persuade me not to enter the monastery. I, however, was determined to go through with it.... I invited certain of my best men friends to a farewell party.... In tears they led me away; and my father was very angry ... yet I persisted in my determination. It never occurred to me to leave the monastery." Luther's break with the Church was an even bigger decision than the one to enter monastic life.

—adapted from *Luther and His Times*, E.G. Schweibert, 1950

Martin Luther

The Renaissance values of humanism and secularism stimulated widespread criticism of the Catholic Church's extravagance. By about 1500, educated Europeans began calling for a reformation—a change in the Church's ways of teaching and practicing Christianity. In Germany the movement for church reform eventually led to a split in the Church that produced a new form of Christianity known as Protestantism. The series of events that gave birth to Protestantism is known as the Protestant Reformation.

Martin Luther

The Protestant Reformation was begun by a German monk named **Martin Luther**, born in 1483, the son of peasants. His father wanted him to become a lawyer, but Luther was interested in religion. In 1505 he was nearly struck by lightning in a thunderstorm. Terrified that the storm was God's way of punishing him, the law student knelt and prayed to Saint Anne. In return for protection, he promised to become a monk. Shortly thereafter, Luther entered a monastery.

As a young monk, Luther struggled to ensure his soul's salvation. He would confess his sins for hours at a time. Yet still he worried that God might not find him acceptable.

Then he read Saint Paul's Epistle to the Romans: "He who through faith is righteous shall live"—and Luther's worries dissolved. He interpreted this to mean that a person could be made just, or good, simply by faith in God's mercy and love. Luther's idea became known as **justification by faith**. Luther later stated that because of this discovery he felt as if he "had been born again and had entered Paradise through wide open gates."

Chapter 16 Section 3

SECTION THEME

▶ **Conflict** Martin Luther's protests against the Catholic Church result in Protestantism.

Find Out

Answer: *When the Catholic Church banned Luther's works and excommunicated him, and the Diet of Worms declared him a heretic, Luther formed a new religion.*

FOCUS

Section Objective

Discuss how Luther's religious reforms led to Protestantism, a new branch of Christianity.

BELLRINGER Motivational Activity

Before taking roll at the beginning of the class period, project Section Focus Transparency 16-3 and have students answer the activity questions. Discuss students' responses.

This activity is also available as a blackline master.

Vocabulary Pre-check

Use Vocabulary Activity 16 to introduce vocabulary terms. **L1 LEP**

SECTION RESOURCES

Reproducible Masters
- Reproducible Lesson Plan 16-3
- Vocabulary Activity 16
- Guided Reading Activity 16-3
- People in World History Profile 29
- Section Quiz 16-3

Transparencies
- Section Focus Transparency 16-3

Multimedia
- Student Self-Test and Review Software
- Testmaker
- Turning Points in World History: *The Reformation*

TEACH

Guided Practice

THEME Conflict

Tell students that important historical events often occur when ideas come into conflict. Ask them to describe some conflicting ideas that led to the development of Lutheranism. **L1**

ABCNEWS INTERACTIVE™

VIDEODISC
Turning Points in World History

Side One
Chapter 8

Title: *The Reformation*
Subject: Martin Luther's questioning led to the founding of numerous Protestant religions.
Ask: Who was Martin Luther? *(a professor and priest who founded Lutheranism)*

Independent Practice

Guided Reading Activity 16-3 **L1**

CONNECTIONS Science and Technology

Many people opposed the printing press. Manuscript copiers lost their jobs. Leaders feared that it would spread subversive ideas.

Answers to Making the Connection

1. *Because books were copied by hand, they were expensive.*
2. *The printing press got Luther's books quickly into readers' hands, thus spreading his religious ideas.*

Protesting Church Abuses

Luther's ideas gradually matured and eventually brought him into conflict with the Church. At this time **Pope Leo X** was trying to raise money to rebuild St. Peter's Basilica in Rome. To this end, the pope sold church positions to his friends and also authorized sales of **indulgences**.

Indulgences were certificates issued by the Church that were said to reduce or even cancel punishment for a person's sins—as long as one also truly repented. People purchased indulgences believing that the document would assure them admission to heaven. John Tetzel, the Church's agent for selling indulgences in northern Germany, even went so far as to promise peasants that indulgences would relieve them of guilt for *future* sins. He also encouraged people to buy indulgences for the salvation of their dead relatives. Tetzel's sale of indulgences inspired a popular jingle: "Once you hear the money's ring, the soul from purgatory is free to spring." (According to church teaching, purgatory is a place in the afterlife where people are made fit for heaven.)

Luther, a professor and priest in the town of **Wittenberg**, preached against the sale of indulgences. He also lectured against other church practices he believed were corrupt. Then, on October 31, 1517, Luther nailed on the door of the Wittenberg Church a placard with 95 theses, or statements, criticizing the sale of indulgences and attacking other church policies.

Breaking With Rome

Printed copies of the Ninety-five Theses spread quickly all over Germany. Sales of indulgences declined sharply. Encouraged by this reaction, Luther published hundreds of essays advocating justification by faith and attacking church abuses.

Pope Leo X responded to the decline in indulgence sales by sending envoys to Germany to persuade Luther to withdraw his criticisms. But Luther refused. In 1520 the pope issued a statement in which he formally condemned Luther and banned his works. In 1521 Pope Leo X excommunicated Luther from the Church.

Shortly after Luther's excommunication, a diet, or council, of German princes met in **Worms**,

CONNECTIONS Science and Technology

Movable Metal Type and Printing

Gutenberg's press

Before the 1400s, books had to be copied by hand—a time-consuming method. Books were rare, and only wealthy people or scholars had access to them or could even learn how to read. Johannes Gutenberg's invention of movable metal type in the 1440s changed all that: Books could be reproduced much faster and much less expensively than ever before. Consequently, more people were able to obtain books and to expand their knowledge. This, in turn, caused them to question age-old traditions and to yearn for change.

German printers quickly adopted Gutenberg's invention and set up similar printing presses in other European countries. In less than 50 years after Gutenberg produced his first book, nearly 10 million books had been printed in Europe.

The German religious reformer Martin Luther was one of the first authors to reap the benefit of this new technology. Since his books could be reproduced inexpensively and in large quantities, they could be easily obtained throughout Europe shortly after Luther completed them. Thus, Martin Luther was able to spread his religious ideas and gain widespread support before the Catholic Church could respond.

MAKING THE CONNECTION

1. Why were scholars and wealthy people the only ones who could obtain books in Europe before Johannes Gutenberg invented his printing press?
2. How did Martin Luther benefit from Gutenberg's invention of movable type?

COOPERATIVE LEARNING ACTIVITY

Role Play Organize the class into five groups and have each group create a short television interview spot in which students interview either Tetzel on the sale of indulgences, Luther on his Ninety-five Theses, Pope Leo X on excommunicating Luther, Prince Frederick of Saxony on hiding Luther, or Luther on the teachings of Lutheranism. Encourage students to conduct research at the library. Have each group select a member to act as an interviewer and another member to be interviewed. All group members should prepare questions for the interview. After all interviews have been presented, have the class summarize the events that led to the Reformation. **L2**

History & Art *Luther Preaching to the Faithful,* (artist unknown). National Museum, Copenhagen, Denmark *What was Luther's view of vocations?* **(below) Indulgence box—an item that Luther opposed.**

Germany, to try to bring Luther back into the Church. They decided that Luther should take back his criticisms of the papacy. Meanwhile, Luther traveled to Worms as crowds of cheering people lined the road. Luther strode into the assembly hall and, when asked to take back his teachings, gave this reply: "I am bound by the Sacred Scriptures I have cited … and my conscience is captive to the Word of God. I cannot and will not recant [take back] anything.… God help me." Luther, condemned as a heretic and outlaw, was rushed out of Worms and hidden at a castle in Wartburg by a friend, Prince Frederick of Saxony.

While in hiding, Luther translated the New Testament into German. Earlier German translations of the Bible were so rare and costly that only priests and teachers had them. With Luther's more affordable translation, the common people could now read the Bible.

Lutheranism

After Worms, Luther made his final break with Rome and formed the first Protestant faith: Lutheranism. Although Lutheranism and Catholicism had many of the same beliefs, Luther stressed several teachings that distinguished his form of Christianity from that of Catholicism. Luther's most important teaching was salvation by faith alone—that no amount of good works can win God's approval for salvation, that only trust in God's love and mercy will win salvation.

Luther's second important teaching was that religious truth and authority lie only in the Bible. As a result, Luther and other Protestant reformers simplified church doctrine and rituals. Protestant leaders, called ministers, preached the Bible, and Protestant worship services were held in the local language instead of Latin. In this way, people could understand and easily share in the services.

Luther also emphasized that the Church was not a hierarchy of clergy, but a community of believers. All useful occupations, not just the priesthood or ministry, were important. They were **vocations**, or callings, in which people could serve God and their neighbors. This view appealed especially to merchants and artisans. Businesspeople were glad to find a religious belief that gave respect to their occupations.

SECTION 3 REVIEW

Recall

1. **Define** justification by faith, indulgences, vocation.
2. **Identify** Protestant Reformation, Martin Luther, Pope Leo X.
3. **Explain** why Luther's translation of the Bible into German influenced the development of European civilization.

Critical Thinking

4. **Synthesizing Information** If you wanted to protest against something today, what medium would you use to communicate your cause? Why?

Understanding Themes

5. **Conflict** Why did the pope ask Luther to recant his beliefs and then excommunicate him when Luther would not do so?

Chapter 16 Section 3

History & Art Tell students that the painting illustrates many of Luther's beliefs: the importance of the sermon in services, having believers physically closer to the minister, baptism and the Lord's Supper as the only sacraments, simplified interior of churches.

Answer to Caption: *All occupations were vocations through which people could serve God and their neighbors.*

ASSESS

Check for Understanding

Assign Section 3 Review as homework or as an in-class activity.

Use Student Self-Test and Review Software to review Section 3.

Evaluate

Section Quiz 16-3

Use the Testmaker to create a customized quiz for Section 3.

Reteach

Ask students to explain the relevance of justification by faith and the sale of indulgences to Luther's break from the Catholic Church.

Enrich

Have students imagine that they are living in Germany in the 1500s. Ask them to assert a Catholic or Lutheran point of view in a letter to the editor about the implications of Luther's reforms on the Catholic Church in Germany.

CLOSE

Have students list reasons that Lutheranism attracted many followers across Germany.

SECTION 3 REVIEW ANSWERS

1. All vocabulary words are defined in the Glossary.
2. Protestant Reformation, 415; Martin Luther, 415; Pope Leo X, 416
3. Luther's German translation was less expensive, so more people could read the Bible on their own, which led people to become more involved in religion.
4. Possible answers might include television and newspapers, but students should give reasons for their choice of medium.
5. **CONFLICT** Possible answer: The pope exercised his authority as head of the Catholic Church in an attempt to stop criticism of a church practice.

Chapter 16 Section 4

SECTION THEME

▶ **Cultural Diffusion** Protestant religious groups spread reform throughout northern Europe.

Find Out

Answer: *Zwinglism, Calvinism, Anabaptism, Anglicanism, and Puritanism*

FOCUS

Section Objective

Identify the different forms of Protestantism that emerged in Europe as the Reformation spread.

BELLRINGER Motivational Activity

Before taking roll at the beginning of the class period, project Section Focus Transparency 16-4 and have students answer the activity questions. Discuss students' responses.

This activity is also available as a blackline master.

Vocabulary Pre-check

Use Vocabulary Activity 16 to introduce vocabulary terms. **L1 LEP**

1500	1525	1550	1575
1509 John Calvin is born.	**1525** Huldrych Zwingli establishes theocracy in Zurich.	**1536** John Calvin publishes *The Institutes of the Christian Religion.*	**1558** Queen Elizabeth I establishes Anglicanism in England.

Section 4

The Spread of Protestantism

Setting the Scene

▶ **Terms to Define**
theocracy, predestination

▶ **People to Meet**
Huldrych Zwingli, John Calvin, the Anabaptists, Henry VIII, Catherine of Aragon, Anne Boleyn, Mary, Elizabeth I

▶ **Places to Locate**
Zurich, Geneva

Find Out What different forms of Protestantism emerged in Europe as the Reformation spread?

The Storyteller

Mary Queen of Scots was a prisoner for seventeen long years. What was she to do, as she and her keeper's wife sat together all that time? She could sew. Over the years, she and her attendant ladies embroidered seas of fabric: tablecloths, cushions, and hangings, every piece scattered with coats of arms and emblems, every piece sprinkled with gold and silver spangles to catch the light. Some became gifts; but occasionally her presents were rudely refused. Her own son, King James VI, returned a vest his mother had embroidered for him because she had addressed it to "The Prince of Scotland."

—adapted from *Mary Queen of Scots*, Roy Strong and Julia Trevelyan Oman, 1972

Mary Queen of Scots

Although the Protestant Reformation spread throughout Europe in the 1500s, divisions began to appear within the movement soon after it had started. Not only did the Protestant reformers not believe in the same methods; they did not even agree on the same goals.

Swiss Reformers

After the rise of Lutheranism in Germany, many preachers and merchants in neighboring Switzerland separated from Rome and set up churches known as Reformed. **Huldrych Zwingli**, a Swiss priest who lived from 1484 to 1531, led the Protestant movement in Switzerland. Like Luther, Zwingli stressed salvation by faith alone and denounced many Catholic beliefs and practices, such as purgatory and the sale of indulgences. Unlike Luther, though, Zwingli wanted to break completely from Catholic tradition. He wanted to establish a theocracy, or church-run state, in the Swiss city of **Zurich**. By 1525 Zwingli had achieved this goal. But in 1531 war broke out over Protestant missionary activity in the Catholic areas of Switzerland. Zwingli and his force of 1,500 followers were defeated by an army of 8,000 Catholics.

In the mid-1500s **John Calvin**, another reformer, established the most powerful and influential Reformed group in the Swiss city of **Geneva**. Here Calvin set up a theocracy similar to Zwingli's rule in Zurich.

Born in 1509, Calvin grew up in Catholic France at the start of the Reformation. He received an education in theology, law, and humanism that prompted him to study the Bible very carefully and to formulate his own Protestant theology. In 1536 Calvin published his theology in *The Institutes of the Christian Religion*, soon one of the most

SECTION RESOURCES

Reproducible Masters
- Reproducible Lesson Plan 16-4
- Vocabulary Activity 16
- Guided Reading Activity 16-4
- Section Quiz 16-4

Transparencies
- Section Focus Transparency 16-4

Multimedia
- Student Self-Test and Review Software
- Testmaker

popular books of its day, influencing religious reformers in Europe and later in North America.

The cornerstone of Calvin's theology was the belief that God possessed all-encompassing power and knowledge. Calvin contended that God alone directed everything that has happened in the past, that happens in the present, and that will happen in the future. Thus, he argued, God determines the fate of every person—a doctrine he called predestination.

To advance his views, Calvin tried to turn the corrupt city of Geneva into a model religious community. He began this project in 1541 by establishing the Consistory, a church council of 12 elders that was given the power to control almost every aspect of people's daily lives. All citizens were required to attend Reformed church services several times each week. The Consistory inspected homes annually to make sure that no one was disobeying the laws that forbade fighting, swearing, drunkenness, gambling, card playing, and dancing. It dispensed harsh punishments to people who disobeyed any of these laws. People convicted of holding Catholic beliefs or of practicing witchcraft might even be executed. This strict atmosphere earned Geneva the title "City of God" and attracted reformers from all parts of Europe.

Visitors to Geneva helped to spread Calvinism, or John Calvin's teaching, throughout Europe. Because the Calvinist church was led by local councils of ministers and elected church members, it was easy to establish in most countries. Furthermore, the somewhat democratic structure of this organization gave its participants a stake in its welfare and inspired their intense loyalty.

The people of the Netherlands and Scotland became some of Calvin's most ardent supporters. John Knox, a leader of the Reformation in Scotland, and other reformers used Calvin's teachings to encourage moral people to overthrow tyrannical rulers. They preached, as Calvin had, "We must obey princes and others who are in authority, but only insofar as they do not deny to God, the supreme King, Father, and Lord, what is due Him." Calvinism thus became a dynamic social force in western Europe in the 1500s and contributed to the rise of revolutionary movements later in the 1600s and 1700s.

Radical Reformers

Several new Protestant groups in western Europe, called **the Anabaptists**, initiated the practice of baptizing, or admitting into their groups, only adult members. They based this practice on the belief that only people who could make a free and informed choice to become Christians should be allowed to do so. Catholic and established Protestant churches, in contrast, baptized infants, making them church members.

Many Anabaptists denied the authority of local governments to direct their lives. They refused to hold office, bear arms, or swear oaths, and many lived separate from a society they saw as sinful. Consequently, they were often persecuted by government officials, forcing many Anabaptists to wander from country to country seeking refuge.

Although most Anabaptists were peaceful, others were fanatical in their beliefs. These zealots brought about the downfall of the rest. When in 1534 radical Anabaptists seized power in the German city of Münster and proceeded to burn books, seize private property, and practice polygamy, Lutherans and Catholics united to crush them. Together they killed the Anabaptist leaders and persecuted any surviving Anabaptist believers.

As a result, many Anabaptist groups left Europe for North America during the 1600s. In the Americas, the Anabaptists promoted two ideas that would become crucial in forming the United States of America: religious liberty and separation of church and state.

England's Church

Reformation ideas filtered into England during the 1500s. A serious quarrel between King **Henry VIII** and the pope, however, brought these ideas to the forefront.

The quarrel arose over succession to the throne. Although Henry's wife **Catherine of Aragon** had borne six children, only one child, Mary, survived. Henry wanted to leave a male heir to the throne so that England might not be plunged into another civil war like the Wars of the Roses. Believing that Catherine was too old to have more children, the king decided to marry **Anne Boleyn**. In 1527 Henry

Footnotes to History

King Henry VIII
Henry VIII was a typical Renaissance ruler who tried to excel in many areas. He enjoyed tennis, jousting, music, and discussions about religion and the sciences. He wrote a book of theology and composed several pieces of music, one of which may have been the song "Greensleeves."

Chapter 16 Section 4

TEACH

Guided Practice

THEME Cultural Diffusion Using a wall map, have students trace the spread of Protestantism from Germany to other European countries. **L1 LEP**

Politics Have students make a chart in which they show the country, leader, relation to government, and basic beliefs of Zwinglism, Calvinism, the Anabaptists, and Anglicanism. *(Example: Zwinglism—Zurich, Switzerland; Huldrych Zwingli; theocracy; salvation by faith alone.)* **L2**

Independent Practice

Guided Reading Activity 16-4 **L1**

Critical Thinking Have students view a film portraying people who are discussed in this section, such as *Anne of the Thousand Days* (Anne Boleyn) or *A Man for All Seasons* (Thomas More). Have them decide from what point of view these people are represented. **L2**

ASSESS

Check for Understanding

Assign Section 4 Review as homework or as an in-class activity.

Use Student Self-Test and Review Software to review Section 4.

COOPERATIVE LEARNING ACTIVITY

Panel Discussion Organize the class into five groups to prepare and present a panel discussion of Reformation movements in one of the following countries: Switzerland, Scotland, the Netherlands, England, or Germany (Anabaptists). Using outside sources, each group member should focus on a specific topic, such as leadership, religious beliefs, relationship to government, or important political events. Have each group appoint a member to serve as moderator or timekeeper. After each group member presents his or her topic, have the moderator summarize the panel's main points. After all panels have made their presentations, encourage the class to compare and contrast these Reformation movements. **L2**

Chapter 16 Section 4

History & Art Henry VIII was an absolute monarch. By placing his allies in positions of power in Parliament, he totally controlled England. **Answer to Caption:** *to show that breaking from the Catholic Church was the will of the English people, not merely a whim of his own*

Evaluate

Section Quiz 16-4

Use the Testmaker to create a customized quiz for Section 4.

Reteach

On the chalkboard, draw a time line from 1500 to 1600. On the time line, have volunteers mark important events from this section.

Enrich

Have students research the more recent history of one of the Protestant groups mentioned in this section. Have them prepare brief reports that include size of the sect today and where most members live, current beliefs and practices, and how the latter have evolved since the group's founding.

CLOSE

Ask students to compare the reasons that England became Protestant with the reasons Switzerland adopted Protestantism. Have students note major points.

History & Art Henry VIII, a portrait by Hans Holbein, shows the king's splendid royal attire, reflecting his authority. *Why did Henry seek Parliament's support in breaking with the Catholic Church?*

asked the pope to agree to a divorce between himself and Catherine. But Catherine's nephew was the powerful Holy Roman Emperor Charles V, upon whom the pope depended for protection. Charles wanted Catherine to remain as queen of England in order to influence the country's policies in favor of his own interests. The pope refused Henry's request.

Henry would not be thwarted. Gradually, and with Parliament's backing, he succeeded in breaking England's ties with the Catholic Church. The English Parliament granted Henry more authority over the English clergy. By rallying Parliament's support, Henry was trying to show that breaking with the Catholic Church was the will of the English people, not merely a whim of his own. In 1534 Parliament finally passed the law that separated the Church of England from Rome and declared Henry head of the English Church.

Henry had the new church grant him his divorce and then married Anne Boleyn. But Anne did not give him the heir he wanted. Instead she gave birth to a daughter, Elizabeth. A few years after Elizabeth's birth, Henry had Anne beheaded for treason. Henry's third wife, Jane Seymour, finally gave birth to a son, Edward, but she herself died 12 days later. The king married three more times before his death in 1547, but none of these marriages produced male heirs.

The sickly 9-year-old Edward VI succeeded his father. Because Edward was too young to rule, a council of lords governed England for him. Since most of the council members were Protestants, they brought Protestant doctrines into the English Church.

Upon Edward's death in 1553, Henry's Catholic daughter **Mary** became queen. Mary tried to restore Catholicism in England by burning hundreds of Protestants at the stake. These atrocities earned her the nickname "Bloody Mary" and only served to strengthen people's support for Protestantism.

Mary's Protestant half sister took the throne in 1558, becoming Queen **Elizabeth I**. To unite her people, she made the English Church Protestant with Catholic features. Anglicanism, as this blend of Protestant belief and Catholic practice was called, pleased most churchgoers. However, some Protestants insisted on removing all Catholic rituals. Because they strove to purge these remnants of Catholicism, or "purify" the Church, these Protestants became known as Puritans. Although at first in the minority, Puritans gradually became influential both in the Church of England and in the English Parliament.

SECTION 4 REVIEW

Recall

1. **Define** theocracy, predestination.
2. **Identify** Huldrych Zwingli, John Calvin, the Anabaptists, Henry VIII, Catherine of Aragon, Anne Boleyn, Edward VI, Mary, Elizabeth I.
3. **Explain** why divisions appeared among the different reformers within the Protestant movement.

Critical Thinking

4. **Making Comparisons** How did the Calvinists and Anabaptists differ in their attitudes toward the government church members participating in government activities?

Understanding Themes

5. **Cultural Diffusion** Why did the Catholic Church want to stop the spread of Protestant ideas?

SECTION 4 REVIEW ANSWERS

1. All vocabulary words are defined in the Glossary.
2. Huldrych Zwingli, 418; John Calvin, 418; the Anabaptists, 419; Henry VIII, 419; Catherine of Aragon, 419; Anne Boleyn, 419; Edward VI, 420; Mary, 420; Elizabeth I, 420
3. The reformers had different goals and ideas about how to reform the Church.
4. The Anabaptists denied the authority of government in their lives and did not take part in government activities; the Calvinists set up a church-run state that had control over people's daily lives.
5. **CULTURAL DIFFUSION** Possible answers: The Catholic Church was losing members, money, and power, as well as influence over European governments.

Critical Thinking

SKILLS

Identifying Evidence

In a geography trivia game, you picked the following question: What is the longest river in the world? The game card says it is the Amazon River, but you think it is the Nile River. Your friends insist that you are wrong. How can you prove you are right?

You must identify evidence that will establish your claim. In the example above, you could consult an atlas, almanac, or encyclopedia to find the lengths of both rivers. In fact, you are correct! The Nile River is 4,160 miles long, while the Amazon is 4,000 miles long.

Learning the Skill

There are four basic kinds of evidence: 1) oral accounts (eyewitness testimony); 2) written documents (diaries, letters, books, articles); 3) objects (artifacts); and 4) visual items (photographs, videotapes, paintings). These kinds of evidence fall into one of two categories—primary evidence and secondary evidence.

Primary evidence is produced by participants or eyewitnesses to events. Eyewitness accounts or photographs of a fire are examples of primary evidence. Secondary evidence is produced later, by those who have not experienced the events directly. Textbooks and encyclopedias are examples of secondary evidence.

To identify evidence that proves a claim, first clearly define the claim. Search available information to find the kind of evidence that can prove or disprove the claim. Compare the pieces of evidence to see if they agree. Also, rate the objectivity of your evidence. In the example above, the sources you consulted—atlas, almanac, or encyclopedia—are all reliable sources of information.

However, if you are using primary sources such as letters, diaries, and news accounts, carefully assess which evidence is most reliable.

Practicing the Skill

Read the claim below. Then read each piece of evidence that follows. Decide which pieces of evidence prove the claim to be true and explain why.

Claim: *Humanism's emphasis on the value of the individual led to artistic flowering in the Renaissance.*

1. In Renaissance Italy humanist scholars opened schools to promote the study of history, philosophy, Latin, and Greek.
2. Renaissance artists used painting and sculpture to convey human emotions and values.
3. In Rome, the pope and cardinals made up the wealthiest and most powerful class of people.
4. In England, William Shakespeare wrote plays that dealt with universal human qualities such as jealousy, ambition, love, and despair.
5. The invention of the printing press spread knowledge of humanism throughout the newly emerging middle class.

Applying the Skill

Think about this claim: The humanist values of the Renaissance still dominate modern American culture. Find at least five pieces of evidence from newspapers, magazines, and other sources to prove or disprove this claim.

For More Practice

Turn to the Skill Practice in the Chapter Review on page 431 for more practice in identifying evidence.

Critical Thinking

SKILLS

TEACH

Identifying Evidence Show students a headline from a newspaper that states a claim or write the following headline on the chalkboard: *Worst Fire in City's History Kills 25.* Ask a student to read the headline aloud. Call on volunteers to explain what the headline is claiming. *(No other fire in the city's history has been as bad and that 25 people died in the fire.)* Ask students what kind of information they need to prove the claim made in the headline. *(information about previous fires; names of people who died in the fire)* Have students discuss where they might find this information. *(city histories, fire department records, interviews with long-time city residents)* Then ask which of these sources would be the most reliable. *(fire department records)* Tell students that identifying sources of evidence and determining their reliability are steps they should take when trying to prove a claim. Then have students read the skill and complete the practice questions.

Additional Practice

Skill Reinforcement Activity 16

ANSWERS TO PRACTICING THE SKILL

1. no
2. yes; tells that Renaissance artists showed human emotions in their works
3. no
4. yes; tells that Shakespeare wrote about human characteristics
5. no

Chapter 16
Section 5

SECTION THEME

▶ **Reaction** The Catholic Church enacts its own reform, the Catholic Reformation.

Find Out

Answer: *The Catholic Church began its own reformation, eliminating abuses, clarifying theology, and sending out missionaries to reclaim Catholic lands.*

FOCUS

Section Objective

Describe how the Catholic Church tried to halt the spread of Protestantism.

BELLRINGER
Motivational Activity

Before taking roll at the beginning of the class period, project Section Focus Transparency 16-5 and have students answer the activity questions. Discuss students' responses.

This activity is also available as a blackline master.

Vocabulary Pre-check

Use the Vocabulary PuzzleMaker to create a puzzle that reinforces the vocabulary terms in this section. **L1**

1525 — 1550 — 1575

1536 Pope Paul III calls for reforms.

1540 Ignatius of Loyola founds Society of Jesus.

1563 Council of Trent ends.

Section 5

The Catholic Reformation

Setting the Scene

▶ **Terms to Define**
seminary, baroque

▶ **People to Meet**
Pope Paul III, Ignatius of Loyola, the Jesuits

▶ **Places to Locate**
Trent

Find Out How did the Catholic Church try to halt the spread of Protestantism?

The Storyteller

The Inquisition sometimes used "ordeals" to determine guilt or innocence, confident that God would give victory to an innocent person and punish the guilty. In the "Trial of the Cross," both parties, accuser and accused, stood before a cross with arms outstretched. The first to drop his arms was judged guilty. In the "Trial by Hot Water," the accused lifted a stone from the bottom of a boiling cauldron. If, after three days, his wound had healed, he was innocent. In the "Trial by Cold Water," the accused was tied up and lowered into water. If he sank, he was innocent. If he floated, he was guilty.

—from *The Medieval Inquisition*, Albert Clement Shannon, 1983

Trial of Books *(detail)*

Most of the people in Spain, France, Italy, Portugal, Hungary, Poland, and southern Germany remained Catholic during the Protestant Reformation. Nevertheless, Catholicism's power was threatened by Protestantism's increasing popularity in northern Europe. To counter the Protestant challenge, Catholics decided to reform church practices. The Catholic Church had had a history of periodic reform since the Middle Ages. Thus, in the movement that came to be known as the Counter-Reformation, or Catholic Reformation, the Catholic Church eliminated many abuses, clarified its theology, and reestablished the pope's authority over church members.

Redefining Catholicism

In 1536 **Pope Paul III** established a distinguished commission of cardinals and bishops to prepare a report on the need for reform and how such reform might be undertaken. The completed report blamed church leaders, including popes, for many abuses. It also called for reforms that would convince Protestants to rejoin the Church.

The reforms undertaken as a result of this report were only partially carried out. The Church's financial problems had increased, and the Church was unable to respond quickly and effectively to the Protestant threat.

By the 1540s Catholic Church leaders, sensing the importance of checking the spread of Protestantism, finally decided to embark on an ambitious reform program. The goals were to eliminate abuses, introduce a rebirth of faith among its followers, reassess the Church's principles, restore the authority of the pope, and halt the spread of Protestantism.

SECTION RESOURCES

Reproducible Masters
- Reproducible Lesson Plan 16-5
- Guided Reading Activity 16-5
- Reteaching Activity 16
- Enrichment Activity 16
- Section Quiz 16-5
- Performance Assessment Activity 16
- Spanish Chapter Summary 16

Transparencies
- Section Focus Transparency 16-5
- World History and Art Transparency 21

Multimedia
- Focus on World Art Print 16
- Vocabulary PuzzleMaker Software
- Student Self-Test and Review Software
- Testmaker

History & Art *The Council of Trent* by Titian. **Held off and on for about 20 years, this church council reaffirmed Catholic doctrine and introduced reforms.** *What Bible was made the only acceptable version?*

The Inquisition

In 1542 the Church gave full powers to an Inquisition, a church court based in Italy, to find, try, and judge heretics—especially Protestants. The purpose of the Inquisition, however, was not merely to rid Italy of non-Catholics. The purge was also intended to restore the pope's authority over church members. With the imposition of rigid repression, the pope succeeded in restoring his authority over the entire Italian Peninsula. The Church also introduced censorship to curtail the humanist thinking that had fueled Italy's Renaissance. In 1543 the Inquisition published the first Index of Prohibited Books.

The Council of Trent

One of the needs of the Church was to clearly state and defend Catholic teaching. In 1545 Pope Paul III called a council of bishops at **Trent**, Italy, to define official doctrine. The Council of Trent met in several sessions from 1545 to 1563.

The Council strictly and clearly defined Catholic doctrine, especially teachings that the Protestants had challenged. Salvation, the Council declared, could not be achieved by faith alone, but only by faith and works together. The Latin Vulgate translation of the Bible was made the only acceptable version of scripture. In addition, the Church hierarchy alone was to decide the interpretation of the Bible.

The Council of Trent also put an end to many church abuses that had been practiced for centuries. It forbade the selling of indulgences. Clergy were ordered to follow strict rules of behavior. The Council decided that each diocese had to establish a seminary, or training school, for the proper education of priests.

The Council decided to maintain the elaborate art and ritual of the Church, and it declared that Mass should be said only in Latin. The Church's art and its Latin ritual were to serve as necessary sources of inspiration for less educated Catholics,

TEACH

Guided Practice

THEME Reaction
Ask students why the Catholic Reformation is also called the Counter-Reformation. *(The Catholic Church reacted to the challenges of the Protestant Reformation.)* **L1**

The Arts Show students examples of work by baroque artists, such as Bernini, Caravaggio, Peter Paul Rubens, and Anthony Van Dyck. Have volunteers describe the works and comment on their effect on the viewer. As students summarize the main points about baroque art, write them on the chalkboard. **L2 LEP**

History & Art Wars, a plague in Trent, and the deaths of three popes, as well as many disagreements between delegates interrupted the sessions of the Council of Trent.
Answer to Caption: *the Latin Vulgate translation*

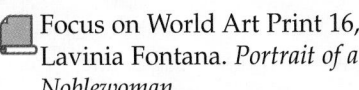

Focus on World Art Print 16, Lavinia Fontana. *Portrait of a Noblewoman*

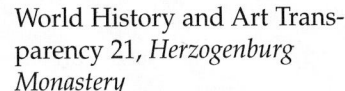

World History and Art Transparency 21, *Herzogenburg Monastery*

Linking Past and Present

The ***Index of Forbidden Books*** issued its last edition in 1948. In 1966 the Church announced that the penalty of excommunication for reading books on the list was lifted.

COOPERATIVE LEARNING ACTIVITY

Visual Reports Organize the class into five groups. Using the map on page 424 as a guide, have one group create a large map showing the distribution of religions in Europe after the Council of Trent. Have the second group research the *Index of Forbidden Books* and make a list of well-known authors and books that were on the list over the years. Have the third group research the Inquisition and make drawings of the trials and punishments. Have the fourth group make an illustrated list of the main outcomes of the Council of Trent. Have the fifth group make a large world map showing areas of Jesuit missionary activities. Remind students to use library resources when needed. Have groups display their work on a Catholic Reformation bulletin-board display. **L1 LEP**

Map Study

Answer

Religious wars broke out.

Map Skills Practice

Reading a Map Which Protestant religion was a significant minority in largely Catholic France? *(Calvinism)*

Independent Practice

Guided Reading Activity 16-5 **L1**

Foreign Affairs Have students choose an area where the Jesuits sent missionaries, such as China, Japan, or North America, and research the Jesuits' activities and accomplishments there. Let students share this information with the class. **L2**

Diplomacy Have students write a brief report on the safe-conducts issued to Protestants who addressed the Council of Trent. **L3**

Cultural Perspectives

No More Latin In the 1960s the Catholic Church convened the Second Vatican Council (the Council of Trent was the First Vatican Council). One result was the decision to say Mass in the vernacular language of each country rather than in Latin.

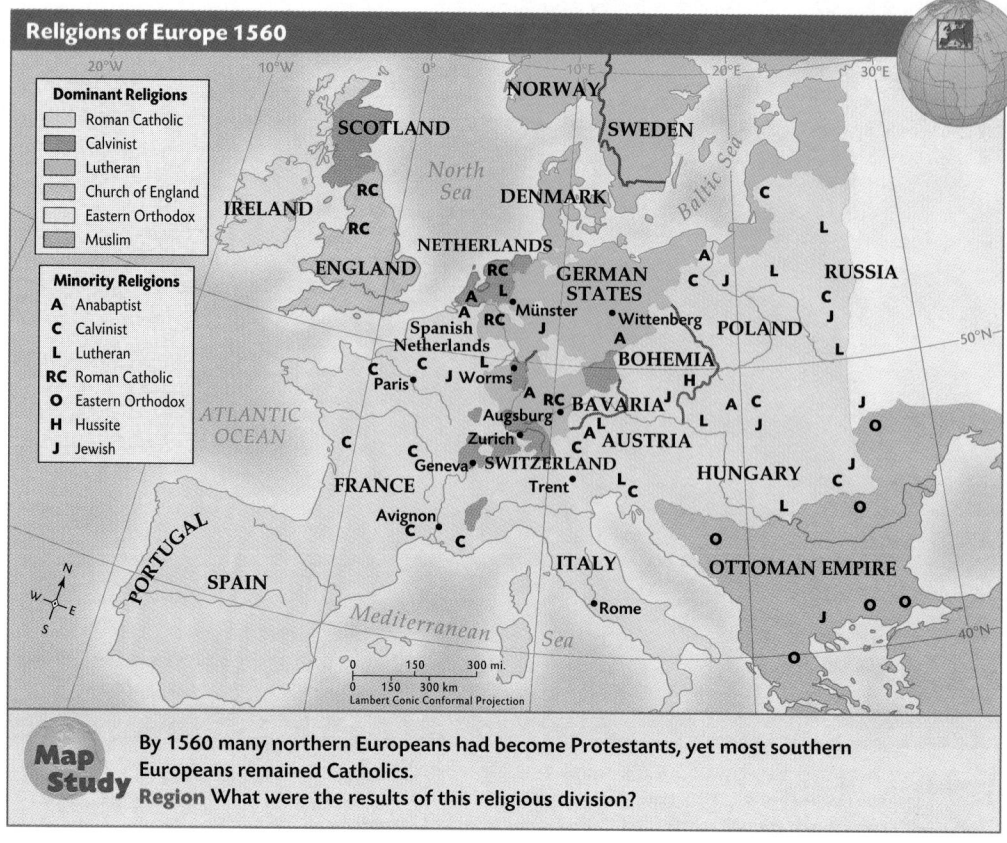

Religions of Europe 1560

Map Study By 1560 many northern Europeans had become Protestants, yet most southern Europeans remained Catholics.
Region What were the results of this religious division?

who had difficulty understanding church teachings by other means. Thus, the Catholic Reformation renewed religious enthusiasm in the arts, sparking a new style of art and music called **baroque** (buh•ROHK). Renaissance art had demonstrated restraint, simplicity, and order, but baroque art emphasized emotion, complexity, and exaggeration for dramatic effect.

Spreading Catholicism

The Church planned to halt Protestantism in two phases. The first was to reform the Church. The second was to launch a missionary offensive against Protestants to reclaim formerly Catholic lands that were now Protestant.

Many religious orders and individuals in the Catholic Church became involved in this missionary effort. One reformer named **Ignatius of Loyola** played a particularly significant role. In 1521 Loyola gave up his life as a Spanish noble to serve the Catholic Church. He developed a set of spiritual exercises to help people achieve inner peace. After a visit to Palestine, he decided to improve his education in order to preach more effectively. While in school, Loyola organized a group of followers to spread Catholic teachings. In 1536 the group went to Rome determined to win souls, not by the sword, but by educating the young.

In 1540 Loyola and his followers founded the Society of Jesus, later known as **the Jesuits**. Organized along military lines, the Jesuits pledged absolute obedience to the pope, wore the black robes of monks, and lived simple lives but did not withdraw from the world. They believed, as Loyola said, "The more universal your work, the more divine it becomes."

The Jesuits preached to the people, helped the poor, and set up schools. They also taught in universities, worked as missionaries, and served as advisers in royal courts. The Jesuits carried their message throughout Europe and in countries as far away as India, China, Japan, Brazil, and Ethiopia

ASSESS

Check for Understanding

Assign Section 5 Review as homework or as an in-class activity.

Use Student Self-Test and Review Software to review Section 5.

MEETING SPECIAL NEEDS ACTIVITY

Study Strategy Have students divide Section 5 into three parts according to the following headings: *Reforms in the Catholic Church*, *Missionary Activity of the Catholic Church*, *Results of the Reformation*. Then have students find similar headings in the text and write at least three outcomes under each heading. *(For example: Missionary Activity—Jesuit order formed; Jesuits retained church members in southern Germany, Bohemia, Hungary, and Poland; Jesuits establish universities throughout Europe.)* Tell students that *Reforms in the Catholic Church* corresponds with "Redefining Catholicism" in the text. **L2**

424 Chapter 16 *Renaissance and Reformation*

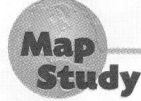

to strengthen the faith of Catholics and bring Protestants back to the Church.

The Jesuits' missionary efforts helped the Catholic Church to retain the loyalty of people in southern Germany, Bohemia, Poland, and Hungary. The Jesuits also established many universities, which remained prominent centers of education in Europe for the next 200 years. At these centers Jesuits not only taught Roman Catholic theology and philosophy but also advanced the study of physics, astronomy, mathematics, archaeology, linguistics, biology, chemistry, and genetics.

Results of the Reformation

By the mid-1500s, the Catholic Church had strengthened its following and reclaimed some territories that had previously been won over by Protestants. This success was due in part to the Catholic Reformation that had increased religious devotion and helped correct many church abuses.

The Catholic Reformation, however, did not succeed in its efforts to eliminate Protestantism. Large areas of Europe remained Protestant—especially in the north. Northern Germany and Scandinavia were mostly Lutheran as a result of the efforts of monarchs and princes. Areas of southern Germany, Switzerland, the Netherlands, and Scotland—with their growing economic wealth based in towns—held to Calvinist beliefs. England, divided in its religious loyalties, developed its own Anglican Church, a mixture of Protestantism and Catholicism under royal control.

There were many reasons why Europeans in large numbers supported Protestantism. One reason was undoubtedly religious conviction. However, nonreligious factors were also involved. German princes often accepted Protestant teachings in order to increase their own power. They made Lutheranism or Calvinism the state religion of their territories, placing it under their protection and control. They also seized lands and wealth owned by the Catholic Church.

Visualizing History **Jesuit missionaries in Japan are depicted by a Japanese painter.** *Who founded the original Society of Jesus?*

Townspeople also rallied to the new faith, which supported their business practices. Many peasants sided with Protestantism as a form of protest against the Catholic nobility. Above all, northern Europeans saw Protestantism as a way to defy an Italian-controlled Catholic Church that drained so much money from their homelands.

For centuries, Europe would be roughly divided into a Protestant north and a Catholic south. During the 1500s and early 1600s this division would especially have catastrophic consequences, with each side wanting to prove that its faith was the true one. These religious claims erupted into full-scale religious wars, which ravaged Europe and brought great hardships to its people.

SECTION 5 REVIEW

Recall

1. **Define** seminary, baroque.
2. **Identify** Pope Paul III, Ignatius of Loyola, the Jesuits.
3. **List** the educational opportunities provided by the Jesuits.

Critical Thinking

4. **Analyzing Information** List any three of the reforms proposed by the Council of Trent. Beside each, give the Protestant viewpoint to which it responded.

Understanding Themes

5. **Reaction** Evaluate the actions the Church took to halt the spread of Protestantism and their effects. Which were successful, and which were not?

Chapter 16 Section 5

Visualizing History In 1549 the Jesuits began their mission to Japan under the Spanish priest Francis Xavier. He learned Japanese and recommended that other missionaries follow local customs and use the native language.
Answer to Caption: *Ignatius of Loyola*

Evaluate

Section Quiz 16-5

Use the Testmaker to create a customized quiz for Section 5.

Reteach

Have students summarize the Catholic Church's activities to halt the Protestant Reformation.

Reteaching Activity 16

Enrich

Have students do research on the Inquisition, the methods it employed, and how and why it eventually ended.

Enrichment Activity 16

CLOSE

Have students make a wall chart summarizing the work of the Inquisition and the Council of Trent.

SECTION 5 REVIEW ANSWERS

1. All vocabulary words are defined in the Glossary.
2. Pope Paul III, 422; Ignatius of Loyola, 424; the Jesuits, 424
3. physics, astronomy, mathematics, archaeology, linguistics, biology, chemistry, and genetics, as well as Roman Catholic theology and philosophy
4. Sample answer: Council of Trent–salvation achieved through faith and works; Protestant viewpoint–salvation achieved by faith alone
5. **REACTION** Sample answer: Catholic missionary activities were successful because they retained many church members; the Inquisition was unsuccessful because it aroused fears in Protestant countries of what might happen if Catholicism were restored.

Bridge to the Past
Literature

Block Schedule

Team Teaching This excerpt from *The Prince* may be presented in a team-teaching context, in conjunction with English or Language Arts.

The Prince

Historical Connection

Machiavelli's advice on how to rule a kingdom helps us to understand the way people in any age compete for power. He emphasizes how rulers really act, not how they should behave, a reflection of the focus on human behavior that began in Europe in the 1400s.

Background Information

Setting Machiavelli lived in a time of political instability in Italy. Tyranny, war, and corruption were common. Machiavelli believed that an effective ruler had to impose peace so that the country could progress.

Literary Elements Tone is the outlook of the writer toward his or her material. Machiavelli tries to achieve an objective tone. For example, when he describes "men in general" as "ungrateful, fickle, and deceitful," he neither condemns nor praises them for these traits.

Machiavelli's theme, the central idea in *The Prince,* is that the end justifies the means. The point of his handbook is to help a ruler stay in power at whatever cost.

Bridge to the Past
Literature

from

The Prince

by Niccolò Machiavelli

Like many other Renaissance thinkers, Niccolò Machiavelli (1469–1527) analyzed human actions rather than spiritual issues. Unlike many of his contemporaries, however, he focused on the selfish side of human nature more than on humanity's potential for progress. Machiavelli observed how successful politicians won and secured power. He sent his thoughts to an Italian prince, hoping to win a position as an adviser. His ruthlessly honest look at how politicians act both confirms and challenges the views we have toward our leaders.

It is the custom of those who are anxious to find favor in the eyes of a prince to present him with such things as they value most highly or in which they see him take delight. Hence offerings are made of horses, arms, golden cloth, precious stones and such ornaments, worthy of the greatness of the Prince. Since therefore I am desirous of presenting myself to Your Magnificence with some token of my eagerness to serve you, I have been able to find nothing in what I possess which I hold more dear or in greater esteem than the knowledge of the actions of great men which has come to me through a long experience of present-day affairs and continual study of ancient times. And having pondered long and diligently on this knowledge and tested it well, I have reduced it to a little volume which I now send to Your Magnificence. Though I consider this work unworthy of your presence, nonetheless I have much hope that your kindness may find it acceptable, if it be considered that I could offer you no better gift than to give you occasion to learn in a very short space of time all that I have come to have knowledge and understanding of over many years and through many hardships and dangers. I have not adorned the work nor inflated it with lengthy clauses nor pompous or magnificent words, nor added any other refinement or extrinsic ornament wherewith many are wont to advertise or embellish their work, for it has been my wish either that no honor should be given it or that simply the truth of the material

About the Author

Machiavelli was born into a poor family in Florence, Italy. For many years he served the ruler of Florence as an ambassador and military adviser. In 1512 Lorenzo de' Medici seized power in Florence and dismissed Machiavelli, who later settled in the countryside where he wrote *The Prince.* Machiavelli dedicated the book to Lorenzo de' Medici in the hope the ruler would forgive him and allow him back into the government.

In *The Prince,* Machiavelli says what many rulers believed but would never have dared declare in public. For centuries *Machiavelli* has been synonymous with amoral cunning.

and the gravity of the subject should make it acceptable....

As for the exercise of the mind, the prince should read the histories of all peoples and ponder on the actions of the wise men therein recorded, note how they governed themselves in time of war, examine the reasons for their victories or defeats in order to imitate the former and avoid the latter, and above all conduct himself in accordance with the example of some great man of the past....

We now have left to consider what should be the manners and attitudes of a prince toward his subjects and his friends. As I know that many have written on this subject I feel that I may be held presumptuous in what I have to say, if in my comments I do not follow the lines laid down by others. Since, however, it has been my intention to write something which may be of use to the understanding reader, it has seemed wiser to me to follow the real truth of the matter rather than what we imagine it to be. For imagination has created many principalities and republics that have never been seen or known to have any real existence, for how we live is so different from how we ought to live that he who studies what ought to be done rather than what is done will learn the way to his downfall rather than to his preservation. A man striving in every way to be good will meet his ruin among the great number who are not good. Hence it is necessary for a prince, if he wishes to remain in power, to learn how not to be good and to use his knowledge or refrain from using it as he may need....

Here the question arises; whether it is better to be loved than feared or feared than loved. The answer is that it would be desirable to be both

Visualizing History Machiavelli advised Lorenzo de' Medici, who became the ruler of Florence in 1513, to be as cunning as his grandfather, Lorenzo the Magnificent, shown here. *Why did Machiavelli believe it is better to be feared than loved?*

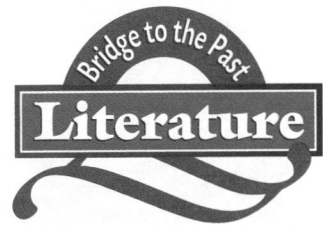

Bridge to the Past
Literature

FOCUS

Have students brainstorm a list of words that can be applied to politicians today. After they have come up with five or more words, ask them whether the connotations of each word are positive or negative.

Visualizing History The Medici were a leading family of Florence. Originally physicians—the family name means "doctors" in Italian—they later founded one of Italy's most important banking houses. **Answer to Caption:** *It is safer to be feared, if one must choose.*

TEACH

Evaluation

Point out that Machiavelli believed rulers could learn lessons from history. Ask students whether they agree with this idea. They may feel that although historical examples are often referred to in contemporary debates, history rarely teaches clear-cut lessons.

Comparison

Ask students to compare their view of human nature with that of Machiavelli. Challenge them to come up with examples that support their views. If they share Machiavelli's pessimism, they might use crime statistics to support the claim that people need to be strictly controlled. If they disagree with Machiavelli, they might point to the amount of charitable work people do.

Other Works Of Or About Machiavelli

Bondanella, Peter, and Mark Musa, trans. *The Portable Machiavelli.* New York: Viking, 1979.

Detmold, Christian, trans. *Discourse on the First Ten Books of Livy.* New York: Modern Library, 1940.

History of Florence and the Affairs of Italy. Washington, DC: M. W. Dunne, 1901.

Hale, J.R., ed. and trans. *The Literary Works of Machiavelli.* New York: Oxford University Press, 1961.

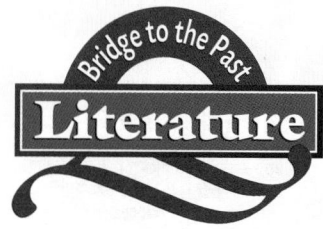

Bridge to the Past

Literature

Visualizing History Cesare Borgia became famous throughout Italy as a brilliant but ruthless military tactician. When Machiavelli held Borgia up as a model ruler, many Italians were appalled.

Answer to Caption: *when it is not to his advantage or when his reasons for giving his word are no longer valid*

Interpretation

Discuss with students the implications of Machiavelli's ideas for a democracy. Some students may argue that if people are deceitful, a democracy is bound to fail. Others may argue that because people are deceitful, a democracy is the best way to check the power of individuals.

World Literature Selection 4

Linking Past and Present

Ethics Machiavelli pioneered the idea that rulers should be held to a looser moral standard because, to stay in power, they had to ignore ethics. Are politicians today held to a looser or stricter moral standard than ordinary citizens?

ASSESS

Assign **Responding to Literature** questions.

Visualizing History This portrait of Cesare Borgia embodies the pride and confidence of the prince about whom Machiavelli wrote his political commentary. Borgia, the son of the controversial Pope Alexander VI, used his position as duke of Romagna to enhance papal political power. *When should a leader not keep his word, according to Machiavelli?*

but, since that is difficult, it is much safer to be feared than to be loved, if one must choose. For on men in general this observation may be made: they are ungrateful, fickle, and deceitful, eager to avoid dangers, and avid for gain, and while you are useful to them they are all with you, offering you their blood, their property, their lives, and their sons so long as danger is remote, as we noted above, but when it approaches they turn on you. Any prince, trusting only in their words and having no other preparations made, will fall to his ruin, for friendships that are bought at a price and not by greatness and nobility of soul are paid for indeed, but they are not owned and cannot be called upon in time of need. Men have less hesitation in offending a man who is loved than one who is feared, for love is held by a bond of obligation which, as men are wicked, is broken whenever personal advantage suggests it, but fear is accompanied by the dread of punishment which never relaxes....

Hence a wise leader cannot and should not keep his word when keeping it is not to his advantage or when the reasons that made him give it are no longer valid. If men were good, this would not be a good precept, but since they are wicked and will not keep faith with you, you are not bound to keep faith with them....

So a prince need not have all the aforementioned good qualities, but it is most essential that he appear to have them. Indeed, I should go so far as to say that having them and always practising them is harmful, while seeming to have them is useful. It is good to appear clement [merciful], trustworthy, humane, religious, and

Additional Literary Works of and About the Period

Cao Xueqin. ***Dream of the Red Chamber.*** New York: Pantheon, 1958. Story of the problems faced by a well-to-do Chinese family in the 1700s.

Shakespeare, William. ***Hamlet.*** *Riverside Shakespeare.* Boston: Houghton Mifflin, 1974. Tragedy written in 1603 about a Danish prince and his Machiavellian uncle.

honest, and also to be so, but always with the mind so disposed that, when the occasion arises not to be so, you can become the opposite. It must be understood that a prince and particularly a new prince cannot practise all the virtues for which men are accounted good, for the necessity of preserving the state often compels him to take actions which are opposed to loyalty, charity, humanity, and religion. Hence he must have a spirit ready to adapt itself as the varying winds of fortune command him. As I have said, so far as he is able, a prince should stick to the path of good but, if the necessity arises, he should know how to follow evil.

A prince must take great care that no word ever passes his lips that is not full of the above mentioned five good qualities, and he must seem to all who see and hear him a model of piety, loyalty, integrity, humanity, and religion. Nothing is more necessary than to seem to possess this last quality, for men in general judge more by the eye than the hand; as all can see but few can feel. Everyone sees what you seem to be, few experience what you really are and these few do not dare to set themselves up against the opinion of the majority supported by the majesty of the state. In the actions of all men and especially princes, where there is no court of appeal, the end is all that counts. Let a prince then concern himself with the acquisition or the maintenance of a state; the means employed will always be considered honorable and praised by all, for the mass of mankind is always swayed by the appearances and by the outcome of an enterprise....

I am not ignorant of the fact that many have held and hold the opinion that the things of this world are so ordered by fortune and God that the prudence of mankind may effect little change in them, indeed is of no avail at all. On this basis it could be argued that there is no point in making any effort, but we should rather abandon ourselves to destiny. This opinion has been the more widely held in our day on account of the great variations in things that we have seen and are still witnessing and which are entirely beyond human conjecture. Sometimes indeed, thinking on such matters, I am minded to share that opinion myself. Nevertheless I believe, if we are to keep our free will, that it may be true that fortune controls half of our actions indeed but allows us the direction of the other half, or almost half....

Visualizing History ***The Pier and the Ducal Palace*** **(detail) by Luca Carlevaris.**
According to the principles of Machiavelli, why should a ruler carefully maintain the exterior of the palace?

RESPONDING TO LITERATURE

1. Describe in your own words Machiavelli's view of human nature.
2. Write a brief essay giving an example that explains whether today's politicians follow Machiavelli's advice.
3. Propose an alternative principle to Machiavelli's view that "where there is no court of appeal, the end is all that counts."
4. **Making Judgments** Do you think individuals should follow Machiavelli's advice in dealing with their family, friends, and classmates? Why or why not?

Bridge to the Past

Literature

Visualizing History

Renaissance architecture revived the simplicity and symmetry of ancient Roman buildings. According to art historian Kenneth Clark, the buildings of Renaissance Italy are "an assertion of the dignity of man."

Answer to Caption: *because the exterior is the basis on which people form judgments about the ruler who lives inside*

CLOSE

Organize the class into small groups. Ask each group to prepare a rebuttal to Machiavelli's ideas. They could address his views of human nature, his analysis of politics, or the long-term effectiveness of his political tactics.

Contemporary Connection

Machiavelli says that a successful ruler must always appear good but can seldom afford to actually *be* good. Have students discuss the idea of appearances versus reality. Then have them write a short essay in which they analyze a person whose appearance belied his or her real nature.

Portfolio Project

Have students write an essay in which they discuss the qualities *they* believe a good political leader should have. Encourage them to support their assertions with examples from history and current events.

ANSWERS TO RESPONDING TO LITERATURE

1. Student answers should recognize that the view is largely pessimistic.
2. Essays should indicate that students understand Machiavelli's belief that politicians' lying is justified.
3. One alternative is the belief that immoral actions cannot lead to a moral end.
4. Answers will vary. Some students may realize that Machiavelli believed standards governing personal relationships differed from those he recommends to princes. Students should give supporting reasons for their views.

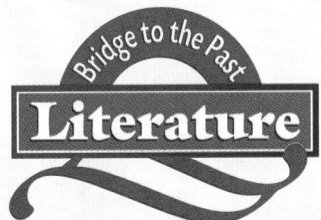

CHAPTER 16 REVIEW

Historical Significance

During the Renaissance, Europeans focused less on religion and the afterlife and more on the individual achievement and on worldly concerns. Like the ancient Greeks and Romans whom they admired, Europe's educated classes stressed human achievement and supported the arts.

With a renewed interest in learning, Europeans began to question age-old traditions and called for church reforms. When changes did not take place, some Europeans broke away from Catholicism and formed Protestant churches. Protestantism—emphasizing individual salvation and the worthiness of ordinary occupations—profoundly influenced the lands and cultures of northern Europe.

Using Key Terms

Write the key term that completes each sentence.

a. baroque
b. humanism
c. seminary
d. vocations
e. indulgences
f. predestination
g. justification by faith
h. theocracy
i. doge
j. sonnet
k. châteaux

1. The Catholic Reformation made use of a new style of art known as _______.
2. Protestantism held that all useful occupations were important _______ in which people could serve God and their neighbors.
3. ________, or the Renaissance interest in the ancient classical writings, sparked an interest in human creativity and fulfillment.
4. A _______ was a Renaissance form of writing that dealt with the theme of love.
5. The Council of Trent declared that each church diocese had to establish a _________ for the proper education of priests.
6. ______________ is the belief that a person could be made good simply by faith in God's mercy and love.
7. The Swiss reformer Huldrych Zwingli set up a __________, or church-run state, in Zurich.
8. French architects combined medieval Gothic styles with classical columns to create ______ for the French king and his nobles.
9. The Italian city of Venice had a republican style of government headed by an elected official called a _______.
10. On October 31, 1517, Martin Luther posted the Ninety-five Theses criticizing the sale of ________, or church certificates that were said to reduce or cancel punishment for sins.

Using Your History Journal

One effect of the Reformation was the migration of thousands of people to colonial America. Research and write a brief history of one religious group's migration. Create a map that shows the origin and destination(s) of that group.

Reviewing Facts

1. **List** the three social classes present in most Italian city-states during the period of the Renaissance.
2. **Describe** how the art and architecture of the Renaissance differed from the art and architecture of the Middle Ages.
3. **Discuss** specific ways in which the Northern Renaissance was different from the Renaissance in Italy.
4. **Explain** why Henry VIII separated from the Catholic Church and created the Church of England.
5. **State** what the Council of Trent did to reform the Catholic Church.

Critical Thinking

1. **Apply** Why did the Medici rulers place a heavy tax burden on the wealthy and use tax revenues to fund public works projects that benefited all the citizens of Florence?
2. **Analyze** What influence did humanism have on literature, architecture, sculpture, and painting during the Renaissance?

Chapter 16 Review

GLENCOE TECHNOLOGY

VIDEODISC
Use MindJogger Videoquiz to review students' knowledge of the chapter.

MindJogger Videoquiz
Chapter 16
Disc 2 Side B

Also available in VHS.

Answers

Using Key Terms

1. a	6. g
2. d	7. h
3. b	8. k
4. j	9. i
5. c	10. e

Using Your History Journal

Suggest that students research one of the following religious groups: Mennonites, Puritans, Huguenots, or Quakers.

Reviewing Facts

1. upper class—merchants and bankers; middle class—shopkeepers and artisans; lower class—laborers and peasants
2. Renaissance art and architecture were based on classical styles and were more realistic and lifelike, and more individualistic and worldly.
3. The Northern Renaissance had a more religious tone and criticized abuses in the Catholic Church.
4. Henry wished to divorce Catherine of Aragon, and the pope denied permission.
5. The Council of Trent defined doctrine, ended the sale of indulgences, established seminaries, and maintained the art, ritual, and Latin language of the Mass.

Critical Thinking

1. Answers may include: to win the loyalty of Florence's lower classes; to make improvements such as sewers and paved streets.
2. Answers may include: encouraged writing in new forms of literature and in vernacular languages; put emphasis on lifelike, individualistic art; accented classical domes, columns, and arches in architecture.
3. Possible answer: Build up a strong following of supporters before challenging the Catholic Church's authority, doctrine, and practices.
4. Possible answer: Another reformer would have come along because Christian humanism made the time right for reform.
5. Answers may include: Figures and horses are

430 Chapter 16 *Renaissance and Reformation*

3. **Synthesize** If you had been a supporter of Martin Luther, how might you have suggested he reform the Church?
4. **Evaluate** What might Europe be like today if Martin Luther had become a lawyer instead of a priest and had never promoted the ideas that inspired the Protestant Reformation?
5. **Analyze** Apollonio Giovanni, an Italian artist, painted the entry of a group of cavaliers into a town in the 1300s, shown below. In what ways does this painting show how Renaissance artists broke away from traditional forms?

Understanding Themes

1. **Innovation** Why do you think Renaissance artists and scholars did not merely imitate Greco-Roman culture?
2. **Cultural Diffusion** How did the people of northern Europe adapt Italian Renaissance ideas to their society?
3. **Conflict** Could the conflict between Luther and the pope have been resolved if either had reacted differently? Explain.
4. **Cultural Diffusion** What factors helped Protestant ideas to spread so rapidly?
5. **Reaction** In what ways could the Catholic Reformation be called the Counter-Reformation?

Linking Past and Present

1. Do you think ancient Greek and Roman culture influences artists, architects, and writers as much today as it did during the Renaissance? Why or why not?
2. Do you think the Inquisition could happen today in the United States? Why or why not?

Skill Practice

Use the information in Chapter 16 to find evidence for each claim below. Then decide which claim you support.

1. Martin Luther was a sincere believer who only wanted to reform the Catholic Church.
2. Martin Luther was a rebel intent on splitting the Catholic Church.

Geography in History

1. **Location** What is the approximate location of the first Spanish bishopric in South America?
2. **Region** In what geographic region were most Spanish missions established during the 1500s?
3. **Human/Environment Interaction** Large areas of South America were unreached by missionaries in the first 200 years of Spanish, Portuguese, and French mission activity. What geographic feature contributed to this?
4. **Place** What river did Jesuit missionaries use as a means of gaining access to the interior of South America?

Catholic Missions in South America

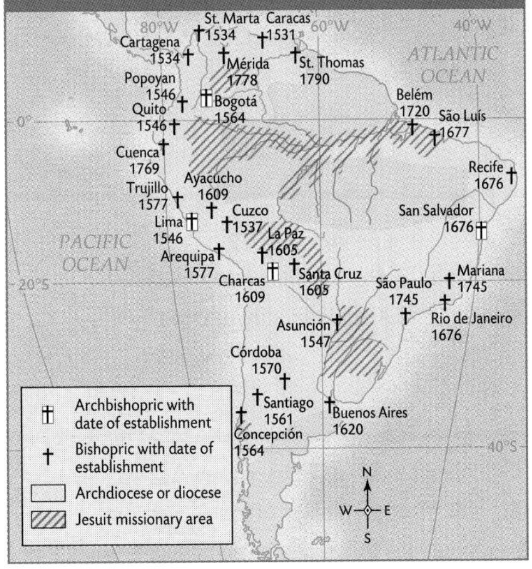

lifelike and set off from the background; subject matter drawn from everyday life.

Understanding Themes

1. **INNOVATION** They adapted classical ideas to suit the needs and values of their day.
2. **CULTURAL DIFFUSION** Many added a religious emphasis to the classical ideals of the Italian Renaissance.
3. **CONFLICT** Possible answer: Luther sought to reform the Church not break from it, and he might not have broken away had the pope responded thoughtfully to him.
4. **CULTURAL DIFFUSION** printing press, vernacular translations of the Bible, peasants wanting freedom from church oppression, and rulers eager to seize church property

Chapter 16 Review

5. **REACTION** The Catholic Reformation was a response or reaction that countered the Protestant Reformation.

Linking Past and Present

1. Answers will vary. Yes: Western art is founded on classical styles developed by the Greeks and Romans. No: artists are exploring diverse non-Western influences and rejecting established rules in favor of individual expression.
2. Most students will say no because of religious diversity, cultural pluralism, secularism in society, and separation of church and state.

Skill Practice

Answers will vary, but evidence for (1) may include the fact that Luther had had sincere struggles of conscience as a monk, had eventually become a priest, and had not proposed leaving the Church until after Worms. Evidence for (2) may include the fact that Luther proclaimed his Ninety-five Theses in a challenging manner and made them as widely known as possible.

Geography in History

1. 66°W, 10°N
2. the northern and western coastal regions
3. tropical rain forests
4. Amazon

Chapter Bonus Test Question

Ask students: Why was the time ripe for the Protestant Reformation? *(Answers will vary but may include the following: Italian humanism brought an emphasis on secular ideas, and Christian humanism in northern Europe focused on criticizing abuses in the Church and returning to the Church's piety.)*

Expanding Horizons

CHAPTER RESOURCES

	Reproducible Resources	Multimedia Resources
Chapter Opener	Chapter Themes: Graphic Organizer 17 Historical Significance Chapter Activity 17	MindJogger Videoquiz
Chapter Enrichment	Vocabulary Activity 17* Time Line Activity 17 Mapping History Activity 17 History Simulation 17 Geography and History Activity 17 Source Reading 17 People in World History Profiles 31, 32 World Art and Music Activity 17 Enrichment Activity 17 Critical Thinking Activity 17 Skill Reinforcement Activity 17 Building Skills in Geography Workbook, Unit 1, Lesson 11 Performance Assessment Activity 17	Focus on World Art Print 1, Jan Vermeer. *The Artist and His Model as Klio* NGS Poster Set: *Age of Exploration* World History and Art Transparencies 22, 23 Mapping History Overlay Transparency 11, *Triangular Trade Routes;* 12, *17th Century Latin American Viceroyalties* Chapter Transparency 17 NGS PicturePack Transparency Set: *Age of Exploration* Vocabulary PuzzleMaker Software NGS PictureShow CD-ROM: *Great Explorers, Parts 1 and 2* Turning Points in World History
Chapter Review/Reteaching	Reteaching Activity 17 Skill Reinforcement Activity 17 Spanish Chapter Summary 17	Chapter 17 Digest Audiocassette, Activity, Test* Vocabulary PuzzleMaker Software Student Self-Test and Review Software MindJogger Videoquiz
Chapter Evaluation/Testing	Performance Assessment Activity 17 Chapter 17 Test, Forms A and B	Testmaker

* *Also available in Spanish*

0:00 **OUT OF TIME?** Assign the Chapter 17 summary in the Unit 4 Digest on pages 506–509, and the Chapter 17 Audiocassettes.

Block Schedule

Block scheduling differs from traditional class scheduling in the amount of time allotted to each period. The extended time frame provided by block scheduling affords you the opportunity to implement a greater number of research-oriented and activity-intense projects to motivate and involve your students. Activities that are particularly suited to use within the block scheduling framework are identified throughout this chapter by the following designation.

KEY TO ABILITY LEVELS

Teaching strategies have been coded for varying learning styles and abilities.

L1 **BASIC** activities for all students
L2 **AVERAGE** activities for average to above-average students
L3 **CHALLENGING** activities for above-average students
LEP **LIMITED ENGLISH PROFICIENCY** activities

A complete, 1-page lesson plan is provided for each section in the *Reproducible Lesson Plans* booklet.

SECTION RESOURCES

Daily Objectives	Reproducible Resources	Multimedia Resources
Section 1 **Early Explorations** Explain why Europeans risked dangerous ocean voyages to discover sea routes to other parts of the world.	Reproducible Lesson Plan 17-1 Vocabulary Activity 17* Guided Reading Activity 17-1* History Simulation 17 Time Line Activity 17 Source Reading 17 Section Quiz 17-1*	Section Focus Transparency 17-1 Chapter Transparency 17 Student Self-Test and Review Software Testmaker Turning Points in World History: *Age of Exploration*
Section 2 **Overseas Empires** Describe how Europeans exploited the lands and the peoples they found in Africa, Asia, and the Americas.	Reproducible Lesson Plan 17-2 Vocabulary Activity 17* Guided Reading Activity 17-2* People in World History Profiles 31, 32 Mapping History Activity 17 Geography and History Activity 17 Section Quiz 17-2*	NGS Poster Set: *Age of Exploration* Section Focus Transparency 17-2 Mapping History Overlay Transparency 11, *Triangular Trade Routes*; 12, *17th Century Latin American Viceroyalties* NGS PicturePack Transparency Set: *Age of Exploration* Student Self-Test and Review Software Testmaker NGS PictureShow CD-ROM: *Great Explorers, Parts 1 and 2* Turning Points in World History: *Age of Exploration*
Section 3 **Changing Ways of Life** Analyze how increased trade and colonial expansion set the stage for a global economy.	Reproducible Lesson Plan 17-3 Guided Reading Activity 17-3* Reteaching Activity 17 Enrichment Activity 17 Section Quiz 17-3* Performance Assessment Activity 17 Spanish Chapter Summary 17	Focus on World Art Print 1, Jan Vermeer. *The Artist and His Model as Klio* Section Focus Transparency 17-3 World History and Art Transparency 22, *View of Toledo*; 23, *Mission San Xavier del Bac* Vocabulary PuzzleMaker Software Student Self-Test and Review Software Testmaker

* *Also available in Spanish*

Chapter Activities

Performance Assessment Activity

A Court Case After students have studied the causes for and results of the era of exploration and mercantilism, have them demonstrate their understanding by taking the roles of modern-day government officials in one of the countries explored by Spain, England, and so on. Students who represent countries of the same empire should form groups to brainstorm ideas and plan a course of action intended to file suit in court and claim damages from the exploring country for lasting harm done to the explored country. Ideas may be presented in the form of a speech to a jury or testimony of experts in a role play, or letters laying out a plan of action.

Possible Rubric Features
Accuracy of content information, concept attainment, collaborative planning, argumentation, clarity of presentation (letter), and impact on audience

• *For an additional activity, refer to Activity 17 in the* Performance Assessment Strategies and Activities *booklet.*

Activity

From the Classroom of...

Scott Shephard
Watertown Senior High School
Watertown, SD

Why We Explore

Encourage students to think about the general reasons humans explore. This activity also encourages students to compare the motives of explorers from the age of exploration with those of explorers from other eras of investigation.

On the board, write the headings *Motives, Risks,* and *Significant Gains*. Ask students what they know about Christopher Columbus and fill in the chart with facts about his explorations.

Next, give students a list of famous explorers such as Neil Armstrong, Lewis and Clark, Yuri Gagarin, Marco Polo, and Edmund Hillary. Have students use classroom resources to find out about these people, then add facts about them to the chart on the board.

As a follow-up to this activity, ask students to draw some generalizations about the following: Why do we explore? Do the risks of exploration ever outweigh the gains? Was Columbus's voyage riskier than the *Apollo 11* moon mission? As a final evaluation, you might ask students to write an essay that compares and contrasts Columbus with another explorer they choose in the areas of motives, risks, and gains.

MULTIPLE LEARNING STYLES

Verbal/Linguistic
During the age of exploration, many Europeans believed in terrible sea monsters and odd beings that inhabited unknown lands. Have students research and report on some of these legends.

Logical/Mathematical
Have students create a time line of all the voyages of exploration and all the colonial activities described in this chapter.

Visual/Spatial
Have students research Columbus's life and create a mural that summarizes its highlights.

Auditory/Musical
Many old folk songs, such as "Upon Sir Francis Drake's Return," relate stories about the sea. Have students locate such folk songs and report on them. Students may refer to the *Oxford Book of Sea Songs*, edited by Roy Palmer (New York: Oxford University Press, 1986) or obtain recordings of some of the songs from the public library and play them for the class.

Additional Resources

TEACHER'S CORNER

NATIONAL GEOGRAPHIC SOCIETY

INDEX TO NATIONAL GEOGRAPHIC MAGAZINE

The following articles may be used for research relating to this chapter:

- "San Diego: An Account of Adventure, Deceit, and Intrigue," by Franck Goddio, July 1994.
- "African Slave Trade: The Cruelest Commerce," by Colin Palmer, September 1992.
- "Portugal's Sea Road to the East," by Merle Severy, November 1992.
- "Search for Columbus," by Eugene Lyon, January 1992.
- "La Isabela: Europe's First Foothold in the New World," by Kathleen A. Deagan, January 1992.
- "Pizarro: Conqueror of the Inca," by John Hemming, February 1992.
- "Track of the Manila Galleons," by Eugene Lyon, September 1990.
- "Nuestra Señora de la Concepción," by William M. Mathers, September 1990.
- "Exploring Our Forgotten Century: Between Columbus and Jamestown," by Joseph Judge, March 1988.
- "Where Columbus Found the New World," by Joseph Judge, November 1986.

NATIONAL GEOGRAPHIC SOCIETY PRODUCTS AVAILABLE FROM GLENCOE

To order the following products for use with this chapter, contact your local Glencoe sales representative or call Glencoe at 1-800-368-7344:

NGS PICTURESHOW CD-ROM
- Great Explorers, Parts 1 and 2

NGS PICTUREPACK TRANSPARENCY SET
- Age of Exploration

NGS POSTER SET
- Age of Exploration

ADDITIONAL NATIONAL GEOGRAPHIC SOCIETY PRODUCTS

To order the following products for use with this chapter, call National Geographic Society at 1-800-368-2728:

- *Digging Up America's Past*, "The First Europeans in the Americas," "Colonization and After." (Filmstrip)
- *Great Explorers*, "Columbus," "Magellan," "Drake." (Filmstrip)

BIBLIOGRAPHY

Literature of the Period

Las Casas, Bartolomé de. ***A Short Account of the Destruction of the Indies.*** Translated and edited by Nigel Griffin. New York: Penguin, 1992. A Dominican missionary's critical account, written in 1552, of the Europeans' brutal treatment of the Native Americans.

Shakespeare, William. ***The Merchant of Venice.*** New York: Oxford University Press, 1993. The moneylender Shylock demands a pound of flesh from the merchant Antonio.

Readings for the Student

Yue, Charlotte and David. ***Christopher Columbus: How He Did It.*** Boston: Houghton Mifflin, 1992. Describes the technology and knowledge on which Columbus's voyages were based.

Readings for the Teacher

The Times Atlas of World Exploration: 3,000 Years of Exploring, Explorers, and Mapmaking. Edited by Felipe Fernandez-Armesto. New York: Harper Collins, 1991. A comprehensive survey.

interNET CONNECTIONS
Columbus Letter Read Christopher Columbus's letter to the king and queen of Spain on this web page.
http://grid.let.rug.nl/~welling/usa/documents/columlet.html

Introducing Chapter 17

CHAPTER THEMES

Chapter Themes are listed by section on this chapter opening page of the Student Edition. A corresponding theme-based activity is available under "TEACH," and a theme-based question is asked in the Section and Chapter Reviews.

The Storyteller

Historical Setting At first Columbus failed to persuade the monarchs of Portugal, England, and France to finance his plan of finding a sea route to Asia by sailing west across the Atlantic Ocean. The deeply religious Catholic queen, Isabella of Spain, was impressed by Columbus's stated intention to use the proceeds of his expedition to seize Jerusalem from the Muslims and to rebuild the Temple of the Jews there. At the queen's insistence, a commission of experts evaluated Columbus's plan but rejected it. Only after Spain's conquest of Granada (January 1492) was Isabella persuaded (April 1492) by royal treasurer Luis de Santangel to seize the opportunity offered by Columbus's plan.

Historical Significance

Answer: *The age of exploration brought the people of Europe, Asia, the Americas, and sub-Saharan Africa into direct contact for the first time and led to a transfer of ideas and products. However, the European process of colonization took a great toll in human life and often had a negative impact on cultures that were conquered.*

Chapter 17

1400–1750

Expanding Horizons

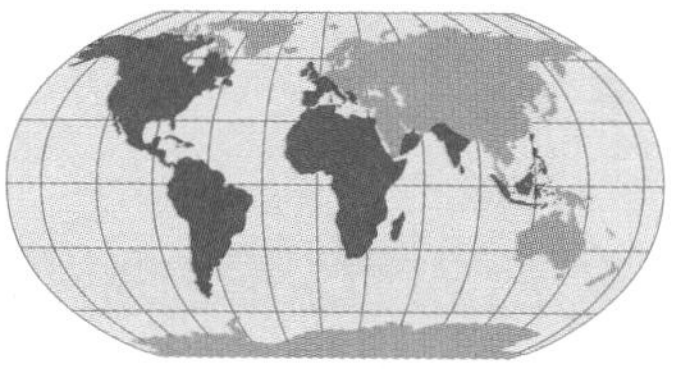

Chapter Themes

- **Innovation** European sailors borrow technological and navigational ideas from Asia. *Section 1*
- **Movement** European nations establish colonies in the lands they explore in Asia, Africa, and the Americas. *Section 2*
- **Change** The wealth of overseas colonies sparks the Commercial Revolution in Europe. *Section 3*

The Storyteller

On the night of October 11, 1492, Christopher Columbus scanned the horizon, praying that landfall was near. "About 10 o'clock at night, while standing on the sterncastle, I thought I saw a light to the west. It looked like a little wax candle bobbing up and down. It had the same appearance as a light or torch belonging to fishermen or travellers...."

The light flickered out, though, and the ship sailed on. The moon rose, but no land appeared. Two hours later, the boom of a cannon roared across the water. A sailor aboard the Pinta, *the fastest of the expedition's three ships, had sighted land. For Spain and other nations of Europe, the land that appeared in the darkness was part of a far greater treasure. As a result of Columbus's voyage, contacts increased among Europeans, Native Americans, Africans, and Asians.*

Historical Significance

How were Europe, Asia, Africa, and the Americas changed as the result of cross-cultural contacts from the 1400s to the 1700s?

1450 — 1500 — 1550 — 1600

- **1492** Christopher Columbus reaches America.
- **1521** Hernán Cortés conquers the Aztec Empire.
- **1599** The Dutch send first expedition to East Asia.
- **1607** The English establish a permanent settlement at Jamestown.

432

GEOGRAPHY CONNECTION

GEOGRAPHIC THEMES

Location Using a world map or globe, have students locate Portugal, Spain, the Netherlands, England, France, North and South America, the islands of the Caribbean, Africa, the East Indies (now Indonesia), India, and the Philippines. Into what three major oceans are the great waters of the world divided? *(Pacific, Atlantic, Indian)* Which ocean is the largest and which the smallest? *(The Pacific is the largest and the Indian the smallest.)* Have students note the distances from Europe to India, the islands of Indonesia, and the coast of the Americas. L1

Visualizing History This busy English port of the 1700s reveals England's position as one of Europe's major seafaring nations.

Your History Journal

Imagine crossing the Atlantic, the Pacific, or the Indian Ocean in the early 1600s. Compared to today, ships were small, and the journey was neither safe nor pleasant. Write a diary of a few days on such a voyage.

Introducing Chapter 17

Visualizing History Although Dutch artists painted pictures with nautical subjects throughout the seventeenth century, English painters began to respond artistically to their country's nautical activity only at the beginning of the eighteenth century. English artists such as Samuel Scott put on canvas faithful depictions of actual scenes in English seaports.

Performance Assessment

Refer to the activity on page 432C of the Planning Guide.

For an additional activity, refer to Activity 17 in the *Performance Assessment Strategies and Activities* booklet.

Using Your History Journal

Suggest that students consider such basic aspects of daily life aboard ship as diet, sleeping conditions, and sanitary facilities.

GLENCOE TECHNOLOGY

VIDEODISC

Use MindJogger to preview chapter content.

MindJogger Videoquiz

Chapter 17
Disc 3 Side A

Also available in VHS.

EXTRA CREDIT PROJECT

Issues in History Historians are still debating whether the early explorers should be viewed primarily as heroes or as exploiters. Have students research this question and report to the class not only on the contributions to knowledge that resulted from the voyages of exploration but also on their negative impact on Native American cultures. Suggested resources: H. Faber, *The Discoverers of America*; M. E. Jones, ed., *Christopher Columbus and His Legacy*; S. E. Morison, *The Great Explorers: The European Discovery of America*; and R. Wright, *Stolen Continents: The Americas Through Indian Eyes Since 1492.*

Chapter 17 Section 1

SECTION THEME

▶ **Innovation** Europeans borrow technological and navigational ideas from Asia.

Find Out

Answer: *Their hopes for profit and for spreading Christianity made the risks seem worthwhile.*

FOCUS

Section Objective

Explain why Europeans risked dangerous ocean voyages to discover sea routes to other parts of the world.

BELLRINGER Motivational Activity

Before taking roll at the beginning of the class period, project Section Focus Transparency 17-1 and have students answer the activity questions. Discuss students' responses.

This activity is also available as a blackline master.

Vocabulary Pre-check

Use Vocabulary Activity 17 to introduce vocabulary terms. **L1 LEP**

1400 **1450** **1500**

1432 Prince Henry the Navigator's explorers reach the Azores.

1488 Bartholomeu Dias of Portugal sails to the tip of Africa.

1519 Magellan expedition sets sail from Seville, Spain.

Section 1

Early Explorations

Setting the Scene

▶ **Terms to Define**
cartographer, line of demarcation, circumnavigation

▶ **People to Meet**
Prince Henry the Navigator, Bartholomeu Dias, Vasco da Gama, Christopher Columbus, Ferdinand Magellan

▶ **Places to Locate**
Cape of Good Hope, Strait of Magellan

Find Out Why did Europeans risk dangerous ocean voyages to discover sea routes to other parts of the world?

The Storyteller

Wealth was on everyone's mind when they thought about the New World. Ferdinand and Isabella wrote, "We have commanded [Columbus] to return … because thereby our Lord God is served, His Holy Faith extended and our own realms increased." The King and Queen offered financial incentives for accompanying Columbus: "Whatever persons wish to … dwell in … Hispaniola … shall pay no tax whatsoever and shall have for their own … the houses which they build and the lands which they work…." As a final enticement, Columbus insisted, "The Indians are the wealth of Hispaniola—for they perform all labor of men and beasts."

Spanish treasure

—adapted from *Ferdinand and Isabella*, Felipe Fernández-Armesto, 1975

In the 1400s European explorers tested uncharted oceans in search of a better trade route to Asia. They left their homelands filled with a desire for gold, glory, and for spreading Christianity. In just over 250 years, their ventures had destroyed and built empires at a great cost in human life. Their efforts, however, linked people of different cultures and ended forever the isolation of the world's major civilizations.

The Quest for Spices

Europe in the 1300s had depended on spices from Asia and India. Such spices as pepper, cinnamon, and nutmeg were in great demand. Used chiefly to flavor and preserve meat, spices were also used for perfumes, cosmetics, and medicine.

The spice trade was controlled in Asia and Europe by Arab and Venetian merchants. Chinese and Indian merchants sold spices to Arab merchants, who then shipped the cargoes overland to Europe and reaped huge profits in the sale of the spices to Venetian merchants. Europeans, eager to amass quick fortunes through direct trade with Asians, began to look for quicker routes to Asia. Because the Mongols by the mid-1300s could no longer guarantee safe passage for traders on overland routes, Europeans were forced to consider the sea as a possible route to Asia.

Several motivations led Europeans into an era of exploration. Not only did merchants seek a profitable trade with Asia, but also Christian religious leaders sought to halt the expansion of Islamic empires and to spread Christian teachings. Learning and imagination also played a part. Renaissance thinkers had expanded the European world view to include new possibilities for exploration and discovery.

Overseas voyages would end Europe's isolation and set it on the path of worldwide expansion.

SECTION RESOURCES

Reproducible Masters
- Reproducible Lesson Plan 17-1
- Vocabulary Activity 17
- Guided Reading Activity 17-1
- History Simulation 17
- Time Line Activity 17
- Source Reading 17
- Section Quiz 17-1

Transparencies
- Section Focus Transparency 17-1
- Chapter Transparency 17

Multimedia
- Student Self-Test and Review Software
- Testmaker
- Turning Points in World History: *Age of Exploration*

434 Chapter 17 *Expanding Horizons*

European Knowledge of the World

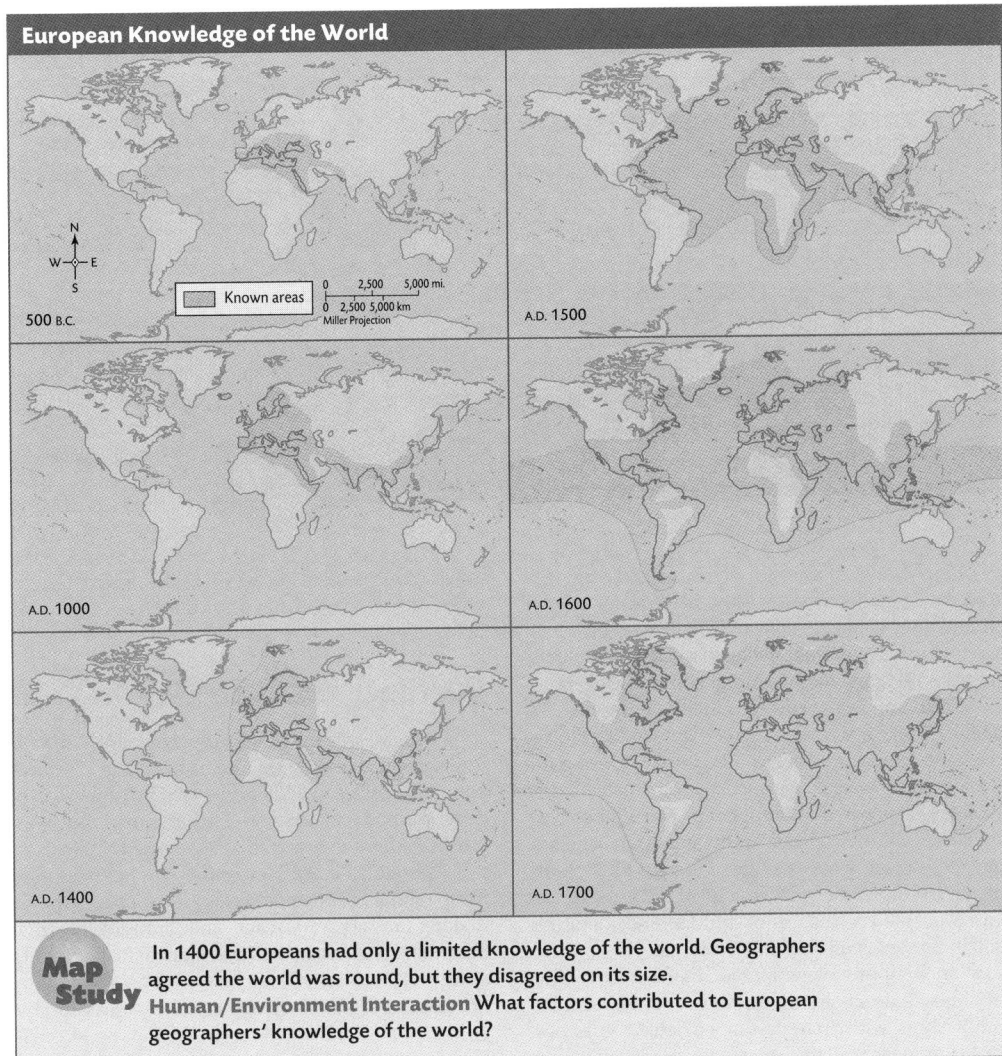

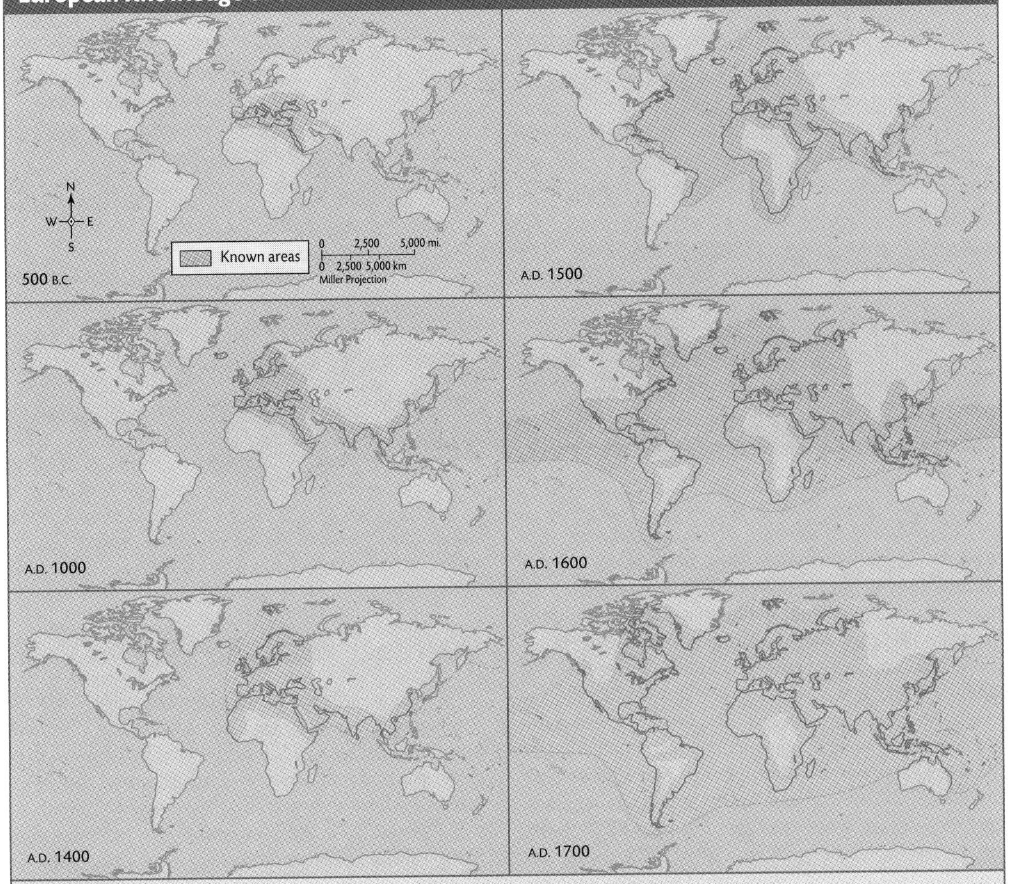

Map Study In 1400 Europeans had only a limited knowledge of the world. Geographers agreed the world was round, but they disagreed on its size.
Human/Environment Interaction What factors contributed to European geographers' knowledge of the world?

They would also prepare the way for the rise of the world's first global age.

Technology of Exploration

Open-water ocean sailing—necessary to find a water route to Asia—requires sailors trained in navigation, accurate maps, and oceangoing ships. For exploration to succeed, ships had to be able both to leave the coastal waters and sight of land and to return home. Ancient navigators stayed close to the coast, using landmarks to determine their position. Later, sailors who traveled beyond sight of land used the positions of stars and the sun to determine in which direction they were traveling. Hourglasses told them how long they had traveled. Keeping track of speed, direction, and time theoretically enabled a captain to tell where the ship was. However, these calculations were very inaccurate.

The compass, of Chinese origin, enabled sailors to determine geographical direction. By 1100, sailors used the astrolabe—perfected by the Arabs—to determine the altitude of the sun or other heavenly bodies. But in practice, standing on the deck of a heaving ship, few ship captains had the skill and patience that the astrolabe required.

COOPERATIVE LEARNING ACTIVITY

Cultural Life Early Spanish and Portuguese explorers encountered many different cultures in the Americas (including Arawak, Carib, Maya, Aztec, Inca). Organize the class into small groups and have each group research and report on one of the indigenous American cultures. Remind students that each group member is responsible for contributing to the overall effort. Each student should be assigned one of the following areas to research: geographic location and method of subsistence, arts and crafts, religious beliefs, customs, and the effect of European contact on the culture. One or more students may illustrate the report. **L2**

TEACH

Guided Practice

THEME Innovation

Have students discuss the design innovations of the caravel that contributed to successful voyages by the Portuguese and Spanish. *(lateen sails, multiple masts, rudder at stern)* Ask why explorers could not have ventured very far into the Atlantic or Pacific without the use of caravels. *(Single-masted ships with one large sail traveled slowly.)* **L1**

Map Study

Answer

inventions such as the compass and the astrolabe, and the reappearance of Ptolemy's maps in Europe

Map Skills Practice

Reading a Map Why are the three maps on the left so similar? *(Until the 1500s, people had unsophisticated navigational instruments and lacked interest in the outside world.)* What changes led to the changes in the maps on the right? *(The Renaissance prompted new curiosity about the world; new navigational instruments and old Ptolemaic maps became available.)*

Literature Have students read an excerpt from one of Columbus's journals. Discuss what the excerpt reveals about Columbus and his times. **L2**

History Simulation 17

Chapter Transparency 17

Visualizing History A true caravel had four masts, one with square sails, the other three with lateen sails. The *Niña* and the *Pinta*, two of Columbus's three ships for the historic 1492 voyage, were caravels. Astrolabes were in use as early as the sixth century but came into wide use by Europeans and Muslims from the early Middle Ages.

Answer to Caption: *Its rudder made it maneuverable, and it drew little water, allowing it to travel in shallow waters.*

Independent Practice

- Guided Reading Activity 17-1 **L1**
- Time Line Activity 17
- Source Reading Activity 17

Daily Life Europe's demand for spices motivated the first voyages of exploration. Have students research and write a report on the use of spices in the 1500s. **L2**

ABCNEWS INTERACTIVE™

VIDEODISC
Turning Points in World History

Side One
Chapter 9

Title: *Age of Exploration*
Subject: As western Europeans sought new routes to Asia, they found lands unknown to them.
Ask: In what ways was the age of exploration a turning point in history? *(Europeans discovered new lands; indigenous peoples were mistreated, killed, or died from disease; new crops were brought to Europe and to the Americas.)*

An astrolabe

Visualizing History **The American artist J.L.G. Ferris painted *The Eve of Discovery*, showing a caravel as it may have appeared in the 1400s.** *Why was the caravel a good ship for sailing up rivers?*

Maps were another problem for early navigators. Most maps were wildly inaccurate, drawn from scattered impressions of travelers and traders. **Cartographers**, or mapmakers, filled their parchments with lands found only in rumor or legend.

Cartographers' skills gradually improved. By about 1300, coastal charts showed the Mediterranean coastline with a great degree of accuracy. During the Renaissance, works by the Egyptian astronomer Ptolemy reappeared in Europe. His maps, improved over the centuries by Byzantine and Arab scholars, gave Europeans a new picture of the world. Ptolemy also introduced the grid system of map references based on the coordinates of latitude and longitude still in use today all over the world.

Innovations were also made in the construction of ships. Late in the 1400s, shipwrights began to outfit ships with triangle-shaped lateen sails perfected by Arab traders. These sails made it possible for ships to sail against the wind, not simply with it. Shipwrights also abandoned using a single mast with one large sail. Multiple masts, with several smaller sails hoisted one above the other, made ships travel much faster. In addition, moving the rudder from the ship's side to the stern made ships more maneuverable.

In the 1400s a European ship called a caravel incorporated all these improvements. The caravel was up to 65 feet (20 m) in length with the capability of carrying about 130 tons (118 metric tons) of cargo. Because a caravel drew little water, it allowed explorers to venture up shallow inlets and to beach the ship to make repairs. A Venetian mariner called the caravels "the best ships that sailed the seas." The caravels also carried new types of weapons—rifles and cannons.

Portugal Leads the Way

Portugal was the first European country to venture out on the Atlantic Ocean in search of spices and gold. Between 1420 and 1580, Portuguese captains pushed farther and farther down the west coast of Africa in search of a sea route to Asia.

Although **Prince Henry the Navigator**, son of King John I of Portugal, was not a sailor—never making an ocean voyage—he brought together mapmakers, mathematicians, and astronomers to study navigation. He also sponsored many Portuguese exploratory voyages westward into the Atlantic and southward down Africa's west coast. In the early 1400s Henry's explorers discovered the Azores, the Madeira Islands, and the Cape Verde Islands. These discoveries were the foundation of what in the 1500s became the Portuguese Empire.

In August 1487 **Bartholomeu Dias** left Portugal, intent upon finding the southern tip of Africa. In 1488 his expedition discovered the southern tip of Africa, which was later renamed the **Cape of Good Hope**. Dias's voyage proved that ships could reach East Asia by sailing around Africa.

In 1497 four ships led by **Vasco da Gama** sailed from Portugal for India. The expedition rounded the Cape of Good Hope, made stops at trading centers along the east coast of Africa, and landed at Calicut on the southwest coast of India in 10 months. There da Gama found Hindus and

MEETING SPECIAL NEEDS ACTIVITY

Learning Style: Visual/Spatial Have students work in pairs or small groups to summarize in pictures on poster board the achievements of Portugal and Spain described in this section. Try to pair competent illustrators with verbally proficient students. Tell students to discuss how the pictures should best convey the information. After the picture or pictures have been sketched and colored in, the groups should write labels summarizing the information the pictures convey. After the posters are completed, display them in the classroom. **L1 LEP**

Richard Schlecht

"Little Girl"

The *Niña*—"Little Girl"—was Christopher Columbus's favorite ship, a small, fast, seaworthy vessel about 67 feet long. Descriptions of the *Niña* discovered in a Spanish document from the period have enabled historians to draw pictures of what the craft actually looked like. In this drawing the lines in red show the *Niña's* sails and riggings. The document also revealed that the *Niña* had four masts, not two or three, as previously believed. Columbus's beloved "Little Girl," the most technically advanced craft of her day, probably made three of his four voyages to the Americas.

The Europe of 1500 was on the brink of the modern era. Monarchs Isabella and Ferdinand of Spain could command Columbus and other explorers, who combined knowledge of sophisticated naval technologies with bravery and determination. In quick succession Columbus (1492), Vasco da Gama (1498), and Magellan (1519–21), among others, linked Europe with the rest of the world. The sea-sheltered Americas were invaded. The slave trade expanded and brought much of Africa into the shadow of the Americas. The Muslim peoples of Africa and Asia lost their central position as guardians of trade between Europe, Asia, and Africa. Within a few centuries, the whole world came within European explorers' reach. ⊕

TEACH

Tell students that the fifteenth-century document describing the *Niña* is only one of many so-called Columbus documents. The documents include more than 2,500 notes Columbus wrote in the margins of his books, about 80 letters and notes, copies of the log from his first trip to the Americas, and his will. Ask students where they think most of the books and manuscripts are located. *(Spain)* Tell them that Columbus documents are also found in Italy, France, and the United States.

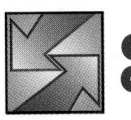

CURRICULUM CONNECTION

GEOGRAPHY

Columbus's seafaring interest may have been shaped by the geography of his birthplace, the seaport Republic of Genoa, in today's Italy. Lacking much fertile land and surrounded by powerful rival cities like Milan and Florence, many inhabitants of Genoa looked to the Mediterranean Sea in search of their fortunes.

you don't say...

Calico, a cotton cloth that began to be used after 1495, is a shortened version of "Calicut cloth." The first place to export calico was the Indian city Calicut.

Global Gourmet

Americas Florida's citrus industry can be traced back to Columbus's second voyage to the Americas in 1493. The citrus seeds the navigator brought to the West Indies took root there and eventually made their way to Mexico and Florida.

ASSESS

Check for Understanding

Assign Section 1 Review as homework or as an in-class activity.

Use Student Self-Test and Review Software to review Section 1.

History & Art After being dismissed in 1487 by advisers to Ferdinand and Isabella, Columbus did not allow the rejection to cause him to abandon his plan.

Answer to Caption: *He made three voyages after the initial voyage.*

Muslims trading fine silk, porcelain, and spices that made the glass beads and trinkets of the Portuguese appear shoddy.

Da Gama tried to persuade the ruler of Calicut and Muslim merchants in India to trade with the Portuguese. He had little success and returned home. In Portugal, however, da Gama was regarded as a national hero. He had pioneered a water route to India, and he had provided a glimpse of the riches that could come from direct trade with the East.

Spain's Quest for Riches

In the late 1400s Spain ended a long period of internal turmoil and wars against the Moors. Under King Ferdinand and Queen Isabella, Spain entered the race for Asian riches by backing the expeditions of an Italian navigator named **Christopher Columbus**.

Columbus Crosses the Atlantic

In 1492 Christopher Columbus approached Queen Isabella with an intriguing plan—to reach India by sailing west across the Atlantic. For years Columbus had tried unsuccessfully to persuade other European rulers to finance his voyage. With Queen Isabella his persistence paid off.

History & Art *Columbus Before the Queen* by Peter Rothermel, 1842. National Museum of American Art, Washington, D.C. **Seven years of persistent pleading earned Spain's support.** *How many voyages did Columbus make seeking proof that he had discovered a new route to India?*

In August 1492 Columbus sailed from Spain with three small ships. He calculated the distance to India to be 700 leagues, about 2,200 nautical miles; he knew that the actual distance might be greater. To calm the crews' fears, he showed them a log that understated the distance they had sailed from home.

The days out of sight of land wore on and on, however, and the terrified sailors begged Columbus to turn back. After a false sighting of land, the crews began to talk of mutiny. Columbus reluctantly agreed to turn back if they did not reach land within three days.

After midnight on the second day, the expedition sighted land. In the morning Columbus and his men went ashore, becoming the first Europeans to set foot on one of the islands of the Bahamas. Columbus wrote of the inhabitants:

> "The islanders came to the ships' boats, swimming and bringing us parrots and balls of cotton thread ... which they exchanged for ... glass beads and hawk bells ... they took and gave of what they had very willingly, but it seemed to me that they were poor in every way. They bore no weapons, nor were they acquainted with them, because when I showed them swords they seized them by the edge and so cut themselves from ignorance."

Believing he was off the coast of India, Columbus called the islanders "Indians." Columbus spent the next three months exploring the islands Hispaniola (present-day Haiti and the Dominican Republic) and Cuba in search of gold. Although he found enough gold to raise Spanish hopes, he saw no evidence of the great civilizations of Asia.

When Columbus returned to Spain, Ferdinand and Isabella gave him the title "Admiral of the Ocean Sea, Viceroy and Governor of the Islands he hath discovered in the Indies." Before he died in 1506, Columbus made three more voyages to the Caribbean islands and South America seeking proof that he had discovered a new route to Asia. He died certain that he had.

Even without sure proof, it was difficult for anyone to dispute Columbus's claim. Maps of the time did not show any landmass between Europe and Asia. It was not until 1507 that another Italian explorer, Amerigo Vespucci (veh•SPOO•chee), suggested that Columbus had discovered a "New World." In honor of Vespucci, the name *America* began to appear on maps that included the newly discovered lands.

MAKING CONNECTIONS ACTIVITIES

Technology Have students research and write a brief illustrated report on developments in ship design and construction from antiquity through the age of exploration. Make sure they include mention of Henry the Navigator's role in encouraging the building of new types of ships. **L2**

Cartography Ask students to research and write a brief report on the history of cartography from antiquity (beginning with Babylonian maps on clay tablets) through the age of exploration. Encourage them to focus on how the discoveries of explorers such as Columbus and Magellan transformed the world maps of those days. **L2**

Dividing the World

Both Spain and Portugal wanted to protect their claims in the Americas and turned to the pope for help. In 1493 the pope drew a line of demarcation, an imaginary line running down the middle of the Atlantic from the North Pole to the South Pole. Spain was to have control of all lands to the west of the line, while Portugal was to have control of all lands to the east of the line.

The Portuguese, however, feared that their line was so far to the east that Spain might take over their Asian trade. As a result, in 1494 Spain and Portugal signed the Treaty of Tordesillas (TAWR•duh•SEE•yuhs), an agreement to move the line of demarcation farther west. The treaty divided the entire unexplored world between just two powers, Spain and Portugal.

History & Art *Discovery of Magellan Strait* (artist unknown). **By this point in Magellan's voyage, one ship foundered on the rocks and another turned back.** *What did the journey prove?*

Voyage of Magellan

In 1519 an expedition led by **Ferdinand Magellan**, a Portuguese soldier of fortune, set sail from Seville under the Spanish flag to find a western route to Asia. The five ships and 260-man crew sailed across the Atlantic and made their way along the eastern coast of South America, searching every bay and inlet for this route.

Along the coast of Argentina, crews of three of the ships attempted a mutiny because Magellan had decided to halt the expedition until spring. Magellan executed the captain who had instigated the mutiny, regained control of the fleet, and resumed the expedition. Finally, near the southern tip of South America, the ships reached a narrow water passageway now called the **Strait of Magellan**. The ships threaded their way through the maze of rocky islands in the 300-mile- (480-km-) long strait. Strong currents and unpredictable gales separated one ship from the others, and its crew forced its return to Spain. Another was shipwrecked.

Magellan's ship and the two other remaining ships finally passed through the strait into the South Sea, which had been discovered and named six years earlier by Vasco Núñez de Balboa. Because the water was so calm, Magellan renamed it the Pacific Ocean. The fleet then sailed nearly four months before reaching land. Water and food ran out, and some sailors died. One of the crew wrote in his journal, "We ate biscuit, which was no longer biscuit, but powder of biscuits swarming with worms, for they had eaten the good."

At last the ships reached the present-day Philippines. Caught in a skirmish between a local chief and his enemy, Magellan was killed. The surviving crew escaped and sailed for Spain.

In 1522, after three years at sea, the last ship with its 18 survivors arrived at Seville, completing the first circumnavigation, or circling of the globe. The spices they brought back barely covered the cost of the voyage, but the expedition had a value far beyond money. It proved that the world was round and much larger than anyone had believed, that the oceans of the world were connected, and that the lands discovered by Columbus were not part of Asia.

SECTION 1 REVIEW

Recall
1. **Define** cartographer, line of demarcation, circumnavigation.
2. **Identify** Prince Henry the Navigator, Bartholomeu Dias, Vasco da Gama, Christopher Columbus, Ferdinand Magellan.
3. **Explain** why Portugal and Spain wanted to find a sea route to Asia.

Critical Thinking
4. **Synthesizing Information** Using the text as a resource, write a journal entry describing your experiences as a sailor on an expedition of Dias, Columbus, Magellan, or da Gama.

Understanding Themes
5. **Innovation** What sciences and new technologies led to voyages of exploration?

SECTION 1 REVIEW ANSWERS

1. All vocabulary words are defined in the Glossary.
2. Henry, 436; Dias, 436; da Gama, 436; Columbus, 438; Magellan; 439
3. quest for riches, desire to spread Christianity
4. Students should include details of the expedition they select.
5. INNOVATION sciences: cartography, math, astronomy; technologies: compass, astrolabe, caravels

Chapter 17 Section 1

History & Art Until the opening of the Panama Canal (1914) shortened the water route from the Atlantic to the Pacific, the Strait of Magellan remained an important sailing-ship route.

Answer to Caption: *that the world was round and larger than previously believed, that the oceans were connected, and that the lands Columbus discovered were not part of Asia*

Evaluate

Section Quiz 17-1

Use the Testmaker to create a customized quiz for Section 1.

Reteach

Organize the class into two groups. Ask both groups to prepare a quiz based on the information discussed in this section. Then have the members of each group take the other group's quiz.

Enrich

Have students use library resources to research the expeditions of Amerigo Vespucci or Vasco Nuñez de Balboa. Then have them prepare a script about the explorer's expedition.

CLOSE

Write these headings on the chalkboard: *Country Financing Voyage, Explorer, Discovery, Date, Result*. Ask volunteers to provide the information for each heading.

SECTION THEME

▶ **Movement** European nations establish colonies in the lands they explore in Asia, Africa, and the Americas.

Find Out

Answer: *They enslaved the peoples and imposed their religion on them and commandeered the lands' valuable resources.*

FOCUS

Section Objective

Describe how Europeans exploited the lands and the peoples they found in Africa, Asia, and the Americas.

BELLRINGER
Motivational Activity

Before taking roll at the beginning of the class period, project Section Focus Transparency 17-2 and have students answer the activity questions. Discuss students' responses.

This activity is also available as a blackline master.

Vocabulary Pre-check

Use Vocabulary Activity 17 to introduce vocabulary terms.
L1 LEP

1500 | 1550 | 1600 | 1650

1500 Pedro Alvares Cabral claims Brazil for Portugal.

1541 Hernando de Soto of Spain reaches the Mississippi River.

1608 France's Samuel de Champlain founds Quebec.

1640 English planters introduce sugarcane in the West Indies.

Section 2

Overseas Empires

Setting the Scene

▶ **Terms to Define**
conquistador, triangular trade, the Middle Passage

▶ **People to Meet**
Pedro Alvares Cabral, Hernán Cortés, Montezuma II, Francisco Pizarro, Atahualpa, Henry Hudson, Jacques Cartier, Samuel de Champlain, John Cabot

▶ **Places to Locate**
Brazil, Peru, West Indies, Quebec, Jamestown

Find Out How did the Europeans exploit the lands and the peoples they found in Africa, Asia, and the Americas?

The Storyteller

John Sparke, who traveled with English admiral John Hawkins, wrote an account of the inhabitants of the Florida coast in 1589: "They have for apothecary [medicine] herbs, trees, roots, and gum, myrrh, and frankincense, with many others, whereof I know not the names.... Gold and silver they want [lack] not, for when the Frenchmen came, they offered it for little or nothing. They received for a hatchet two pounds of gold. The soldiers, being greedy, took it from them, giving them nothing for it. When the Floridians perceived that, they stopped wearing their gold ornaments, for fear that they would be taken away."

—from *The Hawkins Voyages*, edited by Clements R. Markham, reprinted in *The Annals of America*, 1968

Native Americans digging gold

The Treaty of Tordesillas claimed to divide the world between Spain and Portugal. Only Spain and Portugal, however, recognized the treaty. The Netherlands, France, and England soon joined them in a race to exploit wealth from the lands beyond Europe.

Portugal and Spain

Portugal's main interest lay in Africa and Asia, and in trade rather than colonization. When the Portuguese became the first Europeans to reach the Indian Ocean, they found themselves in waters already thoroughly explored by seafarers from Asian lands. Eager to seize control of the spice trade, the Portuguese reacted quickly to Vasco da Gama's voyage to India. In 1500, less than six months after da Gama's return, 13 ships were dispatched to Calicut. Led by **Pedro Alvares Cabral**, the Portuguese won a bloody trade war with Muslim merchants and defeated a large Arab fleet to establish Portuguese control of the Indian Ocean.

The Portuguese then built naval bases along the Indian Ocean—along the Persian Gulf and in Southeast Asia. They soon controlled shipping in the Indian Ocean. Next, they expanded eastward toward the Moluccas, or the Spice Islands. From the Spice Islands, the Portuguese established trading ports in China and Japan.

Portugal also colonized the area of present-day **Brazil**. Cabral claimed this territory as he swung west across the Atlantic to India in 1500. Because this area of South America juts east of the line of demarcation, it became Portuguese. The rest of South America had been claimed by Spain.

Settlers in Brazil grew income-producing crops such as sugarcane, tobacco, coffee, and cotton. Because the local population did not supply enough labor, enslaved people were brought from Africa. By the late 1500s, Brazil was one of Portugal's three remaining colonies.

SECTION RESOURCES

Reproducible Masters
- Reproducible Lesson Plan 17-2
- Vocabulary Activity 17
- Guided Reading Activity 17-2
- People in World History Profiles 31, 32
- Mapping History Activity 17
- Geography and History Activity 17
- Section Quiz 17-2

Transparencies
- Section Focus Transparency 17-2
- Mapping History Overlay Transparencies 11, 12
- Age of Exploration

Multimedia
- Age of Exploration
- Student Self-Test and Review Software
- Testmaker
- Great Explorers, Parts 1 and 2
- Turning Points in World History: *Age of Exploration*

European Voyages of Exploration

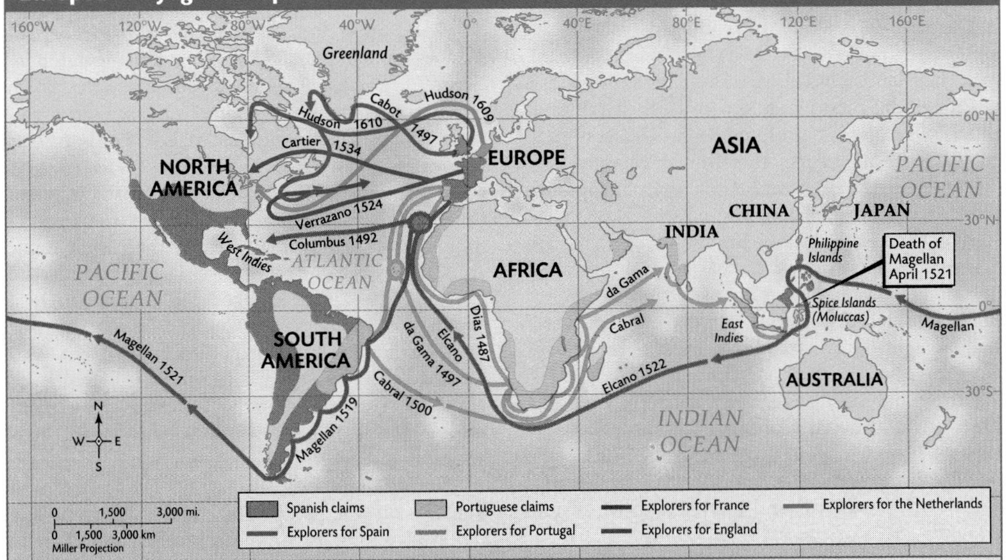

Map Study This map shows nearly 150 years of European voyages.
Location Why are Spanish claims in the Americas and Portuguese claims in Africa and Asia?

Spain

Spanish conquistadors, or conquerors, came to the Americas "to serve God and his Majesty, to give light to those who were in darkness and to grow rich as all men desire to do."

One conquistador, **Hernán Cortés**, left Cuba for Mexico in 1519. Two earlier expeditions brought back enough gold to convince Cortés that more treasure would be found there than on any island. He sailed with 11 ships and more than 500 men.

Cortés landed and marched toward Tenochtitlán, the Aztec capital. Messengers described the approaching army of mounted armed warriors to the Aztec ruler **Montezuma II** as "supernatural creatures riding on hornless deer, preceded by wild animals on leashes, dressed in iron." Believing that the Spaniards had come to fulfill a legendary prophecy, Montezuma offered gifts of gold.

The city's riches were beyond anything the Spaniards had seen. Soon fighting broke out. With the advantage of horses and guns, the Spanish force ultimately slaughtered 50,000 Aztec people. European diseases killed hundreds of thousands more. Within three years Cortés ruled Mexico.

A decade after Mexico's conquest, another conquistador, **Francisco Pizarro**, invaded the Inca Empire in present-day **Peru**. He captured the Inca leader **Atahualpa** (AH•tuh•WAHL•puh) and slaughtered his 2,000 bodyguards. After accepting a ransom in silver and gold for Atahualpa's release, Pizarro executed him. With their leader gone, Inca resistance to the Spaniards evaporated, and Spain controlled a vast territory covering 375,000 square miles (975,000 square kilometers) with some 7 million inhabitants.

Spain also claimed territory in North America. In 1541 Hernando de Soto reached the Mississippi River. Later, Francisco Vásquez de Coronado explored the Grand Canyon.

Building an Empire

By the early 1600s, Spain's empire in the Americas included many islands in the **West Indies**, Central America, much of South America, and parts of the present-day United States. Spain established colonies rather than trading settlements as the Portuguese had. Spanish viceroys ruled the colonies.

Spain had two goals for its American empire—to exploit its wealth and to convert the Native Americans to Christianity. There was conflict, however, over how to treat the inhabitants. In theory the Spanish considered Native Americans their

TEACH

Guided Practice

THEME Movement

Have students discuss the movement of goods and people described in this section. Ask them to name some examples of colonies and trading settlements. *(Portugal: Brazil; Spain: West Indies and the Americas; the Netherlands: Indonesia and Africa)* Have students give examples of some of the goods exported from these areas. *(Brazil: sugarcane, tobacco, coffee, cotton; West Indies and the Americas: animal hides, sugar, tobacco; Indonesia: sugar, spices, coffee, tea)* **L1**

Map Study

Answer

Spain's primary goals were conversion of the Native Americans and exploitation of the Americas' wealth; Portugal was more interested in trade than colonization.

Map Skills Practice

Reading a Map How did the destinations change over time? *(After Columbus crossed the Atlantic, explorers searched for a western, rather than an eastern, route to the East Indies.)*

People in World History Profiles 31, 32

Mapping History Overlay Transparency 11, *Triangular Trade Routes*; 12, *17th Century Latin American Viceroyalties*

COOPERATIVE LEARNING ACTIVITY

Research Organize the class into four research groups and ask each group to become experts on one period in the life of Rembrandt. One group might focus on the artist's early years (1606–1625), another the Leiden years (1625–1631), a third his Amsterdam years (1632–1640), and a fourth his last years (1640–1669). Each group member should have a specific assignment, with some students focusing on specific paintings, etchings, or drawings of each period. After individual students compile their research notes, each group should meet to plan a presentation format—panel discussion, poster presentation, or short dramatic sketch. Each group should make its presentation to the entire class. **L2**

NATIONAL GEOGRAPHIC SOCIETY

Use these materials to enrich student understanding of the age of exploration.

- **NGS PICTURESHOW CD-ROM**
  Great Explorers, Parts 1 and 2
- **NGS PICTUREPACK TRANSPARENCY SET**
  Age of Exploration
- **NGS POSTER SET**
  Age of Exploration

Independent Practice

Guided Reading Activity 17-2 **L1**

Mapping History Activity 17

Geography and History Activity 17

Religion Explain to the class that Spain and France were predominantly Roman Catholic countries. The English and Dutch were primarily Protestant. Ask students how much importance each nation placed on converting the native populations it encountered to Christianity. *(Jesuit missionaries from France and Spain were the most dedicated to conversion.)* **L2**

subjects. They were free and could retain their lands; however, they had to abide by Spanish law and accept Christianity. In reality Spanish plantation owners forced native peoples to work for them, took their lands, and abused them. Spanish priests destroyed their temples and banned their religious rituals. One priest, Bartolomé de Las Casas, tried to protect the Native Americans from such abuses.

Disease was an enemy worse than the Spanish state or church. Isolated for thousands of years, Native Americans lacked immunity to European diseases such as smallpox, measles, and influenza. In the first 50 years under Spanish control, the Inca population fell from about 7 million to just over 1 million. This decline led the Spanish to bring over more enslaved Africans as laborers.

Animal hides, sugar, and tobacco were the heart of the colonial economy. The most valuable exports, however, were silver and gold. The Crown made efforts to retain its one-fifth share of the minerals. Corrupt officials and pirated shipments nevertheless cut into Spanish profits.

Colonies of the Netherlands

The Netherlands was also interested in expansion. In the late 1500s the Dutch won their independence from Spain. This small country on the North Sea had few natural resources and limited farmland. A large Dutch middle class saw commerce as the key to survival.

The period of the 1600s was the golden age of the Netherlands. Dutch ships were efficient, carrying more cargo and smaller crews than other ships. Amsterdam became the world's largest commercial city, and the Dutch enjoyed the world's highest standard of living.

The first Dutch expedition to East Asia returned in 1599. Three years later the Dutch chartered the Dutch East India Company to expand trade and ensure close relations between the government and enterprises in Asia.

In 1619 the company set up headquarters at Batavia on the island of Java in present-day Indonesia. Soon the Dutch controlled island trade

Images of the Times

The Dutch Republic

With no monarchy or aristocracy, the tastes and ideals of society as reflected in Dutch art were determined largely by the middle class.

The World Upside-down by Jan Steen, the son of a brewer, is representative of his earthy, humorous scenes of ordinary people.

The Amsterdam Vegetable Market by Gabriel Metsu focuses on two important themes in Dutch painting of this period—middle-class life and trade.

Images of the Times

The Dutch Republic

The formal name of the Dutch Republic was the United Provinces of the Netherlands. Formed in 1579, the republic experienced a golden age during the seventeenth century, when it was not only the center of a world colonial empire but also a center of international finance and culture. The comic perspective of Jan Steen (1626–1679) makes him unique among leading seventeenth-century Dutch painters. Gabriel Metsu (1629–1667) began painting religious subjects but found the life of the marketplace better suited to his personality. Rembrandt (1606–1669) movingly conveyed the human aspect of all his subjects, whether drawn from the Bible, history, mythology, or everyday life.

in sugar, spices, coffee, and tea. Using Batavia as a base, the Dutch pushed the Portuguese and English out of Asian outposts. After taking Malacca from the Portuguese in 1641, the Netherlands controlled all trade with the Spice Islands. The Dutch also used force against local Muslim rulers to win lands and ports in the region.

At the same time, the Dutch set out for North America. An English navigator, **Henry Hudson**, claimed land for the Dutch along the Atlantic coast of North America, and in 1621 the government chartered the Dutch West India Company to establish colonies in the Americas. The company founded New Amsterdam on Manhattan Island at the mouth of the Hudson River. This settlement was soon a center for European and colonial trade.

The Dutch established a colony in Africa as well. In 1652 Dutch farmers known as Boers settled at the Cape of Good Hope to provide fresh food and water for sailing ships. By the 1700s, however, Dutch power was declining, and England had emerged as Europe's leading maritime nation.

French and English Colonies

The French and the English played only a small part in the early voyages of exploration. Religious conflicts and civil wars kept their interests focused at home. During the 1500s, however, France and England searched for overseas trading colonies.

Thwarted by the Portuguese and later the Dutch control of Asian markets, England and France turned toward North America and the Caribbean. In general, the French companies sought quick profits from trade rather than the long-term investment of farming. For the English, colonies could provide the raw materials—lumber, fish, sugarcane, rice, and wheat—they would otherwise have to purchase from other countries.

France

In 1524 the French hired an Italian captain, Giovanni da Verrazano, to find a Northwest Passage through America to Asia. Da Verrazano explored the North American coast from North

Rembrandt van Rijn, the celebrated Dutch painter, earned fame with his portraits of himself and of his family. Although he died poor and forgotten, his paintings were of more spiritual depth than those of his contemporaries.

REFLECTING ON THE TIMES

1. How does Dutch art compare with art from a nation like France that had a monarch and nobility?
2. Why did Rembrandt's work receive greater acclaim after he died?

ANSWERS TO REFLECTING ON THE TIMES

1. Dutch art focuses on middle-class, not aristocratic, concerns.
2. People later responded to the spiritual depth of his portraits and paintings.

Chapter 17 Section 2

Geography: Movement Have students work in pairs to locate information, including maps, about the explorations of Cartier, Champlain, Marquette, and Joliet. Ask them to draw maps showing each explorer's routes and claims in North America. **L3**

Linking Past and Present

Wall Street, the major financial center of the United States, gets its name from a wall built by the colonists of New Amsterdam in 1653. The wall, meant to protect the colonists from enemy attacks, fell down within a few years. When the colonists built a road in its place, it became known as Wall Street.

ABC NEWS INTERACTIVE™

VIDEODISC
Turning Points in World History

Side One
Chapter 9

Title: *Age of Exploration*
Subject: As western Europeans sought new routes to Asia, they found lands unknown to them; Europeans seeking wealth and power conquered these lands.
Ask: In what ways was the age of exploration a turning point in history? *(Indigenous peoples were mistreated, killed, or died from disease; new crops were brought to Europe, and other crops were introduced to the Americas.)*

Who?What?Where?When?

Virginia Dare, granddaughter of the governor of the Roanoke colony, was the first English child born in the Americas. In May 1587, three months before Virginia's birth, her parents and 115 other settlers left England on an expedition sponsored by Sir Walter Raleigh. Nothing is known about Virginia's life. When English reinforcements arrived in August 1590, they found no trace of the Roanoke settlers.

ASSESS

Check for Understanding

Assign Section 2 Review as homework or as an in-class activity.

Use Student Self-Test and Review Software to review Section 2.

Evaluate

Section Quiz 17-2

Use the Testmaker to create a customized quiz for Section 2.

AROUND THE WORLD **Galileo Improves the Telescope**

Padua, Italy, 1609

Dutch optician Hans Lippershey probably made the first telescope in 1608. The following year Galileo improved Lippershey's design and observed the craters of the moon, the satellites of Jupiter, and the planet Venus. He discovered that Venus underwent periods of light and darkness. From that observation, Galileo concluded that the planets revolved around the sun, reinforcing the theory proposed by Copernicus and disproving Ptolemy's theory that the earth was the center of the universe.

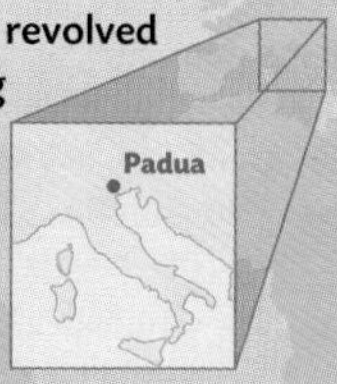

Carolina to Maine without success. Ten years later the French navigator **Jacques Cartier** continued the search and sailed up the St. Lawrence River to the site of the present-day city of Montreal. He claimed much of eastern Canada for France.

In 1608 **Samuel de Champlain**, a French mapmaker, founded **Quebec**, the first permanent French settlement in the Americas. In 1673 missionaries Jacques Marquette and Louis Joliet explored the Mississippi Valley. Later, Robert Cavelier, known as Sieur de La Salle, claimed the entire inland region surrounding the Mississippi River for France.

Like the Spanish, the French sent Jesuit missionaries to convert Native Americans to Christianity. French explorers traded the Native Americans blankets, guns, and wine for animal skins. Trapping, fishing, and lumbering were also profitable.

Some French settlers went to the West Indies, where they claimed the islands of St. Kitts, Martinique, and Guadeloupe. The French brought enslaved Africans to work on sugar and tobacco plantations on the islands. Although most of their interests were in North America, the French also established colonial ports in India.

England

As early as 1497, England began to show an interest in overseas trade. In that year, Henry VII commissioned the Italian-born navigator **John Cabot** to find a northern route to the area reached by Columbus. Cabot explored the coasts of Newfoundland, Nova Scotia, and New England, giving England a claim in the Americas. Because of internal conflict, however, it was 100 years before England established colonies there.

During the 1500s the English harassed their Spanish and Portuguese competitors. Sea captains-turned-pirates raided Spanish ships for gold and silver. In 1580 the most daring of these captains, Francis Drake, became the first Englishman to circumnavigate the globe. Six years later he sacked Spanish seaports in the Caribbean.

In 1600 English expansion was furthered by the founding of the English East India Company. Chartered by Queen Elizabeth I, this trading enterprise set up posts in India and Southeast Asia.

In the West Indies, the English founded settlements on the islands of Jamaica, the Bahamas, and Barbados. In about 1640 they introduced sugarcane. Sugar plantations worked by slave labor made three times as much profit as tobacco plantations did. In the 1600s sugar made Barbados the most profitable English colony.

English merchants also began sending expeditions to North America. In 1606 the Virginia Company of London sent an expedition to America to search for gold and silver. The following year, the company founded the first permanent English settlement at **Jamestown** in what is present-day Virginia. Later, a group of religious dissenters calling themselves Pilgrims founded a second colony, Plymouth, in present-day Massachusetts.

Slave Trade

In the 1600s the colonies in the Americas based their economies on agricultural products that required intensive labor. Enslaved Africans planted and harvested sugar, tobacco, and coffee crops. They also worked silver mines.

The Triangular Trade

The slave trade was part of what was called the triangular trade. Ships sailed the legs of a triangle formed by Europe, Africa, and the Americas. Typically, European ships left their home ports carrying manufactured goods—knives, swords, guns, cloth, and rum. In West Africa the ship captains traded their goods with local rulers for enslaved people. During the second leg of the journey, the ships brought enslaved Africans across the Atlantic to various Caribbean islands or to mainland areas in North America and South America. The enslaved Africans were sold, and the money was used to buy sugar, molasses, cotton, and tobacco. Finally, the ships returned to Europe to sell the goods purchased in America.

MEETING SPECIAL NEEDS ACTIVITY

Learning Style: Auditory/Musical Students with a sensitivity to pitch, melody, rhythm, and tone will deepen their understanding of the African slave experience by being exposed to some well-known spirituals. If recordings are available, play them for students. If not, lead them in singing such familiar spirituals as "Go Down, Moses," "Swing Low, Sweet Chariot," or "Michael, Row the Boat Ashore." Help students understand the relationship between the biblical stories and images and the enslaved peoples' longing for freedom from bondage. **L1**

The Middle Passage

An enslaved person's journey from the west coast of Africa to the lands of the Americas was a ghastly ordeal called **the Middle Passage**. This middle leg of the triangular trade originated from ports along a 3,000-mile (4,800-km) stretch on the west coast of Africa. Often captured by other Africans, enslaved Africans were sold to European slave traders along the coast for transport to American plantations.

Because large cargoes brought large profits, the slave traders packed the captives as tightly as possible. Below deck, each African occupied a space only 4 or 5 feet (122 cm to 153 cm) long and 2 or 3 feet (60 cm to 92 cm) high. Chained together, they could neither stand nor lie at full length. In the darkness and stifling heat, many Africans suffocated or died of disease.

Estimates of the number of enslaved Africans brought to America range from 10 to 24 million. One in five who began the trip did not survive it. Because of the enormous value of their "cargo," however, slave traders made some effort to keep the enslaved people alive. Psychological torment may have been worse than physical conditions. Some Africans committed suicide by jumping overboard. Others simply lost the will to live and refused to eat. Enslaved people on hunger strikes were fed forcibly.

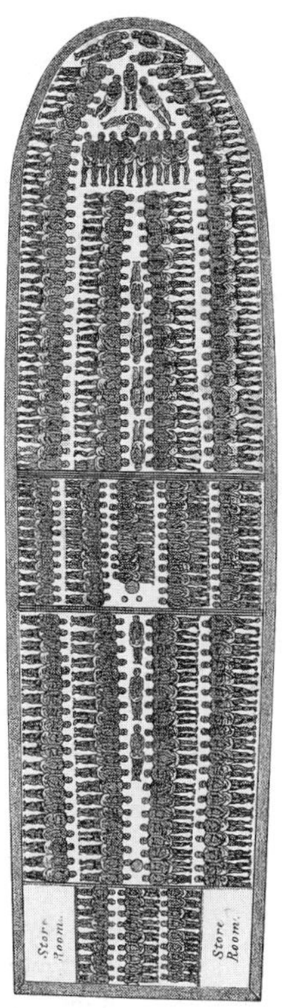

Visualizing History A deck plan shows tightly packed ranks of enslaved people on a ship bound from Africa to the Americas. *What did enslaved people experience on the Middle Passage?*

An Enslaved Person's Life

Africans who survived the long Middle Passage faced another terror when they arrived in American ports: the slave auction. Examined and prodded by plantation owners, most Africans were sold to work as laborers—clearing land, hoeing, planting, weeding, and harvesting. The work was hard, the hours long, and life expectancy short. Because many Europeans believed that Africans were physically suited to hard labor, especially in hot, humid climates, the enslaved people were viewed as nothing more than a unit of labor to exploit for profit.

Resistance

Instead of passively accepting their status, many enslaved people took action to obtain their freedom. Some of them tried to flee their masters. Although most were recaptured, the few enslaved people that did succeed in escaping got far enough away to set up their own free communities.

The ultimate weapon was mass rebellion. In all but the American South, enslaved people rapidly came to outnumber free populations, who often lived in constant fear of uprisings. Most rebellions took place in the Caribbean area, where enslaved people regularly carried out attacks on plantations, burning crops and plotting the murder of their owners. However, only in the French-ruled island of Saint Domingue was an uprising successful. There, a prolonged rebellion by enslaved people in the 1790s led to the eventual proclamation of the independent country of Haiti in 1804. In spite of their limited success, actual or threatened uprisings did give strength to a growing antislavery movement, which saw slavery as a moral evil whose only outcome was violence, oppression, and suffering.

SECTION 2 REVIEW

Recall

1. **Define** conquistador, triangular trade, the Middle Passage.
2. **Identify** Pedro Alvares Cabral, Hernán Cortés, Montezuma II, Francisco Pizarro, Atahualpa, Henry Hudson, Jacques Cartier, Samuel de Champlain, Jacques Marquette, Louis Joliet, John Cabot.
3. **State** the goals that Spain had for its American empire.

Critical Thinking

4. **Making Comparisons** How did treatment of Native Americans differ in the colonies of Spain, France, and England?

Understanding Themes

5. **Movement** What motivated Europeans to move from their countries to the Americas?

Chapter 17 Section 2

Visualizing History Death was common on slave ships. The white spaces on the deck plans denote enslaved persons who died during the crossing. Sharks routinely trailed the slave ships, enticed by the large number of dead or dying Africans who were tossed overboard during the Middle Passage.

Answer to Caption: *Chained together into a tight space in darkness and heat, one in five suffocated or died of disease.*

Reteach

Work with students to make a chart showing European colonial possessions and the major goods each European power received from its colonies.

Enrich

Many students will have seen the animated film very loosely based on the life of Pocahontas. Have students research the actual facts of her life and summarize their findings in short reports. If they have access to the film, have them include its factual inaccuracies in their reports.

CLOSE

Organize the class into five groups; each representing one country: Spain, Portugal, France, England, the Netherlands. Have each group summarize its colonial actions for the others.

SECTION 2 REVIEW ANSWERS

1. All vocabulary words are defined in the Glossary.
2. Cabral, 440; Cortés, 441; Montezuma II, 441; Pizarro, 441; Atahualpa, 441; Hudson, 443; Cartier, 444; Champlain, 444; Marquette and Joliet, 444; Cabot, 444
3. "to serve God and his Majesty, to give light to those who were in darkness and to grow rich as all men desire to do"
4. Spain converted, enslaved, and abused Native Americans; France traded with and converted them.
5. MOVEMENT They sought national prestige, wealth, religious freedom, and religious converts.

Chapter 17 *Expanding Horizons* **445**

Chapter 17
Section 3

SECTION THEME

▶ **Change** The wealth of overseas colonies sparks the Commercial Revolution in Europe.

Find Out

Answer: *They linked the nations of the world economically.*

FOCUS

Section Objective

Analyze how increased trade and colonial expansion set the stage for a global economy.

BELLRINGER Motivational Activity

Before taking roll at the beginning of the class period, project Section Focus Transparency 17-3 and have students answer the activity questions. Discuss students' responses.

This activity is also available as a blackline master.

Vocabulary Pre-check

Use the Vocabulary PuzzleMaker to create a puzzle that reinforces the vocabulary terms in this section. **L1**

1400	1500	1600
c. 1400s Increased trade leads to advanced banking methods.	**c. 1500s** The nation replaces the city and the village as Europe's primary economic unit.	**c. 1600** Europe's population reaches 100 million.

Section 3

Changing Ways of Life

Setting the Scene

▶ **Terms to Define**
joint-stock company, entrepreneur, mercantilism, bullion, balance of trade

▶ **Places to Locate**
Florence, Augsburg

Find Out How did increased trade and colonial expansion set the stage for a global economy?

The Storyteller

The English and French considered piracy against Spain practically a religious crusade. Pirates sometimes held Holy Communion before starting a raid on a Spanish ship! The strangest pirate fleet of all, based in England, attacked Spaniards passing anywhere near, and openly sold their stolen cargo in the market. Even their Spanish prisoners were publicly auctioned for prices set by the ransom money each one might bring. Public opinion finally forced Elizabeth I to put a stop to all this: She declared the pirates public outlaws—"Rascals of the Sea."

—adapted from *The Pirate Picture*, Rayner Thrower, 1980

Pirate ship

The age of exploration brought far-reaching changes to societies and cultures throughout the world. Overseas trade and colonial ventures especially stimulated and expanded the European economy. Business methods and banking practices in various European countries became more sophisticated in order to facilitate profit from the flourishing world trade.

The Commercial Revolution

By the 1600s the nation had replaced the city and village as the basic economic unit in Europe. Nations competed for markets and trade goods. New business methods were instituted for investing money, speeding the flow of wealth, and reducing risks in commercial ventures. These changes, which came to be known as the Commercial Revolution, formed the roots of modern financial and business life.

New Business Methods

Launching an overseas trading venture was a major financial undertaking. The financial backer of the voyage had to raise money to pay for goods and supplies and to hire a captain and crew. Often several years passed as a fleet traveled from port to port, buying and selling, then embarked for the trip home. Only then could the initial investment be recovered. Governments and rich merchants alone had enough money to back such trading voyages, and even they needed financial assistance.

At first merchants turned to bankers for the money to finance their ventures. Families like the Medici of **Florence**, Italy and the Fuggers of **Augsburg**, Germany loaned money as part of their operations. By the 1500s these families were so wealthy that they accepted deposits, made loans, and transferred funds over long distances. Both banking families had branches in several European cities and also made loans to European monarchs.

SECTION RESOURCES

Reproducible Masters
- Reproducible Lesson Plan 17-3
- Guided Reading Activity 17-3
- Reteaching Activity 17
- Enrichment Activity 17
- Section Quiz 17-3
- Performance Assessment Activity 17
- Spanish Chapter Summary 17

Transparencies
- Section Focus Transparency 17-3
- World History and Art Transparency 22, *View of Toledo*; 23, *Mission San Xavier del Bac*

Multimedia
- Focus on World Art Print 1, Jan Vermeer. *The Artist and His Model as Klio*
- Vocabulary PuzzleMaker Software
- Student Self-Test and Review Software
- Testmaker

Visualizing History **This European port scene by Jan Griffier the Elder shows the mix of cultures that resulted from the increased trade between Europeans and the rest of the world.** *How did merchants protect themselves against losses?*

By the 1600s, however, these banking families were beginning to be replaced by government-chartered banks. The banks accepted deposits of money and charged interest on loans. Before long the banks began to provide other services. They issued banknotes and checks, making large payments in heavy coins a thing of the past. They acted as money changers, exchanging currencies from other countries. The banks even provided official exchange rates for foreign currency.

Individual merchants who wanted to invest in exploration often raised money by combining their resources in joint-stock companies, organizations that sold stock, or shares, in the venture, enabling large and small investors to share the profits and risks of a trading voyage. If a loss occurred, investors would lose only the amount they had invested in shares. This sharing of risk provided a stable way of raising funds for voyages.

A few joint-stock companies became rich and powerful through government support. The Dutch government gave the Dutch East India Company a monopoly in trade with Africa and the East Indies. It also gave the company the power to make war, to seize foreign ships, to coin money, and to establish colonies and forts. In return the government received customs duties, or taxes on imported goods, from the company's trade.

Increase in Money

Coins remained the usual means of exchange, so that the gold and silver that flowed into Europe from colonies around the world caused the supply of money to increase. As money became more widely available for large enterprises, ideas changed about the nature and goals of business.

Footnotes to History

Spanish Doubloons and Pieces of Eight

During the 1500s, Spanish ships called galleons sailed the seas loaded with gold doubloons and silver pieces of eight. Minted from the plunder of Central and South American mines, the coins were a favorite target for pirates of other nations. Today, marine archaeologists have explored a number of sunken galleons and recovered hundreds of doubloons and pieces of eight—still worth a fortune.

Chapter 17 Section 3

TEACH

Guided Practice

THEME Change

Discuss how entrepreneurs could change the social structure of a nation that previously had a stable social hierarchy. Ask students what happens when common people can accumulate wealth that had previously been available only to nobility. *(Common people become empowered by wealth; they demand more rights from government.)* **L1**

Focus on World Art Print 1, Jan Vermeer. *The Artist and His Model as Klio*

World History and Art Transparency 22, *View of Toledo*; 23, *Mission San Xavier del Bac*

Visualizing History In the early 1600s, the Dutch Republic modified the port city of Amsterdam to make it more suitable as a base for expanding sea power. Other nations, anxious to emulate the Netherlands' success as a commercial empire, imitated Dutch techniques of planning port cities.

Answer to Caption: *They combined resources in joint-stock companies, enabling them to share profits and risks.*

COOPERATIVE LEARNING ACTIVITY

Research Organize the class into three groups and assign to each group one of the following European banking families: the Medici, the Fuggers, the Rothschilds. Have each group prepare an oral report on the family. Have students include in their report brief biographical sketches of prominent members of the family, aspects of their daily life, what became of the family with time. Each group should decide how best to present to the class the results of its research. Possibilities include a dramatic skit, poster presentation, or panel discussion. **L2**

Independent Practice

Guided Reading Activity 17-3 **L1**

Autobiography Have students work in pairs to find out about life in one of the non-English colonies in North America. Ask them to imagine themselves as colonists and to write brief autobiographies of themselves, telling where they came from, why they chose to become colonists, and what life is like in their colony. **L2**

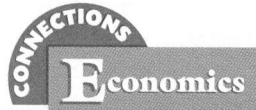

CONNECTIONS **Economics**

The Commercial Revolution

The founder of England's Royal Exchange was merchant and financier Sir Thomas Gresham (1518/19–1579). He had the Royal Exchange built in London in order to provide a convenient place for merchants and traders to conduct business. The Royal Exchange was first called the "Bourse," from the French word for purse. Queen Elizabeth issued a royal proclamation in 1571 that changed its name. Today the London International Financial Futures Exchange stands on the site of the original Royal Exchange.

Answers to Making the Connection

1. *Participation in a joint-stock company helped protect individual merchants from crippling losses by spreading the risk.*
2. *Joint-stock companies could not be set up without a royal charter.*

Gradually, a system based on the belief that the goal of business was to make profits took shape. Individuals known as **entrepreneurs** combined money, ideas, raw materials, and labor to make goods and profits. Profits were then used to expand the business and develop new ventures.

An entrepreneur in the cloth industry, for example, would buy wool and employ spinners to make the wool into yarn. Weavers and dyers would also be hired to turn the yarn into cloth. The entrepreneur would then sell the cloth on the open market for a price that brought a profit. Of course, entrepreneurs took risks when they put up capital for businesses. They could lose their investment if prices fell or workers could not produce goods at a specified time or for a specific market.

In the 1600s the greatest increase in business activity took place in the countries bordering the Atlantic Ocean—Portugal, Spain, England, and the Netherlands—in large part because these countries had the largest colonial empires. Italian cities such as Venice and Genoa, formerly the leading trade centers in Europe, found themselves cut out of overseas trade as trade routes and trade fortunes gradually moved westward toward the Atlantic Ocean and the Americas.

Mercantilism

A new theory of national economic policy called **mercantilism** also appeared. This theory held that a state's power depended on its wealth. Accordingly, the goal of every nation was to become as wealthy as possible.

Europeans believed that the measure of a nation's wealth was the amount of **bullion**, or gold and silver, it owned. One Venetian summed up the general feeling about bullion: "[It is] the sinews of all government, it gives it its pulse, its movement, its mind, soul, and it is its essence and its very life. It overcomes all impossibilities, for it is the master . . . without it all is weak and without movement."

Under mercantilism, nations could gain wealth by mining gold and silver at home or overseas. Thus, Spain sent conquistadors to the Americas to seize the silver and gold mines of the Aztec and Inca Empires. Governments could also gain wealth through trade. Nations sought to create a favorable **balance of trade** by exporting more goods than they imported. The gold and silver received for exports would exceed that paid for imports. This greater wealth meant greater national power and influence in the world.

CONNECTIONS **Economics**

The Commercial Revolution

Queen Elizabeth opens the Royal Exchange

The economic prosperity that resulted from the age of exploration led to a deeper desire by merchants to expand their fortune. Trading with Asia, however, was costly and dangerous. Many independent merchants found it impossible to take the entire burden on themselves. If a voyage failed, the merchant would lose everything. This uncertainty led to the development of joint-stock companies. These companies had profound effects on both trade and colonization.

Joint-stock companies became so popular that stock exchanges where investors could buy and sell stock developed in England and the Netherlands. English monarchs particularly favored these companies. The rulers of England controlled merchant trade, so any system that would make trade more efficient made the government richer and more powerful. The ruler also controlled the company through its charter. In order to set up a joint-stock company, the investors first obtained a charter from the king. These charters became important in the founding of settlements in America. They made the settlements later on the property of the Crown. Joint-stock companies became the model for corporations.

MAKING THE CONNECTION

1. Why were joint-stock companies popular among merchants who wanted to trade overseas?
2. How did the English monarchy control the joint-stock companies?

MEETING SPECIAL NEEDS ACTIVITY

Learning Style: Visual/Spatial Work with students who learn best by producing or decoding graphic information to prepare a balance-of-trade chart of a hypothetical nation's imports and exports. For example, under the heading *Imports*, students might list raw materials and goods. Put a hypothetical dollar value next to each entry. Under the heading *Exports*, they should list items and give a hypothetical dollar value for each item. Have students explain why a nation must have a balance of trade. Ask what happens if more money is spent for imported goods than is received for exported goods. *(The nation goes into debt.)* Ask students how this applies to nations today. **L2**

Visualizing History Coffeehouses, such as this one depicted in London in 1668, were places to converse about the news of the day—fires, feasts, riots, weddings, plays, and scandals. *Besides coffee, what other foods and drinks were introduced to Europe in this period?*

Colonies served a definite purpose in the mercantilist system. They were both the sources of raw materials as well as vital markets for finished goods provided by the parent country. The primary reason for having colonies was to help make the parent country self-sufficient.

Businesses that produced export goods also helped a nation to prosper. For instance, the Dutch exported wool cloth throughout Europe. Governments encouraged manufacturing by setting tariffs, or taxes, on imports and exports. One reason Spain and Portugal went into decline was that they did not build extensive manufacturing industries within their countries. Gold and silver from the Americas flowed to East Asia to pay for spices and silk and to northern Europe to pay for manufactured goods and weapons to send to their colonies. In contrast, mercantilism helped European countries like England amass enormous national wealth that it used to build a colonial empire.

Social and Religious Trends

From the time of the Black Death in the mid-1300s, European populations grew. Towns outgrew their fortifications as more and more people left the countryside to be closer to centers of trade. Europe's population was about 55 million in 1450. By 1650 it was 100 million.

During the years of this population growth, European contact with the rest of the world also increased. New ideas and new products flooded into Europe. New foods, such as corn, chocolate, and potatoes, and new drinks like coffee and tea were introduced. Sugar became widely available. Some people enjoyed the luxuries of African ivory or perfumes, silk, and jewels from East Asia.

Coffeehouses became social gathering places where these new products were tasted and discussed. A Spaniard described a coffeehouse in Amsterdam in 1688:

> "[They] are of great usefulness in winter, with their welcoming stoves and tempting pastimes; some offer books to read, others gaming-tables and all have people ready to converse with one; one man drinks chocolate, another coffee, one milk, another tea and practically all of them smoke tobacco .... In this way they can keep warm, be refreshed and entertained for little expense, listening to the news."
>
> —Joseph de la Vega, *The Wheels of Commerce*, 1817

At first some people rejected foods from the Americas. For example, many believed that potatoes caused leprosy. Eventually new foods and beverages became accepted at European tables. New dress materials, such as calico and muslin, arrived from Asia, and spun cotton clothing came into use.

Merchants prospered most from the trade and colonial expansion of the Commercial Revolution. Living better than the princes of a few centuries earlier, they began to surpass the nobility in both wealth and power. Hereditary nobles had to rely on rents from their lands for wealth, but rents did not rise as fast as prices. The newly rich entrepreneurs used their influence to change European society.

In the countryside, however, peasants lived as meagerly as they ever had. The French writer Jean

Visualizing History Until the middle of the nineteenth century, when daily newspapers and home mail delivery became the norm, London coffeehouses served as informal mail depots and suppliers of both Whig and Tory newspapers.

Answer to Caption: *New foods and drinks included corn, potatoes, chocolate, and tea.*

Linking Past and Present

Modern business **corporations** are the result of the fusion between joint-stock companies and medieval corporations that took place during the first two-thirds of the nineteenth century in Great Britain, the United States, France, and Germany.

ASSESS

Check for Understanding

Assign Section 3 Review as homework or as an in-class activity.

Use Student Self-Test and Review Software to review Section 3.

Evaluate

Section Quiz 17-3

Use the Testmaker to create a customized quiz for Section 3.

MAKING CONNECTIONS ACTIVITIES

Cultural Life Have students research and prepare short reports comparing and contrasting the role of the coffeehouse in the cultural life of London with that of the café in Paris and Vienna. Students who wish to bring their reports up to date may also include speculations on why coffeehouses have become so popular in American cities today. **L2**

Religion Missionary work continues around the world today. Ask students to research and prepare short oral reports describing the nature of contemporary missionary activity. Encourage them to focus not only on Christian missionaries but also on efforts by eastern religions, Lubavitcher Hasidic Jews, and Muslims to attract converts. **L2**

Chapter 17 Section 3

History & Art Man-o'-war is another name for a warship. The Portuguese and Spanish and then the French were probably first to cross the ocean with warships outfitted with cannons.

Answer to Caption: *economic pressure, wars, and religious persecution*

Reteach

Have students work in small groups to list and discuss the most significant changes brought about by overseas empires and the Commercial Revolution.

Reteaching Activity 17

Enrich

Have students research and write short reports on the life of Sir Thomas Gresham, founder of the Royal Exchange.

Enrichment Activity 17

CLOSE

Have students prepare a television talk show about the impact of overseas empires on Europe and on the indigenous peoples. Appoint one student as host and several students as experts. The rest of the class should act as audience. The host should direct a series of questions at the experts and encourage audience participation.

History & Art *Man-o'-War Firing a Salute* by Jan Porcellis. **Building an empire called for military strength in this period of intense European rivalry.** *What caused many Europeans to venture to America?*

de La Bruyère (LAH broo•YEHR) remarked that European peasants worked like animals, lived in hovels, and survived on a diet of water, black bread, and roots.

During the Middle Ages, street beggars were pitied, not scorned, but mercantilist ideas held that those who were idle were a burden to society. Changing religious attitudes also greatly emphasized the value of work. New laws made it a crime not to work. Governments provided some relief to the "worthy poor," not out of charity but because a strong nation needed healthy workers and soldiers.

Later, overseas colonies became an outlet for some of Europe's surplus population. Governments used colonies as a dumping ground for the poor, criminals, and other social outcasts. Some people went voluntarily, drawn by tales of wealth and unlimited free land.

Economic pressure, wars, and religious persecution led many people to venture to the Americas. Most went to Dutch and English colonies because the Spanish barred non-Spaniards and the French banned Huguenots, or French Protestants. With land of their own and economic freedom, colonists prospered and enriched the countries that had cast them out.

Exploration and empires spread European civilization. Christian missionaries brought European culture to Africa, Asia, and the Americas. Traders in colonial ports spread their customs and languages to local populations.

SECTION 3 REVIEW

Recall

1. **Define** joint-stock company, entrepreneur, mercantilism, bullion, balance of trade.
2. **Identify** some of the first banking families to begin to finance trading ventures.
3. **Explain** why a trade voyage overseas required large sums of money.

Critical Thinking

4. **Synthesizing Information** Imagine that you are an entrepreneur living during the 1700s. Invent a way in which you can make profits by using your capital and talents. Appraise the potential risks and profits in your venture.

Understanding Themes

5. **Change** Decide which class of European society benefited most from the Commercial Revolution. Why?

SECTION 3 REVIEW ANSWERS

1. All vocabulary words are defined in the Glossary.
2. Fuggers and Medici
3. Goods and supplies needed to be purchased and crews needed to be hired.
4. Students' answers should reflect a historically accurate assessment of potential risks and gains.
5. **CHANGE** Merchants and bankers probably benefited most. As handlers of financial transactions, they would make sure they received a share of profit. Working classes, lacking the means to invest in business ventures, would benefit least. Workers would be hired at the lowest pay possible to ensure owner profits.

Social Studies
SKILLS

Comparing Thematic Maps

Have you ever gone to a theme party? A theme is a major idea. A theme party has a major idea; everything about the party—food, activities, music—presents the idea.

Learning the Skill

Maps also can have a theme. A thematic map is a map that shows information about a specialized subject. By comparing thematic maps, you can uncover new information about a topic.

To compare thematic maps, read the title of each map to determine its theme. Then interpret the symbols, dates, and map keys. Compare the maps, looking for similarities and differences.

After analyzing this information, look for relationships between the maps. Ask yourself: Do the maps compare the same region in different time periods? Do they compare data for different regions of the world? What has changed from one map to another? What do these changes indicate about the theme?

Practicing the Skill

Compare the thematic maps on this page and answer these questions.

1. What is the common theme of the maps?
2. What do the colors represent?
3. Which nation claimed the most land in North America in 1650?
4. How did European claims in North America change by 1753?

Applying the Skill

Compare the map of North America in 1783 on p. 555 to the map of North America in 1753 shown below. Describe at least three significant changes that occurred in this 30-year period.

For More Practice

Turn to the Skill Practice in the Chapter Review on page 453 for more practice in comparing thematic maps.

European Claims in the Americas 1650–1753

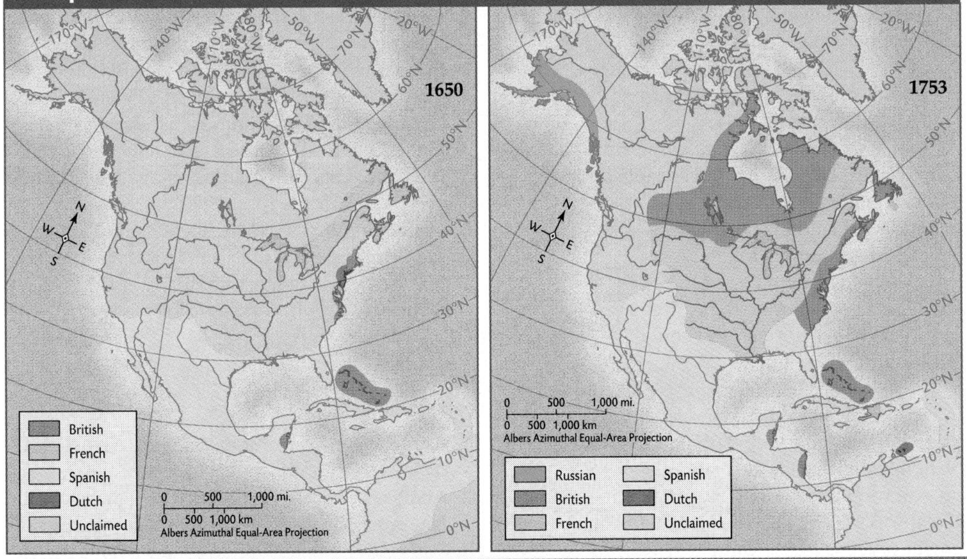

Social Studies
SKILLS

TEACH

Comparing Thematic Maps Before having students read the skill, ask them what maps can show besides geographic features. (Students may mention rainfall, resource, or other types of maps.) Explain that maps that show the overall distribution patterns for a given feature, such as population, rainfall, or a natural resource, are called thematic maps. A single thematic map might show, for example, where the population is densest in the United States or where in Canada the rainfall is greatest. Once students grasp the idea behind individual thematic maps, ask them to consider what might be learned by comparing thematic maps. Then have students read the skill and complete the practice questions.

Additional Practice

Skill Reinforcement Activity 17

Building Skills in Geography Workbook, Unit 1, Lesson 11

ANSWERS TO PRACTICING THE SKILL

1. European claims in North America 1650–1753
2. claims of the different European countries
3. Spain
4. Spanish, British, and French claims grew; Dutch claim disappeared; Russians had a claim

Chapter 17 Review

GLENCOE TECHNOLOGY

VIDEODISC

Use MindJogger to review students' knowledge of the chapter.

MindJogger Videoquiz

Chapter 17
Disc 3 Side A

Also available in VHS.

Answers

Using Key Terms

1. g	**6.** b
2. d	**7.** c
3. j	**8.** e
4. f	**9.** i
5. a	**10.** h

Using Your History Journal

Advise students to find specific data for their journal entries by reviewing the material about these cultures in Chapters 7, 14, and 15.

Reviewing Facts

1. He set up a school for navigators, gathered scientists, and sent ships along the coast.
2. The caravel used triangular sails, multiple masts, a stern-operated rudder, and a shallow draft that enabled it to sail faster, sail against the wind, maneuver better, and go into inlets and to the beach for repairs.
3. They had limited land for agriculture and few natural resources. A large middle class had developed and was ready for commercial expansion.
4. Portugal, Spain, England, the Netherlands
5. It was a terrifying psychological and physical ordeal for the captives, who were crammed into a ship's hold for the transatlantic voyage.
6. The French were interested in trade; the English sought raw materials.
7. It reduced the risk of individual investors.

Critical Thinking

1. Spain sought quicker routes to Asia, where it hoped to increase its wealth.
2. Students should support their position.
3. Possible answers: The colonies would have been less successful economically. Fewer Europeans would have gone there.
4. Portugal had the line of demarcation moved westward less out of a desire to colonize the new lands than out of the desire to protect its trade in Asia.
5. Entrepreneurs needed banking services to help them transact business outside Europe.

Historical Significance

The period from the 1400s to the 1700s is often called the first global age. During this time, the peoples of Europe, Asia, Africa, and the Americas came into direct contact. Through exploration, the size and dimensions of the world and its oceans became known. Europeans established overseas empires, bringing prosperity to their homelands. However, the European process of establishing colonies often left a negative impact on the cultures that Europeans encountered. In the long run, the meeting of civilizations throughout the world laid the foundation of the global community that we know today, with its exchange of ideas and practices among different peoples.

Using Key Terms

Write the key term that completes each sentence.

a. cartographers	g. Middle Passage
b. circumnavigation	h. mercantilism
c. conquistadors	i. balance of trade
d. entrepreneurs	j. bullion
e. joint-stock companies	k. triangular trade
f. line of demarcation	

1. An enslaved person's journey from Africa to the Americas was known as the __________.
2. During Europe's Commercial Revolution, enterprising individuals called _________ made goods and acquired profits.
3. During the 1600s Europeans believed that the measure of a nation's wealth was the amount of ________, or gold and silver, that it owned.
4. To settle the competing land claims of Portugal and Spain, the pope in 1493 drew a _____________, an imaginary boundary down the middle of the Atlantic Ocean from the North Pole to the South Pole.
5. As a result of discoveries made by early European explorers, ______ were able to draw maps with greater accuracy.
6. In 1522 Ferdinand Magellan's crew arrived at Seville, Spain, completing the first ____________, or circling of the globe.
7. Spain won vast lands in the Americas as a result of successful expeditions and conquests carried out by _________.
8. _____________, or organizations that sold stock in ventures, enabled large and small investors to share the risks and profits of a trading voyage.
9. Nations sought to create a favorable _________ by exporting more goods than they imported.
10. The theory of ________ held that a nation's power rested on its accumulated wealth.

Using Your History Journal

Exploration brought people from Europe into contact with the cultures of Asia, Africa, and the Americas for the first time in this period. Imagine and describe such a meeting. Remember that these people did not, when meeting, understand each other's language or culture.

Reviewing Facts

1. **Explain** how Prince Henry the Navigator inspired early Portuguese expeditions along the west coast of Africa.
2. **Describe** the improvements that shipbuilders incorporated in the European caravel.
3. **Explain** why the Dutch turned to commerce instead of agriculture in the late 1500s.
4. **List** the European countries that showed the biggest increase in business activity in the 1600s.
5. **Describe** what the Middle Passage was like for enslaved Africans.
6. **Explain** in what ways the French and the English differed in their aims for their colonies.
7. **State** how a joint-stock company enabled small investors to profit from a major voyage.

Critical Thinking

1. **Apply** Why did Columbus's plan to reach Asia by a western route appeal to Spain?
2. **Analyze** Were the English and the Spanish justified in colonizing the Americas? Why or why not?
3. **Evaluate** How would the colonies have been

different if Europeans had not used slave labor?

4. **Synthesize** Would the Portuguese have tried to colonize North America and South America if the line of demarcation had not been drawn?
5. **Evaluate** How did the influx of wealth from the colonies help bring about the Commercial Revolution in Europe?
6. **Analyze** What were the results of Ferdinand Magellan's circumnavigation?
7. **Apply** Why were the Dutch eager to establish overseas colonies?

Geography in History

1. **Place** What European city was the first to have potatoes for consumption?
2. **Movement** Why were potatoes introduced into Sweden and Finland so much later than they were in other nations?
3. **Human/Environment Interaction** How would new crops such as the potato affect agriculture?

Potato Introduced to Europe

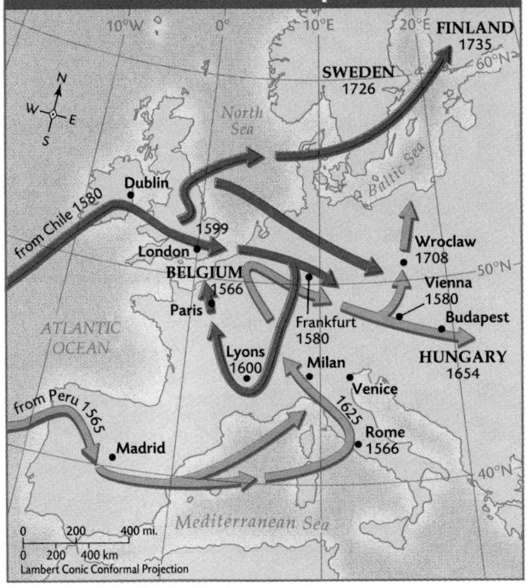

Understanding Themes

1. **Innovation** How did Chinese and Arab discoveries aid European voyages of exploration?
2. **Movement** How did colonization affect changes in world populations?
3. **Change** How did the Commercial Revolution encourage more European voyages of exploration and colonization?

Linking Past and Present

1. History books used to say that Columbus "discovered" America. What did they mean, and why do we no longer see his voyage in this way?
2. Making profits motivated early entrepreneurs. Is this still the goal of entrepreneurs today?
3. The quest for trade in Asian spices was a big motivation behind European exploration in the late 1400s. Today spices are increasingly important in cooking. How many different spices can you name? Research their places of origin.

Skill Practice

Compare the thematic maps below and answer these questions.

1. What is the theme of these maps?
2. What do the colors represent?
3. What changes occurred in the period shown?
4. What conclusion can you draw about the theme?

The Expanding World

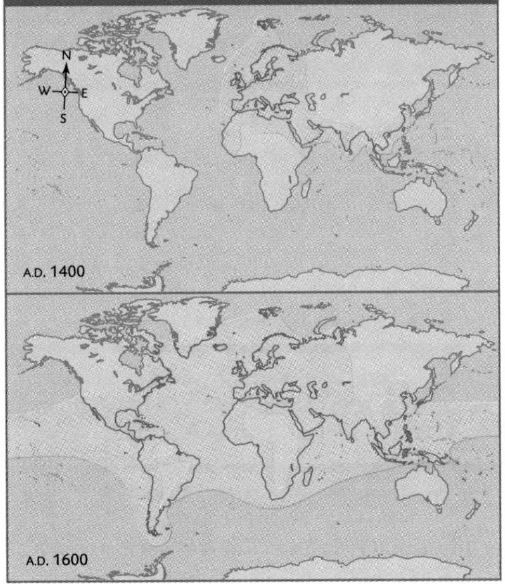

Chapter 17 Review

6. Magellan's voyage proved the world was round and larger than previously believed, that the oceans were connected, and that Columbus had not reached Asia.
7. The Dutch middle class saw trade as a means of survival.

Geography in History

1. Madrid
2. Potatoes came from the west to England and Spain. Sweden and Finland were more isolated from trade with the rest of Europe.
3. They added to, and sometimes replaced, crops that were being grown.

Understanding Themes

1. **INNOVATION** Europeans used the Chinese compass, the astrolabe perfected by Arabs, and lateen sails used by Muslims.
2. **MOVEMENT** Africans were brought to the Americas. Native American populations were reduced.
3. **CHANGE** It made it easier to finance such voyages and for more people to profit from them.

Linking Past and Present

1. Before his voyages, Europeans were unaware of the Americas. Today we have a world perspective rather than a Eurocentric one.
2. Some students may agree, or may argue that entrepreneurs today, regulated by laws and conscience, may base their decisions on factors besides profit.
3. Answers will vary.

Skill Practice

1. the expanding world
2. European knowledge of the existing world
3. The world known to Europeans more than doubled from A.D. 1400 to A.D. 1600.
4. Europeans explored much of the world between A.D. 1400 to A.D. 1600.

Chapter Bonus Test Question

Ask students: How would the world today be different if the age of exploration had never occurred? *(There would be only local or possibly regional economies; there would be no interracial problems; Native Americans would be much more numerous and would constitute the entire population of North and South America; products and ideas would not have spread from one region to others; geographical knowledge would be limited.)*

Teach, Reinforce, and Extend CHAPTER Content

Empires of Asia

CHAPTER RESOURCES

	Reproducible Resources	Multimedia Resources
Chapter Opener	Chapter Themes: Graphic Organizer 18 Historical Significance Chapter Activity 18	MindJogger Videoquiz
Chapter Enrichment	Vocabulary Activity 18* Time Line Activity 18 Mapping History Activity 18 History Simulation 18 Geography and History Activity 18 Source Reading 18 People in World History Profiles 33, 34 World Art and Music Activity 18 Enrichment Activity 18 Critical Thinking Activity 18 Skill Reinforcement Activity 18 Performance Assessment Activity 18	Focus on World Art Print 10, Kitagawa Utamaro. *Reflected Beauty* World History and Art Transparency 24, *Taj Mahal*; 25, *Shah Jahan and One of His Sons Riding in Escort* Chapter Transparency 18 Vocabulary PuzzleMaker Software Picture Atlas of the World World Music: Cultural Traditions, Lessons 7, 8, 9
Chapter Review/Reteaching	Reteaching Activity 18 Skill Reinforcement Activity 18 Spanish Chapter Summary 18	Chapter 18 Digest Audiocassette, Activity, Test* Vocabulary PuzzleMaker Software Student Self-Test and Review Software MindJogger Videoquiz
Chapter Evaluation/Testing	Performance Assessment Activity 18 Chapter 18 Test, Forms A and B	Testmaker

* *Also available in Spanish*

0:00 **OUT OF TIME?** Assign the Chapter 18 summary in the Unit 4 Digest on pages 506–509, and the Chapter 18 Audiocassettes.

Block Schedule

Block scheduling differs from traditional class scheduling in the amount of time allotted to each period. The extended time frame provided by block scheduling affords you the opportunity to implement a greater number of research-oriented and activity-intense projects to motivate and involve your students. Activities that are particularly suited to use within the block scheduling framework are identified throughout this chapter by the following designation.

KEY TO ABILITY LEVELS

Teaching strategies have been coded for varying learning styles and abilities.

- **L1** **BASIC** activities for all students
- **L2** **AVERAGE** activities for average to above-average students
- **L3** **CHALLENGING** activities for above-average students
- **LEP** **LIMITED ENGLISH PROFICIENCY** activities

A complete, 1-page lesson plan is provided for each section in the *Reproducible Lesson Plans* booklet.

SECTION RESOURCES

Daily Objectives	Reproducible Resources	Multimedia Resources
Section 1 Muslim Empires Describe how Muslim rulers controlled and governed much of the Middle East, North Africa, and India between the 1500s and 1800s.	Reproducible Lesson Plan 18-1 Vocabulary Activity 18* Guided Reading Activity 18-1* Time Line Activity 18 History Simulation 18 People in World History Profile 33 Section Quiz 18-1*	Section Focus Transparency 18-1 Chapter Transparency 18 World History and Art Transparency 24, *Taj Mahal*; 25, *Shah Jahan and One of His Sons Riding in Escort* Student Self-Test and Review Software Testmaker World Music: Cultural Traditions, Lesson 7
Section 2 Chinese Dynasties Analyze why China flourished and then declined during the Ming and Qing dynasties.	Reproducible Lesson Plan 18-2 Vocabulary Activity 18* Guided Reading Activity 18-2* Section Quiz 18-2*	Section Focus Transparency 18-2 Student Self-Test and Review Software Testmaker World Music: Cultural Traditions, Lesson 8 Picture Atlas of the World
Section 3 The Japanese Empire Explain why Japan was more adaptable to changes than China before the 1800s.	Reproducible Lesson Plan 18-3 Vocabulary Activity 18* Guided Reading Activity 18-3* Geography and History Activity 18 People in World History Profile 34 Section Quiz 18-3*	Focus on World Art Print 10, Kitagawa Utamaro. *Reflected Beauty* Section Focus Transparency 18-3 Student Self-Test and Review Software Testmaker World Music: Cultural Traditions, Lesson 8
Section 4 Southeast Asia Explain how the Thai kingdom was able to keep its independence while other parts of Southeast Asia gradually came under European control.	Reproducible Lesson Plan 18-4 Guided Reading Activity 18-4* Reteaching Activity 18 Enrichment Activity 18 Section Quiz 18-4* Performance Assessment Activity 18 Spanish Chapter Summary 18	Section Focus Transparency 18-4 Vocabulary PuzzleMaker Software Student Self-Test and Review Software Testmaker World Music: Cultural Traditions, Lesson 9

** Also available in Spanish*

Chapter Activities

Performance Assessment Activity

Creating a Television Series Have students take the roles of producers who want to find the perfect location for a historical television series for a network. Students should work alone or in pairs to study the empires of Asia and develop proposals for the investors for the site they think people of today would find most interesting. The proposals should include descriptions of the setting, possible historical characters, possible problems for episode story lines, and the type of series that would be created. Students might present their proposals orally with visuals or in writing.

Possible Rubric Features
Accuracy of content information, concept attainment, decision-making process skills, creative thinking, clarity and organization of presentation or proposal

• *For an additional activity, refer to Activity 18 in the* Performance Assessment Strategies and Activities *booklet.*

ACTIVITY

From the Classroom of...

Jon Kilgore
Moline High School
Moline, IL

The Quest for Japan
Prepare a list of review questions about Chapter 18. Then divide an outline map of Japan into 10 or 12 sections. Assign each a value between 1 and 5 (representing a number of questions). Organize the class into five groups or families and assign each group one of the sections on the map as its family's home. The families are competing to take over the rest of Japan. Let each group in turn decide which section it wants to "enter." In order to gain that territory, the group must answer correctly the designated number of questions for the section. If a group chooses to enter an occupied section, it must compete with the group already there. The groups take turns answering questions until one answers incorrectly and loses. When all sections have been taken, the "family" with the most territory wins.

MULTIPLE LEARNING STYLES

Verbal/Linguistic
Have students debate the following proposition: Western influence on the countries of East Asia in the early modern period was more helpful than harmful.

Visual/Spatial
Select books on Indian and Persian art from the library and bring them to class. Have each student choose a different miniature painting and write a short description of it.

Kinesthetic
Have students prepare a large map of East and Southeast Asia, indicating on it some of the most important points of contact between Europeans and Asians, such as Macao, the Philippines, and Java. (They might use different colored tacks, push-pins, or labels to represent the various European countries.)

Additional Resources

TEACHER'S CORNER

NATIONAL GEOGRAPHIC SOCIETY

INDEX TO NATIONAL GEOGRAPHIC MAGAZINE

The following articles may be used for research relating to this chapter:

- "Ibn Battuta: Prince of Travelers," by Thomas J. Abercrombie, December 1991.
- "The World of Süleyman the Magnificent," by Merle Severy, November 1987.
- "When the Moguls Ruled India," by Mike Edwards, April 1985.

NATIONAL GEOGRAPHIC SOCIETY PRODUCTS AVAILABLE FROM GLENCOE

To order the following products for use with this chapter, contact your local Glencoe sales representative or call Glencoe at 1-800-368-7344:

CD-ROMS
- NGS PictureShow CD-ROM: India and China
- Picture Atlas of the World

NGS PICTUREPACK TRANSPARENCY SETS
- Ancient India
- Ancient China

ADDITIONAL NATIONAL GEOGRAPHIC SOCIETY PRODUCTS

To order the following products for use with this chapter, call National Geographic Society at 1-800-368-2728:

- *Ancient Civilizations,* "China" (Filmstrip)

BIBLIOGRAPHY

Literature of the Period

Tsao Hsueh-Chin. ***The Dream of the Red Chamber.*** Westport, CT: Greenwood Press, 1975. Written in the eighteenth century, this is considered to be China's greatest novel.

Readings for the Student

Ebrey, Patricia B., ed. ***Chinese Civilization: A Sourcebook, 2nd rev. ed.*** New York: Free Press, 1993.

Readings for the Teacher

Clayre, Alasdair. ***The Heart of the Dragon.*** Boston: Houghton Mifflin, 1985. A look at China today, with reference to its history.

Savory, R.M., ed. ***Introduction to Islamic Civilization.*** New York: Cambridge University Press, 1976. Essays about Islam.

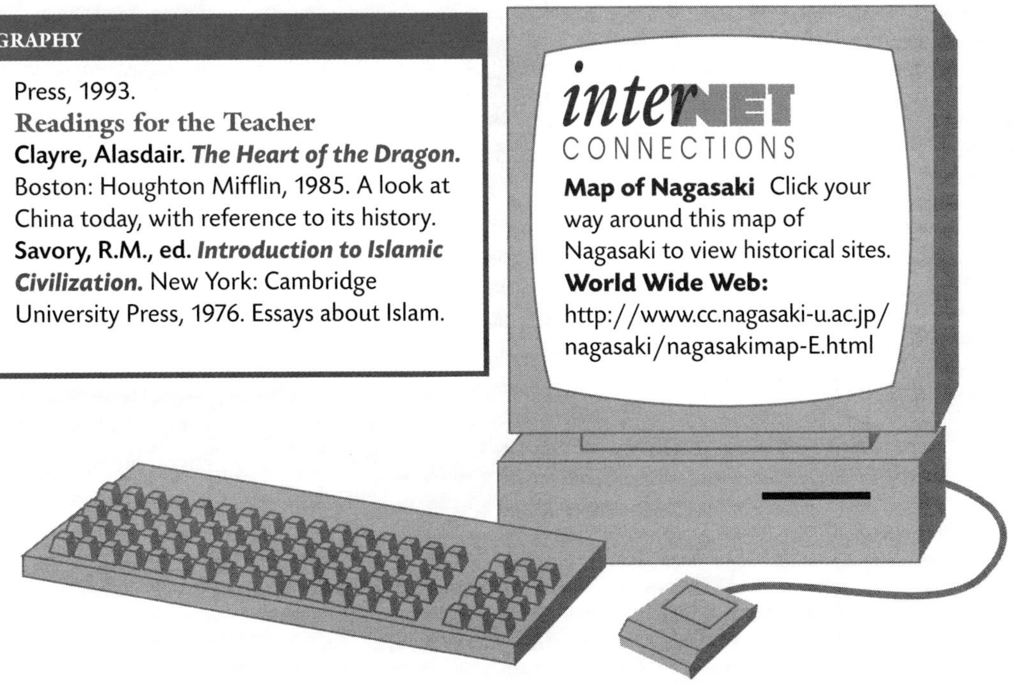
interNET CONNECTIONS
Map of Nagasaki Click your way around this map of Nagasaki to view historical sites.
World Wide Web:
http://www.cc.nagasaki-u.ac.jp/nagasaki/nagasakimap-E.html

Introducing Chapter 18

CHAPTER THEMES

Chapter Themes are listed by section on this chapter opening page of the Student Edition. A corresponding theme-based activity is available under "TEACH," and a theme-based question is asked in the Section and Chapter Reviews.

The Storyteller

Historical Setting Suleiman had begun his campaign against Europe in 1521, soon after coming to power. (It was an Ottoman tradition for a new ruler to celebrate with a military campaign.) Although Suleiman was successful in his attacks on Hungary, well-organized resistance, coupled with supply difficulties and bad weather, contributed to his defeat in Vienna.

Historical Significance

Answers: *One kind–represented by the Ottoman, Persian, and Mogul Empires–was founded by Muslim steppe peoples. New dynasties in China were characterized by a strong central government, while in Japan the ruling shoguns had lost much power to the daimyos. A new type of empire, the European colonial empire, began to transform Southeast Asia, although the Thai emperors managed to preserve their people's independence.*

Asian response to European arrivals ranged from cordial (Philippines) to suspicious (China) to hostile (Japan).

Chapter 18

1350–1850

Empires of Asia

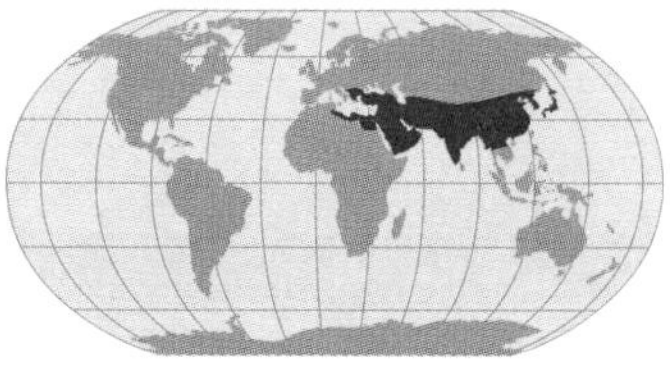

Chapter Themes

- **Movement** Muslim rulers govern empires that cover vast regions of Asia, North Africa, and Europe. *Section 1*
- **Cultural Diffusion** China is directly challenged by its contacts with western European cultures. *Section 2*
- **Reaction** Japan enforces isolationist policy to keep out Western influences. *Section 3*
- **Change** Southeast Asian lands face the growth of European trade and commerce in their region. *Section 4*

The Storyteller

Within the city walls of Vienna, Austria, people quaked as thundering cannonballs signaled the beginning of the Turkish siege of the city on September 27, 1529. Occupying the surrounding hills were 100,000 Turkish soldiers led by their skilled commander Suleiman.

By mid-October, Turkish troops twice had broken through part of Vienna's walls, but failed to capture the city as the Austrians and their allies rushed to plug the breaches. This clash between European and Asian armies was one of many encounters between different civilizations during the early modern period.

Historical Significance

What kinds of empires arose in Asia during the early modern period? How did they respond to the arrival of Europeans in their areas?

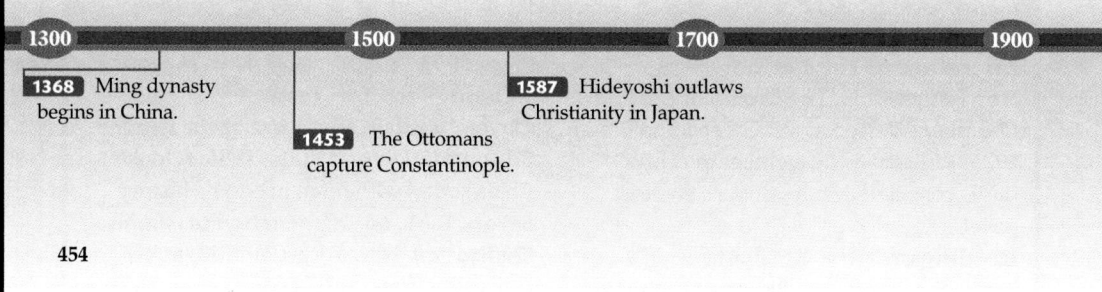

1300 — 1500 — 1700 — 1900

1368 Ming dynasty begins in China.

1453 The Ottomans capture Constantinople.

1587 Hideyoshi outlaws Christianity in Japan.

454

GEOGRAPHY CONNECTION

Region Use a wall map or one of the maps in the Atlas to review with students the distinguishing geographic features of the major regions discussed in this chapter: eastern Europe, western Asia, North Africa, South Asia, East Asia, and Southeast Asia. How might geography make it easier to govern Japan than the Ottoman Empire? *(Japan covers a relatively small area, whereas the Ottoman Empire stretched thousands of miles from the western Mediterranean to the Gulf of Aden.)* **L2**

History & Art *Voyage of the Emperor Qianlong* (detail of a scroll), Qing dynasty. Musée Guimet, Paris, France

Your History Journal

Research one of the following topics, make notes, and write an outline for a short paper: Timur Lenk (Tamerlane), Akbar, The Forbidden City, The Imperial Palace, The Samurai.

EXTRA CREDIT PROJECT

Bulletin Board Have students create a bulletin-board display on one of the great centers of Asian civilization during the period discussed in this chapter, such as Istanbul, Isfahan, Delhi, Beijing, or Kyoto. Their displays should include, if possible, a plan of the city, summaries describing its economic and political importance, pictures of notable buildings and other features, and details on the daily life of its people. The displays should also include a few pictures showing what the city is like today. **L2**

Introducing Chapter 18

History & Art This painting dates from the 1700s, when China was ruled by the Manchus, a non-Chinese people from Manchuria. Their empire—the largest in Chinese history—included Nepal, Outer Mongolia, Taiwan, and parts of Southeast Asia. **What other rulers of China governed large empires?** *(the Han, around 200 B.C.–A.D. 200; and the Mongols, in the 1200s)*

Performance Assessment

Refer to the activity on page 454C of the Planning Guide.

For an additional activity, refer to Activity 18 in the *Performance Assessment Strategies and Activities* booklet.

Using Your History Journal

Headings might include *Early Years* and *Major Achievements* for a person and *When* and *Where Built* and *Description* for a place.

GLENCOE TECHNOLOGY

VIDEODISC
Use MindJogger to preview chapter content.

MindJogger Videoquiz
Chapter 18
Disc 3 Side A

Also available in VHS.

Chapter 18 Section 1

SECTION THEME

▶ **Movement** Muslim rulers govern empires that cover vast regions of Asia, North Africa, and Europe.

Find Out

Answer: *They had absolute power and were aided by the common faith of Islam, large bureaucracies, and powerful military forces.*

FOCUS

Section Objective

Describe how Muslim rulers controlled and governed much of the Middle East, North Africa, and India between the 1500s and 1800s.

BELLRINGER
Motivational Activity

Before taking roll at the beginning of the class period, project Section Focus Transparency 18-1 and have students answer the activity questions. Discuss students' responses.

This activity is also available as a blackline master.

Vocabulary Pre-check

Use Vocabulary Activity 18 to introduce vocabulary terms.
L1 LEP

1500	1700	1900

1526 Babur founds the Mogul dynasty in India.

c. 1740 Nader Shah expands the empire of Safavid Persia.

1856 The Hatt-I Humayun decree sets out reforms for the Ottoman Empire.

Section 1

Muslim Empires

Setting the Scene

▶ **Terms to Define**
sultan, grand vizier, janissary, *millet*

▶ **People to Meet**
Suleiman I, Shah Abbas, Babur, Akbar

▶ **Places to Locate**
Istanbul, Isfahan, Delhi

Find Out How did Muslim rulers control and govern much of the Middle East, North Africa, and India between the 1500s and 1800s?

The Storyteller

On the day that Jahangir was crowned emperor of the Moghuls [Moguls], favorable omens abounded. His coronation was a scene of splendor, illuminated by nearly three thousand wax lights in branches of gold and silver. By his command, the imperial crown was brought to him. On each of the twelve points of this crown was a single diamond.... At the point in the center was a single pearl ... and on different parts of the same were set two hundred rubies. The Emirs of his empire, waiting for Jahangir's commands, were covered from head to foot in gold and jewels.

—adapted from *Memoirs of the Emperor Jahangir Written by Himself*, translated by David Price, reprinted in *The Human Record*, Alfred J. Andrea and James H. Overfield, 1990

Mogul warriors

Between the 1400s and the 1800s, three Muslim empires—the Ottoman Empire, the Persian Empire, and the Mogul Empire—conquered and controlled much of eastern Europe, central Asia, and India respectively. Strong leaders used powerful armies to amass territory that gave them economic control over major trade routes. As these empires spread into new geographic areas, the religion and culture of Islam also expanded.

The Ottoman Empire

During the late 1200s, Turkish clans—calling themselves Ottoman Turks after their first leader, Osman—settled part of Asia Minor and began conquests to build an empire. They conquered much of Byzantine territory, making Constantinople their capital in 1453. Extending their Muslim empire even farther, by the 1500s the Ottomans controlled the Balkan Peninsula and parts of eastern Europe. By the end of their rule in the early 1900s, they had acquired much of the Middle East, North Africa, and the Caucasus region between the Black and Caspian Seas.

The Ottoman Empire maintained a strong navy in the Mediterranean to protect the lucrative trade they controlled there. Alarmed by the threat to their trade and to Christianity, Europeans under Philip II of Spain fought and defeated the Ottoman fleet at the Battle of Lepanto in 1571. But the Ottomans rebuilt their navy and remained a significant seapower until the 1700s.

Suleiman I

Suleiman I was one of the early Ottoman rulers who strengthened Muslim forces prior to the Battle of Lepanto. He was a multitalented man—a heroic military commander, a skillful administrator, and a patron of the arts. Ruling from 1520 to 1566, Suleiman received the name "The Lawgiver" for his

---

SECTION RESOURCES

Reproducible Masters
- Reproducible Lesson Plan 18-1
- Vocabulary Activity 18
- Guided Reading Activity 18-1
- Time Line Activity 18
- History Simulation 18
- People in World History Profile 33
- Section Quiz 18-1

Transparencies
- Section Focus Transparency 18-1
- Chapter Transparency 18
- World History and Art Transparencies 24, 25

Multimedia
- Student Self-Test and Review Software
- Testmaker
- World Music: Cultural Traditions, Lesson 7

Expansion of the Ottoman Empire

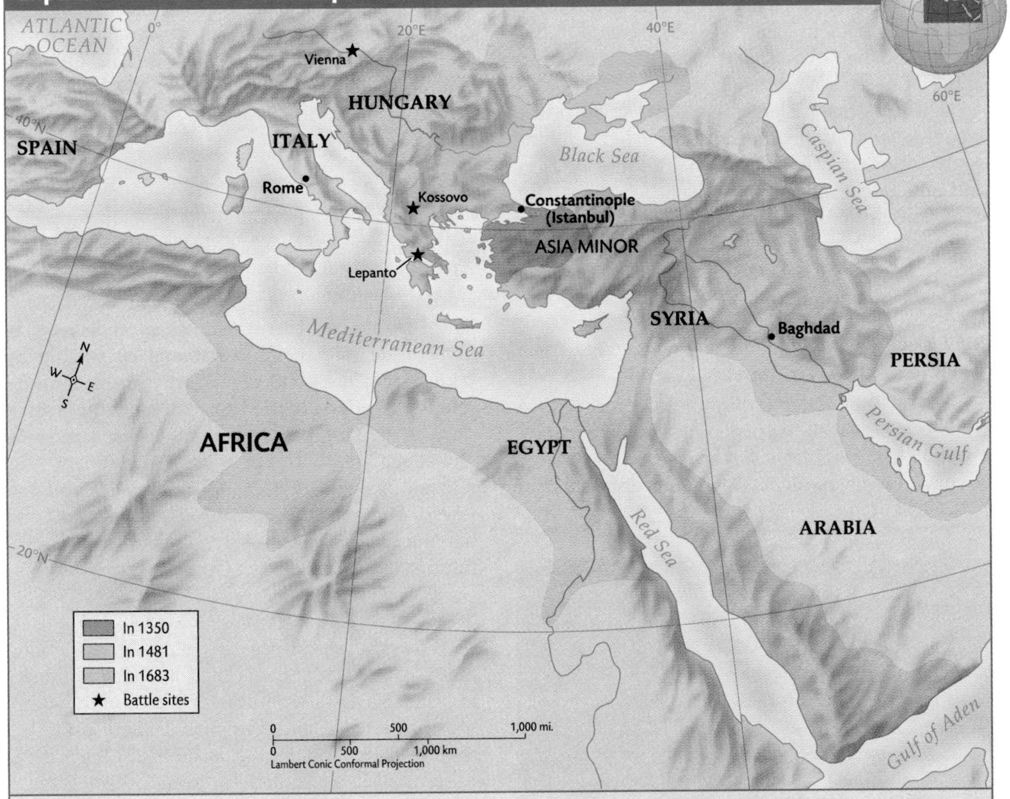

Map Study After making Constantinople their capital in 1453, the Ottoman Turks expanded their empire.
Human/Environment Interaction How do you think the geography of the Ottoman Empire affected conquests after 1481?

work in organizing Ottoman laws. Suleiman boastfully described himself to the French king Francis I: "I, who am the sultan of sultans, the sovereign of sovereigns, the dispenser of crowns to the monarchs on the face of the earth."

Suleiman acted as both the **sultan**, or political ruler, and the caliph, or religious leader; he enjoyed absolute authority. To rule effectively, however, Suleiman needed support from his personal advisers, the bureaucracy, a group of religious advisers known as the Ulema, and a well-trained army. A **grand vizier**, or prime minister, headed the bureaucracy that enforced the sultan's decisions throughout the empire. The Ulema made rulings on questions of Islamic law, and the army held much control within the empire by conquering and controlling new territories. The sultan maintained an elite corps of soldiers called **janissaries**. Rigorous military and religious training made these troops a fierce and loyal fighting force.

Ottoman Law

Because the empire was so large, Ottoman Muslims ruled diverse peoples, including Arabs, Greeks, Albanians, Slavs, Armenians, and Jews. The population was divided into several classes: a ruling class made up of the sultan's family and high government officials; the nobility, which administered agricultural estates; and the largest class, the peasants who worked on those estates.

To accommodate these diverse populations, the government made special laws affecting those who did not practice Islam, the empire's official religion. Non-Muslims were allowed to practice their faith

COOPERATIVE LEARNING ACTIVITY

Quiz Game Organize the class into three groups representing the Ottomans, Safavids, and Moguls. Have each team prepare questions about its empire. Encourage students to ask about the arts, foods, religious beliefs, and social codes of the cultures they represent. Each group should select one person to record the questions on note cards, with the answers on the back. Each team should choose ten questions and present these to the rest of the class as a quiz game. **L1**

TEACH

Guided Practice

THEME Movement
Ask students why Muslim peoples like the Ottomans, Persians, and Moguls might have wanted to expand their territory. *(to gain control of trade routes; to spread their religion; to protect the lands they already governed)* **L1**

Map Study

Answer
Much of Asia Minor is mountainous. Ottoman invaders had to be familiar with mountain passes and inaccessible areas before they attacked their enemies.

Map Skills Practice

Reading a Map **Which modern countries, wholly or in part, were ruled by the Ottoman Empire at its greatest extent?** *(Turkey, Bulgaria, Romania, Greece, Hungary, Egypt, Libya, Tunisia, Algeria, Saudi Arabia, Yemen, Syria, Jordan, Israel, Iraq)*

Religion Have students review the main tenets of Islam, with emphasis on the Five Pillars (Chapter 11). **What is the main difference between Shiite and Sunni Muslims?** *(Shiites believe that only a descendant of Muhammad possesses true spiritual [and political] power; Sunnis believe that any devout Muslim can hold this authority.)* **L2**

History Simulation 18

World History and Art Transparency 24, *Taj Mahal*; 25, *Shah Jahan and One of His Sons Riding in Escort*

Chapter 18 Section 1

Compare Ask students to compare the treatment of subject peoples by the Ottomans, Safavids, and Moguls. *(Ottomans: Non-Muslims could practice their own religion and run their own communities if they paid a tax; Safavids: forced everyone to adopt Shiite Islam; Moguls: Akbar encouraged religious tolerance, but later Moguls persecuted Hindus.)* **L3**

World Music: Cultural Traditions, Lesson 7

Who?What?Where?When?

The Janissaries By 1826 this military force had grown so large—135,000 strong—and so powerful that the sultan was forced to massacre all its members.

Independent Practice

Guided Reading Activity 18-1 **L1**

Time Line Activity 18

People in World History Profile 33

Visualizing History Although Suleiman was credited with many achievements, the governmental reforms of his reign were due largely to his vizier, Ibrahim Pasha, a man of Greek origin.

Answer to Caption: *They could practice their own religion and manage their own affairs if they paid a tax.*

in return for payment of a tax. Ottoman law also permitted the empire's diverse religious groups to run affairs in their own *millets*, or communities, and choose their own leaders to present their views to the Ottoman government.

The Ottoman Islamic civilization borrowed many elements from the Byzantine, Persian, and Arab cultures they had absorbed. Mosques, bridges, and aqueducts reflected this blend of styles. The Christian city of Constantinople was transformed into a Muslim one and renamed **Istanbul**. Islamic architects renovated Hagia Sophia into a mosque and then planned new mosques and palaces that added to Istanbul's beauty.

Decline of the Ottomans

By 1600 the Ottoman Empire had reached the peak of its power; thereafter it slowly declined. Even at its height, however, the empire faced enemies on its borders. Conquests ended as the Ottomans tried to fight both Persians and Europeans. In 1683 Polish King John III Sobieski commanded a brilliant victory over the Turks at Vienna, which dealt a decisive blow to the Ottoman Empire. When military conquests ceased, massive poverty and civil discontent spread throughout Ottoman lands.

Visualizing History **Portrait of Suleiman, "The Lawgiver," from the late 1600s.** *What provision did the Ottoman law make for peoples of diverse religions?*

Reform

During the 1800s, influenced by western European ideas, the Ottoman government attempted to reform the social and economic ills of the empire. In 1856 Sultan Abdul-Mejid I issued the Hatt-I Humayun, a far-reaching reform decree.

The decree created a national citizenship by taking away the political authority of the empire's religious leaders. It tried to remove cultural divisions by making people from all cultures and religions eligible to serve in the government. Tax reform, property rights, and military reforms followed. Between 1856 and 1876, Abdul-Mejid I and his successor, Abdul-Aziz, encouraged liberal reforms and loyalty to the Ottoman dynasty.

Reaction

Powerful resistance to change grew among the religious leaders, who had lost civil authority in their own communities. Although many Muslim, Jewish, and Christian leaders protested reform, merchants and artisans in the individual communities welcomed it. Non-Turkish groups, such as Armenians, Bulgarians, Macedonians, and Serbs, however, had little interest in reforming the empire. They began to think of themselves as separate nationalities and wanted nation-states of their own.

The reform movement lacked strong leadership and broad-based support needed to guarantee its success. To gain public support, determined reformers known as the Young Ottomans overthrew the weak sultan Abdul-Aziz and replaced him with Abdul-Hamid II.

At first the new sultan went along with the reformers. In 1876 he proclaimed a new constitution. He affirmed the unity of the empire and promised individual liberties for his subjects. In 1877 the first Ottoman parliament met in Istanbul. But later that same year Abdul-Hamid II decided to resist reform. He suddenly dissolved the parliament and ended constitutional rule. The sultan believed that moving the Ottoman government toward liberalism would lead to ruin. To further protect the empire from change, he drove many of the Young Ottomans into exile. Then he imposed absolute rule.

MEETING SPECIAL NEEDS ACTIVITY

Study Strategy Have students work alone or in small groups to develop topic sentences for this section—first, for the section as a whole; second, for each of the three peoples discussed; and third, for each paragraph of the section. After they have developed their sentences, each one should be read aloud and discussed briefly. **L1**

Safavid Persia

To the east of the Ottoman Empire lay Persia, a land that had once been part of the Islamic Empire, but which had broken away because of religious differences. In the 1500s Shiite Muslims, bitter enemies of the Ottoman Turks, conquered the land of present-day Iran. The Shiite leader, Ismail (ihs•MAH•EEL), conquered and unified the numerous people living there, declaring himself to be the founder of the Safavid (sah•FAH•weed) dynasty.

Safavid rulers required all of their Persian subjects to accept the Shiite form of Islam. Belief in the Shia branch of Islam distinguished people living in Persia from neighboring Sunni Muslim peoples—the Arabs and Turks.

Shah Abbas

The Safavid leader **Shah Abbas** came to the throne in 1587. His army regained some western territory lost to the Ottomans in previous years. Then the shah sought allies against the Ottomans even among such Christian states as England. The English used their alliance with Persia to seize the strategic Persian Gulf port of Hormuz in 1622, gaining control of the Persian silk and East Indian spice trade.

With his empire secure against the Ottoman forces, Shah Abbas set up his court in **Isfahan**, which became one of the most magnificent cities in the entire Muslim world. Towering above the city was the blue dome of the Imam Mosque, which was covered with lacy white decorations. Near the mosque, Abbas had a three-story palace built for his personal use. He also ordered beautiful streets and parks constructed throughout the city.

During the reign of Abbas, Persian spread as the language of culture, diplomacy, and trade in most of the Muslim world. Later the language spread to India. Urdu, spoken in Pakistan today, is partly based on Persian.

Nader Shah

After the death of Shah Abbas in 1629, inept Safavid rulers weakened the empire, bringing on its decline. In 1736, after the Safavid decline, Nader Shah came to power. He expanded the Persian Empire to its greatest height since Darius. But after his assassination in 1747, territory was lost and the country was divided.

In the late 1700s another Turkic group, the Qajar dynasty, seized the Persian throne and established a new dynasty in Tehran. The Qajars ruled Persia until 1925.

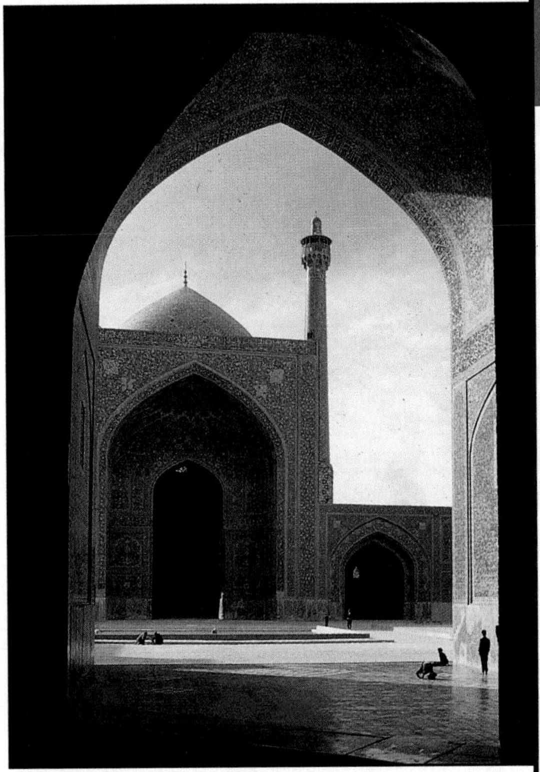

Visualizing History **The Imam Mosque in Isfahan (in present-day Iran) was built by Shah Abbas during the early 1600s.** *What cultural impact did Safavid Persia have on the Muslim world?*

The Mogul Empire

Even before the Ottomans and the Safavids built their empires, Islamic invaders from central Asia had conquered much of northern India by the 1100s. The invaders set up a sultanate, or Muslim kingdom, in **Delhi** in 1206. Once order was restored, northern India prospered economically and culturally. Traditional Hindu culture survived the invasions and blended with Islamic civilization.

Timur Lenk in India

By the late 1300s the Muslim Mongol ruler, Timur Lenk (Tamerlane), had conquered much of central Asia and made Samarkand the capital of his empire. Although a devout Muslim, Timur Lenk was also a ruthless leader. His forces sacked the city of Delhi in 1398, killing thousands and leaving the city in rubble. After Timur Lenk's death, his Islamic

Visualizing History Under Shah Abbas, Isfahan included 162 mosques, 48 schools, 1,802 commercial buildings, and 283 baths, according to one account.
Answer to Caption: *The Persian language spread through much of the Muslim world.*

Biography Have students write an article on Suleiman the Magnificent, Shah Abbas, Babur, or Akbar. Have them assume that they interviewed the ruler in order to write the article in a question-and-answer format. They should include information about the man's interests, religious beliefs, and political goals. **L2**

News Report Have students write a news report on the Battle of Lepanto or the Battle of Panipat. Remind them that news reports tell who, what, where, when, and why. **L3**

you don't say...

Assassin, the English word for a murderer of a politically important person, comes from the name of an Islamic sect, the *hashshashin*, that began in Persia. Its members believed that they had a religious duty to kill their enemies.

MAKING CONNECTIONS ACTIVITIES

Architecture One of Istanbul's most famous buildings, the Christian church of Hagia Sophia, has undergone several changes in its long history. Have students research these changes, ending with a description of the building today. **L2**

Religion Although Sikhs have never been as numerous as Hindus or Muslims in India, their religious group has played an important role in the country. Have students research the basic tenets of Sikhism and summarize the role Sikhs have played in Indian politics, especially in recent years. **L2**

TEACH

Tell students that the name of this tomb comes from the title of Shah Jahan's favorite wife, Mumtazi Mahal, which means "Chosen of the Palace." (Her actual name was Arjumand Banu.) For his own resting place, the emperor planned to build a replica of the Taj Mahal in black marble across the Jumna River from his wife's tomb. He lost his throne, however, before he could do so. Ask students for their responses to Tagore's description of the Taj Mahal.

Who?What?Where?When?

Shah Jahan was a conqueror as well as a builder, extending Mogul rule over areas of central India. But his reign ended unhappily, with his four sons struggling for the throne. His son Aurangzeb declared himself emperor in 1658 and confined his father to a fort for the last six years of his life.

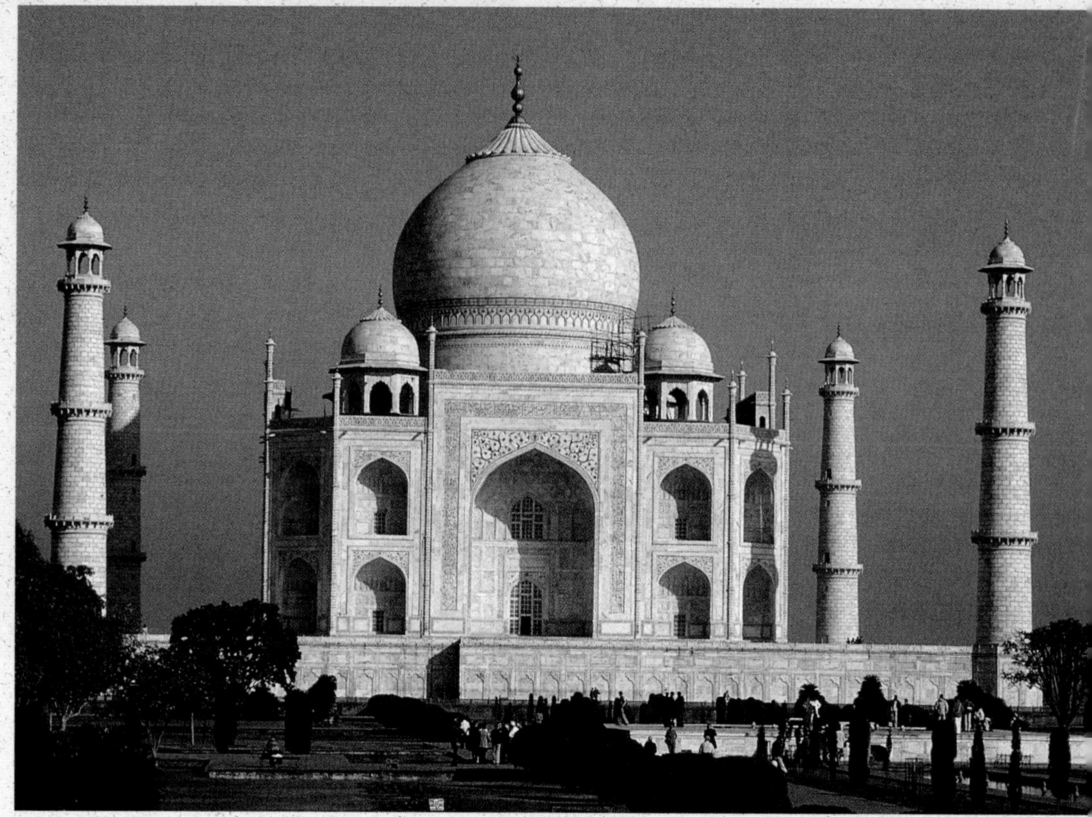

Taj Mahal

The beauty of the Taj Mahal has awed visitors for centuries. A pear-shaped dome crowns the square central building, complete with a reflecting pool. The marble surface glitters with semiprecious stones: jade from China; turquoise from Tibet; lapis lazuli from Afghanistan; chrysolite from Egypt; and mother-of-pearl from the Indian Ocean. Inside all this wealth and beauty lies Mumtazi Mahal, wife of the Mogul emperor of India, Shah Jahan, who ruled from 1628 to 1658. He fell in love with Mumtazi at 16 and adored his queen throughout her life. In 1629, shortly after Shah Jahan's reign began, Mumtazi died in childbirth, after giving birth to their 14th child. Her death left him in black despair, and in his grief he decided to build the world's greatest tomb.

Or so goes the legend. Contemporary scholars argue that Shah Jahan built the Taj Mahal not only as a resting place for his well-loved wife—and later for himself—but also as a symbol of his power and wealth. The Moguls were Muslims—outsiders and conquerors who ruled India in an absolute monarchy. Their administration left India weak and, by the 1800s, vulnerable to British conquest. In their art and architecture they gave India a more lasting legacy. "The Taj Mahal," wrote Indian poet Rabindranath Tagore, is "like a solitary tear suspended on the cheek of time." ⊕

empire disintegrated; yet northern India would face other Muslim invasions.

Akbar the Great

In the early 1500s **Babur**, who was a descendant of Timur Lenk, led another attack on northern India. Using artillery and with cavalry riding elephants and horses, Babur conquered Delhi at the Battle of Panipat in 1526. Then he set up the Mogul dynasty, the Persian name for Mongol, which lasted three centuries in India. Unlike Timur Lenk, the Moguls encouraged orderly government, and they expanded the arts.

Babur's grandson, **Akbar**, was a benevolent ruler who brought peace and order to northern India. Recognizing that most of the people he ruled were Hindus, Akbar encouraged religious tolerance to end quarrels between Hindus and Muslims. Whereas Muslims believed in one God, Hindus worshiped many deities. Hindus and Muslims differed about sacred foods, social organization, and religious customs. To reduce tension among his people, Akbar repealed a tax on Hindus.

Extremely curious about all religions, Akbar invited religious scholars of other faiths to his court to learn about other religions. He concluded that all religions revealed the same divine truth, whatever their external practices were. He tried to set up a new religion that he called Divine Faith. The new religion included features of many of the world's religions such as Islam, Hinduism, and Christianity.

Mogul Civilization

Under Akbar's rule music, painting, and literature flourished in Mogul India. Mogul rulers made their lavish courts centers of art and learning. Although Akbar could not read, he understood the value of education and set up a large library, employing more than 100 court painters to illustrate the elegantly bound books.

Another Mogul ruler, Shah Jahan, created one of the world's most beautiful buildings—the Taj Mahal at Agra—a magnificent example of Muslim architecture. Muslim architects introduced the arch and dome to India, and in trading contacts with China, Muslim merchants brought gunpowder, paper, and Chinese porcelain to Mogul India.

History & Art *Akbar Hunting Tigers Near Gwalior* by Husain Haqqash, c. 1580, from the *Akbar-Nama*. Victoria and Albert Museum, London, England
How did Akbar encourage religious tolerance?

Mogul Decline

In spite of its cultural achievements, Mogul influence in India was weakened at the end of the 1600s by Hindu rebellions and by a new religion, Sikhism (SEE•KIH•zuhm). Led by Nanak, the first of their 10 religious teachers, the Sikhs tried to unite Hinduism with Islam. Most Indians still held onto their Hindu traditions and Hindu customs, and they rebelled against later Mogul rulers, who abandoned the religious tolerance that had been practiced by earlier leaders. Shah Aurangzeb destroyed many Hindu temples and persecuted the Hindus. Local rulers began to grow more independent as the central government lost much of its control over them. Mogul rule continued in a weakened state, with reduced territory, until 1858.

SECTION 1 REVIEW

Recall

1. **Define** sultan, grand vizier, janissary, *millet*.
2. **Identify** Suleiman I, Hatt-I Humayun, Shah Abbas, Babur, Akbar.
3. **Use** the map on page 457 to compare the Ottoman Empire's boundaries in 1481 to those in 1683. How did the growth of the Ottoman Empire lead to decline?

Critical Thinking

4. **Making Comparisons** How did Shah Abbas's patronage of the arts compare to that of a contemporary European monarch?

Understanding Themes

5. **Movement** How do you think the movement of Muslims into northern India affected the people already living there?

Chapter 18 Section 1

History & Art Akbar's interest in religion led him to invite Jesuit missionaries to his court, but they failed to convert him to Christianity.
Answer to Caption: *by repealing a tax on Hindus*

Global Gourmet

Middle East A favorite food for barbecues is shish kebab, meat and vegetables grilled on a skewer. The English term comes from Armenia, whose people adapted it from the Turkish words *sis* ("skewer") and *kebabi* ("roast mutton").

ASSESS

Check for Understanding

Assign Section 1 Review as homework or as an in-class activity.

Use Student Self-Test and Review Software to review Section 1.

Evaluate

Section Quiz 18-1

Use the Testmaker to create a customized quiz for Section 1.

Reteach

Have students review which territories were ruled by each of these peoples at their height: Ottomans, Safavids, Moguls.

Enrich

Have students research a famous landmark in Istanbul, Isfahan, or Delhi and write a description of it.

CLOSE

Ask: **Would you have preferred to live under Suleiman, Shah Abbas, or Akbar? Why?**

SECTION 1 REVIEW ANSWERS

1. All vocabulary words are defined in the Glossary.
2. Suleiman I, 456; Hatt-I Humayun, 458; Shah Abbas, 459; Babur, 461; Akbar, 461
3. It led to border warfare; when military conquests stopped, poverty and discontent spread.
4. Many contemporary rulers also encourage civic improvements and construction of beautiful buildings.
5. MOVEMENT It led to conflicts with the people living there, who were Hindu; eventually it led to the development of a new religion, Sikhism, an attempt to unite Islam and Hinduism.

Chapter 18 Section 2

SECTION THEME

- **Cultural Diffusion** China is directly challenged by its contacts with western European cultures.

Find Out

Answer: *In each dynasty, strong governments were followed by weak and corrupt ones.*

FOCUS

Section Objective

Analyze why China flourished and then declined during the Ming and Qing dynasties.

BELLRINGER Motivational Activity

Before taking roll at the beginning of the class period, project Section Focus Transparency 18-2 and have students answer the activity questions. Discuss students' responses.

This activity is also available as a blackline master.

Vocabulary Pre-check

Use Vocabulary Activity 18 to introduce vocabulary terms. **L1 LEP**

1400 — 1600 — 1800

1405 China begins first seagoing expedition.

1644 The Manchus establish the Qing dynasty.

1800 China's population reaches 350 million.

Section 2

Chinese Dynasties

Setting the Scene

- **Terms to Define**
  junk, queue, labor-intensive farming
- **People to Meet**
  Hong Wu, Yong Le, Zheng He
- **Places to Locate**
  Beijing, the Forbidden City

Find Out Why did China flourish and then decline during the Ming and Qing dynasties?

The Storyteller

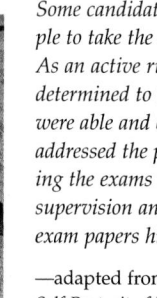

The examination process for civil servants was riddled with corruption. "There are too many men who claim to be pure scholars and yet are stupid and arrogant," K'ang-hsi [Kangxi] fumed. Incompetent examiners were set on memorization instead of independent thinking. Candidate lists were manipulated to favor specific provinces. Some candidates even hired people to take the exams for them. As an active ruler K'ang-hsi was determined to have officials who were able and efficient. He addressed the problems by holding the exams under armed supervision and reading the exam papers himself.

—adapted from *Emperor of China: Self-Portrait of K'ang-hsi*, translated by Johnathan D. Spence, reprinted in *The Human Record*, Alfred J. Andrea and James H. Overfield, 1990

Han civil service exam

In 1368, after the Yuan dynasty fell, a new era of reform began. The Ming and the Qing dynasties built strong central governments that implemented agricultural and public works projects. As food production and trade increased, so did China's population. At the same time, China looked to earlier achievements to invigorate its culture. After years of prosperity, Chinese emperors isolated themselves from their people and the outside, resulting in government corruption, rebellions, and decline.

The Ming Dynasty

After 89 years of Mongol rule, a military officer named Zhu Yuanzhang (JOO YOO•AHN•JAHNG) led a rebellion that overthrew the Yuan dynasty. Born into a poor peasant family, Zhu had been a Buddhist monk before entering the army. In 1368 he became emperor, taking the name **Hong Wu** and establishing his capital at Nanjing. For the first time in more than 1,000 years, the Son of Heaven was of peasant origin. Hong Wu gave the name *Ming* ("brilliant") to his dynasty, which would rule China for nearly 300 years.

Peace and Stability

The Ming dynasty brought peace and stability to China. Hong Wu and the early Ming rulers imposed new law codes, reorganized the tax system, and reformed local government.

The new law codes were harsher than those of previous Chinese dynasties. Scholars, traditionally exempt from corporal punishment, had to endure public whippings if they displeased the emperor and his officials. Formerly, the saying was that "a gentleman could be ordered to die but should never be humiliated."

SECTION RESOURCES

Reproducible Masters
- Reproducible Lesson Plan 18-2
- Vocabulary Activity 18
- Guided Reading Activity 18-2
- Section Quiz 18-2

Transparencies
- Section Focus Transparency 18-2

Multimedia
- Student Self-Test and Review Software
- Testmaker
- World Music: Cultural Traditions, Lesson 8
- Picture Atlas of the World

Visualizing History **The Forbidden City in the heart of the city of Beijing contains hundreds of buildings. Many of these buildings housed the emperors of China and their imperial court from 1421 to 1911.** *How did the Ming Emperor Yong Le contribute to Chinese scholarship?*

Chinese persons replaced Mongols in all civil service posts, and Confucianism again became the empire's official doctrine. The Ming dynasty restored the old examination system, making the tests even stricter than in earlier dynasties.

Strong rulers at the beginning of the dynasty enforced peace throughout the land. With peace and additional revenues from a reformed tax system, economic prosperity came to China. But northern China had been devastated by nomadic invaders. To encourage farmers to move there, the government offered free land, tools, seeds, and farm animals. Farmers reclaimed and restored much of the land in the north, and the policy helped secure the northern frontier from invaders.

With more land under cultivation, farmers could sell their surplus produce at local markets. Government workers repaired and maintained the canal system that connected local markets, an efficient way for bringing farm goods to market. Northern China began to regain its strength and status as a rich farming region.

Increased agricultural productivity also freed workers for nonfarming tasks. Artisans increased in number, expanding production of crafts, silk, tea, porcelain, and cotton cloth. Thus, trade within China expanded, and port cities like Guangzhou (GWONG•JOH) and Shanghai continued to grow. Merchants sold food, textiles, and luxury goods to the growing urban populations.

As city merchants and artisans grew wealthier, they demanded more popular entertainments and learning. The third Ming emperor, **Yong Le**, ordered 2,000 scholars to compile a treasury of Chinese histories and literature. This massive library included neo-Confucian writings from the Song dynasty and also many Buddhist scriptures.

Ming writers preferred the novel to other forms of fiction. Many novelists were students who had failed examinations; thus, many of their works such as *The Scholars* satirize scholars and officials. Novelists ended many chapters on a suspenseful note. However, these tales could hardly rival the real adventures at sea that some sailors lived.

Exploration

The early Ming emperors spent government money on a navy that could sail to foreign ports

Chapter 18 Section 2

TEACH

Guided Practice

THEME Cultural Diffusion

Ask: **How did China's culture spread beyond its boundaries during the Ming and Qing dynasties?** *(by seagoing expeditions and trade)* **How did foreign influences enter China during the Ming dynasty?** *(via Portuguese traders and Jesuit missionaries)* **L1**

Visualizing History The Forbidden City was so called because no one but a member of the imperial household could enter it. Its numerous buildings were erected in only five years but required a million workers to construct.

Answer to Caption: *He had scholars compile a treasury of Chinese history and literature.*

History Review with the class the three dynasties that preceded the Ming: the Tang (618–907), the Song (960–1279), and the Yuan of the Mongols (1260–1368). Ask them to name a well-known ruler from each one. *(Tang: Tai Cong, Empress Wu; Song: Zhao Kuangyin; Yuan: Kublai Khan)* **L2**

COOPERATIVE LEARNING ACTIVITY

Chart Organize students into two teams, one to focus on the Ming dynasty, the other on the Qing. Each team should make a chart organizing the text information about its dynasty. Among the topics to be included are *Leaders*, *Religion*, *Trade Policies*, *Economics*, *European Contacts*, and *Cause of Decline*. Each team member should be responsible for one topic. The team members should jointly decide on the chart's format and organization. After completion, the charts should be displayed for the entire class. **L1**

Chapter 18
Section 2

Government Remind students that the Manchus formed a small minority in China. Ask how these non-Chinese exerted their control. *(by adopting some Chinese traditions, such as Confucian ideals; by favoring Manchus as officers and soldiers; by reserving top government jobs for Manchus and having Manchu supervisors for lesser employees)* **L3**

World Music: Cultural Traditions, Lesson 8

NATIONAL GEOGRAPHIC SOCIETY

CD-ROM
PICTURE ATLAS OF THE WORLD

View traditional ceremonies that open games in Urumqi, a Muslim city deep in Central Asia, by clicking China's "Video" button.

Linking Past and Present

Chinese New Year Although China today uses the Gregorian calendar, its traditional New Year is still celebrated both in China and Chinese communities living outside China. Occurring on the second new moon after the winter solstice, it falls between January 21 and February 19. A time of clearing out the old, Chinese New Year has traditionally been an occasion for thorough housecleaning, paying debts, and giving charity to the poor.

and collect tribute for the emperor. The ships, known as junks, usually traveled along the coastline, but they could also venture into open water.

From 1405 to 1433, Emperor Yong Le sent out seven seagoing expeditions. Their purpose was "glorifying Chinese arms in the remote regions and showing off the wealth and power of the [Middle] Kingdom." The leader of the voyages was a Chinese Muslim named **Zheng He** (JUNG HUH).

Zheng He took his first fleet to the nations of Southeast Asia. In later voyages he reached India, sailed up the Persian Gulf to Arabia, and even visited kingdoms on the east coast of Africa. Everywhere he went, he demanded that the people submit to the emperor's authority. If they refused, he applied force; rulers who accepted were rewarded with gold or silk.

Zheng He brought back trade goods and tribute from many lands. But later Ming emperors did not follow through: ocean voyages were costly, and in the early 1400s China concentrated its funds on military forces to combat threats from nomadic tribes to the north. The emperor's officials saw no great benefit in exploring expeditions and halted them. The government discouraged trade with foreign countries partly because Confucian philosophy regarded trade as the lowest of occupations. The emperor even forbade construction of seagoing vessels.

Inside the Forbidden City

To help defend the northern border, Yong Le shifted his capital from Nanjing to Cambaluc, renaming it **Beijing** (BAY•JING). He ordered the city completely rebuilt, modeled after the great Tang capital of Changan. For 16 years, from 1404 to 1420, workers labored on its construction. On the Chinese New Year's Day in 1421, the government moved to Beijing.

A visitor entering Beijing walked through the great gate in the 30-foot-(9-meter-) high southern wall. If you had government business, you passed through the Gate of Heavenly Peace. There stood the government offices and parks of the Imperial City.

Images of the Times

Chinese Life

Under the stable, centralized rule of the Ming and Qing dynasties, crafts, industry, and agriculture flourished.

Breeding the silkworm required patience, but the reward was income from trade.

The Gate of Supreme Harmony at Beijing's Forbidden City is guarded well by a centuries-old lion.

Images of the Times **Chinese Life**

China generally prospered in the early modern period. One development that helped the economy during the Qing dynasty was the growth of private banks. For the first time in Chinese history, merchants and traders were able to secure loans, transfer funds from one part of the empire to another, and use banknotes—along with coins—as payment.

Farther north, across a moat and through the Meridian Gate, stood **the Forbidden City**, where the emperor and his family lived. The Forbidden City had two main sections: one for the emperor's personal use and another for state occasions. The main courtyard outside the gate held 90,000 people. The emperor sometimes appeared before guests here, but ordinary people stayed out or faced a penalty of death.

The residential section of the Forbidden City consisted of many palaces with thousands of rooms. Pavilions and gardens gave comfort to the imperial family, who spent their days in fabulous splendor. Later Ming emperors devoted much of their time to pleasure. In the last 30 years of one emperor's reign, he met with his closest officials only five times.

Corrupt officials, eager to enrich themselves, took over the country. As law and order collapsed, Manchu invaders from Manchuria attacked the northern frontier settlements. Revenues for military spending were limited by the expenses of the lavish court. The Manchus managed to conquer a weakened China.

The Qing Dynasty

In 1644 the Manchus set up a new dynasty, called the Qing (CHING), or "pure." For only the second time in history, foreigners controlled all of China. The Manchus slowly extended their empire to the north and west, taking in Manchuria, Mongolia, Xinjiang (SHIN•JEE•ONG), and Tibet. The offshore island of Taiwan became part of the empire in 1683. For almost 300 years the Qing dynasty ruled over the largest Chinese empire that ever existed.

Adapting Chinese Culture

The Manchus had already accepted Confucian values before invading China. Their leaders understood that these precepts benefited the ruling class. Ruling over an empire in which Chinese outnumbered Manchus by at least 30 to 1, the Manchu rulers controlled their empire by making every effort to adopt many of the native Chinese customs and traditions.

A Ming porcelain bowl painted in underglaze displays the familiar blue willow pattern.

Iron workers decorate this Chinese vase preserved in the Golestan Palace, Tehran, Iran.

REFLECTING ON THE TIMES

1. What two valuable commodities shown here were in high demand in Europe?
2. Why do crafts and trade flourish under stable government?

Chapter 18 Section 2

Independent Practice

Guided Reading Activity 18-1 **L1**

Daily Life Have students prepare advertisements to encourage farmers during the Ming dynasty to move to northern China. In their ads, students should mention some of these government benefits: free land, tools, seeds, and farm animals. **L2**

Politics Have students brainstorm a list of topics related to the Taiping Rebellion. Examples are: Western reactions, the leader of the rebellion, the government's response to the rebellion. Ask each student to research one topic, taking notes on index cards. Have students make oral reports to the class and turn their cards in to you after the presentation. **L3**

Cultural Perspectives

Foot-binding The Manchus tried unsuccessfully to outlaw an ancient custom of foot-binding of girls. The Chinese not only admired small feet but also believed in restricting women's freedom. Long strips of cloth were used to turn the toes under and keep the feet three or four inches long. For centuries, only women who did heavy work could escape this painful procedure, for normal feet made a woman unfit for marriage. The practice did not die out until the 1900s.

ANSWERS TO REFLECTING ON THE TIMES

1. silk and porcelain
2. In stable times, valuable resources are not diverted to warfare, and there is little danger of attack or invasion; thus people's energies can be devoted to other pursuits, such as industry and trade.

CONNECTIONS

Economics

Feeding the Empire

Providing for China's growing population was made easier by an innovation introduced by the Manchus—the use of storehouses in each province. By storing reserves of grain, these granaries helped avert famine in years when crops were poor.

Answers to Making the Connection

1. *They terraced the land.*
2. *Answers may include: Power-driven machinery helps farmers cultivate more land than ever before. But extensive cultivation can lead to soil erosion, and the chemicals used in fertilizers run off into vital water supplies and contaminate them.*

Who?What?Where?When?

Matteo Ricci—known to the Chinese as Li Ma-tou—was the most famous Jesuit missionary to China. He and his fellow Jesuits impressed the Chinese not only with their knowledge of Chinese but also with their tolerance for Chinese customs. For example, they allowed their congregations to discharge fireworks during Mass, in accordance with Chinese religious practice.

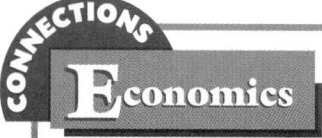

CONNECTIONS

Economics

Feeding the Empire

Chinese irrigation

Both the Ming and the Qing dynasties encouraged agricultural development in China. Rapid population growth, particularly in the Chinese heartland in the eastern part of the empire, made it necessary for farmers to produce more food. The Chinese also had to develop new ways of distributing food to the growing population.

New crops from the Americas arrived in China on Chinese trade ships that traveled regularly to the Philippines and other areas of Southeast Asia. During the mid-1500s Spanish ships brought sweet potatoes, maize, and peanuts as well as silver and gold from the Americas to the Philippines. There Chinese merchants exchanged silk or porcelain for the precious metals and exotic foods. Farmers found that the foreign plants grew well in poor soil. Thus, land that had not been productive in earlier times became a valuable economic resource.

The government continued its efforts to build canals and irrigation systems to help farmers water their crops and transport them to market. Terracing—the flat steplike areas that farmers dug out of the sides of hills—helped them make full use of their lands. All these factors helped make China's population the largest in the world.

MAKING THE CONNECTION

1. How did Chinese farmers change their environment to provide opportunity for agricultural development?
2. How have modern farming practices affected the environment in various parts of the world?

Manchus kept control by naming Manchus to the officer corps and by ensuring that most of the soldiers were Manchus. To control the Chinese civil service, Manchus reserved the top jobs in the government hierarchy for their people. Even Chinese officials in lower positions had a Manchu supervisor monitoring their work. Critical military and government positions thus remained loyal to the Manchu leadership.

In 1645 the Manchu emperor ordered all Chinese men to shave their heads leaving a single **queue**, or braid, at the back of their heads—or be executed. Among the people this order was known as "Keep your hair and lose your head" or "Lose your hair and keep your head." The upper classes had to adopt the Manchu tight, high-collared jacket and abandon their customary loose robes. But in spite of the many-layered controls, the Manchu rulers took on more elements of Chinese culture.

The Qing were fortunate in having able emperors in the first years of their rule. Emperor Kangxi, who ruled from 1661 to 1722, reduced taxes and undertook public works projects, such as flood control. Kangxi, himself a poet, also sponsored Chinese art. Other emperors secured new territory, extending the Qing Empire.

Daily Life

The Manchus made few changes in China's economy. The government-sponsored work projects and internal peace contributed to economic prosperity in the 1700s. Agricultural improvements increased food production, whereupon China's population exploded, from about 150 million in 1600 to 350 million in 1800. China was the most populous country in the world.

More than three-fourths of the Chinese people lived in rural areas. In the south where Chinese farmers worked as tenants, each family farmed its plot and paid rent to a landlord. In the north, more families owned their land. But because a family divided its land among its sons, over the generations the average peasant's share of land shrank.

As population increased, every inch of land had to be made productive. Although the Chinese had invented such simple machines as the wheelbarrow and paddle-wheel pumps, farmers depended on human labor for most farm tasks. In hill country, farm workers dug flat terraces into the hillsides where rice and other crops could be grown. Workers carried pails of water to fill the rice paddies. This **labor-intensive farming**, in which work

MEETING SPECIAL NEEDS ACTIVITY

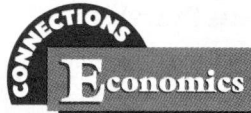

Language Delayed To encourage active participation by students for whom English is a second language, organize the class into two groups. Have one represent a Chinese family in Beijing during the Ming dynasty, the other a Turkish family in Istanbul during the same period. Each group should prepare an itinerary for a visiting student from the other country. Tasks should include gathering information about the places on the itinerary and role-playing an interaction between the hosts and the visitor. Each student should participate by explaining at least one aspect of the culture or describing one historic place to the guest. **L1 LEP**

is performed by human effort, contrasts with agriculture in which the hard work is done by animals or machinery.

Subsistence farming was not a year-round occupation during the Qing dynasty. Many farmers grew cash crops such as cotton, rather than just their own food. A writer in the 1700s described the life of farm families in one district:

> "The country folk only live off their fields for the three winter months.... During the spring months, they ... spin or weave, eating by exchanging their cloth for rice.... The autumn is somewhat rainy, and the noise of the looms' shuttles is once again to be heard everywhere in the villages.... Thus, even if there is a bad harvest ... our country people are not in distress so long as the other counties have a crop of cotton [for them to weave]."

Silk production provided extra income for farm families. They grew mulberry trees, whose leaves provided food for silkworms. From the leaves women and girls plucked the cocoons and carefully unwound them. Then the silk was ready for those who spun it into thread and others who wove it into silk cloth.

Internal trade flourished during the Qing period. There was a lively exchange of goods within and between the various regions of China. Great merchant families made fortunes trading rice, silk, fish, timber, cloth, and luxury goods. The growth of trade prompted specialization. Some regions were famous for textiles; others for cotton, porcelain, tea, or silk. At Jingdezhen, the emperor's porcelain factory employed thousands of workers. Artists painted delicate patterns or scenes on vases, bowls, and plates. Others made chemical glazes that formed a hard, shiny surface on the pottery after it was fired in a hot kiln.

Contacts With Europeans

European demand for Chinese goods such as silk and porcelain was high, attracting European ships to China's coast. The first Europeans arrived in China during the Ming dynasty. In 1514 Portuguese caravels landed near Guangzhou. The Chinese called Portuguese sailors ocean devils, and local officials refused to deal with them. Nonetheless, by 1557 the Portuguese had built a trading base at Macao.

Jesuit missionaries followed the Portuguese traders with the dream of converting China's huge population to Christianity. Although most Chinese officials were not interested in Christianity, the Jesuits' scientific knowledge impressed them. In 1611 the emperor placed a Jesuit astronomer in charge of the Imperial Calendar, and in years to come Jesuits gained other government positions. They also converted some court officials to Christianity. By the 1700s, however, Qing rulers worried that Jesuits were too involved in government affairs and forced the missionaries to leave. The Jesuits had failed to make China a Christian nation.

Qing Decline

During the 1700s corruption and internal rebellions forced the Qing dynasty into a slow decline. As the population grew, the government raised taxes to support public services. High-ranking officials, however, kept much of the revenue. Peasant rebellions followed.

By 1850 the Qing faced the Taiping Rebellion. The leader of this revolt came in contact with Christian missionaries and developed his version of Christianity. He organized many Chinese into a political movement to replace the Qing dynasty with a "Heavenly Kingdom of Great Peace." Lasting 14 years, the rebellion left much of southern China destroyed and the central government weakened. Thus undermined, the Qing faced new threats from foreign imperialistic powers.

SECTION 2 REVIEW

Recall

1. **Define** junk, queue, labor-intensive farming.
2. **Identify** Hong Wu, Yong Le, Zheng He, the Forbidden City, the Manchus.
3. **Use** the world map on pages A4 and A5 in the Atlas to determine the distance Chinese explorers traveled to reach the east coast of Africa. How does this record compare to Prince Henry's expeditions?

Critical Thinking

4. **Evaluating Information** How did the achievements of the Ming and Qing dynasties differ? Did the Qing build on the successes of the Ming, or did they create a completely new civilization?

Understanding Themes

5. **Cultural Diffusion** What might have happened if the Chinese had continued moving westward? Would China have colonized as Europeans did?

Chapter 18 Section 2

ASSESS

Check for Understanding

Assign Section 2 Review as homework or as an in-class activity.

Use Student Self-Test and Review Software to review Section 2.

Evaluate

Section Quiz 18-2

Use the Testmaker to create a customized quiz for Section 2.

Reteach

Have students summarize the similarities between the Ming and Qing dynasties. *(Agricultural development was encouraged, internal trade thrived, the arts flourished, foreigners were met with suspicion, rulers accepted Confucian values.)*

Enrich

Have students research the way silk was produced in the 1500s and 1600s in China. Have them prepare diagrams and oral reports on the process.

CLOSE

Have students summarize relations between China and the rest of the world during the Ming and Qing dynasties.

SECTION 2 REVIEW ANSWERS

1. All vocabulary words are defined in the Glossary.
2. Hong Wu, 462; Yong Le, 463; Zheng He, 464; the Forbidden City, 465; the Manchus, 465
3. Chinese explorers traveled about 5,000 miles (8,000 kilometers) to the east coast of Africa. This was much farther than Prince Henry traveled; his longest expedition was about 2,000 miles (3,200 kilometers), along Africa's west coast.
4. The Ming were known for their overseas voyages, the Qing for conquests that made the Chinese Empire the largest that ever existed. The Qing built on Ming successes.
5. **CULTURAL DIFFUSION** Answers will vary. The Chinese would probably have met stiff resistance from the Ottomans, among others. It is unlikely that they would have set up colonies since they were interested mainly in internal development and protecting their borders.

Chapter 18
Section 3

SECTION THEME

▶ **Reaction** Japan enforces isolationist policy to keep out Western influences.

Find Out

Answer: *This was a period of turmoil for Japan, so people were more open to new social, economic, and religious ideas and practices. By contrast, the 1500s to the 1700s were years of stability in China.*

FOCUS

Section Objective

Explain why Japan was more adaptable to changes than China before the 1800s.

BELLRINGER
Motivational Activity

Before taking roll at the beginning of the class period, project Section Focus Transparency 18-3 and have students answer the activity questions. Discuss students' responses.

This activity is also available as a blackline master.

Vocabulary Pre-check

Use Vocabulary Activity 18 to introduce vocabulary terms.
L1 LEP

1600 — 1700 — 1800

1600 Tokugawa Ieyasu wins the Battle of Sekigahara.

1636 Act of Seclusion forbids Japanese to leave the country.

c. 1700s Japanese cities grow in size and population.

Section 3

The Japanese Empire

Setting the Scene

▶ **Terms to Define**
sankin-kotai, *metsuke*, geisha, haiku

▶ **People to Meet**
Oda Nobunaga, Toyotomi Hideyoshi, Tokugawa Ieyasu, Francis Xavier, Matsuo Basho

▶ **Places to Locate**
Edo, Nagasaki

Find Out Why was Japan more adaptable to changes than China before the 1800s?

The Storyteller

Yamaga Soko bowed deeply. The shogun, Tokugawa Ieyasu, would determine if Yamaga was prepared to assume a samurai's responsibilities. "In peacetime, we should not be oblivious to the danger of war. Should we not then prepare ourselves for it?" asked Tokugawa. Yamaga understood that many considered the use of arms evil. "Beyond these military duties, we have other functions. We are examples for all society, leading simple and frugal lives," Yamaga responded. Not only would the samurai excel at death; they should also cultivate all aspects of life. Tokugawa spoke again, "A samurai's life calls for constant discipline. Are you, Yamaga Soko, prepared to devote yourself to this?"

Samurai in combat

—adapted from *Sources of Japanese Tradition*, reprinted in *The Human Record*, Alfred J. Andrea and James H. Overfield, 1990

While China enjoyed stability in the 1400s and 1500s, Japan experienced a period of turmoil. The shogun was a mere figurehead, and the emperor performed only religious functions. Daimyos, who controlled their own lands, waged war against their neighbors as feudal lords had done in Europe in the 1400s. "The strongest eat and the weak become the meat" was a Japanese expression of the time. Warriors showed no chivalry or loyalty. This time of local wars left Japan with a political system known as the Tokugawa shogunate that combined a central government with a system of feudalism.

Tokugawa Shogunate

Oda Nobunaga (oh•DAH noh•boo•NAH •gah) was the first military leader to begin uniting the warring daimyos. He announced his ambition on his personal seal: "to bring the nation under one sword." After winning control of a large part of central Japan, Nobunaga led his army against the capital city of Kyoto in 1568. Five years later, amid the chaos caused by the weak Ashikaga (ah•shee•KAH •gah) family, Nobunaga deposed the Ashikaga shogun. Meanwhile, his forces had moved against Buddhist military strongholds around Kyoto. After a 10-year siege, he won and so became the most powerful man in the country. In 1582, however, a treacherous soldier murdered him.

Toyotomi Hideyoshi

Power then shifted to Nobunaga's best general, **Toyotomi Hideyoshi** (toh•yoh•TOH•mee HEE•day •YOH•shee), who rose from a peasant family to his high position in the military. By 1590 Hideyoshi had forced Japan's daimyos to pledge their loyalty to him. Acting as a military dictator, Hideyoshi furthered his goal of unity by disarming the peasants to prevent them from becoming warriors. In 1588 he ordered the "great sword hunt," demanding that

SECTION RESOURCES

Reproducible Masters
- Reproducible Lesson Plan 18-3
- Vocabulary Activity 18
- Guided Reading Activity 18-3
- Geography and History Activity 18
- People in World History Profile 34
- Section Quiz 18-3

Transparencies
- Section Focus Transparency 18-3

Multimedia
- Focus on World Art Print 10
- Student Self-Test and Review Software
- Testmaker
- World Music: Cultural Traditions, Lesson 8

all peasants turn in their weapons. To stabilize the daimyo realms he controlled, he imposed laws that prevented warriors from leaving their daimyo's service to become merchants or farmers. The laws also prevented farmers and merchants from becoming warriors.

Hideyoshi, planning to expand Japan's power abroad, invaded Korea as a step toward conquering China. The invasion had another purpose—to rid the country of warriors who could start rebellions at home. However, as you learned in Chapter 14, Admiral Yi's Korean turtle ships thwarted Hideyoshi's conquest.

Tokugawa Ieyasu

After Hideyoshi's death in 1598, a third leader, **Tokugawa Ieyasu** (toh•kuh•GAH•wah ee•YAH •soo), completed the work of unification. At the Battle of Sekigahara (seh•kee•gah•HAR•ah) in 1600, Ieyasu defeated the last of his opponents. Three years later, Ieyasu asked the emperor to make him shogun. The Tokugawa family retained the shogunate for 250 years.

Tokugawa Rule

Ieyasu established his government headquarters at the fishing village of **Edo**, present-day Tokyo. There he built a stone fortress protected by high walls and moats. Today, the fortress is the Imperial Palace, but during the Tokugawa shogunate, the Japanese emperor continued to live in Kyoto. Although the emperor remained the official leader of Japan, the shogun exercised the real power.

After taking control, Ieyasu reassigned the daimyos' lands. He divided the daimyos into three groups: Tokugawa relatives, longtime supporters of the Tokugawa family, and those who came to the Tokugawa side only after the Battle of Sekigahara. He issued the most productive lands near Edo to the Tokugawa relatives. The others—potential enemies—received less desirable lands in outlying areas of Japan.

To ensure daimyo loyalty, Ieyasu set up a system called *sankin-kotai*, or attendance by turn. Each daimyo had to travel to Edo every other year, bringing tribute and remaining in the shogun's service for a full year. Thus, half the daimyos were directly under the shogun's control at any one time. Even when the daimyos returned to their estates, they had to leave their families at Edo as hostages.

The daimyos spent much of their income traveling to and from Edo and maintaining several households. They also had to get the shogun's permission to marry and to repair or build their castles. *Sankin-kotai* kept them weak, obedient to the shogun, and less able to rebel against the government. Much like Louis XIV of France, the shogun turned his aristocracy into courtiers who were carefully watched and controlled.

Political System

The Tokugawa family and a select group of daimyos controlled the government. Together they made up the Council of Elders, the leading administrative body. Assisting the Council, as the "eyes and ears" of the state, was a group of officials known as the *metsuke*. The *metsuke* toured the country and reported on possible uprisings or plots against the shogun. A genuine bureaucracy began to develop, working on the principles of joint decision making and promotion based on talent and success.

Social Classes

Before 1600 there had been some social mobility between classes in Japan. Hideyoshi and Ieyasu

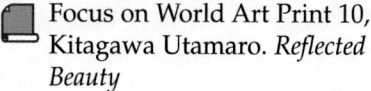

Visualizing History **As a member of a professional class of women, a geisha might serve a samurai in song or dance, by playing a musical instrument, or engaging in stimulating conversation.** *What were the symbols of authority permitted only to a samurai?*

Chapter 18 Section 3

TEACH

Guided Practice

THEME **Reaction**

Ask: **Who were the first Europeans to arrive in Japan? When?** *(the Portuguese; in 1543)*
How did the Japanese react to the Portuguese arrival, both initially and later on? *(Initially they welcomed the Westerners; eventually they forced them to leave and initiated a policy of isolation.)* **L1**

Geography Give each student an outline map of Japan. Have students label the major islands: Hokkaido, Honshu, Kyushu, and Shikoku. Then ask them to add these cities: Edo (Tokyo), Osaka, Kyoto, and Nagasaki. **L1 LEP**

Focus on World Art Print 10, Kitagawa Utamaro. *Reflected Beauty*

World Music: Cultural Traditions, Lesson 8

Visualizing History When a geisha married, she retired from the profession.

Answer to Caption: *a sword and a distinctive topknot in the hair*

COOPERATIVE LEARNING ACTIVITY

Presentation Have students develop presentations on the samurai. Organize the class into small groups and have each one choose a particular topic to research. Possible topics: the rise of samurai, famous samurai, clothing and armor, daily life, combat techniques (such as kendo). Have each group decide on the format of its presentation, such as lecture, bulletin-board display, role play, or drawings. Plan class time for the students to give their presentations. **L2**

Chapter 18 Section 3

Independent Practice

Guided Reading Activity 18-3 **L1**

Geography and History Activity 18

People in World History Profile 34

Art Have students use library resources to prepare a report on one of these Japanese artists: Hiroshige, Hokusai, or Utamaro. In their reports to the class, have them tell something about the artist, the style of art for which he was known, and the subject matter of his work. Encourage students to show examples of the artist's work. **L2**

Linking Past and Present

Kurosawa Feudal Japan has been brought to life in the movies of today. In dramatizing the past, few have excelled more than the great Japanese film director, Akira Kurosawa. His *Seven Samurai* tells the story of poor villagers who hire samurai to fight off bandits. Kurosawa's film was the basis for a popular American Western, *The Magnificent Seven*.

Visualizing History In the early 1700s, Edo's population of more than 1,000,000 made it the largest city in the world.
Answer to Caption: *samurai, farmers, artisans, and merchants*

had both risen to the top from lowly backgrounds. To maintain social stability and limit future rivals, they introduced measures that froze the Japanese social structure.

Under Tokugawa rule, the Japanese were divided into four social classes. At the top were the samurai, including the daimyos, who held all political power. They alone could wear symbols of authority: a sword and a distinctive topknot in their hair. The farmers, as major food producers, were the second-highest class. They were followed by artisans who made goods. Merchants were at the bottom of society, because they only exchanged goods and thus were not productive.

No one could change his social class or perform tasks that belonged to another class. One samurai recalled that his father took him out of school because he was taught arithmetic—a subject fit only for merchants. A character in a popular puppet play, written by the author Chikamatsu, described the proper order of society:

> "A samurai's child is reared by samurai parents and becomes a samurai himself because they teach him the warrior's code. A merchant's child is reared by merchant parents and becomes a merchant because they teach him the way of commerce. A samurai seeks a fair name in disregard for profit, but a merchant, with no thought to his reputation, gathers profit and amasses a fortune. This is the way of life proper to each. This strict social order helped maintain peace and stability throughout Japan."

Visualizing History **In Tokugawa Japan, cities became leading centers of Japanese culture. Artisans began to produce goods for a growing urban market.** *What social classes made up Tokugawa Japan?*

Tokugawa Ethics

Tokugawa ethics placed loyalty to the shogun above the family. Duty and honor became the central values. Individuals had to develop strict inner discipline to live up to the requirements of their assigned place in life. These values gradually spread from the samurai through all social classes in Japan.

Over the course of time, Tokugawa rules for personal conduct evolved into complex rituals and etiquette. Minute details came to have heavy symbolic meaning. They became a way to maintain conformity and control. This was important for a society that had a large population and only a small area of productive land.

Contacts With the West

The peace and order of the Tokugawa shogunate were interrupted when the first Europeans—the Portuguese—arrived in Japan in 1543. Although the Japanese looked upon Europeans as barbarians, the warrior society saw that European weapons meant power. They purchased muskets and cannon to defeat their opponents.

Roman Catholic missionaries soon followed the Portuguese merchants. **Francis Xavier**, the earliest of the Jesuit priests who came to Japan, admired the Japanese people. To convert them, the Jesuits adopted their customs. Jesuit missionaries learned the subtleties of conversing in polite Japanese and set up a tea room in their houses so that they could receive their visitors properly.

After Xavier won the support of some local daimyos, Christianity spread rapidly. Oda Nobunaga himself lent support to the Christians, for during this time he was moving against the Buddhist monasteries that were serving as military strongholds. Jesuits trained Japanese priests to create a strong Japanese Christian church. By 1614 the Jesuits had converted 300,000 Japanese.

Many Japanese welcomed the first contact with Westerners, whose customs and styles became widespread in Japanese society. Even for Japanese who had not converted to Christianity, Christian symbols became fashionable. A missionary described non-Christian daimyos who would wear "rosaries of driftwood on their breasts, hang a

MEETING SPECIAL NEEDS ACTIVITY

Study Strategy Textbooks such as this one often use boldface type to call attention to terms, people, and places students should remember. As students read this chapter, have them make a list of the words in boldface, together with an identifying phrase or sentence to help them recall why the word is important. **L1**

Visualizing History **Merchants from the West arrive in Japan accompanied by Jesuit missionaries.** *How did Christian missionary activity end under Tokugawa rule?*

crucifix from their shoulder or waist ... they think it good and effective in bringing success in daily life."

Hideyoshi began to suspect that Christian influence could be harmful to Japan. He had heard of Spanish missionaries in the Philippines who had helped establish Spain's control over the islands. In 1587 Hideyoshi outlawed Christianity. Although some priests were crucified, Hideyoshi generally did not enforce his ban on the religion.

Tokugawa Ieyasu and his successors also feared that Christianity threatened their power and so continued to persecute Christians, killing them or forcing them to leave Japan. When Japanese Christians in the port city of **Nagasaki** defied authorities and refused to disband, the government attacked their community in 1637 and finally wiped them out in 1638.

Seclusion Policy

The Tokugawa rulers, deciding that contact with outsiders posed too many dangers, laid down edicts. Their seclusion policy lasted 200 years. The Act of Seclusion of 1636 forbade any Japanese to leave the country and added, "All Japanese residing abroad shall be put to death when they return home." As the Chinese had done at an earlier time, the government banned construction of ships large enough for ocean voyages.

Japan barred all Europeans except the Dutch. Unlike the Spanish and the Portuguese, the Dutch were interested only in trade, not conquest or religious conversion of the Japanese. For this reason, after 1641 the Tokugawa government confined the Dutch to a tiny island in Nagasaki harbor where they and a few Chinese carried on a tightly regulated trade. Through the Dutch traders, a trickle of information about the West continued to flow into Japan.

Changes in Japanese Society

Despite Japan's geographic isolation and the Tokugawa policy of isolation, Japan's society and economy continued to change internally. During the early Tokugawa period, agriculture brought wealth to daimyos and samurai, who profited from the rice produced on their lands. Merchants, in turn, grew wealthy by lending money to daimyos and samurai.

Footnotes to History

Karate

Karate is unarmed combat in which a person uses primarily the hands or feet to strike a blow at an opponent. This martial art began on the island of Okinawa near Japan. During the 1600s, Okinawa's Japanese conquerors forbade the local people to own weapons. In response, many Okinawans learned to turn their hands and feet into fighting instruments.

Visualizing History One reason Christianity grew quickly in Japan was that when a daimyo adopted the faith, all the people subordinate to him did so, too.

Answer to Caption: *The shoguns outlawed Christianity, crucified some priests, and killed converts or forced them to emigrate.*

Compare Ask students to compare the Tokugawa period with the Renaissance in Europe. Have them include how the Japanese turned toward pleasure and away from the spirituality of Buddhism. This project can be in the form of a chart or a written report. **L3**

Who?What?Where?When?

Dutch Learning Western knowledge as transmitted through Dutch traders and books interested many Japanese. In 1811 the government established an official translation office, which came to be known as the Institute for the Investigation of Barbarian Books.

MAKING CONNECTIONS ACTIVITIES

Daily Life The Japanese inn, or *ryokan*, preserves many features of Japanese life as they have been for centuries. Have students research the subject and present their findings to the class. Travel guides to Japan would be a good source of information. **L2**

Art Have students research classical Japanese theater, including Noh and Kabuki. Have them use their findings to make a presentation to the class. Encourage students to use visual aids—pictures, photos, and if possible video footage—in their presentations. **L1 LEP**

Chapter 18
Section 3

CURRICULUM CONNECTION

THE ARTS

Japanese prints *(ukiyo-e)* influenced many European artists in the 1800s. Among the painters who admired and imitated their flat, decorative style were Vincent van Gogh, Henri de Toulouse-Lautrec, and Édouard Manet.

ASSESS

Check for Understanding

Assign Section 3 Review as homework or as an in-class activity.

Use Student Self-Test and Review Software to review Section 3.

Evaluate

Section Quiz 18-3

Reteach

Have students make charts for the Tokugawa era (1600–1868). Under headings such as *Government*, *Society*, and *Foreign Relations*, have them summarize the main events of this period.

Enrich

Have students read the classic *A Book of Five Rings* and prepare a brief book report, including biographical material about the author, Miyamoto Musachi.

CLOSE

Discuss Japan's location and how it furthered a policy of isolation. Ask students what would be different in our society if Japan had remained isolated. *(Answers may include that we would lack many innovative electronics products.)*

AROUND THE WORLD

First Public Opera House Opens

Venice, Italy, 1637

The Teatro San Cassano—the world's first public opera house—opened in Venice in 1637. Early baroque operas consisted of recitatives, or informational parts, sung by soloists accompanied by one or two instruments. The arias, or solos expressing a character's feelings, allowed opera singers to show off their vocal skills. By the late 1600s, operas were being written and performed in England, France, and Germany. Italian opera, however, remained the accepted style.

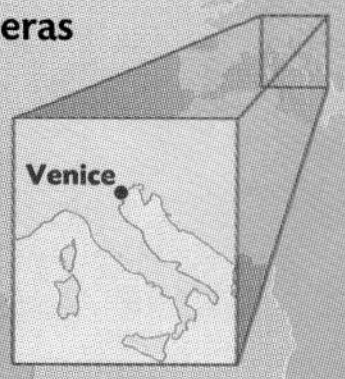

As the daimyos became a debtor class, the merchant class became more powerful.

The system of *sankin-kotai* also helped merchants to prosper and trade to increase, because merchants provided the goods and services that the daimyos needed on their twice-yearly trips to Edo. To smooth the daimyos' journey, the government built roads, which also made it easier for traders to take their goods to distant regions. Rest stations along the roads often grew into trading or administrative towns of considerable size.

At the same time, the demands for increased taxes led the daimyos to increase agricultural yields. As agriculture became more efficient, farming required fewer people. Unemployed farm workers moved to prosperous towns and cities, seeking work as artisans. In urban centers such as Edo, Kyoto, and Osaka, social order began to break down and class distinctions became less rigid.

Social life in the cities converged on bathhouses, restaurants, and theaters. Japanese merchants and samurai could relax in the company of geishas, women who were professional entertainers. Geishas were trained in the arts of singing, dancing, and conversation. Urban amusement centers also provided employment for playwrights, artists, and poets. At this time a new form of theater known as Kabuki developed. Kabuki became popular for its portrayal of historical events and emotion-filled domestic scenes. Another form of drama that arose during this period was the elaborate Japanese puppet theater called Bunraku, in which three-man teams manipulated each puppet as a backstage chorus sang a story.

A popular form of art called ukiyo-e developed from the demand for prints of famous actors and their plays. At first, ukiyo-e prints were black-and-white, but soon ornate, brightly colored prints appeared in street stalls. Printed on delicate rice paper, they are highly prized collectors' items today.

A new form of poetry called haiku (HY•koo) also became popular among city people. In only 17 syllables, the haiku was to express a thought that would surprise the reader. **Matsuo Basho**, one of the great haiku masters, wrote this haiku:

> “In my new clothing
> I feel so different
> I must
> Look like someone else.”

As cities grew in size and population during the 1700s and 1800s, the ban on foreign contacts was gradually relaxed. Some Japanese began to study Western medicine in books that the Dutch brought to Nagasaki. Their interest in the so-called Dutch learning spread to Western science and technology. However, it would not be until the other Europeans arrived in the 1800s that Japan would begin to absorb other Western ideas.

SECTION 3 REVIEW

Recall

1. **Define** *sankin-kotai*, *metsuke*, geisha, haiku.
2. **Identify** Oda Nobunaga, Toyotomi Hideyoshi, Tokugawa Ieyasu, Francis Xavier, Matsuo Basho.
3. **Describe** how the *sankin-kotai* system affected the daimyos. How did shoguns benefit from the system? How was the emperor affected?

Critical Thinking

4. **Synthesizing Information** Imagine that you lived in Japan during the Tokugawa shogunate. Which social class would you have wanted to belong to? Explain.

Understanding Themes

5. **Reaction** Explain why Japan reacted to Western ideas by adopting a policy of isolation. How did this reaction to outside influences affect Japan's development over the next few centuries?

SECTION 3 REVIEW ANSWERS

1. All vocabulary words are defined in the Glossary.
2. Oda Nobunaga, 468; Toyotomi Hideyoshi, 468; Tokugawa Ieyasu, 469; Francis Xavier, 470; Matsuo Basho, 472
3. It weakened the daimyos while strengthening the shoguns. The emperor, having little power to begin with, was probably not much affected.
4. Answers should reflect an understanding of social classes.
5. **REACTION** The Tokugawa rulers believed Western religious ideas were harmful; it prevented the Japanese from acquiring much knowledge of Western ideas and technology until the 1800s.

Critical Thinking SKILLS

Analyzing Primary and Secondary Sources

On the day of an earthquake, you see a television interview with an eyewitness to the event. Later you read a newspaper account of the earthquake. Is one account more accurate than the other?

Learning the Skill

To determine the accuracy of an account, you must analyze its source. There are two main kinds of sources—primary and secondary. Primary sources are accounts or artifacts produced by eyewitnesses to events. Diaries, autobiographies, interviews, artifacts, and paintings are primary sources. Secondary sources use information gathered from others. Textbooks and biographies are secondary sources. Because primary sources convey personal experiences, they often communicate the emotions and opinions of participants in an event. Secondary sources, written at a later time, often help us to understand events in a larger context.

After identifying the type of source, determine its reliability, or accuracy. For a primary source, find out who wrote it and when. An account written during or immediately after an event is more reliable than one written years later. For a secondary source, look for good documentation. In a reliable account, researchers cite their sources of information in footnotes and bibliographies.

For both types of sources, evaluate the author. Is this author biased? What background and authority does he or she have? Finally, compare two accounts of the same event. If they disagree, you should question their reliability.

Practicing the Skill

Read the two sources below and then answer the questions that follow.

> “A. No one can say for certain when or where the first telescope was invented, but everybody agrees that a telescope (Galileo's) existed in Italy by the year 1609. Within a few decades ... one of them was put to highly imaginative use in a piece of fiction ... [written] half a world away, in a provincial city in China ... [by] Li Yu.”
>
> —Patrick Hanan, Introduction to *A Tower for the Summer Heat*, 1992

> “B. One day Jiren went out to buy books with several of his friends. Walking past an antique shop, they noticed a strange-looking object on a stand … bearing a row of tiny characters:
> WESTERN THOUSAND-LI GLASS
> “What's this for?” they asked the shopkeeper.
> “If you look through it from some high place, you'll find that it brings the scenery into view for miles around.”
> “Impossible!” they exclaimed in disbelief.”
>
> —Li Yu, *A Tower for the Summer Heat*, 1657-1658

1. What is the general topic of the two sources?
2. Which is a primary source and which is a secondary source? How can you tell?
3. What does each tell you about this topic?

Applying the Skill

Find two accounts of a recent event or a historical event. The accounts may be primary sources, secondary sources, or one of each. Analyze the reliability of these sources. When were the accounts written? Is the author qualified to write on this topic? Is the account well-documented? Do the two accounts agree?

For More Practice

Turn to the Skill Practice in the Chapter Review on page 479 for more practice in analyzing primary and secondary sources.

Critical Thinking SKILLS

TEACH

Analyzing Primary and Secondary Sources Show the class several print advertisements and have students analyze the accuracy of the claims. **Why is it important to analyze information in advertisements?** *(Because ads try to sell products, they may not present the product objectively.)* Then tell students that, similarly, it is important to analyze the purpose and accuracy of all kinds of information.

Direct students to read the skill on page 473. **What is the difference between a primary and secondary source?** *(Primary sources are accounts or artifacts produced by eyewitnesses to events. Secondary sources use information gathered from others.)* **What are some examples of primary sources?** *(diaries, autobiographies, interviews, artifacts, and paintings)* **How can you analyze the content of a document?** *(Determine who created it, when and where it was created, its topic, and its purpose.)*

Skill Reinforcement Activity 18

ANSWERS TO PRACTICING THE SKILL

1. the "discovery" and use of the telescope by a group of Chinese boys
2. Source B is the primary source; it was excerpted from the actual novel. Source A is the secondary source; it came from the novel's introduction.
3. Source A explains that the telescope existed in China soon after its invention in Europe because the telescope is mentioned in a novel written at the time. Source B confirms the topic by stating Jiren and his friends saw the object in an antique store.

Chapter 18
Section 4

SECTION THEME

▶ **Change** Southeast Asian lands face the growth of European trade and commerce in their region.

Find Out

Answer: *Thai rulers encouraged competition among foreign nations so that no single one could gain control.*

FOCUS

Section Objective

Explain how the Thai kingdom was able to keep its independence while other parts of Southeast Asia gradually came under European control.

BELLRINGER Motivational Activity

Before taking roll at the beginning of the class period, project Section Focus Transparency 18-4 and have students answer the activity questions. Discuss students' responses.

This activity is also available as a blackline master.

Vocabulary Pre-check

Use the Vocabulary PuzzleMaker to create a puzzle that reinforces the vocabulary terms in this section. **L1**

1500	1700	1900
1511 Portuguese seize port of Melaka on the Malay Peninsula.	**1565** Spaniards found first colony in the Philippines.	**1767** Troops from Burma seize Ayutthaya.	**1868** Chulalongkorn becomes king of Siam.

Section 4

Southeast Asia

Setting the Scene

▶ **Terms to Define**
colony, *datus*, animism

▶ **People to Meet**
Trailok, Phraya Chakkri, Mongkut, Chulalongkorn

▶ **Places to Locate**
Manila, Java, Indochina, Bangkok

Find Out How was the Thai kingdom able to keep its independence while other parts of Southeast Asia gradually came under European control?

The Storyteller

The century-old Bayon Temple of Angkor swarmed with workers. Huge stone faces with faint, haunting smiles gazed in all directions. A European merchant stepped closer to examine the temple and nearly collided with a monk. When asked about the faces, the monk replied, "This old Hindu shrine will become a Buddhist temple. Jayavarman, our king, has adopted the Buddhist religion and wishes to introduce its teaching throughout our land. Sculptors have been commissioned to create new images on the temple. Most important is the image of boddhisattva, a compassionate being who looks everywhere for souls to save."

—freely adapted from *World History*, Volume 1, William Duiker and Jackson Spielvogel, 1994

Relief from Bayon Temple of Angkor

By the mid-1400s, Southeast Asia was carrying on extensive trade with other regions. This was partly because of its location on the water route between India and China. In addition, Southeast Asia produced valuable spices and woods that people in other parts of the world wanted to buy.

European Influences

In the early 1500s the first European explorers reached Southeast Asia in search of new trade routes and products. With the coming of the Europeans, Southeast Asian kingdoms faced a growing challenge to their independence and traditional ways of life.

The Portuguese Spice Trade

Coming from India, the Portuguese were the first Europeans to reach Southeast Asia in the early 1500s. They set out to control the region's lucrative spice trade which, for many years, had been controlled by Muslim traders. In 1511 Portuguese soldiers captured the most important of the Muslim ports—Melaka, on the west side of the Malay Peninsula.

During the next 25 years, the Portuguese built a number of new trading posts in Southeast Asia. They patrolled the seas near the islands of present-day Indonesia to keep out the ships of other countries. The Portuguese also tried to spread Catholicism in maritime Southeast Asia. They had little success, however, because most Southeast Asian islanders resented Portuguese disregard for their traditional cultures.

Spanish Rule in the Philippines

The Spaniards were eager to find their own route to the spices of Southeast Asia. In 1519 Ferdinand Magellan, exploring for Spain, reached Southeast Asia by sailing westward around the

SECTION RESOURCES

Reproducible Masters
- Reproducible Lesson Plan 18-4
- Guided Reading Activity 18-4
- Reteaching Activity 18
- Enrichment Activity 18
- Section Quiz 18-4
- Performance Assessment Activity 18
- Spanish Chapter Summary 18

Transparencies
- Section Focus Transparency 18-4

Multimedia
- Vocabulary PuzzleMaker Software
- Student Self-Test and Review Software
- Testmaker
- World Music: Cultural Traditions, Lesson 9

Visualizing History **During the 1600s, the Netherlands reached its height as a seafaring power. Dutch merchant ships sailed the seas from the Caribbean region to the East Indies (Indonesia).** *How did the Dutch win control of the Indonesian island of Java?*

southern tip of South America. Magellan and his crew landed in the Philippines, becoming the first Europeans to visit these islands.

In 1565 the Spanish founded their first colony, or overseas territory ruled by a parent country, in the Philippines. Although the Spanish did not find spices in the Philippines, they did find fertile land and an excellent location for trade. Spanish soldiers and officials established a fortified settlement at **Manila** on the island of Luzon. Manila's magnificent harbor made the Philippines a valuable link in Spain's trade with Asia and the Americas.

The Spaniards gradually expanded their control to other parts of the islands. They persuaded many of the *datus*, or local rulers, to pledge loyalty to Spain in return for keeping their regional powers. Under Spanish rule, most of the people of the Philippines—largely of Malay and Chinese descent—accepted many Spanish customs as well as the Roman Catholic faith. Spanish Roman Catholic clergy established missions, learned the local languages, taught the people European agricultural methods, and introduced new crops—such as maize (corn) and cocoa—from the Americas. Spain's control of the Philippines would last well into the late 1800s.

Dutch Traders in Indonesia

By the end of the 1500s, English and Dutch traders were also wanting a share in the Southeast Asian spice trade. After breaking Portuguese control of the trade, they began to fight each other. During the 1620s, the Dutch finally succeeded in forcing the English to leave the islands that now make up present-day Indonesia. A further step toward Dutch control of the islands came in 1677 when the ruler of Mataram, a kingdom on the island of **Java**, asked the Dutch to help him defeat a rebel uprising. In return for their assistance, the Dutch received important trading rights and

COOPERATIVE LEARNING ACTIVITY

Debate Organize the class into two groups representing advisers to a Southeast Asian ruler. Europeans, who have been trading with their country, now want to establish a colony there. One group should argue in favor of the colony while the other group opposes it. Each participant should contribute specific reasons in support of their group's stand. **L2**

TEACH

Guided Practice

THEME Change

Ask students to list the foreigners who brought change to Southeast Asia beginning in the 1500s. *(Portuguese, Spanish, English, Dutch, French)* What goal did they all have in common? *(trade)* **L1 LEP**

Geography Using a wall map or a map in the Atlas of this book, review with the class the geographical features of the Southeast Asian regions of special concern in this chapter: the Malay Peninsula, Indonesia, the Philippines, Indochina, Siam (Thailand), and Burma (Myanmar). **L2**

Visualizing History During the golden age of the Netherlands—the 1600s—this small country was among the most powerful and influential nations on the earth.
Answer to Caption: *using force to get the English to leave; gaining concessions from local rulers in exchange for their help*

Economics Discuss with students the advantages and disadvantages to a parent country of having colonies. *(advantages: control over subject peoples, assured source of raw materials, assured market for goods from the home country; disadvantages: need for supervision by parent country, drain on parent country's resources)* **L3**

World Music: Cultural Traditions, Lesson 9

Chapter 18 Section 4

Independent Practice

Guided Reading Activity 18-4 **L1**

Daily Life Have students, as Spanish settlers living in the Philippines in the 1600s, write to friends in Spain urging them to emigrate and explaining why life as a colonist offers a good future. **L2**

Government Have students research the present-day Chakkri ruler of Thailand. In brief reports, have them summarize his role and compare it with that of the founder of the dynasty, Phraya Chakkri. **L3**

Linking Past and Present

The King and I In the 1860s King Mongkut employed a Welsh governess, Anna Leonowens, to tutor his children. Her story was told in a popular book of the 1940s, *Anna and the King of Siam*. The book in turn served as the basis for the musical *The King and I*, two movies, and a television serial.

Visualizing History

In a single year, King Trailok had 500 statues of the Buddha cast, hoping to prevent a repetition of the great famine that had devastated his country the year before.

Answer to Caption: *Hinduism and animism*

Javanese lands. Through similar agreements and by force, the Dutch had gained control of most of the other Indonesian islands by the late 1700s.

The French in Vietnam

The French were latecomers in the European pursuit of trade and colonies in Southeast Asia. Beginning in the 1600s, French traders based in India carried out only limited trade with the Vietnamese and other peoples in the Southeast Asian region of **Indochina**. Because of the weakness of this trade link, the Vietnamese and their Indochinese neighbors were able to keep the French from taking control of their area. Roman Catholic missionaries from France, however, settled in Indochina and converted many Vietnamese to Christianity.

By the early 1800s most of Indochina was ruled by local emperors who came from the region of Annam in present-day Vietnam. At this time, Indochina was predominantly Chinese in culture. Devoted to Confucian ideas, the Annamese emperors persecuted their Christian subjects and tried to keep Indochina closed to Europeans. Angered at the policies of the Annamese court, the French in 1858 returned to Southeast Asia in force. Their stated purpose was to protect local Christians from persecution. However, they also wanted to rule Indochina. In the 1860s the French began to colonize the region.

The Thai Kingdom

While European influence grew throughout Southeast Asia, the independent kingdom of Ayutthaya (ah•YU•tuh•yuh) continued to flourish in the area that is present-day Thailand. Under a series of powerful kings, the Thai people of Ayutthaya developed a rich culture based on Buddhism, Hinduism, and animism, the idea that both living and nonliving things have spirits or souls.

Visualizing History **This bronze bas–relief of the Buddha reveals the important role that Buddhism has played in unifying the Thai people and in supporting their rulers.** *What other religious influences shaped the development of Thai culture?*

Trailok's Rule

One of the most powerful Ayutthaya monarchs was King **Trailok**, who ruled from 1448 to 1488. Trailok set up a strong central government with separate civil and military branches directly responsible to him. He also brought local leaders to Ayutthaya and put them in charge of new governmental offices. These officials were required to live in the capital where the king could easily oversee their work.

Trailok set up a rigid class system based on loyalty to the Thai monarchy. All male Thai were given the use of varying amounts of land according to their rank. Nobles and merchants were given as much as 4,000 acres (1,620 ha), while enslaved people, artisans, and other subjects with little status received 10 acres (4 ha) or less. Women were not included in this distribution of land.

Expansion

While the Ayutthaya kingdom set its internal affairs in order, Thai soldiers fought battles with neighboring peoples, such as the Khmer, Burmans, and Malays. Through conquests, the Ayutthaya kingdom grew to almost the size of present-day Thailand. In 1431 Thai soldiers from Ayutthaya captured Angkor Wat and destroyed it. They also overcame the Malays in the south as well as smaller Thai kingdoms in the north.

During the mid-1500s a border dispute led to war between the Ayutthaya kingdom and Burma (Myanmar). Soldiers from Burma briefly captured the city of Ayutthaya in 1569, but the Thai king Naresuan defeated Burma's ruler in the Battle of Nong Sarai in 1593.

European Contacts

The 1500s also saw the beginning of European contacts with Ayutthaya. The Portuguese and later the Dutch and the English sent delegations to the kingdom to encourage trade. For much of the 1600s, Thai rulers allowed Europeans the right to carry out trade in their territory. In 1612

MEETING SPECIAL NEEDS ACTIVITY

Learning Style: Kinesthetic Some students may need help understanding the nature of trade in Southeast Asia in early modern times. Organize the class into small groups and assign each one a Southeast Asian trade item, such as cloves, cinnamon, cassia, nutmeg, ebony, or rosewood. Have each group find an example of its item to bring to class. Also, have each group research its item, finding out where in the region it is from and how it was used by Europeans. **L1**

British traders took a letter from King James I to the Thai monarch. They reported back that the city of Ayutthaya, with its palaces and Buddhist temples, was as large and awesome as London.

The Thai, however, became concerned that Europeans wanted to colonize as well as trade. In 1688 a Thai group that opposed European influences took over the kingdom. The new rulers expelled most of the Europeans except for a few Dutch and Portuguese traders. The kingdom closed its ports to the West until 1826.

The Bangkok Era

Free of European influence, Thai rulers hoped for a period of calm. Burma, however, wanted to resume the conflict with Ayutthaya that it had lost in the late 1500s. In 1767 an army from Burma defeated the Thai and sacked and burned the city of Ayutthaya. The Thai, however, soon rallied after the disaster. Phraya Taksin (PRY•uh tahk•SEEN), a Thai general, led his troops against Burma's army and drove it out of the region.

After proclaiming himself king, Taksin forced rival Thai groups to accept his rule. He reigned until 1782, when rebel leaders overthrew him. The rebels called on General **Phraya Chakkri** (PRY•uh SHAH•kree) to be the new Thai monarch. Chakkri founded the royal dynasty that still rules Thailand today. Chakkri built a new capital called **Bangkok** on the Chao Phraya River. Under Chakkri's rule, the reborn Thai kingdom became known as Siam.

Reforming Monarchs

By the mid-1800s Europeans were pressuring Thai rulers to widen trade opportunities in Siam. King **Mongkut** recognized the threat that Western colonial nations posed to the independence of his kingdom. He moved quickly to protect Siam by setting foreign nations against one another through competition.

Mongkut achieved this goal by allowing many Western nations to have commercial opportunities in the kingdom. The Thai king welcomed what he judged to be the positive influences of Western commerce on his country. He encouraged his people to study science and European languages with the Christian missionaries who had accompanied European traders to the kingdom.

After Mongkut's death in 1868, his son **Chulalongkorn** (choo•lah•LAHNG•kohrn) came to the throne. Like Mongkut, Chulalongkorn worked to modernize Siam while protecting the kingdom from European controls. He ended slavery, founded schools, encouraged his people to study abroad, and built railways and roads.

Visualizing History **King Mongkut ruled Siam from 1851 to 1868. He increased the powers of the monarchy while supporting social reforms to improve the conditions of his subjects.** *How did Mongkut work to preserve Siam's independence?*

SECTION 4 REVIEW

Recall
1. **Define** colony, *datus*, animism.
2. **Identify** Melaka, Manila, Trailok, Phraya Chakkri, Bangkok, Mongkut, Chulalongkorn.
3. **Explain** why Southeast Asia was a region that attracted European explorers, traders, and missionaries during the 1500s and 1600s.

Critical Thinking
4. **Making Comparisons** How do you think the Spanish conquest of the Philippine Islands differed from the Portuguese conquest of the Indonesian islands?

Understanding Themes
5. **Change** How did the Thai kings Mongkut and Chulalongkorn respond to the growth of Western influence in their region?

SECTION 4 REVIEW ANSWERS

1. All vocabulary words are defined in the Glossary.
2. Melaka, 474; Manila, 475; Trailok, 476; Phraya Chakkri, 477; Bangkok, 477; Mongkut, 477; Chulalongkorn, 477
3. It was strategically located between India and China, and it had desirable natural resources.
4. The Spanish established colonies, not just trading posts. Also, they had more success in spreading Christianity.
5. **CHANGE** Both welcomed some Western education and innovations but also protected Siam from foreign control.

Chapter 18 Section 4

Visualizing History Mongkut spent 25 years as a monk before he became king. He also studied Latin, English, mathematics, and astronomy.
Answer to Caption: *By giving commercial opportunities to many different nations, he set them against one another and thus reduced their power.*

ASSESS

Check for Understanding

Assign Section 4 Review as homework or as an in-class activity.

Use Student Self-Test and Review Software to review Section 4.

Evaluate

Section Quiz 18-4

Use the Testmaker to create a customized quiz for Section 4.

Reteach

Have students review the role of European traders in Southeast Asia.

Reteaching Activity 18

Enrich

Have students research and report on the death of Magellan in the Philippine Islands.

Enrichment Activity 18

CLOSE

Have students summarize how Southeast Asia in the late 1800s differed from what it had been in the early 1500s.

Chapter 18 Review

GLENCOE TECHNOLOGY

VIDEODISC

Use MindJogger to review students' knowledge of the chapter.

MindJogger Videoquiz

Chapter 18
Disc 3 Side A

Also available in VHS.

Answers

Using Key Terms

1. h	**6.** d
2. f	**7.** c
3. g	**8.** j
4. e	**9.** b
5. i	**10.** k

Using Your History Journal

Remind students that they should back up any generalizations they make with specific details about the people or places they write about.

Reviewing Facts

1. Ottoman, Safavid (Persian), Mogul
2. The Ottomans were Sunni Muslims; the Persians were Shiites and bitter enemies of the Ottomans.
3. The Moguls were Muslims, unlike their Hindu subjects. Rulers like Akbar were tolerant, but later Moguls persecuted Hindus.
4. to display China's wealth and power and to obtain trade and tribute
5. staffed army with Manchus; reserved top government jobs for Manchus; had Manchus monitor Chinese officials; enforced Manchu hair and clothing styles
6. Oda Nobunaga, Toyotomi Hideyoshi, Tokugawa Ieyasu
7. to ensure the loyalty of the daimyos

Critical Thinking

1. The Safavids, as Shiite Muslims, were bitterly opposed to the Ottomans, who were Sunnis.
2. yes; because of his work in organizing Ottoman laws
3. Akbar invited representatives of all faiths to his court because he was curious about different religions. The Manchus allowed Christian missionaries into China but were only interested in their scientific knowledge.
4. Answers should reflect knowledge of the various governments.
5. The Moguls (who were Muslims) conquered northern India, initiating a continuing

CHAPTER 18 REVIEW

Historical Significance

From 1350 to 1850 many social and political changes came to Asia. Islam continued to expand and reached South Asia as a result of the Mogul invasions. Despite efforts at toleration, conflicts developed between Muslims and Hindus that still divide South Asia today.

During the early modern period, China turned inward instead of meeting the challenge of the West. Japan and Siam at first took the same route; however, they eventually introduced reforms that preserved their freedom. In Japan's case, reforms also enabled it to compete successfully with Western countries.

Using Key Terms

Write the key term that completes each sentence.

a. geisha	g. labor-intensive farming
b. grand vizier	h. sultan
c. haiku	i. queue
d. janissaries	j. *datus*
e. *sankin-kotai*	k. *millets*
f. colony	

1. The Ottoman leader Suleiman I acted as both the ______, or political ruler, and the caliph, or religious leader.
2. In 1565 the Spaniards established their first __________ in the Philippine Islands.
3. During the Manchu dynasty, the Chinese practiced __________ in which workers dug flat terraces into hillsides to grow rice.
4. To ensure daimyo loyalty, shoguns followed a system called _________ that required each daimyo to travel to the capital every other year.
5. In 1645 the Manchu emperor ordered all Chinese men to shave their heads leaving a _____ at the back of their heads.
6. Ottoman sultans maintained a special corps of soldiers known as _________ who were noted as a fierce and loyal fighting force.
7. Japanese writers developed ________, a form of poetry made up of 17 syllables, that became popular among city people.
8. Spaniards made agreements with ______, or local chieftains in the Philippines, in which the chieftains pledged loyalty to Spain in return for keeping their regional powers.
9. A _______ headed the bureaucracy that enforced the ruler's decisions throughout the Ottoman Empire.
10. Ottoman law allowed religious groups to run affairs in their own __________, or communities.

Using Your History Journal

From your notes and outline write a two- to three-page paper on Timur Lenk, Akbar, The Forbidden City, The Imperial Palace, or The Samurai.

Reviewing Facts

1. **Name** the three great Muslim empires in eastern Europe, central Asia, and India.
2. **Define** the relationship between Sunni Muslims and Shiite Muslims living in the Ottoman Empire and the Persian Empire.
3. **Explain** how the Moguls' religion brought them into conflict with the majority of India's people. Describe how Mogul rulers dealt with this conflict.
4. **Explain** the purpose of the voyages of Zheng He.
5. **List** the steps taken by the Manchus to maintain their control over China.
6. **Name** the generals that unified Japan.
7. **Discuss** why the Tokugawa shoguns enforced the policy of *sankin-kotai.*

Critical Thinking

1. **Apply** How did religious differences cause strife between Muslim empires?
2. Would you consider Suleiman I a successful ruler? Why was he called "The Lawgiver" by the Ottomans?
3. **Analyze** How did Akbar's religious tolerance in India differ from that of the Manchus in China?

4. **Evaluate** Which government described in this chapter was most successful in meeting its people's needs? Why?
5. **Evaluate** How did the movement of Islamic peoples affect northern India? What impact did Islam have on religion in this part of India?
6. **Analyze** What factors led to China's growth in both land and population during the Qing dynasty? How did government policies contribute to this growth?
7. **Evaluate** Was the Ming dynasty's policy of isolationism beneficial to China? Explain.
8. **Analyze** How did new urban centers in Japan influence growth in the arts and entertainment?

Geography in History

1. **Region** Refer to the map below that shows the political divisions of Japan about 1560. For more than a century, feudal lords fought for control of territory. How many Daimyo clans ruled in Japan during this period?
2. **Location** What is the relative location of the Takeda domains?
3. **Human/ Environment Interaction** What geographic conditions helped make it possible for Japan to enforce a policy of isolation from the rest of the world in the 1600s?

Civil War in Japan

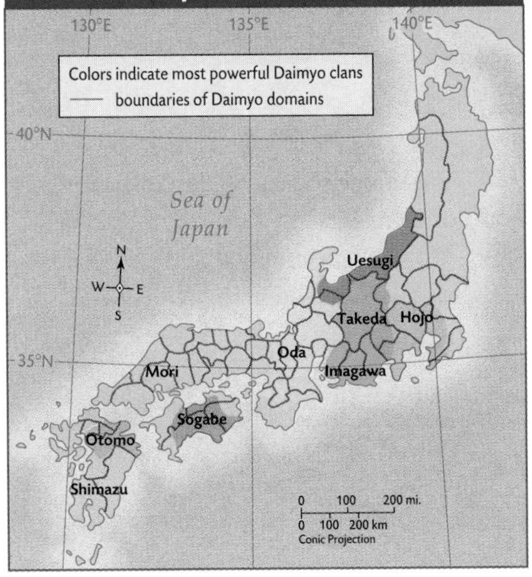

Understanding Themes

1. **Movement** What areas of Asia came under the rule of the Muslim empires?
2. **Cultural Diffusion** How did Christianity spread to China?
3. **Reaction** What good and bad effects resulted from Japan's policy of isolation?
4. **Change** What development was crucial in advancing Dutch control of the islands of Indonesia?

Linking Past and Present

1. Do you think it is possible for today's nations to follow a policy of isolation like Japan's in the early modern period? Have any tried to?
2. From the 1300s to the 1800s powerful Asian rulers took drastic measures to implement changes that they supported. Is a powerful ruler or a strong central government necessary today for technological advance and economic prosperity? Why or why not?

Skill Practice

Read the following excerpt and answer the questions.

> "The Tokugawa rulers officially divided the Japanese people into four classes. At the top were the samurai. The farmers were the second-highest class. They were followed by artisans who made goods. Merchants were at the bottom of society.
>
> A character in a popular puppet play [from that time], written by the author Chikamatsu, described the proper order of society:
>
> 'A samurai's child is reared by samurai parents and becomes a samurai himself because they teach him the warrior's code.'"

1. Which part of this passage is a primary source? How can you tell?
2. Which part of this passage is a secondary source? How can you tell?
3. Do you think Chikamatsu is a reliable source on this topic? Why?
4. Does the information in the two accounts agree?

conflict between Hinduism and Islam.

6. Manchus made conquests in the north and west; its population increased because of peace and improvements in agriculture.
7. yes; the Ming had the funds to fight off nomadic tribes because they had stopped putting money into ocean voyages
8. As cities grew and class divisions weakened, there was a larger market for entertainment.

Geography in History

1. nine
2. south of Uesugi territory, north of Imagawa lands, west of Hojo domains
3. It is an island nation.

Understanding Themes

1. **MOVEMENT** western Asia and South Asia

Chapter 18 Review

2. **CULTURAL DIFFUSION** via Jesuit missionaries
3. **REACTION** Good: internal trade thrived and merchants became wealthy; roads were built; towns grew. Bad: Japan did not absorb many Western ideas until the 1800s.
4. **CHANGE** The ruler of Mataram asked for Dutch help in putting down rebels.

Linking Past and Present

1. Isolation is harder today because of modern communications; Albania, Cambodia, and North Korea.
2. Answers will vary.

Skill Practice

1. the quote; written by the author
2. first paragraph; written by a historian
3. yes; the author lived at that time
4. yes; samurai class stays isolated at the top of society

Chapter Bonus Test Question

Ask students: In your view, what is the most important difference between the Muslim empires of western and South Asia and the older cultures of East Asia? *(Possible answers: In the former, Islam was a driving force, while in the latter, people maintained other religious traditions. The western and South Asian empires, at least in the beginning, resulted from expansive, outward thrusts; in East Asia, civilizations turned inward.)*

Teach, Reinforce, and Extend CHAPTER Content

Royal Power and Conflict

CHAPTER RESOURCES

	Reproducible Resources	Multimedia Resources
Chapter Opener	Chapter Themes: Graphic Organizer 19 Historical Significance Chapter Activity 19	MindJogger Videoquiz
Chapter Enrichment	Vocabulary Activity 19* Time Line Activity 19 Mapping History Activity 19 History Simulation 19 Geography and History Activity 19 Source Reading 19 People in World History Profiles 35, 36 World Art and Music Activity 19 Enrichment Activity 19 Critical Thinking Activity 19 Skill Reinforcement Activity 19 Performance Assessment Activity 19	Focus on World Art Print 19, Jan Steen. *The Dancing Couple*; 20, Jean-Baptiste Simeon Chardin. *The Attributes of Painting* World History and Art Transparency 26, *The French Ambassadors*; 22, *View of Toledo* Chapter Transparency 19 Vocabulary PuzzleMaker Software Picture Atlas of the World World Music: Cultural Traditions, Lesson 3
Chapter Review/Reteaching	Reteaching Activity 19 Skill Reinforcement Activity 19 Spanish Chapter Summary 19	Chapter 19 Digest Audiocassette, Activity, Test* Vocabulary PuzzleMaker Software Student Self-Test and Review Software MindJogger Videoquiz
Chapter Evaluation/Testing	Performance Assessment Activity 19 Chapter 19 Test, Forms A and B	Testmaker

* *Also available in Spanish*

0:00 **OUT OF TIME?** Assign the Chapter 19 summary in the Unit 4 Digest on pages 506–509, and the Chapter 19 Audiocassettes.

Block Schedule

Block scheduling differs from traditional class scheduling in the amount of time allotted to each period. The extended time frame provided by block scheduling affords you the opportunity to implement a greater number of research-oriented and activity-intense projects to motivate and involve your students. Activities that are particularly suited to use within the block scheduling framework are identified throughout this chapter by the following designation.

KEY TO ABILITY LEVELS

Teaching strategies have been coded for varying learning styles and abilities.

- L1 **BASIC** activities for all students
- L2 **AVERAGE** activities for average to above-average students
- L3 **CHALLENGING** activities for above-average students
- LEP **LIMITED ENGLISH PROFICIENCY** activities

A complete, 1-page lesson plan is provided for each section in the *Reproducible Lesson Plans* booklet.

SECTION RESOURCES

Daily Objectives	Reproducible Resources	Multimedia Resources
Section 1 Spain Explain why Philip II and other Spanish monarchs had difficulty ruling the Spanish Empire.	Reproducible Lesson Plan 19-1 Vocabulary Activity 19* Guided Reading Activity 19-1* Time Line Activity 19 Geography and History Activity 19 Section Quiz 19-1*	Section Focus Transparency 19-1 Chapter Transparency 19 Student Self-Test and Review Software Testmaker
Section 2 England Recognize how Tudor monarchs influenced English and European affairs.	Reproducible Lesson Plan 19-2 Vocabulary Activity 19* Guided Reading Activity 19-2* Section Quiz 19-2*	Section Focus Transparency 19-2 World History and Art Transparency 22, *View of Toledo* Student Self-Test and Review Software Testmaker World Music: Cultural Traditions, Lesson 3
Section 3 France Describe the kind of monarchy that developed in France under the Bourbon monarchs.	Reproducible Lesson Plan 19-3 Vocabulary Activity 19* Guided Reading Activity 19-3* Section Quiz 19-3*	Focus on World Art Print 20, Jean-Baptiste Simeon Chardin. *The Attributes of Painting* Section Focus Transparency 19-3 World History and Art Transparency 26, *The French Ambassadors* Student Self-Test and Review Software Testmaker
Section 4 The German States Examine how the Thirty Years' War differed from prior European wars.	Reproducible Lesson Plan 19-4 Vocabulary Activity 19* Guided Reading Activity 19-4* Section Quiz 19-4*	Focus on World Art Print 19, Jan Steen. *The Dancing Couple* Section Focus Transparency 19-4 Student Self-Test and Review Software Testmaker
Section 5 Russia Understand how the power of Russian czars differed from that of other European monarchs.	Reproducible Lesson Plan 19-5 Guided Reading Activity 19-5* History Simulation 19 Reteaching Activity 19 Enrichment Activity 19 Section Quiz 19-5* Performance Assessment Activity 19 Spanish Chapter Summary 19	Section Focus Transparency 19-5 Vocabulary PuzzleMaker Software Student Self-Test and Review Software Testmaker Picture Atlas of the World

** Also available in Spanish*

Chapter Activities

Performance Assessment Activity

A Resume for a Political Candidate After students have studied the leaders in this chapter, have them think about their qualities and actions and then consider what they believe is required of our government leaders today. Each student should create a resume for a candidate for current office based on what they know of the real leaders presented in the chapter, choosing the qualities and actions that best support their vision for modern times. The task may be extended by having students make visual representations of their ideal candidates. Students should include a reflection that defines their vision of those qualities needed in a candidate today and why they chose specific qualities.

Possible Rubric Features
Accuracy of content information, appropriateness of choices for vision communicated, organization and format of resume, argumentation and level of support for qualities and actions chosen

• *For an additional activity, refer to Activity 19 in the* Performance Assessment Strategies and Activities *booklet.*

Activity

From the Classroom of...

Allan Solomonson
West High School
Wausau, WI

Power of Monarchs

Help students understand how monarchs consolidated their power and how they ensured that their monarchies would survive into the next generation.

Write the following words on an overhead transparency, the chalkboard, or a worksheet: *prestige, privilege, organization, personality, diplomacy, opulence, conflict.* Give each student a half sheet of paper or a large note card. Have them select the word that most accurately describes a monarch of their choosing. Using the paper or note card, students should write a short essay explaining why that word is most appropriate. This can be done in class or as a homework assignment.

Use the ideas of the students as a springboard for a discussion on the power of monarchs of this era. For example, ask students to consider what legacy these monarchs left that enabled the monarchy or the nation to survive.

MULTIPLE LEARNING STYLES

Verbal/Linguistic
Have students discuss and evaluate the positive and negative aspects of Louis XIV's reign.

Logical/Mathematical
Have students use the maps in this chapter to compute and compare the approximate areas of the Spanish Hapsburgs, Austrian Hapsburgs, Holy Roman Empire, Dutch Netherlands, and Brandenburg-Prussia at their largest.

Visual/Spatial
Have students create a mural that depicts major events in the reigns of Elizabeth I, Philip II, Louis XIV, and Peter the Great.

Kinesthetic
Have students draw a large outline map of Europe and hang it on the bulletin board. Using tacks and labels, identify the Hapsburg territories.

Additional Resources

TEACHER'S CORNER

NATIONAL GEOGRAPHIC SOCIETY

INDEX TO NATIONAL GEOGRAPHIC MAGAZINE

The following articles may be used for research relating to this chapter:

- "St. Petersburg: Capital of the Tsars," by Steve Raymer, December 1993.
- "Inside the Kremlin," by Jon Thompson, January 1990.
- "Shakespeare Lives at the Folger," by Merle Severy, February 1987.
- "Legacy from the Deep: Henry VIII's Lost Warship," by Margaret Rule, May 1983.

NATIONAL GEOGRAPHIC SOCIETY PRODUCTS AVAILABLE FROM GLENCOE

To order the following products for use with this chapter, contact your local Glencoe sales representative or call Glencoe at 1-800-368-7344:

CD-ROM
- Picture Atlas of the World

BIBLIOGRAPHY

Literature of the Period

Shakespeare, William. ***The Riverside Shakespeare.*** Boston: Houghton Mifflin, 1974. Authoritative collection of Shakespeare's complete works, including historical background.

Readings for the Student

Dumas, Alexandre. ***The Three Musketeers.*** Translated by Jacques Le Clercq. New York: Random House, 1950. Exaggerated tale of swashbucklers in France during the reign of Louis XIII.

Readings for the Teacher

Fraser, Antonia. ***The Weaker Vessel.*** New York: Knopf, 1984. An exploration of women's roles in seventeenth-century England.

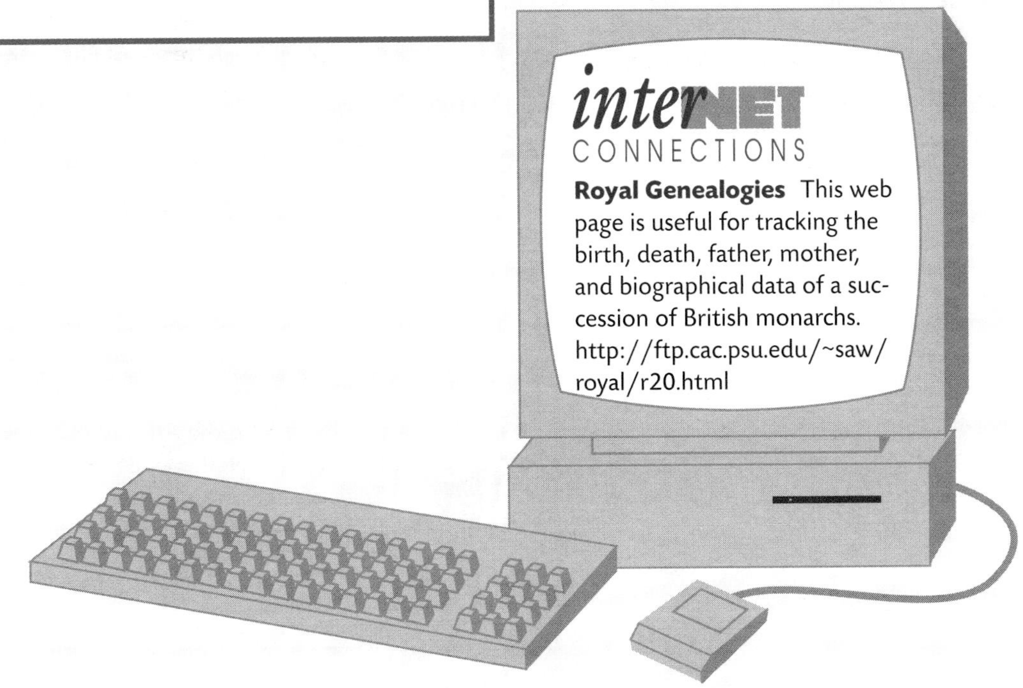
interNET
CONNECTIONS
Royal Genealogies This web page is useful for tracking the birth, death, father, mother, and biographical data of a succession of British monarchs. http://ftp.cac.psu.edu/~saw/royal/r20.html

Introducing Chapter 19

CHAPTER THEMES

Chapter Themes are listed by section on this chapter opening page of the Student Edition. A corresponding theme-based activity is available under "TEACH," and a theme-based question is asked in the Section and Chapter Reviews.

The Storyteller

Historical Setting The opening text reveals one view of the social life of the upper class during the reign of Louis XIV. An evening at Versailles generally began at 6:00 P.M. and could last until 8:00 A.M. the next morning. During that time, activities might include eating two suppers, attending a comedy and a ballet, and dancing at a ball.

It is not surprising that Louis's sister-in-law went hunting—Louis kept 1,000 hounds at Versailles for that sport. France's poor, on the other hand, spent their days working on the estates of the rich, plowing fields, or working in cities at any job that would assure them food to eat and a roof over their heads.

Historical Significance

Answers: *Monarchs tried to strengthen the power of the throne, build up the national economy, and increase military strength. In Spain and France, monarchs also tried to promote a national culture.*

French expansion led to wars with Spain, the Netherlands, and Austria. Russian expansion led to wars with Poland, Sweden, and the Ottoman Empire.

Chapter 19

1500–1750

Royal Power and Conflict

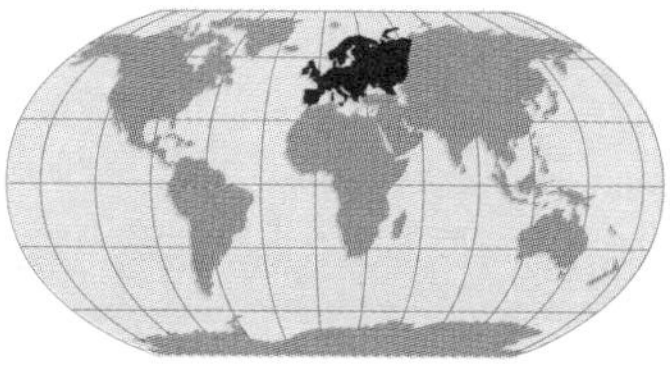

Chapter Themes

- **Conflict** Spanish and English monarchs engage in a dynastic struggle. *Section 1*
- **Change** Tudor monarchs bring stability and prosperity to England. *Section 2*
- **Uniformity** France's Louis XIV strengthens absolute monarchy in France and limits rights of religious dissenters. *Section 3*
- **Conflict** Dynastic and religious conflicts divide the German states. *Section 4*
- **Innovation** Peter the Great attempts to modernize Russian society. *Section 5*

The Storyteller

"We hunted all morning, got back around 3 o'clock in the afternoon, changed, went up to gamble until 7 o'clock, then to the play, which never ended before 10:30, then on to the ball until 3 o'clock in the morning.... So you see how much time I had for writing."

Princess Elizabeth-Charlotte, sister-in-law of France's King Louis XIV, described court life at the Palace of Versailles in a letter to a friend as an endless round of social activities. A man of tremendous energy and drive, Louis routinely devoted eight or nine hours daily to matters of state, regularly rode and hunted, ate with great enthusiasm, and expected courtiers, or members of his court, to do the same as well.

Historical Significance

How did monarchs build strong nation-states in early modern Europe? How did their efforts in national expansion contribute to Europe's legacy of territorial disputes and wars?

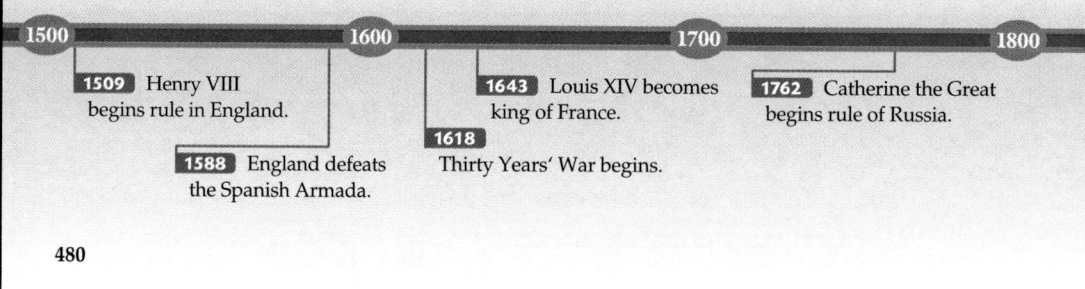

1500 — 1600 — 1700 — 1800

1509 Henry VIII begins rule in England.

1588 England defeats the Spanish Armada.

1618 Thirty Years' War begins.

1643 Louis XIV becomes king of France.

1762 Catherine the Great begins rule of Russia.

480

GEOGRAPHY CONNECTION

Location Use the Atlas to review with students the locations of England, Spain, Prussia, the Netherlands, Russia, Austria, and France. What is unique about England's geographical situation? *(England is an island.)* In what way is Russia different from other European countries? *(Russia covers a vast amount of land.)*

Visualizing History The vast palace and grounds of Versailles lie outside of Paris, France. Versailles was home to France's monarchs and the royal court during the late 1600s and most of the 1700s.

Your History Journal

Choose a country from this chapter. As you read the section, create a time line of important events between 1500 and 1750. Include the reigning monarchs, expansions of territory, laws, and conflicts.

EXTRA CREDIT PROJECT

Essay Many great writers wrote during the period covered here. These include Corneille, Racine, and Molière (France); Shakespeare (England); Cervantes (Spain); and Goethe (Prussia). Have students read excerpts from the works of two of these writers and write an essay comparing and contrasting their style and themes. Students may also draw conclusions, if warranted, about how any differences or similarities in the writers' styles reflect differences or similarities in the political, economic, and social life of the writers' homelands. **L3**

Introducing Chapter 19

Visualizing History Versailles was so expensive to build that Louis XIV destroyed some of the bills to avoid criticism from his ministers. On several occasions during his reign, it was the scene of elaborate and enormously expensive festivals that lasted for as long as a week.

Performance Assessment

Refer to the activity on page 480C of the Planning Guide.

For an additional activity, refer to Activity 19 in the *Performance Assessment Strategies and Activities* booklet.

Using Your History Journal

After students have finished their time lines, have them research the topic they find the most important or most interesting.

GLENCOE TECHNOLOGY

VIDEODISC
Use MindJogger to preview chapter content.

MindJogger Videoquiz
Chapter 19
Disc 3 Side A

Also available in VHS.

Chapter 19
Section 1

SECTION THEME

- **Conflict** Spanish and English monarchs engage in a dynastic struggle.

Find Out

Answer: *There was no uniform system of government; Philip faced opposition from Protestants, and costly wars damaged the economy.*

FOCUS

Section Objective

Explain why Philip II and other Spanish monarchs had difficulty ruling the Spanish Empire.

BELLRINGER
Motivational Activity

Before taking roll at the beginning of the class period, project Section Focus Transparency 19-1 and have students answer the activity questions. Discuss students' responses.

This activity is also available as a blackline master.

Vocabulary Pre-check

Use Vocabulary Activity 19 to introduce vocabulary terms.
L1 LEP

1500	1550	1600	1650

1556 Philip II becomes king of Spain.

1580 Portugal comes under Spanish rule.

c. 1590s Aragon revolts against Castilian control.

1647 Plague kills thousands of Spaniards.

Section 1

Spain

Setting the Scene

- **Terms to Define**
  absolutism, divine right, armada, inflation
- **People to Meet**
  Philip II, the Marranos, the Moriscos, Charles II
- **Places to Locate**
  Madrid

Find Out Why did Philip II and other Spanish monarchs have difficulty ruling the Spanish Empire?

The Storyteller

The Duke of Alva's son, ten-year-old Alejandro, was ecstatic. He had been appointed as a page to King Philip—an excellent beginning to a career with the Spanish court. Alejandro would learn to fence and to perform feats of horsemanship, as well as the rudiments of reading and writing. In five or six years, when he completed his education, Alejandro would become a member of His Majesty's court and would be expected to serve at arms. That position was the fulfillment of most young men's desires. If he proved himself truly outstanding, he might become one of Philip's personal attendants, a position usually reserved for the sons of princes.

—from *Charles V and Philip His Son*, Marino Cavalli, reprinted in *The Portable Renaissance Reader*, Mary Martin McLaughlin, 1977

Philip II

In the 1500s and 1600s, the monarchs of Europe worked to end the independence of cities and feudal territories. They sought to create powerful kingdoms in which the loyalties of all their subjects would be directed to the Crown. The authority of such rule was based on **absolutism**, a form of government with unlimited power held by one individual or a group (such as a monarch and his or her advisers). Its strength came from the political theory popular in the 1500s and 1600s that a king or queen ruled by **divine right**—the belief that a ruler derived absolute, or complete, authority to govern directly from God and was responsible to God alone for his or her actions. Centralized rule, it was reasoned, would serve as a unifying force and bring about greater efficiency and control.

For most of this period, the Hapsburgs of Spain were the leading power of western Europe. They drew their strength from their possessions in the Americas and Europe, which included Spain, the Netherlands, Milan, Burgundy, and after 1580, Portugal. The Spanish Hapsburgs tried to increase their empire's prestige and wealth but faced unrest and opposition to their absolute rule.

Philip II

Philip II, who ruled from 1556 to 1598, was the most powerful monarch in Spanish history. A devout Catholic, Philip saw himself as the leading defender of the faith. His efforts to end Protestantism in his domains made him the enemy of all Protestants. Son of the Holy Roman Emperor Charles V and Isabella of Portugal, Philip worked to increase the Hapsburg family's power throughout Europe. This effort led Philip to involve Spain in a number of costly European wars.

Known as the Prudent King, Philip II was cautious, hardworking, and suspicious of others. He built a granite palace called El Escorial, which

SECTION RESOURCES

Reproducible Masters
- Reproducible Lesson Plan 19-1
- Vocabulary Activity 19
- Guided Reading Activity 19-1
- Time Line Activity 19
- Geography and History Activity 19
- Section Quiz 19-1

Transparencies
- Section Focus Transparency 19-1
- Chapter Transparency 19

Multimedia
- Student Self-Test and Review Software
- Testmaker

served as royal court, art gallery, monastery, and tomb for Spanish royalty. There Philip spent most of his time at his desk, carefully reading and responding to hundreds of documents that poured in from all over the empire. He used councils of bureaucrats to advise him and to handle routine matters, but he made all decisions and signed all papers that he received.

Unrest

Philip II faced many difficulties in ruling Spain and his vast European and overseas empire. The provinces of Spain had been officially united when Ferdinand of Aragon married Isabella of Castile in 1469. A uniform system of government for the country had not been established, however. Separate laws and provincial authorities were allowed to remain. The ways of the Castile region came to dominate Spanish life. In the 1500s Castile had the most territory, the largest population, and the greatest wealth of all the Spanish territories.

Philip II made Castile the center of Spain and the empire. **Madrid**, located in Castile, became the capital. The Castilian, or literary, form of Spanish was spoken at the royal court. Most of Philip's advisers came from Castile. Trade from the overseas empire was controlled by the Castilian city of Seville, and Castilian merchants benefited most from trade. Leaders in Aragon and other Spanish provinces resented the dominance of Castile, and in the 1590s Aragon revolted. The revolt was put down, but discontent continued into the 1600s.

Religious Policy

Philip had to deal with a number of troubling religious issues in his European domains. He was concerned about the loyalty of large religious minorities in Spain. These minorities included Protestants, **the Marranos** (Jews who had converted to Christianity), and **the Moriscos** (Muslims who had become Christians). Philip supported the Inquisition's efforts to uproot the heresies believed to exist among these groups. He personally attended several *autos da fé,* the elaborate public rituals of sentencing usually followed by executions. The Inquisition was so thorough that Protestantism never took hold in Spain. Its actions, however, led to a revolt by the Moriscos in 1569. The revolt was brutally crushed two years later.

In 1567, when Philip had sought to impose Catholicism on the Netherlands, Dutch Protestants rebelled against his rule. This conflict proved to be long, bloody, and complex. The Dutch declared their independence in 1581, but the fighting continued. England gave support to the Dutch and to the English "sea dogs" who raided Spanish ships in their ports.

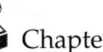

Visualizing History **The Spanish Armada entered the English Channel in late July, 1588.**
Why did the defeat of the Spanish Armada mark a turning point in European history?

Spanish Armada

Philip's empire faced a growing challenge from Protestant England. In the early years of his reign, Philip had supported Elizabeth I as queen of England, in spite of the pope's opposition. When Elizabeth helped Protestant rebels in the Netherlands, Philip decided that to solve his problems with the Netherlands, he had to rid himself of Elizabeth first.

In 1586 Philip laid plans to invade England. For two years the wealth and talent of his empire went toward that effort. On May 30, 1588, a force of 130 ships and 33,000 men, known as the Spanish Armada, sailed for England. An **armada** is a fleet of warships organized to carry out a mission.

In late July the Spanish Armada entered the English Channel in crescent formation. The English had faster, more maneuverable ships and longer-range cannons than did the Spanish. Yet they were unable at first to block the Spanish formation. English fire ships, however, were able to separate the Spanish ships. Running out of shot and desperately short of water, the Spanish fleet was forced to retreat to the stormy North Sea. After circling the northern tip of Great Britain, about 40 Spanish ships later sank in the Irish Sea near the rocky coasts of Scotland and Ireland. As many as 15,000 Spanish soldiers were killed.

TEACH

Guided Practice

THEME **Conflict**

Ask students to identify the conflict that underlay Philip's struggles both at home and abroad. *(the conflict between Philip's Roman Catholic faith and Protestantism)* **L1**

Visualizing History The Spanish ships varied in size and condition. There were transport ships, freighters, dispatch boats, and small cruisers. Still, they made up the greatest sea force Europe had ever seen. **Answer to Caption:** *It marked the beginning of Spain's decline as a European power.*

Geography Have students identify the Holy Roman Empire, Hapsburg holdings, and England on the map on page 484. On the basis of geographic area, ask students to speculate whether the Spanish or English monarchs would be most powerful by the beginning of the 1600s. **L2**

Chapter Transparency 19

Independent Practice

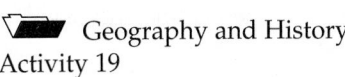

Guided Reading Activity 19-1 **L1**

Time Line Activity 19

Geography and History Activity 19

The Arts Two of Spain's greatest artistic geniuses lived during the reign of Philip II: the writer Cervantes and the painter El Greco. Have students write a brief biography of one of these artists or another artist of the period. **L2**

COOPERATIVE LEARNING ACTIVITY

Research Organize students into three groups. Have each group research and write a report about one of the Spanish minorities during Philip II's reign—Protestants, Marranos, or Moriscos. Reports should include information about the daily life, professions, reasons for conversion or defiance in the face of danger, persecution during the Spanish Inquisition, and decisions people made to flee Spain or to stay in spite of persecutions. Ask the groups to draw some connections between treatment of minorities and the eventual decline of Spain. Students should delegate tasks of finding information, organizing ideas, making outlines and note cards, and writing the drafts. **L2**

Chapter 19
Section 1

Map Study

Answer
Portugal

Map Skills Practice

Reading a Map How far is England from Spain? *(about 450 miles [724 km])*

ASSESS

Check for Understanding

Assign Section 1 Review as homework or as an in-class activity.

Use Student Self-Test and Review Software to review Section 1.

Evaluate

Section Quiz 19-1

Use the Testmaker to create a customized quiz for Section 1.

Reteach

Ask volunteers to give oral summaries of important events during the rule of Philip II and during the decline of the Hapsburg rulers after his death. Assign one student to write the major events on the chalkboard.

Enrich

Have students make a time line reflecting the events of the section. Ask them to chart positive events above the line and negative events below it.

CLOSE

Write *Strengths* and *Weaknesses* on the chalkboard and ask students to list items under each heading for the Spanish Hapsburgs they have studied.

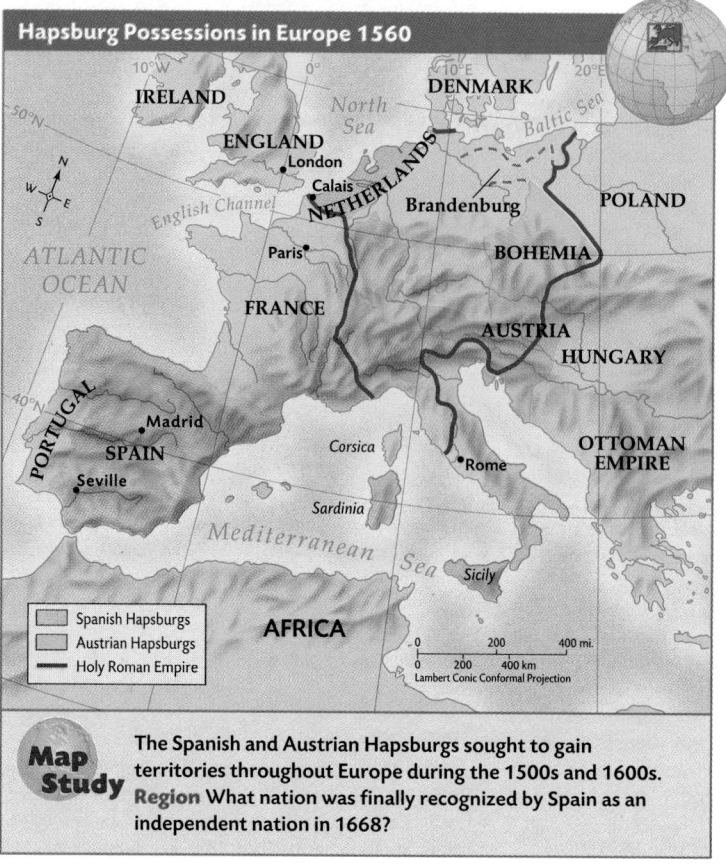

Hapsburg Possessions in Europe 1560

Map Study **The Spanish and Austrian Hapsburgs sought to gain territories throughout Europe during the 1500s and 1600s. Region What nation was finally recognized by Spain as an independent nation in 1668?**

Last of the Spanish Hapsburgs

The defeat of the Spanish Armada marked the beginning of Spain's decline as a European power. Costly wars drained the country's treasury, and the government was forced to borrow from foreign bankers. The Spanish economy suffered **inflation**, an abnormal increase in currency resulting in sharp price rises. In addition, Spain's industry and agriculture deteriorated.

Philip II's successors were not prepared to deal with Spain's decline. Philip's son and grandson, Philip III and Philip IV, lacked his intelligence and interest in politics. They turned over most of the affairs of the government to nobles. Government mismanagement led to widespread corruption. The royal family and nobles retreated from national problems by building extravagant homes and holding lavish parties.

The war with the Dutch was renewed under Philip IV. Spain then became involved in a series of conflicts involving Germany and France. Overburdened and overtaxed, citizens in various parts of the country began to rebel. Portugal, a part of Spain since 1580, was one of those areas. The Portuguese struggle continued until 1668, when Spain finally recognized Portugal's independence.

Philip IV's son **Charles II** was the last of the Spanish Hapsburgs. He became king in 1665 at the age of four, ruling under the regency of his mother. No one expected him to rule long, since he was physically and mentally weak. Although Charles later married, he did not have any children. With no heirs to the throne of Spain, European monarchs plotted to control the succession to the Spanish throne.

SECTION 1 REVIEW

Recall

1. **Define** absolutism, divine right, armada, inflation.
2. **Identify** Philip II, El Escorial, the Marranos, the Moriscos, Spanish Armada, Charles II.
3. **Use** the map of the Hapsburg domains above to locate Spain, Portugal, and the Netherlands. What other areas were under Hapsburg rule?

Critical Thinking

4. **Analyzing Information** Why did Philip II send the Spanish Armada against England? What was the outcome of this effort?

Understanding Themes

5. **Conflict** What were the reasons for internal unrest in the Spanish Empire under Philip II's rule?

SECTION 1 REVIEW ANSWERS

1. All vocabulary words are defined in the Glossary.
2. Philip II, 482; El Escorial, 482; Marranos, 483; Moriscos, 483; Spanish Armada, 483; Charles II, 484
3. Milan, Burgundy, southern Italy, and parts of the Americas
4. Philip was angered by England's support of Protestants in the Netherlands; Spanish Armada was defeated.
5. **CONFLICT** resentment by other provinces of Castile's dominance, religious persecutions, declining economy

1500 — 1550 — 1600

1547 Henry VIII dies.

1558 Elizabeth I becomes queen of England.

1597 Poor Law makes local areas responsible for care of the unemployed.

Section 2

England

Setting the Scene

- **Terms to Define**
  gentry, yeomen, balance of power
- **People to Meet**
  Henry VII, Henry VIII, Elizabeth I, William Shakespeare
- **Places to Locate**
  Scotland, Ireland

Find Out How did Tudor monarchs influence English and European affairs?

The Storyteller

On this day, Elizabeth would be crowned Queen of England. London was arrayed with pavilions and bright banners, and the city's fountains offered wine, not the usual brackish water. Alison Crisp eagerly awaited the royal procession to Westminster Abbey. Although only six years of age, she would present a costly gift to Elizabeth from the Orphans Home board of directors. When the procession neared, the queen commanded her coachmen to stop. Alison flawlessly presented the gift. As the queen prepared to move on, Alison surprised her with another gift, a bouquet of flowers she had picked. With Elizabeth's acceptance of the child's humble offering, the rapport between the queen and her people strengthened.

—from *Description of Elizabeth I's Coronation Procession in 1559*, John Hayward, in *The Past Speaks*, L.B. Smith and J.R. Smith, 1993

Elizabeth I

England, like Spain, developed a strong monarchy. Its Tudor dynasty, which ruled from 1485 to 1603, brought unity to the country after a long period of decline and disorder. Tudor monarchs were hardworking, able, and popular. They greatly expanded the power and authority of the Crown. They were not, however, as absolute in their rule as other European monarchs. Instead, institutions such as Parliament and the courts of law set bounds to the authority that Tudor monarchs could exercise.

Early Tudors

Henry VII, the first Tudor monarch, became king in 1485 after the Wars of the Roses. He used shrewd maneuvering to disarm his rivals and to increase the prestige of his family. Most of Henry's close advisers came from the gentry and merchant classes. Titles were given to these officials, who formed a new aristocracy dependent on the king.

Henry VII helped rebuild England's commercial prosperity. He encouraged the expansion of foreign trade, especially the export of finished woolens to the Netherlands, Germany, and Venice. He promoted the improved collection of taxes as well as careful government spending. In foreign policy Henry avoided war, using diplomacy and the arrangement of suitable royal marriages to strengthen England's interests abroad.

Henry VIII

The second Tudor to rule was **Henry VIII**, son of Henry VII and the most powerful of all Tudor monarchs. Unlike his father, Henry VIII fought wars on the European continent and began to make England a great naval power. His personal life, however, would have a lasting effect on English history. In his pursuit of a male heir, Henry married six times. He worked with Parliament to obtain his personal goals and to break with the Catholic

SECTION THEME

- **Change** Tudor monarchs bring stability and prosperity to England.

Find Out

Answer: *They rebuilt commercial prosperity, expanded the power of the Crown, increased foreign trade, established a balance of power in Europe, and made Scotland and Ireland allies of England.*

FOCUS

Section Objective

Recognize how Tudor monarchs influenced English and European affairs.

BELLRINGER
Motivational Activity

Before taking roll at the beginning of the class period, project Section Focus Transparency 19-2 and have students answer the activity questions. Discuss students' responses.

This activity is also available as a blackline master.

Vocabulary Pre-check

Use Vocabulary Activity 19 to introduce vocabulary terms. **L1 LEP**

SECTION RESOURCES

Reproducible Masters
- Reproducible Lesson Plan 19-2
- Vocabulary Activity 19
- Guided Reading Activity 19-2
- Section Quiz 19-2

Transparencies
- Section Focus Transparency 19-2
- World History and Art Transparency 22

Multimedia
- Student Self-Test and Review Software
- Testmaker
- World Music: Cultural Traditions, Lesson 3

Chapter 19 Section 2

TEACH

Guided Practice

THEME Change

Tudor monarchs used their strong personalities and diplomatic skills to bring about change in England. Write *Henry VII*, *Henry VIII*, and *Elizabeth I* on the chalkboard. Ask students to name some of the changes each of these monarchs brought and list them on the chalkboard. *(Sample answers: Henry VII, expanded foreign trade; Henry VIII, established Anglican Church; Elizabeth I, ushered in one of England's greatest cultural periods.)* **L1 LEP**

Government Tudor rule differed from the absolute rule of Philip II. Both dynasties had successes and failures. Ask students to take a position on whether the Spanish Hapsburgs or the English Tudors were more successful in ruling their kingdoms and why. Students should consider the personal traits and public actions of monarchs. Ask volunteers to judge the positions and point out those with well-supported arguments. **L2**

Critical Thinking Henry VIII used the power of Parliament to help him obtain divorces and break from the Catholic Church. Ask students what advantages this gave Parliament. *(Parliament gained power it had lost to the Church because it helped construct and enforce the laws that allowed Henry to do as he wished.)* **L3**

World History and Art Transparency 22, *View of Toledo*

World Music: Cultural Traditions, Lesson 3

Church. As a result of this cooperation, the House of Commons increased its power during Henry VIII's reign. Henry, however, furthered support for his policies by seizing monastery lands and selling them to wealthy landowners.

Edward VI and Mary I

After Henry VIII's death in 1547, England entered a brief period of turmoil. Edward VI, Henry's son and successor, was only 9 years old when he became king. He died in 1553 after a short reign. Protestant nobles then plotted to prevent Edward's Catholic half-sister, Mary, from becoming queen. The English people, however, supported Mary's claim to the Tudor throne.

Mary's Catholic policies soon offended the English. Despite strong opposition, Mary married Philip II of Spain in 1554. The next year, she restored Catholicism and had about 300 Protestants burned at the stake for heresy. At Philip's urging, Mary involved England in a war with France. As a result, England lost the port of Calais, its final foothold on the European continent. Many English people feared that England would be controlled by Spain. Before this fear could be realized, Mary died childless, and the throne then passed to her Protestant half-sister, Elizabeth.

Elizabeth I

Elizabeth I became queen in 1558, when she was 25 years old. She was shrewd, highly educated, and had a forceful personality. With a sharp tongue she asserted her iron will, causing sparks to fly in exchanges with Parliament. Elizabeth, however, used her authority for the common good of her people. On frequent journeys throughout the kingdom Elizabeth earned the loyalty and confidence of her subjects. During her travels, Elizabeth stayed at the homes of nobles who entertained her with banquets, parades, and dances.

Elizabeth's reign was one of England's great cultural periods. Poets and writers praised

Images of the Times

Tudor England

Under Tudor monarchs, England enjoyed a period of stability and relative prosperity.

Mary I married Philip II of Spain in 1554, against the wishes of her Protestant subjects. This coat of arms represents the marital union of the two monarchs.

Images of the Times — Tudor England

What was life like for the people? Houses of plaster and brick with thatched roofs now had glass windows, but people still needed candles or torches for light at night. Floors had no carpets, but tapestries were hung on walls. Furniture was strong and cut of walnut or oak to last for centuries. People of all classes had a garden by the house. Elizabethan England was an age of fashion. Men wore hats of many shapes and colors outside the home and in church. They wore their hair long and grew beards. Women often wore wigs, used cosmetics, wore jewelry, and had pierced ears. Both men and women wore pleated collars, called ruffs, made of fabric, pasteboard, and wire.

Elizabeth in their works. The theater flourished under playwrights such as **William Shakespeare**. During Elizabeth's reign, English was transformed into a language of beauty, grace, vigor, and clarity.

Marriage

People fully expected that Elizabeth would marry and that her husband would rule. The common attitude of the time was that only men were fit to rule and that government matters were beyond a woman's ability. Elizabeth, however, was slow in seeking a husband. She had learned from the lesson of her sister Mary: to marry a foreign prince would endanger England. At the same time, marrying an Englishman would cause jealousies among the English nobility. In the end, Elizabeth refused to give up her powers as monarch for the sake of marriage. To one of her suitors she stormed, "God's death! My lord, I will have but one mistress [England] and no master." Elizabeth's refusal to marry caused a great deal of speculation as to who would succeed her.

Court and Government

In matters of government, Elizabeth was assisted by a council of nobles. With her approval they drafted proclamations, handled foreign relations, and supervised such matters as the administration of justice and the regulation of prices and wages. These advisers were assisted by small staffs of professional but poorly paid bureaucrats.

Although Parliament did not have the power to initiate legislation, it could plead, urge, advise, and withhold approval. These powers gave Parliament some influence, especially when it was asked to consider tax laws.

The task of enforcing the queen's law was performed by unpaid respected community members known as justices of the peace. Most justices belonged to the rural landowning classes. They knew both the law and local conditions. They maintained peace, collected taxes, and kept the government informed of local problems. Their voluntary participation in support of the government was a key to its success.

The Court of Elizabeth I was known for its love of fashions and style. Noble men and women who served the queen wore elegant clothes and enjoyed music and the arts.

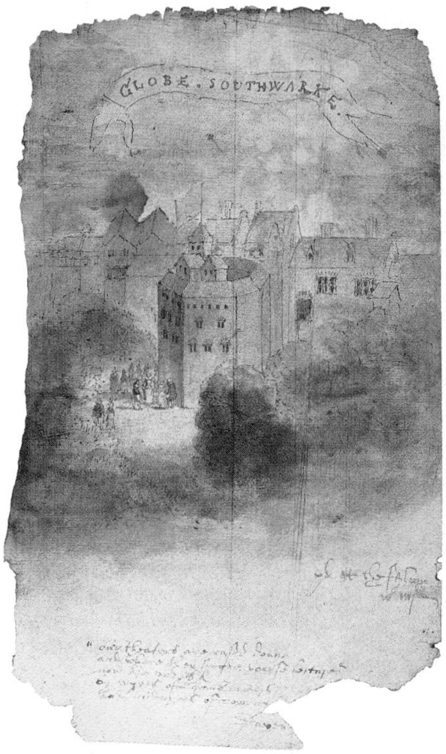

The Globe Theater in London was the site where many of William Shakespeare's plays—tragedies, comedies, and histories—were performed.

REFLECTING ON THE TIMES

1. Why is Elizabeth's reign considered one of England's great cultural eras?
2. Why was Mary I an unpopular ruler?

Chapter 19 Section 2

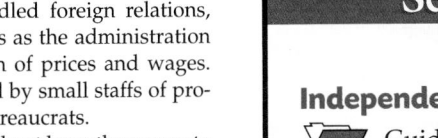

Independent Practice

Guided Reading Activity 19-2 **L1**

Time Line Assign pairs of students to make a biographical time line of Tudor royalty. Using encyclopedias or biographical dictionaries, have them write brief descriptions of each Tudor ruler and place it next to the appropriate birth date on the time line. **L2 LEP**

Women in History Women were very influential during the Tudor reign. Have students research and report on one of the following: a wife of Henry VIII; Mary I; Elizabeth I; Mary, Queen of Scots; Margaret Pole; or Lady Jane Grey. **L3**

Linking Past and Present

Shakespeare's plays are as popular today as they were in Elizabethan England. Through the centuries, directors have adapted productions of the plays to fit contemporary situations. In some cases they have changed everything except the basic plot line. *Romeo and Juliet*, a story of ill-fated lovers in Verona, Italy, was transformed into *West Side Story*, a 1950s musical about lovers caught in the conflict between rival New York City gangs. Changes in time period and culture do not change the universal theme of the original play.

ANSWERS TO REFLECTING ON THE TIMES

1. It was a time when the English language, theater, art, and music all thrived.
2. People feared her Catholic policies and a loss of power because of her marriage to Philip of Spain.

ASSESS

Check for Understanding

Assign Section 2 Review as homework or as an in-class activity.

Use Student Self-Test and Review Software to review Section 2.

you don't say...

"To take the chair," or to preside, is an expression that came from Tudor times. A chair with a back was a luxury then; most people sat on stools or benches. The chair, then, was reserved for the master or mistress of the house or the honored guest.

History & Art Elizabeth Tudor was an extraordinary individual who had had little security, hope, or love in her life. With the freedom of the throne, however, she was able to do as she chose. She chose to appeal to her subjects and earn their love.
Answer to Caption: *England developed a balance of power with European nations.*

CURRICULUM CONNECTION

ASTRONOMY
In his twenties, Edmund Halley published a paper on planetary orbits, financed Newton's first edition of *Principia*, and predicted that in 75 years there would be a reappearance of a comet that appeared in 1682. When the comet returned, it was named Halley's comet.

Social and Economic Policy

Elizabeth believed in the importance of social rank. During the late 1500s, English society was led by the queen and her court. Next were prominent nobles from the great landed families and a middle group of gentry, or lesser nobles, merchants, lawyers, and clergy. This group provided the source of Tudor strength and stability. The lowest social rank was comprised of yeomen, or farmers with small landholdings, and laborers.

Government laws and policies closely regulated the lives of the common people. The Statute of Apprentices of 1563 declared work to be a social and moral duty. It required people to live and work where they were born, controlled the movement of labor, fixed wages, and regulated apprenticeships. The Poor Laws of 1597 and 1601 made local areas responsible for their own homeless and unemployed. These laws included means to raise money for charity and to provide work for vagabonds.

Elizabeth inherited a monarchy that was badly in debt. Royal revenues, which came from rents of royal land, fines in court cases, and duties on imports, barely covered annual expenses. The queen, however, spent lavishly on court ceremonies to show the power and dignity of the monarchy. In other matters, she showed the greatest financial restraint, leading many to call her a "pinchpenny."

To raise funds without relying on Parliament, Elizabeth sold off royal lands, offices, licenses, monopolies, and the right to collect customs. These measures helped but could not solve the problem. England faced the costs of war and mounting inflation. Elizabeth was therefore forced to turn to Parliament for funds. When she ended her reign, England remained badly in debt.

Foreign Policy

By Elizabeth's time, England had lost all of its possessions on the European continent. France was too powerful for England to defeat in order to regain territories. Although England could not completely withdraw from continental affairs, it developed a foreign policy suitable for a small island nation with limited resources.

For security, the English relied on the English Channel to protect their island from European invaders. Building and maintaining a strong navy was therefore important in defending the nation. For that reason, Elizabeth continued the efforts begun by her Tudor predecessors to build such a navy.

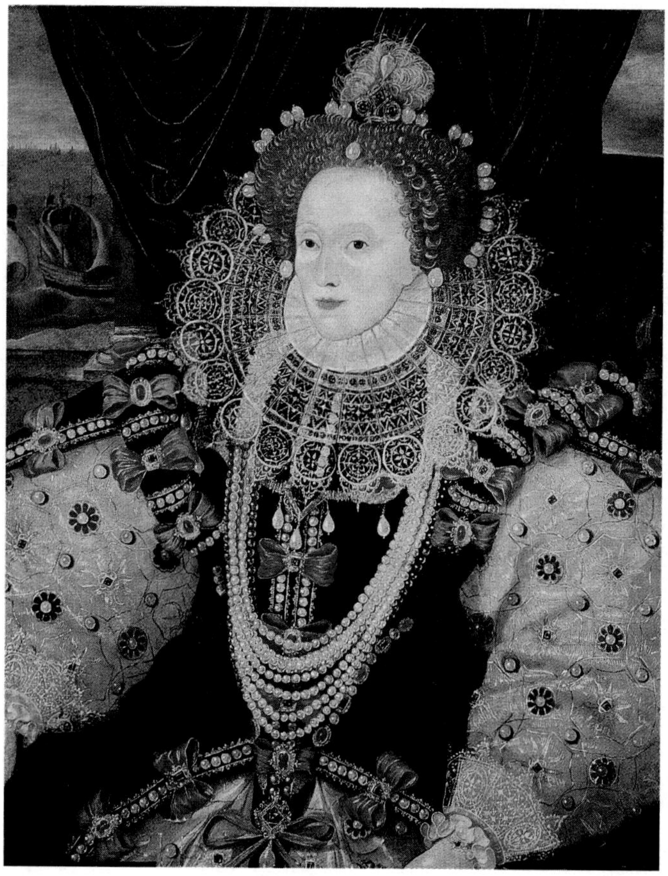

History & Art *Elizabeth I* by George Glower, 1596. National Portrait Gallery, London, England **A woman of keen intellect, Elizabeth I was gifted in music, languages, and the arts. In addition, she was an excellent public speaker.** *What foreign policy strategy did England develop under Elizabeth I's reign?*

COOPERATIVE LEARNING ACTIVITY

Research Have students research Shakespeare, the Elizabethan theater, and London in the middle and late 1500s. Organize the class into several groups and ask each group to choose different tasks: write a biography of Shakespeare; make a model of the Globe or Black Friars theater; give an oral report or write a fictional diary entry describing London in the 1500s—its theater audience and its actors; stage a specific scene from a play (such as *Henry VIII*) to be discussed and performed; make drawings of costumes used on Shakespeare's stage. The class could combine their efforts in creating a Shakespeare Festival, including appropriate musical and dramatic recordings and samples of foods from the 1500s. **L2**

Spain and France posed the greatest naval threats to England. The attack of the Spanish Armada made England realize the dangers of an alliance between Spain and France. England might be able to defeat one power, but certainly not both. As a result, the English relied on diplomacy as well as sea power to protect their interests.

During Elizabeth's reign, England worked to balance the power of European nations. In international affairs, balance of power refers to the system in which each nation helps to keep peace and order by maintaining power that is equal to, or in balance with, rival nations. One nation cannot overpower another. If one nation becomes more powerful than the other, a third nation can reestablish the balance by supporting the second nation.

Under Elizabeth's rule, England operated as the third balancing nation. In the early part of Elizabeth's reign, England and Spain feared the power of the French. England cooperated with Spain in order to keep France out of the Netherlands. Later, when the Netherlands revolted against Philip II, the English supported the rebels and allied with the weaker power against the stronger one.

Scotland was largely Catholic and hostile toward England during the 1550s. Although part of **Ireland** was under English rule, the rest of the country resisted English armies. To protect English interests, Elizabeth sought to solidify her ties with Scotland and Ireland so they could not be used as bases for Spanish and French attacks on England.

In the 1560s, with Elizabeth's help, Scotland became Protestant and an ally of England. Mary Stuart, later known as Mary, Queen of Scots, was Elizabeth's cousin. She was forced to abdicate her position as queen of Scotland in 1567. She later fled to England, where her presence caused controversy. Mary was a Catholic and heir to the English throne. Many English Protestants feared she would try to replace Elizabeth. In 1586 Mary was accused of plotting with English and foreign Catholics against Elizabeth. Public fears of a Catholic monarchy were strong. In 1587 Elizabeth finally agreed to Mary's execution, although she was hesitant to sentence to death another monarch.

Visualizing History **Sir Francis Drake was one of England's most famous explorers and military leaders. After sailing around the world, Drake was knighted in 1581 by Queen Elizabeth I. His naval warfare later helped make England a major sea power.** *What European nation was England's primary enemy during the time of Elizabeth I and Francis Drake?*

In the 1590s, England carried out military campaigns in Ireland to conquer the Irish. With Scotland and Ireland allied with England, a period of temporary peace came to the British Isles.

Elizabeth died in 1603 at the age of 69. With her death came the end of the Tudor dynasty. King James VI of Scotland, the Protestant son of Mary, Queen of Scots, became the new monarch of England. As James I, he founded the Stuart dynasty and united Scotland and England under a common ruler.

SECTION 2 REVIEW

Recall

1. **Define** gentry, yeomen, balance of power.
2. **Identify** Henry VII, Henry VIII, Edward VI, Mary I, Elizabeth I, William Shakespeare, Poor Laws, James I.
3. **Explain** England's foreign policy under Elizabeth I.

Critical Thinking

4. **Evaluating Information** Contrast the effect on English history of Henry's many marriages with the effect of Elizabeth I's refusal to marry.

Understanding Themes

5. **Change** How did the rule of the Tudor monarchs, especially the rule of Elizabeth I, affect the development of England?

Chapter 19 Section 2

Visualizing History Prospects of future Armada attacks on England and the subsequent financial burdens of war led Elizabeth to encourage Drake and his sea captains to attack foreign vessels carrying treasure from the Americas and claim the booty.

Answer to Caption: *Spain*

Evaluate

Section Quiz 19-2

Use the Testmaker to create a customized quiz for Section 2.

Reteach

Ask students to list the political tactics used by Tudor rulers. *(use of Parliament to grant favors, foreign policy based on diplomacy, a balance of power)*

Enrich

Have students assume the role of someone who might have lived between 1485 and 1603. Ask them to choose under which ruler—Henry VIII, Edward VI, Mary I, or Elizabeth I—they would like to have lived and why.

CLOSE

Hold a discussion on how religion affected the policies of the Tudors and whether this influence strengthened or weakened England.

SECTION 2 REVIEW ANSWERS

1. All vocabulary words are defined in the Glossary.
2. Henry VII, 485; Henry VIII, 485; Edward VI, 486; Mary I, 486; Elizabeth I, 486; William Shakespeare, 487; Poor Laws, 488; James I, 489
3. It was a policy of cooperation with Spain to balance the power of France and keep the French out of the Netherlands.
4. Henry's marriages caused a split with the Catholic Church; Elizabeth's refusal to marry prevented foreign claims to the English throne.
5. **CHANGE** Elizabeth strengthened the monarch's ties with Parliament, subdued religious dissent, encouraged cultural development, and established a balance of power among European nations.

1550 — 1600 — 1650 — 1700

1598 Henry IV issues the Edict of Nantes.

1648 Fronde uprising grips Paris.

1661 Louis XIV takes sole charge of the government.

1701 War of the Spanish Succession begins.

Section 3

France

SECTION THEME

▶ **Uniformity** France's Louis XIV strengthens absolute monarchy in France and limits rights of religious dissenters.

Find Out

Answer: *Bourbon kings developed an absolute monarchy in France.*

FOCUS

Section Objective

Describe the kind of monarchy that developed in France under the Bourbon monarchs.

BELLRINGER Motivational Activity

Before taking roll at the beginning of the class period, project Section Focus Transparency 19-3 and have students answer the activity questions. Discuss students' responses.

This activity is also available as a blackline master.

Vocabulary Pre-check

Use Vocabulary Activity 19 to introduce vocabulary terms. **L1 LEP**

Setting the Scene

▶ **Terms to Define**
intendant

▶ **People to Meet**
Henry IV, Cardinal Richelieu, Louis XIV

▶ **Places to Locate**
Versailles

Find Out What kind of monarchy developed in France under the Bourbon monarchs?

The Storyteller

A flourish of trumpets sounded. The crowd of courtiers bowed as King Louis entered the Grand Salon at Versailles, accompanied by his attendants. The Duke of Saint-Simon, one of many noblemen whose power Louis was systematically eclipsing, was nonetheless required to be present. He observed that the king "liked splendor, magnificence, and profusion in everything: you pleased him if you shone through the brilliancy of your houses, clothes, tables, equipages." Because everyone tried to emulate the king, a taste for extravagance and luxury was spreading through all classes of society.

—adapted from *The Memoires of the Duke of Saint-Simon*, reprinted in *Aspects of Western Civilization, Volume II*, Perry M. Rogers, 1988

Louis XIV's lavish court life

After a period of religious conflict, peace was restored to most of France when Henry of Navarre became King **Henry IV** in 1589. He founded the Bourbon dynasty, which ruled France with some interruptions until the early 1800s. During most of that time, Bourbon kings maintained an absolute monarchy that was imitated by monarchs throughout Europe.

Henry IV

Henry IV was a Protestant, but he converted to Catholicism to quiet his Catholic opponents. Believing that people's religious beliefs need not interfere with their loyalty to the government, Henry issued the Edict of Nantes in 1598 to reassure the Huguenots, the name given to France's Protestants. The edict allowed Protestant worship to continue in areas where the Protestants were a majority, but barred Protestant worship in Paris and other Catholic strongholds. The edict granted Huguenots the same civil rights as Catholics.

These actions ended religious strife and enabled France to rebuild itself. With the help of his minister of finance, Henry restored the Crown's treasury, repaired roads and bridges, and supported trade and industry. He also tried to restore discipline in the army and bring order to the government bureaucracy. All of these royal policies were put into effect without the approval of the Estates-General and thus laid the foundation for the absolute rule of later Bourbon monarchs.

Cardinal Richelieu

Henry's son Louis XIII inherited the throne in 1610 at the age of 9. Louis's mother, Marie de Medici, was regent for the next 7 years. In 1617 Louis gained the throne by force and exiled his mother from court. A few years later he recalled

SECTION RESOURCES

Reproducible Masters
- Reproducible Lesson Plan 19-3
- Vocabulary Activity 19
- Guided Reading Activity 19-3
- Section Quiz 19-3

Transparencies
- Section Focus Transparency 19-3
- World History and Art Transparency 26

Multimedia
- Focus on World Art Print 20, Jean-Baptiste Simeon Chardin. *The Attributes of Painting*
- Student Self-Test and Review Software
- Testmaker

490 Chapter 19 Royal Power and Conflict

Marie, and she convinced him to give power to one of her advisers, **Cardinal Richelieu.**

Gradually Louis gave complete control of the government to the cardinal, who set out to build an absolute monarchy in France. To realize this goal, Richelieu had to reduce the power of the nobles and the Huguenots.

When Louis XIII came to the throne, the nobility was in control of the provinces. Nobles collected taxes, administered justice, appointed local officials, and even made alliances with foreign governments. To end the nobles' power, Richelieu destroyed their fortified castles and stripped them of their local administrative functions. The nobility retained social prestige, while authority in local government affairs was given to special agents of the Crown known as **intendants**. Non-nobles, Richelieu believed, would not assert themselves and challenge the king's authority.

Richelieu also sought to take away the military and territorial rights given to the Huguenots by the Edict of Nantes. The Huguenots were seen as a threat to the French state. In 1625 radical Huguenots revolted against Louis XIII. After the defeat of Protestant forces at the seaport of La Rochelle in 1628, Richelieu took away the Huguenots' right to independent fortified towns. The Huguenots were, however, allowed to keep their religious freedom.

Having weakened the monarchy's internal enemies, Richelieu sought to make France the supreme power in Europe. He strengthened the French army and took steps to build up the economy. In order to strengthen national unity, he supported French culture. Under Richelieu's direction, France's leading writers in 1635 organized the French Academy. The Academy received a royal charter to establish "fixed rules for the language ... and render the French language not only elegant but also capable of treating all arts and sciences." In the following century, French became the preferred language of European diplomacy and culture.

Visualizing History **Cardinal Richelieu strengthened France's economy by promoting the manufacture of luxury goods. He also gave charters to commercial companies for overseas trade.** *How did Richelieu encourage the growth of French culture?*

Louis XIV

Louis XIV is recognized as the most powerful Bourbon monarch. He became king in 1643 at the age of 5. At first, France was ruled by his two regents—his mother, Anne of Austria, and Cardinal Mazarin, Richelieu's successor. When Mazarin died in 1661, Louis announced that he would run his own government. He was then 23 years old.

The 72-year reign of Louis XIV was the longest in European history. It set the style for European monarchies during the 1600s and 1700s. During his own lifetime, Louis was known as the Sun King, around whom the royalty and nobility of Europe revolved. He set up a lavish court and surrounded himself with pomp and pageantry. Louis's monarchy had power as well as style. Although Louis relied on a bureaucracy, he was the source of all political authority in France. In one of his audiences, he is said to have boasted, *"L'état, c'est moi!"* ("I am the state!").

Absolute Rule

Louis emphasized a strong monarchy because of his fear of disorder without it. As a child, he had lived through the Fronde, a series of uprisings by nobles and peasants that occurred between 1648 and 1653. During the Fronde, royal troops lost control of Paris and mobs rioted in the streets. The young Louis and his regents were called to give an account of their actions before the *Parlement*, or supreme court of law, in Paris. The Fronde was crushed, but Louis never forgot this attempt to limit royal power. As king, he intended never to let it happen again.

Louis XIV's feelings about absolute monarchy were later supported by Jacques Bossuet (ZHAHK baw•SWAY), the leading church official of France during the 1600s. Bossuet's defense of the divine

TEACH

Guided Practice

THEME **Uniformity**

The efforts of Cardinal Richelieu and Louis XIV brought uniformity of language, government, and religion to France. Discuss the importance of this uniformity and ask which institutions were unified. *(a predominant religion, common language, uniform currency, laws, taxes, culture, customs)* **L1**

Visualizing History Richelieu was devoted to his pursuit of power for France. He taxed the peasantry and used the taxes to build up the military in order to destroy the power of the Hapsburgs in Europe.

Answer to Caption: *He directed the establishment of the French Academy, which helped standardize and refine the French language.*

Science, Technology, and Society Display pictures of the interior and exterior of Versailles from history, art, or architecture books. Ask students to comment on Versailles as a " perfect symbol" for Louis XIV and his court. Contrast Versailles with descriptions of French peasant life. **L1 LEP**

Politics Have students discuss the effects of Cardinal Richelieu's policies on France during the reign of Louis XIII. *(brought stability to government by ending powers of nobility, took away political power of Huguenots, built a strong army, strengthened economy, improved and standardized French language)* **L3**

COOPERATIVE LEARNING ACTIVITY

Research Organize the class into groups of four or five students. Assign a report on the life and actions of Henry Navarre (Henry IV), who converted to Catholicism and issued the Edict of Nantes to restore religious peace to France. Each group should decide on a thesis for their report. Individual students could research Henry's personal and political life, Huguenot beliefs, the St. Bartholomew's Day Massacre, consequences of the Edict of Nantes, or other information that would support the group's thesis. Each member should submit research notes to the person who will write the draft of the report. After group approval and editing, a member should copy the report in final form. **L2**

History & Art Louis XIV was a great patron of the arts and increased the number of paintings in his galleries from 200 to 2,500, many by French artists. He demanded that artists meet classical standards that reflected elegance, self-restraint, and polish. French art became the expression of the nation and the king, but not of the people. Its influence spread to ruling classes all over Europe.

Answer to Caption: *He never forgot the Fronde uprisings that he lived through as a child in Paris and wanted to feel safe from the danger of Paris mobs.*

World History and Art Transparency 26, *The French Ambassadors*

Focus on World Art Print 20, Jean-Baptiste Simeon Chardin. *The Attributes of Painting*

Independent Practice

Guided Reading Activity 19-3 **L1**

Daily Life Ask students to assume the role of an English visitor to the court of Versailles. Have them compose a letter to a friend back home, describing life at court. Their letters could include information about famous acquaintances, fashion, food, the beauty of Versailles, and an audience with the king. **L2 LEP**

Global Gourmet

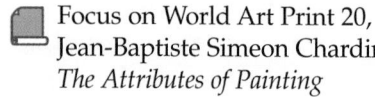

France By the time of Louis XIV, forks were in use, although the king used his fingers all of his life. People began to use napkins, and guests no longer had to use the tablecloth to wipe their fingers.

origins of monarchy became one of the most famous justifications of absolute rule. He wrote:

> “What grandeur that a single man should embody so much! ... Behold this holy power, paternal and absolute, contained in a single head: you see the image of God in the king, and you have the idea of royal majesty.”

According to Bossuet, subjects had no right to revolt even if the king was unjust. Kings need account to no one except God, but they should act with humility and restraint because "God's judgment is heaviest for those who command."

Court Life

After the Fronde, Louis refused to live in Paris. He moved his court and government outside of the city to a new palace that he built at **Versailles**. The Palace of Versailles was a large, splendid structure. No expense was spared, for Versailles was to demonstrate the wealth, power, and glory of France.

The palace had elegant royal apartments, sweeping staircases, mirrored halls, priceless tapestries, and lavish formal salons and dining rooms. There were offices for government bureaucrats as well as tiny, cramped rooms where officials lived. As many as 10,000 people lived at Versailles. Outside the palace were acres of formal gardens, filled with marble sculptures and fountains.

In this setting Louis felt secure from the danger of Parisian mobs. Here he had the nobility attend his court so that he could control them. Instead of using the nobles in government service, Louis had them wait on him in a round of daily court rituals. The nobility depended on the king's favor for pensions, court posts, and protection from creditors.

Louis freed the nobles from paying taxes. To nobles and non-nobles alike, he sold many offices with guaranteed salaries. The sale of offices provided needed royal income but became a long-term drain on the treasury.

Government Policies

Louis continued the efforts of Henry IV and Richelieu to strengthen the power of the monarch and the state. He followed the tradition of Richelieu and chose his top advisers not from the nobility, but from middle-class families. Sons often succeeded their fathers in government service.

Although Louis was an absolute monarch, he was not able simply to change the traditions of his country's feudal past. Legal systems varied throughout France. Private tolls and customs were levied on goods moving from one province to another. Weights and measures were not uniform. There were separate authorities and districts for financial, judicial, religious, and administrative affairs.

History & Art *Louis XIV of France* by Hyacinthe Rigaud, c. 1701, The Louvre, Paris, France **Louis XIV worked six to eight hours a day at what he called "the business of being king."** *Why did the king refuse to live in Paris?*

If Louis had tried to change these practices, it would have disrupted the kingdom and endangered his throne. Instead, the king kept the traditional ways, but added to them new administrative offices and practices. Two key people aided Louis XIV in his efforts—Jean-Baptiste Colbert (kohl•BEHR) and François Michel Le Tellier, the Marquis de Louvois (loov•WAH). Colbert believed that the government had to direct the economy. He became Louis's leading economic and financial adviser. Louvois served as minister of war and improved France's military position.

Economic Policy

While reforming some aspects of government practice, Louis failed to adjust the complicated and unjust tax system. The poor carried most of the tax burden, while nobles, clergy, and government officials were exempt from many payments. Independent tax collectors often made large profits from their work, but they were allowed to continue this practice since the money they provided was needed to support the army.

MEETING SPECIAL NEEDS ACTIVITY

Mixed Learners As a challenge to some students and a help to others, organize the class into two teams. Have students plan a Who? What? When? Where? guessing game about people, places, and events they have studied in this section. Each team should write clues on cards and put the answers on the backs. One team can work on Who? and Where? clues while the other team prepares What? and When? cards. After each team has prepared about ten clue cards, students can take turns guessing the answers. At the end of the game, teams should give answers to clues not guessed. **L1**

492 Chapter 19 *Royal Power and Conflict*

The unreformed tax system heightened the economic differences between the regions of France. Since any visible improvement in one's farm or household might lead to higher tax payments, there was little desire to improve one's output. The tax system encouraged people to move from heavily taxed regions to regions with lower taxes. As a result, heavily taxed regions became poorer.

Religious Policy

Louis regarded the Huguenots as a threat to his absolute monarchy. Many Huguenots were military leaders and prosperous merchants. They often controlled local commerce. In spite of their high social standing, the Huguenots faced mounting persecution from Louis's government. The king wanted the Huguenots to accept Catholicism. He believed that, in this way, they would prove their loyalty to the throne. In 1685 the Edict of Nantes was repealed. Huguenots could no longer practice their religion, and their children had to become Catholics.

The result of the king's policy was the emigration of about 200,000 Huguenots to such places as the Netherlands, England, and England's American colonies. Many of these talented people contributed to the economic growth and prosperity of the lands where they settled.

Expansion

Louis XIV pursued a bold and active foreign policy. His goal was to expand the glory and power of France. Other European rulers were fearful of Louis's desire for expansion, and as a result, allied in opposition to France.

At the end of Louis XIV's reign, Europe was concerned about the succession to the Spanish throne. It was expected that Charles II of Spain would die without an heir. Both France and Austria had claims to the throne. The rest of Europe was alarmed that the balance of power would be disrupted if France inherited Spain's vast empire. Prior to Spanish king Charles II's death, the European powers worked out a plan to divide the Spanish Empire. The will of Charles II upset this plan by stating that the entire empire should remain intact and pass to Louis XIV's grandson, Philip of Anjou. Louis XIV accepted the provisions of the will. When Charles II died in 1700, Philip of Anjou became King Philip V of Spain. As a result, Europe was plunged into a conflict known as the War of the Spanish Succession.

Conflict

The War of the Spanish Succession lasted from 1701 to 1713. During the conflict England, the Dutch Netherlands, and Austria led a Grand Alliance of European nations against France and Spain.

Peace was finally restored with the Treaty of Utrecht in 1713. England and the Dutch Netherlands recognized Philip V as king of Spain, on the condition that France and Spain never be united under one crown. France gained trade advantages with the Spanish colonial empire. France, however, was forced to surrender the North American provinces of Nova Scotia and Newfoundland to England. The War of the Spanish Succession drained the French treasury, brought increased poverty, and created opposition to Louis's rule.

Louis XIV's Legacy

France enjoyed one of its most brilliant cultural periods under Louis XIV. Builders and artisans designed and decorated palaces and churches. Artists and playwrights portrayed the daily life of the king's court, the nobility, and the lower classes. Louis's building projects and his wars, however, had left the country near financial ruin. The ways in which Louis weakened the French nobility also had their costs. The nobles lost their ability to govern, but not the desire for power. The peasants and the middle class resented the privileges and wealth of the nobles. After Louis XIV's death in 1715, the nobility sought to expand its power under Louis's great-grandson, Louis XV. Conflicts between the nobles and the middle and lower classes would bring France to the brink of revolution.

SECTION 3 REVIEW

Recall

1. **Define** intendant.
2. **Identify** Henry IV, Edict of Nantes, Cardinal Richelieu, Louis XIV, Treaty of Utrecht.
3. **Explain** how Henry IV tried to bring religious peace to France.

Critical Thinking

4. **Evaluating Information** What do you think were the successes and failures of Louis XIV's reign?

Understanding Themes

5. **Uniformity** What were Cardinal Richelieu's political goals? How did Richelieu reduce the power of the nobility? Of the Huguenots?

SECTION 3 REVIEW ANSWERS

1. All vocabulary words are defined in the Glossary.
2. Henry IV, 490; Edict of Nantes, 490; Cardinal Richelieu, 490; Louis XIV, 491; Treaty of Utrecht, 493
3. issued the Edict of Nantes
4. Louis XIV elevated French culture and brought every aspect of French life under his control; he antagonized nobility, Huguenots, and the poor, setting the stage for future conflict.
5. **UNIFORMITY** Richelieu sought to build a strong monarchy; he stripped the nobility of their administrative powers and repealed the Edict of Nantes.

Chapter 19 Section 3

ASSESS

Check for Understanding

Assign Section 3 Review as homework or as an in-class activity.

Use Student Self-Test and Review Software to review Section 3.

Linking Past and Present

Molière was a great writer of comic theater during Louis XIV's reign. One of his plays, *L' Ecole des Femmes* or *School for Wives*, is considered the first great comedy of French theater and is still frequently performed. It is said that France loves Molière as England loves Shakespeare.

Reteach

Have students create a biographical outline, chronologically listing the major figures of this section and including examples of how each person helped or hindered France.

Enrich

Have students research the decorative arts of this period in France and make a short oral report, including visuals.

CLOSE

Have students explain how the reign of Louis XIV built on policies begun during the time of Louis XIII, giving specific examples.

SECTION THEME

▶ **Conflict** Dynastic and religious conflicts divide the German states.

Find Out

Answer: *All major European powers except England became involved.*

FOCUS

Section Objective

Examine how the Thirty Years' War differed from prior European wars.

BELLRINGER
Motivational Activity

Before taking roll at the beginning of the class period, project Section Focus Transparency 19-4 and have students answer the activity questions. Discuss students' responses.

This activity is also available as a blackline master.

Vocabulary Pre-check

Use Vocabulary Activity 19 to introduce vocabulary terms.
L1 LEP

1600 — 1700 — 1800

1618 Czechs revolt against Hapsburg rule.

1648 Treaty of Westphalia ends Thirty Years' War.

1740 Maria Theresa becomes empress of Austria.

1763 Seven Years' War ends.

Section 4

The German States

Setting the Scene

▶ **Terms to Define**
pragmatic sanction

▶ **People to Meet**
Maria Theresa, Frederick II

▶ **Places to Locate**
Austria, Prussia

Find Out How was the Thirty Years' War different from prior European wars?

The Storyteller

Thomas Taylor traveled slowly and cautiously from Dresden to Prague. He was overwhelmed by a harshness he had never witnessed in his native England. Life all around him was insecure and uncomfortable. Violent outlaws roamed the highways, torture was part of the judicial process, executions were horrible, famine and disease were evident in every town. Taylor detoured around public refuse heaps, swarming with rats and carrion crows. He dodged the bodies of executed criminals dangling from the gallows. Taylor had heard rumors of war. If the rumors were true, he judged it would be long, brutal and terrible.

—freely adapted from *The Thirty Years' War*, C.V. Wedgwood, 1961

The Thirty Years' War

While the Bourbons were building the strongest monarchy in Europe, the Hapsburgs of Austria were trying to set up their own absolute monarchy in central and eastern Europe. Their efforts renewed tensions between Europe's Catholics and Protestants. This eventually led to yet another conflict—the Thirty Years' War. Though most of the fighting took place in Germany, all the major European powers except England became involved.

The Thirty Years' War

Conflicts between Catholics and Protestants had continued in Germany after the Peace of Augsburg in 1555. These disputes were complicated by the spread of Calvinism, a religion that had not been recognized by the peace settlement. Furthermore, the Protestant princes of Germany resisted the rule of Catholic Hapsburg monarchs.

In 1618 the Thirty Years' War began in Bohemia, where Ferdinand of Styria had become king a year earlier. Ferdinand was also the Hapsburg heir to the throne of the Holy Roman Empire. An enemy of Protestantism who wanted to strengthen Hapsburg authority, Ferdinand began his rule by curtailing the freedom of Bohemian Protestants, most of whom were Czechs. In 1618 the Czechs rebelled and took over Prague. Soon the rebellion developed into a full-scale civil war—Ferdinand and the Catholic princes against the German Protestant princes. Philip III of Spain, a Hapsburg, sent aid to Ferdinand.

The Czech revolt was crushed by 1620 and, over the next 10 years, the Czechs were forcefully reconverted to Catholicism. Instead of ending, however, the war continued. Protestant Denmark now fought against the Hapsburgs, hoping to gain German territory. The Danes were soon defeated and forced to withdraw. Then Sweden entered the war to defend the Protestant cause. By this time the

SECTION RESOURCES

Reproducible Masters
- Reproducible Lesson Plan 19-4
- Vocabulary Activity 19
- Guided Reading Activity 19-4
- Section Quiz 19-4

Transparencies
- Section Focus Transparency 19-4

Multimedia
- Focus on World Art Print 19, Jan Steen. *The Dancing Couple*
- Student Self-Test and Review Software
- Testmaker

war had been going on for 12 years, and religious issues were taking second place to political ones. In 1635, under Cardinal Richelieu, Roman Catholic France took up arms against the Roman Catholic Hapsburgs to keep them from becoming too powerful.

Finally, after another 13 years, the Thirty Years' War ended in 1648. The outcome was the further weakening of Germany and the emergence of France as Europe's leading power. An international peace conference met at Westphalia in Germany to work out a peace agreement. The Treaty of Westphalia extended the Peace of Augsburg by adding Calvinism to the list of recognized religions. The Holy Roman Empire remained divided into more than 300 separate states. Although the Hapsburgs still controlled Austria and Bohemia, they ruled the other German states in name only, thus ending their hope of establishing an absolute monarchy over all of Germany.

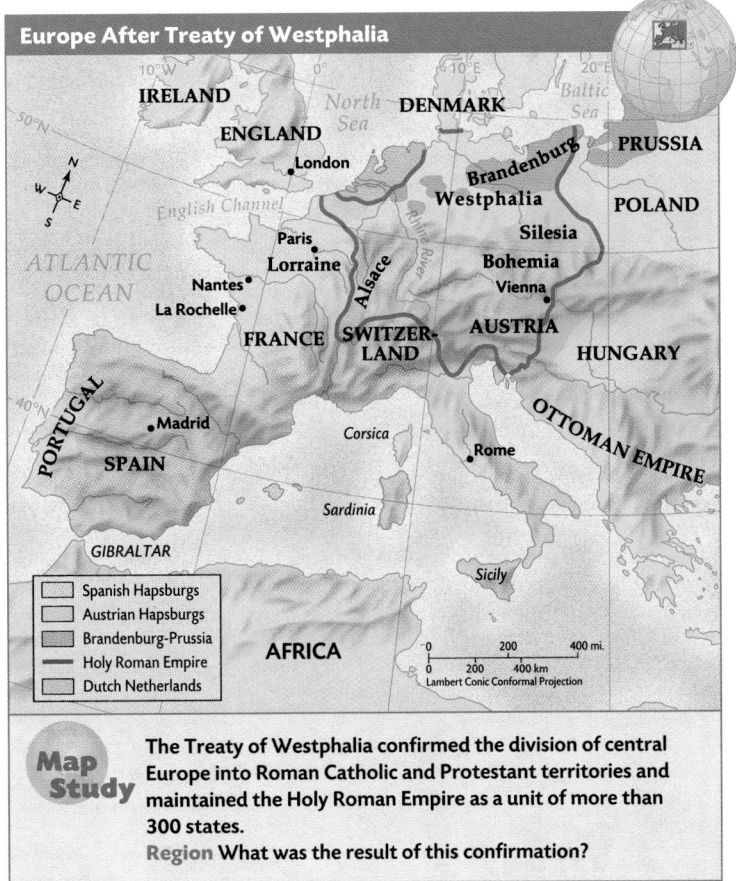

Europe After Treaty of Westphalia

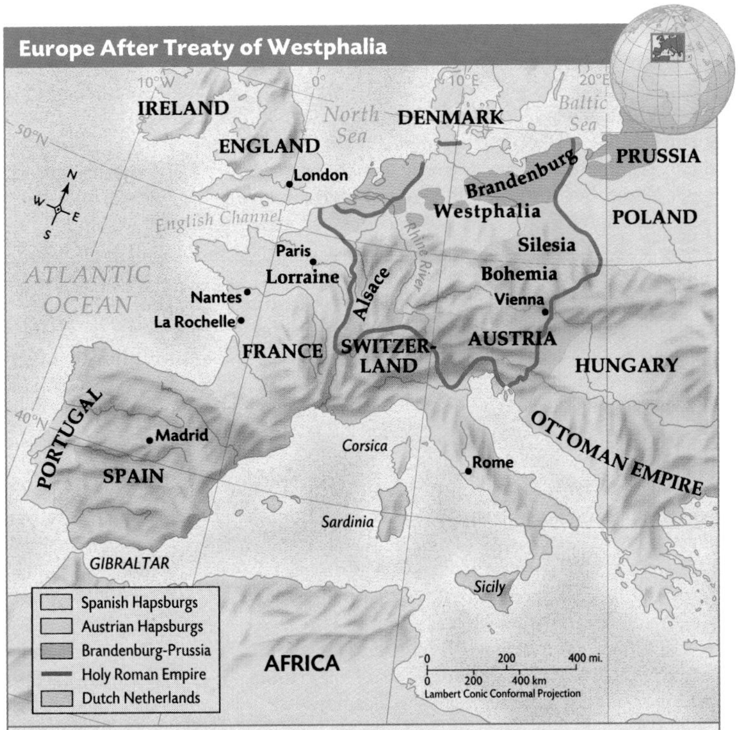

Map Study The Treaty of Westphalia confirmed the division of central Europe into Roman Catholic and Protestant territories and maintained the Holy Roman Empire as a unit of more than 300 states.
Region What was the result of this confirmation?

Austria

After the Thirty Years' War, the Austrian Hapsburgs concentrated on building a strong monarchy in **Austria**, Hungary, and Bohemia. Austria was still the most powerful of the German states. In 1683, the Austrians, with the aid of the Poles, lifted an Ottoman siege of Vienna. By 1739, Austrian armies had regained territory in the Balkan Peninsula from the Ottomans. As a result of the War of the Spanish Succession, the Austrians received the Spanish Netherlands and acquired lands in Italy.

In 1740, 23-year-old **Maria Theresa** inherited the throne of Austria from her father, Holy Roman Emperor Charles VI. According to law and custom, women were not permitted to rule Austria. In 1718 Charles had convinced the monarchs of Europe to accept a pragmatic sanction, or royal decree having the force of law, by which Europe's rulers promised not to divide the Hapsburg lands and to accept

Footnotes to History

Tulip Mania

During the Thirty Years' War, western Europeans fell in love with tulips. Dutch traders brought tulip bulbs into Europe from Ottoman Turkey beginning in the 1500s, and gardeners in the Netherlands and other parts of Europe took a liking to the blossoms. This led to a public craze for tulips that reached a peak in the 1630s.

Chapter 19 Section 4

TEACH

Guided Practice

THEME Conflict

In discussing the conflicts involved in the Thirty Years' War, ask students to recall religious conflicts that were a part of earlier periods. *(Romans and early Christians; Hindus and Muslims in India; Christians and Muslims in the Holy Land)* **L1**

Map Study

Answer

France became the leading power.

Map Skills Practice

Reading a Map What are the major cities in the Hapsburg territories? *(Madrid, Vienna)*

Geography Have students compare the map of the Hapsburg holdings in Section 1 on page 484 to the map in this section. Ask them to identify the changes that took place between the time represented by the earlier map and the time represented by this one. *(Holy Roman Empire is smaller; Hapsburg holdings smaller; Brandenburg-Prussia is new; Switzerland and Dutch Netherlands are now independent states; France is larger.)* **L2**

Focus on World Art Print 19, Jan Steen. *The Dancing Couple*

COOPERATIVE LEARNING ACTIVITY

Debate Have students hold a mock debate centering on Maria Theresa's right to rule the Hapsburg Empire after her father's death. Propose this question to debate: Should the Pragmatic Sanction have been honored by Austria's neighbors? Why or why not? Organize the class into two teams to take opposite positions. Direct each team to delegate a task to each member, such as finding outside resources, organizing data, creating questions and answers, and judging the outcome of the debate. Students should research the life and times of Maria Theresa, her father Charles VI, and also the status of women at that time. **L2**

Who? What? Where? When?

Maria Theresa of Austria not only ruled the foreign affairs of the Holy Roman Empire but also raised 16 children. One of her daughters, Marie Antoinette, became queen of France.

Chapter 19
Section 4

Independent Practice

Guided Reading Activity 19-4 **L1**

Political Cartoon Have students assume the role of a political cartoonist during the Austrian Succession or the Seven Years' War. Have them depict a major event in a cartoon for the *Prussian Press*. Subjects might include the fight over Silesia or alliances formed by different countries. **L2 LEP**

ASSESS

Check for Understanding

Assign Section 4 Review as homework or as an in-class activity.

Use Student Self-Test and Review Software to review Section 4.

CONNECTIONS The Arts

Johann Sebastian Bach

In the Germany of Bach's time, music was taught in schools, and most people could play an instrument. The chief instrument was the organ, but string and keyboard (clavier) instruments were gaining in popularity. Bach favored the organ and composed 143 chorale preludes for it. Of these, 45 were compiled in a "little organ book" for his oldest son and other students. Two famous contemporaries of Bach's time were George Telemann and George Frideric Handel.

Answers to Making the Connection

1. *It was lively and complex in style.*
2. *Few of his compositions were published while he lived.*

female succession to the Austrian throne.

Maria Theresa had not received any training in political matters, yet she proved to be a clever and resourceful leader. Overcoming the opposition of the nobility and most of her ministers, Maria Theresa greatly strengthened the Austrian central government. Under her direction, the central government accepted responsibility for such services as public health, prisons, and roads. Understanding that the unity of her empire depended on a strong economy, Maria Theresa ended trade barriers between Austria and Bohemia and used government funds to encourage the production of textiles and glass.

Prussia

Maria Theresa faced a number of enemies in Europe. One of these was France, the traditional rival of the Hapsburgs. In the 1700s a new European rival rose to prominence in northeastern Germany. Brandenburg-Prussia was ruled by the Hohenzollern family, which had governed the territory of Brandenburg since the 1400s. During the Thirty Years' War, they gained control of **Prussia** and other widely scattered lands in Germany.

Great Elector

One of the greatest of the Hohenzollern monarchs was Frederick William. He held the title "Great Elector." After the Thirty Years' War, Frederick William increased the strength of Brandenburg-Prussia by creating a permanent standing army. To meet the cost of his army, he proposed raising taxes. The Junkers, or nobles, opposed this plan. Frederick William then worked out a compromise with them. He permitted only Junkers to be landowners, freed them from taxes, and gave them full power over the peasants. In return, the Junkers agreed that Frederick William could tax townspeople and peasants. These two groups were too weak to organize and oppose this increased burden. In 1663 the Junkers further strengthened their ties to the Hohenzollerns. They pledged allegiance to Frederick William. As a result of this alliance with the Junkers, Frederick William was able to become an absolute ruler.

Frederick William was succeeded by his son Frederick I. Frederick aided the Austrian Hapsburgs against Louis XIV in the War of the Spanish Succession. As a reward, Frederick was given the title of king. He was, however, a weak ruler who did little to strengthen his country.

CONNECTIONS The Arts

Johann Sebastian Bach

Johann Sebastian Bach

Born in Eisenach, Germany, in 1685, Johann Sebastian Bach was one of the world's most talented composers. During his lifetime, however, Bach was best known for his abilities as a church organist and music director.

Bach wrote music for the Lutheran Church, wealthy nobles, and other musicians. His work reflects the baroque style of music, which reached its height during the early 1700s. Baroque music was characterized by lively dramatic compositions that appealed to the listener's mind and emotions.

Bach is especially known for two types of baroque music—counterpoint and fugue. In counterpoint, two or more melodies are combined. In the fugue, several instruments or voices play together, each playing the same melodies but with variations. Both techniques of composition produce complex and elaborate music.

Although the quantity of work Bach produced is impressive, very few of his compositions were published during his lifetime. It was only years after his death that he was recognized as a masterful composer of baroque music.

MAKING THE CONNECTION

1. Why is Johann Sebastian Bach's work called "baroque"?
2. Why was Bach regarded as a great composer only after his death?

MEETING SPECIAL NEEDS ACTIVITY

Learning Style: Visual/Spatial Help students who learn better visually to understand the conflicts involved between European powers during the Thirty Years' War or the War of the Austrian Succession by guiding them to make diagrams illustrating the actions and reactions, causes and effects, or problems and solutions of that time. For example, students might list problems or causes in one column, effects in another column, then draw arrows between the causes and effects. **L2 LEP**

Frederick William I

Frederick William I, who ruled from 1713 to 1740, was a powerful leader. He centralized the Prussian government, uniting all functions into one bureaucracy under his direct control. He supported production and trade and brought more revenue into the government treasury. Known as the Royal Drill Sargeant, Frederick William devoted his life to the Prussian army and made it the most efficient fighting force in Europe. Royal agents recruited men from rural areas of Germany. Frederick William I especially delighted in recruiting tall soldiers. He formed a special "regiment of giants" that he drilled himself.

Frederick II

In 1740, Frederick II, Frederick William I's son, became king of Prussia. As a boy, Frederick preferred music and art to horseback riding and military drills. However, when he became king, Frederick adopted his father's military ways and set out to expand Prussian territory. Frederick the Great, as he became known, rejected Austria's pragmatic sanction and seized the Austrian province of Silesia.

Frederick's attack on Silesia began a conflict called the War of the Austrian Succession. Prussia's forces were stronger than those of Austria. In spite of Austria's disadvantage, the Austrian empress, Maria Theresa, decided to send her forces into battle. Spain and France backed Prussia, while Great Britain (formed in 1707 as the result of a union between England and Scotland) and the Dutch Netherlands supported Austria.

After seven years of fighting, in 1748 the European powers signed the Treaty of Aix-la-Chapelle, which officially recognized Prussia's rise as an important nation. Frederick was allowed to keep Silesia; Maria Theresa was able to hold the rest of her domain: Austria, Hungary, and Bohemia.

The Austrian ruler, however, was not satisfied with the treaty and was determined to recover Silesia. To this end, Maria Theresa changed her alliance from Great Britain to France. She also gained the support of Russia since Prussia's Frederick II was an archenemy of Empress Elizabeth of Russia. These alliances set the stage for further conflict.

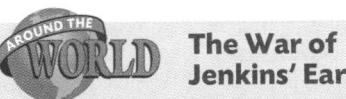

The Seven Years' War—from 1756 to 1763—was a worldwide conflict in which Great Britain and France competed for overseas territory, and Prussia opposed Austria, Russia, France, and other nations. The war between Austria and Prussia erupted in 1756. After victories in Saxony—a German state and an ally of Austria—and after a later victory over the Austrians in Silesia, Frederick II signed a peace agreement that enabled him to retain most of Silesia.

The struggle between Great Britain and France in North America was known as the French and Indian War. The British and French also fought in India. At the Treaty of Paris in 1763, France gave up most of French Canada and its lands east of the Mississippi River to Great Britain. Great Britain also replaced France as the leading power in India. As a result of the Seven Years' War, Great Britain emerged as the strongest colonial empire and Prussia retained the province of Silesia.

AROUND THE WORLD — The War of Jenkins' Ear

Caribbean Sea, 1739

The War of Jenkins' Ear was part of a series of conflicts among European nations in the 1700s. In the waters off Florida, an English smuggler named Robert Jenkins lost his ear in a fight with Spaniards in 1731. Jenkins' appearance in Parliament in 1738 further incited public opinion against Spain. The result was war, declared in June 1739, over possession of Georgia and commercial rivalry at sea. Within a year, the War of Jenkins' Ear had become part of the more serious War of Austrian Succession.

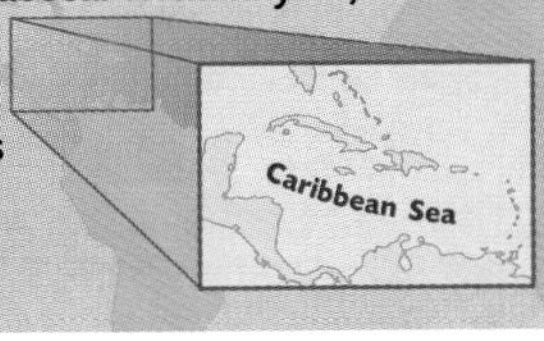

SECTION 4 REVIEW

Recall

1. **Define** pragmatic sanction.
2. **Identify** Ferdinand of Styria, Treaty of Westphalia, Maria Theresa, Frederick II, Silesia.
3. **State** what primary factor caused the Thirty Years' War. What were the war's results?

Critical Thinking

4. **Analyzing Information** How did Maria Theresa strengthen the central government in Austria and in her other domains?

Understanding Themes

5. **Conflict** How did the many conflicts among the German states affect the balance of power?

Chapter 19 Section 4

Who?What?Where?When?

Sans Souci Frederick II planned and had built a one-story summer palace, Sans Souci. French for "without cares," Sans Souci was the king's favorite retreat. It was famous for its midnight suppers, at which Frederick surrounded himself with educated men.

Evaluate

Section Quiz 19-4

Use the Testmaker to create a customized quiz for Section 4.

Reteach

Have students work in small groups to write summaries of conflicts discussed in this section.

Enrich

Have students voice their opinions about the shifting of alliances in order to achieve political goals. **Were these the decisions of a wise monarch or signs of disloyalty and ingratitude?** *(Answers will vary. Students should mention the balance of power theory.)*

CLOSE

Ask students to offer opinions about the justification of war and bloodshed that raged throughout Europe before and during the Thirty Years' War. Ask how they might have reacted if they had lived in the 1600s.

SECTION 4 REVIEW ANSWERS

1. All vocabulary words are defined in the Glossary.
2. Ferdinand of Styria, 494; Treaty of Westphalia, 495; Maria Theresa, 495; Frederick II, 497; Silesia, 497
3. Ferdinand of Styria's attempts to end Protestantism and strengthen Hapsburg rule by curtailing Bohemian Protestants' freedom; ensuing Czech revolt; other Protestant countries became involved
4. Government took responsibilities for services such as public health, prisons, and roads; ended trade barriers; used government funds to encourage production of textiles and glass to build the economy.
5. **CONFLICT** weakened German states and allowed France to become dominant

Chapter 19 Section 5

SECTION THEME

- **Innovation** Peter the Great attempts to modernize Russian society.

Find Out

Answer: *Russian czars were all-powerful and able to crush the nobility, the Church, and the towns.*

FOCUS

Section Objective

Understand how the power of Russian czars differed from that of other European monarchs.

BELLRINGER Motivational Activity

Before taking roll at the beginning of the class period, project Section Focus Transparency 19-5 and have students answer the activity questions. Discuss students' responses.

This activity is also available as a blackline master.

Vocabulary Pre-check

Use the Vocabulary PuzzleMaker to create a puzzle that reinforces the vocabulary terms in this section. **L1**

1500 — 1600 — 1700 — 1800

- **1533** Ivan IV (the Terrible) begins rule.
- **1689** Peter I (the Great) becomes czar.
- **1721** Russia secures areas of Baltic coastline.
- **1796** Catherine II (the Great) dies.

Section 5

Russia

Setting the Scene

- **Terms to Define**
  boyar, *dvorianie*, serf
- **People to Meet**
  Ivan IV, Peter I, Catherine II
- **Places to Locate**
  Poland, St. Petersburg, Siberia

Find Out How did the power of Russian czars differ from that of other European monarchs?

The Storyteller

When first posted, no one could believe the decree. Czar Peter had ordered all children from the nobility and clerical classes [clergy] to study mathematics and geometry. Those who refused were forbidden to marry until they mastered the material. Such commands seemed absurd and many scoffed at the czar's ability to enforce his demands. However, teachers arrived in each district and local taxes were increased for support. Priests likewise received notification and no priest dared solemnize a marriage without proper certification. Father Konstantin looked sadly at the couple before him and explained, "You do not have the proper certification. I cannot marry you."

—adapted from *Decree on Compulsory Education of the Russian Nobility*, reprinted in *The Human Record, Volume 2*, Alfred J. Andrea and James H. Overfield, 1990

Russian Orthodox Priest

Between 1500 and 1800, Russia made tremendous territorial gains and became a major European power. Slavs elsewhere lost ground and were taken over by other powers.

In southeastern Europe, the Ottoman Turks ruled most of the Balkan Peninsula and the Serbs, Bosnians, and Macedonians who lived there. Under the Ottomans, some of these Slavs converted to Islam, while the rest remained Eastern Orthodox. Hungary ruled the Croats (KROH•ATZ), and Austria controlled the Slovenes (SLOH•VEENZ). Both these Slavic peoples remained Roman Catholic and oriented to western Europe.

In central Europe, Austria controlled the Slovaks and the Czechs, whose resistance to Catholicism had sparked the Thirty Years' War. Neighboring **Poland** had been an important Catholic power from the late 1300s. Polish monarchs created one of the larger states of Europe, but by the 1600s Poland gradually weakened. Ukrainian subjects rebelled against Polish rule in the mid-1600s and united with Russia. In the late 1700s Prussia, Austria, and Russia divided Poland among themselves. The region of Belarus and its people, the Belarussians, passed from Polish to Russian control at this time.

Rise of Russia

From the 1200s to the early 1700s, Russia was isolated from western European developments, such as the Crusades, the Renaissance, and the Reformation. Russia developed its own civilization based on the values of the Eastern Orthodox Church and the Byzantine Empire. The Russian monarchy became all-powerful and easily crushed its opponents. The nobility, the established church, and the towns—all of whom had posed repeated opposition to royal power elsewhere in Europe—never posed the same challenge in Russia.

SECTION RESOURCES

Reproducible Masters
- Reproducible Lesson Plan 19-5
- Guided Reading Activity 19-5
- History Simulation 19
- Reteaching Activity 19
- Enrichment Activity 19
- Section Quiz 19-5
- Performance Assessment Activity 19
- Spanish Chapter Summary 19

Transparencies
- Section Focus Transparency 19-5

Multimedia
- Vocabulary PuzzleMaker Software
- Student Self-Test and Review Software
- Testmaker
- Picture Atlas of the World

Ivan IV

The most powerful of the early czars was **Ivan IV**, who ruled from 1533 to 1584. Known as Ivan "the Terrible" or "the Awesome," he was at once learned, religious, and cruel. Ivan became czar at the age of three. While growing up, he was caught between rival groups of nobles who sought to rule the country. He witnessed much cruelty and was never able to rid himself of his early memories. As an adult, Ivan saw treason everywhere and arrested, exiled, or executed many of his closest advisers. In a fit of rage, he even killed his own son.

Ivan took many steps against the **boyars** (boh•YAHRZ), or nobles, to reduce their potential threat to his throne. He seized their scattered lands and placed them under his direct control. The former owners were uprooted and dispersed. On the seized land, which made up about one-half of the country, Ivan placed his own loyal people. They became a secret police force and terrorized the rest of the country.

Russian Expansion

Under Ivan IV, Russia increased its trade and contacts with western Europe. Ivan imported artisans and doctors from Germany and England. He introduced the first printing press into Russia. Russian ties to the West further expanded after English traders found a northern sea route to Russia in 1553. Ivan gave England's Muscovy Company control of Western trade with Russia.

Ivan used his armies to expand Russia's borders in all directions. Despite Russia's vast size, it had few seaports, none of which were free of ice throughout the year. Gaining access to the sea for trade and military security was a long-standing goal of Russian rulers.

During the 1550s Ivan annexed Mongol lands east and south of Moscow. In the west, he waged a 25-year war with Poland, Lithuania, and Sweden for control of territory that would have given Russia an outlet to the Baltic Sea. This effort failed, however, and Russia lost land to Sweden.

The Time of Troubles

After Ivan's death in 1584, Russia entered the Time of Troubles, a period of chaos that lasted from 1598 to 1613. During the Time of Troubles, the succession to the Russian throne was disputed; foreign powers intervened in Russian affairs; and famine, epidemic, and peasant revolts swept through the land. Order was restored in 1613, when Michael Romanov was elected czar. Michael founded the Romanov dynasty, which ruled Russia until 1917.

Visualizing History **Peter the Great, a man of restless energy and sometimes hasty decisions, attempted many reforms.** *What reforms did he introduce to make Russia more like western European nations?*

Peter the Great

In 1689 **Peter I**, known as Peter the Great, came to the throne. He was a towering figure, nearly 7 feet (2 m) tall. Peter had boundless energy and volcanic emotions. During his reign, he sought to bring Russia into the mainstream of European civilization.

Encounter With the West

As a young man, Peter was fascinated with practical subjects, such as mechanics, geography, and military strategy. He sought out tutors among the foreign community in Moscow to learn the basic skills of navigation and shipbuilding. He discovered that Russian knowledge of the outside world was quite limited. Most Russians were illiterate peasants; only a few members of the nobility were well educated.

After becoming czar, Peter took an 18-month study tour of England and the Netherlands. He visited shipyards, factories, mills, and laboratories. He learned carpentry and developed enough skill in

COOPERATIVE LEARNING ACTIVITY

Research Have students work in small groups to research and report on the daily life of women in Russia during the time of Peter the Great and Catherine the Great, as well as women in Russia today. Scholarly works on Russian feminism of the past and the present are available in local libraries. Have groups plan how to delegate the work—some students may research, and others may write the reports. Topics to consider might be family responsibilities, intellectual interests, types of work, and political concerns of the women. Copies of photographs from the resources will help the groups describe the life of women then and now. **L2**

TEACH

Guided Practice

THEME Innovation

Discuss and list on the chalkboard the changes that occurred in Russia between the time of Ivan the Terrible and Catherine the Great. Ask what advances were made in political control, the arts, science, and technology. *(Sample answers: nobility given land in exchange for government service; printing press introduced into Russia; new capital built; army and navy modernized)* **L1 LEP**

Visualizing History Because Peter had such stores of energy, he found relaxation difficult. Although hunting was a favorite sport of many monarchs, Peter refused to hunt; however, he sailed whenever he could. He also enjoyed playing chess and carried a folding leather chessboard with him so he could play with anyone at any time.

Answer to Caption: *required court members to wear Western-style clothes; included women in social gatherings; invited foreign experts to train Russians in sciences, naval warfare, shipbuilding, and foreign languages; increased the power of the central government*

Comparing Catherine the Great has been compared by historians to England's Elizabeth in her ability to rule and in the significance of her reign. Have students prepare a chart comparing the two rulers and their accomplishments. **L2**

History Simulation 19

TEACH

Explain to the class that the building of a city on the marshes of the Neva River was a major project. Peter hired hundreds of foreign architects and thousands of Russian workers to create a city described as the "Venice of the North." **What feature unique to a city like Venice would be useful for a city built on a broad river and marshes?** *(a network of canals)* Tell students that St. Petersburg became the country's main industrial center and one of the world's most brilliant cultural centers.

Who?What?Where?When?

St. Petersburg arrived late as a major city in the world. In the American colonies, New York was already 75 years old, Boston was 73, and Philadelphia was 60. St. Petersburg was the capital of the Russian Empire for 200 years.

NATIONAL GEOGRAPHIC SOCIETY

CD-ROM

PICTURE ATLAS OF THE WORLD

You and your students can see a skyline view of St. Petersburg and the Winter Palace (now the Hermitage Museum) by clicking Russia's "Photos" button.

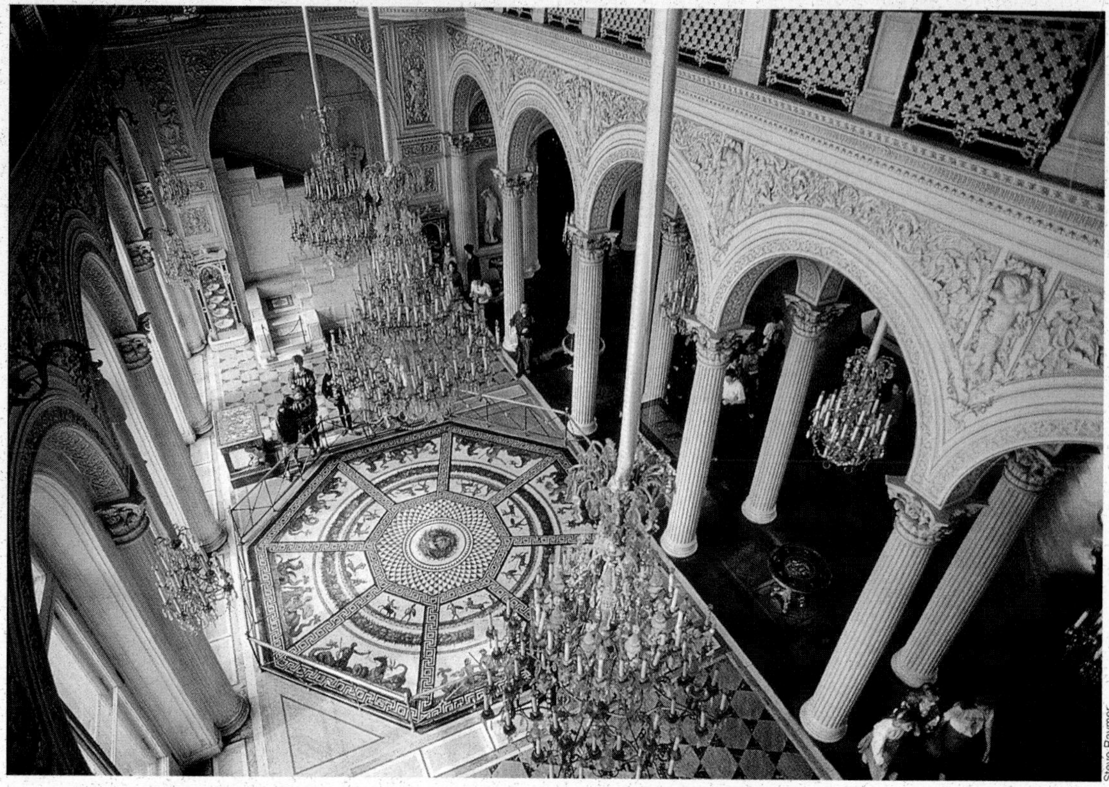

Steve Raymer

Peter's Great City

Where he first set foot on the Baltic coast, legend has it, Peter the Great proclaimed: "Here there shall be a town." On May 16, 1703, Russian workers laid the foundations for a fortress on the Baltic coast. The city of St. Petersburg soon spread out, and in 1712 Peter made it the new capital of Russia. A traveler in his youth, he was determined that his new capital would imitate the imposing European cities he had visited. St. Petersburg did not remain the capital of Russia, but the new city offered Peter the Great a chance to consolidate the power of the Russian central government and to drag Russia into the modern world. Many changes were inaugurated: He forbade men to wear beards or to dress in the traditional long robes called caftans. He simplified the Cyrillic alphabet. He was relentless. At times he even resorted to terror. But he transformed Russia and made his new city on the Baltic Sea a window to the West.

G.D. Talbot

Today Peter's legacy is everywhere: in the shipyards, the research centers, and the architecture of ornate palaces such as the Winter Palace (center), completed during the reign of Catherine the Great in 1762. "I have a whole labyrinth of rooms ... and all of them are filled with luxuries," she wrote of the Winter Palace and the adjoining Hermitage, where Pavilion Hall (top) fills one small corner.

500 Chapter 19 *Royal Power and Conflict*

surgery and dentistry to want to practice on others.

When he returned home, Peter forced the Russian nobility to adopt the ways of western Europe. He ordered members of the court to wear western European clothing. Men entering Moscow were forced to shave their beards or pay a fine. Women, who had always been excluded from social gatherings, were ordered to attend parties.

Peter sent Russians abroad to study shipbuilding, naval warfare, mathematics, and foreign languages. He invited foreign experts to train Russians. His greatest effort to open Russia to Europe was the building of a new capital, which he named **St. Petersburg**. Located at the mouth of the Neva River near the Baltic Sea, St. Petersburg became Russia's "window to the West."

Foreign Policy

Peter's goal was to make Russia a European power. He expanded Russia's boundaries in the south, east, and northwest. In 1689 Russia forced China to recognize Russian claims to **Siberia**, the vast stretch of land east of European Russia. For most of Peter's reign, Russia was at war with Poland, Sweden, or the Ottoman Empire. Peter wanted to win a warm-water port on the Black Sea and control of the Baltic coastline. The Russian failure to defeat the Turks near the Black Sea convinced Peter to modernize the army and navy. His military reforms paid off in 1721, when Russia defeated Sweden and won control of the eastern end of the Baltic region.

Government Administration

Peter made sweeping changes in the Russian government. Borrowing ideas from France, he introduced a central bureaucracy and placed local governments under its control. Peter brought the Eastern Orthodox Church under his direct authority. In place of a single independent church leader, Peter created the Holy Synod, a council of bishops responsible to a secular government official appointed by the czar.

Peter also created a new class of nobles called *dvorianie* (DVOH•ree•YAH•nee•YUH), who, in return for government service, were allowed to own hereditary, landed estates. A noble's duty to the czar started at age 15 and continued until death.

Peter used privileges and force to make the established nobility accept government service. Nobles were given full control over the serfs, or peasant laborers who worked the estates and were bound to the land. While freedom for peasants had gradually increased in western Europe, the opposite was true in Russia.

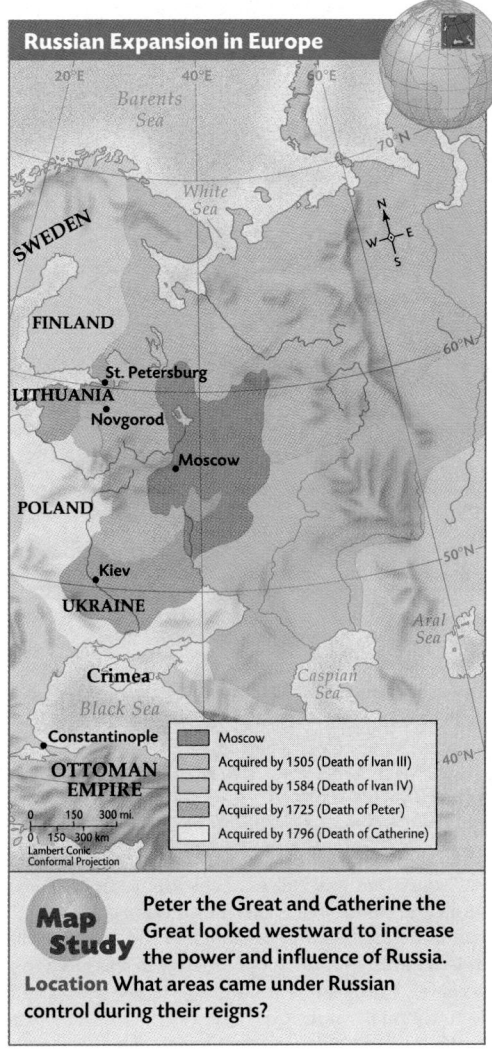

Russian Expansion in Europe

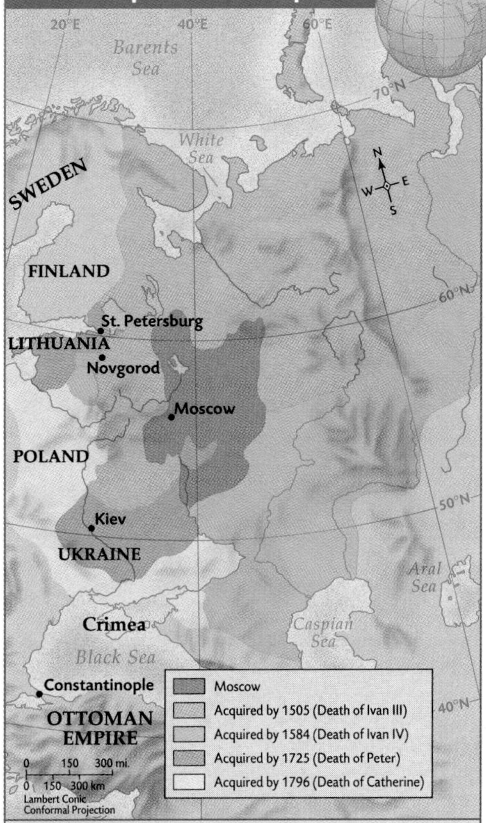

Map Study Peter the Great and Catherine the Great looked westward to increase the power and influence of Russia.
Location What areas came under Russian control during their reigns?

Finally, Peter changed the tax laws to increase government income and efficiency. Under the plan, nobles paid no taxes. As in France, the tax burden fell on the poorest classes.

Economic Changes

To stimulate economic growth, Peter brought agriculture and craft production under strict government control. He gave incentives to increase production in favored areas such as mining and metalworking. New production centers were provided with land, money, and workers. Most of the workers were tied to their trades as the serfs were to the land.

Independent Practice

Guided Reading Activity 19-5 **L1**

Map Study

Answer

Peter the Great: Ukraine and Lithuania; Catherine: Poland and Crimea

Map Skills Practice

Reading a Map The acquisition of Crimea gave Russia access to what important body of water? *(Black Sea)*

Essay Have students assume they are writers during the reign of Peter the Great. Have them write essays expressing their opinions of Peter as the "great innovator of Russia" or as "the oppressor of the people." Suggest that students research to provide concrete examples for their essays. **L3**

Linking Past and Present

City Renamed Peter the Great had the new city named St. Petersburg after himself. Later it was renamed Leningrad after the Communist revolutionary leader Vladimir Lenin. Today the city has been re-renamed and is again called St. Petersburg.

MEETING SPECIAL NEEDS ACTIVITY

Mixed Learners To help students who learn better by discussing a topic and also to help those who have limited use of the language, have students work in groups of three. Each student should select part of the section to study, outline, and then "teach" to the other members of the group. Suggest that they each write a short quiz for the others to take at the end of the teaching session. **L1 LEP**

Chapter 19 *Royal Power and Conflict* **501**

History & Art In the midst of her political and military career, Catherine wrote plays, poems, fairy tales, and memoirs. She encouraged literature and the arts, and architecture flourished under her reign. The famous Hermitage, which became her art gallery, was built as an addition to the Winter Palace.
Answer to Caption: *a peasant rebellion*

ASSESS

Check for Understanding

Assign Section 5 Review as homework or as an in-class activity.

Use Student Self-Test and Review Software to review Section 5.

Evaluate

Section Quiz 19-5

Reteach

Have students work in small groups to summarize the achievements and the acts of oppression of each major ruler in Section 5. Guide a class discussion based on their summaries.

Reteaching Activity 19

Enrich

Have students debate the following: Catherine the Great was not great.

Enrichment Activity 19

CLOSE

Ask students which Russian monarch they would rather serve and in what capacity. *(Answers should reflect the ability and morality of the monarch.)*

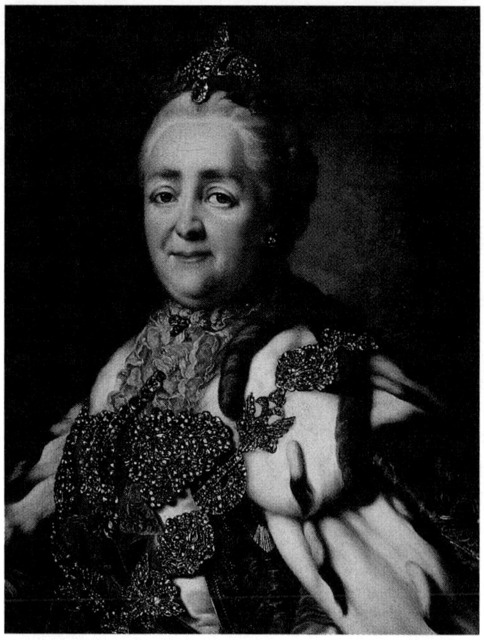

History & Art *Portrait of Catherine the Great* by Alexandre Roslin. Musée des Beaux Arts, La Rochelle, France *What changed Catherine's mind about the equality of all people?*

Effects

Peter's reforms strengthened Russia's role in foreign affairs. In his own country, however, Peter had only limited success. His domestic policies broke the traditional Eastern Orthodox culture that had united nobles and peasants. With Peter's reign, a dangerous split developed between the few who accepted European ways and the many who clung to traditional values. An observer noted: "The tsar pulls uphill alone with the strength of ten, but millions push downhill." Many of Peter's reforms were incomplete and hasty. Yet his measures brought Russia into the mainstream of western European civilization.

Catherine the Great

After Peter's death in 1725, Russia was ruled by a series of weak or ordinary monarchs. The next notable ruler was **Catherine II**. In 1762, Catherine seized the throne from her weak husband, Peter III, and ruled as empress of Russia until 1796. Although born a German princess, Catherine easily adopted Russian ways and earned the respect of her people.

As monarch, Catherine was greatly influenced by leading western European thinkers. She studied their works and corresponded with a number of them. For a time, she believed that all people were born equal and that it was "contrary to the Christian faith and to justice to make slaves of them."

Early in her reign, Catherine considered freeing the serfs. A peasant rebellion that threatened her rule, however, made Catherine change her mind. To ensure the continued support of the nobles, she released them from the government service required by Peter I. Catherine also allowed the nobles to treat their serfs as they pleased. During Catherine's reign, more peasants were forced into serfdom than ever before, and their conditions worsened. The common people of Russia had fewer rights than those in any other part of Europe. When groups of them revolted, Catherine brutally crushed the uprisings.

A successful foreign policy earned her the name Catherine the Great. She significantly expanded Russia's borders to the south and achieved the goal of securing a warm-water port on the Black Sea. In making this gain, Russian armies defeated the Ottoman Turks. In the west, Catherine acquired territory from Poland. Prussia and Austria took the rest of Poland, which then ceased to exist until 1919.

Catherine was the last of the great absolute monarchs of the 1700s. By the time of her death in 1796, new ideas of liberty and equality had spread throughout western Europe. These new ideas directly challenged and questioned the age-old institution of monarchy.

SECTION 5 REVIEW

Recall
1. **Define** boyar, *dvorianie*, serf.
2. **Identify** Ivan IV, the Romanovs, Peter I, Catherine II.
3. **Locate** the cities of Moscow and St. Petersburg on the map on page 501. Why did Czar Peter the Great move the Russian capital from Moscow to St. Petersburg?

Critical Thinking
4. **Synthesizing Information** How did the reigns of Peter the Great and Catherine the Great affect the Russian nobility and the common people?

Understanding Themes
5. **Innovation** How did Peter the Great try to make Russia accept western European ideas and practices?

SECTION 5 REVIEW ANSWERS

1. All vocabulary words are defined in the Glossary.
2. Ivan IV, 499; the Romanovs, 499; Peter I, 499; Catherine II, 502
3. to open Russia to Europe
4. Peter used privileges and force to make the nobility accept government service; bound serfs to the land and granted nobles full control over them; Catherine released the nobles from government service; under her the lot of the common people worsened.
5. INNOVATION He brought foreign experts to teach the European ways and sent Russians abroad.

Study and Writing
SKILLS

Recognizing a Stereotype

Emanuella asks her friend Ashley if she would date a football player. Ashley says, "No way. Football players are all muscle and no brains." Ashley has expressed a stereotype—an oversimplified description of a group. Because stereotypes may be both inaccurate and harmful, we must learn to recognize them in speaking, writing, and thinking.

Learning the Skill

A stereotype can describe any group—a gender, race, religion, country, region, city, neighborhood, school, or profession. Stereotypes blur or ignore the characteristics of individuals within the group. In the example above, Ashley may reject the friendship of a very considerate and intelligent person just because he plays football. While this is a negative stereotype, other stereotypes may have positive or neutral connotations. "Blondes have more fun," for example, is a positive stereotype. Negative stereotypes, however, are the least accurate and most harmful.

Stereotypes can influence not only our attitude about a group's members, but also can affect our behavior toward them. History is full of examples of oppression and persecution directed at particular groups of people. Negative stereotypes usually accompany and support these destructive acts.

Because stereotypes are so common, it is easy to ignore or accept them. Instead, learn how to recognize and evaluate them. Certain words, phrases, and thoughts signal the presence of stereotypes. In any kind of material, written or oral, first notice characteristics attributed to a particular group. Look for exaggerations, often indicated by words such as *all*, *none*, *every*, *always*, and *never*. Identify strong negative adjectives such as *lazy*, *sneaky*, *cruel*, and *corrupt*. Note a consistently positive or negative tone to the description.

Once you recognize a stereotype, then evaluate its accuracy. Think about whether the stereotype puts a positive or negative slant on the information concerning a specific group. Ask yourself: Does this stereotype agree or disagree with what I know about individual members of this group?

Practicing the Skill

Each statement below contains a stereotype held by people from the 1500s to the 1700s. Identify the stereotype in each statement. Identify any words or phrases that helped you recognize the stereotype, and tell whether it has a negative, positive, or neutral connotation.

1. England is an isle fouled by heretics and barbarians. *(Spain, 1554)*
2. It is against the law, human and divine, that a woman should reign and have empire above men. *(England, 1560)*
3. The Italians are so jovial and addicted to music that nearly every countryman plays on the guitar, and will commonly go into the field with a fiddle. *(England, 1600)*
4. Do not put such unlimited power into the hands of husbands. Remember all men would be tyrants if they could. [We ladies] will not hold outselves bound by any laws in which we have no voice, or representation. *(United States, 1776)*

Applying the Skill

Identify three stereotypes about groups within your community. For each stereotype, write a paragraph evaluating its accuracy by recalling your own experiences with individual members of the group.

For More Practice

Turn to the Skill Practice in the Chapter Review on page 505 for more practice in recognizing a stereotype.

Study and Writing
SKILLS

TEACH

Recognizing a Stereotype Most students will understand and be aware of the problem of negative stereotypes. Suggest that they take time to consider positive stereotypes and the actual harm that can come from them, too. Ask students to brainstorm positive stereotype examples from television programs, movies, and magazine advertisements. For example, they might discuss the positive body images portrayed in the media, such as the scent ads, hairstyles, and fashions that are supposed to make life wonderful. Ask students to discuss the impact of these advertisements on young people and the problems they cause for self-esteem in the teenage population.

Additional Practice

Skill Reinforcement Activity 19

ANSWERS TO PRACTICING THE SKILL

1. English people were opposed to Catholicism; words *fouled, heretics*, and *barbarians* are used for their negative connotations; a negative stereotype
2. only men should be rulers of countries; words "against the law" very absolute; a negative stereotype
3. Italians are happy and musical; *every* shows exaggeration; a positive stereotype
4. husbands, men in general, are not to be trusted with power; negative word *tyrants* and use of *all*; a negative stereotype

Chapter 19 Review

GLENCOE TECHNOLOGY

VIDEODISC

Use MindJogger to review students' knowledge of the chapter.

MindJogger Videoquiz

Chapter 19
Disc 3 Side A

Also available in VHS.

Answers

Using Key Terms

1. g	6. k
2. f	7. b
3. j	8. c
4. h	9. d
5. e	10. i

Using Your History Journal

Students should give supporting facts from the text or other resources to explain the reason for their opinion.

Reviewing Facts

1. Hapsburgs, Spain and Austria; Tudors, England; Bourbons, France; Romanovs, Russia; Hohenzollern, Brandenburg-Prussia
2. Catholics and Protestants
3. by cooperating with Parliament and selling monastery lands to wealthy landowners
4. Maria Theresa's claim to Austrian throne through Pragmatic Sanction; Frederick's challenge and invasion of Silesia
5. He built St. Petersburg near the Baltic Sea and made it the capital; expanded Russia's borders; built a navy and factories; introduced newspapers and books and western European styles and customs.

Critical Thinking

1. Similarities: both strong monarchies, sought to increase wealth, faced internal unrest. Differences: Hapsburg Empire vaster; Hapsburgs Protestant and Tudors Catholic; Hapsburgs a larger family with many branches.
2. Possible answer: I joined the army because it was the only way to escape hanging. Conditions during the war were terrible. I was hungry most of the time and often wounded; most of my friends died. I have little hope for the future because my home has been destroyed and the land ruined.
3. Answers will vary. Students may conclude that political leaders today need training in diplomacy and negotiation.
4. Answers will vary. Students should give supporting facts from the text to explain why they admire or do not admire a particular monarch.

CHAPTER 19 REVIEW

Historical Significance

One of the results of the Age of Monarchy was the emergence of strong national states in Europe. Absolute monarchs centralized their governments and established powerful military forces to protect and to expand their countries' natural borders.

Monarchs plunged Europe into wars over territorial, religious, and economic issues. By forcefully asserting their power, monarchs created the national boundaries that would form the basis of modern Europe. Later wars among European nations would modify the boundaries but not change them completely.

Using Key Terms

Write the key term that completes each sentence.

a. absolutism	g. armada
b. balance of power	h. inflation
c. intendants	i. yeomen
d. serfs	j. pragmatic sanction
e. divine right	k. *dvorianie*
f. boyars	

1. In 1558 King Philip II of Spain planned to invade England by sending against it an ______ made up of 130 ships and 33,000 sailors.
2. Ivan IV of Russia took steps against the _____ to reduce their potential threat to his throne.
3. In 1718 the Holy Roman emperor Charles VI convinced Europe's monarchs to accept a __________ in which they promised to accept Maria Theresa as the future Hapsburg monarch.
4. During Spain's decline as a European power, its economy suffered from ________, an abnormal increase in currency resulting in sharp price increases.
5. During the 1600s and the 1700s, European monarchs claimed to rule by __________, the theory that monarchs derive their power from God.
6. Peter the Great of Russia established a new class of nobles, known as ________, who received land and control of peasant laborers.
7. During Elizabeth I's reign, England worked for a ___________ on the Continent to prevent one European power from becoming too strong.
8. Cardinal Richelieu of France gave local government powers to agents of the French crown known as ___________.
9. During the reign of Catherine the Great, conditions worsened for Russia's ______, or peasant laborers bound to the land.
10. During the reigns of the Tudors, ________ were English farmers with small landholdings.

Using Your History Journal

Choose an event from the country time line you created. Write a short opinion paper on why you believe that this was the most significant development, person, or decision in that nation during the period 1500 to 1750.

Reviewing Facts

1. **List** at least four major European royal families and the countries over which they reigned during the period from about 1500 to about 1800.
2. **Identify** two major western European religious groups during the 1500s.
3. **Explain** how England's Henry VIII strengthened support for his policies.
4. **State** what circumstances and events led to the War of the Austrian Succession.
5. **Identify** the changes that Peter the Great brought to Russia.

Critical Thinking

1. **Analyze** How were the Hapsburg and Tudor monarchies of the 1500s similar? How were they different? Which one do you think was more successful?
2. **Synthesize** Imagine you are a soldier during the Thirty Years' War. Describe how you joined the army and what conditions were like during the war. What hopes do you have for the future?
3. **Evaluate** Consider the leadership style of Maria Theresa of Austria, who had no training in political matters. Can a person today be a successful

political leader with no prior training or experience?

4. **Evaluate** Which of the monarchs described in this chapter do you most admire? Which one do you least admire? Explain your reasons.
5. **Evaluate** What does the portrait of Frederick the Great below reveal about the values and characteristics of the Prussian monarchy?

Understanding Themes

1. **Conflict** How did Spain's rivalry with England develop during the period from about 1500 to about 1750?
2. **Change** How did Tudor monarchs bring stability to England?
3. **Uniformity** How did Louis XIV try to strengthen French loyalty to his monarchy?
4. **Conflict** What dynastic and religious issues divided the German states?
5. **Innovation** Why did Peter the Great want to make innovations in government and society?

Linking Past and Present

1. European monarchs in the 1600s and 1700s resolved their territorial disputes and ambitions through war. How do present-day leaders resolve disputes? Explore the similarities and the differences between contemporary world leaders and monarchs in early modern Europe.
2. European monarchs in the 1600s and 1700s were powerful leaders who claimed to rule by divine right. What is the position of monarchs in Europe today? How is power exercised in modern European governments?

Skill Practice

The following lines from William Shakespeare's plays include stereotypes that were common in 16th-century England. Identify each stereotype and any words or phrases that helped you recognize it.

1. "Frailty, thy name is woman!"
2. "These Moors are changeable in their moods."
3. "This Hebrew will turn Christian; he grows kind."
4. "Today the French … all in gold, like heathen gods, shone down the English."

Geography in History

1. **Location** Refer to the map below. Along what body of water did Pomerania lie? What was the population loss over much of its area?
2. **Place** Of Bohemia, Saxony, and Silesia, which area had suffered the least population loss?
3. **Region** In general, what parts of the Holy Roman Empire retained the most population? Why do you think this was so?

Population Loss 1618–1648

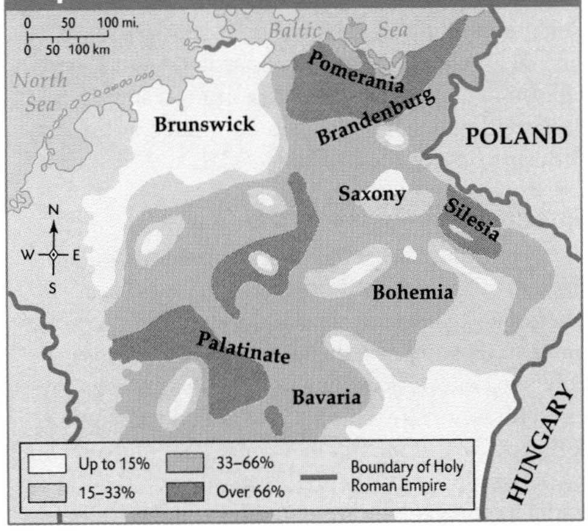

5. reflects a dignified, serious, and strong leader

Understanding Themes

1. **CONFLICT** England supported the Dutch fight for independence against Spain and raided Spanish ships; Philip invaded England with Armada to rid himself of Elizabeth's interference; that defeat led to Spain's decline.
2. **CHANGE** They unified the country, expanded foreign trade, and built a strong navy.
3. **UNIFORMITY** kept nation's traditional ways, chose top advisers from middle classes, repealed Edict of Nantes
4. **CONFLICT** Catholic Hapsburgs fought Protestant German princes; Catholic Bourbons fought Hapsburgs for power; Hohenzollerns of Prussia fought Austrian Hapsburgs.

5. **INNOVATION** He wanted to make Russia more like western Europe.

Linking Past and Present

1. Answers will vary. Today leaders try to resolve disputes through negotiations and diplomacy, but sometimes conflicts still result in war.
2. Most European monarchs today are mainly figureheads with power exercised by a prime minister and national legislature.

Skill Practice

1. all women are weak; woman used to mean "all women"; negative
2. Moors (Africans) are moody people; "these Moors" means "all Moors"; negative
3. Jews are not kind—kindness is a Christian trait; negative
4. the French looked splendid; *all in gold* and *gods* show exaggeration; positive

Geography in History

1. Baltic Sea; over 66 percent
2. Saxony
3. western parts, Brunswick, and Saxony; there were more rebellions and wars in the other territories, depleting the population

Chapter Bonus Test Question

Ask students: If you could spend an evening with one of the rulers you have met in this chapter, who would it be and what would you do? *(Answers will vary but should reflect knowledge of the ruler's life and accomplishments.)*

Unit 4 Digest

The Unit Digest offers a chapter-by-chapter summary that can be used for any of the following teaching purposes:

- ***Preview*** one chapter or an entire unit,
- ***Review*** some or all of the chapters,
- ***Condense*** when specific chapters or units have not been taught, or
- ***Reteach*** chapters that students have studied in the unit.

PREVIEW

Use the Unit 4 Digest Transparencies to preview the highlights of the unit.

History & Art Jan van Eyck (c. 1390–1441) did not invent oil painting but perfected the new technique. This wedding portrait includes many symbols: the dog stands for faithfulness, while the single candle in the chandelier represents Christ's omniscience.

Answer to Caption: *human activities and feelings*

Unit 4 Digest

Throughout the world from 1400 to the mid-1700s, strong rulers increased the power and prestige of their nations. In Europe two major movements—the Renaissance and the Protestant Reformation—resulted in a new European culture that was eager to acquire new knowledge and to spread Christianity.

Religion and politics were also powerful forces in Asia. There, Muslim empires ruled over a vast area between the Mediterranean Sea and South Asia. Other Asian areas—China, Japan, and the lands of Southeast Asia—held fast to traditional ways while facing growing challenges from European voyages of exploration. A new age dawned in which the different civilizations of the world for the first time came into closer contact with each other.

History & Art *The Marriage of Giovanni Arnolfini and Giovanna Cenami* by Jan van Eyck, 1434. National Gallery, London, England *What values were popular throughout Renaissance Europe?*

Chapter 16 Renaissance and Reformation

In the 1300s scholars in the city-states of Italy revived the ancient Greek ideal of individual achievement. This rebirth of interest in the classics, called humanism, sparked a new era of European thought and art known as the Renaissance. For the first time since the fall of Rome, European artists and writers emphasized the value of human activity and feelings in their works. This represented a departure from the medieval preoccupation with religion and spiritual values. During the Italian Renaissance, highly talented people, such as Michelangelo Buonarroti, Leonardo da Vinci, and Filippo Brunelleschi, created paintings, sculptures, and buildings that have been admired throughout the centuries for their technical skill and beauty.

Spread of the Renaissance

From Italy the Renaissance spread north into France, Germany, the Low Countries, and England. There the Renaissance was in many ways more religious in its emphasis than in southern Europe. Scholars, such as Erasmus and Thomas More, criticized abuses in the Church and called for simpler forms of worship. Johannes Gutenberg's use of movable type in printing enabled books to become widely available. Because a larger number of books were published in the everyday languages of the people, the new ideas of the Renaissance spread rapidly and challenged traditional beliefs.

The Protestant Reformation

Religious protests against church abuses soon led to a split in Western Christianity. Martin Luther, a young German monk, led the opposition when he nailed 95 statements to the door of a church in Wittenberg, Germany, on October 31, 1517. Refusing to withdraw his criticisms, Luther was called a heretic and excommunicated by the pope. Nonetheless, Luther's ideas, especially the belief that people could be saved by faith alone, spread throughout northern Europe. By the mid-1500s a new form of Christianity—Protestantism—had emerged. Many people in northern Germany and Scandinavia became followers of Luther's brand of Protestantism known as Lutheranism.

Other Protestant reformers soon put forth their own ideas. John Calvin, a reformer from Switzerland, preached belief in an all-powerful God and favored a church structure made up of local councils of ministers and elected church members. His form of Protestantism, known as Calvinism, spread from Switzerland to the Netherlands, Scotland, and England.

England's King Henry VIII broke his country's ties with the Catholic Church when the pope refused to allow Henry to divorce his wife. Henry

CLASSROOM RESOURCES FOR UNIT 4 DIGEST

Preview
- Unit 4 Digest Transparencies

Review
- Time Line Activities 16, 17, 18, 19
- Student Self-Test Software, Chapters 16, 17, 18, 19
- MindJogger Videoquiz, Chapters 16, 17, 18, 19

Condense
- Chapter Digests Audiocassettes, Chapters 16, 17, 18, 19

Reteach
- Reteaching Activities 16, 17, 18, 19
- Chapter Digests Audiocassettes, Chapters 16, 17, 18, 19
- Turning Points in World History

became head of the English Church, which was similar to Catholicism without the pope. Henry's daughter, Elizabeth I, later made the English Church Protestant with Catholic features.

To counter Protestantism, the Catholic Church began its own reform movement. Between 1545 and 1568, the Council of Trent defined Catholic doctrine and put an end to many church abuses. The Catholic Church tried to block the spread of Protestant ideas by empowering an Inquisition to find heretics and execute them. The pope also sent the Jesuits, a new Catholic religious order, as missionaries to Protestant areas in Europe and non-Christian areas in Asia.

SURVEYING CHAPTER 16

1. **Identifying Trends** How did the use of movable type in printing affect developments in Europe during the early modern period?
2. **Relating Ideas** How did the Renaissance in Italy differ from the Renaissance in northern Europe?

Chapter 17
Expanding Horizons

Because the Italian city-state of Venice controlled the rich overland spice trade from Asia, other European powers looked for a sea route to the spice-producing islands in Southeast Asia. Advances in nautical science made oceangoing voyages possible. The Portuguese prince Henry the Navigator organized maritime explorations along the west coast of Africa. By the 1500s Portugal had discovered a route to South Asia around the southern tip of Africa. Its traders followed the route and founded trading centers in India and Southeast Asia.

Portugal's rival, Spain, supported Christopher Columbus's voyage west to reach Asia. In 1492 Columbus arrived in an area unknown to Europeans that later became known as the Americas. Spain sent other expeditions to find a water route to Asia. Ferdinand Magellan left Spain in 1519; three years later, only 18 of his crew returned, but they had become the first Europeans to completely circle the world.

Spanish explorer-soldiers known as conquistadors destroyed the Native American empires in the Americas and founded a large overseas empire. Using Native American and enslaved African labor, Spanish colonists mined gold and silver, grew sugar and tobacco, and raised cattle—bringing

Visualizing History **During the 1500s and 1600s, European explorers, traders, and missionaries traveled the seas to Africa, the Americas, and Asia.** *What earlier developments in European finance and business encouraged voyages of exploration?*

great wealth to Spain. The Netherlands, France, and England, however, surpassed Spain in the next phase of overseas exploration.

The Dutch took over Portugal's spice trade in Southeast Asia. France began trading with Native Americans in North America and explored the continent's interior lands. England moved into the Americas, India, and Southeast Asia. Like Spain, England brought enslaved people from Africa to work its plantations in the Americas. The slave trade became part of a larger trading network that linked Europe, Africa, and America.

European overseas expansion accompanied a commercial revolution at home. Europeans used new business methods to handle the upsurge in wealth from their overseas trade. Joint-stock companies enabled groups of investors to share both risks and profits. The idea of mercantilism—that a nation's strength depended on its accumulation of wealth in gold and silver—furthered the search for raw materials in the overseas empires.

SURVEYING CHAPTER 17

1. **Determining Cause and Effect** What major factor motivated Europeans to undertake overseas voyages of exploration?
2. **Analyzing Trends** What effect did European expansion have on Europeans at home? On peoples living in the non-European areas?

Unit 4 Digest

REVIEW

GLENCOE TECHNOLOGY

VIDEODISC
Use the MindJogger to review any chapter in Unit 4.

MindJogger Videoquiz

Chapter 16
Disc 2 Side B

Chapter 17
Disc 3 Side A

Chapter 18
Disc 3 Side A

Chapter 19
Disc 3 Side A

Also available in VHS.

Use the Student Self-Test and Review Software to review any chapters that students have studied in Unit 4.

Visualizing History The three-masted caravel was the new type of ship that made voyages of exploration practical. The ship's name actually referred to its method of construction: it has fore-and-aft planks with the edges flush.
Answer to Caption: *Joint-stock companies funded voyages and the theory of mercantilism encouraged them.*

ANSWERS TO SURVEYING THE CHAPTER

CHAPTER 16 ANSWERS

1. Books became cheaper and more common, so new ideas spread rapidly.
2. In northern Europe the Renaissance was more religious; Christian humanists called for reform of the Church, setting the stage for the Protestant Reformation.

CHAPTER 17 ANSWERS

1. Venice's control of the lucrative overland spice trade pushed other European countries to look for a sea route to Asia.
2. led to growth of trade, banking, and joint-stock companies; non-Europeans suffered military conquest and enslavement

Unit 4 *Emergence of the Modern World* 507

Unit 4
Digest

Visualizing History Ottoman rulers such as Selim I supported the arts and public works. One royal architect who worked under Selim and other sultans designed 81 mosques, 50 colleges, 32 public baths, and 3 hospitals, as well as many bridges and canals.
Answer to Caption: *Middle East, North Africa, the Balkans*

Geography: Movement Have students trace European colonization in the Americas and Africa by indicating on outline maps which European languages are spoken in different countries and regions today. **L1**

Role Play Organize the class into four groups and have each group prepare a role play based on discussions between the following: Martin Luther and a Catholic priest; an African king and a slave trader; Louis XIV and a French peasant; a Jesuit missionary and a Japanese lord. Have students present each role play to the class. **L2**

Critical Thinking From the illustrations in this unit, have students choose one example of Western painting or architecture and one example of Eastern art or architecture. Then have students write a short essay comparing the styles of the two works and suggesting what each work reveals about the society that created it. **L3**

CONDENSE

Use Chapter Digests Audiocassettes to introduce chapters that students have not studied in Unit 4. Spanish Chapter Digests Audiocassettes are also available.

Visualizing History **The Ottoman ruler Selim I, who was crowned in 1512, fought wars of expansion against the neighboring Persians and Egyptians.** *What areas eventually made up the territory of the Ottoman Empire?*

Chapter 18
Empires of Asia

From the late 1400s to the early 1700s, powerful empires arose, fell, and arose again throughout Asia. Rooted in the ancient civilizations of the past, these empires made many advances in learning, culture, and government. Some of them, however, faced mounting challenges with the arrival of European explorers.

Muslim Empires

During this period, three Muslim empires—the Ottoman, the Safavid Persian, and the Mogul—conquered and ruled parts of Asia, Europe, and Africa. The culturally diverse Ottoman Empire controlled not only the Middle East, but also much of North Africa and Europe's Balkan Peninsula. Military defeats at Lepanto and Vienna halted the Ottoman advance in Europe.

The Safavids established a dynasty in Persia, or present-day Iran. Because the Safavids followed the Shiite branch of Islam, they were bitter enemies of the Ottomans, whose rulers were Sunni Muslims. Under the leadership of Shah Abbas, Islamic Persia reached the height of its cultural achievements.

Muslims from central Asia conquered northern India and set up the Mogul dynasty. Akbar, a Muslim ruler of the 1500s, fostered religious tolerance between South Asia's Muslims and Hindus. The Moguls encouraged the arts—music, painting, and literature.

Chinese Dynasties

The Ming dynasty ruled China from 1368 to 1644. Early Ming rulers encouraged the development of agriculture and sponsored overseas explorations that sailed as far as Africa and Arabia. Although the expeditions brought back rich tribute from foreign rulers, the Chinese did not continue their voyages of discovery.

In 1644 new invaders from the north, the Manchus, conquered China and set up the Qing dynasty. Internal peace and government-sponsored improvements brought prosperity and increased population. During the 1700s government corruption and internal upheavals, however, forced the Qing dynasty into a slow decline. Meanwhile, the Chinese faced new threats from European explorations in their part of the world.

Japan's Military Government

In the 1500s Japan's warrior classes came under the control of a military government headed by a military leader known as a shogun. From the capital at Edo, the Tokugawa shoguns ruled Japan for 250 years.

Portuguese traders brought Christianity to Japan in 1543. Jesuit missionaries made many converts, but Japan's military rulers feared the influence of foreigners and closed Japan's borders to all except a few Dutch traders.

Southeast Asia

From the 1400s to the 1800s, large areas of Southeast Asia came under European influence as trade and exploration made Southeast Asian riches accessible to the Western world.

The Thai kingdom, known as Ayutthaya and later Siam, was the only Southeast Asian area to remain free of European control. Thai kings built a strong central government and introduced reforms that enabled them to keep their independence.

SURVEYING CHAPTER 18

1. **Making Comparisons** Compare the political power of the Ottomans, Moguls, or Ming dynasty with European absolute monarchs.
2. **Predicting Trends** Would the world be different if China had continued its voyages of exploration? Explain.

Chapter 19
Royal Power and Conflict

During the 1500s and 1600s, European monarchs strengthened their thrones and created

ANSWERS TO SURVEYING THE CHAPTER

CHAPTER 18 ANSWERS

1. European and Asian rulers faced similar problems—how to keep the peace among diverse peoples and how to bring more wealth to their empires. Their tactics were also similar: as absolute monarchs, they created centralized states with large bureaucracies.
2. Answers will vary, but students should recognize that if the advanced civilization of China had been in direct contact with the Middle East and Europe, the development of each region might have been very different.

powerful central governments. Their efforts paved the way for the rise of modern nation-states in Europe.

Hapsburg Spain

In Spain Philip II of the royal house of Hapsburg headed a large bureaucracy that administered a growing empire. To ensure national unity and loyalty to his throne, Philip supported the efforts of the Spanish Inquisition to wipe out heresy among the empire's Protestants, Jews, and Muslims.

Philip's desire to forcibly impose Catholicism, however, sparked a revolt among the Protestant Dutch in the Spanish-ruled Netherlands. The Dutch finally succeeded in winning their independence in 1581, but the fighting continued.

Spanish-English Rivalry

Protestant England gave support to the Dutch and to English "sea dogs," or pirates, who raided Spanish ships in their ports. Philip prepared to invade England, but his mighty fleet of ships, the Spanish Armada, suffered a terrible defeat by the English in 1588. Spain would never recover its old power. By the late 1600s, the Spanish still had their overseas empire in the Americas and Asia. However, they faced the challenges posed by a weakened monarchy and a declining economy.

Tudor England

The Tudor dynasty—Henry VII, Henry VIII, Edward VI, Mary I, and Elizabeth I—brought England peace and stability. Their efforts increased royal power while allowing Parliament and other non-royal institutions to flourish. Meanwhile, the economy prospered, and the first steps were taken toward building an overseas empire based on trade. The Tudor foreign policy followed the principle of a balance of power—seeking to keep the power of opposing European nations equal, or in balance, so that one could not overcome another.

Wars of Religion

Elsewhere in Europe, the new divisions within Christianity led to warfare. France saw years of bloody strife between Catholics and Huguenots (French Protestants). These French wars of religion ended in 1598 when King Henry IV issued the Edict of Nantes, which granted religious freedom to his subjects.

When the Hapsburg monarchs of Austria tried to advance Catholicism and curtail Protestant freedoms, war erupted between central Europe's Protestant and Catholic princes. Other European nations, including Catholic France and Protestant Sweden, entered this conflict known as the Thirty Years' War. The Treaty of Westphalia finally ended the war in 1648. By this time, the concerns of Europe's leaders largely focused on political issues rather than on religious ones.

France's Absolute Monarchy

From 1600 to 1780, European monarchs wielded great power. They believed in the theory of absolute monarchy, which held that kings and queens ruled as representatives of God and were responsible to God alone, not to parliaments or citizens. Louis XIV, the outstanding example of an absolute monarch, occupied the French throne for 72 years (1643–1715). Louis built a magnificent palace at Versailles, where he surrounded himself with courtiers, composers, and writers.

In 1685 Louis XIV revoked the Edict of Nantes, causing thousands of Huguenots to flee France. Louis also sought to expand his territory in a series of wars that cost France thousands of lives and much wealth.

Prussia and Austria

In the 1700s a clash between two other absolute rulers exploded into a major war. Frederick the Great of Prussia forced Maria Theresa, empress of Austria, to yield part of her domains. She formed an alliance with France and Russia to regain the territory. Prussia allied with Great Britain, formed by a union of England and Scotland in 1707. The resulting Seven Years' War (1756–1763) spread to Europe's colonies. Prussia kept its territory, but France lost much of its overseas empire to Great Britain.

Russia

Russia, isolated for centuries, lacked the trade and economic development of western Europe in the 1600s and 1700s. Peter the Great, who became czar at a young age, rebuilt the Russian state, enhanced its military power, and modernized its technology. Peter's reforms, however, created a large gap between the Europeanized upper classes and the lower classes.

SURVEYING CHAPTER 19

1. **Making Comparisons** How did Spain's national power compare to that of England during the period from the late 1500s to the late 1600s?
2. **Analyzing Ideas** What was the major idea promoted by Europe's monarchs during the 1600s and 1700s?

Unit 4 Digest

Discuss Have students read the **Unit Digest** and discuss the **Surveying Chapter** questions.

RETEACH

Review Chart Have students prepare a chart with columns headed *Europe, Asia, Africa,* and *The Americas*. Then have them brainstorm a list of the effects that the Renaissance and the age of exploration had in each region.

Reteaching Activities 16, 17, 18, 19

Chapter Digests Audiocassettes, Chapters 16, 17, 18, 19

ABC NEWS INTERACTIVE™

VIDEODISC
Turning Points in World History

Side One, Chapter 8
Title: *The Reformation*
Ask: Why did Martin Luther begin questioning Church practices? *(He was disturbed by abuses in the Catholic Church.)*

Side One, Chapter 9
Title: *Age of Exploration*
Ask: Why is the age of exploration considered a turning point? *(Europeans came into contact with lands and people unknown to them, irrevocably changing both cultures forever.)*

ANSWERS TO SURVEYING THE CHAPTER

CHAPTER 19 ANSWERS

1. Both countries were strong, with strong monarchs, although the Tudors shared power with Parliament. After the Armada's defeat in 1588, Spain's power declined, making England and France the leading powers of Europe.
2. European monarchs promoted the idea of absolute monarchy and tried to diminish the powers of nobles.

Unit 4 *Emergence of the Modern World* 509

Introducing Unit 5

0:00 **OUT OF TIME?**

If time does not permit teaching each chapter in Unit 5, you may use the Unit Digest beginning on page 590, in conjunction with the Unit Digest Transparencies and Chapter Digest Audiocassettes with accompanying activities and tests.

Introducing the Unit

Unit 5 focuses on the revolutionary changes that transformed early modern Europe, including the Scientific Revolution and political revolutions in England, the United States, and France. The ideas of liberalism, nationalism, and democracy are also explored.

Unit Objectives

After reading Unit 5, students will be able to:

1. explain how the Scientific Revolution changed the way people looked at their world and how the Enlightenment advanced new social and political ideas.
2. compare the causes and results of the English and American Revolutions.
3. understand the different phases of the French Revolution and trace the ways in which that revolution and the Napoleonic period transformed Europe.

Portfolio Project

Student reports should include the major inventions and developments in the technologies they study. This activity may be an appropriate method of authentic assessment.

Unit 5 1500–1830

Age of Revolution

Chapter 20 Scientific Revolution
Chapter 21 English and American Revolutions
Chapter 22 The French Revolution

Then & Now *The discoveries and writings of the Age of Revolution ignited a fuse of knowledge that exploded in a scientific revolution so complete and far-reaching that the years from 1500 to 1830 are often called "the beginning of the modern age."*

Every time you have your temperature taken with a mercury thermometer, receive medication through a fine-needled syringe, let a doctor listen to your heartbeat through a stethoscope, or have your tooth drilled by a dentist, you are seeing instruments invented during the Age of Revolution. When you study a cell through a microscope or a star through a telescope, you are using equipment developed to fill the needs of sixteenth- and seventeenth-century scientists for precise, accurate scientific instruments. Even the simple multiplication symbol × was proposed during this age of scientific revolution.

A Global Chronology

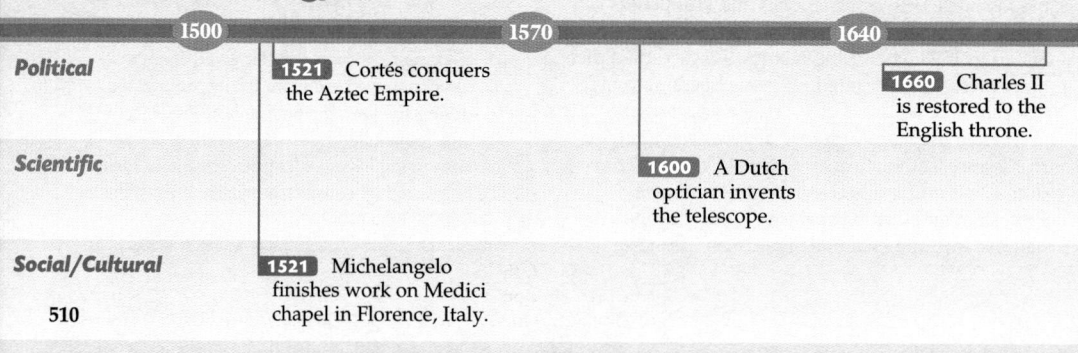

1500 — 1570 — 1640

Political
- **1521** Cortés conquers the Aztec Empire.
- **1660** Charles II is restored to the English throne.

Scientific
- **1600** A Dutch optician invents the telescope.

Social/Cultural
- **1521** Michelangelo finishes work on Medici chapel in Florence, Italy.

510

Then & Now **Science and Society** In this unit students will learn how breakthroughs in science and philosophy—the Scientific Revolution and the Enlightenment—eventually had repercussions on the political and social systems of Europe, North America, and elsewhere.

Have students think about the ways that science and technology influence the way we think and live today. How have scientific breakthroughs by NASA and the space shuttle program influenced our lives? *(Many breakthroughs in telecommunications, air travel, and computer science are*

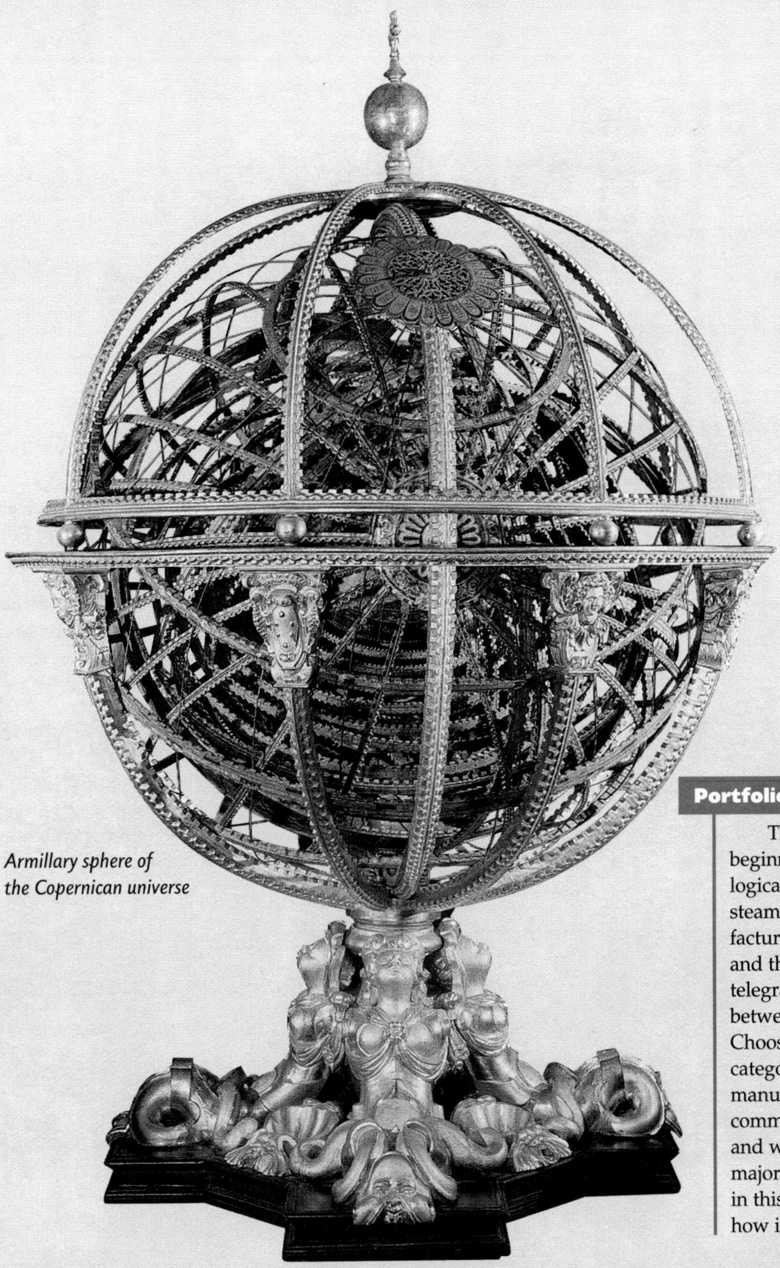

Armillary sphere of the Copernican universe

Portfolio Project

This unit marks the beginning of great technological achievements. The steam engine, textile manufacturing, the electric battery, and the semaphore (visual telegraph) were all developed between 1750 and 1800. Choose one of the following categories—engines, textile manufacturing, electricity, or communications. Research and write a report on the major historical developments in this technology, including how it affects your life today.

1710 · 1780 · 1850

1687 Isaac Newton states the theory of gravity.

1740 Frederick the Great introduces freedom of the press and of worship in Prussia.

1789 The French Revolution begins.

1799 Rosetta stone found in Egypt makes deciphering hieroglyphics possible.

1804 Ludwig van Beethoven composes his Third Symphony, the *Eroica*.

1832 The British Parliament passes the Reform Bill.

511

civilian applications of space program technology.) In what ways have computers and the information superhighway created new possibilities for political activity? *(Through the Internet and E-mail, individuals from around the world can communicate cheaply and instantly about issues that concern them.)* How does our knowledge about the transmission of diseases affect our behavior? *(We take precautions like washing our hands before eating, getting vaccinations, avoiding contact with blood and other body fluids.)*

Introducing Unit 5

History *and the* Humanities

World History and Art Transparencies
- 27 *The Letter*
- 28 *Blue Boy*
- 29 *Napoleon Crossing the Alps*

ABCNEWS INTERACTIVE™

VIDEODISC
Turning Points in World History

Side One, Chapter 11

Title: *French Revolution*
Subject: French Revolution
Ask: What great changes in the way people thought about political rights and freedoms took place in this period? *(The idea of the divine right of monarchs to rule gave way to individual rights and rule by popular consent.)*

History & Art

The Polish astronomer Copernicus (1473–1543) discredited the ancient idea that the earth was at the center of the solar system and that the sun moved around it. "I began to consider the mobility of the Earth," Copernicus wrote, "even though the idea seemed absurd."

The Spread of Ideas

TEACH

Introduction

This feature focuses on the movement of revolutionary ideas between Europe and the Americas. The challenge of early scientists such as Galileo to established authority led to the questioning of long-held ideas about government, religion, and society, as well as science. In the United States, France, and Haiti, revolutionaries tried to put new ideas about government into practice.

Background Notes

Linking Past and Present

Ideas of the 1700s continue to reverberate in this century. When Ho Chi Minh declared Vietnam's independence from France in 1945, his speech began: "All men are created equal. The Creator has given us certain inviolable Rights; the right to Life, the right to be Free, and the right to achieve Happiness. These immortal words are taken from the Declaration of Independence of the United States of America in 1776."

Who?What?Where?When?

Women played an important role in spreading the Enlightenment ideas that helped spark the French Revolution. Parisian intellectuals such as Madame de Pompadour and Madame de Geoffrin brought together writers, artists, and nobles. The lively discussions in these salons helped popularize controversial ideas.

The Spread of Ideas

Revolution

In the 1600s and 1700s, revolution bounced back and forth across the Atlantic. The pattern started with the arrival of the first English colonists in North America. They carried with them ideals born of the English Revolution. They believed that governments existed to protect the rights and freedoms of citizens.

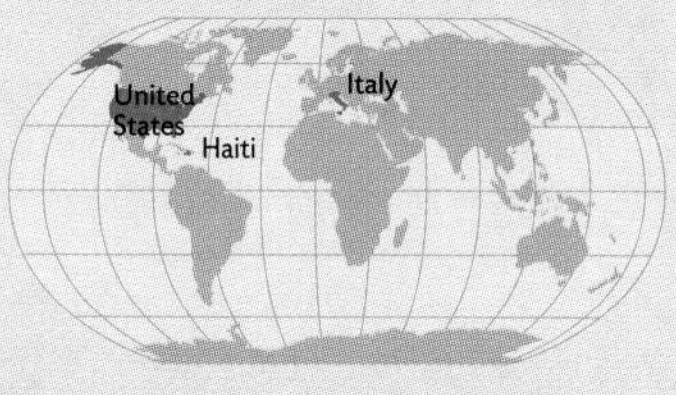

The United States

Revolutionary Ideas

In 1776 the colonists fought a revolution, making clear the principles of freedom and rights in the Declaration of Independence:

> *We hold these truths to be self-evident, that all men are created equal, that they are endowed by their Creator with certain unalienable rights, that among these are life, liberty, and the pursuit of happiness.*

These ideas bounced back across the Atlantic to influence the French Revolution. French rebels in 1789 fought in defense of *Liberté, Egalité, Fraternité* (Liberty, Equality, Fraternity). In drafting their declaration of freedom, French revolutionaries repeated the principles of the American Declaration of Independence: "Men are born and remain free and equal in rights."

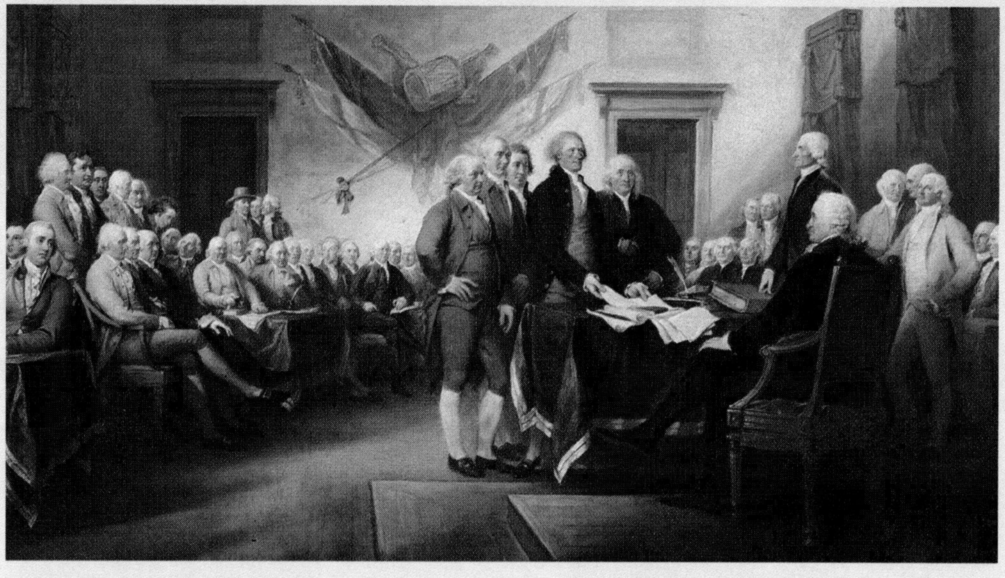

Signing of the Declaration of Independence

COOPERATIVE LEARNING ACTIVITY

Wall Map and Display Have students work together to create a wall map and display that shows the origins of the ideas behind the American, French, and Haitian Revolutions. Organize the class into three groups, letting each group take one of the revolutions. Have members research their revolution, generating a list of philosophers, events, and other specific influences. For each item on the list, students should be sure to name the country of origin. When the lists have been completed, have students organize them by country in a format suitable for display. Have them mount the lists to the sides of a wall map, then use thumbtacks and colored yarn to show how various ideas traveled. **L2**

Italy

The Age of Revolution

The spread of ideas—specifically, revolutionary ideas—forms the subject of Unit 5. The spark that sent the spirit of revolution flashing across Europe and the Americas began in the minds of sixteenth-century European scientists. These thinkers challenged established ideas defended by the Roman Catholic Church. Church officials tried to stop the spread of new scientific ideas. But once unleashed, the ideas respected neither authority nor geographic boundary. Defiance of one authority, in this case, the Church, soon led people to question other authorities as well. The result was the intellectual and political upheavals that historians call the Age of Revolution.

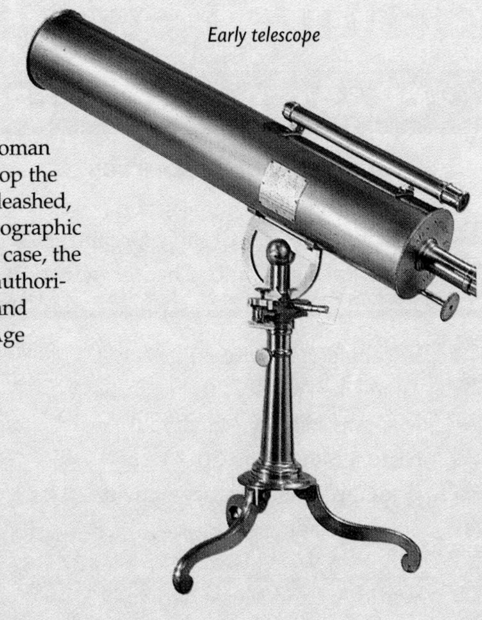

Early telescope

Toussaint-Louverture

Haiti

Exporting Revolution

In 1791 the ideals of the American and French Revolutions traveled across the Caribbean and the Atlantic to the French-held island colony of Saint Domingue. Inspired by talk of freedom, enslaved Africans took up arms. Led by Toussaint-Louverture, they shook off French rule. In 1804 Saint Domingue, present-day Haiti, became the second nation in the Americas to achieve independence from colonial rule. "We have asserted our rights," declared the revolutionaries. "We swear never to yield them to any power on earth."

LINKING THE IDEAS

1. What was the role of government according to the American colonists?
2. What ideals did the Americans and the French share?

Critical Thinking

3. **Cause and Effect** Why do you think revolutionary ideas respect neither authority nor geographic boundaries?

ANSWERS TO LINKING THE IDEAS

1. to protect the rights and freedoms of citizens
2. belief in freedom and equal rights
3. Answers will vary. Students may feel that revolutionary ideas spread quickly when traditional authority has lost touch with the times. The desire for freedom and opportunity motivates people in all times and places.

The Spread of Ideas

Geography

Movement Americans living in France before the French Revolution actively promoted the principles of the new republic across the Atlantic. "Everyone here is trying their hands at forming declarations of rights," wrote Thomas Jefferson, whose advice was often sought by Lafayette and other moderate revolutionaries. Ask students to name other ways ideas of revolution may have traveled between the different locations of revolution shown on the map on page 512. *(Answers may include trade, newspapers, scholars exchanging books.)*

Cultural Diffusion

Containing Antislavery The success of the Haitian Revolution terrified American slaveholders, who feared that the overthrow of slavery in Haiti would inspire their own enslaved people to rebel. In the southern United States, tighter restrictions were placed on both enslaved and free African Americans. In 1802 Jefferson's postmaster general advised a senator from Georgia against letting enslaved people deliver the mail: "After the scenes which St. Domingo has exhibited to the world, we cannot be too cautious in attempting to prevent similar evils.... Everything which tends to increase their knowledge of natural rights ... or that affords them an opportunity ... of establishing a chain and line of intelligence, must increase your hazard."

Scientific Revolution

CHAPTER RESOURCES

	Reproducible Resources	Multimedia Resources
Chapter Opener	Chapter Themes: Graphic Organizer 20 Historical Significance Chapter Activity 20	MindJogger Videoquiz
Chapter Enrichment	Vocabulary Activity 20* Time Line Activity 20 Mapping History Activity 20 History Simulation 20 Geography and History Activity 20 Source Reading 20 People in World History Profiles 37, 38 World Art and Music Activity 20 Enrichment Activity 20 Critical Thinking Activity 20 Skill Reinforcement Activity 20 Performance Assessment Activity 20	World History and Art Transparency 27, *The Letter* Chapter Transparency 20 Vocabulary PuzzleMaker Software Picture Atlas of the World Turning Points in World History: *The Scientific Revolution*
Chapter Review/Reteaching	Reteaching Activity 20 Skill Reinforcement Activity 20 Spanish Chapter Summary 20	Chapter 20 Digest Audiocassette, Activity, Test* Vocabulary PuzzleMaker Software Student Self-Test and Review Software MindJogger Videoquiz
Chapter Evaluation/Testing	Performance Assessment Activity 20 Chapter 20 Test, Forms A and B	Testmaker

* *Also available in Spanish*

0:00 **OUT OF TIME?** Assign the Chapter 20 summary in the Unit 5 Digest on pages 590–593, and the Chapter 20 Audiocassettes.

Block Schedule

Block scheduling differs from traditional class scheduling in the amount of time allotted to each period. The extended time frame provided by block scheduling affords you the opportunity to implement a greater number of research-oriented and activity-intense projects to motivate and involve your students. Activities that are particularly suited to use within the block scheduling framework are identified throughout this chapter by the following designation.

KEY TO ABILITY LEVELS

Teaching strategies have been coded for varying learning styles and abilities.

- **L1** **BASIC** activities for all students
- **L2** **AVERAGE** activities for average to above-average students
- **L3** **CHALLENGING** activities for above-average students
- **LEP** **LIMITED ENGLISH PROFICIENCY** activities

Chapter 20 Planning Guide

A complete, 1-page lesson plan is provided for each section in the *Reproducible Lesson Plans* booklet.

SECTION RESOURCES

Daily Objectives	Reproducible Resources	Multimedia Resources
Section 1 New Scientific Ideas Discuss how scientific thought changed during the 1600s.	Reproducible Lesson Plan 20-1 Guided Reading Activity 20-1* Time Line Activity 20 People in World History Profile 37 Geography and History Activity 20 Section Quiz 20-1*	Section Focus Transparency 20-1 Chapter Transparency 20 Vocabulary PuzzleMaker Software Student Self-Test and Review Software Testmaker Turning Points in World History: *The Scientific Revolution*
Section 2 Impact of Science Analyze the effects that changes in scientific thought had on thinking in other fields.	Reproducible Lesson Plan 20-2 Vocabulary Activity 20* Guided Reading Activity 20-2* History Simulation 20 Section Quiz 20-2*	Section Focus Transparency 20-2 Student Self-Test and Review Software Testmaker Turning Points in World History: *The Scientific Revolution*
Section 3 Triumph of Reason Identify the factors that helped Enlightenment ideas spread throughout Europe.	Reproducible Lesson Plan 20-3 Guided Reading Activity 20-3* People in World History Profile 38 Reteaching Activity 20 Enrichment Activity 20 Section Quiz 20-3* Performance Assessment Activity 20 Spanish Chapter Summary 20	Section Focus Transparency 20-3 World History and Art Transparency 27, *The Letter* Vocabulary PuzzleMaker Software Student Self-Test and Review Software Testmaker Turning Points in World History: *The Scientific Revolution*

* *Also available in Spanish*

Chapter Activities

Performance Assessment Activity

A Last Will and Testament Have students think about the developments that occurred during the Scientific Revolution and list them in order of importance, giving a rationale for their choices. Students should then match each of the items on their list to a current-day group, individual, or country that would be a logical recipient of the invention or development if left to them in a will by the inventor or initiator. Students should then write a collective last will and testament for all of the people highlighted in the chapter. Wills should include a rationale with each beneficiary listed.

Possible Rubric Features

Accuracy of content information, argumentation and level of support, organization and clarity, research skills, ability to make logical connections

• *For an additional activity, refer to Activity 20 in the* Performance Assessment Strategies and Activities *booklet.*

Activity

From the Classroom of...

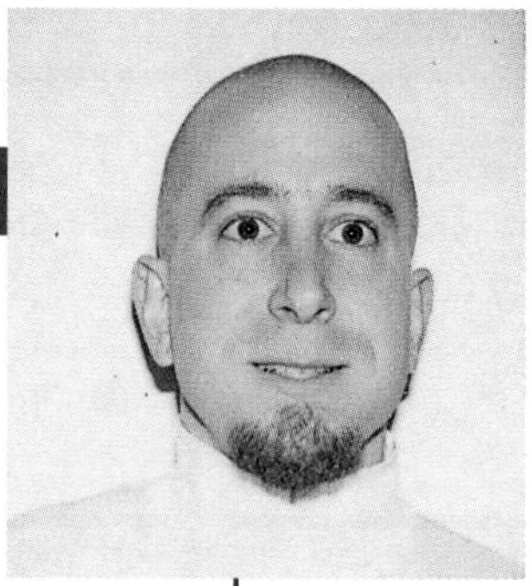

Ross Bennett Brown
Franklin K. Lane High School
Brooklyn, NY

The Scientific Method in Action

Have students employ the scientific method in order to solve a problem. One problem that works well involves a simple chemistry exercise. You will need some filter paper cut into 4-inch strips, paper clips, cups with about 1 inch of water in them, and green felt-tipped pens. Begin by drawing a dot about 1 inch from the end of a strip of filter paper. Ask students what will happen when the dot makes contact with water. This is their *hypothesis*. Most will suggest smearing. Pierce the other end of the filter paper with a paper clip and use the clip to suspend the paper in the cup so that the end with the dot is just touching the water, but the dot remains above the water. This is the *experiment.* The water is drawn up the filter paper, and when it reaches the dot, the green separates into blue and yellow. We could not know this without the process of hypothesis followed by the careful observation of events during the experiment.

Since the result is almost always different from students' hypotheses, it is likely to stimulate in the class the same sort of excitement that seventeenth-century scientists might have felt conducting their own experiments.

MULTIPLE LEARNING STYLES

Verbal/Linguistic
Ask each student to select a discovery or invention of the 1600s and then write a promotional flyer or commercial promoting it. Have students present their commercials to the class.

Visual/Spatial
Have students draw political cartoons illustrating one of the controversies associated with the Enlightenment. Incorporate all the cartoons into a book.

Auditory/Musical
Have students listen to a recording of Leonard Bernstein's musical version of Voltaire's *Candide*. Ask them to write a sentence describing the connection between the lyrics of at least five songs and Enlightenment ideas.

Kinesthetic
Have students prepare models of the universe according to Aristotle and according to Copernicus. Have them use diagrams in astronomy textbooks or other reference books as a guide.

Additional Resources

TEACHER'S CORNER

NATIONAL GEOGRAPHIC SOCIETY

INDEX TO NATIONAL GEOGRAPHIC MAGAZINE

The following articles may be used for research relating to this chapter:

- "Humboldt's Way," by Loren McIntyre, September 1985.

NATIONAL GEOGRAPHIC SOCIETY PRODUCTS AVAILABLE FROM GLENCOE

To order the following products for use with this chapter, contact your local Glencoe sales representative or call Glencoe at 1-800-368-7344:

CD-ROM

- Picture Atlas of the World

BIBLIOGRAPHY

Literature of the Period

Voltaire. ***Candide and Other Stories.*** Translated by Roger Pearson. New York: Oxford University Press, 1990. Voltaire's most popular philosophical novel and other stories.

Readings for the Student

Boorstin, Daniel. ***The Discoverers: A History of Man's Search to Know His World and Himself.*** New York: Random House, 1983. Contains much fascinating and readable information on Copernicus, Kepler, Galileo, Newton, and others.

Readings for the Teacher

Cohen, I. Bernard. ***Science and the Founding Fathers: Science in the Political Thought of Thomas Jefferson, Benjamin Franklin, John Adams and James Madison.*** New York: Norton, 1995. Explains how the Founders incorporated scientific reasoning into the Constitution.

interNET
CONNECTIONS
Galileo Room Surf the web to the Institute and Museum of the History of Science of Florence, Italy, and take a tour of the Galileo Room.
http://galileo.imss.firenze.it/museo/4/index.html

Introducing Chapter 20

CHAPTER THEMES

Chapter Themes are listed by section on this chapter opening page of the Student Edition. A corresponding theme-based activity is available under "TEACH," and a theme-based question is asked in the Section and Chapter Reviews.

The Storyteller

Historical Setting Despite the fact that Leeuwenhoek never attended a university, he became one of the world's greatest scientific pioneers. Though England and Holland were trade rivals and enemies in several wars, Leeuwenhoek shared his scientific ideas with the Royal Society of London, one of the oldest scientific societies in Europe. In October 1678, in his eighteenth letter to the Royal Society, Leeuwenhoek described "these little animals" revealed by his microscope in a drop of water. Today scientists know they are not animals at all but rather bacteria. Leeuwenhoek also discovered red blood cells when he turned his microscope on a drop of human blood.

Historical Significance

Answers: *By introducing a philosophy of knowledge based on observation, experiment, and reason, the Scientific Revolution challenged faith and traditional ideas in many areas.*

New scientific discoveries and new applications continue to challenge accepted ideas and introduce new ways of life.

Chapter 20 1600–1830 Scientific Revolution

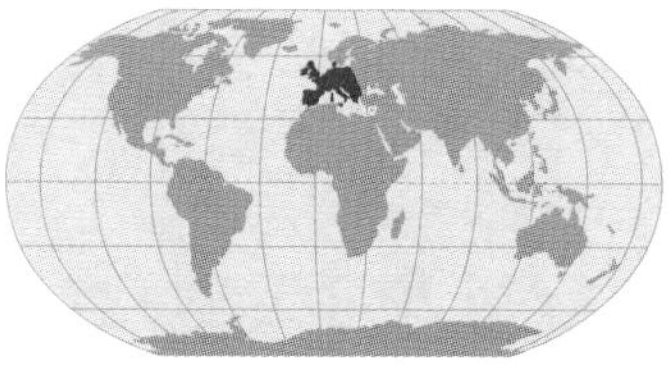

Chapter Themes

- **Innovation** European interest in science leads to discoveries and ideas based on reason. *Section 1*
- **Conflict** Changing views based on science and reason conflict with traditional beliefs. *Section 2*
- **Reaction** Reason and order are applied to many human endeavors. *Section 3*

The Storyteller

Antonie van Leeuwenhoek, a Dutch cloth merchant in the late 1600s, found that his unusual hobby unlocked the door to an unknown world. By carefully grinding very small lenses out of clear glass, van Leeuwenhoek discovered that he could make things look much bigger than they appeared to the naked eye.

Soon the Dutch merchant turned his lenses to everything he could find—from the cloth he had just bought to the scales of his own skin. His most remarkable find was tiny microorganisms, which he described as "wretched beasties" with "incredibly thin feet" swimming through a tiny universe.

New technology such as van Leeuwenhoek's microscope and scientific study in general captured the imagination of many European people in the 1600s. A scientific revolution would lead to a new era in Western thought.

Historical Significance

How did the scientific revolution of the 1600s and 1700s transform European society? What impact has the growth of science had on the world today?

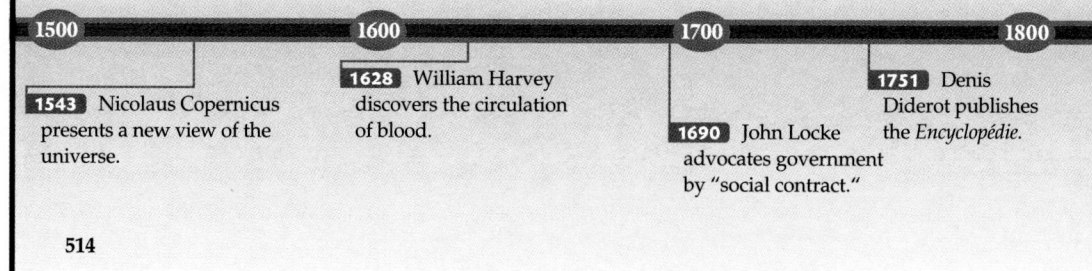

1500 — 1600 — 1700 — 1800

1543 Nicolaus Copernicus presents a new view of the universe.

1628 William Harvey discovers the circulation of blood.

1690 John Locke advocates government by "social contract."

1751 Denis Diderot publishes the *Encyclopédie*.

514

GEOGRAPHY CONNECTION

Movement Point out that scientific ideas traveled quickly and frequently between France, the Netherlands, and England. Have students locate these countries on a map. What route did ideas have to take between the two countries on the European continent and England? *(They had to cross the English Channel.)* How far across is the English Channel at its narrowest? *(about 20 miles [34 kilometers])* How did people cross the Channel at the time of the Scientific Revolution? *(by boat)* What options are available to people crossing the Channel today? *(boat, train, ferry, airplane, Chunnel)* **L1**

History & Art *The Establishment of the Academy of Science and the Foundation of the Observatory by Louis XIV* by Henri Testelin. Musée National du Chateau de Versailles, Versailles, France

Your History Journal

Research a scientific discovery or invention from the 1600s. Write the story of the discovery or invention as it might have appeared in a publication at the time.

EXTRA CREDIT PROJECT

Oral Report Two new instruments, the microscope and the telescope, made possible many of the discoveries of the Scientific Revolution. Since the 1600s many improvements have been made in both. Have students research and report to the class on new types of microscopes developed in the twentieth century, including the electron microscope and the scanning tunneling microscope. Suggested resources: B. J. Ford, *The Leeuwenhoek Legacy*; G. B. Stewart, *Microscopes*. Or have them research and report on twentieth-century improvements in telescopes, such as camera telescopes and radio telescopes. **L2**

Introducing Chapter 20

History & Art Around 1662 a group of French scientists began to hold periodic private meetings in Paris. In 1666 the Royal Academy of Sciences was established to formalize those meetings. Construction of the observatory began the following year. Today the academy's building in Paris is headquarters of the International Time Bureau, which sets standard time for the world's observatories.

Performance Assessment

Refer to the activity on page 514C of the Planning Guide.

Refer to Activity 20 in the *Performance Assessment Strategies and Activities* booklet.

Using Your History Journal

Encourage students to include direct quotations from the scientists whose discoveries or inventions they choose. A good resource is Daniel J. Boorstin, *The Discoverers* (New York: Random House, 1983).

GLENCOE TECHNOLOGY

VIDEODISC

Use MindJogger to preview chapter content.

MindJogger Videoquiz

Chapter 20
Disc 3 Side A

Also available in VHS.

SECTION THEME

▶ **Innovation** European interest in science leads to discoveries and ideas based on reason.

Find Out

Answer: *Observation, experiment, and reason began to replace mysticism and ancient writings as the basis for scientific thought.*

FOCUS

Section Objective

Discuss how scientific thought changed during the 1600s.

BELLRINGER
Motivational Activity

Before taking roll at the beginning of the class period, project Section Focus Transparency 20-1 and have students answer the activity questions. Discuss students' responses.
This activity is also available as a blackline master.

Vocabulary Pre-check

Use the Vocabulary PuzzleMaker to create a puzzle that reinforces vocabulary terms in this section. **L1**

1600 — 1700 — 1800

1632 Galileo Galilei stands trial for his ideas.

1687 Isaac Newton publishes the *Principia.*

1774 Joseph Priestley discovers oxygen.

Section 1

New Scientific Ideas

Setting the Scene

▶ **Terms to Define**
hypothesis, ellipses, scientific method, calculus, alchemist

▶ **People to Meet**
Nicolaus Copernicus, Johannes Kepler, Galileo Galilei, Francis Bacon, René Descartes, Isaac Newton, Andreas Vesalius, William Harvey, Robert Hooke, Robert Boyle, Joseph Priestley, Antoine and Marie Lavoisier

▶ **Places to Locate**
Poland

Find Out How did scientific thought change during the 1600s?

The Storyteller

Christina, Grand Duchess of Tuscany, was intrigued. She had asked the renowned Galileo to describe his studies to her. "Nature," he explained in his letter, "never transgresses the laws imposed upon her, or cares whether her reasons and methods of operation are understandable to men." But Christina knew that others might find Galileo's opinions dangerous, for he also claimed that one could learn truth from these studies as much as from religion. "I do not feel obliged to believe that the same God who has endowed us with senses, reason, and intellect has intended us to forgo their use."

—adapted from *Letter to Christina of Tuscany*, reprinted in *Western Civilization: Sources, Images, and Interpretations*, Dennis Sherman, 1995

Galileo Galilei

Magic, mysticism, and ancient writings ruled scientific thought in Europe throughout the Middle Ages. Scholars based their ideas on theories proposed almost a thousand years before by ancient Greek thinkers such as Aristotle, Ptolemy, and Galen. During the Middle Ages, most Europeans believed that the earth was flat, and they accepted the Catholic Church's view that the earth was the center of the universe. According to church doctrine, God created the universe to serve people. Therefore, the Church reasoned, the people's home—the earth—must be at the center of the universe.

In the 1600s, however, such ideas would topple as a scientific revolution spread throughout Europe. New technology, combined with innovative approaches to seeking knowledge, led to a breakthrough in Western thought. At the forefront of this scientific revolution was a Polish astronomer named **Nicolaus Copernicus.**

A Scientific Revolution

Copernicus started his scientific career at the University of Kraków in **Poland** in 1492—the same year in which Christopher Columbus reached the Americas. Like Columbus, Copernicus began his questioning in a time when few people dared to question age-old beliefs and superstitions.

As Copernicus delved into his studies, he became convinced that ideas commonly accepted about the universe were wrong. Copernicus believed that the earth was round and that it rotated on its axis as it revolved around the sun. The sun stayed still at the center of the universe.

Copernicus realized, however, that his ideas were revolutionary and even dangerous. Disputing or even questioning the Church's views about the universe could mean persecution, excommunication, or even burning at the stake. To avoid this risk, Copernicus worked in privacy, without publishing

SECTION RESOURCES

Reproducible Masters
- Reproducible Lesson Plan 20-1
- Guided Reading Activity 20-1
- Time Line Activity 20
- People in World History Profile 37
- Geography and History Activity 20
- Section Quiz 20-1

Transparencies
- Section Focus Transparency 20-1
- Chapter Transparency 20

Multimedia
- Vocabulary PuzzleMaker Software
- Student Self-Test and Review Software
- Testmaker
- Turning Points in World History: *The Scientific Revolution*

Visualizing History **In 1633, the Inquisition in Rome found Galileo guilty of heresy and sentenced him to life imprisonment.** *Why did church authorities charge Galileo with heresy?*

his ideas. The Polish scientist spent more than 30 years writing his treatise. Friends who realized the significance of Copernicus's ideas helped publish his work just before his death.

New Theories About the Universe

Two other curious scientists took the Polish astronomer's ideas and ventured even further into a scientific understanding of the universe. The German astronomer **Johannes Kepler** and the Italian mathematician **Galileo Galilei** ignited a true revolution in astronomy in the early 1600s.

Early in his studies, Kepler believed in Copernicus's theory. By the end of his career, though, Kepler had refuted all but two of Copernicus's hypotheses, or theories that attempt to explain a set of facts. Copernicus's hypothesis that the earth revolved around the sun was based on study and observations. Copernicus could not prove his hypothesis, however, because the necessary mathematics was not available to him at the time.

A skilled mathematician, Kepler used mathematical formulas to prove that although the sun stays in its place, the planets move in oval paths called ellipses—not in circles as Copernicus had believed. Kepler also found that planets do not always travel at the same speed, but move faster as they approach the sun and slower as they move away from it.

Challenging the Church

Kepler challenged the teachings of many academics and religious leaders. Because Kepler was a Protestant, however, he did not have to fear the Catholic Church. His Catholic contemporary, Galileo, did face considerable opposition from church leaders.

In 1609 Galileo built his own telescope and observed the night skies. His discovery of moons circling a planet convinced him that the Copernican theory about the earth revolving around the sun was correct. Because these moons revolved around Jupiter, Galileo reasoned, not all heavenly bodies revolved around the earth. It was possible that some planets did move around the sun.

In 1632 Galileo published his ideas. Soon afterward, the Catholic Church banned the book. The Church would not tolerate Galileo's spreading of ideas that contradicted its own position. An outraged Pope Urban VIII demanded that Galileo come to Rome and stand trial.

Urban's threats of torture and possible death forced Galileo to recant many of his statements and publicly state that he had gone too far in some of his writing:

COOPERATIVE LEARNING ACTIVITY

Readers' Theater and Discussion Organize the class into four groups. Have the members of three groups prepare five scenes each from Bertolt Brecht's *Life of Galileo* to read dramatically to the class. Have the members of the fourth group make an intensive study of the facts of Galileo's life. After the three groups have completed their classroom reading of the entire play, have members of the fourth group run a panel discussion comparing Brecht's dramatic treatment of characters and events with their actual historical models. **L3**

TEACH

Guided Practice

THEME Innovation

New interest in science led to discoveries and philosophies based on reason. Guide students to a definition of reason. *(the power of acquiring intellectual knowledge based on facts or premises)* Ask students to give an example from this section of an innovator who used reason to advance an idea. *(Possible answer: Galileo reasoned that, as moons circle Jupiter, so planets circle the sun.)* **L1**

Visualizing History Galileo's *Dialogue Concerning the Two Chief World Systems—Ptolemaic and Copernican*, published in 1632, had been approved by the censors. But after the Jesuits claimed that it could do more damage to Catholicism "than Luther and Calvin put together," the pope had Galileo prosecuted for ignoring a warning the Church had made 16 years earlier, prohibiting him from "teaching or discussing Copernicanism in any way."

Answer to Caption: *He published ideas that contradicted the Church's earth-centered view of the universe.*

Critical Thinking Have students list on the chalkboard the stages in the scientific method. *(observation, hypothesis, checking hypothesis)* Then have them suggest the characteristics of a successful scientist. *(observant, systematic, patient, imaginative)* **L2**

Chapter Transparency 20

Chapter 20
Section 1

ABCNEWS INTERACTIVE™

VIDEODISC
Turning Points in World History

Side One
Chapter 10

Title: *The Scientific Revolution*
Ask: What changes took place in European society in the seventeenth century that led to the Scientific Revolution? *(People began to challenge traditional thinking and began to see the world differently.)*

Independent Practice

Guided Reading Activity 20-1 **L1**

Time Line Activity 20

People in World History Profile 37

Geography and History Activity 20

Science, Technology, and Society
Have students pretend that they are university science students in the 1600s. Ask them to write letters home in which they describe discoveries in two of the following areas: astronomy, mathematics, chemistry, anatomy. **L2**

Science Yesterday and Today
Have students prepare an illustrated poster with three types of information: key contributors to the Scientific Revolution, examples of their contributions at the time, and modern machines that may have resulted from their work. *(example: Galileo, telescope, Hubble Space Telescope)* Display completed posters in the classroom. **L3**

"I, Galileo Galilei, ... swear that with honest heart and in good faith I curse ... the said heresies and errors as to the movement of the earth around the sun and all other heresies and ideas opposed to the Holy Church; and I swear that I will never assert or say anything either orally or in writing, that could put me under such suspicion."

Galileo continued his work after the trial. As he experimented with the motion of objects on the earth, he helped to establish the universal laws of physics. Among these discoveries was the law of inertia, which specifies that an object remains at rest or in straight-line motion unless acted upon by an external force. Other investigations into the workings of the pendulum helped to advance its application as a time controller in clocks.

New Ways of Thinking

As European scientists revolutionized the world of astronomy, philosophers such as **Francis Bacon** and **René Descartes** incorporated scientific thought into philosophy. Bacon, an English philosopher, claimed that ideas based solely on tradition or unproven facts should be discarded completely.

To Bacon, truth resulted only from a thorough investigation of evidence. He helped develop what is known today as the scientific method. The scientific method is made up of several steps. The scientist begins with careful observations of facts or things. Then the scientist tries to find a hypothesis to explain the observations. By experimenting, the scientist then tests the hypothesis under all possible conditions and in every possible way to see whether it is true. Finally, if careful and repeated experiments show that the hypothesis does prove true under all conditions, it is considered a scientific law. In other words, a scientific truth is not assumed—it is deduced from observations and a series of thorough experiments.

Like Bacon, French philosopher and mathematician René Descartes believed that truth must be reached through reason. The inventor of analytic geometry, Descartes saw mathematics as the perfect model for clear and certain knowledge. In 1637 he published *Discourse on Method* to explain his philosophy. In the book, Descartes began his search for knowledge by doubting everything except his own existence. He believed he had found one unshakable and self-evident truth in the statement "I think, therefore I am."

New Theories in Physics

In 1642, as Bacon and Descartes transformed European thinking, one of the most influential figures in modern science was born in England. His name was **Isaac Newton**. Newton used the scientific method as he studied science and mathematics. He once commented, "Asking the correct question is half the problem. Once the question is formulated there remains to be found only proof.... "

At Cambridge University, Newton was a below-average student with few friends. He almost left school without realizing his mathematical genius. But one of his teachers recognized his ability and began tutoring him. With this help Newton quickly became an eager and successful student. He explored the most complicated mathematics of his day, reading the writings of Copernicus and Galileo.

In 1665 an outbreak of the plague closed the university and forced Newton to return to his family's farm. There, he laid the foundation for his ground-breaking theories in mathematics and physics. The legend of Newton's apple originated during these years. Newton wrote that while sitting in his garden one day, he watched an apple fall to the ground. The apple's fall led him to the idea of gravity.

Nearly 20 years later, in 1687, Newton published his theories about gravity and other scientific concepts in his book *Mathematical Principles of Natural Philosophy*, often called *Principia*. Newton offered in the *Principia* a new understanding of the universe, explaining and expanding the work of Copernicus, Galileo, and Kepler.

The book stated Newton's theory of universal gravitation, explaining why the planets move as they do. According to this theory, the force of gravity not only prevents objects from flying off the revolving earth, but it also holds the entire solar system together by keeping the sun and the planets

Footnotes to History

The Circus
Identified by Newton, centripetal force pulls an object traveling in a circular path toward the center of the circle. In 1768 the English performer Philip Astley relied on centripetal force to perform stunts on horseback while the horse ran in a circle at full gallop. He took his horse show to Paris in 1774, beginning the first circus. *Circus* is the Latin word for "circle."

MEETING SPECIAL NEEDS ACTIVITY

Attention Deficiency To help students with attention problems organize and remember information about the people in this section, have them list these people's names. Tell students that remembering information is often easier if it is classified in some way. They can classify the names on their lists by scientific field. Organize students into small groups or pairs to identify the scientists' fields and then quiz each other; for example, "Who was Boyle?" "Boyle was a chemist." After students know these facts, have pairs add another fact about each person, then quiz each other again. For example, "Who was Boyle?" "Boyle was a chemist who is often called the founder of modern chemistry." **L1**

CONNECTIONS Science and Technology

Bubbling Waters

Have you ever sipped a fizzy soft drink to settle an upset stomach? People have long believed that bubbling waters contain healing properties. For centuries royalty and wealthy Europeans sought the health benefits of the mineral-rich, bubbling springs scattered throughout Europe.

Soft drink advertisement

Scientists in Europe and the United States attempted to reproduce these effervescent waters. In 1775 the French chemist Antoine Lavoisier identified the gaseous compound as carbon dioxide. In 1782 the English chemist Thomas Henry described how to make artificial carbonated waters commercially. Factories and bottling plants soon began operating in London, Paris, Dublin, and Geneva.

"Soft drinks" were originally sold in drugstores in the United States as syrupy tonics used for medicinal purposes. In the early 1800s it became popular to combine these tonics with carbonated water. Bottled colas appeared on the market in the late 1800s.

Today mineral waters and carbonated beverages are popular throughout the world. People like the tangy, sparkling taste provided by carbonation, which also prevents spoilage.

MAKING THE CONNECTION

1. Do you think carbonated soda has a positive or a negative effect on your health?
2. Can you think of any inventions or technologies that have been produced by the soft-drink industry?

in proper orbits. To prove his theory, Newton developed **calculus**, a system of mathematics that calculates changing forces or quantities.

Newton's work greatly influenced the thinking of his own age and all later scientific thought. It suggested that precise mathematical formulas could be used to describe an orderly world and universe.

Studying the Natural World

As astronomy, philosophy, and mathematics advanced at an incredible pace, so too did the sciences of anatomy and chemistry. Like astronomy and physics, anatomy had been based on ancient works. Most knowledge of anatomy had come from the work of Claudius Galen, an ancient Roman.

Because Roman law forbade the dissection of human corpses, Galen formulated his theories of human anatomy by dissecting dogs and apes. Galen did make many anatomical discoveries, such as the existence of blood within the arteries, but he also held many mistaken views. Galen wrote that human beings have 13 pairs of ribs (they have 12), and he believed that the liver digested food and processed it into blood. A thousand years would pass before anyone began to question his findings.

Investigating the Human Body

French lawmakers in the 1500s also considered dissecting human bodies illegal. This limitation, however, did not stop a young medical student from making great advances in anatomy. Self-assured and outspoken, **Andreas Vesalius** made it clear to his professors that because Galen's views were based on dissected apes and dogs, his beliefs about human anatomy could not be accepted as truth. By dissecting human bodies, Vesalius made ground-breaking discoveries in anatomy. In 1543 he published his work in *The Structure of the Human Body.*

Almost 100 years later, English physician **William Harvey** made a discovery that also disproved many of Galen's hypotheses. From his firsthand observations of human bodies, Harvey announced that blood circulates throughout the body. His findings astonished a medical world that had based their beliefs about circulation on Galen's work.

As Vesalius and Harvey explained the workings of the human body, still another English scientist, **Robert Hooke**, made a more fundamental biological discovery—the cell. Using the newly invented microscope, Hooke recognized cells in vegetable tissue. Hooke decided to call them "cells" because they reminded him of the cells in a honeycomb.

CONNECTIONS Science and Technology

Bubbling Waters

Soft drinks we enjoy today trace back to the eighteenth and nineteenth centuries. Jacob Schweppe, a jeweler in Geneva, began selling artificially carbonated mineral waters by 1794 and later started a carbonated beverage business in London. In 1886 John Pemberton, a pharmacist in Atlanta, Georgia, invented Coca-Cola.

Answers to Making the Connection

1. *Answers will vary. Students may assert that although carbonated beverages may not provide a direct medical benefit, doctors often recommend that patients drink them to help control nausea. They might also suggest that overconsumption of sweetened beverages may increase tooth decay and lead to weight gain.*
2. *Students may mention flavoring syrups; packaging in glass or plastic bottles, aluminum or plastic cans; vending machines.*

ASSESS

Check for Understanding

Assign Section 1 Review as homework or as an in-class activity.

Use Student Self-Test and Review Software to review Section 1.

MAKING CONNECTIONS ACTIVITIES

Mathematics/Science Have students who are talented in math or physics do a demonstration for the rest of the class explaining one of Newton's laws of physics or the basic principle of calculus. Encourage students to use objects or chalkboard diagrams. **L3**

Social Life Antoine and Marie Lavoisier are only one pair of married scientific collaborators. Have students research and write short reports about the fruitful collaborative efforts of other scientist couples, such as Marie and Pierre Curie, Irène and Frédéric Joliot-Curie, or Carolyn and Eugene Shoemaker. **L2**

Who?What?Where?When?

Lavoisier was a friend of the man who invented the guillotine. Ironically, as a member of the detested French tax-collecting agency, in 1794 Lavoisier was himself guillotined. A mathematician noted, "It required only a moment to sever his head, and probably one hundred years will not suffice to produce another like it."

Evaluate

Section Quiz 20-1

Use the Testmaker to create a customized quiz for Section 1.

Reteach

Have students independently review the section and create a time line that lists important discoveries and persons. Discuss the time lines in class and create a class time line.

Enrich

Have students choose an innovator from the section, then choose a pivotal day in that innovator's life and write a journal entry in that person's voice for that day. A suggestion is Galileo's journal on a day during his heresy trial.

CLOSE

Write the words *before* and *after* on the chalkboard. Have students take turns choosing a person mentioned in this section and describing an accepted theory before and after this person's work. For example, having chosen Vesalius, a student would describe anatomy before and after Vesalius.

AROUND THE WORLD

Franklin Experiments With Electricity

Philadelphia, Pennsylvania, 1752

American scientist and inventor Benjamin Franklin performed an experiment to prove his theory that lightning is electricity. During a thunderstorm, Franklin flew a homemade kite with a wire attached to it. A bolt of lightning struck the wire and traveled down the wet kite string to a key fastened at the end, where it caused an electric spark. Franklin reported the results in his pamphlet *Experiments and Observations in Electricity.*

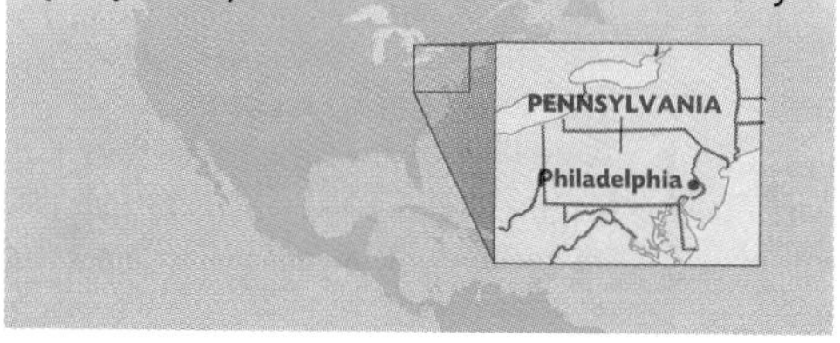

Experimenting With Chemistry

European scientists working in the field of chemistry joined their peers in astronomy, mathematics, and medicine in challenging traditional ideas. By careful scientific experimentation, **Robert Boyle** was primarily responsible for taking chemistry from its mystical and unscientific origins and establishing it as a pure science.

When Boyle was born into an Irish noble family in 1627, the chemistry of the day was alchemy. People who practiced alchemy, called **alchemists**, spent much of their time trying to transform base metals into precious metals such as gold. They also held to the age-old belief that all matter was made up of four elements: earth, fire, water, and air.

Boyle criticized alchemists and attacked the theory of the four elements in his book *The Skeptical Chymist*, published in 1661. Boyle proved that air could not be a basic element because it was a mixture of several gases. He also defined an element as a material that cannot be broken down into simpler parts by chemical means.

A century later, in 1774, an English chemist and clergyman named **Joseph Priestley** conducted further experiments into the properties of air and discovered the existence of oxygen. His study of the properties of carbon dioxide resulted in his invention of carbonated drinks. Toward the end of his career, Priestley wrote, "Every year of the last twenty or thirty has been of more importance to science … than any ten in the preceding century."

Across the English Channel in France, **Antoine Lavoisier** contributed still more to knowledge about oxygen. Lavoisier conducted scientific experiments that probed the nature of air and discovered that materials do not throw off a substance called phlogiston when burned, as commonly believed, but rather they consume oxygen. Lavoisier discovered the nature of combustion, which results from the chemical union of a flammable material with oxygen.

Marie Lavoisier contributed significantly to her husband's work. She learned English and Latin so that she could translate scientific essays and books for him. She also read numerous articles and condensed them so that he could be informed on many scientific subjects. Madame Lavoisier also made illustrations for her husband's writing.

Perhaps more significant than any single discovery in the 1700s was the application of the scientific view to an understanding of the world. Influenced by the discoveries in science, European philosophers in the 1700s began to apply the scientific method to all human ideas and practices. Most people, caught up in the daily struggle for survival, at first took little notice. In the years to come, however, science would profoundly alter humanity's view of the world.

SECTION 1 REVIEW

Recall

1. **Define** hypothesis, ellipses, scientific method, calculus, alchemist.
2. **Identify** Nicolaus Copernicus, Johannes Kepler, Galileo Galilei, Francis Bacon, René Descartes, Isaac Newton, Andreas Vesalius, William Harvey, Robert Hooke, Robert Boyle, Joseph Priestley, Antoine and Marie Lavoisier.
3. **List** three scientific discoveries that were made during the period from 1500 to 1800.

Critical Thinking

4. **Analyzing Information** How did Europeans view the universe and the workings of the human body before the coming of the scientific revolution?

Understanding Themes

5. **Innovation** How did Robert Boyle revolutionize chemistry by applying the scientific method?

SECTION 1 REVIEW ANSWERS

1. The words are defined in the Glossary.
2. Copernicus, 516; Kepler, 517; Galileo, 517; Bacon, 518; Descartes, 518; Newton, 518; Vesalius, 519; Harvey, 519; Hooke, 519; Boyle, 520; Priestley, 520; Lavoisiers, 520
3. sun-centered solar system; universal gravitation; blood circulation; the cell; oxygen
4. People believed the earth was at the center of the universe and that the liver digested food and converted it to blood.
5. **INNOVATION** Boyle used the scientific method to disprove the old theory of the four elements and define the true nature of an element, thereby establishing chemistry as a pure science.

1600 — 1700 — 1800

1651 Thomas Hobbes publishes *Leviathan*.

1662 Charles II establishes the Royal Society of London.

1700s Deism becomes popular in Europe and America.

Section 2

Impact of Science

Setting the Scene

▶ **Terms to Define**
natural law, pacifism, deism

▶ **People to Meet**
Thomas Hobbes, John Locke, Thomas Jefferson, Hugo Grotius, William Penn

▶ **Places to Locate**
Pennsylvania

Find Out What effects did changes in scientific thought have on thinking in other fields?

The Storyteller

Donald MacAdam bent forward to hear better. The lecturer was about to read from a new poem from the pen of Nicolas Boileau-Despreaux.

"What-e'er you write of Pleasant or Sublime,
Always let sense accompany your Rhyme:
Falsely they seem each other to oppose;
Rhyme must be made with Reason's Laws to close:
And when to conquer her you bend your force,
The Mind will Triumph in the Noble Course."

Donald wondered, how would poetry survive if it must always be so rational?

—adapted from *The Reasonableness of Poetry*, reprinted in *From Absolutism to Revolution*, edited by Herbert H. Rowen, 1964

European salon conversation

As scientists made revolutionary discoveries about people, nature, and the universe, popular interest in science spread throughout Europe. Using new technology such as the microscope, scientists and amateurs alike looked with wonder at the world inside a drop of pond water. Others tinkered and prodded in their home laboratories, studying gases and other substances. At social gatherings across Europe, people discussed the latest findings with lively interest.

Monarchs helped the new sciences by supporting scientific academies, observatories, and museums. In England Charles II established the Royal Society of London in 1662. The group included Isaac Newton and Robert Boyle among its members. In 1666 Louis XIV of France supported the founding of the French Academy of Science. These societies provided financial support to scientists and published scientific books and journals.

Exploring Political Ideas

The advances in science led philosophers and other thinkers to believe that if systematic laws governed the workings of nature and the universe, it followed that political, economic, and social relationships could also be understood through reasoned analysis. Scientific thought and method profoundly influenced political theory. Political philosophers believed in the idea of natural law, or a universal moral law that, like physical laws, could be understood by applying reason.

Two English philosophers, **Thomas Hobbes** and **John Locke**, grappled with their ideas of natural law and government during the mid-1600s, as England struggled with the political tensions of a civil war. The country was torn between people who wanted the king to have absolute power and those who thought the people have the right to govern themselves.

Chapter 20 Section 2

SECTION THEME

▶ **Conflict** Changing views based on science and reason conflict with traditional beliefs.

Find Out

Answer: *Thinkers began to use reasoned analysis to scrutinize political theory, legal practice, and religious beliefs.*

FOCUS

Section Objective

Analyze the effects that changes in scientific thought had on thinking in other fields.

BELLRINGER
Motivational Activity

Before taking roll at the beginning of the class period, project Section Focus Transparency 20-2 and have students answer the activity questions. Discuss students' responses.

This activity is also available as a blackline master.

Vocabulary Pre-check

Use Vocabulary Activity 20 to introduce vocabulary terms. **L1 LEP**

SECTION RESOURCES

Reproducible Masters
- Reproducible Lesson Plan 20-2
- Vocabulary Activity 20
- Guided Reading Activity 20-2
- History Simulation 20
- Section Quiz 20-2

Transparencies
- Section Focus Transparency 20-2

Multimedia
- Student Self-Test and Review Software
- Testmaker
- Turning Points in World History: *The Scientific Revolution*

Chapter 20 *Scientific Revolution* **521**

TEACH

Guided Practice

THEME **Conflict**

Ask students how they would react if they encountered ideas that conflicted with their beliefs; for example, if someone argued that we descend from extraterrestrials. Have students list conflicts of ideas in this section. **L1**

History Simulation 20

Picturing History

Tell students that many historians of science challenge claims that Galileo was the first to disprove Aristotle's notions about the relationship between the speed of falling bodies and their weight. Medieval philosophers had pointed out Aristotle's mistake more than 1,000 years before Galileo, and other scientists in the 1500s had also challenged Aristotle's claim. Nonetheless, it is universally agreed that Galileo did make careful experiments of vertically falling objects by rolling balls down inclined planes. Scientists today study falling bodies by using equipment unavailable to Galileo: strobe lights and video cameras.

ABCNEWS INTERACTIVE™

VIDEODISC
Turning Points in World History

Side One
Chapter 10

Title: *The Scientific Revolution*
Ask: What scientist perfected the telescope? *(Galileo)*

NATIONAL GEOGRAPHIC PICTURING HISTORY

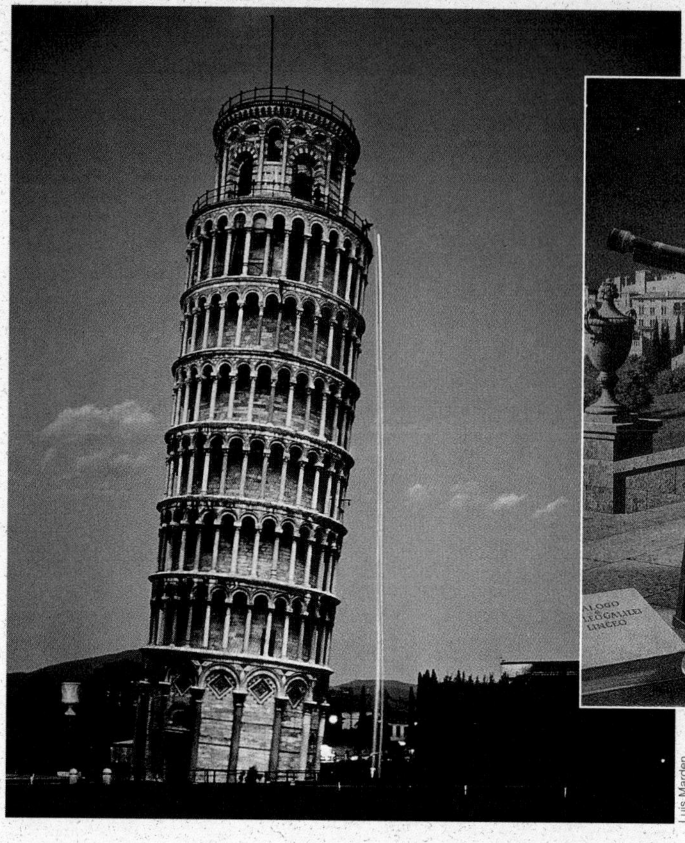

Luis Marden

Tower Physics

In a modern re-creation (left) of Galileo's famous experiment from the Leaning Tower of Pisa, two lighted plastic balls, one heavier than the other, plummet to the ground at once—a result the scientific community of Galileo's day refused to acknowledge. In 1591 Italian scientist Galileo Galilei (right) wanted to test the Aristotelian theory of motion—the idea that when two bodies of unequal weight are dropped simultaneously, the heavier object will hit the ground first. So he dropped a ten-pound weight and a one-pound weight from the top of the bell tower.

Galileo's experiment demonstrated that objects of different weights fell at the same rate—hit the ground at the same time—if one allowed for the impact of air resistance. Galileo proved Greek philosopher Aristotle's theory of motion wrong. In investigating the science of the motion of bodies, Galileo was part of the scientific revolution, a reformulation of ideas that overturned those held by medieval thinkers and the Catholic Church. Scientists began carefully testing old theories of how the material world worked; they used careful measurements, exact observations, and precise experiments. The conflict between these new ideas and the power of the older theories forced the new scientists to develop techniques to prove their claims. Today we call this the scientific method—and admire men like Galileo, who sought to understand motion by dropping things from the tallest building in Pisa. ⊕

522 Chapter 20 *Scientific Revolution*

MORE ABOUT...

Science and Motion In July 1971, *Apollo 15* astronaut David Scott performed Galileo's demonstration on the moon, where there is no air. He dropped a hammer and a feather at the same time to show conclusively that in the absence of air resistance, a heavy object will hit the ground at the same time as a lighter one.

Hobbes Explores Government

Thomas Hobbes used the idea of natural law to argue that absolute monarchy was the best form of government. He believed that violence and disorder came naturally to human beings and that without an absolute government, chaos would occur. In his book *Leviathan*, published in 1651, Hobbes wrote about a state in which people lived without government. The book showed how "nasty, brutish, and short" life in such a world would be.

Hobbes believed that people should form a contract or agreement to give up their freedom and live obediently under a ruler. In this way, they would be governed and ruled by a monarch who would protect them by keeping their world peaceful and orderly. According to Hobbes, people generally do not have the right to rebel against their government, no matter how unjust it might be.

Locke Offers a Different View

Another English philosopher, John Locke, also based his theories on the idea of natural law. He came to an entirely different conclusion, however. Like Hobbes, Locke said that government was based on a contract and that it was necessary to establish order. Unlike Hobbes, he believed that people in a state of nature are reasonable and moral, and that they have natural rights to life, liberty, and property.

Locke believed that these rights exist apart from any government, and people have the right to break their contract if their government fails to uphold their natural rights. According to Locke, if people employed reason, they would arrive at a cooperative and workable form of government.

Locke published his ideas in 1690 in *Two Treatises of Government*. His writings became widely read and were tremendously influential throughout Europe and in England's American colonies. Ironically, the ideas that the American colonists used to justify their independence from Great Britain were formulated by British thinkers. **Thomas Jefferson** based much of the Declaration of Independence on Locke's ideas about the social contract between government and individuals.

Reason Influences Law

As Europeans searched for new principles that would meet the standards of reason, great changes were made in the practice of law. Incorporating scientific or reasoned thought in applying the law helped to end unjust trials. Lawmakers placed less value on hearsay and on confessions made under torture in determining the guilt or innocence of suspected criminals.

In the 1600s several people made the first attempts to create a body of international law. A Dutch jurist named **Hugo Grotius** called for an international code based on natural law. He believed that one body of rules could reduce the dealings of governments to a system of reason and order.

In the American colonies, **William Penn**, founder of the Quaker colony of **Pennsylvania**, believed in pacifism, or opposition to war or violence as a means of settling disputes. Penn advocated an assembly of nations committed to world peace.

Examining Religion

Many Europeans also applied reason to religious beliefs. Members of the upper and middle classes increasingly turned away from traditional religious views, and Europe became a more secular society. In the 1700s a new religious philosophy called deism swept through Europe and America. Although believing in God, Deists often denounced organized religion, declaring that it exploited people's ignorance and superstitions. Deism was intended to construct a simpler and more natural religion based on reason and natural law. Its followers asserted the rightness of humanity's place in an orderly universe.

SECTION 2 REVIEW

Recall

1. **Define** natural law, pacifism, deism.
2. **Identify** Thomas Hobbes, John Locke, Thomas Jefferson, Hugo Grotius, William Penn.
3. **Explain** John Locke's theory of the contract of government.

Critical Thinking

4. **Making Comparisons** Contrast Hobbes's views with Locke's views.

Understanding Themes

5. **Conflict** What was the purpose of the new religious philosophy known as deism, and how did deism conflict with traditional religion?

Chapter 20 Section 2

Independent Practice

Guided Reading Activity 20-2 **L1**

ASSESS

Check for Understanding

Assign Section 2 Review as homework or as an in-class activity.

Use Student Self-Test and Review Software to review Section 2.

Evaluate

Section Quiz 20-2

Use the Testmaker to create a customized quiz for Section 2.

Reteach

Review with students the concept of natural law, the political philosophies of the time, and the political changes that took place.

Enrich

Remind students that ideas covered in this section still affect today's world. Have students make a list of contemporary thinkers, ideas, and technologies they think will still affect the world 300 years from now.

CLOSE

Help students create a flowchart showing how the scientific method affected other areas of thought, such as politics, law, and religion. Incorporate material from Section 1 and leave room for additions from Section 3.

SECTION 2 REVIEW ANSWERS

1. The words are defined in the Glossary.
2. Hobbes, 521; Locke, 521; Jefferson, 523; Grotius, 523; Penn, 523
3. Government was based on a contract, which could be broken if rights were not upheld.
4. Hobbes argued that people need absolute governments to prevent chaos. Locke argued that people may overthrow any government that denies them their natural rights.
5. **CONFLICT** Deism was based on reason and natural law. Deists claimed organized religion exploited people.

SECTION THEME

▶ **Reaction** Reason and order are applied to many human endeavors.

Find Out

Answer: *Enlightenment ideas were spread through the writings of philosophers and other Enlightenment thinkers and through discussions in salons.*

FOCUS

Section Objective

Identify the factors that helped Enlightenment ideas spread throughout Europe.

BELLRINGER
Motivational Activity

Before taking roll at the beginning of the class period, project Section Focus Transparency 20-3 and have students answer the activity questions. Discuss students' responses.

This activity is also available as a blackline master.

Vocabulary Pre-check

Use the Vocabulary PuzzleMaker to create a puzzle that reinforces the vocabulary terms in this section. **L1**

1700 — 1750 — 1800

c. 1736 John Wesley promotes religious revival in Great Britain.

1748 Baron de Montesquieu publishes *The Spirit of Laws.*

1780s Joseph II of Austria introduces Enlightenment reforms.

Section 3

Triumph of Reason

Setting the Scene

▶ **Terms to Define**
philosophe, salon, enlightened despot, classicism, metaphysics, romanticism

▶ **People to Meet**
Madame de Pompadour, Denis Diderot, Baron de Montesquieu, Voltaire, Jean-Jacques Rousseau, Immanuel Kant, John Wesley

▶ **Places to Locate**
Paris

Find Out What factors helped Enlightenment ideas to spread throughout Europe?

The Storyteller

Voltaire

The notorious criminal Jean Chatel had just been executed. Moments before his death, the priests announced that the murderer had confessed all his sins and received absolution. Therefore, he had died in a state of grace and his soul would eventually reach Paradise. The proclamation greatly disturbed Joseph Leveque and his friends. They had just read Voltaire's comments about universal toleration. How could good and bad be defined in such absolute terms? They asked themselves and each other, would the Creator condemn Confucius and Socrates to limitless torment, while blessing a villain simply because he died according to a prescribed formula?

—adapted from *Treatise on Toleration,* Voltaire, reprinted in *The Human Record,* Alfred J. Andrea and James H. Overfield, 1990

Compared to their ancestors, who lived in a world that seemed to be run by inexplicable forces and filled with magic, Europe's new thinkers believed that their scientific approach helped illuminate and clarify both the natural world and the study of human behavior. As a result, the period in Europe from the late 1600s through the 1700s came to be called the Age of Enlightenment.

Men and women of the Enlightenment studied the world as though they were looking at it for the first time. No longer held back by tradition, they defined the world in their own way, using science as their base. Natural scientists analyzed and classified thousands of animals, insects, and plants. Geologists drew maps of the earth's surface. Astronomers continued to make discoveries about the universe.

Largely due to reading Newton's *Principia,* Enlightenment thinkers perceived the universe as a machine governed by fixed laws. They saw God as the master mechanic of the universe—the builder of a machine who provided laws and then allowed it to run on its own, according to these orderly principles. They also believed in progress, or the idea that the world and its people could be improved.

Such radically new perceptions and ideas started a philosophical revolution. Jean Le Rond d'Alembert, a French mathematician, claimed that the new method of thinking and the enthusiasm that accompanied it had "brought about a lively fermentation of minds, spreading through nature in all directions like a river which has burst at its dams."

Spreading Ideas

The thinkers of the Enlightenment who spread these exciting new ideas came to be called **philosophes** (FEE•luh•ZAWFS), the French word for "philosopher." Most philosophes passionately believed in Locke's political philosophy and

SECTION RESOURCES

Reproducible Masters
- Reproducible Lesson Plan 20-3
- Guided Reading Activity 20-3
- People in World History Profile 38
- Reteaching Activity 20
- Enrichment Activity 20
- Section Quiz 20-3
- Performance Assessment Activity 20
- Spanish Chapter Summary 20

Transparencies
- Section Focus Transparency 20-3
- World History and Art Transparency 27

Multimedia
- Vocabulary PuzzleMaker Software
- Student Self-Test and Review Software
- Testmaker
- Turning Points in World History: *The Scientific Revolution*

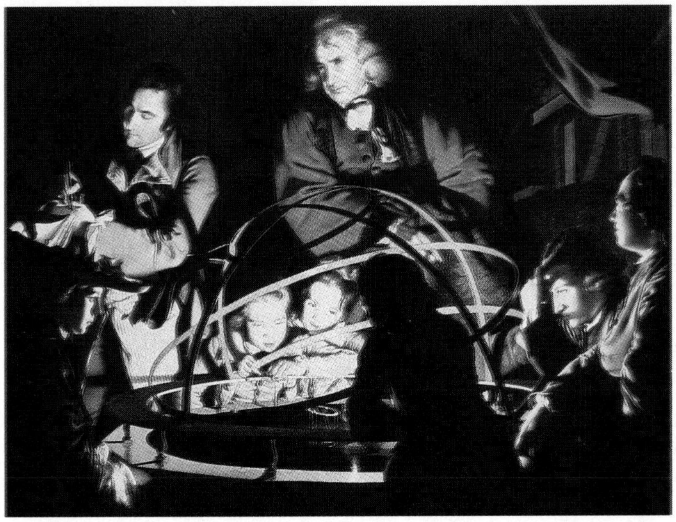

Visualizing History **This device is an orrery, or model of the solar system that demonstrates the motions of the planets about the sun. The typical orrery shows the planets as they appear from outside the solar system and provides an accurate scale model of the planets' periods of revolution. Earth, for example, completes a year's rotation in about 10 minutes. The first orrery was probably invented in England during the 1700s.** *What English mathematician saw the universe as a machine governed by fixed laws?*

Newton's scientific theories. Most disapproved of superstition and religious opposition to new scientific endeavors. They believed in both freedom of speech and the individual's right to liberty. Many philosophes were talented writers whose essays and books helped to spread and popularize ideas and beliefs of the Enlightenment.

Activity in Paris

France was the most active center of ideas. In **Paris** especially, the new intellectuals delighted in gatherings called **salons** held in the homes of wealthy patrons. In a salon, writers, artists, and educated people of the growing middle class mingled with men and women of the nobility. Besides discussing the philosophies of the day, salon guests prized the art of conversation and often engaged in contests to see who had the sharpest wit.

Wealthy and influential women ran many of the popular salons. **Madame de Pompadour** was perhaps the most celebrated. A mistress to Louis XV, Pompadour's intelligence and courtly charm won the admiration of many philosophes.

A remarkable achievement compiled by some of the most prominent philosophes of the Enlightenment was the *Encyclopédie*. First published in 1751, these 28 volumes covered everything then known about the sciences, technology, and history in more than 3,000 pages crammed with illustrations.

The *Encyclopédie* was initially conceived to be simply a French translation of a two-volume English encyclopedia, but its editor, **Denis Diderot** (dee•DROH), had a work of much greater scope in mind. Diderot devoted much of his life to this project. Among other things, the *Encyclopédie* criticized the Church and government and praised religious tolerance.

The Catholic Church banned the *Encyclopédie*. When Diderot discovered that the printer, frightened by the controversial material in the volumes, had omitted passages that might offend the Church's leaders, he became enraged and screamed at the printer:

> "You have massacred ... the work of twenty good men who have devoted to you their time, their vigils, their talents, from a love of truth and justice, with the simple hope of seeing their ideas given to the public...."

For their writings, Diderot and several others went to prison. Still, the *Encyclopédie* was widely read and its ideas spread all through Europe.

Montesquieu

A contributor to the *Encyclopédie* and one of the most learned of the philosophes in political matters was Charles-Louis de Secondat, the **Baron de Montesquieu** (MAHN•tuhs•KYOO). His master work, *The Spirit of Laws*, appeared in two volumes in 1748.

After studying various existing governments, Montesquieu wrote about his admiration for the English government and promoted the idea of separating governmental powers. Montesquieu believed that power should be equally divided among the branches of government: the legislative

Chapter 20
Section 3

TEACH

Guided Practice

THEME Reaction
Have students describe some of the different ways specific people reacted to Enlightenment ideas. Suggest that they consider the reactions of Madame de Pompadour, Diderot, Voltaire, Frederick II, Rousseau, and John Wesley. **L1**

Visualizing History The orrery gets its name from Charles Boyle, fourth earl of Orrery, who probably had the device invented by George Graham. **Answer to Caption:** *Newton*

Global Issues Ask students to restate Voltaire's words: "I disapprove of what you say, but I will defend to the death your right to say it." Then have them identify countries in which Voltaire's approach to free speech could and could not be practiced today. **L2**

Point of View To help students better understand opposition to the ideas of the Enlightenment, have them summarize the nature of the objections of Jean-Jacques Rousseau, Immanuel Kant, Count von Zinzendorf, and John Wesley. **L3**

World History and Art Transparency 27, *The Letter*

COOPERATIVE LEARNING ACTIVITY

Role Play Organize the class into two groups to plan a gathering in a salon. Have each student in one group select a favorite individual from this chapter. Have students in the other group choose roles as members of the middle class or the nobility. Students should research the individuals, the lifestyles of the different social classes, and the salons. They should then plan the setting and select a topic for the gathering. Remind students that salons were places where middle-class writers, artists, and educated people could mingle with the nobility. To stimulate conversation, you may wish to visit the salon in the guise of a noble person. **L2**

Chapter 20 Section 3

ABCNEWS INTERACTIVE™

VIDEODISC
Turning Points in World History

Side One, Chapter 10

Title: *The Scientific Revolution*
Ask: What is your interpretation of this statement, "If there is one evil in the world today for which there is no excuse, it is the evil of stupidity"? *(Students may suggest that the statement seems to say that there is no excuse for lacking knowledge, because everyone has the ability and opportunity to expand their knowledge.)*

Independent Practice

Guided Reading Activity 20-3 **L1**

People in World History Profile 38

Critical Thinking Ask students to write a short paper stating whether they agree or disagree with Rousseau that human beings are naturally good. Ask them to give examples supporting their opinions. **L2**

Linking Past and Present

Encyclopedias—from the Greek words for "general education"—continue to be published along the lines of the French *Encyclopédie*. Although encyclopedias vary in length, format, and content, all aim at presenting up-to-date knowledge in a conveniently accessible form.

branch, which made the laws; the executive branch, which enforced them; and the judicial branch, which interpreted the laws and judged when they were violated.

Montesquieu strongly believed in the rights of individuals. His work powerfully influenced the writing of the constitutions in many countries, including the United States.

Voltaire

Perhaps the most celebrated of the philosophes was François-Marie Arouet, known to the world by his pen name, **Voltaire**. A French author and Deist, Voltaire wrote poetry, plays, essays, and books in a style that was entertaining and often satirical. *Candide*, his most celebrated satire, challenged the notion that everything that happens is for the best in "the best of all possible worlds."

In his youth, Voltaire twice served time in the Bastille, the notorious prison in Paris. His satirical works that mocked the Church and the royal court of France earned him one prison term; he received the other term when he was accused of claiming to be a nobleman. After his second offense, Voltaire was given a choice between further imprisonment and exile from France. He chose the latter. When Voltaire moved to England, he felt unfettered in an atmosphere of political and religious freedom.

During the three years he spent in England, Voltaire wrote books promoting Bacon's philosophy and Newton's science. Voltaire deeply admired the English ideal of religious liberty and its relative freedom of the press. Voltaire is credited with the famous statement in defense of free speech, "I disapprove of what you say, but I will defend to the death your right to say it."

Impact of the Enlightenment

The ideas introduced by the philosophes and other enlightened thinkers spread into the realm of

Images of the Times

Salon Society

During the Enlightenment, Europe's high society gathered in the salons of wealthy patrons to discuss the ideas and events of the day.

Upper class society of the 1700s enjoyed card games as well as intellectual discussions.

Images of the Times **Salon Society**

The salon of Marie-Thérèse Rodet Geoffrin (1699–1777), held in the Hôtel de Rambouillet from 1749 to 1777, drew artists and writers from France and beyond. Although she was the daughter of a valet and lacked a formal education, her native intelligence and her marriage to a rich manufacturer enabled her to be an excellent hostess. Madame Geoffrin underwrote the *Encyclopédie* project.

When Jeanne-Antoinette Poisson (1721–1764) became King Louis XV's mistress in 1745, he made her marchioness of Pompadour. A patron of the arts, Madame de Pompadour also introduced the pompadour hairstyle, in which the hair is raised up over the forehead in a roll.

politics. Philosophes asserted the right of people to speak freely and to disagree with their rulers, and advocated reforms such as ending the use of torture in prisons. Their work influenced rulers in such countries as Prussia, Austria, Spain, Portugal, Denmark, and Sweden. These leaders began to implement humanitarian and social reforms to help their people.

Some Leaders Initiate Reform

Monarchs who attempted to practice some of the political ideas of the Enlightenment were called **enlightened despots**. These leaders aimed to rule according to the principles of the Enlightenment while maintaining their traditional royal powers. They worked hard to improve the performance of government in their countries and promoted agriculture, industry, culture, and education.

Frederick II of Prussia, the most famous of the enlightened despots, played the flute, wrote poems and essays, and earned a reputation as a minor philosophe. Frederick believed that as king, he was the "first servant of the state." He corresponded with Voltaire for many years, and both men greatly admired each other. It was Voltaire who first honored Frederick with the title "the Great." In one letter, Frederick wrote to Voltaire:

> "My chief occupation is to fight the ignorances and the prejudices in this country.... I must enlighten my people, cultivate their manners and morals, and make them as happy as human beings can be; as happy as the means at my disposal permit me to make them."

Frederick's reforms included abolishing the use of torture except for treason and murder, establishing elementary schools, and promoting industry and agriculture. After the Seven Years' War, Frederick tried to help the peasants by giving them seeds to plant and money to rebuild houses and barns.

Madame de Geoffrin's Salon **by Jean-Baptiste Lemoyner** shows one of the Paris salons that influenced art, literature, and politics.

Parisian aristocratic women often posed for their portraits dressed as classical mythological figures.

REFLECTING ON THE TIMES

1. How did salon gatherings in Europe during the 1700s reflect Enlightenment ideals?
2. What role do you think women played in the salon society of the 1700s?

527

ANSWERS TO REFLECTING ON THE TIMES

1. At salons individuals exercised their right to speak freely and to disagree with their rulers, both ideals of the philosophes.
2. Women both hosted salons and participated in salon debates. The salons not only broadened the social views of its female participants but also expanded their role in society.

Chapter 20 Section 3

Literature Have students read English translations of Molière's *Les Précieuses Ridicules* (1659) or *Les Femmes Savantes* (1672). Have them write a short report for class presentation in which they describe how Molière satirizes the pretensions of middle-class women *(les précieuses)* and male participants in salon society. **L3**

Who?What?Where?When?

Marie de Vichy-Chamrond, marchioness of Deffand (1697–1780), was the hostess of another important French salon. Her salon attracted not only writers and socialites but also scientists.

In her mid-fifties, after losing her sight, Madame du Deffand engaged the younger Julie de Lespinasse (1732–1776) to assist her in entertaining. Jealous of Mademoiselle de Lespinasse's popularity with her guests, the older woman dismissed her in 1764. However, that action brought about the end of her salon when many of her former patrons chose to follow the fired cohostess.

Who?What?Where?When?

Rococo During the period of salons, the French decorative arts were characterized by fanciful and intricate decoration in a style that became known as rococo. Furniture, porcelain, clocks, chandeliers, and draperies all were testaments to the middle-class worship of beauty.

Chapter 20 Section 3

Visualizing History The Grand-Théâtre, Bordeaux, was the largest theater in France before the French Revolution. Although Victor Louis (1731–1800) was disliked by many because of his bad temper and conceited nature, his work was admired. Best known for his construction of theaters, Louis also planned the gardens of the Palais Royal.

Answer to Caption: *The classical style often used simple geometric forms and drew on subjects from classical mythology.*

Who?What?Where?When?

Moses Mendelssohn (1729–1786) was an important Jewish figure during the Enlightenment. Son of a poor scribe, the brilliant Mendelssohn taught himself both philosophy and foreign languages by reading the works of John Locke and other Enlightenment figures. Mendelssohn became a renowned philosopher and literary figure. His life demonstrated that religion could coexist with the Enlightenment's emphasis on reason.

Cultural Perspectives

Hasidism was founded by followers of Israel Baal Shem Tov, a Jewish mystic and miracle worker. Although Hasidism was dealt a devastating blow by the murder of millions of European Jews in the Holocaust, it is a growing movement today, with flourishing centers in New York and Israel and active outreach activities around the world.

Visualizing History **The Grand Théâtre was built by the French architect Victor Louis in the mid-1700s. Located in the French city of Bordeaux, this magnificent theater reflects the dominant classical style of the time.** *What were two major characteristics of the classical style?*

Another ruler who introduced several humanitarian reforms was Maria Theresa of Austria. She bore the titles of Holy Roman Empress, Queen of Hungary and Bohemia, and Archduchess of Austria. She was one of Austria's most able rulers. Although as a Catholic she disagreed with much of Enlightenment philosophy, Maria Theresa tried to protect the rights of serfs by issuing codes governing the relationship between them and their lords. She also freed all peasants who lived on land owned by the crown. In 1774 she set up elementary schools supported by local and national funds.

Maria Theresa's son, Joseph II, also admired and followed the ideas of the Enlightenment. After the empress's death in 1780, Joseph II quickly implemented stronger reforms in the kingdom. He abolished serfdom, made land taxes equal for peasants and nobles, and gave freedom to the press. He also took property from the Church and used the money to support hospitals.

Most of Joseph's reforms failed, however. His abrupt changes antagonized too many people. Rebellion by the nobles forced him to repeal many of his reforms. Joseph's brother and successor, Leopold II, revoked most of Joseph's remaining laws, but did allow the peasants to keep their freedom.

Throughout Europe, nobles and church leaders, afraid of losing too much political power to the common people, frustrated many reform efforts made by enlightened despots. In addition, many monarchs backed away from Enlightenment ideals when they realized that their own positions would be threatened by giving too much power to their subjects. In doing so, they struck down many of the political reforms that might have prevented the violent revolutions that were to come.

Classical Movements

The worlds of art, music, and literature also shared in the Enlightenment beliefs. Writers, artists, and architects strove to achieve the ideals of Greek and Roman classicism, which to them represented ultimate order and reason. Using classical titles and imitating classical themes and styles, artists of the Enlightenment attempted to capture the refined and simplified spirit of the ancients.

Architects built palaces, opera houses, and museums based on the architecture of ancient Rome. They used simple forms, such as squares and circles, rather than the elaborate swirls of the baroque style.

Sculptors and painters also emulated the ideals and forms of antiquity. Whereas artists following the baroque style tended to appeal to their viewers with elegant, swirling forms, these artists sought a

MEETING SPECIAL NEEDS ACTIVITY

Learning Style: Auditory/Musical Listening to authentic musical pieces will help students with a sensitivity to harmony, melody, rhythm, and tone better understand the different musical styles of the age of Enlightenment. Play some works from the baroque period (1600–1750) by Bach or Handel, and then some from the classical period (1750–1820) by Haydn or Mozart. Ask students to describe some of the ways the two styles differ. *(Answers may include: the use of repetition in baroque music, and the balance and contrast among movements of a classical work.)* **L2**

528 Chapter 20 *Scientific Revolution*

return to a calm, rational style of art that would appeal to the mind through the logic and geometry of its forms.

Sculptors such as Antonio Canova created works based on subjects from classical mythology. Jean-Antoine Houdon carved sculptures of contemporary figures in poses that recall ancient portraits of philosophers and political leaders.

In the field of painting, Jacques-Louis David (dah•VEED) also drew from classical subjects and forms. His paintings show a concern with geometry and simplicity of form that results in powerful, monumental images. He used clear and uncomplicated primary colors. These reds, yellows, and blues created powerful contrasts and accented the clarity of his forms.

Writers worked to achieve the classical ideal while maintaining their devotion to the concept of reason. Often, imitation of a classical model resulted in an ornate and affected style that was focused more on form than on content. French dramatists Molière, Jean Racine, and Pierre Corneille as well as English poets John Dryden, Alexander Pope, and John Milton mastered the classical tradition.

Musical composers of the Enlightenment also stressed classical elements such as balance, contrast, and refined expression of emotion. At the same time, they witnessed a great evolution in music. Music made the transition from merely supporting religious services and dance and opera companies, to being an "art" in its own right. For the first time, people began going to concerts for the pleasure of listening to the music itself.

The piano, evolving in the late 1600s, allowed musicians to produce much greater ranges of loudness and softness. The violin was perfected at the same time, changing the sound of music. As composers grouped similar instruments, they laid the foundations for chamber music and the modern orchestra. Germany's Johann Sebastian Bach, Great Britain's German-born George Frideric Handel, and Austria's Joseph Haydn and Wolfgang Amadeus Mozart were among the musicians of this era.

Other Views

Not everyone agreed with the ideas of the Enlightenment. Some saw the structured and ordered view of the universe as overly rational and devoid of emotion and feeling. English poet William Blake exclaimed, "God is not a mathematical diagram!"

During the 1700s the French philosopher **Jean-Jacques Rousseau** criticized what he saw as his era's excessive reliance on reason and claimed that people should rely more on instinct and emotion. Born in Geneva, Switzerland to French Huguenot parents, Rousseau led an unhappy life. He suffered from chronic physical ailments and possibly from mental illness. Nevertheless, he became a leading thinker and one of the most profound writers of his day. In Paris in the 1740s, Rousseau's associates included Diderot and the Encyclopedists, and he continued to stay in touch with his Parisian intellectual circle.

Rousseau's unhappy life convinced him that human beings were naturally good but that civilization and institutions made them evil. The inspiration for this philosophy came to him in 1750, when he entered a contest that offered a prize for the answer to the question: Have science and the arts done more to corrupt morals or improve them? Rousseau won the contest with his essay *Discourse on the Effect of the Arts and Sciences on Morals*; his reply that science and the arts did corrupt morals made him famous. Ten years later he published *La Nouvelle Héloïse*, a novel describing the beauties of nature and the pleasures of a simple country life. The popular book influenced people from every level of society to live humbler lives, closer to nature. The fashion spread as far as the French palace of Versailles, where Marie Antoinette, Queen of France, constructed a rural village on royal grounds and pretended to be a milkmaid.

Visualizing History **The Austrian composer Wolfgang Amadeus Mozart died before the age of 36, but he still left the world more than 600 musical works.** *Who were three other noted classical musicians?*

Chapter 20 Section 3

Who?What?Where?When?

Alexander Pope (1688–1744), the English poet, reflected the tenets of the Scientific Revolution in his *An Essay on Man*, in which he described nature as "A mighty maze! but not without plan."

ASSESS

Check for Understanding

Assign Section 3 Review as homework or as an in-class activity.

Use Student Self-Test and Review Software to review Section 3.

Visualizing History A child prodigy, Mozart (1756–1791) began composing music at age five, and at age six he played for the Austrian empress. Among his most popular pieces are the serenade *A Little Night Music* (1787) and the operas *The Marriage of Figaro* (1786) and *Don Giovanni* (1787).

Answer to Caption: *Bach, Handel, and Haydn*

Evaluate

Section Quiz 20-3

Use the Testmaker to create a customized quiz for Section 3.

MAKING CONNECTIONS ACTIVITIES

Religion Hasidism is only one example of a religious movement grounded in mysticism. Have students prepare short oral reports on mysticism in other religions and periods. **L2**

Religion Expressions of religious tolerance proliferated during the Enlightenment. Have students prepare short oral reports on the views on religious tolerance of two or more of these figures: Gotthold Ephraim Lessing, John Locke, William Penn, Voltaire. **L2**

The Arts Not only classicism but also other artistic styles flourished during the Enlightenment. Have students prepare illustrated reports on the baroque style of the 1600s and 1700s or on the rococo style that flourished from about 1700 to 1780. **L1 LEP**

Chapter 20
Section 3

Visualizing History The Methodists got their name from critics who disparaged their belief in methodical study and devotion. Wesley (1703–1791) briefly served as a missionary in the North American colony of Georgia. In 1784 he declared that Methodist societies were completely independent of the Church of England.

Answer to Caption: *the value of personal religious experience*

Reteach

Write on the chalkboard all the terms to define and names of people to meet in this section. Call on different students to identify each term or name.

Reteaching Activity 20

Enrich

During the Enlightenment, with more people reading than ever before, the novel came into its own. Have students read all or part of an English or French novel from this period (for example, Richardson's *Clarissa*, Fielding's *Tom Jones*, Prévost's *Manon Lescaut*) and report to the class on how it compares with more modern novels.

Enrichment Activity 20

CLOSE

Have students write their reactions to the Enlightenment. Ask them to imagine how they might have felt in the 1700s when faced with these new ideas. Collect the papers and then read their ideas aloud. Using the students' ideas as a guide, review the ways people of the time reacted to the ideas of the Enlightenment.

Visualizing History **John Wesley, a clergyman of the Church of England, founded the Protestant movement known as Methodism. His outdoor preaching drew large crowds.** *What value did Methodism stress?*

Rousseau also believed that the power to rule belonged to the people, and that governments should receive their authority from the people. He wrote that people had the right to rise up against their government and carry out needed change.

Rousseau's writings influenced German philosopher **Immanuel Kant**. Kant believed that reason could not explain the problems of metaphysics—the aspects of philosophy that deal with universal, spiritual, and eternal questions, such as the existence of God and the limits of knowledge. In his major work, *The Critique of Pure Reason* (1781), Kant asserted that human feelings about religion, beauty, and morality were real even though science and reason could not explain them.

Kant divided the universe into the realm of physical nature and the realm of ultimate reality. He claimed that the methods for knowing varied greatly in these two worlds. In the physical world, people attained knowledge through the senses such as sight, hearing, and touch, as well as through reason. In the second realm, however, Kant believed that faith, intuition, and conviction were valid instruments for attaining knowledge. For example, the natural sciences, which belonged to the first realm, could not provide a guide for morality, which rested in the second realm.

Religious Movements

Not only philosophers, but ordinary men and women found something lacking in the Enlightenment's emphasis on reason. Many rejected deism, the religion of reason, and searched for a religion that was more emotionally satisfying.

In Germany, Count von Zinzendorf established the Moravian Brethren, which emphasized the emotional and mystical side of Christianity. In England, a movement called Methodism, led by **John Wesley**, also stressed the value of personal religious experience. Methodism was a reaction to the cold formality of the Church of England.

The need for a religion with more feeling also led to a Catholic revival in France. In eastern Europe, Hasidism, which promoted mysticism and religious zeal—as opposed to an emphasis on external ritual—spread among Jews. All of these religious movements rejected reason in favor of an enthusiastic faith.

As people questioned the philosophies of the Enlightenment, classicism in the arts gave way to romanticism, which was a cultural movement that celebrated emotion and the individual. These developments marked the ending of the Age of Enlightenment. Tired of the privileged ruling classes and inspired by new ideas such as the writings of Rousseau, the lower classes began to demand more rights. The sun set on the tranquil world of the Enlightenment as history moved on to a period of tumult and revolution.

SECTION 3 REVIEW

Recall
1. **Define** philosophe, salon, enlightened despot, classicism, metaphysics, romanticism.
2. **Identify** the Enlightenment, Madame de Pompadour, Denis Diderot, Baron de Montesquieu, Voltaire, Jean-Jacques Rousseau, Immanuel Kant, John Wesley.
3. **Describe** some of the main ideas of the Enlightenment thinkers.

Critical Thinking
4. **Making Comparisons** How do John Locke's ideas about government compare with those of Jean-Jacques Rousseau?

Understanding Themes
5. **Reaction** In what ways did Europeans of the 1700s react to Enlightenment ideas and values?

SECTION 3 REVIEW ANSWERS

1. All vocabulary words are defined in the Glossary.
2. Enlightenment, 524; Mme. de Pompadour, 525; Diderot, 525; Montesquieu, 525; Voltaire, 526; Rousseau, 529; Kant, 530; Wesley, 530
3. belief in reason, natural law, classical themes and ideals
4. Both believed that people had the right to revolt against unsatisfactory governments.
5. **REACTION** Some rejected reason in favor of more emotional movements in philosophy, religion, and art.

Critical Thinking SKILLS

Interpreting Point of View

Suppose you are interested in seeing a new science fiction movie, but you are hearing mixed reviews from your friends. Opinions range from "terrific" to "boring." People often have different opinions about the same people, events, or issues because they look at them from different points of view.

Learning the Skill

A point of view is a set of beliefs and values that affects a person's opinion. Many factors affect an individual's point of view including age, sex, racial or ethnic background, economic class, and religion. In order to determine the accuracy of a description or the objectivity of an argument, first you must identify the speaker's point of view.

To interpret point of view in written material, read the material to identify the general subject. Then gather background information on the author that might reveal his or her point of view. Identify aspects of the topic that the author chooses to emphasize or exclude. Look for emotionally charged words such as *cruel, vicious, heartrending, drastic*. Also notice metaphors and analogies that imply an opinion such as, "If this budget can work, then pigs can fly."

If you are uncertain of an author's point of view, read a selection on the same topic by an author with a different background. By comparing works on the same subject, both points of view may become clear. This may not be an easy task in some cases. Alexander Pope, a noted English writer in the 1700s, gave a few words of caution:

> "Some praise at morning what they
> blame at night;
> But always think the last opinion
> right."

Practicing the Skill

Read the following excerpt from Jean-Jacques Rousseau's book *Emile* and then answer these questions.

Alexander Pope

1. What is the general subject of the excerpt?
2. What do you know about Rousseau that might reveal his point of view?
3. What emotionally charged words and phrases indicate his point of view?
4. Which aspects of city life does Rousseau emphasize and which does he exclude?

> "Men are not made to be crowded together in ant-hills, but scattered over the earth to till it. The more they are massed together, the more corrupt they become.... Huddled together like sheep, men would very soon die. Man's breath is fatal to his fellows.... Send your children to renew themselves, so to speak, send them to regain in the open fields the strength lost in the foul air of our crowded cities."

Applying the Skill

In a newspaper, find an editorial, column, or letter to the editor that expresses a point of view that conflicts with your own. Write a brief paragraph analyzing the author's point of view and compare it to your own. Explain why you disagree with the author. If you choose, send your piece to the newspaper.

For More Practice

Turn to the Skill Practice in the Chapter Review on page 533 for more practice in interpreting point of view.

Critical Thinking SKILLS

TEACH

Interpreting Point of View Distribute copies of two reviews of the same movie, one favorable, one critical. After students have read both, ask them what the reviews reveal about the two critics' different perspectives, or points of view. Then have students read the skill and complete the practice questions.

Additional Practice

Skill Reinforcement Activity 20

ANSWERS TO PRACTICING THE SKILL

1. Cities are unhealthful places in which to live.
2. believed in beauties of nature and pleasures of simple country life
3. *crowded together in ant-hills, corrupt, huddled together like sheep, fatal, foul*
4. emphasizes crowding; excludes facts that cities often offer greater employment, business, and cultural opportunities than rural areas

Chapter 20 Review

GLENCOE TECHNOLOGY

VIDEODISC

Use MindJogger to review students' knowledge of the chapter.

MindJogger Videoquiz

Chapter 20
Disc 3 Side A

Also available in VHS.

Answers

Using Key Terms

1. f	6. h
2. e	7. b
3. d	8. j
4. g	9. c
5. a	10. k

Using Your History Journal

Encourage students to include personal as well as scientific details, just as a TV interviewer would ask questions about the scientist's or inventor's private life as well as his or her professional achievements.

Reviewing Facts

1. Copernicus: sun-centered solar system; Galileo: observations with telescope support Copernican model; Kepler: planets move around sun in ellipses; Newton: gravity holds solar system together
2. People learned that the sun is at the center of the solar system and that the earth and other planets move around the sun; that living matter is made up of cells and that blood circulates throughout the body; that truth could be known through reason and the scientific method.

CHAPTER 20 REVIEW

Historical Significance

The scientific revolution and the Enlightenment marked a turning point in the history of human thought. Scientists and thinkers constructed a new understanding of knowledge that stressed observation, experimentation, and reasoning rather than reliance on faith and tradition. Thinkers analyzed the existing political systems and focused on the rights of individuals. Their views challenged the concept of absolute monarchy.

The Age of Enlightenment continues to shape our lives. The United States Constitution incorporates many Enlightenment beliefs, and scientists employ approaches in research today that are based on the scientific method.

Using Key Terms

Write the key term that completes each sentence.

a. philosophes
b. classicism
c. salons
d. hypotheses
e. natural law
f. romanticism
g. pacifism
h. enlightened despots
i. scientific method
j. deism
k. metaphysics

1. _________, with its emphasis on emotion and the individual, opposed the values of the Enlightenment.
2. Political philosophers of the Enlightenment believed in the idea of __________, or a universal moral law that, like physical laws, could be understood by applying reason.
3. Scientists in their work employ _______, or theories that attempt to explain a set of facts.
4. William Penn, founder of the colony of Pennsylvania, believed in _________ and favored the creation of an assembly of nations committed to world peace.
5. __________, as the thinkers of the Enlightenment were called, favored the new scientific endeavors.
6. European monarchs who attempted to practice Enlightenment ideals were called _________.
7. Enlightenment writers, artists, and architects strove to achieve the ideals of ______, which to them represented ultimate order and reason.
8. The philosophy of _______ favored a simpler religion based on reason.
9. In Paris, French Enlightenment thinkers discussed the issues of the day at gatherings called ________.
10. __________ is the branch of philosophy that deals with such issues as the existence of God and the meaning of human life.

Using Your History Journal

Rewrite the story of a scientific discovery or invention from the 1600s as a television news story. Include an interview with the inventor or discoverer.

Reviewing Facts

1. **Explain** how Copernicus, Galileo, Kepler, and Newton each added something new to an understanding of the solar system.
2. **Describe** the ways in which European thinking about the universe, the human body, and philosophy changed during the Enlightenment.
3. **Explain** how the study of history was influenced by the philosophy of the Enlightenment.
4. **State** the political idea advocated by Montesquieu that can be found in the United States Constitution.
5. **Identify** two philosophers in the 1700s who disagreed with Enlightenment ideas. What were their views?

Critical Thinking

1. **Apply** How did classical art reflect the values of the Enlightenment? Give examples to support your answer.
2. **Synthesize** Why do you suppose a belief in witches and ghosts largely became a thing of the past in Europe after the period of the Enlightenment?
3. **Evaluate** Were the 1700s an era of optimism or pessimism? Explain.

3. Answers will vary. Possible answer: Historians began to use the scientific method, posing and testing hypotheses about the past.
4. the separation of powers, rights of individuals
5. Rousseau thought that people should rely more on instinct and emotion than on reason, that people are naturally good, and that they have the right to rise up against a government. Kant believed reason could not explain problems of metaphysics, asserted that human feelings about religion, beauty, and morality are real even though not explainable by reason.

Critical Thinking

1. It emphasized form and order. Examples will vary; students may refer to classical architects' preference for squares and circles rather than elaborate swirls, or to David's concern for simplicity of form.

4. **Synthesize** Do scientific laws apply to human society in the way that they apply to the physical universe? Why or why not?
5. **Analyze** Why were the enlightened despots unable to carry out thorough reforms?
6. **Evaluate** Has science fulfilled the promise of progress that it seemed to hold in the 1700s? Why or why not? Give examples.

Geography in History

1. **Region** Refer to the map below. What conclusion can you draw about European interest in science and learning during the period of the 1500s and 1600s?
2. **Place** In what two nations were organizations founded for people interested in sharing scientific information?
3. **Movement** How do you think scientific ideas and theories spread from one nation of Europe into other nations?

Centers of Science A.D. 1500s and 1600s

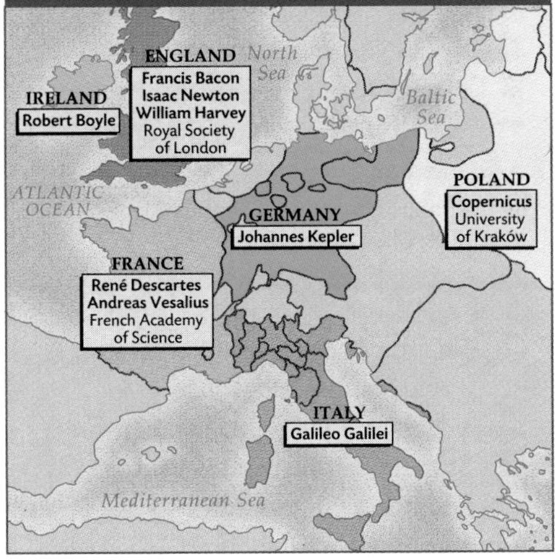

Understanding Themes

1. **Innovation** How did the scientific revolution change the ways in which Europeans investigated the natural world?
2. **Conflict** Catholic Bishop Bossuet said that the skepticism of the philosophes was an "unending error, a risk-all boldness, a deliberate dizziness, in a word, a pride that cannot accept its proper cure, which is legitimate authority." Explain the bishop's view in your own words. What does he mean by "legitimate authority"?
3. **Reaction** What religious movements formed as a reaction to the ideas of the Enlightenment thinkers? Why?

Linking Past and Present

1. William Penn envisioned an assembly of nations working for world peace. What modern organization reflects Penn's idea?
2. Classical movements in music, art, and literature reflected the spirit of the Enlightenment. Does popular music, art, and literature reflect how people feel about society today? Why or why not? Give examples.
3. Do you agree or disagree with Jean-Jacques Rousseau's view that people are naturally good but that civilization and institutions make them evil? Give examples from modern life to support your viewpoint.

Skill Practice

Read the following excerpt from a letter by Frederick II of Prussia to Voltaire. Then answer the questions that follow the excerpt.

> "My chief occupation is to fight the ignorances and the prejudices in this country.... I must enlighten my people, cultivate their manners and morals, and make them as happy as human beings can be; as happy as the means at my disposal permit me to make them."

1. What is the general subject of the passage?
2. What background information do you know about Frederick II that reveals his point of view?
3. What is his viewpoint on his role as a national leader?
4. What statements indicate this point of view?

Chapter 20 Review

2. People began to rely on observation, reason, and the scientific method instead of superstition.
3. Some may argue that it was an optimistic age because people looked favorably on new ideas and believed reason could provide the answers to many of life's problems.
4. Answers will vary. Some may argue that human emotions and actions vary too much to be predictable by law.
5. Many nobles felt threatened by the powers monarchs were giving common people, and so they frustrated reform efforts.
6. Answers will vary. Some may argue that scientific breakthroughs have enhanced the quality of life, others that new technologies have threatened environmental viability.

Geography in History

1. Europeans all over Europe were interested in science.
2. England, France
3. Writers and traveling scholars and scientists spread ideas.

Understanding Themes

1. INNOVATION relied on observation, reason, and the scientific method instead of tradition
2. CONFLICT The philosophes should give up their questioning and accept the views of the Church, the "legitimate authority."
3. REACTION Methodism, the Moravian Brethren, and Hasidism formed. Each emphasized personal faith as opposed to emphasis on reason.

Linking Past and Present

1. the United Nations
2. Students should support claims.
3. Students should support claims.

Skill Practice

1. the king's belief that it is his duty to enlighten his subjects
2. was most famous of the enlightened despots
3. believed he was the "first servant of the state"
4. Both sentences indicate this point of view.

Chapter Bonus Test Question

In 1611 English poet John Donne wrote that "new philosophy calls all in doubt." Similarly, in our times, many people are troubled by the destabilizing effects of new scientific methods. **Ask students:** What are three areas of scientific research today that some people find unsettling? *(Answers will vary but may include: manipulation of human reproduction, tinkering with genetic information.)*

Teach, Reinforce, and Extend CHAPTER Content

English and American Revolutions

CHAPTER RESOURCES	Reproducible Resources	Multimedia Resources
Chapter Opener	Chapter Themes: Graphic Organizer 21 Historical Significance Chapter Activity 21	MindJogger Videoquiz
Chapter Enrichment	Vocabulary Activity 21* Time Line Activity 21 Mapping History Activity 21 History Simulation 21 Geography and History Activity 21 Source Reading 21 People in World History Profiles 39, 40 World Art and Music Activity 21 Enrichment Activity 21 Critical Thinking Activity 21 Skill Reinforcement Activity 21 Writer's Guidebook, Lesson 11 Performance Assessment Activity 21	World History and Art Transparency 28, *Blue Boy* Mapping History Overlay Transparency 13, *European Claims in North America* Chapter Transparency 21 Vocabulary PuzzleMaker Software Picture Atlas of the World World Music: Cultural Traditions, Lesson 1
Chapter Review/Reteaching	Reteaching Activity 21 Skill Reinforcement Activity 21 Spanish Chapter Summary 21	Chapter 21 Digest Audiocassette, Activity, Test* Vocabulary PuzzleMaker Software Student Self-Test and Review Software MindJogger Videoquiz
Chapter Evaluation/Testing	Performance Assessment Activity 21 Chapter 21 Test, Forms A and B	Testmaker

* *Also available in Spanish*

0:00 **OUT OF TIME?** Assign the Chapter 21 summary in the Unit 5 Digest on pages 590–593, and the Chapter 21 Audiocassettes.

Block Schedule

Block scheduling differs from traditional class scheduling in the amount of time allotted to each period. The extended time frame provided by block scheduling affords you the opportunity to implement a greater number of research-oriented and activity-intense projects to motivate and involve your students. Activities that are particularly suited to use within the block scheduling framework are identified throughout this chapter by the following designation.

KEY TO ABILITY LEVELS

Teaching strategies have been coded for varying learning styles and abilities.

- **L1** **BASIC** activities for all students
- **L2** **AVERAGE** activities for average to above-average students
- **L3** **CHALLENGING** activities for above-average students
- **LEP** **LIMITED ENGLISH PROFICIENCY** activities

Chapter 21 Planning Guide

A complete, 1-page lesson plan is provided for each section in the *Reproducible Lesson Plans* booklet.

SECTION RESOURCES

Daily Objectives	Reproducible Resources	Multimedia Resources
Section 1 Civil War Identify factors that led to civil war in England.	Reproducible Lesson Plan 21-1 Vocabulary Activity 21* Guided Reading Activity 21-1* Time Line Activity 21 History Simulation 21 People in World History Profile 40 Section Quiz 21-1*	Section Focus Transparency 21-1 Chapter Transparency 21 Student Self-Test and Review Software Testmaker
Section 2 A King Returns to the Throne Describe how England established a constitutional monarchy.	Reproducible Lesson Plan 21-2 Vocabulary Activity 21* Guided Reading Activity 21-2* Section Quiz 21-2*	Section Focus Transparency 21-2 World History and Art Transparency 28, *Blue Boy* Student Self-Test and Review Software Testmaker
Section 3 Road to Revolt Identify factors that led to disagreement and eventual conflict between the British and the American colonies.	Reproducible Lesson Plan 21-3 Vocabulary Activity 21* Guided Reading Activity 21-3* Geography and History Activity 21 Section Quiz 21-3*	Section Focus Transparency 21-3 Student Self-Test and Review Software Testmaker World Music: Cultural Traditions, Lesson 1
Section 4 A War for Independence Describe the kind of government Americans established after the American Revolution.	Reproducible Lesson Plan 21-4 Guided Reading Activity 21-4* People in World History Profile 39 Reteaching Activity 21 Enrichment Activity 21 Section Quiz 21-4* Performance Assessment Activity 21 Spanish Chapter Summary 21	Section Focus Transparency 21-4 Mapping History Overlay Transparency 13, *European Claims in North America* Vocabulary PuzzleMaker Software Student Self-Test and Review Software Testmaker

* *Also available in Spanish*

Chapter Activities

Performance Assessment Activity

A Time Capsule Have students suppose that they have found a time capsule from the era of the English and American Revolutions. Have them list and make visuals of artifacts they might find inside evoking revolutionary attitudes and events. Have them design a container and make a list with visuals of items they would select for a current-day time capsule representing a revolutionary activity of our time. Students should write a reflection explaining their choices for both capsules.

Possible Rubric Features

Concept attainment, accuracy of content information, decision-making process skills, analytical thinking, research skills, ability to make logical connections, organization and clarity of product

• *For an additional activity, refer to Activity 21 in the* Performance Assessment Strategies and Activities *booklet.*

Activity

From the Classroom of...

Mike Nitzel
Moline High School
Moline, IL

The Revolutionary Times

Organize the class into two groups—one group to write and assemble an American Revolution newspaper, the other group to write and assemble an English Revolution newspaper. Each newspaper should have three sections: Causes of the Revolution; Events of the Revolution; Effects of the Revolution.

Each student should write an article dealing with one of the three topics listed above. Articles should be typed in columns, with titles and by-lines, as in a real newspaper. Each student should also create an advertisement or political cartoon reflective of the period. Let each group put their newspaper together. Students may need to cut and paste and use a copy machine to give their newspapers a professional look. Make a copy of both newspapers for each student and have the class discuss how the American and English Revolutions were similar, how they were different, and how each advanced the ideas of limited government and/or democracy.

MULTIPLE LEARNING STYLES

Verbal/Linguistic
Have students write news reports about the American Revolution as if they were assigned to do a feature on George Washington, the Second Continental Congress, or a town that had been the site of a battle.

Logical/Mathematical
Have students make a time line that shows steps in the English kings' loss of power and Parliament's increase in power. Ask students to display the time line on a bulletin board.

Visual/Spatial
Have students develop pictorial histories of the Glorious Revolution that illustrate the major events before, during, and after this revolution. Remind students to include captions that explain the events. Encourage students to display completed projects in the classroom.

Auditory/Musical
Have students listen to the Chapter 21 Digest Audiocassette, stopping at two-minute intervals to write summary sentences.

Kinesthetic
Have students research life in England under Cromwell. Then ask them to dramatize their research, showing the effects of Puritan rule on daily life.

Additional Resources

TEACHER'S CORNER

NATIONAL GEOGRAPHIC SOCIETY

INDEX TO NATIONAL GEOGRAPHIC MAGAZINE

The following articles may be used for research relating to this chapter:

- "Two Revolutions," by Charles McCarry, July 1989.
- "Yorktown Shipwreck," by John D. Broadwater, June 1988.
- "James Madison, Architect of the Constitution," by Alice J. Hall, September 1987.

NATIONAL GEOGRAPHIC SOCIETY PRODUCTS AVAILABLE FROM GLENCOE

To order the following products for use with this chapter, contact your local Glencoe sales representative or call Glencoe at 1-800-368-7344:

VIDEODISCS
- GTV: The American People
- GTV: A Geographic Perspective on American History

ADDITIONAL NATIONAL GEOGRAPHIC SOCIETY PRODUCTS

To order the following products for use with this chapter, call National Geographic Society at 1-800-368-2728:

- *America: Colonization to Constitution* (Filmstrip)
- *People of the American Revolution* (Filmstrip)

BIBLIOGRAPHY

Literature of the Period

Defoe, Daniel. ***Robinson Crusoe.*** New York: Oxford University Press, 1981. The adventures of a man stranded on an island who survives through ingenuity and hard work.

Readings for the Student

Meltzer, Milton. ***The American Revolutionaries: A History in Their Own Words, 1750–1800.*** New York: Crowell, 1987. Ordinary Americans as well as leaders tell their stories through letters, diaries, and pamphlets.

Readings for the Teacher

Ashley, Maurice. ***The English Civil War.*** London: Thames and Hudson, 1974. A thorough discussion of the causes and battles of the war.

Draper, Theodore. ***A Struggle for Power: The American Revolution.*** New York: Times Books, 1996. A thoroughly researched and penetrating analysis of the struggles that led to the American Revolution.

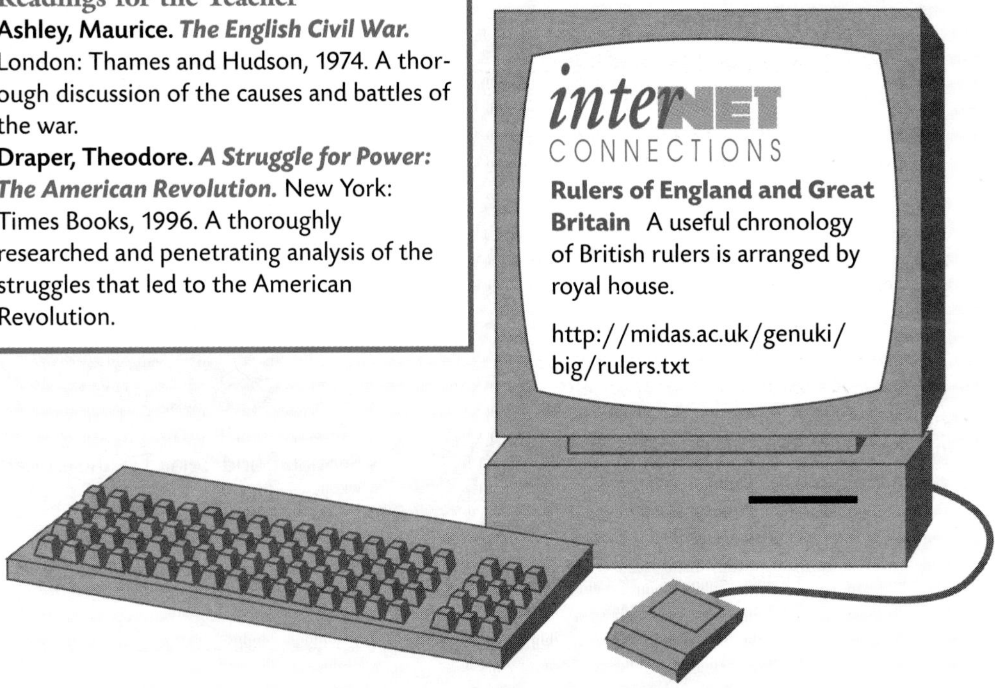

interNET
CONNECTIONS
Rulers of England and Great Britain A useful chronology of British rulers is arranged by royal house.
http://midas.ac.uk/genuki/big/rulers.txt

Introducing Chapter 21

CHAPTER THEMES

Chapter Themes are listed by section on this chapter opening page of the Student Edition. A corresponding theme-based activity is available under "TEACH," and a theme-based question is asked in the Section and Chapter Reviews.

The Storyteller

Historical Setting The death of Charles I in 1649 marked the beginning of a new era in the relationship between the English people and their rulers. Never before had an English monarch been tried and executed by the people. In the past, English monarchs had been murdered or killed in battle, but a monarch's divine right to rule had never been challenged. The idea of the divine right of kings was gradually replaced by the idea of the social contract—that governments are created by an agreement between rulers and their people. In 1776, Great Britain's thirteen colonies declared their independence because Parliament and the king had broken the social contract.

Historical Significance

Answers: *The English Revolution limited the power of the monarchy and increased the power of Parliament and the rights of the people. The American Revolution ended both the power of the king and of Parliament over the thirteen colonies.*

Both the English and American Revolutions led to the development of constitutional government that specified the powers of the government and protected the rights of the governed.

Chapter 21

1600–1800

English and American Revolutions

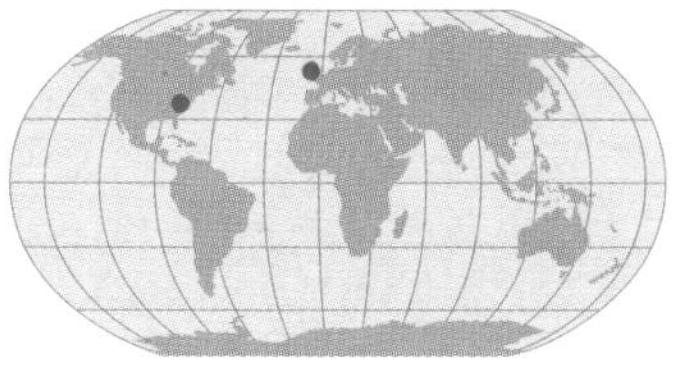

Chapter Themes

- **Conflict** Disputes over the monarchy plunge England into civil war. *Section 1*
- **Change** The English Parliament limits the monarchy's powers. *Section 2*
- **Conflict** The American colonies resist British control. *Section 3*
- **Revolution** The American colonies revolt against Great Britain and form the United States of America. *Section 4*

The Storyteller

In 1649, seventeen-year-old Philip Henry stood near the back of the crowd gathered around a public platform near Whitehall Palace in London. There he watched Charles I, the king of England, prepare to die. The king made a short speech, prayed silently, and then knelt with his head on the block.

With just one blow, the executioner severed the king's head from his body. At that moment, the crowd uttered "such a groan as I never heard before, and desire I may never hear again," Henry wrote in his diary.

By the late 1600s, England would undergo two revolutions limiting the power of the monarch. A new political age was dawning in England and throughout the world.

Historical Significance

How did the English and American Revolutions change government and society in the English-speaking world? What impact did the two revolutions have on the development of democracy?

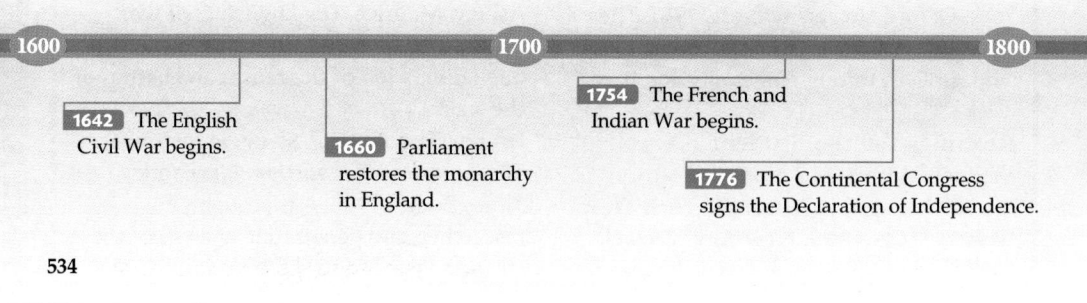

1600 — 1700 — 1800

- **1642** The English Civil War begins.
- **1660** Parliament restores the monarchy in England.
- **1754** The French and Indian War begins.
- **1776** The Continental Congress signs the Declaration of Independence.

534

GEOGRAPHY CONNECTION

Location On a map in the Atlas of their textbook, have students locate England, Scotland, and Ireland in the United Kingdom, and the United States and Canada in North America. Why was England able to exercise control over Scotland and Ireland? *(Both countries were close in distance to England.)* Why did England have difficulty conducting war against the thirteen colonies? *(The long distance across the ocean made it difficult to ship supplies and to issue orders.)* **L1**

History & Art *After Naseby, 1645* by Edgar Bundy, c. 1850. John Noott Galleries, Worcester, England

Your History Journal

In this chapter British and American people make major changes to their governments. What should be the basic ideas upon which government is built? List the ideas you believe to be basic.

Introducing Chapter 21

History & Art

Cromwell's defeat of Charles I at Naseby was important both militarily and politically. Charles lost his infantry, artillery, and most of his cavalry. Most important, he left behind letters that showed his plan to bring Irish troops into England and to repeal laws against Catholics. **How do you think Parliament felt about Charles when they found out about these letters?** *(Parliament probably thought there was no way they could negotiate with Charles; they would have to defeat him.)*

Performance Assessment

Refer to the activity on page 534C of the Planning Guide.

For an additional activity, refer to Activity 21 in the *Performance Assessment Strategies and Activities* booklet.

Using Your History Journal

Encourage students, where possible, to give the origins of the ideas in their list.

GLENCOE TECHNOLOGY

VIDEODISC

Use MindJogger to preview chapter content.

MindJogger Videoquiz

Chapter 21
Disc 3 Side B

Also available in VHS.

EXTRA CREDIT PROJECT

Battle Map Have students research one of the battles from the English Civil War or the American Revolution. Then ask students to draw a map of this battle, showing nearby towns, physical features, the line of approach of the opposing armies, and important points in the battle. Remind students to provide a key to the map and to write a caption that explains the importance of the battle to the war. **L2 LEP**

SECTION THEME

▶ **Conflict** Disputes over the monarchy plunge England into civil war.

Find Out

Answer: *Parliament wanted to limit the monarch's powers, ensure that monarchs would not reestablish the Catholic Church, have more control over taxation and other government policies, and protect individual rights of the people. The religious dispute between Puritans in Parliament and the Church of England was another factor that led to civil war.*

FOCUS

Section Objective

Identify factors that led to civil war in England.

BELLRINGER
Motivational Activity

Before taking roll at the beginning of the class period, project Section Focus Transparency 21-1 and have students answer the activity questions. Discuss students' responses.

This activity is also available as a blackline master.

Vocabulary Pre-check

Use Vocabulary Activity 21 to introduce vocabulary terms. **L1 LEP**

1600	1620	1640	1660
1603 Queen Elizabeth I dies.	**1625** Charles I becomes king of England.	**1640** The Long Parliament meets in London.	**1653** Oliver Cromwell is named Lord Protector.

Section 1

Civil War

Setting the Scene

▶ **Terms to Define**
divine right, martial law, royalist, commonwealth

▶ **People to Meet**
James I, the Puritans, Charles I, the Cavaliers, the Roundheads, Oliver Cromwell

▶ **Places to Locate**
Scotland, Ireland

Find Out What factors led to the outbreak of civil war in England?

The Storyteller

"I say you are no Parliament; I will put an end to your sitting; call them in, call them in." Oliver Cromwell brought in two lines of men armed with muskets, adjourned the session, and locked the doors. That afternoon he intruded upon the Council of State and tried the same. But the chairman, Bradshaw, who had faced worse from King Charles, faced Cromwell. "Sir, we have heard what you did in the morning, and before many hours all England will hear it; but sir, you are mistaken to think that the Parliament is dissolved; for no power under heaven can dissolve them but themselves; therefore take you notice of that."

—from *Oliver Cromwell*, John Morley, M.P., 1901

Oliver Cromwell

Elizabeth I, daughter of Henry VIII and Anne Boleyn, ruled England from 1558 to 1603. She was a strong monarch, but she did not have absolute power. Elizabeth took into consideration the views of Parliament, which grew more politically involved during her reign.

An able leader, Queen Elizabeth recognized the importance of the goodwill of the people—and of Parliament. She once said, "Though God has raised me high, yet this I account the glory of the crown, that I have reigned with your loves." For its part, Parliament was willing to defer to the popular queen. After Elizabeth died in 1603, Parliament, especially the House of Commons, was determined to increase its control over national policy. This move by Parliament resulted in a conflict with the Crown that would eventually tear the nation apart.

Opposition to the Crown

Because Elizabeth died without leaving any children to inherit the throne, **James I**, the son of Elizabeth's cousin, Mary, Queen of Scots, became king in 1603. James, a member of the Stuart family, was the king of **Scotland** when he assumed the English throne.

King and Parliament

Soon after James became king of England, problems arose with the English Parliament. Although James was an educated man, he was a poor judge of people and political situations. His experience in dealing with the weak parliament in Scotland had not prepared him for dealing with the English Parliament.

The rift between Parliament and the king grew even deeper when James professed his belief in divine right—the belief that monarchs derive their power directly from God and that such power is absolute. He lectured the Parliament:

SECTION RESOURCES

Reproducible Masters
- Reproducible Lesson Plan 21-1
- Vocabulary Activity 21
- Guided Reading Activity 21-1
- Time Line Activity 21
- History Simulation 21
- People in World History Profile 40
- Section Quiz 21-1

Transparencies
- Section Focus Transparency 21-1
- Chapter Transparency 21

Multimedia
- Student Self-Test and Review Software
- Testmaker

“Kings are not only God’s lieutenants upon earth and sit upon God’s throne, but even by God himself they are called Gods.... I will not be content that my power be disputed on.”

Such statements only increased the resentment among the members of Parliament.

Problems With Parliament

James I’s greatest political weakness in these conflicts was his constant need to ask Parliament for money. He spent huge sums of money on the government as well as on himself and his advisers. After one of James’s parties, a member of Parliament remarked that James had “given away more plate [money] than Queen Elizabeth did in her whole reign.” When Parliament refused to vote him enough funds, James resorted to other means of raising money, such as selling titles of nobility.

Parliament also criticized the king’s foreign policy. James’s decision to end a war with Spain created outrage in Parliament. The war repayments that were part of the peace treaty put England deep into debt. Opposition to James’s policies grew even stronger when James tried to arrange the marriage of his son, Charles, to a Spanish Catholic princess. Fearing the return of Catholics to power, the people celebrated when James’s marriage plans for his son failed.

Religion and the Monarchy

England’s complicated and unsettled religious issues only added to the tension between Parliament and the Crown. In the 1600s most English people were members of the Church of England, but they had differences of opinion about the doctrine and rituals of the Church. One powerful group of dissenters, or opponents, within the Church was **the Puritans**. They wanted the Church to be “purified” of remaining Catholic rituals and symbols. Many Puritans in Parliament called for these reforms.

James I, as head of both church and government in England, thought that anyone who criticized the Church of England was not a loyal subject. When James had become king, the Puritans presented him with a petition asking for reforms to be made in the Church of England. Not only did James reject the suggested changes, he warned the Puritans that if they did not conform to the Church of England, he would “harry [force] them out of the land.” When the king refused to support the Puritan cause, the Puritans turned against him. Because of James’s policies, many Puritans left England and settled in North America.

History & Art *Portrait of Charles I Hunting* by Anthony Van Dyck, c. 1636. The Louvre, Paris, France *Why were the English Parliament and people unhappy with Charles by 1628?*

Charles Inherits the Throne

When James I died in 1625, his son Charles became king. **Charles I** inherited the country’s religious conflicts and political divisions. Like his father, Charles opposed the Puritans and believed in the divine right of kings. Adding to the tension, Charles eventually married a Catholic woman—Henrietta Maria, sister of France’s King Louis XIII.

Early in his reign, Charles asked Parliament for money to fight a war against Spain and France. When it gave him only a fraction of the sum he had requested, the king dissolved Parliament immediately and tried to raise money without its consent. Charles then forced landowners to give “loans” to the government. When they refused, he put them in jail. People were outraged by the king’s behavior.

People were also angered by Charles’s demand to billet, or board and lodge, his troops in private homes. The king also placed some areas under martial law, or temporary military rule with limitations on individual rights. Thus, discontent ran high when Charles again called Parliament into session in 1628.

TEACH

Guided Practice

THEME Conflict

Tell students that the English Civil War was the result of the deep conflict between Parliament and James I and later Charles I. Help students identify the source of the conflict. *(James and Charles believed in the divine right of kings; Parliament wanted more control over government policy, raising money, and reforms in the Church of England.)* **L1**

History & Art Van Dyck was a Flemish artist who specialized in portraits of Flemish, Italian, Spanish, and English nobles. In 1632 King Charles I made Anton Van Dyck his court painter and knighted him Sir Anthony Van Dyck.

Answer to Caption: *Charles I had dissolved Parliament, tried to raise money without Parliament’s consent, forced landowners to lend him money and put them in jail if they refused, forced people to lodge soldiers in their homes, and placed some areas of England under martial law.*

Politics Have students make a two-column chart that lists Parliament’s grievances against James I and Charles I. **L2**

Chapter Transparency 21

History Simulation 21

COOPERATIVE LEARNING ACTIVITY

Role Play Organize students into three groups to stage the trial of Charles I: the prosecution, the defense, and witnesses for the prosecution and for the defense. Have students choose a classmate to play Charles and another to play Cromwell. Have students from the appropriate group research arguments for the prosecution, arguments for the defense, and background on witnesses. Have each group select a few representatives to work with the other groups’ representatives to prepare dialogue for the role play. Encourage students to ad lib as well. If possible, videotape the students’ presentation. **L2**

Who?What?Where?When?

English Catholics In spite of England’s anti-Catholic laws, about one-fourth of the population was Catholic in 1634.

History & Art The Pilgrims were a dissenting sect that separated from the Church of England and left England on the *Mayflower* to start a new life in New England. In the Mayflower Compact, Pilgrim leaders agreed to form a government for the good of their colony. **How did this differ from government in England?** *(The king claimed to rule by divine right, and ordinary people had no role in government.)*
Answer to Caption: *Leaders of the Church of England persecuted Puritans and Pilgrims.*

Economics Have students discuss how collecting taxes became a point of conflict between Charles I and Parliament. *(When Parliament refused to give King Charles the money he asked for to fight France and Spain, the king tried to raise money without Parliament's consent. In exchange for approval of additional taxes, Parliament forced the king to sign the Petition of Right forbidding him from again collecting taxes without parliamentary consent.)* **L3**

Independent Practice

Guided Reading Activity 21-1 **L1**

Time Line Activity 21

People in World History Profile 40

Political Cartoon Have students draw a political cartoon about the English Civil War, perhaps lampooning Charles I or Cromwell, expressing ideas of Roundheads or Cavaliers, or depicting the tragedy of civil war. **L2 LEP**

History & Art *Pilgrims Signing the Mayflower Compact* by Percy Moran, c. 1900. The Pilgrim Hall Museum, Plymouth, Massachusetts *Why did groups like the Pilgrims and the Puritans leave England?*

By this time England was at war with both France and Spain. Parliament, however, was now ready to press changes on the king. In return for its approval of additional taxes to support the war, Parliament forced Charles to sign the Petition of Right. The Petition severely limited Charles's power in four ways. First, the king was forbidden to collect taxes or force loans without Parliament's consent. Second, the king could not imprison anyone without just cause. Third, troops could not be housed in a private home against the will of the owner. Fourth, the king could not declare martial law unless the country was at war.

Charles's desire to maintain his power, however, was not checked by the Petition of Right. Nearly a year after Parliament had authorized funds in return for his signature on the document, Charles dissolved Parliament and vowed never to call it again. For the next 11 years, Charles ruled without the advice or consent of the Parliament. He continued to collect taxes and imprison opponents—ignoring the Petition of Right he had signed.

At the same time, Charles deepened the religious divisions within England. He named William Laud to be Archbishop of Canterbury, the leading official of the Church of England. Laud and Charles persecuted the Puritans. They denied Puritans the right to preach or to publish. They burned Puritan writings, and punished outspoken Puritans with public whippings.

As a result, thousands of Puritans sought religious freedom in the English colonies in America. Their exodus from England from 1630 through 1643 is known as the Great Migration. Most Puritans, however, remained in their homeland, determined to fight Charles and others who opposed them.

Charles and Archbishop Laud then turned their attention to Scotland. In an effort to establish the Church of England in Scotland, the king and the archbishop tried to force the Calvinist Church of Scotland to accept the Church of England's prayer book. The Scots rejected the new prayer book and formed a National Covenant, or agreement, in which they pledged to preserve their religious freedom. Outraged by the king's actions, they were prepared to go to war to do so.

Beginnings of the Civil War

By 1640 the Scots had invaded England. In dire need of money, Charles was forced to recall a Parliament that he had ignored for 11 years. The members of Parliament, however, refused to discuss anything without first voicing their complaints about Charles's handling of religious and political issues. As a result, Charles dissolved this Parliament, known as the Short Parliament, after only 3 weeks.

Charles became so desperate for money that he had no choice but to summon Parliament once again. By this time members of Parliament were seething with anger and demanded to voice their complaints to the king. Controlled by Puritans, this session of Parliament, called the Long Parliament, would meet for almost 20 years.

The Long Parliament was determined to decrease Charles's power. The members abolished the special courts used to imprison Charles's opponents and passed a law requiring Parliament to be called every 3 years. They ended all forms of illegal taxation and jailed and later executed the hated Archbishop Laud.

While Parliament convened, trouble erupted in **Ireland**. Relations between England and Ireland had been strained since the 1100s. The Irish people remained Roman Catholic and refused to accept the Church of England. What angered the Irish most was the continuing English practice of seizing land from Irish owners and giving it to English and Scots settlers. In 1641 the Irish rebelled. Faced with rebellion in both Scotland and Ireland, Charles was at the mercy of the Puritan-controlled Parliament.

MEETING SPECIAL NEEDS ACTIVITY

Learning Style: Visual/Spatial Collect several portraits of Charles I and Oliver Cromwell for students to analyze. Ask students to list the appearance, characteristics, qualities, and interests of each man as shown in their portraits. Let students discuss similarities and differences that they notice between the two men. Finally, ask students how their differences led to the conflict of the English Civil War. **L1 LEP**

As the Puritans grew stronger, a royalist, or pro-monarchy, group formed in Parliament. It was made up of people who supported the king and opposed Puritan control of the Church of England. As time went on, debates between Puritans and royalists became more heated.

Despite resistance by the royalists, Parliament in June 1642 sent Charles "Nineteen Propositions" that made Parliament the supreme power in England. Charles, however, refused to agree to its demands. With a dramatic personal appearance, Charles led troops into the House of Commons and attempted to arrest five of its leaders. The five were hidden and protected from capture. The king's use of force meant there could be no compromise. Both Charles and Parliament prepared for war.

The English Civil War

Charles gathered an army that included nobles and landowners in the north and west of the country. They were called **the Cavaliers** because many belonged to the king's cavalry, or armed horsemen. Supporters of Parliament and Puritans drew their strength from the south and east of England. They were called **the Roundheads** because many of them had close-cropped hair.

Parliament organized its military forces under the leadership of **Oliver Cromwell**. Cromwell was a very religious man and a brilliant military commander. His rigorous training and firm discipline of the parliamentary forces led to several decisive victories. After nearly four years of conflict, the royalist armies surrendered in May 1646. Parliament had won complete control of the English government. The Puritans removed their remaining opponents from Parliament, leaving behind what was known as the Rump Parliament.

After a failed attempt to escape from his enemies, Charles surrendered in 1647. The army then tried, sentenced, and executed the king in 1649. It was a shocking moment for many English people, no matter how they felt about Charles.

A New Government

After the execution, Parliament abolished both the office of monarch and the House of Lords. With the monarchy ended, parliamentary leaders faced the difficult task of constructing a new republican form of government. England was declared a commonwealth, a state governed by elected representatives. Yet Parliament quarreled about reforming the government and refused to hold new elections. Meanwhile, Cromwell continued to gain power by brutally crushing the revolts in Scotland and Ireland.

Cromwell and his army grew tired of waiting for Parliament's reforms and took Parliament by force in 1653. Named Lord Protector, Cromwell dismissed the Rump Parliament and ruled England for five years as a military dictator. Cromwell enforced strict Puritan rules during this time. Drinking, dancing, and gambling were forbidden; swearing and missing church services were punished with fines.

When Cromwell died in 1658, his son Richard assumed power. Richard, however, lacked his father's leadership ability. The army forced Richard to resign after less than a year.

Many English people were tired of the constant changes in government. They were dissatisfied with military rule, weary of civil wars, and unhappy with Puritan restrictions. The army finally recalled the Long Parliament, which searched for a stable government by negotiating with the son of Charles I, who had been living in Europe during the upheavals. At last, Parliament prepared to reestablish the monarchy. The idea of representative government and many individual rights would survive, however. A king would soon rule England, but no monarch would ever be able to claim absolute power again.

SECTION 1 REVIEW

Recall

1. **Define** divine right, martial law, royalist, commonwealth.
2. **Identify** James I, the Puritans, Charles I, Petition of Right, William Laud, the Cavaliers, the Roundheads, Oliver Cromwell.
3. **Discuss** how the Puritans wanted to change the Church of England.

Critical Thinking

4. **Analyzing Information** How did Elizabeth I and the Stuart monarchs James I and Charles I differ in getting what they wanted from Parliament? Whose methods were more effective? Why?

Understanding Themes

5. **Conflict** What problems did Parliament face before the English Civil War? After the war? Did Parliament achieve its political goals?

Chapter 21 Section 1

ASSESS

Check for Understanding

Assign Section 1 Review as homework or as an in-class activity.

Use Student Self-Test and Review Software to review Section 1.

Evaluate

Section Quiz 21-1

Use the Testmaker to create a customized quiz for Section 1.

Reteach

Organize students into groups of six. Give each group six slips of paper with one of these roles on each slip: *James I, Charles I, Oliver Cromwell, a Puritan, a Cavalier,* and *Archbishop Laud*. Let students play charades with these slips of paper.

Enrich

Have students write a report comparing the structure of government under Charles I with government under Cromwell as Lord Protector.

CLOSE

Have students create a flowchart that traces events in England from 1603 to 1658.

SECTION 1 REVIEW ANSWERS

1. All vocabulary words are defined in the Glossary.
2. James I, 536; the Puritans, 537; Charles I, 537; Petition of Right, 538; William Laud, 538; the Cavaliers, 539; the Roundheads, 539; Oliver Cromwell, 539
3. They wanted the Church of England purified of Catholic rituals and symbols.
4. Elizabeth worked with Parliament; the Stuarts insisted on their divine right as kings. Elizabeth's methods were more successful; Parliament usually did what she wanted whereas the Stuarts brought England into a civil war.
5. **CONFLICT** Answers will vary. Possible answer: No. Before the English Civil War, Parliament faced problems with an overbearing monarchy. After the war, it had to contend with Cromwell's autocratic rule.

SECTION THEME

▶ **Change** The English Parliament limits the monarchy's powers.

Find Out

Answer: *When Parliament restored Charles II to the throne, it kept the limit on the monarch's powers that had been established by the Magna Carta, Petition of Right, and other laws and customs.*

FOCUS

Section Objective

Describe how England established a constitutional monarchy.

BELLRINGER Motivational Activity

Before taking roll at the beginning of the class period, project Section Focus Transparency 21-2 and have students answer the activity questions. Discuss students' responses.

This activity is also available as a blackline master.

Vocabulary Pre-check

Use Vocabulary Activity 21 to introduce vocabulary terms. **L1 LEP**

1650 — 1700 — 1750

1688 The Glorious Revolution brings William III and Mary II to the English throne.

1707 The Act of Union unites England and Scotland.

1714 George I becomes king of Great Britain.

Section 2

A King Returns to the Throne

Setting the Scene

▶ **Terms to Define**
constitutional monarchy, habeas corpus, cabinet, prime minister

▶ **People to Meet**
Charles II, the Whigs, the Tories, William III, Mary II, George I, Sir Robert Walpole

▶ **Places to Locate**
London

Find Out How did England establish a constitutional monarchy?

The Storyteller

"What pillars and arches to be pulled down! What new ones to be erected! What scaffold and engines to lay the foundation of an endless and incalculable future expenditure." The authorities in charge of restoring St. Paul's Cathedral believed Christopher Wren's designs went too far and would cost too much. Just when it seemed as though the great architect would have to change his plans, disaster changed everything. In the Great Fire of London, buildings were demolished overnight. At St. Paul's Cathedral, heated stones flew like grenades and lead ran in rivers down the streets. Wren would design a new cathedral.

—adapted from *The Architecture of Wren*, Kerry Downes, 1982

Christopher Wren

As the son of Charles I, **Charles II** had faced danger throughout the English Civil War and Cromwell's rule. He risked death on the battlefield as he joined the royalist forces in their fight and in their defeat. He saw his father imprisoned and put to death. He narrowly escaped his own capture and execution by disguising himself as a servant and fleeing to the European continent.

In Europe, Charles wandered from country to country. While some European rulers received him as royalty, others threatened him with arrest as a fugitive. In his own country, the Puritans kept a close watch on Charles. Since he was the direct heir to the English throne, Charles posed a threat to their political power. By the time Parliament had restored the monarchy, Charles had learned a good deal about pleasing people he needed for support and safety. Charles willingly accepted a change from the absolute power of his ancestors.

The Merry Monarch

When Charles II returned to **London**, on May 29, 1660, the English people celebrated wildly. They felt released from a violent, unstable period followed by harsh Puritan rule. A court member described the happiness of the English people as they rejoiced in a lavish parade marking the king's return:

> "A triumph of above 20,000 horse and foot soldiers, brandishing their swords and shouting with inexpressible joy; the ways strewed with flowers, the bells ringing, the streets hung with tapestry, fountains running with wine.... I stood and beheld it, and blessed God."

SECTION RESOURCES

Reproducible Masters
- Reproducible Lesson Plan 21-2
- Vocabulary Activity 21
- Guided Reading Activity 21-2
- Section Quiz 21-2

Transparencies
- Section Focus Transparency 21-2
- World History and Art Transparency 28

Multimedia
- Student Self-Test and Review Software
- Testmaker

This period, in which the House of Stuart was returned to the throne, is called the Restoration. In contrast to the severe and religious rule of Cromwell, Charles II was known as the Merry Monarch. He loved social life—parties, games, and witty conversation. He supported the arts, science, and entertainment. People once again danced and enjoyed sports and theater. Charles married a Portuguese princess; and though they had no children, he fathered several illegitimate children by his mistresses.

Dealing With Religious Questions

When Charles accepted the monarchy, he agreed to let Parliament settle the country's raging religious debates. Outwardly, Charles accepted the Church of England. Secretly, however, he leaned toward Catholicism, his mother's religion. Although he hoped for a policy of religious toleration, Charles realized that the decision depended on Parliament.

In 1661 a new Parliament was elected. It was known as the Cavalier Parliament because it contained a majority of royalists. During the next few years, this Parliament passed a series of laws known as the Clarendon Code. These acts made the Church of England once again the state religion. Only Anglicans, or members of the Church of England, could attend the universities, serve in Parliament, or hold religious services. Hundreds of Puritan clergy were driven from their churches.

Limiting Royal Power

The Parliament also maintained its limits on the power of the king. All the acts of Parliament to which Charles I had agreed, such as the Petition of Right, were still in effect. The Restoration thus gave England a **constitutional monarchy**—a form of government in which the monarch's powers are limited by a constitution. Rather than being a single document, however, England's constitution was made up of many documents—such as the Magna Carta and the Petition of Right—plus other laws and customs. Although Charles II disagreed with some of the reforms that limited royal power, he never fought Parliament forcefully. Charles was determined to avoid his father's fate.

The French ambassador to England was astonished at the mood of the country. In France, the king had absolute power. The ambassador commented

CONNECTIONS: The Arts

Rebuilding London

In 1666 a major fire destroyed much of London. Over the next decades, a royal commission worked to rebuild the city and to make it a beautiful capital.

One of the men chosen to work on the commission was Christopher Wren. Although he was a well-respected mathematician and astronomer at Oxford University, Wren is best remembered as the architect of St. Paul's Cathedral, an outstanding London landmark begun in 1675.

The new St. Paul's Cathedral was to be the first major church constructed for the Church of England. As London's principal place of worship, St. Paul's had to be an impressive, monumental structure.

St. Paul's Cathedral

At the same time, Wren—in keeping with English tastes of the period—wanted St. Paul's to be more austere and serious than the ornate Catholic cathedrals in France, Germany, Italy, and Spain.

In his design, Wren used classical and baroque styles of architecture to produce a cathedral that combined a sense of order with dramatic visual effects. His work had an enormous impact on the buildings constructed in central London in the late 1600s. In the end, Wren designed a total of 51 Anglican churches for the city in the period following the fire and was eventually knighted by Charles II for his work as an architect.

MAKING THE CONNECTION

1. Why was London's St. Paul's Cathedral an important building for the Church of England?
2. What architectural sources did Wren use in his design of St. Paul's Cathedral?

TEACH

Guided Practice

THEME Change On the chalkboard, write the following column headings: *Monarchy's Power, Parliament's Power, Religious Problems*. Then write these row headings: *Charles II, James II, William and Mary, Anne, George I, George II*. Help students complete the chart to show how England's government changed between 1660 and 1760. **L1 LEP**

Critical Thinking Lead a discussion about why the English reestablished the monarchy yet limited the ruler's power through a constitutional monarchy. **L2**

World History and Art Transparency 28, *Blue Boy*

CONNECTIONS: The Arts

Rebuilding London

London builders and craftsmen took more than 30 years to complete St. Paul's Cathedral. The dome, its most famous feature, has an inner dome and a much taller outer dome. Light enters the cathedral through an opening in the middle of the inner dome.

Answers to Making the Connection

1. *St. Paul's was the first major church constructed for the Church of England.*
2. *Wren used classical and baroque styles of architecture.*

COOPERATIVE LEARNING ACTIVITY

Documentary Assign the class the task of producing a documentary television show about the London fire of 1666. Have students choose a producer to coordinate the class project. Then organize the class into teams. Have teams research, write, and present "hard news" about the fire, such as its origin, how far it spread, number of casualties, buildings destroyed, or plans for rebuilding. Ask other teams to prepare on-the-scene features about the fire, such as interviews with local residents, firefighters, or government officials. If possible, videotape the presentation for the basis of a class discussion later. **L2**

Cultural Perspectives

Church of England Today in England, the Church of England is also known as the Anglican Church. In the United States, followers of the beliefs of the Church of England belong to the Episcopal Church. The Anglican Church is still the official church in the United Kingdom.

Independent Practice

Guided Reading Activity 21-2 **L1**

Government Have students research to prepare a chart that compares rights in the English Bill of Rights with those in the United States Bill of Rights. Ask students to indicate on their charts the rights common to both countries' bills of rights. **L2**

CURRICULUM CONNECTION

EDUCATION

The College of William and Mary, founded in 1693 in Williamsburg, Virginia, was named for England's king and queen. It is the second oldest institution of higher learning in the United States. Harvard University is the oldest.

you don't say...

Tory comes from an Irish word for "robber" or "royalist outlaw." During the fight for the Exclusion Bill, Tory became an unflattering term for people who supported the monarchy and the Church of England.

AROUND THE WORLD — Religious Revolution in the Colonies

Maryland, 1689

The colony of Maryland had been founded as a refuge for Roman Catholics, with religious freedom for all people. Maryland Protestants resented having Roman Catholic Charles Calvert as the colony's owner. In 1689 Protestants took over Maryland and passed anti-Catholic legislation. The laws required children of mixed marriages to be raised as Protestants and imposed fines for sending children to Catholic schools abroad.

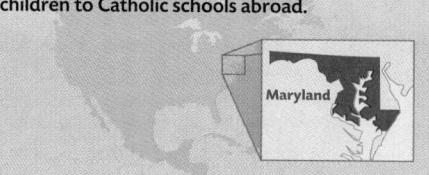

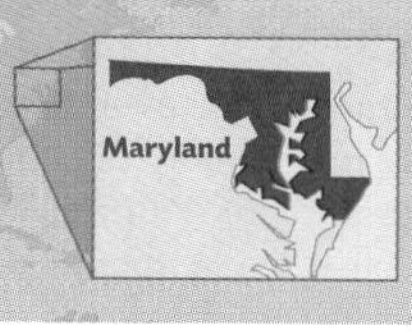

on the changes in England in a letter to the French king, Louis XIV:

> "This government has a monarchical appearance because there is a King, but at bottom it is far from being a monarchy.... The members of Parliament are ... allowed to speak their mind freely...."

While the English celebrated the end of Puritan rule, they were struck by two disasters. In 1665 the plague returned to London for the last time, killing as many as 100,000 people. Later, a terrible raging fire destroyed much of London. Some people falsely blamed Catholics for setting the fire as part of a plan to gain control of the country.

Establishing Political Parties

Opposition to Catholicism helped to spark the growth of England's first political parties. The parties grew out of a debate over who would succeed Charles as the king of England. Because Charles had no legitimate children, James II, Charles's brother, was next in line to be king. James, who was a practicing Catholic, ignited the fears of a revival of Catholic power in England.

In 1679 Parliament tried to pass the Exclusion Bill, which would have kept James from becoming king. During this conflict, those members of Parliament who wanted to exclude James from the throne were known as **the Whigs**. Those who defended the hereditary monarchy were referred to as **the Tories**.

In a compromise, the Tories agreed to defeat the Exclusion Bill by accepting another bill supported by the Whigs. The Whig-proposed bill established the principle of **habeas corpus** as law. According to habeas corpus, a person could not be held in prison by the king (or anyone else) without just cause or without a trial. It was another step that increased individual rights and reduced those of the Crown.

A Bloodless Revolt

When Charles II died in 1685, his Catholic brother, James II, became king, effectively ending the peaceful relations between Parliament and the Crown. James wanted absolute power and claimed he had the right to suspend the law. Ignoring Parliament's religious laws, James appointed Catholics to government and university positions. He also allowed people of all Christian faiths to worship freely.

The Glorious Revolution

These actions alarmed many of the members of Parliament, but they tried to be patient. They were waiting for James to die and for the English throne to pass to his Protestant daughter Mary, who was married to William of Orange, the ruler of the Netherlands.

In 1688, however, a royal birth prompted Parliament to take action. James's second wife bore a son, who would be raised a Catholic. He would inherit the throne, rather than the Protestant Mary. Both Whig and Tory leaders united against James and invited Mary's husband William to invade England and take over the Crown. James fled to France when he realized he had little support in England. **William III** and **Mary II** gained the English throne without battles or bloodshed. This peaceful transfer of power was so welcome and so different from previous struggles that the English called it the Glorious Revolution.

New Limits on Royal Power

At previous coronations, English kings and queens had sworn to observe the laws and customs established by their royal ancestors. In 1689, however, William and Mary swore an oath that they would govern the people of England "according to the statutes in Parliament agreed upon, and the laws and customs of the same."

In that same year, Parliament further strengthened its power by passing the Bill of Rights. According to the Bill of Rights, the king could not

MEETING SPECIAL NEEDS ACTIVITY

Learning Style: Verbal/Linguistic Have students imagine they have been selected by Parliament to write a letter either to Charles II asking him to return as king or to William and Mary inviting them to be monarchs. Remind students to include the conditions under which the monarchs will rule. Suggest that students research styles for writing letters in the 1600s. Encourage students to share their completed letters with the class. **L2**

raise taxes or maintain an army without the consent of Parliament and could not suspend laws. Further, it declared that Parliament should be held often and that there should be freedom of debate in sessions of Parliament.

The Bill of Rights also guaranteed certain individual rights. It guaranteed the right to a trial by jury, outlawed cruel and unusual punishment for a crime, and limited the amount of bail money that could be required for a person to be temporarily released while awaiting trial. Citizens were given the right to appeal to the monarch and to speak freely in Parliament.

In 1689 the exiled James II landed in Ireland and led Irish Catholics in a revolt to recapture the Crown. Although the uprising failed a year later, English Protestants controlling Irish affairs began to exclude the Catholic majority in Ireland from government and business. This action only deepened the hatred Irish Catholics had for English policies.

Anti-Catholic feelings throughout the country also led the English Parliament in London to pass more legislation limiting the Crown's power. In the Act of Settlement (1701), Parliament excluded any Catholic from inheriting the English throne.

Parliament and the Crown

The Bill of Rights and the Act of Settlement made it clear that Parliament had won the long battle with the Crown. England was still a monarchy, but a king or queen could not rule without Parliament's consent.

England was not yet a true democracy, however. Although members of the House of Commons were elected, only male property owners—250,000 people out of 6 million, or 4 percent of the population—had the right to vote. Members of the House of Commons were not paid, so only the wealthy could afford to run for office. Parliament was controlled by people of property—nobles, gentry, wealthy merchants, and clergy.

Succession and Union

The power of Parliament further increased when Mary's sister Anne succeeded William in 1702. (Mary had died in 1694.) At the same time, Parliament had to establish a new order of succession to the throne. Since Anne had no living children to succeed her, she would be succeeded by the children of Sophia, a Protestant granddaughter of James I. Sophia was married to the German elector, or ruler, of Hanover. In short, the English throne would pass to the heirs or heiresses from the German House of Hanover.

Yet there still remained a danger that the Scots might prefer a Stuart monarch to a member of the House of Hanover. Parliament also feared that the Scots would form an alliance with France against England. After negotiations with the Scots, who were militarily and economically weak, the two governments signed the Act of Union in 1707. It united the two countries into a new nation called Great Britain. Both the English and the Scots would now be "British." Although the Scots gave up their own parliament, they were given representation in the English Parliament. Scotland also retained its own Calvinist religion, and its own laws, courts, and educational system as well.

Visualizing History **In 1688 Parliament presented the Crown of England to William and Mary.** *Why did Parliament decide to give the Crown to the royal couple?*

Chapter 21 Section 2

Linking Past and Present

William III At the Battle of the Boyne in Ireland on July 12, 1690, William III defeated the army of James II. He also ended the political power of Irish Roman Catholics. In 1695 Protestants in what is now Northern Ireland formed the Orange Society, named for William III who was also William of Orange.

Visualizing History Sixteen years before the Glorious Revolution, William had gained control of the Netherlands through another revolution. Although by right of birth the office of stadtholder should have been his (his father held it), it had fallen into the hands of Jan de Witt. A revolution in 1672 made William stadtholder.

Answer to Caption: *Parliament wanted England to have Protestant rulers instead of Catholic.*

ASSESS

Check for Understanding

Assign Section 2 Review as homework or as an in-class activity.

Use Student Self-Test and Review Software to review Section 2.

MAKING CONNECTIONS ACTIVITY

The Arts After the long winter of Puritan rule, the arts blossomed in England during the Restoration period. Have students choose an area of the arts, such as architecture, drama, furniture design, music, or painting, and prepare an oral report about it in England from 1660 to 1760. Tell students to describe important people and works, how the works reflected the times, and whether these people and works have any impact on the arts today. Suggest that students illustrate their reports. Then display the illustrations on a classroom bulletin board. **L2**

Chapter 21
Section 2

Visualizing History Robert Walpole wears a powdered wig in this portrait. This fashion spread from France to England in the late 1600s. Men with short hair did not want to be mistaken for Roundheads.
Answer to Caption: *prime minister*

Evaluate

Section Quiz 21-2

Use the Testmaker to create a customized quiz for Section 2.

Reteach

Have students discuss the evolution of England's constitutional monarchy from 1660 to 1760.

Enrich

Have students write a research report on one of England's literary figures of this period, such as Alexander Pope, Jonathan Swift, Daniel Defoe, Richard Steele, or Joseph Addison.

CLOSE

Ask students to create a time line that includes important events and people discussed in Section 2. Have students write a brief explanation next to each event or person.

Visualizing History **Sir Robert Walpole became a close friend of King George II and Queen Caroline. He directed policy as the leading cabinet official.** *What title did the main cabinet official earn?*

Political Parties and the Cabinet

During Anne's reign (1702-1714), Parliament's political powers continued to increase. Anne was unskilled in British politics and sought guidance from a cabinet, a small group of advisers selected from the House of Commons. Because a cabinet made up of both Whigs and Tories often quarreled, it became the custom to choose cabinet members only from the party holding a majority of the seats in Parliament.

Anne died in 1714, and Sophia's son **George I** took the throne according to the Act of Settlement. George had been raised in Germany, and did not speak English very well.

George I relied on the cabinet even more than Anne had. Eventually, **Sir Robert Walpole**, the leader of the Whigs, gained control of the cabinet. Although he spoke no German, Walpole advised the king. Walpole's position as head of the cabinet was later called prime minister, the chief executive of a parliamentary government. Walpole remained prime minister when a new king, George II, took the throne in 1727. With the king's encouragement, Walpole gradually took over many political responsibilities: managing finances, appointing government officials, and requesting the passage of laws. He helped avoid wars and allowed the North American colonies to grow without interference from the British government.

In 1760 George III, grandson of George II, became king at the age of 22. George III greatly expanded the British Empire through victory in a war against France. Great Britain gained Canada and all of France's territory east of the Mississippi River. The cost of waging the war—and the ways in which George III and his ministers tried to deal with that cost—would eventually lead to rebellion in Great Britain's American colonies.

SECTION 2 REVIEW

Recall

1. **Define** constitutional monarchy, habeas corpus, cabinet, prime minister.
2. **Identify** Charles II, the Restoration, the Whigs, the Tories, William III, Mary II, Bill of Rights, George I, Sir Robert Walpole.
3. **Explain** why Charles II was called the Merry Monarch. How was his reign different from that of his father, Charles I?

Critical Thinking

4. **Analyzing Information** How did the royal power of William and Mary compare with that of Charles II? How had Parliament's powers expanded by the time William and Mary came to the throne?

Understanding Themes

5. **Change** Briefly describe how England evolved into a constitutional monarchy. What rights did individual citizens gain as a result of this change?

SECTION 2 REVIEW ANSWERS

1. All vocabulary words are defined in the Glossary.
2. Charles II, 540; the Restoration, 541; the Whigs, 542; the Tories, 542; William III, 542; Mary II, 542; Bill of Rights, 542; George I, 544; Sir Robert Walpole, 544
3. Charles II loved social life, the arts, and entertainment. Charles II accepted limited power; Charles I insisted on the divine right of kings.
4. Charles II accepted the Petition of Right and agreed not to be involved in church affairs; William and Mary agreed to rule only with Parliament's consent.
5. CHANGE Parliament gradually took greater control as it forced monarchs to give up much of their power. Individuals gained the right to a fair trial, freedom from cruel and unusual punishment, and the right to speak freely in Parliament.

1725 — **c. 1730** Colonial assemblies win the right to limit royal governors' salaries.
1750 — **1754** The French and Indian War begins.
1763 British proclamation bans colonial settlement west of the Appalachians.
1775 — **1774** First Continental Congress meets in Philadelphia.

Section 3

Road to Revolt

Setting the Scene

- **Terms to Define**
  duty, direct tax, boycott
- **People to Meet**
  George Grenville, George III, John Adams, Patrick Henry, George Washington, Samuel Adams
- **Places to Locate**
  New York City, Boston, Philadelphia

Find Out What factors led to disagreement and eventual conflict between the British and the American colonies?

The Storyteller

Boston's newspapers announced that a ship bearing tea would arrive soon. All over town, this handbill appeared: "Friends! Brethren! Country-men! That worst of plagues, the detested tea, shipped for this port by the East India Company, is now arrived in this harbor; the hour of destruction or manly opposition to the machinations [schemes] of tyranny stares you in the face; every friend … is now called upon … to make a united and successful resistance. Boston, November 29, 1773."

—adapted from *Tea Leaves, Being a Collection of Letters and Documents Relating to the Shipment of Tea to the American Colonies …*, 1970

Boston Tea Party

While Great Britain struggled through civil war and a changing government, its colonies in America changed as well. By the mid-1700s, 13 colonies thrived on the eastern coast of North America. As more people migrated to North America to escape religious persecution or to gain a new start in life, the population of the colonies grew to more than 1.5 million by 1763.

Since most of the colonists were British, they shared a common language and political background. Although many radical political ideas—ideas about republicanism, universal suffrage, liberty, and equality—had died out in Great Britain, many political radicals had fled to the colonies. Here the old ideas stayed alive. In the colonies, there was no aristocracy. The hardships of life on the frontier and the easy availability of land tended to blur class divisions. Each American colony had a representative assembly, much like Parliament in Great Britain, and the colonists were used to governing themselves.

The British Empire in America

Except for regulating trade, the British government generally left the colonies alone. In the British mercantilist view, the American colonies were valuable to Great Britain only to the extent that they benefited British trade. The role of the colonies was to produce goods—mostly raw materials—that could not be produced in Great Britain, and to provide markets for British manufactured goods.

By the early 1700s, the colonies pulsated with economic activity. In the South, plantations produced tobacco, rice, and indigo with the labor of thousands of enslaved Africans. Settlers in the rich farming land of the Middle Colonies grew enough food to feed their families and trade throughout the year. New England colonists turned to the sea because of their poor soil and harsh climate. In 1673

Chapter 21 Section 3

SECTION THEME

- **Conflict** The American colonies resist British control.

Find Out

Answer: *Britain stopped colonial expansion west of the Appalachians, enforced trade rules, and taxed the colonists without their representation in Parliament.*

FOCUS

Section Objective

Identify factors that led to disagreement and eventual conflict between the British and the American colonies.

BELLRINGER Motivational Activity

Before taking roll at the beginning of the class period, project Section Focus Transparency 21-3 and have students answer the activity questions. Discuss students' responses.

This activity is also available as a blackline master.

Vocabulary Pre-check

Use Vocabulary Activity 21 to introduce vocabulary terms. **L1 LEP**

SECTION RESOURCES

Reproducible Masters
- Reproducible Lesson Plan 21-3
- Vocabulary Activity 21
- Guided Reading Activity 21-3
- Geography and History Activity 21
- Section Quiz 21-3

Transparencies
- Section Focus Transparency 21-3

Multimedia
- Student Self-Test and Review Software
- Testmaker
- World Music: Cultural Traditions, Lesson 1

TEACH

Guided Practice

THEME **Conflict**

Have students recall acts of Parliament that caused conflicts in the colonies. *(Stamp Act, Declaratory Act, Intolerable Acts, Quebec Act, tax on tea)* Encourage students to discuss why the colonists disliked these acts. *(Colonists were not represented in Parliament.)* **L1 LEP**

Geography: Movement Have students locate the thirteen colonies on a historical map. **What hindered communications between northern and southern colonies?** *(few good roads)* **Why were colonists interested in moving west?** *(People wished to acquire land of their own, which, as population grew, was available only in the West.)* **L2 LEP**

Cause and Effect Help students make a flowchart on the chalkboard that shows the sequence of cause and effect from the Stamp Act to the First Continental Congress. *(For example: the Stamp Act caused colonists to call the Stamp Act Congress, whose actions in turn caused Parliament to repeal the Stamp Act.)* **L3**

Geography and History Activity 21

Who?What?Where?When?

Colony Names The colonies of Maryland, Virginia, North and South Carolina, and Georgia were named after the following English rulers: Henrietta Maria, wife of Charles I; Elizabeth I, who was known as the Virgin Queen; Charles I and Charles II; and George II.

a sea captain described busy Boston Harbor, reporting that "ships arrive dayly from Spain, France, Holland & Canarys bringing all sorts of wine, linens, silks, and fruits, which they transport to all the other plantations...."

To protect this profitable trade with its colonies, Parliament passed a series of Navigation Acts in the 1600s. According to these laws, the colonists were required to export certain products only to Great Britain or to other British colonies. In addition, all goods going to the colonies had to first pass through Great Britain, where a **duty**, or tax, had to be paid before shipment to the colonies. Finally, all goods going to or coming from the colonies were to be carried by ships built in British or colonial ports.

The colonists did not suffer as much as one might imagine from the effects these laws had on trade. Actually, the Navigation Acts had some benefits. Some colonies were able to develop a strong shipping industry, and some businesses grew prosperous in the absence of foreign competition. Moreover, the British government was never able to adequately enforce these laws. Smuggling goods in and out of ports along the coast became a major part of colonial trade.

Colonial Political Power

As people in the colonies grew more settled and economically secure, they also became more involved in their government. Most of the colonies were managed by a governor appointed by the king. The royal governor then appointed judges and other officials, but each colony also had an elected assembly. Voting in the colonies was restricted to men who owned property or paid taxes, as it was in Great Britain. In the colonies, however, it was much easier to acquire land. A much greater percentage of the population therefore could vote for their government.

The assemblies often struggled with the royal governors for power in the same way that Parliament and the Crown struggled in Great

Images of the Times

Colonial America

The colonies became prosperous and began to drift away from Great Britain. When the British Parliament tried to take control, Americans revolted.

A creche doll with a wooden face and glass inset eyes looked much like an adult. Colonists treated their children as miniature adults.

A New England dame school fulfilled the Massachusetts General Court's requirement for public school financed by taxes.

546

Images of the Times **Colonial America**

Teaching children how to read so they could understand the Bible on their own was the main purpose of early New England schools. The *New England Primer*, the principal textbook, taught children their ABC's starting with "Adam" and ending with "Zaccheus." Prayers were also part of the *New England Primer*. Both boys and girls went to dame schools. When it came time to learn how to write, however, the boys advanced to grammar schools, whereas education ended for most girls.

Britain. These power struggles were often over money. In the early 1700s assemblies won the right to limit the salaries of governors and judges. If a governor would not do as colonists desired, the assembly would reduce or withhold his salary for the next year. In 1731 the New Hampshire assembly refused to pay the governor's salary for five years.

The assemblies also held fast to their right to approve any taxes requested by the Crown or governors. This issue would become a central point of conflict between the colonies and Great Britain. Just as the British Parliament had fought hard for its right to approve or refuse any taxes, so too would the American colonists.

Tightening Colonial Controls

A bitter rivalry between Great Britain and France for territory in North America would eventually lead the British government to interfere more actively in the colonial economy. A dispute over French and British land claims in North America as well as rights to the rich North American fur trade led France and Great Britain to war in 1754. The conflict, called the French and Indian War, brought French troops and French Canadian colonists against British forces and the American colonists. Some Native Americans fought on behalf of the British, while others supported the French.

After six years of war, the British-led forces finally defeated the French in 1760. Three years later, a treaty was signed in Paris. Under the treaty's terms, Great Britain acquired nearly all of France's possessions in North America, including Canada and lands in the area that lay west of the Appalachian Mountains.

Great Britain's empire had grown both in size and in power, but at a considerable cost. The war strained the British economy, and defending the huge new lands they had gained would cost the British even more.

George Grenville, whom **George III** appointed First Lord of the Treasury in 1763, took the first

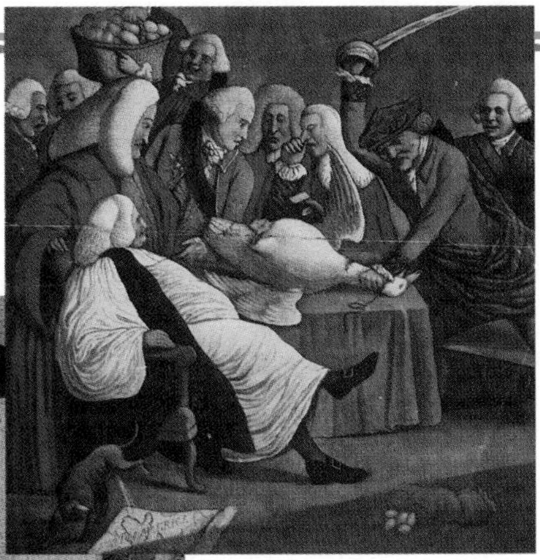

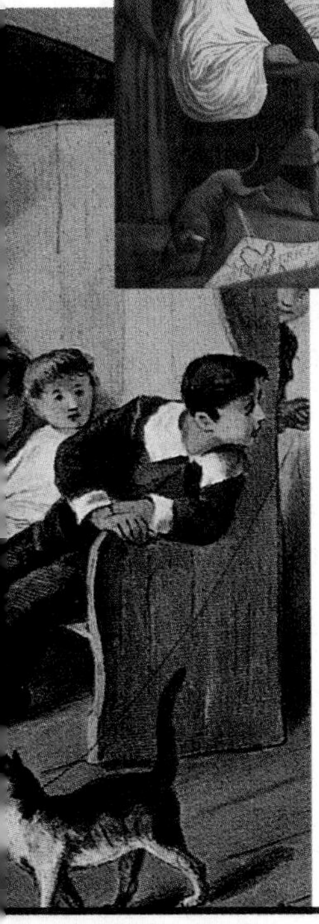

"The Wise Men of Gotham," a political cartoon, appeared in a colonial paper in 1776. It shows the British killing the American goose that laid the golden egg (trade) for the British.

The Stamp Act required stamps such as this on all legal documents. Colonists protested vigorously.

REFLECTING ON THE TIMES

1. Why did colonial legislatures instead of Parliament exercise authority in matters such as education?
2. Why did colonists object to Parliament's authority in the Stamp Act?
3. What attitude toward British policies is reflected in the cartoon "The Wise Men of Gotham"?

547

ANSWERS TO REFLECTING ON THE TIMES

1. Except for regulating trade, the British government generally left the colonies alone.
2. The colonists objected to the Stamp Act because they were not represented in Parliament, who passed the act.
3. opposition to British tax and trade policies

Chapter 21 Section 3

World Music: Cultural Traditions, Lesson 1

Independent Practice

Guided Reading Activity 21-3 **L1**

Economics Have students write paragraphs explaining why Great Britain wanted to control colonial imports and exports. *(to protect colonial trade from competition with other countries)* **L2**

Foreign Affairs Have students use outside resources to write an essay on why the French believed they had a right to the land in the Ohio Valley during the French and Indian War. **L3**

Who?What?Where?When?

Paris has served as the site for the signing of several peace treaties. In addition to the treaty that ended the French and Indian War, the treaties that ended both the American Revolution and United States involvement in the Vietnam War were signed there. The treaty that ended World War I was signed at Versailles, a few miles from Paris.

Global Gourmet

America Native Americans invented succotash, a stew made of corn, lima beans, and meat from bears or wild birds. Colonists soon learned how to make this one-dish meal.

Chapter 21
Section 3

Visualizing History Crispus Attucks, an African American, was one of the five colonists killed during the Boston Massacre.
Answer to Caption: *Parliament repealed most taxes except for the tax on tea.*

Who?What?Where?When?

John Peter Zenger In the early 1700s, colonial newspapers did not criticize government officials. When John Peter Zenger's *New York Weekly Journal* printed letters against New York's governor, Zenger was arrested. When Zenger's lawyer produced evidence proving the truth of the criticisms, a jury acquitted Zenger. Zenger's acquittal is usually viewed as the first American case to uphold freedom of the press.

ASSESS

Check for Understanding

Assign Section 3 Review as homework or as an in-class activity.

Use Student Self-Test and Review Software to review Section 3.

Evaluate

Section Quiz 21-3

Use the Testmaker to create a customized quiz for Section 3.

Visualizing History **Bitter feelings erupted in bloodshed on March 5, 1770, in Boston, when British soldiers fired into a crowd and killed five people. This incident became known to the colonists as the Boston Massacre.** *What happened as a result of the unrest in Boston?*

steps to solve these problems. Grenville issued a proclamation that said the colonists could not, for the time being, settle in the lands west of the Appalachians. This move, he hoped, would avoid wars with Native Americans until Great Britain had the area under control and could gradually open the land to settlers. The colonists, however, were eager to build new settlements in the west, and they were outraged by this attempt to stop them.

Grenville also believed that colonists should help pay the costs of their own defense. He began raising money by enforcing the Navigation Acts with the British navy. British warships hunted down smugglers, who were then tried in British military courts rather than in colonial courts. Another new law allowed British troops to be housed in colonists' homes.

It was the Stamp Act, however, that most infuriated the colonists. Passed in 1765, the Stamp Act was different from previous tax measures because it was a direct tax—a tax paid directly to the government rather than being included in the price of goods. It required that all printed materials, from newspapers and shipping documents to playing cards, bear a stamp to show that a tax had been paid to Great Britain. Colonial lawyers, tavern owners, merchants, and printers were most affected by the Stamp Act.

Colonial Protests

Colonists reacted to these measures quickly. They protested with a boycott—a refusal to buy British goods. They attacked stamp agents and burned stamps in the streets. In 1765 they sent nine representatives to a colonial Stamp Act Congress in **New York City**. The Congress resolved that Parliament could not tax the colonies because the colonies did not have representatives in Parliament. They rallied under the cry "No taxation without representation!" and insisted that only their own colonial assemblies had the right to tax them. The British Parliament repealed the Stamp Act in 1766. The struggle for control of the colonies, however, had begun in earnest. **John Adams**, a colonial leader from Massachusetts, wrote in his diary:

> "The people have become more attentive to their liberties, ... and more determined to defend them.... Our presses have groaned, our pulpits have thundered, our legislatures have resolved, our towns have voted; the crown officers have everywhere trembled, and all their little tools and creatures been afraid to speak and ashamed to be seen."

Unrest in Boston

The British Parliament reasserted its right to pass laws governing the colonies in the Declaratory Act of 1766. The next year Great Britain placed new taxes on glass, lead, paper, and tea coming into the colonies. Royal agents trying to enforce these laws pleaded for British soldiers to protect them from the angry colonists.

In 1770 the first clash between the Americans and British troops took place. Two regiments of British troops had been sent to **Boston** to support the governor. One evening a squad of soldiers was harassed by a Boston crowd throwing snowballs and rotten eggs. Gunfire erupted, and five people died in what became known as the Boston Massacre.

Because of the unrest in Boston, Parliament repealed most of the taxes but kept the tax on tea.

COOPERATIVE LEARNING ACTIVITY

Posters Organize the class into small groups to research and make posters about colonial scientists, doctors, and inventors, such as John Lining, John Winthrop, Benjamin Franklin, James Logan, Benjamin Banneker, Samuel Higby, Thomas Cadwalader, David Rittenhouse, or others that students choose. Ask students to include written information and illustrations about these people's lives, discoveries, and inventions on their posters. When each group has decided on a subject, the tasks of research, writing, and illustration should be divided up among group members. Have students display completed posters around the classroom. Allow time for students to examine the posters and write one interesting fact that they learned from each poster. **L2**

NATIONAL GEOGRAPHIC

PICTURING HISTORY

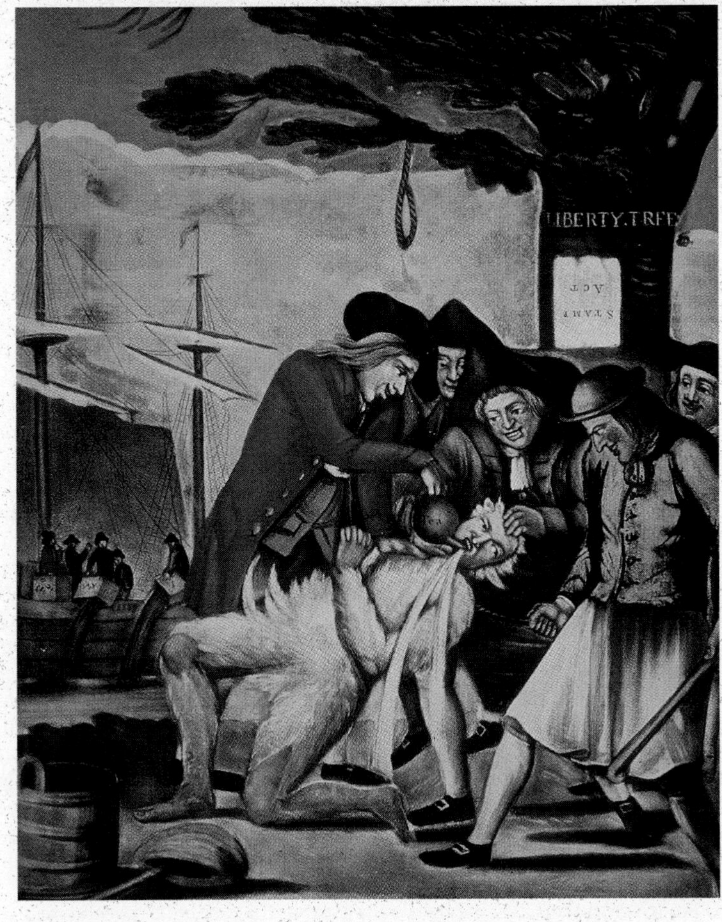

Anne S. K. Brown Military Collection, Brown University Library

Tarred and Feathered

This 1774 British cartoon depicting the tarring and feathering of a British customs officer made a simple point: The American rebels were not men of goodwill simply petitioning r parliamentary representation. The American starts, the cartoon implied, were revolutionaries termined to upset the prevailing order in both the mericas and Europe.

In January 1774 a mob took a customs officer amed John Malcolm, tarred and feathered him, and en beat him with clubs and ropes until he agreed to speak against His Majesty's government. Even then the mob did not let him go but led him half-naked through the snow for four hours. By then the skin hung off his back in strips and his body was frozen solid—or so the British governor of Massachusetts wrote in his report to the British secretary of state. The men of Massachusetts thus earned a reputation for violence and disorder. The cartoon of Malcolm's ordeal made good anticolonial propaganda in Great Britain, and the idea of hot tar on human flesh still sears our imaginations with the violence of the Revolutionary period. ⊕

TEACH

Tell students that the Boston Tea Party took place on December 16, 1773, and that this British cartoon is a response to that event. Have students carefully examine the cartoon. **What activity is going on in the background?** *(the Boston Tea Party)* **What other colonial protest is referred to in the cartoon?** *(protest against the Stamp Act)* **What do you think the noose hanging from the tree might have symbolized?** *(that the cause of liberty might require that people die)*

Linking Past and Present

Propaganda in the form of cartoons and stories is still used to make an enemy look like a monster and to rally citizens behind a cause. During the Persian Gulf War, stories and cartoons showed Saddam Hussein as a baby killer. Iraqi troops were supposed to have killed Kuwaiti babies by taking them out of incubators and removing the incubators to Iraq. The stories were later found to be incorrect.

Linking Past and Present

Patriots and Minutemen Colonists who favored American independence were called Patriots. New England's minutemen were volunteer soldiers who could be assembled quickly. Today *Minuteman* and *Patriot* continue to be used by the United States military as names for modern missile systems. Patriot missiles helped defeat Iraq in the Persian Gulf War in 1991.

Chapter 21 Section 3

Visualizing History During the American Revolution, the states and local militias adopted their own flags. The rattlesnake with the warning "Don't Tread on Me" appeared on several of these flags.
Answer to Caption: *At the Congress, leaders from the different colonies met face to face for the first time and were united for a common cause.*

Reteach

Have students make a chart about events that led to the American Revolution. Help them fill in information under the following headings: *Event, Date, What Happened, Outcome of Event.*

Enrich

Have students read a book—fiction or nonfiction—related to events of this section, write a report, and deliver their report orally to the class.

CLOSE

Ask students to imagine they are attending a protest meeting at the Old South Meetinghouse. Assign one or two students to give brief speeches about the "tyranny" of the British, addressing some specific issue, such as the Boston Massacre. Have other students, acting as participants at the meeting, stand up and "speak their minds" about the issues.

Visualizing History **The Rattlesnake Flag with 13 alternating red and white stripes warns: "Don't Tread on Me."** *What was the significance of the thirteen colonies sending delegates to the First Continental Congress?*

In an effort to keep the British East India Company from going bankrupt, a special law was passed that allowed it to sell tea in the colonies without paying tax. Because their tea could be sold more cheaply, it hurt the business of colonial tea merchants. The Boston colonists decided to retaliate. Disguised as Native Americans, the colonists dumped wooden chests of British tea into Boston Harbor.

The British quickly punished the Massachusetts colonists for the Boston Tea Party by passing what the colonists called the Intolerable Acts. These laws closed Boston Harbor until the tea had been paid for and required colonists to feed and house British soldiers in their homes. The acts also greatly reduced the colonists' right of self-government. Town meetings, for example, could not be held more than once a year without special permission from the royal governor. Parliament also passed the Quebec Act, placing Canada and territories north of the Ohio River under a separate government, thus closing the area to colonists.

The First Continental Congress

The latest repressive measures of the British convinced the thirteen colonies to form a union of resistance. On September 5, 1774, 56 colonial delegates met at **Philadelphia** at the First Continental Congress. The Congress marked an important event in colonial affairs. This was the first time that leaders from different colonies had met face to face. Previously, most colonies had considered their differences with Great Britain individually. Now they were united as a group. **Patrick Henry**, a leading statesman from Virginia, commented: "There are no differences between Virginians, Pennsylvanians, New Yorkers, and New Englanders. I am not a Virginian but an American." **George Washington** of Virginia and **Samuel Adams** of Massachusetts were among the leading members of the Congress.

The Congress, which met for more than 7 weeks, resolved that the "English colonists ... are entitled to a free and exclusive power of legislation in their several provincial legislatures." In other words, only the colonial assemblies should have the right to make laws in the colonies. Although the Congress recognized Parliament's right to regulate trade, the Congress agreed that the colonies would not import goods from Great Britain after December 1774. After September 1775, they resolved not to send colonial goods to Great Britain.

Many colonists, however, were determined to take more radical steps to end British rule. In every colony a volunteer army was organized and weapons collected. In New England, minutemen (so named because they could be ready for battle on a minute's notice) drilled on village greens, while the town officials stored ammunition, weapons, and food. In the Southern Colonies, planters recruited soldiers at their own expense. It began to appear that the dispute between Great Britain and the colonies would be settled only by force.

SECTION 3 REVIEW

Recall

1. **Define** duty, direct tax, boycott.
2. **Identify** Navigation Acts, French and Indian War, George Grenville, George III, Stamp Act, John Adams, First Continental Congress, Patrick Henry, George Washington, Samuel Adams.
3. **Explain** why relations between Great Britain and the colonies worsened after the French and Indian War.

Critical Thinking

4. **Evaluating Information** Do you think that the British monarch and his ministers were right in expecting the colonists to shoulder the burden of defending the American colonies? What other approaches might Grenville have taken?

Understanding Themes

5. **Conflict** Compare and contrast Parliament's struggles for power with the king with the American colonists' later struggle for control of their own affairs. What were the key issues for Parliament? For the colonists?

SECTION 3 REVIEW ANSWERS

1. All vocabulary words are defined in the Glossary.
2. Navigation Acts, 546; French and Indian War, 547; George Grenville, 547; George III, 547; Stamp Act, 548; John Adams, 548; First Continental Congress, 550; Patrick Henry, 550; George Washington, 550; Samuel Adams, 550
3. The British government began to interfere in colonial affairs and to tax the colonies in order to pay for the war.
4. Answers may include that colonists should have paid something for the French and Indian War, but Grenville should have consulted colonial legislatures about acceptable ways to raise money.
5. CONFLICT Both struggles were for more control over the taxing power and for protection of rights. The difference was that Parliament fought to limit the power of the king and change the government, whereas the colonists wanted more representation within the established British government.

Study and Writing SKILLS

Outlining

To sketch a scene, first you would draw the rough shape, or outline, of the picture. Then you would fill in this rough shape with details. Outlining written material is a similar process. You begin with the rough shape of the material and gradually fill in the details.

Learning the Skill

Outlining has two important functions. When studying written material, it helps you identify main ideas and group together related facts. In writing, it helps you put information in a logical order.

There are two kinds of outlines–formal and informal. An informal outline is similar to taking notes. You write only words and phrases needed to remember ideas. Under the main ideas, jot down related but less important details. This kind of outline is useful for reviewing material before a test.

A formal outline has a standard format. In a formal outline, label main heads with Roman numerals, subheads with capital letters, and details with Arabic numerals. Each level would have at least two entries and should be indented from the level above. All entries use the same grammatical form. If one entry is a complete sentence, all other entries at that level must also be complete sentences.

When outlining written material, first read the material to identify the main ideas. In textbooks, section heads provide clues to main topics. Then identify the subheads. Place details supporting or explaining subheads under the appropriate head.

Practicing the Skill

Study the outline below of Chapter 21, Section 1 and then answer these questions.

1. Is this an example of a formal or an informal outline?
2. What are the three main headings?
3. How do subheads under the heading "Commonwealth" relate to this main idea?
4. Give two examples of grammatical consistency in this outline.

I. Monarchy
  A. James I
    1. Believed in the divine right of kings
    2. Fought with Parliament over money and religion
  B. Charles I
    1. Continued to believe in divine right
    2. Tried to rule without Parliament
    3. Lost the Civil War and was beheaded
II. Commonwealth
  A. England ruled by Parliament
  B. Army led by Cromwell
III. Military dictatorship
  A. Headed by Oliver Cromwell
  B. Enforced Puritan rules

Applying the Skill

Write a formal outline for Section 2 of this chapter.

For More Practice

Turn to the Skill Practice in the Chapter Review on page 557 for more practice in outlining.

Oliver Cromwell

Study and Writing SKILLS

TEACH

Outlining On the chalkboard, write the following main headings for an informal outline about activities of a typical school day: *Morning, Afternoon, Evening.* Have students add indented subheads and further indented supporting details under each main head. For example: *At home* and *At school* could be subheads under *Morning. Get up, Get dressed*, and *Eat breakfast* could be details under *At home.* Be sure students have at least two subheads under each head and at least two details under each subhead. Students should maintain grammatical consistency within each level of the outline. Convert students' outline to a formal outline by placing Roman numerals, capital letters, and Arabic numerals in the appropriate places. Then have students read the skill and complete the practice questions.

Additional Practice

Skill Reinforcement Activity 21

Writer's Guidebook, Lesson 11

ANSWERS TO PRACTICING THE SKILL

1. formal outline
2. Monarchy, Commonwealth, Military dictatorship
3. The subheads describe affairs in England during the Commonwealth.
4. The main headings are nouns and the numbered subheads are verb phrases.

Chapter 21
Section 4

SECTION THEME

▶ **Revolution** The American colonies revolt against Great Britain and form the United States of America.

Find Out

Answer: *At first, the Americans had a weak confederacy, but then they wrote a constitution that set up a federal system with a strong central government.*

FOCUS

Section Objective

Describe the kind of government Americans established after the American Revolution.

BELLRINGER
Motivational Activity

Before taking roll at the beginning of the class period, project Section Focus Transparency 21-4 and have students answer the activity questions. Discuss students' responses.

This activity is also available as a blackline master.

Vocabulary Pre-check

Use the Vocabulary PuzzleMaker to create a puzzle that reinforces the vocabulary terms in this section. **L1**

1775 | 1780 | 1785 | 1790

1775 British and American forces exchange fire at Lexington and Concord.

1781 British General Cornwallis surrenders at Yorktown.

1783 Great Britain recognizes American independence.

1787 Delegates in Philadelphia write the United States Constitution.

Section 4

A War for Independence

Setting the Scene

▶ **Terms to Define**
revolution, confederation, federal system

▶ **People to Meet**
Paul Revere, George Washington, Thomas Paine, Thomas Jefferson

▶ **Places to Locate**
Yorktown

Find Out What kind of government did the Americans establish after the American Revolution?

The Storyteller

Mercy Warren lived through the American Revolution and wrote about its horrors. "The roads [were] filled with frighted women and children; some in carts with their tattered furniture, others on foot fleeing into the woods. But what added greatly to the horrors of the scene, was our passing through the bloody field at Monotong, which was strewed with mangled bodies. We met one affectionate father with a cart, looking for his murdered son.… " She concluded one of her letters, "Be it known unto Britain, even American daughters are politicians and patriots, and will aid the good work with their female efforts."

—adapted from *The Women of the American Revolution*, Elizabeth F. Ellet, 1850

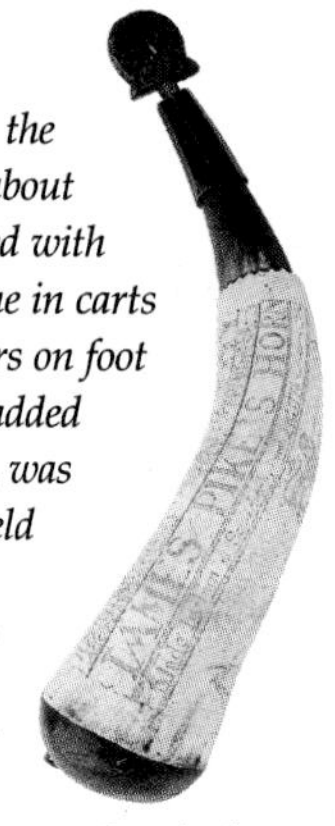

Powder horn

Hostilities between the American colonists and the British broke out near Boston in 1775. People there were outraged by the British government. Their seaport was still closed because of the Boston Tea Party, causing many Bostonians to lose their jobs. As British troops filled the city, rumors accusing the "redcoats" of robberies and murders swept through shops, inns, and other meeting places.

Sensing the tension in the city, the British Parliament ordered the governor of Massachusetts, General Thomas Gage, to seize the colonists' military supplies. Before dawn on April 19, 1775, Gage sent a troop of 700 British soldiers to destroy weapons collected in the town of Concord, about 18 miles (29 km) from Boston.

Colonists **Paul Revere** and William Dawes learned of the British plan and rode to warn the colonial minutemen. As the British marched into Lexington on their way to Concord, they found about 70 farmers and villagers blocking their path. When the colonists refused to put down their guns, a shot was fired, though no one knows which side fired first. In the skirmish, British soldiers killed 8 colonists; later at Concord, the "redcoats" held off a sharp attack by more minutemen.

As the British troops marched back toward Boston, colonists fired at them from behind buildings, trees, and stone walls. The next day, almost 300 British soldiers and nearly 100 colonists lay dead. The British were humiliated. No one expected the colonists to be any match for the professional British soldiers.

Moving Toward Separation

News of the colonial attack on the British troops spread throughout the American colonies.

SECTION RESOURCES

Reproducible Masters
- Reproducible Lesson Plan 21-4
- Guided Reading Activity 21-4
- People in World History Profile 39
- Reteaching Activity 21
- Enrichment Activity 21
- Section Quiz 21-4
- Performance Assessment Activity 21
- Spanish Chapter Summary 21

Transparencies
- Section Focus Transparency 21-4
- Mapping History Overlay Transparency 13

Multimedia
- Vocabulary PuzzleMaker Software
- Student Self-Test and Review Software
- Testmaker

History & Art *Signing of the Declaration of Independence* by John Trumbull, c. 1825. The Yale University Art Gallery, New Haven, Connecticut **To the British, those who signed the Declaration of Independence committed an act of treason.** *How did the document justify revolution?*

When the Second Continental Congress gathered in Philadelphia one month after the battles at Lexington and Concord, it immediately organized an army and named **George Washington** as military commander.

Many colonists, however, still resisted the idea of declaring war on Great Britain. The Congress tried one last time to arrange a peaceful compromise with Parliament and the king. They sent a proposal, called the Olive Branch Petition, to King George III. When the British government refused the petition, chances of a peaceful settlement between Great Britain and the American colonies grew dimmer. To more and more colonists, independence seemed the only answer.

A Call to Part

The most stirring arguments in favor of independence came from the pen of colonist **Thomas Paine**. Paine, who recently had come to the American colonies from Great Britain, wrote a pamphlet called *Common Sense* in January 1776. In it he called upon the colonists to break away from Great Britain. Paine promoted independence for economic, social, and moral reasons:

> "Every thing that is right begs for separation from [Great] Britain. The Americans who have been killed seem to say, 'TIS TIME TO PART. England and America are located a great distance apart. That is itself strong and natural proof that God never expected one to rule over the other."
>
> —Thomas Paine, *Common Sense*, 1776

Common Sense circulated widely and helped to convince thousands of American colonists that it was "time to part." The delegates to the Congress sensed the changing mood in the colonies and assigned five of their best thinkers and writers to prepare a declaration of independence that would clearly state their resolve.

The Declaration of Independence

Thomas Jefferson, a young Virginian, was the principal author of the colonists' declaration of independence. The document set forth the colonists' reasons for separation from Great Britain. Jefferson, like many other colonial leaders, knew and valued the works of John Locke and other Enlightenment thinkers. He incorporated many of their ideas into the Declaration of Independence.

The Declaration stated that individuals have certain basic rights that cannot be taken away by any government. Focusing on John Locke's concept of the "social contract," the Declaration announced that governments are created by an agreement, or contract, between the rulers and those ruled. If a ruler loses the support of the people by taking away basic rights, the people have a right to change the government through rebellion. The beginning of the Declaration reads:

> "We hold these truths to be self-evident, that all men are created equal, that they are endowed by their Creator with certain unalienable Rights, that among these are Life, Liberty, and the pursuit of Happiness. That to secure these rights, Governments are instituted among Men, deriving their just powers from the consent of the governed; that whenever any Form of Government becomes destructive of those ends, it is the Right of the People to alter or to abolish it...."

The Declaration continued with a long list of the ways in which Great Britain and George III had

TEACH

Guided Practice

THEME Revolution

Help students arrive at a definition of revolution as used in this section. *(violent overthrow of the government)* Have them explain how the American Revolution fits their definition. **L1 LEP**

History & Art Trumbull served as George Washington's aide-de-camp during the war and did not start this painting until 1789. To portray Jefferson correctly, Trumbull made sketches of him in France where Jefferson served as United States ambassador.

Answer to Caption: *It said revolution was justified if a ruler took away basic rights of the people, which King George III had.*

Comparison Have students list the advantages and the disadvantages of the Americans and the British during the American Revolution. **L2**

Critical Thinking Help students design a chart that shows the similarities and differences between the American Revolution and the English Civil War (Section 1). Suggest that students use the following headings: *Parties in the Conflict, Issues and Goals, Leaders, Outcomes.* **L3**

Mapping History Overlay Transparency 13, *European Claims in North America*

COOPERATIVE LEARNING ACTIVITY

Dramatization Organize the class into two groups and have each group prepare a play dramatizing the debate about and writing of either the Declaration of Independence or the Constitution. Be sure that each student has a task, such as researching Enlightenment ideas that influenced the documents, investigating background information on the main participants who wrote and debated the documents, writing dialogue that includes a discussion of the Enlightenment ideas, or acting in the drama. After each dramatization has been presented, allow the audience to ask questions. **L2**

Chapter 21 Section 4

Independent Practice

Guided Reading Activity 21-4 **L1**

People in World History Profile 39

Daily Life Have students research the daily routine of American or British soldiers during the American Revolution. Ask them to draw pictures or to write a first-person narrative describing a soldier's experiences. **L2 LEP**

Who?What?Where?When?

Loyalists About one-third of Americans remained loyal to the king during the American Revolution. Called Loyalists, they became targets for Patriot violence. Some were beaten or had their homes damaged. The state governments seized the property of Loyalists and limited their freedom of speech and of movement.

ASSESS

Check for Understanding

Assign Section 4 Review as homework or as an in-class activity.

Use Student Self-Test and Review Software to review Section 4.

Evaluate

Section Quiz 21-4

Use the Testmaker to create a customized quiz for Section 4.

Reteach

Have students make a list of the most significant people and events discussed in this section. Then have students compare their lists and discuss the significance of each person and event.

abused their power and concludes that "these United Colonies are and of Right ought to be Free and Independent States."

On July 4, 1776, the Congress adopted the Declaration of Independence. A few days later, George Washington had the Declaration read to his troops to inspire them and give them hope as war loomed ahead. Cheers went up from the ranks when the reading was done. That night some of the troops joined a crowd of townspeople who pulled down a statue of George III and broke off the head.

The War for Independence

The signing of the Declaration of Independence made war a certainty. The Americans had taken a step that made a peaceful reconciliation with Great Britain impossible. The only course that remained for the colonists was **revolution**, the violent overthrow of a government. For the leaders of the revolution, now seen as traitors to the British king, failure would mean disgrace, imprisonment, and even death. As colonist Benjamin Franklin said, "Yes, we must, indeed, all hang together, or, most assuredly, we shall all hang separately."

The War of Independence was long and bitter. Although the Americans did not have an army that could face the British in the open field, they had a skillful general in Washington. They also had help from the French in the form of arms and ammunition. The French were eager for an American victory, hoping to revenge the losses of the Seven Years' War. They did not, however, actively join forces with the Americans until victory seemed certain.

Footnotes to History

"Yankee Doodle" The song "Yankee Doodle" was first sung by the British to mock the American colonists:

"Yankee Doodle came to town,
Riding on a pony;
He stuck a feather in his cap
And called it macaroni."

"Macaroni" was a term used for British men who thought they dressed in style but actually looked ridiculous. The colonists loved the tune and added verses of their own to make it a song of defiance.

The British had the disadvantage of trying to fight a long-distance war. Also, they had to conquer the whole country to win. The Americans had only to hold out until the British admitted defeat.

The turning point came in October 1777 with a British defeat at Saratoga, New York. The American victory persuaded France to come in on the American side. Spain followed in 1779. Faced with a naval war against France and Spain, Great Britain became less interested in defeating its rebellious colonies. In August 1781 the Americans forced the British army to surrender at **Yorktown**, Virginia.

Forming a New Government

In 1783 Great Britain recognized its former American colonies as an independent nation, the United States of America. The Americans now faced a task more difficult than winning a war: forming a stable government. Between 1781 and 1787, the United States was a **confederation**, or a loose union of independent states, under an agreement called the Articles of Confederation.

The Articles of Confederation

The Confederation had difficulty enforcing what little authority it had. It could not collect taxes. It also could not force the states to pay national debts from the war or to raise armies.

Another of the Confederation's major problems was its failure to regulate the states' economic activities. Soon states began competing against each other economically. At a time when the United States needed to establish its economy and gain recognition from the world as a stable government, the states only quarreled while the country accumulated more debt.

A New Constitution

The Confederation's weaknesses led to calls for a stronger central government that would effectively unite the country. In 1787 the Congress called a convention to revise the Articles. After much discussion and debate, the delegates decided to abandon the Articles and create a new constitution.

After further debates, the states finally ratified the United States Constitution in 1788, and it went into effect the following year. The new constitution set up a **federal system**, or a government in which power is divided between a central government and regional, or state, governments. Following the recommendations in Montesquieu's *The Spirit of Laws* (1748), central political authority was divided

MEETING SPECIAL NEEDS ACTIVITY

Study Strategy Have students outline this section using the following Roman numeral heads: *I. The move toward separation, II. The War of Independence, III. The new government*. Help students correctly place the following subheads in the outline: *Olive Branch Petition, Common Sense, Declaration of Independence, American advantages and disadvantages, British advantages and disadvantages, Articles of Confederation, Constitution.* Then have students find at least two details to place under each subhead. **L1**

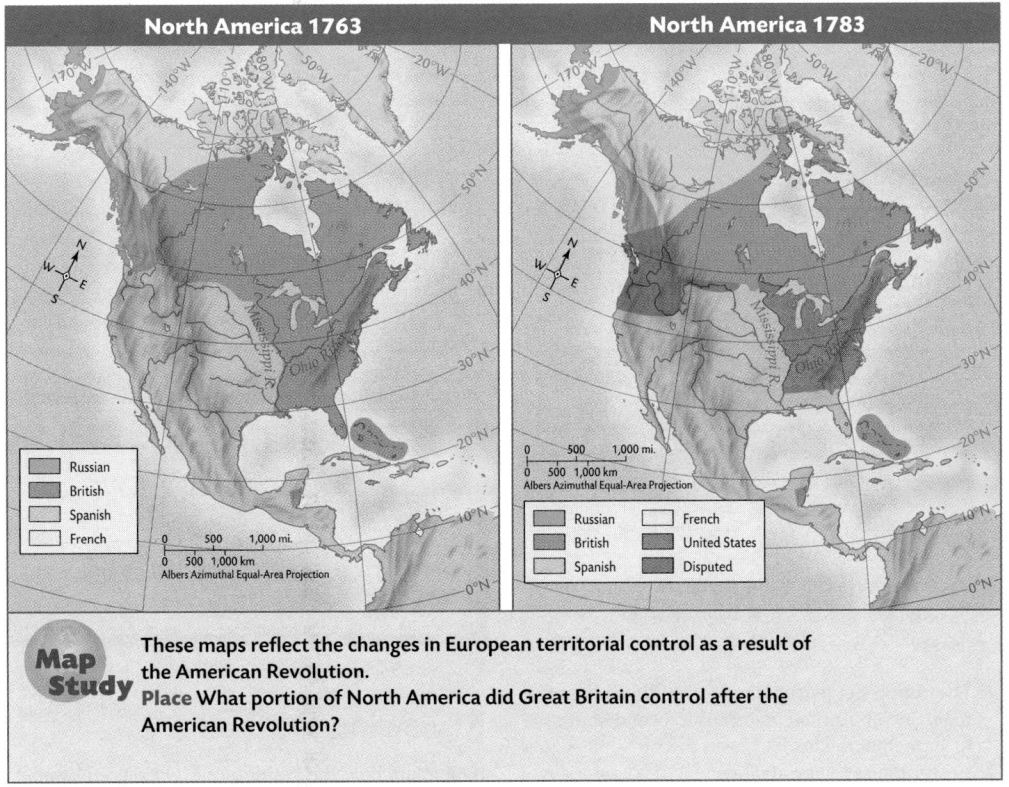

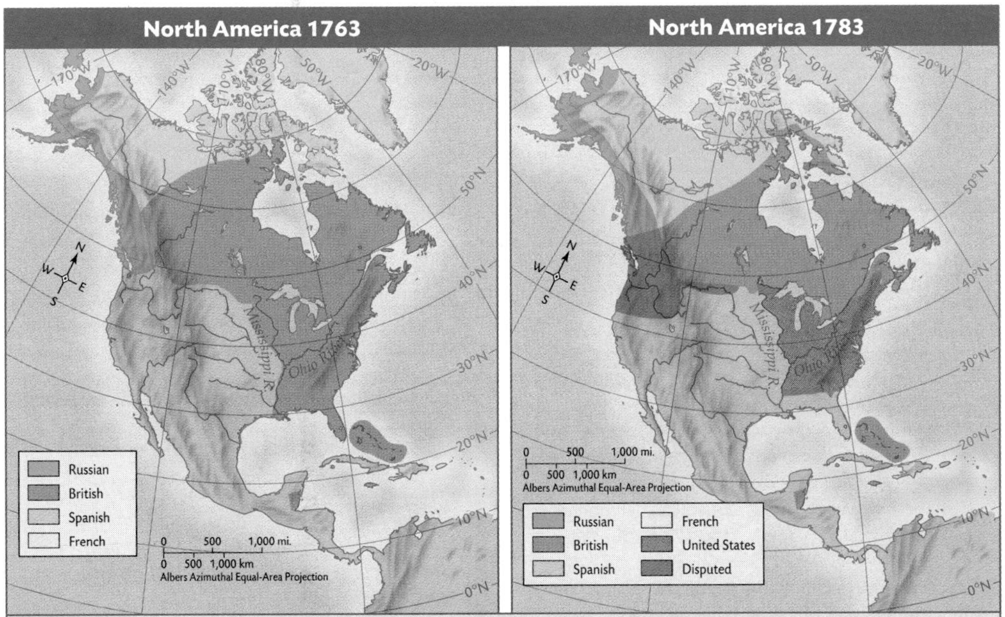

Map Study These maps reflect the changes in European territorial control as a result of the American Revolution.
Place What portion of North America did Great Britain control after the American Revolution?

among executive, legislative, and judicial branches of government, and careful checks and balances were arranged. For example, the President, as head of the executive branch, can appoint judges for the judicial branch, but the legislators in Congress, the legislative branch, must approve them.

Under the new constitution, the United States was a republic with an elected head of state instead of a hereditary monarch. Elections held in 1789 made George Washington the first President of the United States. One of the first steps taken by the United States Congress was the development of a Bill of Rights, which was added to the Constitution in the form of amendments. The Bill of Rights protected personal liberties, such as freedom of religion, freedom of speech, and trial by jury. It also protected the rights of the individual states that made up the new nation.

SECTION 4 REVIEW

Recall

1. **Define** revolution, confederation, federal system.
2. **Identify** Paul Revere, George Washington, Thomas Paine, Thomas Jefferson, the Declaration of Independence.
3. **Explain** the basic message of the Declaration of Independence. Why did the American colonists believe the Declaration was necessary?

Critical Thinking

4. **Evaluating Information** Do you think that if Great Britain had treated the colonists differently, they would have been content to remain under British rule? Support your answer.

Understanding Themes

5. **Revolution** Compare the Americans' attempts to organize a new form of government with those of the English after executing King Charles I. Did both governments ensure representation and individual rights?

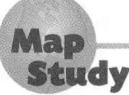

Map Study

Answer

most of Canada and islands in the Caribbean Sea

Map Skills Practice

Reading a Map **What other country had large holdings in North America in 1783?** *(Spain)*

Reteaching Activity 21

Enrich

Have students do further research on how Locke's ideas about the social contract and Montesquieu's ideas about separation of powers became part of American political theory.

Enrichment Activity 21

CLOSE

Have students write a brief summary of the events covered in this section, beginning with the Declaration of Independence. Then have them write what they think is the significance of the events and how those events affect their lives today. Have students discuss what they wrote.

SECTION 4 REVIEW ANSWERS

1. All vocabulary words are defined in the Glossary.
2. Paul Revere, 552; George Washington, 553; Thomas Paine, 553; Thomas Jefferson, 553; Declaration of Independence, 553
3. Individuals have basic rights that government cannot take away. Because the king had taken basic rights from the colonists, they had the right to rebel; they couldn't tolerate the British government any longer.
4. Answers may vary. Possible answer: If the British government had compromised, the Americans would not have revolted.
5. **REVOLUTION** After the English Civil War, Cromwell suspended Parliament, became a military dictator, and placed the people under strict laws. After the American Revolution, Congress wrote a new Constitution to which they added the Bill of Rights to protect individual liberties.

Chapter 21 Review

GLENCOE TECHNOLOGY

VIDEODISC

Use MindJogger to review students' knowledge of the chapter.

MindJogger Videoquiz

Chapter 21
Disc 3 Side B

Also available in VHS.

CHAPTER 21 REVIEW

Historical Significance

The English and American Revolutions helped to establish the rights of citizens within a representative government. In England, and later Great Britain, the monarchy steadily lost power, Parliament became supreme, and legal documents guaranteed certain individual rights.

In the United States, the colonists established a republic with a written constitution and separation of powers. The Bill of Rights spelled out the rights of individual citizens. The American Revolution would become a source of inspiration to people seeking freedom throughout the world.

Using Key Terms

Write the key term that completes each sentence.

a. habeas corpus
b. divine right
c. duty
d. prime minister
e. commonwealth
f. revolution
g. constitutional monarchy
h. federal system
i. royalists
j. direct tax
k. confederation
l. martial law

1. The Stamp Act placed a ______ on the colonists, requiring all printed materials to bear a stamp to show that the tax had been paid.
2. According to the principle of _______, a person cannot be held in prison by the government without just cause or without a trial.
3. During the 1600s, laws of Parliament gradually changed England into a __________, in which the powers of the monarch are limited.
4. A rift between James I and Parliament grew deeper when the king publicly professed his belief in _______.
5. After the signing of the Declaration of Independence, the only course that remained for the American colonists was ________.
6. In Great Britain, the executive leader of the government became known as the ____________.
7. During times of _________, military authorities are given temporary rule and individual rights are limited.
8. In the English Civil War, supporters of the monarchy were known as _________.
9. When the monarchy was abolished in 1649, England became a ________, a state governed by elected representatives.
10. The United States Constitution set up a __________, or a government in which power is divided between a central government and regional, or state, governments.

Using Your History Journal

From your list of key ideas that should be the basis of government, write a short constitution or structure for governing a small group—a club, voluntary organization, or a community.

Reviewing Facts

1. **Explain** how the Petition of Right placed limits on the power of the Crown.
2. **Discuss** how the military rule of Oliver Cromwell helped set the stage for the Restoration in 1660.
3. **Describe** the Glorious Revolution.
4. **Identify** the significance of the colonists' First Continental Congress.
5. **Explain** why Great Britain believed it could easily defeat the colonists at the beginning of the American Revolution.

Critical Thinking

1. **Apply** How did James I and Charles I try to impose the idea of divine right monarchy on the English Parliament?
2. **Analyze** What religious issues affected the growing conflict between Parliament and the Crown in England?
3. **Apply** What were the weaknesses of the Articles of Confederation? Why did the American colonists first choose this type of government? Why did the Articles of Confederation fail?

Answers

Using Key Terms

1. j	**6.** d
2. a	**7.** l
3. g	**8.** i
4. b	**9.** e
5. f	**10.** h

Using Your History Journal

Suggest that students examine bylaws or constitutions from several school or community organizations as models for incorporating their key ideas of government.

Reviewing Facts

1. The monarch could not collect taxes without Parliament's consent, imprison anyone without just cause, force people to house troops, or declare martial law unless there was a war.
2. Harsh Puritan rule made the English people eager to restore the monarchy.
3. Both parties united against James II and invited William and Mary of Orange to rule England according to laws of Parliament.
4. Representatives from all the colonies met together to oppose British rule.
5. The British had a strong army that fought well in the open field.

Critical Thinking

1. They collected taxes and sold titles of nobility without Parliament's consent, imprisoned opponents, and dissolved Parliament when it would not follow the royal command.
2. James I and Charles I both persecuted Puritans, who later gained control of Parliament and led the Parliamentary forces in the English Civil War.
3. The new nation's government could not collect taxes, raise an army, force the states to pay their share of the national debt, or regulate the states' economic activities. Answers should include that the states wanted a loose union after being ruled by the king. The states competed against one another economically, increasing the national debt and failing to gain recognition as a stable government.

4. **Synthesize** How did the Enlightenment influence the American Revolution?

Geography in History

1. **Region** Refer to the map below. One of Great Britain's major challenges in the American Revolution was to control rebellion over a wide area. How far is it from the Battle of Saratoga to the Battle of Camden, South Carolina?
2. **Movement** Why did most British troop movement from one location to another occur by sea?
3. **Region** The dates and stars identify major Revolutionary battles. How do these battles indicate a shift in the region of the most significant battles from the earliest to the latest period?

Major Battles of the American Revolution

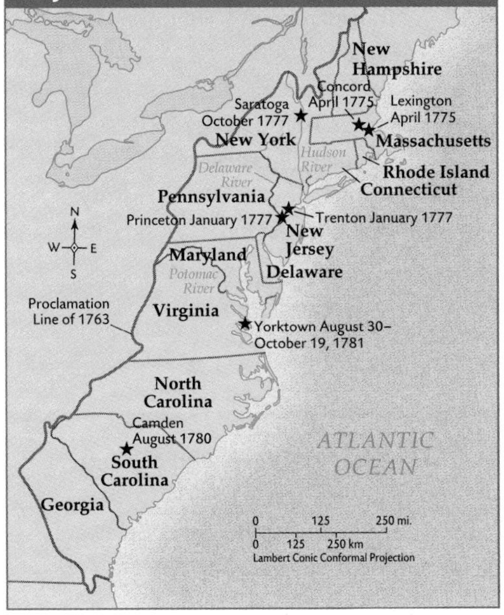

Understanding Themes

1. **Conflict** What factors caused the conflict between Parliament and the Stuart monarchs?
2. **Change** Why do you think the English restored the monarchy after the Commonwealth? What changes came to the monarchy after 1660?

3. **Conflict** How did the British punish Massachusetts colonists after the Boston Tea Party?
4. **Revolution** Why did the American Revolution lead to a stable republic in the colonies, while the English Civil War did not do so in England?

Linking Past and Present

1. Some of the Revolutionary quarrels concerned taxes. In what ways does the United States today struggle with the issue of fair taxation?
2. Religious differences helped fuel the English Civil War. Where do religious differences cause political problems today?
3. The United States and Great Britain today are both democracies. How are their governments similar? How are they different? To what extent do they base their political principles on the events of the 1600s and 1700s?

Skill Practice

Complete the following formal outline for Section 3, "Road to Revolt."

I. Great Britain's American Empire
  A. Economic relationship between Great Britain and colonies
  B. ________________
    1. Some colonial products exported only to Great Britain
    2. ________________
    3. No foreign-made ships in colonies

II. ________________
  A. Structure of colonial governments
    1. ________________
    2. Elected assemblies
  B. Early power struggles
    1. Limited salaries of officials
    2. ________________

III. Tightening British Control
  A. Effects of French and Indian War
    1. ________________
    2. ________________
  B. Stamp Acts

IV. ________________
  A. Boston Massacre
  B. ________________
  C. First Continental Congress

Chapter 21 Review

3. **CONFLICT** passed the Intolerable Acts, required colonists to quarter British soldiers, reduced self-government, and closed land north of Ohio River
4. **REVOLUTION** After the Revolution, the Americans worked together to form a stable government. After the English Civil War, Cromwell ruled as a dictator.

Linking Past and Present

1. Congress makes some changes in the tax laws in response to various groups' calls for fairness.
2. Bosnia, the Middle East, and Northern Ireland
3. Both have representative governments. Britain has a constitutional monarchy; the U.S. is headed by a president. Both are influenced by Enlightenment ideas of individual rights and limited power for government.

Skill Practice

I.B. Navigation Acts
I.B.2. All goods going to colonies first pass through Great Britain
II. Colonial Political Power
II.A.1. Governors appointed by king
II.B.2. Had right to approve taxes requested by the Crown or governors
III.A.1. Land west of the Appalachians closed to colonists
III.A.2. Navigation Acts enforced
IV. Events Leading to War
IV.B. Intolerable Acts

Chapter Bonus Test Question

Ask students: Why did England reestablish the monarchy after the Civil War while the Americans set up a constitutional government after their revolution? *(Between the English Civil War and the American Revolution, the Enlight-enment occurred that brought forth Locke's and Montesquieu's ideas about government.)*

4. John Locke's ideas about the social contract between rulers and the ruled was the basis of the Declaration of Independence.

Geography in History

1. about 700 miles [about 1,126 kilometers]
2. It was easier and faster to move by sea.
3. They show that the war started in the northern colonies and moved south.

Understanding Themes

1. **CONFLICT** The Stuart monarchs believed in the divine right of kings, and Parliament thought the monarch's powers should be limited by law. Parliament and the Stuarts also had conflicts over religion.
2. **CHANGE** The English people were tired of the continued conflicts in Parliament and of harsh Puritan rule. The monarchy became a constitutional monarchy.

The French Revolution

CHAPTER RESOURCES

	Reproducible Resources	Multimedia Resources
Chapter Opener	Chapter Themes: Graphic Organizer 22 Historical Significance Chapter Activity 22	MindJogger Videoquiz
Chapter Enrichment	Vocabulary Activity 22* Time Line Activity 22 Mapping History Activity 22 History Simulation 22 Geography and History Activity 22 Source Reading 22 People in World History Profiles 41, 42 World Literature Selection 5 World Art and Music Activity 22 Enrichment Activity 22 Critical Thinking Activity 22 Skill Reinforcement Activity 22 Building Skills in Geography Workbook, Unit 2, Lesson 8 Performance Assessment Activity 22	World History and Art Transparency 29, *Napoleon Crossing the Alps* Mapping History Overlay Transparency 14, *France and Europe* Chapter Transparency 22 Vocabulary PuzzleMaker Software Turning Points in World History: *French Revolution*
Chapter Review/Reteaching	Reteaching Activity 22 Skill Reinforcement Activity 22 Spanish Chapter Summary 22	Chapter 22 Digest Audiocassette, Activity, Test* Vocabulary PuzzleMaker Software Student Self-Test and Review Software MindJogger Videoquiz
Chapter Evaluation/Testing	Performance Assessment Activity 22 Chapter 22 Test, Forms A and B	Testmaker

* *Also available in Spanish*

0:00 **OUT OF TIME?** Assign the Chapter 22 summary in the Unit 5 Digest on pages 590–593, and the Chapter 22 Audiocassettes.

Block Schedule

Block scheduling differs from traditional class scheduling in the amount of time allotted to each period. The extended time frame provided by block scheduling affords you the opportunity to implement a greater number of research-oriented and activity-intense projects to motivate and involve your students. Activities that are particularly suited to use within the block scheduling framework are identified throughout this chapter by the following designation.

KEY TO ABILITY LEVELS

Teaching strategies have been coded for varying learning styles and abilities.

- L1 **BASIC** activities for all students
- L2 **AVERAGE** activities for average to above-average students
- L3 **CHALLENGING** activities for above-average students
- LEP **LIMITED ENGLISH PROFICIENCY** activities

Chapter 22 Planning Guide

A complete, 1-page lesson plan is provided for each section in the *Reproducible Lesson Plans* booklet.

SECTION RESOURCES

Daily Objectives	Reproducible Resources	Multimedia Resources
Section 1 The Old Order Explain how France's class structure contributed to the French Revolution.	Reproducible Lesson Plan 22-1 Vocabulary Activity 22* Guided Reading Activity 22-1* Time Line Activity 22 People in World History Profile 41 Section Quiz 22-1*	Section Focus Transparency 22-1 Chapter Transparency 22 Student Self-Test and Review Software Testmaker Turning Points in World History: *French Revolution*
Section 2 Constitutional Government List the political reforms the National Assembly adopted for France.	Reproducible Lesson Plan 22-2 Vocabulary Activity 22* Guided Reading Activity 22-2* Source Reading 22 Section Quiz 22-2*	Section Focus Transparency 22-2 Student Self-Test and Review Software Testmaker Turning Points in World History: *French Revolution*
Section 3 Dawn of a New Era Explain why the French Revolution led to war between France and its neighbors.	Reproducible Lesson Plan 22-3 Vocabulary Activity 22* Guided Reading Activity 22-3* History Simulation 22 People in World History Profile 42 Section Quiz 22-3*	Section Focus Transparency 22-3 Student Self-Test and Review Software Testmaker Turning Points in World History: *French Revolution*
Section 4 Napoleon's Empire Relate how Napoleon built and then lost an empire.	Reproducible Lesson Plan 22-4 Vocabulary Activity 22* Guided Reading Activity 22-4* Geography and History Activity 22 World Art and Music Activity 22 Section Quiz 22-4*	Section Focus Transparency 22-4 World History and Art Transparency 29, *Napoleon Crossing the Alps* Mapping History Overlay Transparency 14, *France and Europe* Student Self-Test and Review Software Testmaker
Section 5 Peace in Europe Evaluate the success of the plans of the reactionaries to thwart the spread of liberalism in Europe.	Reproducible Lesson Plan 22-5 Guided Reading Activity 22-5* Reteaching Activity 22 Enrichment Activity 22 Section Quiz 22-5* Performance Assessment Activity 22 Spanish Chapter Summary 22	Section Focus Transparency 22-5 Mapping History Overlay Transparency 14, *France and Europe* Vocabulary PuzzleMaker Software Student Self-Test and Review Software Testmaker

** Also available in Spanish*

Chapter Activities

Performance Assessment Activity

A Concerned Citizen Speaks to the Government This chapter provides an example of how isolated incidents of conflict can spread. Ask students to think of analogous situations today (for example, gangs, crime families, political factions). Have each student assume the role of a citizen who is concerned about one of these situations and would like to bring its seriousness to the attention of the city council, state legislature, or United Nations. In their speeches, students should refer to the French Revolution for historical perspective, making connections with details in their modern-day examples. Have students deliver their speeches to collaborative groups of eight, with the listeners assuming the roles of members of the body being addressed.

Possible Rubric Features

Concept attainment, research skills, ability to make connections, clarity and impact of speech, accuracy of content information, appropriateness of speech to audience

• *For an additional activity, refer to Activity 22 in the* Performance Assessment Strategies and Activities *booklet.*

Activity

From the Classroom of...

Susan E. Szachowicz
Brockton High School
Brockton, MA

The Congress of Vienna Convenes

Organize the class into five groups, representing Austria, Great Britain, Russia, Prussia, and France, and direct each group to select one spokesperson to be Metternich, Castlereagh, Alexander I, Frederick William III, and Talleyrand. Provide each group with an overview of the Congress and its purpose; information specific to their country, which includes their delegate's role at the Congress and their country's goals, vital interests, and demands: and an outline map of Europe at the height of Napoleon's power. Each group should now develop their lists of demands and redraw the map of Europe as they would like to see it. Then convene the Congress by having the representative from each group offer their proposals and maps to the entire class. Questioning and negotiating should proceed until a plan acceptable to all is developed. Finally, the class plan should be compared to the actual decision made at the Congress of Vienna and similarities and differences noted.

MULTIPLE LEARNING STYLES

Verbal/Linguistic
Have students research and then debate the following question: Was Napoleon's legacy positive or negative?

Logical/Mathematical
Have students create a time line of major events that occurred during the French Revolution.

Visual/Spatial
Students may create a comic book that chronicles the life of a French peasant family living outside Paris at the time of the French Revolution. Each section should focus on a particular event that occurred in Paris between 1789 and 1815.

Kinesthetic
Have students draw a large outline map of Europe and hang it on the bulletin board. Using thumbtacks and labels, identify locations of major events during the French Revolution.

Additional Resources

TEACHER'S CORNER

NATIONAL GEOGRAPHIC SOCIETY

INDEX TO NATIONAL GEOGRAPHIC MAGAZINE

The following articles may be used for research relating to this chapter:

- "The Great Revolution," by Merle Severy, July 1989.
- "Two Revolutions," by Charles McCarry, July 1989.
- "Napoleon," by John J. Putman, February 1982.

NATIONAL GEOGRAPHIC SOCIETY PRODUCTS AVAILABLE FROM GLENCOE

To order the following products for use with this chapter, contact your local Glencoe sales representative or call Glencoe at 1-800-368-7344:

CD-ROM

- Picture Atlas of the World

ADDITIONAL NATIONAL GEOGRAPHIC SOCIETY PRODUCTS

To order the following products for use with this chapter, call National Geographic Society at 1-800-368-2728:

- *Democratic Government Series*, "France." (Video)

Bibliography

Literature of the Period

Dickens, Charles. ***A Tale of Two Cities.*** New York: Dutton, 1970. A romantic novel that takes place during the French Revolution.

Readings for the Student

Forester, C. S. ***Mr. Midshipman Hornblower.*** Boston: Little, Brown, 1940. The first of eleven sea stories set in the era of the Napoleonic Wars.

Readings for the Teacher

Evenson, Norma. ***Paris: A Century of Change, 1878–1978.*** New Haven: Yale University Press, 1979. Historical and social changes in France as reflected in the city of Paris, from its rebuilding under Napoleon III.

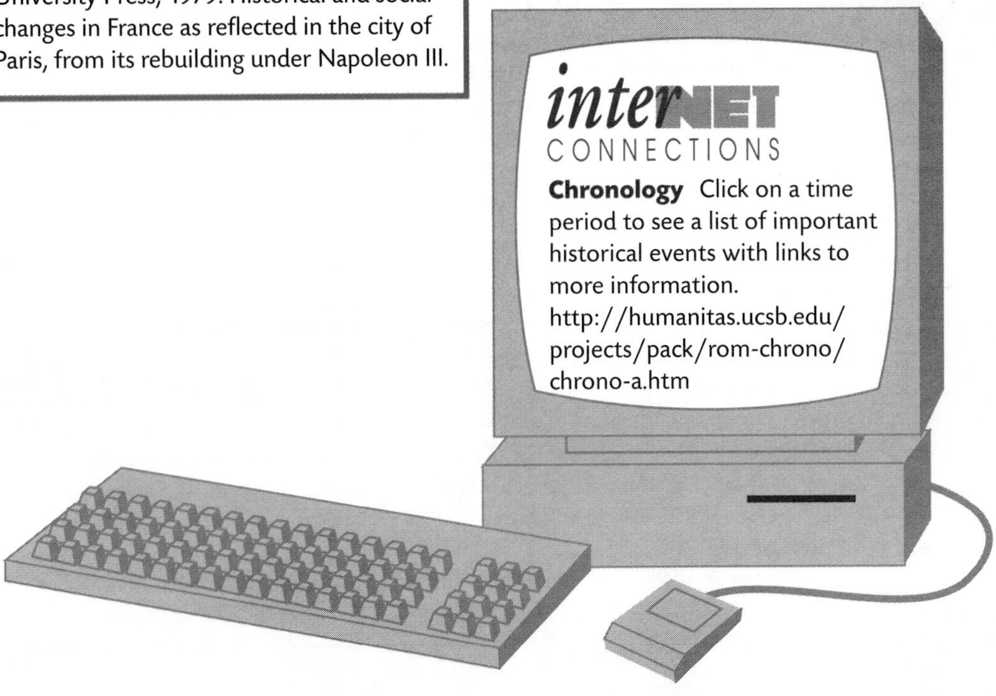
interNET
CONNECTIONS
Chronology Click on a time period to see a list of important historical events with links to more information.
http://humanitas.ucsb.edu/projects/pack/rom-chrono/chrono-a.htm

Introducing Chapter 22

CHAPTER THEMES

Chapter Themes are listed by section on this chapter opening page of the Student Edition. A corresponding theme-based activity is available under "TEACH," and a theme-based question is asked in the Section and Chapter Reviews.

The Storyteller

Historical Setting Marie-Victoire Monnard was one of 15 children in her family. She was also one of thousands of young women who sewed hats and dresses in workshops throughout Paris. Like many of them, she lived in a dormitory for seamstresses.

Monnard is writing during a phase of the French Revolution called the Reign of Terror. From September 1793 to July 1794, revolutionaries declared a policy of terror against anyone who publicly disagreed with their policies. In time, hundreds of thousands of suspects filled French jails, and revolutionary courts handed down more than 17,000 death sentences.

Historical Significance

Answers: *Waves of violence and bloodshed swept across France during the revolution. In time, people became desensitized to the cruelties.*

The French Revolution destroyed the entire structure of royal absolutism and ended the social order based on aristocratic privilege. It set the stage for democratic movements around the world during the next century.

Chapter 22

1700–1830

The French Revolution

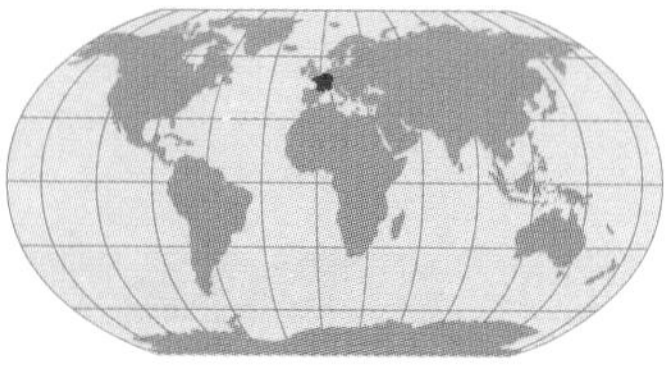

Chapter Themes

- **Revolution** The French overthrow their absolute monarchy. *Section 1*
- **Change** The National Assembly establishes a constitutional government. *Section 2*
- **Conflict** The new French Republic faces enemies at home and abroad. *Section 3*
- **Movement** Napoleon becomes France's emperor and conquers much of Europe. *Section 4*
- **Reaction** European leaders try to reestablish the old order. *Section 5*

The Storyteller

In 1792 the violence of the French Revolution filled the streets of Paris, where a young seamstress named Marie-Victoire Monnard lived and worked. Walking back to her workshop one afternoon, Marie-Victoire saw six large carts coming toward her. The 13-year-old girl later wrote in her diary, "The carts were full of men and women who had just been slaughtered … legs and arms and heads nodded and dangled on either side of the carts."

The next year she wrote again about the carts, "People just went on working in the shops when they passed by, often not even bothering to raise their heads to watch or to turn their backs to avoid the grisly sight."

Historical Significance

What happened during the French Revolution that allowed people to become accustomed to the bloodied bodies? How did the French Revolution alter society in Europe? What lasting effects did it have on the rest of the world?

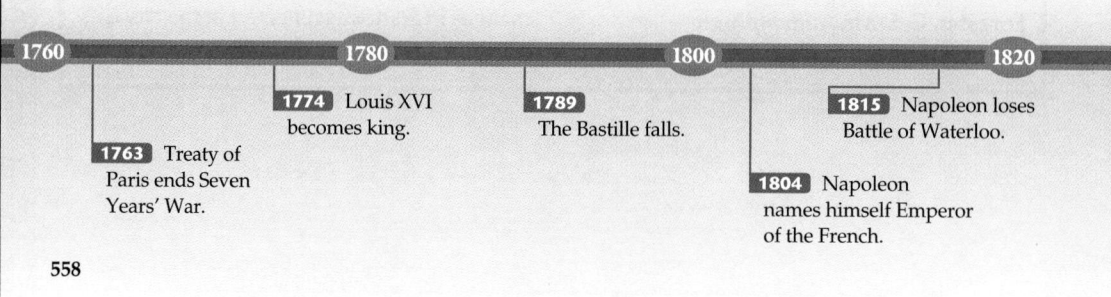

1760 | 1780 | 1800 | 1820

1763 Treaty of Paris ends Seven Years' War.

1774 Louis XVI becomes king.

1789 The Bastille falls.

1804 Napoleon names himself Emperor of the French.

1815 Napoleon loses Battle of Waterloo.

558

GEOGRAPHY CONNECTION

Location Have students locate France, England, Spain, the Netherlands, and their capitals on a map in the Atlas of their textbook. What is the distance from Paris to each of these capitals? Have students compare these distances to those between Washington, D.C., and Cleveland, Ohio; and New York City and Dallas, Texas. How did geography affect relations among these nations in Europe? *(Because the nations were so close together, anything that one nation did affected its neighbors. National rivalries were intense.)* **L2**

History & Art *Assault on the Bastille,* (artist unknown)
Musée National du Chateau de Versailles, Versailles, France

Your History Journal

Imagine living through the tumultuous events of the French Revolution. Choose a point of view represented by one of the following: a Catholic bishop, a landed aristocrat, a wealthy merchant, a poor artisan, or a peasant. From your chosen viewpoint, describe your reactions to three major events of the times as you read the chapter.

EXTRA CREDIT PROJECT

Report Interesting events and first-person accounts of the French Revolution are available in many books. Have students research and report to the class on an event of the French Revolution that is not detailed in the chapter. Suggest that students use vivid quotations from the first-person accounts. **L1**

Introducing Chapter 22

History & Art On July 14, 1789, an angry mob stormed the Bastille, a Paris prison. Bastille Day is a national holiday in France, much like July 4th in the United States, because the revolt that followed overthrew the French monarchy. What evidence of violence does the painting contain? *(The mob has weapons, there are bodies on the ground, and there is smoke in the air.)*

Performance Assessment

Refer to the activity on page 558C of the Planning Guide.

For an additional activity, refer to Activity 22 in the *Performance Assessment Strategies and Activities* booklet.

Using Your History Journal

Journal entries may be in diary form. Have students keep a diary of their reactions to various events of the French Revolution.

GLENCOE TECHNOLOGY

VIDEODISC
Use MindJogger to preview chapter content.

MindJogger Videoquiz
Chapter 22
Disc 3 Side B

Also available in VHS.

Chapter 22 Section 1

SECTION THEME

▶ **Revolution** The French overthrow their absolute monarchy.

Find Out

Answer: *The great inequalities led to resentment among the people.*

FOCUS

Section Objective

Explain how France's class structure contributed to the French Revolution.

BELLRINGER Motivational Activity

Before taking roll at the beginning of the class period, project Section Focus Transparency 22-1 and have students answer the activity questions. Discuss students' responses.

This activity is also available as a blackline master.

Vocabulary Pre-check

Use Vocabulary Activity 22 to introduce vocabulary terms.
L1 LEP

1770 — 1780 — 1790 — 1800

1774 Louis XVI becomes king of France.

1786 Banks refuse to lend money to the government.

1789 Great Fear breaks out.

Section 1

The Old Order

Setting the Scene

▶ **Terms to Define**
estate, tithe, bourgeoisie

▶ **People to Meet**
Louis XVI, Marie Antoinette

▶ **Places to Locate**
Versailles, Paris, the Bastille

Find Out How did France's class structure contribute to the French Revolution?

The Storyteller

Fear tightened young Claudette Leroux's throat as she waited for the questioning. She could not deny that she was smuggling salt. She could only explain that the gabelle—the tax on salt—made the cost ten times what it should be. French peasants simply could not afford the Farmers General's prices. She wondered who gave these corrupt officials the power to store, inspect, tax, register, and force people to buy their salt. Did anyone understand the peasants' plight?

—adapted from *Citizens: A Chronicle of the French Revolution*, Simon Schama, 1989

Peasant woman's burden

At its height, the absolute monarchy in France controlled the richest and possibly the most powerful state in Europe. The French aristocracy set European trends in literature, clothing, art, and ideas for change. Yet the majority of the people did not share the wealth or privileges of the aristocracy. Working men and women who had few rights yearned for a better way of life. The success of the American Revolution fueled their desire for change.

French Society Divided

The source of the unhappiness lay within France's class system, which fostered great inequalities among the French people. All French people belonged to one of three **estates**, or orders of society. The estates determined a person's legal rights and status. The Catholic clergy formed the First Estate. The nobility formed the Second Estate. Everyone else, 97 percent of the French people, made up the Third Estate.

Members of the Third Estate deeply resented the privileges that members of the First and Second Estates enjoyed. For example, neither the First Estate nor the Second Estate was required to pay taxes. The nobility received high positions in the Church, in the government, and in the army, and they could also hunt and carry swords. Third Estate members enjoyed none of these social and political privileges. No matter how successful and well-educated Third Estate members became, they were always excluded from the First and Second Estates—simply because of the families into which they were born.

The First Estate

The First Estate consisted of Roman Catholic clergy and made up about 1 percent of the population. The First Estate comprised two groups: the higher clergy and the lower clergy.

SECTION RESOURCES

Reproducible Masters
- Reproducible Lesson Plan 22-1
- Vocabulary Activity 22
- Guided Reading Activity 22-1
- Time Line Activity 22
- People in World History Profile 41
- Section Quiz 22-1

Transparencies
- Section Focus Transparency 22-1
- Chapter Transparency 22

Multimedia
- Student Self-Test and Review Software
- Testmaker
- Turning Points in World History: *French Revolution*

560 Chapter 22 *The French Revolution*

History & Art *The City and Port of Tolone* (Toulon) by Joseph Vernet. The Louvre, Paris, France **The bourgeoisie in French cities enjoyed wealth and leisure, but few political rights.** *Where had they learned about freedom and social justice?*

Bishops and abbots, noblemen by birth, made up the higher clergy. These powerful men controlled between 5 and 10 percent of the land in France and enjoyed many privileges. At their disposal were the revenues from their land as well as a tithe, or a 10 percent tax on income, from each church member. Although this money was used to support schools, aid poor people, and maintain church property, it also paid for the grand lifestyles the higher clergy enjoyed, often at the expense of their religious duties.

The lower clergy, made up of parish priests, came from poorer backgrounds and were socially more a part of the Third Estate. Many lower clergy members who carried out religious duties, ran schools, and cared for the poor resented the luxurious lifestyles of the higher clergy.

The Second Estate

The nobility, the Second Estate, formed about 2 percent of the population and owned about 25 percent of the land in France. Like the upper clergy, the members of the Second Estate enjoyed many privileges and lived in great style.

The nobility held high posts in the government and the military. Some resided in the palace at **Versailles**. Others lived in lavish homes on inherited land, some of which they rented to peasants to farm. The Second Estate's main income came from the feudal dues they collected from the peasants who lived on and worked their land.

The Third Estate

The Third Estate made up the largest social group in France during the late 1700s. Peasants and artisans, as well as members of the bourgeoisie (BURZH•WAH•ZEE), or middle class, belonged to the Third Estate. Yet they had very few political rights or privileges.

The doctors, lawyers, merchants, and business managers of the bourgeoisie generally lived in the towns and cities. Educated and well-to-do, they had read Enlightenment works and believed in freedom and social justice.

Other members of the Third Estate, such as thousands of poor artisans and their families, also lived in the cities. Artisans worked for low wages and in poor working conditions. Many lived in the slums of **Paris**.

The peasants, the Third Estate's largest group, lived in rural areas. Although they owned 40 percent of the land, they were very poor because of the payments they had to make to the other estates. These payments included a tithe to the clergy; feudal dues, fees, and fines to the nobles; and a taille, or land tax, to the king. Although members of the Third Estate worked hard, they had no voice in the government.

Growing Unrest

Unhappy with this unfair social structure, the people of the Third Estate began to call for change. An Englishman traveling in France saw this growing unrest reflected in a conversation he had with a peasant woman:

> "Walking up a long hill … I was joined by a poor woman who complained of the times, and that it was a sad country; … she said her husband had but a morsel of land, one cow, and a poor little horse, yet they had [42 lbs.] of wheat and three chickens to pay as rent to one [lord], and [4 lbs.] of oats, one chicken and 1s. [shilling] to pay to another, besides very heavy tailles and other taxes."
>
> —Arthur Young, from *Travels,* 1789

TEACH

Guided Practice

THEME Revolution

Ask students to brainstorm definitions of the term *revolution.* When are people justified in choosing revolution as a solution to political problems? **L1**

History & Art Toulon, on the southeast coast of France, is the principal site of modern-day France's Mediterranean fleet.
Answer to Caption: *They had read Enlightenment works.*

ABC NEWS INTERACTIVE™

VIDEODISC
Turning Points in World History

Side One
Chapter 11

Title: *French Revolution*
Ask: Why was 1789 considered "the best of times" for some and "the worst of times" for others in France? *(It was the best of times for the clergy and nobility because they had power and privileges while paying no taxes. It was the worst of times for peasants who went hungry and paid high taxes.)*

Religion Ask students to define the phrase "separation of church and state." *(Religions do not have a formal say in government decisions, and the government has no control over religions.)* Then discuss the relationship between church and state in France and its results. **L3**

COOPERATIVE LEARNING ACTIVITY

Debate Explain that the French government faced heavy debt in 1789. To pay the debt, the king wanted to increase taxes. The clergy and nobility had been exempt from taxation. Would they accept some of the burden now? Organize students into three groups, representing the First, Second, and Third Estates. Each group should prepare a statement and choose a person to present its position on taxation. Allow time for discussion, then vote on each proposal for tax apportionment. Each estate receives one vote. Members of each estate must arrive at a consensus before voting. **L3**

Chapter 22
Section 1

Chapter Transparency 22

Independent Practice

Guided Reading Activity 22-1 **L1**

Time Line Activity 22

People in World History Profile 41

The Bastille Have students research the history of the Bastille—when it was built and some of the famous people imprisoned there. (Built between 1369 and 1383 by Charles V to defend Paris from the English; people imprisoned included the Man in the Iron Mask, a prisoner of Louis XIV and thought by some to be his illegitimate son.) **L2**

Who?What?Where?When?

French aid to the American Revolution represented a large portion of the French government's debt in 1788. Between 1776 and 1781, France lent the American government almost 19 million livres, or about $6 million.

Linking Past and Present

Tricolor The French revolutionaries established the red, white, and blue flag, called the tricolor, that France continues to use today.

As a growing population put increasing demands on resources, and the cost of living in France increased, the peasants' anger rose. Nobles also charged the peasants higher fees for the use of such equipment as mills and wine presses.

At the same time, artisans in the cities faced higher prices while their wages stayed the same. Members of the bourgeoisie also wanted change. Although they were prosperous, they wanted more political power. Nobles, too, were unhappy. They resented the king's absolute power and wanted to increase their political influence in the government.

A growing financial crisis in government only added to the country's problems. The 1700s had begun with debts from the wars waged by Louis XIV. The extravagant court of Louis XV had further enlarged this debt.

In 1774 Louis XV's 19-year-old grandson followed his grandfather to the throne as **Louis XVI**. His wife, **Marie Antoinette**, was a year younger. In spite of his inexperience, the young king recognized the growing financial crisis. Supporting the American Revolution had only increased his debt. After initiating government cost-cutting measures, Louis decided that he had no choice but to begin taxing the nobility and the clergy. Both groups, however, refused to be taxed.

By 1786 banks began to refuse to lend money to the ailing government. The economy suffered a further blow when crop failures caused bread shortages in 1788 and 1789. When the privileged classes refused to aid the government, Louis made a bold choice. He summoned the Estates-General to meet in May 1789 in Versailles. Only in this way could he get additional taxes.

Calling the Estates Together

The Estates-General, which had not met since 1614, was made up of delegates representing each estate. The king hoped that the gathering would agree to new taxes on the First and Second Estates. The nobles, however, intended to use the Estates-General to protect their privileges, weaken royal power, and gain control of the government. Because each estate in the Estates-General had a single vote, the nobles hoped that the First and Second Estates together could easily dominate the Third Estate.

Members of the Third Estate refused this plan. Claiming that they had more right to represent the nation than either the clergy or the nobles, Third Estate delegates called for a meeting of the three estates, with each delegate voting as an individual. The Third Estate was almost as large as the other two combined, and several reform-minded nobles and clergymen supported their views. A mass meeting would give the Third Estate a majority vote. A clergy member who supported the Third Estate, the Abbé Sieyès (see•AY•YEHS), wrote:

> "Therefore, what is the Third Estate? Everything; but an everything shackled and oppressed. What would it be without the privileged order? Everything, but an everything free and flourishing. Nothing can succeed without it, everything would be infinitely better without the others."

The king, however, insisted that the estates meet separately. Refusing the king's demands, the representatives of the Third Estate, most of whom were members of the bourgeoisie, were eventually locked out of the Estates-General. They named themselves the National Assembly and gathered at a nearby indoor tennis court with deputies from the other estates who supported their cause. Here the representatives took an oath, known as the Tennis Court Oath, promising not to disband until they had written a constitution for France.

The king recognized the danger of letting the Third Estate alone draw up a constitution. He ordered the first two estates to join the Third Estate in the National Assembly. Fearing trouble, he also called for troops to concentrate in areas around Paris.

A Call to Revolt

In the National Assembly, delegates loudly voiced their unhappiness with the rigid French social order and the government. While the upper clergy and nobility fought to keep their privileges, some members of the Third Estate called for complete social equality. The spirit of rebellion against the government also spread throughout Paris. Debates raged on streets and in cafes. Some members of the Third Estate even physically attacked people who would not support their cause.

The king only added to the anxiety by gathering more troops at his palace in Versailles. Fearing that he planned to dissolve the National Assembly and halt reforms, the citizens reacted. They focused their action on a Paris prison called **the Bastille** (ba•STEEL).

The Fall of the Bastille

To many French people, the Bastille symbolized the injustices of the monarchy. On July 14, 1789, a huge mob surrounded the Bastille in an attempt to

ASSESS

Check for Understanding
Assign Section 1 Review as homework or as an in-class activity.

Use Student Self-Test and Review Software to review Section 1.

MEETING SPECIAL NEEDS ACTIVITY

Learning Style: Visual/Spatial Encourage students who are strong visual learners to draw pictures of some of the early events of the French Revolution. Drawings might include women protesting the lack of bread, the Tennis Court Oath, the storming of the Bastille, and peasants seizing landlords' property. Then have a group of students arrange the drawings in chronological order along a time line on a bulletin board. **L1 LEP**

History & Art *The Oath of the Tennis Court,* detail from a painting by L.C.A. Couder **The National Assembly, locked out of the meeting hall for three days, resumed their meeting at an indoor tennis court.** *What caused members to fear that the National Assembly would be dissolved by force?*

steal weapons needed to defend the National Assembly. Tensions grew as the angry crowd tried to force its way into the fortress.

Hoping to calm the crowd, the prison commander finally lowered a drawbridge. The mob, however, angrily pressed forward into the main courtyard. Armed with axes, they freed the 7 prisoners held in the Bastille. The soldiers opened fire, and 98 rioters were killed. Several soldiers were also killed as the rioters took over the prison. This outbreak led to the formation of a revolutionary government in Paris.

Violence in the Countryside

The storming of the Bastille released a wave of violence throughout France called the Great Fear. When rumors spread wildly that nobles had hired robbers to kill peasants and seize their property, the peasants armed themselves. No robbers came, but fear fanned the peasants' anxiety into violence. Swearing never again to pay feudal dues, they drove some landlords off their property. Peasants broke into manor houses, robbed granaries, and destroyed feudal records. The first wave of the French Revolution had struck.

SECTION 1 REVIEW

Recall

1. **Define** estate, tithe, bourgeoisie.
2. **Identify** Louis XVI, Marie Antoinette, National Assembly, Tennis Court Oath.
3. **Use** a chart to describe France's class system under the rule of King Louis XVI. What conflicts set the nobility against the members of the Third Estate?

Critical Thinking

4. **Analyzing Information** July 14, Bastille Day, is celebrated in France like an independence day. Why is it an important national event?

Understanding Themes

5. **Revolution** When did events in France become a revolution? Give specific evidence to support your reasoning.

Chapter 22 Section 1

History & Art Some members of the First and Second Estates ioined the Third Estate at the royal indoor tennis court at Versailles. Ask students why they may have decided to do that. *(to show support for the Third Estate or to try to prevent radicals from taking over the National Assembly)*
Answer to Caption: *The king had gathered troops at his palace in Versailles.*

Evaluate

Section Quiz 22-1

Use the Testmaker to create a customized quiz for Section 1.

Reteach

Have students review the groups that made up each of the three estates and the privileges, rights, and responsibilities of each group that led to the revolution.

Enrich

Have students draw a political cartoon depicting a member of the Second Estate responding to Louis XVI's idea of taxing the nobility.

CLOSE

Have students create a flowchart documenting the events in France that led to the storming of the Bastille.

SECTION 1 REVIEW ANSWERS

1. All vocabulary words are defined in the Glossary.
2. Louis XVI, 562; Marie Antoinette, 562; National Assembly, 562; Tennis Court Oath, 562
3. Chart should reflect the rigid and unequally distributed social structure. Conflicts centered on privileges the First and Second Estates enjoyed at the expense of the Third Estate.
4. Bastille Day celebrates the beginning of the revolution that resulted in the overthrow of the monarchy.
5. **REVOLUTION** Possible answer: Events became a revolution with the storming of the Bastille, when the people took violent action against the government.

Chapter 22
Section 2

SECTION THEME

▶ **Change** The National Assembly establishes a constitutional government.

Find Out

Answer: *Reforms included abolition of feudal dues and tithes; taxing of nobles; the opening of government, army, and church offices to all male citizens; the protection of basic civil rights; the confiscation of church lands and government assumption of some church expenses; requirement that parishes elect their own priests; limitation of royal powers; and the establishment of a national legislature whose members would be elected by the people.*

FOCUS

Section Objective

List the political reforms the National Assembly adopted for France.

BELLRINGER
Motivational Activity

Before taking roll at the beginning of the class period, project Section Focus Transparency 22-2 and have students answer the activity questions.

This activity is also available as a blackline master.

Vocabulary Pre-check

Use Vocabulary Activity 22 to introduce terms. **L1 LEP**

1788 — 1790 — 1792 — 1794

1789 National Assembly adopts Declaration of the Rights of Man and of the Citizen.

1791 New French constitution is presented to the people.

1792 France declares war on Austria.

Section 2

Constitutional Government

Setting the Scene

▶ **Terms to Define**
unicameral legislature, émigré

▶ **People to Meet**
Pope Pius VI

Find Out What political reforms did the National Assembly adopt for France?

The Storyteller

Sharp differences of political opinion disrupted the Paris opera. At a performance of Iphigenia *the chorus sang "Let us honor our Queen." Royalists applauded, but the opposing party booed. Lainez, an actor who remarked that "every good Frenchman should love the king and queen," was thrown a laurel wreath. Two days later, the revolutionaries would not let Lainez act until he had trampled that wreath underfoot.*

—adapted from *Blood Sisters, The French Revolution in Women's Memory,* Marilyn Yalom, 1993

French social groups

Violence swept the countryside, while the National Assembly worked to create a new French government. Many delegates wanted the king and a new legislature to rule together. Others, however, supported Louis XVI's belief that he had a God-given right to rule alone. Adding to this tension-filled atmosphere was the refusal of the nobles to give up their privileges. Pitted against the king and nobles, the Third Estate demanded reform.

End of the Old Order

The continuing violence of the Great Fear in the countryside finally convinced the nobles that they could no longer hold back demands for reform. On August 4, 1789, the nobles announced they were ready to give up their privileges. In a session that lasted until 2 A.M., deputies wept and cheered as the National Assembly passed reform after reform, destroying the last remnants of feudalism in France. The reforms included abolition of feudal dues and tithes owed by the peasants. The nobles also agreed to be taxed, and all male citizens could hold government, army, or church office.

The Declaration of Rights

With the old order of estates abolished, the deputies turned to another critical issue—the basic rights due each French citizen. Inspired by the American Declaration of Independence and Constitution, as well as the English Bill of Rights, the National Assembly composed the Declaration of the Rights of Man and of the Citizen in late August 1789. It is in the French Constitution today.

The Declaration of Rights, which incorporated the ideas of Enlightenment writers Locke, Montesquieu, and Rousseau, stated that all people

SECTION RESOURCES

Reproducible Masters
- Reproducible Lesson Plan 22-2
- Vocabulary Activity 22
- Guided Reading Activity 22-2
- Source Reading 22
- Section Quiz 22-2

Transparencies
- Section Focus Transparency 22-2

Multimedia
- Student Self-Test and Review Software
- Testmaker
- Turning Points in World History: *French Revolution*

are equal before the law. It also guaranteed freedom of speech, press, and religion, and protected against arbitrary arrest and punishment.

These principles, however, did not include women. When a group of French women created their own declaration of rights, revolutionary leaders rejected it. They did not believe that women should have equal rights.

March to Versailles

When the king refused to accept the new reforms and the Declaration of Rights, the citizens of Paris feared that he would take action against the National Assembly. The people wanted Louis to move to Paris from his countryside palace in the town of Versailles to show his support for the Assembly.

In October 1789 thousands of women demanding bread marched in the rain to the king's palace in Versailles. Wielding sticks and pitchforks, the angry mob surrounded the palace, shouting for the king and queen. As the cries grew louder and armed guards were not able to hold back the surging crowd, the king declared at last, "My friends, I will go to Paris with my wife and children."

That afternoon, women waving banners and loaves of bread on bayonets surrounded the king's carriage as it drove from Versailles to Paris. In Paris, fervent anti-royalists watched the king, Marie Antoinette, and their two children. A few days later the National Assembly moved to Paris.

A New France

With the king and the National Assembly settled in Paris, government affairs began to move forward again. The delegates could turn their attention to political reforms.

Political Reforms

The National Assembly also faced the practical problem of paying for the government and paying off the national debt. To solve its financial problems and to weaken the power of the Catholic Church, the Assembly decided to confiscate church lands and sell them. In return for the land, the Assembly agreed to assume church expenses such as supporting the clergy and aiding the poor.

In 1790 the Assembly also passed the Civil Constitution of the Clergy, which stated that each parish should elect its own priest. As a result **Pope Pius VI** condemned the revolution. The National Assembly then required clergy to take a loyalty oath; about half of them refused. There were now two Catholic churches in France—one loyal to the government, the other loyal to the pope.

The Constitution of 1791

In 1791 the National Assembly presented a new constitution to the people. The constitution kept the monarchy but limited royal powers. It set up a unicameral legislature, or one-house assembly, whose members were to be chosen by voters.

Visualizing History *Louis XVI Arrested at Varennes* (engraving) **After an attempted escape in June 1791, the royal family was watched closely in Paris.** *Why did revolutionary leaders declare war on Austria?*

Chapter 22 Section 2

TEACH

Guided Practice

THEME Change

Have students create a chart listing changes brought about by the National Assembly in the right-hand column and the corresponding state of affairs before the revolution in the left-hand column. **L1**

Critical Thinking Write the following sentence on the chalkboard: *I am king, and I have the God-given right to rule France. Signed, Louis XVI.* Discuss how this belief influenced events in France. **L2**

ABC NEWS INTERACTIVE™

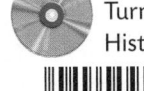

VIDEODISC
Turning Points in World History

Side One
Chapter 11

Title: *French Revolution*
Ask: What American document inspired the "Rights of Man"? *(the Declaration of Independence)*

Visualizing History Louis XVI and his family planned to cross the border into the Austrian Netherlands, northeast of France, and put down the revolution with help from Austrian troops stationed there. Marie Antoinette was from Austria.
Answer to Caption: *They feared Austria would try to reinstate Louis XVI as an absolute monarch.*

COOPERATIVE LEARNING ACTIVITY

Newspaper Have the class work together to plan the front page of *The Revolutionary Times*, a newspaper chronicling the events of the French Revolution through Louis XVI's failed flight to Varennes. After students have read Section 2, organize them into groups and have each group list the stories and visuals they would put on the front page. Students may get ideas for visuals from illustrations in Chapter 22. Groups can decide which event gets the top headline and where the other lead articles and visuals should go. Then, as a class, have groups decide on final placement of stories and visuals. **L2**

Chapter 22
Section 2

Independent Practice

Guided Reading Activity 22-2 **L1**

Source Reading 22

Government Have students research what *left wing* and *right wing* mean in politics today. Then have students write two or three paragraphs in which they define the terms and describe which groups were on the left and on the right in France in 1791. **L3**

ASSESS

Check for Understanding

Assign Section 2 Review as homework or as an in-class activity.

Use Student Self-Test and Review Software to review Section 2.

Evaluate

Section Quiz 22-2

Use the Testmaker to create a customized quiz for Section 2.

Reteach

Have students create a chart on the chalkboard listing the different political groups in France and their goals.

Enrich

Have students prepare speeches that might have been made by women organizing the march to Versailles in 1789. Speeches should include reasons for the march.

CLOSE

Have students name important events in France for each year from 1789 through 1792. Then let them discuss the significance of each event.

AROUND THE WORLD

Revolution in Saint Domingue

August 12, 1791

The French National Assembly, supporting human rights, decided to give the vote to enslaved Africans and people of mixed race in the French colony of Saint Domingue (Haiti). When the planters on the island refused to comply, a major controversy broke out. Enslaved Africans rose in revolt against the plantation owners. Nearly 100,000 of the colony's half million enslaved people participated in the rebellion.

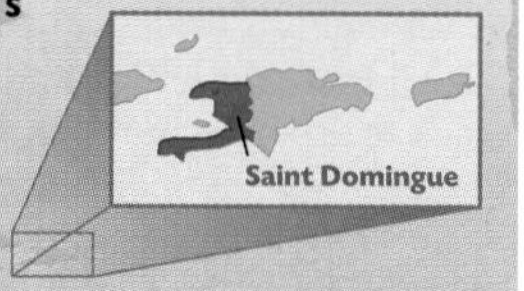

Although equal rights were declared for all, only males who paid a minimum tax could vote.

Many French people were not happy with the Constitution of 1791. For some, the reforms went too far; for others, not far enough. Delegates in the National Assembly were seated according to their political beliefs. The royalists, who supported the king, were seated on the right. Moderates, who favored a limited monarchy, sat in the middle. The radicals, who wanted a republic, sat on the left. Among the radicals were the extremists, who demanded a republic in which all males could vote, whether or not they owned property.

Defending the Revolution

As political groups became more divided, France entered one of the most tumultuous periods in its history. Disagreements led to unrest and violence throughout the country. Many upper-class people feared the breakdown of law and order.

Living in Paris, Louis XVI and Marie Antoinette were aware of the calls for revolution. In June 1791 they decided to flee to Austrian territory, where the French queen's brother was emperor. Disguised as ordinary people, the royal family left Paris in a carriage late at night.

A bystander who recognized the king at a road stop in Varennes, a town east of Paris, foiled the escape plan. Soldiers immediately arrested the royal family, returning them to Paris. A virtual prisoner, Louis reluctantly accepted the limited monarchy established by the National Assembly. The limited monarchy, though, had little chance of success, for the people distrusted the king and were leaning toward a republic.

As news of the revolt against the French monarchy spread to neighboring countries, monarchs in the German states and the Austrian Empire began to worry about the stability of their own governments. French **émigrés** (EH•mih•GRAY), nobles who had fled France, hoped to restore Louis XVI to full power. The émigrés tried to convince the leaders of these governments that their own rule would be threatened unless they smashed the revolution before it spread.

Meanwhile French revolutionary leaders, fearing that Austria would try to reinstate Louis, declared war on Austria in 1792. Austria was soon supported by other monarchies, including Prussia and Sardinia.

War threw France into total upheaval. During the summer of 1792, citizens and troops, frustrated by food shortages caused by the war, attacked the palace where the king and his family were being kept and killed many of the king's guards. The king had fled moments before to the National Assembly for protection. Yet the National Assembly offered him no safety. The radicals suspended the king's powers and voted to imprison the royal family. Then they dissolved the National Assembly. The radicals wanted to replace the limited monarchy established by the National Assembly with a republic. The king and other members of the royal family were clearly in danger.

SECTION 2 REVIEW

Recall

1. **Define** unicameral legislature, émigré.
2. **Identify** the Declaration of the Rights of Man and of the Citizen, Civil Constitution of the Clergy, Pope Pius VI.
3. **List** the reforms the National Assembly made.

Critical Thinking

4. **Analyzing Information** Contrast the views of French moderates and radicals. What type of government did each want?

Understanding Themes

5. **Change** Why were many people unhappy with the Constitution of 1791?

SECTION 2 REVIEW ANSWERS

1. All vocabulary words are defined in the Glossary.
2. Declaration, 564; Civil Constitution, 565; Pope Pius VI, 565
3. abolition of feudal dues and tithes; taxing of the nobles; opening of government, church, and army offices to all male citizens; guarantee of basic civil rights; confiscation of church lands; clergy take a loyalty oath; limitation of royal powers; national legislature elected by the people
4. Moderates favored a limited monarchy; radicals wanted a republic.
5. **CHANGE** Some thought the reforms went too far; others felt they did not go far enough.

566 Chapter 22 *The French Revolution*

1792 — 1794 — 1796 — 1798 — 1800

1793 King Louis XVI is beheaded on the guillotine.

1795 The Directory comes to power in France.

1799 Napoleon helps to overthrow the Directory.

Section 3

Dawn of a New Era

Setting the Scene

- **Terms to Define**
  conscription, coup d'état
- **People to Meet**
  Jacobins, Girondists, Napoleon Bonaparte
- **Places to Locate**
  Prussia, Valmy

Find Out Why did the French Revolution lead to war between France and its neighbors?

The Storyteller

Paul Lemieux was both excited and anxious. At age 16 he had just received a notice that he would be one of the 3,000 young citizens to attend the new School of Mars. The Committee of Public Safety created the new school for learning and public military instruction. He read the Committee's report, "Loyalty to your own families must end when the great family calls you. The Republic leaves to parents the guidance of your first years, but as soon as your intelligence develops, it loudly proclaims the right it has over you. You are born for the Republic and not to be the pride of family despotism or its victims...." Paul wondered how this choice would affect his life.

—from *The Era of the French Revolution, 1789-1799*, Leo Gershoy, 1957

A sans-culottes

In September 1792 the French revolutionary leaders faced the result of their declaration of war on Austria and **Prussia**. Prussian troops had taken the major French fort of Verdun, and the road to Paris was now open for them. As fear gripped the country, Georges-Jacques Danton, a revolutionary orator, exclaimed to the people: "All are burning with a desire to fight! We need boldness ... and France will be saved."

In response to Danton's stirring words, thousands of volunteers came forward to defend the revolution. A week later, thoughts of defeat vanished when the French army won an astonishing victory at **Valmy**, less than 100 miles (161 km) from Paris. After the battle, the French commander wrote in his diary:

> "Our soldiers were badly clothed, they had no straw to sleep on, no blankets, they sometimes went two days without bread. I never once saw them complain.... The tiredness and hardship they have suffered have been rewarded. The enemy has [yielded] to the season, misery, and illness. Its formidable army is in flight, its numbers halved...."
>
> —Commander Dumouriez, 1792

The victory at Valmy boosted the spirits of the revolutionaries. French forces had halted the powerful armies of Europe's monarchs and had saved the revolution for the time being.

Birth of a Republic

As cannons thundered at Valmy, the National Convention met in Paris to create a new government for France. Shouts of "Long live the Nation!" echoed through the chamber as the delegates ended the monarchy and made France a republic.

SECTION THEME

- **Conflict** The new French Republic faces enemies at home and abroad.

Find Out

Answer: *When Europe's monarchies formed an alliance against France's revolutionary government, French leaders responded by forming an army to overthrow royalty and bring people "liberty, equality, and fraternity" all over Europe.*

FOCUS

Section Objective

Explain why the French Revolution led to war between France and its neighbors.

BELLRINGER
Motivational Activity

Before taking roll at the beginning of the class period, project Section Focus Transparency 22-3 and have students answer the activity questions. Discuss students' responses.

This activity is also available as a blackline master.

Vocabulary Pre-check

Use Vocabulary Activity 22 to introduce vocabulary terms. **L1 LEP**

SECTION RESOURCES

Reproducible Masters
- Reproducible Lesson Plan 22-3
- Vocabulary Activity 22
- Guided Reading Activity 22-3
- History Simulation 22
- People in World History Profile 42
- Section Quiz 22-3

Transparencies
- Section Focus Transparency 22-3

Multimedia
- Student Self-Test and Review Software
- Testmaker
- Turning Points in World History: *French Revolution*

TEACH

Guided Practice

THEME **Conflict**

Have students imagine that the classroom is the National Convention. Tell students at the back that they are sitting on high benches. Which groups do you represent? What are the views of these groups? *(sans-culottes and Jacobins; radical)* Tell students at the front that they are Girondists and those in the middle that they are the Plain. Have these two groups explain their views. Then ask students from the front and back to try to persuade the middle to support their points of view on the revolution. **L2**

Literature Write the following quote from the opening of Charles Dickens's *A Tale of Two Cities* on the chalkboard: "It was the best of times, it was the worst of times ..." Discuss how this quote applies to the French Revolution. **L2**

History & Art The Trianon and its gardens, a royal retreat on the grounds at Versailles complete with a theater, lake, river, and village, became a symbol of the excesses of Marie Antoinette. Why did the French people resent the queen's lifestyle? *(She continued her luxurious life while ordinary citizens did not have enough to eat.)*

Answer to Caption: *They began dressing more simply–men wearing long, plain trousers and women wearing long, straight dresses.*

The National Convention met from 1792 to 1795. Its members—who were all male and mostly lawyers, doctors, and other middle-class professionals—passed into law a number of democratic reforms. The Convention wrote France's first democratic constitution. The constitution placed political power in a single national legislature based on universal male suffrage, meaning that every man could vote, whether or not he owned property. Convention members also replaced the monarchy's confusing system of weights and measures with the metric system still used throughout the world today.

The National Convention also adopted a new calendar, naming September 22, 1792—the date of the republic's creation—as the first day of the Year I of Liberty. The year was divided into months with such names as *Nivôse* ("the snowy month"), *Germinal* ("seed time"), and *Thermidor* ("the warm month"). Although this calendar did not last, it and the other democratic reforms expressed the French people's hope that the republic would be the dawn of a new era of freedom.

Death of a King

Before it could forge ahead into the republican era, the Convention had to deal with the legacy of the past. Its first task was to decide Louis XVI's fate. In November 1792 a large iron box holding Louis's secret correspondence with foreign monarchs was found in the royal palace. Although the letters provided little evidence against the former king, the radicals successfully used them to discredit the royal family.

In December 1792 Louis was tried before the Convention and convicted of having "conspired against the liberty of the nation." In January 1793 he was beheaded on the guillotine—a killing machine the revolutionaries had adopted as a humane means of execution. As he faced execution, the king reportedly said:

> "I forgive my enemies; I trust that my death will be for the happiness of my people, but I grieve for France and I fear that she may suffer the anger of the Lord."

Parisian crowds joyously celebrated the king's death. For them, it meant that there was no turning back; the republic would remain.

Toward the Future

In the days that followed, republican enthusiasm swept the country. Parisians were the most fervent. The *sans-culottes*—Paris's shopkeepers, artisans, and workers—saw themselves as heroes and heroines and demanded respect from the upper classes.

Soon even wealthy Parisians addressed each other as "citizen" or "citizeness" rather than "mister" or "madame." They rejected elaborate clothes and powdered wigs in favor of simple styles. Men wore long trousers instead of knee-length breeches (hence the name *sans-culottes*, meaning "without breeches"); women wore long dresses in the style of ancient Rome.

While the nation celebrated the republic, debate over the revolution's future erupted in the Convention. There, supporters of the *sans-culottes* and extreme radicals called the **Jacobins** (JA•kuh•buhns) formed the Mountain, so called because its members sat on high benches at the rear of the hall. Under leaders such as Maximilien Robespierre, Georges-Jacques Danton, and Jean-Paul Marat, the Mountain saw itself as the defender of the revolution and as the voice of the people.

Across the aisle was a group of moderates known as **Girondists** (juh•RAHN•dihsts), because many of them came from the Gironde, a region in southwestern France. The Girondists felt that the revolution had gone far enough and wanted to

History & Art *Marie Antoinette in the Park of Trianon* by Antoine Vestier **Because of her extravagance, the people referred to the queen as "Madame Deficit."** *How did Parisians show their feelings about elaborate clothes?*

COOPERATIVE LEARNING ACTIVITY

Role Play Organize the class into three or four groups and have each group create a television interview program in which ordinary citizens during the French Revolution talk about the times in which they live. Have each group select a television host and individuals to act as guests. The guests could be a shopkeeper, a Jacobin, a Girondist, a *sans-culottes*, a farm woman, a soldier in the French army, and a housewife. The host and students acting as the audience should prepare questions through which the guests reveal important historical developments and how these events affected them. **L2**

Spectrum of Political Opinion

Radical	Liberal	Moderate	Conservative	Reactionary
Favors extreme changes in government policy	Favors some changes in government policy	Open to minor changes in policy	Favors maintaining the status quo	Favors a return to past, traditional policies

Chart Study To the three political groups in the French National Assembly, political scientists today add two—liberal and conservative.
Which group represents those who supported the king in 1791?

protect the wealthy middle class from radical attacks. They organized support to resist the growing strength of the Mountain in Paris.

Seated between these two rivals on the main floor was a group called the Plain. It was made up of undecided deputies who were a majority of the Convention. As the influence of the *sans-culottes* increased during 1793, members of the Plain came to support the Mountain. Together, they helped make the revolution more radical, more open to extreme and violent change.

Spreading the Revolution

Meanwhile, Europe's monarchs viewed events in France with horror. After Louis's execution, they feared democratic revolutions could spread from France and endanger their thrones and their lives. In January 1793 the monarchs of Great Britain, the Netherlands, Spain, and Sardinia joined those of Austria and Prussia in an alliance against the revolutionary government of France.

French Expansion

At the same time, France's leaders were determined to overthrow royalty everywhere. Early in 1793 Danton declared that "the kings in alliance try to frighten us, [but] we hurl at their feet, as a gage of battle, the French king's head." He then called upon French forces to expand France's territories to their natural frontiers: the Alps, the Pyrenees, the Rhine River, and the Mediterranean Sea.

In response to this call, an army made up of volunteers poured outward from France, eager to seize the natural frontiers and to bring "liberty, equality, and fraternity" to Europe's peoples. Although poorly trained, the French forces often caught the enemy off guard and won many battles. The enemy's professional soldiers, however, soon inflicted on the French a string of defeats. In despair, the French commander in chief abandoned his troops and surrendered.

As French forces retreated, the National Convention took steps to repel the foreign invasion. It formed the Committee of Public Safety to direct the entire war effort. In the summer of 1793 the Committee adopted conscription, or the draft, calling up all men between the ages of 18 and 45 for military service. It also called upon the skills and resources of all civilians, both men and women. The Committee turned the conflict into what has been called the world's first "people's war."

The Revolution in Crisis

While waging war, France's revolutionaries had to struggle with problems at home. A fierce civil war raged in western France as royalist peasants revolted against the revolutionaries. They were angered by the drafting of their sons to fight a war they opposed. Mobs in French cities rioted to protest rising food prices and food shortages.

Meanwhile, the government itself was embroiled in a political crisis. The Girondists accused the Jacobins of seeking the favor of the mob. The Jacobins responded by charging that the Girondists were secretly royalists. The Jacobins in the Mountain won control of the Convention and arrested Girondist delegates.

In retaliation Girondist supporters rebelled against the Jacobins in the Convention. During the uprising Charlotte Corday, a loyal Girondist supporter, killed the Jacobin leader Marat and was sent to the guillotine.

Footnotes to History

The Wax Museum
A young Swiss woman living in Paris immortalized the revolution's leaders by making wax models of them. She escaped to London, where she opened a museum—Madame Tussaud's Exhibition—that is open today.

Chapter 22 Section 3

Chart Study

Answer
Conservative

Practice

Reading a Chart Which group held the most political power in France by the summer of 1792? *(the radicals)*

Critical Thinking Ask students to name some of the tactics of the Reign of Terror. *(suspension of rights, neighborhood watch committees)* Then ask them if they can think of any other historical periods when such tactics were used. *(Answers may include Hitler's Germany; Salem, Massachusetts, during the witch trials.)* **L3**

ABCNEWS INTERACTIVE™

VIDEODISC
Turning Points in World History
Side One
Chapter 11

Title: *French Revolution*
Ask: What was the motto for the French Revolution? *("Liberty, Equality, and Fraternity")*

MEETING SPECIAL NEEDS ACTIVITY

Study Strategy Have students work in small groups to outline important events in the French Revolution from September 1792 to October 1799 covered in Section 3. Information in the outline should include dates, people, and places for each event as well as the significance of the event to the revolution as a whole. Let groups share their outlines. **L2**

Chapter 22
Section 3

Independent Practice

Guided Reading Activity 22-3 **L1**

People in World History Profile 42

Time Line Have students create a time line of events in Section 3. Ask students to write a paragraph describing each event and its significance. **L1**

Biography Have students choose a person from the French Revolution and write a short biography of him or her. Tell students to include information from Section 3 as well as from other sources. **L2 LEP**

Global Gourmet

Paris Bread was the mainstay in the diet of the average Parisian in 1789. A typical French worker ate a four-pound loaf a day. Supplying bread for the city's more than 600,000 inhabitants was a major production. It is not surprising that it was often a problem as well. Bread shortages played a significant role in the onset of the French Revolution.

you don't say...

Jacobin was originally used to refer to priests of the Dominican order whose first religious house in Paris was on the Rue St. Jacques. When the radical group made up of Robespierre, Marat, and others met in a former Dominican religious house, the French radicals became known as Jacobins. Today the word is used to refer to people with radical views.

The Reign of Terror

Overwhelmed by enemies at home and abroad, the Jacobins set out to crush all opposition within France. This effort, known as the Reign of Terror, lasted from July 1793 to July 1794.

Crushing Opposition

During the Terror, neighborhood watch committees hunted down suspected traitors and turned them over to the courts. Pressured by mobs, the courts carried out swift trials and handed down harsh sentences. Innocent people often suffered—many of them sentenced because of false statements made by hostile neighbors. Among the victims of the Terror was Marie Antoinette, Louis XVI's wife. Royalty and aristocrats, however, were only a few of those killed. Historians estimate that about 85 percent of the 17,000 people executed were probably commoners—merchants, laborers, and peasants. The Committee of Public Safety ruled France, and Robespierre ruled the committee.

Republic of Virtue

Meanwhile, the Jacobin-controlled Committee of Public Safety went about setting up the "Republic of Virtue." By this the Jacobins meant a democratic republic made up of honest people and good citizens. Because Catholicism was seen as an enemy of the revolution, the Jacobins began a program to do away with Christianity. Churches were closed or turned into "temples of reason." Later this policy was changed to allow worship of a Supreme Being.

Jacobin Struggles

In the spring of 1794 Danton finally decided to call an end to the Terror. Robespierre, however, disagreed and accused Danton of betraying the cause. He had Danton and Danton's followers put to death for disloyalty.

With fanatical zeal Robespierre tried to increase the Terror during the next four months. He had a law passed that gave revolutionary juries the right to convict suspects without hearing evidence or argument.

Images of the Times

Revolutionary Life

Although the causes of the French Revolution had existed for years, the events of 1789 sparked the beginning of the revolution.

After a failed harvest caused bread prices to increase, about 6,000 Parisian women marched on Versailles.

Tri-color badge

570

Images of the Times — Revolutionary Life

The *bonnet rouge* or red liberty cap became a symbol of loyalty to the revolution. The cap came from the head wrap used by enfranchised formerly enslaved Romans. At first, the caps were held high on poles during meetings and ceremonies. Then the Jacobins started wearing them to their meetings. Soon they became the obligatory headgear of all French patriots. Citizens were forced to wear them under pain of beating or death. The king even wore one after the invasion of the Tuileries Palace.

The number of executions increased to about 350 a month. Robespierre's followers—fearing for their lives—had Robespierre arrested and executed on the guillotine. The day after the execution, a Paris newspaper expressed the relief that everyone felt: "We are all throwing ourselves into each other's arms."

End of the Terror

After Robespierre's death, the Jacobins lost power and the Reign of Terror came to an end. A reaction against Jacobin ideas began, and the wealthier middle class took control of the Convention. Even royalists came out of hiding. Fashions changed as people rebelled against the "Republic of Virtue." Once again, people wore knee breeches, luxurious dresses, and wigs. Many Catholic churches reopened. Price controls were relaxed, and prices rose sharply, causing hardship for the poor. Riots broke out, but the leaderless lower classes were easily put down by the army. By mid-1794 many French citizens even favored a restoration of the monarchy.

The Directory

After Robespierre's fall the Convention briefly carried on as France's government. In 1795 it wrote a new constitution. Universal male suffrage was ended; only citizens who owned property could vote. This constitution, in effect, brought the government under the control of the wealthy middle class. The constitution also set up an executive council of five men called directors. The Directory, as the council was called, ruled with a two-house legislature.

Once in power the Directory faced many enemies. Despite the Terror, enough royalists remained to threaten a takeover. Even more alarming was the growing discontent of the radical *sans-culottes*, angered by food shortages and rising prices. During its rule from 1795 to 1799, the Directory used the army to put down uprisings by both groups.

Meanwhile, the Directory made little effort to resolve a growing gap between the rich and the poor people of France. It was having its own problems: the revolutionary government was on the

Symbols of the revolution carried the message of liberty, equality, and fraternity—or death.

REFLECTING ON THE TIMES

1. Why would these images cause European monarchs to react in horror?
2. How might peasants in neighboring European countries react?

571

Cultural Perspectives

Revolutionary Titles Just as the French revolutionaries addressed every person as "Citizen" rather than by titles such as "Sir" or "Madam," the Communists during the Russian Revolution addressed one another as "*Tovarishch*" (meaning "Comrade"). In both cases, the attempt was to show equality of people within a cause. "Comrade" later came to mean a member of the Communist party, not just a citizen of the country.

Who?What?Where?When?

The revolutionary calendar helped secularize revolutionary France by not including Sundays and church feast days. The new calendar contained 12 months, each with 30 days broken into 3 weeks made up of 10 days each. The remaining 5 days of the year were feast days dedicated to the *sans-culottes*. France reverted to the Gregorian calendar on January 1, 1806.

ASSESS

Check for Understanding

Assign Section 3 Review as homework or as an in-class activity.

Use Student Self-Test and Review Software to review Section 3.

Evaluate

Section Quiz 22-3

Use the Testmaker to create a customized quiz for Section 3.

ANSWERS TO REFLECTING ON THE TIMES

1. Seeing citizens rising up in arms against another monarch and willing to die to gain liberty, equality, and fraternity might cause them to worry that these views could spread to their own countries.
2. They might think that they too could rise up against their monarchs.

TEACH

Tell students that the inventor of the guillotine, Dr. Joseph Ignace Guillotin, was a member of the Constituent Assembly and was regarded as a kindly man. Up until the revolution, the punishment of decapitation was viewed as a privilege reserved for nobles. Dr. Guillotin proposed that it be the punishment for anyone accused of a capital crime, regardless of class. He developed his machine to make the process as quick and painless as possible. Point out that people's concepts of "cruel and unusual punishments" have changed over the years. Ask students what they feel constitutes cruel and unusual punishment today.

Linking Past and Present

Guillotine Dr. Guillotin's invention was not the first such machine. Similar decapitating machines had been used in Germany and Italy; in Yorkshire, England; and in Scotland. The guillotine continued to be used in France until 1981, when the French abolished capital punishment.

CURRICULUM CONNECTION

TECHNOLOGY
The Legislative Assembly assigned the guillotine project to a committee that hired a German mechanic to build the machine. To make sure that the new beheading machine worked properly, experiments were conducted on dead bodies at a Paris hospital.

James L. Stanfield

Guillotine

This dreaded machine, pictured here in eerie stillness, embodies the violence and upheaval of the French Revolution. Yet this device used to chop off heads represents not only the terror of the revolution but also its reforms. The guillotine was adopted as a more humane form of capital punishment, a civilized advance over hanging or the executioner's ax. The swift, sharp blade was, according to its French inventor, Dr. Joseph-Ignace Guillotin, "a cool breath on the back of the neck."

A saga of social and political upheaval, the French Revolution transformed the people of France from subjects of an absolute monarch to citizens of a nation. The revolution marked the beginning of the modern age in Europe. "It roused passions," said 19th century French writer Alexis de Tocqueville, that "revolutions had never before excited." In France people still argue over its importance and meaning.

brink of bankruptcy, and the directors were beset by financial and moral scandals in their personal lives. As the Directory appeared more and more inept, French people of all classes looked to the power of the army to save France from ruin.

Napoleon Takes Over

As the Directory faced growing unpopularity at home, the French army won victories in the continuing war with the European monarchies. One of the many able French military leaders who attracted public attention was a young general named **Napoleon Bonaparte**.

Napoleon's Early Fame

During the French Revolution, Napoleon's great military skills won him quick promotion to the rank of general. In 1795, at age 26, he crushed a royalist uprising against the Directory. Napoleon placed his artillery so that he cleared the streets of Paris "with a whiff of grapeshot."

A year later Napoleon married Josephine de Beauharnais, a leader of Paris society. Using Josephine's connections, he won command of the French army that was fighting the Austrians in Italy. Upon arriving, Napoleon improved the soldiers' conditions and mustered their support.

Rapidly moving and massing French forces at weak points on the enemy's line, Napoleon defeated the Austrians. He forced them to sign a peace treaty giving France control over most of northern Italy. Napoleon, France's leading general, was now ready to influence events at home.

Napoleon's Bold Move

In 1799 Napoleon seized his opportunity. For more than a year, he had been fighting the British in Egypt, hoping to cut off Britain's trade with the Middle East and India. Napoleon won victories on land against Egyptian forces. However, the British navy under Admiral Horatio Nelson destroyed the French fleet that was located at a harbor east of Alexandria. French forces were left stranded among the Pyramids. Hearing of the troubled political situation back home, Napoleon abandoned his army in Egypt and returned to France.

Napoleon landed unannounced on the French Mediterranean coast in October 1799. When he entered Paris, he was greeted by cheering crowds. Quickly, Napoleon joined leaders in a coup d'état, or a quick seizure of power, against the Directory.

History & Art *Napoleon Crossing the Great St. Bernard* by Jacques-Louis David. Chateau de Malmaison, Ruiel-Malmaison, France **David's classical style depicts the general larger than life.** *Why was Napoleon able to topple the Directory?*

SECTION 3 REVIEW

Recall

1. **Define** conscription, coup d'état.
2. **Identify** Jacobins, Girondists, Reign of Terror, Napoleon Bonaparte.
3. **Locate** France's "natural frontiers" according to Danton. Why do you think Danton called for France's expansion to its "natural frontiers"?

Critical Thinking

4. **Applying Knowledge** Select a revolutionary leader such as Robespierre and show how he or she succeeded—or failed—in carrying out the ideals of "liberty, equality, and fraternity."

Understanding Themes

5. **Conflict** What conditions led to the Reign of Terror? Why might the French revolutionaries use such violent and drastic measures to advance their cause?

Chapter 22 Section 3

History & Art Napoleon commissioned this painting in 1800. Napoleon spread his image throughout Europe with copies of this portrait and others by David. What might Europeans have thought of Napoleon after seeing this picture? *(Napoleon was tall, strong, masterful, brave, in command.)*

Answer to Caption: *He used his popularity as a military leader to seize political power from a troubled government.*

Reteach

Ask students to explain the relevance of each of the following to the French Revolution: National Convention, death of Louis XVI, Jacobins, Robespierre, Reign of Terror, Directory, Napoleon.

Enrich

Have students explain the political significance of the *sans-culottes'* dress. *(celebration of the common citizen)* Ask students to give modern examples of dress reflecting social change.

CLOSE

Have students summarize the conditions in France that made Napoleon's rise to power possible. List the leading conditions on the chalkboard. *(food shortages, rising prices, growing gap between rich and poor, government financial problems, scandals among the directors)*

SECTION 3 REVIEW ANSWERS

1. All the vocabulary words are defined in the Glossary.
2. Jacobins, 568; Girondists, 568; Reign of Terror, 570; Napoleon Bonaparte, 573
3. the Alps, the Pyrenees, the Rhine River, and the Mediterranean Sea; to increase French lands and to spread revolutionary ideals
4. Answers will vary. Possible answer: Leaders such as Robespierre failed in carrying out the revolutionary ideals because they persecuted many innocent people.
5. **CONFLICT** The Reign of Terror was the outgrowth of the revolutionaries' fears that the revolution would be overthrown. Because they were desperate and the government was in such a chaotic state, the revolutionaries resorted to violence to maintain their power.

Chapter 22 *The French Revolution* 573

Chapter 22 Section 4

SECTION THEME

- **Movement** Napoleon becomes France's emperor and conquers much of Europe.

Find Out

Answer: *He built his empire through military leadership and diplomatic alliances. The empire fell apart when his allies saw him as a threat.*

FOCUS

Section Objective

Relate how Napoleon built and then lost an empire.

BELLRINGER Motivational Activity

Before taking roll at the beginning of the class period, project Section Focus Transparency 22-4 and have students answer the activity questions. Discuss students' responses.

This activity is also available as a blackline master.

Vocabulary Pre-check

Use Vocabulary Activity 22 to introduce vocabulary terms. **L1 LEP**

1800 — 1810 — 1820

1802 France signs Treaty of Amiens with Great Britain.

1804 Napoleon names himself Emperor of the French.

1812 Napoleon invades Russia.

1815 Arthur Wellesley wins Battle of Waterloo.

Section 4

Napoleon's Empire

Setting the Scene

- **Terms to Define**
  dictatorship, plebiscite, nationalism
- **People to Meet**
  Duke of Wellington, Alexander I, Louis XVIII
- **Places to Locate**
  Trafalgar, Moscow, Waterloo

Find Out How did Napoleon build and then lose an empire?

The Storyteller

Carl von Clausewitz, a military theoretician, analyzed the French disaster in Russia: "[Napoleon] had hoped from that centre [Moscow], to influence by opinion [St.]Petersburg and the whole of Russia.... He reached Moscow with 90,000 men, he should have reached it with 200,000. This would have been possible if he had handled his army with more care and forbearance. But these were qualities unknown to him.... It is, moreover, to be considered as a great neglect ... to have made so little preparation as he did for retreat."

—translated from *Campaign of 1812 in Russia,* Carl von Clausewitz, 1835

Napoleon Bonaparte

In 1804 Napoleon named himself Emperor of the French. At the brilliant coronation ceremony in Paris, the people witnessed an astonishing act. Napoleon took the crown from the pope's hands and placed it on his own head. Napoleon's action spoke loudly of his intention to be a strong ruler. How had the French government been transformed from a democracy to an empire in five short years?

The Consulate

After his successful overthrow of the Directory in 1799, Napoleon had proclaimed the new constitution, which theoretically established a republic. The constitution actually set up a **dictatorship**, a government headed by an absolute ruler. The executive branch was a committee of three members, called consuls, who took their title from ancient Rome. Napoleon, however, became First Consul and quickly concentrated power in his own hands.

Restoring Order

Napoleon wanted to bring order to the country. One of his first goals was to restructure the government. Although he tried to keep many of the revolutionary reforms, Napoleon replaced elected local officials with men he appointed himself. He also placed education under the control of the national government, creating technical schools, universities, and secondary schools. The secondary schools, called lycées (lee•SAY), were designed to provide well-educated, patriotic government workers. Although students who attended the lycées came mostly from wealthy families, some poorer students received scholarships. In this way the French schools were a step toward a public school system open to all children.

Napoleon also changed the country's financial system. He created the Bank of France and required that every citizen pay taxes. The collected taxes

SECTION RESOURCES

Reproducible Masters
- Reproducible Lesson Plan 22-4
- Vocabulary Activity 22
- Guided Reading Activity 22-4
- Geography and History Activity 22
- World Art and Music Activity 22
- Section Quiz 22-4

Transparencies
- Section Focus Transparency 22-4
- World History and Art Transparency 29
- Mapping History Overlay Transparency 14

Multimedia
- Student Self-Test and Review Software
- Testmaker

History & Art *The Consecration of Emperor Napoleon I and the Coronation of the Empress Josephine* (detail) by Jacques-Louis David. The Louvre, Paris, France
In imitation of Pepin and Charlemagne, Napoleon seized the crown from Pope Pius VII and placed it on his own head in 1804. A virtual dictator, Napoleon had full support of the people of France. *How had Napoleon earlier made peace with the Catholic Church?*

were deposited in the bank and used by the government to make loans to businesses. These changes gradually brought inflation and high prices under control.

Napoleon's many supporters welcomed his strong government and the peace and order it brought. In 1802 Napoleon named himself Consul for life. This move was overwhelmingly approved by a plebiscite, or popular vote.

The Napoleonic Code

Many historians say that Napoleon made his greatest impact on French law. Old feudal and royal laws were often contradictory and confusing. Napoleon combined these into a unified system. With his knowledge of the Enlightenment, he rewrote the laws to follow principles of natural law.

The Napoleonic Code made French law clear and consistent. Although he put the state above the individual, the new code preserved some revolutionary reforms, such as making all men equal before the law. The code did, however, curtail freedom of speech and press by permitting the censorship of books, plays, and pamphlets. Women, too, found that their rights were curtailed under the Napoleonic Code.

The Church

Napoleon also made peace with the Catholic Church. Realizing that French Catholics had objected to the Civil Constitution of the Clergy, he negotiated an agreement called the Concordat of 1801 with Pope Pius VII. In this agreement Napoleon acknowledged that Catholicism was the religion of the majority of French people but affirmed religious toleration for all. Napoleon did, however, retain the right to name all bishops, who had to swear allegiance to the state. The pope agreed to accept the loss of church lands; in return the state agreed to pay salaries to the Catholic clergy.

Building an Empire

Although Napoleon proved that he was an able administrator, he was more interested in building

TEACH

Guided Practice

THEME Movement
Using the map in their book as a guide, have students identify on a wall map key places in Napoleon's movement through Europe. *(march across the Alps into Italy and Austria, site of Battle of Trafalgar, march into Russia)* **L1 LEP**

History & Art Napoleon's coronation took place in Paris in the cathedral of Notre Dame. Why do you think Napoleon chose to be crowned emperor in a church? *(to show that as emperor he had some control over the Church)*
Answer to Caption: *Napoleon and Pope Pius VII had agreed to the Concordat of 1801.*

Critical Thinking If ever a man has been considered great, it is Napoleon. Historians have traditionally referred to him, like Alexander more than 2,000 years earlier, as Napoleon "the Great." Have students summarize the strengths and accomplishments that earned Napoleon this appellation. Discuss whether, in their opinion, Napoleon was greater than other leaders they have read about. **L3**

- World History and Art Transparency 29, *Napoleon Crossing the Alps*
- Mapping History Overlay Transparency 14, *France and Europe*

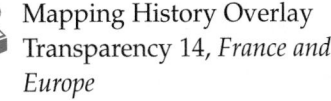

COOPERATIVE LEARNING ACTIVITY

Report Organize the class into groups to research changes Napoleon brought to France and whether these changes are still in effect. Assign each group one of the following topics: restructuring of government, educational system, financial system, legal system (Napoleonic Code), and Concordat of 1801. Have each group present an oral report to the class. Encourage groups to use charts, graphs, and pictures to illustrate their reports. After groups have given their reports, encourage a class discussion about Napoleon's impact on France. **L2**

Chapter 22
Section 4

Independent Practice

Guided Reading Activity 22-4 **L1**

Geography and History Activity 22

World Art and Music Activity 22

Diary Have students write a diary entry or draw an illustration from the viewpoint of a French soldier involved in the march toward Moscow or in the retreat from Russia. **L2 LEP**

Judgment Have students label two columns *Positive* and *Negative* on a sheet of paper. Ask students to list Napoleon's actions, placing them under the appropriate heading. Some actions may be viewed as both positive and negative. *(example: replaced turmoil of revolution with orderly government—positive; put himself at head of a dictatorship —negative)* **L3**

Who?What?Where?When?

Metric System During the revolution French scientists developed the metric system. Before that, France had no uniform system of weights and measures. In 1801 the government made the metric system France's only system of weights and measures. Since then, the metric system has spread to most countries in the world.

an empire. Soon after becoming First Consul, Napoleon commanded the French forces that defeated both Italy and Austria. He also persuaded Russia to withdraw from the war. Though Napoleon was not able to defeat the British navy, the British were ready for peace because their commerce had suffered during the war. The two powers signed the Treaty of Amiens in March 1802.

Over the next few years Napoleon combined his talents as a masterful military leader and brilliant diplomat to build an empire. In 1804 he named himself Emperor of the French and soon set his armies on the road to conquest.

The Battle of Trafalgar

Despite his successes on the continent of Europe, Great Britain remained Napoleon's most tenacious enemy. By 1805 Napoleon felt he was ready to invade Great Britain from the English Channel; his fleet never made it that far, however. In October 1805 at the Battle of **Trafalgar**, off the southern coast of Spain, the British admiral Lord Nelson soundly defeated the French navy, removing once and for all the possibility of a French invasion of Great Britain.

Economic Blockades

After Trafalgar, Napoleon decided to use economic warfare against the British. He believed he could defeat Great Britain by destroying its economic lifeline—trade. In a plan called the Continental System, Napoleon ordered all European nations he had conquered to stop trade with the British. In another decree he forbade British imports entry to the European ports that he controlled. Napoleon also required Russia and Prussia to go along with the blockade of British goods.

Meanwhile, Great Britain responded to the trade blockade with a counterthreat: Any ship on its way to a European port had to stop first at a British port. Napoleon responded that he would seize any ship that did so.

This conflict put the United States and other neutral nations in a difficult position. The United States relied heavily on its trade with both Great Britain and France. If the United States ignored the British threat, American ships would be seized by the British navy. If the United States obeyed the British, the French navy would seize its ships. This conflict on the seas was one of the causes that eventually led to the War of 1812 between the United States and Great Britain.

Despite the blockades, the aggressive British navy did maintain control of the seas, and Napoleon's Continental System failed. French trade suffered, and the French economy worsened. Yet Napoleon's empire kept growing as he continued to win battles on land.

Napoleonic Europe

By 1812 Napoleon controlled most of Europe. France's boundaries now extended to the Russian border. Through successful French military conquests, Napoleon became king of Italy, his brother Joseph became king of Naples and later Spain, and his other brother, Louis, became king of Holland. Napoleon then abolished the Holy Roman Empire and created the Confederation of the Rhine, a loose organization of the German states. This move led Prussia to declare war on France, but the French easily crushed the weak Prussian army.

The people who lived in the countries under Napoleon's rule resented paying taxes to France and sending soldiers to serve in Napoleon's armies. This resentment ignited in the conquered people a feeling of **nationalism**, the yearning for self-rule and restoration of their customs and traditions. Nationalism helped stir revolts against French rule throughout Europe.

The first signs of trouble appeared in Spain. In an attempt to return their king to the throne, Spanish nationalists attacked French soldiers stationed in Spain. In 1812, aided by British troops under the command of Arthur Wellesley (later named **Duke of Wellington**), the Spaniards finally overthrew their hated enemy Napoleon. They reinstated their old king under a system of limited monarchy. Prussia also joined the revolt against Napoleon, as nationalist leaders rebuilt its army and amassed political support in the hope of ridding themselves of French rule.

Downfall of the Empire

When Russia joined the movement against Napoleon, it signaled the end of the empire. Czar **Alexander I** of Russia viewed Napoleon's control of Europe as a threat to Russia. Additionally, Napoleon's Continental System had hurt the Russian economy. In 1811 Alexander withdrew from the Continental System and resumed trade with Great Britain.

The Invasion of Russia

Alexander's withdrawal outraged Napoleon, leading him to invade Russia. Napoleon assembled a massive army of 600,000 soldiers from countries

MEETING SPECIAL NEEDS ACTIVITY

Learning Style: Auditory/Musical Tell students that the composer Beethoven had greatly admired Napoleon, seeing the general as the embodiment of the spirit of the French Revolution. Beethoven originally dedicated his Third Symphony to Napoleon. He retracted the dedication when Napoleon proclaimed himself emperor, renaming the work "Heroic Symphony to celebrate the memory of a great man." It has become known as the *Eroica*. Have students who are strong auditory/musical learners listen to the Third Symphony. Have them select segments that they feel especially express the spirit of Napoleonic or revolutionary France and play these for the rest of the class. **L2 LEP**

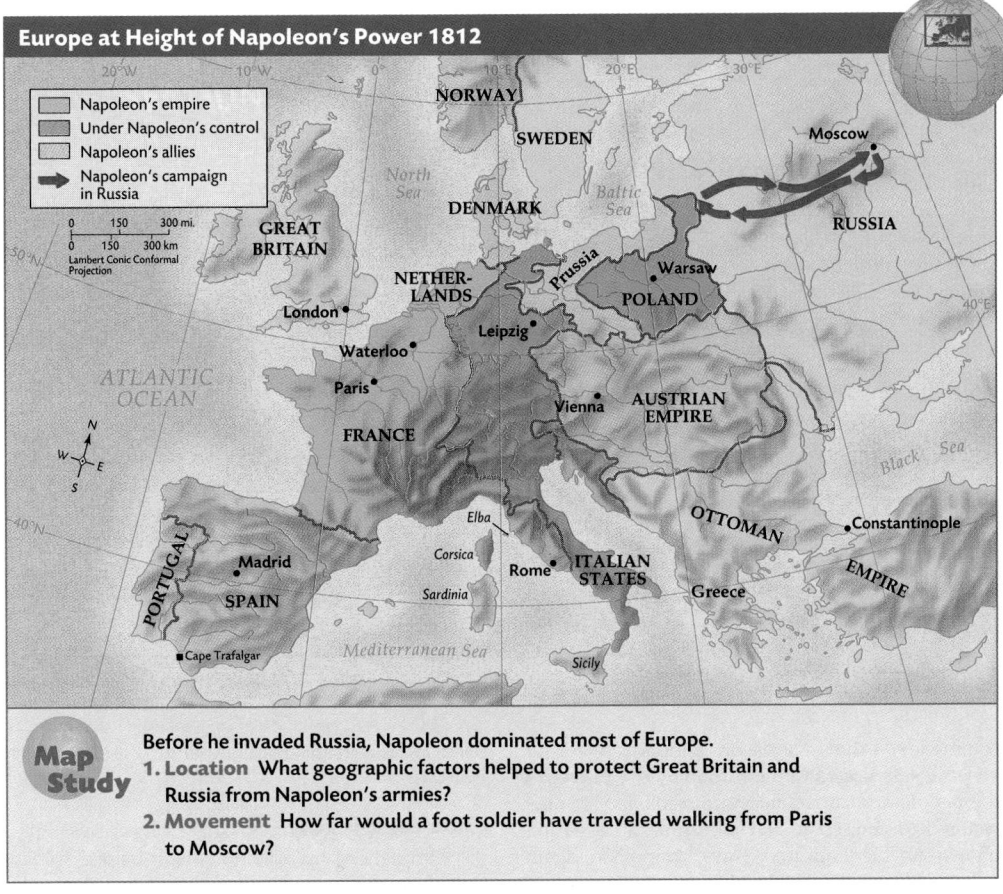

Europe at Height of Napoleon's Power 1812

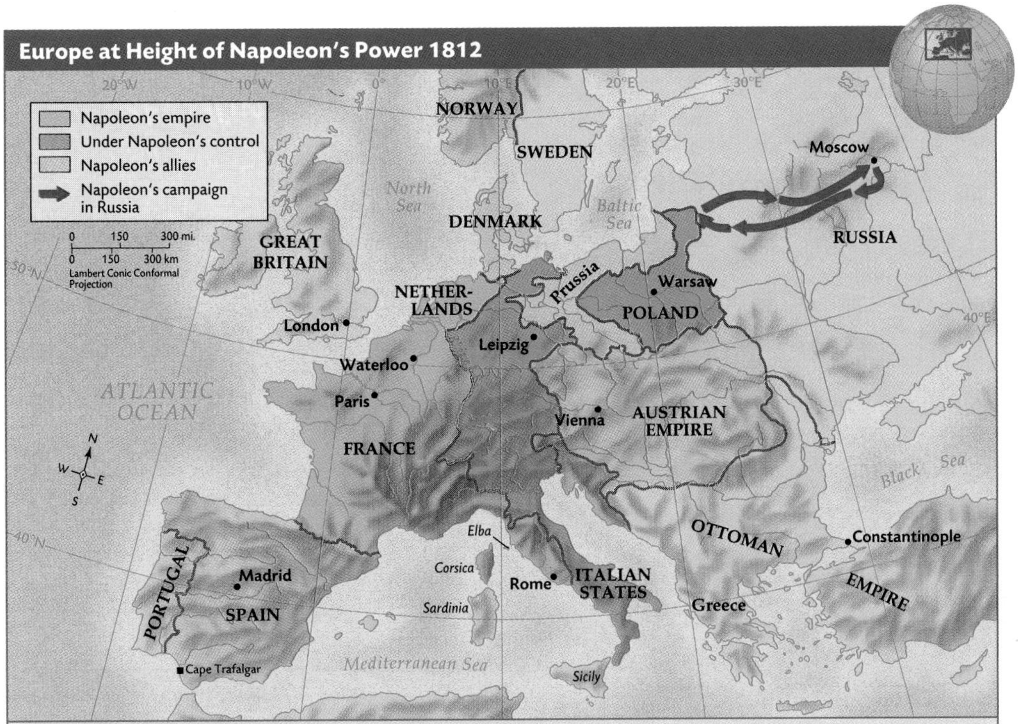

Map Study Before he invaded Russia, Napoleon dominated most of Europe.

1. **Location** What geographic factors helped to protect Great Britain and Russia from Napoleon's armies?
2. **Movement** How far would a foot soldier have traveled walking from Paris to Moscow?

throughout Europe. The long French march toward **Moscow** began in May 1812. The Russians, however, refused to yield to Napoleon's threat. They retreated to central Russia, adopting a "scorched-earth policy" in which they burned everything as they went. On September 14, one of Napoleon's men finally saw the city of Moscow from a nearby hill. But the day after the French entered Moscow, a giant fire, probably started by Russian patriots, destroyed most of the city.

Shortly afterward the harsh Russian winter began to set in, and the French army could not remain in Russia without shelter. Despite the difficult conditions, Napoleon delayed before ordering a retreat. When the French troops finally did withdraw, the Russians relentlessly attacked them. Amid the extreme conditions the retreat became a rout. Five of every six soldiers in Napoleon's army—500,000 men—died in battles or from blizzards.

Defeat

The Russian blow to Napoleon's power ruined him. From all directions his enemies—Russians, Prussians, Spaniards, English, Austrians, Italians—sent armies against Napoleon's forces. Russia and Prussia announced a War of Liberation. Joined by Austria, they defeated Napoleon at Leipzig in Saxony, part of present-day Germany, in October 1813.

By March 1814 the allies were in Paris, forcing Napoleon to surrender and abdicate as emperor. The victors restored the French throne to **Louis XVIII**, a member of the Bourbon family and the brother of Louis XVI. Napoleon was exiled to Elba, an island off the coast of Italy. The boundaries of France were reduced to those of 1792.

Still determined to rule, Napoleon returned to France on March 1, 1815, and easily won widespread popular support. The troops of the restored Bourbon king, Louis XVIII, deserted to their former

Map Study

Answers

1. *Great Britain: the English Channel; Russia: harsh winters*
2. *about 1,700 miles (2,700 kilometers)*

Map Skills Practice

Reading a Map What countries were Napoleon's allies? *(Norway, Denmark, Prussia, Austrian Empire)*

Linking Past and Present

Napoleonic Code France exported the Napoleonic Code to its empire in Europe and its colonies in North America. Today Louisiana, once part of France's lands in America, is the only state with laws still based on the Napoleonic Code.

ASSESS

Check for Understanding

Assign Section 4 Review as homework or as an in-class activity.

Use Student Self-Test and Review Software to review Section 4.

Evaluate

Section Quiz 22-4

Use the Testmaker to create a customized quiz for Section 4.

MAKING CONNECTIONS ACTIVITY

Daily Life During the years of the French Empire, clothing and furniture were made in what became known as the Empire style. Have students prepare an oral report about this style, using reference materials in a local library on the history of fashion and furniture. Encourage them to find out how this style became popular, if it spread to other countries, if it influenced other styles, and if it remained popular in later years. Ask students to make sketches or use pictures showing the Empire style in their reports. **L1 LEP**

CONNECTIONS
The Arts

Music of Revolutions

Claude-Joseph Rouget de Lisle's marching song received the title "The Marseillaise" four months after he wrote it. Troops from Marseilles sang it as they stormed the Tuileries on August 10, 1792.

Answers to Making the Connection

1. *By appealing to people's emotions, music unites them in a common cause.*
2. *Answers will vary but may include high school and college "fight songs" or songs such as "We Are the World."*

Reteach

Have students summarize Napoleon's greatest accomplishments and greatest defeats. *(for example, accomplishments: legal and educational reforms; defeats: defeat at Trafalgar, retreat from Russia)*

Enrich

Have students discuss what Napoleon could have done differently to make his return from Elba a success.

CLOSE

Let students discuss what they consider the most important changes in Europe caused by Napoleon's rule in France.

CONNECTIONS
The Arts

Music of Revolutions

Rouget de Lisle Singing "The Marseillaise" at Dietrich's *by Isidore Pils*

The French Revolution found its voice in a rousing military march written in 1792 by Joseph Rouget de Lisle, a young captain in the army engineers. The march, later known as "The Marseillaise," rallied French citizens by sounding the call to battle:

To arms, citizens!
Form your battalions,
Let us march, let us march!

"The Marseillaise" became the French national anthem in 1795. Because of its revolutionary character, it was banned under the reigns of Napoleon, Louis XVIII, and Napoleon III. It once again became the national anthem in 1879.

The best-known and most enduring song of the American Revolution was "Yankee Doodle." The British had originally used the term "yankee" as an insult. Singing "Yankee Doodle" as they marched, the British showed scorn for the American soldiers. The American colonists, however, turned the insult into a battle cry for freedom.

Revolutionary and protest groups today use music to gain public support. For example, since the 1960s, "We Shall Overcome" has been a unifying force in movements for freedom throughout the world.

MAKING THE CONNECTION

1. How can revolutionary music be used to motivate people?
2. Can you think of cases today where music is used to unite people around a cause?

commander when Napoleon announced, "Your general, summoned to the throne by the prayer of the people and raised upon your shields, is now restored to you; come and join him." In a period known as the Hundred Days, Napoleon again reigned as emperor. To avoid war he announced that France wanted no more territory.

The European governments, however, feared that Napoleon might regain his former strength. Determined to stop him, the armies of Prussia, Great Britain, and the Netherlands advanced toward France under the command of the Duke of Wellington. Napoleon met them at **Waterloo** in the Austrian Netherlands in June 1815; the French troops were decisively defeated. Napoleon was then placed under house arrest on the island of Saint Helena in the South Atlantic. He died there in 1821.

Napoleon's Legacy

Throughout his rule Napoleon helped spread the ideas and reforms of the French Revolution throughout Europe. In the countries that Napoleon conquered, the French established constitutions and enforced the principles of the Napoleonic Code. They also destroyed the remains of feudalism by reforming taxes and agricultural methods.

These reforms helped to modernize the conquered governments, and when Napoleon's empire did eventually collapse, many Europeans wanted to keep the changes that he had introduced—especially the abolition of an absolute monarchy.

SECTION 4 REVIEW

Recall

1. **Define** dictatorship, plebiscite, nationalism.
2. **Identify** the Napoleonic Code, the Continental System, Duke of Wellington, Alexander I, Louis XVIII, Waterloo.
3. **List** three reforms that Napoleon introduced in France.

Critical Thinking

4. **Making Comparisons** Compare Napoleon's rule after the French Revolution to Cromwell's rule after the English Civil War.

Understanding Themes

5. **Movement** How did the principles of the French Revolution spread throughout Europe and contribute to the rise of nationalism?

SECTION 4 REVIEW ANSWERS

1. All vocabulary words are defined in the Glossary.
2. Napoleonic Code, 575; Continental System, 576; Duke of Wellington, 576; Alexander I, 576; Louis XVIII, 577; Waterloo, 578
3. Answers may include placing education under government control, creating a national bank, and establishing the Napoleonic Code.
4. Both were stern military leaders who restored order to countries after a period of political chaos.
5. While emperor, Napoleon helped spread the principles of the French Revolution; however, he also aroused resentment in the peoples he conquered by making them pay taxes to France and provide soldiers for his armies. This resentment, coupled with the inspiration of the new ideals of liberty, led to the development of nationalism.

Social Studies SKILLS

Interpreting Graphs

When you divide a pizza among four people, it is easy to estimate where the circle should be sliced. A circle graph is similar to a round pizza. Circle graphs are useful for showing percentages, such as 25 percent of a pizza. A line or bar graph, however, can be used to show changes over a period of time.

Most graphs also use words to identify or label information. These steps will help you interpret graphs.

- Read the title.
- Read the captions and text.
- Determine the relationships among all sections of the graph.

Learning the Skill

The circle on the right is like a clock. It visually compares the time periods from the following information about revolution and empire in France between 1789 and 1815.

1. **Estates-General and National Assembly**
   May 1789–September 1791
   Limited constitutional monarchy
2. **Legislative Assembly**
   October 1791–September 1792
   New constitution; delegates seated according to political beliefs
3. **National Convention**
   September 1792–October 1795
   King executed; Reign of Terror
4. **Directory**
   October 1795–November 1799
   New constitution with bicameral legislature, five executive directors; Napoleon seizes control
5. **Consulate**
   December 1799–May 1804
   New constitution sets up three consuls; Napoleon rules
6. **Empire**
   May 1804–June 1815
   Napoleon I, emperor until overthrown

Revolution and Empire 1789–1815

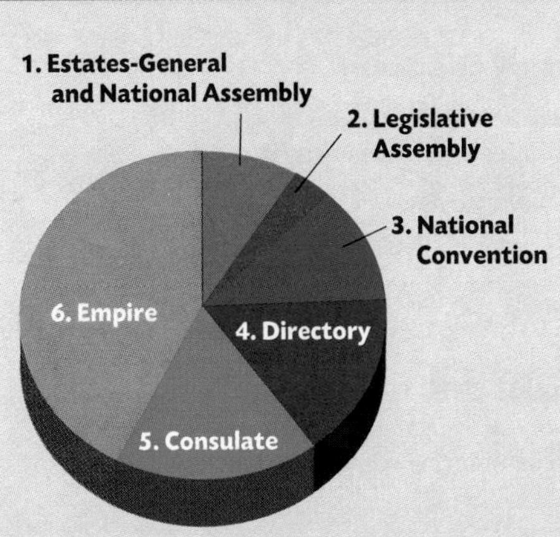

Practicing the Skill

Study the graph and answer the following questions.

1. What was the longest of the six periods of the French Revolution?
2. What was the shortest of the six periods?
3. About what percentage of the total time did Napoleon rule France (during the Consulate and Empire)?
4. About what percentage of the time did the Directory rule?

Applying the Skill

Draw a circle graph showing the major divisions of your day.

For More Practice

Turn to the Skill Practice in the Chapter Review on page 589 for more practice in interpreting graphs.

Social Studies SKILLS

TEACH

Interpreting Graphs Conduct a class survey by counting the number of students who travel to school on foot, by bicycle, on a school bus, by public transportation, or by car. (Have students choose the method they use the most often.) Note the results on the chalkboard and call on volunteers to convert these numbers into percentages. Next, draw a circle on the chalkboard and explain that it represents the whole class, or 100 percent. Divide the circle into sections to represent the percentages of the subgroups. Have students note how the circle illustrates the relationship of the parts to the whole. Then have students read the skill and complete the practice questions.

Additional Practice

Skill Reinforcement Activity 22

Building Skills in Geography Workbook, Unit 2, Lesson 8

ANSWERS TO PRACTICING THE SKILL

1. Empire
2. Legislative Assembly
3. about 66 percent
4. about 15 percent

SECTION THEME

▶ **Reaction** European leaders try to reestablish the old order.

Find Out

Answer: *They were fairly successful, restoring absolute monarchies throughout Europe. However, liberals and nationalists did continue to demonstrate and fight for reforms in several countries.*

FOCUS

Section Objective

Evaluate the success of the plans of the reactionaries to thwart the spread of liberalism in Europe.

BELLRINGER
Motivational Activity

Before taking roll at the beginning of the class period, project Section Focus Transparency 22-5 and have students answer the activity questions. Discuss students' responses.

This activity is also available as a blackline master.

Vocabulary Pre-check

Use the Vocabulary PuzzleMaker to create a puzzle that reinforces the vocabulary terms in this section. **L1**

1810 — 1815 — 1820 — 1825

1814 Congress of Vienna meets.

1819 Carlsbad Decrees impose censorship in Prussia.

1821 Greek nationalists revolt against Turkish rule.

Section 5

Peace in Europe

Setting the Scene

▶ **Terms to Define**
buffer state, reactionary, liberalism

▶ **People to Meet**
Prince Klemens von Metternich

▶ **Places to Locate**
Vienna

Find Out How successful were the plans of the reactionaries to thwart the spread of liberalism in Europe?

The Storyteller

Vienna, native city of Haydn, home of Brahms, and host to Europe's greatest musicians, was known for its opera and its pageantry. The medieval streets of the old city, dominated by the tall Gothic tower of St. Stephen's Cathedral, were once occupied by Napoleon's troops. Now Vienna would host the victorious assembled aristocracies. The czar of Russia, the kings of Prussia, Denmark, Bavaria, and Saxony, and the nobility dined at forty lavish tables in the Hofburg. Colorful military parades, fireworks, balls in the Grand Hall, and Beethoven's concerts all served to disguise the serious discussions that would establish Europe's "balance of power."

—adapted from *Western Civilization, an Urban Perspective*, F. Roy Willis, 1973

The Old University in Vienna

Walking along the streets of **Vienna**, Austria, in the autumn of 1814 were the kings, princes, and diplomats who had gathered for a peace conference known as the Congress of Vienna. With Napoleon in exile, the delegates had come to Vienna to achieve two chief goals: to restore the political balance in Europe and to provide a means of settling disputes among the great powers.

Though nearly every European nation sent representatives, delegations from the great powers of Europe—Great Britain, Prussia, Russia, and Austria—dominated the Congress, which met in September 1814 and lasted nearly eight months.

The Congress of Vienna

Austria's chief minister, **Prince Klemens von Metternich**, served as host to the Congress and presided over it. Metternich believed that in order to establish European stability, Europe should be restored to the way it was before the French Revolution. To achieve his goal, Metternich maintained that settlements reached at Vienna would be guided by three principles: compensation, legitimacy, and balance of power. Compensation meant that all countries should be repaid for the expenses they incurred while fighting the French. By legitimacy, Metternich meant restoring to power the royal families who had ruled before Napoleon. Finally, balance of power meant that no country should ever again dominate continental Europe.

Redrawing the Map

As the victors of the war claimed their rewards, they redrew the map of Europe. France was forced to give up its recently gained territory and to pay a large indemnity, or compensation, to other countries for war damages. Although Great Britain did not gain land in continental Europe, it took from France most of its remaining islands in the West

SECTION RESOURCES

Reproducible Masters
- Reproducible Lesson Plan 22-5
- Guided Reading Activity 22-5
- Reteaching Activity 22
- Enrichment Activity 22
- Section Quiz 22-5
- Performance Assessment Activity 22
- Spanish Chapter Summary 22

Transparencies
- Section Focus Transparency 22-5
- Mapping History Overlay Transparency 14

Multimedia
- Vocabulary PuzzleMaker Software
- Student Self-Test and Review Software
- Testmaker

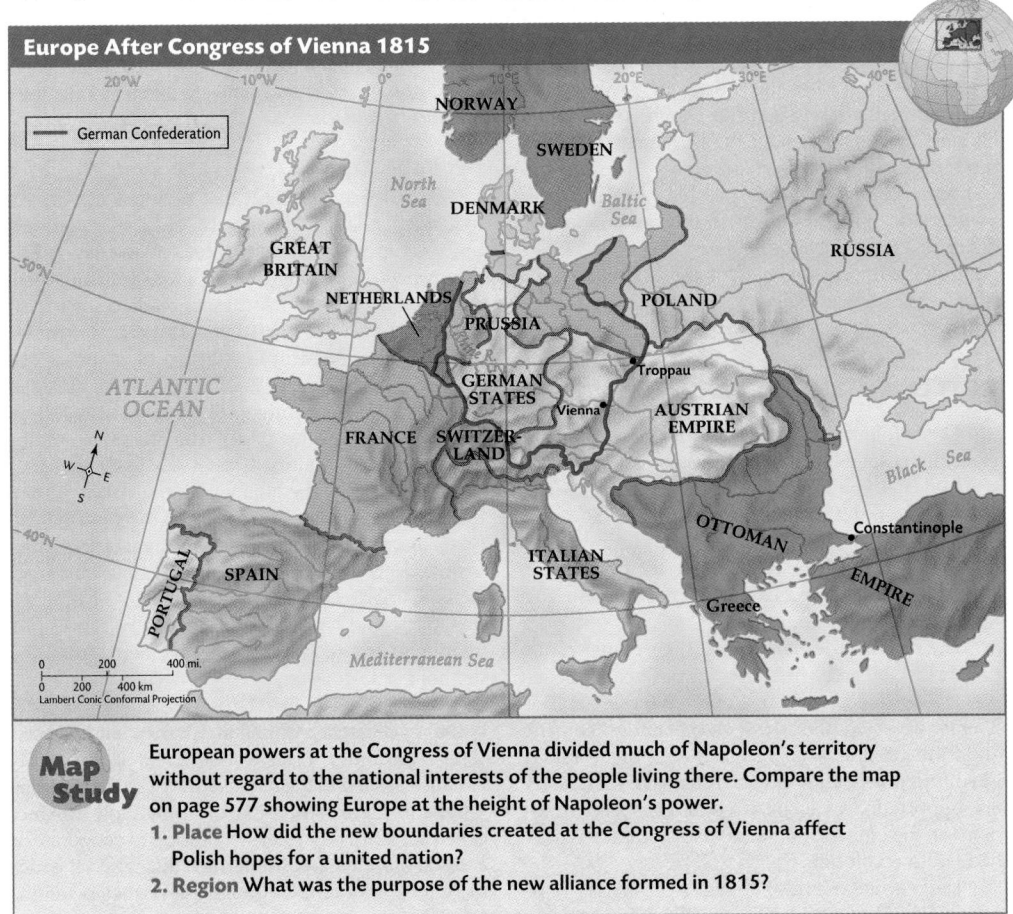

Europe After Congress of Vienna 1815

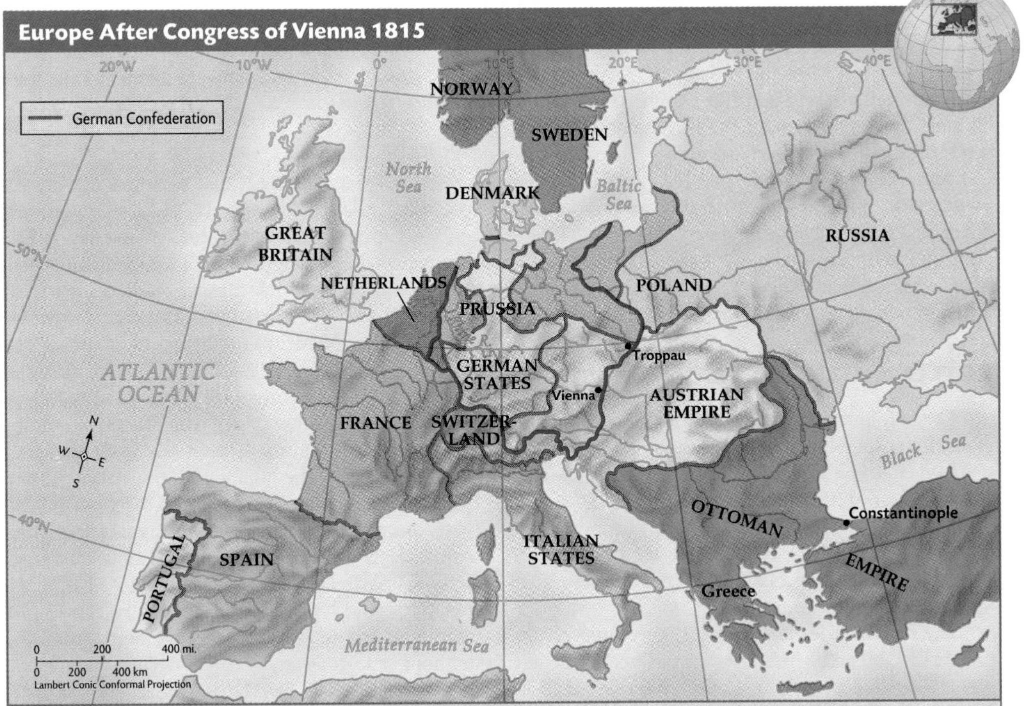

Map Study European powers at the Congress of Vienna divided much of Napoleon's territory without regard to the national interests of the people living there. Compare the map on page 577 showing Europe at the height of Napoleon's power.

1. **Place** How did the new boundaries created at the Congress of Vienna affect Polish hopes for a united nation?
2. **Region** What was the purpose of the new alliance formed in 1815?

Indies. Austria gained the Italian provinces of Lombardy and Venetia as well as territory on the eastern coast of the Adriatic Sea.

At the conference Prussia and Russia also made it known that they wanted to expand their borders by seizing formerly French-held lands. Yet Britain and Austria feared that increased Prussian and Russian influence in central Europe would lead to an imbalance of power on the continent. To put pressure on Prussia and Russia, Great Britain and Austria made an agreement with France. The agreement bound the three powers—Great Britain, Austria, and France—to resist any further Prussian or Russian territorial expansion in Europe by armed force if it was necessary.

In the end a compromise was reached. Prussia received extensive territories along the Rhine River and almost half the kingdom of Saxony for its compensation. Russia received most of the Polish territory formerly held by Prussia and Austria. This increased the Polish territory held by Russia. A new kingdom of Poland was then formed under the czar.

Restoring the Monarchies

Once the territorial compensation was settled, delegates at the Congress of Vienna turned to stabilizing European governments. Believing that divine-right monarchy was necessary for proper order, the delegates made settlements based on legitimate claims to the throne and restored the absolute monarchs who ruled Europe before Napoleon. The Congress reestablished royal dynasties in France, Spain, Portugal, Naples, Sardinia, and Sicily. In France the Congress officially recognized the Bourbon heir Louis XVIII as the legitimate, or legal, ruler.

To safeguard other ruling dynasties, the Congress placed further controls on France. It

TEACH

Guided Practice

THEME **Reaction**

Have students describe reactionary measures taken by the Congress of Vienna to restore Europe to pre-French Revolution status. *(restored absolute monarchies, formed an alliance to keep liberalism and nationalism in check)* **L1**

Map Study

Answers

1. *Poland's hopes were crushed; Polish lands were divided among Russia, Prussia, and Austria.*
2. *to prevent democratic revolutions in Europe*

Map Skills Practice

Reading a Map Compare this map with the map on page 577. Which European states gained French land in 1815? *(the Netherlands, Prussia, German States, and Italian States)*

Geography: Movement Using the map showing Europe after the Congress of Vienna in 1815, have students describe how the map of Europe was redrawn. *(Prussia received territories along the Rhine, almost half of Saxony; Russia received Polish territory formerly held by Prussia and Austria, increased Polish territory held by Russia.)* **L3**

Mapping History Overlay Transparency 14, *France and Europe*

COOPERATIVE LEARNING ACTIVITY

Report Organize the class into three groups. Have one group create a large map of Europe after the Congress of Vienna, using the map in their book as a guide. Have the second group make a wall chart listing countries that participated in the Congress of Vienna, the major leaders who represented each country, and the terms of the Quadruple Alliance. Have the third group make a wall chart listing countries and leaders who reacted against the Congress of Vienna's work and the results of their reactions. Remind students to use library resources when needed. Have groups display their work on a "Congress of Vienna" bulletin-board display. **L2**

Chapter 22 Section 5

Independent Practice

Guided Reading Activity 22-5 **L1**

Foreign Affairs Have students create a chart with three columns titled *Holy Alliance, Quadruple Alliance,* and *Concert of Europe.* In each column, have students write short statements describing the alliance. *(for example: Holy Alliance: by order of Czar Alexander I, called for Christian rulers in Europe to cooperate as a union of monarchs)* **L1**

Essay Have students write a short essay explaining what the Carlsbad Decrees were and why they were instituted. **L3**

Linking Past and Present

Carlsbad Decrees The repressive measures of the 1819 Carlsbad Decrees ended student protests for reform. Students in the 1980s and 1990s also used protests as a way to achieve change. Student protests in China were brutally put down; but in South Africa and Eastern Europe, protests and pressure from other countries helped bring about change.

Visualizing History Parties, balls, and pageantry reminded delegates of what life had been like before the revolution.

Answer to Caption: *to establish peace and stability in Europe*

ASSESS

Check for Understanding

Assign Section 5 Review as homework or as an in-class activity.

reduced French borders to those of 1790 and established **buffer states**, or neutral territories, around French territory. To the north of France, the Austrian Netherlands and the Dutch Netherlands became one country under the Dutch ruler. Thirty-nine independent German states formed the German Confederation, headed by Austria. Switzerland regained its neutrality and independence as a federal league of states. The Italian kingdom of Piedmont united with the Mediterranean island of Sardinia.

Forces Changing Europe

The diplomats responsible for most of the agreements made at the Congress of Vienna were **reactionaries**, people who opposed change and wanted to return things to the way they had been in earlier times. They strongly felt that Europe could maintain peace only by returning to the tradition of strong absolute monarchies in effect before the French Revolution.

The reactionaries hoped that their plans would thwart the spread of **liberalism**, a political philosophy influencing European peoples in the 1800s. The liberals accepted the ideas of the Enlightenment and the democratic reforms of the French Revolution. Believing in individual freedom, liberals supported ideas such as freedom of speech, freedom of the press, and religious freedom—which had led to revolution.

The reactionaries also hoped to crush the rise of nationalism throughout Europe. When they redrew national boundaries, the delegates reflected the wishes of the rulers rather than those of the people they governed. The new boundaries thwarted the nationalistic hopes of many European groups. For example, the boundaries crushed the Polish people's hopes for a united nation of their own. Instead, their land was parceled out among their neighbors: Austria, Prussia, and Russia.

Alliances

The diplomats knew that nationalistic desires for independence, democratic rule, and national unity could well lead to revolution, and revolution threatened everything they believed in. To prevent democratic revolutions, they agreed to form new alliances. Great Britain, Austria, Prussia, and Russia joined in the Quadruple Alliance to maintain the settlements of Vienna. The four powers concluded the alliance in November 1815. France was admitted three years later, when the members of the alliance met for the first time at Aix-la-Chapelle.

According to the alliance agreement, representatives of the great powers were to meet periodically to discuss the security of Europe. Their goals included preservation of territorial boundaries set at the Congress of Vienna, exclusion of Napoleon Bonaparte and his heirs from French rule, and prevention of any revolutionary movements from taking hold in Europe.

With the goals of securing international order based on "Justice, Christian Charity, and Peace," Czar Alexander I of Russia created the Holy Alliance. Issued in the name of the czar, the Prussian king, and the Austrian emperor, the Holy Alliance called for Christian rulers in Europe to cooperate as a union of monarchs. Metternich dismissed the idea as "a loud-sounding nothing." Nevertheless, all the invited rulers joined the Holy Alliance except Pope Pius VII and the British government. The pope had said that "from time immemorial the papacy had been in possession of Christian truth and needed no new interpretation of it." The British government

Visualizing History **The serious work of the Congress of Vienna was nearly overshadowed by lavish entertainment—plays, musicals, and balls.** *What did Metternich want to achieve by a balance of power?*

582

MEETING SPECIAL NEEDS ACTIVITY

Reading Comprehension The principles that guided Metternich at the Congress of Vienna were compensation, legitimacy, and balance of power. Help students find these terms in Section 5. Ask them to explain what Metternich meant by these principles and how he carried them out. Then have students work in pairs to write three original sentences, each using one of these terms. Let students share their sentences. **L1**

excused itself on the grounds that, without approval by Parliament, such an alliance would violate the British constitution.

The Concert of Europe

The two alliances encouraged European nations to work together to preserve the peace. The members decided to have regular meetings to settle international problems. These meetings became known as the Concert of Europe. This system helped to avoid major European conflicts by resolving local problems peaceably.

For nearly 30 years, Metternich used the system set up by the Congress of Vienna to achieve his own political goals: to oppose liberalism and nationalism and to defend absolute monarchies in Europe. His system of beliefs came to be known as the Metternich system.

Metternich's political goals and the Concert of Europe did not go unchallenged, however. In Germany university students demonstrated for liberal reforms and national unity. Alarmed by this revolutionary activity, Metternich persuaded King Frederick William III of Prussia to pass a series of repressive measures in 1819. These so-called Carlsbad Decrees imposed strict censorship on all publications and suppressed freedom of speech. Metternich, with the support of the Prussian king, managed to end student agitation in Germany, but new challenges to the status quo arose in other areas.

Liberal reformers in Spain, for example, forced their monarch to agree to constitutional government in 1820. Metternich pressured members of the Quadruple Alliance to intervene in European countries and their territories to prevent the spread of liberalism. Great Britain, with a tradition of liberalism in government, opposed the action and broke from the alliance. Metternich's system did prevail, however, as French troops restored the Spanish king to full power. But the spirit of revolt did not die, for Spanish colonies in Latin America successfully revolted against Spanish control during the 1820s.

The Greeks also fought for their independence in 1821 when Greek nationalists revolted against Turkish rule. Metternich intervened by attempting to stop other countries from aiding the rebellion. The British and the French provided assistance to the Greek nationalists despite Metternich's threats. Greece finally won independence from the Ottoman Empire in 1829.

The stable political system Metternich envisioned throughout Europe would soon be under attack. The nationalistic spirit fostered by the French Revolution would not die in Europe.

Visualizing History **Metternich pushed for the creation of the Quadruple Alliance.** *What was the alliance's major role?*

SECTION 5 REVIEW

Recall

1. **Define** buffer state, reactionary, liberalism.
2. **Identify** the Congress of Vienna, Prince Klemens von Metternich, Quadruple Alliance.
3. **List** the three guiding principles Metternich used at the Congress of Vienna.

Critical Thinking

4. **Making Comparisons** Compare and contrast the political philosophies of a liberal and a reactionary in the 1800s.

Understanding Themes

5. **Reaction** Why were the countries at the Congress of Vienna mostly represented by reactionaries? What effect did their. views and policies have on the spread of liberalism and nationalism throughout Europe?

Chapter 22 Section 5

Visualizing History Metternich dominated European politics for 30 years after the Congress of Vienna. **Answer to Caption:** *maintaining the settlements made in Vienna*

Use Student Self-Test and Review Software to review Section 5.

Evaluate

Section Quiz 22-5

Use the Testmaker to create a customized quiz for Section 5.

Reteach

Have students summarize how the alliances formed after 1814 contributed to peace in Europe.

Reteaching Activity 22

Enrich

Have students research the effect of Great Britain withdrawing from the Quadruple Alliance.

Enrichment Activity 22

CLOSE

Ask students to make a wall chart summarizing the work of the Congress of Vienna and the Concert of Europe.

SECTION 5 REVIEW ANSWERS

1. All vocabulary words are defined in the Glossary.
2. Congress of Vienna, 580; Prince Klemens von Metternich, 580; Quadruple Alliance, 582
3. compensation, legitimacy, balance of power
4. Liberals accepted the ideas of the Enlightenment and the French Revolution. Reactionaries wanted to reestablish absolute monarchies.
5. **REACTION** Monarchies in the various countries had returned to power. Reactionaries redrew boundaries to reflect the wishes of the rulers rather than the people they governed, thus igniting nationalistic revolts throughout Europe.

Bridge to the Past
Literature

Block Schedule

Team Teaching This excerpt from *Les Misérables* may be presented in a team-teaching context, in conjunction with English or Language Arts.

Les Misérables

Historical Connection

This excerpt from Hugo's novel portrays the social conflicts that wracked France in the 1820s. The bitter argument between the young man and his grandfather reflects the division between monarchists and supporters of the French Republic that persisted long after Napoleon's death.

Background Information

Setting The scene takes place in 1827. Napoleon died in 1821, and the French monarchy has been restored. The spirit of republicanism, here represented by the memory of Marius's father, continues to influence the younger generation.

Characters Monsieur Gillenormand: grandfather of Marius, a bourgeois supporter of the monarchy; Marius: an 18-year-old who is beginning to develop political consciousness.

Plot Marius's grandfather and aunt search his belongings and find a note stating that Napoleon had made Marius's father a baron. When Marius arrives, the grandfather ridicules all republicans as bandits; Marius in turn insults the French monarchy. The scene ends with Gillenormand ordering Marius from his home.

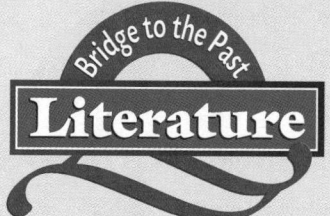

Bridge to the Past
Literature

from Les Misérables

by Victor Hugo

As we have seen, literature can be a bridge to the past, transporting us to a world that may seem strange or obscure at first, but that has much in common with our own. Across the gap between then and now we can see faces that we recognize, situations that are familiar, hopes that we share. The selection that follows was written by one of France's most celebrated writers, Victor Hugo. Hugo lived from 1802 to 1885, a time of dramatic and violent change for France. In this scene, Monsieur Gillenormand snoops through the belongings of his grandson, Marius. Assisting the grandfather is Marius's aunt. Marius's father has recently died.

M. Gillenormand, who had risen early like all the elderly who are in good health, had heard [Marius] come in, and hurried as fast as he could with his old legs, to climb to the top of the stairs where Marius's room was, to give him a kiss, question him while embracing him, and find out something about where he had come from.

But the youth had taken less time to go down than the old man to go up, and when Grandfather Gillenormand went into the garret room, Marius was no longer there.

The bed had not been disturbed, and on it were trustingly laid the coat and the black ribbon.

"I like that better," said M. Gillenormand.

And a moment later he entered the drawing room [room for receiving guests] where Mlle. Gillenormand the elder was already seated, embroidering her carriage wheels.

The entrance was triumphant.

In one hand M. Gillenormand held the coat and in the other the neck ribbon, and cried out, "Victory! We are about to penetrate the mystery! We shall know the end of the mystery, unravel the wanton ways of our rascal! Here we are right to the core of the romance. I have the portrait!"

In fact, a black shagreen box, rather like a medallion, was fastened to the ribbon.

The old man took this box and looked at it for some time without opening it, with that air of desire, delight, and anger, with which a poor,

About the Author

Victor Hugo expressed in his writing his concern for the poor, his belief in democracy, and his desire for social reform. In the mid-1840s, he won election to the French Chamber of Peers, where he advocated public funding of education and the broadening of the voting franchise. After the republican government of France was overthrown, he left the country to live in Belgium and Great Britain. In the middle of his almost twenty-year exile, he published *Les Misérables*. In 1870 he returned to France. By then, he was a successful and well-known writer. When Hugo died, huge throngs of Parisians marched in his funeral procession.

hungry devil sees an excellent dinner pass right under his nose, when it is not for him.

"For it is clearly a portrait. I know all about these things. They are worn tenderly against the heart. What fools they are! Some abominable floozy, probably enough to bring on the shudders! Young people have such bad taste nowadays!"

"Let's see, father," said the old maid.

The box opened by pressing a spring. They found nothing in it but a piece of paper carefully folded.

"More and more predictable," said M. Gillenormand, bursting with laughter. "I know what that is. A love letter!"

"Ah! Then let's read it!" said the aunt.

And she put on her spectacles. They unfolded the paper and read this:

"For my Son.—The emperor made me a baron on the battlefield of Waterloo. Since the Restoration contests this title I have bought with my blood, my son will take it and bear it. I need not say that he will be worthy of it."

The feelings of the father and daughter are beyond description. They felt chilled as by the breath of a death's head [skull]. They did not exchange a word. M. Gillenormand, however, said in a low voice, and as if talking to himself, "It is the handwriting of that bandit."

The aunt examined the paper, turned it over every which way, then put it back in the box.

At that very moment, a little rectangular package wrapped in blue paper fell out of the coat pocket. Mademoiselle Gillenormand picked it up and unwrapped the blue paper. It was Marius's hundred [calling] cards. She passed one of them to M. Gillenormand, who read: *Baron Marius Pontmercy.*

The old man rang. Nicolette [the chambermaid] came. M. Gillenormand took the ribbon, the box, and the coat, threw them all on the floor in the middle of the drawing room, and said:

"Take those things away."

A full hour passed in complete silence. The old man and the old maid sat with their backs turned to one another, and were probably each individually thinking over the same things. At the end of that hour, Aunt Gillenormand said, "Pretty!"

A few minutes later, Marius appeared. He was just coming home. Even before crossing the

Visualizing History **A French salon displays the wealth of the bourgeoisie. With the end of the revolution, the return of social class distinctions accompanied the restoration of the monarchy.** *Why was Monsieur Gillenormand angry about Marius's calling cards?*

Bridge to the Past Literature

Literary Elements Repetition is the use of a word or phrase over and over to achieve some effect. In his tirade against the republicans, the grandfather repeats "I don't know" and "all," revealing that he has strong opinions but little knowledge.

Irony is the use of a word in a way that conveys the opposite of its usual meaning. When Marius's aunt says, "Pretty!" she means that the situation has become unpleasant and uncomfortable.

FOCUS

Point out to students that Gillenormand and Marius still harbor passionate feelings more than a decade after Napoleon's defeat. **By showing that the conflict between monarchists and republicans had not disappeared, what is Hugo saying about the issues at stake in the French Revolution?** *(that they were crucial, life-or-death matters)* **Are there issues or events that arouse such strong emotion today?** *(Answers will vary.)*

Visualizing History The literal meaning of the French word *salon* is "room" or "chamber." Later it came to refer to gatherings of intellectuals.

Answer to Caption: *He probably felt that only the king, not a usurper like Napoleon, had the right to make Marius's father a baron.*

Other Works by Victor Hugo

Cobb, Walter J., trans. ***The Hunchback of Notre Dame.*** New York: New American Library, 1965.

The Works of Victor Hugo. New York: W.J. Black, 1928.

Bridge to the Past

Literature

TEACH

Literary Analysis

Ask students to consider Monsieur Gillenormand's statement that a bourgeois like himself cannot live under the same roof with a baron. **Why is it ironic that Marius would have a higher social position than his grandfather?** *(because Marius and his father are supposedly republicans, not aristocrats)*

Visualizing History In 1848 a wave of rebellions and near-revolutions challenged the old regimes of Europe. In France, the failed popular movement paved the way for the rise of Napoleon III, the nephew of Napoleon Bonaparte, who ruled as emperor from 1852 to 1870.

Answer to Caption: *Gillenormand seems coldhearted.*

Evaluation

To describe the rage that Marius feels when his father is insulted, Hugo compares him to a priest and to a fakir. Discuss with students why Hugo compared Marius to religious figures. Many supporters of the revolution were not religious; Hugo may be implying that their politics had become a religion.

Literary Analysis

Discuss how Hugo builds tension in the final scene in the excerpt. By describing how the grandfather walks across the room, Hugo draws the scene out and involves the reader in the conflict.

World Literature Selection

5

Visualizing History **A republican club meets in Paris in 1848. Victor Hugo's concern for the common people underlies much of his writing. Social commentary and support for democratic movements mark his works in the 1850s and 1860s.** *How does the character of Monsieur Gillenormand portray aristocracy?*

threshold of the drawing room, he saw his grandfather holding one of his cards in his hand; the old man, on seeing him, exclaimed with his crushing air of sneering bourgeois superiority, "Well! Well! Well! Well! Well! So you are a baron now. My compliments. What does this mean?"

Marius blushed slightly, and answered, "It means I am my father's son."

M. Gillenormand stopped laughing, and said harshly, "Your father; I am your father."

"My father," resumed Marius with downcast eyes and stern manner, "was a humble and heroic man, who served the Republic and France gloriously, who was great in the greatest history that men have ever made, who lived a quarter of a century in the camps, under fire by day, and by night in the snow, in the mud, and the rain, who captured colors [flags], who was twenty times wounded, who died forgotten and abandoned, and who had but one fault; that was to have too dearly loved two ingrates [ungrateful persons], his country and me."

This was more than M. Gillenormand could bear. At the word, "Republic," he rose, or rather, sprang to his feet. Every one of the words

Additional Literary Works of the Period

Brontë, Charlotte. ***Jane Eyre.*** New York: Modern Library, 1993. Story of bright, self-possessed young woman of humble origins who falls in love with a troubled, wealthy Englishman.

Dickens, Charles. ***Oliver Twist.*** New York: Penguin, 1966. Novel about a poor English boy struggling to survive in the slums of London.

Stowe, Harriet Beecher. ***Uncle Tom's Cabin.*** New York: Penguin, 1981. Antislavery novel that helped turned Northerners against the institution of slavery.

Swift, Jonathan. ***Gulliver's Travels.*** New York: Oxford, 1977. Biting satire about English society and the human race in general.

586 Chapter 22 *The French Revolution*

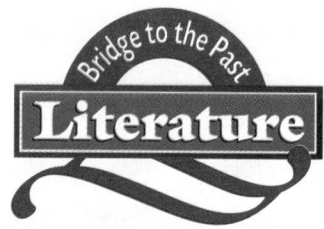

Marius had just spoken, produced on the old royalist's face the effect of a blast from a bellows on a burning coal. From dark he had turned red, from red to purple, and from purple to flaming.

"Marius!" he exclaimed, "abominable child! I don't know what your father was! I don't want to know! I know nothing about him and I don't know him! But what I do know is that there was never anything but miserable wretches among them! That they were all beggars, assassins, thieves, rabble in their red bonnets! I say all of them! I say all of them! I don't know anybody! I say all of them! Do you hear, Marius? Look here, you are as much a baron as my slipper! They were all bandits, those who served Robespierre! All brigands who served Bu-o-na-parté! All traitors who betrayed, betrayed, betrayed! Their legitimate king! All cowards who ran from the Prussians and English at Waterloo! That's what I know. If your father is among them I don't know him, I'm sorry, so much the worse. Your humble servant, sir!"

In turn, it was Marius who now became the coal, and M. Gillenormand the bellows. Marius shuddered in every limb, he had no idea what to do, his head was burning. He was the priest who sees all his wafers thrown to the winds, the fakir [member of a Muslim religious order] seeing a passerby spit on his idol. He could not allow such things to be said before him. But what could he do? His father had just been trodden underfoot and stamped on in his presence, but by whom? By his grandfather. How could he avenge the one without outraging the other? It was impossible for him to insult his grandfather, and it was equally impossible for him not to avenge his father. On one hand a sacred tomb, on the other a white head. For a few moments he felt dizzy and staggering with all this whirlwind in his head; then he raised his eyes, looked straight at his grandfather, and cried in a thundering voice: "Down with the Bourbons, and that great hog Louis XVIII!"

Louis XVIII had been dead for four years; but that made no difference to him.

Scarlet as he was, the old man suddenly turned whiter than his hair. He turned toward a bust of the Duc de Berry that stood on the mantel and bowed to it profoundly with a sort of peculiar majesty. Then he walked twice, slowly and in silence, from the fireplace to the window and from the window to the fireplace, covering the whole length of the room and making the parquet creak as if an image of stone were walking over it. The second time, he bent toward his daughter, who was enduring the shock with the stupor of an aged sheep, and said to her with a smile that was almost calm, "A baron like Monsieur and a bourgeois like myself cannot remain under the same roof."

And all at once straightening up, pallid, trembling, terrible, his forehead swelling with the fearful radiance of anger, he stretched his arm towards Marius and cried out, "Be off!"

Marius left the house.

The next day, M. Gillenormand said to his daughter, "You will send sixty pistoles [old gold coins] every six months to that blood drinker, and never speak of him to me again."

RESPONDING TO LITERATURE

1. What political conflict of the period does the heated clash between Marius and his grandfather represent?
2. What sort of person is Monsieur Gillenormand?
3. If Marius's father had not been a hero at the Battle of Waterloo, do you think Marius still would have become a revolutionary? Explain your answer.
4. **Supporting an Opinion** Was the era of the French Revolution and Napoleon "the greatest history that men have ever made," as Marius claims? Support your answer with evidence.

ANSWERS TO RESPONDING TO LITERATURE

1. Marius was a republican, a supporter of political reform, while his grandfather was a conservative royalist.
2. Answers might include that he is nosy, brash, unprincipled, and insulting, but that he does plan to send money to his grandson after throwing him out.
3. Students may feel that because of his temperament, Marius would be a republican whether or not his father had fought with Napoleon.
4. Answers will vary; students may say that the fact that the revolution dramatically changed not only French but also European history makes this claim justified.

Bridge to the Past

Literature

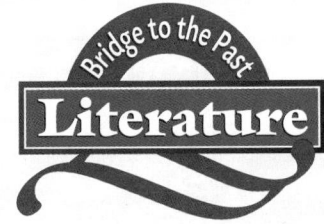

Linking Past and Present

Les Misérables was made into one of the most popular musical plays of the 1990s. Students may be interested in listening to the soundtrack of the play.

ASSESS

Assign **Responding to Literature** questions.

CLOSE

After students have read the excerpt, ask them to discuss the high-handed treatment that Marius receives from his grandfather. **Are conflicts between older and younger people common today? What issues lead to disagreements between them?** *(Answers will vary.)*

Contemporary Connection

The musical *Les Misérables* has been playing on Broadway for more than 10 years. *Les Misérables* has also been made into five movies, including a 1935 version starring Charles Laughton and Fredric March. The universal appeal of its themes has extended for more than 100 years. The themes of Hugo's popular story—conflicting political loyalties and generation gaps—are as applicable today as when the book was published.

Portfolio Project

Write a script for a brief dialogue between a member of the older generation and yourself. The subject could be a political or social issue.

Chapter 22 Review

GLENCOE TECHNOLOGY

VIDEODISC
Use MindJogger to review students' knowledge of the chapter.

MindJogger Videoquiz
Chapter 22
Disc 3 Side B

Also available in VHS.

Answers

Using Key Terms

1. h	6. m
2. j	7. c
3. e	8. k
4. i	9. g
5. b	10. l

Using Your History Journal

Students should consider how the lives of the characters they chose changed as a result of Napoleon's reign. They should also write about Napoleon's effect on France.

Reviewing Facts

1. The First Estate consisted of the Catholic clergy. The nobility formed the Second Estate. The Third Estate consisted of peasants, artisans, bourgeoisie, and everyone else.
2. to destroy the monarchy
3. Answers may include abolition of feudal dues and tithes, taxation of nobles, Declaration of Rights of Man and of the Citizen.
4. The Jacobins wanted to crush all opposition to the revolution within France.
5. meetings of members of the Quadruple Alliance and the Holy Alliance to keep peace in Europe

CHAPTER 22 REVIEW

Historical Significance

Today, the ideals of liberty and equality continue to inspire people around the world. In parts of Africa, China, the Middle East, and Latin America, people of diverse backgrounds struggle for political freedom from oppressive governments.

Many of these struggles have been ignited by feelings of nationalism, as people yearn for self-rule and the return of their traditions. As Napoleon learned in the collapse of his empire, even the strictest military control cannot suppress the power of nationalism.

Using Key Terms

Write the key term that completes each sentence.

a. bourgeoisie	h. liberalism
b. buffer states	i. nationalism
c. conscription	j. plebiscite
d. coup d'état	k. reactionaries
e. émigrés	l. tithe
f. estate	m. unicameral legislature
g. dictatorship	

1. Supporters of the political philosophy of ______ believed in democratic reforms for France.
2. Napoleon Bonaparte's move to become Consul for life was supported by a ______, or popular vote.
3. Many French ______ tried to persuade European leaders to oppose the French Revolution.
4. Intense feelings of ______ caused people to fight for self-rule and a return to their traditional customs.
5. The Congress of Vienna established ______, or neutral areas, around France.
6. In the limited monarchy set up by the Constitution of 1791, a ______ governed the nation.
7. French revolutionaries resorted to ______, or drafting civilians, in their fight against European powers.
8. ______ wanted to return absolute monarchs to Europe after the collapse of Napoleon's empire in 1814.
9. After his successful overthrow of the Directory in 1799, Napoleon established a government based on consuls, but it was a ______ in reality.
10. Before the revolution the Catholic Church in France was supported by a ______, or a 10 percent tax on income.

Using Your History Journal

Napoleon's army lost 500,000 soldiers in the retreat from Russia. Many more died in other battles. Were the reforms of the French Revolution worth its cost? Answer this question from the viewpoint of the character you chose at the beginning of the chapter in an opinion article for a French newspaper to be published upon the death of Napoleon in 1821.

Reviewing Facts

1. **Identify** the groups that formed each of the three estates.
2. **Explain** why the revolutionaries executed King Louis XVI.
3. **List** the three accomplishments of the French National Assembly.
4. **Name** the group responsible for the Reign of Terror and explain what they hoped to gain.
5. **Describe** the Concert of Europe.

Critical Thinking

1. **Apply** How did France's class structure contribute to the French Revolution?
2. **Contrast** How did the ideas of Metternich differ from those of the Enlightenment?
3. **Synthesize** What circumstances, if any, justify a violent revolution? What other means could be used to change an unfair or tyrannical system of government?
4. **Evaluate** In your opinion, did Napoleon's thirst for power help or hurt France?

Critical Thinking

1. Privileges of the First and Second Estates added to the dissatisfaction of the Third Estate.
2. Students may compare Metternich's belief in absolute rule with Montesquieu's belief in republics.
3. Possible answer: suppression of basic rights; work within the system or use of nonviolent protest
4. Possible answer: Napoleon's thirst for power led to France's downfall.

Geography in History

1. about 48°N, about 2°E
2. Poor wheat harvests that made peasants' financial conditions worse and caused bread shortages in cities fueled the discontent.
3. Napoleon wanted to destroy the lifeline of the British economy, which was trade.

CHAPTER 22 REVIEW

Geography in History

1. **Location** Refer to the map below. What is the global address of Paris?
2. **Place** What role did agriculture play in starting the French Revolution?
3. **Movement** Why did Napoleon want to prevent British ships from trading at various European ports?

Western Europe 1789

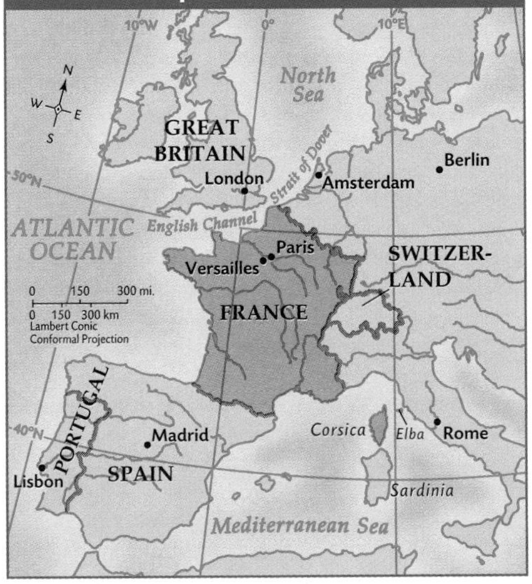

Understanding Themes

1. **Revolution** What similarities and differences do you see between the American and the French Revolutions?
2. **Change** What specific rights did the Declaration of Rights apply to French citizens? Why were these rights not made available to French women?
3. **Conflict** How did violence and fear among the French people contribute to Napoleon's seizure of power?
4. **Movement** How did the desire to expand his European empire help to bring about the downfall of Napoleon?
5. **Reaction** How did the Congress of Vienna show itself to be a strong reaction to revolutionary ideals?

Linking Past and Present

1. Napoleon tried to use military force to unite Europe under his rule. What attempts have been made in this century to forcibly bring Europe or large areas of Europe under one form of government?
2. Unity remains a goal of many Europeans. What recent efforts are peacefully uniting the countries of Europe?

Skill Practice

The diagram below shows the growth of the French army in the early years of the French Revolution. The graph is divided into sizes relative to the additions made to the army between 1791 and 1793. Study the diagram and answer the following questions.

1. How large was the French army in the summer of 1792?
2. How many troops were added to France's army in 1793?
3. What was the total number of French troops called into service during this period?
4. If this information were on a bar graph, the horizontal axis (line) would list the dates. The vertical axis would have labels in units of 100,000 each. What would each bar represent?

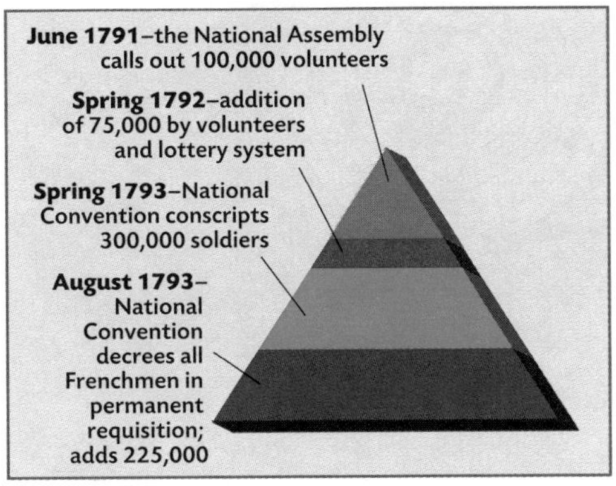

Chapter 22 Review

Linking Past and Present

Answers might mention Hitler's conquest of Europe during World War II and the USSR's control of Eastern Europe after World War II; union of East and West Germany and the European Community.

Skill Practice

1. 175,000 soldiers
2. 300,000 soldiers
3. 700,000 soldiers
4. number of soldiers

Chapter Bonus Test Question

Ask students: Why was the time ripe for revolution in France in 1789? *(Answers will vary but may include the following: widespread knowledge of Enlightenment ideas; example of the successful American Revolution; high national debt plus several poor harvests; seeming indifference of king, queen, and nobles for plight of peasants and workers.)*

Understanding Themes

1. **REVOLUTION** Similarities: People fought for political representation and rights. Differences: Americans did not go through a period of terror or try to spread the revolution to other countries.
2. **CHANGE** All people were equal before the law; freedom of speech, press, religion; freedom from arbitrary arrest and punishment; revolutionary leaders did not think women should have equal rights.
3. **CONFLICT** Napoleon was able to use his popularity and success as a military leader to seize political power.
4. **MOVEMENT** It led to many wars and finally to military defeat.
5. **REACTION** Its actions restored monarchies and built alliances to prevent democratic revolutions.

Unit 5 Digest

The Unit Digest offers a chapter-by-chapter summary that can be used for any of the following teaching purposes:

- ***Preview*** one chapter or an entire unit,
- ***Review*** some or all of the chapters,
- ***Condense*** when specific chapters or units have not been taught, or
- ***Reteach*** chapters that students have studied in the unit.

PREVIEW

Use the Unit 5 Digest Transparencies to preview the highlights of the unit.

Visualizing History In 1590 an English scientist praised Copernicus for overthrowing the "infinite absurdities" of the Ptolemaic system and "by long studye, paynfull practise, and rare invention" devising "a new Theoriick or Model of the world." **Answer to Caption:** *Galileo and Newton*

Unit 5 Digest

From about 1600 to the early 1800s, people in the Western world lived through a time of revolution, or swift and far-reaching change. During this period, Western thinkers laid the foundation of modern science and developed new ideas about society and politics. The two most powerful ideas were democracy—the right of the people to take an active part in government—and nationalism—the right of people who share a common culture to have their own nation. In some areas, people influenced by the new ideas rebelled against monarchs in the hope of creating better societies.

Chapter 20 Scientific Revolution

During the 1500s and 1600s, European thinkers began relying on their own reasoning rather than automatically accepting traditional beliefs. In their investigation of nature, they gradually developed the scientific method. They also developed new instruments, such as the telescope and microscope, to help them in their work. Over time, one discovery or invention led to others, creating an explosion of knowledge known as the Scientific Revolution.

The advance of science transformed the European understanding of the natural world. The work of scientists such as Galileo and Isaac Newton enabled Europeans to view the universe as a huge, orderly machine that worked according to definite laws that could be stated mathematically.

Triumph of Reason

Impressed by scientific findings in the natural world, many European thinkers came to believe that reason could also discover the natural laws governing human behavior. They claimed that once these laws were known, people could use the laws to guide their lives and to improve society. England was an early leader in this effort. There, philosophers such as Thomas Hobbes and John Locke applied scientific reasoning to the study of government. Locke's basic conclusions—that government's authority rested on the people, and that the people had the right to overthrow an unjust government—later were important in the development of democracy in Europe and North America.

During the 1700s Europeans boasted that they had entered an Age of Enlightenment, when the light of reason would free all people from the darkness of ignorance and superstition. They looked to France as the leading center of Enlightenment thought. Through the printed word and at public gatherings, French thinkers called philosophes claimed that science and reason could be used to promote progress in all areas of human life.

SURVEYING CHAPTER 20

1. **Identifying Trends** How did the European view of the natural world change from the 1500s to the early 1800s?
2. **Analyzing Changes** Why did European political thinkers during the Enlightenment stress the importance of natural laws?

Visualizing History **The Copernican model of the universe placed the sun at the center. Ptolemy's second-century model had the sun and the planets revolving around Earth.** *The work of what two scientists enabled Europeans to view the universe as a huge, orderly machine?*

CLASSROOM RESOURCES FOR UNIT 5 DIGEST

Preview
- Unit 5 Digest Transparencies

Review
- Time Line Activities 20, 21, 22
- Student Self-Test and Review Software, Chapters 20, 21, 22
- MindJogger Videoquiz, Chapters 20, 21, 22

Condense
- Chapter Digests Audiocassettes, Chapters 20, 21, 22

Reteach
- Reteaching Activities 20, 21, 22
- Chapter Digests Audiocassettes, Chapters 20, 21, 22
- Turning Points in World History

Chapter 21
English and American Revolutions

While Europe experienced a revolution in science and ideas, its monarchs faced mounting opposition to their methods of rule. The first successful challenge to the power of monarchy came in England. There, during the early 1600s, a bitter quarrel divided the Stuart kings—James I and Charles I—and Parliament.

Monarch and Parliament

The monarchs were determined to impose their absolute rule on the country, while Parliament, under the control of Puritan landowners, wanted to bind royal authority to its will.

During the 1640s, a violent civil war was fought between the supporters of the monarchy and the supporters of Parliament. The conflict finally ended in 1640 with the monarchy's defeat and Charles I's execution—events that shocked the rest of Europe. A republic was then proclaimed under the leading parliamentary general, Oliver Cromwell. Although Cromwell brought reforms and efficient government, most English people grew to resent his strict Puritan rule. Cromwell's death in 1658 was followed two years later by the restoration of the monarchy under Charles II, the son of Charles I.

During Charles II's reign, the monarch and Parliament shared political power in an often uneasy relationship. When Charles died in 1685, his brother, James II, ascended the throne. James, a Roman Catholic, angered the English with his desire to restore Catholicism and absolute monarchy. In 1688 Protestant nobles in Parliament invited Mary, James's Protestant daughter, and William of Orange, her husband and ruler of the Netherlands, to invade England with Dutch troops.

In return for the English throne, William and Mary agreed to accept a Bill of Rights. This document assured the English people basic civil rights and made the monarch subject to the laws of Parliament. During the next 100 years, England developed into a constitutional monarchy. Under this political system, the monarch's powers were gradually reduced, and Parliament became the major power in the government of England.

Visualizing History Mocking King George III, *Horse Throwing His Master* represented **American colonists in revolt against the British monarchy.** *How did colonial economic interests help to ignite the American Revolution?*

The American Republic

By the mid-1700s, Great Britain was trying to tighten its control over its recently acquired overseas empire, especially North America. Enjoying a large measure of self-government, the North American colonies opposed Parliament's efforts to enforce trade laws and impose taxes on them. They began to press for even more freedom from the home country.

History & Art *The Spirit of '76* by Archibald Willard. Abbot Hall, Marblehead, Massachusetts **Revolution was romanticized in the art of the 1800s.** *Why did the American colonies rebel?*

Unit 5 Digest

Visualizing History Was the relation of horse and rider a good metaphor for the relation of the colonies to the English Crown? *(Students may respond that just as a master sees his horse as there to serve him, the British king saw the colonies as there to serve his country.)*
Answer to Caption: *British taxes and trade restrictions angered the colonists.*

GLENCOE TECHNOLOGY

VIDEODISC
Use MindJogger to review any chapter in Unit 5.

MindJogger Videoquiz
Chapter 20 Disc 3 Side A
Chapter 21 Disc 3 Side B
Chapter 22 Disc 3 Side B

Also available in VHS.

REVIEW

Use the Student Self-Test and Review Software to review any chapters that students have studied in Unit 5.

History & Art Romantic representations of the Revolution helped unite Americans from different backgrounds.
Answer to Caption: *for political and economic freedom*

ANSWERS TO SURVEYING THE CHAPTER

CHAPTER 20 ANSWERS

1. In the 1500s Europeans relied mainly on age-old beliefs, traditions, and the teachings of the Church to explain the natural world. From the 1600s to the 1800s, breakthroughs in astronomy, physics, and other sciences moved Europeans toward a more rational and systematic understanding of the natural world.
2. Scientific discoveries convinced European political thinkers that rational laws governed human behavior just as they did the natural world.

Unit 5 Digest

During the 1700s, relations between Great Britain and the North American colonies steadily worsened. The arrival of British troops in North America to put down colonial protests signaled the beginning of what became known as the Revolutionary War. In 1776, 13 of the colonies declared their freedom from British rule and became a new nation—the United States of America. Five years later, the American victory at Yorktown ended the war, and the British officially recognized the independence of their former colonies. From the 1700s to the present century, the success of the American Revolution has inspired colonial peoples struggling to escape from the hold of empires.

Following the Revolutionary War, the United States briefly functioned as a loose union of states with republican governments. In 1788 the nation ratified the United States Constitution. With its blend of European Enlightenment philosophy and American democratic ideals, the United States Constitution served as a model for people in other countries who wanted republican governments.

SURVEYING CHAPTER 21

1. **Relating Ideas** **How was Enlightenment thought reflected in the political events and the political changes that took place in North America during the 1700s?**
2. **Analyzing Events** **Why was William and Mary's acceptance of the Bill of Rights an important event in English history?**

Chapter 22
The French Revolution

The formation of the American republic had a profound impact on the French, who were becoming increasingly critical of their absolute monarchy. Under this system, France's few nobles and clergy—the First and Second Estates—enjoyed power and privilege, while the majority of the people—the Third Estate—paid most of the taxes and had almost no voice in running the nation's government. During the late 1780s, an explosive combination of social injustice, economic distress, and Enlightenment ideas led to the outbreak of the French Revolution.

The revolution began in 1789 when King Louis XVI called a meeting of the Estates-General to solve the government's deepening financial problems. When the monarch refused to reform voting methods, Third Estate delegates took the revolutionary step of meeting separately as the National Assembly. As the government of France from 1789 to 1791, the National Assembly ended the privileges of nobles and clergy, guaranteed basic human rights for all citizens, and established a constitutional monarchy. Louis XVI, however, was not content to rule under a constitution. He plotted with nobles and foreign monarchs to regain his absolute authority. In the summer of 1792, Austria and Prussia responded to Louis's appeals for help and invaded France. In response, angry revolutionaries in Paris arrested the king and called for a democratic government.

After the king's removal, a National Convention elected by all adult males proclaimed France a democratic republic and executed the king. The Convention then drafted a large army to push back the foreign invaders and to spread the revolution throughout Europe. To crush opposition at home, the leaders of the Convention put aside democratic practices and carried out a Reign of Terror, executing thousands of people. The Terror ended in 1794, and the wealthy middle

Visualizing History **Dr. Guillotin's invention of the guillotine, an instrument to make execution more humane, became a symbol of the terror and bloodshed of the revolution.** *How did the radicals bring about King Louis XVI's execution?*

Summarize Have students complete a unit summary chart on the chalkboard that includes the major figures of the unit. In the first column of the chart, list the chapters. The second column should be headed *Major Figures,* and the third *Importance. (example: Chapter 20; Copernicus; developed theory that the earth moves around the sun)* **L1**

Dialogue Organize the class into groups. Have each group pick one intellectual, political, or social change of the time covered in the unit and write a dialogue between a supporter and an opponent of the change. Then have volunteers present the dialogue to the class. Use the dialogues as springboards for discussion. *(examples: for and against the Copernican view of the universe, American independence, or the execution of Louis XVI)* **L2**

CONDENSE

Use Chapter Digests Audiocassettes to introduce chapters that students have not studied in Unit 5. Spanish Chapter Digests Audiocassettes are also available.

Discuss Have students read the **Unit Digest** and discuss the **Surveying Chapter** questions. **L1**

Visualizing History To make sure they would work properly and efficiently, the first guillotines brought to Paris were tested on dead bodies from a local hospital before being used for actual executions.

Answer to Caption: *They used his correspondence with foreign monarchs to convict him of plotting against France.*

ANSWERS TO SURVEYING THE CHAPTER

CHAPTER 21 ANSWERS

1. The Enlightenment ideas that government must serve the people and protect basic rights were reflected in the American Revolution and in the constitutional government the new nation created.
2. The Bill of Rights guaranteed basic rights to English people and made the monarchy subject to the laws of Parliament.

592 Unit 5 *Age of Revolution*

History & Art *Battle at Eylau* by Antoine Jean Gros **Severe November weather froze the French troops as they retreated from Moscow.** *What two factors brought about the downfall of Napoleon's empire?*

class came to power a year later under a new republican government called the Directory. Plagued by scandal and opposed by both conservatives and radicals, the Directory was overthrown by Napoleon Bonaparte in 1799.

Napoleon and Europe

Although Napoleon professed loyalty to the revolutionary ideals, he made himself emperor and imposed strict rule on France. He reformed French law by creating the Napoleonic Code. Although it placed the state above the individual, the new code preserved some revolutionary principles, such as the equality of all men before the law. The code did, however, curtail the rights of women and placed limits on freedom of speech. Napoleon also acknowledged the dominant role of Catholicism in French society but affirmed religious toleration for all.

With a powerful army, Napoleon deposed many foreign monarchs and brought a large part of the European continent under French rule. However, by 1814, Napoleon's empire was falling apart as a result of the combined military might of France's enemies and the growth of anti-French nationalism in the conquered lands.

After Napoleon's defeat, European leaders met in 1814 and 1815 at the Congress of Vienna to determine Europe's future. Opposed to democracy and nationalism, they sought to return to the political and social system that had existed before 1789. They restored monarchs ousted by Napoleon to their thrones and adjusted political boundaries so that France would no longer be able to dominate Europe. Although France never again ruled a European empire, the Congress failed in its efforts to restore absolute monarchy. Democracy and nationalism became powerful forces in the years after the Congress of Vienna and swept aside Europe's traditional social and political order.

SURVEYING CHAPTER 22

1. **Understanding Cause and Effect** What two major factors led to the fall of Napoleon's empire?
2. **Making Comparisons** Compare the political revolutions in England, North America, and France. Which revolution was the most conservative? Which was the most radical? Explain your answers.

ANSWERS TO SURVEYING THE CHAPTER

CHAPTER 22 ANSWERS

1. The combined military power of France's enemies and growing nationalism in the lands conquered by Napoleon undermined the empire.
2. Answers will vary. The American Revolution may be seen as most conservative because fighting was limited, and it was not a social revolution; the French Revolution was the most radical in its goals and methods.

Unit 5 Digest

History & Art During the disastrous retreat from Moscow, Napoleon lost his magnetic appeal. His troops marched "with downcast eyes, as if ashamed and humbled," wrote one French officer.
Answer to Caption: *the combined military might of France's enemies and the growth of anti-French nationalism in conquered lands*

RETEACH

Flowchart Have students create a flowchart that summarizes the major events of each revolution in the unit.

Reteaching Activities 20, 21, 22

Chapter Digests Audiocassettes, Chapters 20, 21, 22

ABCNEWS INTERACTIVE™

VIDEODISC
Turning Points in World History
Side One
Chapter 11

Title: *French Revolution*
Ask: Why did the French revolutionaries storm the Bastille prison? *(The Bastille represented royal authority and the injustice of the government.)*

0:00 OUT OF TIME?

If time does not permit teaching each chapter in Unit 6, you may use the Unit Digest beginning on page 728, in conjunction with the Unit Digest Transparencies and Chapter Digest Audiocassettes with accompanying activities and tests.

Introducing the Unit

Unit 6 focuses on the Industrial Revolution and the rapid political, social, and cultural changes that transformed the world in the 1700s and 1800s.

Unit Objectives

After reading Unit 6, students will be able to:

1. understand the technological innovations and new economic developments of the Industrial Revolution.
2. trace new political, economic, and scientific ideas and the growth of popular culture.
3. describe the revolutionary and reform movements that reshaped politics of Europe and the Americas in the 1800s.
4. explain how nationalists unified Italy and Germany and challenged autocracy in Russia and Austria-Hungary.
5. discuss the effects of European and United States imperialism in Asia, Africa, and Latin America.

Portfolio Project

Students can find information for their graphs in world almanacs and general encyclopedias as well as books such as *The Encyclopedia of American Facts and Dates*. This activity may be an appropriate method of authentic assessment.

Unit 6

1750–1914

Industry and Nationalism

Chapter 23 Age of Industry
Chapter 24 Cultural Revolution
Chapter 25 Democracy and Reform
Chapter 26 Reaction and Nationalism
Chapter 27 The Age of Imperialism

Then & Now *For centuries wealthy landowners in Europe controlled a static agricultural economy. Peasant families farmed strips of land, and small industries and trades met local needs. Then, in England in the late 1700s, innovations in farming made agriculture a profitable business. An agricultural revolution helped start a revolution in industry, beginning in textiles. The factory system expanded the power and wealth of the middle class. While scientific and medical advances improved life for many, in much of Europe the poor remained powerless.*

How long would it take you to walk to school? The railroad began the revolution in transportation. When a German engineer redesigned the internal combustion engine to run on gasoline, the automobile took center stage. Within a few decades the automobile would transform society in every industrial country.

A Global Chronology

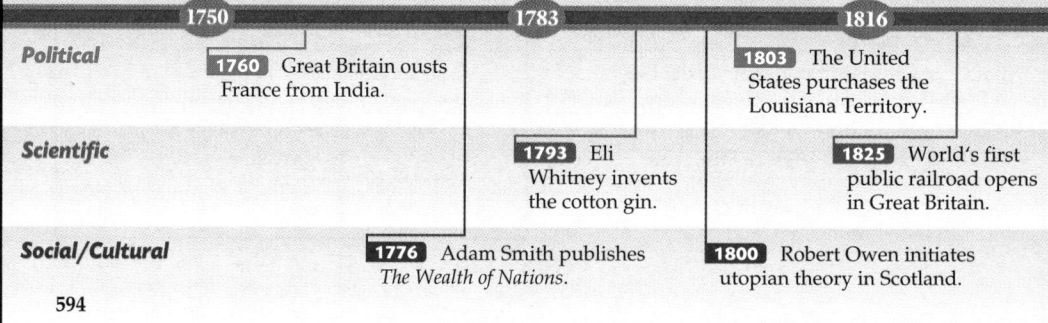

1750 — 1783 — 1816

Political
- **1760** Great Britain ousts France from India.
- **1803** The United States purchases the Louisiana Territory.

Scientific
- **1793** Eli Whitney invents the cotton gin.
- **1825** World's first public railroad opens in Great Britain.

Social/Cultural
- **1776** Adam Smith publishes *The Wealth of Nations.*
- **1800** Robert Owen initiates utopian theory in Scotland.

594

Then & Now **Nationalism** In this unit students will learn about the rise of nationalism in Europe, including nationalist movements in the Balkans (pages 697–698). Ask students to discuss regions of the world where nationalism has led to violence in recent years. **Why is nationalism such a powerful feeling throughout the world?** *(Answers will vary. Some students may feel that nationalism or patriotism is a natural feeling.)* **In what ways has nationalism been a positive force in recent history?** *(It led to dramatic restructuring*

Steam locomotive and wood car

Portfolio Project

Graphs can show the dramatic changes caused by the Industrial Revolution. Create several graphs that illustrate these changes from the early 1800s to the 1900s. Subjects of your graphs for any industrializing nation or group of nations may include: population growth; spread of railroads; production of goods such as cotton, steel, coal, oil, or specific consumer goods; consumption of power such as electricity; output of agriculture; etc. Libraries have good historical references for these statistics.

1849 — 1882 — 1915

1848 Karl Marx publishes *The Communist Manifesto.*

1871 Bismarck unifies Germany.

1874 French impressionists hold first major exhibition in Paris.

1876 Alexander Graham Bell invents the telephone.

1911 Revolution topples Qing dynasty in China.

1914 Panama Canal opens.

1915 Chen Duxiu founds reform journal called *New Youth.*

595

of the Soviet Union and the Communist regimes of Eastern Europe.) Where has nationalism led to violence in recent years? *(former Soviet Union, former Yugoslavia, Rwanda, Liberia)* Why has nationalism sometimes led to violence? *(Answers will vary. Students may mention that political boundaries often do not correspond to distribution of ethnic groups.)* Do you think that every distinct ethnic group should form its own nation? Why or why not? *(Answers will vary. Students may realize that the idea would lead to the splitting up of nearly all nations that now exist.)*

Introducing Unit 6

History *and the* Humanities

Focus on World Art Prints
- 2 *Stables*
- 5 *Palace, Partially Destroyed*
- 22 *Hospital at Saint-Rémy*

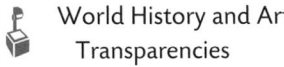

World History and Art Transparencies
- 30 *Le Moulin de la Galette*
- 31 *In the Garden*
- 32 *Sunday Afternoon on the Island of La Grande Jatte*
- 33 *The Banjo Lesson*
- 34 *Starry Night*
- 35 *Ono Waterfall*

World Music: Cultural Traditions, Lessons 2, 3, 4, 6, 9

ABC NEWS INTERACTIVE™

VIDEODISC
Turning Points in World History

Side Two, Chapter 3
Title: *The Industrial Revolution*
Ask: How was the development of the railroad instrumental in the new industrial economy? *(The railroad transported goods being made in the factories.)*

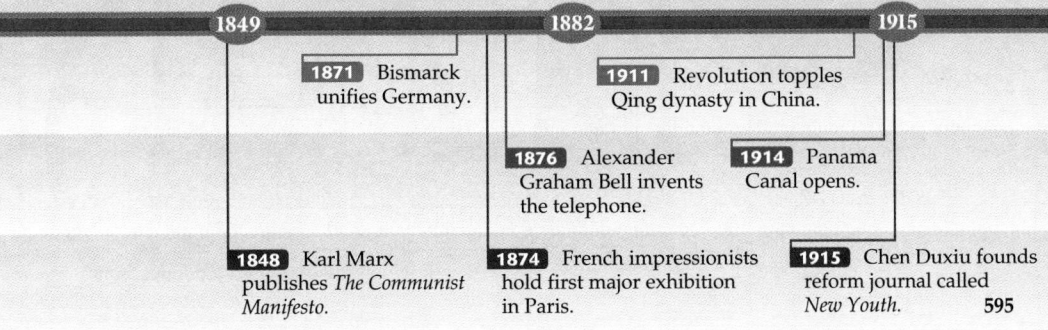

Visualizing History

A network of rail lines spread across Europe and North America after 1820. Railroads opened up vast new markets and spurred the growth of large factories.

The Spread of Ideas

TEACH

Introduction

This feature focuses on the spread of the Industrial Revolution from its beginnings in Great Britain to the United States and Japan.

Background Notes

Linking Past and Present

Today, industrial technology moves quickly from one country to another. For example, computer software, microelectronics, and industrial chemicals, once produced almost entirely in Europe, Japan, and the United States, are now exported from Brazil, India, Korea, and Taiwan. The reduction in trade barriers under GATT (General Agreement on Tariffs and Trade) has made the movement of technology even easier.

Geography

Movement The Industrial Revolution caused unprecedented movement among people as farmers in many lands left their farms to work in factories, often in far-off places. Skilled European workers came to the United States in the early 1800s to work in cotton mills like the one Slater built in Pawtucket. In the 1820s one observer noted that a mix of workers from different parts of Britain made problems for one mill owner: "I cannot conceive a more uncomfortable situation than … to be surrounded by a mixture of Irish, Yorkshire, and west of England workmen. Whatever advice he might receive from the one party would be condemned by the others…."

The Spread of Ideas

Industrialization

The rise of industry changed the world forever. So dramatic were the changes that historians have labeled the period the Industrial Revolution. Although the revolution began in Britain, it respected neither time nor place. The revolution traveled beyond Britain to touch every nation on earth.

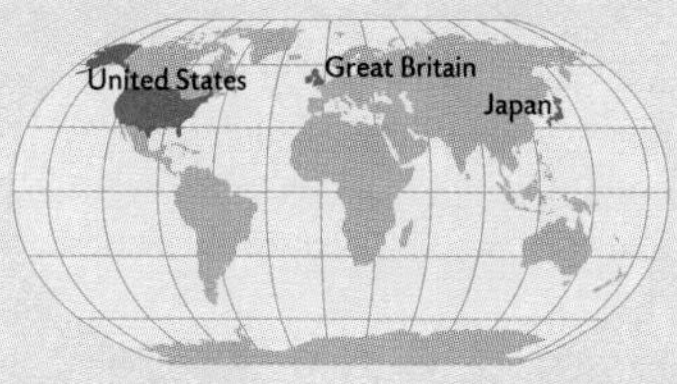

Great Britain

Workshop of the World

The birth of industry needed certain preconditions: the science, incentive, and money capital to build machines; a labor force to run them; raw materials and markets to make the system profitable; and efficient farms to feed a new group of workers. At the start of the 1700s, Great Britain possessed all these conditions. Here industrialism first took root.

As with the development of agriculture, no one person can be credited with the invention of industry. Instead, it grew from the innovations of individuals who developed machines to do work formerly done by humans and animals. One inventor built on the ideas of another. In 1705, for example, Thomas Newcomen devised a crude steam engine to pump water out of coal mines. In 1769 James Watt improved upon Newcomen's work and built a more efficient steam engine. Other inventors adapted Watt's engine to run cloth-making machines. Business owners soon brought machines and workers together in a single place called a factory.

By the 1800s, industry had catapulted Great Britain into a position of world leadership. "[Britain has] triumphantly established herself as the workshop of the world," boasted one leader. It was impossible to monopolize this idea. Workshops began to hum in America.

James Watt

Watt's steam engine

596 Unit 6

COOPERATIVE LEARNING ACTIVITY

Reports Have students brainstorm a list of important technologies today (prompt them if necessary to consider semiconductors, satellites, fiber optics, biotechnology, software, and high-resolution television). Then organize the class into groups and have each group research and prepare an oral report on one technology. Reports should indicate, if possible, where the technology was first developed and where it is produced today. Then have students from each group present their report to the class. Encourage students to include visuals in their reports. **L2**

The Spread of Ideas

The United States

The Revolution Spreads

Great Britain tried to keep the secrets of industry locked up. It forbade the export of industrial machines. It also barred the people who built and operated the machines from leaving the country. In 1787, however, a young factory supervisor named Samuel Slater found a way to escape. He disguised himself as a farmhand and boarded a ship for New York.

Working entirely from memory, Slater built a mill in Pawtucket, Rhode Island. On December 20, 1790, the mill turned out the first machine-made cotton yarn produced in America.

Within two years, Slater had sales offices in Salem, New York City, Baltimore, and Philadelphia. As Slater's mills turned out cotton, the United States began churning out its own brilliant industrial inventors. They produced more than just machines. They came up with new industrial principles such as Eli Whitney's use of standardized parts and Henry Ford's use of the assembly line. Together these two ideas gave the world mass production—a concept that would revolutionize people's lives around the globe.

Samuel Slater's mill

Matthew Perry's steamboat in Tokyo Bay

Japan

The Search for Markets

In 1853, the Industrial Revolution traveled to Japan in the form of a fleet of United States steamships sent to open the island to trade. "What we had taken as a fire at sea," recalled one Japanese observer, "was really smoke coming out of their smokestacks."

The military power produced by United States industry shook the Japanese. Recalled the same observer, "What a joke, the steaming teapot fixed by America—Just four cups [ships], and we cannot sleep at night."

The Japanese temporarily gave in to American demands. But they also vowed that they too would possess industry. By the start of the 1900s, Japan had joined other industrial nations in the search for markets. By 1914 Japan's merchant fleet was the sixth largest in the world and their foreign trade had increased one hundred-fold in value in fifty years.

LINKING THE IDEAS

1. How was the idea for a cotton mill brought from Great Britain to the United States?
2. What feature of the American fleet most impressed the Japanese in 1853?

Critical Thinking

3. **Drawing Conclusions** Why did the British want to control the spread of an idea that made production of goods easier?

Who? What? Where? When?

Women Workers At first, nearly all American factory workers were single women who moved from nearby farms to live in boarding houses owned by the mills. Mary Paul, a mill worker in Lowell, Massachusetts, described her day: "At 5 o'clock in the morning the bell rings for the folks to get up and get breakfast ... at seven they are called into the mill. At half past 12 we have dinner, are called back at one and stay till half past seven." Despite the hard schedule, Paul said, "I think that the factory is the best place for me and if any girl wants employment I advise them to come to Lowell."

Cultural Diffusion

Military-Industrial Complex The Japanese understood that a nation could not have a strong military without industrializing. After Britain defeated China in the Opium War of the 1830s, one Japanese commented: "Why did an upright and righteous great country like China lose to an insolent, unjust, and contemptible country like England? It is because [the rulers of China] prided themselves on their superiority, regarded the outside world with contempt, and paid no heed to the progress of machinery in foreign countries."

ANSWERS TO LINKING THE IDEAS

1. Samuel Slater memorized the mill design and left England by pretending to be a farmer.
2. their steam engines
3. Britain wanted to maintain a monopoly over industrial production.

Teach, Reinforce, and Extend CHAPTER Content

Age of Industry

CHAPTER RESOURCES

	Reproducible Resources	Multimedia Resources
Chapter Opener	Chapter Themes: Graphic Organizer 23 Historical Significance Chapter Activity 23	MindJogger Videoquiz
Chapter Enrichment	Vocabulary Activity 23* Time Line Activity 23 Mapping History Activity 23 History Simulation 23 Geography and History Activity 23 Source Reading 23 People in World History Profiles 43, 44 World Art and Music Activity 23 Enrichment Activity 23 Critical Thinking Activity 23 Skill Reinforcement Activity 23 Performance Assessment Activity 23	World History and Art Transparency 30, *Le Moulin de la Galette* Chapter Transparency 23 Vocabulary PuzzleMaker Software Turning Points in World History: *The Industrial Revolution*
Chapter Review/Reteaching	Reteaching Activity 23 Skill Reinforcement Activity 23 Spanish Chapter Summary 23	Chapter 23 Digest Audiocassette, Activity, Test* Vocabulary PuzzleMaker Software Student Self-Test and Review Software MindJogger Videoquiz
Chapter Evaluation/Testing	Performance Assessment Activity 23 Chapter 23 Test, Forms A and B	Testmaker

* *Also available in Spanish*

0:00 OUT OF TIME? Assign the Chapter 23 summary in the Unit 6 Digest on pages 728–731, and the Chapter 23 Audiocassettes.

Block Schedule

Block scheduling differs from traditional class scheduling in the amount of time allotted to each period. The extended time frame provided by block scheduling affords you the opportunity to implement a greater number of research-oriented and activity-intense projects to motivate and involve your students. Activities that are particularly suited to use within the block scheduling framework are identified throughout this chapter by the following designation.

KEY TO ABILITY LEVELS

Teaching strategies have been coded for varying learning styles and abilities.

- **L1** **BASIC** activities for all students
- **L2** **AVERAGE** activities for average to above-average students
- **L3** **CHALLENGING** activities for above-average students
- **LEP** **LIMITED ENGLISH PROFICIENCY** activities

Chapter 23 Planning Guide

A complete, 1-page lesson plan is provided for each section in the *Reproducible Lesson Plans* booklet.

SECTION RESOURCES

Daily Objectives	Reproducible Resources	Multimedia Resources
Section 1 Living From the Land Describe what daily life was like before the rise of modern industry.	Reproducible Lesson Plan 23-1 Vocabulary Activity 23* Guided Reading Activity 23-1* Time Line Activity 23 Section Quiz 23-1*	Section Focus Transparency 23-1 Chapter Transparency 23 Student Self-Test and Review Software Testmaker Turning Points in World History: *The Industrial Revolution*
Section 2 The Beginnings of Change Explain why the Industrial Revolution began in Great Britain.	Reproducible Lesson Plan 23-2 Vocabulary Activity 23* Guided Reading Activity 23-2* Geography and History Activity 23 Section Quiz 23-2*	Section Focus Transparency 23-2 Student Self-Test and Review Software Testmaker Turning Points in World History: *The Industrial Revolution*
Section 3 The Growth of Industry Analyze how new technology advanced the growth of industry.	Reproducible Lesson Plan 23-3 Guided Reading Activity 23-3* People in World History Profiles 43, 44 History Simulation 23 Section Quiz 23-3*	Section Focus Transparency 23-3 Vocabulary PuzzleMaker Software Student Self-Test and Review Software Testmaker Turning Points in World History: *The Industrial Revolution*
Section 4 A New Society Describe how the Industrial Revolution affected people's lives.	Reproducible Lesson Plan 23-4 Vocabulary Activity 23* Guided Reading Activity 23-4* Reteaching Activity 23 Enrichment Activity 23 Section Quiz 23-4* Performance Assessment Activity 23 Spanish Chapter Summary 23	Section Focus Transparency 23-4 World History and Art Transparency 30, *Le Moulin de la Galette* Student Self-Test and Review Software Testmaker Turning Points in World History: *The Industrial Revolution*

* *Also available in Spanish*

Chapter Activities

Performance Assessment Activity

Students as Inventors Have students assume the roles of modern-day inventors who have identified a clear need for a new product. Ask them to draw up plans for an invention to fill the need, determine an area of the world in which to manufacture it, and suggest possible ways to finance the project. Students will then create a proposal including a diagram and map of manufacturing and distribution. Included in the proposal should be the likely impact of the manufacturing in the area under consideration. As an alternative, you might suggest the type of invention needed, have several groups come up with proposals, then debate the relative merits of their proposals for location and investment.

Possible Rubric Features
Accuracy of research; thoroughness in meeting criteria for labor force, capital, natural resources, and need; organization and clarity of presentation and visuals

• *For an additional activity, refer to Activity 23 in the* Performance Assessment Strategies and Activities *booklet.*

Activity

From the Classroom of...

Edward Thomas
Elmont Memorial High School
Elmont, NY

Analyzing Effects of Industrialization

Ask students what products or inventions have been important during the 1990s. Have students discuss the ways each product or invention has affected their lives and society as a whole, both positively and negatively. Then have students list products and inventions from the Age of Industry, along with their effects in both rural and urban regions. Use these lists as a springboard for a general discussion of the changes in lifestyle brought about by industrialization. Be sure students mention the movement of many people from rural to urban areas. Ask students if any of the problems brought about by industrialization are still present in society.

MULTIPLE LEARNING STYLES

Verbal/Linguistic
Have students read Charles Dickens's *Hard Times* and write a book report analyzing how the novel presents relations between industrialists and workers. Have them consider these questions: Who are the heroes? Who are the villains? How does Dickens's portrayal compare with this chapter's discussion of the situation?

Logical/Mathematical
Have students select one or more stocks and follow their progress on the stock market for several days or weeks. If possible, they should research the companies they select and learn something about their development.

Visual/Spatial
Have students construct a graph showing the growth of Europe's population from 1600 to 1900.

Kinesthetic
Have students select an invention of the period and prepare a model or detailed diagram showing how it works.

Additional Resources

TEACHER'S CORNER

NATIONAL GEOGRAPHIC SOCIETY

INDEX TO NATIONAL GEOGRAPHIC MAGAZINE

The following articles may be used for research relating to this chapter:

- "George Washington's Patowmack Canal," by Wilbur E. Garrett, June 1987.

BIBLIOGRAPHY

Literature of the Period

Trollope, Anthony. ***The Way We Live Now.*** London: Trollope Society, 1992. Witty dissection of English society in the Industrial Age.

Zola, Émile. ***Germinal.*** New York: Vintage Books, 1994. Outspoken attack on harsh conditions in French coal mines.

Readings for the Student

Dickens, Charles. ***Oliver Twist.*** New York: Dodd, Mead, 1984. An orphan's adventures in seamy, industrial London.

Readings for the Teacher

Avery, Gillian. ***The Echoing Green: Memories of Victorian Youth.*** New York: Viking, 1974. Diaries and memoirs re-create life in the 1800s.

interNET
CONNECTIONS
Treasures of the Science Museum Take a tour of land vehicles developed in Great Britain.
World Wide Web:
http://www.nmsi.ac.uk/galleries/plan/gndland.htm

Introducing Chapter 23

CHAPTER THEMES

Chapter Themes are listed by section on this chapter opening page of the Student Edition. A corresponding theme-based activity is available under "TEACH," and a theme-based question is asked in the Section and Chapter Reviews.

The Storyteller

Historical Setting Children had worked for centuries before the onset of the Industrial Revolution. They had worked on their families' farms and had been apprenticed at a variety of skilled crafts. But with the advent of the industrial age, working children's lives were little better than those of enslaved peoples. They worked in factories and in mines. They toiled long hours in the cold and the dark, handling dangerous machinery for very low wages.

Historical Significance

Answers: *Many nations developed urban industrial economies. New inventions led to the growth of factories, and these in turn led to the growth of manufacturing cities. The middle class expanded in size and wealth. Harsh conditions for working people led to the development of labor unions.*

Today industrialized nations have advanced technology and high standards of living; nonindustrialized nations try to gain these benefits by industrializing.

Chapter 23

1700–1914

Age of Industry

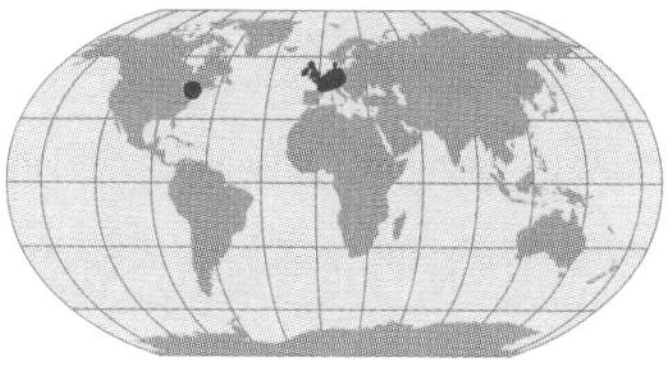

Chapter Themes

- **Relation to Environment** Before the Industrial Revolution of the 1700s and 1800s, most Europeans live in isolated rural villages and depend on the land. *Section 1*
- **Innovation** A series of inventions and new procedures in agriculture and industry transform economies in Europe and North America. *Section 2*
- **Change** Throughout the Western world, new urban centers based on industry develop along with the rise of new social classes. *Section 3*
- **Conflict** Workers in Europe and North America organize to gain better wages and improved working conditions. *Section 4*

The Storyteller

Change swept through Europe and North America as new coal mines and iron works began to dominate rural landscapes. Susan Pitchforth, an 11-year-old British girl, was just one of the millions of men, women, and children who left farming villages to find work in these growing industries.

Like countless others, Susan suffered difficult and dangerous industrial working conditions. When the British Parliament investigated horrible conditions in coal mines, young Susan told them her story:

"I have worked at this pit going on two years … I walk a mile and a half to my work, both in winter and summer. I run 24 [loads] a day; I cannot come up till I have done them all."

Historical Significance

What changes took place in Europe and North America during the Industrial Revolution? How does the Industrial Revolution affect life throughout the world today?

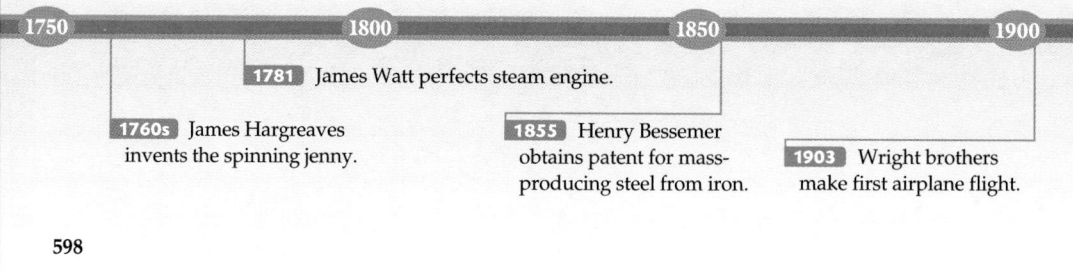

1750 — 1800 — 1850 — 1900

- **1760s** James Hargreaves invents the spinning jenny.
- **1781** James Watt perfects steam engine.
- **1855** Henry Bessemer obtains patent for mass-producing steel from iron.
- **1903** Wright brothers make first airplane flight.

598

GEOGRAPHY CONNECTION

Location Have students locate Great Britain (England, Scotland, Wales) in the Atlas in their textbook or on a wall map. What geographic features do you see? *(Britain is an island nation; there are many harbors and rivers.)* How might these features help stimulate industry? *(Isolation from continental Europe would protect Britain from invasion and warfare; harbors and rivers aid transportation.)* **L1**

History & Art *Coalbrookdale by Night* by Philip de Loutherberg. Science Museum, London, England

Your History Journal

Build a time line of inventions of the Industrial Revolution beginning with John Kay's improved loom and ending with the first airplane.

EXTRA CREDIT PROJECT

Biography Have students investigate one of the men who helped bring about the agricultural revolution: Robert Bakewell, Charles Townshend, or Jethro Tull in England, or John Deere in the United States. Students should report, orally or in writing, on what the man contributed and the difference his contribution made to agricultural production. **L2**

Introducing Chapter 23

History & Art Tell students that Coalbrookdale was an important center of English industrialization. It was here, in the early 1700s, that entrepreneur Abraham Darby first used coke—a coal product—to smelt iron. Previously, manufacturers had used charcoal, a wood product, with the result that England's forests were being depleted.

Performance Assessment

Refer to the activity on page 598C of the Planning Guide.

For an additional activity, refer to Activity 23 in the *Performance Assessment Strategies and Activities* booklet.

Using Your History Journal

Students may use different colors for different industries, such as textiles, iron and steel, and transportation and communication.

GLENCOE TECHNOLOGY

VIDEODISC
Use MindJogger to preview chapter content.

MindJogger Videoquiz
Chapter 23
Disc 3 Side B

Also available in VHS.

Chapter 23 Section 1

SECTION THEME

▶ **Relation to Environment** Before the Industrial Revolution of the 1700s and 1800s, most Europeans live in isolated rural villages and depend on the land.

Find Out

Answer: *Most people lived in small villages and depended mainly on agriculture to make a living. They worked hard, lived always under the threat of disease, seldom ventured far from their village, and expected to die fairly young.*

FOCUS

Section Objective

Describe what daily life was like before the rise of modern industry.

BELLRINGER Motivational Activity

Before taking roll at the beginning of the class period, project Section Focus Transparency 23-1 and have students answer the activity questions. Discuss students' responses.

This activity is also available as a blackline master.

Vocabulary Pre-check

Use Vocabulary Activity 23 to introduce vocabulary terms. **L1 LEP**

1700 — 1750 — 1800

c. 1700s Domestic system is widespread in European towns and villages.

c. 1750 About 75 percent of Europeans live in rural areas.

Section 1

Living From the Land

Setting the Scene

▶ **Terms to Define**
domestic system

▶ **People to Meet**
Charles Dickens

▶ **Places to Locate**
London

Find Out What was daily life like before the rise of modern industry?

The Storyteller

Landlords increased their income by removing common farmers from their rented fields. An anonymous poem passed judgment on the enclosure of Thornborough landlords in 1798:

Ye Thornbro' youths bewail with me;
Ye shepherds lay your pipes aside,
No longer tune the merry glee,
For we are rob'd of all our pride.
The time alas will soon approach,
When we must all our pasture yield;
The wealthy on our rights encroach
And will enclose our common field.

—adapted from *English Parliamentary Enclosure*, Michael Turner, 1980

Haymaking in rural England

During the 1700s and 1800s, a series of innovations in agriculture and industry led to profound economic and social change throughout Europe and the United States. Urban industrial economies emerged in these areas and eventually spread around the world. This transformation, which became known as the Industrial Revolution, began when power-driven machinery in factories replaced work done in homes—altering the way people had lived and worked for hundreds of years.

Cloth making provides a dramatic example of the far-reaching effects of the Industrial Revolution. In the 1700s a home weaver worked many hours to produce a yard of cloth. A century later, a worker operating machines in a textile mill could make 50 times more cloth.

As adventurous businesspeople brought machines and workers together in factories, industries produced mass quantities of goods. Millions of people in search of new opportunities to make a living left rural villages to find factory work in growing towns and cities. A new era of mechanization had arrived.

A Harsh Way of Life

Before the dawn of the Industrial Revolution in the 1700s, people lived in much the same way their ancestors had lived for hundreds of years. Nature's seasons and religious traditions measured time, and social change was rare. Relying almost solely on farming to make a living, people planted and harvested fields, hoped for good weather, and lived always under the threat of disease.

Families, both rich and poor, remained relatively small because of a very high infant death rate. One baby in three died in his or her first year of life,

---

SECTION RESOURCES

Reproducible Masters
- Reproducible Lesson Plan 23-1
- Vocabulary Activity 23
- Guided Reading Activity 23-1
- Time Line Activity 23
- Section Quiz 23-1

Transparencies
- Section Focus Transparency 23-1
- Chapter Transparency 23

Multimedia
- Student Self-Test and Review Software
- Testmaker
- Turning Points in World History: *The Industrial Revolution*

and only one in two people reached age 21. Life expectancy hovered around age 40. People expected life to be short and harsh. As one mother in the 1770s said after her baby's death, "One cannot grieve after her much, and I have just now other things to think of."

Only 25 percent of Europeans lived in towns or cities in the 1700s. **London** was the largest city in Europe in 1750 with about 700,000 people. Yet it too had a rural character. The famous British novelist **Charles Dickens** described the sights of a London morning in the early 1800s:

> ❝By degrees, other shops began to be unclosed, and a few scattered people were met with. Then, came straggling groups of labourers going to their work; then men and women with fish baskets on their heads; donkey carts laden with vegetables; chaise carts filled with live-stock or whole carcasses of meat, milk women with pails; an unbroken concourse of people....❞
>
> —Charles Dickens, *Oliver Twist*, 1837

History & Art *Harvest Scene* by George Vicat Cole. Christie's, London, England *What were the village commons?*

Most people in preindustrial times lived in small country villages consisting of a few hundred people. Many never ventured beyond the village borders. When braver people traveled to other cities and towns, their tales delighted their less worldly neighbors.

Village Life

Virtually all rural villagers were farmers. Wealthy landowners controlled the majority of the village land, renting most of it to small farming families. Families owned or rented small strips of land in several areas of the village. This practice ensured both fair land distribution and economic protection should disaster strike any one field. Farmers worked the land cooperatively, jointly deciding what crops to grow and when to plant and harvest.

In most of the villages, private and public lands were not separated or fenced off. The public lands, called the village commons, consisted of woodlands, pastures, and less fertile land near the village. For centuries, farmers could gather wood and graze their livestock on the commons. Poorer farmers even used these public lands for raising crops.

Village economies were limited largely to the local area because transporting goods to other areas was difficult and unprofitable. Rain turned the few roads into muddy rivers. For this reason, villages had to be nearly self-sufficient. People grew enough food for their families and perhaps a small amount to sell to nearby towns. They made their own homes, clothes, and tools from products raised in the fields or gathered from the land.

The richest rural landowners lived on sprawling country estates with a huge main house, cottages, several barns, and extensive fields. Landowners and their families lived lavishly. Servants ran the households and catered to the families' needs.

People who rented land from the landowners lived quite differently. Most lived in small, smoky, poorly lighted cottages with dirt floors. Since the poorest farming families often did not have barns, they sometimes shared their cramped living quarters with farm animals.

All daily activities revolved around farming, an occupation dominated by tradition. Farmers used the same simple methods and tools their ancestors had used and relied on nature to provide good growing seasons. Nature, however, was never predictable, and harvests ranged from plentiful to disastrously small.

Everyone in the farming family worked hard. From morning to night, husband, wife, and children worked together. Boys helped their fathers in

COOPERATIVE LEARNING ACTIVITY

Demonstration Organize the class into groups and assign each one a crop commonly grown in preindustrial Europe: wheat, rye, barley, and so on. Each group should then research to find out how the crop was planted, cultivated, harvested, and processed in the days before machinery. Groups should present their findings in the form of a demonstration and a report, including information on the agricultural tools used. **L3**

TEACH

Guided Practice

THEME Relation to Environment
Ask students to identify some positive features—perhaps things they lack in their own lives—of life in a preindustrial farm village. *(Answers will vary but might include a feeling of community, little crime, and a sense of accomplishment that comes with self-reliance.)* **L1**

History & Art Before the Industrial Revolution, Britain produced almost all its own foodstuffs except for sugar.
Answer to Caption: *land that all villagers could use*

Daily Life Have half the class take the role of magazine reporter and the other half that of a village inhabitant—landowner, farmer, and so on. Reporters should interview villagers about what it is like to live in the village. **L2**

ABC NEWS INTERACTIVE™

VIDEODISC
Turning Points in World History

Side Two, Chapter 3
Title: *The Industrial Revolution*
Ask: What kinds of power did inventors use to run new machines? *(water, steel, coal)*

Chapter Transparency 23

Chapter 23 Section 1

Independent Practice

Guided Reading Activity 23-1 **L1**

Time Line Activity 23

Technology Have students make a flowchart showing the steps involved in creating a woolen garment under the domestic system. **L2**

ASSESS

Check for Understanding

Assign Section 1 Review as homework or as an in-class activity.

Use Student Self-Test and Review Software to review Section 1.

Evaluate

Section Quiz 23-1

Use the Testmaker to create a customized quiz for Section 1.

Reteach

Organize students into small groups. Each group should list the key characteristics of preindustrial farming, preindustrial mining, and the early wool industry. As the groups share their lists, write major points on the board.

Enrich

Have students draw cartoons showing the best and worst features of rural life in the preindustrial age.

CLOSE

Remind students that people often use the phrase "the good old days" out of nostalgia for the past. Have them write an essay explaining whether the preindustrial era could be considered good.

the fields or at the workbench. Girls helped their mothers with chores such as milking cows and household duties such as churning butter and preparing meals.

Early Industries

In addition to farming, many people worked in small industries or in coal mines. These industries met local needs for goods such as coal, glass, iron, and clothing and employed a small number of workers. Since many workers were also farm workers, work schedules were coordinated with the agricultural cycle.

During harvest time nail makers, glassblowers, ironworkers, and miners helped farmers with the crops; likewise, in the winter farmworkers worked in the mines and in the workshops. This close relationship between farming and industry provided a steadier income to workers than either farming or industry alone.

Making Wool

In Great Britain, the woolen industry had for centuries been second only to farming in the numbers of people it employed and in the volume of trade it created. In the 1700s the demand for wool grew so great that merchants hired workers to produce woolens in their own homes. This system of labor, called the **domestic system**, spread to other industries such as leather working and lace making and was a widespread method used throughout Europe in the 1700s.

The domestic system depended on a network of workers. In the case of wool, a merchant first bought the raw fiber and divided it among several families. Women and children usually cleaned, sorted, and spun the fiber into thread or yarn. Men usually did the actual weaving. Then the merchant collected the yarn, paid the spinner a fee, and took the yarn to a weaver. The material next went to a fuller, who shaped and cleaned the material, and at last to the dyer for coloring. Finally, the merchant took the finished products to market and sold them for the highest possible price.

The domestic system had many benefits. Workers set their own hours and could tend to duties at home during work breaks. Women cared for children, tended vegetable gardens, and cooked meals while they earned money at home. Men carried on farming tasks, such as plowing and planting fields. Children also helped their parents. In one British region, children attended special schools to learn the art of lace making. With this skill they contributed to the family income. The domestic system provided work and income during hard times, saving many families from starvation. Its simple rural domestic practices later became the basis on which the technology and skills of the Industrial Revolution were built.

Mining Coal

The domestic system also had its place in coal mining. Coal fields often lay under farmland. The people who worked the mines often became farm laborers during the harvest, and farm horses pulled coal wagons from the pits. In some coal fields, women and children even hauled baskets of coal from the pits. One observer described these loaded baskets, saying it was "frequently more than one man could do to lift the burden."

With the money earned from mining or farmwork, country people might buy in nearby towns the few things they could not manufacture for themselves. Craftspeople sold handmade guns, furniture, and clothing in their small shops. Some craftspeople sent their goods to foreign markets in exchange for imported goods and traded the rest for food from nearby farmers and products from other local craftspeople.

Yet changes to this way of life were on the horizon. The development of new machinery and sources of power would soon upset the domestic system, transforming forever the way people lived and worked.

SECTION 1 REVIEW

Recall

1. **Define** the domestic system.
2. **Identify** the Industrial Revolution, Charles Dickens.
3. **Describe** the advantage of coordinating the work schedules in small industries with farming cycles.

Critical Thinking

4. **Predicting Trends** During the Industrial Revolution, many traditions were abandoned. How could abandoning tradition help the small farming villages? How might it hurt them?

Understanding Themes

5. **Relation to the Environment** Where did most people live during preindustrial times? What was their most important occupation?

SECTION 1 REVIEW ANSWERS

1. All vocabulary words are defined in the Glossary.
2. Industrial Revolution, 600; Charles Dickens, 601
3. Laborers could earn a steadier income because they could work in industry part-time and farm part-time.
4. It might help them by increasing production and raising the standard of living; it might harm them by weakening community ties.
5. **RELATION TO ENVIRONMENT** in rural villages; farming

1700 | 1750 | 1800 | 1850

c. 1700s British landowners extend enclosures and displace farmers.

1787 Edmund Cartwright develops power loom.

1807 Robert Fulton designs first practical steamboat.

Section 2

The Beginnings of Change

Setting the Scene

▶ **Terms to Define**
enclosure movement, capital, entrepreneur, factory system

▶ **People to Meet**
James Hargreaves, Richard Arkwright, Edmund Cartwright, Eli Whitney, James Watt, Henry Bessemer

Find Out Why did the Industrial Revolution begin in Great Britain?

The Storyteller

About 210,000 men built the first railroads in Britain. They called themselves "navvies." Mostly the men worked in silence. The only British navvies whose singing was noticed were the Welsh, whose songs were mainly hymns. Most other songs that navvies sang while they worked have disappeared. One tune, however, heard on the railway in 1859 gives some insight into the navvies' lives:

...I'm a navvy on the line.
I get me five-and-twenty bob a week,
Besides me overtime.
Roast Beef and boiled beef
An' puddin' made of eggs....

—adapted from *The Victorian Railway*, Jack Simmons, 1991

Early train

For hundreds of years, British farmers had planted crops and kept livestock on unfenced private and public lands. Village society depended on this age-old system of farming and grazing. By the late 1700s, however, wealthy British landowners would end this open-field system, which had been slowly giving way to private ownership since the 1100s.

The landowners felt that larger farms with enclosed fields would increase farming efficiency and productivity. When Parliament endorsed this **enclosure movement**, new laws allowed landowners to enclose private and common lands, combining them into their estates.

The enclosure movement transformed rural areas throughout Great Britain. Many small farmers who had depended on village lands were forced to move to larger towns and cities to find work. At the same time, landowners began to practice new, more effective farming methods.

To achieve the greatest output from their land, these large-scale farmers improved traditional farming methods such as crop rotation systems. Many also experimented with breeding—using larger and stronger animals to produce fatter cattle and more powerful horses. New tools, such as the seed drill, enabled farmers to plant seeds in orderly rows instead of scattering them over the fields. As innovation and competition replaced traditional methods, British agriculture was soon a successful profit-making business, not just a way of life.

Great Britain Leads the Way

This agricultural revolution helped Great Britain to lead the Industrial Revolution. Successful farming businesses provided landowners with money to invest in growing industries. Many

Chapter 23 Section 2

SECTION THEME

▶ **Innovation** A series of inventions and new procedures in agriculture and industry transform economies in Europe and North America.

Find Out

Answer: *because of its supply of capital, its rich natural resources, and its growing population; also, the agricultural revolution provided landowners with money to invest in industry and led farmworkers to leave their homes and look for work in industry*

FOCUS

Section Objective

Explain why the Industrial Revolution began in Great Britain.

BELLRINGER
Motivational Activity

Before taking roll at the beginning of the class period, project Section Focus Transparency 23-2 and have students answer the activity questions. Discuss students' responses.

This activity is also available as a blackline master.

Vocabulary Pre-check

Use Vocabulary Activity 23 to introduce vocabulary terms. **L1 LEP**

SECTION RESOURCES

Reproducible Masters
- Reproducible Lesson Plan 23-2
- Vocabulary Activity 23
- Guided Reading Activity 23-2
- Geography and History Activity 23
- Section Quiz 23-2

Transparencies
- Section Focus Transparency 23-2

Multimedia
- Student Self-Test and Review Software
- Testmaker
- Turning Points in World History: *The Industrial Revolution*

Chapter 23
Section 2

TEACH

Guided Practice

THEME **Innovation**

Ask students why they think textiles were in the forefront of technological innovation. *(A British textile industry already existed but could not meet the increasing demand for cloth.)* **L1**

Visualizing History One indication of the enormous growth of the textile industry was the increase in cotton imports: in the 1760s Britain imported 4 million pounds (1,816 kilograms) of cotton yearly; by the 1830s it was importing 300 million pounds (13,620,000 kilograms).
Answer to Caption: *by passing laws that helped business*

Economics Ask students why the British had surplus capital to invest in the late 1700s. *(Landowners benefited from new large-scale farming; they and others also profited from overseas commerce, including the slave trade.)* **L2**

Time Line Have students construct a time line of important eighteenth-century developments in the textile industry. **L2**

Who?What?Where?When?

James Hargreaves (who may have named the spinning jenny after his wife) tried to keep his invention secret. But other spinners became suspicious because his family produced so much yarn. They burst into his house, destroyed his machine, and forced the family to move away.

Visualizing History **The task of beating cotton by hand was replaced by a beating and lapping machine in the 1700s.** *How did Parliament encourage investment in industry?*

displaced farmers became industrial workers. These factors added to the key elements for industrial success that Great Britain already possessed—capital, natural resources, and labor supply.

Money and Industry

Capital, or money to invest in labor, machines, and raw materials, is essential for the growth of industry. Many British people became very wealthy during the 1700s. Landowners and other members of the aristocracy profited not only from new large-scale farming but also from overseas commerce and the slave trade, as you learned in Chapter 17. At the same time, an emerging middle class of British merchants and shopkeepers had grown more prosperous from trade.

Industry provided the aristocracy and the middle class with new opportunities to invest their money. By investing in growing industries, they stood a good chance of making a profit. Parliament encouraged investment by passing laws that helped the growing businesses.

Natural Resources

Great Britain's wealth also included its rich supply of natural resources. The country had fine harbors and a large network of rivers that flowed year-round. Water provided power for developing industries and transported raw materials and finished goods.

Great Britain also had huge supplies of iron and coal, the principal raw materials of the Industrial Revolution. Iron and the steel made from it proved to be the ideal materials for building industrial machinery. An abundance of coal also helped to fuel industry.

Large Labor Supply

Perhaps the country's greatest natural resource was its growing population of workers. Improvements in farming led to an increased availability of food. Better, more nutritious food allowed people to enjoy longer, healthier lives. In just one century, England's population nearly doubled, growing from about 5 million in 1700 to about 9 million in 1800.

The changes in farming also helped to increase the supply of industrial workers. With the introduction of machinery such as the steel plow, farms needed fewer workers. Former farmworkers left their homes to find jobs in more populated and industrialized areas.

Ambitious British people in the middle and upper classes organized and managed the country's growing industries. These risk-taking entrepreneurs (AHN•truh•pruh•NUHRS), or businesspeople, set up industries by bringing together capital, labor, and new industrial inventions.

By the mid-1700s, the British domestic system was ready for change. The textile industry led the way.

Growing Textile Industries

In the 1700s people in Great Britain and overseas were eager to buy cool, colorful cotton cloth. Since the domestic system could not meet the demand, cotton merchants looked for new ways to expand production. A series of technological advances would revolutionize cloth production.

Advances in Machinery

One of the first innovations in cloth making occurred at the dawn of the Industrial Revolution. Weaving cloth was difficult and time-consuming work. Weavers had to push a shuttle back and forth across a loom by hand. Then they had to beat the

COOPERATIVE LEARNING ACTIVITY

Research Organize the class into groups. Have each group research innovations in one of these areas: farming, textiles, power sources, transportation. Each team member should be assigned a specific topic; for example, a student in the group examining power sources could research the use of wood or coal.

After completing their research, the groups should meet to share their findings. Each team member should summarize his or her research for the group. Then each team should create a general summary, to be delivered orally by one member. **L2** woof—the threads that run crosswise—down tightly against the previous row. The width of the fabric was limited by the distance a weaver could "throw" the shuttle.

In 1733 British clock maker John Kay improved the loom with his "flying shuttle." Instead of pushing the shuttle by hand, the weaver simply pulled sharply on a cord, and the shuttle "flew" across the loom. Wider fabrics could be woven at a faster pace.

Using the flying shuttle, weavers could produce two to three times more material; thus they needed more yarn than ever from the spinners. To answer this need, **James Hargreaves**, a weaver-carpenter, in the 1760s invented a more efficient spinning machine that he called the spinning jenny. Early models of the spinning jenny enabled one person to spin 6 to 7 threads at a time; later refinements increased this number to 80 threads.

While the spinning jenny revolutionized spinning in the home, another invention revolutionized spinning in factories and industrial settings. In 1768 **Richard Arkwright**, a struggling barber with a great interest in machines, developed the water frame, a huge spinning machine that ran continually on waterpower.

By 1779 spinner Samuel Crompton combined the best features of the spinning jenny and the water frame into a new machine called the "spinning mule." It produced strong thread that could be woven into high-quality muslin cloth. Until this time, such fine cloth had to be imported from Asia.

Producing More Cloth

The new spinning machines produced more yarn or thread than there were weavers to use it. In 1787 **Edmund Cartwright**, a British poet and minister, answered this shortage of weavers with the development of a power loom. Running on horse, water, or steam power, the mechanical loom made it possible for weavers to keep up with the amount of yarn produced.

These new inventions created a growing need for raw cotton. Yet raw cotton was expensive because cleaning the seeds out of it was a slow and tedious job. In 1793 **Eli Whitney**, an American inventor, developed a machine that cleaned cotton 50 times more quickly than a person could. The cotton gin helped the booming British textile industry to overcome its last major hurdle on its journey toward full mechanization.

CONNECTIONS

Geography

Development of Industrial Cities

The growth of industrial cities depended on geographic factors such as the availability of raw materials and accessible routes. The city of Manchester in northern England had many geographic advantages. It lies close to two coal fields and at the meeting point of three rivers. A canal connects the city to the Irish Sea, making it an inland port.

Manchester, England

Despite being a wool trade center, Manchester retained a rural atmosphere in the early 1700s. Merchants lived in city townhouses, and people enjoyed sailing on the Irwell River. During the 1800s Manchester grew into a center for textile manufacturing. Mills and warehouses replaced private homes in many areas. The Irwell became so badly polluted that it was described as "a flood of liquid manure."

Many saw Manchester's transformation as evidence of the evils of industrialization. Others, however, saw the change as a symbol of progress. In 1858 editors of the *Edinburgh Journal* wrote:

"Manchester streets may be irregular, its smoke may be dense, and its mud ultra-muddy, but not any or all of these things can prevent the image of a great city rising before us as the very symbol of civilization, foremost in the march of improvement...."

MAKING THE CONNECTION

1. What factors caused Manchester to become a large industrial city?
2. Do you think that what happened to Manchester can be called "progress"? Why or why not?

MEETING SPECIAL NEEDS ACTIVITY

Mixed Learners To help students grasp the timesaving quality of technological innovations, organize the class into three groups. Have one group make up mathematical problems and keep a record of the time spent solving them by members of the second and third groups. The second group should do the math problems with pencil and paper, the third with electronic calculators. Rotate the three tasks, so that each group gets to perform each task. **L2 LEP**

Chapter 23 Section 2

ABCNEWS INTERACTIVE™

VIDEODISC
Turning Points in World History

Side Two, Chapter 3
Title: *The Industrial Revolution*
Ask: How did the Industrial Revolution change population settlement patterns? *(People moved to the cities where they could work in factories.)*

Independent Practice

Guided Reading Activity 23-2 **L1**

Geography and History Activity 23

Telecast Ask students to imagine that they are TV journalists. Instruct them to present a class "telecast" discussing a technological development in Britain. **L2**

CONNECTIONS

Geography

Cities grew at an incredible pace as Britain industrialized. In 1801, at the time of the first census, Manchester was the only city aside from London whose population exceeded 100,000. In only 20 years, it was joined by others—Glasgow, Edinburgh, Liverpool, and Birmingham.

Answers to Making the Connection

1. *It was close to coal fields, at the junction of three rivers, and on a canal that connected to the sea.*
2. *Yes, in purely material terms; no, if quality of life is considered.*

Chapter 23 Section 2

Demonstration Have students research how a waterwheel provides power. Then have them present a class demonstration with a model or drawing. **L3 LEP**

Visualizing History Because the cotton gin made cotton growing more profitable, it stimulated U.S. production of the crop and thus entrenched slavery in the South. **Answer to Caption:** *It removed the seeds from the cotton.*

ASSESS

Check for Understanding

Assign Section 2 Review as homework or as an in-class activity.

Use Student Self-Test and Review Software to review Section 2.

Evaluate

Section Quiz 23-2

Use the Testmaker to create a customized quiz for Section 2.

Reteach

Have students review the three main reasons Britain led the way in industrialization.

Enrich

Have students debate which innovation discussed in this section they think was most important.

CLOSE

Ask students why they think the Industrial Revolution is sometimes called the Machine Age. **Which is the better term? Why?**

Visualizing History **Eli Whitney's original cotton gin was a simple device that one person could turn by hand.** *What task did the cotton gin perform?*

The Factory System

Since the new textile machinery was too large and costly for most workers to use in their homes, industrialists gradually moved cloth production out of workers' cottages and into the large buildings they built near major waterways. This marked the beginning of the factory system, an organized method of production that brought workers and machines together under the control of managers. The waterways powered the machines and provided transportation for raw materials and finished cloth.

As the factory system spread, manufacturers required more power than horses and water could provide. Steam power answered these growing needs. In the 1760s a Scottish mathematician named **James Watt** designed an efficient steam engine. Watt's steam engine helped to set the Industrial Revolution in full motion. Factories that had once closed down when the river froze or flowed too low could now run continuously on steam power. The steam engine also enabled industrialists to build factories in more convenient locations, not just beside waterways.

Industrial Developments

The invention of more factory machinery produced a great demand for iron and steel. Accordingly, the iron industry developed new technologies to keep up with the demand. In the mid-1800s William Kelly, an American ironworker, and **Henry Bessemer**, a British engineer, developed methods to inexpensively produce steel from iron. Steel answered industry's need for a sturdy, workable metal.

At the same time, people worked to advance transportation systems throughout Europe and the United States. Improvements to the slow, often impassable roadways began when private companies began building and paving roads. Two Scottish engineers, Thomas Telford and John McAdam, further advanced road making with better drainage systems and the use of layers of crushed rock.

Water transportation also improved. In 1761 British workers dug one of the first modern canals to link coal fields with the industrial city of Manchester. Because of this efficient transportation system, a canal building craze began both in Europe and the United States.

A combination of steam power and steel would soon revolutionize both land and water transportation. In 1801 British engineer Richard Trevithick first brought steam-powered travel to land. He devised a steam-powered carriage that ran on wheels, and three years later, a steam locomotive that ran on rails. Later, in 1807, Robert Fulton, an American inventor, designed the first practical steamboat. Railroads and steamboats laid the foundations for a global economy and opened up new forms of investment.

SECTION 2 REVIEW

Recall

1. **Define** enclosure movement, capital, entrepreneur, factory system.
2. **Identify** James Hargreaves, Richard Arkwright, Edmund Cartwright, Eli Whitney, James Watt, Henry Bessemer.
3. **List** the factors that favored the early growth of industry in Great Britain.

Critical Thinking

4. **Synthesizing Information** Write a diary entry describing the thoughts of a British farmer who has been forced off his land because of the enclosure movement.

Understanding Themes

5. **Innovation** Is an Industrial Revolution still happening today? If so, name some of today's revolutionary inventions or technological developments. How have these inventions and technological developments changed modern life?

SECTION 2 REVIEW ANSWERS

1. All vocabulary words are defined in the Glossary.
2. James Hargreaves, 605; Richard Arkwright, 605; Edmund Cartwright, 605; Eli Whitney, 605; James Watt, 606; Henry Bessemer, 606
3. surplus capital, ample natural resources, and a growing population of workers
4. Entries might express nostalgia about the "good old days," sadness about leaving the old home, or anger at the landlord.
5. INNOVATION Developments include electronic communication, medical breakthroughs, and high-speed transportation. Results include global interdependence and longer life span.

1800 — 1850 — 1900

1839 Germany builds its first major railway.

c. 1870 The United States becomes an industrial equal of Great Britain and Germany.

1895 Guglielmo Marconi develops wireless telegraph.

Section 3

The Growth of Industry

Setting the Scene

- **Terms to Define**
  industrial capitalism, interchangeable parts, division of labor, partnership, corporation, depression
- **People to Meet**
  Eli Whitney, Frederick Taylor, Henry Ford, Samuel Morse, Guglielmo Marconi, Alexander Graham Bell, Thomas Edison, Rudolf Diesel, Wilbur and Orville Wright

Find Out How did new technology advance the growth of industry?

The Storyteller

The people on the street in Paris waited impatiently for word from inside the store. "It works!" cried a spectator suddenly. Someone held up a hand. "Not so much noise. The people in Brantford [Canada] are talking ... and singing. It can be heard as plain as day." Now everyone wanted a turn at the receiver. Finally, at eleven o'clock the crowd went home. Mr. Bell's telephone was a success.

—adapted from *The Chord of Steel, The Story of the Invention of the Telephone*, Thomas B. Costain, 1960

Alexander Graham Bell's telephone

In 1789 a tall, ruddy young British worker boarded a ship bound for New York, listing his occupation in the ship's record as farmer. Although he looked like the farmer he claimed to be, Samuel Slater was actually a smuggler. Slater was stealing a valuable British commodity—industrial know-how. The 21-year-old spinner headed for the United States with the knowledge of how to build an industrial spinning wheel. When he arrived two months later, Slater introduced spinning technology to the United States.

By keeping spinning and other technologies secret, Great Britain had become the most productive country in the world. To maintain its position, Parliament passed laws restricting the flow of machines and skilled workers to other countries. Until 1824 the law that Samuel Slater had ignored prohibited craftspeople from moving to other countries. Another law made it illegal to export machinery. Nonetheless, by the late 1820s many mechanics and technicians had left Great Britain, carrying industrial knowledge with them.

Spread of Industry

As British workers left the country, Great Britain gave up trying to guard its industrial monopoly. Wealthy British industrialists saw that they could make money by spreading the Industrial Revolution to other countries.

In the mid-1800s, financiers funded railroad construction in India, Latin America, and North America. In Europe, British industrialists set up factories, supplying capital, equipment, and technical staff. The industrialists earned Great Britain the nickname "the workshop of the world." In other lands, however, large-scale manufacturing based on the factory system did not really take hold

SECTION THEME

- **Change** Throughout the Western world, new urban centers based on industry develop along with the rise of new social classes.

Find Out

Answer: *It speeded up communications and transportation and, in electricity, furnished a new source of power.*

FOCUS

Section Objective

Analyze how new technology advanced the growth of industry.

BELLRINGER
Motivational Activity

Before taking roll at the beginning of the class period, project Section Focus Transparency 23-3 and have students answer the activity questions. Discuss students' responses.

This activity is also available as a blackline master.

Vocabulary Pre-check

Use the Vocabulary PuzzleMaker to create a puzzle that reinforces the vocabulary terms in this section. **L1**

SECTION RESOURCES

Reproducible Masters
- Reproducible Lesson Plan 23-3
- Guided Reading Activity 23-3
- People in World History Profiles 43, 44
- History Simulation 23
- Section Quiz 23-3

Transparencies
- Section Focus Transparency 23-3

Multimedia
- Vocabulary PuzzleMaker Software
- Student Self-Test and Review Software
- Testmaker
- Turning Points in World History: *The Industrial Revolution*

TEACH

Guided Practice

THEME Change

Write the headings *Topic* and *Changes* on the chalkboard. Under *Topic*, list *Communications, Energy, Production Methods,* and *Business Organization.* Have a volunteer complete the chart as you elicit information from the class. **L1**

ABCNEWS INTERACTIVE™

VIDEODISC
Turning Points in World History

Side Two, Chapter 3
Title: *The Industrial Revolution*
Ask: What happened to housing as a result of the mass movement of people to cities? *(Housing became hard to find, resulting in the outgrowth of the first slums.)*

History & Art Although Germany and France lagged behind Britain in the Industrial Revolution, they soon made rapid progress. Between 1825 and the 1850s, Germany's annual production of pig iron soared from 40,000 tons to 250,000 tons. At the same time, French iron and coal output doubled.

Answer to Caption: *Great Britain, Germany, and the United States*

until 1870 or later. The major exceptions were France, Germany, and the United States.

Because the French government encouraged industrialization, France developed a large pool of outstanding scientists. In spite of this, France's industrialization was slow-paced. The Napoleonic Wars had strained the economy and depleted the workforce. For a long time the French economy depended more on farming and small businesses than on new industries. Yet with the growth of mining and railway construction, a major network of railway lines radiated in every direction from Paris by 1870.

Germany's efforts to industrialize proved more successful. Before 1830 Germans brought in some machinery from Britain and set up a few factories. In 1839 German industrialists used British capital to build the country's first major railway. In the following decade, strong coal, iron, and textile industries emerged. Even before the German states united in 1871, government funding had helped industry to grow.

At the same time, industrialization increased in the United States, especially in the Northeast. British capital and machinery, combined with American mechanical skills, promoted new industry. In time, shoe and textile factories flourished in New England. Coal mines and ironworks expanded in Pennsylvania. By 1870 the United States ranked with Great Britain and Germany as one of the world's three most industrialized countries.

Growth of Big Business

A major factor in spurring industrial growth was capitalism, the economic system in which individuals and private firms, not the government, own the means of production—including land, machinery, and the workplace. In a capitalist system, individuals decide how they can make a profit and determine business practices accordingly.

Industrialists practiced industrial capitalism, which involved continually expanding factories or investing in new businesses. After investing in a factory, industrial capitalists used profits to hire more workers and buy additional raw materials and new machines.

History & Art *Beirmeister and Wain Steel Forge* by P. S. Kroyer. Statens Museum, Copenhagen, Denmark **Industrialization spread throughout Europe.** *What were the three most industrialized nations in 1870?*

COOPERATIVE LEARNING ACTIVITY

Report Organize the class into groups. Have each group study innovations in transportation during the Industrial Revolution: railroads, steamships, and automobiles. Assign each team member a specific topic, such as method of operation, economic impact, and most common uses. After completing their research, team members should share information. Each team should then combine individual reports into a summary. One member of each team should present the group's summary. **L2**

608 Chapter 23 *Age of Industry*

Mass Production

Looking to increase their profits, manufacturers invested in machines to replace more costly human labor. Fast-working, precise machines enabled industrialists to mass-produce, or to produce huge quantities of identical goods.

In the early 1800s **Eli Whitney**, inventor of the cotton gin, contributed the concept of interchangeable parts that increased factory production. Whitney's system involved machine-made parts that were exactly alike and easily assembled or exchanged. In the past, hand-made parts were not uniform—each differed from the next to some degree.

By the 1890s industrial efficiency had become a science. **Frederick Taylor** encouraged manufacturers to divide tasks into detailed and specific segments of a step-by-step procedure.

Using Taylor's plan, industrialists devised a division of labor in their factories. Each worker performed a specialized task on a product as it moved by on a conveyor belt. The worker then returned the product to the belt where it continued down the line to the next worker. Because products were assembled in a moving line, this method was called the assembly line.

American automobile manufacturer **Henry Ford** used assembly-line methods in 1913 to mass-produce his Model T automobiles. Ford described the assembly line this way:

> "The man who places a part does not fasten it. The man who puts in a bolt does not put in a nut; the man who puts on the nut does not tighten it. Every piece of work in the shop moves; it may move on hooks, on overhead chains.... No workman has anything to do with moving or lifting anything. Save ten steps a day for each of the 12,000 employees, and you will have saved fifty miles of wasted motion and misspent energy."
>
> —Henry Ford, *Ford*, 1913

As Ford produced greater quantities of his cars, the cost of producing each car fell, allowing him to drop the price. Millions of people could then buy what earlier only a few could afford.

Organizing Business

As production increased, industrial leaders developed various ways to manage the growing business world and to ensure a continual flow of capital for business expansion. In addition to individual and family businesses, many people formed partnerships. A partnership is a business organization involving two or more entrepreneurs who can raise more capital and take on more business than if each had gone into business alone. Partners share management responsibility and debt liability.

Corporations take the idea of partnership many steps further. Corporations are business organizations owned by stockholders who buy shares in a company. Stockholders vote on major decisions concerning the corporations. Each vote carries weight according to the number of shares owned. Shares decrease or increase in value depending on the profits earned by the company. In the late 1800s, as industries grew larger, corporations became one of the best ways to manage new businesses.

Business Cycles

As market needs grew more complex, individual businesses concentrated on producing a particular kind of product. This increase in specialization made growing industries dependent on each other. When one industry did well, other related industries also flourished. A great demand for cars, for example, led to expansion in the petroleum industry. Likewise, bad conditions in one industry often spread rapidly to other related industries.

The economic fate of an entire country came to rest on business cycles, or alternating periods of business expansion and decline. Business cycles follow a certain sequence, beginning with expansion. In this "boom" phase, buying, selling, production, and employment rates are high. When expansion ends, a "bust" period of decreased business activity follows. The lowest point in the business cycle is a depression, which is characterized by bank failures and widespread unemployment. As industry increasingly dominated the economy, more people suffered during "bust" periods.

Science and Industry

Amateur inventors relying heavily on trial and error produced most industrial advances at the beginning of the Industrial Revolution. By the late 1800s, manufacturers began to apply more scientific findings to their businesses.

Communications

Science played an important role in the development of communications. In the 1830s **Samuel Morse**, an American inventor, assembled a working model of the telegraph. Using a system of dots and dashes, the telegraph carried information at high speeds. Soon telegraph lines linked most European and North American cities.

Chapter 23 Section 3

History Simulation 23

Independent Practice

Guided Reading Activity 23-3 **L1**

People in World History Profiles 43, 44

Illustration Have students create before-and-after drawings to show changes that occurred during the Industrial Revolution. For example, a *before* picture could show a family in a carriage, while an *after* picture would show a family on a train or in a car. **L1 LEP**

Technology Have students research and present an oral report on the history and uses of Morse code. If possible, have them demonstrate Morse code messages in class. **L2**

Who?What?Where?When?

The corporation had its roots in the joint-stock companies that were formed during the Commercial Revolution of the 1600s. Most joint-stock companies were simple trading companies, however. A corporation, like a person, can own property, buy and sell goods, and bring lawsuits. Its stockholders have limited liability. This means that, if the corporation fails, no stockholder is liable for more than his or her original investment.

Business Have students research and report on a contemporary stock exchange, such as the New York Stock Exchange. Students' reports should summarize how the exchange is organized and how it works. **L3**

MEETING SPECIAL NEEDS ACTIVITY

Language Delayed Have students interview their parents and/or grandparents about technological changes that have occurred during their lifetimes. (They may wish to tape the interviews.) Have them find out what changes have most impressed the interviewees and how the changes have affected their lives. **L1 LEP**

TEACH

Remind students that the chief metal for centuries was iron. But cast iron, though hard, was brittle, and wrought iron was malleable but soft. People knew that steel was better—hard but not brittle—but it was expensive to make. Only with the Bessemer process, developed in the mid-nineteenth century, did cheap steel become widely available. Ask students if they think Benton's mural is a realistic portrayal of steel manufacturing. *(Answers will vary. Some may say it represents a romantic view of a mill.)*

CURRICULUM CONNECTION

MATHEMATICS

As industrialization spread, a common system of weights and measures became necessary. Most countries of the world adopted the metric system, first developed in France in the 1790s. Its basic measurement, the meter, equals one ten-millionth of the distance along a meridian from the Equator to one of the Poles.

NATIONAL GEOGRAPHIC PICTURING HISTORY

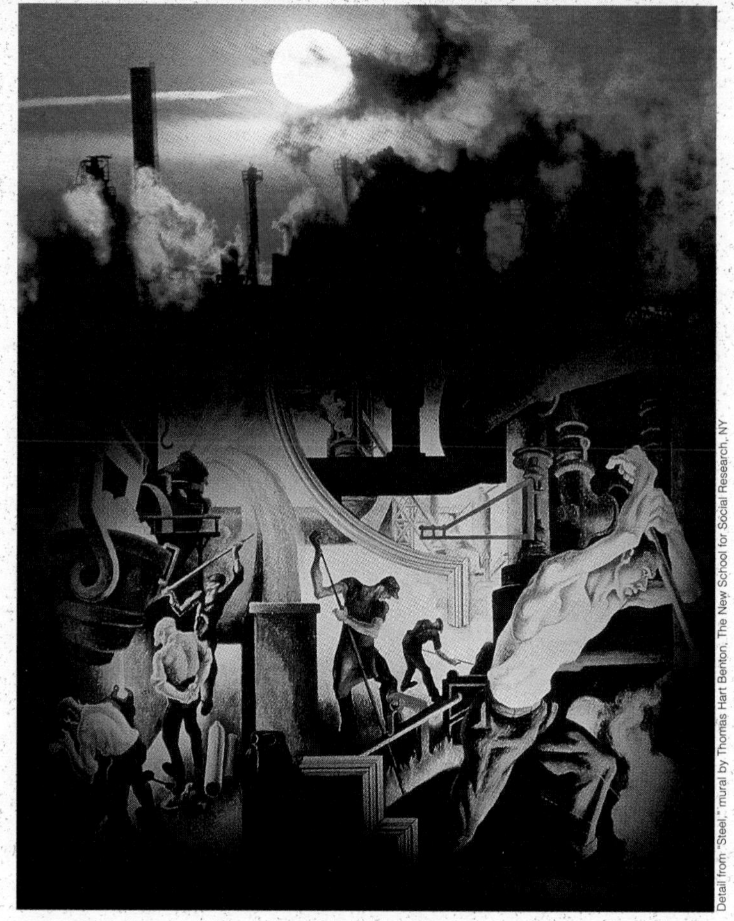

Detail from "Steel," mural by Thomas Hart Benton. The New School for Social Research, NY

Steel

Coal, iron, and steel; railroads, steamships, and airplanes; factories, skyscrapers, and steel forges: This was the new world of the age of industry depicted by artist Thomas Hart Benton in this mural painted in 1930. This section, called "Steel," was taken from a drawing Benton had sketched of a Maryland steel plant. The workers in the mural are skilled and strong, the kind of American citizens who will make the American democracy, originally designed for an agricultural world, thrive in the industrial environment.

The Industrial Revolution began in Great Britain in the late 1700s. By applying steam power to iron machinery the British profoundly transformed how things were made. These new industries began to change how people worked, where they lived, how they ate, and what they needed to know in order to survive. After 1870 the United States and Germany began to take the lead in industrialization, and steel became the most important metal used in industry. In this mural Benton welded a new industrial image to an older republican ideal.

Other advances in communications included the development of the radio. Although British physicist James Clerk Maxwell in 1864 promoted the idea that electromagnetic waves travel through space at the speed of light, it took 30 years to apply this idea to technology. Italian inventor **Guglielmo Marconi** devised the wireless telegraph in 1895. This machine was later modified into the radio.

Development of the telephone in 1876 is credited to **Alexander Graham Bell**, a Scottish-born American teacher of the deaf. Tiny electrical wires carrying sound allowed people to speak to each other over long distances.

Electricity

By the early 1900s, scientists had devised ways to harness electrical power. As a result, electricity replaced coal as the major source of industrial fuel. In 1831 Michael Faraday, a British chemist and physicist, had discovered that moving a magnet through a coil in a copper wire would produce an electric current. Over 40 years later, in the 1870s, an electric motor was based on this principle.

An American inventor made great strides in the development of electricity. In 1877 **Thomas Edison** invented the phonograph, which reproduced sound. Two years later, he made electric lighting cheap and accessible by inventing incandescent lightbulbs.

Energy and Engines

The Industrial Revolution surged forward with advances in engines. In the late 1880s Gottlieb Daimler, a German engineer, redesigned the internal-combustion engine to run on gasoline. The small portable engine produced enough power to propel vehicles and boats. Another German engineer, **Rudolf Diesel**, developed an oil-burning internal-combustion engine that could run industrial plants, ocean liners, and locomotives. These inventions ushered in the age of the motor car.

AROUND THE WORLD

World's Highest Railroad Is Built

Peru, 1870

Henry Meiggs, an American engineer, began building Peru's Central Railway in 1870. Meiggs died before his ambitious project was completed, but the Central Railway remains one of the world's great engineering marvels. The standard-gauge railroad begins at sea level, near Lima, and climbs through the Andes to Huancayo. At its highest point, the Central Railway reaches an altitude of nearly 16,000 feet (5,000 m), higher than the tallest peak in the Alps.

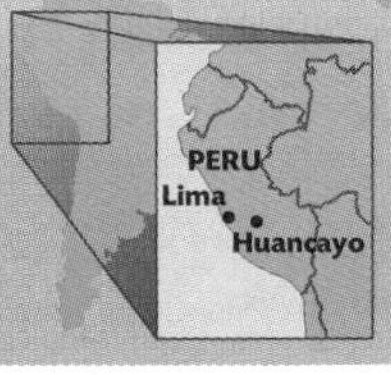

Gasoline engines carried aviation technology to new levels of achievement. In the 1890s Germany's Ferdinand von Zeppelin streamlined the dirigible, a 40-year-old balloonlike invention that could carry passengers. Meanwhile, other scientists experimented with flying heavier aircraft. The American inventors **Wilbur and Orville Wright** achieved success in 1903 with the first flight of a motorized airplane. Although the first flight covered a distance of only 120 feet (37 m), the brothers flew their wooden airplane a distance of 100 miles (161 km) only 5 years later.

The new airplanes and other vehicles needed a steady supply of fuel for power and rubber for tires and other parts. As a result, the petroleum and rubber industries skyrocketed. Innovations in transportation, communications, and electricity changed life at an amazing rate. The world sped forward into an era of ever-increasing mechanization.

SECTION 3 REVIEW

Recall

1. **Define** industrial capitalism, interchangeable parts, division of labor, partnership, corporation, depression.
2. **Identify** Eli Whitney, Frederick Taylor, Henry Ford, Samuel Morse, James Clerk Maxwell, Guglielmo Marconi, Alexander Graham Bell, Michael Faraday, Thomas Edison, Rudolf Diesel, Wilbur and Orville Wright.
3. **List** the major advantages of assembly-line production.

Critical Thinking

4. **Synthesizing Information** Imagine you are a teenager living in the early 1900s. Choose one invention mentioned in this section and describe how it has changed your life.

Understanding Themes

5. **Change** What effects do you think that industrial advancements, such as mass production and the assembly line, have had on workers' lives?

Chapter 23 Section 3

ASSESS

Check for Understanding

Assign Section 3 Review as homework or as an in-class activity.

Use Student Self-Test and Review Software to review Section 3.

Who?What?Where?When?

Guglielmo Marconi, inventor of the wireless telegraph, was inspired to experiment with science after reading a biography of Benjamin Franklin.

Evaluate

Section Quiz 23-3

Use the Testmaker to create a customized quiz for Section 3.

Reteach

Have students review the growth of big business, as described in this section.

Enrich

Ask students to investigate how internal-combustion engines are used today and give brief oral reports on their findings.

CLOSE

Have students show how capital was necessary to develop innovations summarized in this section.

SECTION 3 REVIEW ANSWERS

1. All vocabulary words are defined in the Glossary.
2. Eli Whitney, 609; Frederick Taylor, 609; Henry Ford, 609; Samuel Morse, 609; James Clerk Maxwell, 611; Guglielmo Marconi, 611; Alexander Graham Bell, 611; Michael Faraday, 611; Thomas Edison, 611; Rudolf Diesel, 611; Wilbur and Orville Wright, 611
3. worker efficiency, greater speed, lower costs, more goods produced
4. Answers should reflect a knowledge of inventions in this section.
5. **CHANGE** Students may say that in many cases, industrial advancements have led to boredom and dissatisfaction; however, by lowering product costs, they have enabled more workers to buy more products.

Chapter 23
Section 4

SECTION THEME

▶ **Conflict** Workers in Europe and North America organize to gain better wages and improved working conditions.

Find Out

Answer: *As the middle class expanded, separate spheres developed for men and women. People worked in factories more than on farms. Wages were low, and often the whole family worked. Conditions and pay were so poor that workers formed unions to fight more effectively against factory owners.*

FOCUS

Section Objective

Describe how the Industrial Revolution affected people's lives.

BELLRINGER
Motivational Activity

Before taking roll at the beginning of the class period, project Section Focus Transparency 23-4 and have students answer the activity questions. Discuss students' responses.

This activity is also available as a blackline master.

Vocabulary Pre-check

Use Vocabulary Activity 23 to introduce vocabulary terms. **L1 LEP**

1800 — 1850 — 1900

c. 1800 Combination Acts passed by British Parliament ban labor unions.

1845 Massachusetts mill workers petition state for better working conditions.

1870 British Parliament legalizes labor unions.

c. 1900 Labor union membership grows steadily in Europe and North America.

Section 4

A New Society

Setting the Scene

▶ **Terms to Define**
labor union, collective bargaining

▶ **Places to Locate**
Massachusetts

Find Out How did the Industrial Revolution affect people's lives?

The Storyteller

Factory inspectors interviewed a little boy who worked carrying coal early in the Industrial Revolution:

I don't know how old I am; father is dead; mother is dead also. I began to work when I was about 9. I first worked for a man who used to hit me with the belt or with tools and fling coals at me. I left him and went to see if I could get another job. I used to sleep in the old pits that had no more coal in them; I laid upon the shale all night. I used to eat whatever I could get; I ate for a long time the candles that I found in the pits. I work now for a man who serves me well; he pays me with food and drink.

—freely adapted from *Hard Times, Human Documents of the Industrial Revolution*, E. Royston Pike, 1966

Child at work

Before the Industrial Age, a person's position in life was determined at birth, and most people had little chance of rising beyond that level. Few managed to rise above their inherited place in the rigid European society.

As the Industrial Revolution progressed throughout the 1700s and 1800s, however, new opportunities made the existing social structure more flexible. Many people, such as inventor Richard Arkwright, used their talents and the opportunities presented by the Industrial Age to rise from humble beginnings to material success.

The youngest of 13 children of poor parents, Arkwright trained to become a barber. Yet machines, not his barbershop, occupied his time and energy. Spurred by the developments in the textile industry, Arkwright developed the huge water-frame spinning wheel that was powered by water and spun continuously. Arkwright persuaded investors to join him in establishing textile mills throughout Great Britain.

Soon Arkwright's mills employed more than 5,000 people. He amassed a great fortune, became active in politics, and was eventually knighted by Great Britain's King George III.

The Rise of the Middle Class

Although few businesspeople in Europe and America prospered as Arkwright had, industrialization did expand the size, power, and wealth of the middle class. Once made up of a small number of bankers, lawyers, doctors, and merchants, the middle class now also included successful owners of factories, mines, and railroads. Professional workers such as clerks, managers, and teachers added to the growing numbers.

Many wealthy manufacturers and other members of the middle class strongly believed in education as the key to business success. Politically

SECTION RESOURCES

Reproducible Masters
- Reproducible Lesson Plan 23-4
- Vocabulary Activity 23
- Guided Reading Activity 23-4
- Reteaching Activity 23
- Enrichment Activity 23
- Section Quiz 23-4
- Performance Assessment Activity 23
- Spanish Chapter Summary 23

Transparencies
- Section Focus Transparency 23-4
- World History and Art Transparency 30, *Le Moulin de la Galette*

Multimedia
- Student Self-Test and Review Software
- Testmaker
- Turning Points in World History: *The Industrial Revolution*

active, they became involved in many reform efforts, including education, health care, prison improvements, and sanitation.

Middle-Class Lifestyles

As European and American middle-class men rose in society and assumed the role of sole provider for families, family life began to change. By the end of the late 1800s, stereotypes emerged from the middle class that created and reinforced the idea that men and women occupied different roles based on differences in their characters. Men centered their energy on the workplace, while women concentrated their efforts on maintaining the home and bringing up children.

Visualizing History **During the late 1800s, the middle classes in North America and Great Britain stressed the importance of leisure activities shared by the entire family.** *How did middle-class male and female roles differ?*

As soon as the family could afford it, a middle-class woman would hire domestic help. The number of her servants increased with her wealth. In 1870 an English guidebook listed the sequence in which women hired new help. First she "hires a washerwoman occasionally, then a charwoman, then a cook and housemaid, a nurse or two, a governess, a lady's maid, a housekeeper...." Servants, usually women, did the more difficult and unpleasant household chores, such as carrying loads of wood and coal, washing laundry, and cleaning house.

As middle-class women freed themselves from more tedious labor, they devoted their time to other occupations, such as educating their children, hand-sewing and embroidering, and planning meals. Magazines for women proliferated at this time, instructing housewives in everything from cooking and housekeeping to geography and natural science.

A typical day for one American middle-class woman in the early 1800s began at 6:00 A.M. and lasted until after 10:00 P.M. After waking up the family, the woman fed her infant son and then sat down to breakfast with her family. She read the Bible to her other three children, prayed with the servants, and then ordered the meals for the day. During the day she wrote letters, took one child to the park, and supervised the older daughters in feeding the younger children and folding up the laundry. The woman's schedule continued after nightfall. "After tea," she wrote, "read to [the children] till bedtime...."

Middle-class parents sent their boys to school to receive training for employment or preparation for higher education. Sons often inherited their fathers' positions or worked in the family business. Most daughters were expected to learn to cook, sew, and attend to all the workings of the household so that they would be well prepared for marriage.

Lives of the Working Class

As the middle class in Europe and America grew, so too did the working class in even greater numbers. The members of this class enjoyed few of the new luxuries that the upper and middle classes could now afford. Most people in the working classes had once labored on rural farms and now made up the majority of workers in new industries. Workers depended solely on the money they earned to buy what they needed. Unlike in earlier days, they did not grow or make what their families needed.

Footnotes to History

Shampoo

In the early 1900s, 25-year-old Joseph Breck tried in vain to find a cure for premature baldness. His efforts, however, led to a full line of hair care products that replaced the harsh soaps used at that time. Breck's businesses soon led the United States in shampoo production.

COOPERATIVE LEARNING ACTIVITY

Debate Organize the class into two groups, one representing workers and the other representing factory owners. Workers should present the grievances they have against management (poor working conditions, low pay, dangerous conditions, and so on). Management should counter with the benefits factory owners have conferred on society (wages, lower costs for products, and so on). Each team member should speak when the debate is held. **L2**

TEACH

Guided Practice

THEME Conflict

Discuss the conflicts between industrialists and workers. **Why did conflict arise between mill owners and the workers in their factories?** *(Industrialists wanted to maximize profits by keeping wages low and hours long; laborers wanted to improve their quality of life by doing the opposite.)* **L1**

Visualizing History Along with music, middle-class families enjoyed reading aloud, playing card games such as whist, and acting out charades.

Answer to Caption: *Men focused on the workplace, while women concentrated on the home.*

Role Play Have some students take the role of factory workers and others the role of newspaper or television reporters. The latter should interview the former about a typical day at the factory. **L2 LEP**

Daily Life Ask students to compare the roles of men and women in the middle class with those of working-class men and women. *(Middle-class men and women had very different roles, the men involved in the world of work and the women caring for the children and the house. Among the working classes, both men and women worked long hours.)* **L2**

World History and Art Transparency 30, *Le Moulin de la Galette*

Economics Have students assume the role of entrepreneur, imagining that they are starting their own business. They should choose a form of business organization—individual ownership, partnership, or corporation—and explain why it is best for their particular enterprise. **L3**

ABC NEWS INTERACTIVE™

VIDEODISC
Turning Points in World History

Side Two, Chapter 3
Title: *The Industrial Revolution*
Ask: What were working conditions like for children? *(Children worked long hours for low pay in terrible conditions.)* How did workers express their opposition to work conditions? *(They formed unions and lobbied for government regulation to protect workers.)*

Independent Practice

Guided Reading Activity 23-4 **L1**

Music Have students prepare an oral report on a labor song such as "Sixteen Tons." (Several such songs can be found in the *Folksinger's Wordbook.*) Students should present the lyrics of the songs and summarize the background of the specific events and people mentioned. **L2**

At the Mercy of Machinery

When British and American industrialists first established mill towns such as Lowell, Manchester, Sheffield, and Fall River, work conditions were tolerable. As industrial competition increased, however, work became harder and increasingly more dangerous. Managers assigned workers more machines to operate and insisted that workers perform their tasks as fast as possible throughout the day.

Under the system of division of labor, workers did the same tasks over and over again, and did not have the satisfaction of seeing the completed work. The combination of monotonous work and heavy, noisy, repetitive machinery made the slightest interruption in the work potentially dangerous. Many workers—often children—lost fingers and limbs, and even their lives, to factory machinery.

Time ruled the lives of the industry workers down to the second. On the farms, workers' days had followed the sun and the weather. Now rigid schedules clocked by ringing bells commanded their every minute. One woman who worked in a Lowell, **Massachusetts**, textile mill wrote about her frustration in 1841:

> "I am going home, where I shall not be obliged to rise so early in the morning, nor be dragged about by the factory bell, nor confined in a close noisy room from morning to night. I shall not stay here.... Up before day, at the clang of the bell—and out of the mill by the clang of the bell—into the mill, and at work in obedience to that ding-dong of a bell—just as though we were so many living machines."
>
> —anonymous worker, *The Lowell Offering*

In the textile mills, workers spent 10 to 14 hours a day in unventilated rooms filled with lint and dust. Diseases such as pneumonia and tuberculosis spread throughout the factories, killing many workers. In coal mines, workers faced the danger of working with heavy machinery and of breathing in coal dust in the mines.

Images of the Times

The Industrial Age

Industrialization brought new products and leisure activities to many people. It also produced terrible working conditions that gave rise to labor unions.

A badge of an early labor union represents the cooperative efforts of workers to seek fair wages and a more humane workplace.

614

Images of the Times **The Industrial Age**

The courtyard shown here was ringed by tiny houses. In complexes like this, a house usually had just two rooms, one per family. The only light and air came through the courtyard, for other houses backed up to the ones shown. There was no running water. A common tap and a single toilet in the courtyard served all the families that lived there. In American cities such as New York, old houses were subdivided into tiny, dark apartments. Several families often lived in a single room. In New York's Lower East Side, 290,000 people lived in one square mile. Yet rents were 25 to 30 percent higher than in middle-class neighborhoods uptown.

For these long hours at dangerous work, employees earned little to support themselves and their families. Factory owners kept workers' wages low so that their businesses could make profits. Women often made half the wages as men for the same job. Children were paid even less.

Workers' Lives

To earn enough money, whole families worked in the factories and mines, including small children as young as 6 years old. Children often worked 12-hour shifts, sometimes longer and through the night, with only a short break to eat a small meal.

Working-class children did not usually go to school, spending most of the day working instead. Many became crippled or ill from working under unhealthful and dangerous conditions. In 1843 an observer wrote that a child worker in the brickfields "works from 6 in the morning till 8 or 9 at night … Finds her legs swell sometimes … and [suffers] pains and aches between the shoulders, and her hands swell."

For many women, the industries offered new opportunities for independence. For centuries, women's choices were limited almost entirely either to marriage or to life in a convent. Now they could earn a living. Textile mills in New England, for example, provided young single women an opportunity to make money while making new friends. These "mill girls" lived together in mill boardinghouses where they often gathered in study groups devoted to reading and discussing literature.

Yet for the majority of working-class women and their families, life consisted of a difficult working life and an uncomfortable home life. Workers often lived in crowded, cold apartments in poorly constructed tenement housing near factories. Sometimes whole families lived in one or two rooms.

Because the mill owners often owned the workers' housing, they controlled the rent and decided when and whether to improve living conditions. New urban problems complicated life. Human and industrial waste contaminated water supplies and spread diseases such as cholera and typhoid. In the

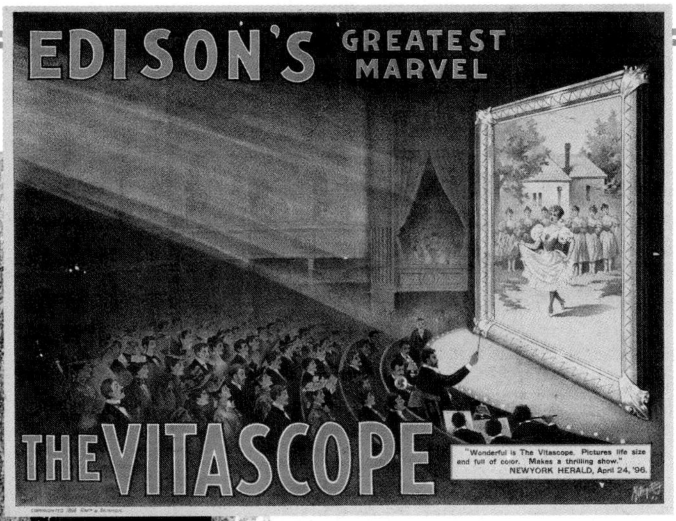

Edison's Vitascope, an early type of motion picture projector, fascinated large audiences.

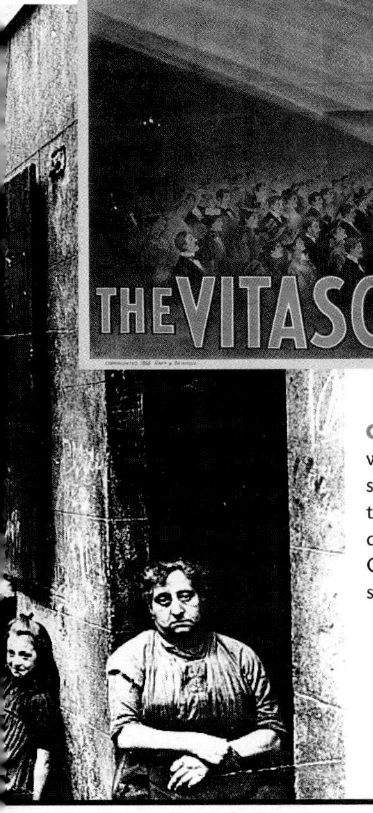

Children of the working class were often underfed and without schooling. Many in this London tenement lived with discouraged parents. Others worked alongside adults.

REFLECTING ON THE TIMES

1. Why did labor unions organize in the industrial period?
2. How did the Industrial Revolution tend to divide people into separate classes?

615

ANSWERS TO REFLECTING ON THE TIMES

1. because workers on their own could not effectively stand up to the powerful mill owners
2. It enabled the middle class to get richer but made workers' lives poorer and harsher; also, the wealth of the middle class was gained by exploiting laborers.

Daily Life Have students research and report on men's and women's clothing during some period of the Industrial Revolution. Their reports should answer such questions as: Did social classes dress differently, and if so, how? Ask students what conclusions they can draw about the period by studying its clothing. **L3**

Who?What?Where?When?

Luddites, who were named after a (probably legendary) worker named Ned Ludd, organized an early protest against industrialization. In the early 1800s, these English laborers smashed textile machines that were putting them out of work. Some of the Luddites were hanged, and others were transported to Australia.

Cultural Perspectives

Women's Rights Middle-class married women during the industrial age benefited from domestic help, but they had few legal rights. In England, for example, a woman forfeited to her husband not only her property but also her right to control it. A man could will his wife's property to someone without her consent.

Chapter 23 Section 4

ASSESS

Check for Understanding

Assign Section 4 Review as homework or as an in-class activity.

Use Student Self-Test and Review Software to review Section 4.

Visualizing History The I.W.W. (Industrial Workers of the World) was a militant American labor organization of the early 1900s. **Answer to Caption:** *Among other things, they circulated blacklists.*

Evaluate

Section Quiz 23-4

Use the Testmaker to create a customized quiz for Section 4.

Reteach

Have students form two groups. Have one group present a skit showing typical middle-class life; have the other group present a skit showing working-class life during the time.

Reteaching Activity 23

Enrich

Have students draw a cartoon expressing a factory worker's dissatisfaction.

Enrichment Activity 23

CLOSE

Have students summarize the social changes that accompanied the Industrial Revolution.

THE I.W.W.
is
COMING!
JOIN THE
ONE BIG UNION

Visualizing History **Through posters, early labor unions called for unity, realizing that the individual worker was powerless.** *How did factory owners try to prevent unionization?*

late 1800s, Holyoke, a Massachusetts mill town, had the highest infant mortality rate in the United States.

Workers Unite

Although governments in Great Britain, Germany, and France began to recognize the workers' complaints and initiate industrial reforms such as better lighting and safety equipment, workers still labored under harsh conditions. Only through forming organized labor groups were workers able to begin to improve their working conditions in the late 1800s and early 1900s.

Workers knew that they could not fight successfully as individuals against the factory owners. They had to join together into groups to make their problems heard. In Great Britain, many workers joined to form worker associations, which were groups dedicated to representing the interests of workers in a specific industry. The associations hoped to improve the wages and working conditions of their members. Eventually these worker associations developed into **labor unions** both in Europe and in the United States in the 1800s.

Union Tactics

Workers in labor unions protested in many ways. They organized strikes, in which every worker refused to work. Other times, in sit-down strikes, workers stopped working but refused to leave their work area.

Despite these efforts, unions faced great opposition. Manufacturers complained that the shorter hours and higher wages would add to production costs, increase the price of goods, and hurt business. To discourage workers from joining unions, factory owners added the names of suspected union members to a blacklist to prevent them from getting jobs throughout the industry. The British Parliament even banned unions in the Combination Acts of 1799 and 1800.

Yet British workers kept their cause alive. They finally won their cause in the 1820s when Parliament agreed that workers could meet to discuss working hours and wages. In the following years, skilled British workers formed unions based on a specific trade or craft, such as woodworking. Because they had valuable skills, these trade union members were able to bargain with employers. When union leaders and an employer meet together to discuss problems and reach an agreement, they practice **collective bargaining**. The British unions' power increased in the 1870s after Parliament legalized strikes.

Following the skilled trade unions' success, unskilled workers such as textile workers and coal miners formed unions in the late 1880s. By the beginning of the 1900s, union membership grew steadily in Europe and the United States.

SECTION 4 REVIEW

Recall

1. **Define** labor unions, collective bargaining.
2. **Identify** Combination Acts.
3. **Discuss** what effect the separation of home and work had on middle-class and working-class people in America and Europe.

Critical Thinking

4. **Analyzing Information** Why were industrialists often able to subject workers to poor working conditions?

Understanding Themes

5. **Conflict** What were some of the problems that factory workers faced? Why did they form labor unions to solve them?

SECTION 4 REVIEW ANSWERS

1. All vocabulary words are defined in the Glossary.
2. Combination Acts, 616
3. effect on middle class: created separate spheres for men and women; effects on working class: both men and women subject to harsh factory conditions much of the day, had impoverished home lives
4. because factory workers were unskilled and many others would be willing to take their place
5. **CONFLICT** Factory workers faced long hours, low pay, and difficult and often dangerous working conditions. They formed unions to gain strength in numbers.

Critical Thinking SKILLS

Detecting Bias

Suppose you see a billboard showing two happy customers shaking hands with "Honest Harry," the owner of a used-car sales business. The ad says, " Visit Honest Harry for the best deal on wheels." That evening you see a television program that investigates used-car sales businesses. The report says that many of these businesses cheat their customers.

Each message expresses a strong bias. A bias is an inclination or prejudice that inhibits impartiality. Most people have preconceived feelings, opinions, and attitudes that affect their judgment on many topics. For this reason, ideas that profess to be facts may turn out to be opinions. Detecting bias enables us to evaluate the accuracy of information.

Learning the Skill

In detecting bias, first identify the writer's or speaker's purpose. For example, the billboard ad is a marketing tool for selling cars. We would expect that it has a strong bias. The television report may also have a bias, because bad news attracts more viewers.

Another clue to identify bias is emotionally charged language such as *exploit*, *terrorize*, and *cheat*. Also look for visual images that provoke an emotional response. For example, in the television report an interview with a person who bought a "lemon" automobile may elicit a strong response.

Look for overgeneralizations such as *unique*, *honest*, and *everybody*. Notice italics, underlining, and punctuation that highlights particular ideas. Watch for opinions stated as facts without substantiating evidence. Finally, examine the material to determine whether it presents equal coverage of differing views.

Practicing the Skill

Industrialization produced widespread changes in society and widespread disagreement on its effects. While many people hailed the abundance of manufactured goods, others criticized its impact on working people. Karl Marx and Friedrich Engels presented their viewpoint on industrialization in the *Communist Manifesto* in 1848. Read the following excerpt and then answer these questions.

1. What is the purpose of this manifesto?
2. What are three examples of emotionally charged language?
3. According to Marx and Engels, which is more inhumane—the exploitation by feudal lords or by the bourgeoisie? Why?
4. What bias about industrialization is expressed in this excerpt?

> "The bourgeoisie *[the class of factory owners and employers]* ... has put an end to all feudal, patriarchal, idyllic relations. It has pitilessly torn asunder the motley feudal ties that bound man to his "natural superiors," and has left remaining no other nexus *[link]* between man and man than naked self-interest, than callous "cash payment." It has drowned the most heavenly of ecstasies of religious fervor, of chivalrous enthusiasm ... in the icy water of egotistical calculation.... In one word, for exploitation, veiled by religious and political illusions, it has substituted naked, shameless, direct, brutal exploitation."

Applying the Skill

Find written material about a topic of interest in your community. Possible sources include editorials, letters to the editor, and pamphlets from political candidates and interest groups. Write a short report analyzing the material for evidence of bias.

For More Practice

Turn to the Skill Practice in the Chapter Review on page 619 for more practice in detecting bias.

Critical Thinking SKILLS

TEACH

Detecting Bias Point out that everyone is biased. Without using reason, people rely on gut emotional reactions, favoring some things—a sports team, a political party—and disapproving of others—a nationality, a breed of dog. Have students list, anonymously, two biases of theirs, either positive or negative. After collecting these, read some of them aloud for class discussion. Which are positive and which negative? How might they be helpful or harmful?

Additional Practice

Skill Reinforcement Activity 23

ANSWERS TO PRACTICING THE SKILL

1. to arouse negative feelings about capitalists and capitalism
2. Emotionally charged language includes: *idyllic, pitilessly, naked, callous, heavenly, ecstasies, chivalrous, egotistical, shameless, brutal.*
3. exploitation by the bourgeoisie; at least feudal relations were accompanied by religious faith and chivalry
4. It is a totally negative force. It has destroyed all ties between people except for the "naked self-interest" expressed through a cash nexus.

Chapter 23 Review

GLENCOE TECHNOLOGY

VIDEODISC

Use MindJogger to review students' knowledge of the chapter.

MindJogger Videoquiz

Chapter 23
Disc 3 Side B

Also available in VHS.

Answers

Using Key Terms

1. l	**6.** f
2. d	**7.** c
3. i	**8.** j
4. h	**9.** k
5. b	**10.** a

Using Your History Journal

Of special interest to students would be the telephone, electricity, and the automobile.

Reviewing Facts

1. Men farmed and wove cloth; women reared children, kept house, gardened, spun thread for weaving; children helped parents.
2. John Kay, James Hargreaves, Richard Arkwright, Samuel Crompton, Edmund Cartwright, Eli Whitney
3. They wanted higher pay, shorter hours, and better working conditions.
4. because it did not want competition from other countries
5. Possible answers: The telephone made personal and business communication easier and faster. The automobile made people more mobile. The harnessing of electricity gave us the electric light and a host of appliances.

Critical Thinking

1. It increased social mobility and enlarged both the middle class and the working class.
2. Farm laborers worked in accordance with the seasons and the days, not a fixed time schedule; they also had greater autonomy.
3. Answers will vary but should focus on capital, natural resources, or a growing labor force.
4. Answers will vary. Possible answers include: positive—growth of cities, higher standard of living; negative—exploitation of labor, degradation of environment.
5. If enough people want an innovative good or service, individuals or businesses will try to develop it.

Geography in History

1. England had resources—plenty of iron ore

CHAPTER 23 REVIEW

Historical Significance

The Industrial Revolution has led to seemingly limitless possibilities. Many of the cities created by the early factories have grown and prospered. International business today is carried on with the aid of computer technology.

At the same time, the Industrial Age has carried with it many social problems as well as a depletion of natural resources. Today, people face the challenge of combining economic development with preservation of the environment.

Using Key Terms

Write the key term that completes each sentence.

a. factory system	g. industrial capitalism
b. partnership	h. entrepreneurs
c. division of labor	i. labor unions
d. corporation	j. domestic system
e. enclosure movement	k. capital
f. collective bargaining	l. depression

1. The lowest point in the business cycle is a ________, which is characterized by bank failures and widespread unemployment.
2. A ________ is a business organization owned by stockholders who buy shares in the company and vote on major decisions concerning the future of the business.
3. During the 1800s workers in Europe and North America joined to form ________, which set out to improve wages and working conditions.
4. Risk-taking ___________ were continually expanding factories or investing in new businesses.
5. A ___________ is a business organization involving two or more people who can raise more capital and take on more business than if each had gone into business alone.
6. When union leaders and an employer meet together to discuss problems and reach an agreement, they practice ________________.
7. Under a ____________, workers peform a particular task on a product as it is moved by on a conveyor belt.
8. Merchants used the _______ to hire workers to produce goods in their own homes.
9. Money invested in labor, machines, and raw materials is known as __________.
10. The ________ is an organized method of production that brings workers and machines together under the control of managers.

Using Your History Journal

From your time line of inventions choose one invention that you believe affects your life every day. How would people live today without this invention? Write a paragraph describing life without it.

Reviewing Facts

1. **Describe** what life was like for a family working under the domestic system.
2. **Name** three inventors who helped revolutionize the textile industry.
3. **List** some reasons why workers organized into labor unions.
4. **Explain** why Great Britain passed strict laws prohibiting skilled craftspeople from leaving the country.
5. **Identify** three important technological inventions of the late 1800s, and state how they affected people's lives.

Critical Thinking

1. **Apply** How did the Industrial Revolution affect Great Britain's social structure?
2. **Analyze** In what ways did the life of a farm laborer differ from the life of a factory worker?
3. **Synthesize** Great Britain had several key elements that led it to industrialize before other nations. Which element do you think was the most critical? Why?
4. **Evaluate** What do you see as the positive and negative effects of the Industrial Revolution?

CHAPTER 23 REVIEW

5. **Evaluate** How can consumer demand influence technological development?

Geography in History

1. **Region** Refer to the map below. Why did England have an advantage in developing heavy industry?
2. **Place** What industrial center is closest to several iron ore and coal fields?
3. **Movement** Railways in northern Scotland and Ireland were not built for transporting iron and coal. How can you tell this from the map? What may have been transported on these railways?

Industrial Revolution: England 1850–1870

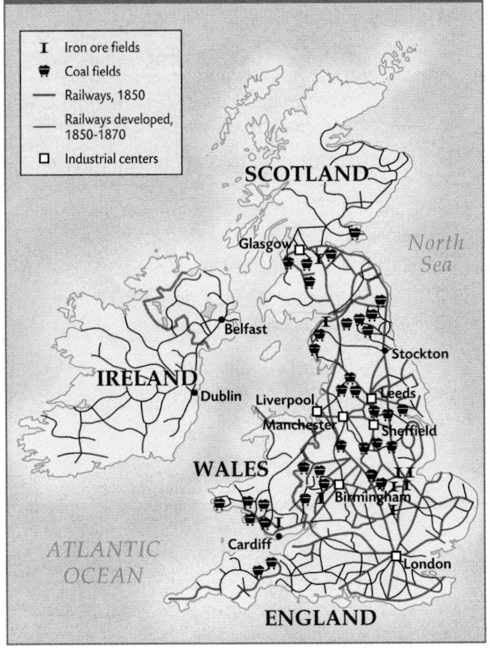

Understanding Themes

1. **Relation to Environment** How were industry and farming related during the period before the Industrial Revolution?
2. **Innovation** It is often said that "necessity is the mother of invention." Using one invention in this chapter, illustrate this statement.
3. **Change** Do you think that progress is a necessary result of change? Give examples.
4. **Conflict** How have differences between employers and workers produced positive effects for workers in the modern world?

Linking Past and Present

1. What effects do you see from the Industrial Revolution in your everyday life?
2. What changes and challenges has industry presented society in recent years?
3. The Industrial Revolution replaced many handcrafted items with mass-produced ones. What things that we use today are made mostly by hand?

Skill Practice

Read the following excerpt from "The Gospel of Wealth," an 1889 essay by Andrew Carnegie. Then answer the questions that follow.

> "The contrast between the palace of the millionaire and the cottage of the laborer with us today measures the changes which had come with civilization. The change, however, is not to be deplored, but welcomed as highly beneficial. It is well, nay, essential for the progress of the race that the houses of some should be homes for all that is highest and best in literature and the arts, and for all the refinements of civilization, rather than that none should be so. Much better this great irregularity than universal squalor."

1. Does the term *cottage* coincide with the description of how workers lived that is found on page 615?
2. How does Carnegie's use of this term indicate bias?
3. How does Carnegie justify large differences in lifestyle between rich and poor?
4. How does Carnegie describe the condition of most of humanity, except the wealthy?

Chapter 23 Review

and coal.
2. Birmingham
3. Neither of these areas has iron or coal fields. The railways may have carried agricultural products to industrial areas and industrial goods to Ireland and Scotland.

Understanding Themes

1. **RELATION TO ENVIRONMENT** Often, families were engaged in both: part-time farming and part-time industry through the domestic system.
2. **INNOVATION** Answers will vary. The textile industry offers many good examples.
3. **CHANGE** Answers will vary. Possible answer: No, the factory system, for example, brought with it exploitation of workers, child labor, and slums.
4. **CONFLICT** In industrialized nations, unions and government regulation have helped workers achieve good wages, benefits, and decent working conditions.

Linking Past and Present

1. Answers will vary but may include rapid transportation, instant communication, and a huge range of inexpensive mass-produced items.
2. Answers will vary but may include the need to adapt to electronic technology, to protect the environment, to lessen the gap between industrialized and nonindustrialized nations.
3. Possible answers: some items of clothing and furnishings (e.g., hand-knit sweaters), works of art (e.g., paintings), some musical instruments (e.g., violins, pianos)

Skill Practice

1. Answers will vary.
2. He infers that all laborers live in cottages or squalor.
3. as a progress of civilization
4. universal squalor

Chapter Bonus Test Question

Ask students: In "exporting" the Industrial Revolution to nonindustrialized nations, what do you think would be the single most important element of the nineteenth-century revolution described in this chapter to introduce? *(Answers will vary. Technological innovations might include steel manufacturing, electric power, good roads. Some students might stress labor unions, in order to prevent exploitation.)*

Teach, Reinforce, and Extend CHAPTER Content

Cultural Revolution

CHAPTER RESOURCES

	Reproducible Resources	Multimedia Resources
Chapter Opener	Chapter Themes: Graphic Organizer 24 Historical Significance Chapter Activity 24	MindJogger Videoquiz
Chapter Enrichment	Vocabulary Activity 24* Time Line Activity 24 Mapping History Activity 24 History Simulation 24 Geography and History Activity 24 Source Reading 24 People in World History Profiles 38, 45, 46 World Literature Selection 6 World Art and Music Activity 24 Enrichment Activity 24 Critical Thinking Activity 24 Skill Reinforcement Activity 24 Performance Assessment Activity 24	Focus on World Art Prints 2, 5, 22 World History and Art Transparency 31, *In the Garden*; 32, *Sunday Afternoon on the Island of La Grande Jatte*; 34, *Starry Night* Mapping History Overlay Transparency 16, *Global Ancestry of Americans* Chapter Transparency 24 Vocabulary PuzzleMaker Software Turning Points in World History: *The Industrial Revolution* Communism and the Cold War: • *Perspectives on Capitalism* • *Perspectives on Communism*
Chapter Review/Reteaching	Reteaching Activity 24 Skill Reinforcement Activity 24 Spanish Chapter Summary 24	Chapter 24 Digest Audiocassette, Activity, Test* Vocabulary PuzzleMaker Software Student Self-Test and Review Software MindJogger Videoquiz
Chapter Evaluation/Testing	Performance Assessment Activity 24 Chapter 24 Test, Forms A and B	Testmaker

* *Also available in Spanish*

0:00 **OUT OF TIME?** Assign the Chapter 24 summary in the Unit 6 Digest on pages 728–731, and the Chapter 24 Audiocassettes.

Block Schedule

Block scheduling differs from traditional class scheduling in the amount of time allotted to each period. The extended time frame provided by block scheduling affords you the opportunity to implement a greater number of research-oriented and activity-intense projects to motivate and involve your students. Activities that are particularly suited to use within the block scheduling framework are identified throughout this chapter by the following designation.

KEY TO ABILITY LEVELS

Teaching strategies have been coded for varying learning styles and abilities.

- **L1** **BASIC** activities for all students
- **L2** **AVERAGE** activities for average to above-average students
- **L3** **CHALLENGING** activities for above-average students
- **LEP** **LIMITED ENGLISH PROFICIENCY** activities

Chapter 24 Planning Guide

A complete, 1-page lesson plan is provided for each section in the *Reproducible Lesson Plans* booklet.

SECTION RESOURCES

Daily Objectives	Reproducible Resources	Multimedia Resources
Section 1 New Ideas Explain why Karl Marx advocated doing away with the capitalist system.	Reproducible Lesson Plan 24-1 Guided Reading Activity 24-1* People in World History Profile 38 Time Line Activity 24 Section Quiz 24-1*	Section Focus Transparency 24-1 Chapter Transparency 24 Vocabulary PuzzleMaker Software Student Self-Test and Review Software Testmaker Communism and the Cold War: • *Perspectives on Communism* • *Perspectives on Capitalism*
Section 2 The New Science List advances made in science between 1750 and 1914 that have improved life today.	Reproducible Lesson Plan 24-2 Guided Reading Activity 24-2* People in World History Profiles 45, 46 Section Quiz 24-2*	Section Focus Transparency 24-2 Vocabulary PuzzleMaker Software Student Self-Test and Review Software Testmaker
Section 3 Popular Culture Analyze why the population grew dramatically in Europe and North America during the 1800s.	Reproducible Lesson Plan 24-3 Vocabulary Activity 24* Guided Reading Activity 24-3* Geography and History Activity 24 Section Quiz 24-3*	Section Focus Transparency 24-3 Mapping History Overlay Transparency 16, *Global Ancestry of Americans* Student Self-Test and Review Software Testmaker Turning Points in World History: *The Industrial Revolution*
Section 4 Revolution in the Arts Describe how writers and artists in Europe and North America reflected changes in society between 1750 and 1914.	Reproducible Lesson Plan 24-4 Guided Reading Activity 24-4* History Simulation 24 Reteaching Activity 24 Enrichment Activity 24 Section Quiz 24-4* Performance Assessment Activity 24 Spanish Chapter Summary 24	Focus on World Art Print 2, Franz Marc. *Stables*; 5, Paul Klee. *Palace, Partially Destroyed*; 22, Vincent van Gogh. *Hospital at Saint-Rémy* Section Focus Transparency 24-4 World History and Art Transparency 31, *In the Garden*; 32, *Sunday Afternoon on the Island of La Grande Jatte*; 34, *Starry Night* Vocabulary PuzzleMaker Software Student Self-Test and Review Software Testmaker

** Also available in Spanish*

Chapter Activities

Performance Assessment Activity

Reform Inquiry and Projection Reforms covered in this chapter took place in government, working conditions, medicine, education, art, and urban life. Have students research reform efforts today in the same areas in order to complete a compare-and-contrast matrix. After students have drawn conclusions about the continuity and change in these areas, ask them to predict the reform movements that might occur after another 50 to 100 years. As a concluding activity, students can create a collage, mural, chart, or multimedia slide show including symbols and illustrations of the past, present, and future reform movements.

Possible Rubric Features

Accuracy of content information; accuracy, relevance, and degree of research; plausibility of predictions; originality, impact, and clarity of visuals

• *For an additional activity, refer to Activity 24 in the* Performance Assessment Strategies and Activities *booklet.*

Activity

From the Classroom of...

Charles Dixon
High School Redirection
Brooklyn, NY

Rise of Socialism Round Robin

Have students read from "Looking for a Better Way" to the end of Section 1 in the text (pages 623–625) and outline the ideas of the different reformers. Ask students to head a sheet of paper *During the 1800s socialism began to ...* , then write an end to the sentence, using information from their outlines.

Have students exchange papers six times (each time with someone new). After each exchange have students add a sentence to the paper they have just received. On the last exchange instruct students to write concluding sentences. Have several student read their completed paragraphs and use these as a springboard for discussion.

MULTIPLE LEARNING STYLES

Logical/Mathematical
Have students create a time line that tracks the major social, cultural, and scientific developments of the period. Students should include details from the text and from class discussions and activities.

Visual/Spatial
Have students produce an art journal filled with their own drawings and paintings done in the different artistic styles presented in this chapter.

Auditory/Musical
Have students listen to Schiller's "Ode to Joy," sung as part of Beethoven's Ninth Symphony. Ask them to write new words of their own that seem appropriate to the music.

Kinesthetic
Have students plan and attend a field trip to a nearby museum whose collection includes works by the artists discussed in this chapter. If possible, arrange to be led through the collection by a docent.

Additional Resources

TEACHER'S CORNER

NATIONAL GEOGRAPHIC SOCIETY

INDEX TO NATIONAL GEOGRAPHIC MAGAZINE

The following articles may be used for research relating to this chapter:

- "Paris: La Belle Epoque," by Eugen Weber, July 1989.
- "The World of Tolstoy," by Peter T. White, June 1986.

ADDITIONAL NATIONAL GEOGRAPHIC SOCIETY PRODUCTS

To order the following products for use with this chapter, call National Geographic Society at 1-800-368-2728:

- *Capitalism, Socialism, Communism Series*, "Communism," "Socialism," "Capitalism." (Videos)

BIBLIOGRAPHY

Literature of the Period

Dreiser, Theodore. ***Sister Carrie.*** Edited by Donald Pizer. New York: Norton, 1970. Includes backgrounds, sources, and criticism in addition to an authoritative text of the naturalist novel.

Readings for the Student

Briggs, Asa. ***A Social History of England: From the Ice Age to the Channel Tunnel.*** London: Weidenfeld and Nicolson, 1994. Offers the human side of change, drawing on artistic, economic, and political developments.

Readings for the Teacher

Heilbroner, Robert L. ***The Worldly Philosophers.*** New York: Simon and Schuster, 1980. Discusses Smith, Ricardo, Malthus, Marx, and the utopian Socialists.

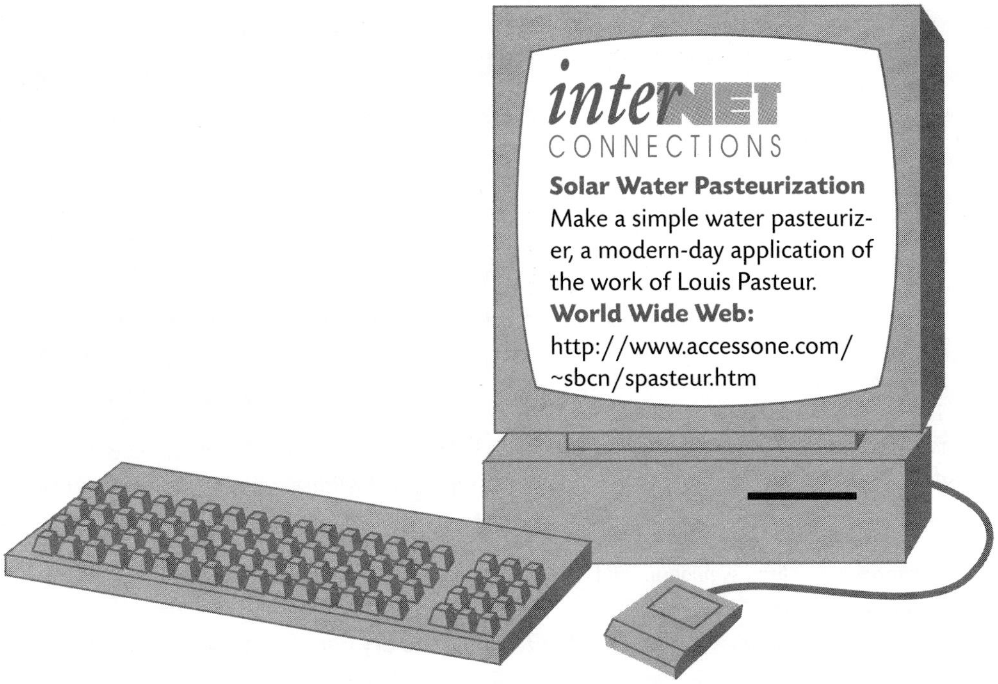
interNET
CONNECTIONS
Solar Water Pasteurization
Make a simple water pasteurizer, a modern-day application of the work of Louis Pasteur.
World Wide Web:
http://www.accessone.com/~sbcn/spasteur.htm

Introducing Chapter 24

CHAPTER THEMES

Chapter Themes are listed by section on this chapter opening page of the Student Edition. A corresponding theme-based activity is available under "TEACH," and a theme-based question is asked in the Section and Chapter Reviews.

The Storyteller

Historical Setting Dreiser (1871–1945) wrote this description of Chicago in his first novel, *Sister Carrie*. Dreiser is considered a member of the literary movement of naturalism, which began in the mid-1800s in France. According to Dreiser and other naturalists, social, economic, and biological forces control human actions and destinies. Dreiser lived and worked in Chicago for several years. He wrote about the city in his autobiographies, journalistic articles, and novels. Although Dreiser believed that cities were the source of power and wealth, he also believed that most city-dwellers were fated to lives of poverty and degradation.

Historical Significance

Answers: *Economic reformers developed theories of socialism and Marxism as alternatives to capitalism; scientists began to understand the nature of living matter and of the atom, and they made advances in medicine.*

Improved nutrition, sanitation, and medical practices resulted in healthier, longer-lived populations. People became more mobile, and many moved to cities. There, leisure-time activities spread, but many people still lived in poverty and in dismal conditions.

Artists reacted to the changes in society through movements such as romanticism, realism, symbolism, and impressionism.

Chapter 24

1750–1914

Cultural Revolution

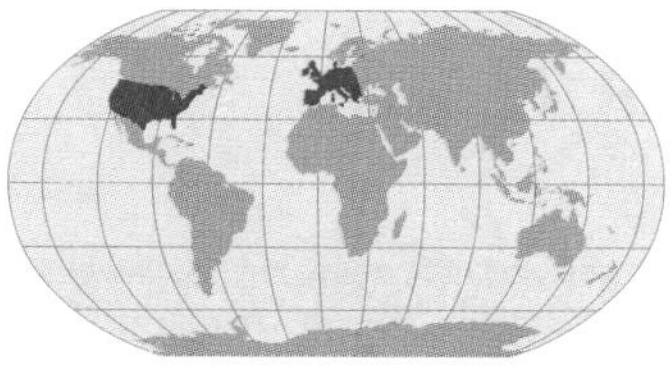

Chapter Themes

- **Change** Political and economic philosophies attempt to make sense of a changing industrial world. *Section 1*
- **Innovation** Scientific discoveries lead to improved health and revolutionary views about the natural world and human society. *Section 2*
- **Movement** People move from rural to urban areas and from continent to continent in search of better lives. *Section 3*
- **Innovation** Artists and writers in the Western world reflect the changes in urban industrial society. *Section 4*

The Storyteller

A new world was in the making. Factories boomed. Cities grew. By the late 1800s, steamships and trains allowed people to move in search of better lives. American novelist Theodore Dreiser described the excitement that drew people to Chicago:

"Its many and growing commercial opportunities gave it widespread fame, which made of it a giant magnet, drawing to itself, from all quarters, the hopeful and the hopeless.... It was a city of over 500,000 with the ambition, the daring, the activity of a metropolis of a million."

The Industrial Revolution also brought challenges to Europeans and North Americans. Cities became overcrowded, and the gap between rich and poor widened. People struggled to make sense of an increasingly complex society.

Historical Significance

What changes occurred in the economics, the sciences, and the arts of the West between 1750 and 1914? How did these changes alter people's values and daily lives?

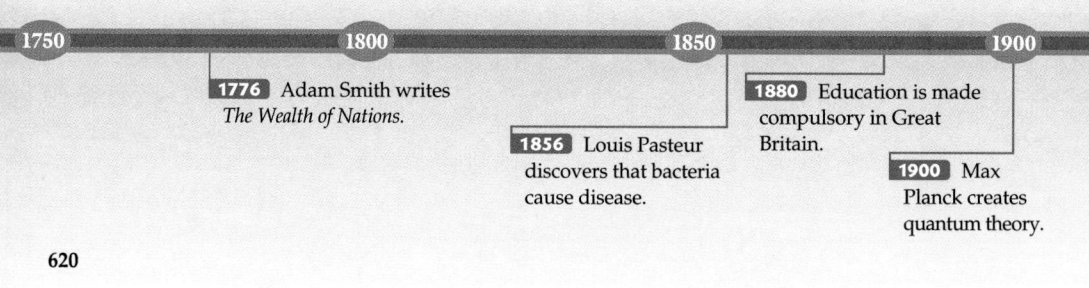

1750 — 1800 — 1850 — 1900

1776 Adam Smith writes *The Wealth of Nations.*

1856 Louis Pasteur discovers that bacteria cause disease.

1880 Education is made compulsory in Great Britain.

1900 Max Planck creates quantum theory.

620

GEOGRAPHY CONNECTION

GEOGRAPHIC THEMES

Location Have students locate Chicago on a map. What two great North American waterways does the Chicago River lie between? *(It empties into Lake Michigan, and its arms nearly reach the drainage basin of the Mississippi River.)* Explain to students that several factors helped transform Chicago into the interior land and water hub of the expanding United States: The opening of the Erie Canal in 1825 connected the Atlantic Ocean and the Great Lakes; the completion of the Illinois and Michigan Canal in 1848 linked the Great Lakes and Mississippi River systems; and the railroad system in 1856 turned the city into the nation's chief rail center.

History & Art *Boulevard Des Capuchines and Théâtre de Vaudeville, 1899,* by Jean Beraud. Musée Carnavalet, Paris, France

Your History Journal

This chapter introduces thinkers and reformers who wanted to create a better society. Write an essay suggesting ways to improve the society in which we live today.

EXTRA CREDIT PROJECT

Socialist Reformers Have students research and report to the class on the life and work of one of the early French utopian Socialist reformers, such as Count Claude Henri de Saint-Simon (1760–1825) or Charles Fourier (1772–1837). Suggested resources: A. J. Booth, *Saint-Simon and Saint-Simonism*; F. E. Manuel, *The Prophets of Paris*; A. Gray, *The Socialist Tradition.*

Introducing Chapter 24

History & Art Tell students that easy movement through the streets of Paris in 1899, as depicted in the painting, was a result of the city planning efforts of Baron Georges-Eugène Haussmann (1809–1891). At the request of Napoleon III, he eliminated constricted streets, cutting large straight boulevards through them.

Performance Assessment

Refer to the activity on page 620C of the Planning Guide.

For an additional activity, refer to Activity 24 in the *Performance Assessment Strategies and Activities* booklet.

Using Your History Journal

Suggest that students research the goals of some reformers active in the United States today, such as Ralph Nader or Amory Lovins.

GLENCOE TECHNOLOGY

VIDEODISC
Use MindJogger to preview chapter content.

MindJogger Videoquiz
Chapter 24
Disc 3 Side B

Also available in VHS.

Chapter 24
Section 1

SECTION THEME

▶ **Change** Political and economic philosophies attempt to make sense of a changing industrial world.

Find Out

Answer: *He believed it exploited workers.*

FOCUS

Section Objective

Explain why Karl Marx advocated doing away with the capitalist system.

BELLRINGER
Motivational Activity

Before taking roll at the beginning of the class period, project Section Focus Transparency 24-1 and have students answer the activity questions. Discuss students' responses.

This activity is also available as a blackline master.

Vocabulary Pre-check

Use the Vocabulary PuzzleMaker to create a puzzle that reinforces the vocabulary terms in this section. **L1**

1800 — 1850 — 1900

1837 David Ricardo writes about the "iron law of wages."

1847 British Parliament passes the Ten Hours Act.

1867 Karl Marx publishes *Das Kapital.*

Section 1

New Ideas

Setting the Scene

▶ **Terms to Define**
laissez-faire, utilitarianism, socialism, proletariat, bourgeoisie, communism

▶ **People to Meet**
Adam Smith, David Ricardo, Jeremy Bentham, John Stuart Mill, Robert Owen, Karl Marx, Friedrich Engels

Find Out Why did Karl Marx advocate doing away with the capitalist system?

The Storyteller

Karl Marx, the chief architect of communism, was always and everywhere a student. At an early age his withdrawal from all university activities except the intellectual brought stern advice from his father:

"My clever and gifted son Karl passes wretched and sleepless nights, wearying body and mind with cheerless study.... But what he builds today he destroys again tomorrow.... At last the body begins to ail and the mind gets confused, whilst ordinary folk ... attain their goal if not better at least more comfortably than those who condemn youthful pleasures and undermine their health...."

—from *The Life and Teaching of Karl Marx*, M. Beer, 1921

Karl Marx

English essayist William Hazlitt, writing in the early 1800s, described Europe in the critical years after the French Revolution:

> "There was a mighty ferment in the heads of statesmen and poets, kings and people. According to the prevailing notions, all was to be natural and new. Nothing that was established was to be tolerated.... The world was to be turned topsy-turvy."

The Western world did appear to be turning upside down, as society underwent a transformation. In little more than 100 years, the Industrial Revolution converted Europe from a farming economy centered in the country to an industrial economy based in urban areas.

Industry produced great wealth for the middle class, but the working class lived in grim, crowded cities and worked in noisy, dirty mills and factories. Many reformers decried a society of "haves" and "have-nots." They argued that the government should regulate working conditions and distribute wealth fairly.

Let Them Be!

The leaders of the Industrial Revolution—owners of railroads, factories, and mines—did not agree with those who called for reform. They believed in **laissez-faire** (LEH•SAY•FAYR) economics. *Laissez-faire* is a French term that means "let do," or "let them alone." Supporters of laissez-faire economics held that people should be able to buy and sell, hire and fire, free from government interference. Only then, they said, was material progress possible. Government interference would only threaten economic growth.

Supporters of laissez-faire knew that business and trade enriched a country, but they did not know how or in what manner.

SECTION RESOURCES

Reproducible Masters
- Reproducible Lesson Plan 24-1
- Guided Reading Activity 24-1
- People in World History Profile 38
- Time Line Activity 24
- Section Quiz 24-1

Transparencies
- Section Focus Transparency 24-1
- Chapter Transparency 24

Multimedia
- Vocabulary PuzzleMaker Software
- Student Self-Test and Review Software
- Testmaker
- Communism and the Cold War:
  - *Perspectives on Capitalism*
  - *Perspectives on Communism*

Adam Smith

Adam Smith, a Scots professor, was the first to explain capitalism and laissez-faire economics. In *The Wealth of Nations*, published in 1776, he spoke out against the policy of mercantilism that dominated the thinking of his time. Basic to the mercantilist system were several beliefs. One was that bullion, or money, was wealth. Another was that national power was more important than individual welfare. The more bullion a country had, the more powerful it was. At the time, most bullion came from foreign trade. As a result, commerce and industry were closely regulated and controlled by the national government.

Smith did not agree with these beliefs. In his view, labor, not money, was the source of wealth. Individual welfare, not national power, should be the goal. Smith argued that the major economic drive of any individual was self-interest. Smith did not think this was necessarily bad. He believed there was a natural order in the universe that made all the individual strivings for self-interest add up to the good of everyone. Competition, along with a free market price system, would act as an "invisible hand" and guide resources to their most productive use. Thus, said Smith, the best economic policy was the one that allowed individuals to act freely without government interference.

Smith's ideas were favorably received by British business leaders. Great Britain, in the early years of the Industrial Revolution, was so much more economically advanced than other nations that its industries did not need government protection or help. In the 1840s the British Parliament finally ended the last remains of the mercantilist system and allowed free trade.

David Ricardo

One leading British economist influenced by Smith was **David Ricardo**. Like Smith, Ricardo believed in laissez-faire; however, he painted a far gloomier picture of the economic future. Ricardo linked the persistence of poverty to what he called the "iron law of wages." According to Ricardo, as the population increased, so did the labor supply. This in turn increased competition for jobs and kept wages low. If the labor supply declined and wages rose, workers would then have more children. This would eventually increase the supply of labor and cause wages to fall once again. Ricardo held that workers could not escape this cycle, which condemned them time and again to periods of low wages and misery.

Visualizing History **Grim-faced young coal mine workers in Kingston, Pennsylvania, pose for the camera.** *How would photographs such as this support criticism of laissez-faire economics?*

Looking for a Better Way

Other thinkers refused to believe that poverty and misery were unavoidable. As more people became aware of working conditions in factories and mines, criticism of laissez-faire economics mounted.

Early Reformers

Humanitarians and religious leaders believed that society should be improved. In the late 1700s and early 1800s, William Wilberforce and other members of Parliament led a reform movement in Great Britain. A devout Anglican, Wilberforce spoke out on behalf of reforms for workers and the abolition of slavery. Another deeply religious political leader, Lord Shaftesbury, organized activities to support factory workers. He promoted legislation to limit working hours for women and children.

The work of these early reformers spurred Parliament to establish commissions to investigate conditions in factories and mines. The commission reports raised a public outcry. As a result, Parliament passed the first factory legislation of the industrial era, an 1833 act regulating the employment of children in factories. An 1842 act prohibited women and children from working in underground

COOPERATIVE LEARNING ACTIVITY

Newsletters Organize the class into several groups. Have each group prepare the front page of a newsletter advocating an economic policy presented in this section, such as laissez-faire or socialist economics. Each group should choose a name for its newsletter that suggests its point of view (for example, *Voice of the People* for a socialist perspective) and select a time period between 1750 and 1914. The groups should research economic issues of that time, which might include unionization, worker strikes, or labor reform. After selecting topics for a number of front-page stories, group members should write the articles or illustrate them. Completed front pages can be displayed in class. **L3**

TEACH

Guided Practice

THEME Change
Have students brainstorm things they would change about present-day society if they could create their own utopian community. At the end of the brainstorming session, have students vote on the changes they would make. **L1**

Visualizing History Not until 1916 did the U.S. Congress pass the first federal child labor law. Among other provisions, that law set the minimum age for work in mines at 16.
Answer to Caption: *It depicts the dismal life of children exploited by the system.*

ABCNEWS INTERACTIVE™

VIDEODISC
Communism and the Cold War

Side One, Chapter 7
Frames 13483–14256
Title: *Perspectives on Capitalism*
Ask: What is the underlying idea behind capitalism? *(individual initiative)*

Side One, Chapter 8
Frames 14264–14893
Title: *Perspectives on Communism*
Ask: In communism, what was "the ideal society"? *(one in which everyone is happy, no competition)*

Chapter 24 Section 1

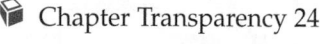

Visualizing History Posters became a popular means of conveying simple messages in the 1860s after the invention of color lithography allowed for inexpensive and easy production.

Answer to Caption: *public control of the means of production and equal distribution of wealth*

Philosophy Work with students to create a chart on the chalkboard that summarizes the philosophies of Smith, Malthus, Owen, and Marx. **L1**

Economics Explain that proponents of laissez-faire economics still believe in a minimum of governmental interference in the economy. They argue that if businesses are allowed to operate freely, competition will keep prices low and quality high. Ask the class to discuss the implications of this policy and ways it might affect today's society. **L3**

Chapter Transparency 24

Independent Practice

Guided Reading Activity 24-1 **L1**

People in World History Profile 38

Time Line Activity 24

Daily Life Have students find out more about the daily life of the working class in the 1800s. They might refer to such books as Charles Dickens's *Hard Times* or Asa Briggs's *The Social History of England*. Have students work in groups to write and present a play about working life. **L2**

Visualizing History Many socialist groups used posters and cartoons to win support for the overthrow of Europe's monarchies as well as the capitalist system. *What were two other goals of the socialist movement?*

mines. The Ten Hours Act of 1847 established a 10-hour working day in textile factories for children under 18 and women.

Other Voices of Reform

Another reformer, British philosopher **Jeremy Bentham**, developed the concept of **utilitarianism**. This philosophy was based on Bentham's belief that the rightness of any action, law, or political institution should be measured by its usefulness. How useful each was could be judged by the contribution it made to human happiness and to the reduction of human misery. Bentham called for a better code of law, education for all, a public health service, and improved prisons.

John Stuart Mill, a follower of Bentham, rejected laissez-faire economics. He argued that the distribution of wealth depended on laws and social customs. Governments could influence the distribution of wealth by taxing income. Mill argued for legislation against monopolies and that protected individual liberties. With free thought and discussion, progress was possible.

Popular English writers also took up the workers' cause. Charles Dickens attacked the misery of industrialization in several novels. In *Hard Times* he described workers' lives:

> ❝It [the city] contained ... people equally like one another, who all went in and out at the same hours, with the same sound upon the same pavements, to do the same work, and to whom every day was the same as yesterday and tomorrow, and every year the counterpart of the last and the next.❞

Rise of Socialism

Not everyone in Europe agreed with the capitalist way of thinking in the early 1800s. Some people believed that ending the misery of workers required eliminating capitalism completely. They advocated **socialism**—the belief that the means of production—capital, land, raw materials, and factories—should be owned and controlled by society, either directly or through the government. In this way, wealth could be distributed equally among all citizens.

Early Socialism

Some early advocates of socialism planned and built communities where everyone was supposed to share equally in the benefits of the industrial age. The first to establish such a community was **Robert Owen**, a wealthy Welsh manufacturer. Owen believed that competition caused society's problems. Thus, he reasoned that if cooperation replaced competition, life would improve.

In 1800 Owen set out to prove his point in New Lanark, a dreary Scottish mill town. In time he reconstructed it into a model industrial community. Although he did not turn the textile mill completely over to the workers, he greatly improved their living and working conditions. In 1825 Owen stopped managing New Lanark and bought New Harmony, Indiana, where he tried to set up a cooperative community. New Harmony, however, did not meet with the same success as New Lanark. Feuding among Owen and the residents led Owen to return to Great Britain.

Marxism

German philosopher **Karl Marx** dismissed the ideas of the early socialists as impractical and set out to provide a scientific basis for socialism. The son of a prosperous German lawyer, Marx received a doctorate in history and philosophy. When his radical views got him into trouble with the Prussian government, he fled to Paris. There in 1844 he met **Friedrich Engels**. Engels was on his way home from one of his father's factories in Manchester, England. Horrified by what he saw there, Engels

MEETING SPECIAL NEEDS ACTIVITY

Language Delayed This chapter will be difficult for students who speak English as a second language. Meet regularly with ESL students as a group to discuss terminology and to clarify concepts. Pair these students with more advanced students and ask each pair to prepare charts, diagrams, time lines, or other graphic organizers for each section to help them master the important data. **L1 LEP**

624 Chapter 24 *Cultural Revolution*

wrote a classic book called *The Condition of the Working Class in England*.

Marx and Engels later settled in London and became lifelong friends and collaborators. Engels, a successful businessman, supported Marx, who devoted his life to writing about economics.

Marx's Theories

Marx based his ideas in part on the teachings of the German philosopher G.W.F. Hegel. Hegel taught that changing ideas were the major force in history. As ideas clashed, new ideas emerged. This produced new changes, conflicts, and ideas.

Like Hegel, Marx believed that history advanced through conflict. In Marx's view, however, economics was the major force for change. Production was at the base of every social order. Laws, social systems, customs, religion, and art all developed in accord with a society's economic base.

The most important aspect of the economic base was the division of society into classes. The class that controlled production became the ruling class. No ruling class would willingly give up its control of production. The only way to make the ruling class give it up was through revolution. Therefore, conflict between classes was inevitable. This conflict, which Marx called "class struggle," was what pushed history forward.

Marx argued that Europe had moved through four stages of economic life—primitive, slave, feudal, and capitalist. During the primitive stage, people produced only what they needed to live. There was no exploitation, or unfair use of a person for one's own advantage. Once tools were developed, however, and people could produce a surplus, they became exploitable. From then on, history was a class struggle. One class was pitted against another—master against slave, lord against serf, capitalist against worker. It was the "haves" against the "have-nots."

Marx believed that capitalism was only a temporary phase. As the makers of goods, the proletariat, or the working class, was the true productive class. An economic crisis in one of the advanced industrial countries would give the proletariat the chance to seize control from the bourgeoisie (BURZH•WAH•ZEE), or middle class. The proletariat would then build a society in which the people owned everything. Without private property, class distinctions would vanish, and the government would wither away. This last stage would be genuine communism, with each individual finding true fulfillment. The governing principle would be "from each according to his ability, to each according to his need."

Marx and Engels published their views in *The Communist Manifesto* in 1848. In it they appealed to the world's workers:

> "Let the ruling classes tremble at a Communist revolution. The proletarians have nothing to lose but their chains. They have a world to win. Working men of all countries, unite!"

The Socialist Legacy

History did not proceed by Marx's plan. When Marx was writing, workers' poverty contrasted sharply with industrialists' wealth. By 1900 conditions had changed in western Europe. Workers could buy more with their wages than they could 50 years earlier. Rather than overthrow their governments, workers gained the right to vote and used it to correct the worst social ills.

In time, democratic socialism developed in western Europe. Democratic Socialists urged public control of some means of production, but they respected individual values and favored democratic means to implement Socialist policies. In the early 1900s, however, revolution swept Russia. Modern Russian communism grew out of Marx's ideas but was imposed by a small elite. Its leaders shunned democratic values and practiced extreme government control.

SECTION 1 REVIEW

Recall

1. **Define** laissez-faire, utilitarianism, socialism, proletariat, bourgeoisie, communism.
2. **Identify** Adam Smith, David Ricardo, Jeremy Bentham, John Stuart Mill, Robert Owen, Karl Marx, Friedrich Engels.
3. **Explain** why, according to Adam Smith, a laissez-faire policy would promote economic progress and social harmony.

Critical Thinking

4. **Making Comparisons** How are the viewpoints of Robert Owen and Karl Marx similar? How are they different?

Understanding Themes

5. **Change** Why did industrialization make people think about the causes and cures of poverty? Can poverty be totally eliminated? Which thinkers of the period would agree with your views?

Chapter 24 Section 1

ASSESS

Check for Understanding

Assign Section 1 Review as homework or as an in-class activity.

Use Student Self-Test and Review Software to review Section 1.

Evaluate

Section Quiz 24-1

Use the Testmaker to create a customized quiz for Section 1.

Reteach

Organize students into small groups. Each group should make lists of the advantages and disadvantages of a socialist and a capitalist society.

Enrich

Have students investigate public reactions to reformers such as Robert Owen and Karl Marx. **Did public support for their ideas grow stronger or weaker during the 1800s?** Have students report to the class.

CLOSE

Tell students to imagine that they are living in 1880 and that a large factory opened in their town a year ago. Have students write a diary entry describing the changes in the town brought about by the factory.

SECTION 1 REVIEW ANSWERS

1. All vocabulary words are defined in the Glossary.
2. Smith, 623; Ricardo, 623; Bentham, 624; Mill, 624; Owen, 624; Marx, 624; Engels, 624
3. Without governmental interference, businesses compete to produce goods as inexpensively as possible, and consumers buy the best goods at the lowest prices. Efficient producers make more profit, hire more workers, and continue to expand, to everyone's benefit.
4. Both called for a system in which all would share equally in society's abundance. Marx, however, believed this would come about only by way of a revolution in which workers seized control from the bourgeoisie.
5. **CHANGE** Industrialization created societies of haves and have-nots. Students should support their answers with explanations.

Chapter 24 Section 2

SECTION THEME

▶ **Innovation** Scientific discoveries lead to improved health and revolutionary views about the natural world and human society.

Find Out

Answer: *The discovery of bacteria; the introduction of vaccines; the introduction of anesthesia; the development of genetics, psychology, and atomic theory have all led to improved lives for people today.*

FOCUS

Section Objective

List advances made in science between 1750 and 1914 that have improved life today.

BELLRINGER Motivational Activity

Before taking roll at the beginning of the class period, project Section Focus Transparency 24-2 and have students answer the activity questions. Discuss students' responses.

This activity is also available as a blackline master.

Vocabulary Pre-check

Use the Vocabulary PuzzleMaker to create a puzzle that reinforces the vocabulary terms in this section. **L1**

1750	1800	1850	1900
1796 Edward Jenner invents smallpox vaccine.	**1803** John Dalton develops atomic theory.	**1859** Charles Darwin publishes *On the Origin of Species.*	**1898** Marie Sklodowska Curie and Pierre Curie discover radium.

Section 2

The New Science

Setting the Scene

▶ **Terms to Define**

cell theory, evolution, genetics, atomic theory, sociology, psychology

▶ **People to Meet**

Charles Darwin, Gregor Mendel, Edward Jenner, Louis Pasteur, John Dalton, Marie Sklodowska Curie, Pierre Curie, Ivan Pavlov, Sigmund Freud

Find Out What advances made in science between 1750 and 1914 have improved life today?

The Storyteller

Dr. Hugh Barrett's hands shook with anger as he met with the industrial board of directors. They had requested his presence because many workers were falling ill and dying, costing them loss of labor. They hoped that modern medicine could offer a cure. Dr. Barrett tried to explain. "Cholera and typhoid will continue to rage as long as elementary hygiene is impossible. The congested, unsanitary housing—all your workers can afford on the wages you give them—is a breeding ground for disease." His persuasive words fell on deaf ears. What good is it, he wondered, to explain how disease is transmitted, if his recommendations were not to be followed?

—freely adapted from *History of Private Life, Volume 4, From the French Revolution to the Great War,* edited by Michelle Perrot, 1987

Family in London slum

During the 1800s and early 1900s, scientific discoveries were beginning to unravel some intriguing mysteries. Not only did discoveries help our understanding of life and the universe, they also led to advances in medical techniques, longer life spans, and cures for deadly diseases.

New Look at Living Things

In the 1600s scientists had observed under a microscope the cells that make up living things, but they did not understand what they saw. It was not until 1838 that German botanist Mathias Schleiden and biologist Theodor Schwann formulated the cell theory: All living things are made up of tiny units of matter called cells. They also discovered that all cells divide and multiply, causing organisms to grow and mature.

The Diversity of Life

Cell theory could not explain why the world has so many kinds of plants and animals. In the 1800s scientists proposed the theory that all plants and animals descended from a common ancestor by evolution over millions of years. During that time, they said, plants and animals had evolved from simple to complex forms.

In France, the scientist Jean-Baptiste de Lamarck observed similarities between fossils and living organisms. He found that an animal's parts—its legs, for example—might grow larger or smaller depending on how much it used them. He suggested that living things adapt to their environment and then pass the changes on to the next generation. Lamarck's theory, though later disproved, influenced **Charles Darwin**, a British naturalist who would build his own theory of evolution.

In December 1831 Charles Darwin set off on a world voyage on HMS *Beagle*, a British naval ship. While traveling he became curious about the great

SECTION RESOURCES

Reproducible Masters
- Reproducible Lesson Plan 24-2
- Guided Reading Activity 24-2
- People in World History Profiles 45, 46
- Section Quiz 24-2

Transparencies
- Section Focus Transparency 24-2

Multimedia
- Vocabulary PuzzleMaker Software
- Student Self-Test and Review Software
- Testmaker

variety of plants and animals. He also wondered why some kinds had become extinct while others lived on.

Darwin developed a theory of evolution based on natural selection. In his book *On the Origin of Species*, Darwin stated that most animal groups increase faster than the food supply and are constantly struggling for survival. The plants and animals that survive are better adapted to their environment, so that they alone live on, producing offspring having the same characteristics. In 1871 Darwin furthered his theories in another book, *The Descent of Man*. In it he traced human evolution from animal species. Darwin's writings created controversy because many religious leaders believed that his views contradicted the biblical account of creation and ignored divine purpose in the universe.

Development of Genetics

In the 1860s **Gregor Mendel** wondered how plants and animals pass characteristics from one generation to another. Mendel, an Austrian monk, experimented with pea plants. He concluded that characteristics are passed from one generation to the next by tiny particles. The particles were later called genes, and Mendel's work became the basis for genetics, the science of heredity.

Medical Advances

Through most of history, diseases have killed more people than famines, natural disasters, and wars. In the 1800s knowledge of living organisms brought medical advances that would give people longer, healthier lives.

Fighting Disease

Smallpox, which killed millions of people over the centuries, was one of the most dreaded diseases. In 1796 **Edward Jenner**, an English doctor, noticed that dairy workers who had contracted cowpox, a mild disease, never caught smallpox. Jenner hypothesized that he could prevent smallpox by injecting people with cowpox. To prove his theory, Jenner injected a boy with cowpox serum and later with smallpox serum. As Jenner expected, the boy contracted cowpox but not smallpox. Jenner had given the world's first vaccination.

About 50 years later, **Louis Pasteur**, a French chemist, learned why Jenner's vaccination worked. In the 1850s Pasteur discovered bacteria, or germs, and proved that they cause infectious diseases. He also discovered that bacteria do not appear spontaneously, but instead reproduce like other living

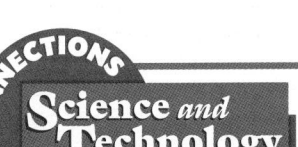

CONNECTIONS Science and Technology

Triumph Over an Ancient Enemy

Louis Pasteur

When a wine maker asked his friend French scientist Louis Pasteur to find out why some wines turned sour as they fermented, science and medicine vaulted into a new era. Pasteur discovered that the wines would not sour if they were heated to a specific temperature and bottled without contact with the air.

With his microscope, Pasteur saw that tiny microbes were destroyed in this heating, later called pasteurization. He had proved that the germs that caused contamination came from an outside source. Pasteur worked to show that bacteria were carried in the air, on hands or clothes, and in other ways. He developed the theory that bacteria can cause disease, and he argued that bacteria could be killed only by heat or other means.

Pasteur then applied his knowledge of bacteria to diseases in animals. He injected chickens with a weakened form of chicken cholera to protect them against the disease. For the first time, a vaccine carried bacteria from the very disease it was meant to prevent.

Understanding human diseases occupied the later years of Pasteur. On Pasteur's seventieth birthday, scientist Joseph Lister praised Pasteur, saying, "You have raised the veil which for centuries had covered infectious diseases.... "

MAKING THE CONNECTION

1. How did Pasteur come to express the germ theory of disease?
2. How did Pasteur change people's understanding of disease?

Chapter 24 Section 2

TEACH

Guided Practice

THEME Innovation

Guide students in a discussion about innovations in today's society caused by modern scientific breakthroughs. **L1 LEP**

CONNECTIONS Science and Technology

Triumph Over an Ancient Enemy

Although as a child Pasteur (1822–1895) seemed interested only in drawing, he went on to become a major contributor to science and industry. In 1854, as dean of the science faculty at the University of Lille, he not only offered evening classes for the workers of that industrial city but also exposed his day students to the factories. In 1857 he became director of scientific studies at France's most prestigious university, the École Normale Supérieure, but after a decade he devoted himself to research. He helped the French economy by finding the bacteria threatening the silk industry. His groundbreaking work in the prevention of rabies led to the opening of the Pasteur Institute in Paris, which he headed until his death. Pasteur and British surgeon Sir Joseph Lister (1827–1912) became good friends, and Lister applied Pasteur's discoveries to surgery.

Answers to Making the Connection

1. *While investigating why some wines turned sour, Pasteur learned that germs that cause contamination come from an outside source.*
2. *Once people knew that bacteria can cause disease, they could take protective measures.*

COOPERATIVE LEARNING ACTIVITY

Poster Display Have students form groups to do additional research into the scientific breakthroughs of the twentieth century. Groups should choose specific areas of science to research; for example, space exploration, medical research, environmental research. Group members should discuss the breakthroughs in their field and develop a poster written and designed by students. The posters should answer such questions as: What was the breakthrough? Who was responsible for it? Why is it important? What effects does it have on our lives today? **L2**

Chapter 24 Section 2

Independent Practice

Guided Reading Activity 24-2 **L1**

People in World History Profiles 43, 44

Geography: Movement Have students research Darwin's voyage. (Refer to his book *Journal of Researches into the Geology and Natural History of the Various Countries Visited by H.M.S. Beagle.*) Have them locate on a world map the stops Darwin made and report his conclusions. **L2**

ASSESS

Check for Understanding

Assign Section 2 Review as homework or as an in-class activity.

Use Student Self-Test and Review Software to review Section 2.

Evaluate

Section Quiz 24-2

Use the Testmaker to create a customized quiz for Section 2.

Reteach

Assign students to work in small groups to create a chart summarizing key information in this section. Have students include these column heads in their charts: *Scientist, Development, Date, Uses.*

Enrich

Have students research a scientist mentioned in the section.

CLOSE

Have students imagine that they are journalists in 1899. Ask them to write an article summarizing the major scientific developments of the past century.

things. Pasteur knew then that they could be killed and that many diseases could be prevented.

New Approaches to Surgery

Surgery benefited from advances in chemistry. Until the mid-1800s, surgeons could operate only when their patients were forcibly held down. The experience was gruesome and often fatal. In the 1840s a Boston dentist demonstrated surgery using ether. When ether was administered, patients slept through their operations, feeling no pain. Sir James Simpson, a professor at the University of Edinburgh, investigated the use of another sleep-producing chemical, chloroform. Using the anesthetics ether and chloroform led to painless surgery.

Still, many people died after surgery because of infection introduced during the procedure. Joseph Lister, an English surgeon, searched for a way to destroy bacteria and make surgery safe. He found that carbolic acid could be used to sterilize medical instruments. Lister's use of an antiseptic moved surgery into a new era.

Breakthroughs in Physics

The explosion of ideas also advanced the physical sciences. Expanding the ideas of Galileo and Newton, scientists created our modern ideas about atomic energy. Atomic theory is the idea that all matter is made up of tiny particles called atoms.

John Dalton, an English chemist, provided proof of this theory. He discovered that elements are composed of atoms, and that all atoms of an element are identical and unlike the atoms of any other element. Dalton then determined chemical formulas showing which atoms make up specific elements.

Until the 1890s scientists believed that atoms were solid and indivisible; then in 1895 German physicist Wilhelm K. Roentgen discovered X rays, or high-energy electromagnetic waves that could penetrate solid matter. Later scientists showed that X rays are made up of particles of electricity called electrons, which are part of every atom.

These beginnings led scientists to frame modern physics. In 1898 the physicists **Marie Sklodowska** (skluh•DAWF•skuh) **Curie** and **Pierre Curie** discovered the highly radioactive element of radium and proved that it emits energy. In 1900 German physicist Max Planck theorized that energy is not continuous, but is released in separate units called quanta. Planck's quantum theory eventually helped Albert Einstein develop his theory of relativity, leading us to the nuclear age.

Social Sciences

Meanwhile, other scientists used the scientific method to study human behavior. This led to the development of two new social sciences—sociology, the study of human behavior in groups, and psychology, the science of human behavior in individuals. The French thinker Auguste Comte (KOHNT) was one of the founders of sociology. Comte believed that society, like nature, operated by certain laws. He stated that once these laws were discovered, people could apply scientific methods to the study of human social groups.

In the 1890s **Ivan Pavlov**, a Russian researcher, experimented with animals to see what effects outside stimuli had on their behavior. His findings suggested that human actions were unconscious reactions to stimuli and could be changed by training. Another researcher who held that an unconscious part of the mind governs human behavior was the Austrian physician **Sigmund Freud** (FROYD). Freud's theories led to psychoanalysis, a method of treatment to discover people's motives.

SECTION 2 REVIEW

Recall

1. **Define** cell theory, evolution, genetics, atomic theory, sociology, psychology.
2. **Identify** Charles Darwin, Gregor Mendel, Edward Jenner, Louis Pasteur, John Dalton, Marie Sklodowska Curie, Pierre Curie, Ivan Pavlov, Sigmund Freud.
3. **Describe** Charles Darwin's theory of natural selection and how it changed thinking about the development of life.

Critical Thinking

4. **Applying Information** Explain in writing how a scientist discussed in Section 2 helped to change the ideas of the day.

Understanding Themes

5. **Innovation** How are the scientific understandings of the 1800s and early 1900s being expanded today? What impact are scientific discoveries having on your life?

SECTION 2 REVIEW ANSWERS

1. All vocabulary words are defined in the Glossary.
2. Darwin, 626; Mendel, 627; Jenner, 627; Pasteur, 627; Dalton, 628; Marie and Pierre Curie, 628; Pavlov, 628; Freud, 628
3. Natural selection, the idea that those species that are best adapted to their environment survive, challenged religious ideas about the divine origins of life.
4. Answers will vary. Students should use specific details to support their answers.
5. **INNOVATION** Answers will vary. Students should use specific details to support their answers.

1800 — 1850 — 1900

1837 Mary Lyon opens the first women's college in the United States.

1858 Frederick Law Olmsted designs New York City's Central Park.

c. 1890s Many Russian Jews flee persecution and settle in the United States.

Section 3

Popular Culture

Setting the Scene

- **Terms to Define**
  emigration, immigration, urbanization
- **People to Meet**
  Frederick Law Olmsted, Mary Lyon
- **Places to Locate**
  London, New York City, Paris

Find Out Why did population grow dramatically in Europe and North America during the 1800s?

The Storyteller

A book titled Host and Guest *described dining for wealthy Europeans in the late 1800s: "The first course consists of soups and fish, followed by boiled poultry, ham or tongue, roasts, stew, etc.; with vegetables ... curries, hashes, cutlets, patties, etc. For the second course, roasted poultry or game at the top and bottom, with dressed vegetables, omelets, macaroni, jellies, creams, salads, preserved fruit, and all sorts of sweet things and pastry are employed.... The third course consists of game, confectionary, the more delicate vegetables dressed in the French way...." Dessert, of course, followed.*

—adapted from *Manners and Morals in the Age of Optimism, 1848-1914*, James Laver, 1966

Dining scene in Victorian England

As the 1900s began, the new science and technology were making a difference throughout Europe and North America. Most people could now expect a longer and healthier life. The rate of infant mortality dropped in the late 1800s, and life expectancy climbed. In 1850 the average person lived about 40 years; by 1900 most people could expect to live beyond 50.

Thus, as industrialization grew, so did world population. At the beginning of the Industrial Revolution, 140 million people lived in Europe. By 1850, about 100 years later, Europe's population had soared to 266 million. In Europe and the United States, the first industrialized areas, the rate of population growth was highest.

Improved Living Conditions

The medical advances of the 1800s were partly responsible for this dramatic growth in population. So too was the availability of more and better food. Before 1740 many people died of starvation and of diseases caused by vitamin deficiency such as rickets. At that time a person's entire daily diet might have consisted of three pounds of bread.

In the 1800s, however, bread ceased to be the staple it had been for centuries. With new machinery and scientific methods, farmers could produce many kinds of foods. Potatoes, nutritious and easy to grow, became popular. Methods for preserving foods, including canning and eventually refrigeration, enabled people to take advantage of the greater variety of food that was available.

One observer of working-class life in London during the late 1890s wrote: "A good deal of bread is eaten and tea is drunk especially by the women and children, but ... bacon, eggs and fish appear regularly in the budgets. A piece of meat cooked on Sundays serves also for dinner on Monday and Tuesday." Some Europeans imported corn from the

Chapter 24 Section 3

SECTION THEME

▶ **Movement** People move from rural to urban areas and from continent to continent in search of better lives.

Find Out

Answer: *Scientific developments led to a decline in infant mortality and a rise in life expectancy. The availability of more and better food also helped people to live longer.*

FOCUS

Section Objective

Analyze why the population grew dramatically in Europe and North America during the 1800s.

BELLRINGER Motivational Activity

Before taking roll at the beginning of the class period, project Section Focus Transparency 24-3 and have students answer the activity questions. Discuss students' responses.

This activity is also available as a blackline master.

Vocabulary Pre-check

Use Vocabulary Activity 24 to introduce vocabulary terms. **L1 LEP**

SECTION RESOURCES

Reproducible Masters
- Reproducible Lesson Plan 24-3
- Vocabulary Activity 24
- Guided Reading Activity 24-3
- Geography and History Activity 24
- Section Quiz 24-3

Transparencies
- Section Focus Transparency 24-3
- Mapping History Overlay Transparency 16, *Global Ancestry of Americans*

Multimedia
- Student Self-Test and Review Software
- Testmaker
- Turning Points in World History: *The Industrial Revolution*

TEACH

Guided Practice

THEME **Movement**

Guide students in discussing the positive and negative aspects of population movement. *(positive: new opportunities; negative: newcomers often face discrimination)* Ask students for examples from other periods and from personal experiences. **L1**

Critical Thinking Organize the class into groups such as the working poor, industrialists, and government officials. Have students role-play a public meeting on urban health and housing during the 1800s. Encourage students to discuss health issues such as housing and clean air. **L3**

ABCNEWS INTERACTIVE™

VIDEODISC
Turning Points in World History
Side Two
Chapter 3

Title: *The Industrial Revolution*
Ask: What was the "price" of the Industrial Revolution? *(Some negative effects include pollution, overcrowding in cities, exploitation of workers.)*

United States and fruit and frozen meat from Australia and New Zealand.

Seeking a Better Life

As the population grew, people became more mobile. Railroads revolutionized not only the food people ate, but also the way they lived. In 1860 London's Victoria Station opened, making it easier for Londoners to leave their crowded city. Steamships carried people to other countries and continents in search of a better life. Between 1870 and 1900, more than 25 million people left Europe for the United States; others moved to South America, South Africa, and Australia.

For a number of reasons, some Europeans chose emigration, leaving their homelands to settle elsewhere. Some looked for higher-paying jobs and better working conditions. Others sought to escape discrimination and persecution by oppressive governments. Still others hoped to escape famine.

Advertisements of steamship companies, along with low fares, lured many immigrants to the United States. Industries looking for cheap labor offered additional encouragement. Some American industrialists sent recruiters whose task was to urge people to leave Europe and obtain permanent jobs and homes in the United States.

Twelve-year-old Mary Antin joined thousands of Russian Jews fleeing persecution in 1894. Many years earlier Mary's father had decided on immigration, or coming to settle permanently in a foreign land. His new homeland was the United States. Mary, her mother, and her brothers and sisters endured a harrowing journey across Europe and the Atlantic Ocean to join him in Boston, Massachusetts. Mary wrote of her experiences: "And so suffering, fearing, brooding, and rejoicing, we crept nearer and nearer to the coveted shore until on a glorious May morning … our eyes beheld the Promised Land and my father received us in his arms."

Most people left their homelands knowing that they would never see their parents or their birthplace again. The ocean voyage often proved a frightening experience. One youngster

Images of the Times

Leisure Time

An urban environment offered many people new opportunities for leisure activities.

A Bicycle was a fashionable new means of getting around, for those who could afford it.

Perth Station, Going South by George Earl captures the happy confusion of a London holiday.

630

Images of the Times **Leisure Time**

Bicycles were exhibited as early as 1818, but the first to become popular was the 1861 machine produced by a French father-and-son team. The bicycle soon gave rise to such leisure-time activities as bicycle touring and bicycle racing.

Railway travel had become very popular in England by the 1840s. British writer Sydney Smith said in an 1842 letter to *The Morning Leader*, "Railway travelling is a delightful improvement of human life."

Iced desserts originated in Asia, but the ice-cream soda was first served in 1874 in Philadelphia, and the ice-cream cone had its debut at the St. Louis World's Fair in 1904.

remembered "the howling darkness, the white rims of the mountain-high waves speeding like maddened dragons toward the tumbling ship."

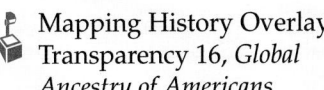

When the immigrants reached their new homes, many learned that their troubles had only begun. Now they had to find housing and jobs in strange surroundings where they did not know the culture or the language. Some people took advantage of the European immigrants, who seemed to them strange "foreigners."

From Country to City

During the 1800s and early 1900s, many people moved within their own country. Cities around the world were absorbing newcomers who were moving from rural villages to find new opportunities. As farms grew larger and more mechanized, they needed fewer workers. The growing industries in or near the cities offered new and challenging ways to make a living.

Although the new city dwellers faced no language barriers, some of their problems were similar to those of the European immigrants. Their old life was gone, with its known boundaries, familiar people, and established routines. Although work was plentiful, living quarters in the cities were often cramped, and neighbors might be less friendly than people they had known. British poet Lord Byron summed up the feelings of many newcomers to the city:

> "I live not in myself, but I become a
> Portion of that around me: and to me
> High mountains are a feeling, but the hum
> Of human cities torture."

Growth of Cities

The movement of people into the cities resulted in the urbanization, or the spread of city life, of the industrialized countries. A country is urbanized when more people live in cities than in rural areas. Great Britain is a prime example. In 1800 **London**

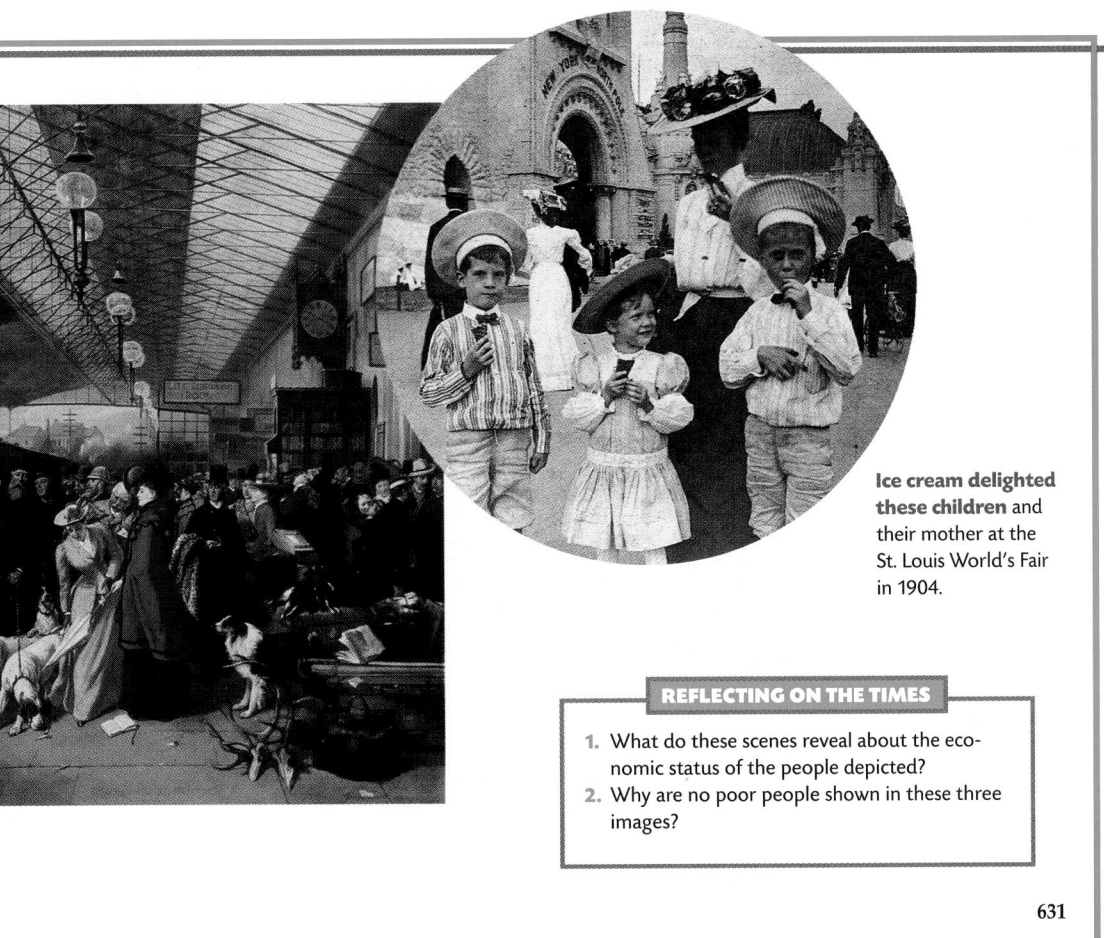

Ice cream delighted these children and their mother at the St. Louis World's Fair in 1904.

REFLECTING ON THE TIMES

1. What do these scenes reveal about the economic status of the people depicted?
2. Why are no poor people shown in these three images?

631

ANSWERS TO REFLECTING ON THE TIMES

1. All the people are sufficiently wealthy to be able to take time off from work and to pay for excursions and treats.
2. The poor had no disposable income to pay for leisure-time activities or treats.

Chapter 24 Section 3

Mapping History Overlay Transparency 16, *Global Ancestry of Americans*

Independent Practice

Guided Reading Activity 24-3 **L1**

Geography and History Activity 24

Brochure Ask students to investigate one of the cultural institutions founded during this period, such as the Louvre or the Albert Hall. Have students create a brochure for the institution, describing its most interesting features and encouraging people to visit it. **L1**

Environmental Issues Have students do further research into the environmental conditions in the large cities of the period, such as London. Have them write letters to the editor as urban dwellers protesting the conditions they see around them. **L2**

Education Have students research and write brief reports on the early public educational system in the United States. Have students investigate classroom structure and school curriculum. The reports should compare and contrast the early system with educational practices today. **L3**

Who?What?Where?When?

Pogroms, or government-sponsored attacks against Jews, led two million East European Jews to seek refuge in the United States between 1881 and the outbreak of World War I. This massive migration accounted for 85 percent of the movement between Europe and America during that period.

Chapter 24
Section 3

Linking Past and Present

Urbanization According to current estimates, about half the world's population will live in urban areas by the year 2000, a sharp contrast with 1800, when less than 3 percent lived in cities of 20,000 or more.

Who?What?Where?When?

Settlement houses, or institutions to improve urban neighborhood living conditions, were founded in the 1880s. The most famous United States settlement house was Hull House in Chicago, founded in 1889 by Jane Addams and Ellen Gates Starr. Although Hull House no longer stands, the Hull House Association still operates about 25 Chicago community centers.

Who?What?Where?When?

Jacob Riis (1849–1914) was a Danish immigrant whose *How the Other Half Lives* (1890), a photojournalistic exposé of the terrible conditions of the urban poor, resulted in improved conditions.

ASSESS

Check for Understanding

Assign Section 3 Review as homework or as an in-class activity.

Use Student Self-Test and Review Software to review Section 3.

was its only city with a population of more than 100,000. By 1851 Britain had 9 such cities. In the same year, and for the first time, slightly more than half of the British people lived in cities. By 1914 that figure had reached 80 percent.

Urbanization was taking place elsewhere as well. In 1914, 60 percent of the Germans, 50 percent of the Americans, and 45 percent of the French were city dwellers.

As people moved to cities, they began to marry earlier. Children could increase a family's income by working in factories. As a result, people had more children, adding to the population.

The cities' growth soon outpaced their ability to provide needed housing and sanitation. Few cities had building codes that mandated adequate housing. Houses were built close together in long rows, one against another. The workers crowded together in damp, cold, unsanitary rooms, with fire a constant danger.

The factories added to the unpleasant city environment. Here is a report on the working conditions of British miners in 1843: "Sheffield is one of the dirtiest and most smoky towns I ever saw. The town is also very hilly, and the smoke ascends the streets, instead of leaving them.... One cannot be long in the town without experiencing the necessary inhalation of soot."

City Services

City governments in Europe and the United States began to look for solutions to the overwhelming troubles. They saw that one of the most pressing problems was sanitation. An observer in the British city of Leeds reported, "The ashes, garbage, and filth of all kinds are thrown from the doors and windows of the houses upon the surface of the streets and courts." Ditches and open sewers carried waste from public toilets. Polluted water encouraged epidemics of cholera and other diseases, especially in the crowded slums.

In the late 1800s, the germ theory and the newly invented iron pipe spurred city leaders to clean up their cities. They installed closed sewer lines and improved garbage collection. Police and fire protection created safer cities.

As city planning progressed, a number of city governments set aside areas as parks. In **New York City**, landscape architect **Frederick Law Olmsted** saw the need for "a simple, broad, open space of clean greensward [grassy turf]" enclosed by a large enough green space to "completely shut out the city." With the architect and landscape designer Calvert Vaux, Olmsted designed Central Park in 1858.

Leisure Time

Leisure time activities expanded for the middle classes and for the working classes. Men and women took more outings and enjoyed more cultural activities. Newspapers helped to make people interested in places and events outside of their own neighborhoods and communities.

In the 1700s the fine arts were available only to the wealthy upper classes. Concerts were performed in palaces and grand homes, or they were performed in churches. Wealthy aristocrats, prosperous merchants, and religious leaders commissioned cultural events and artworks, such as concerts and paintings, to commemorate special events or to honor special people.

In the 1800s, however, fine art and music became available to middle- and working-class people in the city. City governments in Europe and North America built concert halls and opera houses, such as London's vast Albert Hall, erected in 1871. Cities sponsored the opening of art museums, such as the great Louvre (LOOV) Museum in **Paris**.

When people were not visiting libraries and museums, they went to amusement parks, which provided shows, rides, games, and food. Sports such as soccer and rugby began to be organized between cities and around the nation. Many people also enjoyed archery, lawn tennis, and cricket.

Footnotes to History

Moving to the Suburbs During the late 1800s, suburbs, or small communities next to large cities, grew in Europe and the United States along with the development of streetcar lines and railroads. Middle-class people could afford to live in less urban areas and ride the trolley or train to their jobs in the city. In the United States, suburban growth greatly increased in the 1950s as more and more families were able to buy one or two automobiles.

New Interest in Education

In the early 1800s, when governments began to support public schools, their reasons were political. For example, the Prussian government established public schools to train its people in citizenship and in devotion to the monarchy and the army. In the

COOPERATIVE LEARNING ACTIVITY

Interview Assign students to work in pairs to investigate a social issue discussed in this section. Students should take the roles of an interviewer and an interviewee, write a script for an interview, and perform it for the class. Possible interview "pairs" include a journalist and an immigrant discussing the experience of traveling to a new country, a public official and an urban newcomer discussing the difficulty of adjusting to crowded city living and working conditions, or a journalist and Mary Lyon discussing the benefits of education for women. **L2**

United States, government support for public schools grew out of a desire to foster national unity after the Revolutionary War.

By the late 1800s, as people grew more and more interested in improving their lives, they became more actively involved in promoting education. Both in Europe and the United States, they supported education that was funded by the government and available to everyone. Believing education would improve their children's chances for a better life, they voted for increased educational opportunities. Schools and colleges were also established to provide better training for teachers.

The new kind of society—urbanized and industrialized—also benefited from the cause of public education. Industrialists needed employees who could read and write. Advanced technologies based on science depended on workers who had scientific training. Many people came to see that an ever more complex society would demand a well-educated populace. People were needed who could participate intelligently in public affairs.

Education for Women

Education for women was a hotly debated topic in the 1800s. Some felt that women's roles as wives and homemakers did not require education. Others believed women should be given the same educational opportunities as men. Girls were included in the laws providing education to all. Still, they could usually attend only elementary schools. Access to secondary education was limited only to the wealthy few.

Determined to offer higher education to women, some people began to open secondary schools and colleges especially for them. In 1837 American educator **Mary Lyon** opened the first women's college, the Mount Holyoke Female Seminary, which later became Mount Holyoke College in Massachusetts. In 1874 the London School of Medicine was opened, and after two years of bitter debate, the British Parliament finally allowed women to be registered as doctors.

History & Art *Piccadilly Circus, 1912* by Charles Ginner. Tate Gallery, London, England **The circular street of Piccadilly Circus was built near the shopping district of London.** *By 1914, what percent of the British lived in cities?*

Results of Education

The advances in education created a growing demand for accessible reading materials. Magazines and books became popular. Libraries with large collections opened as early as the 1840s in major cities such as Paris and London. Lending libraries loaned books for small fees.

Mass-circulation newspapers were first printed at this time, and by the mid-1800s, more than 500 newspapers were published in the United States. Newspaper publishers benefited from the combination of rapid communication provided by the telegraph, cheaper printing methods, and improved distribution by railroad and steamship.

SECTION 3 REVIEW

Recall

1 **Define** emigration, immigration, urbanization.
2. **Identify** Frederick Law Olmsted, Mary Lyon.
3. **List** three improvements in city life that were made in the 1800s and the early 1900s.

Critical Thinking

4. **Making Comparisons** How do attitudes about women's education today differ from attitudes in the late 1800s? Explain reasons for the differences.

Understanding Themes

5. **Movement** Why did many people in Europe and North America move in the late 1800s and early 1900s? Do the same reasons apply today?

Chapter 24 Section 3

History & Art Tell students that in England, a *circus* is an open circle, square, or plaza where several streets converge. Six busy streets meet at Piccadilly Circus, which, together with Trafalgar Square, is one of two huge intersections in London's West End.
Answer to Caption: *80 percent*

Evaluate

Section Quiz 24-3

Use the Testmaker to create a customized quiz for Section 3.

Reteach

Have students meet in small groups of five or six to discuss the review questions. Circulate to monitor progress.

Enrich

Have students research the popular culture of their town or city during the 1800s and report on topics such as entertainment, economic growth, and population shifts.

CLOSE

Tell students to imagine they are immigrants living in a large city in the late 1800s. Have them write a letter to friends at home describing their new homeland.

SECTION 3 REVIEW ANSWERS

1. All vocabulary words are defined in the Glossary.
2. Olmsted, 632; Lyon, 633
3. sewer lines, improved garbage collection, police and fire protection, development of parks
4. Most people today believe that all opportunities available to men should also be available to women; to enable women to take advantage of these opportunities on equal terms, they need an equivalent education. Many people in the 1800s felt woman's role as wife and homemaker did not require an education. Reasons for the differences will vary but may include that seeing women perform successfully in such formerly all-male roles as doctors, lawyers, and engineers has changed people's thinking.
5. **MOVEMENT** Answers should include the search for better jobs and working conditions and the need to escape from discrimination, famine, and persecution. Similar reasons apply today.

Chapter 24 *Cultural Revolution* **633**

Study and Writing SKILLS

TEACH

Paraphrasing Information Before teaching this skill, make an audiotape or videotape of a presidential address, a political candidate's speech, or remarks made by a school administrator at an assembly. In class, before assigning the skill, play the tape. Then inform students that you would like them to write a paraphrase, or summary, of the remarks they have just heard. Play the tape a second time, stopping at natural breaking points, to allow students time to write a brief summary of each new idea as it is presented. Ask a volunteer to read his or her paraphrase to the class. Have the class comment on the completeness and accuracy of the summary, pointing out any ideas omitted or misconstrued.

Now have the class read the skill silently and complete the practice questions.

Additional Practice

Skill Reinforcement Activity 24

Study and Writing SKILLS

Paraphrasing Information

Like millions of people in the United States, you may have watched the President deliver a State of the Union address. After the speech, suppose a friend should ask, "What did the President say?" Unless you tape-recorded the speech, you would probably *paraphrase*, or put into your own words, the President's remarks.

Learning the Skill

Paraphrasing is a powerful learning tool. It forces us to confront the questions: What do these statements really mean? Can I explain this to someone else? If we cannot, then perhaps we do not fully understand or need more information. Paraphrasing is an effective way to prepare for exams and written reports.

In paraphrasing written material, first read the material to identify main ideas and important details. Then write these main ideas and important details in your own words. Define important terms and explain relationships. If possible, use examples of concepts from your own experience or knowledge base. For example, if you are studying immigration to the United States in the 1800s, you might compare the historical situation with your knowledge of current immigration issues.

Once you have written your version, compare it to the original version to make sure your ideas have the same meaning. Finally, note the source of information on your paraphrased version. If you are writing a research paper, note the title, author, publishing company, date of publication, and page numbers of each source. You will need this information to produce footnotes.

Practicing the Skill

Read the following excerpt about Karl Marx's philosophy.

1. Paraphrase the main idea of the first paragraph.
2. Paraphrase the main idea of the second paragraph.
3. Paraphrase Marx's ideas about class struggle.
4. Give an example from your knowledge of history or personal experience of Marx's ideas in action.

> "Marx believed that history advanced through conflict. But in his view, economics was the major force. Production was at the base of every social order. Laws, social systems, customs, religion, and art all developed in accord with society's economic base.
>
> The most important aspect of the economic base was the division of society into classes. The class that controlled production became the ruling class. No ruling class would willingly give up its control of production. The only way to make the ruling class give it up was through revolution. Therefore, conflict between classes was inevitable. This conflict, which Marx called "class struggle," was what pushed history forward."

Applying the Skill

Choose one of the following subsections in Chapter 24, Section 4: "The Romantic Movement," or "The Turn Toward Realism." Paraphrase your selected material in one paragraph. Be sure to include how the artistic movement reflected changes inherent in the Industrial Revolution.

For More Practice

Turn to the Skill Practice in the Chapter Review on page 645 for more practice in paraphrasing information.

634 Chapter 24 *Cultural Revolution*

ANSWERS TO PRACTICING THE SKILL

1. According to Marx, every historic change results from economic conflict.
2. Conflict between economic classes underlies all historic change.
3. Class struggle is inevitable and occurs when one class revolts and tries to seize control of production from the ruling class.
4. Answers will vary. One example students might mention is described in Chapter 23: the British Parliament's legalization of strikes after decades of labor union activity.

1750 **1800** **1850** **1900**

c. 1780 Romanticism becomes a leading cultural movement.

1852 Ivan Turgenev writes *A Sportsman's Sketches.*

1863 Impressionist artists exhibit paintings in Paris.

c. 1890 Symbolist movement reacts against industrial civilization.

Section 4

Revolution in the Arts

Setting the Scene

- **Terms to Define**
  romanticism, realism, symbolism, impressionism, Postimpressionism
- **People to Meet**
  Peter Tchaikovsky, Johann Wolfgang von Goethe, George Sand, Honoré de Balzac, Charles Dickens, Leo Tolstoy, Claude Monet, Vincent van Gogh
- **Places to Locate**
  Paris

Find Out How did writers and artists in Europe and North America reflect changes in society between 1750 and 1914?

The Storyteller

Gustave frowned as he read his mother's letter. "I am tired of seeing your talent receive no recognition. You must acknowledge what people want. You need to cater to the popular taste ... paint imaginary scenes of Roman or medieval heroes. Then your paintings might win prizes or be purchased by influential collectors." Gustave Courbet would not follow the crowd or popular tastes, just because others were doing it. He would paint images of his own time.

—freely adapted from *Realism*, Linda Nochlin, 1971

After Dinner at Ornans
by Gustave Courbet

European and American artists in the 1800s mirrored society's mixed feelings about the rapid disappearance of the old order and the uncertainty of the new. A growing middle class created a larger audience for music, literature, and poetry. Formerly, artists had depended on patronage by the wealthy. Now, although some artists sought support in the new industrial society, others rebelled against middle-class values and shunned patronage of any kind, preferring to work independently. Those who rebelled would dominate the arts in the late 1700s and early 1800s.

The Romantic Movement

By the late 1700s, artists had begun to react to the Enlightenment's emphasis on order and reason. The French philosopher Jean-Jacques Rousseau taught that people were naturally good and needed only to be free. In rejecting society's formal structures and rules, Rousseau anticipated romanticism, a movement in which artists would emphasize human emotion and imagination over reason.

Romantic artists tried to free themselves from the rigid forms and structures of neoclassical art. Rejecting the mechanization and ugliness of industrialized society, many turned to nature, glorifying its awesome power and quiet beauty.

Many romantic artists looked to the past, admiring the mythical heroes of old. They felt compassion for the weak and oppressed, and they celebrated the lives of "simple peasants." The struggle for personal freedom and heroic rebellion against society's established rules are frequent themes in their works. The French poet Charles Baudelaire described the movement: "Romanticism is precisely situated neither in choice of subject nor in exact truth, but in a way of feeling."

Chapter 24 Section 4

SECTION THEME

▶ **Innovation** Artists and writers in the Western world reflect the changes in urban industrial society.

Find Out

Answer: *Reaction to emphasis on reason led to emotion-filled works of romantics; by the mid-1800s artists rejected romanticism as sentimental and embraced realism. Symbolist writers and painters sought to escape ugly realities by creating images evoked by symbols.*

FOCUS

Section Objective

Describe how writers and artists in Europe and North America reflected changes in society between 1750 and 1914.

BELLRINGER Motivational Activity

Before taking roll, project Section Focus Transparency 24-4 and have students answer the activity questions.

This activity is also available as a blackline master.

Vocabulary Pre-check

Use the Vocabulary PuzzleMaker to create a puzzle that reinforces the vocabulary terms in this section. **L1**

SECTION RESOURCES

Reproducible Masters
- Reproducible Lesson Plan 24-4
- Guided Reading Activity 24-4
- History Simulation 24
- Reteaching Activity 24
- Enrichment Activity 24
- Section Quiz 24-4
- Performance Assessment Activity 24
- Spanish Chapter Summary 24

Transparencies
- Section Focus Transparency 24-4
- World History and Art Transparencies 31, 32, 34

Multimedia
- Focus on World Art Prints 2, 5, 22
- Vocabulary PuzzleMaker Software
- Student Self-Test and Review Software
- Testmaker

Chapter 24 Section 4

TEACH

Guided Practice

THEME **Innovation**

Ask students to scan the section and provide examples of innovations in art. *(They may point out any of the movements discussed or specific examples within them, such as the emphasis on emotion and imagination by the romantics.)* Ask students to cite examples of innovations in art, music, or literature that they have noticed in their lifetimes. **L1**

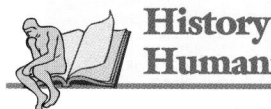

History and the Humanities

Focus on World Art Prints
- 2 Franz Marc. *Stables*
- 5 Paul Klee. *Palace, Partially Destroyed*
- 22 Vincent van Gogh. *Hospital at Saint-Rémy*

World History and Art Transparencies
- 31 *In the Garden*
- 32 *Sunday Afternoon on the Island of La Grande Jatte*
- 34 *Starry Night*

History Simulation 24

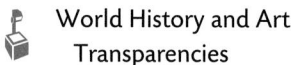

History & Art Tell students that a fjord is a long, narrow arm of the sea bordered by steep cliffs. **Answer to Caption:** *It is dramatic and celebrates nature and freedom of the human spirit.*

Romantic Music

The composers of the Enlightenment had emphasized form and order, but romantic composers departed from traditional forms and styles. They often fused music with imaginative literature, creating operas—dramas set to music—and *lieder* (LEED•uhr)—art songs, or poems set to music.

Romantic music was meant to stir the emotions—whether in large works, such as symphonies by German composer Ludwig van Beethoven (BAY•TOH•vuhn) or Russian composer **Peter Tchaikovsky** (chy•KAWF•skee), or in smaller, more intimate works, such as piano pieces by Poland's Frédéric Chopin (SHOH•PAN) or the *lieder* of Austria's Franz Schubert. Melodies from folk music added emotional power to romantic music, as in works by Czech composer Antonín Dvořák (DVAWR•ZHANK), whose *Symphony From the New World* echoes American spirituals.

Romantic Literature

Like romantic composers, romantic writers created emotion-filled, imaginative works. Early leaders of the romantic movement in literature include German writers Friedrich von Schiller and **Johann Wolfgang von Goethe** (GUHR•tuh). Schiller glorified freedom fighters, such as the legendary hero William Tell. His drama with that title is about the medieval Swiss struggle for freedom. Goethe is best known for *Faust*, a drama about human striving and the need for redemption.

France produced some of the most popular romantic writers. Alexandre Dumas's novel *The Three Musketeers* recounts the exploits of three dashing adventurers in the 1600s. Aurore Dupin, better known as **George Sand**, made peasants and workers heroes in her fiction. The novels of Victor Hugo, the foremost French romanticist, include *The Hunchback of Notre Dame* and *Les Misérables*, tales portraying human suffering with compassion and power.

Romanticism also influenced Great Britain. Scots writer Sir Walter Scott won a huge following with his historical novels *Ivanhoe*, *Quentin Durward*, and *The Talisman*. Another Scot, Robert Burns, showed deep feeling for nature and romantic love in his poetry. English poet and painter William Blake attacked the growing results of industrialization in *Songs of Innocence* and *Songs of Experience*. Similar themes fill the works of English poets Samuel Taylor Coleridge, William Wordsworth, John Keats, Percy Bysshe Shelley, and Lord Byron.

History & Art *Girl With Goats by a Fiord* by Hans Dahl. Christie's, London, England **This painting exemplifies romantic ideals.** *What characteristics of romanticism does the painting show?*

Romantic Painting

Painters, like writers, reflected romantic ideals. Turning from the order, clarity, and balance of the neoclassical style, painters began to portray exotic, powerful subjects in a dramatic and colorful way. For example, the painting *Liberty Leading the People*, by Eugène Delacroix (DEH•luh•KWAH), shows the figure of Liberty as a brave woman carrying a flag and leading patriots through the streets of **Paris**. Like many other romantic works, the painting was meant to stir the emotions, not appeal to the intellect.

The Turn Toward Realism

In the mid-1800s, some artists began to reject the sentimentality of romanticism. They sought to portray life in a realistic manner. In France, painter Gustave Courbet (kur•BAY) expressed the idea behind this style, known as realism: "Painting … does not consist of anything but the presentation of real and concrete things." Realist painters and writers wished to portray life as it was, not to escape from it.

Courbet's own large, somber canvases called attention to the less fortunate members of society and their difficult circumstances. *Burial at Ornans*

COOPERATIVE LEARNING ACTIVITY

Art Magazine Have students work together to produce a magazine displaying their literary and artistic accomplishments. Contributions must be in the style of one of the artistic movements of the period described in this section and may include paintings, drawings, poetry, songs, and so on. Some students should be responsible for assembling and organizing the materials by movement. Others may do interviews of the contributors or write articles evaluating the works. **L2 LEP**

National Gallery of Art

French Impressionists

Purest of the impressionists, Claude Monet captured the essence of light and air. A stiff breeze swirls through "Woman With a Parasol—Madame Monet and Her Son," painted between 1875 and 1878. "His pictures always were too draughty for me!" commented fellow impressionist Edgar Degas. "If it had been any worse, I should have had to turn up my coat collar." Unlike Monet and other French impressionists who insisted on painting from life, Degas was the master of the fleeting moment. He relied on quick sketches and his memory of posture, light, and color, and painted later at his studio.

One of Monet's paintings entitled *Impression—Sunrise*, exhibited in a Paris art show gave impressionism its name. An art critic reviewing the show ridiculed the painting and invented the term "impressionism." French impressionists such as Monet, Degas, and others rebelled against the strict traditions and rules of the art world of the late 1800s to capture the natural appearances of objects. Using dabs and strokes of primary colors, they tried to give the impression of actual reflected light. They often painted outdoors, trying to capture natural light, shadow, and color on canvas.

TEACH

The impressionist style is said to have had its origins at a French riverside café called La Grenouillière, where Monet and Renoir began meeting in 1869. Until that time, both men had employed an ordinary naturalist style in their work. But upon gazing out at the sun sparkling on the rippling river waters, they felt that a new technique was needed to capture that delightful play of light. From then on Monet began to work at finding ways of rendering an *impression* of the many different effects of light. "Light is the principal person in the picture," he once said. **What characteristics of impressionist painting can you see in "Woman With a Parasol"?** *(Students may point to the pattern of separate brushstrokes, the brilliant color, the feathery lightness.)*

CURRICULUM CONNECTION

POLITICS
Many artists of the time took sides in the Dreyfus affair, a military-political scandal that polarized French society during the last half of the 1890s. Monet and Pissarro were among the artists believing that the charge of treason against Captain Alfred Dreyfus, the only Jew on the General Staff of the French army, was unfounded (as in fact it proved to be). Cézanne, Rodin, Renoir, and Degas believed in Dreyfus's guilt.

Independent Practice

Guided Reading Activity 24-4 **L1**

Biography Have students research the life of one of the artists of the period and write a brief biography. Tell students to include information on education, training, major works, and public acceptance. **L1**

The Arts Tell students to imagine they are art critics reviewing the first exhibit of impressionist work. Have students write a review of the exhibit for a local newspaper. They should include in their review a detailed description of at least one impressionist work. **L2**

The Arts Have students assemble copies of paintings from the period covered in this section and report to the class on the techniques and subject matter of the different artists. Instruct them to identify the movement each work represents and to point out characteristics of the movement. **L3**

ASSESS

Check for Understanding

Assign Section 4 Review as homework or as an in-class activity.

Use Student Self-Test and Review Software to review Section 4.

Evaluate

Section Quiz 24-4

Use the Testmaker to create a customized quiz for Section 4.

AROUND THE WORLD

Futabatei Publishes *The Drifting Clouds*

Japan, 1889

Beginning in the 1880s, Western ideas began to influence Japanese writing. A group of Japanese authors, who had been educated in Western languages, broke from traditional forms of literature. These writers believed that Japan's technological development should be accompanied by the development of modern European-style literary works. In 1889 Futabatei Shimei produced a novel titled *The Drifting Clouds* which helped establish the novel as a respected form of Japanese literature.

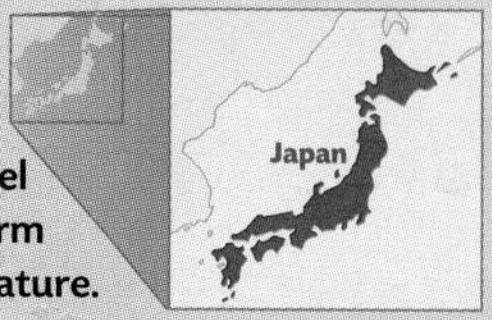

portrayed peasants from his hometown standing around the grave of a loved one. By the end of the 1850s, other French artists had joined Courbet in painting realistically. Among the most notable were Honoré Daumier (doh•MYAY) and Jean-François Millet (mee•YAY).

Realism in Literature

Realism also flourished in literature. French writer **Honoré de Balzac** grouped about 90 of his novels and short stories of French life in the 1800s into a collection he called *The Human Comedy*. Many described frankly the greed and stupidity that Balzac saw in the growing middle class. Gustave Flaubert (floh•BEHR), another French writer, portrayed the conflict between dreary realities and romantic dreams in *Madame Bovary*, the story of a young woman married to a dull provincial doctor.

The English novelist, Mary Ann Evans wrote under the pen name George Eliot. Her novels portrayed the rigidity and senselessness of the British social order. **Charles Dickens**, the foremost English realistic writer, spoke out on behalf of the poor. Dickens focused on the deplorable conditions in the prisons, hospitals, and poorhouses of London. In his novel *Hard Times*, he attacked the materialism of Coketown, a fictional city.

Russian writers came to be known for their penetrating novels about the human spirit. The novels of Russian writer **Leo Tolstoy** also reflected his compassion for the peasants and gave his analysis of social customs. *War and Peace* is a family novel in which Tolstoy takes five families through the stages of life. It is also a historical novel about Napoleon's invasion of Russia in 1812.

The works of American novelist Theodore Dreiser belong to a pessimistic style of realism called naturalism, in which writers tried to apply scientific methods to imaginative writing. In Dreiser's novel *An American Tragedy*, a young man is executed for killing his pregnant girlfriend. To Dreiser, the man is a victim whose tragedy results from circumstances over which he has no control.

Symbolism

Some writers became disgusted with what they viewed as the ugly and brutal realities of European industrial civilization. To escape, they created a world of shadowy images evoked by symbols. This movement, called symbolism, began in France and was led by the poet Stéphane Mallarmé (MA•LAHR•MAY), who believed that "to name an object is to destroy three-quarters of the enjoyment of a poem, which is made up of the pleasure of guessing little by little." He and his followers, Paul Verlaine (vehr•LAYN) and Arthur Rimbaud (ram•BOH), gave impressions by suggestion rather than by direct statement.

Symbolism spread to the other arts and to other countries. The symbolists focused on the exotic, using imagery to suggest the world of the spirit. Intellectuals applauded this effort, but the average person found symbolism difficult to understand.

New Trends in Painting

Intense competition and rigid, traditional standards characterized the artistic world in the 1800s. An artist's works had to be considered "correct" and the subject matter "proper" by judges at London's Royal Academy of Art or Paris's École des Beaux-Arts (School of Fine Arts). Acceptance by those schools and a place in their yearly exhibitions were crucial to a beginning artist's success.

In 1863 the École turned down more than 3,000 of the 5,000 works that were submitted for its approval—the highest proportion of rejections that anyone could remember. Napoleon III, the French emperor at the time, decided to hold an exhibit to let the public see the paintings that had been rejected by the École. Those paintings delighted many people and gave the painters renewed hope that their works would win recognition.

Impressionism

Among the rejected paintings were many by artists who followed a style called impressionism.

MEETING SPECIAL NEEDS ACTIVITY

Learning Style: Logical/Mathematical Have students with good computer skills access information from the World Wide Web on the artistic movements described in this section. Ask them to print out the information they find and distribute it to the class. Then they can explain to the class how they located the information and to point out ways it enhances the coverage available in the text. **L2**

638 Chapter 24 *Cultural Revolution*

The impressionist painters abandoned many of the rules on which earlier painters had based their art—rules about proper subject matter and traditional techniques of line, perspective, and studio lighting. Fascinated by color and light, the impressionists sought to capture the momentary impression a subject made on their senses. They moved out of the studio and into the real world, choosing to work outdoors, in theaters, and in cafes.

Pierre-Auguste Renoir (REHN•WAHR) painted idealized portraits of women and children and outdoor scenes. **Claude Monet** (moh•NAY), one of the most famous impressionists, painted series of paintings on the same subject to show variations in light and color during various times of the day and seasons of the year.

Postimpressionism

In the late 1880s some artists turned away from impressionism. Known as Postimpressionists, they formed their styles independently to express in different ways the chaos and complexity around them. One of their leaders was Paul Cézanne (say•ZAN). Earlier, he had identified with romanticism and impressionism. By the 1880s he had laid the foundation for Postimpressionism when he declared, "I do not want to reproduce nature, I want to recreate it."

Georges Seurat (suh•RAH), another Postimpressionist, applied science to his paintings. He developed a method called pointillism, placing small dabs of color close together to produce a three-dimensional effect. His painting *A Sunday Afternoon on the Island of La Grande Jatte* consists of thousands of different-colored dots.

Paul Gauguin (goh•GAN) moved to the Pacific island of Tahiti, where he painted *Where do we come from? What are we? Where are we going?* It was an attempt to find universal truths in the symbols of a nonindustrial culture.

The son of a Dutch minister, **Vincent van Gogh** (van GOH) led an unhappy life. After failing at the ministry, he turned to painting. Within two years, he produced most of the paintings for which he is known, using brilliant colors and distorted forms to make intense statements.

History & Art *The Swing* by Pierre-Auguste Renoir, 1876. Musée d'Orsay, Paris, France *What did France's impressionist painters, such as Renoir and Monet, seek to capture in their works?*

Henri de Toulouse-Lautrec (tu•LOOZ loh •TREHK) used Paris nightlife as a major subject. He painted with vivid detail, using bright colors to catch the reality of lives he portrayed. His use of line and color in posters of Paris's Moulin Rouge nightclub attracted worldwide attention.

SECTION 4 REVIEW

Recall

1. **Define** romanticism, realism, symbolism, impressionism, Postimpressionism.
2. **Identify** Peter Tchaikovsky, Johann Wolfgang von Goethe, George Sand, Honoré de Balzac, Charles Dickens, Leo Tolstoy, Claude Monet, Vincent van Gogh.
3. **Explain** what factors led to the rise of realism.

Critical Thinking

4. **Analyzing Information** How might the painting *Liberty Leading the People* have influenced French attitudes about revolution?

Understanding Themes

5. **Innovation** How was nature significant in romantic art?

Chapter 24 Section 4

History & Art Tell students that the Musée d'Orsay is situated in the former Gare d'Orsay, a railroad station in Paris. After being remodeled, the building was reopened in 1986 as a museum specializing in the different schools of French art of the middle to late 1800s.

Answer to Caption: *They sought to capture the momentary impression a subject made on their senses.*

Reteach

Ask each student to write three questions on the section's content. Then have students meet in groups and exchange questions.

Reteaching Activity 24

Enrich

Have students who are musically inclined research trends in post-romantic music of the late 1800s and early 1900s. Have them summarize their findings in brief reports to the class that include taped excerpts of compositions.

Enrichment Activity 24

CLOSE

Have students write a brief paragraph explaining which artistic movement described in this section they find most visually pleasing and which they like least.

SECTION 4 REVIEW ANSWERS

1. All vocabulary words are defined in the Glossary.
2. Tchaikovsky, 636; Goethe, 636; Sand, 636; Balzac, 638; Dickens, 638; Tolstoy, 638; Monet, 639; van Gogh, 639
3. Students might mention reactions to romantic sentimentality, to the Industrial Revolution, or to the Scientific Revolution.
4. Answers will vary. Possible answer: The patriotic emotions it stirred might have encouraged people to revolt against a government that seemed unresponsive to the people's needs.
5. INNOVATION Answers will vary but might include the idea that nature's awesome power and quiet beauty inspired artists who rejected industrialized society's mechanization and ugliness.

Bridge to the Past

Literature

Block Schedule

Team Teaching This excerpt from *The Beggar* may be presented in a team-teaching context, in conjunction with English or Language Arts.

The Beggar

Historical Connection

Industrialization increased the number of poor city dwellers. Societies had to decide how to treat those unable to support themselves.

Background Information

Setting The story is set in a Russian city in the late 1800s. During this period many Russians moved to the city to find work and escape the poverty and tedium of rural life.

Characters Lushkoff: a poor alcoholic who survives by begging; Skvortsoff: a wealthy lawyer who prides himself on his compassion for the needy; Olga: Skvortsoff's cook who often supervises Lushkoff

Plot Skvortsoff, though angered by Lushkoff's lies, hires him to cut wood and do other chores. Eventually Lushkoff is able to find a better job as a notary. Years later the two men meet again at the theater, where Skvortsoff takes credit for teaching Lushkoff the value of work. The former beggar confesses that he never chopped any wood; Olga did it all.

Bridge to the Past

Literature

from The Beggar

by Anton Chekhov

Anton Chekhov, who died in 1904 at age 44, wrote several plays and short stories that became classics of Russian literature. The issue he confronts in the following excerpt—how to help those in need—remains a vital issue today. A wealthy lawyer, Skvortsoff, is angered by the lies a beggar tells to win sympathy and money from passersby. Skvortsoff complains to the beggar that "you could always find work if you only wanted to, but you're lazy and spoiled and drunken!"

"By God, you judge harshly!" cried the beggar with a bitter laugh. "Where can I find manual labor? It's too late for me to be a clerk because in trade one has to begin as a boy; no one would ever take me for a porter because they couldn't order me about; no factory would have me because for that one has to know a trade, and I know none."

"Nonsense! You always find some excuse! How would you like to chop wood for me?"

"I wouldn't refuse to do that, but in these days even skilled wood-cutters find themselves sitting without bread."

"Huh! You loafers all talk that way. As soon as an offer is made you, you refuse it. Will you come and chop wood for me?"

"Yes, sir; I will."

"Very well; we'll soon find out. Splendid—we'll see—"

Skvortsoff hastened along, rubbing his hands, not without a feeling of malice, and called his cook out of the kitchen.

"Here, Olga," he said, "take this gentleman into the wood-shed and let him chop wood."

The tatterdemalion [clothed in ragged garments] scarecrow shrugged his shoulders, as if in perplexity, and went irresolutely after the cook. It was obvious from his gait that he had not consented to go and chop wood because he was hungry and wanted work, but simply from pride and shame, because he had been trapped by his own words. It was obvious, too, that his strength had been undermined by vodka and

About the Author

Anton Chekhov grew up in Taganrog, a city on the Black Sea. His father, a recently freed serf, struggled to make a living as a grocer. From this childhood poverty, Chekhov developed a sympathy for the poor and working classes. He worked as a medical doctor among the poor during his adult life. His real interest, however, was writing. As a young man, Chekhov began writing short humorous tales to add to his income. As he grew older, he wrote plays and more serious short stories. He occasionally wrote nonfiction, including an account of convicts on Russia's Sakhalin Island. Often ill, Chekhov died of tuberculosis in 1904.

640 Chapter 24 *Cultural Revolution*

that he was unhealthy and did not feel the slightest inclination for toil.

Skvortsoff hurried into the dining room. From its windows one could see the wood-shed and everything that went on in the yard. Standing at the window, Skvortsoff saw the cook and the beggar come out into the yard by the back door and make their way across the dirty snow to the shed. Olga glared wrathfully at her companion, shoved him aside with her elbow, unlocked the shed, and angrily banged the door.

"We probably interrupted the woman over her coffee," thought Skvortsoff. "What an ill-tempered creature!"

Next he saw the pseudo-teacher, pseudo-student seat himself on a log and become lost in thought with his red cheeks resting on his fists. The woman flung down an ax at his feet, spat angrily, and, judging from the expression of her lips, began to scold him. The beggar irresolutely pulled a billet [log] of wood toward him, set it up between his feet, and tapped it feebly with the ax. The billet wavered and fell down. The beggar again pulled it to him, blew on his freezing hands, and tapped it with his ax cautiously, as if afraid of hitting his overshoe or of cutting off his finger. The stick of wood again fell to the ground.

Skvortsoff's anger had vanished and he now began to feel a little sorry and ashamed of himself for having set a spoiled, drunken, perchance sick man to work at menial labor in the cold.

"Well, never mind," he thought, going into his study from the dining room. "I did it for his own good."

An hour later Olga came in and announced

History & Art *Religious Procession in the Province of Kursk* by Ilya Repin. Tretyakov Gallery, Moscow, Russia **Ilya Repin painted realistic scenes of everyday Russian life.** *How does Chekhov portray Russian life in his story "The Beggar"?*

Bridge to the Past

Literature

Literary Element Irony is the contrast between what is anticipated and what actually occurs. The unexpected twist at the end of the story—that Lushkoff did little work for Skvortsoff—makes the lawyer's comments about the value of hard work ironic.

FOCUS

Ask students how they respond when they see someone asking for money. Discuss how they feel toward the individual and whether they think about why the person might have to beg.

History & Art In the late 1800s when Chekhov wrote, Russia was still a vast, overwhelmingly agrarian society. There was a sharp contrast between the urbane lifestyle of city dwellers in Moscow and St. Petersburg and the way that poor, deeply religious former serfs lived in the countryside.

Answer to Caption: *Students may feel Russia was marked by strong class differences but that members of different classes still had regular contact and that there was some social mobility.*

Other Works by Anton Chekhov

Frayn, Michael, trans. ***Chekhov: Plays.*** Methueun UK: Heinemann, 1988.
Garnett, Constance, trans. ***The Duel and Other Stories.*** New York: Echo Press, 1984.
Garnett, Constance, trans. ***The Steppe.*** Gloucester: Sutton, 1987.
Mamet, David, ed. ***Uncle Vanya.*** New York: Grove Press, 1988.

Chapter 24 *Cultural Revolution* **641**

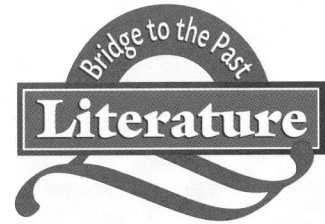

Bridge to the Past
Literature

TEACH

Literary Analysis

Students may recall being told by English teachers to avoid the passive voice, a sentence structure in which the writer does not make clear who carried out an action. However, Chekhov, or the translator of this story, used the passive voice to good effect. When Olga enters, she "announced that the wood had been chopped." The construction avoids stating who actually chopped the wood, which the reader does not learn until the end of the story.

History & Art In the late 1800s Russian women had few rights. A wife had no legal rights except through her husband; a widow was entitled to inherit only one-seventh of her husband's real estate.
Answer to Caption: *Unknown to Skvortsoff, Olga, his cook, played the key role in reforming Lushkoff.*

Interpretation

Point out to students that Skvortsoff obviously considers himself a good judge of character. Yet he misunderstands both his cook, whom he calls "ill-tempered" but who is actually very kind, and Lushkoff, who he believes was reformed by hard work but was actually changed by the cook's sympathy. Ask students what Chekhov might have been saying about how well upper-class Russians understood the poor. *(They did not understand the poor well at all.)*

World Literature Selection 6

History & Art *Female Farmers* by Kazimir Malevich. Russian State Museum, St. Petersburg, Russia **Malevich used modern painting techniques to portray the life of peasant women in rural Russia.** *What role does Olga play in Chekhov's story?*

that the wood had all been chopped.

"Good! Give him half a ruble [the Russian unit of currency]," said Skvortsoff. "If he wants to he can come back and cut wood on the first day of each month. We can always find work for him."

On the first day of the month the waif made his appearance and again earned half a ruble, although he could barely stand on his legs. From that day on he often appeared in the yard and every time work was found for him. Now he would shovel snow, now put the wood-shed in order, now beat the dust out of rugs and mattresses. Every time he received from twenty to forty kopecks [one kopeck equals one-hundredth of a ruble], and once, even a pair of old trousers were sent out to him.

When Skvortsoff moved into another house he hired him to help in the packing and hauling of the furniture. This time the waif was sober, gloomy, and silent. He hardly touched the furniture, and walked behind the wagons hanging his head, not even making a pretense of appearing busy. He only shivered in the cold and became embarrassed when the carters jeered at him for his idleness, his feebleness, and his tattered, fancy overcoat. After the moving was over Skvortsoff sent for him.

"Well, I see that my words have taken effect," he said, handing him a ruble. "Here's for your pains. I see you are sober and have no objection to work. What is your name?"

"Lushkoff."

"Well, Lushkoff, I can now offer you some

Additional Literary Works of the Period

Futabatei, Shimei. ***Ukigumo.*** Novel about Japanese modernization.
Hernandez, José. ***Martin Fierro.*** Epic poem about an Argentinian gaucho.
London, Jack. ***Call of the Wild.*** Tale of a dog that returns to the wilderness.
Wharton, Edith. ***Ethan Frome.*** Tragic novel set in rural New England.

other, cleaner employment. Can you write?"

"I can."

"Then take this letter to a friend of mine tomorrow and you will be given some copying to do. Work hard, don't drink, and remember what I have said to you. Good-bye!"

Pleased at having put a man on the right path, Skvortsoff tapped Lushkoff kindly on the shoulder and even gave him his hand at parting. Lushkoff took the letter, and from that day forth came no more to the yard for work.

Two years went by. Then one evening, as Skvortsoff was standing at the ticket window of a theater paying for his seat, he noticed a little man beside him with a coat collar of curly fur and a worn sealskin cap. This little individual timidly asked the ticket seller for a seat in the gallery and paid for it in copper coins.

"Lushkoff, is that you?" cried Skvortsoff, recognizing in the little man his former wood-chopper. "How are you? What are you doing? How is everything with you?"

"All right. I am a notary [a clerk who certifies legal documents] now and get thirty-five rubles a month."

"Thank Heaven! That's fine! I am delighted for your sake. I am very, very glad, Lushkoff. You see, you are my godson, in a sense. I gave you a push along the right path, you know. Do you remember what a roasting I gave you, eh? I nearly had you sinking into the ground at my feet that day. Thank you, old man, for not forgetting my words."

"Thank you, too," said Lushkoff. "If I hadn't come to you then I might still have been calling myself a teacher or a student to this day. Yes, by flying to your protection I dragged myself out of a pit."

"I am very glad, indeed."

"Thank you for your kind words and deeds. You talked splendidly to me then. I am very grateful to you and to your cook. God bless that good and noble woman! You spoke finely then, and I shall be indebted to you to my dying day; but, strictly speaking, it was your cook, Olga, who saved me."

"How is that?"

"Like this. When I used to come to your house to chop wood she used to begin: 'Oh, you sot [drunkard], you! Oh, you miserable creature! There's nothing for you but ruin.' And then she would sit down opposite me and grow sad, look into my face and weep. 'Oh you unlucky man! There is no pleasure for you in this world and there will be none in the world to come. You drunkard! You will burn in hell. Oh, you unhappy one!' And so she would carry on, you know, in that strain. I can't tell you how much misery she suffered, how many tears she shed for my sake. But the chief thing was—she used to chop the wood for me. Do you know, sir, that I did not chop one single stick of wood for you? She did it all. Why this saved me, why I changed, why I stopped drinking at the sight of her I cannot explain. I only know that, owing to her words and noble deeds a change took place in my heart; she set me right and I shall never forget it. However, it is time to go now; there goes the bell."

Lushkoff bowed and departed to the gallery.

RESPONDING TO LITERATURE

1. Explain how the beggar Lushkoff's character and behavior change between the beginning of Chekhov's story and the conclusion of the story.
2. Contrast Skvortsoff's plan for helping Lushkoff improve his life and what actually helped Lushkoff.
3. What advice do you think Chekhov would give to people today who want to help the poor?
4. **Predicting an Outcome** What might have happened if Skvortsoff had found out immediately that Olga was chopping the wood for Lushkoff?

ANSWERS TO RESPONDING TO LITERATURE

1. Lushkoff stops drinking and begging and takes a respectable job as a notary.
2. Skvortsoff thought he would help Lushkoff by giving him work. Instead, Olga helped him by showing real concern.
3. Students may feel Chekhov was saying that people should help the poor out of genuine compassion, not a sense of superiority.
4. He probably would have stopped hiring Lushkoff. He probably would have scolded Olga.

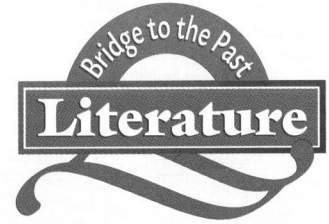

Bridge to the Past

Literature

ASSESS

Assign **Responding to Literature** questions.

CLOSE

After students have read the excerpt, point out to them that Chekhov came from a very humble background. Ask them to discuss whether Chekhov was sympathetic to Lushkoff when he was a beggar. **Does Chekhov seem to blame society in general or Lushkoff himself for Lushkoff's poverty?** *(Since Lushkoff reforms through his own efforts, Chekhov seems to point to individual responsibility for poverty in this story.)*

Contemporary Connection

The Cherry Orchard and other Chekhov plays are often presented by regional theater companies. Students may also be interested in watching the film *Uncle Vanya on 42nd Street*, a play within a play that deals with a production of the famous drama by Chekhov, directed by Louis Malle.

Portfolio Project

Have students interested in issues of unemployment, poverty, and substance abuse choose and research a specific topic in one of these areas and write a brief essay.

Chapter 24 Review

GLENCOE TECHNOLOGY

VIDEODISC

Use MindJogger to review students' knowledge of the chapter.

MindJogger Videoquiz

Chapter 24
Disc 3 Side B

Also available in VHS.

Answers

Using Key Terms

1. f	6. k
2. j	7. a
3. b	8. l
4. g	9. c
5. i	10. e

Using Your History Journal

Encourage students to comment on the universality of Chekhov's subject by including in their reviews allusions to contemporary situations in real life or fiction.

Reviewing Facts

1. They preferred not to have the government restrict their ability to make money.
2. Building on Pasteur's work with bacteria, Lister introduced antiseptics.
3. Comte urged the application of scientific methods to the analysis of human behavior.
4. advances in atomic theory, discovery of X rays and radioactivity, quantum theory, theory of relativity
5. the desire for better pay and working conditions, oppressive regimes, and famine
6. Millet: realism; Monet: impressionism; van Gogh: postimpressionism
7. Hugo's *Les Misérables*: romantic novel portraying human suffering with compassion; Tolstoy's *War and Peace*: realistic historical novel about Napoleon's 1812 invasion of Russia; Dreiser's *An American Tragedy*: naturalistic novel about a young man executed for killing his pregnant girlfriend

Critical Thinking

1. Answers will vary and may include examples from painting, literature, or music.
2. Darwin wondered why there was such a great variety of plants and animals and why some had become extinct. Natural selection explained that only those species best adapted to their environment survive.
3. Answers will vary but should point out strengths and weaknesses in each system.
4. Answers will vary but may focus on the equality of men and women.

CHAPTER 24 REVIEW

Historical Significance

The Industrial Revolution created new businesses and social classes. Living standards improved for many people, although a wide gap separated rich and poor.

Today capitalism is the world's dominant economic system. Since the 1930s, democratic societies have combined capitalism with social welfare policies. The role of government in social affairs, however, currently provokes much debate, and there are calls for greater personal responsibility and less government involvement.

Using Key Terms

Write the key term that completes each sentence.

a. atomic theory	g. socialism
b. evolution	h. sociology
c. laissez-faire	i. genetics
d. immigration	j. emigration
e. impressionism	k. urbanization
f. realism	l. psychology

1. In the mid-1800s artists and writers in Europe and North America developed a style called __________ that often called attention to the less fortunate members of society.
2. Wanting a better life, many Europeans in the 1800s chose __________, leaving their homelands to settle elsewhere.
3. In the mid-1800s scientists proposed the theory that all plants and animals developed from simple to complex forms by ______ over millions of years.
4. Supporters of ________ believe that society, directly or through the government, should own the means of production.
5. The research of Gregor Mendel laid the foundation for the development of _________, the science of heredity.
6. The movement of people into the cities resulted in the __________, or the spread of city life, of the industrialized countries.
7. The English chemist John Dalton provided proof of the __________, the belief that matter is made up of tiny particles called atoms.
8. Freud's theory that human actions grew out of subconscious motives led to the development of the science of ___________.
9. Supporters of ________ believed that people should be able to buy and sell, hire and fire, free from government interference.
10. Artists following a style called __________ tried to capture the momentary impact of objects on the senses.

Using Your History Journal

After reading the literature selection from "The Beggar" by Anton Chekhov, write a review of the piece. Do you agree or disagree with Chekhov's assumptions about the poor? Why?

Reviewing Facts

1. **Explain** why business leaders during the early 1800s promoted laissez-faire economics.
2. **Discuss** Joseph Lister's contribution to science. Upon whose ideas did he base his work?
3. **State** how Auguste Comte's ideas encouraged the rise of the social sciences in the 1800s.
4. **Identify** the major discoveries made in physics in the 1800s and early 1900s.
5. **List** three reasons why people left Europe in the late 1800s.
6. **Identify** the movement associated with each of the following artists: Jean-François Millet, Claude Monet, Vincent van Gogh.
7. **Describe** one work by each of the following writers: Victor Hugo, Leo Tolstoy, Theodore Dreiser.

Critical Thinking

1. **Apply** What are three examples of the romantics' emphasis on emotion?
2. **Analyze** How did Charles Darwin's theories answer his question about the great variety of living things?
3. **Synthesize** Imagine that you have decided to create a self-sufficient community like New Lanark near your town or city. Would you

advocate public or private ownership of the means of production? Why?

4. **Evaluate** Write a letter to the editor of an 1800s newspaper, expressing your views on secondary-school education for women.
5. **Analyze** The painting *Dinner at Haddo House* shows the lifestyle of the wealthy. How did this show of wealth further separate social classes?

Understanding Themes

1. **Change** According to Karl Marx, what steps would societies follow in moving toward the goal of communism?
2. **Innovation** Describe one innovation of the 1800s and early 1900s in each of these sciences: biology, physics, psychology. How did each innovation affect people's lives?
3. **Movement** How did improved methods of transportation affect the movement of people and products?
4. **Innovation** Select a cultural movement such as romanticism, realism, symbolism, impressionism, or Postimpressionism, and explain how the movement reflected the way people felt about changes in the 1800s.

Linking Past and Present

1. Explain why Russia turned away from the radical Socialist movement born during the Industrial Revolution.
2. Choose a writer from Section 4, and tell how his or her work reflected the broad changes of the day. Compare the writer with a modern writer, and explain how both reflect their eras.

Skill Practice

Reread Chapter 24, Section 1, "Looking for a Better Way," on pages 623-624. Then paraphrase the information from each subhead in separate paragraphs. Include main ideas, important details and events, and key individuals.

1. Early Reformers:
2. Other Voices of Reform:

Geography in History

1. **Place** Refer to the map "Population Growth in the United Kingdom." What were the major industrial cities of the United Kingdom by 1900?
2. **Place** How much did the population per square mile in the London and Bristol areas grow during this period?
3. **Region** What areas of the United Kingdom were not heavily industrialized during this period?

Population Growth in the United Kingdom

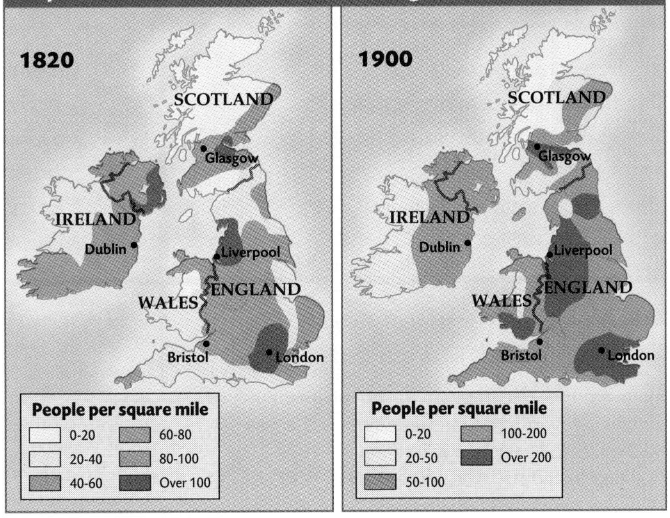

Chapter 24 Review

Linking Past and Present

1. Answers should touch on the failure of the Russian economy and the hope that capitalism will bring a better standard of living.
2. Answers should show knowledge of writers and social issues.

Skill Practice

1. The first reformers were humanitarians and religious leaders who believed that society should be improved. Their work led Parliament to investigate conditions in factories and mines. Parliament then passed legislation setting limits on the employment of women and children.
2. The utilitarian philosopher Jeremy Bentham argued that the rightness of an action should be judged by its usefulness. Bentham called for such reforms as education for all and improved prisons. John Stuart Mill, a follower of Bentham, argued for legislation against monopolies and laws protecting individual liberties.

Geography in History

1. London, Bristol, Liverpool, Glasgow, Dublin
2. London: from over 100 people per square mile to over 200 per square mile; Bristol: increased no more than 20 people per square mile
3. western Ireland, northern Scotland

5. It emphasized the great gap between rich and poor.

Understanding Themes

1. **CHANGE** primitive, slave, feudal, and capitalist—before the proletariat seized control, creating a society without private property, class distinctions, or government
2. **INNOVATION** discovery of bacteria led to new approaches in disease prevention; discovery of X rays led to new diagnostic methods in medicine; theory of the unconscious led to psychoanalysis
3. **MOVEMENT** People became more mobile. Railroads enabled people to eat food grown elsewhere and encouraged travel.
4. **INNOVATION** Answers should reflect an understanding of cultural movements.

Chapter Bonus Test Question

Ask: How would you respond to the romantic poet Keats's famous statement, "Beauty is truth, truth beauty,—that is all/Ye know on earth, and all ye need to know"? *(Answers will vary but should include that Keats's statement reflects the romantics' rejection of the increasing mechanization of industrialized society.)*

Democracy and Reform

CHAPTER RESOURCES

	Reproducible Resources	Multimedia Resources
Chapter Opener	Chapter Themes: Graphic Organizer 25 Historical Significance Chapter Activity 25	MindJogger Videoquiz
Chapter Enrichment	Vocabulary Activity 25* Time Line Activity 25 Mapping History Activity 25 History Simulation 25 Geography and History Activity 25 Source Reading 25 People in World History Profiles 47, 48 World Art and Music Activity 25 Enrichment Activity 25 Critical Thinking Activity 25 Skill Reinforcement Activity 25 Performance Assessment Activity 25	World History and Art Transparency 33, *The Banjo Lesson* Mapping History Overlay Transparency 16, *Global Ancestry of Americans* Chapter Transparency 25 Vocabulary PuzzleMaker Software World Music: Cultural Traditions, Lessons 1, 2, 3, 10 Lessons of War: *Why Soldiers Fight*
Chapter Review/Reteaching	Reteaching Activity 25 Skill Reinforcement Activity 25 Spanish Chapter Summary 25	Chapter 25 Digest Audiocassette, Activity, Test* Vocabulary PuzzleMaker Software Student Self-Test and Review Software MindJogger Videoquiz
Chapter Evaluation/Testing	Performance Assessment Activity 25 Chapter 25 Test, Forms A and B	Testmaker

** Also available in Spanish*

0:00 **OUT OF TIME?** Assign the Chapter 25 summary in the Unit 6 Digest on pages 728-731, and the Chapter 25 Audiocassettes.

Block Schedule

Block scheduling differs from traditional class scheduling in the amount of time allotted to each period. The extended time frame provided by block scheduling affords you the opportunity to implement a greater number of research-oriented and activity-intense projects to motivate and involve your students. Activities that are particularly suited to use within the block scheduling framework are identified throughout this chapter by the following designation.

KEY TO ABILITY LEVELS

Teaching strategies have been coded for varying learning styles and abilities.

- **L1** **BASIC** activities for all students
- **L2** **AVERAGE** activities for average to above-average students
- **L3** **CHALLENGING** activities for above-average students
- **LEP** **LIMITED ENGLISH PROFICIENCY** activities

A complete, 1-page lesson plan is provided for each section in the *Reproducible Lesson Plans* booklet.

SECTION RESOURCES

Daily Objectives	Reproducible Resources	Multimedia Resources
Section 1 **Reform in Great Britain** Describe how political change came to Great Britain during the 1800s.	Reproducible Lesson Plan 25-1 Vocabulary Activity 25* Guided Reading Activity 25-1* Time Line Activity 25 History Simulation 25 Section Quiz 25-1*	Section Focus Transparency 25-1 Chapter Transparency 25 Student Self-Test and Review Software Testmaker World Music: Cultural Traditions, Lesson 3
Section 2 **The Dominions** Relate how new societies emerged in Canada, Australia, and New Zealand.	Reproducible Lesson Plan 25-2 Vocabulary Activity 25* Guided Reading Activity 25-2* Geography and History Activity 25 Section Quiz 25-2*	Section Focus Transparency 25-2 Student Self-Test and Review Software Testmaker World Music: Cultural Traditions, Lesson 10
Section 3 **Political Struggles in France** Identify the changes in government that France underwent during the 1800s.	Reproducible Lesson Plan 25-3 Vocabulary Activity 25* Guided Reading Activity 25-3* Section Quiz 25-3*	Section Focus Transparency 25-3 Student Self-Test and Review Software Testmaker
Section 4 **Expansion of the United States** Explain how the United States changed during the 1800s.	Reproducible Lesson Plan 25-4 Vocabulary Activity 25* Guided Reading Activity 25-4* People in World History Profile 47 Section Quiz 25-4*	Section Focus Transparency 25-4 World History and Art Transparency 33, *The Banjo Lesson* Mapping History Overlay Transparency 16, *Global Ancestry of Americans* Student Self-Test and Review Software World Music: Cultural Traditions, Lesson 1 Lessons of War: *Why Soldiers Fight*
Section 5 **Latin American Independence** Relate how the countries of Latin America won independence.	Reproducible Lesson Plan 25-5 Guided Reading Activity 25-5* People in World History Profile 48 Reteaching Activity 25 Enrichment Activity 25 Section Quiz 25-5* Performance Assessment Activity 25 Spanish Chapter Summary 25	Section Focus Transparency 25-5 Vocabulary PuzzleMaker Software Student Self-Test and Review Software Testmaker World Music: Cultural Traditions, Lesson 2

** Also available in Spanish*

Chapter Activities

Performance Assessment Activity

An Import/Export Company Organize students into groups that will assume the roles of owners of an import/export company. First, each group will review the expansions and reforms of the era and predict how various parts of the world would be different today if none of these had occurred—including differences today in government, foreign affairs, trade, language, travel and tourism, and economics. Each group will then create five scenarios of how they would acquire merchandise for their companies from different parts of the world studied in this chapter. Each scenario should reflect the long-term effects of one of the expansions or reforms.

Possible Rubric Features
Accuracy of content information; collaborative skills; logical predicting; plausibility of scenarios; and thoroughness in including criteria related to government, trade, language, foreign affairs, economics, and tourism

• *For an additional activity, refer to Activity 25 in the* Performance Assessment Strategies and Activities *booklet.*

Activity

From the Classroom of...

Chuck Kloes
Beverly Hills High School
Beverly Hills, CA

The Irish Question: A Solution Satisfactory to Whom?

Prepare "point of view" sheets for both sides of the Irish question—Sheet A listing four to five arguments in support of granting home rule to all of Ireland, and Sheet B listing four to five arguments in support of maintaining English control over Northern Ireland. Organize the class into A and B groups to debate the question and pass out the sheets. Give the groups 15 minutes to study the sheets, collect data, and prepare their presentations. Have each group select two students to be spokespersons, with you acting as moderator. After the debate, hold a class discussion about what students learned from the exercise.

MULTIPLE LEARNING STYLES

Verbal/Linguistic
Tell students to imagine going on a tour of Europe and North and South America during the 1800s. Have them keep a journal of their travels and record their impressions of culture, environment, society, and special events.

Logical/Mathematical
Have students create a time line that tracks the major political, social, and cultural struggles of the period. Ask students to include details from the text as well as class presentations.

Visual/Spatial
Have students make a large wall map of the Oregon, Santa Fe, and California Trails. Have them mark key physical geographic features and main stopping places.

Auditory/Musical
Ask students to research and report on the music of this period in Europe, the British dominions, the United States, or Latin America. They might select a sample from each area or concentrate on just one location. They may present their findings to the class.

Additional Resources

TEACHER'S CORNER

NATIONAL GEOGRAPHIC SOCIETY

INDEX TO NATIONAL GEOGRAPHIC MAGAZINE

The following articles may be used for research relating to this chapter:

- "El Libertador: Simón Bolívar," by Bryan Hodgson, March 1994.
- "The Itch to Move West: Life and Death on the Oregon Trail," by Boyd Gibbons, August 1986.
- "The Travail of Ireland," by Joseph Judge, April 1981.

NATIONAL GEOGRAPHIC SOCIETY PRODUCTS AVAILABLE FROM GLENCOE

To order the following products for use with this chapter, contact your local Glencoe sales representative or call Glencoe at 1-800-368-7344:

VIDEODISCS
- GTV: The American People
- GTV: A Geographic Perspective on American History

ADDITIONAL NATIONAL GEOGRAPHIC SOCIETY PRODUCTS

To order the following products for use with this chapter, call National Geographic Society at 1-800-368-2728:

- *Building a Nation: The Story of Immigration*, "From the Beginnings Through the 1880s," "From the 1880s to Recent Times." (Filmstrip)
- *Nations of the World Series*, "Australia." (Video)
- *The Westward Movement*, "Into the Wilderness," "Spanning the Continent." (Filmstrip)

BIBLIOGRAPHY

Literature of the Period

Eliot, George. *The Mill on the Floss.* New York: Bantam, 1987. Novel explores family relationships while taking a critical look at British middle-class values.

Readings for the Student

Davis, William C., ed. *Touched by Fire: A Photographic Portrait of the Civil War*. Boston: Little, Brown, 1985. Portrays the tragedy of the American Civil War.

Readings for the Teacher

Hoppen, K. Theodore. *Ireland Since 1800: Conflict and Conformity.* White Plains, NY: Longman, 1989. This survey of Irish history examines the social, economic, and political aspects of recent Irish history.

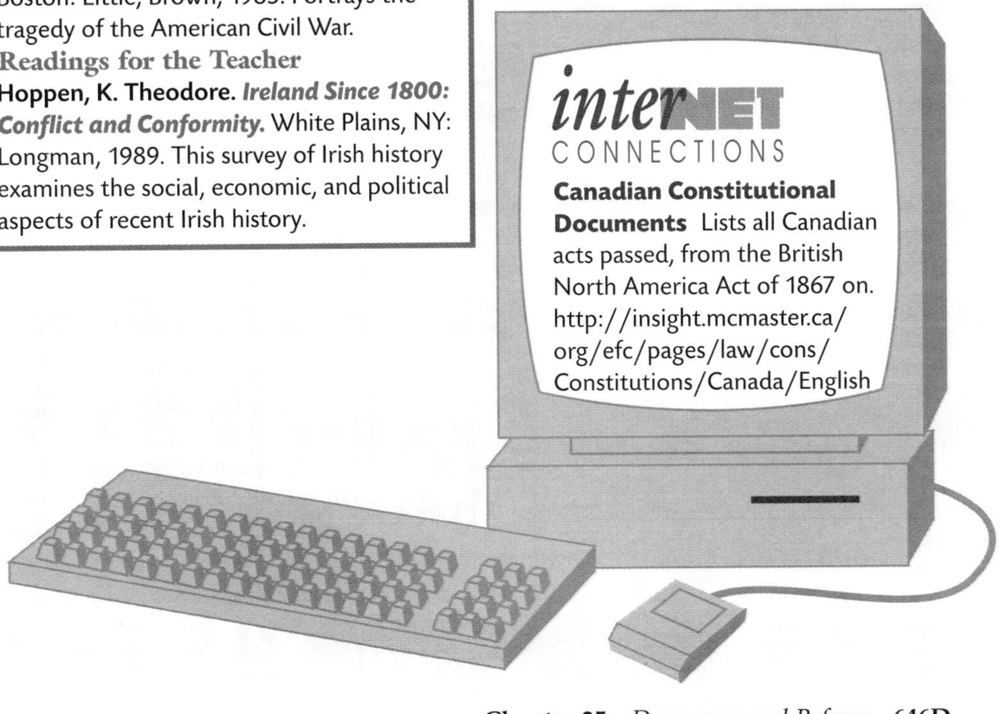

interNET
CONNECTIONS
Canadian Constitutional Documents Lists all Canadian acts passed, from the British North America Act of 1867 on.
http://insight.mcmaster.ca/org/efc/pages/law/cons/Constitutions/Canada/English

Introducing Chapter 25

CHAPTER THEMES

Chapter Themes are listed by section on this chapter opening page of the Student Edition. A corresponding theme-based activity is available under "TEACH," and a theme-based question is asked in the Section and Chapter Reviews.

The Storyteller

Historical Setting Richard Cobden, an English political leader and economist, became a great supporter of the democratic movement and of laws to protect the interests of the middle class. Cobden worked for peace and argued against the British foreign policy of intervention to maintain the balance of power. He was a strong advocate of free trade and played a key role in the fight to repeal the Corn Law.

Historical Significance

Answers: *Democratic reform came about through both peaceful and violent means. Although some reform movements were unsuccessful, they set the stage for later successes in democracy and self-government.*

With Latin American independence came rivalry among countries, political instability, and the challenge of facing continuing social and economic problems.

Chapter 25

1800–1914

Democracy and Reform

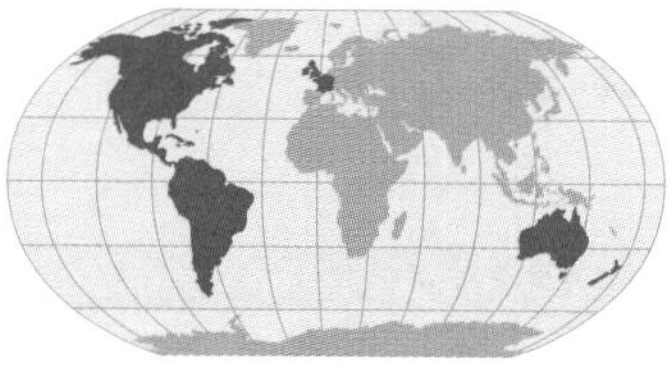

Chapter Themes

- **Change** Great Britain carries out democratic reforms. *Section 1*
- **Movement** Immigrants from Great Britain and other countries settle Canada, Australia, and New Zealand. *Section 2*
- **Revolution** France undergoes political upheaval during the 1800s. *Section 3*
- **Change** The United States extends its borders and develops its economy. *Section 4*
- **Nationalism** Latin American nations achieve self-government. *Section 5*

The Storyteller

British politician Richard Cobden stood before the House of Commons in 1845. In a loud voice, he demanded that the middle and working classes be given more representation in a government that unfairly favored the landed aristocracy. Cobden declared:

"I say without being revolutionary ... that the sooner the power of this country is transferred from the landed ruling class, which has so misused it, and is placed absolutely ... in the hands of the intelligent middle and industrious classes, the better for the condition and destinies of this country."

While Cobden worked for change within the British political system, people in Europe and Latin America faced fiercer and often bloody struggles for democratic reform. By the end of the 1800s, democracy had triumphed in many parts of the world.

Historical Significance

In what ways did democratic reform movements develop and flourish in Europe and other parts of the world? What changes did independence bring to the peoples of Latin America?

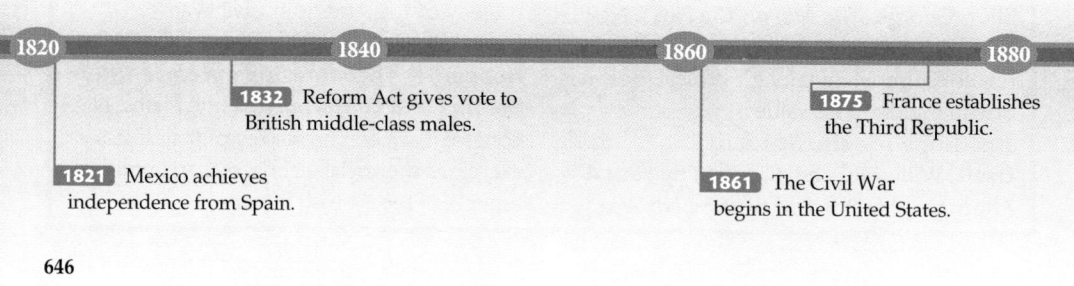

1820 | 1840 | 1860 | 1880

1821 Mexico achieves independence from Spain.

1832 Reform Act gives vote to British middle-class males.

1861 The Civil War begins in the United States.

1875 France establishes the Third Republic.

646

GEOGRAPHY CONNECTION

Location Using a world map, have students use a scale of miles to estimate distance between Great Britain and Australia *(approximately 8,000 miles [13,000 km])* and the distance between Spain and Ecuador *(approximately 6,000 miles [10,000 km])*. Ask students what effect these distances might have on the relationship between the country and the colony. *(It might have made it difficult for the countries to govern their distant colonies efficiently or knowledgeably; it might have increased the colonies' desire for independence.)*

History & Art *Celebration of the Concorde of May 21, 1848* by Jean Jacques Champin. Musée de la Ville de Paris, Musée Carnavalet, Paris, France

Your History Journal

On an outline map of the world, draw and label all the territories once held by Great Britain and the dates when they became self-governing, or independent.

EXTRA CREDIT PROJECT

Research To further their understanding of the period covered in this chapter, have students investigate one of the following topics: the potato famine of 1845–1847, schools and education on the frontier, the California gold rush, the Dreyfus affair, or the penal colonies of Australia. Ask students to prepare an outline first, then write the report and present it to the class. **L2**

Introducing Chapter 25

History & Art

The work to build the Place de la Concorde began in 1755. Almost a hundred years later, during the reign of Louis Philippe, it was completed with the addition of the Egyptian obelisk. The Place de la Concorde has been the arena for many historic events including guillotine executions in the 1790s.

Performance Assessment

Refer to the activity on page 646C of the Planning Guide.

For an additional activity, refer to Activity 25 in the *Performance Assessment Strategies and Activities* booklet.

Using Your History Journal

Suggest that students use colored pencils or pens to color code the territories on their maps. They should label neatly with black pen.

GLENCOE TECHNOLOGY

VIDEODISC

Use MindJogger to preview chapter content.

MindJogger Videoquiz

Chapter 25
Disc 4 Side A

Also available in VHS.

Chapter 25
Section 1

SECTION THEME

▶ **Change** Great Britain carries out democratic reforms.

Find Out

Answer: *Electoral reform, the reorganization of political parties, and the dynamic leadership of prime ministers Gladstone and Disraeli brought peaceful change in government in Britain during the 1800s.*

FOCUS

Section Objective

Describe how political change came to Great Britain during the 1800s.

BELLRINGER Motivational Activity

Before taking roll at the beginning of the class period, project Section Focus Transparency 25-1 and have students answer the activity questions. Discuss students' responses.

This activity is also available as a blackline master.

Vocabulary Pre-check

Use Vocabulary Activity 25 to introduce vocabulary terms. **L1 LEP**

1825	1850	1875	1900
1837 Victoria becomes queen of Great Britain.	**1867** Reform Act extends vote to all male homeowners and renters.	**1886** Gladstone introduces Irish home rule legislation.	**1900** Trade unionists and Socialists begin to form the Labour party.

Section 1

Reform in Great Britain

Setting the Scene

▶ **Terms to Define**
apportion, disenfranchised, suffragette, home rule

▶ **People to Meet**
the Chartists, Queen Victoria, William Gladstone, Benjamin Disraeli, the Fabians, Emmeline Pankhurst, Charles Stewart Parnell

▶ **Places to Locate**
Ireland

Find Out How did political change come to Great Britain during the 1800s?

The Storyteller

When women first lobbied for voting rights, some critics feared that if they won the vote, men would become women's servants. Political cartoons and works of art appeared that showed sour-faced men caring for babies and wringing out dirty laundry, while women happily rode around in carriages or talked excitedly around the ballot box. Other opponents claimed that if women won the vote, they would spend all their time at the polls. One poster nicknamed a woman who ran for office "Susan Sharp-Tongue, the Celebrated Man Tamer."

—adapted from *On To Victory, Propaganda Plays of the Woman Suffrage Movement*, edited by Bettina Friedl, 1987

Woman suffrage rally

Political change in Great Britain took place gradually and peacefully. The British government moved toward greater democracy through evolution rather than revolution. By the 1800s Great Britain was a limited constitutional monarchy. The monarch's authority consisted only of the rights to encourage, to warn, and to be consulted by those who really governed Great Britain. Actual executive power belonged to the Cabinet led by the prime minister, while Parliament maintained legislative control.

Although all British people in theory were represented in the House of Commons, the British government was not a true democracy in the early 1800s. Political power remained with the landed aristocracy, while the middle and working classes had no voting rights.

Electoral Reforms

In the early 1800s some rural districts were well represented in the House of Commons, while growing industrial areas had little representation. Factory workers, farm laborers, and the middle class began to demand that they receive a greater political voice. The liberal minority party, the Whigs, continually introduced bills to give voting rights to more people and to apportion, or divide and share, electoral districts more fairly. The Whigs' efforts were repeatedly defeated by the Tory party, which opposed such bills.

When the Whigs came to political power in 1830, however, their demands could no longer be ignored. In 1832 the Whigs forced the king to announce that he would create as many new lords as necessary to give the reform bill a majority in the House of Lords. To avoid this action, the lords gave in and passed the bill.

SECTION RESOURCES

Reproducible Masters
- Reproducible Lesson Plan 25-1
- Vocabulary Activity 25
- Guided Reading Activity 25-1
- Time Line Activity 25
- History Simulation 25
- Section Quiz 25-1

Transparencies
- Section Focus Transparency 25-1
- Chapter Transparency 25

Multimedia
- Student Self-Test and Review Software
- Testmaker
- World Music: Cultural Traditions, Lesson 3

The Reform Act of 1832

The Reform Act of 1832 lowered the property qualifications for voting and gave more middle-class males the right to vote. The proportion of voters increased from 1 in 100 to 1 in 32 men. The act also took representation rights away from areas that had declined in population. With 143 seats freed in the House of Commons, the heavily populated cities finally increased their representation. One observer recalled the moments after the passing of the reform bill:

> "We shook hands and clapped each other on the back, and went out laughing, crying ... into the lobby. And no sooner were the outer doors opened than another shout answered that within the House. All the passages ... were thronged by people who had waited till four in the morning to know the issue [outcome]."

Reform Movements

While the Reform Act gave middle-class men the right to vote, it only frustrated the industrial and farm workers, who remained disenfranchised, or deprived of the right to vote. These disenfranchised citizens banded together to demand further reforms. In a document called *A People's Charter*, **the Chartists**, an important reform group of the working class, proposed political changes. The Chartists' demands included voting rights for all adult men, no property qualifications for voting, a secret ballot, salaries for members of Parliament so that the middle and lower classes could take seats, and equal electoral districts.

The Chartists submitted two petitions to Parliament, one with more than a million signatures and the other with more than 3 million. Parliament rejected both petitions. After the defeat, the Chartists had little success and their movement faded by the 1840s. Parliament did, however, eventually pass many of their reforms.

Another reform movement, the Anti-Corn Law League, was supported by the middle class. The aim of the League was to repeal the Corn Law, which since 1815 had severely limited and taxed the importation of foreign grain. Wealthy landowners benefited from the law, as it ensured them a profitable hold on the grain market. Middle-class industrialists fought the Corn Law because it forced them to pay higher wages to workers to enable them to buy bread.

The League—the first major political pressure group in Great Britain—captured public attention with lectures, pamphlets, books, and meetings.

Visualizing History **In this British cartoon, Prime Minister Benjamin Disraeli presents the crown of India to Queen Victoria.** *What other noted prime minister served during Victoria's reign?*

When an Irish crop failure forced Great Britain to import much grain, Parliament responded to the pressure and repealed the Corn Law.

Political Parties

One result of electoral reform was more elaborate organization of political parties. Before 1800 both parties—the Tories and the Whigs—represented wealthy landowners. They had no formal organization. They were actually loose groups of politicians with common interests. As more middle-class men gained voting rights, the old parties reorganized to win support from the new voters. After 1832 the Tory and Whig parties began to change into the modern Conservative and Liberal parties.

Support for the Conservative party came largely from the aristocracy and members of the old Tory party. The industrial and commercial classes and members of the old Whig party supported the Liberal party. Both parties eventually competed for middle-class and working-class votes.

Political Leadership

This era of political reform took place during the reign of **Queen Victoria**. She came to the throne in 1837 at age 18 and reigned for 64 years. Two brilliant prime ministers—**William Gladstone** and **Benjamin Disraeli**—served during Victoria's reign. Both men offered dynamic leadership for the

TEACH

Guided Practice

THEME Change

Work with students to create a chart on the chalkboard listing the changes caused by the Reform Act of 1832. **L1 LEP**

Visualizing History The rise of British political cartoons came with the movement toward greater democracy. These caricatures became a popular way to communicate political messages and influence voters. In this cartoon the artist is commenting on the well-known fact that Queen Victoria was very fond of Disraeli and had offered him a peerage.

Answer to Caption: *William Gladstone*

Diagram Have students list events that influenced the democratic reform movement in Great Britain during the 1800s. *(Whigs coming to power in 1830, formation of the Chartists)* Help students make a diagram showing the cause-and-effect relationships between these events and specific reforms. **L2**

Debate Have students take the following roles: industrial workers, middle-class landowners, and members of the House of Lords. Lead an impromptu debate on the Reform Act of 1832. **L3**

History Simulation 25

Chapter Transparency 25

World Music: Cultural Traditions, Lesson 3

COOPERATIVE LEARNING ACTIVITY

Role Play Have students form groups to role-play a visit to Ireland by members of the British Parliament. Tell students to imagine that they are living in the mid-1800s and that some members of Parliament are visiting Ireland to hear the people's views on home rule. Select one group of five or six students to be observers. Have remaining students represent: members of Parliament who oppose or favor home rule, Irish Catholics, and a group of Irish Protestants. Have students who have assumed roles debate the issue of home rule. At the conclusion of the debate, have the observers comment on the effectiveness of each faction's arguments. **L2**

Chapter 25 Section 1

Independent Practice

Guided Reading Activity 25-1 **L1**

Time Line Activity 25

Geography: Location Using the Atlas in their textbook, have students locate Ireland and write a brief paragraph about the conflict between the Irish and the British, focusing especially on the locations of the places involved. **L1 LEP**

Women Ask students to investigate the Women's Social Political Union or the lives of Emmeline, Christabel, and Sylvia Pankhurst and report on the women's rights movements. Ask them to describe the strategies used to gain public attention and support and then tell whether they agree with the strategies. **L2**

Critical Thinking Have students recall the cultural, economic, and political history of Great Britain and how it may have contributed to a male, landowner-dominated political system. Ask them to list specific changes that may have brought about the reevaluation of this political system in the 1800s. *(the Industrial Revolution)* **L3**

Linking Past and Present

Protests To publicize their cause, British suffragists went to extraordinary lengths, including arson, bombing of monuments, window smashing, and hunger strikes. These tactics were also used by Vietnam War protesters in the 1960s.

emerging Liberal and Conservative parties. Through their efforts Great Britain continued toward full democracy.

William Gladstone

William Gladstone of the Liberal party served 4 times as prime minister between 1868 and 1894. His first term, from 1868 to 1874, became known as the Great Ministry because of his many social reforms. Deeply religious, Gladstone always sought to apply morality to politics.

Gladstone directed reforms in such areas as government administration, education, and elections. A civil service reform of 1870 made appointments to most civil service positions dependent on competitive examinations. The Education Act of 1870 divided the country into school districts, which were maintained by local control. With the Ballot Act of 1872, Gladstone satisfied the old Chartist demand for the secret ballot. He also changed election districts. The Redistribution Act of 1885 divided Britain into electoral districts almost equal in population.

Benjamin Disraeli

Benjamin Disraeli of the Conservative party first gained fame in Great Britain as a novelist and later as a politician. He served two terms as prime minister—his first term briefly in 1868 and his second term from 1874 to 1880.

Disraeli believed that the Conservative party could save aristocratic traditions while cautiously adopting democratic reforms. He realized that blocking change would be damaging to the Conservative party, which began to base its primary support among the upper middle class.

In 1867 Disraeli introduced a Conservative-backed reform bill. By lowering property qualifications for voters, the Reform Bill of 1867 extended the vote to all male homeowners and most men who rented property. The bill increased the electorate by about 1 million men, adding to it many working-class voters.

Growth of Democracy

The British government changed in the last quarter of the 1800s. As steps were taken toward democracy, the working class, women, and Irish Catholics began to influence political life.

Rise of Labor

Political reforms inspired many groups to fight for increased rights. Labor unions had been steadily growing and gaining political strength since the mid-1700s. By the time of Gladstone's Great Ministry, unions had become a way of life among the working classes. Laborers from nearly every trade organized into unions, which achieved great gains by staging strikes and demonstrations.

At the same time that labor unions were growing stronger, socialism was also gaining followers. In 1884 a group of middle-class intellectuals formed the Fabian Society, an organization whose aim was to peacefully and gradually prepare the way for a Socialist government. Through education, its members promoted social justice such as improved conditions and fair wages for workers. Unlike labor unions, **the Fabians** favored parliamentary action over strikes and demonstrations.

In 1900 trade unionists and Socialists laid the foundation for a new political party—the Labour party—to speak for the working class. Labour party supporters backed the reform-minded Liberal government elected in 1906. Together the Liberal and Labour members of Parliament promoted government reform to improve workers' lives. Between 1906 and 1914, new legislation provided the working classes with old-age pensions, a minimum wage, unemployment assistance, and health and unemployment insurance.

A Constitutional Crisis

To finance these measures, the Liberal government called for higher taxes in the budget of 1909. The largely Conservative House of Lords vehemently opposed the proposed taxation, because it directly threatened the wealth of the aristocracy.

The contest ended in victory for the House of Commons when the 1911 Parliament Act narrowed the powers of the House of Lords by removing money bills from their control. This action symbolized the aristocracy's political decline.

Women Demand Greater Rights

Women also sought to benefit from Great Britain's move toward more representative democracy. British women, mostly from the middle class, spoke out for political and social equality in the mid-1800s. In the 1850s women's rights activist Barbara Leigh Smith fought to win property rights for married women. Her efforts led to the passage of the Married Women's Property Acts of 1870 and 1882, which gave women increased legal control over a family's earnings and property.

Achieving women's voting rights came more slowly. Although women had gained the right to vote in local elections in 1869, they still could not vote on a national level. In 1903 **Emmeline**

MEETING SPECIAL NEEDS ACTIVITY

Mixed Learners Because of the large amount of information conveyed in this chapter, allow students with learning disabilities to work in study groups. Help them to graphically organize the material by using time lines, charts, and diagrams to show relationships and to serve as study aids. Encourage students who need challenges to explore the section topics in detail. Direct them to key events that had major repercussions or that typify other similar situations. Have students look for cause-and-effect relationships. Establish a forum by which students can share their research with the class in a meaningful way, such as by a panel discussion. **L2**

Pankhurst and her two daughters, Christabel and Sylvia, founded the Women's Social Political Union (WSPU). They led a voting rights campaign on behalf of all British women and became known as **suffragettes**. The WSPU attracted attention to its cause by staging street demonstrations and hunger strikes. The violence cost the cause much political support. Nevertheless, the movement grew. In 1918, after World War I, Parliament finally granted British women over 30 the right to vote; 10 years later, in 1928, it gave the vote to all women over 21.

Ireland

Like others in the British Isles, Irish Catholics sought greater participation in the government. Their ultimate goal, however, was to govern themselves. For centuries, English and Scots Protestants in **Ireland** enjoyed almost total political and economic control of Ireland. This privileged minority owned large amounts of land. They rented it at high prices to Irish Catholic peasants, who were prohibited from purchasing land. Most Irish people lived in poverty. Ireland was predominantly Catholic, and a law requiring Catholics to pay taxes to the Anglican Church of Ireland only intensified anti-British feeling.

In 1801 Parliament had passed the Act of Union, joining Ireland and Great Britain. This union entitled Ireland to representation in Parliament, but it was not until 1829 that Catholics in the British Isles won the right to vote and hold office. Although these acts increased their rights, most Irish people still demanded to rule themselves.

Irish hatred of British rule heightened when a disastrous potato famine hit the country in the 1840s. Because peasants were forced to export the grain they grew in order to pay their high rents, they came to rely on the potato as their main source of food. In 1845 a deadly fungus destroyed much of the potato crop, and the British government sent inadequate aid to Ireland during the famine. Thousands of people died of starvation; over a million more, weakened by malnutrition, died of disease. Roughly a million others fled Ireland altogether; many people fled to the United States.

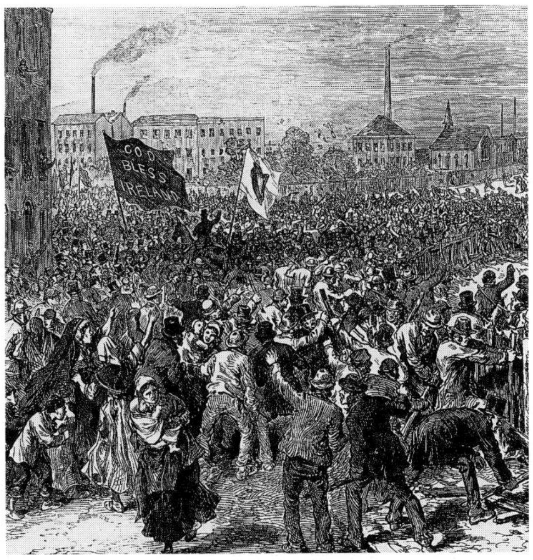

Visualizing History **Irish activists seeking home rule riot in Belfast in 1872.** *What minority group controlled most of the land in Ireland for centuries?*

Various groups fought for Irish rights. **Charles Stewart Parnell**—Irish-born member of a Protestant family—led Irish nationalists who sought to have the question of **home rule**, or self-government, heard in Parliament. Liberal Prime Minister Gladstone tried to pass legislation granting Irish home rule. His action split the Liberal party, and the measure was defeated. In 1914 Parliament finally passed a home rule bill, but it never went into effect. Irish Protestants threatened to fight British troops if Parliament enforced it.

SECTION 1 REVIEW

Recall

1. **Define** apportion, disenfranchised, suffragette, home rule.
2. **Identify** the Chartists, Anti-Corn Law League, Queen Victoria, William Gladstone, Benjamin Disraeli, the Fabians, Emmeline Pankhurst, Charles Stewart Parnell.
3. **List** three democratic reforms that occurred in Great Britain during the 1800s.

Critical Thinking

4. **Synthesizing Information** Imagine that you are an Irish Catholic farmworker living in Ireland in the 1800s. Express your feelings and attitudes about the British government.

Understanding Themes

5. **Change** What might have happened if Parliament had opposed democratic reform?

Chapter 25 Section 1

ASSESS

Check for Understanding

Assign Section 1 Review as homework or as an in-class activity.

Use Student Self-Test and Review Software to review Section 1.

Visualizing History The population of the city of Belfast in 1872 was largely Protestant with much opposition to home rule.
Answer to Caption: *English and Scots Protestants*

Evaluate

Section Quiz 25-1

Use the Testmaker to create a customized quiz for Section 1.

Reteach

Have students review the material and write one sentence that summarizes the key idea under each heading in the section.

Enrich

Have students imagine that they are journalists working for a political magazine in the 1830s. Have them write an article on the growth of democracy in Great Britain, focusing on the people who have recently been given the vote and those who are still struggling to obtain it.

CLOSE

Have students write six newspaper headlines that report the main ideas discussed in this section.

SECTION 1 REVIEW ANSWERS

1. All vocabulary words are defined in the Glossary.
2. Chartists, 649; Anti-Corn Law League, 649; Queen Victoria, 649; William Gladstone, 649; Benjamin Disraeli, 649; the Fabians, 650; Emmeline Pankhurst, 651; Charles Stewart Parnell, 651
3. Reform Act of 1832, civil service reform of 1870, Ballot Act of 1872
4. Answers will vary but should include a sense of anger and frustration.
5. **CHANGE** Answers will vary. Possible answer: British lower classes might have staged a revolution against the wealthy ruling classes.

Chapter 25 Section 2

SECTION THEME

▶ **Movement** Immigrants from Great Britain and other countries settle Canada, Australia, and New Zealand.

Find Out

Answer: *Settlers in Canada, Australia, and New Zealand sought self-government, developed the natural resources, and enlarged the areas of British settlement.*

FOCUS

Section Objective

Relate how new societies emerged in Canada, Australia, and New Zealand.

BELLRINGER Motivational Activity

Before taking roll at the beginning of the class period, project Section Focus Transparency 25-2 and have students answer the activity questions. Discuss students' responses.

This activity is also available as a blackline master.

Vocabulary Pre-check

Use Vocabulary Activity 25 to introduce vocabulary terms. **L1 LEP**

1850 · 1875 · 1900 · 1925

1840 Treaty of Waitangi guarantees Maori rights in New Zealand.

1867 British North America Act forms the Dominion of Canada.

1885 Canadian Pacific Railway links eastern and western parts of Canada.

1901 Australia becomes a dominion in the British Empire.

Section 2

The Dominions

Setting the Scene

▶ **Terms to Define**
dominion

▶ **People to Meet**
the Loyalists, Lord Durham, John A. Macdonald, the Aborigines, the Maori

▶ **Places to Locate**
Canada, Australia, New Zealand

Find Out How did new societies emerge in Canada, Australia, and New Zealand?

The Storyteller

On the long sea voyage to Australia, first-class passengers could go anywhere on board; other passengers, traveling more cheaply, were more restricted. Seamen were most restricted of all, and after three months on board, got their revenge for staying belowdeck in curious ways. Sometimes the crew would protest their rights by tossing a pig or sheep down among the cabins at night, to invade the passengers' space and keep them awake. One emigrant wrote in her diary: "From every quarter of the cabin you could hear the 'Ma, Ma' during the greater part of the night."

—adapted from *Sailing to Australia*, Andrew Hassam, 1994

Immigrant mother and children

As Great Britain moved toward greater democracy, the British Empire reached its height. With its colonies making up one-fourth of the world's land and people, Great Britain became the richest and most powerful country in the world. Political changes also took place in the empire, especially in territories largely inhabited by British settlers. Colonies such as **Canada**, **Australia**, and **New Zealand** sought self-government.

Canada

By the mid-1800s, Canada consisted of a number of British colonies dependent on the British government. The colonial population was ethnically divided. One part was French, another immigrant British, and a third part descendants of **the Loyalists**—Americans loyal to Great Britain during the American Revolution. Most Britons and Loyalists lived in Nova Scotia, New Brunswick, and near the Great Lakes. The French were concentrated in the Saint Lawrence River valley.

In 1763, as a prize for their victory in the French and Indian War, the British gained control of Quebec, which included most of French Canada. From that time, the French in Quebec firmly resisted British colonial rule. The predominantly Catholic French population were irritated by the influx of British immigrants, English-speaking and Protestant, that began about 1760.

To solve the growing English and French problem, the British government passed the Constitutional Act of 1791. This law divided Quebec into two colonies: Lower Canada and Upper Canada. Lower Canada remained French-speaking, but Upper Canada became English. Each colony had an assembly whose laws were subject to veto by a governor-general appointed by the British government. This arrangement worked until political differences brought rebellion in each colony.

SECTION RESOURCES

Reproducible Masters
- Reproducible Lesson Plan 25-2
- Vocabulary Activity 25
- Guided Reading Activity 25-2
- Geography and History Activity 25
- Section Quiz 25-2

Transparencies
- Section Focus Transparency 25-2

Multimedia
- Student Self-Test and Review Software
- Testmaker
- World Music: Cultural Traditions, Lesson 10

Visualizing History **Quebec City, founded in 1608, is Canada's oldest city. Located on the St. Lawrence River, Quebec City was a major lumber and ship-building center during the 1800s.** *What three groups contributed to the founding of Canada?*

By the late 1830s the French began to feel threatened by the growing English-speaking minority. Meanwhile, the British-Loyalist community was divided by disagreements between the conservative upper-class leadership and a group of liberal reformers who wanted a share in government. In 1837 unrest triggered rebellions in both colonies.

Canadian Self-Government

Uprisings in both Upper Canada and Lower Canada convinced the British that they had a serious problem in North America. In 1838 the British Parliament ordered **Lord Durham** to Canada to investigate. In a report to Parliament, Durham urged granting virtual self-government to Canada. Durham insisted that the real authority should be an elected assembly, not a British-appointed governor-general or the British government in London. With acceptance of the Durham report by the British Parliament, self-government developed in Canada. This pattern was later adopted by other territories of the British Empire.

In 1867 the British Parliament passed the British North America Act. This law established Canada as a **dominion**, or a self-governing territory owing allegiance to the British king or queen. The British North America Act joined Upper Canada (Ontario), Lower Canada (Quebec), Nova Scotia, and New Brunswick in a confederation called the Dominion of Canada. This act became the basis of the modern nation of Canada. In that same year, Canadian voters elected their first parliament. The first Canadian prime minister was **John A. Macdonald**, a Scottish-born lawyer.

Expanding Canadian Territory

At first the Dominion of Canada consisted of four provinces in the southeast, extending from the Great Lakes to the Atlantic Ocean. Then, in 1869 the dominion acquired the Northwest Territory, which extended west across vast prairies and forestlands and north to the Arctic wilderness. Most of this area was populated by Native Americans and European and American fur traders. Following sporadic violence between traders and Native Americans, the Canadian government set up and sent westward a special law-keeping force known as the Northwest Mounted Police. The police largely won the respect and loyalty of the Native Americans before the arrival of large numbers of Canadian settlers.

Canada further expanded its territory during the late 1800s. From the eastern part of the Northwest Territory, the province of Manitoba was formed in 1870. In 1871 British Columbia, a separate British colony on the Pacific coast, became a province. In 1873 tiny Prince Edward Island near the Atlantic Ocean joined Canada. To link the eastern provinces with the western provinces, the Canadian Pacific Railway was completed in 1885. This made possible the development of the Canadian prairies. In 1905 the prairie provinces of Saskatchewan and Alberta were added to the dominion.

Australia and New Zealand

On the other side of the world—in the south and southwest Pacific—the British colonies of Australia and New Zealand also sought self-government.

Chapter 25 Section 2

TEACH

Guided Practice

THEME Movement

Ask students to recall other periods or places where two cultures clashed as a result of colonization. *(the Spanish and the Aztec; British colonists and Native Americans)* Point out that culture clashes occurred in the British dominions. Ask students to predict how these clashes might affect the indigenous peoples in the Dominions. *(Colonization usually results in negative effects on native peoples.)* **L2**

Visualizing History It was in the mid-1820s that unemployment in Britain and Ireland spurred a great migration to Canada. Many of the people who came were fairly wealthy and educated.
Answer to Caption: *French-speaking settlers, American Loyalists and their descendants, and British settlers*

Critical Thinking Organize students into two groups to take the roles of the French-speaking residents of Lower Canada (Quebec) and the English-speaking citizens of Upper Canada (Ontario). Have the groups discuss their views on nationalism, language, and immigration. **L3**

World Music: Cultural Traditions, Lesson 10

COOPERATIVE LEARNING ACTIVITY

Documentary Have students work in groups to develop a television documentary on the settlement of Australia or New Zealand. In each group (one for Australia and one for New Zealand) have students take on the roles of writers, researchers, on-location reporters, British settlers, native groups, and British government officials. Other students in each group may produce maps and other graphic materials. Have students research information as necessary and then write and produce the documentary. If possible, record the performance on videotape. **L2**

Chapter 25 Section 2

Independent Practice

Guided Reading Activity 25-2 **L1**

Geography and History Activity 25

Multicultural Have students imagine themselves as settlers in one of the Dominions. Ask them to write letters describing their lives to friends in Great Britain. Suggest that students describe their work, their relationship with native people and other settlers, their remoteness from England, and the rigors of living on a frontier. **L2**

ASSESS

Check for Understanding

Assign Section 2 Review as homework or as an in-class activity.

Use Student Self-Test and Review Software to review Section 2.

Evaluate

Section Quiz 25-2

Use the Testmaker to create a customized quiz for Section 2.

Reteach

Have students create a time line documenting the development of the British dominions.

Enrich

Have students research the working of modern government in Canada, Australia, or New Zealand.

CLOSE

Ask students to write an essay summarizing changes in the Dominions during the 1800s.

Footnotes to History

Australian Language

Australian English has its own unique words: some come from the Aboriginal languages; others from the experiences of European settlers in the outback—the dry, open Australian interior. "Waltzing Matilda," Australia's best-known song, captures the flavor of Australian speech in this region:

"Once a jolly swagman [hobo] camped by a billabong [waterhole]
Under the shade of a coolibah tree,
And he sang as he watched and waited till his billy [milkpail] boiled
Who'll come a-waltzing Matilda [tramp the roads carrying a blanket roll] with me?"

Australia

Initially, Great Britain established Australia as a prisoners' colony to relieve overcrowded British jails. By 1860, after a gold rush lured new immigrants, the population reached 1 million, and the practice of transporting prisoners to Australia was abolished.

In settling the land, Europeans came into contact with **the Aborigines**, the original people of Australia. Many early European settlers treated the Aborigines badly, occupied their land, and killed many of them. Large numbers of Aborigines died from diseases introduced by the Europeans.

The increase in European settlement called for a better administration of colonial Australia. By the late 1800s Australia was made up of six British colonies—New South Wales, Victoria, Queensland, Tasmania, Western Australia, and South Australia. In 1901 Parliament made Australia a dominion that included the colonies plus a region known as the Northern Territory.

New Zealand

The first Europeans to settle in New Zealand were from James Cook's expedition in 1770. Hunters from Great Britain and the United States set up whaling stations during the 1790s. New Zealand also attracted timber traders.

Foreigners brought many problems to the original inhabitants, known as **the Maori**. Firearms, for example, increased warfare among the Maori tribes. Foreigners also brought diseases to which the Maori had no immunity, causing an almost 50 percent reduction in the Maori population in 20 years.

In an effort to provide law for the Maori and the settlers, British naval officers and Maori chiefs concluded the Treaty of Waitangi in 1840. The treaty protected Maori rights, including property rights, while the Maori gave the British sovereignty over New Zealand. In 1840 the first permanent British settlements were founded at Wellington and Wanganui. Their economies were based on wool exports to British markets.

As with Australia, New Zealand's British population was small until the discovery of gold. The gold discovery also brought conflict between the newcomers and the Maori.

Prospectors unsuccessful in finding gold in New Zealand remained to farm. To gain more land, they violated those Maori land rights guaranteed by the treaty with the British. During the Maori Wars in the mid-1800s, the New Zealand government sided with the newcomers and seized some Maori land for public use.

New Zealand received a constitution from Great Britain in 1852 and became a largely self-governing colony. In the 1890s, the New Zealand government carried out an extensive program of social reforms, such as pensions for the elderly and protection of workers' rights. At this time Great Britain itself had not yet introduced many of these reforms. In 1907 New Zealand finally became a dominion within the British Empire.

SECTION 2 REVIEW

Recall

1. **Define** dominion.
2. **Identify** the Loyalists, Lord Durham, John A. Macdonald, British North America Act, Northwest Mounted Police, the Aborigines, the Maori, Treaty of Waitangi.
3. **State** the terms of the Treaty of Waitangi. Were its terms carried out?

Critical Thinking

4. **Evaluating Information** The Canadians at first wanted to call their confederation "the Kingdom of Canada." The British government, however, suggested the term *dominion* because they felt *kingdom* would be offensive to the United States. Why might Americans find *kingdom* an offensive title?

Understanding Themes

5. **Movement** What was the original purpose for British settlement of Australia?

SECTION 2 REVIEW ANSWERS

1. All vocabulary words are defined in the Glossary.
2. Loyalists, 652; Durham, 653; Macdonald, 653; British North America Act, 653; Mounted Police, 653; Aborigines, 654; Maori, 654; Waitangi, 654
3. The treaty protected Maori rights, including property rights, and gave the ownership of New Zealand to the British. The terms were violated; British settlers later took Maori lands with the backing of the government.
4. Americans had fought to be independent from the "kingdom" of Great Britain and favored republican governments.
5. **MOVEMENT** Australia was a prisoners' colony.

1800 | 1850 | 1900

1830 Revolution overthrows Bourbon dynasty.

1848 Voters elect Louis-Napoleon president.

1870 Revolutionaries establish Commune of Paris.

1890s The Dreyfus affair divides French society.

Section 3

Political Struggles in France

Setting the Scene

- **Terms to Define**
  ultraroyalist, coup d'état, plebiscite
- **People to Meet**
  Charles X, Louis Philippe, Louis-Napoleon, General Georges Boulanger, Alfred Dreyfus
- **Places to Locate**
  Paris

Find Out What changes in government did France undergo during the 1800s?

The Storyteller

Louis-Napoleon Bonaparte (Emperor Napoleon III) had grand ideas for the government of France—including a grand role for himself. Of course, he would not revive the excesses of royalty that France had groaned under before. Still, Frenchmen could not help but notice that his plans for the new constitution of France included the following ideas: "The executive power vests in the Emperor alone. The Emperor is the supreme head of the state; he commands the national forces both on land and sea; declares war, makes treaties of peace, of alliance, and of commerce...."

—adapted from *The Political and Historical Works of Louis Napoleon Bonaparte*, Volume 1, 1852

Louis-Napoleon Bonaparte

When the Congress of Vienna placed Louis XVIII on the throne in 1815, the Bourbon monarchy once again ruled France. In the beginning of Louis XVIII's reign, the French enjoyed relative calm under the constitutional monarchy. This calm did not last long because conservative aristocrats tried to reestablish the old order. Called ultraroyalists, these aristocrats even sought to create courts to punish radicals. The ultraroyalists grew stronger when their leader, **Charles X**, became king after Louis's death in 1824.

After a splendid coronation reminiscent of earlier times, Charles X set out to restore absolute royal authority to France. When he passed a bill to repay aristocrats for the property they had lost during the French Revolution, he set in motion a storm of rebellion.

Revolt in France

The legislative assembly passed a vote of no-confidence in the government after this unpopular act. Undaunted, the king dissolved the assembly and held new elections. This proved fruitless, however, when voters elected more liberals who rejected Charles's policies.

In response to this election, Charles issued the July Ordinances. The ordinances proposed to dissolve the newly elected assembly, abolish freedom of the press, and restrict voting rights. Several journalists, however, ignored the restrictions and wrote fiery tracts urging rebellion.

On July 27, 1830, angry Parisian workers and students thundered through the streets, as they had done in 1789. By July 29, after *Les Trois Glorieuses* (three glorious days), triumphant revolutionaries forced Charles X to give up his right as monarch

SECTION THEME

Revolution France undergoes political upheaval during the 1800s.

Find Out

Answer: *France went from a monarchy to the Second Empire, to the Commune, and finally to a republic in the 1800s.*

FOCUS

Section Objective

Identify the changes in government that France underwent during the 1800s.

BELLRINGER Motivational Activity

Before taking roll at the beginning of the class period, project Section Focus Transparency 25-3 and have students answer the activity questions. Discuss students' responses.

This activity is also available as a blackline master.

Vocabulary Pre-check

Use Vocabulary Activity 25 to introduce vocabulary terms. **L1 LEP**

SECTION RESOURCES

Reproducible Masters
- Reproducible Lesson Plan 25-3
- Vocabulary Activity 25
- Guided Reading Activity 25-3
- Section Quiz 25-3

Transparencies
- Section Focus Transparency 25-3

Multimedia
- Student Self-Test and Review Software
- Testmaker

Chapter 25
Section 3

TEACH

Guided Practice

THEME Revolution

Based on their knowledge of the French Revolution, guide students in a discussion about how the events described in this section can be called a continuation of the original French Revolution of 1789. *(French people revolted against monarchy installed after Napoleon's downfall.)* **L1 LEP**

Visualizing History The 1848 uprising lasted three days. Louis Philippe had called the National Guard to keep order, but they sided with the rioters, and the municipal police force was too small to control the citizens. The mobs took over. This was considered a fairly bloodless revolution as revolutions go. **Answer to Caption:** *It was replaced by an empire headed by Louis-Napoleon Bonaparte.*

Chart Guide students in making a chart to organize the succession of French governments presented in this section. Use the following heads: *French Leader, Form of Government, Cause of Downfall.* **L2**

Critical Thinking History has been described as a pendulum. Guide a discussion of the meaning of this idea using the French government after the French Revolution as an example. *(revolution against monarchy, followed by Napoleonic dictatorship, followed by reinstatement of the monarchy, followed by revolution against monarchy)* **L3**

Visualizing History **The Revolution of 1848 that began in France triggered revolts throughout Europe.** *What happened to the Second Republic within four years of its constitution?*

and abdicate the throne. The fallen king fled to Great Britain.

The "Citizen-King"

After the chaos had subsided, revolutionary leaders set up a new constitutional monarchy that did not have close ties to the old aristocracy. **Louis Philippe**, a cousin of Charles, accepted the throne. Because he dressed and behaved like a middle-class person, Louis Philippe became known as the "Citizen-King" and won the support of the growing middle class.

From 1830 to 1848, however, many French people became discontented with Louis Philippe's government. At heart, the "Citizen-King" favored the wealthy, and many working-class citizens began to demand political reforms, especially voting rights.

Louis Philippe refused their demands. When they appealed to Prime Minister François Guizot (gee•ZOH), he too refused. Frustrated, leaders organized political banquets, where they called for an extended vote and Guizot's resignation.

The Revolution of 1848

In 1848 Guizot canceled a banquet, fearing a demonstration. This order, however, came too late. On February 22, crowds flooded the streets, singing "The Marseillaise" and shouting protests against Guizot. Louis Philippe called in troops, but the soldiers sympathized with the rebels and joined them. Over the next days, at least 52 civilians were killed or wounded. The disturbances forced Louis Philippe to abdicate and flee to Great Britain. The Revolution of 1848 ended with the rebels proclaiming France a republic.

Inspired by events in France, revolutionaries in other European countries also fought for greater political rights. Political discontent in Austria, Italy, and Prussia was particularly significant in the changing political climate on the Continent. In these areas, however, the political status quo was more or less maintained despite the uprisings.

The Second Empire

When the political turmoil in France had finally subsided, the revolutionary leaders proclaimed the Second Republic of France and set out to create a new constitution. The French constitution featured many democratic reforms, including a legislative branch called the National Assembly, the election of a president, and an extension of voting rights to all adult men. Eight million men eagerly set off to the polls to elect a new National Assembly in the spring of 1848. Only briefly, however, would the French enjoy the freedoms brought by the Second Republic.

The Rise of Louis-Napoleon

In presidential elections held in December 1848, French voters gave **Louis-Napoleon** Bonaparte, the nephew of Napoleon Bonaparte, an overwhelming victory. Louis-Napoleon's popularity came more from his name than from his political skills. The name "Napoleon" reminded the French people of the greatness their nation had once enjoyed under Napoleon I.

Although Louis-Napoleon presented himself as a democratic reformer, the president hoped to use his popularity to make himself an emperor. To guarantee victory, Louis-Napoleon worked to win

COOPERATIVE LEARNING ACTIVITY

News Broadcast Organize students into broadcast teams to provide coverage of the revolutions in France. Each team should divide up responsibility to research and prepare stories that provide a rounded picture of events in one of the revolutions. Each team member should have a role as a news anchor, on-the-scene reporter, or subject of an interview. Have teams report on events, reactions of royalists, republicans, leaders, and the person-in-the-street. Remind students to base their reports on actual events and actual people when possible. Have them write scripts and present their broadcasts to the class. You may want to videotape the presentations. **L2**

the support of powerful groups in France—the army, the Church, the middle class, and the peasants. For example, in 1849 he won the confidence of French Catholics by ordering French troops to help the pope suppress an attempt by Italian nationalists to set up a republic in Rome. He also gave the Church more control over French education.

This support for the Catholics, however, created an uproar in **Paris**. Demonstrators opposing support for the pope filled the streets. Alarmed by the mob action, the National Assembly restricted people's rights in order to keep law and order. They also revoked voting rights for about a third of the voters.

Louis-Napoleon used this uproar to his advantage by convincing the French people that the republic was a failure. Deciding to take control of the French government, Louis-Napoleon directed a **coup d'état**, or a quick seizure of power, on December 2, 1851. He dissolved the National Assembly and arrested 70 of his opponents. With shrewd planning, he won popular support by reestablishing voting rights for all French men.

Louis-Napoleon then called for a **plebiscite**, or national vote, asking the people to give him the power to create a new French constitution. The people enthusiastically gave him their support. Now Louis-Napoleon had complete legislative and executive control, and the people appeared happy with the order and stability he provided. In a second plebiscite, 95 percent of the people approved the transformation of the French republic into a hereditary empire. In 1852 Louis-Napoleon became Napoleon III, Emperor of France.

Although Napoleon III restricted the press and limited civil liberties, he had a successful economic program. During the 1850s French industrial growth doubled and foreign trade tripled. France built new railroads and roads, including Paris's famous wide boulevards.

The Crimean War

In 1854 Napoleon III led France into the Crimean War. The war pitted France and Great Britain against Russia. All three countries had interests in the Ottoman Empire. When a dispute arose over whether France or Russia had the right to protect Christians in the empire or visiting the Holy Land, the Ottoman emperor sided with the French.

Angered by the decision, Russian czar Nicholas I decided to try to extend the Russian Empire by encroaching upon Ottoman land. Nicholas's invasion of Ottoman territory in the Balkans upset both Great Britain and France, who wanted to protect their trade and financial interests in the Middle East. When the Ottoman Empire declared war on Russia in 1854, Great Britain, France, and the tiny Italian kingdom of Sardinia joined the battle.

French and British armies invaded Russian-controlled territory, setting up posts on the Crimean Peninsula, where most of the fighting took place. This peninsula juts into the Black Sea from southern Ukraine. During the winter of 1854–1855, little fighting took place as armies battled cold, violent storms, and especially disease. Frostbite, cholera, and other diseases weakened and depleted the ranks on both sides and caused more deaths than war-related injuries. Finally, in the early fall of 1855, weakened British troops captured the port of Sebastopol, forcing the Russian government to make peace. Early in 1856 the Crimean War came to an end.

End of the Empire

In 1870 conflict with Prussia ended Napoleon III's empire. Alarmed by Prussia's growing power, Napoleon made his most costly error in judgment: he declared war on the Prussians on July 19, 1870.

Few French or foreign observers anticipated the quick and relatively easy defeat of France in the Franco-Prussian War. The French armies were slow to mobilize, and German forces crossed into France with little armed resistance. The Prussians defeated the French in just over six weeks. On September 2, after winning a decisive victory at Sedan, the Prussians took Napoleon III as prisoner.

History & Art *The Siege of Paris* by Ernest Meissonier. The Louvre, Paris, France *What impact did the Franco-Prussian conflict of 1870–1871 have on France and the government of Napoleon III?*

Chapter 25 Section 3

Independent Practice

Guided Reading Activity 25-3 **L1**

Campaign Have students imagine that they are citizens supporting the election of Louis-Napoleon. Tell students to prepare campaign materials, such as posters and pamphlets, encouraging others to support their candidate. **L1 LEP**

Daily Life Have students work in small groups and take the roles of ordinary French people in the late 1800s. Have them role-play casual conversations in which they reveal the average person's thoughts about the political events of the day. **L2**

Critical Thinking Ask students to list factors that contributed to the revolutions described in this section. **L3**

History & Art Two million Parisians were cut off from all contact with the outside world during the siege. The Prussians formed a continuous front of about 52 miles with 150,000 men and 700 guns. **How might the four-month siege have affected people's daily lives?** *(They would have been cut off from food and fuel supplies and suffered severe hardships.)*

Answer to Caption: *France was easily defeated by Prussia, and the government of Napoleon III collapsed.*

MEETING SPECIAL NEEDS ACTIVITY

Study Strategy To help students learn the information in this section, suggest that they outline it. They should list each major head and any subheads, leaving space under these heads to write the key figures, dates, and events as they read about them. They should look up words they do not understand and write the definitions to reinforce remembering them. They might continue this strategy with other chapters. **L1**

ASSESS

Check for Understanding

Assign Section 3 Review as homework or as an in-class activity.

Use Student Self-Test and Review Software to review Section 3.

Chapter 25 *Democracy and Reform* **657**

CURRICULUM CONNECTION

LITERATURE
The author of *Les Misérables*, Victor Hugo, was banished to the Channel Island of Guernsey for opposing Louis-Napoleon. His famous novel portrays nineteenth-century problems and events of France during the post-Napoleonic period.

CONNECTIONS Science and Technology

The Development of Photography

Tell students that in 1839 in France, photographs were displayed for the first time. By the 1850s, photographers were heading west in the United States and recording the frontier. They carried bulky cameras and used glass plates for negatives instead of small rolls of film as are used today. The photographer's covered wagon served as a darkroom.

Answers to Making the Connection

1. *Photography provided them with exact images of people and events.*
2. *Answers will vary. Possible answer: Photography has a major influence on people's lives given the importance of television.*

When the news of the emperor's capture reached Paris on September 4, crowds filled the streets and forced the collapse of the Second Empire. The people of Paris endured a Prussian siege for four months before a truce was signed.

Making Peace With Prussia

The French people elected a new National Assembly, dominated by royalists, to make peace with Prussia. The Assembly surrendered the provinces of Alsace and Lorraine and agreed to pay 5 billion francs—the equivalent of 1 billion dollars—to Prussia. Prussian forces further humiliated France by staging a victory march through Paris. The people of Paris, strong republicans who wanted a renewal of the war with Prussia instead of peace, were angered by the peace terms. They sank into despair after their loss.

In March the National Assembly set about restoring order in France, particularly in Paris. The provisional government inspired an angry outcry when it demanded that Parisians pay the rents and the debts that had been suspended during the siege. At the same time, the Assembly stopped payments to the National Guard, which many Parisian workers had joined during the Prussian siege. These drastic measures led to unrest and to an uprising in Paris.

The Commune of Paris

During the revolt, the workers established a Socialist government known as the Commune of Paris. The leaders of the Commune refused to recognize the National Assembly and called for the conversion of France into a decentralized federation of independent cities. The Commune declared war on the propertied classes and the Church. It advocated an end to government support for religion, the adoption of a new revolutionary calendar, and the introduction of a 10-hour workday.

In a bitter civil war, the National Assembly took the offensive and reasserted its control over Paris. Armies pushed past the Commune's barricades throughout the strife-ridden city. In defiance, the supporters of the Commune burned public buildings, including the Tuileries Palace and the City Hall. During the "Bloody Week" in May 1871, the Assembly's powerful military forces arrested nearly 40,000 people and killed more than 20,000. The horror of rebellion set back the political and social advances made by workers and caused distrust between France's middle and working classes.

CONNECTIONS Science and Technology

The Development of Photography

People experimented with photography long ago. In ancient Greece, Aristotle noticed that light shining through a small hole made an upside-down image of an object. In the early 1500s Italians built the first darkroom, which was large enough for a person to walk into. It projected an image onto a wall. Artists then traced the image's outline and colored the picture.

Camera obscura

For centuries scientists tried to record lasting images. In 1826 Joseph Niépce, a French inventor, produced the world's first photograph—a blurry farmyard view—by coating a metal plate with a light-sensitive chemical. In 1837 Louis Daguerre perfected Niépce's methods and fixed an image on silver-coated copper. Daguerreotypes, as these images were called, produced detailed pictures.

Photography progressed rapidly throughout the 1800s. Some photographers took portraits of wealthy families. Others risked their lives photographing the horrors of war. In 1888 George Eastman developed the box camera. Small and lightweight, the camera was relatively inexpensive and easy to use. The mass-produced box cameras put photography into the hands of millions.

MAKING THE CONNECTION

1. How did photography help people record their lives in the 1800s?
2. In what ways does photography affect events today? Think about the power of the media.

MAKING CONNECTIONS ACTIVITIES

Science and Technology Have students investigate the photographic process. Have them present their findings to the class in the form of a detailed diagram that shows the stages of the printing process. **L2**

Photography Students can research the lives and the work of pioneers in photography. Examples include Mathew Brady and his photographs during the Civil War, George Eastman and the development of the Eastman-Kodak company, or Julia Cameron, a British pioneer of portrait photography. Have students present their findings to the class. **L2**

The Third Republic

After the fall of the Commune, the dispirited French again tried to rebuild their government. This proved to be a difficult task, as royalists and republicans alike fought bitterly over the form the government should take.

Finally, in 1875 a new constitution made France once again a republic. The Third Republic's constitution provided for a two-house legislature. The two houses elected a president, who served for four years and who had little real power. Every official act required the full support of both houses of the legislature to be signed into law. A cabinet of ministers was responsible for government policy, and the post of premier was created to handle all executive business.

Threats to the Republic

Although France had finally established itself as a republic, the new government was particularly vulnerable to attack. One of its greatest threats came from **General Georges Boulanger** (BOO•lahn•ZHAY), who was a popular war hero. Boulanger urged the French people to seek revenge against Prussia. He launched a campaign to demand the election of a new legislature in 1888.

Boulanger won great support from royalists and others who opposed the republic. In 1889 his supporters urged him to overthrow the Third Republic with a coup d'état. When the government ordered him arrested for treason, Boulanger fled the country to Belgium. Without the direction of its popular leader, the Boulanger movement collapsed.

A second threat to the republic in the early 1890s centered around the construction of a canal through Panama. The canal would provide France with a waterway connecting the Atlantic and Pacific Oceans.

When the Panama Company collapsed and the Panama project failed, thousands of French stockholders lost all of the money they had invested. Charges of dishonesty and poor managerial practices erupted. The scandal spread to the highest government offices, as members of both houses were accused of accepting bribes to get more funding for the troubled project. The Panama scandal partly benefited France's growing Socialist movement. In 1893 nearly 50 Socialists won seats in the national legislature.

The Dreyfus Affair

The 1890s saw the Third Republic's greatest crisis—the Dreyfus affair. **Alfred Dreyfus**, a Jewish army officer, was arrested and charged with selling military secrets to the Germans. A military court convicted Dreyfus and sentenced him to a life term on Devil's Island, a prison colony off the coast of South America.

Yet Dreyfus's family and many supporters maintained his innocence. In 1897 growing evidence pointed to the fact that much of the original evidence against Dreyfus had been forged. Dreyfus's supporters demanded a retrial, but army officials refused, arguing that to do so would undermine military authority.

The Dreyfus affair became a national issue that divided France, because the honor of the military, the security of the country against Germany, the reputation of the republic, as well as Dreyfus's life, seemed to be at stake. While the media popularized the issue, republicans, Socialists, writers, and artists rallied to support Dreyfus. In 1906 pro-republic forces finally prevailed. A civil court pardoned Dreyfus on all charges and reinstated him into the French army.

The Dreyfus affair was an important event in modern French history. Although it deeply split a generation of French people, it also proved that the republican form of government was able to survive in France. After the Dreyfus affair, republicans directed their attention to other reforms, among them the separation of church and state in 1905.

SECTION 3 REVIEW

Recall

1. **Define** ultraroyalist, coup d'état, plebiscite.
2. **Identify** Charles X, Louis Philippe, Louis-Napoleon, Commune of Paris, General Georges Boulanger, Alfred Dreyfus.
3. **Explain** how the French government changed under the rule of Louis-Napoleon.

Critical Thinking

4. **Analyzing Information** Why was the government of the Third Republic especially vulnerable to political opposition?

Understanding Themes

5. **Revolution** Trace France's political history during the 1800s. What events led the French people to revolt against their government in 1830? What events led the French people to revolt in 1848?

Chapter 25 Section 3

Evaluate

Section Quiz 25-3

Reteach

Have students review the section and create an outline of events.

Enrich

Ask students to write a short story about France during the nineteenth century. They should use historical events as the backdrop for their stories.

CLOSE

Have students draw a series of political cartoons reflecting the changes in French government from the Revolution of 1830 to the creation of the Third Republic in 1875.

Who?What?Where?When?

Florence Nightingale became a nurse at a time when it was not considered a noble profession, and in 1854 led a group of British nurses to the Crimean War. Her efforts at the battle zone transformed the appalling conditions and won her worldwide fame. In 1864 she helped inspire the organization of the International Red Cross.

SECTION 3 REVIEW ANSWERS

1. All vocabulary words are defined in the Glossary.
2. Charles X, 655; Louis Philippe, 656; Louis-Napoleon, 656; Commune of Paris, 658; General Georges Boulanger, 659; Alfred Dreyfus, 659
3. It became an empire under an autocratic emperor.
4. It was young and unstable.
5. REVOLUTION In 1830 French people revolted against Charles X and the ultraroyalists after Charles passed a bill to repay aristocrats for property they lost during the French Revolution; in 1848 they revolted against Louis Philippe because he favored the wealthy and refused working-class demands for reform.

Chapter 25 Section 4

SECTION THEME

▶ **Change** The United States extends its borders and develops its economy.

Find Out

Answer: *The United States grew in size, wealth, and power during the 1800s and went through a civil war that resulted from sectional conflicts.*

FOCUS

Section Objective

Explain how the United States changed during the 1800s.

BELLRINGER Motivational Activity

Before taking roll at the beginning of the class period, project Section Focus Transparency 25-4 and have students answer the activity questions. Discuss students' responses.

This activity is also available as a blackline master.

Vocabulary Pre-check

Use Vocabulary Activity 25 to introduce vocabulary terms. **L1 LEP**

1800		1850		1900
1803 The United States gains the Louisiana Purchase.	**1846** War begins between the United States and Mexico.	**1865** The Civil War ends.	**c. 1890s** Immigrants arrive in the United States from eastern and southern Europe.	

Section 4

Expansion of the United States

Setting the Scene

▶ **Terms to Define**
sectionalism, secede, ratify

▶ **People to Meet**
Thomas Jefferson, Abraham Lincoln, Elizabeth Cady Stanton, Woodrow Wilson

▶ **Places to Locate**
Louisiana Purchase, Gadsden Purchase

Find Out How did the United States change during the 1800s?

The Storyteller

During the Civil War when Confederate casualties returned in large numbers from the front, buildings quickly became makeshift hospitals. Miss Sally Tomkins was one of the most tireless workers among the many brave women who served in the overcrowded places of mercy. As a "soldier without a gun," she received a commission in the Confederate Army as well as a commendation—the only such commission ever issued to a woman, and a unique "first" for any American army. In a note to the War Department, she said: "I accepted the commission … but would not allow my name to be placed on the payroll of the army."

—adapted from *A Pictorial History of the Confederacy*, Lamont Buchanan, 1951

Civil War nurse and patient

While many political upheavals shook Europe during the 1800s, the United States grew in size, wealth, and power. The vast area of forests and plains west of the original colonies lured American settlers by the thousands, and no European powers with colonial interests blocked their westward drive. The conflicts between European countries during the early years of the nation had created opportunities for the United States to acquire more territory.

The Young Nation Grows

The United States gained its biggest territorial prize as a result of Napoleon I's desire to conquer his most hated enemy, Great Britain. In 1803 Napoleon was preparing to go to war against Great Britain and needed money to finance it. Desperate for money, Napoleon offered to sell the French-owned Louisiana territory to the United States. With a quick stroke of the pen and a payment of $15 million, President **Thomas Jefferson** acquired the **Louisiana Purchase**—all the land between the Mississippi River and the Rocky Mountains. The area eventually formed 13 states.

The United States also gained land as a result of Spain's internal conflicts. Weakened by political and financial problems, Spain ceded, or gave up, Florida in 1819.

Later acquisitions of new land from other nations proved to be not so easy or peaceful. In 1845 the Republic of Texas was annexed to the United States. By 1846 this territorial gain resulted in a conflict between the United States and Mexico that escalated into war. The United States defeated the Mexicans in 1848, and in the resulting treaty Mexico gave up a vast area that later formed all of California, Utah, and Nevada and parts of

SECTION RESOURCES

Reproducible Masters
- Reproducible Lesson Plan 25-4
- Vocabulary Activity 25
- Guided Reading Activity 25-4
- People in World History Profile 47
- Section Quiz 25-4

Transparencies
- Section Focus Transparency 25-4
- World History and Art Transparency 33
- Mapping History Overlay Transparency 16, *Global Ancestry of Americans*

Multimedia
- Student Self-Test and Review Software
- Testmaker
- World Music: Cultural Traditions, Lesson 1
- Lessons of War: *Why Soldiers Fight*

Denver Public Library, Western History Department

Pioneers

You can see the fatigue in the faces of these pioneers, moving West in Conestoga wagons. Prairie stretched behind them, mountains ahead—and an unbearable distance to go. From the settlement of Jamestown in 1607 to the settlement of the West two centuries later, Americans explored, moved, and endured unspeakable hardships. Their journeys stretched their endurance, as they battled hunger, Native Americans, and the difficulties of the terrain itself. The West was dry: Wood shrank; wheels fell off wagons; and the hooves of oxen split. "Dust is two or three inches in depth and as fine as flour," one pioneer wrote. "We cannot see the wagons next to us...." Settled into new homes, the pioneers' hardships did not end. Families lived through winters so harsh that cows, sheathed in ice, had to be brought inside. Summers brought plagues of grasshoppers and prairie fires. And always there was isolation and loneliness.

By 1860 the United States stretched from the Atlantic to the Pacific. But expansion brought problems for the nation as well as benefits. The territory won in the Mexican-American War (1846–1848) shifted the issue of slavery into the political mainstream with such force that it took the Civil War to resolve the conflict between North and South.

TEACH

Tell students that the first wagon trains to go West set out in 1841 from one of a number of towns in Missouri along the Missouri River called "jumping-off places." They headed toward Oregon or California. Supplies were fresh, animals were healthy, the Kansas prairie was flat, and this beginning part of the trip was the easiest. Hardships and fatigue came later on the trails. **How do you think this pioneer life affected the lives of children?** *(Answers will vary but may include that children grew up faster because they faced so many dangers and hardships at a young age and because they had to shoulder adult responsibilities for the good of their families.)*

Who?What?Where?When?

Willa Cather was a journalist and novelist who wrote many stories about the plains of Nebraska. At the age of nine, she had to move with her parents from Virginia to the West. She portrays the psychological trauma of that move in *My Ántonia*.

TEACH

Guided Practice

THEME Change

Discuss with students the changes that occurred in the United States as it expanded rapidly. Emphasize especially the impact of rapid expansion and westward migration on daily life. Help them to visualize packing up and heading West without knowing much about your destination. **L1**

Time Line To help students understand the swiftness of the expansion of the United States, have them work as a class to develop a time line showing the acquisition of territory. **L2 LEP**

Geography: Movement Have students recall how the colonists slowly expanded their settlements along the east coast. Have students describe the stages in westward expansion. Point out that between 1607 and 1890, the idea of expansion was part of the American consciousness. Ask students what people mean today when they think of expansion. **L3**

World Music: Cultural Traditions, Lesson 1

World History and Art Transparency 33, *The Banjo Lesson*

Mapping History Overlay Transparency 16, *Global Ancestry of Americans*

Colorado, Arizona, Wyoming, and New Mexico. This large acquisition of territory added a sizable Hispanic population to the United States.

Farther north, the United States argued with Great Britain over the exact borders of the Oregon Country. In a treaty with Great Britain, the United States gained this vast region. Oregon, Washington, and Idaho, as well as parts of Wyoming and Montana, were later created from this territory.

By the mid-1800s the young country had grown to 3 million square miles (8 million sq. km). Only one step remained in the country's move across the continent. In 1853 James Gadsden, the American ambassador to Mexico, gave Mexico $10 million for 45,000 square miles (116,550 sq. km) of land in southern New Mexico and Arizona, south of the Rio Grande.

With the **Gadsden Purchase**, the United States finally stretched from "sea to shining sea." This westward expansion brought new opportunities to settlers, who forged communities and built states in the new lands. The expansion also brought suffering—loss of land, culture, and often life—to Native Americans who had inhabited lands in the West for centuries.

Rise of the United States

As Americans moved westward, democratic rights in the United States expanded. When the nation was first founded, the right to vote and hold public office was generally restricted to white male property owners.

The people of the West sought to extend these voting rights. All of the new states adopted constitutions that granted the right to vote to all men. These new states gradually gained power in Congress, and, over time, their liberal policies influenced the country. By 1856 every state had granted all white men the vote.

An Expanding Economy

Many factors contributed to the rapid growth of the American economy. The Industrial

Images of the Times

The Civil War

There had always been economic and cultural differences between the North and the South. In 1861 these differences led to the American Civil War, or the War Between the States.

Union naval forces took New Orleans in May 1862. In the Civil War, both North and South suffered heavy losses, but the North's industrial strength gave it an advantage over the agricultural South.

135,000 SETS, 270,000 VOLUMES SOLD.
UNCLE TOM'S CABIN
FOR SALE HERE.
AN EDITION FOR THE MILLION, COMPLETE IN 1 Vol., PRICE 37 1-2 CENTS.
" " IN GERMAN, IN 1 Vol., PRICE 50 CENTS.
" " IN 2 Vols., CLOTH, 6 PLATES, PRICE $1.50.
SUPERB ILLUSTRATED EDITION, IN 1 Vol., WITH 153 ENGRAVINGS,
PRICES FROM $2.50 TO $5.00.
The Greatest Book of the Age.

Antislavery feeling in the North was stimulated by Harriet Beecher Stowe's *Uncle Tom's Cabin*, a novel portraying slavery at its worst. The book sold 300,000 copies in 1852, its first year of publication.

662

Images of the Times — The Civil War

Harriet Beecher Stowe wrote most of *Uncle Tom's Cabin* in Brunswick, Maine; she had spent exactly one weekend in a slave state. Stowe said that the powerful death scene of Uncle Tom came to her in a vision while she was in church.

Although slavery was the primary moral issue dividing the North and the South, the abolition of slavery was not the main reason that hundreds of thousands of men joined the Northern army in the early days of the war. Most of them did not agree with the abolitionists; they viewed their own efforts as a struggle to preserve the Union.

Revolution, which began in Great Britain, spread to the United States. Busy commercial regions filled with factories and heavily populated cities characterized the North. Irish, German, and Scandinavian immigrants joined the Northern workforce, settling in cities and farmlands. Northern workers received pay for their labor, as well as the right to leave their jobs for better ones. This system of work was called free labor.

In contrast, the South became the chief producer of raw cotton for the booming British textile industry. The South's economy remained primarily agricultural and depended on the labor of enslaved African Americans. Most white Southerners, even those who held no enslaved people, believed in slave labor. As the United States expanded, it was clear that the different economic interests of the two regions would cause conflict.

A Nation Divided

The differences in their economies led the two regions, the North and the South, to take widely different positions on many political and economic issues. The result was **sectionalism**, the devotion to the political and economic interest of a region or a section of the country. The most divisive issue, however, was slave labor. The South wanted to expand slavery into the territories gained during the Mexican War. The North wanted these new western areas to remain territories employing free labor.

By 1860 the United States consisted of 18 free states and 15 slave states. In the presidential election of 1860, proslavery and antislavery forces vied for power. When **Abraham Lincoln** won the presidency, the South feared he would abolish slavery.

To protest the election, South Carolina decided to **secede**, or withdraw, from the Union. Other Southern states followed suit. By February 8, 1861, seven states had joined to form their own nation, the Confederate States of America. In Washington, D.C., Congress worked on a compromise, but to no avail. When Lincoln was sworn in as President in March, he declared that "no state, upon its own mere motion, can lawfully get out of the Union."

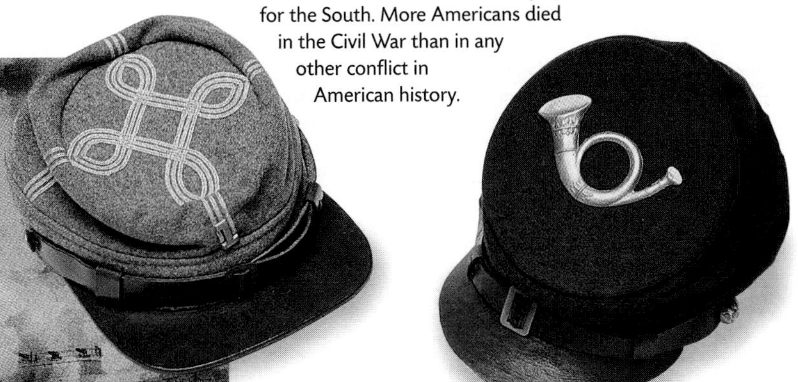

Union and Confederate caps reveal the war's colors: blue for the North, and gray for the South. More Americans died in the Civil War than in any other conflict in American history.

REFLECTING ON THE TIMES

1. What major issue helped spark conflict between the North and the South?
2. Why was the Civil War unique in American history?

663

ANSWERS TO REFLECTING ON THE TIMES

1. slavery
2. It was a war fought on American soil.

Chapter 25 Section 4

Independent Practice

Guided Reading Activity 25-4 **L1**

People in World History Profile 47

Diary Tell students to imagine that they are Europeans preparing to emigrate to the United States in the late 1800s. Have them write a brief diary entry describing their hopes and fears about the new land. Have them include the things they will miss when they leave their native country. **L2 LEP**

Critical Thinking Organize students into small groups to consider whether a state should have the right to withdraw from the United States. Have each group take one side of the issue and gather information. Then each group should choose a member to participate in a class debate on the issue. **L3**

Linking Past and Present

States' Rights Today United States government officials continue to disagree about whether certain issues, such as school integration, should be controlled by the federal or by the state government.

Map Study

Answer
France, Spain, Britain, Russia

Map Skills Practice

Reading a Map Which acquisitions allowed the United States to stretch from "sea to shining sea"? *(Oregon Country, 1846; Mexican Cession, 1848; Gadsden Purchase, 1853)*

ABCNEWS INTERACTIVE™

VIDEODISC
Lessons of War

Side One, Chapter 4
Frames 8662–11204
Title: *Why Soldiers Fight*
Subject: Discussion and images of what motivates soldiers to fight
Ask: What motivates people to volunteer in the armed services? *(Most volunteer because they feel a sense of patriotic duty and loyalty to their country.)*

ASSESS

Check for Understanding

Assign Section 4 Review as homework or as an in-class activity.

Use Student Self-Test and Review Software to review Section 4.

Evaluate

Section Quiz 25-4

Territorial Expansion of the United States

Map Study The United States stretched from the Atlantic Ocean to the Pacific Ocean by 1848. Territory was added by purchase, conquest, and treaty. **Region** From what four European nations did the United States acquire most of its territory?

By April the divided nation was at war. The Civil War, lasting from 1861 to 1865, was one of the bloodiest struggles of the 1800s.

Although the North had a population of 22 million people and the South had only 9 million, of which nearly a third were enslaved, Northern forces had a difficult time defeating the Confederacy. In brutal warfare, the two sides sent volleys of shells as soldiers advanced within yards of each other.

After four years of war that claimed the lives of more than 500,000 Americans, the Northern forces defeated the Confederate forces. After the war, Congress passed three amendments to the Constitution of the United States. These amendments abolished slavery and gave formerly enslaved African Americans citizenship and equal protection under the law, as well as the right to vote. The nation set about to rebuild itself.

A New Society

After the Civil War, the growth of industries and cities in the United States continued with new vigor. Across the country textile mills, lumberyards, mines, and factories increased their output. In 1900 oil fields provided about 130 times more oil than they had in 1860, ironworks 10 times more iron, and steelworks almost 60 times more steel. The "captains of industry" who developed and invested in these thriving industries amassed great fortunes and gained widespread admiration.

COOPERATIVE LEARNING ACTIVITY

Discussion Groups Organize the class into groups to discuss the ways American life might be different if the Civil War had not been fought and the country had remained divided into two separate nations. Have each group focus on a different topic, such as economy, international relations, labor, government, or culture. One person from each group should take notes on the discussion and report the group's ideas to the class. Encourage students from the other groups to ask questions after each presentation. **L1**

664 Chapter 25 *Democracy and Reform*

Immigration

As industry grew, so did the nation's population. Between 1870 and 1900, the population of the United States doubled, rising from 38 million to 76 million. Immigrants contributed significantly to this growth.

In the years before the Civil War, most immigrants to the United States had come from Great Britain, Ireland, Germany and Scandinavia. The Irish potato famine of the 1840s had caused nearly 1 million Irish people to immigrate to the United States. The failed German revolution of 1848 had prompted many disappointed liberals and intellectuals to leave their homeland. They carried with them their knowledge in the fields of science, medicine, agriculture, music, and crafts.

After the Civil War, the flow of immigrants from northern European countries decreased. Immigrants from eastern and southern Europe—especially from Italy, Russia, and Austria-Hungary—began to arrive in the United States in increasing numbers. By 1900, immigrants from these three countries made up more than three-fourths of the United States's immigrant population.

After landing at Ellis Island in New York, most immigrants headed for urban areas to work. Cities pulsed with the energy of different nationalities. By 1900 one in four city dwellers had been born outside of the United States.

Visualizing History **During the late 1800s and early 1900s, suffragists pushed for an amendment to the Constitution granting women the right to vote.** *By 1918, in which of the states could women vote?*

Women's Rights

Thriving American industries employed a large number of the nation's women. As women gained economic opportunities, they also demanded political equality.

Like British women, American women fought hard for the vote and became known as suffragists. Led by **Elizabeth Cady Stanton**, suffragists formed the National Woman Suffrage Association (NWSA). They traveled across the land, speaking in cities, towns, and rural areas for women's right to vote. They stood before members of state legislatures, wrote books, and tried to convince the nation that female suffrage was vital.

Slowly women achieved the right to vote at the state level, beginning with Wyoming, Colorado, and Utah. By 1918 women had gained full suffrage in every Western state, Michigan, and New York. Finally, because of women's contribution in World War I, it became impossible for politicians to ignore women's demands. In September 1918 President **Woodrow Wilson** asked Congress to pass a constitutional amendment guaranteeing the vote to all United States citizens 21 years of age and older regardless of their sex. In 1920 Congress decided to ratify, or approve, the Nineteenth Amendment.

SECTION 4 REVIEW

Recall

1. **Define** sectionalism, secede, ratify.
2. **Identify** Thomas Jefferson, Louisiana Purchase, Abraham Lincoln, the Civil War, Elizabeth Cady Stanton, Woodrow Wilson.
3. **Explain** how the United States acquired territory to achieve its present-day continental borders.

Critical Thinking

4. **Analyzing Information** How did the Industrial Revolution in the North contribute to the outbreak of the Civil War?

Understanding Themes

5. **Change** Describe the changes to the economy of the United States in the late 1800s. What caused these changes?

Chapter 25 Section 4

Visualizing History Susan B. Anthony joined Elizabeth Cady Stanton in working for women's rights and forming the NWSA. They fought for other legal rights in addition to suffrage.

Answer to Caption: *in every Western state, Michigan, and New York*

Use the Testmaker to create a customized quiz for Section 4.

Reteach

Have each student write a question about the material under each head in this section. Then have students work in pairs to answer each other's questions, looking up answers as necessary.

Enrich

Ask students to assess how one of the territorial acquisitions benefits the United States today. Suggest that they look at the population, economy, political leadership, and cultural diversity. Have students write an editorial on the merits of the acquisition.

CLOSE

Have students write one-paragraph summaries of how the United States changed in each of the following areas during the 1800s: territory, economy, industry, population, human rights.

SECTION 4 REVIEW ANSWERS

1. All vocabulary words are defined in the Glossary.
2. Thomas Jefferson, 660; Louisiana Purchase, 660; Abraham Lincoln, 663; the Civil War, 664; Elizabeth Cady Stanton, 665; Woodrow Wilson, 665
3. Louisiana Purchase; annexation of Texas; territory gained through Mexican-American War; Oregon Country; Gadsden Purchase
4. It caused the North to build factories and rely on free labor. Cotton farming boomed in the South to meet demands from British textile industry. The South relied on slave labor. These economic differences led to the Civil War.
5. **CHANGE** The economy boomed in the late 1800s; it was caused by the increase in production that began during the Civil War.

SECTION THEME

▶ **Nationalism** Latin American nations achieve self-government.

Find Out

Answer: *Revolts and uprisings and, in the case of Brazil, a constitutional convention brought independence to Latin American countries.*

FOCUS

Section Objective

Relate how the countries of Latin America won independence.

BELLRINGER
Motivational Activity

Before taking roll at the beginning of the class period, project Section Focus Transparency 25-5 and have students answer the activity questions. Discuss students' responses.

This activity is also available as a blackline master.

Vocabulary Pre-check

Use the Vocabulary PuzzleMaker to create a puzzle that reinforces the vocabulary terms in this section. **L1**

1800 — 1820 — 1840

1804 Haiti proclaims its independence.

1819 Simón Bolívar ends Spanish rule in Venezuela.

1825 Portugal recognizes Brazil's independence.

Section 5

Latin American Independence

Setting the Scene

▶ **Terms to Define**
peninsulares, Creoles, mestizos

▶ **People to Meet**
François Toussaint-Louverture, Miguel Hidalgo, Simón Bolívar, José de San Martín, Pedro I

▶ **Places to Locate**
Haiti, Mexico, Central America, Venezuela, Argentina, Chile, Peru, Brazil

Find Out How did the countries of Latin America win independence?

The Storyteller

Simón Bolívar sent a joyous letter to a fellow general on January 8, 1822, displaying his belief in a unified America. He wrote, "America's greatest day has not yet dawned. We have indeed driven out our oppressors, smashed the tablets of their tyrannical laws, and established legitimate institutions; but we have yet to lay the foundation … that will make of this part of the world a nation of republics." Bolívar was confident that this unified America would impress Europe: "Who shall oppose an America united in heart, subject to one law, and guided by the torch of liberty?"

—adapted from *Selected Writings of Bolívar*, compiled by Vicente Lecuna and edited by Harold A. Bierck, Jr., 1951

Simón Bolívar

For 300 years Spain and Portugal held colonies in the Americas without facing serious threats to their rule. In the early 1800s, however, the situation changed. Inspired by the American and French Revolutions, Latin Americans sought an end to colonial rule and joined independence movements.

Ruling the Colonies

Like other European nations, Spain and Portugal regarded their Latin American colonies with a mercantilist view—the idea that colonies existed chiefly to increase the home countries' wealth. Mexico, Peru, and Brazil contained large deposits of gold and silver as well as forests that yielded valuable exotic woods such as mahogany and ebony.

Farming provided another major source of colonial income. Spanish and Portuguese monarchs granted huge tracts of fertile land to explorers and nobles for the growing of cash crops, such as corn, sugar, and cocoa. The landowners then forced the Native Americans to work the farms. When they died from forced labor and diseases that the Europeans had introduced to the Americas, the Spanish and the Portuguese imported large numbers of enslaved Africans.

The Catholic Church also played a critical role in the colonial economies, strengthening Spanish and Portuguese rule in Latin America. Both the Spaniards and the Portuguese brought the Catholic religion with them to the Americas. Priests and monks converted the Native Americans who worked on the farms to Catholicism and taught them loyalty to the Crown.

The colonial governments and the clergy worked very closely together. Clergymen held high

---

SECTION RESOURCES

Reproducible Masters
- Reproducible Lesson Plan 25-5
- Guided Reading Activity 25-5
- People in World History Profile 48
- Reteaching Activity 25
- Enrichment Activity 25
- Section Quiz 25-5
- Performance Assessment Activity 25
- Spanish Chapter Summary 25

Transparencies
- Section Focus Transparency 25-5

Multimedia
- Vocabulary PuzzleMaker Software
- Student Self-Test and Review Software
- Testmaker
- World Music: Cultural Traditions, Lesson 2

government offices. The government, in turn, supported the Church. By 1800 the Catholic Church controlled almost half the wealth of Latin America.

Over the years, colonists became increasingly unhappy with colonial rule. They resented the trade restrictions and high taxes Spain and Portugal imposed upon them. Most of all, they resented the rigid colonial social structure.

A Rigid Social Order

Social classes based on privilege divided colonial Latin America. Colonial leaders, called **peninsulares**, were born in Spain or Portugal and stood at the top level of the social order. Appointed by the Spanish and Portuguese governments, the *peninsulares* held all important military and political positions. Below them were the colonial-born white aristocrats, called **Creoles**. Although they controlled most of the land and business in the colonies, the Creoles were regarded as second-class citizens by the *peninsulares*. The Creoles envied the privileged leadership positions that were held exclusively by the *peninsulares*.

At the bottom of the colonial social pyramid were the majority of Latin Americans. Some were Native Americans. Others were of African or African and European ancestry. The largest of this group, however, were **mestizos** (meh•STEE•zohz), Latin Americans of mixed Native American and European ancestry. Spurned by the ruling white classes, these Latin Americans faced social and racial barriers in colonial society. They worked as servants for *peninsulares* and Creoles, and as unskilled laborers and carpenters. Some worked as plantation overseers and farmhands.

Growing Discontent

In the 1800s Latin Americans began to challenge the rigid social order and its controls with revolts throughout Latin America. The Creoles played the largest leadership roles in these conflicts. Wealthy and well educated, many were well versed in the liberal political philosophies of the Enlightenment, but their colonial birth prevented them from holding the highest government positions. The Creoles were eager to take control of Latin American affairs.

Uprising in Haiti

Although the Spanish and Portuguese colonies were ripe for revolt, the first successful uprising in the Latin American colonies took place in the French colony of **Haiti** (Saint Domingue), on the island of Hispaniola in the Caribbean Sea. Huge plantations of sugar, cotton, and coffee spread across the mountains and valleys of the lush tropical land. France and many other countries depended on the tiny colony for their supply of sugar and coffee.

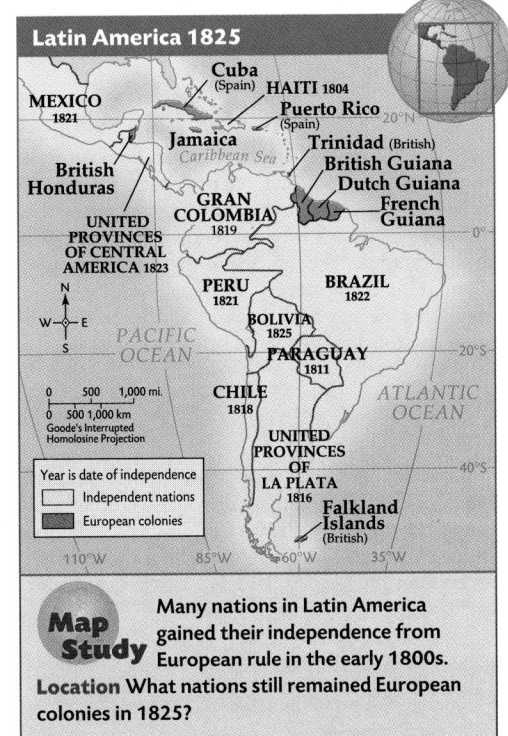

The plantations were owned by French planters and worked by the colony's enslaved African population. More than 500,000 of the 560,000 people living in Haiti in the late 1700s were enslaved or had been. The few French planters who controlled the French colony often went to severe and brutal extremes to control the African majority.

Unrest erupted in the early 1790s when enslaved Africans led by a formerly enslaved man named **François Toussaint-Louverture** (TOO•SAN LOO•vuhr•TYUR) revolted, setting fire to plantation homes and fields of sugarcane. One observer described the horrifying scene:

> "Picture to yourself the whole horizon a wall of fire, from which continually rose thick vortices [whirling columns] of smoke, whose huge black volumes could be likened only to those frightful storm-clouds ... for nearly three weeks we could

Map Study Many nations in Latin America gained their independence from European rule in the early 1800s.
Location What nations still remained European colonies in 1825?

Chapter 25 Section 5

TEACH

Guided Practice

THEME Nationalism

Review with students the definition of *nationalism*. *(the feeling that people of the same culture should have their own nation)* Ask students how nationalism can lead to revolution. *(People revolt against foreign governments in an effort to rule themselves.)* Have students cite examples of present-day or historic nationalistic struggles. *(Answers may include: Palestinian Arabs; Bosnians in former Yugoslavia.)* **L1**

Map Study

Answer

Cuba, British Honduras, Trinidad, British Guiana, Dutch Guiana, French Guiana, Falkland Islands, Puerto Rico

Map Skills Practice

Reading a Map **What is the only Latin American country that is completely landlocked?** *(Paraguay)*

Multicultural Discuss the rigid social order in South American colonies. Ask students to compare this with the Estate system that existed before the French Revolution of 1789. *(Both were rigid social orders that a person was born into; the small number of people in the top classes created discontent.)* **L3**

World Music: Cultural Traditions, Lesson 2

COOPERATIVE LEARNING ACTIVITY

Creating a Constitution Organize students into teams: priests, *peninsulares*, mestizos, and Creoles. Tell students that their colony has just achieved independence from Spain and they now have the opportunity to form a new government. Have students research the social and economic interests and goals of their groups. Next have the groups discuss their concerns and draw up a platform stating their positions and their goals for the new government. Then have the teams meet in a constitutional convention to create the laws for their new government. Allow students to debate their needs and draw up a constitution. Emphasize the importance of negotiation and compromise throughout the activity. **L2**

History & Art Hidalgo angered Spanish authorities by violating their prohibition of independent manufacturing that competed with Spanish industry. Hidalgo ran pottery and leather factories, made silk, and cultured grapes. How does this fresco portray him? *(determined and strong)*
Answer to Caption: *Native Americans and mestizos*

Independent Practice

Guided Reading Activity 25-5 **L1**

People in World History Profile 48

Geography: Location Have students imagine that they are on a journey through Latin America. Tell them to keep a journal in which they record their impressions of the geography. Ask them to draw conclusions about the difficulties early Latin Americans may have had in communicating and transporting goods. **L1**

Broadcast Have students investigate the revolution in Haiti. Then have students form news teams to report key events throughout the period. Students may write news stories or produce a news broadcast. **L2**

Linking Past and Present

Mexican Independence On September 16, 1810, Father Hidalgo rang the bells in his small church in the village of Dolores and shouted the *Grito de Dolores* (Cry of Dolores) in which he demanded independence. To this day, the president of Mexico rings a bell in Mexico City each September 16 and repeats the *Grito de Dolores.*

barely distinguish between day and night, for so long as the rebels found anything to feed the flames, they never ceased to burn.... ”

In 1802 Napoleon sent forces to take control of the colony. Captured by French officers, Toussaint-Louverture was imprisoned in France, where he died in 1803. Then a wave of yellow fever aided the revolutionaries. The epidemic swept across the colony, killing thousands of French soldiers. The rebel army defeated the French, and in 1804 Haiti proclaimed its independence.

Mexico Struggles for Freedom

One of the earliest uprisings against Spanish rule occurred in **Mexico**, which at that time was part of New Spain. In 1810 a Catholic priest named **Miguel Hidalgo** led the fight against the Spanish government in Mexico. Hidalgo cared deeply for the poverty-stricken Native Americans and mestizos in his parish. To Hidalgo, revolt was the only way to bring democracy to Mexico.

History & Art *Father Miguel Hidalgo, a fresco by José Clemente Orozco, 1937. Governor's Mansion, Guadalajara, Mexico* *What two groups made up the rebel force that Hidalgo led against the Spanish army?*

In September 1810 Hidalgo led Native Americans and mestizos on a freedom march. They headed to Mexico City, gathering recruits along the way. The army plundered cities and killed those who defended Spain. Finally, they arrived in Guadalajara (GWAH•duhl•uh•HAHR•uh), where Hidalgo based his government.

In January Spanish forces attacked the rebels. The 80,000 Native Americans and mestizos greatly outnumbered the 6,000-man Spanish army. When a wild shot hit the rebels' store of ammunition, however, the well-trained Spanish army quickly overtook the confused rebels in the ensuing fire. Spanish authorities charged Hidalgo with heresy and executed him in 1811.

Another priest, José María Morelos, took charge of the revolution after Hidalgo died. Morelos captured a large portion of southern Mexico. In 1813 he called a conference that declared Mexico's independence from Spain. Morelos's forces fought the Spaniards but were defeated in 1815.

Despite many battles, Mexico did not gain full independence until 1821. That year, a liberal revolt in Spain threatened to overthrow the monarchy and establish a constitution. This reform frightened wealthy Mexican Creoles, who feared such a change might infringe on their own privileges. To make sure this did not happen, they declared independence from Spain in 1821.

Ironically, their leader was Agustín de Iturbide (EE•TUR•BEE•thay), the army officer who had crushed Morelos's movement. Iturbide made himself emperor in 1822, but opposition to his oppressive rule developed. The Mexican people soon deposed Iturbide and declared their country a republic in 1823.

When Mexico became a republic, the Central American provinces in New Spain declared their independence. In Guatemala, representatives established the United Provinces of **Central America**. In the 1830s leaders divided the region into the countries of Costa Rica, El Salvador, Guatemala, Honduras, and Nicaragua.

Spanish South America

Creoles in the Spanish colonies of South America gained an opportunity for independence in 1808 when Napoleon seized control of the Spanish government. The refusal of the Spanish

MEETING SPECIAL NEEDS ACTIVITY

Study Strategy Reading comprehension is often greatly aided by presentation of background information or "schema." The schema is developed from the reader's current knowledge and then extended with new information from text, lecture, pictures, and media. Have students with comprehension problems research the meeting between San Martín and Bolívar in Guayaquil in July 1822, or the meeting between O'Higgins and San Martín in Chile in 1818. Have students take the roles of these leaders and reproduce a probable conversation from each point of view. **L2**

American colonists to acknowledge Napoleon's government resulted in revolts throughout the empire. In addition, Spain's fight against France, together with the colonies' isolation from their home country, left the Spanish weak and vulnerable to attack. Three outstanding leaders—Simón Bolívar, José de San Martín, and Bernardo O'Higgins—led South American colonies in their fight against Spanish rule.

Simón Bolívar, a Creole from **Venezuela**, led many colonies to independence. Bolívar believed in equality and saw liberty as "the only object worth a man's life." Bolívar had witnessed the reforms of the French Revolution. Called "the Liberator," Bolívar devoted his life to freedom for Latin Americans.

In 1810 Bolívar started a revolt against the Spanish in Caracas. After nearly 9 years of fighting, Bolívar succeeded in crushing Spain's power in Venezuela in 1819. After a series of battles over the next 20 years, Bolívar and his forces won freedom for the present-day countries of Venezuela, Colombia, Panama, Bolivia, and Ecuador.

While Bolívar fought in Venezuela, another revolutionary leader, **José de San Martín** of **Argentina**, led Latin American armies over the Andes Mountains and into **Chile**. In Chile, San Martín joined Bernardo O'Higgins. Together, their forces successfully achieved independence for Chile in 1818. San Martín then set off to free **Peru** in 1820. Within a year he captured Lima and declared Peru independent.

In July 1822 San Martín and Bolívar met in the Ecuadorian port of Guayaquil (GWY•uh•KEEL) to discuss the future of Latin America. Though they shared a common goal, they could not agree on strategy and policy. San Martín finally decided to withdraw from the revolt and allowed Bolívar to take command. By 1826 Bolívar and his armies had liberated all of South America.

Brazil Gains Independence

Brazil achieved its independence without the bloodshed that accompanied the liberation of Spanish America. In 1808 Napoleon's French army had invaded Portugal, causing the Portuguese royal family to flee to Brazil.

King João transferred his monarchy to Brazil, declaring Rio de Janeiro capital of the Portuguese Empire. João immediately introduced governmental reforms in Brazil. He reinstated more favorable trade laws by opening Brazil's ports to the world. João also worked to make the agriculture and mining industries more profitable. Soon both industry and commerce were flourishing.

The liberal ruler brought Brazilians increasing opportunities by funding public education, including military academies, an art school, and medical schools. With these reforms Brazil moved quickly toward independence, and in 1815 João made Brazil a self-governing kingdom within the Portuguese Empire.

King João came to love the semitropical land of mountains and endless forests; he chose to remain there after Napoleon was defeated in 1815. In 1820, however, liberals took over the Portuguese government. Determined to save his throne, he returned to Portugal. He left Brazil in the hands of his 23-year-old son, Dom Pedro.

The new Portuguese government fought to make Brazil a colonial possession again. Leaders ended free trade and many of the other advantages Brazil had enjoyed under João's monarchy. They also demanded that Dom Pedro abandon his rule and immediately return to Portugal. Supported by his father, Dom Pedro declared that he would remain in Brazil. Dom Pedro defied Portuguese leaders by calling a constitutional convention and answered their angry response with a cry of "Independence or death!"

In September 1822 Brazil won full independence from Portugal. Three months later Dom Pedro was

AROUND THE WORLD — Greeks Fight for Independence

Greece, 1821

Greece's struggle for independence from the Ottoman Turks began in 1821 when Greek fighters gained control of the Peloponnesus and many islands in the Aegean Sea. But in 1825, a combined army of Turks and Egyptians regained these regions. France, Great Britain, and Russia came to Greece's aid in 1827 and defeated the Turkish-Egyptian fleet in the Battle of Navarino. By 1829 both the Turks and the Egyptians left Greece, and Greece became independent that year.

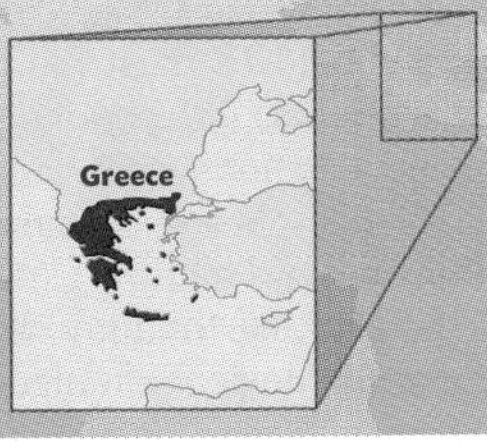

Cultural Perspectives

Other Revolts The spirit of revolt also swept through China during the 1800s. The Taiping Rebellion (1851–1864) tore the country apart when a group combining Christian and ancient Chinese beliefs attempted to create a perfect society with an equal division of land among the people. In 1899–1900, a Chinese group led the Boxer Rebellion in which they tried to protect their traditions against Western influences.

Who?What?Where?When?

Brazil is the fifth-largest country in the world. It encompasses an area greater than that of the 48 contiguous states of the United States.

ASSESS

Check for Understanding

Assign Section 5 Review as homework or as an in-class activity.

Use Student Self-Test and Review Software to review Section 5.

MAKING CONNECTIONS ACTIVITY

Religion The Roman Catholic Church was extremely powerful in Latin America in the nineteenth century. Have students investigate the role of the Church in Latin America today and answer the question: How has the role of the Church changed in Latin America during the past 150 years? Students should research the Church's role in the social affairs of the people, in economics, and in political affairs. After doing the research, students should present the information in a panel presentation. **L2**

Chapter 25 Section 5

Evaluate

Section Quiz 25-5

Use the Testmaker to create a customized quiz for Section 5.

Reteach

Ask students to imagine they have to write a history of the Latin American independence movement. Ask them to create an outline of the topics and key information they would include in their book.

Reteaching Activity 25

Enrich

Remind students that the main reason European powers wanted colonies was for their raw materials. Ask students to report on how the economies of selected Latin American countries have changed since the days of colonialism.

Enrichment Activity 25

CLOSE

Have students make lists of general causes for revolutions based on revolutions they have studied thus far. Have them write a brief explanation of how the Latin American revolutions were similar to and different from others they have studied.

crowned Emperor **Pedro I** of Brazil. With Pedro ruling the empire under a constitution, Brazil became the only independent country in South America to freely choose a constitutional monarchy as its form of government.

Meanwhile, João maintained his support of his beloved Brazil by refusing to allow the Portuguese government to send new military forces to fight the rebels. Great Britain also pressured Portugal to end its battle. In 1825 Portugal finally recognized Brazil's independence.

Challenges to Growth

By the mid-1820s most Latin American countries had won their independence. Their next task was to achieve national unity and a stable government. These goals, however, were difficult to reach. Simón Bolívar, who had dreamed of uniting all of northern South America into one large and powerful state, became so disappointed and disillusioned that he wrote, "Those who have toiled for liberty in South America have plowed the sea."

Common Problems

In trying to build stable and prosperous nations, Latin Americans faced a number of challenges. One obstacle was the geography of Central and South America. High mountains and thick jungles made transportation and communication difficult, hindering trade and economic growth. Vast areas of fertile land remained undeveloped. Population centers, separated by physical barriers, became rivals instead of allies.

Other problems were part of Latin America's colonial heritage. Spanish and Portuguese rule had given the Latin Americans little practice in self-government. Instead, they were used to authoritarian government, which was not responsible to the people and demanded obedience from them.

In the colonial system, political power was in the hands of the executive branch of government. The judicial branch was weak and limited, and the legislative branch was practically nonexistent. Latin Americans had strong, well-educated leaders, but they had no experience in the legislative process. Simón Bolívar complained that the colonial system had kept his people in a state of "permanent childhood" with regard to knowledge of running a government. "If we could have at least managed our domestic affairs and our internal administration, we could have acquainted ourselves with the process and machinery of government," he wrote.

Independence did not bring about much change in social conditions in Latin America. Catholicism remained the official religion, and Church and government continued to be closely tied. The new countries also continued to maintain a separation between upper and lower classes. The dominant group was now the Creoles instead of the *peninsulares*. Creoles owned the best land and controlled business and government. Their privileged position was resented, especially by the mestizos.

Continuing Political Conflicts

Soon after independence, political conflicts increased. Liberals called for separation of Church and state, the breakup of large estates, higher taxes on land, public social services, and civilian control of the government. Most of the liberals were mestizos, intellectuals, or merchants who wanted free trade. Opposed to this group were the Creoles, most of whom were rich landowners, church leaders, and military officers. These conservatives favored strong central government and a powerful Church and army.

The decades that followed the wars for independence saw an ongoing struggle for economic strength and social justice. Although many South American governments were republics in appearance, many actually were military dictatorships. Today, there still remains in many Latin American countries a vast gap between the ruling rich and the underprivileged poor.

SECTION 5 REVIEW

Recall

1. **Define** *peninsulares*, Creoles, mestizos.
2. **Identify** François Toussaint-Louverture, Miguel Hidalgo, Simón Bolívar, José de San Martín, Pedro I.
3. **Explain** why Creoles were strong supporters of independence movements in Latin America.

Critical Thinking

4. **Making Comparisons** How did the independence movement in Mexico differ from that in Brazil?

Understanding Themes

5. **Nationalism** Did independence bring social advances in Latin American countries? Why or why not?

SECTION 5 REVIEW ANSWERS

1. All vocabulary words are defined in the Glossary.
2. François Toussaint-Louverture, 667; Miguel Hidalgo, 668; Simón Bolívar, 669; José de San Martín, 669; Pedro I, 669
3. They were educated in the political philosophies of the Enlightenment and frustrated by the rigid social order imposed by the ruling Spaniards and Portuguese.
4. The independence movement in Mexico was violent; in Brazil, the king granted independence without violence.
5. NATIONALISM Answers will vary. Possible answer: No, there was still separation between upper and lower classes; Creoles assumed the positions formally held by the *peninsulares* and ignored the needs of the mestizos.

Social Studies SKILLS

Reading a Cartogram

On most maps, land areas are drawn in proportion to the actual surface areas on the earth. On some maps, however, a small country may appear much larger than usual, and a large country may look much smaller. Even the shapes of the countries may look different. If maps are supposed to outline the earth's features, why are these maps so distorted?

Learning the Skill

Maps that distort country size and shape are called **cartograms**. In a cartogram, country size reflects some value *other* than a land area, such as population or gross national product. For example, on a conventional map Canada appears much larger than India. In a cartogram showing world population, however, India would appear larger than Canada because it has a much larger population. The cartogram is a tool for making visual comparisons. At a glance, you can see how each country or region compares with another in a particular value.

To use a cartogram, first read the title and key to identify what value the cartogram illustrates. Then examine the cartogram to see which countries or regions appear. Find the largest and smallest countries. Compare the cartogram with a conventional land-area map to determine the degree of distortion of particular countries. Finally, draw conclusions about the topic.

Practicing the Skill

Study the cartogram shown at the top right and answer these questions.

1. What is the subject of the cartogram?
2. Which country appears largest on the cartogram? Which appears smallest?
3. Compare the cartogram to the map of Europe found in the Atlas. Which countries are most distorted in size compared to a land-area map?

European Immigration to the U.S. 1890

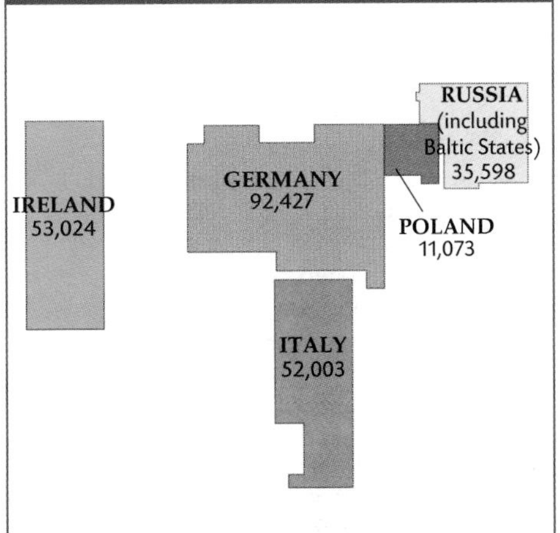

Historical Statistics of the United States, Colonial Times to 1970, Part 1, U.S. Department of Commerce, Bureau of Census, Washington D.C.

4. What accounts for these distortions?

Applying the Skill

At the library, find statistics that compare some value for different states or countries. For example, you might compare the number of farms in each state, or annual oil consumption of countries in North America. Be creative in your choice of value.

Convert these statistics into a simple cartogram. Determine the relative size of each country or state according to the chosen value. If the United States consumes five times more oil than does Mexico, then the United States should appear five times larger.

For More Practice

Turn to the Skill Practice in the Chapter Review on page 673 for more practice in reading a cartogram.

Social Studies SKILLS

TEACH

Reading a Cartogram Suggest that students pretend they are members of a city school board charged with the responsibility of planning where the city needs new schools. The standard city map shows the various residential areas and the borders of school districts. Ask students to consider how a cartogram would help them. Suggest that if it showed at a glance the relative numbers of school-age children in each district, this would help them to judge the capacity needs. Ask students to brainstorm other situations where a cartogram would be helpful.

Additional Practice

Skill Reinforcement Activity 25

ANSWERS TO PRACTICING THE SKILL

1. European immigration to the United States in 1890
2. Germany; Poland
3. Ireland and Russia
4. the number of immigrants these nations sent to the United States relative to their size

Chapter 25 Review

GLENCOE TECHNOLOGY

VIDEODISC

Use MindJogger to review students' knowledge of the chapter.

MindJogger Videoquiz

Chapter 25
Disc 4 Side A

Also available in VHS.

CHAPTER 25 REVIEW

Historical Significance

The 1800s saw the growth of democracy and nationalism in Europe and the Americas. In Great Britain, the British dominions, and the United States, democracy came peacefully. In France and Latin America, violent upheavals led to democracy or independence.

Although some revolts of the 1800s were unsuccessful, they planted the seeds of self-government. Today, many of the world's countries are democracies with guarantees of protection for citizens' rights.

Using Key Terms

Write the key term that completes each sentence.

a. Creoles
b. disenfranchised
c. dominion
d. home rule
e. seceded
f. ratify
g. *peninsulares*
h. sectionalism
i. ultraroyalists
j. suffragettes
k. plebiscite
l. mestizos

1. A self-governing country other than Great Britain that recognizes the British monarch as its head of state is called a ____________.
2. To protest the election of Abraham Lincoln as President, various Southern states ________ from the Union.
3. ________ are Latin Americans of mixed Native American and European ancestry.
4. In 1920 the United States Congress decided to ________ the Nineteenth Amendment, which guarantees all United States citizens 21 years of age and older the vote regardless of their sex.
5. Conservative aristocrats who wanted to restore the old monarchical order in France were called ____________.
6. Women in Great Britain and the United States who led a voting rights campaign for women became known as ____________.
7. Charles Stewart Parnell and other Irish nationalists wanted the question of __________ for Ireland to be discussed in the British Parliament.
8. In 1851 Louis-Napoleon called for a _______, or national vote, asking the French people to give him support to create a new constitution.
9. While the Reform Act of 1832 gave middle-class men the right to vote, agricultural laborers, factory workers, and women remained ____________.
10. In colonial Latin America, ___________ born in Spain or Portugal stood at the top level of the social order.

Using Your History Journal

Write a short report on a political issue in one of Great Britain's former territories, such as Hong Kong's return to Chinese rule in 1997, or the movement for an independent Quebec.

Reviewing Facts

1. **List** the social groups in Great Britain that gained the right to vote in national elections under the Reform Act of 1832. What social groups were still excluded from voting?
2. **Explain** why many French people came to oppose the constitutional monarchy of Louis Philippe, the "Citizen-King." How did this opposition affect Louis Philippe's rule?
3. **Explain** why France went to war in 1870. What was the result of the conflict?
4. **Identify** three land acquisitions that significantly expanded the territorial borders of the United States in the 1800s.
5. **Name** three leaders who helped win independence for Latin American countries.

Critical Thinking

1. **Apply** Compare the movement toward democratic reform in Great Britain with similar movements in France under Louis Philippe. How were they alike? How did they differ?
2. **Synthesize** What factors in French society enabled Napoleon III to name himself emperor of France?

Answers

Using Key Terms

1. c
2. e
3. l
4. f
5. i
6. j
7. d
8. k
9. b
10. g

Using Your History Journal

Have students refer to the maps they made of Britain's territories and choose one to write about. Be sure they supply details and sources.

Reviewing Facts

1. most British middle-class men; British working-class men, women
2. Middle-class French people felt that Louis Philippe favored the rich; they overthrew his government.
3. Napoleon felt that Prussia was gaining too much power; the Prussians defeated the French, and Napoleon's empire collapsed.
4. Louisiana Purchase; Mexican Cession; Oregon Country; Gadsden Purchase
5. Toussaint-Louverture, Hidalgo, Bolívar, San Martín, O'Higgins

Critical Thinking

1. Alike: Both had a monarchy that people wanted to change. Different: The British democratic movements were peaceful; the French movement was violent.
2. The political situation had been so tumultuous that strong leadership under Louis-Napoleon might have seemed welcome.
3. With European nations involved in conflict, the United States was able to expand its territory with few prohibitions. European countries were willing to sell North American land to raise money for their wars at home.

Geography in History

1. Great Britain
2. United States
3. the potato famine
4. Answers will vary. Possible answers: the revolts in Europe; economic instability; colonization of territory.

672 Chapter 25 *Democracy and Reform*

3. **Evaluate** How did conflict in Europe in the 1800s contribute to the development of the United States?

Geography in History

1. **Movement** Refer to the map below. Which European nation lost the most emigrants in this period?
2. **Movement** To which nation did most Europeans migrate during this period?
3. **Human/Environment Interaction** What caused many Irish people to migrate to the United States in the 1840s?
4. **Region** What circumstances in Europe caused millions of people to migrate during this period?

European Emigration 1821–1910

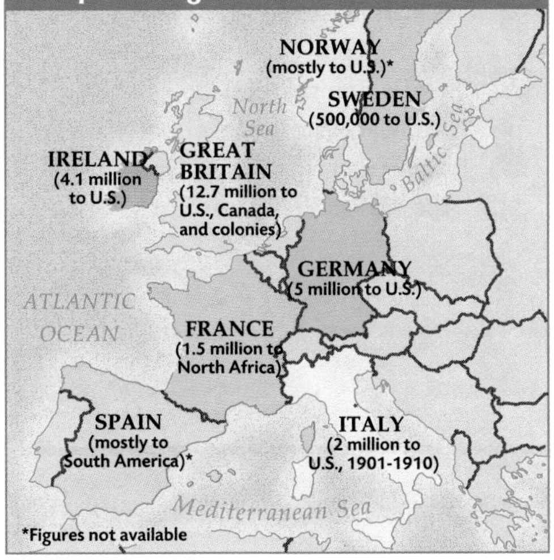

Understanding Themes

1. **Change** From your reading, would you say that the method of gradual reform was the best way that the British could have taken to change their government and society in the 1800s?
2. **Movement** How did British settlement of the dominions affect the original inhabitants?
3. **Revolution** Why do you think revolutions are often followed by governments led by dictators?
4. **Change** How did immigration affect the economic growth of the United States?
5. **Nationalism** How has social conflict affected political stability in Latin America?

Linking Past and Present

1. British and American women fought for many years to win the right to vote. What rights do women continue to seek today? Are their methods today similar to or different from past methods?
2. After slavery was abolished in the United States, African Americans and other groups still had to struggle for equality. What educational and employment opportunities do some Americans seek today?
3. The Irish were granted home rule in 1914, but it never went into effect. How does this relate to the political situation in Ireland today?

Skill Practice

Study the cartogram below and then answer these questions.

1. What is the subject of the cartogram?
2. Which country appears largest on the cartogram? Which appears smallest?
3. Compare the cartogram to a world map or globe. Which countries are most distorted in size compared to a land-area map?
4. What accounts for these distortions?

Value of U.S. Merchandise Exports 1870

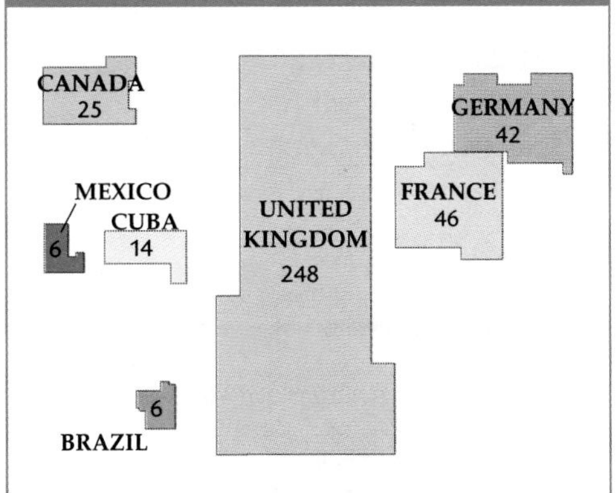

(Value of exports in millions of dollars)

Understanding Themes

1. **CHANGE** Answers will vary. Possible answer: It seems that Great Britain's way of achieving democracy was the smoothest, most stable, and longest lasting.
2. **MOVEMENT** It brought them deadly diseases, took away their land, and led to conflicts that killed many native peoples.
3. **REVOLUTION** Answers will vary. Possible answer: The people have been used to being ruled by an autocratic government and may not know how to go about ruling themselves. It may be difficult for opposing factions to agree on the best way of establishing the new government.
4. **CHANGE** Immigrants provided the workforce for the expanding United States industries.
5. **NATIONALISM** Latin America has failed to achieve political stability because of the tension between classes. Instead of uniting to forge strong nations, the classes fight among themselves.

Linking Past and Present

1. Possible answer: Women still seek equal pay for equal work and an end to sex discrimination. Methods used today by the women's movement are less dramatic and violent.
2. Possible answer: African Americans continue to seek legislation to fight discrimination.
3. The Irish Catholics in Northern Ireland continue to resent British rule and use terrorist tactics to protest.

Skill Practice

1. value of United States merchandise exports in 1870
2. United Kingdom; Mexico or Brazil
3. Canada, the United Kingdom, Brazil
4. the value of these countries' United States merchandise exports relative to their size

Chapter Bonus Test Question

Ask students: What political, social, economic, or other conditions make it easiest for a country to achieve democratic government with civil rights for all citizens? What conditions make it most difficult? *(Answers will vary but may include that some history of self-government or of limitations on the power of the monarch make it easiest; while traditions of absolute rule and a rigid social class structure make it most difficult.)*

Chapter 25 *Democracy and Reform* 673

Teach, Reinforce, and Extend CHAPTER Content

Reaction and Nationalism

CHAPTER RESOURCES

	Reproducible Resources	Multimedia Resources
Chapter Opener	Chapter Themes: Graphic Organizer 26 Historical Significance Chapter Activity 26	MindJogger Videoquiz
Chapter Enrichment	Vocabulary Activity 26* Time Line Activity 26 Mapping History Activity 26 History Simulation 26 Geography and History Activity 26 Source Reading 26 People in World History Profiles 49, 50 World Art and Music Activity 26 Enrichment Activity 26 Critical Thinking Activity 26 Skill Reinforcement Activity 26 Writer's Guidebook, Lesson 9 Performance Assessment Activity 26	Mapping History Overlay Transparency 17, *Revolutionary Centers in Europe 1820–1848* Chapter Transparency 26 Vocabulary PuzzleMaker Software Turning Points in World History: *The Russian Revolution*
Chapter Review/Reteaching	Reteaching Activity 26 Skill Reinforcement Activity 26 Spanish Chapter Summary 26	Chapter 26 Digest Audiocassette, Activity, Test* Vocabulary PuzzleMaker Software Student Self-Test and Review Software MindJogger Videoquiz
Chapter Evaluation/Testing	Performance Assessment Activity 26 Chapter 26 Test, Forms A and B	Testmaker

* *Also available in Spanish*

0:00 OUT OF TIME? Assign the Chapter 26 summary in the Unit 6 Digest on pages 728–731, and the Chapter 26 Audiocassettes.

Block Schedule

Block scheduling differs from traditional class scheduling in the amount of time allotted to each period. The extended time frame provided by block scheduling affords you the opportunity to implement a greater number of research-oriented and activity-intense projects to motivate and involve your students. Activities that are particularly suited to use within the block scheduling framework are identified throughout this chapter by the following designation.

KEY TO ABILITY LEVELS

Teaching strategies have been coded for varying learning styles and abilities.

L1 **BASIC** activities for all students
L2 **AVERAGE** activities for average to above-average students
L3 **CHALLENGING** activities for above-average students
LEP **LIMITED ENGLISH PROFICIENCY** activities

Chapter 26 Planning Guide

A complete, 1-page lesson plan is provided for each section in the *Reproducible Lesson Plans* booklet.

SECTION RESOURCES

Daily Objectives	Reproducible Resources	Multimedia Resources
Section 1 The Unification of Italy Explain how nationalism led to a united Italy in the 1860s.	Reproducible Lesson Plan 26-1 Vocabulary Activity 26* Guided Reading Activity 26-1* History Simulation 26 Time Line Activity 26 Section Quiz 26-1*	Section Focus Transparency 26-1 Chapter Transparency 26 Student Self-Test and Review Software Testmaker
Section 2 The Unification of Germany Identify the methods Bismarck used to unite the German states.	Reproducible Lesson Plan 26-2 Vocabulary Activity 26* Guided Reading Activity 26-2* Section Quiz 26-2*	Section Focus Transparency 26-2 Student Self-Test and Review Software Testmaker
Section 3 Bismarck's Realm Analyze how Bismarck's policies affected the German Empire.	Reproducible Lesson Plan 26-3 Vocabulary Activity 26* Guided Reading Activity 26-3* Section Quiz 26-3*	Section Focus Transparency 26-3 Student Self-Test and Review Software Testmaker
Section 4 Empire of the Czars Explain why revolutionary movements developed in Russia.	Reproducible Lesson Plan 26-4 Guided Reading Activity 26-4* Geography and History Activity 26 Section Quiz 26-4*	Section Focus Transparency 26-4 Vocabulary PuzzleMaker Software Student Self-Test and Review Software Testmaker Turning Points in World History: *The Russian Revolution*
Section 5 Austria-Hungary's Decline Describe how the growth of nationalistic feelings affected the empire of Austria-Hungary.	Reproducible Lesson Plan 26-5 Vocabulary Activity 26* Guided Reading Activity 26-5* Reteaching Activity 26 Enrichment Activity 26 Section Quiz 26-5* Performance Assessment Activity 26 Spanish Chapter Summary 26	Section Focus Transparency 26-5 Mapping History Overlay Transparency 17, *Revolutionary Centers in Europe 1820–1848* Student Self-Test and Review Software Testmaker

* *Also available in Spanish*

Chapter Activities

Performance Assessment Activity

A Portfolio of Examples The concepts featured in this chapter include sectionalism, nationalism, and empire. Ask students to make connections with their own lives by creating a portfolio of contemporary examples of these concepts. For each example, have students discuss the positive and negative roles played by diversity and unity in the situation. Students may include examples from politics, business, city, and the family. As a concluding activity, have students write a reflection in their portfolios in which they explain how diversity and unity affect their lives.

Possible Rubric Features
Concept attainment for concepts and themes studied, organization and classification of portfolio, analytical skills, clarity and detail of reflection

• *For an additional activity, refer to Activity 26 in the* Performance Assessment Strategies and Activities *booklet.*

Activity

From the Classroom of...

Kimberly C. Felder
Frederick Douglass Academy
New York, NY

Nationalism Then and Now
Organize students into four groups: Germany, Italy, Russia, and Austria-Hungary. Have each group use the text to review the nationalistic struggle in its country, or provide groups with fact sheets. Then have each group write a letter to the editor of a newspaper in their country, arguing a nationalistic position.

Distribute magazine and newspaper articles about current nationalistic struggles (try to include letters to the editor). Have the entire class compare the late twentieth-century struggles with the nationalistic movements of the nineteenth century.

MULTIPLE LEARNING STYLES

Verbal/Linguistic
Have students write an essay comparing the effects of war on the governments of Italy, Germany, Russia, Austria-Hungary, and the Ottoman Empire during the last half of the 1800s. Ask students to consider how war strengthened or weakened the existing governments and what political changes war brought about.

Logical/Mathematical
Have students make a time line that shows the main events in the spread of nationalism through Italy, Germany, Russia, Austria-Hungary, and the Ottoman Empire.

Visual/Spatial
Have students create a picture gallery of the many personalities mentioned in the chapter. Have them accompany each copy of a portrait with a thumbnail sketch that provides the person's nationality and principal accomplishments.

Auditory/Musical
Have students develop a musical collage of works by Richard Wagner, Giuseppe Verdi, and Modest Mussorgsky that show the spirit of nationalism.

Kinesthetic
Have students create a board game that uses Bismarck's domestic and foreign strategies to bring about a unified Germany.

Additional Resources

TEACHER'S CORNER

NATIONAL GEOGRAPHIC SOCIETY

INDEX TO NATIONAL GEOGRAPHIC MAGAZINE

The following articles may be used for research relating to this chapter:

- "St. Petersburg: Capital of the Tsars," by Steve Raymer, December 1993.

Bibliography

Literature of the Period

Dostoyevsky, Fyodor. ***The Possessed.*** Translated by Constance Garnett. New York: Modern Library, 1963. A Russian novel about nineteenth-century revolutionaries.

Readings for the Student

Snyder, L. L. ***A Comparative History of Nationalism.*** New York: Holt, 1976. An introduction to the different varieties of nationalism.

Readings for the Teacher

Knapton, Ernest John, and Thomas Kingston Derry. ***Europe: 1815–1914.*** New York: Scribners, 1965. Comprehensive history of Europe that includes cultural, social, and economic trends as well as political, diplomatic, and military themes.

interNET
CONNECTIONS
Treasures of the Czars Take a tour of this virtual museum.
World Wide Web:
http://www.times.st-pete.fl.us/Treasures/TC.Lobby.html

Introducing Chapter 26

CHAPTER THEMES

Chapter Themes are listed by section on this chapter opening page of the Student Edition. A corresponding theme-based activity is available under "TEACH," and a theme-based question is asked in the Section and Chapter Reviews.

The Storyteller

Historical Setting Giuseppe Mazzini, born in Genoa in 1805, founded Young Italy, a secret society whose goal was the unification of Italy. Mazzini spent most of his life in exile under a sentence of death. While in Switzerland, he and exiles from Poland and Germany founded Young Europe. Their vision was a Europe of many free nations coming together through an elected assembly that would regulate matters of common interest. Mazzini helped form other nationalist groups across Europe, such as Young Switzerland, Young Germany, Young Poland, Young Spain, and Young Russia.

Historical Significance

Answers: *French nationalism under Napoleon brought parts of Europe into the French Empire. When the Congress of Vienna broke up the French Empire and divided much of Europe among Prussia, Russia, and Austria, it set the stage for nationalist movements among groups in lands controlled by those nations.*

Nationalist feelings in the Balkans led to World War I and to the recent war in Bosnia; Hitler's nationalistic program to unite the German people and create a German Empire led to World War II; nationalist feelings in Africa and Asia led to the breakup of the British and French Empires.

Chapter
26
1815–1914
Reaction and Nationalism

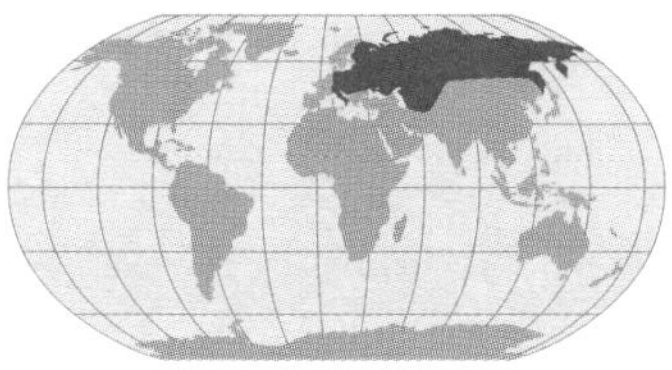

Chapter Themes

- **Nationalism** The rise of nationalism contributes to the unification of Italy. *Section 1*
- **Conflict** Bismarck uses war and diplomacy to bring unity to Germany. *Section 2*
- **Change** Bismarck's German Empire allows for economic growth but limits political freedoms. *Section 3*
- **Reaction** Russian czars oppose the forces of liberalism and nationalism in the Russian Empire. *Section 4*
- **Diversity** The large empire of Austria-Hungary contains many different nationalities seeking self-rule. *Section 5*

The Storyteller

One Sunday in 1821, 16-year-old Giuseppe Mazzini walked along a street in Genoa, Italy. Suddenly a tall, black-bearded stranger approached him. With a piercing look, the stranger held out his hand for money and said, "for the refugees of Italy." Everyone knew that the refugees were those who had recently rebelled against the Austrians to win independence for Italy.

Forty years later, Mazzini—now a leader of the Italian nationalist movement—wrote of this incident: "That day was the first in which ... [I realized that] ... we Italians could and therefore ought to struggle for the liberty of our country." During the early 1800s feelings of nationalism similar to Mazzini's began to stir all across Europe.

Historical Significance

How has the force of nationalism repeatedly changed the map of Europe? What impact has nationalism had on European and world developments in the twentieth century?

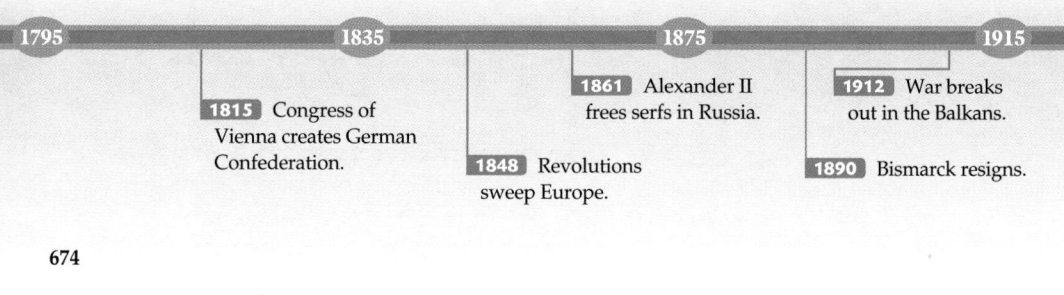

1795 — 1835 — 1875 — 1915

- **1815** Congress of Vienna creates German Confederation.
- **1848** Revolutions sweep Europe.
- **1861** Alexander II frees serfs in Russia.
- **1890** Bismarck resigns.
- **1912** War breaks out in the Balkans.

GEOGRAPHY CONNECTION

Location On a historical map of Europe of about 1860, have students locate the independent Italian states and German states, the Russian Empire, Austria, Hungary, and the Ottoman Empire. Why would Austria-Hungary and Russia be interested in land in the Ottoman Empire? *(The Ottoman Empire bordered both Austria-Hungary and Russia.)* Then have students compare the historical map with a present-day map of Europe. What area in present-day Italy remains part of the Papal States? *(Vatican City)*

History & Art *Meeting at Teano* by Cesare Maccari. Palazzo Pubblico, Siena, Italy
A desire to unite Italy brought together Sardinia's King Victor Emmanuel I (left) and the revolutionary leader Giuseppe Garibaldi (right).

Your History Journal

Write a report on a subtopic from "Powder Keg in the Balkans" in Section 5 of this chapter. Suggested titles: Decline of the Ottoman Empire, The Crimean War, Russo-Turkish War, The Congress of Berlin, Russian Objectives in the Balkans, British Objectives in the Balkans.

Introducing Chapter 26

History & Art

In 1860 Giuseppe Garibaldi had conquered the Kingdom of the Two Sicilies in southern Italy, while Victor Emmanuel II had brought most of northern Italy into his kingdom. When the two men met at the bridge of Teano, Garibaldi surrendered his conquests to Victor Emmanuel and hailed him as king of Italy.

Performance Assessment

Refer to the activity on page 674C of the Planning Guide.

For an additional activity, refer to Activity 26 in the *Performance Assessment Strategies and Activities* booklet.

Using Your History Journal

Have students research one of the suggested report topics by using outside sources. Suggest that they take notes for their report in their journals.

GLENCOE TECHNOLOGY

VIDEODISC
Use MindJogger to preview chapter content.

MindJogger Videoquiz
Chapter 26
Disc 4 Side A

Also available in VHS.

EXTRA CREDIT PROJECT

Oral Report Have students use outside sources to do in-depth research on one of the people mentioned in this chapter or on a person or group not mentioned in the chapter that was involved in a European nationalist movement during the 1800s. Suggest that they cover the background, education, social position, political ideas, and political actions of the person or group. Ask them to analyze the success or failure of their person or group.

SECTION THEME

▶ **Nationalism** The rise of nationalism contributes to the unification of Italy.

Find Out

Answer: *The desire for a politically united Italy caused the Italians to overthrow Austrian rule and look to the king of Sardinia as a unifying force. After fighting started, people in many regions of Italy overthrew their rulers and united with the Kingdom of Sardinia to become the nation of Italy.*

FOCUS

Section Objective

Explain how nationalism led to a united Italy in the 1860s.

BELLRINGER Motivational Activity

Before taking roll at the beginning of the class period, project Section Focus Transparency 26-1 and have students answer the activity questions. Discuss students' responses.

This activity is also available as a blackline master.

Vocabulary Pre-check

Use Vocabulary Activity 26 to introduce vocabulary terms. **L1 LEP**

1820 — 1860 — 1900

1831 Giuseppe Mazzini founds Young Italy.

1861 Italians establish a united kingdom.

1871 Victor Emmanuel II moves the capital from Florence to Rome.

Section 1

The Unification of Italy

Setting the Scene

▶ **Terms to Define**
nationalism, nation-state, guerrilla warfare

▶ **People to Meet**
Giuseppe Mazzini, Charles Albert, Victor Emmanuel II, Count Camillo di Cavour, Giuseppe Garibaldi

▶ **Places to Locate**
Florence, Genoa, Sicily, Sardinia, Rome

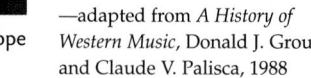

Find Out How did nationalism lead to a united Italy in the 1860s?

The Storyteller

As the crowd shouted "Viva Verdi!", *Giuseppe Verdi smiled. He understood the phrase's double meaning. Although the throng appreciated his operas, they were actually demonstrating for a unified Italy. The* Risorgimento, *those wishing for a unified Italy, adopted Verdi's music as a rally-cry supporting Victor Emmanuel, the king of Sardinia. When people cheered* "Viva Verdi," *the occupying Austrians thought they were praising the musician. But the words meant* Viva Vittorio Emanuele, Re D'Italia*—long live Victor Emmanuel, king of Italy.*

—adapted from *A History of Western Music,* Donald J. Grout and Claude V. Palisca, 1988

The Musician Giuseppe Verdi *by Boldini*

From about the 1100s to the 1800s, central Europe was made up of numerous kingdoms, principalities, and free cities. Stimulated by the desire for economic growth, by the success of the American Revolution, and by the experience of the Napoleonic Wars, a small but dedicated group of Italians and Germans worked to unify these territories into nations in the 1800s. The desire for national independence that inspired them, known as nationalism, became one of the most powerful forces at work in Europe during the 1800s.

In 1815 the modern nation of Italy did not yet exist. At that time the Italian Peninsula was divided into a number of independent states, many of which had foreign rulers. A French Bourbon monarch ruled the Kingdom of the Two Sicilies, while Austria controlled Lombardy and Venetia and the pope controlled the Papal States.

In addition to political divisions, cultural and economic differences divided the regions of the Italian Peninsula. Not only did people speak different dialects of the Italian language, but trade barriers and poor transportation discouraged the flow of goods and people. To move goods the 200 miles (322 km) from **Florence** to Milan often took 8 weeks.

While cultural and economic divisions continued into the 1900s, a growing unification movement eventually swept aside the political divisions on the Italian Peninsula. By the 1860s, Italy had become a single country.

Early Attempts

The name given to the movement for Italian unity was *Risorgimento* (ree•ZAWR•jih•MEHN•toh), meaning the "resurgence" or "revival."

SECTION RESOURCES

Reproducible Masters
- Reproducible Lesson Plan 26-1
- Vocabulary Activity 26
- Guided Reading Activity 26-1
- History Simulation 26
- Time Line Activity 26
- Section Quiz 26-1

Transparencies
- Section Focus Transparency 26-1
- Chapter Transparency 26

Multimedia
- Student Self-Test and Review Software
- Testmaker

Giuseppe Mazzini was its most effective speaker. A native of **Genoa** and a bold and active leader in the fight for Italian independence, Mazzini founded in 1831 a secret society called Young Italy. The goal of this society was to transform Italy into an independent sovereign nation. According to Mazzini, the nation-state, a political organization consisting of one nationality rather than several nationalities, was very important. Through it, people in one unified country with common ideals could best contribute their efforts to the well-being of all its citizens.

In January 1848, Mazzini-inspired nationalists led a republican revolution in **Sicily**. Some weeks later, news of larger revolutions in France and Austria sparked uprisings throughout the Italian Peninsula. When fighting began against Austrian forces in Lombardy and Venetia, King **Charles Albert** of the Kingdom of **Sardinia** joined the war to expel the foreigners. Nationalists pressured the rulers of Naples, Tuscany, and the Papal States to send troops against the Austrians.

By April 1848 the united Italian forces had almost succeeded in driving the Austrians from the peninsula. Then, saying that he opposed a war with another Catholic country, Pope Pius IX suddenly withdrew his troops. Naples followed suit. Their withdrawal enabled Austria to defeat the army of Charles Albert and reestablish its control over Lombardy and Venetia.

The pope's decision infuriated Italian nationalists. In November 1848 angry mobs forced the pope to flee the city. Nationalists proclaimed **Rome** a republic and summoned Mazzini to the capital to head the government. The expulsion of the pope, however, aroused the Catholic governments of Naples, Spain, and France. As a result, Louis-Napoleon sent a French army to Rome. His troops occupied the city and restored the pope to power.

The events of 1848 caused Italian nationalists to lose faith in Mazzini. Charles Albert, on the other hand, earned their respect with his brave stand against the Austrians. Consequently, nationalists now looked to Sardinia to lead the struggle for Italian unification.

Count Cavour's Diplomacy

In 1849 **Victor Emmanuel II**, Charles Albert's son, became king of Sardinia. During the next few years Victor Emmanuel II toiled to keep popular support for the unity movement alive. He was greatly helped in his efforts by a shrewd and determined adviser named **Count Camillo di Cavour**.

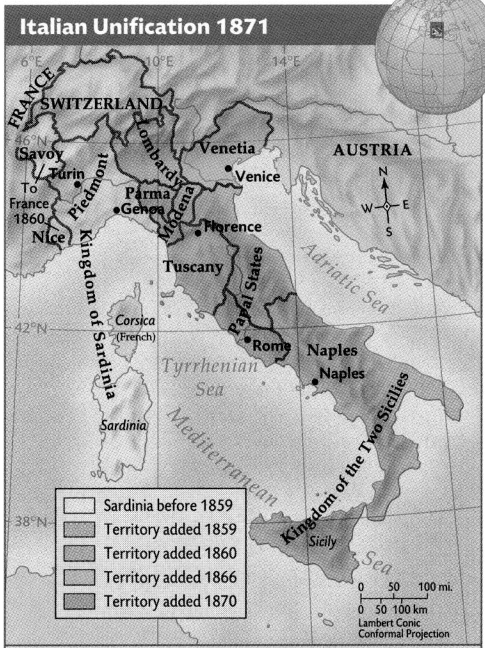

Map Study The unification of Italy was largely accomplished between 1859 and 1870.

Place What territories were added in 1860?

Physically, Cavour was not impressive, as this description by a contemporary illustrates:

> "The squat ... pot-bellied form; the small, stumpy legs; the short, round arms, with the hands stuck constantly in the trousers' pockets ... and the sharp grey eyes, covered by the goggle spectacles ... The dress itself seemed a part and property of the man."

Cavour's looks were deceptive, however. Hidden behind the rumpled clothes and strange appearance was a bold, intelligent man of great personal charm. By the time of the Crimean War in 1854, Cavour dominated Sardinia's council of ministers. His major goals were the promotion of rapid industrial growth, the reduction of the Catholic Church's influence, and the advancement of Sardinia's national interests in foreign affairs.

The defeat of Sardinia in 1848 convinced Cavour that the kingdom needed the aid of a foreign power to expel Austria and achieve Italian

TEACH

Guided Practice

THEME Nationalism

Help students define *nationalism.* Discuss how nationalism can unify people in a country or can lead to war and to discrimination against minority groups. Conclude by asking students to give examples of nationalism at work in the world today. **L1**

Map Study

Answer

Parma, Modena, Tuscany, part of the Papal States, and the Kingdom of the Two Sicilies

Map Skills Practice

Reading a Map When did Venetia become part of Italy? *(1866)*

Geography: Place Refer students to the map on this page. Have students identify the changing political loyalties of the major islands west of Italy. Which ones became part of a unified Italy? *(Sardinia and Sicily)* Which one did not? *(Corsica)* Let students discuss the importance of political loyalties of islands. *(important for trade and military strategy)* **L2**

Critical Thinking Have students discuss whether Cavour's problems with Garibaldi were justified. *(No; Garibaldi surrendered his conquests to Victor Emmanuel II.)* **L2**

Chapter Transparency 26

History Simulation 26

COOPERATIVE LEARNING ACTIVITY

Time Line Organize students into three groups to construct a chronology showing the unification of Italy. Have one group gather information on key people, writing short descriptions of their roles. Have the second group prepare short written descriptions about key events and their dates. Have the third group design and draw the time line, incorporating information from the other two groups. Have this group post the time line on a classroom bulletin board or wall. Encourage the class to use the time line as a reference. **L1**

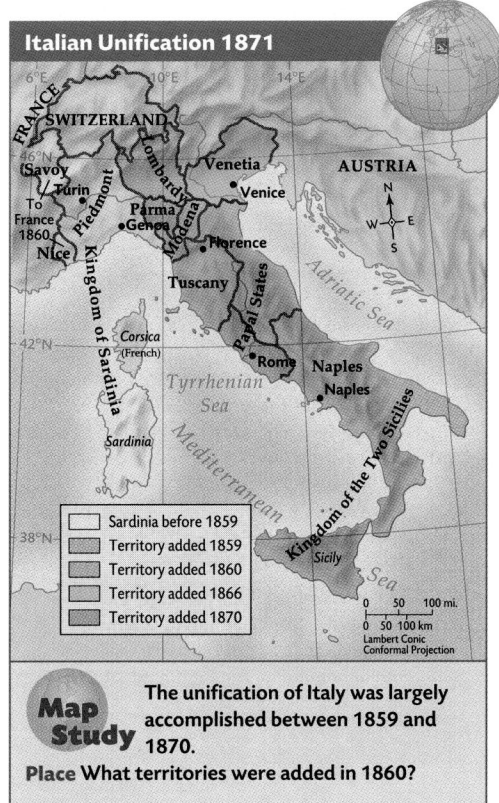

Chapter 26
Section 1

Independent Practice

Guided Reading Activity 26-1 **L1**

Time Line Activity 26

Chart Have students create a chart with the following column headings: *Mazzini, Count Cavour, Victor Emmanuel II, Garibaldi.* Include the following topics for rows: *Goals and Ideals, Events and Dates, Impact on Unification.* Suggest students use outside sources to complete the chart. **L2 LEP**

Biography Have students research the life of Pope Pius IX and write a short biography. Suggest that students include the following topics in their biographies: Pius IX's early reforms, his views on and role in Italian unification, his removal from Rome, the doctrine of papal infallibility. **L3**

you don't say...

Carbonari means "charcoal burners" in Italian. It was the name of one of the first Italian secret societies for the overthrow of foreign governments in Italy. Although charcoal is black, it gives off a bright glow when burning. This was associated with the light of freedom and liberty.

unity. To win such aid, Cavour decided to support France and Britain in the Crimean War. One historian later called this action "one of the most brilliant strokes of statecraft in the nineteenth century."

By sending an army to the Crimea in 1854, Sardinia established a claim to equality with the other warring nations. Participating in the war also won Sardinia admittance to the Congress of Paris, which settled treaty matters after the war.

War With Austria

Not long after the Crimean War, in the summer of 1858, Cavour met secretly with Napoleon III at Plombiéres-les-Bains in France. There Napoleon III promised to aid Sardinia in expelling Austria if Sardinia found itself at war. In return, Sardinia agreed that it would give the provinces of Savoy and Nice to France in the event of an Italian-French victory over Austria. Cavour next forced Austria to declare war against Sardinia. He did this by encouraging nationalist groups in Lombardy to revolt. When Austria demanded that Sardinia withdraw its support of the rebels, Sardinia refused. Austria declared war in April 1859. As he had promised, Napoleon III led a force of 120,000 French soldiers to aid Sardinia.

The combined forces of France and Sardinia defeated the Austrians at Magenta and Solferino in June 1859. Austria was on the run. The French suffered heavy losses, however, and Napoleon III feared the loss of public support at home if the fighting in Italy continued.

Without consulting Cavour, Napoleon III withdrew from the fighting in July and signed a treaty with Emperor Francis Joseph of Austria. By the terms of the treaty, Austria gave Lombardy to Sardinia but retained control of Venetia. When Cavour read these terms, he became furious. He insisted that Victor Emmanuel II continue to fight. Believing that victory was impossible without France, the king refused.

The fighting, however, did not stop. People in Tuscany, Parma, Modena, and the papal province of Romagna overthrew their rulers in late 1859 and

Images of the Times

Uniting Italy

Before 1860 Italy was made up of many separate states. After 1860 it became a united kingdom but remained culturally and economically divided. The deepest division was between northern and southern parts of the country.

Southern Italy remained a leading rural and agricultural area. Traditional customs were strong, and artisans excelled in various crafts.

678

Images of the Times **Uniting Italy**

"We have made Italy, now we have to make Italians," remarked Massimo d'Azeglio, a former prime minister of the Piedmont, after 1860. This task was especially hard to accomplish in southern Italy, where few local people had actively taken part in the fight for unification. Many of the peasants who lived in this region had to scratch out a living working as laborers or as tenants on large estates. Poverty and unemployment were common throughout the south, and the new government lacked revenue for relief, job programs, and education. Because of lack of work, many southern Italians migrated to North Africa and the Americas. From there, they sent money home to their families.

early 1860. Their new governments demanded the right to unite with Sardinia. To gain Napoleon III's consent for this unification, Cavour gave Savoy and Nice to France. In April 1860 Victor Emmanuel II accepted the territories into his kingdom.

Garibaldi Seizes the South

Southern Italy remained isolated from the revolutionary fever sweeping the rest of the peninsula, but at the death of Ferdinand II, ruler of the Kingdom of the Two Sicilies, Italian nationalists prepared for a revolution. Their leader was a charismatic military commander and adventurer named **Giuseppe Garibaldi**.

As a young man, Garibaldi had joined Young Italy. Forced into exile after taking part in the 1830 uprisings, he went to South America, where he fought in several revolutionary wars. As a result of this experience, Garibaldi became an expert in guerrilla warfare, a method of warfare using hit-and-run tactics. Garibaldi returned to Italy in 1848 and took part in Mazzini's short-lived Roman Republic. When the Roman Republic fell in 1849, Garibaldi again fled his homeland, this time to the United States.

Sensing that the people of the Kingdom of the Two Sicilies were ready to revolt, Garibaldi returned to Italy in 1860. After collecting a thousand volunteers in Genoa, he set out for Sicily. When his troops faltered in the midst of the first battle of the Sicilian campaign, Garibaldi rallied them to victory. In a few weeks, he gained total control of the island.

He then crossed to the mainland and advanced toward Naples. The army of the Kingdom of the Two Sicilies proved no match for the guerrilla tactics of Garibaldi's Red Shirts, so called because of the color of their uniforms. Naples fell, and the king of the Two Sicilies fled.

Garibaldi's successes in the south made Cavour nervous. He worried about his fellow countryman's political ambitions. To prevent Garibaldi

Northern Italy became a highly urbanized and industrialized region. The city of Milan was known both for its economic prosperity and its festive outdoor celebrations.

Tuscany, a region in north-central Italy, was known for its picturesque villages and vineyards as well as the cultural city of Florence.

REFLECTING ON THE TIMES

1. How was Italy organized politically before 1860?
2. What economic and social differences distinguished northern Italy from southern Italy?

Chapter 26 Section 1

Who?What?Where?When?

Giuseppe Garibaldi Between 1850 and 1860, Garibaldi lived on Staten Island in New York City. He made a meager living working in a friend's candle factory.

Linking Past and Present

Guerrilla warfare, such as that which Garibaldi's Red Shirts were known for, has been used since biblical times. During the American Revolution, Francis Marion, the "Swamp Fox," led guerrilla groups against the British in South Carolina. More recently, guerrilla warfare proved effective during the Vietnam War.

ASSESS

Check for Understanding

Assign Section 1 Review as homework or as an in-class activity.

Use Student Self-Test and Review Software to review Section 1.

ANSWERS TO REFLECTING ON THE TIMES

1. Italy was divided into several independent states.
2. Northern Italy became highly industrialized and urbanized; southern Italy remained a rural, agricultural area.

Chapter 26 Section 1

Visualizing History Tell students that Garibaldi left Sicily at Messina, crossed the Straits of Messina, and entered the mainland at Reggio. The army of the Kingdom of the Two Sicilies—although 30,000 strong—offered little resistance to Garibaldi's 4,000 men.

Answer to Caption: *guerrilla warfare*

Evaluate

Section Quiz 26-1

Use the Testmaker to create a customized quiz for Section 1.

Reteach

Have students write five paragraphs summarizing information in Section 1. Suggest that students organize each paragraph around one of the section's headings.

Enrich

Have students discuss the role foreign nations played in the unification of Italy. Ask students to decide which nation had the most influence in the unification process.

CLOSE

Use the map on page 677 to summarize the steps by which Italian unification was achieved.

Visualizing History **After gaining control of Sicily in 1860, Giuseppe Garibaldi and his forces left the island for the Italian mainland.** *What type of warfare did Garibaldi carry out on behalf of Italian national unity?*

from further victories, Cavour sent an army into the Papal States. On September 18 the forces of Sardinia defeated the papal army at Castelfidaro. The victory kept Cavour in control of the campaign for national unity.

When voters in southern Italy supported union with Sardinia in October 1860, Garibaldi surrendered his conquests to Victor Emmanuel II. By February 1861 the whole peninsula, with the exception of Rome and Venetia, was united under one government. Victor Emmanuel II was now king of the newly created constitutional monarchy of Italy.

Building a New Nation

Three months after the unification of Italy, Count Cavour died. His last words were "Italy is made. All is safe." Despite Cavour's optimism, many difficult problems faced the new nation. For example, national unification had not erased the profound cultural and economic divisions that separated the south and north of Italy. The south was poor and agricultural, while the north had begun to industrialize. The gap in the standards of living between the two regions fueled discontent and hampered unification efforts.

In the name of national unity, Sardinia often tried to force its laws and customs onto the other Italian states. This tactic only fanned resentment. Former rulers also encouraged discontent. When some of these rulers tried to regain their thrones, bloody civil wars erupted.

Gradually the Italian government developed a unified military force and a national educational system. It built railroads, linking not only the south with the north but also Italy with the rest of Europe. While these developments were important steps in the process of unification, cultural and economic barriers remained.

Another problem concerned the location of the nation's capital. Most Italians thought that **Rome** should be the capital of the new nation. During the 1860s, however, the pope still ruled the city. In addition, the Austrians continued to control Venetia.

Italy again sought foreign help to solve a political problem. In 1866 Italy allied itself with Prussia in a war against Austria. In return, Prussia promised to give Venetia to Italy. Although Austria defeated Italian forces in the conflict, the Prussian victory was so overwhelming that Prussia gave Venetia to Italy anyway.

Foreign intervention also played a role in helping Italy win Rome. When war broke out between France and Prussia in 1870, Napoleon III withdrew French troops that had been protecting the pope. Italian troops then entered Rome and conquered the pope's territory. In 1871 Victor Emmanuel II moved the national capital from Florence to Rome. The political unification of Italy was finally complete.

SECTION 1 REVIEW

Recall

1. **Define** nationalism, nation-state, guerrilla warfare.
2. **Identify** Giuseppe Mazzini, Charles Albert, Victor Emmanuel II, Count Camillo di Cavour, Giuseppe Garibaldi.
3. **List** three problems Italy faced after unification.

Critical Thinking

4. **Applying Information** Select a leader in the movement for Italian unification and show how that leader furthered the aims of the movement.

Understanding Themes

5. **Nationalism** Explain how the papacy and the Catholic Church responded to the rise of nationalism in the Italian Peninsula.

SECTION 1 REVIEW ANSWERS

1. All vocabulary words are defined in the Glossary.
2. Mazzini, 677; Charles Albert, 677; Victor Emmanuel II, 677; Cavour, 677; Garibaldi, 679
3. cultural and economic differences between northern and southern Italy; attempts by former rulers of Italian states to regain their thrones; Venetia and Rome were not part of the new Italy
4. Answers will vary but should reveal an understanding of how selected leader furthered Italian unification.
5. NATIONALISM At first Pope Pius IX supported the war against Austria, but later he withdrew the forces of the Papal States, opposing warfare with another Catholic state. This earned him the dislike of Italian nationalists, who staged an uprising against the pope in Rome.

1820 — 1840 — 1860 — 1880

1834 German states create the *Zollverein.*

1866 Prussia and Austria fight Seven Weeks' War.

1871 William I becomes emperor of a united Germany.

Section 2

The Unification of Germany

Setting the Scene

- **Terms to Define**
  realpolitik, kaiser, chancellor
- **People to Meet**
  William I, Otto von Bismarck
- **Places to Locate**
  Frankfurt, Austria, Prussia, Schleswig, Holstein

Find Out What methods did Bismarck use to unite the German states?

The Storyteller

Klaus von Erlach was impressed by Otto von Bismarck's message, although many of Klaus's fellow aristocrats disliked the Iron Chancellor, considering him a traitor to his class. Who other than a great leader, Klaus wondered, would be able to defend a change of political opinion? As Bismarck stated, "The man who does not learn also fails to progress and cannot keep abreast of his time. People are falling behind when they remain rooted in the position they occupied two years ago." If Germany was to progress, the old systems would have to adapt.

—adapted from "Professorial Politics," Otto von Bismarck, reprinted in *Sources of World History*, Mark A. Kishlansky, 1995

Otto von Bismarck

Germany was the last of the great European powers to achieve complete political unity. In 1815, 39 independent German states stretched north and south from the Baltic Sea to the Alps, and east and west from the Rhine River to the Russian Empire. Political rivals Austria and Prussia were the most powerful of these German states.

While Great Britain and France were developing as strong industrial nations, Germany remained divided and economically disadvantaged. The Reformation and the Thirty Years' War contributed to Germany's social and political divisions. Antagonisms between Protestant and Catholic states ran deep. By 1871, however, the German states—excluding Austria and Switzerland—had united into a single nation.

Steps Toward Unity

The Congress of Vienna had created the German Confederation in 1815 as a buffer against possible future French expansion. This first major step toward German unity established closer economic ties between the German states and helped pave the way for greater political union.

The German Confederation loosely tied together the numerous German states with a diet, or assembly, sitting at **Frankfurt**. **Austria** dominated the confederation. Its position as head of the diet eventually brought it into conflict with **Prussia**. Neither Austria nor the smaller German states wanted to see a united Germany. Austria feared the economic competition, while the smaller states feared domination by Prussia.

The largest of the German states, Prussia had a well-organized government and a strong economy. Political power in Prussia lay in the hands of

SECTION THEME

- **Conflict** Bismarck uses war and diplomacy to bring unity to Germany.

Find Out

Answer: *war and diplomacy*

FOCUS

Section Objective

Identify the methods Bismarck used to unite the German states.

BELLRINGER
Motivational Activity

Before taking roll at the beginning of the class period, project Section Focus Transparency 26-2 and have students answer the activity questions. Discuss students' responses.

This activity is also available as a blackline master.

Vocabulary Pre-check

Use Vocabulary Activity 26 to introduce vocabulary terms. **L1 LEP**

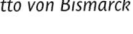

SECTION RESOURCES

Reproducible Masters
- Reproducible Lesson Plan 26-2
- Vocabulary Activity 26
- Guided Reading Activity 26-2
- Section Quiz 26-2

Transparencies
- Section Focus Transparency 26-2

Multimedia
- Student Self-Test and Review Software
- Testmaker

Chapter 26 Section 2

TEACH

Guided Practice

THEME Conflict

Have students make a chart on the chalkboard that shows the participants, purpose, and outcomes of the war against Denmark, the Seven Weeks' War, and the Franco-Prussian War. **L1 LEP**

Map Study

Answers

1. *Prussia*
2. *a well-organized government and a strong economy*

Map Skills Practice

Reading a Map For what practical reason would Prussia want a united Germany? *(to unite the two parts of Prussia)*

Economics Lead a discussion about economic issues involved in unification. Have students include the *Zollverein* and Bismarck's budget for the army. **L2**

Government Hold an informal class debate on the advantages and disadvantages of Bismarck's policy of realpolitik. Conclude the debate by having students discuss whether realpolitik is a force in political policy today. Encourage students to give examples of realpolitik from current events. **L3**

influential aristocratic landowners called Junkers (YUN•kuhrs), but members of the rising business class demanded a share of political power. To reduce trade barriers among German lands, the Prussian Junkers called for a *Zollverein*, or economic union. Formed in 1834, the *Zollverein* reduced tariffs and other trade barriers between most of the German states, resulting in lower and more uniform prices of goods throughout the confederation. The *Zollverein* also standardized systems of currency and weights and measures, and strengthened the business class.

By forming this close economic union, Prussia won an important political victory over Austria. Just as Sardinia led Italy toward unification, Prussia now directed military and political events that would eventually unite Germany.

Map Study The German Confederation consisted of many small independent states in 1815.
1. Location Which was the largest and most important of these states?
2. Place What characteristics of the largest state in the German Confederation made it so important?

Rise of Bismarck

In 1861 **William I** became king of Prussia, succeeding his brother Frederick William IV. Opposed to liberal ideas, William supported the military. Believing that Prussia could establish its position of leadership in Germany by means of a powerful military force, William planned to expand the army.

Liberal German nationalists, however, saw no use for a strong military except to control the Prussian people. They wanted the king to adopt democratic policies to gain support from the other German states. As a result, liberal deputies in the Prussian assembly overwhelmingly defeated new taxes to support a larger army.

Frustrated by the defeat, the king appointed as his new prime minister a man who shared his views on army reconstruction. That man was **Otto von Bismarck**. A Junker himself, Bismarck had served in the Prussian assembly and as ambassador to Russia and France. He shared the king's view that Prussia needed a strong government and army to achieve German unity. A brilliant negotiator, Bismarck embraced the policy of realpolitik, the right of the nation-state to pursue its own advantage by any means, including war and the repudiation of treaties.

In September 1862 Bismarck defied the finance committee of the Prussian assembly. He declared that the great issues of the times would not be decided "by speeches and majority decisions ... but by blood and iron." When the lower house again refused to approve the new army budget, Bismarck pushed the program through by simply collecting the necessary taxes without authorization.

Three Wars

Bismarck once said, "Show me an objective worthy of war and I will go along with you." As prime minister, he found several worthy objectives. His initial goal was to raise money for army expansion. Then he wanted Prussia to use its military and economic power to reduce Austrian influence among the German states. Finally, he planned to arrange the unification of all German states except Austria and Switzerland under Prussian domination. To accomplish these objectives, Bismarck went to war three times.

War Against Denmark

By inheritance, the king of Denmark ruled the territories of **Schleswig** and **Holstein**. Schleswig's population was part German and part Danish; Holstein's population was entirely German. When King Christian IX proclaimed Schleswig a Danish province in 1863, Germans in both territories appealed to the larger German states for support.

COOPERATIVE LEARNING ACTIVITY

Role Play Organize the class into six groups to role-play the diplomatic stands taken by Germany and its rivals in the war with Denmark, the Seven Weeks' War, and the Franco-Prussian War. Have three groups research Germany's position in each war and the other three groups each research Denmark's, Austria's, and France's positions. Suggest that students gather data about their assigned country's goals and relations with their opposing country. Then have each pair of rival groups present their dramatizations in the order in which they occurred: the war with Denmark, the Seven Weeks' War, and the Franco-Prussian War. **L2**

To prevent Danish annexation of Schleswig, Bismarck persuaded Austria to join Prussia in declaring war against Denmark in 1864. Prussia and Austria soon won this war and forced Denmark out of the disputed provinces. By mutual agreement, Prussia took control of Schleswig, and Austria took over the administration of Holstein. This arrangement strained the relationship between these rival powers.

The war accomplished two of Bismarck's objectives. First, it made Europe aware of Prussia's military might and influence. Second, the tension resulting from the war settlement gave Bismarck the excuse he wanted for going to war with Austria.

Seven Weeks' War

One month before the invasion of Schleswig, Bismarck wrote to his envoy in Paris:

> "You do not trust Austria. Neither do I. But I consider it the correct policy at present to have Austria with us. Whether the moment of parting will come, and on whose initiative, we shall see.... I am not in the least afraid of war, on the contrary ... you may very soon be able to convince yourself that war also is included in my program."

Bismarck prepared for war by stripping Austria of possible allies. He gained Russia's goodwill by offering the czar aid against Polish rebels in 1863. He offered France possible "compensations" for its neutrality in case of an Austro-Prussian war. He also forged an alliance with Italy by supporting its claim to Venetia in return for military support against Austria.

Bismarck gained public support for his actions when Austria sided with the duke of Augustenburg, who claimed title to Schleswig and Holstein. To prevent an alliance between Austria and the duke, Bismarck ordered Prussian troops into Austrian-occupied Holstein. When Austria then asked the German Confederation to take military action against Prussia for this invasion, Bismarck responded by declaring war against Austria.

The war between Austria and Prussia began on June 15, 1866, and ended in a Prussian victory just seven weeks later. For Bismarck, the conflict had been a limited war with limited objectives. Its purpose was to separate Austria from Germany and

CONNECTIONS

Geography

A Divided Land

Germany's geography has made it a country of distinct regions. Throughout German history, rivers have drawn people in different directions. The north-flowing Rhine, Weser, and Oder Rivers have linked the peoples of these river valleys to the northern plains. In southern Germany, the Danube River has oriented people of that region to the southeast.

Rhineland Industry

Mountains and highland areas—especially the Alps and the Central Highlands—have isolated populations and strengthened local dialects and traditions.

In the past, revolutions, civil wars, and religious strife heightened a sense of separation among people of various regions, so that Swabians considered Westphalians as foreigners, and Bavarians regarded Prussians as archrivals.

This spirit of regional allegiance led the Germans to resist political centralization to a much greater extent than the Spaniards, the French, and the British. In Germany, power remained largely in the hands of the many territorial princes until the mid-1800s.

MAKING THE CONNECTION

1. What geographical factors contributed most to the growth of regionalism in Germany?
2. How did physical barriers delay the growth of nationalism in Germany?

Chapter 26 Section 2

Linking Past and Present

German Unification Bismarck used three wars to unify Germany, but another German-caused war—World War II—left Germany divided for 45 years. In 1990 West Germany and East Germany were reunited as one country.

Independent Practice

Guided Reading Activity 26-2 **L1**

Comic Strip Have students draw an action comic strip of the major events that led to German unification. Suggest that they include the German Confederation, *Zollverein*, rise of Bismarck, the three wars, William I, the Ems telegram, and the government of the empire. **L2**

CONNECTIONS

Geography

A Divided Land

Germany is made up of three major geographic areas: the northern Lowlands, the Central Highlands, and the southern mountains. These physical divisions hindered political unification of the German states.

Answers to Making the Connection

1. *the mountains, highlands, and flow of major rivers*
2. *They kept people in the different regions of Germany isolated from one another and strengthened local dialects and traditions.*

MEETING SPECIAL NEEDS ACTIVITY

Study Strategy Organize students into four groups, with the most students in group three. Assign each group one of the four main headings in the section. Ask each group to prepare an outline of its part of the section. Remind students to include important dates and explanations of why certain people, places, and events were important to German unification. Make photocopies of each group's outline to distribute to students in all the groups. **L2**

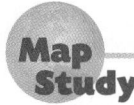

Map Study

Answer

to unite the eastern and western parts of Prussia

Map Skills Practice

Reading a Map To which central European country did a united Germany pose the biggest threat? *(Austria-Hungary)*

CURRICULUM CONNECTION

MILITARY HISTORY

In 1841 Johann Nikolas Dreyse designed the Prussian needle gun. Using this breech-loading rifle, the Prussian army defeated the Austrian army at the Battle of Sadowa in 1866 during the Seven Weeks' War. Lying down on the ground, Prussian soldiers outfired the standing Austrians who used muzzle-loading rifles.

Cultural Perspectives

German Dialects The German language has many dialects. When Germany was first united, speakers of Low German dialects had trouble understanding Swabians in southern Germany. Eastern Rhinelanders could not easily communicate with southwestern Saxons. In addition, minority groups spoke French, Lithuanian, Polish, and Danish.

ASSESS

Check for Understanding

Assign Section 2 Review as homework or as an in-class activity.

end the chance for a united Germany under Austrian control. In the end, Bismarck did not want to destroy Austria with a harsh peace settlement. He knew that he would probably need an alliance with Austria in the future.

The treaty ending the war was negotiated in the city of Prague. The settlement dissolved the German Confederation and gave Holstein to Prussia and Venetia to Italy. The treaty also called for "a new organization of Germany without the participation of Austria."

This "new organization" became the North German Confederation in 1867. It embraced all the German states north of the Main (MYN) River. The Confederation's constitution gave each state the right to manage its domestic affairs, but put foreign policy and national defense in the hands of Prussia. Legislative authority was vested in a federal council composed of representatives from the various governments and a diet, or assembly, elected by universal male suffrage.

The establishment of a strong confederation by Prussia made Bismarck a hero among German nationalists. Bismarck's work of uniting Germany, however, was not finished.

The Franco-Prussian War

The southern German states, which were largely Catholic, remained outside the new German confederation. Most of them feared Protestant Prussia's military strength and its control of Germany. The kingdoms of Bavaria and Württenberg (WUHR•tehm•BUHRG), in particular, steadfastly opposed German unification under Prussian rule. They would accept German unification only if Prussia gave up some of its authority in a united government. Prussia would not agree to this, however.

France posed the most serious obstacle to a united Germany. Napoleon III would not accept German unification unless France received some territory—its compensation for not joining Austria in the Seven Weeks' War. To resolve the situation, Bismarck again chose war.

Some historians believe that Bismarck was responsible for the Franco-Prussian War. In his memoirs, Bismarck had written that "a Franco-German [Prussian] war must take place before the construction of a united Germany could be realized." If Napoleon III had not wanted war as much as Bismarck, however, the war may never have taken place. Bismarck knew that he could not invade France without public support. Instead, he had to lure France into war, taking advantage of Napoleon III's weakness in foreign policy and of the French public's current anti-Prussian feeling.

Map Study Bismarck succeeded in unifying Germany in just 15 years. **Location** Why do you think it was important to Prussia to add northern Germany to its territory?

Bismarck's chance came in 1870 in connection with the Hohenzollern candidacy for the Spanish throne.

A revolution in 1868 had deposed Queen Isabella of Spain. The Spanish government offered the throne to Prince Leopold of Hohenzollern, a Catholic cousin of William I of Prussia. Fearing a Spanish-German alliance against France, Napoleon III protested the offer. William brushed aside this protest, but Leopold later voluntarily declined the throne.

In July 1870, France demanded a promise from William that a Hohenzollern would never sit on the Spanish throne. William, who was vacationing at the German resort of Ems, refused. In a telegram to Bismarck, he described the details of his meeting with the French ambassador. To make it appear that William had deliberately insulted the French envoy, Bismarck altered the Ems telegram and released it to the press. Newspaper coverage of the supposed insult enraged the French, leading Napoleon to declare war on Prussia.

The fighting began on July 19, 1870. Because they were more anti-French than anti-Prussian, the southern German states allied with Prussia. With the easy defeat of the French, Bismarck gained

MAKING CONNECTIONS ACTIVITY

Music and Literature Have students research and write brief reports on one of the following German composers or writers: Richard Wagner, Johannes Brahms, Gustav Mahler, Anton Bruckner, Friedrich Nietzsche, Gustav Freytag, Leopold von Ranke, or Heinrich von Treitschke. Ask students to include the major works and main ideas of the person chosen and to discuss the person's views about the unification of Germany. **L2**

History & Art *Otto von Bismarck* by Franz von Lenbach, Art History Museum, Vienna, Austria **Otto von Bismarck poses in military uniform with a Prussian helmet. He came from the Junker class of Prussia and supported a strong monarchy.** *What does Bismarck's style of dress reveal about the German Empire formed in 1871?*

support from all the German states for the unification of Germany under Prussian rule.

Formation of an Empire

On January 18, 1871, William I assumed the title of kaiser, or emperor, of a united Germany. He ruled over a domain that stretched from the Baltic sea in the north to the Alps in the south. Bismarck became the German chancellor, or chief minister.

The new empire united 25 German states into one federal union. Although each state had its own ruler, and some had their own armies and diplomatic staffs, the kaiser headed the national government. He had authority to make appointments, command the military in time of war, and determine foreign policy. Prussian Junkers now shared power with wealthy industrialists. Unification did not make Germany a model democratic state.

William's son, Crown Prince Frederick of Prussia, was a liberal and a supporter of reform. He deplored the means Bismarck used to bring about the unification of Germany. In his diary, he wrote of his despair: "We are no longer looked upon as the innocent victims of wrong, but rather as arrogant victors." While he foresaw many of the consequences of Bismarck's policies, Frederick did nothing to change them.

SECTION 2 REVIEW

Recall

1. **Define** realpolitik, kaiser, chancellor.
2. **Identify** William I, Otto von Bismarck.
3. **Locate** Schleswig and Holstein on the map on page 684. Why do you think the Danish king claimed Schleswig and not Holstein as a Danish province?

Critical Thinking

4. **Synthesizing Information** Imagine that you are a member of the Prussian assembly opposed to Bismarck's policy for German unification. What alternative policy would you have suggested to William I?

Understanding Themes

5. **Conflict** Compare Bismarck's methods for achieving the unification of Germany with Cavour's methods for bringing about the unification of Italy.

Chapter 26 Section 2

History & Art Fashionable parties in the German Empire were not complete without officers splendidly attired in imperial uniforms. Bismarck even wore his uniform in the parliament.
Answer to Caption: *It shows that the German Empire was founded on militaristic, authoritarian values.*

Use Student Self-Test and Review Software to review Section 2.

Evaluate

Section Quiz 26-2

Use the Testmaker to create a customized quiz for Section 2.

Reteach

Have students orally summarize material under each of the section's major headings.

Enrich

Have students write a brief essay on why the Junkers felt that Bismarck had betrayed his class by giving the industrial, business class a share in political power.

CLOSE

Have students discuss whether Germany could have been unified without war.

SECTION 2 REVIEW ANSWERS

1. All vocabulary words are defined in the Glossary.
2. William I, 682; Otto von Bismarck, 682
3. Schleswig is directly south of Denmark and part of the same peninsula. Holstein is more a part of the mainland.
4. Answers will vary but may include that offering people greater participation in government rather than threats of force might have gained their support for unification.
5. **CONFLICT** Both Cavour and Bismarck planned the unification of their respective countries; both used military means to achieve their objective; both used foreign help to achieve unification—although Bismarck relied more on his own Prussian army than on foreign troops.

Chapter 26
Section 3

SECTION THEME

▶ **Change** Bismarck's German Empire allows for economic growth but limits political freedoms.

Find Out

Answer: *Bismarck's policies left Germany militarily and economically strong but prevented the development of a parliamentary democracy. Also, the working class was disgruntled about poor working and living conditions.*

FOCUS

Section Objective

Analyze how Bismarck's policies affected the German Empire.

BELLRINGER Motivational Activity

Before taking roll at the beginning of the class period, project Section Focus Transparency 26-3 and have students answer the activity questions. Discuss students' responses.

This activity is also available as a blackline master.

Vocabulary Pre-check

Use Vocabulary Activity 26 to introduce vocabulary terms. **L1 LEP**

1870 1885 1900 1915

1872 Bismarck expels Jesuits from Germany.

1883 German government provides health insurance to workers.

1888 William II becomes emperor of Germany.

1913 Germany's standing army numbers more than 800,000 soldiers.

Section 3

Bismarck's Realm

Setting the Scene

▶ **Terms to Define**
papal infallibility, militarism

▶ **People to Meet**
Pope Pius IX, Ferdinand Lassalle, William II

Find Out How did Bismarck's policies affect the German Empire?

The Storyteller

Erich Klein's Uncle Karl enjoyed talking politics and was eager to explain the German political system to his American nephew. "Germany consists of twenty-six different states that were once independent but now are united. Each state has its own governmental officials and hereditary princes, but they are all subject to Kaiser [William] I." Erich remarked, "This government sounds similar to the United States." Uncle Karl agreed, but mentioned an important difference: "The Kaiser was not elected. He was acclaimed by the various princes who were willing to concede their power so that aristocracy by birth would remain within the German government."

—adapted from *Im Vaterland [In the Fatherland]*, Paul V. Bacon, 1910

Kaiser William I

Victory on the battlefield brought about Germany's political unity, but the Germans were not united as a people. Religious, economic, social, and political divisions remained. German leaders now had to encourage a sense of common purpose in the population.

Bismarck became the key figure in early German nation building. With the support of Kaiser William I, Bismarck took charge of policy in the German Empire. Over the years, he faced several direct challenges to the German nation-state and his own political authority.

Bismarck and the Church

One of the first challenges Bismarck faced was with the Catholic Church in the so-called Kulturkampf (kul•TUR•KAHMF), or cultural struggle, between Church and state. After German unification, Catholics in Germany organized the Center party to represent their interests in opposition to the predominantly Protestant Prussians.

Bismarck viewed Catholicism as an antinationalist force and consequently supported the Protestants in political affairs. In part, he was annoyed at the popularity of the Center party. He was also worried about an 1870 proclamation by Catholic bishops in Rome declaring **papal infallibility**—the doctrine that the pope, when speaking on matters of faith and morals, is infallible, or free from error.

Since the Jesuits, in Bismarck's eyes, were papal agents working to destroy the German Empire, the chancellor launched his campaign against the Church by expelling the Jesuits from Germany in 1872. One year later, the German legislature began passing a series of laws aimed at destroying Catholic influence in Germany. These so-called May Laws deprived Catholic bishops of much of their authority and even required that weddings be performed by secular officials. In response,

SECTION RESOURCES

Reproducible Masters
- Reproducible Lesson Plan 26-3
- Vocabulary Activity 26
- Guided Reading Activity 26-3
- Section Quiz 26-3

Transparencies
- Section Focus Transparency 26-3

Multimedia
- Student Self-Test and Review Software
- Testmaker

Pope Pius IX declared the laws invalid and broke diplomatic ties with Germany.

Bismarck soon realized that he was fighting a losing battle. Instead of weakening the Center party, Bismarck's repressive measures strengthened it. In the legislative elections of 1877, the Center party gained even more seats. Even the Junker-controlled Conservative party began to oppose Bismarck's policies. Knowing that he needed the support of the Center party to defeat a serious challenge from the Socialists, Bismarck sought to make peace with the Catholics.

When Pope Pius IX died in 1878, his successor, Leo XIII, made an effort to heal the rift with Germany. Eventually, the German legislature repealed most laws directed against Catholics. By 1881 the Kulturkampf was over.

Germany's Industrial Growth

Prior to unification, Germany was not a great industrial nation. Primarily agricultural, the German states lagged far behind Great Britain in the production of textiles, coal, iron, and steel. Knowing that Germany's position as a major political and military power depended on a strong economy, German political and business leaders worked to expand the nation's industry. By the mid-1800s, advances in many areas began to transform Germany's economy. The establishment of the *Zollverein* had already encouraged economic growth and spurred efforts to improve transportation. After unification, investment capital from Great Britain, France, and Belgium helped to modernize industrial production and establish a mechanized factory system.

The development of deep-pit coal mining in the provinces along the Rhine and the opening of new coal mines in the Saar made available large reserves of cheap fuel for the new plants. Cities grew rapidly. Many young men and women streamed in from the villages to work in the new factories. As a result, at the end of the 1800s, Germany finally became a major industrial power.

The economic changes sweeping Germany conferred on at least some of its people the highest standard of living in Europe. The middle class and the business leaders benefited enormously from the rapid industrialization of the country. Every improvement in factory machinery, however, resulted in lower wages and higher unemployment for many German workers. They lived in crowded, filthy tenements and toiled long hours under dangerous working conditions.

Visualizing History **Pope Leo XIII took a more conciliatory approach to new forms of secular government than did earlier popes.** *What effect did Leo's papacy have on church relations with Bismarck's Germany?*

Workers and Socialism

Poor wages, long workdays, and job uncertainty made German workers receptive to a more hopeful vision of the future. They looked forward to a democratic social order in which they would no longer be exploited. To help bring about this new order in Germany, **Ferdinand Lassalle**, a writer and labor leader, founded the Universal German Workingmen's Association in 1863. Although he called himself a Socialist and a disciple of Karl Marx, Lassalle did not preach revolution. Whereas Marx called for the workers of the world to revolt against capitalism, Lassalle advocated mass political action to change the system.

Lassalle was a national celebrity who knew Bismarck and lectured him on the workers' plight. He did not live long enough, however, to finish the fight, for he was killed in a duel in 1864. The party he founded grew slowly until it merged with the Social Democratic party in 1875 and became a major political force.

COOPERATIVE LEARNING ACTIVITY

Research Organize the class into five groups to research the reign of Kaiser William II. Have each group select one of the following topics to research: economic growth, William II and chancellors after Bismarck, the growth of the German navy, foreign affairs, and the rise of anti-Semitism. Ask each group to compile a written report of their research and to choose one group member to present the group's findings to the class. After all groups have given their reports, encourage students to compare Germany under William II with Germany under Bismarck. **L3**

Chapter 26
Section 3

TEACH

Guided Practice

THEME Change

Have students make two lists, one showing economic changes in the German Empire under Bismarck, the other showing social changes. **L1 LEP**

Visualizing History Although Leo XIII worked to reconcile with Germany, he continued to support the papacy's conservative political views, remaining opposed to freedom of speech, freedom of conscience, freedom of worship, and separation of church and state.

Answer to Caption: *Leo XIII worked to heal the rift between the papacy and Germany. German laws against Catholics were repealed and Kulturkampf ended by 1881.*

Religion Have students discuss the goals and outcome of Bismarck's Kulturkampf with the Catholic Church. **L2**

Cause and Effect Have students identify the causes and effects of the rise of socialism in the German Empire. **L3**

Independent Practice

Guided Reading Activity 26-3 **L1**

ASSESS

Check for Understanding

Assign Section 3 Review as homework or as an in-class activity.

Use Student Self-Test and Review Software to review Section 3.

TEACH

Tell students that to get Ludwig II to join the German Empire, Bismarck promised Bavaria its own post office and a separate peacetime army. Bismarck also had Ludwig send William I a letter inviting him to be emperor of Germany. Ludwig received the equivalent of $45,000 a year in exchange for the letter. **What do you think he spent the money on?** *(castles)* Within a week of being declared insane and losing his throne in 1886, Ludwig was found drowned in a lake near Neuschwanstein.

Linking Past and Present

Neuschwanstein Today nearly one million people tour Neuschwanstein each year. Many more people see a model of Ludwig's famous castle at the Disney theme parks. Cinderella's castle, the heart of Fantasyland, was patterned after Neuschwanstein.

Richmond Crawford, Jr.

Mad Ludwig's Castle

Ludwig II, King of Bavaria, ruled the independent German kingdom of Bavaria until 1871 and built for himself the storybook Neuschwanstein castle. He came to the throne unprepared to rule but enthusiastic about indulging his two passions: opera and palaces. Ludwig's castles were based on his romantic vision of the past. In each new mansion, rooms were decorated to look like scenes from the famous operas of nineteenth-century composer Richard Wagner. Ludwig's dreamy castles glorified and enshrined a bygone Germany. Ludwig's ministers, who had to find th cash to pay for his follies, finally had him declare insane and removed from power. Today his castle one of Germany's leading tourist attractions.

While Ludwig dreamed and listened to romanti operas, Count Otto von Bismarck set about unitin the German Confederation and creating a moder German nation through military strength. "The gre questions of the age," Bismarck once remarked, "ar not settled by speeches and majority votes ... but b iron and blood." ⊕

Bismarck and the Socialists

Despite his association with Lassalle, Bismarck believed that any Socialist party was out to change the government and that it therefore posed a serious threat to the German Empire. To destroy the Socialist movement in Germany, he set out to crush its organization. In 1878 the German legislature passed an anti-Socialist bill introduced by Bismarck. Although the bill did not outlaw the party itself, it banned all Socialist meetings and publications.

Bismarck's efforts to suppress the Socialists met with only temporary success. Consequently, Bismarck changed his tactics. He tried to show the workers that the government, and not the Socialists, had their true interests at heart. He directed the passage of several bills that gave workers some measure of comfort and security. In 1883, for example, the Sickness Insurance Law gave limited compensation to those who missed work because of illness. In 1889 the Old Age Insurance Law protected industrial workers in retirement.

Bismarck's reform efforts, however, did not go far enough to end the popularity of the Socialists. In 1890 the Social Democratic party won 35 seats in the legislature. With strong Socialist backing, the legislature refused to renew Bismarck's anti-Socialist law.

The Fall of Bismarck

In 1888 Kaiser William I died at the age of 91. Crown Prince Frederick, his liberal-minded son, succeeded him. Frederick III, however, died about 100 days after his coronation. **William II**, his son, succeeded him as emperor in 1888.

Only 29 years old at the time of his coronation, William II was a man of great energy and strong conservative opinions. Like his grandfather, William I, he favored **militarism**, or support for a powerful military prepared for war. His belief in the absolute authority of the emperor immediately brought him into conflict with Bismarck. Bismarck wanted the kaiser to leave political affairs to him.

Under William I, Bismarck often got his way by threatening to resign. When Bismarck offered his resignation in 1890, the kaiser accepted it. Much to Bismarck's surprise, William II "sent the veteran pilot over the side," as a popular cartoon of the time illustrated Bismarck's dismissal.

Bismarck's policies had left Germany strong, but they frustrated the German people. His strict rule prevented the development of a parliamentary democracy. With Bismarck gone, William II was free to pursue his own policies. During his reign Germany became one of the world's major industrial and military powers.

Visualizing History **After steering the German ship of state for thirty years, Bismarck resigned in 1890. This cartoon was published upon Bismarck's departure from office.** *What is the cartoon saying about Bismarck's relationship with Kaiser William II?*

SECTION 3 REVIEW

Recall

1. **Define** papal infallibility, militarism.
2. **Identify** Kulturkampf, Pope Pius IX, Ferdinand Lassalle, William II.
3. **List** the economic and technological advances that contributed to the growth of industry in Germany.

Critical Thinking

4. **Evaluating Information** Predict what might have happened if Frederick III had not died so soon after becoming kaiser.

Understanding Themes

5. **Change** What tactics did Bismarck use in his attempt to block challenges from Catholicism and the Socialist movement?

Chapter 26 Section 3

Visualizing History Tell students that after William II accepted Bismarck's resignation, William made Bismarck a duke, offered him a gift of cash, and sent Bismarck a portrait. Bismarck accepted the title and portrait but refused the money.

Answer to Caption: *Bismarck, the dignified elder statesman, is being dismissed by the young, upstart kaiser.*

Evaluate

Section Quiz 26-3

Use the Testmaker to create a customized quiz for Section 3.

Reteach

Have students make a chart that shows how Bismarck influenced political, economic, social, and religious developments in the German Empire.

Enrich

Have students write a brief essay on Bismarck's Kulturkampf, which includes their views of separation of church and state.

CLOSE

Have students discuss struggles Bismarck had with the legislature during his years as chancellor. *(Kulturkampf alienated many legislators; legislature refused to renew anti-Socialist laws introduced by Bismarck.)*

SECTION 3 REVIEW ANSWERS

1. All vocabulary words are defined in the Glossary.
2. Kulturkampf, 686; Pope Pius IX, 687; Ferdinand Lassalle, 687; William II, 689
3. the earlier establishment of the *Zollverein*; influx of investment capital from Britain, France, and Belgium; establishment of a modern factory system; the development of deep-pit coal mining along the Rhine; opening of new coal mines in the Saar; growth of cities
4. Answers may vary but should include that since Frederick was liberal-minded, he might have promoted liberal reforms.
5. CHANGE Bismarck expelled the Jesuits and deprived bishops of their authority, encouraged passage of anti-Catholic and anti-Socialist laws, and directed passage of laws that gave workers some measure of comfort and security as a way to blunt the Socialist challenge.

Chapter 26
Section 4

SECTION THEME

▶ **Reaction** Russian czars oppose the forces of liberalism and nationalism in the Russian Empire.

Find Out

Answer: *Few Russians were satisfied with the czars' halfway reforms. Students and intellectuals with strong ideals but little practical political experience espoused revolutionary and violent measures.*

FOCUS

Section Objective

Explain why revolutionary movements developed in Russia.

BELLRINGER
Motivational Activity

Before taking roll at the beginning of the class period, project Section Focus Transparency 26-4 and have students answer the activity questions. Discuss students' responses.

This activity is also available as a blackline master.

Vocabulary Pre-check

Use the Vocabulary PuzzleMaker to create a puzzle that reinforces the vocabulary terms in this section. **L1**

1815 — 1845 — 1875 — 1905

1825 The Decembrist uprising fails.

1855 Nicholas I dies.

c. 1870 Populist movement reaches out to peasants.

1905 Nicholas II issues the October Manifesto.

Section 4

Empire of the Czars

Setting the Scene

▶ **Terms to Define**
autocracy, emancipation, zemstvo, anarchy, nihilist, Russification, pogrom, soviet, duma

▶ **People to Meet**
Alexander I, Nicholas I, Alexander II, Nicholas II, Empress Alexandra, Mensheviks, Bolsheviks, Lenin

▶ **Places to Locate**
Poland, St. Petersburg

Find Out Why did revolutionary movements develop in Russia?

The Storyteller

Prince Peter Kropotkin, a student in the Corps of Pages for the sons of the aristocracy, went to the opera with his friends the evening after Czar Alexander proclaimed an end to serfdom. The students planned to sing the hymn "God Save the Czar," and expected that everyone would join them. When they arrived they found the band of the opera was already playing the hymn, which was drowned immediately in enthusiastic cheers from all parts of the hall. This night, Prince Kropotkin thought, was undoubtedly the czar's finest hour.

—adapted from *A Source Book for Russian History from Early Times to 1917*, reprinted in *Sources of World History*, Mark A. Kishlansky, 1995

Czar Alexander II

In the early 1800s the Russian Empire stretched from Europe to the Pacific Ocean. More than 60 nationalities, speaking over 100 different languages, populated this vast territory. Although Slavs, including Russians, comprised nearly two-thirds of the population, many other European, Middle Eastern, and Asiatic peoples lived within the empire.

The agricultural economy of the Russian Empire was more oppressive but not much more effective than it had been during the Middle Ages. Serfdom, long in decline in western Europe, still bound the peasants living and working in rural areas. As a result of this entrenched agricultural system, Russia's level of industrialization remained lower than that of western Europe.

As an **autocracy**, a government in which one person rules with unlimited authority, the political structure of the Russian Empire had also remained much as it was in the days of Peter the Great. The forces of reform, already at work in western Europe in the early 1800s, soon threatened this traditional economic and political order of the Russian Empire.

Autocracy on the Defensive

Alexander I, who ruled from 1801 to 1825, dreamed of improving Russia's system of government and even granted a constitution to Russian-ruled **Poland** for a brief period of time. Convinced by the Napoleonic Wars that he was the savior of Europe, Alexander soon lost his desire to improve social, political, and economic conditions within his country.

The Russian officers who fought in the Napoleonic Wars were impressed by the reforms they saw in western Europe. Many of these officers joined secret societies to discuss the need in their country for economic reform, for a constitutional government, and for freeing the serfs. In December

SECTION RESOURCES

Reproducible Masters
- Reproducible Lesson Plan 26-4
- Guided Reading Activity 26-4
- Geography and History Activity 26
- Section Quiz 26-4

Transparencies
- Section Focus Transparency 26-4

Multimedia
- Vocabulary PuzzleMaker Software
- Student Self-Test and Review Software
- Testmaker
- Turning Points in World History: *The Russian Revolution*

Russian Expansion 1801–1914

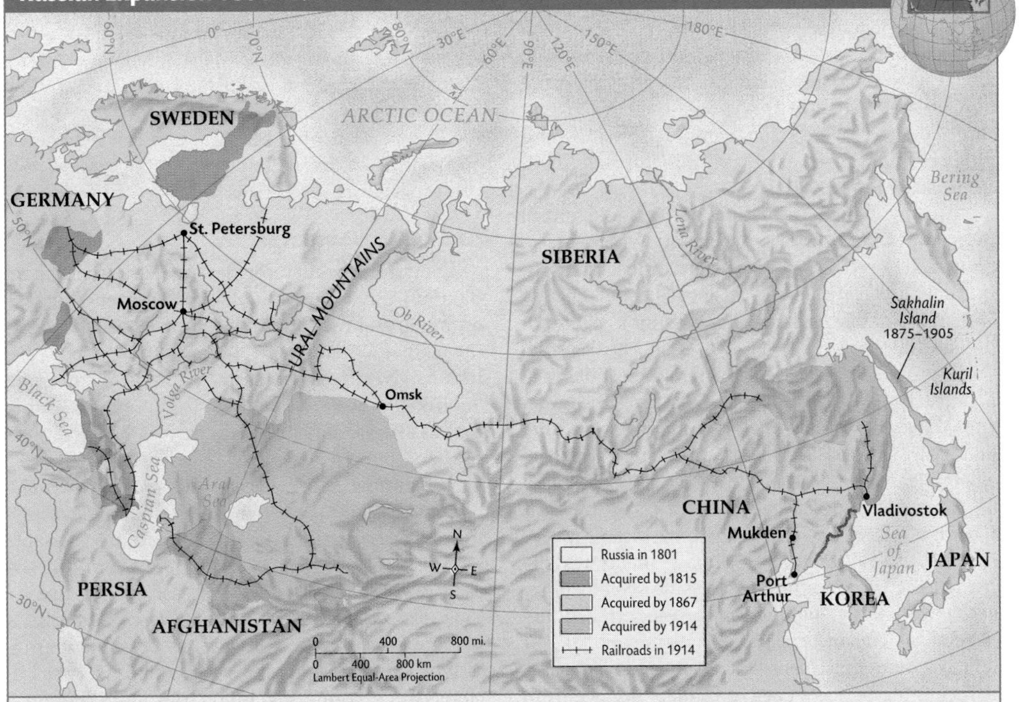

Map Study Russia expanded its borders in every direction between 1801 and 1914. **Region** How many different languages and nationalities were a part of Russia's vast territory?

1825, some of these officers took advantage of the uncertainty about the transfer of power after Alexander I's death and staged a military revolt.

Although the government quickly crushed the so-called Decembrist Revolt, the uprising had two very different effects. Its leaders were seen as martyrs and inspired later generations of revolutionaries. In the short term, however, the uprising hardened the determination of Alexander I's successor, **Nicholas I**, to strengthen the autocracy and suppress all opposition.

Under Nicholas I, the secret police had unlimited power to arrest and imprison people without trial and to censor the press. Despite Nicholas I's efforts to resist change, demands for reform persisted during the 1830s and 1840s. Russian losses in the Crimean War underscored the fact that the Russian Empire was in serious trouble. Nicholas, however, was too ill to begin any reforms. Following Nicholas I's death in 1855, his son **Alexander II** undertook the task of saving the autocracy and preventing a revolution.

Alexander II and Reforms

Russia's humiliating defeat in the Crimean War revealed the extent to which the nation lagged behind the other European powers militarily and economically. One major reason for Russia's backwardness was its system of serf labor. To progress, Russia needed to industrialize, but to industrialize, the factories needed a steady source of cheap labor. Only the serfs could provide this labor force, but they were not free to leave the land.

On March 3, 1861, Alexander II decreed the emancipation, or freeing, of the serfs. Although the serfs attained legal freedom, they received no land individually. Their village communities, called mirs, were granted varying amounts of the landlords' holdings, for which they had to undertake a 50-year mortgage. Peasants could not leave the mirs without paying their share, so they were still bound to the worst land and had an additional tax to pay. The landlords kept the best land and

Chapter 26 Section 4

TEACH

Guided Practice

THEME Reaction

Help students recall the definition of *reaction* as it applies to government and politics. *(a maintenance of or return to a former political or social order)* Have students discuss how this definition fits the Russian czars. *(The czars suppressed all opposition to the autocracy.)* **L1 LEP**

Map Study

Answer

People of 60 nationalities speaking 100 different languages lived in the Russian Empire.

Map Skills Practice

Reading a Map What does the heavy concentration of railroads in the western part of the empire indicate? *(That part of Russia was the most heavily populated, the most urban, and the most industrial.)*

Government Have students make a chart that shows the acts of reform and repression of Alexander I, Nicholas I, Alexander II, Alexander III, and Nicholas II. **L2**

Critical Thinking Have students compare the methods of Russia's anarchists, nihilists, Mensheviks, and Bolsheviks. Ask what goal all four groups had in common. *(ending the autocracy)* **L3**

COOPERATIVE LEARNING ACTIVITY

Panel Discussion Organize the class into five groups and have each group research the following groups of Russian society: the aristocracy, the landowners, the intellectuals, the urban workers, and the peasants. Have each group assemble a composite portrait of its class. Suggest that students include in their portraits the major characteristics, occupations, interests, and problems of the class. Have each group assign one of those topics to one or more group members to present in a panel discussion. After each group has presented its panel, encourage students to predict possible outcomes of these class differences for Russia. **L2**

Chapter 26
Section 4

VIDEODISC
Turning Points in World History

Side Two
Chapter 5

Title: *The Russian Revolution*
Ask: Why was the Russian Revolution a turning point in history? *(A Communist government was established.)*

Independent Practice

Guided Reading Activity 26-4 **L1**

Geography and History Activity 26

Religion Have students research and write a brief report on the Jewish pogroms of the nineteenth century and why the pogroms increased during this time. **L2**

Daily Life Have students research to write several journal entries from the point of view of a peasant after Alexander II emancipated the serfs. Suggest that students include information about daily life, such as food, clothing, housing, work, education, and recreation, as well as views on political and economic conditions in rural areas and the effect of the military draft on peasant families. **L3**

received compensation from the government for their losses.

Many peasants gave up farming rather than return to bondage. Landless peasants moved from the farms to the cities, adding to the growing numbers of unskilled urban workers. Their discontent revealed itself in occasional minor uprisings and produced new stirrings of revolutionary activity in the Russian Empire.

Because the emancipation decree took control of the provinces away from the landowners, it also created the need for a new system of local government. An 1864 law created this new system. Locally elected assemblies called **zemstvos** took charge of provincial matters such as schools and health care. Three groups could vote in zemstvo elections: the nobility, the wealthy townspeople, and the peasants. The vote was weighted, however, so that noblemen and rich taxpayers dominated the local assemblies.

Czar Alexander II became known as the Czar Liberator for freeing the serfs and for his many reforms. In addition to those already mentioned, he limited the use and authority of the secret police, eased restrictions on the press, modernized the judicial system, and expanded the educational system. Alexander also reorganized the Russian army, reducing the period of active military service from 25 years to 6 years.

Unfortunately, the reforms of Alexander II satisfied few Russians. The landowners had lost both land and power. The peasantry had made few economic gains. Conservatives feared weakening of the autocracy, while reformers pushed for even greater changes. Designed to stem discontent, the reforms failed to halt the growth of revolutionary movements.

Footnotes to History

A Sickly Prince
In 1904 Czar Nicholas II and Empress Alexandra finally had a son—an heir to the throne— after four girls. Tragically, Alexis suffered from hemophilia, an inherited disease preventing the normal clotting of blood. To ease her son's agonies, Alexandra relied on a mystic healer named Grigori Rasputin (ra•SPYOO•tuhn). Rasputin's apparent success in helping Alexis gave him great political influence over the czar. This in turn increased Nicholas's isolation from his people and the forces of change sweeping his empire.

Terror and Reaction

Among the most vocal critics of the Russian government during Alexander II's reign were intellectuals and students from the upper and middle classes. Although these reformers had strong ideals, they had little practical political experience and almost no direct contact with the Russian people, especially the peasants.

Radical Movements

Some radical reformers, such as Michael Bakunin, advocated **anarchy**, or the absence of government, and called for the complete destruction of the state, the family, law, property, and other institutions. **Nihilists** (from the Latin *nihil*, meaning "nothing") also rejected all traditions, believing that Russia would have to destroy the czarist autocracy and build a completely new society.

Beginning in the early 1870s, many reformers became active in a new movement known as populism. The populists believed that the peasants would eventually lead a revolution, overthrow the czar, and establish a socialist society. To further their cause, groups of students and intellectuals went to the villages to prepare the peasants for revolution. The peasants, however, often grew suspicious of the young revolutionaries and sometimes even turned them over to the police. Frustrated by their lack of success, many populists turned to violent tactics.

The most radical faction of the revolutionaries plotted the assassinations of key officials in order to frighten the government into making radical reforms. Beginning in 1866, revolutionaries made several attempts to assassinate Alexander II. Although Alexander insisted that these radicals be crushed, he eventually responded to popular pressure by drafting a plan to establish a national assembly. Before the plan could be enacted, however, a young revolutionary killed the czar with a bomb in 1881.

Alexander III

Alexander III, who succeeded his father, vowed to maintain the old order and crush revolutionaries. He warned that he would not tolerate a constitution and reduced the powers of the zemstvos. Reversing his father's reforms, he abolished autonomy in the schools, restored censorship of the press, and extended the powers of the secret police.

To protect the autocracy, Alexander III used a resurgence of nationalism to promote a policy of **Russification**. Designed as an attempt to unite the empire's many provinces, Russification instead

Global Gourmet

Russia Beef stroganoff, made of thinly sliced beef, onions, sour cream, and seasonings served with egg noodles, is a popular dish in Europe and the United States. It was created for Count Paul Stroganov, a liberal adviser of Alexander I.

MEETING SPECIAL NEEDS ACTIVITY

Learning Style: Visual/Spatial Have students who are visual learners research outside sources and then draw a picture depicting one of the following people in czarist Russia: a member of the imperial family, a wealthy landowner, a revolutionary intellectual, an urban worker, or a peasant. Suggest that students characterize the position of the person through clothing, hairstyle, facial expression, surroundings, and tools or equipment. Set aside space on a bulletin board for completed drawings. **L1 LEP**

Visualizing History **Moscow workers, students, and intellectuals fought czarist troops during the 1905 Revolution.** *How did the czarist government under Alexander III and Nicholas II deal with its opponents?*

became an official policy of intolerance and persecution of non-Russian peoples. Anyone who questioned the czar's authority, who spoke a language other than Russian, or who followed a religion other than Eastern Orthodoxy risked prosecution.

Russification singled out the Jews in particular for persecution. Government decrees deprived Jews of the right to own land and forced them to live in a certain area of the empire called the Pale. The government also encouraged bloody pogroms, or organized massacres of a minority group, in Jewish communities.

The Revolution of 1905

When Alexander III died in 1894, most Russians expected his son, **Nicholas II**, to pursue more liberal policies. Nicholas, however, continued his father's rigid defense of the autocracy. Nicholas, however, lacked the strong will needed to make absolute rule effective. He was easily influenced by those around him, particularly his wife, **Empress Alexandra**, whose chief aim was for her son to inherit an undiminished autocracy.

During the reign of Nicholas II, a revolutionary mood swept over Russia. Peasants grew increasingly dissatisfied; national minorities called for an end to persecution; and middle-class reformers pushed for a constitutional monarchy. At the same time, the emancipation of the serfs and rapid industrialization had resulted in a marked increase in the size of the urban working class. Russian factories at the turn of the century lacked proper lighting, ventilation, and sanitation. Workers toiled long hours for little pay and lived in terrible, overcrowded housing. Not surprisingly, then, urban workers joined the ranks of the dissatisfied.

Russian Marxists

By the early 1900s several revolutionary groups in Russia followed the teachings of Karl Marx. Their members believed that the working class, not the peasants, would lead the revolution. The **Mensheviks** believed that Russia needed to develop into an industrial state with a sizable working class before a socialist revolution could occur. The more radical **Bolsheviks**, led by Vladimir Ilyich Ulyanov—commonly known as **Lenin**—believed that a small party of professional revolutionaries

MAKING CONNECTIONS ACTIVITY

Literature Have students research and present an oral report on one of the following Russian writers: Aleksandr Pushkin, Mikhail Lermontov, Nikolay Gogol, Ivan Turgenev, Fyodor Dostoyevsky, or Leo Tolstoy. Ask students to include the following information in their reports: the writer's education and social, economic, and political background; titles of major works; how the writer portrayed Russian history and society in the works; and the writer's lasting impact on Russian culture. **L3**

Visualizing History In August 1905 the czar proposed to give peasants but not urban workers the right to vote for duma representatives. In response, urban workers and students led a general strike for 10 days in October that has been described as the most effective strike in history. **Why was this a successful strike?** *(The czar issued the October Manifesto making Russia a constitutional monarchy.)*

Answer to Caption: *It vowed to maintain the old order and cracked down on revolutionary opposition, extending the powers of the secret police.*

Who?What?Where?When?

Fabergé Eggs In the 1880s, Alexander III appointed Peter Carl Fabergé jeweler to the imperial court. Each Easter, Fabergé's workshop designed a special Easter egg for the czar to present to the czarina. These eggs, made of jewels and precious metals, opened to reveal a surprise, such as a miniature peacock or basket of flowers.

Linking Past and Present

Secret police have been known since Greek and Roman times. In 1825 the Russian czar established the first modern version of the secret police, giving them the power not only to arrest but also to try and to punish anyone who opposed the czar's power. From 1954 to 1991, the KGB was the Soviet Union's secret police, questioning and trying suspects and sending those with questionable loyalty to forced labor camps, psychiatric hospitals, and prisons. With the USSR's collapse, the KGB was disbanded.

Chapter 26 Section 4

ASSESS

Check for Understanding

Assign Section 4 Review as homework or as an in-class activity.

Use Student Self-Test and Review Software to review Section 4.

Evaluate

Section Quiz 26-4

Use the Testmaker to create a customized quiz for Section 4.

Reteach

Have students make an outline of Section 4 showing czarist reforms and reactions. Tell students to use the names of the five czars discussed in this section as the main headings for their outlines.

Enrich

Have students do further research and then write an essay about the events and outcome of the Revolution of 1905.

CLOSE

Have students draw evidence from Section 4 to support the following statement: Czarist reforms were incomplete, aroused opposition, and were always followed by reactionary measures.

could use force to bring about a socialist society in the near future.

Upheavals

War between Russia and Japan in 1904 over control of Manchuria furthered the Socialists' cause. Russian land forces suffered major setbacks, and a Russian fleet attempting to deliver supplies lost many ships in a Japanese attack. With the mediation of the United States, the war-exhausted empires finally concluded a peace agreement in 1905.

Russia's humiliating military performance heightened already mounting opposition to the czar's government by urban workers, middle-class thinkers, and peasants. The war had strained the Russian economy, raising food prices while keeping wages low.

Spontaneous strikes began to break out in many cities throughout the empire. On Sunday, January 22, 1905, about 200,000 workers marched in a peaceful procession to the czar's palace in **St. Petersburg** to present a petition for reform. Palace soldiers opened fire on the crowd, killing hundreds of workers. Bloody Sunday, as the demonstration was called, sparked riots and strikes in most industrial centers and set off a wave of political protests.

Middle-class organizations drew up programs for political reform. The zemstvos issued lists of demands. In the spring of 1905, the first **soviets**, or workers' councils, formed to voice workers' grievances. From all reformist and revolutionary groups came the cry for the establishment of a representative government elected by universal suffrage.

In October 1905, angry workers seized control of the major cities in a general strike. As disorder and violence in the cities and rural areas continued, Nicholas II announced a law providing for the election of a national **duma**, or legislature. The czar, however, proposed that the Duma serve as an advisory council rather than a genuine legislative body. Instead of appeasing the Russian people, the measure set off more nationwide strikes.

> AROUND THE WORLD
>
> **Slavery Is on Its Way Out**
>
> **Washington, D.C., 1863**
>
> **During the American Civil War, President Abraham Lincoln issued the Emancipation Proclamation that eventually led to the end of slavery in the United States. This historic document declared freedom for all enslaved people in the Confederacy—the states that were in rebellion against the Union. The Emancipation Proclamation strengthened the Union's war effort and made the war a fight against slavery. It also weakened the Confederacy by discouraging France and England from entering the war.**
>
> 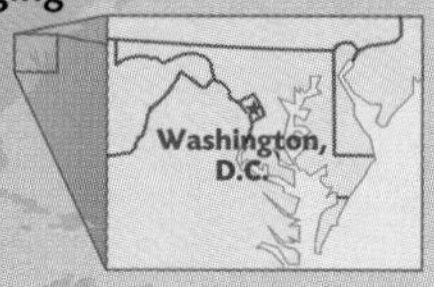
>

The events of October forced Nicholas to yield reluctantly to the demands of his people. The czar issued the October Manifesto, granting civil rights to citizens and allowing the Duma to make laws. In theory, Russia had become a constitutional monarchy; however, in practice, Nicholas continued to keep his powers. Stern measures to restore order, including pogroms against the Jews and the arrest of peasant and labor leaders, remained in place. When the Duma tried to act independently of the czar, Nicholas quickly dissolved it.

Nicholas II's ability to silence opposition was only temporary. Russia's many serious troubles had not been resolved. On the eve of World War I, growing numbers of peasants, workers, national minorities, and middle-class reformers supported an immediate end to the autocracy. Their demands and the stress of war would soon bring revolution to Russia.

SECTION 4 REVIEW

Recall

1. **Define** autocracy, emancipation, zemstvo, anarchy, nihilist, Russification, pogrom, soviet, duma.
2. **Identify** Alexander I, Nicholas I, Alexander II, Nicholas II, Empress Alexandra, Mensheviks, Bolsheviks, Lenin.
3. **Name** the two major Russian revolutionary groups that followed the teachings of Karl Marx, and explain the differences between the two.

Critical Thinking

4. **Applying Information** Select one of the Russian czars and tell how his policies affected the Russian Empire.

Understanding Themes

5. **Reaction** Why was effective reform difficult to achieve in Russia during the reign of Nicholas II?

SECTION 4 REVIEW ANSWERS

1. All vocabulary words are defined in the Glossary.
2. Alexander I, 690; Nicholas I, 691; Alexander II, 691; Nicholas II, 693; Empress Alexandra, 693; Mensheviks, 693; Bolsheviks, 693; Lenin, 693
3. Mensheviks and Bolsheviks: The Mensheviks believed that a revolution would take place when Russia was industrialized and had a large working class. The Bolsheviks believed that a small revolutionary party using force could bring about a socialist society.
4. Answers may vary but should include both the reforms and reactionary measures.
5. **REACTION** Answers may vary but should include that Nicholas II gave in to reforms only when he was forced to but remained determined to maintain his power and the autocracy of the czars.

1855 — 1875 — 1895 — 1915

1867 Austria and Hungary form a dual monarchy.

1878 Congress of Berlin settles Russo-Turkish War.

1913 Treaty of Bucharest ends Balkan conflict.

Section 5

Austria-Hungary's Decline

Setting the Scene

▶ **Terms to Define**
dual monarchy, jingoism

▶ **People to Meet**
Francis Joseph, Francis Deak

▶ **Places to Locate**
Austria, Vienna, Hungary, Bohemia, Moravia, Serbia, Bulgaria, Romania, Montenegro, Bosnia and Herzegovina

Find Out How did the growth of nationalistic feelings affect the empire of Austria-Hungary?

The Storyteller

Josef Heismann knew that the army was edgy. Once a powerful force, Austria was now regarded as second-rate. Inflammatory newspaper articles called for Austria to annex Bosnia, Serbia, and other Slav republics. Josef read an army newspaper article calling for an immediate invasion: "On us depends the future of our Empire. If we return victorious, we shall not only have conquered a foreign land: we shall have won back Austrian self-respect, given new life to the Imperial idea and vanquished … the enemy in our midst."

—adapted from *The Origins of World War I*, Roger Parkinson, 1970

Austrian soldiers of the 1860s

In the early 1800s, in addition to Russia and the Ottoman Empire, there was a third dominant power in eastern Europe: **Austria**. The Austrian Empire at this time contained more than 12 different national groups, including the Germans of Austria and the Magyars of Hungary.

Like Russia, Austria lacked national and geographical unity. Also as in Russia, life in Austria remained almost feudal at the beginning of the 1800s. A powerful landed nobility controlled a large peasant population and resisted any change in the old agricultural system. Through strict censorship and the arrest and intimidation of protesters, the government sought to stem the forces of nationalism and revolution sweeping through Europe.

The Revolution of 1848

As you learned in Chapter 22, the principal political figure in Austria during the early 1800s was Prince Klemens von Metternich, who held the office of minister of foreign affairs from 1809 to 1848. Metternich believed that democratic and nationalist movements would destroy the Austrian Empire and threaten peace in Europe. As a result, Metternich worked to crush all revolutionary activity, both within and outside the empire.

Despite Metternich's conservative policies, however, the revolutionary movement that had begun in France in 1848 spread to Austria the same year. Throughout the empire, nationalist groups demanded freedom of speech and press, peasant relief from feudal dues, and a representative government. The Austrian Empire seemed on the verge of collapse.

The tide of revolutionary activity was to turn once more, however. Infighting among nationalist groups and within radical factions with different

Chapter 26
Section 5

SECTION THEME

▶ **Diversity** The large empire of Austria-Hungary contains many different nationalities seeking self-rule.

Find Out

Answer: *The growth of nationalistic feelings led to infighting among the various national groups and eventually to the restoration of conservative government as a reaction.*

FOCUS

Section Objective

Describe how the growth of nationalistic feelings affected the empire of Austria-Hungary.

BELLRINGER
Motivational Activity

Before taking roll at the beginning of the class period, project Section Focus Transparency 26-5 and have students answer the activity questions. Discuss students' responses.

This activity is also available as a blackline master.

Vocabulary Pre-check

Use Vocabulary Activity 26 to introduce vocabulary terms. **L1 LEP**

SECTION RESOURCES

Reproducible Masters
- Reproducible Lesson Plan 26-5
- Vocabulary Activity 26
- Guided Reading Activity 26-5
- Reteaching Activity 26
- Enrichment Activity 26
- Section Quiz 26-5
- Performance Assessment Activity 26
- Spanish Chapter Summary 26

Transparencies
- Section Focus Transparency 26-5
- Mapping History Overlay Transparency 17, *Revolutionary Centers in Europe 1820–1848*

Multimedia
- Student Self-Test and Review Software
- Testmaker

TEACH

Guided Practice

THEME Diversity

Have students list the national groups that were part of Austria-Hungary by 1914. **L1 LEP**

Geography: Regions Have students use the map on page 697 to name the areas that bordered the Austro-Hungarian Empire. *(Germany, Russia, Romania, Serbia, Montenegro, Italy, Switzerland)* Have students discuss how cultural ties between these neighbors and ethnic groups within Austria-Hungary could threaten the coherence of the empire. **L2**

Analyzing Information Have students explain how the Congress of Berlin and the Treaty of Bucharest set the stage for further conflict in the Balkans. **L3**

Mapping History Overlay Transparency 17, *Revolutionary Centers in Europe 1820–1848*

Visualizing History Although Francis Joseph was both an emperor and a king, he has been described as being at heart "a simple soul with Spartan tastes." Francis Joseph was usually painted wearing the white jacket and red trousers of the Austrian army.

Answer to Caption: *the transformation of Austria-Hungary into a dual monarchy, with Hungary as an independent kingdom on an equal level with Austria*

political ideas enabled conservative forces to strike back. In **Vienna**, for example, conflict between middle-class moderates who wanted to reform the political system and radical workers who wanted to overthrow it weakened the revolutionary movement. By October 1848, the government once more occupied the capital. When Emperor Francis Ferdinand resigned his throne, his nephew, **Francis Joseph**, became emperor at the age of 18.

Francis Joseph moved quickly to restore the conservative order. He dissolved the revolutionary assembly and rejected the new constitution. Although threatened, the old regime had managed to withstand revolutionary change by playing one nationalist faction against another.

Throughout his 68-year reign, Francis Joseph struggled to maintain a unified empire. Neither repressive measures nor reforms, however, helped ease the nationalist tensions that threatened Austria. At the same time, a series of foreign crises further weakened the empire. In 1859 Austria was forced to give up the Italian province of Lombardy. Then in 1866, during the Seven Weeks' War with Prussia, Austria lost its influence over its German states as well.

The Dual Monarchy

Francis Joseph's efforts to strengthen his authority were most effectively challenged by the Magyars of **Hungary**. After Austria's defeat in the Seven Weeks' War, Francis Joseph sought a compromise with Hungary. Hungary agreed to this compromise because it seemed the only way to preserve its own national existence.

Soon after the Seven Weeks' War, Francis Joseph sent for **Francis Deak**, the Hungarian leader, and asked him what the people of Hungary wanted. When Deak answered that they wanted their rights, the emperor is said to have replied, "I suppose it must be as you insist."

After months of negotiations, Austria and Hungary finally reached an agreement in 1867. The *Ausgleich* (OWS•glyk), or Compromise, restored Hungary's independence and divided the Austrian Empire into a **dual monarchy**: the empire of Austria and the kingdom of Hungary. Francis Joseph remained ruler of both areas. He kept his title as emperor of Austria, and the Hungarians crowned him king of Hungary.

In addition to sharing a monarch, the two states had common ministries of foreign affairs, war, and finance. A system of committees handled other matters of mutual concern. In internal affairs, however, Austria and Hungary were completely independent of each other. Each had its own constitution, prime minister, and parliament.

While Austria and Hungary were independent politically, they were dependent on each other economically. Industrialized Austria supplied manufactured goods for the peoples of the dual

Visualizing History **Francis Joseph ruled the Austrian Empire for 68 years. When he came to the throne in 1848, Europe was in the midst of revolutions. When he died in 1916, Europe was in the midst of World War I.** *What change did Francis Joseph agree to in 1867 in order to save his empire?*

696 Chapter 26 *Reaction and Nationalism*

COOPERATIVE LEARNING ACTIVITY

Fact File Organize the class into groups of two or three students to research and prepare fact files on the following ethnic groups in the Austro-Hungarian Empire: Germans, Magyars, Italians, Romanians, Czechs, Serbs, Croatians, Slovaks, Poles, Slovenes, and Ukrainians. Have each group gather information on the culture, language, religion, traditions, national dress, and political goals of one ethnic group. Tell students to organize this information on no more than two sheets of paper. Choose a few students to compile each group's information into a "Fact File on Ethnic Groups in Austria-Hungary." Make the Fact File available to the class as a source of information. **L1**

monarchy. Agricultural Hungary supplied food products. Their cooperation, however, was not without conflict. Disputes inevitably developed between Austria and Hungary over foreign trade, tariffs, and currency.

During the mid-1800s, Austrian industrial growth had been slow. After the creation of the dual monarchy, however, the empire's production of coal, iron, steel, and manufactured goods grew rapidly. The territories of **Bohemia** and **Moravia** became the empire's leading industrial centers, producing machine tools, textiles, armaments, shoes, and chemicals. The concentration of industry in Bohemia and Moravia caused a more rapid urbanization in those areas.

Peoples of Austria-Hungary 1914

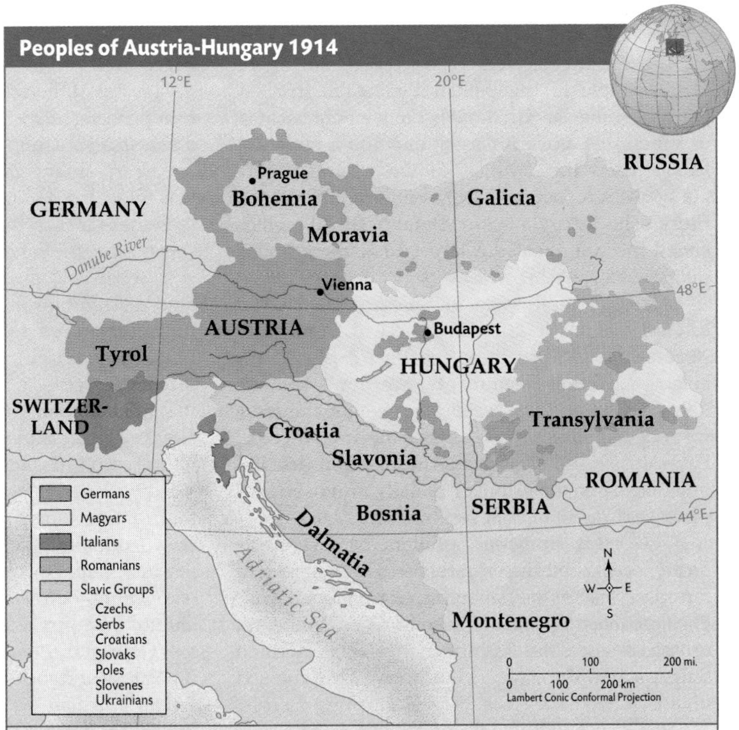

Map Study Although Germans held the dominant position in Austria-Hungary in 1914, they still made up less than one-half of the total population. **Place** What was the social and political status of the many Slavic peoples who lived in Austria-Hungary?

The dual monarchy was satisfactory to both the Austrian-Germans, who maintained power in Austria, and the Magyars, who controlled Hungary. Other nationalities remained discontented. Three-fifths of the population of Austria-Hungary were Slavs—Poles, Czechs, Slovaks, Serbs, and Bosnians— who had no voice in the government. Many Slavic nationalist groups dreamed of breaking free from the Austro-Hungarian Empire and forming a large Slav kingdom. Their discontent became a threat to the empire's unity.

Powder Keg in the Balkans

By the mid-1800s, the Ottoman Empire had declined to a weakened and diminished state. In 1829 Greece won its independence. By 1850 the Ottomans had lost the provinces of Moldavia and Wallachia to Russia and Algeria to France. In addition, Egypt, Arabia, and several Balkan territories had gained their autonomy.

Foreign powers watched the decline of the Ottoman Empire closely. Austria hoped to expand into the Balkan region. France sought to protect persecuted Catholics within the empire. Great Britain feared disruption of its Mediterranean trade. The primary objective of these foreign powers, though, was to prevent Russian expansion into the region. "We have a sick man on our hands," declared Czar Nicholas I, referring to Turkey, and Russia stood ready to contribute to its final collapse.

During the Crimean War, from 1854 to 1856, France, Great Britain, and Sardinia helped defend the Ottoman Empire against Russia's advances. Although the Ottoman allies defeated Russia in this war, the empire continued to lose power and territory. In 1875 nationalists in the Balkan states of **Serbia**, **Bulgaria**, and **Romania** rose up in revolt, demanding immediate independence from Turkey. The Turks brutally suppressed these revolts with widespread massacres.

MEETING SPECIAL NEEDS ACTIVITY

Learning Style: Visual/Spatial To help students better visualize the location of ethnic groups in the Austro-Hungarian and Ottoman Empires, have them work in pairs using a historical atlas to draw a map of these areas. Ask students to label the map with the ethnic groups. Then have students compare their maps with a map of present-day Europe. Help students identify the countries in which these ethnic groups now live. **L2 LEP**

Map Study

Answer

They had no voice in their government.

Map Skills Practice

Reading a Map Which nationality group lived throughout Austria-Hungary? *(the Germans)*

Independent Practice

Guided Reading Activity 26-5 **L1**

Multicultural Have students research and write a brief history on one of the following ethnic groups from early times through the present: Magyars, Romanians, Serbs, Croatians, Bosnians, Poles, Lithuanians, Slovaks, Bohemians, Moravians, or Slovenes. **L2**

Global Gourmet

Hungary Hungary's first people, the Magyars, were nomads. As such they needed food that traveled well without spoiling. *Gulyás*, cubes of seasoned, cooked, dried meat added to hot water and any local vegetables, became an instant soup or stew. Today the ingredients in *gulyás*, or goulash, are fresh.

ASSESS

Check for Understanding

Assign Section 5 Review as homework or as an in-class activity.

Use Student Self-Test and Review Software to review Section 5.

Chapter 26 Section 5

Linking Past and Present

Ethnic Cleansing From the 1890s to the 1920s, Ottoman Turk rulers led massacres to suppress the Christian Armenians. During this time more than one million Armenians died. In the 1990s, Bosnian Serbs who followed Orthodox Christianity led a similar program of "ethnic cleansing" against the Muslims who lived in Bosnia.

Evaluate

Section Quiz 26-5

Use the Testmaker to create a customized quiz for Section 5.

Reteach

Have students make a time line from 1848 to 1913 of major events covered in Section 5.

Reteaching Activity 26

Enrich

Have students redraw the map on page 697 to show how they would have divided Austria-Hungary into independent countries based on nationality.

Enrichment Activity 26

CLOSE

Have students discuss why the Balkans were called "the powder keg of Europe."

The Congress of Berlin

In 1877 Russia went to war on behalf of the Slavic people in the Balkan Peninsula. Publicly embracing the Slavic nationalist movement because it suited the government's imperial ambitions, Russia used the conflict known as the Russo-Turkish War to justify its expansion into Balkan territory. The Treaty of San Stefano (1878), which ended the war, created a large Russian-controlled Bulgarian state.

As news of Russian victories reached Great Britain, the public cried out for war. A popular slogan in Great Britain at the time captured the heightened public sentiment: "We don't want to fight, but by jingo, if we do, we've got the men, we've got the ships, we've got the money, too." From this slogan came the term jingoism, used to describe extreme patriotism, usually provoked by a perceived foreign threat.

The great European powers protested the Treaty of San Stefano. In the end a congress of European leaders met in Berlin, Germany, to revise it. At the meeting, which began in June 1878, representatives of the European powers divided Bulgaria into three parts, one of which remained under Ottoman rule. Neighboring Serbia, **Montenegro**, and Romania, on the other hand, won their complete independence. Britain gained control of Cyprus, and Austria-Hungary won the Balkan provinces of **Bosnia and Herzegovina**.

The Congress of Berlin satisfied few. Russia lost its war gains, and the Ottoman Empire lost much of its European territory. In addition, the congress dealt with the Balkan states inequitably, granting independence for some, but not all, of the people of any given nationality.

Balkan Conflict

By 1912 the Balkan states had joined forces and moved to free members of their respective nationalities from Ottoman rule. Encouraged by Italy's easy victory over the Turks in North Africa, the Balkan League—consisting of Bulgaria, Greece, Montenegro, and Serbia—declared war on Turkey in 1912. As a result of the war, the Ottomans lost all of their European territory with the exception of Istanbul and a small surrounding area.

Unity among members of the Balkan League was short-lived. No sooner had the Balkan states won the war than they began to fight among themselves over the lands they had gained. Before the war, Serbia and Bulgaria had secretly arranged for land distribution in case of victory. After the war, Bulgaria refused to go along with the plan. The Bulgarians did not want to give up territory won directly in battle.

To keep their land, the Bulgarians in June 1913 attacked Greek and Serb forces in the disputed area. In this second Balkan War, Montenegro and Greece sided with Serbia against Bulgaria. Romania joined the fighting when it saw the opportunity to win land from Bulgaria. The Balkan conflict brought new hope to the Ottomans. Seeing the chance to recover its own lost European territory, the Ottoman Empire attacked Bulgaria.

The fighting ended in 1913 with the Treaty of Bucharest, and the disputed land was redistributed. Bulgaria, which lost the war, surrendered much of the land it had won from the Ottomans in the previous Balkan conflict.

The Treaty of Bucharest did not bring lasting peace to the Balkans. Serbia's increased power encouraged nationalism among Slavs and threatened Austria-Hungary. Russia, in supporting the pan-Slavic movement, sought to extend its own influence in the Balkans. The French, British, and German governments tried to preserve the existing balance of power to prevent either Austria-Hungary or Russia from gaining greater influence in the area. It is not difficult to see why writers of the time called the Balkans "the powder keg of Europe." It seemed inevitable that events in the Balkans would sooner or later explode into a major European war.

SECTION 5 REVIEW

Recall

1. **Define** dual monarchy, jingoism.
2. **Identify** Francis Joseph, Francis Deak, the Congress of Berlin.
3. **List** two ways in which Austria and Hungary were dependent upon each other in the dual monarchy. List two ways they were independent of each other.

Critical Thinking

4. **Analyzing Information** How did Austria-Hungary and Russia differ from the Balkan countries in their reasons for intervening in the Ottoman Empire's problems?

Understanding Themes

5. **Diversity** Explain how ethnic diversity contributed to the decline of Austria-Hungary. Could this decline have been avoided? Why or why not?

SECTION 5 REVIEW ANSWERS

1. All vocabulary words are defined in the Glossary.
2. Francis Joseph, 696; Francis Deak, 696; Congress of Berlin, 698
3. Austria and Hungary were dependent on each other in matters of foreign affairs and finance; they were independent in internal affairs, and each had its own constitution, prime minister, and parliament.
4. The Balkan countries wanted to win independence from the Ottoman Empire. Austria-Hungary and Russia wanted to expand their control into the Balkans.
5. DIVERSITY Answers will vary but should include that the many ethnic groups in the empire had more allegiance to their own group than to the empire. Because nationalism was spreading across Europe, the Austrian Empire's decline probably could not have been avoided.

Study and Writing
SKILLS

Selecting and Using Research Sources

You have to write a report, so you head off to the library. There you are surrounded by bookshelves filled with books. Where do you begin?

Learning the Skill

Libraries contain many kinds of research sources. Understanding the content and purpose of each type will help you find relevant information more efficiently. Here are brief descriptions of important sources:

Reference Books Reference books include encyclopedias, biographical dictionaries, atlases, and almanacs.

An encyclopedia is a set of books with short articles on many subjects arranged alphabetically. General encyclopedias present a wide range of topics, while specialized encyclopedias have articles on a theme—i.e., an encyclopedia of music.

A biographical dictionary provides brief biographies listed alphabetically by last names. Each biography gives data such as the person's place and date of birth, occupation, and achievements.

An atlas is a collection of maps and charts for locating geographical features and places. An atlas can be general or thematic. An atlas contains an alphabetical index of place names that directs you to the map(s) where that place appears.

An almanac is an annually updated reference that provides current statistics together with historical information on a wide range of subjects.

Card Catalog The library's catalog, on computer or cards, lists every book in the library. Search for books by author, title, or subject. Each listing gives the book's call number and location. Computer catalogs also show whether the book is currently available.

Many libraries have joined networks. A library network usually has a single computer catalog listing all the books in the network. A patron can borrow any book in the system. Find out whether your library is part of a network.

Periodical Guides A periodical guide is a set of books listing topics covered in magazine and newspaper articles.

Computer Databases Computer databases provide collections of information organized for rapid search and retrieval.

If you have trouble finding the needed information, ask the librarian for help.

Practicing the Skill

Suppose you are going to Germany and want to learn more about the country before you go. Read the research questions below. Then decide which of the following sources you would use to answer each question and why.

a. encyclopedia
b. atlas
c. historical atlas
d. almanac
e. biographical dictionary
f. catalog entry: Germany—travel
g. catalog entry: Germany—modern history
h. periodical guide

1. Where is each city on the trip itinerary located?
2. What are the places of interest in each city?
3. What have been the major events in German history since 1800?
4. What political issues face Germany today?

Applying the Skill

Use research resources from your school or local library to research the following topic:

What medical treatment was given to Czarevitch Alexis, son of Nicholas II and Alexandra? How has medical care of hemophiliacs improved since 1910? List your sources.

For More Practice

Turn to the Skill Practice in the Chapter Review on page 701 for more practice in selecting and using research sources.

Study and Writing
SKILLS

TEACH

Selecting and Using Research Sources Make arrangements with the director of the school's resource center to have the class use the center to review various kinds of research sources: general and specialized encyclopedias, atlases, dictionaries, almanacs, periodical guides, the card catalog, and computerized databases such as Infotrak. Organize the class into several groups. Have each group familiarize itself with one of the above kinds of sources. Have each group describe to the class how to use the source and the kinds of information that can be found in that source. Then have students read the skill and complete the practice questions.

Additional Practice

Skill Reinforcement Activity 26

Writer's Guidebook, Lesson 9

ANSWERS TO PRACTICING THE SKILL

1. atlas; provides collection of maps
2. catalog entry: Germany—travel; entry deals with travel in Germany
3. encyclopedia; provides information on many subjects; catalog entry: Germany—modern history
4. periodical guide; lists article topics covered in current magazines and newspapers

CHAPTER 26 REVIEW

Historical Significance

The forces of nationalism changed the map of Europe dramatically in the 1800s. In the 1860s, the independent states on the Italian Peninsula united into the nation of Italy. About 10 years later, a loose confederation of states in the heart of Europe became the modern nation of Germany.

Nationalism, however, weakened the Austrian Empire, where various ethnic groups wanted independence. Nationalist tensions increased throughout Europe during the late 1800s and early 1900s. They pushed European nations closer to an all-out war.

Using Key Terms

Write the key term that completes each sentence.

a. anarchy
b. duma
c. jingoism
d. nationalism
e. Russification
f. autocracy
g. dual monarchy
h. nihilists
i. kaiser
j. pogroms
k. emancipation
l. zemstvo

1. In March 1861, Czar Alexander II decreed the __________, or freeing, of the serfs.
2. In the 1800s some radical reformers in Russia called for __________, the complete destruction of the government, the family, law, property, and other institutions.
3. In 1867 Austria and Hungary reached an agreement to transform the Austrian Empire into a ____________, consisting of two separate but interrelated kingdoms.
4. After the unification of the German states, Prussia's King William I assumed the title of __________, or emperor.
5. During the 1800s the Russian Empire was an __________, a government in which one person rules with unlimited authority.
6. __________ is the desire for national independence.
7. Among Russian revolutionaries, the _________ rejected all traditions, believing that Russia would have to completely build a new society.
8. The term __________ describes an extreme form of patriotism, usually caused by a perceived foreign threat.
9. The Russian government encouraged bloody ______, or organized massacres, in Jewish communities of the Russian Empire.
10. To protect his throne, Czar Alexander III used nationalism to promote a policy of ______.

Using Your History Journal

Read two or three recent news magazine reports on Bosnia and Herzegovina. Write an essay about how to achieve lasting peace in the Balkans.

Reviewing Facts

1. **Explain** how Sardinia gained control of the Italian struggle for unification.
2. **Identify** the leaders of Italy's unification movement.
3. **Describe** the *Zollverein*. How did it help Prussia gain leadership of the German Confederation?
4. **List** the challenges that faced the new German state.
5. **Explain** why the reforms of Alexander II satisfied few Russians.
6. **State** what interests foreign powers had in the Balkans.

Critical Thinking

1. **Apply** How did foreign powers help Italians achieve independence?
2. **Contrast** How did the problems that Italy faced after unification differ from the problems that Germany faced?
3. **Synthesize** Why do you think Austria agreed to the compromise with Hungary that established the dual monarchy?
4. **Evaluate** What do you think might have happened if Russia's Czar Nicholas II had given the Duma full legislative power?

Chapter 26 Review

GLENCOE TECHNOLOGY

VIDEODISC

Use MindJogger to review students' knowledge of the chapter.

MindJogger Videoquiz

Chapter 26
Disc 4 Side A

Also available in VHS.

Answers

Using Key Terms

1. k	6. d
2. a	7. h
3. g	8. c
4. i	9. j
5. f	10. e

Using Your History Journal

Suggest that students use the encyclopedia to gain an understanding of the history of the conflict in Bosnia.

Reviewing Facts

1. After the events of 1848, Italian nationalists lost faith in Mazzini and turned to the king of Sardinia, respected for his brave stand against the Austrians, to lead the struggle for unification.
2. Mazzini, Cavour, Victor Emmanuel II, Garibaldi
3. The *Zollverein* was an economic union that established a uniform tariff among the German states. Because Prussia formed the *Zollverein* and was the largest of the German states, Prussia was able to outmaneuver Austria.
4. economic, social, religious, political, and cultural divisions
5. Landowners lost land and power; peasants made few gains; conservatives feared autocracy was weakened; reformers wanted greater reforms.
6. Austria and Russia hoped to expand into the Balkans; France sought to protect Catholics in the Ottoman Empire; Britain wanted to protect its Mediterranean trade.

Critical Thinking

1. Britain and France recognized Italy's sovereignty because Italy supported them in the Crimean War; France agreed to help the Italians expel Austria from the peninsula; Prussia agreed to give Italy Venetia for Italy's help in defeating Austria in the Seven Weeks' War.
2. Germany faced divisions based on religion and dialects; Italy was threatened by former rulers of the Italian states and Austria still controlled some Italian land.
3. After losing the Seven Weeks' War, Austria

700 Chapter 26 *Reaction and Nationalism*

Geography in History

1. **Place** In what two areas was most of the fighting during the Russo-Japanese War?
2. **Movement** Across what three bodies of water were Japanese troops transported to the war zone?
3. **Movement** What railway helped in moving Japanese forces north to Mukden?
4. **Region** What effect did Russia's setback in this region have on the czar's government?

Russo–Japanese War

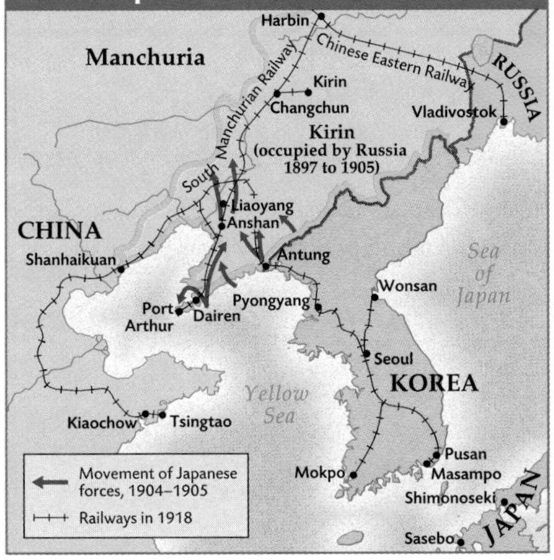

Understanding Themes

1. **Nationalism** How did the rise of nationalism spur the unification movement in Italy?
2. **Conflict** How did Bismarck promote his goal of German unification?
3. **Change** What changes came to Germany's economy after unification?
4. **Reaction** How did the policies of Alexander II differ from those of Alexander III in dealing with mounting opposition to autocracy?
5. **Diversity** How did the great diversity of nationalities in the Austrian Empire lead to the establishment of the dual monarchy in the mid-1800s?

Linking Past and Present

1. Bismarck had the difficult task of forging a strong, united German nation. What problems did he face? What problems have confronted German leaders since the early 1990s in reuniting Germany today after nearly 50 years of division into Communist and democratic areas?
2. Alexander III carried out a policy of Russification that led to intolerance and persecution of non-Russian groups in the Russian Empire. Are similar policies carried out today in Russia and the other countries of the former Soviet Union? Explain your answer.

Skill Practice

For each research question below, decide which of these sources would provide relevant information.

a. encyclopedia
b. atlas
c. historical atlas
d. almanac
e. biographical dictionary
f. catalog entry: European history 19th century
g. catalog entry: nationalism
h. periodical guide

1. How have the borders of the countries discussed in Chapter 26 changed since World War I?
2. What are the latest population statistics for Germany, Italy, Austria, Hungary, and Russia?
3. What were Otto von Bismarck's greatest accomplishments?
4. What nationalist struggles have occurred in Europe in the last decade?

Chapter 26 Review

was in a weakened bargaining position
4. Russia might have evolved into a constitutional monarchy.

Geography in History
1. along the coast of the Yellow Sea; along the South Manchurian Railway
2. Sea of Japan, Yellow Sea
3. South Manchurian Railway
4. It weakened the government.

Understanding Themes
1. **NATIONALISM** caused the Italian people to move toward independence from foreign countries and to unite the Italian states into one country
2. **CONFLICT** He carried out a policy of realpolitik, using a combination of war and diplomacy to advance the interests of the Prussian state.
3. **CHANGE** Germany developed a strong and prosperous industrial economy.
4. **REACTION** Alexander II allowed reforms such as emancipation of the serfs, the creation of zemstvos, and an improved legal system; Alexander III rigidly resisted any reforms, cracked down on dissent, and imposed a harsh policy of Russification.
5. **DIVERSITY** The nationalist movements of the empire's many ethnic groups had left Austria in a weakened position. When the Magyars in Hungary asked for greater independence, Francis Joseph agreed to the dual monarchy.

Linking Past and Present
1. Bismarck faced problems with the Catholic Church and Socialists. Since 1990, Germany has faced economic differences between former East and West Germans and has had to protect foreign minority workers.
2. yes; Russia's move against the Chechen independence movement

Skill Practice
1. c
2. d
3. e
4. g, h

Chapter Bonus Test Question

Ask students: How did the goals of nationalism differ between the people in Italy and Germany and the people in the Austrian, Russian, and Ottoman Empires? *(Answers may vary but should include that nationalism in Italy and Germany sought to unite the separate states in each of those countries, but that nationalism in the Austrian, Russian, and Ottoman Empires sought independence for their various ethnic groups.)*

Teach, Reinforce, and Extend CHAPTER Content

The Age of Imperialism

CHAPTER RESOURCES

	Reproducible Resources	Multimedia Resources
Chapter Opener	Chapter Themes: Graphic Organizer 27 Historical Significance Chapter Activity 27	MindJogger Videoquiz
Chapter Enrichment	Vocabulary Activity 27* Time Line Activity 27 Mapping History Activity 27 History Simulation 27 Geography and History Activity 27 Source Reading 27 People in World History Profiles 51, 52 World Art and Music Activity 27 Enrichment Activity 27 Critical Thinking Activity 27 Skill Reinforcement Activity 27 Performance Assessment Activity 27	World History and Art Transparency 35, *Ono Waterfall* Chapter Transparency 27 Vocabulary PuzzleMaker Software
Chapter Review/Reteaching	Reteaching Activity 27 Skill Reinforcement Activity 27 Spanish Chapter Summary 27	Chapter 27 Digest Audiocassette, Activity, Test* Vocabulary PuzzleMaker Software Student Self-Test and Review Software MindJogger Videoquiz
Chapter Evaluation/Testing	Performance Assessment Activity 27 Chapter 27 Test, Forms A and B	Testmaker

** Also available in Spanish*

0:00 **OUT OF TIME?** Assign the Chapter 27 summary in the Unit 6 Digest on pages 728–731, and the Chapter 27 Audiocassettes.

Block Schedule

Block scheduling differs from traditional class scheduling in the amount of time allotted to each period. The extended time frame provided by block scheduling affords you the opportunity to implement a greater number of research-oriented and activity-intense projects to motivate and involve your students. Activities that are particularly suited to use within the block scheduling framework are identified throughout this chapter by the following designation.

KEY TO ABILITY LEVELS

Teaching strategies have been coded for varying learning styles and abilities.

- L1 **BASIC** activities for all students
- L2 **AVERAGE** activities for average to above-average students
- L3 **CHALLENGING** activities for above-average students
- LEP **LIMITED ENGLISH PROFICIENCY** activities

Chapter 27 Planning Guide

A complete, 1-page lesson plan is provided for each section in the *Reproducible Lesson Plans* booklet.

SECTION RESOURCES

Daily Objectives	Reproducible Resources	Multimedia Resources
Section 1 Pressures for Expansion Identify the political, economic, and social causes of imperialism.	Reproducible Lesson Plan 27-1 Vocabulary Activity 27* Guided Reading Activity 27-1* Time Line Activity 27 Section Quiz 27-1*	Section Focus Transparency 27-1 Chapter Transparency 27 Student Self-Test and Review Software Testmaker
Section 2 The Partition of Africa List the effects imperialism had on the continent of Africa.	Reproducible Lesson Plan 27-2 Vocabulary Activity 27* Guided Reading Activity 27-2* People in World History Profile 52 History Simulation 27 Section Quiz 27-2*	Section Focus Transparency 27-2 Student Self-Test and Review Software Testmaker
Section 3 The Division of Asia Describe how the countries of Asia responded to imperialism.	Reproducible Lesson Plan 27-3 Guided Reading Activity 27-3* Geography and History Activity 27 People in World History Profile 51 Section Quiz 27-3*	Section Focus Transparency 27-3 World History and Art Transparency 35, *Ono Waterfall* Vocabulary PuzzleMaker Software Student Self-Test and Review Software Testmaker
Section 4 Imperialism in the Americas Explain how Latin Americans responded to the growth of American influence in their region.	Reproducible Lesson Plan 27-4 Vocabulary Activity 27* Guided Reading Activity 27-4* Reteaching Activity 27 Enrichment Activity 27 Section Quiz 27-4* Performance Assessment Activity 27 Spanish Chapter Summary 27	Section Focus Transparency 27-4 Student Self-Test and Review Software Testmaker

** Also available in Spanish*

Chapter Activities

Performance Assessment Activity

Conducting a Draft Assign students to cooperative groups, with each group representing a world power of the era discussed in the chapter. The whole class should brainstorm a list of all of the areas of the world that once were under the control of these powers. Then give each group approximately 30 minutes to organize a strategy for drafting countries or areas from this list for their empires. On the second day, the actual draft will occur. It should be patterned after the NFL or NBA drafts, where each group has a limited amount of time to make a choice, at which time the country is removed from the list. Groups of world powers may work out trades among themselves as well, following any agreed-upon rules of the drafting system. As a final product, the groups should submit a record sheet of each of their transactions and drafts with a rationale for each.

Possible Rubric Features

Accuracy of content information, decision-making skills, collaborative skills, concept attainment for imperialism and empires, organization of plan

• *For an additional activity, refer to Activity 27 in the* Performance Assessment Strategies and Activities *booklet.*

Activity

From the Classroom of...

Scott L. Miles—Teacher of the Year, Wisconsin Council for the Social Studies Wausau West High School Wausau, WI

Establishing Colonies in Africa

Assign small groups a European nation and give them a list of goals for the country's colonial activities in Africa. (For example, Portugal: secure African coastal areas to help develop secure trade routes with Asia.)

Spread out a large piece of paper on the classroom floor and draw a large outline map of Africa. Provide each nation (small group) with a length of yarn based on their relative strength. Some suggested lengths are: Portugal (9 ft.), England (26 ft.), France (22 ft.), Germany (12 ft.), Spain (6 ft.), and Italy (6 ft.). You may wish to use a separate color for each nation. Then ask students to place the yarn on the map to mark off territory in such a way as to meet their country's objectives.

Compare the map with an actual colonial map of the continent. How accurate was your country in fulfilling its objectives? How do colonial boundaries (maps) compare with current national boundaries? What problems would this cause for African nations?

Multiple Learning Styles

Verbal/Linguistic
Have students assume the role of a newspaper editor during the 1800s. Have them prepare editorials entitled either "The Case for Imperialism" or "The Case Against Imperialism." Their editorials should include examples that support their opinion.

Logical/Mathematical
Have students create a circle graph showing how much of Africa was controlled by the various colonial powers during the Age of Imperialism. Have them obtain rough area figures by comparing colonial boundaries with those of modern nations and then consulting an almanac or encyclopedia. Areas can be converted to percentages of the total area of the continent.

Visual/Spatial
Have students trace the continents of Europe, Asia, Africa, and the Americas, including the Pacific islands. Have them label countries discussed in the chapter and create a key using different colors to indicate the European power that ruled each country. Then have students color their maps accordingly, creating a map for the Age of Imperialism.

Auditory/Musical
Have students prepare a short musical skit about one of the events described in this chapter, such as the Sepoy Rebellion or U.S. involvement in Mexico from 1914 until 1917.

Additional Resources

TEACHER'S CORNER

NATIONAL GEOGRAPHIC SOCIETY

INDEX TO NATIONAL GEOGRAPHIC MAGAZINE

The following articles may be used for research relating to this chapter:

- "Hagi: Where Japan's Revolution Began," by N. Taylor Gregg, June 1984.

Bibliography

Literature of the Period

Forster, E. M. ***A Passage to India.*** New York: Harcourt Brace, 1989. A novel about life in India under British rule.

Readings for the Student

Conrad, Joseph. ***Heart of Darkness.*** New York: Norton, 1987. Conrad's grim 1902 story of one man's journey up the Congo River, accompanied by backgrounds, sources, and critical essays.

Readings for the Teacher

Said, Edward W. ***Culture and Imperialism.*** New York: Knopf, 1993. A literary critic's interpretation of the relationship between imperialism and literature.

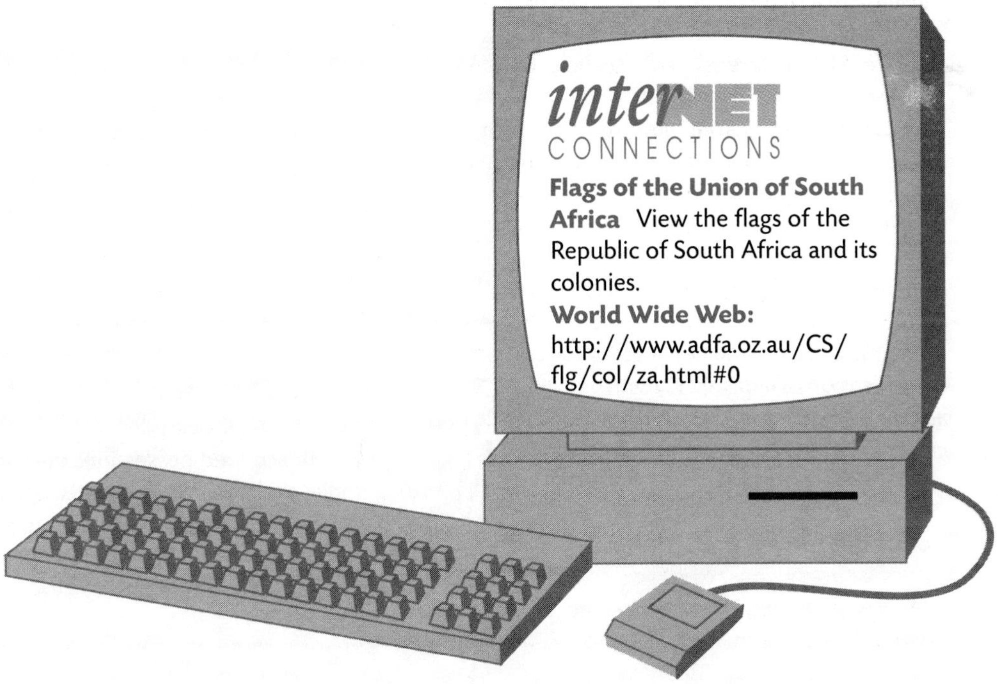
interNET
CONNECTIONS
Flags of the Union of South Africa View the flags of the Republic of South Africa and its colonies.
World Wide Web:
http://www.adfa.oz.au/CS/flg/col/za.html#0

Introducing Chapter 27

CHAPTER THEMES

Chapter Themes are listed by section on this chapter opening page of the Student Edition. A corresponding theme-based activity is available under "TEACH," and a theme-based question is asked in the Section and Chapter Reviews.

The Storyteller

Historical Setting The incident that led to the Sepoy Rebellion reveals how Great Britain, like many of the imperialist powers in the 1800s, imposed its own culture and values on its colonized peoples. Imperialists were often contemptuous of the sacred beliefs and rituals of the people in their colonies, often to the point of wiping out other cultures in the name of progress. Where colonized peoples tried to resist imperialist pressures to discard traditional ways of life, tension—and sometimes fighting—occurred. In many cases, such as the Sepoy Rebellion, simple ignorance or thoughtlessness about local customs and beliefs created hostile feelings between imperialists and colonial peoples.

Historical Significance

Answers: *Colonized people in those regions were introduced to Western traditions and technologies for the first time—sometimes against their will. Often, they were also led to reject native customs and beliefs. Imperialists exploited laborers in colonial areas and sometimes split up families and villages.*

Western rule inspired the rise of nationalist movements that ultimately brought independence.

Chapter 27

1800–1914

The Age of Imperialism

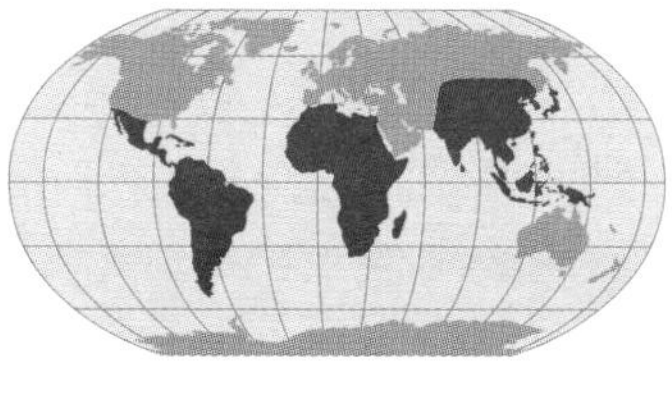

Chapter Themes

- **Movement** Political, economic, and social factors lead to a new period of expansion known as the Age of Imperialism. *Section 1*
- **Change** European powers divide most of Africa into colonies, and Africans resist European intervention and colonialism. *Section 2*
- **Reaction** India and China come under European control or influence, while Japan adopts reforms to meet the Western challenge. *Section 3*
- **Nationalism** Nationalism intensifies in Latin America as United States involvement in the region increases. *Section 4*

The Storyteller

No one knows how the rumor started, but it spread quickly. The bullets for the new rifles, the story went, were greased with the fat of cows and pigs. The sepoys, Indian soldiers in the British army, were outraged. Because Hindus regarded the cow as sacred and Muslims could not touch pork, using these bullets would violate the beliefs of both groups. As a result, the sepoys started a rebellion in May 1857 that soon engulfed much of India.

The Indian Revolt of 1857 was not an isolated incident. As European powers acquired new territories in the 1800s, conflicts between colonial rulers and colonial peoples developed. By the early 1900s European nations ruled large parts of Asia and Africa, while the United States was expanding its interests in Latin America.

Historical Significance

How did the spread of empires affect peoples in Asia, Africa, and Latin America? How did colonial peoples respond to Western rule?

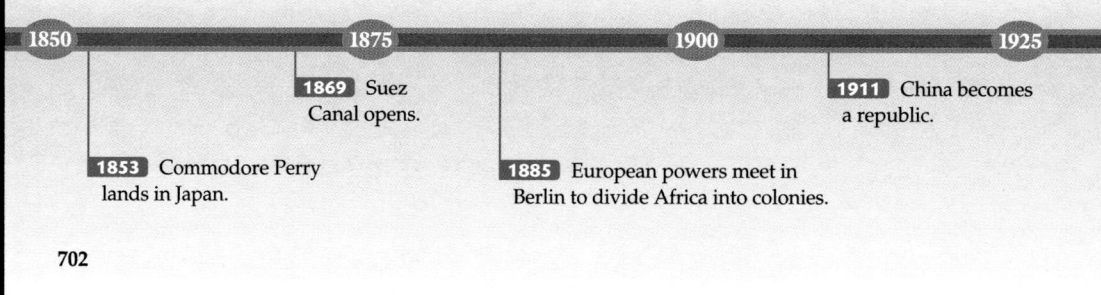

1850 — 1875 — 1900 — 1925

1853 Commodore Perry lands in Japan.

1869 Suez Canal opens.

1885 European powers meet in Berlin to divide Africa into colonies.

1911 China becomes a republic.

702

GEOGRAPHY CONNECTION

Location Have students locate on a world map some of the regions in which the British acquired possessions during the Age of Imperialism, including South Africa, India, and the Pacific islands. Then have them locate the British dominions they studied in Chapter 25, including Canada, Australia, and New Zealand. What was required to rule such a large and far-flung empire? *(Answers may include: a large navy and merchant fleet, a sizable army, many adventurous and loyal citizens.)* **L1**

Visualizing History An Indian prince hosts a British officer at a nautch (a form of entertainment by professional dancers).

Your History Journal

Draw or copy the map "Imperialism in Africa 1914" on page 710 of this chapter. Then, using the map of modern Africa in the Atlas as a guide, write in the new national names and draw in present boundaries.

Introducing Chapter 27

Visualizing History

Lower-ranking Indian princes were called rajas, while higher-ranking ones were known as maharajas. Unlike Western ballet, which emphasizes the action of the legs, in Indian dance the legs are usually bent and the feet flat.

Performance Assessment

Refer to the activity on page 702C of the Planning Guide.

For an additional activity, refer to Activity 27 in the *Performance Assessment Strategies and Activities* booklet.

Using Your History Journal

Suggest that students choose any single African country (for example, Bechuanaland), research its history, and summarize in their journals what interest imperialist powers had in it and how the country attained independence.

GLENCOE TECHNOLOGY

VIDEODISC
Use MindJogger to preview chapter content.

MindJogger Videoquiz
Chapter 27
Disc 4 Side A

Also available in VHS.

EXTRA CREDIT PROJECT

Oral Report Ask students to search for an explanation of why India's struggle for independence lasted 90 years. To find their answers, students should research the phases of that struggle. Have them summarize their findings for the class in a brief oral report. Suggested resources: C. A. Galbraith and R. Mehta, *India: Now and Through Time;* S. Ashton, *Indian Independence;* S. Wolpert, *A New History of India.* **L2**

Chapter 27
Section 1

SECTION THEME

▶ **Movement** Political, economic, and social factors lead to a new period of expansion known as the Age of Imperialism.

Find Out

Answer: *competition for international power and prestige, desire for new markets and sources of raw materials, religious fervor, and feelings of racial and cultural superiority*

FOCUS

Section Objective

Identify the political, economic, and social causes of imperialism.

BELLRINGER
Motivational Activity

Before taking roll at the beginning of the class period, project Section Focus Transparency 27-1 and have students answer the activity questions. Discuss students' responses.

This activity is also available as a blackline master.

Vocabulary Pre-check

Use Vocabulary Activity 27 to introduce vocabulary terms. **L1 LEP**

1800 **1850** **1900**

c. 1800 Age of Imperialism begins.

c. 1840s French citizens settle in Algeria.

1899 British author Rudyard Kipling writes the poem "The White Man's Burden."

Section 1

Pressures for Expansion

Setting the Scene

▶ **Terms to Define**
imperialism, colony, protectorate, sphere of influence

▶ **People to Meet**
Cecil Rhodes, Rudyard Kipling

▶ **Places to Locate**
Algeria, Australia, New Zealand, Rhodesia (Zimbabwe)

Find Out What were the political, economic, and social causes of imperialism?

The Storyteller

In India, British schools taught English and required students to adopt Christianity. The wife of a British official described attending a graduation ceremony in the year 1886. "The proceedings began with a hymn. The children sang pretty well, though in a harsh voice.... Then a boy stood up, put his hands together, and repeated the Lord's Prayer. Others followed him, and then Mr. Summers [the teacher] read a chapter from the Old Testament about Adam and Eve.... We could just tell he was speaking of the various nations—English, Parsee, [Muslim], Hindu, all came from Adam and Eve, we were all one family here."

—adapted from *An Indian Journal*, Nora Scott, 1994

Indians and British

The term imperialism is a Latin word from the days of the Roman Empire. Imperialism means one country's domination of the political, economic, and social life of another country. About 2,000 years ago, imperial Rome controlled most of the Mediterranean world. By the end of the 1800s, a handful of European countries, together with the United States, controlled nearly the entire world. Not surprisingly, the era between 1800 and 1914 has come to be known as the Age of Imperialism.

The imperialism of the 1800s resulted from three key factors. First, nationalism prompted rival European nations to build empires in their competitive quests for power. Second, the Industrial Revolution created a tremendous demand for raw materials and expanded markets, which prompted industrialized nations to seek new territories. Finally, both religious fervor and feelings of racial and cultural superiority inspired Europeans to impose their cultures on distant lands.

Political Rivalries

In the mid-1800s European countries saw themselves as actors on the world stage, and each country wanted to play a starring role. If Great Britain started a small colony in distant Asia or Africa, France had to start one too—and so did Belgium, Germany, Italy, Holland, Spain, Portugal, and Russia.

Once begun, the quest for colonies became a continuing enterprise that seemed to have no limits. Slow and difficult communication between remote territories and European capitals often enabled colonial governors and generals to take matters into their own hands. If a colony's borders did not provide military security, for instance, military officials

SECTION RESOURCES

Reproducible Masters
- Reproducible Lesson Plan 27-1
- Vocabulary Activity 27
- Guided Reading Activity 27-1
- Time Line Activity 27
- Section Quiz 27-1

Transparencies
- Section Focus Transparency 27-1
- Chapter Transparency 27

Multimedia
- Student Self-Test and Review Software
- Testmaker

Visualizing History **In this cartoon Bismarck (representing Germany), John Bull (representing Great Britain), and Uncle Sam (representing the United States) decide the fate of Samoa.** *What phrase described Great Britain's vast overseas holdings?*

based in the colony used their armies to expand the colony's borders. This strategy worked well enough until colonial governments started claiming the same territories. Then new conflicts arose, and European troops found themselves facing off on remote battlefields in Africa and Asia.

Desire for New Markets

The Industrial Revolution of the 1800s knew no borders. Factories in Europe and the United States consumed tons of raw materials and churned out thousands of manufactured goods. The owners and operators of these factories searched constantly for new sources of raw materials and new markets for their products. They hoped to find both in foreign lands.

Rubber, copper, and gold came from Africa, cotton and jute from India, and tin from Southeast Asia. These raw materials spurred the growth of European and American industries and financial markets, but they represented only the tip of the iceberg. Bananas, oranges, melons, and other exotic fruits made their way to European markets. People in Paris, London, and Berlin drank colonial tea, coffee, and cocoa with their meals and washed themselves with soap made from African palm oil.

The colonies also provided new markets for the finished products of the Industrial Revolution. Tools, weapons, and clothing flowed out of the factories and back to the colonies whose raw materials had made them possible.

Seeking New Opportunities

Imperialism involved more than just guns, battles, raw materials, and manufactured goods. Colonies needed people who were loyal to the imperialist country. Great Britain, France, and Germany needed British, French, and German citizens to run their newly acquired territories and keep them productive.

Throughout the 1800s European leaders urged their citizens to move to far-off colonies. Many of them responded. In the 1840s, for example, thousands of French citizens sailed across the Mediterranean Sea to **Algeria**, where they started farms and estates on lands seized from local Algerian farmers.

The British, meanwhile, emigrated to the far corners of the globe, hoping to find opportunities not available at home. Many rushed to **Australia** and **New Zealand** in the 1850s in search of gold. As the British government continued to acquire vast tracts of land in Africa, Asia, and the Pacific, the phrase "the sun never sets on the British Empire" became a popular way of describing Great Britain's vast holdings.

Strong-minded individuals saw emigration as a chance to strike it rich or make a name for themselves. Perhaps the most spectacular success story of the era belonged to **Cecil Rhodes**, a British adventurer who made a fortune from gold and diamond mining in southern Africa. Rhodes went on to found a colony that bore his name: **Rhodesia** (now **Zimbabwe**).

COOPERATIVE LEARNING ACTIVITY

Oral Reports Organize students into groups of three or four. Assign each group a topic that has something to do with daily life in India under the British (for example, Indian ceremonies, Indian religious life, the role of Indian women, transportation, agriculture, tiger hunts). Have each group member take on a specific task, such as library work, note taking, or presenting. Have the spokesperson for each group present a 10-minute report. Then open the topic for class discussion. **L2**

Chapter 27 Section 1

TEACH

Guided Practice

THEME Movement

Have students begin a discussion of the concept of movement during the Age of Imperialism by first considering their own personal travels. Ask them how traveling to new places has changed their views of the world, of other people, and of themselves. **L1**

Visualizing History John Bull, who first appeared as a literary character in 1712, later became the caricaturist's symbol for England. He was usually portrayed as a solid and jovial figure. The original Uncle Sam is said to have been Samuel Wilson, a businessman from Troy, New York, who supplied beef to the army during the War of 1812. **Why are the three men not looking at one another?** *(The cartoonist seems to imply that each country stubbornly resisted the others' arguments.)*
Answer to Caption: *"The sun never sets on the British Empire."*

Economics Discuss the close connection between the Industrial Revolution in Europe and America and the rise of imperialism. Review the effects of industrialization discussed in Chapter 23. Include the idea that the colonies that provided raw materials also became new markets for mass-produced goods. **L3**

Chapter Transparency 27

Independent Practice

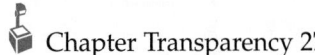

Guided Reading Activity 27-1 **L1**

Time Line Activity 27

Chapter 27 Section 1

Essay Have students write an essay summarizing the causes and effects of imperialism. The essays should include an introduction; a paragraph each for political, economic, and social causes and effects; and a conclusion. **L1**

ASSESS

Check for Understanding

Assign Section 1 Review as homework or as an in-class activity.

Use Student Self-Test and Review Software to review Section 1.

Evaluate

Section Quiz 27-1

Use the Testmaker to create a customized quiz for Section 1.

Reteach

Have students create an outline for Section 1 using the main headings and subheadings as a guide. Go over the outlines in class, creating a group outline on the chalkboard so that students can check their understanding of major ideas.

Enrich

Assign each student a person or event to research (for example, Cecil Rhodes or Perry's opening of Japan). Have them summarize their research in a three-minute class presentation.

CLOSE

Ask students how their own views on imperialism have changed after reading Section 1. **Is it possible that imperialism led to progress? How? Why? For whom?**

"Civilizing" Mission

Some emigrants had motives that went beyond mere personal glory and profit. Religious and humanitarian impulses inspired many individuals to leave their secure lives at home and head for the distant colonies. The desire to spread Western technology, religion, customs and traditions also fueled colonial expansion.

During the Age of Imperialism, growing numbers of Catholic and Protestant missionaries decided to bring the Christian message to the most remote corners of Africa and Asia. Over the decades they set up hundreds of Christian missions and preached to thousands of Africans and Asians throughout these two continents. Like many other Europeans and Americans of this period, these missionaries believed that Christianity and Western civilization together could benefit and transform the world.

The missionaries were not military conquerors, but they did try to change people's beliefs and practices. They believed that, in order to become "civilized," the people of Africa and Asia would have to reject their old religions and convert to Christianity. To achieve this goal, missionaries built churches and taught Christian doctrine. Missionaries often set up schools and hospitals as well.

Other Europeans also believed that Western civilization was superior to the civilizations of colonial peoples. As a result, colonial officials tried to impose Western customs and traditions on the people they conquered. These officials insisted that their colonial subjects learn European languages, and they encouraged Western lifestyles as well. They also discouraged colonial peoples from practicing traditional customs and rituals.

Some Europeans seized on the theory of social Darwinism as proof of their cultural superiority. This theory adapted Darwin's ideas about the evolution of animals—particularly his notion of "the survival of the fittest"—to explain differences among human beings. Social Darwinists believed that white Europeans were the "fittest" people in the world and that Western nations had a duty to spread Western ideas and traditions to "backward" peoples living overseas.

In 1899 the British writer **Rudyard Kipling** captured the essence of the imperialist attitude in his famous poem "The White Man's Burden." Kipling addressed the poem to the United States, which at this time had just begun to acquire and govern colonies of its own:

> "Take up the White Man's burden—
> Send forth the best ye breed—
> Go bind your sons to exile
> To serve your captives' need;
> To wait in heavy harness
> On fluttered folk and wild—
> Your new-caught, sullen peoples,
> Half-devil and half-child."

Forms of Imperialism

Imperialist nations used a variety of means to gain new land. Sometimes they made treaties with the people who lived there. Sometimes they bought the land from another imperialist country. More often than not, however, they simply conquered the area with military force.

Imperialists used several types of territorial control. The first of these, a **colony**, was a territory that an imperialist power ruled directly. A **protectorate** had its own government, but officials of a foreign power guided its policies, particularly in foreign affairs. A **sphere of influence** was a region of a country in which an imperialist power held exclusive investment or trading rights.

The type of government an imperialist power chose for a region depended on the size of the area and the number of people living there. The main idea behind all three forms of imperialism was to give the imperialists firm control over the conquered territory.

SECTION 1 REVIEW

Recall

1. **Define** imperialism, colony, protectorate, sphere of influence.
2. **Identify** Cecil Rhodes, Rudyard Kipling.
3. **List** five raw materials that imperialists took from their colonies. What did they send to these colonies?

Critical Thinking

4. **Evaluate** What does the Kipling poem reveal about his attitude toward Africans and Asians?

Understanding Themes

5. **Movement** Explain the main reasons for the growth of imperialism in the 1800s.

SECTION 1 REVIEW ANSWERS

1. All vocabulary words are defined in the Glossary.
2. Rhodes, 705; Kipling, 706
3. Raw materials included rubber, copper, cotton, jute, tin, gold, bananas and other exotic fruits, coffee, tea, cocoa, and palm oil. The colonies were sent manufactured goods such as tools, weapons, and clothing.
4. The colonists were childlike, in need of discipline and instruction.
5. **MOVEMENT** Political rivalries, the search for new markets and sources of raw materials, religious fervor, and feelings of cultural and racial superiority were the main reasons for the growth of imperialism.

1870 — 1890 — 1910

c. 1870 David Livingstone explores Africa.

1896 The Ethiopians defeat the Italians in the battle of Adowa.

1905 The French win special rights in Morocco.

1910 The British form the Union of South Africa.

Section 2

The Partition of Africa

Setting the Scene

- **Terms to Define**
  partition
- **People to Meet**
  David Livingstone, Abd al-Qadir, Muhammad Ali, Samory Touré, Menelik II, the Afrikaners, Shaka
- **Places to Locate**
  Morocco, Egypt, the Sudan, Liberia, Ethiopia, Union of South Africa

Find Out What effects did imperialism have on the continent of Africa?

The Storyteller

An eyewitness to the opening ceremonies for the Suez Canal reported: "Fireworks in front of the Viceroy's Palace. Open house everywhere.... Luxurious dinners, vintage wines, exquisite fish, partridges, wild duck. Seven or eight thousand people sitting down to dinner in the middle of the desert. It was like something out of the Arabian Nights*.... At last I got back to my houseboat.... All through the night I could hear the noise of the fair—the sound of music, the banging of fireworks, and the shouting of happy revelers."*

—adapted from *World Ditch, The Making of the Suez Canal*, John Marlowe, 1964

Opening of Suez Canal

Until the 1800s Europeans knew little of Africa beyond its northern, western, and southern coasts. Then, in the mid-1800s, a few brave explorers began to venture into the African interior. The most famous of these was Scottish doctor and missionary **David Livingstone**, who first went to Africa in 1840. For the next 30 years, Livingstone explored wide tracts of central and eastern Africa, setting up Christian missions and sending back to Great Britain detailed reports of his discoveries.

When Europeans temporarily lost touch with Livingstone late in the 1860s, the *New York Herald* hired a British journalist and explorer named Henry M. Stanley to track him down. Their famous meeting in 1871 is best remembered for Stanley's understated greeting, "Dr. Livingstone, I presume?" With help from European financial backers, Stanley went on to lead several major expeditions through central Africa himself.

The publicity surrounding the explorations of Livingstone and Stanley generated new interest in Africa throughout Europe. This interest swelled when subsequent explorers sent back excited reports about the continent's abundance of resources. Reports such as these helped set off a mad European scramble for Africa between 1880 and 1914. One European country after another laid claim to parts of Africa. In 1885, 14 nations met in Berlin, Germany, and agreed to **partition**, or divide, the prize King Leopold II of Belgium called "this magnificent African cake." By 1914 European nations controlled 90 percent of the continent.

North Africa

The world's largest desert—the Sahara—stretches across North Africa from the Atlantic

Chapter 27 Section 2

SECTION THEME

- **Change** European powers divide most of Africa into colonies, and Africans resist European intervention and colonialism.

Find Out

Answer: *By 1914 European nations controlled 90 percent of Africa, whose native populations and resources they exploited. In some places families and even whole villages were split up. Africans were taught to reject their own customs and beliefs in favor of European ways.*

FOCUS

Section Objective

List the effects imperialism had on the continent of Africa.

BELLRINGER Motivational Activity

Before taking roll at the beginning of the class period, project Section Focus Transparency 27-2 and have students answer the activity questions. Discuss students' responses.

This activity is also available as a blackline master.

Vocabulary Pre-check

Use Vocabulary Activity 27 to introduce vocabulary terms. **L1 LEP**

SECTION RESOURCES

Reproducible Masters
- Reproducible Lesson Plan 27-2
- Vocabulary Activity 27
- Guided Reading Activity 27-2
- People in World History Profile 52
- History Simulation 27
- Section Quiz 27-2

Transparencies
- Section Focus Transparency 27-2

Multimedia
- Student Self-Test and Review Software
- Testmaker

Chapter 27
Section 2

TEACH

Guided Practice

THEME **Change**

Discuss the changes brought to Africa as a result of imperialist expansion and conflict. Focus on changes involving local inhabitants, land, and culture. Ask students to explain which changes they perceive as good and which they view as bad. *(Students may point to new products and the establishment of better transportation and trade routes as good; they may point to the inhumane treatment of Africans by people such as Leopold II and the land devastation caused by wars as bad.)* **L1**

Visualizing History The historic meeting between Livingstone and Stanley took place in Ujiji, in Central Africa, on November 10, 1871.
Answer to Caption: *British recognition of French control of Morocco*

Critical Thinking Ask students to speculate on Italy's reasons for "settling" Libya. **Why was controlling Libya better than having no imperialist claim at all?** *(Possible answer: It gave Italy a foot in the door to further expansion in Africa—to Ethiopia, for example.)* **L3**

History Simulation 27

Independent Practice

Guided Reading Activity 27-2 **L1**

People in World History Profile 52

Visualizing History **British explorer Sir Henry Morton Stanley finds missionary David Livingstone in Africa.** *What ended Britain's imperialist dispute with France over the Sudan?*

Ocean to the Red Sea. Most of the people in North Africa live on a thin strip of land located north of the Sahara along the Mediterranean coast. Here the land is fertile and the climate mild. In the early 1800s Muslim Arabs under the authority of the Ottoman ruler governed the large territories west of Egypt, which at that time were called Tripoli, Tunis, Algiers, and **Morocco**. Today Tripoli, Tunis, and Algiers are the North African countries of Libya, Tunisia, and Algeria.

The French in North Africa

In 1830 King Charles X of France ordered an invasion of Algiers with the aim of colonizing that country. French troops encountered stiff resistance from the native Algerians, whose leader was **Abd al-Qadir** (AB•duhl KAH•duhr). About 10 years passed before 100,000 French soldiers finally subdued the determined Algerians.

After conquering Algiers, the French went on to seize neighboring Tunis in 1881 and secured special rights in Morocco by 1905. About 1 million French people settled in North Africa during these years of struggle.

Britain and Egypt

During the early 1800s, **Egypt** was an independent kingdom under a ruler named **Muhammad Ali**. Hoping to build Egypt into a strong, modern state, Ali carried out many building projects with European assistance. Egypt's debts rose, however, and European political and economic influence in the country increased.

Between 1859 and 1869, a French company headed by Ferdinand de Lesseps built the Suez Canal. Cutting through Egyptian territory to connect the Mediterranean Sea and the Red Sea, the canal was a vital shortcut between Europe and Asia. During the next 10 years, Egypt sold some of its holdings in the canal company to Great Britain to pay off its debts.

Egypt's worsening financial situation eventually provided Great Britain with an excuse to intervene militarily. In 1882 a British force moved into Egypt. It defeated an Egyptian army led by the nationalist leader Ahmed Arabi. After this victory, Egypt became a British protectorate.

Having subdued Egypt, the British looked southward to a region called **the Sudan**. In 1898 British forces defeated the Sudanese at the battle of Omdurman. No sooner was the battle over than the British learned of a rapidly advancing French force that also was laying claim to the Sudan. The two armies met at the Sudanese town of Fashoda, where for several weeks they stared at each other across the Nile. An imperialist dispute had brought Great Britain and France to the brink of war. In the end, the French withdrew their army and their Sudanese claim when the British recognized French control of Morocco.

Italy Seizes Libya

Libya lies between Egypt on the east and Algeria and Tunisia on the west. Known as Tripoli in the late 1800s, the country had almost no economic value, but it was coveted by Italy, the nearest European nation. Having entered the imperialist race late, however, Italy was eager to establish an African empire. After seeking guarantees of neutrality from several other European nations, Italy in 1911 declared war on the Ottoman Empire, which

COOPERATIVE LEARNING ACTIVITY

News Report Have students prepare an in-depth news report on the Boer War in the style of a prime-time television news program. Organize students into four groups—those who will gather information about the war and the issues surrounding it, those who will prepare written copy for the telecast, those who will represent the Afrikaners and the British in interviews, and those who will serve as reporters and anchors for the show. If possible, videotape the show for presentation to other classes. **L2**

controlled Tripoli. Italy easily defeated the Ottoman Turks and took Tripoli as a colony, renaming it Libya. Libya was the last country in North Africa to be conquered by Europeans.

Dividing Sub-Saharan Africa

Sub-Saharan Africa consists of all the land between the Sahara and the southern tip of the continent. It is an immensely varied land of mountains and plains, deserts and rain forests. In the 1800s it was home to dozens of kingdoms and states, each of which had its own rich and complicated history. The imperialist powers of Europe swallowed up most of these small countries in the late 1800s.

West Africa

As early as the 1400s, Portuguese sailors had explored the west coast of Africa. During the next hundred years, the Portuguese, Dutch, British, and French set up trading posts and forts along the coast. By the 1600s these outposts had become the center of a booming transatlantic slave trade.

Although the West African states traded salt, gold, and iron wares, they were also involved in the slave trade. Their economies declined rapidly when key European countries abolished the slave trade in the early 1800s. They then began to rely on cash crops such as cotton and cacao beans. They also exchanged natural products such as palm oil, ivory, and rubber for European manufactured goods.

In an effort to control this trade, and with the further aim of expanding their coastal possessions, European nations began to push inland in the 1870s. By 1900 the French had conquered a vast territory they called French West Africa. During this same period, the British acquired the Gold Coast, the kingdom of Ashanti, and parts of Nigeria. While Spain and Portugal expanded older claims, Germany staked out new colonies in the region.

European expansion in West Africa, however, did not go unchallenged. In the 1890s, **Samory Touré** (sah•MOHR•ree too•RAY), ruler of a kingdom centered in present-day Senegal, led armies against the French who had seized control of land. Another African ruler, King Behanzin of the coastal state of Dahomey, also battled French forces. In the Gold Coast, the Ashanti stubbornly resisted British expansion. All of these African efforts, however, were defeated by well-armed European forces. By the early 1900s, many West Africans had reluctantly accepted agreements with European powers that gave them some limited self-rule under European supervision.

At this time, **Liberia** was the only remaining independent state in West Africa. Established in 1822 by freed Americans who were once enslaved, Liberia had become an independent republic in 1847. The support Liberia received from the United States discouraged European powers from attempting to seize it as a colony.

Central and East Africa

In 1877 the explorer Henry M. Stanley reached the mouth of the Congo River. He later described the river as a "grand highway of commerce to … Central Africa." As a result of Stanley's exploration, Belgium's King Leopold II claimed the Congo region as his own private plantation. He enslaved the Congolese people and had them cut down forests for rubber trees and kill elephant herds for ivory tusks. In pursuing his ambitions, Leopold stripped the Congo of many people and resources.

Leopold's brutal control of the Congo lasted about 20 years, despite the world's outrage. In 1908 he finally agreed to give his plantation to the Belgian government in return for a large loan. Thus,

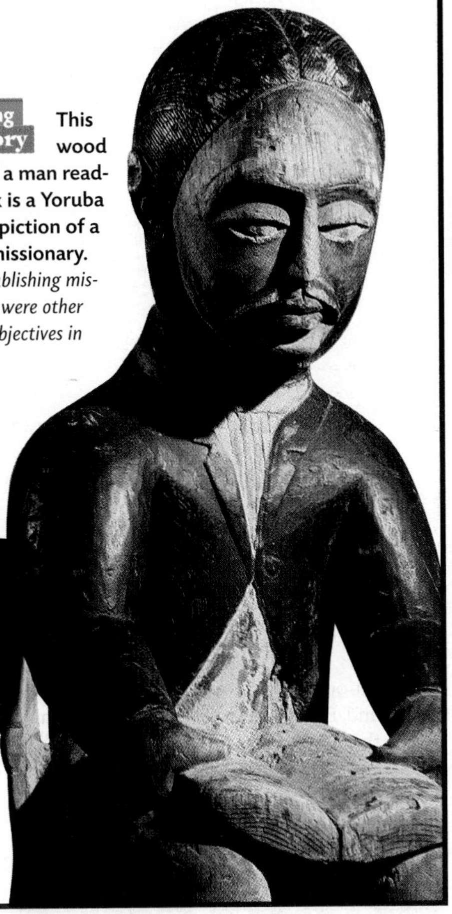

Visualizing History **This wood carving of a man reading a book is a Yoruba artist's depiction of a Swedish missionary.** *Besides establishing missions, what were other European objectives in Africa?*

Chapter 27 Section 2

Role Play Ask students to assume the persona of Henry Stanley, David Livingstone, or Cecil Rhodes and write letters describing the details of everyday life and their discoveries. **L2**

Multicultural The imperialists, with their desire to colonize and control Africa, often clashed with the diverse indigenous groups. Have students research some of the original inhabitants of Africa and their relations with the imperialists and report to the class on their findings. This exercise may be done in small groups. **L3**

Cartoon Have students prepare political cartoons or comic strips entitled "Effects of Imperialism in Africa." Have them depict one specific incident in Section 2, such as Menelik's defeat of the Italians in Ethiopia. **L2 LEP**

Literature Have students read Joseph Conrad's *Heart of Darkness* as background for studying imperialism in the Congo. Have them prepare written reports. Some may wish to work together to prepare a class presentation on different aspects of imperialism as presented in Conrad's story. **L3**

Visualizing History Southwestern Nigeria is home to the Yoruba peoples. Yoruba sculptures of humans are distinctive for their bulging eyes and flat lips.

Answer to Caption: *to exploit the continent's resources for their own purposes, to control trade to their own advantage, and to enhance their national prestige by increasing their overseas possessions*

MEETING SPECIAL NEEDS ACTIVITY

Learning Disability For the benefit of students with learning problems, organize the entire class into five groups, making sure that each group has a similar mix of students of different abilities. Assign each group one area of Africa covered in the section: North Africa (including Egypt and Libya), West Africa, Central Africa, East Africa, and southern Africa. Have the students in each group use the material in the chapter and an encyclopedia to prepare a brief oral report on the history of their region. Then ask one person in each group to present its oral report to the other groups. **L1**

in that year, the Congo region owned by Leopold became the Belgian Congo.

While the Belgians were claiming the Congo Basin, the British, the Germans, and the Italians were doing the same in East Africa. The only country in East Africa to remain independent during this period was **Ethiopia**, located in a remote region known as the Horn of Africa. Beginning in the 1880s, Italy tried to conquer this country, but the Italians underestimated the determination of their opponent, Ethiopia's Emperor **Menelik II**. As emperor, Menelik had conquered many small kingdoms and succeeded in reunifying the Ethiopian Empire.

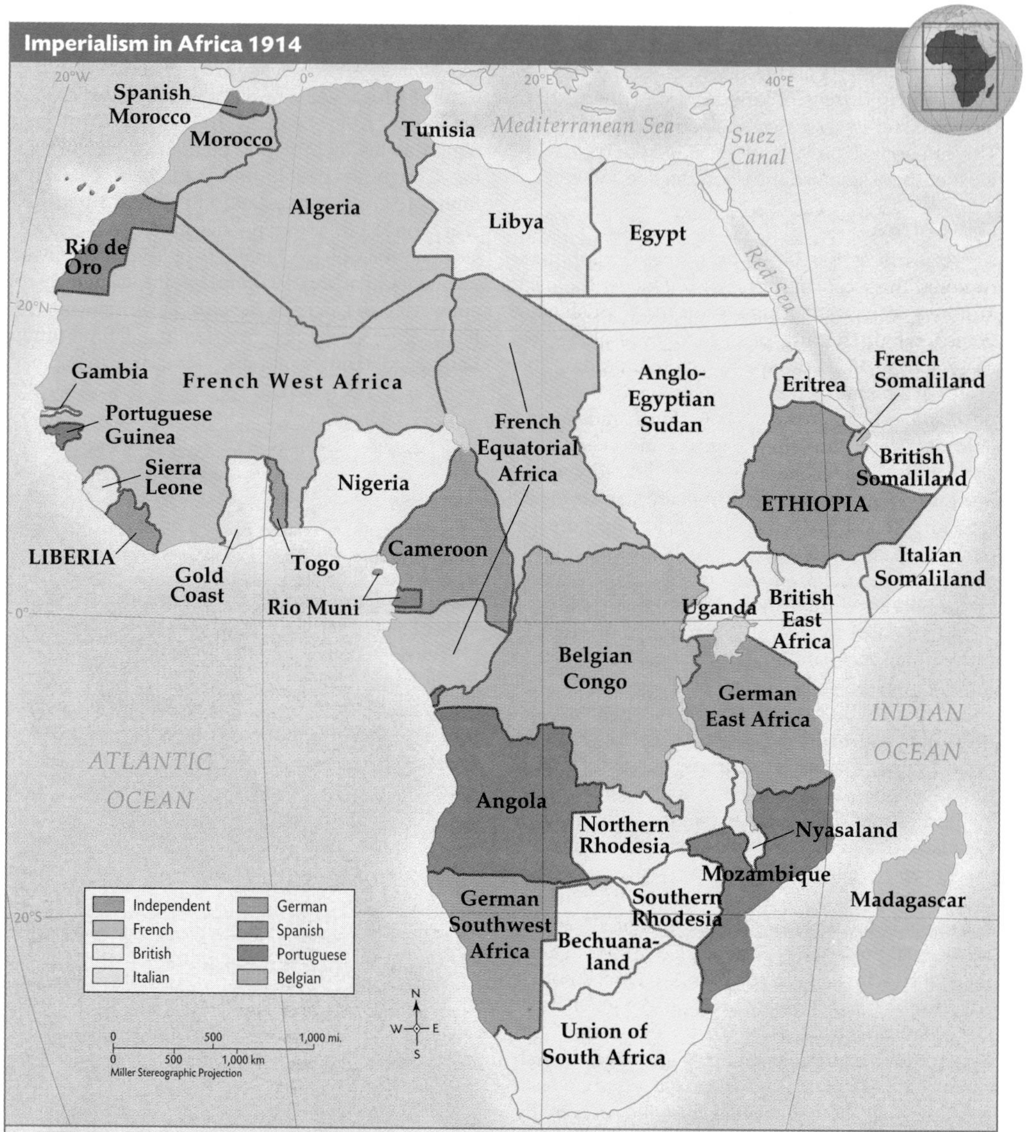

Map Study By 1914 only two independent countries remained in all of Africa.
Location What is the location of each of those nations?

Who?What?Where?When?

South Africa's Orange Free State and **Transvaal** provinces both get their names from rivers. The Orange River forms part of the Orange Free State's southern boundary, and the Vaal River forms part of the Transvaal's southern boundary. Transvaal means "across the Vaal." Afrikaners first crossed both rivers in the early 1800s.

you don't say...

Trek, an arduous journey, comes from the Afrikaans word meaning "to draw a vehicle or to migrate." In South Africa a trek is also a stage of a journey, between two stopping places.

Map Study

Answers

Liberia: West Africa; Ethiopia: East Africa

Map Skills Practice

Reading a Map Which two European imperialist powers controlled the most territory in Africa in 1914? *(France, Great Britain)*

MAKING CONNECTIONS ACTIVITY

The Arts Have some students watch the video *Out of Africa* (1985), which takes place around the time of World War I, when discontented European settlers moved in waves to East Africa. Ask students to summarize what the film shows about the effects of imperialism on both Africans and Europeans of the time. Have other students watch movies set in South Africa, such as *Sarafina!* (1992), *A World Apart* (1988), *Overindulgence* (1987), and the more recent *Cry, the Beloved Country* (1996). Ask them to write brief reviews of the movies, focusing on the long-lasting effects of imperialism on the country's inhabitants. Use students' reactions to the various movies as a springboard for a general discussion of the effects of imperialism in Africa. **L2**

Visualizing History King Menelik is shown here with his chiefs. *How did Ethiopia's emperor prevent Italy and other nations from establishing imperialist control of Ethiopia?*

When the Italians attacked Ethiopia in 1896, Menelik's well-trained forces crushed the invaders at the battle of Adowa. His victory was so devastating that no Europeans dared invade his country again during his lifetime. Ethiopia and Liberia were the only two African nations to escape European domination completely during the Age of Imperialism.

Southern Africa

Dutch settlers came to southern Africa in 1652 and established the port of Cape Town. For the next 150 years, **the Afrikaners**, as these settlers came to be called, conquered the lands around the port. The lands they eventually acquired became known as Cape Colony.

Before construction of the Suez Canal, the quickest sea route to Asia from Europe was around the Cape of Good Hope at the southern tip of Africa. Sensing the strategic value of Cape Colony, the British seized it during the Napoleonic Wars in the early 1800s. The Afrikaners resented British rule, particularly laws that forbade the enslaving of black Africans. The white Afrikaners believed that they were superior to black Africans and that God had ordained slavery.

In the 1830s about 10,000 Afrikaners, whom the British called *Boers* (the Dutch word for "farmers"), decided to leave Cape Colony rather than live under British rule. In a move known as the Great Trek, the Afrikaners migrated northeast into the interior. Here they established two independent republics, the Transvaal and the Orange Free State. The constitution of the Transvaal stated, "There shall be no equality in State or Church between white and black."

The Afrikaners fought constantly with their neighbors. First they battled the powerful Zulu nation for control of the land. Under their king **Shaka**, the Zulu in the early 1800s had conquered a large empire in southern Africa. The Zulu and Boers were unable to win a decisive victory. Finally, in 1879, the British became involved in battles with the Zulu. Under their king, Cetywayo, the Zulu at first defeated British forces. With superior weapons and numbers, however, the British eventually destroyed the Zulu Empire.

Conflict also developed between the British and the Boers. During the 1880s, British settlers moved into the Boer-ruled Transvaal in search of gold and diamonds. Eager to acquire this mineral wealth for Great Britain, Cecil Rhodes—now prime minister of Cape Colony—and some other British leaders wanted all of South Africa to come under British rule. They began pressuring the Boers to grant civil rights to the British settlers in the Transvaal. Growing hostility between the British and the Boers finally erupted in 1899 into the Anglo-Boer War, which the British won three years later.

In 1910 Great Britain united the Transvaal, the Orange Free State, Cape Colony, and Natal into the **Union of South Africa**. The constitution of this British dominion made it nearly impossible for nonwhites to win the right to vote. As one black African writer of the time said, "The Union is to be a Union of two races, namely the British and the Afrikaners—the African is to be excluded."

Racial equality became a dominant issue in South African affairs after the formation of the Union. Several nonwhite South African groups tried to advance their civil rights against the white minority government. Mohandas K. Gandhi, a lawyer from India, worked for equality for Indians in South Africa. He urged the Indians to disobey laws that discriminated against them. Gandhi's efforts brought some additional rights for the Indian community.

Chapter 27 Section 2

Visualizing History Sahle Miriam (1844–1913) took the title Menelik II when he assumed the imperial crown of Ethiopia in 1889. Menelik I was the son of the Bible's Solomon and the queen of Sheba.
Answer to Caption: *Menelik crushed the invading Italians so effectively that no Europeans dared invade Ethiopia again during his lifetime.*

Linking Past and Present

Apartheid, the South African policy of segregation, has taken on a more general meaning. The word is sometimes used to refer to any practice anywhere that separates people by race, social class, gender, and so on.

ASSESS

Check for Understanding

Assign Section 2 Review as homework or as an in-class activity.

Use Student Self-Test and Review Software to review Section 2.

Evaluate

Section Quiz 27-2

Use the Testmaker to create a customized quiz for Section 2.

Reteach

Ask students to identify the role each of the following played in the imperialist expansion in Africa: Stanley and Livingstone, Suez Canal, Leopold II, Afrikaners, gold and palm oil, Liberia.

CRITICAL THINKING ACTIVITY

Recognizing Ideologies On the chalkboard write these statements quoted on page 711: "There shall be no equality in State or Church between white and black" and "The Union is to be a Union of two races, namely the British and the Afrikaners–the African is to be excluded." Without glossing over American racial problems, ask students to suggest some aspects of American national ideology that enabled more rapid advances in the civil rights movement in this country than in South Africa. *(Students may point to the assertion in the Declaration of Independence "that all Men are created equal, that they are endowed by their Creator with certain unalienable Rights....")* **L3**

CONNECTIONS

Geography

Coastal Trading Centers

Scottish-born Mungo Park (1771–1806) was trained as a surgeon and began his explorations in 1792 as medical officer of a ship bound for trade in the East Indies. Park survived many adventures, which he recounted in the popular book *Travels in the Interior Districts of Africa* (1797). He died by drowning in 1806, when his second expedition to the Niger was attacked.

Answers to Making the Connection

1. *establishing the Niger River as a trading route for the British*
2. *They were places where European trading ships could unload manufactured goods in exchange for raw materials transported from the African interior.*

Enrich

Have each student select an important figure from the section to impersonate. Have each student use information from the text to prepare a brief speech to deliver in class, taking the role of that individual. Challenge the class to identify the person each student represents.

CLOSE

Many countries vied for Africa during the Age of Imperialism. Have students summarize five or six main reasons for the scramble for Africa.

CONNECTIONS

Geography

Coastal Trading Centers

West African Port

"The king of the white people wishes to find out a way by which we may bring our own merchandise to you and sell everything at a much cheaper rate," said British explorer Mungo Park to a West African king in 1805. Park was interested in the possibilities of trade on the Niger River.

Like the other great rivers of Africa—the Congo, the Nile, and the Zambezi—the Niger flows to the sea. To the European traders of the 1800s, few places were more important than the mouth of a river. These were the only places where the large trading ships could unload European manufactured goods in exchange for African raw materials.

At the mouth of the Niger in the late 1800s, trade centered on palm oil. The British used the oil for making soap. Barrels of the precious oil were floated down the Niger and collected at depots, or ports, with names like Calabar and Port Harcourt.

Today these ports are growing cities that draw people from all parts of Nigeria. Port Harcourt now has a population of 400,000 inhabitants, while Calabar has about 160,000. Both ports still provide oil to the world, but today it is crude oil, the lifeblood of the world's industries and transport.

MAKING THE CONNECTION

1. What was Mungo Park interested in doing in Africa?
2. Why did the mouths of African rivers become centers for trade with Europeans?

South Africa's black majority also was stirred into action against racial injustices. In 1912 black South Africans founded the South African Native National Congress (SANNC). The SANNC's goal was to work for black rights in South Africa. In 1923 the SANNC shortened its name to the African National Congress (ANC).

Effects of Imperialism

Imperialism had profound and lasting effects on the African continent. These effects varied from colony to colony, but they centered mainly on economic and social life.

The imperialists profited from the colonies by digging mines, starting plantations, and building factories and ports. They hired Africans at extremely low wages and imposed taxes that had to be paid in cash. Men were often housed in dormitories away from their families and subjected to brutal discipline.

Although schools were few, they taught Africans that European ways were best. Missionaries taught them to reject African customs and beliefs. Africans learned to read European books and to wear European clothes. Under some colonial governments, entire villages broke up, families came apart, and ancient traditions withered and disappeared.

SECTION 2 REVIEW

Recall

1. **Define** partition.
2. **Identify** David Livingstone, Abd al-Qadir, Muhammad Ali, Samory Touré, Menelik II, the Afrikaners, Shaka.
3. **Locate** the countries of North Africa on the map on page 710. What geographical feature separates these countries from the rest of Africa?

Critical Thinking

4. **Analyzing Information** How did British attitudes toward black Africans differ from those of the Afrikaners? Find evidence to support your answers.

Understanding Themes

5. **Change** What were the main causes and effects of the European partition of Africa?

SECTION 2 REVIEW ANSWERS

1. All vocabulary words are defined in the Glossary.
2. Livingstone, 707; al-Qadir, 708; Muhammad Ali, 708; Touré, 709; Menelik, 710; Afrikaners, 711; Shaka, 711
3. the Sahara
4. The British passed laws forbidding the possession of enslaved blacks. The Afrikaners included in the constitution of the Transvaal assertions of racial inequality.
5. **CHANGE** The partition of Africa resulted from European rivalries and interest in Africa's resources and potential markets. The imperialists hired Africans at low wages, laid waste their land, and destroyed traditional ways of life.

1850 | 1875 | 1900 | 1925

1851 Taiping Rebellion begins in China.

1868 The Meiji era begins in Japan.

1885 Indian leaders form the Indian National Congress.

c. 1914 Japan emerges as a leading industrial nation.

Section 3

The Division of Asia

Setting the Scene

- **Terms to Define**
  sepoy, viceroy, sphere of influence, culture system, westernization
- **People to Meet**
  Ci Xi, Sun Yat-sen, Matthew C. Perry, Mutsuhito, Diponegoro
- **Places to Locate**
  Beijing, the East Indies, the Philippines, Indochina

Find Out How did the countries of Asia respond to imperialism?

The Storyteller

"Until the year 1924 I was the only foreigner privileged to witness and to participate in the great ceremonies.... " So wrote Reginald Johnston, Professor of Chinese at the University of London, and witness to the end of an empire in the "Palace of Cloudless Heaven" within the Forbidden City. "It was not without difficulty that even the emperor was able to ... invite a few 'ocean-men' to witness the New Year ceremonial which took place on February 5, 1924. It turned out to be the last occasion on which the ceremony was performed. Before another year had passed, the life of the Manchu court had come to an end."

—adapted from *Twilight in the Forbidden City*, Reginald F. Johnston, 1934

China's Forbidden City

In his book *Description of the World*, written in 1298, Italian explorer Marco Polo relates the many stories he heard about Zipangu, an East Asian island with a supposedly inexhaustible supply of gold. Polo never did visit Zipangu, now called Japan, but his description of its imagined treasures, and of the Asian riches he did see, inspired generations of Europeans. They looked eastward to Asia, dreaming of wealth.

The British in India

European trade with Asia opened up in the 1500s as sea routes began to replace the difficult overland route Marco Polo had taken. British involvement in India dates back to this period, when English traders first sailed along India's coast. In 1600 some of these traders banded together and formed the East India Company. It later became one of the richest and most powerful trading companies the world has ever known.

After its founding the East India Company built trading posts and forts in strategic locations throughout India. The French East India Company did the same and challenged the British for control of the India trade. In 1757 the British defeated French-trained Indian forces at the battle of Plassey. During the next hundred years, the British expanded their territory in India through wars and commercial activity.

The Sepoy Rebellion

As a result of steady expansion, the East India Company came to control most of India by 1857. Their power was tested that year, however, when the sepoys, or Indian soldiers, rebelled against their British commanders. Long before the greased bullet rumor discussed at this chapter's beginning triggered the Indian Revolt of 1857, sepoy resentment had been growing over British attempts to impose Christianity and European customs on them.

Chapter 27 Section 3

SECTION THEME

- **Reaction** India and China come under European control or influence, while Japan adopts reforms to meet the Western challenge.

Find Out

Answer: *In India and China, nationalist movements developed; Japan industrialized and became a major world power.*

FOCUS

Section Objective

Describe how the countries of Asia responded to imperialism.

BELLRINGER Motivational Activity

Before taking roll at the beginning of the class period, project Section Focus Transparency 27-3 and have students answer the activity questions. Discuss students' responses.

This activity is also available as a blackline master.

Vocabulary Pre-check

Use the Vocabulary PuzzleMaker to create a puzzle that reinforces the vocabulary terms in this section. **L1**

SECTION RESOURCES

Reproducible Masters
- Reproducible Lesson Plan 27-3
- Guided Reading Activity 27-3
- Geography and History Activity 27
- People in World History Profile 51
- Section Quiz 27-3

Transparencies
- Section Focus Transparency 27-3
- World History and Art Transparency 35, *Ono Waterfall*

Multimedia
- Vocabulary PuzzleMaker Software
- Student Self-Test and Review Software
- Testmaker

TEACH

Guided Practice

THEME Reaction

Write the words *China* and *Japan* on the chalkboard. Lead students in a comparison and contrast of Chinese and Japanese reactions to Western influence. Summarize student comments on the appropriate place on the chalkboard. *(China: People rebelled, first in the Opium War, then in the Boxer Rebellion, but foreign influence increased; Japan: New leaders worked to make Japan a great power capable of competing with modern, industrialized Western nations.)* **L1**

Map Study

Answer

Kashmir, the Rajput States, Hyderabad, Mysore

Map Skills Practice

Reading a Map In which period did Great Britain seize the largest amount of territory in India? *(1805–1856)*

Economics Discuss the importance of the Chinese opium trade to the merchants in imperialist countries. What were the effects of smuggling opium into China besides the exchange of merchandise? *(war between Britain and China)* What effects do you think this trade had on the Chinese people? *(The use of opium led to illness and less productive lives.)* **L2**

India Under British Rule

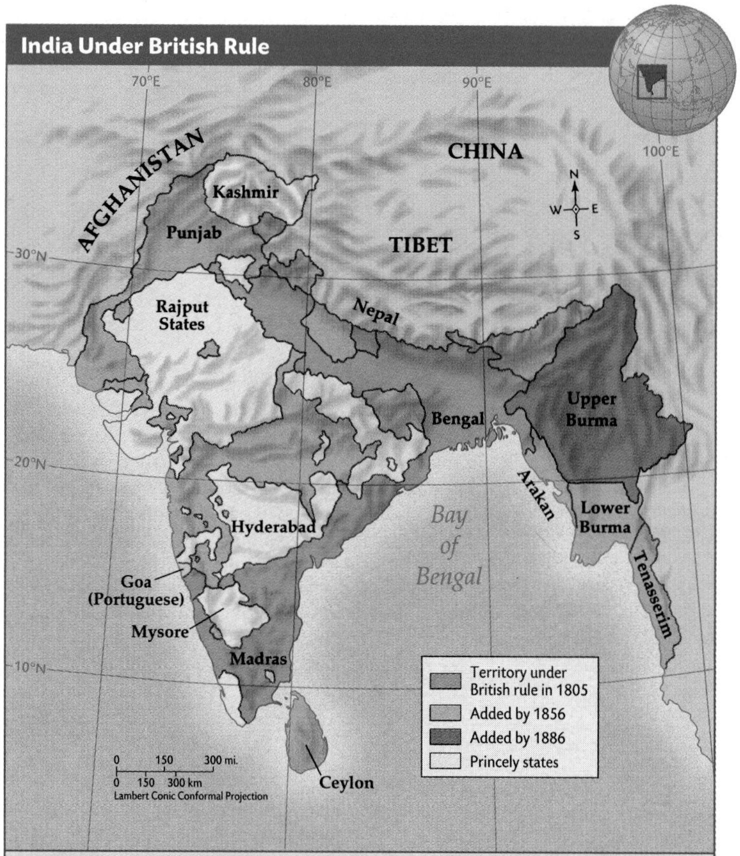

Map Study By 1886 the British had gained control of most of India. **Region** What areas remained free of British rule?

telegraph lines and dug irrigation canals; and it established schools and universities.

At the same time, British colonial officials discriminated against Indians and forced them to change their ancient ways, often with tragic results. Indian farmers, for example, were told to grow cotton instead of wheat, because British textile mills needed cotton. The lack of wheat then led to severe food shortages that killed millions of Indians during the 1800s.

Outraged by the food shortages and other problems, many Indians demanded more power for Indian leaders. In 1885 some of them formed the Indian National Congress, a political group that eventually led the long struggle for Indian independence. Continued protests and scattered violence led to a few political reforms, but at the beginning of the 1900s Great Britain still held India firmly in its grasp.

The Indian Revolt of 1857 lasted for about a year. Although the uprising failed, it forced the British government to tighten its control of India. In 1858 the British Parliament dissolved the East India Company and sent a viceroy, or governor ruling as a royal representative, to take over the company's territory. A viceroy soon won the loyalty of the few remaining independent Indian states by signing agreements with their rulers. In 1877 British Prime Minister Disraeli conferred upon Queen Victoria the title "Empress of India."

Indian Nationalism

The British government tried to quell further unrest in India by spending vast amounts of money on India's economic development. It built paved roads and an extensive railway system; it installed

China Faces the West

While the British were establishing an empire in India, they and other Europeans also developed trade with China. During the 1500s Chinese civilization had been highly advanced, and the Chinese at that time showed little interest in acquiring European products. There was only limited trade between China and Europe during the next 300 years. During this period, however, China's political, military, and economic position weakened under the rule of the Qing dynasty. Qing emperors ruled the country from 1644 to 1911.

The Unequal Treaties

In the early 1800s British merchants found a way to break China's trade barriers and earn huge

COOPERATIVE LEARNING ACTIVITY

Debate Have students prepare a debate between the British officials who ruled India and the Indian National Congress. Have students on one team portray members of the British government and defend their rule in India by citing the progress they have brought to the country. Have students on the other team portray the Indians who dispute this assertion and cite the problems they face as a result of British rule. Have each group member contribute by gathering data, forming arguments, or suggesting practice questions. **L3**

profits. In exchange for Chinese tea, silk, and porcelain—and to avoid paying cash—the merchants smuggled a drug called opium, which they obtained from India and Turkey, into China. In 1839 Chinese troops tried to stop the smuggling. When the British resisted, war broke out.

Great Britain won the Opium War in 1842 and signed the first of many foreign treaties with the Qing dynasty. Because the treaties took advantage of China's weakness, the Chinese called them the unequal treaties. Over the next 60 years, Great Britain, France, Germany, Japan, Russia, and the United States all signed unequal treaties with China. In general, these treaties increased foreign power in China and weakened the Qing dynasty. Civil wars such as the Taiping Rebellion (1851–1864) did even more to erode the dynasty's control of the country.

By the end of the century, the imperialist nations had won their struggle for power in China. Great Britain, France, Germany, Russia, and Japan claimed large sections of China as spheres of influence—areas where they had exclusive trading rights. Because it came late to the imperialist scramble, the United States did not claim a sphere of influence. Instead, it tried to open China to the trade of all nations through the Open Door Policy. Deadlocked by their own intense rivalries, the European nations reluctantly agreed to this policy in 1899.

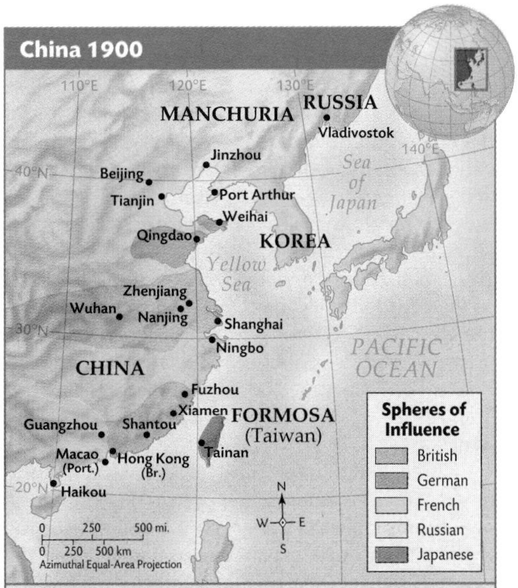

Map Study The European powers divided China into spheres of influence in the late 1800s.
Location Which of these powers controlled Manchuria in 1900?

By 1900 foreign power in China was at a high point. This influence infuriated Empress **Ci Xi** (TSUH•SEE), the domineering mother of the Qing emperor, who opposed all foreigners and modernization. She wrote her thoughts on China's dilemma in her diary: "The various Powers cast upon us looks of tiger-like voracity [intense hunger], hustling each other in their endeavors to be the first to seize upon our innermost territories."

The Boxer Rebellion

Ci Xi prevented the emperor from ruling in his own right and encouraged Chinese antiforeigner groups that gathered in secret to plot ways of driving out the imperialists. One such group called itself the Society of Righteous and Harmonious Fists because it also practiced a Chinese form of boxing. Its members became known as the Boxers.

The Boxers gained strength from their belief in Chinese rituals and traditions and their hatred of foreigners. In June 1900 they launched a series of attacks that killed several hundred foreigners and thousands of Chinese Christians. They besieged the foreigners in **Beijing**, the capital of China.

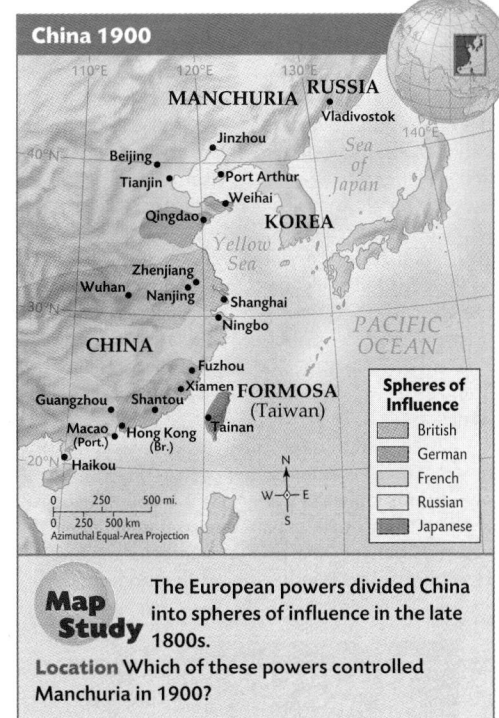

The foreign powers responded quickly and decisively. Their governments formed a combined army of 25,000 troops, which marched on Beijing and quelled the rebellion with a hail of bullets. When the fighting was over, thousands of Chinese lay dead in the streets. The empress, who had praised the "patriotic Boxers" and ordered them to kill foreign officials, fled the city.

Foreign troops crushed the Boxers in a few weeks. The Qing dynasty continued to rule, but only with the backing of the foreign powers. This settlement further undermined Chinese respect for the dynasty and set the stage for an even greater revolt.

The Revolution of 1911

After the Boxer Rebellion, Ci Xi struggled to hold on to power. She agreed to allow foreign troops to remain in China and gave in to some of her people's demands for change. For example, she established schools and reorganized the government. But it was too little, too late. Many Chinese believed that a modern republic should replace the Qing dynasty. In their view, the only way to achieve this goal was through revolution.

Map Study

Answer

Russia controlled Manchuria in 1900.

Map Skills Practice

Reading a Map Which non-European nation had a sphere of influence in China? *(Japan)*

Critical Thinking Have students analyze and discuss the reasons the British dissolved the East India Company. What were their main concerns? *(fear of rebellion and of conflict with local inhabitants)* What seems to have concerned them least about the Sepoy Rebellion? *(the feelings and sacred beliefs of the sepoys)* **L3**

World History and Art Transparency 35, *Ono Waterfall*

Who?What?Where?When?

Surendranath Banerjea The history of the brilliant Indian Surendranath Banerjea (1848–1946) sheds light both on imperialist oppression and on the rise of colonial nationalism. Although Banerjea scored higher on the Indian Civil Service exam than most British test takers, every effort was made to prevent him from having a successful career. After giving up on British justice, Banerjea founded a nationalist political organization. His political persistence combined with the pronunciation of his first name led to his nickname, "Surrender Not."

MEETING SPECIAL NEEDS ACTIVITY

Learning Style: Visual/Spatial Ask students who learn best by producing and decoding graphic information to depict events such as the Sepoy Rebellion or the Dutch presence in Southeast Asia in drawings, graphs, or political cartoons. Encourage them to share their work with the class as a way of reinforcing the section's main ideas. **L2**

Chapter 27 *The Age of Imperialism* 715

Chapter 27 Section 3

Independent Practice

Guided Reading Activity 27-3 **L1**

Geography and History Activity 27

People in World History Profile 51

Interview Have students research Matthew Perry's dealings with the Japanese and prepare a television interview with questions and answers for Perry and the Japanese shoguns who signed treaties with him. Have students prepare and present a "Special News Report" for U.S. citizens eager to know the outcome of Perry's dealings with the Japanese. Some students can take the role of reporters and others can represent Perry, members of his crew, and the Japanese. **L2**

Linking Past and Present

Hong Kong In 1898 Britain acquired from China a 99-year lease on Hong Kong, which is located off the southern coast of Guangdong Province, China. Over the years, Hong Kong developed into a major trading center. In 1997 Britain's lease will expire, and Hong Kong will become a special administrative region of China.

Global Gourmet

India Chutney, whose name comes from the Hindi word *chatni*, is a relish that originated in east India. Chutney, which has remained popular in Great Britain since the Age of Imperialism, usually combines mangoes or other fruits with onions, raisins, sugar, and spices. Indian curry is typically served with one or more chutneys.

The revolutionaries wanted China to regain its former power and influence. One of them, a doctor named **Sun Yat-sen**, wrote in the early 1900s: "Today we are the poorest and weakest nation in the world and occupy the lowest position in international affairs. Other men are the carving knife and serving dish; we are the fish and the meat."

The revolutionaries came together to form the United League (later called the *Guomindang*, or "Nationalist Party") in 1905, choosing Sun Yat-sen as their leader. They soon attacked troops loyal to the Qing dynasty, but without success. Then the empress died in 1908, and by law two-year-old Prince Pu Yi became the new emperor of China. The resulting confusion further weakened the dynasty.

Three years later Sun Yat-sen was raising money in the United States when the emperor's own troops joined in a successful revolt against the dynasty. Sun hurried back home and became the first president of the new Republic of China in 1911. His country had finally entered the modern age.

Modernization of Japan

Japan's dealings with the European powers began in much the same way as China's, but they ended differently. European traders first came to the island country in the 1500s. Like the Chinese, the Japanese were uninterested in European products, and they cut off almost all trade with Europe in the early 1600s. At the time a military commander called a shogun ruled Japan. Although the country also had an emperor, he had no real power.

Japan did not trade again with the outside world until 1853, when four American warships commanded by Commodore **Matthew C. Perry** sailed into the bay at Edo (present-day Tokyo). Perry wanted Japan to begin trading with the United States. The shogun, knowing what had happened to China in the recent Opium War, decided early in 1854 to sign a treaty with Perry.

The Meiji Leaders

In the first five years after Perry's arrival, the

Images of the Times

The British Empire

From the late 1700s to the early 1900s, Great Britain ruled the world's largest overseas empire. British territories were found in every continent.

British naval forces demonstrated British power in countries that were not directly under Queen Victoria's crown. Here a British ship attacks Chinese warships off the coast of China.

716

Images of the Times **The British Empire**

The period of British rule in India is often called the Raj, from the Sanskrit word for "rule" or "king." It comes from the same root as *raja*, an Indian prince, yet during the Raj, the princes' powers were limited by the British. India was considered "the jewel in the crown," that is, Great Britain's prize possession.

The canopied elephant saddle is called a howdah. The Australian outback is called the bush.

shogun signed trade treaties with Britain, France, Holland, Russia, and the United States. Since the treaties favored the imperialist powers, the Japanese people called them unequal treaties, just as the Chinese had. Unhappiness with the treaties led to the overthrow of the shogun in 1868. A group of samurai put a new emperor, **Mutsuhito**, on the Japanese throne, but kept the real power to themselves. Because Mutsuhito was known as the Meiji (MAY•jee), or "Enlightened" emperor, Japan's new rulers were called the Meiji leaders.

The Meiji leaders tried to make Japan a great power capable of competing with Western nations. Adopting the slogan "Rich country, strong military" they brought the forms of parliamentary government to Japan, strengthened the military, and worked to transform the nation into an industrial society. The Meiji leaders established a system of universal education designed to produce loyal, skilled citizens who would work for Japan's modernization. In this way, the Japanese hoped to create a new ruling class based on talent rather than birth.

Industrialization

In the 1870s Japan began to industrialize in an effort to strengthen its economy. The Japanese did this with little outside assistance. They were reluctant to borrow money from the West, fearing foreign takeovers if loans could not be repaid. In any case, most Western banks were not interested in making loans to Japan, because they considered the country a poor financial risk.

The Japanese government laid the groundwork for industrial expansion. It revised the tax structure to raise money for investment. It also developed a modern currency system and supported the building of postal and telegraph networks, railroads, and port facilities.

Beginning in the late 1880s, Japan's economy grew rapidly. A growing population provided a continuing supply of cheap labor. The combination of new technological methods and cheap labor allowed Japan to produce low-priced goods. Wars at the turn of the century further stimulated Japan's economy and helped it enter new world markets.

India was the most important British possession. This painting shows a British military officer traveling by elephant through northern India with his cavalry and foot soldiers.

Australia drew many British settlers, who made their homes in the harsh outback, or semi-dry interior, as well as in coastal areas.

REFLECTING ON THE TIMES

1. What types of British people were found throughout Great Britain's empire?
2. In the 1800s, people often said that "the sun never sets on the British Empire." What do you think this phrase meant?

ANSWERS TO REFLECTING ON THE TIMES

1. military officials, adventurers, missionaries, and ordinary settlers who worked hard to make homes for themselves
2. Britain's imperial holdings covered such a vast portion of the globe that, when it was nighttime in one part of the holding (Canada and the Caribbean), it was daytime in another part (India and Australia).

Literature Have students choose a work by Rudyard Kipling, such as *Plain Tales from the Hills, Kim, Soldiers Three and Other Stories, The Man Who Would Be King*, or a collection of his poems. Have them write a report on the work, concentrating on Kipling's literary uses of Indian culture, people, and geography. **L3**

Cultural Perspectives

Madama Butterfly Puccini's popular opera *Madama Butterfly*, which was first performed in 1904, dramatizes some of the consequences of Japan's relationship with the West. It is the tragic story of the love affair between a young Japanese girl and Lieutenant Pinkerton, an officer in the United States Navy. The opera provided the model for the modern musical *Miss Saigon*, though set in a different location and historical period.

Who?What?Where?When?

Shogun James Clavell's novel *Shogun*, and the 10-hour television miniseries based on it, tell the story of Blackthorne, an English sailor shipwrecked among the feudal Japanese.

Chapter 27
Section 3

ASSESS

Check for Understanding

Assign Section 3 Review as homework or as an in-class activity.

Use Student Self-Test and Review Software to review Section 3.

Evaluate

Section Quiz 27-3

Use the Testmaker to create a customized quiz for Section 3.

Reteach

Create a group outline of the section on the board. Have students contribute oral summaries of each part for a class discussion.

Who?What?Where?When?

The Philippines Spanish explorers who colonized the Philippines in the 1500s named the island country after King Philip II of Spain (1527–1598).

Global Gourmet

The Philippines Typical of Filipino food are two items made of fermented seafood: *bagoong* is a fish paste, and *patis* is a flavoring sauce. Both have a sour-salty taste.

By 1914 Japan had become one of the world's leading industrial nations.

Japan as a World Power

By the 1890s the Meiji leaders had taken great strides toward creating a modern nation. Japan had acquired an efficient government, a vigorous economy, and a strong army and navy. Needing more natural resources to increase its strength, the Japanese government began to establish its own overseas empire. The first prize it attempted to take was Korea.

When the people of Korea revolted against their Chinese rulers in 1894, Japan decided to intervene. Japanese troops easily defeated the Chinese army in the Sino-Japanese War. Although Korea officially became a separate and independent country, Japan gained partial control of its trade. Over the next few years, thousands of Japanese settled in Korea.

Korea also figured in Japan's next war. The Russian Empire had interests in Korea as well, and its interests began to clash with Japan's. Even more important was neighboring Manchuria, where the Russians kept troops and had a naval base at Port Arthur. In 1904 the Japanese navy launched a surprise attack on Port Arthur. Few people expected Japan to win the Russo-Japanese War, but the Japanese piled up victory after victory. The conflict ended in 1905, when Russia signed a treaty granting the country of Japan control over Korea and other nearby areas.

Japan's victory over Russia inspired non-Western nationalist leaders throughout the world. It proved that the European empires could be defeated if one had the will and determination. On the other hand, Japan had now become an imperialist country itself. It annexed Korea as a colony in 1910 and continued to expand its empire for the next 35 years.

Footnotes to History

A Teenage Emperor
Mutsuhito was only 15 when he became Japan's emperor in 1867. During his 44-year reign, he often led the way in adopting Western customs. He cut his traditional topknot, a tuft of hair on the top of the head, and wore European-style clothes. While previous emperors lived apart from the people, Mutsuhito rode around Tokyo in an open carriage and toured the countryside.

Southeast Asia

Southeast Asia consists of two distinct geographic areas. Island Southeast Asia is made of two archipelagos, or groups of islands: **the East Indies** and **the Philippines**. To the north and west lies mainland Southeast Asia. It includes all of the territories that occupy the Indochinese and Malay Peninsulas.

The growth of imperialism in these areas followed a familiar pattern. Beginning in the 1500s, imperialist powers came, saw, and conquered. Over the next 400 years Portugal, Spain, the Netherlands, Great Britain, France, and the United States all set up colonies in that region. They ranged in size from the huge Dutch East Indies that included thousands of islands to the tiny British settlements on the island of Singapore.

The Islands of Southeast Asia

For centuries, the island region of Southeast Asia had attracted foreign traders and colonizers. At the beginning of the 1800s, the Dutch controlled most of the East Indies and Spain controlled the Philippines.

The Dutch East Indies, present-day Indonesia, had many natural resources, including rich soil. Farmers grew coffee, pepper, cinnamon, sugar, indigo, and tea; miners dug for tin and copper; loggers cut down ebony, teak, and other hardwood trees. The Dutch government used a method of forced labor called the culture system to gather all these raw materials. The Dutch also discouraged westernization, or the spread of European civilization. The enormous profits the Dutch received from the East Indies made the colony the envy of the imperialist powers.

Diponegoro, a native prince from the East Indian island of Java, started a revolt against the Dutch in 1825. Although it lasted 10 years, this revolt eventually ended in failure, and the Dutch encountered little real opposition for the next 80 years. One of the Dutch governors put it this way: "We have ruled here for 300 years with the whip and the club and we shall still be doing it in another 300 years."

The Spanish rule of the Philippines resembled the Dutch rule of the Dutch East Indies. Native Filipinos worked for very low wages, if any, on tobacco and sugar plantations owned by wealthy Spaniard landowners. During the 1800s the Filipinos' resentment grew until it finally exploded into revolution in 1896.

When the United States declared war on Spain in 1898, the American government promised to

MAKING CONNECTIONS ACTIVITIES

Daily Life Ask students to research and then write short reports on the similarities and differences among the cuisines of China, Japan, India, and Southeast Asia. **L1**

Science, Technology, and Society Have students research the improvements made by the Japanese under the Meiji leaders. Have students pay particular attention to modern Japanese business philosophy and its influence on American corporations. **L2**

Visualizing History **This view of Whampoa Reach in China (about 1860) shows an English barque and an American ship.** *How did Western trade and commerce affect Southeast Asia?*

make the Philippines an independent country in return for the rebels' help against the Spanish. When the United States won the Spanish-American War later that year, however, it broke its promise and instead ruled the Philippines as a colony. The Filipinos then arose against American rule, but United States troops defeated them two years later.

Mainland Southeast Asia

The mainland region of Southeast Asia consisted of several large territories in the early 1800s, including Burma (Myanmar) and Malaya in the west, Vietnam in the east, and Siam (Thailand), Cambodia, and Laos in the middle. All through the 1800s, the British and French struggled for domination of the area, more for military than for economic reasons.

The British swept into Burma from India in the 1820s. Over the next 60 years, they took full control of Burma and neighboring Malaya. Meanwhile, the French were slowly conquering **Indochina**, the region that includes present-day Vietnam, Cambodia, and Laos. They, too, established complete control in the 1880s.

Squeezed between the two growing blocks of British and French territory lay the kingdom of Siam. In 1893 the French invaded Siam, sending forces into Bangkok, the capital city. Great Britain and France avoided armed conflict, however, when they agreed to define their spheres of influence in Southeast Asia. As a result of the agreement, Siam remained independent.

Struggles between Europeans for control of economic resources brought much destruction and disturbance to mainland Southeast Asia. Western products and business practices also changed the traditional ways of life of the people who lived there. Colonial landowners and trading companies forced local farmers and workers to grow cash crops, usually rice. They also hired them to mine coal and cut teak trees. These raw materials and cash crops interested Western capitalists.

SECTION 3 REVIEW

Recall

1. **Define** sepoy, viceroy, sphere of influence, culture system, westernization.
2. **Identify** Ci Xi, Sun Yat-sen, Matthew C. Perry, Mutsuhito, Diponegoro.
3. **Explain** why the British government dissolved the East India Company.

Critical Thinking

4. **Synthesizing Information** How did European imperialism differ in India, China, and Southeast Asia?

Understanding Themes

5. **Reaction** How did the Japanese succeed in avoiding extensive Western interference in its affairs, while China could not?

SECTION 3 REVIEW ANSWERS

1. All vocabulary words are defined in the Glossary.
2. Ci Xi, 715; Sun Yat-sen, 716; Perry, 716; Mutsuhito, 717; Diponegoro, 718
3. because of the Sepoy Rebellion
4. In India, Britain ruled closely and developed Western institutions. In China, various European powers held spheres of influence. In Southeast Asia, a number of European powers ruled colonies in a variety of ways; make sure students use specific facts.
5. REACTION Japan industrialized and created a strong military, becoming a power in its own right.

Chapter 27 Section 3

Visualizing History In 1844 China and France signed the Treaty of Whampoa, which expanded French rights within that port.
Answer to Caption: *Colonial landowners and trading companies changed traditional ways of life and damaged the landscape.*

Enrich

Have students prepare comic strips depicting a specific event in this section, such as the Sepoy Rebellion, the Boxer Rebellion, or the colonization of the Dutch East Indies. After students present their work in class, display the comic strips until completing Chapter 27.

CLOSE

Have students hold a class discussion on the topic "Positive and Negative Outcomes of Imperialism in Asia." Have them decide whether imperialism was a constructive or destructive force in the late 1800s and early 1900s.

Critical Thinking SKILLS

TEACH

Analyzing Political Cartoons
Bring some political cartoons to class, such as the ones that appear on the editorial page of many newspapers. Before having the class read the skill, distribute copies of the cartoons. **What is each cartoon's point and how did you figure it out?** After a short class discussion, ask students to read the skill and complete the practice questions.

Additional Practice

Skill Reinforcement Activity 27

Critical Thinking SKILLS

Analyzing Political Cartoons

Do you enjoy reading the comics section in the newspaper? Most people enjoy reading comic strips. Cartoons, however, also appear on the editorial page. These are called political cartoons because they express opinions on political issues. Political cartoons are good sources of historical information because they reflect opinions on current affairs.

Learning the Skill

A political cartoonist relies mostly on images to communicate a message. Using caricature and symbols, political cartoons help readers see relationships and draw conclusions about events. A caricature is a drawing that exaggerates a subject's distinctive features. Cartoonists use caricature to create a positive or negative impression of a subject. For example, if a cartoon shows one figure three times larger than another, it implies that one figure is more powerful than the other.

A symbol is an image or object that represents something else. For example, a cartoonist may use a crown to represent monarchy. Symbols often represent nations or political parties. The bald eagle and Uncle Sam are common symbols for the United States. A bear often stands for Russia.

To analyze a political cartoon, first identify the topic and principal characters. Read labels and messages. Note relationships between the figures and symbols. Review your knowledge of the cartoon's topic to determine the cartoonist's viewpoint and message.

Practicing the Skill

The political cartoon on this page, published in 1900, makes a statement about China after the Boxer Rebellion. Study the cartoon and then answer these questions.

1. How is China represented in the cartoon?
2. What do the other figures represent?
3. Why are the bear and the lion so large? Why are they holding weapons?
4. What is the message of the cartoon?

Applying the Skill

Choose a current issue on which you hold a strong opinion. It can be a school, local, national, or international issue. Draw a political cartoon expressing your opinion on this issue. Show it to a friend to find out if the message is clear. If not, revise the cartoon to clarify its point.

For More Practice

Turn to the Skill Practice in the Chapter Review on page 727 for more practice in analyzing political cartoons.

ANSWERS TO PRACTICING THE SKILL

1. as a dragon
2. bear: Russia; eagle: United States; lion: Austria; leopard: Japan
3. because Russia and Austria were powerful
4. China has been defeated by the imperialist nations, each of which wants to expand its sphere of influence.

720 **Chapter 27** *The Age of Imperialism*

1820 — **1823** The United States proclaims the Monroe Doctrine.
1870 — **1898** The United States declares war on Spain.
1920 — **1914** The Panama Canal opens.

Section 4

Imperialism in the Americas

Setting the Scene

- **Terms to Define**
  arbitration
- **People to Meet**
  James Monroe, José Martí, William McKinley, Theodore Roosevelt, Benito Juárez, Porfirio Díaz, Woodrow Wilson, Venustiano Carranza, Francisco "Pancho" Villa, Emiliano Zapata
- **Places to Locate**
  Cuba, Puerto Rico, the Virgin Islands, Isthmus of Panama, Mexico

Find Out How did Latin Americans respond to the growth of American influence in their region?

The Storyteller

Frederic Remington was one of the first "foreign correspondents"—a journalist in Cuba during the Spanish-American War. He wrote: "At night I lay up beside the road outside of Siboney, and cooked my supper by a soldier fire, and lay down under a mango-tree on my raincoat, with my haversack for a pillow. I could hear the shuffling of the marching troops, and see by the light of the fire near the road the ... sweaty men."

—adapted from *Frederic Remington and the Spanish-American War*, Douglas Allen, 1971

Teddy Roosevelt and the Rough Riders

On the floor of the Senate in 1898, United States Senator Albert J. Beveridge delivered a stirring speech on America's growing role as a world power:

> "Fate has written our policy for us; the trade of the world must and shall be ours. We will establish trading-posts throughout the world as distributing-points for American products.... Great colonies governing themselves, flying our flag and trading with us, will grow about our posts of trade."

Senator Beveridge's grand ambition capped a half-century of growing American influence in world affairs. The imperialist powers of Europe had already laid claim to much of the world. Now that the United States had grown considerably in size, wealth, and power, it was determined to use the Monroe Doctrine to block the spread of European imperialism in neighboring Latin America, an area that includes Mexico, the Caribbean islands, Central America, and South America. In doing so, the United States was also promoting its own brand of imperialism that involved the penetration of new economic markets and the acquisition of overseas territories.

The Monroe Doctrine

Even before the independence of all the Latin American countries was well established, Spain had sought the support of other European powers in reconquering its former colonies. Both the United States and Great Britain opposed Spain's plan. The United States did not want a strong European power so close to its borders. Great

Chapter 27
Section 4

SECTION THEME

- **Nationalism** Nationalism intensifies in Latin America as United States involvement in the region increases.

Find Out

Answer: *They rebelled against American rule.*

FOCUS

Section Objective

Explain how Latin Americans responded to the growth of American influence in their region.

BELLRINGER
Motivational Activity

Before taking roll at the beginning of the class period, project Section Focus Transparency 27-4 and have students answer the activity questions. Discuss students' responses.

This activity is also available as a blackline master.

Vocabulary Pre-check

Use Vocabulary Activity 27 to introduce vocabulary terms. **L1 LEP**

SECTION RESOURCES

Reproducible Masters
- Reproducible Lesson Plan 27-4
- Vocabulary Activity 27
- Guided Reading Activity 27-4
- Reteaching Activity 27
- Enrichment Activity 27
- Section Quiz 27-4
- Performance Assessment Activity 27
- Spanish Chapter Summary 27

Transparencies
- Section Focus Transparency 27-4

Multimedia
- Student Self-Test and Review Software
- Testmaker

Chapter 27 *The Age of Imperialism* 721

TEACH

Guided Practice

THEME **Nationalism**

Ask students to write a definition of *nationalism*. Discuss students' ideas about nationalism and refer to nationalist leaders discussed in the section (Martí, Juárez, Díaz, Carranza, "Pancho" Villa, Zapata). Then ask students to name some locations where nationalist movements have arisen recently. *(former Yugoslav republics, republics of the former Soviet Union, the West Bank and Gaza Strip under Israeli control, Basque separatists in Spain)* **What do nationalist movements hope to gain or preserve?** *(cultural and political independence)* **L1**

Visualizing History A U.S. military government controlled Cuba from 1898 to 1902. In 1903 Cuba signed a treaty granting the United States a permanent lease on Guantánamo Bay, where it built a large naval base. From 1906 to 1909, American forces occupied Cuba again.
Answer to Caption: *Cuba's sugar and tobacco plantations were important to Spain's economy.*

History Have students examine the events leading to the outbreak of the Spanish-American War. **What reasons did politicians and businesspeople have for wanting war with Spain?** *(voter popularity; a show of strength; fear that investments would be worthless if the revolutionaries lost to the Spanish)* **Do you think that U.S. involvement in the conflict was a rational decision, an emotional response, or a combination of both?** **L2**

Visualizing History **United States Marines hoist the American flag in Cuba.** *What was Spain's economic interest in Cuba?*

Britain had developed good trade relations with the Latin Americans and did not feel that its commercial interests would be served by the return of Spanish control to the Americas.

Proclamation

Great Britain suggested to the United States that a joint warning be issued to the various European powers. However, President **James Monroe** and Secretary of State John Adams decided to act alone. In 1823 Monroe warned the European powers not to interfere in the countries of the Western Hemisphere. The Monroe Doctrine, as it was later called, contained two major points:

> "1. The American continents, by the free and independent condition which they have assured and maintain, are hence forth not to be considered as subjects for future colonization by any European powers.
>
> 2. We should consider any attempt on their part to extend their system to any portion of this hemisphere as dangerous to our peace and safety."

At the time the Monroe Doctrine was declared, it was not clear what the United States would do if European powers tried to conquer any part of Latin America. The support of the British Royal Navy, however, ensured that the infant states of Latin America would remain free to determine their own political destinies.

Growing Involvement

As the United States grew in strength during the late 1800s and early 1900s, it began to make its power felt in Latin America. In 1895, when Great Britain was in conflict with Venezuela over the boundaries of British Guiana, the United States urged that the dispute be submitted to **arbitration**, or settlement by a third party that is agreeable to both sides. Appealing to the Monroe Doctrine, the United States Department of State issued a strong warning to the British to pressure them into accepting arbitration. Aware of the power of the United States and involved with problems in its empire, Great Britain agreed to a peaceful settlement.

In 1904 President Theodore Roosevelt extended the Monroe Doctrine in what became known as the Roosevelt Corollary. Under this addition, the United States government would actively intervene to force Latin American countries to honor their foreign debts.

The Spanish-American War

Soon after the Guiana border dispute was settled, the United States turned its attention to **Cuba**. Cuba and the neighboring island of **Puerto Rico** were still Spanish colonies in the late 1800s. Cuba was particularly important to Spain, which reaped huge profits from the island's many sugar and tobacco plantations.

In 1895 **José Martí**, a writer and political activist, led Cubans in a revolution against Spanish rule. Cuba's Spanish leaders embarked on a bloody attack on the rebel forces. Martí was killed in a battle against the Spaniards, and Spanish troops rounded up thousands of Cubans and sent them to prison camps where conditions were brutal. Disease and starvation soon claimed more than 400,000 Cuban lives.

Remember the *Maine*!

The struggle of the Cubans for freedom attracted much sympathy in the United States. American newspapers printed vivid stories describing the cruelty and killings in Cuba. Soon, prominent American politicians began clamoring for war with Spain. Businesspeople who had invested in Cuba also joined in. Finally, in January 1898, President **William McKinley** ordered the battleship *Maine* to Havana, the capital of Cuba, to demonstrate growing American interest in Cuban affairs. A few weeks later, an explosion ripped through the *Maine* while it was still anchored in Havana harbor, sinking the ship and killing 260 American sailors.

COOPERATIVE LEARNING ACTIVITY

Research Organize students into several small groups. Have each group research U.S. relations with the Philippines during one of these time periods: immediately after the Spanish-American War (the period discussed in this section), during World War I, during World War II, during the cold war, and at the present time. Have each group divide the tasks of gathering data, preparing summaries of the material, providing a time line to accompany the summaries, and exhibiting the material in a class presentation. **L2**

ettmann

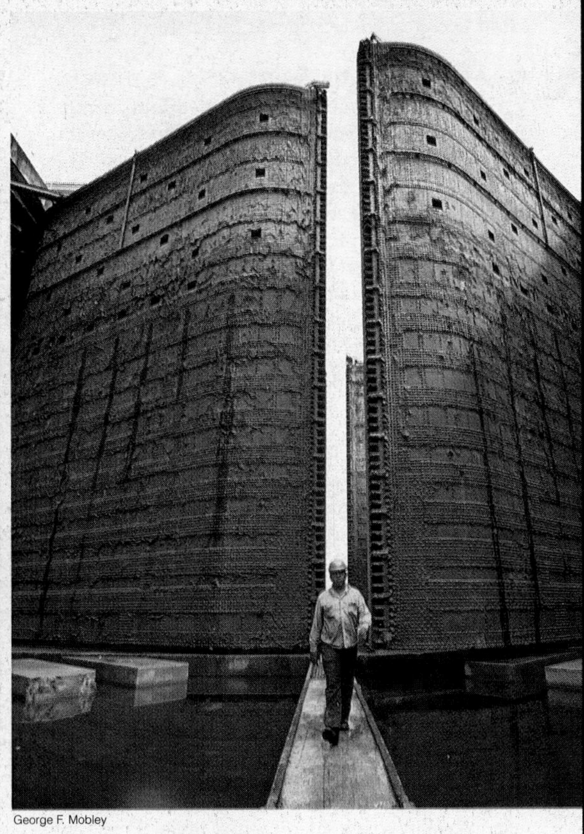

George F. Mobley

Panama Canal

Harvard College Library

The Panama Canal was a testament to the skill of American engineers. The enormous lock gates (under construction, left) were made of steel plates attached to a skeleton of steel girders. (Note the size of the men working around these gates.) Each gate weighed 700 tons (784 short tons) but was hollow and could float. Because they were buoyant, the gates exerted less stress on their hinges as the gates were opened and closed. Without the significant advances made in technology during the 1800s, this canal could not have been built.

Without President Theodore Roosevelt (center) the Panama Canal would not have been built. During his presidency he decided that the United States would build a canal across the Isthmus of Panama—and he made it happen. Roosevelt wanted to boost American power and to compete more effectively with the imperial powers of Europe and Japan. The Panama Canal helped accomplish this goal by strengthening the military posture of the United States. The canal eliminated 7,800 miles (12,550 km) from the sea voyage between New York and San Francisco. It cost $380 million and tens of thousands of lives, and took ten years to complete.

TEACH

Tell students that there were several reasons for Lesseps's failure to built a Panama Canal. The French not only did not have the necessary tools for implementing such a huge task of digging but also lacked the medical knowledge needed to control the epidemics of tropical disease that decimated the laborers. In addition, dishonest political backers of Lesseps siphoned off cash from the company, which went bankrupt in 1889.

CURRICULUM CONNECTION

MEDICINE
Beginning in 1904, Colonel William C. Gorgas, the U.S. physician who had wiped out yellow fever in Havana, Cuba, after the Spanish-American War, began an effort to eliminate malaria, yellow fever, and bubonic plague from the Isthmus of Panama. By destroying the mosquitoes that carry the first two diseases and the rats that carry the third, Gorgas dramatically lowered the death toll.

Linking Past and Present

Teddy Bears The stuffed bears that generations of children have cherished are named for President Theodore Roosevelt. After a cartoonist depicted him with a bear cub, toymakers began to produce the stuffed animals that are still called teddy bears.

Chapter 27
Section 4

Independent Practice

Guided Reading Activity 27-4 **L1**

Cartoon Have students draw political cartoons depicting a major event from the section and present them to the class. **L2**

Foreign Policy Have students research and write short reports on public reaction to a more recent attempt by the United States to shape political events in Latin America by supporting the Nicaraguan *contras*. Ask students to consider how attitudes toward American intervention have changed over the century. **L3**

ASSESS

Check for Understanding

Assign Section 4 Review as homework or as an in-class activity.

Use Student Self-Test and Review Software to review Section 4.

The cry "Remember the *Maine!*" swept across the United States. American newspapers left little doubt that Spain was responsible for the disaster. In April 1898, under pressure from all sides, McKinley asked Congress to declare war on Spain.

American Territorial Gains

The Spanish-American War lasted four months and ended with a victory and new territories for the United States in the Pacific and the Caribbean. The Philippine Islands, the Pacific island of Guam, and Puerto Rico became American territories. Cuba was recognized as independent but came under American protection. Nearly two decades later, the United States acquired its last territorial gain in the Caribbean, when Congress in 1917 ratified the purchase of **the Virgin Islands** (St. Thomas, St. John, and St. Croix) from Denmark for $25 million.

The Panama Canal

Victory in the Spanish-American War made the United States a world power. It became important for the United States to be able to move its fleet quickly between the Pacific and Atlantic Oceans. What was needed was a canal across the **Isthmus of Panama**, a narrow neck of land that linked Central America and South America.

For centuries, Europeans and Americans had dreamed of building a canal across Central America. In the 1880s the Frenchman Ferdinand de Lesseps, who had built the Suez Canal, tried to build a Central American canal in Panama. He failed. Twenty years later, United States President **Theodore Roosevelt** found a way to succeed.

In 1903 Panama was part of Colombia. Roosevelt tried to negotiate a treaty with Colombia that year that would allow the United States to build a canal through Panama. When Colombia refused to sign the treaty, Roosevelt and the American public were outraged.

Roosevelt soon developed a plan, however. With his approval, American agents encouraged the people of Panama to revolt against the government of Colombia. They did so on the night of November 3, 1903, with the help of the United States Navy, which prevented Colombian troops from landing. The rebellion was over by the next day, and the new Republic of Panama quickly signed a treaty granting the United States the right to build the Panama Canal.

Construction of the canal began in 1904 and took 10 years to complete. More than 40,000 workers cut through hills, built dams, and drained swamps until the two mighty oceans were connected. Many of the workers, however, died of malaria and yellow fever. This problem eventually was solved by implementing a sanitation program to control disease-carrying mosquitoes. When the first ship finally steamed through the canal in August 1914, the canal was hailed as one of the world's great engineering feats.

The Roosevelt Corollary

Possession of the Panama Canal gave the United States even more of a stake in Latin America. Thus, the United States continued to exert its power in the region throughout the early 1900s. In 1904 the Monroe Doctrine was extended by President Theodore Roosevelt in what became known as the Roosevelt Corollary. Some Latin American countries had been unable to pay back foreign loans, and European powers threatened to collect their debts by force. Roosevelt announced that the United States would act as a police power to force Latin American countries to honor their debts. The United States made it clear that it would not only stop European powers from intervention, but would itself actively intervene in Latin America.

The Roosevelt Corollary, or addition to, the Monroe Doctrine was first applied in 1905. At that time the United States took charge of the customs service of the Dominican Republic, receiving duties and distributing them to that country's creditors. Beginning in 1916, United States Marines occupied the Dominican Republic for 8 years to keep order. During the next 3 decades, the United States intervened in a similar manner in such countries as Nicaragua and Haiti.

The United States hoped that its Marines would provide stability and prepare the way for democracy. However, most Latin Americans interpreted American actions as moves to turn their countries into "colonies" of the United States and to protect foreign businesses that were exploiting their resources.

Mexico

During the late 1800s the United States cautiously watched developments in its southern neighbor, **Mexico**. Since winning its independence in 1821, Mexico had seen conflict between liberals and conservatives who competed for control of the country. Conservatives favored an orderly government in the hands of the wealthy, the Catholic Church, and the military. Liberals, by contrast,

MEETING SPECIAL NEEDS ACTIVITY

Language Delayed Some students who speak English as a second language may come from families with personal experiences in countries fighting against outside intervention. Ask these students to interview a parent or an acquaintance with such experience. Have them write the interviews in their native language. Then work with them individually as they translate their interviews into English. Read some of the translated interviews to the class as a basis for class discussion. **L1 LEP**

supported limits on the power of the military and the Church. They also wanted to break up the large estates of the Creoles and return the land to poor mestizo and Native American farmers.

Reform and Stability

In 1855 Mexican voters chose **Benito Juárez**, a lawyer of Native American background, as president. Juárez immediately introduced a program of wide-ranging liberal reforms, but his administration was hampered by conservative opposition, civil war, and the intervention of French forces.

In 1872 a mestizo general named **Porfirio Díaz** succeeded Juárez as president. Díaz's presidency was one of the longest in Mexican history, lasting until 1911. To ensure law and order, Díaz relied on the army and often stifled individual freedoms. He also encouraged foreign investors to bring their capital to Mexico. The foreign companies that took advantage of Díaz's offers made good profits and enjoyed stable political conditions. Unfortunately for the Mexican people, most profits were sent outside the country.

The Mexican Revolution

In 1910 a bloody revolution supported by mestizos and Native Americans led to the overthrow of Díaz. For several years civil war raged throughout Mexico. After Díaz's overthrow, a new government came to power under the liberal politician Francisco Madero. Two years later, one of Díaz's generals, Victoriano Huerta, assassinated Madero and seized the reins of power himself.

The United States despised Huerta and immediately began looking for a way to topple him from power. After the Mexican police arrested some disorderly American soldiers visiting Mexico in 1914, President **Woodrow Wilson** saw his chance. He ordered United States Marines to seize the Mexican port of Veracruz and shut off Huerta's flow of guns and supplies.

Although uprisings by the Mexican people soon toppled Huerta from power, no strong leader emerged to take his place. Instead, three rival revolutionary leaders—**Venustiano Carranza**, **Francisco "Pancho" Villa**, and **Emiliano Zapata**—competed for power. When the United States recognized Carranza as president in 1915, Villa launched a series of anti-American raids. He not only removed 17 American citizens from a Mexican train and had them shot, but also killed 19 more Americans in a raid on a New Mexico border town. In response, President Wilson sent American troops into Mexico in 1916 to capture Villa.

The entry of the United States into World War I in 1917 led to the withdrawal of these troops, and a probable war with Mexico was avoided. That same year, Carranza adopted a new constitution, and launched liberal reforms. Although tension between Mexico and the United States decreased sharply, the memory of United States intervention lingered in the minds of Latin Americans for years to come.

AROUND THE WORLD

The Hague Peace Conference

The Netherlands, 1899

Representatives from 26 nations attended a peace conference at The Hague in 1899 to deal with arms limitation. While no arms limitation agreement was made, the Hague Conference accomplished other goals, such as the creation of the Permanent Court of Justice. The Hague Conference also prohibited the use of chemical and biological weapons.

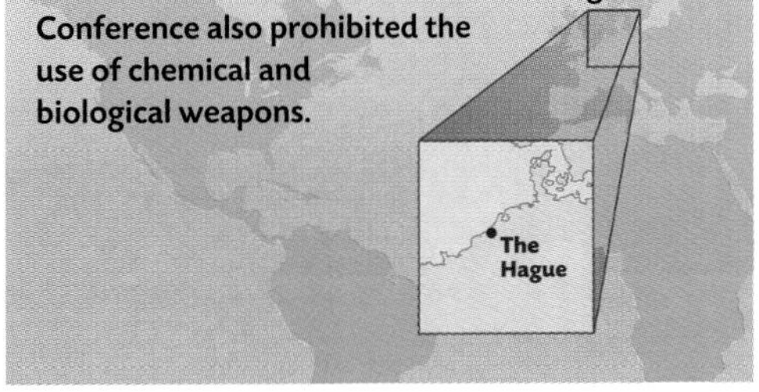

SECTION 4 REVIEW

Recall

1. **Define** arbitration.
2. **Identify** James Monroe, Monroe Doctrine, José Martí, William McKinley, Theodore Roosevelt, Benito Juárez, Porfirio Díaz, Woodrow Wilson, Venustiano Carranza, Francisco "Pancho" Villa, Emiliano Zapata.
3. **Explain** the purpose of the Roosevelt Corollary to the Monroe Doctrine.

Critical Thinking

4. **Analyzing Information** Why do you think the United States government was so concerned about maintaining its influence in Latin America during the late 1800s and early 1900s?

Understanding Themes

5. **Nationalism** What factors led to the Mexican Revolution that began in 1910?

Chapter 27 Section 4

Evaluate

Section Quiz 27-4

Use the Testmaker to create a customized quiz for Section 4.

Reteach

Ask students to explain the importance of the Monroe Doctrine and the Roosevelt Corollary to U.S. imperialism. Have them provide examples of the influence each had on the events covered in Section 4.

Reteaching Activity 27

Enrich

Arrange for students to see a video of *Viva Zapata!*, the 1952 film chronicling the life of the Mexican revolutionary leader. Ask students to pretend they are newspaper or television movie critics and to write a review of the film for submission or for class presentation.

Enrichment Activity 27

CLOSE

Have students divide a sheet of paper into three columns. In one column have them summarize their reactions to imperialism as if they were supporters of Woodrow Wilson in 1914–1916. In the second column have them summarize their reactions to imperialism as if they were supporters of "Pancho" Villa in 1914–1916. In the third column have them summarize their reactions to imperialism in their own voices.

SECTION 4 REVIEW ANSWERS

1. All vocabulary words are defined in the Glossary.
2. Monroe, 722; Monroe Doctrine, 722; Martí, 722; McKinley, 722; Roosevelt, 724; Juárez, 725; Díaz, 725; Wilson, 725; Carranza, 725; "Pancho" Villa, 725; Zapata, 725
3. to justify U.S. involvement in Latin American countries with debts to Europe
4. It wanted to establish itself as a contender in the imperialist competition.
5. **NATIONALISM** pent-up grievances after years of dictatorship under Díaz; demands for social justice for mestizos and Native Americans

Chapter 27 Review

GLENCOE TECHNOLOGY

VIDEODISC

Use MindJogger to review students' knowledge of the chapter.

MindJogger Videoquiz

Chapter 27
Disc 4 Side A

Also available in VHS.

Answers

Using Key Terms

1. a	**6.** e
2. b	**7.** i
3. j	**8.** c
4. f	**9.** g
5. d	**10.** h

Using Your History Journal

Suggest that students update the history of the same nation they chose to highlight in their journal when they began the chapter. The new journal entry should review the country's history since independence as well as make some predictions for its future that are grounded in specifics.

Reviewing Facts

1. France (Algeria, Morocco, Tunis, French West Africa); Britain (Egypt, Gold Coast, Ashanti, Nigeria, South Africa); Italy (Libya); Belgium (Congo)
2. Puerto Rico, the Philippines, and Guam
3. revised the tax structure; created modern currency system; supported the building of postal and telegraph networks, railroads, and port facilities
4. Siam

Critical Thinking

1. It created a demand for raw materials and expanded markets.
2. It transformed itself into a modern society by reforming its government and educational system, industrializing, and building a strong military.
3. They might force you to grow crops for export, to work for low wages, and to pay special taxes.
4. It promoted unity by bringing people from around the world into closer contact; it promoted disunity by sparking wars and other conflicts.

Geography in History

1. Atlantic and Pacific Oceans
2. The distance across the continent is shortest there.
3. because the isthmus makes a bend at the

CHAPTER 27 REVIEW

Historical Significance

The Age of Imperialism brought much of the globe under Western control. An unparalleled exchange of ideas and products resulted. European ways, however, often disrupted many cultures.

By the mid-1900s, after two world wars and many smaller conflicts, Europe saw its world leadership pass to the United States. Meanwhile, nationalist movements in Africa, Asia, and Latin America challenged the West's control of global events.

Using Key Terms

Write the key term that completes each sentence.

a. sepoys	f. imperialism
b. protectorate	g. spheres of influence
c. partition	h. viceroy
d. arbitration	i. culture system
e. westernization	j. colony

1. Before revolting in 1857, ______ had resented British attempts to impose Christianity and European customs on them.
2. In 1882 the British invasion of Egypt led to the establishment of a ____________, in which Egypt kept its government but had to follow British direction in its foreign affairs.
3. A _________ is a territory that an imperial power rules directly.
4. _______ means one country's control of the political, economic, and social life of another country.
5. In the 1895 border dispute between British Guiana and Venezuela, the United States urged the British to settle the dispute by __________, a process involving judgment by an impartial third party.
6. The acquisition of colonies by Europeans led to ___________, or the spread of European civilization to other parts of the world.
7. In the East Indies, the Dutch used a method of forced labor called the ________ to gather raw materials and harvest crops.
8. In 1885, 14 nations met in Berlin, Germany, and agreed to ___________ the continent of Africa among themselves.
9. By the end of the 1800s, many European nations and Japan claimed large sections of China as ___________, areas where they had exclusive trading rights.
10. In 1858 the British government sent a _________, or representative of the monarch, to govern the area of India formerly controlled by the East India Company.

Using Your History Journal

Choose one nation in Africa and research its history from the colonial era to the present. Write a short paper about your chosen country's independence and its prospects for the future.

Reviewing Facts

1. **Name** four European powers that participated in the partition of Africa. For each European power, name at least one African territory that it conquered.
2. **Identify** the three territories the United States gained as a result of the Spanish-American War.
3. **Describe** three policies that the Meiji leaders introduced to promote industrial growth.
4. **Name** the Southeast Asian kingdom that remained free of European control during the Age of Imperialism.

Critical Thinking

1. **Apply** How did the Industrial Revolution promote the growth of imperialism?
2. **Evaluate** Why was Japan able to establish itself as an imperial and military power, unlike other Asian countries?
3. **Synthesize** Imagine that your country is under the control of a foreign power. What steps might the colonial rulers take to make your country profitable?
4. **Analyze** Contrast the ways in which the Age of Imperialism contributed to the growth of unity in the world with the ways in which it contributed to disunity.

726 Chapter 27 *The Age of Imperialism*

CHAPTER 27 REVIEW

Geography in History

1. **Place** Refer to the map below. What two large bodies of water does the Panama Canal connect?
2. **Human/Environment Interaction** Why do you think engineers chose this particular location in which to build the canal?
3. **Location** Why is the Pacific Ocean located on the southeast side of this map?
4. **Region** What geographic features of this region made building the canal difficult?

The Panama Canal

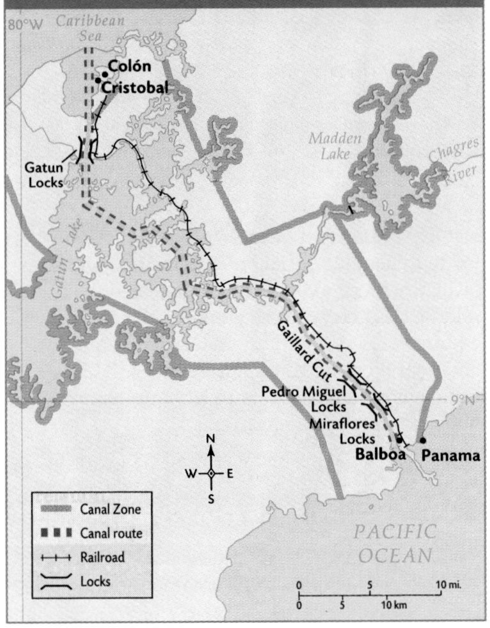

Understanding Themes

1. **Movement** What factors stimulated outward expansion by the European powers in the Age of Imperialism?
2. **Change** How did Africans react to the changes brought by the spread of imperialism in Africa?
3. **Reaction** In what two ways did Indian nationalists respond to British rule in India?
4. **Nationalism** Give an example of how the United States used Latin American nationalism to promote American national interests.

Linking Past and Present

1. Since the mid-1900s, peoples in Asia, Africa, and the Americas have won their independence from colonial rule. What remains of the empires created during the Age of Imperialism?
2. Throughout the 1900s the United States continued to intervene in Latin America. Investigate and explain three of these interventions.
3. Have attitudes about imperialism changed from the 1800s to the present time? Explain.
4. Does imperialism exist in some form today? If imperialism exists today, does it differ from the imperialism of the 1800s?

Skill Practice

Study the political cartoon on this page and then answer the following questions.

1. Who is the figure in the cartoon?
2. How has the cartoonist used caricature?
3. How has the cartoonist used symbols?
4. What is the message of the cartoon?

point where the Panama Canal was dug, putting the Pacific Ocean south and east of the Atlantic
4. its jungles, hills, and swamps

Understanding Themes

1. **MOVEMENT** national rivalries, the desire for raw materials and markets, individuals' search for new opportunities, a "civilizing" mission
2. **CHANGE** In various parts of Africa, leaders such as Samory Touré, Abd al-Qadir, and Shaka fought unsuccessfully against European control; some Africans accepted European rule with allowances for limited self-government.
3. **REACTION** Indians revolted during the Sepoy Rebellion, and they later formed the Indian National Congress to fight for Indian independence.

Chapter 27 Review

4. **NATIONALISM** The United States supported a revolt in Panama against Colombian rule. Unlike Colombia, the new Republic of Panama allowed the United States to build the Panama Canal across the isthmus.

Linking Past and Present

1. the independent member countries of the Commonwealth of Nations; the worldwide possessions of the United States
2. Answers may focus on Panama, Grenada, and Nicaragua.
3. Students might refer to Russian people's objections to Soviet involvement in Afghanistan and to American people's objections to the U.S. in Nicaragua.
4. Responses could include the view that imperialism still exists in an economic sense, because many politically independent but economically weak nations rely on wealthier nations for some kind of economic assistance.

Skill Practice

1. Cecil Rhodes
2. Rhodes appears to be a giant.
3. The cartoonist has made Rhodes look like the Colossus of Rhodes, one of the Seven Wonders of the Ancient World.
4. Rhodes's imperialist activities in Africa made him powerful.

Chapter Bonus Test Question

Ask students: How did the motives behind the age of exploration differ from those behind the Age of Imperialism? *(There was less pressure to find sources of raw materials and new markets for products during the age of exploration than during the Age of Imperialism, because the latter was in part an outgrowth of the Industrial Revolution.)*

Unit 6 Digest

The Unit Digest offers a chapter-by-chapter summary that can be used for any of the following teaching purposes:

- ***Preview*** one chapter or an entire unit,
- ***Review*** some or all of the chapters,
- ***Condense*** when specific chapters or units have not been taught, or
- ***Reteach*** chapters that students have studied in the unit.

PREVIEW

Use the Unit 6 Digest Transparencies to preview the highlights of the unit.

History & Art In the late 1800s, innovations such as gas and electric lighting, streetcars, and telephones revolutionized life in cities around the world.

Answer to Caption: *The middle class grew, but life for factory workers worsened.*

Unit 6 Digest

In the 1800s a new and vigorous spirit of change and progress enveloped the world. Great Britain led the way in the late 1700s, as inventors and industrialists helped to transform primarily rural, agricultural economies into industrial economies based on cites, factories, and manufactured goods. This swift advance of industry throughout western Europe and North America was accompanied by discoveries in science and medicine, as well as changing cultural and political attitudes. In many countries people were inspired to fight for political reform. At the same time, increasingly industrialized nations competed to establish themselves as world powers.

History & Art *The Gas Factory at Courcelles* by Ernest Jean Delahae. Museé du Petit Palis, Paris, France *How did increasing industrialization affect the social order?*

Chapter 23
Age of Industry

Before the 1700s, long-established traditions ruled daily living in Europe, and change was slow. Most people lived in rural villages and farmed small tracts of land. They were generally self-sufficient farmers who grew the food or made the things their families needed.

Agricultural Improvements

In the late 1700s, however, great changes began to occur. Wealthy landowners took control of land that for centuries had been open to all villagers, forcing many small farmers to move to the cities to find work.

As landowners gained control of greater tracts of land, they worked to get the highest possible crop yield and devised such techniques as crop rotation and fertilization. The increased food supply enabled people to live healthier, longer lives. As a result, Europe's population grew dramatically.

The Industrial Revolution

A growing population looking for work in cities, coupled with abundant natural resources such as coal, iron, and water power, helped to ignite the Industrial Revolution in Great Britain, which eventually spread throughout the world. Power-driven machinery took the place of handwork done in the home. As industry came to dominate economies, inventors developed technology for industrialists to increase and speed production.

Expanding and increasingly complex industries led to a changing social order in the mid-1800s. As factory owners and managers prospered, a sizable middle class grew. Many workers, however, endured crowded and unsanitary living quarters and poor working conditions. In the late 1800s some workers joined to form labor unions in the hope of improving their lives.

SURVEYING CHAPTER 23

1. **Identifying Trends** How did the Industrial Revolution transform European society in the 1800s?
2. **Relating Ideas** What social groups emerged as industry developed in Europe and North America?

Chapter 24
Cultural Revolution

The Industrial Revolution brought about many changes in the social and cultural life of the West. In their daily lives, Western Europeans and North Americans were forced to grapple with the challenges posed by the new industrial society.

CLASSROOM RESOURCES FOR UNIT 6 DIGEST

Preview
- Unit 6 Digest Transparencies

Review
- Time Line Activities 23, 24, 25, 26, 27
- Student Self-Test and Review Software, Chapters 23, 24, 25, 26, 27
- MindJogger Videoquiz, Chapters 23, 24, 25, 26, 27

Condense
- Chapter Digests Audiocassettes, Chapters 23, 24, 25, 26, 27

Reteach
- Reteaching Activities 23, 24, 25, 26, 27
- Chapter Digests Audiocassettes, Chapters 23, 24, 25, 26, 27
- Turning Points in World History

New Ideas

Economists such as Adam Smith and David Ricardo pointed out the basic principles of capitalism and held that businesses should operate without governmental interference. Other thinkers, including British philosophers Jeremy Bentham and John Stuart Mill, favored capitalism but called for government supervision and reforms to provide social justice. Still others, such as the German philosopher Karl Marx, opposed capitalism and supported socialism, believing that workers either by themselves or through the government should control industry.

Scientific Advances

The Age of Industry also saw many exciting scientific advances. In the 1850s British naturalist Charles Darwin proposed a theory of evolution to explain the origins of life. About the same time, medical pioneers such as Louis Pasteur used new scientific knowledge to conquer diseases such as smallpox and rabies that had plagued humankind for thousands of years.

Medical discoveries meant a better quality of life. Meanwhile, improved means of transportation enabled people to venture from their native lands to seek new opportunities in other parts of the world. Increased interest in education led to the spread of literacy as public schools and libraries were established throughout Europe and the United States.

The Arts

The rapid pace of social changes in Europe and North America was reflected in the arts. Painters and writers expressed a diversity of approaches. Romantics reacted to industrialization by glorifying nature, the emotional, the spiritual, and the ideal. Realists rejected the idealism of the romantics and vividly portrayed the lives of ordinary people and the problems of urban industrial life that they wanted to change. Impressionists and their artistic successors abandoned the rules governing traditional art and focused on colors, light, and the structure of objects.

SURVEYING CHAPTER 24

1. **Making Comparisons** How did Adam Smith and Karl Marx differ in their views about the way economic affairs should be handled?
2. **Relating Ideas** What impact did industrial and scientific advances have on the daily lives of people?

Chapter 25
Democracy and Reform

Economic and social transformation inspired the growth of democracy in various parts of the world. In some places, the political changes were gradual and peaceful; in other places, they were sudden and violent.

Great Britain

Great Britain was the world's strongest economic and imperial power during most of the 1800s. The British government moved slowly toward democracy as more people gained voting rights and election districts were redistributed to give equal representation. Electoral reform in Great Britain brought about the rise of political parties that represented certain well-defined beliefs.

While democracy evolved in Great Britain, the working class, women, and Irish Catholics often used pressure to speed up the reform process. Meanwhile, overseas colonies, such as Canada, Australia, and New Zealand, benefited from the era of reform and achieved self-rule within the British Empire.

France

In France, political changes did not come so easily. The 1800s was a century of turmoil, as the French government changed in form from monarchy to republic to empire to republic.

The Second Republic of France, created by a revolution in 1848, served as a stepping-stone from which Louis-Napoleon launched the Second Empire of France. The most striking achievement of the Second Empire was economic growth. The Second Empire collapsed as a result of French defeat in a war with Prussia. The Third Republic of France, created in 1875, lacked stability, but managed to survive several crises that threatened its collapse. The most enduring achievements of the Third Republic were its safeguards of civil liberties and educational reforms.

The United States

As the countries of Europe struggled with demands for reform, the United States in the early 1800s more than doubled in size. As new states entered the Union, the slavery issue began to divide public opinion. The South favored the protection and expansion of slavery, while the North argued for either limiting slavery to the South or abolishing it altogether.

The slavery debate drew the country into a bloody civil war in 1861. President Abraham Lincoln led the United States through this bitter conflict as he strove to save the Union. After the Civil War, the United States, once more reunited, began to develop into a strong industrial nation.

ANSWERS TO SURVEYING THE CHAPTER

CHAPTER 23 ANSWERS

1. As power-driven machines replaced handwork done in the home, large factories grew. Many people left their farms to work in the factories, and cities grew. The middle class expanded as more and more factory owners and managers prospered. The conditions of the working classes worsened.
2. A sizable middle class and a large working class developed in industrialized nations.

Unit 6 Digest

REVIEW

GLENCOE TECHNOLOGY

VIDEODISC
Use MindJogger to review any chapter in Unit 6.

MindJogger Videoquiz

Chapter 23
Disc 3 Side B

Chapter 24
Disc 3 Side B

Chapter 25
Disc 4 Side A

Chapter 26
Disc 4 Side A

Chapter 27
Disc 4 Side A

Also available in VHS.

Use the Student Self-Test and Review Software to review any chapters that students have studied in Unit 6.

ABCNEWS INTERACTIVE™

VIDEODISC
Turning Points in World History

Side Two
Chapter 3

Title: *The Industrial Revolution*
Ask: What kind of revolution are we experiencing today? *(a technological revolution)*

Unit 6 Digest

History Lead students in a discussion of the power of nationalism to prompt political change. Have the class agree on a definition of nationalism. *(the desire of people sharing a common culture to have their own nation-state)* Then have students write two or three paragraphs about the role nationalism played in European political events during the 1800s. **L2**

The Arts Guide students in a discussion about movements in literature and art during the 1800s. What effect did the movements have on views of the working class? *(Romantic writers portrayed workers positively and made them into heroes.)* What effect do you think these cultural movements had on society as a whole? *(Possible answer: Realists and naturalists portrayed the suffering of exploited workers and may have gained support for efforts to improve their condition.)* **L3**

CONDENSE

Use Chapter Digests Audiocassettes to introduce chapters that students have not studied in Unit 6. Spanish Chapter Digests Audiocassettes are also available.

Discuss Have students read the **Unit Digest** and discuss the **Surveying Chapter** questions. **L1**

Latin America

Farther south, the Enlightenment ideas of freedom and equality influenced the peoples of Latin America. Beginning in the late 1700s, Latin American colonists began to fight for independence from Spanish or Portuguese rule. Dedicated leaders such as Simón Bolívar and José de San Martín helped Latin Americans achieve this goal by the mid-1820s.

The newly independent Latin American countries, however, lacked experience in self-government, and military dictators frequently came to power during the 1800s. Economic advancement was hampered by the huge social gap that divided wealthy landowners from impoverished farmers.

SURVEYING CHAPTER 25

1. **Making Comparisons** How did Great Britain differ from France in the advance toward democracy?
2. **Relating Ideas** What ideas had an impact in promoting the cause of independence in Latin America?

Chapter 26 Reaction and Nationalism

The desire for national independence, known as nationalism, became one of the most powerful forces in Europe during the 1800s. In some areas people struggled to unify small, individual states into one nation. In others people fought to break free from large empires.

Italy

Following the Congress of Vienna in 1815, a movement for Italian unity grew and spread across Italy. To achieve political unification, the Italians had to expel Austria from the Italian Peninsula and overcome the opposition of the pope. Giuseppe Mazzini, Giuseppe Garibaldi, and Count Camillo di Cavour were key figures in generating interest in the cause of unity and gained the military support needed to expel Austria and unite southern Italy with the rest of the peninsula. In 1861 Italy became a constitutional monarchy under the leadership of Sardinia.

Germany

A similar quest for political unification took place in the much larger area of central Europe known as Germany. The main figure in German political unification was Otto von Bismarck, the prime minister of Prussia. In the early 1860s Bismarck directed the development of a strong Prussian army. Prussia's military victories helped to win the support of Germans for the cause of unity.

In 1871 Germany finally became one nation under William I of Prussia, who served as kaiser, or emperor. Bismarck, however, discouraged the growth of democracy and tried in vain to destroy the Catholic and Socialist political parties. Conflict between Bismarck and the new kaiser, William II, led to Bismarck's resignation in 1890.

The Russian Empire

Russian czars generally resisted the forces of nationalism, democracy, and social change that were affecting the Russian Empire. As these forces transformed Europe during the 1800s, Russia's rulers strove to keep their absolute powers.

After 25 years of repressive rule by Nicholas I, Alexander II undertook major reforms, including the emancipation of serfs in 1861. For many liberals these reforms did not go far enough. When radicals assassinated Alexander II in 1881, political repression returned in full force under Alexander III, but revolutionary groups continued to grow.

Preservation of the old order was the objective of Alexander III's successor, Nicholas II. The urban working class, in spite of its small size, became a major political force during Nicholas' reign. Strikes and protests following Russia's defeat in the Russo-Japanese War forced limited political concessions from the czar.

Austria-Hungary

The Austrian Empire also tried to maintain its old order. As the empire's diverse nationalities rallied for independence and reform in 1848, Emperor Francis Joseph was able to retain power only by playing one national group against another. In 1867, after Austria's defeat in the Seven Weeks' War, Francis was forced to accept the dual monarchy that gave Hungary equal standing with Austria in the empire. Meanwhile, the Slavic peoples of the empire continued to push for greater political rights.

SURVEYING CHAPTER 26

1. **Making Comparisons** How did the influence of nationalism on Italy in the mid-1800s differ from its influence on Austria-Hungary during the same period?
2. **Identifying Trends** How did Russian czars of the 1800s and early 1900s respond to the forces of change that were affecting their empire?

ANSWERS TO SURVEYING THE CHAPTER

CHAPTER 24 ANSWERS

1. Smith believed that an unregulated market would bring prosperity to all; Marx felt that inequality and conflicts between classes were inevitable—until the revolution of the proletariat.
2. Medical breakthroughs conquered diseases such as smallpox; better transportation and communication opened new possibilities for ordinary people.

CHAPTER 25 ANSWERS

1. Britain democratized slowly by giving more people voting rights; France went back and forth between republic and monarchy or empire.
2. Enlightenment ideas of freedom and equality and the examples of the American and French Revolutions promoted Latin American independence.

Chapter 27
The Age of Imperialism

Three key factors led to the rise of imperialism in the 1800s. First, European nationalism prompted rival countries to engage in competition for overseas territory. Second, the Industrial Revolution created a great demand for more raw materials and new markets. Finally, feelings of cultural and racial superiority also influenced Europeans to impose their cultures on distant lands.

Imperialism in Africa and Asia

Africa was especially affected by the European zeal to found new colonies. Beginning around 1870, the major European powers divided the continent among themselves, established colonies, and exploited the continent's natural resources. By 1914 only two African nations—Liberia and Ethiopia—had managed to escape European control.

In India, the British East India Company established a strong hold over the subcontinent and its abundant resources in the 1700s. Following the Sepoy Rebellion in 1857, the British government took direct control of India's affairs. To quell further unrest in India, the British spent vast amounts of money on the country's economic development. Most Indians, however, still resented British rule. In 1885 the Indian National Congress was formed, signaling the start of the long struggle for independence.

Also during the 1800s, the major European powers began to intervene in the internal affairs of China. Using military power or the threat of it, they forced China to accept trade agreements that favored Western interests. These agreements allowed the Europeans to carve out economically valuable spheres of influence in China. When the Chinese fought back in the Boxer Rebellion of 1900, the Europeans quickly crushed the revolt. Eleven years later, Chinese revolutionaries overthrew the corrupt Qing dynasty and established a republic.

The United States forced Japanese leaders to open their doors to trade when it sent Commodore Matthew C. Perry to Japan in 1853. As a result, the Meiji leaders who took control of Japan in the late 1860s decided to make Japan a great power capable of competing with the West. They reformed Japan's government and began a program to modernize and industrialize the nation. Partly as a result of this program, Japan defeated Russia in 1905 in the Russo-Japanese War. By 1914 Japan had emerged as a modern industrial nation and world power.

The United States and Latin America

Like the European powers, the United States in the late 1800s wanted to exercise influence on world affairs. During these decades the United States used the Monroe Doctrine to oppose European involvement in Latin America. At the same time, the United States government and American businesses were becoming increasingly involved in the affairs of Latin American nations. This trend increased following the Spanish-American War and construction of the Panama Canal. Tension between Latin American nations and the United States grew as a result of the United States government's repeated interventions in the region during the first two decades of the 1900s.

Meanwhile, United States intervention was accompanied by an upsurge of nationalism in Latin America. A revolution swept Mexico from 1910 to about 1920. During this upheaval, the dictatorship of Porfirio Díaz was overthrown, and various rebel leaders competed for power. The final outcome of the struggle was a new constitution and social reforms.

Visualizing History **The Boxers in China launched a series of attacks against foreigners in 1900.** *What were "spheres of influence"?*

SURVEYING CHAPTER 27

1. **Identifying Trends** What factors led to the growth of imperialism as a significant force in the world during the 1800s?
2. **Making Comparisons** How was the influence of imperialism in India different from the influence of imperialism in China?

Unit 6 Digest

RETEACH

Review Chart Have students create a review chart that summarizes the goals of colonizing nations and the resistances made by those colonized.

Reteaching Activities 23, 24, 25, 26, 27

Chapter Digests Audiocassettes, Chapters 23, 24, 25, 26, 27

Visualizing History An American missionary living in provincial China during the Boxer Rebellion wrote: "We are shut in this province with no communication with the coast for weeks....It gives one the feeling of being caught in a trap ... and the feeling will come, in spite of trying to be brave, that the Shansi missionaries may need to give their lives." **Answer to Caption:** *Spheres of influence were areas of China where European powers had exclusive trading rights.*

ANSWERS TO SURVEYING THE CHAPTER

CHAPTER 26 ANSWERS

1. The leadership of Mazzini and the spread of nationalist ideas united Italy, whereas nationalism helped to break apart Austria-Hungary.
2. Czar Alexander II undertook major reforms, but the other czars of the period used repression to preserve the old order.

CHAPTER 27 ANSWERS

1. Nationalism prompted European nations to compete for new lands; industrialization led to a search for new markets and new raw materials; and ideas of superiority inspired Europeans to bring Western ways to other cultures.
2. India was ruled first by the East India Company and then by Britain directly, which worked to develop the Indian economy; China remained independent but conceded unequal treaties and spheres of influence to the Europeans.

Introducing Unit 7

0:00 OUT OF TIME?

If time does not permit teaching each chapter in Unit 7, you may use the Unit Digest beginning on page 854, in conjunction with the Unit Digest Transparencies and Chapter Digest Audiocassettes with accompanying activities and tests.

Introducing the Unit

Unit 7 focuses on the political movements and global conflicts that gripped the world between 1914 and 1945, including the rise of fascism and communism in Europe, the growth of nationalism in the developing world, and World War I and World War II.

Unit Objectives

After reading Unit 7, students will be able to:

1. discuss the causes, events, and results of World War I.
2. trace the growth of fascist and Communist dictatorships in Italy, Germany, and the Soviet Union.
3. explain the upsurge of nationalism in Asia, Africa, and Latin America from 1919 to 1939.
4. discuss the causes of World War II and the major political realignments that followed the war.

Portfolio Project

For their radio news reports, have students choose events from the time lines on pages 732–33, 736, 768, 794, and 824. Tell them that their reports should begin with a catchy opener and be brief and lively. This activity may be an appropriate method of authentic assessment.

Unit 7 **1914–1945**

World in Conflict

Chapter 28 World War I
Chapter 29 Between Two Fires
Chapter 30 Nationalism in Asia, Africa, and Latin America
Chapter 31 World War II

Then & Now *Nationalism and imperialism had dire consequences for Europe and the world. When national pride and the scramble for overseas territories dictated foreign relations among industrial states, conflict was inevitable. Two world wars resulted. Never before in the history of civilization had the world endured devastation on such a massive scale.*

When you climb aboard a jetliner, you may reflect on the technology of air travel developed in this period. After World War II, many people hoped that the refined instruments of war could be turned to peaceful purposes. The power of the atom could be used to produce energy rather than bombs. Airplanes, developed in World War I and refined in World War II, could become a major means of transportation.

A Global Chronology

1915 — 1921 — 1927

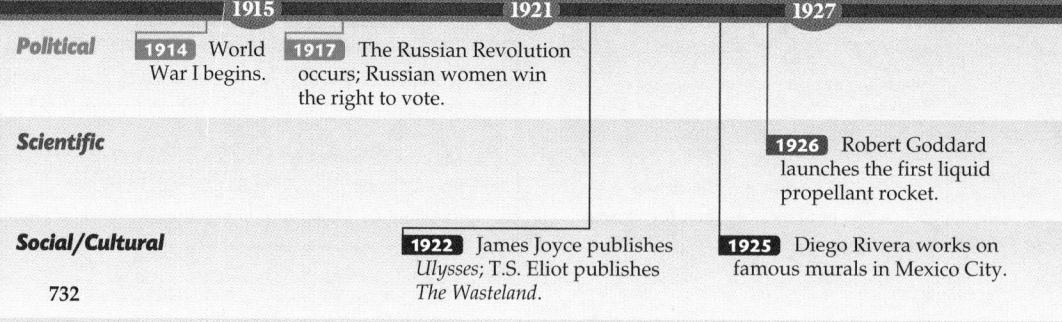

Political
- **1914** World War I begins.
- **1917** The Russian Revolution occurs; Russian women win the right to vote.

Scientific
- **1926** Robert Goddard launches the first liquid propellant rocket.

Social/Cultural
- **1922** James Joyce publishes *Ulysses*; T.S. Eliot publishes *The Wasteland*.
- **1925** Diego Rivera works on famous murals in Mexico City.

732

Then & Now **Why War?** In this unit, students will learn how democracy and peace broke down twice in Europe during the first half of the twentieth century, leading to the bloodiest conflicts in world history.

Ask students to think about the causes of war in general, particularly more recent conflicts involving the United States such as the Vietnam War and the Persian Gulf War. **What are the main reasons that nations go to war?** *(Answers will vary. Students may feel that*

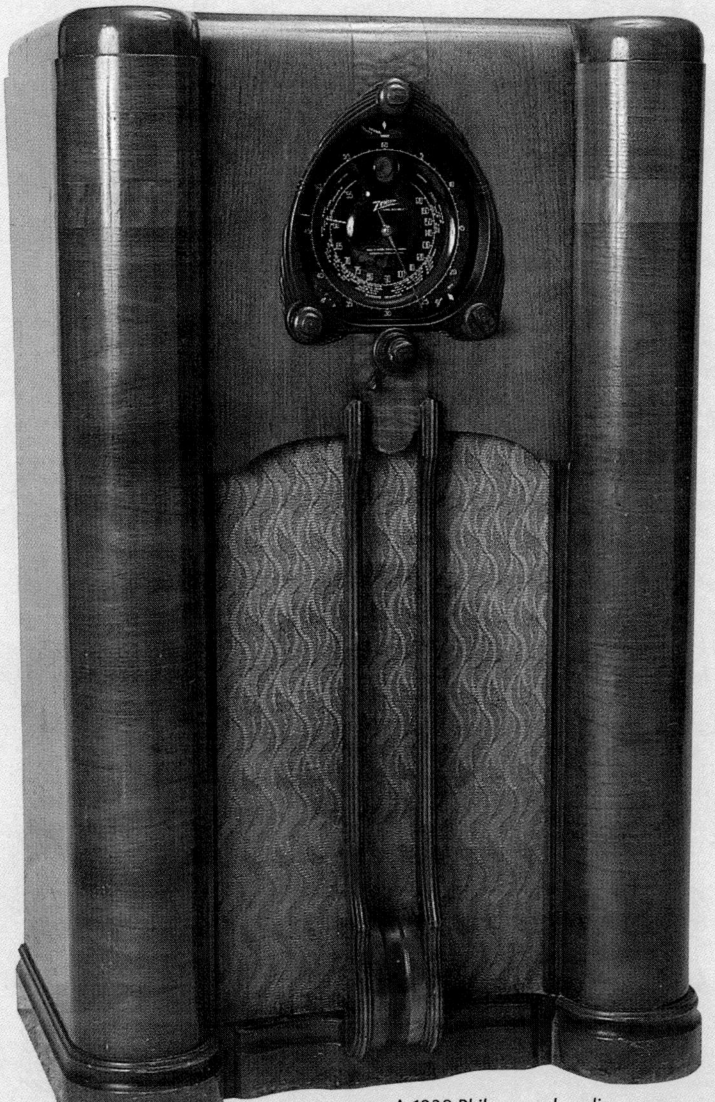

A 1938 Philco console radio

Portfolio Project

In the 1930s and 1940s radio reported dramatic news to anxious listeners. At first radio news was simply newspaper-style writing that was read on the air. Soon radio news developed a style of its own. Listen to a few radio news stories. How do they lead in? How much detail is given? How long is the typical report? From the dramatic developments of 1930–1945, compose several radio news reports and read them as an announcer on audiotape.

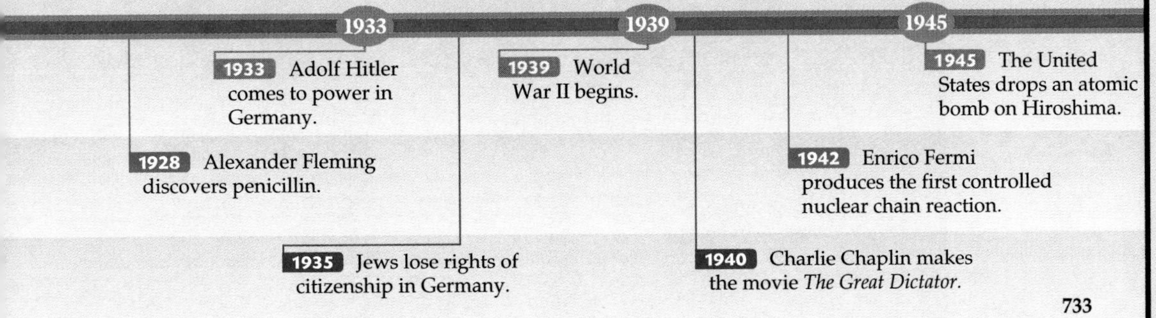

1933
1939
1945
1928 Alexander Fleming discovers penicillin.
1933 Adolf Hitler comes to power in Germany.
1935 Jews lose rights of citizenship in Germany.
1939 World War II begins.
1940 Charlie Chaplin makes the movie The Great Dictator.
1942 Enrico Fermi produces the first controlled nuclear chain reaction.
1945 The United States drops an atomic bomb on Hiroshima.

733

conflicting ideologies or interests between two nations, or aggressive actions by one nation, are the main causes of war.) Are democratic governments more or less likely to go to war than dictatorships? Why? *(Some students may feel that democracies are less likely to resort to war; others may point out that Britain and the United States, the world's oldest democracies, have fought many wars.)* Is war ever justified as a way of achieving foreign policy goals? *(Answers will vary; some students may feel that at times war cannot be avoided or is the lesser of two evils; others may respond that war is never justified.)*

Introducing Unit 7

History *and the* Humanities

World History and Art Transparencies
- 36 *Three Musicians*
- 37 *I Want You for the U.S. Army*
- 38 *Migrant Mother*
- 39 *Bird in Space*
- 40 *Zapatistas*
- 41 *Turkestan Oriental Rug*
- 42 *The Red Stairway*

World Music: Cultural Traditions, Lessons 1, 2, 6, 9

ABCNEWS INTERACTIVE™

VIDEODISC
Turning Points in World History

Side Two
Chapter 4

Title: *Assassination Ignites World War I*
Ask: Why did the assassination of the archduke plunge Europe into war? *(A web of European alliances caused most major nations to declare war.)*

Visualizing History

The first commercial radio station began to broadcast in the United States in 1920; only two years later more than 500 stations were broadcasting throughout the country. With radio, human society entered the modern era of instant communications, including special reports and live, on-the-scene broadcasting.

The Spread of Ideas

TEACH

Introduction

This feature focuses on efforts by the international community to achieve collective security, first through the League of Nations, established after World War I, and later through the United Nations, set up in the aftermath of World War II.

Background Notes

Linking Past and Present

As students will read on pages 762–764, American President Woodrow Wilson was the prime mover of the League of Nations; the failure of the Senate to approve American participation was a blow to Wilson and the League. In contrast, today the United States is a leading funder and supporter of the United Nations, even though there is often heated debate in Congress about American participation in UN peacekeeping missions.

Geography

Movement Since 1989, troops from around the world have participated in UN observer and peacekeeping missions in Latin America, Africa, and Europe. Among the most important have been observer groups to monitor elections in Nicaragua, Haiti, and South Africa and peacekeeping missions in the former Yugoslavia, the republic of Georgia, and Somalia. Ask students what problems the growing number of UN missions in recent years may have created. *(The UN has been burdened with ballooning costs and funding shortages.)*

The Spread of Ideas

International Peacekeeping

The 1900s taught people the meaning of world war. No previous century in history had ever seen conflicts that literally spanned the globe. In addition to numerous regional conflicts, the 20th century witnessed two world wars. As the scope of war grew, so did the commitment to collective security—the principle in which a group of nations join together to promote peace.

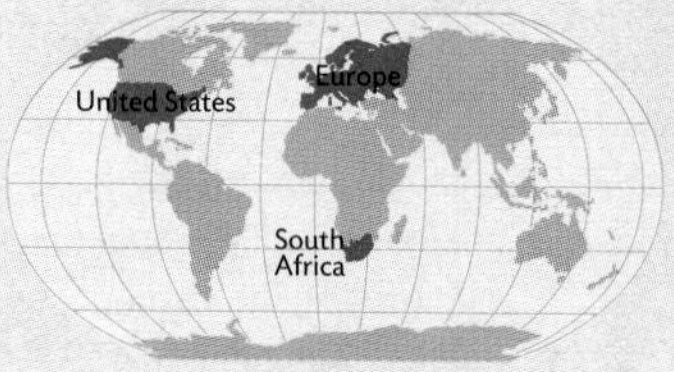

Europe

The League of Nations

As early as 1828, an American named William Ladd sought to establish a Congress of Nations to settle international disputes and avoid war. Nearly a century later, at the end of World War I, the victorious nations set up a "general association of nations" called the League of Nations.

By 1920 42 nations had sent delegates to the League's headquarters in Geneva, Switzerland. Another 21 nations eventually joined, but conspicuously absent was the United States. Opponents in the United States Senate had argued that membership in the League went against George Washington's advice against "entangling alliances."

When the League failed to halt warlike acts in the 1930s, these same opponents pointed to the failure of collective security. The League was a peacekeeper without a sword—it possessed neither a standing army nor members willing to stop nations that used war as a method of diplomacy.

UN distribution center in the Gaza Strip

COOPERATIVE LEARNING ACTIVITY

Role Play Have students brainstorm a list of international conflicts today. Then organize students into small groups. Assign each group a conflict from the list. Have them role-play an attempt by the United Nations to resolve the situation. In each group, have some students represent the two parties in conflict and others represent UN mediators. Have students discuss the sources of the conflict, then draw up and if possible agree to a peace treaty. Each group can describe its dilemma to the class and explain whether—and why—they could or could not resolve it. **L3**

Rwandan child at a refugee camp

The United States

The United Nations

Non-membership in the League did not protect the United States from the horrors of war. The Japanese air attack on Pearl Harbor, Hawaii, ended the notion that the United States could isolate itself from the rest of the world.

As World War II drew to a close, the United States hosted a meeting in San Francisco to create a new global peacekeeping organization. Here delegates from 50 nations hammered out the Charter of the United Nations. The document's Preamble sets forth a formula for international peace:

> *We the peoples of the United Nations, determined to save succeeding generations from the scourge of war, which twice in our lifetime has brought untold sorrow to mankind and to reaffirm faith in fundamental human rights ... and to promote social progress and to better standards of life and to promote our strength to maintain international peace and security, and to ensure ... that armed force shall not be used, save in the common interest ... have resolved to combine our efforts to accomplish these aims.*

In the years following, the United Nations (UN) attempted to eliminate the root causes of war. In 1946 it founded the UN Educational, Scientific, and Cultural Organization (UNESCO) and the UN Children's Fund (UNICEF). These agencies promoted global education and the well-being of children. Two years later, in 1948, United States delegate Eleanor Roosevelt convinced the UN to adopt The Universal Declaration of Human Rights. This committed the UN to the elimination of oppression wherever it existed.

South Africa

The Power of World Opinion

Like the League of Nations, the UN could be only as strong as its members were prepared to make it. The development of atomic weapons, however, was a powerful incentive for members to cooperate. By 1995, the UN had taken part in 35 peacekeeping missions—some successful, some failures. It also had provided protection for more than 30 million refugees.

The UN's ability to use world opinion to promote justice was perhaps best tested in South Africa. In 1977 the UN urged nations to use an arms embargo and economic sanctions against South Africa until apartheid was lifted. In 1994 South Africa held its first all-race elections. Many believed this was a major triumph for collective international action.

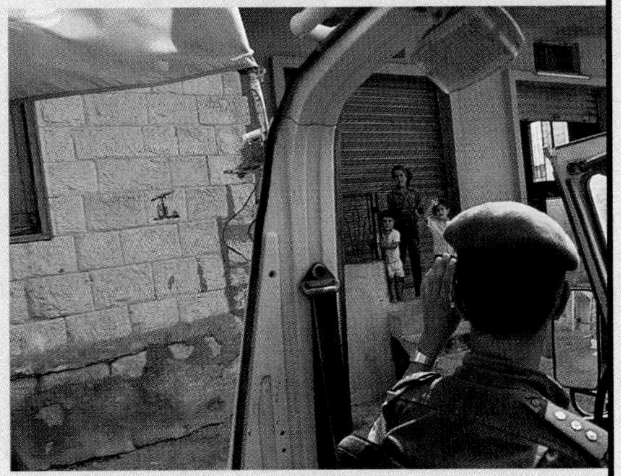

UN troops in Beirut, Lebanon

LINKING THE IDEAS

1. What factors made it difficult for the League of Nations to promote world peace?
2. What methods has the United Nations used to encourage peace?

Critical Thinking

3. **Forming Opinions** The United Nations Declaration of Human Rights sees injustice in one part of the world as a threat to peace in all parts of the world. Do you agree? Why or why not?

The Spread of Ideas

Who? What? Where? When?

Eleanor Roosevelt As the first U.S. representative to the UN Commission on Human Rights, Eleanor Roosevelt was the moving force behind the creation of the Universal Declaration of Human Rights. When the Soviet Union called for a provision against racial discrimination, Mrs. Roosevelt reluctantly opposed it, since racial segregation was still the law in much of the United States. She did, however, support the change in the first article, suggested by Hansa Mehta of India, from "All men are created equal" to "All human beings are born equal."

Cultural Diffusion

International Cooperation and Popular Music Since the 1970s the spirit of international cooperation has influenced the world of rock music. In the early 1970s, a number of rock musicians, including George Harrison and Bob Dylan, held a concert to raise money for famine victims in the newly created nation of Bangladesh (formerly part of Pakistan). In the 1980s Bob Geldof of the Boomtown Rats organized Band Aid, featuring many recording artists such as Sting and Phil Collins, to raise money for famine relief in Ethiopia.

ANSWERS TO LINKING THE IDEAS

1. It had no army, and its members were not willing to use force to stop aggression.
2. The UN has tried to eliminate the causes of war through UNESCO and UNICEF and has used peacekeeping missions, arms embargoes, and economic sanctions to promote peace.
3. Answers will vary. Some students may feel that injustice creates instability that can lead to war.

Unit 7 *World in Conflict* 735

Teach, Reinforce, and Extend CHAPTER Content

World War I

CHAPTER RESOURCES

	Reproducible Resources	Multimedia Resources
Chapter Opener	Chapter Themes: Graphic Organizer 28 Historical Significance Chapter Activity 28	MindJogger Videoquiz
Chapter Enrichment	Vocabulary Activity 28* Time Line Activity 28 Mapping History Activity 28 History Simulation 28 Geography and History Activity 28 Source Reading 28 People in World History Profiles 53, 54 World Art and Music Activity 28 Enrichment Activity 28 Critical Thinking Activity 28 Skill Reinforcement Activity 28 Performance Assessment Activity 28	World History and Art Transparency 36, *Three Musicians*; 37, *I Want You for the U. S. Army* Mapping History Overlay Transparency 18, *World War I* Chapter Transparency 28 Vocabulary PuzzleMaker Software Turning Points in World History: *Assassination Ignites World War I* Lessons of War: *How Wars Begin—World War I* Communism and the Cold War: *Perspectives on Communism*
Chapter Review/Reteaching	Reteaching Activity 28 Skill Reinforcement Activity 28 Spanish Chapter Summary 28	Chapter 28 Digest Audiocassette, Activity, Test* Vocabulary PuzzleMaker Software Student Self-Test and Review Software MindJogger Videoquiz
Chapter Evaluation/Testing	Performance Assessment Activity 28 Chapter 28 Test, Forms A and B	Testmaker

* *Also available in Spanish*

0:00 **OUT OF TIME?** Assign the Chapter 28 summary in the Unit 7 Digest on pages 854–857, and the Chapter 28 Audiocassettes.

Block Schedule

Block scheduling differs from traditional class scheduling in the amount of time allotted to each period. The extended time frame provided by block scheduling affords you the opportunity to implement a greater number of research-oriented and activity-intense projects to motivate and involve your students. Activities that are particularly suited to use within the block scheduling framework are identified throughout this chapter by the following designation.

KEY TO ABILITY LEVELS

Teaching strategies have been coded for varying learning styles and abilities.

- **L1** **BASIC** activities for all students
- **L2** **AVERAGE** activities for average to above-average students
- **L3** **CHALLENGING** activities for above-average students
- **LEP** **LIMITED ENGLISH PROFICIENCY** activities

Chapter 28 Planning Guide

A complete, 1-page lesson plan is provided for each section in the *Reproducible Lesson Plans* booklet.

SECTION RESOURCES

Daily Objectives	Reproducible Resources	Multimedia Resources
Section 1 The Seeds of War Identify the underlying causes of World War I.	Reproducible Lesson Plan 28-1 Vocabulary Activity 28* Guided Reading Activity 28-1* Time Line Activity 28 Section Quiz 28-1*	Section Focus Transparency 28-1 Chapter Transparency 28 Student Self-Test and Review Software
Section 2 The Spark Describe the series of events that provided the spark that ignited World War I.	Reproducible Lesson Plan 28-2 Vocabulary Activity 28* Guided Reading Activity 28-2* Section Quiz 28-2*	Section Focus Transparency 28-2 Student Self-Test and Review Software Turning Points in World History: *Assassination Ignites World War I*
Section 3 The War Specify where and how World War I was fought.	Reproducible Lesson Plan 28-3 Guided Reading Activity 28-3* History Simulation 28 Geography and History Activity 28 Section Quiz 28-3*	Section Focus Transparency 28-3 Mapping History Overlay Transparency 18, *World War I* World History and Art Transparency 36, *Three Musicians*; 37, *I Want You for the U. S. Army* Vocabulary PuzzleMaker Software Student Self-Test and Review Software Lessons of War: *How Wars Begin—World War I*
Section 4 The Russian Revolution Summarize the events that led to the Russian Revolution.	Reproducible Lesson Plan 28-4 Vocabulary Activity 28* Guided Reading Activity 28-4* Section Quiz 28-4*	Section Focus Transparency 28-4 Student Self-Test and Review Software Communism and the Cold War: *Perspectives on Communism*
Section 5 Peace at Last Explain why the Treaty of Versailles was ultimately unsuccessful.	Reproducible Lesson Plan 28-5 Guided Reading Activity 28-5* Reteaching Activity 28 Enrichment Activity 28 Section Quiz 28-5* Performance Assessment Activity 28 Spanish Chapter Summary 28	Section Focus Transparency 28-5 Vocabulary PuzzleMaker Software Student Self-Test and Review Software Testmaker

* *Also available in Spanish*

Chapter Activities

Performance Assessment Activity

A Chain of Events Have students assume the role of scriptwriters for a television episode about a time traveler. Each student will think of one event of the World War I era to change, then predict the chain of events that would have flowed from the changed event and describe how the war would have been different because of it. Then have students write a brief summary of the chain of events, choose real actors to play the parts of the significant individuals, decide on how the time traveler will be able to make the proposed change, and choose locations for the scenes (either real or with designed sets). Students will then present their ideas to a group whose members play the roles of producers.

Possible Rubric Features

Accuracy of content information, logical predictions, appropriateness of sets and locales for events, clarity of presentation, originality, and summarization skills

• *For an additional activity, refer to Activity 28 in the* Performance Assessment Strategies and Activities *booklet.*

ACTIVITY

From the Classroom of...

Kathleen M. Slane
Rockville High School
Vernon, CT

World War I Propaganda Posters

Show the class a number of World War I propaganda posters, designed by members of both the Allied Powers and the Central Powers. Explain to students that they will design propaganda posters for either the Allied forces or the Central forces. Number slips of paper with a 1 or 2, representing the Allied or Central forces. Place the slips of paper in a container and have each student (or group of students) pick one to determine the alliance system for which they will create a poster.

Students may create posters that demonstrate the following: (1) support for the Red Cross, (2) women's roles in wartime, (3) financial support through the purchase of war bonds, (4) fear of the opposing forces, (5) savagery of the opposing forces, (6) patriotism for their country and loyalty to the cause.

Display the completed posters in the classroom. Have students study each poster and answer the following questions: Which country or alliance system designed this propaganda poster? How do you know? What was the important message of the poster? Can you think of examples of propaganda that present-day countries utilize?

MULTIPLE LEARNING STYLES

Verbal/Linguistic
Have students select poems from the World War I era and read them aloud in class as a basis for discussion.

Logical/Mathematical
Have students debate the following proposition: War unites the people of a country as nothing else can.

Auditory/Musical
Have students listen to a tape or CD of World War I songs. On the basis of these, ask what generalizations they can make about the armies and/or civilians of the time.

Kinesthetic
Have students use models or diagrams to explain to the rest of the class the workings of one of the new pieces of military technology used in World War I. They might choose machine guns, tanks, submarines, or fighter planes.

Additional Resources

TEACHER'S CORNER

NATIONAL GEOGRAPHIC SOCIETY

INDEX TO NATIONAL GEOGRAPHIC MAGAZINE

The following articles may be used for research relating to this chapter:

- "Riddle of the Lusitania," by Robert D. Ballard, April 1994.
- "The Bolshevik Revolution: Experiment That Failed," by Dusko Doder, October 1992.

NATIONAL GEOGRAPHIC SOCIETY PRODUCTS AVAILABLE FROM GLENCOE

To order the following products for use with this chapter, contact your local Glencoe sales representative or call Glencoe at 1-800-368-7344:

VIDEODISCS

- GTV: The American People
- GTV: A Geographic Perspective on American History

ADDITIONAL NATIONAL GEOGRAPHIC SOCIETY PRODUCTS

To order the following products for use with this chapter, call National Geographic Society at 1-800-368-2728:

- *1914-1918: World War I* (Video)
- *1917: Revolution in Russia* (Video)
- *The Rise and Fall of the Soviet Union* (Video)
- *Last Voyage of the* Lusitania (Video)

BIBLIOGRAPHY

Literature of the Period

Hemingway, Ernest. ***A Farewell to Arms.*** New York: Macmillan, 1988. A romantic novel by a writer who served as an ambulance driver during the war.

Remarque, Erich Maria. ***All Quiet on the Western Front.*** New York: Fawcett, 1987. A novel about the destruction of a generation of young German soldiers in World War I.

Readings for the Student

Taylor, A.J.P. ***The First World War: An Illustrated History.*** New York: Perigee, 1980. Includes many photographs and an informative commentary.

Readings for the Teacher

Tuchman, Barbara W. ***The Guns of August.*** New York: Bantam, 1980. A vivid account of the crucial first six weeks of World War I.

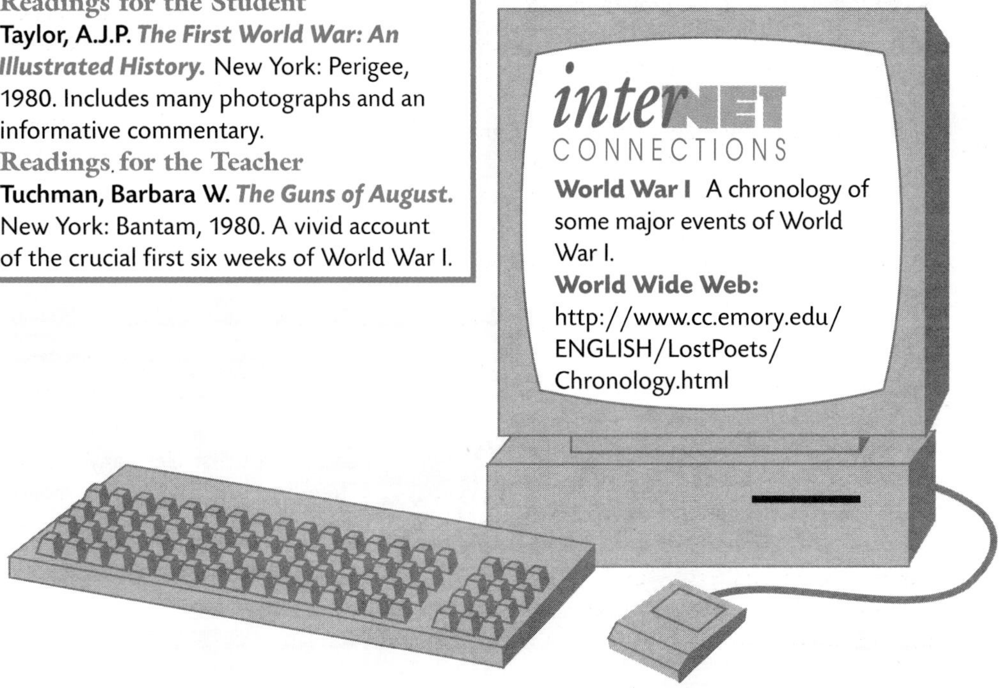
interNET
CONNECTIONS
World War I A chronology of some major events of World War I.
World Wide Web:
http://www.cc.emory.edu/ENGLISH/LostPoets/Chronology.html

Introducing Chapter 28

CHAPTER THEMES

Chapter Themes are listed by section on this chapter opening page of the Student Edition. A corresponding theme-based activity is available under "TEACH," and a theme-based question is asked in the Section and Chapter Reviews.

The Storyteller

Historical Setting Erich Maria Remarque, author of *All Quiet on the Western Front*, was 18 when he was drafted into the German army. He saw action on the Western Front, where he was wounded.

The novel's hero, Paul Baumer, volunteers enthusiastically for the army but is soon disillusioned by the carnage. "How senseless is everything," he says, "when such things are possible.... A hospital alone shows what war is." Baumer is killed on the Western Front, on a day that is otherwise "all quiet."

Historical Significance

Answers: *It differed in scope (fought on several continents), scale (heavy casualties), and the destructiveness of the weapons used, including poison gas and machine guns.*

The war ended several empires and created many small countries. Among its legacies were the decimation of a generation of young men, widespread impoverishment, and lasting resentments and animosities.

Chapter 28

1914–1920

World War I

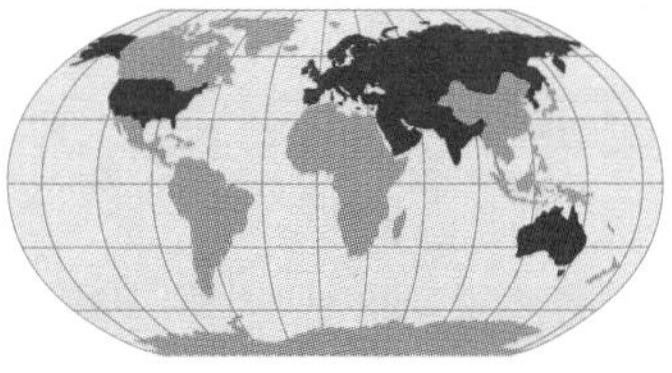

Chapter Themes

- **Cooperation** European powers form a series of alliances before World War I. *Section 1*
- **Conflict** Tensions between the two European alliances erupt into a European-wide conflict. *Section 2*
- **Conflict** The European war is transformed into a war that engulfs much of the world; the global conflict directly affects many civilians as well as soldiers. *Section 3*
- **Revolution** Revolution in Russia overthrows the czar and brings Lenin and the Bolsheviks to power. *Section 4*
- **Internationalism** The Treaty of Versailles provides for the creation of a League of Nations to mediate international disputes. *Section 5*

The Storyteller

To survive days of bombardment on the Western Front during World War I, men crouched down in deep ditches. During these times there was nothing to do but wait and watch. Finally, they would receive orders to attack:

"Suddenly the nearer explosions cease. The shelling continues but it has lifted and falls behind us, our trench is free. We seize the hand-grenades, pitch them out in front of the dug-out and jump after them. The bombardment has stopped and a heavy barrage now falls behind us. The attack has come."

In this passage from All Quiet on the Western Front, *Erich Maria Remarque captures the chaos and horror of what is now called World War I. When this war broke out in the summer of 1914, most Europeans thought it would be over by Christmas. Instead, it lasted four long years and changed Europe and the world forever.*

Historical Significance

In what ways was World War I different from previous wars? How did it affect the countries and peoples involved? What impact did it have on the future course of the 1900s?

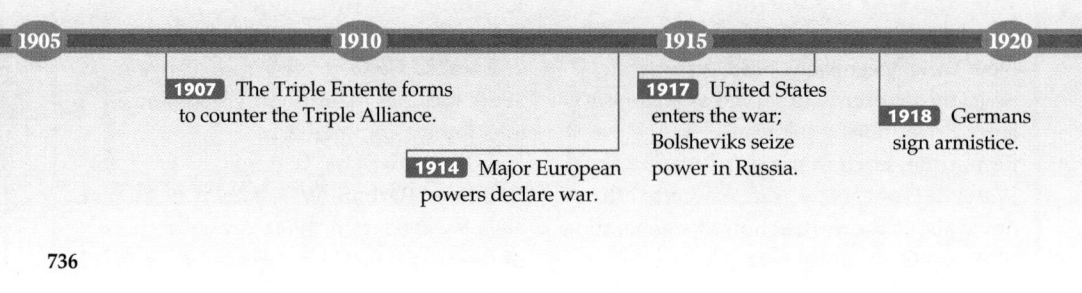

1905 — 1910 — 1915 — 1920

1907 The Triple Entente forms to counter the Triple Alliance.

1914 Major European powers declare war.

1917 United States enters the war; Bolsheviks seize power in Russia.

1918 Germans sign armistice.

GEOGRAPHY CONNECTION

GEOGRAPHIC THEMES

Location On a wall map, have students locate the countries that became the Central Powers: Germany, Austria-Hungary, the Ottoman Empire, and Bulgaria. Then have them locate the countries that became the (European) Allies: Britain, France, Russia, Belgium, Serbia, Montenegro, and later, Romania, Greece, Portugal, and Italy. **L1 LEP**

History & Art *American Troops Arriving in Paris July 14, 1918* by J. F. Foucher. West Point Museum, West Point, New York

Your History Journal

Write a letter home as a first-person account of one of the following events: Poison gas at Ypres, the Sinking of the* Lusitania, *the Battle of Verdun.

Introducing Chapter 28

History & Art Tell students that although the United States was late in entering World War I, its participation made a big difference. Note that this parade is being held on Bastille Day, the French national holiday. What is the mood of this painting? *(upbeat, excited, with bands playing and flags flying)*

Performance Assessment

Refer to the activity on page 736C of the Planning Guide.

For an additional activity, refer to Activity 28 in the *Performance Assessment Strategies and Activities* booklet.

Using Your History Journal

The main participants were Ypres: Germans and British; *Lusitania*: Germans, British, Americans; Verdun: Germans, French.

GLENCOE TECHNOLOGY

VIDEODISC
Use MindJogger to preview chapter content.

MindJogger Videoquiz
Chapter 28
Disc 4 Side A

Also available in VHS.

EXTRA CREDIT PROJECT

Deadly Influenza In the last months of the war, the world was struck by a pandemic of influenza that killed more people than the war itself. Have students research and report on the pandemic: where and when it began; how the disease manifested itself; and the total number of casualties.

SECTION THEME

▶ **Cooperation** European powers form a series of alliances before World War I.

Find Out

Answer: *The main causes were competition for resources and territories, nationalism, and militarism.*

FOCUS

Section Objective

Identify the underlying causes of World War I.

BELLRINGER Motivational Activity

Before taking roll at the beginning of the class period, project Section Focus Transparency 28-1 and have students answer the activity questions. Discuss students' responses.

This activity is also available as a blackline master.

Vocabulary Pre-check

Use Vocabulary Activity 28 to introduce vocabulary terms. **L1 LEP**

1880 | 1890 | 1900 | 1910

1882 Italy joins Germany and Austria-Hungary to form the Triple Alliance.

1894 France and Russia become allies to counter the Triple Alliance.

c. 1900 Germany has the most powerful weapons and the best army in Europe.

1905 Conference averts war between France and Germany over Morocco.

Section 1

The Seeds of War

Setting the Scene

▶ **Terms to Define**
militarism, conscription, alliance system, *entente*

▶ **People to Meet**
Otto von Bismarck

▶ **Places to Locate**
Morocco, Alsace-Lorraine, Bosnia-Herzegovina

Find Out What were the underlying causes of World War I?

The Storyteller

Herbert Marlow, foreign editor for a large United States newspaper, was amazed. His correspondents in Paris, Vienna, and Berlin had all wired similar reports concerning European nationalism and attitudes favoring war. Roland Doregelès wrote, "No more poor or rich ... there were only Frenchmen." Stefan Zweig in Vienna observed, "As never before, thousands and hundreds of thousands felt what they should have felt in peacetime, that they belonged together." Marlow reread Philipp Scheidermann's dispatch from Berlin, resolving to use it as his headline. Scheidermann had noted Germans proclaiming "It is the hour we yearned for."

German military parade

—adapted from articles reprinted in *Sources of the Western Tradition*, edited by Marvin Perry, 1991

In the summer of 1914, an assassination took place in the Austro-Hungarian province of Bosnia in the Balkans. Although some people mourned, there was no broad sense of outrage or alarm. There had been other assassinations in the recent past with no major consequences.

Within weeks, it became apparent that this assassination was different. By August, the major European powers were at war with each other. The war was to last from 1914 to 1918; it led to the development of new weapons that changed warfare forever. By the time it was over, the war had involved most nations of the world and was the largest that the world had ever seen.

It was known as the Great War, the "war to end all wars." The name by which it was called was not important. The changes it brought about were. The way of life that had existed before the war was destroyed. Empires were swept away, and governments toppled. European dominance of the world was shaken. The war marked the close of a long era of international peace.

European Rivalries

Since the mid-1800s, rivalries had been building up and intensifying among some of the countries of Europe. As Western nations industrialized, each sought the most favorable conditions for economic growth. This led to intense competition. As industrialization spread, the competition grew keener. One by one, Great Britain, France, Germany, Austria-Hungary, Russia, and Italy sought to acquire new markets and to establish and expand global empires.

Great Britain wanted to maintain the lifelines of its empire and keep open the sea-lanes it needed for trade. It also wanted to make sure no other nation became strong enough to attack it. France was intent on adding mineral-rich **Morocco** to its gains.

SECTION RESOURCES

Reproducible Masters
- Reproducible Lesson Plan 28-1
- Vocabulary Activity 28
- Guided Reading Activity 28-1
- Time Line Activity 28
- Section Quiz 28-1

Transparencies
- Section Focus Transparency 28-1
- Chapter Transparency 28

Multimedia
- Student Self-Test and Review Software
- Testmaker

AROUND THE WORLD Race to the South Pole

Antarctica, 1911

Two European explorers–Roald Amundsen of Norway and Robert Scott of Great Britain–became engaged in a dramatic race to reach the South Pole. Amundsen and his companions began crossing the Ross Ice Shelf on October 19, 1911. They traveled on skis and used dogsleds to carry their supplies. They arrived at the South Pole on December 14. Scott and his party reached the Pole in January to find a Norwegian flag and a message from Amundsen. Then tragically, Scott and all his companions died on the return trip.

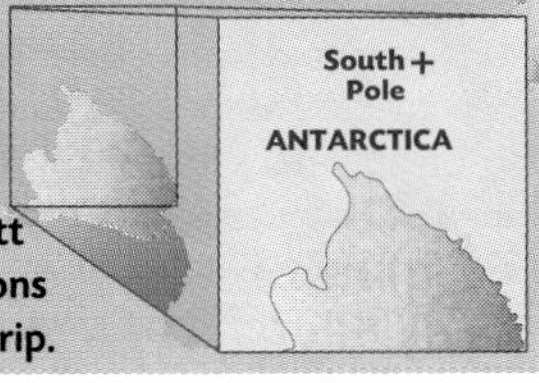

Germany hoped to gain economic control of the declining Ottoman Empire. Austria-Hungary set out to gain territorial access through the Balkans to the Aegean Sea. Russia aspired to take control of the Bosporus and the Dardanelles near the Black Sea and to extend the influence it already had over Manchuria in East Asia.

Competition turned to hostility as one power crossed another in its efforts to accomplish its goals. In 1898, for example, Great Britain and France confronted one another over rival claims in Egypt and the Sudan. The following year, Germany started to build the Berlin-Baghdad railway, which created resentment among both the British and the Russians. The British feared that the railroad would interfere with their interests in India and reduce traffic through the Suez Canal. The Russians thought the railroad interfered in their traditional areas of interest. In 1905, 1908, and 1911, Germany and France came close to war over control of Morocco.

Nationalism

Contributing to the tension was a growing spirit of nationalism. Nationalism had unified Germany and was rapidly becoming popular in France. There, French nationalists sought revenge against Germany for depriving France of the border provinces of **Alsace-Lorraine** in the 1870–1871 Franco-Prussian War.

The French novelist Victor Hugo urged France to "have but one thought: to reconstitute her forces, gather her energy, nourish her sacred anger.... Then one day she will be irresistible. Then she will take back Alsace-Lorraine." This put the Germans on their guard. They were well aware that the issue of Alsace-Lorraine was not settled permanently.

Slavic Nationalism

In Austria-Hungary, nationalism was creating the most violent tensions in Europe. The empire's Slavs were attracted to Pan-Slavism, the idea that the Slavs had a historic mission to develop their culture and unite into an empire. Slavic nationalists in neighboring Serbia supported the Slavs of Austria-Hungary. They wanted their own country to be the center of a South Slav, or Yugoslav, nation. This new Slavic state would be formed out of Slavic territories in Austria-Hungary.

Austria-Hungary was alarmed by Serbian activities in the Balkans. It feared that the idea of a Yugoslav state would attract restless Slavic groups in Austria-Hungary. Such a development would harm the security of the empire and lead to its eventual breakup.

In 1908 Austria-Hungary annexed the Slavic territories of **Bosnia-Herzegovina**, once the provinces of the Ottoman Empire. Angered at the Austro-Hungarian move, Serbia called on Russia, its traditional protector, for help. Russia, however, was still weak from the Russo-Japanese War and was not ready to fight again. In addition, Russia had made a secret deal with the Austro-Hungarians. The Russians had agreed to let Austria-Hungary have Bosnia-Herzegovina in exchange for the right for Russian warships to go through the Dardanelles. So, Russia persuaded the Serbs to restrain themselves. Then, Russia discovered that Austria-Hungary had made its move before Russia could get its part of the deal. As a result, the Russians were bitter.

Balkan Wars

The first Balkan war in 1912 further inflamed the Serbs. One of Serbia's war aims had been to acquire Albania, a small territory along the coast of the Adriatic Sea, an arm of the Mediterranean Sea. This would give Serbia the water outlet it desired. When, after winning the war, Serbia did not get Albania, Serb resentment grew even stronger.

In 1913 a second Balkan war broke out. Albania was made independent, frustrating once again Serbian ambitions. In this war, as in the last one, the Russians had not been able to support Serbia. This upset the Serbs and humiliated the Russians. Austria-Hungary, meanwhile, became increasingly worried about its future role in European affairs.

Chapter 28 Section 1

TEACH

Guided Practice

THEME Cooperation

Ask students to suggest different reasons why nations cooperate. *(Possible answers: for protection against mutual enemies, to help poorer nations, to increase trade and wealth, to manage common natural resources wisely.)* Ask which of these reasons are most likely to lead to war. *(protection against mutual enemies)* **L1**

Militarism Have students name the main components of militarism in the period before World War I. *(winning allies, increasing military spending, stockpiling arms, conscription, universal military training)* Ask which of these elements can be found in societies today. *(Answers will vary, but students may mention high levels of military spending.)* **L2**

Time Line Have students create a time line of the alliance systems formed between 1872 and 1907. Ask a volunteer to record the time line on the chalkboard. **L2**

Chapter Transparency 28

Who?What?Where?When?

Slavs, modern descendants of an ancient people, are related mainly by their similar languages. Slavs include the Russians, Ukrainians, Poles, Czechs, Slovaks, Bulgarians, Croatians, Slovenes, Serbs, and Macedonians.

COOPERATIVE LEARNING ACTIVITY

Roundtable Organize the class into small groups. Each group should represent one of the major nations that eventually became the Central Powers and the Allies. Have each "nation" list its grievances and fears vis-à-vis the others. Then have them reevaluate their lists in light of one factor changing—for example, if Germany agreed to return Alsace-Lorraine to France. Discuss how small incidents can lead to major shifts in alignments. **L3**

Chapter 28
Section 1

Independent Practice

Guided Reading Activity 28-1 **L1**

Time Line Activity 28

Competition Have students explain briefly why each of the following caused tension among the European powers: Berlin-Baghdad railway; Morocco; Alsace-Lorraine; Dardanelles. **L2**

ASSESS

Check for Understanding

Assign Section 1 Review as homework or as an in-class activity.

Use Student Self-Test and Review Software to review Section 1.

Evaluate

Section Quiz 28-1

Use the Testmaker to create a customized quiz for Section 1.

Reteach

Have students summarize the chief factors that constituted the "seeds" of war.

Enrich

Have students list the alliances the United States maintains today.

CLOSE

Have students point out on a map the main areas of tension in Europe, the Middle East, and Africa in 1914. For each area, have students indicate whether the tensions were due principally to nationalistic feelings or imperialist rivalries.

Militarism

As tensions began to rise, so did **militarism**, the glorification of war and the military. The European powers assessed each other's military strength. They compared military training programs and levels of spending. They also looked at levels of industrialization and tried to estimate how fast a nation could ready its troops for battle.

Diplomats manuevered to win new allies. Military leaders argued for increased military spending and more arms. After 1870, all the powers except Great Britain adopted **conscription**, the compulsory call-up of civilians for military service, and universal military training. They were sure that their national security depended almost entirely on the technology, skill, and readiness of their military forces.

Each nation's actions caused a reaction in the other nations. For example, when Germany decided in 1898 to expand its navy, Great Britain felt threatened. The Germans argued that they needed a larger navy to protect colonial and merchant shipping and "for the general purpose of greatness." Great Britain claimed that as an island nation that depended on trade for many vital supplies, it had to be able to control the seas. To do this, said the British, they had to maintain a navy as large as the combined fleet of their two nearest rivals.

Alliances

Along with militarism came a hardening of the **alliance systems**, or the defense agreements among nations. In 1872 **Otto von Bismarck** created the Three Emperors' League, which united Germany, Austria-Hungary, and Russia. His purpose was to isolate France by attaching all of its possible friends to Germany. The Emperors' League, however, did not last very long because of Austrian-Russian rivalry in the Balkans. Bismarck then created a new and stronger alliance with Austria-Hungary.

In 1882 Italy joined the Austrian-German alliance, and it became known as the Triple Alliance. Italy joined because it wanted allies against France. The Italians were angry with the French for occupying Tunis, or present-day Tunisia, in North Africa. They also were afraid that the French might send an army to defend the pope, with whom they were having a dispute. The three powers of the Triple Alliance agreed that if any one member became involved in a war with two or more enemies, the others would provide support.

In 1890 another alliance began to evolve as Russia and France developed friendlier relations. In 1894 Russia and France signed a military alliance in which they agreed to come to each other's aid in case of an attack by either Germany or Austria-Hungary, or by both powers. This was followed in 1904 by the Entente Cordiale between France and Great Britain. The term ***entente*** refers to a friendly understanding between two nations that, at the same time, lacks the binding commitments of a full-fledged alliance. Three years later, Great Britain and Russia settled their conflicting ambitions in the Middle East and central Asia.

All of these agreements developed into the Triple Entente, a loose alliance between France, Russia, and Great Britain. Russia, an autocratic monarchy, and France, a democratic republic, were willing to ally out of a common fear of Germany and Austria-Hungary. Great Britain, a democratic monarchy, was willing to join because it was alarmed by Germany's naval-building program. It felt hard pressed to protect its empire on its own.

Thus, by 1907, the great powers of Europe had aligned themselves in two opposing combinations. On one side stood the Triple Alliance. On the other stood the Triple Entente. Instead of making their members more secure, however, these alliances threatened the peace of the continent. Given the conditions of the Triple Alliance and the Triple Entente, a minor conflict between rival nations had the potential to involve all major European powers in war.

SECTION 1 REVIEW

Recall

1. **Define** militarism, conscription, alliance system, *entente*.
2. **Identify** Otto von Bismarck, Triple Alliance, Triple Entente.
3. **Locate** Germany on the map on page 742. Why was Germany at a disadvantage in fighting an all-European war?

Critical Thinking

4. **Evaluating Information** What were the factors that led to alliances before the outbreak of World War I?

Understanding Themes

5. **Cooperation** Given the conditions that existed in Europe before 1914, could the nations of that continent have avoided a major war? If so, how?

SECTION 1 REVIEW ANSWERS

1. All vocabulary words are defined in the Glossary.
2. Otto von Bismarck, 740; Triple Alliance, 740; Triple Entente, 740
3. Its central location meant that it had to fight on two fronts.
4. fear of military threats from rival powers; nationalistic rivalries; imperialistic rivalries
5. **COOPERATION** Answers will vary. Possible answer: They probably could have avoided a major war if some differences had been negotiated.

JUNE, 1914 — JULY, 1914 — AUGUST, 1914

JUNE 28, 1914 Slav nationalist assassinates Austria's Archduke Francis Ferdinand.

JULY 28, 1914 Austria-Hungary declares war on Serbia.

AUGUST 1, 1914 Germany declares war on Russia.

AUGUST 4, 1914 Great Britain declares war on Germany.

Section 2

The Spark

Setting the Scene

- **Terms to Define**
  ultimatum, mobilization
- **People to Meet**
  Francis Ferdinand, Gavrilo Princip, William II, Nicholas II
- **Places to Locate**
  Sarajevo, Serbia

Find Out What series of events provided the spark that ignited World War I?

The Storyteller

Nearly one month after Archduke Francis Ferdinand was assassinated at the Bosnian capital of Sarajevo, some European leaders suspected that the crisis would pass. Newspaper headlines carried other stories. Cabinet minister Lloyd George of Britain told the House of Commons: "I cannot help thinking that civilization which is able to deal with disputes among individuals and small communities ... should be able to extend its operations to the larger sphere of disputes among states." Before he finished his address, Austria had delivered an ultimatum to Serbia. World War I was about to begin.

—adapted from *The Modern World*, edited by Esmond Wright, 1979

Assassination at Sarajevo

Until 1914, a false optimism prevailed in Europe regarding peace. Although the arms race and the military buildup continued, most Europeans did not really think there would be a major war. Almost a century of relative peace had followed the Congress of Vienna. The absence of a major war for so long a period had lulled many Europeans into believing that such a war would not ever happen again.

Major social reforms and important scientific advances during the 1800s reinforced a widespread belief that as time passed, the world was improving steadily and that people had outgrown the need for war to solve their problems. Most countries were enjoying the fruits of industrialization and economic prosperity. A war would destroy what had been built up over the years.

Despite this optimism, war did come, triggered by the assassination in the Balkans. That event set in motion the diplomatic moves that ended in war.

Trouble in the Balkans

On June 28, 1914, Archduke **Francis Ferdinand**, nephew and heir to Austro-Hungarian Emperor Francis Joseph, paid a visit to **Sarajevo** (SAR•uh•YAY•voh), the capital of Bosnia-Herzegovina. Francis Ferdinand planned, upon becoming emperor, to give the Slavs of Bosnia-Herzegovina and other parts of the empire a voice in the government equal to that of the Austrians and Hungarians. This political action might have defused the movement for a separate Slavic state.

Before the archduke and his wife, Sophie, began their ride through the streets of Sarajevo in an open car, seven young assassins had already taken their places along the route. All were members of a secret nationalist group based in **Serbia** known as the Black Hand, or Union of Death. Although the archduke and Sophie survived the first assassin's attempt, their luck did not hold.

Chapter 28 Section 2

SECTION THEME

- **Conflict** Tensions between the two European alliances erupt into a Europe-wide conflict.

Find Out

Answer: *the assassination of Archduke Francis Ferdinand, followed by declarations of war and mobilizations by Austria-Hungary, Russia, Germany, France, and Britain*

FOCUS

Section Objective

Describe the series of events that provided the spark that ignited World War I.

BELLRINGER Motivational Activity

Before taking roll at the beginning of the class period, project Section Focus Transparency 28-2 and have students answer the activity questions. Discuss students' responses.

This activity is also available as a blackline master.

Vocabulary Pre-check

Use Vocabulary Activity 28 to introduce vocabulary terms. **L1 LEP**

SECTION RESOURCES

Reproducible Masters
- Reproducible Lesson Plan 28-2
- Vocabulary Activity 28
- Guided Reading Activity 28-2
- Section Quiz 28-2

Transparencies
- Section Focus Transparency 28-2

Multimedia
- Student Self-Test and Review Software
- Testmaker
- Turning Points in World History: *Assassination Ignites World War I*

TEACH

Guided Practice

THEME **Conflict**

Have students study the map on page 742, then create a list of all the possible sources of conflict between the major powers in Europe at this time. Discuss how one of these sources of conflict might have led to World War I if Archduke Ferdinand had not been assassinated. **L1**

Map Study

Answer

Triple Entente countries, they surrounded the Triple Alliance countries and had better access to the sea

Map Skills Practice

Reading a Map What geographic advantages did the Central Powers have over the Allied Powers? *(They had better access to western Asia; also, because they were centrally located, they could move troops quickly from one theater of war to another.)*

ABCNEWS INTERACTIVE™

VIDEODISC
Turning Points in World History

Side Two
Chapter 4

Title: *Assassination Ignites World War I*
Ask: Why did the assassination of the archduke plunge Europe into war? *(A web of European alliances caused most major nations to declare war.)*

Europe in 1915

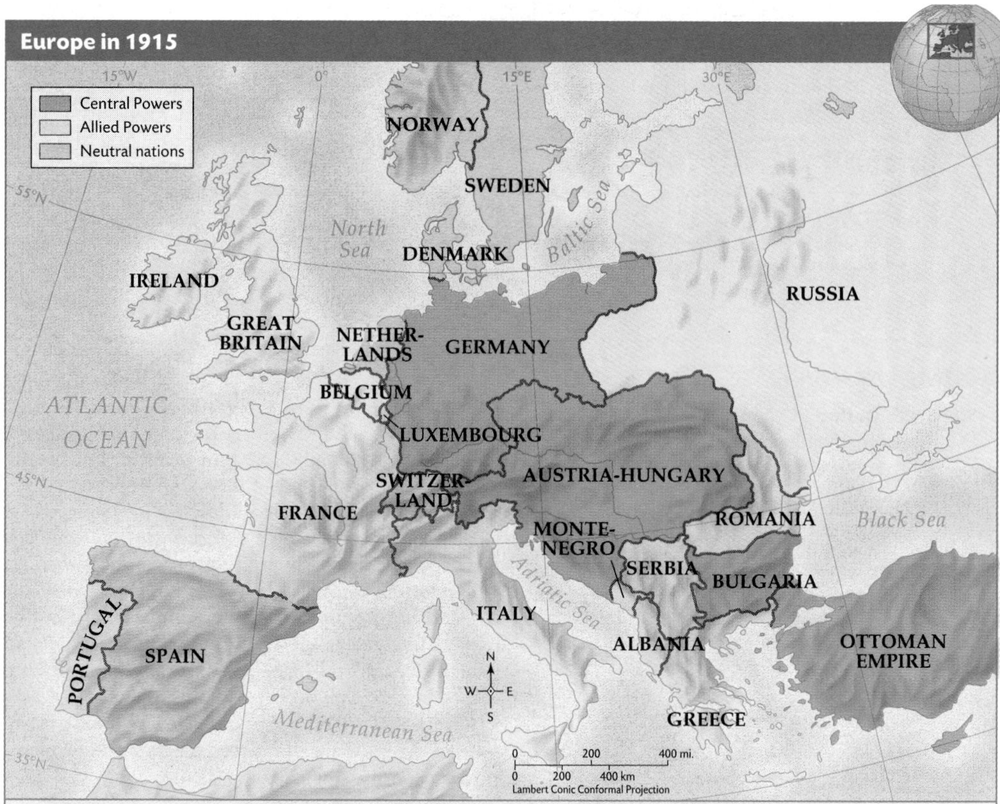

Map Study **World War I split Europe into two armed camps.**
Location Which side do you think had the better strategic location: the Triple Alliance or the Triple Entente countries?

When the couple's car took a wrong turn, 19-year-old **Gavrilo Princip** (gah•VREE•loh PREEN•seep) fired his gun, fatally wounding them both.

German Support

Although the assassination had not occurred in Serbia, Austro-Hungarian leaders held the Serbians responsible. They were encouraged in this line of thinking by their German allies and by Count Leopold Berchtold, the Austro-Hungarian foreign minister. On July 5, Berchtold sent an envoy to Berlin to talk to the German emperor, **William II**. William assured the envoy that Germany would give its full support to any actions Austria-Hungary might take against Serbia. The next day, the German chancellor officially repeated this promise to the Austro-Hungarian government. In effect, Germany gave Austria-Hungary permission to do with Serbia as it pleased.

Declaration of War

On July 23, Austria-Hungary gave Serbia an ultimatum, a set of final conditions that must be accepted to avoid severe consequences. The ultimatum demanded that Serbia allow Austro-Hungarian officials into the country to suppress all subversive movements there and to lead an investigation into the archduke's murder. Austria-Hungary gave Serbia 48 hours to agree to these terms or face war. Berchtold knew, however, that the ultimatum "would be wholly impossible for the Serbs to accept."

Although the ultimatum outraged Serbian leaders, they knew that their nation was not ready for war with Austria-Hungary. Therefore, on July 25, they responded in a conciliatory manner. They rejected, however, the demand that Austro-Hungarian officials take part in the investigation and trial of those involved in the assassination.

COOPERATIVE LEARNING ACTIVITY

Dramatization Organize students into small groups and have them stage a series of radio or television newscasts devoted to the outbreak of World War I. Each group should select a critical date from June 28 to August 4. They should incorporate researched information with the text material. Have groups include comments by participants, descriptions of citizen responses, and speculation as to what will happen next. **L3**

The Serbian answer did not satisfy Austria-Hungary. Consequently, on July 28, 1914, exactly one month after the assassination of Archduke Ferdinand, Austria-Hungary declared war on Serbia. Both countries immediately issued general orders for **mobilization**, the gathering and transport of military troops and fighting equipment in preparation for war. News of these mobilizations spread quickly across the European continent.

A European War

Many Europeans still believed war could be avoided. The major European powers pushed each other to the brink of war, believing that the other side would back down at the last minute. They were tragically mistaken.

Russia was the first to act once Austria-Hungary declared war. Knowing it had lost face often in the past, the Russian government had to support Serbia now or risk the bitter hatred of all the Slavs in the Balkan region. Although the czar was convinced that Germany would fight, he had also been assured through diplomatic channels that France would support Russia.

Consequently, on July 30, Czar **Nicholas II** ordered a general mobilization of his armed forces against both Austria-Hungary and Germany. Austria-Hungary mobilized against Russia the following day. Once Russia's intentions were clear, France and Great Britain showed their hands.

On July 31, Germany issued Russia an ultimatum to cancel its mobilization order or face war. On the same day, Germany also delivered an ultimatum to France. France had 18 hours to decide whether or not it would remain neutral if Germany went to war with Russia. France's answer was to give its support to Russia. When Czar Nicholas did not even reply to Germany's ultimatum, Germany declared war on Russia on August 1. Two days later, Germany declared war on France as well.

The British, meanwhile, were divided on the question of going to war. They still hoped to avoid conflict through negotiations. They did not make it clear whether or not they would support France and Russia. Germany hoped that Great Britain would stay neutral.

The same day that Germany declared war on Russia, however, the German army marched into Luxembourg. The Germans then demanded passage across Belgium, claiming that France intended to invade that country at any moment. Belgium was a neutral country whose borders and neutrality had been guaranteed in an 1839 treaty signed by Great Britain, Russia, France, and Germany.

The Belgians refused the Germans entry into their territory and appealed to Great Britain for help. When the Germans went ahead and invaded Belgium on August 3, Britain protested and sent an ultimatum to the German government that demanded withdrawal of German forces from Belgium. The German chancellor responded by calling the 1839 treaty "a scrap of paper." This left the British little choice. On August 4, Britain declared war on Germany.

The outbreak of war in August 1914 was generally greeted with confidence and rejoicing by the peoples of Europe. In an outburst of patriotic enthusiasm, crowds gathered in the streets, squares, and railway stations of European cities to cheer on the military forces of their respective nations. As the conflict unfolded, most Europeans believed in the war as a matter of defending their country's honor or upholding "right against might."

Few people, however, imagined how long or how devastating a war between the powers of Europe could be. Designed to protect nations against their enemies, the European alliance systems not only dragged a whole continent into war. What began as a local dispute between Austria-Hungary and Serbia eventually became a global conflict that had no clear, limited objective.

SECTION 2 REVIEW

Recall

1. **Define** ultimatum, mobilization.
2. **Identify** Francis Ferdinand, Gavrilo Princip, William II, Nicholas II.
3. **Locate** Serbia on the map on page 742. How did Serbia's location affect its relations with Austria-Hungary?

Critical Thinking

4. **Evaluating Information** Historians have long argued over which European nation was most responsible for the start of World War I. Using examples to support your statements, explain which country you think was most responsible for the war.

Understanding Themes

5. **Conflict** Why do you think World War I came as a surprise to many Europeans?

Chapter 28 Section 2

Time Line Have students create a time line on the chalkboard listing events from the assassination of Francis Ferdinand (June 28) to Britain's declaration of war against Germany (August 4). **L2**

Independent Practice

Guided Reading Activity 28-2 **L1**

Biography Have students research Gavrilo Princip and write a short biographical sketch of him, including what happened to him after the assassination of Archduke Francis Ferdinand. **L2**

ASSESS

Check for Understanding

Assign Section 2 Review as homework or as an in-class activity.

Use Student Self-Test and Review Software to review Section 2.

Evaluate

Section Quiz 28-2

Use the Testmaker to create a customized quiz for Section 2.

Reteach

Have students recount in their own words the causes of World War I.

Enrich

Have students write an essay on how World War I might have been avoided.

CLOSE

Have students discuss why the Balkans have been called "the powder keg of Europe."

SECTION 2 REVIEW ANSWERS

1. The words are defined in the Glossary.
2. Francis Ferdinand, 741; Gavrilo Princip, 742; William II, 742; Nicholas II, 743
3. Overshadowed by its neighbor, Serbia was either dependent on Austria-Hungary for protection or vulnerable to attack.
4. Answers will vary. Possibilities: Austria-Hungary, because of its rigid ultimatum; Germany, because of the tacit permission it gave Austria-Hungary.
5. **CONFLICT** The period preceding it was one of optimism. Europeans were proud of their material progress. Also, there had been no major wars since the time of Napoleon.

Chapter 28
Section 3

SECTION THEME

▶ **Conflict** The European war is transformed into a war that engulfs much of the world; the global conflict directly affects many civilians as well as soldiers.

Find Out

Answer: *the Western and Eastern Fronts in Europe, in western Asia, and at sea; infantry attacks, trench warfare, naval battles, blockades, tanks, airplanes, and submarines*

FOCUS

Section Objective

Specify where and how World War I was fought.

BELLRINGER
Motivational Activity

Before taking roll at the beginning of the class period, project Section Focus Transparency 28-3 and have students answer the activity questions. Discuss students' responses.

This activity is also available as a blackline master.

Vocabulary Pre-check

Use the Vocabulary PuzzleMaker to create a puzzle that reinforces the vocabulary terms in this section. **L1**

1914 | 1915 | 1916 | 1917

1914 French and German armies collide in the Battle of the Marne.

1915 German submarine sinks British passenger liner *Lusitania.*

1916 Allies withdraw forces from the Gallipoli Peninsula.

1917 American newspapers publish the Zimmermann telegram.

Section 3

The War

Setting the Scene

▶ **Terms to Define**
belligerent, propaganda, war of attrition, trench, contraband

▶ **People to Meet**
Alfred von Schlieffen, Helmuth von Moltke, Joseph Jacques Joffre, Henri-Philippe Pétain, Winston Churchill, Woodrow Wilson

▶ **Places to Locate**
Paris, Tannenberg, Verdun, Gallipoli

Find Out Where and how was World War I fought?

The Storyteller

François was only 8 years old when war's realities entered his small French village. Gendarmes delivered the official notice of death on the field of honor to the towns, villages, and farms. A hush fell when the names were read. Then the word spread. "Gustave was killed, the little clerk who had looked so handsome in his cavalryman's uniform. Alcide, Jules, Léon, Maurice, Rèmi, Raoul—all killed." In horror, François watched his neighbors' grief. Childhood playmates, cousins, the only sons of families, and brothers all perished in battle. "They remained on their battlefields in the great military cemeteries, neat and orderly, hidden forever."

—adapted from "World War I: A Frenchman's Recollections," reprinted in *The Global Experience*, vol. 2, 1987

French soldiers in the trenches

By August 1914 the major powers of Europe had lined up against each other. Germany and Austria-Hungary, joined by the Ottoman Empire and Bulgaria, became known as the Central Powers. Great Britain, France, Russia, Serbia, Belgium, and, later, Japan and Montenegro, became known as the Allied Powers, or Allies. Claiming that Austria-Hungary and Germany had acted aggressively rather than defensively, Italy remained neutral.

In spite of their military buildups, none of the European powers was fully prepared for what lay ahead. For example, cavalry and horse-drawn vehicles still played an important role in each nation's army—traditions that were quickly discarded. Nations from both sides also seriously underestimated the length of the war. No country had stockpiled enough war materials or ammunition to last more than six months. The widespread feeling among Europeans was that the war would be over by Christmas.

The Schlieffen Plan

Germany's invasion of Belgium on August 3 had been part of the Schlieffen Plan, a war strategy that German General **Alfred von Schlieffen** (SHLEE•fuhn) drew up in 1905. Germany's main problem was that it had enemies in both the east and the west. Schlieffen assumed, however, that Russia would be slow to mobilize. As a result, Schlieffen believed that the Germans could reach Paris and defeat the French in six weeks and then move on to the Eastern Front and fight against Russian forces.

Schlieffen's plan ran into problems from the beginning. First, German Commander **Helmuth von Moltke** led his troops through an area of Belgium that proved to be heavily fortified. Second, Moltke encountered far stronger resistance than anyone had expected; the German advance was

SECTION RESOURCES

Reproducible Masters
- Reproducible Lesson Plan 28-3
- Guided Reading Activity 28-3
- History Simulation 28
- Geography and History Activity 28
- Section Quiz 28-3

Transparencies
- Section Focus Transparency 28-3
- Mapping History Overlay Transparency 18, *World War I*
- World History and Art Transparencies 36, 37

Multimedia
- Vocabulary PuzzleMaker Software
- Student Self-Test and Review Software
- Testmaker
- Lessons of War: *How Wars Begin—World War I*

744 Chapter 28 *World War I*

delayed until August 20. Third, the Russian army mobilized far more quickly than Schlieffen had estimated, necessitating the movement of two German divisions to the Eastern Front.

The Germans were held up further when they met British forces in the north of France. British troops eventually had to retreat, but they fought expertly and inflicted heavy losses on the Germans. At the same time, the French attacked another wing of the German army in Alsace-Lorraine. The French offensive eventually collapsed but not before delaying the German advance yet again.

The Battle of the Marne

France struggled to recover after the defeat at Alsace-Lorraine. The French chief of command, General **Joseph Jacques Joffre**, pulled back his troops to protect **Paris**. While many Parisians fled the city, General Joseph Simon Gallieni strengthened the army in Paris to the point that it was able to launch a counterattack. To speed troops into position, the French army requisitioned several hundred Parisian taxis.

On September 5 the French and German armies collided in northeastern France in the Battle of the Marne. After four days of shelling, the French finally pushed the Germans back a distance of about 50 miles (80 km) from Paris. The attack saved Paris from the Germans and boosted French morale. Although German forces continued to hold much of France's heavily industrialized areas, the German retreat from the Battle of the Marne signified the abandonment of the Schlieffen Plan. It also made it clear that neither side was capable of defeating the other quickly or easily.

A Russian Disaster

Russia, meanwhile, kept its word to the French and sent troops into battle even before its military was fully mobilized. The speed with which the Russians moved surprised Germany and Austria-Hungary. By August 13 the Russians had invaded East Prussia from the south and from the east. This attack diverted German troops from the attack against the French and British during the first critical weeks of the war.

Russia's success did not last long. At the end of August, Russian and German troops met at **Tannenberg** in present-day Poland. There the Russians suffered a disastrous defeat from which they never fully recovered. At Tannenberg, the Germans were able to encircle and destroy the Russian army. They killed more than 30,000 Russian soldiers and took 92,000 prisoners. German casualties numbered only about 13,000.

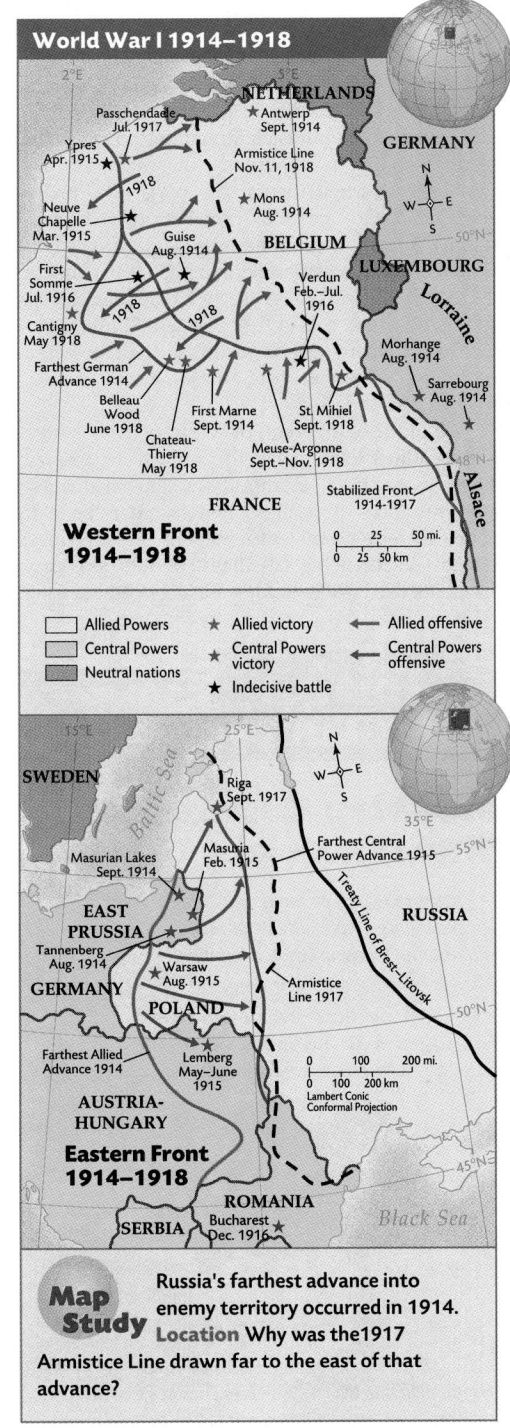

World War I 1914–1918

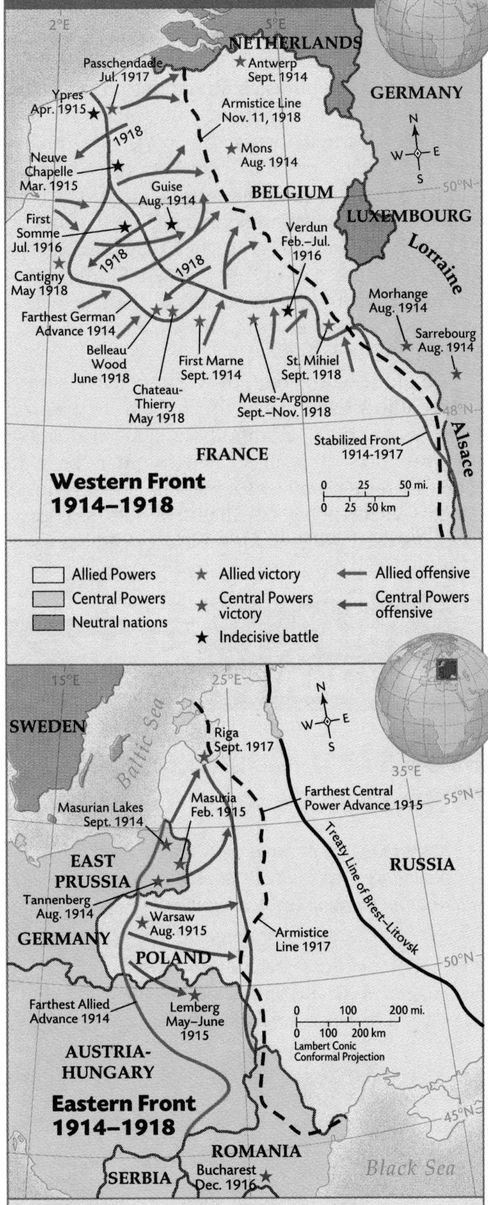

Map Study Russia's farthest advance into enemy territory occurred in 1914. **Location** Why was the1917 Armistice Line drawn far to the east of that advance?

COOPERATIVE LEARNING ACTIVITY

Report Have students research and present an oral report on the first six weeks of World War I. Assign each of five groups one of the following: the invasion of Belgium, the German sweep through France toward Paris, the retreat of the Allies, Russian mobilization and early victories ending at Tannenberg, and the Battle of the Marne. Individual students should gather information on a specific topic within his or her group. Then ask each group to present its report to create a composite picture. **L2**

TEACH

Guided Practice

THEME Conflict
Have students write several reasons trench warfare was so deadly. Discuss these reasons as a class. Focus especially on how trench warfare resulted in a state of deadlock. *(Machine guns made successful offenses almost impossible; neither side had a way to break through the other's lines.)* **L1**

Military History Have students explain the significance of the Battle of the Marne. *(It signified the end of the Schlieffen Plan and also showed that the war would not end quickly.)* **L2 LEP**

Geography: Location Ask students why they think the Germans attacked the Allies through Belgium rather than more directly across Alsace and Lorraine. *(France probably expected a German attack from the east and so fortified its eastern boundary more heavily than its northern border with Belgium. Also, Alsace and Lorraine, once French, might have been more hostile to the Germans than Belgium was.)* **L3 LEP**

Map Study

Answer
By 1917 the Central Powers had pushed the front that far to the east.

Map Skills Practice
Reading a Map What aspects of fighting on the Western Front did not characterize the Eastern Front? *(indecisive battles, a stabilized front)*

Chapter 28 *World War I* 745

Chapter 28
Section 3

History Simulation 28

World History and Art Transparency 36, *Three Musicians*; 37, *I Want You for the U.S. Army*

Mapping History Overlay Transparency 18, *World War I*

ABCNEWS INTERACTIVE™

VIDEODISC
Lessons of War

Side One, Chapter 5
Frames 11214-15727
Title: *How Wars Begin—World War I*
Subject: Exploration of the reasons behind war, specifically World War I
Ask: What did Germany wish to accomplish in World War I? *(Germany wanted to become a world power.)* What did Austria-Hungary want to acquire? Who helped them to accomplish this? *(Austria-Hungary wanted to acquire Serbian territory and asked Germany for help.)*

Years of Deadlock

After the Battle of the Marne, the Germans and the Allies began a series of battles known as "the race to the sea," with each attempting to reach the North Sea first and outflank the other. As the Germans advanced toward the ports of Dunkirk and Calais, they ran into British troops at Ypres (EEPR), a town in southwestern Belgium. The battle that followed cost the Germans 130,000 men, but the victorious British lost nearly 60,000 themselves. At this point the war in the west settled into a stable front from the Swiss border to the North Sea coast. By November 1914, the war had already reached a stalemate.

All of the **belligerent**, or warring, nations now had to adjust their plans. To produce the needed ships, guns, food, ammunition, and medicines, large numbers of civilians had to enter the war effort. To raise morale, newspapers gave even the smallest victories big headlines. In addition, governments used **propaganda**—ideas or rumors used to harm an opposing cause—to portray the enemy as beastly and inhuman. Making peace with such an enemy seemed unthinkable.

Trench Warfare

By early 1915 the war on the Western Front had turned into a deadly **war of attrition**, in which each side tried to wear down the other side by constant attacks. To protect themselves, soldiers on both

Footnotes to History

Holiday Cheer
On Christmas Day, 1914, fighting stopped, and British and German soldiers met in "no-man's-land" to chat, play soccer, and pose for photographs! Officers, however, quickly ended these goodwill meetings, and the soldiers returned to their positions to take up firing at one another again.

Images of the Times

Industry Generates War Materials

More than any previous war, World War I demanded large-scale industrial production of military and transportation equipment.

This German officer's helmet and the English gas mask and pack were produced by their respective war industries.

746

Images of the Times **Industry Generates War Materials**

The Allies faced problems in supplying their troops because they had expected the war to be short and mobile. But when soldiers dug in on the Western Front, they needed much bigger quantities of war materials, especially ammunition, than had been foreseen. Not only were supplies short, but hundreds of the skilled male workers needed to produce more shells had volunteered for or been drafted into the army. For many of the belligerent nations, women workers provided vital help in war industries.

sides dug trenches, or ditches. Eventually, two parallel trenches stretched for about 500 miles (805 km) in an unbroken line from Switzerland to the North Sea. Land mines and barbed wire protected the area in front of each trench. The desolate area that separated the two sides, which could vary from a half a mile to a few yards, was known as "no-man's-land."

Soldiers lived in the trenches for weeks at a time, fighting boredom and terror. They endured cold, mud, rats, and disease. To attack, the soldiers charged "over the top" of their own trenches and ran across "no man's land" to the enemy's trenches. As attackers struggled through the barbed wire, their opponents mowed them down with heavy artillery and machine guns.

Throughout 1915, battle followed battle, and casualties mounted. At the battle of Ypres, the Germans introduced a new weapon—poison gas. From cylinders in their trenches, they released yellow-green chlorine gas. The wind carried the gas into French trenches, causing blindness, choking, vomiting, torn lungs, and death. Wilfred Owen, an English poet and soldier, described the horrors of poison gas in his poem "Dulce et Decorum Est" (1916):

> "Gas! Gas! Quick, boys!—An ecstasy of
> fumbling,
> Fitting the clumsy helmets just in time;
> But someone still was yelling out and
> stumbling
> And flound'ring like a man in fire or lime …
> Dim, through the misty panes and thick
> green light,
> As under a green sea, I saw him drowning."

Verdun and the Somme

The year 1916 opened with the war on the Western Front still stalemated. Although Italy had denounced the Central Powers six months earlier and entered the war on the side of the Allies, it had gained little ground after four battles against the Austro-Hungarians. Then in February 1916, the Germans made a move. They staged a surprise

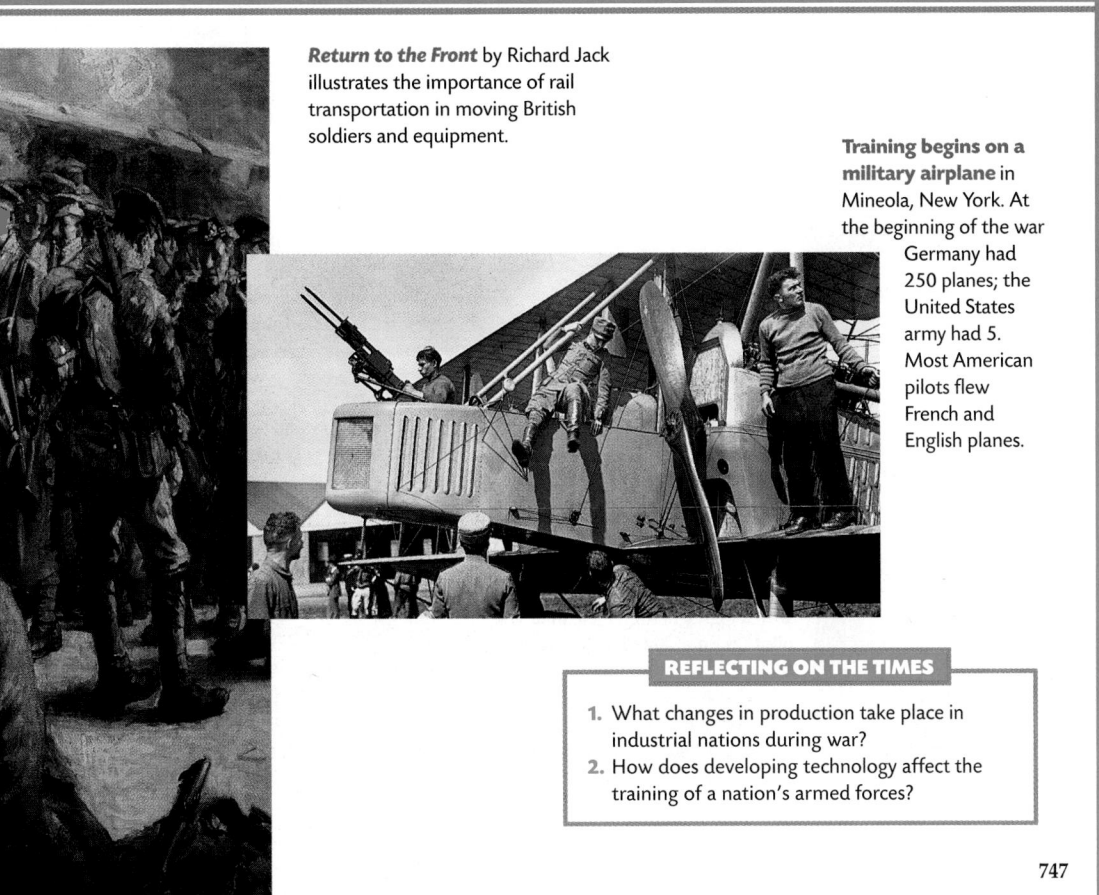

Return to the Front by Richard Jack illustrates the importance of rail transportation in moving British soldiers and equipment.

Training begins on a military airplane in Mineola, New York. At the beginning of the war Germany had 250 planes; the United States army had 5. Most American pilots flew French and English planes.

REFLECTING ON THE TIMES

1. What changes in production take place in industrial nations during war?
2. How does developing technology affect the training of a nation's armed forces?

747

ANSWERS TO REFLECTING ON THE TIMES

1. They must switch from making peacetime goods to meeting wartime needs. They have to do so quickly, since lives are at stake.
2. Troops must be trained in the use of new and unfamiliar technologies; specialization is often the result, with specific personnel trained to use specific equipment.

Who? What? Where? When?

"Dulce et Decorum Est" The title of Wilfred Owen's poem is the first phrase of a line from the Latin poet Horace, "Dulce et decorum est pro patria mori," meaning "It is sweet and honorable to die for one's country." Owen's use is ironic—fitting for a man who himself was killed on the battlefield.

Independent Practice

Guided Reading Activity 28-3 **L1**

Geography and History Activity 28

Science, Technology, and Society Have students research and report on the use of poison gas in World War I—the different types used, when and where employed, effects, and effectiveness. **L2**

Who? What? Where? When?

Edith Cavell, an English nurse working in Belgium, was an Allied heroine of World War I. After the Germans occupied the country, she helped Belgian, French, and British soldiers escape. Arrested in 1915, she confessed and was sentenced to die by the firing squad. Her execution in October, though legally justified, aroused worldwide condemnation.

Propaganda Have students research and report on the propaganda issued by both sides during World War I. If possible, they should bring examples, such as posters, to class. **L2**

Chapter 28
Section 3

Literature Have students read the entire Owen poem, "Dulce et Decorum Est,"and comment on its meaning. In particular, ask them to speculate what effect Owen hoped to achieve through his choice of title. **L3**

you don't say...

Blimp The German dirigibles known as zeppelins, which were used to drop bombs on London, had their counterpart in British balloons known as blimps. The English word comes from the original designation—*B* for balloon and *limp* indicating that the gas bag was not rigid, having no metal framework.

CONNECTIONS
Science *and* Technology

Flaming Coffins

Because World War I aircraft were so vulnerable, the men who flew them were widely admired. Pilots who shot down five enemy planes were known as "aces." Among the best-known aces of the war were Georges Guynemer of France, Manfred von Richthofen of Germany, "Mick" Mannock of England, and Eddie Rickenbacker of the United States.

Answers to Making the Connection

1. *They were flimsily built and had no brakes. There was no radio communication, either.*
2. *extremely dangerous; the average life expectancy was three to six weeks*

attack against French forces at **Verdun**, a massive fortress in northeastern France on the Meuse River. The French, under General **Henri-Philippe Pétain** (PAY•TAN), rallied to the cry "They shall not pass." More than 2 million soldiers took part in this battle, one of the longest and bloodiest of the war. Before it was over, more than 750,000 French and German soldiers had lost their lives. When the fighting stopped, the Western Front had moved less than 10 miles (16 km).

Later that year the British, aided by a small French force, launched a similar offensive against the Germans in the valley of the Somme River in northern France. The Battle of the Somme turned out to be as terrible and inconclusive as the one at Verdun. Although the British introduced another new weapon during this battle—an armored vehicle called the tank—it made little difference to the outcome of the struggle. Tanks were still too clumsy and slow to be an effective weapon, and the generals on both sides did not yet understand how best to use them.

The Eastern Front

The Eastern Front in Russia was less entrenched than the Western Front in France; the war there was far more mobile, involving constant changes in battlefield positions. Neither side, however, was able to achieve a complete victory.

By mid-1915, the Russians had been forced to give up territory greater than the whole of France. In addition to suffering a staggering number of casualties, they had lost ammunition and guns equal to the amount they had possessed when the war began. Russia was doing so badly at this point that the Allies feared Nicholas II would make a separate peace with the Central Powers. As a result they promised the Russian government that if the Allies won the war, they would give Russia Constantinople and control of the Dardanelles, a strait that connects the Mediterranean and Black Seas.

Inspired by this agreement, the Russians went to work rebuilding their army. In March 1916 they launched an offensive against the Germans but made little headway. A few months later, however, they fared much better against Austria-Hungary. In addition to capturing many cities, they took several hundred thousand prisoners. They paid a heavy toll in the process, however, losing more than a million men and most of their supplies.

Although morale in the Russian army suffered greatly as a result of the 1916 offenses, their efforts

CONNECTIONS
Science *and* Technology

Flaming Coffins

Airplanes added a new dimension to fighting in World War I. For the first time, combat took place not only on land and at sea but also in the air. Crude but operational, these noisy, pitching, and bucking machines were not built with the pilot's safety foremost in mind. The typical plane was made of thin wood reinforced by steel wire. Its body and wings were covered by cloth coated with a highly flammable liquid. The pilot sat on a seat directly over the fuel tank. Fire was such a constant danger that airplanes were often referred to as "flaming coffins."

Battle between German and British planes

Brakes did not exist on World War I-era planes. On takeoff, the crew had to hold the plane back while the pilot revved the engine. On landing, the pilot had to turn the engine off and on to slow the approach. Once the pilot was airborne, contact with the ground was possible only if an unwieldy Morse code transmitter was on board. Sometimes, pilots would release carrier pigeons to convey messages or to stage a rescue.

The pilot's life was glamorized, but the statistics were grim. The average life expectancy of a new pilot was from 3 to 6 weeks. High losses of life resulted from accidents as well as from enemy action.

MAKING THE CONNECTION

1. In what sense were World War I airplanes "crude" vehicles?
2. How dangerous was the life of a World War I pilot? Explain.

MEETING SPECIAL NEEDS ACTIVITY

Mixed Learners Encourage students needing extra reinforcement to summarize the material under each subhead in this section in a manner of their own choosing. Some students may elect to prepare oral summaries. Students may be divided into small groups. Each group would assign a subsection to pairs of students who would prepare the summaries.

Visual learners might draw a series of cartoons depicting such subjects as the battles, the weapons used, or trench warfare. Gifted students may use outside resources to enhance their summaries. This activity may be done in groups or individually. **L2 LEP**

748 Chapter 28 *World War I*

Visualizing History **These heavy guns were not enough to overcome the resistance of the Turks at Gallipoli.** *What were Churchill's three main goals in attacking Turkey?*

helped the Allies on the Western Front. The Germans had to transfer several divisions from the west to the east, hampering the effectiveness of their attack at Verdun.

Gallipoli Campaign

As the war dragged on and casualties soared, each side tried to find ways to turn the war in its favor. In Great Britain, First Lord of the Admiralty **Winston Churchill**—head of the British navy—asked, "Are there not other alternatives than sending our armies to chew barbed wire in Flanders?" Churchill favored opening an offensive on the Dardanelles strait, which Turkey controlled. This strait was the only practical means of supplying Russia and of strengthening Serbia. From there, the Allies could take Constantinople and possibly put the Ottoman Empire out of the war. This offensive, Churchill believed, might also lead to the collapse of Austria-Hungary.

Churchill's idea had merit. The Allies' initial offensive in early 1915 nearly succeeded, but a lack of coordination, planning, and reinforcements gave the Turks time to rearm. When the Allies followed up in April with a land attack on the peninsula of **Gallipoli** (guh•LIH•puh•lee), the Turks drove them back. On January 9, 1916, the Allies finally gave up the effort and withdrew the last of their troops from the area.

On the Seas

The British, meanwhile, had been using their naval superiority to dominate the seas. They were determined to keep the Germans from invading Great Britain and to keep war materials from reaching the Central Powers by sea. The Germans were just as determined to disrupt Allied shipping. Both Great Britain and Germany depended heavily on the seas for their food and war materials. Without those goods, neither country could continue the war.

Great Britain blockaded all ports under German control at the start of the war. The blockade was so effective that Germany had to receive most of its supplies through the neutral countries of Holland, Denmark, Sweden, and Norway. The

Chapter 28 Section 3

Visualizing History The Gallipoli Campaign took a savage toll on both sides. The Allies lost a quarter of a million men as casualties or prisoners. Turkish losses—including 66,000 killed—were almost as great.
Answer to Caption: *to supply Russia and strengthen Serbia through the Dardanelles; to take Constantinople and thus end Ottoman participation in the war; to precipitate the collapse of Austria-Hungary*

Who?What?Where?When?

Mustafa Kemal was the commander of the Turkish forces at Gallipoli. After the war he became the first president of the newly created nation of Turkey.

Linking Past and Present

Wristwatches were first introduced in Switzerland in 1790. For over a century, however, they were worn only by women. Men traditionally used pocket watches. It was not until World War I, when pocket watches were impractical at the front, that men started to wear wristwatches.

MAKING CONNECTIONS ACTIVITIES

Daily Life Have students research and report on the effects of the war on civilians. Among the subjects they might investigate are: rationing; restrictions on transportation; and the role of popular entertainment. **L2**

Economics Have students research and report on how the war was paid for, with special attention to the sale of war bonds. **L3**

TEACH

Tell students that the main line of trenches on the Western Front was established by November 1914. It ran almost 500 miles from the North Sea to Switzerland. One reason it became relatively fixed as soon as it did was that both sides were too exhausted and too short of war materials to launch major offensives in the fall; over the winter, troops had an opportunity to dig in and make their positions more defensible. Ask students why both sides were in such bad shape after only four months of war. *(They expected a short war and had not stockpiled enough arms and ammunition.)*

Linking Past and Present

Gallipoli One of the most effective movies ever made about World War I is *Gallipoli* (1981). It tells the story of two Australian soldiers who take part in the unsuccessful Allied attack on the Turkish peninsula.

NATIONAL GEOGRAPHIC PICTURING HISTORY

In the Trenches

In the Dardanelles Campaign of 1915 these soldiers of the British Empire fought to capture Gallipoli. Held by the Ottoman Empire, Gallipoli was a strategic location for supplying Russia and the Eastern Front of the war. These troops have hastily dug a trench on their way up a hillside. There they could make use of periscopes and wait for their officers to decide whether they should go "over the top." Three of the men in this photo are Australian. The heavy losses sustained by Australian troops in the Gallipoli Campaign fostered a new sense of Australian identity.

It was on the Western Front, however, in France and Belgium, that trench warfare was most gruesome. In ditches and tunnels called trenches the armies of the Allies and the Central Powers settled into a war of position. The units of horse cavalry that had pranced proudly into war were replaced by foot soldiers hunkered into trenches, facing the enemy across a no-man's-land of barbed wire. Stuck in mud and water, soldiers lived alongside lice and rats amid the smell of dead horses and dead men. It was a war, British poet Wilfred Owen wrote, "obscene as cancer" and "bitter as ... vile."

Germans protested that the blockade violated international law and called it "the hunger blockade." Ignoring these protests, the British also stopped ships they suspected of carrying **contraband**, or prohibited goods. They escorted these ships into port and seized their cargoes.

Submarine Warfare

The Germans eventually found a new way to counter the British blockade and to wear down British sea power. They instituted a policy of submarine warfare. At first, German submarines, or U-boats, struck only warships. In 1915 they also began to strike civilian and commercial ships without warning, disregarding all rules of naval warfare. The Allies were particularly enraged when the Germans sank the British passenger liner *Lusitania* in May 1915, killing over 1,000 people.

At this time the naval code stated that enemy ships had to give warning before attacking a nonmilitary target so the passengers and crew could be evacuated. The attacking ship was expected to take the evacuees on board. The Germans said that their submarines would be easy targets if they surfaced to give warning. In addition, they had no space for passengers or contraband cargo.

By March 1916, German U-boats had sunk other British and French ships. This led the United States to issue an ultimatum to the Germans. It threatened to sever diplomatic relations if Germany did not agree to stop attacking passenger and freight vessels. The Germans responded by ending unrestricted submarine warfare for a while.

United States Enters War

One of the most important events of 1917 was the decision of the United States to enter the war. Until this point, American public opinion was divided about the conflict in Europe. For example, many Irish Americans were staunchly anti-British, and many German Americans sided with the Central Powers. Many other Americans, mostly of British or French descent, favored the Allies. The majority of Americans, however, agreed with President **Woodrow Wilson** that the war was strictly a European conflict. While incidents such as the sinking of the *Lusitania* in 1915 angered them, Americans were not ready to take an active part in the war.

Meanwhile, in Europe, the Germans did not want the Americans to enter the war. At the same time, they were determined to break British control of the seas. They believed that the way to do this was by resuming a policy of unrestricted submarine warfare. As a result, Germany announced that beginning February 1, 1917, it would sink any merchant ships heading to British or western European ports. President Wilson responded to this announcement by breaking off diplomatic relations with Germany.

Tensions between the two countries grew worse in March 1917 when American newspapers published the Zimmermann telegram, a message sent to the Mexican government by Arthur Zimmermann, the German foreign minister. The British had found and passed on the note to the Americans. In this telegram, Zimmermann proposed a deal with Mexico. He promised that if Mexico joined Germany in the war, Mexico would receive New Mexico, Texas, and Arizona after a German victory. Zimmermann also proposed that Mexico talk to Japan about joining the Central Powers alliance.

That same month the Germans sank four American merchant ships. Thirty-six lives were lost. For the United States, this was the final provocation. On April 2, 1917, President Wilson asked Congress for a declaration of war. Wilson also called upon Americans to help "make the world safe for democracy."

SECTION 3 REVIEW

Recall

1. **Define** belligerent, propaganda, war of attrition, trench, contraband.
2. **Identify** Alfred von Schlieffen, Helmuth von Moltke, Joseph Jacques Joffre, Henri-Philippe Pétain, Winston Churchill, Woodrow Wilson.
3. **List** the nations that made up the Central Powers and the Allied Powers during World War I.

Critical Thinking

4. **Synthesizing Information** Create your own strategy for avoiding a stalemate in trench warfare. Determine the main factors working against a breakthrough in this type of warfare.

Understanding Themes

5. **Conflict** Explain how World War I was a new kind of war. Consider objectives, strategy, and technology in the course of your explanation.

Chapter 28 Section 3

ASSESS

Check for Understanding

Assign Section 3 Review as homework or as an in-class activity.

Use Student Self-Test and Review Software to review Section 3.

Evaluate

Section Quiz 28-3

Use the Testmaker to create a customized quiz for Section 3.

Reteach

Discuss the following topics with students: the major events on the Western Front, on the Eastern Front, and at sea; technological advances used, and their effects; events prior to and following the entrance of the United States into the war.

Enrich

Have students read Mark Helprin's *A Soldier of the Great War* for a vivid account of an Italian soldier's experiences. Have them select several passages and present an oral reading to the rest of the class.

CLOSE

Have students summarize the situations of the Allies and the Central Powers in the spring of 1917. *(The prospect of victory was slim for both sides at this point.)*

SECTION 3 REVIEW ANSWERS

1. All vocabulary words are defined in the Glossary.
2. Alfred von Schlieffen, 744; Helmuth von Moltke, 744; Joseph Jacques Joffre, 745; Henri Pétain, 748; Winston Churchill, 749; Woodrow Wilson, 751
3. Central Powers: Germany, Austria-Hungary, Ottoman Empire, Bulgaria; Allies: Britain, France, Russia, Serbia, Belgium, Italy (after 1915), Japan, Montenegro, the United States (after 1917)
4. Answers will vary but should show an understanding of trench warfare.
5. **CONFLICT** Old strategies did not take into account the contingencies of war and surprise moves by the enemy. In World War I, strategists had to react to many new situations as they arose; new technology—machine guns, land mines, submarines, tanks, airplanes—made it possible to kill people in unprecedented numbers.

Special Report Summary

In 1915 a German submarine sank the British luxury liner *Lusitania*, killing more than 1,000 people and helping draw the United States into World War I.

↓

To clear up questions about the sinking, scientists used a robot vehicle to examine the wreck on the ocean floor.

↓

Although the ship was carrying arms, the team found that the weapons had not exploded when a torpedo struck the *Lusitania*. This disproved a once-popular theory of why the ship sank so fast.

↓

The team hypothesized that the powerful secondary explosion that caused the ship to sink in only 18 minutes was probably caused by the ignition of coal dust in a storage compartment.

NATIONAL GEOGRAPHIC Special Report

Bettmann

The Lusitania

Passengers boarding the British liner R.M.S. *Lusitania* in New York on May 1, 1915, for the voyage to Liverpool, England, knew of Germany's threat to sink ships bound for the British Isles. England and Germany had been fighting for nine months. Still, few passengers imagined that a civilized nation would attack an unarmed passenger steamer without warning.

Built eight years earlier, the *Lusitania* was described as a "floating palace." German authorities, however, saw her as a threat. They accused the British government of using the *Lusitania* to carry ammunition and other war materials across the Atlantic.

With her four towering funnels, the liner looked invincible as she left New York on her last voyage. Six days later, at 2:10 p.m. on May 7, 1915, Walther Schwieger, the 30-year-old commander of the German submarine U 20, fired a single torpedo at the *Lusitania* from a range of about 750 yards.

Captain William Turner of the *Lusitania* saw the torpedo's wake from the navigation bridge just before impact. It sounded like a "million-ton hammer hitting a steam boiler a hundred feet high," one passenger said. A second, more powerful explosion followed, sending a geyser of water, coal, and debris high above the deck.

Listing to starboard, the liner began to sink rapidly at the bow, sending passengers tumbling down her slanted decks. Lifeboats on the port side were hanging too far inboard to be readily launched, while those on the starboard side

TEACHER NOTES

NGS Cartographic Division

Boston Evening Globe

EVENING EDITION—7:30 O'CLOCK—LATEST

LUSITANIA SUNK

Not Known How Many Passengers Saved

TORPEDOED BY GERMANS, REMAINED AFLOAT 12 HOURS

TORPEDOED OFF THE IRISH COAST

Left New York Last Saturday With 1253 Passengers

Titanic Historical Society Inc.

were too far out to be easily boarded. Several overfilled lifeboats spilled occupants into the sea. The great liner disappeared under the waves in only 18 minutes, leaving behind a jumble of swimmers, corpses, deck chairs, and wreckage. Looking back upon the scene from his submarine, even German commander Schwieger was shocked. He later called it the most horrible sight he had ever seen.

News of the disaster raced across the Atlantic. Of 1,959 people aboard, only 764 were saved. The dead included 94 children and infants.

Questions were immediately raised. Did the British Admiralty give the *Lusitania* adequate warning? How could one torpedo have sunk her? Why did she go down so fast? Was there any truth to the German claim that the *Lusitania* had been armed?

From the moment the *Lusitania* sank, she was surrounded by controversy. Americans were outraged by the attack, which claimed the lives of 123 U.S. citizens. Newspapers called the attack "deliberate murder" and a "foul deed," and former President Theodore Roosevelt demanded revenge against Germany. The attack on the *Lusitania* is often credited with drawing the United States into

The** Lusitania **arrives in New York on her maiden voyage in 1907 (opposite page).

In the two days prior to the attack on the** Lusitania**, the German submarine U 20 had sunk three ships off Ireland's southern coast. Yet the captain of the** Lusitania**, who had received warnings by wireless from the British Admiralty, took only limited precautions as he approached the area. Headlines in Boston and New York report the terrible news of the sinking of the** Lusitania **on May 7, 1915 (above).

TEACH

Points to Discuss

After students have read the feature, ask the following: Why did the sinking of the *Lusitania* anger many Americans? *(because sinking the unarmed passenger vessel killed more than 1,000 civilians, including 123 Americans)* What questions were raised about the sinking? *(Was the ship warned about German submarines? Why did one torpedo sink it so fast? Was it armed, as Germany claimed? What caused a second explosion?)* What did researchers learn by examining the wreck with a robot vehicle? *(They found that weapons carried by the* Lusitania *had not exploded, and they hypothesized that the second explosion was caused by the ignition of coal dust.)*

Cultural Perspectives

Rules of War Although the *Lusitania* carried arms in its hold, under the rules of war at the time, it was not considered a legitimate target. Even so, before the *Lusitania* sailed, Germany published a warning in American newspapers: "NOTICE! Travellers ... are reminded that a state of war exists ... that the zone of war includes the waters adjacent to the British Isles; that ... vessels flying the flag of Great Britain, or of any of her allies, are liable to destruction."

FUN FACTS

- Woodrow Wilson's secretary of state, William Jennings Bryan, resigned rather than sign a strongly worded protest Wilson sent to Germany after the *Lusitania*'s sinking.
- The name of the ship came from the ancient Roman province of Lusitania, which made up the region that is now Portugal and western Spain.
- The cargo of arms and ammunition that the *Lusitania* was carrying weighed about 173 tons.
- The British admiralty had recommended that the *Lusitania* follow a zigzag course, changing direction every few minutes, to avoid torpedo attacks.

Linking Past and Present

Shipwrecks In recent years a number of wrecked ships have been raised from the ocean bottom by scientists and entrepreneurs. The salvage operations have generated controversy about the ownership of the materials recovered, which can be worth millions of dollars.

Among the better-known cases are the Padre Island wrecks in Texas and the case of *Nuestra Señora de la Atocha* in Florida.

CURRICULUM CONNECTION

SCIENCE AND TECHNOLOGY

The first submarine to be used in combat was built by an American, David Bushnell, in 1776, and was used during the Revolutionary War. It was made of wood and moved by means of a hand-turned propeller. (The craft was used in an unsuccessful attempt to blow up a British warship in New York harbor.) By the late 1800s, an American engineer named Simon Lake had made considerable advances in submarine technology, including the use of horizontal rudders for diving and water ballast for submergence. However, the U.S. Navy was slow to see the merits of Lake's work. It wasn't until several European governments had made use of Lake's ideas in the early 1900s that he was hired by the United States.

NATIONAL GEOGRAPHIC Special Report

World War I. President Woodrow Wilson—though he had vowed to hold Germany responsible for its submarine attacks—knew that the American people were not ready to go to war. It was almost two more years before the United States joined the conflict in Europe.

A British judge laid full blame on the German submarine commander, while the German government claimed that the British had deliberately made her a military target. Tragically, inquiries following the sinking of the *Lusitania* revealed that Captain Turner had received warnings by wireless from the British Admiralty, but took only limited precautions as he approached the area where U 20 was waiting.

Rumors of diamonds, gold, and valuables locked away in *Lusitania's* safes have prompted salvage attempts over the years. To date, no treasure has ever been reported.

Perhaps the biggest puzzle has been the hardest to solve: Why did the liner sink so fast? Newspapers speculated that the torpedo had struck ammunition in a cargo hold, causing the strong secondary explosion. Divers later reported a huge hole in the port side of the bow, opposite where munitions would have been stored.

HOPING TO SETTLE the issue, a team from the Woods Hole Oceanographic Institution, sponsored by the National Geographic Society, sent their robot vehicle Jason down to photograph the damage. Fitted with cameras and powerful lights, the robot sent video images of the wreck by fiber-optic cable to a control room on the surface ship, *Northern Horizon*. A pilot maneuvered Jason with a joystick, while an engineer relayed instructions to the robot's computers. Other team members watched for recognizable objects on the monitors. In addition to using Jason to make a visual survey of the *Lusitania*, the team of researchers and scientists also used sonar to create a computerized, three-dimensional diagram of how the wreck looks today.

From this data, it was discovered that the *Lusitania's* hull had been flattened—in part by the force of gravity—to half its original width. When Jason's cameras swept across the hold, looking for the hole reported by divers shortly after the sinking, there was none to be found. Indeed, no evidence was found that would indicate that the torpedo had detonated an explosion in a cargo hold, undermining one theory of why the liner sank.

Questions about her cargo have haunted the *Lusitania* since the day she went down. Was she carrying illegal munitions as the Germans have always claimed? In fact, she was. The manifest for her last voyage included wartime essentials such as motorcycle parts, metals, cotton goods, and food, as well as 4,200 cases of rifle ammunition, 1,250 cases of shrapnel (not explosive), and 18 boxes of percussion fuses. The investigation conducted by the Woods Hole team and Jason suggested that these munitions did not cause the secondary blast that sent the *Lusitania* to the bottom. So what did?

One likely possibility was a coal-dust explosion. The German torpedo struck the liner's starboard side about ten feet below the waterline, rupturing one of the long coal bunkers that stretched along both sides. If that bunker, mostly empty by the end of the voyage, contained explosive coal dust, the torpedo might have ignited it. That would explain all the coal found scattered on the seafloor near the wreck.

The *Lusitania's* giant funnels have long since turned to rust, an eerie marine growth covers her hull, and her superstructure is ghostly wreckage. Yet the horror and fascination surrounding the sinking of the great liner live on. With today's high-technology tools, researchers and scientists at Woods Hole and the National Geographic Society have provided another look—and some new answers—to explain the chain of events that ended with the *Lusitania* at the bottom of the sea.

Brown Brothers

UPI/Bettmann

754 Chapter 28 World War I

MORE ABOUT...

German U-Boat Attacks After the sinking of the *Lusitania*, German submarines continued to torpedo merchant vessels without warning. In March 1910, fearing the United States would enter the war, Germany stopped the attacks. With the war stalemated, however, Germany resumed unrestricted submarine attacks in February 1917, sinking four American ships in just two months. Wilson cited German violations of "freedom of the seas" as a reason for entering the war in April 1917.

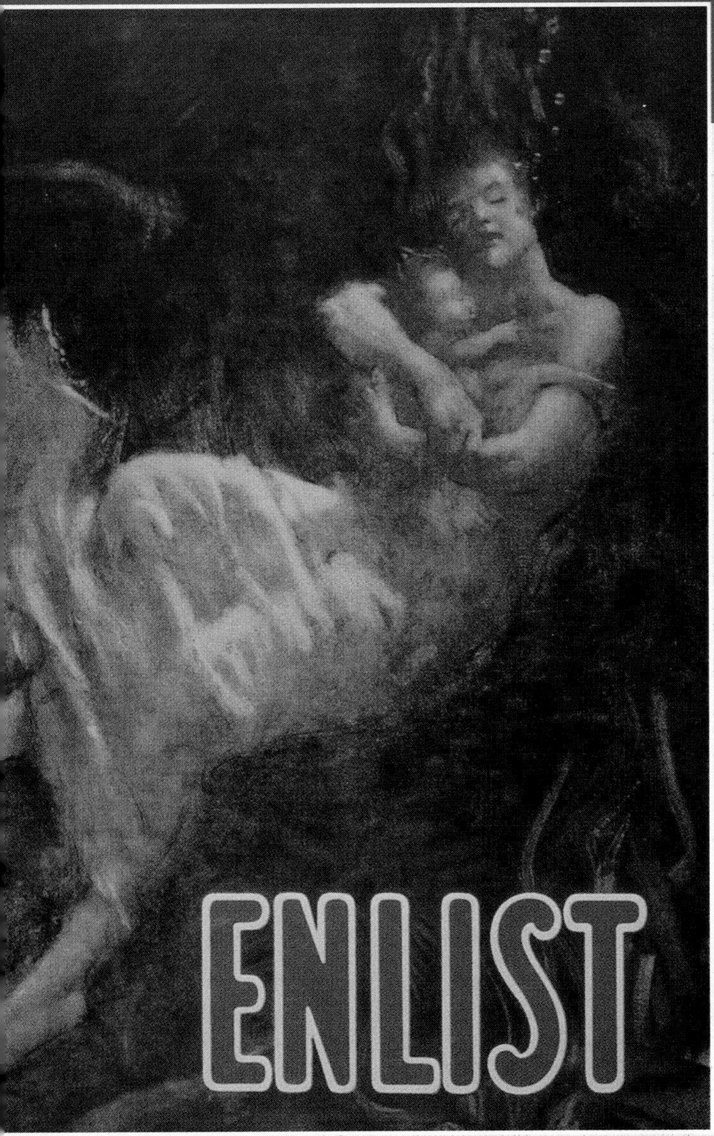

Bowman Gray Collection, University of North Carolina, Chapel Hill

Jonathan Blair

A provocative poster (left) depicted drowning innocents and urged Americans to enlist in the armed forces. For the women pictured above, the image was all too real. Alice Drury (above left) was a young nanny for an American couple on the Lusitania. She and another nanny were caring for the couple's children: Audrey, Stuart, Amy, and Susan. Alice was about to give Audrey a bottle when the torpedo hit. Alice wrapped Audrey in a shawl, grabbed Stuart, and headed for the lifeboats. A crewman loaded Stuart, but when Alice tried to board, the sailor told her it was full. Without a life jacket and with Audrey around her neck, Alice jumped into the water. A woman in the lifeboat grabbed her hair and pulled her aboard. Audrey's parents were rescued too, but Amy, Susan, and the other nanny were lost. Alice and Audrey Lawson Johnston (above right) have remained close ever since.

Jonathan Blair

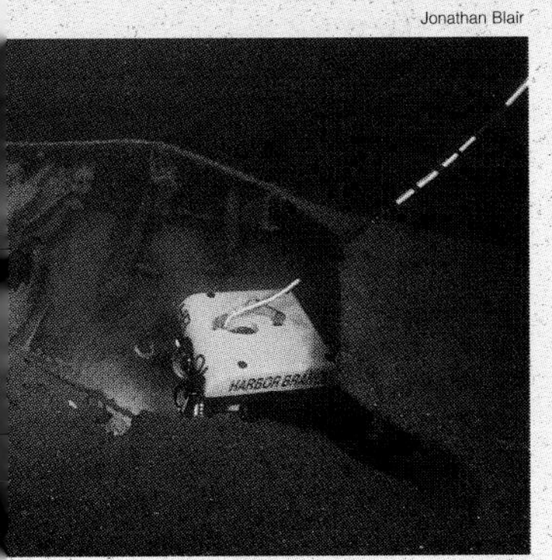

Captain William Turner of the Lusitania, (opposite page, top); Walther Schwieger, commander of the German submarine U 20 (opposite page, bottom).

Homer, a small robot, (left) explores a hole in the stern of the Lusitania that was cut by a salvage crew to recover silverware and other items.

TEACHER NOTES

CURRICULUM CONNECTION

GEOGRAPHY

Have students study the map on page 753. How far was the *Lusitania* from the Irish coast when it was sunk? *(about 10 miles [16 km])* How far apart were the two ships sunk by U 20 on May 6, 1915? *(about 10 miles [16 km])* What is the approximate distance between Ireland and Wales? *(about 35 miles [56 km])*

you don't say...

"There is such a thing as a man being too proud to fight," President Wilson explained on May 10. Although Wilson had sent several stern diplomatic notes to Germany following the *Lusitania*'s sinking, he had stopped short of delivering an ultimatum that would lead to war. Most Americans were horrified by the attack, but they supported Wilson's measured response.

Portfolio Project

Have students discuss the effect of the *Lusitania*'s sinking on U.S. public opinion. Organize the class into two groups and have each write a short newspaper editorial either for or against going to war with Germany as a result of the attack on the *Lusitania.*

SECTION THEME

▶ **Revolution** Revolution in Russia overthrows the czar and brings Lenin and the Bolsheviks to power.

Find Out

Answer: *Russia's participation in World War I, with its hardships for both soldiers and civilians; the unpopularity of Czar Nicholas II*

FOCUS

Section Objective

Summarize the events that led to the Russian Revolution.

BELLRINGER
Motivational Activity

Before taking roll at the beginning of the class period, project Section Focus Transparency 28-4 and have students answer the activity questions. Discuss students' responses.

This activity is also available as a blackline master.

Vocabulary Pre-check

Use Vocabulary Activity 28 to introduce vocabulary terms. **L1 LEP**

1916 — 1918 — 1920

1917 Czar Nicholas II abdicates.

1918 Bolshevik Russia and Germany sign Treaty of Brest-Litovsk.

1919 Reds and Whites fight civil war.

Section 4

The Russian Revolution

Setting the Scene

▶ **Terms to Define**
provisional government, communism

▶ **People to Meet**
Nicholas II, Grigori Rasputin, Alexander Kerensky, Vladimir Ilyich Lenin, Leon Trotsky

▶ **Places to Locate**
Petrograd, Siberia, Ukraine, Poland

Find Out What events led to the Russian Revolution?

The Storyteller

Thousands filled the hall, waiting for Trotsky's speech. The crowd was tense, waiting. When Trotsky appeared, they applauded, but briefly, so as to hear that much sooner what he would say. Trotsky spoke of current conditions, and then continued. "The Soviet government will give everything the country contains to the poor and the men in the trenches. You, bourgeois, have two fur caps!—give one of them to the soldier, who's freezing in the trenches." The crowd surrounding Trotsky was aroused almost to ecstasy. This, actually, was already an insurrection. A transformation had begun.

Leon Trotsky

—adapted from *The Russian Revolution*, N. N. Sukharov, translated by Joel Carmichael, 1917

World War I proved to be the breaking point for czarist rule in Russia. By 1917, morale in the Russian army had reached bottom. As many as one-fourth of the Russian soldiers, having no weapons of their own, had to pick up the guns of dead soldiers. Inadequate transport made grave food shortages even worse. Almost all of the country's resources went to supply the army, making the human and financial costs of war increasingly unbearable.

A nurse at the Russian front in 1917 described the situation that helped bring about the collapse of the autocracy and the establishment of a Communist state:

> "Discontent among the masses in Russia is daily becoming more marked. Disparaging statements concerning the Government are being voiced.... "Bring the men home!" "Conclude peace!" "Finish this interminable war once and for all!" Cries such as these penetrate to the cold and hungry soldiers in their bleak earthworks, and begin to echo among them. Now that food has grown scarce in Petrograd (St. Petersburg) and Moscow, disorder takes the shape of riots and insurrections. We are told that mobs of the lower classes parade the streets shouting 'Peace and Bread!'"

Fall of the Czar

Events leading to the fall of the czar began to accelerate in the last half of 1916. Czar **Nicholas II** and his wife, Alexandra, had already become unpopular because of the czar's political incompetence and the couple's reliance on the mystic healer **Grigori Rasputin** (rah•SPOO•teen). Wanting to

SECTION RESOURCES

Reproducible Masters
- Reproducible Lesson Plan 28-4
- Vocabulary Activity 28
- Guided Reading Activity 28-4
- Section Quiz 28-4

Transparencies
- Section Focus Transparency 28-4

Multimedia
- Student Self-Test and Review Software
- Testmaker
- Communism and the Cold War: *Perspectives on Communism*

save the monarchy, two relatives of the czar assisted in killing Rasputin in December 1916.

Rasputin's death did not solve the monarchy's problems. Public anger against the government mounted as a result of food and fuel shortages, and strikes erupted across the country. On March 8, 1917, and for the next few days, hundreds of thousands of men and women gathered in the streets of **Petrograd** (the Russian name given to St. Petersburg). Demanding food and an end to the war, the crowds shouted, "Down with the czar!" On March 11 and 12, the troops the government ordered to put down the riots refused to fire on the crowds. Many soldiers joined the protesters.

When the czar ordered his generals at the front to crush the rebellion, they told him that any troops they might send to the capital would also join the rioters. With the country sinking into chaos, the czar finally abdicated on March 15, ending the 300-year-old Romanov dynasty. The March revolution was a spontaneous uprising of working people and soldiers. It caused the loss of relatively few lives and took place, surprisingly, without the leadership of its revolutionary intellectuals, most of whom were living in exile abroad.

The Provisional Government

After Czar Nicholas II's abdication, political authority in Russia passed into the hands of a temporary central government known as the **provisional government**. This new regime called for elections later in the year to choose a constituent, or constitutional, assembly. The constituent assembly would then establish a permanent government.

The provisional government, which consisted of middle-class Duma representatives, soon had a rival for power—the Petrograd Soviet of Workers' and Soldiers' Deputies. Members of the Petrograd Soviet were workers and peasants belonging to different socialist groups. The majority were either Mensheviks or Social Revolutionaries, the political heirs of the Populists. A smaller, more radical group was the Bolsheviks.

One man who moved easily between the provisional government and the Petrograd Soviet was **Alexander Kerensky** (keh•REHN•skee). A moderate socialist, Kerensky served first as the provisional government's minister of justice and then as its prime minister. He also belonged to the executive committee of the Petrograd Soviet.

The Petrograd Soviet became a model for the founding of other soviets throughout Russia. Together, the soviets called for an immediate peace, the transfer of land to the peasants, and the control of factories by workers. As the Russian economy continued to collapse under the war effort, this three-point program gained great popularity among the Russian masses.

In spite of the suffering and anger of the Russian people, however, the provisional government did not withdraw from the war. Desertion, worsening transportation problems, and a drop in already low armament production plagued the Russian army. Preoccupied with war policy, the provisional government could not carry out the social reforms proposed by the soviets. As a result, the government lost much of its popular support, a factor that contributed to its eventual downfall.

Lenin

As the provisional government struggled to maintain order, a variety of revolutionary groups vied to fill the power vacuum. Since their split into two factions in 1903, the Mensheviks and the Bolsheviks had competed for control of Russia's revolutionary movement. By 1917 the Mensheviks far outnumbered the Bolsheviks. Because they believed that a socialist revolution would be the work of the masses, however, the Mensheviks did not make concrete plans to seize control of the Russian government.

The more radical Bolsheviks, on the other hand, believed that a socialist society could be introduced immediately by force. They claimed that a small group of dedicated revolutionaries could carry out the revolution with the help of a relatively small working class and the peasants. They also believed that Russia's revolution would spread worldwide. Their leader, **Vladimir Ilyich Lenin**, urged them to make plans to topple the provisional government from power.

Born in 1870, Lenin came from a middle-class provincial background. When Lenin was in high school, his older brother, Alexander, became involved in a plot to assassinate Czar Alexander III, the father of Nicholas II. The attempt failed, however, and the government hanged Lenin's brother and four fellow conspirators in 1887. Alexander's death made a powerful impression on Lenin, who dedicated his life to promoting a revolution.

In 1895 the Russian government arrested Lenin for his activities and exiled him to **Siberia**. After his release, he went to Germany, Great Britain, and Switzerland, where he wrote revolutionary articles and kept a close eye on the political situation in

TEACH

Guided Practice

THEME **Revolution**

Have students review the earlier Russian Revolution, that of 1905. **How was the situation different in 1917?** *(widespread dissatisfaction caused by Russian participation in World War I)* **L1**

Analyze Discuss the reasons the provisional government of Russia failed to win public support. *(Its leaders did not withdraw Russia from the war, nor did they carry out the social reforms proposed by the soviets.)* **L2**

Chart Have students make a chart listing the three groups in Russia that opposed the Bolsheviks after their takeover and what each group wanted. *(royalists: restoration of the czar; liberals: capitalist democracy; socialists: democratic socialist government)* **L3**

Who?What?Where?When?

Rasputin was a hard man to kill. The conspirators who murdered him first tried poison wine and cakes. When these methods did not work, Prince Felix Yusupov, organizer of the plot, shot Rasputin. The bullets did not kill him either. He was finally drowned by plotters in the Neva River.

Independent Practice

Guided Reading Activity 28-4 **L1**

Cartoon Have students draw cartoons, dating from the summer of 1917, representing the point of view of the Mensheviks, the Bolsheviks, a Moscow worker, or a Russian farmer. **L2 LEP**

COOPERATIVE LEARNING ACTIVITY

Biographies Organize the class into four groups and assign each one a major figure in the Russian Revolution: Czar Nicholas II, Kerensky, Lenin, and Trotsky. Have each group research its assigned individual—his background, education, beliefs, and so on—and prepare a written or oral report to present to the class. If possible, the report should be accompanied by illustrations. **L2**

ABCNEWS INTERACTIVE™

VIDEODISC
Communism and the Cold War

Side One, Chapter 8
Frames 14264–14893
Title: *Perspectives on Communism*
Subject: Discussion of the ideals of communism
Ask: What did the Soviet Union feel it could teach the world? *(It felt the world needed to be taught to work collectively.)*

Literature Have students research and report on one of the following: Maksim Gorky, a champion of the revolutionary movement in Russia; Alexander Blok, who wrote "The Twelve," a poem about the revolution; or Vladimir Mayakovsky, who popularized the revolution. **L3**

CURRICULUM CONNECTION

SCIENCE
After the execution of Czar Nicholas II and his family, their bodies were disfigured by acid and thrown into unmarked graves. Not until the 1990s were systematic efforts made to locate and identify the Romanovs. When some likely remains were found, they were subjected to DNA analysis. Prince Philip, husband of Britain's Queen Elizabeth II, also was tested. DNA from his blood matched DNA from a bone fragment, proving that one of the bodies was that of Philip's relative, Czarina Alexandra.

Russia. After hearing the news of the March 1917 revolution, he wanted to return to Russia as soon as possible. Since Germany wanted Russia out of the war and knew that Lenin would promote a withdrawal, it provided him with a special "sealed" train that allowed no one to enter or exit during the trip. Lenin's goal upon his arrival in Russia was to organize the Bolsheviks and seize power from the provisional government.

Lenin realized that the provisional government could not maintain the support of the soldiers, peasants, and workers. His slogan, "Peace, Land, and Bread," promised the Russian people that Russia would withdraw from the war, that the peasants would be given land, and that everyone would have enough to eat. Another point in Lenin's program was that the soviets should become the nation's only government. This goal was summed up in the slogan "All power to the soviets!"

The Bolshevik Revolution

During the summer of 1917, a number of demonstrations against the provisional government broke out across Russia. Blaming these demonstrations on the Bolsheviks and calling Lenin a German agent, the government issued arrest warrants for all Bolshevik leaders, forcing Lenin into hiding. By late August, however, the Bolsheviks started to show new strength in local elections, and by mid-September they had gained control of the Petrograd Soviet.

Two months later, in November 1917, the Bolsheviks staged a coup d'etat in Petrograd, overthrowing the provisional government in the name of the soviets. Bolshevik soldiers, workers, and sailors took over the main post office, the telephone system, electrical generating plants, and train stations. When the Bolsheviks turned the guns of the battleship *Aurora* against the Winter Palace, the former home of the czar, the ministers of the provisional government quickly surrendered. As a result, the revolution was relatively bloodless.

In spite of the Bolshevik coup, the election for the constituent assembly still took place in late November. Of those elected, 420 seats went to the Social Revolutionaries and only 225 to the Bolsheviks. When the assembly met in Petrograd in January 1918, however, the Bolsheviks dissolved it after only one day.

Lenin's first goal after seizing power was to end Russian involvement in World War I. After the Allies rejected the Bolshevik proposal for a general armistice, however, Lenin realized that Russia would have to negotiate a separate peace with Germany. Russia eventually signed the Treaty of Brest-Litovsk in March 1918, in which the Bolsheviks gave up the Baltic provinces, **Ukraine,** and **Poland**. Lenin was not worried about these losses; he believed that a revolution would soon sweep Germany, too.

Civil War

After dissolving the constituent assembly, the Bolsheviks faced challenges from many different groups within Russia. Royalists favored the restoration of the czar, middle-class liberals supported a capitalist democracy, and moderate Socialists wanted both democracy and a government-controlled economy. During the early months of 1918, Russia slipped into a devastating civil war between the Bolsheviks and their opponents.

Reds and Whites

The various groups opposed to the Bolsheviks came to be called the Whites. The Bolsheviks at this time began to call themselves Communists. Because they favored the red flag of revolution, they were also called the Reds. The Bolsheviks and their supporters throughout the world founded an international revolutionary movement. Their political viewpoint, based on the ideas of Marx and Lenin, became known as **communism**.

The Allies wanted to overthrow the Bolsheviks and get Russia back into the war against the Central Powers. As a result, they sent soldiers and military aid to help the Whites, who promised to defeat the Reds quickly and then to begin helping with the war effort again. Lenin's government, however, was determined not to yield power. Under the Communist leader **Leon Trotsky**, the Red Army was organized to defend the Communist state. Trotsky restored discipline to Russian military ranks and fostered loyalty to communism by teaching soldiers, many of whom were illiterate, how to read and write.

Although the Whites had many soldiers and arms, they suffered from a lack of unity among their royalist, liberal, and moderate Socialist supporters. As a result, the Whites were not able to work together to inflict a quick defeat on the Reds as they had planned.

For three grim years, the fighting raged across the vast landscape of Russia. Both sides burned villages and slaughtered civilians. When the Whites captured an area, they killed all suspected Bolsheviks. The Reds did the same to "counter-revolutionaries," or

MEETING SPECIAL NEEDS ACTIVITY

Study Strategy Students may have trouble following the events in the chaotic period of the Russian Revolution. Have them construct a chart with dates (from 1916 to 1922) along the side and these headings across the top: *Leader(s) of Government; Political/Social Events.* **L3**

Russian Civil War 1918–1922

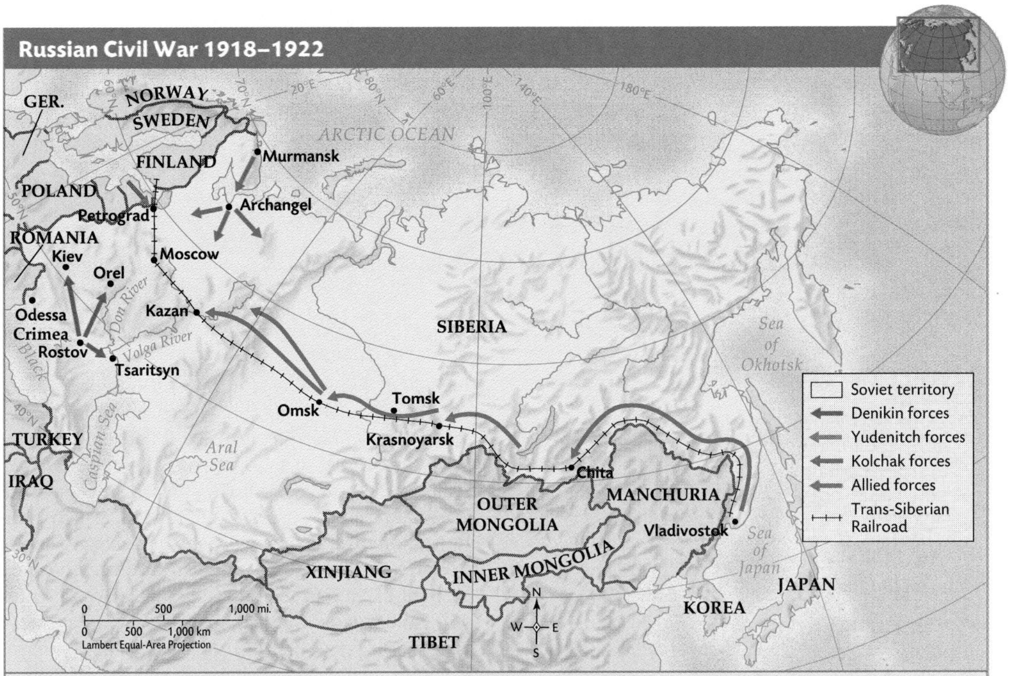

Map Study The leaders of the White forces during the Russian Civil War included General Anthony Denikin, General Nicholas Yudenitch, and Admiral Alexander Kolchak. **Movement** Why do you think Kolchak chose the strategy indicated by the map to attack Moscow?

those believed to be opposed to communism. In the meantime, workers and peasants were starving and the nation's economy was disintegrating.

The Terror

During the upheaval, Lenin used terror as a political weapon against his opponents. In July 1918, Communist soldiers killed the imprisoned czar and his family. To further strengthen his control, Lenin set up the Cheka, a secret police force that arrested anyone considered an "enemy of the revolution." In keeping with communism's antireligious viewpoint, Lenin also placed severe restrictions on the Russian Orthodox Church.

Many Socialists who had backed Lenin's revolution now withdrew their support and fled Russia. By 1921 Lenin had extended Communist control throughout the country. Outnumbered, disorganized, and poorly equipped, the White armies finally admitted defeat.

SECTION 4 REVIEW

Recall

1. **Define** provisional government, communism.
2. **Identify** Nicholas II, Grigori Rasputin, Alexander Kerensky, Vladimir Ilyich Lenin, Leon Trotsky.
3. **Discuss** the main differences that separated the Mensheviks and the Bolsheviks.

Critical Thinking

4. **Evaluating Information** Do you think Lenin was justified in closing down the democratically elected constituent assembly in January 1918? Why or why not?

Understanding Themes

5. **Revolution** What were the reasons for Russia's withdrawal from World War I? How did the war lead to the collapse of czarist autocracy and the birth of a radical Socialist state?

SECTION 4 REVIEW ANSWERS

1. The words are defined in the Glossary.
2. Nicholas II, 756; Rasputin, 756; Kerensky, 757; Lenin, 757; Trotsky, 758
3. Mensheviks: revolution should be the work of the masses; Bolsheviks: revolution could occur by force by a small group of revolutionaries plus workers and peasants
4. Answers should show understanding of Bolsheviks' political beliefs.
5. **REVOLUTION** The war was destroying the country's army, economy, and morale. Both the czar and the provisional government insisted on continuing to fight; the Bolsheviks promised peace and enough to eat.

Map Study

Answer

He hoped that if he could seize control of the Trans-Siberian Railroad, he could control an important supply line and transport his troops to the main theater of action.

Map Skills Practice

Reading a Map From what regions did Denikin and Yudenitch attack? *(Denikin: from the Crimea, south of Moscow; Yudenitch: from the Baltic region, in the north)*

ASSESS

Check for Understanding

Assign Section 4 Review as homework or as an in-class activity.

Use Student Self-Test and Review Software to review Section 4.

Evaluate

Section Quiz 28-4

Use the Testmaker to create a customized quiz for Section 4.

Reteach

Have students review the goals of the Bolsheviks and discuss why they appealed to the Russian people.

Enrich

Have the class watch the film *Dr. Zhivago* and discuss its message and impact.

CLOSE

Have students summarize the effects of World War I on the Russian Revolution.

Chapter 28 Section 5

SECTION THEME

▶ **Internationalism** The Treaty of Versailles provides for the creation of a League of Nations to mediate international disputes.

Find Out

Answer: *because it left Germany weakened, humiliated, and resentful*

FOCUS

Section Objective

Explain why the Treaty of Versailles was ultimately unsuccessful.

BELLRINGER Motivational Activity

Before taking roll at the beginning of the class period, project Section Focus Transparency 28-5 and have students answer the activity questions. Discuss students' responses.

This activity is also available as a blackline master.

Vocabulary Pre-check

Use the Vocabulary PuzzleMaker to create a puzzle that reinforces the vocabulary terms in this section. **L1**

1917 | **1918** | **1919**

1917 United States declaration of war raises Allied morale.

1918 President Woodrow Wilson presents Fourteen Points.

1919 Allies sign Treaty of Versailles.

Section 5

Peace at Last

Setting the Scene

▶ **Terms to Define**
convoy, armistice, reparation, mandate, cordon sanitaire

▶ **People to Meet**
T.E. Lawrence, Ferdinand Foch, Woodrow Wilson, Georges Clemenceau, David Lloyd George, Vittorio Orlando

▶ **Places to Locate**
Fiume

Find Out Why was the Treaty of Versailles ultimately unsuccessful?

The Storyteller

Four officers of France, Great Britain, America, and Italy marched into the Palace of Versailles to sign the treaty ending World War I. Harold Nicholson described the ceremony in his diary: "And then, isolated and pitiable, come the two German delegates, Dr. Muller and Dr. Bell. The silence is terrifying.... They keep their eyes fixed away from those two thousand staring eyes, fixed upon the ceiling. They are deathly pale.... Suddenly from outside comes the crash of guns thundering a salute. It announces to Paris that the second Treaty of Versailles had been signed.... We kept our seats while the Germans were conducted like prisoners from the dock, their eyes still fixed upon some distant point of the horizon."

—adapted from *Peacemaking*, Harold Nicholson, reprinted in *Western Civilization, an Urban Perspective*, F. Roy Willis, 1973

German officer's helmet

Russia's withdrawal from the war in 1918 might have proved a disaster for the Allied cause if it had not been offset by the entry of the United States into the war. American intervention took some of the pressure off the British navy and strengthened French positions along the Western Front. Although no single decisive victory turned the war around, what had seemed like a permanently stalemated war eventually gave way in 1918 to an Allied victory.

The American Contribution

The American entry into the war raised Allied morale. It also gave the Allies much needed resources, both industrial and human. The Americans threw themselves into the war effort. A Selective Service System was instituted to draft soldiers into the army. The British and the French urged the Americans to speed up their arrival in Europe. It took time for the Americans to build and train an army. The American navy, however, was of immediate help.

The German U-boat campaign had been increasingly effective in late 1916 and early 1917. As a result, American Admiral William S. Sims went to London to discuss with the British how to deal with the German submarines. In London, Sims introduced the idea of the **convoy**. Under this system, merchant ships crossed the Atlantic in clusters surrounded by a small number of warships for protection. Before long, the Allies were using the convoy system for all ships crossing the Atlantic.

At the same time, mines and underwater explosives began to be used more effectively. So did air reconnaissance, or surveying. The airplane had started to come into its own earlier in the war. At first, airplanes had been used only for scouting, photography, and dropping markers. In time, they came to be used to bomb enemy military and civilian positions.

SECTION RESOURCES

Reproducible Masters
- Reproducible Lesson Plan 28-5
- Guided Reading Activity 28-5
- Reteaching Activity 28
- Enrichment Activity 28
- Section Quiz 28-5
- Performance Assessment Activity 28
- Spanish Chapter Summary 28

Transparencies
- Section Focus Transparency 28-5

Multimedia
- Vocabulary PuzzleMaker Software
- Student Self-Test and Review Software
- Testmaker

Turning the Tide

Until American forces arrived, the fighting along the trench lines in the Western Front continued without lasting gains for either side. In April 1917, a French offensive stalled. It led to losses so great that French troops mutinied. The British, in order to keep the Germans from taking advantage of the French weakness, launched an offensive into Flanders, a coastal region of northern France and eastern Belgium. Heavy rains, however, made the clay soil of Flanders an impassable expanse of mud. In November, the fighting finally came to an end at Passchendaele (PAH•shehn•dayl). Casualties were enormous, and both the British and the Germans were reaching the end of their reserves.

The Middle East

The war was also being carried on in the Middle East. The Arabs, seeking independence from the Ottomans, turned to the British for help. In October 1915, Great Britain had pledged its support for an independent Arab state. The following year, however, the British had signed the Sykes-Picot Agreement with the French and the Russians. It provided for the division of the Ottoman Empire among three powers.

While the war on the Western Front was deadlocked, the Allies advanced in the Middle East. There the British stopped a Turkish drive on the Suez Canal and then went on to destroy the Ottoman Empire. In December 1917, they occupied Jerusalem. British efforts in the Middle East were aided by Arab fighters who sought independence from the Ottoman Empire. Arab guerrilla raiders, led by a young British officer named **T.E. Lawrence**, harassed the Ottoman Turks and gave the British valuable information about important Turkish locations.

End of Fighting

In the spring of 1918, the Allies created their first unified command in the west under French General **Ferdinand Foch** (FAWSH). At about the same time, the Germans mounted a series of offensives. Their aim was to split the Allies and drive the British into the sea. They almost succeeded. They came to within 37 miles (60 km) of Paris before the Allies finally stopped them.

By that time, the Germans had lost valuable time and were out of reserves. The Allies, however, were bolstered by the arrival each month in France of 250,000 fresh American troops. General Foch ordered a counterattack in July that pushed the Germans back to the border of Germany. With the British advancing in the north, and the Americans and French attacking through the Argonne region of France, the offensive continued into September.

Visualizing History **More than 2 million American soldiers made up of 42 infantry divisions served in France before the war ended in 1918.** *How did the arrival of American troops affect the war's outcome?*

The resistance of the other Central Powers collapsed in other areas. In southeastern Europe, Allied troops drove the Balkans. Within a few weeks, Turkey asked for peace. In November, Italian forces, rallying after a long period of retreat, defeated the Austro-Hungarians at Vittorio Veneto, and Austria-Hungary surrendered.

Although the German army stood firm, morale in Germany gave way. On November 9, 1918, Emperor William II abdicated and fled to the Netherlands. On November 11, the Germans signed an armistice, or agreement to end the fighting.

Effects of the War

The fury of the war had shattered Europe. Governments were almost bankrupt, and revolution threatened much of eastern Europe. The old aristocratic political order was dead. A new Europe had to be forged. Boundaries of parts of the Middle East, Asia, and Africa had to be redrawn.

As a result of the war, human misery had become commonplace. Nearly 9 million soldiers were dead, and another 21 million were wounded.

Chapter 28 Section 5

TEACH

Guided Practice

THEME Internationalism

Ask students to define *internationalism. (having to do with two or more nations)* Then have them list the goals of the United States, Britain, and France in drafting a peace settlement after World War I. **L1 LEP**

Visualizing History U.S. soldiers, known as the American Expeditionary Force, were commanded by General John J. Pershing. This was the first American army ever sent to Europe.

Answer to Caption: *They helped bolster Allied morale and provided much needed human and industrial resources.*

Geography: Location Have students look at the map on page 764 and locate the new European nations created after the war. *(Finland, Estonia, Latvia, Lithuania, Poland, Czechoslovakia, Austria, Hungary, Yugoslavia)* **L2 LEP**

Linking Past and Present

Lafayette After the first U.S. troops landed in France, an American officer announced: "Lafayette, we are here." He was referring to the services rendered to the colonists during the American Revolution by a French aristocrat, the Marquis de Lafayette, who served as a valuable aide to George Washington.

COOPERATIVE LEARNING ACTIVITY

Presentation Organize the class into three groups to research and report on World War I in the Middle East. One group should research the life of T. E. Lawrence. The second group should research Britain's role on the Middle Eastern front, including its broken promise of Arab independence. The third group should research the goals and participation of the Arab peoples involved. All three groups should then meet to share their data in a presentation to the rest of the class. **L3**

Chapter 28
Section 5

Chart Study

Answers

1. *Russia*
2. *the United States*

Practice

Reading a Chart Which side had the heavier casualties, the Allies or the Central Powers? *(the Allies)*

Independent Practice

Guided Reading Activity 28-5 **L1**

Time Line Ask students to create a time line of events that led to Allied victory. They should begin with May 1917 (the first convoy) and end with the armistice in November 1918. **L2 LEP**

Biography Ask students to write a brief biography of Woodrow Wilson. They should concentrate on his role at the Paris Peace Conference and his belief in international negotiations as a basis for future world peace. **L3**

Linking Past and Present

November 11, 1918—the day World War I ended—is a time when members of the armed services are honored in many of the former Allied countries. It is called Veterans Day in the United States, Remembrance Day in Canada, and Armistice Day in Britain.

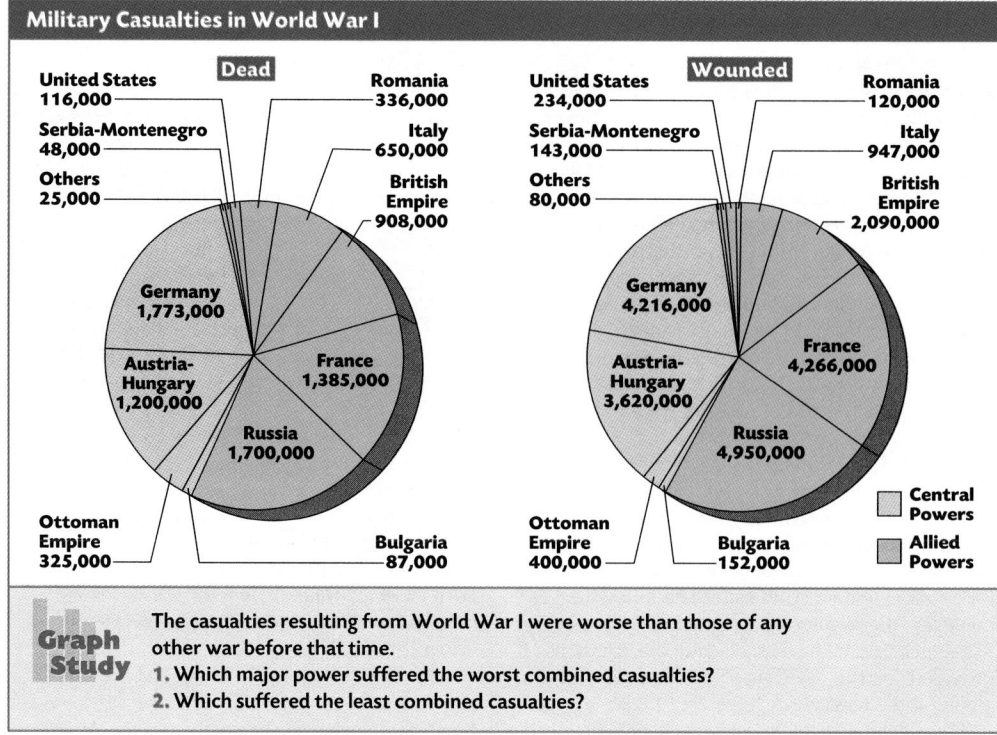

Military Casualties in World War I

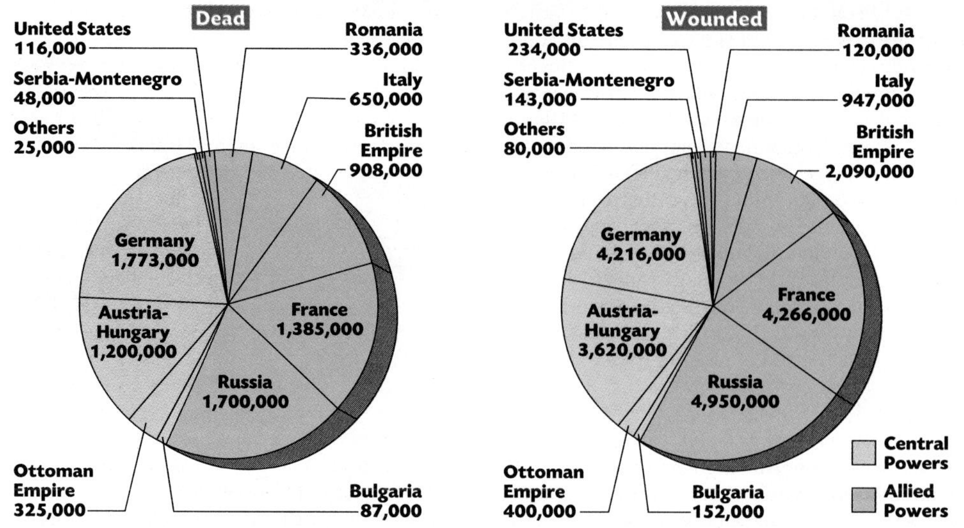

Graph Study The casualties resulting from World War I were worse than those of any other war before that time.

1. Which major power suffered the worst combined casualties?
2. Which suffered the least combined casualties?

In addition, about 13 million civilians were dead of disease and starvation. Mass deaths or killings on a grand scale, such as those of the Armenians under the rule of the Ottoman Turks in 1915, added to the list of horrors.

Angry at Armenian support for the Allies and fearful of Armenian nationalism, the Turkish government decided to use the war as an excuse to end the long history of animosity between Turks and Armenians. The Turkish army first removed all Armenian soldiers from its ranks and deported them to labor camps. Then they rounded up Armenian civilians, roped them together, and drove them into the desert to starve. In other cases they destroyed whole Armenian villages and shot the inhabitants. Some historians have estimated that more than 1 million Armenians lost their lives in this slaughter.

Restoring the Peace

The hopes of many Europeans and North Americans focused on United States President **Woodrow Wilson**. Even before the war ended, Wilson had put forth his Fourteen Points, a peace plan whose terms included international recognition of freedom of the seas and of trade, limitations on arms, and an end to all secret alliances. Wilson's plan also called for just settlements of colonial claims, the right of self-rule for all nations, and the establishment of a "general assembly of nations" to settle future problems peacefully. It was these points that Germany thought would be the basis of peace negotiations.

For the most part, everyone seemed to agree that Wilson's points should be the guiding framework for the peace settlement. There were only two major reservations—one was Great Britain's. Control of the seas had been a major British war aim vital to British interests. Great Britain depended on foreign trade for its survival and still ruled a vast overseas empire. The British, therefore, objected to the idea of open seas. The other reservation was held by France. Wilson had stated that there should be "no annexations, no contributions, and no punitive damages" as a result of the war. France believed that some statement demanding reparations, or payments for damages, should be included in any peace settlement.

MEETING SPECIAL NEEDS ACTIVITY

Learning Style: Visual/Spatial Have students compare the map of Europe in 1919 on page 764 with the map of Europe in 1915 on page 742. Ask them to make a list of all the ways Europe changed as a result of World War I. **L1 LEP**

The Paris Peace Conference

In January 1919, delegates from 27 nations gathered in Paris to work out 5 separate peace treaties known as the Peace of Paris. The Allies did not invite representatives from the defeated Central Powers or Russia. In a break with tradition, heads of state attended the conference. President Wilson represented the United States; Prime Minister **Georges Clemenceau** (KLEH•muhn•SOH), France; Prime Minister **David Lloyd George**, Britain; and Prime Minister **Vittorio Orlando**, Italy. Most of the decisions were made by these "Big Four."

It soon became clear that there was a large gap between the idealistic goals of Wilson and the nationalistic goals of the French, British, and Italian leaders. Lloyd George and Clemenceau wanted to make Germany pay for the war. Wilson's chief aim was to win support for his idea of an international assembly of nations. The League of Nations, as Wilson called it, became a bargaining point. Again and again, Wilson gave in on other issues to ensure the acceptance of the League of Nations.

The Treaty of Versailles

The Treaty of Versailles, the most important treaty of the Peace of Paris, spelled out the details of the Allied settlement with Germany. Lloyd George and Clemenceau prevailed in their goal to punish Germany. Militarily, the treaty reduced the German army and banned conscription and the manufacture of major war weapons.

The treaty reduced Germany in size as well. Germany had to return Alsace-Lorraine, seized in the Franco-Prussian War of 1870, to France. For a period of 15 years, France would also control the coal-rich Saar Basin, while Allied forces together would occupy the Rhineland region of Germany.

In the east, Germany had to renounce the Treaty of Brest-Litovsk. The Allies also reestablished an independent Poland out of lands held by Germany, Austria-Hungary, and Russia. So that it had access to the Baltic Sea, Poland received the Polish Corridor, a strip of land separating East Prussia from the rest of Germany.

The Treaty of Versailles stripped Germany of all of its overseas colonies as well. The Allies received all of Germany's overseas possessions as mandates, territories administered by other countries. Great Britain and France divided Germany's African colonies, Australia and New Zealand split the German Pacific islands south of the Equator, and Japan took the German Pacific islands north of the Equator.

Although these terms were harsh, France and Great Britain were still not satisfied. The Allies also demanded that Germany pay reparations for the property damage it caused during the war and for the costs to the Allies of fighting the war.

The Allies signed the treaty at the Palace of Versailles on June 28, 1919. Only four of Wilson's Fourteen Points and nine supplementary principles emerged intact in the treaty. The most important of these was the Covenant of the League of Nations.

Other Settlements

The Allied Powers signed separate peace agreements with Austria, Bulgaria, Hungary, and Turkey. In them, the greatest attention was given to territorial matters. The Allies recognized the breakup of Austria-Hungary. Austria was left a small, economically weak country. Italy received from Austria German-speaking areas near the Brenner Pass in the Alps. Italy also wanted the port of **Fiume** on the Adriatic, but Wilson refused to agree.

New nations emerged in eastern Europe from the ashes of the old German, Russian, and Austro-Hungarian empires. These included Finland, Estonia, Latvia, Lithuania, Poland, Czechoslovakia, and Yugoslavia. The Allies, particularly France, regarded these countries as a cordon sanitaire (kawr•DOHN sah•nee•TEHR), or quarantine line, that would serve as a buffer against any potential threat from Russia or Germany. In creating Yugoslavia, the Serbs achieved their goal of forming a nation of South Slavic peoples. Hungary lost territory to Yugoslavia, Czechoslovakia, and Romania, while Bulgaria lost land to Yugoslavia, Greece, and Romania.

In the Middle East, the Allies divided what was left of the Ottoman Empire. The Arabs did not receive the independence that Great Britain had promised them. Instead, Palestine, Transjordan, and Iraq became British mandates. At the same time, Lebanon and Syria became French mandates.

Bitter Fruits

A general disillusionment set in after World War I. Slogans such as "the war to end all wars" and "to make the world safe for democracy" rang hollow after years of slaughter. In addition to killing millions of people, the war destroyed the homes and lives of millions more. Many people suddenly found themselves to be minorities within newly formed nations. Others who believed they would become the citizens of independent nations found their hopes dashed by the settlements. Those whose lands were defeated were embittered by the loss of territory and prestige.

Cultural Perspectives

Anti-German feeling reached near-hysteria in many of the Allied countries during World War I. In the United States, German-language instruction was dropped from schools. In Britain, King George V changed his family name from Wetlin to Windsor, and the Battenberg family changed theirs to Mountbatten.

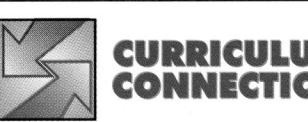

CURRICULUM CONNECTION

SCIENCE

Vitamins had been isolated before World War I. Only with the war, when medical examinations of draftees revealed widespread malnourishment, did people realize how important they were. Of 2.5 million British draftees examined in 1917–1918, 41 percent were in poor health, mainly because of inadequate nutrition.

ASSESS

Check for Understanding

Assign Section 5 Review as homework or as an in-class activity.

Use Student Self-Test and Review Software to review Section 5.

MAKING CONNECTIONS ACTIVITY

Literature For writers who took part in World War I, the war was an unforgettable experience. Have students research and write brief biographies of writers who wrote fiction or memoirs about their experiences. Possible subjects include Robert Graves, Siegfried Sassoon, e. e. cummings, John Dos Passos, and Ernest Hemingway. Encourage students to read an actual work by their subject as well. **L2**

Chapter 28 Section 5

Map Study

Answer

Russia

Map Skills Practice

Reading a Map What European countries created after World War I no longer exist today? *(Czechoslovakia, Yugoslavia)*

Evaluate

Section Quiz 28-5

Use the Testmaker to create a customized quiz for Section 5.

Reteach

Have students list the major participants at the Paris Peace Conference and summarize the aims of each.

Reteaching Activity 28

Enrich

Have students research and write an essay on the history and activities of the present-day United Nations as an outgrowth of the earlier League of Nations. Ask students to compare the UN and the League in terms of their effectiveness.

Enrichment Activity 28

CLOSE

Have a roundtable discussion about the ways the Treaty of Versailles prepared the way for World War II. Include the provisions of the treaty and the role that U.S. isolationism played in the aftermath.

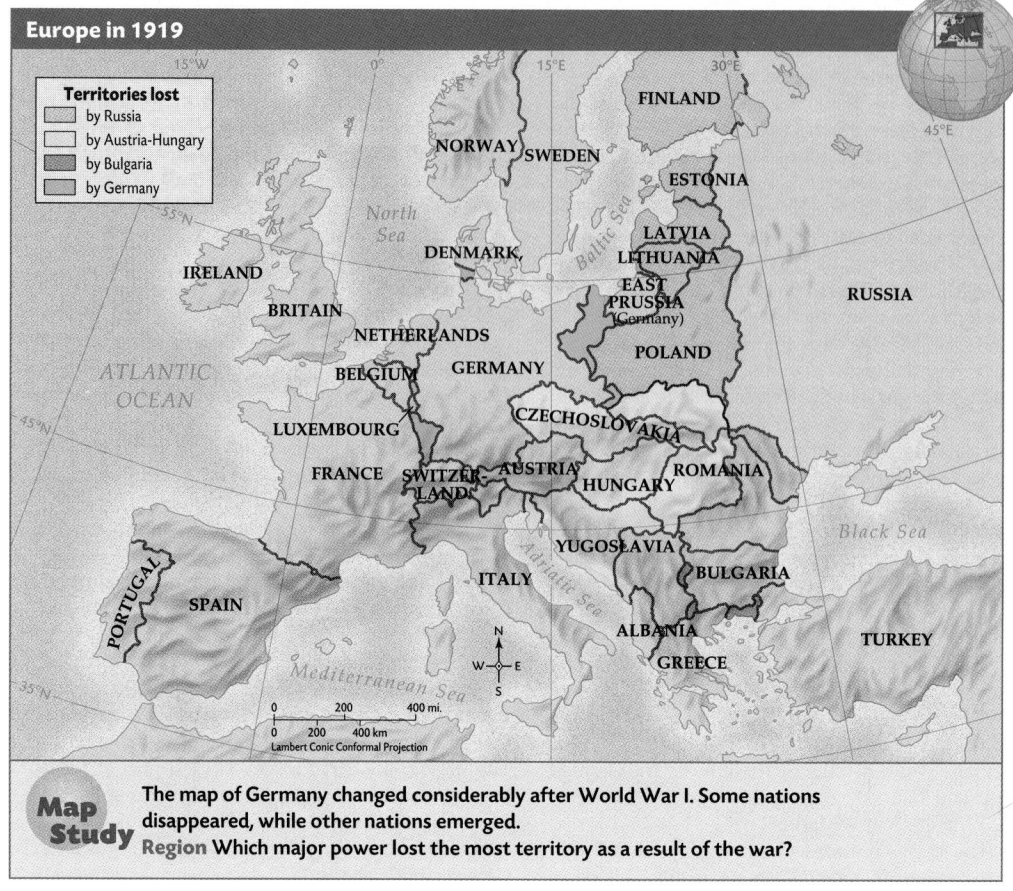

Europe in 1919

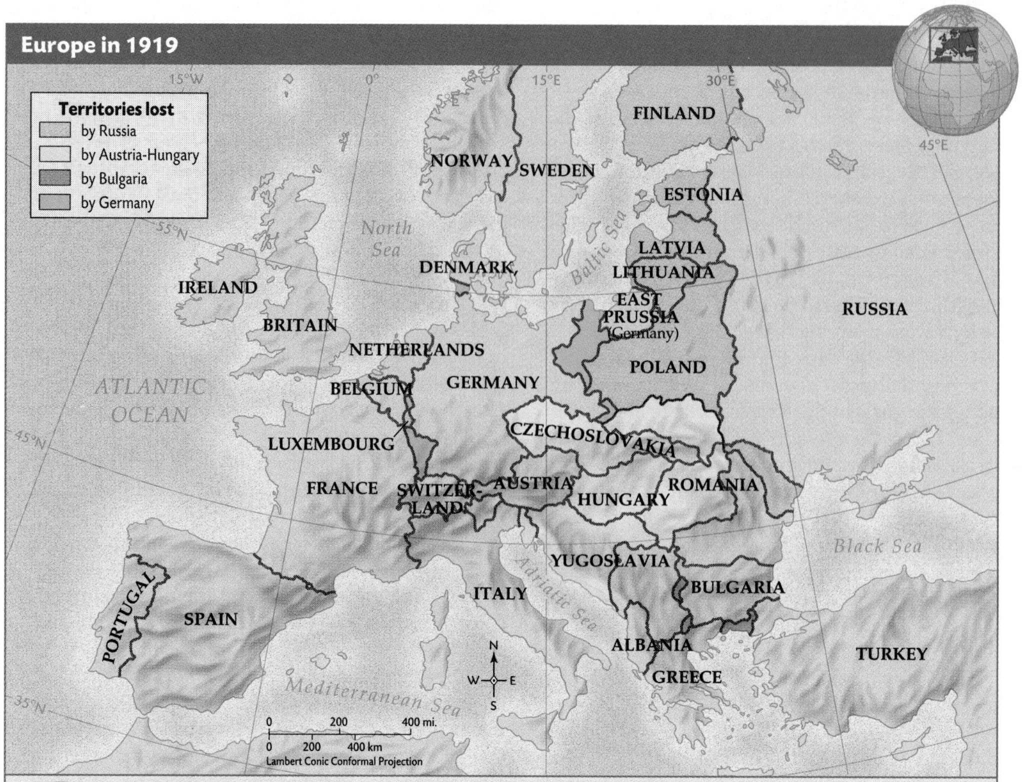

Map Study The map of Germany changed considerably after World War I. Some nations disappeared, while other nations emerged.
Region Which major power lost the most territory as a result of the war?

The Germans felt an especially deep sense of resentment about their loss in World War I. Because they had fought mostly on foreign territory and used resources from other countries to supplement their own, German economic strength remained largely intact. The harsh provisions of the Treaty of Versailles, however, left Germany weakened and humiliated as well as deprived of great-power status. This made reconciliation with the Allies very difficult. The Germans' festering resentment burst forth upon the world with an even greater violence two decades later in the form of Nazism.

SECTION 5 REVIEW

Recall

1. **Define** convoy, armistice, reparation, mandate, cordon sanitaire.
2. **Identify** Woodrow Wilson, Ferdinand Foch, T. E. Lawrence, the Fourteen Points, Georges Clemenceau, David Lloyd George, Vittorio Orlando.
3. **List** the terms of the Treaty of Versailles that was concluded as part of the Peace of Paris.

Critical Thinking

4. **Analyzing Information** How do you think a German citizen in 1919 would have felt about the provisions of the Treaty of Versailles?

Understanding Themes

5. **Internationalism** Explain some of the problems created by the Treaty of Versailles. How did this treaty lay the foundation for another international conflict? How could it have been written to prevent this?

SECTION 5 REVIEW ANSWERS

1. The words are defined in the Glossary.
2. T. E. Lawrence, 761; Foch, 761; Wilson, 762; the Fourteen Points, 762; Clemenceau, 763; George, 763; Orlando, 763
3. It reduced the size of Germany's army and banned conscription and the manufacture of war materials; reduced Germany's European territories and took away all its colonies; set reparations.
4. angry, humiliated, vengeful
5. **INTERNATIONALISM** Because of its harsh terms, it caused bitter resentment; if punishments had been lessened, or if Germany had been present at the peace conference, future conflict might have been avoided.

Social Studies
SKILLS

Interpreting Military Movements on Maps

Although wars begin over many different issues, they all end up as fights to control territory. Because wars are basically fought over land, maps are particularly good tools for seeing the "big picture" of a war.

Learning the Skill

The map key is essential in interpreting military maps. The key explains what the map's colors and symbols represent. Use the following steps to study the key:

- Determine what color scheme appears on the map. Usually, colors represent different sides in the conflict.
- Identify all symbols. These may include symbols for battle sites, victories, types of military units and equipment, fortifications, and so on.
- Study the arrows, which show the direction of military movements. Because these movements occur over periods of time, some maps give dates showing when and where the troops advanced and retreated.

Once you have carefully studied the key and the map, try to follow the progress of the battle or campaign that is shown. Notice where each side began, in which direction it moved, where the two sides met and fought, and which side claimed victory.

Practicing the Skill

The map on this page shows the Middle East front during World War I. Study the map and then answer the following questions.

1. On which side did Arabia and Egypt fight?
2. Which side won the crucial battle of the Dardanelles?
3. Describe the movement of the Central Powers offensive.
4. When did the Allied Powers win the most battles in the Middle East?

The Middle East in World War I

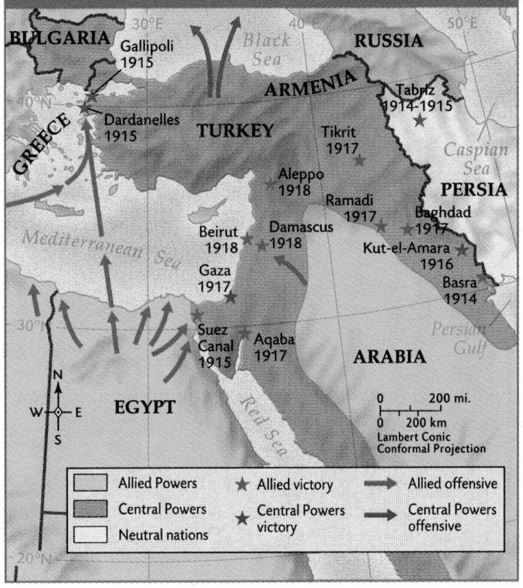

Applying the Skill

Choose one of the maps (showing the Western Front and the Eastern Front of World War I) on page 745. Study your map selection carefully. Then write a paragraph answering the following questions.

1. Where did most of the fighting occur?
2. Which side made the most significant advance in 1914?
3. How did each side progress on this front as the war continued?
4. Did either side win a decisive victory on this front?

For More Practice

Turn to the Skill Practice in the Chapter Review on page 767 for more practice in interpreting military movements on maps.

ANSWERS TO PRACTICING THE SKILL

1. on the Allied side
2. the Central Powers
3. from the Ottoman Empire north across the Black Sea toward Russia
4. 1917

Social Studies
SKILLS

TEACH

Interpreting Military Movements on Maps Ask students to make their own military maps of an engagement in an imaginary war. They should use two different colors to represent the opposing sides; different symbols or colors for the victories of each side; and arrows to show the direction of troop movements. The students should label land and water areas and a few important towns or cities. The map should also include a key explaining what the various colors and symbols represent.

Additional Practice

Skill Reinforcement Activity 28

Chapter 28 Review

GLENCOE TECHNOLOGY

VIDEODISC

Use MindJogger to review students' knowledge of the chapter.

MindJogger Videoquiz

Chapter 28
Disc 4 Side A

Also available in VHS.

Answers

Using Key Terms

1. i
2. g
3. d
4. l
5. b
6. k
7. j
8. c
9. e
10. f

Using Your History Journal

Remind students to write their letters at the appropriate time; for example, soon after May 7, 1915, for the sinking of the *Lusitania.*

Reviewing Facts

1. Germany and France
2. It abandoned the Schlieffen Plan.
3. About 30 million soldiers were killed or wounded. About 13 million civilians died of disease or starvation.
4. Peace: Russian withdrawal from the war; Land: land to the peasants; Bread: enough food for everyone. "All power to the soviets" meant that these local organizations would govern Russia.
5. freedom of the seas; freedom of trade; arms limitations; an end to secret alliances; just settlement of colonial claims; self-rule for all nations; "general assembly of nations"
6. Finland, Estonia, Latvia, Lithuania, Poland, Czechoslovakia, Austria, Hungary, Yugoslavia

Critical Thinking

1. The alliance systems transformed what might have been a local conflict into a major war.
2. The British, who dominated the seas, maintained an extremely effective blockade of Germany. Germany's submarine warfare did extensive damage but also brought the United States into the war.
3. Machine guns and heavy artillery, combined with trenches, made it very hard for either side to mount a decisive offensive attack on the other.

Understanding Themes

1. **COOPERATION** because they were all afraid of Germany
2. **CONFLICT** Serbia: to be the cen-

Historical Significance

World War I brought weapons of mass destruction. The resulting slaughter on the battlefields destroyed the image of war as a heroic undertaking.

Many people also became disillusioned about the war's aftermath. World War I swept away the old order in Europe and redrew the map of the continent.

It caused widespread economic suffering and ended in a controversial peace settlement that sowed the seeds for another, even more destructive, war.

Using Key Terms

Write the key term that completes each sentence.

a. armistice
b. contraband
c. convoy
d. entente
e. propaganda
f. mobilization
g. trenches
h. alliance system
i. provisional government
j. reparations
k. communism
l. ultimatum

1. After Czar Nicholas's abdication, political authority in Russia passed into the hands of a __________.
2. By early 1915, soldiers on the Western Front dug __________, or ditches, that stretched from Switzerland to the North Sea.
3. In 1904, Great Britain and France signed an ________ that settled key colonial disputes.
4. On July 23, 1914, Austria-Hungary gave Serbia an ____________, a set of final conditions that must be accepted to avoid severe consequences.
5. The British stopped ships on the high seas that they suspected carried __________, or prohibited goods.
6. The Bolsheviks founded an international revolutionary movement based on __________, the political viewpoint stemming from the ideas of Marx and Lenin.
7. After World War I, France demanded that the peace settlement have a statement requiring __________, or payments for damages, from Germany.
8. Under the _______ system, merchant ships crossed the Atlantic in clusters surrounded by a small number of warships for protection.
9. During World War I, governments used _______ to portray the enemy as beastly and inhuman.
10. Warring countries issued general orders for ______________, the gathering and transport of military troops and fighting equipment.

Using Your History Journal

Take the role of a parent and answer the letter you wrote as a first-person account of the war. Include words of encouragement and try to explain the significance of the war effort.

Reviewing Facts

1. **Identify** the European nations who disputed control of Morocco.
2. **Explain** how Germany's war strategy changed after the Battle of the Marne.
3. **State** how many soldiers were killed or wounded in World War I. How many civilians died of disease or starvation?
4. **Explain** the social changes promised by the Bolshevik slogans.
5. **List** five of the Fourteen Points that United States President Woodrow Wilson presented at the Paris peace conference in 1919.
6. **Identify** seven new European nations that emerged from the empires that collapsed as a result of defeat in World War I.

Critical Thinking

1. **Analyze** In what sense were the European alliance systems more responsible for starting World War I than any specific event?
2. **Apply** How did sea power have a major effect on the outcome of World War I?
3. **Analyze** How were technological advances in weaponry most responsible for the military stalemate during much of World War I?

766 Chapter 28 *World War I*

CHAPTER 28 REVIEW

Understanding Themes

1. **Cooperation** Why do you think Great Britain, France, and Russia put aside their differences to form the Triple Entente?
2. **Conflict** Name a war goal for each of these countries: Serbia, Austria-Hungary, Russia, and France. Discuss a situation today where a conflict over national goals might lead to war.
3. **Conflict** What key events turned the tide in World War I? Why were these events or developments important to the war's outcome?
4. **Revolution** Name the main causes of the Russian Revolution of 1917. Compare these causes with the causes of recent changes in the former Soviet Union.
5. **Internationalism** Do you think the peace settlement after World War I promoted the success of the League of Nations? Explain.

Skill Practice

Study the map "Russian Civil War 1918–1922" and answer the questions that follow.

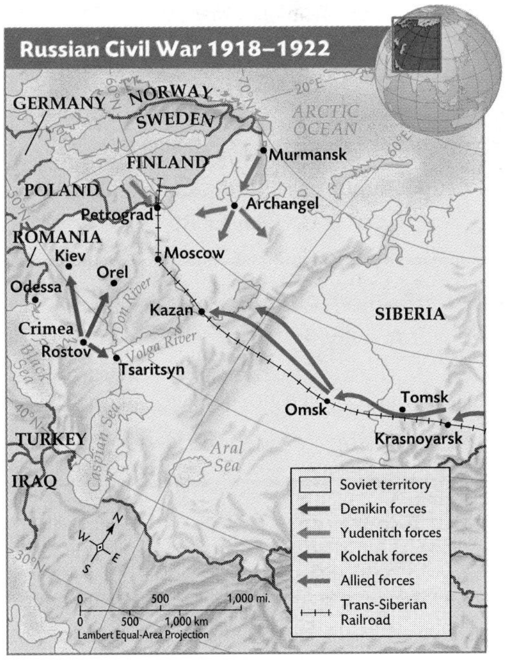

1. From which direction did the Allied forces invade Russia?
2. Where did Denikin's forces begin and in what direction did they move?
3. Why do you think Kolchak chose his route to Moscow?
4. Which military group advanced on Russian territory from Poland?

Geography in History

1. **Place** Refer to the map below. What five European nations had built up the largest standing armies during World War I?
2. **Location** How do you think Germany's location affected its military strategy?
3. **Movement** When war broke out, which side had the more challenging task of moving troops and materials, the Allies or the Central Powers? Why?

Linking Past and Present

1. Where in Europe have nationalist tensions recently sparked conflict?
2. The ideal of self-determination was not granted to European colonies after World War I. Where do struggles for self-determination continue today?

Chapter 28 Review

ter of a new South Slav nation; Austria-Hungary: to gain territory through the Balkans to the Aegean Sea and to contain Slavic nationals; Russia: an Adriatic port; France: return of Alsace-Lorraine. Answers will vary, but possibilities include the former Yugoslavia and the former Soviet Union.

3. **CONFLICT** a unified command for the Allies in the west, the arrival of 250,000 fresh American troops
4. **REVOLUTION** Shortages of food and fuel, dissatisfaction with the monarchy, war casualties. Answers will vary but might mention a common element of dissatisfaction with the regime in power.
5. **INTERNATIONALISM** No, it created too much resentment and bad feeling.

Skill Practice

1. from the northwest
2. Denikin's forces began in the Crimea and moved north.
3. He hoped to seize control of the Trans-Siberian Railroad, which would give him control of an important supply line into Russia and enable him to use the railroad to transport his troops.
4. Yudenitch forces

Geography in History

1. Germany, Russia, Great Britain, France, Austria-Hungary
2. It had to worry about two fronts of fighting.
3. the Allies, because their territories were split in two by the Central Powers

Linking Past and Present

1. Russia, the former Yugoslavia, Northern Ireland
2. Chechnya; the Basque region of Spain; Quebec; among the Kurds in the Middle East, Tamils in Sri Lanka, Kashmiris in South Asia, and Tibetans

Chapter Bonus Test Question

Ask students: One clause of the Versailles Treaty put all the blame for causing World War I on Germany. Do you think this was just? *(Yes: War might have been avoided if Germany had not given Austria-Hungary permission to do with Serbia as it pleased. No: The intransigence of Austria-Hungary was also to blame, and without the terrorism of Serbian nationalists, the war might not have broken out at all.)*

Teach, Reinforce, and Extend CHAPTER Content

Between Two Fires

CHAPTER RESOURCES

	Reproducible Resources	Multimedia Resources
Chapter Opener	Chapter Themes: Graphic Organizer 29 Historical Significance Chapter Activity 29	MindJogger Videoquiz
Chapter Enrichment	Vocabulary Activity 29* Time Line Activity 29 Mapping History Activity 29 History Simulation 29 Geography and History Activity 29 Source Reading 29 People in World History Profiles 55, 56 World Art and Music Activity 29 Enrichment Activity 29 Critical Thinking Activity 29 Skill Reinforcement Activity 29 Writer's Guidebook, Lesson 10 Performance Assessment Activity 29	Focus on World Art Print 3, Thomas Hart Benton. *The Wreck of the Ole '97*; 4, Sargent Johnson. *Forever Free*; 23, René Magritte. *The Human Condition 1* World History and Art Transparency 38, *Migrant Mother*; 39, *Bird in Space*; 43, *The Persistence of Memory* Chapter Transparency 29 Vocabulary PuzzleMaker Software World Music: Cultural Traditions, Lesson 1 Lessons of War: *The Enemy* Communism and the Cold War: *Growing Up Communist*
Chapter Review/Reteaching	Reteaching Activity 29 Skill Reinforcement Activity 29 Spanish Chapter Summary 29	Chapter 29 Digest Audiocassette, Activity, Test* Vocabulary PuzzleMaker Software Student Self-Test and Review Software MindJogger Videoquiz
Chapter Evaluation/Testing	Performance Assessment Activity 29 Chapter 29 Test, Forms A and B	Testmaker

* *Also available in Spanish*

0:00 OUT OF TIME? Assign the Chapter 29 summary in the Unit 7 Digest on pages 854-857, and the Chapter 29 Audiocassettes.

Block Schedule

Block scheduling differs from traditional class scheduling in the amount of time allotted to each period. The extended time frame provided by block scheduling affords you the opportunity to implement a greater number of research-oriented and activity-intense projects to motivate and involve your students. Activities that are particularly suited to use within the block scheduling framework are identified throughout this chapter by the following designation.

KEY TO ABILITY LEVELS

Teaching strategies have been coded for varying learning styles and abilities.

- L1 **BASIC** activities for all students
- L2 **AVERAGE** activities for average to above-average students
- L3 **CHALLENGING** activities for above-average students
- LEP **LIMITED ENGLISH PROFICIENCY** activities

Teach and Reinforce SECTION Content

Chapter 29 Planning Guide

A complete, 1-page lesson plan is provided for each section in the *Reproducible Lesson Plans* booklet.

SECTION RESOURCES

Daily Objectives	Reproducible Resources	Multimedia Resources
Section 1 **The Postwar World** Describe the trends that dominated the arts and popular culture from 1919 to 1939.	Reproducible Lesson Plan 29-1 Vocabulary Activity 29* Guided Reading Activity 29-1* Time Line Activity 29 Chapter Themes: Graphic Organizer 29 Section Quiz 29-1*	Focus on World Art Print 3, Thomas Hart Benton. *The Wreck of the Ole '97*; 4, Sargent Johnson. *Forever Free*; 23, René Magritte. *The Human Condition 1* Section Focus Transparency 29-1 Chapter Transparency 29 World History and Art Transparency 39, *Bird in Space*; 43, *The Persistence of Memory* Student Self-Test and Review Software Testmaker World Music: Cultural Traditions, Lesson 1
Section 2 **The Western Democracies** Explain why democratic government survived in the United States, Great Britain, and France during the post-World War I era.	Reproducible Lesson Plan 29-2 Vocabulary Activity 29* Guided Reading Activity 29-2* Section Quiz 29-2*	Section Focus Transparency 29-2 World History and Art Transparency 38, *Migrant Mother* Student Self-Test and Review Software Testmaker
Section 3 **Fascist Dictatorships** Identify the factors that led to the rise of Fascist dictatorships in Italy and Germany after World War I.	Reproducible Lesson Plan 29-3 Guided Reading Activity 29-3* History Simulation 29 Geography and History Activity 29 Section Quiz 29-3*	Section Focus Transparency 29-3 Vocabulary PuzzleMaker Software Student Self-Test and Review Software Testmaker Lessons of War: *The Enemy*
Section 4 **The Soviet Union** Examine how Joseph Stalin's rule transformed the Soviet Union.	Reproducible Lesson Plan 29-4 Guided Reading Activity 29-4* Reteaching Activity 29 Enrichment Activity 29 Section Quiz 29-4* Performance Assessment Activity 29 Spanish Chapter Summary 29	Section Focus Transparency 29-4 Vocabulary Puzzlemaker Software Student Self-Test and Review Software Testmaker Communism and the Cold War: *Growing Up Communist*

** Also available in Spanish*

Chapter Activities

Performance Assessment Activity

Newsreel Explain that in the 1920s and 1930s (before television), movie theaters showed newsreels along with the feature films. They included narration and footage of what was happening nationally and around the world, and they often included propaganda. Have small groups of students choose an important event and write newsreel scripts, including headlines and visuals. Then groups can combine their scripts into a 10- or 15-minute production. One student from each group may narrate its segment.

Possible Rubric Features

Accuracy of content information, concept attainment, originality and creativity of product, clarity, organization of ideas, and collaborative skills

• *For an additional activity, refer to Activity 29 in the* Performance Assessment Strategies and Activities *booklet.*

Activity

From the Classroom of...

Loretta Smithson
Elsinore High School
Lake Elsinore, CA

Experiencing the Holocaust

Organize the class into small groups to research the roots and results of anti-Semitism. Assign each group a different area to research: (1) a history of the Hebrew people, including the Diaspora (A.D. 70); (2) a history of Jewish expulsion from European countries (e.g., Spain, 1493); (3) excerpts of writings or speeches by famous people (e.g., Martin Luther); (4) excerpts from books or stories of the Holocaust (e.g., *The Blue Tattoo*); (5) reasons given by Nazis for their treatment of European Jews; and (6) world reactions to Nazi treatment of the Jews.

Provide students with the condensed materials they need for their categories, and encourage them to prepare their information in interesting ways for group presentations, such as charts, maps, diagrams, slides.

After group presentations, let students share their analyses of the materials provided, then conduct a class discussion on the meaning of genocide and its implications for world events today (in Bosnia, for example).

MULTIPLE LEARNING STYLES

Verbal/Linguistic

Have students create a front page for a newspaper of the postwar period. Allow students to divide the work for the page: research and writing, editing, laying out the copy, printing, and distributing to the class.

Visual/Spatial

For a mock international TV news special, have students pretend they are news reporters on assignments in one of the following countries: Great Britain, France, Germany, Italy, or the Soviet Union. They are to cover an event in postwar Europe, or a special feature on daily life in their country.

Auditory/Musical

Suggest that students collect music from the 1920s and present a sampling as a concert for the class. They should include both popular and classical selections. Part of the project should include a program for the audience that lists the composers, songwriters, and musicians along with brief biographical sketches, and the names of the works.

Kinesthetic

Ask students to research the currency of each of the countries mentioned in the chapter. Have students collect samples, either real or photocopied, of the currencies. Remind students that some of the nations may have had a change in currency during the postwar period. Have students create a display for the class.

Additional Resources

TEACHER'S CORNER

NATIONAL GEOGRAPHIC SOCIETY

INDEX TO NATIONAL GEOGRAPHIC MAGAZINE

The following articles may be used for research relating to this chapter:

- "U.S.S. Macon: Lost and Found," by J. Gordon Vaeth, January 1992.

NATIONAL GEOGRAPHIC SOCIETY PRODUCTS AVAILABLE FROM GLENCOE

To order the following products for use with this chapter, contact your local Glencoe sales representative or call Glencoe at 1-800-368-7344:

VIDEODISCS
- GTV: The American People
- GTV: A Geographic Perspective on American History

ADDITIONAL NATIONAL GEOGRAPHIC SOCIETY PRODUCTS

To order the following products for use with this chapter, call National Geographic Society at 1-800-368-2728:

- *1929-1941: The Great Depression* (Video)
- *Decades of History: The 20th Century–The Early Years*, "The 1920s: Prosperity to Panic," "The 1930s: Days of Depression." (Filmstrip)

Bibliography

Literature of the Period

Hemingway, Ernest. *The Sun Also Rises.* New York: Scribner, 1926. A novel about English and American expatriates in France and Spain after World War I.

Readings for the Student

Laqueur, Walter. *Stalin: The Glasnost Revelations.* Scribner, 1990. A review of a new body of evidence about Stalin and modern-day Russia.

Readings for the Teacher

Garraty, John. *The Great Depression.* San Diego: Harcourt, 1986. Focuses on the Great Depression from a global perspective.

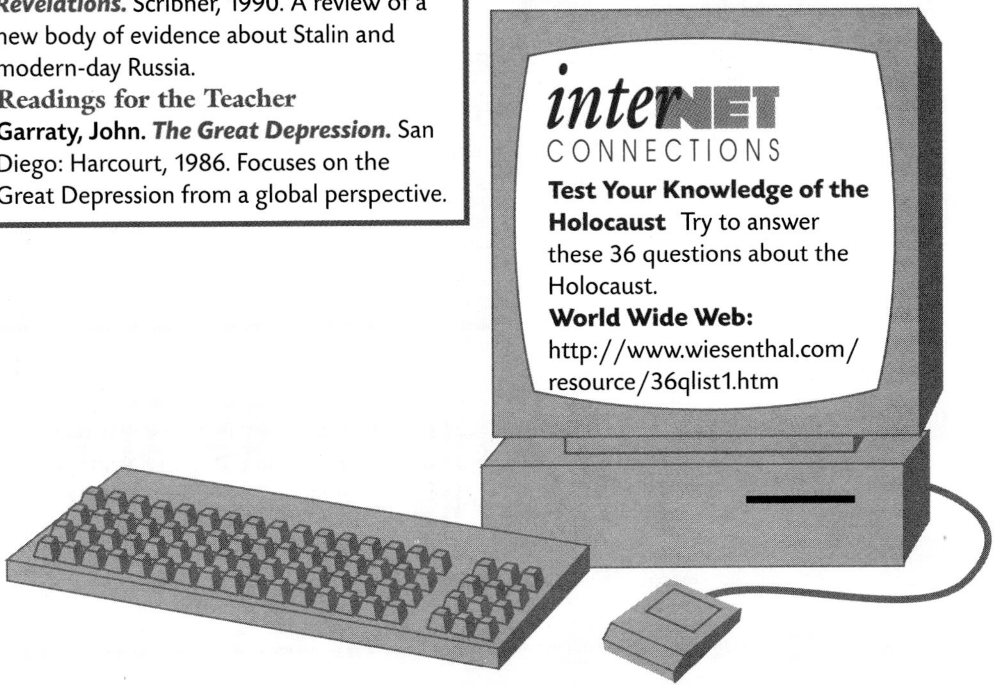

interNET
CONNECTIONS
Test Your Knowledge of the Holocaust Try to answer these 36 questions about the Holocaust.
World Wide Web:
http://www.wiesenthal.com/resource/36qlist1.htm

Introducing Chapter 29

CHAPTER THEMES

Chapter Themes are listed by section on this chapter opening page of the Student Edition. A corresponding theme-based activity is available under "TEACH," and a theme-based question is asked in the Section and Chapter Reviews.

The Storyteller

Historical Setting Joachim's devotion to a movement that he really knew little about was common during Hitler's reign. Hitler was a master speechmaker. His personal architect, Albert Speer, recalled in his memoirs that when he first heard Hitler speak, he was immediately charmed by his style. He had expected a fanatic man dressed in uniform. Instead Hitler appeared in a blue suit and seemed almost shy. He had a gift for adjusting to his audience. Hitler spoke with hypnotic persuasiveness that cast a mood that transformed his listeners.

Historical Significance

Answers: *Economic depressions, unemployment, and social unrest led to the rise of dictatorships in postwar Europe.*

Democratic governments had to become involved in social reforms, adapt to changing technology, and (except for the United States) deal with major debts and rebuild damaged territory.

Chapter 29

1919–1939

Between Two Fires

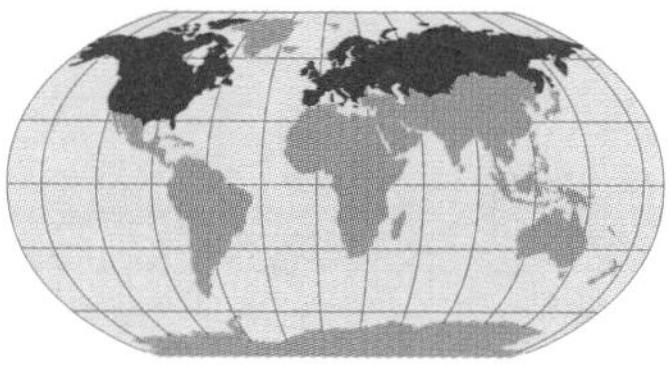

Chapter Themes

- **Innovation** The period after World War I brings revolutionary changes in science, the arts, and popular culture. *Section 1*
- **Change** The Great Depression forces governments in Europe and North America to increase their involvement in social and economic affairs. *Section 2*
- **Uniformity** Fascist governments in Italy and Germany limit individual liberties and stress loyalty to the state. *Section 3*
- **Uniformity** Communist leaders in the Soviet Union impose state control on society and crush opposition. *Section 4*

The Storyteller

From early evening until long past midnight, Nazi stormtroopers and youth groups marched in disciplined columns through Berlin. Joachim, now a priest and medical missionary, took part in that torchlight parade in the early 1930s:

"When I marched in that parade, I thought it was only the beginning. I had been privileged to be an important person in helping to create the Thousand Year Reich, the great new Germany that Hitler would bring forth out of the chaos and trouble around us."

Looking back on that night, Joachim is appalled at how little he really knew about the Nazis. But the economic and political chaos caused by World War I and the Great Depression led many Europeans to support powerful dictators during the 1920s and 1930s.

Historical Significance

What factors led to the rise of dictatorships in Europe after World War I? How were democratic nations affected by the social and economic crises that came after the end of World War I?

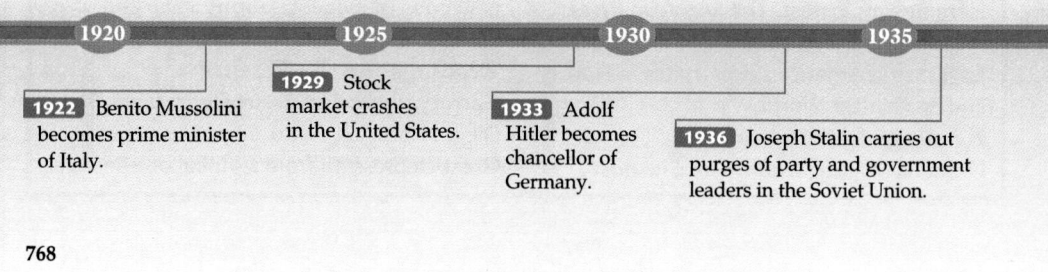

1920 — 1925 — 1930 — 1935

1922 Benito Mussolini becomes prime minister of Italy.

1929 Stock market crashes in the United States.

1933 Adolf Hitler becomes chancellor of Germany.

1936 Joseph Stalin carries out purges of party and government leaders in the Soviet Union.

768

GEOGRAPHY CONNECTION

GEOGRAPHIC THEMES

Location To help students realize where events of this chapter took place, have them find the United States, Great Britain, France, Germany, the Commonwealth of Independent States, and Italy on a world map. What geographic factor made it possible for the United States to escape economic problems and get on with life immediately after World War I? *(Its distance from battle sites kept it from being physically damaged and allowed people to isolate themselves from Europe's problems.)*

History & Art *Automat,* Edward Hopper, 1927. Des Moines Art Center Permanent Collection, Des Moines, Iowa

Your History Journal

Interview an older person about his or her feelings and perceptions in the period between 1930 and 1941. Use the chapter to formulate questions about events. Take notes during the interview, or write down your impressions soon afterward.

Introducing Chapter 29

History & Art

Edward Hopper (1882–1967) was an American artist known for his realistic paintings of loneliness and boredom. He depicted characters in all-night restaurants or in lonely settings such as this automat. The world he revealed was stark and impersonal. What detail in this picture tells you that the setting is not a modern fast-food restaurant? *(radiator)*

Performance Assessment

Refer to the activity on page 768C of the Planning Guide.

For an additional activity, refer to Activity 29 in the *Performance Assessment Strategies and Activities* booklet.

Using Your History Journal

Students might find it helpful to tape-record the interview. This will allow them to capture all of the details and get accurate quotes.

GLENCOE TECHNOLOGY

VIDEODISC

Use MindJogger to preview chapter content.

MindJogger Videoquiz

Chapter 29
Disc 4 Side B

Also available in VHS.

EXTRA CREDIT PROJECT

The Commonwealth Students might research the history of Canada or Australia during the postwar years. They should find out about the relationship with Great Britain, the economies, social issues, Canadians' relationship with France, and developments in literature, the arts, and sciences in those countries. Have students prepare reports to share with the whole class.

Chapter 29 *Between Two Fires* **769**

Chapter 29
Section 1

SECTION THEME

▶ **Innovation** The period after World War I brings revolutionary changes in science, the arts, and popular culture.

Find Out

Answer: *Breaking with tradition and experimenting with new styles dominated the arts and popular culture of the 1920s and 1930s.*

FOCUS

Section Objective

Describe the trends that dominated the arts and popular culture from 1919 to 1939.

BELLRINGER Motivational Activity

Before taking roll at the beginning of the class period, project Section Focus Transparency 29-1 and have students answer the activity questions. Discuss students' responses.

This activity is also available as a blackline master.

Vocabulary Pre-check

Use Vocabulary Activity 29 to introduce vocabulary terms.
L1 LEP

1920	1930	1940
1920 United States women win the vote.	**1926** Ernest Hemingway writes *The Sun Also Rises.*	**1935** Dance bands reach height of popularity.

Section 1

The Postwar World

Setting the Scene

▶ **Terms to Define**
cubism, surrealism, jazz, choreographer

▶ **People to Meet**
Albert Einstein, Sigmund Freud, T.S. Eliot, Pablo Picasso, Sergey Prokofiev, Walter Gropius

▶ **Places to Locate**
Hollywood

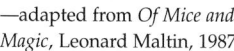

Find Out What trends dominated the arts and popular culture from 1919 to 1939?

The Storyteller

There was trouble in Hollywood. One of Tinseltown's biggest names, with a bigger screen following than 90 percent of the stars, according to columnist Louella Parsons, had "fallen afoul of the censors in a big way." Censor boards throughout the nation were receiving vigorous complaints about the "devilish, naughty" behavior of this national celebrity. Terry Ramsaye wrote in the Motion Picture Herald, *"It's the old, old story. If nobody knows you, you can do anything, and if everybody knows you, you can't do anything—except what everyone approves." The star was Mickey Mouse.*

—adapted from *Of Mice and Magic*, Leonard Maltin, 1987

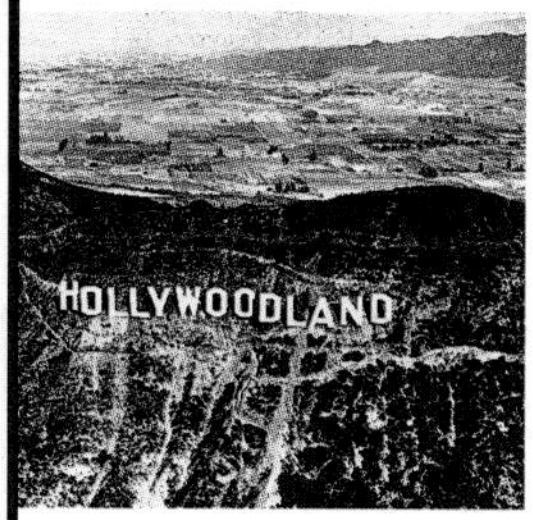

Hollywood landmark

"ARMISTICE SIGNED, END OF THE WAR!" proclaimed *The New York Times* headline on November 11, 1918. In the United States and Europe, people exploded in a frenzy of celebration. The critic and author Malcolm Cowley wrote later of the feeling of euphoria that marked the end of the war: "We danced in the streets, embraced old women and pretty girls, swore blood brotherhood with soldiers in little bars...." But the excitement did not last. "On the next day," continued Cowley, "...we didn't know what to do."

World War I marked the great divide between the old and the new. The war changed the way many people looked at the world, and the disillusionment it caused led artists and intellectuals on a restless search for something new. The postwar period was a time for breaking with tradition and experimenting with new styles in politics and culture.

Changing Patterns of Life

Warren Harding was elected President of the United States in 1920, promising a "return to normalcy." But there was no going back to the past. The war had changed the world too much for that to be possible. Instead, people in both North America and Europe began to experiment with new customs and ways of life.

New Trends in Culture and Style

In the postwar era, women gained a new level of independence. With the ratification of the Nineteenth Amendment in 1920, women in the United States won the right to vote at last. Women also won the vote in most other Western countries following the war.

SECTION RESOURCES

Reproducible Masters
- Reproducible Lesson Plan 29-1
- Vocabulary Activity 29
- Guided Reading Activity 29-1
- Time Line Activity 29
- Chapter Themes: Graphic Organizer 29
- Section Quiz 29-1

Transparencies
- Section Focus Transparency 29-1
- Chapter Transparency 29
- World History and Art Transparencies 39, 43

Multimedia
- Focus on World Art Prints 3, 4, 23
- Student Self-Test and Review Software
- Testmaker
- World Music: Cultural Traditions, Lesson 1

770 **Chapter 29** *Between Two Fires*

Many women now demanded other freedoms as well. Throwing off the inhibitions of the prewar era, some women in the United States and western Europe began to use rouge and lipstick openly. Their skirts rose from a few inches above the ankle to an inch above the knee. They cropped their hair to a shingle bob and aimed for a carefree, little-boy look. Thus attired, the "flapper" created a revolution in manners and morals.

In the postwar era, not only the flapper but people in general disdained the familiar and the commonplace. They wanted heroes who were larger than life. Babe Ruth, the "Sultan of Swat," was the king of baseball. Tennis champions Big Bill Tilden and Helen Wills Moody became national heroes. When Gertrude Ederle swam the English Channel and Charles Lindbergh flew nonstop from Long Island to Paris, the public saluted them with tumultuous ticker-tape parades on Broadway.

Amid all the hoopla, bankers and business leaders were having a heyday. The war had opened new prospects for economic development. President Calvin Coolidge neatly summed up the nation's focus in the 1920s when he said, "The business of America is business."

The Impact of Technology

New forms of technology altered people's lifestyles and brought people closer together in the 1920s. The decade following the war witnessed a revolution in transportation and communication.

The automobile had perhaps the greatest impact on European and American society. A network of highways began to crisscross Europe and the United States. People could now move easily from place to place, and move they did. The United States, in particular, became an increasingly mobile society. Americans traveled farther afield on vacations and moved from rural areas to cities.

Radio also brought about dramatic changes. By exposing millions of people to the same news and entertainment shows, radio helped to produce a more homogeneous, or uniform, culture. Through its advertisements, radio also stimulated the public's desire for consumer goods. Advertisers learned the art of motivation, and ads now played on people's insecurities and self-doubts. "Why had he changed so in his attentions?" queried a forlorn-looking woman in an ad for a leading mouthwash.

Many products of the new technology eased the burden of the homemaker. With the advent of packaged foods, refrigerators, vacuum cleaners, and electric irons, people had more leisure time. Instead of working at home, they could take a drive, listen to the radio, or go out dancing. Millions spent their idle moments with another new product of technology: the movies.

A Revolution in Ideas

New inventions had an enormous impact on people's daily lives in the postwar period. At the same time, exciting new ideas in physics and psychology transformed the way people looked at themselves and the world.

Physics

In 1905 German physicist **Albert Einstein** published three papers in a German scientific periodical that became the basis of a new branch of physics. His theories radically altered scientific thought with new conceptions of time, space, mass, and motion. The theory of relativity provided the groundwork for controlling the release of energy from the atom. With this theory, Einstein launched the Atomic Age.

Einstein started a revolution that has now affected almost every branch of science and technology. Since he first advanced his theories, scientists have harnessed the atom in nuclear bombs. They have also used atomic energy to generate electricity and improve agricultural and industrial techniques.

Psychology

The Austrian physician **Sigmund Freud** (FROYD) revolutionized people's ideas about how the human mind works. After observing many patients, Freud concluded that the unconscious mind plays a major role in shaping behavior. The unconscious, he said, is full of memories of events from early childhood. If the memories are especially painful, people sometimes suppress them. Such suppression may lead to a variety of mental disorders.

When Freud first introduced his theories in the late 1800s, many people ridiculed or attacked them. By the 1920s, however, his ideas about human

Footnotes to History

Fads

The 1920s was a time when many fads swept the United States. These ranged from crossword puzzles, to stunts, such as sitting on the top of flagpoles for days at a time, to parlor games, such as mah-jongg, a Chinese version of rummy played with tiles.

Chapter 29 Section 1

TEACH

Guided Practice

THEME **Innovation**

Ask students to review the section and identify the innovations of the postwar years. *(automobile, radio, refrigerator, new ideas in science and the arts)* Discuss with the class how these changes made a difference in people's lives. **L1 LEP**

Economics Initiate a class debate focused on Calvin Coolidge's words, "The business of America is business." Ask students to analyze whether his words are still applicable today. Should economic development be the main focus of the United States? What else are Americans concerned about? *(peace, human rights, the environment)* **L2**

Chapter Transparency 29

History *and the* Humanities

- World Music: Cultural Traditions, Lesson 1
- World History and Art Transparency 39, *Bird in Space;* 43, *The Persistence of Memory*
- Focus on World Art Print 3, Thomas Hart Benton. *The Wreck of the Ole '97*; 4, Sargent Johnson. *Forever Free*; 23, René Magritte. *The Human Condition 1*

COOPERATIVE LEARNING ACTIVITY

Bulletin Board Organize the class into small groups and have each group select a topic, such as science, literature, music, art, or technology. They should plan a display of the innovations in that field during the time period of this section. Groups can gather copies of examples from library books and magazines or do their own illustrations. Each group should be responsible for an overall design for their part of the bulletin board and for written copy or labels to describe the samples they display. **L1 LEP**

Independent Practice

Guided Reading Activity 29-1 **L1**

Time Line Activity 29

Chapter Themes: Graphic Organizer 29

History & Art Picasso did not complete Stein's face during the actual sitting. When he did finish it, he painted the face from memory in a sculptural, masklike style. This was indicative of the move Picasso would soon make into cubism.
Answer to Caption: *Artists and writers broke with long-established traditions and experimented with new styles, media, and subject matter.*

Economics Show students how to read and follow stock market reports in the newspaper. Have them select one or two companies to follow for a month. Suggest that they notice political trends as well. At the end of the month, ask them to report on their shares and on how they would feel if the stock market crashed as it did in 1929. **L3**

you don't say...

Cubism, as a name, had its origin in a comment by art critic Louis Vauxhouses. Vauxhouses described Georges Braque's works as reducing things to "geometrical schemas, to cubes." Although there were no cubes in cubist painting, the name stuck.

History & Art *Gertrude Stein* by Pablo Picasso, 1906. The Metropolitan Museum of Art, New York, New York **The Spanish painter Pablo Picasso and the American writer Gertrude Stein were two of the major cultural figures of the 1920s and 1930s.** *What were two major characteristics of the arts during the period between the world wars?*

psychology had become more accepted and influential. Freud's theories eventually led to new approaches in the treatment of mental illness, in child rearing, and in education.

Upheaval in the Arts

The break between old and new following World War I was perhaps most sharply defined in the arts. In painting, music, literature, and dance, artists abandoned long-accepted traditions. The avant-garde experimented with new styles, media, and subject matter. Often the public greeted their pioneering efforts with cries of shock and protest.

Literature

Many of the period's most thoughtful writers had been disillusioned by World War I and its aftermath. The war had destroyed their belief in the traditional values of middle-class society. In expressing that disillusionment, they broke new literary ground.

In his poems *The Waste Land* and "The Hollow Men," for example, American-born poet **T.S. Eliot** used a patchwork style that juxtaposed different literary, religious, and historical references to convey a sense of despair about life. German novelist Thomas Mann, Austrian novelist Franz Kafka, and British novelist Virginia Woolf also experimented with new literary techniques. Both in terms of their style and content, all of these writers represented a sharp break with the literature of the past.

While they echoed Eliot's sense of disenchantment, American writers such as Ernest Hemingway and F. Scott Fitzgerald developed markedly different literary styles. For instance, in his 1926 novel *The Sun Also Rises*, Hemingway used a lean, straightforward style to tell the tale of Americans and Britons who roamed France and Spain, living for the moment while trying to find meaning in their lives. In contrast, Fitzgerald used a more elaborate poetic style in his 1925 novel *The Great Gatsby* to explore the atmosphere and excesses of the Roaring Twenties.

Several years earlier, in 1922, Irish novelist James Joyce had published *Ulysses*, an in-depth account of a day in the lives of three ordinary people in Dublin. *Ulysses* was a landmark in the development of the modern novel. Influenced by Freud's theories, Joyce developed a style known as "stream of consciousness" in which he presented the inner thoughts—rather than just the external actions—of his characters. Joyce's psychological emphasis and his earthy language caused a storm of protest, which led to a number of court battles over the publication of his novel.

In the late 1920s and the 1930s, many writers

MEETING SPECIAL NEEDS ACTIVITY

Mixed Learners Review the headings that appear in Section 1. Help students understand that each heading introduces the specific topic or change that will be covered. Organize the class into small groups. Ask each group to select a heading and prepare an oral presentation about that topic for the class. Encourage students to find ways to illustrate the topic either with photographs from books or magazines or with drawings. These oral presentations should provide additional help in reviewing the material for students. **L2 LEP**

772 Chapter 29 *Between Two Fires*

became interested in important social issues of the day. Langston Hughes, Claude McKay, and Zora Neale Hurston, who belonged to an African American literary movement known as the Harlem Renaissance, explored the African American experience in America. In *The Grapes of Wrath*, John Steinbeck described the plight of Oklahoma farmers who, in the midst of a severe drought, abandoned their farms and moved to California. John Dos Passos's *U.S.A.* trilogy was a broader social criticism of conditions in American society during the postwar period.

Painting

The postwar period also witnessed a revolution in the visual arts. Artists no longer tried to be realistic or tell a story in their paintings. Instead, they developed radical new styles and redefined the nature of painting.

Pablo Picasso, a Spanish painter, was one of the most influential artists of the period. Picasso constantly experimented with new styles, new techniques, and new media. In 1907 he created a commotion in the art world when he painted *Les Demoiselles d'Avignon*. The painting was the earliest example of cubism, an abstract art form that employs intersecting geometric shapes. Cubist painters transformed their subjects by flattening them, cutting them up, rearranging different portions of them, and altering their shapes and colors to fit their own vision. As Picasso explained: "Art is a lie that makes us realize the truth."

Another startling artistic development was surrealism, an art form that used dreamlike images and unnatural combinations of objects. Influenced by Freud, surrealist painters tried to find a new reality by exploring the unconscious mind. The Spanish painter Salvador Dali created such realistically impossible images as limp watches set in bleak landscapes. The bizarre, often haunting quality of these paintings shocked the public.

In the tradition of Steinbeck and Dos Passos, other artists used their talents to attack social problems. Ben Shahn, Moses Sayer, Peter Blume, and Dorothea Lange made a name for themselves as social realists. In their paintings and photographs, they showed the human suffering caused by the Depression of the 1930s.

Music and Dance

Composers also broke new ground after the war. Several eastern European composers transformed the classical form. **Sergey Prokofiev** (sehr•GAY pruh•KAWF•yuhf), a Russian, composed driving and dissonant music that lacked the familiar harmonies of traditional forms. Critics dubbed him the "age of steel composer."

Arnold Schoenberg (SHUHN•BUHRG), a self-taught Austrian composer, made radical changes in music theory. Instead of harmonies based on the traditional eight-note scale, he proposed new musical arrangements based on 12 equally valued notes. In his groundbreaking composition, *Pierrot Lunaire* (1912), Schoenberg used harsh, dissonant music to express what he regarded as the decay of civilization. His composition outraged conservative audiences.

Meanwhile, in the United States, musicians were creating their own distinctive sound. The 1920s was "the golden age of jazz." What some have called the only art form to originate in the United States, jazz is a mixture of American folk songs, West African rhythms, harmonies from European classical music, and work songs from the days of slavery. Trumpet player Louis Armstrong, blues singer Bessie Smith, and pianist Jelly Roll Morton popularized the new music.

The postwar era also saw a transformation in the art of dance. Performing barefoot in a loose tunic, the American dancer Isadora Duncan changed people's ideas about dance. Another American, Martha Graham, expanded on Duncan's style and turned modern dance into a striking new art form.

Visualizing History **Young people of the 1920s enjoyed a fast dance called the Charleston. They often held dance marathons, or contests to see who could dance the longest.** *What two women contributed greatly to modern dance?*

Chapter 29 Section 1

ASSESS

Check for Understanding

Assign Section 1 Review as homework or as an in-class activity.

Use Student Self-Test and Review Software to review Section 1.

Evaluate

Section Quiz 29-1

Use the Testmaker to create a customized quiz for Section 1.

Reteach

Have students independently review the section and list important dates, discoveries, movements, and people on a time line. Some students may wish to do additional research to fill in gaps. Discuss the time lines in class and combine them to make a class time line.

Visualizing History A sense of freedom and rebellion against the old ways was particularly evident in the carefree new dance styles. This was the era of dancers such as Fred and Adele Astaire, big bands such as that of Paul Whiteman, and musicians such as Duke Ellington.
Answer to Caption: *Isadora Duncan and Martha Graham*

MAKING CONNECTIONS ACTIVITY

The Arts Motion pictures became a major industry in the 1920s. One of the earliest silent film stars was British comedian Charlie Chaplin. Sound was added to films in the late 1920s. Have students research the movie industry and the technological advances it made during the postwar decade. Have students work in pairs to write a report on their findings and then design a poster advertising a movie of the era. This was the time of *Dracula* with Bela Lugosi, Greta Garbo in *Mata Hari*, Jeanette MacDonald and Nelson Eddy in *Rose Marie*, and Fred Astaire and Ginger Rogers in *Top Hat*. Suggest that students bring to class a video of one of the old films; groups of students could plan a small film festival. **L2**

TEACH

Point out that the people in the status symbol cars wearing fancy dresses and tuxedos were the wealthy set. Entertainment for millions of others often centered around a more modest piece of technology—the radio. By 1925 the listening audience was put at 50 million, and radio advertising was making an incredible impact. **What radio shows or stars have you heard about from that era?** *(some shows: "Fibber McGee and Molly," "Baby Snooks," "Flash Gordon," "Little Orphan Annie," "Inner Sanctum"; stars: Jack Benny, Burns and Allen, Edgar Bergen and Charlie McCarthy, Kate Smith)*

you don't say...

Clarence Darrow also defended Nathan Leopold and Richard Loeb, two university students accused of murdering a classmate, in 1924. Darrow did not believe in capital punishment, even though the men admitted to the murder. Darrow introduced psychiatrists and neurologists to the courtroom battle and opened a new era in murder trials by entering the first "temporary insanity" plea.

NATIONAL GEOGRAPHIC PICTURING HISTORY

Flying High

Racing down a dark road, the young men and women in this photograph enjoy a new freedom. Cars were important throughout the industrialized world of Europe and North America, and the American auto industry led the global market. The automobile brought mobility to many Americans during the years following World War I. It was all part of a new lifestyle called the Roaring Twenties.

Behind the gaiety and frivolity, however, the 1920s was a decade in which a new urban style of living came into conflict with an older rural way of life. In the United States this conflict was played out again and again: Politician and orator William Jennings Bryan battled lawyer Clarence Darrow in the famous Scopes trial over whether or not public schools should teach Darwinian science. Farms failed and farmers lost their land, while the sounds of the new prosperity played on radios in their living rooms. The new city slickers were jazz age flappers, like the ones here, racing along unpaved roads in a fancy new Stutz Bearcat. ⊕

Sergey Diaghilev (dee•AH•guh•LEHF), the Russian impresario, or sponsor, developed modern ballet, which blended modern dance with classical ballet. When Russian composer Igor Stravinsky wrote *The Rite of Spring* (1913) for Diaghilev and his company of dancers, the Ballets Russes, it was a turning point for ballet. The leaping dance steps that ballet star Vaslav Nijinsky (VAHT•slahv nuh •ZHIHN•skee) performed to Stravinsky's music created a sensation. George Balanchine, who had been a choreographer, or dance arranger, with the Ballets Russes, expanded on Diaghilev's work after moving from the Soviet Union to the United States.

Architecture

The 1920s and 1930s saw striking new designs in buildings and furnishings. **Walter Gropius** founded the Bauhaus (BOW•HOWS) school of design in Weimar (VY•MAHR), Germany. He and his followers created a simple, unornamented style of design. Linking beauty to practicality, Gropius pioneered geometric concrete and glass structures in both Germany and the United States.

In the United States, Frank Lloyd Wright blended his structures with their natural surroundings. Because of their low horizontal form, his houses seem to grow out of the ground. Instead of creating boxlike rooms, Wright reduced the number of walls so that one room flowed into another.

Popular Culture

While the revolutionary developments taking place in art and music may not have had an immediate effect on the lives of ordinary people, films and big bands did. In the postwar era, **Hollywood** productions dominated the movie screens of the world. The movies reflected the new morality of the "Jazz Age" and the doctrine of living for the moment. During the 1930s the public flocked to movie theaters, where for 10 cents they could escape the harsh realities of hard economic times.

In the early part of the century, the creative use of the camera elevated the motion picture to an art form. In *The Last Laugh*, a silent film directed by German filmmaker F.W. Murnau, the camera work is so expressive that the story is told entirely without subtitles. British actor and director Charlie Chaplin also broke new ground in his films while delighting millions of moviegoers with his humor.

But in 1927 motion pictures found their voice. *The Jazz Singer*, starring American actor Al Jolson, changed motion pictures overnight and signaled the beginning of the end of the era of silent films. During the early 1930s American musicals, gangster movies, and horror movies were popular. However, some filmmakers tried to educate as well as entertain their audiences. *I Am a Fugitive From a Chain Gang* (1932) was a forceful indictment of the Southern penal system, while *Mr. Smith Goes to Washington* (1939) showed the effects of political corruption.

The public also sought escape from their troubles on the ballroom floor. In the 1930s and 1940s, dance bands reached their greatest popularity. Tommy Dorsey, Count Basie, Benny Goodman, Duke Ellington, Artie Shaw, and their swing bands performed in ballrooms and hotels all across America. Swing was the new word for music played with a happy, relaxed jazz beat. But if swing was not everyone's cup of tea, there were alternatives. The bands of Guy Lombardo and Sammy Kaye played traditional waltzes and fox-trots.

Obviously, the social upheavals and economic hardships that World War I created did not dampen the creative spirit following the war. During this era artists introduced new styles in every major art form. They took little interest in politics and reform. Many cried out against conformity and retreated into individualism. At times it seemed as if they were transforming the world with their radical new visions of life. But the euphoria did not last. The stock market crash that took place on Wall Street in late October 1929 signaled for the United States and much of the world an economic depression that had devastating and deadly consequences.

SECTION 1 REVIEW

Recall

1. **Define** cubism, surrealism, jazz, choreographer.
2. **Identify** Albert Einstein, Sigmund Freud, T.S. Eliot, Pablo Picasso, Sergey Prokofiev, Walter Gropius.
3. **Explain** how the events and aftermath of World War I affected the way many people looked at the world.

Critical Thinking

4. **Analyzing Information** The era after World War I was a time for breaking with tradition. How could abandoning traditions help a society? How might it harm a society?

Understanding Themes

5. **Innovation** What impact did technological advances in transportation and communication have on American culture in the 1920s?

Chapter 29 Section 1

Cultural Perspectives

Jazz, created by African American musicians in the United States, incorporated many sources. It grew out of spiritual music, old ballads, children's jingles, minstrel music, and the ragtime piano music of the early 1920s. In New Orleans it was common for bands in funeral processions to play hymns on the way to the funeral and then break out in joyful jazz tunes afterward. Singing and dancing crowds would tag along after the band. Today jazz is a popular form of music throughout the world.

Enrich

Have students choose one of the literary works or paintings mentioned in the section, read or study it, and report on it to the class.

CLOSE

Discuss with students how World War I changed the way people viewed the world. Review the artistic and scientific advances and cultural movements of the time. Help students conclude that the postwar world had adopted a style of "living for the moment."

SECTION 1 REVIEW ANSWERS

1. All vocabulary words are defined in the Glossary.
2. Albert Einstein, 771; Sigmund Freud, 771; T. S. Eliot, 772; Pablo Picasso, 773; Sergey Prokofiev, 773; Walter Gropius, 775
3. Disillusioned and restless after the war, people broke with tradition and looked for something new.
4. Answers will vary. Possible answer: New creative spirit can spur inventions and improvements; however, some traditions are still valuable and should not be abandoned.
5. **INNOVATION** They made society more homogeneous, brought people together more easily, and made life easier so there was more leisure time.

SECTION THEME

▶ **Change** The Great Depression forces governments in Europe and North America to increase their involvement in social and economic affairs.

Find Out

Answer: *because the governments in these nations intervened in new ways in social and economic affairs, taking steps to improve life for people suffering in the Great Depression*

FOCUS

Section Objective

Explain why democratic government survived in the United States, Great Britain, and France during the post-World War I era.

BELLRINGER Motivational Activity

Before taking roll at the beginning of the class period, project Section Focus Transparency 29-2 and have students answer the activity questions. Discuss students' responses.

This activity is also available as a blackline master.

Vocabulary Pre-check

Use Vocabulary Activity 29 to introduce vocabulary terms. **L1 LEP**

1920 1925 1930 1935

1926 The General Strike paralyzes Great Britain.

1933 Franklin D. Roosevelt introduces the New Deal.

1936 French voters elect a Socialist government.

Section 2

The Western Democracies

Setting the Scene

▶ **Terms to Define**
disarmament, general strike, coalition

▶ **People to Meet**
Franklin D. Roosevelt, Ramsay MacDonald, Eamon De Valera, Léon Blum

▶ **Places to Locate**
Washington, D.C., Irish Free State

Find Out Why did democratic government survive in the United States, Great Britain, and France during the post-World War I era?

The Storyteller

Throughout 1932 the lines had grown. They formed at banks, as investors tried to withdraw their savings before the bank collapsed. They formed at factory gates and employment offices. Men lost their jobs, lost their homes. They swallowed their pride and formed another line—for relief. If there was none to be found, another line waited. As one eyewitness reported, "We saw a crowd of some 50 men fighting over a barrel of garbage which had been set outside the back door of a restaurant."

—adapted from *Since Yesterday*, Frederick Lewis Allen, 1939

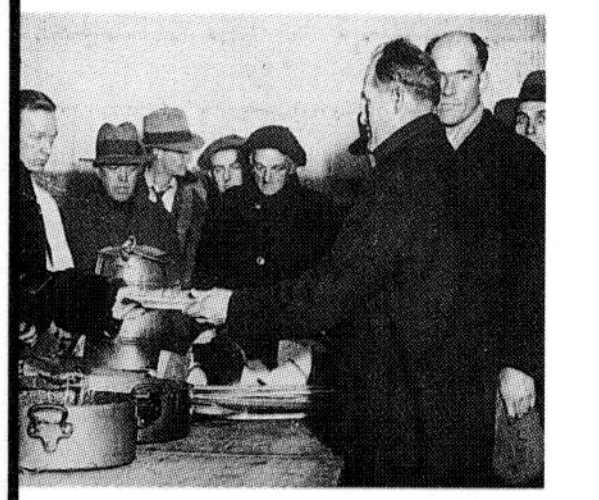

Depression-era food line

Peace brought neither stability nor lasting prosperity to the Western democracies, which paid a heavy price for their victory in World War I. Although the United States suffered comparatively minor financial losses, huge war debts threatened the economic and political stability of Great Britain and France. The West did enjoy a brief period of prosperity in the 1920s, but a global economic depression soon followed. This depression further weakened the Western democracies in the 1930s, making it difficult for them to counter the rising totalitarian threat in Italy and Germany.

The United States

The United States emerged from World War I in better shape than its allies. No battles were fought on American soil, and because of its late entry into the conflict, America suffered far fewer casualties than the other nations. Moreover, unlike the economies of many European countries, the American economy remained strong until 1929.

Cutting Foreign Ties

President Woodrow Wilson wanted the United States to assume a greater role in world affairs following the war. Americans, however, were weary of war and of the foreign entanglements that had dragged the nation into war. They wanted to return to a life of isolation, free from international problems.

An idealistic man, Wilson had seized on the notion of a League of Nations as the cornerstone of a lasting peace. But the newly elected Republican majorities in both the Senate and the House of Representatives had no wish to accommodate the Democratic President. When Congress failed to ratify the Treaty of Versailles in 1919, it also rejected American membership in the League. The absence

SECTION RESOURCES

Reproducible Masters
- Reproducible Lesson Plan 29-2
- Vocabulary Activity 29
- Guided Reading Activity 29-2
- Section Quiz 29-2

Transparencies
- Section Focus Transparency 29-2
- World History and Art Transparency 38, *Migrant Mother*

Multimedia
- Student Self-Test and Review Software
- Testmaker

of the United States significantly weakened the League's effectiveness as a strong international peacekeeping organization.

Economic Boom

Unlike Europe, the United States had come out of World War I with a dynamic industrial economy. In addition, the Allies owed the United States huge sums of money, and these loans more than canceled out America's prewar debt of $4 billion. The war had transformed the United States from a debtor nation, which owed money, into a creditor nation, to which money was owed.

The 1920s were boom years for many American industries. Factories turned out millions of automobiles, radios, vacuum cleaners, and refrigerators. The United States was soon producing 40 percent of the world's manufactured goods. Employment was rising, and many workers' wages reached the highest levels ever paid in the history of the nation.

As a result of this economic prosperity, more and more people entered the stock market. In the hope of doubling and tripling their money in a rising market, schoolteachers, cabdrivers, shoe clerks, doctors, and lawyers gambled their life savings. But despite the soaring "bull market," the economy was shaky.

Crash and Depression

On Tuesday morning, October 29, 1929, the crash came. In that one day, the value of stocks listed on the New York Stock Exchange dropped $14 billion. In the next three years, as prices continued to fall, thousands of businesses and banks closed. Sales dropped off, forcing a curtailment of production. Salaries and wages also fell, and many workers lost their jobs. By 1933 more than 13 million American workers were unemployed—nearly one-fourth of the nation's workforce.

As property owners defaulted on taxes, hundreds of small towns found themselves unable to pay their teachers or sanitation workers. Schools shut down, garbage rotted in the streets, and people went hungry. Since state and local governments could provide little relief, private businesses and organizations sometimes stepped in to help care for the needy.

In the opinion of many political leaders, direct relief was not the responsibility of the national government but of the individual, the family, and the local community. Government-funded relief, they believed, would destroy American self-reliance and would lead to socialism. However, in these desperate times not everyone agreed.

CONNECTIONS Geography

The Dust Bowl

Dust Bowl scene

American farmers in the 1930s suffered greatly from the Great Depression, but their hardships also came from a devastating drought that afflicted the central United States from 1933 to 1937. As the Great Plains became powder-dry, winds lifted vital topsoil in clouds of dust that turned day into night. Dust storms had swept over the area before, but never on such a large and destructive scale.

The roots of this disaster lay well in the past. Ranchers' cattle overgrazed an area that experienced scant rainfall. The ranchers were followed by farmers, who planted wheat. These early settlers plowed land that should never have been cultivated, and they farmed it badly. They did not use contour plowing to check erosion, rotate their crops, or plant trees as windbreaks to hold the soil.

Ruined by drought, about 200,000 farmers and their families packed up their belongings and headed West, especially to California. However, they found little relief in their new homes. Only low-paying seasonal jobs were available, and local residents resented the intrusion. It took many years of normal rainfall and improved farming techniques to transform the Great Plains from a Dust Bowl into productive land again.

MAKING THE CONNECTION

1. What factors created the Dust Bowl?
2. What did many Dust Bowl farmers do in the 1930s?

TEACH

Guided Practice

THEME Change

Discuss how the aftermath of the war changed the economies in France, Great Britain, and the United States. Ask students to comment on the drastic change in the United States when the stock market crashed. **L1**

Government Lead a discussion of how the existence of many political parties in France weakened democracy in the nation. Have students discuss the effect that more than two main political parties would have on democracy in the United States. **L2**

Economics Hold a class discussion about the benefits and drawbacks of labor strikes. Ask what can be accomplished. *(Employees gain benefits and are more satisfied.)* What are some reasons for striking? *(to gain pay increases, better hours and conditions)* **L2**

CONNECTIONS Geography

The Dust Bowl

Lead students in a discussion of how the weather and other natural phenomena affect business, the economy, and daily life. Ask them to consider how heavy rains and flooding, unexpected snow and freezing, and hurricanes affect farmers and orchard growers.

Answers to Making the Connection

1. *overgrazing of land, drought, poor farming methods*
2. *packed up and headed west to find work as migrants in California*

COOPERATIVE LEARNING ACTIVITY

Interviews Organize the class into small groups. Ask students in each group to interview people who lived through the Great Depression of the 1930s. (If some students have no such contacts, direct them to local retirement or nursing homes.) Within each group, students should choose a topic (memories of Hoover and Roosevelt, New Deal programs, family experiences) and assign tasks such as planning the interview questions, selecting people to be interviewed, and deciding how to present the interviews. Remind students to have questions ready, listen well, and take accurate notes. If possible, students should tape-record the interviews. Have each group share the interviews with the class. **L2**

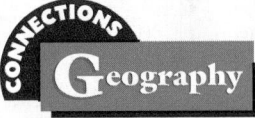

Chapter 29 Section 2

World History and Art Transparency 38, *Migrant Mother*

Independent Practice

Guided Reading Activity 29-2 **L1**

Visualizing History A general strike is labor's strongest weapon, and when it occurs society can be thrown into upheaval. Winston Churchill had prepared for such a strike in 1926. Police were mobilized, troops dispatched, and thousands of upper- and middle-class volunteers drove trucks, taxis, and locomotives. It was an emergency, but one with little violence. **Answer to Caption:** *The war had reduced Great Britain's standing in world markets; its privileged standing in foreign trade was upset by challenges from new competitors; it became a debtor nation.*

Broadcast Have students write the script for a 1930s radio news broadcast. They may use facts from the text or conduct additional research. The broadcast should also include weather or sports or some other feature related to the country of origin of the broadcast. **L2 LEP**

Linking Past and Present

"Happy Days Are Here Again," the popular jingle that Franklin D. Roosevelt used as his 1932 campaign song, is still played today at the Democratic party's national conventions.

Visualizing History **During the 1920s and 1930s, economic downturns led to labor unrest in many western democracies. British workers especially carried out strikes for better wages.** *What was Great Britain's economic standing after World War I?*

The New Deal

In 1932 voters elected a new President, former New York governor **Franklin D. Roosevelt.** Roosevelt had campaigned on the promise of "a new deal" for the American people. He believed that the federal government had to aid the stricken economy and provide relief for the unemployed.

In the first 100 days of his administration, in the spring and early summer of 1933, Roosevelt sent a number of bills to Congress that quickly became laws. These measures regulated the banks and stock market and established production guidelines for industry and agriculture. To put people back to work, the government established public works projects to build roads, dams, bridges, homes, and parks. Later New Deal legislation provided for social security and unemployment insurance. Although Roosevelt's New Deal policies were not entirely successful in ending the Depression, they did much to restore the confidence of the nation.

Foreign Affairs

The American government was concerned with more than just domestic affairs during the 1920s and 1930s. Despite its rejection of the League of Nations and binding alliances, the United States did take steps to prevent a future world war. In 1921 it played host in **Washington, D.C.,** to an international conference on disarmament, the reduction of military weapons. At this conference, the United States signed a treaty with Japan and Great Britain limiting the number of naval warships each could stockpile. The leading powers at the conference also agreed to seek peaceful rather than military solutions to disagreements.

In 1928 the United States and France signed the Kellogg-Briand Pact, which denounced war as a means of settling disputes. Eventually, nearly all the nations of the world signed this agreement. Unfortunately, it was nothing more than a statement of intentions and had no powers of enforcement.

Great Britain

Although World War I increased the United States's economic and political influence, it cost Great Britain its position as a leading economic power in the world. Before the war British banks lent money to nations all over the globe. But the war

MEETING SPECIAL NEEDS ACTIVITY

Physical Disability For students who have chronic illnesses and are absent from classes fairly often, it is helpful to provide materials that can be used at home or in the hospital. If there are special oral class presentations, tape them for home use. Assign a special book report or research project to make up for missed class lectures. When a cooperative learning activity has a task that can be done at home, assign it to the student who must be absent often. If the student is willing and interested, suggest a science presentation or special report on his or her health problem. **L2**

was costly, and Great Britain was forced to borrow heavily from the United States. As a result, Great Britain became a debtor instead of a creditor nation.

The war also cost Great Britain its privileged position in world trade. American and Japanese companies captured many British overseas markets during the war. In addition, Great Britain's factories were old and the equipment outdated. Countries like the United States and Japan, which had industrialized later, had newer factories and more modern equipment. Consequently, they could produce goods at a lower cost. Many factories in Great Britain closed or cut back production after the war. By 1921 more than 2 million workers had lost their jobs.

The General Strike

Great Britain's economic woes reached a crisis point in 1926. Coal miners were engaged in a bitter strike for higher wages that year. For months the coal companies had refused to give in to their demands. In an effort to end the stalemate, the coal miners convinced many other trade union workers to join in a general strike, a strike involving all or a large number of a nation's workers. On May 4 all transport workers, dockers, public utility employees, and workers in the building trades and heavy industry walked off their jobs. The government declared a state of emergency and called out the troops to run essential services.

In the end, the General Strike was a failure. By December 1926 the coal strike had also collapsed. In 1927 Parliament passed the Trade Disputes Act, which made general strikes illegal.

Rise of the Labour Party

Despite the failure of the General Strike, British workers gained political strength during the 1920s. During this decade the Labour party became the second leading party in the country after the Conservatives. In 1924 and again in 1929, Labour governments were elected to office. Each time, King George V named Scottish Labour leader **Ramsay MacDonald** prime minister. Because the Labour party supported Socialist policies, its rise to power alarmed the Conservatives and their wealthy supporters. However, once in power, MacDonald and other Labour leaders tempered many of their radical demands.

From Empire to Commonwealth

In the 1920s and 1930s, Great Britain retained control of many of its colonial territories. However, the dominions, like Canada and Australia, became completely independent states. In 1931 Parliament passed the Statute of Westminster, which established the Commonwealth of Nations, a voluntary association linking Great Britain and its former colonies on an equal basis.

Visualizing History **Irish nationalist leader Michael Collins, speaking here to crowds in the Irish capital of Dublin, negotiated a 1921 treaty with the British.** *What changes did the treaty bring to Ireland?*

One of Great Britain's major postwar problems was its relationship with Ireland. After an unsuccessful rebellion by Irish nationalists, the British government and the Irish agreed to a compromise that moved Ireland toward independence.

A treaty signed in 1921 granted dominion status to the Catholic southern part of Ireland, which became known as the **Irish Free State**. The largely Protestant northern counties remained part of Great Britain. They were known as Ulster, or Northern Ireland.

Wanting complete independence for all of Ireland, a radical group, led by **Eamon De Valera**, revolted against the new Irish Free State. The Irish government suppressed this rebellion, but economic distress brought De Valera to power in 1932. Five years later, the name of the country was changed to Eire, and a president replaced the British monarch as the head of state.

France

World War I had an even more devastating effect on France than on Great Britain. In the four years of fighting, the combatants had destroyed thousands of square miles of farmland and forests and reduced villages and cities to rubble. French casualties were enormous. Half of the males

Visualizing History Michael Collins was a courageous and a very popular Irish leader. He was successful in raising funds for the Irish war for independence and organized an intelligence service for the Irish Republican Army. As commander of the Free State army, Collins took strong actions to end fighting but was killed in an ambush in County Cork in 1922.

Answer to Caption: *It divided the island of Ireland into two parts: the southern part became known as the Irish Free State, a dominion separate from Great Britain; the northern counties remained part of Great Britain and were known as Ulster or Northern Ireland.*

CURRICULUM CONNECTION

LITERATURE

In the postwar world of Great Britain, A. A. Milne offered a protected and imaginary world for children in *Winnie-the-Pooh* and *The House at Pooh Corner*. Two other well-known children's stories of the time were Margery Williams Bianco's *The Velveteen Rabbit* and Hugh Lofting's *The Story of Doctor Doolittle.*

MAKING CONNECTIONS ACTIVITIES

Literature Have students read John Steinbeck's novel *The Grapes of Wrath* about farmers making the journey from the Dust Bowl area to California. Have them report to the class on how Steinbeck portrayed the life these people led. **L2**

The Arts Movies were an extremely popular form of entertainment for Americans in the 1930s. Suggest that students view a video of one or two hit films from the era, such as *It Happened One Night* or *Footlight Parade*. Discuss as a class what sorts of movies appealed to people during the time of the Depression. **L1 LEP**

Chapter 29
Section 2

ASSESS

Check for Understanding

Assign Section 2 Review as homework or as an in-class activity.

Use Student Self-Test and Review Software to review Section 2.

Evaluate

Section Quiz 29-2

Use the Testmaker to create a customized quiz for Section 2.

Reteach

Write the headings *Causes* and *Effects* on the chalkboard and create a class chart to help students review the causes and effects of World War I.

List students' comments under the proper heading and suggest that they copy the chart for a study aid.

Enrich

Have students use the chart from **Reteach** to write a short report on what they think were the most important effects of World War I on the Western democracies.

CLOSE

Lead a discussion about why democracy survived in the United States, Great Britain, and France after World War I despite serious economic and political problems.

AROUND THE WORLD

Jordan Gains Independence

Jordan, 1921

After World War I, lands east and west of the Jordan River were administered by Great Britain. In 1921 the territory east of the Jordan gained partial self-government. This land—then called Transjordan—won full independence in 1946 as a monarchy under King Abdullah. The country was renamed Jordan after it annexed the West Bank of the Jordan River following the 1948–1949 Arab-Israeli war.

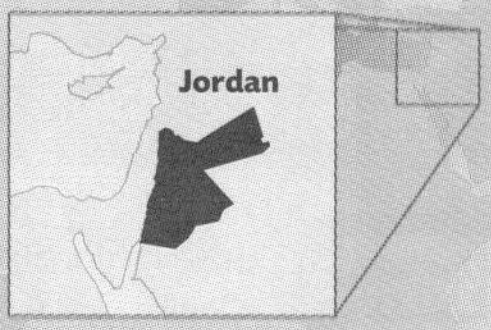

between the ages of 18 and 32 were killed in the fighting.

Troubled Years

Like Great Britain, France faced severe economic problems after the war. High unemployment and soaring inflation caused terrible hardships. The French government was nearly bankrupt, and its war debts were staggering. As a result of these financial problems, France's factories, railways, and canals could not be quickly rebuilt.

The political picture was as bleak as the economic one. Many political parties competed for votes. Since each party received seats in the national legislature according to its percentage of the vote, no party ever won a majority of seats. In order to form a government, several parties had to band together into a coalition, or alliance of factions, but the coalition governments often fell apart soon after they were formed.

Extremist groups on both the left and the right also threatened the political stability of the nation. Communists and Socialists struggled for power against Fascists, extreme nationalists favoring a strong government, and outbreaks of violence were common.

The Popular Front

In 1934 the political crisis reached a head. Fascist groups rioted in Paris, killing several people. Fearing a Fascist takeover, the Communists appealed to leaders of the Socialist party for "a broad Popular Front to combat fascism and for work, liberty, and peace."

The new coalition won enough votes in a 1936 election to form a government. **Léon Blum**, the Socialist leader, became prime minister. The Popular Front was in power for about a year, but in that short time it passed many new laws that benefited workers and farmers.

Foreign Policy

Exhausted and drained by World War I, France wanted, above all else, to prevent another war. Consequently, the French government supported the League of Nations in the postwar years and worked to create a series of alliances to contain Germany. But it also sought friendly ties with Germany's new democratic Weimar Republic. In 1925 France signed the Locarno Agreements with Germany, Italy, Belgium, and Great Britain that appeared to ensure a lasting peace.

As added insurance against a future German invasion, France built a series of fortifications that were 200 miles (320 km) long called the Maginot (MA•zhuh•NOH) Line. This stretch of concrete bunkers and trenches extended along France's border with Germany. French military leaders boasted that the Maginot Line could never be crossed. What they failed to consider was that past German invasions had come through Belgium, whose border with France remained virtually undefended.

SECTION 2 REVIEW

Recall

1. **Define** disarmament, general strike, coalition.
2. **Identify** Franklin D. Roosevelt, Ramsay MacDonald, Commonwealth of Nations, Eamon De Valera, Léon Blum.
3. **Explain** how World War I affected the economies of the United States, Great Britain, and France.

Critical Thinking

4. **Evaluating Information** Why do you think the democracies of the United States, Great Britain, and France survived despite postwar political, economic, and social problems?

Understanding Themes

5. **Change** How did President Franklin D. Roosevelt's New Deal change the role the federal government played in American society after 1933?

SECTION 2 REVIEW ANSWERS

1. All vocabulary words are defined in the Glossary.
2. Roosevelt, 778; MacDonald, 779; Commonwealth of Nations, 779; De Valera, 779; Blum, 780
3. It had a devastating effect on the economies of Great Britain and France; the United States emerged with a strong economy.
4. Answers will vary. Students may conclude that democracy was more firmly established in these countries or that the governments of these nations took bold new steps to meet citizens' needs.
5. **CHANGE** The federal government became more actively involved in domestic affairs.

1920 — 1925 — 1930 — 1935

1924 Italy's Benito Mussolini assumes dictatorial powers.

1932 The Nazis become the largest party in Germany's parliament.

1935 Nuremberg Laws in Germany deprive Jews of rights.

Section 3

Fascist Dictatorships

Setting the Scene

- **Terms to Define**
  fascism, corporate state, syndicate, *Kristallnacht*, concentration camp
- **People to Meet**
  Benito Mussolini, Adolf Hitler
- **Places to Locate**
  Weimar

Find Out What factors led to the rise of Fascist dictatorships in Italy and Germany after World War I?

The Storyteller

Alice Hamilton was dismayed. Twenty-five years earlier, she had spent a year in Frankfurt as a student. She now returned to visit the city only to find the lovely Römer Platz draped with Nazi flags. The city's children and young people also had changed. Formerly they played games; now they marched in regular ranks. Where tuneful songs had been sung in public houses, militant music blared forth. Mrs. Hamilton understood why this transformation had taken place. Hitler was inspiring Germany's impoverished, hopeless youth to believe they were the elect of the earth.

—adapted from "The Youth Who Are Hitler's Strength," *New York Times Magazine*, October 8, 1933. Alice Hamilton. Reprinted in *Sources of the Western Tradition*, Marvin Perry, 1991

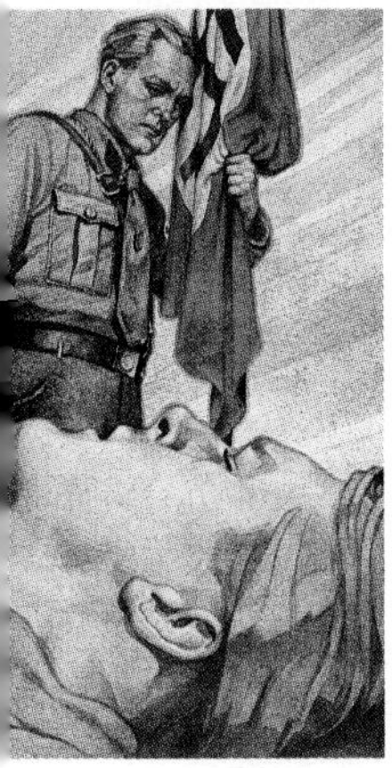

Nazi poster

World War I shattered the economic and political stability of many European nations. For example, it caused staggering inflation in Germany in the early 1920s. The situation in Italy during this period was equally serious, causing workers there to stage lengthy nationwide strikes. When the United States stock market crashed in October 1929, the worldwide economic depression that followed wreaked havoc on the already weakened German economy. The economic and social chaos created by war and depression made both Italy and Germany ripe for revolution in the postwar period.

Rise of Fascism in Italy

A general mood of dissatisfaction permeated Italy after the war. Although it had fought on the side of the Allies, Italy did not gain all that the Allies had promised. It had expected to receive huge portions of territory from the Central Powers. Instead, it only gained a small piece of Austrian territory, leaving many Italians with bitter feelings.

The war had also aggravated Italy's economic woes. War debts were staggering. When millions of Italian soldiers returned home, they found no jobs. The nation's industries lacked raw materials. But even if it had possessed the materials, Italy had no market for its products. Its best customers, Germany and Austria, had no money to buy anything.

Conditions were perfect for an opportunistic leader, and one soon emerged on the political horizon. His name was **Benito Mussolini** (MOO•suh•LEE•nee). Born in 1883, Mussolini came from a working-class family. As a young man, he worked as a journalist and was active in Socialist politics. But after the war, he attacked the Socialists for failing to put forward a policy of social reform. He eventually abandoned socialism and became an ardent nationalist.

Mussolini formed a new political party in 1919

SECTION THEME

- **Uniformity** Fascist governments in Italy and Germany limit individual liberties and stress loyalty to the state.

Find Out

Answer: *Economic problems, social chaos, and unemployment led to the rise of dictatorships in Italy and Germany.*

FOCUS

Section Objective

Identify the factors that led to the rise of Fascist dictatorships in Italy and Germany after World War I.

BELLRINGER
Motivational Activity

Before taking roll at the beginning of the class period, project Section Focus Transparency 29-3 and have students answer the activity questions. Discuss students' responses.

This activity is also available as a blackline master.

Vocabulary Pre-check

Use the Vocabulary PuzzleMaker to create a puzzle that reinforces the vocabulary terms in this section. **L1**

SECTION RESOURCES

Reproducible Masters
- Reproducible Lesson Plan 29-3
- Guided Reading Activity 29-3
- History Simulation 29
- Geography and History Activity 29
- Section Quiz 29-3

Transparencies
- Section Focus Transparency 29-3

Multimedia
- Vocabulary PuzzleMaker Software
- Student Self-Test and Review Software
- Testmaker
- Lessons of War: *The Enemy*

Chapter 29 *Between Two Fires* 781

TEACH

Guided Practice

THEME Uniformity

Ask students if they would like to live in a uniform society. Have them give examples from Fascist Italy and Nazi Germany to illustrate the effects of imposed uniformity. List these examples on the chalkboard as they are given. **L1**

Visualizing History Point out what effect Mussolini's military attire and disciplined stance would have on the people. When *Il Duce* was in power there were no purges, but he was able to intimidate people with the threat of terror.

Answer to Caption: *Mussolini promised "something to everyone," then used street violence and political pressure to destroy his opponents and get himself named prime minister.*

Recognizing Ideologies Write two headings on the chalkboard: *What the People Wanted* and *What Mussolini Had to Offer.* Encourage students to fill in the chart during class discussion. Ask students to make a similar chart for Adolf Hitler. **L2**

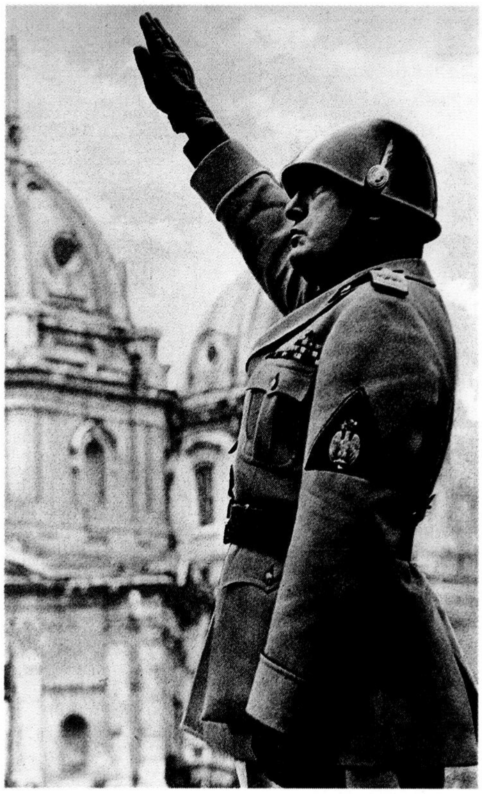

Visualizing History **Italian dictator Benito Mussolini salutes soldiers at a military parade. He dreamed of making Italy a great nation and reviving the Roman Empire.** *How did Mussolini come to power in Italy?*

called the *Fasci di Combattimento*, or Fascist party. Fascism (FA•SHIH•zuhm) is a political philosophy that advocates the glorification of the state, a single-party system with a strong ruler, and an aggressive form of nationalism. Like communism, fascism was a totalitarian system of government, meaning that it gave the state absolute authority. But fascism defended private property and the class structure. According to its principles, the cause of the nation was to be advanced at all cost. War and conquest were glorified to achieve national goals.

Mussolini's Road to Power

Conditions in Italy continued to deteriorate in the months following the war. The value of the lira declined steadily, the price of bread rose, and a shortage of coal hampered industrial production. To express their dissatisfaction, workers staged a series of strikes that paralyzed the country. In September 1920, workers in Lombardy and Piedmont took over the factories. Mussolini showed his support for the strikers in a speech at Trieste:

> "I demand that the factories increase their production. If this is guaranteed to me by the workers in place of the industrialists, I shall declare without hesitation that the former have the right to substitute themselves ... [for] the latter."

The unrest spread to rural Italy. Peasants seized land from wealthy landowners, and tenant farmers refused to pay their rents. The situation was so chaotic that the middle and upper classes feared a Communist revolution. Ever the politician, Mussolini offered "a little something to everyone." To appease the landowners, he vowed to end the unrest and protect private property. To woo the workers, he promised full employment and workers' benefits. He pleased nationalists by pledging to restore Italy to its former greatness.

By 1921 fascism had become a major political force in Italy. But the Blackshirts, as Mussolini's followers were called, did not rely on verbal assaults alone to achieve their goals. They physically attacked political opponents in the streets and drove elected officials from office.

Believing that fascism was a useful way of controlling the Socialists and workers, the democratic government did nothing to stop the Blackshirts. As a result, Mussolini grew bolder. In October 1922 the Fascists staged a march on Rome. Mussolini waited in Milan to see how the government would react. Believing that the Fascists were planning to seize power, the cabinet asked King Victor Emmanuel III to declare martial law. The king refused, and the cabinet resigned. Instead of calling for new elections, the monarch named Mussolini prime minister.

Mussolini's Dictatorship

Mussolini quickly put an end to democratic rule in Italy. In a 1924 election, Blackshirts used their now familiar brutal tactics to make sure that Italians voted for Fascist candidates. As a result, Fascists won a majority of seats in the Italian parliament. The Fascist-controlled parliament gave Mussolini sweeping new powers. After this election Mussolini began calling himself *Il Duce* (eel DOO•chay), "The Leader."

COOPERATIVE LEARNING ACTIVITY

Debate Organize the class into two groups to debate this statement: Mussolini's rule was good for Italy. Have the members of each group agree on assignments within the group as they prepare for the debate. Inform them that they will need to conduct research to support their positions. Remind students that to hold a good debate, statements must be based on fact, not opinion. Be sure to allow both sides time to make rebuttal arguments. Explain to students the bases on which you determine the winning team (thoroughness of research, clarity and force of arguments, presentation, and so forth). **L3**

To consolidate his power, Mussolini reorganized the Italian government and established a corporate state. Under the corporate state, Mussolini hoped to bring workers and employers together and consequently to end the political quarreling that he associated with a democratic, multiparty system. To this end, he banned non-Fascist parties and ordered that syndicates, or corporations of workers and employers, be formed in each industry. Each syndicate sent representatives to a legislature in Rome that set policies on wages, production, and distribution. In theory, the corporate state was a new form of democracy; in practice, it was a political tool expressly designed for strengthening Mussolini's power.

Many Italians bitterly opposed fascism. They mourned the loss of democracy and individual freedoms. The Fascists arrested, assaulted, and murdered any who dared speak out against the abuses. "The masses must obey," thundered Mussolini. "They cannot afford to waste time searching for truth."

A majority of Italians, however, supported Mussolini. They believed he had done Italy a great service by preventing a Communist revolution and had brought order to the nation. After all, they said, he "made the trains run on time."

By building up Italy's armed forces, Mussolini did solve the unemployment problem. Even more important, he rekindled the feelings of patriotism and nationalism that had lain dormant in the Italian people. He made it clear to Italians that it was in their destiny to recapture all the greatness that had made the glory of ancient Rome. He would use all the economic and human resources available to make Italy a great power again.

The Weimar Republic

While Mussolini was founding the Fascist party in Italy, the Allies were preoccupied with making sure that Germany would never again threaten the peace in Europe. As a result, the Versailles Treaty limited the size of Germany's armed forces and required the Germans to form a democratic government. While many Germans believed that democracy had become inevitable after the breakdown of the monarchy, few really believed in it.

In early 1919 Germans went to the polls and elected delegates to a national assembly. Meeting in **Weimar**, the assembly drafted a constitution for Germany establishing a democratic republic. The republic, which lasted from 1919 to 1933, was called the Weimar Republic.

Soon after the Weimar Republic became a reality, political instability and violence threatened to overwhelm it. In 1920 nationalist army officers tried to overthrow the government in a coup d'état. Like many other Germans, they claimed that Weimar leaders had betrayed the nation by accepting the Versailles Treaty. Although the revolt was suppressed, the government failed to overcome widespread opposition to its policies.

Reparations

More than just political problems threatened Germany. Great Britain and France promised their citizens that the German government would pay reparations for the full cost of the war. The Allies set this cost at $35 billion. Already beset by serious economic problems, the German government in 1922

Visualizing History **The blockade of Germany in World War I and postwar reparations on Germany brought hardships to many German citizens. These women in Berlin are searching in a garbage pile for food.** *What form of government did Germany have between 1919 and 1933?*

Chapter 29 Section 3

ABCNEWS INTERACTIVE™

VIDEODISC
Lessons of War

Side Two, Chapter 11
Frames 40065-44679
Title: *The Enemy*
Subject: A discussion of the process of "demonization," which causes people to see their enemies not as human beings
Ask: Why is it important for governments to "dehumanize" the enemy? *(When the enemy is dehumanized, soldiers and others are justified in their killing of the "monsters.")*

Daily Life Ask students to list some freedoms that we take for granted that would be suppressed under Fascist rule. Have a student read the United States Bill of Rights to stimulate a follow-up discussion. **L3**

History Simulation 29

Visualizing History German citizens struggled to survive in a time of increasing inflation. People in the United States were also finding food hard to get and spent hours waiting in breadlines or at soup kitchens.
Answer to Caption: *a democratic republic*

MEETING SPECIAL NEEDS ACTIVITY

Reading Comprehension Suggest that students who have difficulty reading the text take notes as they read. Have them list the headings and write any important ideas, events, and people under the headings. They should also write words they are unsure of and look them up in a dictionary as they study. By the end of the chapter, students will have completed a guide for studying. **L1**

Chapter 29 Section 3

Independent Practice

Guided Reading Activity 29-3 **L1**

Geography and History Activity 29

Biography Have students list the steps in Hitler's rise to power. They may begin with his forming the Brownshirts and conclude with his taking the title of *Der Führer*. **L1 LEP**

Critical Thinking Have students write short essays comparing and contrasting the ways Hitler and Mussolini rose to power. Instruct students to include the conditions that favored each ruler's coming to power. **L2**

Economics Ask students to research the topic of inflation. Have them find or calculate what the inflation rate of the German mark was in 1923, then compare that figure to the current inflation rates in Germany and the United States. **L3**

Global Gourmet

Italy is known for its traditional pasta dishes but it also has some foods that reflect German influence. Northeastern Italy has such dishes as sauerbraten, wurst, and strudel (marinated meat, sausage, and a pastry).

ASSESS

Check for Understanding

Assign Section 3 Review as homework or as an in-class activity.

Use Student Self-Test and Review Software to review Section 3.

announced that it could not meet its obligations.

France, however, insisted that Germany pay its debt. To ensure this result, French troops marched into Germany's industrial Ruhr Valley in 1923 and took control of the coal mines and steel mills. Angered at the French invasion, German workers went on strike while their government paid them. With income from Ruhr industries going to France, Germany had lost an important asset.

Inflation

To meet its growing expenses, the German government printed more and more paper money. As a result, inflation soared. Before the war, 4 marks equaled 1 American dollar. By the end of 1923, it took 4 trillion marks to equal 1 dollar. For members of the middle class, inflation was a disaster. It wiped out all their savings.

In the mid-1920s, Germany finally saw ahead some relief from its troubles. The French reached a compromise with the Germans that eased payments, and they left the Ruhr. Freed of debt and strengthened by American loans, Germany entered a five-year period of relative prosperity. But the seeds of discontent had already been sown.

Rise of Nazism

Among the many new political parties challenging the Weimar Republic's authority was the National Socialist Workers' party, or Nazi party. One of the first recruits to this new party was a World War I veteran named **Adolf Hitler**. Born in Austria in 1889, Hitler failed in his efforts to become a successful artist. After the war, he settled in Munich and joined the Nazi party.

Hitler soon formed the Brownshirts, a private army of young veterans and street thugs. During the inflationary crisis of 1923, Hitler made an attempt to seize power. With armed Brownshirts outside, Hitler jumped on a table in a Munich beer hall and announced, "The revolution has begun!" When the police intervened and arrested Hitler,

Images of the Times

Life in Nazi Germany

During the 1930s, Hitler's National Socialist party ruled Germany with an iron hand. Many Germans accepted the Nazi dictatorship, believing that it would solve the country's problems. Other Germans, however, suffered under Hitler's rule.

Adolf Hitler at a Nazi rally accepts flowers from a German child. German children were taught in schools to honor Hitler as Germany's savior.

German young people joined Nazi youth groups where they participated in parades and athletics and learned Nazi ideas.

784

Images of the Times **Life in Nazi Germany**

When the Nazis took power in 1933, terror against the Jews escalated. November 9, 1938—*Kristallnacht* (named "The Night of Broken Glass" because of the shattered glass strewn all over German cities)—marked the beginning of the Nazis' open persecution of the Jews. Almost 8,000 Jewish businesses were destroyed, homes were broken into and looted, and 177 synagogues were gutted. Main streets everywhere were littered with glass. This night of terror was the start of massive arrests and transportation of Jews to concentration camps.

however, the revolt quickly collapsed.

While in prison, Hitler wrote his autobiography, *Mein Kampf* (My Struggle). In Hitler's view, the Germans were not responsible for losing the war. He blamed the Jews and the Communists for the German defeat. He also declared that the Germans were a "master race" whose destiny was to rule the world. Hitler saw himself as the leader who would unite all German-speaking people into a new empire that would dominate other groups.

During the economic boom of the mid-1920s, the Nazis' influence declined. When the worldwide depression struck in 1929, however, the fortunes of the Nazi party revived. After listening to Hitler blame the depression on the Jews for three years, many Germans began to believe him. In 1932 the Nazis won 229 seats and became the largest party in the Reichstag (RYKS•tahg), the German parliament. On January 30, 1933, German President Paul von Hindenburg asked Hitler to become chancellor. Through entirely legal means, the Nazis had come to power.

Hitler in Power

Hitler's goal all along was the creation of a totalitarian state. Because the Nazis were still a minority in the Reichstag, however, he planned to hold a new election. But a week before it was to be held, the Reichstag building mysteriously caught fire and burned to the ground. Hoping to reduce Communist support among the workers, Hitler blamed the Communists for the fire. In the election, the Brownshirts forced German voters to back the Nazis. When the Nazi-dominated Reichstag met after the election, it voted Hitler emergency powers to deal with the "Communist threat."

Hitler used his new powers to crush his opponents and consolidate his rule. He banned all political parties except the Nazi party. He discarded constitutional guarantees of freedom of speech, assembly, religion, and press. He placed labor unions under Nazi control. The Nazi government regulated wages, working hours, housing, and the production of goods.

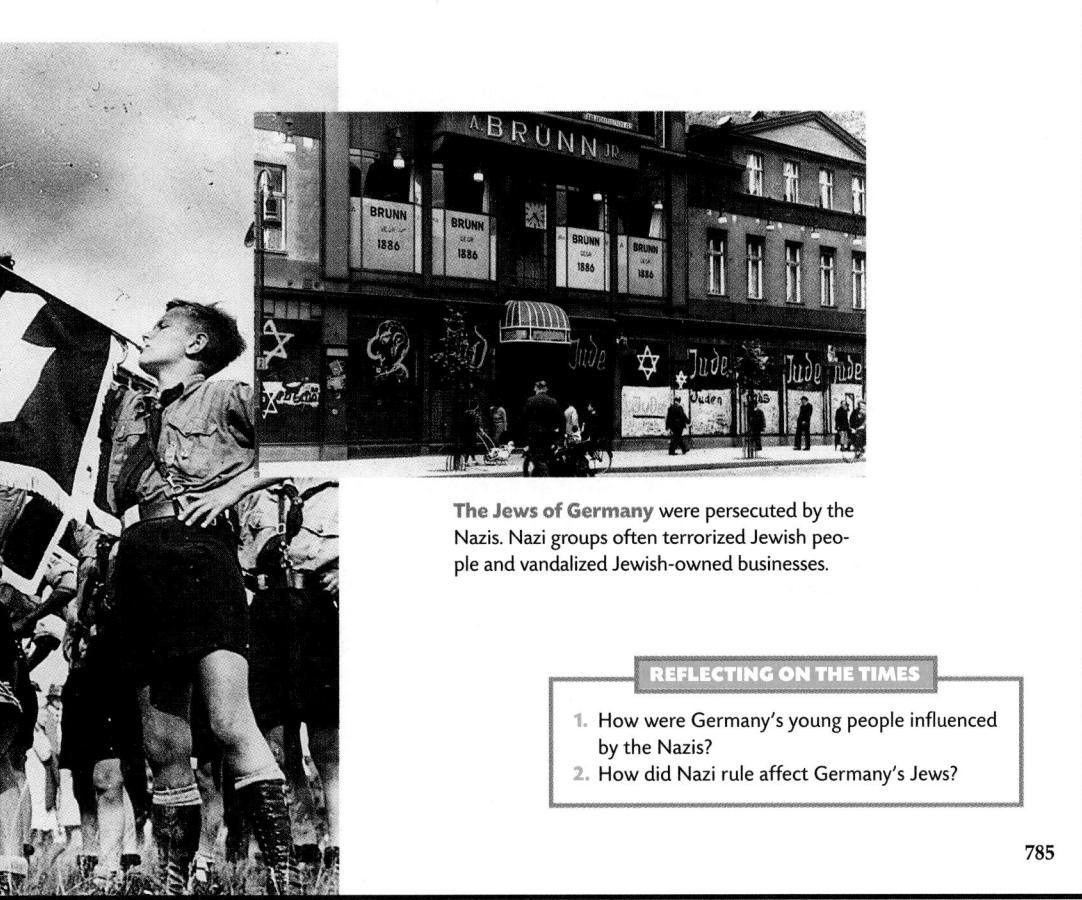

The Jews of Germany were persecuted by the Nazis. Nazi groups often terrorized Jewish people and vandalized Jewish-owned businesses.

REFLECTING ON THE TIMES

1. How were Germany's young people influenced by the Nazis?
2. How did Nazi rule affect Germany's Jews?

785

ANSWERS TO REFLECTING ON THE TIMES

1. Young people were taught Nazi ideas at school and in youth groups.
2. Hitler's rule led to the persecution of Germany's Jews.

Chapter 29 Section 3

Evaluate

Section Quiz 29-3

Reteach

Review with students the differences in postwar life in the United States, Great Britain, France, Italy, and Germany. Discuss the reasons democracy continued in the United States, France, and Great Britain, but not in Italy and Germany.

Enrich

Show students a documentary film of Nazi rallies in the 1930s such as the Nazi propaganda film *Triumph of the Will* or the American propaganda film *Nazi Strike*. Discuss the feelings they have after seeing and hearing Hitler speak.

Who?What?Where?When?

The Sound of Music, the Rodgers and Hammerstein musical, depicts the Nazi takeover of Austria.

Linking Past and Present

Anne Frank was a Jewish girl who kept a diary during the two years she spent hiding with her family in an attic in Amsterdam. She was arrested in 1944 and sent to the Nazi death camp at Bergen-Belsen, where she died at the age of 15. Her account, *The Diary of a Young Girl*, was published in 1952. More than thirty years later, in 1987, Miep Gies, the woman who hid the Frank family, wrote her own story, *Anne Frank Remembered*, about life under Nazi occupation and what she remembers of Anne Frank.

Chapter 29 Section 3

Visualizing History Point out the Hitler salute in the photo and explain that this "Heil Hitler" salute became a famous gesture associated with Hitler.

Answer to Caption: *Hitler wanted to expand German territory and make it into a mighty world power.*

CLOSE

Hold a class discussion to help students outline what led to the rise of Fascist dictatorships in Italy and Germany. For each country, have students create a flowchart of the events on the chalkboard. Encourage students to copy the flowchart and use it for reference.

Visualizing History After becoming dictator of Germany in 1933, Adolf Hitler often held large rallies to inspire the loyalty of Germans. Hitler also adopted the slogan *Ein Volk, Ein Reich, Ein Führer* (One People, One Empire, One Leader). *What ambitions did Adolf Hitler have for Germany?*

Attacks on the Jews

Hitler directed his most bitter attacks against the Jews. In 1935 the Nuremberg Laws stripped Jews of their citizenship and their right to hold public office. The laws barred Jewish students from schools and destroyed Jewish businesses. The Nazis forced Jews to wear yellow badges on their clothing. In the *Kristallnacht*, members of the Nazi party attacked Jews on the streets and vandalized Jewish businesses, homes, and synagogues. Hitler's secret police, the Gestapo, arrested Jews and other opponents of the government by the thousands. Many of these opponents were shot. Others were sent to concentration camps, large prison camps where political prisoners or refugees were confined.

Hitler was suspicious of even his closest supporters. He particularly feared radical members among the Brownshirts and set out to purge their ranks. In 1934 Hitler had hundreds of Brownshirts and their leaders shot.

The Third Reich

Assured of absolute power, Hitler took the title of *der Führer* (duhr FYUR•uhr), "the Leader." He called his government the Third Reich (RYK), or Third Empire, and boasted it would last 1,000 years. To reach this end, he set about restoring Germany's military might. He ignored the provisions of the Versailles Treaty, which limited the size of the German army, and ordered German factories to begin turning out guns, ammunition, airplanes, tanks, and other weapons. He made no secret of his ambitions to expand Germany's territory: "Today, Germany; tomorrow, the world!"

Hitler also brought all intellectual and artistic activity in Germany under his control and imposed his own ideas on the arts. To glorify Nazism, he made plans to rebuild Berlin in the style of monumental classical architecture. He discouraged the artistic experimentation that had flourished during the 1920s. As a result, many of Germany's most talented artists and scientists—among whom were Walter Gropius, Arnold Schoenberg, Sigmund Freud, and Albert Einstein—fled the country.

Hitler actively used the press, radio, and movies to flood Germany with propaganda praising the Nazi cause. In its propaganda, the government stressed the importance of a strong military and devotion to the nation and its leader. Hitler also set up organizations for young people between the ages of 6 and 18. These organizations aimed to mold German youth to accept Nazi ideas.

SECTION 3 REVIEW

Recall

1. **Define** fascism, corporate state, syndicate, *Kristallnacht*, concentration camp.
2. **Identify** Benito Mussolini, Adolf Hitler, Weimar.
3. **Explain** how World War I affected Italy economically.

Critical Thinking

4. **Analyzing Information** Why did fascism appeal to many Italians and Germans in the decade following World War I?

Understanding Themes

5. **Uniformity** Describe the way Hitler treated Germany's Jewish population during the 1930s.

SECTION 3 REVIEW ANSWERS

1. All vocabulary words are defined in the Glossary.
2. Benito Mussolini, 781; Weimar, 783; Adolf Hitler, 784
3. Italy had huge war debts, unemployment was high, and its economy was seriously damaged.
4. because the economic and social chaos created by war and depression made both Italy and Germany ripe for Fascist-style revolution
5. UNIFORMITY He took away their citizenship and right to hold office; barred them from schools; destroyed their businesses; and had them attacked, arrested, shot, or sent to concentration camps.

Study and Writing

SKILLS

Preparing Note Cards for a Research Report

Writing a research report can be a difficult task or a fascinating adventure. It depends on two main factors: your attitude and your level of organization.

Attitude is important. If possible, select a topic that interests you. Then approach your research as a detective approaches a mystery. Pose questions and look for answers. This process requires both time and patience. Good organization can make research easier and exciting.

Learning the Skill

Note cards are a great tool for preparing a research report. They let you record and combine related facts and ideas from several sources.

Suppose your research topic is "The Growth of the Aviation in the 1920s." First, list some main idea questions such as, "What technological advances were made in this decade?" "What were the most popular aircraft?" "What was the life of a barnstormer like?" "Who were the most famous pilots and why?"

At the library, search for books and other materials about early aviation. In each source, skim the table of contents and index for sections referring to your questions. Do not try to read entire books! This will distract you from the focus of your report.

Suppose you find the book, *The Sound of Wings, The Life of Amelia Earhart* by Mary Lovell. On a note card, write the main idea: "Most famous pilots." Then write information about the source: the book's title, author, publisher, and the page numbers where relevant information appears. Take notes on the information explaining how Earhart became the most famous woman pilot of the decade.

If you find answers to other main idea questions in the same book, write these facts on separate cards. Each card should begin with a main idea and source information. You need source information for two reasons: 1) you may have to find the information again to clarify points, and 2) you will need it to create a bibliography for your report.

As your research proceeds, group together note cards from different sources on the same main idea. When you leave the library, you should have enough information to write about each subtopic.

Practicing the Skill

Suppose you are researching a report on the rise of fascism in Europe between the two World Wars. For each numbered note card below, complete the missing information. Use your textbook as the source for all cards.

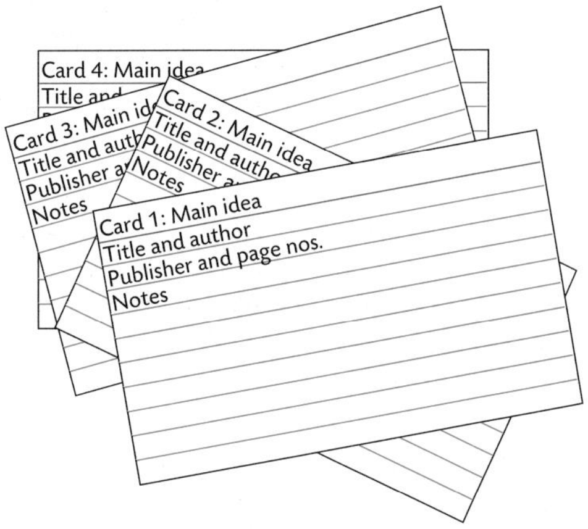

Applying the Skill

Choose a topic and write six main idea questions about it. At the library, find sources on this topic and prepare at least one note card on each main idea. Be sure to include source information.

For More Practice

Turn to the Skill Practice in the Chapter Review on page 793 for more practice in preparing note cards for a research report.

Study and Writing

SKILLS

TEACH

Preparing Note Cards for a Research Report Remind students to put only key words and ideas on the cards. Too much information on one card will be confusing. They should, however, include some quotes on the cards, especially when a famous person's exact words are revealing of his or her character. Suggest to students that when creating a number of cards from the material in a single source, it can be helpful to use an abbreviation for the source on all cards after the first one, which should always contain complete source information. Or they might want to write a special bibliography card for the source, which gives its bibliographical information.

Additional Practice

Skill Reinforcement Activity 29

Writer's Guidebook, Lesson 10

ANSWERS TO PRACTICING THE SKILL

Answers will vary. Possible main ideas include: conditions in Italy that led to the rise of fascism; how Mussolini gained power; conditions after World War I that made Germany ripe for racism; how Hitler and the Nazis came to power. All cards should give correct bibliographic information for this textbook. Notes should reflect an accurate reading of the text.

Chapter 29 *Between Two Fires* 787

Chapter 29 Section 4

SECTION THEME

▶ **Uniformity** Communist leaders in the Soviet Union impose state control on society and crush opposition.

Find Out

Answer: *Stalin's rule created a climate of repression and terror, purged the nation of those who opposed him, and put all artistic and cultural activities under the Communist party's control.*

FOCUS

Section Objective

Examine how Joseph Stalin's rule transformed the Soviet Union.

BELLRINGER Motivational Activity

Before taking roll at the beginning of the class period, project Section Focus Transparency 29-4 and have students answer the activity questions. Discuss students' responses.

This activity is also available as a blackline master.

Vocabulary Pre-check

Use the Vocabulary PuzzleMaker to create a puzzle that reinforces the vocabulary terms in this section. **L1**

1920 — 1930 — 1940

1921 Lenin announces New Economic Policy.

1928 Stalin promotes collective farms.

1932 "Terror famine" sweeps Ukraine.

Section 4

The Soviet Union

Setting the Scene

▶ **Terms to Define**
nationalization, dictatorship of the proletariat, collectivization, kulak, purge, Socialist realism

▶ **People to Meet**
Vladimir Ilyich Ulyanov (Lenin), Leon Trotsky, Joseph Stalin, Maksim Gorky

▶ **Places to Locate**
Georgia, Ukraine

Find Out How did Joseph Stalin's rule transform the Soviet Union?

The Storyteller

It was 35 degrees below zero when the team set out for work at Magnitogorsk. They would weld fittings to the blast furnaces 100 feet off the ground. It was hazardous work, for ice coated every surface. Three hours into the day a rigger fell off the scaffolding. Badly injured, he was carried to the first-aid station. His shaken companions talked of the need to improve the scaffolding. The foreman, however, blamed the workers. "You ploughboys don't know how to be careful. You don't pay as much attention as you should. People will fall, but we are building blast furnaces all the same, aren't we?"

Soviet construction project

—adapted from *Behind the Urals: An American Worker in Russia's City of Steel*, John Scott, reprinted in *The Global Experience*, Volume 2, 1987

By 1921 Russia had endured the horrors of world war, revolution, and civil war. In the course of seven years of conflict, 27 million Russians had perished. Most had died on the battlefields and in countless guerrilla engagements, but millions had died of disease and starvation as well. In addition, the nation's transport system was in ruins, the peasants were in open revolt, and the economy was plunging toward collapse. At the Tenth Party Congress, Red Army director Leon Trotsky proclaimed: "We have destroyed the country in order to defeat the Whites."

Lenin in Power

In their struggle for survival during the civil war, **Vladimir Ilyich Ulyanov** (ool•YAH•nuhf), also known as **Lenin**, and the Bolsheviks had introduced an economic policy called war communism in 1918. Under war communism, the government carried out a policy of nationalization, in which it brought under state control all major industries. Applying the principle that those who would eat must work, the government required everyone between the ages of 16 and 50 to hold a job. It also erected a huge bureaucratic administration that wielded tremendous power but was extremely inefficient.

In 1921 Lenin tried to bring order out of the chaos that both war and government policy had caused. He announced a plan called the New Economic Policy, or NEP. Major industries such as steel, railroads, and large-scale manufacturing remained under government control. But in an attempt to stimulate the economy, Lenin allowed some private businesses to operate. In a startling departure from Marxist theory, NEP permitted small manufacturers and farmers to own their own businesses and to sell what they produced for a profit.

In 1922 the Communists changed the official name of the country from Russia to the Union of

SECTION RESOURCES

Reproducible Masters
- Reproducible Lesson Plan 29-4
- Guided Reading Activity 29-4
- Reteaching Activity 29
- Enrichment Activity 29
- Section Quiz 29-4
- Performance Assessment Activity 29
- Spanish Chapter Summary 29

Transparencies
- Section Focus Transparency 29-4

Multimedia
- Vocabulary PuzzleMaker Software
- Student Self-Test and Review Software
- Testmaker
- Communism and the Cold War: *Growing Up Communist*

Soviet Socialist Republics (USSR), or the Soviet Union. During this time, Lenin and other Communist leaders also completed a new constitution. This constitution stated that the USSR was a Socialist state, meaning that the government controlled the means of production.

In theory this state, called the dictatorship of the proletariat, was controlled by workers. But in practice the leadership of the Communist party controlled the workers. It was, as German Communist party member Rosa Luxemburg observed: "... a dictatorship, to be sure, not the dictatorship of the proletariat, however, but only the dictatorship of a handful of politicians." The classless society envisioned by Marx was, in the Soviet Union, a pyramid, with the party boss at the top and the peasants at the bottom.

The non-Russian nationalities in the USSR did not fare much better than the peasants. Because Lenin did not want to break up the old Russian Empire into independent states, he gave each major nationality its own republic with its own bureaucracy. In reality, however, the central government in Moscow still made the important decisions for these republics. In spite of the government's talk about equality for all nationalities, the Russians remained the dominant group in the Soviet Union and largely determined its policies.

Visualizing History **Lenin's New Economic Policy (NEP) helped put the Soviet Union's economy back on its feet in the early 1920s.** *In what way did NEP depart from Marxist theory?*

Trotsky and Stalin

In 1922 Lenin suffered two strokes that left him permanently disabled. He died two years later at the age of 54.

The struggle to succeed Lenin began during his final illness. The two main contenders for the position were **Leon Trotsky** and **Joseph Stalin**. Next to Lenin, Trotsky had been the most important person in the Communist party. He had played a key role in the Bolshevik Revolution and had built the Red Army into a powerful fighting force. Trotsky came from a middle-class background and was a scholar who contributed many new ideas to the Marxist movement. He was also a speaker of great power and eloquence.

Born in **Georgia**, a territory south of Russia, Stalin was the son of artisans. A seminary student in his youth, Stalin was punished for reading books about revolution and social conditions, including novels such as *Les Misérables*. Stalin later renounced Russian Orthodoxy and became a Marxist revolutionary. Unlike Trotsky, Stalin was a skilled administrator. In 1922 he rose to the important post of secretary general of the Communist party.

Trotsky and Stalin held fundamentally different views about the path the Soviet Union should follow. Like Lenin, Trotsky believed in the theory of a "permanent revolution." He believed that only when the Russian Revolution had touched off uprisings all over the world could Socialists build an ideal society in the Soviet Union. Stalin, in contrast, declared it possible and necessary to "build socialism in a single country." By this he meant that the Soviet Union should concentrate on growing strong first, before it tried to spread revolution around the world.

Trotsky was better known than Stalin, both at home and in the Comintern (Communist International), an organization of Communist parties from all over the world. Moreover, Trotsky had been closer to Lenin. Nevertheless, Stalin managed to outmaneuver Trotsky politically. As secretary general, Stalin had the authority to appoint and remove officials. He gradually gained control of the party bureaucracy. As soon as he was securely in power, Stalin exiled Trotsky to Siberia and then expelled him from the Soviet Union. Trotsky eventually settled in Mexico City, where he continued to write about communism and the Soviet Union. An assassin acting on Stalin's orders murdered him in 1940.

TEACH

Guided Practice

THEME Uniformity

Ask students to imagine the United States government taking total control of all industrial and agricultural production. Have students tell ways such control would change daily life. *(Average citizens could not own businesses; the government would control the supply of food and industrial products.)* Ask students how they would react to such a government. **L1**

Visualizing History Lenin's New Economic Policy was a radical change that opened the way for a modified form of capitalism. Whereas selling for profit had once been a crime against the state, it was now officially encouraged. However, along with Lenin's strategy to get the economy moving came a new tightening of discipline.

Answer to Caption: *It allowed small manufacturers and farmers to own businesses and sell their products for a profit.*

Literature Lead a discussion on Socialist realism, or the literary and artistic style that became obligatory under Stalin's rule. Ask what the aim of art was under Socialist realism. Discuss how this style stifled artistic expression. **L3**

Independent Practice

Guided Reading Activity 29-4 **L1**

COOPERATIVE LEARNING ACTIVITY

Advertising Plans Organize the class into three groups and have each group create an advertising plan. One group's plan should promote the Bolshevik policy of communism, or government control over all major industries; another group should promote Lenin's New Economic Policy (NEP), which allowed some private businesses to operate but maintained government control over steel, railroads, and large-scale manufacturing; the last group should create an advertisement to support Stalin's Five-Year Plan, which set Soviet economic goals for that period and brought industrial and agricultural production under government control. Each group should research its topic, create an advertisement, and select someone to present it. **L2**

ABCNEWS INTERACTIVE™

VIDEODISC
Communism and the Cold War

Side One, Chapter 9
Frames 14929–17326
Title: *Growing Up Communist*
Subject: Soviet journalists describe what it was like growing up in a Communist society
Ask: What did the leaders of the Soviet Union feel they could teach the world? *(to work collectively)*

Daily Life Have students imagine that they are Soviet citizens under Stalin's rule. Have them write letters describing life in the Soviet Union to relatives who live in the United States. **L2 LEP**

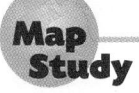

Map Study

Answer

This land gave Russia greater access to the Black Sea and created a larger buffer between Germany and Russia.

Map Skills Practice

Reading a Map What countries on the Baltic Sea did Russia lose in 1918? *(Estonia, Latvia, Lithuania)*

ASSESS

Check for Understanding

Assign Section 4 Review as homework or as an in-class activity.

Use Student Self-Test and Review Software to review Section 4.

Russia 1914–1922

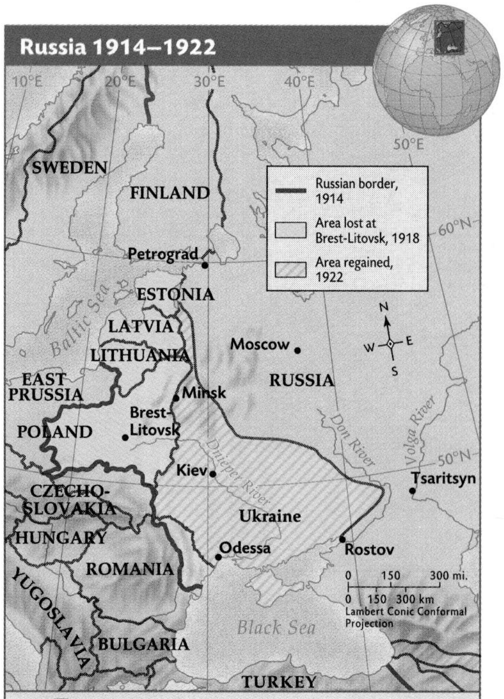

Map Study Russia gave up a vast amount of territory in the 1918 Treaty of Brest-Litovsk.
Region Why was the land Russia regained by 1922 particularly valuable to the nation?

Five-Year Plans

Fearing war with the Western democracies, Stalin wanted to rapidly transform the Soviet Union into a leading industrial power. In 1928 he declared an end to NEP and announced the first of his Five-Year Plans, a program that set economic goals for a five-year period. The plan brought all industrial and agricultural production under government control. It also provided for housing, health care, and other services.

While promising a better future, Stalin demanded sacrifices from the Soviet people. The first Five-Year Plan concentrated on building heavy industry. Consumer goods were produced in small amounts and were of inferior quality.

Responsibility for administering the plan lay in the hands of bureaucrats in Moscow. Theirs was a difficult task requiring tight control and careful planning. Not surprisingly, they made plenty of mistakes. For example, one Soviet enterprise purchased its nail supply from a nail factory many miles away, while a nail factory across the street was shipping its goods a similar distance. Despite the mistakes, the first Five-Year Plan was a success in spurring industrial growth.

Collective Farms

In agriculture, Stalin's plan called for collectivization, a system of farming in which the government owned the land and used peasants to farm it. Stalin believed that collective farms would be more efficient. They would not only produce food for the Soviet people but produce it for export as well. By increasing agricultural exports, Stalin hoped to pay for Soviet industrialization without borrowing from the capitalist West.

Stalin also planned to use collectivization to intimidate the Soviet Union's peasant majority, most of whom were fiercely anti-Communist. Kulaks, or the most prosperous peasants, especially opposed collectivization. They had prospered under NEP and did not want to give up their land, livestock, and machinery. Fighting broke out in the countryside when the government tried to impose its plans. Thousands of peasants and their families were killed or arrested and sent to labor camps in Siberia. Stalin also took measures to crush anti-Communist resistance in **Ukraine**. By seizing the region's grain during the terrible winter of 1932, Stalin promoted a "terror famine," causing the deaths of more than 5 million Ukrainian peasants.

Results

The first Five-Year Plan transformed the Soviet Union into an industrial power, but the human cost of the plan was enormous. Industrial workers received low wages, or none at all, and food was often limited in quantity. Millions of people died because of rural unrest, and collective farms were often unable to provide enough grain to feed the nation's population.

Stalin's Dictatorship

Stalin ruled the Soviet Union from the mid-1920s until his death in 1953. During this period he established one of the most brutal dictatorships the world has ever seen.

Secret Police

Stalin demanded complete obedience from the people he ruled and got it through an effective use of terror. He granted the secret police immense power, which they used to scrutinize every aspect

MEETING SPECIAL NEEDS ACTIVITY

Study Strategy To visually clarify the information in this section, have students create a chart that summarizes the changes brought about by Lenin and Stalin in the Soviet Union. Headings for one axis of the chart might include *Major Industries, Small Businesses, Agriculture, Non-Russian Nationalities, Communist Party, The Arts, Comintern*. Headings for the other axis would be *Stalin, Lenin*. **L2**

of the nation's social and political life. Agents of the secret police encouraged workers to spy on each other and children to spy on their parents. Those accused of disloyalty were either shot or sent to labor camps in Siberia. The secret police and their activities helped to create a climate of fear in Soviet society.

Visualizing History **The Soviet government used posters to glorify Soviet achievements and to urge people to carry out the goals of the Communist party.** *How did Stalin strengthen his hold on the Soviet Union and the Communist party?*

Purges

In the 1930s Stalin began a methodical attack upon his potential enemies. Even members of the Communist party did not escape the reach of Stalin and his secret police. In 1934 an unknown assailant, probably acting on Stalin's orders, assassinated a high party official. Stalin used the event to rid himself of opponents and strengthen his hold on the party. He had millions of Communist party members expelled from the party, arrested and put in labor camps, or shot.

Stalin then turned against the Old Bolsheviks. These officials had been associates of Lenin and Stalin in the early days of the movement. Because some of them had sided with Trotsky, Stalin moved in 1936 to purge, or remove, them from any position where they could threaten his leadership. He had them arrested and put on trial. In open court in Moscow, with foreign reporters looking on, they pleaded guilty to false charges of treason, murder, and other crimes. Although these prisoners showed no signs of mistreatment, many Western experts have since concluded that the secret police used psychological torture to break their wills.

The Arts

Stalin also set out to put all artistic and cultural activities under the Communist party's control. In 1934 he put **Maksim Gorky**, one of the Soviet Union's leading writers, in charge of all Soviet culture. Gorky promoted a new literary style that soon became obligatory in the arts: Socialist realism. Writers and artists created a "new reality" by glorifying Soviet heroes and achievements, while denouncing the rumors about forced labor and terror. Artists who violated these dictates faced exile or imprisonment in labor camps.

Stalin's restrictions had a chilling effect on Soviet artists. Although talented writers and artists struggled to survive, most official artistic works were predictable and uninspiring.

The Comintern

In 1919 Lenin had established the Communist International, or Comintern. The goal of the Comintern was to encourage Communist parties in other countries to overthrow their governments by legal or illegal means and to establish Soviet-style regimes. While Stalin at first gave low priority to Comintern affairs, he later took more seriously the relations of the Soviet Union to the Communist parties in other countries. Stalin eventually decided to dissolve the Comintern in 1944, to win the favor and approval of the Western Allies during World War II.

SECTION 4 REVIEW

Recall

1. **Define** nationalization, dictatorship of the proletariat, collectivization, kulak, purge, Socialist realism.
2. **Identify** Vladimir Ilyich Ulyanov (Lenin), Leon Trotsky, Joseph Stalin, Maksim Gorky, Georgia, Ukraine.
3. **Explain** why Lenin began the New Economic Policy.

Critical Thinking

4. **Analyzing Information** How did Stalin transform the Soviet economy? What effects did Stalin's economic policies have on the Soviet people? Are these effects still felt today? Explain.

Understanding Themes

5. **Uniformity** Predict what might have happened if Trotsky—and not Stalin—had succeeded Lenin.

SECTION 4 REVIEW ANSWERS

1. All vocabulary words are defined in the Glossary.
2. Lenin, 788; Trotsky, 789; Stalin, 789; Georgia, 789; Ukraine, 790; Gorky, 791
3. Lenin wanted to revive the economy, which had been devastated by war.
4. Stalin's Five-Year Plan brought all major industries and agriculture under government control. The plan caused the people to have to sacrifice with fewer and inferior consumer goods and low wages. There are still serious shortages of foods and other goods today.
5. **UNIFORMITY** Answers will vary. Students may conclude that Trotsky's regime may have been less repressive.

Visualizing History Stalin also spread propaganda by bombarding the Soviets with his portraits—they were hung in schoolrooms and every public building.

Answer to Caption: *He used terror tactics to demand obedience. He expelled millions of Communists from the party. All Soviet citizens accused of disloyalty were arrested and either placed in labor camps or shot.*

Evaluate

Section Quiz 29-4

Use the Testmaker to create a customized quiz for Section 4.

Reteach

Review with students the economic and cultural changes that took place under Lenin and Stalin. Discuss these items from the points of view of the leaders and the general public.

Reteaching Activity 29

Enrich

Books and music can bring the period to life. Suggest that students read *And Quiet Flows the Don* by Mikhail Sholokov or listen to the music of Rimsky-Korsakov or Shostakovich.

Enrichment Activity 29

CLOSE

Have students discuss what postwar life was like for the average citizen in the Soviet Union. Have students compare this picture to postwar life in Italy, Germany, and the Western democracies.

Chapter 29 Review

GLENCOE TECHNOLOGY

VIDEODISC

Use MindJogger to review students' knowledge of the chapter.

MindJogger Videoquiz

Chapter 29
Disc 4 Side B

Also available in VHS.

Answers

Using Key Terms

1. f	**6.** d
2. g	**7.** k
3. i	**8.** c
4. l	**9.** j
5. b	**10.** a

Using Your History Journal

Be sure students have used some quotes from the interviews.

Reviewing Facts

1. automobiles, radios, vacuum cleaners, packaged foods, refrigerators, movies, and electric irons
2. T. S. Eliot, new style of writing; Pablo Picasso, introduced cubism, Salvador Dali, surrealist paintings; Arnold Schoenberg, brought 12-note scale to music.
3. Americans were weary of war and international problems.
4. war debts, unemployment, inflation, charismatic leader
5. war debts, inflation, unemployment, political instability, charismatic leader (Hitler) fostered belief in supremacy of Germans
6. Mussolini formed the Fascists, gave the state absolute authority; Hitler joined the new Nazi party and crushed Communist opponents until he gained control.
7. put major industries under government control but permitted small manufacturers and farmers to own businesses
8. Stalin was a more skilled administrator and used his post to gain control politically.

Critical Thinking

1. It radically changed the way people looked at the world.
2. caused Dali to try a new art form named surrealism and Joyce to explore inner thoughts by writing in a style called "stream of consciousness"
3. League of Nations; United States and France signed Kellogg-Briand Pact denouncing war; an international conference on disarmament
4. It describes the terrorizing and assault on Jews and their property by the Nazis.
5. Possible answer: the Allies should have

CHAPTER 29 REVIEW

Historical Significance

After World War I, scientists and artists in the West broke with old traditions and sought a "new reality." Meanwhile, economic and political instability posed challenges to democratic societies, which took emergency steps to save their economies. In lands where democracy was weak, such as Italy and Germany, social and economic upheaval led to the rise of Fascist governments. At the same time, a brutal Communist dictatorship emerged in the Soviet Union. Tensions between totalitarian and democratic nations paved the way for a new global conflict.

Using Key Terms

Write the key term that best completes each sentence.

a. cubism	g. concentration camps
b. coalition	h. disarmament
c. surrealism	i. corporate state
d. fascism	j. nationalization
e. purge	k. *Kristallnacht*
f. kulaks	l. general strike

1. Stalin imposed harsh measures on the ________, prosperous peasants who opposed the introduction of collective farms.
2. Many opponents of the Nazi government in Germany were sent to __________.
3. Under the ________, Mussolini hoped to bring workers and employers together.
4. In 1926 Great Britain faced a ________, which involved a large number of workers from many different trade unions.
5. Because there were numerous political parties, the formation of a government in France required a ___________ of several parties.
6. ________ is a political philosophy that glorifies the state, supports a single-party system under a strong leader, and promotes an aggressive form of nationalism.
7. In the __________, members of the Nazi party attacked Jews on the streets and vandalized Jewish businesses, homes, and synagogues.
8. The art form of __________ used dreamlike images and unnatural combinations of objects.
9. Under war communism, the Bolshevik government carried out a policy of ____________, in which it brought all major industries under government control.
10. _______ is an abstract art form that uses combinations of geometric shapes.

Using Your History Journal

Use your notes from the interview of a person who lived through the period between the wars. Write an account of how events affected ordinary people's lives.

Reviewing Facts

1. **List** the technological advances in the 1920s and 1930s that had an important impact on people's lives.
2. **Identify** three artists who produced revolutionary changes in literature, art, music, or architecture. Describe the contributions each made.
3. **Explain** why the United States retreated into a period of isolationism after World War I.
4. **Explain** the factors that led to the rise of fascism in Italy.
5. **Discuss** the rise of Nazism in Germany.
6. **Explain** how Hitler and Mussolini strengthened their political power.
7. **Identify** Lenin's New Economic Policy (NEP).
8. **Describe** how Stalin was able to defeat Trotsky in their struggle for power.

Critical Thinking

1. **Apply** Why was World War I a watershed event in the twentieth century?
2. **Apply** How did Freud's theories affect the work of James Joyce and Salvador Dali?
3. **Analyze** What steps did Americans and Europeans take in the 1920s to prevent another world war?

792 **Chapter 29** *Between Two Fires*

4. **Analyze** How does the term "Night of Terror" describe *Kristallnacht*?
5. **Synthesize** To aid Germany's economic recovery after World War I, how might the Allies have structured the peace settlements?
6. **Compare** How does fascism differ from communism?
7. **Analyze** Salvador Dali, a surrealist, was influenced by Sigmund Freud. How is Freud's influence evident in *The Persistence of Memory*, painted in 1931?

The Persistence of Memory, Salvador Dali. *Museum of Modern Art, New York, New York*

Understanding Themes

1. **Innovation** How did new movements in literature, art, and music reflect the change in the way many people viewed the world following World War I?
2. **Change** How was Roosevelt's New Deal similar to Stalin's Five-Year Plan? How was it different?
3. **Uniformity** How and why did the leaders of Nazi Germany suppress opponents and minorities?
4. **Uniformity** How did Lenin try to unify all non-Russian republics under one government?

Linking Past and Present

1. During the 1920s and 1930s the automobile, motion pictures, and the radio transformed the way Americans lived. What technological advances shape our lives today? Do they have a negative or a positive impact on society? Explain.

2. Fascist regimes came to power in Italy and Germany primarily because of political and economic weakness. Name a country that today is ruled by a dictator or a one-party system. How did this person or party come to power?

Skill Practice

Using Chapter 29 of this text as a source, prepare one note card on each main idea below.

1. How did technology change people's lives in the postwar era?
2. What new artistic forms emerged after World War I?
3. What was the New Deal?
4. What were Lenin's greatest achievements?

Geography in History

1. **Location** Refer to the map below. What are the relative locations of Estonia, Latvia, and Lithuania?
2. **Place** In which countries did fascist governments come to power during the 1930s?
3. **Region** In what region of Europe were 10 of the 11 democracies in the 1930s?

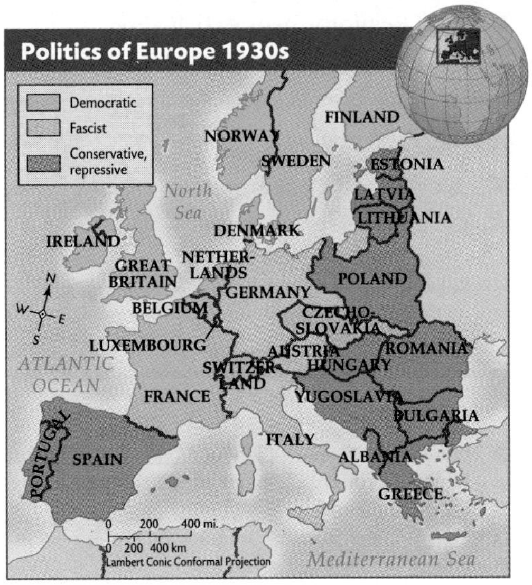

Chapter 29 Review

imposed milder terms on Germany and reduced its war debt payments.

6. Fascism defended private property and the class structure and made the cause of the nation supreme. Communism, at least theoretically, did away with private property and class distinction and worked for an international proletarian revolution.
7. Answers should mention that the bizarre images reflect Dali's attempt to explore the unconscious mind.

Understanding Themes

1. **INNOVATION** reflected disillusionment and search for new ideas and ways of portraying the world
2. **CHANGE** Both plans brought enormous changes in the two countries and increased the governments' involvement in social and economic affairs. The New Deal did not demand great sacrifices from the people.
3. **UNIFORMITY** Hitler used the Gestapo to terrorize the people. He purged dissidents to secure his dictatorship.
4. **UNIFORMITY** gave each nationality its own republic but had Moscow make the important decisions

Linking Past and Present

1. the computer, lasers, microwaves, and televisions
2. Answers may detail Castro's Cuba and Saddam Hussein's Iraq.

Skill Practice

1. technology: automobiles, radios, home appliances; results—more mobility, better communication, more leisure
2. literary styles—stream of consciousness and James Joyce; art—Dali and surrealism, Picasso and cubism; music—jazz with Louis Armstrong, 12 notes of Schoenberg; architecture—Walter Gropius and Bauhaus school
3. Franklin D. Roosevelt, 1933, regulated banks, people back to work, attempt to end Depression
4. NEP, helped economy, new constitution

Geography in History

1. Lithuania lies just north of Poland, Latvia just above Lithuania, and Estonia just above Latvia; all three border the Baltic Sea.
2. Germany, Italy
3. northwestern Europe

Chapter Bonus Test Question

Ask students: Given the state in which Germany, Italy, and Russia found themselves after World War I, could they have achieved economic health and national self-respect by any means other than totalitarianism? Explain your answer.

Teach, Reinforce, and Extend CHAPTER Content

Nationalism in Asia, Africa, and Latin America

CHAPTER RESOURCES

	Reproducible Resources	Multimedia Resources
Chapter Opener	Chapter Themes: Graphic Organizer 30 Historical Significance Chapter Activity 30	MindJogger Videoquiz
Chapter Enrichment	Vocabulary Activity 30* Time Line Activity 30 Mapping History Activity 30 History Simulation 30 Geography and History Activity 30 Source Reading 30 People in World History Profiles 57, 58 World Literature Selection 7 World Art and Music Activity 30 Enrichment Activity 30 Critical Thinking Activity 30 Skill Reinforcement Activity 30 Performance Assessment Activity 30	World History and Art Transparency 40, *Zapatistas*; 41, *Turkestan Oriental Rugs* Chapter Transparency 30 Vocabulary PuzzleMaker Software In the Holy Land: *Arab violence 1919–1921* Lessons of War: *Philosophy of Nonviolence*
Chapter Review/Reteaching	Reteaching Activity 30 Skill Reinforcement Activity 30 Spanish Chapter Summary 30	Chapter 30 Digest Audiocassette, Activity, Test* Vocabulary PuzzleMaker Software Student Self-Test and Review Software MindJogger Videoquiz
Chapter Evaluation/Testing	Performance Assessment Activity 30 Chapter 30 Test, Forms A and B	Testmaker

* *Also available in Spanish*

0:00 OUT OF TIME? Assign the Chapter 30 summary in the Unit 7 Digest on pages 854–857, and the Chapter 30 Audiocassettes.

Block Schedule

Block scheduling differs from traditional class scheduling in the amount of time allotted to each period. The extended time frame provided by block scheduling affords you the opportunity to implement a greater number of research-oriented and activity-intense projects to motivate and involve your students. Activities that are particularly suited to use within the block scheduling framework are identified throughout this chapter by the following designation.

KEY TO ABILITY LEVELS

Teaching strategies have been coded for varying learning styles and abilities.

- **L1** **BASIC** activities for all students
- **L2** **AVERAGE** activities for average to above-average students
- **L3** **CHALLENGING** activities for above-average students
- **LEP** **LIMITED ENGLISH PROFICIENCY** activities

A complete, 1-page lesson plan is provided for each section in the *Reproducible Lesson Plans* booklet.

SECTION RESOURCES

Daily Objectives	Reproducible Resources	Multimedia Resources
Section 1 New Forces in the Middle East and Africa Identify how the forces of nationalism affected events in the Middle East and Africa after World War I.	Reproducible Lesson Plan 30-1 Vocabulary Activity 30* Guided Reading Activity 30-1* People in World History Profile 58 Section Quiz 30-1*	Section Focus Transparency 30-1 Chapter Transparency 30 Student Self-Test and Review Software Testmaker In the Holy Land: *Arab violence 1919–1921*
Section 2 India's Struggle for Independence State the methods Gandhi used in India's struggle for independence from British rule.	Reproducible Lesson Plan 30-2 Vocabulary Activity 30* Guided Reading Activity 30-2* Section Quiz 30-2*	Section Focus Transparency 30-2 Student Self-Test and Review Software Testmaker Lessons of War: *Philosophy of Nonviolence*
Section 3 China's Drive for Modernization Explain the factors that divided and the factors that united nationalist forces in China.	Reproducible Lesson Plan 30-3 Vocabulary Activity 30* Guided Reading Activity 30-3* Time Line Activity 30 Section Quiz 30-3*	Section Focus Transparency 30-3 Student Self-Test and Review Software Testmaker
Section 4 Militarism in Japan Describe how militarism shaped the development of Japan after World War I.	Reproducible Lesson Plan 30-4 Vocabulary Activity 30* Guided Reading Activity 30-4* History Simulation 30 Mapping History Activity 30 Section Quiz 30-4*	Section Focus Transparency 30-4 Student Self-Test and Review Software Testmaker
Section 5 Nationalism in Latin America Analyze why nationalism in Latin America brought conflict with the United States.	Reproducible Lesson Plan 30-5 Vocabulary Activity 30* Guided Reading Activity 30-5* World Art and Music Activity 30 People in World History Profile 57 Reteaching Activity 30 Enrichment Activity 30 Section Quiz 30-5* Performance Assessment Activity 30 Spanish Chapter Summary 30	Section Focus Transparency 30-5 World History and Art Transparency 40, *Zapatistas* Student Self-Test and Review Software Testmaker

** Also available in Spanish*

Chapter Activities

Performance Assessment Activity

Point/Counterpoint For the concepts of pacifism and militarism, organize students into groups of four to role-play a point/counterpoint segment on public television. Each group will research a current problem that has led to violence or that threatens to erupt in violence in Asia, Africa, the Middle East, or Latin America. After groups have gathered information from newspapers or magazines, have two students from each group present the pacifist response to solving the problem and two students present the militarist perspective. During the role play, students should refer to principles or historical examples to justify their positions.

Possible Rubric Features

Concept attainment, accuracy of content information, clarity of oral presentation, effect on audience, collaborative skills, persuasion and argumentation skills

• *For an additional activity, refer to Activity 30 in the* Performance Assessment Strategies and Activities *booklet.*

ACTIVITY

From the Classroom of...

James Kim
Polytechnic
Preparatory Country
Day School
Brooklyn, NY

China's Drive for Modernization

Have students create either a Nationalist (Guomindang) or Communist newspaper. Once they have read the chapter, have each student select a topic for an article. After researching their topics at the library, students should write rough drafts, then use peer editing to edit the drafts and prepare final versions of their articles. Have students type the articles, select a name for their paper, and lay out the copy. The newspaper can be photocopied or printed for distribution and display.

MULTIPLE LEARNING STYLES

Verbal/Linguistic

Have students select one of the countries discussed in this chapter and imagine that they live in that country during the time period under study. Ask them to write a letter to the editor of a newspaper in which they express their opinions about an incident described in the chapter.

Visual/Spatial

Give students an outline map of the world. As they read the chapter, have them fill in the names of the countries, continents, and regions they are studying. At the end of the chapter, put up an enlarged version of the outline map on the bulletin board. Organize the class into two teams and hold a geography bee. Have teams take turns trying to identify places mentioned in the chapter. Whichever team correctly identifies the most places wins.

Auditory/Musical

Have students write and present a short class musical based on the rise of nationalism in one of the countries described in this chapter.

Kinesthetic

Have students choreograph and perform a dance that displays through movement the struggle for independence in one of the countries described in this chapter.

Additional Resources

TEACHER'S CORNER

NATIONAL GEOGRAPHIC SOCIETY

INDEX TO NATIONAL GEOGRAPHIC MAGAZINE

The following articles may be used for research relating to this chapter:

- "Who Are the Palestinians?" by Tad Szulc, June 1992.

NATIONAL GEOGRAPHIC SOCIETY PRODUCTS AVAILABLE FROM GLENCOE

To order the following products for use with this chapter, contact your local Glencoe sales representative or call Glencoe at 1-800-368-7344:

- *The Middle East,* "The 20th Century: Imperialism, Nationalism, and Independence." (Filmstrip)

Bibliography

Literature of the Period

Malraux, André. ***Man's Fate.*** Translated by Haakon M. Chevalier. New York: Random, 1990. First published in 1933, this French novel is based on the struggle between the Communist Reds and Chiang Kai-shek's Blues in the Shanghai insurrection of 1927.

Readings for the Student

Paz, Octavio. ***The Labyrinth of Solitude: The Other Mexico, Return to the Labyrinth of Solitude, Mexico and the U.S.A., The Philanthropic Ogre.*** Translated by Lysander Kemp, Vara Milos, and Rachel Phillips Belash. New York: Grove Press, 1985. Perceptive studies of Mexican character and culture by the acclaimed poet.

Readings for the Teacher

Rose, Norman. ***Chaim Weizmann: A Biography.*** New York: Viking, 1986. Life of the Zionist leader whose work in England led to the Balfour Declaration.

interNET
CONNECTIONS
Mohandas K. Gandhi Institute Photos, writing, and an interview with Gandhi's grandson.
World Wide Web: http://www.cbu.edu/Gandhi/Welcome.html

Introducing Chapter 30

CHAPTER THEMES

Chapter Themes are listed by section on this chapter opening page of the Student Edition. A corresponding theme-based activity is available under "TEACH," and a theme-based question is asked in the Section and Chapter Reviews.

The Storyteller

Historical Setting U.S. Marines had occupied Nicaragua since 1912. In 1927 the United States backed Emiliano Chamorro, who had seized power from the elected president. Sandino (1893–1934) refused to accept the U.S.-imposed regime and led several hundred followers to the mountains of northern Nicaragua. His ability to evade capture by U.S. forces and the Nicaraguan National Guard not only turned Sandino into a popular hero but also encouraged anti-American sentiment throughout the hemisphere. After the Marines withdrew in 1933, Sandino attended a peace conference with the head of the National Guard, Anastasio Somoza, who abducted and murdered the guerrilla leader. In 1962 the Sandinista National Liberation Front was formed with the goal of overthrowing the Somoza family dictatorship. The Sandinistas overthrew Somoza in July 1979 and governed Nicaragua until 1990.

Historical Significance

Answer: *World War I shattered the old order in Europe while the Versailles peace conference raised hopes for self-determination in many colonies, leading to the growth of nationalist and independence movements between 1919 and 1939.*

Chapter 30

1919–1939

Nationalism in Asia, Africa, and Latin America

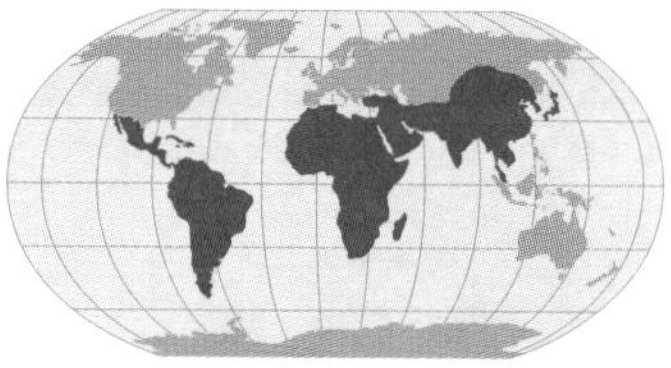

Chapter Themes

- **Nationalism** Hope for a new world after World War I leads to the rise of nationalism in the Middle East and Africa. *Section 1*
- **Change** Gandhi calls for nonviolence in India's struggle for independence from British rule. *Section 2*
- **Conflict** Nationalists, Communists, and the Japanese compete for control of China. *Section 3*
- **Conflict** Japan's militarism and expansionism place it on a collision course with the West. *Section 4*
- **Change** Nationalist forces in Latin America oppose increased American intervention in the region. *Section 5*

The Storyteller

"I swear before country and history that my sword will defend our nation's dignity, that it will be a sword for the oppressed. I accept the invitation to fight.... The last of my soldiers, the soldiers of freedom for Nicaragua, may die; but before that, more than a battalion of your blond invaders will have bitten the dust of my wild mountains."

With these fighting words, General Augusto César Sandino challenged the United States Marines in 1927. Sandino was trying to drive out the "blond invaders" who had occupied Nicaragua for 15 years. In the years following World War I, nationalist leaders such as Sandino struggled to end foreign control and win independence for their countries around the globe.

Historical Significance

What factors led to the growth of nationalist and independence movements in Asia, Africa, and Latin America between 1919 and 1939?

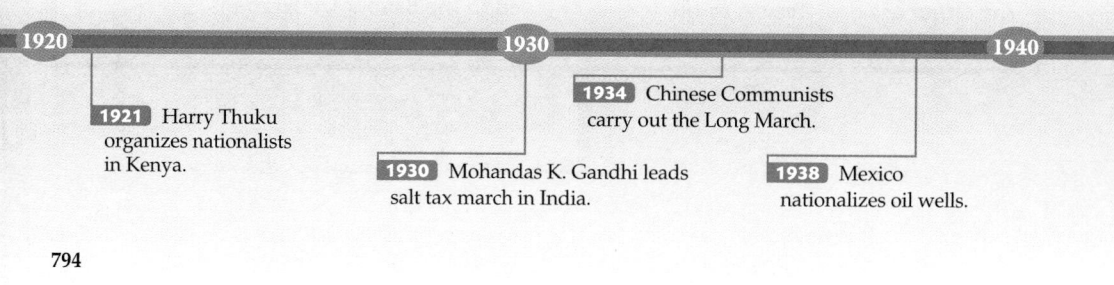

1920 — 1930 — 1940

1921 Harry Thuku organizes nationalists in Kenya.

1930 Mohandas K. Gandhi leads salt tax march in India.

1934 Chinese Communists carry out the Long March.

1938 Mexico nationalizes oil wells.

794

GEOGRAPHY CONNECTION

GEOGRAPHIC THEMES

Location Have students use a globe to locate the Middle East, Africa, India, China, Japan, and Central America. In which hemisphere does each region or country lie? *(Central America is in the Western Hemisphere; all the other locations are in the Eastern Hemisphere.)*

History & Art *The Destruction of the Old Order* by José Clemente Orozco. National Preparatory School, Mexico City, Mexico

Your History Journal

Choose a major event that occurred after 1930 in one of the nations featured in this chapter. Write a short radio news report describing the event for broadcast in the United States.

Introducing Chapter 30

History & Art Orozco is considered the most important modern muralist to work in fresco, the technique of applying watercolors to a moist plaster surface. While he did not fight in the Mexican Revolution, his political cartoons rallied support for General Venustiano Carranza. Orozco lived in the U.S. on several occasions, and in 1932–1934 he painted a series of frescoes at Dartmouth College in Hanover, New Hampshire.

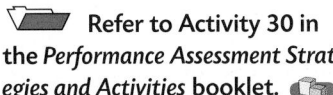

Performance Assessment

Refer to the activity on page 794C of the Planning Guide.

Refer to Activity 30 in the *Performance Assessment Strategies and Activities* booklet.

Using Your History Journal

If possible, have students listen to Edward R. Murrow's radio broadcasts on the recording, *I Can Hear It Now, 1919–1949: 30 Years of Audible History.*

GLENCOE TECHNOLOGY

VIDEODISC

Use MindJogger to preview chapter content.

MindJogger Videoquiz

Chapter 30
Disc 4 Side B

Also available in VHS.

EXTRA CREDIT PROJECT

Oral Report Ask students to research the events leading to the Balfour Declaration, the importance of that document in the establishment of Israel, and Britain's short-lived commitment to it. Have students summarize their findings in a brief oral report. Suggested resources: R. Sanders, *The High Walls of Jerusalem: A History of the Balfour Declaration and the Birth of the British Mandate for Palestine;* W. Laqueur, *A History of Zionism.*

Chapter 30 Section 1

SECTION THEME

▶ **Nationalism** Hope for a new world after World War I leads to the rise of nationalism in the Middle East and Africa.

Find Out

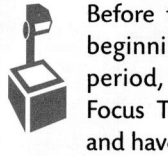

Answer: *Nationalist movements caused economic, political, and cultural ferment in Turkey, Iran, Palestine, Egypt, Kenya, and Nigeria.*

FOCUS

Section Objective

Identify how the forces of nationalism affected events in the Middle East and Africa after World War I.

BELLRINGER Motivational Activity

Before taking roll at the beginning of the class period, project Section Focus Transparency 30-1 and have students answer the activity questions. Discuss students' responses.

This activity is also available as a blackline master.

Vocabulary Pre-check

Use Vocabulary Activity 30 to introduce vocabulary terms. **L1 LEP**

1917 — 1927 — 1937

1917 The British issue the Balfour Declaration.

1929 Nigerian women oppose British tax.

1936 Egypt becomes independent.

Section 1

New Forces in the Middle East and Africa

Setting the Scene

▶ **Terms to Define**
self-determination, fez, shah

▶ **People to Meet**
Kemal Atatürk, Reza Shah Pahlavi, Theodor Herzl, Saad Zaghlul, Harry Thuku, Jomo Kenyatta, Nnamdi Azikiwe

▶ **Places to Locate**
Turkey, Iran, Palestine, Egypt, Kenya, Nigeria

Find Out How did the forces of nationalism affect events in the Middle East and Africa after World War I?

The Storyteller

Fawaz Khourey listened as a delegate at the Arab Students Congress in Paris read the committee report. "I am an Arab. I believe Arabs constitute one nation. This nation's sacred right is to be sovereign in her own affairs. Her ardent nationalism drives her to liberate our homeland, uniting all parts, and finding political, economic, and social institutions more sound and more compatible than existing ones."

—adapted from *Arab Nationalism: An Anthology*, edited by Sylvia G. Haim, reprinted in *Documents in World History*, Volume 2, 1988

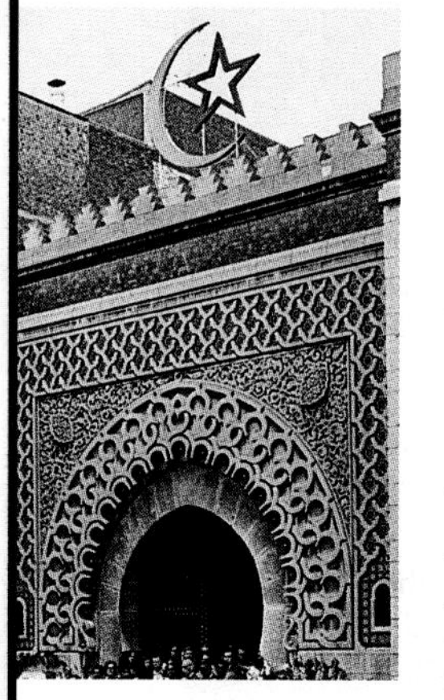

Paris mosque

At the end of World War I, European powers continued to control most of the Middle East and Africa. Many colonies had assisted the Allies during the war, hoping to gain their independence as a reward. President Woodrow Wilson of the United States raised their hopes in 1918 by endorsing the concept of self-determination: the right of national groups to set up independent nations.

But instead of relaxing their grip, the European powers tightened it. Nationalists prepared to fight for independence and organized political demonstrations. They were eager to establish modern countries where their own cultures could flourish.

Turkey

For nearly 500 years, Turkish emperors called sultans ruled the vast Ottoman Empire, which at one time included parts of eastern Europe, the Middle East, and North Africa. During the 1800s, however, large sections of this empire broke away or were conquered. When World War I began, the Ottomans joined forces with Germany, hoping to save their remaining lands.

War With Greece

The Allied victory in World War I dashed Ottoman hopes. The Ottoman sultan, or ruler, lost all of his lands except the area of present-day **Turkey**. In 1919 the Greeks invaded Turkey in an attempt to complete the destruction of the Ottoman Empire. Turkish general Mustafa Kemal, however, rallied forces to his country's defense. Kemal led a political group known as the Young Turks who wanted reforms to modernize Turkey. Turkish armies under Kemal counterattacked and defeated the Greeks in 1922.

SECTION RESOURCES

Reproducible Masters
- Reproducible Lesson Plan 30-1
- Vocabulary Activity 30
- Guided Reading Activity 30-1
- People in World History Profile 58
- Section Quiz 30-1

Transparencies
- Section Focus Transparency 30-1
- Chapter Transparency 30

Multimedia
- Student Self-Test and Review Software
- Testmaker
- In the Holy Land: *Arab violence 1919–1921*

796 **Chapter 30** *Nationalism in Asia, Africa, and Latin America*

The Turkish victory led to dramatic changes. The sultan gave up his throne, and the Turks formed a new country, the Republic of Turkey. Kemal became its first president. The new government moved the capital from Istanbul to Ankara, a city near the center of the country. Believing that Turkey needed to industrialize in order to assert its role in world affairs, Kemal's government established industries and planned their growth. Tariffs on imports were raised to protect the new industries from foreign competition and to reduce dependence on foreign countries.

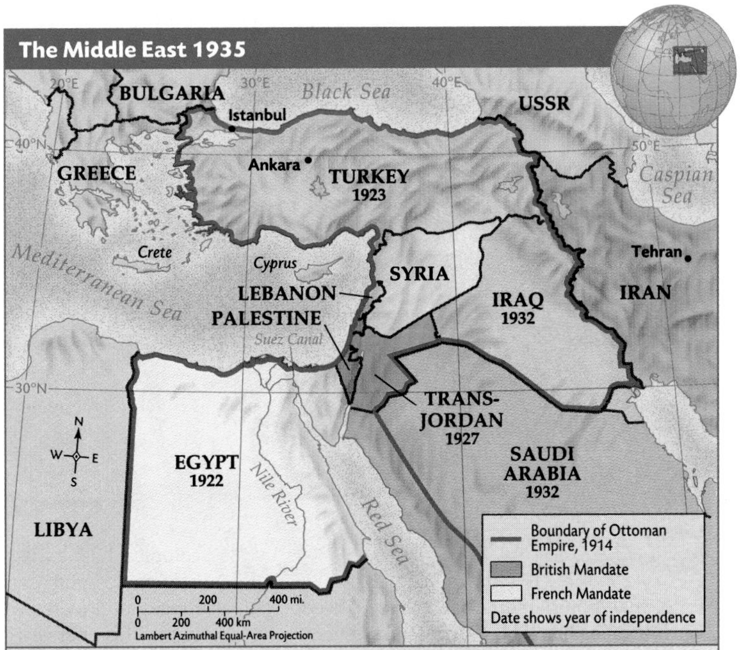

Map Study **The destruction of the Ottoman Empire was part of a global trend away from large empires. Nationalism disrupted imperial rule in eastern Europe, Africa, and southern Asia following World War I.**
Region Based on this map, how many countries contain territory that was part of the Ottoman Empire in 1914?

Kemal's Reforms

Kemal carried out a number of radical reforms in Turkish society. As a result of Kemal's policies, Turkey adopted a Western way of life. The Turks began using the Western calendar, the Latin alphabet, and the metric system. Kemal ordered men to stop wearing the fez, a traditional hat, and he allowed women to remove their veils. He also urged Turks to use Western-style last names. To modernize the government along Western lines, he reformed the legal code and separated government and religion.

Some of Kemal's changes were designed to promote national pride among the Turks. For example, he urged Turks to "purify" their language by ridding it of all words that had Persian or Arabic origins. He also changed his own name to **Kemal Atatürk** (keh•MAHL AT•uh•TUHRK), which means "father of the Turks."

In defense of his reforms, Kemal said: "We have suffered much. This is because we have failed to understand the world. Our thoughts and our mentality will become civilized from head to toe." Kemal ruled Turkey with an iron fist until his death in 1938. His policies were not always popular, but he changed Turkey from an ancient empire into a modern nation.

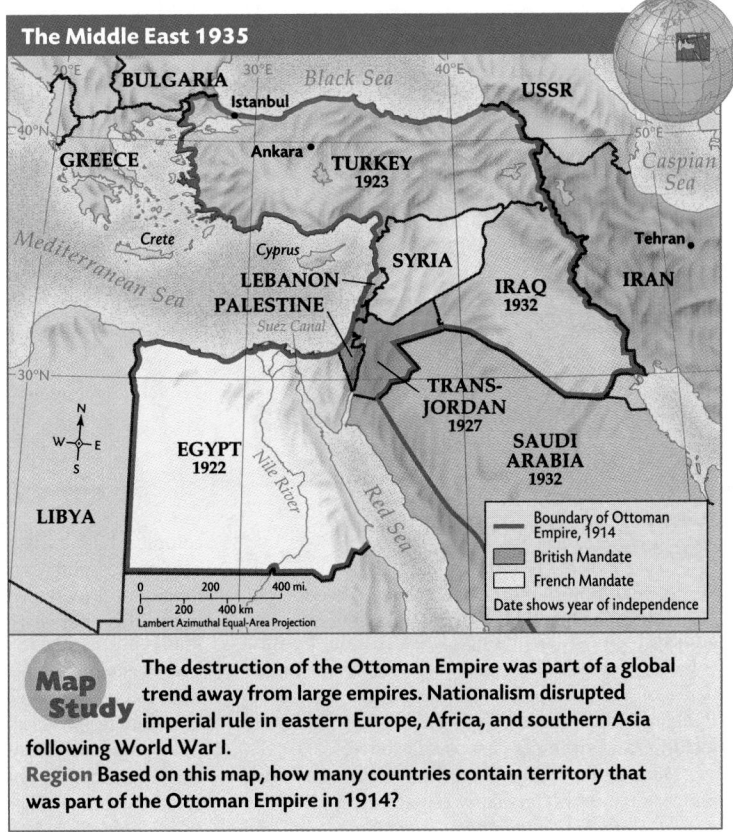

Iran

Located between Turkey and Pakistan, **Iran** is a land of mountains, deserts, and oil. At the end of World War I this land, known by its historic name of Persia, was ruled by a shah, or king. However, Great Britain and the Soviet Union each had controlling interests in Persia's oil fields.

In 1921 nationalist forces led by Reza Khan wanted to cut back the foreign influence on their government and economy. The nationalists overthrew the shah and set up a new government. Like Atatürk, Reza Khan built schools, roads, and hospitals, and he allowed women more freedom. Improved communications helped unite the diverse groups in the country. Although adopting many Western ways, he tried to reduce Western political influence in Persia.

Reza wanted to change the Persian monarchy into a republic. However, traditional Muslim leaders opposed this change, so Reza ruled as a dictator. Later, in 1925, he declared himself shah and

TEACH

Guided Practice

THEME Nationalism

Write on the chalkboard Sandino's statement quoted on page 794: "I swear before country and history that my sword will defend our nation's dignity, that it will be a sword for the oppressed." Although the statement was made by a Nicaraguan general, it may have been echoed by nationalist leaders in other areas of the world. Have students explain how Sandino's statement might have rallied the support of Nicaraguans. **L1**

People in World History Profile 58

Map Study

Answer
eight countries

Map Skills Practice

Reading a Map **Which region did Britain control through a mandate?** *(Palestine)*

Geography: Location Have students study the map on this page. **What body of water lies west of Palestine?** *(Mediterranean Sea)* **What country now exists in the area that was a British mandate?** *(Israel)* **What nations bordered Syria in 1935?** *(Turkey, Iraq, Transjordan, Palestine, Lebanon)* **L2**

Chapter Transparency 30

Independent Practice

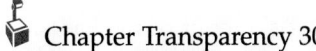

Guided Reading Activity 30-1 **L1**

COOPERATIVE LEARNING ACTIVITY

Posters Organize the class into two groups and assign one group Turkey and the other Iran. Have each group list the ways its country modernized and adopted certain elements of Western countries following World War I. Then ask the groups to research the subsequent history of each country, including the reaction against westernization in Iran. Have students create posters illustrating daily life in Turkey and Iran today. Encourage students to use photographs from magazines or newspapers to illustrate their posters. When the posters are completed, have students discuss how life in secular Turkey differs from life in Iran's Islamic republic. **L3**

Chapter 30 *Nationalism in Asia, Africa, and Latin America* **797**

Chapter 30
Section 1

Visualizing History Although he served in a series of governments that collaborated with the British, Zaghlul (1857–1927) became a nationalist when he realized that Britain had no intention of granting independence to Egypt.

Answer to Caption: *Kemal Atatürk of Turkey and Reza Shah Pahlavi of Iran*

Linking Past and Present

Iran In 1979 a revolutionary movement led by Muslim religious leader Ayatollah Ruholla Khomeini overthrew Reza Shah's son, Mohammad Reza Pahlavi, and declared Iran an Islamic republic. Although Khomeini died in 1989, Iran continues to follow his anti-Western orientation and commitment to Muslim fundamentalism.

ABCNEWS INTERACTIVE™

VIDEODISC
In the Holy Land

Side One, Chapter 15
Frame: 20841
Title: *Arab violence 1919–1921*
Subject: Jewish and Palestinian perspectives of anti-Jewish rioting and violence
Ask: As a result of the Balfour Declaration, Jewish immigration to Israel increased. What was the effect of this on the Arabs? *(They felt threatened because others were claiming their homeland. This resulted in riots, strikes, and violence.)*

Visualizing History **In 1919 Egyptian nationalists protested the arrest of their leader Saad Zaghlul by the British.** *What two other nationalist leaders rose to prominence in the Middle East after World War I?*

adopted the new name **Reza Shah Pahlavi** (rih•ZAH SHAH PAL•uh•vee). Pahlavi was the name of the ancient Persian language. Reza Shah Pahlavi earned money from Persia's oil fields and factories and from his vast royal estates.

During the 1930s, Reza Shah Pahlavi aligned his country with Germany. He admired Hitler, in part because he believed that Germans and Persians shared a common ancestry in the ancient Aryan, or Indo-European, peoples. In 1935 he changed the country's name from Persia to Iran, a variation of the word *Aryan*. In 1941, when Great Britain and the Soviet Union were at war with Germany, British and Soviet forces deposed Reza Shah Pahlavi and replaced him with his son, Mohammad Reza Pahlavi. The new ruler permitted British and Soviet troops to remain in Iran.

Palestine

While Iran was trying to free itself from European control, another Middle Eastern region was just coming under British domination. After World War I, the newly formed League of Nations gave Great Britain a mandate to control **Palestine**. This region had been part of the Ottoman Empire. Britain was eager to benefit from control of Palestine's fine ports and strategic location at the eastern end of the Mediterranean Sea.

In Palestine, the nationalism of two groups—Jewish and Arab—came into conflict. Jews recalled that centuries before, the ancient state of Israel had been located there. Arabs pointed out that the region had been inhabited by Muslim and Christian Palestinians whose ancestors had lived there for many centuries also. During this period, Palestine's small number of Jews and large number of Arabs coexisted peacefully most of the time.

Beginning in the late 1800s, the number of Jews in Palestine began increasing. European Jews, facing harsh anti-Jewish pogroms in Russia and stirred by a growing sense of nationalism, believed they should reestablish a Jewish national homeland in Palestine. This movement, known as Zionism, became an organized political force in the late 1890s under the leadership of **Theodor Herzl**, a prominent Austrian Jewish writer and journalist. By World War I, about 500,000 Arabs and 85,000 Jews lived in Palestine.

During World War I, the British government promised independence to the Arabs in return for their help against the Ottoman Turks and also promised a homeland to the Jews. The Balfour Declaration—a letter from British Foreign Secretary Arthur Balfour in 1917 to the English Zionist Federation—promised Great Britain's help in establishing "a national home for the Jewish people" in Palestine. Great Britain's pledge of support, however, was on the condition that the civil and religious rights of non-Jewish Palestinians be protected. In September 1923, the British mandate officially came into force in Palestine in spite of Great Britain's conflicting promises to the area's Jewish and Arab communities.

MEETING SPECIAL NEEDS ACTIVITY

Learning Disability To check the progress of students with learning problems, ask them to identify the country described in each of the following statements:

1. In 1922 the British granted this country limited independence. *(Egypt)*
2. It was originally known as Persia. *(Iran)*
3. Greece invaded this country in 1919. *(Turkey)*
4. Reza Khan became its leader and eventually declared himself shah. *(Iran)*
5. Mustafa Kemal introduced radical reforms here. *(Turkey)* **L1**

Under the British mandate, tensions heightened between Arabs and Jews. As the persecution of Jews in Nazi Germany increased, so did Jewish immigration to Palestine. As more Jews moved into a region long inhabited by Arabs, the two groups clashed. Riots broke out, resulting in hundreds of casualties. When Great Britain tried to limit Jewish immigration, Zionists responded in anger. By the end of the 1930s, Great Britain's ambiguous promises had angered both Jews and Arabs, and the conflict in Palestine was worsening.

Egypt

Palestine's neighbor **Egypt** also confronted troubles after World War I. Under British occupation since 1882, Egypt was beginning to feel the power of nationalism. **Saad Zaghlul** (zag•LOOL) led the nationalist forces in Egypt demanding independence. The British tried to weaken the nationalist cause by arresting Zaghlul, but their action only sparked riots and violence. Finally, in 1922, Great Britain granted Egypt limited independence. However, the British kept control of the Suez Canal.

Tensions continued over the next decade between Egypt and Great Britain. But when Italy invaded Ethiopia in 1936, the British decided they needed Egypt's help to prevent further Italian aggression. As a result, the British government granted Egypt its complete independence in 1936 and helped it become a member of the League of Nations the following year. Great Britain also withdrew all British troops from Egypt, except for those in the Suez Canal zone.

Kenya

South of Egypt, in central East Africa, lay another part of Great Britain's empire: **Kenya**. During World War I, about 45,000 Kenyans died while helping the British fight the Germans in East Africa. The survivors returned home after the war with dreams of independence and a new life. However, instead of granting Kenya its independence, the British allowed European settlers to seize the land of many Kenyans in order to start large coffee plantations and other agricultural operations. The settlers hired Kenyans at low wages and made them work under harsh conditions. Resentment of British rule in Kenya gave rise to a

CONNECTIONS

Geography

Imperialist Boundaries

During the late 1800s, European powers carved up Africa without respect to the continent's historic ethnic boundaries. Colonial boundary lines split groups of people and joined them to other groups with different religious beliefs, customs, and languages. This often led to unwanted rivalries and hostilities. Nowhere was this problem more evident than in Nigeria.

Nigerian nationalist Nnamdi Azikiwe

Nigeria is home to more than 250 separate ethnic groups. The three largest are the Hausa, the Yoruba, and the Ibo. In the days before colonial rule, each group controlled its own territory. When the British united the region in 1914, Hausa, Yoruba, and Ibo peoples were part of the same country for the first time. They eyed each other with suspicion.

After independence arrived in 1960, the struggle for unity continued in Nigeria. However, hostilities flared into warfare in 1967. Eastern Nigeria seceded and established the independent state of Biafra. The Nigerian government eventually won the war and reclaimed Biafra, but the country remains haunted by the prophetic words that nationalist leader Obafemi Awolowo spoke in 1947: "Nigeria is not a nation. It is a mere geographical expression."

MAKING THE CONNECTION

1. How did colonial boundaries cause dissension among ethnic groups?
2. Why were Nigerians reluctant to unite?

Chapter 30 Section 1

CONNECTIONS

Geography

Imperialist Boundaries

Awolowo (1909–1987) himself was a leader of the Yoruba people. He studied law in London, where he wrote *Path to Nigerian Freedom* (1947), a call for his homeland's independence. Upon his return to Nigeria, he founded the Action Group, a Yoruba political party. After Nigeria attained independence in 1960, Awolowo turned to socialism and spent some years in prison.

Answers to Making the Connection

1. *Colonial boundaries often led to rivalries and hostilities by joining ethnic groups with different religious beliefs, customs, and languages.*
2. *Ethnic groups formerly in control of their own territories were reluctant to live as one people.*

ASSESS

Check for Understanding

Assign Section 1 Review as homework or as an in-class activity.

Use Student Self-Test and Review Software to review Section 1.

MAKING CONNECTIONS ACTIVITIES

The Arts Have students watch videos of *Lawrence of Arabia*, the 1962 screen biography of T. E. Lawrence, the English leader of the Arab revolt against the Ottoman Empire, and *Exodus*, the 1960 film about the last days of the British mandate in Palestine and the clash of Arab and Zionist nationalists there after the birth of Israel.

Have students write brief reports in which they evaluate the complex British role in the region as depicted in the two films. **L2**

Politics Have students research and write brief reports comparing the lives and political goals of Theodor Herzl, founder of political Zionism, and Yasir Arafat, leader of the Palestine Liberation Organization. **L2**

Chapter 30
Section 1

Visualizing History Kenyatta (1894–1978) first came into contact with Europeans when, at the age of ten, he underwent surgery at a mission in East Africa. *Facing Mount Kenya* was based on his graduate thesis in anthropology at the London School of Economics. After its publication he changed his name from Kamau Ngengi to Jomo ("Burning Spear") Kenyatta.
Answer to Caption: *by talking with British officials in London*

Evaluate

Section Quiz 30-1

Use the Testmaker to create a customized quiz for Section 1.

Reteach

Have students explain why the experience of World War I promoted the concept of self-determination among colonial peoples of Africa and the Middle East. *(Many hoped to receive their independence in exchange for fighting with the Allies.)*

Enrich

Ask students to imagine that they are one of the nationalist leaders described in this section. Have them write a short speech directed at a European audience, demanding independence for their homeland.

CLOSE

Write the following on the chalkboard: *No matter how small or weak, every nation has the right to decide its own form of government and to manage its own affairs.* Ask students to discuss whether they agree with this statement in principle and if they think it is practical in real life.

protest movement in 1921 led by **Harry Thuku** (THOO•koo). The protesters complained about high colonial taxes and strict British labor laws. Colonial officials promptly arrested Thuku, and in the riot that followed, British troops killed about 25 Kenyans. The British government then exiled Thuku from Kenya.

In Thuku's absence, **Jomo Kenyatta** took over the growing nationalist movement. Instead of fighting the British in Kenya for independence, Kenyatta took his struggle to the center of British power in London. By meeting with government officials in the 1920s and 1930s, he succeeded in making progress—but at a very slow pace. He later recalled his frustrations:

> "By driving [the African] off his ancestral lands, the Europeans have robbed him of the material foundations of his culture, and reduced him to a state of serfdom incompatible with human happiness.… It is not in his nature to accept serfdom forever. He realizes that he must fight unceasingly for his own complete emancipation; for without this he is doomed to remain the prey of rival imperialisms."
>
> —Jomo Kenyatta, *Facing Mount Kenya*, 1938

Visualizing History **Jomo Kenyatta wrote a book, *Facing Mount Kenya*, that explained how British rule had disrupted his country's culture.** *How did Kenyatta try to obtain Kenya's independence?*

In spite of Kenyatta's efforts for independence, when World War II began in 1939, Kenya remained firmly in British hands.

Nigeria

Across the continent from Kenya, on the west coast of Africa, lies **Nigeria**. The British controlled this region of Africa as well, and they made large fortunes from Nigeria's rubber, oil, and tin. As in Kenya, the British imposed heavy taxes on men and strict labor laws.

In 1929 Nigerian women learned that they too would be taxed. When a group of unarmed women protested by attacking British goods and property, police fired on them, killing 50.

The violent ending of the women's uprising drove many Nigerians to adopt nonviolent methods in their struggle for independence. One of these Nigerian nationalists was **Nnamdi Azikiwe** (eh •nahm•dee ah•zee•KEE•WEE), who started the newspaper *The West African Pilot* in 1937. He wrote many articles in favor of independence, not only for Nigeria but for all of Africa. "Africa needs a pilot," he wrote once. "Those who follow the true pilot, believing they are on the right track, will find their way to their destination."

SECTION 1 REVIEW

Recall
1. **Define** self-determination, fez, shah.
2. **Identify** Kemal Atatürk, Reza Shah Pahlavi, Theodor Herzl, Saad Zaghlul, the Balfour Declaration, Harry Thuku, Jomo Kenyatta, Nnamdi Azikiwe.
3. **List** three reforms introduced in Turkey by Kemal Atatürk.

Critical Thinking
4. **Evaluating Information** The British in Kenya said they were "exercising a trust on behalf of the African population." What does that phrase imply about Great Britain's attitude toward Africans?

Understanding Themes
5. **Nationalism** What were the reasons for the rise of nationalism in the Middle East and Africa at the end of World War I?

SECTION 1 REVIEW ANSWERS

1. All vocabulary words are defined in the Glossary.
2. Atatürk, 796–797; Reza Shah, 797–798; Balfour Declaration, 798; Zaghlul, 799; Thuku, 800; Kenyatta, 800; Azikiwe, 800
3. use of the Western calendar, Latin alphabet, metric system, and Western-style last names; ban on the fez for men and encouragement of women not to wear the traditional veil
4. The British thought they knew what was best for Africans.
5. NATIONALISM Colonial peoples wanted to establish modern nations where their own cultures could flourish.

1919 1929 1939

1919 The Amritsar Massacre heightens anti-British feeling in India.

1930 Mohandas K. Gandhi leads protest against British rule.

1935 The British Parliament passes the Government of India Act.

Section 2

India's Struggle for Independence

Setting the Scene

- **Terms to Define**
  pacifist, civil disobedience, satyagraha
- **People to Meet**
  Mohandas K. Gandhi, Mohammed Ali Jinnah, Jawaharlal Nehru
- **Places to Locate**
  India, Amritsar, Ahmadabad

Find Out What methods did Gandhi use in India's struggle for independence from British rule?

The Storyteller

Riswati and Kamala, once friendly neighbors in Bombay, had not spoken to each other for months—since relations between Muslims and Hindus had deteriorated. The British could use the problem as an excuse for delaying Indian independence. The two women had argued over which group, Muslims or Hindus, was more to blame. Kamala recalled the example of Mohandas Gandhi and resolved to visit Riswati and renew their friendship. Perhaps she could quote Gandhi saying, "It does not matter to me that we see things from different angles of vision." Kamala caught sight of Riswati at the market. Quickly she crossed the square toward her old friend.

—adapted from *Communal Unity*, M.K. Gandhi, reprinted in *World Civilizations*, Volume 2, 1994

Mohandas Gandhi

When World War I began, the most important colony in the British Empire was **India**. As in the Middle East and Africa, nationalism was spreading in India. Some Indians wanted independence. Many were willing to remain in the British Empire but demanded home rule. Two of the largest nationalist organizations were the Indian National Congress and the Muslim League.

During World War I, Indian nationalists supported Great Britain and its allies. More than a million Indian soldiers fought on the battlefields of the Middle East and Africa. Indian wheat fed the Allied troops, and Indian cotton kept them clothed. In return for this aid, Great Britain promised in 1917 to support "the gradual development of self-governing institutions" in India.

The Amritsar Massacre

Independence did not come easily to India. After the war, the Indian National Congress staged demonstrations to protest British rule. The nationalist movement, however, was divided by religion. The Hindu majority and the Muslim minority did not trust each other. The British authorities in India encouraged that distrust.

A second difficulty was British opposition. Many Britons were unwilling to see their empire's power reduced and staunchly opposed granting India its independence. In 1919 Great Britain imposed on India harsh laws intended to stifle opposition to British rule. British officials could arrest Indian nationalists without cause and jail them without trial.

British repression reached an extreme in the northern city of **Amritsar** in April 1919. The British had outlawed all large gatherings and declared that

Chapter 30 Section 2

SECTION THEME

- **Change** Gandhi calls for nonviolence in India's struggle for independence from British rule.

Find Out

Answer: *Gandhi used nonviolent methods such as protest marches and boycotts of British goods.*

FOCUS

Section Objective

State the methods Gandhi used in India's struggle for independence from British rule.

BELLRINGER
Motivational Activity

Before taking roll at the beginning of the class period, project Section Focus Transparency 30-2 and have students answer the activity questions. Discuss students' responses.

This activity is also available as a blackline master.

Vocabulary Pre-check

Use Vocabulary Activity 30 to introduce vocabulary terms. **L1 LEP**

SECTION RESOURCES

Reproducible Masters
- Reproducible Lesson Plan 30-2
- Vocabulary Activity 30
- Guided Reading Activity 30-2
- Section Quiz 30-2

Transparencies
- Section Focus Transparency 30-2

Multimedia
- Student Self-Test and Review Software
- Testmaker
- Lessons of War: *Philosophy of Nonviolence*

Chapter 30 *Nationalism in Asia, Africa, and Latin America* **801**

TEACH

Guided Practice

THEME **Change**

Have students discuss the purpose of the boycott led by Gandhi. Ask them to explain why this tactic might be more effective at achieving change than a march or demonstration. Ask students to describe how the boycott attacked the underlying logic of imperialism. *(The empire was supposed to benefit England economically.)* **L1**

Visualizing History The Indian National Congress, founded in 1885, led not only the movement for independence from Great Britain but was also India's ruling party from 1947 to 1977.
Answer to Caption: *South Africa*

ABCNEWS INTERACTIVE™

VIDEODISC
Lessons of War

Side Two, Chapter 6
Frames 12636–20751
Title: *Philosophy of Nonviolence*
Subject: The philosophies of Mohandas Gandhi and Martin Luther King, Jr.
Ask: Identify two people in history who exemplified nonviolent protest. *(Mohandas Gandhi and Martin Luther King, Jr.)*

Independent Practice

Guided Reading Activity 30-2 **L1**

Visualizing History **During the 1920s and 1930s, Gandhi was India's leading nationalist. He worked to promote unity between Hindus and Muslims in the Indian National Congress party.** *Where did Gandhi first use nonviolent methods to protest injustices?*

they would respond to any violation with force. When 10,000 unarmed Indians assembled in a walled garden in Amritsar for a political meeting, the local commander decided that the British needed to demonstrate their authority. Without warning, British troops blocked the only entrance to the garden and began firing into the trapped crowd. When the firing ceased, nearly 400 people, including many children, lay dead. Another 1,200 people were wounded. Criticized for his action, the British commander declared:

> "I fired and continued to fire until the crowd dispersed, and I consider this is the least amount of firing which would produce the necessary moral effect.... If more troops had been at hand, the casualties would have been greater."

Footnotes to History **Gandhi and the West** Mohandas K. Gandhi has had a profound influence on people in the West. He served as a model for Martin Luther King, Jr. King led the African American civil rights struggle until his assassination in 1968. Like Gandhi, King protested injustice with nonviolent boycotts and marches.

Indians across the country were shocked by the brutal massacre and the general's justification of it. In large numbers, they came together in meeting after meeting, more determined than ever to drive the British out of their land. However, they needed a strong leader to spearhead their struggle.

Gandhi

In the months following the Amritsar Massacre, **Mohandas K. Gandhi** became the leading Indian nationalist. Born in India of middle-class parents in 1869, Gandhi had been educated in England. He later practiced law in South Africa, where he and other Indians experienced mistreatment because of their dark skin.

Until 1914 Gandhi lived in South Africa and led protests against racial discrimination. He was a **pacifist**, a person opposed to using war and other violence to settle disputes. In keeping with his beliefs, Gandhi used protest methods based on **civil disobedience**, or the refusal to obey laws that are considered unjust.

When Gandhi returned to India, he began working with the Indian National Congress and led a nonviolent movement for self-government and for greater tolerance among the country's many social and religious groups. Gandhi urged Indians to reject much of Western civilization for its use of brute force, its worship of money, and its prejudicial attitudes toward non-Western peoples. Gandhi's understanding of India's problems made him popular throughout the country. The Indian people called Gandhi *Mahatma*, meaning "great soul."

Gandhi's doctrine of moral nonviolent protest won him international attention. He believed that one could force an evil person or government to change by challenging it directly, but without violence. Gandhi used the term **satyagraha** (suh •TYAH•gruh•huh), which means "truth force," to describe the nonviolent protests he led after the Amritsar Massacre. One effective form of protest was the boycott, in which Indians refused to buy British cloth and other manufactured goods. As a step toward independence, Gandhi urged Indians to begin spinning their own cloth.

Gandhi practiced what he preached by spinning cloth for a half hour every day. He made the spinning wheel the symbol of the National Congress, and he wore nothing but simple homespun clothes for the rest of his life.

COOPERATIVE LEARNING ACTIVITY

Debate Organize the class into two groups to debate the following statement: "Gandhi's nonviolent philosophy made India's independence movement less effective than it would have been, had force been used." Each group should research the issue and organize its argument before the debate takes place, dividing the work into research, organization of information, and presentation of information, and assigning these tasks to subgroups. You might want to have students conduct this debate before another class and let the members of that class vote on the more persuasive argument. **L2**

Gandhi's courage inspired millions of Indians to join in protests. In 1922, however, the British arrested Gandhi, and he disappeared from active protest for the rest of the decade. Undaunted, the Indian National Congress continued to protest, but it achieved very little success until Gandhi's return in 1930.

Toward Independence

Gandhi planned his next major protest around salt. In India's hot climate, the millions of people who worked in fields and factories needed salt to replace what they lost daily in sweat. The British controlled the salt mines and the ocean salt fields. They taxed every grain of salt they sold and jailed Indians who gathered salt on their own.

In 1930 Gandhi protested the salt tax. First he led thousands of his followers on a 200-mile (322-km) march from **Ahmadabad** to the sea, where they made salt from sea water. One month later, Gandhi openly defied British authority by wading into the sea and picking up a lump of salt. The British did not dare arrest him, but they did arrest thousands who followed his example. To quell the mounting protests, they arrested him a month later, but the protests only increased. Webb Miller, a British journalist, described one such protest, in which a group of Indians marched on a heavily guarded salt mine: "Although every one knew that within a few minutes he would be beaten down, perhaps killed, I could detect no signs of wavering or fear.... There was no fight, no struggle; the marchers simply walked forward until struck down."

This pattern continued throughout the 1930s. As Indians protested, the British responded with guns and clubs. Their violence could not stop the millions of people motivated by nationalism.

Limited Self-Rule

Under pressure from the nationalist movement, the British began to give Indians more political power. In 1935 the British Parliament passed the Government of India Act, which created a constitution for India. This measure gave provincial legislatures control over the making of law in the provinces. Areas such as agriculture, education, public health, and public works came under the control of the provincial governments. The British government retained control of national lawmaking, finance, defense, and foreign affairs.

The majority of Indian nationalists rejected the act, wanting complete independence. However, the Indian National Congress, at the insistence of Gandhi, finally accepted it as the first step toward self-rule. The Indian historian K.M. Panikkar states that with the Government of India Act, "British authority in India was in full retreat, in the administrative field no less than in the political and economic fields." Nevertheless, independence was not yet won.

Hindu-Muslim Relations

Even as India moved toward independence in the 1930s, conflicts among Indians increased. For every Muslim, India had three Hindus. As independence approached, the Muslims began worrying about their future treatment by the Hindus, and many joined the Muslim League.

In 1936 the Indian National Congress, controlled by Hindus, won election majorities in 7 out of 11 provinces. Muslims came to power in the others. This heightened bitter feelings. The Muslim League, headed by **Mohammed Ali Jinnah**, split with the Congress party. It demanded a separate Muslim nation for the millions of Muslims in India. The Hindus, led by **Jawaharlal Nehru**, a follower of Gandhi, wanted a united India.

Although a Hindu, Gandhi was concerned about the deepening rift between Hindus and Muslims. His pleas for toleration were largely ignored by both groups. As 1939 ended, India continued its long struggle for freedom. But now the nationalist movement had split in two, and not even Gandhi could put it together again.

SECTION 2 REVIEW

Recall

1. **Define** pacifist, civil disobedience, satyagraha.
2. **Identify** Mohandas K. Gandhi, Mohammed Ali Jinnah, Jawaharlal Nehru.
3. **List** the three countries in which Gandhi spent most of his life. Locate these countries on the Atlas map on pages A-5 and A-6.

Critical Thinking

4. **Synthesizing Information** What could Hindus have done to keep Muslims united with them against the British?

Understanding Themes

5. **Change** What nonviolent methods did Mohandas K. Gandhi use to bring about change?

Chapter 30 Section 2

Critical Thinking Have students discuss under what conditions, if any, it is proper to break the law. Ask them to consider whether someone who breaks an unjust law should accept punishment, and what moral point a person makes by intentionally breaking the law.

ASSESS

Check for Understanding

Assign Section 2 Review as homework or as an in-class activity.

Use Student Self-Test and Review Software to review Section 2.

Evaluate

Section Quiz 30-2

Use the Testmaker to create a customized quiz for Section 2.

Reteach

Have each student write one review question for each of the three major parts of this section. Ask students to exchange their questions with a classmate, write the answers to the questions they receive, and return them to the student who wrote them for review.

Enrich

Have students watch a video of the 1982 screen biography *Gandhi*. Ask them to write a brief review as if they were a critic.

CLOSE

Have students create two lists on the chalkboard, one of British actions to prevent Indian independence, and the other of measures taken by Indian nationalists to win self-rule.

SECTION 2 REVIEW ANSWERS

1. All vocabulary words are defined in the Glossary.
2. Gandhi, 802; Jinnah, 803; Nehru, 803
3. Gandhi was born in India, educated in Great Britain, and worked in South Africa before returning to India.
4. Answers will vary but may include the guarantee of a voice for Muslims in political decisions or support of strong civil rights laws.
5. **CHANGE** He led marches and urged Indians to boycott British goods and to make their own cloth and salt.

Chapter 30 *Nationalism in Asia, Africa, and Latin America* **803**

SECTION THEME

▶ **Conflict** Nationalists, Communists, and the Japanese compete for control of China.

Find Out

Answer: *They were united in their wish to control the threat from Japan but divided by political conflicts.*

FOCUS

Section Objective

Explain the factors that divided and the factors that united nationalist forces in China.

BELLRINGER
Motivational Activity

Before taking roll at the beginning of the class period, project Section Focus Transparency 30-3 and have students answer the activity questions. Discuss students' responses.

This activity is also available as a blackline master.

Vocabulary Pre-check

Use Vocabulary Activity 30 to introduce vocabulary terms.
L1 LEP

1919 | 1929 | 1939

1919 Chinese students protest Treaty of Versailles.

1925 Chiang Kai-shek sets up government at Nanjing.

1939 Japan controls most of eastern China.

Section 3

China's Drive for Modernization

Setting the Scene

▶ **Terms to Define**
warlord

▶ **People to Meet**
Sun Yat-sen, Yuan Shigai, Chiang Kai-shek, Mao Zedong

▶ **Places to Locate**
Nanjing, Guangzhou, Manchuria

Find Out What divided nationalist forces in China, and what united them?

The Storyteller

Wai Zhou watched a small man addressing a group in the square. "China has become a colony of all the Powers," he proclaimed. This was nothing new, Wai Zhou thought, just another agitator seeking an audience. But the man continued, "Foreigners often refer to the Chinese nation as a bowl of loose sand. To revive nationalism we must expand our small group loyalty to a very large group. The people must learn to read and write. China must become a democracy. Those who till the soil should own it." The speaker outlined a plan for Chinese independence. Completely won over, Wai Zhou asked a bystander who the speaker was. "I heard him called Sun Yat-sen," the man replied.

—adapted from *Lectures on Nationalism*, Sun Yat-sen, reprinted in *Lives and Times*, James P. Holoka and Jiu-Hwa Lo Upshur, 1995

Sun Yat-sen

Unlike India, China was never entirely controlled by a European country. However, despite its independence and size, China did not have the military power to command respect. That they lacked the respect of Europeans was shown by the final terms of the Versailles peace conference that followed World War I. The Versailles Treaty had a provision granting Japan economic control of the Shandong (SHON•DOONG) Peninsula of northeastern China. This provision was a humiliating and surprising blow to the Chinese. During and after World War I, China was torn apart by internal divisions, and the foreign powers took advantage of China's weakness.

The Chinese Republic

As you read in Chapter 27, the Chinese revolutionary leader **Sun Yat-sen** formally declared China a republic in January 1912. Sun dreamed of a free, democratic society. However, just two months after taking office, he was ousted by a military strongman, **Yuan Shigai** (YOO•AHN SHUR•GIE). Yuan quickly turned the new republic into a dictatorship. Meanwhile, Sun organized and formed the nationalist Guomindang (KWOH•MIHN•DAHNG) party, tried and failed to overthrow Yuan, and then fled to Japan.

When Yuan died in 1916, China slipped into chaos. Local military leaders called warlords divided the vast country among themselves. An almost continual state of civil war followed.

Sun Yat-sen returned to China in 1917 and tried in vain to restore strong central government to China and rebuild the Guomindang party. Then in 1923, with aid from the Soviet Union and an ambitious young officer named **Chiang Kai-shek**

SECTION RESOURCES

Reproducible Masters
- Reproducible Lesson Plan 30-3
- Vocabulary Activity 30
- Guided Reading Activity 30-3
- Time Line Activity 30
- Section Quiz 30-3

Transparencies
- Section Focus Transparency 30-3

Multimedia
- Student Self-Test and Review Software
- Testmaker

Visualizing History **Chiang Kai-shek was appointed commander of the National Revolutionary Army in 1926. By the end of 1928 the last major faction of warlords pledged obedience to the National Government.** *What other party opposed the warlords?*

(JEE•AHNG KY•SHEHK), the Guomindang army grew rapidly in strength. Three years after Sun's death in 1925, Chiang led the army to victory over the warlords and established a government in the city of **Nanjing**.

Though undemocratic, government under the Guomindang promoted economic development by building schools, roads, and railways. However, the Guomindang did very little to raise the living standards of the peasants who comprised the vast majority of the population of China.

Rivalry With the Communists

Many peasants, along with intellectuals and urban workers, supported another party that opposed the warlords: the Communists. During Chiang's drive against the warlords, Communist soldiers provided him with crucial military support. But in 1927 the Communists attempted to take over the Guomindang party and failed. Chiang turned against the Communists and tried to wipe them out. In the city of **Guangzhou** (GWAHNG •JOH), Guomindang soldiers killed 6,000 suspected Communists in just three days.

As Chiang began his purge, tens of thousands of Communists fled to the mountains in the southern province of Jiangxi (jee•AHNG•SHEE). Here they gathered their strength and formed the Red Army, led by the son of a prosperous peasant family, **Mao Zedong** (MOW DZUH•DOONG). Mao believed that the Communists could still triumph with the help of China's millions of peasants:

> "In a very short time, in China's central, southern, and northern provinces, several hundred million peasants will rise like a mighty storm, like a hurricane, a force so swift and violent that no power, however great, will be able to hold it back."
>
> —Mao Zedong, *Report on an Investigation*, 1926

Living conditions for China's peasants had changed little over the centuries. They worked small plots of land and turned over most of their crops to wealthy landlords. The Red Army gained popular support in rural areas of the country by overthrowing local landlords and distributing their land to the peasants. Before long, the Red Army included nearly 250,000 peasant troops.

The success of the Red Army worried Chiang. In the early 1930s he ordered a series of "extermination campaigns" in an attempt to destroy this rival army. Mao fought back, however, using his own strategies: "The enemy advances, we retreat; the enemy camps, we harass; the enemy tires, we attack; the enemy retreats, we pursue."

Mao's military plans worked at times, but by October 1934, the Guomindang had nearly surrounded the Communists with a million troops. Mao decided to retreat once again, leading about 100,000 followers out of Jiangxi Province in a desperate gamble for survival.

TEACH

Guided Practice

THEME Conflict
Have students discuss the difficulties faced by Sun Yat-sen in creating a new China. *(ousted by Yuan Shigai shortly after taking office; failed in his attempt to overthrow Yuan with his Guomindang party; failed to restore strong central government)* **L1**

Visualizing History To strengthen the moral fiber of the nation, Chiang (1887–1975) encouraged a movement to teach Confucian morals.
Answer to Caption: *the Communists*

Independent Practice

Guided Reading Activity 30-3 **L1**

Time Line Activity 30

Politics Have students imagine that they are members of the Red Army trying to gain the support of peasants in the countryside. Have them write a short speech that deals with issues of concern to Chinese peasants. **L2**

Linking Past and Present

Taiwan After Mao won control of the Chinese mainland, Chiang headed the Nationalist government in exile on Taiwan from 1949 until his death in 1975. China continued to regard Taiwan as a renegade province. Although tensions between the two eased in the late 1980s, they intensified again in the 1990s.

COOPERATIVE LEARNING ACTIVITY

Reports Organize the class into two groups to report on the influence of Chinese students on the politics of China. Each group member should have a specific task, such as researching, organizing, or summarizing. Have one group examine the political role Chinese students played in the early part of this century and the other group research the role Chinese students have played in politics in recent years, including the Tiananmen Square demonstrations of June 1989. **L2**

Chapter 30 *Nationalism in Asia, Africa, and Latin America* **805**

Visualizing History Communist troops on the Long March crossed 18 mountain ranges and 24 rivers to reach northwest China.
Answer to Caption: *the Guomindang headed by Chiang Kai-shek*

ASSESS

Check for Understanding

Assign Section 3 Review as homework or as an in-class activity.

Use Student Self-Test and Review Software to review Section 3.

Evaluate

Section Quiz 30-3

Use the Testmaker to create a customized quiz for Section 3.

Reteach

Have students list statements on the chalkboard summarizing the main events in China's drive for unity and modernization.

Enrich

Have students watch a video of the 1987 film *The Last Emperor*. Have them write reports analyzing the way the film uses the story of Pu Yi as a mirror reflecting China's passage from feudalism through revolution toward a modern society.

CLOSE

Have students create a time line covering the key events in Chinese history from 1919 to 1939. Have them write summary statements describing the political situations in China in 1919 and 1939.

Visualizing History **Mao Zedong led the Communist retreat known as the Long March. Some Communists survived the ordeal in spite of harsh weather and rugged terrain.** *From what Chinese force were the Communists fleeing?*

The Long March

Mao's retreat from Jiangxi lasted for one year and covered about 6,000 miles (9,600 km). During that time the Red Army marched an average of 16 miles (26 km) a day, across rivers and mountains, and defeated 10 provincial armies—all the while being chased by Guomindang military forces. The Chinese Communists called the arduous undertaking the Long March.

At times the line of marching Communist soldiers stretched out for nearly 50 miles (80 km). One of these soldiers later recalled the march:

> "If it was a black night and the enemy far away, we made torches from pine branches or frayed bamboo, and then it was truly beautiful. At the foot of a mountain, we could look up and see a long column of lights coiling like a fiery dragon up the mountainside. From the summit we could look in both directions and see miles of torches moving forward like a wave of fire. A rosy glow hung over the whole route of the march."

Conditions on the Long March were far from rosy, however. Thousands of soldiers froze or starved to death, and others died in battle. Of the original 100,000 troops, fewer than 8,000 remained at the end of the march in 1935.

Threat From Japan

While Chiang and Mao battled each other in 1931, the Japanese had conquered the large section of northeast China known as **Manchuria**. Now it appeared that Japan wanted even more land, and Chiang's advisers urged him to confront the Japanese. Mao offered assistance but was rejected by Chiang. Members of the Guomindang then kidnapped Chiang and held him prisoner until he finally agreed to end his war with the Communists.

However, unity between Chiang and Mao could not stop the Japanese invasion that came eight months later. By 1939 Japan controlled most of eastern China. Chiang withdrew to the interior of the country, where Mao was awaiting the proper moment to strike back. Before that moment arrived, the entire world was at war.

SECTION 3 REVIEW

Recall
1. **Define** warlord.
2. **Identify** Sun Yat-sen, Yuan Shigai, Chiang Kai-shek, Mao Zedong.
3. **List** the groups of Chinese who supported the Communists most strongly.

Critical Thinking
4. **Analyzing Information** Why do you think Mao decided to undertake the Long March? What other choices did he have?

Understanding Themes
5. **Conflict** What conflicts kept China in turmoil after World War I?

SECTION 3 REVIEW ANSWERS

1. All vocabulary words are defined in the Glossary.
2. Sun Yat-sen, 804; Yuan Shigai, 804; Chiang Kai-shek, 804; Mao Zedong, 805
3. The Communists attracted support from peasants, urban workers, and intellectuals.
4. Answers will vary. Possible answer: Mao may have believed the Long March would build solidarity among members of the Red Army.
5. CONFLICT Fighting occurred among the warlords, between the Guomindang and the Communists, and against the Japanese.

1915 | 1925 | 1935

1915 Japan forces China to accept the Twenty-One Demands.

1925 Japanese parliament grants vote to all males.

1932 Army officers assassinate Japanese prime minister.

Section 4

Militarism in Japan

Setting the Scene

▶ **Terms to Define**
population explosion, heavy industry, *zaibatsu*

▶ **People to Meet**
Hirohito

▶ **Places to Locate**
Manchuria

Find Out How did militarism shape Japan during the period after World War I?

The Storyteller

Japan's Total War Research Institute drafted a secret strategy for the Japanese government. Called the "Greater East Asia Co-Prosperity Sphere," the plan outlined the establishment of a "zone of peaceful living and common prosperity for the peoples of East Asia." Japan would be the stabilizing power. The influence of all other nations would be driven out. The "New Order of East Asia" was an idea that did not include independence based on national self-determination. Instead, Japan would establish a new morality whose basic principle would be the Imperial Way.

—adapted from *Sources of the Japanese Tradition*, edited by W.T. deBary, reprinted in *Sources of World Civilization*, Volume 2, 1994

Japanese cavalry in China

Like China, Japan, an independent country, had fought on the side of the Allies in World War I. During the conflict, the Japanese supplied weapons to their European partners, particularly to Russia. At the same time, they took advantage of the war to expand their economic and political influence in East Asia. In addition to ruling Korea and Taiwan, Japan pressed for an enlargement of its role in China. In 1915 Japanese diplomats forced the Chinese government to accept a list of terms known as the Twenty-One Demands. The Twenty-One Demands, in effect, made China a Japanese protectorate.

Japan and the West

When World War I ended, Japan received Germany's Pacific islands north of the Equator as mandates from the League of Nations. The Japanese also entered into a series of military and commercial agreements with the Western powers. A disarmament conference held in Washington, D.C., in 1922 led to a five-power agreement among Japan, Great Britain, the United States, Italy, and France that allowed Japan to become the world's third-largest naval power after Great Britain and the United States. Yet, in spite of this and other gains, the Japanese were bitter toward the West.

First, Japan felt that the West did not accept it as an equal. In 1919 the League of Nations, dominated by Western powers, refused to accept Japan's demand for a statement on racial equality in the League's charter. The Japanese regarded this rejection as a humiliation. In 1924 the United States banned further Japanese immigration to its shores. In response, the Japanese staged demonstrations and boycotted American goods.

The Japanese were angered further by the West's refusal to support Japanese policy in China. Japan wanted to tie China closer to itself; the West wanted to retain the Open Door policy. As a result

Chapter 30 Section 4

SECTION THEME

▶ **Conflict** Japan's militarism and expansionism place it on a collision course with the West.

Find Out

Answer: *Militarism pervaded all aspects of Japanese life–from foreign policy to education.*

FOCUS

Section Objective

Describe how militarism shaped the development of Japan after World War I.

BELLRINGER
Motivational Activity

Before taking roll at the beginning of the class period, project Section Focus Transparency 30-4 and have students answer the activity questions. Discuss students' responses.

This activity is also available as a blackline master.

Vocabulary Pre-check

Use Vocabulary Activity 30 to introduce vocabulary terms. **L1 LEP**

SECTION RESOURCES

Reproducible Masters
- Reproducible Lesson Plan 30-4
- Vocabulary Activity 30
- Guided Reading Activity 30-4
- History Simulation 30
- Mapping History Activity 30
- Section Quiz 30-4

Transparencies
- Section Focus Transparency 30-4

Multimedia
- Student Self-Test and Review Software
- Testmaker

Chapter 30 *Nationalism in Asia, Africa, and Latin America* **807**

Chapter 30 Section 4

TEACH

Guided Practice

THEME Conflict To help students understand how population density encouraged Japanese expansionism, have them consider the relative areas of Japan (145,856 square miles [377,767 square km]) and California (158,706 square miles [411,049 square km]). By 1925 Japan's population was about 60 million; have students find out the current population of California. Ask students to discuss how Japan's growth led to aggressive policies. **L1**

Visualizing History After Chiang Kai-shek's Nationalist government made Nanking (now Nanjing) the capital of a united China in 1928, the city thrived. When the city fell to the Japanese in 1937, between 40,000 and 300,000 civilians were killed. From then until Japan's defeat in World War II, Nanjing was ruled by puppet governments. **Answer to Caption:** *His advisers feared the emperor would be removed and that extremism would increase if he opposed militarism.*

Independent Practice

Guided Reading Activity 30-4 **L1**

History Simulation 30

Mapping History Activity 30

Writing Have students discuss the influence of the military on Japan in the 1930s. Then have them write a news article as if they were reporting on events in Japan from 1931 to the end of the decade. **L2**

Visualizing History **Young Japanese students celebrate the fall of Nanking to Japanese forces in 1938.** *Why was Emperor Hirohito unable to thwart the spread of militarism in Japan?*

of Western pressure, Japan had to abandon the Twenty-One Demands and recognize Western interests in China.

Social and Political Tensions

After World War I, Japan faced social and economic challenges at home. Of major concern was a **population explosion**, or dramatic increase in population. Japan's population had increased from nearly 35 million in 1872 to about 60 million in 1925. This rate of increase was a challenge because of the already high density of population on the Japanese islands.

Japan's Industrial Growth

Since emigration was cut off to such places as the United States, the Japanese looked for other ways to cope. They placed new emphasis on manufacturing and foreign trade. It was hoped that new factories and markets would provide employment for large numbers of people.

Government-controlled banks provided the needed capital to encourage the expansion of **heavy industry**, or the manufacture of machinery and equipment needed for factories and mines. Industries important to national defense, especially steel and the railroads, were owned by the government, but most of the Japanese economy was in the hands of large privately owned businesses known together as the ***zaibatsu*** (zy•BAHT•soo).

During the 1920s and 1930s Japan's industry grew rapidly, and Japanese manufactured goods began to flood world markets. Increased manufacturing, however, stimulated the desire for raw materials. Since Japan had few mineral resources of its own, it was forced to look overseas for them.

Social and Political Changes

Meanwhile, Japan's working class increased in importance. Because of overpopulation in the countryside, land already scarce was continually subdivided among farmers. Rural economic woes enabled farm villages to provide the bulk of labor for the new urban industries. Along with male workers, many young women from rural areas found jobs in the factories.

Labor unions became more powerful and increased their membership to more than 300,000 members by the end of the 1920s. The growth of the urban, working-class population produced movements demanding social changes. Several efforts by intellectuals to organize Socialist groups, however, were speedily met with police repression.

During this period, the urban middle class expanded as well. Japanese cities became great metropolitan areas and centers of middle-class culture. The Tokyo-Yokohama area, devastated by a terrible earthquake in 1923, took on a new appearance as Western influences increasingly shaped the tempo of urban life. American music, dancing, and sports especially became popular, and rising standards of living and expectations produced the need for more and better higher education.

With the growth of the working and middle classes, steps were taken toward greater political democracy. In 1925 the Japanese parliament granted universal male suffrage; voters increased from 3 million to 14 million. Japanese women, however, did not receive the right to vote until 1947.

Political Weaknesses

In spite of these gains, democracy remained very limited in Japan. Political power was actually in the hands of nobles and urban industrialists. The emperor, **Hirohito**, was a constitutional monarch. However, he was a powerful symbol of traditional authority. Behind the emperor was an influential group of military leaders, who were opposed to democratic reforms.

The appeal of antidemocratic nationalist groups increased as the economy deteriorated in

COOPERATIVE LEARNING ACTIVITY

Roundtable Discussion Have students make a list of the social and economic problems that Japan faced after World War I. The list should include rapid population growth, need for raw materials, scarce farmland, limited democracy, and political repression. Organize the class into groups and have each group think of several possible solutions to one problem. Then hold a roundtable discussion in which representatives from each group try to work out peaceful solutions to Japan's challenges. **L2**

the 1930s. A worldwide fall in prices caused by the Great Depression devastated Japan's silk factories and other industries. Millions of workers lost their jobs and could not find new ones. Some began to starve, and children went begging in the streets. In November 1930 an assassin from a secret society shot Prime Minister Osachi Hamaguchi (oh•SAH •chee hah•mah•GOO•chee). Teetering on the brink of economic chaos, many impoverished farmers and workers in Japan looked to strong-minded military leaders such as Hashimoto Kingoro (hah•shee•MOH•toh keen•GOH•roh) for answers:

> "We are like a great crowd of people packed into a small and narrow room, and there are only three doors through which we might escape, namely emigration, advance into world markets, and expansion of territory. The first door ... has been barred to us by the anti-Japanese immigration policies of other countries. The second door ... is being pushed shut by tariff barriers.... Japan should rush upon the last door [expansion of territory]."
>
> —Hashimoto Kingoro, *Addresses to Young Men*

Militarism and Daily Life

During the 1930s, militarism began to influence all aspects of Japanese life—from foreign policy to education. Supporters of the military program opposed the spread of Western lifestyles in Japan and favored traditional Japanese ways. Military dress, including items such as the samurai swords, appealed to nationalist sentiments. Young children even carried out military drills in schools and participated in parades.

Military Expansion

In September 1931 the Japanese military demonstrated just how powerful it had become. Without seeking approval from the government, army leaders decided to invade the northeastern region of China known as **Manchuria**. In short order, they launched an invasion. It was clear that the Japanese government could no longer control its own army. In five months the powerful Japanese army had conquered Manchuria.

The conquest of Manchuria was a clear sign of the plans of the military to dominate the Japanese government at home and expand Japanese influence abroad. The principal opposition to democratic government came from young military officers. Largely from rural backgrounds, they opposed the urban luxuries of the politicians and readily accepted extremist ideas.

By the early 1930s extremist groups in the military were ready to use violence to bend the government to their will. In 1932 army officers assassinated a prime minister who dared to oppose their views. Then, in 1936, another group of officers led an armed revolt against the government. Although the revolt collapsed, it did not halt the steady takeover of government policy making by the military. By early 1937 the army and the government had become one and the same.

Many democratically-minded Japanese hoped that Emperor Hirohito would try to thwart the spread of militarism. As a crown prince, the emperor had traveled in the West and had a keen appreciation of Western ways. Palace advisers, however, feared that any strong stand by the emperor would only increase the extremism of the military leaders. Above all, they feared that the emperor would be removed from office and that the Japanese monarchy would be abolished.

As international criticism of Japan's expansion grew, many Japanese rallied to the support of their soldiers and the military leaders. With no powerful political opposition at home, Japan's military leaders looked forward to conquering all of Asia. Their dreams of a mighty Japanese empire—like the dreams of German and Italian rulers—brought the world to war.

SECTION 4 REVIEW

Recall

1. **Define** population explosion, heavy industry, *zaibatsu*.
2. **Identify** Hirohito.
3. **Locate** the Manchurian Plain on the map on pages A-17 and A-18 of the Atlas. Explain why the location of this region made it valuable to the Japanese.

Critical Thinking

4. **Synthesizing Information** Imagine you are an unemployed worker in Japan in the 1930s. Would you support the new military powers? Why or why not?

Understanding Themes

5. **Conflict** What steps did the military take to increase its hold on the Japanese government?

SECTION 4 REVIEW ANSWERS

1. All vocabulary words are defined in the Glossary.
2. Hirohito, 808
3. It was a nearby region and China was preoccupied with internal conflicts.
4. Answers will vary. Students might suggest that a strong military government might provide work through expanding war industries.
5. CONFLICT invaded Manchuria without government approval in 1931, assassinated a prime minister who opposed it in 1932, rebelled against the government in 1936, and steadily took over government policy making

Chapter 30 Section 4

Linking Past and Present

Japan's Military The Japanese Constitution of 1947 not only abolished the country's army and navy but also pledged that Japan would abandon war as a political tool. The prohibition was observed so strictly that it was not until February 1996 that 45 Japanese soldiers—the first Japanese troops to participate in peacekeeping operations—joined UN forces in the Golan Heights.

ASSESS

Check for Understanding

Assign Section 4 Review as homework or as an in-class activity.

Use Student Self-Test and Review Software to review Section 4.

Evaluate

Section Quiz 30-4

Use the Testmaker to create a customized quiz for Section 4.

Reteach

Have students state how Japan's geography contributed to its problems during the late 1800s and early 1900s.

Enrich

Have students imagine that they are Japanese civilians opposed to militarism living in Tokyo during the 1930s. Have them write diary entries responding to key events during the decade.

CLOSE

Have students make two lists, one of the problems that Japan confronted in the 1920s and 1930s, and one of solutions pursued by Japanese militarists.

Critical Thinking SKILLS

TEACH

Identifying an Argument In preparation for this lesson, find two newspaper editorials or opinion pieces that make opposing arguments on the same issue. Before having the class read the skill, distribute copies of the pieces. After students have read the editorials, ask them to identify the argument and supporting reasons in each piece. Now have students read the skill and complete the practice questions.

Additional Practice

Skill Reinforcement Activity 30

Critical Thinking SKILLS

Identifying an Argument

Have you ever argued with someone about a political or social issue? In everyday conversation, the word *argument* refers to a conflict involving two or more opinions. However, in writing and in formal debate, an argument is the full presentation of a single opinion. It is important to learn how to identify a writer's or speaker's argument to fully understand and evaluate the position.

Learning the Skill

The main idea of an argument is its thesis, or the writer's basic position or viewpoint on the subject. In some arguments the thesis is stated explicitly. In others, you must read carefully to determine the writer's position.

The writer supports the thesis with reasons and supports the reasons with examples or facts. For instance, suppose your parents have said that it would be better if you did not have a car to drive until after your 18th birthday. They support their thesis with these reasons: 1) other forms of transportation are available; and 2) you will be a more mature and better driver by that age. They support the first reason with these facts: you live in a city with good public transportation; your best friend has a car and frequently drives you to school. They support the second reason with accident statistics of younger and older drivers.

Before accepting or rejecting an argument, evaluate its strengths and weaknesses. Determine the validity of each reason. How well is each reason supported by facts and examples? Does the author's bias invalidate the argument? In the above example, your parents may be biased; they may want to protect your safety and keep their car insurance rates low for another year. Despite this bias, however, they still may have a strong argument if the supporting facts are true.

Practicing the Skill

Read the quotation from Jomo Kenyatta below, and review the discussion of Kenya in Section 1, pages 799-800. Then answer the following questions.

1. What is Kenyatta's thesis in this quotation?
2. What reasons does Kenyatta give to support this thesis?
3. What facts support Kenyatta's statement that Europeans have robbed Africans of their birthright?
4. What bias does Kenyatta show in his statement? Do the facts outweigh his bias? Why or why not?

> "By driving [the African] off his ancestral lands, the Europeans have robbed him of the material foundations of his culture, and reduced him to a state of serfdom incompatible with human happiness.... It is not in his nature to accept serfdom forever. He realizes that he must fight unceasingly for his own complete emancipation; for without this he is doomed to remain the prey of rival imperialisms."
>
> —Jomo Kenyatta, *Facing Mount Kenya*, 1938

Applying the Skill

Find an article in a recent newspaper or magazine that states an argument about a political or historical issue. Identify the thesis of the argument and major reasons and evidence supporting it. Decide whether you accept or reject this argument and explain why.

For More Practice

Turn to the Skill Practice in the Chapter Review on page 823 for more practice in identifying an argument.

ANSWERS TO PRACTICING THE SKILL

1. Europeans have robbed Africans of the material foundations of their culture.
2. Europeans drove Africans from their lands, reducing them to serfdom. Unless Africans emancipate themselves, they will continue to be subject to outside powers.
3. Britain refused to grant independence to Kenya and violently suppressed protests; Europeans settled on African lands and employed Africans on plantations for very low wages.
4. Kenyatta reveals an anti-European bias with emotional words such as *robbed, serfdom, emancipation, prey*. Student evaluations may differ, but point out that, despite his bias, the facts support Kenyatta's thesis.

1915 — 1925 — 1935

1917 Mexico ratifies a new constitution.

1930 José F. Uriburu leads successful coup in Argentina.

1934 Lázaro Cárdenas becomes president of Mexico.

Section 5

Nationalism in Latin America

Setting the Scene

- **Terms to Define**
  cooperatives, nationalization
- **People to Meet**
  Lázaro Cárdenas, Juan Vicente Gómez, Hipólito Irigoyen, José F. Uriburu, Getúlio Vargas, Augusto César Sandino
- **Places to Locate**
  Mexico, Venezuela, Argentina, Brazil, Nicaragua

Find Out Why did nationalism in Latin America bring conflict with the United States?

The Storyteller

"Let us forget the marble of the Acropolis and the towers of the Gothic cathedrals. We are the sons of the hills and the forests. Stop thinking of Europe. Think of America!" The words of Ronald de Carvallo, a Brazilian nationalist, rang in Lucio Costa's ears. He resolved to break with traditional forms and create architecture appropriate for Brazil. He visualized a style integrating art and nature—murals, sculptures, and tiles with gardens and decorative painting.

—adapted from *Latin America, A Concise Interpretive History*, E. Bradford Burns, 1994

Modern Brazilian architecture

After World War I, economic change and nationalism swept Latin America. Although the region's economy remained basically agricultural, the oil and mineral industries became increasingly important. Much of the investment that developed these resources was from the United States, Great Britain, France, Germany, and Italy. Anger at foreign influence led to growing nationalism among Latin Americans of all backgrounds. Rubén Darío, a noted Nicaraguan writer, had expressed the view of many Latin Americans:

> “The United States is grand and powerful.
> Whenever it trembles, a profound shudder
> runs down the enormous backbone of the
> Andes.
> If it shouts, the sound is like the roar of a
> lion....
> But our own America, which has had poets
> since the ancient times ...
> and has lived, since the earliest moments
> of its life,
> in light, in fire, in fragrance, and in love—
> the America of Moctezuma and Atahualpa,
> the aromatic America of Columbus,
> Catholic America, Spanish America ...
> our America lives. And dreams. And loves.
> And it is the daughter of the Sun. Be
> careful.
> Long live Spanish America!”
>
> —Rubén Darío, "To Roosevelt," 1903

Economic Changes

In the 20 years following World War I, Latin Americans continued to grow coffee, bananas,

SECTION THEME

▶ **Change** Nationalist forces in Latin America oppose increased American intervention in the region.

Find Out

Answer: *Nationalism in Latin America brought conflict with the United States because of increased American intervention.*

FOCUS

Section Objective

Analyze why nationalism in Latin America brought conflict with the United States.

BELLRINGER
Motivational Activity

Before taking roll at the beginning of the class period, project Section Focus Transparency 30-5 and have students answer the activity questions. Discuss students' responses.

This activity is also available as a blackline master.

Vocabulary Pre-check

Use Vocabulary Activity 30 to introduce vocabulary terms. **L1 LEP**

SECTION RESOURCES

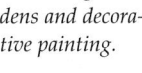

Reproducible Masters
- Reproducible Lesson Plan 30-5
- Vocabulary Activity 30
- Guided Reading Activity 30-5
- World Art and Music Activity 30
- People in World History Profile 57
- Reteaching Activity 30
- Enrichment Activity 30
- Section Quiz 30-5
- Performance Assessment Activity 30
- Spanish Chapter Summary 30

Transparencies
- Section Focus Transparency 30-5
- World History and Art Transparency 40, *Zapatistas*

Multimedia
- Student Self-Test and Review Software
- Testmaker

Chapter 30 *Nationalism in Asia, Africa, and Latin America* **811**

Chapter 30
Section 5

TEACH

Guided Practice

THEME Change

Write on the chalkboard the following line from Rubén Darío's poem quoted on page 811: *"Whenever it trembles, a profound shudder runs down the enormous backbone of the Andes."* Ask students to interpret the sentence. **How did economic changes in Latin America after World War I make the poem even more relevant?** *(Latin America became even more tied to global markets.)* **L1**

Global Issues Ask students to discuss the ways in which the United States was involved in Latin America following World War I. *(It kept a military presence in Nicaragua, Haiti, the Dominican Republic, Panama; it was involved in the economies of many countries through ownership of oil wells and other businesses.)* **L2**

Politics Have students explain what the United States promised to do under the Good Neighbor policy. *(not to interfere militarily in the affairs of other countries)* Initiate a discussion of why this was a change from the actions of the United States before this time. *(The United States had formerly kept a strong military presence in Latin America.)* **L3**

World Art and Music Activity 30

World History and Art Transparency 40, *Zapatistas*

wheat, corn, beans, sugarcane, and other crops in large amounts. However, industrial growth—particularly in the United States and western Europe—increased the demand for tin, copper, silver, oil, and other raw materials from Latin America. As mineral exports increased, Latin Americans had more cash with which to buy imports. More and more of the Latin American economy became tied to global markets.

When world prices for raw materials increased, Latin American economies improved. However, in the 1920s, prices for coffee, sugar, and other raw materials plunged. The price declines foretold the global economic depression that was soon to occur. Like much of the world, Latin America suffered high unemployment and low prices for its products in the decade of the Great Depression, 1929–1939.

Mexico's Oil Economy

Oil was one of the vital resources for growing industries, and **Mexico** was an important source of oil. Mexico entered the postwar era, still reeling from its own bloody and divisive revolution that had begun in 1910. However, a stable, one-party system was evolving that seemed able to maintain order and unity. Mexico's constitution, ratified in 1917, authorized the government to protect workers from exploitation and to require private property owners to act in the public interest.

Despite the constitution, reforms came slowly until 1934. In that year, **Lázaro Cárdenas** (KAHR•duhn•AHS) was elected to the presidency. Over the next six years, his government carried out other reforms in the spirit of the 1910 revolution. First, Cárdenas directed the redistribution of vast tracts of land to landless peasants. To increase agricultural production, the Mexican government also encouraged the formation of cooperatives, farm organizations operated by and for the peasants. By 1940 more than half of all Mexicans farmed land they could finally call their own.

Cárdenas's main goal, however, was to make Mexico economically independent of foreign countries. His government especially wanted to bring

Images of the Times

Mexican Murals

During the 1930s, Mexican artists painted colorful murals showing key themes and events in Mexico's history. Many of these murals still decorate outer and inner walls of government buildings, theaters, universities, and hospitals throughout the country.

Distribution of the Land by Diego Rivera. Court of Fiestas, Secretaria de Educacion Publica, Mexico City, Mexico

812

Images of the Times **Mexican Murals**

Mexican murals won world renown after World War I, and controversy made Diego Rivera (1886–1957) the best-known Mexican muralist. A mural he was commissioned to paint for the Detroit Institute of Arts was attacked for being antireligious, and a fresco he did for New York's Rockefeller Center was ultimately destroyed because it included a portrait of the Bolshevik leader Lenin.

Siqueiros (1896–1974) also used his art to convey his radical political beliefs. Over the course of his lifetime, his Communist sympathies and work for labor unions landed him in jail and drove him into exile at different times.

the industrial economy under Mexican control. In 1937 Cárdenas supported an oil workers' strike. At the time, about 17,000 Mexican workers had gone on strike against their British and American employers, demanding higher wages and better working conditions. Cárdenas urged the oil companies to meet their demands, but the companies refused. After a year of futile negotiations, Cárdenas carried out a policy of nationalization of foreign-owned oil wells on March 18, 1938, declaring them the property of the government. He explained his actions by reaching all the way back to a colonial law written by the Spanish king in 1783, which had been retained in the new constitution: "The Mines are the property of My Royal Crown, [including] all bitumens [minerals] and juices of the earth."

The British and American companies were furious, but the Mexican people were ecstatic. They celebrated March 18 as the day of their "Declaration of Economic Independence." Cárdenas, meanwhile, defused the crisis by offering to pay a fair price for the oil wells. With World War II looming on the horizon, Great Britain and the United States soon accepted this offer. They did not want an angry Mexico to sell its oil to Japan and Germany.

The nationalization of Mexico's oil fields signaled the arrival of economic nationalism in Latin America. For Mexico it was a clean break from the economic dependence of the past.

Changes in Venezuela

Another oil-rich country, **Venezuela**, followed a course unlike that of Mexico, but more like that of other Latin American countries that had a single source of wealth. Between 1908 and 1935, President **Juan Vicente Gómez** ruled Venezuela as a dictator. During this period, engineers discovered oil along Venezuela's Caribbean coast. By the late 1930s Venezuela was the third-largest oil-producing country in the world. However, British, Dutch, and American oil companies controlled the Venezuelan oil industry. Gómez, instead of nationalizing the oil companies, worked closely with them. He, his

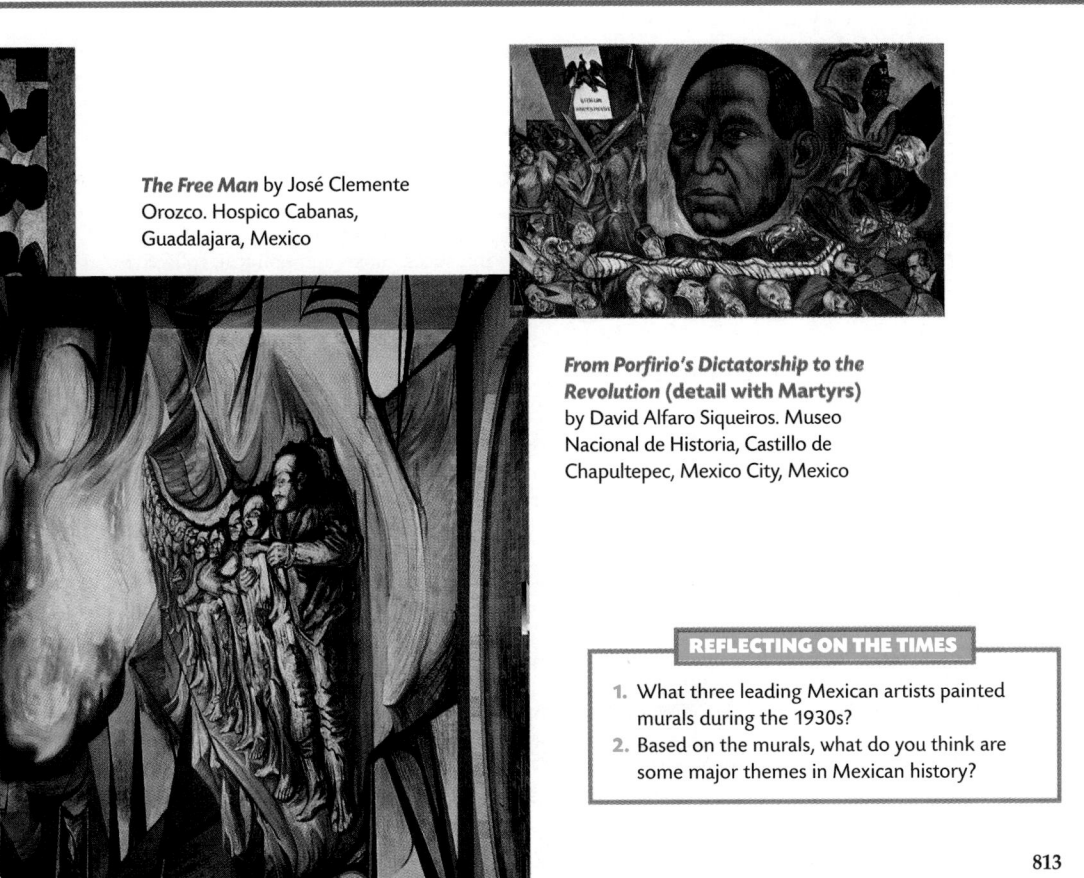

The Free Man by José Clemente Orozco. Hospico Cabanas, Guadalajara, Mexico

***From Porfirio's Dictatorship to the Revolution* (detail with Martyrs)** by David Alfaro Siqueiros. Museo Nacional de Historia, Castillo de Chapultepec, Mexico City, Mexico

REFLECTING ON THE TIMES

1. What three leading Mexican artists painted murals during the 1930s?
2. Based on the murals, what do you think are some major themes in Mexican history?

813

ANSWERS TO REFLECTING ON THE TIMES

1. Diego Rivera, José Clemente Orozco, and David Alfaro Siqueiros
2. transforming Mexico into a more independent and equitable society, economically as well as politically

Chapter 30 Section 5

Independent Practice

Guided Reading Activity 30-5 **L1**

Economics Organize students into two groups. Have one group write a pamphlet in favor of the nationalization of foreign-owned oil wells in Mexico, and the other a pamphlet against nationalization. Tell students to support their arguments by forecasting the long-term effects of state ownership of the wells. **L2**

The Arts Have students research Latin American artists and writers whose work dealt with nationalist issues. Then ask students to deliver brief oral reports describing how the artists' political beliefs shaped their work. Suggest that they bring in reproductions of artwork if possible. **L3**

People in World History Profile 57

you don't say...

Latin America The region consisting of Mexico, Central America, South America, and the islands of the Caribbean gets its name from the Latin language. When Europeans began to settle the area during the late 1400s, they brought their languages and customs with them. These languages—Spanish, Portuguese, and French—all derived from ancient Latin. They are the main languages of Latin America to this day.

Visualizing History The city's main avenue, named 9 de Julio after the official independence day, was patterned on the Champs-Élysées in Paris and was claimed as the broadest avenue in the world. It was built in the 1930s and officially opened in October 1937.

Answer to Caption: *divided between Socialist and Fascist movements, with the army playing an important role in government*

Who?What?Where?When?

Uriburu (1868–1932), like other Latin American military officers of the time, was an admirer of German militarism. He became a member of the kaiser's imperial guard during a visit to Germany in 1902. He made another visit to Germany in 1908, a year after becoming director of Argentina's war college.

Linking Past and Present

OPEC In 1960, Venezuela joined Iran, Iraq, Kuwait, and Saudi Arabia in founding OPEC, the Organization of Petroleum Exporting Countries. It remains the only Latin American country among OPEC's 12 current members. In the early 1990s, OPEC's members produced more than half of all oil traded internationally.

Visualizing History **By the 1930s, Buenos Aires had become a city of wide avenues and public buildings. Its prosperity rested on the export of beef and other agricultural products.** *How did the Great Depression affect Argentina's political life during the 1930s?*

political allies, and oil companies prospered, but most Venezuelans did not.

Gómez used the oil profits to strengthen his government. He paid off his country's huge national debt to European bankers and created a strong army. He also used some of the profits for his personal benefit.

After Gómez died in 1935, workers and students around the country rioted to protest the domination of their country by foreign oil companies and their Venezuelan partners. The army intervened to stop the protests and remained in charge of the country for the next several decades.

Democracy and the Military

Venezuela was one of many Latin American countries in which a small group of people prospered from the natural wealth found in the country. It was also typical in that the military intervened to put down protests that threatened business interests. Argentina and Brazil are two of the other countries in which democracy failed to take hold.

Argentina Becomes Fascist

In 1916 **Argentina** held its first open presidential election in which every male could vote. The winner, **Hipólito Irigoyen** (ee•PAW•lee•TOH IHR•ih•GOH•YEHN), obtained most of his support from urban workers and the middle class. They elected him because of his party's success in achieving electoral reforms. During his first administration, Irigoyen carried through social reforms that improved factory conditions, boosted workers' wages, and regulated working hours. He advocated other democratic reforms and efforts to help the poor. After serving six years as president, Irigoyen proudly claimed:

> "We have held public office in obedience to the popular mandate and inspired by the duty to make reparation ... for all the injustices, moral and political, collective and individual, that have long dishonored the country."

In 1928 Irigoyen was again elected president. His second term, however, aroused widespread opposition, and he did not complete his term in office. Although he was personally popular, his government had often been ineffective. He was slow to make decisions, so that official documents needing his attention piled up on his desk awaiting action. More important, corrupt aides stole money from the national treasury. In addition, few Argentinians believed any more in the democratic process by which Irigoyen had won office.

Angered by inefficiency and corruption and opposed to democracy, General **José F. Uriburu** led a successful coup against Irigoyen in 1930. With the coming of the Great Depression, Argentina was divided between Socialist and Fascist political

COOPERATIVE LEARNING ACTIVITY

Research Ask students to research U.S. involvement in Nicaragua in the 1920s and 1930s. Organize the class into research groups of four to six students. The groups should gather information about important dates, events, and policies in U.S.-Nicaraguan relations during this period, beginning with facts from this section. A good work on the topic is *The Sandino Affair* by Neill Macaulay. Have students create a chart that includes significant dates and events concerning U.S. involvement in Nicaragua. Post the chart on a bulletin board and conclude the activity by discussing students' opinions about the ethics and practical results of U.S. involvement in Nicaragua between the wars. **L2**

PICTURING HISTORY

National Archives

Sending in the Marines

National Archives

American marines in Nicaragua unload a cannon to help defend their military position. The United States has a history of military intervention in the Central American nation of Nicaragua. In the early years of the 1900s American interest in Nicaragua increased with the building of the Panama Canal, with growing pressure to defend the hemisphere against British and German threats, and with expanding United States involvement in Central American trade.

In 1912, U.S Marines landed in Nicaragua to ensure the payment of its debts and remained there for the next 13 years. In 1927, American forces again intervened to put down an uprising by nationalist leader Augusto César Sandino (left, center figure). Sandino fought American involvement in his country's domestic affairs—and failed. American forces remained in Nicaragua until 1933.

During the years between the two world wars the empires of Europe began to crumble. In the Western Hemisphere President Hoover pulled American troops out of Nicaragua, and President Franklin D. Roosevelt declared a Good Neighbor policy with Latin America. Nevertheless, imperialism endured until after World War II. ⊕

TEACH

Tell students that for many years before the United States began construction of the Panama Canal, Americans had hoped to build a canal across Nicaragua to link the Atlantic and Pacific Oceans. **What was the political group that controlled Nicaragua from 1979 until 1990 called, and why?** *(They were called Sandinistas in honor of Nicaragua's nationalist hero, Sandino.)*

CURRICULUM CONNECTION

THE ARTS

Nicaraguan poet and essayist Rubén Darío (1867–1916) was a founder of the literary movement called modernism. Many literary historians date the birth of modernism to the 1888 publication of *Azul*, Darío's first major work, and the movement's peak to the 1896 publication of his *Prosas profanas*.

Chapter 30 *Nationalism in Asia, Africa, and Latin America* **815**

Chapter 30
Section 5

Who?What?Where?When?

Getúlio Vargas Even after being forced out of office, Vargas remained popular. He became president of Brazil again in 1951. By the middle of 1954, however, criticism of his government was so intense that, rather than be forced out of office a second time, Vargas committed suicide.

ASSESS

Check for Understanding

Assign Section 5 Review as homework or as an in-class activity.

Use Student Self-Test and Review Software to review Section 5.

Evaluate

Section Quiz 30-5

Use the Testmaker to create a customized quiz for Section 5.

Reteach

Write this heading on the chalkboard: *Latin America and the Global Economy.* Have students list facts that show how the world market affected Latin America. *(Lists might include increased U.S. and European demand for raw materials from Latin America; sale of exports increased Latin American purchases of imports; U.S. investment in Latin America led to interventions to protect American interests.)*

AROUND THE WORLD **Major Oil Discovery**

Saudi Arabia, 1938

In 1933 the government of Ibn Saud granted an American oil company the right to explore for oil in the newly united kingdom of Saudi Arabia. After a major oil deposit was discovered on the Arabian Peninsula, other oil companies joined to form the Arabian American Oil Company (Aramco) in 1944. After World War II, large-scale oil production brought immense wealth to Saudi Arabia and enabled Ibn Saud's government to build roads, schools, and hospitals throughout the country.

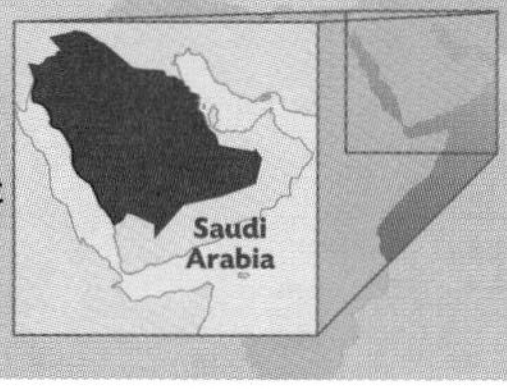

movements. To maintain social order, the army began to assume an important role in the Argentine government.

Uriburu, like Italy's Mussolini, believed in fascism. He cancelled elections and tried to abolish the congress. For the remainder of the 1930s, military men and their sympathizers ruled Argentina. They faked elections, suppressed their opponents, and consolidated their power. Democracy was dead in Argentina, destroyed by the military.

Brazil's Popular Dictator

Brazil, like Argentina, fell under an authoritarian government. In 1930 President **Getúlio Vargas** took power. Seven years later, Vargas proclaimed a new constitution that made him a virtual dictator. He strengthened the government by transferring powers from the cities and states to the national government. He won support from many Brazilians for his willingness to oppose the interests of large businesses. To gain working- class support, Vargas's administration increased wages, shortened working hours, and gave unions the right to organize. Vargas's supporters called him "father of the poor" for these efforts.

Vargas, with the support of the military, was able to keep Brazil united and stable until 1945. In that year, a democratic revolt threw him out of power. When Vargas refused to leave office, military leaders stepped in and forced Vargas out of office. Although the military did not actually rule in Brazil, their support was crucial in deciding who did.

Ties With the United States

During the 1920s and 1930s, the mineral wealth of Latin America attracted American businesses, which invested heavily in the region. To protect American economic interests, the United States intervened militarily in Central America and the Caribbean countries.

Increased American Intervention

In 1912 United States Marines had invaded **Nicaragua** when the country failed to pay its debts. American forces landed again during the 1920s to protect United States interests. Rebel forces led by General **Augusto César Sandino** resisted the Americans and tried to force a United States withdrawal. To help the American soldiers, the United States government trained a loyal Nicaraguan army called the National Guard. By the mid-1930s the National Guard was able to defeat the rebels. Its leader, Anastasio Somoza, seized power in 1936. From that time until 1979, the Somoza family ruled Nicaragua with American support.

During the early 1900s, American troops also occupied Haiti and the Dominican Republic as well as Nicaragua. This American military intervention, as well as the growth of American economic influence, was deeply resented by many Latin Americans. Latin American nationalists particularly opposed the Roosevelt Corollary. They stated that no country had the right to intervene in the affairs of another. They also claimed that, while the United States was exploiting their raw materials, Latin America was getting few economic benefits in return. Anti-Americanism was especially strong during the Great Depression. At this time, world market prices for raw materials fell sharply. This decline increased hardships among Latin Americans dependent on trade with North America and Europe.

Good Neighbor Policy

Aware of growing resentment, the United States tried to improve relations with its southern neighbors. Following his election in 1928, United States President Herbert Hoover went on a goodwill tour of Latin America. He hoped to show that the United States regarded its Latin American neighbors as equals. At the same time, Secretary of State Joshua Reuben Clark began to restate the meaning of the Monroe Doctrine. In a memorandum issued in December 1928, Clark held that the Monroe Doctrine's warning that European powers could not interfere in Latin America did not mean that the United States had the right to interfere.

MEETING SPECIAL NEEDS ACTIVITY

Language Delayed Ask students whose first language is Spanish, Creole, or Portuguese to interview a grandparent or other adult who lived through some of the events described in this section. To prepare for their interviews, help students organize a list of questions to ask the interviewee. Have them write the interview in their first language. After they have completed the write-up, help them prepare an English translation. Select the best of these interviews for presentation to the class. **L1**

United States Involvement in Latin America 1903–1922

Map Study The United States intervened in the affairs of Latin American nations in the early 1900s. **Region** How did Latin Americans view United States intervention in their affairs?

In 1933 President Franklin D. Roosevelt, Hoover's successor, announced the Good Neighbor policy toward Latin America. He declared, "I would dedicate this nation to the policy of the good neighbor—the neighbor who resolutely respects himself, and because he does so, respects the rights of others." The Good Neighbor policy renounced past United States military intervention in the region. To prove his good intentions, Roosevelt ended American restrictions on the sovereignty of Cuba. He also ordered the withdrawal of American troops from Haiti and Nicaragua.

In 1933 the United States took another step toward improving its relationship with Latin America. Diplomats from the United States joined with their Latin American counterparts at the Pan American conference in Montevideo, Uruguay. After much discussion, all parties signed an agreement stating: "No state has the right to intervene in the internal or external affairs of another."

SECTION 5 REVIEW

Recall
1. **Define** cooperatives, nationalization.
2. **Identify** Lázaro Cárdenas, Juan Vicente Gómez, Hipólito Irigoyen, José F. Uriburu, Getúlio Vargas, Augusto César Sandino, the Good Neighbor policy.
3. **List** three Latin American countries in which American military forces intervened between 1890 and 1940.

Critical Thinking
4. **Making Comparisons** How did Mexico and Venezuela differ in their response to European and American control of their oil industries?

Understanding Themes
5. **Change** Does the United States have the right to intervene in the affairs of other countries? Explain, using recent examples.

Chapter 30 Section 5

Map Study

Answer
Latin Americans resented U.S. interference in their national affairs.

Map Skills Practice
Reading a Map **What nations border Costa Rica?** *(Nicaragua and Panama)*

Reteaching Activity 30

Enrich

Have students select one leader from this section and research his life. Have them write a brief essay about the leader that focuses on whether he was good or bad for his country.

Enrichment Activity 30

CLOSE

Review with students the political and economic changes that were occurring in Latin America during the period after World War I. *(the revolution in Mexico, struggles for economic independence, conflicts over freedom from interference by the United States)*

SECTION 5 REVIEW ANSWERS

1. All vocabulary words are defined in the Glossary.
2. Cárdenas, 812; Gómez, 813; Irigoyen, 814; Uriburu, 814; Vargas, 816; Sandino, 816; the Good Neighbor policy, 817
3. Haiti, the Dominican Republic, Panama, Nicaragua, Mexico, Cuba
4. Mexico nationalized its oil industry; Venezuela worked closely with foreign oil companies.
5. **CHANGE** Answers will vary but might include discussions of U.S. intervention in Somalia, Haiti, or Bosnia.

Bridge to the Past
Literature

Block Schedule

Team Teaching This excerpt from *Gifts of Passage* may be presented in a team-teaching context, in conjunction with English or Language Arts.

Gifts of Passage

Historical Connection

British rule dramatically affected Indian society. In British schools, government offices, and elsewhere, the diverse peoples of India met and interacted with the British but not on terms of equality.

Background Information

Setting The incident takes place in the Indian city of Zorinabad about 1928. The British still ruled India, but the Indian independence movement was growing stronger.

Characters Santha: a five-year-old girl from whose point of view the story is told; Premila: Santha's eight-year-old sister; Headmistress: the Englishwoman who runs the Anglo-Indian school; Mother: the mother of Santha and Premila

Plot Santha and Premila start to attend an Anglo-Indian school, where the headmistress assigns them British names because she does not think she can pronounce Indian names. When Premila takes her first test, her teacher separates the Indian students because she thinks they will cheat. Premila, with Santha, leaves the school in anger.

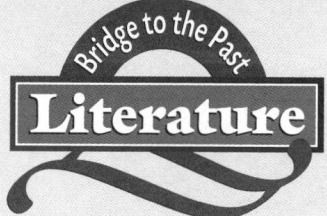

Bridge to the Past
Literature

from Gifts of Passage

by Santha Rama Rau

Santha Rama Rau, born in Madras, India, in 1923, spent her childhood in India, England, and South Africa. In each place, she closely watched the way people from different backgrounds related with one another. Advances in transportation and communication have sharply increased the interactions of people from different cultures. Today these interactions shape the world more than ever before. In the following excerpt, Rau recalls her early experiences at a school for English and Indian children in India.

At the Anglo-Indian day school in Zorinabad to which my sister and I were sent when she was eight and I was five and a half, they changed our names. On the first day of school, a hot, windless morning of a north Indian September, we stood in the headmistress's study and she said, "Now you're the *new* girls. What are your names?"

My sister answered for us. "I am Premila, and she"—nodding in my direction—"is Santha."

The headmistress had been in India, I suppose, fifteen years or so, but she still smiled her helpless inability to cope with Indian names. Her rimless half-glasses glittered, and the precarious bun on the top of her head trembled as she shook her head. "Oh, my dears, those are much too hard for me. Suppose we give you pretty English names. Wouldn't that be more jolly? Let's see, now—Pamela for you, I think." She shrugged in a baffled way at my sister. "That's as close as I can get. And for *you*," she said to me, "how about Cynthia? Isn't that nice?"

My sister was always less intimidated than I was, and while she kept a stubborn silence, I said "Thank you," in a very tiny voice....

That first day at school is still, when I think of it, a remarkable one. At that age, if one's name is changed, one develops a curious form of dual personality. I remember having a certain detached and disbelieving concern in the actions of "Cynthia," but certainly no responsibility. ...

About the Author

Santha Rama Rau is the daughter of an Indian government official. When she was young, India was still part of the British Empire. Many Indian leaders and administrators, including Rau's father, were strongly influenced by British culture. Her father, for example, was educated in England. Rau herself attended Wellesley College in Massachusetts. She has written a number of novels and nonfiction works, including essays about her childhood and her extensive travels, as well as a stage play based on the novel *A Passage to India*, by E. M. Forster.

Visualizing History **During the years of British rule, the Indian subcontinent had a wealthy upper class of princes and their families. This upper-class Indian family of the 1940s practiced traditional ways but was also familiar with the customs of the British aristocracy.** *What are the British teachers' attitudes toward ordinary Indians in the story by Santha Rama Rau?*

Accordingly, I followed the thin, erect back of the headmistress down the veranda [porch] to my classroom feeling, at most, a passing interest in what was going to happen to me in this strange, new atmosphere of School....

I can't remember too much about the proceedings in class that day, except for the beginning. The teacher pointed to me and asked me to stand up. "Now, dear, tell the class your name."

I said nothing.

"Come along," she said, frowning slightly. "What's your name, dear?"

"I don't know," I said, finally.

The English children in the front of the class—there were about eight or ten of them—giggled and twisted around in their chairs to look at me. I sat down quickly and opened my eyes very wide, hoping in that way to dry them off. The little girl with the braids put out her hand and very lightly touched my arm. She still didn't smile.

Most of the morning I was rather bored. I looked briefly at the children's drawings pinned to the wall, and then concentrated on a lizard clinging to the ledge of the high, barred window behind the teacher's head. Occasionally it would shoot out its long yellow tongue for a fly, and then it would rest, with its eyes closed and its belly palpitating, as though it were swallowing several times quickly. The lessons were mostly concerned with reading and writing and simple numbers—things that my mother had already taught me—and I paid very little attention. The teacher wrote on the easel blackboard words like

Other Works by Santha Rama Rau

The Adventuress. New York: Harper, 1970.
East of Home. New York: Harper, 1950.
Home to India. New York: Harper, 1945.
My Russian Journey. New York: Harper, 1959.
Remember the House. New York: Harper, 1956.
This Is India. New York: Harper, 1954.
View to the Southeast. New York: Harper, 1957.

Bridge to the Past

Literature

Visualizing History Many upper-class Indians strongly supported the movement for independence. Like the Latin American Creoles who fought for independence from Spain in the early 1800s, members of this upper class had the most to gain from independence since they would become the ruling elite of the new nation.

Answer to Caption: *superficially friendly but condescending and mistrustful*

Literary Element Imagery consists of the words and phrases that a writer uses to evoke particular sights, sounds, smells, or other sensations for the reader. In this excerpt, for example, Rau helps readers picture the headmistress by describing her "rimless half-glasses" and "precarious bun."

FOCUS

As students read, ask them to think about the importance of name giving in the story. Santha and her sister are given British names, as is Santha's friend, Nalini. But other characters, such as the headmistress and the teachers, are not referred to by name at all. Discuss what Rau may have intended by not giving names to certain characters. **Why might Rau have chosen to focus on names, and their significance, at this moment in Indian history?** *(Names establish identity, and the struggle for an Indian identity was part of the independence movement.)*

Bridge to the Past

Literature

TEACH

Literary Analysis

Rather than simply tell the reader that she was bored during her first day in school, Rau describes a lizard on the wall in vivid detail. The description of the lizard takes the reader's mind off the classwork, just as the actual lizard distracted Santha.

Comparison

Discuss the difference between Santha's view of games and that of the British children. The way the children played reflected their basic values about individual achievement and group cooperation. Discuss how games today may reflect the values of students in schools in the United States.

Clarification

Discuss how social-class relationships affect even school students. Rau, even as a five-year-old child, knew that friendship between Indian and British or Anglo-Indian children was "out of the question." Have students consider how Rau knew that social equality between British and Indian students was impossible.

World Literature Selection 7

"bat" and "cat," which seemed babyish to me; only "apple" was new and incomprehensible.

When it was time for the lunch recess, I followed the girl with braids out onto the veranda. There the children from the other classes were assembled. I saw Premila at once and ran over to her, as she had charge of our lunchbox. The children were all opening packages and sitting down to eat sandwiches. Premila and I were the only ones who had Indian food—thin wheat chapatties [a type of bread], some vegetable curry, and a bottle of buttermilk. Premila thrust half of it into my hand and whispered fiercely that I should go and sit with my class, because that was what the others seemed to be doing....

I had never really grasped the system of competitive games. At home, whenever we played tag or guessing games, I was always allowed to "win"—"because," Mother used to tell Premila, "she is the youngest, and we have to allow for that." I had often heard her say it, and it seemed quite reasonable to me, but the result was that I had no clear idea of what "winning" meant.

When we played twos-and-threes that afternoon at school, in accordance with my training, I let one of the small English boys catch me, but was naturally rather puzzled when the other children did not return the courtesy. I ran about for what seemed like hours without ever catching anyone, until it was time for school to close. Much later I learned that my attitude was called "not being a good sport," and I stopped allowing myself to be caught, but it was not for years that I really learned the spirit of the thing....

It was a week later, the day of Premila's first test, that our lives changed rather abruptly. I was sitting at the back of the class, in my usual inattentive way, only half listening to the teacher. I had started a rather guarded friendship with the girl with the braids, whose name turned out to be Nalini (Nancy, in school). The three other Indian children were already fast friends. Even at that age it was apparent to all of us that friendship with the English or Anglo-Indian children was out of the question. Occasionally, during the class, my new friend and I would draw pictures and show them to each other secretly.

The door opened sharply and Premila marched in. At first, the teacher smiled at her in a kindly and encouraging way and said, "Now, you're little Cynthia's sister?"

Premila didn't even look at her. She stood with her feet planted firmly apart and her shoulders rigid, and addressed herself directly to me. "Get up," she said. "We're going home."

I didn't know what happened, but I was aware that it was a crisis of some sort. I rose obediently and started to walk toward my sister.

"Bring your pencils and your notebook," she said.

I went back for them, and together we left the room. The teacher started to say something just as Premila closed the door, but we didn't wait to hear what it was.

In complete silence we left the school grounds and started to walk home. Then I asked Premila what the matter was. All she would say was "We're going home for good."...

When we got to our house the ayah [maid] was just taking a tray of lunch into Mother's room. She immediately started a long, worried questioning about what are you children doing back here at this hour of the day.

Mother looked very startled and very concerned, and asked Premila what had happened.

Premila said, "We had our test today, and she made me and the other Indians sit at the back of the room, with a desk between each one."

Mother said, "Why was that, darling?"

"She said it was because Indians cheat," Premila added. "So I don't think we should go back to that school."

Mother looked very distant, and was silent a long time. At last she said, "Of course not, darling." She sounded displeased.

We all shared the curry she was having for lunch, and afterward I was sent off to the beautifully familiar bedroom for my siesta. I could hear Mother and Premila talking through the open door.

Mother said, "Do you suppose she understood all that?"

Additional Literary Works of the Period

Mistral, Gabriela. ***Feeling.*** Poems for children by one of Chile's most famous writers.

Natsume, Sóseki. ***The Three-Cornered World.*** Story of a Japanese artist who visits a small village.

Tagore, Rabindranath. ***Gitanjali.*** Poetry about India, religion, and nationalism.

820 Chapter 30 *Nationalism in Asia, Africa, and Latin America*

Visualizing History **These Indian women are dressed in the sari, a garment of several yards of material draped so that one end forms a skirt and the other a shoulder or head covering.** *How do you think the two Indian girls in the story dressed for their classes at the British school?*

Premila said, "I shouldn't think so. She's a baby."

Mother said, "Well, I hope it won't bother her."

Of course, they were both wrong. I understood it perfectly, and I remember it all very clearly. But I put it happily away, because it had all happened to a girl called Cynthia, and I never was really particularly interested in her.

RESPONDING TO LITERATURE

1. Why did Santha and her sister leave school?
2. Explain why Santha was unable to tell the class her name.
3. When the headmistress gives Santha and her sister new names, what can you determine the headmistress thought of Indian culture?
4. **Demonstrating Reasoned Judgment** Explain why Santha's mother would or would not keep her children home permanently from the Anglo-Indian school.

ANSWERS TO RESPONDING TO LITERATURE

1. because a British teacher assumed that Indian students cheated
2. Answers may vary but might suggest that Santha had not accepted her British name but realized her real name would not be accepted by the teacher.
3. The headmistress does not value Indian culture and feels it should be replaced by British customs.
4. Answers will vary. Students may say that the mother is forced to face the fact that to get a good, that is British, education, her daughters must confront British racism.

Bridge to the Past

Literature

Visualizing History Clothing can make a powerful statement about identity. A woman's decision to wear a veil in secular Muslim nations like Egypt and Turkey, for example, is a way to identify with traditional Muslim values.

Answer to Caption: *Answers will vary but may include Western styles of dress, especially uniforms.*

ASSESS

Assign **Responding to Literature** questions.

CLOSE

After students have read the excerpt, ask them how they would react if they were Indian students in Premila's classroom. Discuss what other ways they might have found to protest their treatment by the British teachers.

Contemporary Connection

Students interested in learning more about India might wish to see the films of the great Indian director Satyajit Ray, including *The World of Apu* and *Pather panchali*.

Portfolio Project

Have students write an essay in which they tell what steps they think a teacher ought to take to overcome or prevent prejudice among the different ethnic groups represented in his or her classroom.

Chapter 30 *Nationalism in Asia, Africa, and Latin America* 821

CHAPTER 30 REVIEW

Historical Significance

World War I shattered the old order in Europe and stirred nationalist feelings in lands under Western colonial rule. During the 1900s dozens of new nations in Asia, Africa, and the Americas either emerged from the ashes of old empires or asserted their independence from powerful neighbors. In addition, newly developing countries began to follow economic policies based on nationalism. Governments in these lands sometimes took over foreign-owned industries and limited foreign investment when national sovereignty seemed threatened.

Using Key Terms

Write the key term that completes each sentence.

a. warlords
b. nationalization
c. pacifist
d *zaibatsu*
e. cooperatives
f. heavy industry
g. shah
h. population explosion
i. self determination
j. civil disobedience

1. During the 1930s the Mexican government encouraged peasants to form ______ to boost agricultural production.
2. One of Japan's major social problems after World War I was a __________ that raised the number of its people from nearly 35 million in 1872 to about 60 million in 1925.
3. After Yuan Shigai's death in 1916, local military leaders called _______ divided China among themselves.
4. Mohandas K. Gandhi carried out a campaign of __________ against British rule.
5. United States President Woodrow Wilson raised the hopes of colonial peoples by endorsing the principle of ___________.
6. In 1938 the Mexican government carried out a policy of __________ in which it took over the foreign-owned oil industries.
7. In 1921 Reza Khan led nationalists in overthrowing the Iranian _____, or king.
8. To boost its economy, Japanese leaders in the 1920s encouraged the growth of _________, the manufacture of machinery and equipment needed for factories and mines.
9. Mohandas K. Gandhi was a ________, a person opposed to using war and other means of violence to settle disputes.
10. The privately owned part of the Japanese economy in the 1920s and 1930s was largely in the hands of large companies known as _________.

Using Your History Journal

Write a three-minute radio news feature about the setting and causes of the event you described in Your History Journal news report at the beginning of the chapter.

Reviewing Facts

1. **Name** the major contributions that India made to the British war effort in World War I. What did Great Britain promise India in return?
2. **Identify** three nationalist leaders who would probably agree with the statement "Political power grows out of the barrel of a gun."
3. **Describe** two nonviolent tactics for social change used by Gandhi.
4. **List** the modernization reforms ordered by Kemal Atatürk.
5. **Describe** the problems that colonial boundaries created in Africa. Discuss the West African nation of Nigeria as an example.
6. **Identify** the major event in 1938 that marked the arrival of economic nationalism in the countries of Latin America.

Critical Thinking

1. **Apply** How does political control relate to economic control? Give examples from Egypt or India.
2. **Apply** How did religious differences hamper the Indian independence movement? Give examples to support your opinion.

Chapter 30 Review

GLENCOE TECHNOLOGY

VIDEODISC
Use MindJogger to review students' knowledge of the chapter.

MindJogger Videoquiz
Chapter 30
Disc 4 Side B

Also available in VHS.

Answers

Using Key Terms

1. e
2. h
3. a
4. j
5. i
6. b
7. g
8. f
9. c
10. d

Using Your History Journal

Suggest that students model their feature on those presented on all-news radio broadcasts.

Reviewing Facts

1. soldiers, wheat, and cotton; greater control over their government
2. Kemal Atatürk, Reza Shah, Chiang Kai-shek, Mao Zedong, and José Uriburu, among others
3. a boycott and a march
4. the Western calendar, Latin alphabet, metric system, Western-style last names; men stopped wearing the fez, and women, the veil.
5. Boundaries split traditional homelands and forced confrontations between ancient enemies. In Nigeria, the Hausa, Yoruba, and Ibo peoples became citizens of the same nation, resulting in many conflicts.
6. Mexican President Cárdenas nationalized foreign oil wells.

Critical Thinking

1. The two forms work together. In Egypt, Britain asserted political control in order to retain the Suez Canal. In India, Britain's political control maintained a profitable trade in cotton, wheat, and other raw materials.
2. Differences split the independence movement just as it was gaining power.
3. Nationalist movements had to grow stronger so that the cost of retaining colonial control outweighed the profits of imperialism.
4. by nonviolent means and challenging one another through marches, boycotts, and other forms of protest
5. Possible answer: While Egypt, India, and other countries either won or moved toward breaking free of the West's political control,

3. **Analyze** In 1939 most of Africa and much of Asia were European colonies. What conditions needed to change before self-determination could be achieved by all countries? Give examples to support your answer.
4. **Synthesize** Instead of warlords, imagine "peacelords." How would they acquire their power? How would they use it? What would they accomplish?
5. **Evaluate** Did the global influence of the West become more or less widespread in the two decades after World War I? Give examples to support your opinion.

Geography in History

1. **Location** Refer to the map below. What is the relative location of the Sea of Japan?
2. **Movement** Approximately how many miles would the Japanese military have had to transport troops across the Sea of Japan to invade Manchuria (Northeast Plain) in 1931?
3. **Region** Along what major rivers might the Japanese have traveled to gain access to central China?

China and Japan

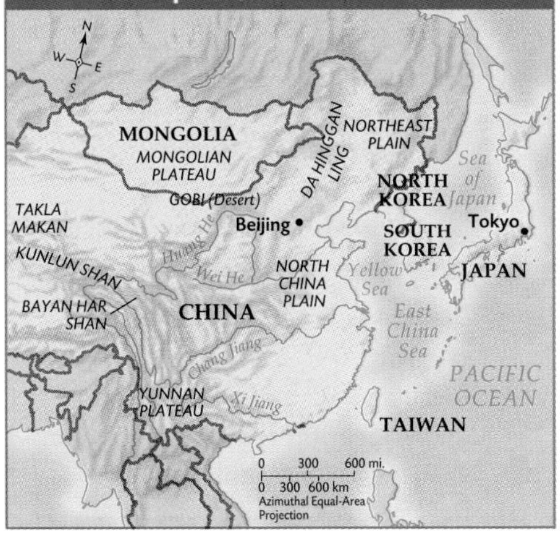

Understanding Themes

1. **Nationalism** In what countries of Africa and the Middle East did nationalism lead to self-determination in the period 1919 to 1939?
2. **Change** How did the British respond to Gandhi's campaign for Indian independence?
3. **Conflict** Do you think Mao Zedong and Chiang Kai-shek were wise to put aside their differences and unite against Japan? Explain.
4. **Conflict** What were the main areas of disagreement that resulted in conflict between Japan and the West after World War I?
5. **Change** How did nationalism change Latin America following World War I?

Linking Past and Present

1. Review Gandhi's major criticisms of Western civilization. Were they accurate? Do they apply today?
2. Do you think nationalism is stronger or weaker throughout the world today than it was in the 1920s and 1930s? Give examples from current events that support your opinion.

Skill Practice

Read the quotation below by Hashimoto Kingoro and review the discussion of Japan in Section 4, pages 807-809. Then answer the questions below.

> "We are like a great crowd of people packed into a small and narrow room, and there are only three doors through which we might escape, namely emigration, advance into world markets, and expansion of territory. The first door … has been barred to us by the anti-Japanese immigration policies of other countries. The second door … is being pushed shut by tariff barriers … Japan should rush upon the last door [expansion of territory]."
>
> —Hashimoto Kingoro, *Addresses to Young Men*

1. What is Kingoro's thesis in this argument?
2. What reasons does he give to support this thesis?
3. What evidence in Section 4 supports Kingoro's thesis?
4. Do you accept or reject Kingoro's argument? Explain your answer.

Chapter 30 Review

countries such as Iran and Turkey adopted many elements of Western culture.

Geography in History
1. It lies between Japan to the east and Korea and China to the west.
2. about 600 miles (965 km)
3. Huang He, Wei He, Chang Jiang, Xi Jiang

Understanding Themes
1. **NATIONALISM** Turkey, Iran, and Egypt
2. **CHANGE** They arrested Gandhi, keeping him from active protest and weakening the Indian National Congress.
3. **CONFLICT** Even though the Chinese were unable to stop the invasion, they were more likely to prove effective as a united force.
4. **CONFLICT** Japan felt humiliated by the League of Nations' rejection of its demand for a statement on racial equality, by the U.S. ban on Japanese immigration, and by the West's insistence that Japan abandon the Twenty-One Demands and recognize Western interests in China.
5. **CHANGE** Mexico nationalized its oil fields, breaking with past economic dependence; Nicaraguans fought U.S. Marines; anti-Americanism spread throughout the region.

Linking Past and Present
1. the West's violence, materialism, and self-righteousness, compared with the spirituality of India Answers will vary.
2. Answers will vary. Students should support their answers.

Skill Practice
1. In order to support its large population, Japan must expand its territory.
2. Japan is overcrowded. The only solutions are emigration, capturing world markets, or expanding its territory. The first two options are closed by hostile foreign powers, leaving only the third.
3. Japan had a population explosion; the United States banned Japanese immigration in 1924; Western countries forced Japan to abandon the Twenty-One Demands on China.
4. Answers may vary.

Chapter Bonus Test Question

Ask students: How does Mao's statement, "Political power grows out of the barrel of a gun," apply to the revolutions discussed in this chapter? *(Answers may include: Not all the revolutions were violent, but brute force played a key role in many of them.)*

Teach, Reinforce, and Extend CHAPTER Content

World War II

CHAPTER RESOURCES

	Reproducible Resources	Multimedia Resources
Chapter Opener	Chapter Themes: Graphic Organizer 31 Historical Significance Chapter Activity 31	MindJogger Videoquiz
Chapter Enrichment	Vocabulary Activity 31* Time Line Activity 31 Mapping History Activity 31 History Simulation 31 Geography and History Activity 31 Source Reading 31 People in World History Profiles 59, 60 World Art and Music Activity 31 Enrichment Activity 31 Critical Thinking Activity 31 Skill Reinforcement Activity 31 Performance Assessment Activity 31	World History and Art Transparency 42, *The Red Stairway* Mapping History Overlay Transparencies 19, 20, 21 Chapter Transparency 31 Vocabulary PuzzleMaker Software Turning Points in World History: • *The Holocaust* • *Dropping the Atomic Bomb* In the Holy Land: *The Holocaust: 1938–1945* Lessons of War: • *Can a Battle Change History?* • *Appeasement: Munich Pact* • *At the Front* • *Laws of War*
Chapter Review/Reteaching	Reteaching Activity 31 Skill Reinforcement Activity 31 Spanish Chapter Summary 31	Chapter 31 Digest Audiocassette, Activity, Test* Vocabulary PuzzleMaker Software Student Self-Test and Review Software MindJogger Videoquiz
Chapter Evaluation/Testing	Performance Assessment Activity 31 Chapter 31 Test, Forms A and B	Testmaker

* *Also available in Spanish*

0:00 **OUT OF TIME?** Assign the Chapter 31 summary in the Unit 7 Digest on pages 854–857, and the Chapter 31 Audiocassettes.

Block Schedule

Block scheduling differs from traditional class scheduling in the amount of time allotted to each period. The extended time frame provided by block scheduling affords you the opportunity to implement a greater number of research-oriented and activity-intense projects to motivate and involve your students. Activities that are particularly suited to use within the block scheduling framework are identified throughout this chapter by the following designation.

KEY TO ABILITY LEVELS

Teaching strategies have been coded for varying learning styles and abilities.

L1 **BASIC** activities for all students
L2 **AVERAGE** activities for average to above-average students
L3 **CHALLENGING** activities for above-average students
LEP **LIMITED ENGLISH PROFICIENCY** activities

A complete, 1-page lesson plan is provided for each section in the *Reproducible Lesson Plans* booklet.

SECTION RESOURCES

Daily Objectives	Reproducible Resources	Multimedia Resources
Section 1 The Path to War Explain in what sense World War II was a product of World War I.	Reproducible Lesson Plan 31-1 Vocabulary Activity 31* Guided Reading Activity 31-1* Chapter Themes: Graphic Organizer 31 People in World History Profile 59 Time Line Activity 31 Section Quiz 31-1*	Section Focus Transparency 31-1 Chapter Transparency 31 Student Self-Test and Review Software Lessons of War: *Appeasement: Munich Pact*
Section 2 War in Europe Describe how Hitler took over most of Europe and how Great Britain and the United States responded to German expansion.	Reproducible Lesson Plan 31-2 Vocabulary Activity 31* Guided Reading Activity 31-2* People in World History Profile 60 Section Quiz 31-2*	Section Focus Transparency 31-2 Mapping History Overlay Transparency 19, *Europe in June, 1942* Student Self-Test and Review Software Lessons of War: *Laws of War*
Section 3 A Global Conflict Describe how the Soviet Union and the United States entered World War II.	Reproducible Lesson Plan 31-3 Vocabulary Activity 31* Guided Reading Activity 31-3* History Simulation 31 Section Quiz 31-3*	Section Focus Transparency 31-3 Student Self-Test and Review Software Lessons of War: *At the Front*
Section 4 Turning Points Explain how the tide of war turned in favor of the Allies during 1942 and 1943.	Reproducible Lesson Plan 31-4 Vocabulary Activity 31* Guided Reading Activity 31-4* Geography and History Activity 31 Section Quiz 31-4*	Section Focus Transparency 31-4 Mapping History Overlay Transparency 20, *Southeast Asia Prior to World War II* Student Self-Test and Review Software Lessons of War: *Can a Battle Change History?*
Section 5 Allied Victories Understand how new technology affected the conduct and outcome of World War II.	Reproducible Lesson Plan 31-5 Guided Reading Activity 31-5* Reteaching Activity 31 Enrichment Activity 31 Section Quiz 31-5* Performance Assessment Activity 31 Spanish Chapter Summary 31	Section Focus Transparency 31-5 Mapping History Overlay Transparency 21, *Battle Sites in the Pacific* World History and Art Transparency 42, *The Red Stairway* Vocabulary PuzzleMaker Software Student Self-Test and Review Software Testmaker Turning Points in World History: • *The Holocaust* • *Dropping the Atomic Bomb* In the Holy Land: *The Holocaust: 1938-1945*

* *Also available in Spanish*

Chapter Activities

Performance Assessment Activity

World War III After studying the factors contributing to the two world wars, have students predict the likelihood of a third world war. Organize students into small groups to develop a scenario including real countries, leaders, and plausible issues they believe have the potential to trigger a third world war. Students then should write a treaty or suggest some other plan they think could avert the crisis. Have each group present its detailed scenario as well as its treaty or plan to the rest of the class. Then have the class discuss and vote on which scenario for World War III is the most plausible and which treaty or plan would be most effective in averting war.

Possible Rubric Features
Accuracy of information, plausibility of predictions, problem-solving skills, research skills

• *For an additional activity, refer to Activity 31 in the* Performance Assessment Strategies and Activities *booklet.*

Activity
From the Classroom of...

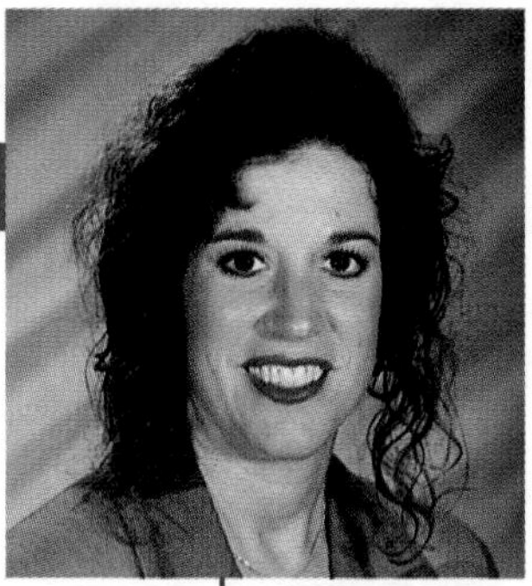

Jill M. Frimel and Gene A. Brunswick
Solon High School
Solon, OH

Atomic Bombs
Students will experience the complex decision-making process that led to the dropping of atomic bombs on Japan. Students will need to be familiar with the events of the Pacific theater of World War II, including Japanese resistance in Okinawa, kamikaze attacks on U.S. ships, and projections of massive casualties in a direct invasion of Japan.

Have partners discuss what they know about the decision to use atomic weapons against Japan. Then assign students one of the following roles: member of U.S. Congress today; member of U.S. Congress in 1945; U.S. civilian in 1945; Japanese civilian in 1945; U.S. military officer in 1945; U.S. soldier in 1945; and a human rights activist today. Have students present their different views to the class. Then have the class discuss Truman's decision and vote for or against the use of atomic bombs.

Multiple Learning Styles

Verbal/Linguistic
Have students interview family or community members who remember World War II. Suggest that students make a list of questions before conducting their interviews. Have students present oral reports to the class based on their interviews.

Logical/Mathematical
Have students make a time line that shows the main events of World War II. Suggest that they record European events on one side of the time line and Asian events on the other.

Visual/Spatial
Have students design a bulletin board that depicts the battles and destruction of World War II.

Auditory/Musical
Have students make a tape recording of the voices of World War II. Suggest that they locate recordings of Edward R. Murrow's reports on the war; wartime speeches by Roosevelt or Churchill; songs popular during the war; and any other recordings they can find. Remind them to record the voices in chronological order before they present their tapes to the class.

Kinesthetic
Have students construct a model that shows the strategies and outcome of one of the following events of World War II: D-Day landing, Battle of the Bulge, Battle of Guadalcanal, or the Battle of Stalingrad.

Additional Resources

TEACHER'S CORNER

NATIONAL GEOGRAPHIC SOCIETY

INDEX TO NATIONAL GEOGRAPHIC MAGAZINE

The following articles may be used for research relating to this chapter:

- "Hiroshima," by Ted Gup, August 1995.
- "Blueprints for Victory," by John F. Shupe, May 1995.
- "The Wings of War," by Thomas B. Allen, March 1994.
- "Douglas MacArthur: An American Soldier," by Geoffrey C. Ward, March 1992.
- "Pearl Harbor: A Return to the Day of Infamy," by Thomas B. Allen, December 1991.
- "Remembering the Blitz," by Cameron Thomas, July 1991.
- "The Bismarck Found," by Robert D. Ballard, November 1989.
- "Ghosts of War in the South Pacific," by Peter Benchley, April 1988.
- "Remnants: The Last Jews of Poland," by Malgorzata Niezabitowska, September 1986.
- "Corregidor Revisited: 43 Years After the Siege," by William Graves, July 1986.

NATIONAL GEOGRAPHIC SOCIETY PRODUCTS AVAILABLE FROM GLENCOE

To order the following products for use with this chapter, contact your local Glencoe sales representative or call Glencoe at 1-800-368-7344:

VIDEODISCS
- GTV: The American People
- GTV: A Geographic Perspective on American History

ADDITIONAL NATIONAL GEOGRAPHIC SOCIETY PRODUCTS

To order the following products for use with this chapter, call National Geographic Society at 1-800-368-2728:

- *Decades of History: The 20th Century–The Early Years,* "The 1940s: War and Recovery." (Filmstrip)
- *Lost Fleet of Guadalcanal* (Video)
- *Search for Battleship Bismarck* (Video)

BIBLIOGRAPHY

Literature of the Period
Frank, Anne. *The Diary of a Young Girl.* New York: Doubleday, 1972. First-person account of a young Jewish girl and her family who spent years hiding from the Nazis.

Readings for the Student
Ryan, Cornelius. *The Longest Day.* New York: Simon and Schuster, 1984. Detailed, exciting account of D-Day and the Normandy invasion.

Readings for the Teacher
Leckie, Robert. *Delivered from Evil: The Saga of World War II.* New York: Harper, 1987. A complete history of World War II told in the style of a novel.

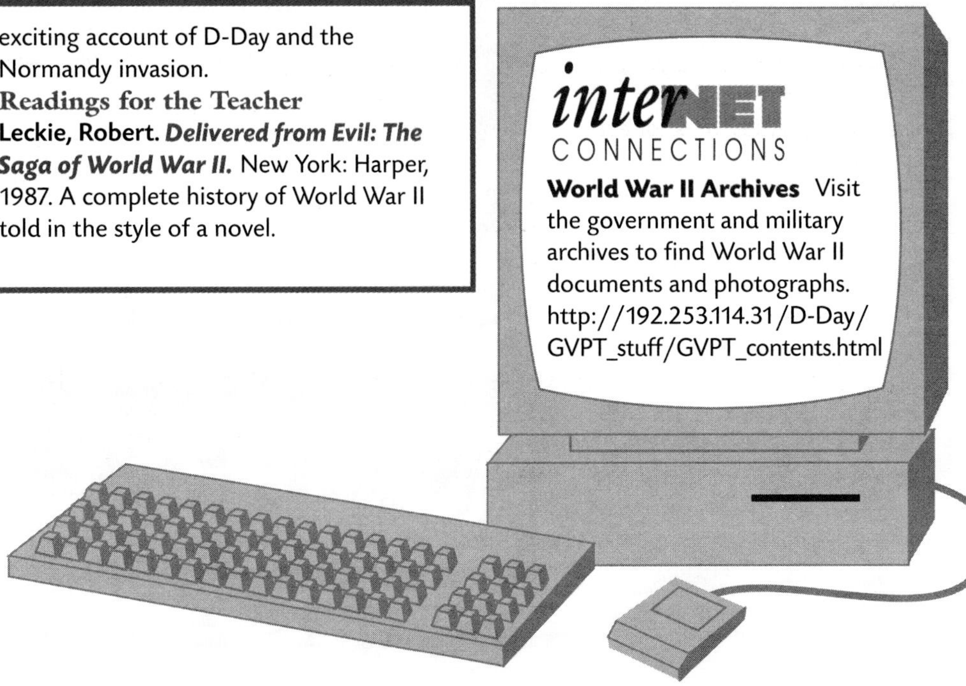
interNET
CONNECTIONS
World War II Archives Visit the government and military archives to find World War II documents and photographs.
http://192.253.114.31/D-Day/GVPT_stuff/GVPT_contents.html

Introducing Chapter 31

CHAPTER THEMES

Chapter Themes are listed by section on this chapter opening page of the Student Edition. A corresponding theme-based activity is available under "TEACH," and a theme-based question is asked in the Section and Chapter Reviews.

The Storyteller

Historical Setting The invasion of Normandy launched by the Allies in June 1944 was not their first invasion of German-occupied France. In 1942 the Allies launched a raid on the seaport town of Dieppe. About two-thirds of the 6,000 soldiers who took part in this attack were killed, wounded, captured, or reported missing. However, the defeat at Dieppe did provide the Allies with valuable information that was used two years later when planning the D-Day invasion.

Historical Significance

Answers: *By the end of World War II, the balance of power had shifted away from Europe.*

The United States and the Soviet Union held the balance of power.

Chapter 31

World War II

1930–1945

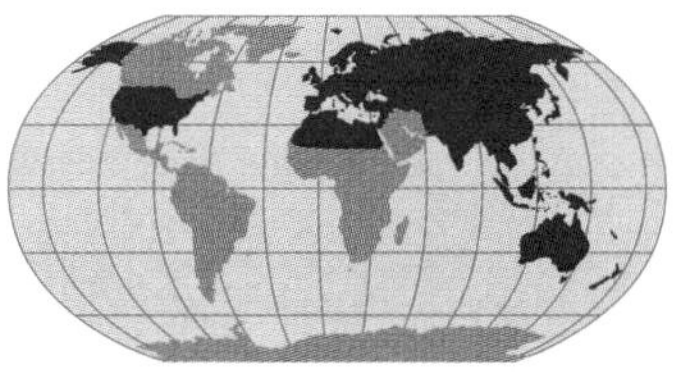

Chapter Themes

- **Movement** Japan, Italy, and Germany carry out expansionist policies. *Section 1*
- **Cooperation** The United States and Great Britain move slowly toward an alliance, while Germany and Italy make major territorial gains in Europe and the Mediterranean. *Section 2*
- **Conflict** Two separate and opposing alliances, the Allies and the Axis, wage a worldwide war. *Section 3*
- **Conflict** The Allies make major gains against the Axis powers. *Section 4*
- **Innovation** New military technologies, such as the atomic bomb, affect the outcome of World War II. *Section 5*

The Storyteller

On June 6, 1944, the Allies mounted an all-out attack against German forces in Normandy, France. Years later an American soldier named Elliott Johnson could still vividly recall the events of the day:

"I remember going up to the highest part of that ship and watching the panorama around me unfold. In my mind's eye, I see one of our ships take a direct hit and go up in a huge ball of flames. There were big geysers coming up where the shells were landing and there were bodies floating, face down, face up."

The invasion of Normandy was one of the key events of World War II. Although the war began in 1939, it had its roots in the peace treaties that settled World War I.

Historical Significance

How did World War II affect the world balance of power? What nations emerged from conflict as world powers?

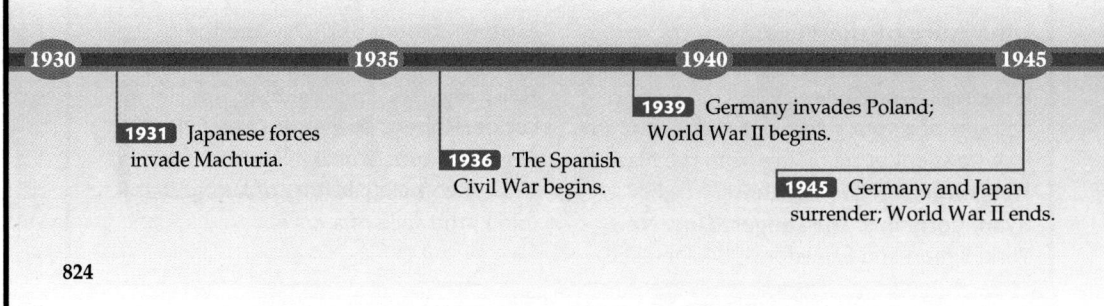

1930 — 1935 — 1940 — 1945

1931 Japanese forces invade Machuria.

1936 The Spanish Civil War begins.

1939 Germany invades Poland; World War II begins.

1945 Germany and Japan surrender; World War II ends.

GEOGRAPHY CONNECTION

Location On a large wall map of the world or on the world map in the Atlas of their textbook, have students locate the following countries that took part in World War II: Germany, Italy, Japan, China, Poland, Finland, Norway, Denmark, France, Germany, the former Soviet Union (now the Commonwealth of Independent States), the United States, Egypt, Libya, and the Philippines. Why was this war called a world war? *(World War II involved countries in all parts of the world.)*

Visualizing History Allied forces led by the United States land in the Pacific island of Bougainville, the largest of the Solomon Islands.

Your History Journal

Create a two-column chart that shows the significance of ten key events in World War II. In column one list the event and date. In column two write a short statement of why the event was important to the outcome of the war.

EXTRA CREDIT PROJECT

Prisoners of War Have students use outside sources to do in-depth research on a prisoner-of-war camp run by the Germans, the Japanese, or the Allies. Have them write a report that includes information on general living conditions, work done by prisoners, chances for recreational activities, escape attempts, and compliance with international law on treatment of prisoners of war.

Introducing Chapter 31

Visualizing History The United States entered World War II on December 8, 1941, one day after Japan's surprise attack on the American naval and air base at Pearl Harbor in Hawaii. The victory at Bougainville was part of America's strategy of "island-hopping" to capture Japanese-held islands in the Pacific.

Performance Assessment

Refer to the activity on page 824C of the Planning Guide.

Refer to Activity 31 in the *Performance Assessment Strategies and Activities* booklet.

Using Your History Journal

Tell students to note major events and turning points in World War II as they read the chapter. Then, from their notes, ask them to select the ten most significant events and tell why they were important to the outcome of the war.

GLENCOE TECHNOLOGY

VIDEODISC

Use MindJogger to preview chapter content.

MindJogger Videoquiz

Chapter 31
Disc 4 Side B

Also available in VHS.

Chapter 31
Section 1

SECTION THEME

▸ **Movement** Japan, Italy, and Germany carry out expansionist policies.

Find Out

Answer: *The peace treaties that ended World War I left Italy, Germany, and Japan dissatisfied, laying the groundwork for another world war.*

FOCUS

Section Objective

Explain in what sense World War II was a product of World War I.

BELLRINGER
Motivational Activity

Before taking roll at the beginning of the class period, project Section Focus Transparency 31-1 and have students answer the activity questions. Discuss students' responses.

This activity is also available as a blackline master.

Vocabulary Pre-check

Use Vocabulary Activity 31 to introduce vocabulary terms. **L1 LEP**

1930 — 1935 — 1940

1933 Japan withdraws from the League of Nations.

1936 Germany occupies the Rhineland.

1938 European powers meet at the Munich Conference.

Section 1

The Path to War

Setting the Scene

▸ **Terms to Define**
collective security, sanctions, appeasement

▸ **People to Meet**
Chiang Kai-shek, Benito Mussolini, Haile Selassie, Francisco Franco, Adolf Hitler, Joseph Stalin, Neville Chamberlain

▸ **Places to Locate**
Manchuria, Ethiopia, Spain, the Rhineland, Austria, Czechoslovakia

Find Out In what sense was World War II a product of World War I?

The Storyteller

Joseph Stalin sent an invitation to formal negotiations to Adolf Hitler, the Nazi dictator. Hitler read the note and drummed both fists against the wall, exclaiming, "Now I have the world in my pocket." German Foreign Minister Joachim von Ribbentrop and Stalin arranged the division of Europe and agreed never to attack each other, then celebrated with an elaborate dinner. Each side toasted the other and told jokes the other side did not find funny. After dinner, in a final show of hospitality, Stalin drew the German foreign minister aside and told him that he personally could guarantee, on his word of honor, that the Soviet Union would not betray its partner.

Joseph Stalin

—adapted from *Joseph Stalin: Man and Legend*, Ronald Hingley, 1974

In the 1930s the Western democracies watched uneasily as militaristic dictatorships came to power in Europe and Asia. Despite their fears, Britain, France, and the United States could not agree on what steps to take to ensure their collective security, or what was needed to defend their common interests against enemy attack. Much of the unrest in Europe and Asia can be traced to the peace settlements made at the end of World War I. Great Britain, France, and the United States were substantially satisfied with these settlements; however, Japan, Italy, and Germany were not.

Japan's Expansion in Asia

Japan was the first of the nondemocratic powers to reveal its territorial ambitions in the interwar period. With limited natural resources of its own, Japan depended heavily on foreign sources for raw materials and on foreign markets for finished goods. To acquire more of these materials and markets, Japan sought new territories for conquest.

The Japanese military used a bomb explosion on the South Manchurian Railway in September 1931 as an excuse to overrun **Manchuria**. The following year Japan established Manchuria as an independent state, renamed it Manchukuo, and set up former Chinese emperor Pu Yi as puppet ruler.

When China protested in the League of Nations about Japan's actions, the League ordered a commission under British statesman Lord Lytton to investigate the affair. Lytton's commission laid the blame squarely on Japan and ordered the Japanese government to return Manchuria to China. The League voted overwhelmingly in favor of this recommendation, to which Japan responded in March 1933 by withdrawing from the League. The Manchurian incident not only revealed that the League of Nations was powerless, but also boosted the expansionist ambitions of Italy and Germany.

SECTION RESOURCES

Reproducible Masters
- Reproducible Lesson Plan 31-1
- Vocabulary Activity 31
- Guided Reading Activity 31-1
- Chapter Themes: Graphic Organizer 31
- People in World History Profile 59
- Time Line Activity 31
- Section Quiz 31-1

Transparencies
- Section Focus Transparency 31-1
- Chapter Transparency 31

Multimedia
- Student Self-Test and Review Software
- Testmaker
- Lessons of War: *Appeasement: Munich Pact*

In the early 1930s, the Japanese military hoped to gain control of the East Indies and its oil reserves, which would supply Japan's ships and airplanes. But to control the East Indies, Japan needed ports on the South China coast.

Consequently, during the summer of 1937, the Japanese launched a full-scale invasion of China. In August Japanese armies attacked Shanghai and began a bold drive up the Chang Jiang to Nanjing, the Chinese capital. After seizing Nanjing, Japan went on to invade South China, but the Japanese armies soon lost their momentum in the struggle against the Chinese nationalist forces under **Chiang Kai-shek.**

Visualizing History **Haile Selassie (center) appealed to the League of Nations for action against Italian aggression in Ethiopia. The League's failure to halt Axis expansion led to its own downfall.** *Why were the League's sanctions against Italy ineffective?*

Italy's Conquest of Ethiopia

The relative ease with which Japan acquired Manchuria encouraged Italy to make a similar move. Italy's goal was to secure control of the ancient kingdom of **Ethiopia** in East Africa. In 1934 Italian and Ethiopian forces clashed in a disputed zone on the border of Ethiopia and Italian Somaliland. When the Italian dictator, **Benito Mussolini**, demanded an apology and reparations, the Ethiopians responded by asking the League of Nations to investigate the matter. The League decided that because each side viewed the area where the incident took place as its own territory, neither side was to blame.

The League's decision did not satisfy Mussolini, who thought an Ethiopian colony would enhance Italy's image as a world power. Consequently, in October 1935, Mussolini ordered the Italian army to invade Ethiopia. In a dramatic appearance at the League of Nations, Ethiopian Emperor **Haile Selassie** appealed for help. This time the League condemned the action and voted to impose economic sanctions, measures designed to stop trade and other economic contacts, against Italy. The League forbade its members to sell Italy arms and certain raw materials. But the sanctions did not include oil, coal, and iron, all vital to Italy's war efforts.

Once again the League's actions were ineffective. Mussolini completed his conquest of Ethiopia, and in May 1936 he formally annexed the African nation.

Spanish Civil War

A civil war in **Spain** further inflamed the international situation in the 1930s. After presiding over years of social and economic chaos, King Alfonso XIII abdicated in 1931, and Spain became a republic. The new republican government immediately began a program of social reforms. It ended the Catholic Church's role in educating Spanish youth and redistributed land from nobles to peasants.

As a result of these and other reforms, many right-wing groups in Spain opposed the republic and wished to restore the old order. In July 1936 right-wing army chiefs staged an uprising in Spanish Morocco that soon spread to Spain. For three years the conservative Spanish Nationalists, led by General **Francisco Franco**, and the left-wing Loyalists, or Spanish Republicans, battled for control of Spain.

Early in the fighting several foreign powers intervened in the Spanish war. The Soviets supported the Loyalists, while the Germans and Italians aided the Nationalists. Volunteers from Britain, France, the United States, and other countries around the world flocked to Spain to join the International Brigade and fight for the Republican cause against fascism. The governments of the Western democracies, however, refused to intervene because they feared a general European war.

Germany's dictator, **Adolf Hitler**, viewed German participation in the Spanish Civil War as a

COOPERATIVE LEARNING ACTIVITY

Oral Report Organize students into groups of four to six to research how the world reacted to the expansion of Japan, Italy, or Germany into Manchuria, Nanjing, Ethiopia, the Rhineland, Austria, and Czechoslovakia, respectively. Have each group choose one area and find reports about that conquest. Encourage them to use quotations that reveal the point of view of the reporter toward the conquest. Then have each group present its report to the class. **L2**

TEACH

Guided Practice

THEME Movement

Ask several students to point out on a wall map the areas that Japan, Italy, and Germany invaded. *(Japan: Manchuria and China; Italy: Ethiopia; Germany: the Rhineland, Austria, Czechoslovakia)* **L1 LEP**

Visualizing History After Italy invaded Ethiopia, Haile Selassie lived in England for several years, helping plan the liberation of Ethiopia. When he returned to power, he wrote a new constitution that provided for universal suffrage. In 1974, with drought and starvation plaguing the country, Ethiopians deposed the aging ruler. A year later, Ethiopia's last emperor died.

Answer to Caption: *The sanctions did not include oil, coal, and iron—all of which helped Italy's war effort.*

Economics Have students discuss the economic reasons for Japan's expansionism. *(the need for raw materials, markets, and ports)* **L2**

Global Issues Tell students that the Spanish Civil War is sometimes called a rehearsal for World War II. Have them discuss why. *(Italy and Germany backed the Nationalists and later became the Axis powers; the Soviet Union and individuals from Great Britain, France, and the United States backed the Loyalists and became the Allies.)* **L3**

Chapter Transparency 31

Chapter Themes: Graphic Organizer 31

Chapter 31
Section 1

ABC NEWS INTERACTIVE™

VIDEODISC
Lessons of War

Side Two, Chapter 3
Frames 3466-5635
Title: *Appeasement: Munich Pact*
Subject: British Prime Minister Neville Chamberlain's attempt to keep peace with Germany in 1938
Ask: What did Hitler demand at the Munich Conference? *(that the Sudetenland be given to Germany)*

Independent Practice

Guided Reading Activity 31-1 **L1**

People in World History Profile 59

Time Line Activity 31

Art Have students research and write a short report on Pablo Picasso's famous painting *Guernica*, which he painted in 1937 after the German aircraft bombed civilians in the town of Guernica during the Spanish Civil War. **L2 LEP**

Global Issues Have students imagine that they are newspaper editors in 1938. Ask them to list the events that have pushed the world toward another war. Then have them write an editorial titled "On the Brink of War" that offers suggestions on how to diffuse the powder keg. **L3**

way to strengthen ties with Italy and to secure a vital supply of Spanish iron ore and magnesium. Hermann Goering, head of the Luftwaffe—or German air force—saw an opportunity "firstly, to prevent the further spread of Communism; secondly, to test my young Luftwaffe in this or that technical aspect." To accomplish these goals, Goering formed the Condor Legion, an all-German air and ground force. They used Spanish towns and cities as testing grounds for new weapons and military tactics, such as the combined use of fire and high-explosive bombs.

By the summer of 1936, the Nationalists had taken most of western Spain. When the Soviets stopped sending aid to the Loyalists in 1938, Franco launched his final offensive. In March 1939 Franco entered Madrid, the last of the Loyalist strongholds. The civil war had ended, but more than half a million Spaniards had died, and much of the country lay in ruins. Although Spain joined Italy and Germany as countries headed by fascist dictators, Franco did not ally himself with Italy and Germany.

Hitler on the Offensive

The same year the Spanish Civil War broke out, Hitler made his move in Germany. The German dictator was convinced that Germany needed more *lebensraum*, or living space, for its expanding population. In his book, *Mein Kampf (My Struggle)*, Hitler wrote:

> "Only an adequate large space on this earth assures a nation freedom of existence....We must hold unflinchingly to our aim ... to secure for the German people the land and soil to which they are entitled...."

Footnotes to History

Writers at War
The Spanish Civil War became a crusade for many writers. In *For Whom the Bell Tolls*, American writer Ernest Hemingway describes an idealistic American fighting the Fascist forces in Spain. The English novelist George Orwell, in *Homage to Catalonia*, presents his experiences on the Aragon front and his nearly fatal gunshot wound.

Occupying the Rhineland

Since 1919, the Versailles Treaty had forbidden German troops in **the Rhineland**, a German region between the Rhine and the French border. This ban was designed to provide security to France. Hitler gambled that if he violated the treaty, France and Great Britain would do nothing to stop him. In March 1936, therefore, Hitler sent troops into the Rhineland. France had the right to take military action, and Britain had the obligation to back France with its own armed forces. Neither country acted, however, because neither was willing to risk a war.

In October 1936 Hitler signed a political and military agreement with Mussolini called the Rome-Berlin Axis. As a result of this treaty, Italy and Germany became known as the Axis powers. The next month Hitler signed the Anti-Comintern Pact, an anti-Communist alliance that included Germany, Italy, and Japan. The Soviet Union's dictator, **Joseph Stalin**, was afraid that the new alliance would threaten Soviet security and urged the Western powers to unite against Germany and its allies. But the West, fearing that such a union would lead to war, refused.

Seizing Austria

Hitler, meanwhile, grew bolder. For a long time he had dreamed of *Anschluss* (ANSH•luhs)—the joining of **Austria** to Germany. "German-Austria must return to the great mother country," he wrote. "One blood demands one Reich."

In 1934 Hitler had tried to take over Austria but backed down when Mussolini responded by mobilizing Italy's troops. In 1938, now that Germany and Italy were allies, Hitler tried again. He invited the Austrian chancellor to Berchtesgaden, his mountain retreat in the German Alps, and bullied him into appointing Nazis to key posts in Austria. The Austrian chancellor appealed to Britain and France for help, but once more the two major democracies in Europe did nothing. In March 1938 Hitler sent German troops into Austria and then proclaimed it part of Germany. He insisted that he was only promoting political stability in central Europe by uniting German-speaking peoples into one country. The Western democracies, however, refused to take military action.

Tension Builds in Europe

Austria was the first victim of Hitler's policy of expansion. **Czechoslovakia** was the next. In the late 1930s, Czechoslovakia was the only democratic nation in central Europe. It held a key strategic position in the

MEETING SPECIAL NEEDS ACTIVITY

Learning Style: Visual/Spatial Have students who are strong visual learners work together to review information in Section 1 and plan political cartoons based on these topics: Japan sets up puppet government in Manchuria; Italy takes Ethiopia; Condor Legion bombs Spain; League of Nations fails to stop aggression; Hitler grabs Austria. Display completed cartoons on the bulletin board and hold a class discussion on what the cartoons say about events of the 1930s. **L2**

region. Its standard of living was second only to that of Germany. Czechoslovakia also had a strong army and alliances with France and the Soviet Union.

The nation of Czechoslovakia was created by treaty at the end of World War I. In addition to Czechs and Slovaks, it had 1 million Hungarians, half a million Ruthenians, and more than 3 million Germans. During the 1930s these minorities began to demand more freedom than they had received under the terms of the treaties, creating serious problems for the Czechoslovak government. Hitler took advantage of Czechoslovakia's ethnic problems to destroy the country.

Visualizing History **In May 1938 Adolf Hitler (left) visited Rome, Italy to meet with his Italian ally Benito Mussolini (right). The visit was designed to demonstrate the unity of the Rome-Berlin Axis.** *What role did Mussolini play in the Czech crisis later that year?*

Sudeten Crisis

On September 12, 1938, Hitler demanded that the Germans of the Sudetenland, a heavily fortified region in northwestern Czechoslovakia, be given the right of self-determination. The Czechoslovak government responded by proclaiming martial law. In an effort to avert an international crisis, British Prime Minister **Neville Chamberlain** suggested to Hitler that they meet to discuss the matter. France supported his request.

Chamberlain met with Hitler in Germany on September 15, 1938. There Hitler demanded that the Sudetenland be given to Germany. At a second meeting a week later, Chamberlain accepted Hitler's demands. He thought that a policy of appeasement, granting concessions to maintain peace, would stabilize Europe. But Hitler responded by saying that the "plan is no longer of any use" and raised his demands. After further talks the two failed to reach any accord. Czechoslovakia, meanwhile, called for the full mobilization of its troops.

The Munich Conference

On September 29, Chamberlain met with Hitler a third time at a conference in Munich, Germany. Also attending were French Premier Édouard Daladier and Italy's dictator Benito Mussolini. Czechoslovakia and the Soviet Union were not represented.

Mussolini offered a "compromise" that gave Germany control over the Sudetenland. In return, Hitler promised to respect Czechoslovakia's sovereignty. He also promised not to take any more European territory and to settle future disputes by peaceful negotiation. Still hoping to avoid war, Great Britain and France accepted the terms. On September 30, Czechoslovakia reluctantly accepted the Munich Agreement.

Chamberlain returned home to cheering crowds, proclaiming that he had ensured "peace in our time." He trusted Hitler and believed that the Nazis would cause no more trouble. Events soon proved him wrong. On March 15, 1939, Hitler sent his armies into Czechoslovakia and took control of the western part of the country. The eastern part, Slovakia, became a German puppet state. After the takeover the Western democracies could no longer maintain their illusions about Hitler's plans and began to prepare for war.

The Nazi–Soviet Pact

More German demands followed the Munich agreement. In March 1939 Hitler turned his attention to eastern Europe. He forced Lithuania to give up the German-speaking city of Memel.

MAKING CONNECTIONS ACTIVITY

Foreign Affairs Have students choose one of the following topics and write a brief report on it: Japan's attack on Nanjing, Haile Selassie and the League of Nations, Germany's advance into the Rhineland, the Nationalist victory in the Spanish Civil War, or the Munich Agreement. Tell students to use issues of popular magazines from the 1930s, such as *The Saturday Evening Post, Time,* and *Life* for their research. Have them include quotes and copies of pictures in their reports. **L2**

Visualizing History Hitler and Mussolini first met in Venice in 1934, but little came of that first encounter. Mussolini remarked to an aide, "I don't like the look of him." Yet, two years later, the two men formed the Rome-Berlin Axis.
Answer to Caption: *Mussolini offered a compromise that gave the Sudetenland to Germany in return for Hitler's promise to respect Czechoslovakia's sovereignty, to take no more European territories, and to settle future disputes by peaceful negotiation.*

Cultural Perspectives

Ethnic Ties In 1918 representatives of the large Slovak population of Pittsburgh, Pennsylvania, asked the provisional Czech government to sign the Pittsburgh Agreement. It guaranteed that Slovaks, who made up only 12 percent of Czechoslovakia's population, would enjoy self-government in that new nation. However, Czechoslovakia's constitution created a single state with no special voice for the Slovaks. Today the Czech and Slovak republics are separate nations.

Linking Past and Present

Realpolitik, the idea that a state should pursue its own interests without regard for ethics or morality, was first used in the 1860s and 1870s when Bismarck united the German states into the German Empire. Hitler applied realpolitik ruthlessly in the 1930s as he conquered neighboring countries. Today the term is often employed to mean "power politics."

Chapter 31
Section 1

ASSESS

Check for Understanding

Assign Section 1 Review as homework or as an in-class activity.

Use Student Self-Test and Review Software to review Section 1.

Evaluate

Section Quiz 31-1

Use the Testmaker to create a customized quiz for Section 1.

Reteach

Have students explain the connection of the following people to acts of aggression in the 1930s: Pu Yi, Benito Mussolini, Haile Selassie, Francisco Franco, Adolf Hitler, Joseph Stalin, and Neville Chamberlain.

Enrich

Have students write a paragraph explaining why Germany, Italy, and Japan eventually became allies.

CLOSE

Have students summarize how aggressive expansion, a weak League of Nations, appeasement, and secret treaties led to the outbreak of war in 1939.

Next the German dictator put pressure on Poland, threatening to take over the Baltic port of Danzig and the Polish Corridor, a narrow strip of Polish land that separated the German region of East Prussia from the rest of Germany. Great Britain and France promised to help Poland defend its borders if it became necessary. The Polish government accepted the support of the Western democracies and firmly rejected Hitler's demands.

The West and the Soviets

To defend Poland, the democracies had to consider the Soviet Union, Poland's neighbor but also its traditional enemy. During the late 1930s, Stalin had urged the Western powers to do something about Hitler. He suspected that the Munich Agreement was an attempt by the British and the French to turn Hitler's attention away from the West and toward the Soviet Union. Chamberlain, on the other hand, did not trust Stalin. He suspected that the Soviet leader wanted to extend his influence in eastern Europe. This confusion as to whether the Fascists or the Communists were the greater enemy contributed to the coolness of the British and the French toward Stalin.

Despite Chamberlain's suspicions and his lack of faith in the fighting ability of the Soviet army, he asked the Soviets to join Britain and France in an alliance to contain Nazism. Stalin agreed on the condition that the Western powers acknowledge the Soviet right to occupy a broad zone stretching from Finland to Bulgaria. Chamberlain refused Stalin's request, deepening Stalin's suspicion that the West would like nothing better than to see Germany and the Soviet Union destroy each other.

Nazi-Soviet Talks

Stalin believed that Hitler's desire for "living space" would eventually lead the German dictator to move into the rich agricultural areas of eastern Europe. Because he doubted that the West would come to his country's aid if Germany threatened it, Stalin began secret talks with the Germans. On August 23, 1939, the Soviet Union and Germany signed the Nazi-Soviet Nonaggression Pact.

According to the agreement, Germany and the Soviet Union pledged that they would never attack each other. Moreover, each would remain neutral if the other became involved in a war. Stalin and Hitler also secretly agreed to create spheres of influence in eastern Europe. Germany would occupy the western part of Poland, while the Soviet Union would govern the eastern part. They agreed to include Finland, part of Romania, and the Baltic republics of Estonia, Latvia, and Lithuania in the Soviet sphere of influence.

Neither Stalin nor Hitler had any illusions about their agreement. They were long-term enemies who, for their own purposes, needed a short-term alliance. Stalin still believed that war with Germany was inevitable. But he thought that the pact would improve Soviet security. If nothing else, it would buy the Soviets time to prepare for war. Hitler saw the pact as a means of securing Germany's eastern border. If he did not have to worry about fighting the Soviets, he would be free to act as he wanted.

The pact shocked and outraged Western leaders, who realized that it destroyed the last barrier to war. The West had also lost a potential ally, and Hitler had won a pledge of neutrality that freed him to pursue his military objectives regarding Poland. Hitler remained convinced, however, that the West would do nothing if he moved against Poland. "The men of Munich," he said, "will not take the risk." With this thought in mind, Hitler sent his armies across the Polish frontier on September 1, 1939. However, he had finally misjudged what the Western leaders would do. Two days after Hitler's invasion of Poland, Great Britain and France declared war on Germany. World War II had begun.

SECTION 1 REVIEW

Recall

1. **Define** collective security, sanctions, appeasement.
2. **Identify** Chiang Kai-shek, Benito Mussolini, Haile Selassie, Francisco Franco, Adolf Hitler, Joseph Stalin, Neville Chamberlain.
3. **Locate** Czechoslovakia on the map on page 832. What about this country's location gave it such strategic value in Hitler's eyes?

Critical Thinking

4. **Evaluating Information** How did the West's policy of appeasement contribute to the start of World War II?

Understanding Themes

5. **Movement** How was the response by the League of Nations to Japanese expansion in 1933 similar to the response by the Western democracies to German expansion in 1938? How was it different? Explain your response.

SECTION 1 REVIEW ANSWERS

1. All vocabulary words are defined in the Glossary.
2. Chiang Kai-shek, 827; Benito Mussolini, 827; Haile Selassie, 827; Francisco Franco, 827; Adolf Hitler, 827; Joseph Stalin, 828; Neville Chamberlain, 829
3. Czechoslovakia separated Germany from Austria, which had already been conquered by Germany.
4. By failing to take strong action when Hitler invaded the Rhineland and Austria and by giving in to his demands at Munich, the Western powers convinced Hitler that they would never take a stand against him.
5. MOVEMENT The response of both the League of Nations and the Western democracies was so weak and ineffective that it encouraged more aggression.

1939 The Soviet Union fights Finland.

1940 France surrenders to Germany; the Battle of Britain begins.

1941 Franklin D. Roosevelt and Winston Churchill issue the Atlantic Charter.

Section 2

War in Europe

Setting the Scene

▶ **Terms to Define**
blitzkrieg, blitz, cash-and-carry policy, lend-lease

▶ **People to Meet**
Winston Churchill, Charles de Gaulle, Franklin D. Roosevelt

▶ **Places to Locate**
Finland, Norway, London, Libya

Find Out How did Hitler take over most of Europe, and what was the response of Great Britain and the United States to German expansion?

The Storyteller

Saturday night, August 24th, 1940, the first German bombs fell on London. That September, bombing became more frequent and deadly as waves of planes came over the city. For hours bombers would attack; then, to fight the fires, thousands of firefighters went into action. Many Londoners lost their homes. An observer reported that boats normally used by tourists on vacation became evacuation boats "chugging along the riverside ... defying high explosive and incendiary bombs, walls of flame, and clouds of choking fumes.... With a few bundles of clothes the refugees climbed aboard and were taken by river to the safety zone or ferried across to the opposite bank."

—adapted from *The Lost Treasures of London*, William Kent, 1947

German bombers

On September 1, 1939, the German Luftwaffe roared toward its targets in Poland, spreading panic and confusion with its bombs. At the same time, armored tank divisions known as panzers swept across the Polish border. Next came the infantry, a million and a half strong, in motorized vehicles. This was blitzkrieg, or "lightning war," a new German strategy aimed at taking the enemy by surprise.

The blitzkrieg worked with speed and efficiency, devastating Poland in a few weeks. Great Britain and France could not move fast enough to send troops to Poland. The Soviet Union, meanwhile, quickly moved its forces to occupy the eastern half of that nation.

Stalin also forced the Baltic republics of Latvia, Lithuania, and Estonia to accept Soviet military bases. When he tried to do the same with **Finland**, war broke out. The Finns held out heroically until March before the Soviets forced them to surrender. As a result of their victory, the Soviets moved their frontier 70 miles (112 km) to the west, making the city of Leningrad less vulnerable to German attack.

Hitler Looks to the West

All through the winter and spring of 1939–1940, the western front was quiet. The Germans called this period the "sit-down war," or *Sitzkrieg*, while the West dubbed it the "phony war." Many hoped that an all-out war could still be avoided.

When Finland capitulated to the Soviets, however, the British took steps to ensure that the same fate would not befall **Norway**. In early April 1940, they mined Norwegian waters to block any ships trading with Germany. Hitler used the mining to support his claim that the Allies were about to invade Scandinavia. He delivered an ultimatum to Norway and Denmark, demanding that they accept the "protection of the Reich." The Danes accepted his demands; the Norwegians did not.

Chapter 31 Section 2

SECTION THEME

▶ **Cooperation** The United States and Great Britain move slowly toward an alliance, while Germany and Italy make major territorial gains in Europe and the Mediterranean.

Find Out

Answer: *Hitler quickly took over Poland, Denmark, Norway, the Low Countries, and France. Britain declared war on Germany. The United States supplied Britain with food and weapons.*

FOCUS

Section Objective

Describe how Hitler took over most of Europe and how Great Britain and the United States responded to German expansion.

BELLRINGER Motivational Activity

Before taking roll at the beginning of the class period, project Section Focus Transparency 31-2. This activity is also available as a blackline master.

Vocabulary Pre-check

Use Vocabulary Activity 31 to introduce vocabulary terms. **L1 LEP**

SECTION RESOURCES

Reproducible Masters
- Reproducible Lesson Plan 31-2
- Vocabulary Activity 31
- Guided Reading Activity 31-2
- People in World History Profile 60
- Section Quiz 31-2

Transparencies
- Section Focus Transparency 31-2
- Mapping History Overlay Transparency 19, *Europe in June, 1942*

Multimedia
- Student Self-Test and Review Software
- Testmaker
- Lessons of War: *Laws of War*

TEACH

Guided Practice

THEME **Cooperation**

Have students find examples in Section 2 of countries cooperating, or working together for their common good. *(Britain mined Norwegian waters to keep German ships out, helped the French, and sent troops to Belgium; the United States supplied food and weapons to Britain; Hitler sent Rommel to help the Italians in Libya.)* **L1**

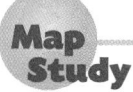

Map Study

Answer

Ireland, Portugal, Spain, Switzerland, Turkey, Sweden

Map Skills Practice

Reading a Map What countries did Germany invade in 1941? *(Yugoslavia, Lithuania, Latvia, Estonia, the Soviet Union)*

Military History Have students compare the fall of France with the Battle of Britain. **L2**

Politics Have students examine the reasons for the downfall of Neville Chamberlain and discuss why Great Britain's attitude toward Germany changed when Winston Churchill became prime minister. **L3**

Axis Expansion Into Europe 1935–1941

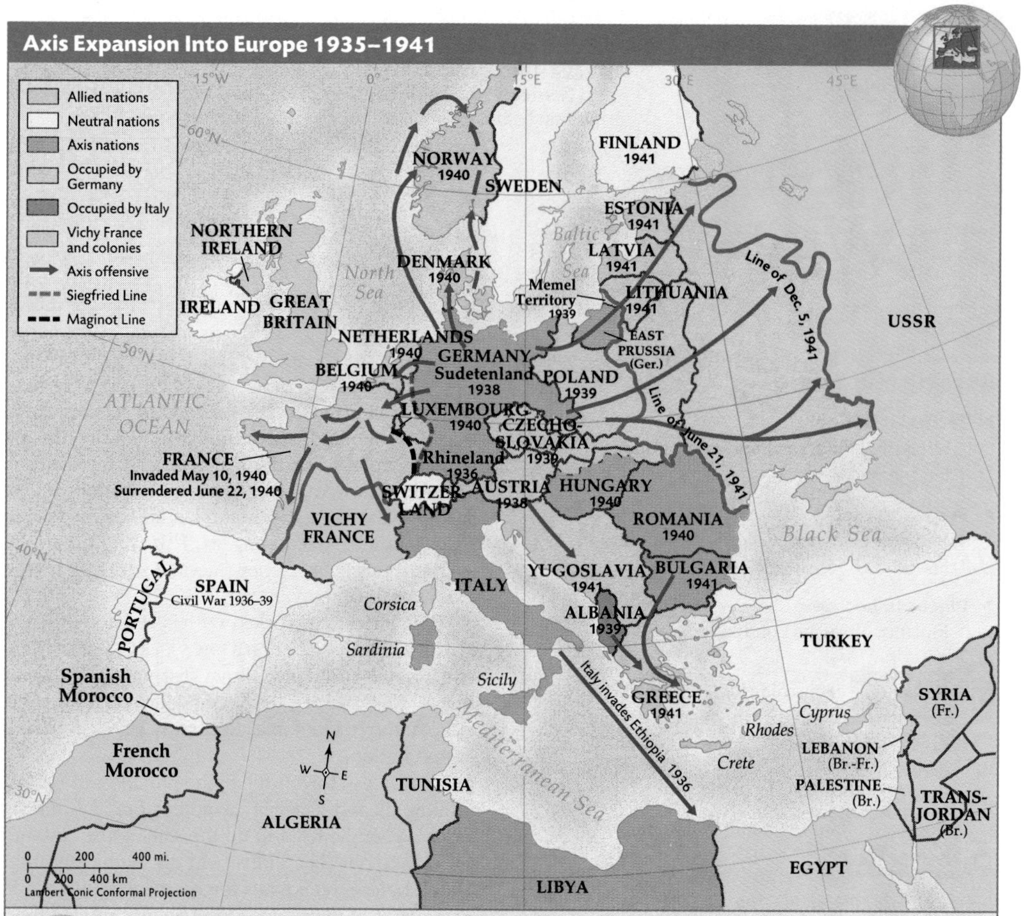

Map Study By the end of 1941, Germany had seized control of much of Europe.
Location Which European nations chose to remain neutral during the war?

The Invasion of Scandinavia

In the early morning hours of April 9, three small German transports steamed into the harbor of Copenhagen. After meeting only token resistance from the Danes, the Germans took control of Denmark.

That same morning German forces landed all along the Norwegian coast. Within hours the Germans had seized the important Baltic Sea ports of Narvik and Trondheim. Bergen, the second-largest city, put up more resistance, but it too fell, as did Oslo.

Although Germany now controlled Norway, the Norwegian invasion had proved costly. Germany lost 10 of 20 destroyers and 3 of 8 cruisers—a large segment of its navy. On the other hand, Hitler had won the outlet to the Atlantic that he needed to ensure that the German navy would not be bottled up in the Baltic Sea.

News of the fall of Norway and Denmark caused an uproar in the British House of Commons. The Labour and Liberal opposition strongly attacked Prime Minister Neville Chamberlain and his policies. Knowing that he had lost the confidence of his own Conservative party as well, Chamberlain stepped down. On May 10, 1940, King George VI summoned **Winston Churchill** to Buckingham Palace and asked him to form a new

COOPERATIVE LEARNING ACTIVITY

Video Presentation Organize the class into three groups to create a 15-minute video documentary about Germany's early military offensives in World War II. Assign each group one of the following topics: the conquest of Poland, fall of France (include the Low Countries and Dunkirk), or the Battle of Britain. Suggest that students use pictures of events and people, sound effects, "interviews," speeches, and songs in their films. Each group should choose a narrator for its segment, and one student to act as a coordinator with the other groups. When the documentaries are completed, have students present them to other classes. **L3**

government. Churchill, one of the few politicians to warn of the Nazi danger in the 1930s, was now prime minister.

The Fall of France

On that same momentous date, the war began in earnest on the western front. Along the Maginot Line, the British and French watched and waited. The Maginot Line was impressive, but it had one major flaw. It had a 50-mile (80-km) gap in the Ardennes. Although the Germans had invaded through Belgium and the Ardennes during World War I, the French still believed that the forests, swamps, and hills of that region were a sufficient barrier. A French tank commander, **Charles de Gaulle**, pleaded for more tanks and planes, but the French command insisted that the Maginot Line was impenetrable.

Hitler, meanwhile, carried out a massive attack on the Low Countries—Luxembourg, the Netherlands, and Belgium. Before dawn on May 10, 1940, German troops parachuted into the Netherlands. It was the first large-scale airborne attack in the history of warfare and caught the Dutch by surprise. Five days after the start of the invasion, the Dutch capitulated.

On the same day that Germany invaded the Netherlands, Britain and France moved their best troops into Belgium. German panzers swept into the Ardennes and began to encircle them. Other panzer divisions drove through Luxembourg and raced toward France.

Dunkirk

Although the Belgian forces fought valiantly, they did not hold out as long as had been expected. The Germans were now rolling through undefended open country. They pushed westward toward the English Channel, trapping the Belgian, British, and French forces in the northwest corner of France. The only hope for the Allies was an evacuation by sea from the French port of Dunkirk. With German forces within sight of the coast, the rescue of 300,000 Allied soldiers seemed impossible. But for reasons never entirely understood, Hitler ordered his forces to halt.

The British Admiralty began a desperate rescue operation at Dunkirk on May 26. A ragtag armada of 850 vessels, ranging from destroyers and cruisers to trawlers, tugs, yachts, and fishing boats, left England and set sail for Dunkirk. Civilians operated many of the smaller boats. Over the next nine days, under fierce air and ground attack, this hastily assembled fleet rescued the Allied armies.

The evacuation of Dunkirk was a stunning military achievement, but as Churchill said, "wars are not won by evacuations." Faced with an unprepared French army and a confused French government, the Germans continued their sweep into France and on June 14 entered Paris. A week later France signed an armistice with Germany.

Vichy and the Free French

By the terms of the armistice, the Germans occupied all of northern France and the Atlantic coastline to the Spanish border. In southern France, the Nazis set up a puppet government in the city of Vichy under French Marshal Henri Pétain. Pétain and other officials in the so-called Vichy government collaborated with the Germans. Many French citizens, on the other hand, continued to fight for freedom. In Britain, de Gaulle organized a Free French government, while in France many joined the French Resistance, an underground movement that opposed the German occupation.

Battle of Britain

All that stood between Hitler and German domination of western Europe was Winston Churchill and the determined British people. Hitler expected that Britain would seek peace with Germany, but he misjudged the resolve of the British. Alone and only partially prepared, Britain faced the mightiest military machine the world had ever seen.

AROUND THE WORLD

Chemist Invents Nylon

Wilmington, Delaware, 1938

Wallace H. Carothers, a chemist at the DuPont Company in Wilmington, Delaware, created fiber from coal or petroleum in a solution form in the early 1930s. These early products melted at a temperature that was too low to make them useful for textiles. Carothers came up with a product called nylon 66–the first completely synthetic textile fiber. One of its most common uses was in women's stockings. During World War II, nylon was widely used for making parachutes.

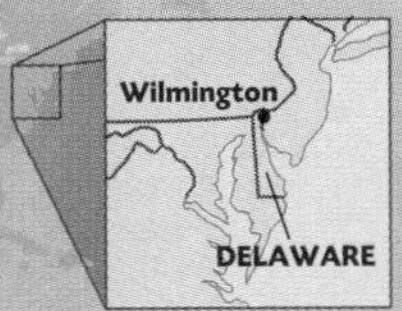

Chapter 31 Section 2

Mapping History Overlay Transparency 19, *Europe in June, 1942*

Independent Practice

Guided Reading Activity 31-2 **L1**

People in World History Profile 60

Art Have students use outside sources to research and write a brief report on the work of a World War II correspondent or photojournalist such as Edward R. Murrow, Alan Moorehead, Robert Capa, Margaret Bourke-White, Max Alpert, or Henri Cartier-Bresson. **L2**

Literature Have students research Winston Churchill's World War II speeches and write a brief report that explains how Churchill's oratory rallied the British people. Ask students to use quotations from Churchill in their reports. **L3**

Cultural Perspectives

Finland In the war between Finland and the Soviet Union (November 1939–March 1940), Finnish ski patrols in white camouflage maneuvered over Finland's snow-covered fields. They cut off Soviet supplies, isolated Soviet patrols, and stranded entire brigades. Eventually, 400,000 Soviet troops were massed against Finland's army of 33,000.

MEETING SPECIAL NEEDS ACTIVITY

Study Strategy To help students better understand terms used in Section 2, have them make a minidictionary for the following words: *blitzkrieg, sitzkrieg, capitulate, ultimatum, panzer, armada, Luftwaffe, neutrality, cash-and-carry policy,* and *lend-lease*. Tell them first to alphabetize the words, then find them in Section 2 and either determine their meaning from context or look them up in the dictionary or the Glossary of their textbook. Then have students write a good definition for each word and use each in a sentence. **L1**

ABC NEWS INTERACTIVE™

VIDEODISC
Lessons of War

Side One, Chapter 12
Frames 46153-50167
Title: *Laws of War*
Subject: A review of the rules that place limits on the types of weapons that can be used in war and against whom they can be used
Ask: What rule is supposed to protect civilians? *(Civilians should not be "injured or killed on purpose"; there should be no attacks on residential areas.)*
Ask: How did Japan break laws of war? *(The Japanese killed thousands of civilians in the places they occupied.)*

you don't say...

Quisling, a word that means "traitor," comes from the name of Vidkun Quisling, a Norwegian Nazi who helped the Germans take over Norway in 1940. During the war Quisling headed Norway's government under direction from Germany.

Who? What? Where? When?

Radar The invention of radar, an early-warning system against incoming aircraft, by physicist Robert Watson-Watts in 1935 helped the British defeat the German Luftwaffe in the Battle of Britain. By 1939 there was a chain of radar stations strung along England's southern and eastern coasts.

On May 13, 1940, Churchill delivered his first speech before the House of Commons. He told the Commons that he had "nothing to offer but blood, toil, tears, and sweat." He ended the speech with these words:

> "You ask, what is our policy? I will say: it is to wage war, by sea, land, and air, with all our might and with all the strength that God can give us: to wage war against a monstrous tyranny, never surpassed in the dark, lamentable catalogue of human crime. That is our policy. You ask, what is our aim? I can answer in one word: Victory—victory at all costs, victory in spite of all terror, victory, however hard and long the road may be; for without victory, there is no survival."

Immediately after France fell, Hitler began making plans to invade Great Britain. Hitler and the German High Command soon realized that this invasion depended on winning air supremacy over the English Channel and destroying British airfields and vital industries. To accomplish this goal, the Luftwaffe began bombing the southern coast of Britain in early August 1940. The bombings damaged four aircraft factories and five Royal Air Force (RAF) airfields, but British fighter planes known as Hurricanes and Spitfires shot down 75 German planes. From then on, Hermann Goering, head of the German air force, focused his attacks on the RAF. From August 24 to September 6, Goering sent over 1,000 planes a day. The RAF lost 466 fighters and 103 pilots, but it inflicted even heavier losses on the Germans.

Seeking to do better, the Luftwaffe changed tactics once again, switching its attack to massive night bombings of **London**. For 57 consecutive nights, from September 7 to November 3, German bombers pounded London in its great blitz, or series of air raids. In one night alone, the Luftwaffe dropped 70,000 fire bombs on Britain's capital. The devastation was enormous, killing and injuring thousands of

Images of the Times

The Blitz

During World War II, German bombers rained destruction on London and strategic targets in an attempt to knock out Great Britain's defenses and force the British to surrender.

Many London school children were evacuated to safer parts of Great Britain and even overseas to escape the bombing.

Public shelters were set up throughout London in subway tunnels and other protected areas. At the height of the blitz, 1 out of 7 Londoners slept in a shelter.

834

Images of the Times

The Blitz

During the war, about two million children were evacuated to the countryside from London and other British cities. There, many of these city children played on grass and climbed trees for the first time. The government paid the children's hosts for their care. Some children lived in cottages, while others stayed at large country estates. Parents and children were reunited periodically when the government offered reduced train fares to the country. Knowing that their children were safe helped parents carry on with the war effort.

civilians, damaging light, power, and gas lines and destroying buildings, roads, and railways. But the bombings did not break the British people's morale.

The Luftwaffe never did gain air supremacy over Britain. While incurring heavy losses of its own, the RAF downed more than 1,700 German aircraft during the Battle of Britain, and in so doing, blocked Hitler's invasion. Churchill spoke for all Britons when he said of the RAF pilots: "Never in the field of human conflict was so much owed by so many to so few."

Anglo–American Cooperation

Throughout the early phase of the war, the United States expressed its determination to remain neutral. Even before the fighting began, the United States Congress had enacted laws designed to prevent American involvement in the war. The Neutrality Acts, passed in 1937, prohibited arms shipments, loans, and credit to belligerent nations. Congress later banned the export of armaments, "for the use of either of the opposing forces" in the Spanish Civil War.

President **Franklin D. Roosevelt,** however, became convinced that Germany's expansion endangered American security and that Britain and France could not stop Hitler without American aid. Throughout his campaign for the presidency in 1940, Roosevelt tried to rally national opinion. And as they listened to news reports of German aggression, Americans became more sympathetic to Britain's plight.

After Dunkirk, Churchill appealed to the United States for help. Roosevelt gave the British 50 old American naval destroyers in return for the right to maintain American bases in Newfoundland, Bermuda, and the British West Indies. He also convinced Congress that a cash-and-carry policy—a program in which Great Britain traded cash for desperately needed supplies—would allow the United States to supply the British without risking the loss

The Royal Air Force (RAF) won the Battle of Britain, the first battle ever fought to control the air. RAF pilots intercepted German planes with the help of ground radar stations that warned of the German planes' approach.

The bombing of London, which lasted nightly beginning in September 1940, caused much ruin, but failed to break the determined spirit of the British people.

REFLECTING ON THE TIMES

1. What did the Germans achieve by bombing London during World War II?
2. How did the British people respond to the German attacks?

Chapter 31 Section 2

Linking Past and Present

Blitz The British shortened the German word *blitzkrieg* to *blitz* to describe the intensive German bombing of London during the Battle of Britain. Today the word *blitz* is used for a defensive maneuver in American football, in which one or more defensive linebackers charge through the offensive line and try to tackle the quarterback before he can pass the ball.

Who?What?Where?When?

A Controversial Ambassador Joseph Kennedy, father of President John F. Kennedy, was appointed U.S. ambassador to England in 1937 by President Roosevelt. His view that Hitler should be appeased because Britain could not win a war ran counter to Roosevelt's belief. Kennedy resigned in December 1940.

ASSESS

Check for Understanding

Assign Section 2 Review as homework or as an in-class activity.

Use Student Self-Test and Review Software to review Section 2.

ANSWERS TO REFLECTING ON THE TIMES

1. They destroyed some of Britain's aircraft factories and airfields and damaged light, power, and gas lines as well as buildings, roads, and railways.
2. The German air attacks pulled the British people together and made them more determined to defeat the Nazis.

Visualizing History Rommel had trained his troops for desert warfare on a sandy peninsula on the Baltic Sea. To prepare them for desert conditions, Rommel housed them in overheated barracks and held them to strict rations of food and water.
Answer to Caption: *to stop German troops that were sweeping through Yugoslavia and Greece*

Evaluate

Section Quiz 31-2

Use the Testmaker to create a customized quiz for Section 2.

Reteach

Have students write paragraphs that summarize the information under each main heading in Section 2.

Enrich

Have students write short essays about the resistance movement against the Nazis in occupied France.

CLOSE

Call on volunteers to trace the major events in World War II from September 1939 to April 1941 in chronological order on a map of Europe and North Africa. Ask other students to tell the significance of each event.

Visualizing History **In the spring of 1941, Erwin Rommel, "The Desert Fox" drove the British out of Libya into Egypt.** *Why had Churchill diverted some troops from Africa to southeast Europe?*

of American neutrality. Throughout 1940 this policy enabled the British to import American food and armaments. They paid cash and transported the goods in their own ships.

But the cost of the war drained the British treasury. Britain ordered 12,000 airplanes from the United States in 1940 but could not pay for them. On Roosevelt's urging, Congress approved a policy of lend-lease. It authorized the President to lend war equipment to any country whose defense he deemed vital to the national security of the United States.

On August 9, 1941, Churchill met with Roosevelt on a British battleship off the Newfoundland coast to discuss war aims. The leaders issued a joint declaration called the Atlantic Charter. It upheld freedom of trade and the right of people to choose their own government. But it also called for the "final destruction of Nazi tyranny."

Eastern Europe and Africa

While Hitler was conquering much of western Europe, Mussolini was dreaming of building a Mediterranean empire for his own country—Italy. On June 10, 1940, Mussolini declared war on France and Britain. Italy's armies in **Libya** were poised for an attack on the British forces guarding Egypt and the Sudan. Although vastly outnumbered, the British attacked the Italians on December 9. In the following weeks they scored victory after victory against the Italians stationed along Libya's north coast.

Churchill, however, halted this advance and diverted some of the troops to stop a German advance in southeast Europe that had already claimed Romania, Bulgaria, and Hungary. It was a fatal decision. German forces, sweeping through Yugoslavia and Greece in April 1941, forced the British into a second Dunkirk. Although most British troops escaped by sea, they left behind their tanks and 12,000 men. Meanwhile, Hitler sent Erwin Rommel, a brilliant general who had led the 7th Panzer Division in France, to take command of a tank force in Libya and rescue the Italians. By April 11, Rommel had pushed the British out of northern Libya, except for a small force at Tobruk.

SECTION 2 REVIEW

Recall

1. **Define** blitzkrieg, blitz, cash-and-carry policy, lend-lease.
2. **Identify** Winston Churchill, Charles de Gaulle, Franklin D. Roosevelt.
3. **Explain** why Neville Chamberlain stepped down as British prime minister in 1940.

Critical Thinking

4. **Analyzing Information** What mistakes did French military leaders make that led to the fall of France?

Understanding Themes

5. **Cooperation** How did the United States government in the early 1940s move from a policy of isolationism to a policy of openly assisting the British in the war effort against the Nazis?

SECTION 2 REVIEW ANSWERS

1. All vocabulary words are defined in the Glossary.
2. Winston Churchill, 832; Charles de Gaulle, 833; Franklin D. Roosevelt, 835
3. The German conquest of Norway and Denmark showed that appeasement had failed, and Chamberlain lost the support of all three political parties.
4. French military leaders assumed that the Maginot Line would stop an invasion even though Germany had invaded through Belgium in World War I.
5. **COOPERATION** Because Roosevelt believed that German aggression threatened American security, he convinced Congress to adopt the cash-and-carry and lend-lease policies.

Critical Thinking SKILLS

Synthesizing Information

If you want to play the guitar, you must learn different skills: how to hold the instrument, play various chords, and read music. By putting together, or synthesizing, this information, you will learn to play the guitar.

Learning the Skill

When synthesizing information, we combine information obtained from separate sources. To write a research report, for example, you study the topic in several sources—encyclopedias, books, articles, and so on. Eventually, you synthesize this information and write the report.

Before synthesizing information, first analyze each source separately. Determine the value and reliability of each source. Then, look for connections and relationships among the different sources. Some information may conflict with your existing knowledge, or may present exceptions to the general rule.

Practicing the Skill

Study the passage and the map on this page. Then answer the following questions.

1. What is the main idea of the passage?
2. What information does the map add to your knowledge of this topic?
3. By synthesizing the two sources, what conclusion can you draw about the extent of the Nazis' "final solution" of the Jewish problem?

> "I have received a report which is of the greatest importance.... It is stated in this report that very large numbers of ... Jews first deported to Poland or directly sent to [Auschwitz-] Birkenau in the well-known cattle-trucks from Germany, France, Belgium, Holland, Greece, etc. have been killed in these establishments. The bodies have been burnt in specially constructed stoves and the ashes have been used as fertilizers. All those who died by starvation or ill-treatment in the various labour-camps nearby were also burned in these stoves."
>
> —Letter from Richard Lichtheim of the Jewish Agency, June 19, 1944

Applying the Skill

Find two sources of information on the same topic and write a short report. In your report, answer these questions: What kinds of sources did you use—primary or secondary? What are the main ideas in these sources? How does each source add to your understanding of the topic? Do the sources support or contradict each other?

For More Practice

Turn to the Skill Practice in the Chapter Review on page 853 for more practice in synthesizing information.

Nazi Concentration and Death Camps

ANSWERS TO PRACTICING THE SKILL

1. It describes the systematic extermination of Jews in Nazi concentration camps.
2. The map shows the location of Auschwitz-Birkenau and other concentration camps and killing centers.
3. This was happening not only at Auschwitz but also at camps throughout occupied Europe.

Critical Thinking SKILLS

TEACH

Synthesizing Information Ask students to write detailed directions from your classroom to the principal's office, to the cafeteria, or to the gym. Have students exchange directions with a classmate. Then pass out copies of a school map. Have students compare the written directions with the map. How do the two sources differ? *(For example: The written directions are more personal; the map gives options of other routes.)* Does the information from each source lead to the same locations? *(yes)* Tell students that when they prepare material for reports, they must first synthesize, or combine, information from several sources. Then have students read the skill and complete the practice questions.

Additional Practice

Skill Reinforcement Activity 31

Chapter 31
Section 3

SECTION THEME

▸ **Conflict** Two separate and opposing alliances, the Allies and the Axis, wage a worldwide war.

Find Out

Answer: *The Soviet Union fought back after Germany invaded in June 1941. When the United States declared war on Japan after Pearl Harbor, Germany and Italy declared war on the United States.*

FOCUS

Section Objective

Describe how the Soviet Union and the United States entered World War II.

BELLRINGER
Motivational Activity

Before taking roll at the beginning of the class period, project Section Focus Transparency 31-3 and have students answer the activity questions. Discuss students' responses.

This activity is also available as a blackline master.

Vocabulary Pre-check

Use Vocabulary Activity 31 to introduce vocabulary terms. **L1 LEP**

MAY 1941 — **JUNE 1941** German forces invade the Soviet Union.

AUG. 1941 — **JULY 1941** The Nazis order the mass killing of Europe's Jews.

NOV. 1941 — **NOV. 1941** German forces reach the outskirts of Moscow.

FEB. 1942 — **DEC. 1941** Japan stages surprise attack on Pearl Harbor; the United States enters World War II.

Section 3

A Global Conflict

Setting the Scene

▸ **Terms to Define**
scorched-earth policy, Holocaust

▸ **People to Meet**
Isoroku Yamamoto

▸ **Places to Locate**
Moscow, Kiev, Leningrad, Dachau, Auschwitz, Pearl Harbor

Find Out How did the Soviet Union and the United States enter World War II?

The Storyteller

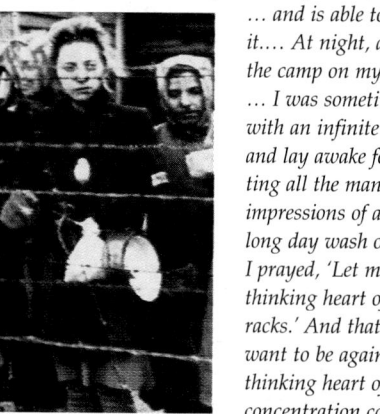

In 1942 a young Jewish woman wrote: "Of course, it is our complete destruction they want! But let us bear it with grace.... And a camp needs a poet, one who experiences life there, even there ... and is able to sing about it.... At night, as I lay in the camp on my plank bed ... I was sometimes filled with an infinite tenderness, and lay awake for hours letting all the many, too many impressions of a much too long day wash over me, and I prayed, 'Let me be the thinking heart of these barracks.' And that is what I want to be again. The thinking heart of a whole concentration camp."

—from *An Interrupted Life, the Diaries of Etty Hillesum, 1941–1943*, translated by Arno Pomerans, 1983

Surviving in a concentration camp

In the spring of 1941, Great Britain stood alone against Nazi Germany, which now controlled almost all of western Europe. In Africa, the Nazi General Erwin Rommel had succeeded in pushing the British back and had taken control of most of Libya. In Asia, meanwhile, the Japanese held Manchuria and controlled much of China. By the end of 1941, the expansive war would grow even larger. Events since June drew two more major powers into the conflict: the Soviet Union and the United States.

Invasion of the Soviet Union

Having failed in his attempt to defeat Great Britain, Hitler now turned his attention to the Soviet Union. Only by conquering the vast Soviet steppe, Hitler reasoned, could the "living space" believed vital to Germany's future be gained. He also wanted the wheat of Ukraine and the oil reserves of the Caucasus region.

On June 22, 1941, Hitler launched a massive attack on the Soviet Union. Despite British warnings and the massing of German troops along the border, the invasion took Stalin by surprise. In the first few days of fighting, the Germans destroyed the greater part of the Soviet air force, disabled thousands of Soviet tanks, and captured half a million Soviet soldiers. As German divisions advanced deeper into Soviet territory, Stalin appealed to his people to resist the invasion and issued his famous scorched-earth policy. If the Germans forced Soviet forces to retreat, Stalin ordered, Soviet citizens should destroy everything that could be of use to the invaders.

By November 1941 German armies had pushed 600 miles (960 km) inside the Soviet Union to the outskirts of **Moscow**. In addition to controlling 40 percent of the Soviet population, the Germans had captured **Kiev** and begun the siege of **Leningrad**. Yet the Soviets refused to surrender. Young Soviet

---

SECTION RESOURCES

Reproducible Masters
- Reproducible Lesson Plan 31-3
- Vocabulary Activity 31
- Guided Reading Activity 31-3
- History Simulation 31
- Section Quiz 31-3

Transparencies
- Section Focus Transparency 31-3

Multimedia
- Student Self-Test and Review Software
- Testmaker
- Lessons of War: *At the Front*

soldiers rallied to the cry, "Behind us is Moscow—there is no room left for retreat!" The Germans faced not only a steely Soviet resistance but another equally formidable foe—the Russian winter. A German soldier described the conditions:

> "We had no gloves. We had no winter shoes. We had no equipment whatsoever to fight or withstand the cold.... We lost a considerable part of our equipment.... Due to the cold we lost a lot of people who got frost-bitten, and we had not even the necessary amount of ointments, or the most simple and primitive things to fight in.... Guns didn't fire anymore. Even our wireless equipment didn't work properly anymore because the batteries were frozen hard...."

On December 2, 1941, German troops began an assault on Moscow, and in just one day they drew within sight of the city's center. It was as far as they ever got. When all seemed lost, the Soviets staged a counterattack and forced a German retreat.

The Nazi Order

Hitler wanted to conquer the Soviet Union as part of his plan to create a "New Order" in Europe. In the new world that Hitler envisioned, the Nazis would rule Europe and exploit its resources. In addition to enslaving the conquered peoples and forcing them to work for the German "master race," the Nazis would exterminate "undesirable elements" such as the Jews and the Slavs.

The Nazis began to implement Hitler's plan by plundering the occupied countries. They seized art treasures, raw materials, and factory equipment. At the same time, the Nazis drove millions into forced labor and concentration camps and massacred millions more. Between 1939 and 1944, about 7.5 million people were deported to Germany and put to work in factories, fields, and mines. Many people in the occupied countries, however, joined underground resistance movements to combat the Nazis.

The Holocaust

In July 1941, Nazi leaders implemented a plan that called for the complete extermination of all Jews in Europe. In the next four years, the Nazis rounded up Jews by the hundreds of thousands and sent them to concentration camps and death camps such as **Dachau** (DAH •KOW) in Germany and **Auschwitz** (AUSH•VIHTS) in Poland. Those who did not work as slave laborers were shot or were poisoned in gas chambers.

Visualizing History **The powerful German panzers were no match for the harsh Soviet winter of 1941. The intense cold froze lubricating oil and cracked engine blocks.** *What other problems did the German invaders encounter during that winter?*

Altogether, the Nazis murdered more than 6 million Jews during the war. This mass destruction of the Jewish people based on racial grounds has become known as the **Holocaust**. Another 6 million people, including the Slavs and Gypsies, also were slaughtered at the hands of the Nazis.

Japanese Expansion

After seizing much of China in the 1930s, Japan shifted its attention to the European colonies in East and Southeast Asia and their stores of raw materials. Taking advantage of Hitler's offensive in Europe, the Japanese acquired many of these territories. The collapse of France and the Low Countries left French Indochina and the Dutch East Indies virtually defenseless. And when the Germans threatened to invade Great Britain, the British withdrew their fleet from Singapore, leaving that colony open to attack as well.

In July 1940 the Japanese government announced its plan to create a "new order in greater East Asia." Proclaiming "Asia for the Asiatics," Japan moved to establish the "Greater East Asia Co-prosperity Sphere," an appeal to Asians who wanted to rid their lands of European rule. First, it asked France for the right to build airfields and station troops in northern Indochina. After gaining this foothold, Japan invaded southern Indochina.

COOPERATIVE LEARNING ACTIVITY

Panel Discussion Assign small groups of students to research one of the following topics: *Kristallnacht*; the Warsaw ghetto; German use of slave labor; artworks stolen by Germany from occupied countries. Have each group present a panel discussion based on their research. After all panels have been presented, have the class discuss how Hitler's "New Order" was carried out through these various activities. **L2**

TEACH

Guided Practice

THEME **Conflict**

Remind students that World War II began as a European conflict but expanded to become a global conflict by the end of 1941. Have students take turns pointing out on a wall map of the world the various areas involved in the war by December 8, 1941. **L1 LEP**

Visualizing History Have students review Napoleon's invasion of Russia in the winter of 1812 (pages 576–577). Remind students that geography often plays a vital role in war. In what ways did Napoleon and Hitler make the same mistakes? *(They underestimated the effects of the Russian winter and the resistance of the Russian people.)*

Answer to Caption: *They were without winter clothing and medical supplies.*

Linking Past and Present

Genocide Since World War II, the German people have accepted collective responsibility for the campaign of genocide carried out by the Nazis. In 1996 Germany's head of state, President Roman Herzog, proclaimed January 27 a national day of commemoration for the victims of National Socialism. That day is the anniversary of the liberation of the Auschwitz concentration camp.

TEACH

Tell students that on February 19, 1942, President Roosevelt signed Executive Order 9066, which authorized the War Department to move 112,000 Japanese American men, women, and children from the West Coast to crude internment camps farther inland. These Americans lost their constitutional rights, property, businesses, and homes. Despite this policy, Japanese Americans remained loyal to the United States. None was ever brought to trial for espionage or sabotage. Why do you think Roosevelt signed this order?

Linking Past and Present

Reparations Not until 1988 did the U.S. government acknowledge the wrong done to Japanese Americans during World War II. That year, President Ronald Reagan signed a bill that gave surviving internees a formal apology and reparations for their suffering during internment.

ABCNEWS INTERACTIVE™

VIDEODISC
Lessons of War

Side Two, Chapter 8
Frames 25814-28652
Title: *At the Front*
Subject: Contributions of minorities in World War II
Ask: How did the Japanese American 442nd Regimental Combat Team of World War II prove themselves during the war? *(This regiment was even more successful than the other units.)*

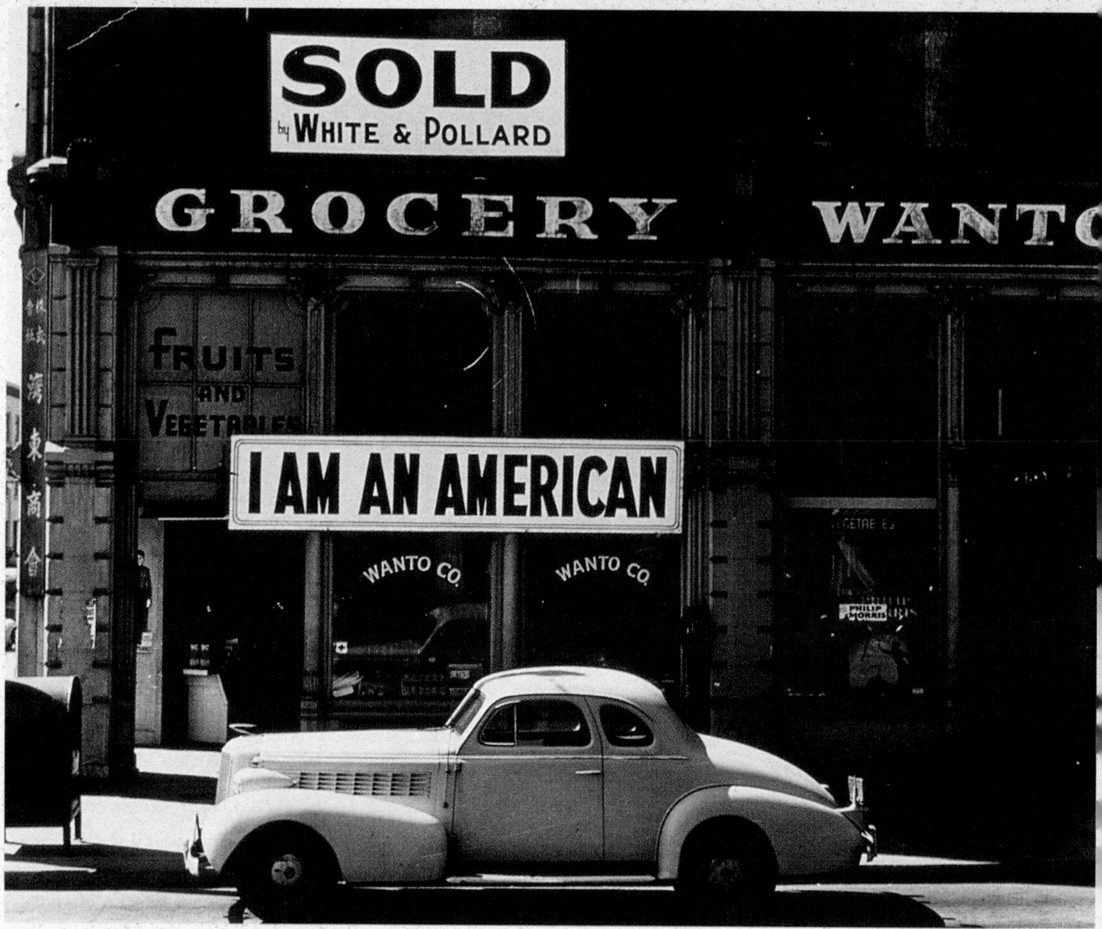

Japanese Americans

During World War II Japanese Americans were feared and hated by many other Americans, especially those living on the West Coast. In Oakland, California, the Japanese American owner of this small store—in an attempt to prevent its burning or looting—put up a sign asserting his loyalty: "I am an American." This very American scene emphasizes the cruelty of persecuting Japanese American businessmen. After the Japanese bombed Pearl Harbor, U.S. politicians spoke with fiery rhetoric, and newspapers ran hate stories that fanned the fear and antagonism against Japanese Americans.

This campaign of hate was a symptom of the brutality of the war in the Pacific. Both sides, Japanese and American, found it necessary to demonize the enemy so that their own soldiers could fight a long and hard war, and their own civilian populations could fully support their country's war effort, despite wartime shortages, extra-long working hours, or family members killed in the war. ⊕

MORE ABOUT...

Japanese American Soldiers The 442nd Regimental Combat Team, a Japanese American unit, helped the Allies win control of Italy. Altogether, almost 26,000 Japanese Americans fought for the United States during World War II.

The United States retaliated by placing an embargo, or ban, on the sale of scrap iron to Japan. In response, Japan signed the Tripartite Pact with Germany and Italy on September 27, 1940. Under this pact, the three powers affirmed the right of every nation to "receive the space to which it is entitled" and pledged to cooperate to reach that goal as well as to come to one another's aid if attacked.

Pearl Harbor

When the Japanese invaded southern Indochina on July 24, 1941, President Roosevelt demanded that they withdraw—not only from Indochina but also from China. To back up his demands, Congress placed an embargo on oil and froze all Japanese assets in the United States. Negotiations with the Japanese government continued during the summer and fall.

The Japanese government decided to go to war with the United States because it believed the United States stood in the way of its plans for expansion in the East. To defeat American military forces, however, Japanese leaders knew they had to destroy the American Pacific fleet based at **Pearl Harbor** in Hawaii. Although most American and Japanese leaders believed that Pearl Harbor was safe from attack, Admiral **Isoroku Yamamoto**, the commander of the Japanese navy, did not agree. He convinced Japanese leaders that bombers taking off from aircraft carriers and equipped with newly designed torpedos for use in shallow water could effect a successful surprise attack on Pearl Harbor. In November 1941 Yamamoto's plan was put into effect, and the Japanese fleet set sail for Hawaii.

Meanwhile, negotiations between the United States and Japan had broken down. By now Roosevelt knew that the Japanese were "poised for attack," but was convinced that Japan's move would be in Southeast Asia. As a precaution, United States military leaders sent all aircraft carriers and half the army's planes from Pearl Harbor.

On the morning of December 7, the Japanese attack squadron took off from their carrier decks and began the attack on Pearl Harbor. Within the first 25 minutes of the attack, they sank or damaged the battleships *Arizona, Utah, Oklahoma, West Virginia,* and *California*. The Japanese success was even greater than they had hoped. In all, they sank or disabled 19 American ships and destroyed 188 airplanes. They also killed more than 2,400 people and wounded 1,100. Fortunately for the United States, its aircraft carriers were at sea and escaped the attack. Calling December 7 "a date which will live in infamy," President Roosevelt, in an appearance before Congress the next day, asked for and received a declaration of war against Japan.

The Allies

The United States was now officially at war. On December 11, 1941, Germany and Italy honored their pledge to Japan in the Tripartite Pact by declaring war on the United States. Great Britain, backing the United States, declared war on Japan.

Although mistrust still lingered between the Western democracies and the Soviet Union, they put aside their differences in their resolve to defeat their common enemy. Meanwhile, the fighting in the Soviet Union remained fierce. Vast areas of the country were under German occupation. The Germans had completely surrounded Leningrad, trapping 3 million people. When the Germans cut the main railway line and supplies could no longer get through to Leningrad, many starved.

Stalin urged the Allies to open a "second front" in Europe as quickly as possible. Although President Roosevelt was open to the idea of creating a second front, Winston Churchill was opposed to it. He knew that Great Britain would have to bear the brunt of any second-front operation. Consequently, the two Allied leaders postponed plans for an invasion of Europe. Instead, they laid plans for military campaigns in North Africa and the Mediterranean area.

SECTION 3 REVIEW

Recall

1. **Define** scorched-earth policy, Holocaust.
2. **Identify** Isoroku Yamamoto.
3. **Explain** Adolf Hitler's reasons for attacking the Soviet Union in June 1941.

Critical Thinking

4. **Analyzing Information** How did the "New Order" that Germany's Adolf Hitler wanted to create in Europe affect different groups of people living on that continent?

Understanding Themes

5. **Conflict** How did World War II turn into a large-scale global conflict?

SECTION 3 REVIEW ANSWERS

1. All vocabulary words are defined in the Glossary.
2. Isoroku Yamamoto, 841
3. Hitler wanted "living space" for Germany as well as the Soviet Union's farmland and oil deposits.
4. Hitler's "New Order" exploited the resources of the conquered countries and enslaved or exterminated the conquered people.
5. **CONFLICT** Germany invaded the Soviet Union and Japan attacked Pearl Harbor, causing the United States to enter the war.

Chapter 31 Section 3

Political Policies Have students compare the goals and methods of Hitler's "New Order" with Japan's plans to create an "Asia for Asians." **L2**

History Simulation 31

Independent Practice

Guided Reading Activity 31-3 **L1**

ASSESS

Check for Understanding

Assign Section 3 Review as homework or as an in-class activity.

Use Student Self-Test and Review Software to review Section 3.

Evaluate

Section Quiz 31-3

Use the Testmaker to create a customized quiz for Section 3.

Reteach

Have students summarize the events that brought the Soviet Union and the United States into World War II.

Enrich

Have students research the raw materials Japan gained by invading French Indochina and the Dutch East Indies.

CLOSE

Have students discuss how the entry of the Soviet Union and the United States into the war changed the balance of forces between the Allies and the Axis.

SECTION THEME

▶ **Conflict** The Allies make major gains against the Axis powers.

Find Out

Answer: *The Soviet victory at Stalingrad, the German surrender in North Africa, the Allied invasion of Italy, and the American victories in the Pacific turned the tide of the war.*

FOCUS

Section Objective

Explain how the tide of war turned in favor of the Allies during 1942 and 1943.

BELLRINGER
Motivational Activity

Before taking roll at the beginning of the class period, project Section Focus Transparency 31-4 and have students answer the activity questions. Discuss students' responses.

This activity is also available as a blackline master.

Vocabulary Pre-check

Use Vocabulary Activity 31 to introduce vocabulary terms. **L1 LEP**

1941 — **MAY 1941** British naval forces sink German battleship *Bismarck.*

1942 — **JULY 1942** British halt German advance in North Africa at El Alamein, Egypt.

1943 — **FEB. 1943** German forces at Stalingrad surrender to the Soviets.

Section 4

Turning Points

Setting the Scene

▶ **Terms to Define**
kamikaze

▶ **People to Meet**
Erwin Rommel, Bernard Montgomery, Dwight D. Eisenhower, Douglas MacArthur, Chester W. Nimitz

▶ **Places to Locate**
Stalingrad, Casablanca, Sicily, Guadalcanal

Find Out How did the tide of war turn in favor of the Allies during 1942 and 1943?

The Storyteller

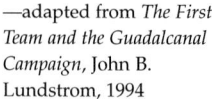

A kamikaze attack on an American aircraft carrier, the Hornet, *was recorded in photographs and by eyewitness accounts such as this one: "His [plane] already with flame blossoming on its underside, appeared high above the* Hornet*'s starboard quarter. Perhaps dead or dying, [the pilot] did not release his bomb but kept coming directly at the carrier. He did not miss.... Ruptured fuel tanks sprayed the signal bridge with burning gasoline, while the wrecked airplane smashed into the flight deck...." The impact and burning fuel killed and maimed many men, and fires blazed for two hours.*

—adapted from *The First Team and the Guadalcanal Campaign*, John B. Lundstrom, 1994

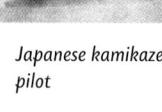

Japanese kamikaze pilot

In the early months of 1942, the war was going badly for the Allies. By destroying much of the American fleet at Pearl Harbor, Japan had gained control of the Pacific Ocean and cleared the way for a seaborne invasion of American, British, and Dutch territories in that region. In December 1941 Japanese forces had captured the British colony of Hong Kong and invaded the Malay Peninsula. In the West, meanwhile, Rommel controlled a large area of North Africa, and German forces held the upper hand in the Soviet Union as well.

Despite these successes, the Axis powers would never again enjoy such a strong position. By the end of 1942, the tide of the war had begun to turn in favor of the Allies.

Sea and Air Battles

Even before the United States entered the war, it was shipping food and war supplies to Britain under the Lend-Lease Act. But German submarines, or U-boats, threatened this vital lifeline across the Atlantic. By the end of 1939, U-boats had already sunk 114 Allied and neutral ships. German air attacks also took their toll.

To make matters worse for the Allies, the new German battleship *Bismarck*, accompanied by the new cruiser *Prinz Eugen*, entered the fight in May 1941. With 11 Allied convoys either at sea or about to sail, the British hastily dispatched several ships to intercept the Nazis. On May 23 they sighted the two German ships in the Denmark Strait between Iceland and Greenland and opened fire. In the battle that followed, the *Bismarck* sank the British battle cruiser *Hood* and damaged a new British battleship before slipping away to safety.

Three days later, on May 26, a British patrol plane spotted the *Bismarck* about 600 miles (965 km) off the French coast. In the battle that followed, the *Bismarck* sustained at least eight

SECTION RESOURCES

Reproducible Masters
- Reproducible Lesson Plan 31-4
- Vocabulary Activity 31
- Guided Reading Activity 31-4
- Geography and History Activity 31
- Section Quiz 31-4

Transparencies
- Section Focus Transparency 31-4
- Mapping History Overlay Transparency 20, *Southeast Asia Prior to World War II*

Multimedia
- Student Self-Test and Review Software
- Testmaker
- Lessons of War: *Can a Battle Change History?*

torpedo hits before it finally sank. With this crucial victory, the British put an end to German efforts to win the Battle of the Atlantic with surface ships. Gradually, the Allies devised new methods for protecting their convoys against U-boats as well.

As they fought for control of the Atlantic, the Allies launched a sustained air offensive against Germany in May 1940. In August, the RAF bombed Berlin for the first time. During the next five years, the Allies flew mission after mission against Germany, destroying factories, oil refineries, and railways and leveling entire cities.

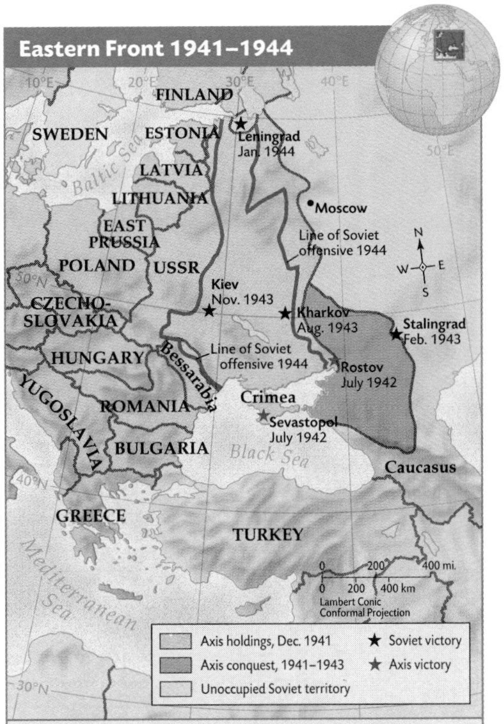

Map Study Some of the fiercest battles of World War II took place on the eastern front in the Soviet Union.
Location Which battle proved to be a major turning point of the war?

The Soviet Offensive

In July 1942 the military situation in the Soviet Union looked desperate. With the Soviet army in full retreat, the Germans were approaching **Stalingrad**, a major industrial center on the Volga River. In angry exchanges with Churchill, Stalin continued to press for a second front in the West to take some of the military pressure off his nation. But in August Churchill went to Moscow to tell Stalin that there would be no second front in 1942.

On August 22 the Germans attacked Stalingrad. Because it was named after Stalin, losing the city would have been a blow to Soviet morale. As determined to protect Stalingrad as Hitler was to take it, Stalin ordered that the city be held at all costs.

The Soviets launched a counterattack in September and encircled the German troops threatening the city. They cut off German supply lines. Although the Soviets and the frigid winter weather were closing in on the Germans, Hitler refused to allow his troops to retreat. By the time German officers finally surrendered in February 1943, the German army had lost the best of its troops. Many historians now view the Soviet victory at Stalingrad as the major turning point of World War II. By killing about 100,000 German soldiers, capturing 80,000 more, and seizing large quantities of German military equipment, the Soviet Union broke the back of the Nazi military machine.

War in the Desert

In January 1942 Allied forces in North Africa were struggling to regain ground lost to the Germans. They faced a formidable foe. **Erwin Rommel,** commander of the Afrika Korps, applied blitzkrieg tactics to warfare in the desert. His exploits earned him the nickname "the Desert Fox."

In the spring of 1942, Rommel pushed the British two-thirds of the way back to the Egyptian frontier. He struck again at the end of May, but the British, under General **Bernard Montgomery**, stopped him two months later at El Alamein (EL A•luh•MAYN), a railway junction about 70 miles (112 km) from Alexandria. In October Montgomery launched a counterattack that forced the Germans back across the Egyptian-Libyan frontier and ended with the British capture of Tripoli, the capital of Libya, in January 1943.

As Montgomery was advancing westward, the Allies were landing troops in Morocco and Algeria as part of a planned offensive against Rommel. By advancing from the east and from the west, the Allies hoped to trap Rommel with their "pincers" strategy. But the Allied landings met with heavy resistance from the Vichy French, who governed French North Africa. To end the fighting, Allied commander **Dwight D. Eisenhower** struck a deal with Admiral François Darlan, a Vichy official. In

COOPERATIVE LEARNING ACTIVITY

Biographies Organize the class into two groups. Have one group use outside sources to prepare a biography of Franklin Roosevelt, and the other group to do the same for Winston Churchill. Tell students to focus on how each man developed the qualities he needed to serve as a wartime leader. Students should examine factors such as education, military experience, personality traits, charisma, oratory skills, and ideals. Have both groups present their reports and then have them draw up a list of leadership qualities shared by FDR and Churchill. **L2**

TEACH

Guided Practice

THEME **Conflict**

List the following events on the chalkboard: the sinking of the *Bismarck*; victory at Stalingrad; the battle of El Alamein in North Africa; the invasion of Sicily; the capture of Malaya, Singapore, Burma, Dutch East Indies, Guam, Wake Island, and the Philippines; Battles of the Coral Sea, Midway, and Guadalcanal. Have students identify the combatants and the victors of each event. **L1 LEP**

Map Study

Answer
the Battle of Stalingrad

Map Skills Practice

Reading a Map Which Russian city is near 50°N latitude and 30°E longitude? *(Kiev)*

ABC NEWS INTERACTIVE™

VIDEODISC
Lessons of War

Side One, Chapter 6
Frames 15755-18472
Title: *Can a Battle Change History?*
Subject: The Battle of Midway
Ask: Why was the Battle of Midway considered a turning point in World War II history? *(Japan was winning, and Midway was a strategic attempt to shut off U.S. supply lines. Stopping Japan at Midway changed the direction of the war.)*

Chapter 31
Section 4

Map Study

Answer

The Allies invaded Italy from Tunisia because it was the closest point to Italy.

Map Skills Practice

Reading a Map **Where in North Africa did the Allies win victories in 1943?** *(Tripoli, Kasserine Pass, Tunis, Bizerte)*

Military Strategies Have students describe the strategies that led to the victory at Stalingrad, the defeat of the Germans in North Africa, the invasion of Italy, and the Battle of Guadalcanal. **L3**

Mapping History Overlay Transparency 20, *Southeast Asia Prior to World War II*

Independent Practice

Guided Reading Activity 31-4 **L1**

Geography and History Activity 31

Daily Life Have students research the effect of the attack on Stalingrad on its citizens. Ask them to imagine they are students in Stalingrad in the summer of 1942. Have them write a letter to relatives in the United States describing what is happening and how they feel about it. **L2**

ASSESS

Check for Understanding

Assign Section 4 Review as homework or as an in-class activity.

Use Student Self-Test and Review Software to review Section 4.

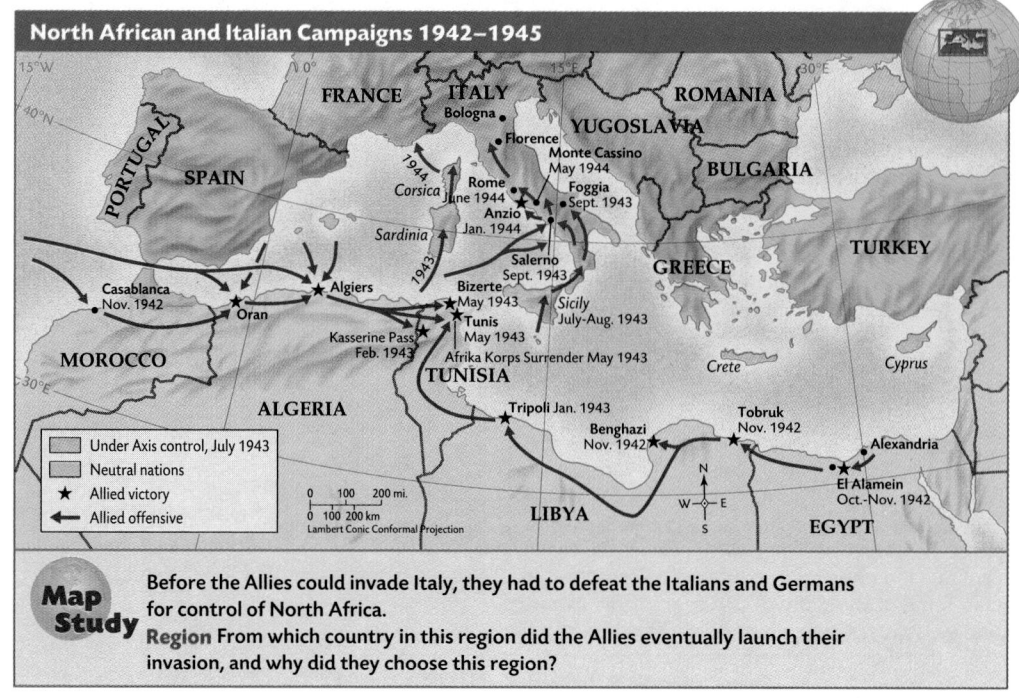

North African and Italian Campaigns 1942–1945

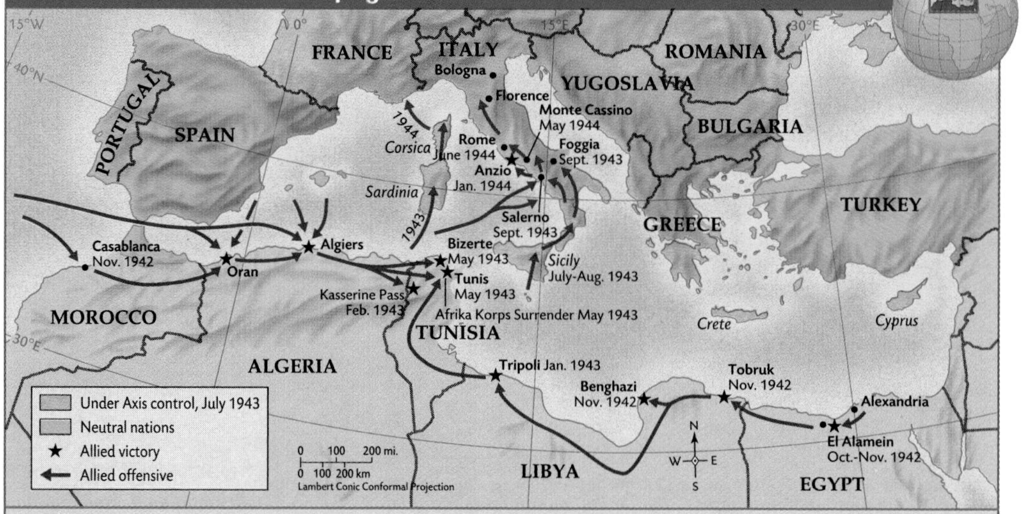

Map Study **Before the Allies could invade Italy, they had to defeat the Italians and Germans for control of North Africa.**
Region From which country in this region did the Allies eventually launch their invasion, and why did they choose this region?

return for Allied support of his claim to French North Africa, Darlan ordered an end to the resistance. With the armistice concluded in November 1942, the Free French, under Charles de Gaulle, joined the Allies in Africa. Meanwhile, in a series of powerful attacks, the Allies began closing the pincers. When Rommel flew to Berlin to tell Hitler that the situation was hopeless, the Nazi dictator rejected his general's assessment and barred Rommel from returning to Africa. But Rommel was right. In May 1943, General von Arnim, the new commander of the German forces in Tunisia, surrendered. The Allies now controlled all of North Africa.

Invasion of Italy

In early 1943, the American and British chiefs of staff and political leaders met at **Casablanca** in Morocco to discuss their next move. Because they wanted to secure communications in the Mediterranean and intensify the pressure on Italy, they decided to invade **Sicily**, the large island near the southern tip of the Italian Peninsula.

Under the command of General Eisenhower, the Allies began a combined air and sea attack on **Sicily** in July 1943. The seaborne landings met little resistance at first, but when the Allies approached Messina, on the extreme northeastern tip of the island, the Germans put up a stronger fight to cover their withdrawal across the Strait of Messina. In six days nearly 40,000 German and 70,000 Italian troops escaped to Italy.

The conquest of Sicily led quickly to Mussolini's downfall. On July 25, King Victor Emmanuel III, pressed into action by antiwar factions, fired Mussolini and had him arrested. The new prime minister, Marshal Pietro Badoglio, soon dissolved the Fascist party and on September 3 signed a secret act of surrender.

That same day, Allied forces crossed the Strait of Messina and landed in Calabria on the Italian mainland. The broadcast announcement of Badoglio's unconditional surrender caught the Germans by surprise, but they recovered in time to occupy Rome two days later, forcing the king and Badoglio to withdraw to the south. The Germans later rescued Mussolini and put him in control of northern Italy.

For the remaining months of 1943 and early months of 1944, the Allies fought their way up the Italian Peninsula. Allied troops could not penetrate the German defenses at Monte Cassino, a sixth-century monastery located on a mountaintop that dominated the road to Rome. In the end it took a

MEETING SPECIAL NEEDS ACTIVITY

Learning Style: Kinesthetic Have students who are kinesthetic learners create a "war map" showing one of the following conflicts of the war: the Soviet offensive, the war in the desert, the invasion of Italy, or the war in the Pacific. Tell students to re-create the area of conflict and then illustrate how the Allied forces took the offensive and achieved victory. Suggest that they use markers, flags, or pictures to illustrate the actions in the conflict. Display completed maps in the classroom and encourage students to explain their maps. **L2 LEP**

massive artillery bombardment and almost five months for the Allies to dislodge the Germans in May 1944. One month later, on June 4, Allied forces entered Rome.

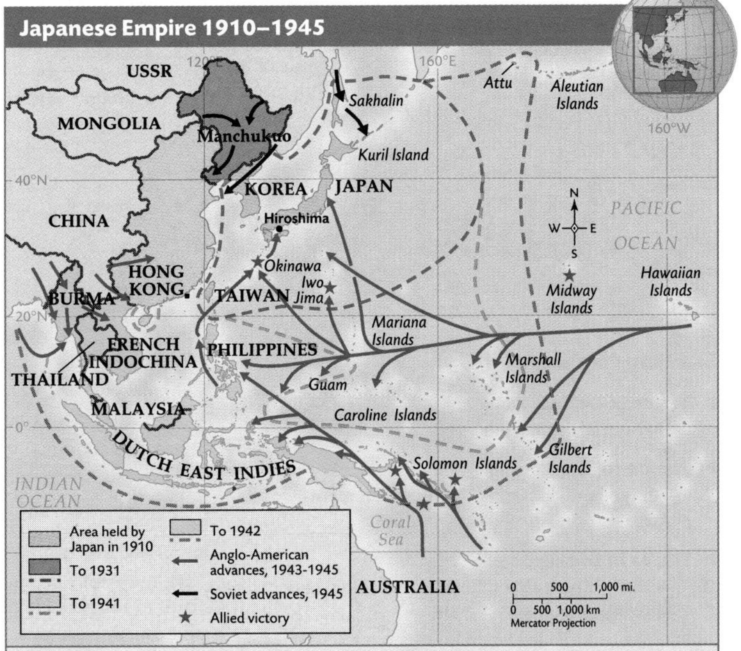

Map Study Between 1931 and 1942, Japan took over large areas of East Asia, Southeast Asia, and the Pacific.
Region Why were the Japanese able to seize the European colonies in this region so easily in 1941 and 1942?

War in the Pacific

While the war raged in Europe, the Japanese were having great success in Asia. In the months following Pearl Harbor, they captured Malaya, Singapore, and Burma. In the Pacific, they seized the Dutch East Indies, Guam, Wake Island, and the Philippines.

The Allies were able to make some gains. In May 1942, in the Battle of the Coral Sea, the Allies claimed a victory. And in June, at the Battle of Midway, the Americans defeated the Japanese navy and ended Japanese naval superiority in the Pacific.

To follow up this victory, the Americans launched an attack against **Guadalcanal** in early August. While troops under General **Douglas MacArthur** attacked the Japanese on land, naval forces under Admiral **Chester W. Nimitz** confronted them at sea. The six-month land, sea, and air battle for control of the island ended in victory for the Allies. Guadalcanal was the first in a series of island battles the Americans fought as they leapfrogged their way north to Japan. Their strategy was to capture some islands and bypass others. Those bypassed would be cut off from supplies and made to "wither on the vine."

After Guadalcanal, the Americans paused to build up their Pacific forces. When the American advance resumed in November 1943, Japanese leaders called upon their soldiers to die for their homeland. Japanese pilots known as kamikazes volunteered for suicide missions, crashing their bomb-laden aircraft into Allied bases and ships. The Japanese were far from ready to surrender.

SECTION 4 REVIEW

Recall

1. **Define** kamikaze.
2. **Identify** Erwin Rommel, Bernard Montgomery, Dwight D. Eisenhower, Douglas MacArthur, Chester W. Nimitz.
3. **Locate** Stalingrad on the map on page 843. Why was the Battle of Stalingrad a major turning point in World War II?

Critical Thinking

4. **Synthesizing Information** How did Hitler's decisions contribute to Germany's defeats in both Stalingrad and North Africa?

Understanding Themes

5. **Conflict** Why did the Allies decide to "leapfrog" their way to Japan rather than launch a direct attack?

SECTION 4 REVIEW ANSWERS

1. The words are defined in the Glossary.
2. Erwin Rommel, 843; Bernard Montgomery, 843; Dwight D. Eisenhower, 843; Douglas MacArthur, 845; Chester W. Nimitz, 845
3. In the Battle of Stalingrad, the best of the German army was destroyed.
4. Hitler refused to allow the German forces to withdraw from Stalingrad and refused to end the North African campaign even after it had become hopeless.
5. **CONFLICT** By capturing some islands and leapfrogging over others, the Allies hoped to cut off supplies to the bypassed islands, forcing them to surrender.

Chapter 31 Section 4

Map Study

Answer

The European powers were preoccupied with Hitler.

Map Skills Practice

Reading a Map Where did the Soviets advance in 1945? *(Manchukuo and the Kuril Islands)*

Evaluate

Section Quiz 31-4

Use the Testmaker to create a customized quiz for Section 4.

Reteach

Using a large wall map, have students show Allied progress in the Atlantic, Soviet Union, North Africa, Italy, and the Pacific in 1942–1943.

Enrich

Have students watch the film *North Star* (also called *Armored Attack*), made in 1943, which shows the German invasion of the Soviet Union. Have students write a short essay describing the attitude toward the Soviet Union reflected in the film.

CLOSE

Organize the class into two groups. Have each group make a list in chronological order of ten key events from this section. Then as a class combine the two lists into one top-ten list.

Chapter 31
Section 5

SECTION THEME

▶ **Innovation** New military technologies, such as the atomic bomb, affect the outcome of World War II.

Find Out

Answer: *The use of the atomic bomb, developed secretly by the United States, quickly ended the war.*

FOCUS

Section Objective

Understand how new technology affected the conduct and outcome of World War II.

BELLRINGER
Motivational Activity

Before taking roll at the beginning of the class period, project Section Focus Transparency 31-5 and have students answer the activity questions. Discuss students' responses.

This activity is also available as a blackline master.

Vocabulary Pre-check

Use the Vocabulary PuzzleMaker to create a puzzle that reinforces the vocabulary terms in this section. **L1**

JUNE 1944 — DEC. 1944 — JUNE 1945 — DEC. 1945

JUNE 6, 1944 (D-Day) Allies land in Normandy.

DEC. 16, 1944 Battle of the Bulge begins.

MAY 8, 9, 1945 V-E (Victory in Europe) Day celebrated in Allied countries.

AUG. 6, 1945 The United States drops atomic bomb on Hiroshima, Japan.

Section 5

Allied Victories

Setting the Scene

▶ **Terms to Define**
D-Day, partisan, genocide

▶ **People to Meet**
George Patton, Harry S Truman, Clement Attlee

▶ **Places to Locate**
Warsaw, Rhine River, Berlin, Yalta, Potsdam, Hiroshima, Nagasaki

Find Out How did new technology affect the conduct and outcome of World War II?

The Storyteller

An American woman, living in Russia, later recalled how hope for Allied rescue was everywhere in Russia during the spring of 1944:

"They knew it must come this summer, for the war was already in Europe.... On a day in early June the air was split by a radio announcement: 'Stand by for a special broadcast at 1:45.' We knew what it would be. Everybody knew. 'Today, June 6, 1944, early in the morning, General Eisenhower's forces began landing operations on the northern coast of France.'" The long-awaited second front was a reality. People laughed and slapped each other on the back.

—adapted from *Fifty Russian Winters, An American Woman's Life in the Soviet Union*, Margaret Wettlin, 1992

American troops land in Normandy

At a conference in Washington, D.C., in May 1943, Franklin D. Roosevelt and Winston Churchill decided that the Allies would invade Normandy, a province of northwestern France on the English Channel, the following spring. When Roosevelt and Churchill met with Joseph Stalin in Tehran (TAY•RAN), Iran, in November of that year, the Soviet leader learned that the Allies would finally be opening a second front in Europe. He promised to start a Soviet offensive on the eastern front at the same time as the invasion of France occurred.

D-Day

No other offensive in history was as large and carefully planned as Operation Overlord, the Allied plan to land troops in France. Under the direction of General Eisenhower, the Allies assembled a force of 150,000 soldiers, 5,000 ships, and 11,000 planes in southern England in early 1944 in preparation for the invasion. Although the Germans expected an invasion, they did not know when or where it would occur. As a result, they spread their forces thinly along the Channel coast of France.

The Allies set D-Day, or the day of attack, for June 5, but bad weather forced a 24-hour postponement. Finally, in the early morning of June 6, large convoys sailed from England to the Normandy coast. Royal Air Force (RAF) bombers attacked the German coast-defense guns, and at midnight three Allied airborne divisions parachuted into France to assist the seaborne assault. At dawn, landing craft with infantry, tanks, and other weapons moved toward the coast as destroyers and battleships pounded the beaches. Then the infantry waded ashore.

Despite the confusion of the fighting and the heavy German resistance, the invasion was a great success. The Allies now had a foothold in western Europe from which they could launch an effective drive against Germany. By the beginning of July

SECTION RESOURCES

Reproducible Masters
- Reproducible Lesson Plan 31-5
- Guided Reading Activity 31-5
- Reteaching Activity 31
- Enrichment Activity 31
- Section Quiz 31-5
- Performance Assessment Activity 31
- Spanish Chapter Summary 31

Transparencies
- Section Focus Transparency 31-5
- Mapping History Overlay Transparency 21, *Battle Sites in the Pacific*
- World History and Art Transparency 42, *The Red Stairway*

Multimedia
- Vocabulary PuzzleMaker Software
- Student Self-Test and Review Software
- Testmaker
- Turning Points in World History
- In the Holy Land

Allied Offensive in Europe June 1944–May 1945

Map Study From D-Day in June 1944 to its surrender in May 1945, Germany was in full retreat on both the western and eastern fronts.
Location Where did the one German offensive occur during this period?

1944, more than 1 million troops and massive amounts of supplies poured into northern France.

On July 25 the Americans broke through the German line. By early August, American tank commander General **George Patton** and his forces were racing across northern France through open countryside. At the same time, General de Gaulle ordered his Free French forces to advance on Paris, where members of the French Resistance had risen up against their German occupiers. On August 25, 1944, de Gaulle entered Paris, a free city for the first time in four years.

Victory over Germany

Months before the Allies invaded Normandy, the Soviet army was advancing steadily toward Germany from the east, recovering one Soviet city after another. In January 1944, it finally broke the siege of Leningrad. During the 890-day siege, more than 800,000 of the city's inhabitants had died from cold, starvation, or German bombs. By the spring of 1944 the Soviets had liberated Ukraine as well. In July they crossed the Polish frontier and soon approached Poland's capital city, **Warsaw**.

TEACH

Guided Practice

THEME **Innovation**

Have students describe how strategies used in the D-Day invasion and in capturing Pacific islands helped the Allies, and how the atomic bomb quickly ended the war. **L1**

Map Study

Answer
the Battle of the Bulge

Map Skills Practice

Reading a Map What countries were affected by the Allied offensives? *(France, Italy, Austria, Germany, Poland, Hungary)*

International Relations Have students summarize the agreements made at Yalta and then compare the Yalta and Potsdam conferences. **L2**

Mapping History Overlay Transparency 21, *Battle Sites in the Pacific*

World History and Art Transparency 42, *The Red Stairway*

CURRICULUM CONNECTION

TECHNOLOGY
After D-Day, PLUTO (Pipe-Line Under The Ocean), a pipeline under the English Channel, supplied 700 tons of gasoline a day for Allied trucks and tanks advancing across Europe.

COOPERATIVE LEARNING ACTIVITY

Mapmaking Organize the class into five groups. Each group will be responsible for mapping one of the following military campaigns from June 1944 to August 1945: Operation Overlord, the Battle of the Bulge, the Soviet advances, the Pacific Campaign, and the bombing of Japan. Instruct each group to create a map of their campaign using poster paper and markers. Suggest that they use maps from the text as well as from other sources as guides. Tell them to show the locations of battles, troop movements, flight patterns, and strategies. Have each group prepare a brief written summary that explains the campaign. When the maps are completed, ask each group to present its map and summary to the class. **L3 LEP**

Chapter 31
Section 5

VIDEODISC
Turning Points in World History

Side Two
Chapter 6

Frames 15755-18472
Title: *The Holocaust*
Ask: What lessons can we learn from the Holocaust? *(Ethnic and racial prejudices have no foundation; genocide must be prevented.)*

Side Two
Chapter 7

Title: *Dropping the Atomic Bomb*
Ask: What cities were bombed? *(Hiroshima and Nagasaki, Japan)*

Independent Practice

Guided Reading Activity 31-5 **L1**

Technology Have students find out more about the work of Enrico Fermi and J. Robert Oppenheimer that led to the development of the atomic bomb. **L2**

Visualizing History The Soviet army, aided by the Royal Air Force, fought for nine days to win control of Berlin. On the last morning, April 30, 1945, Soviet tanks reached the Reichstag, the German parliament building, which they bombarded until afternoon.
Answer to Caption: *The Western Allies crossed the Rhine and by April 11 reached the Elbe, where they later met Soviet armies coming from the east.*

With Soviet troops approaching the city, the Polish Resistance rose up against the Germans on August 1 and fought them in the streets of the capital. In retaliation, the Germans destroyed much of the city and killed more than 250,000 Poles. Because the Polish resisters were anti-Communist, Stalin did nothing to help them, nor would he allow the British to airlift in supplies. This action embittered the Poles and renewed the West's suspicions that the Soviet Union wanted to extend its control over eastern Europe.

On August 23 Romania surrendered to the Soviets. This victory opened the Balkans to the advancing Soviet forces. Shortly thereafter, Bulgaria sued for peace and joined the war on the Soviet side. By October 1944, the Soviets controlled almost all of east-central Europe.

While the Soviets advanced through eastern Europe, the Allies attacked Germany itself in September 1944. Despite the Allied gains and the devastating bombing of Germany, Hitler insisted that Germany would never surrender. Although most of the German people remained loyal to Hitler, resistance to his leadership had grown among his top military leaders. Two months earlier, several of his generals had even plotted to take his life. One anti-Nazi military official placed a bomb under a conference table in Hitler's military headquarters in East Prussia. Although the bomb exploded just a few feet away, the Führer escaped serious injury.

Despite the increasing certainty of an Allied victory, Hitler was convinced that a surprise offensive might still reverse the Allied advance. Over his generals' objections, he ordered a last, desperate offensive in mid-December 1944. In the famous Battle of the Bulge, the Germans cut through the center of the American forces, creating a great bulge in the Allied line of troops. The Allies finally checked the German drive at Bastogne, Belgium, and in March 1945 they stormed across the **Rhine River**, Germany's historic defensive barrier. By April 11, they had reached the Elbe River. Eight days later, the Soviets fought their way into the city of **Berlin**, and on April 25, advance units of the American and Soviet armies met on the Elbe at the town of Torgau (TOHR•gow).

On May 7, 1945, the Germans surrendered unconditionally. The next day was proclaimed V-E (Victory in Europe) Day in Great Britain, France, and the United States; May 9 was celebrated as V-E Day in the Soviet Union. With the German surrender, the war in Europe had finally come to an end. The end had also come for the Fascist dictators. Italian partisans, or resistance fighters, had shot Mussolini, and Hitler had committed suicide in a fortified underground chamber in Berlin.

Visualizing History **Celebrating the Red Army's capture of Berlin, a group of Soviet troops unfurl the Soviet flag over the ruins of the German parliament building.** *What advances were made by the Western Allies during the spring of 1945?*

Yalta and Potsdam

In February 1945 Roosevelt, Churchill, and Stalin had met at **Yalta**, a Soviet resort on the Black Sea in Crimea. Because it was clear that the end of the war was at hand, the participants discussed issues affecting the postwar world.

The Allied leaders agreed to divide Germany, as well as the capital city of Berlin, into four zones that Great Britain, France, the United States, and the Soviet Union would occupy and administer. They also agreed "to disarm and disband all German armed forces ... to remove or destroy all German military equipment ... to bring all war criminals to just and swift punishment and ... wipe out the Nazi party."

At Yalta, the Allies proposed that France and China help the United States, the Soviet Union, and

MEETING SPECIAL NEEDS ACTIVITY

Reading Comprehension Have students reread the information under the main heading "Effects of the War." Then let them work in pairs to summarize in one sentence the main idea of each paragraph. *(For example, the first paragraph: There were about 55 million military and civilian deaths because of the war.)* Have pairs of students exchange their summaries and comment on those of others. **L1**

Visualizing History **In February 1945, Allied leaders Winston Churchill, Franklin D. Roosevelt, and Joseph Stalin met at Yalta on the USSR's Crimean Peninsula. They discussed a number of issues related to the postwar Europe.** *What major agreement was made at Yalta regarding the war against Japan?*

Great Britain in forming the United Nations. This permanent international organization would maintain peace and security after the war. Delegates from the three major Allied countries had laid the groundwork for a United Nations charter in October 1944 at Dumbarton Oaks near Washington, D.C. Because Winston Churchill and Franklin Roosevelt feared that Stalin intended to establish Communist governments in eastern Europe, they pressured him to hold free elections in the Soviet-occupied countries. In return, they gave Stalin the eastern part of Poland. Poland would receive former German land in return for yielding its eastern territory.

The Western leaders were also eager to get Stalin to declare war on Japan. They feared that unless the Soviet Union joined the Japanese war, the war in the Pacific would last an additional two years. Stalin agreed to declare war on Japan, but in return he asked for and got the Kuril Islands and the southern part of Sakhalin Island. These islands, located off the coast of Siberia in the northern Pacific Ocean, were ruled by Japan.

Six months later the three Allied leaders met again at **Potsdam** in Germany, but by this time some of the key participants had changed. After Franklin D. Roosevelt died in April, **Harry S Truman** succeeded him as President. Although Churchill was there at the opening, his Conservative party lost the general election, and **Clement Attlee** of the Labour party replaced him as prime minister halfway through the conference.

The atmosphere at Potsdam was also quite different from that at Yalta. Although the Allies made plans for the occupation of Germany and issued an ultimatum to Japan demanding unconditional surrender, more issues were raised than were settled. New tensions over the future of the European continent were beginning to pull apart the wartime alliance.

Victory Over Japan

By the early summer of 1945, it was clear that an Allied victory over Japan was inevitable. American planes had been bombing Japanese cities since the end of 1944. In October, at the Battle of Leyte Gulf in the Philippines, Japan lost most of what remained of its naval power.

Still the Japanese fought on. In early 1945 Japanese and American troops engaged in two of the fiercest battles of the Pacific campaign for control of two islands: Iwo Jima and Okinawa. Iwo Jima, the largest of the Volcano Islands, was 750 miles (1,200 km) from Tokyo; Okinawa, the largest of the Ryukyu Islands, was only 360 miles (576 km) off the southern tip of Japan. Despite putting up fierce resistance, the Japanese lost both battles. The victories were extremely important to the Allies because they now controlled air bases within reach of Japan.

On July 26, 1945, the United States issued another ultimatum to Japan demanding unconditional surrender. When the Japanese refused to accept defeat, the United States decided to use a new secret weapon—the atomic bomb—to swiftly end the war. Earlier, President Truman had received news that the bomb had been tested successfully while he was at the Potsdam conference. Before

Visualizing History At Yalta, Churchill, Roosevelt, and Stalin also agreed that each of the five permanent members of the United Nations Security Council would have veto power over matters brought before the Council. During the early years of the United Nations, the Soviet Union often used its veto to prevent UN action against Soviet actions in Eastern Europe.

Answer to Caption: *The Soviets agreed to join the war against Japan. In return they received the Japanese-owned Kuril Islands and the southern part of Sakhalin Island.*

Cultural Perspectives

Navajo Code Talkers In 1943 the U.S. Marines recruited the Navajo to develop a military code that the Japanese could not break. Based on their oral language, the Navajo code talkers created the only unbreakable code in military history.

ABCNEWS INTERACTIVE™

VIDEODISC
In the Holy Land

Side One, Chapter 17
Frame 22795
Title: *The Holocaust: 1938–1945*
Ask: Why did Jewish people feel insecure after the Holocaust? *(They had suffered terrible persecution and loss. They wanted to live where they could be safe from any such persecution ever again, and they felt that place was Israel.)*

MAKING CONNECTIONS ACTIVITY

Women's Roles The day-to-day activities of women in Allied, Axis, and occupied countries changed during the war. Have students research and write a report on how the war affected women's daily lives in the United States, Great Britain, France, Germany, Italy, the Soviet Union, or Poland. Suggest that students include in their reports changes in home life, work opportunities, and military roles as well as popular images of women's roles. **L1**

you don't say...

Gobbledygook was the term applied to the hard-to-understand rules, regulations, and orders that came from the U.S. government during the war as well as the abbreviations for new government boards and agencies. For example, PWPGSJ-SISACWPB stood for the Pipe, Wire Product, and Galvanized Steel Jobbers Subcommittee of the Iron and Steel Advisory Committee of the War Production Board.

CONNECTIONS The Arts

Let Us Never Forget

Controversy surrounded some of the exhibits in the Holocaust Memorial Museum. Jews and non-Jews, concentration camp survivors, and others, all agreed on the need for a museum that accurately portrayed the horrors of the Holocaust. Such items as actual collections of the shoes, teeth, and hair taken from prisoners were, however, deeply disturbing to some visitors. A few compromises were made, but the museum stands as a truthful account of millions of people who will not be forgotten.

Answers to Making the Connection

1. *They created artwork as an outlet for some of their pain.*
2. *in books, artwork, movies, memorials*

ASSESS

Check for Understanding

Assign Section 5 Review as homework or as an in-class activity.

Use Student Self-Test and Review Software to review Section 5.

reaching the fateful decision to use the bomb against Japan, Truman wrote his family:

> "I certainly regret the necessity of wiping out whole populations because of the 'pig-headedness' of the leaders of a nation and, for your information, I am not going to [use the atomic bomb] unless it becomes absolutely necessary. My object is to save as many American lives as possible…."

On August 6, 1945, the Americans dropped the first atomic bomb used in warfare on **Hiroshima**, a center of the Japanese munitions industry. The blast leveled more than 60 percent of the city. When no immediate response from the Japanese was forthcoming, the Americans dropped another atomic bomb on the port city of **Nagasaki**. The bomb devastated almost 2 square miles (5 sq km). Altogether, nearly 200,000 Japanese lost their lives in three days.

After the bombings, Japan's Emperor Hirohito proclaimed that "the unendurable must be endured," and on August 14, 1945, Japan surrendered. Truman declared August 15 V-J (Victory over Japan) Day. On September 2, Japan officially surrendered. The war was over.

Effects of the War

More than 70 million people fought in World War II. The casualties were staggering. Altogether, some 55 million people perished because of the conflict. The Soviet Union lost 22 million people, Germany almost 8 million, and Japan 2 million. In addition, 6 million Jews died in a Nazi campaign of **genocide**, or the deliberate killing of a racial, political, or cultural group.

The Holocaust

The Nazis had tried to keep the killings and death camps secret from the world. Even European Jews at first had been unaware of the fate in store for them. But once they became aware of Nazi intentions, Jews fought back in Warsaw and other European cities. However, Jewish resistance groups were outnumbered and lacked the arms to fight the Germans. In spite of their heroic efforts, Jewish resisters were easily defeated.

During the war, rumors had reached the Allies about the Nazi treatment of Jews and other groups. However, little action was taken, because many governments disbelieved the rumors and devoted their primary attention to winning the war. The

CONNECTIONS The Arts

Let Us Never Forget

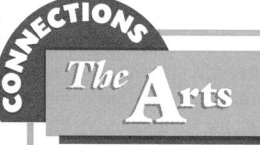

From 1941 to 1945, Jewish artists, musicians, and writers in the Theresienstadt concentration camp created moving artistic expressions of their Holocaust experiences. Since World War II, their works—and those of others—have stirred hearts and consciences of people everywhere about one of the most horrifying events of our century.

Concentration camp survivors

In his memoir called *Night* (1958), the Romanian-born writer Elie Wiesel (vee•ZEHL), a Holocaust survivor, described the horrors he witnessed in the Auschwitz and Buchenwald camps. Another writer, the Australian Thomas Keneally, in his 1982 novel *Schindler's List*, tells a powerful true story about Oskar Schindler, a German manufacturer who saved his Jewish workers from the Holocaust. The American filmmaker Steven Spielberg later turned Keneally's novel into an Oscar Award-winning movie in 1993.

Another 1993 event relating to the Holocaust was the opening of the United States Holocaust Memorial Museum in Washington, D.C. Through exhibits, videos, and special lectures, the museum commemorates the millions of Jews and others murdered by the Nazis during World War II.

MAKING THE CONNECTION

1. How did people in the Theresienstadt concentration camp try to cope with their ordeal?
2. How has the Holocaust been artistically commemorated since World War II?

850 Chapter 31 World War II

CRITICAL THINKING ACTIVITY

Identifying Alternatives Remind students that Churchill and Roosevelt feared that Stalin would impose Communist governments on the countries liberated by the Soviets from German control. Have students research the events in East Germany, Poland, Hungary, Czechoslovakia, Romania, Bulgaria, and Yugoslavia from 1945 to 1950. Encourage them to discuss other ways the fate of Eastern Europe might have been handled at the Yalta Conference. **L3**

Visualizing History **When the Nazis advanced throughout Europe in 1939 and 1940, they rounded up Jews—such as these residents of Warsaw, Poland—and forced them to work as slave laborers. Later, the Nazis killed or imprisoned millions of Jews.** *How did the Allies react to the Nazi persecution and killing of Europe's Jews?*

truth about the Holocaust became clearly known when Allied forces liberated the concentration camps and death camps.

The horrors the Allies uncovered sickened and outraged the world. Many people in the camps had died of starvation and disease; others were the victims of cruel experiments carried out by Nazi doctors. A large number of prisoners had been killed in poison gas chambers.

After the war, the Allies began to address the wrongs committed by the Axis powers. Between November 1945 and September 1946, trials held at Nuremberg, Germany, brought many Nazi leaders to justice for pursuing "aggressive war" and for committing "crimes against humanity." In addition to the millions of casualties, many areas of Europe and Asia lay in ruins.

A Time of Hardship

The use of deadly new weapons made World War II the most destructive war in history. Heavy aerial bombing and shifting battlelines destroyed cities and countryside, leaving as many as 12 million people homeless. Food, medicine, and clothing were in short supply. One Japanese student recalls life after the war:

> "When winter came we were really miserable. We had neither food nor clothing.... We were told to go to the countryside and find food wherever we could. There was nothing in Tokyo."

For millions of people the suffering and hardships lasted long after the war's end.

SECTION 5 REVIEW

Recall

1. **Define** D-Day , partisan, genocide.
2. **Identify** George Patton, Harry S Truman, Clement Attlee.
3. **Explain** why Operation Overlord has been called "unmatched in history."

Critical Thinking

4. **Analyzing Information** Why do you think the Allies made the decision to divide Germany and Berlin into four sectors administered by the United States, the Soviet Union, Great Britain, and France?

Understanding Themes

5. **Innovation** World War II was even more costly in the destruction of human life and property than World War I. What factors made World War II the most destructive war in the history of the world?

SECTION 5 REVIEW ANSWERS

1. The words are defined in the Glossary.
2. George Patton, 847; Harry Truman, 849; Clement Attlee, 849
3. No other military operation was as large or as carefully planned.
4. Answers will vary but might include that the Allies wanted to postpone deciding what permanent political arrangement would be made for Germany.
5. **INNOVATION** Answers will vary but should include that World War I was mainly a trench war fought between armies. In World War II, both the Axis and Allied powers used tanks and air power, especially aerial bombing against civilian as well as military targets.

Visualizing History In October 1940 the Nazis forced all 400,000 of Warsaw's Jews to move into a walled, 1-square-mile (2.6-square-kilometer) area known as the Warsaw Ghetto. Warsaw's Jews resisted the Nazis, but more than 300,000 died in the ghetto or were deported to Nazi labor or death camps. On April 18, 1943, Nazi forces blew up the ghetto's synagogue, killing 14,000 people. The remaining 42,000 Jews were sent to labor camps.

Answer to Caption: *Rumors of Nazi atrocities had reached the Allies, but little action was taken on behalf of the Jews. Many governments did not believe the rumors and devoted their main attention to winning the war.*

Evaluate

Section Quiz 31-5

Use the Testmaker to create a customized quiz for Section 5.

Reteach

Have students compare the end of the European war with the conclusion of the war in the Pacific.

Reteaching Activity 31

Enrich

Have students research the controversy surrounding the commemoration of the dropping of atomic bombs on Hiroshima and Nagasaki on the fiftieth anniversary of those events in 1995.

Enrichment Activity 31

CLOSE

Have students discuss why World War II is seen as a turning point in United States history.

Chapter 31 Review

GLENCOE TECHNOLOGY

VIDEODISC

Use MindJogger to review students' knowledge of the chapter.

MindJogger Videoquiz

Chapter 31
Disc 4 Side B

Also available in VHS.

Answers

Using Key Terms

1. d
2. c
3. e
4. g
5. j
6. l
7. a
8. h
9. b
10. k

Using Your History Journal

Remind students to use examples to show how the event affected other developments in the war.

Reviewing Facts

1. The League of Nations could only make recommendations and impose sanctions.
2. Austria and Czechoslovakia
3. Germany's invasion of Poland
4. The U.S. stood in the way of Japan's expansionist policy. Realizing that war with the U.S. was inevitable, Japan wanted to destroy its Pacific fleet.
5. The Nazis would rule Europe and exploit its resources. They would enslave the conquered peoples, forcing them to work for the German "master race," and would exterminate undesirable peoples.

Critical Thinking

1. They thought that by appeasing Hitler they could maintain peace.
2. German pressure would be relaxed and Stalin's army could push the Germans out.
3. Yes; because the Atlantic Charter called for the destruction of Nazi tyranny.
4. Students should explain their opinions.

Understanding Themes

1. **MOVEMENT** Hitler wanted to control all of Europe, including the Soviet Union, to obtain "living space" for the "master race." Japan wanted to establish a "Greater East Asia Co-Prosperity Sphere."
2. **COOPERATION** The United States gave the British old destroyers, supplied food and weapons through the cash-and-carry policy, and lent war equipment through the lend-lease policy.
3. **CONFLICT** because the Soviet Union was fighting the Nazis alone

CHAPTER 31 REVIEW

Historical Significance

World War II dramatically shifted the world balance of power. Weakened by the conflict, European nations lost their empires and their dominance of world affairs. In their place emerged the United States and the Soviet Union—superpowers and rivals with nuclear arsenals capable of unleashing global mass destruction. Meanwhile, scores of newly independent nations arose from the ashes of the European empires and presented their own distinct outlooks on world affairs. One hopeful development in the crisis-prone postwar world was the work of the United Nations, an international organization dedicated to preserving and protecting world peace.

Using Key Terms

Write the key term that completes each sentence.

a. blitzkrieg
b. sanctions
c. lend-lease
d. appeasement
e. kamikazes
f. partisan
g. D-Day
h. scorched-earth policy
i. genocide
j. Holocaust
k. collective security
l. cash-and-carry policy

1. British Prime Minister Chamberlain pursued _________ with Nazi Germany in hopes of stablilizing Europe.
2. On President Roosevelt's urging, the United States Congress approved _________, which enabled the President to loan war equipment to any country whose protection was important to the United States.
3. Japanese pilots known as ________ crashed their bomb-laden aircraft into Allied ships.
4. On _______, Allied forces landed on the coast of Normandy, France.
5. In the _________, the Nazis murdered almost 6 million Jews during the war.
6. The ________ allowed the United States to supply the British in return for payment without risking American neutrality.
7. _________ was the Germany strategy of quickly striking an enemy with masses of troops and mechanized vehicles.
8. Joseph Stalin tried to thwart the German invasion of his country by a ____________.
9. After the invasion of Ethiopia, the League of Nations voted to impose economic ________ against Italy.
10. During the 1930s, the Western democracies were unable to agree on what steps to take to ensure their ___________.

Using Your History Journal

Select one event from your chart about important events in World War II. Write a paragraph showing how the event affected other developments in the war.

Reviewing Facts

1. **Explain** why the League of Nations was ineffective in stopping Japanese and Italian expansion.
2. **List** the countries that Germany occupied before the outbreak of war.
3. **Identify** the immediate cause of World War II.
4. **Explain** why the Japanese attacked the American base at Pearl Harbor.
5. **Describe** the "New Order" that Hitler set out to create in Europe.

Critical Thinking

1. **Apply** Why did the Western democracies let Hitler overrun much of Europe before trying to stop him?
2. **Analyze** Why did Stalin want the Allies to speed the opening of a second front?
3. **Synthesize** If the Japanese had not bombed Pearl Harbor, would the United States have entered the war? Explain your position.
4. **Evaluate** Was the United States justified in using the atomic bomb to end the war with Japan?

CHAPTER 31 REVIEW

Understanding Themes

1. **Movement** What were Hitler's objectives in Europe? What were Japan's objectives in Asia?
2. **Cooperation** What assistance did the United States provide to Great Britain before American entry into the conflict?
3. **Conflict** Why did Stalin press the Allies to establish a second front in Europe?
4. **Conflict** Why did the Western Allies at Yalta agree to give Stalin the Kuril Islands and the southern part of Sakhalin Island?
5. **Innovation** What effect did new technology have on the war?

Geography in History

1. **Location** Refer to the map below. What were the relative locations of territories held in France by the Allies in September 1944?
2. **Region** What areas touching the Mediterranean Sea were in Allied control by September 1944?
3. **Movement** Beginning in June 1944, the Allied strategy was to pressure Germany on two fronts —East and West. How does the map show that the plan was a successful way to end the war?
4. **Location** Where did Soviet and American forces meet in April 1945?

The Allies Regain Europe

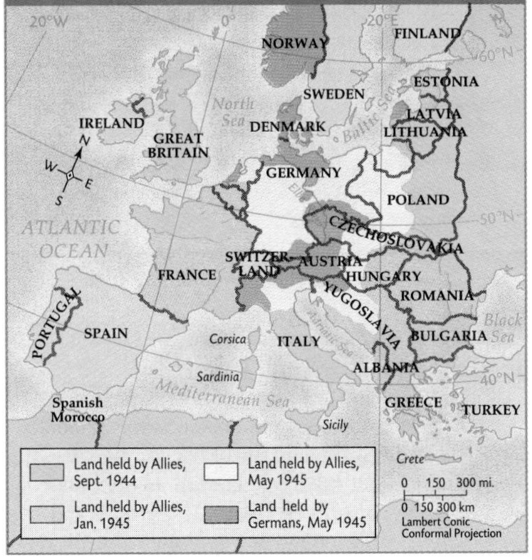

Linking Past and Present

1. To avert war with Germany, the European democracies allowed Hitler to occupy Czechoslovakia. How did the United Nations react to Iraq's occupation of Kuwait in 1990? Do you think the United Nations made the correct decision? Explain.
2. After World War II, several historians and publications bestowed on Churchill the title "Man of the Century." Do you think he still deserves the title? Explain.

Skill Practice

Reread the section of Chapter 31 that describes the bombing on Hiroshima, page 850. Then read the passage on this page written six years later by a survivor. Use the two sources to answer the questions below.

> "I was eating breakfast ... when there was bright light in front of my eyes and an indescribable orange light surged in.... It must have been ten or fifteen minutes later when I recovered consciousness.... but I could see nothing because the place was filled with white smoke.... I tried to stand up and fell again.... What on earth had happened? ...
>
> I looked over my shoulder and saw our house was a flattened wreck, and at the back waves of swirling flames were threatening to sweep down on us at any moment.... I suddenly heard my sister's voice calling, 'Someone help me! ...' She was my own sister but the sight of her was horrifying. Her dark hair which reached her shoulders, that hair was now pure white. At the side of her mouth was a crescent-shaped gash through which her gums were pitifully exposed, and from which bright red blood flowed... When I saw this figure my sister had been transformed into, for a fleeting moment, I just couldn't think that it was her. I was afraid even to go near her."
>
> —Eiko Matsunaga, 11th grade girl, 1951

1. What is the topic of the two sources?
2. What information does the textbook give about this topic?
3. How does the passage add to your understanding of this topic?

Chapter 31 Review

4. **CONFLICT** in exchange for Stalin's promise to enter the war against Japan
5. **INNOVATION** New technology extended the scope of the war and increased its devastation.

Geography in History

1. northwest France and southeast France
2. southeastern France, Corsica, Sardinia, Italy, Sicily, North Africa
3. It shows that the Allies steadily gained territory on both the eastern and western fronts throughout late 1944 and late 1945, thus reducing German control.
4. in Germany

Linking Past and Present

1. The United Nations sent a multinational force to Saudi Arabia to prevent Iraq from invading that country and authorized the use of force to expel Iraq from Kuwait. Answers will vary but should include that Iraq's aggressive behavior might have continued had the international community not responded as it did.
2. Answers will vary but should recognize that without Churchill's firm stand against Germany in the Battle of Britain, Great Britain could have fallen to Nazi Germany.

Skill Practice

1. the dropping of the atomic bomb on Hiroshima
2. The textbook explains why the bomb was dropped and gives facts about the time, place, extent of damage, and political outcome.
3. Matsunaga's account describes the bombing firsthand. It tells what she saw, heard, and felt both physically and emotionally. It makes the personal suffering very real.

Chapter Bonus Test Question

Ask students: How were the gains made by Stalin at Yalta similar to those made by Hitler at the Munich conference? *(Answers should include that both men got what they wanted in exchange for promises they didn't keep: Hitler got the Sudetenland and then took over the rest of Czechoslovakia; Stalin got Poland but instead of holding free elections made Poland a Communist state.)*

Unit 7 Digest

The Unit Digest offers a chapter-by-chapter summary that can be used for any of the following teaching purposes:

- **Preview** one chapter or an entire unit,
- **Review** some or all of the chapters,
- **Condense** when specific chapters or units have not been taught, or
- **Reteach** chapters that students have studied in the unit.

PREVIEW

Use the Unit 7 Digest Transparencies to preview the highlights of the unit.

ABC NEWS INTERACTIVE™

VIDEODISC
Turning Points in World History

Side Two
Chapter 4

Title: *Assassination Ignites World War I*
Ask: Why did the assassination of the archduke plunge Europe into war? *(A web of European alliances caused most major nations to declare war.)*

Unit 7 Digest

Two destructive wars engulfed the world in the first half of the 1900s. World War I brought about the collapse of many European royal dynasties, triggered a Communist revolution in Russia, and left many countries in political and economic chaos. This turmoil, the bitterness created by the peace treaties that ended the war, and the worldwide economic depression that started in 1929 led to the rise of dictatorships in Germany, Italy, and Japan.

During the 1930s, the world once again was set on a course toward war. When it arrived, World War II proved to be the most destructive in history. At its end, European dominance of world affairs had ended, with many new nations arising from the ashes of the overseas European empires. Above all, two superpowers—the United States and the Soviet Union—were extending their power and struggling for global influence.

Chapter 28 World War I

In the late 1800s, nationalism and imperialism created intense rivalries among European powers. To secure protection, the nations of Europe formed two rival alliances. France, Great Britain, and Russia formed the Triple Entente in the early 1900s to offset the Triple Alliance concluded in the late 1870s and early 1880s by Germany, Italy, and Austria-Hungary.

The Conflict

The conflict between the two armed camps began on June 28, 1914, when a member of a Serb nationalist group assassinated Archduke Francis Ferdinand, the heir to the Austro-Hungarian throne. Austria-Hungary thereupon declared war on Serbia, and bound by their alliances, the other European powers entered the conflict.

For four years war raged on land, at sea, and in the air. The belligerents used sophisticated new weapons, such as machine guns, tanks, airplanes, and poison gas. In the west the war quickly settled into a stalemate along two parallel lines of trenches stretching from Switzerland to the North Sea.

To try to win control of the seas and cut off Germany's supply lines, Great Britain blockaded all German ports. The Germans struck back, however, with U-boats, or submarines. After German U-boats sank four American merchant ships in 1917, President Woodrow Wilson asked Congress for a declaration of war. It was America's intervention that proved to be the turning point of the war, as the United States gave the Allies much-needed human and material resources. In November 1918, Germany finally surrendered.

The war changed the map of Europe. The Ottoman and the Austro-Hungarian empires ceased to exist, and new European nations rose from the breakup. The peace settlements signed at Versailles, moreover, made Germany responsible for the war and imposed a heavy financial penalty on its people.

The Russian Revolution

In Russia, the war brought about the fall of the czarist autocracy. The Russian people had endured great hardships in the war, and public anger against the government mounted. In early 1917 spontaneous demonstrations forced Czar Nicholas II to abdicate. Later that year the Bolsheviks, a Marxist political party led by Vladimir Ilyich Lenin, overthrew the provisional government that had replaced the czar. The Bolsheviks were eventually victorious in the civil war that followed, and Russia became a Communist state.

SURVEYING CHAPTER 28

1. **Relating Ideas** What general factors led to the outbreak of World War I?
2. **Identifying Trends** What new inventions made World War I a more destructive conflict than previous wars?

Chapter 29 Between Two Fires

World War I was an important turning point in the 1900s. It carried away the old political order, shattered traditions, and ushered in an era of experimentation in culture. The war also changed the way many people looked at the world, destroyed

CLASSROOM RESOURCES FOR UNIT 7 DIGEST

Preview
- Unit 7 Digest Transparencies

Review
- Time Line Activities 28, 29, 30, 31
- Student Self-Test and Review Software, Chapters 28, 29, 30, 31
- MindJogger Videoquiz, Chapters 28, 29, 30, 31

Condense
- Chapter Digests Audiocassettes, Chapters 28, 29, 30, 31

Reteach
- Reteaching Activities 28, 29, 30, 31
- Chapter Digests Audiocassettes, Chapters 28, 29, 30, 31
- Turning Points in World History

854 Unit 7 *World in Conflict*

Visualizing History **Lenin guided the affairs of the Soviet state through civil war and economic collapse until his death in January 1924.** *What changes did Lenin's successor, Joseph Stalin, bring to the Soviet Union?*

their faith in progress and creating feelings of disillusionment instead. In the postwar era, artists experimented with new styles and subject matter. Innovative forms of technology, such as the automobile and the radio, changed people's lives and brought the world closer together.

The Western Democracies

The United States came out of the war in far better shape than its allies. The 1920s were boom years for the American economy, and an atmosphere of exuberance and frivolity earned the decade the name "Roaring Twenties." But when the stock market crashed in 1929, the nation fell into a major economic depression that had worldwide repercussions.

Although the war and the depression had a terrible effect on Great Britain and France, democratic traditions in these nations were firmly entrenched. Their governments were able to survive assaults from the political extremists on the left and right. Great Britain, however, lost its privileged position in world trade and was no longer a leading economic power. France, too, faced severe economic problems after the war, and Communist, Fascist, and Socialist parties vied for power. In 1934, however, the Communists joined forces with the Socialists to thwart a Fascist takeover. While in power, the Popular Front, as it was called, instituted many social reforms.

The Rise of Dictators

World War I shattered the economies of Germany and Italy, but these countries did not have strong democratic traditions. Amid political and economic chaos in Italy, Benito Mussolini seized power and in 1922 established a Fascist dictatorship. In Germany Adolf Hitler and the Nazi party gained an audience by blaming the Communists and Jews for Germany's economic woes. In 1933 Hitler became German chancellor and moved quickly to crush his opponents and establish a dictatorship.

Dramatic changes were also occurring in the Soviet Union. Seven years of world and civil war had devastated the country. After seizing power, Lenin tried to quickly impose a new socialist order but faced widespread opposition. In 1921 he finally consolidated Communist power under the New Economic Policy (NEP) that allowed limited capitalism. After Lenin's death in 1924, Joseph Stalin won a political struggle with his rival, Leon Trotsky, and established a brutal dictatorship.

Beginning in the late 1920s, Stalin set about putting all Soviet industries and agriculture under state control. In a succession of purges in the 1930s, Stalin also eliminated suspected opponents from positions of leadership. Many ordinary Soviet citizens also suffered imprisonment, exile, and death during this grim period.

SURVEYING CHAPTER 29

1. **Analyzing Ideas** Why is World War I considered an important turning point in the 1900s?
2. **Identifying Trends** What common problems did many nations face in the 1920s and 1930s? Why did democracy survive in Great Britain and France, while it collapsed in Italy and Germany?

Chapter 30
Nationalism in Asia, Africa, and Latin America

In spite of the turmoil created by World War I, the European powers retained control of their colonial territories in the Middle East and Africa. But in the years following World War I, nationalist forces in these Middle Eastern and African territories began the long struggle for independence.

Unit 7 Digest

Visualizing History During World War I, the German government allowed Lenin to travel across Germany to reach Russia, hoping he would further disrupt the Russian war effort. Lenin's fame as a rousing orator was so great, however, that the Germans sealed Lenin's train so he could not speak to crowds.
Answer to Caption: *Stalin put industry and agriculture under state control, eliminated political opposition, and set up a brutal dictatorship.*

REVIEW

GLENCOE TECHNOLOGY

VIDEODISC
Use MindJogger to review any chapter in Unit 7.

MindJogger Videoquiz

Chapter 28 Disc 4 Side A

Chapter 29 Disc 4 Side B

Chapter 30 Disc 4 Side B

Chapter 31 Disc 4 Side B

Also available in VHS.

ANSWERS TO SURVEYING THE CHAPTER

CHAPTER 28 ANSWERS

1. Nationalism and imperialism led to rivalries among European powers, which in turn led to the formation of competing alliances.
2. machine guns, tanks, airplanes, and poison gas

CHAPTER 29 ANSWERS

1. The war destroyed several empires and marked the beginning of a new social, political, and cultural era.
2. The war and Great Depression strained all nations; Italy and Germany did not have the strong democratic traditions of Britain and France.

Use the Student Self-Test and Review Software to review any chapters that students have studied in Unit 7.

Unit 7 Digest

Visualizing History Diego Rivera's artwork depicted real people in real-life struggles. He believed that his art belonged to the people and, therefore, the best place for it was on the walls of public buildings.
Answer to Caption: *Mexico nationalized American and other foreign-owned oil industries.*

Cause and Effect Ask students to give examples of some of the indirect results of World War I and its aftermath that destabilized both Europe and the rest of the world. *(the Russian Revolution; the rise of dictators in Italy and Germany; the growth of nationalist movements in Asia, Africa, and Latin America)* Then discuss how World War I contributed to these developments and decide which were the most important in causing World War II. **L1**

Geography: Location Ask students to write a short essay explaining how Germany's geographical position in Europe caused strategic problems during both world wars. Read and discuss the essays as a class. **L2**

Biography Have students choose the leader of a nationalist movement in Asia, Africa, or Latin America from the interwar period and research that leader's life. Then ask them to prepare oral reports in which they describe the leader and the goals of the national movement and evaluate the success of the movement this person led. **L3**

Visualizing History **During the 1930s, Mexico's government broke up many estates and gave the land to peasant groups.** *What action taken by the Mexican government at this time affected ties to the United States?*

The Middle East, Africa, and India

The old Ottoman Empire of Turkey, weakened by discord and external threats, crumbled during the war. After General Mustafa Kemal repulsed a Greek invasion in 1922, the Turks deposed the Ottoman sultan and formed the Republic of Turkey with Kemal as president. Persians, too, asserted their independence and gave Persia a new name—Iran.

Although Great Britain granted Egypt complete independence in 1936, it controlled neighboring Palestine and continued to rule African colonies, such as Kenya and Nigeria. Despite India's contributions to the British war effort, Great Britain refused to grant independence and moved to stifle a growing nationalist movement. As a result, Mohandas K. Gandhi and other nationalists organized nonviolent protests against British rule, including strikes and a refusal to buy British goods.

East Asia

In China the nationalist Guomindang army led by Chiang Kai-shek overthrew the local military leaders who had ruled the country since 1916. After acquiring power, Chiang turned on Chinese Communist allies, many of whom fled to the mountainous interior of China. When the Japanese invaded China in the 1930s, however, Chiang again joined with the Communists in an effort to repulse the invaders.

In Japan military leaders became a powerful force in the 1920s and 1930s. Believing that Japan could solve the problems of an expanding population and limited resources by acquiring new territories, these leaders launched a program of territorial expansion without their government's approval. By the late 1930s, Japan's government was controlled by the increasingly powerful military, and the Asian country was on a collision course with the Western powers.

Latin America

Although most Latin American countries had achieved political independence long before the 1920s, they remained economically dependent on the United States. They also faced United States military intervention whenever American economic interests were threatened by internal political discord. In the early 1930s President Franklin D. Roosevelt proclaimed the Good Neighbor policy and withdrew American troops from Nicaragua and Haiti, where they were protecting American business interests. This policy eased Latin America's fears of the United States, but tensions increased again in 1938 when Mexico took over foreign-owned oil industries.

SURVEYING CHAPTER 30

1. **Identifying Trends** What kind of protest did Mohandas K. Gandhi direct against British rule in India?
2. **Relating Ideas** How did nationalism in Latin America differ from nationalism in other parts of the world?

Chapter 31
World War II

The expansionist policies of the Fascist dictatorships that came to power in the 1920s and 1930s increasingly threatened world peace. The League of Nations, which had been formed after World War I to preserve peace, proved powerless to stop the drift toward war.

Failure of Appeasement

Adolf Hitler aimed to bring much of Europe under Nazi control. When the German leader threatened to invade Czechoslovakia in 1938, British Prime Minister Neville Chamberlain

ANSWERS TO SURVEYING THE CHAPTER

CHAPTER 30 ANSWERS

1. Gandhi organized nonviolent protests, including strikes and a refusal to buy British goods.
2. Most of Latin America was already independent; nationalists protested economic dependence and frequent U.S. military interventions in the region.

negotiated the Munich Agreement that gave Hitler the part of Czechoslovakia that he demanded. This policy of appeasement, or compromise with the dictatorships, only whetted Hitler's appetite. Six months later, he seized all of Czechoslovakia. Convinced that the West would do nothing to stop him, Hitler secured the help of the Soviet Union in attacking Poland in September, 1939. The Nazi assault on Poland led Britain and France to declare war on Germany.

Waging War

After taking control of Norway and Denmark in the spring of 1940, German troops invaded the Netherlands, raced through Belgium and northern France, and pushed the British and French forces to the English Channel. France surrendered in June, leaving the British to fight Hitler alone.

In the summer and fall of 1940, Great Britain won a crucial victory over Germany in the air conflict known as the Battle of Britain. In spite of widespread American sympathy for Great Britain, isolationists in the United States kept the nation out of the war. The American government was, however, supplying the British with equipment to fight the war. By 1941 Nazi Germany ruled large areas of Europe, and in June of that year, Germany invaded the Soviet Union.

To prevent the United States from interfering with its expansionist aims in East Asia and the Pacific, Japan engaged in an attack on the United States fleet at Pearl Harbor. This attack on Pearl Harbor brought the United States into the war. The United States joined with the Allies—Great Britain, the Soviet Union, the Free French, and other anti-Fascist governments and nations.

Allied Victory

Not until 1942 did the tide begin to turn in favor of the Allies. Americans defeated Japanese naval forces at the Battle of Midway. In 1943, Soviet forces repulsed a German offensive at Stalingrad, and British and American forces pushed the Germans out of North Africa. From there, the Allies launched an invasion of Sicily and the Italian Peninsula.

On June 6, 1944, Western Allied forces invaded Normandy in France and pushed toward Germany as Soviet troops advanced from the east. In April 1945 Western and Soviet Allies met at the Elbe River, and the following month Germany surrendered. When Japanese leaders refused to surrender, the United States dropped its new secret weapon, the atomic bomb, on Hiroshima and Nagasaki in August. Days later Japan surrendered.

World War II was over, but much of Europe and Asia lay in ruins, and tens of millions of people had died. The Allies divided Germany and its capital of Berlin into four sections, each of which was occupied by one of the powers. Tensions between the Soviet Union and the Western Allies increased, however, and the fragile wartime alliance began to unravel.

SURVEYING CHAPTER 31

1. **Making Comparisons** How were the causes of World Wars I and II different? How were they similar?
2. **Relating Ideas** What were the major turning points of World War II?

Visualizing History **After Pearl Harbor, San Francisco prepared for possible Japanese air attacks by sandbagging buildings.** *Why was the Japanese attack on Pearl Harbor a significant event?*

ANSWERS TO SURVEYING THE CHAPTER

CHAPTER 31 ANSWERS

1. The causes of World War I included nationalist tensions, imperialist rivalries, militarism, and the alliance system. Militarism and the territorial ambitions of European dictators caused World War II.
2. By 1940 Germany had won control of Europe but failed to conquer Britain; in 1941 Japan bombed Pearl Harbor, and the United States entered the war; in 1943 the Soviet Union repulsed the German attack on Stalingrad; in 1944 the Allies invaded and liberated France; in 1945 the United States used atomic bombs against Japan.

Unit 7 Digest

CONDENSE

Use Chapter Digests Audiocassettes to introduce chapters that students have not studied in Unit 7. Spanish Chapter Digests Audiocassettes are also available.

Discuss Have students read the **Unit Digest** and discuss the **Surveying Chapter** questions. **L1**

RETEACH

Review Chart Organize the class into two groups. Have one group prepare a review chart featuring the causes, main events, and consequences of World War I, and the other group do the same for World War II. **L1**

Reteaching Activities 28, 29, 30, 31

Chapter Digests Audiocassettes, Chapters 28, 29, 30, 31

Visualizing History Fear of Japanese attack prompted one of the most shameful episodes of World War II—the internment of Japanese Americans in concentration camps. In the 1990s the U.S. government began to pay a settlement to survivors of the internment.
Answer to Caption: *The attack brought the United States into World War II on the side of the Allies.*

Introducing Unit 8

0:00 Out of Time?

If time does not permit teaching each chapter in Unit 8, you may use the Unit Digest beginning on page 1026, in conjunction with the Unit Digest Transparencies and Chapter Digest Audiocassettes with accompanying activities and tests.

Introducing the Unit

Unit 8 focuses on the political trends of the post-World War II era, including the origins and effects of the cold war; decolonization in Asia, Africa, and the Middle East; and the decline of communism and the end of the cold war since 1989.

Unit Objectives

After reading Unit 8, students will be able to:

1. summarize the causes and impact of the cold war.
2. describe conflicts in Asia and the region's emergence as an economic powerhouse.
3. analyze the legacy of colonial rule in Africa and the challenges facing that continent.
4. examine the rival nationalisms of the Middle East and the region's search for peace.
5. identify political and economic trends in Latin America.
6. analyze factors that are leading toward globalization.

Portfolio Project

Have students work together in groups on related topics such as debt, poverty, and urbanization in developing countries. This activity may be an appropriate method of authentic assessment.

Unit **8** 1945–Present

The Contemporary World

Chapter 32 The Cold War

Chapter 33 Asia and the Pacific

Chapter 34 Africa

Chapter 35 The Middle East

Chapter 36 Latin America

Chapter 37 The World in Transition

Then & Now *International tension continued after World War II. Two blocs of nations aligned themselves behind the United States and the Soviet Union to dominate world politics. The two sides fought a cold war using economic powers, diplomacy, espionage, and the threat of nuclear war. When the cold war ended, leaders struggled to address the long-standing problems of nationalism, poverty in the developing nations, distribution of resources, and environmental damage.*

The pace of scientific and technological change quickened. Satellite communications and computers linked in a global network offered undreamed of challenges and opportunities. When you turn on your computer, remember that it has been just a few years since this technology was invented. No one can guess the nature or degree of change it will bring to your future.

A Global Chronology

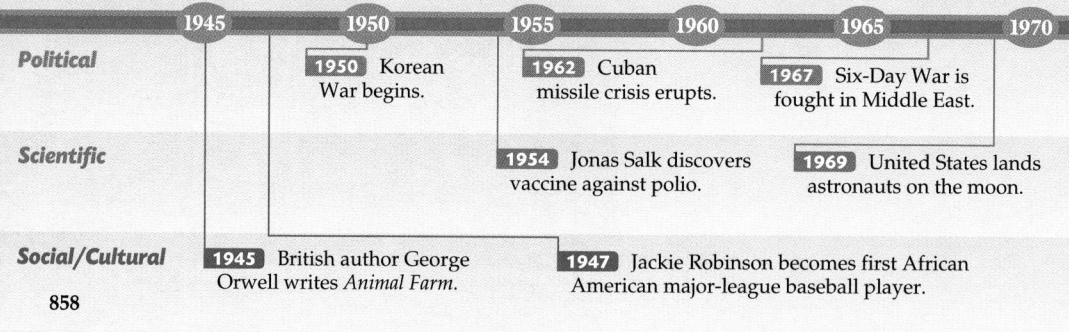

1945 — 1950 — 1955 — 1960 — 1965 — 1970

Political
- **1950** Korean War begins.
- **1962** Cuban missile crisis erupts.
- **1967** Six-Day War is fought in Middle East.

Scientific
- **1954** Jonas Salk discovers vaccine against polio.
- **1969** United States lands astronauts on the moon.

Social/Cultural
- **1945** British author George Orwell writes *Animal Farm.*
- **1947** Jackie Robinson becomes first African American major-league baseball player.

858

Then & Now **Declaring Independence** In this unit, students will learn about the problems faced by the newly independent nations of Africa, the Middle East, and Asia, as well as efforts by Latin American countries to end their economic dependency on the industrialized nations.

Point out to students that the nations that have emerged from colonial rule since World War II won their independence nearly 200 years after the United States became the first colony in modern history to become a sovereign nation. What are the main problems that newly independent nations face in the modern world? *(Answers will vary. Students may say that setting up a representative*

Computer pentium chip

Portfolio Project

Choose an ongoing worldwide problem or situation such as ethnic wars or rivalries, the conflict between Arabs and Israelis, economic difficulties in former Soviet states, population growth in overcrowded cities, oil or other resource shortages, debt in developing nations, the spread of arms, hunger and homelessness, or terrorism. Collect and study news articles about this subject. Write a one-page essay offering suggestions for dealing with the issue.

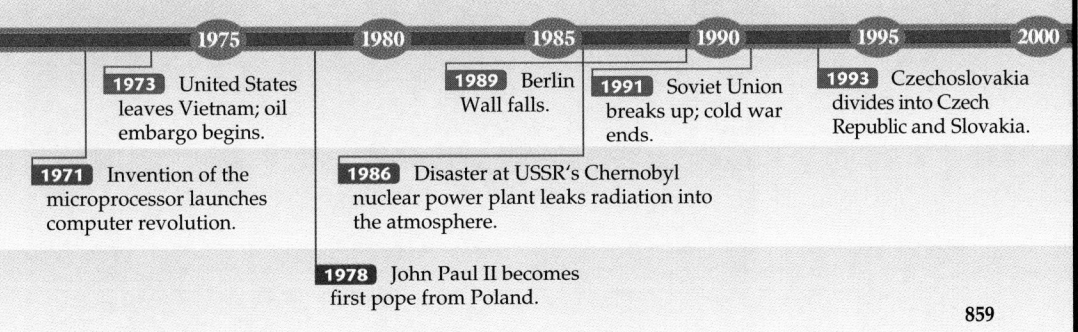

1975 1980 1985 1990 1995 2000

1971 Invention of the microprocessor launches computer revolution.

1973 United States leaves Vietnam; oil embargo begins.

1978 John Paul II becomes first pope from Poland.

1986 Disaster at USSR's Chernobyl nuclear power plant leaks radiation into the atmosphere.

1989 Berlin Wall falls.

1991 Soviet Union breaks up; cold war ends.

1993 Czechoslovakia divides into Czech Republic and Slovakia.

Introducing Unit 8

History *and the* Humanities

Focus on World Art Print
- 24, Bridget Riley. *Current*

World History and Art Transparencies
- 43 *The Persistence of Memory*
- 44 *Sydney Opera House*
- 45 *The Liberated African Woman*
- 46 *Bedouin Woman's Headpiece*
- 47 *Iranian Mihrab*
- 48 *The Twelve Tribes of Israel*
- 49 *Figura*
- 50 *Diego and I*
- 51 *Vietnam Memorial*
- 52 *Sky Above Clouds II*

World Music: Cultural Traditions, Lessons 1, 2, 3, 4, 5, 6, 8

ABCNEWS INTERACTIVE™

VIDEODISC
Turning Points in World History

Side Two
Chapter 8

Title: *The Moon Landing*
Ask: Competition between what two countries led to the space race? *(the United States and Soviet Union)*

government and creating a vigorous, independent economy are main challenges.) How do the challenges facing new nations today differ from those faced by the United States after 1776? *(Answers will vary. Students may say that the economy was simpler in the 1700s; the United States did not have to worry about the technology gap. On the other hand, as the world's first democracy the United States had to pioneer an untested system of government.)* How did the cold war affect the transition of many colonies to independence? *(Answers will vary. Some students may realize that in Vietnam, Algeria, and elsewhere independence movements backed by the Soviet Union were opposed by the United States and its allies, leading to bloody wars.)*

Visualizing History Since World War II, computers have revolutionized the world economy. A single pentium chip holds more computing capacity than did the earliest mainframe computers.

The Spread of Ideas

TEACH

Introduction

This feature focuses on the political consequences of the development of modern international communications through satellite broadcasting and the Internet.

Background Notes

Linking Past and Present

The early days of the space race that was triggered by the Soviet launching of *Sputnik I* were the subject of Tom Wolfe's recent novel *The Right Stuff* and the popular film by the same title. Students interested in learning more about the period may want to read the book or watch a video of the movie.

Geography

Movement The United States is the leading source of television programs and films for the world market. Many countries have taken steps to limit the consumption of American cultural products in order to support their own film and television industries. Attempts by European nations to limit imports from the United States have led to conflicts under GATT (General Agreement on Tariffs and Trade), which seeks to open markets and reduce trade restrictions.

The Spread of Ideas

Communications

The invention of writing reshaped history. So did Johannes Gutenberg's use of movable type. Today, however, electronics technology is moving communications forward at a startling rate. Two of the biggest changes have been the linking of people around the world via satellite broadcasts and the creation of a vast computer network known as the "information highway."

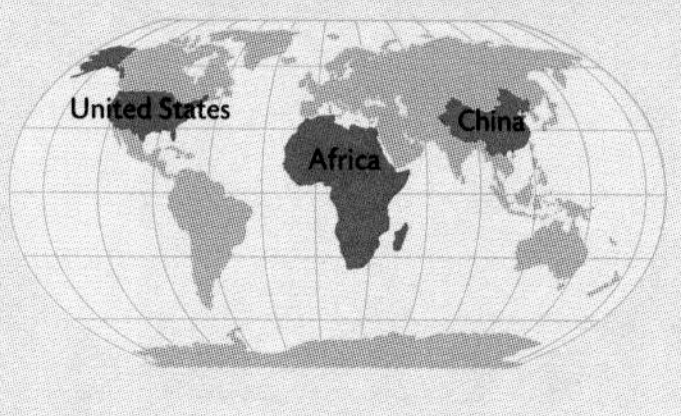

The United States

Satellite Communications

In October 1957, a special announcement interrupted radio broadcasts across the United States. "Listen now … for the sound which forever separates the old from the new," said the broadcaster. Then a voice from outer space—and eerie beep … beep … beep.

The former Soviet Union had taken the lead in space exploration by launching a tiny communications satellite named *Sputnik I*. A crudely simple device by today's standards, the first satellite could do little more than beam back radio signals. In the cold war era, however, it sent shock waves through American society.

Three years later, the United States launched *Echo* and *Courier*. Instead of beeps, these satellites relayed telephone calls between Europe and the United States. In 1962, the United States launched *Telstar*—the first satellite to relay live television programs from one place to another. By the 1980s people around the world with satellite dish antennas could tune in to hundreds of television programs. The effect was revolutionary. Repressive governments in Eastern Europe and elsewhere could not legislate against free speech beamed down from the skies.

Telstar

Scientist and Soviet Sputnik I

COOPERATIVE LEARNING ACTIVITY

Multimedia Presentation Organize students into small groups and have each group select one medium of communication, such as films, television, radio, newspapers, CD-ROM, or the Internet. Then ask each group to choose a current international news story and create a news feature on that topic for the medium they have chosen. Have each group present its report, explaining the features of the presentation that were specially adapted to the medium they chose, and estimating the size and nature of the audience they hoped to reach. **L3**

China

Satellite Dishes

In the 1990s, satellite dishes sprouted like mushrooms across the People's Republic of China. Star TV, a pan-Asian satellite service, boomed down Mandarin-speaking rappers out of Hong Kong, English broadcasts of CNN News, NFL football games, and movies from Japan. The uncensored broadcasts enraged government officials. However, a 1993 ban against satellite dishes proved nearly impossible to enforce. Even while officials tried to dismantle the thousands of large dishes, kits for smaller dishes were being smuggled into the country.

The example of China was repeated in other repressive nations. Iran, Myanmar (Burma), and other countries tried and failed to ban satellite reception. Even free governments, such as India, expressed concern about the "cultural invasion," but satellite television, a part of the information age, was here to stay.

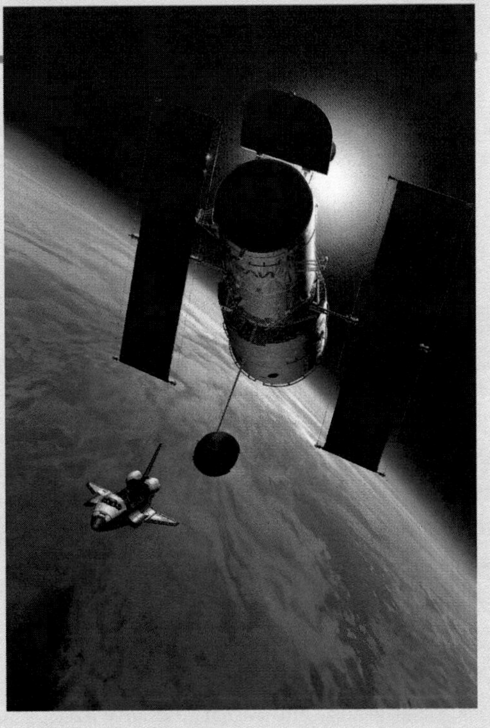

Communications satellite

Africa

The Internet

A telephone line and a personal computer—that is all someone needs to jump on the information highway. Internet Web sites exist globally, putting individuals in touch with databases and other computer users on every continent.

In Africa, the least electronic continent, UNESCO is helping the Pan-African News Agency to link up with the Internet. The project will help Africans overcome one of the legacies of imperialism—a communications system that linked African nations with European capitals rather than with each other. The driving force behind the project, a Senegalese journalist named Babacar Fall, sees the Internet as one of the keys to unlocking Africa's economic potential. "Without information," explained Fall, "there can be no development."

High school students on the Internet

LINKING THE IDEAS

1. How did the revolution in satellite communications get its start?
2. How has this revolution affected nondemocratic political systems?

Critical Thinking

3. **Drawing Conclusions** How has the revolution in communications made our world more interdependent?

The Spread of Ideas

Who?What?Where?When?

Sputnik I The launching of *Sputnik I* in 1957 created near-panic in the United States. One senator called the Soviet breakthrough "a devastating blow to the prestige of the United States as the leader in the scientific and technical world," while *The New Republic* said it proved "that the Soviet Union gained a commanding lead in certain vital sectors of the race for world scientific and technological supremacy."

Cultural Diffusion

Hollywood Abroad The internationalization of the film industry has changed the content of Hollywood films. Many American films now earn as much or more money in foreign distribution as they do inside the United States. Since these films are either dubbed or subtitled, those based on action and adventure rather than dialogue tend to be more successful. This phenomenon in part explains the trend toward producing Hollywood blockbuster action thrillers.

ANSWERS TO LINKING THE IDEAS

1. The Soviet Union launched *Sputnik I* in 1957.
2. They have been unable to stop the flow of information from democratic nations that comes via satellites and the Internet.
3. Sharing of information has been greatly enhanced by satellite technology and the Internet, bringing all parts of the world into closer communication. Development and growth are frequently dependent on this shared information.

Teach, Reinforce, and Extend CHAPTER Content

The Cold War

CHAPTER RESOURCES

	Reproducible Resources	Multimedia Resources
Chapter Opener	Chapter Themes: Graphic Organizer 32 Historical Significance Chapter Activity 32	MindJogger Videoquiz
Chapter Enrichment	Vocabulary Activity 32* Time Line Activity 32 Mapping History Activity 32 History Simulation 32 Geography and History Activity 32 Source Reading 32 People in World History Profiles 61, 62 World Art and Music Activity 32 Enrichment Activity 32 Critical Thinking Activity 32 Skill Reinforcement Activity 32 Building Skills in Geography Workbook, Unit 1, Lesson 10 Performance Assessment Activity 32	Focus on World Art Print 24, Bridget Riley. *Current* World History and Art Transparency 43, *The Persistence of Memory* Mapping History Overlay Transparency 22, *The United Nations*; 23, *The Commonwealth of Nations* Chapter Transparency 32 Vocabulary PuzzleMaker Software World Music: Cultural Traditions, Lessons 3, 4 Turning Points in World History Lessons of War Communism and the Cold War
Chapter Review/Reteaching	Reteaching Activity 32 Skill Reinforcement Activity 32 Spanish Chapter Summary 32	Chapter 32 Digest Audiocassette, Activity, Test* Vocabulary PuzzleMaker Software Student Self-Test and Review Software MindJogger Videoquiz
Chapter Evaluation/Testing	Performance Assessment Activity 32 Chapter 32 Test, Forms A and B	Testmaker

* *Also available in Spanish*

0:00 OUT OF TIME? Assign the Chapter 32 summary in the Unit 8 Digest on pages 1026-1029, and the Chapter 32 Audiocassettes.

Block Schedule

Block scheduling differs from traditional class scheduling in the amount of time allotted to each period. The extended time frame provided by block scheduling affords you the opportunity to implement a greater number of research-oriented and activity-intense projects to motivate and involve your students. Activities that are particularly suited to use within the block scheduling framework are identified throughout this chapter by the following designation.

KEY TO ABILITY LEVELS

Teaching strategies have been coded for varying learning styles and abilities.

- **L1** **BASIC** activities for all students
- **L2** **AVERAGE** activities for average to above-average students
- **L3** **CHALLENGING** activities for above-average students
- **LEP** **LIMITED ENGLISH PROFICIENCY** activities

A complete, 1-page lesson plan is provided for each section in the *Reproducible Lesson Plans* booklet.

SECTION RESOURCES

Daily Objectives	Reproducible Resources	Multimedia Resources
Section 1 The East-West Split Identify the events that caused and heightened the cold war.	Reproducible Lesson Plan 32-1 Guided Reading Activity 32-1* Time Line Activity 32 Geography and History Activity 32 Section Quiz 32-1*	Section Focus Transparency 32-1 Chapter Transparency 32 World History and Art Transparency 43, *The Persistence of Memory* Mapping History Overlay Transparency 22, *The United Nations* Vocabulary PuzzleMaker Software Student Self-Test and Review Software Testmaker World Music: Cultural Traditions, Lesson 4 Communism and the Cold War
Section 2 The Communist Bloc Explain how the Soviet Union carried out Communist policies after the death of Stalin.	Reproducible Lesson Plan 32-2 Vocabulary Activity 32* Guided Reading Activity 32-2* Section Quiz 32-2*	Section Focus Transparency 32-2 Student Self-Test and Review Software Testmaker Communism and the Cold War
Section 3 Western Europe Describe how Western Europe moved toward greater political and economic unity during the cold war.	Reproducible Lesson Plan 32-3 Vocabulary Activity 32* Guided Reading Activity 32-3* History Simulation 32 Section Quiz 32-3*	Focus on World Art Print 24 Section Focus Transparency 32-3 Mapping History Overlay Transparency 23, *The Commonwealth of Nations* Student Self-Test and Review Software Testmaker
Section 4 The United States and Canada Trace the political and social changes that the people of the United States and Canada experienced during the cold war years.	Reproducible Lesson Plan 32-4 Guided Reading Activity 32-4* Reteaching Activity 32 Enrichment Activity 32 Section Quiz 32-4* Performance Assessment Activity 32 Spanish Chapter Summary 32	Section Focus Transparency 32-4 Vocabulary PuzzleMaker Software Student Self-Test and Review Software Testmaker Communism and the Cold War Turning Points in World History Lessons of War

* *Also available in Spanish*

Chapter Activities

Performance Assessment Activity

Another Berlin Wall Assign students to groups of four to create an expressive version of the Berlin Wall. Give each group a piece of poster board to use for their wall. On one side of the wall, have students use visuals, words, and graffiti to represent sentiments and beliefs held by the Soviet Union. On the other side, have students represent beliefs held by the West. Important events of the era should also be included. Have the students write an individual reflection listing and explaining each item included on their wall.

Possible Rubric Features

Accuracy of content information, concept attainment, originality and creativity of product, collaborative skills, thoroughness of explanation

- *For an additional activity, refer to Activity 32 in the* Performance Assessment Strategies and Activities *booklet.*

ACTIVITY

From the Classroom of...

Robert W. Gardner
New Canaan High School
New Canaan, CT

Preventing the Cold War

On the chalkboard, list the leaders of the United States and the Soviet Union who played key roles during the cold war era: Harry Truman, Joseph Stalin, Nikita Khrushchev, Leonid Brezhnev, Dwight Eisenhower, John Kennedy, Lyndon Johnson, and Richard Nixon.

Have partners pick an issue, event, or crisis faced by these leaders during the cold war. One student analyzes the problem from the point of view of the American president at the time, the other from the perspective of the Soviet leader. Have students attempt to negotiate a solution to the problem and describe it in a paragraph.

Have pairs present the problem, the world leaders they represent, and the solution they agreed on. Then have the class discuss whether the cold war could have been avoided, or at least ameliorated.

MULTIPLE LEARNING STYLES

Verbal/Linguistic

Have students obtain and read short selections from a collection of *samizdat*—underground literature circulated by Soviet dissidents.

Logical/Mathematical

Have students debate the following proposition: The United States and the Soviet Union were equally to blame for the cold war.

Visual/Spatial

Have students create a poster, based on conditions in the early days of the cold war, warning Americans against the "Communist menace."

Auditory/Musical

Have students listen to a tape or CD of music from the early era of rock and roll, featuring such performers as Chuck Berry and Elvis Presley. Discussion might focus on why this music aroused so much opposition from mainstream America at the time.

Additional Resources

TEACHER'S CORNER

NATIONAL GEOGRAPHIC SOCIETY

INDEX TO NATIONAL GEOGRAPHIC MAGAZINE

The following articles may be used for research relating to this chapter:

- "Are the Soviets Ahead in Space?" by Thomas Y. Canby, October 1986.
- "Bikini: A Way of Life Lost," by William S. Ellis, June 1986.
- "Two Berlins: A Generation Apart," by Priit J. Vesilind, January 1982.

NATIONAL GEOGRAPHIC SOCIETY PRODUCTS AVAILABLE FROM GLENCOE

To order the following products for use with this chapter, contact your local Glencoe sales representative or call Glencoe at 1-800-368-7344:

VIDEODISCS
- GTV: The American People
- GTV: A Geographic Perspective on American History

ADDITIONAL NATIONAL GEOGRAPHIC SOCIETY PRODUCTS

To order the following products for use with this chapter, call National Geographic Society at 1-800-368-2728:

- *1945–1989: The Cold War* (Video)
- *Capitalism, Socialism, Communism Series,* "Communism." (Video)
- *Nations of the World Series*, "East Germany." (Video)
- *The Changing Faces of Communism Series*, "Poland." (Video)
- *Europe: The Road to Unity* (Video)
- *Decades of History: The 20th Century—The Middle Years*, "The 1950s: Prosperity and Cold War." (Filmstrip)

Bibliography

Literature of the Period

Ellison, Ralph. ***The Invisible Man.*** New York: Random House, 1952. An idealistic young black man meets disappointment in Harlem.

Grass, Günter. ***The Tin Drum.*** New York: Pantheon, 1962. Picaresque novel about the German wartime and postwar experience of a veteran and former prisoner of war.

Solzhenitsyn, Alexander. ***One Day in the Life of Ivan Denisovich.*** New York: Dutton, 1963. The story of an inmate in one of Stalin's forced-labor camps.

Readings for the Student

le Carré, John. ***The Spy Who Came in from the Cold.*** New York: Coward-McCann, 1964. Classic espionage fiction set in postwar Europe.

Readings for the Teacher

Patterson, Thomas G. ***On Every Front: The Making and Unmaking of the Cold War.*** New York: Norton, 1992. Objective explanation of the motives and tactics of both sides.

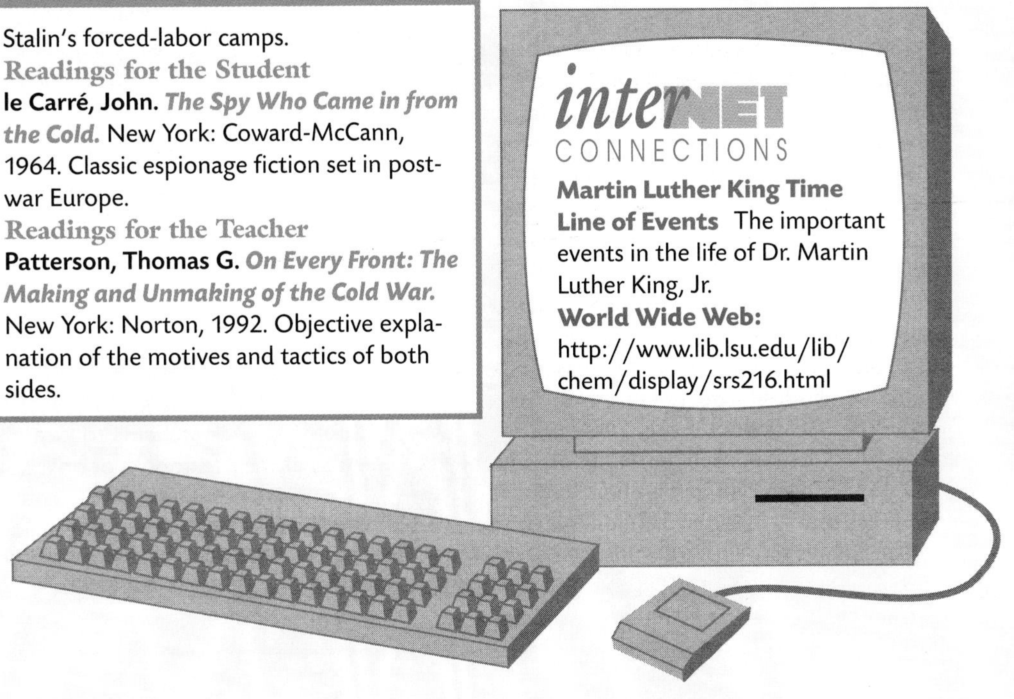

Martin Luther King Time Line of Events The important events in the life of Dr. Martin Luther King, Jr.
World Wide Web: http://www.lib.lsu.edu/lib/chem/display/srs216.html

Introducing Chapter 32

CHAPTER THEMES

Chapter Themes are listed by section on this chapter opening page of the Student Edition. A corresponding theme-based activity is available under "TEACH," and a theme-based question is asked in the Section and Chapter Reviews.

The Storyteller

Historical Setting The Allies had made a mistake by failing to arrange for a safe land corridor through East Germany to West Berlin. But their prompt, decisive action in supplying the city by airlift during the Berlin blockade was an important cold war victory for the West.

Historical Significance

Answers: *the lowering of the iron curtain in Eastern Europe; the division of Germany; the Berlin blockade; the formation of rival military and economic alliances*

It led to an arms race and to competition by the superpowers for power and influence on a global scale.

Chapter 32

1945–1979

The Cold War

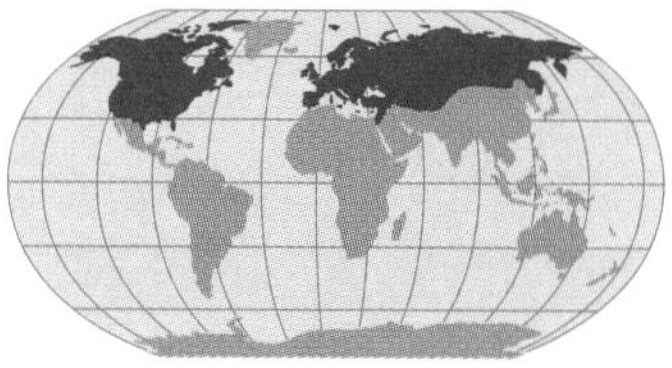

Chapter Themes

- **Conflict** A cold war develops between the United States and the Soviet Union, the two superpowers that emerged after World War II. *Section 1*
- **Change** The Soviet Union tries to move away from the legacy of Stalin while maintaining its control over Eastern Europe. *Section 2*
- **Regionalism** Western European democracies develop closer regional unity. *Section 3*
- **Cooperation** The United States and Canada build strong economies and forge closer ties. *Section 4*

The Storyteller

In 1948 the city of West Berlin was an island in the middle of a hostile sea. The Soviets had cut off all land routes into the German city in the hope of driving out the Western Allies. For 11 months the United States airlifted food to 2 million stranded residents in West Berlin.

One day while his plane was on the ground in West Berlin, an American pilot, Lieutenant Gale S. Halvorsen, met a group of German children. Although they had received few sweets to eat during the blockade, they did not beg. He told them to wait for his plane at the end of the airport runway the next day. The children came, and, to their delight, packets of gum and chocolate showered down from Halvorsen's plane.

Soon other pilots joined "Operation Little Vittles," and the crowds of children grew. The children named Halvorsen "the Chocolate Pilot."

Historical Significance

What developments led to a cold war between the Western democracies and the Soviet Union? How did this East-West split affect world affairs during the next 40 years?

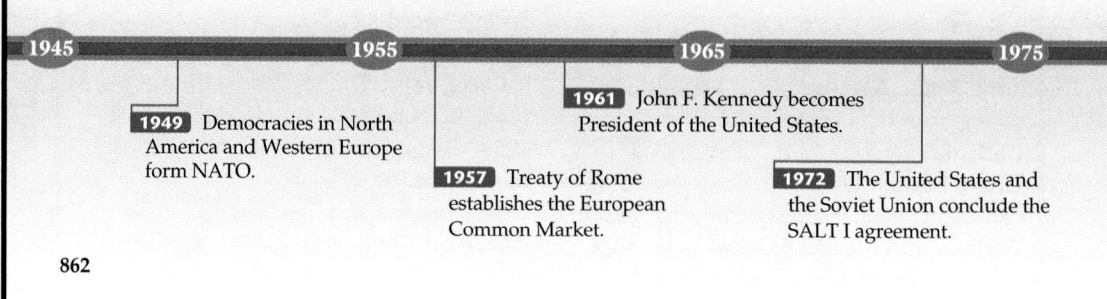

1945 · 1955 · 1965 · 1975

1949 Democracies in North America and Western Europe form NATO.

1957 Treaty of Rome establishes the European Common Market.

1961 John F. Kennedy becomes President of the United States.

1972 The United States and the Soviet Union conclude the SALT I agreement.

GEOGRAPHY CONNECTION

Location Ask students to locate Moscow, Berlin, Bonn, Paris, and London in the Atlas of their textbooks or on a wall map. What were the Eastern European countries that fell behind the iron curtain? *(Albania, Bulgaria, Czechoslovakia, East Germany, Hungary, Poland, Romania, Yugoslavia)* **L1**

Visualizing History During the Soviet era, vast numbers of military vehicles and marchers paraded past Soviet leaders in Moscow's famous Red Square to celebrate May Day (May 1st), the Communist workers' holiday.

Your History Journal

Interview someone who can remember the events of the 1950s or early 1960s. Ask them to relate their emotions and concerns regarding communism and the threat of war with the Soviet Union.

EXTRA CREDIT PROJECT

Report Almost as soon as the war ended, the Allies began trials of several leading Nazis at Nuremberg, Germany. The men were accused of murder, enslavement, and other crimes against humanity. Have students research and report on the Nuremberg trials and their outcome. They should also deal with the controversy surrounding the trials—the first in which a nation's leaders were tried for war crimes.

Introducing Chapter 32

Visualizing History

Point out that May Day has been the "labor day" for Socialist and Communist countries since 1889. What message is conveyed by a parade like this one? *(that the country is prepared militarily; it has the latest weapons; its people are united behind it)* Kremlinologists used to study the lineup of leaders at these parades to see, by their positions (or nonappearance), who was in favor and who was not.

Performance Assessment

Refer to the activity on page 862C of the Planning Guide.

For an additional activity, refer to Activity 32 in the *Performance Assessment Strategies and Activities* booklet.

Using Your History Journal

Students may want to make an audiocassette or videotape of their interview.

GLENCOE TECHNOLOGY

VIDEODISC

Use MindJogger to preview chapter content.

MindJogger Videoquiz

Chapter 32
Disc 4 Side B

Also available in VHS.

Chapter 32
Section 1

SECTION THEME

- **Conflict** A cold war develops between the United States and the Soviet Union, the two superpowers that emerged after World War II.

Find Out

Answer: *the extension of Soviet control over Eastern Europe; the division of Germany; the Berlin blockade; the formation of rival military and economic alliances*

FOCUS

Section Objective

Identify the events that caused and heightened the cold war.

BELLRINGER
Motivational Activity

Before taking roll at the beginning of the class period, project Section Focus Transparency 32-1 and have students answer the activity questions. Discuss students' responses.

This activity is also available as a blackline master.

Vocabulary Pre-check

Use the Vocabulary PuzzleMaker to create a puzzle that reinforces the vocabulary terms in this section. **L1**

1945 — 1955 — 1965

1947 The United States announces the Truman Doctrine and the Marshall Plan.

1955 West Germany joins NATO.

1961 Soviets and East Germans build the Berlin Wall.

Section 1

The East-West Split

Setting the Scene

- **Terms to Define**
  superpower, cold war, satellite, iron curtain, containment, arms race, ideology, bloc
- **People to Meet**
  Joseph Stalin, Harry S Truman, George C. Marshall
- **Places to Locate**
  San Francisco, Greece, West Berlin

Find Out What key events caused and heightened the cold war?

The Storyteller

Nikita Khrushchev recalled the beginning of the arms race: "We are surrounded by American air bases.... For many years after the war, bombers were to represent the major threat in our enemy's arsenal of weapons. It took time and a great deal of work for us to develop a bomber force on our own.... Two of our famous designers ... developed the MiG-15, which in time was acknowledged as the best jet fighter in the world.... However, our superiority was short-lived. During the Korean War the U.S. started making a jet fighter that was better than the MiG-15, and soon the Americans ruled the air over Korea."

—from *Khrushchev Remembers, The Last Testament*, translated and edited by Strobe Talbott, 1974

Nikita Khrushchev

The United States and the Soviet Union emerged from World War II as the world's two superpowers. No other countries were equal to them in military power or political influence. Differences in political beliefs and policies soon pulled the two superpowers apart and led to a struggle between them known as the cold war. In the cold war, each superpower sought world influence by means short of total war. This was because the possibility of nuclear war made the costs of a "hot" war too high. The "weapons" used in the cold war included the threat of force, the use of propaganda, and the sending of military and economic aid to weaker nations.

The United Nations

In the closing months of World War II, the Allies started planning for the postwar world. To handle future global problems, they had agreed at Yalta to replace the League of Nations with the United Nations, a new, permanent international organization. The purpose of the United Nations (UN) was to maintain peace by guaranteeing the security of member nations. It would foster good relations among nations based on the principles of equal rights and self-determination. It would also encourage cooperation on economic, cultural, and humanitarian problems.

In April 1945, representatives from 50 nations gathered in **San Francisco** to draft the Charter of the United Nations, which was completed and signed in June. The United Nations, headquartered in New York City, held its first sessions in 1946.

Although the UN Charter provided for six major bodies, it assigned the bulk of power to only two of them—the Security Council and the General Assembly. The Security Council, which decided diplomatic, political, and military disputes, was made up of 11 members. The five permanent members were Great Britain, China, France, the

SECTION RESOURCES

Reproducible Masters
- Reproducible Lesson Plan 32-1
- Guided Reading Activity 32-1
- Time Line Activity 32
- Geography and History Activity 32
- Section Quiz 32-1

Transparencies
- Section Focus Transparency 32-1
- Chapter Transparency 32
- World History and Art Transparency 43, *The Persistence of Memory*
- Mapping History Overlay Transparency 22, *The United Nations*

Multimedia
- Vocabulary PuzzleMaker Software
- Student Self-Test and Review Software
- Testmaker
- World Music: Cultural Traditions, Lesson 4
- Communism and the Cold War

864 Chapter 32 *The Cold War*

Visualizing History **All seemed well when American and Soviet forces met at the Elbe River in April 1945.** *What events in Eastern Europe changed the American attitude toward the Soviet Union?*

United States, and the Soviet Union. Each was given the right to veto any Security Council decision. The other six members served two-year terms. The General Assembly, the policy-making body, was made up of representatives from all UN member nations. Each nation had one vote.

The third body, the Economic and Social Council, oversaw the fights against poverty, ignorance, and disease. The fourth, the International Court of Justice, handled international legal disputes. The fifth, the Trusteeship Council, promoted the welfare of people in colonial territories and helped them toward self-rule. The sixth, the Secretariat, handled the UN's administrative work.

During the postwar period, the UN effectively resolved many crises. However, the right of veto granted the Security Council's permanent members made the UN powerless to resolve any dispute involving the United States and the Soviet Union. The United Nations became deadlocked. It was criticized as being a "debating society"—far from what the signers of the Charter had hoped it would be.

From Allies to Arch Enemies

After World War II, the Western Allies—the United States, Great Britain, and France—believed the best way to achieve security was to strengthen democracy and to build prosperous economies in Europe. The Soviets, however, had different goals. Historically, they had well-justified fears of invasion and had lost 20 million people in World War II. The Soviet dictator **Joseph Stalin** wanted to establish pro-Soviet governments in Eastern Europe not only to prevent any future attacks but also to expand his empire. Democracy, which might result in governments unfriendly to the Soviets, was not what Stalin had in mind for Eastern Europe.

President Franklin D. Roosevelt had believed that postwar cooperation with Stalin was possible, although he was starting to change his mind shortly before his death in April 1945. In the months afterward, Roosevelt's successor, President **Harry S Truman**, and other leaders adopted a much darker view of Stalin. They concluded that the Soviet dictator wanted to control Eastern Europe with the same ruthlessness that he used to govern the Soviet Union.

The Iron Curtain

Eastern Europe thus became the first region where Soviet and Western interests came into conflict. In Albania and Yugoslavia, local Communist parties, which had led the resistance against Axis forces in their countries, took control with little help from the Soviets. In Poland, Romania, and Bulgaria, where Soviet troops were in full command, the Soviet Union made sure that government ministries included Communists. Later, breaking his promise made at Yalta, Stalin refused to allow free elections. Non-Communists were ousted from governments, and Communists took charge. By 1947, most of the nations of the region had become Soviet satellites, controlled by the Soviet Union.

COOPERATIVE LEARNING ACTIVITY

Debate After the war, the Russians stripped East Germany of its industrial resources and equipment, while the Allies helped their three zones—what later became West Germany—toward economic recovery. Organize the class into two groups for a debate, one side representing the Soviet Union and the other the Allies. Each side should present its case for acting as it did. Students should try to answer why the differing policies were adopted and what their long-term effects were. **L3**

TEACH

Guided Practice

THEME Conflict

Review with students the important differences between the Soviet Union and the United States that predated the end of World War II. *(different political systems: totalitarian versus democratic; different economic systems: planned Communist economy versus market capitalism; also, far different wartime experiences)* **L1 LEP**

Visualizing History At this time, Russian troops were poised to push on to Berlin. American troops did not join them because American generals feared that casualties would be too high, and in fact Soviet casualties may have reached 100,000 in the assault on Berlin.

Answer to Caption: *the extension of Soviet control over Poland and other Eastern European countries*

Politics Review with the class the main agreements made at the Yalta conference in February 1945. *(The Allies agreed to divide Germany and Berlin. Stalin agreed to hold free elections in Soviet-occupied countries and to aid the Allies against Japan; in return, he received eastern Poland and territories in Asia.)* **L2**

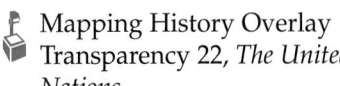

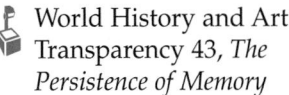

- Mapping History Overlay Transparency 22, *The United Nations*
- Chapter Transparency 32
- World History and Art Transparency 43, *The Persistence of Memory*
- World Music: Cultural Traditions, Lesson 4

Map Study

Answer

Austria, Finland, Republic of Ireland, Spain, Sweden, Switzerland

Map Skills Practice

Reading a Map What Communist nation did not join the Warsaw Pact? *(Yugoslavia)*

Regionalism Ask students to explain how the circumstances of Soviet expansion differed in these three sets of examples: (1) Albania, Yugoslavia, and Czechoslovakia; (2) Poland, Romania, Bulgaria, and Hungary; and (3) East Germany. *(1: Local Communists took control; 2: Soviet troops occupied during the war; 3: originally agreed on as the Soviet zone.)* **L3**

Who?What?Where?When?

Harry Truman, a little-known senator from Missouri before he became Franklin Roosevelt's Vice President, had relatively little experience in foreign affairs. When he succeeded to the presidency on Roosevelt's death, he had been Vice President only 82 days and had met with the President just twice.

Independent Practice

Guided Reading Activity 32-1 **L1**

Time Line Activity 32

Geography and History Activity 32

Europe 1945–1955

Map Study After World War II, Europe became divided between the Soviet and Western spheres of influence.
Place What nations of Europe remained neutral?

Stalin's actions in Eastern Europe convinced President Truman that the United States had to resist further Soviet moves. Truman was backed by British statesman Winston Churchill. In March 1946, Churchill had first used the phrase "iron curtain" in a speech in Fulton, Missouri: "From Stettin in the Baltic to Trieste in the Adriatic an iron curtain has descended across the continent of Europe." Thereafter, iron curtain referred to the Soviet-made barrier that split Europe into non-Communist Western Europe and Communist Eastern Europe.

Containing Communism

To counter any expansionist threat from the Soviet Union, the United States developed a new foreign policy in 1947. The idea for the new policy was presented in early 1947 by George Kennan, a State Department expert on the Soviet Union. Believing that the Soviets sought to expand their territory without war, he suggested a policy of containment—holding back the spread of communism. By standing firm, the United States hoped to keep communism inside its existing borders.

The Truman Doctrine

In the spring of 1947, President Truman applied the containment policy for the first time in the eastern Mediterranean. In **Greece**, local Communists were fighting a guerrilla war against the pro-Western monarchy. They were aided by Communists from neighboring Yugoslavia and Albania. The West feared that the fall of Greece to

MEETING SPECIAL NEEDS ACTIVITY

Study Strategy Events unfolded rapidly in the early years of the cold war. To understand the events that were happening in many parts of Europe, students can construct a chart. Along the side, suggest that they put the years 1945 to 1947, divided into two- or three-month intervals. Along the top, students should enter the names of the countries most involved in the cold war, either alphabetically or by region. At the appropriate place, they should then indicate important events in the cold war. **L2**

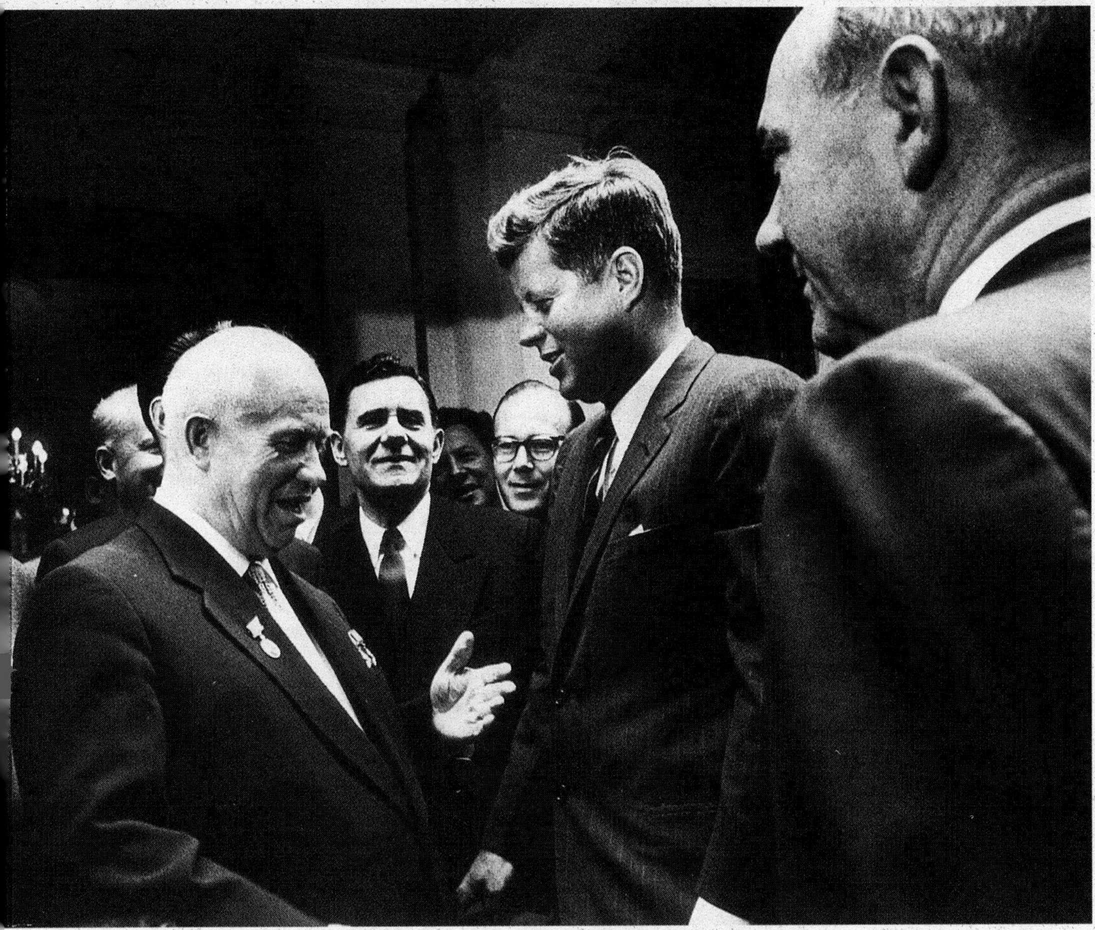

Cornell Capa, Magnum

Cold War

In 1961 Soviet Premier Nikita Khrushchev (left) and United States President John F. Kennedy held a cold war meeting. Khrushchev insisted that troops of the Soviet Union's former World War II Allies—France, Great Britain, and the United States—must leave West Berlin. The Allies' sector of Berlin was entirely inside East Germany, a separate nation from West Germany and an ally of the Soviet Union. Kennedy refused, believing that the Soviets would take control over West Berlin if the Allies departed. Two months later the Soviets shocked the people of both Berlins—and the world—by building the Berlin Wall.

The Berlin Wall became an important symbol of the cold war. For nearly a half century after the end of World War II the world's two superpowers, the United States and the Union of Soviet Socialist Republics, dominated the world and fought a "cold" war. In fact, it was not always cold. The two powers fought a number of regional conflicts either directly or through allies, including the Korean and Vietnam Wars. In 1989 the Berlin Wall was torn down; a year later the Soviet Union crumbled and the cold war came to an end. ⊕

TEACH

Tell students that, although the United States could not prevent the building of the Berlin Wall, American leaders never abandoned their goal of reuniting Germany. Two years after this meeting, in June 1963, Kennedy appeared before a huge outdoor rally in West Berlin and delivered an address that included this famous declaration: "All free men, wherever they may live, are citizens of Berlin, and, therefore, as a free man, I take pride in the words 'Ich bin ein Berliner' (I am a Berliner)."

Linking Past and Present

Green Berets One tactic advanced by the West against the East during the cold war was counterinsurgency—organized military action to counteract revolutionary activity. A prime U.S. counterinsurgent force, the Green Berets, received its name because of its distinctive headgear, specifically authorized by President Kennedy.

ABCNEWS INTERACTIVE™

VIDEODISC
Communism and the Cold War

Side One, Chapter 15
Frames 26867–29413
Title: *Berlin Wall*
Ask: What reason did the Soviets give for blockading East and West Berlin? *(They were attempting to keep agents from the West from coming into the Soviet Union.)*

Chapter 32 Section 1

Literature Have students read George Orwell's *Animal Farm*, the satire of Russian totalitarianism. Some of them may want to read selected portions to the class for discussion. **L2**

you don't say...

"Iron curtain" was an expression that Churchill popularized but did not originate. As long ago as the early 1800s, it was used to refer to a fireproof curtain in theaters, installed to prevent the spread of flames between the stage area and the audience.

ABCNEWS INTERACTIVE™

VIDEODISC
Communism and the Cold War

Side One, Chapter 3
Frames 2488–7305
Title: *End of Alliance*
Subject: Summary of events near end of World War II, which led to the cold war
Ask: Why did the United States view the Soviet Union as a threat? *(believed the Soviet Union was trying to spread communism)* Why did the Soviet Union view the United States as a threat? *(believed the United States was an imperialistic power that wanted to destroy communism)*

communism would endanger Western influence in the eastern Mediterranean region.

Great Britain was the traditional defender of the eastern Mediterranean. Economic weaknesses at home, however, prevented the British from continuing their commitment. In February 1947, Great Britain informed President Truman of this fact and asked the United States to assume British responsibilities in the area. A month later, Truman asked Congress for a $400 million aid program for Greece and Turkey. In asking Congress for support, Truman made a new statement of foreign policy that became known as the Truman Doctrine. He stated:

> "I believe that it must be the policy of the United States to support free peoples who are resisting attempted subjugation by armed minorities or by outside pressures.... [W]e must assist free peoples to work out their own destiny in their own way."

Congress approved Truman's aid request. With the acceptance of the Truman Doctrine, the United States took on international responsibilities as the leader of the Western world. American military aid would now be available to any nation threatened by communism. As a result of American assistance, Greece was able to defeat the Communist guerrillas and the spread of communism in the eastern Mediterranean was blocked.

The Marshall Plan

Conditions in Europe posed immediate and long-term challenges for the United States. World War II had severely weakened European economies. The Truman administration feared that a European economic collapse would open Europe to communism. It believed that the military and economic security of the United States depended on a strong and democratic Europe.

Therefore, the United States government devised a new approach to provide aid to Europe. Speaking at Harvard University on June 5, 1947,

Images of the Times

Rebuilding Europe

Fearing the spread of communism, the United States adopted strong economic programs to rebuild Europe after World War II. The Soviets responded with a rival plan in Eastern Europe.

Devastation in the divided city of Berlin challenged the resolve of the West to restore not only the structures but the spirit of the people.

868

Images of the Times **Rebuilding Europe**

By 1945 and 1946, Europe had begun to recover from the war. But an extremely harsh winter in 1947 caused a setback. For this reason, economic aid such as the Marshall Plan was crucial. By the mid-1960s, European industrial output totaled more than two and a half times what it had been before the war.

Secretary of State **George C. Marshall** proposed a European aid program that became known as the Marshall Plan. Its purpose, he said, was to restore "the confidence of European people in the economic future of their own countries." For the plan to work, Marshall urged a united effort to determine where Europe's economic needs lay and how the United States could help.

Western European countries responded enthusiastically to the Marshall Plan; however, the Soviet Union refused to participate in the plan and forced its Eastern European allies to do the same. Despite their great need for economic aid, the Soviets felt they could not afford to give out information about their economy. They also opposed linking their Communist economy with the largely capitalist ones of Western Europe.

The Marshall Plan was a great success. Western European nations worked together to boost productivity, reduce trade barriers, and use resources efficiently. They received about $13 billion in aid from the United States during the next four years. By 1951, Western Europe's economies were prospering, and Communist prospects in these countries had declined.

The Marshall Plan extended American influence in Western Europe and helped unite the region into a single economic group to counter the Soviets. In reaction to the Marshall Plan, in 1949 the Soviet Union set up a rival plan known as the Council of Mutual Economic Assistance, or COMECON. Eastern Europe was thus formed into a competing economic group led by the Soviet Union.

Germany Divided

In 1945, Germany had been divided into four zones, controlled by Great Britain, France, the United States, and the Soviet Union. The zones of the Western Allies included the western part of Germany, while the Soviet zone encompassed eastern Germany. The city of Berlin, deep within the Soviet zone, was also divided into four sectors.

Modern Warsaw finally emerged from behind the iron curtain when Poland overthrew its Communist government in 1989.

Threatened by revolt, Greece received economic aid under the Truman Doctrine until the Marshall Plan went into effect.

REFLECTING ON THE TIMES

1. Why was it difficult for the United States to send supplies into Berlin in 1948?
2. What is the purpose of the large sign on the railway car delivering goods in Greece?
3. Why did the Soviet Union prevent its allies from participating in the Marshall Plan?

ANSWERS TO REFLECTING ON THE TIMES

1. The Soviet Union had cut off access by land.
2. to publicize the role of the United States in bringing about European recovery
3. The Soviets did not want to give out information about their economy, and they did not want to link their economies with the non-Communist West.

Cooperation The UN, which began with 51 members, now has 184. Have students research the changes in membership and what these changes have meant to the operation of the United Nations. **L3**

Who?What?Where?When?

George F. Kennan, a counselor at the American embassy in Moscow, first advanced the idea of containment. In February 1946, he sent a lengthy telegram to the State Department in Washington outlining his approach. "Soviet pressure," he wrote, "is something that can be contained by the adroit and vigilant application of counterforce at ... shifting geographical and political points." The policy led the United States toward opposing revolutions anywhere in the world.

ABC NEWS INTERACTIVE™

VIDEODISC
Communism and the Cold War

Side One, Chapter 6
Frames 11768–13455
Title: *The Arms Race*
Subject: Development of the arms race between the United States and the Soviet Union
Ask: What was the arms race? *(The arms race was a competition between the United States and the Soviet Union in the development of high-tech weaponry.)*

Map Study

Answer

The Soviets stripped resources from its occupied zone, while the Allies aided economic recovery in their zones.

Map Skills Practice

Reading a Map In what zone was the port city of Bremen? *(U.S. zone)*

Who?What?Where?When?

Denazification After the war the Allies agreed that Nazis should be punished—a process called denazification. One aspect of this process consisted of trials of wartime leaders. But many low-level collaborators were also purged—some tried and executed or imprisoned, many simply fired from their jobs.

Linking Past and Present

NATO Although the Warsaw Pact came to an end in 1991, NATO continues to flourish. Representatives of its 16 member nations form the North Atlantic Council, with headquarters in Brussels, Belgium. Since its beginnings, NATO has been dominated by the United States, and its supreme allied commander in Europe has always been an American.

Map Study The Soviets and the West had different priorities for rebuilding their occupied zones.
Place What were the differences?

Zones of Occupation

The Western Allies and the Soviets could not reach agreement on a final peace treaty for Germany. As relations with Stalin soured, the United States, Great Britain, and France decided to include their zones in the Marshall Plan as means to contain communism.

While the Soviets stripped their German zone of its industrial resources and equipment, the three Western powers aided their zones toward economic recovery. Free elections for local governments were held in the Western zones. The United States, Great Britain, and France also agreed to combine their sectors of Berlin to form what became known as the city of **West Berlin**. They also planned to form an independent West German state by joining their zones of occupation.

The Berlin Blockade

In June 1948, the Soviets tried to block this merger plan by cutting all land access from the West into West Berlin. Two million Berliners depended on the Western Allies for all their food, fuel, and other needs. The United States and other Western countries considered and rejected the idea of using force to regain access to Berlin. Instead, they came up with a plan to airlift needed supplies to the isolated city.

To keep the city alive, at least 4,000 tons of supplies were needed every day. Airplanes surpassed this goal by landing every 3 minutes at West Berlin's 2 airports. At the peak of the airlift, 13,000 tons were landed in one day. The airlift would continue for 11 months. Its success finally forced the Soviets to lift the blockade in May 1949.

That same month, the Western Allies went ahead with their plans to form an independent West German state. A constitution was approved that set up a federal system of 10 states. In the fall of 1949, the Federal Republic of Germany, or West Germany, was proclaimed. Its capital was at Bonn. The Soviets then set up the German Democratic Republic, or East Germany, with its capital at East Berlin. Thus, Germany was divided into 2 separate countries.

New Alliances

Just before the Berlin blockade, another crisis had occurred in Europe. In February 1948, Czechoslovakia was taken over by Communists and incorporated into the Soviet alliance system. The Czechoslovak and Berlin crises heightened Western concerns about military defense. In April 1949, shortly before the end of the Berlin blockade, the North Atlantic Treaty Organization (NATO) was formed by the United States, Great Britain, France, Belgium, the Netherlands, Luxembourg, Italy, Portugal, Denmark, Iceland, Norway, and Canada. NATO expanded to include Greece and Turkey in 1952 and West Germany in 1955. Members of this military alliance agreed that an attack on one would be considered an attack on all. In response to NATO, the Soviet Union and its Eastern European allies signed a military agreement known as the Warsaw Pact.

Later events showed that the purpose of the Warsaw Pact was as much to strengthen the Soviet

MAKING CONNECTIONS ACTIVITIES

Military History The United States has stationed troops in Germany ever since the end of World War II. Have students research and report on the reasons for their presence; the location of the main bases; and troop totals and how they have varied over the years. **L2**

Daily Life At its height the cold war had a strong impact on many nonpolitical aspects of life, including sports. Have students research and report on how the cold war affected the Olympic Games. **L1**

hold on Eastern Europe as to defend it. Soviet troops stationed in Hungary under the terms of the Warsaw Pact were used to suppress a 1956 uprising there. In 1968 the Soviet Union appealed to the treaty to justify its invasion of Czechoslovakia, which had introduced a liberal form of communism.

Worldwide Struggle

The cold war soon turned into a global struggle. In 1949, the Soviets successfully exploded their first atomic bomb. International tensions further increased as the two superpowers engaged in an **arms race**, or a competition to strengthen their armed forces and weapons systems.

Meanwhile, communism made rapid advances in Asia. In the late 1940s, Communist governments came to power in China and North Korea. In 1950, the North Koreans, allied to the Soviet Union and Communist-ruled China, attacked South Korea, a pro-Western republic. Although the North Koreans were forced back to their territory, the Korean conflict fed Western fears that in communism, it faced a single, powerful enemy that sought to conquer the world.

Beginning in the 1950s, the cold war also came to be not only a test of military strength, but also a test of the superpowers' competing **ideologies**, or political and economic philosophies—democratic capitalism on the part of the United States, and communism on the part of the Soviet Union. Military buildups, space exploration, and local and regional conflicts around the globe became entangled in the cold war as the two superpowers sought to win support and to block gains by the other.

Germany

Germany became a critical flash point in the cold war during the 1950s and 1960s. Nikita Khrushchev (krush•CHAWF), who became Soviet leader in the mid-1950s, set out to test the resolve of the new United States President John F. Kennedy in 1961 by threatening to force the Allies out of West Berlin. Stating that the West would defend West Berlin's freedom, Kennedy bolstered the United States military presence, and Khrushchev did not act on his threats.

Meanwhile, large numbers of East Germans were fleeing to West Berlin, which was easily accessible to them. In an effort to halt the drain of its workforce, the East German government, with Soviet backing, built a concrete wall across the divided city in August 1961. The Berlin Wall stemmed the flow of East Germans fleeing communism and raised East-West tensions. It became a symbol of the cold war and the hostile confrontation between democracy and communism.

The Developing World

After the early 1960s, superpower competition directly affected newly independent or economically developing nations in Asia, Africa, and Latin America. In most areas, such as in Africa and the Caribbean area, the superpowers provided aid to their allies in the particular region. Sometimes—as in the case of the Soviet Union in Afghanistan and the United States in Vietnam—they became militarily involved themselves.

By the late 1970s, however, the division of the world into two **blocs**, or groups of nations, each headed by a superpower, was coming to an end. The United States, wary of military involvements, faced growing challenges to its hold on world markets. Western Europe and Japan, less dependent on the United States, were prosperous economic powers in their own right. The Soviet Union, faltering economically, was facing internal pressures for change. Finally, many smaller nations, aligned with neither superpower, were following their own paths of development. All of these events marked the move away from a world dominated by the superpowers to one in which there were many competing groups of countries.

SECTION 1 REVIEW

Recall

1. **Define** superpower, cold war, satellite, iron curtain, containment, arms race, ideology, bloc.
2. **Identify** Joseph Stalin, Harry S Truman, George C. Marshall, the Marshall Plan, NATO, Warsaw Pact.
3. **Use** the map on page 866 to name the European nations under Soviet control.

Critical Thinking

4. **Evaluating Information** Why do you think Stalin risked a war with the West by blockading Berlin?

Understanding Themes

5. **Conflict** What were some of the political and economic "weapons" of the cold war? What goals did the superpowers hope to accomplish using these varying strategies?

Chapter 32 Section 1

ASSESS

Check for Understanding

Assign Section 1 Review as homework or as an in-class activity.

Use Student Self-Test and Review Software to review Section 1.

Evaluate

Section Quiz 32-1

Use the Testmaker to create a customized quiz for Section 1.

Reteach

Have students review the events that precipitated the cold war by brainstorming a list on the chalkboard and then putting the events in chronological order.

Enrich

Have students watch a video of a film made during the cold war such as *Fail Safe, Dr. Strangelove,* or *The Russians Are Coming! The Russians Are Coming!* Have them write a brief analysis of the view of U.S.-Soviet relations in the film they see.

CLOSE

Have students list, in order, the American Presidents who held office during the cold war and the major events related to the cold war that took place during their administrations.

SECTION 1 REVIEW ANSWERS

1. All vocabulary words are defined in the Glossary.
2. Joseph Stalin, 865; Harry Truman, 865; George C. Marshall, 869; Marshall Plan, 869; NATO, 870; Warsaw Pact, 870
3. East Germany, Poland, Czechoslovakia, Hungary, Romania, Bulgaria, Albania
4. He may have thought that the West was too afraid of war to stand up to him; in any case, he believed that war with the West was inevitable.
5. **CONFLICT** Political weapons: transforming governments into Communist or democratic states; active military intervention. Economic weapons: aid and trade links. Goals included extending actual rule or at least influence.

Chapter 32 Section 2

SECTION THEME

▶ **Change** The Soviet Union tries to move away from the legacy of Stalin while maintaining its control over Eastern Europe.

Find Out

Answer: *Along with maintaining its authoritarian system of Communist rule, it continued the arms race and exercised tight control over its Eastern European satellites.*

FOCUS

Section Objective

Explain how the Soviet Union carried out Communist policies after the death of Stalin.

BELLRINGER Motivational Activity

Before taking roll at the beginning of the class period, project Section Focus Transparency 32-2 and have students answer the activity questions. Discuss students' responses.

This activity is also available as a blackline master.

Vocabulary Pre-check

Use Vocabulary Activity 32 to introduce vocabulary terms. **L1 LEP**

1955 | 1965 | 1975

1955 Nikita Khrushchev becomes the dominant leader in the Soviet Union.

1968 The Soviets invade Czechoslovakia.

1972 Soviet and American leaders hold summit meeting in Moscow.

Section 2

The Communist Bloc

Setting the Scene

▶ **Terms to Define**
peaceful coexistence, intercontinental ballistic missile (ICBM), dissident, detente

▶ **People to Meet**
Nikita Khrushchev, Leonid Brezhnev, Josip Broz Tito, Alexander Dubček

▶ **Places to Locate**
Yugoslavia, East Germany, Poland, Hungary, Czechoslovakia

Find Out How did the Soviet Union carry out Communist policies after the death of Stalin?

The Storyteller

Peter Hauptman and Willi Pfeiffer had been best friends since childhood. Although their homes were only two blocks apart, they lived in different sectors of Berlin. Now, literally overnight, their frequent visits ended. The Soviet sector was walled off. Not just a barricade or a lowered gate, it was a wall, protected by barbed wire and concrete blocks. Peter stood on the western side of the wall, straining to catch a glimpse of Willi. But it was to no avail. Everyone living near the wall's eastern side had been forcibly relocated, and the nearby apartment doors and windows were sealed shut.

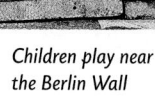

—adapted from *People and Politics: The Years 1960–1975,* translated and edited by Strobe Talbott, 1974

Children play near the Berlin Wall

The cold war affected the internal policies of the Soviet Union and its Eastern European satellites. During the late 1940s and early 1950s, Joseph Stalin believed that a full-scale conflict with the West was inevitable. To confront the West, the Soviet leader increased his control over the Soviet Union and Eastern Europe. He purged Communist parties of officials suspected of disloyalty. He also forbade writers and artists to use Western ideas in their works.

The Soviet Union

After World War II, Stalin worked to rebuild the Soviet Union's heavy industry and to boost its military strength. The Soviet Union surpassed its prewar rates of production in several major products, including coal, steel, and oil. It continued a high level of military spending and exploded its first nuclear bomb. In spite of the country's military prestige, life for the average Soviet citizen was difficult. Towns and cities destroyed by the war were rebuilt. Consumer goods, food, and clothing, however, remained in short supply because of high military spending.

Stalin died in March 1953. He was succeeded by a collective leadership of top Communist officials. **Nikita Khrushchev**, who served as Communist party secretary, emerged as the dominant leader in 1955.

De-Stalinization

In the following year, the 20th Congress of the Soviet Communist Party was held in Moscow. At a secret session, Nikita Khrushchev gave a controversial speech about Stalin. He denounced the Soviet dictator for the purges in the 1930s, in which thousands of loyal party members had been tortured

SECTION RESOURCES

Reproducible Masters
- Reproducible Lesson Plan 32-2
- Vocabulary Activity 32
- Guided Reading Activity 32-2
- Section Quiz 32-2

Transparencies
- Section Focus Transparency 32-2

Multimedia
- Student Self-Test and Review Software
- Testmaker
- Communism and the Cold War:
  - *Rebellion Behind the Iron Curtain*
  - *Sputnik Launches the Space Race*
  - *Cuban Missile Crisis*

Visualizing History **President Eisenhower hosts Premier Nikita Khrushchev in Washington, D.C., in 1959.** *What prevented the four-power summit meeting planned for May 1960 from taking place?*

and condemned to death or sent to labor camps. He also accused Stalin of creating a "cult of personality," in which he boosted his own image at the expense of the Communist party.

Khrushchev's anti-Stalin speech was part of a broader program of de-Stalinization, which he undertook from 1956 to 1964 to reverse some of the policies that had existed under Stalin. Khrushchev understood that many Soviet citizens wanted a relaxation of government controls and an improved standard of living. While keeping Stalin's Five-Year Plans and collective farms, he promised better wages and more consumer goods. He gave artists and intellectuals more freedom. He also reduced the terror of the secret police and freed many political prisoners from labor camps.

Cold War "Thaw"

By the mid-1950s, both American and Soviet leaders were interested in reducing cold-war tensions. Khrushchev called for a policy of **peaceful coexistence** in which the Soviets would compete with the West but avoid war. He stated the Soviet Union would surpass the West economically and encouraged other countries to follow the Communist model.

To make the Soviet Union more economically competitive, Khrushchev tried to boost production by improving working conditions. He sought to improve housing and to increase the production of consumer goods. The Soviet leader also put new emphasis on technological research. This paid off in 1957 with the launch of *Sputnik I*, the world's first space satellite. *Sputnik* stunned the United States and boosted the prestige of the Soviet Union and its leader.

Despite the cold-war "thaw," both superpowers continued a massive military buildup. In the late 1950s, the Soviets successfully tested long-range rockets known as **intercontinental ballistic missiles**, or ICBMs, which for the first time could target locations in the United States. Likewise, American missiles were pointed at the Soviet Union. A nuclear war would result in what was known as mutual assured destruction—that is, the certain destruction of both nations.

Even as they pursued this deadly race, United States and Soviet leaders sought to maintain peace. Summit meetings were the most visible of many contacts between Soviets and the United States. United States President Dwight Eisenhower and Soviet Premier Khrushchev met in Geneva, Switzerland, in 1955 and again in 1959 at Camp David, in Maryland. They recognized the deadly threat of nuclear war and agreed on the need to end the arms race. They planned a four-power summit for Paris in May 1960 and Khrushchev invited Eisenhower to visit the Soviet Union later in the year. But shortly before the Paris summit, the Soviets shot down an American U-2 spy plane over their territory and captured its pilot. Facing criticism from the Soviet military, Khrushchev strongly

Footnotes to History

The Kitchen Debate
In 1959, Vice President Richard M. Nixon, on a tour of the Soviet Union, visited an exhibition of American products with Soviet leader Nikita Khrushchev. The two leaders soon got into a heated argument on the merits of capitalism versus communism. The argument became known as the "kitchen debate" because the two men were standing in front of a model kitchen display.

COOPERATIVE LEARNING ACTIVITY

Press Conference Organize the class into two groups, one to represent reporters and the other to play the roles of President Eisenhower and his staff. The teams should research to plan questions and answers for a news conference after the announcement of the shooting down of the U-2 spy plane. Encourage students to address the larger issues of the cold war. The conference should be enacted as if it were actually happening, and you may want to videotape it. **L3**

TEACH

Guided Practice

THEME Change

After Stalin's death in 1953, the Soviet leadership instituted some changes to ease living conditions. **What were the most important aspects of de-Stalinization?** *(promises of higher wages and more consumer goods; more freedom for artists and intellectuals; a lessening of secret police activities; and the release from labor camps of many political prisoners)* **L1 LEP**

Visualizing History On this 1959 trip, Khrushchev dined at the White House, visited a farm in Iowa, and dropped in on a supermarket in San Francisco. In Hollywood he watched a rehearsal of the movie *Can Can*, later criticizing it as immoral.
Answer to Caption: *An American U-2 spy plane was shot down by Soviets.*

ABCNEWS INTERACTIVE™

VIDEODISC
Communism and the Cold War

Side One, Chapter 14
Frames 24964–26834
Title: *Sputnik Launches the Space Race*
Subject: The beginning of the space race
Ask: **Why did the United States panic when the Soviet Union unveiled *Sputnik*?** *(The U.S. feared that the enemy was more technologically prepared.)*

Politics Ask students when and how the Soviet Union dealt with reactions against its rule in East Germany, Hungary, and Czechoslovakia. *(East Germany: military intervention in 1953, built the Berlin Wall in 1961; Hungary, armed force in 1956; Czechoslovakia, armed force in 1968)* **L3 LEP**

ABC NEWS INTERACTIVE™

VIDEODISC
Communism and the Cold War

Side One, Chapter 16
Frames 29427–32782
Title: *Cuban Missile Crisis*
Subject: Summary and different perspectives of the Cuban missile crisis
Ask: Why did the United States panic when the Soviet Union put missiles in Cuba? *(The U.S. felt threatened because Cuba was located so close to the United States.)*

Independent Practice

Guided Reading Activity 32-2 **L1**

CURRICULUM CONNECTION

SCIENCE
Under Stalin every aspect of intellectual life was scrutinized and controlled. Biology fell under the control of an eccentric scientist named T. D. Lysenko. Among other things, he taught that acquired characteristics could be inherited and that wheat plants could produce rye seeds.

denounced the United States and canceled Eisenhower's visit. Relations soon worsened further.

The Cuban Missile Crisis

The Soviet Union and the United States came to the brink of nuclear war in 1962. In 1961, Eisenhower was succeeded as United States President by John F. Kennedy, who adopted a dynamic foreign policy to impress the Soviets with American strength and boost American prestige abroad. Testing Kennedy's resolve, Khrushchev pressured the Allies to get out of Berlin. Then in 1962, he secretly began to install nuclear missiles on Cuba, 90 miles (145 km) from Florida. Khrushchev gambled, hoping to offset American missiles based in Turkey which were aimed at the Soviet Union. Devising a strong response short of attack, Kennedy blockaded Cuba and forced Khrushchev to withdraw the missiles.

The Cuban missile crisis was one of the significant events of the cold war. Having come so close to nuclear disaster, the superpowers worked to establish a better relationship. In 1963, a telephone "hot line" linked Washington and Moscow, so that the leaders of both nations could instantly communicate with each other. That same year, the Soviet Union and the Western Allies also signed a treaty banning the testing of nuclear weapons in the atmosphere. For the next few years, the superpowers, although disagreeing sharply on many issues, avoided direct confrontations.

Meanwhile, Khrushchev's position within the Soviet Union weakened. In addition to his poor handling of the Cuban missile crisis, relations with China had soured, and Khrushchev's economic policies were in trouble. Heavy spending on technology, defense, and heavy industry had left little for improving agriculture and consumer goods. Far from surpassing the United States, the Soviet Union was forced to import grain from the United States. Sharply rising meat and butter prices provoked angry public demonstrations. In October 1964, Khrushchev was removed from office.

The Brezhnev Era

The Communist party chose a new collective leadership: Aleksei Kosygin (kuh•SEE•guhn) was premier and **Leonid Brezhnev** (BREHZH•NEHF) was general secretary of the party. By the mid-1970s, Brezhnev emerged as the dominant leader. He remained in control until his death in 1982.

Cautious and traditional, Brezhnev reversed Khrushchev's de-Stalinization policies. He clamped down again on intellectuals and dissidents—those who criticized the party or regime. Two prominent dissidents refused to be silenced. Alexander Solzhenitsyn (SOHL•zhuh•NEET•suhn), author of many works including *The Gulag Archipelago*, an account of the horrors of Soviet prison camps, was eventually deported and settled in the United States. Dr. Andrei Sakharov (SAH•kuh•RAWF), scientist and developer of the Soviet hydrogen bomb, later denounced the arms race and was sentenced to internal exile in Gorki.

Brezhnev's military and economic policies were similar to Khrushchev's. Concerned that there was a missile gap with the United States, he greatly increased the Soviet nuclear arsenal and its supplies of conventional weapons. He felt that military power gave the Soviet Union a stronger position in world diplomacy.

Under Brezhnev, economic conditions, however, worsened in the Soviet Union. Heavy military spending stifled growth in other sectors of the economy. Soviet workers had to make do with outdated equipment. Technologically, many industries were at least 20 years behind the times. Consumer goods were shoddy and in short supply. Farmers were only one-sixth as productive as their American counterparts. Poor harvests forced the Soviet Union to again import grain from the West.

Detente

By 1972, Brezhnev was ready to reduce tensions with the West. He hoped to find a way to cut military spending without falling behind the United States militarily. He also needed access to Western technology, grain, and consumer goods.

The United States was ready for Brezhnev's policy of detente. Derived from the French word meaning "relaxation," detente referred to an improvement of American-Soviet relations. A 1972 summit meeting between Brezhnev and United States President Richard Nixon in Moscow began a period of detente that lasted seven years. The Brezhnev-Nixon summit led to the signing of the Strategic Arms Limitation Agreement (SALT) Treaty, under which both sides agreed to limit the number of nuclear warheads and missiles each country could maintain. SALT did not reduce the number of weapons or end the arms race; it did slow it significantly.

Detente did not end the rivalry between the United States and the Soviet Union. The countries continued to compete for influence in various parts of the world. In 1979, the Soviets invaded neighboring Afghanistan to reinforce local Communist control. The move shocked the West and marked the end of detente. It also drew the Soviet Union into a 10-year guerrilla war against tough Afghan

MEETING SPECIAL NEEDS ACTIVITY

Attention Deficiency To help students understand the many personalities and events discussed in this section, make out a card for each key person, from Stalin to Dubček.Then organize the class into two teams and have students from each team take turns picking a card, sight unseen. Have that team identify the person, citing his nationality and an event associated with him. Give points based on correct answers. **L1 LEP**

Visualizing History **While the Soviets constructed the Berlin Wall in 1961, Russian and American tanks maneuvered within sight of each other.** *What was the real purpose of the wall?*

nationalists. The occupation of Afghanistan drained the national treasury, brought about the deaths of thousands of young Soviet soldiers, and became extremely unpopular at home.

Soviet Satellites

For most of the cold war, the Soviet Union maintained tight control over its Eastern European satellites. The peoples of these nations resented Soviet domination, but were largely powerless against the secret police and Soviet troops.

Yugoslavia

After World War II, **Yugoslavia** became the only large Communist state in Eastern Europe to resist Soviet control. Its leader, **Josip Broz Tito**, had participated in the resistance against the Nazis. As much a nationalist as a Communist, Tito insisted on developing his own national policies. Angered by Tito's independence, Stalin expelled Yugoslavia from the international Communist movement. Throughout Eastern Europe, Stalin waged a propaganda war against what he called Titoism, or the tendency of some Communists to place their national interests above those of the Soviet Union. With the support of his people, Tito resisted Soviet pressure, developed his own form of communism, held together the different religious and ethnic groups of the country, and won aid from the West. He led Yugoslavia until his death in 1980.

East Germany

Although it recovered from World War II more slowly than West Germany, **East Germany** became the most prosperous of the Soviet satellites. Its people deeply resented Soviet controls, however. In the aftermath of Stalin's death in 1953, East German workers struck and rioted when the government tried to lengthen the work day without an increase in wages. Soviet troops and tanks easily put down the revolt.

In the years that followed, nearly 3 million East Germans migrated to West Germany, by way of West Berlin, the only safe access available once the Soviets sealed the East German-West German border. A large percentage of the migrants were well-educated professionals who were attracted by West Germany's higher standard of living and greater

Visualizing History When the Berlin Wall was first erected, it bisected some buildings. Thus people were able to enter the premises in East Berlin and leave—jumping out a window if necessary—in West Berlin. East German authorities acted quickly, however, to brick up escape routes of this sort.
Answer to Caption: *to stop the flow of people from East Berlin to West Berlin*

Report Have students research and report on the pilot of the U-2 mission in 1960, Francis Gary Powers, explaining what happened to him after he was shot down over the Soviet Union. **L2**

Diary Have students write diary entries before and after the Soviet crackdowns in Hungary (1956) or Czechoslovakia (1968). They should describe the hopes and fears of typical citizens in these satellite countries during the anti-Soviet uprisings. **L3**

Who?What?Where?When?

Soviet Firsts The launching of *Sputnik I* in October 1957 was followed by other Russian scientific achievements. Just a month later, *Sputnik II* carried a dog named Laika, the first animal launched into space. In 1961, Russian cosmonaut Yuri Gagarin became the first person to orbit the earth.

MAKING CONNECTIONS ACTIVITIES

Music Artistic activity was closely regulated in the Soviet Union. Even composers were expected to glorify the Communist state. Have students research and report on what this meant for such important composers as Sergey Prokofiev, Dmitry Shostakovich, and Aram Khachaturian. **L3**

Religion Although the Soviet Union officially embraced atheism and placed many restrictions on the Russian Orthodox Church, religion survived and even flourished. Have students research and report on religion in the Soviet Union during the cold war and its role in Russian or Eastern European societies today. **L2**

Cultural Perspectives

Daring Dancers Since the late 1800s, Russians have excelled in the art of classical ballet. Russian ballet companies toured the world, winning wide acclaim for their creativity and energy. Tours continued during the cold war, but dancers were closely supervised to prevent them from defecting. Several did manage to escape, including two of the greatest male dancers of modern times. Rudolf Nureyev defected in 1961 while on tour in Paris; Mikhail Baryshnikov made his escape in 1974 in Toronto. Both men went on to have lengthy and productive careers with Western dance companies.

ABCNEWS INTERACTIVE™

VIDEODISC
Communism and the Cold War

Side One, Chapter 10
Frames 17333–20021
Title: *Rebellion Behind the Iron Curtain*
Subject: Discussion of rebellions in Soviet satellite nations, Soviet reaction, and why the United States did not support the rebellion acts
Ask: Why would the Soviet Union not allow democratic reforms in Czechoslovakia and Hungary? *(due to the fear that the reform movements would spread into the Soviet Union)*

freedoms. This "brain drain" was an embarrassment to the Soviets and an economic blow to the nation.

East Germany's problems contributed to a new cold war crisis in 1959. By then, West Germany had recovered from the war and was fully armed with tanks, bombs, and guns. It also had nuclear weapons on its soil under the control of NATO command. Alarmed at this development, Khrushchev called for negotiations on European security and on a nuclear-free Germany. He also demanded that the Western powers withdraw from Berlin.

Frustrated by the lack of a settlement and the continuing flight of East Germans, Khrushchev ordered the construction of what became the notorious Berlin Wall. In 1961, East German soldiers began work on the wall, a massive concrete structure 26 miles (42 km) long and up to 15 feet (4.6 m) high, topped with electrified wire.

The stated purpose of the wall was to keep Westerners out, but its true purpose was to halt the exodus of East Germans from East Berlin. To escape to West Berlin, people now had to survive mined trenches, guard dogs, and self-activating guns. Then they had to scale the wall itself. Stories reached the West of heroic escapes, but scores of East Germans died trying to run to freedom. Although the Berlin Wall did halt the flow of East German refugees, it became the most visible and powerful physical symbol of the iron curtain.

Poland

Under Communist rule, **Poland** industrialized and, among the satellites, became second in manufacturing only to East Germany. Poles, however, resented Soviet controls. They were angered by the government's efforts to collectivize farms and by its anti-Catholic policies. In June 1956 workers demanding better wages rioted in the city of Poznan. Upheavals in other cities forced Poland's Communist leaders to remove hard-line officials from office.

Poland's new leader was Wladyslaw Gomulka (VLAH•dee•slah goh•MUL•kuh), a popular Communist who had been accused of anti-Soviet activities and jailed during the late 1940s. Gomulka freed political prisoners, ended forced collectivization, and eased relations with the Catholic Church. He retained close ties with the Soviet Union, however. By the mid-1960s many of the Polish freedoms had again been lost.

In the 1970s, there was a new wave of anti-government strikes, with workers demanding better living conditions, and political and economic reforms. Gomulka resigned under the pressure. Continued economic problems led to food riots in 1976 and the growth of an underground anti-Soviet movement, aided by the Catholic Church.

Hungary

Hungary, a largely agricultural nation, experienced harsh Communist rule after 1947. The Hungarian government required peasants to join collective farms, and nationalized banking, trade and industry. Central planners emphasized heavy industry, at the expense of consumer goods. The Communist leadership silenced or disbanded potential opposition groups, such as trade unions or other political parties. Catholic Church property was seized, and Church schools taken over by the government. Opponents within the Communist party were purged and executed.

After Stalin's death in 1953, Hungary's Communist leaders eased controls for two years and then reimposed them when the economy did not reach its goals. Bitter opposition turned into full revolt in the fall of 1956. As in Poland, worker uprisings brought a liberal Communist government to power. However, Imre Nagy, the new Hungarian prime minister, went further than the Polish leaders. He announced Hungary's neutrality and its withdrawal from the Warsaw Pact. This raised the danger the Soviet Union feared most—the loss of Soviet control over Eastern Europe.

Two days after Nagy's announcement, Soviet tanks and troops poured into Hungary to crush the revolt. Realizing that intervention could cause World War III, the West sympathized with the Hungarians, but did nothing to help. Order in Hungary was restored under a Soviet-controlled government led by János Kádár. More than 200,000 Hungarian refugees fled to the West.

During the 1960s and 1970s, Hungary's Communist government tried to increase production, sometimes tightening controls, while at other times encouraging initiative through small private enterprises. Support of economic reform would eventually spur political reform efforts in the 1980s.

Czechoslovakia

Czechoslovakia, with its developed industry and democratic traditions, was the last Eastern European country to become Communist. After the Communist takeover in 1948, the country was forced to conform to the Soviet model, like Hungary. Purges against officials in Czechoslovakia were the bloodiest outside of the Soviet Union. The Czechoslovak leader, Antonin Novotny, kept the country under such rigid control that

CRITICAL THINKING ACTIVITY

Identifying Cause and Effect The cold war period was one of shifting policies and frequent international crises. Identifying cause-and-effect relationships makes these events easier to understand. For example, the death of Stalin and Khrushchev's desire to lessen discontent were causes that led to the effect of de-Stalinization. Have students write short essays that identify the causes of each of the following: the policies of peaceful coexistence and of détente and Soviet military intervention in East Germany, Hungary, and Czechoslovakia; the building of the Berlin Wall. **L2**

Visualizing History Czech citizens reacted in anger and defiance when Soviet and other Warsaw Pact troops invaded Prague. *How did the Soviets justify the invasion?*

de-Stalinization did not begin in Czechoslovakia until the 1960s.

At this time, public pressure for reform finally gained strength because of Czechoslovakia's economic stagnation. A liberal Communist reformer, **Alexander Dubček** (DOOB•chehk), replaced Novotny as leader in 1968 when Brezhnev signaled his approval. For a brief time, known as "the Prague spring," reform was allowed. Dubček eased press censorship and began to allow some political groups to meet freely.

Although Dubček assured the Soviets that Czechoslovakia was still loyal to the Warsaw Pact and to communism, the Soviets became alarmed at the direction the reform movement was taking. Many Czechoslovak thinkers wanted more freedom, and there were hints that opposition parties might be allowed to operate. To the Soviets, their hold on Eastern Europe again seemed threatened.

On August 20, 1968, about 500,000 troops from the Soviet Union and its Warsaw Pact allies invaded Czechoslovakia. They took control of Prague and sent Dubček and other Czechoslovak leaders to Moscow. Most of Dubček's reforms were withdrawn and a new constitution put into effect. In April 1969, Dubček was replaced as party leader. In 1970 he was expelled from the party entirely.

The Soviet Union justified the invasion by declaring its right to intervene in Communist states to counter anti-Communist uprisings. This principle, known as the Brezhnev Doctrine, was the basis for relations between the Soviet Union and its Eastern European satellites for the next 20 years.

SECTION 2 REVIEW

Recall

1. **Define** peaceful coexistence, intercontinental ballistic missile (ICBM), dissident, detente.
2. **Identify** Nikita Khrushchev, Leonid Brezhnev, Josip Broz Tito, Alexander Dubček, the Brezhnev Doctrine.
3. **Explain** why the Soviet Union and East Germany built the Berlin Wall.

Critical Thinking

4. **Analyzing Information** Why do you think the Soviet Union under Leonid Brezhnev pursued detente while it also carried out a huge military buildup?

Understanding Themes

5. **Change** What impact do you think Nikita Khrushchev's 1956 de-Stalinization speech had in the satellites of Eastern Europe?

SECTION 2 REVIEW ANSWERS

1. All vocabulary words are defined in the Glossary.
2. Nikita Khrushchev, 872; Leonid Brezhnev, 874; Josip Broz Tito, 875; Alexander Dubček, 877; the Brezhnev Doctrine, 877
3. The Berlin Wall was built to restrict the flow of people from East Berlin to West Berlin.
4. The Russian leadership wanted to reduce military spending; they also needed technology, grain, and consumer goods from the West.
5. **CHANGE** It probably raised hopes for greater freedom and may have encouraged dissident activities.

Visualizing History The strongest Czech resistance centered on the Prague radio station. Students barricaded it to keep the Russians out and thus enable Czech broadcasters to continue informing people about what was happening.
Answer to Caption: *The Russians claimed the right to intervene in Communist countries to counteract anti-Communist revolts.*

ASSESS

Check for Understanding

Assign Section 2 Review as homework or as an in-class activity.

Use Student Self-Test and Review Software to review Section 2.

Evaluate

Section Quiz 32-2

Use the Testmaker to create a customized quiz for Section 2.

Reteach

Have students use an outline map of the world to locate, date, and label hot spots during the cold war.

Enrich

Have students draw political cartoons criticizing Soviet control over its satellites.

CLOSE

Have students create a time line that includes the major events discussed in this section.

Chapter 32
Section 3

SECTION THEME

▶ **Regionalism** Western European democracies develop closer regional unity.

Find Out

Answer: *by joining NATO and by forming the European Coal and Steel Community and the Common Market*

FOCUS

Section Objective

Describe how Western Europe moved toward greater political and economic unity during the cold war.

BELLRINGER
Motivational Activity

Before taking roll at the beginning of the class period, project Section Focus Transparency 32-3 and have students answer the activity questions. Discuss students' responses.

This activity is also available as a blackline master.

Vocabulary Pre-check

Use Vocabulary Activity 32 to introduce vocabulary terms.
L1 LEP

1945 Great Britain elects a Labour party government.

1958 Charles de Gaulle heads France's Fifth Republic.

1963 Konrad Adenauer retires as West German chancellor.

1978 Spain introduces a new democratic constitution.

Section 3

Western Europe

Setting the Scene

▶ **Terms to Define**
welfare state, coalition

▶ **People to Meet**
Clement Attlee, Charles de Gaulle, Valéry Giscard d'Estaing, Konrad Adenauer, Willy Brandt

▶ **Places to Locate**
Rome

Find Out How did Western Europe move toward greater political and economic unity during the period of the cold war?

The Storyteller

Jacques LeMoine nervously held the rifle issued to him just that morning. Like many other citizens of Paris, the 17-year-old had been pressed into service, guarding the city's perimeter. President de Gaulle's announced plans to guide Algeria to independence had aroused furious opposition. In reaction to the independence policy for Algeria, a threat had been received: Paris would be invaded. Paratroopers under the leadership of four retired French generals had seized key overseas bases and planned to bring citizens like Jacques LeMoine to defend the city.

—adapted from *The 1962 World Year Book,* "France," Fred J. Pannwitt, 1962

Paris street disturbance

After World War II, the non-Communist nations of Western Europe were concerned about two major issues: economic recovery and military security. They came to realize that only through united action would they be able to improve their economies, strengthen the Western Alliance, and contribute to world affairs.

Great Britain

After World War II, Great Britain's position as a world power further declined. The British had bankrupted themselves to win the war. Therefore, they had to sharply reduce their worldwide military, political, and economic role.

A Reduced Role

Even with financial cutbacks, Great Britain's recovery was slow. Many British industries were too inefficient and outdated to compete successfully in world markets that were increasingly dominated by the United States, Japan, and other Western European nations.

Because of economic weakness, the British passed on many of their international obligations to the United States. To maintain its pride and a level of independent security, Great Britain, however, developed its own nuclear force. It also maintained a close relationship with other members of the Western Alliance.

Loss of Empire

The British also could no longer afford to support a vast global empire. During the 1950s and 1960s, many of Great Britain's important Asian and African colonies became independent. Most of these new nations joined as equals with Great Britain in the Commonwealth of Nations, an organization that promoted cooperation among the nations of the former British Empire.

SECTION RESOURCES

Reproducible Masters
- Reproducible Lesson Plan 32-3
- Vocabulary Activity 32
- Guided Reading Activity 32-3
- History Simulation 32
- Section Quiz 32-3

Transparencies
- Section Focus Transparency 32-3
- Mapping History Overlay Transparency 23, *The Commonwealth of Nations*

Multimedia
- Focus on World Art Print 24, *Current*
- Student Self-Test and Review Software
- Testmaker

The Welfare State

Internally, Great Britain underwent many changes after World War II. In 1945 Churchill and the Conservatives were voted out of office. They were replaced by the Labour party, which appealed to many Britons who wanted greater social equality. Under Prime Minister **Clement Attlee**, the Labour government continued wartime restrictions to improve the economy. However, it also promised a better standard of living for all British citizens.

Carrying out a moderate Socialist program, the Labour government nationalized the coal, steel, and transportation industries. Greater freedom was given to labor unions to strike and to participate in political activities. Like many other Western European governments, Britain's Labour government created a welfare state, a system in which the national government provides programs for the well-being of its citizens. Social security was expanded to provide lifetime benefits for the needy. Free education was provided to all children up to the age of 16. The government also introduced a national health service that provided free medical care for everyone.

As the economic situation improved in the early 1950s, the Conservatives returned to power and ruled until 1964. Although they ended many government controls over the economy, Conservative prime ministers, such as Winston Churchill, Anthony Eden, and Harold Macmillan did not eliminate the social welfare programs introduced by the Labour party.

The Monarchy

In 1952, the popular wartime monarch, George VI, died and was succeeded by his elder daughter, Elizabeth. As queen, Elizabeth II had little, if any, power. But, for many Britons, she served as a reassuring symbol of traditional British values during a period of rapid, and sometimes discouraging, change. For other Britons, however, the monarchy represented all that they believed was wrong with Great Britain—its preoccupation with past imperial glories and its failure to discard the trappings of an outdated class system.

France

Germany's occupation of France during World War II had ended the Third French Republic created in 1870. After the war, a new constitution established the Fourth French Republic. Like the Third Republic, it, too, had a strong legislature and a weak presidency.

Visualizing History **Riots between Hindus and Muslims led to the division of British India in 1947 into two nations: India and Pakistan. Both joined the Commonwealth of Nations.** *What was the Commonwealth of Nations?*

The Fourth French Republic

In spite of economic growth, France in the 1950s was plagued with domestic and international problems. The existence of many political parties undermined hopes for a stable government. No single political party was strong enough to obtain a working majority in the National Assembly. Cabinets were formed by coalitions, or temporary alliances, of several parties. When one of the parties disagreed with policy, the cabinet members had to resign and form a new government.

Overseas, France's Asian and African colonies demanded their independence. Unlike Great Britain, France at first clung to its empire. It fought, and lost, expensive and bloody wars in Indochina and North Africa.

The Fifth French Republic

In 1958, the threat of civil war in the North African colony of Algeria resulted in the downfall of France's ineffective Fourth Republic. **Charles de Gaulle**, leader of the French Resistance during World War II, was called from retirement to head an emergency government. De Gaulle asked the

Chapter 32 Section 3

TEACH

Guided Practice

THEME Regionalism

Ask students to discuss what regionalism means to them. They should focus on the concept as it applies to their own area. What region do you live in? How do people in this region cooperate with one another? With other regions? **L1 LEP**

Visualizing History In a 1942 speech, Prime Minister Winston Churchill declared proudly: "I have not become the King's First Minister in order to preside over the liquidation of the British Empire." But the process began under his successor and was almost complete by the mid-1960s.

Answer to Caption: *an organization to promote cooperation among former nations of the British Empire*

Who?What?Where?When?

Vatican II This general council of the Roman Catholic Church, held from 1962 to 1965, had far-reaching consequences for Catholics worldwide. Among the changes it instituted was the substitution, in the Mass, of people's native languages for the Latin that had been used for centuries.

Economics Britain, France, and West Germany all instituted programs to promote citizens' well-being during the cold war period. What programs in the United States provide for our well-being? *(Answers might include Social Security, Medicare, Medicaid, and welfare.)* **L2**

COOPERATIVE LEARNING ACTIVITY

Debate Organize the class into two groups and have students debate this proposition: The British monarchy should be abolished. Both sides should gather information to bolster their cases. Possible points to discuss include cost of the monarchy and functions of the royal family. **L3**

Chapter 32 Section 3

Movement Since World War II, millions of Africans, Asians, and West Indians have resettled in the former colonial powers, especially Britain and France. At the same time, Germany allowed millions of Turks to ease labor shortages. Today the presence of non-Europeans in these countries has led to racist violence. Have students investigate and report on the situation of immigrants in Europe. **L3**

History Simulation 32

Focus on World Art Print 24, Bridget Riley. *Current*

Mapping History Overlay Transparency 23, *The Commonwealth of Nations*

Independent Practice

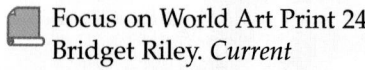

Guided Reading Activity 32-3 **L1**

Biography Have students prepare brief reports on one of these European leaders: Clement Attlee, Charles de Gaulle, Georges Pompidou, Konrad Adenauer, Willy Brandt. **L2**

Regionalism Have students research and report on the following European regions in the cold war period: Scandinavia, Italy, Spain. **L3**

Visualizing History De Gaulle saw himself as the personification of France. "There were many things I would have liked to do but could not," he once said, "for they would not have been fitting for General de Gaulle."
Answer to Caption: *He allowed Algeria to become independent.*

French people to approve a new constitiution providing for a strong presidency. French voters overwhelmingly responded to de Gaulle's appeal. Thus, the Fifth French Republic was born.

De Gaulle became the first president of the Fifth Republic. His political party, the Gaullist Union, formed a working majority in the National Assembly. As president, de Gaulle recognized that France could not stubbornly hold on to its empire against strong nationalist opposition. In the early 1960s, he allowed France's African colonies, including Algeria, to become independent.

With the loss of France's empire, de Gaulle worked to strengthen French cultural and economic influence in Europe and throughout the rest of the world. His strongly nationalistic policies angered France's allies, especially Great Britain and the United States. In 1963, de Gaulle blocked Great Britain's application for membership in the European Common Market. Three years later, the French president decided to withdraw all French troops from NATO's military command and requested that all NATO bases and headquarters be removed from French soil. At the same time, he insisted on maintaining France's political ties to NATO. De Gaulle's ultimate expression of nationalism was the building of an independent French nuclear force.

De Gaulle's successor, Georges Pompidou (PAHM•pih•DOO), by contrast, worked to build closer relations with Great Britain and the United States. He also focused on economic growth rather than on nationalistic projects. After Pompidou's death in 1974, **Valéry Giscard d'Estaing** (zhihs •KAHR dehs•TAN) was elected president. Giscard continued Pompidou's domestic and international policies. He set out to lessen state economic controls and to encourage the expansion of French private enterprise. Giscard's pro-business policies, however, were crippled by the worldwide economic downturn of the 1970s.

Visualizing History **France gave Charles de Gaulle broad presidential powers and election by direct popular vote.** *How did de Gaulle solve the problem of nationalist opposition in Algeria?*

Germany

During the postwar years, West Germany rebuilt its economy and became Western Europe's leading industrial nation. Many experts called West Germany's reconstruction an "economic miracle." New industries used the latest in modern equipment, and industrial production more than tripled in the 1950s. Prosperity enabled West Germany to create a welfare state closely resembling that in Great Britain and France. West Germany also absorbed 10 million refugees from Eastern Europe. Another 1 million people settled in Germany from other parts of the continent.

The Adenauer Years

West Germany's democratic political system was dominated by two parties: the Christian Democrats and the Social Democrats. In 1949, the Christian Democrats, led by **Konrad Adenauer** (A•duhn•OWR), formed the first West German government. They created a capitalist economy with close ties to the West. In 1955 West Germany joined NATO and developed its own armed forces.

As chancellor, Adenauer was known as a strong leader devoted to the Western Alliance, European unity, and the reunification of Germany under a democratic government. During his tenure, West Germany became one of the world's most stable democracies. Adenauer retired in 1963. He was succeeded as chancellor by the economic minister Ludwig Erhard, who served until 1966.

Willy Brandt

During the 1960s, the Christian Democrats lost support to the Social Democrats, a moderate socialist party led by West Berlin's mayor, **Willy Brandt**. The Social Democrats maintained strong support for NATO while seeking improved relations with the Soviet bloc.

Brandt became chancellor of Germany in 1969. During the 1970s, he worked to reduce tensions

MEETING SPECIAL NEEDS ACTIVITY

Reading Comprehension Organize the class into four groups, one for each major subsection of Section 3. Then have each group develop a topic sentence for each paragraph in its subsection. After completing the sentences, each group should share its list with other students, then review and comment on their topic sentences. **L2**

880 Chapter 32 *The Cold War*

between West Germany and the Soviet bloc. This policy, known as *Ostpolitik* (German for "Eastern policy") led West Germany to reach agreements to normalize relations with the Soviet Union and Poland in 1972. Brandt's initiative eventually led to the establishment of diplomatic ties between West Germany and East Germany a year later.

European Unity

Throughout Europe's history, local disputes between two or more nations often drew the entire continent into war. In the twentieth century, developments in technology, such as nuclear weapons, made it clear that future wars could lead to global catastrophe. This possibility prompted leaders to seek regional solutions to European issues.

As World War II ended, European leaders discussed plans for the postwar unification of European countries. These plans included organizations for economic cooperation and the resolution of disputes. Some even raised the idea of a United States of Europe. Others proposed that each nation retain its national identity but hand over control of defense and foreign policy to an all-European government. This arrangement, it was felt, would prevent European nations from waging war on each other.

To coordinate economic policies, six nations—France, Italy, West Germany, Belgium, the Netherlands, and Luxembourg established the European Coal and Steel Community in 1952. The organization's goal was to create a tariff-free market for European coal and steel products. By ending trade barriers and developing uniform standards, the European Coal and Steel Community would further European industrial growth.

The Community was so successful that the same countries decided to bring together the rest of their economies. In 1957, representatives of the six nations meeting in **Rome**, Italy, signed the Treaty of Rome. This agreement created the European Economic Community, also known as the Common Market. The six members of the Common Market planned to abolish all tariffs among themselves and form a single economic market by 1970. During the 1960s and 1970s, Great Britain, attracted by the Common Market's success, ended its traditional aloofness from European affairs and sought membership in the European organization.

The Common Market benefited Western Europe in several ways. By promoting economic cooperation among individual European nations, it reduced the threat of conflict and contributed to European prosperity. It also enabled Western Europe to pursue cooperative technological programs in fields such as space research and nuclear energy. These programs were too expensive for any one nation to pursue on its own. Finally, it enabled Europe to compete on an equal basis with North America and East Asia in world markets.

AROUND THE WORLD

Edmund Hillary Climbs Mount Everest

Nepal-Tibet, 1953

Located in the Himalayas, on the Nepal-Tibet border, Mount Everest is the world's highest peak. A British expedition set out in 1953 to scale the south slope, which was considered unclimbable. The climbers established a series of camps as they advanced up the mountain. The last camp was set up by Edmund Hillary of New Zealand and Tenzing Norgay of Nepal. On May 29, 1953, they became the first climbers to reach the top of Mount Everest. Queen Elizabeth II knighted Hillary for his achievement.

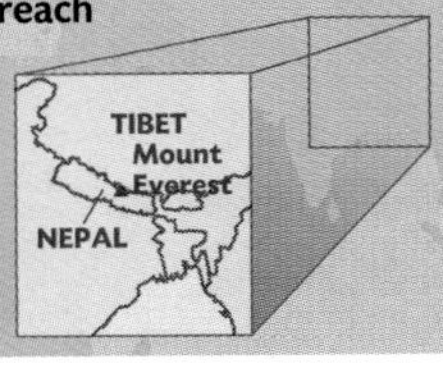

SECTION 3 REVIEW

Recall
1. **Define** welfare state, coalition.
2. **Identify** Clement Attlee, Charles de Gaulle, Valéry Giscard d'Estaing, Konrad Adenauer, Willy Brandt, *Ostpolitik*, European Economic Community (Common Market).
3. **Explain** why Charles de Gaulle of France was considered an independent leader.

Critical Thinking
4. **Synthesizing Information** Why was a strong European economy vital to world peace after World War II? What factors contributed to the economic recovery of Western Europe during the postwar years?

Understanding Themes
5. **Regionalism** What do you think would be the advantages and disadvantages of a United States of Europe?

Chapter 32 Section 3

ASSESS

Check for Understanding

Assign Section 3 Review as homework or as an in-class activity.

Use Student Self-Test and Review Software to review Section 3.

Evaluate

Section Quiz 32-3

Use the Testmaker to create a customized quiz for Section 3.

Reteach

Have students review the factors that moved Western Europe toward greater cooperation in the postwar period.

Enrich

Have students watch a video of the film *The Mouse That Roared* and then discuss the European attitude toward the United States that is reflected in the film.

CLOSE

Have students summarize the ways Western democracies cooperated during the cold war era.

SECTION 3 REVIEW ANSWERS

1. All vocabulary words are defined in the Glossary.
2. Clement Attlee, 879; Charles de Gaulle, 879; Valéry Giscard d'Estaing, 880; Konrad Adenauer, 880; Willy Brandt, 880; *Ostpolitik*, 881; European Economic Community (Common Market), 881
3. He relinquished France's African colonies and pursued a nationalistic policy toward the Common Market and NATO.
4. It contributed to political stability and decreased the likelihood of future conflicts. Economic recovery was aided by the Marshall Plan, the European Coal and Steel Community, and the Common Market.
5. **REGIONALISM** Answers will vary but might include the following ideas. Advantages: lower trade barriers, cooperative research and development in industry, pooling of resources. Disadvantages: loss of sovereignty, weakening of national identity.

Chapter 32
Section 4

SECTION THEME

▶ **Cooperation** The United States and Canada build strong economies and forge closer ties.

Find Out

Answer: *United States: political: anti-Communist crusade, new foreign alliances, arms race, strong presidency, social: domination of automobile, growth of suburbs, civil rights movement. Canada: political: increased independence from Britain, new foreign alliances, social: search for national identity in face of separatism.*

FOCUS

Section Objective

Trace the political and social changes that the people of the United States and Canada experienced during the cold war years.

BELLRINGER
Motivational Activity

Before taking roll at the beginning of the class period, project Section Focus Transparency 32-4. This activity is also available as a blackline master.

Vocabulary Pre-check

Use the Vocabulary PuzzleMaker to create a puzzle that reinforces the vocabulary terms in this section. **L1**

1945 — 1955 — 1965 — 1975

1947 U.S. Congress conducts hearings on Communist influence in American life.

1955 Martin Luther King, Jr., begins nonviolent civil rights campaign for African Americans.

1967 Canada celebrates 100th anniversary of nationhood.

1974 Richard M. Nixon becomes the first United States President to resign his office.

Section 4

The United States and Canada

Setting the Scene

▶ **Terms to Define**
automation, racial segregation, imperial presidency, stagflation, embargo, double-digit inflation, trade deficit, middle power, multicultural, separatism

▶ **People to Meet**
Dwight D. Eisenhower, John F. Kennedy, Lyndon B. Johnson, Richard M. Nixon, Martin Luther King, Jr., Gerald R. Ford, Jimmy Carter, Lester B. Pearson, Pierre Elliott Trudeau

▶ **Places to Locate**
Vietnam, Cambodia, Washington, D.C., St. Lawrence Seaway, Toronto, Montreal, Quebec

Find Out What political and social changes did the people of the United States and Canada experience during the cold war years?

The Storyteller

By the time President Eisenhower began his first term, 33,629 Americans had been killed in the Korean War. Then on March 5, 1953, Joseph Stalin died. Hearing of Stalin's death, Eisenhower asked his associates, "Well, what do you think we can do about this?" He was advised to seek improved relations with Russia. The new Soviet leaders also wanted reduced tensions. As a result, a truce ending the war in Korea was signed on July 28th.

—adapted from *The Glorious Burden*, Stefan Lorant, 1968

President Dwight D. Eisenhower

Because they were spared the destruction of their territory in World War II, the United States and Canada emerged from the war with prosperous economies. During the postwar era, the stunning technological achievements of the United States, its high standard of living, and business success were admired and envied around the globe.

In the 1960s and the 1970s, however, the United States was shaken by domestic political crises, economic difficulties, and its involvement in the Vietnam War. By the 1980s other nations were catching up economically, but the United States retained its role as the leader of the non-Communist world.

During this time, the United States' northern neighbor, Canada, sought to maintain unity between its French-speaking and English-speaking populations. It also attracted immigrants from all parts of the world. Moving away from its traditional British connection, Canada sought a new identity in international affairs and developed closer economic ties with the United States.

American Prosperity

After World War II, the United States entered an era of economic growth that brought material wealth to a larger group of Americans. Demand for American goods was high, and business responded to meet this need. Production soared, and new industries appeared. Higher wages and better benefits gave Americans more money to spend. American shoppers pushed up demand as they eagerly purchased consumer goods that had been scarce during the war. Future prospects were also bright. The postwar "baby boom," or soaring birthrate, added to the potential number of consumers and promised increased economic growth.

SECTION RESOURCES

Reproducible Masters
- Reproducible Lesson Plan 32-4
- Guided Reading Activity 32-4
- Reteaching Activity 32
- Enrichment Activity 32
- Section Quiz 32-4
- Performance Assessment Activity 32
- Spanish Chapter Summary 32

Transparencies
- Section Focus Transparency 32-4

Multimedia
- Vocabulary PuzzleMaker Software
- Student Self-Test and Review Software
- Testmaker
- Communism and the Cold War
- Turning Points in World History
- Lessons of War

Science and Technology

During the postwar years, the United States made spectacular leaps in the field of science and technology. With more money to spend, an increase in the number of university-trained scientists, and a growing commitment to the future, the United States led the world in new technological developments.

During the 1950s and 1960s, American factories and industries began to use automation, the technique of operating a production system using mechanical or electronic devices. With automated methods of production, goods could be produced more efficiently than with human workers.

Beginning in the 1950s, the use of computers began to revolutionize American industry. Businesses used computers for many purposes, including billing and inventory control. Computers were also used for such things as making hotel reservations, sorting bank checks, tracking space satellites, forecasting weather conditions, and setting type for printing. Automation and computers in the workplace caused many workers to lose their jobs. In the long run, however, computers and automation created more jobs than they eliminated. In addition, the new jobs usually demanded a higher level of education.

American technological skills brought the United States into competition with the Soviet Union in space exploration and missile development. The two superpowers experimented with moon probes, weather and communications satellites, and extended flights of humans orbiting the earth. The grand prize of the "space race" was putting a human on the moon. United States astronaut Neil Armstrong won that honor on July 20, 1969.

Social Changes

Many social changes came to the United States during the period from the late 1940s to the late 1970s. In the 1950s the automobile changed the face of America. No longer did people have to live near their places of work. Those who lived and worked in the city could move to less-crowded places. This migration of city residents caused the rapid growth of suburbs.

In the years after World War II, American cities became ringed by seemingly endless housing developments carved out of the less densely settled country land. Shopping centers with vast parking lots were built to serve the new suburban population. Businesses and factories also began relocating from the cities to the suburbs, where their workers now lived. The Highway Act of 1956 contributed to the growth of the suburbs by adding 41,000 miles (66,000 km) to the interstate highway system.

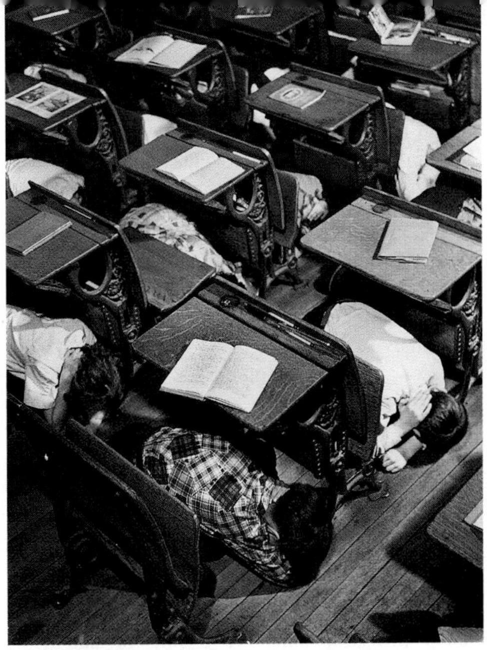

Visualizing History **Cold war tensions and fear of nuclear attack led to "duck and cover" drills in public schools.** *How did the government react to the fear of the "enemy within"?*

In addition to the automobile, another symbol of American prosperity was the television set. In 1945, fewer than 1 in every 20,000 people had a television. But within a few years, televisions were everywhere, and they were almost as common as telephones. Some critics worried that television would make Americans desire entertainment more than solid information. However, other experts pointed out the positive impact of television in making people directly aware of national and international events.

The Cold War at Home

Despite this time of prosperity, the cold war created deep political divisions in the United States. During the late 1940s and early 1950s, conservatives blamed President Harry S Truman and State Department officials for allowing the Communists to make gains in Eastern Europe and Asia. They also charged that Communists were serving in high government positions. A "red scare" swept the country. The growing fear of the "enemy within"—of subversion within the United States government and society—helped to launch a controversial anti-Communist crusade to discover and expose

Chapter 32
Section 4

TEACH

Guided Practice

THEME **Cooperation**
The United States and Canada have had a cooperative relationship throughout the twentieth century. What factors have served to promote this relationship? *(geographic proximity, a common language, and similar political and social institutions based on British models)* **L1 LEP**

Visualizing History In the late 1950s, some Americans called for the construction of an extensive network of fallout shelters to protect civilians in case of atomic attack. Congress and state legislatures, however, refused to appropriate the massive funds needed.
Answer to Caption: *Congress investigated suspected Communists, and many people lost their jobs.*

Daily Life Fear of Communist influence was very strong in American society during the cold war years. Ask students whether they think attitudes are different today, and if so, why. **L2**

ABC NEWS INTERACTIVE™

VIDEODISC
Turning Points in World History

Side Two, Chapter 8
Title: *The Moon Landing*
Ask: Who was aboard *Apollo 11* in 1969 when it headed to the moon? *(Neil Armstrong, Edwin "Buzz" Aldrin, and Michael Collins)*

COOPERATIVE LEARNING ACTIVITY

The Anti-Communist Crusade Organize the class into small groups, one for each year from 1947 through 1954, the years of the post-World War II "red scare." Have each group research and report on relevant anti-Communist activities in its year. Then have groups work together to agree on a format to present their information; suggest either radio or TV reports. **L3**

ABCNEWS INTERACTIVE™

VIDEODISC
Communism and the Cold War

Side One, Chapter 11
Frames 20050–21335
Title: *Communists in Our Midst: McCarthyism*
Ask: How were Americans who believed in Communist ideas treated in the 1940s and 1950s? *(They were investigated, shunned, and considered treasonous.)*

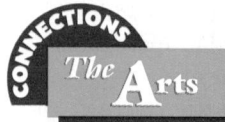

CONNECTIONS The Arts

Abstract Painting

European abstract painting of the early 1900s tended to be cool and geometrical. What was new in the 1940s, when American painters set the trend, was a heightened, energetic emotionalism—in other words, abstract *expressionism*. While some artists dripped paint on canvas (Pollock), others experimented with wild colors (Willem de Kooning) or used thin washes that allowed the canvas to show through (Mark Rothko).

Answers to Making the Connection

1. *It was a highly emotional form of abstract (nonobjective) painting.*
2. *Answers will vary but might include dissatisfaction with realism and reaction against European traditions.*

suspected Communists. The search was concentrated on diplomats, intellectuals, liberals, and other leaders of public opinion whose views could be interpreted as sympathetic toward, or even tolerant of, communism.

Congressional Investigations

Both houses of Congress set up panels to investigate suspected Communists. In 1947, the House Committee on Un-American Activities held hearings on suspected Communist influence in the entertainment industry and in labor unions. As a result, several well-known writers were jailed or found their careers ruined.

The Senate Committee on Investigation was headed by Senator Joseph McCarthy of Wisconsin. In the early 1950s, McCarthy charged there was a vast Communist conspiracy within the State Department and called government employees before the committee to defend themselves. He never proved a single case. But the climate of opinion was such that the accusation alone was enough to label someone a Communist, and many lost their jobs. The term *McCarthyism* came to mean the leveling of public accusations of political subversion without regard to evidence.

Forming Alliances

Between the 1950s and the 1980s, the cold war influenced national political campaigns, and many aspects of domestic policy, as well as most major foreign policy decisions of the United States. In its dealings with Eastern Europe, Africa, the Middle East, Latin America, and Asia, the United States saw its diplomacy as an extension of the struggle against communism.

During the 1950s, the United States expanded the nation's network of alliances in order to contain communism. In Western Europe, the Americans took a leading role in NATO. In Southeast Asia, the United States helped to create the Southeast Asian Treaty Organization (SEATO). In the Middle East, the United States counted on the cooperation of the Central Treaty Organization (CENTO), and in Latin America, the United States promoted the Organization of American States (OAS). These alliances created a formidable counterbalance to the influence of the Soviet Union.

Military Buildup

When necessary, American Presidents also used espionage and military power to fight the cold war. During the 1950s, the effort to contain

CONNECTIONS The Arts

Abstract Painting

Abstract expressionism was a movement in American painting that flourished from the mid-1940s to the mid-1950s. Abstract expressionist artists rejected many of the rules of earlier art. Instead of showing recognizable subject matter in their works, they emphasized the techniques or basic elements of painting, such as color, brushstrokes, lines, and shapes.

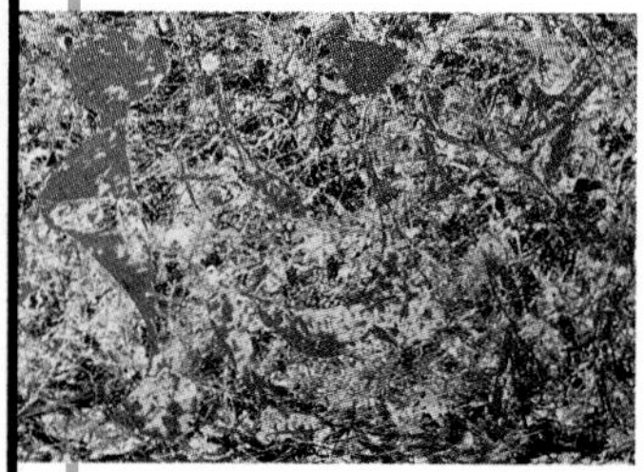
Out of the Web *by Jackson Pollock*

One of the important abstract expressionist painters was Jackson Pollock. His usual painting technique involved placing a huge canvas on the floor and then dripping paint from above onto it. The drippings formed sweeping, rhythmic patterns that seemed to move across the surface. About his highly unusual method of painting, Pollock said, "I feel nearer, more a part of the painting, since this way I can walk around it, work from the four sides, and literally be in the painting."

Although abstract expressionist styles differed, all of the artists in the movement believed that art should express immediate personal feelings and attitudes toward life. Their nontraditional, revolutionary approach to art influenced painters throughout the world.

MAKING THE CONNECTION

1. How did abstract expressionist painting differ from traditional forms of art?
2. Why do you think abstract expressionist art developed in the United States during the cold war era?

MEETING SPECIAL NEEDS ACTIVITY

Mixed Learners List on the chalkboard some key terms that occur in this section, including all or some of the following: *baby boom, computers, television, Communist subversion, McCarthyism, abstract expressionism, military-industrial complex, teach-ins, Vietnamization, Watergate scandal.* Have students define each term and tell why it is relevant to a discussion of the cold war period. **L2 LEP**

communism, strongly backed by the American public, caused the United States to send troops to fight Communist forces in Korea. It also led President **Dwight D. Eisenhower** in 1954 to agree to shoulder France's efforts to stop Communist military activity in **Vietnam**. The United States engaged in an unprecedented military buildup during this time, even during the cold war "thaw" in the late 1950s.

By the closing months of his presidency, Dwight D. Eisenhower, though a proponent of a strong military, was deeply concerned about the global arms race, or the competition between the superpowers for new and better weapons. On leaving office in 1960, he warned of a growing "military-industrial complex" in the United States. The American fear of communism, the armed services' enthusiasm for sophisticated weapons, and the large profits earned by weapons manufacturers had created a built-in incentive to increase military spending and build more machines of war.

Nuclear Battlefield

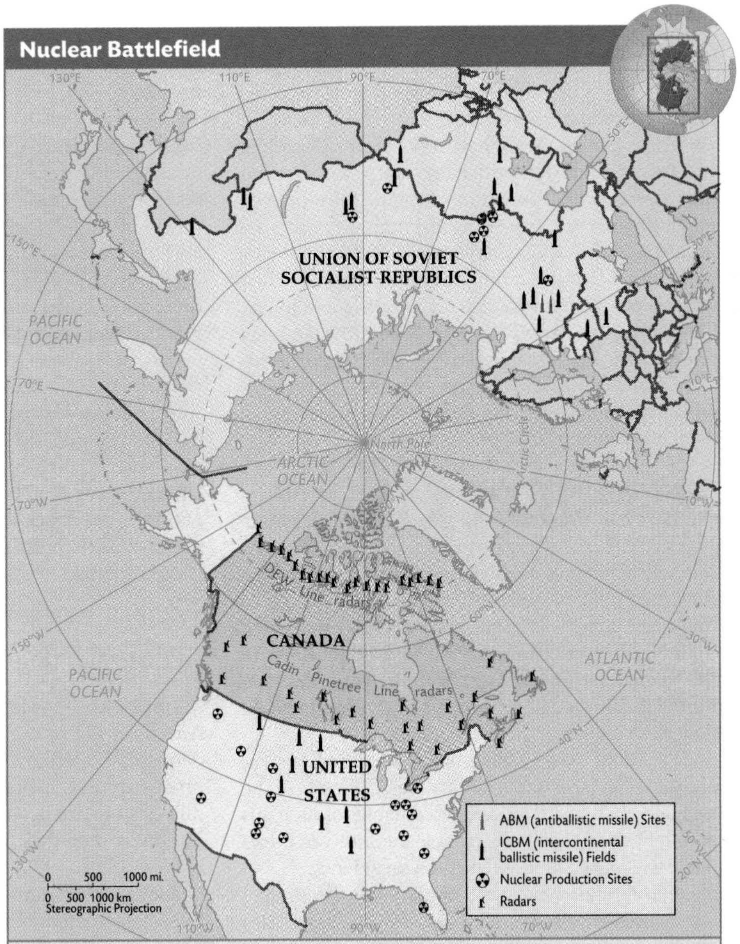

Map Study By the 1980s the United States and the Soviet Union each had more than 12,000 ICBMS aimed at the other. The Distant Early Warning Line (DEW Line)was a radar system built in 1957 to detect incoming missiles. It was replaced in 1994 with a more sophisticated North Warning System.

Region Why were DEW Line radars placed in northern Canada rather than along the east and west coasts of the United States?

Battle of Ideas

John F. Kennedy, a young senator from Massachusetts, succeeded Eisenhower as President in 1961. During the 1960 presidential race, Kennedy had campaigned on the theme of restoring the strength and prestige the United States had lost after the embarrassments of the U-2 spying incident and *Sputnik*.

Kennedy engaged in cold-war maneuvering on several fronts. He acted quickly to create the Peace Corps, a program that sent young American volunteers overseas to help impoverished countries that were open to Communist influence. Kennedy's cold-war views influenced his actions in several major foreign policy crises, including the building of the Berlin Wall and the Cuban missile crisis.

The Vietnam War

Kennedy's assassination in 1963 brought **Lyndon B. Johnson** to the White House. Johnson supported civil rights laws and reforms in education and social welfare to achieve what he

Chapter 32 Section 4

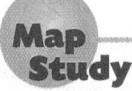

Map Study

Answer

the most direct path of the missiles would be over the North Pole

Map Skills Practice

Reading a Map Why are the Soviet Union's missile sites located mostly on its western borders? *(located near Europe and NATO forces)*

Independent Practice

Guided Reading Activity 32-4

Who?What?Where?When?

Eleanor Roosevelt A moderate voice in the controversial postwar period was that of Eleanor Roosevelt, who continued her public career after the death of her husband, Franklin, in 1945. As a member of the UN Commission on Human Rights, she tried to meet the Russians halfway. "All of us are going to die together or we are going to learn to live together," she said, "and if we are to live together we have to talk."

Biography Have students research and report on some of the most popular television performers of the medium's early days, such as Milton Berle, Sid Caesar, and Lucille Ball. **L2**

MAKING CONNECTIONS ACTIVITIES

Military History One of the most notorious incidents of the Vietnam War was the My Lai massacre of 1968. Have students research and report on the event and on the subsequent trial of William L. Calley, Jr., the American officer accused of responsibility for it. **L2**

Architecture Few war monuments have moved and inspired Americans as much as the Vietnam Veterans Memorial in Washington, D.C. Have students research and report on this structure: who designed it, what it looks like, when it was dedicated, and the controversy about its design. If possible, they should include illustrations to show the class or post on the bulletin board. **L2**

Chapter 32 *The Cold War* **885**

Chapter 32
Section 4

ABCNEWS INTERACTIVE™

VIDEODISC
Communism and the Cold War

Side Two, Chapter 8
Frames 18729–22891
Title: *Vietnam War*
Ask: In what way did the United States view Vietnam as a conflict not between North and South Vietnam but rather between the United States and the Soviet Union? *(The United States believed they were also fighting the Soviet Union because of the Soviet military and economic support for North Vietnam.)*

Who?What?Where?When?

Jackson State Another antiwar demonstration against the bombing of Cambodia also had tragic results. At Jackson State College in Mississippi, police fired on a women's dormitory, killing 2 students and wounding 12. After this incident, more than 125 colleges suspended classes for a week.

you don't say...

Hawks and doves are terms that were used widely in the 1960s. Supporters of the Vietnam War were called hawks, while opponents were known as doves. The use of *hawk* to describe a warlike person goes back to the War of 1812. Doves have long been thought of as peaceful; the symbolism was reinforced by a poster by Pablo Picasso that was popular during the 1950s and 1960s.

called the Great Society. However, the consuming issue during Johnson's five years in office became the Vietnam War, in which the United States assisted South Vietnam in resisting a Communist takeover.

American involvement in Vietnam, described in Chapter 33, began under Presidents Eisenhower and Kennedy and grew out of their desire to keep communism from spreading throughout Southeast Asia. During the Eisenhower and Kennedy years, American civilian and military advisers had arrived in Vietnam to aid the South Vietnamese. The role of the United States in the Southeast Asian nation was later expanded into full-scale participation by President Johnson. During Johnson's administration, large numbers of American combat soldiers were sent to fight in Vietnam.

Opposition to the War

By 1968, domestic opposition to the Vietnam War had become widespread, and Vietnam became the central issue in the presidential race of that year. President Johnson, condemned for his handling of the lengthy, costly, and indecisive war, decided not to run for reelection. Former Vice President **Richard M. Nixon**, a strong anti-Communist, won the election with his pledge to stop the war and to restore American self-esteem.

President Nixon soon found that ending the war and "saving face" for America was difficult. As he struggled to find a politically acceptable solution, his administration was besieged by the antiwar forces that had overwhelmed Johnson's presidency.

Young men who were eligible for the draft—the mandatory enrollment in the United States armed services—burned their draft cards, which was an illegal act. Many young men fled to Canada to avoid the draft, choosing to spend years in exile from their families and country rather than fight in the war. Demonstrators marched in front of the White House, carrying signs and shouting antiwar slogans. College professors cancelled classes and held antiwar protests called "teach-ins." Most protests across the country were peaceful, but many incidents of violence occurred, including the bombing of military facilities and other institutions that symbolized America's political and military power.

Ending the War

President Nixon's plans for ending the war respectably for the United States was called "Vietnamization"—a gradual withdrawal of American troops while handing over control of war operations to South Vietnam. In a November 1969 speech, the President tried to counter the antiwar protests by appealing to what he called the silent majority of Americans whom he said supported his policies.

Simultaneously with the American withdrawal from Vietnam, Nixon ordered fierce bombing raids on neighboring **Cambodia**. The bombings prompted renewed protests, creating a superheated atmosphere of anger and distrust between supporters and opponents of the war. The situation exploded tragically in May 1970, when National Guard soldiers fired into a crowd of demonstrators at Kent State University in Ohio, killing four students.

In 1973, the last of the active American forces withdrew from Vietnam, and the Paris Accords were signed. Of the 500,000 United States troops that had fought in Southeast Asia, about 58,000 died and 365,000 were wounded. The war cost the United States $150 billion. In addition, it made the nation more cautious of foreign involvement and shook world confidence in United States military commitments.

Struggle for Civil Rights

Even as the cold war was shaping so much of American life in the 1950s and 1960s, other issues demanded attention. Despite the general economic prosperity of the United States after World War II, millions of Americans continued to live in poverty. The poor included members of all ethnic groups, but the plight of the nation's poor in the African American community seemed especially critical. Ever since emancipation in the 1860s, African Americans in both the North and the South had faced discrimination in jobs, housing, education, and other areas. After World War II, an increasing number of Americans realized that continuing poverty and racial discrimination were at odds with the basic American values of equality and justice for all. A civil rights movement begun by African Americans in the early 1900s gained momentum and affected many areas of American life.

Changing Social Attitudes

Changing social attitudes helped civil rights advances. The war against Germany played a part. The horrifying racism of the Nazis helped to make some Americans more sensitive to racism in their own country. They began to realize that not only African Americans, but also Asian Americans, Hispanic Americans, and other ethnic groups had been treated unfairly and denied social and educational opportunities.

CRITICAL THINKING ACTIVITY

Making Comparisons Write two headings on the chalkboard, *United States* and *Canada*. Under each, have students enter data given in this section, supplemented by research in reference works. Data should include size, population, major resources, and main ethnic groups. **L2**

Court Decisions

During the 1940s and 1950s, African Americans worked hard to gain civil rights. The war years saw the membership of the National Association for the Advancement of Colored People (NAACP) increase from 100,000 to 351,000. In the late 1940s, the NAACP hired teams of able lawyers to bring a series of lawsuits to the federal courts to end violations of the constitutional rights of African American citizens.

This effort resulted in several United States Supreme Court decisions that attacked discrimination. In the best known case, *Brown* v. *Board of Education of Topeka, Kansas* (1954), the United States Supreme Court ruled that racial segregation, or the separation of the races, in public schools was illegal. President Eisenhower used federal agencies to enforce the Court's decision.

Martin Luther King, Jr.

In the following years, the civil rights movement broadened and changed tactics. **Martin Luther King, Jr.**, a Baptist minister, advocated the use of nonviolent sit-ins and marches to focus attention on discrimination in housing, public facilities, and voting. Media coverage of the segregationist opposition to the movement's efforts helped convince many Americans of the injustice of discrimination.

In 1963, more than 200,000 African Americans, whites, and people of other ethnic groups converged on Washington, D.C., for the largest civil rights demonstration in the nation's history. At the Lincoln Memorial, the marchers heard eloquent speeches, especially from Martin Luther King, Jr., who, in a famous address, described his dream of freedom and equality for all people:

> "I have a dream that one day this nation will rise up and live out the true meaning of its creed: 'We hold these truths to be self-evident; that all men are created equal'.... And when this happens, and when we allow freedom to ring, when we let it ring from every village and hamlet, from every state and every city, we will be able to speed up that day when all God's children ... [will] join hands and sing in the words of the old ... spiritual: 'Free at last, Free at last, Thank God Almighty, we're free at last.'"

The civil rights movement peaked in the 1960s with the passage of major civil rights laws under President Johnson. These measures banned discrimination in public places and education as well as strengthening the right to vote. In addition to helping African Americans, the civil rights legislation also advanced opportunities for other groups, such as Hispanic Americans.

After Martin Luther King, Jr.'s assassination in 1968, the civil rights movement faced the loss or delay of some of its hard-won gains. Beginning in the late 1960s, much of the United States government's social policies shifted to the right, away from earlier liberal policies. However, despite the setback, the movement for civil rights continued. It strongly influenced other groups in the United States—women, Hispanic Americans, and Native Americans—that wanted better opportunities and social equality. It also was an inspiration to civil rights groups in other parts of the world.

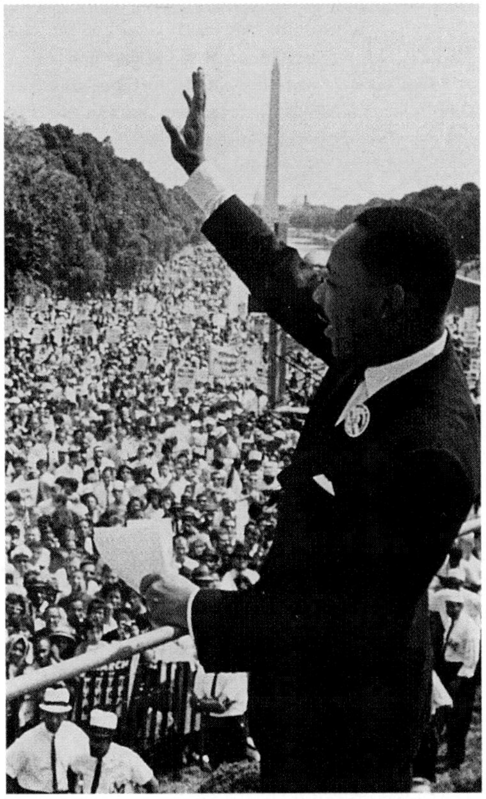

Visualizing History **Dr. Martin Luther King, Jr., spoke to more than 200,000 people on the 100th anniversary of the Emancipation Proclamation.** *What civil rights did legislation in the 1960s address?*

Chapter 32 Section 4

Biography The career of Senator Joseph McCarthy was relatively short. Have students write a brief account of when and why McCarthy's career came to an end. **L2**

Report Two notable trials of the cold war era were those of Alger Hiss, accused of Communist ties, and Julius and Ethel Rosenberg, convicted of spying for Russia. Have students research and report on one of these trials. **L3**

CURRICULUM CONNECTION

SCIENCE

A great scientific breakthrough of the cold war period was the conquest of polio. This disease had menaced both children and adults all over the world for centuries. (Franklin D. Roosevelt was one of its most prominent victims.) An inoculation, pioneered by Jonas Salk, was pronounced safe in 1955. An oral vaccine, developed by Albert Sabin, was approved in 1961. Today polio has been all but eliminated globally.

Visualizing History

King came to prominence in 1955, when African Americans in Montgomery, Alabama, began a boycott against the local bus company, which practiced discrimination in seating and hiring. **Answer to Caption:** *the right to vote, the right to education, and the use of public accommodations without discrimination*

MORE ABOUT...

The Civil Rights Struggle Students and other young people played a key role in the civil rights struggle. In 1960 college students in North Carolina organized the first sit-ins, occupying seats at a segregated lunch counter as a form of protest. The following year many students took part in freedom rides, demonstrating against segregated buses. In 1964 three young men—two white (Michael Schwerner and Andrew Goodman) and one black (James Chaney)—were murdered while organizing voter registration in Mississippi.

Chapter 32 Section 4

Visualizing History The embargo affected many sectors of the American economy, from home heating to a range of products that depended on petroleum—synthetic fabrics, plastics, cosmetics, and even toothpaste. **Answer to Caption:** *It made them rise.*

Who?What?Where?When?

Accidental Executives When Gerald Ford became President, he named Nelson Rockefeller, former governor of New York, as his Vice President. For the first time in history, the two Chief Executives of the United States occupied their offices by appointment rather than by election.

ABCNEWS INTERACTIVE™

VIDEODISC
Lessons of War

Side Two, Chapter 6
Frames 12636–20751
Title: *Philosophy of Nonviolence*
Subject: The philosophies of Mohandas Gandhi and Martin Luther King, Jr., and how their philosophies were used in protests and demonstrations
Ask: For what cause did Martin Luther King, Jr., peacefully protest? *(civil rights)*

Visualizing History **Long lines formed at gasoline stations because of shortages when OPEC placed an embargo on oil exports.** *How did the embargo affect the prices of other goods?*

The Changing Presidency

During the cold war, United States Presidents gradually began to exercise powers beyond those spelled out in the United States Constitution. Claiming a need for a quick military response to counter communism, Presidents began to assume the war-making powers of Congress, committing American military forces to combat without congressional approval. The two largest commitments to undeclared wars were in Korea and Vietnam.

The Imperial Presidency

As the cold war continued into the 1960s and 1970s, many people felt that the increased presidential power was subject to abuses and a violation of the Constitution. The term **imperial presidency** came into use, reflecting this concern.

The term was most often applied to Presidents Lyndon B. Johnson and Richard M. Nixon, both of whom expanded the conflict in Vietnam without a congressional declaration of war, as called for in the Constitution, and often kept their actions secret from Congress. In 1973 Congress overrode Nixon's veto to pass the War Powers Limitation Act. The measure required the President to consult Congress before committing United States troops to combat.

The Watergate Scandal

Political scandals rocked the United States during the 1970s. Investigations revealed many cases of corruption in local and state government, but the country's attention focused primarily on charges of corruption in the federal government. Early in President Nixon's second term, scandal engulfed his administration. Vice President Spiro Agnew was accused of taking bribes when he was governor of Maryland and was forced to resign. Then the President himself came under fire in a scandal that became known as Watergate.

The Watergate scandal began on June 17, 1972, when five men were caught trying to plant electronic listening devices in the offices of the Democratic National Committee, located in the Watergate building in downtown **Washington, D.C.** The break-in was traced to Nixon's reelection committee.

A congressional probe revealed that the White House knew of the burglary and tried to cover it up. The President denied the charges at first, but tape recordings of Oval Office conversations proved that he had participated in the cover-up. Under the threat of impeachment, Nixon resigned on August 9, 1974. He was the first United States President ever to do so.

Gerald R. Ford, the Republican congressman from Michigan who had replaced Spiro Agnew as Vice President, became President when Nixon stepped down. Ford was the first United States President not to have been elected to either of the nation's top two offices. He assumed a presidency that had been weakened and tarnished. Watergate had shaken public confidence in the American political system. In addition, Ford had no personal mandate from the voters, since he had not been elected. As a former congressman, Ford maintained close ties with Congress. That, coupled with his acknowledged personal integrity, enabled him to function effectively. Both Ford and his Democratic successor, **Jimmy Carter**, a former governor of Georgia, worked to restore ethics to the presidency. In addition, as a result of Watergate, the media became far more vigilant in pursuing wrong-doing of public officials.

The Economy

During the late 1960s and 1970s, the United States economy was buffeted by the effects of the cold war and a changing world economy. The country suffered serious inflation in the 1970s as a result of the costs of the Vietnam War and increased

888 Chapter 32 *The Cold War*

TEACHER NOTES

government spending for social programs. Administrations and congressional leaders were reluctant to offset spiraling costs with either cuts in programs or tax increases. Meanwhile, inflation combined with high unemployment to produce an economic trend called **stagflation**. Low productivity in factories and increased competition from foreign companies also slowed the American economy.

Soaring gas prices were part of an energy crisis that crippled economies around the world during the 1970s. In the United States, rapid economic growth had been dependent on cheap, abundant oil. Wanting to gain from increased world oil prices, OPEC (Organization of Petroleum Exporting Countries) countries in 1973 refused to ship oil to foreign customers. This oil **embargo** was damaging to American—and world—economic stability because it increased the cost of producing a wide range of goods.

Sharp rises in the price of oil and gasoline contributed to **double-digit inflation**, or a rise in the general level of prices of 10 percent or more. By 1980 it cost more than $200 to purchase the same goods that $100 would have bought only 10 years earlier. At the same time, the United States government raised interest rates to all-time highs in an effort to discourage borrowing and bring the economy under control. These policies helped reduce inflation but caused a severe recession.

During the 1970s, the United States also experienced a **trade deficit**, or importing more goods than it was exporting, and the steady loss of American jobs. As other nations in the world became more industrialized, they began to compete with American companies for sales to American consumers. In the late 1970s for example, rising gasoline prices led Americans to buy more fuel efficient Japanese cars rather than larger American cars. The shift of American factories abroad to take advantage of cheaper, talented labor also had a chilling impact on the employment situation in the United States.

Canada

Canada thrived economically after World War II. By 1960, it had changed from a primarily agricultural country to one of the world's most important industrial nations. Like the United States, production in Canada boomed after World War II as consumers demanded household goods and new homes. The exploitation of Canada's rich mineral resources also enabled the Canadian economy to flourish. Foreign investors, mainly from the neighboring United States, financed the development of many new industries.

Improved communications and transportation strengthened Canada's trade links with the United States. One significant joint venture of both countries in the 1950s was the completion of the **St. Lawrence Seaway**, a system of locks and canals that allows ships to travel between the Great Lakes and the Atlantic Ocean.

Canada's World Role

Traditionally linked to Great Britain, Canada's loyalties to the parent country gradually diminished as British global influence plummeted after World War II. Canada's new and growing economic strength convinced many Canadians that their country needed to play a more active, independent role in world affairs. In 1945, Canada became a founding member of the United Nations and sent troops to Korea as part of the UN forces in 1950. Canada also joined NATO when it was formed in 1949. During the 1950s, cold war tensions brought the United States and Canada into a close defensive partnership.

In pursuing their foreign policy, Canadians were suspicious of a world dominated by superpowers. Over time, Canada advanced a role for itself as a **middle power**—that is, one that is strong economically, if not militarily. The Canadians used what military strength they had to promote peace. In 1956, Canada helped to bring about peace in the Middle East after Great Britain, France, and Israel had invaded Egypt. **Lester B. Pearson**, Canada's secretary of state for external affairs, won the 1957 Nobel Peace Prize for proposing and organizing a UN peacekeeping force for the troubled area.

A National Identity

In internal affairs, Canada struggled to find its own national identity during the period after World War II. While breaking many of their traditional ties to Europe, Canadians found themselves increasingly influenced by American ideas and practices. Most Canadians favored a continued close relationship to the United States. However, there were growing concerns that the "Americanization" of Canada posed a threat to Canada's newly emerging culture. In 1963, Pearson became Canada's prime minister. His administration expanded the country's social welfare programs and worked to strengthen Canadian national identity. Pearson achieved a personal goal when the Canadian parliament in 1965 adopted a new national flag, one that featured a red maple leaf as a symbol of Canada. The maple leaf soon became very popular

Global Gourmet

United States An American innovation that has spread around the world is the fast-food restaurant. From humble origins in hot-dog stands in the 1950s, fast-food outlets began to grow into a multibillion-dollar industry. Although their staple fare has been the American hamburger with fries and soft drinks, they now sell everything from minestrone soup to burritos. One of the factors encouraging fast-food growth has been an increase in the number of women who work outside the home.

Who?What?Where?When?

Ice Hockey More than 25 countries now play ice hockey, a game that originated in Canada. The sport began in military garrisons in the 1800s, when soldiers had time—and a lot of winter weather—on their hands.

ASSESS

Check for Understanding

Assign Section 4 Review as homework or as an in-class activity.

Use Student Self-Test and Review Software to review Section 4.

TEACHER NOTES

Visualizing History In a referendum held in Quebec in 1995, citizens narrowly defeated a proposal that would have led to independence for the province.

Answer to Caption: *Sixty-five percent are of British or French descent, and the rest come from many different backgrounds.*

Evaluate

Section Quiz 32-4

Use the Testmaker to create a customized quiz for Section 4.

Reteach

Have students brainstorm a list of similarities and differences between the experiences of the United States and Canada during the cold war years.

Reteaching Activity 32

Enrich

Have students view one or more episodes of *Eyes on the Prize*, the public television series about the civil rights movement. Then have them describe their reactions to the video.

Enrichment Activity 32

CLOSE

Have students discuss which they think was the most important event or development in the United States and in Canada during the cold war period.

Visualizing History **The movement for an independent Quebec continued to gain strength through the 1990s.** *How ethnically diverse is the population of Canada?*

among Canadians, who for years had honored some form of the Union Jack, or the British flag, as their national flag.

In 1967, Pearson presided over celebrations marking Canada's 100th anniversary of its nationhood. Many Canadians were especially proud of the fact that Canada had become a **multicultural** country, made up of people from many different ethnic groups. From 1945 to 1956, more than a million people from Germany, Italy, and other war-torn European countries had moved to farms or to **Toronto**, **Montreal**, and other large Canadian cities. In addition, other Canadians claimed Native American, Asian, African, or Latin American ancestry. Canada's two major ethnic groups, however, were still people of British descent, who make up about 35 percent of the population, and those of French descent, who make up about 30 percent.

Separatism

While celebrating their nationhood, Canadians also faced a growing challenge to their country's unity. During the 1960s, French Canadians began a movement to defend their rights throughout Canada. They also wanted English-speaking Canadians to recognize and respect their culture in the province of **Quebec**, where 80 percent of the people are French-speaking.

A growing debate arose over the issue of **separatism**, a movement favoring the establishment of Quebec as an independent country. The issue gave rise to the Parti Quebecois (kay•beh•KWAH), or Quebec party, sometimes known as the Separatist party. Opposing the separatist drive for Quebec independence was Canadian Prime Minister **Pierre Elliott Trudeau**, himself a French Canadian, who had been elected to office in 1968. Trudeau promised to protect French Canadian language and cultural rights while supporting a strong united Canada. In 1969, he had the Canadian parliament pass the Official Languages Act. This law required federal government offices to provide service in both French and English if 10 percent of the people in a particular area spoke either language.

The Official Languages Act brought many changes to Canada's government. However, it had little effect on the growing separatist movement. In 1976, the Parti Quebecois won control of Quebec's government and declared French the province's official language. It also promised to hold an election to decide Quebec's future.

SECTION 4 REVIEW

Recall

1. **Define** automation, racial segregation, imperial presidency, stagflation, embargo, double-digit inflation, trade deficit, middle power, multicultural, separatism.
2. **Identify** Dwight D. Eisenhower, John F. Kennedy, Lyndon B. Johnson, Richard M. Nixon, Martin Luther King, Jr., Gerald R. Ford, Jimmy Carter, Lester B. Pearson, Pierre Elliott Trudeau.
3. **Describe** the Supreme Court ruling in *Brown* v. *Board of Education of Topeka, Kansas.*

Critical Thinking

4. **Analyzing Information** Why did President Eisenhower believe that the military-industrial complex was dangerous? Has his warning been borne out by history?

Understanding Themes

5. **Cooperation** Why did the United States and Canada develop close ties after 1945?

SECTION 4 REVIEW ANSWERS

1. All vocabulary words are defined in the Glossary.
2. Dwight D. Eisenhower, 885; John F. Kennedy, 885; Lyndon B. Johnson, 885; Richard M. Nixon, 886; Martin Luther King, Jr., 887; Gerald R. Ford, 888; Lester B. Pearson, 889; Pierre Elliott Trudeau, 890
3. This decision held that racial segregation in public schools was unconstitutional.
4. He believed that it created an incentive to increase military spending and expand the arms race. Answers will vary.
5. **COOPERATION** As Canada's ties with Europe weakened, its relationship with the United States intensified.

Critical Thinking SKILLS

Understanding World Time Zones

Imagine that you work in an office in New Jersey. Your boss asks you to place a telephone call to a client in London. At 2:00 P.M. you place the call, but no one answers. Why? When it is 2:00 P.M. in New Jersey, it is already 7:00 P.M. in London. The times differ because the world is divided into time zones.

Learning the Skill

In 1884 an international conference established standard time zones around the world. The Prime Meridian (0° longitude), which runs through Greenwich, England, became the reference point for measuring time. The conference divided the world into 24 time zones, each 15° of longitude apart. Traveling east from Greenwich, the time is one hour later in each time zone. Traveling west from Greenwich, the time is one hour earlier.

The conference also established the International Date Line at 180° longitude. When crossing this line from west to east, you lose one day; when crossing in the opposite direction, you gain a day.

The map on this page illustrates the world time zones. To use this map, locate a reference point and note its time. Then locate the place for which you wish to know the time. Determine whether this place lies east or west of the reference point. Then count the number of time zones and add or subtract as needed. If the International Date Line lies between two points, add or subtract a day.

Practicing the Skill

Use the map to calculate these times.

1. If it is 3:00 P.M. in Greenwich, what time is it in Moscow?
2. If it is 9:00 A.M. in Cape Town, what time is it in Washington, D.C.?
3. If it is Tuesday, 4:30 P.M. in Japan, what day and time is it in Honolulu?
4. If it is Friday, 8:15 A.M. in Rio de Janeiro, what day and time is it in Beijing?

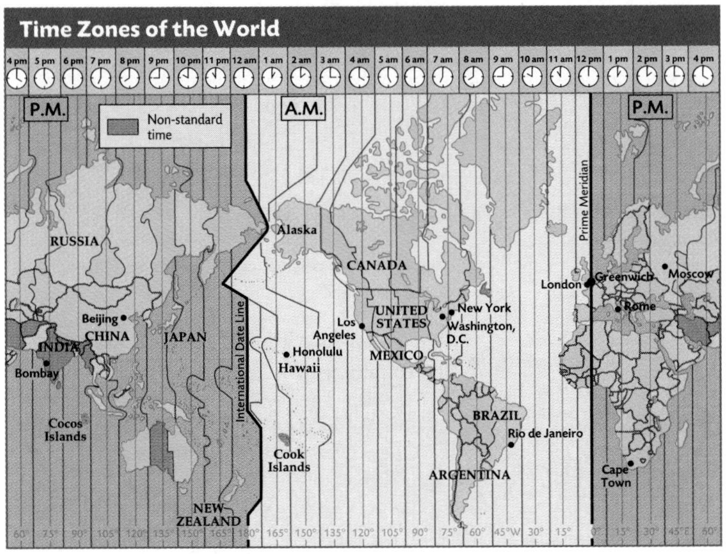

Applying the Skill

Make up four time zone problems and compute the answers. Exchange your problems with a friend. See who can answer them most quickly.

For More Practice

Turn to the Skill Practice in the Chapter Review on page 893 for more practice in understanding world time zones.

Critical Thinking SKILLS

TEACH

Understanding World Time Zones
Point out that the United States has had standard time zones only since 1883, when they were instituted by America's railroads, which found the 100 different time zones in that era too difficult to cope with. Have students use the hour your class begins and then figure out what the time would be in the following places: Washington, D.C.; Toronto, Ontario; Budapest, Hungary; and Cairo, Egypt.

Additional Practice

Skill Reinforcement Activity 32

Building Skills in Geography Workbook, Unit 1, Lesson 10

ANSWERS TO PRACTICING THE SKILL

1. 5 P.M.
2. 3 A.M.
3. Students will either answer Monday, 9:00 P.M. or Monday, 9:30 P.M. depending on which Japanese island student is using to count.
4. Saturday, 6:15 P.M.

Chapter 32 Review

GLENCOE TECHNOLOGY

VIDEODISC

Use MindJogger to review students' knowledge of the chapter.

MindJogger Videoquiz

Chapter 32
Disc 4 Side B

Also available in VHS.

CHAPTER 32 REVIEW

Historical Significance

The cold war between the United States and the Soviet Union divided Europe and the large areas of the rest of the world into two camps. Long-range nuclear weapons made the superpowers' quarrel dangerous because of the threat of nuclear war that would destroy civilization.

Gradually, this realization compelled the superpowers to seek ways of reducing tensions. Ultimately, the economic strength and democratic principles of the United States and Western Europe undermined communism and stimulated demands for change within the Communist bloc.

Using Key Terms

Write the key term that completes each sentence.

a. cold war	g. dissidents
b. containment	h. separatism
c. ICBMs	i. racial segregation
d. iron curtain	j. imperial presidency
e. welfare states	k. peaceful coexistence
f. stagflation	l. middle power

1. After World War II, Great Britain and other Western European countries became ________ in which the government provided social programs for the well-being of their citizens.
2. The term ___________ referred to the Soviet-made barrier that divided Europe into non-Communist and Communist areas.
3. To counter any expansionist threat from the Soviet Union, the Truman administration in 1947 developed a policy known as ________.
4. During the Vietnam War era, historians referred to increased presidential powers not specified in the United States Constitution as the _____________.
5. In the 1970s, inflation combined with high unemployment to produce _________.
6. In its foreign policy, Canada after World War II aimed to be a ___________, a country that had economic, if not military, influence in world affairs.
7. In the ________, the superpowers competed with each other by means short of total war.
8. Nikita Khrushchev adopted a new policy toward the West known as ___________.
9. Soviet leader Leonid Brezhnev applied harsh measures to ___________ who criticized the Communist party or the Soviet government.
10. In *Brown v. Board of Education of Topeka, Kansas*, the United States Supreme Court ruled that _________ in public schools was illegal.

Using Your History Journal

From your notes on the interview with a person who remembers the events of the 1950s or early 1960s, write a newspaper feature piece titled "Living Through the Cold War."

Reviewing Facts

1. **Explain** the purpose of the Marshall Plan. In what ways was the plan effective?
2. **Explain** why Joseph Stalin ordered the Berlin blockade.
3. **List** the names of the Soviet satellite countries in Eastern Europe.
4. **Identify** the reforms that Dubček introduced in Czechoslovakia.
5. **Explain** the meaning of the term *McCarthyism*.
6. **Discuss** what happened at Kent State University in May 1970.

Critical Thinking

1. **Apply** What postwar developments launched the cold war?
2. **Analyze** In your view, why did the United States assume global responsibility for containing communism?
3. **Synthesize** The Western Allies saw the Soviet takeover of Eastern Europe as brutal aggression. Did the Soviets have any justification for their actions? Explain.
4. **Evaluate** Was Americans' fear of communism during the 1950s justified? Do you think the actions that Congress took to counter

Answers

Using Key Terms

1. e	6. l
2. d	7. a
3. b	8. k
4. j	9. g
5. f	10. i

Using Your History Journal

Students might organize their notes and/or tapes under such headings as *Politics*, *The Economy*, and *Daily Life*.

Reviewing Facts

1. It provided financial aid to Europe in order to further economic and political stability. It succeeded in spurring economic recovery.
2. to try to force the Western powers out of Berlin
3. Poland, East Germany, Czechoslovakia, Hungary, Romania, Bulgaria, and Albania
4. He eased censorship and allowed some political groups to meet freely.
5. publicly accusing people of political subversion without regard to evidence
6. National Guard troops killed four students demonstrating against the bombing of Cambodia.

Critical Thinking

1. the Soviet imposition of communism in Eastern Europe; the division of Germany; the Berlin blockade; the formation of military and economic alliances
2. because it was a democratic superpower, firmly opposed to the spread of communism
3. Answers will vary, but students may feel the Soviets had a right to establish a buffer zone between themselves and Western Europe, from which they had been invaded.
4. Some students may feel communism posed little threat to the United States; others may say the Soviet Union was engaged in aggression. Congressional actions seem inappropriate because they exposed minimal Communist danger while destroying many careers.
5. It heightened fears of Soviet intervention

communism were appropriate? Explain your reasoning.
5. **Apply** How do you think the cold war affected politics in Western European countries?
6. **Evaluate** the effect of Watergate on the United States presidency.
7. **Apply** Is the United States presidency today an imperial presidency? Why or why not?
8. **Apply** What was the major source of tension that led to the French Canadian separatist movement?

Understanding Themes

1. **Conflict** By the 1950s the superpowers had enough nuclear weapons to eliminate each other. What effect did this power have on superpower relations during the cold war?
2. **Change** What might have happened if the Soviet Union had not used force to keep its Eastern European satellite countries under control?
3. **Regionalism** How did the European Common Market benefit member countries?
4. **Cooperation** How did the foreign policy of Canada compare and contrast with that of the United States during the cold war era?

Linking Past and Present

1. Key cold war issues continued until about 1989, when they reached a dramatic conclusion. Name these issues and explain their link to recent events.
2. Name a previous period in history when Europe was united. When did the continent become fragmented again?
3. Is containment an important or pressing issue in American foreign policy today? Explain your reasoning.

Geography in History

1. **Location** Refer to the map of Berlin on this page. What side of the city of Berlin became the Soviet sector after World War II?
2. **Place** What nations maintained army headquarters in Berlin following the war?

Berlin After World War II

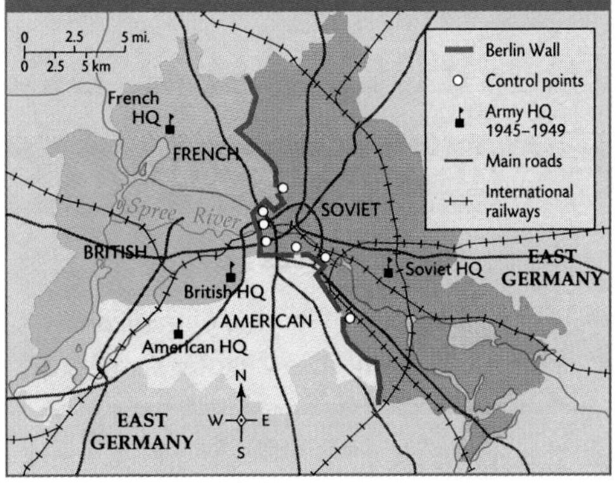

3. **Movement** Approximately how long was the wall that the Soviets built to keep East Germans from crossing to the West?
4. **Location** How many control points were located along the Berlin Wall?

Skill Practice

Refer to the map of World Time Zones on page 891 to answer the following questions.

1. In what areas of the world do you find nonstandard time?
2. You are in New York and you want to call someone in Rome, Italy, at noon Rome time. When would you call?
3. Assume that flying from New York to London requires 6 hours. When would a flight leaving New York on a Wednesday at 6:00 P.M. arrive in London?
4. You are flying from Los Angeles to Moscow. You leave Los Angeles at 10:00 A.M. on Saturday and you arrive in Moscow on Sunday at 9:00 A.M. How many hours did you actually spend flying?
5. You are planning a flight from Bombay, India, to Washington, D.C., that must connect through several cities. You will leave Bombay on August 2, at 8:00 A.M., and will continue directly through Beijing and Los Angeles to Washington, D.C. What time is it in Washington, D.C., when you begin your trip? What will be the date when you arrive in Washington, D.C.?

Chapter 32 Review

while encouraging moves toward European unity.
6. It led to a lessening of respect for the office on the part of the American people.
7. Some students may feel the President still has a great deal of power; others may say the system of checks and balances works to limit the presidency.
8. Quebecois fears that their culture would not be recognized and respected

Understanding Themes
1. **CONFLICT** Both sides, realizing that using nuclear weapons was unacceptable, sought ways to limit the arms race.
2. **CHANGE** broken away from its influence and become independent or allied themselves with the West
3. **REGIONALISM** It reduced conflict, lessened trade barriers, and helped raise the standard of living.
4. **COOPERATION** Although Canada, like the United States, joined the UN and NATO, it saw itself not as a superpower obliged to join the arms race but as a middle power and thus a peacekeeper.

Linking Past and Present
1. The iron curtain lifted and the Berlin Wall fell in 1989; Eastern Europe abandoned communism and instituted democratic reforms; the Warsaw Pact was dissolved.
2. Much of it was united under the Roman Empire. It became fragmented after the death of Charlemagne.
3. No, because the cold war is over and the threat of Soviet expansion appears to have ended.

Geography in History
1. east
2. France, Britain, United States, Soviet Union
3. approximately 26 miles (42 km)
4. 7

Skill Practice
1. Cook Islands, Newfoundland, Suriname, area north of Iceland, Saudi Arabia, Afghanistan, India and the Bay of Bengal, Cocos Islands, central Australia
2. 6:00 A.M.
3. 5:00 A.M. Wednesday
4. 12 hours
5. 10 P.M. August 1; August 2

Chapter Bonus Test Question

Ask students: Do you think the cold war could have been prevented? *(Yes, the West gave away too much at Yalta and/or that it should have acted quickly after Stalin's first takeovers in Eastern Europe; no, Stalin was willing to risk war to get what he wanted.)*

Teach, Reinforce, and Extend CHAPTER Content

Asia and the Pacific

CHAPTER RESOURCES

	Reproducible Resources	Multimedia Resources
Chapter Opener	Chapter Themes: Graphic Organizer 33 Historical Significance Chapter Activity 33	MindJogger Videoquiz
Chapter Enrichment	Vocabulary Activity 33* Time Line Activity 33 Mapping History Activity 33 History Simulation 33 Geography and History Activity 33 Source Reading 33 People in World History Profiles 63, 64 World Art and Music Activity 33 Enrichment Activity 33 Critical Thinking Activity 33 Skill Reinforcement Activity 33 Performance Assessment Activity 33	World History and Art Transparency 44, *Sydney Opera House* Mapping History Overlay Transparency 24 Chapter Transparency 33 Vocabulary PuzzleMaker Software World Music: Cultural Traditions, Lessons 7, 8, 9, 10 Lessons of War: *Philosophy of Nonviolence* Communism and the Cold War: • *Revolution in China* • *Korean War* • *Vietnam War* • *Tiananmen Square*
Chapter Review/Reteaching	Reteaching Activity 33 Skill Reinforcement Activity 33 Spanish Chapter Summary 33	Chapter 33 Digest Audiocassette, Activity, Test* Vocabulary PuzzleMaker Software Student Self-Test and Review Software MindJogger Videoquiz
Chapter Evaluation/Testing	Performance Assessment Activity 33 Chapter 33 Test, Forms A and B	Testmaker

* *Also available in Spanish*

0:00 **OUT OF TIME?** Assign the Chapter 33 summary in the Unit 8 Digest on pages 1026–1029, and the Chapter 33 Audiocassettes.

Block Schedule

Block scheduling differs from traditional class scheduling in the amount of time allotted to each period. The extended time frame provided by block scheduling affords you the opportunity to implement a greater number of research-oriented and activity-intense projects to motivate and involve your students. Activities that are particularly suited to use within the block scheduling framework are identified throughout this chapter by the following designation.

KEY TO ABILITY LEVELS

Teaching strategies have been coded for varying learning styles and abilities.

- **L1** **BASIC** activities for all students
- **L2** **AVERAGE** activities for average to above-average students
- **L3** **CHALLENGING** activities for above-average students
- **LEP** **LIMITED ENGLISH PROFICIENCY** activities

Chapter 33 Planning Guide

A complete, 1-page lesson plan is provided for each section in the *Reproducible Lesson Plans* booklet.

SECTION RESOURCES

Daily Objectives	Reproducible Resources	Multimedia Resources
Section 1 Japan's Economic Rise List the factors that have contribut-edto the economic success of Japan.	Reproducible Lesson Plan 33-1 Vocabulary Activity 33* Guided Reading Activity 33-1* History Simulation 33 Section Quiz 33-1*	Section Focus Transparency 33-1 Mapping History Overlay Transparency 24, *Trade Between the U.S. and Japan* Chapter Transparency 33 Student Self-Test and Review Software World Music: Cultural Traditions, Lesson 8
Section 2 China in Revolution Explain how communism has affected the domestic and international affairs of China since the late 1940s.	Reproducible Lesson Plan 33-2 Vocabulary Activity 33* Guided Reading Activity 33-2* Geography and History Activity 33 Section Quiz 33-2*	Section Focus Transparency 33-2 Student Self-Test and Review Software World Music: Cultural Traditions, Lesson 8 Communism and the Cold War
Section 3 A Divided Korea Describe how South Korea and North Korea have differed in their political and economic development.	Reproducible Lesson Plan 33-3 Vocabulary Activity 33* Guided Reading Activity 33-3* Section Quiz 33-3*	Section Focus Transparency 33-3 Student Self-Test and Review Software Communism and the Cold War
Section 4 Southeast Asia Explain how nationalism, the cold war, and the rise of a global economy have affected Southeast Asia.	Reproducible Lesson Plan 33-4 Vocabulary Activity 33* Guided Reading Activity 33-4* Section Quiz 33-4*	Section Focus Transparency 33-4 Student Self-Test and Review Software World Music: Cultural Traditions, Lesson 9 Communism and the Cold War
Section 5 South Asia Identify the challenges that have faced the countries of South Asia since independence.	Reproducible Lesson Plan 33-5 Vocabulary Activity 33* Guided Reading Activity 33-5* Section Quiz 33-5*	Section Focus Transparency 33-5 Student Self-Test and Review Software World Music: Cultural Traditions, Lesson 7 Lessons of War
Section 6 The Pacific List the factors that have helped Pacific nations develop prosperous economies and new national identities since World War II.	Reproducible Lesson Plan 33-6 Guided Reading Activity 33-6* Reteaching Activity 33 Enrichment Activity 33 Section Quiz 33-6* Performance Assessment Activity 33 Spanish Chapter Summary 33	Section Focus Transparency 33-6 World History and Art Transparency 44, *Sydney Opera House* Vocabulary PuzzleMaker Software Student Self-Test and Review Software Testmaker World Music: Cultural Traditions, Lesson 10

* *Also available in Spanish*

Chapter Activities

Performance Assessment Activity

A Page on the Internet **Many of the physical and ideological conflicts in Korea, Vietnam, and China, as well as the economic conflicts the United States has had with Japan, still affect Americans today. Many people have lived through these times, and others have strong opinions about them. Have students design a page for the Internet giving information about one of these historical conflicts, their own opinions, information regarding interviews they have had with Americans who have experiences to share, and current laws or reforms that can be traced back to these conflicts.**

Possible Rubric Features

Research skills, interviewing techniques, accuracy of content information, appropriateness to audience and purpose, clarity and organization, and use of technology

- *For an additional activity, refer to Activity 33 in the* Performance Assessment Strategies and Activities *booklet.*

ACTIVITY

From the Classroom of...

Anna Mae Grimm
Homestead High School
Mequon, WI

Leading a Developing Republic

Students will play the roles of the newly elected president and cabinet of a fictitious developing country, to gain a perspective on the complexities involved in national development. Students should take the roles of president; military leader; ministers of health, industry, finance, trade, agriculture, public works; leaders of two religious groups; farmers; businesspeople; feminists; and the unemployed—all of them with competing interests.

Have students participate in a roundtable discussion and try to create a national structure that keeps everyone happy. Students should keep in mind that their country is poor, with health and literacy problems. It does, however, have abundant untapped natural resources. Remind students that their contribution to the discussion should reflect the interests of their chosen role. Ask students to discuss whether their discussion gave them insight into the complexities involved in industrializing a developing country.

MULTIPLE LEARNING STYLES

Verbal/Linguistic
Ask students to conduct an interview of a veteran of the Korean or Vietnam War, focusing on wartime experiences and postwar reflections. Have students write up the interview for possible classroom presentation.

Visual/Spatial
Have students draw the national flag for each country in this chapter. Ask them to research the meaning of any symbols, colors, and wording on the flags.

Auditory/Musical
Have the class listen to a tape or CD of *Miss Saigon*, the musical about the relationship between a young Vietnamese woman and an American soldier in 1975 at the end of the Vietnam War.

Kinesthetic
Have students investigate the degree to which Western styles of dress have been adopted in the countries discussed in this chapter and the extent to which traditional styles are still worn. Suggest that students make drawings illustrating existing traditional styles.

Additional Resources

TEACHER'S CORNER

NATIONAL GEOGRAPHIC SOCIETY

INDEX TO NATIONAL GEOGRAPHIC MAGAZINE

The following articles may be used for research relating to this chapter:

- "Shanghai: Where China's Past and Future Meet," by William S. Ellis, March 1994.
- "Kyushu: Japan's Southern Gateway," by Tracy Dahlby, January 1994.
- "Taiwan: The Other China Changes Course," by Arthur Zich, November 1993.
- "Japan's Sun Rises Over the Pacific," by Arthur Zich, November 1991.
- "China's Youth Wait for Tomorrow," by Ross Terrill, July 1991.
- "Missing in Action," by Peter T. White, November 1986.

ADDITIONAL NATIONAL GEOGRAPHIC SOCIETY PRODUCTS

To order the following products for use with this chapter, call National Geographic Society at 1-800-368-2728:

- *Capitalism, Socialism, Communism Series*, "Communism." (Video)
- *Democratic Governments Series*, "Japan." (Video)
- *The Vietnam War*, "Introduction to the Region," "Chronicle of Conflict: 1954-1964," "Chronicle of Conflict: 1965-1975," "Legacies of War." (Filmstrip)
- *The Changing Faces of Communism Series*, "Vietnam." (Video)
- *Nations of the World Series*, "Japan." (Video)

BIBLIOGRAPHY

Literature of the Period

Lau, Joseph S. M., and Howard Goldblatt, eds. ***The Columbia Anthology of Modern Chinese Literature.*** New York: Columbia University Press, 1995. A selection from the best modern Chinese writing.

Oe, Kenzaburo. ***Nip the Buds, Shoot the Kids.*** Translated by Paul St. John Mackintosh and Maki Sugiyama. New York: Marion Boyars, 1995. This first novel by the winner of the 1994 Nobel Prize in literature tells the story of a band of teenage delinquents in wartime.

Readings for the Student

Marrin, Albert. ***America and Vietnam: The Elephant and the Tiger.*** New York: Viking, 1992. The causes and effects of the Vietnam War.

Readings for the Teacher

Paik, Sun Yup. ***From Pusan to Panmunjom.*** New York: Macmillan, 1992. A South Korean commander describes his involvement in the Korean War.

interNET
CONNECTIONS
Pictorial History of Tiananmen 1989 View a photo journal of the events that took place in Tiananmen Square in 1989.
World Wide Web:
http://www.christusrex.org/www1/sdc/tiananmen.html

Introducing Chapter 33

CHAPTER THEMES

Chapter Themes are listed by section on this chapter opening page of the Student Edition. A corresponding theme-based activity is available under "TEACH," and a theme-based question is asked in the Section and Chapter Reviews.

The Storyteller

Historical Setting Although the kimono is universally recognized as a Japanese garment, this familiar ankle-length gown with long, wide sleeves actually derives from a Chinese robe. The transformation of the kimono into a work of art, however, is attributable to Japanese designers of the 1600s and 1700s. Their stylistic prowess turned a simple garment into one of the world's most beautiful articles of clothing. Although Japanese men and women have worn the kimono since the Early Nara period (A.D. 645–724), the broad sash, or obi, that holds the buttonless garment together is of more recent origin, dating from the 1700s.

Historical Significance

Answers: *The countries of Asia play an important role in world politics, economics, and culture.*

Several Asian nations have emerged as economic models; Asian cinema, music, and religion have had a growing influence; and world peace has been affected by Asia since 1945.

Chapter 33 1945–Present Asia and the Pacific

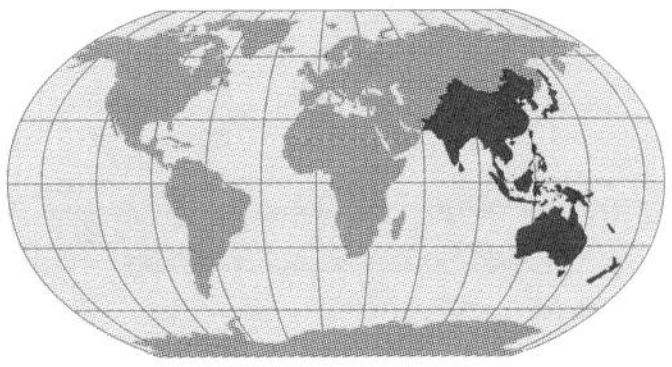

Chapter Themes

- **Change** Japan builds a democracy and becomes a global economic power. *Section 1*
- **Revolution** Communists in China introduce socialist measures, and then promote a limited free enterprise economy. *Section 2*
- **Regionalism** After decades of conflict and cold war tensions, North Korea and South Korea take first steps toward unification. *Section 3*
- **Conflict** The rise of nationalism and cold war competition leads to conflict in post-World War II Southeast Asia. *Section 4*
- **Diversity** A diversity of religious and ethnic groups challenges the unity in South Asia. *Section 5*
- **Cultural Diffusion** Changing political and economic roles open the nations of the Pacific to other parts of the globe. *Section 6*

The Storyteller

"My methods are old, " declares Japanese artist Kako Muriguchi, "but my designs are new." Muriguchi designs innovative patterns for kimonos, the traditional Japanese garment for women. The people of Japan have such respect for his contributions to their heritage that they have declared him a "living national treasure." As a result of this designation, Muriguchi is entitled to lifetime national support for his art. Like Muriguchi, Japan and other countries in Asia have found success by combining old and new. Traditional values that encourage education and hard work, combined with modern developments, such as computer technology, have brought prosperity to many countries in Asia since the end of World War II.

Historical Significance

What role do the countries of Asia and the Pacific play in the contemporary world? How have they contributed to the world's economy, culture, and politics since 1945?

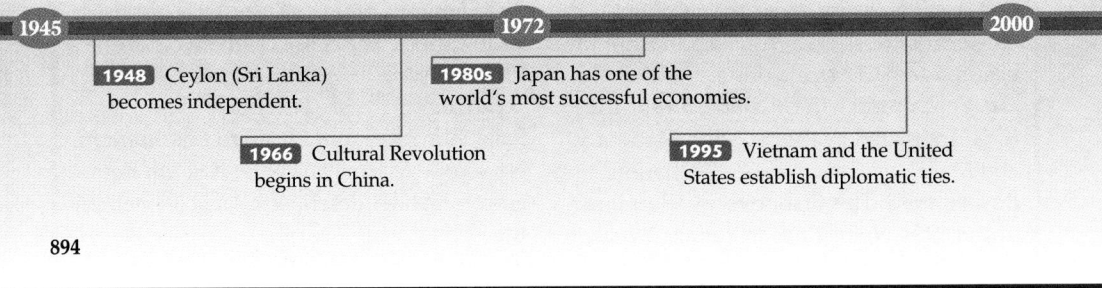

1945 — 1972 — 2000

- **1948** Ceylon (Sri Lanka) becomes independent.
- **1966** Cultural Revolution begins in China.
- **1980s** Japan has one of the world's most successful economies.
- **1995** Vietnam and the United States establish diplomatic ties.

894

GEOGRAPHY CONNECTION

GEOGRAPHIC THEMES

Location Have students use a globe to locate the countries discussed in this chapter: Japan, China, Taiwan, North Korea, South Korea, India, Pakistan, Bangladesh, Myanmar, Sri Lanka, Vietnam, Cambodia, Laos, Thailand, Indonesia, Singapore, the Philippines, Australia, and New Zealand. Which of the countries are large? *(China, India, Australia)* Do you think that size is a measure of a country's power or importance? *(No. India is relatively big, but much of its population is poor. Japan is small but economically advanced.)*

Visualizing History Today a giant sculpture of Chinese workers stands above the railroad in Nanjing, the capital of Nationalist China from 1946 to 1949.

Your History Journal

Interview someone who migrated to the United States from an Asian or Pacific nation, or research the culture of an Asian or Pacific nation. Write a short report on the cultural adjustments a person from that nation would make to live in the United States.

Introducing Chapter 33

Visualizing History The name Nanjing, which means "southern capital," was introduced in 1421 under the Ming dynasty. Nanjing served seven times as the capital of regional empires and twice as the capital of a united China (most recently from 1928 to 1937). The Nationalist government transformed the city into a modern industrial center, specializing in the manufacture of farm equipment, vehicles, chemicals, and weapons. Nonetheless, there is still a large rural population within the city.

Performance Assessment

Refer to the activity on page 894C of the Planning Guide.

For an additional activity, refer to Activity 33 in the *Performance Assessment Strategies and Activities* booklet.

Using Your History Journal

Advise students to prepare a specific list of questions they want to have answered before they begin their interviews.

GLENCOE TECHNOLOGY

VIDEODISC
Use MindJogger to preview chapter content.

MindJogger Videoquiz
Chapter 33
Disc 5 Side A

Also available in VHS.

EXTRA CREDIT PROJECT

Oral Report Ask students to research the industrial and economic development of China from the Communist takeover to the present. Advise them to consider the effects of the First Five-Year Plan, the Great Leap Forward, the Cultural Revolution, and the reform measures introduced following Mao's death. Have students summarize their findings in a brief oral report. Suggested resources: J. K. Fairbank, *China: A New History*; Feng Jicai, *Voices from the Whirlwind: An Oral History of the Chinese Cultural Revolution*; W. Overholt, *The Rise of China*; R. Terrill, *China in Our Time.*

Chapter 33 Section 1

SECTION THEME

▶ **Change** Japan builds a democracy and becomes a global economic power.

Find Out

Answer: *MacArthur's postwar reform policies, America's need for supplies in the vicinity during the Korean War, Japanese government-business cooperation, political stability, and normalization of relations with China have contributed to the economic success of Japan.*

FOCUS

Section Objective

List the factors that have contributed to the economic success of Japan.

BELLRINGER Motivational Activity

Before taking roll at the beginning of the class period, project Section Focus Transparency 33-1 and have students answer the activity questions. Discuss students' responses.

This activity is also available as a blackline master.

Vocabulary Pre-check

Use Vocabulary Activity 33 to introduce vocabulary terms. **L1 LEP**

1945 — 1972 — 2000

1947 Japan adopts democratic constitution.

1980s Japan has one of the world's most successful economies.

1995 Severe earthquake strikes Kobe area.

Section 1

Japan's Economic Rise

Setting the Scene

▶ **Terms to Define**
gross domestic product, pollution, sect, quota

▶ **People to Meet**
Douglas MacArthur, Hirohito

▶ **Places to Locate**
Tokyo, Kobe

Find Out What factors have contributed to the economic success of Japan?

The Storyteller

Kyoichi Tabuchi's plane landed in Bangkok, the city he would now call home. He had accepted a position as manager of an industrial complex. The Thai government eagerly received Tabuchi and his fellow Japanese for establishing economic opportunities. The age of Heisei, or peaceful achievement, had begun. Japan's economy was booming; her industry was welcomed throughout the region she had occupied militarily just 50 years earlier. As Tabuchi drove to the Japanese district, he heard the radio play a song that clearly defined the beneficial situation: "The Samurai Are Here."

—adapted from "Japan's Sun Rises Over the Pacific," *National Geographic*, November, 1995, Arthur Zich

Ascendant electronics

The end of World War II brought dramatic changes to Asia; Japan lost much of the territory it had acquired. Great Britain, France, and the Netherlands were forced to withdraw from their Asian colonies, and new nations arose. Communists won control in China and North Korea, and the cold war affected the entire region. Out of the turmoil, vigorous industrial powers have emerged. Japan's transformation into a global economic giant has been one of the most important changes of the post-World War II era.

Occupation and Reform

Japan, a proud nation with a long history of self-reliance, ended World War II with its pride crushed, its economy wrecked, and its people demoralized by the humiliating defeat. The victorious countries established an occupation government, the Supreme Command of the Allied Powers (SCAP), to govern Japan after the war. Although planned as a joint venture of the Allies, the occupation government became entirely a United States enterprise, headed by General **Douglas MacArthur**. The general was determined not to plant the seeds of future war by imposing an unjust and unworkable system on the Japanese. MacArthur's reform policies affected Japan's political and economic spheres, and Japan made a remarkable recovery.

A New Constitution

SCAP required Japan to adopt a new constitution in 1947. The constitution stripped the imperial family of its political power and gave it to the Japanese citizens. No longer could Japanese emperors rule by their claim to divine authority. Instead, the constitution allowed Emperor **Hirohito** to remain in office as a symbol of the state. Moreover, he was encouraged to renounce any claims to divine origins. The constitution established a cabinet based on the British model. Both houses of the

SECTION RESOURCES

Reproducible Masters
- Reproducible Lesson Plan 33-1
- Vocabulary Activity 33
- Guided Reading Activity 33-1
- History Simulation 33
- Section Quiz 33-1

Transparencies
- Section Focus Transparency 33-1
- Mapping History Overlay Transparency 24, *Trade Between the U.S. and Japan*
- Chapter Transparency 33

Multimedia
- Student Self-Test and Review Software
- Testmaker
- World Music: Cultural Traditions, Lesson 8

Diet, or legislature, were made elective, and citizens over the age of 20 could vote. A bill of rights guaranteed basic freedoms.

The new constitution included an unusual provision. Article 9 barred Japan from all warfare except for defense—"The Japanese people forever renounce war as a sovereign right of the nation.... Land, sea, and air forces, as well as other war potential, will never be maintained." SCAP hoped that this would prevent Japan from ever threatening its neighbors again. The United States agreed to protect Japan militarily. In the early 1990s, the United States still had troops—40,000 in all—stationed on Japanese territory, most of them on the island of Okinawa. This military arrangement enabled Japan to concentrate more of its resources on consumer goods than on military equipment. It also reassured other nations of the region who feared the revival of a militarily strong Japan.

Economic Reform

SCAP also set out to decentralize Japanese agriculture and industry. Landlords not living on their property could own only 2.5 acres (1.1 ha) of land. The law required them to sell off holdings above this figure at very low prices. Those who actually farmed the soil were permitted to own up to 7.5 acres (3.1 ha). Decentralization changed the face of Japanese agriculture, resulting in the transfer of more than 5 million acres (2 million ha). Although Japanese farmers have prospered, small-scale farming has been costly and inefficient. Today, the Japanese government subsidizes farmers by buying their crops at high prices to cover farmers' costs and then resells the crops to consumers at a loss.

SCAP took steps to decentralize the *zaibatsu*, the giant industrial and banking organizations that controlled Japanese industry. General MacArthur believed that removal of *zaibatsu* control would prevent Japan from rearming. The Korean War, however, led the United States to change this policy and gave renewed life to Japan's large industrial organizations. It was hoped by the United States that a strong Japanese economy would help in the effort to contain the spread of communism in Asia.

Japan's Dramatic Recovery

Japan's shattered economy recovered quickly in the early 1950s with assistance from the United States. The Korean War created a vast need for all kinds of war supplies, ranging from trucks to uniforms and medical supplies. To have sources of supply close at hand, the United States poured $3.5 billion into Japan—an amount nearly equal to what the United States gave Germany under the Marshall Plan. The United States also provided training in management skills so that Japan was able to rebuild its factories to the latest standards. Japanese shipbuilders, car manufacturers, electronics and pharmaceutical industries all benefited from American aid and later became major leaders in the global economy.

As part of its recognition of Japan's support to the United States during the Korean War, a formal peace treaty with Japan was reached in 1951 and the American occupation of Japan ended.

Visualizing History **Emperor Hirohito (center) began his rule in 1926 and held the title of Emperor of Japan until he died in 1989.** *How did Japan's government change in 1947?*

Government-Business Cooperation

The Japanese government and Japan's well-educated workforce took advantage of the boom created by the United States. Although Japan had to import most of its raw materials, the Japanese economy expanded quickly. Japan's engineers, managers, and laborers worked hard to boost the country's prosperity. The Japanese government worked closely with large corporations to plan and promote

Chapter 33 Section 1

TEACH

Guided Practice

THEME Change

Have students give examples of political, economic, and cultural reforms instituted by MacArthur in Japan. Ask students if they think making these changes was easy. **L1**

Visualizing History Hirohito was the longest-reigning ruler in Japan's history. From the outset, the period of his rule was named *Showa*, or "Enlightened Peace." Even though World War II took place during Hirohito's reign, he wound up accepting the Allied terms of surrender. A few months later he renounced the tradition of conferring divine status on Japan's emperors.

Answer to Caption: *A new constitution stripped the imperial family of its political power, established a cabinet based on the British model, and barred Japan from all warfare except for defense.*

The Arts Arrange a classroom showing of the Japanese director Akira Kurosawa's *Rhapsody in August*, about the bombing of Nagasaki during World War II. After viewing the film, have the class discuss it. **L2**

Geography: Location Have students locate Japan, China, Taiwan, Korea, and Indonesia on a map. Point out how proximity would cause these countries to be involved in one another's affairs. Have students note examples of this involvement as study of the chapter proceeds. **L2 LEP**

COOPERATIVE LEARNING ACTIVITY

TV Interview Organize the class into two groups: one group to prepare interview questions to ask General MacArthur, the other group to prepare questions for Emperor Hirohito. Questions should be based on research of topics such as demilitarization, government, economic reform, and world affairs. Have students from both groups meet to combine their questions into a satisfactory list. Then appoint students to act as MacArthur, Hirohito, and an interviewer, and have them practice role-playing a TV interview. When students are prepared, invite another class or families to attend the mock broadcast. **L3**

Visualizing History By 1980, Japan had overtaken West Germany, France, Great Britain, and the United States to become the world's leading automotive producer.
Answer to Caption: *Japan increased its share of world automobile production from 3 percent in 1960 to 29 percent in 1980.*

Mapping History Overlay Transparency 24, *Trade Between the U.S. and Japan*

Chapter Transparency 33

History Simulation 33

World Music: Cultural Traditions, Lesson 8

Independent Practice

Guided Reading Activity 33-1 **L1**

Politics Ask students to use *Readers' Guide to Periodical Literature* to find articles that give more details about the collapse of the Liberal Democratic party in 1993. Have them summarize their research in a short written report. **L2**

Science, Technology, and Society Have students use *Readers' Guide to Periodical Literature* to find articles about Japan's program to use plutonium-based fast-breeder reactors to relieve itself from dependence on imported oil and uranium. Ask them to prepare a short written report summarizing the status of Japan's energy program and the reaction of the Japanese people and of other Asian nations to it. **L3**

Visualizing History **Production of automobiles became the heart of Japan's industrial expansion in the 1960s.** *How fast did Japanese auto production grow?*

industrial growth. They brought vision to long-range planning and then followed through on their decisions. For example, in the late 1950s government and industry agreed to invest heavily in research and development in the home electronics field. By the early 1970s, Japanese radios, televisions, stereos, and other items were challenging American dominance in the world market.

Similarly, the Japanese government and industrial leaders targeted the automobile industry as one they thought could help bring prosperity to Japan. The government helped fund researchers who developed dependable, high-mileage automobiles. Managers and laborers worked together to develop newer and more efficient production techniques. As a result of these innovations, Japan began producing high-quality cars at competitive prices, and sales of Japanese automobiles around the world soared. Japan increased its share of world automobile production from 3 percent in 1960 to a full 29 percent in 1980.

By 1980 Japan had one of the most successful economies in the world. Although only as big as California, Japan's gross domestic product (GDP)—the sum value of all goods and services it produced—was half that of the United States. Its per capita GDP, the amount of production per individual, surpassed that of any other industrialized country.

Japan's rapid growth continued through the 1980s. Between 1988 and 1992, the annual growth rate was 5 percent, one of the highest rates in the world. Japanese businesses invested heavily overseas in real estate, banks, and factories.

In 1992, Japan was hit by a recession that lasted into the mid-1990s. The value of many of its foreign investments dropped, and Japanese banks were hard hit. Day laborers were badly hurt by the recession. Even some salaried workers who previously had lifetime employment with large corporations lost their jobs. The long-term prospects for Japan remain very strong despite the downturn.

Side Effects of Growth

Like many other industrialized countries, Japan had solid economic growth that raised the standard of living of its citizens. However, the spread of industry also caused environmental damage. Japan's industries clustered along a narrow coastal belt between the city of **Tokyo** and the southernmost Japanese island, Kyushu. Along with industry came a dense concentration of people and automobiles and pollution, or the release of impure or poisonous substances into land, water, and air. In addition, rapid industrial development had created severe housing shortages in urban areas. Government and business leaders began to take steps to balance industrial growth with environmental protection.

Politics and Government

Japan's economic growth has been bolstered by an extraordinary level of political stability. From 1955 to 1993, one political party dominated the Japanese government. Despite its name, the **Liberal Democratic party** (LDP), is a conservative, probusiness party that has had broad Japanese support. The LDP has traditionally been strong among Japan's farming population, but it also receives heavy financial support from the country's large corporations. Voters liked the party's dependability, especially during the uncertainty of the cold war.

MEETING SPECIAL NEEDS ACTIVITY

Learning Style: Logical/Mathematical Have students create a time line of important events in Japan's history between World War II and the present. Before advising students on the appropriate scale to use (for example, three inches per year), determine how much wall space you have available to display the five time lines that students will generate as they study other sections in this chapter. Tell students to include political, religious, economic, and cultural events, as well as natural disasters such as the 1995 Kobe earthquake. **L1**

In 1993, Japanese voters defeated the scandal-weakened LDP. With the collapse of the Soviet Union, and the end of the cold war, it seemed safe to support the chief opposition party, the Social Democratic Party of Japan (SDPJ). The splintered SDPJ was forced to form a coalition government and to include many LDP leaders in the cabinet.

Because of its political diversity, the new government had difficulty steering Japan through a number of crises. In January 1995, a severe earthquake struck the area around the port city of **Kobe**. It was the deadliest natural disaster to hit Japan since World War II. Political opponents criticized the government for not responding rapidly to provide relief to the quake victims. In addition many SDPJ members, unhappy about their party's linkage to the LDP were leaving the party to form another political party: the New Democratic League.

Japan also encountered the ugly face of terrorism. In March 1995, a Japanese sect, or small religious group, carried out a nerve gas attack in Tokyo's subway system, leaving 11 people dead and 5,000 injured. A month later, another gas attack in a railroad station in the city of Yokohama injured more than 300 people. The two attacks stunned most Japanese, who considered their society violence-free, and heightened security concerns among government officials and business leaders.

In early 1996, the LDP regained its influence over Japanese politics. A new prime minister, Ryutaro Hashimoto (ree•you•TAH•roh hah•shee•MOH•toh), promised to rid Japan's government of corruption and promote economic growth.

Japan in World Affairs

As a result of its economic growth since World War II, once self-reliant and isolated Japan became tightly interwoven into the world economy. Economic power has made Japan a world political leader as well, but the Japanese have been unsure how to use their power in world affairs.

Trade Tensions

One cause of conflict was Japan's trade imbalance with other countries. A trade deficit occurs when a country imports more than it exports. Because Japan sold far more goods to other countries than it purchased, many countries, including the United States, had trade deficits with Japan.

CONNECTIONS

Economics

Rebuilding Japan's Steel Industry

Japan's steel industry was devastated by World War II. Steel, like other Japanese industries, needed a major rebuilding effort.

Japanese steel mill

Beginning in the 1950s Japan poured capital into new steelmaking facilities. An efficient method of continuous casting, computer-controlled production systems, and speed smelting made Japanese plants the most efficient in the world.

With the advantage of greater productivity, Japan began to sell steel at lower prices on the world market. By the 1980s, American steelmakers who had dominated world production were complaining that the Japanese were dumping underpriced steel on the market.

The United States responded with voluntary restraint agreements to hold imported steel to 20 percent of its domestic market. Japanese companies began to buy into United States steel companies, partially owning several by the 1990s.

By 1990, however, American steel companies had regained the lead in productivity. Then Japanese and American steelmakers started joint ventures to find even more efficient methods of making steel.

MAKING THE CONNECTION

1. What three methods enabled Japan to become the most efficient steel producer?
2. How did competition in steelmaking change from the 1980s to the 1990s?

Chapter 33 Section 1

Linking Past and Present

Religion and Government In 1868 the Japanese government set up an official religion, State Shinto, which emphasized loyalty to the nation and worship of the emperor as a god. When the government abolished State Shinto after World War II in a historic radio broadcast on January 1, 1946, Hirohito claimed that the emperor was not a divine being. Thirteen years later, in 1959, Hirohito's son, Akihito, broke a 1,500-year-old tradition when he married a commoner, Shoda Michiko. Akihito became emperor upon Hirohito's death in 1989.

CONNECTIONS

Economics

Rebuilding Japan's Steel Industry

Japan has proved that by industrializing, non-Western nations can become not only the equals of the Western powers but also economically superior to some of the strongest.

Answers to Making the Connection

1. *continuous casting, computer-controlled production systems, and speed smelting*
2. *Japanese and American steelmakers competed against each other in the 1980s, but in the 1990s they began joint steelmaking ventures.*

MAKING CONNECTIONS ACTIVITIES

Science, Technology, and Society The Japanese have a deep reverence for nature and longevity. Both are reflected in the ancient Japanese art of bonsai, in which trees are carefully pruned to be no more than a few feet tall and may live for centuries. Have students research the techniques used in bonsai and do a demonstration for the class. **L3**

Earthquakes Have students use *Readers' Guide to Periodical Literature* to find articles about Japan's reaction to the 1995 Kobe earthquake and the United States's reaction to the 1989 San Francisco earthquake. Ask them to write a comparison and contrast of the national responses to the two events. **L2**

Chapter 33
Section 1

ASSESS

Check for Understanding

Assign Section 1 Review as homework or as an in-class activity.

Use Student Self-Test and Review Software to review Section 1.

Evaluate

Section Quiz 33-1

Use the Testmaker to create a customized quiz for Section 1.

Reteach

Ask students to explain the relevance of each of the following to the modern history of Japan: SCAP, 1947 constitution, and decentralization. *(The Supreme Command of the Allied Powers, or SCAP, governed postwar Japan; the new constitution provided democratic reforms; business and agricultural monopolies were decentralized right after the war, dramatically changing the face of Japanese agriculture.)*

Enrich

Have students write short biographical sketches of the two recent Japanese winners of the Nobel Prize in literature: Yasunari Kawabata (1968) and Kenzaburo Oe (1994).

CLOSE

Have students write one or two paragraphs assessing whether it was right for MacArthur to impose his political views on an entire nation. *(Answers will vary. Students may point to the great success Japan enjoys today and say that the end justifies the means.)*

Trade Issues

Japan's economic prosperity has created tensions with other countries. Since Japan sells more products than its buys, many countries now have trade deficits with Japan. A trade deficit occurs when a country imports more than it exports. The United States, Europe, and Japan's Asian neighbors have deficits with Japan. They have pressured Japan to change its trade laws to make it easier for their companies to reach Japanese consumers.

Japanese government regulations limit the ability of foreign companies to sell goods in Japan. Japanese retailers have long-standing ties with local producers that they want to maintain. Japanese farmers want to continue trade protection for their crops and livestock rather than face competition with lower-priced imports. Japanese consumers prefer to purchase goods made in Japan because the goods are well made and because they wish to protect the jobs of Japanese citizens.

Overcoming these barriers has been difficult and frustrating for foreigners. In May 1995, the United States threatened to impose high tariffs on Japanese-made luxury cars. It wanted to pressure Japan to open its domestic automobile and auto-parts markets to foreign competition. A trade war between the two countries seemed likely until a compromise agreement was reached between them a month later. In the accord, the United States agreed not to impose trade **quotas**, or specified limits on the amount of imports or exports, on Japan. In return, Japan's major auto companies agreed to follow "voluntary plans" to increase purchases of American parts and step up production at their plants in the United States.

Military Issues

In 1990, the Middle Eastern country of Iraq invaded its tiny neighbor Kuwait, threatening the vital flow of oil to Japan, Europe, and the United States. The United States called upon Japan to help force Iraq out of Kuwait. After considerable debate, Japan decided to contribute financially to the military effort, but refused to send troops itself, in part because of Article 9 in the Japanese constitution. Referring to World War II, one member of Japan's parliament said, "After that experience, we should never again aim a gun at foreign peoples—even the people of Iraq."

Japan's military policy has been a sensitive issue in Japan and abroad. Some American leaders have argued that Japan should contribute more to the defense of its own vital interests. They claim Japan's low defense budget (about 1 percent of its GDP in 1995-1996) gives Japan an economic advantage in nondefense industries. Japanese voters have resisted changing Article 9. Nevertheless, the Japanese government in 1992 decided to send Japanese troops overseas as part of a United Nations peacekeeping mission.

Japan and Its Neighbors

Japan normalized relations with China in 1978. It quickly became China's second-largest trading partner after the United States. Japan also has relations with South Korea, but not North Korea. Concerns that North Korea's nuclear weapons program may threaten Japan's security have made Japan cautious in dealing with North Korea. Since the collapse of the Soviet Union in 1991, Japan's relations with Russia have improved. However, a territorial dispute with Russia over the Kuril Islands north of Japan remains unresolved, and Japan refuses to aid Russia's economic development until the issue is settled.

Foreign Aid

Japan's growing prosperity has brought demands that it spread its wealth to other countries. In 1990, South African leader Nelson Mandela stated bluntly that Japan's aid to African nations trying to overcome poverty was insignificant. Japan has committed itself to raising its aid levels and to widening the scope of its aid beyond Asia, which has received the bulk of Japanese foreign aid in the past.

SECTION 1 REVIEW

Recall
1. **Define** gross domestic product, pollution, sect, quota.
2. **Identify** Douglas MacArthur, Hirohito, Liberal Democratic party.
3. **Describe** two major reforms instituted during the Allied occupation of Japan after World War II.

Critical Thinking
4. **Synthesizing Information** Imagine how Japan's modern history might have been different if General MacArthur had wanted to punish Japan for its actions in World War II.

Understanding Themes
5. **Change** What economic policies have promoted Japan's prosperity since World War II?

SECTION 1 REVIEW ANSWERS

1. All vocabulary words are defined in the Glossary.
2. MacArthur, 896; Hirohito, 896; LDP, 898
3. Answers might include a new constitution and land redistribution.
4. Answers will vary. Students might suggest that Japan may have resented MacArthur and returned to militarism.
5. **CHANGE** Japan has focused on building a strong economy rather than a strong military, and the government has worked closely with large corporations to plan and promote industrial growth.

1945 — 1972 — 2000

1949 Communists proclaim the People's Republic of China.

1972 United States President Richard M. Nixon visits China.

1989 Chinese students in Beijing call for democracy.

Section 2

China in Revolution

Setting the Scene

▶ **Terms to Define**
communes, pragmatists, special economic zone

▶ **People to Meet**
Chiang Kai-shek, Mao Zedong, Zhou Enlai, Deng Xiaoping, Jiang Jing, Li Peng, Dalai Lama

▶ **Places to Locate**
Beijing, Taiwan, Taipei, Shanghai, Tibet, Hong Kong

Find Out How has communism affected the domestic and international affairs of China since the late 1940s?

The Storyteller

Wang Xin had heard his father and grandfather talk about the old days in China. As peasants, they owned no land. If someone was unable to work, he was dismissed by the landlord and had to beg or live off his family. But when Wang was a small boy, things changed. The peasants became masters, receiving shares of farmland. They were no longer starving. Wang's family of 10 people moved from a three-room house to one with seven rooms and a tile roof. For the rest of his life, Wang Xin would remember how happy the peasants were that spring of 1950.

—adapted from "A Peasant Maps His Road to Wealth," *Beijing Review*, reprinted in *Documents in World History*, Peter Stearns, 1988

Chinese peasant's house

The Allied defeat of Japan in World War II removed the last foreign power from China. Without a common enemy, the Soviet-backed Communists and the Western-backed Nationalists fought a bitter civil war for control of China. In 1949, the Communists won control of the mainland of China and proclaimed the People's Republic of China, with **Beijing** as the capital. The defeated Nationalist leader, **Chiang Kai-shek**, and nearly 2 million of his followers retreated to the island of **Taiwan**, where they set up the new capital of the Republic of China at **Taipei**.

Over the next four decades, China underwent dramatic changes. The Communists under **Mao Zedong** radically transformed China. Then, after Mao's death in 1976, new Communist leaders decided to allow Western-style economic reforms while maintaining their tight political control of the country.

The People's Republic

In the early 1950s, China's Communist leaders worked to strengthen their control of the countryside. They carried out land reform, a promise that had attracted many peasants to the Communist cause. In often bloody struggles, the Communists drove large landlords from their property and redistributed the land to the peasants. Between 50,000 and several million people may have died in the process. Communist party leaders then established firm control over local governments.

Building a New Society

In 1950, although relations between Mao's government and Stalin's Soviet Union were cool, the Chinese and the Soviets signed a treaty of friendship, alliance, and mutual assistance. The treaty was followed by economic agreements between the two Communist countries in which the Soviet Union promised to give China economic aid.

SECTION THEME

▶ **Revolution** Communists in China introduce socialist measures and then promote a limited free enterprise economy.

Find Out

Answer: *Domestically, Communist rule encourages some privately owned business, but government repression continues; internationally, Communists have increased trade and cultural contact with the West.*

FOCUS

Section Objective

Explain how communism has affected the domestic and international affairs of China since the late 1940s.

BELLRINGER
Motivational Activity

Before taking roll at the beginning of the class period, project Section Focus Transparency 33-2 and have students answer the activity questions.

This activity is also available as a blackline master.

Vocabulary Pre-check

Use Vocabulary Activity 33 to introduce vocabulary terms. **L1 LEP**

SECTION RESOURCES

Reproducible Masters
- Reproducible Lesson Plan 33-2
- Vocabulary Activity 33
- Guided Reading Activity 33-2
- Geography and History Activity 33
- Section Quiz 33-2

Transparencies
- Section Focus Transparency 33-2

Multimedia
- Student Self-Test and Review Software
- Testmaker
- World Music: Cultural Traditions, Lesson 8
- Communism and the Cold War:
  - *Revolution in China*
  - *Tiananmen Square*

Chapter 33 *Asia and the Pacific* **901**

TEACH

Guided Practice

THEME **Revolution**

Write *Five-Year Plan, Great Leap Forward, Red Guards, Gang of Four, Four Modernizations,* and *Tiananmen Square* on the chalkboard. Ask students to describe the role each played in initiating or preserving revolutionary change in China. **L1**

Economics On the chalkboard write the heading *Economic Change under Mao Zedong*. Then label two columns *Mao's Goals and Methods* and *Effects of Mao's Policies*. Ask volunteers to insert information in the appropriate column. **L2**

Critical Thinking Ask students to compare and contrast the 1964 Berkeley Free Speech Movement and the 1989 Tiananmen Square student protests. Ask them what cultural differences account for the different outcomes. **L3**

ABCNEWS INTERACTIVE™

VIDEODISC
Communism and the Cold War

Side Two, Chapter 4
Frames 5825-7229
Title: *Revolution in China*
Subject: Transformation of China into a Communist country
Ask: Why was it a shock to the U.S. when China became Communist? *(During World War II, the U.S. backed the Nationalist Chiang Kai-shek and believed that China would be an ally after the war.)*

In 1953, the Chinese launched their first Soviet-style Five-Year Plan. This ambitious program stressed the development of heavy industry and promoted agriculture. It brought private industries under government control and had peasants unite their landholdings into cooperatives. Under the Plan, industrial output increased an average of 15 percent, a phenomenal rate. Agricultural production, however, increased more slowly than industrial output.

Promoting Revolution

After the Communists' victory in 1949, Mao followed the Soviet example and opposed the United States and other capitalist countries. In 1950 China and the Soviet Union both supported the Communist government of North Korea in its war against American-backed South Korea. In 1954 Chinese Prime Minister **Zhou Enlai** (joe ehn•LY) took part in a peace conference at Geneva, Switzerland, that ended French rule in Vietnam and indirectly led to involvement of the United States in Vietnam a few years later.

During the late 1950s, relations between China and the Soviet Union soured and led to an open split. Mao was appalled at Nikita Khrushchev's de-Stalinization campaign, the low level of Soviet aid to China, and the Soviet Union's support of peaceful coexistence with the West. The Soviets for their part were concerned about Mao's carefree attitude toward nuclear weapons. In 1960 the Soviet Union withdrew its technical advisers from China, taking with them plans for many vital projects.

AROUND THE WORLD **Free Speech Movement**

Berkeley, California, 1964
In 1964 officials at the University of California at Berkeley prohibited political activities on campus, including the distribution of literature promoting various causes near the school's main gate. The Free Speech Movement was a reaction against these restrictions. In December, students took over the college administration building, then proclaimed a strike. More than 800 students were arrested, but the movement succeeded in forcing the school's president and chancellor out of office.

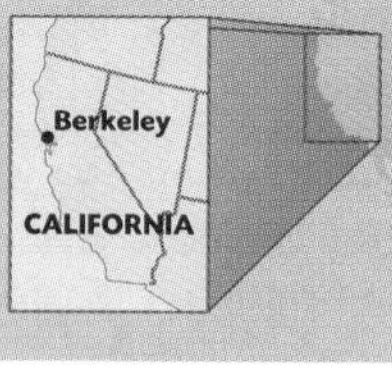

The Great Leap Forward

In 1958 the Chinese launched a more ambitious economic plan known as the Great Leap Forward. Under this plan, collectives were merged into larger government-controlled units called communes that combined the production of goods, administration of laws, and distribution of social services. In industrial production, the plan stressed human labor rather than complex technology. Factory workers were forced to work long hours to meet goals.

Within two years, it became clear that the Great Leap Forward was a disaster. Food shortages, industrial mismanagement, and peasant resistance to communes brought the program to a halt. The damage was done, however. The Great Leap Forward had caused massive suffering. As many as 20 million people died of starvation

The Cultural Revolution

The failure of the Great Leap Forward and the Chinese-Soviet split led to a deep division within the Chinese Communist party. Pragmatists, headed by **Deng Xiaoping** (DENG SHOW•PIHNG), party secretary general, wanted practical reforms. Radicals, led by Mao and his wife **Jiang Jing**, insisted on strict obedience to revolutionary principles. To end the influence of the pragmatists, Mao in 1966 began a movement known as the Cultural Revolution. Pragmatists, accused of betraying communism, were removed from office. People in all levels of society were encouraged to denounce their relatives, friends, and coworkers for suspected disloyalty to Communist goals.

Mao encouraged radical students and young adults, known as the Red Guards, to spread the Cultural Revolution thoughout the country. Rampaging Red Guards burned books and destroyed treasures of traditional Chinese culture. They harassed and arrested local politicians, teachers, and other leaders.

The Cultural Revolution was a time of disorder and confusion throughout China. Schools closed, factory production dropped, and violence erupted. Finally, in 1968, Mao called on the army to restore order. By the time Mao acted, however, the education and careers of millions of people had been disrupted, and tens of thousands of people had died.

Reform and Reaction

In the early 1970s, fighting within the party leadership continued as Mao's health declined.

COOPERATIVE LEARNING ACTIVITY

Oral-Visual Presentations Have students form five groups to research one of the following topics: the 1949 civil war, the Five-Year Plans of the 1950s, the Cultural Revolution of the 1960s, the pragmatists versus the Gang of Four in the 1970s, and the Tiananmen Square crackdown in 1989.

Tell students to use their texts as well as outside research materials. After they have completed their research, they can make charts and other visuals to present their findings. Each group should then choose one student to present its research orally, using the visual materials. **L2**

902 Chapter 33 *Asia and the Pacific*

Survivors of the Cultural Revolution returned to public life, but the struggle for control continued between radicals, who supported a rigid Communist approach, and pragmatists, who wanted to try any new methods that would help to advance China's economy. Instead of supporting hostility toward the capitalist countries, the pragmatists believed that the way to modernization was through closer ties with the West to gain needed technology and to promote trade.

New Global Contacts

Desire for advanced technology was one reason China began to reach out to other countries. Another reason was China's worsening relations with the Soviet Union. In the 1960s, China and the Soviet Union had disagreed over their roles in Vietnam. By 1969, Chinese–Soviet relations had deteriorated so much that the two countries began shooting at each other over a border dispute.

The Chinese-Soviet split gave the United States an opportunity to reestablish relations with China. Since 1949, the United States had opposed all ties to the Chinese Communists and instead recognized the Nationalist government on Taiwan as the legitimate ruler of all of China. In 1971 United States Secretary of State Henry Kissinger made a secret trip to China, which was followed by the historic visit of President Richard Nixon in 1972. This marked the beginning of a new era in global politics. China, long viewed by the United States as an ally of the Soviet Union against the United States, had begun to side with the United States against the Soviets.

Communist Feuds

When Mao and Zhou each died in 1976, the struggle for control of the Chinese Communist party increased dramatically. Mao's widow, Jiang Jing, leader of a group of radicals, sought to discredit the pragmatists. With crucial military support, in a secret coup in October 1976, the pragmatists arrested Jiang Jing and three of her main supporters, a group known as the Gang of Four. In 1977 longtime Communist leader, Deng Xiaoping, who had been expelled from the party during the Cultural Revolution, was rehabilitated. He soon became the leading force in China's pragmatic effort to modernize.

Four Modernizations

The pragmatists put into effect a plan for economic renewal developed earlier by Zhou Enlai. Known as the Four Modernizations, the plan stressed new approaches in the four areas of agriculture, industry, science and technology, and national defense. All were essential areas of development for China.

The essence of the plan was to abandon longheld Chinese notions of self-reliance. It sought instead to build on the growing relationship with the West. Under the pragmatists light industry prospered, led by the textile and food-processing groups. Today China produces significant quantities of consumer goods, many of which were not produced before 1950.

Visualizing History **Students at a commune perform a play supporting Mao Zedong.** *What was the contribution of the Red Guards to the Cultural Revolution?*

Crackdown

While the pragmatists encouraged economic incentives and market reforms, they opposed greater political freedoms—a difficult course of action.

Tiananmen Square Demonstrations

Under the pragmatists, government corruption increased and pressure for political change mounted. In April 1989 more than 100,000 student

Footnotes to History **Chinese Students Abroad** In the spirit of improving and expanding relations with Western countries, the Chinese government allowed more students to study in foreign countries. By the early 1900s there were about 40,000 Chinese students studying in American universities.

Chapter 33 Section 2

Visualizing History The Red Guards were named for the real army units Mao had organized in 1927. Formed into paramilitary units in 1966, the Red Guard movement subsided by 1969.
Answer to Caption: *They spread the Cultural Revolution throughout the country, using such methods as burning books and destroying treasures of traditional Chinese culture, as well as harassing and arresting their opponents.*

World Music: Cultural Traditions, Lesson 8

Independent Practice

Guided Reading Activity 33-2 **L1**

Geography and History Activity 33

Literature Have students read a work by a Chinese American writer, such as Betty Bao Lord, Amy Tan, or Maxine Hong Kingston. Ask them to write a short report that illuminates how the writer incorporates Chinese historical events from this period in her work. **L2**

Political Dissent Have students use *Readers' Guide to Periodical Literature* to find articles about China's treatment of political dissenters. Ask students to describe the ordeals that such recent dissenters as Harry Wu or Fang Lizhi have undergone, as well as the personal outcome for the individual dissenters. **L3**

Who? What? Where? When?

Dalai Lama For his nonviolent struggle to end China's rule of Tibet, the Dalai Lama was awarded the 1989 Nobel Peace Prize.

MEETING SPECIAL NEEDS ACTIVITY

Learning Style: Logical/Mathematical Have students work together to create a time line of important events in China's history between World War II and the present. This time line will be displayed along with the time line they completed for Japanese history of the same period, so students should use the same scale for this project. Tell students to include political, economic, and cultural events. **L1**

Chapter 33
Section 2

Visualizing History Tiananmen Square has been used for student demonstrations since 1919. Ironically, the square's name means "Gate of Heavenly Peace." It is named for the huge stone (formerly the main gate of the Imperial Palace) located at its northern end.

Answer to Caption: *Deng sent in tanks and troops to break up the demonstration, killing or wounding many protesters.*

ABCNEWS INTERACTIVE™

VIDEODISC
Communism and the Cold War

Side Two, Chapter 19
Frames 46766-49626
Title: *Tiananmen Square*
Ask: What were the protests in Tiananmen Square about? *(students and others protesting for democratic reform in China)*

Linking Past and Present

"Ownership" of Taiwan Taiwan, originally called Formosa, was "discovered" by Portugal, then controlled by the Dutch and later by Spain. Still later it was acquired by China, then Japan, then China again. Taiwanese moves toward independence are strongly resisted by China. In early March 1996, as a threat, China launched 3 unarmed missiles in the water only 20 miles (32 km) from Taiwan's coast.

Visualizing History **Demonstrating for more freedoms, students carry a hastily constructed model of the Statue of Liberty through Tiananmen Square.** *How was this demonstration broken up?*

demonstrators gathered in Beijing's Tiananmen Square. They protested against official corruption and demanded more civil liberties and better conditions at Chinese universities. In the following weeks factory workers joined the students. Demonstrations spread to the port of **Shanghai** and other Chinese cities. Communist party members began to express support for the students.

After 6 tense weeks, fearing that the party was losing control of the country, Deng sent in tanks and troops to break up the demonstration in Tiananmen Square. Many students were killed or wounded. Other protestors, mostly workers, were also killed. The government then hunted down those dissidents advocating free speech, heightening fear and stifling political discussion.

Effects of the Crackdown

The crackdown on students and workers set back China's economic development and damaged its prestige abroad. Fearing political instability, foreign investors backed off for a time. By 1990, a new prime minister, **Li Peng**, again appealed for Western investment in China. The Chinese government tolerated and even encouraged free market activities. This created an economic boom, especially in southeastern China, where foreign businesses were allowed to flourish without government interference in special economic zones. Between 1990 and 1994, China's annual economic growth rate averaged nearly 10 percent.

Many difficulties, however, remain for China and its 1.2 billion people. Economic growth has been uneven, and the gap has widened between the richer industrial areas on the coast and the largely agricultural regions of the interior. In recent decades, millions of peasants have migrated to the cities seeking work. This mass movement of people has put pressure on housing and various city social services.

Meanwhile, unrest has grown among China's many non-Chinese ethnic groups. Opposition to Chinese Communist rule is particularly strong in **Tibet**, a mountainous region in the southwestern part of the country. Once an independent Buddhist kingdom, Tibet came under direct Chinese control in 1950. Since an unsuccessful Tibetan rebellion in 1959, the **Dalai Lama**, the spiritual leader of Tibet, has led a worldwide movement in support of Tibetan rights from his place of exile in India.

Overall, in recent years, the Communist government's control of China has weakened, and the country's future is somewhat uncertain. Much will depend on the new rulers who succeed Deng Xiaoping.

International Relations

Since the Tiananmen Square crackdown, China has worked to maintain good relations with other countries without backing down on its tough stand at home.

MAKING CONNECTIONS ACTIVITY

International Affairs Have students research to find out about China's behavior as a permanent member of the United Nations Security Council. Ask them to write short reports summarizing their findings. Make sure they include information comparing China's use of the veto with that of the Soviet Union and the United States. **L3**

904 Chapter 33 *Asia and the Pacific*

China and the United States

During the early 1990s, China's relations with the United States were strained. Although China is interested in substantial trade and investment from the United States, it resents American pressures on human rights issues and continuing American support for the Nationalists on Taiwan. Chinese sales of missiles and nuclear technology to nationalistic governments in the Middle East and South Asia have also been a troublesome issue dividing China and the United States. In 1995, China moved toward improving relations by releasing a Chinese-American dissident it had imprisoned. China has also moved to develop more trade with European nations to offset its reliance on the United States.

China and Its Neighbors

To encourage regional trade and investment, China has reached out to its neighbors in East Asia. Although some Chinese remain bitter about Japan's 1937 invasion of China, Japan has now become China's third largest trading partner. In 1992, China and South Korea established full diplomatic relations and now trade extensively with each other. China still has close links with Communist North Korea, and has developed friendlier approaches to Russia since the collapse of the Soviet Union. China has also developed links with the Southeast Asian countries of Myanmar, Thailand, and Singapore.

Hong Kong

The year 1997 will be a momentous year for **Hong Kong**, the bustling international port on China's south coast. At that time Great Britain's control of Hong Kong will end and Hong Kong will become part of China.

Hong Kong is one of the world's largest financial centers, a leading exporter of manufactured goods, and a popular tourist attraction. Since the late 1970s, Hong Kong has become closely linked with the prosperous economy of southern China. It has also served as an important link in the substantial trade between Taiwan and the mainland of China.

Although China has pledged to allow Hong Kong to keep its capitalist system, Hong Kong's citizens have been greatly concerned about how their city will fare under Communist control. The Chinese crackdown on Tiananmen Square had a chilling effect on Hong Kong. Hong Kong businesses and professionals have gone abroad or are considering overseas locations in light of the uncertainty about capitalism's future in Hong Kong.

Taiwan

The status of Taiwan has been a prominent issue in Chinese affairs since 1949. Both the Chinese Nationalists and the Chinese Communists believe that Taiwan is a province of China. Each government claims to be the legal ruler of all of China.

Under the rule of Chiang Kai-shek, Taiwan's export of manufactured goods grew rapidly, and Taiwan prospered. After Chiang's death in 1975, his son Chiang Ching-kuo became the leader of the country and ruled until 1988. Vice President Lee Teng-hui succeeded Chiang as president.

In the late 1980s, relations between Taiwan and China began to improve, and Taiwan even allowed its citizens to visit China. Also, during this decade, the Nationalist government allowed more democracy, ending martial law and permitting opposition political parties.

Today, Taiwan's economy remains strong, but its political future is uncertain. In recent years, many people in Taiwan have come to accept separation from China as a fact and want to declare Taiwan an independent country. This demand has soured Taiwan's relations with China. The Chinese government in Beijing has stepped up pressure on Taiwan by trying to isolate it internationally. It also threatens to use force against Taiwan if the island declares its independence.

SECTION 2 REVIEW

Recall

1. **Define** communes, pragmatists, special economic zone.
2. **Identify** Chiang Kai-shek, Mao Zedong, Zhou Enlai, Great Leap Forward, Cultural Revolution, Deng Xiaoping, Jiang Jing, Tiananmen Square, Li Peng, Dalai Lama.
3. **Describe** the changes that occurred in China's relations with the United States and with the Soviet Union between 1949 and 1973.

Critical Thinking

4. **Making Comparisons** How did Mao's policies for the economic development of China differ with those of MacArthur in Japan?

Understanding Themes

5. **Revolution** Can political struggles within a country always be viewed as a battle between pragmatists and radicals? In your answer use different historical examples.

Chapter 33
Section 2

ASSESS

Check for Understanding

Assign Section 2 Review as homework or as an in-class activity.

Use Student Self-Test and Review Software to review Section 2.

Evaluate

Section Quiz 33-2

Use the Testmaker to create a customized quiz for Section 2.

Reteach

Assign one student to be timekeeper and organize the rest of the class into two teams. Play a game in which you give the teams names or terms such as Mao Zedong, Taipei, and the First Five-Year Plan. Have students explain the importance of each term or name within 10 seconds. Score one point for a correct answer.

Enrich

Have students write and perform skits that dramatize events in this section. Each scene should show how the event affected a segment of society, such as students, peasants, or factory workers.

CLOSE

Have students write a paragraph summarizing China's current position in world affairs.

SECTION 2 REVIEW ANSWERS

1. All vocabulary words are defined in the Glossary.
2. Chiang Kai-shek, 901; Mao Zedong, 901; Zhou Enlai, 902; Great Leap Forward, 902; Cultural Revolution, 902; Deng Xiaoping, 902; Jiang Jing, 902; Tiananmen Square, 903; Li Peng, 904; Dalai Lama, 904
3. Relations with the Soviets worsened, and those with the United States improved.
4. Each promoted equality and economic reform. Unlike MacArthur's policies, Mao's were harsh and repressive.
5. **REVOLUTION** Answers should include examples from earlier periods, such as the French Revolution or the Russian Revolution.

Chapter 33 Section 3

SECTION THEME

- **Regionalism** After decades of conflict and cold war tensions, North Korea and South Korea take first steps toward unification.

Find Out

Answer: *North Korea, led by a Communist dictator, has focused on the development of heavy industry and military expenditures; South Korea, which moved from repressive military government to greater democracy, has a more technologically advanced economy and higher standard of living than North Korea.*

FOCUS

Section Objective

Describe how South Korea and North Korea have differed in their political and economic development.

BELLRINGER Motivational Activity

Before taking roll at the beginning of the class period, project Section Focus Transparency 33-3 and have students answer the activity questions.

This activity is also available as a blackline master.

Vocabulary Pre-check

Use Vocabulary Activity 33 to introduce terms. **L1 LEP**

1945 — 1972 — 2000

- **1945** Soviets and Americans divide Korea at the 38th parallel.
- **1950** North Koreans invade South Korea.
- **1953** Korean War ends.
- **1990** North Korea and South Korea hold talks on unification.

Section 3

A Divided Korea

Setting the Scene

- **Terms to Define**
  stalemate, referendum
- **People to Meet**
  Kim Il Sung, Roh Tae Woo, Kim Young Sam, Kim Il Jong
- **Places to Locate**
  Pyongyang, Seoul

Find Out How have South Korea and North Korea differed in their political and economic development?

The Storyteller

President Roh Tae Woo watched as teams from 161 nations marched into the stadium. It was a proud day for South Korea, host of the 1988 Olympic games. North Korea's Kim Il Sung had called for a boycott, had even threatened violence, but only 6 national teams had chosen to stay at home. In fact, the leaders of most communist states had openly supported the Seoul Olympics. Even now, as the torch entered the stadium, American, Japanese, and Soviet ships off the peninsula kept North Korea under surveillance. As Roe watched 300 of China's finest athletes in the opening ceremonies, he wondered, was it a sign of a new era dawning?

—adapted from "The Politics of the Olympics," *The World and I*, October 1988

1988 Olympics in Seoul

Korea's modern history has been heavily shaped by international politics. In 1910 the Korean Peninsula was annexed by the Japanese, who ruled it as a colony until the end of World War II, when Japan was stripped of its territorial possessions.

After the war the United States occupied Korea south of the 38th parallel while the Soviet Union occupied the north. Thereafter Korea became the scene of a major cold war struggle. Koreans expected that the division of their country would be temporary, lasting only until UN-supervised elections could be held and a new government established. However, with the coming of the cold war, the Soviets refused to cooperate with the UN election procedures. As a result, Korea remained divided along the 38th parallel.

Two separate governments took shape in Korea, each claiming to be the legal ruler of all of the entire country. North Korea, officially called the Democratic People's Republic of Korea, with its capital at **Pyongyang**, kept close ties with the Soviet Union and China. South Korea, officially the Republic of Korea, established its capital at **Seoul**. It maintained links with the United States. The Soviets withdrew their troops from North Korea in late 1948, the United States from South Korea in mid-1949.

The Korean War

On June 25, 1950, North Korea, hoping to unify the country under a Communist government, invaded South Korea. The United Nations Security Council, in the absence of the Soviet Union, immediately voted to condemn the invasion and organized an army to oppose it. While 16 countries contributed troops to the UN force, more than 90 percent of the soldiers came from the United States.

In the first months of the war, the North Koreans swept southward, conquering almost all of

SECTION RESOURCES

Reproducible Masters
- Reproducible Lesson Plan 33-3
- Vocabulary Activity 33
- Guided Reading Activity 33-3
- Section Quiz 33-3

Transparencies
- Section Focus Transparency 33-3

Multimedia
- Student Self-Test and Review Software
- Testmaker
- Communism and the Cold War: *Korean War*

South Korea. However, on September 15, 1950, the UN troops counterattacked, led by General Douglas MacArthur of the United States. MacArthur launched a surprise invasion at **Inchon**, along Korea's west coast and far behind the North Korean front lines. The daring move gave the UN forces the offensive they needed. Within six weeks, MacArthur's troops had retaken all of South Korea and had conquered most of North Korea.

The Chinese then came to the aid of their ally, North Korea. Chinese troops forced the UN army to retreat southward. By the middle of 1951, after one year of fighting, each army dug in along a line not far from the 38th parallel. There the fighting reached a stalemate, a situation in which two opponents are unable to move significantly or make further gains. Truce talks began on July 10, 1951. The armies continued to attack one another, but neither side advanced very far.

On July 27, 1953, the two sides agreed to stop fighting and accept a temporary armistice line that divided Korea along the existing battlefront. After the deaths of nearly 5 million people and the devastation of much of Korea, the war ended with Korea still divided not far from where it had been divided three years earlier.

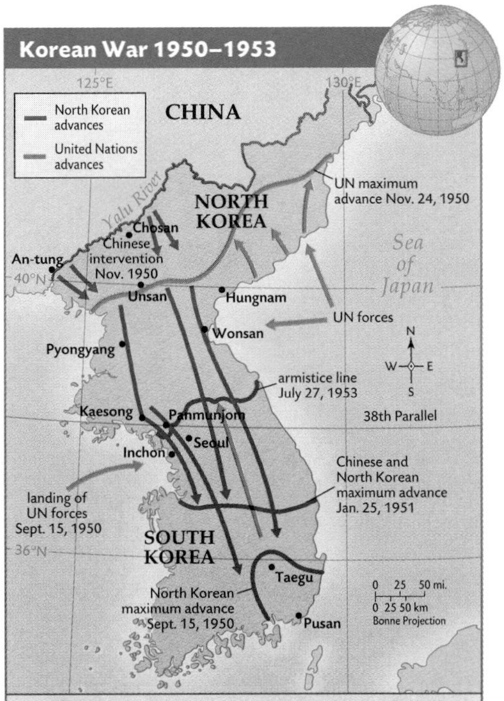

Map Study Each side of the Korean War occupied virtually the entire Korean Peninsula at various times.
Movement Why was MacArthur's Inchon landing so effective?

Korea Since 1953

The stalemate in the Korean War for a long time was matched by a stalemate in diplomacy. The two Koreas continued to draw economic and military aid from their respective sponsors, the United States and China.

North Korea

From 1948 to 1994, North Korea was led by the Communist dictator, **Kim Il Sung**. A cult of personality developed around Kim, and North Koreans revered him as a god-like figure. Called the "Great Leader," Kim established a repressive and tightly controlled government that largely isolated North Korea from the rest of the world.

Like the Soviet Union and China, North Korea implemented a Communist program of economic development. Under Kim's direction, all of the country's farmland was organized into collective farms between 1953 and 1956. In 1954, the North Korean government announced the first Five-Year Plan for building an industrial economy. North Korea stressed the growth of heavy industry and built up its military power.

Until the early 1990s, North Korea made some progress in developing its economy, but it did not match South Korea's growth. About 20 percent of North Korea's gross domestic product (GDP) was annually devoted to military expenditures, including the development of nuclear capabilities. Improvements in the standard of living were limited by this heavy military spending.

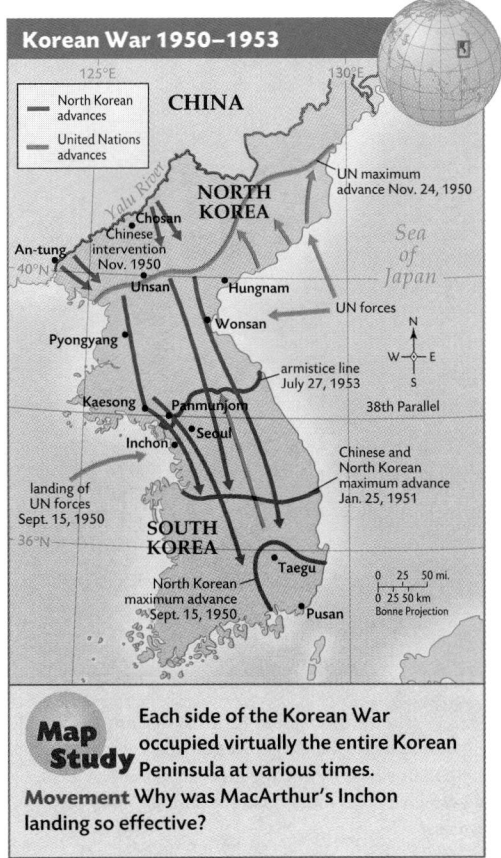

In the mid-1990s, another factor limiting North Korea's growth was widespread crop failure. The resulting food shortages threatened to bring starvation to many of North Korea's people. As catastrophe loomed on the horizon, the Communist government reluctantly sought limited amounts of aid from foreign sources.

South Korea

By contrast, South Korea made tremendous strides in a number of industrial fields and has had impressive economic growth since the mid-1960s. Between 1983 and 1987, the South Korean economy grew at a remarkable rate of 10 percent a year. To promote prosperity, the South Korean government

TEACH

Guided Practice

THEME **Regionalism**

Discuss ways that life in North Korea and South Korea are different as a result of their different forms of government.

Map Study

Answer

The surprise attack cut off enemy troops behind their front lines.

Map Skills Practice

Reading a Map What two South Korean cities did the North Koreans approach in September 1950? *(Taegu and Pusan)*

ABCNEWS INTERACTIVE™

VIDEODISC
Communism and the Cold War

Side Two, Chapter 7
Frames 16806-18713
Title: *Korean War*
Ask: What was the policy of containment? *(U.S. policy to stop the spread of communism)*

Independent Practice

Guided Reading Activity 33-3 **L1**

COOPERATIVE LEARNING ACTIVITY

An Exchange of Letters One of the most controversial episodes of the Korean War was President Truman's firing of General Douglas MacArthur, head of the UN forces in Korea. Organize students into two groups, one to research Truman's role in the war and the other to research MacArthur's role. Direct them to study the two men's personalities, political views, and leadership styles. Then have the groups plan and write mock dispatches between the two men—one exchange following the Inchon landing and another during the dismissal. The letters should contain historical detail and reflect knowledge of war strategy. Choose students to read the letters to the class. **L3**

Visualizing History Although Kim Young Sam won the presidency in 1992 by allying himself with the political party of his two predecessors, Chun Doo Hwan and Roh Tae Woo, he later put them on trial for taking bribes and for staging a coup in December 1979.

Answer to Caption: *Despite some setbacks, it maintains one of the highest economic growth rates in the world.*

ASSESS

Check for Understanding

Assign Section 3 Review as homework or as an in-class activity.

Use Student Self-Test and Review Software to review Section 3.

Evaluate

Section Quiz 33-3

Use the Testmaker to create a customized quiz for Section 3.

Reteach

Write the following dates on the chalkboard and ask students to identify their significance in Korean history: June 25, 1950 *(North Korea invades South Korea)*; September 15, 1950 *(Inchon invasion)*; July 27, 1953 *(both sides accept a temporary armistice line)*; October 1990 *(unification talks begin)*; December 1991 *(a treaty is signed, officially ending the state of war)*.

Enrich

Have students research the life and career of Douglas MacArthur in a brief biographical essay.

CLOSE

Have students write a summary of Korea's history from 1945 to the present.

Visualizing History **President Kim Young Sam fought hard against political corruption and helped business by cutting interest rates.** *How does South Korea's economic growth compare to that of other nations?*

has strongly encouraged exports. Recently, South Korean electronics products, automobiles, and other goods have begun to compete in world markets with those made in Japan.

South Korea's economic growth, however, was achieved under a series of repressive governments. Beginning in the early 1960s, the military used the Communist threat to play a strong role in the government. Despite elections, the president of South Korea was essentially a military-backed dictator, limiting speech, press, and opposition. However, throughout the 1980s, massive student protests demanded and led to greater democracy. In 1987, South Korean voters for the first time elected a new president—**Roh Tae Woo**—by direct vote instead of indirectly by an electoral college. Five years later, the same method of direct vote was used in the selection of **Kim Young Sam** as president.

The greatest breakthrough to democracy, however, came in 1987, when a new constitution was adopted by a **referendum**, an election in which all voters approve or disapprove a measure. The new constitution allowed almost complete political freedom. Since its adoption, students and workers have pressed for social reforms, higher wages, and better working conditions. Government efforts to satisfy these demands, however, has caused inflation and slowed economic growth. In spite of some setbacks, South Korea still maintains one of the highest economic growth rates in the world.

North—South Relations

The end of the cold war in the early 1990s raised hopes for uniting the two Koreas. Unification talks began in October 1990. In December 1991 the two countries signed a reconciliation and nonaggression treaty, which officially ended the state of war between them. Efforts to work out the agreement's details on specific military, political, economic, and social issues has been halted by continuing suspicions.

South Korea was fearful that North Korea was developing nuclear weapons. The North Korean government refused to permit international inspections of its nuclear facilities and resisted United States pressures on the issue. The death of Kim Il Sung in 1994 and uncertainty about the intentions of his son and successor, **Kim Il Jong**, delayed progress toward peace. In the spring of 1995, a breakthrough on the nuclear issue finally was achieved with the United States agreeing to supply North Korea's energy needs in exchange for inspections and for ending its nuclear program.

SECTION 3 REVIEW

Recall

1. **Define** stalemate, referendum.
2. **Identify** Inchon, Kim Il Sung, Roh Tae Woo, Kim Young Sam, Kim Il Jong.
3. **Explain** the political significance of the 38th parallel in the history of modern Korea.

Critical Thinking

4. **Making Comparisons** How are North Korea and South Korea similar? In what ways are the two Koreas different?

Understanding Themes

5. **Regionalism** How might the two Koreas' futures be influenced by the end of the cold war?

908 Chapter 33 *Asia and the Pacific*

SECTION 3 REVIEW ANSWERS

1. All vocabulary words are defined in the Glossary.
2. Inchon, 907; Kim Il Sung, 907; Roh Tae Woo, 908; Kim Young Sam, 908; Kim Il Jong, 908
3. The UN divided Korea at the end of World War II at the 38th parallel, and the current north-south border is close to this line.
4. Both have had stable, authoritarian governments. South Korea has prospered more than North Korea and has also moved toward democracy.
5. REGIONALISM The easing of tensions and weakening of communism might promote reunification.

1945 — 1972 — 2000

1949 Indonesia wins its independence from Dutch rule.

1954 Vietminh defeats French forces at Dien Bien Phu.

1965 U.S. President Johnson sends first American ground troops to Vietnam.

1994 Cambodia establishes a democracy.

Section 4

Southeast Asia

Setting the Scene

- **Terms to Define**
  domino theory, refugee
- **People to Meet**
  Ho Chi Minh, Norodom Sihanouk, Pol Pot, Daw Aung San Suu Kyi, Achmed Sukarno, Suharto, Lee Kuan Yew
- **Places to Locate**
  Vietnam, Cambodia, Laos, Thailand, Myanmar, Indonesia, Malaysia, Singapore

Find Out How have nationalism, the cold war, and the rise of a global economy affected Southeast Asia?

The Storyteller

Once again it was Tet. Tran Van Dinh could recall when that most joyous of Vietnamese holidays was the background for twenty-six days of bloody fighting between American and Viet Cong forces. Thousands had died. But throughout Vietnam's history, whether independent or under foreign domination, Tet was an occasion to meditate on the past, enjoy the present, and contemplate the future. Tran, who had made his life in France since 1968, bought flowers from the street vendor to mark the new beginning. It was deeply satisfying to return to his native city of Hue for the celebration.

—adapted from "Hue: My City, Myself," *National Geographic*, November, 1989, Tran Van Dinh.

Celebrating Tet

During the cold war years, Southeast Asia was thrust into the middle of the superpower contest and also suffered because of regional hostilities. The ongoing struggle between Communists and anti-Communists brought instability and war to much of the region of Southeast Asia known as Indochina. Only in recent years have Indochinese countries such as **Vietnam** and **Cambodia** begun to recover from earlier conflicts.

Struggle for Indochina

Before Japan conquered Southeast Asia in World War II, France ruled most of Indochina as a colony. When Japanese forces withdrew following the war, France attempted to reestablish its control. By then, however, nationalist movements demanding independence had gained strength. Vietnamese nationalists in the Indochinese Communist party, later known as the Vietminh, declared the formation of the independent Democratic Republic of Vietnam in 1945. The Vietminh were supported by the Soviet Union and the Communist Chinese.

The Vietminh, under the leadership of **Ho Chi Minh**, and the French could not reach an agreement on how to share power. In 1946 the two sides went to war. The United States, fearing Ho's Communist ties and wanting to support its ally France, provided military and financial aid to France to subdue the Vietminh. Despite American aid, the French could not win a military victory. In May 1954 the Vietminh defeated French forces in the decisive battle at Dien Bien Phu. After their loss, the French agreed to a cease-fire and decided to pull out of Vietnam completely.

A month before the battle, the Vietminh, the French, the United States, and several other countries had agreed to meet in Geneva, Switzerland, to negotiate a settlement to the Vietnam conflict. Negotiators divided Vietnam along the 17th parallel, creating a Communist North Vietnam and a

Chapter 33 Section 4

SECTION THEME

▶ **Conflict** The rise of nationalism and cold war competition leads to conflict in post-World War II Southeast Asia.

Find Out

Answer: *Nationalism and the cold war brought instability and war to the region, but in recent years parts of the region have become prosperous participants in the global economy.*

FOCUS

Section Objective

Explain how nationalism, the cold war, and the rise of a global economy have affected Southeast Asia.

BELLRINGER
Motivational Activity

Before taking roll at the beginning of the class period, project Section Focus Transparency 33-4 and have students answer the activity questions. Discuss students' responses.

This activity is also available as a blackline master.

Vocabulary Pre-check

Use Vocabulary Activity 33 to introduce vocabulary terms. **L1 LEP**

SECTION RESOURCES

Reproducible Masters
- Reproducible Lesson Plan 33-4
- Vocabulary Activity 33
- Guided Reading Activity 33-4
- Section Quiz 33-4

Transparencies
- Section Focus Transparency 33-4

Multimedia
- Student Self-Test and Review Software
- Testmaker
- World Music: Cultural Traditions, Lesson 9
- Communism and the Cold War: *Vietnam War*

Chapter 33 Section 4

TEACH

Guided Practice

THEME Conflict

Have students examine the map of Vietnam on page 912. Describe the physical outline of the country. *(long and narrow)* What influence might Vietnam's shape have had on its conflicts? *(It was difficult to integrate the territory of Vietnam. Few roads or railroads connected the north with the south. Internal divisions within the nation increased.)* **L1**

Daily Life Have students plan a reenactment of a 30-minute radio broadcast on a particular day in the United States in the late 1960s or early 1970s. Advise them to look through old newspapers to find the events of the day they want to report. In addition to news bulletins reporting that day's significant events, have students include popular music and ads for foods, fashions, and fads. **L2**

ABCNEWS INTERACTIVE™

VIDEODISC
Communism and the Cold War

Side Two, Chapter 8
Frames 18729–22891
Title: *Vietnam War*
Ask: What did North Vietnam represent to the United States? *(the threat of Communist expansion)* Why was Vietnam known as a television war? *(For the first time, a war was televised. Showing the reality of war proved detrimental to public support.)*

pro-Western South Vietnam. This arrangement was to last only until elections could be held in 1956. But the elections never took place. They were scuttled by the new leader in South Vietnam, Ngo Dinh Diem, a staunch anti-Communist who feared that elections would demonstrate Ho's popularity. Guerrillas in South Vietnam, known as Viet Cong, continued to fight against the Diem government, hoping to unify the country under Ho. The United States government sent financial aid and several hundred military advisers to bolster Diem.

However, Diem was a weak and unpopular leader. In 1963 the South Vietnamese military, despairing of Diem's leadership and fearing that the South would fall to the Communists, staged a coup in which Diem was killed. This was done with the quiet approval of the United States government and President John F. Kennedy.

Reflecting on France's earlier troubles in Vietnam, French President Charles de Gaulle urged Kennedy to withdraw. "I predict you will sink step by step into a bottomless quagmire," he warned.

The Vietnam War

In its zeal to contain the spread of communism, the United States ignored de Gaulle's advice and moved deeper into the conflict. The growing American role in Vietnam was justified by those who accepted the domino theory—the belief that if one country in a region fell to communism, its neighbors would fall as well. American military and political advisers since the early 1950s had believed in this theory. By the end of 1963, the number of American advisers in Vietnam rose to 16,000.

Gulf of Tonkin

In August 1964, United States President Lyndon Johnson announced that North Vietnam had fired on two American destroyers in the Gulf of Tonkin off the coast of Vietnam. Johnson seized on this incident to increase American involvement in the war. He ordered air strikes on North Vietnam. At his request Congress passed the Gulf of Tonkin Resolution, which gave the President broad powers

Images of the Times

Vietnam War, 1964–1975

Americans, forced to consider the cost of war in terms of human and economic sacrifice, debated for years before withdrawing troops in 1973.

United States troops searched the hills and rice paddies for Viet Cong guerrillas, the hidden enemy.

910

Images of the Times **Vietnam War, 1964–1975**

The human costs of the war included 47,000 Americans killed in action and an additional 305,000 wounded. Vietnamese casualties were much higher (400,000 in North Vietnam; 900,000 in South Vietnam), and many civilians were killed by American bombs. The economic costs of the war were also high. For the United States, the cost of the war has been estimated at $200 billion. The war also had devastating effects on Vietnamese agriculture, business, and industry.

The Vietcong concentrated their efforts on the countryside, where their guerrilla tactics included ambush, terrorism, and sabotage.

to conduct war. In March 1965 Johnson sent the first ground troops to South Vietnam. By the middle of the year, the United States had 60,000 troops serving in Vietnam.

Over the next three years, the war escalated sharply. By 1968 United States troops numbered more than 500,000, and United States planes were bombing Vietnam heavily. The South Vietnamese army numbered about 800,000. The number of Viet Cong and their North Vietnamese allies was about 300,000. Despite numerical superiority, the United States and South Vietnamese forces did not seem close to victory. As the American role in Vietnam increased, so did opposition to the war within the United States and in other countries.

The Tet Offensive

The turning point in the war came in early 1968. The Viet Cong launched a major military offensive during the Vietnamese New Year holiday, Tet. Although they failed to capture any major cities, the bitter fighting made more and more Americans realize that several years of United States involvement had failed to significantly weaken the Viet Cong. Opposition to Johnson's war policy became so fierce that Johnson decided not to seek reelection in 1968.

Ending the War

As the antiwar movement grew stronger, the United States began withdrawing its troops. In 1973, South Vietnam, the United States, and the Communists agreed to a cease-fire, and the last United States combat troops left Vietnam. However, the war continued until 1975, when the Viet Cong successfully defeated the South Vietnamese army.

After more than 20 years of fighting, Vietnam was unified under a Communist government. However, at least 2 million people, including 58,000 Americans, had died in the conflict. Half of South Vietnam's population, 10 million people, were **refugees**, people who flee to another country for safety from danger or disaster. In addition, large areas of Vietnam lay devastated.

South Vietnamese villagers from Quang Tri Province assemble at a refugee camp. Many hope to leave Vietnam.

Student war protest demonstrations on United States college campuses became common in the early 1970s.

REFLECTING ON THE TIMES

1. Why did college students play a significant role in the antiwar protest movement?
2. Why was the war so difficult for a powerful nation like the United States to win?

911

ANSWERS TO REFLECTING ON THE TIMES

1. Many college students who opposed the war did not want to serve in the army.
2. American soldiers did not know the terrain of Vietnam as well as the Vietcong—a necessity for the guerrilla-style war the Vietcong waged.

Chapter 33 Section 4

Critical Thinking Have students explain the domino theory and cite specific examples of its occurrence in Southeast Asia. **L3**

World Music: Cultural Traditions, Lesson 9

Independent Practice

Guided Reading Activity 33-4 **L1**

The Arts Have students watch films involving the Vietnam War, such as *Apocalypse Now; Born on the Fourth of July; The Deer Hunter; Good Morning, Vietnam;* and *Platoon*. Then have them write reports that compare and contrast the points of view of the different directors. **L2**

Critical Thinking Have students compare and contrast the Vietnam War with the Korean War. As resources, suggest J. C. Goulden, *Korea: The Untold Story of the War* and S. Karnow, *Vietnam: A History*. Ask students to write a short report summarizing the similarities and differences between the two conflicts. **L3**

Global Gourmet

Indonesia *Nasi goreng* is similar to Chinese fried rice, but instead of the meat and vegetables being cooked together with the rice, the individual ingredients surround a pile of fried rice. In the course of eating, the diner mixes them together.

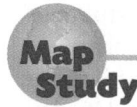

Map Study

Answer

Cambodia and Laos

Map Skills Practice

Reading a Map What is the name of the trail used by North Vietnam and Vietcong forces for transport and communication among North and South Vietnam, Laos, and Cambodia? *(Ho Chi Minh Trail)*

Linking Past and Present

Cambodia The 1984 film *The Killing Fields* told the story of the relationship between an American reporter covering the invasion of Cambodia and a local translator, Dith Pran, who was caught and tortured by the Khmer Rouge but escaped. Even though Haing S. Ngor, the Cambodian refugee who played the latter role, was a physician with no acting experience, his portrayal was so convincing that he won an Academy Award for best supporting actor. In February 1996, Ngor was shot to death outside his Los Angeles home. He had spent his years in the United States helping survivors of the Khmer Rouge and trying to bring to justice those responsible for the Cambodian massacres.

Who?What?Where?When?

The Year of Living Dangerously (1983) was set in Indonesia in the mid-1960s, when the Sukarno regime was unstable and the war in Vietnam was intensifying. The film stars Mel Gibson as a foreign correspondent from Australia and Sigourney Weaver as a British attaché.

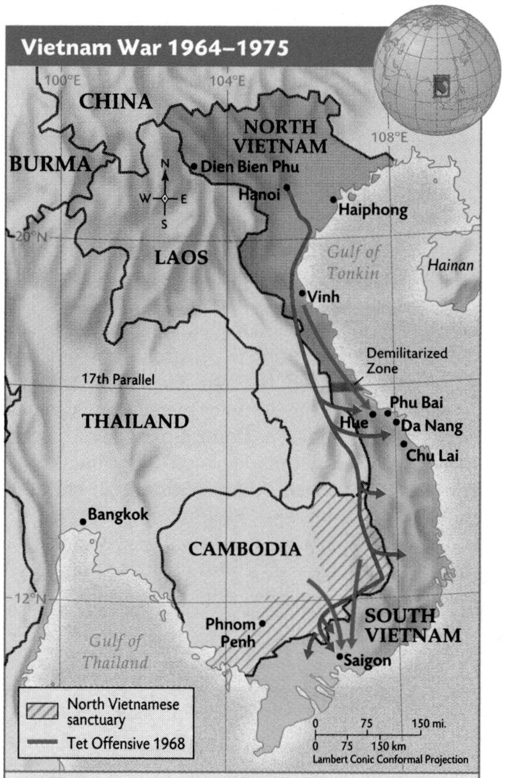

Map Study **The negotiated division of Vietnam, unlike Korea, did not hold.** **Place In what two countries did the Viet Cong find sanctuary to stage their attacks on South Vietnam?**

Vietnam's Relations with the West

Since the war, Vietnam has faced economic difficulties. To improve the economy, the government in the late 1980s encouraged limited private enterprise and sought contacts with the West.

In recent years, relations between the United States and Vietnam have begun to improve. The Vietnamese government has helped locate and return many of the bodies of American soldiers killed in Vietnam. Unfortunately, the remains of many United States soldiers have not been found. Some former American soldiers have returned to Vietnam to help disarm land mines they planted during the war.

A major step toward normal relations was made in 1994 when the United States ended its trade embargo against Vietnam, which had been in place since 1975. Vietnam also moved to improve its relations and trade with the industrialized nations of western Europe as a way to gain funds to rebuild and strengthen its desperately poor economy.

A Legacy of Violence

The Vietnam War affected many areas of Southeast Asia other than Vietnam. Fighting and civil war engulfed Vietnam's neighbors, Laos and Cambodia. Other countries of Southeast Asia, such as Thailand, escaped combat but were flooded by refugees. Since the late 1970s, the region has slowly recovered from the effects of conflict.

Cambodia

In 1953, Cambodia won its independence from France. The country became a constitutional monarchy led by King **Norodom Sihanouk** (noo•roh•DAHM SEE•ah•nuk), a member of Cambodia's historic ruling family. In 1955 Sihanouk abdicated the Cambodian throne in order to become prime minister.

Sihanouk refused to take sides in cold war power struggles. However, as the war intensified in Vietnam, Cambodia became an unwilling participant. In 1969, American planes began to bomb Cambodia in an effort to destroy Viet Cong bases there. The bombings were also intended to stop the flow of supplies and troops moving through Cambodia from North Vietnam to South Vietnam.

The bombing failed to achieve its objectives but did intensify the conflict between Cambodian Communists and Sihanouk's government. In 1970 an American-backed army officer, Lon Nol, ousted Sihanouk. Lon Nol charged that Sihanouk was not battling the Communists aggressively enough.

Civil war broke out after the American bombings and Lon Nol's seizure of power. Cambodian Communists, known as the Khmer Rouge, finally defeated Lon Nol's forces in 1975. Khmer Rouge troops, under the leadership of **Pol Pot**, took control of Cambodia's capital, Phnom Penh.

The Khmer Rouge wanted Cambodia, which they renamed Kampuchea, to become an independent, self-sufficient agricultural country. In the attempt to achieve this goal, the Khmer Rouge devastated the country. They destroyed all money and books. Soldiers forced city residents into the countryside to work on farms. Troops murdered civil servants, teachers, and students who may have supported the old system. Starvation, torture, and executions by the brutal government killed more than 3 million people—nearly one-third of the entire Cambodian population.

COOPERATIVE LEARNING ACTIVITY

Research Organize students into groups. Assign each group one of the countries studied in this chapter. Tell them to research types of arts and crafts produced in these countries. As much as possible, divide each country's art forms and crafts among group members. Make sure that each student has a specific role to play in the research effort. Have each group prepare a short presentation summarizing its findings, using visual examples wherever possible. **L1 LEP**

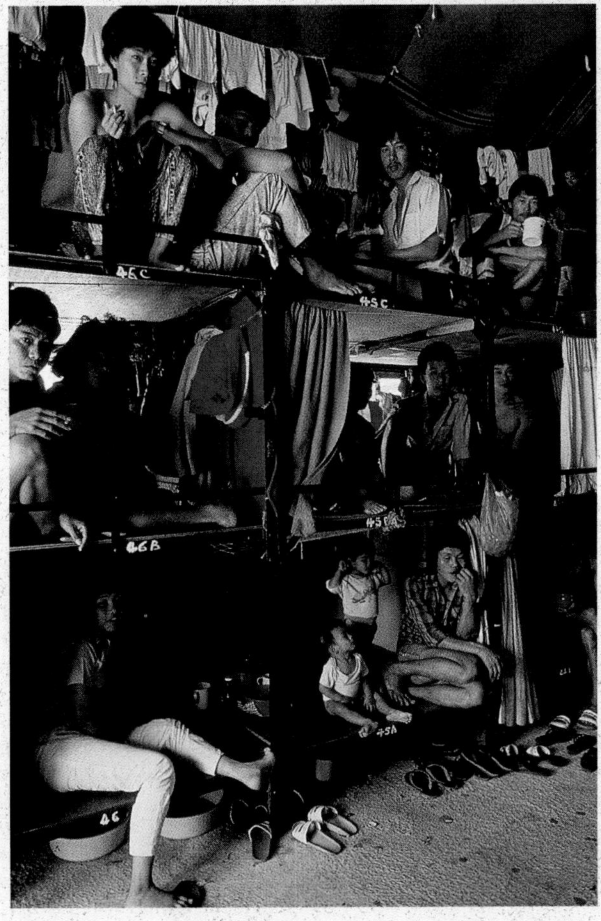

National Geographic photographer Jodi Cobb

Boat People

Even today, two decades after the Vietnam War, Vietnamese refugees waiting to go elsewhere remain stranded in Hong Kong. In this photograph, Vietnamese refugees in Hong Kong live inside huge concrete-and-metal dormitories where whole families sleep together in shelf-like bunks.

Vietnam suffered decades of war. In the 1800s the area was colonized by the French, who often proved to be brutal masters of rubber plantations and tin works. By the beginning of the 1900s an independence movement had begun in Vietnam. Not until 1975 did Vietnam free itself from foreign interference. But the price was high: economic devastation and domination of South Vietnam by North Vietnam. During the second half of the 1970s—years of poverty and political persecution—hundreds of thousands of Vietnamese left their country, many by boat. Untold numbers died. Some came to the United States; others scattered across Asia; some remain in detention camps in Hong Kong, where they are not allowed to settle, still awaiting their destiny.

TEACH

Tell students that sometimes the boat people fled political tensions only to find themselves caught up in racial tensions. For example, in 1979, Vietnamese boat people who were mostly ethnic Chinese arrived in Malaysia, already an ethnically diverse country. So intense was the fear that the arrival of the Vietnamese would upset the country's ethnic balance that, instead of welcoming the newcomers, the Malaysian government issued orders to shoot any boat person found landing on Malaysian shores. **What current movement in the United States reflects Malaysia's response to the boat people?** *(the movement to put an end to immigration)*

Linking Past and Present

Racial tensions between Malays and ethnic Chinese have been a problem in Malaysia since its formation in 1963. In May 1969, racial riots between Malays and Chinese led to a state of emergency that lasted for nearly two years, with the suspension of parliamentary rule. Differences in income between the two groups remain a serious problem, with Malays forming a majority in five of Malaysia's six poorest states.

Chapter 33 *Asia and the Pacific* 913

Chapter 33
Section 4

Visualizing History *Bangkok,* the name foreigners use for the city, may derive from the Thai words meaning "village of wild plums." The Thai people themselves call their capital Krung Thep. Krung Thep is only the first part of the long official name, which translates into "the City of Gods, the Great City, the Residence of the Emerald Buddha, the Impregnable City of God Indra, the Grand Capital of the World Endowed with Nine Precious Gems, the Happy City Abounding in Enormous Royal Palaces Which Resemble the Heavenly Abode Wherein Dwell the Reincarnated Gods, a City Given by Indra and Built by Vishnukarm."
Answer to Caption: *It survived a military government that abolished the constitution and dissolved the parliament.*

ASSESS

Check for Understanding

Assign Section 4 Review as homework or as an in-class activity.

Use Student Self-Test and Review Software to review Section 4.

Visualizing History **Home to about 6 million people, Bangkok, the capital of Thailand, thrives on tourism and a diverse economy.** *What difficulties did Thailand's government survive in 1991–1992?*

In 1978, after a series of border incidents, Vietnam invaded Cambodia and ousted Pol Pot. Cambodian Communists friendly to Vietnam took control of the government, but other Communist groups continued the civil war. In October 1991, representatives of the four major political groups in Cambodia signed an agreement that ended the civil war and called for an election under UN supervision. The United Nations sent 20,000 soldiers in 1992 to maintain peace and to supervise the promised elections.

The 1993 elections brought a democratic government to power in Cambodia. Stability was restored, though groups linked to the Khmer Rouge remained hostile. Cambodia's leaders have won foreign aid and investments by restoring free market policies. The country is handicapped by a shortage of trained professionals, however.

Laos

Laos became independent of France in 1954. While war raged in neighboring Vietnam, Laos had its own civil war between Laotian Communists and the American-backed government.

After United States forces withdrew from the region, Laos fell under the domination of Vietnam in 1975. A Communist government was formed, and the economy was reorganized along socialist lines. The Lao People's Revolutionary party abandoned those policies 20 years later after the collapse of the Soviet Union. They have reintroduced private land ownership and free markets. With investments from Thailand, Australia, and other foreign countries, the Lao government has built new roads, bridges, and railroads to advance regional trade and to gain access to timber and mineral resources.

Thailand

Thailand's post-World War II history was less violent than that of its neighbors because it had not been a European colony. It did not have to fight a war of national independence or struggle to forge a new national identity. The monarchy continues as a stabilizing force in Thai society, but the real power is now held by top military leaders.

During the Vietnam War, Thailand held to a firm anti-Communist policy, aligning itself decisively with the United States. In recent years, Thailand has adopted a more relaxed policy toward China and its neighbors, while remaining an ally of the United States.

In 1991 a new military government took over the country. It abolished the constitution and dissolved the parliament. A year later, widespread demonstrations forced the military government to resign and new elections were held. Pro-military parties, however, won most seats. Despite the political unrest, the Thai economy and the nation's standard of living have continued to grow rapidly.

Myanmar

Myanmar is the northernmost country of Southeast Asia. Once called Burma, it was for many years part of British India but became a separate independent republic in 1948. The new Burmese government faced opposition from Communists and various ethnic groups. To restore order, military leaders took control of the country in 1962.

During the 1960s and 1970s, the military leadership turned Myanmar into a dictatorship. The government took control of the economy and forbade any criticism of its policies. It also limited Myanmar's contacts with the outside world.

During the late 1980s, large numbers of Burmese began to protest the government's policies and call for democracy. Military leaders finally promised free elections in 1990, but before the voting took place, they arrested the leader of the main opposition party, **Daw Aung San Suu Kyi**. In spite of her arrest, her party won the elections.

The military leaders, however, refused to accept the election results and drafted a new con-

MEETING SPECIAL NEEDS ACTIVITY

Learning Style: Logical/Mathematical Have students work together to create a time line of important events in Vietnam's history from World War II to the present. Advise students to use the same scale for this project, so that their time lines for Japanese, Chinese, and Vietnamese history can be juxtaposed, making simultaneous events easy to see. **L1**

stitution that emphasized the power of the military in the government. The Burmese struggle for freedom, however, gained much international support. For her nonviolent struggle for democracy and human rights, Daw Aung San Suu Kyi won the 1991 Nobel Peace Prize.

Rim of Southeast Asia

Indonesia, Malaysia, Singapore, and the Philippines won their independence following World War II. They went through periods of turmoil and have emerged 50 years later with stable, booming economies. Their people and leaders are optimistic about the future of their countries.

Indonesia

Ruled by the Dutch for nearly 350 years, **Indonesia** gained its independence in 1949. Forging a national identity was an early goal, because the new nation consisted of a string of 13,000 islands stretching 3,000 miles (4,827 km) as well as 200 million people of many different cultures, languages, and religions. Indonesia's first president, **Achmed Sukarno**, did much to unite the country. He ensured the adoption of a national language that put all Indonesians on an equal footing.

Indonesia's progress was set back in 1965 when Communists tried to seize control of the government. In a bloody rampage, about 300,000 ethnic Chinese suspected of Communist loyalties were killed. Sukarno was forced out of office, and General **Suharto**, a staunch anti-Communist, took control of the country.

In 1975 Indonesia seized the former Portuguese colony of East Timor. It has refused to grant East Timor independence despite the resistance of the island's people. Some 200,000 citizens of East Timor have died as a result of Indonesia's use of force and intimidation to maintain control.

In the early 1990s, Suharto continued to lead Indonesia. During his term of office, he brought political stability and pushed forward the economic development of the country, although his critics brought charges of corruption. With oil and many other natural resources, Indonesia is expected to have continuing rapid economic growth. European, Japanese, and American businesses are competing for a share of the Indonesian market.

Malaysia

Created by the merger of several former British colonies in 1963, **Malaysia** is made up of territory on the Malay Peninsula and on the island of Borneo. Conflict between Malays and Chinese—the country's two largest ethnic groups—has been a frequent source of tension.

Since the early 1970s, however, Malaysia has been relatively stable. Like other nations on the rim of Southeast Asia, Malaysia has enjoyed an economic boom. Its well-educated labor force, good transportation networks, and tax incentives have helped attract foreign investment.

Singapore

Singapore is a small island republic off the tip of the Malay Peninsula. Independent since 1965, Singapore is a leading international port and commercial center, involved in shipping, banking, insurance, and telecommunications. Today, Singapore's people are well-educated and prosperous. Their standard of living is second only to Japan's in Asia.

Singapore's modern economic growth occurred under the authoritarian leadership of **Lee Kuan Yew** (lee kwahn yoo), who was prime minister from 1965 to 1990. Closely involved with Singapore's economic development, the government focused on encouraging high-technology industries and welcomed foreign business investment. A prosperous economy and the high rate of savings by Singapore citizens helped finance quality housing, health care, and education. In spite of having these benefits, Singapore's people have had limits placed on their freedom of speech and other civil liberties.

SECTION 4 REVIEW

Recall

1. **Define** domino theory, refugee.
2. **Identify** Ho Chi Minh, Norodom Sihanouk, Pol Pot, Daw Aung San Suu Kyi, Achmed Sukarno, Suharto, Lee Kuan Yew.
3. **Locate** the Ho Chi Minh Trail on the map on page 912. Through which countries did it cross?

Critical Thinking

4. **Analyzing Information** How have the economies of Southeast Asian nations changed since the end of World War II?

Understanding Themes

5. **Conflict** Evaluate whether the domino theory was proven correct by events in Southeast Asia. Explain your reasoning.

Chapter 33 Section 4

Evaluate

Section Quiz 33-4

Use the Testmaker to create a customized quiz for Section 4.

Reteach

Organize the class into eight groups and assign each group one of the countries covered in this section: Vietnam, Cambodia, Laos, Thailand, Myanmar, Indonesia, Malaysia, and Singapore. Ask each group to write a succinct paragraph summarizing the information in this section about their country. Reproduce the eight summaries and distribute them as study aids.

Enrich

Ask students to research the role played by Henry Kissinger in the events covered in this section. Have them summarize their findings in brief written reports.

CLOSE

Have students write a paragraph in which they explain whether and why they would have supported or opposed American military involvement in Vietnam if they had been of college age at the time.

SECTION 4 REVIEW ANSWERS

1. All vocabulary words are defined in the Glossary.
2. Ho Chi Minh, 909; Norodom Sihanouk, 912; Pol Pot, 912; Daw Aung San Suu Kyi, 914; Achmed Sukarno, 915; Suharto, 915; Lee Kuan Yew, 915
3. North Vietnam, South Vietnam, Laos, Cambodia
4. Vietnam has encouraged limited private enterprise; Cambodia has restored free market policies; Laos has reintroduced private land ownership and free markets; Thailand's economy and standard of living have grown rapidly; Myanmar's military dictatorship has taken control of the economy; Indonesia, Malaysia, and Singapore have experienced an economic boom.
5. **CONFLICT** Answers will vary. Laos and Cambodia became Communist soon after Vietnam did, but Cambodia might not have if the United States had not bombed it.

SECTION THEME

▶ **Diversity** A diversity of religious and ethnic groups challenges the unity in South Asia.

Find Out

Answer: *Since independence, the countries of South Asia have struggled with religious and ethnic unrest, cold war tensions, and economic problems.*

FOCUS

Section Objective

Identify the challenges that have faced the countries of South Asia since independence.

BELLRINGER
Motivational Activity

Before taking roll at the beginning of the class period, project Section Focus Transparency 33-5 and have students answer the activity questions. Discuss students' responses.

This activity is also available as a blackline master.

Vocabulary Pre-check

Use Vocabulary Activity 33 to introduce vocabulary terms.
L1 LEP

1945 — 1972 — 2000

1947 India and Pakistan become independent nations.

1971 Civil war in Pakistan leads to independence of Bangladesh.

1984 Sikh unrest leads to assassination of Indira Gandhi.

Section 5

South Asia

Setting the Scene

▶ **Terms to Define**
nonaligned

▶ **People to Meet**
Jawaharlal Nehru, Indira Gandhi, Benazir Ali Bhutto

▶ **Places to Locate**
India, Pakistan, Kashmir, Bangladesh, Sri Lanka

Find Out What challenges have faced the countries of South Asia since independence?

The Storyteller

Pradeep Bandhari was deeply shaken. Yet another Indian leader had been assassinated. Confused and distressed, he asked his professor to explain why visionary leaders were repeatedly struck down. "I have no immediate answer to give," replied the professor. "However, you might find some meaning in the eulogy for Mohandas Gandhi written by Jawaharlal Nehru." Pradeep was struck by the timeliness of the message:

"Long ages afterwards history will judge of this period we have passed through. We are too near to be proper judges and to understand what has happened and what has not happened."

—adapted from *Independence and After*, "A Glory Has Departed," Jawaharlal Nehru, reprinted in *Great Speeches from Pericles to Kennedy*, 1965

Nehru and Mohandas Gandhi

British rule of South Asia came to an end after World War II. The creation of independent states in the region, however, was marred by religious and ethnic conflicts. The cold war also had an impact. In recent years, dramatic changes in the world have made South Asian nations rethink their policies and relationships.

Dividing the Subcontinent

After World War II ended, the British agreed to give **India** its freedom. While independence was being planned, however, violent riots between Hindus and Muslims erupted across the country. This led to the creation of two countries out of British India in August 1947. Heavily Muslim areas in the far west and far east became **Pakistan**. The vast area in between, where most of the people were Hindus, became India. One Indian leader, **Jawaharlal Nehru** (jah•wah•HAR•lahl NAY•roo), delivered a moving radio address in which he expressed the hope that independence gave him:

> "A moment comes, which comes but rarely in history, when we step out of the old to the new, when one age ends, and when the soul of a nation, long suppressed, finds utterance."

Independence came, but not peace. The division of British India led to one of the largest single mass movements of people in history. Hindus from Pakistan flocked to India, while Muslims from India flocked to Pakistan. This migration of nearly 10 to 12 million people led to violence that resulted in the deaths of hundreds of thousands of people. Tragically, another casualty of the conflict was Hindu leader Mohandas Gandhi. A Hindu extremist, angered at Gandhi's acceptance of India's division, assassinated him on January 30, 1948.

The migrations and the killings did not end the

SECTION RESOURCES

Reproducible Masters
- Reproducible Lesson Plan 33-5
- Vocabulary Activity 33
- Guided Reading Activity 33-5
- Section Quiz 33-5

Transparencies
- Section Focus Transparency 33-5

Multimedia
- Student Self-Test and Review Software
- Testmaker
- World Music: Cultural Traditions, Lesson 7
- Lessons of War: *Philosophy of Nonviolence*

conflicts between Hindus and Muslims. More than 60 million Muslims remained in India, ensuring future tensions. Bitter hostilities between India and Pakistan would also continue.

India

India's first prime minister was Jawaharlal Nehru. Aristocratic and British-educated, Nehru had led the fight for independence along with Gandhi. He continued to head the Indian government until his death in 1964.

The Nehru Era

Under Nehru, India became a leader among the emerging countries of Asia and Africa. Nehru argued that newly independent countries such as India should not ally with either superpower and refrain from participating in the cold war. By remaining nonaligned—that is, tied to neither superpower—the less powerful countries of the world could provide alternatives to the United States and the Soviet Union.

In domestic affairs Nehru believed in following a democratic path to socialism. In 1950 the Indian government introduced a series of Five-Year Plans for economic development. The plans set up a mixed economy of privately owned and government-run businesses. Nehru's government also promoted greater social equality. India's new constitution granted universal suffrage and aimed to ban caste distinctions and improve the status of women.

Indira Gandhi

In 1966, Nehru's daughter, **Indira Gandhi**, was elected prime minister. Gandhi, a member of the Congress party, was the first woman to lead the Indian government. By the mid-1970s, Indira Gandhi became more committed to keeping power for herself and her family. When convicted of corruption in 1975, she suspended the constitution, issued a state of emergency, and arrested thousands of her political opponents. In 1977, she called for new elections. Unexpectedly she lost and was briefly jailed by the new prime minister Morai Desai (moh•RAY deh•SY), leader of the opposition Janata party. Due to divisions among her opponents, Indira was reelected prime minister in 1980.

Religious Strife

During the 1980s, India was troubled by increasing religious and ethnic unrest. In addition to Muslims, India has other religious minorities: Buddhists, Sikhs, Jains, Parsis, Christians, and

Visualizing History **Indira Gandhi had been a leader in the Congress party and minister of information and broadcasting in India before becoming prime minister.** *Why did she lose the 1977 election?*

Jews. Although the constitution defended religious freedom, religious intolerance was widespread. In 1983, over 2,000 people died in clashes between Hindus and Muslims in Assam in eastern India. In the northern part of the country, Sikhs pressed for greater freedom for their state of Punjab. In 1984, Indira Gandhi crushed a rebellion of Sikhs by sending tanks and troops into the holiest Sikh shrine. Outraged at the violation of the shrine, two of Gandhi's personal bodyguards, themselves Sikhs, assassinated her.

Foreign and Military Policies

In foreign affairs, India has faced periodic conflict with Pakistan since 1947. A major source of hostility between India and Pakistan has been the northern territory of **Kashmir**. Although most of Kashmir's people are Muslim, two-thirds of the territory is governed by India. Since the 1980s, Muslims in the Indian section of Kashmir have increased their protests against Indian rule.

In 1962, China invaded India over a border dispute. Stunned and feeling the need for protection, India turned toward the Soviet Union for military aid. It also began to develop its own nuclear weapons. In 1974, India tested its first atomic bomb. In reaction, Pakistan is believed to have developed its own nuclear capability. In 1995, the United States tried to get India and Pakistan to agree to the Nuclear Non-Proliferation Treaty, an international

Chapter 33 Section 5

TEACH

Guided Practice

THEME **Diversity**

Ask students to read the section, looking for signs of how diversity contributed to developments in this region. *(Not only did British India break up into India and Pakistan because of religious differences, but Bangladesh later broke off from Pakistan because of language and cultural differences. Religious and ethnic diversity within India, Pakistan, and Sri Lanka continues to create unrest.)* **L1**

Visualizing History One of Indira Gandhi's assassins died soon after the assassination. The second, as well as a third coconspirator, was tried and sentenced to death.

Answer to Caption: *She had moved away from democracy toward authoritarian rule.*

ABC NEWS INTERACTIVE™

VIDEODISC
Lessons of War

Side Two, Chapter 6
Frames 12636–20751
Title: *Philosophy of Nonviolence*
Subject: The philosophies of Mohandas Gandhi and Martin Luther King, Jr., and how their philosophies were used in protests and demonstrations
Ask: What form of demonstration did Mohandas Gandhi stress? *(nonviolent protest)*

COOPERATIVE LEARNING ACTIVITY

Research Organize the class into four teams, one for each country being studied–India, Pakistan, Bangladesh, and Sri Lanka. Each team should assign individual members to research one of the following topics: religion, economy, language, education, government (type, current leadership, and perceived strengths and weaknesses). Instruct each team to create a chart in poster form that will summarize what they learn about their assigned country. Have students display the completed charts and compare and contrast the four nations. **L1**

Map Study

Answer

The large number of island nations made regional unity difficult to achieve.

Map Skills Practice

Reading a Map Which country achieved independence most recently? *(Brunei)*

World Music: Cultural Traditions, Lesson 7

Independent Practice

Guided Reading Activity 33-5 **L1**

Religion Have students choose one of the religions mentioned in this section to research and report on in an oral presentation. Tell them to give a brief general overview, then focus on one aspect of the religion. Have them supplement their oral commentary with visual material showing religious symbols, statues, or places of worship. **L2**

Critical Thinking Have students research the militant activities of the Sikhs since Indian independence in order to explain the Sikh wish to establish a separate nation. Ask them to summarize their findings in a brief written report. **L3**

ASSESS

Check for Understanding

Assign Section 5 Review as homework or as an in-class activity.

Use Student Self-Test and Review Software to review Section 5.

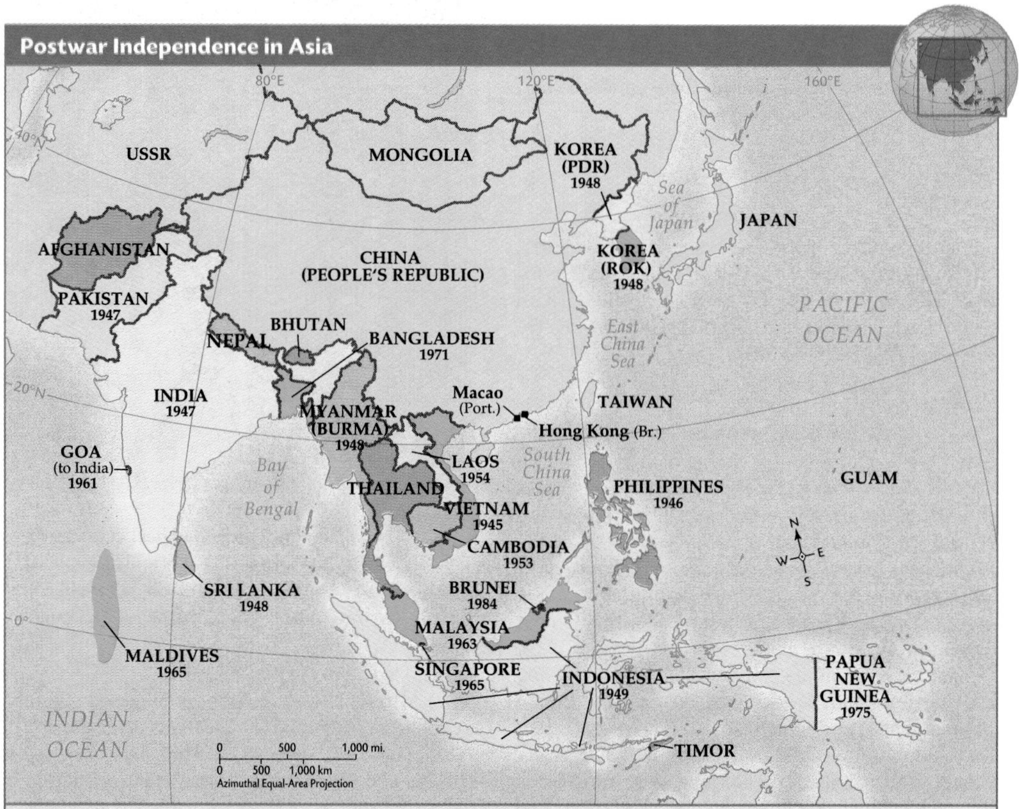

Map Study With the crumbling of the European colonial empires after World War II, a large portion of the world's population came under self-rule.
Region Why would regional cooperation in Asia be difficult for these nations to achieve?

agreement designed to halt the spread of nuclear weapons. Both countries have resisted signing.

A New Direction

Since Indira Gandhi's assassination, India has had several prime ministers, including her son Rajiv Gandhi. He was assassinated in 1991 during an election campaign. After the collapse of the Soviet Union India adopted economic reforms to sell off government-owned industries and has worked to attract new foreign investors. However, continuing ethnic and religious differences endanger its stability.

Pakistan and Bangladesh

After independence in 1947, Pakistan faced difficulties in joining two distinct regions separated by over 1,000 miles (1,609 km) of Indian territory. West Pakistan was a dry, mountainous region in which most people spoke Urdu. East Pakistan was a wet lowlands region in which most people spoke Bengali. The religion of Islam was their only common bond.

In March 1971, civil war broke out between the two regions. In December 1971, India joined the war in support of East Pakistan. This action spread the fighting to West Pakistan and Kashmir. The war ended quickly, and East Pakistan won its independence as the republic of Bangladesh.

Bangladesh

Bangladesh is one of the most densely populated nations of the world. More than 125 million people live in an area about the size of New York State. Most people are located in rural areas where

MEETING SPECIAL NEEDS ACTIVITY

Learning Style: Logical/Mathematical Have students work together to create two time lines, one of important events in India's history between World War II and the present, and the second of important events in Pakistan's history over the same period. Tell students to include political, economic, and cultural events. Advise students to use the same scale for this project so that their five time lines can be studied together. **L1**

918 Chapter 33 *Asia and the Pacific*

illiteracy and the birthrate are high and the life expectancy is low.

Achieving stable rule has been difficult in Bangladesh. The first two prime ministers of Bangladesh were assassinated. Between 1975 and 1990, army generals controlled the government. In 1991, popular demonstrations forced the government to hold free elections. Leaders of the two major parties were women. Khalida Zia, the leader of the winning party, became prime minister.

In spite of economic growth and substantial foreign aid, the future of Bangladesh remains uncertain. Its gross domestic product (GDP) is one of the lowest in the world. The country is vulnerable to extreme drought and floods.

Pakistan Since 1971

Pakistan suffered from political instability and military rule after 1971. Only in the elections of 1993 did a strong two-party system of democracy appear. **Benazir Ali Bhutto**, from a leading political family, was again elected prime minister after having been out of office for three years.

During the 1970s and 1980s, Pakistan allied with the United States in order to counter India's close military and economic ties with the Soviet Union. The Pakistani government allowed the Americans to channel military arms to anti-Soviet rebels in neighboring Afghanistan. It also permitted Afghani fighters to use Pakistan as a base of operations, and sheltered 3 million Afghani refugees. Despite massive United States aid, the presence of so many refugees was costly and worsened ethnic tensions within Pakistan.

Military spending has taken a large share of Pakistan's budget because of tensions with India. This has drained resources that could have been used for the economic development of the country. Pakistan's efforts to develop nuclear weapons led the United States to cut economic aid to Pakistan in 1990, a situation that Pakistan has been trying to reverse.

Visualizing History **Benazir Ali Bhutto was first elected in 1988, replacing the military government that had executed her father, a previous prime minister.** *What is the recent hopeful sign of democracy in Pakistan?*

Sri Lanka

In 1948, the year after the partition of India, Great Britain granted independence to Ceylon, known since 1972 as **Sri Lanka**. This beautiful island off the southeast coast of India has been the site of ethnic civil war since the 1980s. The Sinhalese, who make up about about 75 percent of the population, are Buddhists. The Tamils, who make up about 20 percent, are Hindus. In recent years the Tamils, complaining of discrimination against them by the Sinhalese, have demanded their own state within Sri Lanka. Hundreds of people have died in conflicts between government troops and Tamil guerrillas. Efforts to improve the economy have been helped by developing privately owned businesses and by attracting foreign investments.

SECTION 5 REVIEW

Recall

1. **Define** nonaligned.
2. **Identify** Jawaharlal Nehru, Indira Gandhi, Benazir Ali Bhutto.
3. **Explain** the consequences of Great Britain's withdrawal from South Asia.

Critical Thinking

4. **Analyzing Information** What do you think are the underlying causes of continuing political strife in India?

Understanding Themes

5. **Diversity** Has the division of the Indian subcontinent into separate countries been beneficial? Explain your answer.

Chapter 33 Section 5

Visualizing History Benazir Bhutto is the first woman in modern history to lead a predominantly Muslim country. A 1973 graduate of Harvard and Radcliffe Colleges, she also holds a 1977 degree from Oxford University, where she studied philosophy, political science, and economics.
Answer to Caption: *As of the elections of 1993, a strong two-party system seemed to be developing.*

Evaluate

Section Quiz 33-5

Use the Testmaker to create a customized quiz for Section 5.

Reteach

Have students locate India, Pakistan, Bangladesh, and Sri Lanka on a map. Ask them to identify the year each country achieved independence and to summarize the contemporary challenges each country faces.

Enrich

Have students each choose one of the 22 states of India and write a short report on its ethnic, cultural, and religious aspects. Some students may organize the class findings visually as a poster.

CLOSE

Have students write a short paragraph summarizing modern history and contemporary problems of each of the four countries studied in this section.

SECTION 5 REVIEW ANSWERS

1. All vocabulary words are defined in the Glossary.
2. Jawaharlal Nehru, 916; Indira Gandhi, 917; Benazir Ali Bhutto, 919
3. violence between Hindus and Muslims and the division of the Indian subcontinent
4. Answers will vary but should refer to religious and ethnic conflict.
5. DIVERSITY Answers will vary. The division allowed groups more autonomy but left a legacy of conflict.

Chapter 33 *Asia and the Pacific* 919

Chapter 33
Section 6

SECTION THEME

▸ **Cultural Diffusion** Changing political and economic roles open the nations of the Pacific to other parts of the globe.

Find Out

Answer: *foreign investment, close trading ties to Pacific Rim and other Asian nations, economic diversification; a rethinking of military relationships with the United States, and concern over nuclear proliferation*

FOCUS

Section Objective

List the factors that have helped Pacific nations develop prosperous economies and new national identities since World War II.

BELLRINGER
Motivational Activity

Before taking roll at the beginning of the class period, project Section Focus Transparency 33-6 and have students answer the activity questions.

This activity is also available as a blackline master.

Vocabulary Pre-check

Use the Vocabulary PuzzleMaker to create a puzzle that reinforces the vocabulary terms in this section. **L1**

1945 — 1972 — 2000

1946 The Philippines wins independence from the United States.

1970s Australia admits non-British European and Asian immigrants for the first time.

1995 Pacific nations protest French nuclear testing.

Section 6

The Pacific

Setting the Scene

▸ **Terms to Define**
archipelago

▸ **People to Meet**
Ferdinand Marcos, Corazon Aquino, Paul Keating, David Lange, Jim Bolger

▸ **Places to Locate**
The Philippines, Australia, New Zealand, Papua New Guinea

Find Out What factors have helped Pacific nations develop prosperous economies and new national identities since World War II?

The Storyteller

Toby Doust knew what to expect between the Great Sandy Desert and the Gibson Desert in northwestern Australia—and it wasn't water. Earlier explorers had expected water, but Lake Disappointment had water only when a rare inland cyclone brought a spattering shower to the dry bed. Toby, however, was prospecting for more commercial materials—iron, zinc, bauxite—to sell throughout the Pacific Basin. Perhaps there was even gold or uranium. One thing Toby never lacked was nerve. Nearing a remote outcrop, he unstrapped his bag and got out his metal detector, ready to strike it rich.

—adapted from "Journey into the Daytime," *National Geographic*, January 1991

Australia's Uluru (Ayers Rock)

The Pacific region east and south of Asia contains Australia, the world's only island continent, and numerous other islands that spread out across millions of miles of the Pacific Ocean. Until recently, long distances and rugged landscapes kept many parts of the region isolated from each other and the rest of the world. Beginning in the 1700s, Western powers exercised a strong influence in the region. Since World War II, the Pacific countries, now mostly independent, have forged new identities from a mix of European, traditional Pacific, and Asian cultures. Many of them have close trading ties to Japan, Singapore, and other nations of the Pacific Rim, a region of economically prosperous countries bordering the Pacific Ocean.

The Philippines

The Philippines is an archipelago, or group of islands, in the Pacific Ocean east of Vietnam. The Philippines faced severe challenges when it became independent from the United States in 1946. Philippine Communists, known as the Huks, pressed for land reform and tried to take over the government. The Philippine army defeated them in 1954, but the Huks have arisen periodically to challenge later leaders.

Between 1965 and 1986, the Philippines was led by President **Ferdinand Marcos**. Marcos at first was popular because he tried to improve education and transportation. Evidence of corruption later fueled bitter protests against him. Marcos's downfall finally came about as a result of his suspected involvement in the killing of the political opposition leader, Benigno Aquino, Jr.

A massive public outcry over the assassination forced new elections, which Marcos won by fraud. Popular outrage at his deceit forced Marcos to flee the country. **Corazon Aquino**, the widow of the assassinated opposition leader, became the new president.

SECTION RESOURCES

Reproducible Masters
- Reproducible Lesson Plan 33-6
- Guided Reading Activity 33-6
- Reteaching Activity 33
- Enrichment Activity 33
- Section Quiz 33-6
- Performance Assessment Activity 33
- Spanish Chapter Summary 33

Transparencies
- Section Focus Transparency 33-6
- World History and Art Transparency 44, *Sydney Opera House*

Multimedia
- Vocabulary PuzzleMaker Software
- Student Self-Test and Review Software
- Testmaker
- World Music: Cultural Traditions, Lesson 10

Visualizing History **President Corazon Aquino pledged to restore democracy to the Philippines under a new constitution in 1987.** *What four groups opposed her rule?*

Optimism that Corazon Aquino would begin a new era of reform and economic growth soon faded. She faced opposition from Marcos supporters, the Huks, the military, and nationalist Filipinos opposed to American military bases in the Philippines. An attempt to overthrow her failed due to American support. In 1992, Fidel Ramos succeeded her as president.

That same year, the United States withdrew from its last military base in the Philippines. Although this was the desire of the Philippine government, the loss of revenue to the Philippine economy was substantial. Japan has since become the foreign country with the most economic influence in the Philippines.

Australia

Before World War II, **Australia** was a largely agricultural country dependent on Great Britain. Beef, wool, wheat, and dairy products were the country's main exports. Since 1945, Australia has changed to an industrial economy with close links to the United States and Asian countries. With the help of foreign investment, Australians have developed assembly and manufacturing plants for consumer goods, processed foods, paper, textiles, and transportation equipment.

Since the 1970s, Australia has strengthened ties with its Asian neighbors. In 1973, Australian Prime Minister Gough Whitlam traveled to China for a visit with Mao Zedong. Under **Paul Keating**, who became prime minister in 1991, Australia has increased economic links to Japan and Southeast Asia. Today more than 60 percent of Australia's exports and imports are with Asian countries.

Australia's turning from Great Britain to its Asian and Pacific neighbors has been influenced by the country's changing population. After World War II, large numbers of southern and eastern Europeans—Greeks, Italians, and Slavs—made new homes in Australia. Then, in the 1970s, the Australian government liberalized its immigration laws and allowed Asian immigrants into the country. Today, about 50 percent of immigrants to Australia each year come from neighboring Asian countries. By the 1990s only about 35 percent of Australians were of British descent; this was down from 75 percent in 1949.

On the World Stage

Since World War II Australia has also sought a greater role in world affairs. It became a founding member of the United Nations in 1945. Five years later, Australian troops joined the UN forces fighting in the Korean War. In 1951 Australia signed the ANZUS treaty, which linked Australia, New Zealand, and the United States in a mutual defense pact. As part of the effort to contain communism, Australia sent forces to fight alongside the United States in the Vietnam War. It later backed the UN effort against Iraq in 1990 by sending Australian warships to the Persian Gulf.

Australians continue to support close military ties with the United States but are concerned about

COOPERATIVE LEARNING ACTIVITY

The Arts Organize the class into four groups to research Australian, Melanesian, Polynesian, and Micronesian art. Each group member should have a specific area to research, such as visual art, music, dance, literature, or specific crafts. When the groups have completed their research, ask them to prepare class presentations combining oral commentary with visual and aural examples. After all the groups have made their presentations, hold a class discussion in which students compare and contrast Australian, Melanesian, Polynesian, and Micronesian arts and crafts. **L2**

TEACH

Guided Practice

THEME Cultural Diffusion

Ask students to list the cultural influences that have affected the development of Australia *(population: Aborigines, British, southern and eastern European; military: United States; trade: Japan, Southeast Asia),* New Zealand *(population: Maori, British, other European; military: United States; trade: Japan, Australia, United States, Europe),* and Papua New Guinea *(population: ethnic groups speaking nearly 700 different languages).* **L1**

Visualizing History Corazon Aquino called for only nonviolent demonstrations, boycotts, and strikes to protest the corrupt Marcos regime.

Answer to Caption: *Marcos supporters, the Huks, the military, and nationalist Filipinos opposed to American military bases in the Philippines*

World History and Art Transparency 44, *Sydney Opera House*

World Music: Cultural Traditions, Lesson 10

Linking Past and Present

Philippine Government In February 1986, Marcos dispatched columns of tanks against a group of rebel soldiers in Manila. They were stopped by the crowds assembled at the corner of Ortigas Avenue and the highway. In February 1996, Filipinos celebrated the tenth anniversary of the "People Power" revolution against Marcos. President Fidel V. Ramos addressed a rally at that corner.

Chapter 33 *Asia and the Pacific* **921**

Chapter 33
Section 6

Independent Practice

Guided Reading Activity 33-6 **L1**

Literature Have students choose a book by Australian novelist Patrick White, who won the 1973 Nobel Prize in literature. Ask them to write a book report that focuses on life in Australia. **L2**

ASSESS

Check for Understanding

Assign Section 6 Review as homework or as an in-class activity.

Use Student Self-Test Software to review Section 6.

Evaluate

Section Quiz 33-6

Use the Testmaker to create a customized quiz for Section 6.

Reteach

Have students write one-sentence identifications of each of the terms, people, and places listed in "Setting the Scene," on page 920.

Reteaching Activity 33

Enrich

Have students locate articles about recent antinuclear activities in the Pacific region. Ask them to summarize their findings in a brief written report.

Enrichment Activity 33

CLOSE

Have students write a short paragraph for each of the countries covered in this section (the Philippines, Australia, New Zealand, and Papua New Guinea) summarizing recent developments.

the presence of nuclear weapons in the Pacific region. Australia has been a major sponsor of a South Pacific Nuclear-Free Zone. Even so, it sided with the United States in the United States's dispute with New Zealand about American nuclear-armed vessels entering into New Zealand waters.

New Zealand

Consisting of two major islands and many small ones, **New Zealand** lies about 1,000 miles (1,600 km) to the southeast of Australia. Most of New Zealand's 3.5 million people are of British, other European, or Maori descent. Like Australia, New Zealand traditionally was joined by trade, politics, and culture to Great Britain. After the war, it began to ally itself more closely with the United States and Asian countries.

New Zealand also added more variety to its economy. While agriculture—mainly sheep and dairy farming—remain important, New Zealand now has many manufacturing and service industries. It trades with Japan, Australia, the United States, and the countries of Western Europe.

Fear of Japanese attack during World War II made New Zealand turn to the United States for defense when the war was over. In 1951, New Zealand welcomed the creation of the ANZUS alliance and participated in the Korean and Vietnam conflicts.

Since the 1980s, however, New Zealand's opposition to nuclear weapons has strained its relationship with the United States and has drawn it closer to other Pacific countries that also oppose nuclear weapons. In 1985, New Zealand Prime Minister **David Lange** announced that ships carrying nuclear weapons, including those from the United States, could no longer enter New Zealand ports. In the early 1990s, Lange's successor as prime minister, **Jim Bolger**, worked to improve relations with the United States on the nuclear issue.

South Pacific Island Countries

Thousands of islands dot the Pacific Ocean. Many are small and uninhabited. Others were first settled thousands of years ago by various Asian and Pacific peoples. Their descendants today belong to three major groups: Melanesians, Micronesians, and Polynesians.

Nations and Colonies

Since World War II, some of the islands—such as Fiji—have become independent of Western rule. Other islands—such as Tahiti—continue to be held by Western powers as colonial territories valued for military reasons. France, for example, in 1995 conducted nuclear tests on an atoll, or ring-shaped coral island, in French Polynesia. French actions have aroused antinuclear protests in the Pacific region and throughout other parts of the world.

Papua New Guinea

Among the larger island countries in the Pacific region is **Papua New Guinea**. Made up of 700 islands, Papua New Guinea has most of its territory on the eastern half of the island of New Guinea. Formerly held by Germany and Great Britain, and later by Australia, Papua New Guinea became independent in 1975.

Papua New Guinea faces many challenges in its efforts to achieve national unity. Its population is made up of many ethnic groups that speak nearly 700 different languages. Because of this ethnic diversity, Papua New Guinea has little sense of nationhood. Tensions and conflict between ethnic groups is common.

In addition, most of Papua New Guinea's people are poor and illiterate. Copper and gold mining has boosted the economy since the 1980s, but other economic sectors remain to be developed. The government of Papua New Guinea is working to interest companies in Japan, the United States, Hong Kong, and Singapore to invest in the country.

SECTION 6 REVIEW

Recall

1. **Define** archipelago.
2. **Identify** Ferdinand Marcos, Corazon Aquino, ANZUS, Paul Keating, David Lange, Jim Bolger.
3. **Explain** what events led to Marcos's downfall in the Philippines.

Critical Thinking

4. **Analyzing Information** How has the economy of Australia changed since World War II?

Understanding Themes

5. **Cultural Diffusion** What cultural influences have affected the development of South Pacific island countries?

SECTION 6 REVIEW ANSWERS

1. All vocabulary words are defined in the Glossary.
2. Ferdinand Marcos, 920; Corazon Aquino, 920; ANZUS, 921; Paul Keating, 921; David Lange, 922; Jim Bolger, 922
3. his suspected involvement in the killing of Benigno Aquino, Jr., and his corrupt government
4. It has changed from a largely agricultural country dependent on Great Britain to an industrial economy with close links to the United States and Asia.
5. **CULTURAL DIFFUSION** Melanesian, Micronesian, and Polynesian influences have affected the development of South Pacific island countries.

Study and Writing
SKILLS

Conducting Interviews

Reading about an event informs us, but hearing about it from someone who was directly involved can provide invaluable personal insights. Interviews are a good way to obtain this kind of information. An interview is a conversation in which one person asks for information from another.

Interviews provide insight into both current and historical events. Every community has members who have lived through important moments of history. Interviewing these people creates the primary source materials of our collective past. By conducting interviews, you may help to build the historical record.

Learning the Skill

Conducting a successful interview requires preparation. First, invite your subject to the interview by letter or telephone. Explain why you seek the interview. What aspects of the person's life and experience interest you? Be sure the subject agrees to discuss these topics. If you want to tape-record the interview, get permission in advance.

Before the interview, gather background information. Using the library, find out all you can about the event your subject has experienced. If the subject is a public figure, find biographical information about the person's life and work.

Use your research to develop a list of questions. Think about what unique information this person has. For example, suppose you interview a Vietnamese American who survived the Vietnam War. What do you want to know about this experience? Avoid asking questions that lead to yes or no answers. Plan follow-up questions to elicit more information.

Assemble your equipment—audio or video cassette recorder, notepad, pencils, and your list of questions. Conduct the interview in a quiet comfortable place with no disruptions. Be punctual and courteous.

Begin by asking your prepared questions, but stay flexible. Your subject's answers may lead to unexpected but valuable topics. Trust your intuition to follow new thoughts. Later, you can return to your list of questions.

Listen carefully to all responses. Your mind may race ahead to the next question instead of absorbing the subject's response to the last one. If you need an explanation, ask for it. Take notes. It is all right to pause to finish writing something important, or to ask your subject to repeat an important idea. Even if using a tape recorder, take some notes in case the recorder malfunctions.

After the interview, transcribe your notes or recording into a written transcript. If you will publish the interview, provide a preview copy to your subject for an accuracy check.

Practicing the Skill

Imagine that you want to interview a member of your community who was one of the Cambodian "boat people." Answer the following questions about conducting this interview.

1. In your invitation, what would you say to the subject?
2. What research would you do to prepare for the interview?
3. Write two questions for this interview.
4. Write two follow-up questions.

Applying the Skill

Conduct an oral history interview of a member of your family or community. Gather background information about the person and the historical events that he or she witnessed. Prepare questions and conduct the interview. Afterward, make a written transcript.

For More Practice

Turn to the Skill Practice in the Chapter Review on page 925 for more practice in conducting interviews.

Study and Writing
SKILLS

TEACH

Conducting Interviews Before students read the skill, discuss how interviewing different kinds of people requires different approaches and techniques. As an example, focus on the special techniques required when interviewing political leaders. **What do the "People to Meet" on page 920 have in common?** *(They all were or are political leaders.)* **What special problems might be involved in interviewing political leaders?** *(They might try to use the interviewer as a mouthpiece for their ideas and for publicizing their goals; they might be evasive on tough questions; they might simply lie.)* **What steps might an interviewer take to steer such an interview in a desired direction?** *(If the subject takes off on an irrelevant line of conversation, interrupt politely but firmly and guide the discussion back to the proper topic. Beware of grandstanding and posturing and demand specific answers to your questions. If the answer is vague, follow up by repeating the question or making it more specific. Confront the subject with any evidence that will expose lies or half-truths.)* Now have the class read the skill and complete the practice questions.

Additional Practice

Skill Reinforcement Activity 33

ANSWERS TO PRACTICING THE SKILL

1. Answers will vary but might include introducing oneself and explaining the purpose of the interview and who will read it or see it.
2. Answers will vary but should indicate that the student will find out as much as possible about the Cambodian boat people in advance.
3. Answers will vary but should reflect student preparation.
4. Answers will vary but should reflect student preparation.

Chapter 33 Review

GLENCOE TECHNOLOGY

VIDEODISC

Use MindJogger to review students' knowledge of the chapter.

MindJogger Videoquiz

Chapter 33
Disc 5 Side A

Also available in VHS.

CHAPTER 33 REVIEW

Historical Significance

The most dramatic change in Asia since 1945 is the dazzling economic achievements of Japan, South Korea, Hong Kong, Taiwan, and Singapore. In these nations, stable governments have worked with private companies to foster economic growth. Experts from around the world study Japan and other prosperous Asian countries to learn the reasons for their success.

Meanwhile, India and other Asian countries are developing their economies. While the gap between rich and poor remains wide in many areas, standards of living are rising.

Using Key Terms

Write the key term that completes each sentence.

a. referendum	g. sect
b. stalemate	h. special economic zones
c. archipelago	i. domino theory
d. refugee	j. nonaligned
e. quota	k. pollution
f. pragmatists	l. gross domestic product

1. In the 1960s the growing American role in Vietnam was justified by those who accepted the ________.
2. Jawaharlal Nehru believed if India and other less powerful countries remained _________ in the cold war, they could provide alternatives to the superpowers.
3. By 1951, the Korean War had reached a ________, a situation in which two opponents are unable to move significantly or make further gains.
4. In China, a group known as _______ favored modernizing China through increased trade and contacts with the West.
5. By 1980, Japan's _________indicated that it had one of the world's most successful economies.
6. The turmoil in Southeast Asia during the 1970s forced many people to flee their homes and settle in ________ camps.
7. The Philippines, Japan, and Indonesia each is made up of an __________, or chain of islands.
8. The Chinese government has allowed foreign privately owned businesses to flourish in ___________ located in southeastern China.
9. Industrialized countries face challenges from ________, or the release of impure or poisonous industrial wastes into water, air and land.
10. In a __________, voters are asked to accept or reject a measure.

Using Your History Journal

Imagine that you and your family have moved to live in an Asian country. Write a letter back to your friends in the United States about your experiences during the first year in your new country.

Reviewing Facts

1. **List** the major areas of reform in Japan during the American occupation after World War II.
2. **Explain** why India was partitioned in 1947.
3. **Identify** the American Presidents who were in office during the United States direct involvement in Vietnam 1964–1973.
4. **Discuss** why Australia and New Zealand have shifted their focus away from Great Britain and toward Asia and the United States.
5. **Identify** the boat people.
6. **Explain** the goals of China's Red Guards during the Cultural Revolution.

Critical Thinking

1. **Apply** Using examples from Asia, explain whether a country's economic progress is related to its form of government.
2. **Analyze** Why was General MacArthur's occupation of Japan so successful?
3. **Synthesize** Explain how events in Asia since 1945 have influenced the population profile of the people of the United States.
4. **Analyze** Why did Pakistan as created in 1947 split into two separate nations?

Answers

Using Key Terms

1. i	6. d
2. j	7. c
3. b	8. h
4. f	9. k
5. l	10. a

Using Your History Journal

Suggest that students reflect on political, cultural, and economic changes they confront as new immigrants, as well as possible discrimination.

Reviewing Facts

1. politics, cultural change, economics
2. because of violent confrontations between Hindus and Muslims
3. Kennedy, Johnson, Nixon
4. defense links with the United States; economic ties to the United States and Asia
5. Southeast Asian refugees who fled by sea to escape war and political turmoil
6. to enforce pure communism in China by arresting those suspected of Western sympathies and by destroying books that were vehicles of traditional Chinese culture

Critical Thinking

1. Answers will vary. Possible answer: Countries with relatively stable governments—such as the sometimes authoritarian Singapore and democratic Japan—have had the greatest economic success.
2. MacArthur sought to rebuild, not to exact revenge from, Japan.
3. Turmoil in Southeast Asia caused a large immigration to the United States.
4. because of civil war between Urdu-speaking West Pakistan and Bengali-speaking East Pakistan (now Bangladesh)
5. It led to the establishment of diplomatic relations with the People's Republic of China.

Understanding Themes

1. **CHANGE** MacArthur's postwar policies, American need for nearby supplies during Korean War, Japanese government-

5. **Analyze** United States President Richard Nixon visited China in 1972. What historic change in United States policy did this visit signal?

Understanding Themes

1. **Change** What factors account for Japan's economic recovery and prosperity since World War II?
2. **Revolution** What changes did the Communist takeover of 1949 bring to China during the 1950s? How have policies changed since the 1970s?
3. **Regionalism** What basic reason keeps Korea divided into two nations?
4. **Conflict** How did the United States get involved in the war in Vietnam?
5. **Diversity** What religious groups other than Hindus and Muslims form part of India's diverse population?
6. **Cultural Diffusion** What new national and ethnic groups have come to once predominately British Australia as a result of changes in immigration since World War II?

Linking Past and Present

1. The era from about 1950 to the present and on into the twenty-first century has been called the Asian Century. Explain what name you would give to the 100 years prior to 1950.
2. The involvement by the United States in Vietnam was based on the domino theory and the Truman Doctrine, both of which declared the United States commitment to containing communism. What circumstances, if any, do you think would justify United States involvement overseas today?

Geography in History

1. **Region** Refer to the map on this page. What generalization describes the diverse economies of East Asia and the Pacific?
2. **Movement** By what type of transportation is most trade among nations in this region conducted?
3. **Place** What five nations make up the low-income economies group?
4. **Place** What nations make up the middle-income economies groups?
5. **Region** What do the economies of Japan and Australia have in common according to the map?

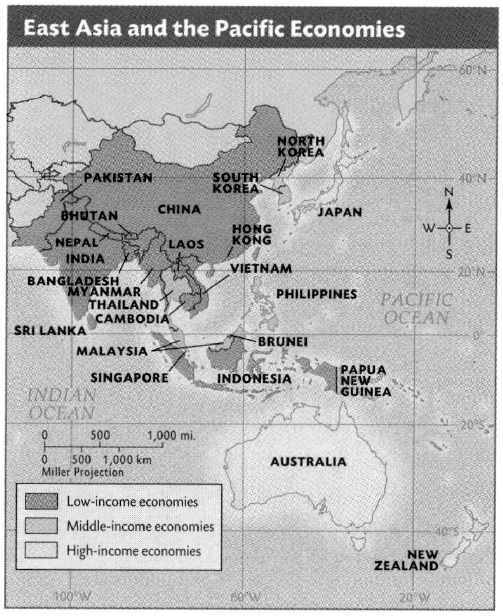

Skill Practice

Watch or listen to an experienced interviewer conduct an interview on a television or radio program. If possible, tape-record the interview. Then answer the following questions.

1. Name the date and time of the interview, the interviewer, and the subject.
2. Did the interviewer prepare for the interview? How could you tell?
3. On what topics did the interview concentrate?
4. What were the most interesting questions asked by the interviewer?
5. What new things did you learn about the subject from this interview?

business cooperation, political stability, normalization of relations with China

2. **REVOLUTION** the 1950s: land reform, firm control over local governments, Five-Year Plan to develop heavy industry and agriculture, the Great Leap Forward, close relations with the Soviet Union; since the 1970s: split with the Soviet Union, closer ties with United States and East Asian neighbors, development of light industry and consumer goods, some free market activity, creation of special economic zones
3. **REGIONALISM** North Korea remains a Communist dictatorship, and South Korea fears its military threat.
4. **CONFLICT** support of its ally, France, the colonial ruler of most of Indochina
5. **DIVERSITY** Buddhists, Sikhs, Jains, Parsis, Christians, Jews
6. **CULTURAL DIFFUSION** southern and eastern Europeans, Asians

Chapter 33 Review

Linking Past and Present

1. Some students might call it the American Century or the European Century, because of the economic and political dominance of these regions.
2. Students may mention prevention of genocide and other types of humanitarian aid.

Geography in History

1. Most are low-income; only 3 high-income
2. ship
3. China, Pakistan, Bhutan, Nepal, India, Bangladesh, Myanmar, Cambodia, Laos, Vietnam, Indonesia
4. South Korea, Thailand, Malaysia, Philippines, Brunei, Papua New Guinea
5. Both have high-income economies.

Skill Practice

Answers will vary but should be supported by specific details gleaned from the interview.

Chapter Bonus Test Question

Ask students: How convincing are arguments by developing nations that democracy should be sacrificed in the name of promoting economic growth and public safety? Support your answer with examples from specific countries studied in this chapter. *(Answers will vary but may include: The end justifies the means, and countries such as Singapore are cleaner and safer than the United States, with a higher general standard of living, even if there is political repression; or, the end does not justify the means, and people are better served by democratic countries, even if some citizens do not have an economic safety net.)*

Teach, Reinforce, and Extend CHAPTER Content

Africa

CHAPTER RESOURCES

	Reproducible Resources	Multimedia Resources
Chapter Opener	Chapter Themes: Graphic Organizer 34 Historical Significance Chapter Activity 34	MindJogger Videoquiz
Chapter Enrichment	Vocabulary Activity 34* Time Line Activity 34 Mapping History Activity 34 History Simulation 34 Geography and History Activity 34 Source Reading 34 People in World History Profiles 65, 66 World Art and Music Activity 34 Enrichment Activity 34 Critical Thinking Activity 34 Skill Reinforcement Activity 34 Writer's Guidebook, Lesson 12 Performance Assessment Activity 34	World History and Art Transparency 45, *The Liberated African Woman;* 46, *Bedouin Woman's Headpiece* Chapter Transparency 34 NGS PicturePack Transparencies: Physical Geography of the World Vocabulary PuzzleMaker Software Picture Atlas of the World World Music: Cultural Traditions, Lesson 6 Turning Points in World History: *End of Apartheid* STV: World Geography, Vol. 2, *Africa*
Chapter Review/Reteaching	Reteaching Activity 34 Skill Reinforcement Activity 34 Spanish Chapter Summary 34	Chapter 34 Digest Audiocassette, Activity, Test* Vocabulary PuzzleMaker Software Student Self-Test and Review Software MindJogger Videoquiz
Chapter Evaluation/Testing	Performance Assessment Activity 34 Chapter 34 Test, Forms A and B	Testmaker

* *Also available in Spanish*

0:00 **OUT OF TIME?** Assign the Chapter 34 summary in the Unit 8 Digest on pages 1026–1029, and the Chapter 34 Audiocassettes.

Block Schedule

Block scheduling differs from traditional class scheduling in the amount of time allotted to each period. The extended time frame provided by block scheduling affords you the opportunity to implement a greater number of research-oriented and activity-intense projects to motivate and involve your students. Activities that are particularly suited to use within the block scheduling framework are identified throughout this chapter by the following designation.

KEY TO ABILITY LEVELS

Teaching strategies have been coded for varying learning styles and abilities.

- **L1** **BASIC** activities for all students
- **L2** **AVERAGE** activities for average to above-average students
- **L3** **CHALLENGING** activities for above-average students
- **LEP** **LIMITED ENGLISH PROFICIENCY** activities

A complete, 1-page lesson plan is provided for each section in the *Reproducible Lesson Plans* booklet.

SECTION RESOURCES

Daily Objectives	Reproducible Resources	Multimedia Resources
Section 1 African Independence Describe how African nations won their independence after World War II.	Reproducible Lesson Plan 34-1 Vocabulary Activity 34* Guided Reading Activity 34-1* Time Line Activity 34 People in World History Profile 65 Section Quiz 34-1*	Section Focus Transparency 34-1 Chapter Transparency 34 World History and Art Transparency 46, *Bedouin Woman's Headpiece* NGS PicturePack Transparencies: Physical Geography of the World Student Self-Test and Review Software Testmaker Picture Atlas of the World
Section 2 Africa Today Explain what kinds of governments ruled in Africa from the 1970s to the 1990s.	Reproducible Lesson Plan 34-2 Vocabulary Activity 34* Guided Reading Activity 34-2* People in World History Profile 66 Section Quiz 34-2*	Section Focus Transparency 34-2 Student Self-Test and Review Software Testmaker World Music: Cultural Traditions, Lesson 6 Picture Atlas of the World Turning Points in World History: *End of Apartheid*
Section 3 Africa's Challenges Identify the challenges faced by modern African nations in their quest for political and economic independence.	Reproducible Lesson Plan 34-3 Guided Reading Activity 34-3* Reteaching Activity 34 Enrichment Activity 34 Section Quiz 34-3* Performance Assessment Activity 34 Spanish Chapter Summary 34	Section Focus Transparency 34-3 World History and Art Transparency 45, *The Liberated African Woman* Vocabulary PuzzleMaker Software Student Self-Test and Review Software Testmaker Picture Atlas of the World STV: World Geography, Vol. 2, *Africa*

** Also available in Spanish*

Chapter Activities

Performance Assessment Activity

A Letter to a Young African Have students write letters to a high school student in Africa who is living with the challenges addressed in this chapter. Have students organize their letters around the question of why political independence was easier to achieve than economic independence for most African nations. Ask students to suggest reasons why it is sometimes easier to solve political problems than economic problems and have them give examples from their own experiences or from recent United States history.

Possible Rubric Features

Concept attainment, critical thinking, elaboration and organization of letter, analysis of relationships, persuasion

• *For an additional activity, refer to Activity 34 in the* Performance Assessment Strategies and Activities *booklet.*

Activity

From the Classroom of...

Anna Mae Grimm
Homestead High School
Mequon, WI

Experiencing Apartheid

For one class period, designate about half the students in the class to be part of an "underclass" that will not be allowed to participate in activities with the rest of the class. Have the "underclass" sit at the back of the room. Provide an interesting activity for the rest of the class, and assign the separated students routine worksheets. Hold an election during the class period (for example, elect a discussion leader) and exclude the separated students from the voting.

During the next class period, discuss how students felt during the simulation—both those in the "underclass" and those in the mainstream. Use this as a springboard for discussing apartheid in South Africa.

Multiple Learning Styles

Verbal/Linguistic
Have students read and write brief reviews of a short story, play, novel, or poem by a contemporary African author.

Visual/Spatial
Have students create a piece of art based on an African model.

Auditory/Musical
Have students find recordings of modern African music by such popular artists as King Sunny Ade and Babatunde Olanji of Nigeria, Baaba Maal or Youssou N'Dour of Senegal, Ladysmith Black Mambazo of South Africa, or Thomas Mapfumo of Zimbabwe and play selected songs for the class.

Kinesthetic
Have students plan and attend a field trip to a nearby museum that displays African art and artifacts.

Additional Resources

TEACHER'S CORNER

NATIONAL GEOGRAPHIC SOCIETY

INDEX TO NATIONAL GEOGRAPHIC MAGAZINE

The following articles may be used for research relating to this chapter:

- "The Mountain Gorillas of Africa," by Paul F. Salopek, October 1995.
- "The Dawn of Humans," by Meave Leakey, September 1995.
- "The African Roots of Voodoo," by Carol Beckwith and Angela Fisher, August 1995.
- "Ndoki—The Last Place on Earth," by Douglas Chadwick, July 1995.
- "Fantasy Coffins of Ghana," by Carol Beckwith and Angela Fisher, September 1994.
- "The Twilight of Apartheid," by Charles E. Cobb, Jr., February 1993.
- "The Stricken Land: Africa's Sahel," by William S. Ellis, August 1987.

NATIONAL GEOGRAPHIC SOCIETY PRODUCTS AVAILABLE FROM GLENCOE

To order the following products for use with this chapter, contact your local Glencoe sales representative or call Glencoe at 1-800-368-7344:

VIDEODISC
- STV: World Geography, Vol. 2, *Africa*

CD-ROM
- PICTURE ATLAS OF THE WORLD

PICTUREPACK TRANSPARENCIES
- Physical Geography of the World

ADDITIONAL NATIONAL GEOGRAPHIC SOCIETY PRODUCTS

To order the following products for use with this chapter, call National Geographic Society at 1-800-368-2728:

- *South Africa: After Apartheid* (Video)
- *Baka: People of the Forest* (Video)

BIBLIOGRAPHY

Literature of the Period

Achebe, Chinua, and C. L. Innes, eds. ***Heinemann Book of Contemporary African Short Stories.*** Portsmouth, NH: Heinemann, 1992. Fiction about African social life and customs.

Soyinka, Wole. ***Death and the King's Horseman.*** New York: Norton, 1990. Short historical drama by the Nigerian who won the 1986 Nobel Prize in literature.

Readings for the Student

Davidson, Basil. ***The Black Man's Burden: Africa and the Curse of the Nation-State.*** New York: Times Books, 1992. Underlying causes of political conflict and instability in Africa since independence.

Readings for the Teacher

Malan, Rian. ***My Traitor's Heart: A South African Exile Returns to Face His Country, His Tribe, and His Conscience.*** New York: Atlantic Monthly Press, 1990. Personal reflections on South Africa by a descendant of one of the builders of apartheid.

interNET
CONNECTIONS
Biography of Nelson Mandela A description of the major events in Nelson Mandela's life.
World Wide Web:
http://www.polity.org.za/people/mandela.html

Introducing Chapter 34

CHAPTER THEMES

Chapter Themes are listed by section on this chapter opening page of the Student Edition. A corresponding theme-based activity is available under "TEACH," and a theme-based question is asked in the Section and Chapter Reviews.

The Storyteller

Historical Setting Mandela, born in 1918, spent 28 years (1962–1990) in prison for conspiring to overthrow the white-minority government of South Africa. During those years, his wife, Winnie, helped focus the world's attention on Mandela and make him a symbol of the struggle against apartheid. After his release from prison, his negotiations with white leaders led to the end of apartheid and establishment of a nonracial government system. For their joint efforts to end apartheid, Mandela and F. W. de Klerk, his predecessor as president of South Africa, shared the 1993 Nobel Peace Prize.

Historical Significance

Answers: *The European colonial empires in Africa were replaced by independent nations.*

Africa has become an international force, wielding more than a third of the votes in the United Nations General Assembly.

Using Your History Journal

Advise students, as they begin their clipping or paraphrasing, to concentrate on a single country or region of Africa about which they would like to learn more after concluding the chapter.

Chapter

34 1945–Present Africa

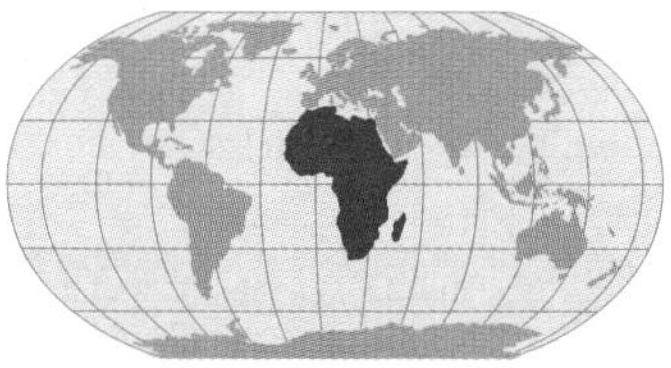

Chapter Themes

- **Nationalism** European empires crumble, and independent nations emerge in Africa. *Section 1*
- **Change** Some African nations move toward democracy and free enterprise economies. *Section 2*
- **Change** Ethnic, cultural, environmental and economic challenges face newly independent African nations. *Section 3*

The Storyteller

From April 26 to 29, 1994, South Africa held its first election in which all of its citizens, regardless of race, could vote. The outcome was a landslide victory for nationalist leader Nelson Mandela and his African National Congress party.

On May 10, during his inauguration as South Africa's first black president, Mandela declared, "The people of South Africa ... want change.... Our plan is to create jobs, promote peace and reconciliation and to guarantee freedom for all South Africans." Mandela's rise to office signaled a joyous dawn of freedom after decades of white-minority rule and racial discrimination in South Africa.

By the early 1990s nearly 700 million people in more than 50 African countries had thrown off various forms of colonial rule and were charting new courses as independent nations.

Historical Significance

What sweeping changes came to Africa after World War II? What role does Africa play in world affairs today?

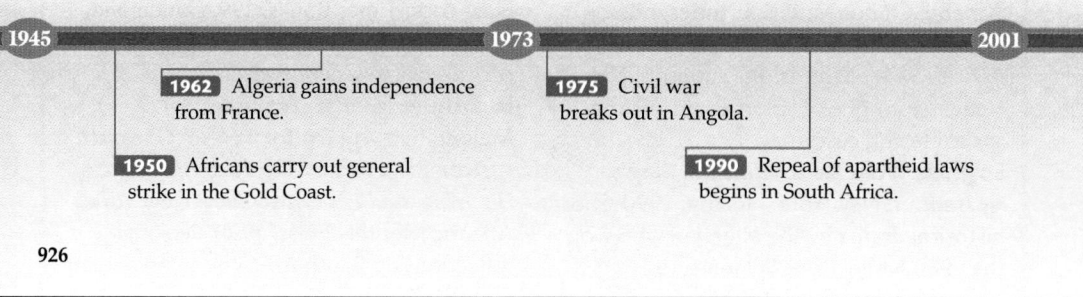

1945 — 1973 — 2001

1950 Africans carry out general strike in the Gold Coast.

1962 Algeria gains independence from France.

1975 Civil war breaks out in Angola.

1990 Repeal of apartheid laws begins in South Africa.

926

GEOGRAPHY CONNECTION

GEOGRAPHIC THEMES

Location Have students use a world map to locate Africa. Compare the size of Africa with the size of the United States. *(It is much larger, closer to the size of North America.)* Show students a landform or vegetation map of Africa and ask them to describe the continent. *(About one-third is desert; it has grasslands, rain forests, and hot, dry savannas.)*

Visualizing History Children in Somalia, like this student, were doing their daily school work in the midst of civil war, when United Nations troops arrived in 1992.

Your History Journal

Watch for current articles about African nations in newspapers and magazines. Clip and paste or write headlines and paraphrase short excerpts from these articles in your History Journal.

EXTRA CREDIT PROJECT

Oral Report Ask students to choose three African countries, one in western Africa, one on the Mediterranean Sea, and one in eastern or central Africa. Have them research the economic problems each country faces and the policies each country is adopting to solve them. Have students summarize their findings in a brief oral report. Suggested resources: C. Wekesser and C. Pierce, *Africa: Opposing Viewpoints*; S. Baynham, *Africa from 1945*; B. Davidson, *The Black Man's Burden: Africa and the Curse of the Nation-State*; S. J. Ungar, *Africa: The People and Politics of an Emerging Continent*.

Introducing Chapter 34

Visualizing History In 1991 fighting broke out among rebel groups in Somalia. By late 1992 the fighting had led to the deaths of about 30,000 people and had disrupted food production, threatening millions with starvation. With UN authorization, a coalition of military forces from several countries, led by the United States, went into Somalia to provide security for relief organizations distributing food. U.S. troops were withdrawn in March 1994, and the remaining UN forces left Somalia in March 1995.

Performance Assessment

Refer to the activity on page 926C of the Planning Guide.

For an additional activity, refer to Activity 34 in the *Performance Assessment Strategies and Activities* booklet.

GLENCOE TECHNOLOGY

VIDEODISC
Use MindJogger to preview chapter content.

MindJogger Videoquiz
Chapter 34
Disc 5 Side A

Also available in VHS.

Chapter 34 Section 1

SECTION THEME

▶ **Nationalism** European empires crumble, and independent nations emerge in Africa.

Find Out

Answer: *Relatively small prewar efforts for freedom swelled into powerful mass movements.*

FOCUS

Section Objective

Describe how African nations won their independence after World War II.

BELLRINGER Motivational Activity

Before taking roll at the beginning of the class period, project Section Focus Transparency 34-1 and have students answer the activity questions. Discuss students' responses.

This activity is also available as a blackline master.

Vocabulary Pre-check

Use Vocabulary Activity 34 to introduce vocabulary terms. **L1 LEP**

1945 — 1960 — 1975

1948 South Africa introduces apartheid politics.

1957 Ghana becomes independent.

1970 Biafran conflict ends in Nigeria.

Section 1

African Independence

Setting the Scene

▶ **Terms to Define**
colons, general strike, apartheid

▶ **People to Meet**
Muammar al-Qatar Qaddafi, Kwame Nkrumah, Ahmed Sékou Touré, Jomo Kenyatta, Nelson Mandela

▶ **Places to Locate**
Sudan, Algeria, Ghana, Congo (Zaire), Nigeria, Kenya, Angola, Mozambique, Malawi, Zambia, Zimbabwe, South Africa

Find Out How did African nations win their independence after World War II?

The Storyteller

Meeting in an open field at Kliptown, South Africa, 3,000 delegates adopted the Freedom Charter in 1955. The Charter held out hope for a democratic nation: "We the people of South Africa, declare for all our country and the world to know: that South Africa belongs to all who live in it, black and white, and that no government can claim authority unless it is based on the will of all the people ... that our country will never be prosperous and free until all people live in brotherhood, enjoying equal rights and opportunities."

—from *South Africa, Challenge and Hope*, American Friends Service Committee, Lyle Tatum, editor, 1987

First free election in South Africa

After World War II, the desire for liberation that found expression in Asia also spread to Africa. On the vast African continent in 1945, only Egypt, Ethiopia, and Liberia were independent states. South Africa, although independent, was governed by a white minority that withheld freedom from most of the country's population. In other areas, Great Britain, France, Portugal, Spain, and Belgium still exercised direct colonial rule.

By the mid-1960s, these European countries had freed most of their African colonies. The southern part of Africa remained the only area of the continent where liberation movements encountered obstacles—in this case, from sizable European settler populations. The path to independence in Africa was often bloody, and once free, the new nations faced the enormous task of building modern societies. Civil wars and economic and political crises often complicated this effort.

Winds of Change

Since the beginning of the colonial era, nationalist groups in Africa had resisted European rule, often violently. But following World War II, these relatively small efforts for freedom swelled into powerful mass movements.

Opposition to Empire

The democratic ideals for which the Allies fought in the war—self-rule and freedom from tyranny—inspired Africans, many of whom had fought in the Allied armies. "[We] overseas soldiers are coming back home with new ideas," wrote Nigerian Theo Ayoola, stationed with British troops in India. "We have been told what we fought for. That is freedom! We want freedom, nothing but freedom!"

Many people throughout the world were recognizing the hypocrisy and injustice of European

SECTION RESOURCES

Reproducible Masters
- Reproducible Lesson Plan 34-1
- Vocabulary Activity 34
- Guided Reading Activity 34-1
- Time Line Activity 34
- People in World History Profile 65
- Section Quiz 34-1

Transparencies
- Section Focus Transparency 34-1
- Chapter Transparency 34
- World History and Art Transparency 46
- NGS PicturePack Transparencies: *Physical Geography of the World*

Multimedia
- Student Self-Test and Review Software
- Testmaker
- Picture Atlas of the World

nations continuing to rule African populations while professing democratic values. In addition to the moral argument against colonialism, European nations faced political and economic changes that made it impractical to retain their African possessions. The European continent itself was devastated by World War II, and debt-ridden Europeans could scarcely afford to maintain empires abroad. Even so, the imperial nations of Europe as a matter of pride clung stubbornly to the idea of empire, making the inevitable changes more painful.

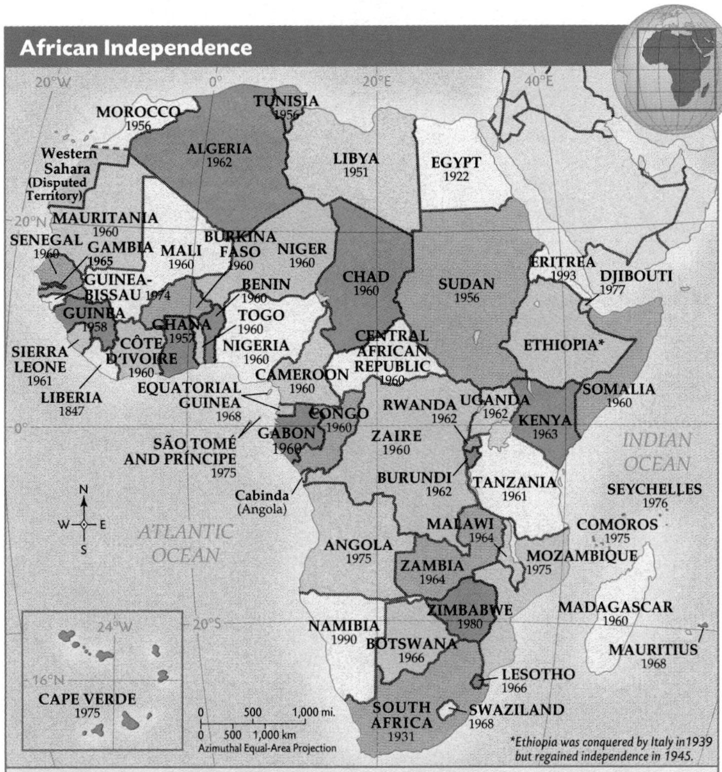

Map Study Between 1951 and 1993 more than 50 African colonies achieved independence.
Place What four African nations were independent before 1950?

African Nationalism

What European imperial nations did not recognize were the changes occurring throughout Africa. In many colonies, nationalism was growing among the European-educated African elite who worked in colonial governments and in businesses. In the late 1940s, leaders emerged among this group. In speeches and at conferences, they rallied support for African independence.

Nationalist leaders found a ready audience for their ideas among workers in the fields, mines, and factories owned by overseas investors. World demand for African minerals and crops boomed after World War II, but Africa's European-owned industries appropriated the profits. Africans saw little change in their conditions, and their resentment of foreign rule grew.

North Africa

The movement for independence saw its first successes in North Africa. Italy ruled Libya, a large country west of Egypt, under a UN trusteeship. France owned colonial possessions—Tunisia, Algeria, and Morocco—in the rest of North Africa. All of the territories of North Africa were Islamic and shared in a common Arab culture.

The only exception was **Sudan**—ruled jointly by Great Britain and Egypt—which had a large non-Muslim African population in its southern part. Sudan eventually became independent in 1956.

Libya

In 1951, Italy conceded independence to Libya, which became a monarchy. The discovery of oil in Libya in 1959 transformed the country from a poor, desert nation into one of the wealthiest in the world. Widespread discontent against the monarchy and the ruling class owning the oil wealth led to a military takeover in 1969 under Colonel **Muammar al-Qatar Qaddafi** (kuh•DAH•fee). Qaddafi established a socialist government to redistribute the national wealth. He also sought to spread his brand of nationalism to other parts of Africa and the Arab world.

COOPERATIVE LEARNING ACTIVITY

Geographical Map Have students separate the countries of Africa into five regions: north, west, central, east, and south. Organize the class into five teams, assigning one region to each team. Have the class create a wall-size map of the African continent, with each group researching its area and coordinating with other groups to produce the final map. Students should research the climate, landforms, and waterways of their region. Have team members illustrate the map and present a short oral presentation about their region. **L2**

Chapter 34
Section 1

TEACH

Guided Practice

THEME **Nationalism**

Write on the chalkboard the following sentence from the statement of Theo Ayoola quoted on page 928: "[We] overseas soldiers are coming back home with new ideas." Ask students to describe some of the postwar ideas that led to the rise of African nationalism. *(realization that ideals for which the Allies fought the war were not being applied to Africans; realization that Africans were not sharing in wealth resulting from postwar demands for African resources)* **L1**

Map Study

Answer

Liberia, Egypt, Ethiopia, South Africa

Map Skills Practice

Reading a Map What African nations have gained their independence in the 1990s? *(Eritrea, Namibia)*

Compare Remind students that American colonists had to fight for their independence from Britain and that Latin Americans fought Spain to create independent nations in the early 1800s. By the 1950s, why had European powers not learned that colonized people prefer independence over foreign rule? *(Students may realize that imperialism brought economic and other advantages that Europeans would not easily give up.)* **L2**

Chapter Transparency 34

World History and Art Transparency 46, *Bedouin Woman's Headpiece*

Chapter 34 *Africa* 929

TEACH

Tell students that the city of Banjul was formerly called Bathurst, after Henry Bathurst, who was British colonial secretary in 1816. In that year the British established a military post on the Gambia River to stop the slave trade and to serve as a trade center. **Why does the Gambian woman's dress include the portrait of a Senegalese leader?** *(The Gambia is completely surrounded by Senegal, and relations between the two countries have always been close.)*

CURRICULUM CONNECTION

THE ARTS

Tell students that only recently has the influence of African art on modern European art been fully recognized. Have students look at reproductions of traditional African sculptures and masks and then compare these works with the sculpture and painting of European modernists such as Picasso, Matisse, Brancusi, and Braque.

NATIONAL GEOGRAPHIC SOCIETY

PHYSICAL GEOGRAPHY OF THE WORLD TRANSPARENCIES

Display and discuss the physical features of the following transparencies:

41. Atlas Mountains, Morocco
42. Sahara in North Africa
44. Nile River, Egypt
51. Namib Desert, Namibia
53. Rain Forest, Zaire
57. Lake Victoria in East Africa

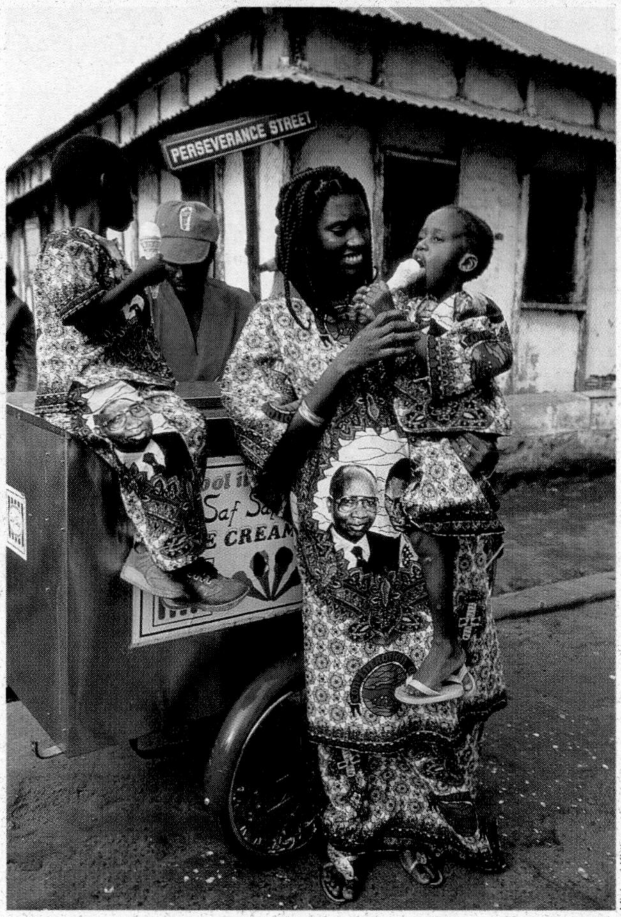

Michael Kirtley

Africa and Independence

This mother in Banjul, capital of The Gambia, combines something old and something new. She wears a traditional West African dress stamped with the colors of Africa: red, black, yellow, and green. Printed on the fabric is a portrait of two of Africa's independence leaders. On the left is Sir Dawda Jawara, who led The Gambia to independence in 1965. He remained president until 1994, when Captain Yahya Ajj Jammeh took power. On the right is President Abdou Diouf, who succeeded Senegal's great independence leader Leopold Senghor in 1981.

Keeping local traditions and languages—the pride in being African—while discarding the years of colonial rule and white supremacy became the task of the new leaders of West Africa. Where once there were 3 colonial empires, today there are 14 sovereign states in the region.

Independence from France, Great Britain, and Portugal was won peacefully. The task that now remains is to create and to sustain expanding economies. This is the hope of all West Africans, including this young mother and her children on Perseverance Street in The Gambia's capital.

Algeria

The French colonies of Morocco, Tunisia, and Algeria also wanted independence. France reluctantly granted independence to Morocco and Tunisia in 1956, but refused to do so in the case of Algeria.

Freedom for **Algeria** came only after one of the most costly wars in African colonial history. French settlers, called colons, had been coming to Algeria since the 1830s. By 1940 nearly 1 million colons had taken the best land and jobs in Algeria, ignoring the needs of 9 million Muslim Algerians.

Backed by Egypt, Morocco, and Tunisia, Algerian guerrilla fighters launched a war for independence in 1954. In response to guerrilla raids, French troops destroyed Algerian property, herded people into concentration camps, and used helicopters and heavy artillery to hunt down the rebels.

Despite French firepower, the guerrillas fought on. The controversial war forced the collapse of France's government, the Fourth Republic. After General Charles de Gaulle became president in May 1958, he promised self-determination for Algeria. Despite fierce resistance from the colons, de Gaulle arranged talks with the rebels that led to independence on July 3, 1962. The price of freedom had been eight years of warfare and more than 250,000 deaths.

Visualizing History **Kwame Nkrumah celebrates independence. Ten years of struggle had won freedom for Ghana and inspired other African nations to form national movements.** *What led to Nkrumah's loss of power in Ghana?*

Ghana

In sub-Saharan Africa, mass independence movements pressured the colonial powers to relinquish control. Great Britain's richest colony, the Gold Coast, traveled a relatively easy road to independence, raising the hopes of other sub-Saharan African nations for a smooth transition.

Before World War II ended, the British had begun to give the Africans of the Gold Coast more political rights. By then, well-educated African leaders had organized an independence movement. In 1947 the group asked the political activist **Kwame Nkrumah** (kwah•may ehn•KROO•muh) to lead them. Three years later, Nkrumah led a general strike, in which a large number of workers pressured the British for independence.

For his role in the strike, Nkrumah was jailed, but his efforts were effective. He soon moved from his jail cell to head a new government. In 1957 the Gold Coast, now renamed **Ghana**, became the first sub-Saharan African nation to gain full independence after World War II.

The Nkrumah years came to represent the best and the worst in African leadership after independence. Ghana got off to a strong start, exporting cocoa, gold, and diamonds. It also had a literate and skilled labor force. The Nkrumah government, however, mismanaged the economy. After Nkrumah was ousted by the army in 1966, one regime after another ruled Ghana, forcing the nation into a slow decline.

Guinea

Nationalist movements also took hold in France's sub-Saharan African colonies. Seeking to head off another "Algeria-like" conflict, France's President de Gaulle in 1958 proposed the creation of a French Community. Under this plan, France's sub-Saharan African colonies could choose to remain linked to France, with their foreign and economic policies under French control. The other option was for them to become completely

Chapter 34 Section 1

Visualizing History After the army deposed Nkrumah, President Sékou Touré of Guinea not only gave him political asylum but also declared him cohead of state.

Answer to Caption: *He was ousted by the army in 1966.*

Independent Practice

Guided Reading Activity 34-1 **L1**

Time Line Activity 34

People in World History Profile 65

Biography Have students research one of the outstanding leaders from this section and summarize their findings in a one-page biographical sketch that discusses the leader's major challenges and successes. **L2**

Literature Have students read Wole Soyinka's short drama *Death and the King's Horseman* and write a brief report describing the contrast it develops between Yoruba culture and British power. **L3**

Who? What? Where? When?

Buchi Emecheta was born in 1944 near Lagos, Nigeria, and moved to London in 1962. Her 1976 novel, *The Bride Price*, focuses on an intelligent Nigerian girl who confronts conflicts with her family when she elopes with a low-caste schoolmaster.

MEETING SPECIAL NEEDS ACTIVITY

Learning Style: Visual/Spatial Have students who learn best by producing graphic information create a "home page" for several African nations. Each page should consist of the country's flag, a picture of its ruler, a map and legend showing the major cities and geographic features, and other references appropriate to a web site. Have students share their home pages with the class. **L2**

Chapter 34 Section 1

Visualizing History Although Lagos is Nigeria's largest city and chief commercial center, it was replaced as the capital in 1991 by Abuja, a new city built in the 1980s near the country's center.
Answer to Caption: *Few Europeans had settled there during the colonial period, so there was little internal resistance to independence.*

Apartheid Have students research the policy of apartheid as practiced in South Africa from the 1940s until the 1990s. Ask them to write short reports explaining how the racial laws developed; how they affected the civil, human, and economic rights of black South Africans; and how they were ultimately abolished. **L3**

NATIONAL GEOGRAPHIC SOCIETY

CD-ROM

PICTURE ATLAS OF THE WORLD

Click the "Video" button of Botswana to see the wildlife of the Linyanti River.

Linking Past and Present

Ecological Imperialism The centuries of white settlement in South Africa have affected the region's ecology and worsened its droughts. The native thorn trees and baobabs resist drought, as do traditional crops such as sorghum and tubers. The European settlers, however, planted crops that required more water and put in lawns and swimming pools. They also imported pine and eucalyptus trees, which use great amounts of water.

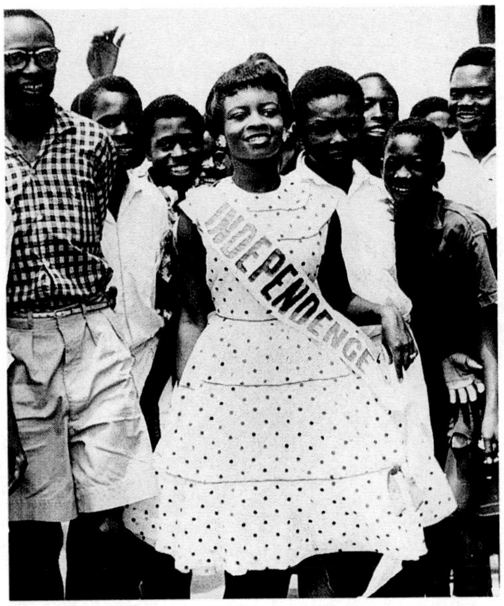

Visualizing History **After winning a contest as "Miss Independence," Rosemary Anieze celebrates Nigerian independence in Lagos.** *Why was the path to Nigerian independence easier than that of other African countries?*

independent—with no economic support from France.

Only Guinea (GIH•nee) under its nationalist leader, **Ahmed Sekou Touré** (ah•MEHD SEH•koo TOO•ray), wanted full independence. De Gaulle swiftly ordered all French officials out of Guinea and vowed not to help the new nation. The Soviet Union, however, promised aid to the new nation.

In a world dominated by the cold war, Sekou Touré's link to the Soviets angered de Gaulle, who feared that other sub-Saharan African colonies would follow suit. To prevent this, France gave its remaining African colonies independence in 1960, this time with French help.

Nigeria

In the West African country of **Nigeria**, Africa's most populous nation, few Europeans had settled during the period of British colonial rule. The path to independence was therefore easier there than in the colonies that had sizable European minorities. With little resistance, the Nigerians won independence from Great Britain in 1960. Creating a stable democratic nation was far more difficult, however.

Because Nigeria was contained within old colonial boundaries, the country's population consisted of 250 ethnic groups speaking 395 languages, as well as 3 major religious groups. Muslims dominated the north, followers of traditional African religions the east, and Christians the west. From 1960 to 1965, first one group, then another seized control of the central government.

By the mid-1960s, ethnic conflict drove the Ibo to set up the independent Republic of Biafra in the eastern part of Nigeria. After the creation of Biafra, civil war ravaged Nigeria for three years, killing more than 600,000. About 2 million Biafrans died of hunger as a result of the fighting. Biafra surrendered in January 1970. The Nigerian government then turned to rebuilding the country, developing the nation's rich oil reserves.

Congo

By the late 1950s the vast Belgian Congo in central Africa was ready for change. Belgian authorities, however, responded slowly to the independence movement and imprisoned nationalist leaders who demanded radical changes. Following riots in 1959, however, Belgium hastily granted independence in June 1960. The new country was called Congo. In the 1970s, it became known as Zaire.

Civil war broke out in Congo following independence between rival political groups and different regions. The rich copper-mining province of Katanga (now the Shaba region) seceded from the new nation in July 1960. UN peacekeeping forces arrived in Congo to prevent the superpowers from becoming involved. After settling differences with the central government, Katanga finally returned to Congolese rule, and UN forces withdrew in 1964. However, conflicts among rival political and ethnic groups continued to divide the country. Not until General Joseph D. Mobutu became dictator in 1965 was order restored.

East Africa

After World War II, nationalism also swept the East African countries of Uganda, Tanzania, and Kenya, all ruled by Great Britain. Uganda, which won independence in 1963, fell prey to ethnic conflicts and brutal military dictatorship.

By contrast, Tanzania, independent in 1961, developed a stable government that followed

MAKING CONNECTIONS ACTIVITY

Flora and Fauna Have students research to find out about the native plants and animals of Africa and how human behavior has affected them. Ask them to summarize their research in a brief written report in which they also consider the effect on the environment of the plants and animals introduced from elsewhere. **L2 LEP**

socialist principles. **Kenya**, however, attracted considerable global attention because of a combination of unique geographic and political characteristics.

Under British colonial rule, Kenya was dominated by European settlers who held the control of the fertile highlands of central Kenya. The Kikuyu, the local African ethnic group, regarded this region as their homeland. Moreover, the Europeans banned all Africans from owning land. This discrimination fanned the flames of nationalism in Kenya.

During the postwar period, the nationalist leader **Jomo Kenyatta**, who had been living in Great Britain, brought his battle for independence home to Kenya. By this time, nationalist feelings in Kenya had become intense. A political movement for independence—the Kenya African Union—was formed, and it chose Kenyatta as its president in 1947.

Meanwhile, some Kenyans had formed an underground freedom movement, which the Europeans called the Mau Mau. The movement sought to unite Kenya's many African ethnic groups against British rule. In the early 1950s, it carried out attacks on European settlers, and the British government took military action against the movement. British authorities jailed thousands of nationalists, including Kenyatta, whom they accused of leading the rebellion. By 1956, the uprising had been crushed, but calls for freedom continued. The British finally granted Kenya its independence in 1963.

Kenyatta was elected Kenya's first president in 1964 and held office until 1978. He maintained a free market economy and made Kenya a popular spot for tourists and international businesses.

Angola and Mozambique

Portugal ruled the southern African countries of **Angola** and **Mozambique** with an iron hand. The Portuguese, governed by a dictatorship at home, refused to listen to nationalist demands and created conditions for brutal uprisings.

Starting in 1961 in Angola and 1964 in Mozambique, rebel groups waged guerrilla wars against Portugal. For over a decade, Portuguese troops were able to suppress the guerrillas. In 1974, however, Portugal itself underwent a revolution that overthrew the dictatorship. The new democratic Portuguese government, facing many problems at home, freed Angola and Mozambique in 1975. Both African countries eventually came under Marxist governments that took complete control of their economies.

Malawi, Zambia, and Zimbabwe

Throughout the late 1950s and early 1960s, Great Britain slowly gave up control of its other African colonies. In 1964, Nyasaland became **Malawi** (mah•LAH•wee), and Northern Rhodesia became **Zambia**. The future, however, remained uncertain for Rhodesia, with 4 million Africans and 250,000 Europeans.

As European Rhodesians saw new African nations coming into existence in the 1960s, they formed a party called the Rhodesian Front. Two years later, the Front took control of Rhodesian politics to keep Africans from gaining power.

Great Britain opposed the Front's goals and asked that Africans be given a greater share of political power. White Rhodesians were enraged. In 1965 Rhodesian Prime Minister Ian Smith declared Rhodesia independent. Although most of the world refused to recognize or trade with Rhodesia, the country did get support from South Africa, where a white minority also ruled.

In the 1970s, bands of guerrilla fighters began attacking Rhodesia's Europeans. European settlers began to flee, and the nation's economy was disrupted. In 1979 Smith agreed to negotiate with the African majority, and in 1980, Rhodesia—renamed **Zimbabwe**—won its freedom.

South Africa

After World War II, independent **South Africa** was governed by a white minority—most of British and Afrikaner descent—that denied basic freedoms to other minorities and the majority African population. British and pro-British Afrikaner South Africans controlled the government until elections in 1948 brought to power the nationalist Afrikaners. The nationalist Afrikaner government opposed

Footnotes to History

The Great Zimbabwe Once winning freedom, many African nations took new names with great meaning for their people. Zimbabwe, for example, refers to the 1,000-year-old city of Great Zimbabwe. Massive, protective stone walls gave the city its name—*zimbabwe*—which means "stone enclosure."

Chapter 34 Section 1

Global Gourmet

South Africa Among the traditional specialties eaten by white South Africans is *boerewors*, an Afrikaner sausage dish. A staple food for black South Africans is *mealies*, a corn porridge.

Who? What? Where? When?

The ***lukasa***, or memory board, is a small rectangular wooden panel produced by the Luba people of southeastern Zaire. Each *lukasa* is used to store the history of the Luba kings, who reigned from the 1600s to the early 1900s.

NATIONAL GEOGRAPHIC SOCIETY

CD-ROM

PICTURE ATLAS OF THE WORLD

You and your students can see and read about the physical features of Africa by clicking the "Photos" and "Essay" buttons of individual countries in the region.

ASSESS

Check for Understanding

Assign Section 1 Review as homework or as an in-class activity.

Use Student Self-Test and Review Software to review Section 1.

Evaluate

Section Quiz 34-1

Use the Testmaker to create a customized quiz for Section 1.

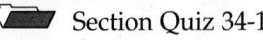

CRITICAL THINKING ACTIVITY

Synthesizing Information Have students reread the section and write two sentences for each of the countries discussed, summarizing how each attained independence. Then ask students to write a paragraph that answers the "Find Out" question on page 928. **L2**

Visualizing History The Soweto uprising began as a protest against a government order that students in the township's high schools be taught in Afrikaans, which blacks associated with their oppressors. **Answer to Caption:** *The inhabitants of the township, like other black South Africans, were oppressed economically and politically.*

Reteach

Have students state the country associated with the following names or terms: colons *(Algeria)*; Nkrumah *(Ghana)*; Sékou Touré *(Guinea)*; Lumumba, Tshombe, Mobutu *(Zaire)*; Ibo, Biafra *(Nigeria)*; Kenyatta *(Kenya)*; Smith, Mugabe *(Zimbabwe)*; apartheid, Afrikaners, ANC, Mandela, Botha, de Klerk *(South Africa)*.

Enrich

Have students write a report on *Things Fall Apart*, the first novel of Nigerian author Chinua Achebe, or watch the film *The Camp at Thiaroye* by Ousmane Sembene, Africa's premier director.

CLOSE

Have students write one paragraph in which they describe the main differences between pre-World War II Africa and Africa today. *(Answers should include mention of independence and the independent nations' attempts to establish more economic autonomy and diversification, increased political involvement of the population, and accelerated modernization of national infrastructures.)*

Visualizing History **Smoke rises from a burning tanker, set aflame by rioting students in Soweto, outside Johannesburg, South Africa.** *What conditions in Soweto led to student protests and riots?*

South Africa's remaining ties to Great Britain and had strong belief in its divine right to rule the country. Committed to white supremacy, the nationalist Afrikaners legalized and strengthened a policy of racial separation between blacks and whites called apartheid.

Enforcement of Apartheid

Under apartheid—meaning "apartness"—white, black, and mixed races were strictly segregated. Black South Africans suffered the worst under this legalized segregation. Apartheid laws defined whom blacks could marry and where they could travel, eat, and go to school. Blacks could not vote or own property. To enforce separation of the races, the government moved thousands of blacks to desolate rural areas that it called "homelands," where jobs and food were scarce. Those who were able to get low-paying jobs in the cities were forced to live in wretched, fenced-in townships like Soweto, on the outskirts of Johannesburg. Blacks had to carry identity cards at all times. Under the repressive police state, blacks could be jailed indefinitely without cause.

African Resistance

Black nationalist groups, such as the African National Congress (ANC), and other movements staged strikes and demonstrations to press for reforms, but the government repeatedly crushed the resistance. By the 1960s ANC leader **Nelson Mandela** had formed a military operation to press for change. In 1962 officials charged Mandela with treason and sabotage, and jailed him for life. From his prison cell, Mandela became a world-renowned symbol of the fight for freedom in South Africa.

In the face of strong criticism from Great Britain, South Africa angrily withdrew from the Commonwealth of Nations in 1961, increasing its political isolation. In 1974 South Africa was barred from the United Nations. World condemnation grew, especially after police fired on a student protest march in the black township of Soweto in 1976, provoking riots. South African athletes that year were barred from the Olympics. In the 1980s, the United States and other nations halted investment in South Africa until the government freed political prisoners and ended apartheid. These economic sanctions crippled the nation's once-booming economy.

SECTION 1 REVIEW

Recall

1. **Define** colon, general strike, apartheid.
2. **Identify** Muammar al-Qatar Qaddafi, Kwame Nkrumah, Ahmed Sekou Touré, Jomo Kenyatta, Nelson Mandela.
3. **Explain** How did Ghana serve as a model for nationalists in other African countries?

Critical Thinking

4. **Applying Information** How did the presence of large populations of European descent in Algeria, Kenya, Zimbabwe, and South Africa affect the African nationalist movement?

Understanding Themes

5. **Nationalism** Why did nationalist movements gain appeal in Africa after World War II?

SECTION 1 REVIEW ANSWERS

1. The words are defined in the Glossary.
2. Qaddafi, 929; Nkrumah, 931; Sékou Touré, 932; Kenyatta, 933; Mandela, 934
3. the first sub-Saharan colony to gain full independence; it did so with relative ease, encouraging other nationalists
4. White colonists resisted efforts to give black majorities political control. In Algeria and Rhodesia, colonists even defied their home countries' demands for political change.
5. **NATIONALISM** Africans saw the hypocrisy of Europe professing democracy but ruling an empire in Africa; they also resented foreign companies that exploited Africa's resources.

1970 | 1980 | 1990 | 2000

1978 Daniel T. arap Moi becomes president of Kenya.

1994 African National Congress wins South Africa's first open, multiracial elections.

Section 2

Africa Today

Setting the Scene

- **Terms to Define**
  genocide, clan
- **People to Meet**
  Muammar al-Qatar Qaddafi, Mobutu Sese Seko, Daniel T. arap Moi, F.W. de Klerk, Nelson Mandela
- **Places to Locate**
  Namibia, Eritrea, Libya, Zaire, Rwanda, Burundi, Somalia

Find Out What kinds of governments ruled in Africa from the 1970s to the 1990s?

The Storyteller

Fidele Nshogoza has been monitoring gorillas for 18 years. In the gorilla parks of the Virunga volcano range that borders Rwanda, Zaire, and Uganda, he works to prevent war and poaching from wiping out the animals he loves. "Gorillas are better than us," he explains. "They are peaceful. They have no tribes. When they fight, it is for good reason." Fidele knows the horror of warfare. An ethnic Hutu, he fled over the volcanoes after the 1994 Tutsi victory. Two of his children almost died in a Zairean refugee camp—one of seven huge camps in Zaire that sheltered more than 700,000 ethnic Hutu.

—adapted from "Gorillas and Humans: An Uneasy Truce," by Paul F. Salopek in *National Geographic*, October 1995.

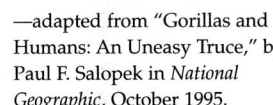

Hutu children in Zaire refugee camp

By the mid-1990s, Africa had experienced both setbacks and gains. Beginning in the early 1980s, devastating droughts ravaged large areas of the continent. The ups and downs of the world economy as well as political and ethnic conflict also negatively affected African nations.

Still there were reasons for celebration. Since the late 1970s, three new nations had emerged—Zimbabwe and **Namibia** in southern Africa (1980 and 1990), and **Eritrea** in the northeastern part of the continent (1993). Progress also was made in settling some of the civil wars that ravaged the continent. The most remarkable achievement was the dismantling of apartheid in the Republic of South Africa.

North Africa

The 1980s and 1990s saw widespread economic and political unrest in the North African countries of Algeria, Morocco, and Tunisia. A soaring population and increased industrialization led to the growth of the cities. Urban growth rates were further heightened as people from the countryside crowded into urban areas in hope of finding food, shelter, and work. When governments proved unable to provide decent housing and steady jobs, many people turned to a strict practice of Islam or to radical political movements in an effort to solve their problems.

Algeria

The greatest challenge to established government in the region took place in Algeria. In a free election in 1992, the people of Algeria elected to the national legislature a majority of members who favored a strict application of Islamic laws and values. The more moderate government, however, ignored the election results and dissolved the legislature. Military leaders then took control of Algeria.

Chapter 34 Section 2

SECTION THEME

- **Change** Some African nations move toward democracy and free enterprise economies.

Find Out

Answer: *African governments from the 1970s to the 1990s included one-party dictatorships, military rule, and multiparty systems.*

FOCUS

Section Objective

Explain what kinds of governments ruled in Africa from the 1970s to the 1990s.

BELLRINGER Motivational Activity

Before taking roll at the beginning of the class period, project Section Focus Transparency 34-2 and have students answer the activity questions. Discuss students' responses.

This activity is also available as a blackline master.

Vocabulary Pre-check

Use Vocabulary Activity 34 to introduce vocabulary terms. **L1 LEP**

SECTION RESOURCES

Reproducible Masters
- Reproducible Lesson Plan 34-2
- Vocabulary Activity 34
- Guided Reading Activity 34-2
- People in World History Profile 66
- Section Quiz 34-2

Transparencies
- Section Focus Transparency 34-2

Multimedia
- Student Self-Test and Review Software
- Testmaker
- World Music: Cultural Traditions, Lesson 6
- Picture Atlas of the World
- Turning Points in World History: *End of Apartheid*

Chapter 34 Section 2

TEACH

Guided Practice

THEME Change

On the chalkboard copy the section's opening sentence from page 935: "By the mid-1990s, Africa had experienced both setbacks and gains." Underneath it, create two columns headed *Setbacks* and *Gains*. As you work through the section with the class, have students enter events in the appropriate columns. **L1**

Government Ask students to discuss the aftermath of the elections of 1992 in Algeria as described on pages 935–936. Can the military's banning of the Islamic movement be justified in any way? *(Some students might argue that the end—the suppression of theocratic rule—justifies the means. Others might argue that denying power to the Islamic movement can only further radicalize its supporters, and any subversion of democracy is wrong.)* **L2**

ABCNEWS INTERACTIVE™

VIDEODISC
Turning Points in World History

Side Two
Chapter 10

Title: *End of Apartheid*
Ask: What did the international community do to show disapproval of South African apartheid policies? *(South Africa was banned from the UN and Olympic Games and boycotted.)*

They banned the Islamic movement and arrested many of its members.

Armed conflict soon developed between the government and the Islamic opposition. By 1995, the unrest had claimed more than 40,000 lives. Hoping to defuse the situation, the government allowed multiparty elections that year, but the major opposition groups boycotted the contest. The election results confirmed the military's candidate as president.

Libya

During the 1980s, Colonel **Muammar al-Qatar Qaddafi** of **Libya** aroused great resentment among Western countries because of his foreign policy. The United States, accusing Qaddafi of aiding international terrorists, broke economic ties with Libya in 1986. Qaddafi in turn charged the United States with attempting to overthrow his government. Military encounters in the air between aircraft of the two countries were accompanied by United States bombing of Libyan military installations. Since the mid-1980s, declining oil revenue and a worsening Libyan economy have prompted Qaddafi to improve his relations with neighboring countries. Libya's suspected involvement with terrorist bombings of civilian airlines, however, has kept Libya isolated from the international community.

Nigeria

After independence, Nigeria and many of the nations of West Africa faced political stalemates, ethnic conflicts, and economic hardships. Some relied on military leaders or one-party systems to maintain order. By the late 1980s, however, authoritarian governments had fallen out of favor, and a trend toward democracy began to emerge in the region. An example was Ghana, which became a multiparty democracy in 1992 after years of military rule.

Nigeria, however, continued to remain under its military leaders. Following the destructive Biafran war of the 1960s, the military government

Images of the Times

Toward a New Africa

Beyond independence, African nations work to promote economic growth, while preserving cultural traditions and developing democracy.

An earth satellite station 30 miles (48 km) from Nairobi, Kenya, signals Africa's connection to the telecommunications revolution.

Images of the Times **Toward a New Africa**

As in other parts of the developing world, Africans experience sharp contrasts between older ways of life and the latest technological developments. In the continent's rapidly growing cities, newcomers from small villages encounter movies, fax machines, and computers for the first time.

One sign that the telecommunications revolution has not yet saturated the African countryside is the fact that on average, there is only one television set for every 25 Africans. In the United States, by contrast, more than 98 percent of households have at least one television. In most of rural Africa, radios, not televisions or computers, are the lifeline to the rest of the world.

of Nigeria worked to rebuild the country. It relied on oil for the country's economic prosperity. As oil prices rose in the 1970s, Nigeria grew wealthy. Its military leaders set as their goals industrial development, new schools, improved transportation, and development programs to raise the standard of living of all Nigerians.

World oil surpluses in the 1980s, however, dealt crippling blows to the Nigerian economy and weakened the military government. When oil revenues moved upward during the early 1990s, pressures mounted for political reform. Nigeria's military leadership at first seemed willing to cooperate and even permitted elections. But it later refused to allow the freely elected civilian government to take power and cracked down on critics of its policies. In 1995, ignoring international protests, the military authorities hanged 9 opposition leaders, including Ken Saro-Wiwa, a respected author and candidate for the Nobel Peace Prize. Saro-Wiwa had led a grass-roots movement to improve human rights in Nigeria. Following the executions, the international community mobilized an effort to impose economic sanctions on Nigeria.

Zaire

From the 1970s to the 1990s, Congo continued under the rule of the Mobutu government. Mobutu encouraged his people to honor their heritage by taking African names. He himself took the name **Mobutu Sese Seko** (SAY•say SAY•koh). In 1971 Mobutu changed the name of the country to **Zaire** (zah•IHR).

During the early 1970s, high copper prices produced an economic boom in Zaire. Unrest grew, however, as Mobutu strengthened his power and cracked down on opposition groups. To acquire revenues for his building projects, the Zairian leader also expelled profitable foreign businesses and seized their property.

When copper prices plunged in the late 1970s, Zaire's economy and standard of living declined

Modern office buildings rise above a newly built monument and public garden in Pretoria, South Africa.

Tea pickers toil on a plantation in Kenya. Tea is one of Kenya's chief cash crops and a major export.

REFLECTING ON THE TIMES

1. In what ways could the connection to global telecommunications affect African economies? Cultural traditions?
2. Why are export products key to economic development?

ANSWERS TO REFLECTING ON THE TIMES

1. Access to global telecommunications might make Africa a more inviting place for international business and thus might strengthen African economies. The widespread exposure to foreign media might further erode African cultural traditions.
2. Exports bring in foreign capital and strengthen a country's balance of trade, although reliance on a single export makes the economies of some African countries dangerously sensitive to changes in world market prices.

World Music: Cultural Traditions, Lesson 6

Independent Practice

Guided Reading Activity 34-2 **L1**

People in World History Profile 66

Human Rights Have students use *Readers' Guide to Periodical Literature* to find articles about the execution of Ken Saro-Wiwa and the role played by the oil industry in that controversial event. Ask them to summarize their findings in a brief oral report. **L2**

Government Ask students to find out about United States support for the Mobatu regime and the reasons for it. Have them research not only public policy but also the involvement of the CIA in Zaire. Have students summarize their findings in a brief written report. **L3**

Linking Past and Present

Asylum In February 1995, Zaire announced its intention to close camps inside its borders that housed Rwandan refugees who had fled civil war in that neighboring nation. This action was condemned by many human rights groups.

NATIONAL GEOGRAPHIC SOCIETY

CD-ROM

PICTURE ATLAS OF THE WORLD

You can view the "Zaire Highway" by clicking the "Video" button of Zaire.

Visualizing History In 1991 representatives of Zaire's opposition parties held a national conference to move the country in the direction of democracy, but Mobutu broke up the conference several times. **Answer to Caption:** *In the early 1970s, he expelled foreign businesses and seized their property; in the late 1970s, he invited European businesses to return to Zaire to help steady the country's development.*

NATIONAL GEOGRAPHIC SOCIETY

CD-ROM

PICTURE ATLAS OF THE WORLD

Click the "Video" button of Tanzania to view the Masai people and Serengeti National Park.

Global Gourmet

Ethiopia A popular Ethiopian food now being served in Ethiopian restaurants in the United States is a thick stew called *wat*. Vegetarian *wats* are made with lentils or chickpeas flavored with spices. Other *wats* contain chicken or meat and are sometimes served with hard-cooked egg. Most *wats* are flavored with a very spicy berbere sauce.

Who? What? Where? When?

The Nobel Prize in literature was awarded to two Africans in recent years, Nigeria's Wole Soyinka (1986) and South Africa's Nadine Gordimer (1991).

Visualizing History **General Joseph Mobutu, who suppressed the rebels in Katanga, took the name Mobutu Sese Seko and ruled Zaire.** *How did Mobutu deal with foreign-owned businesses?*

sharply. Mobutu then asked European businesses to return to Zaire to help steady the country's development. By the early 1990s, public pressure had forced Mobutu to allow opposition political parties, but he was reluctant to relinquish any of his powers to a democratically elected government.

East Africa

East Africa was torn by ethnic unrest, especially in the inland countries of **Rwanda** and **Burundi**. Political stability, however, characterized some countries in the region. After decades of turmoil, Uganda enjoyed peace under military leaders, who promoted free enterprise and economic development. Uganda's southern neighbor, Tanzania, continued its tradition of stable government, but economic difficulties in the early 1990s made it abandon socialism for free enterprise.

Kenya

From the early 1960s to the late 1970s, Kenya enjoyed political stability and economic prosperity under the one-party system of President Jomo Kenyatta. After Kenyatta's death in 1978, **Daniel T. arap Moi** became president. In the 1980s, Moi put down demonstrations by political opponents who wanted a multiparty system. Finally, a decade later, he allowed a multiparty election in which the voters endorsed Moi's party and presidency. In 1995, however, Moi began arresting opposition leaders in parliament, leading human rights activists to question the sincerity of Moi's commitment to democratic reform.

Rwanda and Burundi

During the 1990s, long-standing ethnic unrest in Rwanda and Burundi led to one of the most violent conflicts in postindependence Africa. Most people in Rwanda and Burundi belong to two ethnic groups—the Hutu and the Tutsi. The Hutu are the largest group in both countries. Under the colonial rule of Belgium, the Tutsi were favored over the Hutu. Since the independence of Rwanda and Burundi in 1962, the Hutu have worked to regain power and prestige.

In 1994 civil war broke out in Rwanda between the Hutu and Tutsi. Fighting developed the day after the presidents of Rwanda and Burundi, both Hutus, were killed in a suspicious plane crash in Rwanda. Forces loyal to the Hutu-led Rwandan government battled the Tutsi-led Rwandan Patriotic Front (RPF). In what has been called a **genocide**, or the deliberate killing of a racial, ethnic, or cultural group, some 500,000 people, mostly Tutsis, were killed by Hutus in savage ethnic violence before the RPF declared victory. An additional 2 million people, fearful of losing their lives, fled from their homes. These refugees settled in huge camps on the border of Zaire and neighboring countries.

Ethiopia and Somalia

In Ethiopia, military leaders in 1974 ousted the ancient monarchy of Emperor Haile Selassie I and replaced it with a Marxist dictatorship. While implementing land reforms, the new government persecuted and killed many of its opponents. These policies led to civil war. Movements for independence arose in the regions of Tigre and Eritrea.

By the early 1990s, widespread suffering caused by drought and civil war led to the fall of

COOPERATIVE LEARNING ACTIVITY

The Arts Have students form five teams, one for each region of Africa: north, west, central, east, and south. Individual team members should choose different types of African art to research within their region, such as painting, pottery, metal and wood sculpture, textiles, body ornamentation, and music. Have students find examples of each type of art and copy or record them to bring to class. Have the teams work together to create a classroom or hallway exhibit, complete with captions explaining the display. Organize the exhibit by region or by type of art. **L2 LEP**

the military dictatorship. In 1991, rebel forces took control of the government and moved Ethiopia onto the path toward democracy. As a result of their victory, Eritrea became independent in 1993.

Drought and civil war also ravaged Ethiopia's neighbor, **Somalia**. There, in the 1980s, rival clans, or groups of people related to one another, fought for control of the government. When a drought struck a few years later, hundreds of thousands of Somalis starved. Other countries sent food, but the fierce fighting kept much of it from reaching the starving.

In 1992, a UN-sponsored coalition of military forces led by the United States arrived in Somalia to protect relief organizations that were distributing food to needy Somalis. A year later, UN forces replaced most of the coalition troops. Tensions heightened when fighting broke out between the UN soldiers and the forces of one of the Somali clan leaders. By 1995, foreign troops, including United States forces, had withdrawn from Somalia after the worst of the famine had ended, and rival clan leaders had signed a peace settlement. Continued fighting, however, delayed progress on the formation of a stable government.

South Africa

From the 1970s to the 1990s, South Africa and its neighbors Mozambique, Angola, and Zimbabwe experienced many sweeping changes. After a period of civil wars between Marxist and non-Marxist groups, Mozambique, Angola, and Zimbabwe moved toward peace and gradually abandoned socialism for free enterprise.

In South Africa, mounting pressure from the antiapartheid movement and from foreign countries brought a gradual end to apartheid. During the 1980s, the white-dominated South African government lifted the ban on interracial marriage, and the nation's sizable population of Asian and mixed-race people won voting rights.

In February 1990, South African President **F. W. de Klerk** surprised the world by releasing the black nationalist leader **Nelson Mandela** from prison. During the next few years, the South African government repealed the remaining apartheid laws. Talks began in 1992 between white and black political groups that paved the way for a constitution, ending apartheid, and granting political equality to all South Africans regardless of race. A year later, black South Africans won full voting rights.

In April 1994, South Africa held its first election open to all races. The African National Congress won nearly two-thirds of the seats in the national legislature, and the legislature then elected Nelson Mandela president. Mandela recognized the importance of reconciling racial and ethnic groups and bridging the social and economic gap that separated white and nonwhite South Africans. He faced the challenge of raising the standard of living of disadvantaged South Africans while maintaining economic growth.

AROUND THE WORLD: Kwanzaa Celebrates African American Culture

United States, 1966

Kwanzaa is a holiday based on a traditional African harvest festival. Developed in the United States in 1966 by Maulana Karenga, an African American cultural leader, Kwanzaa begins on December 26 and lasts for seven days. Each day is dedicated to one of the seven principles of African American culture that Karenga established. African American families celebrate Kwanzaa by lighting candles and exchanging gifts.

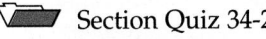

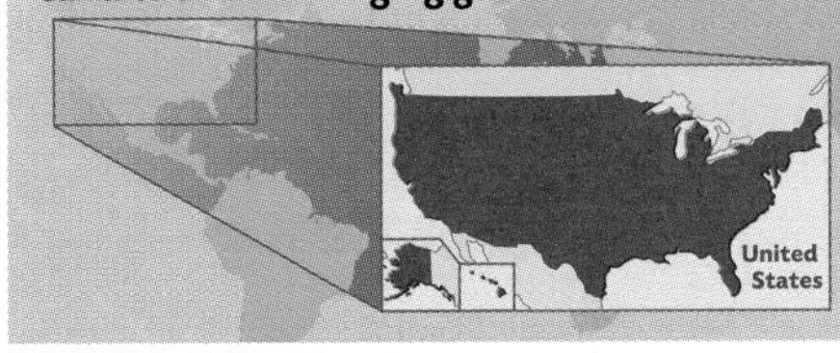

SECTION 2 REVIEW

Recall

1. **Define** genocide, clan.
2. **Identify** Muammar al-Qatar Qaddafi, Mobutu Sese Seko, Daniel T. arap Moi, F.W. de Klerk, Nelson Mandela.
3. **Explain** the causes of the civil war in Rwanda.

Critical Thinking

4. **Synthesize** If you were a citizen of South Africa today, how would you describe recent changes there?

Understanding Themes

5. **Changes** What worldwide factors do you think account for the recent trend toward democracy in Africa?

Chapter 34 Section 2

ASSESS

Check for Understanding

Assign Section 2 Review as homework or as an in-class activity.

Use Student Self-Test and Review Software to review Section 2.

Evaluate

Section Quiz 34-2

Use the Testmaker to create a customized quiz for Section 2.

Reteach

Have students write a sentence to define each term and to identify each individual and each country listed in "Setting the Scene" on page 935.

Enrich

Have students watch the 1992 film *Sarafina!*, based on a popular antiapartheid stage musical, and write a brief review.

CLOSE

Have students list the ten countries discussed in this section *(Algeria, Libya, Nigeria, Zaire, Kenya, Rwanda, Burundi, Ethiopia, Somalia, South Africa)* and write a sentence for each that summarizes the changes it has undergone since the 1980s.

SECTION 2 REVIEW ANSWERS

1. All vocabulary words are defined in the Glossary.
2. Qaddafi, 936; Mobutu Sese Seko, 937; Daniel T. arap Moi, 938; F. W. de Klerk, 939; Nelson Mandela, 939
3. The immediate cause was the suspicious plane crash in Rwanda that killed the Hutu presidents of Rwanda and Burundi. The underlying cause was the ethnic tensions between the Hutu majority and the Tutsi.
4. Answers will vary depending on the race of the South African citizen students describe.
5. **CHANGE** Answers will vary. Students might feel that the democratic trend has been encouraged by the end of the cold war.

Study and Writing SKILLS

TEACH

Writing a Research Report Have students review the process of choosing a topic. Practice this process with them by suggesting a number of general topics about Africa that students must narrow down. General topics might include Africa since the cold war, Africa's natural resources, democracy in Africa, or the role of women in Africa. These could be narrowed down to Angola since the cold war, northern Africa's natural resources, democracy in Algeria, and African women in politics.

Additional Practice

Skill Reinforcement Activity 34

Writer's Guidebook, Lesson 12

Study and Writing SKILLS

Writing a Research Report

Writing a research report is similar to most other complex tasks. There are tools to use, skills to master, and steps to follow. You have already mastered many of the steps: taking notes, outlining, selecting and using sources, and preparing note cards. In this lesson, you will put them all together.

Learning the Skill

Select an interesting topic. Brainstorming, skimming books and magazines, and talking with classmates can help.

Do preliminary research to determine whether your topic is too broad or too specific. Suppose you've chosen "Problems Facing Africa Today." The library's computers list more than 100 books on this topic. A more manageable topic might be: "Environmental Problems in the Sahara."

As early as possible, write a statement defining what you want to prove, discover, or illustrate in your report. For this topic, your statement might be: "Deforestation is the greatest environmental threat to North Africa."

- **Prepare to do research.** Formulate a list of main idea questions.
- **Research your topic and take notes.** At the library, use the computerized referral service to find suitable research sources. Prepare note cards on each main idea question listing the source information. Keep all the facts for each main idea together.
- **Organize your information.** Build an outline or another kind of organizer. Follow your outline or organizer in writing a rough draft.
- **Write a rough draft.** A research report should have three main parts: the introduction, the body, and the conclusion. The introduction briefly presents the topic and gives your thesis statement. In the body, follow your outline to develop the important ideas in your argument. Connect these ideas with transitions. The conclusion summarizes and restates your findings.

In writing the rough draft write as quickly as possible without editing. Imagine that you are explaining your findings and ideas to an interested listener.

Revise the draft into a final report. Put it away for a day or so; then reread it with the cold, clear eye of an editor. Does the report have a clear structure—an introduction, a body, and a conclusion? Does the body contain all the main ideas arranged logically? Are there transitions to lead the reader from one thought to the next? If not, revise it and repeat the writing process. Correct spelling, punctuation, and grammar. Finally, make a clean copy.

Practicing the Skill

Suppose you are writing a report on recent changes in South Africa. Answer the following questions about the writing process.

1. How could you narrow this topic?
2. What are three main idea questions to use?
3. Name three possible sources of information.
4. What are the next two steps in the process of writing a research report?

Applying the Skill

In the Chapter 29 skill lesson, you chose a topic and prepared note cards. Continue your research on this topic and write a short report.

For More Practice

Turn to the Skill Practice in the Chapter Review on page 947 for more practice in writing a research report.

ANSWERS TO PRACTICING THE SKILL

1. Answers will vary. Possible answers include: end of apartheid; voting rights for black South Africans; the African National Congress; Nelson Mandela; challenges for future government
2. Answers will vary depending on the topic.
3. Sources include books, magazines, and newspapers.
4. After selecting sources, students should prepare note cards, organize them, and then write a rough draft.

1945 — 1973 — 2001

1963 African nations form Organization of African Unity (OAU).

1980s Famine ravages Ethiopia, Somalia, and other areas of Africa.

1990 A trend develops in Africa away from military and one-party rule toward democracy.

Section 3

Africa's Challenge

Setting the Scene

- **Terms to Define**
  Pan-Africanism, cash crop, subsistence farmer, desertification, literacy rate, negritude
- **People to Meet**
  Julius Nyerere, Léopold Sédor Senghor
- **Places to Locate**
  the Sahel

Find Out What challenges have modern African nations faced in their quest for political and economic development?

The Storyteller

The Sahara has its own voices. The abrupt changes from darkness to daylight are often accompanied by the shattering of the desert rocks, with a grating sound or a loud noise. Even the sand dunes talk: wind or even the pressure of a human foot will cause shocks and tremblings; then the countless grains of sand, rubbing gently together, will make a strange snoring noise.

According to legend, these mysterious noises are the bursts of laughter of a genie named Rul—the bad angel of strayed travelers. When the wanderer has lost his way, when fatigue and thirst begin to confuse the mind, then the traveler is tormented by "the laughter of Rul."

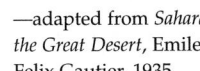

—adapted from *Sahara, the Great Desert*, Emile Felix Gautier, 1935

Desert oasis

African nations have seen enormous changes in less than half a century. In that short time, a largely rural continent has become increasingly urban, with ties to all parts of the globe. In 44 African nations, the number of children in school soared from 18 million to 38 million in just 12 years. Africa also has become an international force, wielding more than a third of the votes in the United Nations General Assembly.

Yet huge challenges remain. "Africa has its feet in the neolithic age and its head in the thermonuclear age," wrote African expert Elliott Skinner. "Where is the body? It is managing as best it can."

Search for Unity

After the excitement of independence celebrations had passed, Africa's new nations entered a difficult period. Many of them adopted the political borders that had been drawn by the colonial powers. These boundaries divided people with similar customs and faiths. Old ruling families and ethnic groups began to struggle for power, and civil wars often erupted.

National Unity

African politicians and parliaments were unable to stop the violence that sprang from these ethnic divisions. At first, many leaders in Africa governed through political systems inherited from their colonial predecessors—systems that were unfamiliar to many Africans. Often these systems did not work for African countries in the postindependence years. All too often, a nation's most powerful group, the military, stepped in to restore order.

By the 1970s, military leaders or one-party dictatorships ruled about half of Africa's newly freed nations. In some, like Nigeria, dividing strong regional groups into smaller states helped to break down some regional rivalry. By the late 1980s, however, military rule and one-party political systems

SECTION THEME

- **Change** Ethnic, cultural, environmental, and economic challenges face newly independent African nations.

Find Out

Answer: *They have faced ethnic and cultural division, environmental obstacles, and economic development.*

FOCUS

Section Objective

Identify the challenges faced by modern African nations in their quest for political and economic independence.

BELLRINGER
Motivational Activity

Before taking roll at the beginning of the class period, project Section Focus Transparency 34-3 and have students answer the activity questions. Discuss students' responses.

This activity is also available as a blackline master.

Vocabulary Pre-check

Use the Vocabulary PuzzleMaker to create a puzzle that reinforces the vocabulary terms in this section. **L1**

SECTION RESOURCES

Reproducible Masters
- Reproducible Lesson Plan 34-3
- Guided Reading Activity 34-3
- Reteaching Activity 34
- Enrichment Activity 34
- Section Quiz 34-3
- Performance Assessment Activity 34
- Spanish Chapter Summary 34

Transparencies
- Section Focus Transparency 34-3
- World History and Art Transparency 45, *The Liberated African Woman*

Multimedia
- Vocabulary PuzzleMaker Software
- Student Self-Test and Review Software
- Testmaker
- Picture Atlas of the World
- STV: World Geography, Vol. 2

TEACH

Guided Practice

THEME **Change**

Write on the chalkboard each of the terms listed in "Setting the Scene" on page 941. Ask students to explain the relationship between each term and a change Africa has undergone in recent times. **L1**

Visualizing History The modern city takes its name from *Enkare Nairobi*, or "cold water," referring to a freshwater spring that used to be located on the site.

Answer to Caption: *the creation of an all-African common market to promote Africa's economic growth and development*

NATIONAL GEOGRAPHIC SOCIETY

VIDEODISC
STV: WORLD GEOGRAPHY, VOLUME 2

Side 1
Frames 00001-49739
Title: *Africa* (in its entirety)
Subject: Describes the geographic contrasts and how people and animals have affected the natural environment of Africa
Ask: What desert in Africa is the world's largest? *(the Sahara)* What kind of technique is used to clear the land for planting? *(slash-and-burn)*

World History and Art Transparency 45, *The Liberated African Woman*

Visualizing History **The promise of a brighter future—a rainbow glistens over high-rise buildings at dawn in Nairobi, Kenya. Founded in the late 1890s as a small colonial railway settlement, Nairobi today is a busy metropolis of more than 1.5 million people.** *What goal has the Organization of African Unity set for the year 2000?*

had failed to fulfill their promises of order and economic progress. They were in decline in certain countries of Africa. Meanwhile, the end of the cold war and the collapse of the Soviet Union discredited the socialist economic model once popular among many African leaders. By the early 1990s, some African countries had adopted multiparty systems and free enterprise approaches to economic development.

Pan-Africanism

Besides the challenge of providing national unity, African leaders had long worried about harmony among African nations. Through a movement called Pan-Africanism, they sought to promote a feeling of oneness and cooperation among all the nations on the continent. In 1963 Kwame Nkrumah of Ghana and Ahmed Sekou Touré of Guinea took the idea of unity a step further and invited 32 countries to form the Organization of African Unity (OAU). Nkrumah hoped the organization would be the first step in creating a United States of Africa. That idea failed, but the OAU did dedicate itself to building a strong African identity and coordinating national defense, health, and other policies.

Since its founding in Addis Ababa, Ethiopia, in 1963, the OAU has increased its influence in African and global affairs. During the 1970s and 1980s, member nations of the OAU pledged to remain neutral in cold war politics. In a concerted effort to rid Africa of remaining colonialism, the OAU backed pro-independence movements in Angola, Mozambique and Zimbabwe (formerly Rhodesia). As part of this undertaking, OAU members put pressure on white-ruled South Africa to end the apartheid system. A major achievement of the OAU during this period was settlement of boundary disputes among member nations.

As it looks to the twenty-first century, the OAU has set as its major goal Africa's economic growth and development. Its members plan to create an all-African common market by the year 2000.

Economic Development

In addition to creating a united continent, post-independence leaders of Africa worked to build strong economies in their nations. To move Africa's rural economies into the world of mining, manufacturing, and service industries, millions of people

COOPERATIVE LEARNING ACTIVITY

Debate Have pairs of students select one African country to represent at a mock session of the UN General Assembly. Before the session, have students brainstorm a list of issues they will discuss; these should include economic development, the environment, foreign aid, free trade, and urbanization. Have students research their country so they can represent its interests at the General Assembly session. **L2**

had to learn to read and write. Workers who made a living with their hands had to learn to operate machines in factories. Governments had to repair aging phone lines, railroads, and highways. Tanzania's President **Julius Nyerere** in the 1960s stated "while the great powers are trying to get to the moon, we are trying to get to the village."

Legacy of Colonialism

After independence, most African countries suffered from the economies created by colonial rule. As you remember from Chapter 27, Europeans obtained raw materials in Africa for their home industries and developed little industry in Africa. Under colonial rule, some Africans worked on European-owned plantations that produced cash crops, or crops grown for profit and exported. Most, however, were subsistence farmers, who grow only enough food to meet the needs of a family or village.

After independence, African leaders tried to remedy the imbalance between farming and industry. Many African countries were rich in one or two key resources or crops, but their economies could not provide the basic needs of their populations. One-product economies, such as Ghana with cocoa and Burundi with coffee, were constantly at the mercy of changing prices for products on world markets. In addition, internal conflicts left some countries with ruined land and heavy war debts.

Economic Challenges

To bring economic advancement, African leaders decided to push the export of cash crops and raw materials while promoting industrialization. A lack of capital, skilled workers, and transportation systems, however, stood in the way of industrial growth. Seeking to overcome these obstacles, African countries turned to foreign governments and banks for loans to build factories, airports, harbors, and roads.

Reliance on foreign aid, however, provoked different reactions among Africans. Some nations followed a capitalist model and developed close ties with the West. Resource-rich nations, such as Nigeria with its oil wealth, tried to fund development from their exports of minerals and other raw materials. To assert their sovereignty, other nations decided to organize various kinds of

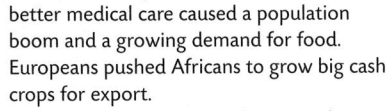

CONNECTIONS **Geography**

The Moving Sahara

Deep in the Sahara, ancient rock paintings show grazing cattle and grasses where now there is only rock and sand. In recent times, farmers also grazed cattle in areas bordering the Sahara. But now those grasslands too are giving way to desert.

The encroaching desert

Before Africa was colonized, farmers cultivated fields until the soil was exhausted. When they moved to new plots of land, they let the old ones lie fallow, replenishing the soil. Under colonialism, better medical care caused a population boom and a growing demand for food. Europeans pushed Africans to grow big cash crops for export.

Destruction of the land increased. Farmers cut down trees to open up new fields and farmed land year after year without allowing the fields to lie fallow. Droughts in the 1980s brought disaster. People had to use grains for food instead of for seed. Without plants to anchor the soil, tons of topsoil disappeared. The mixture of overfarming, overgrazing, cutting trees, and drought pushed the Sahara south as fast as 90 miles (145 km) a year.

The solution to this problem lies with individual farmers. By planting trees, terracing fields, and fertilizing the soil, they may be able to slow the shifting of the Sahara.

MAKING THE CONNECTION

1. What is causing the Sahara to spread south?
2. Why do you think it is difficult to get individual farmers to change their practices?

MEETING SPECIAL NEEDS ACTIVITY

Mixed Learners Have language-delayed students and visual learners identify the different African nations by researching the current flags of several nations from different African regions. On a large sheet of paper or poster board, have students draw and color each nation's flag and describe briefly what the colors and the symbols mean. Encourage students to display their completed work in the classroom. **L1 LEP**

Chapter 34 Section 3

CONNECTIONS **Geography**

The Moving Sahara

Tell students that the name *Sahara* comes from *sahrá*, the Arabic word for "desert." From the late 1800s through the mid-1900s, France, Spain, Italy, and Britain occupied parts of the Sahara. In 1976 Spain became the last European country to give up control of the portion of the Sahara it claimed as its own.

Answers to Making the Connection

1. *drought and poor farming practices*
2. *Students may suggest that individual farmers may not understand the larger problems caused by their methods.*

Independent Practice

Guided Reading Activity 34-3 **L1**

Economics Have students compare the current economic situations in five African countries. Students should look up such information as per capita income and percentage of the labor force in agriculture and industry in a current almanac or other reference work. Have students display the data they have collected in chart form. **L2**

NATIONAL GEOGRAPHIC SOCIETY

CD-ROM

PICTURE ATLAS OF THE WORLD

You and your students can see apartheid's legacy by clicking the "Video" button of South Africa.

Chapter 34 Section 3

Visualizing History The attempt to improve educational opportunities in Africa is challenged in a variety of ways. New schools cannot be built quickly enough to keep up with the population growth, there is a shortage of trained teachers in many regions, and many families cannot afford to send their children to school instead of to work.
Answer to Caption: *Literacy rates are rising.*

Linking Past and Present

African Music American singer, songwriter, and performer Paul Simon has helped to popularize African pop music around the world. Simon worked with black South African musicians to create his 1986 album, *Graceland*.

ASSESS

Check for Understanding

Assign Section 3 Review as homework or as an in-class activity.

Use Student Self-Test and Review Software to review Section 3.

Evaluate

Section Quiz 34-3

Use the Testmaker to create a customized quiz for Section 3.

Visualizing History **The education of children like these kindergarten students in Angola is the key to the nation's future.** *What is happening with literacy rates in Africa?*

government-controlled economies. This turn to socialism pleased many nationalists, who equated capitalism with colonialism.

No matter how they organized their economies, however, many countries failed to develop agriculture in their push to industrialize. Soon food crops for the domestic markets began to suffer and thousands of unskilled rural people moved to the cities, searching in vain for jobs. With many people out of work and unable to buy the products of new African industries, economies suffered.

Africa's soaring population also caused problems for economic growth. With economies geared for export, not enough food was produced for domestic needs. Governments had to increase borrowing from foreign sources, often to buy food, and their debts grew. As a result, not enough money was available to develop health care, food production, and industry necessary to improve overall standards of living.

Famine

Severe droughts in Africa also hindered economic development, causing food shortages and starvation in various parts of western, central, and eastern Africa. The causes of famine in Africa, as in other parts of the world, are complex and varied. In the case of Africa in the 1980s, growing populations, a lack of capital, and overdependence on cash crops all contributed to this problem.

Another factor was the expansion of desert into formerly fertile areas. Countries crossed by the Sahara, Africa's largest desert, particularly faced the effects of desertification, or the transformation of fertile land into desert land. The worst occurrence of desertification took place in **the Sahel**, a West African grassland area bordering the Sahara. In addition to the ravages of nature, human activities, such as grazing livestock, planting, and the harvesting of trees, left the land in this environmentally fragile area dangerously exposed to erosion.

Signs of Hope

In the 1980s, Africa was a continent in crisis. A World Bank study showed that 21 of the world's 34 poorest countries were in Africa. More than 60 percent of all Africans received too little food each day, and more than 5 million children died every year. Relying on foreign help to remedy these problems, sub-Saharan African nations by the mid-1980s were $130 billion in debt.

As the year 2000 approaches, the problems of inadequate food, growing populations, and foreign debt still plague Africa, but some hopeful signs exist. More Africans than ever are attending school. Literacy rates, or the percentages of people who can read and write, have risen. Through education, many Africans are developing the skills needed to improve their standard of living.

In various parts of the continent, Africans are cooperating to improve their economies. To break their dependency on foreign countries, some African nations have formed regional associations that promote trade and economic contacts. An example of this type of organization is the West African Economic Community, in which a number of West African nations have agreed to barter among themselves, trading products for oil instead of for scarce cash. In late 1992 Ugandan President Yoweri Museveni expressed a viewpoint that had become increasingly widespread throughout Africa: "We have to go back to the year 1500 [prior to colonialism], where we left off building an African economy, able to produce its own food, its own tools, its own weapons.... In short, we have to rely on ourselves."

MAKING CONNECTIONS ACTIVITIES

Languages More than 800 languages are spoken in Africa. Ask students to research and write a short report on Swahili or other native African languages; Amharic or other Afro-Asian languages; or Afrikaans, which is an Indo-European language. **L2**

Marriage Ask students to research and write a short report on marriage practices in different parts of Africa, including dowries and bride wealth. **L1**

Visualizing History **African American children celebrate Kwanzaa, a festival held in late December since 1972.** *What is the purpose of such poems as "My Africa"?*

African Identity

> "I love a world,
> This priceless world,
> Sweet home of haunting melodies
> And roll of tom-toms—
> My Africa."
>
> —Michael Dei-Anang, from the poem "My Africa"

In 1963 the African American poet Langston Hughes gathered nearly 100 African poems into a collection called *Poems from Black Africa*. It includes this one by Dei-Anang, a poet and government official in Ghana.

"Usually," Hughes wrote in the foreword, "poets have their fingers on the emotional pulse of their peoples." The poetry of Dei-Anang, like that of other Africans, had begun to rekindle a deep pride among Africans in their heritage.

During the colonial era, Africans had learned much, both good and bad, from Europeans. There remained the idea, although not accepted by all Africans, that European culture was superior to African culture in art, music, literature, and technology.

As independent nations emerged on the continent, many African leaders stressed the need to take pride in Africa. In Senegal, a former French colony, President **Léopold Sédar Senghor** published poems that expressed his love of Africa. Because Africans had never lost touch with nature, he thought, they could help restore "a world that has died of machines and cannons." Senghor helped found a poetry movement called **negritude**, an effort to recapture black Africa's past dignity.

During the decades since independence, African artists and writers have built on this foundation of pride. Theater groups, filmmakers, novelists, painters, and others have explored the pain of colonialism as well as the modern problems of corruption and hunger. Music, in particular, developed as a a form of social protest in countries such as South Africa.

Open now to influences from around the globe, Africans have also created exciting new art forms. Congolese music, for instance, a mix of African, Latin American, and Caribbean styles, brings pleasure and delight to people in all of Africa and around the world.

SECTION 3 REVIEW

Recall

1. **Define** Pan-Africanism, cash crop, subsistence farmer, desertification, literacy rate, negritude.
2. **Identify** Organization of African Unity (OAU), Julius Nyerere, West African Economic Community, Léopold Sédar Senghor.
3. **Discuss** the goal the OAU has for the future development of African economies.

Critical Thinking

4. **Evaluating Information** What might have happened if African nations had spent funds producing more food for their people instead of growing cash crops and industrializing their economies?

Understanding Themes

5. **Change** What trend influenced African political systems by the early 1990s? How do you think this will affect the political future of African nations?

SECTION 3 REVIEW ANSWERS

1. The words are defined in the Glossary.
2. OAU, 942; Nyerere, 943; Economic Community, 944; Senghor, 945
3. promote Africa's economic growth and development by creating an all-African common market by the year 2000
4. Students may feel that a better balance between food and export crops might have reduced hunger and lessened dependence on foreign governments and banks for loans.
5. **CHANGE** The new trend favored multiparty systems and free enterprise approaches. Students may feel that these changes promise to improve life for Africans.

Visualizing History The word *Kwanzaa* comes from a Swahili phrase meaning "first fruits." The holiday, based on a traditional harvest festival, celebrates seven principles of African culture: unity, self-determination, collective work and responsibility, cooperative economics, purpose, creativity, and faith. Holiday customs include candle lighting and the exchange of gifts.

Answer to Caption: *to instill pride in African culture*

Reteach

Ask students to explain (1) the relevance of the Pan-African movement and the OAU to Africa's search for political unity; (2) the causes and significance of drought in Africa; and (3) the role of negritude in the formation of an African identity.

Reteaching Activity 34

Enrich

Have students read a work by Nobel laureates Wole Soyinka or Nadine Gordimer and write a short report describing the novel's treatment of challenges facing Africa in recent times.

Enrichment Activity 34

CLOSE

Have students write one paragraph in which they summarize the main challenges facing African countries today. *(Answers should include a search for unity, economic development, and the preservation of an African identity.)*

Chapter 34 Review

GLENCOE TECHNOLOGY

VIDEODISC

Use MindJogger to review students' knowledge of the chapter.

MindJogger Videoquiz

Chapter 34
Disc 5 Side A

Also available in VHS.

Answers

Using Key Terms

1. e	**6.** h
2. f	**7.** g
3. d	**8.** i
4. b	**9.** c
5. a	**10.** j

Using Your History Journal

Suggest that students write their essay as if it were the year 2020 and that they are looking back on how their chosen nation has fared over the previous two decades.

Reviewing Facts

1. The democratic ideals for which the Allies fought in the war inspired Africans. African nationalists found support among workers who resented foreign exploitation of Africa.
2. Ghana
3. Oil was discovered there in 1959.
4. The Rhodesian Front thwarted Britain's wish to share political power with Africans and in 1965 declared independence; guerrilla warfare caused European settlers to flee and the economy to crumble, driving the Front to negotiate with the African majority and leading to the emergence of a free Zimbabwe.
5. ANC, economic sanctions
6. Rival clans fought for control of the government, keeping food aid from reaching famine victims. UN forces sent in to protect the distribution of food were withdrawn because they were becoming involved in the fighting.
7. African artists have been developing art expressing pride in their heritage.

Critical Thinking

1. Benefits may include a variety of perspectives with which to approach problems. Drawbacks include conflict and a lack of unity.
2. Solutions may include short-term relief efforts or long-term agricultural reform.
3. Old boundaries often divided ethnic and religious groups; divisions created factionalism.
4. Answers should reflect familiarity with South Africa's former racial policies.

CHAPTER 34 REVIEW

Historical Significance

The nations of Africa are very old—and very new. They have ancient cultures, but their political systems are still young. Most have been independent for only a generation. Their efforts to forge effective governments are complicated by debt, hunger, and ethnic strife.

Some factors weighed on the side of progress and peace. Nations, such as Angola, South Africa, and Zimbabwe, have developed peaceful ways of dealing with their challenges. Also, education and a higher standard of living are being enjoyed by more people now than in the past.

Using Key Terms

Write the key term that completes each sentence.

a. general strike	f. desertification
b. colons	g. cash crops
c. clans	h. apartheid
d. negritude	i. genocide
e. Pan-Africanism	j. literacy rate

1. Through the movement of ________, African nations seek to promote oneness and cooperation throughout the continent.
2. ________, or the transformation of fertile land into desert land, affected countries near the Sahara.
3. __________ is a poetry movement established to recapture black Africa's past dignity.
4. From the 1830s to the early 1960s, French settlers known as _________ played an important role in Algeria's political and social life.
5. In 1950, Kwame Nkrumah led the workers of the Gold Coast in a __________ against British colonial authorities.
6. In 1948, the South African government began legalizing and strengthening a policy of racial separation known as __________.
7. Under colonial rule, many Africans worked on European-owned plantations that produced _________ grown for profit and exported.
8. The deliberate killing of a racial, ethnic, or national group is known as ________.
9. During the late 1980s, Somalia was divided by conflict among _______, or groups of related peoples.
10. ________, the percentage of people who can read and write, has increased in Africa in recent years.

Using Your History Journal

Review your news clippings on Africa. Write a short essay on the future of an African nation. What are the challenges that your chosen nation faces? What are the prospects for peace and progress?

Reviewing Facts

1. Discuss the reasons for the strong growth of nationalism in Africa after World War II.
2. Identify the first sub-Saharan African country to win independence.
3. Explain the reason for Libya's postwar economic prosperity.
4. Discuss the events leading to Zimbabwe's late independence in 1980.
5. Identify the two major forces that challenged the long-standing apartheid policy of the South African government.
6. Discuss developments in Somalia during the 1980s and early 1990s.
7. Identify the changes that are occurring in African culture.

Critical Thinking

1. **Analyze** What are the benefits and drawbacks of Africa's cultural and ethnic diversity?
2. **Apply** How would you solve the problem of food shortages in various parts of Africa?
3. **Analyze** How did the political boundaries drawn by European colonial powers cause problems for many African nations after they

gained independence?
4. **Synthesize** How would you respond if you had lived under the system of apartheid?
5. **Apply** How has migration of people from the countryside to cities affected many African countries?
6. **Analyze** In the photograph below Nigerian farmers irrigate a field. How does this show the transition to a new Africa?

Understanding Themes

1. **Nationalism** What was the purpose of the African National Congress (ANC) in South Africa? How has its role changed since 1994?
2. **Change** What political changes came to Angola and Mozambique between the 1970s and 1990s?
3. **Change** How has the Organization of African Unity (OAU) affected African affairs since its founding in 1963?

Skill Practice

Exchange with another student the research reports you completed in "Applying the Skill" for this chapter. Critique the reports using the following questions. For each question, find examples in the report and present them to the author.

1. Does the report have an introduction, body, and conclusion?
2. Does the introduction define the writer's thesis or main point of the report?
3. Is the body of the report organized in a logical way?
4. Are there clear transitions between ideas? Give an example of a good transition and a weak one.
5. Does the conclusion restate and summarize the thesis of the report?

Geography in History

1. **Region** What is the largest uninhabited region of Africa?
2. **Human/Environment Interaction** Why is a narrow strip of land in northeast Africa heavily populated?
3. **Location** Near what city in South Africa is the heaviest population?

Population Density of Africa

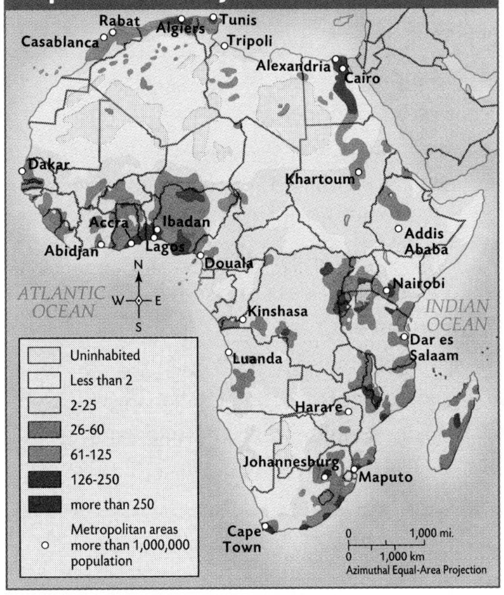

Linking Past and Present

1. In the 1980s, droughts brought widespread famine to Africa. What efforts to relieve food shortages continue there today?
2. In 1994, power passed relatively peacefully from the white minority government of South Africa to an all-racial government that includes black South Africans. How might the South Africa solution serve as model for solving political problems in other countries that are torn by ethnic unrest?

Chapter 34 Review

5. Unskilled rural people remain unemployed and unable to buy African products, weakening national economies.
6. shows more advanced agricultural techniques

Understanding Themes

1. **NATIONALISM** The ANC's original purpose was to press the white government for reform. Since 1994 it has been the country's ruling party, with many new responsibilities.
2. **CHANGE** After a period of civil war between Marxist and non-Marxist groups, Angola and Mozambique moved toward peace and gradually abandoned socialism for free enterprise.
3. **CHANGE** Although it failed in creating a United States of Africa, it urged its members to remain neutral during the cold war, put pressure on South Africa to end apartheid, supported pro-independence movements, settled boundary disputes among member nations, and has set as a major goal the creation of an all-African common market by the year 2000.

Skill Practice

Answers will vary but should be based on critical evaluation of the written report and on the elements of the lesson on page 940.

Geography in History

1. North Africa
2. It borders the Nile River.
3. Johannesburg

Linking Past and Present

1. Students might mention international relief programs and attempts to improve agricultural productivity in the Sahel.
2. Students might argue that if blacks and whites can overcome the racial divide, Hutus and Tutsis and different Somali clans should be able to live in peace also.

Chapter Bonus Test Question

Ask students: What situations elsewhere in the world suggest that optimism about Africa's future is warranted? What situations suggest otherwise? *(Answers will vary but may include: Peace developments in the Middle East and the movement toward peace in the Balkans suggest that optimism is warranted; ongoing ethnic conflicts elsewhere suggest otherwise.)*

The Middle East

CHAPTER RESOURCES

	Reproducible Resources	Multimedia Resources
Chapter Opener	Chapter Themes: Graphic Organizer 35 Historical Significance Chapter Activity 35	MindJogger Videoquiz
Chapter Enrichment	Vocabulary Activity 35* Time Line Activity 35 Mapping History Activity 35 History Simulation 35 Geography and History Activity 35 Source Reading 35 People in World History Profiles 67, 68 World Literature Selection 8 World Art and Music Activity 35 Enrichment Activity 35 Critical Thinking Activity 35 Skill Reinforcement Activity 35 Writer's Guidebook, Lessons 9, 13 Performance Assessment Activity 35	World History and Art Transparency 47, *Iranian Mihrab*; 48, *The Twelve Tribes of Israel* Chapter Transparency 35 Vocabulary PuzzleMaker Software World Music: Cultural Traditions, Lesson 5 Turning Points in World History: *Middle East Peace Accords* In the Holy Land: • *State of Israel Proclaimed: 1948* • *Six-Day War: Scenes* • *Intifadah (The Uprising)*
Chapter Review/Reteaching	Reteaching Activity 35 Skill Reinforcement Activity 35 Spanish Chapter Summary 35	Chapter 35 Digest Audiocassette, Activity, Test* Vocabulary PuzzleMaker Software Student Self-Test and Review Software MindJogger Videoquiz
Chapter Evaluation/Testing	Performance Assessment Activity 35 Chapter 35 Test, Forms A and B	Testmaker

* *Also available in Spanish*

0:00 **OUT OF TIME?** Assign the Chapter 35 summary in the Unit 8 Digest on pages 1026–1029, and the Chapter 35 Audiocassettes.

Block Schedule

Block scheduling differs from traditional class scheduling in the amount of time allotted to each period. The extended time frame provided by block scheduling affords you the opportunity to implement a greater number of research-oriented and activity-intense projects to motivate and involve your students. Activities that are particularly suited to use within the block scheduling framework are identified throughout this chapter by the following designation.

KEY TO ABILITY LEVELS

Teaching strategies have been coded for varying learning styles and abilities.

L1 **BASIC** activities for all students
L2 **AVERAGE** activities for average to above-average students
L3 **CHALLENGING** activities for above-average students
LEP **LIMITED ENGLISH PROFICIENCY** activities

Teach and Reinforce SECTION Content

Chapter 35 Planning Guide

A complete, 1-page lesson plan is provided for each section in the *Reproducible Lesson Plans* booklet.

SECTION RESOURCES

Daily Objectives	Reproducible Resources	Multimedia Resources
Section 1 **Nationalism in the Middle East** Explain how nationalism established independent nations and created conflict in the Middle East after World War II.	Reproducible Lesson Plan 35-1 Vocabulary Activity 35* Guided Reading Activity 35-1* Time Line Activity 35 Section Quiz 35-1*	Section Focus Transparency 35-1 Chapter Transparency 35 Student Self-Test and Review Software Testmaker In the Holy Land: *State of Israel Proclaimed: 1948*
Section 2 **War and Peace in the Middle East** Summarize how issues of peace and war have been decided in the Middle East since the mid-1960s.	Reproducible Lesson Plan 35-2 Vocabulary Activity 35* Guided Reading Activity 35-2* People in World History Profile 68 Geography and History Activity 35 Section Quiz 35-2*	Section Focus Transparency 35-2 World History and Art Transparency 47, *Iranian Mihrab*; 48, *The Twelve Tribes of Israel* Student Self-Test and Review Software Testmaker World Music: Cultural Traditions, Lesson 5 Turning Points in World History: *Middle East Peace Accords* In the Holy Land: • *Six-Day War: Scenes* • *Intifadah (The Uprising)*
Section 3 **Challenges Facing the Middle East** Describe how people in the Middle East have handled the conflict between traditional ways and modern values.	Reproducible Lesson Plan 35-3 Guided Reading Activity 35-3* People in World History Profile 67 Reteaching Activity 35 Enrichment Activity 35 Section Quiz 35-3* Performance Assessment Activity 35 Spanish Chapter Summary 35	Section Focus Transparency 35-3 Vocabulary PuzzleMaker Software Student Self-Test and Review Software Testmaker

**Also available in Spanish*

Chapter Activities

Performance Assessment Activity

An Awareness Campaign Events in the Middle East affect the United States in major ways. Have students work through the following steps: (1) list Middle East conflicts and events that have affected the United States in the past; (2) list the areas and issues of continued tensions in the region; (3) for each tension, predict future problems or implications for Americans; and (4) prioritize the list according to the degree of impact on Americans.

Have students work in groups to create an awareness campaign to inform Americans about the severity of the issues. This campaign may include talk-shows, leaflets, newspaper ads, interviews on the evening news, and so on. For each venue chosen, have students explain what would be said or shown, or have them actually create the visual product.

Possible Rubric Features

Concept attainment, accuracy of content information, plausibility of predictions, analysis skills, originality of products, elaboration and detail, persuasion, and collaborative skills

• *For an additional activity, refer to Activity 35 in the* Performance Assessment Strategies and Activities *booklet.*

Activity

From the Classroom of...

Peter Twomey
Brockton High School
Brockton, MA

Israel/Palestine—A Solution?

Assign each student a Middle Eastern or North African country to research. Then, utilizing the text, library books, and current newspaper articles, each student should write a brief history of his or her country from the end of World War II to the present, including an economic profile. Supply each student with a summary sheet of Arab-Israeli conflicts from 1948 to the present accompanied by maps of the Israeli-Palestinian area in 1948, 1967, and today. When students' research is completed, call a peacekeeping meeting. In round one, each country introduces itself and gives an oral summary of its recent history, including an economic profile. In round two, the countries give their views on the question at hand: What should be the nature of the Israeli and Palestinian states? Why?

To conclude, students should compare their views with current Israeli and Palestinian politicians.

MULTIPLE LEARNING STYLES

Verbal/Linguistic
Have students find examples of different types of literature from modern Middle Eastern writers, including myths, folktales, poetry, drama, novels, and short stories. Have students present to the class oral reports that include brief readings from the literature and that explain how the literature reflects the history and/or current conditions in the Middle East.

Logical/Mathematical
Have students make charts that show the per capita income and the literacy rate of each country in the Middle East. Ask students to compare the charts of several Middle Eastern countries to see if any conclusions can be drawn about the relationship between per capita income and literacy.

Visual/Spatial
Students may research the current flags of each country in the Middle East and then draw or reproduce the flags on poster board. Ask students to include in their posters the meaning of each flag's colors and symbols. Display the posters around the classroom.

Auditory/Musical
Have students collect representative recordings of secular and religious music from the Middle East and play them for the class. Ask students to point out similarities and differences between this music and Western music.

Kinesthetic
Ask students to construct a model that shows the strategies and outcome of the following Middle East conflicts: the Six-Day War, the October War, and the Persian Gulf War.

Additional Resources

TEACHER'S CORNER

NATIONAL GEOGRAPHIC SOCIETY

INDEX TO NATIONAL GEOGRAPHIC MAGAZINE

The following articles may be used for research relating to this chapter:

- "Israel's Galilee: Living in the Shadow of Peace," by Don Belt, June 1995.
- "Oman," by Peter Ross Range, May 1995.
- "Water: The Middle East's Critical Resource," by Priit J. Vesilind, May 1993.
- "Cairo: Clamorous Heart of Egypt," by Peter Theroux, April 1993.
- "Struggle of the Kurds," by Christopher Hitchens, August 1992.
- "Who Are the Palestinians?" by Tad Szulc, June 1992.
- "Living in Harm's Way: The Persian Gulf," by Thomas J. Abercrombie, May 1988.
- "The Stricken Land: Africa's Sahel," by William S. Ellis, August 1987.
- "Iran Under the Ayatollah," by Michael Coyne, July 1985.
- "Iraq at War: The New Face of Baghdad," by William S. Ellis, January 1985.

ADDITIONAL NATIONAL GEOGRAPHIC SOCIETY PRODUCTS

To order the following products for use with this chapter, call National Geographic Society at 1-800-368-2728:

- *Nations of the World Series*, "Egypt." (Video)
- *Nations of the World Series*, "Israel." (Video)
- *The Middle East* (Filmstrip)

BIBLIOGRAPHY

Literature of the Period

Yesoshea, A. B. ***Mr. Mani.*** Translated by Hillel Halkin. New York: Harcourt, 1992. This contemporary Israeli novel gives a great deal of history on the Zionist movement and Israel today.

Readings for the Student

Moore, Molly. ***A Woman at War: Storming Kuwait with the U.S. Marines.*** New York: Macmillan, 1993. Eyewitness account from the battlefield of the Persian Gulf War by a reporter.

Readings for the Teacher

Decosse, David E., ed. ***But Was It Just? Reflections on the Morality of the Persian Gulf War.*** New York: Doubleday, 1992. Five essays from differing points of view on the war's justness.

Peres, Shimon. ***The New Middle East.*** New York: Henry Holt, 1993. An analysis of how the Middle East can achieve a social and economic revival based on peace.

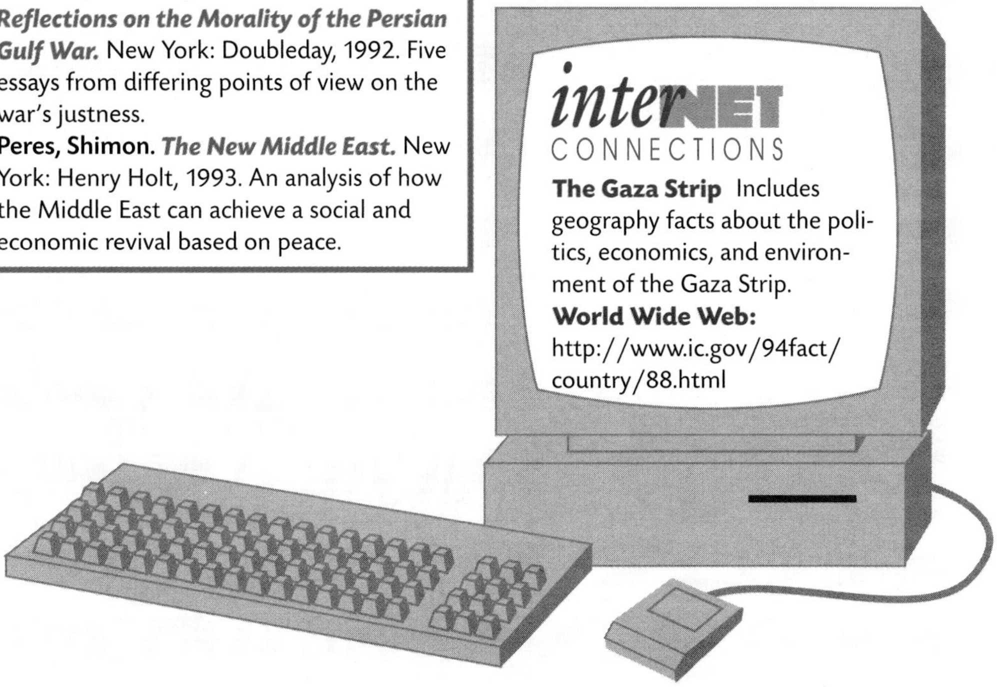
interNET
CONNECTIONS
The Gaza Strip Includes geography facts about the politics, economics, and environment of the Gaza Strip.
World Wide Web:
http://www.ic.gov/94fact/country/88.html

Introducing Chapter 35

CHAPTER THEMES

Chapter Themes are listed by section on this chapter opening page of the Student Edition. A corresponding theme-based activity is available under "TEACH," and a theme-based question is asked in the Section and Chapter Reviews.

The Storyteller

Historical Setting Both Yitzhak Rabin and Yasir Arafat were born in Jerusalem, Palestine. Rabin fought the British to form an independent Israeli state and led the defense of Jerusalem during Israel's war for independence (1947–1949). Rising through the ranks of the army, Rabin later became a leader of Israel's Labor party and a forceful opponent of the PLO.

Yasir Arafat left Jerusalem in 1948 when Israel became a nation. He led raids into Israel, became a leader of the PLO, and dreamed of establishing a new state of Palestine. In 1993 after secret negotiations, these two old enemies sat down at a special ceremony at the White House, signed a peace accord, and shook hands as the world watched.

Historical Significance

Answers: *Protecting the Middle East's waterways and oil resources caused the Western powers and the Soviet Union to back opposing Middle Eastern countries during the cold war. The United Nations administered the partition of Palestine in 1947 and has sent troops in peacekeeping roles to many places in the Middle East since then. The United States played an important role in the negotiation of peace between Israel and its Arab neighbors.*

Egypt, Jordan, and the Palestinians have signed peace agreements with Israel, and Syria has begun negotiations.

Chapter 35

1945–Present

The Middle East

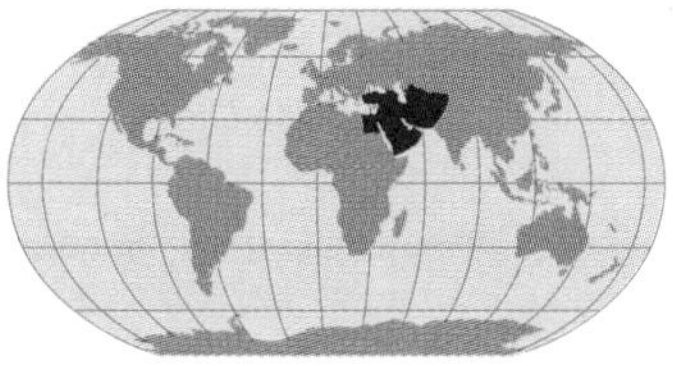

Chapter Themes

- **Nationalism** The cold war and rival nationalisms affect the politics of the Middle East. *Section 1*
- **Cooperation** Middle Eastern nations take steps toward peace after years of conflict. *Section 2*
- **Cultural Diffusion** Middle Eastern countries search for a reconciliation between traditional and modern values. *Section 3*

The Storyteller

In the fall of 1993, a remarkable event occurred that, to many people, seemed like a miracle. Yitzhak Rabin, the prime minister of Israel, and Yasir Arafat, the chairman of the Palestine Liberation Organization (PLO) signed an agreement to end the decades-long conflict between Israel and the Arabs, known as Palestinians.

In 1995, Rabin's assassination stunned Israel and the world, revealing that the quest for peace is often an uphill struggle marked by tragedy. Since 1945, the Middle East has shown itself to be a complex region where violence has been a constant feature of life but where hopes for peace remain unquenchable.

Historical Significance

How have Middle Eastern developments affected world affairs since 1945? What steps have the nations of the Middle East taken to resolve their differences?

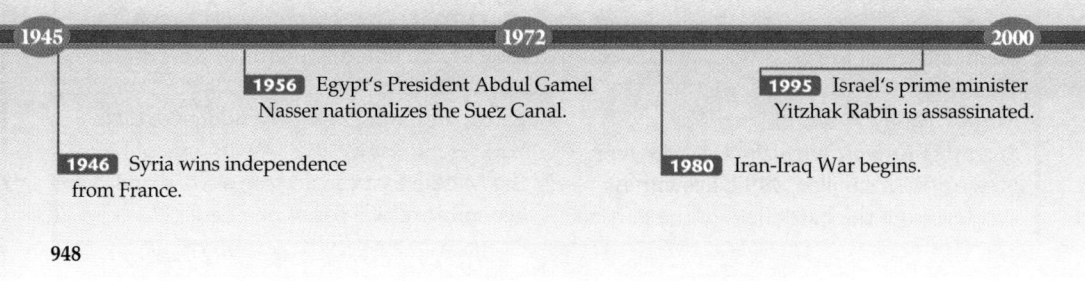

1945 — 1972 — 2000

- **1946** Syria wins independence from France.
- **1956** Egypt's President Abdul Gamel Nasser nationalizes the Suez Canal.
- **1980** Iran-Iraq War begins.
- **1995** Israel's prime minister Yitzhak Rabin is assassinated.

GEOGRAPHY CONNECTION

Region Point out the locator map of the Middle East on page 948. What has long made the Middle East an important region of the world? *(The Middle East links Europe, Asia, and Africa.)* What makes it an especially important region today? *(its plentiful oil reserves)* Have students turn to the map of the Middle East in the Atlas in their textbook. Ask them to make a list of the 15 countries in the Middle East and their capitals. Also ask them to write down one characteristic of each country. *(For example: The Nile River flows through Egypt; Kuwait borders the Persian Gulf.)*

Visualizing History Istanbul (formerly Constantinople) is Turkey's largest city and one of the busiest ports in the Middle East.

Your History Journal

Create an illustrated time line of conflicts and peace conferences or accords in the Middle East beginning in 1948 and ending at the present. Illustrate your time line with symbols of peace and war.

EXTRA CREDIT PROJECT

Country Fact Booklet Have students select one of the Middle Eastern countries, conduct in-depth research on it, and compile a fact booklet. Tell students to include the following types of information in their booklets: geography (bordering countries, physical features, plants, animals); government, politics, and army; economy (agriculture, natural resources, industry, trade); society (social classes, religion, education, daily life, literature, the arts, sports and recreation, role of women, role of children and teens); and history.

Introducing Chapter 35

Visualizing History Tell students that Istanbul straddles the Bosporus Strait that divides Europe from Asia. As Constantinople, the city was once the capital of the Byzantine Empire and then the Ottoman Empire. Today the city is a shipbuilding center and a major center for the manufacture of cement, cigarettes, and leather products. **Why has Istanbul's location made it an important city throughout history?** *(It has been a link between Europe and Asia.)*

Performance Assessment

Refer to the activity on page 948C of the Planning Guide.

Refer to Activity 35 in the *Performance Assessment Strategies and Activities* booklet.

Using Your History Journal

Suggest that students also include on their time lines the names, and if possible the pictures, of people important in the conflicts and peace conferences.

GLENCOE TECHNOLOGY

VIDEODISC

Use MindJogger to preview chapter content.

MindJogger Videoquiz

Chapter 35
Disc 5 Side A

Also available in VHS.

Chapter 35 Section 1

SECTION THEME

▸ **Nationalism** The cold war and rival nationalisms affect the politics of the Middle East.

Find Out

Answer: *led to the establishment of the independent states of Lebanon, Syria, Transjordan (present-day Jordan), and Israel; led to conflicts between Israel and the ousted Palestinians, between Israel and its Arab neighbors; nationalism in Egypt, Lebanon, and Iran led to anti-Western feelings.*

FOCUS

Section Objective

Explain how nationalism established independent nations and created conflict in the Middle East after World War II.

BELLRINGER Motivational Activity

Before taking roll at the beginning of the class period, project Section Focus Transparency 35-1 and have students answer the activity questions.

This activity is also available as a blackline master.

Vocabulary Pre-check

Use Vocabulary Activity 35 to introduce vocabulary terms. **L1 LEP**

1945 — 1955 — 1965

1948 Israel and Arab states fight first conflict.

1951 Iran nationalizes foreign-owned oil industries.

1958 Political crisis engulfs Lebanon.

Section 1

Nationalism in the Middle East

Setting the Scene

▸ **Terms to Define**
Pan-Arabism, kibbutzim, nationalize, pact

▸ **People to Meet**
David Ben-Gurion, Gamal Abdel Nasser, Hussein I, Mohammed Reza Pahlavi, Mohammed Mossadeq

▸ **Places to Locate**
Egypt, Iraq, Lebanon, Syria, Jordan, Saudi Arabia, Yemen, Israel, Suez Canal, Turkey, Iran

Find Out How did nationalism establish independent nations and create conflict in the Middle East after World War II?

The Storyteller

In spite of the separate living arrangements, members of a kibbutz family do not become strangers to one another.... Kibbutz parents spend a great deal of their free time with their children.... Parents and children enjoy each other all the more when they meet just for fun and companionship. Kibbutz-niks [residents of a kibbutz] *take good care of their elderly parents, too. There is less friction among kibbutz grandparents, parents, and children.... There is less divorce—fewer marriage problems.*

—adapted from *Israel Today*, Harry Essrig and Abraham Segal, 1977.

Children in a kibbutz

In the decades after World War II, nationalist movements took hold in the Middle East. For more than 20 years, Great Britain and France had governed much of the area under the terms of post–World War I agreements. Gradually the presence of foreign officials and troops on Middle Eastern soil revived the desire for independence, as it did in Asia and Africa.

While most Middle Eastern countries shook off European control in the postwar years, foreign influence in the region remained strong. With its valuable waterways and oil reserves, the Middle East became the scene of superpower maneuvering for influence during the cold war.

Arab Independence

Several Arab countries, such as **Egypt** and **Iraq**, had achieved independence before World War II. During the 1940s, other European-ruled Arab territories followed. The Mediterranean coastal lands of **Lebanon** and **Syria** won their freedom from France. In Lebanon, Christian and Muslim leaders agreed to share power under a new constitution, while Syria elected its first parliamentary government. The largely desert kingdom of Transjordan (present-day **Jordan**) gained its independence from Great Britain. In all of these new states, however, Western influences remained strong after independence.

As independent Arab states emerged, Pan-Arabism, a movement aimed at building closer cultural and political ties among Arabs, grew stronger, especially among the educated urban middle class. In 1945, leaders of Egypt, Iraq, Transjordan, Syria, Lebanon, **Saudi Arabia**, and **Yemen** formed the Arab League. Its mission was to unify the Arab world.

SECTION RESOURCES

Reproducible Masters
- Reproducible Lesson Plan 35-1
- Vocabulary Activity 35
- Guided Reading Activity 35-1
- Time Line Activity 35
- Section Quiz 35-1

Transparencies
- Section Focus Transparency 35-1
- Chapter Transparency 35

Multimedia
- Student Self-Test and Review Software
- Testmaker
- In the Holy Land: *State of Israel Proclaimed: 1948*

Formation of Israel

By 1947, Palestine remained the only significant European-ruled territory in the region. Arabs, who had lived in Palestine for centuries, wanted the British to honor their promise of freedom made in the early 1900s. Zionist Jews wanted to build a Jewish state on the same land—land that their ancestors had claimed since Biblical times and that the British had also promised to them.

The Holocaust in Nazi-occupied Europe had boosted support in Western countries for the Zionist movement. Fearing that the British would allow increased Jewish immigration, Arabs in Palestine began to attack Jewish settlers. Many of Palestine's Jews lived on kibbutzim, or collective farms, where they struggled to turn swamps and boulder-strewn hillsides into productive farms. To defend themselves, Jewish settlements relied on a military force called the Haganah. Meanwhile, Jewish underground forces carried out attacks on British soldiers and Palestinian Arabs. As hostilities mounted, Great Britain admitted its inability to keep the peace and turned Palestine over to the United Nations in 1947.

For months, world leaders debated the future of Palestine. The United States and much of the West wanted to divide Palestine into a Jewish and an Arab state. Arab nations, along with several European and Pacific nations, rejected the idea and called for a single Palestinian state. At a meeting of the General Assembly on November 29, 1947, the United Nations voted to partition Palestine and to place Jerusalem under UN administration.

Jewish leaders were quick to accept the UN partition plan, while embittered Arab leaders rejected it. Great Britain relinquished control of Palestine on May 14, 1948, as Prime Minister **David Ben-Gurion** proclaimed the new state of **Israel**. Within 24 hours, the armies of Syria, Lebanon, Iraq, Egypt, and Transjordan attacked the new Jewish state. With foreign aid and effective civilian and military organization, the Israelis defeated the Arab forces in nine months.

When the fighting ended in early 1949, Israel held most of Palestine. Jerusalem was divided, with the eastern part of the city in Arab hands. Transjordan annexed East Jerusalem and the West Bank of the Jordan River. Egypt held the Gaza Strip. The war was a resounding victory for Israel. To the Arabs, the war spelled disaster. As a result of partition, more than 700,000 Palestinians became homeless. Many fled to neighboring Arab lands, where a large number settled in refugee camps hoping to eventually return home.

Visualizing History **Despite British restrictions on immigration, Jews aboard the *Exodus* migrated to Palestine in 1947.** *Why did Great Britain turn Palestine over to the United Nations in 1947?*

Arab Unity

The 1948–1949 war had other serious consequences for the Arab world. In Egypt, many people blamed rich, corrupt King Farouk for the Arab defeat and the country's weak economy. In 1952 army officers seized control of the government and proclaimed a republic. Within a year, Colonel **Gamal Abdel Nasser**, a leader of the coup, took over as president.

Nasser profoundly disliked Western influence in the Middle East, and quickly launched new policies through which he hoped Egypt would lead the Arab world to greatness. In an extremely popular move, Nasser broke up the estates of wealthy Egyptian landowners and gave plots of land to the peasants. Then he negotiated the British withdrawal from the **Suez Canal**. Finally, he set out to modernize Egypt and build up its military muscle to confront Israel.

The Suez Crisis

Nasser wanted to help Egypt by building a dam at Aswan in the Upper Nile River valley. Known as the Aswan High Dam, the massive structure—36 stories high and more than 2 miles (3 km) wide—would end flooding, increase irrigation, and give farmers two extra harvests a year. Electricity generated by the dam would power new industries.

Seeking political influence in the economic development of Egypt, the United States offered Egypt a $270 million loan to build the dam. However, Nasser's growing Soviet leanings, including a major arms deal with the Soviet Union, caused the United States to angrily withdraw

TEACH

Guided Practice

THEME Nationalism

Help students recall the meaning of *nationalism. (the desire of a people to achieve independence from foreign control and to govern themselves)* Lead students in a discussion on how Egypt's seizure of the Suez Canal increased the spirit of Arab nationalism in the Middle East. *(Nasser emerged from the Suez crisis as a powerful Arab leader and his brand of nationalism spread throughout the Arab world.)* **L1**

Visualizing History Tell students that the British did not allow the *Exodus* to disembark its 4,500 Jewish refugee passengers in Palestine. After the ship was badly damaged by British destroyers, its passengers were taken by other ships to France and Germany.

Answer to Caption: *Great Britain was unable to keep the peace between Jewish settlers and Arabs in Palestine.*

Politics Have students make a chart that shows the parties involved, the goals, and the outcomes of the following events in the Middle East: the Arab-Jewish War (1948–1949), the Suez crisis, the civil war in Lebanon (1958), the crisis in Iran (early 1950s). **L2**

Chapter Transparency 35

International Relations Have students compare the role the United States played in Turkish affairs with its role in Iranian affairs. **L3**

Independent Practice

Guided Reading Activity 35-1 **L1**

Time Line Activity 35

COOPERATIVE LEARNING ACTIVITY

Time Line Organize students into nine groups and assign each group one of the following countries mentioned in this section: Egypt, Iraq, Lebanon, Syria, Jordan, Saudi Arabia, Israel, Turkey, Iran. Have each group make a horizontal time line of significant events that occurred in the country from the 1940s to the present. Have representatives from each group get together to determine a standard length for the time lines. Remind the groups to assign members to research or to place information on the time lines. Display completed time lines one above the other so that students can determine what occurred in each country at a particular time. **L2**

Map Study

Answer
because of the oil reserves found there

Map Skills Practice

Reading a Map What nations border Israel? *(Egypt, Jordan, Lebanon, Syria)*

Daily Life Have students research life in a Palestinian refugee camp or in an Israeli kibbutz. Ask students to write diary entries for a week from the point of view of a teenager in a camp or on a kibbutz. **L2**

Geography: Movement Have students draw a map that shows the route of a ship from Jiddah, Saudi Arabia, to Marseilles, France, before and after the closing of the Suez Canal. Ask students to estimate the difference in distance between the two routes and research the difference in travel time. **L3 LEP**

ABC NEWS INTERACTIVE™

VIDEODISC
In the Holy Land

Side One, Chapter 20
Frame: 27441
Title: *State of Israel Proclaimed: 1948*
Subject: David Ben-Gurion issued a proclamation of Israel's independence over Jewish-controlled areas of Palestine.
Ask: What was the significance of the founding of the State of Israel? *(Now there was a Jewish nation.)*

The Middle East

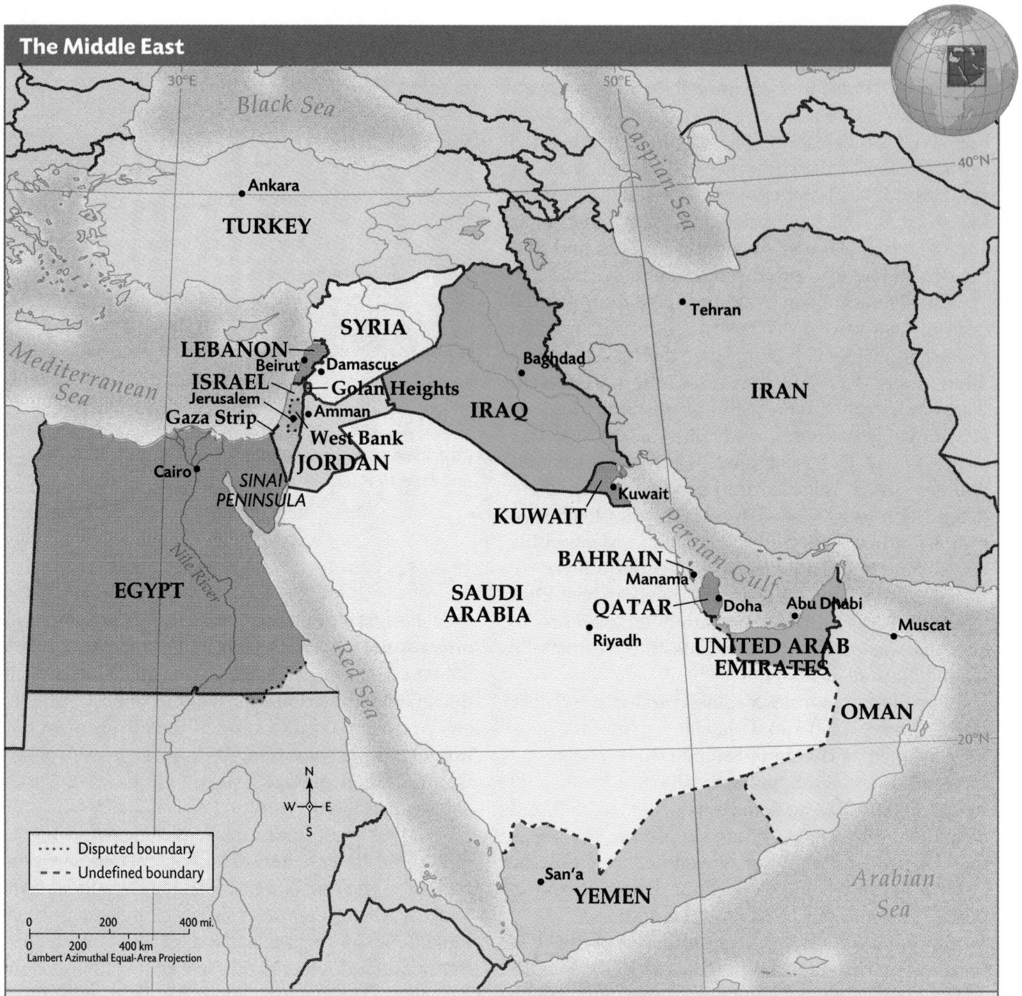

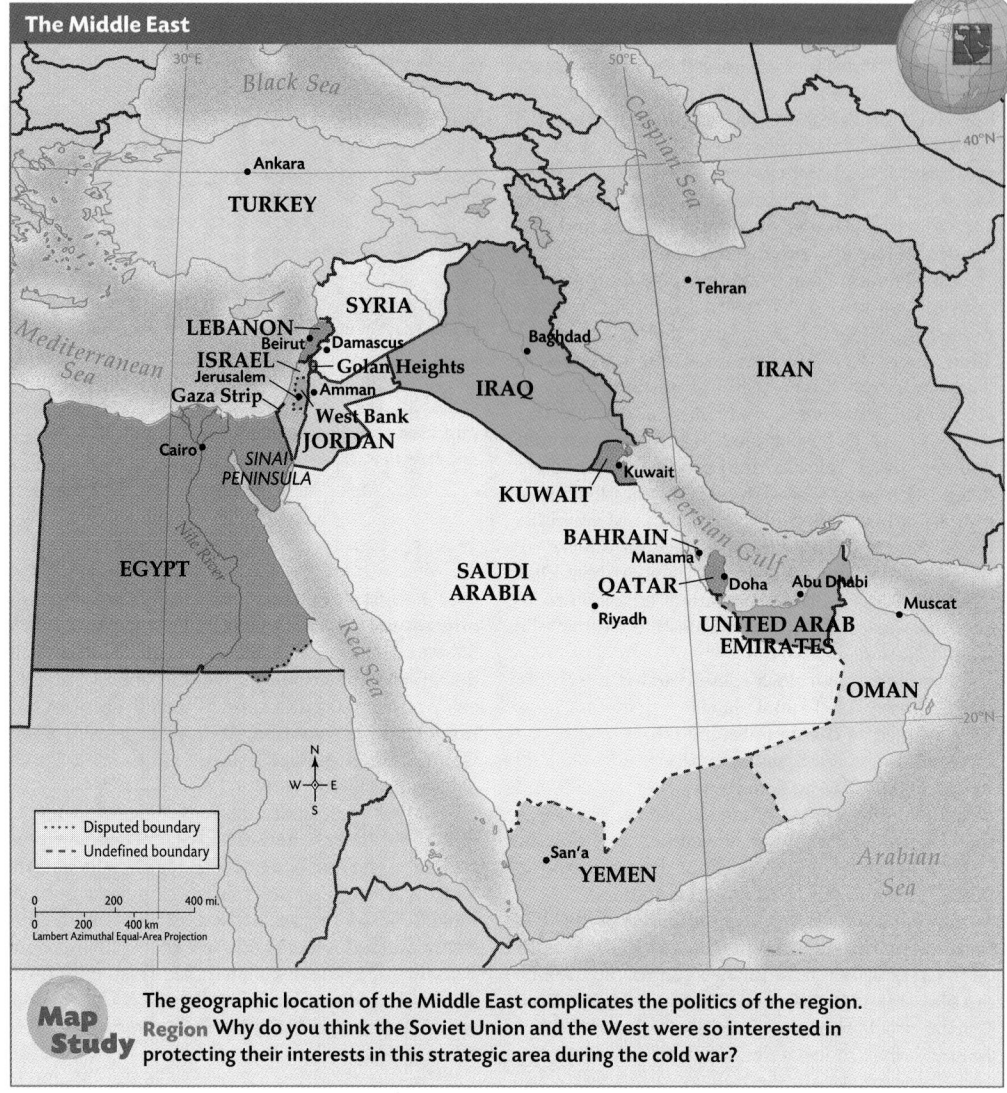

Map Study **The geographic location of the Middle East complicates the politics of the region.**
Region **Why do you think the Soviet Union and the West were so interested in protecting their interests in this strategic area during the cold war?**

its offer. In July 1956 Nasser retaliated against the Western powers by nationalizing, or bringing under government control, the Suez Canal. He vowed to use millions of dollars in canal fees to finance the building of the dam.

President Eisenhower was opposed to Western intervention, and the United States tried to negotiate an end to the crisis. Great Britain and France, however, feared that Nasser might close the canal and cut off shipments of oil between the Middle East and Western Europe. In October, the two European powers joined Israel in invading Egypt. Great Britain and France hoped to overthrow Nasser and seize the canal. Israel wanted to end Egyptian guerrilla attacks on its borders. The United States immediately sponsored a United Nations resolution calling for British and French withdrawal from Egypt. The Russians threatened rocket attacks on British and French cities. Eisenhower, opposed to Soviet interference, put the Strategic Air Command on alert. In face of this pressure, the three nations pulled out of Egypt. United Nations forces were sent to patrol the Egyptian-Israeli border. Nasser then accepted the Soviet offer to build the Aswan High Dam.

MEETING SPECIAL NEEDS ACTIVITY

Study Strategy Have students make a flash card for each of the following countries: Egypt, Iraq, Syria, Lebanon, Jordan, Israel, Turkey, and Iran. Tell students to write the country's name on one side of the card. On the other side, they should write the names of the main leaders from 1948 to 1960; the leaders' positions—pro-Western or pro-Arab, pro-Nasser, and so forth; and main crises or events for the country during those years. **L2**

Middle East Crises

Nasser emerged from the Suez crisis as a powerful Arab leader. He had embarrassed Great Britain and France, won control of the Suez Canal, and had stopped Israel from taking more territory. Pro-Nasser parties began forming throughout the Arab world. It seemed that Nasser might rise to lead a unified Arab world.

In early 1958 Syria and Egypt merged to form a Nasser-led state called the United Arab Republic (UAR). The union lasted about three years. At that point, Syrian leaders had grown resentful of the loss of their power, and Syria withdrew from the UAR.

That same year, Nasser's brand of Arab nationalism seemed to be taking hold in Iraq. There, King Faisal II, Nasser's strongest Arab opponent and a friend of the West, was killed by radical political and military forces in his country. They set up a one-party regime like Nasser's and broke ties with the West.

In the face of pro-Nasser pressure, some Arab leaders turned to the West for support. Jordan's **Hussein I** asked for British and American help when pro-Nasser forces threatened his government. In Lebanon, violence broke out between the Christians, who dominated the nation, and a huge Muslim population that sympathized with Nasser and the UAR. Christian President Camille Chamoun, a supporter of the West, sought re-election to a new term. Anti-Western elements revolted, and a civil war followed. Chamoun asked for Western help to stop the violence. At first, Eisenhower refused. However, when the unexpected coup overthrew the government of Iraq, Eisenhower decided to uphold political stability in the region. He sent 15,000 Marines to Lebanon in July 1958. When order was restored that fall, the troops pulled out.

By 1960 Arab nationalism had made gains, but the Middle East was in a state of uncertainty. A fragile truce held between Arabs and Israelis; competing Arab groups were at an impasse; and neither superpower had managed to achieve dominance in the region.

Pro-Western Tier

Two other Middle Eastern countries, **Turkey** and **Iran**, experienced the upheaval of nationalism and rapid modernization. Both bordered the Soviet Union, making them pawns in cold-war struggles.

Turkey

At the end of World War II, Turkey received American aid to modernize its economy and to ward off Soviet advances. During the 1950s, the Turks joined NATO and the Baghdad Pact, alliances aimed at blocking Soviet expansion. Turkey also made strides toward democracy, encouraged foreign investment, and strengthened its capitalist economy. By the 1960s, however, government corruption, inflation, and a huge international debt discredited Turkey's ruling politicians and increased the political influence of the military.

Iran

By contrast, Western influence in oil-rich Iran was shaken after World War II. The young shah, **Mohammed Reza Pahlavi**, relied on Western help to block Soviet influence. Many Iranian people, however, resented the West. For decades, the British had grown rich on Iranian oil at Iran's expense.

In 1951, a wealthy politician, **Mohammed Mossadeq**, became prime minister. He nationalized the British-owned oil industry and declared that all oil money would be used for social and economic reforms. Great Britain called for a world boycott of Iranian oil. As Iranians began to suffer, their hatred of the West and the shah grew.

In 1953 growing support for Mossadeq forced the shah to flee the country. He returned after a military coup—promoted by the United States—deposed Mossadeq. The shah increased his ties to the United States and signed the Baghdad Pact. A pact is a treaty between two or more nations. He also signed an agreement with Western oil companies. Backed by the army and Western powers, the shah was firmly in control by the 1960s.

SECTION 1 REVIEW

Recall

1. **Define** Pan-Arabism, kibbutzim, nationalize, pact.
2. **Identify** David Ben-Gurion, Gamal Abdel Nasser, Arab League, Hussein I, Mohammed Reza Pahlavi, Mohammed Mossadeq.
3. **Explain** why the United Nations divided Palestine into an Arab and a Jewish state.

Critical Thinking

4. **Applying Information** How did the Holocaust in Europe contribute to the development of the Jewish state in Palestine?

Understanding Themes

5. **Nationalism** How was Nasser viewed by the Arab world after his nationalization of the Suez Canal?

SECTION 1 REVIEW ANSWERS

1. The words are defined in the Glossary.
2. Arab League, 950; Ben-Gurion, 951; Nasser, 951; Hussein I, 953; Pahlavi, 953; Mossadeg, 953
3. The United Nations divided Palestine in order to grant freedom and independence to the Palestinian Arabs and to create a Jewish state in Palestine for Zionist Jews.
4. boosted support among Western countries for the Zionist movement
5. **NATIONALISM** Nasser was viewed as a great Arab leader because he had embarrassed Great Britain and France and had stopped Israel from taking more territory.

Chapter 35 Section 1

ASSESS

Check for Understanding

Assign Section 1 Review as homework or as an in-class activity.

Use Student Self-Test and Review Software to review Section 1.

Global Gourmet

Middle East Pita bread, or pocket bread, began with nomads in the Middle East. After pitching their tents at the end of the day, they mixed powdered grain and water to form a dough, patted it into flat rounds, and baked them over an open fire.

Evaluate

Section Quiz 35-1

Use the Testmaker to create a customized quiz for Section 1.

Reteach

Have students identify the relation of the following people to a Middle Eastern country and to major events in the Middle East: David Ben-Gurion, King Farouk, Gamal Abdel Nasser, Hussein I, Camille Chamoun, Mohammad Reza Pahlavi, and Mohammad Mossadeg.

Enrich

Have students research and write a short report explaining how and why Lebanon's government was divided between Christians and Muslims.

CLOSE

Have students summarize the results of anti-Western feelings in Egypt, Iraq, Lebanon, and Iran.

Chapter 35 Section 2

SECTION THEME

▶ **Cooperation** Middle Eastern nations take steps toward peace after years of conflict.

Find Out

Answer: *Syria's threat led Israel to respond with force in the Six-Day War. Resentment over Israel's occupation of Palestinian lands led Egypt to strike back in the Yom Kippur War. Peaceful resolution to Arab-Israeli conflicts was finally achieved in the Camp David Accords and the 1993 peace treaty. Whether armed members of the PLO should be allowed in Lebanon led to fighting in that country. An Iraqi invasion of Kuwait was resolved by the use of force.*

FOCUS

Section Objective

Summarize how issues of peace and war have been decided in the Middle East since the mid-1960s.

BELLRINGER
Motivational Activity

Before taking roll at the beginning of the class period, project Section Focus Transparency 35-2 and have students answer the activity questions.

This activity is also available as a blackline master.

Vocabulary Pre-check

Vocabulary Activity 35

1965 | 1975 | 1985 | 1995

- **1967** Israel and Arab nations fight Six-Day War.
- **1979** Revolution establishes Islamic republic in Iran.
- **1990** Iraq invades Kuwait.
- **1993** Israelis and Palestinians agree to end their conflicts.

Section 2

War and Peace in the Middle East

Setting the Scene

▶ **Terms to Define**
disengagement, cartel, *intifada*, embargo

▶ **People to Meet**
Yasir Arafat, Anwar al-Sadat, Menachem Begin, Hosni Mubarak, Yitzhak Rabin, Shimon Peres, Ayatollah Ruhollah Khomeini, Saddam Hussein

▶ **Places to Locate**
Gaza Strip, Golan Heights, West Bank, Beirut, Kuwait

Find Out How have issues of peace and war been decided in the Middle East since the mid-1960s?

The Storyteller

When Shah Mohammed Reza Pahlavi was overthrown in 1979, Iran had male tailors fitting women's clothes and male teachers in girls' classrooms. The revolutionaries, however, refused to allow unrelated men and women to work closely together. The result: many more job opportunities for women. In the media, for example, the need for women to cover women's sports opened jobs for directors and reporters.

—adapted from *Nine Parts of Desire, The Hidden World of Islamic Women*, Geraldine Brooks, 1995

Shah Mohammed Reza Pahlavi

From the 1960s to the 1990s, many sweeping changes came to the Middle East. Wars broke out between various nations and groups in the region, but hopes for peace were also high, especially in the early 1990s.

As the 1960s opened, the most prolonged and bitter dispute was between Israel, its Arab neighbors, and the Palestinians. Within Israel, Palestinians struggled to win nationhood. In 1964 the Palestine Liberation Organization (PLO) was formed to eliminate Israel and to create a Palestinian state. Later, however, many Palestinians and Israelis came to accept a two-state solution: a state for Israelis and a state for Palestinians.

Arab-Israeli Conflict

The cease-fire between Israel and its Arab neighbors fell apart during the 1960s. A new radical regime in Syria sought the end of Israel and the creation of an Arab Palestine. Syrian and Israeli troops engaged in border clashes in early 1967. Egypt's President Nasser aided Syria by closing the Gulf of Aqaba to Israel and by having United Nations forces removed from the Israeli-Egyptian border.

Six-Day War

Fearing possible attack, Israel responded with force on June 5, 1967. At 8:45 A.M., Israeli fighter jets bore down on 17 Egyptian airfields, destroying 300 of Egypt's 350 warplanes. Hundreds of miles away, Israeli jets also demolished the air forces of Iraq, Jordan, and Syria.

In the Six-Day War, Israeli forces tripled Israel's land holdings, seizing the Sinai Peninsula and the **Gaza Strip** from Egypt, and the **Golan Heights** from Syria. When Jordan entered the war, Israeli troops also took East Jerusalem.

SECTION RESOURCES

Reproducible Masters
- Reproducible Lesson Plan 35-2
- Vocabulary Activity 35
- Guided Reading Activity 35-2
- People in World History Profile 68
- Geography and History Activity 35
- Section Quiz 35-2

Transparencies
- Section Focus Transparency 35-2
- World History and Art Transparency 47, *Iranian Mihrab*; 48, *The Twelve Tribes of Israel*

Multimedia
- Student Self-Test and Review Software
- Testmaker
- World Music: Cultural Traditions, Lesson 5
- Turning Points in World History
- In the Holy Land

In a move that spawned decades of upheaval, Israel occupied the **West Bank** of the Jordan River. The West Bank was land that had been designated as part of Arab Palestine in the United Nations partition plan in 1947. Palestinian Arabs had never achieved self-rule, however; they had been under Jordanian rule ever since 1949, when Jordan annexed the West Bank. Now, as a result of the Six-Day War, the area's more than one million Palestinians found themselves under Israeli military occupation.

Thousands more Palestinians fled to neighboring countries such as Lebanon. They turned more than ever to the PLO and its militant leader, **Yasir Arafat**, who vowed to use armed struggle to establish a Palestinian state.

The United Nations asked Israel to pull out of occupied territories and asked Arab nations to recognize Israel's right to exist. Both sides refused. Terrorist attacks and border raids continued for several years.

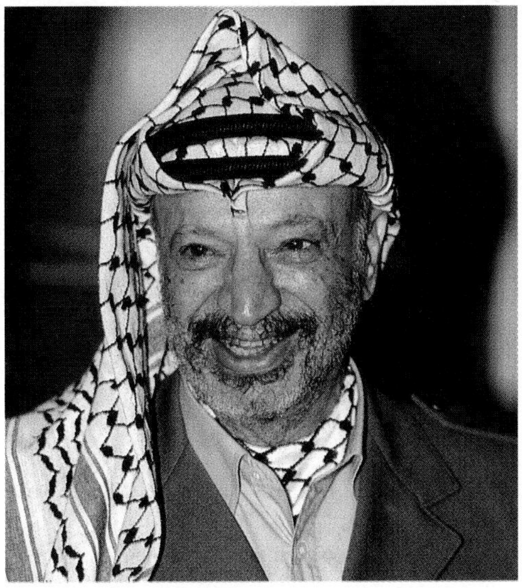

Visualizing History **Yasir Arafat became chairman of the Palestine Liberation Organization (PLO) in 1969. The PLO, formed in 1964, is a confederation of various Palestinian Arab groups.** *Why was the PLO formed?*

Oil and Conflict

Nasser died in 1970. His successor, President **Anwar al-Sadat**, led Arab forces in a new war against Israel. On October 6, 1973, Egyptian and Syrian forces launched a surprise attack on Israel on the Jewish holy day of Yom Kippur and during the Muslim holy month of Ramadan. In early battles, many Israeli planes were shot down. Egyptian troops crossed over into the Sinai, and Syria moved into the Golan Heights. With an American airlift of weapons, Israel struck back. Israeli troops crossed the Suez Canal and occupied Egyptian territory. The fighting raged until the UN negotiated a cease-fire. Secretary of State Henry Kissinger negotiated a disengagement, or military withdrawal, agreement in late 1973.

American support of Israel during the 1973 war angered Arab countries. Attempting to halt Western support, Arab oil countries imposed an embargo on oil sales to Israel's allies in 1973. Additional pressure came from the Organization of Petroleum Exporting Countries (OPEC), a cartel, or group of businesses formed to regulate production and prices among its members. OPEC, which included Arab and non-Arab oil producers, quadrupled the price of oil. However, the embargo threatened such dire economic problems for the world, including Arab countries, that it was lifted in 1974.

The Camp David Accords

In 1977, Egypt's President Sadat acted independently to break the deadlock. He accepted an invitation to visit Israel, becoming the first Arab leader to step in peace on Israeli soil. In a speech before Israel's parliament, Sadat called for Arab acceptance of Israel, a just solution to the Palestinian problem, and an end to hostilities between Israelis and Arabs.

The next year Sadat accepted an invitation from United States President Jimmy Carter to meet with Israeli Prime Minister **Menachem Begin** (BAY•gihn). The 12 days of meetings at Camp David in Maryland resulted in the Camp David Accords, the basis for an Arab-Israeli peace treaty.

Sadat and Begin signed the treaty in March 1979—the first time an Arab nation recognized Israel's right to exist. In return, Israel gave up the Sinai Peninsula. Many nations applauded Sadat's actions, but several Arab states broke ties with Egypt. Sadat's separate peace with Israel, they said, threatened Arab unity.

In 1981 Muslim extremists assassinated Sadat, and **Hosni Mubarak** succeeded him as president. Mubarak supported Egypt's peace with Israel but also worked to improve Egypt's relations with other Arab nations in the region. At home, he faced economic pressures caused by Egypt's soaring population and lack of resources. Another challenge to Mubarak came from a growing opposition movement led by strict Islamic groups that wanted to end Western influences in Egypt.

Chapter 35 Section 2

Guided Practice

THEME Cooperation Have students find examples in Section 2 of countries or political groups cooperating, or working together for their common good. *(Answers may include: Arab countries aiding one another against Israel in the Six-Day and Yom Kippur Wars; OPEC oil embargo; Camp David Accords; peace accords between Israel and PLO; Arab-Western coalition in Persian Gulf War.)* **L1**

Visualizing History Tell students that Yasir Arafat, who once backed the destruction of Israel through terrorist acts, denounced the acts of violence perpetrated by Muslim extremists against Israel civilians in February and March 1996. Why do you think he did this? *(to further the peace process aimed at achieving the establishment of a Palestinian state as outlined in the 1993 peace agreement)* **Answer to Caption:** *to eliminate Israel and establish a Palestinian state*

Time Line Have students make a time line that shows Arab-Israeli relations in the following years: 1967, 1973, 1978, 1987, and 1993. **L2 LEP**

Cultural Perspectives

Religions Ramadan and Yom Kippur are both periods of atonement and fasting. During Ramadan, the ninth month of the Islamic year, Muslims fast from sunrise to sunset. Each evening they recite long passages from the Quran. The most sacred of Jewish holidays, Yom Kippur, falls in late September or early October. Jews spend the day fasting and praying for the forgiveness of sins committed during the year.

COOPERATIVE LEARNING ACTIVITY

Group Presentations Organize the class into five groups. Have each group choose a slip of paper from a box with one of the following types of people on it: Palestinians who took part in the *intifada*; Israelis who participated in the Six-Day War; Lebanese Christian merchants during Lebanon's civil war; American hostages during Iran's revolution; or Kuwaiti civilians during the Persian Gulf War. Have each group research to present its people's view of the cause of violence in the Middle East. Let each team decide the format of its presentation–skit, interview, role playing, or lecture. Suggest that one person from the group record on the chalkboard the main points of the presentation. **L2**

Chapter 35
Section 2

Politics Have students compare the reasons for and the outcomes of the assassinations of Anwar al-Sadat and Yitzhak Rabin. *(Both men were assassinated by extremists who opposed the Israeli-Arab peace process; both men's successors pledged to support the peace, although Sadat's successor, Mubarak, also worked to improve Egypt's relations with other Arab nations.)* **L3**

ABC NEWS INTERACTIVE™

VIDEODISC
In the Holy Land

Side One, Chapter 26
Frame: 36164
Title: *Six-Day War: Scenes*
Ask: In 1967, which areas were captured by Israeli forces? *(the Sinai Peninsula, West Bank of Jordan River, and Jerusalem)*

Side Two, Chapter 6
Frame: 9840
Title: *Intifadah (The Uprising)*
Subject: Two different perspectives of the *intifada*
Ask: What were the Palestinians' reasons for the uprising? *(They felt that Israeli policies had been repressive.)* How did the Israeli soldier feel about putting down the Palestinian uprising? *(He said he had been trained to fight military enemies, not civilians, and that it was very difficult.)*

The Palestinian Uprising

For 20 years after the 1967 war, Arabs and Israelis could not agree on the future of the Israeli-occupied territories. Resenting Israeli rule, Palestinians lived in a smoldering rage. Most could get only low-paying jobs. Those who protested could be arrested. During this time, the PLO staged hijackings and bombings in Israel and abroad.

In December 1987, a traffic accident in the Gaza Strip sparked Palestinian protests. In one incident, Israeli soldiers sent to maintain order were surrounded by a group of angry Palestinians. In the confusion, one soldier fired, killing a 17-year-old boy. This confrontation led to the *intifada*, an uprising that spread from the Gaza Strip to the West Bank. Workers went on strike, and thousands of demonstrators hurled stones at Israeli soldiers and civilians. The *intifada* focused world attention on the Palestinian issue.

In late 1988 the PLO's Arafat stated that he would renounce terrorism and accept Israel's right to exist as an independent nation. However, distrusting Arafat's motives, Israel refused to negotiate with the PLO and to halt the growth of Jewish settlements in the West Bank.

Making Peace

Tension and often violent confrontations between Palestinians and Israelis continued into 1991. The United States, with cooperation from the former Soviet Union, applied pressure on the Arabs and the Israelis to begin negotiations that, hopefully, would lead to peace in the region. Representatives of Israel and its Arab neighbors and Palestinians met in Madrid in October 1991 for the first round of talks. More meetings were held later in Moscow and Washington, D.C.

The prospect for success improved when the Israelis elected a new government in the summer of 1992. The new prime minister, **Yitzhak Rabin** (YIHT•zahk rah•BEEN), agreed in principle to

Images of the Times

Living in the Middle East

Daily life in the Middle East today is a blend of modern and traditional ways as well as urban and rural lifestyles.

Beirut, Lebanon, is rebuilding its neighborhoods after a long period of civil war.

Jiddah, Saudi Arabia, is a modern port city on the Red Sea that has prospered from the country's oil wealth.

956

Images of the Times — Living in the Middle East

Money from oil provides most of Kuwait's income. These oil revenues pay for medical care, education, and social security for the Kuwaitis. Kuwaitis pay no taxes other than customs duties. Because Kuwaiti families share in the country's oil wealth, they can afford to hire household help. This help and workers in other service industries come from immigrants from Asian and other Arab countries. As a result of immigration, the ethnic Kuwaiti population now makes up a minority of only 45 percent. To keep Kuwait for the Kuwaitis, the government limits voting rights to Kuwaiti males over 21 years of age who can trace their families' residence in the country back to 1921.

exchange some of the occupied land for security guarantees and to accept self-rule by the Palestinians. Delegates from Jordan, Syria, and other Arab countries also showed a new flexibility in their positions.

The Peace Process

In September 1993, Israel and the PLO recognized each other and agreed to eventual self-government for Palestinians in the West Bank and the Gaza Strip. The agreement also provided for a gradual Israeli military withdrawal from both areas. In May 1994, the agreement went into effect in the West Bank city of Jericho and in the Gaza Strip. A year later, Israel and the PLO agreed on the removal of Israeli forces from other Palestinian areas and for the grant of significant self-rule to the Palestinians by mid-1996. Palestinians voting in January 1996 elections chose Yasir Arafat as their first president.

Meanwhile, the peace process also reached out to Israel's Arab neighbors: Jordan and Syria. In July 1994 Jordan's King Hussein and Israeli Prime Minister Rabin signed a declaration ending the state of war that had technically existed between Jordan and Israel since 1948. Syria and Israel also carried out direct talks aimed at reaching a peace treaty between them. A major obstacle, however, were the terms and extent of an Israeli withdrawal from the Golan Heights, occupied by Israel since the 1967 Arab-Israeli war.

Rabin's Assassination

Although many Israelis and Palestinians supported the peace process, a large number on both sides opposed it. Many Palestinians feared that peace would lead to a less-than-independent Palestinian state subject to Israeli restrictions. By contrast, Israeli opponents of the process feared that a self-governing Palestinian state could be a threat to Israel. In addition, some Jewish settlers in the occupied territories believed that the West Bank—which they called by the Biblical names Judea and Samaria—was given by God to the

Kuwait on the Persian Gulf has an economy based on oil. An increasing number of women in the Middle East, as in other areas of the world, earn university degrees and work in businesses.

The Galilee region of Israel has areas where swamps and lakes have been drained to create productive farmlands.

REFLECTING ON THE TIMES

1. What impact has oil had on various countries of the Middle East?
2. What country in the Middle East is rebuilding after a long period of civil war?

ANSWERS TO REFLECTING ON THE TIMES

1. The economies of countries such as Kuwait and Saudi Arabia are based on oil. Oil production has brought prosperity to these countries.
2. Lebanon

Chapter 35 Section 2

World Music: Cultural Traditions, Lesson 5

World History and Art Transparency 47, *Iranian Mihrab*; 48, *The Twelve Tribes of Israel*

ABCNEWS INTERACTIVE™

VIDEODISC
Turning Points in World History

Side Two
Chapter 11

Title: *Middle East Peace Accords*
Ask: Why is it likely that the Middle East peace talks will be ongoing? *(The disputes are centuries old and many difficult issues are involved; thus, negotiations will likely take a long time.)*

you don't say...

Intifada literally translated means "shaking off." The Palestinians in the Israeli-controlled East Jerusalem, the Gaza Strip, and the West Bank tried to "shake off" Israeli control and end the expansion of Jewish settlements in these areas.

Who?What?Where?When?

Nobel Peace Prizes were awarded in 1978 to Anwar al-Sadat and Menachem Begin for signing the Camp David Accords and in 1994 to Yasir Arafat, Yitzhak Rabin, and Shimon Peres for starting the peace process between Israel and the PLO.

Visualizing History Tell students that the ayatollah had been an opponent of the Pahlavi dynasty in Iran since the 1930s. In 1963 he was arrested and exiled. He spent a year in Turkey before finding asylum in Iraq, where he lived until he was expelled in 1978. From there he went to France, where he made tape recordings calling for the overthrow of the shah. These recordings were smuggled into Iran and broadcast over shortwave radio.
Answer to Caption: *Iran's hatred of the shah turned against the United States, culminating in the taking of American hostages at the United States embassy.*

Independent Practice

Guided Reading Activity 35-2 **L1**

Multicultural Have students research to make a chart that shows the majority religion, official language, and current leader of Egypt, Israel, Iran, Iraq, Jordan, Lebanon, and Syria. **L2**

Literature Have students write a one-page report on the extent of censorship under the Shiite regime in Iran, using as an example the case of the novelist Salman Rushdie. **L3**

Linking Past and Present

The Hanging Gardens of Babylon, one of the Seven Wonders of the Ancient World, were built about 4,000 years ago by Nebuchadnezzar. In the 1980s, Saddam Hussein had started rebuilding the gardens using 15 million bricks baked in the ancient way. The Persian Gulf War ended this ambitious project.

Visualizing History **In 1979, after the Islamic Revolution overthrew the shah, Ayatollah Ruhollah Khomeini returned in triumph to Iran from exile in France.** *How did the Islamic Revolution affect Iran's relations with the United States?*

Israelites centuries ago and that no political agreement could give it away.

During 1995, tensions steadily mounted in Israel between supporters and opponents of the peace process. Tragically, in November of that year, Rabin was shot to death by an Israeli student who opposed Rabin's policies. The assassination shocked and saddened Israelis and also many Arabs. Rabin's successor as Israeli prime minister, **Shimon Peres** (shee•MOHN PEHR•ehs), pledged not only to continue, but also to speed up, the peace process.

Lebanon

The status of the Palestinians also affected neighboring Lebanon. In 1975, a civil war broke out between Lebanon's Christian and Muslim groups over the presence of armed PLO members in the country. Most Lebanese Muslims supported the PLO. The majority of Lebanese Christians did not.

As full-scale fighting erupted, the weakened Lebanese government asked Syria to send in troops to keep order. In 1982, the Israelis invaded southern Lebanon in an effort to wipe out PLO bases, which had been staging attacks on Israel. The PLO agreed to withdraw from Lebanon, and a multinational peacekeeping force supervised the PLO pullout. Christian, Muslim, and other groups, however, continued fighting among themselves. After foreign troops became victims of terrorist bombings, the peacekeeping force departed by 1985.

In the early 1990s some signs of hope appeared. Syrian forces ousted a Christian general who stood in the way of an Arab peace plan for Lebanon. Meanwhile, a newly elected Lebanese president won solid international support. In 1991 various Christian and Muslim armies in **Beirut** pulled out of the city, allowing the Lebanese government to restore order. However, by the mid-1990s, Israeli troops still remained in the south, and Syrian troops continued to occupy some northern areas of Lebanon.

Iran's Revolution

Throughout the 1960s and 1970s, Iran grew into a major military power in the Persian Gulf region. Shah Mohammed Reza Pahlavi built a capitalistic economy based on oil revenues. Muslim religious leaders resented his emphasis on Western materialism and values and sought a return to Muslim traditions. Through his hated secret police force, SAVAK, the shah silenced all protests and dissent.

During the late 1970s, opposition to the shah grew. Anti-shah forces rallied around 76-year-old **Ayatollah Ruhollah Khomeini** (koh•MAY•nee), a powerful Iranian Shiite Muslim leader living in exile in France. The ayatollah had long preached the overthrow of the shah and a return to Muslim traditions. By January 1979, widespread unrest forced the shah to flee the country. Khomeini triumphantly returned to form a new government run according to Islamic principles. He destroyed his enemies and kept power in his hands.

Iranian hatred for the shah then turned against the United States, where the shah had gone to receive medical help. Iran demanded that the United States return the shah to stand trial for his "crimes against the Iranian people." The United States refused, and the shah took refuge in Egypt, where he died in 1980. Anti-American sentiment in Iran exploded. On November 4, 1979, Iranians stormed the United States embassy and took American diplomats hostage. The captives were not freed until January 1981.

During most of the 1980s, Iran fought a devastating war with neighboring Iraq. In 1988, a UN

MEETING SPECIAL NEEDS ACTIVITY

Study Strategy Give students outline maps of the Middle East. Have them locate and label the following places mentioned in this section: Syria, Israel, Egypt, Lebanon, Iran, Iraq, Kuwait, Saudi Arabia, Sinai Peninsula, Golan Heights, Gaza Strip, West Bank, Gulf of Aqaba, Suez Canal, Persian Gulf, Beirut, and Baghdad. Remind students to title their map and to make a legend. **L1 LEP**

958 Chapter 35 *The Middle East*

PICTURING HISTORY

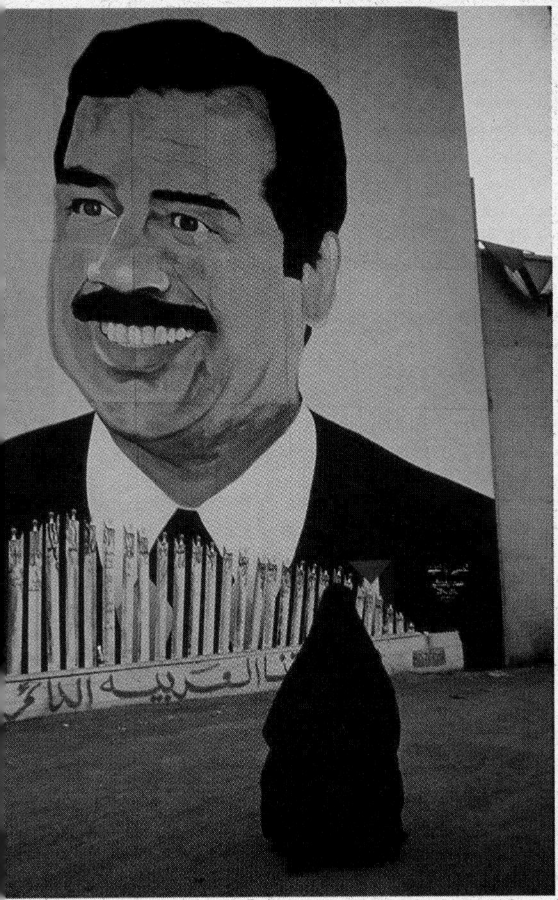

Steve McCurry, Magnum

Mohsen Shandiz, SYGMA

Mortal Enemies

This giant portrait of Iraqi President Saddam Hussein (left) overlooks a Baghdad street. An inscription under the portrait in red Arabic characters praises the Arab forces in Iraq's struggle with its Islamic but non-Arab enemy neighbor, Iran. In Iran the stern gaze of the Ayatollah Ruhollah Khomeini peers from a mural behind women attending the departure of soldiers for the battlefront in September 1988. With his zealous view of Islam, Khomeini, who died in 1989, regarded the secular Saddam Hussein as both an enemy and an infidel.

The Middle East has changed profoundly since World War II. What was once an area largely held by the Ottoman Empire and then by European colonial powers is now a region of independent nations. With the end of imperialism came the rise of nationalism. At the same time parts of the Islamic world have witnessed the rise of a fiercely held fundamentalism that views the secular world, even the Muslim secular world, as evil and corrupt. In this context Iran and Iraq fought a long and devastating war that lasted from 1980 to 1988. ⊕

TEACH

Tell students that the dispute between Iran and Iraq was about religious and political issues more than it was a struggle over territory. Before the ayatollah came to power in Iran, he listed his enemies as, "First the Shah; then the American Satan; then Saddam Hussein and his infidel Ba'ath party." Iraq's Ba'ath party was made up of Sunni Muslims and promoted pan-Arabism. It was also the party in charge of expelling Khomeini in 1978 at the request of the shah of Iran. Because Iran is not an Arab country, the fundamentalist Shiite Muslims promote a universal Islam that is indifferent to nationality and aims to unite all Muslim peoples.

Linking Past and Present

Iran and Iraq The present-day countries of Iran and Iraq were sites of ancient empires and kingdoms that are often called "cradles of civilization." Iran was part of the Persian Empire; and Iraq, known as Mesopotamia, is heir to the civilizations of Sumer, Akkad, Babylonia, and Assyria. The two peoples clashed in ancient times also. In 539 B.C., Cyrus the Great, founder of the Persian Empire, captured the present-day Iraqi city of Babylon and conquered the Babylonian Empire.

Chapter 35
Section 2

People in World History Profile 68

Geography and History Activity 35

ASSESS

Check for Understanding

Assign Section 2 Review as homework or as an in-class activity.

Use Student Self-Test and Review Software to review Section 2.

Evaluate

Section Quiz 35-2

Use the Testmaker to create a customized quiz for Section 2.

Reteach

Have students take turns summarizing major events in Israel, Egypt, Lebanon, Iran, and Iraq from 1967 to 1996.

Enrich

Have students research and give a short oral report on how the 1973 oil embargo affected daily life in the United States.

CLOSE

Have students create a time line on the chalkboard that shows major events in the Middle East from 1967 to 1996.

Footnotes to History

War and the Environment

During the Persian Gulf War, Iraqi troops spilled an estimated 250 million gallons (947 million l) of Kuwait's oil into the Persian Gulf. Thousands of birds, fish, and other marine life perished when the oil spill spread for 350 miles (563 km) along the Persian Gulf coastline.

cease-fire ended the fighting. A year later, Ayatollah Khomeini died. Iran's new leader, Hashemi Rafsanjani (hah•SHEH•mee RAHF•sahn•JAH •nee), then turned to rebuilding Iran's crippled economy. Under Rafsanjani, Iran continued its revolutionary fervor but worked to improve relations with neighboring countries, such as Russia and the Central Asian republics. The United States and other Western nations, however, were concerned about the sale of Soviet nuclear technology to Iran following the collapse of the Soviet Union.

Iraq's Bid for Power

The war with Iran also left Iraq's economy near collapse. To boost oil revenues and divert attention from Iraq's economic woes, Iraqi President **Saddam Hussein** invaded neighboring **Kuwait** in 1990. He claimed that Kuwait was a historic part of Iraq and that Kuwait had unfairly drilled Iraqi oil.

Fearing an Iraqi attack, oil-rich Saudi Arabia asked the United States for protection. United States President George Bush responded by sending troops to the Saudi desert. Eight Arab nations also sent forces to Saudi Arabia. Western nations, the Soviet Union, and Japan imposed a trade embargo, or a ban on the export of goods, against Iraq.

The United States threatened to use force against the Iraqis, but Saddam Hussein vowed not to leave Kuwait until Israel pulled out of its occupied territories and Syria left Lebanon. He further threatened to attack Israel if Iraq were attacked.

War Breaks Out

In January 1991, after a UN deadline for an Iraqi withdrawal expired, the United States rained medium-range missiles on the Iraqi capital of Baghdad. During the next month coalition forces from the United States, Great Britain, France, Syria, Saudi Arabia, Egypt, and Kuwait conducted a massive air war against Iraq. Saddam Hussein responded by launching missiles at Israel, hoping to draw Israel into the war and splinter Arab support for the coalition. Israel did not retaliate, however, and the United States provided Israel with an antimissile defense system.

With Iraq's war-making abilities checked, the coalition began bombing Iraqi ground forces in Kuwait. In desperation, Iraq set hundreds of Kuwaiti oil fields afire to provide smokescreens. When Iraq still refused to leave Kuwait, the coalition staged a massive ground attack on Iraqi forces. In a campaign that took only 100 hours, coalition troops swept into Kuwait, meeting only minor resistance from the Iraqis. With Kuwait freed, a cease-fire went into effect. Allied war deaths totaled just over 100, with tens of thousands of Iraqi soldiers believed killed.

Iraq After the War

Shortly after Iraqi forces left Kuwait, coalition troops withdrew from Iraq. Meanwhile, Saddam Hussein used brutal force to put down rebellions by Kurds and Shiites in Iraq. World public opinion condemned Hussein's attacks on his civilian population. In late 1994, Iraq once again threatened an invasion of Kuwait, but the prompt arrival of American forces made Iraq pull back its forces. As the mid-1990s approached, Iraq still had not fulfilled the cease-fire agreement, and the UN continued its trade embargo.

SECTION 2 REVIEW

Recall

1. **Define** disengagement, cartel, *intifada*, embargo.
2. **Identify** PLO, OPEC, Yasir Arafat, Anwar al-Sadat, Menachem Begin, Camp David Accords, Hosni Mubarak, Yitzhak Rabin, Shimon Peres, Ayatollah Ruhollah Khomeini, Saddam Hussein.
3. **Explain** the outcome of the Six-Day War.

Critical Thinking

4. **Analyzing Information** How has the Persian Gulf war affected the Middle East?

Understanding Themes

5. **Cooperation** What were the major points of the 1993 agreement between Israel and the Palestinians?

SECTION 2 REVIEW ANSWERS

1. All vocabulary words are defined in the Glossary.
2. PLO, 954; OPEC, 955; Arafat, 955; Sadat, 955; Begin, 955; Camp David Accords, 955; Mubarak, 955; Rabin, 956; Peres, 958; Khomeini, 958; Hussein, 960
3. Israel seized the Sinai Peninsula and the Gaza Strip from Egypt, the Golan Heights from Syria, and East Jerusalem and the West Bank from Jordan. Arab nations refused to recognize Israel's right to exist. Terrorist attacks continued.
4. A coalition of Middle Eastern countries worked with Western forces to stop a common enemy; Israel, by accepting protection from the United States instead of responding to Iraqi attacks, helped hold the coalition together, thus leading the way to peace accords.
5. COOPERATION Israel and the PLO recognized each other and agreed to eventual self-government for Palestinians in the West Bank and the Gaza Strip and a gradual withdrawal of Israeli forces.

Study and Writing

SKILLS

Preparing a Bibliography

In the last chapter, you wrote a research report on some topic of interest. To complete your report, you have one more step—preparing a bibliography.

Learning the Skill

A bibliography is a list of sources used in a research report. These sources include: books; articles from newspapers, magazines, and journals; interviews; films, videotapes, audiotapes, and compact discs. Why do you need a bibliography? What purpose does it serve?

There are two main reasons to write a bibliography. First, those who read your report may want to learn more about the topic. Second, a bibliography supports the reliability of your report.

A bibliography should follow a definite format. The entry for each source must contain all the information needed to find that source: author, title, publisher information, and publication date. You should have this information already on note cards. If you neglected this step earlier, you must return to the library to find the sources again.

In a bibliography, arrange entries alphabetically by the author's last name. The following are accepted formats for bibliography entries, followed by sample entries. Note the form of punctuation used between parts of the entry.

Books

Author's last name, first name. Full Title. Place of publication: publisher, copyright date.

Hay, Peter. Ordinary Heroes: The Life and Death of Chana Szenes, Israel's National Heroine. New York: Paragon House, 1986.

Articles

Author's last name, first name. "Title of Article." Name of Periodical in which article appears, Volume number (date of issue): page numbers.

Watson, Bruce. "The New Peace Corps in the New Kazakhstan." Smithsonian, Vol. 25 (August 1994): pp.26–35.

Other Sources

For other kinds of sources, adapt the format for book entries.

Practicing the Skill

Review the sample bibliography below for a report on Mexico. Then answer the questions that follow.

Caste–eda, Jorge G. The Mexican Shock: Its Meaning for the United States. New York: The New Press, 1995.

Marquez, Viviane Brachet de. The Dynamics of Domination: State, Class and Social Reform in Mexico, 1910–1990. Pittsburgh, Penn., University of Pittsburgh Press, 1994.

Cockburn, A., "The Fire This Time." Cond—Nast Traveler, Vol. 30 (June 1995): pp. 104–113.

Smith, G. "The Brave New World of Mexican Politics." Business Week (August 28, 1995) pp. 42–44.

1. Are the bibliography entries in the correct order? Why or why not?
2. What is missing from the second book listing?
3. What is missing from the second article listing?

Applying the Skill

Compile a bibliography for your research report. Include at least five sources, preferably a mix of books and articles. Exchange bibliographies with another student and check each other for proper format and arrangement.

For More Practice

Turn to the Skill Practice in the Chapter Review on page 971 for more practice in preparing a bibliography.

Study and Writing

SKILLS

TEACH

Preparing a Bibliography Write the following list on the chalkboard: *Author's name, Title, Place of publication, Publisher, Date of publication*. Ask students to find this information for their textbook. If necessary, guide students to the title and copyright pages. Have volunteers write the correct information from their text opposite the five categories on the chalkboard. Then tell students that this information is required for books in a bibliography. Direct students to read the skill and complete the practice questions to learn more about the purposes and formats of a bibliography.

Additional Practice

Skill Reinforcement Activity 35

Writer's Guidebook, Lessons 9, 13

ANSWERS TO PRACTICING THE SKILL

1. No; the entries should be in alphabetical order by author's last name.
2. The title of the book should be underlined.
3. The volume number is missing, and the title of the periodical should be underlined.

Chapter 35
Section 3

SECTION THEME

▶ **Cultural Diffusion** Middle Eastern countries search for a reconciliation between traditional and modern values.

Find Out

Answer: *Some have welcomed the changes brought by modernization. Others have greeted them with mistrust, often blaming the West for the social problems brought by modernization.*

FOCUS

Section Objective

Describe how people in the Middle East have handled the conflict between traditional ways and modern values.

BELLRINGER
Motivational Activity

Before taking roll at the beginning of the class period, project Section Focus Transparency 35-3 and have students answer the activity questions.

This activity is also available as a blackline master.

Vocabulary Pre-check

Use the Vocabulary PuzzleMaker to create a puzzle that reinforces the vocabulary terms in this section. **L1 LEP**

1945 — 1972 — 2000

1945 Arab nations form the Arab league.

1979 Israel and Egypt sign peace treaty.

1994 Jordan and Israel end their state of war.

Section 3

Challenges Facing the Middle East

Setting the Scene

▶ **Terms to Define**
sovereignty, desalination, fundamentalism

▶ **People to Meet**
Shimon Peres, Hafez al-Assad, Golda Meir, Tansu Çiller

▶ **Places to Locate**
West Bank, Gaza Strip, Jerusalem, Golan Heights, Saudi Arabia, Cairo, Turkey, Euphrates River

Find Out How have people in the Middle East handled the conflict between traditional ways and modern values?

The Storyteller

An Israeli observer records the expulsion of Arabs from Israeli-held territory: "Masses of people marched on behind the next. Women bore bundles and sacks on their heads; mothers dragged children after them. From close up it was sad to watch this trek of thousands going into exile. As soon as they left the city, they began to divest themselves of things ... and the roads were cluttered with the belongings that people had abandoned to make their walk easier."

—from *The People of Nowhere*, Danny Rubenstein, 1991

Palestinian Arabs in exile

The tragic cycle of violence, wars between nations, and civil wars within nations have brought much suffering to the people of the Middle East since the end of World War II. Besides the lost lives, billions of dollars of precious resources are spent each year on weapons. If you speak to Middle Easterners about their hopes for the future, they consistently include peace and stability. But peace and stability have been hard to achieve.

War and Peace

Since Egypt and Israel agreed to peace in 1979, major steps have been taken in ending the state of war between Israel and the rest of the Arab world. In 1993, the Israelis and the Palestinians came to an agreement, and a year later, Jordan and Israel finally ended their conflict. Contacts also began between Israel and Syria for the settlement of issues stemming from the Six-Day War of 1967.

West Bank and Gaza Strip

After years of bitterness, Israel and the PLO have recognized each other, and the Israeli government has gradually yielded control of Palestinian areas in the **West Bank** and the **Gaza Strip** to the Palestinians living there. Major issues still to be resolved between Israel and the PLO are the ownership of **Jerusalem**, the status and security of Israeli Jewish settlers living on the West Bank, and the drawing up of borders between Israel and the yet undefined Palestinian state.

Still another major issue is the resettlement of Palestinians who fled their homes beginning in the 1948 Arab-Israeli conflict. Today there are more than 6 million Palestinian Arabs scattered throughout the Middle East, North Africa, Europe, and the

SECTION RESOURCES

Reproducible Masters
- Reproducible Lesson Plan 35-3
- Guided Reading Activity 35-3
- People in World History Profile 67
- Reteaching Activity 35
- Enrichment Activity 35
- Section Quiz 35-3
- Performance Assessment Activity 35
- Spanish Chapter Summary 35

Transparencies
- Section Focus Transparency 35-3

Multimedia
- Vocabulary PuzzleMaker Software
- Student Self-Test and Review Software
- Testmaker

Americas. About 850,000 Israeli Arabs live inside Israel itself and consider themselves Palestinians, but try to combine Israeli citizenship with their Arab heritage. However, about 2 million Palestinians live in the West Bank and Gaza Strip, many of them living in crowded refugee camps.

Golan Heights and Lebanon

Relations between Israel and its northern neighbors, Syria and Lebanon, also need to be normalized before a comprehensive peace can be achieved. The **Golan Heights** is a major area of contention. Peace between Syria and Israel depends, in part, on the future of this territory, which has been in Israel's hands since 1967. Nevertheless, Israeli Prime Minister **Shimon Peres** and Syria's President **Hafez al-Assad** both have committed themselves to settling this issue according to the principle of land for Syria in exchange for the promise of security for Israel.

Lebanon's civil war has ended, but Israeli troops in the south and Syrian troops in other regions still have an influence on the internal affairs of the country. A truly free and prosperous Lebanon must be able to govern itself without foreign troops. Then, the massive effort to reconstruct the country and to restore its democratic system will proceed more effectively.

The Elusive Dream

Unity among Arab people has long been a powerful desire. For many centuries, millions of people throughout the Arab world have shared strong cultural ties, such as the Arabic language, traditions, religious beliefs, and a common history. British and French imperialism in the 1800s and 1900s increased division among the Arabs and created numerous states with artificial boundaries. Many Arabs thought that with independence from foreign powers they would be able to achieve unity. They began to take steps to strengthen the common links among them.

In 1945 political unity seemed within reach when Egypt, Transjordan (present-day Jordan), Syria, Lebanon, Iraq, **Saudi Arabia**, and Yemen formed the Arab League, a step toward unity. By 1995 membership in the Arab League had grown to 22 participants (including the PLO) covering an area larger than the United States, with a population of about 200 million. But disagreements among governments and the unwillingness of some Arab nations to give up their **sovereignty**, or independent decision-making powers, frustrated any move toward further unity.

Visualizing History **Banking and financial services are important to the economies of many Middle Eastern countries.** *In what other ways have Middle Eastern economies changed in the past 40 years?*

Some political leaders and government officials have advocated a cautious move toward unity. They formed cooperative councils among their countries to coordinate trade, economic development, and travel. Peoples' aspirations and political realities, in time, may lead to some type of loose union in which each state would retain independence and contribute to stability in the region.

Economic Developments

In the past 40 years the Middle East has seen greatly changed economic conditions. Light and heavy industry has been developed in most countries. Irrigation for agriculture spread as hydroelectric projects were constructed on major rivers, such as the Nile and the Euphrates. At the same time as production rose and jobs became available, the region's population grew rapidly. If the current rate of increase continues, the population will double in the next 25 years. The increase has been most apparent in major urban centers. By the early 1990s, more than 15 cities had populations exceeding 1 million each. The largest is **Cairo**, Egypt's capital, with 12 million people. It is also the largest in the whole African continent. The needs and the challenges of rapidly growing populations are on the minds of every major leader in the Middle East.

TEACH

Guided Practice

THEME Cultural Diffusion

Remind students that cultural diffusion is the spread of ideas or ways of living from one culture to another. Help students find examples of cultural diffusion in this section. *(Palestinians in Israel combining Israeli citizenship with Arabic heritage; goods and ideas from the West changing Islamic society)* **L1 LEP**

Visualizing History Have students differentiate between the modern and traditional styles of clothing shown in the picture. Tell students that the long, loose robe, called a *thwab*, and the head covering, a *kef-fiyah*, are suited to the climate of the Middle East.

Answer to Caption: *Industry has developed in most Middle Eastern countries. Agricultural production has increased because of irrigation.*

Economics Have students make a flowchart that shows how economic development (industrialization, improved agriculture) in the Middle East has led to challenges (increase in population, gap between oil-producing and non-oil-producing countries, water shortages). **L2**

COOPERATIVE LEARNING ACTIVITY

Panel Discussions Organize the class into five groups. Have each group choose one of the following topics: role of women in Muslim nations; dam building on the Nile and Euphrates Rivers; Middle Eastern desalination projects; dispersal of oil wealth among citizens in oil-producing countries; or the debate about moving toward more democratic government in Kuwait and Saudi Arabia. Tell students to research their topic using recent newspaper, magazine, and journal indexes. Suggest that each group break its topic into subtopics so that each group member has a specific topic to research. Before each group presents its panel discussion, have students choose a moderator for their panel. **L3**

Chapter 35 *The Middle East* **963**

Chapter 35
Section 3

Economics Have students discuss how a Middle East common market might arise if peace between Israel and its neighbors is attained. **L3**

Independent Practice

Guided Reading Activity 35-3 **L1**

People in World History Profile 67

CONNECTIONS Science and Technology

Water from the Euphrates

Because Turkey had not worked out an agreement with Syria and Iraq for sharing water from the Euphrates, the World Bank refused to extend Turkey a loan to build Ataturk Dam. Turkey obtained independent financing to build the dam.

Answers to Making the Connection

1. *Turkey, Syria, Iraq*
2. *Answers will vary. Yes: Turkey needs water to irrigate farmland in order to supply food for its people, and the dams are on its territory. No: Turkey's dams should not hurt the people of Iraq and Syria.*

CURRICULUM CONNECTION

GOVERNMENT
The royal family of Saudi Arabia holds daily *majlis*, audiences with ordinary citizens who come to petition for help in settling a dispute or to receive special aid from the government. The royal princes receive up to 300 people a day; the king, far fewer and on a less regular basis.

Oil Wealth

Oil-producing countries of the Middle East have become well-developed and wealthy in recent years. Their wealth, however, contrasts sharply with the poverty of other countries in the region. The per capita income of some Persian Gulf countries is about 15 times that of Egypt. Oil-producing countries have invested in and loaned large sums of money to the non-oil-producing countries. The poorer countries are asking for more assistance. They do not want the gap between the rich and the poor to be so wide.

Water Problem

As the Middle East develops industrially and faces population increases, various nations in the region are working to overcome critical water shortages caused by an uneven distribution of water. For example, **Turkey** has built dams and other water facilities on the **Euphrates River** to irrigate fertile, but dry, areas.

Another country with a water shortage is Israel. The Israelis have been using their water resources and those of the West Bank and Gaza Strip close to their maximum capacity. Extensive settlement of the West Bank and Gaza Strip would require quantities of water that the regions do not have. Israel's neighbors Syria and Jordan have themselves been experiencing shortages of water. If all three countries settle their political differences, they will be able to coordinate their water resources and build plants for **desalination**, the removal of salt from sea water to make it usable for drinking and farming.

Social Change

Throughout the Middle East, modernization has turned traditional desert societies upside down. With the discovery of oil, desert cities boomed and new industrial areas were created. Urban areas now contain high-rise offices, shopping centers, luxury apartments, and freeways. People in Middle Eastern countries have viewed these new influences in different ways.

CONNECTIONS Science and Technology

Water From the Euphrates

To ensure its water supply, Turkey is building a series of huge dams on the Euphrates River. The dams' reservoirs provide water for Turkey's fertile but dry southeastern corner. The dams' power stations generate electricity for Turkey's expanding industry and cities.

Turkish dam on the Euphrates River

Turkey's solution for its water problem, however, deprives Syria and Iraq of water from the same river. Iraq would be especially worse off because it is the last country that is situated along the river.

The Turks defend their right to use the river to better economic and social conditions. They hope to turn more of the Anatolian Peninsula into farmland. Crops grown there are necessary to feed Turkey's growing population, they say.

Syria and Iraq claim that Turkey does not own the entire Euphrates River. Their officials point out that not only will their countries lose water from the reduced flow, but that more will be lost through evaporation from the Turkish reservoirs.

Experts point out that a number of practices could ease this crisis. They state that all three countries need to repair existing equipment, improve their irrigation and water conservation methods, and expand their water recycling. The countries also need to grow some crops that do not require so much water. Above all, experts state that the countries need to better manage their population growth.

MAKING THE CONNECTION

1. What Middle Eastern countries are concerned about the water supply from the Euphrates River?
2. Does Turkey have the right to build dams on the Euphrates River?

MEETING SPECIAL NEEDS ACTIVITY

Learning Style: Visual/Spatial Have students create a bulletin-board display of various aspects of traditional Islamic life. They might include drawings of traditional dress for both men and women and photographs of Islamic religious rituals or such rituals of daily life as eating, entertaining, and shopping. Be sure all images are clearly labeled with explanatory captions. **L1 LEP**

964 Chapter 35 *The Middle East*

Progress

Middle Easterners welcomed some of the changes. Foreign investment created new jobs and raised living standards. New wealth enabled countries to establish better education and health care systems, to build roads, and to provide utilities. In addition, women in the region made a growing impact on the traditionally masculine worlds of business and politics. In politics, for example, **Golda Meir** (meh•IHR), who served as Israeli prime minister from 1969 to 1974, was the modern Middle East's first female head of government. In 1993, **Tansu Çiller** (TAHN•soo see•LAHR) of Turkey became the first female prime minister to govern a Middle Eastern Muslim country.

Challenges

In other ways, however, Middle Easterners were dissatisfied with the rapid pace of change. In the cities they saw rising crime and violence. In business life they observed greed, abuse of workers, and a growing gap between rich and poor. Traditional family structure and authority were shattered by changing values among women and young people. Foreign influences, especially from the West, were seen as the cause of many new social problems.

In addition, people in the Middle East found themselves surrounded by more material goods such as cars, television sets, VCRs, and personal computers. The influence of these things became a source of resentment to conservative Middle Easterners who feared the spread of materialism. They blamed the West for this new emphasis in Middle Eastern society.

In Saudi Arabia, the birthplace of Islam, the majority of people have fiercely resisted undesirable Western cultural influences, despite the influence of enormous oil wealth flowing into the country. Saudis are shielded from exposure to many Western ideas through tight censorship. By contrast more liberal lifestyles are permitted in Iraq, Lebanon, Syria, Jordan, Egypt, and Israel.

AROUND THE WORLD

SALT II Pact Signed

Vienna, Austria, 1979

A second round of Strategic Arms Limitation Talks (SALT) led to a United States-Soviet treaty in 1979. U.S. President Jimmy Carter and Soviet leader Leonid Brezhnev signed SALT II in Vienna, Austria. The pact limited both nations to a maximum number of long-range missiles and bombers. SALT II did not officially take effect because the U.S. Senate refused to ratify the treaty. But the agreed limits were observed until 1986.

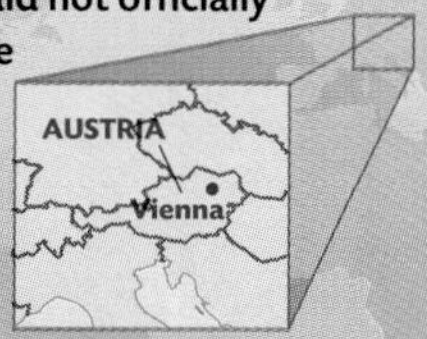

A Return to Religion

In recent years many Middle Easterners have sought solutions to their problems in fundamentalism, or adherence to traditional religious values and practices. Movements for reviving religious values have been active in many Middle Eastern nations. In Iran, Shiite Muslim leaders are in control of the country. In Turkey, Egypt, Algeria, and Jordan, the political power of Muslim fundamentalist groups poses a serious challenge to secular governments. Israel's Jewish right-wing religious parties, although small in size, have contributed to the rising strength of political conservatism there.

Some observers view support for fundamentalism as a natural reaction by people who are overwhelmed by massive change and desire to seek security in long-valued traditions. Other experts, however, point out that the continued growth of religious fundamentalism in the Middle East will deepen mistrust and harden prejudices at a time when efforts toward peace are moving forward.

SECTION 3 REVIEW

Recall

1. **Define** sovereignty, desalination, fundamentalism.
2. **Identify** Arab League, Shimon Peres, Hafez al-Assad, Golda Meir, Tansu Çiller.
3. **Explain** three challenges to stability in the Middle East today.

Critical Thinking

4. **Applying Information** What impact has religious fundamentalism had on the Middle East?

Understanding Themes

5. **Cultural Diffusion** How have Middle Easterners responded to the growth of foreign influences in their region?

Chapter 35 Section 3

ASSESS

Check for Understanding

Assign Section 3 Review as homework or as an in-class activity.

Use Student Self-Test and Review Software to review Section 3.

Evaluate

Section Quiz 35-3

Use the Testmaker to create a customized quiz for Section 3.

Reteach

Have students make charts that describe the positive and the negative aspects of the political, economic, and social changes that have taken place since the 1970s in the Middle East.

Reteaching Activity 35

Enrich

Have students write a short report on the effect of the Islamic militant groups Hamas and Jihad on the Israel-PLO peace process since 1994.

Enrichment Activity 35

CLOSE

Have students hold a mock UN meeting in which they offer possible solutions to Middle East problems.

SECTION 3 REVIEW ANSWERS

1. All vocabulary words are defined in the Glossary.
2. Arab League, 963; Peres, 963; Assad, 963; Meir, 965; Ciller, 965
3. disagreements between Israel and the PLO; Muslim and Israeli religious fundamentalism; the gap between the oil-rich and non-oil countries; the increasing population; water shortages
4. Muslim fundamentalists have taken control of the government in Iran and pose a challenge to secular governments in other nations. Fundamentalist Jewish parties have contributed to the rise of political conservatism in Israel.
5. **CULTURAL DIFFUSION** Answers will vary but should include that some people have welcomed the Western influences while others blame Western influences for the rise of crime, the growing gap between rich and poor, and the decrease in traditional values.

Bridge to the Past
Literature

Block Schedule

Team Teaching This selection of modern poems may be presented in a team-teaching context, in conjunction with English or Language Arts.

Modern Poems

Historical Connection

The three poems in this feature were written by poets from developing countries: Mexico, Turkey, and Nigeria. The increasing prominence in the West of literature from developing nations suggests that people in Europe and the United States are more aware of the achievements of people in other parts of the world.

Background Information

Setting The setting for each poem appears to be the homeland of the poet. Students may wish to discuss, however, whether these poems could be set in another country just as well.

Literary Elements Personification means giving human characteristics to an inanimate object. For example, in "The Window," Torres Bodet talks about the world issuing a "great, rough, hoarse cry." Giving the world the power of speech is personification.

A stanza is a collection of lines in a poem, separated from other lines or stanzas. In "Once Upon a Time," most stanzas are six lines long. In modern poetry, stanza length varies.

Metaphor is a comparison of two objects. For example, Nazim Hikmet compares the earth to "a mere toy next to the sun."

Bridge to the Past
Literature

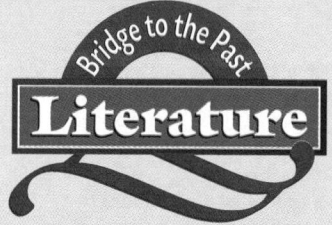

from Modern Poems

by Jaime Torres Bodet, Nazim Hikmet, and Gabriel Okara

Modern poets have continued to explore both universal themes, such as friendship and loneliness, as well as individual preferences for a particular place or group of people.

The following poem was written by one of Mexico's greatest writers, Jaime Torres Bodet, who was born in 1902 and was active in politics. Bodet served the government as an administrator and diplomat. In this poem, Bodet urges people to take risks in their lives. Bodet died in 1974.

The Window

Translated from Spanish by George Kearns

You closed the window, And it was the world,
the world that wanted to enter, all at once,
the world that gave that great shout,
that great, deep, rough cry
you did not want to hear—and now
will never call to you again as it called today,
asking your mercy!

The whole of life was in that cry:
the wind, the sea, the land
with its poles and its tropics,
the unreachable skies,
the ripened grain in the resounding wheat field,
the thick heat above the wine presses,
dawn on the mountains, shadowy woods,
parched lips stuck together longing for
cool water condensed in pools,
and all pleasures, all sufferings,
all loves, all hates,
were in this day, anxiously
asking your mercy …

But you were afraid of life,
And you remained alone,
behind the closed and silent window,
not understanding that the world calls to a man
only once that way, and with that kind of cry,
with that great, rough, hoarse cry!

ABOUT THE AUTHORS

Jaime Torres Bodet was supervisor of Mexico's libraries in the 1920s. Later he served as director-general of the United Nations Educational, Scientific, and Cultural Organization (UNESCO).

Nazim Hikmet's outspoken views on behalf of the poor and oppressed in Turkey led to his imprisonment by the government. When he was released in 1951, he left the country. Many of his works were not published in Turkey during his lifetime, yet he became a popular hero there.

Gabriel Okara received little formal schooling in Nigeria. He learned enough on his own, however, to become a widely respected writer. He usually writes in his native language, Ijaw.

Nazim Hikmet, who lived from 1902 to 1963, often criticized the government of his native Turkey for serving only the wealthy. In 1951 he left Turkey, never to return, and settled in Europe. His sympathy for the peasants of his country, his love of nature, and his hope for humanity are all suggested in the following poem.

The World, My Friends, My Enemies, You, and the Earth

Translated from the Turkish by
Randy Blasing and Mutlu Konuk

Nazim Hikmet

I'm wonderfully happy I came into the world,
I love its earth, its light, its struggle, and its bread.
Even though I know its dimensions from pole to pole to the
  centimeter,
and while I'm not unaware that it's a mere toy next to the sun,
the world for me is unbelievably big.
I would have liked to go around the world
and see the fish, the fruits, and the stars that I haven't seen.
However,
I made my European trip only in books and pictures.
In all my life I never got one letter
        with its blue stamp canceled in Asia.
Me and our corner grocer,
we're both mightily unknown in America.
Nevertheless,
from China to Spain, from the Cape of Good Hope to Alaska,
in every nautical mile, in every kilometer, I have friends and
  enemies.
Such friends that we haven't met even once—
we can die for the same bread, the same freedom, the same dream.
And such enemies that they're thirsty for my blood,
            I am thirsty for their blood.
My strength
is that I'm not alone in this big world.
The world and its people are no secret in my heart,
        no mystery in my science.
Calmly and openly
        I took my place
              in the great struggle.
And without it,
        you and the earth
          are not enough for me.
And yet you are astonishingly beautiful,
          the earth is warm and beautiful.

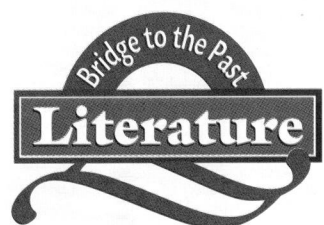

Bridge to the Past
Literature

FOCUS

Before students read the poems, have them speculate about what writers from such different countries as Mexico, Turkey, and Nigeria might have in common. Have them read the biographical statement about each poet and then ask them to consider what the poets' attitudes might be toward European culture, political change, economic development, and nationalism. After they have read the poems, ask them if the works have anything in common. *(Students may say that, in distinct ways, each poet deals with his attitude toward the wider world.)*

CURRICULUM CONNECTION

POLITICS
Many writers from developing countries are actively involved in their countries' politics. Other politically active Latin American, Middle Eastern, and African writers include Mario Vargas Llosa, Carlos Fuentes, Naguib Mahfouz, Chinua Achebe, and Wole Soyinka.

Other Works by the Authors

Other Works by Jaime Torres Bodet
Karser, Sonja, trans. *Selected Poems.* Bloomington: Indiana University Press, 1964.

Other Works by Nazim Hikmet
The Moscow Symphony and Other Poems. Chicago: Swallow Press, 1971.
Blasing, Randy, and Mutlu Konuk, trans. *Things I Didn't Know I Loved.* New York: Persea Books, 1975.

Other Works by Gabriel Okara
The Voice. New York: Africana Publishing Corp., 1970.

Chapter 35 *The Middle East* **967**

Bridge to the Past

Literature

TEACH

Interpretation

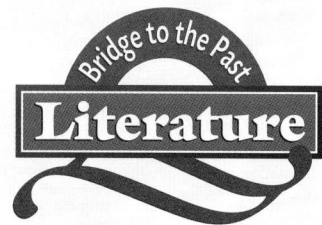

Ask students to decide for which age group Torres Bodet wrote this poem. *(Possible answer: Young people trying to choose a direction in life might benefit from the challenge he presents, but the message can apply to people of any age.)*

Definition

Hikmet's claim to know the dimensions of the world "to the centimeter" is an example of hyperbole. Discuss with students how Hikmet uses overstatement as a way of suggesting his love of the world.

Literary Analysis

Okara effectively uses the technique of repetition when he lists the many faces that one must learn to wear as one grows older. Ask students to cite other examples of repetition in the poem. Have volunteers read the verses aloud and guide them to see how repetition gives the verses a certain rhythm.

Evaluation

Ask students to choose their favorite poem of the three and to write a paragraph on why they like it. Tell them to support their view with specific details.

World Literature Selection 8

Gabriel Okara, born in 1921, is one of many Nigerian writers to achieve international acclaim since the 1960s. Others include Chinua Achebe, Christopher Okigbo, and Wole Soyinka. Some of Okara's poems deal with the problems of living in a country that is influenced by European culture. Others deal with family, friends, and daily life.

Once Upon a Time

Once upon a time, son,
they used to laugh with their hearts
and laugh with their eyes;
but now they only laugh with their teeth,
while their ice-block-cold eyes
search behind my shadow.

There was a time indeed
they used to shake hands with their hearts;
but that's gone, son.
Now they shake hands without hearts
while their left hands search
my empty pockets.

"Feel at home," "Come again,"
they say, and when I come
again and feel
at home, once, twice,
there will be no thrice—
for then I find doors shut on me.

So I have learned many things, son.
I have learned to wear many faces
like dresses—homeface,
officeface, streetface, hostface, cock-
tailface, with all their conforming smiles
like a fixed portrait smile.

And I have learned, too,
to laugh with only my teeth
and shake hands without my heart.
I have also learned to say, "Goodbye,"
when I mean, "Good-riddance";
to say "Glad to meet you,"
without being glad; and to say "It's been
nice talking to you," after being bored.

Additional Literary Works of the Period

García Márquez, Gabriel. ***One Hundred Years of Solitude.*** A mystical novel by a prominent Colombian writer about life in a Latin American village.

Head, Bessy. ***A Question of Power.*** A powerful and disturbing novel by one of South Africa's leading women writers.

Mahfouz, Naguib. ***The Beginning and the End.*** A novel by one of Egypt's greatest writers, winner of the 1988 Nobel Prize in literature.

Senghor, Léopold Sédar. ***Poems.*** Poetry about African culture by a West African.

968 Chapter 35 *The Middle East*

Visualizing History **National unity has been difficult for Nigeria to achieve because of its diverse ethnic groups.** *How does the author remember his childhood years before strife divided the country?*

But believe me, son.
I want to be what I used to be
when I was like you. I want
to unlearn all these muting things.
Most of all, I want to relearn
how to laugh, for my laugh in the mirror
shows only my teeth like a snake's bare fangs!

So show me, son,
how to laugh; show me how
I used to laugh and smile
once upon a time when I was like you.

RESPONDING TO LITERATURE

1. In your own words, define "the great struggle" that Hikmet refers to near the end of his poem.
2. Explain whether you think the poem by Bodet is written just to the people of Mexico or whether it applies to people throughout the world.
3. What is the main point of the poem by Okara?
4. **Demonstrating Reasoned Judgment** How does each poet view individuals who are willing to act boldly?

ANSWERS TO RESPONDING TO LITERATURE

1. Answers will vary. Some students may feel Hikmet means that life itself is a struggle, while others may feel he refers to class struggle between the rich and poor.
2. Torres Bodet's challenge seems directed to people everywhere but may have special significance for people in Mexico and other developing countries.
3. Students may feel the poet is reflecting on the insincerity that comes with success in the world.
4. Each poet seems to value boldness: Torres Bodet criticizes one who is "afraid of life"; Hikmet praises those who dared to struggle; Okara is nostalgic for the honesty of his early years.

Bridge to the Past
Literature

Visualizing History Nigeria's people belong to more than 250 ethnic groups.
Answer to Caption: *as happy times*

ASSESS

Assign **Responding to Literature** questions.

CLOSE

After students have read the poems, ask them if they think that writers and artists in the developing world have special responsibilities to their people.

Contemporary Connection

Students interested in learning more about the culture of Nigeria can listen to the music of such world-famous "Afropop" musicians as King Sunny Ade, Fela Anikulapo Kuti, Babatunde Olatunji, or Shina Peters.

Portfolio Project

Have students read a poem on one of the themes touched on in these selections but written by a Western poet. Walt Whitman and T.S. Eliot are two possible choices. Then have students write an essay comparing the two poems. Have them answer these questions: **Do you think any of the differences between the two poems can be traced to the differences in the poets' backgrounds? Is poetry a universal language?**

Chapter 35 Review

GLENCOE TECHNOLOGY

VIDEODISC

Use MindJogger to review students' knowledge of the chapter.

MindJogger Videoquiz

Chapter 35
Disc 5 Side A

Also available in VHS.

Answers

Using Key Terms

1. h	**6.** i
2. a	**7.** e
3. k	**8.** j
4. g	**9.** c
5. b	**10.** d

Using Your History Journal

Have students use their time lines on conflicts, peace conferences, and accords as a basis for essays.

Reviewing Facts

1. Palestinians resented Israeli rule and low-paying jobs. After a traffic accident in the Gaza Strip sparked Palestinian protests, an Israeli soldier fired a gun, killing a young Palestinian.
2. When the United States withdrew its offer of a loan to build the Aswan High Dam, Nasser nationalized the Suez Canal.
3. He invited the leaders of Egypt and Israel to meet at Camp David where they worked out the Camp David Accords.
4. Israel emerged victorious and holding most of Palestine; Transjordan annexed East Jerusalem and the West Bank of the Jordan River; Egypt held the Gaza Strip. Nasser rose to power in Egypt. More than 700,000 Palestinians were left homeless.
5. to ward off the influence and possible military advances of the Soviet Union
6. He claimed that Kuwait was part of Iraq and that Kuwait had unfairly drilled Iraqi oil.
7. They resented his emphasis on Western values.
8. Israel and Jordan in 1994 signed a declaration ending the state of war.

Critical Thinking

1. Acts of terrorism occurred in the struggle for American independence.
2. They caused a rift between Lebanese Muslims who supported the PLO and Lebanese Christians who did not. Once a PLO pullout had been supervised by a multinational force, Lebanon's Christian, Muslim, and other groups continued fighting.
3. Answers might mention that thus far, all

CHAPTER 35 REVIEW

Historical Significance

The nations of the Middle East have ancient cultures, but their political systems are still being developed. This undertaking has often been complicated by conflicts among themselves and by the great difficulties of reconciling traditional and modern ways of life.

Solutions for the challenges facing the Middle East often seem elusive, and progress has to be measured in gradual steps. An example is the complicated peace process among Israel and its Arab neighbors. In spite of setbacks, some factors weigh on the side of progress and peace. The end of the cold war has made cooperation among Middle Eastern nations a greater possibility.

Using Key Terms

Write the key term that completes each sentence.

a. disengagement	g. sovereignty
b. nationalized	h. Pan-Arabism
c. fundamentalism	i. pact
d. *intifada*	j. desalination
e. kibbutzim	k. cartel
f. embargo	

1. _______ is a movement to build close political and cultural ties among Arab nations.
2. In late 1973, United States Secretary of State Henry Kissinger negotiated a ______, or military withdrawal, agreement between Egypt and Israel.
3. The Organization of Petroleum Exporting Countries (OPEC) is a _________ formed to regulate production and prices among some of the world's oil-producing nations.
4. In the quest for regional unity, some Arab nations refuse to yield their _______ to an international body.
5. In 1951, Iranian Prime Minister Mohammed Mossadeq _______ foreign-owned oil companies in Iran.
6. A ______ is a agreement binding nations.
7. Some Jewish immigrants to Palestine settled on ________, or collective farms.
8. Some Middle Eastern countries have built _____ plants to remove salt from sea water for purposes of drinking and farming.
9. In recent years, some Middle Easterners have supported religious _______ in their efforts to defend traditional values and to oppose governments they dislike.
10. In 1987, Palestinians in the West Bank and Gaza Strip carried out an _______ to oppose Israeli rule of their areas.

Using Your History Journal

Write an essay concerning peace and progress in the Middle East. Include your suggestions for a resolution of the Arab-Israeli differences and economic progress that does not disrupt cherished traditions.

Reviewing Facts

1. **Discuss** the factors that sparked the outbreak of the Palestinian *intifada.*
2. **Explain** the link between the building of the Aswan High Dam and the Suez crisis of 1956.
3. **Describe** United States President Jimmy Carter's role in improving relations between Israel and Egypt.
4. **List** the results of the 1948 conflict between Israel and its Arab neighbors.
5. **Explain** why the United States gave money and political support to Turkey and to Iran after World War II.
6. **State** the reasons for Saddam Hussein's invasion of Kuwait in 1990.
7. **Discuss** why Iran's Muslim leaders opposed the rule of the shah.
8. **Describe** how relations between Israel and Jordan have changed in recent years.

Critical Thinking

1. **Evaluate** Do you think that terrorism can be justified as a means of attaining political goals? Why or why not?

970 **Chapter 35** *The Middle East*

2. **Apply** How did Palestinian refugees in Lebanon contribute to the outbreak of civil war in that country? What aspects of the war distinguished it from other modern-day conflicts?
3. **Evaluate** Which do you think inspires the most loyalties in the Arab Middle East—Pan-Arabism or the individual nation-state?
4. **Evaluate** Saddam Hussein justified Iraq's invasion of Kuwait, in part, on the grounds of nationalism and Arab unity. Analyze this reasoning. Do you think it is justified?

Geography in History

1. **Place** Refer to the map below. What country of the Middle East produced the most oil in 1990?
2. **Location** The four main producers of oil in the Middle East all border what body of water?
3. **Region** What correlation is there between the size, in area, and the amount of oil produced in the countries shown?

Major Oil Producers in the Middle East

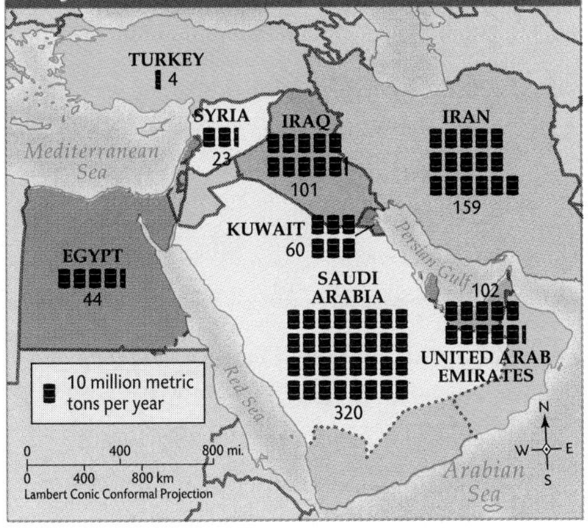

Understanding Themes

1. **Nationalism** How did the cold war contribute to the development of the Suez crisis in 1956?
2. **Cooperation** What areas in 1994 did Israel first withdraw from under the terms of the 1993 agreement between Israel and the PLO?
3. **Cultural Diffusion** What Middle Eastern country in recent years has firmly resisted many Western ways and practices despite its enormous oil wealth?

Linking Past and Present

1. When the state of Israel was founded in 1948, Israelis and Palestinians were bitter enemies. What was the basic issue that divided them in 1948? By 1995, how had their relationship changed? What issues continued to divide them?
2. Religious fundamentalism is not only a Middle Eastern development; it also has been growing in other parts of the world. What do you think accounts for the growth of fundamentalist religion elsewhere? Are the causes the same as those in the Middle East?

Skill Practice

Review the sample bibliography below for a report on the South American country of Brazil. Then answer the questions that follow.

Page, Joseph A. The Brazilians. Addison-Wesley Publishing Company, 1995.

Kirch, John. Why is This Country Dancing: One-Man Samba to the Beat of Brazil. New York: Simon & Schuster, 1993.

Rambali, Paul. In the cities and the Jungles of Brazil. New York, 1994.

J. F. Hage, "Fulfilling Brazil's Promise: a Conversation with President Cardoso." Foreign Affairs, Vol. 74, July–August 1995: pp. 62–75.

Levine, J. "The Dance Drink: Brazil's Samba Soft Drink to be Marketed in the U.S." Vol. 154: p. 232.

1. The entries presented above are not listed in the correct order. What author do you think should be listed first?
2. What is missing from the Joseph A. Page book listing?
3. What is wrong or missing in the Paul Rambali book listing?
4. Rewrite the J.F. Hage article listing correctly.
5. What do you think is missing from the J. Levine listing?

Chapter 35 Review

efforts at Arab political unity have been frustrated by individual Arab nations.

4. No country or people should be forced to become part of another country.

Geography in History
1. Saudia Arabia
2. Persian Gulf
3. The larger the country, the more oil it produces.

Understanding Themes
1. NATIONALISM Both the U.S. and Soviet Union wanted to gain influence in Egypt. When the U.S. found out that the Soviet Union's aid to Egypt included weapons, the U.S. withdrew its offer of a loan to build the Aswan High Dam. Nasser nationalized the Suez Canal so he could raise funds with canal fees.
2. COOPERATION the West Bank city of Jericho and the Gaza Strip
3. CULTURAL DIFFUSION Saudi Arabia

Linking Past and Present
1. the partition of Palestine into an Arab and a Jewish state; by 1995, the Israelis and Palestinians had begun the process of setting up a Palestinian state in the Gaza Strip and the West Bank. Some Palestinians still fear that a Palestinian state would be subject to Israeli restrictions, and some Israelis still feel that a Palestinian state would be a threat to Israel's security.
2. Fundamentalist religions are reactions to changing social values. Fundamentalists believe that problems can be solved by returning to traditional beliefs.

Skill Practice
1. J. F. Hage
2. The title should be underlined, and the place of publication is missing.
3. The author's name should not be underlined, the word *cities* should be capitalized, and the publisher is missing.
4. Hage, J. F. "Fulfilling Brazil's Promise: A Conversation with President Cardoso." Foreign Affairs, Vol. 74 (July–August 1995): pp. 62–75.
5. the title of the periodical and the date

Chapter Bonus Test Question

Ask students: What role did the end of the cold war play in the formation of the coalition of nations that opposed Iraq in the Persian Gulf War? *(If the cold war had not ended, the Soviet Union might have backed Iraq against the United States, Saudi Arabia, and Kuwait.)*

Teach, Reinforce, and Extend CHAPTER Content

Latin America

CHAPTER RESOURCES

	Reproducible Resources	Multimedia Resources
Chapter Opener	Chapter Themes: Graphic Organizer 36 Historical Significance Chapter Activity 36	MindJogger Videoquiz
Chapter Enrichment	Vocabulary Activity 36* Time Line Activity 36 Mapping History Activity 36 History Simulation 36 Geography and History Activity 36 Source Reading 36 People in World History Profiles 69, 70 World Art and Music Activity 36 Enrichment Activity 36 Critical Thinking Activity 36 Skill Reinforcement Activity 36 Performance Assessment Activity 36	World History and Art Transparency 49, *Figura*; 50, *Diego and I* Chapter Transparency 36 Vocabulary PuzzleMaker Software Communism and the Cold War: • *Perspectives on Communism* • *Bay of Pigs* • *Cuban Missile Crisis* • *Revolution in Cuba* • *Nicaragua* • *El Salvador* • *Chile*
Chapter Review/Reteaching	Reteaching Activity 36 Skill Reinforcement Activity 36 Spanish Chapter Summary 36	Chapter 36 Digest Audiocassette, Activity, Test* Vocabulary PuzzleMaker Software Student Self-Test and Review Software MindJogger Videoquiz
Chapter Evaluation/Testing	Performance Assessment Activity 36 Chapter 36 Test, Forms A and B	Testmaker

* *Also available in Spanish*

0:00 **OUT OF TIME?** Assign the Chapter 36 summary in the Unit 8 Digest on pages 1026–1029, and the Chapter 36 Audiocassettes.

Block Schedule

Block scheduling differs from traditional class scheduling in the amount of time allotted to each period. The extended time frame provided by block scheduling affords you the opportunity to implement a greater number of research-oriented and activity-intense projects to motivate and involve your students. Activities that are particularly suited to use within the block scheduling framework are identified throughout this chapter by the following designation.

KEY TO ABILITY LEVELS

Teaching strategies have been coded for varying learning styles and abilities.

- L1 **BASIC** activities for all students
- L2 **AVERAGE** activities for average to above-average students
- L3 **CHALLENGING** activities for above-average students
- LEP **LIMITED ENGLISH PROFICIENCY** activities

Teach and Reinforce SECTION Content

Chapter 36 Planning Guide

A complete, 1-page lesson plan is provided for each section in the *Reproducible Lesson Plans* booklet.

SECTION RESOURCES

Daily Objectives	Reproducible Resources	Multimedia Resources
Section 1 **Latin American Challenges** List the social and political challenges facing Latin America after World War II.	Reproducible Lesson Plan 36-1 Vocabulary Activity 36* Guided Reading Activity 36-1* Time Line Activity 36 Section Quiz 36-1*	Section Focus Transparency 36-1 Chapter Transparency 36 Student Self-Test and Review Software Testmaker Communism and the Cold War: *Perspectives on Communism*
Section 2 **Mexico and the Caribbean** Describe the political and economic crises faced by Mexico and the Caribbean after World War II.	Reproducible Lesson Plan 36-2 Vocabulary Activity 36* Guided Reading Activity 36-2* History Simulation 36 People in World History Profile 70 Section Quiz 36-2*	Section Focus Transparency 36-2 World History and Art Transparency 49, *Figura*; 50, *Diego and I* Student Self-Test and Review Software Testmaker Communism and the Cold War: • *Bay of Pigs* • *Cuban Missile Crisis* • *Revolution in Cuba*
Section 3 **Central America** Summarize the factors that led to conflicts in Central America from the 1970s to the 1990s.	Reproducible Lesson Plan 36-3 Vocabulary Activity 36* Guided Reading Activity 36-3* Mapping History Activity 36 Section Quiz 36-3*	Section Focus Transparency 36-3 Student Self-Test and Review Software Testmaker Communism and the Cold War: • *Nicaragua* • *El Salvador*
Section 4 **South America** Explain how democracy has advanced in South America since the late 1980s.	Reproducible Lesson Plan 36-4 Vocabulary Activity 36* Guided Reading Activity 36-4* People in World History Profile 69 Reteaching Activity 36 Enrichment Activity 36 Section Quiz 36-4* Performance Assessment Activity 36 Spanish Chapter Summary 36	Section Focus Transparency 36-4 Student Self-Test and Review Software Testmaker Communism and the Cold War: *Chile*

* *Also available in Spanish*

Chapter Activities

Performance Assessment Activity

A Conversation Among Immigrants Have students list situations and locations from the postwar era that produced refugees or immigrants. In each instance have them identify reasons people would want to immigrate to the United States. Students should then role-play a conversation among a group of refugees representing several of the countries from their list. In the conversation students should use information from their lists, from the chapter, and from their own research. The conversation should include opinion statements about standing policies or potential laws that could affect them.

Possible Rubric Features

Accuracy of content information, concept attainment, elaboration and detail, research skills, analytical skills, and persuasion

• *For an additional activity, refer to Activity 36 in the* Performance Assessment Strategies and Activities *booklet.*

Activity

From the Classroom of...

Mark Manning
Egg Harbor Township High School
Egg Harbor Township, NJ

Value of the Amazon Rain Forest

After students have read about the Amazon region, organize the class into two groups. Have one group research the economic potential of the rain forest, while the other investigates the region's unique ecology. Then have the class generate two lists comparing the economic and ecological worth of the Amazon region.

Have the full class discuss both sides of the issue of developing the Amazon rain forest. Given the struggling economies of the nations of the region, should economic development be a priority? Can economic development and ecological preservation be balanced?

Multiple Learning Styles

Verbal/Linguistic
Have students locate Latin American literature, including folktales, poetry, drama, nonfiction, novels, and short stories. Direct them to create an annotated bibliography.

Visual/Spatial
Have students draw or reproduce the flag of each nation studied. Ask them to find out what the flag symbols mean and to provide a key to them. They should then display the flags to the class.

Auditory/Musical
Play recordings of the music of several of the countries studied and ask students to compare musical styles. Possible examples include reggae from Jamaica, merengue from the Dominican Republic, tango from Argentina, and samba from Brazil.

Kinesthetic
Show the class examples of murals by such Latin American artists as Diego Rivera and José Orozco. Have students choose aspects of life in Latin America and illustrate them. Create a colorful classroom mural, using all of the illustrations.

Additional Resources

TEACHER'S CORNER

NATIONAL GEOGRAPHIC SOCIETY

INDEX TO NATIONAL GEOGRAPHIC MAGAZINE

The following articles may be used for research relating to this chapter:

- "Buenos Aires: Making Up for Lost Time," by John J. Putman, December 1994.
- "Mexico City: An Alarming Giant," by Bart McDowell, August 1984.

ADDITIONAL NATIONAL GEOGRAPHIC SOCIETY PRODUCTS

To order the following products for use with this chapter, call National Geographic Society at 1-800-368-2728:

- *Capitalism, Socialism, Communism Series*, "Communism." (Video)
- *The Changing Faces of Communism Series*, "Cuba." (Video)
- *Nations of the World Series*, "Mexico." (Video)
- *Nations of the World Series*, "Central America." (Video)

BIBLIOGRAPHY

Literature of the Period

García Márquez, Gabriel. *One Hundred Years of Solitude.* New York: Harper, 1970. The rise and fall of the fictional town of Macondo is an allegory of Colombian history.

Vargas Llosa, Mario. *The Time of the Hero.* New York: Grove Press, 1966. Adolescents struggle for survival in a military school.

Readings for the Student

Guillermoprieto, Alma. *The Heart That Bleeds: Latin America Now.* New York: Knopf, 1994. Personal encounters in major cities.

Readings for the Teacher

Winn, Peter. *Americas: The Changing Face of Latin America and the Caribbean.* New York: Pantheon, 1992. Past and present, with an emphasis on human interest.

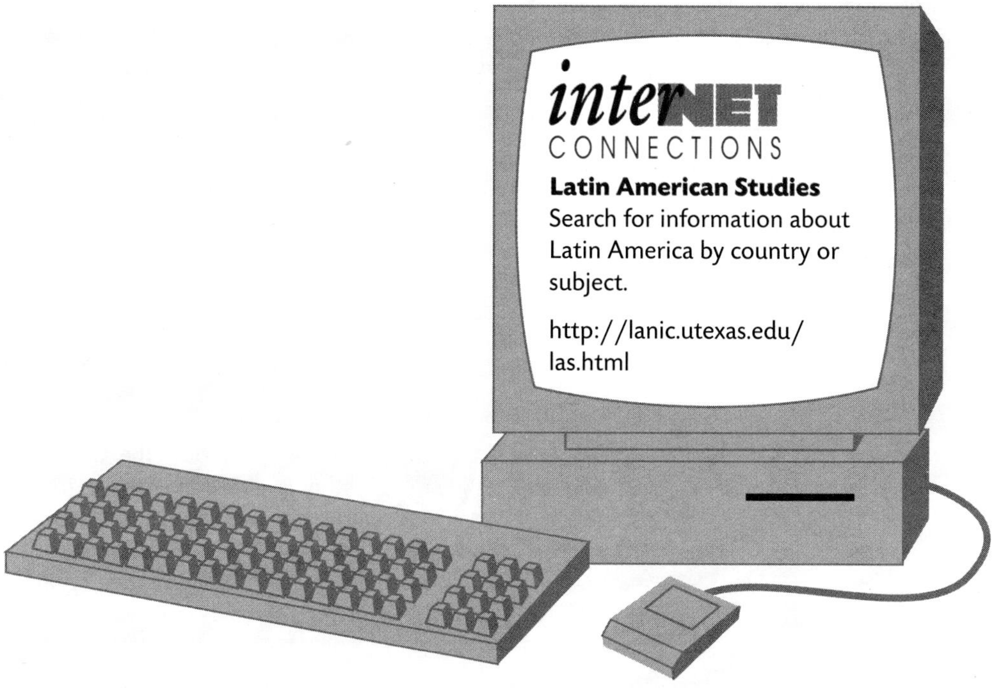

interNET
CONNECTIONS
Latin American Studies
Search for information about Latin America by country or subject.
http://lanic.utexas.edu/las.html

Introducing Chapter 36

CHAPTER THEMES

Chapter Themes are listed by section on this chapter opening page of the Student Edition. A corresponding theme-based activity is available under "TEACH," and a theme-based question is asked in the Section and Chapter Reviews.

The Storyteller

Historical Setting Fidel Castro came from a family of well-to-do landowners. But he claimed that his "vocation" was "being a revolutionary." As a young man, he took part in an unsuccessful invasion of the neighboring Dominican Republic to try to overthrow that nation's dictator, and he organized riots that disrupted the 1948 Pan-American Conference at Bogotá, Colombia.

Historical Significance

Answers: *They have tried to institute democratic reforms and industrialize their countries, as well as joining economic and political alliances.*

Countries have become more democratic, and their economies have grown. Their populations have also skyrocketed.

Chapter

36 Latin America

1945–Present

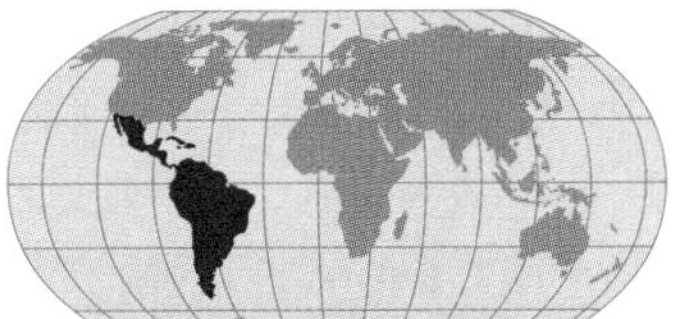

Chapter Themes

- **Cooperation** New organizations promote economic ties in Latin America. *Section 1*
- **Revolution** The overthrow of dictatorial government in Cuba opens the door to communism in the Western Hemisphere. *Section 2*
- **Conflict** Calls for land reform and political freedom lead to civil wars in Latin America. *Section 3*
- **Change** Latin American countries work to develop their struggling economies and to establish democracies. *Section 4*

The Storyteller

On New Year's Day, 1959, the island of Cuba went mad with joy. Tall, bearded Fidel Castro, a lawyer turned soldier, and his band of guerrillas had overthrown dictator Fulgencio Batista.

Along the road to Santiago, crowds of people waved and cheered as Castro's ragtag troops passed by in battered jeeps and trucks. "Viva, Fidel! Viva la revolución!" they cried. So delirious were the throngs, so swept away by the power of the moment, that a friend of Castro's later recalled, "It was like a messiah arriving. We were walking on a cloud."

Castro's revolution was not the first in Latin America, nor the last. Over the next few decades, tensions between rich and poor would erupt in violence repeatedly as the nations of Latin America struggled toward economic and political development.

Historical Significance

How have Latin American countries worked toward political reform and economic growth? What changes have come to Latin America since the end of the cold war?

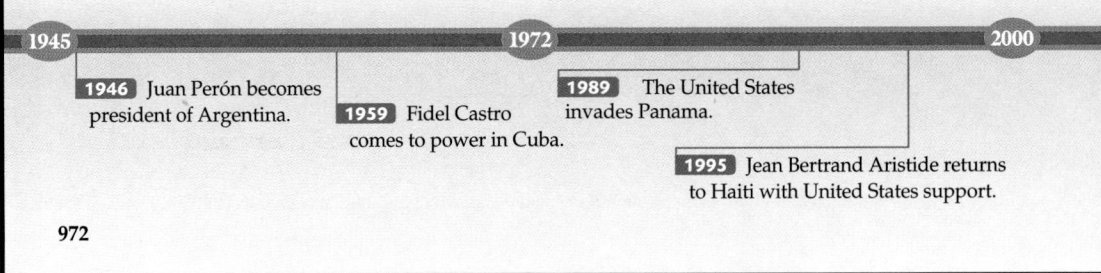

1945 — 1972 — 2000

- **1946** Juan Perón becomes president of Argentina.
- **1959** Fidel Castro comes to power in Cuba.
- **1989** The United States invades Panama.
- **1995** Jean Bertrand Aristide returns to Haiti with United States support.

972

GEOGRAPHY CONNECTION

GEOGRAPHIC THEMES

Location Have students locate Latin America on a map. Ask them to point out the following: Mexico; the Caribbean region; Central America; South America; the Isthmus of Panama. What major American cities are closest to the Caribbean, Mexico, and Central America? *(Answers include Miami, New Orleans, Houston, San Antonio, and Los Angeles.)* Why is this region called Latin America? *(Except for indigenous people, most of the inhabitants of this region speak Spanish, Portuguese, or French—languages based on Latin.)*

Visualizing History Amid the glow of night lights, Sugarloaf Mountain overlooks the city of Rio de Janeiro, Brazil.

Your History Journal

Research population statistics of either Central or South American nations. Draw a cartogram that shows the relative population sizes of these nations today.

EXTRA CREDIT PROJECT

Native Americans In pre-Columbian times, Latin America had the most advanced Native American cultures in the Western Hemisphere and the largest population of Native Americans. Ask students what has happened to the descendants of the Maya, Aztec, Inca, and other indigenous peoples. Have them research and report on the Native Americans of Latin America today—where most of them are concentrated and how they live.

Introducing Chapter 36

Visualizing History Portuguese sailors named Rio de Janeiro; the words mean "river of January." Arriving on January 1, 1502, they thought that Guanabara Bay was the mouth of a river. **What is special about the culture of Brazil?** *(Brazil is the only South American country where Portuguese, not Spanish or French, is spoken.)*

Performance Assessment

Refer to the activity on page 972C of the Planning Guide.

For an additional activity, refer to Activity 36 in the *Performance Assessment Strategies and Activities* booklet.

Using Your History Journal

Suggest that students use a current almanac or recent encyclopedia for up-to-date statistics.

GLENCOE TECHNOLOGY

VIDEODISC
Use MindJogger to preview chapter content.

MindJogger Videoquiz
Chapter 36
Disc 5 Side A

Also available in VHS.

SECTION THEME

▶ **Cooperation** New organizations promote economic ties in Latin America.

Find Out

Answer: *social: population growth, urbanization, gap between elites and rest of population; economic: large foreign debt, industrialization; political: conflicts between conservatives and liberals, guerrilla movements*

FOCUS

Section Objective

List the social and political challenges facing Latin America after World War II.

BELLRINGER Motivational Activity

Before taking roll at the beginning of the class period, project Section Focus Transparency 36-1 and have students answer the activity questions. Discuss students' responses.

This activity is also available as a blackline master.

Vocabulary Pre-check

Use Vocabulary Activity 36 to introduce vocabulary terms. **L1 LEP**

1945 — 1972 — 2000

1948 The United States and Latin American nations form the Organization of American States (OAS).

1968 Catholic clergy in Latin America support social reform efforts.

1990s Civilian democratic governments begin to replace military rule throughout Latin America.

Section 1

Latin American Challenges

Setting the Scene

▶ **Terms to Define**
campesino, elite, liberation theology, free trade

▶ **People to Meet**
Luis Echeverría, Javier Pérez de Cuéllar, Jacobo Arbenz Guzmán

▶ **Places to Locate**
Mexico City, Brazil, Rio de Janeiro

Find Out What social and political challenges did Latin America face after World War II?

The Storyteller

The university student volunteers reached the Guatemalan Indian village after nightfall. Eating tortillas and drinking fresh milk around the fire came first; then the cursillo *began—city and mountain people coming together to talk about liberation. The program included talks about the common good, the right of people to organize, and how to organize for greater strength. Standing before the gathering, Juan took a stick and snapped it. "Alone we are like this," he said. Then he picked up a bundle of sticks that he could not break. "Together we are like this. You and I and your children."*

—adapted from *Guerrillas of Peace, Liberation Theology and the Central America Revolution*, Blase Bonpane, 1985

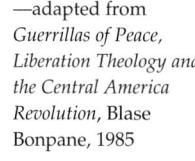

Guatemalan village

In the years after World War II, powerful changes began to reshape Latin America. Between 1940 and 1970, many Latin American nations industrialized as rapidly as did the United States in the late 1800s. Social changes followed this economic transformation. For example, schools and health-care facilities spread, and women won the right to vote.

Yet a dark cloud hung over these bright and hopeful achievements. Much of the region's newfound wealth flowed into the hands of the well-to-do, leaving millions of farmers and workers in the grip of desperate poverty. As the gap between rich and poor widened, the huge peasant class grew hungry and angry. Communism, with its appeal to the oppressed and its promise of social and economic equality, won many converts. As the peasants' demands increased, strong military dictators emerged to quell political upheaval through repression and terror.

These military leaders, in turn, were unable to solve mounting political and economic problems during the 1970s, and their failures inspired calls for democratic reform. By the early 1990s, new civilian democratic governments had replaced many of the old, harsh regimes in a number of Latin American countries.

Population Growth

Since World War II, Latin America's population has skyrocketed. In 1940 Latin America's population was 126 million. With a growth rate of about 2.3 percent a year—about three times the rate of the United States and other industrialized countries—the region's population may expand to nearly 600 million by the year 2000.

Rapid growth has resulted from a combination

SECTION RESOURCES

Reproducible Masters
- Reproducible Lesson Plan 36-1
- Vocabulary Activity 36
- Guided Reading Activity 36-1
- Time Line Activity 36
- Section Quiz 36-1

Transparencies
- Section Focus Transparency 36-1
- Chapter Transparency 36

Multimedia
- Student Self-Test and Review Software
- Testmaker
- Communism and the Cold War: *Perspectives on Communism*

Visualizing History **Deforestation by slash-and-burn methods and by excessive logging threatens the rainforests of Latin America. Despite increased agricultural acreage, there are not enough jobs in rural areas.** *Where do people from these areas go to find work?*

of tradition and progress. Traditionally, families had many children. But because so many died in infancy, the population grew slowly. Latin American women still have many children. The average number of births per 1,000 Latin American women is twice the number in the United States, but improved health care has sharply lowered the infant mortality.

The rate of infant deaths, though five times that in the United States, is lower than in the past. Thus, more babies live to adulthood, and Latin America's population is increasing.

The population growth of Latin America has strained its economic and political systems. The expanding population requires increased supplies of food, clean drinking water, housing, schools, health care, jobs, and transportation.

Urbanization

As the population of rural areas expanded, the poor farmers—known as campesinos—headed to cities in search of work in factories or stores and of better living conditions. With more schools, medical facilities, and other social services than rural areas have, larger cities continue to attract many rural people. In the 1950s about 10 percent of Latin Americans lived in a city of at least 1 million people. Today, over 25 percent do; another 45 percent live in smaller cities.

Cities, however, could not absorb easily the heavy flow of campesinos. The new residents clustered in sprawling, dilapidated shantytowns, many with no electricity, running water, or sanitary facilities. In his 1969 book *A Death in the Sanchez Family*, Oscar Lewis captured the bleakness of life in one such **Mexico City** slum:

> "The [place] where she [Guadalupe] lived consisted of a row of 14 one-room adobe huts about 10 feet by 15 feet, built along the left side and across the back of a 30-foot-wide bare lot.... Five of the dwellings had makeshift sheds, constructed by setting up two poles and extending the kitchen roofs of tarpaper, tin, and corrugated metal over the low front doorways.... Toward the rear of the yard, two large cement water troughs, each with a faucet, were the sole sources of water for the 84 inhabitants."

Such miserable surroundings offered little comfort or hope for the future. Even so, thousands of campesinos kept coming. The president of Venezuela observed, "The poor country peasant would rather come to the city and try to make a living selling lottery tickets than remain in the [countryside] where he has absolutely nothing."

Social Inequalities

Latin America's social structure—masses of poor people dominated by a small but wealthy class of elite—was established during the colonial period. Today the elite includes large landowners, industrialists, top church officials, and military leaders. Many of the elite in Latin America today

COOPERATIVE LEARNING ACTIVITY

Posters Have students form five teams, each one to make a poster graphically representing one of the challenges faced by Latin America: population growth, urbanization, economic development, the growth of democracy, and foreign relations. Students should focus on these aspects: background of the challenge, a clear statement of the issue, key individuals or countries involved with the issue, and possible solutions. **L2**

TEACH

Guided Practice

THEME Cooperation
Have students list ways the United States and Latin America can cooperate and the benefits that would result for each region. *(The United States can help Latin American nations become economically stable, enabling them to improve living conditions, prevent environmental degradation, and repay their debts to U.S. banks. Cooperating to curb the drug trade would reduce crime in both regions.)* **L1 LEP**

Visualizing History In some cases, deforestation is aimed at clearing land on which to graze cattle (often for export to the Northern Hemisphere). Elsewhere, it is done to create more farmland; unfortunately, much of the cleared soil lacks fertility.
Answer to Caption: *to cities*

Population A major challenge to development in Latin America has been its growing population. **How does population growth in Latin America compare with that in the United States?** *(It is about three times as great in Latin America.)* **L2**

Chapter Transparency 36

Independent Practice

Guided Reading Activity 36-1 **L1**

Time Line Activity 36

Cooperation The Organization of American States (OAS), formed in 1948, has worked to encourage political and economic ties among its members. Have students research and report on how this organization is set up and how it operates. **L2**

Economics Land reform has been a controversial issue in many Latin American countries for many years. Have students research and report on land-reform efforts since World War II. They may wish to choose a specific country. **L3**

Who?What?Where?When?

Woman Suffrage For decades, left-wing politicians in Latin America opposed woman suffrage because they thought that women would vote for right-wing candidates. In Ecuador, the first Latin American country to give women the vote, voting was mandatory for men but optional for women.

Connections Geography

Booming Buenos Aires

Visitors to the city enjoy shopping, especially fine woolens and leather goods; eating steak dinners at reasonable prices (Argentina remains a major beef producer); and dancing the tango, the Argentine national dance.

Answers to Making the Connection

1. *its pleasant climate and its prosperity as a commercial and industrial center*
2. *Students may suggest that growth will likely increase pollution and strain city services.*

are the descendants of the Europeans who colonized the region centuries ago. The increase in wealth brought by industrialization in this century simply made these families richer. By the late 1980s, 50 percent of the newly generated wealth in **Brazil** flowed into the hands of the wealthiest 10 percent of the people. As of 1992, 33 million Brazilians, about 21 percent of the population, lived in extreme poverty.

The majority of Latin America's population consists of poor people: peasants, landless farm workers, and factory workers. Many countries in recent decades have a small but growing middle class consisting of professionals, managers, clerks, and government workers.

A more important change has been in the development of the role of women in Latin America. Traditionally women had important but restricted roles in society. They were expected to work at home and raise children. In the late 1800s, women established their right to get an education and to enter a variety of careers. However, not until the mid-1960s did all Latin American women win the right to vote.

Economic Development

In recent decades many Latin American leaders pushed for increased industrialization. They hoped that their countries could manufacture their own products instead of importing them, thereby reducing their trade deficits. In just a few decades, Latin American steel production grew by 20 percent, while the production of metals, machines, and energy rose by 10 percent. Manufacturers flooded the markets with consumer products aimed at the upper and middle classes—fashions, sports cars, toys, and appliances. Since industrialization did little to increase the buying power of the poor, the market for consumer goods was limited to the small elite. Latin American firms quickly produced more than they could sell at home, so they turned to exporting goods to stay in business.

The efforts at industrialization brought results. Between 1950 and 1995, Latin America achieved a remarkable economic growth rate. Much of the money to finance industrial growth, however, came from large multinational corporations and banks. For every dollar they invested in Latin America,

Connections Geography

Booming Buenos Aires

Latin America is one of the world's most rapidly urbanizing continents. For example, today more than 12 million people—well over one-third of all Argentinians—live in the port city and capital of Buenos Aires. One attractive feature of the city is the pleasant, temperate climate. The people of Buenos Aires, called *porteños*, or port dwellers, are descendants of immigrants from all over the world—Spain, Italy, England, France, Poland, and the Middle East.

Downtown Buenos Aires

In the mid-1800s, British and Argentinian investors built a network of rail lines spreading outward from Buenos Aires. On these rail lines, wheat, corn, cattle, and sheep are now sent to Buenos Aires for export. Building on its foundation of trade in agricultural products, Buenos Aires grew into a prosperous industrial center. Among the major industries are food processing and textiles.

Buenos Aires' rapid growth typifies the recent expansion of cities throughout the region. In 1909 Buenos Aires topped the 1 million mark. Immigration from overseas and from rural areas in Argentina added to the population in the succeeding decades. During the 1940s, Buenos Aires had 4.5 million people, and in forty years the population had nearly tripled, reaching over 12 million.

MAKING THE CONNECTION

1. What features of Buenos Aires have attracted immigrants?
2. Predict the consequences of growth on Buenos Aires' future.

MEETING SPECIAL NEEDS ACTIVITY

Mixed Learners Students with learning disabilities and those with limited English proficiency will benefit from organizing the chapter information in a visual way. Have students create wall maps of Latin America to reinforce the location of each country. Have students find, copy, or create images of important aspects of life in the various countries: people, places, farming, industry, and so on. Gifted students may write captions explaining the meaning and importance of the images for each country. **L1 LEP**

976 Chapter 36 *Latin America*

these business and banking enterprises took out more than three dollars in profits and dividends.

Agricultural growth did not match industrial growth. More land was allocated for growing cash crops for export, such as coffee, bananas, and coca, which is used to make cocaine. But as farmers converted more land to growing cash crops, they grew less food for the local population. Although the landowners prospered from selling their crops abroad, local people had to pay more to buy food from farther away. Most campesinos remained poor.

Hoping to stimulate economic growth, many Latin American leaders borrowed heavily from large banks in wealthy countries such as the United States. Between 1975 and 1985, Latin American debt to other parts of the world increased 318 percent.

By the 1980s a worldwide recession made matters worse. It cut the demand for Latin American exports, forcing plants to slow production and lay off workers. At the same time, interest rates—and Latin American debts—rose disastrously. By 1984 the region's debt totaled $350 billion; by 1993, it had climbed to over $465 billion.

In spite of some economic improvements, many observers believe that Latin American debt remains one of the major problems for the region. If the debts are not paid, many banks may fail, threatening the stability of the global economy. Two major debt crises have occurred in Brazil and Mexico. In early 1987 Brazil stated it would suspend payment on its massive debt and interest payments. This action had a chilling effect on American banks, which held about 25 percent of the loans. The United States government began working with Brazilian and other Latin American leaders to encourage an equitable rescheduling of loan payments to avoid future crises. In late 1994 and early 1995, a political and economic crisis in Mexico nearly led to Mexico's failure to meet its international debt payments. The United States came to Mexico's rescue with a $20 billion aid package that aimed for a gradual recovery of the country's economy.

Visualizing History **Workers load bananas for shipment in Ecuador, where petroleum and agricultural products are the main exports.** *How did the emphasis on production of cash crops affect the campesinos?*

Growth of Democracy

The economic problems of Latin America made the growth of democracy almost impossible. In most countries, the elite controlled the government as well as the economy. The elite did not trust the masses enough to allow any form of majority rule to take hold. The majority of people, long dominated by a few powerful leaders, had little experience in making decisions or choosing leaders.

Political conflicts in most of Latin America were between liberals and conservatives. Liberals tried to help the masses through land and tax reforms. Conservatives wanted to maintain the traditional social structure and opposed any redistribution of wealth. Clashes between liberals and conservatives have often been bloody.

The failure of democracy and social reform prompted calls for more radical change. Armed guerrilla movements, that sought to change society by force, emerged in many countries. These groups often relied on the support and protection of campesinos. Many guerrilla organizations included at least some Communists. In countries such as Cuba and Nicaragua, guerrilla movements successfully overthrew governments and took power themselves.

Fear of communism combined with outrage at the poverty of so many people caused changes in the Catholic Church. Since colonial times, the Church had generally supported rule by elites in most Latin American countries. Individual priests sometimes called for reforms to help the poor, but they were exceptions. After a meeting of Latin American bishops in Colombia in 1968, however, an increasing number of Catholic clergy began supporting land reform, democracy, and other changes that campesinos and workers had long demanded. They began emphasizing the role of Christianity in liberating people from oppression. Their beliefs

Visualizing History Agriculture continues to be the leading occupation in most of Latin America. Have students use an almanac or encyclopedia to identify which nations in Latin America have economies based on agriculture and what crops they export.

Answer to Caption: *They grew less food for their own use and thus had to buy it, increasing their need for income.*

ABCNEWS INTERACTIVE™

VIDEODISC
Communism and the Cold War

Side One, Chapter 8
Frames 14264–14893
Title: *Perspectives on Communism*
Subject: Discussion of the ideals of communism
Ask: In Communist philosophy, what was the ideal society? *(The ideal society was one in which everyone was happy; in which all were "master and owner of everything" with no competition.)*

MAKING CONNECTIONS ACTIVITIES

Literature Latin American literature has gained worldwide fame in recent decades. The first writer from this region to win the Nobel Prize was the Chilean poet Gabriela Mistral, in 1945. Have students research her work or the poetry of such writers as Pablo Neruda, Octavio Paz, or Derek Walcott and then present selections to the class, reading in both Spanish (where relevant) and English if possible. **L3**

History Several Nazi leaders fled to South America after the defeat of Germany in World War II. One of the best known was Adolf Eichmann, who was arrested in Argentina in 1960. Have students research and report on how he was found and captured and his subsequent fate. **L3**

Chapter 36
Section 1

ASSESS

Check for Understanding

Assign Section 1 Review as homework or as an in-class activity.

Use Student Self-Test and Review Software to review Section 1.

Evaluate

Section Quiz 36-1

Use the Testmaker to create a customized quiz for Section 1.

Reteach

Have students brainstorm a list of the main challenges facing Latin America in the post-World War II period and then rank them by importance.

Enrich

Have students watch the 1983 movie *El Norte*, a moving depiction of illegal immigrants who make a dangerous journey from Guatemala to California, and write a short essay on why immigrants are willing to take great risks to reach the United States.

CLOSE

Have students list all the organizations through which Latin American nations cooperate for economic, social, and political progress.

became known as liberation theology. One Latin American religious worker explained the new movement this way:

> "For example, if, as the book of Genesis teaches, human beings have been created in God's image, they have a great dignity; hence, to torture another human being is to disfigure God's image. If the Lord gave the Earth to Adam and Eve, he meant it for all—not just a few plantation owners."
>
> —Philip Berryman, *Inside Central America*, 1985

The combined pressure of guerrillas, liberal Catholic clergy, and organized citizens began to bring changes in the 1980s. Argentina, Brazil, Chile, and other countries threw off their dictators and adopted democratic governments. However, these young democracies inherited international debts, widespread poverty, and social unrest. The most controversial issue in many countries has been land reform, which is still opposed by the military and wealthy landowners.

International Relations

Since the end of World War II, Latin America has become involved with the rest of the world. Latin American nations have forged new trading relationships with Western Europe, Asia, Africa, and Japan.

In addition, many Latin American leaders have taken leadership positions in world diplomacy. For example, in the 1970s, Mexico's president, **Luis Echeverría** (AY•chuh•vuh•REE•uh), was a leader in the nonaligned movement. Peruvian diplomat, **Javier Pérez de Cuéllar** (kway•YAHR), served as the secretary general of the United Nations from 1982 to 1991.

The most important relations of Latin American nations, however, have been with each other and with the United States. In **Rio de Janeiro**, Brazil, in 1947, representatives of the United States and most of the Latin American nations signed the Rio Treaty. This defense pact provided that any attack on one member would be considered an attack on all members.

A year later, the Organization of American States (OAS) was set up to develop political and economic ties among the nations of the Western Hemisphere. One of its most important successes was in 1995, when OAS members Brazil, the United States, Argentina, and Chile intervened to stop a war between Peru and Ecuador.

Relations between Latin America and the United States were shaped by the cold war. The United States often provided military aid to conservative regimes while undermining left-wing governments. In 1954 the U.S. CIA helped overthrow a left-wing government in Guatemala led by **Jacobo Arbenz Guzmán**. Guzmán's efforts to redistribute land to the peasants was viewed as a threat to American business interests.

Another way to fight communism was through financial assistance. In 1961 President John F. Kennedy launched the Alliance for Progress. It provided $10 billion for Latin American industry, housing, medical care, and military development. However, much of the money sent to Latin America was used to buy American-made goods.

As the cold war ended in the 1980s nations in the Americas began working toward free trade, or the elimination of trade barriers among countries. Throughout the Western Hemisphere, groups of countries formed regional economic pacts, such as the North American Free Trade Agreement (NAFTA), the Andean Pact, the Southern Common Market (Mercosur), the Caribbean Community and Common Market (Caricom), and the Central American Common Market.

Western Hemisphere governments also took steps to bring together all of the region's free trade organizations. In 1994 leaders from 34 Western Hemisphere nations planned for a free trade area by the year 2005.

SECTION 1 REVIEW

Recall
1. **Define** campesino, elite, liberation theology, free trade.
2. **Identify** Luis Echeverría, Javier Pérez de Cuéllar, Jacobo Arbenz Guzmán, Alliance for Progress, NAFTA.
3. **Explain** How did fast-growing populations and cities cause problems for Latin American nations?

Critical Thinking
4. **Analyzing Information** How has the role of the Catholic Church in Latin America changed since World War II?

Understanding Themes
5. **Cooperation** How might increased United States–Latin American trade affect the campesinos of Latin America?

SECTION 1 REVIEW ANSWERS

1. All vocabulary words are defined in the Glossary.
2. Luis Echeverría, 978; Javier Pérez de Cuéllar, 978; Jacobo Arbenz Guzmán, 978; Alliance for Progress, 978; NAFTA, 978
3. Both trends strained their economic and political systems.
4. It has been influenced by liberation theology to advocate reform, especially liberation of the oppressed.
5. COOPERATION It might benefit them if the increased income is distributed more widely than in the past; if only the rich profit, campesinos will make no progress.

1945 — 1972 — 2000

1961 U.S.-trained exiles stage Bay of Pigs invasion in Cuba.

1971 The first Duvalier presidency ends in Haiti.

1993 United States, Mexico, and Canada enact NAFTA.

Chapter 36
Section 2

Section 2

Mexico and the Caribbean

Setting the Scene

- **Terms to Define**
  standard of living, privatization
- **People to Meet**
  Carlos Salinas de Gortari, Zapatistas, Ernesto Zedillo Ponce de Léon, Fidel Castro, Jean Bertrand Aristide
- **Places to Locate**
  Mexico, Cuba, Dominican Republic, Haiti

Find Out How did Mexico and the Caribbean face political and economic crises after World War II?

The Storyteller

The revolutionary leader Fidel Castro spoke of revolutionaries: "Whoever stops to wait for ideas to triumph among the majority of the masses before initiating revolutionary action will never be a revolutionary.... It is obvious that in Latin America there are already in many places a number of men who ... have started revolutionary action. And what distinguished the true revolutionary from the false revolutionary is precisely this: one acts to move the masses, the other waits for the masses to have a conscience already before starting to act."

—*Fidel Castro Speaks*, edited by Martin Kenner and James Petras, 1969

Castro as a young rebel fighter

After World War II, Mexico and the Caribbean nations of Cuba, the Dominican Republic, and Haiti were ruled frequently by either a single political party or by dictators. Mexico's single-party government controlled much of its economy, while American businesses played an important role in the Caribbean economies. In Cuba, a Communist government took power in 1959, bringing the cold war to the Western Hemisphere. In recent decades, Mexico and the Caribbean countries have tried to reform their political systems and develop their economies. Growing populations and political turmoil, however, have made these goals difficult to reach.

Mexico

Of all the countries in Latin America, **Mexico** was among the most stable after World War II. Since 1929, it had been dominated by one political party, the Institutionalized Revolutionary Party (PRI). Restricted by the constitution to single, six-year terms, strong PRI presidents, using their appointment powers, kept tight control over national and local governments. State-controlled businesses produced rapid industrialization and a growing middle class.

From the late 1940s to the 1960s, Mexico's standard of living—the overall wealth of its people—increased. Industrial growth was concentrated in the central region of the country around Mexico City. There, more goods and services were available to a growing number of people. Rural areas, especially in the south, lagged far behind, and millions of peasants remained desperately poor. Today 40 percent of Mexico's population lives in poverty.

SECTION THEME

- **Revolution** The overthrow of dictatorial government in Cuba opens the door to communism in the Western Hemisphere.

Find Out

Answer: *Mexico devalued the peso, ran up a huge foreign debt, privatized some industries, and joined NAFTA. In the Caribbean, responses varied: Cuba adopted communism, with heavy reliance on the Soviet Union; Haiti tried to institute democratic reforms.*

FOCUS

Section Objective

Describe the political and economic crises faced by Mexico and the Caribbean after World War II.

BELLRINGER
Motivational Activity

Before taking roll at the beginning of the class period, project Section Focus Transparency 36-2 and have students answer the activity questions. Discuss students' responses.

This activity is also available as a blackline master.

Vocabulary Pre-check

Use Vocabulary Activity 36 to introduce vocabulary terms. **L1 LEP**

SECTION RESOURCES

Reproducible Masters
- Reproducible Lesson Plan 36-2
- Vocabulary Activity 36
- Guided Reading Activity 36-2
- History Simulation 36
- People in World History Profile 70
- Section Quiz 36-2

Transparencies
- Section Focus Transparency 36-2
- World History and Art Transparency 49, *Figura*; 50, *Diego and I*

Multimedia
- Student Self-Test and Review Software
- Testmaker
- Communism and the Cold War:
  - *Bay of Pigs*
  - *Cuban Missile Crisis*
  - *Revolution in Cuba*

Chapter 36 Section 2

TEACH

Guided Practice

THEME **Revolution**

Cuba's government was overthrown in 1959. What dissatisfactions led to this uprising? *(foreign domination of the economy, together with Batista's repressive and corrupt rule)* **L1 LEP**

Linking Past and Present

Three Cultures Mexico City boasts a dramatic example of how the present builds on the past. The Plaza of the Three Cultures contains the ruins of Aztec temples, the remains of a Spanish colonial church, and a modern housing complex.

Politics In spite of economic progress under Mexico's President Salinas, his regime faced opposition. What were three causes of this opposition? *(Economic benefits were slow to reach the poor; many resented the political domination of the PRI; many opposed NAFTA, fearing the loss of their lands.)* **L2**

History Simulation 36

World History and Art Transparency 49, *Figura*; 50, *Diego and I*

Who?What?Where?When?

Zapata The name of Emiliano Zapata is written in gold in Mexico's chamber of deputies. An uneducated, landless Native American, Zapata became a powerful spokesperson for others like himself. In 1919, during the violence of the Mexican Revolution, he was assassinated by political foes.

Economic Problems

In the 1970s, oil seemed to offer Mexico the solution to its economic problems. New oil discoveries suggested that Mexico had three times as much oil as previously thought. With rising prices due to turmoil in the Middle East, the state-owned Mexican oil industry prospered and so did the rest of the Mexican economy. The government borrowed money to finance economic development, assuming that oil revenues would make repaying the loans easy.

Worldwide recession in the early 1980s and a sudden glut of oil caused world oil prices to plunge. The Mexican government was forced to cut back jobs and services to save money. To stimulate exports, the government cut the value of the peso, the Mexican unit of currency, by 47 percent. Some wealthy Mexicans responded by fleeing the country with their money.

Mexico's economic troubles worsened during the 1980s. Mexico owed foreign investors $100 billion, one of the highest debts of developing countries. The gap between the rich and the poor widened, as the population continued to grow rapidly. The growing demand of jobs, goods, and services could not be met. Then in 1985, a devastating earthquake hit Mexico, killing 7,200 people and causing $4 billion in damages.

Relations worsened with the United States during this period, too, as a result of differences over drug smuggling and illegal immigration. The United States wanted the Mexican government to do more to stop the flow of illegal drugs from South America through Mexico into the United States. In addition, growing numbers of Mexicans and Central Americans were crossing the United States-Mexico border without visas in hopes of finding work.

A New Era

In 1988 Mexico's new president, **Carlos Salinas de Gortari**, began broad reforms to help solve

Images of the Times

Mexico Today

Mexico faces economic, social, and political change as the nation attempts to provide a better living for its growing population.

Native Mexican crafts delight shoppers in the Sunday craft market in Oaxaca.

Petroleum and petroleum products play an important role in Mexico's trade. World oil prices affect the nation's economy.

980

Images of the Times **Mexico Today**

Every year some 800,000 people move to Mexico City. This migration has made the city the largest metropolitan area in the world. Almost one-fourth of the Mexican people live in the *distrito federal*—on less than one-half of one percent of the country's land.

Mexico's problems. To improve relations with the United States, he worked to crack down on drug smuggling and illegal immigration. He reversed the 50-year-old policy of state ownership of major industries, such as oil, railroads, and communication. With privatization, or a shift to private ownership of businesses, Salinas hoped that these industries would be run more efficiently.

Salinas also sought to boost Mexico's economy by attracting more foreign investment that would create more jobs. The centerpiece of his effort was NAFTA, the North American Free Trade Agreement. Implemented in 1993, NAFTA committed Mexico, Canada, and the United States to remove all quotas, tariffs, and other trade barriers among the three countries over a 15-year period.

While Salinas's reforms were expected to succeed in the long run, Mexico immediately faced a variety of setbacks. Economic benefits were slow to reach the poorest Mexicans. In addition, there was growing opposition to the PRI's hold on political power. In 1994, a guerrilla army of Native American peasants in the southern Mexican state of Chiapas rebelled against the government. Calling themselves the **Zapatistas**, after the early 1900s Mexican revolutionary leader Emiliano Zapata, they demanded a stronger government commitment to aid the poor and advance democracy. They also vehemently opposed NAFTA, which they feared would force them to hand their lands over to large corporations.

In the same year, the PRI candidate for president was assassinated during the campaign. **Ernesto Zedillo Ponce de Léon**, the new PRI candidate, won easily, but there was widespread disatisfaction about the extent of government corruption.

As president, Zedillo continued Salinas's economic reforms while promising to improve the lot of the poor. He also began to open the political system to opposition parties and carried out negotiations with the Zapatistas. A worsening trade deficit, however, forced Mexico to devalue the peso in late 1994. The move shook international business confidence in Zedillo's government.

Mexico City, home to more than 20 million people and one of the world's most rapidly growing cities, faces pollution, crime, and inadequate housing.

Ballet Folklórico enhances the cultural life of Mexico City, the nation's leading business, industrial, and cultural center.

REFLECTING ON THE TIMES

1. How do world oil prices affect Mexico's economy?
2. What problems does Mexico City face because of its rapidly growing population?

ANSWERS TO REFLECTING ON THE TIMES

1. Since Mexico is a prime oil producer, high world prices help its economy and low ones harm it.
2. pollution, crime, and inadequate services

Chapter 36 Section 2

Independent Practice

Guided Reading Activity 36-2 **L1**

People in World History Profile 70

you don't say...

Buckaroos—and more Mexicans were the first cowboys, so many of the words we associate with the American West are of Spanish origin. They include *buckaroo* (vaquero, cowboy), *bronco* (rough, unruly), *chaps* (chaparejos), *corral* (enclosed yard), *lariat* (*la reata*), and *ranch* (rancho).

Immigration Illegal immigration from Mexico to the United States has long been an issue between the two countries. Have students investigate this issue—the reasons for the migration, numbers in recent years, and policies of both governments—and present their findings to the class. **L2**

Who?What?Where?When?

Ernesto "Che" Guevara, an Argentinian, was one of Castro's ablest guerrilla fighters. After Castro came to power, Guevara occupied several important posts until 1965, when he dropped out of public life in Cuba. Apparently Guevara went to South America to preach revolution. He was captured and shot in Bolivia in 1967. His eloquent writings made him a hero to revolutionaries everywhere.

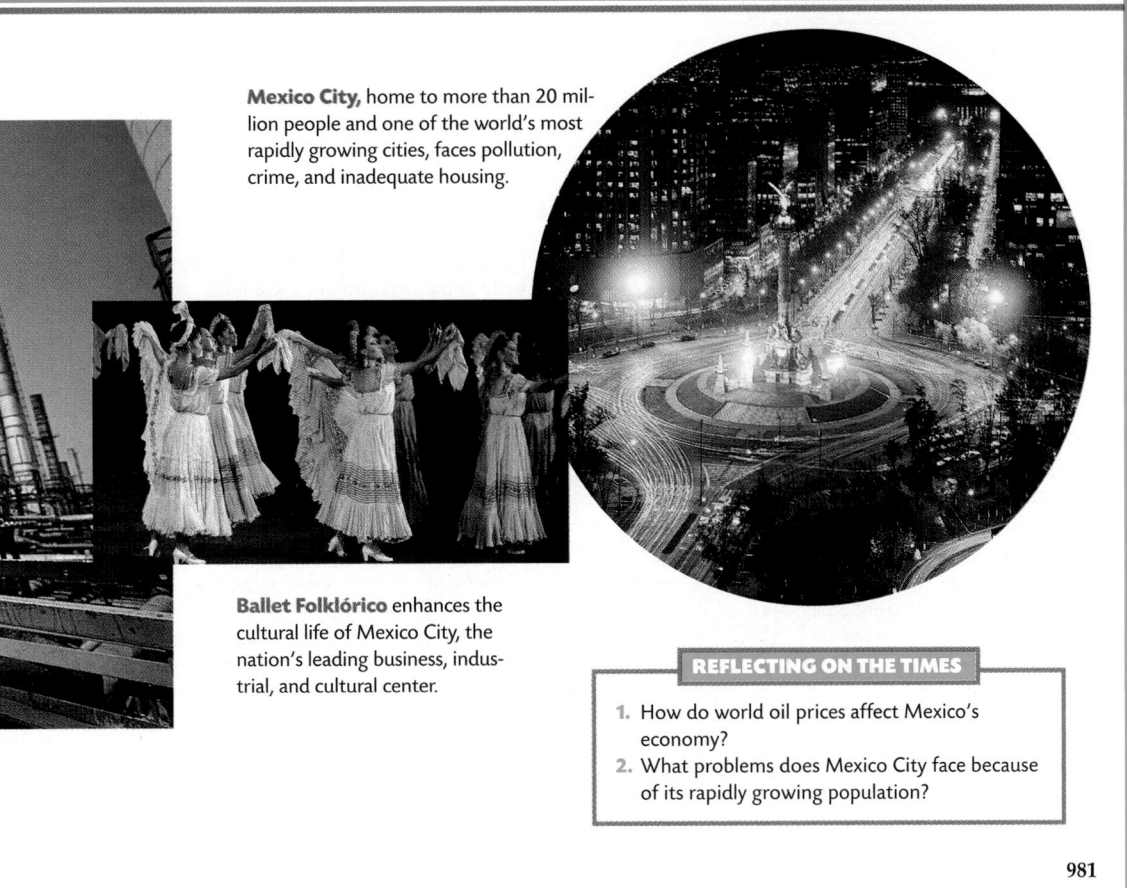

Chapter 36
Section 2

Map Study

Answer

about 2,300 miles (3,700 kilometers)

Map Skills Practice

Reading a Map

How far from mainland Florida were the Soviet missile sites? *(about 350 miles [563 kilometers])*

Interventions Often in this century, the United States has intervened politically and militarily in the Caribbean region. Have students research and report on some of these interventions. Examples include the Dominican Republic, 1916 and 1965; Haiti, 1915; and Cuba, 1906 and 1917.
L3

ABCNEWS INTERACTIVE™

VIDEODISC
Communism and the Cold War

Side Two, Chapter 13
Frames 30190–31200
Title: *Bay of Pigs*
Ask: What does this footage portray? *(American forces in Cuba as a result of the threat of communism.)*

Side One, Chapter 16
Frames 29427-32782
Title: *Cuban Missile Crisis*
Ask: What part of the United States was in the most danger from the missiles? *(the southeastern United States)*

Map Study The Cuban missile crisis frightened the United States and the Soviet Union into improving relations with each other.
Region From east to west, how large was the area covered by the United States blockade of Cuba?

With financial aid from the United States, Mexico was able to weather the crisis. To receive the aid package, however, the Mexican government had to promise a reduction in spending, which threatened to impose hardships on Mexicans of all income levels. Many observers feared that, while the Mexican economy would eventually improve under these terms, government cutbacks in jobs and services would in the short term contribute to further social unrest.

Cuba

From 1952 to 1959, the Caribbean island nation of **Cuba** was ruled by the dictator Fulgencio Batista. Batista's government—often accused of employing corrupt practices—allowed American corporations to dominate the Cuban economy. By the early 1950s, United States companies, taking full advantage of this policy, owned or controlled many of Cuba's mines and ranches as well as much of the oil and sugar industries.

In 1956 a young lawyer named **Fidel Castro** began a guerrilla movement against Batista. Castro opposed Batista's repressive and corrupt practices and called for political reforms. For three years, he and his soldiers carried out attacks on Batista's forces. On January 1, 1959, Batista fled the country, and Castro took control. Many former political officials and army officers were tried and executed. Independent newspapers were closed. Many Cubans who opposed Castro left the country and settled in the United States.

Castro's Domestic Policies

Castro promised democratic reforms and a better standard of living for the Cuban people. Instead of establishing a democracy, however, Castro suspended elections. He did push through reforms to improve wages, health care, and basic education. He took control of the land and nationalized plantations and major industries. Castro's seizure of American-owned property and his disregard of Cuban civil liberties angered the United States.

In retaliation, the United States cut off all sugar imports from Cuba in 1960. Castro meanwhile allied Cuba with the Soviet Union. Soviet Premier Nikita Khrushchev agreed to buy Cuban sugar and to sell arms to Cuba. Castro's dictatorship was openly Communist two years after the revolution.

Cuba and the Cold War

Castro's friendship with the Soviet Union made Cuba the focal point of the cold war in the Western Hemisphere. Castro supported revolutions in Latin America and Africa by supplying military aid and troops and by urging people to join the cause:

> "The revolution will triumph in America and throughout the world, but it is not for revolutionaries to sit in the doorways of their houses waiting for the corpse of imperialism to pass by."
>
> —From a 1962 speech by Fidel Castro

Castro's defiance of the United States put him in danger. During this period the Central Intelligence Agency (CIA), the intelligence-gathering agency of the United States government, made many attempts to assassinate Castro.

In April 1961 the United States tried and failed to overthrow Castro in a secretly planned invasion. About 1,500 anti-Castro exiles trained by the CIA landed in Cuba at the Bay of Pigs, hoping to rally the Cubans to revolt and topple Castro. At the last moment, United States President John F. Kennedy barred open American military support for the effort. The Cuban people failed to revolt, and Castro's forces captured or killed most of the invaders within a few days. Kennedy's new presidency and the global image of the United

COOPERATIVE LEARNING ACTIVITY

Debate Have students hold a debate about the Cuban missile crisis of 1962. Organize the students into two groups, one taking the position that Soviet missiles had to be removed from Cuba at any cost, the other defending a negotiated settlement or even allowing the missiles to remain. Refer students to Samuel Dinerstein, *The Making of a Missile Crisis*, October 1962; Robert A. Divine, *The Cuban Missile Crisis*; and Robert F. Kennedy, *Thirteen Days: A Memoir of the Cuban Missile Crisis.*
L2

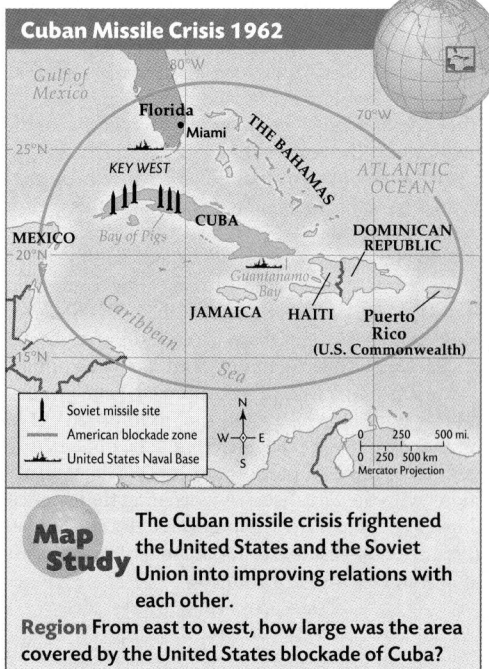

982 Chapter 36 *Latin America*

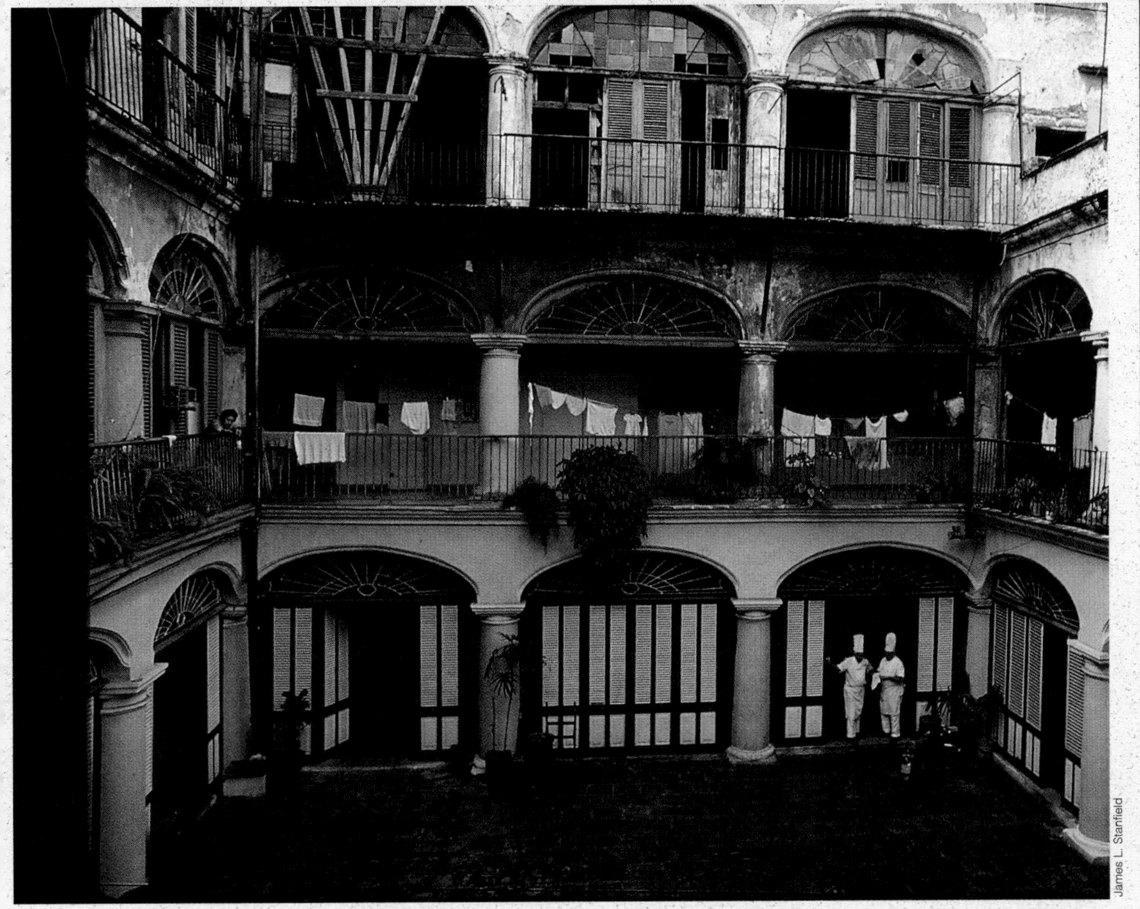
James L. Stanfield

Rich Heritage

Havana, the capital city of Cuba, dates to the 1500s. The Old City has endured, essentially unchanged for four centuries. Today more than 900 buildings—including palaces, churches, mansions, and humble dwellings—remain so uniquely preserved that the United Nations has classified Old Havana as a world heritage site. This palace, being restored from the ground up, reveals the faded grandeur and splendor of the colonial era. Once home to a Spanish conquistador's widow and later to orphans, the building now houses one of the few restaurants in Old Havana.

In 1959 Fidel Castro led a successful Cuban Revolution. After the United States rejected Castro, he turned to the Soviet Union, and for the next 30 years Cuba was a critical stronghold of communism in the Western Hemisphere. Castro's revolution kept out modern developers—along with tourist dollars. But it is partly as a result of Cuba's poverty and relative isolation that the island has preserved its heritage of architectural wonders like the building above. ⊕

TEACH

Tell students that Havana is also famous for fortresses originally built by Spain to defend the port city. One of them, Morro Castle, has become the symbol of Havana. Another, the Castillo de la Fuerza, was begun in 1538 and is the oldest colonial military building in the Americas. What historic sites are preserved in or near your community? *(Examples might include birthplaces or residences of famous people; forts or other military installations; and buildings of architectural interest.)*

Linking Past and Present

Cuban Exiles More than half a million Cubans fled to the United States after the Cuban Revolution. The vast majority settled in south Florida, where they transformed Miami into "Little Havana." The annual Calle Ocho (formerly Eighth Street) Festival draws as many as a million visitors.

ABCNEWS INTERACTIVE™

VIDEODISC
Communism and the Cold War

Side Two, Chapter 12
Frames 28259–30174
Title: *Revolution in Cuba*
Ask: According to Gennadi Gerasimov, how did the United States push Fidel Castro toward communism? *(by trying to stop the revolution instead of supporting it)*

Chapter 36
Section 2

ASSESS

Check for Understanding

Assign Section 2 Review as homework or as an in-class activity.

Use Student Self-Test and Review Software to review Section 2.

Evaluate

Section Quiz 36-2

Use the Testmaker to create a customized quiz for Section 2.

Reteach

Review with the class key events in relations between the United States and Cuba since the 1950s.

Enrich

Have students draw a cartoon from the point of view of another Latin American country that reacts to the Cuban missile crisis.

CLOSE

Have students discuss whether the United States should lift the economic embargo it placed on Cuba in 1962.

States were badly damaged by the disaster.

A year later, the Cuban missile crisis brought the world to the brink of nuclear war. Soviet leader Khrushchev's installation of nuclear missiles on Cuba met with stiff American opposition. President Kennedy ordered nearly 200 American warships to blockade Cuba and stop military shipments from the Soviet Union. American B-52 bombers with nuclear warheads took to the skies, and American forces worldwide went on full alert. As Soviet ships steamed toward Cuba, a tense world watched and waited.

Four days later, after sleepless nights and tense negotiations, the crisis ended. Khrushchev agreed to dismantle the bases and withdraw the missiles, if the United States promised never to attack Cuba again. Separately the United States agreed to remove American missiles in Turkey aimed at the Soviet Union. The most dangerous confrontation of the cold war left the world shaken but relieved. Castro, however, was outraged at Khrushchev's yielding to American pressure.

United States-Cuban relations also continued to be icy. In 1962, the United States imposed an economic embargo on Cuba. Travel between the two countries was tightly restricted. Due to its ties with the Communist world, Cuba was isolated by other countries in the Western Hemisphere.

For brief periods, in 1980 and 1994, Castro allowed thousands of Cubans to sail to the United States. Most of these people were opponents of Castro's authoritarian rule. Others were criminals, mentally ill, or impoverished peasants.

Cuba After the Cold War

With the fall of communism and the collapse of the Soviet Union, Cuba was devastated economically. Due to loss of Soviet aid, poor sugar harvests, and the continuing American embargo, Cuba's economy shrank 60 percent since 1989.

Despite strong pressures from the United States, Castro resisted abandoning his Communist political system. However, he permitted limited capitalist reforms to encourage needed foreign investment. He also allowed some private enterprise, especially in mining and tourism. Castro improved ties with Canada and the other countries in the Western Hemisphere. The United States, however, refused to end the embargo as long as Castro remained in power. As a result, Cuba continued as the last remnant of the cold war.

Haiti

East of Cuba is the large, mountainous island of Hispaniola, which is divided into two nations. The eastern two-thirds of the island is the **Dominican Republic**, a Spanish-speaking country. The western third is French-speaking **Haiti**. The two countries are among the poorest in the Western Hemisphere. Relations between the two countries have often been tense because of their cultural differences.

Economically poorer than the Dominican Republic, Haiti has been ruled by dictatorships during much of its recent history. The dictator François Duvalier (du•VAL•YAY) ruled Haiti from 1957 to 1971. His son, Jean-Claude Duvalier, then became Haiti's leader but was overthrown in 1986. After four years of strife, **Jean Bertrand Aristide** (ah•reh•STEED), a popular reform-minded priest, was elected president. A military coup forced Aristide to flee the country in 1991. With broad international support, and the intervention of American military forces, Aristide returned to power in 1994. A United Nations peacekeeping mission helped in the country's transition from military rule to democracy. Mistrust and violence among rival political groups, however, slowed progress toward stable government and economic recovery. In December 1995, however, a peacefully conducted election brought René Preval to power as Aristide's successor to the presidency.

SECTION 2 REVIEW

Recall

1. **Define** standard of living, privatization.
2. **Identify** Carlos Salinas de Gortari, Zapatistas, Ernesto Zedillo Ponce de Léon, Fidel Castro, Jean Bertrand Aristide.
3. **Locate** Cuba on the map on page 982. Why might people in the United States have felt threatened by Castro?

Critical Thinking

4. **Applying Information** Why did Mexico's huge oil reserves cause as many problems for Mexico as they solved?

Understanding Themes

5. **Revolution** Explain why revolutions have been so common in the Caribbean and in other parts of Latin America since 1945.

SECTION 2 REVIEW ANSWERS

1. All vocabulary words are defined in the Glossary.
2. Carlos Salinas de Gortari, 980; Zapatistas, 981; Ernesto Zedillo Ponce de León, 981; Fidel Castro, 982; Jean Bertrand Aristide, 984
3. Cuba is only 90 miles (145 kilometers) from Miami; also, Castro hoped to export revolution, which worried Americans.
4. Oil revenues fueled the country's development but subjected it to fluctuations in the oil market. Also, borrowing against undeveloped oil indebted Mexico to foreign investors.
5. **REVOLUTION** The region has been dominated, politically and economically, by elites or dictators; it has also been subject to foreign intervention.

1970 — 1980 — 1990 — 2000

1979 The Sandinistas overthrow Somoza rule in Nicaragua.

1981 United States begins aid to the contras in Nicaragua.

1999 U.S.-owned Panama Canal to come under Panamanian control.

Section 3

Central America

Setting the Scene

- **Terms to Define**
  covert, death squad
- **People to Meet**
  Anastasio Somoza Debayle, Sandinistas, contras, Oscar Arias, Violeta Chamorro, Oscar Romero, Manuel Noriega
- **Places to Locate**
  Nicaragua, El Salvador, Panama

Find Out What factors led to conflicts in Central America from the 1970s to the 1990s?

The Storyteller

An American journalist interviewed a Nicaraguan mother whose daughter, a schoolteacher, had been killed. The teacher, who had volunteered to help young children in a small remote village in the war zone, was ambushed by the contras. "My daughter gave her life fighting for freedom, like my son who died in the insurrection. Losing a child is like losing your life." She stopped for a moment to wipe her cheeks, and then looked up again. "My children were my whole life," she said. "My daughter never hurt anyone. All she was doing was teaching poor children in the mountains how to read."

—adapted from *Blood of Brothers, Life and War in Nicaragua*, Stephen Kinzer, 1991

Contra soldiers

Although independent since the 1800s, the nations of Central America have suffered from wars, civil unrest, and interference by foreign powers. Ruled by wealthy elites, several nations were gripped by revolution and civil war from the late 1970s. Only in the early 1990s was some stability restored to the region. This achievement gave hope that the desperate needs of the people could finally be addresssed.

Revolution in Nicaragua

Nowhere was the hold of the wealthy elite tighter than it was in **Nicaragua**. There the Somoza family took power in 1937, and, with the exception of one four-year period, remained in control, backed by the American-trained army known as the National Guard until 1979. By 1967, when **Anastasio Somoza Debayle** took over the presidency from his older brother, the Somoza family owned one-quarter of the land in Nicaragua and most of the country's industries, banks, and businesses.

The Somozas' domination of Nicaragua caused increasing resentment until 1978, when civil war broke out. A broad coalition of groups, including peasants, Catholic priests, middle-class merchants, socialists, and Communists, united to challenge Somoza. Leading the coalition was the Sandinista National Liberation Front (FSLN). The **Sandinistas** took their name from General Augustino Sandino, the popular hero who had waged guerrilla attacks on the U.S. occupation forces in Nicaragua in the 1920s. Sandino had been executed by the father of Anastasio Somoza in 1934.

After the Revolution

The rebel coalition succeeded in overthrowing Somoza in 1979. Although the majority of Nicaraguans cheered the revolution, they differed on how the new government should operate. Some Nicaraguans believed in capitalism and wanted to

Chapter 36 Section 3

SECTION THEME

▶ **Conflict** Calls for land reform and political freedom lead to civil wars in Latin America.

Find Out

Answer: *domination by elites; political control by Communists or Socialists; foreign intervention; drug trafficking*

FOCUS

Section Objective

Summarize the factors that led to conflicts in Central America from the 1970s to the 1990s.

BELLRINGER
Motivational Activity

Before taking roll at the beginning of the class period, project Section Focus Transparency 36-3 and have students answer the activity questions. Discuss students' responses.

This activity is also available as a blackline master.

Vocabulary Pre-check

Use Vocabulary Activity 36 to introduce vocabulary terms. **L1 LEP**

SECTION RESOURCES

Reproducible Masters
- Reproducible Lesson Plan 36-3
- Vocabulary Activity 36
- Guided Reading Activity 36-3
- Mapping History Activity 36
- Section Quiz 36-3

Transparencies
- Section Focus Transparency 36-3

Multimedia
- Student Self-Test and Review Software
- Testmaker
- Communism and the Cold War:
  - *Nicaragua*
  - *El Salvador*

Chapter 36
Section 3

TEACH

Guided Practice

THEME **Conflict**

The United States played a key part in the conflicts in both Nicaragua and El Salvador. **Which side did the United States aid in Nicaragua?** *(the* contras*)* **Which side did the United States help in El Salvador?** *(the government)* **What was its motive in both cases?** *(fear of communism)* **L1 LEP**

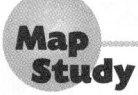

Map Study

Answer

Nicaragua, El Salvador, Panama

Map Skills Practice

Reading a Map **Besides the three countries that experienced fighting in the 1980s, what nations are located in Central America?** *(Guatemala, Honduras, Costa Rica, Belize, Mexico)*

Who?What?Where?When?

Mayan Activist Another Central American country that has been in turmoil since the 1970s is Guatemala. Death squads have killed thousands, especially among the Maya. Rigoberta Menchu—whose father, mother, and brother were killed by security forces—organized resistance among her people and was finally forced to flee for her life. She was awarded the Nobel Peace Prize in 1992.

Independent Practice

Guided Reading Activity 36-3 **L1**

Map Study Powerful wealthy minorities ruled Central American countries, fueling revolutions.

Region What three nations experienced political upheavals that led to fighting in the 1980s?

maintain close ties with the United States. Others called for socialism and a lessening of dependence on the United States.

The Sandinistas, many of whom were Socialists or Communists, held control and began a series of popular reforms. They seized land that belonged to Somoza supporters and turned it over to peasant groups. With Castro's help, they taught people to read and write and improved rural health care.

Within a year after taking power, however, the new Nicaraguan government faced growing opposition. Upper- and middle-class Nicaraguans who had lost property to the Sandinistas opposed the creation of what they saw as a socialist dictatorship. Many of them fled to the United States. Meanwhile, disgruntled former allies of the Sandinistas joined forces with former Somoza supporters to try to overthrow the government. These opponents were called the **contras**, from the Spanish word meaning "against."

Civil War

The Nicaraguan government received financial and military aid from Cuba, the Soviet Union, and many western European countries. However, the United States, fearing the influence of the Soviets and the Cubans, decided to support the contras. In 1981 the United States government sent $19.5 million to the contras, the first official aid to the rebels. By 1985 contra forces numbered 12,000. From bases in Honduras and Costa Rica, they attacked Nicaraguan military bases and businesses.

By 1985 the American public began to fear that the United States would be drawn into another conflict like that in Vietnam. The United States Congress banned military aid to the contras. Despite the ban, members of President Ronald Reagan's staff continued to send covert, or secret, funds to the contras. This illegal use of funds was part of the so-called Iran-Contra scandal that became public in 1987, embarrassing the Reagan administration and leading to indictments of some of the President's staff. Critics charged that an undercover foreign policy was being carried out against the express will of Congress.

Through negotiations, which were led by Costa Rican president **Oscar Arias**, the contras and the Nicaraguan government agreed to a cease-fire and to hold presidential elections in 1990. **Violeta Chamorro**, the widow of a popular newspaper editor killed by Somoza in 1978, won the election. Chamorro, with financial and political backing by the United States, led a wide-ranging coalition of parties. After her election, Chamorro faced immense challenges. Her keeping of key Sandinistas in her government cost her support among the conservative opposition and the suspension of aid from the United States. Despite efforts to introduce reforms, Nicaragua declined economically. By the mid-1990s, it had a staggering foreign debt, high inflation, a large trade deficit, and massive unemployment. In 1993 almost 70 percent of the population was living belowing the poverty line.

Footnotes to History

Nicaragua's Literacy Campaign In 1980 over one-half of adult Nicaraguans were unable to read or write. The Nicaraguan government decided that those who were literate must help those who were not literate. Over the next 5 months, almost 100,000 students helped teach 500,000 people, most of whom were peasants. At the end of the period, Nicaragua's illiteracy rate was less than 15 percent.

COOPERATIVE LEARNING ACTIVITY

News Coverage Organize students into three teams, one each for Nicaragua, El Salvador, and Panama. Have each team investigate news coverage about its country. Students should listen to radio news broadcasts, watch TV news broadcasts, and read newspapers and newsmagazines. They may use *Readers' Guide to Periodical Literature* to find stories that have appeared recently. Students should summarize the information they gather and share it with the class. As a wrap-up, have the class discuss how well and how fairly these countries are covered by the media. **L2**

Conflict in El Salvador

During the 1960s and the early 1970s, **El Salvador** showed some signs of progress. The second most industrialized nation in Central America, El Salvador boasted modern highways, railroads, hotels, and airports. However, the wealth of the country was held by a tiny elite group of people. One study in 1963 estimated that a group of 25 families, many of whom were related to one another by marriage, controlled about 90 percent of the wealth of El Salvador. And while the country seemed to be growing more prosperous as a whole, the number of landless peasants increased from 12 percent in 1961 to 40 percent in 1970.

The unequal distribution of wealth brought growing demands for change. Fearing a popular revolution like the one in Nicaragua, wealthy landowners hired death squads—bands of killers who murdered their political opponents. As many as 1,000 protesters, popular leaders, and their supporters were being killed a month. One of the leading critics of the murder of innocent civilians was El Salvador's Roman Catholic archbishop, Monsignor **Oscar Romero**. When a death squad killed him as he celebrated Mass on March 24, 1980, the country erupted into a civil war. In her poem "Because I Want Peace," Claribel Alegría described the feelings of many Salvadorans:

> "Because there are clandestine
> cemeteries
> and Squadrons of Death
> drug-crazed killers
> who torture
> who maim
> who assassinate
> I want to keep on fighting. . . .
> Because there are liberated
> territories
> where people
> learn how to read
> and the sick are cured
> and the fruits of the soil
> belong to all
> I have to keep on fighting.
> Because I want peace
> and not war."

To stop the uprising, the military appointed José Napoleón Duarte as president in 1980. Duarte supported land reform, but he was powerless to stop the death squads. As the killing continued, the Farabundo Martí National Liberation Front (FMLN)–a coalition of guerrilla groups opposing the death squads and the military–won greater popular support. The United States, fearing Communist influence within the FMLN, gave military aid to the conservative governments of Duarte and his successor, Alfredo Cristiani.

In 1992 with pressure from the United States, Cristiani agreed to a UN-mediated peace settlement with the FMLN, and the FMLN agreed to demobilize. Over 70,000 people had died in the 12-year civil war. Another 1.5 million became refugees.

Since the peace agreement, the government has made progress towards economic recovery and has supported renewed efforts for economic cooperation with its Central American neighbors.

In 1994, another conservative, Armando Calderon Sol, won the presidential elections and succeeded Cristiani to the presidency.

Visualizing History **Civil war in El Salvador claimed more than 70,000 lives before the 12-year war ended in 1992.** *What was the FMLN?*

MEETING SPECIAL NEEDS ACTIVITY

Study Strategy To help students understand recent conflicts in Central America, have them construct a time line of events in Nicaragua, El Salvador, and Panama. (They may wish to add entries for incidents in other Central American countries, such as Guatemala or Honduras.) **L2**

Chapter 36 Section 3

Critical Thinking One of the slogans of FMLN supporters was "no justice, no peace." Ask students what the slogan meant in the context of El Salvador's civil war and whether it might be relevant in other parts of Latin America. **L2**

Mapping History Activity 36

Visualizing History During this period, the United States gave El Salvador more than $5 billion in aid; these funds allowed the government's armed forces to quadruple in size and modernize their tactics and weaponry.

Answer to Caption: *a coalition of guerrilla groups*

ABCNEWS INTERACTIVE™

VIDEODISC
Communism and the Cold War

Side Two, Chapter 15
Frames 33016–35726
Title: *Nicaragua*
Ask: Why did Nicaragua *contra* rebels fight? *(because they believed the Communist regime was taking over Nicaragua)*

Side Two, Chapter 16
Frames 35749-38013
Title: *El Salvador*
Ask: What threat did San Salvador represent to the United States, according to President Reagan? *(Communist influence in close proximity to the United States)*

Visualizing History During the U.S. invasion, Noriega took refuge with the Vatican's representative in Panama. U.S. troops tried to drive him out by playing loud rock music over loudspeakers (Noriega was said to be an opera lover). He finally surrendered after 11 days.
Answer to Caption: *Florida*

ASSESS

Check for Understanding

Assign Section 3 Review as homework or as an in-class activity.

Use Student Self-Test and Review Software to review Section 3.

Evaluate

Section Quiz 36-3

Use the Testmaker to create a customized quiz for Section 3.

Reteach

Review with the class the various motives behind U.S. intervention in Central America.

Enrich

Have students watch the 1989 film *Romero*, starring Raul Julia, which tells the story of the Salvadoran archbishop murdered in 1980, and write a short essay on the role of the Catholic Church in El Salvador's civil war.

CLOSE

Have students debate whether they think U.S. intervention helped or harmed the three Central American countries discussed in this section.

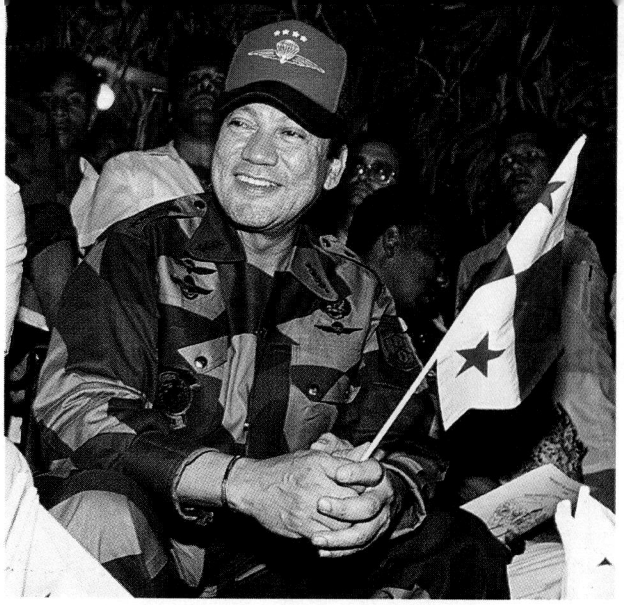

Visualizing History **General Manuel Noriega temporarily controlled Panama until he was arrested and brought to trial for drug trafficking.** *Where was the trial held?*

Power Struggles in Panama

Compared with Nicaragua and El Salvador, **Panama** has been relatively peaceful and prosperous since World War II. From 1968 to 1981, dictator Omar Torrijos (toh•REE•hohs) ruled Panama, bringing stability to the country. He gave government jobs to the country's poor, enabling them to move up the economic ladder. Under his rule, Panama became the most prosperous country in Central America.

Much of Panama's prosperity came from the American-owned Panama Canal. Many Panamanians, however, resented what they saw as foreign domination. In 1977 United States leaders and representatives of 23 Latin American nations signed the Panama Canal Treaty. They agreed that Panama would take control of the canal by December 31, 1999, and that the canal would remain open to the ships of all nations. This marked a new United States approach to Latin American relations.

After Torrijos died in a plane crash in 1981, Panama entered a period of political instability. In 1988 General **Manuel Noriega**, head of the National Guard, took power. A Panamanian CIA agent known for his brutality and his drug trafficking activities, Noriega put the National Guard on full alert, suppressing all protests.

Despite Noriega's ties with the CIA, tensions between Panama and the United States grew. Aware that Noriega was helping to smuggle drugs to the United States, an American grand jury indicted him under international law. In response, Noriega arrested a group of United States citizens in Panama. In December 1989 United States President George Bush sent 9,000 American troops into Panama, where they seized Noriega in January 1990 and brought him to Florida to stand trial. In 1992 Noriega was convicted of drug trafficking. Panama's new President Ernesto Pérez Balladares worked to attract foreign investment and to get rid of the legacy of drug trafficking.

SECTION 3 REVIEW

Recall
1. **Define** covert, death squad.
2. **Identify** Anastasio Somoza Debayle, Sandinistas, contras, Oscar Arias, Violeta Chamorro, Oscar Romero, Manuel Noriega.
3. **List** the terms of the 1977 Panama Canal Treaty.

Critical Thinking
4. **Applying Information** President Kennedy once said of Central America: "Those who make peaceful change impossible make violent change inevitable." Show how events in El Salvador supported this observation.

Understanding Themes
5. **Conflict** What role do you think the United States should play in Central America? What role do you think other countries should play?

SECTION 3 REVIEW ANSWERS

1. All vocabulary words are defined in the Glossary.
2. Anastasio Somoza Debayle, 985; Sandinistas, 985; *contras*, 986; Oscar Arias, 986; Violeta Chamorro, 986; Oscar Romero, 987; Manuel Noriega, 988
3. Panama would take control of the canal by the end of 1999, and the canal would remain open to the ships of all nations.
4. The elite resisted demands for change and used death squads to silence opposition; the result was a violent revolution.
5. CONFLICT Answers should consider the security of other Western Hemisphere nations, fears of elites, and poverty of the masses.

988 Chapter 36 *Latin America*

Social Studies

SKILLS

Analyzing Trends

In the last few years, more and more people have been communicating over the Internet. This indicates a trend. A trend is a general movement of society in a certain direction.

Learning the Skill

Trends exist in all aspects of society—fashion, housing, finance, communications, education, and politics. Analyzing trends allows us to identify and perhaps benefit from patterns of change within a society. Suppose, for example, that you have identified a trend among colleges to award scholarships to students who have performed community service. Knowing this trend, you can improve your chances of winning a scholarship by doing community service while still in high school.

To analyze a trend, first read the material or study the statistics that describe the changes. Identify these changes and patterns of changes. Use this information to project the trend into the future. Ask yourself: What will happen if current patterns continue? What factors could alter this trend?

Sometimes it is hard to distinguish a trend from a fad. A fad is an activity, product, or style that becomes popular for a brief period of time. In the 1990s many people started drinking gourmet coffee. Coffee houses selling specialized coffee sprang up in many cities. Will this be a trend or a fad? Only time will tell.

Practicing the Skill

Study the passage and the table on this page. Then answer the following questions.

1. What world population trends are described in these sources?
2. In which regions is population growing faster than the world average?
3. What are some possible consequences of these trends?

> "One of the most important findings of the *Global 2000 Study* is that enormous growth in the world's population will occur by 2000.... The rate of growth per year in 1975 was 1.8 percent; the projected rate for 2000 is 1.7 percent.... Most of the population growth (92 percent) will occur in the less developed countries rather than in the industrialized countries."

Applying the Skill

From your observations of society, identify a trend in a field that interests you—sports, arts, politics, or health. At the library, find information that provides evidence of this trend. Write an essay predicting the consequences of this trend and its impact on society.

For More Practice

Turn to the Skill Practice in the Chapter Review on page 995 for more practice in analyzing trends.

World Population Projections

	1975	2000	Percent Increase by 2000	Average Annual Percent Increase	Percent of World Population in 2000
	Millions				
World	4,090	6,351	55	1.8	100
More developed regions	1,131	1,323	17	0.6	21
Less developed regions	2,959	5,028	70	2.1	79
Major regions					
Africa	399	814	104	2.9	13
Asia and Oceania	2,274	3,630	60	1.9	57
Latin America	325	637	96	2.7	10
Russia, Commonwealth States. and Eastern Europe	384	460	20	0.7	7
North America, Western Europe, Japan, Australia and New Zealand	708	809	14	0.5	13

Source: Global 200 Technical Report, Table 2-10

ANSWERS TO PRACTICING THE SKILL

1. There will be tremendous growth in the world's population by the year 2000, and most of that growth will occur in less-developed regions.
2. Africa, Asia and Oceania, Latin America
3. Answers will vary but may include overcrowding in the cities, shortages of food and drinking water, and inability to supply basic human services in developing regions.

Social Studies

SKILLS

TEACH

Analyzing Trends Write this heading on the chalkboard: *Hispanic Members of U.S. Congress.*
Beneath it write these figures:

1981	6
1985	10

What is the change here? *(an increase of 4)* **Could it be called a trend?** *(Not necessarily; there are not enough examples, and they do not cover a long enough period to be sure.)*
Then add the following figures:

1987	11
1991	11
1995	17

Ask students whether this addition creates a trend. *(yes)* **How would you explain it?** *(There are several possibilities: The number of Hispanics in the United States is growing; more Hispanics are voting; more money is available for Hispanic candidates; voting districts have been altered to favor Hispanic blocs.)*

Additional Practice

Skill Reinforcement Activity 36

Chapter 36 Section 4

SECTION THEME

▶ **Change** Latin American countries work to develop their struggling economies and to establish democracies.

Find Out

Answer: *In several countries—notably Argentina, Chile, and Brazil—authoritarian governments have been replaced by more democratic regimes.*

FOCUS

Section Objective

Explain how democracy has advanced in South America since the late 1980s.

BELLRINGER Motivational Activity

Before taking roll at the beginning of the class period, project Section Focus Transparency 36-4 and have students answer the activity questions. Discuss students' responses.

This activity is also available as a blackline master.

Vocabulary Pre-check

Use Vocabulary Activity 36 to introduce vocabulary terms. **L1 LEP**

1945 — 1972 — 2000

1973 Military forces overthrow Allende presidency in Chile.

1982 Argentina and Great Britain fight the Falkland Islands War.

Section 4

South America

Setting the Scene

▶ **Terms to Define**
hyperinflation, cartel

▶ **People to Meet**
Juan Perón, Eva Perón, Carlos Menem, Salvador Allende, Augusto Pinochet, Alberto Fujimori

▶ **Places to Locate**
Argentina, Falkland Islands, Chile, Colombia, Peru, Brazil

Find Out How democracy has advanced in South America since the late 1980s?

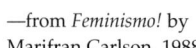

The Storyteller

Eva Perón expressed herself about many topics, including feminismo, *the women's movement in Argentina: "I felt that the women's movement in my country and all over the world had a sublime mission to fulfill … and everything I knew about feminism seemed to me ridiculous. For, not led by women but by those who aspired to be men, it ceased to be womanly and was nothing: feminism had taken the step from the sublime to the ridiculous. And that is the step I always try to avoid taking."*

—from *Feminismo!* by Marifran Carlson, 1988

Eva Perón

Since the end of World War II, South America has become a region of sharp contrasts. Rapidly growing cities have sprawling slum areas as well as suburbs for the well-to-do and glamorous tourist resorts. While new industries have developed in the coastal urban areas, traditional forms of agriculture still dominate much of the interior of the continent. Despite areas of modernization and prosperity, widespread poverty continues to shape the politics and social structures of South American nations.

Argentina

Before a world depression and the rise of fascism in **Argentina** in the 1930s, the country was one of the 10 wealthiest in the world. Since then, the country has often been under military rule, and its prosperity has declined.

The Perón Era

The dominant political figure in Argentina from the 1940s to the 1970s was Colonel **Juan Perón** (pay•ROHN). When he was first elected president in 1946, Perón enjoyed great popularity, even though he was an authoritarian ruler. Perón and his glamorous wife, **Eva Perón**, a former film and radio star, became the heroes of the downtrodden. By increasing the military budget and supporting pay raises for union members, Perón won the loyalty of soldiers and workers. By nationalizing foreign-owned industries, he appealed to Argentinian pride over controlling its own resources. Eva supported construction of hospitals, schools, clinics, and nursing homes and distributed millions of shoes, sewing machines, and other household goods to the poor.

However, Perón's popularity began to wane in the 1950s. The much-loved Eva died in 1952. Perón's policy of taxing agriculture to fuel industrial growth led to a decline in food production. As the economy declined, anti-Perón protests increased.

SECTION RESOURCES

Reproducible Masters
- Reproducible Lesson Plan 36-4
- Vocabulary Activity 36
- Guided Reading Activity 36-4
- People in World History Profile 69
- Reteaching Activity 36
- Enrichment Activity 36
- Section Quiz 36-4
- Performance Assessment Activity 36
- Spanish Chapter Summary 36

Transparencies
- Section Focus Transparency 36-4

Multimedia
- Student Self-Test and Review Software
- Testmaker
- Communism and the Cold War: *Chile*

Visualizing History **More than 100,000 people rally in Buenos Aires, Argentina, in support of democratic government in 1987. The nation has had long periods of military rule interrupted by brief intervals of constitutional government.** *Why has the military often seized power?*

He responded by imprisoning more of his opponents. In 1955 the military forced him to leave office.

In 1973, after almost 20 years of military rule, Perón returned briefly to power. When he died in 1974, his new wife Isabel took over, becoming the first woman president in the Western Hemisphere. Economic problems continued, and a coup ousted her in 1976.

Once again Argentina was under military rule. The generals who jointly ruled Argentina managed to spark an economic turnaround but ruled the country brutally. Death squads roamed the country, torturing and killing those who dissented. Thousands of people died or simply disappeared.

Falkland Islands War

In 1982, in an effort to unite Argentina and to end one of the last outposts of colonialism, the military leadership sent Argentinian troops to seize the **Falkland Islands**, also known as the Malvinas. These islands off the coast of Argentina had been controlled by the British since 1833. Seventy-four days later, the Argentinians returned home defeated by the British forces.

After the Falklands humiliation, the military was discredited, and democracy was gradually restored. Economically, Argentina came dangerously close to collapse. In 1989 inflation reached 5,000 percent. This hyperinflation—extremely sharp and rapid price increases—caused a severe depression, and much of the middle class fell into poverty.

In 1989 Argentinians elected **Carlos Menem** as president and in 1995 re-elected him. Menem brought inflation under control, reducing it to about 4 percent in 1994, while keeping the economy growing at a healthy rate. Regionally he worked to create a tariff-free common market called Mercosur with neighboring Brazil, Paraguay, and Uruguay. To advance Argentina's international standing and attractiveness to investors, Menem improved relations with the United States, Great Britain, and the United Nations, joining in UN peacekeeping missions.

Chile

The long coastal country of **Chile** has one of the strongest traditions of democracy in Latin America. In 1970 the voters elected socialist **Salvador Allende** (ah•YEHN•day) to the presidency. He was the first Marxist in the Western Hemisphere to come to power through peaceful means.

COOPERATIVE LEARNING ACTIVITY

Debate Organize the class into two teams to debate this proposition: The U.S. war on Colombian drug lords is proving successful. Students on each team should research such factors as American drug dealers and users, the U.S. Drug Enforcement Agency, the Colombian suppliers, and Colombian efforts to stop the drug traffic. Students who argue that the war on drugs is not working should suggest alternatives to current policies. **L3**

TEACH

Guided Practice

THEME Change

Beginning in the late 1980s, many South American countries formerly controlled by the military changed to civilian rule. What factors led to this change in Argentina, Chile, and Brazil? *(Argentina: Falklands defeat discredited the military; Chile: popular dissatisfaction with repression; Brazil: military agreed to democratic rule.)* **L1 LEP**

Visualizing History In 1987 Argentine army officers staged an antigovernment revolt, but it was quelled, with strong public support.

Answer to Caption: *because of the country's economic problems and political turmoil*

Economics High inflation rates affect the price of everything. In Argentina in 1989, the annual inflation rate was 5,000 percent. What would this mean for a $5 movie ticket? *(Within a year it would cost $225.)* How would people cope with increases like this? *(Wages would also rise, but usually not enough to compensate.)* **L2**

CURRICULUM CONNECTION

SCIENCE

Charles Darwin's study of animals in the Galápagos Islands, an Ecuadorean possession in the Pacific, were crucial to his theory of evolution. In his journal, Darwin noted that animal species he observed there were the "origin of all my views."

Visualizing History Bolivia is one of two landlocked countries in South America. This geographic isolation, coupled with the Andes barrier, has made economic progress difficult.
Answer to Caption: *Chile*

Independent Practice

Guided Reading Activity 36-4 **L1**

People in World History Profile 69

Daily Life In most Latin American countries, the period before Lent is a time of parades, entertainment, and feasting. Have students research and report on the most famous carnival of all, that of Rio. **L2**

ABCNEWS INTERACTIVE™

VIDEODISC
Communism and the Cold War

Side Two, Chapter 14
Frames 31217–32996
Title: *Chile*
Subject: Inauguration of President Salvador Allende
Ask: To what does President Nixon refer by saying that Latin America will be all "red" eventually due to the election of a Marxist leader in Chile? *(He believes Chile will spread communism across Latin America.)*

Visualizing History **From 1965, when Cuba sponsored guerrilla fighters against the government, to the1990s, Bolivia has had an unstable political system.** *What neighboring country also faced struggles between the military and socialists in this period?*

To stimulate the faltering economy, Allende nationalized businesses, including American copper-mining companies, and distributed land to the poor. He also boosted wages by 35 percent and put a ceiling on prices. In two years, the economy grew 13.5 percent and unemployment was cut in half.

Not all of Allende's policies were successful, however. For example, the breakup of big farms resulted in a decline in food production, which in turn caused food shortages. And the increased wages led to inflation.

More important, though, Allende's policies made him powerful enemies. Wealthy Chileans, frightened by Allende's ties to Castro's Cuba, took their money out of Chile and invested it in other countries. In addition, the United States decided to undermine the Allende government by funding opposition candidates, promoting strikes and protests, and convincing the World Bank to halt loans to Chile. By 1972 Chile's economy was near collapse.

In 1973 Chilean military leaders who had worked closely with the CIA led a coup against Allende. After the successful uprising, Allende was found dead in his office. The military leaders claimed Allende had killed himself with a machine gun that Castro had given him as a gift. It was reported that thousands of people died during and after the coup.

The new government was led by a ruthless and powerful dictator, General **Augusto Pinochet** (PEE •noh•CHEHT). Immediately, Pinochet put an end to Chile's long-standing democracy. He dissolved the congress, censored the press, canceled civil liberties, and issued a new constitution. He killed or imprisoned as many as 1 in every 100 Chileans.

To improve the Chilean economy, Pinochet imposed higher taxes and encouraged foreign investment. Inflation, which had reached 600 percent in 1973, fell to 10 percent by 1981. Soon, store shelves were filled with consumer goods.

Popular opposition to Pinochet, however, remained strong. Many Catholic leaders continued to risk arrest, torture, and death by protesting against Pinochet's cruelty. In 1988, at long last Pinochet gave in to mounting pressure and allowed the people to have elections, which brought Patricio Aylwin to power. With the threat of another military coup still strong, Aylwin tried to revive Chile's democratic tradition.

In 1993, Eduardo Frei Ruiz-Tagle suceeded Aylwin as Chile's president. He has continued many of Aylwin's policies: decreasing the number of people in poverty by increased spending on education, health, and housing; and achieving steady economic growth. By the mid-1990s, Chile had one of the strongest economies in Latin America and prepared to join NAFTA.

Colombia

Since World War II, **Colombia** has had long periods of instability. Between the late 1940s and the mid-1960s, battles between liberals and conservatives caused the deaths of about 200,000 people. Colombians refer to this period as *La Violencia*, or the violence.

During the 1970s and 1980s, the ever-growing power of drug dealers infected Colombian politics. Drugs, including marijuana and cocaine, became Colombia's largest export. Drug barons in the city of Medellin amassed tremendous fortunes. They murdered more than 350 judges and prosecutors who tried to stop the drug business. By the

MEETING SPECIAL NEEDS ACTIVITY

Learning Disability Students who have difficulty reading and understanding standard text material may respond well to music. Play selections from the works of the Brazilian composer Heitor Villa-Lobos and have students create drawings to illustrate their responses to the music. **L1 LEP**

mid-1990s, some progress was made in curtailing the power of the Colombian drug cartels, associations formed to establish an international monopoly by price fixing and regulating production. Yet, the illegal trade continued to flourish. In 1996, President Ernest Samper resigned because of charges that he had accepted campaign contributions from drug barons.

Peru

Since the end of World War II, **Peru** has been run by military or by civilian dictators. One official who took bold steps to improve Peru's economy was General Juan Velasco, who ruled from 1968 to 1975.

General Velasco distributed land to the peasants, nationalized foreign-owned companies, and provided aid to the urban poor. By so doing, he hoped to unite Peruvians and to stimulate economic growth. However, inflation and unemployment continued to remain high. Military leaders removed Velasco from power in 1975.

In 1990 **Alberto Fujimori** was elected Peru's president. Two years later, Fujimori suspended the constitution and ruled as a dictator, before gradually restoring democracy. In 1995, he succeeded in ending a 15-year civil war with a Marxist guerrilla group known as the Shining Path, and he was re-elected president. Fujimori still faced massive social and economic challenges with more than 50 percent of Peruvians living in poverty.

Brazil

For two decades following World War II, **Brazil** was generally governed by freely elected leaders. Under their leadership, foreign investors opened auto factories and steel plants. However, when Jõao Goulart became president in 1961 with the support of organized labor, the military feared he would begin reforms that would lead to communism. Military leaders, therefore, took control of the national government in 1964.

AROUND THE WORLD — Live Aid Concert

Philadelphia and London, 1985

A rock concert, organized by Irish singer Bob Geldof, raised money to help feed starving people in Africa. The day-long event was held simultaneously in Philadelphia and London on July 13, 1985. Performers included Paul McCartney, Bob Dylan, Mick Jagger, Madonna, and Joan Baez. Live Aid drew crowds in excess of 160,000. It was televised worldwide to an audience estimated at 1.5 billion people.

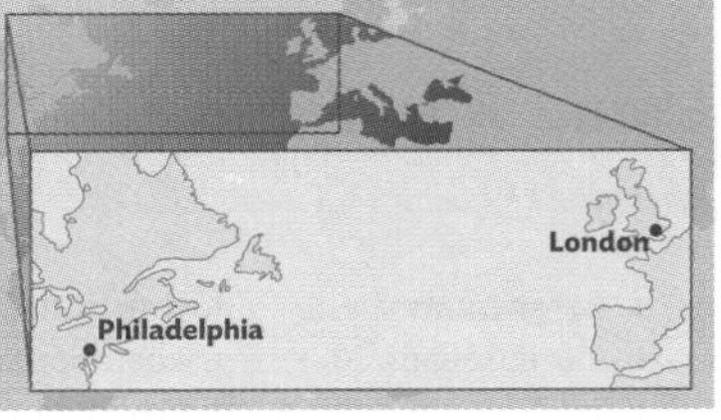

In 1968 the military government launched a program to industrialize Brazil. Over the next seven years, they reduced social programs, sought investments by foreign companies, weakened the unions, and fixed wages at 50 cents an hour. With the economy growing 11 percent a year, businesses prospered. With wages kept low, however, workers remained poor.

In 1985 the military agreed to permit Brazil to return to democratic rule. Since then, political leaders have succeeded in winning sufficient popular support to reduce the military's influence in the government.

Hopes for economic improvement were heightened with the election of Fernando Collor de Mello as president in 1990. His concern for the environment, including efforts to slow destruction of the Amazon rain forest, won him international support. In 1992, Collor resigned, however, following charges of corruption. The new president Fernando Henrique Cardoso faced substantial economic problems, among them reducing inflation and government waste.

SECTION 4 REVIEW

Recall

1. **Define** hyperinflation, cartel.
2. **Identify** Juan Perón, Eva Perón, Carlos Menem, Salvador Allende, Augusto Pinochet, Alberto Fujimori.
3. **Describe** political conditions in Chile under the dictatorship of Augusto Pinochet.

Critical Thinking

4. **Analyzing Information** Why was Juan Perón's government so popular in Argentina?

Understanding Themes

5. **Change** How did military governments both improve and damage various South American nations?

Chapter 36 Section 4

ASSESS

Check for Understanding

Assign Section 4 Review as homework or as an in-class activity.

Use Student Self-Test and Review Software to review Section 4.

Evaluate

Section Quiz 36-4

Use the Testmaker to create a customized quiz for Section 4.

Reteach

Have students review the changes in government in Argentina, Chile, and Brazil since the 1980s.

Reteaching Activity 36

Enrich

Have students watch the 1982 film *Missing*, starring Jack Lemmon and Sissy Spacek, based on the true story of an American who disappeared in Chile after Allende's overthrow in 1973.

Enrichment Activity 36

CLOSE

Have students list the challenges facing the countries of South America today.

SECTION 4 REVIEW ANSWERS

1. All vocabulary words are defined in the Glossary.
2. Juan Perón, 990; Eva Perón, 990; Carlos Menem, 991; Salvador Allende, 991; Augusto Pinochet, 992; Alberto Fujimori, 993
3. Congress was dissolved, the press was censored, civil liberties were nonexistent, and one in every 100 Chileans were killed or imprisoned.
4. It increased funds for the military and unionized workers, built public facilities, aided the poor, and stimulated national pride.
5. **CHANGE** They improved them by making economic reforms and encouraging development; they damaged them by discarding democratic institutions and carrying out reigns of terror.

Chapter 36 Review

GLENCOE TECHNOLOGY

VIDEODISC

Use MindJogger to review students' knowledge of the chapter.

MindJogger Videoquiz

Chapter 36
Disc 5 Side A

Also available in VHS.

Answers

Using Key Terms

1. j	6. g
2. b	7. a
3. c	8. i
4. f	9. h
5. e	10. d

Using Your History Journal

Point out that gross domestic product (GDP) is the total goods and services produced by an economy in a year, while gross national product (GNP) is GDP plus the income from foreign investments.

Reviewing Facts

1. population growth, urbanization, domination by elites, foreign intervention and debt
2. Politically, PRI control has somewhat relaxed; economically, it has privatized some industries and joined NAFTA.
3. Nicaragua: Somoza family owned one-quarter of the land and most industry, banks, and businesses. El Salvador: A small group of families controlled 90 percent of the country's wealth.
4. After four years of turmoil, Aristide was elected president but was then forced to flee; reinstated in 1994, he served until 1995, when a successor was elected.
5. the Soviet Union
6. to develop political and economic ties among nations of Western Hemisphere
7. Britain defeated Argentina, causing the military to be discredited and democracy to be restored.
8. a straining of economic and political systems; need for increased food, water, housing, jobs, and services

Critical Thinking

1. Answers will vary. Positive: suppressing communism and protecting U.S. interests; negative: maintaining dictatorships and inequitable distribution of wealth.
2. Suggestions should reflect independent thinking and may include education,

CHAPTER 36 REVIEW

Historical Significance

The history of Latin America since World War II shows the challenge of establishing democracy in societies traditionally ruled by a small elite. In most countries, the bitter conflict between the rich and the poor has limited the development of stable democracies.

A second significant challenge in Latin America is economic development. Increasing agricultural exports and building industry have brought increases in total national wealth. However, the majority of the population has not always benefited from these changes.

Using Key Terms

Write the key term that completes each sentence.

a. campesinos	f. free trade
b. death squads	g. liberation theology
c. elite	h. covert
d. privatization	i. cartel
e. standard of living	j. hyperinflation

1. During the 1980s, the economy of Argentina was dangerously close to collapse because of _________, extremely sharp and rapid price increases.
2. Fearing a popular revolution, landowners in El Salvador hired _________ to murder their political opponents.
3. Since colonial times, Latin America society has consisted of masses of poor people dominated by a small but wealthy ______________.
4. By the mid-1990s, many countries in the Americas were members of economic organizations that promoted _________, or the elimination of trade barriers.
5. From 1945 to the 1960s, Mexico's __________—the overall wealth of its people—increased.
6. Beginning in the 1960s, many Catholics in Latin America supported social change and promoted the ideas of ______________.
7. Since 1945, poor farmers, or _________, have left rural villages to find work in Latin America's urban areas.
8. Since the 1970s, Colombia has been affected by the drug _________, who control the illegal drug trade by fixing prices and regulating production.
9. The United States participated in the ______ planning of the 1961 Bay of Pigs invasion.
10. By the mid-1980s, Mexico and other Latin American countries were supporting programs of __________, shifting control of industry from governments to private owners.

Using Your History Journal

Research statistics about the gross national (or gross domestic) product of Central American or South American nations. Draw a cartogram that shows the relative economic strength of these nations.

Reviewing Facts

1. **List** various political and economic problems that have confronted Latin American countries in recent decades.
2. **Describe** Mexico's political and economic system as developed since the 1980s.
3. **List** the causes of the civil wars in Nicaragua and El Salvador.
4. **Discuss** political developments in Haiti since the fall of the Duvaliers.
5. **Identify** the major ally of Fidel Castro after 1960.
6. **Explain** the purpose of the Organization of American States (OAS).
7. **Discuss** the outcome of the Falkland Islands War in 1982.
8. **List** the challenges posed by rapid population growth in Latin America.

Critical Thinking

1. **Evaluate** Have the policies of the United States government had a positive or negative effect on the development of Latin America?
2. **Apply** How would you solve the problem of the illegal drug trade between Colombia and criminals in the United States?

994 Chapter 36 *Latin America*

3. **Synthesize** Imagine that you were a citizen of El Salvador in 1980. How would you feel about the United States providing support to your military government?
4. **Synthesize** Why do you think so many Latin American governments have become dictatorships?

Geography in History

1. **Region** Refer to the map below. What large area of South America has an economy largely based on hunting, fishing, and gathering?
2. **Movement** Why are most manufacturing and commercial areas located along the seacoast?
3. **Place** Judging from the type of economic activity, where are South America's largest plains?

Economic Activity in South America

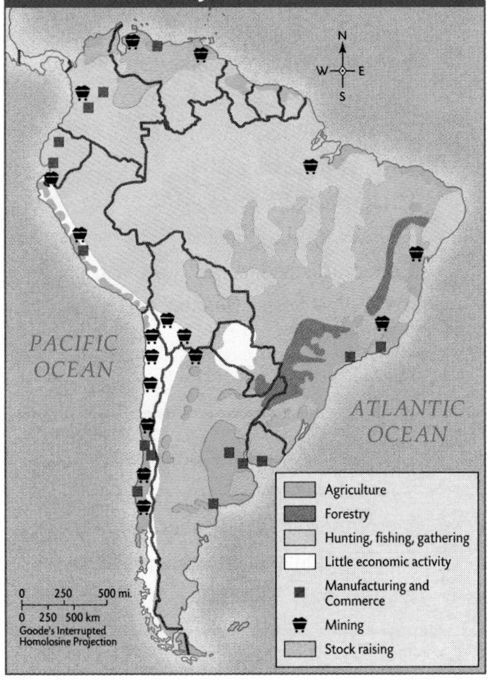

Understanding Themes

1. **Cooperation** How has Latin America's interdependence with global and hemispheric markets affected its ability to develop economically?
2. **Revolution** How did Cuba's revolution affect relations between Cuba and the Soviet Union?
3. **Conflict** How did the cold war affect revolutions and civil wars in Central America?
4. **Change** How have South American countries changed politically and economically since the late 1980s and early 1990s?

Linking Past and Present

1. How might the economic crises in Latin America cause problems for the United States in years to come?
2. In both the Monroe Doctrine and the Rio Treaty of 1947, the United States pledged to protect Latin American nations from outside powers. In the Falkland Islands War, however, the United States supported Great Britain. How do you think Latin Americans responded to this?

Skill Practice

Read the passage below and then answer the questions that follow.

> "If present trends continue, both forest cover and growing stocks of commercial-size wood in the less developed regions ... will decline 40 percent by 2000.... Deforestation is projected to continue until about 2020....
>
> The real prices of wood products—fuelwood, sawn lumber, wood panels, paper, wood-based chemicals, and so on—are expected to rise considerably as ... world supplies tighten.... Loss of woodlands will force people ... to pay steeply rising prices for fuelwood and charcoal."

1. According to this passage, what is the trend in the world's forest cover?
2. How will this trend affect the price of wood products in the 21st century? Why?
3. What factors might alter the course of this trend?

interdiction, eradication, or legalization.

3. Answers will vary depending on perspective. A wealthy person might welcome protection of his or her property, while a campesino might resent U.S. support of a repressive regime.
4. Possible causes: need for force to keep money and power in the hands of the elite; external interference; inability of democratic governments to provide stability.

Geography in History

1. the north
2. This gives them access to the sea for easy transport of raw materials and finished goods.
3. east and southeast

Understanding Themes

1. **COOPERATION** It has brought industrialization and boosted exports but has not resulted in a higher standard of living for most workers or campesinos.
2. **REVOLUTION** Because the United States broke off trade, Cuba turned to the Soviet Union for trade and aid.
3. **CONFLICT** U.S. fear of communism led it to intervene in the internal affairs of many Latin American countries.
4. **CHANGE** Several countries—notably Argentina, Chile, and Brazil—have become more democratic. But many countries have relied heavily on foreign investors.

Linking Past and Present

1. Possible answers: U.S. bank failures resulting from defaults on Latin American debts; loss of trade; more illegal immigration.
2. Some saw it as a violation of U.S. pledges, but others did not object since they had not supported Argentina's move in the first place.

Skill Practice

1. deforestation
2. Price will rise because of a decrease in supply.
3. Students may suggest that if less forest is cut down, or if more trees are planted, deforestation could be prevented.

Chapter Bonus Test Question

Ask students: Which of the three regional groupings in this chapter—Mexico and the Caribbean, Central America, or South America—do you think has the best prospects for the future? *(Answers will vary. When predicting, students should keep in mind the region's history, governmental organization, economic resources, and social structure.)*

The World in Transition

CHAPTER RESOURCES	Reproducible Resources	Multimedia Resources
Chapter Opener	Chapter Themes: Graphic Organizer 37 Historical Significance Chapter Activity 37	MindJogger Videoquiz
Chapter Enrichment	Vocabulary Activity 37* Time Line Activity 37 Mapping History Activity 37 History Simulation 37 Geography and History Activity 37 Source Reading 37 People in World History Profiles 71, 72 World Art and Music Activity 37 Enrichment Activity 37 Critical Thinking Activity 37 Skill Reinforcement Activity 37 Building Skills in Geography Workbook, Unit 2, Lesson 11 Performance Assessment Activity 37	World History and Art Transparencies 51, 52 Mapping History Overlay Transparency 25 Chapter Transparency 37 Vocabulary PuzzleMaker Software Picture Atlas of the World Turning Points in World History: *Fall of the Berlin Wall* Lessons of War: *The Nature of Violence* Communism and the Cold War: • *A New Soviet Union: Communist Rule Ends* • *Challenge of Reform*
Chapter Review/Reteaching	Reteaching Activity 37 Skill Reinforcement Activity 37 Spanish Chapter Summary 37	Chapter 37 Digest Audiocassette, Activity, Test* Vocabulary PuzzleMaker Software Student Self-Test and Review Software MindJogger Videoquiz
Chapter Evaluation/Testing	Performance Assessment Activity 37 Chapter 37 Test, Forms A and B	Testmaker

* *Also available in Spanish*

0:00 **OUT OF TIME?** Assign the Chapter 37 summary in the Unit 8 Digest on pages 1026–1029, and the Chapter 37 Audiocassettes.

Block Schedule

Block scheduling differs from traditional class scheduling in the amount of time allotted to each period. The extended time frame provided by block scheduling affords you the opportunity to implement a greater number of research-oriented and activity-intense projects to motivate and involve your students. Activities that are particularly suited to use within the block scheduling framework are identified throughout this chapter by the following designation.

KEY TO ABILITY LEVELS

Teaching strategies have been coded for varying learning styles and abilities.

- **L1** **BASIC** activities for all students
- **L2** **AVERAGE** activities for average to above-average students
- **L3** **CHALLENGING** activities for above-average students
- **LEP** **LIMITED ENGLISH PROFICIENCY** activities

A complete, 1-page lesson plan is provided for each section in the *Reproducible Lesson Plans* booklet.

SECTION RESOURCES

Daily Objectives	Reproducible Resources	Multimedia Resources
Section 1 **The End of the Cold War** Identify the developments that changed the relationship of the superpowers by the mid-1990s.	Reproducible Lesson Plan 37-1 Guided Reading Activity 37-1* Section Quiz 37-1*	Section Focus Transparency 37-1 Chapter Transparency 37 World History and Art Transparency 51, *Vietnam Memorial* Vocabulary PuzzleMaker Software Student Self-Test and Review Software Communism and the Cold War: *A New Soviet Union: Communist Rule Ends*
Section 2 **The Crumbling Wall** Describe how Soviet Communist controls came to an end in Eastern Europe.	Reproducible Lesson Plan 37-2 Vocabulary Activity 37* Guided Reading Activity 37-2* People in World History Profile 71 Section Quiz 37-2*	Section Focus Transparency 37-2 Student Self-Test and Review Software Turning Points in World History: *Fall of the Berlin Wall* Communism and the Cold War: *Challenge of Reform*
Section 3 **Toward a European Union** Identify the steps western European nations have taken to unify their governments and economies.	Reproducible Lesson Plan 37-3 Vocabulary Activity 37* Guided Reading Activity 37-3* Section Quiz 37-3*	Section Focus Transparency 37-3 Student Self-Test and Review Software Testmaker Picture Atlas of the World
Section 4 **National and Ethnic Conflicts** Recognize the areas of the world that have been in ethnic discord since the end of the cold war.	Reproducible Lesson Plan 37-4 Vocabulary Activity 37* Guided Reading Activity 37-4* People in World History Profile 72 Section Quiz 37-4*	Section Focus Transparency 37-4 Student Self-Test and Review Software Testmaker Lessons of War: *The Nature of Violence*
Section 5 **Global Interdependence** Explain how recent advances in technology have affected the world's cultures.	Reproducible Lesson Plan 37-5 Guided Reading Activity 37-5* Geography and History Activity 37 History Simulation 37 Reteaching Activity 37 Enrichment Activity 37 Section Quiz 37-5* Performance Assessment Activity 37 Spanish Chapter Summary 37	Section Focus Transparency 37-5 World History and Art Transparency 52, *Sky Above Clouds II* Mapping History Overlay Transparency 25, *World Population Growth* Vocabulary PuzzleMaker Software Student Self-Test and Review Software Testmaker

** Also available in Spanish*

Chapter Activities

Performance Assessment Activity

An Awards Ceremony Have the students take the roles of producers and judges of a competition of persons and developments of the last 20 years. Have students create a name for the awards ceremony and identify the different types of awards that might be given, the nominees for each award (based on accomplishments found in the chapter or researched), and the winners (as determined by greatest impact). As a final product, students should create one of the following: (1) a newspaper article summarizing the awards ceremony, giving the categories, nominees and winners; (2) a videotape of the actual awards program; or (3) a set of radio interviews with the winners.

Possible Rubric Features

Accuracy of content information, decision-making skills, originality, ability to analyze relationships and classify information, oral presentation skills (if applicable), clarity of writing (if applicable)

• *For an additional activity, refer to Activity 37 in the* Performance Assessment Strategies and Activities *booklet.*

Activity

From the Classroom of...

Trent Steele
Kearney High School
Kearney, NE

[Name]'s Excellent Adventure!

Organize the class into five teams and give each team a current physical/political map of Europe with roads and train routes. Each team must plan a trip across modern-day Europe; for example, from London to Athens. Each group must plot the route on a map, following major roadways, trains, and water routes. Then, on poster paper, each group should list all countries, major cities, and major physical geographic features they will encounter on their journey, as well as at least ten major points of interest. Finally, each group should provide an approximate mileage [kilometer] figure for the entire trip. Have each group present the details of their journey to the class. After comparing current maps of Europe with some older ones, have the class draw conclusions about European geography. How has Europe changed? What features have stayed the same?

Multiple Learning Styles

Verbal/Linguistic
Have students choose one of the global concerns covered in this chapter (political, economic, social, or environmental), research the problem, and prepare a report to share with the class.

Logical/Mathematical
Have students who are computer buffs create a "bibliography" of interesting and useful web sites from around the world.

Visual/Spatial
Have students create a series of cartoons focusing on global environmental problems.

Kinesthetic
Ask students to make a time line banner for the bulletin board or wall that covers the years 1980 to 2000. They should fill in events and places from this chapter and leave spaces for filling in current events and predictions.

Additional Resources

TEACHER'S CORNER

NATIONAL GEOGRAPHIC SOCIETY

INDEX TO NATIONAL GEOGRAPHIC MAGAZINE

The following articles may be used for research relating to this chapter:

- "Information Revolution," by Joel L. Swerdlow, October 1995.
- "Crimea: Pearl of a Fallen Empire," by Peter T. White, September 1994.
- "New Eyes on the Universe," by Bradford A. Smith, January 1994.
- "Czechoslovakia: The Velvet Divorce," by Thomas J. Abercrombie, September 1993.
- "Sweden: In Search of a New Model," by Don Belt, August 1993.
- "Europe Faces an Immigrant Tide," by Peter Ross Range, May 1993.
- "A Broken Empire: After the Soviet Union's Collapse," by Mike Edwards, March 1993.
- "Persian Gulf Pollution: Assessing the Damage One Year Later," by Sylvia A. Earle, February 1992.
- "DNA Profiling: The New Science of Identity," by Cassandra Franklin-Barbajosa, May 1992.
- "Georgia Fights for Nationhood," by Angus Roxburgh, May 1992.

NATIONAL GEOGRAPHIC SOCIETY PRODUCTS AVAILABLE FROM GLENCOE

To order the following products for use with this chapter, contact your local Glencoe sales representative or call Glencoe at 1-800-368-7344:

VIDEODISCS
- GTV: The American People
- GTV: A Geographic Perspective on American History

CD-ROM
- Picture Atlas of the World

ADDITIONAL NATIONAL GEOGRAPHIC SOCIETY PRODUCTS

To order the following products for use with this chapter, call National Geographic Society at 1-800-368-2728:

- *The Changing Faces of Communism Series*, "Poland." (Video)
- *Voices of Leningrad* (Video)
- *The Rise and Fall of the Soviet Union* (Video)
- *Russia: After the U.S.S.R.* (Video)
- *Europe: The Road to Unity* (Video)
- *Democratic Governments Series*, "Germany." (Video)
- *Decades of History: The 20th Century–The Middle Years, "The 1960s: Turbulent Times."* (Filmstrip)
- *The Robotic Revolution* (Video)
- *Computer: Tool for the Future* (Video)
- *Lasers* (Video)
- *Medical Technology* (Video)

BIBLIOGRAPHY

Literature of the Period

Shields, Carol. *The Stone Diaries.* New York: Penguin Books, 1993. A novel of a woman's journey through life in the changing twentieth century.

Readings for the Student

Weiner, Jonathan. *The Next One Hundred Years.* New York: Bantam Books, 1990. Prospects for life on this planet in light of the accelerated changes of the twentieth century.

Readings for the Teacher

Walker, Martin. *The Cold War.* New York: Henry Holt, 1993. An overview of the origins and course of the cold war and related foreign policy challenges of the future.

Kennedy, Paul. *Preparing for the Twenty-First Century.* New York: Random House, 1993. An analysis of the world's great powers and the problems they face.

interNET
CONNECTIONS
Bosnia Link Information from the U.S. government and NATO headquarters about the peace-keeping mission in Bosnia
World Wide Web:
http://www.dtic.dia.mil/bosnia/index.html

Introducing Chapter 37

CHAPTER THEMES

Chapter Themes are listed by section on this chapter opening page of the Student Edition. A corresponding theme-based activity is available under "TEACH," and a theme-based question is asked in the Section and Chapter Reviews.

The Storyteller

Historical Setting More than a year had passed since a group of Soviet economists had prepared a 500-day plan for transition to a semifree market that was based on Western economic support and cuts in Soviet defense spending. Opposition to this plan came from the senior ranks of the Soviet military and from directors of the defense industries. Gorbachev also failed to get the Western financial support he counted on, and by August 1991, a coup could not be held off. When Gorbachev spoke over television, the Soviet Union had ended.

Historical Significance

Answers: *Gorbachev's policies of glasnost, perestroika, and military concessions to the West, together with the growing world influence of blocs of nations other than the United States and the Soviet Union, helped bring about the end of the cold war.*

The Soviet Union broke up, and in its place the former Soviet republics formed a commonwealth. Communist systems collapsed in most Eastern European nations. Nationalist sentiments grew, leading to war in the Balkans and ethnic conflicts in CIS republics and elsewhere. The movement for European unity took on increased momentum, resulting in the formation of the European Union.

Nations became more interdependent economically. European and Pacific Rim nations are now economic giants.

Chapter 37

1980–Present

The World in Transition

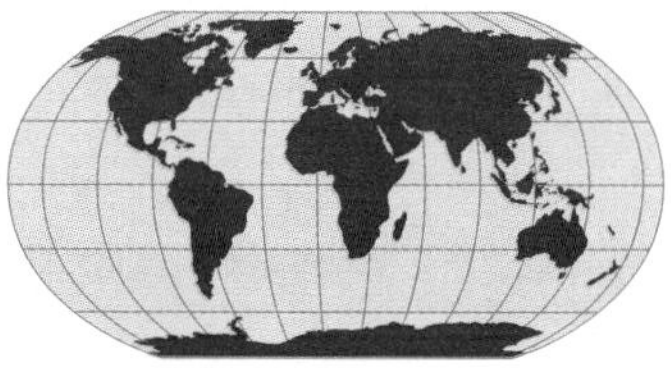

Chapter Themes

- **Change** The end of the cold war and the collapse of communism transform the relationship of the United States and the Soviet Union. *Section 1*
- **Change** The weakening of the Soviet Union and the rise of reform movements bring an end to Soviet control in Eastern Europe. *Section 2*
- **Cooperation** The European Union works to create a united Europe that will be a major economic power. *Section 3*
- **Conflict** National and ethnic conflicts intensify worldwide after the end of the cold war. *Section 4*
- **Cultural Diffusion** New technology and an integrated world communications system speed the transfer of ideas and practices throughout the world. *Section 5*

The Storyteller

On December 25, 1991, Soviet President Mikhail Gorbachev resigned his office in a speech on national television:

"We live in a new world. The Cold War has ended, the arms race has stopped, as has the insane militarization that mutilated our economy, public psyche and morals. The threat of world war has been removed....

We opened ourselves to the rest of the world, abandoned the practices of interfering in others' internal affairs ..., and we were reciprocated with trust, solidarity, and respect.... "

With these words, Gorbachev pronounced the end of the cold war. The road that had led to the end of this war was long and dangerous. The last ten years were no exception. Now, amid the jubilation and hope, the question was raised: "Where do we go from here?"

Historical Significance

What developments brought about the end of the cold war? How has the world changed politically and economically since the beginning of the 1980s?

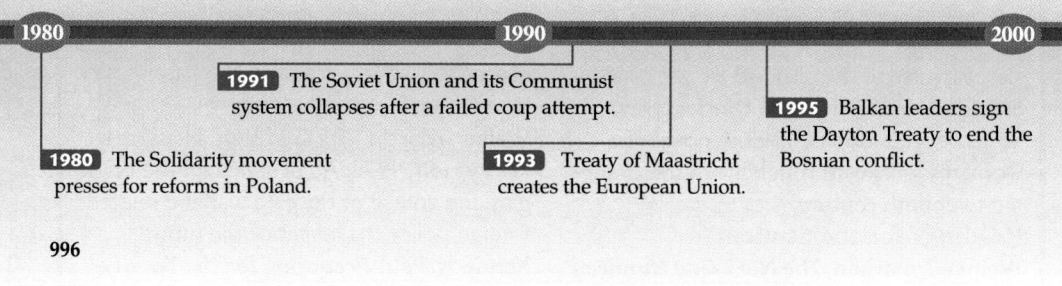

1980 — 1990 — 2000

1980 The Solidarity movement presses for reforms in Poland.

1991 The Soviet Union and its Communist system collapses after a failed coup attempt.

1993 Treaty of Maastricht creates the European Union.

1995 Balkan leaders sign the Dayton Treaty to end the Bosnian conflict.

GEOGRAPHY CONNECTION

Location Display a world map. Before studying each section of the chapter, ask students to find the region covered on the map. Have students put markers on the map for the areas of ongoing conflict as they study them. How does the location of European countries present a special problem not encountered by the United States? *(They are so close together that they are in the midst of each other's conflicts; uprisings can easily spread beyond national boundaries. The United States, by contrast, is physically removed.)*

Visualizing History New technology has helped advance space exploration. The earth's people now can view the earth as a single unit with a shared environment.

Your History Journal

Choose a region of the world that is having difficulty keeping peace. Imagine that you are part of a delegation of diplomats from the United States who have been sent to the region to talk with leaders. Write your opening statement.

Introducing Chapter 37

Visualizing History

Space has become a laboratory in which scientists can assess what is happening to our planet. Spacecraft can orbit the earth and photograph areas of the planet to monitor changes. Scientists hope to be able to "watch the planet breathe" and study global change with the aim of preventing more damage to the earth.

Performance Assessment

Refer to the activity on page 996C of the Planning Guide.

For an additional activity, refer to Activity 37 in the *Performance Assessment Strategies and Activities* booklet.

Using Your History Journal

Remind students to think first about how the people native to the region they are visiting differ from them culturally. Remind them of the need to be sensitive to and respect their values and needs.

GLENCOE TECHNOLOGY

VIDEODISC

Use MindJogger to preview chapter content.

MindJogger Videoquiz

Chapter 37
Disc 5 Side B

Also available in VHS.

EXTRA CREDIT PROJECT

Global Issues Daily newspapers, television broadcasts, and newsmagazines cover and update most of the topics in this chapter. Have students gather up-to-the-minute information on the issues, people, and places they study and compile articles to put into a "Global Issues" newspaper. They can work in groups or individually; one or two students might volunteer to be the editors and oversee the articles coming in. By the end of the chapter, they should have current information on most of the topics to print in the newspaper for class distribution.

SECTION THEME

▶ **Change** The end of the cold war and the collapse of communism transform the relationship of the United States and the Soviet Union.

Find Out

Answer: *Domestic problems and the growing influence of other blocs of nations changed the relationship of the superpowers.*

FOCUS

Section Objective

Identify the developments that changed the relationship of the superpowers by the mid-1990s.

BELLRINGER
Motivational Activity

Before taking roll at the beginning of the class period, project Section Focus Transparency 37-1 and have students answer the activity questions. Discuss students' responses.

This activity is also available as a blackline master.

Vocabulary Pre-check

Use the Vocabulary PuzzleMaker to create a puzzle that reinforces the vocabulary terms in this section. **L1**

1980 1990 2000

1980 Ronald Reagan is elected President of the United States.

1985 Mikhail Gorbachev becomes leader of the Soviet Union.

1991 Former Soviet republics form the CIS.

1995 Russian and American soldiers take part in NATO-led Bosnian peacekeeping mission.

Section 1

The End of the Cold War

Setting the Scene

▶ **Terms to Define**
trade deficit, budget deficit, glasnost, perestroika, privatization

▶ **People to Meet**
Ronald Reagan, George Bush, Bill Clinton, Mikhail Gorbachev, Boris Yeltsin

▶ **Places to Locate**
Moscow, Latvia, Lithuania, Estonia, Russia, Ukraine, Belarus, Kazakstan, Georgia, Armenia, Azerbaijan, Uzbekistan, Tajikistan, Turkmenistan

Find Out What developments changed the relationship of the superpowers by the mid-1990s?

The Storyteller

As the U.S. government's deficit soared out of control, the budget became the focus of debate. Aaron Wildavsky explained what may be the heart of the problem: "There are times when an agency wishes to cut its budget.... If the agency [has] effective clientele groups (special interests), however, it may not only fail in this purpose but may actually see the appropriation increased as this threat mobilizes the affected interests."

—from "Political Implications of Budgetary Reform," Aaron Wildavsky in *Classic Readings in American Politics*, 1986

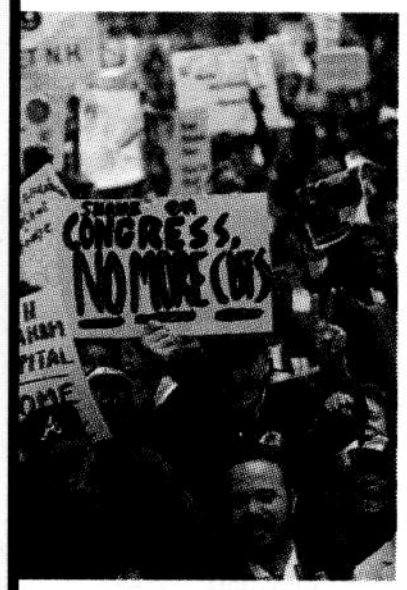

U.S. group protesting budget cuts

In the early 1980s, cold war tensions between the United States and the Soviet Union increased dramatically. However, the world had changed since the 1950s when the superpowers competed alone in the arena of world affairs. Now other blocs of nations, with their own separate concerns, were influencing global developments. In addition, the two superpowers faced growing political and economic problems at home. Together, domestic and international changes would lead to the end of the cold war.

The United States

In the early 1980s, the United States faced a trade deficit, or an economic imbalance that occurs when a country imports more than it exports. As western Europe, Japan, and other countries developed more powerful economies, their industries competed with American industries in sales to American consumers. In the automobile market, for example, rising gasoline prices caused Americans to choose more fuel-efficient cars from Japan, instead of larger American models. This trend contributed strongly to the United States trade deficit and continued into the early 1990s. By 1995, however, improved American-made cars and the removal of some of Japan's import restrictions helped slow the growth of the American trade deficit.

The Reagan-Bush Era

Meanwhile, the United States government found it difficult to live within its means. In 1980 **Ronald Reagan** was elected President in a campaign in which he promised to reduce the budget deficit, the condition in which the government spends more money than it earns in revenues, thus going into debt. As President, Reagan cut

SECTION RESOURCES

Reproducible Masters
- Reproducible Lesson Plan 37-1
- Guided Reading Activity 37-1
- Section Quiz 37-1

Transparencies
- Section Focus Transparency 37-1
- Chapter Transparency 37
- World History and Art Transparency 51, *Vietnam Memorial*

Multimedia
- Vocabulary PuzzleMaker Software
- Student Self-Test and Review Software
- Testmaker
- Communism and the Cold War: *A New Soviet Union: Communist Rule Ends*

998 Chapter 37 *The World in Transition*

government spending on social programs and lowered taxes to stimulate economic growth. During the course of his two terms in office, inflation began to slow and the economy began to improve. However, increased military spending by Reagan and his successor as President, **George Bush**, pushed the budget deficit to new heights. The view of some of Reagan's advisers was that high military spending would force the Soviet Union to spend more on its military than it could afford.

The Clinton Years

By 1992, the United States economy was in a deep recession. Consumer confidence was low, and voter dissatisfaction was high. Running against President Bush, the Democratic presidential candidate, Governor **Bill Clinton** of Arkansas, called for change and a renewed attention to domestic needs. An independent candidate, Ross Perot, a Texas businessman, called for deep cuts in spending to reduce the budget deficit. In a three-way election, Clinton was elected President with 43 percent of the popular vote.

In the first two years of his presidency, Clinton did not reduce the budget deficit as much as many people wanted him to do. The President was concerned that a deep and rapid cut would hurt the poor and other disadvantaged groups. Although the American economy grew and unemployment was relatively low, popular pressure for greater cuts in spending continued to rise. In 1994 American voters elected, for the first time in forty years, a Republican majority in both the Senate and the House of Representatives. The new Congress pushed for deeper cuts in government spending and vowed to work for a balanced budget by the year 2002. By 1996, the federal government was paying nearly $600 million per day as interest on its debt, and the amount continued to grow.

American-Soviet Relations

During the early 1980s, United States-Soviet relations were embittered by a Soviet military buildup and the Soviet army's occupation of Afghanistan. Ronald Reagan took a hard-line anti-Communist stand, calling the Soviet Union an "evil empire," and greatly increased American military spending. By the mid-1980s, however, the Soviet Union's new leader **Mikhail Gorbachev** indicated a willingness to make weapons cuts and to reform the Soviet system. Reagan responded positively and developed a good working relationship with Gorbachev.

President George Bush continued warm relations with Gorbachev. As the Soviet Union collapsed, Bush shifted American support from Gorbachev to the new democratic Russian leader **Boris Yeltsin**. Later, President Clinton also backed economic reform and democratic change in Russia and the other former Soviet republics.

AROUND THE WORLD

Castro Allows Flood of Refugees

Havana, August, 1994
Cuban leader Fidel Castro suddenly allowed a wave of refugees to head for the United States. Castro hoped that the flood of refugees would force President Bill Clinton to reconsider lifting the United States trade embargo against Cuba. President Clinton, however, reacted by refusing to accept refugees, and by calling for a United Nations condemnation of Cuban human rights abuses. After negotiations, Fidel Castro agreed to limit the exodus, and the United States agreed to accept 20,000 Cuban immigrants each year.

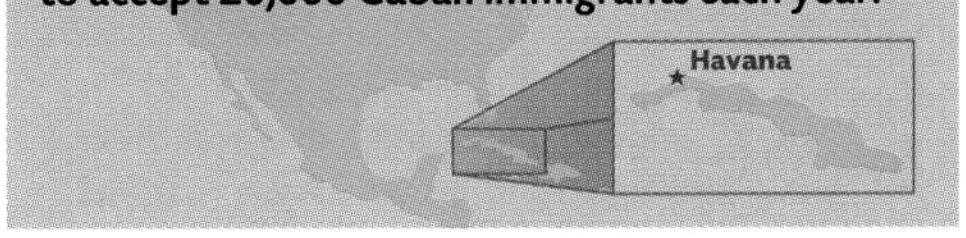

Gorbachev's USSR

Until Mikhail Gorbachev became the Soviet leader in 1985, Soviet rulers had followed hard-line Communist policies, refusing to publicly acknowledge the Soviet Union's problems. Gorbachev, by contrast, realized that the only way to transform the inefficient, sluggish economy and to halt the decay of Soviet society was to expose the hidden problems and to discuss them freely. "I do not pretend to know the absolute truth," he said. "We have to search for truth together."

Gorbachev's Domestic Reforms

Gorbachev was willing to take risks and make drastic changes. Under his policy of glasnost, meaning "openness," Gorbachev permitted new freedom of expression for Soviet citizens and eased harsh measures against opponents of the Soviet system.

There were other changes as well. Departing from rigid state controls, Gorbachev pushed for a rebuilding of the Soviet economy, a policy the Soviets called perestroika (PEHR•uh•STROY •kuh), or "restructuring." Gorbachev gradually encouraged limited moves toward private

TEACH

Guided Practice

THEME **Change**

Put the heads *U.S.* and *USSR* on the chalkboard and ask students to list the economic problems these countries faced in the 1980s and the changes leaders sought. **L1 LEP**

Politics Ask students what caused Gorbachev to return to tightening controls. *(criticism from conservatives, fear of breakup of Soviet Union)* **L2**

Critical Thinking With the freedom to leave the Soviet Union, Soviet Jews poured into Israel in the early 1990s. Ask students to suggest what problems Israel faced as a result of this influx. *(shortage of jobs, newcomers don't understand the language or such basic things as the banking system; inadequate housing)* **L3**

ABCNEWS INTERACTIVE™

VIDEODISC
Communism and the Cold War

Side One, Chapter 21
Frames 38662–44504
Title: *A New Soviet Union: Communist Rule Ends*
Subject: Chronicles the rise of Gorbachev and the end of the Soviet Union
Ask: What changes were made by Gorbachev's reforms? *(The people were allowed to vote, political prisoners were set free, and the ruling party was no longer required to be Communist.)*

COOPERATIVE LEARNING ACTIVITY

Geography: Place Organize the class into small groups. Assign each group one of the republics of the Soviet Union to research and prepare an oral report. Students should find out about the geographic features, the people, the resources, the cities, and daily life. Suggest that each group divide the tasks and prepare information, including a map or copies of photographs, about one aspect of their republic. When the research is complete, ask each group to give a class presentation on its assigned republic. **L2**

Chapter 37 *The World in Transition* **999**

Chapter 37 Section 1

Chapter Transparency 37

World History and Art Transparency 51, *Vietnam Memorial*

Independent Practice

Guided Reading Activity 37-1 **L1**

Visualizing History By speaking directly with citizens and listening to their complaints and hopes, Gorbachev sought to soften the government's image and encourage greater citizen participation.

Answer to Caption: *He wanted to publicly acknowledge the nation's problems and rebuild the Soviet economy, moving toward greater reliance on free enterprise.*

The Arts Have students prepare an oral or written report on the Bolshoi opera and ballet companies, the State Museums of the Moscow Kremlin, or another artistic institution of the region. **L2**

Critical Thinking Gorbachev has written that the end of the cold war "… has also brought to the fore tensions that were latent, frozen as it were, during the confrontation between global alliances. Many of these tensions have exploded into bloody conflicts." Have students comment on this statement in view of material in this section. **L3**

Visualizing History **Soviet leader Mikhail Gorbachev (right) and his wife Raisa (center) greet Soviet citizens at a public meeting.** *What changes did Gorbachev want to make in 1985?*

enterprise and began to dismantle the national bureaucracy that controlled industrial production, allowing more decisions to be made at the local level.

Gorbachev's Foreign Policy

Facing the enormous American military buildup under President Reagan, Gorbachev needed to negotiate new arms-reduction agreements with the United States. Since Soviet economic progress depended on military cutbacks, Gorbachev made large concessions to settle long-stalled treaty negotiations. His offers to cancel nuclear tests and to withdraw Soviet missiles from Eastern Europe were so sweeping that they took Western leaders by surprise. To further ease global tensions, Gorbachev withdrew Soviet troops from Afghanistan.

Gorbachev also encouraged Eastern European leaders to carry out reforms. His policies of glasnost and perestroika inspired discontented majorities in these repressed countries. Scattered demands for democracy grew into a wave of anti-Communist protest that eventually brought down the Iron Curtain.

New Challenges

Gorbachev's fresh outlook and friendly personality made him a popular figure in the Western countries he visited. At home, however, Gorbachev was increasingly criticized. The promised perestroika came slowly. The enormous Soviet bureaucracy and the military resisted change, fearing the loss of jobs and the weakening of Soviet might. Gorbachev had to move carefully to avoid backlash from hard-line Communists. He often zigzagged between reformist and hard-line positions, creating uncertainty throughout government and business. Economic problems continued, and worsened, while reforms were put in place. People became impatient, and Gorbachev's popularity declined.

Rise of Yeltsin

Another problem facing Gorbachev was one of his own making. Before glasnost, he had no political rivals, because dissent was not allowed. By 1990, however, the slow results of perestroika brought forward new challengers to Gorbachev's leadership. Ironically, Gorbachev's most visible rival was a former ally, **Boris Yeltsin**. Yeltsin felt perestroika was moving too slowly. His vocal criticism of Gorbachev eventually earned him a severe reprimand and dismissal from party positions. Yeltsin took his case to the people, winning election to the presidency of the Russian Republic, the largest of the Soviet republics. As an elected leader, Yeltsin had a stronger base of support than did Gorbachev, and he enjoyed greater popularity.

The Soviet Breakup

While Gorbachev faced mounting opposition from political rivals, nationalist and ethnic unrest began to sweep the Soviet Union. As its name reflected, the Union of Soviet Socialist Republics (USSR) was a union of 15 separate republics, or states. The largest was Russia, which included the Soviet capital, **Moscow**. The non-Russian republics resented the dominance of the Russians over their affairs. A strong Soviet secret police and army had long kept opposition and nationalist groups under control. But in the relaxed atmosphere of glasnost, old hatreds resurfaced. Throughout the republics there were strong demands for self-rule, if not outright secession. In 1990 **Latvia**, **Lithuania**, and **Estonia** became the first republics to declare their independence from the Soviet Union.

A Dangerous Course

To appease the conservatives who feared a breakup of the Soviet Union, Gorbachev began a rollback of glasnost in the early 1990s and adopted new hard-line positions. Among them were the tightening of controls on the Soviet press to curb dissent and the restoration of powers to the secret

you don't say...

Babushka, the name for a woman's head scarf, comes from the Russian term for "grandmother."

MEETING SPECIAL NEEDS ACTIVITY

Physical Disability Students with a hearing loss are usually stronger visual learners. To help them study this section, encourage them to write down the main ideas under each of the section headings and to copy any charts or words put on the chalkboard. Have students who give oral reports provide copies for these students so they can highlight important facts and learn visually. **L1**

1000 Chapter 37 *The World in Transition*

police. Some of Gorbachev's reform-minded political aides resigned in protest, and Soviet citizens, led by Yeltsin, called for Gorbachev to step down.

The Coup Attempt

In August 1991 events in the Soviet Union finally reached a climax. Hard-liners in the military and secret police staged a coup to remove Gorbachev from power and to restore the old order. In three tense days the coup un-raveled. Early support for the coup evaporated in the face of the heroic leadership of Boris Yeltsin in Moscow. Resistance spread to other parts of the country. Military units refused to carry out the orders of the coup leaders.

The coup turned out to be the turning point for the Soviet Union. Gorbachev was seen as unable to solve the country's problems and unable to shake off his Communist roots. Yeltsin became the real leader. Popular anger at the Communist party and the secret police swept the land, and the party dissolved. Statues of party leaders were torn down; cities chose to return to their pre-1917 names.

Russia and the Independent Republics

Map Study By December 1991 all the republics had declared their independence from the Soviet Union. Russia invaded Chechnya in December 1994.
Place What independent republic has the best access to warm water ports?

The New Commonwealth

By the end of September all the Soviet republics had announced their independence from the Soviet Union. Gorbachev failed to win their support for a Union Treaty guaranteeing the republics greater self-rule within the old Soviet framework. Yeltsin, however, chose an alternative plan. In December 1991, the three Slavic republics—**Russia**, **Ukraine**, and **Belarus**—announced the formation of the Commonwealth of Independent States (CIS), a loose association of republics to take the place of the Soviet Union. Other republics quickly joined.

Military Issues

Of immediate concern following the collapse of the Soviet Union was the security of its nuclear arsenal. Russian President Boris Yeltsin moved quickly to allay Western fears. In agreements with Ukraine, Belarus, and **Kazakstan**, the republics where Soviet nuclear weapons had been based, nuclear weapons were shifted to the command of

Chapter 37 Section 1

Map Study

Answer
Russia

Map Skills Practice

Reading a Map **What bodies of water does Russia border?** *(Baltic Sea, Barents Sea, Black Sea, Caspian Sea, Sea of Japan, Sea of Okhotsk, Bering Sea, Arctic Ocean)*

ASSESS

Check for Understanding

Assign Section 1 Review as homework or as an in-class activity.

Use Student Self-Test and Review Software to review Section 1.

Who?What?Where?When?

Soviet Exodus With glasnost came the freedom for Soviet Jews to emigrate. Half a million Jews moved to Israel between 1989 and 1992.

Linking Past and Present

Alexander Pushkin, perhaps Russia's greatest poet, was born in 1799 and lived only 37 years, but he is an enduring part of Russian culture. He was a champion of liberty and wrote drama and some prose as well as poetry. His masterpiece, *Eugene Onegin*, inspired an opera by Tchaikovsky and was translated into English by Vladimir Nabokov. Russian poet Yevgeny Yevtushenko, a modern-day champion of freedom, says, "Pushkin stands out as that rare Russian, an independent man."

MAKING CONNECTIONS ACTIVITY

Environment One of the largest lakes in the world, the Aral Sea, is located in the republics of Uzbekistan and Kazakstan and is drying up. Many have recognized this as a major environmental tragedy. The Aral Sea has already lost a volume of water equal to one and a half times that of Lake Erie and continues to shrink. Have students research this topic and prepare a written report on the problem and the environmental impact it is having on the inhabitants of the area. **L2**

TEACH

Explain that the new freedom of expression allowed under Gorbachev opened a floodgate after years of repression. Ask students to try to imagine the courage it took, after such ingrained habits of watching one's words, to openly confront a Russian colonel as the man in this photograph is doing. **What other forms of protest could people make under glasnost?** *(open display of banners of protest, telegrams of criticism to politicians, publicly airing grievances through demonstrations, publishing books critical of the government, even jokes about the system)*

Who?What?Where?When?

Mikhail Gorbachev, who is now chairman of the International Institute for Social, Economic, and Political Studies in Moscow, has written a book called *The Search for a New Beginning: Developing a New Civilization*. The views expressed in the book reflect a man who has taken a careful look at the past, has learned from it, and has changed. About the early years of glasnost and perestroika, he says: "... we formulated the principle 'Start perestroika with yourself.' In fact, however, we rushed to change society while leaving the change of ourselves for later ... the root cause of many of our ... failures."

NATIONAL GEOGRAPHIC PICTURING HISTORY

Steve Raym

Seeing Red

Traitor! A flag-waving Russian colonel shouts at a demonstrator who wants to end the 70-year-long rule of communism in the Soviet Union. Opposing visions divided the Russian people as they faced their uncertain future in the spring of 1990. Would their children live in the Union of Soviet Socialist Republics where they had grown up? Would communism prevail, after all the sacrifices made in the name of Lenin or Stalin? Would the state plan a national economy, or would the forces of the market prevail? Who would win and who would lose?

Communism first began to crumble in the satellit nations of Eastern Europe. As early as 1956 th Hungarians revolted, and in 1968 the Czechs rebelled In these early years of the cold war the Communis regime was strong enough to withstand those assaults In 1989 Germany's Berlin Wall crumbled. In 1990 th Soviet Union itself began to fall apart, first in th Baltic States and then throughout the country as th various republics proclaimed their independence. N wonder anger and fear line the faces of the two me pictured above, as they confront the end of the worl they know.

1002 Chapter 37 *The World in Transition*

the Russians, although a nuclear attack could be launched only with the approval of all four republic presidents. In the following year, Ukraine signed the Nuclear Nonproliferation Treaty, designed to stop the spread of nuclear weapons, and declared its intention to become a nuclear-free zone by dismantling its arsenal of nuclear warheads.

A further nuclear arms agreement between Russia and the United States was reached. The two nations agreed on a mutual reduction in the number of nuclear weapons that each had.

After the fall of the Soviet Union, the United States and western Europe started to reconsider the future of NATO and the number of American troops stationed in Europe. The role of NATO underwent a gradual change from a military alliance against possible Communist attack to an alliance of collective security that aimed to include much of Europe. In 1995 Russia announced its intention of joining NATO's Partnership for Peace, a program that gave former Soviet-bloc countries a limited role in NATO without granting them full membership. This plan was implemented in 1995 and 1996 by the deployment of NATO-led forces, to keep the peace in the war-torn Balkan Peninsula.

Economic and Social Changes

Yeltsin and other Commonwealth leaders also introduced economic reforms to speed the transition from communism to free enterprise. The removal of price controls, the closing of inefficient factories, and the movement toward privatization, or the setting up of privately owned businesses, increased both prices and unemployment in the short term. By the mid-1990s, however, inflation seemed to be slowing down, and new businesses and a new middle class were growing in the former Soviet republics. Yet the reforms were bypassing large numbers of people. Workers, the aged, and the poor faced continuing economic hardships. Street violence, organized crime, and ethnic unrest increased public fears about the collapse of law and order. Pollution caused by Soviet-era industrialization presented a major health risk.

Taking advantage of widespread dissatisfaction, nationalists and Communists in Russia forced Yeltsin to slow the pace of his reforms. In 1993 Yeltsin succeeded in blocking a Communist attempt to seize control of the government. However, Russia faced continued political instability as Yeltsin and his Communist-nationalist foes in the Russian parliament competed for control of the country. Many of the other CIS countries—for example, Ukraine, **Georgia**, **Armenia**, **Azerbaijan**, **Uzbekistan**, **Tajikistan**, and **Turkmenistan**—also pushed economic reforms while facing political and social unrest among their populations.

Visualizing History **Soviet President Boris Yeltsin tried to promote free enterprise reforms but faced powerful opposition.** *What two groups opposed Yeltsin's reforms?*

SECTION 1 REVIEW

Recall

1. **Define** trade deficit, budget deficit, glasnost, perestroika, privatization.
2. **Identify** Ronald Reagan, George Bush, Bill Clinton, Mikhail Gorbachev, Boris Yeltsin.
3. **Explain** the issues facing many of the republics of the CIS by the mid-1990s.

Critical Thinking

4. **Applying Information** Why do you think the transition from communism to free enterprise has been difficult in the former Soviet republics?

Understanding Themes

5. **Change** How did Gorbachev's policy of glasnost contribute to ethnic unrest in the former Soviet republics and open the way for independence movements there?

Chapter 37 Section 1

Visualizing History Yeltsin had the support of both urban and rural sectors in the 1990 elections. In the 1991 coup, he showed the courage and populist instincts that made them rally behind him.

Answer to Caption:
nationalists and Communists

Evaluate

Section Quiz 37-1

Use the Testmaker to create a customized quiz for Section 1.

Reteach

Lead the class in discussing the main points covered in this section about the United States, the Soviet breakup, and the new Commonwealth. Ask volunteers to name the key people involved and write them on the chalkboard.

Enrich

Have students find music, art, or literature from Eastern European artists of the late twentieth century and compile a resource list for the class.

CLOSE

Ask students to consider what problems they think the end of the cold war solved and what new problems it may have created.

SECTION 1 REVIEW ANSWERS

1. All vocabulary words are defined in the Glossary.
2. Ronald Reagan, 998; George Bush, 999; Bill Clinton, 999; Mikhail Gorbachev, 999; Boris Yeltsin, 999
3. economic reforms not reaching enough people, crime and ethnic unrest, and pollution creating health risks
4. Answers will vary. Possible answer: Not all people favor the change and some have wanted to block the transition.
5. CHANGE It allowed people to express discontent and admit problems; rigid controls were dropped and old resentments resurfaced.

Chapter 37 Section 2

SECTION THEME

▶ **Change** The weakening of the Soviet Union and the rise of reform movements bring an end to Soviet control in Eastern Europe.

Find Out

Answer: *When the Soviet Union began to change under Gorbachev and signaled that it would not object to changes in Eastern Europe, the Communist systems there collapsed.*

FOCUS

Section Objective

Describe how Soviet Communist controls came to an end in Eastern Europe.

BELLRINGER Motivational Activity

Before taking roll at the beginning of the class period, project Section Focus Transparency 37-2 and have students answer the activity questions. Discuss students' responses.

This activity is also available as a blackline master.

Vocabulary Pre-check

Use Vocabulary Activity 37 to introduce vocabulary terms. **L1 LEP**

1980 — 1990 — 2000

1983 Polish labor leader Lech Walesa is awarded the Nobel Peace Prize.

1989 Uprisings topple Communist governments in Eastern Europe.

1993 Czechoslovakia divides into the Czech Republic and the Republic of Slovakia.

Section 2

The Crumbling Wall

Setting the Scene

▶ **Terms to Define**
autonomy

▶ **People to Meet**
Pope John Paul II, Lech Walesa, Nicolae Ceaușescu, Helmut Kohl, Václav Havel, Aleksander Kwasniewski

▶ **Places to Locate**
Poland, Gdansk, East Germany, Hungary, Romania, Bulgaria, Berlin, the Czech Republic, Slovakia, Albania, Bosnia-Herzegovina, Croatia, Macedonia, Slovenia, Serbia, Montenegro, Dayton

Find Out How did Soviet Communist controls come to an end in Eastern Europe?

The Storyteller

The wall was coming down. West Berliners chipped away at it with hammers and chisels, while impatient East Berliners used heavy equipment. Finally a gap opened and a crowd of people surged through. Young people who had never visited the West sampled the goods of a market economy. Older people looked for friends whom they had not seen for nearly three decades. "It's been so long, it's a wonder we recognized each other!" With joyful exclamations, two old friends met by the ruins of the wall that had separated them as teenagers.

—adapted from "Berlin's Ode to Joy," Prit J. Vesilind in *National Geographic*, April 1990

Fall of the Berlin Wall

During the 1980s, the Communist nations of Eastern Europe, like the Soviet Union, faced massive problems. Their government-controlled economies failed to produce high-quality consumer goods and had fallen far behind the economies of the West. Reform had to be tried, but the Communist system was too flawed. When the Soviet Union began to change and signaled that it would not object to changes in Eastern Europe, the Communist systems collapsed.

The Rise of Solidarity

The final round of unrest in Eastern Europe began in the 1970s and continued into the 1980s. In **Poland**, the antigovernment movement had received a strong boost in 1978, when the Roman Catholic Church selected a Polish church leader, Karol Wojtyla (voy•TEE•wah), as its pope. The elevation of **Pope John Paul II**, a staunch anti-Communist, inspired confidence among the largely Catholic Poles and enabled them to take further steps toward liberation from Communist control.

In 1980 Polish workers in the Baltic port of Gdansk organized a trade union called Solidarity. **Lech Walesa** (lehk vah•LEHN•suh), an electrical worker at the Lenin Shipyard in **Gdansk**, was a founder and leader of Solidarity.

Solidarity backed up its demands for better living and working conditions with strikes, including one led by Walesa at the Gdansk shipyards. In a remarkable victory, the strikers forced the Polish government to recognize Solidarity in October 1980. Until this time, self-governing trade unions independent of Communist control had not been allowed to exist in Communist countries.

Under Walesa's leadership, Solidarity demanded free elections and a voice for workers in forming government policy. The Polish government responded by demanding that strikes and other "antistate" activities be ended. Under pressure

SECTION RESOURCES

Reproducible Masters
- Reproducible Lesson Plan 37-2
- Vocabulary Activity 37
- Guided Reading Activity 37-2
- People in World History Profile 71
- Section Quiz 37-2

Transparencies
- Section Focus Transparency 37-2

Multimedia
- Student Self-Test and Review Software
- Testmaker
- Turning Points in World History: *Fall of the Berlin Wall*
- Communism and the Cold War: *Challenge of Reform*

Visualizing History **Lech Walesa began his career as an electrician and eventually became Poland's first democratically elected president of the post-Communist era.** *What role did Walesa have in Polish affairs during the early 1980s?*

from the Soviet Union, Polish authorities outlawed the union 16 months later and jailed many of its leaders. Despite this, Walesa and others continued their activities underground.

Although Solidarity's activities were not immediately successful, the courage of its members inspired people in other Eastern European countries. Walesa became a symbol of freedom and an international hero. He was awarded the Nobel Peace Prize in 1983. By the end of the decade, the Soviet Union itself was changing under Gorbachev, and unrest had spread across Eastern Europe.

A Year of Miracles

By the late 1980s, reduced production, decreases in labor productivity, high inflation, and trade deficits had virtually paralyzed the economies of Eastern Europe. This meant fewer goods at ever-increasing prices. The highly centralized economies, out of touch with consumer needs, caused widespread food shortages. Dissent against communism reached its peak in 1989.

Soviet Policies

As democratic movements gathered force across Eastern Europe during the late 1980s, many people wondered: Would Mikhail Gorbachev exercise the terms of the Brezhnev Doctrine and put down rebellions? In a speech in January 1989, Gorbachev announced that he had ordered a cutback of 500,000 troops in the Soviet army—about half of that number to come from troops stationed in Eastern Europe. The troops had been put there to enforce the Warsaw Pact and keep the Soviet satellites in line.

In March he pledged not to interfere with democratic reforms in Hungary. Referring to the 1956 and 1968 invasions of Hungary and Czechoslovakia, Gorbachev declared that "all possible safeguards should be provided so that no external force can interfere in the domestic affairs of socialist countries."

Gorbachev decided that most Eastern-bloc governments—which lacked popular support—would continue to provoke opposition. The Soviet Union would be forced to intervene militarily at great cost. Soviet interests would be better served if he simply let these governments fall. Gorbachev would then establish friendly relations with new governments.

Collapse of Communism

In 1989 Communist governments in Eastern Europe crumbled under the weight of staggering problems. All the satellite countries had ruined economies. Many had terrible environmental damage that had been ignored in the push to industrialize. Other countries, such as Yugoslavia, were being shaken by internal ethnic conflicts.

As economic and political instability increased, Communist regimes either resigned or were overturned in **East Germany**, Czechoslovakia, **Hungary**, Poland, **Romania**, and **Bulgaria**. Throughout this remarkable year of 1989, Gorbachev astounded the world by not only refusing to intervene in democratic uprisings, but actually encouraging reform in the region.

In mid-1989 Hungary, which had been quietly moving toward democratic reform for more than a decade, opened its sealed borders. A flood of East German refugees poured through this new "hole" in the Iron Curtain, seeking sanctuary in the West. The exodus called attention to the failed government of East Germany's aging leader, Erich Honecker.

The Wall's Fall

Amid mass demonstrations and calls for democratic reform, Honecker's government was toppled in October and replaced by a more moderate Communist administration. The move did not satisfy the reform movement but made its supporters bolder and more demanding. The next month, in an attempt to defuse the situation, the government lifted all travel restrictions between East and West. It

Chapter 37 Section 2

TEACH

Guided Practice

THEME **Change**

Write *A Year of Miracles* on the chalkboard and ask students to list the events and changes from this section that made 1989 a year of "miracles." **L1 LEP**

Visualizing History Walesa was jailed for his involvement with Solidarity, and after his release suffered harassment from the government. Influenced by its economic problems, however, in 1988 the government agreed to recognize Solidarity and to allow the union to have seats in the legislature.

Answer to Caption: *He led the drive for free elections and became a symbol of freedom.*

ABCNEWS INTERACTIVE™

VIDEODISC
Communism and the Cold War

Side Two, Chapter 17
Frames 38033–42654
Title: *Challenge of Reform*
Subject: Challenges facing Eastern European countries
Ask: What happened as Poland tried to establish a free market system? *(Prices and unemployment rose.)*

COOPERATIVE LEARNING ACTIVITY

Television Broadcast Organize the class into news teams and assign one team to cover West Germany, one to cover East Germany, and one to represent the team in the news studio in the United States. Each team will need to research the November 1989 reuniting of Berlin as the wall came down. They are to conduct interviews to get firsthand reactions and accounts of united families and friends. (Teams should decide what parts each member will play.) The studio team should research details about the people in the West and the East and alert news teams about the questions they might ask when they air the show. If possible, have a video camera available to tape the broadcast. **L2**

Chapter 37
Section 2

Government Guide students in naming the different countries mentioned in this section whose Communist regimes ended. *(Poland, East Germany, Hungary, Romania, Bulgaria, Czechoslovakia, Albania, Yugoslavia)* Have students create a chart on the chalkboard that lists the names of the rulers involved in each country and that tells whether the change in each country was peaceful or violent. **L2 LEP**

Critical Thinking Ask students to discuss the issues of freedom and control. Point out how difficult it has been for the newly freed countries to build democracies and stability without new outbreaks of fighting and chaos. Ask students to give examples from this section of the results of too much control and of the results of sudden freedom. **L3**

ABCNEWS INTERACTIVE™

VIDEODISC
Turning Points in World History

Side Two
Chapter 9

Title: *Fall of the Berlin Wall*
Subject: The building of the Berlin Wall, its symbolic and literal 28-year division between East and West Germany, the fall of the wall as a symbol of the failure of communism
Ask: What was desirable about the West for East Germany's people? *("Good wages, affordable homes, and most of all freedom.")* What did the fall of the wall represent to Germany? *(that East and West Germany were unified once again)*

hoped the refugees would remain in East Germany under a reformed but still Communist government.

On the evening of November 9, 1989, the famous Brandenburg Gate at the **Berlin** Wall was opened. All through the night East Germans and West Germans, hearing the wall had been opened, rushed there to see for themselves, overwhelming the guards and passing through the gate in both directions. Others swarmed over the wall, dancing and singing atop it.

In the following days, people on both sides of the wall attacked it with picks and shovels, opening huge holes—even selling chunks as souvenirs. More gates were opened, and the flow of people increased. Families and friends who had not seen each other in decades were reunited. The government, helpless before this popular uprising, ordered the rest of the wall torn down.

Violence in Romania

The overthrow of Communist governments in Eastern Europe was, for the most part, nonviolent. The one grim chapter in the story took place in Romania, where dictator **Nicolae Ceauşescu** (NEE•koh•lay chow•SHEHS•koo) had ruled for 24 years. Ceauşescu's methods had become increasingly brutal over the years, and his reaction to freedom protests in his country was violent. Hundreds of people were killed before the Romanians revolted and ousted the dictator in December 1989. Ceauşescu and his wife, Elena, were tried and shot.

Throughout Europe and the West, crowds celebrated the fall of Ceauşescu. They were also celebrating the end of Soviet domination in Eastern Europe and, in a larger sense, the end of the cold war.

New Leaders in a New Age

Following the downfall of Communist governments, reformers looked for new leaders to bring democracy and stability to their countries. They wanted leaders who had not been tainted by collaboration or membership in the Communist

Images of the Times

A New Era

A wave of unrest swept Eastern Europe in the late 1980s, leading to the fall of hard-line Communist governments. By the mid-1990s, some countries in the region had become sound democracies; others, plagued by economic uncertainties, turned to nationalist or former Communist leaders.

Solidarity led the movement for democracy in Poland. The labor union began in the shipyards of the Baltic port of Gdansk and soon spread to other parts of the country.

Images of the Times **A New Era**
With the fall of communism and rise of nationalism came ethnic conflicts that have resulted in a major international problem: refugees. The UN founded an agency known as the United Nations High Commission for Refugees (UNHCR) after World War II. Its mission is to assist people who are refugees, including those living like refugees in their own country. The UNHCR staff attempts to get food and medicine to refugees. The Yugoslavian breakup had created nearly 4 million refugees by 1994, 600,000 of them children. The UNHCR has airlifted supplies to Kurds, Rwandans, residents of Sarajevo, and to the people in Bosnia-Herzegovina.

party—a particularly difficult task in East Germany and Romania.

In East Germany, the fall of the Berlin Wall quickly led to calls for the reunification of Germany. On December 2, 1990, **Helmut Kohl**, riding a wave of pro-unification sentiment, was elected in a landslide as the first chancellor of a reunited Germany. Other countries looked to their national heroes to lead their new regimes. Czechoslovakia elected a dissident playwright, **Václav Havel** (VAHT•SLAHF HAH•vehl), who had been in jail only months before. Then, in 1992, Czech and Slovak leaders agreed to split Czechoslovakia into two separate nations. **The Czech Republic** and the Republic of **Slovakia** became separate sovereign nations in January 1993. The countries maintain close economic and political ties. In Poland, voters made a choice that surprised no one: Lech Walesa was elected president in 1990.

Even staunchly Communist **Albania**, the lone holdout against the reforms of 1989, was finally swept up in the wave of protests. It opened its sealed borders, allowed opposition parties to form, and held elections in 1991. Other nations, such as Romania, organized coalition governments from a multitude of political parties.

Facing Challenges

After the excitement of the rebellions had cooled, the new governments of Eastern Europe faced daunting problems. Making a complete transformation from communism to private enterprise would take years. The infant free enterprise economies did not have enough capital investments to boost production and employment. Communism had left Eastern Europe and the former Soviet Union with their economic, political, and social structures in shambles. The new governments inherited inefficient or outdated industries, huge government debts, workforces paid regardless of the quality of their work, artificially low prices for basic goods, and currencies considered

Refugees push across the border from Hungary into Austria after Hungary in 1989 became the first Communist state to open its sealed borders.

A reunited Germany was celebrated by throngs of people near Berlin's Brandenburg Gate on October 3, 1990.

REFLECTING ON THE TIMES

1. How did the fall of communism in Eastern Europe affect Germany?
2. What movement rallied public support for democracy in Poland?

1007

ANSWERS TO REFLECTING ON THE TIMES

1. It led to the reunification of Germany.
2. Solidarity movement

Independent Practice

Guided Reading Activity 37-2 **L1**

People in World History Profile 71

Daily Life Have students research and depict in a letter to a newspaper what everyday life is like in one of the Eastern European countries studied in this section. **L2**

Linking Past and Present

Nazi War Crimes Germans have decided to remember the victims of Nazi war crimes by establishing January 27, the anniversary of the liberation of Auschwitz by Red Army troops, as a national day of commemoration. In establishing this day, the German president expressed the desire that young people who did not experience the Nazi regime maintain awareness of racism and totalitarianism in order to resist them.

Critical Thinking Have students research Yugoslavia and its collapse. Ask them to study resources other than newspapers and to analyze the factors that led to its collapse. **L3**

Chapter 37 Section 2

Who?What?Where?When?

Women from East Germany have lost benefits with reunification. They were used to working with a year's paid maternity leave and free day-care centers. The unemployment after unity has left many jobless.

ASSESS

Check for Understanding

Assign Section 2 Review as homework or as an in-class activity.

Use Student Self-Test and Review Software to review Section 2.

Evaluate

Section Quiz 37-2

Use the Testmaker to create a customized quiz for Section 2.

worthless by the rest of the world. The challenges before the new leaders were great.

Citizens expressed a willingness to wait for reforms to work. But, as Mikhail Gorbachev had found out, the patience of impoverished people has its limits. In May 1994 the Hungarian people elected a majority of Socialists and former Communists to the parliament. The new Socialist government, however, promised to maintain democracy and a free market economy. In November 1995 a 41-year-old former Communist, **Aleksander Kwasniewski** (kvash •NYEHF•skee) defeated Lech Walesa for the presidency of Poland. President Kwasniewski pledged to support democracy, economic freedom, and privatization. He also wanted Poland to join NATO and the unification movement of western Europe.

Democracy and the free market are taking root in Eastern Europe. The road may be rough, but the direction seems irreversible. Today, even Eastern Europe's former Communists accept the changes made since 1989. Perhaps the main differences separating them from their opponents are their support for a slower approach to privatization and their desire to protect social welfare programs from drastic government spending cuts.

Rise of Nationalism

After the fall of communism, Eastern Europe experienced a rebirth of nationalist feeling that has lasted into the late 1990s. Many observers consider the growth of nationalism in Eastern Europe a mixed blessing. Nationalism provides a unifying force that joins together people sharing the same language and culture. However, in the past, nationalism has often led to conflicts among peoples of the region that have sharp ethnic and cultural differences.

Today, many Eastern European countries consist of a major ethnic group (or groups) and a number of smaller ethnic communities. Tensions between dominant ethnic groups and smaller ethnic communities sometimes have developed into larger disputes involving neighboring countries. Often such disputes occur when a smaller group in one country has close ethnic and cultural ties with a dominant group in a neighboring country. Among Eastern Europe's smaller ethnic communities at the center of ongoing disputes between countries of the region are the Hungarian communities in southern Slovakia and northern Romania, the Greeks in Albania, the Turks in Bulgaria, and the Albanians in Macedonia and in Kosovo, a province of Serbia.

War in the Balkans

The most serious outbreak of ethnic conflict occurred in Yugoslavia. Here, the breakup of the Communist Yugoslav state was accompanied by extreme violence and cruelty.

For many years before the breakup, tensions had existed between the many ethnic groups in Yugoslavia, especially between the Serbs and Croats. However, these feelings were muted during the harsh rule of Communist leader Josip Broz Tito. After the death of Tito in 1980, communism gradually weakened, and by the late 1980s many Yugoslavs were calling for a multiparty political system. In January 1990 the Yugoslav Communist party finally ended its control of the country, and many new political parties formed.

Breakup of Yugoslavia

Each of Yugoslavia's individual republics held multiparty elections in 1990. Non-Communist parties won a majority of seats in the parliaments of **Bosnia-Herzegovina**, **Croatia**, **Macedonia**, and **Slovenia**. In **Serbia** and **Montenegro** the former Communist parties, renamed as Socialist parties, won majorities.

Meanwhile, the end of communism led to the airing of long-suppressed nationalist demands. The industrialized republics of Yugoslavia—Croatia and Slovenia—charged that the national government located in the capital of Belgrade in Serbia taxed them too heavily and that Serbia sought to control the rest of Yugoslavia. Demands for independence were also heard among ethnic Albanians in the less developed Serb province of Kosovo in the south.

In May 1991 Serbia refused to accept the election of a Croat to the presidency of Yugoslavia. Serbia also balked at any restructuring of Yugoslavia that would give the other republics more **autonomy**, or self-rule. A month later, Slovenia and Croatia declared their independence.

Fighting in Croatia

Fighting then broke out between the Croat army and the ethnic Serbs in Croatia who refused to be under Croat rule. Serbia and Montenegro, which made up the remainder of Yugoslavia, supplied troops and arms to the ethnic Serbs of Croatia. With this aid, ethnic Serb forces gained control of about one-third of Croatia's territory.

A cease-fire in January 1992 finally ended much of the fighting in Croatia. The borders between Serb-held and Croat-held areas were patrolled by United Nations (UN) peacekeeping forces. A Croat

MEETING SPECIAL NEEDS ACTIVITY

Reading Comprehension To help students who learn best by hearing words and information first and then writing, organize the class into small study groups. Suggest that each group list the names of the people and places in this section. Have them first say the names aloud, practicing difficult pronunciations, before they write their lists. You may also want to have students read the sections aloud and discuss them in their study groups. **L1 LEP**

Visualizing History **On November 21, 1995, the leaders of Serbia, Bosnia-Herzegovina, and Croatia joined U.S. Secretary of State Warren Christopher in initialing an accord.** *What decision was reached at the Dayton peace talks?*

offensive in August 1995 finally brought the Serb-held territory back into Croatia.

Bosnia-Herzegovina

In the fall of 1991, another republic, Macedonia, declared its independence. In March 1992 most of the Muslim population and the ethnic Croats in still another republic—Bosnia-Herzegovina—voted for independence from Serb-controlled Yugoslavia. Ethnic Serbs living in Bosnia-Herzegovina opposed the election and its outcome.

Fighting then broke out between the ethnic Serbs in Bosnia-Herzegovina and the rest of the population—the Bosnian Muslims and the Croats. Yugoslavia, which was now Serbia and Montenegro, provided troops and equipment to the Bosnian Serbs, who soon gained control of most of Bosnia-Herzegovina.

In March 1994 the exhausted Bosnian Croats and Muslims finally agreed to form a federation, and the United States a few months later asked the Bosnian Serbs to end the fighting and join as well. After military pressure from Croat land attacks and NATO air strikes, the Bosnian Serbs accepted a cease-fire and peace talks sponsored by the United States. In November 1995 the leaders of Bosnia-Herzegovina, Yugoslavia (Serbia and Montenegro), and Croatia met at **Dayton**, Ohio, and reached a settlement that established a Bosnian state divided into two separate Croat-Muslim and Serb regions.

SECTION 2 REVIEW

Recall

1. **Define** autonomy.
2. **Identify** Pope John Paul II, Solidarity, Lech Walesa, Nicolae Ceausescu, Helmut Kohl, Václav Havel, Aleksander Kwasniewski.
3. **Explain** Why were some of the revolutions in Eastern Europe more violent than others?

Critical Thinking

4. **Applying Information** What kinds of changes have occurred rapidly in Eastern European countries? Which changes are occurring slowly?

Understanding Themes

5. **Change** What changes came to the Yugoslav area with the fall of communism in the late 1980s and early 1990s?

Chapter 37 Section 2

Visualizing History After this accord, Bosnian Muslims began returning to the ruins of their homes in Sarajevo. The Dayton agreement brought change, but it does not prevent countries from seeking assistance in military training. In 1996 the Bosnian government sent soldiers to Iran for more training.

Answer to Caption: *A Bosnian state divided into a Croatian-Muslim and a Serb region was established.*

Reteach

Have the class make a flowchart documenting what happened to Eastern Europe after the collapse of the Soviet Union.

Enrich

Ask students to collect information from the library or a travel agency about the historic sights and the natural beauties of the Eastern European countries before civil wars changed some of them.

CLOSE

Ask students to summarize the recent changes in the Balkans and predict what might change in Eastern Europe in the next decade.

SECTION 2 REVIEW ANSWERS

1. All vocabulary words are defined in the Glossary.
2. Pope John Paul II, 1004; Solidarity, 1004; Lech Walesa, 1004; Nicolae Ceaușescu, 1006; Helmut Kohl, 1007; Václav Havel, 1007; Aleksander Kwasniewski, 1008
3. The Romanian dictator resisted the freedom protests and had hundreds of people killed, whereas most other Communist regimes responded to protests peacefully.
4. The collapse of Communist systems and establishment of new governments has been rapid; privatization and the establishment of a free market has been a slower process.
5. **CHANGE** Individual republics declared independence, fighting broke out in Croatia and Bosnia-Herzegovina, and a Bosnian state with two separate regions was established.

Chapter 37
Section 3

SECTION THEME

▸ **Cooperation** The European Union works to create a united Europe that will be a major economic power.

Find Out

Answer: *The Common Market was transformed into the European Community. Members signed the Maastricht Treaty establishing the European Union. The Single Europe Act ended most obstacles to trade and movement among European Union members.*

FOCUS

Section Objective

Identify the steps western European nations have taken to unify their governments and economies.

BELLRINGER
Motivational Activity

Before taking roll at the beginning of the class period, project Section Focus Transparency 37-3 and have students answer the activity questions.

This activity is also available as a blackline master.

Vocabulary Pre-check

Use Vocabulary Activity 37 to introduce vocabulary terms. **L1 LEP**

1980 · 1990 · 2000

1981 France elects its first Socialist president.

1986 Spain and Portugal join the European Community.

1990 East Germany and West Germany reunite.

1995 The British and Irish governments announce talks to resolve Northern Ireland's future.

Section 3

Toward a European Union

Setting the Scene

▸ **Terms to Define**
referendum, collective security

▸ **People to Meet**
Margaret Thatcher, John Major, François Mitterrand, Jacques Chirac, Helmut Kohl, Juan Carlos I, Felipe González

▸ **Places to Locate**
Northern Ireland, Cyprus

Find Out What steps have western European nations taken to unify their governments and economies?

The Storyteller

Paddy Ashdown believed in the European Union. As a businessman and a member of Parliament, he saw the benefits of Britain's participation. Already he had seen imports and exports move more freely, unhampered by restrictive tariffs. The last remaining hurdle was that of a common currency. Ashdown took the floor of Parliament to argue for the proposition. "We face the prospect of either joining an imperfect monetary union at a later date, or staying out altogether. This is exactly what happened over the EU itself. We must not make the same mistake twice."

—adapted from "The Case for a Single Currency," Paddy Ashdown, in *The Economist Newspaper, Ltd.*, March 4, 1995

Members of the British Parliament

Since the 1970s, western European nations have faced economic recession, budget deficits, and high unemployment. However, they also have worked to modernize their societies and to balance economic growth with the social needs of their peoples. By 1995, western Europe as a whole had made great strides toward full economic and political unity. Yet it faced a number of economic and political challenges resulting from economic restructuring, increasing immigration, the reunification of Germany, the collapse of the Soviet bloc, and the outbreak of fierce ethnic conflict in the Balkans.

Great Britain

The severe economic problems that plagued Great Britain after 1945 worsened during the 1970s. In 1979 voter dissatisfaction with high taxes, trade union strikes, and Labour government paralysis brought the Conservative party into a long period of power.

Margaret Thatcher

The Conservative party leader, **Margaret Thatcher**, became Great Britain's first woman prime minister. To lower inflation and promote economic growth, Thatcher introduced free-market economic measures. She sold nationalized industries to private owners, dismantled welfare programs, and limited the power of the trade unions.

Thatcher's popularity slowly declined during the late 1980s. Her policies had reduced inflation and aided business growth, but high unemployment continued in hard-pressed industrial areas. In addition, Thatcher faced difficulties at home and abroad with her European policies. Although Great Britain had joined Europe's Common Market in

---

SECTION RESOURCES

Reproducible Masters
- Reproducible Lesson Plan 37-3
- Vocabulary Activity 37
- Guided Reading Activity 37-3
- Section Quiz 37-3

Transparencies
- Section Focus Transparency 37-3

Multimedia
- Student Self-Test and Review Software
- Testmaker
- Picture Atlas of the World

Visualizing History Political murals cover buildings in both Protestant and Catholic Northern Ireland neighborhoods.
What issue has led to conflict in Northern Ireland?

1973, Thatcher opposed any future European union that would mean a loss of British independence. When she lost the backing of many of her government colleagues, Thatcher resigned in 1990.

John Major

Margaret Thatcher's successor, **John Major**, supported a closer link between Great Britain and the rest of the European Community (EC). In 1993 Great Britain and the other EC countries formed the European Union to increase their economic and political cooperation. By 1995, the issue of Great Britain's future role in Europe, however, had nearly split the Conservative party and seriously weakened Major's government.

Ireland

A major European issue from the 1970s to the 1990s was the status of **Northern Ireland**, the British-ruled province torn by sometimes violent disagreement. Northern Ireland's Protestant majority favored union with Great Britain; its sizable Catholic minority, however, wanted to join Northern Ireland to the predominantly Catholic Republic of Ireland to the south.

Clashes between Catholics and Protestants during the 1960s and 1970s caused Great Britain to suspend the government of Northern Ireland and impose direct rule. The outlawed Irish Republican Army (IRA), a group of Irish radicals opposing British rule in Northern Ireland, stepped up its attacks on British military forces in the province and on civilians in Great Britain.

In the early 1980s, Margaret Thatcher took strong measures to stem the IRA. Her government suspended many civil liberties for suspected IRA terrorists, such as the right to a trial by jury.

Under John Major, the British government made contact with the IRA in an effort to end the violence in Northern Ireland. By 1995, both the IRA and Protestant militants in Northern Ireland had accepted a cease-fire and peace talks. The talks stalled, however, over a British demand that the IRA disarm. In February 1996 the IRA rejected the demand, ended the cease-fire, and began bombing attacks in London.

France

France experienced political stability from the 1970s to the 1990s. In 1981 French voters elected their country's first Socialist president, **François Mitterrand**. Mitterrand nationalized major industries and increased taxes to pay for new social programs. His measures, however, heightened inflation, and he eventually was forced to cut government spending.

By the mid-1990s, Mitterrand's brand of socialism was in full retreat. Conservatives won a large majority in parliamentary elections in 1993, and Mitterrand appointed a conservative as prime minister. Concern about government corruption, unemployment, high taxes, and increasing immigration from northern Africa and southern Europe remained high.

In May 1995 **Jacques Chirac**, the conservative mayor of Paris, was elected president of France. Chirac pledged to reduce France's unemployment rate and to hold a referendum, or popular vote, on the issue of France's further integration into the European Union. By late 1995, another of Chirac's plans—to make further government cuts in social programs and government employee benefits—had led to nationwide strikes by workers and students. Chirac also faced protests over France's policy of conducting nuclear tests in the South Pacific.

Germany

During the 1970s West Germany, under Chancellor Willy Brandt and his successor, Helmut Schmidt, enjoyed prosperity. The West German economy, however, faced mounting difficulties

TEACH

Guided Practice

THEME Cooperation

Have students list the ways members of the European Union cooperate now or hope to cooperate in the future. *(cooperation in areas of defense policy, crime, immigration; ending most obstacles to trade and movement among member nations; establishing a common currency and a central bank)* **L1**

Visualizing History Point out the open hostility the murals on the buildings portray. Militaristic murals and street decorations can be seen in the cities of Northern Ireland, but by contrast, the countryside is a place of peace and natural beauty. **Answer to Caption:** *The Protestant majority in Northern Ireland favors continued union with Great Britain, while the Catholic minority there wants to join the Republic of Ireland.*

Critical Thinking Explain that *xenophobia* means "fear of foreigners." Tell students that German reunification caused an upsurge of xenophobia in the early 1990s. Neo-Nazi sects preached German superiority and targeted foreigners. Ask students to comment on why this might have occurred. *(new problems of housing shortages and public deficit blamed on refugees from Eastern Europe)* **L3**

COOPERATIVE LEARNING ACTIVITY

Panel Presentations Organize students into small groups. Have each group choose one of the countries studied in this section to research in depth. Have individual students in each group look at the people and culture, the music and literature, places of interest to visit, the politics, economics, and social conditions. They should try to collect any visual materials they feel will help the presentation. Have them present these reports as panels of experts. **L2**

Cultural Perspectives

London There is a mix of cultures in this city that is unparalleled in Europe. Each of 34 countries ranging from Ireland and the United States to Mauritius and Malaysia are represented in London communities.

Chapter 37 Section 3

Independent Practice

Guided Reading Activity 37-3 **L1**

Politics Have students draw cartoons about one of the political situations discussed in this section. Each cartoon should express a specific point of view. **L2 LEP**

Linking Past and Present

Madrid's Plaza Mayor This Spanish city square was built in the seventeenth century and served as the site for public tortures during the Spanish Inquisition. Today it is a place of pleasure; where people enjoy refreshments and conversation at its courtyard cafés.

Civil Strife Ask students to look at a map showing Turkey and Greece in relation to Cyprus. Ask volunteers to research and report to the class about the conflicts in Cyprus between the Greek and Turkish communities. **L2**

NATIONAL GEOGRAPHIC SOCIETY

CD-ROM

PICTURE ATLAS OF THE WORLD

You and your students can view the streets of London, the moors of the United Kingdom, the vineyards of Germany, and the hillsides of Greece by clicking the "Video" button of selected countries.

with inflation and unemployment in the early 1980s. Promising better times, a conservative chancellor, **Helmut Kohl**, came to power in 1982.

With the downfall of the Communist government in East Germany in 1989, the reunification of Germany, which many had hoped for but few dreamed possible, was finally realized in 1990. When the excitement of reunification wore off, however, Germans found that the costs of reunification were far higher than anyone had foreseen. Economic and social levels in the eastern parts of Germany, held back by years of Communist rule, had to be raised to the economic and social levels of the western areas of the country. The closing of inefficient eastern German industries caused unemployment to soar, and the arrival of refugees from Eastern Europe placed a strain on social services.

Social and political unrest accompanied the economic difficulties. Germans in western parts complained about paying high taxes to support economic and social restructuring in the eastern parts. Neo-Nazis and other right-wing Germans protested against immigration from southern Europe and Turkey. Some of them attacked foreigners, resulting in a number of deaths. Large numbers of Germans took part in demonstrations to protest the attacks, but the German parliament in 1993 finally amended the German constitution to reduce the flow of immigrants into Germany.

That same year, Germany's highest court ruled that German armed forces, with parliamentary approval, could participate in international peacekeeping missions. Until then, the German constitution had banned all military activities except those related to collective security, or joint agreement by nations to protect themselves from attack. The court ruling permitted a German role in overseas peacekeeping activities in places such as Somalia and Bosnia-Herzegovina.

Footnotes to History

The Chunnel

In 1994 Great Britain and France, separated for thousands of years by the English Channel, were once again joined. The Channel Tunnel, nicknamed the Chunnel, linked the island country to mainland Europe. By the year 2003 the Chunnel is expected to carry more than 120,000 people between Great Britain and France each day. At night, tons of freight will move through the Chunnel.

Mediterranean Europe

Mediterranean Europe made great strides in political and economic development from the 1970s to the 1990s. Dictatorships fell and democracies arose in Spain and Portugal. Economic recession, however, created hard times for the Mediterranean countries of Europe.

Italy

From the 1970s to the 1990s, a variety of economic, social, and political problems plagued Italy. Among these were the uneven distribution of wealth, especially between north and south, an inefficient government bureaucracy, and constantly changing governments.

During the 1970s, Italy had the largest Communist party in western Europe. The party was popular in part because it promoted a less authoritarian view of communism. It sought to share power with the ruling conservative Christian Democrats. Many conservative Italians, however, were alarmed at this prospect. Adding to the political uncertainty was a wave of murders, kidnappings, and bombings by leftist groups.

Christian Democrats held control of the government during the late 1980s and early 1990s. During this time, the leftist parties—Communists and Socialists—suffered from policy disputes and political scandals. By the mid-1990s, however, the Christian Democratic party, renamed the Populist party, lost influence to even more conservative parties. The leaders of these parties sought drastic spending cuts to shrink Italy's enormous budget deficit. Charges of corruption, however, ended their careers in early 1995, and a government run by independent civil servants took power.

Spain and Portugal

After nearly 35 years of dictatorship under Francisco Franco, Spain in the late 1970s entered a new era of democracy guided by its new king, **Juan Carlos I**. For most of the 1980s and 1990s, Spain's democratic government was in the hands of the Socialists and their leader, **Felipe González**. The Spanish government granted the Basque Provinces and other regions of Spain increased self-rule after years of Basque repression by Franco. Nevertheless, it was unable to stop terrorist attacks by Basques wanting independence for their provinces. In foreign affairs, Spain strengthened its links to other European countries and in 1986 joined the European Community.

A turn toward democracy also occurred in neighboring Portugal. Decades of dictatorship in

MEETING SPECIAL NEEDS ACTIVITY

Language Delayed Have students trace an outline map of Europe. Ask them to label the countries studied in this section and then color-code each country. Have them make a color-code key for the map and in the key give specific information about each country, such as political leaders, important dates and events, and any other details they want to include. **L1 LEP**

1012 Chapter 37 *The World in Transition*

Portugal ended with a military coup in 1974, and in 1976 the nation held its first free elections in 50 years. During this time Portugal finally freed its African and Asian colonies. The Socialist party, elected in 1983, attempted to deal with the persistent unemployment and inflation. In 1986 Portugal joined the European Community.

Greece

From the late 1960s to the early 1970s, Greece was ruled by a repressive military government. In 1974 democracy was restored, and the country's first free elections in 10 years brought to power the conservative New Democratic party. A Socialist government followed in the 1980s and 1990s. The Socialists brought Greece into the European Community in 1981. Greece continued to have border disputes with neighboring Turkey and disagreement over the status of **Cyprus**.

A United Europe

During the 1980s and 1990s the Common Market broadened its activities to include political and financial affairs and was transformed into the European Community.

In February 1992, representatives of the member countries of the European Community signed the Treaty on European Union in Maastricht, the Netherlands. This pact, also known as the Treaty of Maastricht, set up the European Union, which went into effect in November 1993. The European Union aimed to extend cooperation among the community's members in such areas as defense policy, crime, and immigration.

In 1993 another measure—the Single Europe Act—ended most obstacles to trade and movement among European Union members. Two years later, seven European Union nations allowed their citizens to freely travel from one member country to another without a passport. The year 1995 also saw the admission of Austria, Finland, and Sweden to the European Union.

The European Union looked ahead to even closer unity among its members. Plans were underway to include Eastern European countries and to create an Economic and Monetary Union (EMU) by the year 2002. The principal features of the EMU would be a common currency known as the euro and a central bank for all European Union nations.

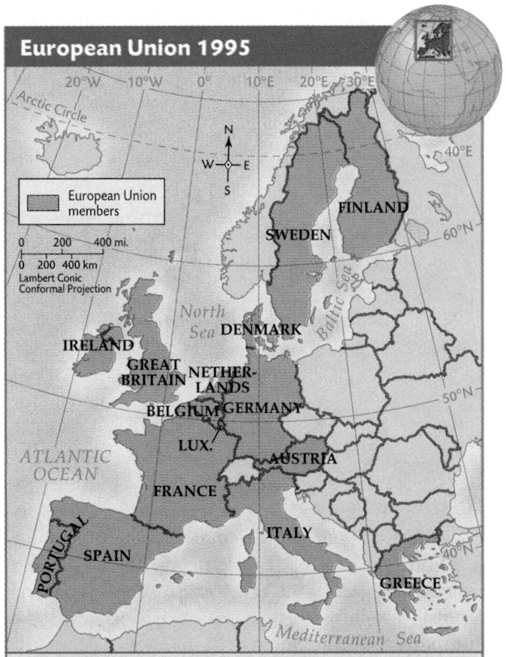

Map Study The European Union includes most western European countries. **Region** How many member nations were there in 1995?

SECTION 3 REVIEW

Recall

1. **Define** referendum, collective security.
2. **Identify** Margaret Thatcher, John Major, the Irish Republican Army, François Mitterrand, Jacques Chirac, Helmut Kohl, Juan Carlos I, Felipe González, Treaty of Maastricht.
3. **Explain** the purpose of the European Union.

Critical Thinking

4. **Applying Information** Explain why Great Britain has shown reluctance to fully participate in plans for full European unity.

Understanding Themes

5. **Cooperation** How do relationships among countries in the European Union compare with those among states in the United States?

SECTION 3 REVIEW ANSWERS

1. The words are defined in the Glossary.
2. Thatcher, 1010; Major, 1011; IRA, 1011; Mitterrand, 1011; Chirac, 1011; Kohl, 1012; Juan Carlos I, 1012; González, 1012; Maastricht, 1013
3. to increase the cooperation among members of the European Community
4. Great Britain fears a loss of independence.
5. **COOPERATION** Countries in European Union do not share a common government, legal system, or currency as the states in the United States do. Free trade and movement among member nations resemble the same freedoms among the states of the United States.

Map Study

Answer

15

Map Skills Practice

Reading a Map What nation in the center of western Europe is not a member of the European Union? *(Switzerland)*

ASSESS

Check for Understanding

Assign Section 3 Review as homework or as an in-class activity.

Use Student Self-Test and Review Software to review Section 3.

Evaluate

Section Quiz 37-3

Reteach

Create a diagram or chart with the students identifying the countries and the leading political groups discussed in this section and the problems they faced in the 1980s and 1990s.

Enrich

Have students research the European Union and create a chart of its current members. Summarize any goals it has for further unity.

CLOSE

Ask students to write a brief summary of the evidence of growing cooperation among European countries since 1990.

Chapter 37 *The World in Transition* 1013

SECTION THEME

▶ **Conflict** National and ethnic conflicts intensify worldwide after the end of the cold war.

Find Out

Answer: *The Balkans, southern Russia and the Caucasus, the Middle East, Sri Lanka, and Canada have suffered ethnic discord in the 1990s.*

FOCUS

Section Objective

Recognize the areas of the world that have been in ethnic discord since the end of the cold war.

BELLRINGER
Motivational Activity

Before taking roll at the beginning of the class period, project Section Focus Transparency 37-4 and have students answer the activity questions. Discuss students' responses.

This activity is also available as a blackline master.

Vocabulary Pre-check

Use Vocabulary Activity 37 to introduce vocabulary terms. **L1 LEP**

1980 — **1982** Canada enacts new constitution.
1990 — **1992** Civil war begins in Bosnia.
1994 Russian troops enter Chechnya. — 2000

Section 4

National and Ethnic Conflicts

Setting the Scene

▶ **Terms to Define**
ethnic cleansing, atrocity, embargo, enclave

▶ **People to Meet**
Slobodan Milosevic, Alija Izetbegovic, Franjo Tudjman, the Chechens, the Ossetians, the Abkhazians, the Kurds, the Sinhalese, the Tamils, Brian Mulroney, Jean Chretien

▶ **Places to Locate**
Sarajevo, Dayton, Chechnya, Nagorno-Karabakh, Sri Lanka, Quebec

Find Out What areas of the world have been in ethnic discord since the end of the cold war?

The Storyteller

Zahid Olorcic remembered how things had been just a few years ago. People in Sarajevo had gotten along with their neighbors. Even though coming from diverse backgrounds, the city's multiethnic population lived in harmony. Then the situation changed as radical groups stirred up ethnic hatred. Zahid recalled earlier times:

"Funerals, weddings, birthdays, we never counted how many Muslims were there, how many Serbs, how many Croats. The only important thing was to be together.... "

—adapted from "Bosnians Recall Karadzic, a Neighbor Turned Enemy," Tracy Wilkinson, in *The Los Angeles Times*, July 23, 1995

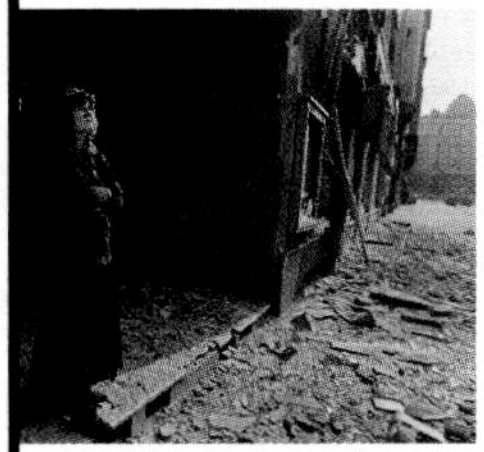

War damage in Sarajevo

The end of the cold war brought about the fall of communism and the triumph of democracy and free enterprise. A new world was at hand—or so it seemed. The aftermath has proven to be more complex. During the cold war, all global conflicts were somehow easily linked to the East-West struggle. Now that the superpower rivalry was over, each problem stood on its own terms, and predictability and stability had given way to uncertainty and confusion.

During the 1990s, long-standing national and ethnic rivalries flared into violence along Russia's southern borders and in the Balkans, South Asia, Africa, and other areas. The threats to peace included not only fighting but also human tragedies such as starvation and the flow of refugees.

The stark reality of the 1990s was the seeming inability of the global community, through the United Nations and other organizations, to respond effectively to these and other crises. However, there were bright spots—for example, South Africa, the Balkans, and the Middle East. In all three places, the mid-1990s saw efforts—either fulfilled or in progress—to peacefully resolve differences or deeply rooted injustices.

Fighting in Bosnia

The most serious ethnic conflict continued in the Balkan republic of Bosnia-Herzegovina. In the late 1980s, relations among the Serbs, Croats, and Muslims living in the republic had steadily worsened. In 1992 most of the republic's Croats and Muslims voted for independence from Yugoslavia. But ethnic Serbs, a minority in Bosnia, boycotted the vote and rejected its outcome. They feared domination by the Croats and Muslims if a separate Bosnian nation were established.

SECTION RESOURCES

Reproducible Masters
- Reproducible Lesson Plan 37-4
- Vocabulary Activity 37
- Guided Reading Activity 37-4
- People in World History Profile 72
- Section Quiz 37-4

Transparencies
- Section Focus Transparency 37-4

Multimedia
- Student Self-Test and Review Software
- Testmaker
- Lessons of War: *The Nature of Violence*

Outbreak of War

The creation of an independent Bosnia led to war among the republic's Serbs, Croats, and Muslims. With the support of Serbia and Montenegro, all that was left of Yugoslavia, the ethnic Serbs were able to conquer two-thirds of Bosnia-Herzegovina. In April 1992 the Serbs began a siege of **Sarajevo**, the Bosnian capital, which was largely controlled by Muslims. Following a policy called ethnic cleansing, the Serbs ruthlessly expelled rival ethnic groups from the areas taken by their army. The Croats and Muslims also carried out atrocities, or cruel actions, against the Serbs.

International Response

The United Nations imposed an embargo, a ban on trade, against Serbia in May 1992, hoping to get the Serbs to stop sending supplies to Serbs in Bosnia-Herzegovina. A month later, UN peacekeeping forces began arriving in the republic to protect shipments of food and medicine to the people of Bosnia. Since the war began, thousands of Bosnians, including many civilians, had been killed, and hundreds of thousands left homeless.

In October 1992 the United States and other UN members reported extensive human rights abuses in Bosnia. The reports indicated that Bosnian Serbs had tortured and killed Bosnian Muslims and Croats in detention camps. In July 1995 a UN-sponsored international court charged Bosnian Serb leaders with genocide for operating thousands of Nazi-style concentration camps and ruthlessly attacking civilian populations.

Steps Toward Peace

In 1994 Serbia, hurting from the effects of the UN embargo, called on Bosnian Serbs to cease fighting. Later in the year, the United States offered a peace plan that would divide Bosnia between the Serbs and a new Muslim-Croat federation. A cease-fire, begun in January 1995, brought a temporary halt to the fighting.

After fighting broke out again in July 1995, Bosnian Serbs seized a number of UN peacekeepers as hostages, throwing in doubt the future of the UN's role in Bosnia. A month later, the Bosnian Serbs stepped up their attacks on Sarajevo, and NATO responded with air attacks on Serb positions around the city.

The NATO air strikes signaled for the first time that the Western powers were united in their support of action in the Balkans. Meanwhile, Croatia completed a massive land offensive to regain land held by its own Serb minority. With a possible defeat looming, the Bosnian Serbs decided to negotiate as a way of preserving some of their earlier gains.

In November 1995, three presidents—**Slobodan Milosevic** (swoh•boh•dahn mee•LAH•soh•veech) of Serbia, **Alija Izetbegovic** (ah•LEE•hah ee•zeht•BEH•goh•veech) of Bosnia-Herzegovina, and **Franjo Tudjman** (FRAHN•hoh TOOZH•mahn) of Croatia—met in **Dayton**, Ohio, and agreed to the partition of Bosnia into distinct Serb and Muslim-Croat areas. In December the Dayton Treaty was signed in Paris, ending the Bosnian conflict. In response to the agreement, the UN Security Council voted to lift the embargo on Serbia. By the time of the Dayton agreement, the Bosnian conflict had resulted in the deaths of 200,000 people and the forced removal of 3 million people from their homes.

Keeping the Peace

One major point of the Dayton Treaty—the reunification of Sarajevo under Muslim-Croat control—was not acceptable to many Bosnian Serbs. To safeguard the peace, a 60,000-strong NATO-led force was sent to Bosnia to replace the exhausted United Nations troops. In spite of opposition at home, United States President Bill Clinton pledged 20,000 American troops to serve as part of the peacekeeping force. Other nations, including Russia, also made troop commitments.

Ethnic Unrest in the CIS

With the collapse of Communist rule, fierce ethnic hatreds boiled to the surface in Russia and the other CIS republics. During the Communist era, the Russian-dominated government of the Soviet Union had repressed the nationalism of non-Russian ethnic groups. This policy increased resentment among many peoples.

Even after the collapse of the Soviet Union, relations among the Commonwealth republics were strained. Although Russia was clearly the most powerful, European republics, such as Ukraine and Moldova, were reluctant to concede their hard-won independence to a Russian-dominated association. Wary of Russia, the central Asian republics and those in the Caucasus region balanced ties to Russia with new links to Middle Eastern and Western countries.

Ethnic unrest was also found within some of the individual CIS republics. Each republic had dominant ethnic groups and many smaller ethnic groups. Many of these groups were concentrated in a particular area and had their own local

TEACH

Guided Practice

THEME Conflict

Trace the steps of the Bosnian conflict with the class, making a time line on the chalkboard as students list events from this section. Start the time line with Bosnian independence in 1992. **L1 LEP**

Summarize Ask students to summarize the pressures applied by the UN against Serbia and the peace plan that was finally agreed on. **L2**

Critical Thinking Have students discuss the stand Boris Yeltsin took against Chechnya. Have them suggest how they think Yeltsin should have responded to the Chechens. **L3**

ABCNEWS INTERACTIVE™

VIDEODISC
Lessons of War

Side Two, Chapter 10
Title: *The Nature of Violence*
Subject: Various perspectives concerning the nature of violence
Ask: Is violence inherent in human nature? *(Answers will vary, but one theory is that if provoked, all humans are capable of violence.)* How can violence be stopped? *(perhaps through peaceful negotiations)*

COOPERATIVE LEARNING ACTIVITY

Global Peace Union Organize students into small groups to plan and organize a cooperative international effort to educate people in techniques for peaceful resolution of conflicts. First students should brainstorm ideas in their small groups, then have a joint meeting of all the groups and write guidelines for the organization and a plan of action for use in future conflicts. **L2**

Independent Practice

Guided Reading Activity 37-4 **L1**

People in World History Profile 72

Visualizing History The Russian military took over Grozny and expanded into the countryside. According to some reports, the Russians' "total-war strategy" in Chechnya made it a terrifying war zone. **Answer to Caption:** *He wanted to prevent the breakup of Russia that might occur if other ethnic groups followed the example of the Chechens.*

Culture Have students research Sri Lanka and prepare a bulletin-board display of the land, its people, and its culture. **L2**

Who?What?Where?When?

Village Divided On the border between the United States and Canada, a village is divided. On the United States side, in Escourt Station, Maine, live five French-speaking families and an American wildlife warden. On the Canadian side is Escourt, Quebec. One of the households in the village is bisected by the border line.

ASSESS

Check for Understanding

Assign Section 4 Review as homework or as an in-class activity.

Use Student Self-Test and Review Software to review Section 4.

Visualizing History **In December 1994, Russian soldiers with tanks (above) attacked Chechen fighters (left), some of whom were dressed in traditional Chechen clothing.** *Why did Yeltsin send troops to Chechnya?*

governments. After the fall of the Soviet Union, they asserted pride in their traditional cultures and demanded greater self-rule.

The Chechens

The Chechens are among the ethnic groups of Russia. Their republic, **Chechnya** (chehch•NYA), lies in southern Russia near the Caspian Sea. In 1994, against the wishes of the Russian government in Moscow, the Chechens declared their full independence from Russia.

Fearing the breakup of Russia if other ethnic groups did the same, Russian leader Boris Yeltsin sent Russian troops into Chechnya in December 1994. In a full-scale attack, Russian forces bombarded the Chechen capital, Grozny, which was fiercely defended by Chechen rebel forces. Russian President Yeltsin was widely criticized at home and abroad for the invasion, in which hundreds of civilians were killed in bombing attacks.

The Chechens fought extremely well against the poorly trained and disheartened Russian forces. By mid-January 1995, however, Chechen resistance had weakened as more experienced Russian soldiers were rushed to the front. Within a month, Russian forces had won nearly all of Grozny, forcing residents to flee and reducing the city to smoldering ruins.

In June 1995 the Russians and Chechens agreed to a cease-fire, and Chechen fighters retreated to the mountains. Although the Russians claimed victory, Chechen hit-and-run attacks indicated that the war was far from over.

The Caucasus Republics

Ethnic conflicts troubled other republics in the CIS. In the Caucasus region, Armenia and Azerbaijan both claimed ownership of the enclave of **Nagorno-Karabakh**. An enclave is a small territory entirely surrounded by another territory. Nagorno-Karabakh lies entirely within Azerbaijan, but its majority population of Armenians wanted it to separate from Azerbaijan and join Armenia. In 1993 Armenia and Azerbaijan went to war over Nagorno-Karabakh. Armenian forces made significant advances and took control of much of the disputed territory.

Neighboring Georgia has faced separatist uprisings by minority ethnic groups, such as **the Ossetians** and **the Abkhazians**. In 1994 the Abkhazians declared their region an independent republic. Meanwhile, Georgia has received support from Russia in the effort to preserve its national unity. The Russians hold three military bases in Georgia and train and equip the Georgian army.

The Kurds

In the Middle East, one of the most divisive ethnic disputes was between **the Kurds** and the governments of Iraq and Turkey. The Kurds, who live in mountainous areas of Armenia, Iran, Iraq, Syria, and Turkey, number about 20 million and are Sunni Muslims.

The Kurds have never had their own nation, but have long sought their freedom. In 1988 and 1991, the Kurds in Iraq revolted against the government of Saddam Hussein. The Iraqi army quickly put down these uprisings, bombing Kurdish villages and forcing over 1 million Kurds to flee to remote mountain areas or to neighboring countries.

Beginning in the mid-1980s, the Kurds in Turkey carried out a guerrilla war against the

MEETING SPECIAL NEEDS ACTIVITY

Attention Deficiency Suggest that students who find it easier to break up study into short sessions concentrate on the information under one subhead for a short time, then go to the resource center and find additional information about that subject. This physical activity will help them to focus again when they return to studying. These students could be responsible for gathering current information about conflicts for the newspaper project suggested for this chapter. **L1**

Turkish government. In 1994 the Turkish army staged an offensive to destroy Kurdish guerrilla bases. During the Turkish attack, Western nations expressed concern about Turkey's use of force.

The Tamils

Another place torn by ethnic discord was the beautiful Indian Ocean island country of **Sri Lanka**. Sri Lanka's 18 million people largely belong to two ethnic groups, **the Sinhalese** and **the Tamils**. The Sinhalese, who make up about 75 percent of the population, are Buddhist. The Tamils, most of whom are Hindus, form about 18 percent of the population and live in northern and eastern areas of Sri Lanka.

In 1993 violence broke out between Tamil guerrillas and Sinhalese government troops. The Sinhalese controlled most posts in the Sri Lankan government, and the Tamils believed that Sinhalese-controlled governments blocked Tamil opportunities for education and employment. Despite peace efforts, the fighting continued through the 1980s and into the 1990s. Nearly 40,000 people were killed, and hundreds of thousands of Tamil refugees fled to India.

By late 1995, Sri Lankan government troops had gained the upper hand. After a two-month siege, they captured the city of Jaffna, the leading Tamil stronghold. The government offered the guerrillas a plan that would give greater self-rule to Tamil areas. The guerrillas, however, wanted complete independence and rejected the plan.

Canada's Fragile Unity

During the 1980s and 1990s, Canada faced growing uncertainty about its future. Many French-speaking people in the province of **Quebec** continued to feel that their language and culture were threatened by English-speaking Canada. In 1980 Quebec held another referendum to seek voter approval for Quebec independence. Amid widespread controversy, the plan for Quebec independence was defeated at the polls.

Meanwhile, the Canadian government in Ottawa set out to strengthen national unity while respecting regional differences. In 1982 Prime Minister Pierre Trudeau had the British government relinquish its constitutional control of Canada. A new Canadian constitution granted more powers to the provinces and guaranteed the language and cultural rights of all Canadians.

Quebec, however, refused to accept the new constitution because it did not allow individual provinces to have veto power over future amendments. Prime Minister **Brian Mulroney**, whose Conservative party came to power in 1984, tried—and failed—to convince English-speaking Canada that Quebec needed to have a special status within the Canadian nation.

In 1994 the Liberal party won parliamentary elections, and **Jean Chretien** (cray•TYEHN) became prime minister. Although a French-speaking Quebecer, Chretien was a firm believer in Canadian national unity and opposed Quebec separatism.

Sensing growing support for independence, Quebec's separatist leaders held another referendum in November 1995. In this election, Quebec voters, by a margin of only a little over 1 percent, rejected independence for the province. However, nearly 60 percent of Quebec's French-speaking population voted in favor of independence.

Canada in theory remained united, but the referendum left Canada's people deeply divided. Hoping to dampen separatist fervor, Prime Minister Chretien stated that his government would favor giving Quebec more power in deciding Canadian constitutional issues.

SECTION 4 REVIEW

Recall

1. **Define** ethnic cleansing, atrocity, embargo, enclave.
2. **Identify** Slobodan Milosevic, Alija Izetbegovic, Franjo Tudjman, the Chechens, the Ossetians, the Abkhazians, the Kurds, the Sinhalese, the Tamils, Brian Mulroney, Jean Chretien.
3. **List** the ethnic groups in the Commonwealth of Independent States that have been or are involved in nationalistic conflicts.

Critical Thinking

4. **Making Comparisons** How was Quebec's expression of dissatisfaction with Canada different from that of the Tamils with Sri Lanka? What do you think accounts for the differences between the two disputes?

Understanding Themes

5. **Conflict** Why did the Bosnian Serbs in 1992 oppose the creation of an independent Bosnia? Why did they agree to peace talks in 1995?

Chapter 37 Section 4

Linking Past and Present

United Nations Fiftieth Anniversary On June 26, 1945, fifty nations joined to sign the UN Charter. Fifty years later there were 185 members planning a celebration in New York City at the UN headquarters. This organization has received the Nobel Peace Prize numerous times. Although it has not succeeded in resolving some major conflicts, most members believe that the problems countries face are too great for any one nation to solve alone.

Evaluate

Section Quiz 37-4

Use the Testmaker to create a customized quiz for Section 4.

Reteach

Ask students to write five opening statements for a national TV news broadcast covering issues in this section.

Enrich

Have students scan newspapers and magazines for articles related to the regions or issues mentioned in this section. Then have them share the articles with the class.

CLOSE

Ask students to discuss which conflicts that they have studied in this section cause them the greatest concern and why.

SECTION 4 REVIEW ANSWERS

1. All vocabulary words are defined in the Glossary.
2. Milosevic, 1015; Izetbegovic, 1015; Tudjman, 1015; Chechens, 1016; Ossetians, 1016; Abkhazians, 1016; Kurds, 1016; Sinhalese, 1017; Tamils, 1017; Mulroney, 1017; Chretien, 1017
3. Chechens, Armenians, Azerbaijanis, Ossetians, Abkhazians
4. Quebec sought separation from Canada through the election process; the Tamils' discord was expressed through violent fighting. Answers will vary. Possible answer: responding to an unjust blocking of basic opportunities for education and employment; people in Quebec were not having rights withheld.
5. **CONFLICT** Bosnian Serbs feared domination by the Croatians and Muslims if Bosnia became independent. Bosnian Serbs agreed to peace talks because it looked like they would be defeated and would lose territory.

SECTION THEME

▶ **Cultural Diffusion** New technology and the emergence of an integrated world communications system speed the transfer of ideas and practices throughout the world.

Find Out

Answer: *Advanced technology has hastened the growth of a global culture and has motivated people to fight against injustices and to expand rights and opportunities for women and oppressed peoples throughout the world.*

FOCUS

Section Objective

Explain how recent advances in technology have affected the world's cultures.

BELLRINGER Motivational Activity

Before taking roll at the beginning of the class period, project Section Focus Transparency 37-5 and have students answer the activity questions.

This activity is also available as a blackline master.

Vocabulary Pre-check

Use the Vocabulary PuzzleMaker to create a puzzle that reinforces terms. **L1**

1980 — 1990 — 2000

1987 The Montreal Protocol calls for global reduction of chemical pollutants.

1992 The first Earth Summit is held in Rio de Janeiro, Brazil.

1995 The United States space shuttle *Atlantis* docks with the Russian space station *Mir*.

Section 5

Global Interdependence

Setting the Scene

▶ **Terms to Define**
interdependent, developing nations, developed nations, deforestation, information superhighway, genetic engineering

▶ **People to Meet**
Neil Armstrong, Edwin Aldrin, Jr.

▶ **Places to Locate**
Montreal, Rio de Janeiro

Find Out How have recent advances in technology affected the world's cultures?

The Storyteller

With small bursts from the thrusters Robert "Hoot" Gibson, the American astronaut, carefully maneuvered Atlantis *closer and closer to* Mir, *the Russian space station. Finally, just after 9:00 A.M. eastern standard time, June 29, 1995, Gibson gently docked the 100-ton shuttle with the* Mir's *central docking port. On Earth, at the Russian mission control, NASA chief Dan Goldin leaped from his seat to hug his Russian counterpart, Yuri Koptev. When the hatch was opened, Gibson floated along the pathway into the Russian ship. After decades of competition, American and Russian space programs had launched a promising partnership.*

—adapted from "Mir Reflections," Frank Sietzen, in *Final Frontier*, November/December 1995

Partnership in space

At the dawn of the twentieth century, most of the world's people were relatively uninformed about the lives and activities of other people living in distant places on the planet. As the twenty-first century approaches, however, people communicate instantly with others thousands of miles away and access vast amounts of information with their fingertips. Today, we are participants in a technological and communications revolution that has made people increasingly interdependent, or reliant on each other.

World Trade

Today's nations have become economically interdependent through trade. The volume of world trade now exceeds $8 trillion per year. This means that about $900 million worth of goods and services are bought and sold among nations every hour. Consequently, one region experiencing an economic boom will stimulate the economies of other regions by increasing its purchases from them. The reverse could also happen too. One region suffering an economic downturn will reduce imports from other regions and these areas, too, will face economic difficulties because of a decline in trade.

About 50 years ago, the United States was by far the economic superpower of the world. Today, it no longer has unchallenged supremacy in world markets. Other countries or regions of the world have developed to the point of competing successfully with the United States. Western Europe and the countries of Asia's Pacific Rim are now economic giants, and their trade with the United States has grown rapidly. Although this growth benefits consumers, it also requires some painful adjustments. Trade can mean the loss of certain jobs and the creation of others. An increase in imports, for example, may raise demands for protective tariffs and other trade restrictions.

SECTION RESOURCES

Reproducible Masters
- Reproducible Lesson Plan 37-5
- Guided Reading Activity 37-5
- Geography and History Activity 37
- History Simulation 37
- Reteaching Activity 37
- Enrichment Activity 37
- Section Quiz 37-5
- Performance Assessment Activity 37
- Spanish Chapter Summary 37

Transparencies
- Section Focus Transparency 37-5
- World History and Art Transparency 52, *Sky Above Clouds II*
- Mapping History Overlay Transparency 25, *World Population Growth*

Multimedia
- Vocabulary PuzzleMaker Software
- Student Self-Test and Review Software
- Testmaker

1018 Chapter 37 *The World in Transition*

Developing Nations

Despite increasing interdependency, many countries still are struggling to meet the basic needs of their citizens. The gap between rich and poor nations is a pressing global issue that concerns world leaders.

Developing nations in Asia, Africa, and Latin America are newly industrializing countries, and many of their people still follow traditional ways of earning a living. These developing nations are dependent on the economic systems of **developed nations**, countries like the United States that have long been industrialized and have the technology to produce a great quantity and variety of goods. Many developing countries supply raw materials to developed nations in exchange for manufactured goods.

Building Strong Economies

A developing nation often will try to raise its standard of living by diversifying, or increasing the variety of, the types of goods it supplies to the world. This helps protect a nation's economy from depending on a single crop or product for its economic well-being. The transition to a diversified economy, however, can be long and difficult because of lack of funds and skilled workers.

The financial demands of such an economic transformation often lead developing countries to seek outside sources for funding. The World Bank and the International Monetary Fund (IMF) are financial organizations that were established after World War II to provide a strong foundation for international trade. They, along with private banks, have loaned money to countries in need. Foreign corporations also have invested in developing nations.

The World Debt Crisis

Borrowing the money needed for economic growth has caused monumental debt in many parts of the world. Today, developing countries such as Mexico and Brazil are struggling to pay the interest charges on their loans. When loans cannot be repaid, banks often suffer huge losses. These losses can sometimes hurt business in the country in which a bank is located.

World leaders are working to solve the international debt crisis. Many strategies have been tried. In some cases, the banks involved have issued new loans to enable developing countries to pay off old debts. While such practices have helped to offset immediate problems, the debt crisis remains a grave threat to the world's economic health.

Visualizing History **Hong Kong is one of the busiest ports of Asia's Pacific Rim.** *In addition to Asia's Pacific Rim, what other prosperous area of the world trades extensively with the United States?*

Population Growth

The number of people on our planet affects both human well-being and the environment. Developed nations point to the rapid growth of population in developing countries as a major cause in straining world resources. As much as 97 percent of the world's population growth occurs in the developing world. Families are large in very poor countries because many children are needed to help earn money and to assist parents in their old age. At the present rate of growth, the world's population is expected to increase from the present 5.7 billion to more than 6 billion by 2000 and about 12 billion by 2050.

Developing nations blame environmental problems on the high consumption of resources by people in the developed world. One person in a developed country consumes 10 to 35 times more energy than a person in a developing country. The United States creates twice as much garbage as any other nation.

TEACH

Guided Practice

THEME Cultural Diffusion
Have students discuss how increasing economic interdependence can hasten the spread of different cultures. *(Answers may include that an increase in international trade encourages foreign travel by the businesspeople of many nations and brings people into contact with the goods from other countries.)* **L1**

Visualizing History Hong Kong is a 400-square-mile (1,036-sq.-km) area with a population of 6 million. It is one of the world's largest financial centers. Life expectancy there is higher than in the United States.
Answer to Caption: *western Europe*

Economics Explain that the World Bank is a specialized agency of the United Nations which was founded to provide loans to developing countries to finance investments that will help their economic growth. Discuss the issues this bank would have to consider in making such loans. *(environmental concerns, human rights, political upheavals)* **L2**

Critical Thinking Ask students to consider the problem and effects of overpopulation at the individual and family level. Have some students participate in an impromptu panel discussion about how overcrowding can affect people's daily lives. **L3**

History Simulation 37

COOPERATIVE LEARNING ACTIVITY

Environmental Responsibilities Display Have students choose an environmental concern (for example, energy conservation, deforestation, species extinction) and make one poster graphically dramatizing the problem and another poster displaying a possible solution. Have students gather visual materials to go with the posters and make a wall display to promote environmental awareness. They should include global as well as local examples. **L1 LEP**

Chapter 37 *The World in Transition* 1019

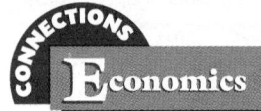

World History and Art Transparency 52, *Sky Above Clouds II*

Mapping History Overlay Transparency 25, *World Population Growth*

Independent Practice

Guided Reading Activity 37-5 **L1**

Geography and History Activity 37

Economics Have students do a survey of where the foods they eat and other things they purchase or consume are produced. Have them bring labels to class and use these as a basis for making a rough assessment of how the world is catching up to the United States in trade. **L2**

CONNECTIONS **Economics**

Global Economy

China is another Asian nation on its way to becoming an economic giant. Its economy is expected to boom in the next century. It has been growing rapidly and is expected to expand to $6 trillion over the next 25 years, a nearly tenfold growth since 1994. With this explosion of growth, however, has come increased pollution; in 1991, industries there created more polluted water than in the entire Western world.

Answers to Making the Connection

1. *to increase trade and coordinate economic growth among members*
2. *Possible answer: They help the global economy since they help member nations achieve economic health and stability.*

While consuming far less per person, however, the large populations in the developing world are exhausting the resources of many areas. In Africa and Asia, for example, population pressures have forced farmers to make a living on fragile, poorly productive lands. In some places erosion and landslides have caused irreversible environmental damage. Throughout the developing world, millions of people leave the countryside each year and crowd into the cities in the hope of improving their lives. Urban growth has been so rapid that cities cannot keep up with the needs for shelter, food, and jobs. To remedy these problems, countries must link population, development, and environmental needs in their planning.

The Environment

Protecting the environment is another challenge facing the planet as the twenty-first century approaches. For much of human history, the abundance of the planet's resources was taken for granted. Today, however, human use and abuse of resources has reached such levels that the planet may no longer be able to heal itself. Damage to the atmosphere, land, water, and air has an impact on all living things.

Land and Water

Vast areas of the earth's land have been destroyed by overgrazing, pesticides, and **deforestation**, the widespread clearing of forests for logging or farming. Particularly at risk are semiarid areas located at the edge of deserts. Between 1970 and 1990, developing countries lost 40 percent of their farmland. This loss will make it increasingly difficult for poorer countries to raise enough food for their growing populations.

The oceans and freshwater supplies of the planet also are showing signs of overuse and abuse. Coastal waters are heavily polluted with chemicals and litter. The bulk of contamination comes from poisonous industrial wastes, municipal sewage, and runoffs of fertilizers, pesticides, and salts. Instead of being swept out to sea, most of this

CONNECTIONS **Economics**

Global Economy

Japanese cars for export

Since 1945, many of the world's nations have joined together to create large regional economic markets. The goal of each of these markets is to increase trade and to coordinate economic growth among member nations.

In North America the United States, Canada, and Mexico have implemented the North American Free Trade Agreement (NAFTA). In southern South America several nations participate in the Southern Common Market (Mercosur), while in the Caribbean region a number of countries form the Association of Caribbean States (ACS).

Western European nations have not only promoted economic interdependence among themselves. In the 1993 Treaty of Maastricht, they also took steps toward political unity by creating the European Union.

The creation of large economic blocs in the Americas and in Europe in part stems from the increasing competition these two regions have faced from the growing economic might of the countries of Asia's Pacific Rim. During the past few decades Japan, South Korea, Taiwan, and Hong Kong have become economic giants and are very active in world trade. In addition, another potentially powerful Asian economic bloc is emerging in the Association of Southeast Asian Nations (ASEAN).

MAKING THE CONNECTION

1. Why have individual countries joined in forming large regional economic markets?
2. Do you think regional economic blocs benefit or hinder the global economy?

MEETING SPECIAL NEEDS ACTIVITY

Language Delayed Students with a need for help with language would benefit by making a set of flash cards for the names of places and the special vocabulary in this section. They might want to go on to compile a set of cards for the entire chapter and use them in studying the material. **L1 LEP**

contamination settles into the coastal soil. Environmental damage is reflected in epidemics spread by contaminated fish, in increasing numbers of diseased wildlife, and in the decay of coral reefs.

Meanwhile, demand for fresh water has grown. Conflicts over the distribution of limited water supplies have already developed in the southwestern United States, the Middle East, and North Africa. Efforts will be needed to achieve some fair distribution of scarce water supplies among countries, as well as between rural and urban areas.

Environmental Awareness

Since the 1970s, the world's people have become increasingly aware of environmental issues, and a number of international gatherings have stressed the urgency of dealing effectively with the environmental crisis. In 1987 representatives from 46 countries meeting in **Montreal**, Canada, signed the Montreal Protocol, which urged the world's nations to significantly reduce the use of chemicals damaging to the earth's ozone layer. Located 14 to 15 miles (23 to 24 km) up in the atmosphere, the ozone layer protects the earth from the sun's deadly ultraviolet rays. Scientists have recorded a steady loss of ozone, linking the decline to chemical pollutants.

Another important international gathering on the environment was the UN-sponsored Earth Summit, held in 1992 in **Rio de Janeiro**, Brazil. This conference called on nations and industries to plan economic growth to meet present global needs without sacrificing the environmental needs of future generations.

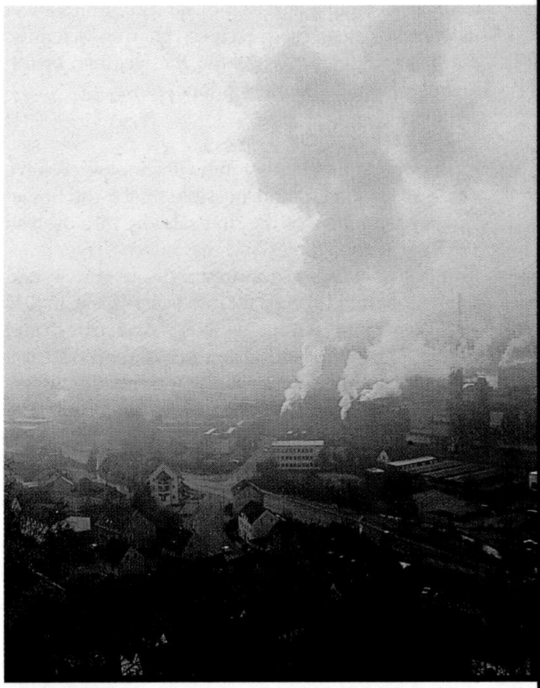

Visualizing History **Air pollution from factories is a problem in industrialized countries. In this scene, clouds containing industrial pollutants cover an area in Germany.** *How has pollution affected the planet's water?*

The Technological Revolution

Since 1945, the world has undergone a technological revolution as significant as the Industrial Revolution of the early 1800s. Computers are at the heart of this transformation. They process information that can analyze a nation's economy, forecast the weather, interpret public opinion polls, or calculate the flight path of a rocket. Nations that can afford the latest computer technology gain a distinct advantage—whether through increased productivity or ultimately a higher standard of living—over those still struggling with outdated equipment.

The applications of computer technology are varied. The "brain" driving the computer is the microchip, a mesh of circuits etched on a silicon wafer. In medicine, doctors use these chips to power artificial limbs worn by people who need them. Industrial robots programmed to assemble machines and perform tasks such as welding and painting represent another application of microchip technology.

The Information Superhighway

Computers are playing an important role in the expansion of global communications. The most dramatic leap in communications in recent years has been the development of the National Information Infrastructure, commonly known as the **information superhighway**. Using a computer and a modem, a device linking two compatible computers together by a direct connection to the telephone line, the user can have access to the screens of millions of participants around the globe. One can send a message through E-mail, or electronic mail, to any place in the world in seconds. The World Wide Web is a network of computer connections that allows the participant to transmit or receive information ranging from the availability of

Chapter 37 Section 5

Visualizing History One of the problems facing a unified Germany was that of serious air and water pollution in former East Germany. The cleaning of the air is a costly and important task for all industrialized countries.

Answer to Caption: *It has contaminated much freshwater.*

Science, Technology, and Society Although scientists are developing new drugs all of the time, a problem of drug-resistant diseases now confronts modern medicine. Have students research drug-resistant viruses and share their findings with the class. **L3**

Linking Past and Present

Forests The North American continent was once covered with great forests. With the movement west, rising populations, and decades of logging, these temperate rain forests that are home to many plants, fish, and wildlife are shrinking.

Global Gourmet

Ethnic Foods Checking the restaurant listing in any major city will show how multicultural the world's cities have become. Menus list Italian risotto, Mexican salsa, Japanese nori, and Indian samosas.

MAKING CONNECTIONS ACTIVITY

Science, Technology, and Society Every day new and more advanced forms of technology are produced, such as computers, diagnostic equipment for medical problems, and video and audio equipment. Have students interview people who grew up in the 1950s or earlier to find out how daily life then, without this technology, differed from life today. For example, students can find out whether their subjects have learned to use a computer. Then ask students to write the interview as a magazine article and include an assessment of how their own lives would be different without the technology they use every day. **L1**

Chapter 37 Section 5

ASSESS

Check for Understanding

Assign Section 5 Review as homework or as an in-class activity.

Use Student Self-Test and Review Software to review Section 5.

Evaluate

Section Quiz 37-5

Reteach

Lead a class discussion on developments of the last decade in communications technology, medicine, environment, and cultural global interdependence.

Reteaching Activity 37

Enrich

Have students prepare written reports on an international environmental issue. Allow an opportunity for them to share these studies.

Enrichment Activity 37

CLOSE

Have students create a wall chart showing the major technological changes in communication and transportation that have occurred in the twentieth century.

a certain book in a library thousands of miles away to learning new food recipes, sharing scientific data, playing games, checking the weather, or following national and international news.

Space Exploration

Computer and other new technologies have made space exploration possible. Since the Soviet Union's launching of the first satellite into orbit in 1957, the United States and the Soviet Union (later Russia) have sent hundreds of satellites and human-operated spacecraft into outer space. In July 1969 American astronauts **Neil Armstrong** and **Edwin Aldrin, Jr.,** landed on the moon. In the early 1980s American scientists developed the first operational space shuttle, a reusable spacecraft that takes off like a rocket and lands like an airplane. From the shuttle, astronauts can launch, retrieve, and repair satellites. In 1995 the United States space shuttle *Atlantis* docked with the Russian space station *Mir*. Symbolizing the end of the cold war and the start of a new era of international cooperation, this linkage opened the way for the eventual building of an internationally operated space station.

Medical Advances

Medical science also has benefited from technological progress. Lasers, or devices that emit narrow, powerful beams of light, allow doctors to perform delicate surgery with minimal discomfort to patients. Current medicines can even correct chemical imbalances in the brain, thereby treating the severe depression that can cripple some people's lives. Organ transplants, too, have benefited from new technologies. Kidneys and livers are among the most commonly transplanted organs, and many people now live for years with transplanted hearts as well.

Recent DNA (desoxyribonucleic acid) technology has led to the new field of genetic engineering, a process that involves the alteration of cells to produce new life-forms. Further molecular research may yield insights into the origins and cure of diseases such as cancer and AIDS that affect millions of people worldwide.

The Global Culture

Technological advances have hastened the growth of a global culture. Jet travel, television, and communications satellites have spread ideas and practices from one part of the globe to another. Today the cultures of various regions meet and blend in a variety of ways. Rock music from the United States now echoes in clubs around the world. Folk dancers from Indonesia perform their traditional artistry on tour in Scandinavia, while Latin American poets recite their works before audiences in Japan.

Under the impact of the new technology, social roles have changed as people have sought a new degree of individual freedom. Throughout the world, women as well as people from various oppressed ethnic and social groups have pressed for an end to long-standing injustices. Even though many injustices still occur, the push for change has expanded human rights and opportunities in many parts of the world.

In 1948 the United Nations adopted what has become the most important human-rights document of the postwar years—the Universal Declaration of Human Rights. The document addresses social and economic as well as political rights. It is a statement not of the way things are, but of the way things should be. As new technologies develop, more will have to be done to provide the basic needs and a decent quality of life for the planet's inhabitants. As the year 2000 quickly approaches, the Universal Declaration of Human Rights gives the world a common goal and the people of the earth an ideal to bring them closer together.

SECTION 5 REVIEW

Recall

1. **Define** interdependent, developing nations, developed nations, deforestation, information superhighway, genetic engineering.
2. **Identify** NAFTA, ASEAN, Montreal Protocol, Neil Armstrong, Edwin Aldrin, Jr.
3. **Explain** how population growth and movement have affected lifestyles in developing countries.

Critical Thinking

4. **Analyze** Why do environmental dangers to the planet require global solutions?

Understanding Themes

5. **Cultural Diffusion** What is the most powerful source of cultural diffusion today? Explain the reasoning behind your answer.

SECTION 5 REVIEW ANSWERS

1. All vocabulary words are defined in the Glossary.
2. NAFTA, 1020; ASEAN, 1020; Montreal Protocol, 1021; Neil Armstrong, 1022; Edwin Aldrin, Jr., 1022
3. Large populations in developing nations are consuming natural resources, including land; the movement of people from countryside to cities has exhausted urban resources.
4. Possible answer: Damage to one part of the planet affects other parts of the planet, as all environments are interconnected.
5. **CULTURAL DIFFUSION** Answers will vary. Possible answer: Computer technology has made instant global communication possible, which has allowed the sharing of art, language, and science within seconds.

Social Studies
SKILLS

Interpreting Statistics

Statistics seem to support a claim or an opinion with a ring of authority. We have heard that statistics can be misleading, but do we really understand how to interpret statistics?

Learning the Skill

Statistics are sets of tabulated information that may be gathered through surveys and other sources. When studying statistics, consider each of the following:

Biased sample A sample, or group of the total population surveyed, may affect the results. A sample that does not represent the entire population is called a biased sample. An unbiased sample is called a representative sample.

Correlation Two sets of data may be related or unrelated. If they are related, we say that there is a correlation between them. For example, there is a positive correlation between academic achievement and wages. There is a negative correlation, however, between smoking and life expectancy. Statistics may seem to show a correlation when none exists. For example, a report that "people who go fishing are less likely to get cancer" may be statistically true but lack any correlation.

Statistical Significance Using statistics, researchers determine whether the data support a generalization or whether the results are due to chance. If the probability that the results were due to chance is less than 5 percent, researchers say that the result is statistically significant.

Practicing the Skill

Study the table below (the amount of economic freedom is shown on a scale from 0–8, with 8 being most free). Then answer the questions that follow.

1. Is there a correlation between wage rates and the percentage of government employees? Explain.
2. What statistics deny a correlation between the percentage of government employees and the index of economic freedom?

Applying the Skill

Create a survey with two questions for which you believe the answers may show a correlation. For example, "How many hours of television do you watch per day?" and "How many hours of sleep do you average per night?" Gather a representative sample of responses. Tabulate and evaluate your statistics.

Wages, Government Employment, and Economic Freedom

Nation	Hourly Wage Rate (1994)	Government employees as percent of total	Index of Economic Freedom 1993–1995*
Germany	$27	16.2	6.5
Japan	$21	8.4	7.0
Sweden	$19	33.2	5.5
United States	$17	15.4	7.5
Great Britain	$14	18.1	7.0
New Zealand	$10	15.3	8.0
South Korea	$6	na	7.0
Mexico	$5	31.8	5.5

* Index compiled by survey of economists for "Economic Freedom of the World: 1975–1995," James Gwartney, Robert Lawson, and Walter Block.

For More Practice

Turn to the Skill Practice in the Chapter Review on page 1025 for more practice in interpreting statistics.

ANSWERS TO PRACTICING THE SKILL

1. No; wages are highest in Germany, but percentage of government employees is highest in Sweden.
2. They all do. For example, Sweden has the highest percentage of government employees but its index is 5.5; Japan has the lowest percentage of government employees and its index is high, 7.0.

Social Studies
SKILLS

TEACH

Interpreting Statistics Explain to students that finding a correlation does not mean you have found its cause. When two things are correlated, you cannot tell whether one factor causes the other. For example, if students who did particularly well on an exam were found to have consumed more caffeine the night before, it would not mean that this was the reason for the better performance. The real reason might have been that these students spent more time studying. Remind students to be on guard against inferring a causative relationship where none exists when analyzing statistical data.

Additional Practice

Skill Reinforcement Activity 37

Building Skills in Geography Workbook, Unit 2, Lesson 11

Chapter 37 Review

GLENCOE TECHNOLOGY

VIDEODISC

Use MindJogger to review students' knowledge of the chapter.

MindJogger Videoquiz

Chapter 37
Disc 5 Side B

Also available in VHS.

Answers

Using Key Terms

1. a
2. b
3. f
4. d
5. l
6. c
7. e
8. g
9. h
10. k

Using Your History Journal

Students should include several specific issues with their effects.

Reviewing Facts

1. trade deficit and budget deficit
2. He was willing to reform the Soviet system and to make military concessions to the West.
3. East Germany, Czechoslovakia, Hungary, Poland, Romania, Bulgaria
4. Yeltsin removed price controls, closed inefficient factories, and pushed toward privatization; this increased prices and caused job losses at first, then led to gradual new business and middle-class growth.
5. It led to the reunification of Germany.
6. Anti-Communist Polish Pope John Paul II inspired Catholic Poles to resist Communist control. They inspired people in other European nations to do the same.
7. Developed nations have blamed overpopulation; developing nations have blamed high consumption of resources.
8. The United States is no longer the economic giant; western Europe and Asia's Pacific Rim now compete.
9. Developing nations have large interest charges on their loans; banks suffer losses when debts can't be paid, and businesses suffer.
10. Serbs, Muslims, Croatians

Critical Thinking

1. Answers may vary. Students may say yes, because the new freedom caused many uprisings and ethnic conflicts.
2. French-speaking people in Canada felt that their language and culture were threatened by English-speaking Canada.
3. Developing nations supply raw materials to

CHAPTER 37 REVIEW

Historical Significance

Since World War II, the world has undergone tremendous changes. The cold war between the United States and the Soviet Union was resolved peacefully, and the global supremacy of the superpowers has given way to a world of regional blocs. Capitalist economies have triumphed over Communist ones, and efforts toward democracy are yielding results in many parts of the world. New technology also has linked world regions more closely together, creating a global economy and culture. Facing complex economic and environmental problems, the world's nations must learn to cooperate to find solutions and to meet the needs of all the planet's people.

Using Key Terms

Write the key term that completes each sentence.

a. interdependent
b. glasnost
c. privatization
d. genetic engineering
e. developing nations
f. ethnic cleansing
g. information superhighway
h. referendum
i. perestroika
j. trade deficit
k. enclave
l. deforestation

1. The growth of technology, communications, and transportation since 1945 has made the regions of the world increasingly ____________.
2. Mikhail Gorbachev's policy of ________ allowed Soviet citizens to express their opinions about the problems of their society.
3. In the war in Bosnia, ethnic Serb forces carried out ____________, a policy of forcibly removing rival ethnic groups.
4. Through ____________, scientists can now alter cells to produce new life-forms.
5. Environmental damage in part has been caused by __________.
6. Since the 1980s, Eastern European countries have carried out programs of ____________ to raise incentives and attract foreign investment.
7. ___________ have established new industries, but many of their people still follow traditional ways of earning a living.
8. The widespread use of computers has led to the development of a communications network known as the _______________.
9. In 1995 the people of Quebec held a _________ to determine if they wanted their province to become independent from Canada.
10. The territory of Nagorno-Karabakh is an _______ completely surrounded by Azerbaijan.

Using Your History Journal

How will world events affect your future? Write an essay entitled "The World's Future and My Own" identifying important international issues and explaining how events could affect your life.

Reviewing Facts

1. **List** two major economic challenges faced by the United States during the 1980s and 1990s.
2. **Explain** how Mikhail Gorbachev differed from earlier Soviet leaders.
3. **List** three Eastern European countries that overthrew Communist rule in the late 1980s and early 1990s.
4. **Discuss** Boris Yeltsin's economic policy and its effects on Russia.
5. **Describe** how the collapse of communism in Eastern Europe affected Germany.
6. **Explain** the role of religion in the anti-Communist movements of Eastern Europe during the late 1970s and early 1980s.
7. **Explain** how developed nations and developing nations differ in their analysis of the causes of the world's environmental problems.
8. **Describe** how the role of the United States in world trade has changed in recent decades.
9. **Explain** the international debt crisis, and discuss its costs to both borrowing countries and lending countries.
10. **List** the three major ethnic communities that live in Bosnia-Herzegovina.

CHAPTER 37 REVIEW

Critical Thinking

1. **Analyze** Is Europe less stable now than it was during the cold war? Why or why not?
2. **Analyze** What factors led to the separatist movement in Quebec?
3. **Evaluate** How does a global economy affect developing nations?
4. **Analyze** How have recent developments in medical technology affected humans?

Geography in History

1. **Region** Refer to the map below. What continent has the largest population?
2. **Place** Why do economists believe that the Pacific Rim is likely to become the world's fastest-growing market in the next decades?
3. **Human/Environment Interaction** How does this map help to identify regions of extreme climate and unsuitable living conditions?

Eastern Hemisphere Population Density

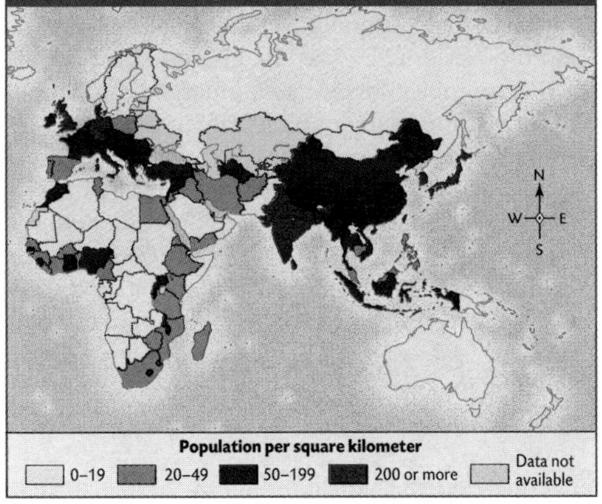

Understanding Themes

1. **Change** What factors do you think led both superpowers to seek an end to the cold war?
2. **Change** Evaluate Mikhail Gorbachev's response to the uprisings in Eastern Europe. What might have happened if he had tried to stop the changes? How were changes in the Soviet Union and its satellites linked?
3. **Cooperation** What are two future goals of the European Union that was created by the 1993 Treaty of Maastricht?
4. **Conflict** How did the Dayton peace settlement attempt to bring peace to Bosnia?
5. **Cultural Diffusion** What factors have led to the emergence of a global culture?

Linking Past and Present

1. How have many people's attitudes toward natural resources and their use changed over the past fifty years?
2. Placing a person on the moon was the primary goal of the space race between the United States and the Soviet Union. Has a new goal for the space programs of the United States and Russia emerged? Explain.

Skill Practice

Study the statistics in the chart below and answer the questions that follow.

1. Is there a correlation between energy consumed and per capita GDP? Explain.
2. What factors may explain the correlation between energy consumption and GDP?
3. Is the sample of countries used in the chart statistically significant? Explain.

Energy Use and Per Capita GDP

Country	Energy Consumed* per capita (kilograms)	GDP** per capita
Bahrain	15,608	$12,000
United States	10,798	$24,000
Netherlands	7,248	$9,700
New Zealand	5,838	$15,700
Poland	3,167	$4,400
Argentina	1,977	$5,500
Thailand	833	$5,500
India	336	$1,300
Sudan	62	$750

* figures for 1991
** Gross Domestic Product: the sum of all goods and services produced within the country (1993).

Chapter 37 Review

developed nations in exchange for manufactured goods.

4. Lasers allow doctors to perform delicate surgery with minimal discomfort; drugs can help relieve depression; organs can be transplanted; genetic engineering may lead to cures for diseases such as cancer and AIDS.

Geography in History

1. Asia
2. because it has such a large population
3. Those are the regions where population is least dense.

Understanding Themes

1. **CHANGE** political and economic problems at home; other nations were influencing world affairs
2. **CHANGE** Answers may include that the uprisings would have occurred anyway but would have been violent if Gorbachev had tried to stop them.
3. **COOPERATION** to include Eastern European nations and to create an Economic and Monetary Union featuring a common currency and a central bank
4. **CONFLICT** by partitioning Bosnia into distinct Serb and Muslim-Croatian areas
5. **CULTURAL DIFFUSION** jet travel, television, communications satellites, computers

Linking Past and Present

1. Students may say that people have become concerned about using up the world's resources.
2. Students may say that the new goal is advancing scientific knowledge or developing space stations.

Skill Practice

1. Yes: in most cases, the higher a country's GDP, the more energy it consumes.
2. The higher the GDP, the better off the population is likely to be, thus the more energy-consuming devices they are likely to use.
3. It looks like a fairly good cross section from all over the world.

Chapter Bonus Test Question

Ask students: What do you think is the future of communism as an international political ideology? *(Answers should reflect an understanding of the overthrowing of Communist regimes in the former Soviet Union and Eastern Europe and of more recent events in these countries, such as the election of former Communists in Hungary and Poland.)*

Unit 8 Digest

The Unit Digest offers a chapter-by-chapter summary that can be used for any of the following teaching purposes:

- **Preview** one chapter or an entire unit,
- **Review** some or all of the chapters,
- **Condense** when specific chapters or units have not been taught, or
- **Reteach** chapters that students have studied in the unit.

PREVIEW

Use the Unit 8 Digest Transparencies to preview the highlights of the unit.

Visualizing History When the Soviet Union dissolved, the newly independent nation of Ukraine became the possessor of a large nuclear stockpile. Today Ukraine is negotiating with the international community to destroy these deadly weapons. **Answer to Caption:** *They formed the NATO alliance.*

REVIEW

Use Student Self-Test and Review Software to review any chapters that students have studied in Unit 8.

Unit 8 Digest

The period from 1945 to the present brought a major political realignment among the nations of the world. Weakened by World War II, European colonial nations withdrew from Asia and Africa. New nations arose from the remains of the European empires and struggled to establish their roles in the global community of nations.

The United States and the Soviet Union emerged from World War II as superpowers and became locked in a struggle for global influence known as the cold war. As the Soviet Union sought to spread communism worldwide, the United States tried to resist its spread and to promote democracy. For the most part, the cold war was not fought on battlefields, although armed conflicts did occur. The main weapons in this struggle were propaganda, espionage, diplomacy, and the threat of nuclear war.

By the 1980s, the Soviet Union and the Eastern European nations under its sway faced severe economic difficulties. Communism proved incapable of reform, in spite of concerted efforts by Mikhail Gorbachev to introduce drastic changes and improve relations with the West. With the Soviet Union moving away from strict communism, popular uprisings succeeded in toppling Communist governments in Eastern Europe without the fear of Soviet intervention. The collapse of the Soviet Union itself and the emergence of new republics in 1991 signaled the end of the cold war. The complexities of the transition from communism to free enterprise soon became apparent, and hope for a new era of global cooperation faded as ethnic rivalries led to bloody conflicts in various parts of the world.

Visualizing History **The cold war led to an arms race between the United States and the Soviet Union. This Soviet rocket launcher was based in Ukraine.** *What major step did the Western allies take in 1949 to contain communism?*

Chapter 32
The Cold War

The World War II alliance quickly dissolved when conflict arose over the postwar reorganization of Europe. As a result, Europe was divided into the Eastern bloc, dominated by the Soviet Union, and the Western bloc, tied to the United States.

Communist governments emerged throughout Eastern Europe, either voluntarily or by force. The economies of Eastern European countries were government-controlled and tied to the Soviet Union. The Soviets regarded the Eastern bloc as a buffer zone against Western influences. In 1955 the Soviet Union created the Warsaw Pact to maintain its control in the region. Uprisings in Hungary and Czechoslovakia against Soviet domination were put down by force.

After World War II, the United States, as the leader of the non-Communist world, issued the Truman Doctrine, which promised aid to countries fighting Communist takeover. Western Europe's democratic nations rebuilt their shattered economies under the United States-sponsored Marshall Plan. With the United States and Canada, they formed the NATO alliance in 1949 for mutual defense against Soviet attack. Economic prosperity came to western Europe by 1960, and a movement for European unification led to the formation of a free trade area known as the Common Market.

The United States and Canada developed strong economies after World War II. The cold war

CLASSROOM RESOURCES FOR UNIT 8 DIGEST

Preview
- Unit 8 Digest Transparencies

Review
- Time Line Activities 32, 33, 34, 35, 36, 37
- Student Self-Test and Review Software, Chapters 32, 33, 34, 35, 36, 37
- MindJogger Videoquiz, Chapters 32, 33, 34, 35, 36, 37

Condense
- Chapter Digests Audiocassettes, Chapters 32, 33, 34, 35, 36, 37

Reteach
- Reteaching Activities 32, 33, 34, 35, 36, 37
- Chapter Digests Audiocassettes, Chapters 32, 33, 34, 35, 36, 37

affected American politics during the 1950s, when concern arose about Communist influences in American government and society. During the 1960s women, African Americans, Hispanic Americans, and Native Americans began to make advances in civil rights. The Vietnam War divided American society and led to a questioning of the United States's military role in world trouble spots.

SURVEYING CHAPTER 32

1. **Relating Ideas** How did the cold war affect the continent of Europe?
2. **Analyzing Information** How did the United States largely view its role in world affairs after World War II?

Chapter 33
Asia and the Pacific

The post–World War II period brought profound changes to the nations of Asia and the Pacific. Japan arose from the ashes of defeat to become one of the world's major economic and trading nations. European colonies became independent nations and faced the problems of building united societies and developing successful economies. In South Asia, ethnic and religious rivalries led to the creation of three new nations: India, Pakistan, and later, Bangladesh.

After World War II, China was torn by civil war between Nationalists and Communists. The Communist victory in 1949 established the People's Republic of China on the mainland, with the Nationalist government based on the island of Taiwan. Beginning in the 1970s, China maintained its Communist system while encouraging limited free enterprise and contacts with the West.

Korea and Vietnam, both divided into Communist and non-Communist states, became hot spots in the cold war. The Korean War, fought from 1950 to 1953, saw American-led United Nations forces fight back a Communist advance, but the conflict ended in stalemate, with Korea returning to its divided status at the 38th parallel. In Vietnam, however, Communist forces defeated American and anti-Communist Vietnamese forces and united the entire country under Communist rule. The Vietnam conflict lasted from the 1950s to the mid-1970s, with direct American military involvement beginning in the mid-1960s.

Visualizing History **Since the 1960s, Taiwan has developed a booming economy that exports goods to other parts of the world.** *How was Taiwan affected by events in China during the late 1940s?*

Since the Korean and Vietnam conflicts, economic prosperity has come to the nations along Asia's Pacific Rim, stretching from South Korea through Japan, Taiwan, and Hong Kong to Southeast Asia. Australia, New Zealand, and other South Pacific nations are increasingly involved in trade with their Asian neighbors.

SURVEYING CHAPTER 33

1. **Relating Ideas** What impact did communism have in Asia after 1945?
2. **Identifying Trends** What area of Asia is entering a new era of economic prosperity?

Chapter 34
Africa

World War II weakened Europe's hold on Africa and led to the rise of nationalist movements. From about 1956 to 1993, a number of new nations arose throughout the continent. Newly independent African nations worked to build stable governments, resolve ethnic conflicts, and create modern economies.

Unit 8 Digest

Visualizing History Both Nationalists and Communists believe that Taiwan is part of China, and each government claims to rule all China. That conflict has made relations between China and Taiwan difficult, as was seen in March 1996, when China conducted missile tests just a few miles from Taiwan. The United States responded by sending aircraft carriers to the region as a gesture of support to Taiwan.

Answer to Caption: *Chiang Kai-shek and two million followers retreated to Taiwan and created the Republic of China after Mao Zedong won control of the mainland in 1949.*

GLENCOE TECHNOLOGY

VIDEODISC

Use MindJogger to review any chapter in Unit 8.

MindJogger Videoquiz

Chapter 32 Disc 4 Side B

Chapter 33 Disc 5 Side A

Chapter 34 Disc 5 Side A

Chapter 35 Disc 5 Side A

Chapter 36 Disc 5 Side A

Chapter 37 Disc 5 Side B

Also available in VHS.

ANSWERS TO SURVEYING THE CHAPTER

CHAPTER 32 ANSWERS

1. It divided Europe into a pro-Soviet eastern bloc and a pro-American western bloc.
2. to rebuild wartorn Europe and contain communism worldwide through Truman Doctrine, Marshall Plan, and NATO

CHAPTER 33 ANSWERS

1. Communists came to power in China; Communist advances in Korea and Vietnam led to war.
2. the Pacific Rim

Unit 8 *The Contemporary World* **1027**

Unit 8
Digest

Visualizing History Rabin's assassination, like the bombing of the federal building in Oklahoma City in 1995, reminded Americans that terrorism is a weapon of right-wing as well as left-wing fanatics.
Answer to Caption: *Israel agreed to withdraw from the Gaza Strip and the West Bank and to grant eventual self-government to Palestinians in these areas.*

Environment Have students work in small groups to design a "Plan for the Planet," suggesting ten steps that the nations of the world could take to improve and protect the global environment. Remind students to consider not only technical steps, such as cleaning up toxic waste, but political and economic changes as well. Have them present their plan as an illustrated booklet. **L1**

Time Capsule Have students create a time capsule representing the state of the world at the end of its second millennium. Have students work together in small groups based on their interests: technology, politics, economics, human rights, the environment, the arts, sports, and so on. If actual articles cannot be obtained, students may list items to be included in the capsule. **L2**

Critical Thinking Point out to students that the post-World War II era saw the end of two phenomena that profoundly influenced the development of the world: European colonialism and Soviet-style communism. Ask students to imagine what the world might be like now if neither of these political systems had existed. Have students write a one-page sketch explaining their hypotheses. **L3**

The legacy of colonialism, however, often interfered with these efforts. Some African countries, based on boundaries established by the European powers without regard to ethnic loyalties, experienced internal unrest. Others, forced by European colonial rulers to rely on a single crop or product, had difficulty protecting their economies from sharp declines in world commodity prices.

Many Africans sought to reestablish their cultural identity and began to throw off reminders of the colonial past. A movement for African unity created new political and economic links among the nations on the continent. Meanwhile, after years of struggle against racial segregation, South Africa in the mid-1990s became a full democracy open to all its races, especially the black majority.

SURVEYING CHAPTER 34

1. **Analyzing Information** How has the colonial legacy affected modern Africa?
2. **Identifying Trends** What change came to South Africa in the mid-1990s?

Visualizing History **Israeli Prime Minister Yitzhak Rabin was assassinated in 1995 by a young Israeli opposed to the peace process.** *What did Israel agree to do as a result of the peace process?*

Chapter 35
The Middle East

After 1945, fully independent nations arose in the Middle East as European influence declined. Huge oil reserves brought tremendous economic growth to some Middle Eastern nations, but the attractiveness of its oil wealth also drew the Middle East into the cold war struggle between the superpowers.

Arabs united in opposing the formation of the Jewish state of Israel in 1948. During the years of the Arab-Israeli conflict, the Israelis were able to preserve their independence and even extend their territory. A major issue related to the fighting was the status of the Palestinian Arabs, who claimed the land which Israel occupied.

After years of struggle, Israel and its Arab neighbors began to make peace in the 1970s and 1980s. With the end of the cold war, this task became somewhat less complicated. By the early 1990s, Israel had agreed to give back some of the territory it had taken in the 1967 war in return for guarantees of peace and security from the Arabs. The peace process, however, was often marred by violence from opponents of peace on both sides.

SURVEYING CHAPTER 35

1. **Relating Ideas** What natural resource made the Middle East a place of confrontation between the superpowers during the cold war?
2. **Identifying Trends** How has the relationship between Israel and the Arab nations evolved since 1948?

Chapter 36
Latin America

The nations of Latin America faced many challenges during the postwar period. Rapid industrialization brought new wealth to the region, but the population was sharply divided between rich and poor. Social inequality often led to political unrest and civil war.

In the late 1950s, Fidel Castro's revolution in Cuba brought communism and the influence of the cold war to the Western Hemisphere. To contain the spread of communism, the United States often supported military dictatorships in various Latin

ANSWERS TO SURVEYING THE CHAPTER

CHAPTER 34 ANSWERS
1. Borders ignored ethnic groups, leading to internal unrest, and one-crop agriculture made economies vulnerable.
2. Apartheid ended and full democracy began.

CHAPTER 35 ANSWERS
1. oil
2. After two wars and years of conflict, Israel and its Arab neighbors have signed several peace agreements and are moving toward peace.

American countries. During the 1970s and 1980s, civil wars developed in Central America and South America between military dictators calling for social order and left-wing forces supporting radical social reforms. Many civilians were killed either by repressive governments or guerrilla forces.

During the 1980s and 1990s, pro-democracy movements overturned dictatorships in several Latin American countries. Today the region faces rapid population growth and heavy foreign debt. Mexico especially has faced economic crisis and internal upheaval as it tries to integrate its economy with those of the United States and Canada.

Visualizing History **This leftist mural in Bolivia reflects the political conflicts dividing many Latin American countries.** *What two groups fought civil wars in Latin America during the 1970s and 1980s?*

SURVEYING CHAPTER 36

1. **Analyzing Information** How has Latin America changed economically since 1945?
2. **Identifying Trends** How has democracy fared in Latin America in recent years?

Chapter 37
The World in Transition

After a tense beginning in the early 1980s, superpower relations warmed considerably by the end of the decade, signaling the end of the cold war. In 1985 the new Soviet leader Mikhail Gorbachev departed from hard-line Communist rule and introduced the policies of glasnost (openness) and perestroika (restructuring) that set out economic and social reforms for the Soviet Union. This resulted in the collapse of the Soviet Union and the end of its Communist system in 1991. Russia's leader Boris Yeltsin and the other leaders of the now independent republics of the Commonwealth of Independent States (CIS) faced challenges from internal unrest as they attempted to move their economies toward free enterprise.

The reform movement spread to the countries of Eastern Europe, which threw off Soviet domination and launched new governments. East Germany and West Germany reunited in 1990. Meanwhile, the nations of western Europe moved forward toward economic and political unity as members of the European Union (EU).

During the mid-1990s, ethnic and national divisions affected peoples and governments in various parts of the world. In places such as Czechoslovakia and Canada, disputes split or nearly split countries in two. The bloodiest encounters took place along the southern borders of the former Soviet Union and in the Balkans. Former Yugoslavia in the Balkans was torn apart by civil war, especially in the republic of Bosnia-Herzegovina, where Serbs, Croats, and Muslims fought for control of territory. In 1995 a peace agreement sent in a NATO-led peacekeeping force that included soldiers from the United States, Russia, and European Union countries.

As the world heads into the twenty-first century, the interdependence and common purpose of nations and peoples are gradually being recognized. Space exploration has permitted us to see the earth as a single unit with a shared environment. Advances in technology have enabled instantaneous communication across the globe, creating an electronic neighborhood of the world's people.

Such advances, however, are offset by rapid increases in world population and industrial growth. These trends have created critical environmental problems that now affect the entire world. It is now apparent that global cooperation is essential to protecting the future of the planet.

SURVEYING CHAPTER 37

1. **Identifying Trends** Have the 1980s and 1990s seen a shift toward political freedom throughout the world? Explain, using examples from two continents.
2. **Relating Ideas** How have global environmental problems such as deforestation changed people's thinking about the political relationships among nations?

ANSWERS TO SURVEYING THE CHAPTER

CHAPTER 36 ANSWERS

1. It has industrialized rapidly, but gaps between rich and poor remain, and the region has a heavy foreign debt.
2. Despite civil wars in Central America, democracy has taken hold in Chile, Argentina, Brazil, and elsewhere.

CHAPTER 37 ANSWERS

1. Possible answer: Yes; since the cold war democracy has come to Eastern Europe, Russia, and South Africa.
2. Isolationist and nationalist views have given way to more global views.

Unit 8 Digest

CONDENSE

Use Chapter Digests Audiocassettes to introduce chapters that students have not studied in Unit 8. Spanish Chapter Digests Audiocassettes are also available.

Discuss Have students read the **Unit Digest** and discuss the **Surveying Chapter** questions. **L1**

Visualizing History Bolivia, one of the poorest countries in South America, has an economy based largely on the export of tin and other minerals. More than half its people are Native Americans, mainly from the Quechua and Aymará peoples.

Answer to Caption: *military dictators and left-wing guerrillas*

RETEACH

Review Chart Organize the class into two groups. Have one group prepare a list of challenges facing the contemporary world, and the other group suggest possible solutions to each challenge. **L1**

Reteaching Activities 32, 33, 34, 35, 36, 37

Chapter Digests Audiocassettes, Chapters 32, 33, 34, 35, 36, 37

APPENDIX

Glossary	**1030**
Index	**1040**
Spanish Glossary	**1073**
Acknowlegments	**1086**

GLOSSARY

A

abbess the director of a convent (p. 305)
abbot the head of a monastery (p. 304)
absolutism political system in which a monarch (or group) holds supreme, unlimited power or theory that supports such a system (p. 482)
acupuncture traditional technique of Chinese medicine using thin needles at vital body points (p. 232)
age set in traditional Africa, a group of males or females of similar age who learn skills and go through life stages together (p. 188)
ahimsa (uh•HIHM•sah) Hindu doctrine of nonviolence toward all living things (p. 207)
alchemist person who practiced alchemy, an early form of chemistry emphasizing changes in substances, such as lead into gold (p. 520)
alliance system series of defense agreements involving two or more nations (p. 740)
alphabet system of symbols or characters that represent the sounds of a language (p. 82)
amphora a tall, two-handled Greek vase (p. 131)
anarchy absence of political authority (p. 692)
animism belief that spirits are found in both living and nonliving things (pp. 351, 476)
anthropologist (an•thruh•PAH•luh•jihst) scientist who studies physical and cultural characteristics of humans and their ancestors (p. 20)
apartheid official policy of strict racial separation and discrimination practiced in South Africa from 1948 to the early 1990s (p. 934)
appeasement policy of granting concessions to a potential enemy in order to maintain peace (p. 829)
apportion to divide into assigned shares (p. 648)
apprentice person who works for a master to learn a trade, art, or business (p. 325)
aqueduct a channel built to carry water (p. 168)
arabesque (ar•uh•BEHSK) complex designs typical of Islamic art, combining intertwining plants and geometric patterns (p. 286)
"Arabic numerals" counting symbols (1-9) devised by mathematicians in Gupta India (p. 214)
arbitration process of settling a dispute by submitting it to an impartial third party (p. 722)
archaeologist (ahr•kee•AHL•uh•jihst) scientist who studies earlier peoples and cultures (p. 20)
archipelago a group or chain of islands (pp. 351, 920)
aristocrat member of the nobility or the upper class (p. 113)
armada (ahr•MAH•duh) a fleet of warships (p. 483)
armistice an agreement to stop fighting (p. 761)
arms race the cold war competition between the U.S. and Soviet Union to build up their respective armed forces and weapons (p. 871)
artifact a historic object made or used by humans, such as a tool, ornament, or pottery (p. 20)
artisan person skilled in a craft (p. 33)
atomic theory scientific idea that all matter is made up of tiny particles called atoms (p. 628)
atrocity a cruel and evil action, such as torture (p. 1015)
autocracy government ruled by one person with unlimited authority (p. 690)
automation process in which electronic devices or machines do work once done by humans (p. 883)
autonomy self-government (p. 1008)

B

balance of power the distribution of power among rival nations so that no one is dominant (p. 489)
balance of trade difference in value between what a nation imports and what it exports over a period of time (p. 448)
bard a poet who tells stories by singing (p. 108)
baroque (buh•ROHK) ornate, dramatic artistic style developed in Europe in the 1550s (p. 424)
barter a system of trade in which goods, not money, are exchanged (p. 82)
bazaar marketplace in an Islamic city (p. 284)
belligerent engaged in fighting or war (p. 746)

bishop a regional leader of the early Christian Church, with authority over a diocese and other clergy (p. 174)
blitz a series of intensive air raids (p. 834)
blitzkrieg (German, "lightning war") a swift, sudden Nazi offensive (p. 831)
bloc a group of political factions or nations acting together (p. 871)
bourgeoisie (boorzh•wah•ZEE) the middle class, between aristocrats and workers (pp. 561, 625)
boyar a landowning noble of early Russia (pp. 260, 499)
boycott a refusal to buy or use certain goods as a protest against an action (p. 548)
budget deficit the amount by which government spending exceeds government income (p. 998)
buffer state neutral territory between rival powers, intended to prevent conflict (p. 582)
bullion gold or silver in the form of bars or plate (p. 448)
bureaucracy a group of government officials headed by an administrator (p. 48)

C

cabinet group of advisers to a ruler or head of state (p. 544)
calculus system of mathematics developed by Newton to analyze changing quantities (p. 519)
caliph (KAY•lihf) supreme leader of Islam, chosen as the "successor" of Muhammad (p. 277)
calligraphy the art of beautiful handwriting (p. 286)
campesino (kahm•puh•SEE•noh) a poor Latin American farm worker (p. 975)
capital money available to invest in business (p. 604)
cardinal high-ranking official of Roman Catholic Church, appointed by the pope (p. 306)
cartel (kahr•TELL) an association of businesses supplying the same product that regulates its members' prices and production (pp. 955, 993)
cartographer person who makes maps (p. 436)
cash-and-carry policy World War II program allowing Great Britain to pay cash and transport needed supplies from the U.S. (p. 836)
cash crop farm product grown to be sold or traded, not used by the farmer (p. 943)
cavalry soldiers mounted on horseback (p. 221)
celi theory scientific theory that small units called cells make up all living things (p. 626)
chancellor title of the chief minister of some European countries (p. 685)
charter formal document granting the right of self-rule (p. 326)
châteaux (sing., chateau [Fr.]) castles (p. 413)
chinampas artificial islands built by the Aztecs for use as gardens (p. 388)
chivalry code of conduct for medieval knights, based on ideals of honor and courtesy (p. 301)
choreographer person who creates dances (p. 775)
chronicle an account that records events in the order in which they happened (p. 288)
circumnavigation sailing completely around something, such as the world (p. 439)
citizen in ancient Greece, a person who took part in the government of a city-state (p. 112)
city-state an independent state consisting of a city and the surrounding land and villages (p. 59)
civil disobedience nonviolent refusal to obey a law or practice thought unjust (p. 802)
civil service system by which government offices are given on the basis of examinations (p. 224)
civilization highly organized society marked by advanced knowledge of trade, government, arts, science, and often written language (p. 32)
clan group based on family ties (pp. 342, 939)
classical describing the artistic style of ancient Greece and Rome, characterized by balance, elegance, and simplicity (p. 130)
classicism style and attitudes derived from the ideals of ancient Greece and Rome (p. 528)
clergy persons, such as priests, given authority to conduct religious services (p. 249)
coalition a temporary alliance of differing political factions (pp. 780, 879)
cold war era of political tension in which the United States and the Soviet Union competed for world influence without actual armed conflict (p. 864)
collective bargaining negotiations between union representatives and employers (p. 616)
collective security the common defense interests of several nations against an enemy (pp. 826, 1012)
collectivization under Stalin, a system to combine land into large farms owned by the government and worked by peasants (p. 790)
colon (koh•LOHN) a French settler in the colony of Algeria (p. 931)
colony a settlement of people outside their homeland, linked with the parent country by trade and direct government control (pp. 82, 475, 706)
comedy story or play intended to entertain and amuse, usually with a happy ending (p. 134)
common law body of English law based on tradition and court decisions, not specific laws (p. 309)
commonwealth a nation or state governed by the people or their representatives (p. 539)

commune a group of people who live communally, with collective ownership and use of property (p. 902)
communism in the theories of Marx and Engels, a society without class distinctions or private property (pp. 625, 758)
concentration camp prison camp where political prisoners or refugees are held (p. 786)
confederation a loose alliance or union of several states or groups (pp. 82, 378, 554)
conquistador (kon•KEES•tuh•dohr) a Spanish "conqueror" or soldier in the Americas (p. 441)
conscription compulsory call to military service; the draft (pp. 569, 740)
constitutional monarchy state in which a monarch's power is limited by a constitution (p. 541)
consul in ancient Rome, one of two officials who headed the executive branch (p. 157)
containment U.S. policy designed to prevent the spread of communism (p. 816)
contraband goods that may not legally be transported, particularly during wartime (p. 749)
convoy group of merchant ships traveling together with warships for safety (p. 760)
cooperative a farm organization owned and managed by members, who share profits (p. 812)
cordon sanitaire (kawr•dahn sah•nee•TEHR) a line of "quarantine" or buffer states (p. 764)
corporate state Mussolini's concept of a government with representation by industrial corporations, not political parties (p. 783)
corporation business organization that is owned by stockholders who buy shares, and is run by professional managers (p. 609)
cortes (KOR•tays) assembly of nobles, clergy, and town officials in medieval Spain; also, the parliament of modern Spain (p. 333)
count a noble who acted as a local official within the Frankish empire (p. 295)
coup d'état (koo day•TAH) sudden overthrow of government leaders by a small group (pp. 525, 657)
covenant a solemn pledge or agreement (p. 83)
covert (KOH•vert) secret (p. 986)
Creole a person of European ancestry born in colonial Latin America (p. 667)
Crusades military expeditions by European Christians in the 11th–13th centuries to regain the Holy Land from the Muslims (p. 318)
cubism 20th-century art style that abstracts natural forms into geometric shapes (p. 773)
cultural diffusion the exchange of goods, ideas, and customs among different cultures (p. 27)
culture the way of life of a given people at a given time, including language, behavior, and beliefs (p. 24)
culture system in Dutch colonies in Asia, a system of forced labor to get raw materials (p. 718)
cuneiform (kyoo•NEE•uh•fawrm) Sumerian system of writing using wedge-shaped markings (p. 60)
czar (from "caesar") title taken by rulers of Russia beginning in the late 1400s (p. 264)

D

D-Day the day of the Allied invasion of Normandy, France (June 6, 1944)(p. 846)
daimyo (DY•mee•oh) a powerful local noble in feudal Japan (p. 363)
datus local rulers in the Philippines (p. 475)
death squad in Central America, a band of killers hired by landowners to murder political opponents (p. 987)
deforestation process of cutting trees and clearing forests on large areas of land (p. 1020)
deism religious philosophy of the 1700s based on reason and the idea of natural law (p. 523)
deity a god or goddess (p. 31)
democracy form of government in which the citizens hold power (p. 114)
depression economic situation characterized by a business slump and unemployment (p. 609)
desalination process of removing salt from seawater to produce drinkable water (p. 964)
desertification process of fertile land becoming desert (p. 944)
developed country an industrialized nation with advanced technology (p. 1019)
developing country a country in the process of industrializing, where people often follow traditional lifestyles (p. 1019)
détente (day•TAHNT) the relaxing of tensions between the United States and the Soviet Union in the 1970s (p. 874)
dharma duties and rights of members of each class in traditional Hindu society (p. 173)
Diaspora (dye•AS•pur•uh) term for the scattering of communities of Jews outside their original homeland after the Babylonian captivity (p. 86)
dictator in ancient Rome, a leader given temporary absolute power during a crisis (p. 157)
dictatorship government headed by a ruler with absolute authority (p. 574)
dictatorship of the proletariat in the former Soviet Union, theoretical control of the state by the working class (p. 789)

direct tax a tax paid directly to the government (p. 548)
disarmament limiting or reducing military forces and weapons (p. 778)
disciple an active follower of a teacher (p. 172)
disenfranchised denied the right to vote (p. 649)
disengagement act of freeing oneself or withdrawing from a situation (p. 955)
dissident a person who openly criticizes the policies of his or her government (p. 874)
divine right political theory that a ruler derives his or her power directly from God and is accountable only to God (pp. 482, 536)
division of labor production technique in which each worker does one specialized task (p. 609)
doge (DOHJ) the elected leader of the republic in the city-states of Venice and Genoa (p. 408)
domain territory held by a ruler (p. 143)
domesticate to tame animals or plants to serve human needs (p. 30)
domestic system early industrial labor system in which workers produced goods at home (p. 602)
dominion a self-governing nation within the British Empire, later the Commonwealth (p. 654)
domino theory cold war belief that if one nation became Communist, its neighbors would follow (p. 910)
double-digit inflation a quick rise in prices of 10 percent or more (p. 889)
dual monarchy two states with one monarch (p.696)
duma the Russian national legislature (p. 694)
duty a tax on imports (p. 546)
dvorianie (dvoh•ree•YAH•nee•yuh) new class of Russian landed nobility established by Peter the Great (p. 501)
dynasty a line of rulers who belong to the same family (p. 47)

E

economy system by which goods and services are produced and distributed to meet people's needs (p. 33)
ellipse an oval (not round) closed curve (p. 517)
elite a select group of people (p. 975)
emancipation legally granting freedom (p. 691)
embargo an order restricting trade (pp. 889, 960, 1015)
emigration leaving one's home country or region to settle elsewhere (p. 630)
émigré (EH•mih•GRAY) person who fled France during the Revolution (p. 566)
empire group of territories or nations ruled by a single ruler or government (p. 49)
enclave (EHN•klayv) a small territory entirely surrounded by the territory of another country or group (p. 1016)
enclosure movement the trend for large landowners gradually to fence and include public and private common lands in their own estates (p. 603)
enlightened despot a monarch who began social changes based on Enlightenment ideas (p. 527)
entente (ahn•TAHNT) an agreement, but not a formal alliance, between nations (p. 740)
entrepreneur person who undertakes risks to establish a business (pp. 448, 556, 604)
epic long poem celebrating the deeds of a legendary or historical hero (p. 203)
estate one of three distinct social classes in France during the 1700s: clergy, nobility, and commoners (the Third Estate) (p. 560)
ethics a system of moral principles that guide behavior (p. 225)
ethnic cleansing term used in the Bosnian conflict for a policy of forcibly removing or killing members of another ethnic group (p. 1015)
evolution theory that species of living things change over long periods of time (p. 626)
excommunication formal exclusion from membership or participation in a church (p. 306)
exodus the departure of a large group of people (p. 84)
extended family family group including several generations as well as other relatives (p. 229)

F

factory system method of production in which goods are made by workers and machines in one location (a factory) outside their homes (p. 606)
fascism (FASH•ihz•uhm) political philosophy based on nationalism and an all-powerful state (p. 782)
federal system form of government in which power is divided between a central authority and its political subdivisions (p. 534)
feudalism medieval political system in which monarchs and lesser nobles made alliances based on exchanging land grants for loyalty (p. 298)
fez traditional hat worn by Turkish men (p. 797)
fief under feudalism, an estate with its peasant workers granted to a noble in exchange for loyalty and military help (p. 298)
filial piety children's respect for their parents, an important principle in Confucian ethics (p. 225)

free trade the elimination of trade barriers between nations (p. 978)
friar member of a Catholic order who preached in towns and practiced poverty (p. 307)
fundamentalism movement emphasizing adherence to traditional religious laws and practices (p. 965)

G

geisha Japanese woman trained as a professional entertainer (p. 472)
general strike a strike involving workers from many parts of a nation's economy (pp. 779, 931)
genetics the study of biological heredity (p. 627)
genetic engineering scientific field in which cell structures can be altered to produce new or different organisms (p. 1022)
genocide deliberate attempt to kill all members of a racial, cultural, or ethnic group (pp. 850, 938)
gentry in Elizabethan England, the social group including minor nobility and landowners (p. 488)
ghana title of the ruler of a region in ancient Africa, later applied to the kingdom (p. 189)
glasnost Russian term for the policy of "openness" and free expression introduced by Mikhail Gorbachev (p. 999)
grand jury in English law, group of people who decide whether the evidence of a crime justifies bringing a person to trial (p. 309)
grand vizier (vih•ZEER) prime minister to the sultan of a Muslim country (p. 457)
gross domestic product (GDP) total value of goods and services produced within a country in a year (p. 898)
guerrilla warfare method of fighting in which small groups strike unexpectedly (p. 679)
guild medieval business association of merchants or craftsworkers (p. 324)

H

habeas corpus legal principle that requires authorities to show reasons why a person should be held in custody and to provide a speedy trial (p. 542)
haiku (HY•koo) Japanese poetry form with 17 syllables, usually in three lines (p. 472)
hajj pilgrimage to Makkah that every able-bodied Muslim is expected to make at least once (p. 276)
heavy industry the manufacture of machines and equipment for factories and mines (p. 808)
heresy disagreement with or denial of the basic teachings of a religion (p. 306)
hierarchy group of people organized according to levels of rank or importance (pp. 228, 389)
hieroglyphics ancient Egyptian writing system using picture symbols for ideas or sounds (p. 52)
Holocaust name given to the Nazis' mass murder of European Jews in World War II (p. 839)
homage formal ceremony establishing feudal ties between a lord and a vassal (p. 299)
home rule self-government, especially when granted to a dependent country (p. 651)
hominid (HAH•muh•nihd) member of the group that includes human beings and earlier human-like creatures (p. 20)
humanism Renaissance movement based on the literature and ideas of ancient Greece and Rome, such as the worth of each individual (p. 404)
hygiene the science of good health (p. 138)
hyperinflation an extreme form of inflation, with sharp, rapid price increases (p. 991)
hypothesis solution proposed to explain a set of facts, which can be tested (p. 517)

I

icon a Christian religious image or picture of a saint or other holy person (p. 249)
iconoclast ("image breaker") an opponent of the use of icons in Byzantine churches, who thought they encouraged the worship of idols (p. 250)
ideology the system of beliefs and attitudes that guides the actions of a group or nation (p. 871)
illuminated manuscript book page decorated by hand with elaborate designs, beautiful lettering, or miniature paintings (p. 253)
imam (ih•MAM) a Muslim prayer leader (p. 276)
immigration entering a new country or region to settle permanently there (p. 630)
imperialism policy of building an empire to extend a nation's power and territory (p. 704)
imperial presidency term for a President and executive branch who assume powers beyond those defined in the Constitution (p. 888)
impressionism artistic style of the late 1800s in which painters tried to capture quick impressions and the effects of light (p. 638)
indemnity payment for damages or losses (p. 160)
indulgence pardon sold by the Catholic Church to reduce one's punishment for sins (p. 416)
industrial capitalism economic system in which individuals continually reinvest profits and expand their businesses (p. 608)
inflation situation in which prices rise quickly while the value of money decreases (pp. 176, 484)

information superhighway popular term for the advanced communications network linking people and computers around the world (p. 1021)

intendant an agent representing the king of France in local government (p. 491)

interchangeable parts production method using identical, easy-to-assemble parts (p. 609)

intercontinental ballistic missile (ICBM) a long-range rocket carrying a warhead (p. 873)

interdependent relying on one another (p. 1018)

intifada the 1987 uprising by Palestinians against Israeli occupation (p. 956)

iron curtain term coined by Winston Churchill for the political barrier isolating Soviet-dominated Eastern Europe from Western Europe (p. 866)

J

jaguar spotted wild cat of Mesoamerica (p. 380)

janissary member of an elite corps of soldiers in the Ottoman Empire (p. 440)

jati groups based on occupation formed within larger social classes (varna) in ancient India, each with its own rules and customs (p. 204)

jazz American musical style incorporating African rhythms with American and European sounds (p. 773)

jihad (jih•HAHD) Muslim struggle to introduce Islam to other lands (p. 278)

jingoism attitude of extreme patriotism, usually directed toward a foreign power (p. 698)

joint-stock company trading venture that sold shares to divide costs and profits (p. 447)

journeyman craftsworker who has finished an apprenticeship and works for pay (p. 325)

junk a Chinese sailing ship (p. 464)

justification by faith Martin Luther's concept that faith alone is enough to bring salvation (p. 415)

K

kaiser title of the German emperor (p. 685)

kamikaze in World War II, the Japanese pilots who crashed bomb-filled planes in suicide attacks on Allied targets (p. 845)

karma in Hinduism, the idea that one's actions in life determine one's destiny and future (p. 207)

khan an absolute ruler of the Mongols (p. 344)

kibbutz (pl. kibbutzim) a collective farm community in Israel (p. 951)

Kristallnacht ("night of broken glass") Nazi terrorist attacks, November 9-10, 1938, on Jewish property in Germany and Austria (p. 786)

kulak a well-to-do peasant in the USSR (p. 790)

L

labor-intensive farming agriculture that relies on human labor, not animals or machines (p. 466)

labor union organization of workers formed to pressure business owners to improve wages and working conditions (p. 616)

labyrinth a complex, confusing series of connected passages (p. 107)

laissez-faire (leh•say•FAYR) economic principle that government should not regulate businesses (p. 622)

laity church members who are not clergy (p. 249)

lay investiture medieval practice in which secular rulers appointed and inaugurated church officials such as bishops (p. 306)

lend-lease World War II policy allowing the loan of equipment to friendly countries (p. 836)

liberalism political philosophy that promotes social change and individual freedoms (p. 582)

liberation theology movement led by Catholic clergy in Latin America emphasizing the Church's role in improving people's lives (p. 978)

line of demarcation imaginary line in the Atlantic Ocean, drawn by the pope in 1493 to divide the world's lands between Spain and Portugal (p. 439)

literacy rate the percentage of a country's adult population who can read and write (p. 944)

logic the science of reasoning and establishing proof for arguments (p. 135)

M

madrasa Muslim school of theology and law (p. 283)

maize corn native to the Americas (p. 374)

mandarin member of the elite class of civil servants in Chinese government (pp. 224, 348)

mandate (1) in ancient China, authority granted by heaven to deserving rulers, called the Mandate of Heaven (p. 71); (2) a territory administered by another nation before independence (p. 763)

manorialism medieval economic system linking nobles and the peasants on their land (p. 301)

martial law temporary military rule, limiting rights such as free speech (p. 537)

martyr person who suffers and dies for a belief (p. 173)

master skilled artisan who owned a shop and employed other craftsworkers (p. 325)

matrilineal tracing family descent through the mother and her ancestors (p. 187)
mayor of the palace Frankish official who, by A.D. 700, held real power in government (p. 294)
mercantilism economic policy of European nations in the 1600s, equating wealth and power (p. 448)
mercenary a soldier who serves a foreign country for pay (p. 124)
meritocracy system in which people gain success on the basis of ability and performance (p. 347)
messiah in Judaism, a savior promised by the Hebrew prophets, who would bring peace (p. 171)
mestizo (meh•STEE•zoh) in Latin America, a person of Native American and European ancestry (p. 667)
metaphysics aspects of philosophy dealing with basic questions of existence and reality (p. 530)
metsuke group of officials who gathered information for the Tokugawa shoguns (p. 469)
middle class class of society that originally fell between nobility and peasants, earning their income from business and trade (p. 310)
Middle Passage middle section of the triangular trade, in which enslaved Africans were brought by ship to the Americas (p. 445)
middle power a nation that is economically strong but not a military power (p. 889)
militarism national policy based on military strength and glorification of war (pp. 689, 740)
millet community of non-Muslims within the Ottoman Empire (p. 458)
missionary person who travels to carry the ideas of a religion to others (p. 254)
mobilization act of assembling and preparing troops and equipment for war (p. 742)
monarchy rule by a king or a queen (p. 47)
monastery a community of men who have taken religious vows (p. 254)
money economy economic system in which money (not barter) is used to buy and sell (p. 323)
monopoly control of all (or almost all) trade or production of a given good (p. 194)
monotheism belief in one God (pp. 83, 189)
monsoon seasonal wind that affects climates and ways of life in southern Asia (p. 67)
mosaic picture made up of tiny pieces of colored glass, tile, or stone set in mortar (p. 253)
mosque a Muslim house of worship (pp. 191, 276)
multicultural representing several different cultural and ethnic groups (pp. 195, 889)
myth a traditional story that explains natural events (p. 35)

N

nationalism pride in one's own nation or group and its traditions; desire for independence from outside rule (pp. 576, 676)
nationalization placing a privately owned business under government ownership (pp. 737, 813)
nationalize to bring a private industry under government control (p. 952)
nation-state a political state whose people also share the same language and culture (p. 677)
natural law a universal truth or principle that 17th-century thinkers believed could be found through reason (p. 521)
negritude a literary movement that emphasizes and takes pride in Africa's cultural heritage (p. 945)
nihilist member of a Russian political movement of the late 1800s that rejected all authority and advocated terrorism (p. 692)
nirvana in Buddhism, a state of oneness with the universe, the end of the cycle of rebirth (p. 210)
nomad member of a group of people with no fixed home, who travel constantly to find food and water (p. 22)
nonaligned not taking sides with either of the superpowers in the cold war (p. 917)
nuclear family family group consisting only of parents and children (p. 229)

O

obsidian black volcanic glass (p. 383)
oligarchy form of government in which a small group holds political power (p. 114)
oral tradition the legends and history of a culture preserved by word of mouth (p. 184)

P

pacifism opposition to war or violence as a way to settle disputes (p. 523)
pacifist a believer in pacifism (p. 802)
pact a treaty between several nations (p. 953)
paleontologist (pay•lee•ahn•TAH•luh•jihst) scientist who studies fossil remains (p. 20)
Pan-Africanism movement encouraging unity and cooperation among African nations (p. 942)
Pan-Arabism mid-1940s movement intended to build cultural and political ties among Arabs (p. 950)
papal infallibility Roman Catholic doctrine that the pope cannot make an error in speaking about faith and morals (p. 686)

partisan World War II term for an underground resistance fighter, especially in Italy and Yugoslavia (p. 848)
partition to divide a region (p. 707)
partnership business owned by two or more entrepreneurs who share management, profits, and losses (p. 609)
patriarch in the early Christian Church, one of five powerful bishops in major cities (p. 174)
patrician a member of the wealthy aristocratic class of ancient Rome (p. 156)
peaceful coexistence Soviet policy of competing with the United States while avoiding war (p. 873)
peninsulares officials born in Spain or Portugal who led society in colonial Latin America (p. 667)
perestroika (pehr•uh•STROY•kuh) Russian term for "restructuring," the changes in the Soviet economy begun by Mikhail Gorbachev (p. 999)
perspective an artistic technique for showing relationships and space between objects (p. 131)
petit jury group of people who determine the guilt or innocence of a person on trial (p. 309)
phalanx in ancient Greece, a military formation in which foot soldiers stood so that their shields overlapped (p. 114)
pharaoh title of rulers of ancient Egypt (p. 49)
philosophe (fee•luh•ZAWF) a social or political thinker of the Enlightenment (p. 524)
philosopher a thinker or lover of wisdom (p. 135)
pilgrimage journey to a holy place (p. 334)
plateau a relatively flat region of land higher than the surrounding area (p. 185)
plebeian (plih•BEE•uhn) a citizen of ancient Rome who was not an aristocrat (p. 156)
plebiscite (PLEB•uh•syt) a direct popular vote on a program or issue (pp. 575, 657)
pogrom organized persecution of a minority group, usually Jews, in czarist Russia (p. 693)
polis city-state of ancient Greece (p. 112)
pollution putting toxic or impure substances into the air, land, or water (p. 898)
polytheism worship of many gods (p. 52)
pope the bishop of Rome, later the head of the Roman Catholic Church (p. 174)
population explosion a large, sudden increase in the human population (p. 808)
Postimpressionism artistic movement whose members experimented with form and color (p. 639)
potlatch feast held by Native Americans of the Pacific Northwest to display their wealth (p. 376)
pragmatic sanction decree issued by a ruler on an important question (p. 495)
pragmatist in China, a moderate who advocated economic reform and trade with the West (p. 903)
predestination doctrine of John Calvin that each person's fate is predetermined by God (p. 419)
prehistory time before written history (p. 20)
prime minister the chief executive of a parliamentary government (p. 544)
principality territory ruled by a prince (p. 260)
privatization the return of government-owned industries to private ownership (pp. 981, 1003)
proletariat in Marxist theory, the working class (p. 625)
propaganda news and information intended to influence people's feelings about a cause (p. 746)
prophet a person who preaches or interprets what are thought to be messages from God (p. 85)
protectorate a country whose policies are guided by a foreign nation (p. 706)
provisional government a temporary government set up while waiting for elections (p. 757)
psychology study of behavior and its causes (p. 628)
purge an official effort to remove people that a government considers undesirable (p. 791)

Q

queue (KYOO) single braid of hair at the back of the head (p. 466)
quinoa grain grown in the Andes (p. 390)
quota a specified number or amount (p. 900)

R

racial segregation the social separation of people according to their race (p. 887)
radiocarbon dating method for telling the age of once-living material by measuring the amount of radioactive carbon remaining in it (p. 21)
rajah an Aryan tribal chief in ancient India; later the ruler of an Indian state (p. 202)
ratify to give formal approval (p. 665)
reactionary one who opposes progress or change and wants to return to earlier ways (p. 582)
realism artistic and literary style of the mid-1800s that pictured the realities of everyday life (p. 636)
realpolitik political theory that national success justifies the use of any means (p. 682)
referendum a direct popular vote on a measure or proposed law (pp. 908, 1011)
refugee person who must leave his or her home and flee elsewhere for safety (p. 911)
reincarnation the rebirth of the soul or spirit in different bodies over time (p. 175)

reparation compensation for war damage (p. 763)
republic a government in which citizens elect the leaders (p. 156)
regent person who acts as temporary ruler (p. 251)
revelation a vision of divine truth, such as those attributed to Muhammad (p. 272)
revolution a sudden, radical change; change of government by force (p. 554)
rhetoric art of effective public speaking (p. 119)
romanticism artistic movement of the early 1800s emphasizing individuality and emotion (pp. 530, 635)
royalist person who supports a monarchy (p. 539)
Russification policy of imposing Russian language and customs on other peoples (p. 692)

S

sacrament one of the established formal rituals of the Roman Catholic Church, such as baptism, holy communion, or matrimony (p. 303)
salon in France, a gathering where Enlightenment intellectuals met for conversation (p. 525)
samurai class of landowning warriors in feudal Japan, who pledged loyalty to a daimyo (p. 363)
sanctions penalties and restrictions imposed on a nation for breaking international law (p. 827)
sanctuary building considered sacred and used for worship (p. 130)
sankin-kotai ("alternate attendance") in feudal Japan, system in which a daimyo had to spend every other year at the shogun's court (p. 469)
satellite a country politically dominated by a nearby power (p. 866)
satrap the governor of a province in the Persian Empire (p. 91)
satyagraha ("truth force") term for nonviolent protests led by Gandhi (p. 802)
savanna a flat grassland, with few trees, in tropical or subtropical regions (p. 185)
schism (SIH•zuhm) the division of the Christian Church in 1054 that separated the Roman Catholic Church and the Eastern Orthodox Church (p. 250)
scholasticism medieval school of thought that tried to bring together Aristotle's philosophy and the teachings of Church scholars (p. 326)
scientific method steps to find scientific truth through observation and experiments (p. 518)
scorched-earth policy Stalin's order for the Soviet people to destroy buildings, land, and anything that Nazi invaders could use (p. 839)
secede to withdraw formally from membership in a political organization (p. 663)
sect a subgroup with distinct beliefs within a larger religious group (pp. 157, 899)
sectionalism overemphasis on the political and economic interests of one's own region (p. 663)
self-determination the right of a people to decide their own political status or government (p. 796)
seminary school for educating priests, as ordered by the Council of Trent (p. 423)
separatism in Canada, a political movement favoring the independence of Quebec (p. 890)
sepoy an Indian soldier in the British army (p. 713)
serf a peasant laborer legally bound to the lands of a noble (pp. 302, 501)
shah the ruler of a Middle Eastern country (p. 797)
shamanism belief that spirits inhabit living and nonliving things, communicating with humans through priests called shamans (p. 358)
shari'ah (shuh•REE•uh) Islamic code of law that includes rules for all aspects of life (p. 275)
sheikh (SHAYK) chief of a bedouin tribe (p. 271)
shogun military ruler of feudal Japan (p. 363)
shogunate government established by a shogun's family and followers in feudal Japan (p. 363)
simony the selling of official positions in the medieval Roman Catholic Church (p. 335)
slash-and-burn farming farming method in which land for crops is cleared by cutting and burning trees to fertilize the soil (p. 380)
socialism political theory that society as a whole should control the means of production, such as factories and land (p. 624)
Socialist realism under Stalin, an artistic style that glorified the Soviet way of life (p. 791)
sociology study of human group behavior (p. 628)
sonnet poetry form with 14 lines and a fixed pattern of rhyme and meter (p. 405)
sovereignty the independent decision-making power of a group or nation (p. 963)
soviet a workers' council formed early in the Russian Revolution; later, a unit of government in the Soviet Union (p. 694)
special economic zone areas of China where foreign businesses and a free market were allowed to operate in the 1990s (p. 905)
sphere of influence area in a country where a foreign power has exclusive rights to trade or invest (pp. 706, 715)
stagflation economic trend combining slow growth with high inflation and unemployment (p. 889)
stalemate a deadlock, or situation in which neither of two opponents can move further (p. 907)

standard of living a general measure of people's overall wealth and quality of life (p. 979)
steppe wide, grassy, semiarid plains of Eurasia, from the Black Sea to the Altai Mountains (p. 258)
stupa a dome-shaped Buddhist shrine built over relics or bones of a holy person (p. 210)
subcontinent landmass that is part of a continent but distinct from it, such as India (p. 66)
subsistence farmer farmer who grows only enough to supply a family or village (p. 943)
suffragette woman who actively worked to win voting rights for women (p. 651)
sultan political leader with absolute authority over a Muslim country (p. 457)
superpower a powerful, influential nation with a bloc of allies; specifically, the United States and the Soviet Union during the cold war (p. 864)
surrealism 20th-century art movement using distorted, surprising images (p. 773)
symbolism antirealism artistic movement that focused on dreamlike images and symbols (p. 638)
symposium in ancient Athens, a gathering of men that featured eating, drinking, entertainment, and intellectual discussions (p. 123)
syndicate under fascism, an organization of workers and employers in an industry (p. 783)

T

technology the skills and knowledge used by people to make tools and do work (p. 24)
theocracy government headed by religious leaders or a leader regarded as a god (pp. 48, 418)
theology study of religious questions (p. 251)
tithe a 10 percent tax on income, paid to the clergy (p. 561)
tournament medieval sport in which knights competed to show their fighting skills (p. 299)
trade deficit the economic imbalance when a country's imports exceeds its exports (pp. 889, 998)
tragedy story or play in which the central character struggles against destiny but meets an unhappy end (p. 132)
trench a ditch dug to protect soldiers (p. 747)
triangular trade three-directional trade route between Europe, Africa, and America in the 1600s (p. 444)
tribune in ancient Rome, an official who represented the plebeians (p. 157)
triumvirate in ancient Rome, a three-person ruling group (p. 163)
troubadour poet-musician of the Middle Ages, who traveled from court to court (p. 327)
tyrant in ancient Greece, a person who seized power and established one-man rule (p. 114)

U V

ultimatum a final demand or statement of terms, implying a threat of serious penalties (p. 742)
ultraroyalist an extremely conservative aristocrat in France in the 1820s (p. 655)
unicameral legislature assembly or lawmaking body with one house (p. 565)
urbanization the spread of cities and city living (p. 631)
utilitarianism economic philosophy, developed by Jeremy Bentham, that social and political actions should be useful and helpful to humanity (p. 624)
vassal in feudalism, a noble who held land from and served a higher-ranking lord (p. 299)
varna one of four main social classes in Aryan society of ancient India (p. 203)
vernacular the language of everyday speech, not of scholars, in a country or region (p. 328)
viceroy governor representing a monarch (p. 714)
vocation a calling from God to take up certain work (p. 417)

W X Y Z

war of attrition conflict in which each side tries to win by wearing down the other (p. 747)
warlord local military leader in China (p. 804)
weir net or trap placed across a river to catch fish (p. 376)
welfare state government system in which the state provides programs to protect people's social and economic well-being (p. 879)
westernization the spread of European culture (p. 718)
yasa Mongol law code of Genghis Khan (p. 344)
yeoman (YOH•mun) in English society, a farmer who owned land (p. 488)
yin and yang in Chinese thinking, the opposing principles present in all nature (p. 227)
yurt large, round, portable tent used by nomads of central Asia (p. 343)
zaibatsu (zy•BAHT•soo) large Japanese industrial firms owned by a few families (p. 808)
zemstvo local assembly in czarist Russia (p. 692)

Italicized page numbers refer to illustrations. Preceding the page number, abbreviations refer to a map (m), chart (c) photograph or other picture (p), graph (g), cartoon (crt), painting (ptg). Quoted material is referenced with the abbreviation (q) before the page number.

A

Abbas, Shah, 459
Abbasid dynasty, *m284,* 274, 280–81; cultural life, 282, 285; establishment, 277, 280; Turk mercenaries, 342
abbesses, 305
abbots, 304
Abdul-Aziz, 458
Abdul-Hamid II, 458
Abdul-Mejid I, 458
á Becket, Thomas, 309–10
Aborigines, 654
Abraham, 83, 84, 275
absolutism, 482, 492; end of, in England, 539; in France, 655
abstract expressionism, 884
Abu Bakr, 273, 277
Abu'l-'Abbas, 280
Abu (Sumerian god), *p36*
Achebe, Chinua, 968
acid rain. *See* pollution
Acre, 321
Acropolis, *p116–17,* 112, 130
Actium, 163
Act of Seclusion, 468, 471
Act of Settlement, 543, 544
Act of Supremacy. *See* Church of England
Act of Union, 540, 543, 651
acupuncture, *p228,* 232
Adams, John, *q548,* 722
Adams, Samuel, 550
Adena culture, *p326*
Adenauer, Konrad, 878, 880
adobe, 377
Adowa, Battle of, 711
Adrianople, *m177*
Adulis, 186
advertising, 771
Aegean civilizations, *m107;* culture, 108–10; deities, 110–11; festivals, 111; Minoan civilization, 107–11; Mycenaean civilization, 107–08; religion, 110–11
Aeneid, 170
Aeschylus, 132
Aesop's fables, 229
Afghanistan; Pakistan, relations with, 919; Seleucus, rule of, 143; Soviet invasion of, 871, 874–75
Africa, *m199,* 184–96; agriculture, 17, 943–44; arts, 945; climate, 184–85; cold war, 871; colonialism, 928–29; colonialism 942, 943, legacy of, 943; common market, 942; digest, 238; East Africa. *See* East Africa; economic development, 942–43; exploration, 434, 436, 707; food production, 944; foreign aid, 943–944; future challenges, 941–45; geography, 184–85; human prehistory, 20; imperialism, social effects, 799; independence, 928–29; Internet, 861; kingdoms, *m193;* military rulers, 941–42; national borders, 942; nationalism, 856, 929; national unity, 941–42; North Africa. *See* North Africa; Pan-Africanism, 942; population growth, 944; post-World War II period, 1027; pride, 930, 941–45; regional economic cooperatives, 944; religion, 190–91; socialism, 943; Southern Africa. *See* Southern Africa; Sub-Saharan African. *See* Sub-Saharan Africa; trade with Muslims, 284; West Africa. *See* West Africa. *See also* individual countries
African Americans; citizenship, 664; civil rights movement, 886–88; literature, 773; identity, 945; music, 401
African National Congress (ANC), 712, 926, 934, 935, 939
Afrika Korps, 843
Afrikaners, 709, 934
Afro-Caribbean music, 401
After Dinner at Ornans, ptg635
After Naseby, 1645, *ptg535*
Afternoon, ptg373
Agamemnon, *p101, p110,* 132
age sets, 187–88
Agincourt, Battle of, 330
Agnew, Spiro, 888
Agni, 206
agora, 112, 119
agriculture; as a business, 603; cash crops, 943; civilization, influence on, 31; collectivization, 790; development of, 16–17, 18, 30; enclosure movement, 603; food distribution, 34; labor-intensive farming, 466; in Middle Ages, 302; pre-Industrial Revolution, 601–02; rotation of crops, 298; slash-and-burn, 380; subsistence farming, 467, 943
Aguateca, 386
ahimsa, 207
Ahmose, 49
Ahriman, 92–93
Ahura Mazda, 92–93
AIDS, 1022
airplanes, 611; in cold war, 864; first flight, 598; reconnaissance aircraft, 760; in World War I, 748
Aix-la-Chapelle, Treaty of, 497
Ajanta caves, 213
Akan culture, 191
Akbar, 461
Akbar Hunting Tigers Near Gwalior, ptg461
Akhenaton, 51, 52
Akkadian Empire, *m60,* 62, 63
Aladdin and His Lamp, 287
Alaric, 178
Alaska, Native Americans, 375
Albania, 739; communism, 865; communism, end of, 1007
Alberta, Canada, 653
Albert Hall, 632
Albigensians, 306–07
alchemy, 285, 520
Alcuin, 303
Aldren, Edwin, Jr., 1022
Alegría, Claribel, *q987*
Alejandro of Alva, 482
Alemanni, 175
Alexander I, Czar, 576, 582, 690–91
Alexander II, Czar, *p690,* 674, 691–92
Alexander III, Czar, 692–93, 757
Alexander the Great, *p141, p142,* 141–42, 237; becomes king of Macedonia, 128; empire, *m141, m151;* education by Aristotle, 137; invasion of Indus River valley, 211; Pachacuti, compared to, 389; Persepolis, destruction of, 90; Persian Empire, conquest of, 93, 256. *See also* Macedonian Empire
Alexander VI, Pope, 428
Alexandra, Empress, 692, 693, 756–57
Alexandria, Egypt, 100, 142, 143–44
Alexis, son of Czar Nicholas II, 692
Alexius I Comnenus, 343
Alfonso XIII, King of Spain, 827
Alfred of Wessex, 308
Alfred the Great, 308
algebra, 243, 285
Algeria, 708; French imperialism, 697, 704, 705; fundamentalism, Muslim, 965; independence, 879–80, 926, 931; Islamic state, 936; in the 1990s, 935–36
Algiers, 708
Alhambra, *p279*
Ali, Muhammad, 708
Ali, son-in-law of Muhammad, 277, 278
Ali, Sunni, 193
Ali Baba and the Forty Thieves, 287
al-jabr w'al-muqabalah, 243
Allah, 272, 275
Allen, Douglas, 721
Allen, Lewis, 776
Allende, Salvador, 991
Alliance for Progress, 978
alliance systems; as a cause of World War I, 740, 743; defined, 740
Allied Powers (World War I), 744
alloys, 34
All Quiet on the Western Front, 736
Almoravids, 190
alms, 276
alphabet, 78, 82; Cyrillic, 255; Ionians, use by, 108; Japanese, 250
Alps; Hannibal's crossing, 160
Alsace-Lorraine, 739, 763
Alsace province, 658
al Tabari, 282, 288
Altar of the Hand, *p190*
Amaterasu, 360, 361
Amazon River, 421
Amen-hir-khopshef, 55
Amenhotep, 49, 51
America; Cro-Magnon migration into, 35; name derivation, 438. *See also* North America. *See also* South America
American colonies. *See* English colonies
American Revolution; anthems, 578; battles, *m557;* Boston Massacre, 548; Boston Tea Party, 550, 552; British view, 549; Continental Congress, First, 550; Continental Congress, Second, 553; Declaration of Independence, 553–54; events leading to, 545–50; French Revolution, influence on, 560, 562; Revolutionary War. *See* Revolutionary War; women, 552
American Tragedy, An, 638
Amiens, Treaty of, 574, 576
Amon, 52
Amon-Ra, 52
Amorites, 63
amphitheaters, 111
amphora, 131
Amritsar Massacre, 801–02
Amsterdam, Netherlands, 442
Amsterdam Vegetable Market, The, ptg442–43
Anabaptists, 419
Analects, 225, 231
anarchy, defined, 692
Anasazi. *See* Pueblo
Anatolia, 88
anatomy, 519
ANC; *See* African National Congress (ANC)
Ancient Records of Assyria and Babylonia, q69, q88
Andean Pact, 978
Andes Mountains, 389

Andrea, Alfred J., 277, 456, 462, 468, 498, 524
angels, *ptg287*
Angkor, 351, 352
Angkor Wat, *p352–53,* 353, 476
Angles, 178, 308
Anglican Church, 420, 425
Anglicanism, 418
Anglo-Boer War, 711
Anglo-Saxon Chronicle, 308
Anglo-Saxons, 305
Angola; civil war, 926; independence, 933; Marxism and free enterprise, 939
Animal Farm, 858
animals, domestication of, 26, 30
animism, 351, 353; in Japan, 361; in Korea, 358; in Thailand, 476
Ankara, Turkey, 797
Annals of America, The, 440
Annam, Vietnam, 476
Anne, Queen of England, 335–36, 543–44
Anne, Saint, 415
Anne of Austria, 491
Annunication, Church of the, *p264*
Anschluss, defined, 828
anthems, musical, 578
anthropology, 20–21
Anti-Comintern Pact, 828
Anti-Corn Law League, 649
Antigone, 146–49
Antigonus, 142, 143
Antin, Mary, *q630,* 630
Antioch, *m320*
Antiochus IV, 143
anti-semitism; *See* Jews; Nazi Persecution; Persecution in Russia. *See* Holocaust
antiseptics, 628
antislavery movement, 445
Antony, Marc, *p159,* 159, 163
Anyang, 71
ANZUS Treaty, 921, 922
Apache, 377–78
Apadana Hall, 91
apartheid, 934. *See also* South Africa
Aphrodite, 110, 157–58
Apocryphal Life of All, *ptg269*
Apollo (deity), 111
Apology, 171
appeasement, 829
Appian Way, 168
apportion, 648
apprentices, 325
Apsu, 35
aqueducts, 168, 170
Aquinas, Thomas, 327
Aquino, Benigno, Jr., 920
Aquino, Corazon, *p921,* 920–21
arabesques, 286
Arabi, Ahmed, 708
Arabia; independence, 697; trade, 81, 214
Arabian Nights, The, 283, 287
Arabian Peninsula, 270–71
Arabic language, 80, 273, 285
Arabic numerals, 214, 243, 285
Arab-Israeli conflict; in 1948, 950, 951; *intifada,* 955; Six-Day War, 954–55; trends, 962; Yom Kippur War, 955
Arab League, 950, 962, 963
Arab Nationalism: An Anthology, 796
Arabs; Armenia, invasion of, 257; Byzantine Empire, conquest of, 255; independence denied, 764, 951; Jerusalem, conquest of, 240; Jews, relations with, 798–99; Ottoman Empire, influence on, 458; unity, 951, 963; in World War I, 761, 798
Arafat, Yasir, *p955,* 948, 955; renunciation of terrorism, 956
Aragon, Kingdom of, 333, 482
Aramaeans, 80, 88, 89; summary, 98
Aramaic language, 80
Aramis, Ethiopia, 21
arbitration, defined, 722
arch, 61
archaeology, *p96,* 20–21
Archbishop of Canterbury, 538
Archimedes, 145
archipelagos, defined, 351, 920
architecture; classicism, 528; French, 413; Gothic, *p328,* 322, 328; Greek, 130–31, 409; Hindu, 204–05, 353; Hitler's plans, 786; London, England, 541; medieval, 328; Muslim, 286; Persian Empire, 132; Roman Empire, 168–69; Romanesque, 328; Twenties, 775
Architecture of Wren, The, 540
Arctic, Native Americans in, 375
Ardashir I, King of Persis, 178
Ares, 158
Argentina, 990–91; democracy, 814; dictatorship, 978; fascism, 814–16; Inca Empire, 390; independence, 669; women, 990
argument, 810
arias, defined, 472
Arias, Oscar, 986
Aristarchus, 145
Aristide, Jean Bertrand, 972, 984
Aristides, Aelius, *q164*
aristocracy; British, 650; Greek, 113
Aristophanes, 134
Aristotle, 101, 135, 137, 141, 522; study by Muslims, 287; taught in medieval universities, 326
Arizona; German promise to Mexico, 751; Native Americans, 377; U.S. acquisition, 662
***Arizona* (battleship),** 841
Arjuna, 200, 205
Arkwright, Richard, 605, 612
armada, defined, 483
Armenia, 256–57; Nagorno-Karabakh, claim of, 1016; reforms and unrest, 1003
Armenians; mass killing by Ottomans, 762
armistice, 761
armor, *p301*
arms race, 871, 873, 874, 885
Armstrong, Louis, 773
Armstrong, Neil, 883, 1022
Arouet, François-Marie. *See* Voltaire
Articles of Confederation, 554
artifacts, 20–21
artisans, 33
arts; advances in 19th and 20th centuries, 635; Greek, 131–32; neoclassical, 635; painting, 638; realism, 636, 638–39; romanticism, 635–36; Socialist realism, 791; symbolism, 638; Twenties, 772–75. *See also* individual countries, empires, etc.
Artz, Frederick B., 282
Aryans, 100, 202–07; defined, 798; duty, 205; India, invasion of, 200; language, 203; social structure, *c203,* 203–05
Ashanti, 709
Ashdown, Paddy, *q1010*
Ashikaga family, *q468,* 358, 363, 469
Ashinto, Lake, *p360*
Ashurbanipal, *p79,* 78
Ashurbanipal II, 88
Asia; agriculture development, 17; imperialism, 713–19; nationalism, 856; postwar independence, *m918;* post-World War II period, 1027; superpower rivalry, 871. *See also* individual countries
Asia Minor, 456
Asoka, Mauryan king, 211–12
Aspasia, 123
Assad, Hafez al-, 963
Assault on the Bastille, *ptg559*
Assemblée Nationale, *p103*
Assembly (Athens), 117, 118, 119
assembly lines, 597, 609
Assembly of Centuries, 157
Assembly of Tribes, 157, 162
Association of Caribbean States (ACS), 1020
Association of Southeast Asian Nations (ASEAN), 1020
Assyrian Empire, *m89,* 78, 85, 89; invasion of Egypt, 186; summary, 99
Astley, Philip, 518
astrolabe, *p282, p436,* 240, 285, 435
astrology, 90
astronomy, 101, 524; Chinese development, 228, 231; Chaldean development of, 90; Greek development, 128; mathematics, use of, 242; Maya, 381; model of Copernican universe, *p511;* Roman development, 170; 1600s, 516–17; solar system, model, *p525*
Aswan High Dam, 47, 952
Atahualpa, 441
Atatürk, Kemal, 796–97
Athena, *p117;* Alexander's homage to, 141; aspects, 110; Athens named for, 117; in *Oresteia,* 132; Parthenon dedication, 130; statue, 131
Athenian Empire, 123
Athens, 117–19; Athenian Empire, 123; citizenship, 117, 118; daily life, 122–23; democracy, 114, 115, 118–19; education, 119; Golden Age. *See* Greece, Golden Age; Persian Empire, war against, 120–22; reforms, 118; slavery, 122–23; Sparta, war against, 123–24; women, 119, 123
Athens (city), 122
Athir, Ibn al-, 288
Atlantic Charter, 831, 836
***Atlantis* (space shuttle),** 1018, 1022
atom, 137
atomic bomb, 733; dropped on Japan, 849–50; Soviet Union, 871
atomic energy, 771; Chernobyl nuclear power plant disaster, 859
atomic theory, 626, 628
Aton, 51
Attica, 117
Attila, 178
Attlee, Clement, 849, 879
attrition, war of, 747
Augsburg, Germany, 446
Augustine, *q173,* 173–74
Augustus, *p164, p237,* 101, 159, 163, 164–65, 171
Aurangzeb, Shah, 460
Aurelius, Marcus, *q165–66, p175,* 165, 175
***Aurora* (ship),** 758
Auschwitz, 839
Ausgleich, 696
Australia, *p717,* 653–54; British imperialism, 705; dominion status, 652, 654; foreign relations, 921–22; in Gallipoli Campaign, 750; human prehistory, 24; immigration to, 630, 920, 921; industrialization, 921; language, 654; mandates, 763; natural resources, 920
Australopithecus, 22, 25
Austria, 495–96; Congress of Vienna involvement, 580; Denmark, war against, 683; dual

monarchy, 696–97; in European Union, 1013; France, war against, 564, 566, 567, 573, 576, 577, 678; French Revolution, policy toward, 566; German Confederation, 582, 681; German invasion, 828; Hungary, compromise with, 696–97; immigration from, 665; industrialization, 697; Italy, expulsion from, 678–79; Lombardy, loss of, 696; Lombardy and Venetia, control of, 676; monarchy, 495–96; Ottomans, defeat of, 495; Poland, absorption, 399, 502; Poland, relations with, 582; Prussia, war against, 683–84; Quadruple Alliance membership, 582–83; reform, political, 656; reform, resistance to, 695–96; in Seven Years' War, 497, 696; in Seven Weeks War, 696, soldiers, *p696;* in War of the Spanish Succession, 493
Austria-Hungary; Archduke Ferdinand's assassination, reaction to, 742; Balkans, expansion in, 739; Bosnia-Herzegovina, annexation of, 739; breakup of, 763; digest, 730; in League of Three Emperors, 740; population groups, m697; Russia, agreement with, 739; Serbia, war against, 741, 742; World War I surrender, 761
autocracy, defined, 690
Automat, ptg769
automation, 883
automobile industry, 998; in Japan, *p898,* 898
automobiles, 594, 771; influence on society, 774, 883; influence on suburbs, 632
autonomy, defined, 1008
autos de fé, 483
Avarair, Battle of, 257
Avars, 255
Avesta, 93
Avignon, France, 334
Awolowo, Obafemi, *p799*
axes, *p41,* 28
Axis powers, 828
Axum, *m187,* 184, 186–87
Aylwin, Patricio, 992
Ayoola, Theo, *q928*
Ayutthaya, 351, 355
Ayutthaya kingdom, 476
Azerbaijan; Nagorno-Karabakh, claim of, 1016; reforms and unrest, 1003
Azikiwe, Nnamdi, 800
Azores, 434, 436
Aztec Empire, *m390,* 388–89; markets, 389; population, 389; religion, 383, 389; social order, 389; Spanish conquest, 388, 389, 441; Tenochtitlán established, 372; wealth, removal from, 448

B

Baal, 83
Babur, 456, 460
baby boom, 882
Babylon, *m95*
Babylonian Captivity, 334
Babylonian Empire, *m60,* 63–64, 85; Alexander, occupation by, 142; calendar, 85, 100; Chaldeans descendants of, 89; exile of Jews, 334; first cities, 16; Hittite conquest, 64, 88; rebuilding, 90; social structure, 64
Babylonian Wisdom Literature, *q58*
Bach, Johann Sebastian, *p496,* 529
Bach Dang River, Battle of, 351, 354
Bacon, Francis, 518, 526
Bacon, Paul V., 686
bacteria, 620, 627–28
badge, French Revolution, *p570*
Badoglio, Pietro, 844
Baghdad, Iraq, *m281,* 274, 280–81, 282; bombing of, 960; Mongol conquest, 344
Baghdad Pact, 953
Bahamas, 444; discovery by Columbus, 438
baileys, 299
Bailkey, Nels M., 171
bakeries, *p56*
Bakunin, Michael, 692
balance of power, 489, 580
balance of trade, 448
Balanchine, George, 775
Balboa, Vasco Núñez de, 439
Balfour Declaration, 796, 798
Bali, 355
Balkan League, 698
Balkans; Austrian occupation, 495; Avar invasion, 255; Bulgar occupation, 256; Russian invasion, 698; Second Balkan War, 698; Serb occupation, 256
Balkan War, Second, 698
ballet, 775
Ballot Act of 1872, 650
ballroom dancing, 775
Baltic Sea, Russian ports on, 499
Balzac, Honoré de, 638
banana industry, *p977*
Bandhari, Pradeep, 916
Bangkok, Thailand, 355, 477, 914
Bangladesh, 919
Banjul, Gambia, *p930*
banking, *p323,* 323, 398, 446–47; government-chartered banks, 447
Bangkok, Thailand, 914
Bantu-speaking peoples, 187–88; arts, 188; kingdoms, 195–96; migrations, 187; religion, 188; social life, 187–88
baptism, 419
Barbados, 444
barbarians, 177–78
Barbarossa, Frederick, Holy Roman Emperor, 320
Barber, Elizabeth Wayland, 26
bards, 108
barley, 17
baroque style, 424, 528; in music, 496
Barrett, Hugh, *q626*
barter system, 82, 323
baseball, 858
Basho, Matsuo, 472
Basic Writing of Mo Tzu, Hsun Tzu, and Han Fei Tzu, 220
Basie, Count, 775
Basque separatism, 1012
Bastille, storming of, 558, 562–63
Bastogne, Belgium, 848
Batavia, 442–43
batik, 351
Batista, Fulgencio, 972, 982
Battuta, Ibn, 192
Batu, 344
Baudelaire, Charles, *q635*
Bauhaus school, 775
Bavaria, 684; Mad Ludwig, 688
Bayeaux Tapestry, *p309*
Bay of Pigs invasion, 979, 982–84
Bayon Temple of Angkor, *p474*
bazaars, 284
Beagle, **H.M.S.,** 626
Beatles, 21
Beauharnais, Josephine de, 573
beauty, pursuit of, 363
Because I Want Peace, 987
Becket, Thomas á, 309–10
bedouins, 270–71
Beethoven, Ludwig von, 511, 580, 635
Beggar, The, 639
Begin, Menachem, 955
Behanzin, King of Dahomey, 709
Beijing, China, 349, 715, 901; construction, 464
Beirmeister and Wain Steel Forge, *p608*
Beirut, Lebanon, 958
Belarus, 247; in Commonwealth of Independence States, 1001; ethic origins, 259
Belgian Congo, 709, 932. *See also* Congo
Belgium, 413; in Common Market, 881; Congo, colonization of, 932; German invasion, 743, 833; law, 103; Locarno Agreements, 780
Belisarius, Byzantine general, 248
Belize, Native Americans, 379
Bell, Alexander Graham, 595, 611
belligerents, defined, 746
Benedict, *p304,* 303, 304
Benedictine Rule, 304, 305
Ben-Gurion, David, 951
Benin, 189, 190
Bentham, Jeremy, 624
Benton, Thomas Hart, 608
Beowulf, 327
Beraud, Jean, 621
Berbers, 193
Berchtold, Leopold, 742
Beringia, 35
Bering Strait, 35, 374
Berlin, Germany, 786; division after World War II, *m893,* 869–70; Krushchev demands Western withdrawal, 876; postwar division of, 848. *See also* West Berlin
Berlin airlift, 862, 870
Berlin-Baghdad railway, 739
Berlin's Ode to Joy, 1004
Berlin Wall, 871, 876; fall of, 859, *p1006–07,* 1004, 1005–06; symbolism, 867
Bermuda, U.S. military bases, 835–36
Bernard of Clairvaux, 320
Berytus, 82
Bessemer, Henry, 598, 606
Beveridge, Albert J., *q721*
Bhagavad Gita, 205
Bhutto, Benazir Ali, 919
Biafra, 799, 928, 932
bias, detecting, 617
Bible, *q82;* books of, 86; conflict with evolution, 627; Deborah, story of, 206; as historical source, 83, 84; illustrated in Sistine Chapel, 411; interpretation, 249; interpretation by Catholic hierarchy, 423; language, 80; Latin Vulgate version, 423; *Mahabharata,* compared to, 205; New Testament, 172; printed, 241; Quran, compared to, 275; Septuagint translation, 140, 144; source of truth and authority, 417; translation into Cyrillic, 255, 262; translation into English, 335; translation into German, 417
Bible as History, The, 80
bibliographies, 961
bicycles, *p630*
Bierck, Harold A., Jr., 666
Bill of Rights, English, 564
Bill of Rights, U.S., 555
Bimbisara, Magadha king, 211
biology, 626-27; botany, cell theory, evolution, genetics, 626-27
birth rate, in Latin America, 975
bishops, 174
Bismarck, Otto von, *p681, q683, q684,* 595,

682–89, 740; conflict with Church, 686–87; conflict with Socialists, 689; Franco-Prussian War, 684; militarism, *q682;* resignation, *crt689,* 674; Seven Weeks' War, 683
***Bismarck* (battleship),** 842
bison, 378
Black Death, *m339,* 241, 322, 324, 327
Blackfoot, 378
Black Hand, 741
Black Sea, 252
Blackshirts, 782
blacksmith's guild, *p325*
Blake, William, *q529,* 636
blitz, 834–35
blitzkrieg, 831
Bloodax, Eric, 296
Blood of Brothers, Life and War in Nicaragua, 985
Blood Sisters, The French Revolution in Women's Memory, 564
Bloody Mary, 420
Bloody Sunday, 694
blue collar workers. *See* working class
Bluetooth, Harald, 296
Blum, Léon, 780
Blume, Peter, 773
boat building, 28, 34
Boat People, 913
Bodet, Jaime Torres, 966
Boers, 443, 711; Anglo-Boer War, 711
Bohemia, 697; church reform, 336; Jesuit missionaries, 425
Boileau-Despreaux, Nicolas, 521
Boleyn, Anne, 419–20, 536
Bolger, Jim, 922
Bolívar, Simón, *q666, q670,* 669
Bolivia; Inca Empire, 390; independence, 669
Bologna, Italy, 326
Bolshevik Revolution, 736, 758–59
Bolsheviks, 693, 757; Reds and Whites, 759
bombers, 864
Bonaiuto, Andrea de, 317
Bonaparte, Joseph, 576
Bonaparte, Louis-Napoleon. *See* Napoleon III
Bonaparte, Napoleon. *See* Napoleon Bonaparte
Boniface VIII, Pope, 312
Bonn, Germany, 153
Bonpane, Blase, 974
Book of Changes, 231, 233
Book of Documents, 230–31
Book of Songs, 228, 230
Book of the Dead, *p97,* 53
book printing, 416; first, 232
book publishing, 413
Borgia, Cesare, *p428*
Borneo, 915
Bosnia-Herzegovina; Austria-Hungary, annexation by, 698, 739; Dayton Treaty, 1015; ethnic conflict, 1008, 1009, 1014–15; independence, 1008–09; partition, 1015; peace agreement, 996, 1009. *See also* Yugoslavia
Bosnians, 498; ethnic origins, 259
Bosnians Recall Karadzic, a Neighbor Turned Enemy, 1014
Bosporus, 246, 252
Bossuet, Jacques, 491–92
Boston Massacre, *p548,* 548
Boston Tea Party, *p542,* 550, 552
Boulanger, Georges, 659
Boulevard Des Capuchines and Theatre de Vaudeville, *ptg621*
Bourbon dynasty, 490, 655, 676
bourgeoisie, 325, 561, 625; wealth of, *p585*
Boxer Rebellion, *p731,* 715
Boxers, 715
boyars, 260, 499
boycotts, 802; defined, 548
Boyle, Robert, 520, 521
Brahma, 204
Brahman Nerguna, 206, 212
Brahmans, 203, 204, 207
Brahmaputra River, 66
Brahms, Johannes, 580
Brandenburg-Prussia, 496
Brandt, Willy, 880–881
Brazil, 993; dictatorship, 816, 978; foreign debt, 977; independence, 666, 669–70; Jesuit missionaries, 424; natural resources, 666; Portuguese colonization, 440; wealth, distribution of, 976
bread, 56, 629
Brest-Litovsk, Treaty of, 756, 759, 763
Brezhnev, Leonid, 874
Brezhnev Doctrine, 877, 1005
bricks, 66
bridges, suspension, 232
Britain, Battle of, 833–35
British Columbia, Canada, 653
British Empire. *See* Great Britain
British Guiana, 722
British Isles; Phoenician contact, 82
British North America Act, 652, 653
British West Indies; U.S. military bases, 835–36
bronze, 61
Bronze Age, 34
bronze casting, 232
Brown, Ford Madox, 336
Brownshirts, 784
Brown v. Board of Education of Topeka, Kansas, 887
Brueghel, Pieter, 414
Brunelleschi, Filippo, 404, 408, 409
Brutus, Marcus, 163
Bryan, William Jennings, 774
bubonic plague, 324, 327
Buchanan, Lamont, 660
Bucharest, Treaty of, 696, 698
buckle, Merovingian, *p295*
Buddha, the, 207–10; death, *p362;* teachings, *q210*
Buddhism, *m235,* 207–10, 239; in China, 225, 227, 347; compared to Shinto, 362; influence on neo-Confucianism, 348; influence on the common man, 364–65; introduced, 200; in Japan, 362, 364–65; in Korea, 359; in Myanmar, 354; principles, 210; in Southeast Asia, 351, 355; split, 210; spread in Asoka, 212; in Sri Lanka, 919, 1016; in Thailand, 355; varieties, 364; in Vietnam, 353
budget deficit, U.S., 998–99
Buenos Aires, Argentina, *p976, p991;* population, 976
buffalo, 378
buffer states, 581
Bukhara, 281
Bulgaria; in Balkan League, 698; communism, end of, 1005; division, 698; losses in Second Balkans War, 698; loss of territory, 764; nationalism, 697; Soviet liberation of, 848
Bulgars, 255, 256
Bulge, Battle of the, 846, 848
bullion, 448, 623
bull leaping, 104
Bundy, Edgar, 535
Bunraku, 472
Buonarroti, Michelangelo. *See* Michelangelo
buoyancy, 145
bureaucracy, 48
burgesses, 325
burghers, 325
Burgundy, 332–33
Burial at Ornans, 636, 638
Burma; Ayutthaya, conflict with, 474; British imperialism, 719; Japanese capture of, 845; Thailand, conflict with, 476–77. *See also* Myanmar
Burns, E. Bradford, 811
Burundi, 938
Bush, George, 960, 988
Bush administration, 999; Soviet Union, relations with, 999
Bushido, 364
business; business cycles, 609; Commercial Revolution, 446–50; corporations, 609; development of, 82; export goods, 449; goals of, 448; partnerships, 609; stockholders, 609
Byblos, 82
Byron, Lord, 631, 636
Byzantine Empire, *m247,* 177, 178, 246–56; art, 252–53; bureaucrats, 280; Christianity, 254–55; Constantinople, 246–47; construction, 249; culture, 247; decline, *m254, 278;* economy, 251–52; education, 253–54; Europe, influence on, 321; Islamic conquest, 277; Justinian, 247–49; legal code, 248; lifestyle, 251; military conquests, 248; Ottoman conquest, 456; Ottoman Empire, influence on, 458; religion, 249–50; Renaissance, influence on, 404; Roman Catholicism, break with, 295; Russia, influence on, 498; Seljuk Turks, threat from, 319, 343; Slavs, influence on, 258, 262, 264; social structure, 251; Empress Theodora, 247; threat to Arab land, 271; women, 247, 251
Byzantium. *See* Constantinople

C

cabinet, defined, 544
Cabot, John, 444
Cabral, Pedro Alvares, 440
Caesar, Augustus. *See* Augustus
Caesar, Julius, *p162,* 159, 163, 165; influence on calendars, 85
Cairo, Egypt; founded, 311; population, 963
Calabar, Nigeria, 712
Calais, France, 486
calculus, 519
Calderon Sol, Armando, 987
calendars, 31; ancient Egypt, 53; Aztec, *p388;* development of, 85; French Revolution, 568; Julian, 85, 163; Maya, 381; Muslim, 273; Navajo, 374; Sumerian, 61
Calicut, India, 436
***California* (battleship),** 841
California; Native Americans, 376; U.S. acquisition, 660
Caligula, 165
caliphate, 278
caliphs, 277, 279, 342, 457
calligraphy, *p346,* 286; in Japan, 363
Calvin, John, 418
Calvinism, 418–19, 538; in Germany, 494, 495; influence of revolution, 419; in Scotland, 543
Cambaluc. *See* Beijing
Cambodia; bombing of, 886, 912; cold war, 912, 914; democracy, 909; French imperialism, 719; Khmer people, 352–53; Khmer Rouge, 912; Vietnam, invasion by, 912
Cambridge University, 518

Cambyses, 91
camel, *p342*
camera obscura, *p658*
cameras, 658
Campaign of 1812 in Russia, 574
Camp David Accords, 955
campesinos, 975
Canaan, *m84,* 80, 82, 83, 91
Canaanites, 84
Canada, 652–53, 882; Constitutional Act of 1791, 652; Dominion of, 652, 653; economy, 889; French exploration, 444; Great Britain, acquisition by, 544, 547, 652; language, 890; multiculturalism, 889–90; national identity, 889; Native Americans, 375, 653; post-World War II development, 889–90; Quebec separatism, 890, 1016–17; role in world affairs, 889; self government, 653; 100th anniversary, 882; United States, relations with, 889; Upper and Lower Canada, 652
Canadian Pacific Railway, 652, 653
canals, 606
Cancuén, 386
Candide, 526
Cannae, 160
canning, 629
cannon, 330
Canon of Medicine, 285
Canova, Antonio, 529
Canterbury, Archbishop of, 537
Canterbury, England, 328
Canterbury Tales, The, 322, 328
Cape Colony, 709
Cape of Good Hope, 436, 443, 711
Capet, Hugh, 311
Capetian dynasty, 311
Cape Town, South Africa, 711
Cape Verde Islands, 436
capital, defined, 604
capitalism; criticism of, 624; defined, 608
capital punishment, 572
caravans, 284, 342
caravels, *p436*
carbolic acid, 628
carbonation, 519
carbon dating. *See* radiocarbon dating
carbon dioxide, 520; in beverages, 519
Cárdenas, Lázaro, 811, 812–13
cardinals, 306
Cardoso, Henrique, 993
Caribbean; music, 401; piracy, 444; resistance to slavery, 445; superpower rivalry, 871
Caribbean Community and Common Market (Caricom), 978
Carlevaris, Luca, 429
Carlsbad Decrees, 580, 583
Carmichael, Joel, 756
Carolingian, *See* Charlemagne
carpets, *p278–79,* 283
Carranza, Venustiano, 725
cartels, defined, 955, 993
Carter, Howard, 54
Carter, Jimmy, 888, 955
Carthage, 81; Roman Republic, war against, 159, 160; trading center, 82
Cartier, Jacques, 444
cartograms, 671
cartography, 436
cartoons; political, 720
Cartwright, Edmund, 603, 605
Carvallo, Ronald de, 811
Casablanca, Morocco, 844
Case for a Single Currency, The, *q1010*
cash-and-carry policy, 835–36
Cassandra, 132
Cassius, Dio, 159
Cassius, Gaius, 163
caste system, 204; the Buddha's rejection of, 210
Castile, kingdom of, 333
Castile, Spain, 483
castles, *p300,* 299
Castor, Temple of, *p169*
Castro, Fidel, *p979;* Batista, overthrow of, *q982,* 972
catacombs, *ptg174*
Çatal Hüyük, 31
Catherine II. *See* Catherine the Great
Catherine of Aragon, 419–20
Catherine the Great, *q499,* 480, 498, 502
Catholicism. *See* Roman Catholicism
Catholic Reformation, 422–25; doctrine, 423
cattle, *p217,* 202
Caucasus, 456
cause and effect, 215
Cavalier Parliament, 541
Cavaliers, 538
Cavalli, Marino, 482
cavalry; defined, 221; economic development of, 298; Mongol, 344
cave dwellers, 18
Cavelier, Robert, 444
cave paintings, *p19,* 14, 29; Algeria, 183; in India, 213; in Korea, 359
Cavour, Camillo de, 677–80
Cayuga, 378
Ceausescu, Elena, 1006
Ceausescu, Nicolae, 1006
Celebration of the Concorde of May 21, 1848, *ptg647*
Cellini, Benvenuto, 405
cells, 519
cell theory, 626
Celts, 92, 163, 308
censors, 157
censorship; by Catholic Church, 423; in China, 222
census, first in Europe, 309
Center party, 686, 687
CENTO. *See* Cooperation of the Central Treaty Organization
Central America; modern era, 985–88. *See also* individual countries
Central America, United Provinces of, 668
Central American Common Market, 978
Central Intelligence Agency (CIA), 982
central issues identification, 233
Central Park, 629, 632
Central Powers, 744
centripetal force, 518
Cetywayo, King of the Zulu, 711
Ceylon. *See* Sri Lanka
Cézanne, Paul, *q639*
Chac, 380
Chaghatai, *q342*
Chakkri, Phraya, 477
Chaldean Empire, *m89,* 64, 85, 89–90; summary, 99
chalices, *p107, p391*
Chamberlain, Neville; appeasement of Germany, 829; resignation, 832
Chambord, chateau of, 413
Chamorro, Violeta, 986
Chamoun, Camille, 953
Champagne, France, 323
Champin, Jean Jacques, 647
Champlain, Samuel de, 440, 444
Champollion, Jean-François, 53
chancellor, defined, 685
Chandragupta I, 212
Chandragupta II, 211, 213, 214
Chandragupta Maurya, 211
Changamire Empire, 196
Changan, China, 346, 347, 362, 464
Chang Jiang River, 17, 69, 347, 421
chansons de geste, 327
Chao Phraya River, 355
Chaplin, Charlie, 733, 775
chariots, *p90,* 88, 89
charity, in Islam, 276
Charlemagne, 294
Charlemagne, *p294,* 292, 295–96, 575; defense of Christianity, 327; love of learning, 294
Charles Albert, King of Sardinia, 677
Charles I, king of England, 536; execution, 534, 538; relations with Parliament, 537–39
Charles II, king of England, 510, 521, 540–42; relations with Parliament, 541–42
Charles II, king of Spain, 484, 493
Charles V, Holy Roman Emperor, 420, 482
Charles V and Philip His Son, 482
Charles VI, Holy Roman Emperor, 495
Charles VII, king of France, 332
Charles X, king of France, 655–56, 708
Charles the Bald, 296
Charles the Bold, 332–33
Charleston (dance), *p773*
charters, 326, 333, 448
Chartists, 649
Chartres Cathedral, *p331*
châteaux, 413
Chatel, Jean, 524
Chaucer, Geoffrey, 322, 328
Chechnya, *p1017,* 1016
checks; development, 447; first used, 399
checks and balances, 555
Cheka, 759
Chekov, Anton, *p639*
chemical warfare, 254
chemistry, 285, 520
Chernobyl nuclear power plant disaster, 859
Chiang Ching-kuo, 905
Chiang Kai-shek, 804–06, 905; Japan, defeat of, 827; Taiwan, relocation, 901
Chiapas, Mexico, 981
Chicago, Illinois, 620
Chichén Itzá, *p379*
Ch'ien Lung, 341
Chikamatsu, *q470*
child labor, 632; in industry, 614–15; mining coal, 602, *p623;* wool industry, 602
Children's Crusade, 318
Chile, 991–92; Allende overthrow, 992; dictatorship, 978; Inca Empire, 390; independence, 669
China, *m350, m715, m823,* 220–32, 346–50, 462–67; agriculture, 463, 466; ancient. *See* China, ancient; art, *p464–65;* becomes republic, 702; Boxer Rebellion, 715; Buddhism, 227; Byzantine expedition to, 251, 252; Christianity, 467; civil liberties, 904–05; civil service, 222–24, 462; communes, 902; communism, 804–06, 871, 903–05; Confucianism, 209, 225–26; consumer goods, 904; Cultural Revolution, *p903,* 902–03; Daoism, 226–27; digest, 239; ethnic groups, 905; European contact, 467; family, 228–29; Five-Year Plan, 902; foreign relations, 905; Great Leap Forward, 902; Great Wall, 222; Han dynasty, *m221,* 222–24; imperialism in, 714–16; India, invasion of, 918; Japanese invasion, 827; Jesuit missionaries, 424; Korea, invasion,

358; in Korean War, 907; land reform, 901; literature, 230–31; Long March, 806; Mao Zedong era, 901–03; Marco Polo visit, 241; Ming dynasty, 462–65; mining, 232; Mongol rule, 344–45; poetry, 366; population, 462, 466; prodemocracy movement, *p904*, 901, 903–05; Qin dynasty, *m221*, 221–22; Qing dynasty, 465–67; Rebellion of 1911, 715–16; Red Guards, 902; religions, 347; republic, 804–06; satellite television, censorship, 860; science and technology, 231–32; sculpture, *p895;* social structure, 229–30; Song dynasty, 348–50; Soviet Union, relations with, 901–02, 903; Tang dynasty, 346–48; Tiananmen Square crackdown, 904–05; trade, 223, 232, 347; trade with East Africa, 195; trade with India, 214; trade with Japan, 364; trade with Muslims, 284; trade with Portugal, 440; transportation development, 347; Treaty of Versailles, protest, 804; United States, relations with, 905; UN Security Council, 865; Vietminh, support for, 909; Vietnam, influence on, 353–54; women, 229; writing, 221; Yuan dynasty, 350; Zhou dynasty, *m221*, 220–21
China, ancient; agriculture, development of, 30; climate, 70; cultural diffusion, 69; early civilization, 69–71; geography, 69–70; metalwork, 71; myths, 70; Neolithic period, 70; religion, 70–71; summary, 98; writing, 70–71
China, Republic of. *See* Taiwan
chinampas, 388
china (pottery), 348
Ching Hao, 346
Chirac, Jacques, 1011
chivalry, 301, 327
chloroform, 628
Chocolate Pilot, The, 862
Chopin, Frédéric, 635
Chord of Steel, the Story of the Invention of the Telephone, The, 607
choreographer, 775
Choson, 359
Chosroes I, Emperor of Persia, 248
Chretien, Jean, 1017
Christ. *See* Jesus
Christian Democrats (Italy), 1012
Christian humanism, 413–14
Christianity, 171–74, 173–74; Arabs, impact on, 271; Aristotle, opposition to, 326; in Armenia, 257; in Axum, 186-87; in Byzantine Empire, 249, 254–55; Charlemagne's defense of, 327; in China, 347, 467; conflict between Rome and Constantinople, 250; development of, 99; digest, 237; early variations, 173; French Revolution, policy of, 570; in Georgia, 257; Golden Rule, 226; in India, 210; intent to block Islam, 434; under Islamic law, 273, 280, 319; in Japan, 470–71; Jerusalem, importance of, 318; Judaism, influence of, 83, 171; legal system, 166; missionary work in Africa, 706; motivation for exploration, 434; Native Americans, conversion of, 441–42, 444; in North Africa, 184, 186–87; Persian Empire, influence of, 93; Roman Empire, policy of, 173; spread, *m181*, 172–73; Viking acceptance of, 296
Christian IX, King of Denmark, 682–83
Christian Roman Empire, 295
Christians, defined, 172
Christina, Grand Duchess of Tuscany, *q516*
Christopher, Warren, *p1009*
Chronicle of the Seeker, The, 277
chronicles, defined, 288
Chulalongkorn, King of Thailand, 474, 477
Chumash, 376–77
Chunnel, 1012
churches; defined, 172; medieval architecture, 328
Churchill, Winston; appeal to U.S. for aid, 835–36; "blood, sweat and tears" speech, *q834;* Conservative prime minister, 833, 879; Dunkirk evacuation, *q833;* Iron Curtain speech, *q866;* RAF pilots, *q835;* in World War I, *q749*
Church Militant and Triumphant, The, *ptg317*
Church of England, 420; reaction against, 530; reform movement, 537; in Scotland, 538; St. Paul's Cathedral, 541
Church of the Annunciation, *p264*
Cicero, *p102*, 103, 170
Çiller, Tansu, 965
circulation of blood, 514, 519
circumnavigation, 439
circus, derivation, 518
Circus Maximus, *p168*, 167
CIS. *See* Commonwealth of Independent States
cities; development of, 16, 32; fine arts, 632; government, 326; growth in Europe, 323–26; industrial cities, 605; leisure in, 632; Neolithic, 34; political representation, 649; self government in France, 311; services, 632; urbanization. *See* urbanization. *See also* villages
Citizen-King, 656
Citizens: A Chronicle of the French Revolution, 560
City and the Port of Tolone, The, *ptg561*
City of God, 174
city-states, 58, 59, 82; in East Africa, 194; in Italy, 405–06; in Medieval Europe, 326. *See also* polis
Civil Constitution of the Clergy, 565, 575
civil disobedience, 802
civilization, development of, 32–35, 97
civil rights movement, 886–88
civil service, 100, 230; basis in Confucianism, 226; in China, 222, 224; examinations, *p230*, 340, 346; in Korea, 359; reform in Britain, 650; in Song dynasty, 348
Civil War, U.S., 646, 661, 663–64; nursing, *p660*
Ci Xi, Empress of China, *q715*
clans; defined, 342, 938; in Japan, 361, 362
Clarendon Code, 541
Clark, Joshua Reuben, 816
classical style, 130; in Renaissance, 404
classicism, 528–29; Charlemagne's support for, 295
Classic Readings in American Politics, 998
class struggle, 625
Claudius, 165
Clausewitz, Carl von, 574
clay tablets, *p61*, 60
Cleisthenes, 118
Clèmanges, Nicholas de, 334
Clemenceau, Georges, 763
Clement V, Pope, 334
Cleopatra, 142, 163
Clermont, France, 319
Clinton, Bill, 999
Clinton administration, 999; Bosnia-Herzegovina, policy toward, 1015
clothing, 25
Clouds, The, 134
Clovis, Frankish king, 294
Cluny, France, 306
Clusium, 154
Clytemnestra, 132
coal; in Great Britain, 604; replacement by electricity, 611
Coalbrookdale by Night, *ptg599*
coalitions, defined, 780, 879
coal mining, *p623*, 602; in Germany, 687; strike in Britain, 779; working conditions, *q599*, 614
coat of arms, *p486*
Cobden, Richard, *q646*
Code of Hammurabi. *See* Hammarubi's Code
coffeehouses, *p449*
coins, 82, 447; ancient Greece, 112, 113; Macedonian, *p144*
Colbert, Jean-Baptiste, 492
Colchis, 257
cold war, 858–71; Cuba, 982; detente, 874; digest, 1026–27; domino theory, 910; end of, 996; Latin America, influence on, 978; thaw, 873
Cole, George Vicat, 601
Coleridge, Samuel Taylor, 636
collective bargaining, 616
collective farms, 790
collective security, 734, 826; defined, 1012
Collor de Mello, Fernando, 993
Colombia, 992–93; independence, 669; Panama, loss of, 724
coloniae, 159
colonialism. *See* individual countries, regions, etc.
colonies, 82; defined, 475, 706; immigration to, 450, 705; purpose in mercantilism, 448–49; 19th century, 704
colons, 931
Colorado; **Native Americans,** 377; U.S. acquisition, 662; women's vote, 665
Colosseum, *p169*, 167
Columbus, Christopher, *q438*, 437; reaches America, 398, 432
Columbus Before the Queen, *ptg438*
Combination Acts, 612, 616
combustion, 520
COMECON, 869. *See* Council of Mutual Economic Assistance
comedies, 134
Comintern (Communist International), 789, 791
Commercial Revolution, 446–50
Committee of Public Safety, 567, 569, 570
Committee on Un-American Activities, 884
Commodus, 175
common law, 103
Common Market, 862, 881, 1010–11, 1013
Commons, House of, 311. *See also* House of Commons
Common Sense, 553
commonwealth, defined, 538
Commonwealth of Independent States(CIS), 1001; ethnic conflict, 1015–16; formed, 998; free enterprise, transition to, 1003; privatization, 1003
Commonwealth of Nations, 779, 878; South African participation, 934
Communal Unity, 801
Commune of Paris, 655, 658
communes, 326, 405, 902
communications, 860–61, 1018; computer-linked, 1021; hot line, 874
communism, 625; anticommunist resistance, 790; anticommunist sentiment in U.S., 883–84; in China, 804–06, 903–05; containment, 866, 884; containment, in

Vietnam, 885, 886; domino theory, 910; in East Africa, 934; in Eastern Europe, 865–66; end of, in Eastern Europe, 1005–06; end of, in Soviet Union, 1001, 1002; established in Russia, 759; in Italy, 1012; in Laos, 914; in Latin America, 977; Nazi policy toward, 784–85; in North Korea, 907; poster, *p791;* private businesses under, 788; Truman Doctrine, 866, 868; war communism, 788
Communist Manifesto, The, 595, 625
comparisons, 125
compasses, 321, 435; invention of, 232, 348
compensation, 580
competition, 623
computers, 883, 1021; revolution begins, 859
Comte, Auguste, 628
concentration camps, 786, 839, 850–51; prisoners, 838
Concerning the Soul, *q167*
Concert of Europe, 583
Concord, Massachusetts, 552
Concordat of 1801, 575
Concordat of Worms, 292, 312
concrete, 168
Condition of the Working Class in England, The, 624–25
Condor Legion, 828
condottieri, 406
Confederate States of America, 663
confederation, 82; defined, 378, 554
Confederation of the Rhine, 576
Confessions, 173
conformal maps, 37
Confucianism, 209, 225–26; in civil service examinations, 346–47; Daoism, compared to, 227; in Ming dynasty, 463; neo-Confucianism, 348; in Vietnam, 353; women, 359
Confucius, *p225, q226, q228, q231,* 101, 225–26; birth, 218; family, attitude toward, *q218,* 225–26; government, attitude toward, 226; women, attitude toward, *q229*
Congo; Belgian imperialism, 709; independence, 932. *See also* Belgian Congo, Zaire
Congo River. *See* Zaire River
Congress of Berlin, 696, 698
Congress of Nations, 734
Congress of Paris, 678
Congress of Vienna, *p582,* 580-82, 655, 674, 681
conquistadors, 441
conic projection, 37
Conrad III, Holy Roman Emperor, 320
conscription, 569, 740. *See also* Selective Service System
Consecration of Emperor Napoleon I and the Coronation of the Empress Josephine, The, *ptg575*
conservatism, defined, 569
Conservative party, British, 649, 650, 879
Conservative party, German, 687
Consistory, 419
Constantine, *p173;* begins rule, 152, 171; establishes Constantinople, 175, 246; reforms, 176, 177; Roman Emperor, 246
Constantine IX, Byzantine Emperor, *p251*
Constantine VII, Byzantine Emperor, *q253*
Constantinople, 175, 177; architecture, 244; crusader conquest, 318; establishment, 175, 246; fall of, 251, 256, 264; Ottoman capital, 456; Persian Empire, attack by, 255; Seljuk Turks, threat from, 319; Slavs, raids by, 260; strategic position, 246–47, 252. *See also* Istanbul, Turkey
Constantinople, University of, 253
Constitutional Act of 1791, 652
constitutional law, 103
constitutional monarchy, 541, 648; in Brazil, 670; in Italy, 680
Constitution of the United States, 552, 554–55; amendments, 664; basis in Roman law, 103; Bill of Rights, 555; influence on French Revolution, 564
construction; in Cambodia, 352
Consulate, 579
consuls; French, 574, 575; consuls; Roman, 157
containment, 866, 884; in Vietnam, 886
Continental Congress, First, 545, 550
Continental Congress, Second, 553
contraband, defined, 749–51
Contras, *p985,* 986
convents. *See* monastic life
convoys, 760
Cook, James, 654
Coolidge, Calvin, *q771*
Cooperation of the Central Treaty Organization (CENTO), 884
cooperatives. in Mexico, 812
Copernicus, Nicolaus, 514, 516, 518
copper, 34
Copper Age, 40–41
copper industry, 937
copper mining, 992; in East Africa, 195
Coral Sea, Battle of the, 845
Corday, Charlotte, 569
Córdoba, Spain, 284, 287
cordon sanitaire, defined, 764
corn, 629–30
Corn Dance, *ptg17*
Corneille, Pierre, 529
Corn Law, 649
Cornwallis, General, 552
Coronado, Francisco Vásquez de, 441
corporate state, 782
corporations, 448, 609
Corpus of Civil Law, 248
cortes, 333
Cortés, Hernán, 432, 441, 510
Cossack Tales, 258
Costain, Thomas B., 607
Costa Rica, 668
cotton, 663
cotton gin, *p606,* 594, 605
Coubet, Gustave, *q635, q636*
Couder, L.C.A., 563
Council of 400, 118
Council of 500, 118–19
Council of Elders, 469
Council of Mutual Economic Assistance (COMECON), 869
Council of Ten, 408
Council of Trent, 402, 422, 423
Council of Trent, The, *ptg423*
counterpoint, 496
Counter-Reformation. *See* Catholic Reformation
counts, in Frankish Empire, 295–96
coup d'état, 573, 657
Courbet, Gustave, *636, 638*
Court, The, *ptg403*
courtiers, defined, 480
Court of the Myrtles, *p279*
covenant, 83
covert, defined, 986
Cowley, Malcolm, *q770*
Coyote (mythical Navajo creature), 374
Craig, Franck, 330
Crassus, Marcus Licinius, 163
Crean, 146
creation myths, 35–36; Japan, 360
Crécy, France, 330
Crécy, Battle of, 329
Creoles, 667, 670
Crete, *m127,* 104, 107
Crimean War, 657, 697; Russian defeat, 691; Sardinia, 678
Crisp, Alison, 485
Cristiani, Alfredo, 988
critical thinking; argument, 810; cause and effect, 215; central issues, 233; comparisons, 125; detecting bias, 617; evidence, 421; fact and opinion, 265; generalizations, 356; hypothesizing, 391; inferences, 313; information classification, 65; information synthesis, 837; point of view, 531; relevant information, 179; stereotypes, 473
Critique of Pure Reason, The, 530
Croatia, independence, 1008–09
Croats, 247, 1014–15; ethnic origins, 259
Cro-Magnons, 14, 27–29
Crompton, Samuel, 605
Cromwell, Oliver, *p536,* 538; dissolution of Parliament, 536
Cromwell, Richard, 538
crossbow, 221
Crow, 378
crucifix, *p251*
Crusade of Kings, 320
Crusades, *m320, p318,* 318–21; beginning, 241; Europe, influence on, 321; First Crusade, 319; Second Crusade, 320; Third Crusade, 320–21
Ctesiphon, 178
Cuba, 722–23, 982–84; architecture, *p983;* Bay of Pigs invasion, 982, 984; Cuban Missile Crisis, 858, 874, 984; discovery, 438; economy after communism, 984; reforms under Castro, 982, 984; Sandinistas, support for, 986; Soviet Union, relations with, 982; U.S., relations with, 984
Cuban missile crisis, *m982,* 858, 874, 984
cubism, 773
cultural differentiation, 375
cultural diffusion, 34, 412, 449
Cultural Revolution, 894, 903
culture; beginnings of, 24; differentiation, 375, diffusion, 34, 412, 449; global, 1022; hominid, *c30,* 26–27; influence of language, 25
culture, popular; Twenties, 775
culture system, 718
cuneiform, *p29, p61,* 44, 60, 242
Cunningham, Alexander, 66
Cupid, *p140*
Curie, Marie and Pierre, 626, 628
currency, 447
Cuzco, 389, 390
cylinder-screw, 145
cylindrical projection, *m37*
Cynicism, 144
Cyprus, 1013; acquisition by Britain, 698
Cyril, monk, 252, 255
cyrillic alphabet, 252, 255
Cyrus II, 90, 91, 120
czar, derivation, 264
Czar Liberator, 692
Czechoslovakia; communism, 870–71, 876–77; communism, end of, 1005; division after communism, 859, 1004, 1007; established, 764; ethnic groups, 828–29; German invasion, 828–29; Soviet invasion, 872, 877
Czech Republic, 859; ethnic origins, 259; formation, 1007

Czechs, 247; church reform, 336; revolt against Hapsburgs, 494

D

Dachau, 839
da Gama, Vasco, 436, 437, 438, 440
Daguerre, Louis, 658
daguerrotypes, 658
Dahl, Hans, 636
Dahomey, 709
Daimler, Gottlieb, 611
daimyos, 364, 468; clans, *m479;* duties in Tokugawa shogunate, 469
Daladier, Edouard, 829
Dalai Lama, 904
d'Alembert, Jean Le Rond, 524
Dali, Salvador, 773
Dalton, John, 626, 628
Damascus, Syria, 80, 279; trade center, 283
damasks, 231
dance; ballroom dancing, 775; Twenties, 773–75
dancer, Hellenistic, *p142*
Daniel, son of Alexander Nevsky, 263
Dante Alighieri, *q137,* 328
Danton, Georges-Jacques, *q567, q569,* 568, 570
Danube River, 683
Dao De Jing, 227
Daoism, *m235,* 225, 226–27; Confucianism, compared to, 227; neo-Confucianism, influence on, 348; in Vietnam, 353
Dardanelles, 246, 252, 739
Darío, Rubén, *q811*
Darius I, *p93, q93;* death, 78; government, 91–2; Greeks, war against, 140; Indus River valley, invasion of, 211; Ionians, defeat of, 120; palace at Persepolis, 90
Darius III, 141, 142
Dark Ages. *See* Middle Ages
Darlan, François, 843–44
Darrow, Clarence, 774
Darwin, Charles, 626–27
Das Kapital, 622
dating artifacts, 20–21
datus, 475
Daumier, Honoré, 638
David, (king), 83, 85
David (statue), 406, 411
David, Jacques-Louis, 529, 573, 575
da Vinci, Leonardo, *q410,* 407, 411, 412
Daw Aung San Suu Kyi, 914–15
Dawes, William, 552
Dayton Treaty, 1015
D-Day, 824, 846–47; witnessed in Russia, 846
Deak, Francis, 696
Death in the Sanchez Family, A, 975
death squads, 987
deBary, W.T., 807
Deborah, 84, 205
debt; international crisis, 1019. *See also* individual countries
Deccan, 212
Decembrist Revolt, 690, 691
Declaration of Independence, 512, 534, 553–54; French Revolution, influence on, 564; John Locke, influence of, 523
Declaration of the Rights of Man and of the Citizen, 564
Declaratory Act of 1766, 548
Decree on Compulsory Education of the Russian Nobility, 498
deforestation, defined, 1020
Degas, Edward, *q637*
de Gaulle, Charles, 833, 844; Algeria, policy toward, 931; Fifth Republic, 878; French president, 879–80; Paris, liberation of, 847; Vietnam, *q910*
Dei-Anang, Michael, 945
Deism, 521, 523
deities; *See* religion
de Klerk, F.W., 939
Delacroix, Eugène, 636
Delahae, Ernest Jean, 728
de la Vega, Joseph, 449
Delhi, India, 459; conquest by Babur, 460
Delian League, 123
Delos, 123
de Loutherberg, Philip, 599
Delphi, oracle at, 111
demarcation, line of, 439
Demeter, 110
democracy, 114; African trend, 941; Athens, 118–19; development of, 106; in Roman Republic, 157
Democratic People's Republic of Korea. *See* North Korea
Democratic Republic of Vietnam. *See* Vietnam
democratic socialism, 625
Democritus, 137
demographic data, interpretation, 289. *See also* population growth
Demoiselles d'Avignon, 773
de Montaigne, Michel, *q413*
Demosthenes, 140
Deng Xiaoping, 903, 904
Denmark; German invasion, 831–82; Germany, war against, 682–83; Hapsburgs, war against, 494; Virgin Islands, sale of, 724
depression, treatment of, 1022
depressions (economic), defined, 609, 776-80, 785
Desai, Morai, 917
desalination, defined, 964
Descartes, René, 518
Descent of Man, The, 627
Description of Elizabeth I's Coronation Procession in 1559, 485
Description of the World, 713
Desert Fox. *See* Rommel, Erwin
desertification, 943, 944
de Soto, Hernando, 440, 441
d'Estaing, Válery Giscard, 880
de-Stalinization, 872–73; Chinese reaction to, 902
d'Este, Isabella, 402
Destruction of the Old Order, The, *ptg794*
detente, 874
de Tocqueville, Alexis, *q572*
Deuteronomy, 85
Devil's Island, 659
De Valera, Eamon, 779
developed nations, 1019
developing nations, 1019
dharma, 205, 206, 207
Diaghilev, Sergey, 775
Dias, Bartholomeu, 434, 436
Diaspora, 85
Díaz, Porfirio, 725
dicasteries, 118
Dickens, Charles, *q601, q624,* 638
Dickinson, J.C., 303
dictatorship, 157, 574; in Latin America, 670
dictatorship of the proletariat, 789
Diderot, Denis, *q525,* 514, 529
Diehl, Charles, 246
Dien Bien Phu, Vietnam, 909
Diesel, Rudolf, 611
Diet at Worms, 416–17
dinh, 353
diocese, 174
Diocletian, 175, 176–77
Diogenes, 144
Dionysus, *p111, p142,* 111, 132
Diouf, Abdou, 930
diplomacy, 406–07
Diponegoro, Prince of Java, 718
Directory (French Revolution), 567, 571, 573, 574, 579
dirigibles, 611
disarmament, defined, 778
disciples, 172
Discourse on Method, 518
Discourse on the Effect of the Arts and Sciences, 529
Discovery of Magellan Strait, *ptg439*
discrimination, racial, 886–87
Discus Thrower, 131
discus thrower, *p134*
disenfranchisement, 649
disengagement, defined, 955
Disraeli, Benjamin, *crt649,* 649–50, 714
dissidents, 874
diversified economies, 1019
Divine Comedy, 328
Divine Faith, 460
divine right, 482, 536
division of labor, 614
divorce, 420
Djenné, Mali, *p193,* 192
Djoser, King, 48
Dnieper River, 252, 260
doctrines, 174
Documents in World History, 796, 901
doge, 408
dogs, domestication of, 26
doll, creche, *p546*
domains, 142
Domesday Book, 309
domestication of animals, 26, 30
domestic system, 600, 602, 606
Dominic, 307
Dominican order, 307
Dominican Republic, 984; discovery, 438; U.S. interventions, 816
domino theory, 910
Domremy, France, 330
Donatello, 409
Doregelès, Roland, *q738*
Dorian civilization, 104, 108, 115, 140
Dorsey, Tommy, 775
Dos Passos, John, 773
Dos Pilas, Guatemala, *m387, p385,* 384–86
double-digit inflation, 889
doubloons, 447
Doust, Toby, 920
Downes, Kerry, 540
Draco, 115, 118
draconian, 118
draft. *See* conscription
Drake, Francis, *p487,* 444
drama; *See* theater
Dream and the Tomb, The, 318
Dreiser, Theodore, *q620,* 638
Dreyfus, Alfred, 659
Dreyfus Affair, 655, 659
drug smuggling, 980, 988, 993
drum, African, *p400*
Drury, Alice, *p755*
Dryden, John, 529
dual monarchy, 695, 696

Duarte – English Channel

Duarte, Jose Napoleón, 987
Dubcek, Alexander, 877
Duce, Il, 782. *See* Mussolini, Benito
Dulce et Decorum Est, 747
dumas, 694
Dumas, Alexandre, 635
Dumouriez, Charles François, *q567*
Duncan, Isadora, 773
Dunkirk, evacuation, 833
Duo Fu, 348
Dupin, Aurore, 636
Durham, Lord, 653
dust bowl, 777
Dutch East India Company, 442, 447
Dutch East Indies, 718, 839; Japanese capture of, 845
Dutch language, 413
Dutch West India Company, 443
duty (moral); in Aryan culture, 205; in China, 226
duty (tax), 546
Duvalier, François, 979, 984
Duvalier, Jean-Claude, 984
Duxiu, Chen, 595
Dvorák, Antonin, 635
dvorianie, 501
dwellings, 28–29
dye, 80
dynasties, 47, 71

E

Earl, George, 630
Early Civilizations of Europe, The, q32
Early History of Rome, 154
Earth Mother, 107, 108, 110
earthquakes, 104, 226, 896, 899, 980
Earth Summit, 1018, 1021
East Africa, 194–96; British imperialism, 709; European arrival, 196; German imperialism, 709; independence, 932–33; Italian imperialism, 709; Marxism, 939; in the 1990s, 938; trade, 195
East Berlin, 870
Eastern Europe; communism, end of, 1004, 1005–06; democracy, 1008; ethnic tensions, 1008; free enterprise transition, 1007–08; leadership, 1006–07; nationalism, 1008
Eastern Orthodox Church, 144, 247; establishment, 174; in Kievan Rus, 262; in Moscow, 264; Roman Catholicism, split with, 250; in Russia, 501; Russia, influence on, 498; Slavs, 247; source of education, 253; spread, 251
Eastern Slavs, 259–64; early culture, 259; isolation, 262, 263; Kievan Rus. *See* Kievan Rus; land, *m259*
Eastern Woodlands, Native Americans, 378
East Germany; communism, 875–76; communism, end of, 1005; formation, 870; migration from, 875–76
East India Company, 398, 444, 550, 713–14
East Indies. *See* Dutch East Indies
East Pakistan, 918-19
Eastman, George, 658
East Timor, 915
Ea (Sumerian deity), 35
Eberle, Gertrude, 771
Ebla, 62–63
Echeverriia, Luis, 978
École des Beaux-Arts, 638
Economic and Monetary Union (EMU), 1013
economics; competition, 623; economic nationalism, 812–13; hyperinflation, 991; Marxist stages, 625; standard of living, 979; theory, 622–23, 624–26
Economist Newspaper Ltd., The, 1010
economy; barter system, 323; capital, 604; depressions, defined, 609; development of, 33–34; diversified economies, 1019; global, 1020; gross domestic product, 898; investment, 604; market economies, 623; money economies, 323; one-product economies, 943; regional economic markets, 1020
Ecuador; Inca Empire, 390; independence, 669; Peru, war against, 978
Eddas, 296
eddubas, 61
Eden, Anthony, 879
Ederly, Gertrude, 771
Edict of Milan. *See* Constantine
Edict of Nantes, 490, 491; repeal, 493
Edict of Prices, 176
Edison, Thomas, 611
Edo, Japan. *See* Tokyo, Japan
education; advances in 19th and 20th centuries, 632–33; for women, 633. *See also* individual countries
Education Act of 1870, 650
Edward I, king of England, 311
Edward III, king of England, 330
Edward IV, king of England, 333
Edward the Confessor, 308
Edward VI, king of England, 420, 486
Effect of Good Government on a City, The, ptg293
Egypt, *m77,* 15; ancient. *See* Egypt, ancient; in Arab League, 950; Axum, trade with, 186; British imperialism, 708, 799; early civilization, 15; Fatimid dynasty, 281; Fatimids, conquest by, 311; France, war against, 573; fundamentalism, Muslim, 965; Gaza Strip, annexation of, 951; independence, 697, 796, 799, 950; Islamic state, conquest by, 277, 278; Israel, relations with, 955, 962; Kush, contact with, 185–86; Nasser era, 951–53; in Roman Republic, 161; Soviet Union, relations with, 952; Sudan, government of, 929; Syria, support for, 954; in United Arab Republic, 953
Egypt, ancient, *m48,* 46–57; afterlife, 48, 50; Alexander, conquest by, 142; archeology, 54–57; bakery, *p56;* daily life, 56; empire building, 49; family life, 51–52; flood control, 47; foreign rule, 46; government, 47; Greece, trade with, 107; Hittite culture, influence on, 88; Israelites, 84; Middle Kingdom, 48–49; New Kingdom, 49, 51; Nile River, importance of, 46–47; Old Kingdom, 47–48; Persian Empire, conquest by, 91; population, 51; Ptolemy, rule by, 142; religion, 51, 52, 56; Roman Empire, conquest by, 142; science, 53; settlement of, 44, 47; social organization, 51; summary, 97; tomb art, *ptg45, ptg54–55;* trade, 49, 81; women, 52; writing, 52–53
Eightfold Path, 210, 227
Einhard, *q295*
Einstein, Albert, 628, 771; flight from Nazism, 786
Eire. *See* Irish Free State
Eisai, 365
Eisenhower, Dwight D., 843, 953; with Krushchev, 873; Vietnam, policy toward, 884
Eisenhower administration; desegregation, policy toward, 887
El Alamein, Battle of, 843
Elba, 577
Eleanor of Aquitaine, 329
electrical power, 611
electromagnetic waves, 611
electronic mail, 1021
Elements of Geometry, The, 145
Eliot, George, 638
Eliot, T.S., 732, 772
Elizabeth, Empress of Russia, 497
Elizabeth-Charlotte, Princess, 480
Elizabeth I, ptg487
Elizabeth I, Queen of England, *p448, p485,* 486–89; Anglicanism established, 418; ascension to the throne, 420; attitude toward piracy, 446; coronation, 485; domestic policy, 488; East Indian Company chartered, 444; foreign policy, 488–89; marriage, *q487;* Parliament, relations with, 536
Elizabeth II, Queen of Great Britain, 879
Ellet, Elizabeth F., 552
Ellington, Duke, 775
ellipses, defined, 517
Ellis Island, 665
El (Phoenician deity), 83
El Salvador, 987–88; establishment, 668; guerrillas, 987; Native Americans, 379
emancipation; Russian Serfs, 691; United States ends slavery, 664
embalming, 48, 50
embargo; defined, 841, 1015; of Iraq, 960; of Vietnam, 912
embroidery, 309
emigration, 630
émigrés, 566
emmer, 16, 57
Emperor of China: Self-Portrait of K'ang-hsi, 462
Emperor of the Romans, 312
Emperor Who Never Sleeps, 247
empires, 49
enclave, defined, 1016
enclosure movement, 603
Encyclopédie, 514, 525
Engels, Friedrich, 624–25
England; American colonies. *See* English colonies; Anglicanism, 420; anti-Catholic sentiment, 537, 542, 543; Bill of Rights, 542–43; Catholicism under Mary I, 486; Church of England, 420, 537; civil war, 332, 521, 534, 538–39; colonies, 443–44, 450; commerce, growth of, 448; commonwealth, 538; Cromwell dictatorship, 538; debt under Elizabeth I, 488; Dutch, conflict with in Asia, 443; Elizabethan period, 486–89; exploration by, *m441;* fashion under Elizabeth I, *p487;* France, relations with, 489; France, war against, 329–32, 537; government under Elizabeth I, 487–88; immigration to North America, 537, 538; Jenkins' Ear war, 497; monarchy, 308–11, 333, 485–89; monarchy, abolition and restoration of, 538; name derivation, 308; naval power, 488–89; Netherlands, relations with, 489; Parliament, 311; piracy, 446; political parties, 542; Puritans, 537; Renaissance, 412; Restoration, 534, 540–41; Russia, trade with, 499; Safavid dynasty, relations with, 459; settlement by Danes, 296; social structure, 488; in Southeast Asia, 475; Spain, relations with, 489; Spain, war against, 483, 537; stock exchanges, 448; support for Dutch against Spain, 483; in Thailand, 476–77; in War of the Spanish Succession, 493. *See also* Great Britain
English Channel, 88, 1012

English colonies, 545–50; colonial assemblies, 542, 546, 550; colonial assemblies and governors, relations between, 546–47; Great Britain, trade with, 545–46, 550; political power, 546–47; public education, *p546–47;* taxation, protests against, 548–50; western settlement, restrictions on, 545, 548
English language, 170; Australian version, 654; Elizabethan period, 487; Old English, 327
English Parliamentary Enclosure, The, 600
English Zionist Federation, 798
Enkidu, 72
enlightened despots, 527
Enlightened One, The. *See* Buddha, the
Enlightenment, 365, 524–30, 564; American Revolution, influence on, 553; end, 530; liberalism, support of, 582; Napoleonic Code, influence on, 575; reaction against, 529–30; social reform, influence on, 526–27
Enlightenment, Age of. *See* Enlightenment
enslaved persons; population, 445; revolt in Saint Domingue, 566. *See also* slavery. *See also* slave trade
entente, defined, 740
Entente Cordiale, 740
entrepreneurs, 448, 604; social status, 449
environment; awareness of, 1021; damage in Persian Gulf War, 960; protection, 1020–21
ephors, 116
epic poems, 108, 20
Epicureanism, 144
Epicurus, 144
equal-area maps, 37
Equiano, Olaudah, *q400*
equites, 162
Era of the French Revolution, The, 567
Erasmus, *ptg413*
Erasmus, Desiderius, *q414,* 412, 413–14
Eratosthenes, 145
Erechtheum, *p127*
Erhard, Ludwig, 80
Eridu, 59
Eritrea; independence, 935, 938–39
Eroica **symphony,** 511
erosion in Africa, 944
Escorial, El, 482–83
Esdraelon, Battle of, 206
Eskimos, 35. *See also* Inuit
essay, personal, 413
Establishment of the Academy of Science ..., *ptg515*
estates, French, 560–61
Estates-General, 312, 562, 579
Estonia, 1000; established, 764; in Nazi-Soviet Nonaggression Pact, 830; Soviet military bases, 831
Eteocles, 146
ether, 628
Ethiopia; Italian imperialism, 707, 709, 827; Jesuit missionaries, 424; in the 1990s, 938–39
Etruria, 155–56
Etruscans, *p158,* 155–56; alphabet, *p181*
eucharist, 303
Euclid, 145
Eugenius IV, pope, 320
Euphrates River, 964. *See also* Tigris and Euphrates Rivers
Euripides, 128, 132, 134
euro (currency), 1013
Europe; 1789, *m589;* after Roman Empire, 294; after Treaty of Westphalia, *m495;* agriculture, 322–23; Byzantine culture, influence of, 319, 321; Chinese inventions, influence of, 321; Common Market, 862, 1013; competition among nations, 738; Crusades, influences of, 321; cultural diffusion, 449; Economic and Monetary Union (EMU), 1013; economic growth, 322–26; economic unity, 880; European Union, 1013; exploration by Vikings, 296; High Middle Ages, 318–36; invasion by Slavs, 296; invasions, *m297;* kingdoms, *m310;* knowledge of the world, *m435;* life expectancy, 629; Marshall Plan, 868–69; Muslim culture, influence of, 319, 321; political alignment after Napoleon, *m581,* 580–83; population, 446, 449; religions, *m424;* Roman Catholicism, 295; social structure, 449–50; spread of civilization, 450; trade, 323; trade with China, 350; unification, *m1013,* 1013; Viking invasion, 296–97; World War I, influences of, 764. *See also* individual countries, World War II. *See* World War II
European Community. *See* Common Market
European Union, 996, 1013; Treaty on, 1013
Evans, Arthur, 107
Evans, Mary Ann, 638
Eve of Discovery, The, *ptg436*
evidence, 421
evolution, 626–27
Exchequer, 309
excommunication, 306
Exodus, 85
Exploration, Age of, 434–44; motivations for, 434. *See also* individual countries
export goods, 449
extended family, 229
Eyck, Jan and Herbert van, 414
Ezana, Axum king, 187

F

Fabian Society, 650
fact and opinion, 265
factories, 596, 606
factory system, 606
fads, 771
Faisal II, king of Iraq, 953
faith, in Islam, justification by, 415; as religion, Judaism, 83; Christianity, 171-74, 275
Falkland Islands, 990, 991
Fall, Babacar, 861
family; among bedouins, 271; in China, 228–29; Confucius' teachings, 225–26; extended, 229; middle class, 613; Muslim, 282; nuclear, 229; Roman Republic, 158
famine, 941, 944
Farabundo Martí National Liberation Front (FMLN), 987
Faraday, Michael, 611
farming. *See* agriculture
Farouk, king of Egypt, 951
fascism; in Argentina, 814–816; in France, 780; in Italy, 781–83; philosophy, 782; in Spain, 827–28
fasting, in Islam, 276
Father Miguel Hidalgo, *ptg668*
Fatima, daughter of Muhammad, 277, 311
Fatimid dynasty, 281, 311
Faust, 635
Faxian, *q213*
Federal Republic of Germany. *See* West Germany
federal system, defined, 554
Female Farmers, *ptg642*
Femenismo!, 990
Ferdinand and Isabella, 434
Ferdinand, Archduke Francis, 695, 741-42
Ferdinand II, 679
Ferdinand of Aragon; Columbus, instructions to, 434, 437, 438; marries Isabella, 329, 333; Spain, unification of, 483
Ferdinand of Styria, 494
Fermi, Enrico, 733
Fernández-Armesto, Felipe, 434
Ferris, J.L.G., 436
Fertile Crescent, *m59;* civilizations, 98; early civilizations, 58–64; empires of, *m89,* 78–93; settlement, 58; water supply, 58
fertilization, 232
feudalism, 298–302; castles, 299; church, relationship with, 306; daily life, 301–02; decline, 321, 329, 332; development of, 298; in Japan, 364; Japanese art, 361; manorialism, compared to, 301; middle class, conflict with, 326; monarchy, influence of, 311; social structure, 298–99
fez, 797
Fidel Castro Speaks, 979
fiefs, 298
field hollers, 401
Fiero, Gloria K., 184, 189
Fifty Russian Winters, 846
Fiji, 922
filial piety, 225
Finland; established, 764; in European Union, 1013; in Nazi-Soviet Nonaggression Pact, 830; Soviet Union, resistance of, 831
Finlayson, Donald Lord, 404
fire, 14, 25
fireworks, 348
First Angry, 374
First Consul, 574
First Crusade, 343
First Emperor, 221
First Estate, 560–61
First Man, 374
First Team and the Guadalcanal Campaign, The, 842
First Woman, 374
First World War. *See* World War I
Fitzgerald, F. Scott, 772
Five Classics, 230
Five-Year Plans, 790
flag, rattlesnake, *p550*
Flanders, 312, 323, 333; in World War I, 761
flappers, 771
Flaubert, Gustave, 638
Fleming, Alexander, 733
flood control, 33; in China, 221
Florence, Cathedral of, 404, 409
Florence, Italy, 404, 407–08, 446; bans Arabic numerals, 243
Florida; Native Americans, 440; U.S. acquisition of, 660
flower arranging, 365
flying coffins, 748
"flying shuttle," 605
Foch, Ferdinand, 761
food; from America, 449; developments in 19th and 20th centuries, 629–30; preservation, 629; variety, 629
Forbidden City, *p463, p713,* 464–65, 713
Ford, Gerald R., 888
Ford, Henry, *q609*
fortune tellers, 157
Forum, *p154, p169,* 156
For Whom the Bell Tolls, 828
fossils, *p23, p27*
Four Modernizations, 903
Four Noble Truths, 210

Fourteen Points, 760, 762
Four Travelers on Horseback, *p347*
France; Algeria, policy toward, 879–80; Algiers, colonization of, 708; Austria, war against, 564, 566, 573, 576, 577, 578, 678; Bismarck's relations with, 683; Cambodia, colonization of, 719; Canada, loss of, 544, 547; Catholicism, 422; China, unequal treaties with, 715; civil war, 569, 658; class system, 560–61; colonial possessions, 879; colonies, 443–44, 450; in Common Market, 881; Commune of Paris, 658; constitutional monarchy, 656; constitution of 1791, 564, 568; constitution of 1795, 571; Crimean War, 657, 697; Dreyfus Affair, 658; economy, post-World War I, 780; economy under Napoleon III, 657; education, 567, 574; Egypt, colonization of, 739; Egypt, invasion of, 953; Egypt, war against, 573; England, war against, 329–32, 446, 537; expansion under Louis XIV, 493; fascism, 780; Fifth Republic, 879–80; Fourth Republic, 879, 931; Franco-Prussian War, 657–58, 684–85; French Revolution. *See* French Revolution; German invasion, 831, 833; Germany, war against, 830; Germany declares war, 743; Great Britain, 1904 alliance with, 740; Great Britain, blockade of, 576; Great Britain, defeat by in India, 713; Great Britain, war against, 573, 576, 577, 578; Hapsburgs, war against, 494; Huguenots, 450, 490–91, 493; impressionist art, 595; India, loss of, 497, 594; Indochina, colonization of, 719; Industrial Revolution, 608; Islamic state, invasion by, 279; Italy, invasion by, 412; Italy, war against, 576, 577; Japan, unequal treaties with, 717; Kellogg-Briand Pact, 778; Laos, colonization of, 719; Locarno Agreements, 780; mandates, 763; monarchy, 311–12, 332–33, 490–93; monarchy, restoration of, 577, 581; Morocco, imperialism toward, 708, 738, 739; Napoleonic Era. *See* Napoleonic Era; Napoleon III, 656–57; nationalism, 880; NATO, policy toward, 880; Netherlands, war against, 578; nobles, 491; North African colonization, 929; North American provinces, loss of, 493; nuclear weapons tests, 920, 922, 1011; Panama Canal scandal, 659; Poland, defense of, 829–30; political conflict, 655–59; Popular Front, 780; Protestantism, 490; Prussia, war against, 567, 577; Quadruple Alliance membership, 582–83; Renaissance, 412; reparations, policy on, 762–63; Resistance, 833; restrictions after Napoleon, 580–81; in Revolutionary War, 554; Revolution of 1848, 656; Roman Catholic Church, status of, 560–61; Ruhr Valley, seizure of, 783–84; Russia, 1894 alliance with, 740; Russia, war against, 577; 1400s, *m332;* Second Republic, 656–57; in Seven Years' War, 497; social groups, *p564;* socialism, 776, 780, 1010, 1011; Southeast Asia, colonization of, 718–19; South Pacific, colonies, 922; Spain, war against, 577; Sudan, colonization of, 708, 739; taxation, 561; Third Republic, 646, 658, 879; in Triple Entente, 740; Tunis, colonization of, 708; UN Security Council, 865; urbanization, 632; Vichy government, 833; in Vietnam, 476, 719; voting rights, 657; in War of the Spanish Succession, 493; in War of the Austrian Succession, 497; Weimar Republic, relations with, 780; World War I, after, 779–80
Franciscan order, 307
Francis I, King of France, 412, 413, 457
Francis Joseph, emperor of Austria, *p695,* 678
Francis of Assisi, 292, 307, 411
Franco, Francisco, 827–28
Franco-Prussian War, 657–58, 684–85, 739
Frankish period, *m296,* 294–96
Franklin, Benjamin, *q554*
Franks, 175, 178, 250
Frederick, crown prince of Prussia, *q685*
Frederick, prince of Saxony, 417
Frederick I, king of Prussia, 496
Frederick II, king of Prussia; *See* Frederick the Great
Frederick III, kaiser, 685
Frederick the Great, *q527,* 497, 511
Frederick William, 496
Frederick William I, king of Prussia, 497
Frederick William III, king of Prussia, 583
Frederick William IV, king of Prussia, 682
Frederic Remington and the Spanish-American War, 721
Free French, 844
freeholders, 322
Freeman, Edward A., 308
free trade, defined, 978
French Academy of Science, 491, 521
French and Indian War, 497, 534, 542, 547, 652
French Community, 931
French East India Company, 713
French language, 170, 491; in Canada, 890
French Protestants. *See* Huguenots
French Revolution, 511, 512, 560–73; anthems, 578; army, *c589,* 569; Bastille, storming of, 562; causes, 560–61; Christianity, policy toward, 570; civil war, 569; class warfare, 563; Constitution of 1791, 565–66; Directory, 571, 573; Enlightenment, influence of, 582; Estates-General, 562; Europe, influence on, 566, 569; government, *g579;* legacy, 578; Louis XVI, policy toward, 565, 566, 568; military aspects, 569; monarchy, policy toward, 566; Napoleonic Era, influence of, 578; National Assembly, 562–66; National Convention, 567–69, 571; peasants, influence on, 560, 563; political reform, 565–66; popular reaction, 564, 568; principles, 564–65; Reign of Terror, 570–71; republic, establishment, 567; Republic of Virtue, 570–71; Roman Catholic Church, influence on, 565; symbols, *p571;* women, 565; women's march, *p570–71*
French West Africa, 709
frescoes, 411
Freud, Sigmund, 628, 771–72; flight from Nazism, 786; influence on art, 773
friars, 307
Friedl, Bettina, 648
Fritze, Ronald H., 228
Froissart, Jean, *q330*
From Absolutism to Revolution, 521
Fronde, 490, 491
Fugger family, 446
fugue, 496
Führer, 786
Fuji, Mount, *p360*
Fujimori, Alberto, 993
Fujiwara family, 362
Fulton, Robert, 603, 606
fundamentalism, 959, 965

G

gabelle, 560
Gabriel (angel), *p244,* 273
Gadsden, James, 662
Gadsden Purchase, 662
Gage, Thomas, 552
Galen, Claudius, 170, 519
Galileo Galilei, *p516, q518,* 517–18, 522
galleons, 447
Gallieni, Joseph Simon, 745
Gallipoli, 738, 744, 749, 750
Gambia, The, 930
games; Maya, 381, 382; Sumerian, *p58*
Gandhi, Indira, *p917,* 917–18; assassination, 916
Gandhi, Mohandas K. (also known as Mahatma) , *p916, q801,* 801–03; assassination, 916; salt tax march, 794, 803; in South Africa, 711
Gandhi, Rajiv, 919
Ganesha, 205
Ganges River plain, 66, 202
Gaozong, 347
gardens, *p371;* meditation, *p365*
Garibaldi, Giuseppe, 679–80
Gas Factory at Courcelles, The, 728
Gate of Supreme Harmony, *p464*
Gaugamela, Battle of, 142
Gauguin, Paul, 639
Gaul, 160, 163, 178
Gaullist Union, 880
Gautama, Siddhartha, *p208, p238,* 200, 208–10
Gautier, Emile Felix, 941
Gaza Strip; Egyptian annexation of, 951; Israeli withdrawal from, 957, 962; settlement, 964; Six-Day War, 954–55
Gdansk, Poland, 1004
geishas, *p469,* 472
General Assembly (UN), 864–65. *See also* United Nations
generalizations, 356
general strike, 776, 779, 926, 931
Genesis, 85
genetic engineering, 1022
genetics, 627
Geneva, Switzerland, 418, 419
Genghis Khan, 342, 344, 345, 350
Genji, 363
Genoa, Italy, 321, 323; decline in trade, 448
genocide, 938; in Bosnia-Herzegovina, 1014–15; defined, 850
gentry, defined, 488
geography, study of, 285
geology, 524
geometry, 100, 242, 285, 518; Hellenistic, 145
George, David Lloyd, *q741,* 763
George I, king of Great Britain, 540, 544
George II, king of Great Britain, 544
George III, king of Great Britain, 544, 553
George V, king of Great Britain, 779
George VI, king of Great Britain, 832–33, 879
Georgia (Europe), 256, 257, 789; ethnic groups, 1016; reforms and unrest, 1003
Georgia (U.S.); Jenkins' Ear war, 497
German Confederation, *m682,* 582, 674, 681, 684
German Democratic Republic. *See* East Germany
German Empire, *m684,* 686–89; army, 686; conflict with Catholicism, 686–87; industrialization, 687; labor legislation, 686, 689; political structure after unification, 685, 686. *See also* Germany
Germania, 170
Germanic peoples; 177–78; invasions, *m177*
German language, 413

Germany; after World War I, 764; anti-immigrant sentiment, 1012; armed forces after World War I, 783; Austria, invasion of, 828; Austria-Hungary, support for, 742; Belgium, invasion of, 833; Berlin-Baghdad railway, 739; Catholicism, 422; China, unequal treaties with, 715; civil wars, 312; Confederation, 1815, *m682;* Denmark, war against, 682–83; division after World War II, 848, 869–70; Eastern Slavs, war against, 263; expansion, 828–30; first railroad, 607; France, invasion of, 833; France, war against, 743; immigration from, 665; Industrial Revolution, 608; inflation, 784; Iran, relations with, 798; Italy, treaty with, 828; Japan, treaty with, 828; Jesuit missionaries, 425; in League of Three Emperors, 740; London bombing campaign, 834–35; Low Countries, invasion of, 833; Lutheranism, 425; Manchurian invasion, influence of, 826–27; Mexico, proposal to, 751; monarchies, 312; Morocco, intent toward, 739; navy, expansion of, 740; Nazism, 784–86; Norway and Denmark, invasion of, 831–32; Ottoman Empire, relations with, 739; Papua New Guinea, colonization of, 922; Poland, invasion of, 824, 830; Prussian leadership in unification, 682; regionalism, 683; religious conflict, 494; reparations, 783–84; reunification, *p1006–07,* 1007, 1010, 1011–12; Ruhr Valley seizure by France, 783–84; Russia, treaty with, 759; Russia, war against, 743; Slavic states, wars against, 312; Slavs, war against, 259; Soviet Union, invasion of, 838–39; Soviet Union, nonaggression pact with, 830; Spain civil war, policy toward, 827–28; Third Reich, 786; Thirty Years' War, 494–95; unification, *m684,* 595, 681–85, 730; urbanization, 632; U.S., war declared, 841; Weimar Republic, 783–84; West Africa, colonization of, 709; World War II surrender, 848; World War I reparations, 763. *See also* East Germany. *See also* German Empire. *See also* West Germany

Germinal, 568

Gershoy, Leo, 567

Gertrude Stein, *ptg772*

Gestapo, 786

Ghana, 189–90, 191; democracy, 936; independence, 928, 931. *See also* Gold Coast

Ghiberti, Lorenzo, 409

Gibson, Robert, 1018

Gidwani, Ashim Kumar Ron N.N., 66

Gifts of Passage, 818–21

Gilgamesh, *p74*

Gilgamesh, *q72–75,* 15, 61

Gillenormand, Marius, 584

Gimbutas, Marija, 32

Ginner, Charles, 633

Giotto, 411

Girl with Goats by a Fiord, *ptg636*

Gironde, France, 568

Girondists, 568, 569

Giza, 44, 48

gladiators, 167, 169

Gladstone, William, 647, 649–50, 651

glasnost, 999–1001

Glaukos, 106

global culture, 1022

global economy, 898-99, 915, 942-44, 964, 976-78, 980, 1013, 1020

Global Experience, The, 154, 220, 744, 788

global warming. *See* environment, Montreal Protocol

Globe Theater, *p487*

Glorious Revolution, 540, 542

glory, 106

Glory Had Departed, A, 916

Glower, George, 487

glyphs, 385

Gobi (desert,) 69

God; Abraham, covenant with, 84; in African oral tradition, 184; Allah, compared to, 275; in Byzantine culture, 249; Calvin's interpretation, 419; icon symbolism, 250; influence on Martin Luther, 415; Israelites' belief in, 83; Jesus' teaching, 172; as master mechanic, 524; monotheism, 189; obedience to, 253; prophets of, 85; role in Inquisition, 422

Goddard, Robert, 732

God Save the Czar, 690

Godwinson, Harold, 309

Goering, Hermann, 828, 834

Goethe, Johann Wolfgang von, 635

Gogol, Nikolay, *q258*

Golan Heights; future of, 963; Israeli withdrawal from, 957; Six-Day War, 954

gold; in Australia, 654; in East Africa, 195; in New Zealand, 654; Spanish search for, 438, 441, 442

Gold Coast, 926; British imperialism, 709. *See also* Ghana

Golden Fleece, 257

Golden Horn, 252

Golden Mean, 131

Golden Rule, 226

Goldin, Dan, 1018

gold trading; in Africa, 182, 189–90

Goliath, 85

Gómez, Juan Vicente, 813–14

Gomulka, Wladyslaw, 876

González, Felipe, 1012

Good Emperors, 165–66, 175

Goodman, Benny, 775

Good Neighbor policy, 817

Gorbachev, Mikhail, *p1000, q996;* attitude toward fall of Eastern Europe, 1005; comes to power, 998; U.S., relations with, 999

gorillas, 935

Gorillas and Humans: An Uneasy Truce, 935

Gorky, Maksim, 791

Gothic architecture, *p328,* 322, 328

Goths, 175

Goulart, João, 993

government; constitutional, 102; development of, 32, 34; federal system, defined, 554; the governed, relationship to, 523; home rule, 651; responsibility to protect citizens, 64; separation of powers, 525–26; social welfare, role in, 778

Government of India Act, 803

Gracchus, Gaius, 162

Gracchus, Tiberius, 159, 162, 165

Graham, Martha, 773

Granada, Spain, 333

Grand Canyon, 441

grand jury, 309

Grand Théâtre of Bourdeaux, *p528*

grand vizier, 457

Granicus River, 141

Grapes of Wrath, The, 773

graphs, 579

gravitation, 511, 518

Gray, Tom, 21

Great Basin, Native Americans, 377

Great Britain; Anglo-Boer War, 711; Arabs, support for, 761; Ashanti, colonization of, 709; Battle of Britain, 833–35; Berlin-Baghdad railway, resentment toward, 739; blockade by France, 576; British Empire, end of, 878; Burma, colonization of, 719; Canada, acquisition of, 544, 547, 652; Cape Colony, colonization, 711; China, unequal treaties with, 715; coal, 604; colonial power, 497; in Common Market, 880, 881; Commonwealth of Nations, 779; competition, 738; Congress of Vienna involvement, 580; creation, 497, 543; Crimean War, 657, 697; Cyprus, acquisition of, 698; defeat of France in India, 713; democracy, 650–51; disarmament treaty, 778; Dunkirk evacuation, 833; economy, post-World War I, 778–79; education, 650; education, compulsory, 620; Egypt, colonization, 708; Egypt, colonization of, 739; Egypt, invasion of, 953; electoral reform, 650; Europe, closer ties to, 1010–11; France, 1904 alliance with, 740; France, war against, 573, 576, 577, 578; French Revolution, policy toward, 569; Germany, war against, 741, 743, 830; Gold Coast, colonization of, 709; Holy Alliance, policy toward, 582–83; immigration from, 665; India, colonization of, 594, 713–14; Industrial Revolution, 603–06; industry, 596; Iran, colonization, 797–98; Japan, unequal treaties with, 717; Labour party, 647, 650, 779, 878, 879; Libya, evacuation of, 836; Locarno Agreements, 780; Malaya, colonization of, 719; mandates, 763; Monroe Doctrine, role in, 722; natural resources, 604; naval power, 716–17; Nigeria, colonization, 709; North Africa campaign, 843–44; open seas, policy on, 762; opium trade, 715; Oregon Country, 662; Palestine, government of, 951; Palestine, mandate in, 798–99; Papua New Guinea, colonization of, 922; Poland, defense of, 829–30; political parties, 649; political reform, 648–51; population, 604; post-World War II, 878–79; Quadruple Alliance membership, 582–83; Russo-Turkish War, reaction to, 698; 1980s and 1990s, 1010–11; in Seven Years' War, 497; social reform, 623; Southeast Asia, colonization, 718–19; Southeast Asia, colonization of, 916; Sudan, colonization of, 708, 739, 929; in Triple Entente, 740; UN Security Council, 865; U.S. aid for, 835–36; U.S. policy toward, 576; Venezuela, dispute with, 722; voting rights, 649–50; in War of the Austrian Succession, 497; welfare state, 879; women's vote, 651; World War I, after, 778–79; Zulu, battle with, 711. *See also* England

Great Canal, 346

Great Charter. *See* Magna Carta

Great Council, 309, 311

Great Depression. *See* depressions (economic)

Great Dictator, The, 733

Great Elector. *See* Frederick William

Greater East Asia Co-Prosperity Sphere, 807, 839–841

Great Fear, 560, 563, 564

Great Gatsby, The, 772

Great Leap Forward, 902

Great Migration, 537

Great Ministry, 650

Great Mosque of Timbuktu, *p190*

Great Mother, 262

Great Plains; dust bowl, 777; Native Americans, 378

Great Pyramid, 44, 48

Great Rift Valley, 185

Great Schism, 335

Great Society, 885
Great Speeches from Pericles to Kennedy, 916
Great Serpent Mound, The, *ptg. 376-77*
Great Trek, 711
Great Wall of China, *p219,* 222, 346, 347
Great Zimbabwe, *p194, p196,* 195–96, 933
Greece; ancient civilization. *See* Greece, ancient; Axum, trade with, 186; in Balkan League, 698; climate, 106; democracy, 1013; geography, 106; independence, 580, 583, 697; Persian Empire, conquest by, 91; Persian Empire, war against, 92; territorial gains, 764; Truman Doctrine, 866, 868; Turkey, invasion of, 796
Greece, ancient, *m114,* 106–24; Aegean civilizations, 107–14; archeology, 108; Athens, 117–19, 122–23; citizenship, 112; city-states relations, 120, 123; civil rights, 112; colonies, 104, 112–13; dark age, 108; decline, 124, 140; deities, 110–11; digest, 236; economy, 113; festivals, 111; Golden Age. *See* Greece, Golden Age; government, 113–14; influence on Muslim literature, 286; influence on Muslim science, 285; influence on Renaissance, 404–05; literature, 108; organization, 112–14; Peloponnesian War, 123–24; Persian Wars, 119–22; religion, 110–11; Roman Empire, conquest by, 143; Roman Empire, contributions to, 152; rule by Antigonus, 143; sculpture, *p116;* social structure, 113–14; Sparta, 115–17; trade, 107, 112–13; values, 110; women, *p148,* 107
Greece, Golden Age, 104, 122–23, 130–38; architecture, 130–31; Byzantine Empire, preservation by, 254; digest, 236–37; drama, 132–34; fine arts, 131–32; history, study of, 137–38; mathematics, 138; medicine, 138; Olympic Games, 134; painting, 131; philosophy, 135–37, 209, 287; physical fitness, 134; sculpture, 131–32
Greek fire, 254
Greek language, 82, 152, 170, 178
Greek Pastoral Poetry, 140
Greenland, 296
Greensleeves, 419
Greenwich, England, 139
Gregory I, pope, 175, 305
Gregory the Illuminator, 257
Gregory VII, pope, 306, 312
Gregory XI, pope, 335
Gregory XIII, pope; influence on calendars, 85
Grendel, 327
Grenville, George, 547–48
grid system, global, 139, 436
Griffier, Jan, the Elder, 447
Gropius, Walter, 775; flight from Nazism, 786
gross domestic product (GDP), defined, 898
Grotius, Hugo, 523
Grout, Donald J., 676
Grozny, Chechnya, 1016
Guadalajara, Mexico, 668
Guadalcanal, 845
Guadeloupe, 444
Guam; Japanese capture of, 845; U.S. acquisition of, 724
Guangzhou, China, 463
Guatemala, 668, 978; Maya ruins, 384; Native Americans, 379
Guerrillas of Peace, Liberation Theology, and The Central American Revolution, 974
guerrilla warfare, 679
Guide of the Perplexed, The, 288
guilds; craft, 325; in Japan, 364; merchant, 324
Guillotin, Joseph-Ignace, 572
guillotine, *p572,* 568
Guinea, 931–32
Gui Xi, 346
Guizot, François, 656
Gulag Archipelago, The, 874
Gulf of Tonkin Resolution, 910–11
gunpowder, 240
gunpowder, invention of, 232, 348
Guomindang, 716, 804–806
Gupta Empire, 212–14; art, 214; beginning, 200; religion, 212; science, 214; social life, 213–14; women, 213–14
Gurche, John, 41
Gutenberg, Johannes, 241, 412, 413, 416
Guzmán, Jacobo Arbenz, 978
Gypsies, in Holocaust, 839

H

habeas corpus, 542
Hadar, Ethiopia, 21
Hadith, 275
Hadrian, 165, 167
Haganah, 951
Hagia Sophia, *p249,* 244
haiku, 472
Haim, Sylvia G., 796
Haiti; discovery, 438; modern era, 984; revolt and independence, 666; uprising and independence, 445, 513, 667–68; U.S. interventions, 816. *See also* Saint Domingue
hajj, 276
Halley's Comet, 228, 231
Hall of One Hundred Columns, 132
Hallstatt Celts, 92
Hamaguchi, Osachi, 809
Hamilton, Alexander, *q103*
Hamlet, 412
Hammurabi, king, *p64,* 63
Hammurabi's code, 58, 63–64, 88
Handel, George Frideric, 529
Han dynasty, *m221, m224,* 222–24; agriculture, 232; civil service system, 226; Confucian values, impact of, 228; founded, 218; Korea, invasion of, 358; literature, 231; pottery, *p231;* renewal by Emperor Wen, 346
Hanging Gardens, 90
hangul, 359
Hangzhou, 348
hanifs, 271
Hannibal, 160
Hanover, House of, 543
Hanukkah, 143
Hanyang, Korea, 359
Hapsburg dynasty, *m484,* 482; Denmark, war against, 494; in Spain, 482, 484; Sweden, war against, 494
Haqqash, Husain, 460
Harappa civilization, *m67,* 44, 67–68; summary, 98
Harappan Civilization, q66
Harding, Warren G, *q770*
Hard is the Journey, 367
Hard Times, Human Documents of the Industrial Revolution, 612, 624, 638
Hargreaves, James, 598, 605
Harlem Renaissance, 773
harnesses, 322
Harun al-Rashid, 281
Harvest Scene, ptg601
Harvey, William, 514, 519
Hasidism, 530
Hashimoto, Ryutaro, 899
hasidism, 530
Hastings, Battle of, 308, 309
Hatshepsut, queen, *ptg49,* 46, 49, 52
Hatt-I Humayun, 456, 458
Hattusas, 88
Hausa, 799
Havana, Cuba, 983
Havel, Václav, 1007
Hawass, Zahi, 56
Hawkins, John, 440
Hawkins Voyages, The, 440
Haydn, Joseph, 529, 580
haymaking, *p600*
Haytham, Ibnal, 285
Hayward, John, 485
Hazlitt, William, *q622*
Hebrews, 80. *See* Israelites
Hegel, G.W.F., 625
Heian Kyo, 362
Heisei, 896
Heismann, Josef, 696
Helagu, 344
Helen of Troy, 108
Hellenes, 107
Hellenistic culture, 108, 143–45; arts and sciences, 145; Byzantine Empire, influence on, 178; culture, 143–44; philosophy, 144
Hellespont, 109
helots, 115. *See also* enslaved persons
Hemingway, Ernest, 770, 772, 828
hemophilia, 692, 757
Henrietta Maria, 537
Henry, Patrick, *q550*
Henry, Philip, 534
Henry, Thomas, 519
Henry I, king of England, 309
Henry II, king of England, 309–10, 329
Henry III, king of England, 310–11
Henry IV, king of France, 312, 490, 492
Henry of Navarre; *See* Henry IV, king of France
Henry the Navigator, Prince, 434, 436
Henry VII, king of England, 329, 333, 414, 444, 485
Henry VIII, ptg420
Henry VIII, king of England, 419–20, 480, 485–86, 536; death, 485
Hera, 134
heresy, 174, 306, 307
Hermitage (St. Petersburg), *p499*
Hermit Kingdom, 359
Herodotus, *q122,* 120, 135, 137
heroes, 771
Herzegovina; acquisition by Austria-Hungary, 698
Herzl, Theodor, 798
Heurlimann, Martin, 251
Hidalgo, Miguel, 668
Hideyoshi, Toyotomi, 454, 468–69, 471
hierarchy, defined, 228, 389
hieratic writing, 52
hieroglyphics, 52–53, 511
Highway Act of 1956, 883
Hijrah, 270, 272–73
Hikmet, Nazim, 967
Hildebrand, 303, 306
Himalayas, 66
Hindenburg, Paul von, 785
Hinduism, 206–07; architecture, 204–05, 353; attempt to unite with Islam, 460; the Buddha's rejection of, 210; deities, 204; Islam, compared to, 460; Islam, conflict with, in India, 801, 803; Muslim literature, influence on, 286; in Southeast Asia, 351, 355; in Sri Lanka, 919, 1016

Hindu Kush, *p202,* 66
Hingley, Ronald, 826
Hippias, 112
Hippocrates, *q138*
Hippolochios, 106
hiragana, 250
Hiram, King, 80
Hirohito, emperor of Japan, *p897;* constitutional monarch, 808; divinity, 360–61; militarism, policy toward, 809; under occupation constitution, 896; World War II surrender, 850
Hiroshige, A., 363
Hiroshima, Japan, 733, 846, 849–50
Hispanic Americans, 662; civil rights, 887
Hispaniola, 667–68, 984; discovery, 438
Historia, 137
Historial Record, 231
Histories, The, 120
history; beginning of, 32, 96; study of, 137–38, 287–88
History of Private Life, Volume 4, From the French Revolution..., 626
History of Western Music, A, 676
Hitler, Adolf, *p784, p786, q826;* chancellor of Germany, 768; comes to power, 733; death of, 848; rise to power, 784–85; Spanish civil war, policy toward, 828
Hitler Youth, *p784–85,* 786
Hittite Empire, *m89,* 64, 88, 89; hunting scene, *p88;* summary, 99
Hobbes, Thomas, 521–22
Ho Chi Minh, 909
Hohenzollern family, 496
Hohokam, 372, 377
Hokkaido, 359
Holbein, Hans, 420
Holden, Anthony, 140
Hollywood, 770
Holocaust, *p838, p851,* 838, 839, 850–51
Holoka, James P., 225, 804
Holstein, 682–83, 684
Holy Alliance, 582
Holy Bible. *See* Bible
Holy Roman Empire; abolition by Napoleon, 576; conflict with papacy, 312; in Germany, 495
Holy Synod, 501
homage (medieval ceremony), 299
Homage to Catalonia, 828
home electronics, 898
Homer, *p110,* 106, 108, 109
Homer (robot), *p755*
home rule, 651
Homiliarum in Ezechielem, 175
hominids, *c30,* 20–25; discovery of, 20–21, 23, 25; earliest, 22; fossils, *p23;* groupings, 22, 24; language development, 25; migrations, 20, 25, 27; summary, 96–97; time line, 18. *See also* human prehistory
Homo, 22
Homo erectus, 20, 24, 25
Homo habilis, 18, 20, 22, 24, 25
Homo neanderthalensis, 27
Homo sapiens, 18, 24, 26–27; migration, *m22*
Homo sapiens sapiens, 27
Honduras; establishment, 668; Native Americans, 379
Honecker, Enic, 1005
Hong Kong, *p1019,* 905; boat people, 913; Japanese invasion of, 842
Hong Wu, 462
honor, in Olympic Games, 120
Honshu, 359, 360
Hood **(battleship),** 842
Hooke, Robert, 519
Hoover, Herbert, 816–17
Hopper, Edward, 769
Hotmuz, 459
Hornet **(battleship),** 842
horsemen, terra-cotta, *p231*
horses, use in agriculture, 322
Horus, *p52*
hot line, 874
Houdon, Jean-Antoine, 529
House of Commons; election, 543; under Henry VIII, 486; representation in, 648
House of Lords, 538
House of Wisdom, 268, 285
housing, 28–29
Huang He River valley, 17, 32, 69
Hua Tho, 228
Hudson, Henry, 443
Hudson River, 443
Hue: My City, Myself, 909
Huerta, Victoriano, 725
Hughes, Langston, *q945,* 773
Hugo, Victor, *q739,* 584, 586, 636
Huguenots, 450, 490–91; emigration, 493
Huks, 920
Human Comedy, The, 638
humanism, 404–05, 409, 412; Catholic censorship, 423; Christian humanism, 413–14
Humanistic Tradition, The, 184, 189
human origins. *See* human prehistory
human prehistory, *m30,* 18–31; climate, influence of, 24; culture, 24; paleontology, 23; population, 28, 31; summary, 196–97. *See also* hominids
Human Record, The, 277, 456, 462, 468, 498, 524
human rights, 523, 530, 1022; under Magna Carta, 310
human sacrifices. *See* sacrifices, human
Hunchback of Notre Dame, The, 636
Hundred Years' War, 316, 329–32
Hungary; Austria, compromise with, 696–97; Catholicism, 422; communism, 876; communism, end of, 1005; immigration from, 665; Jesuit missionaries, 425; loss of territory, 764; open borders, *p1007;* rule of Croats, 247; socialism, 1008; Soviet invasion, 876
Huns, 177–78, 178
hunting-gathering, 16, 25, 28, 374; in Japan, 361
Hurston, Zora Neale, 773
Hus, Jan, 334, 336
Husayn, son of Ali, 278–79
Hussein, King of Jordan, 953
Hussein, Saddam, *p959,* 960; Kurds, policy toward, 1016
Hussites, 334, 336
Hutus, 938
hygiene, 138, 626
Hygiene and Preventive Medicine in Ancient China, 228
Hyksos, 46, 49, 84
hyperinflation, defined, 991
hypotheses, 391; defined, 517

I

I Am a Fugitive from a Chain Gang, 775
Iberia, 257
Ibn-Rushd, 287
Ibo, 799
ICBMs *See* Intercontinental ballistic missiles
ice ages, 24
Iceland, 296
Iceman, *p41,* 38–41
iconoclasts, 250
icons, *p244;* approved, 246; as art, 252–53; controversy, 249–50; defined, 249
Idaho, 662
ideologies, 871
idol, Neolithic, *p15*
Idylls of Theocritus, The, 140
Ieyasu, Tokugawa, *q468,* 469, 471
Ignatius of Loyola, *q424,* 422
ikebana, 365
Iliad, *q110,* 108, 109, 119
Iliad, The, *q106*
illuminated manuscripts, *p253,* 328
Imam Mosque, *p459*
imams, 276, 279
immigration, *p652,* 630–31; to colonies, 450; illegal, 980; internal, 631; to U.S., 660, 665
imperialism; cultural reasons for, 704; defined, 704; immigration to colonies, 705; legacy, 712; morality, 929; reasons for, 704; territorial control, kinds of, 706
Imperialism, Age of, 704–25; digest, 731
Imperial Palace (Japan), 469
imperial presidency, 888
impressionism, 595, 635, 637, 638–39
Impression–Sunrise, 637
Im Vaterland, 686
Inca Empire, *m390,* 389–90; creation myth, 372; population, 442; removal of wealth from, 448; Spain, conquest by, 390, 441
incensario, *p382*
Inchon, Korea, 907
Incontro di Teano, *ptg675*
indemnity, 160, 580
Independence Hall, *p103*
Index of Prohibited Books, 423
India, *m217,* 202–14; Alexander, conquest by, 142; Aryan invasion, 200; Aryans, 202–07; atomic bomb, 917; Axum, trade with, 186; British acquisition, *crt649;* British dominance, *m714,* 497, 594; British imperialism, 713–14; Buddhism, 207–10; caste system, 917; China, invasion by, 918; China, trade with, 347, 348; digest, 238–39; East Africa, trade with, 194, 195; economic development, 714; ethnic minorities, 918; French colonization, 444; Golden Age, 212; Gupta Empire, *m212,* 212–14; Hindu-Muslim conflict, 801, 803, 916; Hindu period, 202–07; independence, 916–18; independence movement, 801–03; influence on Southeast Asia, 351; invasion by Timur Lenk, 459–60; Jesuit missionaries, 424; Mauryan Empire, *m212,* 211–12; migration to India and Pakistan, 916; Mogul Empire, 459–61; Muslim science, influence on, 285; nationalism, 714, 856; Portugal, trade with, 438; religious conflict, 918; Roman Empire, trade with, 211; satellite television, censorship, 860; social equality, 917; socialism, 917; social structure, *c203;* Soviet support, 918
Indian Journal, An, 704
Indian National Congress, 713, 714, 801, 803
Indian Ocean; Portuguese exploration, 436, 438, 440; trade routes, 195
Indian Revolt of 1857, 702
Indians, name derivation, 438, Indians, American. *See* Native Americans
Indochina, 476; cold war, 909; French imperialism, 719; Japanese invasion of, 841. *See also* Vietnam
Indo-European language family, 203

Indo-Europeans, 90, 163; in Italy, 90
Indonesia, 355–56, 475, 915; Dutch colonization, 442; Dutch imperialism, 718; East Timor, repression of, 915; independence, 909; natural resources, 718
Indra (Aryan deity), 206
indulgences, 415, 416, 423
Indus River, 32, 66
Indus River valley, 66–68; Aryan settlement, 202; climate, 66–67; early civilizations, 67–68; geography, 66; invaders, 211
industrial capitalism, 608
industrialization, 596–97; assembly lines, 597, 609; automation, 883; mass production, 597, 609; specialization, 609; standardized parts, 597, 609. *See also* Industrial Revolution
Industrial Revolution, 600–16; cities, 605; digest, 728; early industry, 602; imperialism, influence on, 704; labor, 604; new markets, 705; preindustrial society, 600–02; raw materials, 705; social changes, 610, 612–16, 620, 728–29; spread outside Great Britain, 607–08; United States, 662–63, 664–65
Indus Valley Civilization, *q66*
inertia, 518
infant mortality, in Latin America, 975
inferences, 313
inflation, 176, 888–89; defined, 484; double-digit inflation, 889; hyperinflation, 991
information classification, 65
information superhighway, 860, 1021
information synthesis, 837
Innocent III, pope, *q255,* 306, 307
In Praise of Folly, 414
Inquisition, 303, 307, 422, 423
Inquisition, Spanish, 333, 483
Institutes of the Christian Religion, The, 418–19
Institutionalized Revolutionary Party (PRI) (Mexico), 979
intendants, 491
interchangeable parts, 609
intercontinental ballistic missiles (ICBMs), 873
interdependence, 1029; defined, 1018; global, 1018–22
internal-combustion engines, 611
International Brigade, 827
International Court of Justice, 865
international law, 523
International Monetary Fund, 1019
Internet, 861
Interrupted Life, the Diaries of Etty Hillesum, An, 838
interstate highway system, 883
intifada, 956
Intolerable Acts, 550
Inuit, 35
investment, 604
invisible hand, 623
Ionia, 108, 113, 123; conquest by Persian Empire, 120
Iphigenia, 132
Iphigenia, 564
IRA. *See* Irish Republican Army
Iran, 91; American hostage crisis, 958; Iraq, war against, 948, 959; Islamic revolution, 954, 958, 960; nuclear weapons, 960; oil field nationalization, 950, origin of name, 798; reform, 797–98; rule by Seleucus, 143; satellite television, censorship, 861; Shah, era of, 953; Shah, restoration of, 953
Iran-Contra scandal, 986
Iraq; in Arab League, 950; British mandate, 764; independence, 950; Iran, war against, 948, 959; Islamic state, conquest by, 277, 278; Kurds, policy toward, 1016; Kuwait, invasion of, 900, 954, 960; nationalism, 953; Turkey, conflict over water, 964
Ireland; defeat by Cromwell, 538; dominion status, 779; England, alignment with, 489; England, conflict with, 538, 543; Great Britain, conflict with, 779, 1011; home rule, *p651,* 647; immigration from, 651, 665; missionaries, 303, 305; Northern Ireland, 1011; religious conflict, 651; Republic of, 1011
Irene, Byzantine empress, 250
Irigoyen, Hipólito, *q816*
Irish Free State, 779
Irish Republican Army (IRA), 1011
iron casting, 232
iron curtain, 866
iron industry, 664
iron mining, 186, 194; in Spain, 828
Iroquois League, 374, 378
Irrawaddy River, 354
irrigation, 48; in China, *p466,* 221, 232; development of, 33; Native American, 377
Irwell River, 605
Isaac, sacrifice of, *p408*
Isabella, queen of Spain, 684
Isabella of Castile; Columbus, instructions to, 434, 437; Columbus, support for, 438; Ferdinand, marriage to, 329; unites Spain, 333, 483
Isabella of Portugal, 482
Isfahan, Iran, *p288,* 459
Isipatana, India, 209
Isis, 52
Islam; acceptance by Makkah, 270; attempt to unite with Hinduism, 460; beliefs, 273, 275–76; China, introduction into, 347; Christianity, compared to, 275; Christianity's intent to block, 434; development of, 99; in East Africa, 195; emergence, 271; examination by Slavic Vikings, 262; Five Pillars, 275–76; fundamentalism, 959; in Ghana, 190; Hinduism, compared to, 460; Hinduism, conflict with, in India, 801, 803; importance of Jerusalem, 318; in Indonesia, 355; Islamic law, 275; Islamic state, 273, 277–81; Judaism, compared to, 275; Judaism, influence of, 83; in Malay Peninsula, 355; in Mali, 191; Mongol conversion to, 345; in North Africa, 190–91; Persian Empire, influence of, 93; Slavic culture, influence of, 259, 498; spread, 189; spread by Timur Lenk (Tamerlane), 345; spread in 7th century, *m280,* 255, 257, 273, 274; spread in 13th century, 456. *See also* Muslims
Islamic government, modern, 935–36
Islamic state; Abbasid dynasty, 280–81; breakup, 281; decline, 437; defeat by Charles Martel, 295; defeat by Portugal, 440; established, 268; Italy, seizure of, 296; Mongol invasion, 344; Rightly Guided Caliphs, 277–79; taxation of non-Muslims, 280; Umayyad dynasty, 279–80
Ismail, Shiite leader, 459
Ismene, 146
isolationism, 772
Israel; creation, 951; Egypt, invasion of, 953; Egypt, relations with, 955, 962; established, 951; Jordan, relations with, 957, 962; Lebanon, occupation of, 958, 963; peace process, opposition to, 957–58; in Persian Gulf War, 960; PLO, relations with, 948, 954, 956–57, 962; religious fundamentalism, 965; Syria, relations with, 957, 962–63; U.S. support for, 955; water shortage, 964. *See also* Arab-Israeli conflict. *See also* Israelites. *See also* Palestine
Israel, son of Abraham, 84
Israeli-Arab conflict; *See* Arab-Israeli conflict
Israelites, 83–86; in Babylon, 85–86; in Canaan, 84–85, 206; in Egypt, 78, 84; in Jerusalem, 85–86; legacy, 86, 88; religion, 83; summary, 98–99; 12 tribes of, 83, 84, 85. *See also* Jews. *See also* Judaism
Issus, Syria, 141
Istanbul, 251
Istanbul, Turkey, *p949;* establishment of, 458. *See also* Constantinople
Italian language, 170
Italian Renaissance, *m405,* 404–11; art, *p406,* 409–10; education, 405; English Renaissance, influence on, 414; Florence, 407–08; government, 405–07; literature, 405; northern Europe, influence on, 412; Rome, 408; scholarship, 405; social structure, 405–06; Venice, 408–09
Italy; Age of Revolution, 513; Allies, surrender to, 844; Austrian acquisition, 495; barbarian invasion, 177–78; barriers to unification, 676, 680; Bismarck's relations with, 683; Catholicism, 422; climate, 154; in Common Market, 881; Communist party, 1012; constitutional monarchy, 680; cultural divisions, 678; dictatorship, 782; early people, 155; entry into World War I, 748; Ethiopia, colonization of, 711; Ethiopia, occupation of, 827; fascism, 781–83; France, war against, 576, 577; French invasion, 412; gains after World War I, 763, 781; geography, 154; Germany, treaty with, 828; Greek colony, 154; immigration from, 665; Libya, colonization, 708–09, 929; Locarno Agreements, 780; Lombard invasion, 255; Manchurian invasion, influence of, 826–27; Napoleon as king, 576; Neolithic people, 155; Norman invasion, 255; northern Italy, 679; Ottoman Empire, war against, 708–09; political reform, 656; Prussia, alliance with, 680; Renaissance, *m405,* 404–11; before Roman Republic, *m156;* southern Italy, 678; Spanish civil war, policy toward, 827–28; in the 1970s-90s, 1012; trade center, 154; in Triple Alliance, 740; unification, *m677,* 676–80, 730; U.S. missiles, 984; U.S., war declared, 841, World War II, 836, 844–45
Iturbide, Agustín de, 668
Ivanhoe, 636
Ivan I, Prince of Moscow, 263
Ivan III, 244, 258, 263–64
Ivan IV. *See* Ivan the Terrible
Ivan the Great, 263–64
Ivan the Terrible, 498, 499
ivory trade, 186
Iwo Jima, 849
Izanagi, 360
Izanami, 360
izbas, 259
Izetbegovic, Alija, 1015

J

Jacob, 4
Jacobins, 568, 569, 570–71
jade ax, *p380*
jade dragon, *p220*
Jael, 83

Jaffna, Sri Lanka, 1016
jaguars, 380
Jahan, Shah, 460
Jahangir, Moghul emperor, 456
Jains, 210
Jamaica, 444
James I, king of England, 477, 489; debt, 537; relations with Parliament, 536–37
James II, king of England, 542; Irish revolt, 543; overthrow, 542
Jamestown, Virginia, 432, 444
James VI, king of England, 418
Jammeh, Yahya Ajj, 930
Janata party (India), 917
janissaries, 457
Japan, 359–65; agriculture, 897; arts, *p361,* 365; atomic bomb, 849–50; automobile industry, *p898,* 998; China, influence of, 362; China, invasion of, 804, 827, 838; China, relations with, 905; China, trade with, 347; China, unequal treaties with, 715; Christianity, 470–71; civil service, 340; civil war, *m479;* constitution, 362, 896–97; creation myth, 360; daily life, 472; disarmament treaty, 778; early man, 361; economy, 894; education, 717; emperors, 360–61; empire 1910-1945, *m845;* European influence, 470–72; expansion in Asia, 826–27, 841; feudalism, 364; foreign aid, 900; foreign relations, 900; geography, 360; Germany, treaty with, 828; growth in 18th century, 468; Heian period, 362–63; imperialism in, 716–17; Indochina, invasion of, 841; industrialization, 713, 717–18, 808, 897–98; Industrial Revolution, 597; islands, 359; isolation, 360; Jesuit missionaries, *p425,* 424; Korea, attack on, 359; Korea, colonization of, 718; Korea, influence of, 361; Korea, invasion of, 469; Latin America, trade with, 978; in League of Nations, 807; League of Nations, withdrawal from, 826; literature, 363; Manchuria, occupation of, 806, 809, 826; mandates, 763; Meiji leaders, 716–17; merchant class, 364; militarism, rise of, 807–09; military *versus* consumer spending, 897, 900; Mongol attack, 350, 358; Noh theater, 358; North Korea, relations with, 900; opening by Admiral Perry, 702; Philippines, relations with, 921; pollution, 898; population growth, 808; Portugal, trade with, 440; postwar economy, 851, 896–900; postwar government, 898–99; postwar military policy, 896–97; postwar occupation, 896–97; recession, 898; religion, 364–65; rise of merchants, 471–72; Russia, relations with, 900; Russia, war against, 694, 718; samurai, 363–64; seclusion policy, 471; Shandong Peninsula, control of, 804; social changes, 808; South Korea, relations with, 900; steel industry, 899; terrorism, 899; Tokugawa shogunate, 468–72; trade protection, 900; United Nations, military involvement in, 900; U.S., attack upon, 734, 841; U.S. economic support for, 897; U.S., investment in, 899; West, resentment toward, 807–08; women, 808; world trade, 899–900; World War II involvement, 824, 841, 845, 849-50; Yamato clan, 361–62
Japanese Americans, *p840,* 840
Japan's Sun Rises Over the Pacific, 896
jar, Greek, *p16*
jar, Harappan, *p66*
Jason (robot), 753
jati, 204
Java, 355, 442, 475; revolt against Dutch imperialism, 718
Jawara, Dawda, 930
Jayavarman, 474
jazz, 773
Jazz Singer, The, 775
Jefferson, Thomas, 523, 553, 660
Jenkins, Robert, 497
Jenkins' Ear, War of, 497
Jenner, Edward, 626, 627
Jeremiah, 85
Jericho, 16, 31, 957
Jerusalem; Arab conquest, 240, 318; archaeology, *p96;* Chaldean conquest, 90; Crusader conquest, 319; crusades for, 318–21; David's capital, 85; Jewish rebellion against Rome, 171; Maccabean reconquest, 143; Muslim reconquest, 320; partition, 951; religious importance, 318; Roman Republic, destruction by, 161; Six-Day War, 955. *See also* Israel
Jesuit order, 424, 444; in China, 467; expulsion from German Empire, 686; in Japan, 470
Jesus, *p171,* 172; in Byzantine literature, 249, 254; choice of Peter to lead the church, 303; crucifixion, 101, 152; death, 253; Francis of Assisi, 307; Islamic view, 275; in Jerusalem, 318; Last Supper, *q410;* in *Pietá,* 411; preaches in Palestine, 171
jewelry, Harappan, *p68*
jewelry making, 31
Jews, 84; Arabs, relations with, 798–99; Crusaders, persecution by, 319; genocide, 850–51; Holocaust, 839; influence on calendars, 85; Nazi persecution, *p785,* 733, 781, 784–86; origin of name, 85; Palestine, immigration to, *p951,* 798–99; persecution in Russia, 693; Rome, rebellion against, 171–72; in Spain, 333; U.S., immigration to, 629. *See also* Israelites. *See also* Judaism
Jiang Jing, 903
Jiangxi, China, 805
jihad, 278
Jimmu, 360
Jingdezhen, China, 467
jingoism, defined, 698
Jinnah, Mohammed Ali, 803
Jiu-Hwa Lo Upshur, 804
Joan of Arc, 316, 330, 332
João, King of Portugal, 669
Joffre, Joseph Jacques, 745
Johannesburg, South Africa, *p934,* 934
Johanson, Donald C., 21
John, king of England, 241, 308, 310, 329
John I, king of Portugal, 436
John III Sobieski, Polish king, 458
John of Damascus, 250
John Paul II, Pope, 859, 1004
Johnson, Elliot, *q824*
Johnson, Lyndon B.; Great Society, 885; imperial presidency, 888
Johnson administration; civil rights legislation, 887; Vietnam policy, 886, 909, 910
Johnston, Audrey Lawson, *p755*
Johnston, Reginald, 713
John Wycliffe Reading His Translation of the Bible to John of Gaunt, *ptg336*
John XII, Pope, 312
joint-stock companies, 447, 448
Joliet, Louis, 444
Jolson, Al, 775
Jordan; in Arab League, 950; British mandate, 764; East Jerusalem, annexation of, 951; fundamentalism, Muslim, 965; independence, 950; Israel, relations with, 957, 962; water shortage, 964; West Bank, annexation of, 951; Western support for, 953
Jordan River, 83
Joseph II of Austria, 524, 528
Joseph Stalin: Man and Legend, 826
Joshua, 84
Journal of Near Eastern Studies 4, 46
Journey into the Daytime, 920
journeymen, 325
Joyce, James, 732, 772
Juan Carlos I, king of Spain, 1012
Juárez, Benito, 725
Judah, 85, 171; Roman conquest, 143
Judah Maccabees, 143
Judaism; Arabs, impact on, 271; beginnings, 83; development of, 99; examination by Slavic Vikings, 262; Golden Rule, 226; Hasidism, 530; under Islamic law, 273, 280, 319; Jerusalem, importance of, 318; Moses Maimonides, 287–88; Persian Empire, influence of, 93. *See also* Jews. *See also* Israelites
Judea, 171
Judges (book of Bible), 206
judges (Jewish leaders), 84
Julian emperors, 164–65
Julius, Pope, 404
Julius II, Pope, 407, 411
July Ordinances, 655
Junkers, 496, 682, 685
junks, 464
Jupiter, 158
Jurchen, 348, 350
Jurjis ibn Bakhtishu, 286
jury system, 118–19, 309
jus civile, 166
jus gentium, 166
justices of the peace, 487
justification by faith, 415
Justin, 171
Justin I, Byzantine emperor, 247
Justinian, Byzantine emperor, *p248,* 247–49; becomes emperor, 240, 246; Christianity, influence on, 249; flight from Constantinople, 246, 247–48; silk industry, influence on, 252
Justinian Code, 102, 248
Jutes, 308

K

Kaaba, 268; attack on, 272; destruction, 273; before Islam, 271; pilgrimage to, 276
Kabuki theater, 472
Kádár, János, 876
Kafka, Franz, 772
Kaifeng, 348
Kailasa Temple, 364
kaiser, defined, 685
Kalila and Dimna, 286
Kamakura, Japan, 363
kami, 361
kamikazes, 363, 842, 845
Kampuchea, 912. *See also* Cambodia
Kangxi, 462, 466
kanji, 250
Kant, Immanuel, 530
Kantanga, Congo, 932
kaolin, 71
Karanga, 193, 196
karma, 207
Kashmir, 917
Kassites, 63
Kati, Mahmud, 277
Kay, John, 605
Kaye, Sammy, 775
Kazakhstan, 1001

Keating, Paul, 921
Keats, John, 636
keeps, 299
Keller, Werner, 80
Kellogg-Briand Pact, 778
Kelly, William, 606
Kemal, Mustafa; *See* Ataturk, Kemal
Kemet, 46
Keneally, Thomas, 850
Kennan, George, 866
Kennedy, John F., *p867,* 871; Cuban Missile Crisis, 984; elected, 862
Kennedy administration; foreign policy, 885–86; Latin America, policy toward, 978; Vietnam policy, 910
Kenner, Martin, 979
Kent, William, 831
Kent State University, 886
Kenya; British control, 799–800; democracy and repression, 938; independence, 932–33
Kenya, Mount, 185
Kenya African Union, 933
Kenyatta, Jomo, *q800,* 933
Kepler, Johannes, 517
Kerensky, Alexander, 757
Khadija, 271, 272
Khaldun, Ibn, 288
Khalid ibn al-Walid, *q280*
khalifah, 277
khan, defined, 344
Khan, Reza; *See* Pahlavi, Reza Shah
Kharar-nama, 269
Khitan, 348
Khmer, 340; conflict with Thailand, 476
Khmer people, 351, 352–53
Khmer Rouge, 912
Khomeini, Ruhollah, Ayatollah, *p958, p959,* 958, 960
Khourey, Fawaz, 796
Khowarizmi, al-, 243
Khrushchev, Nikita, *p867, q864,* 871; Cuban Missile Crisis, 984; de-Stalinization, 872–73; with Eisenhower, *p873;* removal from office, 874
Khufu, 44
kibbutz, 951
Kiev, Russia, 260, 261, 838; Mongol destruction of, 244
Kievan Rus, 244, 260–63; Christianity, 262; culture, 262; decline, 263; golden age, 262–63; government, 260; legal system, 262
Kikuyu, 933
Kilimanjaro, Mount, *p184,* 185
Kilwa, 194, 195
Kim Il Jong, 908
Kim Il Sung, 907, 908
kimonos, 894
Kim Young Sam, *p908,* 908
King, Martin Luther, Jr., *q887,* 882; Gandhi, influence of, 802
Kingdom of the Two Sicilies, 676, 679
Kingoro, Hashimoto, *q809*
kings; ancient Greece, 112, 113; position in government, 34
Kinneret, Lake, Galillee, *p20*
Kiowa, 378
Kipling, Rudyard, 704, 706
Kishlansky, Mark A., 270, 358, 379, 690
Kissinger, Henry, 903, 955
Kiyomatsu, *p361*
Klein, Erich, 686
knights, 292, 298, 301
Knossos, 104
Knox, John, 419
Kobe, Japan, 226, 896, 899
Koguryo, 358
Kohl, Helmut, 1007, 1012
Kongzi. *See* Confucius
Koptev, Yuri, 1018
Koran. *See* Quran
Korea, *m371,* 358–59, 906–08; civil service, 340; division, 906; Japan, trade with, 364; Japanese occupation, 469, 718, 906; Korean War, 906–07; Mongol Empire, capture by, 350; Soviet occupation, 906; U.S. occupation, 906; writing, 359. *See also* North Korea. *See also* South Korea
Korea, Republic of. *See* South Korea
Korean War, *m907,* 858, 906–07
Kosygin, Aleksei, 874
Kraków, University of, 516
krater, 131
Kremlin, *p264,* 188
Krishna, Emperor, 64
Krishna (Indian deity), 200
Kristallnacht, 785–86
Kropotkin, Peter, 690
Kroyer, P.S., 608
Kshatriyas, 203, 204, 207
Kublai Khan, *p349,* 350, 354; attack on Japan, 363
Kufa, Iraq, 283
Kulaks, 790
Kulikovo, Battle of, 258, 263
Kulturkampf, 686
Kunlun Shan mountains, 69
Kurds, 960, 1016
Kuril Islands, 849, 900
Kush, *m187,* 182, 184, 185–86
Kushite merchants, 101
Kuwait; Iraqi invasion, 900, 960
Kwakiutl, 375–76
Kwanza, 945
Kwasniewski, Aleksander, 1008
kylix, 131
Kyoto, Japan, 362
Kyushu, 359

L

labor; child labor, *p612, q599, q612,* 602, 615, 623; division of, 609; domestic system, 602, 606; labor unions. *See* labor unions; legislation, in Germany, 689; Massachusetts mill workers, 612; natural resource, 604; source of power, 623; specialization of, 32, 33–34; technological unemployment, 883; working class. *See* working class; working conditions, 622
labor-intensive farming, 466
labor unions, 616; badge, *p614;* in Great Britain, 612, 650; growth, 612; poster, *p616*
Labour party, 647, 650, 779, 878, 879
La Bruyere, Jean de, 449–50
labyrinth, 107
Ladd, William, 734
ladies (feudal noblewomen), 299
Lady Fujitsubo Watching Prince Genju Departing in the Moonlight, The, *ptg363*
laissez-faire, 622–23; criticism of, 623–24
laity, 249
Lakhshamana, *p214*
Lamarck, Jean-Baptiste de, 626
Lambert, W.B., 58
lamp, Islamic, *p276*
Lamsa, George M., 270
Lamu, Kenya, *p195*
Lancaster, House of, 333
land bridges, 24, 35
land ownership, 31
Lange, David, 922
Lange, Dorothea, 773
language; development of, 14; in humanism, 405; *lingua franca,* 170; vernacular, 328. *See also* specific languages
Lao People's Revolutionary party, 914
Laos, 914; conquest by Khmer, 352; French imperialism, 719
Laozi, *p227,* 226
La Pietá, *p411*
"La Pucelle!" Jeanne d'Arc Leads Her Army, *ptg330*
La Salle, Sieur de, 444
Las Casas, Bartolomé de, 442
Lascaux, France, 29
lasers, 1022
Lassalle, Ferdinand, 687, 689
Last Laugh, The, 775
Last Supper, *p174*
Last Supper, The, *ptg410,* 411
Latham, Ronald, 342
latifundia, 161–62
Latin America, *m667;* agriculture, 977; birth rate, 975; Catholicism, role of, 666–67; cold war influences, 978; communism, 974, 977, 978, 991; democracy, 974, 977–78; economy, 976–77; European imperialism, 721; foreign debt, 722, 977; guerrilla movements, 977; imperialism, 721–25; independence, 583, 666–70; industrialization, 976–77; infant mortality, 975; Japan, trade with, 978; land reform, 978; law, 103; modern era, 974–93; nationalism, 811–17, 856; obstacles to stability, 670; population, 974; post-World War II period, 1028; raw materials, source of, 812; regional economic pacts, 978; self government, 670; social reform, 974, 977–78; social structure, 667, 974, 975–76; superpower rivalry, 871; urbanization, 975; U.S. interventions in, 816–17; U.S., relations with, 811–17; women, 976. *See also* Central America. *See also* South America. *See also* individual countries
Latin America, A Concise Interpretive History, 811
Latin language, 152, 170, 178, 328; use in Roman Catholicism, 423–24
Latins (Indo-European people), 155, 156
latitude, 139, 436
Latium, 155
Lattimore, Richmond, 106
Latvia; established, 764; independence, 1000; in Nazi-Soviet Nonaggression Pact, 830; Soviet military bases, 831
Laud, William, 537
Laue, Theodore Von, 175
La Venta, 379
Lavoisier, Antoine, 519, 520
Lavoisier, Marie, 520
law, 102; Byzantine, 248; common, 103; constitutional, 103; development of, 63–64; English common law, 309; influence of reason, 523; international, 523; Islamic, 275; jury system, 118–19, 309; Ottoman, 457–58; Roman, 102, 166; Slavic, 262
Lawrence, T.E., 761
lawyers, 326
lay investiture, 306, 312
League of Nations; development, 734; Ethiopian invasion, 827; French involvement, 780; Japan, censure of, 826; Japanese involvement, 807; replaced by United

Nations, 864; U.S. rejection of, 776; in Wilson's Fourteen Points, 763
League of Three Emperors, 740
Leakey, Louis, 23, 25
Leakey, Mary, *p21,* 23, 25
Leakey, Meave, *p23*
Leakey, Richard, 25
Leaning Tower of Pisa, *p522*
leap years, 85
Lebanon; in Arab League, 950; Christian-Muslim conflict, 950, 953, 958; French mandate, 764; independence, 950; Israeli occupation, 958, 963; Syrian occupation, 958, 963; U.S. occupation, 953
lebensraum, defined, 828
Lechfeld, Battle of, 312
Lectures on Nationalism, 804
Lecuna, Vicente, 666
Leeds, England, 632
Lee Kuan Yew, 915
Lee Teng-hui, 905
Leeuwenhoek, Antonie van, 514
legionnaires, *p160,* 159
legions, Roman, 159
legitimacy (Congress of Vienna), 580
Leipzig, Germany, 577
leisure, 632, 771
Lemoyner, Jean-Baptiste, 527
Lenbach, Franz von, 685
lend-lease, 836
Lend-Lease Act, 842
Lenin, Alexander, 758
Lenin, Vladimir Ilyich, *p789,* 693, 758–59, 788–89
Leningrad, Soviet Union; 838–39, siege of, 831, 841, 847
Leo III, Byzantine Emperor, 250
Leo III, Pope, 295
Leo XIII, Pope, 687
Leonidas, 120, 122
Leopold, Prince of Hohenzollern, 684
Leopold II, King of Belgium, 709
Leopold II of Austria, 528
Lepanto, Battle of, 456
Lepidus, Marcus, 159, 163
leprosy, beliefs about, 449
Les Misérables, 584–87, 636, 789
Lesseps, Ferdinand de, 708, 724
Lessing, Karl Friedrich, 321
Le Tellier, François Michel, 492
Letter to His Two Small Children..., 368–69
Leveque, Joseph, 524
lever, 145
Leviathan, 521, 523
Leviticus, 85
Lewis, Oscar, *q975*
Lexington, Massachusetts, 552
Leyte Gulf, Battle of, 849
leythos, 131
Liberal Democratic Party (Japan), 898–99
liberalism, 582, 583; defined, 569
Liberal party, 649, 650, 651
liberation theology, 978
Liberator, the, 669
Liberia, 709
Liberty Leading the People, 636
Li Bo, *p366,* 348
libraries, 100, 698; how to use, 633; Ming dynasty, 463; Muslim, 282, 287; resources, 698
Libya, 708; Great Britain, attack on Italy, 836; independence, 929; Italy, colonization by, 929; Ptolemy, rule by, 142; in the 1990s, 936; terrorism, links to, 936; in World War II, 836, 838
Lichtheim, Miriam, 46
lieder, 636
life expectancy, 629
lightbulbs, incandescent, 611
Lincoln, Abraham, *q663*
Lindbergh, Charles, 771
lineages, 376
line of demarcation, 439, 440
lingua franca, 170
Li Peng, 904
Lisle, Joseph Rouget de, 578
Lister, Joseph, *q627,* 628
literacy campaign, in Nicaragua, 986
literature; personal essay, 413; reason, influence of, 529; romantic, 635; stream of consciousness, 772; Twenties, 772–73; value as history, 584
literature, oral, 188
Lithuania, 829, 1000; established, 764; in Nazi-Soviet Nonaggression Pact, 830; Russia, war against, 499; Soviet military bases, 831
Little Diomedes Island, *p35*
Liu Bang, 218, 222
Lives and Times: A World History Reader, 225, 804
Livingstone, David, *p708,* 707
Livy, Titus, *q156,* 154, 170
Li Yuan, 346
Lloyd George, David, 763
Locarno Agreements, 780
Locke, John, 514, 521–22, 524–25, 564; influence on the Declaration of Independence, 553
loess, 70
Lollards, 335
Lombardo, Guy, 775
Lombards, 250, 255, 295
Lombardy, 580, 676, 677; revolt against Austria, 678
London, England, 153; architecture, 541; blitz, 831, 834–35; great fire, 540, 542; urbanization, 631–32
London School of Medicine, 633
longbow, 330
longitude, 139, 436
Long March, 794, 806
Long Parliament, 536, 538
Lon Nol, 912
loom, 31
Lop, Desert of, 342
Lords, House of, 311
lords (medieval gentlemen), 299
Lorenzetti, Ambrogio, 293
Lorenzo the Magnificent, *p427*
Lorraine province, 658
Los Angeles, California, 226
Los Angeles Times, The, 1014
Lost Treasures of London, The, 831
Lothair, 296
Louis, Victor, 528
Louisiana Purchase, 594, 660
Louis Philippe, king of France, 656
Louis the German, 296
Louis the Pious, 296
Louis VI, king of France, 311
Louis VII, king of France, 320
Louis IX, king of France, *q311*
Louis XI, king of France, 332–33, 525
Louis XIII, king of France, 490–91, 537
Louis XIV, king of France, 491–93, 521, 562; becomes absolute monarch, 490; becomes king, 480; court life, *p490,* 492; domestic policies, 492–93; foreign policy, 493; legacy, 493; Palace of Versailles, 480; taxation, 492–93
Louis XIV of France, *ptg492*
Louis XV, king of France, 562
Louis XVI, king of France, *q568;* attempted flight, 566; becomes king, 558, 560; belief in divine right of rule, 564; Estates-General, relations with, 562; execution, 567, 568; move to Paris, 565
Louis XVI Arrested at Varennes, *ptg565*
Louis XVIII, king of France, 577, 581, 655
Louvre Museum, 632
Low Countries; German invasion, 833; Renaissance, 413–14
Loyalists, 652
Lu (Chinese state), 231
Luckenbill, Daniel David, 69, 88
Lucy (hominid), 21
Ludwig II, king of Bavaria, 688
Luftwaffe, 828, 834
Lundstrom, John B., 842
Lung-shan culture, 69, 70
Lusitania, *p752,* 738, 744, 751, 752–53; salvage, 753
Luther, Martin, *p415, q417,* 398, 402, 415–17
Lutheranism; justification by faith, 415; principles, 417; reaction to Anabaptists, 419; spread through printing, 416
Luther Preaching to the Faithful, *ptg417*
Luxembourg, 413; in Common Market, 881; German invasion, 743
Luxor, Egypt, 50, 54
Luzon, Philippines, 475
lycées, 574
Lyceum, 135, 137
Lydians, 80, 82, 88, 91, 112
Lyon, Mary, 629, 633
lyre, *p59*
Lytton, Lord, 826

M

Maastricht Treaty of, 996, 1013, 1020
MacAdam, Donald, 521
Macao, 467
MacArthur, Douglas, 896; in Korean War, 907; in the Pacific, 845
Maccabees, Judah, 143
Maccari, Cesare, 675
MacDonald, John A., 653
MacDonald, Ramsay, 779
Macedonia, 498, 1008–09
Macedonian Empire, *m141,* 140–43; Antigonus, rule by, 143; division after Alexander, m151, 142–43; economic aspects, 144; goals, 142; Greeks, conquest of, 119, 124; Roman Empire, conquest by, 143. *See also* Alexander the Great
Machiavelli, Niccolò, 405, 426
Machu Pichu, *p393*
Macmillan, Harold, 879
Madagascar, 184
Madame Bovary, 638
Madame de Geoffrin's Salon, *p526–27*
Madame Tussaud's Exhibition, 569
Madero, Francisco, 725
Madeira Islands, 436
Madinah; establishment, 273; pilgrimage to, 276
Madinah Compact, 273
Madinat al-Nabi. *See* Madinah
madrasas, 283
Madrid, Spain, 483; Franco, conquest by, 828
Maecenas, 159
Maffeo, 342
Magadha, 211

Magellan, Ferdinand, 434, 437, 439, 474–75
Magellan, Strait of, 439
Maginot Line, 780, 833
Magna Carta, 241, 308, 310, 541
magnesium, 828
Magyars, 296, 312, 695, 697
Mahabharata, 200, 205, 212
Mahal, Mumtazi, 460
Mahatma, 802
Mahayana, 210
Mahmet II, Ottoman sultan, *p256*
Maid of Orléans, 332
Maimonides, Moses, 282, 287–88
Maine **(battleship),** 722–24
Maisuna, *q283*
maize, 15, 17, 374
Majapahit, 355
Major, John, 1011
Makkah, 191, 268; direction of, 285; establishment of, 271; Islam, emergence of, 272; in Islamic prayers, 276
Malacca, Strait of, 355
Malawi, 933
Malaya; British imperialism, 719; conflict with Thailand, 476; Japanese capture of, 845
Malay Peninsula, 915; conquest by Thai people, 355; Japanese invasion of, 842
Malaysia, 915
Malcolm, John, 549
Malevich, Kazimir, 642
Mali, 182, 189, 191–93; poetry, 189
Malindi, 194, 195
Mallarmé, Stéphane, 638
Mallows, Wilfrid, 194
Maltin, Leonard, 770
Malvinas Islands, 991
Mamikonian, Vartan, 257
Mamluks, 344
Ma'mun, 268, 285
Manchester, England, *p605*
Manchukuo; *See* Manchuria
Manchuria; Japanese occupation, 806, 809, 824, 826; Manchu occupation, 465; Russian occupation, 739; war for control of, 694
Manchus, 462, 465–67
mandarins, 224, 348
Mandate of Heaven, 71, 220, 222, 231
mandates, defined, 763
Mandela, Nelson, *q926,* 934, 939; criticism of Japanese foreign aid, 900
Manhattan Island, 443
manifest destiny. *See* imperialism; United States, expansion
Manila, Philippines, 475
Man in the Ice, The, q20
Manitoba, Canada, 653
Mann, Thomas, 772
manners, development of, 301
manorialism, 301–02; compared to feudalism, 301; social structure, 302
Man-o'-War Firing a Salute, ptg450
Mansa Musa, 182, 191, 193, 277
Mansur, 286
Mantegna, Andrea, 403
Mantua, Italy, 402
manuscripts, illuminated, *p253, p304,* 328
Manzikert, Battle of, 343
Maori, 652, 654, 922
Mao Zedong, *q805,* 804–06; Long March, 806
map making, 321
map projections, 37
maps, 37, 436; historical, 337; military, 765; thematic, 451
Marat, Jean-Paul, 568, 569
Marathon, Battle of, 120, 121, 137
marathon race, 121
March on Washington; (1963), 887
Marconi, Guglielmo, 607, 611
Marcos, Ferdinand, 920
Marduk, 35–36
Maria Theresa, Archduchess of Austria, 494, 495–96, 497, 528
Marie Antoinette, Queen of France, 529, 562, 565, 566, 570
Marie Antoinette in the Park of Trianon, ptg568
Marine Corps, U.S., *p815*
Marius, Gaius, 162
market, medieval, *p324–25*
market economy, 623
Markham, Clements R., 440
Marlow, Herbert, 738
Marlowe, Christopher, 414
Marlowe, John, 707
Marne, Battle of the, 738, 744, 745–46
Marquette, Jacques, 444
Marranos, 483
Married Women's Property Acts of 1870, 650
Mars, 158
Marseillaise, The, 578
Marshall, George C., 869
Marshall Plan, 868–69
Martel, Charles, 279, 295, 298
Martí, Jose, 722
martial law, defined, 537
Martinique, 444
Martin V, Pope, 335
martyrs, 173
Marx, Karl, *p622,* 595, 624, 687; influence on Russian revolution, 693
Marxism, 624–25
Mary, daughter of Charles VII, 333
Mary, mother of Jesus, 253; in *Pietá,* 411
Mary I, queen of England, 486; coat of arms, *p486*
Mary II, queen of England, *p543,* 542
Mary Queen of Scots, *p418,* 419, 420, 489, 536
Masaccio, 411
Mask of Apollo, The, 130
Mason, Herbert, 72
Mass, Roman Catholicism, 303, 423
mass production, 597, 609
masterpieces, craftsman's, 325
masters, guild, 325
Masudi, *q190*
Massachusetts, 444
Mataram, Java, 475
Mathematical Principles of Natural Philosophy, 518
mathematics; Egyptian, 53; Greek, 138; in Gupta Empire, 214, 285; invention, 242; Maya, 381; Muslim, 285; philosophic expression, 518
Matilda, wife of William the Conqueror, 309
matrilineal societies, 187
Matthew, Apostle, 410
Mau Mau, 933
Maurya, Chandragupta. *See* Chandragupta Maurya
Mauryan Empire, 200, 211–12
Maximian, 176
Maxwell, James Clark, 611
Maya Empire, *m390,* 380–87; archaeology, *m385,* 384–86; art, *p241;* astronomy, 381; Aztec culture, influence on, 389; collapse, 386; creation myth, 379; decline, 379, 383; economy, 381; expansion, 379; games, 381; height, 372; king, *p385;* pyramids, *p381;* religion, 380; warfare, 386; writing, 383
May Laws, 686
Mayflower Compact, 538
mayors of the palace, 294
Mazarin, Cardinal, 491
Mazzini, Giuseppe, *q674,* 676, 677, 679
McCarthy, Joseph, 884
McCarthyism, 884
McKay, Claude, 773
McKinley, William, 722, 724
McLaughlin, Mary Martin, 482
Mecca. *See* Makkah
Medellín, Colombia, 993
Medes, 89, 90, 91
Medici, Cosimo de', 407
Medici, Lorenzo de', 398, 402, 407
Medici, Marie de, 490–91
Medici family, 446–47
medicine; advances in 19th and 20th centuries, 627–28; Chinese development, 232; Neanderthal development, 27; Egyptian development, 53; Greek development, 138; modern advances, 1022; Muslim development, 285–86; Roman development, 170
medieval, origin, 294
Medieval Europe. *See* Middle Ages
Medieval Inquisition, The, 422
Medina. *See* Madinah
meditation, 365
meditation gardens, *p365*
Meditations, 165–66
Mediterranean, 80–82
Mehsana Sun Temple, 204–05
Meiji leaders, 713, 716–17
Mein Kampf, q828, 784
Meir, Golda, 965
Meissonier, Ernest, 657
Melaka, 355, 474
Melanesians, 922
Melqart, 83
Memel, Lithuania, 829
Memoirs of the Emperor Jahangir Written by Himself, 456
Memphis, Egypt, 47, 48, 51
Menander, 145
Mendel, Gregor, 627
Menelik I, king of Axum, 186
Menelik II, emperor of Ethiopia, *p711,* 709
Menem, Carlos, 991
Menes, 47
Mensheviks, 693, 757
Mercosur. *See* Southern Common Market
Meroë, 186
mercantilism, 448–49, 623, 666
Mercator projection; *See* cylindrical projection
mercenaries, 124
merchants; in China, 229; rise of, 34
meridians, 139
meritocracy, defined, 347
Merovingian kings, 294–95
Merowig, Merovingian king, 294
Merry Monarch. *See* Charles II, king of England
Mesoamerica; Native Americans, 379–83; Spanish conquest, 441; trade, 381. *See also* Central America
Mesolithic period, 24
Mesopotamia, *m43,* 61–64; Alexander, conquest by, 142; art, *p62–63;* early settlement, 58; Greece, trade with, 107; Hittite culture, source of, 88; Persian Empire, conquest by, 91; Seleucus, rule by, 143; summary, 98; trade, 81

Mesorb, monk, 257
messiah, 171
mestizos, 667
metalworking, 31, 33–34
Metamorphoses, 170
metaphysics, 530
Methodism, 530
Methodius, monk, 255
metic class, 123
metics, 117
metric system, 568
metropolitan, 263
Metsu, Gabriel, 442
metsuke, 469
Metsys, Quentin, 413
Metternich, Klemens von, Prince, *p583,* 580, 695
Mexican War, 660, 661
Mexico; agriculture development, 17; early civilization, 15; economy, 981–82; foreign debt, 977, 980; foreign investment, 981; Germany, proposal from, 751; guerrillas, 981; illegal immigration, 980; independence, 646, 668; modern era, 979–82; Native Americans, 374, 377, 379, 388–89; natural resources, 666; new constitution, 811; oil, nationalization of, 794, 812–13; oil industry, 980; political system, 979; Spanish conquest, 441; U.S. intervention in, 724–25; U.S., war against, 660, 661
Mexico City, Mexico, 388, 975, 979
Micah, *q85*
Michelangelo Buonarroti, *q404,* 402, 406, 409, 411, 510
Michelangelo the Man, 404
Michigan, 665
Mickey Mouse, 770
Micronesians, 922
microprocessor, 859
microscopes, 514, 519, 521
Middle Ages, 294–312; agriculture, 302; art, *p309;* cultural mix, 294; feudalism, 298–303; Frankish period, 294–96; Medieval Church, 303–07; monarchy, 307–12; monastics, role of, 305; science, 516; Viking invasions, 296–97; women's rights, 298. *See also* Middle Ages, High
Middle Ages, High, 318–36; the Church, 334–36; Crusades, 318–21; economic expansion, 321–26; education, 326–27; literature and art, 327–28; monarchies, 329–33; philosophy, 326–27
middle class, *p613,* 325–26; in Dutch art, 442–43; emergence of, 412; in England, 310, 604; factory system, influence on, 594; lifestyles, 613; monarchy, relations with, 326; voting rights, 646, 649
Middle East, *m952;* agriculture, development of, 30; Arab unity, 950, 951; China, trade with, 347, 350; economy, 963; fundamentalism, 959, 965; future challenges, 962–65; human prehistory, 14; independence, 950; Mongol conquest, 344; nationalism, 856, 950; oil, 964; Ottoman conquest, 456; population, *c289,* 963; post-World War II period, 1028; social changes, 965; water, 964; Western influence, 950, 965; women, 965; World War I, 761. *See also* Arab-Israeli conflict
Middle Kingdom (China), 69
Middle Kingdom (Egypt), 48–49
Middle Passage, 445
middle power, defined, 889
Middle Stone Age. *See* Mesolithic period
Midway, Battle of, 845
MiG-15, 864
mihrabs, 284
Miletus, 138
militarism, 685; as a cause for World War I, 740
military; art, 361; development, 34; tactics development, 321; weapons development, 330, 332
military-industrial complex, 885
military rulers, 941–42
Mill, John Stuart, 624
Miller, Webb, *q803*
millet, 17
Millet, Jean-François, 638
Milosevic, Slobodan, 1015
Milton, John, 529
Minamoto family, 340, 363
minarets, 284
Mind of the Middle Ages, The, 282
Ming dynasty, 454, 462–65; art, *p465;* collapse, 465; construction of Beijing, 464; East Africa, contact with, 195; seagoing exploration, 462, 463–64
ministers, 417
Minoan civilization, 104, 107, 108, 110; art, *p105*
Minos, 104, 107
minutemen, 550, 552
mirs, defined, 691
Mir **(space station),** 1018, 1022
Mishne Torah, 287
missionaries, 254–55, 422; in Japan, 470; relation to imperialism, 706
Mississippi River; exploration by de Soto, 441; exploration by France, 444
Mitterrand, François, 1011
Mobutu, Joseph D., 932. *See also* Seko, Mobutu Sese
Moche, 389
Moctezuma. *See* Montezuma II
Model Parliament, 311
Modena, 678
moderate, defined, 569
modernization. *See* economics, economy, education, industrialization, urbanization
Modern World, The, 741
Mogul Empire, 459–61
Moguls, *p456*
Mohammad, 271–73
Mohawk, 378
Mohenjo-Daro, *p33,* 67, 68
Moi, Daniel T. arap, 935, 937
moksha, 207
Moldavia, 697
Molière, Jean Baptiste, 529
Moltke, Helmuth von, 744
Moluccas; *See* Spice Islands
Mombasa, 194
Mona Lisa, *ptg407,* 411
monarchies, 47, 329–33, 480–502; abolition in England, 538; absolutism, 482, 492; in Austria, 495–96; constitutional monarchy, 541, 648, 656; control of trade, 448; development of, 93; divine right, *q536–37,* 482; dual monarchy, 696; in England, 333, 485–89; enlightenment, attitude toward, 528; feudalism, influence on, 311; in France, 332–33, 490–93; in Great Britain, 879; growth after Crusades, 321; Magna Carta, 310; during Middle Ages, 308–12; middle class, relations with, 326; papacy, conflict with, 312; in Prussia, 496–97; public opinion on, 879; restoration after Napoleon, 581–82; in Russia, 498–502; in Spain, 333, 482–84
monasteries. *See* monastic life
monastic life, *p304–05,* 254, 304–05; role in Middle Ages, 305
Monastic Life in Medieval England, 303
Monet, Claude, 637, 639
money; ancient Greece, 113; development, 82; as source of power, 623
money economy, 323
money supply, 447
Mongkut, king of Thailand, 477
Mongol Empire, *m343,* 343–45; Baghdad, sack of, 268, 281; China, rule over, 342, 350; Eastern Slavs, rule over, 262; Georgia, attacks on, 257; Moscow, war against, 258; Myanmar, invasion of, 354
Mongolia, 343; occupation by Manchus, 465
monks, 254
Monomotapa Empire, 196
monopoly, defined, 194
monotheism, 83, 189; in Arab world, 271, 272
Mon people, 354
Monroe, James, 722
Monroe Doctrine, 721–22; re-interpretation, 817; Roosevelt Corollary, 722, 816
monsoons, 66–67
Montagu, Mary Wortley, 399
Montana, 662
Monte Albán, 119
Monte Cassino, Italy, 304
Montenegro, 1008–09, 1015; in Balkan League, 698; independence, 698
Montesquieu, Baron de, 524, 525–26, 554, 564
Montezuma II, 441
Montgomery, Bernard, 843
months; creation myth, 374; development of, 85
Montreal, Quebec; establishment, 444; immigration to, 890
Montreal Protocol, 1018, 1021
Mont St. Michel, *p304–05*
Moody, Helen Willis, 771
moon landing, 858, 883, 1022
Moors, 438
Moran, Percy, 538
Moravia, 697
Moravian Brethren, 530
More, Thomas, 414
Morelos, José María, 668
Moriscos, 483
Morley, John, 536
Morocco; French imperialism, 707, 708, 738; trade with Ghana, 189
Morse, Samuel, 609
Morton, Jelly Roll, 773
mosaic, 253
Moscow, Muscovy culture, *m267,* 263–64; beginnings, 263; Byzantine influence, 264; culture, 264; independence, 244; Mongols, war against, 258, 263; religion, 264
Moscow, Soviet Union, 574, 838–39; French invasion, 577
Moses, 84, 275
Mosque, Tower, *p274*
mosques, *p288,* 191, 276, 409
Mossadeq, Mohammed, 953
mother goddess, *p32*
Motion Picture Herald, 770
motion pictures, 770, 771, 775
Motokiyo, Zeami, 358
Moulin Rouge, 639
Mound Builders, 378
Mountain (French National Convention), 568, 569
Mount Holyoke College, 633

Mount Holyoke Female Seminary, 633
Mount Kenya, 185
Mount Kilimanjaro, 185
movies. *See* motion pictures
Mozambique; early city-states, 194; independence, 933; Marxism and free enterprise, 939
Mozart, Wolfgang Amadeus, *p529,* 399
Mr. Smith Goes to Washington, 775
Mu'awiyah, 278, 279, 283
Mubarak, Hosni, 955
Mucius, Gaius, 154
Muhammad, 240; ascent into heaven, 318; born, 268; death, 270, 274; descendants, 277, 279; divinity, 275; *Hijrah,* 270; revelation, 270
Muhammad, Askia, 189, 193
Mughal Empire. *See* Mogul Empire
Mulroney, Brian, 1017
multiculturalism, 890; defined, 195
multinational corporations. *See* global economy
mummies, 48
Munich Conference, 826, 829
Münster, Germany, 419
murals, 732; Greek, 131
Muriguchi, Kato, 894
Murnau, F.W., 775
Muscovy. *See* Moscow
Muscovy Company, 499
Museveni, Yoweri, *q944*
music; anthems, 578; baroque, 496; classicism, 529; folk music, 635; jazz, 773; romantic, 635; in sub-Saharan Africa, 188; swing, 775; twelve tone row, 773; Twenties, 773–75; in West Africa, 400
Muslims, 189, 257; agriculture, 284; architecture, 460; art, 278–79, 286–87; in Bosnia-Herzegovina, 1014–15; calendar, 273; cultural life, 282–88; education, 282; Europe, influence on, 321; family life, 282–83; first, 272; in India, 803; intellectual life, 285; literature, 286; philosophy, 287–88; science, 285–86; Shiites, 278–79, 459; Sunnis, 279, 459; trade, *m284;* unity, 276; urban life, 283–84; women, 282–83. *See also* Islam
Muslim League, 803
Mussolini, Benito, *p782, q782, q783,* 781–83; arrest of, 844; death of, 848; Ethiopia, policy toward, 827; prime minister of Italy, 768
Mutsuhito, Emperor of Japan, 717, 718
mutual assured destruction, 873
My Africa, 945
Myanmar, 354–55; conquest by Thai people, 355; militarism, 914–15; satellite television, censorship, 860. *See also* Burma
Mycenaean civilization, 107–10, 108; beginning, 106; chalices, *p236;* Greek descent from, 117; pottery, 113; Troy, war against, 109
Myron, 131, 132, 134
Mystery of the Great Zimbabwe, The, 194
mythology, 35; Greek, 110–11; Navajo, 374; Roman, 157–58

N

NAACP, *See* National Association for the Advancement of Colored People
Nader Shah, 456, 459
NAFTA. *See* North American Free Trade Agreement (NAFTA)
Nagasaki, Japan, 471, 850
Naga serpent, *p352*
Nagorno-Karabakh, 1016
Nagy, Imre, 876
Nairobi, Kenya, 942
Namibia, 935
Nanak, Sikh leader, 460
Nanjing, China, 805, 827
Napata, 185–86
Naples, 677; Bonaparte king, 576; monarchy re-establishment, 581
Napoleon Bonaparte, *p574, q577;* coronation as Emperor, 558, 574, 576; early life, 573; exile, 577; Napoleon III, emulation by, 656; return from Elba, 578; rise to power, 567, 573
Napoleon Crossing the Great St. Bernard, *ptg573*
Napoleonic Code, 103, 575, 578; influence of Roman law, 103
Napoleonic Era, *g579, m577,* 574–78; Continental System, 576; defeat, 577; Europe, conquest of, 575–76; European revolt against, 576; finance, 574–75; Hundred Days, 578; legacy, 578; Napoleonic Code, 103, 575; Quadruple Alliance policy, 582; Roman Catholic Church, policy toward, 575; Russia, campaign against, 574, 576–77
Napoleonic Wars; industrialization, influence on, 608; Russian reform movement, influence on, 690–91
Napoleon III, 656–57; art exhibition, 638; attitude toward German unification, 684; elected president, 655; relations with Cavour, 678; support of pope, 677, 680
Nara, Japan, 362
Naresuan, King of Thailand, 476
Narmer, *p46,* 15, 47
Nasser, Gamal Abdel, 951–53
National Assembly, French, 562, 564, 565, 579, 656
National Association for the Advancement of Colored People (NAACP), 887
National Convention, French, 567–69, 571, 579
National Covenant, 538
National Geographic Society, 384, 753
National Information Infrastructure, 1021
nationalism, 576, 582, 676, 855–56; in Africa, 929, as a cause for World War I, 739; economic nationalism, 812–13; in Russia, 692–93
Nationalist China. *See* Taiwan
nationalization, defined, 813
National Socialist Worker's Party. *See* Nazism
National Woman Suffrage Association (NWSA), 665
nations, replace cities, 446
nation-states, 677
Native Americans, *p440,* 547; agriculture, 374; archeology, 375, 376; Arctic region, 375; California, 376; in Canada, 653; civil rights, 887; cultures, *m375;* disease, effects of, 442; Eastern Woodlands, 378; in Florida, 440; Great Basin, 377; Great Plains, 378; in Latin America, 667; migration to Americas, 374; Pacific Northwest, 375–76; pre-Columbian population, 375; religion, 376, 377; Spain, relations with, 441–42; trade, 376; western expansion, effect of, 662
NATO (North Atlantic Treaty Organization), 862, 884; in Balkans, 1003; in Bosnia-Herzegovina, 1015; formation, 870; role change, after communism, 1003; Turkish membership, 953; in Yugoslavia, 1009
naturalism, 638
natural law, 521, 523
natural resources; exhaustion of, 1020; importance in industrialization, 604
natural science, 524
natural selection, 626
nature, harmony with, 227
nautch, 703
Navajo, mythology, 374
navigation, 23, 82, 435
Navigation Acts, 546, 548
navvies, 603
Nazareth, 172
Nazism, 784–86; concentration camps, *m837;* refugee flight from, 786; persecution of Jews, 784–86; plans for conquest, 839; propaganda, 786; in Reichstag, 781. *See also* Germany, World War II
Nazi-Soviet pact, 829–30
Neanderthals, 14, 26–27; fossils, *p27*
Neander Valley, Germany, 23, 26
Nebuchadnezzar, 88, 90
Nefertari, queen of Egypt, 51
Nefertiti, queen of Egypt, 49, 52
negritude, 945
Nehru, Jawaharlal, *p916, q916,* 803, 916–17
Neil, William, 80
Nelson, Horatio, 573, 576
neoclassical art, rejection of, 635
neo-Confucianism, 348; in Korea, 359
Neolithic period, 24; in Italy, 155
Neolithic Revolution, 29–31
Nero, *q165,* 175
Nerva, 165
Netherlands, 413; in Africa, 443; art, 442–43; Austria, acquisition by, 495; Bonaparte as king, 576; Calvinism, 419, 425; colonization, 442–43; in Common Market, 881; East Asia, exploration of, 432; exploration by, *m441;* France, war against, 578; French Revolution, policy toward, 569; growth of commerce, 448; imposition of Catholicism, 483; in Japan, 471; Japan, unequal treaties with, 717; in North America, 443, 450; Renaissance, 412; Renaissance art, 414; sea power, *p475;* in Southeast Asia, 475, 718–19; Southeast Asia, colonization of, 718–19; stock exchanges, 448; in Thailand, 476–77; unification, 582; in War of the Spanish Succession, 493; in War of the Austrian Succession, 497
Neuschwanstein castle, *p688*
Neutrality Acts, 835
Nevada, 660
Neva River, 501
Nevsky, Alexander, *p263,* 258
New Amsterdam, 443
New Babylonians. *See* Chaldean Empire
Newcomen, Thomas, 596
New Deal, 776, 778
New Democratic League (Japan), 899
New Economic Policy (NEP), 788–89
New England, exploration by England, 444
Newfoundland; acquisition by England, 493; exploration, 444; U.S. military bases, 835–36
New Guinea, human prehistory, 24
New Harmony, Indiana, 624
New Kingdom (Egypt), 49, 51
New Lanark, Scotland, 624
New Mexico; German promise to Mexico, 751; Native Americans, 377; U.S. acquisition, 662
New Orleans, Louisiana, *p662–63*
New Rome, 246
news media, 888
New South Wales, Australia, 654
New Spain. *See* Spain, colonies

newspapers, 632, 633
New Stone Age. *See* Neolithic period
New Testmaent, 172
Newton, Isaac, *q518,* 518–19, 524–25; *Principia* published, 516; promotion by Voltaire, 526; in Royal Society, 521; theory of gravity, 511
New York, women's suffrage, 665
New York, New York; immigrant destination, 665; parks, 632
New York Herald, 707
New York Stock Exchange, 777
New York Times, The, 770
New Youth, 595
New Zealand, 653–54, 922; British imperialism, 705; mandates, 763
Ngo Dinh Diem, 910
Ngo Quyen, 354
Nicaea; Council at, 250
Nicaragua, 794, 985–86; civil war, 986; establishment, 668; literacy campaign, 986; U.S. intervention in, *p815,* 816
Nice, France, 678, 679
Nicholas I, czar of Russia, 657, q697, 690, 691
Nicholas II, czar of Russia, 690, 692, 693–94, 743; abdication, 756, 757; closes Duma, 756
Nicholson, Harold, *q760*
Niepce, Joseph, 658
Nigeria; British imperialism, 709, 800; ethnic conflict, 799; independence, 932; repression, 936–37; in the 1990s, 936; women, 796
Niger River, 185, 712
nihilism, defined, 692
Nijinsky, Vaslav, 775
Nile River valley, 17, 46–47; early civilization, 32, 185; flood control, 47
Nimitz, Chester W., 845
Niña, p437
Nineteen Propositions, 538
Nineteenth Amendment, 665, 770–71
Ninety-Five Theses, 398, 416
Nineveh, 78, 89
Ninigi, 360
Nino, 257
nirvana, 210, 227
Nivôse, 568
Nixon, Richard M.; China, visit to, 903; imperial presidency, 888; resignation, 882, 888; role in detente, 874; visits China, 901
Nixon administration; Vietnam policy, 886
Nkrumah, Kwame, *p931,* 931, 942
Nobel Peace Prize, 889, 915, 1005
nobility, 298-301
Nobunaga, Oda, *q468,* 470
Nochlin, Linda, 635
Noh mask, *p358*
Noh theater, 358
Nok culture, 182, 187
nomads, 22, 33; Central Asia, 342; Mongols, 343
nonaligned nations, 917
Nong Sarai, Battle of, 476
nonviolent protest, 802
noodles, 348
Noriega, Manuel, *p988,* 988
Norman conquest, 308-09, 329
Normandy, 329; settlement by Danes, 296
Normandy invasion. *See* D-Day
Normans, 255
North Africa; Arab occupation, 255; climate, 184; democratic trend, 936; early cultures, 185–87; France, colonization by, 929; imperialism, 707–09; independence, 929–31; Islamic conquest, 279; Ottoman conquest, 456; in the 1990s, 935, Nshogoza, Fidele, *q935;* in World War II, 842, 843–44
North America; *m555;* French exploration, 443–44; life expectancy, 629; Native Americans, 375–78; wildlife, 378
North American Free Trade Agreement (NAFTA), 978, 979, 981, 1020
North Atlantic Treaty Organization (NATO). *See* NATO
Northern Horizon (ship), 753
Northern Ireland, 779, 1010, 1011
Northern Renaissance, 412-14
Northern Rhodesia. *See* Zambia
Northern Territory, Australia, 654
North German Confederation, 684
North Korea; China, relations with, 905; communism, 871; postwar status, 907
Northwest Mounted Police, 653
Northwest Passage, 443
Northwest Territory, Canada, 653
Norway, German invasion, 831–32
note cards in research papers, 787
note taking, 87
Nouvelle Héloise, 529
Nova Scotia, 444; acquisition by England, 493
novels; first, 363; Ming dynasty, 463
Novgorod, 260, 263, 264
Novotny, Antonin, 876–77
Nubia, *ptg185,* 48, 185
nuclear family, 229
Nuclear Nonproliferation Treaty, 917–938, 1003
nuclear weapons, 734, *m885;* Australia and New Zealand, policy toward, 921–22; in Commonwealth of Independent States, 1001–1003; French, 880; French tests, 920, 1011; in India and Pakistan, 918–19; in Iran, 960; test ban treaty, 874; U.S.-Russian agreements, 1003; in West Germany, 876
numbering systems, 214, 242–43, 381
Numbers (book of Bible), 85
nuns, 254, 305
Nuremberg Laws, 781, 785
Nuremberg trials, 851
nursing, *p660*
Nyasaland. *See* Malawi
Nyerere, Julius, *q943*

O

OAS. *See* Organization of American States (OAS)
Oath of the Tennis Court, The, ptg563
OAU; *See* Organization of Africa Unity (OAU)
Oaxaca, Mexico, 119
oba, 190
observatories, *p359,* 359
obsidian, 383
Oceania. *See* Australia, New Zealand, selected Pacific islands
Octavian. *See* Augustus
October Manifesto, 690, 694
Oder River, 683
Odessa, 261
Odoacer, 175, 178
Odysseus, *p131,* 110
Odyssey, 108, 110, 119
Oedipus, 132
Oedipus Rex, 132
Official Languages Act (Canada), 890
Of Mice and Magic, 770
Of the Disadvantages of Greatness, 413
Ogadai Khan, 344
Ogun, 182
O'Higgins, Bernardo, 669
oil; and embargo, 889; in Kuwait, 960; in Latin America, 812-13; in Middle East economy, 764; Persian Gulf War, 955; production, 1990, *m971*
Okara, Gabriel, 968
Okigbo, Christopher, 968
Okinawa, 849
Oklahoma **(battleship),** 841
Old Kingdom, 47–48
Old Stone Age. *See* Paleolithic period
Olduvai Gorge, 25
Oleg, Kievan prince, 260
Olga, Kievan princess, 262
oligarchy, 114
olive oil, 154
Oliver Branch Petition, 553
Oliver Cromwell, 536
Olmecs, 15, 372, 379–80
Olmsted, Frederick Law, 629, 632
Olorcic, Zahid, 1014
Olson, James S., 228
Olympia, 111, 134
Olympic Games, 111, 120, 134; first, 128; South African participation, 934
Olympus, Mount, 111
Omar Khayyám, 287
On a Quiet Night, 366
Once Upon a Time, 968
Oneida, 378
Onondaga, 378
On the Origin of Species, 626, 627
On the Ruin and the Repair of the Church, 334
On to Victory, Propaganda Plays of the Woman Suffrage Movement, 648
Ontario, Canada, 653
OPEC. *See* Organization of Petroleum Exporting Countries
Open Door Policy, 715
opera, 472, 635
Operation Desert Storm. *See* Persian Gulf War
Operation Overlord, 846-47
opinion and fact, 265
Opium War, 715, 716
optics, 285
oracle at Delphi, 111, 120
oracle bones, *p69, p70,* 15, 70–71
oral literature, 188
oral traditions, 184, 203
Orange Free State, 711
Oration on the Pax Romana, 164
Oregon, 662
Oregon Country, 662
Oresteia, 132
Orestes, 132
Organization of African Unity (OAU), 941, 942
Organization of American States (OAS), 884, 974, 978; intervenes in Ecuador-Peru war, 978
Organization of Petroleum Exporting Countries (OPEC), 889, 955
organ transplants, 1022
Origins of World War I, The, 696
orishas, 182
Orlando, Vittorio, 763
Orléans, France, 332
Orozco, José Clemente, 668, 794
orrery, *p525*
Orwell, George, 828, 858
Oscans, 155
Osiris, 50, 52
Osman, Ottoman leader, 456

Ostia, 167
Ostpolitik, 880
ostracism, 119
ostracon, 119
Ostrogoths, 248
Ottoman Empire, *m457,* 456–58; in Armenia, 256; art, *p273;* Byzantine Empire, attack upon, 255; Constantinople, conquest of, 264, 454; Crimean War, 657; decline, 458; defeat by Tamerlane, 345; destruction by Allies, 761; end, 796; Gallipoli, 749; Greece, freedom of, 583; Italy, war against, 708–09; law, 457–58; navy, 456; reform, 458; revolt by Young Ottomans, 458; Russia, threat from, 697; Russia, war against, 501, 502; Vienna, siege, 454
Otto the Great, 308, 312
Otto von Bismarck, *ptg685*
outlining, 551
Overfield, James H., 277, 456, 462, 468, 498, 524
Ovid, 170
Owen, Robert, 594, 624
Owen, Wilfred, *q750,* 747
oxen, 31
oxygen, 520
ozone layer, 1021

P

Pachacuti, 388, 389, 390
Pacific Ocean, 439
Pacific Rim, 920
pacifism, 523, 802
pact, defined, 953
Paekche, 358
Pagan, 351, 354
pages, 301
Pahlavi, Mohammed Reza Shah, 953; overthrow, 958
Pahlavi, Reza Shah, 798
Paine, Thomas, 553
painting, 638; abstract expressionism, 884; classicism, 529; Greek, 131; romanticism, 636; social realism, 773; techniques, 409; Twenties, 772–73; use of oil, 414
Pakistan; civil war, 916; formation, 916; independence, 916, 919; migration to, 917; U.S., relations with, 919
Palace of Persepolis, 132
palazzos, 409
Pale, Russia, 693
Paleolithic period, 14, 24
paleontology, 20–21
Palestine, 798–99, 951; Arab occupation, 255; British mandate, 764; capture by Arabs, 318; feudal states, 319; Islamic conquest, 277; Jewish immigration to, *p951;* Muslim recapture of, 321; name derivation, 82; partition, 951; Romans, resistance to, 161; Turkish conquest, 320, 343. *See also* Israel. *See also* Palestinians
Palestine Liberation Organization (PLO), 948; formation, 954; Israel, relations with, 948, 954, 956–57, 962
Palestinians; *intifada,* 956; under Israeli military occupation, 955; peace process, opposition to, 957; refugees in 1947, *p951;* resettlement, 962–63; separate state, 954
Palisca, Claude V., 676
palm oil, 712
Pamir Mountains, 223
Pan-Africanism, 942
Pan-African News Agency, 861
Panama, Isthmus of, 724
Panama, Republic of, 988; creation, 724; independence, 669
Panama Canal, *p723, m727,* 595, 721, 724; French scandal, 659; Panamanian control, 985, 988
Pan-Arabism, 950
Panchatantra, 214
Pan Gu, 70
Panikkar, K.M., *q803*
Panipat, Battle of, 460
Pankhurst, Christobel and Sylvia, 651
Pankhurst, Emmeline, 650–51
Pan-Slavism, 739
Pantheon, 167, 170
panzers, 831
papacy, 174; criticism of, 414; election of popes, 312; expulsion by Italian nationalists, 677; Great Schism, 335; Holy Roman Empire, conflict with, 312; monarchies, conflict with, 312; move to Avignon, 334; papal infallibility, 686; power, 306; during Renaissance, 408
Papal States, 676, 677, 680
paper, invention of, 228, 232
papers, research writing, 787
Papua New Guinea, 922
papyrus, 47
parables, 172
parallels, 139
paraphrasing, 634
pariahs, 204, 210
Paris, France, 108, 153; Age of Enlightenment, 525; Allied liberation of, 847
Paris, Peace of, 763
Paris, Treaty of , 497, 558
Paris, University of, 326
Paris Accords, 886
parishes, 174
Park, Mungo, *q712*
Parkinson, Roger, 696
parks, 632
Parlement, 491
Parliament, British; Cavalier Parliament, 541; Charles II, relations with, 541–42; development of, 311; dissolution by Charles I, 537; Elizabeth I, relations with, 536; Estates-General, compared to, 312; James I, relations with, 536–37; labor legislation, 623; Long Parliament, 536, 537, 538; reform, 650; role in English civil war, 538; royalists, 538; Rump Parliament, 538; Short Parliament, 537; Tudor dynasty, relations with, 485
Parliament Act, 650
Parma, 678
Parnell, Charles Stewart, 651
Parsons, Louella, *q770*
Parthenon, *p112, p116–17,* 122, 123, 130
Parthians, 178
Parti Quebecois, 890
partisans, defined, 848
Partnership for Peace, 1003
partnerships, 609
passive resistance, 802
Passover, 83, 84
pasta, 348
Pasteur, Louis, *p627,* 620, 627
pasteurization, 627
Past Speaks, The, 485
patriarchs, 174
patricians, 156
Patton, George, 847
Paul, *p172*
Paul III, pope, 422, 423
Pavlov, Ivan, 628
Pax Romana, 164; effect of, 167; end, 152, 175; established, 101; *Pax Sinica,* compared to, 222
Pax Sinica, 222, 224
Payne, Robert, 318
Peace Corps, The, 885
peaceful coexistence, 873
Peacemaking, *q760*
Peace of Augsburg, 494
Peace of Paris, 399
Pearl Harbor, Hawaii. Japanese attack upon, 838, 841
Pearson, Lester B., 889
peasant, French, *p560*
peasant life; in China, 229; under enlightenment, 528; in Middle Ages, 301–02
Peasant Maps His Road to Wealth, A, 901
Peasant's Dance, *ptg414*
Peden, Joseph, 175
Pedro I, Emperor of Brazil, 669–70
Peisistratus, 118
Peloponnesian War, *m124,* 120, 123–24, 132, 140; Thucydides' history of, 137
Peloponnesian War, The, *q112*
Peloponnesus peninsula, 115
pendulum, 518
penicillin, 733
peninsulares, 667
Penn, William, 523
Pennsylvania, 523
pentathlon, 134
People's Charter, A, 649
People's Republic of China; *See* China
Pepin, 575
Pepin the Short, 250, 295
Péres, Shimon, 958, 963
perestroika, 999–1000
Perez Balladares, Ernesto, 988
Pérez de Cuéllar, Javier, 978
Pericles, *p122,* 130; Athenian leadership, 123; death of, 124; rebuilding of Athens, 120, 122
perioeci, 115
Perón, Eva, *p990*
Perón, Isabel, 991
Perón, Juan, 972, 990–91
Perot, Ross, 999
Perrot, Michelle, 626
Perry, Marvin, 164, 175, 738, 781
Perry, Matthew C., 702
Persepolis, *p90–91,* 132, 142
Persia; Arab occupation, 255; Armenia, war against, 257; Axum, trade with, 186; Byzantine Empire, war against, *m121,* 248; empire, *m92,* Islamic conquest, 277, 281; Mongols, influence on, 345; Safavid dynasty, 458; Sassanian Empire, 248
Persian Empire, *m92,* 90–93; architecture, 132; Armenia, occupation of, 256; bureaucrats, 280; Byzantine Empire, attacks upon, 255; Chaldeans, conquest of, 86; decline, 278; defeat by Alexander, 141; Egypt, conquest of, 88; gods and goddesses, *p91;* government, 91; Greece, relations with, 119–22, 132,140; Islamic conquest, 277; Muslim literature, influence on, 286; Ottoman Empire, influence on, 458; relations with conquered peoples, 91; religion, 92–93; Sparta, relations with, 123; summary, 99; in 17th century, 459; threat to Arab land, 271; trade, 92
Persian Gulf, 440
Persian Gulf War, 960; Australian involvement, 921; environmental damage, 960
Persian language, 287

Persian Wars, *m121,* 120–22; Herodotus' history, 135, 137
personal essay, 413
perspective, 131
Perth Station, Going South, *ptg630–31*
Peru, 993; agriculture development, 17; Ecuador, war against, 978; Inca Empire, 390; independence, 669; Native Americans, 389; natural resources, 666; Spanish conquest, 441
Perun, 262
Pétain, Henri, 748, 833
Peter, *p172,* 172
Peter I. *See* Peter the Great
Peter III, 502
Peter the Apostle, 303
Peter the Great, *p499,* 498, 499–502; education, compulsory, 498; legacy, 499, 502; St. Petersburg, *q499*
Petexbatún, 384, 385
Petexbatún, Lake, *p387*
Petition of Right, 537, 541
petit jury, 309
Petrarca, Francesco, *q334–35,* 405, 413
Petrarch, *See* Petrarca Manesco
Petras, James, 979
Petrograd Soviet of Workers' and Soldiers' Deputies, 757, 758
petroleum industry, 611, 664; in Mexico, 980; nationalization in Mexico, 812–13; nationalization in Iran, 953; oil embargo, 889. *See also* OPEC (Organization of Petroleum Exporting Countries)
phalanxes, 114, 140
pharaohs, 49
Phidias, 131, 132
Philip Augustus, king of France, 308, 311, 320
Philip II, king of France, 311, 329
Philip II, king of Macedonia, 140–41
Philip II, king of Spain, *p482,* 456, 482–84; ally of Ferdinand of Styria, 494; coat of arms, *p486;* marries Mary I of England, 486
Philip III, king of Spain, 484
Philip IV, king of France, 312
Philip IV, king of Spain, 484
Philip V, king of Spain, 493
Philip of Anjou. *See* Philip V, king of Spain
Philip of Macedonia; compared to Inca leaders, 389
Philip of Valois, 330
Philippines, 475; after independence, 920; American imperialism, 719; discovery, 439; Japanese capture of, 845; Spanish imperialism, 718–19; U.S. acquisition of, 724
Philip the Fair. *See* Philip IV, king of France
Philistines, 80, 82, 83, 84, 85
philosophes, 524–25
philosophy; Greek, 135–37; Hellenistic, 144–45; medieval, 326–27; Muslim, 287; science-based, 518
phlogiston, 520
Phoenicians, 80–82; defeat by Alexander, 142; exploration, 80, 82; Persian Empire, conquest by, 91; religion, 83; spread of trade, 81–82; summary, 98
phonographs, 611
photography, 658
physics, 518, 628, 771
Piankhi, Kushite king, 186
piano, 529
Picadilly Circus, *ptg633*
Picasso, Pablo, *q773,* 772
pictograms, 34
Pictorial History of the Confederacy, A, 660
pieces of eight, 447
Piedmont, 582
Pier and the Ducal Palace, The, *ptg429*
Pierrot Lunaire, 773
Pike, E. Royston, 612
Pilate, Pontius, 172
pilgrimages, 268, 334; in Islam, 276
Pilgrims, 444
Pilgrims Signing the Mayflower Compact, *ptg538*
Pinochet, Augusto, 992
Pinta, 432
pioneers, American West, *p661*
piracy, 444, 446; pirate ship, *p446*
Pirate Picture, The, 446
Pisa, Italy, 323
Pitchforth, Susan, *q599*
Pitt, William, *q102*
Pius, Antoninus, 165
Pius VI, Pope, 565
Pius VII, Pope, *q582,* 575
Pius IX, Pope, 677, 686–87
Pizarro, Francisco, 441
plague, 542
Plain (French National Convention), 569
Planck, Max, 620, 628
plateau, defined, 185
Plato, *p136, p145, q136,* 135, 136–37
plays. *See* theater
plebeians, 156
plebiscite, 575; defined, 657
PLO. *See* Palestine Liberation Organization (PLO)
plows, 31, 41, 302, 322; invention, 221
Pluto, 111
Plymouth, Massachusetts, 444
Poems from Black Africa, 945
poetry; Chinese, 366; Mali, 189; Middle Ages, 328; modern, 772; 966–69; romantic, 636. *See also* individual poets
pogroms, defined, 693
pointillism, 639
point of view, 531
poison gas, 747
pok-a-tok, *p382,* 381
Poland; Catholicism, 422; communism, 865, 876; communism, end of, 1005; creation, 581; decline, 247; defense against Germany, 829–30; divided among Russia, Prussia, and Austria, 399, 502; establishment, 582; ethnic origins, 259; German acquisition, 759; German invasion, 824, 830; Jesuit missionaries, 425; postwar borders, 849; re-established, 763; reform, pressure for, 1004–05; Russia, occupation by, 690; Russia, war against, 499, 501; Solidarity, 1004–05; Soviet policy toward, 847–48; Soviet Union, occupation by, 831
polio vaccine, 858
polis, 112. *See also* city-states
Polish Corridor, 763, 830
political cartoons, 720
political science, 136, 137, 405
Politics (Aristotle), 137
politics, 569
Pollock, Jackson, *q884*
pollution; of the air, *p1021;* of the environment, 1020–21; in Japan, 898; in Persian Gulf War, 960
Pollux, Temple of, *p169*
Polo, Marco, *p349,* 350; Ibn Battuta, compared to, 192; journal entry, 342; reaches China, 241, 346; search for gold, 713
Pol Pot, 912
polygamy, 282
Polyneices, 146
Polynesians, 922
polytheism, 52, 61
Pomerans, Arno, 838
Pompadour, Madame de, 525
Pompeii, *p165,* 164
Pompey, Gnaeus, 163
Pompidou, Georges, 880
pontifex maximus, 166
Poor Laws, 485, 488
pope, 174
Pope, Alexander, *p531,* 529
population explosion, defined, 808
population growth, 1019–20
population of the world, *m989,* 629
populism, 690, 692
porcelain, *p342, p347,* 359, 467
Porcellis, Jan, 450
Porsena, 154
Portable North American Indian Reader, The, 374
Portable Renaissance Reader, The, 482
Port Harcourt, Nigeria, 712
Portrait of Catherine the Great, *ptg502*
Portrait of Charles I Hunting, *ptg537*
Portugal, 333; Catholicism, 422; China, contact with, 467; colonies, 440, 666; democracy, 1012–13; East African colonization, 933; exploration by, *m441,* 436, 438; growth of commerce, 448; independence, 484; India, trade with, 438; Japan, relations with, 470; joins European Community, 1010; lack of export goods, 449; liberal government, 669–70; line of demarcation, 439; in Malay Peninsula, 474; monarchy re-establishment of, 581; Netherlands, conflict with in Asia, 443; in Southeast Asia, 474, 718–19; under Spanish control, 482; in Thailand, 476–77; West Africa, colonization of, 709
Portuguese language, 170
Possehl, Gregory, 66
postimpressionism, 639
potatoes, 17, 629
potato famine, 651, 665
potlatches, 376
Potsdam Conference, 849
potter's wheel, 61
pottery, 30; ancient Africa, 185; ancient Greece, *p113;* Chinese, 348; Native American, 375, 381
poverty, theory of, 623
powder horn, *p552*
praetors, 157
Pragmatic Sanction, 495–96
Praise of Folly, The, 412, 414
Praxiteles, 132
predestination, 419
prehistory. *See* human prehistory
preindustrial society, daily life, 600–02
premier, French, 659
presidency, United States, 888
Preval, Rene, 984
PRI. *See* Institutionalized Revolutionary Party
Price, David, 456
Priestley, Joseph, 516, 520
priests, 34; Christian, 174
Primary Chronicle, 260
Prime Meridian, 139
prime ministers (British), 648; first, 544
Prince, The, 405, 426–29
Prince Edward Island, Canada, 653
Prince of the Humanists, 413

Princip, Gavrilo, 742
principalities, 260
Principia, 516, 518, 524
printing; invention, 101, 348, 412, 413; during Italian Renaissance, 409; moveable type, 416
Prinz Eugen (battleship), 842
privatization; in Commonwealth of Independent States, 1003; defined, 981
proconsuls, 161
Procopius, *q244*
progress, 524
Prokofiev, Sergey, 773
proletariat. *See* working class
proletariat, dictatorship of the, 789
propaganda, defined, 746
prophets, 85–86
protectorates, defined, 706
Protestantism, 415–20; Catholic reaction to, 422, 424; conflict with Catholicism in Germany, 494, 681; in England, 420; in Spain, 482; spread of, 418–20
Protestant Reformation, 415–17; Germany, influence on, 681
provinces, of Roman Republic, 161
provisional government, defined, 757
Prudent king. *See* Philip II, king of Spain
Prussia, 496, 576; Austria, conflict with, 681, 683-84; Carlsbad Decrees, 583; Congress of Vienna involvement, 580–81; educational goals, 632; France, war against, 567, 577, 578; Franco-Prussian War, 657–58, 684–85; French Revolution, policy toward, 566; Italy, alliance with, 680; leadership in German unification, 682; monarchy, 496–97; Poland, division of, 399, 502; Poland, relations with, 582; political reform, 656; Quadruple Alliance membership, 582–83; in Seven Years' War, 497; in War of the Spanish Succession, 496
psychology, 628, 771–72
Ptolemy, astronomer, 101, 436
Ptolemy, kings of Egypt, 142, 170
publicans, 161
public health, 632
Pueblo, 377, 378
Puerto Rico, 722–24; U.S. acquisition of, 724
pulley, 145
Punici. *See* Carthage
Punic Wars, 152, 160
puppetry, 351
purdah, 274
purgatory, 416
purges, defined, 791
Puritanism, 420
Puritans, 540; in England, 537; persecution, 537, 541
purple dye, 80
Pu Yi, prince of China, 716, 826
Pyongyang, North Korea, 906
pyramids, 48; construction, 44, 55
Pythagoras, 135, 138

Q

Qaddafi, Muammar al-Qatar, 929, 936
Qadir, Abd, al- 708
Qahira, El, 311
Qajar dynasty, 459
Qin dynasty, *m221,* 221–22, 230; sculpture, *p239*
Qing dynasty, 465–67, 595; Europeans, relations with, 714–16
Qin Shihuangdi, 220, 221
Quadruple Alliance, 582–83
quantum theory, 620, 628
Quebec, 652; founded, 440, 444; law, 103; separatism, 890, 1016–17
Quebec Act, 550
Quechua language, 390
Queensland, Australia, 654
Quentin Durward, 636
Quetzalcoatl, 383
queues, 466
quinoa, 390
quotas, defined, 900
Quran, 193, 273; Bible, compared to, 275; compiled, 282; Greek philosophy, compared to, 287; role in military success, 278; used as art, 286

R

Ra, 52
rabbis, 172
Rabelais, François, 413
Rabin, Yitzhak, 956–57; assassination, 948, 958
Racine, Jean, 529
racism, 886
radicalism, defined, 569
radio, 611, 771
radiocarbon dating, 20–21
radium, 626, 628
Rafsanjani, Hashemi, 960
railroads, *p603;* in Canada, 653; first locomotive, 606; first public, 594; in Germany, 607
rain measurement, 359
rajahs, 202
Rama, *p214, q206*
Rama Rau, Santha, *p818*
Ramadan, 276
Ramathibodi, 355
Ramayana, 206, 212, 351
Ramkhamhaeng, Thai ruler, 355
Ramos, Fidel, 921
Ramsaye, Terry, *q770*
Ramses II, *p51,* 51, 54
Ramses III, 51
Ramses the Great, *p50, See* Ramses II
Raphael, 407
Rashtrakuta dynasty, 364
Rasputin, Grigori, 692, 757
ratification, defined, 665
Rau, Santha Rama, 818
Ravana, 206
Razi, al-, 285
razors, 27
reactionaries, 582, 583; defined, 569
Readings in Ancient History from Gilgamesh to Diocletian, 58, 159, 171
Readings in Western Civilization, 334
Reagan, Ronald; communism, attitude toward, 999; election, 998
Reagan administration, 998–99; Nicaragua policy, 986
Realism, 635
realism, 636, 638
realpolitik, defined, 682
reason, 523, 529
Reasonableness of Poetry, The, 521
recession, 889
reciprocity, 226
reconnaissance aircraft, 760
Reconquista, 333
Record of Brush Methods: Essay on Landscape Painting, 346
Red Army, 805-06
Red Guards, 902
Redistribution Act of 1885, 650
Reds (Bolsheviks), 759
referendum, defined, 908, 1011
Reflections on World Civilization, 228
reform; Armenia, 1003; Athens, 118; Azerbaijan, 1003; Church of England, 537; Cuba, 982; Georgia (Russia), 1003; Iran, 797–98; Ottoman Empire, 458; Poland, 1004–05; Russian Empire, 730; Tajikistan, 1003; Turkmenistan, 1003; Ukraine, 1003; Uzbekistan, 1003
reform, land; China, 901; Latin America, 978; Roman Republic, 162
reform, political; Austria, 656; Europe, 729; Italy, 656; Latin America, 730; Prussia, 656; United States, 729
reform, social, 623–24; Great Britain, 623; Latin America, 974, 977–78
Reform Act of 1832, 646, 647, 649
Reform Bill of 1867, 511, 650
reformation. *See* Catholic Reformation; Protestant Reformation
Reformed church, 418
refrigeration, 629
refugees, 734
regents, 251
Reichstag, 785
Reign of Terror, 570–71
Reims, France, 332
Reims Cathedral, *p322*
reincarnation, 207
relativity, 628; theory of, 771
relevant information, 179
religion, 31; development of, 34; in Africa, 188; in Asia, 83, 92, 172–74, 206–10, 225–27; 273–76; in Europe, *m424;* freedom of, 419; good and evil, 92–93; influence of reason, 523; liberation theology, 978; Native American, 377, 380, 383, 389, 390; reaction against reason, 530; separation of church and state, 419. *See also* individual religions
Religious Healing in the Veda, 202
Religious Procession in the Province of Kursk, *ptg641*
Remarque, Erich Maria, 736
Rembrant van Rijn, *ptg443*
Remember the *Maine!,* 724
Remington, Frederic, *q721*
Remus, 156
Renaissance, 404–14; Age of Exploration, influence on, 434; baroque, compared to, 424; defined, 402; in England, 414; in France, 413; in Northern Europe, 412–14. *See also* Italian Renaissance
Renault, Mary, 130
Renneville, Geoffrey de, 318
Renoir, Pierre-Auguste, 639
reparations, World War I, 762–63
Repin, Ilya, 641
report writing, 940
republic, 156
Republic, The, 136
Republic of China. *See* Taiwan
Republic of Korea. *See* South Korea
Republic of Virtue, 570, 571
research reports; bibliographies, 961; note cards, 787; note taking, 87; outlining, 551; report writing, 940; sources, research, 633
resistance movements, 839, 850
Return from the Crusade, *ptg321*
revelation, 272
Revere, Paul, 552
Revolutionary War, 554; major battles, *m557. See also* American Revolution

Revolution of 1848, *p656*
Revolution of 1905, *p693,* 693–94
rhetoric, 119
Rhineland, 826, 828
Rhine River, 683
Rhodes, Cecil, 705, 711
Rhodesia, 705. *See also* Zimbabwe
Rhodesian Front, 934
Ribbentrop, Joachim von, 826
Ricardo, David, 622, 623
rice, 17
rice production; in Cambodia, 352; Chinese development, 347; in Japan, 361
Richard I, king of England, 310, 320
Richard II, king of England, 336
Richard III, king of England, 333
Richelieu, Cardinal, *p491,* 492, 494
Rigaud, Hyacinthe, 492
Rightly Guided Caliphs, 277–79
rights, human, 523, 530, 1022; under Magna Carta, 310
Rig-Veda, 200, 202, 203
Rimbaud, Arthur, 638
Rio de Janeiro, Brazil, *p973*
Rio Treaty, 978
Risorgimento, 676
Rite of Spring, The, 775
Rivera, Diego, 732
river valley civilizations, 32
road building, 92; Great Britain, 606; Roman Republic, 159, 168
Roaring Twenties. *See* Twenties
Roberts, Randy W., 228
Robertson, Charles, 278
Robespierre, Maximilien, 568, 570–72
Robinson, Jackie, 858
Rock Edicts, *p211,* 212
rockets, 348, 732
Roentgen, Wilhelm K., 628
Roh Tae Woo, 908
Romagna, 678
Roman Catholicism; Anabaptists, reaction to, 419; arrest of Galileo, 517; in Bohemia, 336; Catholic Reformation, 422–25; criticism of, 415–16, 513; decline of influence, 334; doctrine during Reformation, 423; Eastern Orthodox Church, split with, 247, 250; *Encyclopedie,* influence on, 525; in England, 420; establishment, 174; examination by Slavic Vikings, 262; expansion, *m165,* feudal system, relationship with, 306; in France, 490; Franks, influence on, 294; French Revolution, influence of, 565; in French Second Republic, 657; German Empire, conflict with, 686; Great Schism, 335; Henry VIII, conflict with, 420; imposition on Netherlands, 483; in Indochina, 476; intoleration in Spain, 333; Ireland, conflict in, 651; in Latin America, 666–67, 977–78; lay investiture, 306, 312; in Middle Ages, 303–07, 334–36; missionary work, 305; missions in South America, *m431;* monastic life, 304–05; Napoleonic France, policy of, 575; organization, 304; in Philippines, 475; political role, 303; in prerevolutionary France, 560–61; Protestantism, reaction to, 422, 424; Protestantism in Germany, conflict with, 494, 681; reforms, 306, 335–36, 413–14; revival in France, 530; science, policy toward, 516; in Scotland, 489; Slavic culture, influence on, 259; Slavs, 247; in Southeast Asia, 474; use of images, 303–04. *See also* papacy
Romance languages, 170
Roman Empire, *m165,* 101, 164–70; architecture, 168; Armenia, conquest of, 256–57; army, 167; barbarian invasion, *m177,* 177–78; China, contact with, 222; Christianity, 173; citizenship, 166; civil rights, 166; daily life, 168; decline, 175–78; digest, 237–38; division, 175, 177, 244; economic decline, 175–76; economic reforms, 176–77; economy, 167; education, 170; Egypt, defeat of, 142; emperors, 164–66; end, 178; Georgia, conquest of, 257; government, 166–67; Greece, conquest of, 143; Greece, contributions of, 170; Hellenistic culture, conquest of, 140; imperialism, 704; Judah, conquest of, 143; law, 102; literature, 170; Macedonia, conquest of, 143; preservation by Byzantine Empire, 247, 254; religion, 171, 173; Renaissance, influence on, 404; science, 170; tax collection, *p176;* trade, 167. *See also* Roman Republic
Romanesque architecture, 328
Roman History, 159
Romania; communism, 865; communism, end of, 1005; government, 1006–1007; independence, 698; nationalism, 697; in Nazi-Soviet Nonaggression Pact, 830; Soviet liberation of, 848; territorial gains, 764; violence, 1006
Romanian language, 170
Roman numerals, 243
Romanov, Michael, 499
Romanov dynasty, 499, 757
Roman Republic, 156–63, 677, 679; army, 159, 162; Carthage, war against, 159, 160; citizenship, 156–57; conquest, 159; corruption, 161–62; democracy, 157; dining, 157; end, 163; established, 152; family life, 158; funeral, *p161;* government, 156–57; Greek contributions, 152, 157; land reform, 162; law, 157; migration to cities, 162; navy, 160; provinces, relations with, 161; religion, 157–58; road building, 159; social conflict, 157; values, 158; women, *p153,* 158. *See also* Roman Empire
romanticism, 636; defined, 635; development of, 530; rejection of, 636
Rome, Treaty of, 881
Rome-Berlin Axis, 828
Rome (city); Allied liberation, 845; Axum, trade with, 186; barbarian sack of, 178; Christianity, 172; development, 164; establishment, 156; under Etruscan control, 156; Frankish support for, 295; outside unified Italy, 680; Renaissance, 404, 408
Romero, Oscar, 987
Rommel, Erwin, 836, 838, 843; Allied defeat of, 844
Romulus, 156
Ronsard, Pierre, 413
Roosevelt, Eleanor, 734
Roosevelt, Franklin D., 776, 778; German expansion, policy toward, 835; Good Neighbor policy, *q817;* Stalin, opinion of, 865
Roosevelt, Theodore, *p723,* 722, 724; reaction to *Lusitania* sinking, 753
Roosevelt Corollary, 722, 816–17
Roses, Wars of the, 316, 333, 414, 419
Rosetta stone, 53, 511
Roslin, Alexandre, 502
Rothermel, Peter, 438
Rough Riders, *p721*
Roundheads, 538
Rousseau, Jean-Jacques, 529–30, 564, 635
Rowen, Herbert H., 521
Royal Academy of Art, 638
Royal Air Force (RAF), 834, 843, 846
Royal Drill Sargeant. *See* Frederick William I
Royal Road, 92
Royal Society of London, 521
Rubaiyat, 287
rubber industry, 611
Rubicon River, 163
rug, Navajo, *p374*
rugby, 632
Ruiz-Tagle, Eduardo Frei, 992
Rump Parliament, 538
Runnymeade, 310
rural life, pre-Industrial Revolution, 600–01
Rurik the Rus, *p261,* 260
Russia, 498–502; Austria, support for, 497; Austria-Hungary, agreement with, 739; Balkan expansion, 698; Baltic coast, acquisition of, 498; Berlin-Baghdad railway, resentment toward, 739; Bismarck, relations with, 683; Black Sea, expansion toward, 739; Chechnya, 1016; China, trade with, 350; China, unequal treaties with, 715; civil war, *m759,* 756, 759; in Commonwealth of Independent States, *m1001,* 1001; communism, 625; Congress of Vienna involvement, 580–81; creation, 264; Crimean War, 657, 697; Decembrist Revolt, 691; England, trade with, 499; ethic origins, 259; expansion, *m501, m691;* expansion under Catherine, 502; expansion under Ivan, 499; expansion under Peter, 501; France, 1894 alliance with, 740; France, war against, 576–77, 577; Germany, treaty with, 759; Germany declares war, 743; government under Peter, 501; immigration from, 665; isolation, 498; Japan, unequal treaties with, 717; Japan, war against, *m701,* 694, 718; Jewish immigration to U.S., 629; Jews, persecution of, 693; in League of Three Emperors, 740; monarchy, 498–502; Mongol conquest, 344; Napoleon, invasion by, 574; Napoleonic France, revolt against, 576; Ottoman Empire, policy toward, 697; Poland, division of, 399, 502; Poland, relations with, 582; Quadruple Alliance membership, 582–83; radicalism, 692; reform movements, 690–94; revolution of 1917, 756–59, revolution of 1905, 693–94; seaports, 499; secret police, 759; Serbia, support for, 739, 743; serfs, emancipation of, 691–92; settlement by Swedes, 296; in Seven Years' War, 497; social structure under czars, 691–92; strikes, 694; taxation, 501; in Triple Entente, 740; Vikings, occupation by, 261; Western influence, 499–502; women, voting rights, 732; World War I, Eastern front, 748–49; World War I, entry into, 746. *See also* Russian Empire. *See also* Russian Revolution (1917), Soviet Union
Russia, name, 260
Russian Empire; Armenia, acquisition of, 257; Georgia, acquisition of, 257; reform, 730
Russian Orthodox Church, 264; persecution under Lenin, 760
Russian Republic, 1000
Russian Revolution (1917), 732, 756–59; Bolshevik Revolution, 758–59; civil war, 756, 759; events leading to, 756–57; provisional government, 757–58
Russian Revolution, The, 756
Russification, 692–93
Russo-Japanese War, 718
Russo-Turkish War, 696, 698
Ruth, Babe, 771
Ruthenians, 829

Rwanda; ethnic civil war, 938; Rwandan Patriotic Front, 938

S

Saar Basin, 687, 763
Sabbath, 86
sacraments, 303
Sacred Mosque, 268
sacrifices, human; Aztec, 389; Inca, 390; Maya, 381
Sadat, Anwar al-, 955
Safavid dynasty, 458
sagas, 296
Sahara, 184, 707–08, 941, 943
Sahara, The Great Desert, 941
Sahel, 185, 944
Sahul, 24
Saint Augustine, 173-74
Saint Domingue, 445, 513, 566. *See also* Haiti
Saint Helena, 578
Saint Paul's Epistle to the Romans, 415
Saint-Simon, Duke of, *q490*
Sakhalin Islands, 849
Sakharov, Andrei, 874
Saladin, 320–21
Salamis, 122
Salinas de Gortari, Carlos, 980–81
Salk, Jonas, 858
salons, *p521, p526–27,* 525
Salopek, Paul F., 935
salt, 182, 189–90; in India, 803
SALT I treaty, 862
Samanid dynasty, 281
Samarkand, 281, 342, 409; establishment, 345
Samarra, Iraq, 274
Samoa, *crt705*
samurai, *p468,* 363–64, 365; ethics, 470
Samurai are Here, The, 896
sanctuaries, 130
Sand, George, 636
Sandinista National Liberation Front (FSLN), 985
Sandino, Augusto, *p815,* 794, 816, 985
Sanin, Joseph, *q264*
sankin-kotai, 469, 472
San Francisco Conference, 864
San Lorenzo, 379
San Martín, José de, 669
sans-culottes, *p567,* 568, 569, 571
Sanskrit, 203, 351
San Stefano, Treaty of, 698
Sarajevo, Bosnia-Herzegovina, *p1014,* 741–42, 1015
Saratoga, New York, 554
Sardinia, 582, 657; Crimean War, 697; French Revolution, policy toward, 566, 569; monarchy, re-establishment of, 581; role in Italian unification, 677–80
Sargon I, 58, 62
Sarnath, India, 209
Saro-Wiwa, Ken, 937
Sarpedon, *q106*
Saskatchewan, Canada, 653
Sassanid Empire, 178, 248
satellite communications, 860
satellite countries, 866, 875–77. *See also* individual countries
satellite dishes, 860
satellite television, 860
satraps, 91
satyagraha, 802
Saudi Arabia, 960; in Arab League, 950; censorship, 965
Saul, 85
SAVAK, 958
savannas, defined, 185
Savonarola, Girolamo, *q407–08*
Savoy, 678, 679
Saxons, 175, 178, 308
Saxony, 577, 581
Sayer, Moses, 773
Scandinavia; immigration from, 665; Lutheranism, 425; Slavs, war against, 259; Viking origin, 296
Schama, Simon, 560
Scheidermann, Philipp, *q738*
Schiller, Friedrich von, 635
Schism, Great, 335
schisms, 250
Schleiden, Mathias, 626
Schleswig, 682–83
Schlieffen, Alfred von, 744
Schlieffen Plan, 744
Schliemann, Heinrich, 108
Schindler's List, 850
Schoenberg, Arnold, 773; flight from Nazism, 786
Scholars, The, 463
scholasticism, 326
School of Athens, *ptg406–07*
School of Mars, 567
schools; under Charlemagne, 295; public, 528, 574
Schubert, Franz, 635
Schwann, Theodor, 626
Schwieger, Walther, 752
science; advances in 1600s, 516–23; advances in 19th and 20th centuries, 626–28; Greek development, 138; Hellenistic, 145; Muslim, 326
scientific method, 518, 520, 522, 524
Scipio, Publius, 160, 162
Scopes evolution trial, 774
scorched-earth policy, 577, 838
Scotland; becomes Protestant, 489; Calvinism, 419, 425; Church of England, 538; Cromwell, defeat by, 538; England, alignment with, 489; England, war against, 538
Scott, Nora, 704
Scott, Walter, 636
scraper, Neolithic, *p26, p28*
scribes, 52, 61, 82
sculpture, 29; classicism, 529; Greek, 131–32; Hellenistic, *p143,* 145; Italian Renaissance, 409; in sub-Saharan Africa, 188; West Africa, *p189*
seas, freedom of the, 762
SEATO. *See* Southeast Asia Treaty Organization (SEATO)
Sebastopol, 657
secession, defined, 663
Secondat, Charles-Louis de. *See* Montesquieu, Baron de
Second Estate, 561, 562
Second Republic, French, 656–58
Secretariat (UN), 865
sect, defined, 899
sectionalism, 663
secularism, 415
Security Council (UN), 864
Segovia, Spain, 170
segregation, defined, 887
Seibal, 386
seismographs, 226
Sejong, King, 359
Sekigahara, Battle of, 469
Seko, Mobutu Sese, *p938,* 937. *See also* Mobutu, Joseph
Selassie, Haile I, Emperor of Ethiopia, 186, 827, 938
Selected Writings of Bolívar, 666
Selective Service System, 760. *See also* conscription
Seleucus, 142, 143
self-determination, 796
Selincourt, Aubrey de, 120
Seljuk Turks. *See* Turks, Seljuk
seminaries, 423
Senate (Roman), 157, 162
Seneca, 378
Senegal, 709
Senghor, Léopold Sédar, 930, 945
Seoul, South Korea, 906
separation of powers, 525–26
Sepoy Rebellion, 713–14
sepoys, 702
Septuagint, 144
Serbia, 739, 1008–09, 1014–15; Austria-Hungary declares war, 742; in Balkan League, 698; independence, 698; nationalism, 697
Serbs, 256, 498, 1014–15; ethnic origins, 259; Slavic nation, 764
serfs, 501, 502; emancipation in Russia, 691–92
servants, of the middle class, 613
Seurat, Georges, 639
Seventh Panzer Division, 836
Seven Weeks' War, 681, 683–84, 696
Seven Wonders of the World, 90
Seven Years' War, 494, 497, 527, 554, 558; end, 399
Seville, Spain, 284
Seymour, Jane, 420
Shaba province, Congo, 932
shadoof, 47
Shaftesbury, Lord, 623
shah, 797
Shahn, Ben, 773
Shaka, king of the Zulu, 711
Shakespeare, William, *p412,* 414, 487
Shakuntala, 214
shamanism, 358
Shamash, 58
Shandong Peninsula, 804
Shang dynasty, *m67,* 44, 69, 70–71, 111, 220
Shanghai, China, 463, 827
Shannon, Albert Clement, 422
shari'ah, 275
shaving, 27
Shaw, Artie, 775
Sheffield, England, 632
sheikh, 271
Shelley, Percy Bysshe, 636
sheriffs, 309
Shiite Muslims, 278–79, 459; Iraq, suppression by, 960; opposition to Umayyad dynasty, 280
Shikibu Murasaki, 363
Shikoku, 359
Shining Path guerrillas, 993
Shinto, 361; Buddhism, compared to, 362
ship, Phoenician, *p80, p81*
ship building, 82, 321, 409, 436
ships, 113; ironclad warships, 359
Shoes of the Faithful, *ptg278*
shogunate, 363, 716
shopping centers, 883
Short Koran, The, 270
Short Parliament, 538
Shotoku, Japanese prince, 362
Siam. *See* Thailand
Siberia, 501

Siboto of Falkenstein, 299
Sic et Non, 327
Sicily, 154, 679; Allied invasion, 844; Carthage's colonies, conquest of, 160; monarchy, re-establishment of, 581; 1848 revolution, 677
sickle, 30
Sidon, 82
Siege of Paris, The, *p657*
siege techniques, 321, 344
Sieyès, Abbé, *q562*
Signing of the Declaration of Independence, *ptg553*
signori, 406
Sihanouk, Norodom, 912
Sikhs, 460, 916, 917
silent majority, 886
Silesia, 497
silk production, *p232, p464–65,* 252, 467
Silk Road, *m223, p223,* 222, 257, 347; blockade by Turks, 348
Silla, 358, 359
silver mining, 442
Sima Qian, 231
Simmons, Jack, 603
Simon, Apostle, 410
Simon, Helmut and Erika, 38
simony, 335
Simpson, James, 628
Sims, William S., 760
Sina, Ibn, 285, 287
Sinai, Mount, *p83*
Sinai Desert, 84
Sinbad the Sailor, 287
Since Yesterday, 776
Singapore, 839; economic development, 915; Japanese capture of, 845
Single Europe Act, 1013
Sinhalese, 919, 1016
Sino-Japanese War, 718
Siphnos, *p106*
Siqueiros, David Alfaro, *ptg813*
Sirens, *p131*
Sirius, 53
Sisera, 206
Sistine Chapel, *p404,* 404, 411
Sita, 206
sit-down war, 831
Sitzkrieg, 831
Siva, *p207,* 204, 364
Six-Day War, 858, 954–55
Skeptical Chymist, The, 520
Skinner, Elliott, *q941*
Sklodowska, Marie, 626, 628
slash-and-burn farming, 380
Slater, Samuel, 597, 607
slavery; abolished, 664; Athens, 122–23; in Cape Colony, 711; effect of textile industry, 663; in Latin America, 666; living conditions, 445; reaction against, 662; resistance, 445; revolt, 513. *See also* enslaved persons. *See also* slave trade
slaves. *See* enslaved persons
slave trade; auction block, 445; Middle Passage, 445; slave ship, *p445;* Spanish, 442; in West Africa, 709. *See also* enslaved persons. *See also* slavery
Slavs, 255, 258–59; in Balkan Peninsula, 698; groups, 259; in Holocaust, 839; invasion of Europe, 296; Islam, 498; loss of power, 498; nationalism, 739; Pan-Slavism, 739; in Russia, 690. *See also* Eastern Slavs
Slovakia, Republic of; formation, 859, 1007; ethnic origins, 259
Slovaks, 247
Slovenes; ethnic origins, 259
Slovenia; independence, 1008–09
smallpox; 626, 627; inoculation, 399
Smith, Adam, 594, 620, 623
Smith, Barbara Leigh, 650
Smith, Bessie, 773
Smith, Ian, 933
Smith, J.R., 485
Smith, L.B., 485
smuggling, 546
Sobieski, King John III. *See* John III Sobieski
soccer, 632
social classes, 34, 625
social contract, 514, 523, 553
social Darwinism, 705
Social Democratic party (Germany), 687
Social Democratic party (Japan), 899
socialism, *ctn624,* 624; democratic socialism, 625; in France, 658, 659; in Germany, 687, 689; in Great Britain, 650; in India, 917
Socialist realism, 791
social mobility, 612
social organization; development of, 28
social realism, 773
Social Revolutionaries, 757
Society of German Maidens, 786
Society of Jesus, 422, 424. *See also* Jesuit Order
Society of Righteous and Harmonious Fists, 715. *See also* Boxers
sociology, 628
Socrates, *p135, q136,* 128, 135–36
Socratic method, 136
Sofala, 194
soft drink advertisement, *p519*
Soga family, 361–62
Soko, Yamaga, *q468*
solar system, model, *p525*
soldier, Spartan, *p123*
soldiers, terra-cotta, *p239*
Solidarity, *p1006,* 996, 1004–05
Solomon, 85, 318
Solon, 115, 118
Solzhenitsyn, Alexander, 874
Somalia, *p927;* United Nations intervention, 939
Somme, Battle of the, 748
Somoza Debayle, Anastasio, 816, 985
Sondok, Korean queen, 359
Song dynasty, 348–50; economic development, 348; Vietnam, relations with, 354
Songhai, 189, 193
Song of Roland, 327
Song of the Harper, 46
Songs of Experience, 636
Songs of Innocence, 636
sonnets, 405
Son of Heaven, 220
soothsayers, 157
Sophia, granddaughter of James I, 543
Sophia, wife of Ivan III, 264
Sophie, wife of Archduke Francis Ferdinand, 741
Sophists, 135
Sophocles, 132, 146
Source Book for Russian History from Early Times to 1917, A, 690
Source Book in Chinese Philosophy, A, 225
sources, research, 633
Sources in World History, 690
Sources of Japanese Tradition, 358, 468, 807
Sources of the Western Tradition, 164, 175, 738, 781
Sources of World Civilization, 807
Sources of World History, 270, 358, 379
South Africa; apartheid, end of, 926, 934, 935, 939; apartheid introduced, 928; civil rights, 711–12; elections, 926; formation, 707; immigration to, 630
South African Native National Congress (SANNC), 712
South America; Catholic missions, *m431;* exploration, 439; immigration to, 630; modern era, 990–93. *See also* Latin America
Southampton, England, 324
South Asia, British colonialism, 916
South Australia, 654
South Carolina, 663
Southeast Asia, *m354,* 351–56, 474–77; China, relations with, 348, 905; countries of, 351; European arrival, 355; European influence, 474–76; imperialism in, 718–19; India, influence of, 351; Khmer, 352–53; Mongol Empire, attack by, 350; Myanmar, 354–55; Portuguese arrival, 440; seafaring kingdoms, 355–56; Thai, 355; Vietnam, 353–54. *See also* individual countries
Southeast Asia Treaty Organization (SEATO), 884
Southern Africa, 933–34
Southern Common Market (Mercosur), 978, 1020
South Korea; China, relations with, 905; government, 907–08; industrialization, 907–08
South Pacific, 922
South Pacific Nuclear-Free Zone, 922
South Sea. *See* Pacific Ocean
sovereignty, defined, 963
soviets, defined, 694
Soviet Union, 788–91, 872–75; agriculture, 790; arts, under Stalin, 791; atomic bomb, 871; breakup, 859, 1000–01; China, relations with, 901–03; collectivization, 788, 790; communism, 788–90; Cuba, support for, 982; Czechoslovakia, invasion of, 877; de-Stalinization, 872–73; dissidents, 874; Eastern Europe, noninterference, 1005; Egypt, relations with, 951–52; end of, 996, 999–1003; Five-Year Plans, 790; German invasion, 838; Germany, nonaggression pact with, 830; Gorbachev, foreign policy, 1000; Gorbachev era, 999–1001; Hungary, invasion of, 876; India, support for, 917; industrialization, 790; Iran, relations with, 797–98; Leningrad, siege of, 839–840, 847–48; loss of satellites, 1005; Marshall Plan, policy toward, 869; militarism, 874; military bases in eastern Europe, 831; name change from Russia, 788–89; New Economic Policy (NEP), 788–89; Poland, defense of, 830; reforms, 999–1000; republics, 789; Sandinistas, support for, 986; secret police, 790–91; Spanish civil war, policy toward, 827–28; Sputnik I, 860; Stain, rise of, 790–91; standard of living, 873; UN Security Council, 865; Vietminh, support for, 909. *See also* Russia
Soweto, South Africa, 934
Soyinka, Wole, 968
space exploration, *p997,* 1022
space shuttle, 1022
Spain; Basque separatism, 1012; Bonaparte king, 576; under Carthage, 160; Catholic intoleration, 333; Catholicism, 422; Catholicism, imposition on Netherlands, 483; civil war, 824, 827–28; colonies, 441–42, 450, 666; commerce, growth of, 448; decline of power, 484; democracy, 878, 1012;

England, war against, 483, 537; in European Community, 1010; exploration by, *m441,* 438–42; fascism, 827–28; Florida, loss of, 660; France, war against, 577; French Revolution, policy toward, 569; Inca Empire, conquest of, 390, 441; Jenkins' Ear war, 497; lack of export goods, 449; law, 103; liberalism, 583; line of demarcation, 439; mercantilism, 448; Mesoamerica, conquest of, 388, 389, 441; monarchy, 333, 482–84; monarchy re-establishment of, 581; Muslim eviction, 333; Muslim occupation, 279, 284; Napoleonic France, revolt against, 576; North American claims, 441; Philippines, colonization of, 474, 718–19; Phoenician contact, 82; plague, 482; Protestantism, 482; religious minorities, 483; republic, 827; in Revolutionary War, 554; in Southeast Asia, 474–75, 718-19; Spanish-American War, 718–19, 721, 724; Spanish Armada, 480, 483, 489; Spanish Inquisition, 333; Spanish Succession, War of the, 493; succession after Charles II, 493; Umayyad dynasty, 281; unity, 483; in War of the Austrian Succession, 497; West Africa, colonization of, 709
Spanish-American War, 718–19, 721, 724
Spanish Armada, *p483,* 480, 483, 489
Spanish Inquisition, 333
Spanish language, 170
Spanish Succession, War of the, 493
Sparke, John, *q440*
Sparta, 114, 115–17, 136; Athens, war against, 123–24; culture, 117; government, 116; militarism, 115–16, 117; navy, 123; Persian Empire, war against, 120; social structure, 115–16; women, 116
special economic zones, 904
Spence, Johnathan D., 462
spheres of influence, 706, 830; in China, 715
Sphinx, *p55,* 46
Spice Islands, 440, 443
spice trade, 434, 440, 474
Spielberg, Steven, 850
Spindler, Konrad, 20
spinning jenny, 598, 605
spinning mule, 605
Spirit of Laws, The, 524, 525, 554–55
spirituals, 401
spoons, silver, 335
sports, 632
Sportsman's Sketches, A, 635
Spring and Autumn Annals, 231
Sputnik I, 860, 873, 885
squires, 301
Sri Lanka, 919; independence, 894; religious conflict, 1016
Srivijaya Empire, 355–56
St. Croix, 724
St. Dominic and Albigensians, *ptg307*
St. Jacob, *p255*
St. John, 724
St. Kitts, 444
St. Lawrence River, 444
St. Lawrence Seaway, 889
St. Mary of Zion Church, *p186*
St. Paul's Cathedral, *p541,* 540
St. Peter's Basilica, 408, 411, 416
St. Petersburg, Russia, 499, 501, 694
St. Stephen's Cathedral, 580
St. Thomas, 724
stagflation, 889
stained glass, *p325*
stained glass windows, 303–04
stala, *p385*
stalemate, 907
Stalin, Joseph, 789–91; de-Stalinization, 872–73; dictatorship, 790–91; Germany, alliance with, 826; Germany, policy toward, 828; postwar plans, 865; at Potsdam, 849; purges, 768, 791; Trotsky, Leon, struggle with, 789; world opinion, 865
Stalingrad, Soviet Union, 842, 843
Stamp Act, 548
standardization of parts, 597
standard of living, defined, 979
Stanley, Henry M., *p708, q709,* 707
Stanton, Elizabeth Cady, 665
starvation, 629
statistics, 1023
statue, Spartan, *p115*
Statute of Apprentices, 488
Statute of Westminster, 779
steam boats, 603, 606; in Japan, 597
steam engine, 596, 598, 606
Stearns, Peter, 901
Steel, *ptg608*
steel drums, p401
steel industry, 598, 606, 610, 664; Japan, 899; Latin America, 976
Steen, Jan, 442
Stein, Gertrude, 772
Steinbeck, John, 773
steppe, 258–59
Step Pyramid, 48
stereotypes, 473, 503
sterilization, 628
Stoa Poikile, 144
stock exchanges, 448
stockholders, 609
stock market, 775; crash, 768, 777
Stoicism, 144, 165
Stone Age, 24
Stonehenge, *m53,* 15
Stowe, Harriet Beecher, 662
Strategic Arms Limitation Agreement (SALT); *See* SALT I Treaty
Stravinsky, Igor, 775
stream of consciousness, 772
Strepsiades, 134
strikes, *p778,* 616; general strikes, 779
Structure of the Human Body, The, 519
Stuart, Mary; *See* Mary Queen of Scots
stupas, *p209,* 210
subcontinent, 66
submarine warfare, 751, 760, 842
Sub-Saharan Africa, 187–88; climate and geography, 184–85; European imperialism, 709–10; independence, 931–32
suburbs, 632, 883
Sudan; British imperialism, 708, 929; early civilization, 185
Sudetenland, 829
Sudras, 204
Suez Canal, 702, 707, 708; British control, 799; nationalization of, 948, 953
Suez crisis, 953
suffering, in Buddhism, 210
suffrage. *See* voting rights, women
suffragists, 650-51, 665
sugarcane, 440, 444
Suharto, General, 915
Sui dynasty, 346
Sukarno, Achmed, 915
Sukhanov, N.N., 756
Sukhothai Historic Park, *p355*
Sukhothai kingdom, 355
Sulayman, Mansa, 192
Suleiman I, *p458, q457,* 454, 456–57
Sulla, Lucius Cornelius, 162
sultan, defined, 457
sultanates, 459
Sumatra, 355
Sumer. *See* Sumerian civilization
Sumerian civilization, *m60,* 59–61; afterlife, 61; art, *p59;* cuneiform, invention of, 44; first cities, 15; government, 59–60; kings, 60; mythology, 35; number system, 242; religion, 61; social structure, 60; summary, 98; technology, 61; writing, 60
Summa Theologica, 327
summit meetings, 872, 873
Sun Also Rises, The, 770, 772
Sunday Afternoon on the Island of La Grande Jatte, A, 639
sundial, *p85,* 61
Sundiata: An Epic of Old Mali, 189
Sundiata Keita, 191
Sung, Kim Il, 906-07
Sun King. *See* Louis XIV, king of France
Sunni Muslims, 279, 342, 459; Kurds, 1016
Sun Yat-sen, *q716,* 804
superpowers; arms race, 873; defined, 864; nonaligned nations, 917, 942; rivalry, 871, 874
Supreme Command of the Allied Powers (SCAP), 896
Supreme Court, ruling on segregation, 887
surgery, 628; Muslim development, 286
surrealism, 773
Survival of the fittest; *See* Darwin, Charles
Suryavarman II, Khmer king, 352, 353
Susa, 142
Susanowo, 360
Suwa, Gen, 21
Swahili language, 195
Sweden; in European Union, 1013; Hapsburgs, war against, 494; Russia, war against, 499, 501
Swedes; Eastern Slavs, war against, 258, 263
Swing, The, *ptg639*
swing music, 770, 775
Switzerland, 681; Burgundy, war against, 333; Calvinism, 425; Protestantism, 418
Sykes-Picot Agreement, 761
syllogism, 137
symbolism, 635, 638
Symonds, Stacy, *p386*
symphonies, 635
Symphony From the New World, 635
symposium, 123
synagogues, 86
syndicates, 783
Syria, 48, 80, 91; in Arab League, 950; Arab occupation, 255; feudal states, 319; French mandate, 764; independence, 948, 950; Islamic conquest, 277; Israel, relations with, 954, 957, 962–63; Lebanon, occupation of, 958, 963; in Roman Republic, 161; rule by Ptolemy, 142; rule by Seleucus, 143; travel from China, 347; Turkey, conflict over water, 964; in United Arab Republic, 953; water shortage, 964

T

Tabor, Mount, 84
Tabuchi, Kyoichi, 896
Tacitus, 170
Taft, William Howard, 815
Tagore, Rabindranath, *q460*
Tahiti, 639, 922
Tai Cong, 346, 347, 354

Taika reforms, 362
Taiping Rebellion, 467, 713, 715
Taira family, 363
Taiwan, 716, 901; occupation by Manchus, 465; status, 905
Tajikistan, 1003
Taj Mahal, *p460,* 460
Taking Leave of a Friend, 366
Taksin, Phraya, 477
Tale of Genji, The, 363
Tale of the Heike, The, 364
Talisman, The, 636
Talmud, 172
Tamara, Queen of Georgia, 252, 257
Tamarindito, 386
Tamerlane. *See* Timur Lenk
Tamils, 919, 1016
Tang dynasty, 69, 340, 346–48, 354; decline, 346, 348; establishment, 346
Tangun, 358
tanks, 748, 831
Tanzania, 932; early trade, 195; in the 1990s, 938
Tao, 225
tapestries, *p309*
Tarquins, 156
Tarquin the Proud, 156
tarring and feathering, *ctn549*
Tashkent, 281
Tasmania, 654; human prehistory, 24
Tatars. *See* Mongol Empire
tattoos, 41
taxation; direct tax, 548; duties, 546; of English colonial goods, 546–50; France, 561; income taxes, 407; Indian salt tax, 794; under Louis XIV, 492–93; in medieval France, 312; of non-Muslims, 458; by popes, 408; Roman Empire, *p176;* in Russia, 501; in Turkey, 797
Taylor, Frederick, 609
Tchaikovsky, Peter, 635
tea ceremony, Japanese, 365
Teatro San Cassano, 472
technology, 14, 18, 20, 24; Cro-Magnon, 28; development of, *c30;* hominid, 26–27; household, 771; since 1945, 1021
Tehran, 459
telegraph, 609; wireless, 607, 611
telephone, *p607,* 611
telescope, *p513,* 510
Telestar, 860
television, impact on society, 883
Tell, William, 635
Temple in Jerusalem, 83, 85; rededication by Maccabees, 143
Temujin. *See* Genghis Khan
Ten Commandments, 84, 249
Ten Hours Act, 622, 624
Tennis Court Oath, 562
Tenochtitlán, 372, 388–89, 441
Teotihuacán, 383
terra-cotta, *p191,* 187
terror famine, 788
terrorism; Japan, 899; Libyan links, 936
Tertullian, *q167*
Testelin, Henri, 515
test taking, 197
Tet, 909
Tetzel, John, 416
Texacatlipoca, 383
Texas, 751
Texas, Republic of, 660
Texcoco, Lake, 388
textile industry, 604–05; demand for cotton, 663; first mill, *p597;* introduction in U.S., 607; inventions, 605; mill girls, 615; working conditions, 614; working hours, 624
textiles, ancient Greece, 113
Thaddeus, Apostle, 410
Thailand, 476–77, 914; Burma, conflict with, 477; European contact, 476–77; Khmer people, conquest by, 352; Thai people, 355
Thai people, 351, 355; capture of Angkor Wat, 353
Thales of Miletus, 128, 138
Thatcher, Margaret, 1010–11
theater, development of, 111; English Renaissance, 412, 414; Greek, *p129,* 132–34; Hellenistic, 145; Japanese, 358
Thebes, 48, 124, 140–41
thematic maps, 451
Themistocles, *p120,* 120, 122
theocracy, 48; defined, 418
Theodora, Byzantine Empress, *p246,* 247, 251
Theodora, Empress of Byzantium, 246
Theodosius I, 173, 175, 177
theology, 251
Theravada Buddhism, 210
Thermidor, 568
Thermopylae, 120
thespian, 129
Third Estate, 561, 562
Third Reich, 786
Third Republic, French, 646, 659
Thirteen Classics, 231
Thirty Years' War, *p494,* 247, 480, 494–95; influence on Germany, 681
Thousand and One Nights, A, 287
Three Kingdoms, *m371,* 358
Three Musketeers, The, 635
Thrower, Rayner, 446
Thucydides, *q122,* 112, 137–38
Thuku, Harry, 794, 800
Thutmose III, 49
Tiamat, 35
Tiananmen Square, 904–05
Tian Shan mountains, 69
Tiberius. *See* Gracchus, Tiberius
Tiber River, 156
Tibet, 904; China, war against, 348; occupation by Manchus, 465
Tibeto-Burmans, 354
Tigran II, king of Armenia, 256
Tigre, Ethiopia, 938
Tigris and Euphrates Rivers, 32, 58
Tikal, 385–86
Tilden, Bill, 771
tile, Turkish, *p272*
Timbuktu, 191, 192, 193; Great Mosque, *p190*
Time of Troubles, 499
time zones, 891
Timur Lenk, *p345,* 342, 409; invasion of India, 459–60
tin, 34
Tiridates III, king of Armenia, 257
tithes, 561
Titian, 423
Tito, Josip Broz, 875, 1008–09
Titoism, 875
Titus, Arch of, *p169*
Tlaloc, *p382*
Tlateloco, 389
tobacco, 444
Todaiji Temple, 362
Tokugawa shogunate, 468–72; ethics, 470; relations with daimyos, 469; social structure, 469–70
Tokyo, Japan, 469
Tolstoy, Leo, 638
Toltec, 383; influence on Aztec culture, 389
Tomkins, Sally, 660
toolmaking. *See* technology
tools, Neolithic, *p31*
Topa Inca Yupanqui, 389
Torah, *p86,* 86, 172
Tordesillas, Treaty of, 439, 440
Tories, 542; in Great Britain, 649
Toronto, Ontario; immigration to, 890
Torrijos, Omar, 988
totalitarianism, 782
Total War Research Institute, 807
totems, *p378*
Toulouse-Lautrec, Henri de, 639
Touré, Ahmed Sékou, 931–32, 942
Toure, Samory, 709
tournaments, *p298,* 299–300
Tours, Battle of, 277, 279, 295
Toussaint-Louverture, François, *p513,* 667–68
Tower Mosque, *p274*
Tower of London, *p329*
towns. *See* cities
Toyokuni, U., 363
trade; balance of, 448; barter system, 82, 323; deficit, 889, 899, 900, 998; development of, 34, 80–82; export goods, 449; free trade, 978; protectionism, 900; quotas, 900; routes, *m339,* 434; by sea, *p433,* 113; special economic zones, 904; trade deficit, 998; triangular, 444; triangular route, *m393;* world trade, 1018. *See also* individual countries, empires, etc.
Trade Disputes Act, 779
Trafalgar, Battle of, 576
tragedies, 132, 134
Trailok, King of Thailand, 476
trains. *See* railroads
Trajan, 165
Transjordan. *See* Jordan
Transvaal, 711
Tran Van Dinh, 909
travel, 630–31; Ibn Battuta, 192; use of mathematics, 242
Travels, *q561*
Travels of Marco Polo, The, 342
treasure, *p434,* 447
Treatise on Toleration, 524
Treaty of. *See* specific locations: (Paris, Treaty of)
trench warfare, 747, 750
Trés Riches Heures du Duc de Berry, *ptg299*
Trevithick, Richard, 606
triangular trade route, *m393,* 444
Tribonian, 248
tribunes, 157
trigonometry, 285
trilogy, 132
Tripartite Pact, 841
Tripitaka Koreana, 359
Triple Alliance, 736, 740
Triple Entente, 736, 740
Tripoli; British capture of, 843; Italian imperialism, 708–09
triumvirate, 163
Trois Glorieuses, Les, 655
Trojan horse, 108–10
Trojan Women, The, 128, 132, 134
Trotsky, Leon, *q756,* 759; philosophy toward revolution, 789; Stalin, struggle with, 789
troubadours, *p325,* 327
Troy, 108, 109, 132
Trudeau, Pierre Elliott, 890, 1017
Truman, Harry S; at Potsdam, 849; Stalin, opinion of, 865; Truman Doctrine, *q868*

Truman administration; communism, policy toward, 866, 868; foreign policy, 866–69
Truman Doctrine, 866, 868
Trumbull, John, 553
Trung sisters, 354
Trusteeship Council, 865
truth, 135–37
tsar. *See* czar
Tsuki-yumi, 360
Tsunoda, Ryusaku, 358
Tudjman, Franjo, 1015
Tudor, Henry. *See* Henry VII, king of England
Tudor dynasty, 329, 333, 414, 485
Tula, 383
tulips, 495
Tunis, 708
Tunisia, 82, 708
Turgenev, Ivan, 635
Turkana, Lake, Kenya, 23
Turkey, 697; after World War II, 953; Balkan League, war against, 698; fundamentalism, Muslim, 965; Iraq, conflict over water, 964; irrigation, 964; Kurds, policy toward, 1016; reform, 796–97; republic declared, 797; Syria, conflict over water, 964; Truman Doctrine, 868; U.S. missiles in, 874, 984
Turkish language, 345
Turkmenistan, 1003
Turks; conquest by Mongols, 344; revolt against Chinese, 348
Turks, Ottoman. *See* Ottoman Empire
Turks, Seljuk, 255, 257, 281, 342–43; Byzantine Empire, threat to, 319; crusader Palestine, conquest of, 320; Jerusalem, conquest of, 319
Turner, Frederick W. III, 374
Turner, Michael, 600
Turner, William, 752
Tuscany, 677, 678
Tussaud, Madame, 569
Tutankhamen, 51, 54
Tutsi, 938
Twelve Tables, 157
Twenties, 770–75; changing national lifestyle, 774; digest, 854–55; fads, 771; France, 779–80; Germany, 783–86; Great Britain, 778–89; Italy, 781–83; Soviet Union, 788–91; United States, 776–78
Twenty-One Demands, 807
Twilight in the Forbidden City, 713
Two Treatises of Government, 523
type, moveable, 416
tyranny, 112, 114
Tyre, 80, 82, 90

U

Ubadah, *q270*
U-boats. *See* submarine warfare
Uganda, 932; in the 1990s, 938
ukiyo-e, 472
Ukraine, 247, 759, 790; in Commonwealth of Independent States, 1001; ethic origins, 259; Nuclear Nonproliferation Treaty, 1003; reforms and unrest, 1003; settlement by Swedes, 296; Soviet liberation of, 847; terror famine, 790
Ulema, 457
Ullah, Najib, *q283*
Ulster, 779
ultimatum, defined, 742
ultraroyalists, 655
Ulu Danua temple, *p356*
Ulyanov, Vladimir Ilyich. *See* Lenin, Vladimir Ilyich
Ulysses, 732, 772
Umayyad Empire, 278–80; established, 268
umbrellas, 61
Umbrians, 155
UN; *See* United Nations
UN Children's Fund (UNICEF), 734
Uncle Tom's Cabin, 662
UN Economic and Social Council, 865
UN Educational, Scientific, and Cultural Organizations (UNESCO), 734, 861
unicameral legislatures, 565
UNICEF. *See* UN Children's Fund
Union of South Africa. *See* South Africa
Union of Soviet Socialist Republics (USSR); *See* Soviet Union
United Arab Republic, 953
United League, 716
United Nations (UN), 734, 848–849, 864–65; Australian participation, 921; in Bosnia-Herzegovina, 1015; in Cambodia, 914; Charter, 864; in Congo, 932; in Egyptian-Israeli border, 952–53; in Haiti, 984; human rights declaration, 1022; in Iraq, 960; Japanese military participation, 900; in Korea, 906–07; major bodies, 864–65; in Palestine, 951; peacekeeping missions, 734; South African participation, 934; in Yugoslavia, 1008–09
United Provinces of Central America, 668
United States; Allende, overthrow of, 991–92; alliances, 884; American Revolution, 512; anti-communist sentiment, 882, 883–84; atomic bomb drop, 849–50; Bill of Rights, 555; China, relations with, 903, 905; China, unequal treaties with, 715; civil rights movement, 886–87; Civil War, 646, 663–64; cold war foreign policy, 883–84; computers, 883; Cuba, relations with, 984; disarmament treaty, 778; economy, 777, 888–89; economy, after World War II, 882; economy, 19th century, 663; educational goals, 632–33; expansion, *m664*, 660–62; foreign affairs, 778; France, support for in Vietnam, 909; freedom of religion, 419; global economy, part of, 1018; government spending, 999; Great Britain, policy toward, 576; immigrants, 663; immigration, 630, 660, 665; industrialization, 607, 664; Industrial Revolution, 608; Japan, economic support for, 897; Japan, unequal treaties with, 717; Japan, war against, 841; Japanese investment, 899; Kellogg-Briand Pact, 778; Latin America, interventions in, 816–17; Latin America, relations with, 811–17, 978; League of Nations, rejection of, 734, 776; Lebanon, occupation of, 953; Liberia, influence in, 709; manufacturing, 596–97, 777, 889; Mexico, intervention in, 725; moon landing, 858; Napoleonic France, policy toward, 576; Nicaraguan contras, support for, 986; Pakistan, relations with, 919; Panama, invasion of, 972; Philippines, colonization of, 719; Philippines, military bases in, 921; presidency, 888; recognition of, 552, 554; 1980s and 1990s, 998–99; social changes, 883; in Somalia, 939; Southeast Asia, colonization of, 718–19; Soviet Union, relations with, 999; space program, 883; Taiwan, policy toward, 903; technological development, 883; UN Security Council, 865; urbanization, 632; women's voting rights, 665; World War I, after, 772; World War I, entry into, 736, 751, 760; World War II, entry into, 841; World War II neutrality, 835–36
Universal Declaration of Human Rights, 734, 1022
Universal German Workingman's Association, 687
universities, 316, 326
Upanishads, 202, 206, 207, 212
Upshur, Jiu-Hwa L., 225
Ur, 16, 59, 63, 83
Urban, Pope, 333
Urban II, Pope, *p319*, *q319*, 318, 343
Urban VIII, Pope, 517
urbanization, 631–32
urban planning, 67–68
Urdu, 459
Uriburu, José F., 811, 814–16
Uruk, 59, 61
U.S.A., 773
Usha, 206
U-2 spy plane, 873, 885
USSR. *See* Soviet Union
Utah; Native Americans, 377; U.S. acquisition, 660; women's vote, 665
***Utah* (battleship),** 841
Uthman, 278
utilitarianism, 624
Utnapishtim, 72
Utopia, 414
utopian theory, 594
Utrecht, Treaty of, 493
Uzbekistan, 1003

V

vaccination, 627
Vaisyas, 203
Valla, Lorenzo, 405
Valley of the Kings, 49, 54
Vallon-Pont-d'Arc, France, *p19*, 29
Valmy, France, *q567*
value systems, development of, 35
Vandals, 178, 248
Vanderbilt University, 384
Van Dyck, Anthony, 537
van Eyck, Hubert and Jan, 414
van Gogh, Vincent, 639
Varanasi, India, 209
Vargas, Getúlio, 816
Varieties of Visual Experience, 346
varna, 203, 205, 207; the Buddha's rejection of, 210
vases, Greek, *p109*, *p130*, *p131*, 131
vassals, 299
Vatican, 408
Vaux, Calvert, 632
Vedas, 203, 204
V-E Day, 846, 848. *See also* World War II
Vedic Age, 100, 202, 203
Velasco, Juan, 993
Venetia, 580, 676, 677, 684; control by Austria, 678; unification with Italy, 680
Venezuela; Great Britain, dispute with, 722; independence, 666, 669; oil industry, 813–14
Venice, Italy, 255, 321, 323, 408–09; decline in trade, 448; opera house, 472
Venus, 158
Veracruz, Mexico, 725
Verdi, Giuseppe, *p676*
Verdun, France, 567; attack on, 748
Verdun, Treaty of, 294, 296
Verlaine, Paul, 638
vernacular language, 328
Vernet, Joseph, 561

Verrazano, Giovanni de, 443
Versailles, France, 561, 565
Versailles, Palace of, *p481,* 492
Versailles, Treaty of, 760, 763, 776; Hitler's policy toward, 786; Japan mandates, 804; leading to World War II, 826
Vesalius, Andreas, 519
Vesilind, Prit J., 1004
Vespucci, Amerigo, 438
Vesta, 158
Vestier, Antoine, 568
Vesuvius, Mount, 165–66
veterinary medicine, 232
veto, 157
viceroys, 441, 714
Vichy France, 843
Victor Emmanuel II, king of Sardinia, 676, 677, 678–79; rule over unified Italy, 680
Victor Emmanuel III, king of Italy, 782, 844
Victoria, Australia, 654
Victoria, Queen of Great Britain, 647, 649, 714
Victorian Railway, The, 603
Vienna, Austria, 153, 580; siege by Ottomans, 454
Vienna, Congress of, *p582,* 580–82, 655, 674, 681
Vienna, Old University, *p580*
Viet Cong, 911
Vietminh, 909
Vietnam, 353–54, 909–13; Cambodia, invasion of, 912; conquest by Khmer, 352; division, 909–10; foreign relations, 912; French colonialism, 719, 909; French influence, 476; U.S. direct involvement, 871; U.S., postwar relations with, 894; Vietnam War. *See* Vietnam War. *See also* Indochina
Vietnamization, 886
Vietnam War, *m912, p910,* 910–11; Australian involvement, 921; casualties, 886, 911; Johnson administration policy, 886; opposition to, *p911,* 886, 911; South Vietnam, defeat, 911; Tet offensive, 911
Vikings, 294, 296–97; exploration, *m315;* influence on European economy, 297; leadership of Slavs, 260, 261
Villa, "Pancho", 725
village commons, 601
villages; development of, 31; village life, pre-Industrial Revolution, 601–02. *See also* cities
violin, 529
Virajas, 206
Virgil, *q170*
Virginia Company, 444
Virgin Islands; U.S. acquisition of, 724
Vishnu, *q206,* 204, 353
Visigoths, 178, 248
Visvamitra, *p214*
vitamins, 232
vitascope, *p615*
vizier, grand, 457
V-J Day, 850
Vladimir, Grand Prince of Kiev, 258, 262
Vladimir-Suzdal, 263
Vladimir the Russian Viking, 258
vocations, 417
volcanos, 164-66
Volga River, 258
Volkoff, Vladimir, 258
Voltaire, *p524, q526,* 527
von Arnim, General, 844
von Erlach, Klaus, *q681*
von Zinzendorf, Count, 530
voting rights; African Americans, 664; in France, 657; in Great Britain, 649–50; middle class, 649; secret ballot, 650; western United States, 662; women, 648, 650–51; women, U.S., 665; working class, 625
Voyage of the Emperor Qianlong, p455

W

Wagner, Richard, 688
Waitangi, Treaty of, 652, 654
Wake Island, 845
Walesa, Lech, *p1005,* 1004–05; presidency of Poland, 1007
Wall, Berlin. *See* Berlin Wall
Wallachia, 697
Wall of China; *See* Great Wall of China
Walpole, Robert, *p544*
Waltzing Matilda, 654
Wanganui, New Zealand, 654
Wang Xin, 901
War and Peace, 638
war communism, 788
warfare, 31, 88; advances in, 49, 89; chemical, 254; guerrilla warfare, 679; scorched-earth policy, 577, 838; siege techniques, 344
warlords, 804
War of 1812, 576
War of the Austrian Succession, 497
War of the Spanish Succession, 490, 495
War Powers Limitation Act, 888
Warren, Mercy, *q552*
Warsaw, Poland, 847–48
Warsaw Pact, 870–71
Wars of the Roses, 316, 333
Washington, George, 550, 553, 555
Washington (state), 662
Wasteland, The, 732, 772
water; conservation, 964; demand, 1021; pollution, 1020–21
water frame, 605, 612
Watergate, 888
Waterloo, Battle of, 558, 574, 578
Wat Mahathat, *p355*
Watt, James, 596, 598, 606
wax museums, 569
wealth; accumulation of, 448; distribution of, 624
Wealth of Nations, The, 594, 620, 623
weapons, 14, 28, 31, 254
week, development of, 85
Weeks, Kent, 54
Wei-hui, Prince, 225
Weimar Republic, 775; French ties to, 780
welfare, need for, 777
welfare state, defined, 879
Wellesley, Arthur. *See* Wellington, Duke of
Wellington, Duke of, 574, 576, 578
Wellington, New Zealand, 654
Wen, Emperor, 346
Weser River, 683
We Shall Overcome, 578
Wesley, John, *p530,* 524
West Africa, 189–93; architecture, 192; digest, 238; European imperialism, 709; French West Africa, 709; geography and climate, 185; Ghana, 189–90; Mali, 191–93; music, 400; sculpture, *p189;* self-rule, 709; Songhai, 193; trade, 189, 712
West African Economic Community, 944
West African Pilot, The, 800
West Bank, 962–63; Israeli withdrawal from, 957, 962; Jordanian annexation of, 955; settlement, 964; Six-Day War, 955
West Berlin, 870
Western Australia, 654
Western Civilization, an Urban Perspective, 580, 760
westernization, 718
West Germany; in Common Market, 881; formation, 870; post-World War II development, 880; Soviet Union, relations with, 880–881
West Indies, 441, 444
Westphalia, Treaty of, 494
West River. *See* Xi Jiang
West Virginia (battleship), 841
Wettlin, Margaret, 846
Whampoa Reach, China, *p719*
wheat, 16, 17
wheel, 31, 61
wheelbarrow, invention of, 232
Wheels of Commerce, The, 449
Where do we come from? What are we? Where are we going?, 639
Whig party, 542, 648
White, Tim D., 21
White (Mensheviks), 759
White Man's Burden, The, 706
Whiteside, Frank Reed, 17, 373
Whitlam, Gough, 921
Whitney, Eli, 594, 605, 609
Wick, T.E., 112
Wiesel, Elie, 850
Wilberforce, William, 623
Wildavsky, Aaron, 998
Wilkinson, Tracy, 1014
William I, kaiser, *p686,* 681, 685, 689
William I, king of Prussia, 682, 684
William II, kaiser, 686, 689, 742, 761
William III, kaiser, 686
William III, king of England, *p543,* 542
William of Normandy, 329
William of Orange; *See* William III, king of England
William the Conquerer, 308
William the Conquerer, *p308,* 292, 308–09
Willis, F. Roy, 580
Wilson, Woodrow, 665, 725, 751; Fourteen Points, 760, 762; Peace of Paris, 763; reaction to *Lusitania* sinking, 753; self-determination, 796
Window, The, 966
wine, 154
Winged Victory of Samothrace, *p143*
Winston, Richard, 294
Winter Palace, *p500*
Wise Men of Gotham, The, ctn547
Wittenberg, Germany, 416
Woman With a Parasol–Madame Monet and Her Son, ptg637
women; in ancient Egypt, 52; in Argentina, 990; in Athens, 119, 123; in China, 229; civil rights, 887; in Confucianism, 359; education, 633; first college for, 629; in French Revolution, 565; in the global culture, 1022; in Gupta Empire, 213–14; in Hellenistic culture, 144; in Japan, 808; in Latin America, 976; in Middle Ages, 298; in Middle East, 965; in Minoan civilization, 107; as monarchs, 495–96; in Muslim society, 282–83; in Nigeria, 800; Olympic Games alternative, 134; role in early civilization, 32; in Roman Republic, 158; in Sparta, 116; in Sumerian civilization, 60; in Twenties, 770–71; voting rights, 648, 650–51, 770; voting rights, U.S., 665; working women, 615

Women of the American Revolution, The, 552
Women's Social Political Union (WSPU), 651
Women's Work: The First 20,000 Years, *q26*
Wood, Edward, *p57*
Woods Hole Oceanographic Institution, 754
woof, defined, 605
woolen industry, 602
Woolf, Virginia, 772
Wordsworth, William, 636
work, attitude toward, 450
workers; *See* working class
working class, 613–16; Germany, 687; living conditions, 615–16; political growth, 650; syndicates with employers, 783; theory, 625; voting rights, 625. *See also* labor unions
working conditions; coal mining, *q598,* 614; government regulation of, 622; textile industry, 614
World, My Friends, My Enemies, You, and the Earth, The, 967
World Bank, 1019
World Civilizations, 801
World Ditch, The Making of the Suez Canal, 707
World Upside-down, *ptg442*
World War I, 738–64; begins, 732; Christmas truce, 746; digest, 854; direct cause, 741–42; Eastern front, 748–49; effects of, 770, 738; end, 761; events leading to, 738–40; Germany, blockade of, 749–51; postwar period. *See* Twenties; propaganda, 746–47; reparations, 762–63; Russian involvement during revolution, 757, 759; Schlieffen Plan, 744; sea power, 749–51; stalemate, 746–50, 761; submarine warfare, 751; U.S. entry, 736, 751, 760
World War I: A Frenchman's Recollections, 744
World War II; begins, 733; Britain, Battle of, 833–35; Bulge, Battle of the, 848; casualties, 850; D-Day, 846–47; digest, 856–57; Dunkirk evacuation, 833; events leading to, 826–30; France declares war, 830; German expansion, 828–30; German surrender, 848; Germany invades Austria, 828; Germany invades Czechoslovakia, 828–29; Germany invades France, 833; Germany invades Poland, 830; Germany invades Scandinavia, 831–32; Germany invades Soviet Union, 838; Great Britain, campaign against Italy, 836; Great Britain declares war, 830; Holocaust, 839; Italian campaign, 844–45; Japanese involvement, 824, 841, 845, 849-50; Munich Conference, 829; Nazi-Soviet pact, 829–30; North Africa campaign, 843–44; Pearl Harbor attack, 841; propaganda, 840; resistance movements, 839; roots in World War I, 764; sea warfare, 842–43; submarine warfare, 842; Stalingrad, siege of, 843; strategy, 841; U.S. entry, 838, 841; U.S., support for Britain, 835–36
World Wide Web, 1021–22
Worms, Concordat of. *See* Concordat of Worms
Wren, Christopher, *p540,* 541
Wright, Esmond, 741
Wright, Frank Lloyd, 775
Wright, Orville and Wilbur, 598, 611
writing; in China, 221; development of, 34–35; in East Africa, 195; glyphs, 385; Korean, 359; Maya, 383; Thai, 355
Wu, 71
Wu, Empress, 346, 347
Wudi, 220, 221, 222, 226, 231
Wu Phu, *q228*
Württenberg, 684
Wycliffe, John, 335
Wyoming; U.S. acquisition, 662; women's vote, 665

X

Xavier, Francis, 470
Xerxes, *p93,* 90, 92, 120, 140
Xia dynasty, 69, 70
Xi Jiang River, 69
Xinjiang, occupation by Manchus, 465
X rays, 628
Xuanzang, 348

Y

Yahweh, 83
Yalom, Marilyn, 564
Yalta Conference, 848
Yamamoto, Isoroku, 841
Yamato family, 358
Yang Jian, 346
Yang-shao culture, 70
Yangtze River. *See* Chang Jiang River
Yankee Doodle, 554, 578
Yao, 70
yarn, 597
Yaroslav, 262
yasa, 344
Yathrib, 272, 273
Yellow River, 70. *See also* Huang He
Yeltsin, Boris, *p1003;* Chechnyan separatism, policy toward, 1016; against 1991 coup attempt, 1001; rise to power, 1000; U.S., relations with, 999
Yemen, 950
yeshivas, 172
Yi dynasty, 340, 359
yin and yang, 227, 232
Yi-Sun-Shin, 359
yoga, 207
Yong Le, 463–64
Yoritomo Minamoto, 363
York, House of, 333
York family, 414
Yorktown, Virginia, 552, 554
Yoruba, 182, 799; art, *p709*
Young, Arthur, *q561*
Young Italy, 676, 677, 679
Young Ottomans, 458
Young Turks, 796
Yu, 69
Yuan dynasty, 346, 350; overthrow, 462
Yüan Shigai, 804
Yucatan Peninsula, 380
Yugoslavia, 739; breakup, 1008–09; communism, 865; established, 763; under Tito, 875
yurts, *p344,* 343
Yu the Great, 70

Z

za, 364
Zaghlul, Saad, 799
Zagros Mountains, *p16*
zaibatsu, 808, 897
Zaire; copper industry, 937–38; in the 1990s, 937–38
Zaire River, 185, 709
Zama, 159, 160
Zambia, 933
Zanzibar, 195
Zapata, Emiliano, 725, 981
Zapatistas, 981
Zapotec culture, 119
Zedillo Ponce de Léon, Ernesto, 981
zemstvos, 692
Zen, 365
Zeno, 144
Zeppelin, Ferdinand von, 611
zero, 243, 285
Zeus; chief Greek deity, 110; Jupiter, compared to, 158; oaths sworn to, 119; Olympic Games honoring, 134; role, 111
Zhang Heng, 226
Zhang Qian, 218, 222
Zhao Kuangyin, 348
Zheng He, 464
Zhong Guo, 69
Zhou, Wai, 804
Zhou Dakuan, *q352*
Zhou dynasty, *m221,* 69, 71, 220–21
Zhou Enlai, 902
Zhu Yuanzhang, 350, 462
Zia, Khalida, 919
ziggurat, 59
Zimbabwe, 705; independence, 933; Marxism and free enterprise, 939. *See also* Rhodesia
Zimmermann telegram, 744, 751
Zinzendorf, Count von, 530
Zion, 318
Zionism, 798, 951
Zipangu. *See* Japan
Zollverein, 681, 682, 687
Zoroaster, 92–93
Zoroastrianism, 132, 178
Zulu, 711
Zurich, Switzerland, 418
Zweig, Stefan, *q738*
Zwingli, Huldrych, 418
Zysk, Kenneth, 202

A

abbess/abadesa superiora de un convento (pág. 305)
abbot/abad superior de un monasterio (pág. 304)
absolutism/absolutismo sistema político en el cual un monarca (o grupo) tiene poder supremo e ilimitado, o teoría que sustenta tal sistema (pág. 482)
acupuncture/acupuntura técnica tradicional de la medicina china que utiliza agujas finas en puntos vitales del cuerpo (pág. 232)
age set/grupo etario en el África tradicional, un grupo de varones o hembras de edad semejante que adquieren destrezas y siguen juntos a través de las distintas etapas de la vida (pág. 188)
ahimsa/ahimsa doctrina hindú de no-violencia hacia todo lo que tiene vida (pág. 207)
alchemist/alquimista persona que practica la alquimia, forma primitiva de la química, que enfatizaba cambios en las sustancias, como la conversión del plomo en oro (pág. 520)
alliance system/sistema de alianzas serie de acuerdos sobre la defensa en que participan dos o más naciones (pág. 740)
alphabet/alfabeto sistema de símbolos o caracteres que representan los sonidos de un lenguaje (pág. 82)
amphora/ánfora jarrón griego alto, de dos asas (pág. 131)
anarchy/anarquía ausencia de autoridad política (pág. 692)
animism/animismo creencia de que los espíritus residen tanto en los seres vivos como en las cosas inanimadas (págs. 351, 476)
anthropologist/antropólogo científico que estudia las características físicas y culturales de los seres humanos y sus antecesores (pág. 20)
apartheid/apartheid política oficial de estricta segregación y discriminación racial practicada en África del Sur desde 1948 hasta principios de la década de 1990 (pág. 934)
appeasement/apaciguamiento la política de hacer concesiones a un enemigo en potencia a fin de mantener la paz (pág. 829)
apportion/prorratear dividir en partes proporcionales (pág. 648)
apprentice/aprendiz persona que trabaja para un maestro a fin de aprender un oficio, arte o negocio (pág. 325)
aqueduct/acueducto canal construido para conducir las aguas (pág. 168)
arabesque/arabesco complejos diseños típicos del arte islámico que combinaban plantas entrelazadas y patrones geométricos (pág. 286)
"Arabic numerals"/números arábigos símbolos de numeración diseñados por matemáticos en Gupta, India (pág. 214)
arbitration/arbitraje proceso de poner fin a una disputa sometiéndola a una tercera parte imparcial (pág. 722)
archaeologist/arqueólogo científico que estudia pueblos y culturas de la Antigüedad (pág. 20)
archipelago/archipiélago grupo o cadena de islas (págs. 351, 920)
aristocrat/aristócrata miembro de la nobleza o de la clase alta (pág. 113)
armada/armada escuadra de buques de guerra (pág. 483)
armistice/armisticio acuerdo para dar fin a una guerra (pág. 761)
arms race/carrera armamentista la competencia durante la Guerra Fría entre Estados Unidos y la Unión Soviética para fortalecer sus respectivas fuerzas militares y armamentos (pág. 871)
artifact/artefacto histórico objeto fabricado o usado por los humanos, tal como una herramienta, adorno o artículo de alfarería (pág. 20)
artisan/artesano persona diestra en un arte manual (pág. 33)
atomic theory/teoría atómica idea científica de que la materia está hecha de partículas pequeñas llamadas átomos (pág. 628)
atrocity/atrocidad acción cruel y maligna, tal como la tortura (pág. 1015)
autocracy/autocracia gobierno regido por una persona con poder ilimitado (pág. 690)
automation/automatización proceso por el cual dispositivos electrónicos o máquinas hacen el trabajo antes realizado por humanos (pág. 883)
autonomy/autonomía gobierno propio (pág. 1008)

B

balance of power/equilibrio de poder la distribución del poder entra naciones rivales de modo que ninguna predomine (pág. 489)
balance of trade/equilibrio comercial diferencia en valor entre lo que una nación importa y lo que exporta durante un período de tiempo (pág. 448)
bard/bardo poeta que narra cuentos por medio del canto (pág. 108)
baroque/barroco estilo artístico recargado y dramático, desarrollado en Europa a mediados del siglo XVI (pág. 424)
barter/trueque sistema de comercio en el cual se

intercambiaban bienes y no dinero (pág. 82)

bazaar/bazar mercado público en una ciudad islámica (pág. 284)

belligerent/beligerante enfrascado en una guerra (pág. 746)

bishop/obispo jefe regional de la Iglesia Cristiana primitiva, con autoridad sobre una diócesis y otros miembros del clero (pág. 174)

blitz/ataque relámpago serie de ataques aéreos intensos (pág. 834)

blitzkrieg/guerra relámpago ofensiva nazi rápida e inesperada (pág. 831)

bloc/bloque grupo de facciones políticas o agrupación de naciones que actúan conjuntamente (pág. 871)

bourgeoisie/burguesía la clase media, entre los aristócratas y los trabajadores (págs. 561, 625)

boyar/boyardo un noble propietario de tierras en la Rusia primitiva (págs. 260, 499)

boycott/boicot rechazo a comprar ciertos productos como protesta por alguna acción (pág. 548)

budget deficit/déficit presupuestario la cantidad por la cual los gastos del gobierno exceden a sus ingresos (pág. 998)

buffer state/estado parachoques territorio neutral entre potencias rivales, destinado a prevenir un conflicto (pág. 582)

bullion/lingote oro o plata en forma de barras o planchas (pág. 448)

bureaucracy/burocracia un grupo de funcionarios del gobierno encabezado por un administrador (pág. 48)

C

cabinet/gabinete grupo de consejeros de un gobernante o jefe de estado (pág. 544)

calculus/cálculo sistema de matemáticas desarrollado por Newton para analizar cantidades variables (pág. 519)

caliph/califa líder supremo de Islam, escogido como sucesor de Mahoma (pág. 277)

calligraphy/caligrafía el arte de escribir con letra hermosa (pág. 286)

campesino/campesino agricultor pobre de Latinoamérica que trabaja en una finca (pág. 975)

capital/capital dinero disponible para invertir en negocios (pág. 604)

cardinal/cardenal eclesiástico de alto rango en la Iglesia Católica designado por el Papa (pág. 306)

cartel/cartel convenio entre empresas que ofrecen el mismo producto, que regula los precios de sus miembros y su producción (págs. 955, 993)

cartographer/cartógrafo persona que dibuja mapas (pág. 436)

cash-and-carry policy/política de compra al contado programa de la Segunda Guerra Mundial que permitía a Gran Bretaña pagar en efectivo y transportar desde los Estados Unidos las mercancías que necesitara (pág. 836)

cash crop/cosecha comercial producto agrícola cultivado para la venta o el intercambio, no usado por el agricultor (pág. 943)

cavalry/caballería cuerpo de soldados a caballo (pág. 221)

cell theory/teoría celular teoría científica que sostiene que las pequeñas unidades llamadas células constituyen todas las cosas vivas (pág. 626)

chancellor/canciller título del primer ministro en algunos países europeos (pág. 685)

charter/carta constitucional documento formal que concede el derecho al gobierno propio (pág. 326)

chateaux/castillos un tipo de fortaleza (pág. 413)

chinampas/chinampas islas artificiales construidas por los aztecas para utilizar como jardines (pág. 388)

chivalry/caballería código de conducta de los caballeros medievales basado en ideales de honor y cortesía (pág. 301)

choreographer/coreógrafo persona que crea bailes (pág. 775)

chronicle/crónica relación que registra eventos en el orden en que éstos sucedieron (pág. 288)

circumnavigation/circunnavegación viaje marítimo completamente alrededor de algo, como por ejemplo, el mundo (pág. 439)

citizen/ciudadano en la antigua Gracia, persona que participaba del gobierno en una ciudad-estado (pág. 112)

city-state/ciudad-estado un estado independiente que consistía en una ciudad y las tierras y aldeas que la rodeaban (pág. 59)

civil disobedience/desobediencia civil rechazo sin violencia a obedecer una ley o práctica considerada injusta (pág. 802)

civil service/servicio civil sistema mediante el cual puestos del gobierno son concedidos mediante exámenes (pág. 224)

civilization/civilización sociedad altamente organizada caracterizada por el conocimiento avanzado del comercio, gobierno, artes, ciencia y a menudo, lenguaje escrito (pág. 32)

clan/clan grupo unido por lazos familiares (págs. 342, 939)

classical/clásico que describe el estilo artístico de las antiguas Gracia y Roma, caracterizado por el equilibrio, la elegancia y la simpleza (pág. 130)

classicism/clasicismo estilo y actitudes derivadas de los ideales de las antiguas Gracia y Roma (pág. 528)

clergy/clero personas, tales como los sacerdotes, que tienen autoridad para conducir servicios religiosos (pág. 249)

coalition/coalición alianza temporal de facciones políticas en desacuerdo (págs. 780, 879)

cold war/Guerra Fría período de tensión política en el que Estados Unidos y la Unión Soviética rivalizaron por obtener el dominio mundial sin llegar a un conflicto armado real (pág 864)

collective bargaining/convenios colectivos negociaciones entre los delegados sindicales y los patronos acerca de asuntos (pág. 616)

collective security/seguridad colectiva los intereses de defensa comunes a varias naciones frente a un enemigo (págs. 826, 1012)

collectivization/colectivización bajo Stalin, sistema de unificar tierras en grandes fincas que pertenecían al gobierno y las trabajaban los campesinos (pág. 790)

colon/colon colonizador francés en la colonia de Algeria (pág. 931)

colony/colonia establecimiento de personas que están fuera de su país, enlazado a la madre patria por el comercio y el control directo del gobierno (págs. 82, 475, 706)

comedy/comedia historia o representación que se propone entretener y divertir usualmente con un desenlace feliz (pág. 134)

common law/derecho consuetudinario sistema de leyes inglesas basadas en la tradición y decisiones de la corte, no en leyes específicas (pág. 309)

commonwealth/mancomunidad nación o estado gobernado por el pueblo o representantes del mismo (pág. 539)

commune/comuna Un grupo de personas que viven en comuna, con posesión y uso colectivo de la sociedad (pág. 902)

communism/comunismo según las teorías de Marx y Engels, una sociedad sin distinciones de clases ni propiedad privada (págs. 625, 758)

concentration camp/campo de concentración recinto donde se encierra a prisioneros políticos o a refugiados (pág. 786)

confederation/confederación alianza flexible o unión de varios estados o grupos (págs. 82, 378, 554)

conquistador/conquistador aventurero o soldado español en las Américas (pág. 441)

conscription/reclutamiento llamado obligatorio al servicio militar (págs. 569, 740)

constitutional monarchy/monarquía constitucional estado en el cual el poder del monarca está limitado por una constitución (pág. 541)

consul/cónsul en la antigua Roma, uno de los dos magistrados que dirigían al poder ejecutivo (pág. 157)

containment/contención política de Estados Unidos proyectada para prevenir la propagación del comunismo (pág. 816)

contraband/contrabando mercancías que no pueden ser transportadas legalmente, particularmente en tiempo de guerra (pág. 749)

convoy/convoy grupo de naves mercantes que viajan junto a buques de guerra para su seguridad (pág. 760)

cooperative/cooperativa sociedad de fincas que pertenece y es administrada por sus miembros, los cuales comparten sus ganancias (pág. 812)

cordon sanitaire/cordón sanitario línea de cuarentena o estados "parachoques" (pág. 764)

corporate state/estado corporativo concepto de Mussolini de un gobierno con representación de corporaciones, y no de partidos políticos (pág. 783)

corporation/corporación organización de empresas que es propiedad de socios que compran acciones y que es dirigida por administradores profesionales (pág. 609)

cortes/cortes asamblea de los nobles, el clero y los funcionarios del pueblo en la España medieval; también, el parlamento en la España moderna (pág. 333)

count/conde noble que actuaba como funcionario local dentro del imperio de los francos (pág. 295)

coup d'état/golpe de estado derrocamiento repentino de líderes del gobierno por un pequeño grupo (págs. 525, 657)

covenant/convenio pacto o acuerdo solemne (pág. 83)

covert/encubierto secreto (pág. 986)

Creole/criollo persona de ascendencia europea nacida en la América Latina colonial (pág. 667)

Crusades/Cruzadas expediciones militares por cristianos europeos en los siglos XI al XIII para conquistar la Tierra Santa de manos de los musulmanes (pág. 318)

cubism/cubismo estilo artístico del siglo XX que representa las formas naturales por medio de formas geométricas (pág. 773)

cultural diffusion/difusión cultural intercambio de bienes, ideas y costumbres entre diferentes culturas (pág. 27)

culture/cultura modo de vida de un pueblo en un tiempo determinado, que incluye su lenguaje, conducta y creencias (pág. 24)

culture system/sistema de cultivo en las colonias holandesas en Asia, sistema de trabajos forzados para obtener materias primas (pág. 718)

cuneiform/cuneiforme sistema de escritura sumerio que utilizaba símbolos en forma de cuña (pág. 60)

czar/zar (de "caesar") título adoptado por los gobernantes de Rusia desde finales del siglo XV (pág. 264)

D

D-Day/Día D día de la invasión de Normandía, Francia por los Aliados (junio 6 de 1944)(pág. 846)

daimyo/daimyo poderoso noble local en el Japón feudal (pág. 363)

datus/datus gobernantes locales en las Filipinas (pág. 475)

death squad/escuadrón de la muerte en la América Central, una banda de asesinos contratados por terratenientes para asesinar a sus contrincantes políticos (pág. 987)

deforastation/deforestación proceso de talar los árboles y desmontar los bosques en grandes extensiones de tierra (pág. 1020)

deism/deísmo filosofía religiosa del siglo XVIII basada en la razón y en la idea de leyes naturales (pág. 523)

deity/deidad un dios o diosa (pág. 31)

democracy/democracia forma de gobierno en la cual los ciudadanos ejercen el poder (pág. 114)

depression/depresión situación económica caracterizada por la quiebra de los negocios y el desempleo (pág. 609)

desalination/desalinización proceso de extraer la sal del agua de mar para producir agua potable (pág.964)

desertification/desertización proceso por el cual una tierra fértil se convierte en un desierto (pág. 944)

developed country/país desarrollado nación industrializada, con una tecnología avanzada (pág. 1019)

developing country/país en desarrollo país en proceso de industrialización, donde el pueblo mantiene frecuentemente los estilos de vida tradicionales (pág. 1019)

détente/detente la relajación de las tensiones entre los Estados Unidos y la Unión Soviética en la década de 1970 (pág. 874)

dharma/dharma deberes y derechos de los miembros de cada clase en la sociedad hindú tradicional (pág. 173)

Diaspora/Diáspora término que se refiere a la dispersión de las comunidades judías fuera de su patria original después de la Cautividad de Babilonia (pág. 86)

dictator/dictador en la antigua Roma, líder a quien se daba poder temporal absoluto durante una crisis (pág. 157)

dictatorship/dictadura gobierno encabezado por un gobernante con poder absoluto (pág. 574)

dictatorship of the proletariat/dictadura del proletariado en la antigua Unión Soviética, control teórico del estado por la clase trabajadora (pág. 789)

direct tax/impuesto directo impuesto pagado directamente al gobierno (pág. 548)

disarmament/desarme limitación o reducción de las fuerzas militares y de las armas (pág. 778)

disciple/discípulo activo seguidor de un maestro (pág. 172)

disenfranchised/privado del derecho al sufragio negado el derecho al voto (pág. 649)

disengagement/desembarazo acto de liberarse o retirarse uno mismo de una situación (pág. 955)

dissident/disidente persona que critica abiertamente las maneras de actuar de su gobierno (pág. 874)

divine right/derecho divino teoría politica que mantiene que un gobernante deriva su autoridad directamente de Dios y es responsable de sus actos sólo ante Dios (págs. 482, 536)

division of labor/división del trabajo técnica de producción en la cual cada obrero realiza un trabajo especializado (pág. 609)

doge/dux líder electo de la república en las ciudades-estados de Venecia y Génova (pág. 408)

domain/dominio territorio perteneciente a un gobernante (pág. 143)

domesticate/domesticar adiestrar animales o adaptar plantas para satisfacer necesidades humanas (pág. 30)

domestic system/sistema doméstico sistema primitivo de trabajo industrial en el cual los obreros producían los bienes en sus hogares (pág. 602)

dominion/dominio nación de gobierno propio dentro del Imperio Británico; más tarde, mancomunidad (pág. 654)

domino theory/teoría del dominó creencia de la época de la Guerra Fría por la que si una nación se hacía comunista, sus vecinos seguirían el ejemplo (pág. 910)

double-digit inflation/inflación de dos dígitos rápida elevación de los precios en un diez por ciento o más (pag. 889)
dual monarchy/monarquía dual dos estados con un solo monarca (pág. 696)
duma/duma legislatura nacional rusa (pág. 694)
duty/arancel de aduana impuesto sobre productos importados (pág. 546)
dvorianie/dvorianie nueva clase de nobleza rusa dueña de tierras, establecida por Pedro I el Grande (pág. 501)
dynasty/dinastía sucesión de gobernantes que pertenecen a la misma familia (pág. 47)

E

economy/economía sistema por el cual bienes y servicios son producidos y distribuidos para satisfacer las necesidades del pueblo (pág. 33)
ellipse/elipse curva cerrada ovalada (no redonda) (pág. 517)
elite/elite un grupo de personas selecto (pág. 975)
emancipation/emancipación acción de conceder la libertad legalmente (pág. 691)
embargo/embargo orden restringiendo el tráfico comercial (págs. 889, 960, 1015)
emigration/emigración abandono del país o región natal para establecerse en otro lugar (pág. 630)
émigré/émigré emigrado o persona que huyó de Francia durante la Revolución (pág. 566)
empire/imperio grupo de territorios o naciones regidos por un solo emperador o gobierno (pág. 49)
enclave/enclave pequeño territorio completamente rodeado por el territorio de otro país o grupo (pag. 1016)
enclosure movement/expansión por apropiación tendencia de los grandes terratenientes a cercar e incluir tierras comunes públicas y privadas en sus propios terrenos (pág. 603)
enlightened despot/déspota iluminista monarca que comenzaba cambios sociales basados en las ideas del iluminismo (pág. 527)
entente/entente acuerdo, pero no alianza formal, entre naciones (pág. 740)
entrepreneur/empresario persona que corre riesgos para fundar un negocio (págs. 448, 556, 604)
epic/poema épico poema extenso que celebraba las hazañas de un héroe legendario o histórico (pág. 203)
estate/estado una de las tres clases sociales distintas en Francia durante el Siglo XVIII: el clero, la nobleza y los plebeyos (el Tercer Estado) (pág. 560)
ethics/ética sistema de principios morales que guían la conducta (pág. 225)
ethnic cleansing/limpieza étnica término usado en el conflicto de Bosnia, para referirse a una política de traslado forzoso o de dar muerte a los miembros de otro grupo étnico (pág. 1015)
evolution/evolución teoría de que las especies de seres vivos se transforman a través de largos períodos de tiempo (pág. 626)
excommunication/excomunión exclusión formal de la membresía o de su participación en una iglesia (pág. 306)
exodus/éxodo emigración de un grupo numeroso de personas (pag. 84)
extended family/familia completa grupo familiar que incluye a varias generaciones así como a otros parientes (pág. 229)

F

factory system/sistema de fábrica método de producción en el cual los bienes son producidos por obreros y máquinas en un local (una fábrica) fuera de sus hogares (pág. 606)
fascism/fascismo filosofía política basada en el nacionalismo y en un estado todopoderoso (pág. 782)
federal system/sistema federal forma de gobierno en la cual el poder se halla dividido entre la autoridad central y sus subdivisiones políticas (pág. 534)
feudalism/feudalismo sistema político medieval en el cual los monarcas y los nobles menores hacían alianzas basadas en el intercambio de concesiones de tierras por lealtad (pág. 298)
fez/fez sombrero tradicional usado por los hombres turcos (pág. 797)
fief/feudo bajo el feudalismo, una tierra con sus labriegos concedida a un noble a cambio de lealtad y ayuda militar (pág. 298)
filial piety/piedad filial respeto de los hijos hacia sus padres, un principio importante en la filosofía moral de Confucio (pág. 225)
free trade/comercio libre la eliminación de barreras comerciales entre naciones (pág. 978)
friar/fraile miembro de una orden religiosa católica que predicaba en los pueblos y practicaba la pobreza (pág. 307)
fundamentalism/fundamentalismo movimiento que enfatiza el cumplimiento de las leyes y prácticas religiosas tradicionales (pág. 965)

G

geisha/geisha mujer japonesa adiestrada profesionalmente para entretener (pág. 472)

general strike/huelga general huelga en que participan obreros de muchas áreas de la economía de la nación (págs. 779, 931)

genetics/genética el estudio de la herencia biológica (pág. 627)

genetic engineering/ingeniería genética campo científico en el cual la estructura de las células puede ser alterada para producir organismos nuevos o distintos (pág. 1022)

genocide/genocidio intento deliberado de matar a todos los miembros de un grupo racial, cultural o étnico (págs. 850, 938)

gentry/gentry en la Inglaterra isabelina, el grupo social que incluía a la nobleza menor y a los terratenientes (pág. 488)

ghana/ghana título del gobernante de una región en el África antigua, que más tarde fue aplicado al reinado (pág. 189)

glasnost/glasnost palabra rusa aplicada a la política de "apertura" o "transparencia" y de libre expresión, introducida por Mijail Gorbachov (pág. 999)

grand jury/gran jurado en la ley inglesa, grupo de personas que deciden si la evidencia de un crimen justifica llevar a una persona a juicio (pag. 309)

grand vizier/gran visir primer ministro del sultán de un país musulmán (pág. 457)

gross domestic product/producto territorial bruto valor total de las mercancías y los servicios producidos en un país en un año (pág. 898)

guerrilla warfare/guerra de guerrillas método de lucha en el cual pequeños grupos atacan de modo inesperado (pág. 679)

guild/gremio asociación comercial medieval de mercaderes o artesanos (pág. 324)

H

habeas corpus/hábeas corpus principio legal que requiere que las autoridades muestren las razones por las cuales una persona debe ser detenida y garanticen un juicio rápido (pág. 542)

haiku/hai kai forma de poesía japonesa generalmente con tres versos de 17 sílabas (pág. 472)

hajj/hajj peregrinación a La Meca que todo musulmán en buenas condiciones físicas se supone realice por lo menos una vez en su vida (pág. 276)

heavy industry/industria pesada la manufactura de máquinas y equipo para fábricas y minas (pág. 808)

heresy/herejía desacuerdo con la enseñanzas básicas de una religión o negación de las mismas (pág. 306)

hierarchy/jerarquía grupo de personas organizadas de acuerdo con niveles de rango o importancia (págs. 228, 389)

hieroglyphics/jeroglíficos sistema egipcio antiguo de escritura que utilizaba símbolos pictóricos para representar ideas o sonidos (pág. 52)

Holocaust/Holocausto nombre dado al asesinato en masa de judíos europeos por los nazis en la Segunda Guerra Mundial (pág. 839)

homage/homenaje ceremonia formal que establecía lazos feudales entre un señor y un vasallo (pág. 299)

home rule/autonomía local gobierno propio, especialmente cuando se concede a un país dependiente (pág. 651)

hominid/homínido miembro del grupo que incluye a los seres humanos y a las criaturas primates primitivas (pág. 20)

humanism/Humanismo movimiento renacentista basado en la literatura e ideas de las antiguas Grecia y Roma, tales como el valor de cada individuo (pág. 404)

hygiene/higiene la ciencia de la buena salud (pág. 138)

hyperinflation/hiperinflación forma extrema de inflación, con aumentos violentos y rápidos de los precios (pág. 991)

hypothesis/hipótesis solución propuesta para explicar una serie de hechos, que puede ser probada (pág. 517)

I

icon/ícono imagen religiosa cristiana o cuadro que representa a un santo u otra persona sagrada (pág. 249)

iconoclast/iconoclasta ("destructor de imágenes") un opositor al uso de íconos en las iglesias bizantinas, que pensaba que éstos estimulaban la adoración de ídolos (pág. 250)

ideology/ideología sistema de creencias y actitudes que guían las acciones de un grupo o nación (pág. 871)

illuminated manuscript/manuscrito iluminado página de un libro, decorada con elaborados diseños, hermosas letras, o pinturas en miniatura (pág. 253)

imam/imán un guía de oraciones musulmanas (pág. 276)

immigration/inmigración entrada a un nuevo país o región para asentarse allí permanentemente (pág. 630)

imperialism/imperialismo política de erigir un imperio para extender el poderío y el territorio de una nación (pág. 704)

imperial presidency/presidencia imperial término aplicado a un presidente y al poder ejecutivo que asumen poderes que van más allá de los estipulados en la Constitución (pág. 888)

impressionism/impresionismo estilo artístico del Siglo XIX en el cual los pintores trataban de captar impresiones rápidas y los efectos de la luz (pág. 638)

indemnity/indemnización pago por daños y pérdidas (pág. 160)

indulgence/indulgencia perdón vendido por la Iglesia Católica para reducir el castigo de pecados (pág. 416)

industrial capitalism/capitalismo industrial sistema económico en en cual individuos continuamente reinvierten sus ganancias y expanden sus negocios (pág. 608)

inflation/inflación situación en la cual los precios suben rápidamente mientras que el valor del dinero disminuye (págs. 176, 484)

information superhighway/supercarretera informática término popular para referirse a la avanzada red de comunicaciones que enlaza a las personas y a las computadoras alrededor del mundo (pág. 1021)

intendant/intendente agente que representaba al rey de Francia en el gobierno local (pág. 491)

interchangeable parts/piezas intercambiables método de producción que utiliza piezas idénticas, fáciles de ensamblar (pág. 609)

intercontinental ballistic missile (ICBM)/misil balístico intercontinental un cohete de combate de largo alcance que lleva una carga explosiva en la punta (pág. 873)

interdependent/interdependiente confianza mutua (pág. 1018)

intifada/intifada el levantamiento de los palestinos contra la ocupación israelita (pág. 956)

iron curtain/Cortina de Hierro término acuñado por Winston Churchill para referirse a la barrera política que aislaba a la Europa Oriental dominada por los soviéticos de la Europa Occidental (pág. 866)

J

jaguar/jaguar gato salvaje con manchas en la piel, de América Central (pág. 380)

janissary/jenízaro miembro del cuerpo más selecto de soldados del Imperio Otomano (pág. 440)

jati/jati grupos formados dentro de las mayores clases sociales *(varna)* en la antigua India según las ocupaciones de sus miembros y con sus propias reglas y costumbres (pág. 204)

jazz/jazz estilo de música de Estados Unidos que incorpora ritmos africanos a sonidos estadounidenses y europeos (pág. 773)

jihad/jihad lucha mahometana para introducir el islamismo en otras tierras (pág. 278)

jingoism/jingoísmo actitud de patriotismo extremo, usualmente dirigida hacia un poder extranjero (pág. 698)

joint-stock company/compañía por acciones empresa comercial que vende acciones para dividir entre los participantes los costos y las ganancias (pág. 447)

journeyman/jornalero artesano que ha terminado su aprendizaje y trabaja por un jornal (pág. 325)

junk/junco embarcación china (pág. 464)

justification by faith/justificación por la fe concepto de Martín Lutero de que la fe por sí sola es suficiente para alcanzar la salvación (pág. 415)

K

kaiser/káiser título del emperador de Alemania (pág. 685)

kamikaze/kamikaze en la Segunda Guerra Mundial, pilotos japoneses que hacían estallar aviones llenos de bombas en ataques suicidas contra objetivos Aliados (pág. 845)

karma/karma en el hinduismo, la idea de que las acciones de los hombres en la vida determinaban sus destinos y sus futuros (pág. 207)

khan/kan gobernante absoluto de los mongoles (pág. 344)

kibbutz/kibbutz comunidad de granjas colectivas en Israel (pág. 951)

***Kristallnacht*/la noche de las vidrieras rotas** ataques terroristas nazis en noviembre 9 y 10 de 1938, contra propiedades judías en Alemania y Austria (pág. 786)

kulak/kulak labriego en la Unión Soviética que vivía holgadamente (pág. 790)

L

labor-intensive farming/agricultura manual intensiva agricultura que confía en el trabajo humano, no en animales o máquinas (pág. 466)

labor union/sindicato obrero organización de obreros formada para presionar a los dueños de los negocios a que mejoren los salarios y las condiciones en el trabajo (pág. 616)

labyrinth/laberinto conjunto complejo y confuso de pasajes que se conectan (pág. 107)

laissez-faire/laissez-faire doctrina económica según la cual el gobierno no debe regular los negocios (pág. 622)

laity/el estado seglar miembros de una iglesia que no pertenecen al clero (pág. 249)

lay investiture/investidura seglar práctica medieval en la cual las autoridades seglares designaban e investían a funcionarios de la iglesia tales como los obispos (pág. 306)

lend-lease/préstamo-arriendo política de la Segunda Guerra Mundial de permitir el préstamo de equipo a países amigos (pág. 836)

liberalism/liberalismo filosofía política que promueve el cambio social y las libertades individuales (pág. 582)

liberation theology/teología de la liberación movimiento dirigido por el clero católico en la América Latina que enfatizaba el papel de la Iglesia en el mejoramiento de las vidas humanas (pág. 978)

line of demarcation/línea de demarcación línea imaginaria en el Océano Atlántico, trazada por el papa en 1493 para dividir las tierras del mundo entre España y Portugal (pág. 439)

literacy rate/tasa de alfabetización el porcentaje de población adulta de un país que sabe leer y escribir (pág. 944)

logic/lógica la ciencia del razonamiento y del establecimiento de pruebas en los debates (pág. 135)

M

madrasa/madrasa escuela musulmana de teología y leyes (pág. 283)

maize/maíz el maíz nativo de la América (pág. 374)

mandarin/mandarín miembro de la clase más selecta de funcionarios en el gobierno chino (págs. 224, 348)

mandate/mandato (1) en la antigua China, la autoridad concedida por el cielo a gobernantes merecedores de ello, llamada el Mandato del Cielo (pág. 71); (2) territorio administrado por otra nación antes de su independencia (pág. 763)

manorialism/economía feudal sistema económico medieval que ataba a los nobles y a los campesinos a su tierra (pág. 301)

martial law/ley marcial ley militar temporal, que limita derechos tales como la libertad de expresión (pág. 537)

martyr/mártir persona que sufre y muere por una creencia (pág. 173)

master/maestro artesano hábil que era el propietario de un taller y empleaba a otros artesanos (pág. 325)

matrilineal/línea materna que traza el origen de una familia a través de la madre y los ancestros de ésta (pág. 187)

mayor of the palace/jefe del palacio dignatario franco que, alrededor del siglo VIII d.C. tenía poder en el gobierno (pág. 294)

mercantilism/mercantilismo política económica de las naciones europeas en el Siglo XVII, que igualaba la riqueza al poder (pág. 448)

mercenary/mercenario soldado que sirve a un país extranjero por dinero (pág. 124)

meritocracy/sistema de ascenso por méritos sistema en el cual las personas obtienen éxito a base de su habilidad y actuación (pág. 347)

messiah/mesías en el judaísmo, el salvador prometido por los profetas hebreos, quien traería la paz (pág. 171)

mestizo/mestizo en América Latina, persona de ancestro indígena americano y europeo (pág. 667)

metaphysics/metafísica aspectos de la filosofía relativos a los problemas básicos de la existencia y la realidad (pág. 530)

metsuke/metsuke grupo de funcionarios que recolectaban información para los shogúnes de Tokugawa (pag. 469)

middle class/clase media clase social que originalmente estaba entre la nobleza y el campesinado, y que se ganaba la vida por medio de actividades comerciales (pág. 310)

Middle Passage/Paso Central sección intermedia del comercio triangular, en el cual los africanos esclavizados eran traídos a la América por barco (pág. 445)

middle power/potencia mediana nación que es fuerte económicamente pero que no es una potencia militar (pág. 889)

militarism/militarismo política nacional basada en la fuerza militar y la glorificación de la guerra (págs. 689, 740)

millet/millet comunidad de los no-musulmanes dentro del imperio otomano (pág. 458)

missionary/misionero persona que viaja para llevar las principios de una religión a otras personas (pág. 254)
mobilization/movilización acción de reunir y preparar tropas y equipo para la guerra (pág. 742)
monarchy/monarquía gobierno de un rey o una reina (pág. 47)
monastery/monasterio comunidad de hombres que han tomado votos religiosos (pág. 254)
money economy/economía monetaria sistema económico en el cual se usa el dinero y no el trueque para comprar y vender (pág. 323)
monopoly/monopolio control de todo (o casi todo) el comercio o la producción de un producto determinado (pág. 194)
monotheism/monoteísmo creencia en un solo dios (págs. 83, 189)
monsoon/monzón viento periódico que afecta el clima y las formas de vida en el sur de Asia (pág. 67)
mosaic/mosaico cuadro hecho de pedazos de vidrio de colores, barro cocido o piedra unidos con mortero (pág. 253)
mosque/mezquita templo mahometano (págs. 191, 276)
multicultural/multicultural que representa varios grupos culturales y étnicos diferentes (págs. 195, 889)
myth/mito relato tradicional que explica sucesos naturales (pág. 35)

N

nationalism/nacionalismo orgullo en la nación o grupo propios y sus tradiciones; deseo de independencia de un gobierno extranjero (págs. 576, 676)
nationalization/nacionalización traspaso de un negocio de propiedad privada al gobierno (págs. 737, 813)
nationalize/nacionalizar traspasar una industria privada al control del gobierno (pág. 952)
nation-state/estado-nación un estado político cuyos habitantes comparten también el mismo idioma y la misma cultura (pág. 677)
natural law/ley natural verdad o principio universal que los pensadores del Siglo XVII creían podía ser hallado mediante la razón (pág. 521)
negritude/negritud movimiento literario que enfatiza y se enorgullece de la herencia cultural del África (pág. 945)
nihilist/nihilista miembro de un movimiento político ruso de finales del Siglo XIX que rechazaba toda autoridad y abogaba a favor del terrorismo (pág. 692)
nirvana/nirvana en el budismo, estado de unidad con el universo; el final del ciclo de renacimiento (pág. 210)
nomad/nómada miembro de un grupo de personas sin hogar fijo, que viajan constantemente para buscar comida y agua (pág. 22)
nonaligned/no alineado que no toma partido con ninguna de las superpotencias en una guerra fría (pág. 917)
nuclear family/núcleo familiar grupo familiar que incluye sólo a padres e hijos (pág. 229)

O

obsidian/obsidiana cristal volcánico negro (pág. 383)
oligarchy/oligarquía forma de gobierno en la cual un grupo pequeño ejerce el poder político (pág. 1114)
oral tradition/tradición oral las leyendas e historia de una cultura preservada de viva voz (pág. 184)

P

pacifism/pacifismo oposición a la guerra o a la violencia como medio de resolver disputas (pág. 523)
pacifist/pacifista creyente en el pacifismo (pág. 802)
pact/pacto tratado entre varias naciones (pág. 953)
paleontologist/paleontólogo científico que estudia los fósiles (pág. 20)
Pan-Africanism/Panafricanismo movimiento que aboga por la unidad y la cooperación entre las naciones africanas (pág. 942)
Pan-Arabism/Panarabismo movimiento de mediados del siglo XX que pretendía construir lazos culturales y políticos entre los árabes (pág. 950)
papal infallibility/infalibilidad papal doctrina católica romana que sostiene que el papa no puede cometer un error al hablar acerca de la fe y la moral (pág. 686)
partisan/partisano en la Segunda Guerra Mundial, término aplicado a un guerrillero de la resistencia clandestina, especialmente en Italia y Yugoeslavia (pág. 848)
partition/partición división de una región (pág. 707)
partnership/sociedad negocio que es propiedad de

dos o más empresarios que comparten el manejo, las ganancias y las pérdidas (pág. 609)

patriarch/patriarca en la Iglesia cristiana primitiva, uno de los cinco obispos poderosos en las ciudades importantes (pág. 174)

patrician/patricio miembro de una clase aristocrática acaudalada en la antigua Roma (pág. 156)

peaceful coexistence/coexistencia pacífica política soviética de competir con los Estados unidos para evitar la guerra (pág. 873)

peninsulares/peninsulares funcionarios nacidos en España o Portugal que dirigían la sociedad en la América Latina colonial (pág. 667)

perestroika/perestroika término ruso que significa "reestructuración"; los cambios en la economía soviética iniciados por Mikhail Gorbachev (pág. 999)

perspective/perspectiva técnica artística que muestra las relaciones y el espacio entre los objetos (pág. 131)

petit jury/jurado menor grupo de personas que determinan la culpabilidad o la inocencia de una persona procesada (pág. 309)

phalanx/falange en la antigua Grecia, una formación militar en la cual soldados de infantería se colocaban de tal modo que sus escudos quedaban superpuestos (pág. 114)

pharaoh/faraón título de los gobernadores del antiguo Egipto (pág. 49)

philosophe/filósofo pensador social o político del Siglo de las Luces (pág. 524)

philosopher/filósofo un pensador o un amante de la sabiduría (pág. 135)

pilgrimage/peregrinación viaje a un lugar sagrado (pág. 334)

plateau/altiplanicie región relativamente llana más elevada que el área circundante (pág. 185)

plebeian/plebeyo ciudadano de la antigua Roma que no era un aristócrata (pág. 156)

plebiscite/plebiscito voto popular directo sobre un programa o asunto (págs. 575, 657)

pogrom/pogrom persecución organizada de un grupo minoritario, usualmente judíos, en la Rusia de los zares (pág. 693)

polis/polis ciudad-estado de la antigua Grecia (pág. 112)

pollution/contaminación incorporación de sustancias tóxicas o impuras en el aire, tierra o agua (pág. 898)

polytheism/politeísmo adoración de varios dioses (pág. 52)

pope/papa el obispo de Roma, más tarde el jefe de la Iglesia Católica Romana (pág. 174)

population explosion/explosión demográfica aumento grande y repentino de la población humana (pág. 808)

Postimpressionism/Posimpresionismo movimiento artístico cuyos miembros experimentaban con la forma y el color (pág. 639)

potlatch festín celebrado por los americanos nativos del Noroeste del Pacífico (pág. 376)

pragmatic sanction/sanción pragmática decreto emitido por un gobernante sobre un asunto importante (pág. 495)

pragmatist/pragmatista en China, una persona moderada que abogaba por reformas económicas y por el comercio con Occidente (pág. 903)

predestination/predestinación doctrina de John Calvin (fundador del calvinismo) que predicaba que el destino de una persona estaba predeterminado por Dios (pág. 419)

prehistory/prehistoria tiempo anterior a la historia escrita (pág. 20)

prime minister/primer ministro jefe ejecutivo de un gobierno parlamentario (pág. 544)

principality/principado territorio gobernado por un príncipe (pág. 260)

privatization/privatización la devolución de industrias que eran propiedad del gobierno, a dueños privados (págs. 981, 1003)

proletariat/proletariado según la teoría marxista, la clase trabajadora (pág. 625)

propaganda/propaganda noticias e información destinadas a influir en los sentimientos de las personas hacia una causa (pág. 746)

prophet/profeta persona que predica o interpreta lo que se cree son mensajes de Dios (pág. 85)

protectorate/protectorado país cuya política es dirigida por una nación extranjera (pág. 706)

provisional government/gobierno provisional gobierno temporal establecido mientras se espera por un proceso electoral (pág. 757)

psychology/psicología estudio del comportamiento y sus causas (pág. 628)

purge/purga esfuerzo oficial para eliminar a las personas que un gobierno considera indeseables (pág. 791)

Q

queue/coleta trenza de pelo única en la parte posterior de la cabeza (pág. 466)

quinoa/quinua grano cultivado en los Andes (pág. 390)

quota/cuota número o cantidad específica (pág. 900)

R

racial segregation/segregación racial separación social de las personas de acuerdo a su raza (pág. 887)

radiocarbon dating/datación de carbono radioactivo método para determinar la edad de un sustancia que tuvo vida, midiendo la cantidad de carbono que permanece en ella (pág. 21)

rajah/rajá jefe tribal ario en la antigua India; más tarde el gobernante de un estado indio (pág. 202)

ratify/ratificar dar aprobación oficial (pág. 665)

reactionary/reaccionario el individuo que se opone al progreso o al cambio y desea retornar a costumbres antiguas (pág. 582)

realism/realismo estilo y literatura de mediados del Siglo XIX, que reflejaba las realidades de la vida cotidiana (pág. 636)

realpolitik/realpolitik teoría política según la cual el éxito nacional justifica el uso de cualquier medio (pág. 682)

referendum/referéndum voto popular directo para ratificar una disposición o una ley propuesta (págs. 908, 1011)

refugee/refugiado persona que tiene que abandonar su patria y escapar a otro lugar buscando seguridad (pág. 911)

reincarnation/reencarnación el renacimiento del alma o el espíritu en diferentes cuerpos a través del tiempo (pág. 175)

reparation/indemnización de guerra compensación por daños producidos durante una guerra (pág. 763)

republic/república gobierno en el cual los ciudadanos eligen a sus dirigentes (pág. 156)

regent/regente persona que actúa como gobernante temporal (pág. 251)

revelation/revelación visión de una realidad divina, como las atribuidas a Mahoma (pág. 272)

revolution/revolución cambio de gobierno mediante la fuerza (pág. 554)

rhetoric/retórica el arte de hablar en público de manera efectiva (pág. 119)

romanticism/romanticismo movimiento artístico de principios del siglo XIX, que enfatizaba la individualidad y la emoción (págs. 530, 635)

royalist/realista persona que apoya una monarquía (pág. 539)

Russification/rusificación política de imponer la lengua y costumbres rusas a otros pueblos (pág. 692)

S

sacrament/sacramento uno de los rituales formales establecidos por la Iglesia Católica Romana, tales como el bautismo, la sagrada comunión o el matrimonio (pág. 303)

salon/salón en Francia, tertulia donde los intelectuales del Siglo de las Luces se reunían para conversar (pág. 525)

samurai/samurai clase de guerreros terratenientes en el Japón feudal que juraban lealtad a un *daimyo* (pág. 363)

sanctions/sanciones penalidades y restricciones impuestas a una nación por haber infringido la ley internacional (pág. 827)

sanctuary/santuario edificio considerado sagrado, usado para la adoración (pág. 130)

sankin-kotai/sankin-kotai ("presencia alterna") en el Japón feudal, el sistema en el cual un *daimyo* tenía que residir en años alternos en la corte de un shogún (pág. 469)

satellite/satélite país dominado políticamente por un poder vecino (pág. 866)

satrap/sátrapa el gobernador de una provincia en el Imperio Pérsico (pág. 91)

satyagraha/satyagraha ("fuerza de la verdad") término para referirse a las protestas no violentas guiadas por Ghandi (pág. 802)

savanna/sabana llanura cubierta de vegetación, con pocos árboles, en las regiones tropicales o subtropicales (pág. 185)

schism/Cisma de Oriente la división de la Iglesia cristiana en 1054, que separó a la Iglesia Católica Romana de la Iglesia Ortodoxa Oriental (pág. 250)

scholasticism/escolasticismo enseñanza medieval que trataba de combinar la filosofía de Aristóteles con las enseñanzas de los sabios de la Iglesia (pág. 326)

scientific method/método científico pasos para descubrir la verdad científica por medio de la observación y la experimentación (pág. 518)

scorched-earth policy/política de tierra arrasada orden dada por Stalin para que el pueblo soviético destruyera edificios, tierras y cualquier cosa que pudiera ser usada por los invasores nazis (pág. 839)

secede/separarse retirarse formalmente de la membresía de una organización política (pág. 663)

sect/secta subgrupo con sus propias creencias dentro de un grupo religioso mayor (págs. 157, 899)

sectionalism/regionalismo énfasis exagerado en los intereses políticos y económicos de la región propia (pág. 663)
self-determination/autodeterminación el derecho de un pueblo de decidir su propio gobierno o estado político (pág. 796)
seminary/seminario escuela destinada para la enseñanza de los sacerdotes, según ordenó el Concilio de Trento (pág. 423)
separatism/separatismo en el Canadá, movimiento político que favorecía la independencia de Quebec (pág. 890)
sepoy/cipayo soldado natural de la India en el ejército británico (pág. 713)
serf/siervo campesino labrador que dependía de las tierras de un noble (págs. 302, 501)
shah/sha el soberano de un país del Oriente Medio (pág. 797)
shamanism/chamanismo creencia de que los espíritus habitan en cosas vivas y muertas, y que se comunican con los humanos a través de unos sacerdotes llamados chamanes (pág. 358)
shari'ah/shari ah código islámico de leyes que contiene reglas para todos los aspectos de la vida (pág. 275)
sheikh/jeque jefe de una tribu beduina (pág. 271)
shogun/shogún gobernador militar en el Japón feudal (pág. 363)
shogunate/shogunado gobierno fundado por la familia de un shogún y sus seguidores en el Japón feudal (pág. 363)
simony/simonía venta de cargos oficiales en la Iglesia Católica Romana medieval (pág. 335)
slash-and-burn farming/sistema de quema y siembra método de labranza en el cual la tierra cosechable se limpia talando y quemando los árboles para fertilizar el terreno (pág. 380)
socialism/socialismo teoría política que propugna que la sociedad como un todo debe tener el control de los medios de producción, tales como las fábricas y la tierra (pág. 624)
Socialist realism/realismo socialista bajo Stalin, un estilo artístico que glorificaba el modo de vida soviético (pág. 791)
sociology/sociología el estudio del comportamiento de grupos humanos (pág. 628)
sonnet/soneto composición poética de 14 versos y con un patrón de rima y métrica (pág. 405)
sovereignty/soberanía el poder independiente de un grupo o nación de tomar sus propias decisiones (pág. 963)
soviet/soviet un consejo de trabajadores formado al principio de la Revolución Rusa; más tarde, una unidad del gobierno en la Unión Soviética (pág. 694)
special economic zone/zona económica especial áreas de China donde se han permitido que negocios extranjeros y un mercado libre desarrollaran sus actividades en la década de 1990 (pág. 905)
sphere of influence/esfera de influencia área de un país donde una potencia extranjera tiene derechos exclusivos para comerciar o hacer inversiones (págs. 706, 715)
stagflation/estanflación tendencia económica que combina el estancamiento con la elevada inflación y el desempleo (pág. 889)
stalemate/estancamiento una detención o una situación en la que ninguna de las dos partes opuestas pueden avanzar (pág. 907)
standard of living/nivel de vida la medida general de la riqueza global de las personas y su calidad de vida (pág. 979)
steppe/estepa llanuras de Eurasia, extensas, herbáceas, semiáridas, que se extienden desde el Mar Negro hasta los montes Altai (pág. 258)
stupa/estupa capilla budista con bóveda semiesférica, construida sobre las reliquias o los huesos de un santo (pág. 210)
subcontinent/subcontinente porción de tierra que es parte de un continente pero bien diferenciada del mismo, tal como la India (pág. 66)
subsistence farmer/agricultor de subsistencia campesino que cultiva sólo lo suficiente para mantener a su familia o a una aldea (pág. 943)
suffragette/sufragista mujer que trabajaba activamente para obtener el derecho al voto femenino (pág. 651)
sultan/sultán líder político con autoridad absoluta sobre un país mahometano (pág. 457)
superpower/superpotencia nación poderosa e influyente, con un bloque de aliados, específicamente, los Estados Unidos y la Unión Soviética durante la Guerra Fría (pág. 864)
surrealism/surrealismo movimiento artístico que utilizaba sorpresivas imágenes distorsionadas (pág. 773)
symbolism/simbolismo movimiento artístico antirrealista que se centraba alrededor de imágenes y símbolos fantásticos (pág. 638)
symposium/simposio en la antigua Atenas, reunión que se celebraba con banquetes, entretenimiento y discusiones literarias (pág. 123)
syndicate/sindicato bajo el fascismo, agrupación de obreros y patronos en una industria (pág. 783)

T

technology/tecnología las habilidades y conocimientos empleados por las personas para fabricar herramientas y trabajar (pág. 24)

theocracy/teocracia gobierno encabezado por líderes religiosos o por un líder considerado como un dios (págs. 48, 418)

theology/teología el estudio de temas religiosos (pág. 251)

tithe/diezmo contribución de un 10 por ciento de los ingresos que se pagaba al clero (pág. 561)

tournament/torneo deporte medieval en el cual los caballeros competían para mostrar sus habilidades en la lucha (pág. 299)

trade deficit/déficit comercial el desequilibrio económico que ocurre cuando el valor de las importaciones excede el valor de las exportaciones (págs. 889, 998)

tragedy/tragedia historia o representación teatral en la que el personaje central lucha contra el destino pero que desemboca en un final trágico (pág. 132)

trench/trinchera zanja cavada para dar protección a los soldados (pág. 747)

triangular trade/comercio triangular ruta de tres direcciones entre Europa, África y América en el Siglo XVII (pág. 444)

tribune/tribuna en la antigua Roma, magistrado que representaba a los plebeyos (pág. 157)

triumvirate/triunvirato en la antigua Roma, grupo de tres personas gobernando (pág. 163)

troubadour/trovador músico y poeta de la Edad Media que viajaba de corte en corte (pág. 327)

tyrant/tirano en la antigua Grecia, persona que usurpaba el poder y establecía un gobierno unipersonal (pág. 114)

U V

ultimatum/ultimátum última disposición o declaración de condiciones, que implica una amenaza de penalidades severas (pág. 742)

ultraroyalist/ultrarrealista aristócrata extremadamente conservador en la Francia de principios del Siglo XIX (pág. 655)

unicameral legislature/legislatura unicameral asamblea o cuerpo legislativo de una sola cámara (pág. 565)

urbanization/urbanización la expansión de las ciudades y la vida citadina (pág. 631)

utilitarianism/utilitarismo filosofía económica desarrollada por Jeremy Bentham que considera que las acciones sociales y políticas deben ser de utilidad y ayuda a la humanidad (pág. 624)

vassal/vasallo en el feudalismo, noble que ocupaba la tierra de un señor de más alto rango y le servía (pág. 299)

varna/varna una de las cuatro clases sociales principales en la sociedad aria de la antigua India (pág. 203)

vernacular/vernáculo el lenguaje del habla diaria, no de los eruditos, en un país o región (pág. 328)

viceroy/virrey gobernante que representa a un monarca (pág. 714)

vocation/vocación llamado de Dios para asumir cierto trabajo (pág. 417)

W X Y Z

war of attrition/guerra de desgaste conflicto en el cual cada bando trata de ganar agotando al contrario (pág. 747)

warlord/señor de la guerra líder militar local en China (pág. 804)

weir/nasa red o trampa colocada a lo ancho de un río para coger peces (pág. 376)

welfare state/estado de proteccionismo social sistema de gobierno en el cual el estado provee programas para proteger el bienestar económico y social del pueblo (pág. 879)

westernization/occidentalización la expansión de la cultura europea (pág. 718)

yasa/yasa código de leyes de Gengis Kan (pág. 344)

yeoman/campesino propietario en la sociedad inglesa, un campesino que poseía tierras (pág. 488)

yin and yang/yin y yan en el pensamiento chino, los principios opuestos presentes en toda naturaleza (pág. 227)

yurt/yurta tienda de campaña portátil grande y redonda que usaban los nómadas del Asia central (pág. 343)

zaibatsu/zaibatsu grandes firmas industriales japonesas que pertenecían a varias familias (pág. 808)

zemstvo/zemstvo asamblea local en la Rusia zarista (pág. 692)

Text

Grateful acknowledgment is given authors and publishers for permission to reprint the following copyrighted material.
58 W.G. Lambert, Shamash Hymn from Babylonian Wisdom Literature, Copyright © 1960. Reprinted by permission Oxford University Press; **72** Herbert Mason, *Gilgamesh*, translated by Herbert Mason. Copyright © 1970 by Herbert Mason. Reprinted by permission of Houghton Mifflin Company; **146** Sophocles, "The Antigone of Sophocles," an English version translated by Dudley Fitts and Robert Fitzgerald. Copyright 1939 by Harcourt Brace Jovanovich, Inc.; renewed 1967 by Dudley Fitts and Robert Fitzgerald. Caution: All rights, including professional, amateur, motion picture, recitation, lecturing, performance, public reading, radio broadcasting, and television are strictly reserved. Inquiries on all rights should be addressed to Harcourt Brace Jovanovich, Inc., Copyrights and Permissions Department, Orlando, Florida 32887; **366** Li Bo, "On a Quiet Night" from *The Works of Li Bo the Chinese Poet*, translated by Shigeyoshi Obata. Published in 1965 by Paragon Book Reprint Corp.; **366** Li Bo, "Taking Leave of a Friend" from *Personae* by Ezra Pound. Copyright 1926 by Ezra Pound. Reprinted by permission of New Directions Publishing Corporation; **367** "Hard Is the Journey" and **368** Li Bo, "Letter to His Two Small Children Staying in Eastern Lu at Wen Yang Village Under Turtle Mountain" from *Li Bo and Tu Fu*, translated by Arthur Cooper. Translation copyright © 1973 by Arthur Cooper. Reprinted by permission of Viking-Dutton, Inc.; **388** from "The Broken Spears" by Miguel Leon-Portilla, Copyright (1962, 1990 by Beacon Press, Reprinted by permission of Beacon Press; **426** Niccolò Machiavelli, *The Prince*, translated and edited by Thomas G. Bergin. Copyright © 1947 by F. S. Crofts & Co. Inc. Reprinted by permission of Viking-Dutton, Inc.; **584** Victor Hugo, *Les Misérables* translated by Lee Fahnestock and Norman MacAfee. Copyright © 1987 by Lee Fahnestock and Norman MacAfee. Copyright © 1985 by Cameron Mackintosh (Overseas) Ltd. Reprinted by permission of Viking-Dutton, Inc.; **640** Anton Chekhov, "The Beggar," translated by Marian Fell. Reprinted by permission of Random House, Inc.; **747** Wilfred Owen, "Dulce et Decorum Est" from *Collected Poems*, edited by C. Day Lewis. Copyright © 1963 by Chatto & Windus Ltd. Reprinted by permission of New Directions Publishing Corporation; **818** Santha Rama Rau, "By Any Other Name" from *Gifts of Passage*. Copyright © 1961 by Vasanthi Rama Rau Bowers; copyright © renewed 1989 by the author. Reprinted by permission of Harper & Row, Publishers, Inc.; **945** Michael Dei-Anang, "My Africa" from *Poems from Black Africa*, edited by Langston Hughes. Copyright © 1963 by Langston Hughes. Reprinted by permission of Indiana University Press; **966** Jaime Torres Bodet, "The Window," translated by George Kearns. Translation copyright © 1974, 1963 by the McGraw-Hill Book Company, Inc.; **967** Nazim Hikmet, "The World, My Friends, My Enemies, You, and the Earth" from *Things I Didn't Know I Loved*. Copyright © 1975 by Randy Blasing and Mutlu Konuk. Reprinted by permission of Persea Books, Inc.; **968** Gabriel Okara, "Once Upon a Time," from *African Voices*, edited by Howard Sergeant. Copyright © 1973 by Howard Sergeant. Used by permission of Evans Brothers Ltd, London; **987** Claribel Alegría, "Because I Want Peace" from *El Salvador: Testament of Terror*, edited by Joe Fish and Cristina Sganga. Copyright © 1988. Reprinted by permission of Olive Branch Press, an imprint of Interlink Publishing Group, Inc.

Maps

Cartographic Services provided by Ortelius Design, and GeoSystems Global Corp.

Photographs

Cover i Mark D. Phillips/Photo Researchers; **iv** Erich Lessing/Art Resource, NY; **v** (t)Palazzo Ducale, Mantua, Italy/M. Magliari/SuperStock, (b)National Gallery of Art, Washington DC; **vi** (t)Scala/Art Resource, NY, (b)Christies, London/SuperStock; **vii** AFP/Bettmann; **viii** (t)Heraklion Museum, Crete/Kurt Scholz/ SuperStock, (b)David David Gallery, Philadelphia/ SuperStock; **ix** Scala/Art Resource, NY; **x** Mark Burnett; **xvi** Lauros-Giraudon/ Art Resource, NY; **2** NASA; **8** Simon Fraser/Science Photo Library/Photo Researchers; **10** (t)NASA, (b)Edna Douthout; **11** (t)Bosvieux/Explorer/Photo Researchers, (c)David R. Frazier, (b)Jeff Greenberg/Photo Researchers; **12** (t)SuperStock, (b)Musee de Petit Palais, Paris/Bridgeman Art Library/SuperStock; **15** National Museum, Belgrade/E.T. Archives, London/SuperStock; **16-17** Anthony Howard/Woodfin Camp & Associates; **16** Heraklion Museum, Crete/Kurt Scholz/ SuperStock; **17** (t)David David Gallery, Philadelphia/SuperStock, (b)National Museum, Lagos, Nigeria/Kurt Scholz/SuperStock; **19** Jean Clottes/Sygma; **20** Esias Baitel/Gamma-Liaison; **21** John Reader/Science Photo Library/ Photo Researchers; **26** Boltin Picture Library; **27** John Reader/Science Photo Library/Photo Researchers; **28-29** Erich Lessing/Art Resource, NY; **28** Boltin Picture Library; **29** Scala/Art Resource, NY; **31** Ara Guler/ Magnum; **32** Scala/Art Resource, NY; **33** Borromeo/Art Resource, NY; **35** Ira Block/The Image Bank; **36** Scala/Art Resource, NY; **45** The British Museum, London/Bridgeman Art Library/SuperStock; **46** Giraudon/Art Resource, NY; **47** (t)Sylvain Grandadam/Photo Researchers, (c)Carl Purcell/Photographic Resources, (b)Erich Lessing/Magnum; **49** N. Nuccio/ SuperStock; **51** Michael Holford; **52 through 63** Boltin Picture Library; **63** (l)Aleppo Museum, Syria/E.T. Archives, London/SuperStock, (r)Museum of Baghdad, Iraq/Silvio Fiore/SuperStock; **64** Musee de Louvre, Paris/E.T. Archives, London/SuperStock; **66** Borromeo/Art Resource, NY; **68** Scala/Art Resource, NY; **69** Giraudon/Art Rersource, NY; **70-71** Bridgeman/Art Resource, NY; **72 74 79** Michael Holford; **80** Giraudon/Art Resource, NY; **83** Laura Zito/Photo Researchers; **85** David Forbert/SuperStock; **86** SuperStock; **88** Hittite Museum, Ankara/E.T. Archives, London/ SuperStock; **90-91** SEF/Art Resource, NY; **90 91** Erich Lessing/Art Resource, NY; **93** H. Linke/SuperStock; **96** Jerry Bergman/ Gamma-Liaison; **97** Scala/Art Resource, NY; **98** Laurie Platt Winfrey, Inc. **99** SuperStock; **101** Scala/Art Resource, NY; **102 103** Bettmann Archive; **103** Joseph Nettis/Photo Researchers; **105 106** Erich Lessing/Art Resource, NY; **107** SuperStock; **108** Alberto Incrocci/The Image Bank; **110** Museo Capitolino, Rome/E.T. Archives, London/SuperStock; **111** House of Masks, Delos, Greece/Bridgeman Art Library/SuperStock; **112** William Katz/ Photo Researchers; **113** Giraudon/Art Resource, NY; **115** Michael Holford; **116-117** Bill Bachmann/Photo Researchers; **116** Nimatallah/Art Resource, NY; **117** Art Resource, NY; **118** The Brooklyn Museum, Charles Wilbour Fund; **120 122** Scala/Art Resource, NY; **123** Art Resource, NY; **125** Scala/Art Resource, NY; **127** Bettmann Archive; **129** Scala/Art Resource, NY; **130** Statliche Antikensammlung, Munich, Germany/Bridgeman Art Library/Superstock; **131** Werner Forman Archive/Art Resource, NY; **134** Museo Delle Terme, Rome/E.T. Archives, London/SuperStock; **135** Scala/Art Resource, NY; **136** Museo Capitolino, Rome/E.T. Archives, London/SuperStock; **138** Erich Lessing/Art Resource, NY; **140** Scala/Art Resource, NY; **141** Musee du Louvre, Paris/E.T. Archives, London/SuperStock; **142-143** Erich Lessing/Art Resource, NY; **142** (l)The Metropolitan Museum of Art, Bequest of Walter C. Backer, 1972 (1972.118.95) **143** (l)Art Resource, NY, (r)Giraudon/Art Resource, NY; **144** Boltin Picture Library; **145** Giraudon/Art Resource, NY; **146** Scala/Art Resource, NY; **147 148** Art Resource, NY; **153** Erich Lessing/Art Resource, NY; **154 through 159** Scala/ Art Resource, NY; **160** Prenestino Museum, Rome/E.T. Archives, London/SuperStock; **161** Scala/Art Resource, NY; **162** Archaeological Museum, Venice/E.T. Archives, London/SuperStock; **164** Robert Emmett Bright/Photo Researchers; **166-167** Scala/Art Resource, NY; **166** (c)Villa of the Mysteries, Pompeii/Euramax/ SuperStock, (l)The Metropolitan Museum of Art, Rogers Fund, 1903 (03.14.5); **167** Alinari/Art Resource, NY; **168 171** Scala/Art Resource, NY; **172** Erich Lessing/Art Resource, NY; **173** Art Resource, NY; **174** Scala/Art Resource, NY; **175** Robert Frerck/ Tony Stone Images; **176** (l)Erich Lessing/Art Resource, NY, (r)John Bigelow Taylor/Art Resource, NY; **181** The Metropolitan Museum of Art, Fletcher Fund, 1924 (24/97.21ab) **183** Tassili N'Ajjer Plateau, Algeria/ Holton Collection/SuperStock; **184** Roger K. Burnard; **185** Egyptian Expedition of The Metropolitan Museum of Art, The Rogers Fund, 1930 (30.4.21); **186** file photo; **189** The Metropolitan Museum of Art, The Michael C. Rockefeller Collection, Gift of Nelson A. Rockefeller, 1972 (1978.412.310); **190** The British Museum, London/Bridgeman Art Library/SuperStock; **190-191** The Elliott Elisofon Archives, Museum of African Art, The Smithsonian Institution; **191** The Metropolitan Museum of Art, The Michael C. Rockefeller Memorial Collection, Gift of Nelson A. Rockefeller, 1964 (1978.412.352). Photo by Schecter Lee;

194 H. von Meiss/ Photo Researchers; **195** Larry Hamill; **196** M.P. Kahl/Photo Researchers; **199** The Metropolitan Museum of Art, The Michael C. Rockefeller Collection, Gift of Nelson A. Rockefeller, 1972 (1978.412.310); **201** Scala/Art Resource, NY; **202** Toby Molenaar/ The Image Bank; **204** Robert Harding Picture Library; **204-205** B. Kapbor/SuperStock; **205** Art Resource, NY; **207** Victoria & Albert Museum, London/Art Resource, NY; **208** Christies, London/ Bridgeman Art Library/SuperStock; **211 213** Ancient Art & Architecture Collection; **214** Lauros-Giraudon/Art Resource, NY; **215** Ancient Art & Architecture Collection; **217** Jon Gardey/Robert Harding Picture Library Ltd.; **219** Tony Stone Images; **220** Bettmann Archive; **225** Bibliotheque Nationale, Paris/Bridgeman Art Library /SuperStock; **226** Michael Holford; **227** Giraudon/Art Resource, NY; **228** Paul Biddle & Tim Malyon/Science Photo Library/Photo Researchers; **230** Bibliotheque Nationale, Paris; **231** (l)Giraudon/Art Resource, NY, (r)Bettmann Archive; **232** Bettmann Archive; **233** Mark Burnett; **236** SuperStock; **237** Robert Emmett Bright/Photo Researchers; **238** Christies, London/Bridgeman Art Library/ SuperStock; **241** Jacksonville Museum of Contemporary Art, FL/SuperStock; **242** (t)Archive Photos, (cl, c)The Smithsonian Institution, (cr)Ancient Art & Architecture Collection, (b)Erich Lessing/Art Resource, NY; **245 246 248** Scala/Art Resource, NY; **249** SuperStock; **251** Hagia Sophia, Istanbul, Turkey/E.T. Archives, London/SuperStock; **252** (l)Michael Holford, (r)Ancient Art & Architecture Collection; **253 255** Ancient Art & Architecture Collection; **256** SEF/Art Resource, NY; **258** Roy/Explorer/Photo Researchers; **260** Art Wolfe/Tony Stone Images; **262 263** Bettmann Archive; **264** Richard Bergman/Photo Researchers; **265** Michael Holford; **267** Ancient Art & Architecture Collection; **269** Bettmann Archive; **270** Christies, London/Bridgeman Art Library/SuperStock; **272** AKG Berlin/SuperStock; **273** Ancient Art & Architecture Collection; **275 276** Michael Holford; **277** Ancient Art & Architecture Collection; **278-279** Lerner Fine Art Collection/SuperStock; **278** Christies, London/Bridgeman Art Library/SuperStock; **279** Ancient Art & Architecture Collection; **282 286** Bettmann Archive; **287** Michael Holford; **288** SuperStock; **293** Scala/Art Resource, NY; **294** Bettmann Archive; **295** Scala/Art Resource, NY; **298** British Library, London/Bridgeman Art Library/SuperStock; **299** Ancient Art & Architecture Collection; **301** The Metropolitan Museum of Art, Munsey Fund, 1932(32.130.6); **303** Robert Smith/Ancient Art & Architecture Collection; **304-305** Art Resource, NY; **304** (t)Abbey of Monteoliveto Maggiore, Sienna/E.T. Archives, London/ SuperStock, (b)Ronald Sheridan/Ancient Art & Architecture Collection; **305 306** Ronald Sheridan/Ancient Art & Architecture Collection; **307** Museo del Prado, Madrid/E.T. Archives, London/SuperStock; **308** Ronald Sheridan/Ancient Art & Architecture Collection; **309** Erich Lessing/Art Resource, NY; **312** George Holton/Photo Researchers; **313** Robert Smith/Ancient Art & Architecture Collection; **317** Scala/Art Resource, NY; **318** Ancient Art & Architecture Collection; **319** Giraudon/Art Resource, NY; **321** Erich Lessing/Art Resource, NY; **322** O. Troisfontaines/SuperStock; **323** The British Library, London/ Bridgeman Art Library/SuperStock; **324-325** Scala/Art Resource, NY; **325** Ancient Art & Architecture Collection; **327** Giraudon/Art Resource, NY; **328** Scala/Art Resource, NY; **329** British Library, London/E.T. Archives, London/SuperStock; **330** Erich Lessing/ Art Resource, NY; **334** Ancient Art & Architecture Collection; **336** Bridgeman Art Library/Art Resource, NY; **341** Bibliotheque Nationale, Paris/AKG Berlin/SuperStock; **342** Laurie Platt Winfrey, Inc.; **344** J. Bertrand/Photo Researchers; **345** SEF/Art Resource, NY; **346** Naomi Duguid/Asia Access; **347** Laurie Platt Winfrey, Inc.; **351** Wolfgang Kaehler; **352-353** Ernest Manewal/ SuperStock; **352** Frederick Ayer/Photo Researchers; **353** R. Rowan/Photo Researchers; **355** A. Hubrich/H. Armstrong Roberts; **356** Jim Steinberg/Photo Researchers; **358** T. Iwamiya/ Photo Researchers; **359** Rick Browne/Photo Researchers; **360** Masao Hayashi/Dunq/Photo Researchers; **361** Bettmann Archive; **363** Private Collection/ Bridgeman Art Library/SuperStock; **364** Freer Gallery; **365** Paul Chesley/Tony Stone Images; **366** Mary Evans Picture Library; **367 368** Bettmann Archive; **371** file photo; **373** David David Gallery, Philadelphia/SuperStock; **374** Steve Smith/Westlight; **376-377** Mark Burnett; **376** Georgia Department of Natural Resources; **377** (l)Cranbrook Institute of Science, (r)Bettmann Archive; **378** J. Warden/SuperStock; **379** S. Vidler/SuperStock; **380** Museum of Mankind/E.T. Archives, London/ SuperStock; **381** W. Bertsch/H. Armstrong Roberts; **383** Jacksonville Museum of Contemporary Art, FL/SuperStock; **388** Michael Zabe/Art Resource, NY; **391** Woodfin Camp & Associates; **393** Loren McIntyre/Woodfin Camp & Associates; **394** Art Resource, NY; **395** Bridgeman/Art Resource, NY; **396** Giraudon/ Art Resource, NY; **399** Scala/Art Resource, NY; **400** The British Museum; **401-402** Scala/Art Resource, NY; **401** Wolfgang Kaehler; **403** SuperStock; **404** Sistine Chapel, Vatican, Rome/ Bridgeman Art Library/SuperStock; **406-407** Scala/Art Resource, NY; **406** Galleria Dell'Academia, Florence/Scala/ SuperStock; **407** Erich Lessing/ Art Resource, NY; **408** Scala/Art Resource, NY; **411** St. Peter's Basilica, Vatican, Rome/SuperStock; **412** AKG, Berlin/ SuperStock; **413** Scala/Art Resource, NY; **414** Erich Lessing/Art Resource, NY; **415** SuperStock; **416** Erich Lessing/Art Resource, NY; **417** (l)Erich Lessing/Art Resource, NY, (r)National Museum, Copenhagen/E.T. Archives, London/SuperStock; **418** Mary Evans Picture Library/ Photo Researchers; **420** Scala/Art Resource, NY; **421** Erich Lessing/Art Resource, NY; **422** Michael Holford; **423** Giraudon/ Art Resource, NY; **425** Werner Forman Archive/Art Institute of Chicago/Art Resource, NY; **426 through 429** Scala/Art Resource, NY; **431** Erich Lessing/Art Resource, NY; **433** National Maritime Museum; **434** Karen Kasmauski/Woodfin Camp & Associates; **436** (l)SuperStock, (r)Michael Holford; **438** National Museum of American Art, Washington DC/Art Resource, NY; **439 440** AKG, Berlin/ SuperStock; **442-443** Scala/Art Resource, NY; **442** Erich Lessing/ Art Resource, NY; **443** (l)Brent Turner/BLT Productions, (r)Scala/ Art Resource, NY; **445** Bettmann Archive; **446 447** SuperStock; **448** Bridgeman/Art Resource, NY; **449** Michael Holford; **450** Bridgeman/Art Resource, NY; **455 456** Giraudon/Art Resource, NY; **458** Art Resource, NY; **459** Adam Woolfitt/Woodfin Camp & Associates; **461** by courtesy of the Board of Trustees of the Victoria & Albert Museum, London/Bridgeman Art Library/SuperStock; **462** Bibliotheque Nationale, Paris; **463** Dallas & John Heaton/Westlight; **464-465** Philadelphia Free Library/AKG, Berlin/SuperStock; **464** G. Hunter/SuperStock; **465** (l)Art Trade, Bonhams, London/ Bridgeman Art Library/SuperStock, (r)SEF/Art Resource, NY; **466** D.E. Cox/Tony Stone Images; **468** Werner Forman Archive/Art Resource, NY; **469** Culver Pictures Inc./SuperStock; **470** Kita-In Saitumi/Werner Foreman Archive/Art Resource, NY; **471** Michael Holford; **474** George Holton/Photo Researchers; **475** SuperStock; **476** Scala/Art Resource, NY; **477** Bettmann Archive; **481** Giraudon/Art Resource, NY; **482** Bridgeman Art Library, London/SuperStock; **483** Bettmann Archive; **485** Victoria & Albert Museum/Art Resource, NY; **486** Michael Holford; **487** (l)Bridgeman/Art Resource, NY, (r)National Portrait Gallery, London; **488 489** National Portrait Gallery, London/ SuperStock; **490** Giraudon/ Art Resource, NY; **491** Lauros-Giraudon/Art Resource, NY; **492** A&F Pears Ltd., London/ SuperStock; **494** Museum of Art History, Vienna/AKG, Berlin/ SuperStock; **496** AKG, Berlin/SuperStock; **498** Novosti from Sovfoto; **499** Michael Holford; **502** Giraudon/Art Resource, NY; **505** Bridgeman/Art Resource, NY; **506** National Gallery, London/ SuperStock; **507** Bridgeman/Art Resource, NY; **508** Giraudon/Art Resource, NY; **511** Scala/Art Resource, NY; **512** Architect of the Capitol, Washington D.C.; **513** Bettmann Archive; **515** Giraudon/Art Resource, NY; **516** Royal Society of London **517** Private Collection/Bridgeman Art Library/SuperStock; **519** Bettmann Archive; **521** (detail)Erich Lessing/Art Resource, NY; **524** Giraudon/ Art Resource, NY; **525** Derby Museum and Art Gallery, England/ Bridgeman Art Library/SuperStock; **526** Christies, London/ SuperStock; **526-527** Erich Lessing/Art Resource, NY; **527** Bettmann Archive; **528 529** Ronald Sheridan/Ancient Art & Architecture Collection; **530 531** Archive Photos; **535** Bridgeman/Art Resource, NY; **536** Ronald Sheridan/Ancient Art & Architecture Collection; **537** Bettmann Archive; **538** courtesy The Pilgrim Society; **540** National Portrait Gallery, London/SuperStock; **541 543** Ronald Sheridan/ Ancient Art & Architecture Collection; **544** Bettmann Archive; **545** Scala/Art Resource, NY; **546-547** Bettmann Archive; **546** Historic Deerfield Inc.: photo by Amanda Merullo; **547** (l)John Carter Brown Library, Brown University, (r)Massachusetts Historical Society; **548** Bettmann Archive; **550** Archive Photos; **551** Ronald Sheridan/Ancient Art & Architecture Collection; **552** Chicago Historical Society; **553** Yale University Art Gallery; **559** AKG, Berlin/SuperStock; **560** Bettmann Archive; **561** Scala/Art Resource, NY; **563** Mary Evans Picture

Library/Photo Researchers; **564** Bettmann Archive; **565** Giraudon/Art Resource, NY; **567** Photo Researchers; **568** AKG, Berlin/SuperStock; **570-571** Stock Montage; **570** Photo Researchers; **571** Archiv/Photo Researchers; **573** Erich Lessing/Art Resource, NY; **574** Bettmann Archive; **575 578** Giraudon/Art Resource, NY; **580** Photo Researchers; **582 583** Bettmann Archive; **584** Giraudon/Art Resource, NY; **585** The Metropolitan Museum of Art, Gift of Mrs. Herbert N. Straus, 1942 (42.203.1) Photo by Derry Moore; **586** Mary Evans Picture Library/Photo Researchers; **590** (l)Stock Montage, (r)Scala/Art Resource, NY; **591** (t)Bettmann Archive, (b)Original painting hangs in the Selectmen's Meeting Room, Abbot Hall, Marblehead MA; **592** (l)Stock Montage, (r)Giraudon/Art Resource, NY; **593** Scala/Art Resource, NY; **595** L. Berger/SuperStock; **596** Stock Montage; **597** (t)Library of Congress, (b)Laurie Platt Winfrey, Inc.; **599** The Science Museum, London; **600** Waterhouse and Dodd, London/Bridgeman Art Library/SuperStock; **601** Christies, London/SuperStock; **603** Archive Photos; **604** Ronald Sheridan/ Ancient Art & Architecture Collection; **605** file photo; **605** North Wind Pictures; **606 607** The Smithsonian Institution; **608** Royal Museum of Fine Arts, Copenhagen/Bridgeman Art Library/ SuperStock; **612** International Museum of Photography/George Eastman House; **613 614** Collection of Picture Research Consultants; **614-615** Snark/Art Resource, NY; **615** Library of Congress; **616** Courtesy Labor Archives and Research Center, San Francisco State University; **621 622** Giraudon/Art Resource, NY; **623** Library of Congress; **624** file photo; **626** Bettmann Archive; **627** Erich Lessing/Art Resource, NY; **629** National Portrait Gallery, London/SuperStock; **630-631** Christies, London/SuperStock; **630** Library of Congress; **631** Missouri Historical Society; **633** Tate Gallery, London/Art Resource, NY; **635** (detail)Giraudon/Art Resource, NY; **636** Christies, London/SuperStock; **638** Art Resource, NY; **639** Erich Lessing/Art Resource, NY; **640** Archive Photos; **641** Scala/ Art Resource, NY; **642** Russian Sate Museum, St. Petersburg/Bourkatouskey/SuperStock; **645** National Portrait Gallery, London/SuperStock; **647** Giraudon/Art Resource, NY; **648** Library of Congress; **649** Snark/Art Resource, NY; **651 652** Bettmann Archive; **653** Archive Photos; **655** Erich Lessing/Art Resource, NY; **656** Stock Montage; **657** Giraudon/Art Resource, NY; **658 660 662** Bettmann Archive; **662-663** Scala/Art Resource, NY; **663** Mark Burnett; **665** Library of Congress; **666** Bettmann Archive; **668** Schalkwijk/Art Resource, NY; **675 676** Scala/Art Resource, NY; **678-679** Giraudon/Art Resource, NY; **679** (l)Scala/Art Resource, NY, (r)Vince Streano/Tony Stone Images; **680** Bettmann Archive; **681** Archive for Art & History, Berlin/AKG, Berlin/SuperStock; **683** National Gallery, Berlin/AKG, Berlin/ SuperStock; **685** Erich Lessing/Art Resource, NY; **686** FPG International; **687** SuperStock; **689** Bettmann Archive; **690** FPG International; **693** Bettmann Archive; **695** Corbis-Bettmann; **696** SEF/Art Resource, NY; **701** Mark Burnett; **703** Bridgeman/Art Resource, NY; **704** Laurie Platt Winfrey, Inc.; **705** Bettmann Archive; **707** Archive Photos/Popperfoto; **708** Bettmann Archive; **709** Werner Forman Archive/Art Resource, NY; **711** Bettmann Archive; **713** Stock Concepts; **714-715** Bridgeman/ Art Resource, NY; **715** (l)Bettmann Archive, (r)Bridgeman Art Library/Art Resource, NY; **719** Bettmann Archive; **720** file photo; **721 722** Bettmann Archive; **727** Historical Picture Service; **731** Stock Montage; **733** Aaron Haupt; **734** UPI/Bettmann Archive; **735** AP/Wide World Photos; **737** West Point Museum/Joshua Nefsky; **738** SuperStock; **741** Bettmann Archive; **744** Archive Photos; **746-747** Bridgeman/Art Resource, NY; **746** Collection of Colonel Stuart S. Corning. Photo: Rob Huntley:Lightstream; **747** UPI/Bettmann Archive; **748** Erich Lessing/Art Resource, NY; **749** Bettmann Archive; **756** Snark/Art Resource, NY; **757** AP/Wide World Photos; **760** Collection of Colonel Stuart S. Corning. Photo: Rob Huntley:Lightstream; **761** Bettmann Archive; **769** Des Moines Art Center Permanent Collection, 1958.2. Photo: Craig Anderson; **770** Archive Photos; **772** The Metropolitan Museum of Art, bequest of Gertrude Stein, 1946(47.106); **773** Bettmann Archive; **776** Archive Photos; **777** National Museum of American Art/Art Resource, NY; **778** Bettmann Archive; **779** UPI/Bettmann; **781** AKG, Berlin/SuperStock; **782** L'Illustration/Sygma; **783 784** Bettmann Archive; **784-785** AP/Wide World Photos; **785** Bettmann Archive; **786** Hugo Jaeger/LIFE Magazine, Time Inc.; **788** Sovfoto; **789 791** Bettmann Archive; **793** Museum of Modern Art, New York/Bridegeman Art Library/SuperStock; **795** Schalkwijk/Art Resource, NY; **796** Archive Photos; **798** UPI/Bettmann; **799** Eliot Elisofon National Museum of African Art, Eliot Elisofon Archives, Smithsonian Institution; **800** David Keith Jones/Images of Africa Photobank; **801** Bridgeman/Art Resource, NY; **802** file photo; **804** Keystone, Paris/ Sygma; **805** AP/Wide World Photos; **806** SIPA Press; **807 808** Bettmann Archive; **810** David Keith Jones/Images of Africa Photobank; **811** Luis Veiga/The Image Bank; **812 813** Schalkwijk/Art Resource, NY; **814 818** UPI/Bettmann; **819** Laurie Platt Winfrey, Inc.; **821** Rudi Von Briel; **825** U.S. Naval Photographic Center; **826** UPI/Bettmann; **827** AP/Wide World Photos; **829** Sygma; **831** Archive Photos; **834-835** UPI/ Bettmann; **834** AP/Wide World Photos; **835** (l)Bettmann Archive, (r)Archive Photos; **836** Popperfoto/ Archive Photos; **838 839 842** UPI/Bettmann; **846** Archive Photos; **848** RIA-Novosti/Sovphoto; **849** UPI/Bettmann; **850** Archive Photos; **851** UPI/Bettmann; **855** B. Swersey/Gamma-Liaison; **856** Schalkwijk/Art Resource, NY; **857** AP/Wide World Photos; **859** Chuck O'Rear/Westlight; **860** (l)UPI/Corbis-Bettmann, (r)Sovfoto/Eastfoto; **861** (l)T. Rosenthal/ SuperStock, (r)NASA; **863** Sovfoto/Eastfoto; **864** Archive Photos; **865** SuperStock; **868-869** AP/Wide World Photos; **868** UPI/Bettmann; **869** S. Vidler/SuperStock;**872** Archive Photos; **873** UPI/Bettmann; **875** Black Star; **877** UPI/Bettmann; **878** Roger-Viollet; **879** AP/Wide World Photos; **880** UPI/Bettmann; **882** Bettmann Archive; **883** UPI/ Bettmann; **884** SIPA Press; **887** AP/Wide World Photos; **888** UPI/Corbis-Bettmann; **889** A. Keller/Sygma; **890** Reuters/Bettmann; **895** Eugene Gilliom; **896** P. Amranand/SuperStock; **897** T. Matsumoto/Sygma; **898** Tom Wagner/SABA;**899** Michael Yamashita /Westlight; **901** George Matchneer; **903** Bettmann Archive; **904** Langevin/Sygma; **906** Duclos/Guichard/Gouver/Gamma-Liaison; **908** Haruyoshi Yamaguchi/ Sygma; **909** UPI/Bettmann; **910-911** file photo; **911** UPI/Bettmann; **914** Ben Simmons/SIPA Press; **916** Sygma; **917** UPI/Bettmann; **919** D. Hudson/Sygma; **920** G.R. Robert; **921 925** Sygma; **927** Klaus Reisinger/Black Star; **928** Louis Gubb/JB Pictures; **931** UPI/Bettmann; **932** AP/Wide World Photos; **934** David Keith Jones/Images of Africa Photobank; **935** Haviv/SABA; **936** (l)David Keith Jones/Images of Africa Photobank, (r)Tony Stone Images; **936 937** David Keith Jones/Images of Africa Photobank; **938** UPI/Bettmann; **940** Mark Burnett; **941** J.M. Bertrand/SuperStock; **942** Carla Signori Jones/Images of Africa Photobank; **943** Doug Menuez/SABA; **944** P. Schmidt/SuperStock; **945** Lawrence Migdale/Tony Stone Images; **947** Betty Press/ Woodfin Camp & Associates; **949** Robert Frerck/Woodfin Camp & Associates; **950** Jesse Nemerofsky/Photoreporters; **951** Sygma; **954** L. de Raemy/Sygma; **955** UPPA/Photoreporters; **956 957** Barry Iverson/Woodfin Camp & Associates; **957** (l)Penny Tweedie/ Woodfin Camp & Associates, (r)Esaias Baitel/Gamma-Liaison;\ **958** Alain Dejean/Sygma; **962** Reuters/Bettmann; **963** Paul E. Korn/Photoreporters; **964** Ed Kashi; **967** AP/Wide World Photos; **969** Dennis Stock/Magnum; **973** Ary Diesendruck/Tony Stone Images; **974** Alain Keler/Sygma; **975** David L. Perry; **976** Neil Beer/Tony Stone Images; **977** Carrion/Sygma; **979** Bettmann Archive; **980-981** Sergio Dorantes/Sygma; **980** Robert Frerck/Tony Stone Images; **981** (l)Robert Frerck/Woodfin Camp & Associates, (r)Russell Cheyne/Tony Stone Images; **985** Javier Bauluz/SABA; **987** Sygma; **988** Susan Meiselas/Magnum; **990** UPI/Bettmann; **991** Reuters/Bettmann; **992** David L. Perry; **997** NASA; **998** Les Stone/ Sygma; **1000** Novosti/Gamma-Liaison; **1003 1004** Reuters/ Bettmann; **1005** AP/Wide World Photos; **1006 1007** Reuters/ Bettmann; **1009** AFP/Bettmann; **1010** Archive Photos; **1011** Peter Turnley/Black Star; **1014** AP/Wide World Photos; **1016** (l)AP/Wide World Photos, (r)Reuters/Bettmann; **1018** NASA/Gamma-Liaison; **1019** SuperStock; **1020** J.L. Atlan/Sygma; **1021** Hans Peter Merten/Tony Stone Images; **1026** Epix/Sygma; **1027** Adrian Bradshaw/SABA; **1028** Black Star; **1029** David L. Perry.